The

Bessie Parmet Kannerstein '32

Memorial Fund

Established by

MR. JOSEPH PARMET

for the purchase of

REFERENCE BOOKS

for the

CEDAR CREST COLLEGE

LIBRARY

Encyclopedia of
World Literature
in the 20th
Century

Encyclopedia of World Literature in the 20th Century

VOLUME 2: E–K

ST. JAMES PRESS

Steven R. Serafin, *General Editor*

Laura Standley Berger, *Project Coordinator*

Joann Cerrito, Dave Collins, Nicolet V. Elert,
Miranda Ferrara, Kristin Hart, Margaret Mazurkiewicz, Michael J. Tyrkus
St. James Press Staff

Peter M. Gareffa, *Managing Editor, St. James Press*

Mary Beth Trimper, *Production Director*
Deborah Milliken, *Production Assistant*

Cynthia Baldwin, *Product Design Manager*
Eric Johnson, *Art Director*
Pamela A. Reed, *Photography Coordinator*
Randy Bassett, *Image Database Supervisor*
Robert Duncan, Mike Logusz, *Imaging Specialists*

Susan Trosky, *Permissions Manager*
Kelly A. Quin, *Permissons Associate*

Copyright © 1999
St. James Press
27500 Drake Road
Farmington Hills, MI 48331

Encyclopedia of World Literature / Steven R. Serafin, general editor. — 3rd ed.
    p.   cm.
Includes bibliographical references and index.
Contents: v. 1. A-D — v. 2. E-K — v. 3. L-R — v. 4. S-Z and indexes
ISBN 1-55862-373-6 (set). — ISBN 1-55862-374-4 (v. 1). — ISBN 1-55862-375-2 (v. 2). — ISBN 1-55862-376-0 (v. 3). — ISBN 1-55862-377-9 (v. 4).
1. Literature, Modern—20th century—Bio-bibliography.
2. Literature, Modern—20th century—Encyclopedias   I. Serafin, Steven.
PN771.E5   1998
803—dc21   98-40374
                                                                CIP

Printed in the United States of America
St. James Press is an imprint of Gale

10 9 8 7 6 5 4 3 2

BOARD OF ADVISORS

PERIODICALS USED

A&E	Anglistik & Englischunterricht		*AL*	American Literature
AAS	Asian and African Studies			Alaluz: Revista de Poesia, Narracion y Ensayo
AAW	Afro-Asian Writing		*AL&C*	African Languages & Cultures
ABnG	Amsterdamer Beiträe zur Neueren Germanistik		*ALEC*	Anales de la Literatura Española Contemporánea
ACLALSB	ACLALS Bulletin		*ALHis*	Anales de Literatura Hispanoamericana
	Actualidades: Consejo Nacional de la Cultura, Centro de Estudios Latinoamericanos "Romulo Gallegos"/Caracas, Venezuela		*ALR*	American Literary Realism, 1870-1910
			ALS	Australian Literary Studies
ADP	Arbeiten zur deutschen Philologie		*ALT*	African Literature Today
	Africa: Rivista Trimestrale di Studi e Documentazione		*AmerD*	American Drama
AfricaL	Africa: Journal of the International African Institute/Revue de l'Institut Africain International		*AmerP*	American Poetry
			AmerT	American Theatre
AfricaR	Africa Report		*AmLH*	American Literary History
AfrLJ	African Journal		*AmRev*	Americas Review
AfrLS	African Language Studies		*AN*	Acta Neophilologica
AfrSR	African Studies Review		*ANP*	Anales de la Narrative Española Contemporánea
AGald	Anales Galdosianos			
AGR	American-German Review		*AnUs*	Annual of Urdu Studies
AHR	Afro-Hispanic Review		*ANZSC*	Australian and New Zealand Studies in Canada
AICRJ	American Indian Culture and Research Journal		*APR*	American Poetry Review
AIPHOS	Annuaire de l'Institut de Philologie et d'Histoire Orientales et Slaves		*AQ*	American Quarterly
			AR	Antioch Review
AIQ	American Indian Quarterly			Arabica: Revue d'Études Arabes
AJFS	Australian Journal of French Studies		*ARD*	African Research and Documentation
AJPh	American Journal of Philology		*ArielE*	Ariel: A Review of International English Literature
AJS	American Journal of Semiotics			

ArielK	Ariel
ArO	Archív Orientální: Quarterly Journal of African, Asian, and Latin-American Studies
ArQ	Arizona Quarterly
ASch	American Scholar
ASEER	American Slavic and East European Review
	Asemka: A Literary Journal of the University of Cape Coast
ASPAC	Asian Pacific Quarterly of Cultural and Social Affairs Quarterly
ASQ	Arab Studies Quarterly
ASR	American Scandinavian Review
	Atenea: Revista de Ciencia, Arte y Literatura de la Universidad de Concepción
AUB-LLR	Analele Universităţii, Bucureşti, Limbă şi Litereră Română
AUC	Anales de la Universidad de Chile
AUMLA	AUMLA: Journal of the Australasian Universities Language and Literature Association—A Journal of Literary Criticism and Linguistics
AWR	Anglo-Welsh Review
BA	Books Abroad
BAALE	Bulletin of the Association for African Literature in English
BAC	Boletín de la Academia Colombiana
BALF	Black American Literature Forum
BalSt	Balkan Studies
BB	Bulletin of Bibliography
BeneN	Bete Noire

BEPIF	Bulletin des Etudes Portugaises et Brésiliennes
BF	Books from Finland
BHe	Baltische Hefte
BHS	Bulletin of Hispanic Studies
BlackI	Black Images: A Critical Quarterly on Black Arts and Culture
BMMLA	Bulletin of the Midwest Modern Language Association
BO	Black Orpheus
Boundary	Boundary 2: A Journal of Postmodern Literature and Culture
BRMMLA	Rocky Mountain Review of Language and Literature
BRP	Beiträge zur Romanischen Philologie
BR/RB	Bilingual Review/La Revista Bilingüe
BSIS	Bulletin of the Society for Italian Studies
BSS	Bulletin of Spanish Studies
BSUF	Ball State University Forum
BUJ	Boston University Journal
BuR	Bucknell Review
BW	Black World
CA	Cuadernos Americanos
CALC	Cahiers Algériens de Littérature Comparée
	Callaloo: A Black South Journal of Arts and Letters
CalSS	California Slavic Studies
CanL	Canadian Literature
CARHS	Canadian-American Review of Hungarian Studies
CarQ	Caribbean Quarterly

CasaA	Casa de las Américas		*CJItS*	Canadian Journal of Italian Studies
CAsJ	Central Asiatic Journal		*CL*	Comparative Literature
CASS	Canadian-American Slavic Studies		*CLAJ*	College Language Association Journal
CatR	Catalan Review		*CLAQ*	Children's Literature Association Quarterly
CBAA	Current Bibliography on African Affairs		*CLC*	Columbia Library Columns
CBC	Cesare Barbieri Courier		*CLEAR*	Chinese Literature: Essays, Articles, Reviews
CCrit	Comparative Criticism			
CCur	Cross Currents: A Yearbook of Central European Culture		*CLQ*	Colby Library Quarterly
CE	College English		*CLS*	Comparative Literature Studies
CE&S	Commonwealth Essays and Studies		*CML*	Classical and Modern Literature
CEA	CEA Critic		*CMo*	Creative Moment
CEAfr	Cahiers d'Études Africaines		*CMRS*	Cashiers du Monde Russe et Soviétique
CelfanR	Revue Celfan/Celfan Review		*CNIE*	Commonwealth Novel in English
CentR	Centennial Review		*CNLR*	CNL/Quarterly World Report
CFM	Canadian Fiction Magazine		*CollG*	Colloquia Germanica
CFR	Canadian Fiction Review		*Colóquio*	Colóquio/Letras
CFrC	Contemporary French Civilization		*ColQ*	Colorado Quarterly
CH	Crítica Hispánica		*CompD*	Comparative Drama
CHA	Cuadernos Hispanoamericanos		*ComQ*	Commonwealth Quarterly
	Chasqui: Revista de Literatura Latinoamericana			Confluencia: Revista Hispánica de Cultura y Literatura
ChicL	Chicano Literature		*ConL*	Contemporary Literature
ChinL	Chinese Literature		*ContempR*	Contemporary Review
ChiR	Chicago Review		*CP*	Concerning Poetry
CJAS	Canadian Journal of African Studies		*CQ*	Cambridge Quarterly
CJLACS	Canadian Journal of Latin American and Caribbean Studies		*CR*	Critical Review
			CRCL	Canadian Review of Comparative Literature
CJIS	Canadian Journal of Irish Studies			

CREL	Cahiers Roumains d'Études Littéraires: Revue Trimestrielle de Critique, d'Esthétique et d'Histoire Littéraires
CRevAS	Canadian Review of American Studies
Crit	Critique: Studies in Modern Fiction
CritI	Critical Inquiry
	Critique: Revue Générale des Publications Françaises et Étrangères
CritQ	Critical Quarterly
CS	Cahiers du Sud
CSP	Canadian Slavonic Papers
CSR	Christian Scholar's Review
CSS	Canadian Slavic Studies
CTR	Canadian Theatre Review
CV II	Contemporary Verse II
Dada	Dada/Surrealism
DASDJ	Deutsche Akademie für Sprache und Dichtung, Darmstadt, Jahrbuch
DeltaES	Delta: Revue du Centre d'Études et de Recherche sur les Écrivains du Sud aux États-Unis
	Diacritics: A Review of Contemporary Criticism
	Dimension: Contemporary German Arts and Letters
DLB	Dictionary of Literary Biography
DLit	Discurso Literario: Revista de Temas Hispánicos
DQ	Denver Quarterly
DQR	Dutch Quarterly Review of Anglo-American Letters
DR	Dalhousie Review

DSt	Deutsche Studien
DU	Der Deutschunterricht: Beiträge zu Seiner Praxis und Wissenschaftlichen Grundlegung
DUJ	Durham University Journal
DUR	Dublin University Review
DutchS	Dutch Studies
DVLJ	Deutsche Vierteljahrsschrift für Literaturwissenschaft und Geistesgeschichte
EA	Études Anglaises
	Eco: Revista de la Cultura de Occidente
ECr	L'Esprit Créateur
ECW	Essays on Canadian Writing
	Edebiyat: A Journal of Middle Eastern Literatures
EF	Études Françaises
EG	Études Germaniques
EI	Études Irlandaises
EinA	English in Africa
Éire	Éire-Ireland: A Journal of Irish Studies
EJ	English Journal
ELH	English Literary History (formerly Journal of English Literary History)
ELit	Études Littéraires
ELT	English Literature in Transition
ELWIU	Essays in Literature
	English: The Journal of the English Association
Ensayistas	Los Ensayistas: Georgia Series on Hispanic Thought

ES	English Studies
ESA	English Studies in Africa
ESC	English Studies in Canada
	Escritura: Revista de Teoría y Crítica Literarias
ETJ	Educational Theatre Journal
ETR	East Turkic Review
Evergreen	Evergreen Review
ExTL	Explicación de Textos Literarios
FE	France-Eurafrique
FI	Forum Italicum
FLS	French Literature Series
FMLS	Forum for Modern Language Studies
	Folio: Essays on Foreign Languages and Literatures
FR	French Review
FS	French Studies
Francofonia	Studi e Ricerche Sulle Letterature di Lingua Francese
FrF	French Forum
	Frontiers: A Journal of Women Studies
FSt	Feminist Studies
GaR	Georgia Review
GerSR	German Studies Review
GettR	Gettysburg Review
GL&L	German Life and Letters
GN	Germanic Notes
GQ	German Quarterly
GR	Germanic Review

GRM	Germanisch-Romanische Monatsschrift
GSlav	Germano-Slavica: A Canadian Journal of Germanic and Slavic Comparative Studies
HAHR	Hispanic American Historical Review
HAR	Hebrew Annual Review
HC	Hollins Critic
HisJ	Hispanic Journal
Hispam	Hispamérica: Revista de Literatura
	Hispania: A Journal Devoted to the Interests of the Teaching of Spanish and Portuguese
Hispano	Hispanófila
HJAS	Harvard Journal of Asiatic Studies
	Horizontes: Revista de la Universidad Católica de Puerto Rico
HR	Hispanic Review
HSL	University of Hartford Studies in Literature
HSS	Harvard Slavic Studies
HudR	Hudson Review
HungQ	Hungarian Quarterly
I&FR	Indian & Foreign Review
I&L	Ideologies and Literature
Ibero	Iberoromania
	IBLA: Revue de l'Institut des Belles Lettres Arabes
IBSB	International P.E.N. Bulletin of Selected Books
IC	Islamic Culture
IFR	International Fiction Review
IFRev	International Folklore Review

IJMES	International Journal of Middle East Studies
IJSLP	International Journal of Slavic Linguistics and Poetics
	Imagine: International Chicano Poetry Journal
IndL	Indian Literature
IndSch	Indian Scholar
	Inti: Revista de Literatura Hispánica
IonC	Index on Censorship
IowaR	Iowa Review
IQ	Italian Quarterly
IranS	Iranian Studies: Journal of the Society for Iranian Studies
IRLI	Italianistica: Rivista di Letteratura Italiana
IS	Italian Studies
ItalAm	Italian Americana
Italianist	The Italianist: Journal of the Department of Italian Studies, University of Reading
ItC	Italian Culture
IUR	Irish University Review: A Journal of Irish Studies
IWT	Indian Writing Today
JAAC	Journal of Aesthetics and Art Criticism
JAC	Journal of American Culture
JAOS	Journal of the American Oriental Society
JapQ	Japan Quarterly
JAPS	Journal of the American Portuguese Society
JArabL	Journal of Arabic Literature
JARCE	Journal of the American Research Center in Egypt
JASO	Journal of the Anthropological Society of Oxford
JASt	Journal of Asian Studies
JATJ	Journal of the Association of Teachers of Japanese
JBalS	Journal of Baltic Studies
JBlS	Journal of Black Studies
JBRS	Journal of the Burma Research Society
JByelS	Journal of Byelorussian Studies
JCF	Journal of Canadian Fiction
JCH	Journal of Contemporary History
JCL	Journal of Commonwealth Literature
JCLTA	Journal of the Chinese Language Teachers Association
JCS	Journal of Croatian Studies
JCSR	Journal of Canadian Studies/Revue d'Études Canadiennes
JCSt	Journal of Caribbean Studies
JEGP	Journal of English and Germanic Philology
JES	Journal of European Studies
JEthS	Journal of Ethnic Studies
JFCS	Journal of Feminist Cultural Studies
JGE	Journal of General Education
JHD	Journal of the Hellenic Diaspora
JHI	Journal of History of Ideas
JIAS	Journal of Inter-American Studies
JIL	Journal of Irish Literature
JIWE	Journal of Indian Writing in English

JJS	Journal of Japanese Studies		*L&P*	Literature and Psychology
JLSTL	Journal of Literary Studies		*LAAW*	Lotus: Afro-Asian Writing
JMAF	Journal of Modern African Studies		*LALR*	Latin American Literary Review
JNALA	Journal of the New African Literature and the Arts			Landfall: A New Zealand Quarterly
JNT	Journal of Narrative Technique		*Lang&S*	Language and Style
JNZL	Journal of New Zealand Literature		*LangF*	Language Forum
JOL	Journal of Oriental Literature		*LangQ*	USF Language Quarterly
JPalS	Journal of Palestinian Studies		*LARR*	Latin America Research Review
JPC	Journal of Popular Culture		*LATR*	Latin American Theatre Review
JPrag	Journal of Pragmatics		*LBR*	Luso-Brazilian Review
JRS	Journal of Russian Studies		*LCUT*	Library Chronicle of the University of Texas
JSoAL	Journal of South Asian Literature		*LE&W*	Literature East and West
JSS	Journal of Semitic Studies		*LHY*	Literary Half-Yearly
JSSB	Journal of the Siam Society		*LitG*	Literary Griot
JSSE	Journal of the Short Story in English		*LitR*	Literary Review
JSSTC	Journal of Spanish Studies: Twentieth Century			Lituanus: Baltic States Quarterly of Arts & Sciences
JTamS	Journal of Tamil Studies		*LJ*	Library Journal
JUkGS	Journal of Ukrainian Graduate Studies		*LJGG*	Literaturwissenschaftliches Jahrbuch im Auftrage der Görres-Gesellschaft
JUkS	Journal of Ukrainian Studies		*LM*	London Magazine
JWIL	Journal of West Indian Literature		*LOS*	Literary Onomastics Studies
KanQ	Kansas Quarterly		*LPer*	Literature in Performance: A Journal of Literary and Performing Art
KFLQ	Kentucky Foreign Language Quarterly		*LQ*	Literary Quarterly
KFQ	Keystone Folklore		*LuK*	Literatur und Kritik
	Kiabàrà: Journal of the Humanities		*LWU*	Literatur in Wissenschaft und Unterricht
KR	Kenyon Review		*MAL*	Modern Austrian Literature
KRQ	Romance Quarterly (formerly Kentucky Romance Quarterly)			

MAPS	Memoirs of the American Philosophical Society
MarkhamR	Markham Review
MAWAR	MAWA Review
MBL	Modern Black Literature
MCL	Modern Chinese Literature
MD	Modern Drama
MEF	Middle Eastern Forum
MEJ	Middle East Journal
MelbSS	Melbourne Slavonic & East European Studies (formerly Melbourne Slavonic Studies)
	Merkur: Deutsche Zeitschrift für europäisches Denken
MES	Middle Eastern Studies
MFS	Modern Fiction Studies
MGS	Michigan Germanic Studies
MHL	Modern Hebrew Literature
MHRev	Malahat Review
MichA	Michigan Academician: Papers of the Michigan Academy of Science, Arts, and Letters
MinnR	Minnesota Review
MissQ	Mississippi Quarterly
ML	Modern Languages
MLF	Modern Language Forum
MLJ	Modern Language Journal
MLN	Modern Language Notes
MLQ	Modern Language Quarterly
MLR	Modern Language Review

MLS	Modern Language Studies
MMisc	Midwestern Miscellany
MN	Monumenta Nipponica
ModA	Modern Age
	Monatshefte: Für Deutschen Unterricht, Deutsche Sprache und Literatur
	Mosaic: A Journal for the Interdisciplinary Study of Literature
MP	Modern Philology: A Journal Devoted to Research in Medieval and Modern Literature
MPS	Modern Poetry Studies
MQ	Midwest Quarterly: A Journal of Contemporary Thought
MQR	Michigan Quarterly Review
MR	Massachusetts Review: A Quarterly of Literature, the Arts and Public Affairs
MRRM	Monographic Review/Revista Monográfica
MSFO	Mémoires de la Société Finno-Ougrienne
MSpr	Moderna Språk
MuK	Maske und Kothurn
MV	Minority Voices: An Interdisciplinary Journal of Literature and the Arts
MW	Muslim World
NAR	North American Review
NConL	Notes on Contemporary Literature
NDEJ	Notre Dame English Journal
NDH	Neue Deutsche Hefte
NDL	Neue Deutsche Literatur
	Neohelicon: Acta Comparationis Litterarum Universarum

Neophil	Neophilologus		*NTQ*	New Theatre Quarterly
NEQ	New England Quarterly		*NWR*	Northwest Review
NER	New England Review and Bread Loaf Quarterly		*NYHT*	New York Herald Tribune
NewA	New African		*NYHTBR*	New York Herald Tribune Books Review
NewC	New Criterion		*NYLF*	New York Literary Forum
NewL	New Letters: A Magazine of Fine Writing		*NYRB*	New York Review of Books
NewR	New Republic		*NYT*	New York Times
NewS	New Scholar		*NYTBR*	New York Times Book Review
NFS	Nottingham French Studies		*NYTMag*	New York Times Magazine
NGC	New German Critique: An Interdisciplinary Journal of German Studies		*NZSJ*	New Zealand Slavonic Journal
			O&C	Œuvres & Critiques
				Obsidian II: Black Literature in Review
NGS	New German Studies		*ÖGL*	Österreich in Geschichte und Literatur
NHQ	New Hungarian Quarterly		*OJES*	Osmania Journal of English Studies
NL	Nouvelles Littéraires		*OL*	Orbis Litterarum
NLH	New Literary History: A Journal of Theory and Interpretation		*OLR*	Oxford Literary Review
NLitsR	New Literatures Review		OnsE	One Erfdeel: Algemeen-Nederlands Tweemaandelijks Cultureel Tijdschrift
NMAL	Notes on Modern American Literature		*OntarioR*	Ontario Review
NME	New Middle East		*OSP*	Oxford Slavonic Papers
NMQ	New Mexico Quarterly		*P&R*	Philosophy and Rhetoric
NorS	Northern Studies		*PA*	Présence Africaine
NorthwestR	Northwest Review		*PAJ*	Pan-African Journal
	Novel: A Forum on Fiction		*PakR*	Pakistan Review
NR	New Republic			Paragraph: The Journal of the Modern Critical Theory Group
NRF	Nouvelle Revue Française			Parnassus: Poetry in Review
NRs	Neue Rundschau			
NS	New Statesman		*PCL*	Perspectives on Contemporary Literature

PCLS	Proceedings of the Comparative Literature Symposium	*PSMLAB*	Pennsylvania State Modern Language Association Bulletin
PCP	Pacific Coast Philology	*PStud*	Portuguese Studies
PEGS	Publications of the English Goethe Society	*QI*	Quaderni d'Italianistica
PFr	Présence Francophone: Revue internationale de langue et de littérature	*QIA*	Quaderni Ibero-Americani
		QL	La Quinzaine Littéraire
	Plaza: Revista de Literatura	*QQ*	Queen's Quarterly
PLL	Papers on Language and Literature	*QRFS*	Quarterly Review of Film Studies
	Ploughshares	*QRL*	Quarterly Review of Literature
	Plural: Revista Cultural de Excelsior		Quimera: Revista de Literatura
	PMLA: Publications of the Modern Language Association of America	*RaJAH*	Rackham Journal of the Arts and Humanities
PoetryR	Poetry Review	*RAL*	Research in Africa Literatures
PolP	Polish Perspectives	*RALS*	Resources for American Literary Study
PolR	Polish Review	*RCB*	Revista de Cultura Brasileña
POMPA	Publications of the Mississippi Philological Association	*RCEH*	Revista Canadiense de Estudios Hispánicos
PoT	Poetics Today	*RCF*	Review of Contemporary Fiction
PPNCFL	Proceedings of the Pacific Northwest Conference on Foreign Languages	*RChL*	Revista Chilena de Literatura
PQ	Philological Quarterly	*RCL*	Revue de Littérature Comparée
PQM	Pacific Quarterly (Moana)	*RCLL*	Revista de Crítica Literaria Latinoamericana
PR	Partisan Review	*RC-R*	Revista Chicano-Riqueña
PRev	Poetry Review	*RCSCSPL*	Russian, Croatian and Serbian, Czech and Slovak, Polish Literature
	Prismal/Cabral: Revista de Literatura Hispánica/Caderno Afro-Brasileiro Asiático Lusitano	*REH*	Revista de Estadios Hispánicos
PRL	Puerto Rican Literature	*RELC*	RELC Journal
PrS	Prairie Schooner		Renascence: Essays on Value in Literature
PSA	Papeles de Son Armandans		Renditions: A Chinese-English Translation Magazine
PSM	Philippine Studies	*RevB*	Revista Bilingüe

RevI	Revista/Review Interamericana		*RRWC*	Renaissance and Renascences in Western Literature
	Review: Latin American Literature and Arts		*RS*	Research Studies
RG	Revue Générale		*RSI*	Revista Storica Italiani
RH	Revue Hebdomaire		*RUO*	Revue de l'Université d'Ottawa
RHL	Revue d'Histoire Littéraire de la France		*RUS*	Rice University Studies
RHLQCF	Revue d'Histoire Littéraire du Québec et du Canada Français		*RusL*	Russian Literature
			RusR	Russian Review
RHM	Revista Hispánica Moderna		*SAB*	South Atlantic Bulletin
RI	Revista Iberoamericana		*SAD*	Studies in American Drama
RIB	Revista Interamericana de Bibliografía/ Inter-American Review of Bibliography		*SAF*	Studies in American Fiction
RLA	Romance Language Annual		*SAIL*	Studies in American Indian Literature
RLC	Revue de Littérature Comparée		*SAJL*	Studies in American Jewish Literature
RLJ	Russian Language Journal		*SAQ*	South Atlantic Quarterly
RLI	Rassegna della Letteratura Italiana		*SatR*	Saturday Review
RLMC	Rivista di Letterature Moderne e Comparate		*SBL*	Studies in Black Literature
			SBR	Swedish Book Review
RLT	Russian Literature Triquarterly		*Scan*	Scandinavica
RLV	Revue des Langues Vivantes		*ScanR*	Scandinavian Review
RMS	Renaissance & Modern Studies		*SCB*	South Central Bulletin
RNL	Review of National Literatures		*SchM*	Schweizer Monatshefte
RO	Revista de Occidente		*SCL*	Studies in Canadian Literature
ROMM	Revue de l'Occident Musulman et de la Méditerranée		*ScotIR*	Scottish International Review
			ScotR	Scottish Review
RomN	Romance Notes		*SCR*	South Carolina Review
RoR	Romanian Review		*SDR*	South Dakota Review
RPh	Romance Philology		*SEACS*	South East Asian Cultural Studies
RR	Romanic Review		*SEEA*	Slavic and East European Arts

SEEJ	Slavic and East European Journal		*SSF*	Studies in Short Fiction
SEER	Slavonic and East European Review		*SSl*	Scando-Slavica
SFC	Science Fiction Chronicle		*SSL*	Studies in Scottish Literature
SFR	Stanford French Review		*SSLit*	Soviet Studies in Literature
SHEH	Stanford Honors Essays in the Humanities		*SSMLN*	Society for the Study of Midwestern Literature Newsletter
SHR	Southern Humanities Review		*SSR*	Scottish Slavonic Review
Siglo	Siglo XX/20th Century		*StBL*	Studies in Black Literature
	Signs: Journal of Women in Culture and Society		*StIsl*	Studia Islamica
SlavonicR	Slavonic Review		*StTCL*	Studies in Twentieth Century Literature
SlavR	Slavic Review			Studies: An Irish Quarterly Review
SLitI	Studies in the Literary Imagination			SubStance: A Review of Theory and Literary Criticism
SLJ	Southern Literary Journal		*SuF*	Sinn und Form
	Slovo: Časopis Staroslavenskog Zavoda u Zagrebu		*Sur*	Revista Sur
SlovLit	Slovenská Literatúra: Revue Pre Literárnu Vedu		*SUS*	Susquehanna University Studies
SlovS	Slovene Studies		*SWR*	Southwest Review
SNNTS	Studies in the Novel		*SXX*	Secolul XX
SoQ	Southern Quarterly			Symposium: A Quarterly Journal in Modern Foreign Literatures
SoR	Southern Review (Baton Rouge, LA)		*T&K*	Text & Kontext
SoRA	Southern Review (Adelaide, Australia)		*TA*	Theatre Annual
	Southerly: A Review of Australian Literature		*TAH*	The American Hispanist
SovL	Soviet Literature		*TamR*	Tamarack Review
SPFA	Bulletin de la Société des Professeurs Français en Amérique		*TC*	Twentieth Century
SPHQ	Swedish Pioneer Historical Quarterly		*TCL*	Twentieth Century Literature
SR	Sewanee Review		*TCrit*	Texto Crítico
			TDR	Tulane Drama Review/The Drama Review
SS	Scandinavian Studies		*TheatreQ*	Theatre Quarterly

	Theoria: A Journal of Studies in the Arts, Humanities and Social Sciences
TJ	Theatre Journal
TkR	Tamkang Review
TLS	[London] Times Literary Supplement
TM	Temps Modernes
TQ	Texas Quarterly
Transatlantic	Transatlantic Review
TRev	Translation Review
TriQ	TriQuarterly
TSAR	Toronto South Asian Review
TSLL	Texas Studies in Literature and Language
TSWL	Tulsa Studies in Women's Literature
TuK	Text + Kritik: Zeitschrift für Literatur
TWQ	Third World Quarterly
TxSE	Texas Studies in English
UDQ	Denver Quarterly
UDR	University of Dayton Review
UES	Unisa English Studies
UHSL	University of Hartford Studies in Literature
UkrR	Ukrainian Review: A Quarterly Magazine Devoted to the Study of the Ukraine
UQ	Ukrainian Quarterly: Journal of East European and Asian Affairs
UR	University Review
UTQ	University of Toronto Quarterly
UWR	University of Windsor Review (Windsor, Ontario)
V&I	Voix et Images: Littérature Québécoise

VLang	Visible Language
VQR	Virginia Quarterly Review
W&L	Women & Literature
WAJML	West African Journal of Modern Languages
WAL	Western American Literature
WascanaR	Wascana Review
WB	Weimarer Beiträge
WCR	West Coast Review
	Westerly: A Quarterly Review
WHR	Western Humanities Review
WI	Die Welt dea Islams
WIRS	Western Illinois Regional Studies
WLT	World Literature Today
WLWE	World Literature Written in English
WR	Western Review
WS	Women's Studies: An Interdisciplinary Journal
WSCL	Wisconsin Studies in Contemporary Literature
WSJ	Wiener Slavistisches Jahrbuch
WSl	Die Welt der Slaven
WSlA	Wiener Slawistischer Almanach
WVUPP	West Virginia University Philological Papers
WZ	Wort in de Zeit
WZUG	Wissenschaftliche Zeitschrift der Ernst Moritz Arndt-Universität Greifswald
YCC	Yearbook of Comparative Criticism

YCGL	Yearbook of Comparative and General Literature	*Y/T*	Yale/Thestre
YES	Yearbook of English Studies	*ZAA*	Zeitschrift für Anglistik und Amerikanistik
YFS	Yale French Studies	*ZS*	Zeitschrift für Slawistik
YItS	Yale Italian Studies	*ZSP*	Zeitschrift für Slavische Philologie
YR	Yale Review		

ACKNOWLEDGMENTS

For permission to reproduce the illustrations in this edition of the *Encyclopedia of World Literature in the 20th Century,* the publisher is indebted to the following:

Abe, Kōbō, photograph by Jerry Bauer. © Jerry Bauer. Reproduced by permission.—Achebe, Chinua, photograph. AP/Wide World Photos. Reproduced by permission.—Adams, Henry S., photograph. AP/Wide World Photos. Reproduced by permission.—Adorno, Theodore W., photograph. Archive Photos, Inc. Reproduced by permission.—Agee, James, photograph. The Library of Congress.—Akhmatova, Anna Andreevna, photograph. The Library of Congress.—Albee, Edward, photograph. The Library of Congress.—Alegría, Fernando, photograph. Arte Publico Press Archives, University of Houston. Reproduced by permission.—Aleixandre, Vicente, photograph. AP/Wide World Photos. Reproduced by permission.—Algren, Nelson, photograph. The Library of Congress.—Allende, Isabel, photograph. AP/Wide World Photos. Reproduced by permission.—Amado, Jorge, photograph. AP/Wide World Photos. Reproduced by permission.—Amichai, Yehuda, photograph by John Reeves. Reproduced by permission.—Amis, Kingsley, photograph. AP/Wide World Photos. Reproduced by permission.—Anderson, Sherwood, photograph. Archive Photos, Inc. Reproduced by permission.—Angelou, Maya, photograph. AP/Wide World Photos. Reproduced by permission.—Anouilh, Jean, photograph. AP/Wide World Photos. Reproduced by permission.—Aragon, Louis, photograph. The Library of Congress.—Ashbery, John, photograph. AP/Wide World Photos. Reproduced by permission.—Atwood, Margaret, photograph. The Library of Congress.—Auchincloss, Louis, photograph by Jerry Bauer. © Jerry Bauer. Reproduced by permission.—Auden, W. H., photograph. Corbis-Bettmann. Reproduced by permission.—Audiberti, Jacques, photograph. AP/Wide World Photos. Reproduced by permission.—Azuela, Mariano, photograph. The Library of Congress.—Baraka, Imamu Amiri (LeRoi Jones), photograph. Corbis-Bettmann. Reproduced by permission.—Barnes, Djuna, photograph. UPI/Corbis-Bettman. Reproduced by permission.—Baroja, Pìo, photograph. AP/Wide World Photos. Reproduced by permission.—Barrie, Sir James M., photograph. AP/Wide World Photos. Reproduced by permission.—Barth, John, photograph. AP/Wide World Photos. Reproduced by permission.—Barthelme, Donald, photograph by Jerry Bauer. © Jerry Bauer. Reproduced by permission.—Bates, H. E., photograph. Mark Gerson Photography. Reproduced by permission.—Beattie, Anne, photograph by Jerry Bauer. © Jerry Bauer. Reproduced by permission.—Beckett, Samuel, photograph. Archive Photos, Inc. Reproduced by permission.—Behan, Brendan, photograph. AP/Wide World Photos. Reproduced by permission.—Bellow, Saul, photograph. Archive Photos, Inc. Reproduced by permission.—Benét, Stephen Vincent, photograph by Pirie MacDonald. The Library of Congress.—Bergson, Henri, photograph. The Library of Congress.—Berryman, John, photograph. AP/Wide World Photos. Reproduced by permission.—Betjeman, Sir John, photograph. Archive Photos, Inc. Reproduced by permission.—Bialik, Hayyim N., photograph. The Library of Congress.—Bierce, Ambrose, photograph. Corbis-Bettmann. Reproduced by permission.—Bishop, Elizabeth, photograph. AP/Wide World Photos. Reproduced by permission.—Blaise, Marie Claire, photograph by John Reeves. Reproduced by permission.—Blasco Ibáñez, Vicente, photograph. AP/Wide World Photos. Reproduced by permission.—Bloom, Harold, photograph by Jerry Bauer. © Jerry Bauer. Reproduced by permission.—Böll, Heinrich, photograph. Archive Photos, Inc. Reproduced by permission.—Borges, Jorge Luis, photograph. The Library of Congress.—Bowen, Elizabeth, photograph. The Library of Congress.—Breton, André, photograph. Archive Photos, Inc./AFP. Reproduced by permission.—Brookner, Anita, photograph by Jerry Bauer. © Jerry Bauer. Reproduced by permission.—Brooks, Gwendolyn, photograph. The Library of Congress.—Brutus, Dennis, photograph. AP/Wide World Photos. Reproduced by permission.—Buber, Martin, photograph. The Library of Congress.—Bullins, Ed, photograph by Marva Rae. Helen Merrill Ltd. Reproduced by permission of the photographer.—Bunting, Basil, photograph by Thomas Victor. Copyright © 1986 by Thomas Victor. All rights reserved. Reproduced by permission of the Estate of Thomas Victor.—Burgess, Anthony, photograph. AP/Wide World Photos. Reproduced by permission.—Burke, Kenneth, photograph. The Library of Congress.—Burroughs, William S., photograph. AP/Wide World Photos. Reproduced by permission.—Caldwell, Erskine, photograph. The Library of Congress.—Čapek, Karel, photograph. AP/Wide World Photos. Reproduced by permission.—Capote, Truman, photograph. The Library of Congress.—Cardenal, Ernesto, photograph by Lou Dematteis. Reuters/Corbis-Bettmann. Reproduced by permission.—Carpentier, Alejo, photograph. Archive Photos, Inc. Reproduced by permission.—Carver, Raymond, photograph. Archive Photos, Inc. Reproduced by permission.—Cather, Willa, photograph by Carl Van Vechten. The Library of Congress.—Cela, Camilio José, photograph by Jerry Bauer. © Jerry Bauer. Reproduced by permission.—Celine, Louis F., photograph. Archive Photos, Inc. Reproduced by permission.—Chandler, Raymond, photograph. The Library of Congress.—Cheever, John, photograph. The Library of Congress.—Chekov, Anton, photograph. International Portrait

Gallery/Library of Congress.—Chesterton, G. K., photograph. Archive Photos, Inc. Reproduced by permission.—Claudel, Paul, photograph. The Library of Congress.—Cocteau, Jean, photograph. AP/Wide World Photos. Reproduced by permission.—Cortázar, Julio, photograph. AP/Wide World Photos. Reproduced by permission.—Coward, Sir Noel (Peirce), photograph. AP/Wide World Photos, Inc. Reproduced by permission.—Crane, Hart, photograph by Walker Evans. The Library of Congress.—cummings, e. e., photograph. The Library of Congress.—Day Lewis, Cecil, photograph. Archive Photos, Inc. Reproduced by permission.—de Beauvoir, Simone, photograph. AP/Wide World Photos. Reproduced by permission.—de la Mare, Walter, photograph. The Library of Congress.—Derrida, Jacques, photograph. Archive Photos, Inc. Reproduced by permission.—Dickey, James, photograph. AP/Wide World Photos. Reproduced by permission.—Didion, Joan, photograph by Jerry Bauer. © Jerry Bauer. Reproduced by permission.—Doctorow, E. L., photograph by Horst Tappe. Archive Photos, Inc. Reproduced by permission.—Doolittle, Hilda, photograph. The Library of Congress.—Dos Passos, John, photograph. The Library of Congress.—Drabble, Margaret, photograph. AP/Wide World Photos. Reproduced by permission.—Dreiser, Theodore, photograph by Pirie MacDonald. The Library of Congress.—DuBois, W. E. B., photograph. The Library of Congress.—Ehrenburg, Ilya Grigoryevich, photograph. The Library of Congress.—Eliot, T. S., photograph. The Library of Congress.—Ellison, Ralph, photograph. AP/Wide World Photos. Reproduced by permission.—Elytis, Odysseus, photograph. AP/Wide World Photos. Reproduced by permission.—Farrell, James T., photograph. The Library of Congress.—Faulkner, William, photograph by Carl Van Vechten. The Library of Congress.—Fitzgerald, F. Scott, photograph by Carl Van Vechten. The Library of Congress.—Fo, Dario, photograph. © Jerry Bauer. Reproduced by permission.—Forster, E. M., photograph. Archive Photos, Inc. Reproduced by permission.—France, Anatole, photograph. The Library of Congress.—Freire, Romulo Gallegos, photograph. The Library of Congress.—Freud, Sigmund, photograph. The Library of Congress.—Frost, Robert, photograph. The Library of Congress.—Fuentes, Carlos, photograph. AP/Wide World Photos. Reproduced by permission.—Furphy, Joseph, photograph. The Library of Congress.—Gaines, Ernest, photograph. AP/Wide World Photos. Reproduced with permission.—Gaitán Durán, Jorge, photograph. The Library of Congress.—García Lorca, Federico, photograph. Archive Photos/Popperfoto. Reproduced by permission.—García Márquez, Gabriel, 1982, photograph. AP/Wide World Photos. Reproduced by permission.—Gass, William, photograph by Miriam Berkley. © Miriam Berkley. Reproduced by permission.—Genet, Jean, photograph. Archive Photos, Inc. Reproduced by permission.—Gibran, Kahlil, photograph. UPI/Corbis-Bettman. Reproduced by permission.—Gide, André, photograph. UPI/Corbis-Bettman. Reproduced by permission.—Glissant, Edouard, photograph. AP/Wide World Photos. Reproduced by permission.—Golding, William, photograph by Caroline Forbes. The Library of Congress.—Gordimer, Nadine, photograph. AP/Wide World Photos. Reproduced by permission.—Gordon, Caroline, photograph. The Library of Congress.—Gorky, Maxim, photograph. The Library of Congress.—Grass, Günter, photograph by Fred Stein. The Library of Congress.—Graves, Robert, photograph. AP/Wide World Photos, Inc. Reproduced by permission.—Greene, Graham, photograph. AP/Wide World Photos, Inc. Reproduced by permission.—Hammett, Samuel D., photograph. The Library of Congress.—Hamsun, Knut, photograph. The Library of Congress.—Handke, Peter, photograph by Jerry Bauer. © Jerry Bauer. Reproduced by permission.—Hansberry, Lorraine V., photograph. The Library of Congress.—Hardy, Thomas, photograph. Archive Photos, Inc. Reproduced by permission.—Hauptmann, Gerhart, photograph. The Library of Congress.—Head, Bessie, photograph. Reproduced by the kind permission of the Estate of Bessie Head.—Hellman, Lillian, photograph. AP/Wide World Photos. Reproduced by permission.—Hemingway, Ernest, photograph. Archive Photos, Inc. Reproduced by permission.—Housman, A. E., photograph. Archive Photos, Inc. Reproduced by permission.—Hughes, James Langston, photograph by Carl Van Vechten. The Library of Congress.—Hughes, Ted, photograph by Mark Gerson. Mark Gerson Photography. Reproduced by permission.—Hurston, Zora Neale, photograph. AP/Wide World Photos. Reproduced by permission.—Inge, William R., photograph. The Library of Congress.—Ionesco, Eugéne, photograph. The Library of Congress.—Irving, John, photograph. AP/Wide World Photos. Reproduced by permission.—Isherwood, Christopher, photograph. Archive Photos, Inc. Reproduced by permission.—James, Henry, photograph. The Library of Congress.—Jarry, Alfred, drawing by F. A. Cazalz, 1897, photograph. Corbis-Bettmann. Reproduced by permission.—Jeffers, Robinson, photograph. The Library of Congress.—Jiménez, Juan Ramón, photograph. AP/Wide World Photos. Reproduced by permission.—Johonson, James Weldon, photograph. The Library of Congress.—Jones, James, photograph. Corbis-Bettmann. Reproduced by permission.—Joyce, James (Ulysses), photograph. The Library of Congress.—Jung, Carl, photograph. The Library of Congress.—Jünger, Ernst, photograph. Archive Photos/Camera Press. Reproduced by permission.—Kafka, Franz, photograph. AP/Wide World Photos. Reproduced by permission.—Kawabata Yasunari, photograph. AP/Wide World Photos. Reproduced by permission.—Kerouac, Jack, photograph. Archive Photos. Reproduced by permission.—Killens, John O., photograph by Carl Van Vechten. The Library of Congress.—Kristeva, Julia, photograph by Jerry Bauer. © Jerry Bauer. Reproduced by permission.—Kumin, Maxine, photograph. AP/Wide World Photos. Reproduced by permission.—Kundera, Milan, photograph. Archive Photos.

Reproduced by permission.—Lagerkvist, Pär F., photograph. The Library of Congress.—Lawrence, D(avid) H(erbert), photograph. AP/Wide World Photos. Reproduced by permission.—Lessing, Doris, photograph by Jerry Bauer. © Jerry Bauer. Reproduced by permission.—Levi, Carlos, photograph. Archive Photos, Inc. Reproduced by permission.—Levi, Primo, photograph. The Library of Congress.—Lewis, Sinclair, photograph. The Library of Congress.—Lindsay, Vachel, photograph. Corbis-Bettmann. Reproduced by permission.—London, Jack, photograph. The Library of Congress.—Lowell, Amy, photograph. UPI/Corbis-Bettman. Reproduced by permission.—Lowell, Robert, photograph. The Library of Congress.—Lukács, György, photograph. Hulton-Deutsch/Corbis-Bettmann. Reproduced by permission.—Macleish, Archibald, photograph. The Library of Congress.—MacLennan, Hugh, photograph. AP/Wide World Photos. Reproduced by permission.—Maeterlinck, Maurice, photograph. The Library of Congress.—Mailer, Norman, photograph by Carl Van Vechten. The Library of Congress.—Malamud, Bernard, photograph. The Library of Congress.—Mamet, David, photograph by Brigitte Lacombe. Grove/Atlantic, Inc. Reproduced by permission.—Mann, Luiz Heinrich, photograph. The Library of Congress.—Mann, Thomas, photograph. The Library of Congress.—Mansfield, Katherine, photograph. Corbis-Bettmann. Reproduced by permission.—Marcel, Gabriel, photograph. Archive Photos, Inc. Reproduced by permission.—Marquand, John, photograph. Archive Photos, Inc. Reproduced by permission.—Masefield, John, photograph. The Library of Congress.—Maugham, W. Somerset, photograph by Carl Van Vechten. The Library of Congress.—Mauriac, François, photograph. The Library of Congress.—McCarthy, Mary, photograph. The Library of Congress.—McCullers, Carson, photograph. AP/Wide World Photos. Reproduced by permission.—McKay, Claude, photograph. The Library of Congress.—Mencken, Henry Louis, photograph. The Library of Congress.—Merrill, James, photograph. AP/Wide World Photos. Reproduced by permission.—Millay, Edna St. Vincent, photograph. The Library of Congress.—Miller, Arthur, photograph. Archive Photos, Inc. Reproduced by permission.—Miller, Henry, photograph. The Library of Congress.—Milosz, Czeslaw, photograph by Jerry Bauer. © Jerry Bauer. Reproduced by permission.—Mishima, Yukio, photograph. AP/Wide World Photos. Reproduced by permission.—Mistral, Gabriela, photograph. The Library of Congress.—Momaday, N. Scott, photograph. AP/Wide World Photos. Reproduced by permission.—Moore, Marianne, photograph. The Library of Congress.—Moravia, Alberto, photograph. The Library of Congress.—Morrison, Toni, photograph. AP/Wide World Photos. Reproduced by permission.—Mukherjee, Bharati, photograph. AP/Wide World Photos. Reproduced by permission.—Nabokov, Vladimir, photograph. AP/Wide World Photos. Reproduced by permission.—Naipaul, V. S., photograph. AP/Wide World Photos. Reproduced by permission.—Narayan, R. K., photograph. The Library of Congress.—Nemerov, Howard, photograph by Margaret Nemerov. Reproduced with permission.—Neruda, Pablo, photograph by Jerry Bauer. © Jerry Bauer. Reproduced by permission.—Nin, Anaïs, photograph. The Library of Congress.—O'Casey, Sean, photograph. The Library of Congress.—O'Connor, Flannery, photograph. Corbis-Bettmann. Reproduced by permission.—O'Hara, Frank, photograph. AP/Wide World Photos. Reproduced by permission.—O'Hara, John, photograph. The Library of Congress.—O'Neill, Eugene G., photograph. The Library of Congress.—Oates, Joyce Carol, photograph. UPI/Corbis-Bettmann. Reproduced by permission.—Odets, Clifford, photograph. AP/Wide World Photos, Inc. Reproduced by permission.—Ōe Kenzaburō, photograph. Reuters/Kyodo/Archive Photos. Reproduced by permission.—Ortega y Gasset, José, photograph. AP/Wide World Photos. Reproduced by permission.—Orwell, George, photograph. AP/Wide World Photos. Reproduced by permission.—Osborne, John, photograph. AP/Wide World Photos. Reproduced by permission.—Ozick, Cynthia, photograph. Corbis-Bettmann. Reproduced by permission.—Parra, Nicanor, photograph by Miriam Berkley. © Miriam Berkley. Reproduced by permission.—Pasolini, Pier Paolo, photograph. AP/Wide World Photos, Inc. Reproduced by permission.—Paton, Alan, photograph. The Library of Congress.—Pavlović, Miodrag, photograph by John Reeves. Reproduced by permission.—Paz, Octavio, photograph. AP/Wide World Photos. Reproduced by permission.—Percy, Walker, photograph by Jerry Bauer. © Jerry Bauer. Reproduced by permission.—Pérez Galdós, Benito, photograph. The Library of Congress.—Perse, Saint John, photograph. AP/Wide World Photos. Reproduced by permission.—Pietri, Dr. Arturo Uslar, photograph. AP/Wide World Photos. Reproduced by permission.—Pinter, Harold, photograph. AP/Wide World Photos. Reproduced by permission.—Pirandello, Luigi, photograph. AP/Wide World Photos. Reproduced by permission.—Plath, Sylvia, photograph. Corbis-Bettmann. Reproduced by permission.—Porter, Katherine Anne, photograph. Archive Photos, Inc. Reproduced by permission.—Pound, Ezra, photograph. The Library of Congress.—Pritchett, V. S., photograph by Jerry Bauer. © Jerry Bauer. Reproduced by permission.—Proust, Marcel, photograph. The Library of Congress.—Puig, Manuel, photograph by Jerry Bauer. © Jerry Bauer. Reproduced by permission.—Purdy, James, photograph. The Library of Congress.—Pynchon, Thomas R., photograph. UPI/Corbis-Bettmann. Reproduced by permission.—Quasimodo, Salvatore, photograph. Corbis-Bettmann. Reproduced by permission.—Remarque, Erich M., photograph. The Library of Congress.—Renault, Mary, photograph. AP/Wide World Photos. Reproduced by permission.—Rexroth, Kenneth, photograph. AP/Wide World Photos. Reproduced by permission.—Rice, Elmer, photograph. AP/Wide World Photos.

Reproduced by permission.—Rich, Adrienne, photograph. AP/Wide World Photos. Reproduced by permission.—Richler, Mordecai, photograph by John Reeves. Reproduced by permission.—Robbe-Grillet, Alain, photograph by Jerry Bauer. © Jerry Bauer. Reproduced by permission.—Robinson, Edwin Arlington, photograph. AP/Wide World Photos. Reproduced by permission.—Roethke,Theodore, photograph by Imogen Cunningham. AP/Wide World Photos, Inc. Reproduced by permission.—Roth, Philip, photograph. Corbis-Bettmann. Reproduced by permission.—Rukeyser, Muriel, photograph. AP/Wide World Photos. Reproduced by permission.—Rulfo, Juan, photograph. AP/Wide World Photos. Reproduced by permission.—Rushdie, Salman, photograph. Archive Photos, Inc. Reproduced by permission.—Russell, George William, photograph. The Library of Congress.—Salinger, J. D., photograph. AP/Wide World Photos, Inc. Reproduced by permission.—Sandburg, Carl, photograph. The Library of Congress.—Santayana, George, photograph. The Library of Congress.—Saroyan, William, photograph. The Library of Congress.—Sarraute, Nathalie, photograph. AP/Wide World Photos. Reproduced by permission.—Sarton, May, photograph. UPI/Corbis-Bettmann. Reproduced by permission.—Sassoon, Siegfried, photograph. The Library of Congress.—Schnitzler, Arthur, photograph. Archive Photos, Inc. Reproduced by permission.—Sexton, Anne, photograph. AP/Wide World Photos. Reproduced by permission.—Shaw, George Bernard, photograph. The Library of Congress.—Shepard, Sam, photograph. Archive Photos, Inc. Reproduced by permission.—Simenon, Georges, photograph. AP/Wide World Photos, Inc. Reproduced by permission.—Sinclair, Upton, photograph. AP/Wide World Photos, Inc. Reproduced by permission.—Singer, Isaac Bashevis, photograph. UPI/Corbis-Bettmann. Reproduced by permission.—Sitwell, Edith, photograph. UPI/Corbis-Bettman. Reproduced by permission.—Škvorecký, Josef, photograph by John Reeves. Reproduced by permission.—Snow, Charles Percy, photograph. Corbis-Bettmann. Reproduced by permission.—Snyder, Gary, photograph. AP/Wide World Photos. Reproduced by permission.—Sontag, Susan, photograph. AP/Wide World Photos. Reproduced by permission.—Soto, Pedro Juan, photograph. Arte Publico Press Archives, University of Houston. Reproduced by permission.—Soyinka, Wole, photograph. Archive Photos/Trappe. Reproduced by permission.—Spark, Muriel, photograph. AP/Wide World Photos. Reproduced by permission.—Stein, Gertrude, photograph by Carl Van Vechten. The Library of Congress.—Steinbeck, John, photograph. Archive Photos, Inc. Reproduced by permission.—Stevens, Wallace, photograph. The Library of Congress.—Strachey, Lytton, photograph by E. O. Hoppe. Corbis-Bettmann. Reproduced by permission.—Strand, Mark, photograph. The Library of Congress.—Szymborska, Wislawa, photograph. AP/Wide World Photos. Reproduced by permission.—Tate, Allen, photograph. UPI/Corbis-Bettman. Reproduced by permission.—Thomas, Dylan, photograph. AP/Wide World Photos. Reproduced by permission.—Thurber, James, photograph. AP/Wide World Photos. Reproduced by permission.—Tolkien, J. R. R., photograph. AP/Wide World Photos. Reproduced by permission.—Tremblay, Michel, photograph by Yves Renaud. Agence Goodwin. Reproduced by permission of the photographer.—Trevor, William, photograph by Kristin Morrison. Mark Gerson Photography. Reproduced by permission.—Tyler, Anne, photograph. AP/Wide World Photos. Reproduced by permission.—Unamuno, Miguel de, photograph. Corbis-Bettmann. Reproduced by permission.—Undset, Sigrid, photograph. AP/Wide World Photos. Reproduced by permission.—Updike, John, photograph. AP/Wide World Photos. Reproduced by permission.—Valéry, Paul, photograph. Archive Photos, Inc. Reproduced by permission.—Vargas Llosa, Mario, photograph. AP/Wide World Photos. Reproduced by permission.—Vidal, Gore, photograph. AP/Wide World Photos. Reproduced by permission.—Villa, José Garcia, photograph. AP/Wide World Photos. Reproduced by permission.—Vonnegut, Kurt, Jr., photograph. Archive Photos/Saga 1991 Frank Capri. Reproduced by permission.—Walcott, Derek, photograph by Jerry Bauer. © Jerry Bauer. Reproduced by permission.—Walker, Alice, photograph. Archive Photos, Inc. Reproduced by permission.—Warren, Robert Penn, photograph. The Library of Congress.—Wassermann, Jakob, photograph. Archive Photos, Inc. Reproduced by permission.—Waugh, Evelyn, photograph. Mark Gerson Photography. Reproduced by permission.—Wedekind, Frank, photograph. Hulton-Deutsch Collection/Corbis-Bettmann. Reproduced by permission.—Weiss, Peter, photograph. AP/Wide World Photos. Reproduced by permission.—Weldon, Fay, photograph. AP/Wide World Photos. Reproduced by permission.—Wells, H. G., photograph. The Library of Congress.—Welty, Eudora, photograph. AP/Wide World Photos. Reproduced by permission.—Wesker, Arnold, photograph. UPI/Corbis-Bettman. Reproduced by permission.—Wharton, Edith, photograph. AP/Wide World Photos. Reproduced by permission.—White, E. B., photograph. AP/Wide World Photos. Reproduced by permission.—White, Patrick, photograph. AP/Wide World Photos. Reproduced by permission.—Wiesel, Elie, photograph by Nancy Rica Schiff. Archive Photos, Inc. Reproduced by permission.—Wilbur, Richard, photograph. AP/Wide World Photos. Reproduced by permission.—Wilder, Thornton, photograph by Carl Van Vechten. The Library of Congress.—Williams, Tennessee, photograph. AP/Wide World Photos. Reproduced by permission.—Wilson, August, photograph. AP/Wide World Photos. Reproduced by permission.—Wodehouse, P. G., photograph. AP/Wide World Photos. Reproduced by permission.—Wolfe, Thomas, photograph by Carl Van Vechten. The Library of Congress.—Wolfe, Tom, photograph. AP/Wide World Photos. Reproduced by permission.—Woolf, Virginia, photograph. AP/Wide World Photos. Reproduced by permission.—Wright, James, photograph by Ted Wright. Reproduced by permission of the Estate of James Wright.—Wright, Richard, photograph by Carl Van Vechten. The Library of Congress.—Yeats, William Butler, photograph. The Library of Congress.—Yourcenar, Marguerite, photograph. AP/Wide World Photos. Reproduced by permission.

INTRODUCTION

This four-volume third edition of the *Encyclopedia of World Literature in the 20th Century* is designed as a comprehensive survey of significant literary activity of international scope and proportion extending from the beginning of the century to the present. The breadth and complexity of this activity demands progressive study, analysis, and evaluation, and the *Encyclopedia* serves as an inclusive and authoritative guide for this purpose. Responsive to the needs of scholarly and general readers alike, the *Encyclopedia* provides in a reference work of singular importance the most extensive treatment of information necessary to the assessment and appreciation of the growth and development of modern world literature.

The twentieth century represents a period of extraordinary literary productivity and proliferation realized within the framework of unprecedented historical transformation and challenge. The decades preceding the publication of the *Encyclopedia* have produced global transition, dominated by the impact of social and political upheaval and the redefinition of national boundaries and identities. We have witnessed events that have altered the shape of the world in which we live and the terms by which we discuss literature. Although the sociopolitical as well as cultural ramifications of these alterations have yet to fully realize themselves and be understood, we have made every effort to incorporate these developments within the context of the *Encyclopedia,* thus enhancing the reader's perception of the relationship between literature and society.

This edition is a collaborative effort to cover, in more than 2,300 article entries in four volumes, the major aspects of world literature in the twentieth century. To this end, nearly all the literatures of the world with claim to a substantial productivity within the century are discussed in survey articles. Likewise, in their relationship to the literature of the century, literary movements of consequence (e.g., expressionism, futurism, surrealism) are covered in separate topical articles, as are movements in ideas (e.g., existentialism, historicism, postmodernism). The core of the *Encyclopedia* consists of separate articles on major and representative writers incorporating salient biographical information and critical analysis of the writer's major themes and works.

Bases of Selection: The selection of individual entries represents extensive assessment and evaluation of critical recognition earned from the international literary community as well as endorsement as figures of substantial literary importance from specialists of representative national literatures. In order to fulfill its purpose as a reference work, the *Encyclopedia* attempts to be as comprehensive as possible within the limitations imposed by the span of the edition. It is also important to maintain the international scope of the *Encyclopedia.* Thus, many authors—American, British, European—who are well known to English-speaking readers do not receive individual entries but are instead treated within the survey articles of national literatures. Many of the authors receiving individual entries are from less familiar literatures who have limited exposure to English-speaking readers, and a significant number to date have not been translated into English or have not generated criticism in English of scholarly merit. For these authors, the *Encyclopedia* serves as the primary source of reference to English-speaking readers.

Omissions: Despite the scope and magnitude of the *Encyclopedia,* it is inevitable that an appreciable number of writers have been omitted. In works of this kind, with claims of a wide coverage, the inclusion of some writers as against others is of course subject to debate. Regrettably, it was not always possible to identify a specialist of sufficient expertise to prepare individual author entries or to compile and research a national literature. As a result, there is unfortunately at times insufficient coverage of writers deserving of inclusion from relatively obscure or isolated literatures.

Entries: Organization and Data—Individual author entries have been arranged into four parts: a headnote containing vital statistics; a body that includes biographical information and a critical assessment of the author's achievement; a section titled *Further Works* containing publications not mentioned in the body of the article; and a final section titled *Bibliography* comprising selective bibliographical material concerning the author and his or her work. A list of periodicals and their abbreviations cited will be found at the front of Volume 1, and an index to the entries will be included at the end of Volume 4. In a very few of the headnotes the statistics are incomplete, owing to the difficulty of obtaining conclusive confirmation from accessible, reliable sources.

Works featured in the body of the article, as well as in the *Further Works* section, carry their full title and, wherever possible, their original year of publication. In the case of authors writing in languages other than English, titles of published English translations are cited in parentheses, along with their original publication dates. Where several translations of a non-English work have been made under the same title in English, only the publication date of the earliest translation is given. With those works that have been translated under more than one English title, we have tried to feature the titles of all such translations. For non-English works that have not been translated into English, original titles will appear followed by the year of publication and the title's literal translation in parentheses.

Cross References and Pseudonyms: Extensive cross-references to other authors, literatures, and movements appear wherever appropriate in the texts of articles. Where a writer with an individual entry is referred to in another entry, at the first mention his or her last name appears in small capital letters. Likewise, where a movement with a separate entry is referred to in another entry, at the first mention the topic appears in small capital letters. The survey articles on national literatures are cross-referenced by language so that the reader will be directed to the appropriate national literature or literatures (e.g., under Bengali Literature will be found "See Bangladeshi Literature and Indian Literature").

Authors known primarily by their *non de plume* will be listed under their pseudonym (e.g., Blixen under *Dinesen,* Gorenko under *Akhmatova,* Hadjiandreas under *Tsirkas*). For the convenience of readers certain of these names have been cross-referenced, but the abiding principle in this regard has been to avoid overelaboration.

Transliterated and Romanized Languages: As an international reference work, the *Encyclopedia* attempts to be as consistent as possible with the transliteration and romanization of non-English names, most notably those in Arabic, Chinese, Japanese, and Russian. In Arabic, prefixes that are part of the surname will be retained when the surname is used for alphabetizing (e.g., 'Abd al-Hamīd ibn Hadūga under *Ibn Hadūga*). In Chinese practice, the family name comes before the given name, which usually has two elements. The family name and the first element of the given name are capitalized, and the given name is hyphenated (e.g., Kao Hsiao-sheng). Chinese names wherever necessary are cross-referenced in the index by their updated romanization (e.g., Gao Xiaosheng. *See* Kao Hsiao-sheng). In Japanese practice, the family name also comes before the given name (e.g., Ōe Kenzaburō rather than Kenzaburō Ōe). While there are many systems for transliterating Russian names, the phonetic method adopted was considered the most appropriate for a general reader, and the most easily recognizable from the viewpoint of common usage (e.g., see *Gorky,* not Gorki, Gorkii, or Gor'kiy).

Quotations: To some entries, primarily authors of international repute, the *Encyclopedia* appends a selection of critical excerpts to further enhance the reader's understanding and perception of the author's productivity and contribution to world literature. The excerpts are cited by author, source, year of publication, and page number(s).

The Contributors: These have been drawn from a wide sphere of literary authorities, both from the United States and abroad, most often based on the recommendation of the advisers in national literatures. The name of the contributor appears at the end of each article in the *Encyclopedia.*

The general editor wishes to express his appreciation, first, to the hundreds of individuals whose contributions have helped to make the *Encyclopedia* a reference work of distinction. He is most indebted to those individuals listed in the board of advisers, whose generosity of time and expertise provided proportion, balance, and consistency in the preparation of the edition. He also expresses his appreciation to Peter M. Gareffa, managing editor of St. James Press, and Laura Berger, senior editor.

Assisting the general editor, Madeline D. Murray was the senior editor and production coordinator of the *Encyclopedia.* Production editors were Sonya Collins, Victoria Eng, and Matthew Miller. Technical assistance was provided by Enercida Guererro, Ana Angelillo, and Harlan Cayetano. Editorial assistance was provided by Carina Garcia, Bonnie MacSaveny, Denise Galang, Sean O'Hanlon, Chriscita Corbin, Rachel Shook, Michelle Gonzalez, Christine Cifra, Anna Degrezia, Francesca Fiore, Rebecca Lawson, Jill Bauer, Lisa Butler, Michelle Cutler, Julie Miele, Anna Gross, Karma Cloud, Nancy Moore, Joseph Weissman, Rose Sung, Jason Berner, and Greta Wagle.

STEVEN R. SERAFIN
HUNTER COLLEGE OF THE CITY UNIVERSITY OF NEW YORK

E

EBEJER, Francis

Maltese dramatist and novelist, b. 28 Aug. 1925, Ħad-Dingli; d. 10 June 1993, St. Julians

E. studied medicine at the University of Malta between 1942 and 1943, but he abandoned the course to work as an English-Italian interpreter with the 8th Army of the British Forces in Tripolitania, North Africa (1943-44). He then became a teacher, and after completing studies at St. Mary's Training College, Middlesex (1948-50), he was appointed a primary school head teacher, a post he held until 1977. In 1961 he received an international PEN Fellowship and remained a member of this international society for novelists. Between 1961 and 1962 he became a Fulbright Scholar in the U.S. E. has received numerous awards and titles in Malta and abroad for his work in drama. He was a member of the Academy of Maltese Writers and an honorary member of the Accademia de Vaucluse (France).

E. wrote all his novels except one in English, but the majority of his plays were written in Maltese. His theatrical activities often involved him in directing his own plays. He became Malta's leading dramatist after his notorious revolutionary contribution to local drama in which he introduced a deep introspection of Maltese society. He used an elegant style that proved him to be a master of the language. In the 1950s he wrote mostly for the radio, and the 1960s and the 1970s saw the more mature E. writing his major dramatic works. His three most significant works, *Vaganzi tas-Sajf* (1962; Summer Holidays), *Boulevard* (1964; Boulevard), and *Menz,* (1967; Menz), were successful because they gave the public something that was missing from the Maltese society: intellectual drama. Many other plays followed and E. translated several of them into English. He also wrote a number of novels: *A Wreath of Maltese Innocents* (1958), *Wild Spell of Summer* (1968), *In the Eye of the Sun* (1969), *Come Again in Spring* (1973), *Requiem for a Malta Fascist* (1980), and *Leap of Malta Dolphins* (1982). An unpublished novel, *The Maltese Baron . . . and I Lucien*, was left to his son.

E. always defined the Maltese as Mediterranean, and most of his plays deal with aspects of humanity and therefore treat universal themes. The universal is often applied to a specific environment within a cosmopolitan atmosphere so as to explain that life on tiny Malta is steeped in history but the island is alive in a modern world. Thematically, he is concerned with the future of the Central Mediterranean through geopolitical, economic, and cultural concerns. A recurrent theme in his works is the interaction of past and present as alternative glimpses into the future. His characters with all their psychological structure represent the self-flawed image of the nation and the context is a search for identity and cultural continuity that reveals a society interlocked in religion. Character is explored in existential terms, and he often feels the oppression of guilt, exploitation, aspects of freedom, conscience, impotence, destiny, loneliness, self-delusion, and contradiction. Stylistically, he fluctuates from one mode to another even in a single work. He depicts the natural to show deterministic attitudes, uses expressionism to reveal psychological workings, applied symbolism to relate the social with the political, and finds the absurd convenient to discuss his themes philosophically.

E. is the most important Maltese dramatist of the second half of the 20th c. His plays are often discussions on a theme or presentations of a problem, and his characters develop in response to the circumstances they encounter. In *Menz*, E. discusses the usefulness of individual freedom within a social system that imposes rigidity; in *Vaganzi tas-Sajf* man has to look for internal peace within the bounds of his own experience and maturity; and in *L-Imwarrbin* (1973; The Cliffhangers) he puts the past in confrontation with the present to reveal the workings of the individual conscience—here he makes use of the play-within-a-play technique to retain the link with reality. All the theatrical techniques that E. uses—roleplaying, use of symbolism, emotional displays, stylized dialogue, lighting, setting—are indicative of his experience as a director and an actor. His drama is self-conscious in its external manifestation but analytical of the human state in its thematic structures.

BIBLIOGRAPHY: Friggieri, J., "Drama—F. E.," in England, R., ed., *Contemporary Art in Malta* (1973): 19-28; Pollard, A., "F. E.: Novelist of Malta," *ACLLSB*, 2 (Jan. 1979): 73-79; Hopkins, K., and R. van Roekel, eds., *Crosswinds: An Anthology of Post-War Maltese Poetry* (1980); King, B., "F. E.," in Kirkpatrick, D. L., ed., *Contemporary Dramatists* (1988): 138-40

—CHARLES BRIFFA

ECHEGARAY, José

Spanish dramatist, b. 19 Apr. 1832, Madrid; d. 27 Sept. 1916, Madrid

Trained as a mathematician and an engineer, E. taught at the School of Civil Engineering until the revolution of 1868. Subsequently, he was elected to the Spanish Parliament and became the minister of finance. He was the founder of the Modern Bank of Spain and held other prominent public posts. He began to write plays while in exile. In 1875 he became extremely popular with his *En el puño de la espada* (1875; at the hilt of the sword). In fact, he clearly dominated the Spanish stage until the end of the 19th c. In 1904 he shared the Nobel Prize for literature with Frédéric Mistral (1830–1914). The literary generation that followed E., the so-called Generation of 1898, reacted negatively to this award in that to this group he represented Spain's decadence in political, social, and literary terms.

In 1874, under the pseudonym/anagram of Jorge Hayaseca, he published *El libro talonario* (the checkbook), a drawing-room comedy in which a young wife ingeniously turns tables on her unfaithful husband and in so doing demonstrates that crime is always punished. Even though after the staging of this play he held other important government positions, E. devoted himself almost exclusively to the theater as evidenced by the scores of plays he wrote.

A master of melodrama, E. brought new life to the dull Spanish stage that preceded him. At times, his characters are mere cardboard representations of human beings. His major virtue lies in the power to create and maintain suspense despite the relatively simple plots of his works, a trait that explains to an extent his association by critics with romantic drama. E.'s theater is one of extreme exaggeration. According to him, he often began his plays at the end in order to find very theatrical and, at times, high-handed conclusions to plots that were to him of secondary importance to the overall effect provoked by what he wrote. Generally speaking, it is accepted that E.'s theater lacks authenticity (referentiality) as it portrays a humanity possessed and dominated by unsubstantial—unauthentic—passion and truth. Thus, critics confront special difficulties in discussing his favorite themes (among them, honor, love, duty, religion, hypocrisy, and envy) in that their portrayal by E. had little to do with their exploration; they were used as excuses to awaken the interest of a public concerned with experiencing extreme superficial emotions during a given theatrical representation. In this sense, E. not only provided a useful indication of artistic sensitivity in Spain during the late 19th and the early years of the 20th c. (that is, after the revolution of 1868), but of a phenomenon labeled by the Spanish philosopher José ORTEGA Y GASSET "the revolt of the masses," a concept that is nowadays very much valued by those interested in, among others, the influence of mass communication in the postmodern era. E., to the extent that he successfully wrote dramatic texts appealing to the masses of his day, was a craftsman in that he was very much aware of the effect provoked by his plays; he was someone who calmly calculated the best way possible to appeal to his audience.

Among E.'s best plays is *O locura o santidad* (1887; *Madman or Saint*, 1912), a work that attempts to make a moral statement as its protagonist, Lorenzo Avendaño, does his best to surrender a fortune he has inherited after discovering he is not the real heir of this wealth. His actions are, however, frustrated by greedy relatives who declare him insane and, therefore, place him in an asylum. All of this is communicated by means of the extreme verbiage so typical of E., speech excesses that were much welcomed by Spanish audiences of the time.

E.'s masterpiece was *El gran galeoto* (1881; *The World and His Wife*, 1908), a work with clear connections with high comedy. In this play, society is blamed for the tragic developments that befall the play's main character as a result of the apparent unlimited power of public opinion. As is the case with many of his other works, this play documents E.'s tendency to juxtapose oversimplified and exaggerated themes in order to achieve intense theatrical effects. Thus, it is not surprising that the great Spanish playwright Ramón del VALLE-INCLÁN used *El gran galeoto* as a source of inspiration as to the lack of authenticity prevailing in the modern world, a world in which human beings were mere types, generic entities with passions that were mere abstractions, individuals who spoke words that were empty rhetoric.

E.'s style and approach to drama changed little during his career. In his case, the significance of his theatrical works lies not so much in the contribution made by a specific play but on his overall impact on the Spanish stage for several decades. From the 1870s to 1904, when he was awarded the Nobel Prize, E. was the fundamental Spanish dramatist, one able and willing to speak to the feelings of the Spanish masses, one in full communion with their views on the cosmos. Thus, E.'s theater is extremely significant in sociological terms as one attempts to understand a period of transition in Spanish history and aesthetics.

FURTHER WORKS: *La esposa vengador* (1874); *En el seno de la muerte* (1879); *La muerte en los labios* (1880); *Lo sublime en lo vulgar* (1890); *Un crítico incipiente* (1891); *El hijo de Don Juan* (1892; *The Son of Don Juan*, 1895); *Malas herencias* (1892);

Mariana (1892; *Mariana*, 1895); *El estigma* (1895); *Mancha que limpia* (1895); *La duda* (1898); *El loco dios* (1900; *The Madman Divine,* 1908); *Recuerdos* (1917)

BIBLIOGRAPHY: Olmet, L. Antón del, and Carraffa, A. García, *Los grandes españoles: E.* (1912); Curzon, H. de, *Un théâtre d'idées en Espagne: le théâtre de J. E.* (1912); Olmedilla, A. Martínez de, *J. E.* (1947); Newberry, W., "E. and Pirandello," *PMLA*, 81 (1966): 123–29; Mathías, J., *E.* (1970); Sánchez, R. G., "Mancha que no se limpia, o el dilema de E., " *CHA*, 297 (1975): 601–12; Sobejano, G., " E. Galdós y el melodrama, " *A Gald* (1978): 94–115; Fernandez, M.I. Martín, *Lenguaje dramático y lenguaje retórico* (1981); Ramón, F. Ruiz, *Historia del teatro español (desde sus orígenes hasta 1900)*, rev. ed., (1986): 350–58

—LUIS T. GONZÁLEZ-DEL-VALLE

ECO, Umberto

Italian semiotician and novelist (writing in Italian and English), b. 5 Jan. 1932, Allesandria, Piedmont

E. studied philosophy at the University of Turin, receiving his doctorate in 1954. In 1956 he published his thesis, *Il problema estetico in San Tommaso* (repub. as *Il problema estetico in Tommaso d'Aquino,* 1970; *The Aesthetics of Thomas Aquinas*, 1988). From 1954 to 1959, E. helped elaborate cultural programs in the Milan office of the RAI, the Italian state television network, an experience that contributed to his understanding of the mass media, which was to become a major subject of his writing. He was assistant lecturer of aesthetics from 1956 to 1963, and lecturer in 1963–1964, at the University of Torino. In 1964–1965 he was a lecturer in the architecture department of the University of Milano. From 1959 to 1976, E. was also a nonfiction editor for Bompiani Publishing House. He founded and now edits the journal of semiotics, *VS,* is the secretary general of the International Association for Semiotic Studies, and occupies the first chair of semiotics at the University of Bologna. Although a variety of interests made demands on his attention, E. was always attracted to the medieval world. In 1969 he published *Sviluppo dell'estetica madioevale* (development of medieval aesthetics), and his analysis of the Beato of Leibana's medieval manuscript was published in 1973 as *Beatus Apocalypses* (the apocalypses according to Beato of Leibana).

E. is internationally known for his contribution to the theoretical study of signs encompassing all cultural phenomena. Much of his study, including *A Theory of Semiotics* (1976), has been on the development of a methodology of communication. In 1980 and 1988, with the publications of *Il nome della rosa* (1980; *The Name of the Rose*, 1983) and *Il pendolo di Foucault* (1988; *Foucault's Pendulum,* 1989), E. extended the use of semiotics to the fiction genre. He has also demonstrated the practical applications of his theories in literary essays as well as newspaper and magazine articles.

At one time E. wrote for the literary magazine *Il Menabò,* edited by the socialist novelist Elio VITTORINI. One of the articles E. wrote for this magazine is "Del modo al formare come impengno sulla realtà" ("Form and Social Commitment"), since collected in *Opera Aperta* (1962; rev. ed, 1972; *The Open Work,* 1989). In this article E. expresses the desire that contemporary art seek solutions to contemporary crises by offering new ways of seeing, feeling, and understanding the universe. Art, therefore, in its special way is seen as an instrument for social change. A concern for social betterment is also E.'s leitmotiv in *Apocalittici e Integrati* (1964, rev. ed., 1977; the apocalyptic and the integrated). For E., the apocalyptic view is that of the intellectuals who think culture has been debased by mass media; and the integrated view is that of those intellectuals who see the nature of mass media as necessary and even desirable. E. takes an in-between position. He discusses the concepts of "Kitch" (which he defines as nonart that aspires to artistic status) and of entertainment (which acknowledges the complexity of the world in which we live). He advocates a form of entertainment that does not have a false artistic pretension. For E. entertainment must allow the viewers to be critical and to generate in themselves a sense of freedom of choice.

E. contributes regularly to daily newspapers (*Corriere della Sera*), weekly magazines (*L'Espresso,*) and artistic and intellectual periodicals (*Quindici, Il Verri,* et al.). Some of his articles have been collected in books such as *Diario minimo* (1963; rev. ed., 1976; minimal diary), *Il costume di casa* (1973; the habits of home), and *Dalla periferia dell'impero* (1977; from the periphery of the empire). In these books the reader can enjoy E.'s journalistic style—extremely humorous with a number of parodies.

E. knows several languages. He is married to Renate Ramge, a German-born graphic artist, who helped translate *Il pendolo di Foucault* into German. Among English-speaking writers E. feels a special affinity with James JOYCE. Like Joyce, E. was raised a Catholic and then left the church. In 1989, during an interview with Thomas Stauder, E. said, "The person who lived the religious experience can lose God, but not the religious dimension."

E.'s *Opera Aperta* collects his major presemiotic writings on modern art and literature. *Opera Aperta* served as a theoretical manifesto for the Grupo '63. This group created an avant-garde literary movement that flourished in Italy during the late 1950s and 1960s. *Opera Aperta* is a work on general questions of aesthetics in marked conflict with the Crocean concept of pure intuition-expression. It explains and justifies the difference between modern and traditional art. In the former, the artists leave the arrangement of some of their works' consituencies to the public, or to chance. On the contrary, classical or traditional art is unambiguous (even if it can elicit various responses). In fact, there is only one way to understand the text of a classical work. But modern forms of art require a much greater degree of collaboration and personal involvement on the part of the public. Modern art is associated with deliberate and systematic ambiguity. The whole notion of plurality of meaning overturns the Cartesian axes of the vertical and the horizontal, paradigm and syntagm. For E., a work of modern art is aesthetically successful when it produces "controlled disorder, organic fusion of multiple elements." For E., the modern open work is not entirely free. A formative intention is manifest in every work, and this intention must be a determining factor in the interpretative process. For E. modern art conveys a much higher degree of information, though not necessarily a higher degree of meaning. His interest in information theory was one of the factors that led to the study of semiotics.

While taking over many of the fundamentals of the structuralistic theory of Claude LÉVI-STRAUSS and Roman Jacobson (1896–1982) and of the theories of structural linguistics of Ferdinand de Saussure, E. drastically differs from them. For Saussure, meaning is the production of structure. E., however, maintains that structures are only methodological in the sense that they are provisional, hypothetical products of the mind and that they may only partially reflect the nature of things. E.'s first work on semiotics was *La struture assente* (1968, rev. ed., 1983; the absent structure), followed by *Le forme del contenuto* (1971; the form of the content) and *Il segno* (1973; sign). E.'s most advanced and systematic semiotic work is *A Theory of Semiotics,* written originally in English and then translated into Italian as *Trattato di semiotica general* (1975). *A Theory of Semiotics* was supplemented by the collection of essays *Semiotics and the Philosophy of Language* (1984).

Semiotics is the science of signs. All forms of intellectual, social, and cultural life can be viewed as sign systems. E.'s theory is mainly concerned with the general theory of signs. E. wants to develop a single framework for a comprehensive conceptual theory of signs within which all sign systems may be studied to facilitate a growing interaction among all of them.

For E. the process of communication entails a theory of "signs production:" that depends upon a system of signification entailing a theory of codes. The latter are sets of conventions that connect systems of expression to systems of content. Through codes we recognize a gesture, a picture, or a word as standing for a particular meaning.

Although not a science, semiotics can nevertheless be used in a rational way to critize literature, art, and films. In *Lector in fabula* (1979; reader in fable) E. gives a detailed study of reader responses to a work of art. In this work he develops general groups of categories that describe the process of interpretative cooperation between the text and the reader. At the same time E. attacks the STRUCTURALISM of the 1960s that attributes objective properties to works of literary art. According to E., the reader uses two main concepts in the process of interpretative cooperation: the "frames" and the "possible worlds." The former are several situations or sequences of action the reader inserts in the text in order to complete its meaning. The latter are possible worlds the reader projects into the text. *Lector in fabula* concludes with an analysis of an "open work," *Un drame bien parisien* (a very Parisian drama) by Alphonse Allais (1854–1905).

E.'s first novel, *Il nome della rosa,* is written in the genre of the detective novel, with appeal to the general reader. On the jacket of the first Italian edition E. writes that his novel may be read by three different groups of readers: The first group will be involved with the plot; the second group "will attempt to establish connections with the present"; and the third group "will realize that this text is a textile of other texts, a 'whodunit of quotations,' a book built of books." *Il nome della rosa* pays homage to Leibniz, as it is a book we read long before it was written. Undoubtedly it sheds light on how modern people might read the Middle Ages. Our reading of the past cannot be innocent, because it is "produced by the discourse upon it." In *Postille a Il nome della rosa* (1983; *Postscript to The Name of the Rose,* 1984) E. claims that the title came by chance: "I liked it because the rose is a symbolic figure so rich in meanings that by now it hardly has any meaning left."

Il nome della rosa is an electric literary work. In it are present history and semiotics, biblical exegesis and anthropology, medieval studies and literary theory. The story is told by the eighty-year-old Adso of Melk, who narrates what happened sixty-two years before during one week in 1327. He was the Dr. Watson of Brother William of Baskerville, a Franciscan from England who was visiting a wealthy Benedictine abbey in northern Italy. William went to the monastery to mediate a discussion between representatives of the Avignon Pope John XXII and the leaders of the Franciscan order regarding their differences in approaching the Franciscan vow of poverty. William finds the abbey in turmoil over the sudden and violent death of a monk. William is asked to revive his once famous gift for investigation. He solves the murder, though not before several other monks have been killed. The murders are all connected with the labyrinthine library of the abbey. In it is preserved the manuscript of the lost second book of Aristotle's *Poetics*, which deals with the subject of comedy. The monks who died had read the book and aspirated the poison smeared on it by Jorge de Burgos, an elderly blind monk who believed Aristotle's text was corrupt, and wanted to prevent its release. In the struggle that follows the discovery of the murderer, the monastery catches fire and burns down.

In the book two themes are clear: the conflict between intellectual freedom and repression; and the urge toward intellectual freedom. In *Il nome della rosa* the reader gets to know E.'s culture, love, doubts, sense of humor, and aesthetic tastes. The book is very humorous in the sense that it makes people laugh at the truth, as the only truth lies in learning to free ourselves from insane passion caused by truth. In the novel the Italian language is influenced by the languages in which E. reads, teaches, lectures, writes, and thinks. Latin is the common denominator, but if the readers do not understand the Latin, the detective plot still makes sense. *Il nome della rosa* has been translated into more than sixteen languages. In 1981 it won two of Italy's main literary awards, the Premio Viareggio and the Premio Strega, and France's Medici Prize. In the summer of 1983 the American edition topped the *New York Times* bestseller list, and a film version of the novel was made by French director Jean Jacques Arnaud.

In 1988 E. published his second novel, *Il pendolo di Foucault*. While the action of *Il nome della rosa* takes place in the Middle Ages, E.'s second novel displays the scenery of the modern world from 1968 to 1984. However, through numerous references to past centuries, *Il pendolo di Foucault* encompasses the whole history of the world. The narrator is Casaubon, a young philosophy professor. While he is writing his thesis on the process to the Templarians, he meets Jacobus Belbo, who works for Garamond Publishing House. Belbo invites Casaubon and his colleague Diotallevi to select the most scientific manuscripts on the secret of the Templarians for the publisher. Within a few years, the three friends realize there was no such secret. In a playful way they decide to invent the secret of the Templarians by themselves. They make believe the Templarians had elaborated a plan that was going to lead them to the control of all the energy in the universe. The friends invent a map that six different diabolical groups had supposedly put together and placed under Foucault's pendulum in the Conservatoire des Arts et Métiers in Paris. Here they are waiting unsuccessfully to find the center of the world's energy. The plan, which had started as an ironic and playful mimesis of diabolic argumentation, leads the three friends to their deaths. E. apparently wants to teach his readers that there is no other reality than the one offered by the immanent world. It seems that the novel deals with the hazards of intellectual overreaching and the impossibility of achieving definite answers to questions that beset us all. However, throughout the book E. tries to come closer to the unreachable and authentic reality of the mystery of our human existence, as when he writes about the "epiphanic moment" Bembo felt while playing the trumpet during a funeral in the presence of the town's authorities.

In E.'s two novels we find the Peircian theory of unlimited semiosis and the Bakhtinian views of the novel as an incorporation of various genres and a linguistic hybrid. In the two novels we can trace theories and comments from E.'s essays on different aspects of modern culture ranging from Woody Allen and Snoopy to Jorge

Luis BORGES and John BARTH and so on. E.'s novels are also books about books. In *Il nome della rosa* Adso says, "Now I realize that not infrequently books speak of books: it is as if they spoke among themselves."

In 1991, E.'s *Sguardi venuti da lontano* (looks come from afar) was published, launching a new discipline, "reciprocal anthropology." it is the result of a convention held in Italy. There a group of scholars from the African and Asian countries observed carefully the Western people and came to the conclusions that Westerners are barbaric. So the westerners, who used to pay little or no attention to the way others understood them, now must come to grips with this new historical reality.

E. is now in his sixties, and he is an energetic man with a prolific literary activity. We can expect many more books in the near future from him. However, he may not write any more novels. In a 1989 interview E. says in his usual playful manner, "to write the second novel means to show that I am able to produce more than one novel. To write a third novel is like to write thirty of them, and it doesn't make much sense."

FURTHER WORKS: *Filosofi in libertà* (1958); *Le poetiche di Joyce* (1965; repub. as *Le poetiche di Joyce dalla "Summa" al "Finnegan's Wake,"* 1966; repub. in English as *The Aesthetics of Chaosmos: The Middle Ages of James Joyce*, 1982); *La definizione dell'arte* (1968); *Il superuomo di massa* (1976; rev. ed., 1978); *Come si fa una tesi di laurea* (1977); *Sette anni di desiderio* (1983); *Sugli specchi e altri saggi* (1985). FURTHER WORKS IN ENGLISH: *Carnival!* (with V. V. Ivanov and Monica Rector, 1984); *Art and Beauty in the Middle Ages* (1986); *The Limits of Interpretation* (1990)

BIBLIOGRAPHY: Benson, T. W., on *A Theory of Semiotics, P&R,* 10 (Summer 1977): 214–16; Bruss, E., and M. Waller, "Interview with *U. E.*," MR, 19 (Summer 1978): 409–20; De Lauretis, T., *U. E.*, (1981); Robey, D., "U. E.," in Caesar, M. and Hainsworth, P., eds., *Writers and Society in Contemporary Italy* (1984); Lewis, T. E., "Semiotics and Interpretation: Before or After the Fact? U. E.'s *Semiotics and the Philosophy of Language*," PoT, 6, 3 (1985): 503–20; special E. issue, *SubStance*, 47 (1985); Richter, D. H., "E.'s Echoes: Semiotic Theory and Detective Practice in *The Name of the Rose*," StTCL, 10, 2 (Spring 1986): 213–36; Haft, A. J., J. G. White, and R. J. White, *The Key to the Name of the Rose* (1987); Frentz, T. S., "Resurrecting the Feminine in *The Name of the Rose*," *Pre/Text: A Journal of Rhetorical Theory*, 9, 3–4 (Fall–Winter 1988): 123–45; Inge, M. T., ed., *Naming the Rose: Essays on E.'s The Name of the Rose* (1988); Capozzi, R., "Palimpsests and Laughter: The Dialogical Pleasure of Unlimited Intertextuality in *The Name of the Rose*," *Italica*, 66, 4 (Winter 1989): 412–28; Luke, A., "Open and Closed Texts: The Ideological/Semantic Analysis of Textbook Narratives," JPrag, 13, 1 (Feb. 1989): 53–80; Viegnes, M., "Interview with U. E., " *L'Anello Che Non Tienne: Journal of Modern Literature* 2, 2 (Fall 1990): 57–75; Weaver, W., "Pendulum Diary," SWR, 75, 2 (Spring 1990): 150–78

—MICHELA MONTANTE

"Semiotics," says U. E., the world's first professor of semiotics, "is concerned with everything that can be taken as a sign. A sign is everything which can be taken as significantly substituting for something else. This something else does not necessarily have to exist or to actually be somewhere at the moment in which a thing stands in for it. Thus *semiotics is in principle the discipline studying everything which can be used in order to lie,"* But this is not a work of ethics or metaphysics. E. proceeds with order, lucidity, and tact to define the boundaries of semiotics (all of culture, from zoosemiotics to rhetoric) and to elaborate two semiotic processes—communication and signification—and their associated methodological approaches.

E. defines communication as "the passing of a signal . . . from a source . . . to a destination." Acts of human communication are made possible by signification, the process by which a code links "present entities with absent units." From this distinction, E. bases a theory of codes which is in turn the foundation for a theory of sign production (and interpretation).

E. proposes a theory of codes in which the semantics has to do with the content, understood as a unit of culture. Hence, meaning is a matter of cultural conventions and not of states of an objective world. This distinction requires, for instance, definitions of denotation and connotation that do not make them extensional versus international processes.

Thomas W. Benson, on *A Theory of Semiotics,*
P&R, 10 (Summer 1977), pp. 214–15

U.E.'s *Semiotics and the Philosophy of Language* engages readers in a discussion that is at once more and less ambitious than its title suggests. For many readers, the phrase "Philosophy of language" will serve to designate those writings associated with Anglo-American analytic philosophy. Yet E. devotes only eight and seven pages respectively to an examination of the work of Hilary Putnam and of Saul Kripke; only once or twice each does he mention an idea put forward by Carnap, Quine, Russell, Searle, or Wittgenstein. Parts of the book do facilitate a future encounter between semiotics and analytic philosophy, however, while the book as a whole contributes immediately to clarifying and developing some of the most fundamental areas of *Semiotics and the Philosophy of Language* surfaces as an attempt to wrest control of a series of key concepts from those who would wish to pursue semiotics exclusively as a formalist enterprise. I believe that the book generally succeeds in this endeavor because its arguments may be seen to accord methodological privilege to a semiotics of signification over a semiotics of communication. . . .

E. never asserts explicitly in this book that he now considers that a semiotics of signification should be made to govern a semiotics of communication. That he has finally come to enact this view in his most recent work, however, need provoke little surprise. Of course, in *A Theory of Semiotics* (1976), even as he stresses the interdependence of a theory of codes and a theory of sign production, E. exercises great care in attempting to establish the relationship between a semiotics of signification and a semiotics of communication on the basis of their relative autonomy and lack of hierarchy. Yet there occur several moments in *Theory* in which such happy relations verge upon collapse.

Thomas E. Lewis, "Semiotics and Interpretation: Before or After the Fact? U. E.'s *Semiotics and the Philosophy of Language,*" *PoT*, 6, 3 (1985), pp. 503–04

In U. E.'s *The Name of the Rose*, a murder mystery set in a medieval monastery, the learned Franciscan, Brother William of Baskerville, discovers that his misguided interpretation of the significance of a series of clues has led him to erroneously link several deaths that have taken place in the abbey. He comes to realize that there is ultimately no "right way" through and out of any labyrinth of clues, or signs. Although the signs themselves can be useful and valid, the idea that it is possible to create an enduring thread of meaning by linking them together and following them to a permanent truth is an illusion. "I have never doubted the truth of signs," says William to Adso, his young novice assistant; "they are the only things man has with which to orient himself in the world. What I did not understand was the relation among signs. . ."

The pursuit of signs in the quest for truth—the structure of every detective novel—is most metaphorically embodied in *The Name of the Rose* by the monastery's library. A huge labyrinthine construction with secret passageways, cryptic indices, and rooms within rooms of ancient books and scrolls holding diverse cultures and philosophies, it is guarded by zealous monks and is open only to a select few. Through the twists and truns of a plot that is yet another maze, William and Adso end up trying to utilize the library's winding structure and coded contents to lead them to the murderer.

In this novel, a parallel search to the hunt for the murderer goes on at the same time. Casually introduced in the first few pages as the purported subject of the frame story, in this optional search (the whodunit can be enjoyed without undertaking it), the reader is the detective, and the discovery he or she seeks is no less than the text itself. In an attempt to learn the nature and authority of its creator and its ultimate truth and reality, if any, the reader must penetrate the labyrinth of the novel's structure, find a way through and, by its twists and turns of signs, genres, translated codes, parodies, and intertextual culture clashes, to an awareness of the shape of the novel's universe.

Jocelyn Mann, "Traversing the Labyrinth: The Structures of Discovery in E.'s *The Name of the Rose,*" in M. Thomas Inge, ed., "Naming the Rose Essays on E.'s *The Name of the Rose*" (1988), pp. 130–31

The difficulties in trying, for nearly a decade, to classify *The Name of the Rose* under a specific label (metaphysical, mystery, detective or anti-detective story, post-modern, historiographic metafiction; historical, gothic or essay novel; *bildungsroman*, etc.) derive primarily from the plurality of meanings, and the plurality of texts, implanted in E.'s first bestselling novel. Even before the novel reached the public, privileged critics and friends of the author, such as Maria Corti, were already debating whether or not *The Rose* was an open or closed work. My conviction is that E.'s semiotic fabula, from its very structure, proves that texts are made of unlimited semiosis and unlimited intertextuality, and that a narrative is essentially a literary and linguistic pastiche of signs and systems of signs from the great encyclopedia of literature and language(s). *The Rose* illustrates the notion that with an aesthetic test the semiotic practice of writing and reading, coding and decoding, constructing and deconstructing (in short: the whole process of signification, communication, and interpretation) is an "interdisciplinary dissemination" of linguistic and cultural codes and of encyclopedic competence, of both writers and readers. His second novel, just published, *Il pendolo di Foucault*, certainly reconfirms this.

The Rose seems to have been written to demonstrate both the Peircean theorization of unlimited semiosis and the Bakhtinian views of the novel as a "developing genre" and as a linguistic and literary hybrid. . . . In fact, E.'s novel is a perfect example of conscious (and unconscious) "hybridization"; it is a text in which many other texts merge, fuse, collide, intersect, speak to, and illuminate, one another—each with its own language and "idealogue." *The Rose*, succinctly put, is a skillful (con)structure of an intentionally ambiguous, polyvalent, and self-reflexive novel intended to generate multiple meanings. Moreover, it is a novel which wishes to be: an intersection of textual "traces" and "textures"; a dialogue with many texts; and a literary text generated through the endless process of writing and reading, re-writing and re-reading, etc.

Rocco Capozzi, "Palimpsests and Laughter: The Dialogical Pleasure of Unlimited Intertextuality in *The Name of the Rose*," Italica, 66, 4 (1989), pp. 412–13

ECUADORIAN LITERATURE

Ecuador won its independence from Spain on May 24, 1822, and during the rest of the 19th c. many of the country's leading intellectuals devoted their efforts to defining and consolidating the newly formed Ecuadorian nation. Two of the country's principal figures of that period were Juan León Mera (1832-1894) and Juan Montalvo (1832-1889), a political conservative and a political liberal whose literary works illustrate the ideological conflicts of the times. Mera's Indianist novel, *Cumandá* (1879; Cumandá), considered one of Latin America's principal examples of romanticism, defined the nation in terms of its supposed Christian and *mestizo* nature and argued for the assimilation of Ecuador's native

peoples (the "savage" majority) by its European-bred leaders (the "civilized" minority). At the same time Montalvo unleashed his anticlerical and liberal teachings in his volatile essays that denounced the abuses of power characteristic of the political and ecclesiastical leadership of the period. Montalvo claimed that his essays were responsible for the assassination in 1875 of Gabriel García Moreno, Ecuador's principal conservative president and dictator of the period.

The social and political orientation in much of the literature published by Mera and Montalvo continued to influence Ecuador's major writers of the 20th c. The literature of protest written within the tradition of social realism was an offshoot of Montalvo's libelous writings while the modern works that have stressed Ecuador's search for a national *mestizo* identity were grounded in Mera's contributions. In either case, Ecuador's principal writers of the 20th c produced a literature of social commitment, calling for social justice, freedom and democracy.

Fiction

Ecuadorian narrative of the 20th c. flourished from the 1930s to the 1970s. With the founding in the 1920s of the Socialist and Communist Parties, along with numerous labor strikes, economic failures, and the general political upheaval of the decade, a group of young intellectuals believed they could contribute to the much-needed revolution through their literature. In 1930 a collection of short stories entitled *Los que se van* (Those Who Go Off) was published by three writers from Guayaquil: Joaquín GALLEGOS LARA, Enrique Gil Gilbert (1912-1973), and Demetrio AGUILERA MALTA. With their frank use of language and honest depiction of the social conditions in which most Ecuadorians lived, they revolutionized the way writers would portray the country's downtrodden and oppressed masses. Together with José de la Cuadra (1903-1941) and Alfredo PAREJA DIEZCANSECO, these five writers formed El Grupo de Guayaquil (the Guayaquil Group); their works generally focused on the lives and mores of the Ecuadorian coast, and a modest sampling of their major publications would include such novels as *Cruces sobre el agua* (1946; Crosses on the Water) by Gallegos Lara, a novel about the tragic 1922 labor strike in Guayaquil; Gil Gilbert's *Nuestro pan* (1942; Our Daily Bread) deals with the workers of the rice fields; Aguilera Malta's *Don Goyo* (1933; *Don Goyo*, 1980) describes in mythical terms the relationship between man and nature, revealing the extent to which uncontrolled capitalist investment brings about ecological disaster; Pareja Diezcanseco's *El muelle* (1933; The Dock) protests the exploitation and injustice suffered by a prototypical Ecuadorian worker; de la Cuadra's *Los Sangurimas* (1934; The Sangurimas Family), frequently cited as a forerunner of Latin American MAGIC REALISM, explores the superstitions and struggles of Ecuador's *montuvios*, a group of rural people from the Pacific coast.

Fictional writing also flourished outside of Guayaquil during this period. Jorge ICAZA wrote Ecuador's most internationally acclaimed novel, *Huasipungo* (1934; *The Villagers*, 1964), and set the tone for Latin America's *Indigenista* narrative that championed Indian rights. Adalberto Ortiz (b. 1914) authored *Juyungo* (1943; *Juyungo*, 1982), a novel about Ecuador's Afro community from Esmeraldas, which many consider a major example of Afro-Hispanic narrative. Nelson Estupiñán Bass (b. 1912) wrote *Cuando los guayacanes florecían* (1954; *When the Guayacanes Were in Bloom*, 1987) and has established himself as one of Latin America's most prominent Afro writers.

By the 1950s, when Ecuador's social protest literature had become stale and predictable, writers began to look for new themes and forms of expression. Curiously, it would be a writer of the 1930s who would inspire much of Ecuadorian fiction's resurgence of the 1970s. Unlike his contemporaries who emphasized overt protest and concentrated their attention on the country's rural and poor, Pablo Palacio (1906-1947) created a fictional world of irony and ambiguity as he dissected the tragically petty and uninspired lives of the urban middle class in *Débora* (1929; Debora) and *Vida del ahorcado* (1932; The Life of the Man Who Was Hung), key novels of Latin American vanguard fiction of the 1920s and 1930s.

Although Ecuadorian writers continued honoring their predecessors' socially committed themes, with the advent of the 1970s, the younger writers would be characterized by their use of parody, irony, history, and language. Eliécer Cárdenas (b. 1950) wrote *Polvo y ceniza* (1978; Dust and Ashes), a novel about a popular Robin Hood-type bandit, who instead of being depicted as a social misfit is seen as an epic hero. Jorge Velasco Mackenzie (b. 1949) has written about the conflicts and changing demographics of Guayaquil, Ecuador's largest city, in *El Rincón de los Justos* (1983; The Corner of the Just); he has also concentrated his literary talents on rewriting/deconstructing segments of Ecuador's official history: *Tambores para una canción perdida* (1986; Drums for a Lost Song) deals with a runaway slave and *En nombre de un amor imaginario* (1996; In Name of an Imaginary Love) revisits the period when a scientific team measured the Equator from the Ecuadorian Andes. Other major fiction writers of the last quarter of the 20th c. are Iván Egüez (b. 1944), author of *La Linares* (1976; The Linares); Abdón Ubidia (b. 1944) who wrote *Sueño de lobos* (1986; Wolves' Dreams, 1997); Alicia Yánez Cossío (b. 1929) whose *Bruna, soroche y los tíos* (1973; Bruna, Soroche, and Relatives) reclaimed a prominent place in literature for women writers and female protagonists; and Raúl Pérez Torres (b. 1941), one of Ecuador's principal short-story writers, recipient of such prestigious literary awards as the Casa de las Américas Prize (1980) and the Juan Rulfo Prize (1994), and author of *Los últimos hijos del bolero* (1997; The Last Sons of Love Ballads).

Poetry

Although Ecuador's modernist poets of the beginning of the 20th c. have traditionally been criticized as escapist and decadent, and thus, not central to the development of Ecuadorian letters, they were very much a part of a general rethinking of the role of the writer and literature in society that took place throughout Latin America, particularly in light of the growing influence of capitalism in the region.

New imagery and stylistic experimentation of the period would bear fruit among later poets. Gonzalo Escudero (1903-1971) was noted for his formalized poetry that tested each reader's ability to comprehend unexpected metaphors as in *Altanoche* (1947; High Night). Jorge Carrera ANDRADE is Ecuador's most renowned poet; his uniqueness lies in his ability to celebrate the simple things of life in a poetry that is full of visual images and metaphors clearly evident in *Hombre planetario* (1959; Planetary Man). Jorge Enrique Adoum (1923) also wrote about his surrounding world, but with a deeply critical eye and a strong voice of social protest visible in *Ecuador amargo* (1949; Bitter Ecuador) and in *Dios trajo la sombra* (1959; God Brought the Shadow), which won the first Casa de Américas Prize for poetry in 1959. Other notable poets are Efraín Jara Idrovo (b. 1926), who experimented with musical forms

and the auditory effects of language that characterize *Sollozo por Pedro Jara* (1978; Sob for Pedro Jara), and Euler Granda (b. 1935), who wrote *La inútilmanía y otros nudos* (1973; The Useless Mania and Other Knots), poetry of social protest against the ruling class and the excesses of capitalism. Julio Pazos (b. 1944) won the Casa de las Américas Prize for poetry in 1982 for his *Levantamiento del país con textos libres* (The Lifting of the Country with Free Texts).

Drama

Unlike the other literary genres in Ecuador, drama has not enjoyed wide support. Although one can name individuals who have written dramatic pieces, generally they have not done so with any consistency or long-term commitment. Among Ecuador's best-known dramatists, albeit few in number, is Francisco Tobar García (b. 1928), author, actor, director, and promoter, who wrote such plays as *Parábola* (1958; Parable) and *La noche no es para dormir* (1960; Night Time Is Not for Sleeping), plays that are Kafkaesque, ironic, and deeply cynical. José Martínez Queirolo (b. 1931) has also been relentless in his efforts to write short dramatic works and to stage them. His theater is marked by satire and humor and a keen interest in local customs apparent in works such as *Cuestión de vida o muerte* (1970; A Question of Life or Death) and *Q. E. P. D.* (1970; May You Rest in Peace). Alvaro San Félix (b. 1931) has specialized in historical drama that focuses on some of Ecuador's major political figures such as Gabriel García Moreno in *La herida de Dios* (1979; God's Wound) and Eloy Alfaro in *Caudillo en llamas* (1979; Leader in Flames). Hugo Salazar Tamariz (b. 1923) is known for his social and political theater exemplified in *El habitante amenazado* (1973; The Threatened Inhabitant).

The Essay

The Ecuadorian essay has a long and rich tradition covering all topics pertinent to national life and culture. Seminal works include *El indio ecuatoriano* (1922; The Ecuadorian Indian) by Pío Jaramillo (1894-1978), *Ecuador: drama y paradoja* (1948; Ecuador: Drama and Paradox) by Leopoldo Benites Vinueza (1905-1995), *Cartas al Ecuador* (1943; Letters to Ecuador) by Benjamín Carrión (1897-1979), *Entre la ira y la esperanza* (1976; Between Wrath and Hope) by Agustín Cueva (1937-1992), and *Aproximaciones y distancias* (1986; Approximations and Distances) by Fernando Tinajero (b. 1940). As has been the case throughout Latin America, Ecuador's essayists have devoted their energies and talents to examining and defining their national identity. While many of the earlier writers tended to be generalists who would write about any and all national themes, after World War II essayists became more specialized and concentrated their writings on topics related to their particular areas of professional expertise—history, sociology, literature, and politics. Regardless of the genre, Ecuadorian literature stands out for an unfailing commitment to create a more just society and to offer testimony on behalf of those people who continue to be voiceless and powerless.

BIBLIOGRAPHY: Sacoto, A., *Sobre el ensayo ecuatoriano contemporáneo* (1988); Varas, P., *Narrativa y cultura nacional* (1993); Castelo, H. R., *Lírica ecuatoriana contemporánea* (2 vols., 1979); Universidad de Cuenca y Casa de la Cultura, *La literatura ecuatoriana de las dos últimas décadas: 1970-1990* (1993); Handelsman, M., *Amazonas y artistas: Un estudio de la prosa de la mujer ecuatoriana* (2 vols., 1978); Harrison, R., *Entre el tronar épico y el llanto elegíaco: simbología indígena en la poesía* *ecuatoriana de los siglos XIX-XX* (1996); Robles, H., *La noción de vanguardia en el Ecuador* (1998)

—MICHAEL HANDELSMAN

EDGELL, Zee

Belizean novelist (writing in English), b. 10 Oct. 1940, Belize City, British Honduras (now Belize)

Born Zelma Inez Tucker, E. grew up in Belize City where she developed a passion for writing while in grade school at Holy Redeemer. Nurtured by Sister Andretta Reyes, principal of the school, E. wrote an essay on why she wanted to become a writer when she grew up. E. explains that in those days women didn't have a lot to do outside of the home, church, and school, so she was always delighted to have a book, and when she discovered that one could write about very ordinary things, she was even happier. In the early 1960s E. wrote for the *Daily Gleaner*, a newspaper in Kingston, Jamaica. Later she went to London to study journalism and returned to Belize where she edited a small newspaper and taught at her former high school, St. Catherine Academy. She began writing fiction seriously at the age of thirty-five and published her first novel, *Beka Lamb*, in 1982. Though still writing, E. entered academic life in 1993, and she currently teaches at Kent State University in Kent, Ohio.

E. is the first Belizean writer of international renown and her three novels, *Beka Lamb*, *In Times Like These* (1991), and *The Festival of San Joaquin* (1997), have been published to notable critical and popular acclaim. Her works express the extent to which Belize is a multicultural and multiracial society, the extent to which the women of the society from the various groups are connected, and the extent to which Belize's nationalistic impulses have the ability to mend fractures. She writes about ordinary people whose lives play out against the backdrop of political and social issues affecting the county. And in this way, she has made a lasting contribution to literature, history, and sociology. Principally known for her novels, she has recently begun to write short stories for publication. Her first two short stories, "The Longtime Story" and "My Uncle Theophilus," were published in 1998 and continue her expose of ordinary people caught up in the drama of society.

Beka Lamb assured E. a place in the annuals of Caribbean and world literature. The novel took some seven years to complete. The wife of a diplomat and mother of two children, E. began the novel in Afghanistan, continued it in the U.S., and completed it in Bangladesh. The first novel written by a Belizean writer to reach an international audience, *Beka Lamb* is the story of a fourteen-year-old girl, Beka Lamb, who grows into maturity during the turbulent years of the 1950s in Belize. At fourteen Beka is completely immersed in her multiracial society. There are at least six racial groups inhabiting the country: African, West Indian, Central American, European, North American, and Asian. Beka hails from a middle-class, Creole family. The Caribs are a mixture of African and Caribbean Indians, Bakras are local whites, and Panias are Mexican. Early, the reader understands the traditional social standing of each group as Beka discovers where and how she fits into her world. Beka's dream of being left on the wrong side of town is central to her movement into womanhood. In her dream she goes to that side of town where the govern house is located, where the sailors work, and where the library of Bliss Institute is located.

While "that side" holds the appeal of the seat of government, commerce/travel, and knowledge, it is also the seedy side and a place where her father would chide her for being. The dream signals the destruction of the illusion of security, a necessary occurrence for the onset of womanhood/adulthood. E. engages the memory as a means of explaining how the character has arrived at the present. It features the events that led to the death of a dear friend, Beka's decision to stop lying and to channel her energies to story writing/creation against the backdrop of the nationalistic movement in Belize.

In Times Like These might be read as a companion piece to *Beka Lamb*. Together the two novels chart, in miniature, the development of Belize during a thirty-year period, from 1951 to 1981, years in which the former British colony experienced sweeping social and political changes. The novel begins with the return of Pavana Leslie, the central character who had been absent from Belize for some fifteen years. Like many of the educated class of Belize, after completing one phase of education, residents would set off to do advance work in the seat of the empire and absent themselves from society for many years. Pavana, a former member of the internal set, decides to return home to reconnect to lost values. She returns with her twins who had been conceived by a now prominent member of the Belizean ruling class during her student days in London. Set principally in Belize in March 1981, the novel examines Belize's bid for independence from both British and Guatemalan claims, the preoccupation of the émigré attempting to readjust to Belizean society, and the question of women and development, among others.

The Festival of San Joaquin is set in the small Mestizo community of San Joaquin, seventy-two miles from Belize City, where residents believe in spirits, ghosts, Catholicism, evangelism, and the sanctity of the home. It is the story of Luz Marina Figueroa, a descendant of a poor Indian family, and her relationship with the son of a powerful landowning family who takes Luz Marina as his common law wife. The work is something of a departure from E.'s first two novels in that the plight of the uneducated Mestizo woman is central to the plot. After years of abuse, Luz Marina murders her abusive spouse, serves fifteen months in jail for his murder, and returns to her community in the hopes of regaining her children. This is the story of a woman who fights back against a community in which women are expected to passively endure the whims of their men. As with her other novels, this work also considers the political realities of the time such as the land grabbing deals executed by foreign investors.

In his "Introduction to Belize" written for *Latin American Research Review*, Bruce Ergood decries Belize's lack of presence in scholarship written about Central America, stating that a real difference exists between viewpoints of Belizean and U.S. analysts. E.'s literature offers a balanced portrait of the country and its residents' preoccupations. E.'s genius rests with her ability to call on the people themselves to tell their stories. As medium, she assumes the persona of the varied residents of the country to record the story and perspectives for prosperity.

BIBLIOGRAPHY: Hunter, C., "Literature: Belize's First Novel, *Beka Lamb*," *Belizean Studies*, 10 (1982): 14-21; Bromley, R., "Reaching a Clearing: Gender and Politics in *Beka Lamb*," *Wasafiri*, 2 (1985): 10-14; Blain, V., P. Clements, and I. Grundy, "Z. E.," *The Feminist Companion to Literature in English* (1990): 328; Ergood, B., "Belize: An Introduction," *LARR*, 26 (1991): 257-65; Shea, R. H., "The Person She Wants to Be," *Bell Lettres*, 8 (1992): 38;

Wilentz, G., "'One Life is not Enough': An Interview with Z. E.," *Obsidian II*, 9 (1994): 27-45

—ADELE S. NEWSON

EDWARDS, Jorge

Chilean novelist, short-story writer, and essayist, b. 29 July 1931, Santiago

Born into a prominent bourgeois family of English ancestry, E. graduated with a degree in law from the University of Chile and subsequently studied international relations at Princeton University. From 1957 until 1973 he was a member of the Chilean diplomatic corps. After his resignation he moved to Spain and in 1978 returned to Chile where he still maintains his residence. Known throughout the Hispanic world as a journalist, E. also served as president of the Chilean Commission on Human Rights during the Pinochet dictatorship.

E. is perhaps best known for his *Persona non grata* (1973; *Persona non grata: An Envoy in Castro's Cuba*, 1977). This volume of memoirs chronicles his experiences as the Chilean government's chargé d'affaires in Havana, where he was sent in 1970 by socialist President Salvador Allende to reopen diplomatic relations between the two countries. After three frustrating months in Havana, E. became disillusioned with the Cuban revolution and was asked by the Cuban government to leave his post.

With the publication of *Persona non grata,* E. came under attack from the Latin American intellectual community because his book appeared at approximately the same time as the military coup in Chile, when unity among leftists was considered essential. E.'s memoirs, however, do not constitute a political tract inspired by right-wing sympathies, but rather a soul-searching quest undertaken by an intellectual who confronts the realities of a police state and expresses his negative reactions. In his short stories E. broke with the traditional depictions of Chilean rural life and introduced universal themes such as middle-class decadence and alienation stemming from dehumanizing government bureaucracy. Evident also in his stories are his experiments with innovative techniques and his explorations of the elusive boundaries between reality and fantasy.

E.'s first novel, *El peso de la noche* (1964; the weight of the night), portrays a conservative bourgeois family whose decline symbolizes middle-class decadence within Chile's rigidly stratified society. *Los convidados de piedra* (1978; the stone guests), E.'s most complex novel, is a mosaic of modern Chilean society. Its foreground action represents a fiesta in the home of Sebastián Agüero during the month of October 1973. Although it is Sebastián's birthday, the real occasion for the celebration is the recent overthrow of the socialist régime of Salvador Allende whose policies the host and his guests, all archconservatives, detest. The fiesta lasts an entire night during which the revelers evoke in desultory fashion episodes from the past involving characters from various levels of society. This intricate work unveils the political and social tensions that festered for decades prior to the military coup.

El museo de cera (1981; the wax museum) is best described as a political allegory, with occasional flights of fantasy, whose plot parallels events in Chile during the years immediately before and after Allende's fall from power. In the opening pages the aging Marqués de Villa Rica discovers his young wife Gertrudis and her Italian piano teacher Sandro making love in the music room of his mansion. Outraged, he expels the couple and hires a sculptor to create life-size wax figures of Gertrudis and Sandro making love, and another of the Marqués himself surprising them in their illicit act. The Marqués then places the wax figures in the music room of his mansion, which has remained unoccupied since the day Gertrudis and her lover left. The subsequent surrealistic episodes—an example is a modern dictator's television appearance in a medieval city—suggest that Chile under Pinochet was an anachronism and the Marqués de Villa Rica's wax museum, the symbol of a nation frozen in time.

In his most recent novel, *El anfitrión* (1987; the host), E. continues to quarry the rich vein of recent Chilean history, this time presenting a modern version of the Faust legend. Faustino Piedrabuena, a Chilean socialist exile bored with his life in East Berlin, meets Apolinario Canales (Mephistopheles), who treats him to the debauchery of capitalism in West Berlin and then offers him a new past, making him a noncontroversial figure and thus qualifying him to become Chile's post-Pinochet leader. E. has invented this fantasy as a vehicle for satirizing the political maneuvers in his native land along with the obstacles to healing old wounds. *Adios, poeta* (1990; Good-bye, poet) is not only E.'s highly readable memoir of his friendship with Pablo NERUDA, but also a fascinating view of contemporary Chilean society.

Although E.'s fiction concentrates on recent Chilean history, his sensitively drawn characters, dreamlike fantasies, and complex structural techniques all but eliminate the national boundaries of his settings. One of Chile's most talented and widely read writers today, E. is steadily broadening his reputation both throughout and beyond the Hispanic world.

FURTHER WORKS: *El patio* (1952); *Gente de la ciudad* (1961); *Las máscaras* (1967); *Temas y variaciones. Antología de relatos* (1969); *Desde la cola del dragón Chile y España, 1973–1977* (1977); *La mujer imaginaria* (1985)

BIBLIOGRAPHY: Dorfman, A., "¿Volar?: Un estudio de la narrativa de Skármeta y E.," *RChL*, 1 (1970): 133–54;; Turner, J. H., on *Persona non grata, Chasqui*, 4, 1 (1974): 84–85; Llosa, M. Vargas, "Un francotirador tranquilo," *Contra viento y marea (1962–1982)* (1984): 201–12; Moody, M., "J. E., Chile, and *El museo de cera,*" *Chasqui*, 14: 2–3 (Feb.–May 1985): 37–42; Alegría, F., "J. E," *Nueva historia de la novela hispano americana* (1986): 385–90; McMurray, G. R., on *La mujer imaginaria* by J. E., *WLT*, 61, 1 (Winter 1987): 93; Otero, J., "Subjetividad y mito como medos narratives en *Personal non grata* de J. E.," *Confluencia*, 5, 1 (1990): 47–53

—GEORGE R. MCMURRAY

EEDEN, Frederik Willem van

Dutch novelist, dramatist, and poet, b. 3 May, 1860, Haarlem; d. 16 June, 1932, Bussum

In his parents' home and at school E. was steeped in the positivistic, materialistic atmosphere prevalent in the second half of the 19th c. But as he reached adulthood, he developed a mystical outlook, which in 1922 culminated in his conversion to Roman Catholicism. He also took a strong interest in social issues, which induced him to establish a short-lived communal living project named Walden, in honor of Thoreau. In 1908–9 E., who was on friendly terms with Upton SINCLAIR, made a trip to the U.S., in the course of which he founded another commune in North Carolina.

A psychiatrist by profession, E. nonetheless vigorously pursued his literary career. He belonged to the generation of the "Movement of '80," and was involved in its journal, but his religious and political preoccupations were irreconcilable with the movement's predominantly aesthetic orientation. He had a greater affinity with such foreign authors as Tolstoy and the German romantics, whose favorite motifs—the mysterious, hypnosis, dreams, the Orient, death, spiritism, demons, lunacy—he incorporated into his own books. The novel which established him as a writer and which remains his best-known work, *De kleine Johannes* (3 vols., 1887, 1905, 1906; *The Quest*, 1907), is based on a narrative by E. T. A. Hoffmann (1776–1822). It relates the evolution of a child's ineradicable idealism, which in defiance of the rationalistic pressures of the modern world matures into faith in man's eternal soul.

Van de koele meren des doods (1900; *The Deeps of Deliverance*, 1902) is E.'s most significant novel, the one he himself considered to be a synthesis of all his main themes. The plot, dealing with a woman's erotic misadventures, decline into drug addiction and prostitution, and eventual religious salvation, was derived from an actual case history. The outspoken treatment of female sexuality was sufficiently daring to create a stir, but formally the novel lacks sophistication.

E.'s literary output was by no means limited to novels. Besides prodigious translating activity, which included nine volumes of Rabindranath TAGORE'S work, E. wrote copious amounts of poetry. Many of his contemporaries considered his writing for the theater to be particularly important. He had, in fact, started his literary career with some comedies, and he went on to write historical plays, as well as social satires for the stage. E.'s work in the drama—a relative rarity in modern Dutch literature—was in great demand, especially in German theaters. Although his work lacks enduring aesthetic value, E. was a major figure in the literary renewal in the Netherlands, which began in the late 19th c.

FURTHER WORKS: *Het rijk der wijzen* (1882); *Het poortje of de duivel in Kruimelburg* (1884); *Het sonnet* (1884); *Panopticum* (1884); *Frans Hals* (1884); *Grassprietjes* (1885, under pseud. Cornelis Paradijs); *De student thuis* (1885); *Kunstmatige voeding bij tuberculose* (1886); *De psychische geneeswijze* (1888); *Don Torribio* (1890); *Aan den keizer aller Russen* (1890); *Ellen* (1890); *Studies* (6 vols., 1890, 1894, 1897, 1904, 1908, 1918); *Johannes Viator* (1892); *Het beginsel der psychotherapie* (1892); *De broeders* (1894; also known as *De broederveete*); *Het lied van schijn en wezen* (3 vols., 1895, 1910, 1922); *Lioba* (1897); *Enkele verzen* (1898); *Twaalf sonnetten* (1898); *Waarvoor werkt gij?* (1899); *Waarvan leven wij?* (1899); *Van de passieloooze lelie* (1901); *De blijde wereld* (3 vols., 1903, 1905, 1906; *Happy Humanity*, 1908); *In kenterend getij* (1906); *De vrije arbeid op Walden* (1906); *Brieven* (1907); *Minnestral* (1907); *IJsbrand* (1908; *Ysbrand*, 1910); *Dante en Beatrice* (1908); *De nachtbruid* (1909; *The Bride of Dreams*, 1913); *De idealisten* (1909); *Het paleis van Circe* (1910); *Welt-Eroberung durch Heldenliebe* (1911); *Open brief aan de padvinders* (1911); *Sirius en Siderius* (3 vols., 1912, 1914, 1924); *Nieuwe nederlandsche dichtkunst* (1913); *Paul's ontwaken* (1913); *Aan de vrije jeugd* (1914); *Bij 't licht van de oorlogsvlam* (1915); *De heks van Haarlem* (1915); *De bokkenrijder* (1918); *Jezus' leer en verborgen leeven* (1919); *Literatuur en leeven*

(1920); *Kerk en communisme* (1921); *Het roode lampje* (1921); *Het godshuis in de lichtstad* (1921); *Uit Jezus' oopenbaar leeven* (1922); *Aan mijn engelbewaarder, en andere gedichten* (1922); *Isméa of de stervende vlinder* (1923); *De geest der waarheid* (1923); *Deutsch-Chinesische Liebes-Mosaik* (1923); *Eucharistie* (1924); *Langs de weg* (1925); *De legende van Sancta Sura* (1926); *Jeugdverzen* (1926); *Mijn dagboek* (9 vols., 1931–1945); *Over dromen* (1956); *De briefwisseling tussen F. v. E. en Lod. van Deyssel* (1964)

BIBLIOGRAPHY: Macdonald, M. I., "Poet, Novelist, and Practical Communist," *Craftsman*, 14 (1908), 126–36; Meijer, R. P., *Literature of the Low Countries* (1978): 248–50 and passim

—EGBERT KRISPYN

EGYPTIAN LITERATURE

As with other literary traditions within the Arab world, modern Egyptian literature is the product of two major forces: the revival of the great Arabic heritage of the past and the influence of modernization through contact with Europe and America. The force of the impact between these two phenomena varied considerably according to time and place. In the case of Egypt, the process was abrupt, resulting from Napoleon's invasion in 1798. This military incursion served both to rid Egypt of its Mamlūk rulers and to expose its intellectual leaders to European thought. The process was further stimulated after 1860 by the arrival of numerous writers from Syria, where civil war had forced many Christian families to flee to Europe and the Americas as well as to Egypt. Many members of those families had already been involved in the revival of interest in the Arabic language and its literature. These and other Syrians were now to join Egyptian writers in making major contributions to the emergence of an indigenous modern Arabic literature in Egypt and of the press (which has always been and remains the principal means of propagating literature in Egypt).

At the turn of the century, the prevalence of the "traditional" or the "modern" varied according to genre. It is hardly surprising that poetry, by far the most prevalent medium of literary expression in the "classical" period, should have produced a modern neoclassical revival, the more conservative proponents of which carefully watched and often vigorously resisted attempts at change well into the 1950s. Pride of place as pioneer in this movement must go to Mahmūd Sāmī al-Bārūdī (1839–1904), while the patriotic fervor and violent attacks on the British occupying forces guaranteed Hāfiz Ibrāhīm (1871–1932) a warm place in Egyptian hearts. However, it is Ahmad Shawqī (1868–1932) who is undoubtedly the greatest poet of the period. While some commentators have rightly drawn attention to glimmerings of a more individual vision that can occasionally be seen in poems of these and other poets like them, it remains true that the vast bulk of their writings are occasional verse *(shi'r al-munāsabāt)*, a fact that elicited the wrath of later critics.

While both fiction and drama may have had precedents of one kind or another in the earlier tradition of Arabic literature, the beginnings of both genres in the modern period point to their derivative origins in the West. While poets were imitating the stentorian tones of earlier exemplars, pioneers in fiction and drama translated and imitated European models, before attempting their own creative offerings. 'Uthmān Jalāl (1828–1898) translated some of Molière's plays into colloquial Egyptian. An Egyptian Jew, Ya'qūb Sanū' (1839–1912), began to write a series of satirical playlets poking fun at the aristocracy and the Khedive Ismā'īl (ruled 1863–79). Drama at this time was very much a "popular" phenomenon, with much melodrama, and singing and dancing almost as a *sine qua non*. The tradition was carried on into this century by Najīb al-Rīhānī (1891–1949), who followed Sanū's example by writing comedies that poked fun at the foibles of various segments of society.

The rise of fiction is closely associated with the rapid expansion of the press in the 1880s and 1890s. Newspapers would regularly publish stories and novels in serial form. It was in this way that Jurjī Zaydān (1861–1914) published a whole series of historical novels dealing with Islamic history; these had a plainly educational purpose, but were "spiced" with local interest and romance so as to make them at least somewhat similar to the love, murder, and intrigue narratives that characterized other fictional writings of the era. Equally educational but more topical was Muhammad al-Muwaylihī's (1868–1930) *Hadīth 'Īsā ibn Hishām* (1898–1902; *Hadīth 'Īsā ibn Hishām*, 1974, also pub. as *A Period of Time*, 1992), which provided a marvelous exposé of the many faults of Egyptian society and its institutions under British administration. More straightforward in both style and sentiment were the series of essays on a variety of topics by Mustafā Lutfī al-Manfalūtī (1876–1924), which have remained popular among adolescents for many decades.

These writers and others were to carry out the vital tasks of adapting the older tradition to the needs of modern times, of experimenting with new genres, and of applying new language to the older genres. All this was an essential preliminary to the emergence of an indigenous tradition of modern Egyptian literature.

During the past two decades Egypt has gone through a process of rapid social, economic, and political change and development, something that has produced a variety of effects within the cultural sector. The move to a more open, market-oriented economy and the development of a parliamentary system, with a number of political parties and press organs to reflect their points of view, has offered Egyptian citizens new opportunities and challenges, not all of them regarded as favorable and beneficial by the indigenous populace. The ever-growing size of the population and the problems of housing and agriculture, while long anticipated, continue to impinge upon the life-style and expectations of most Egyptian families. These issues form an often problematic backdrop to literary creativity within the country.

In the specific area of literary genres, the two spheres in which change is most noticeable are those of fiction and criticism. That is not, of course, to maintain that everything has remained static in the realm of poetry and drama, but rather to suggest that a number of factors, some involving the more overtly political aspects of the cultural sector, others more subtle and complex, has led to a gradual but perceptible realignment in the relative prominence accorded the different literary genres in Egypt and the attention that each receives from critics, whether Egyptian or non-Egyptian. A younger generation of poets and dramatists continues to produce large quantities of work, but the cultural press will often contain articles whose authors allude to problems associated with the publication and reception of poetry and drama in Egypt today.

Among significant trends in contemporary Western literary criticism and theory that are providing new insights into the Egyptian literary tradition, one of the most interesting is that of women's literature and FEMINIST CRITICISM. On the public level, the role of Qāsim Amīn (1865–1908) as the pioneer in the process of raising the consciousness of his countrymen regarding the status of women in Egyptian society has long been acknowledged. At the turn of the century he published two famous works on the subject: *Tahrīr al-mar'a* (1899; women's liberation) and *Al-Mar'a aljadīda* (1901; modern woman). Within the more literary realm, recent research has shown that women writers were recording their creative output, sending it to each other, and publishing their views in a number of women's journals in the 19th c. However, it was not until the emergence of a series of women's movements throughout the region in the 1920s and the concomitant growth in educational opportunities that women were to be able to emerge as full contributors to the literary tradition of Egypt. The increasing number of women writers in Egypt who are making notable contributions to the literary tradition are successors and beneficiaries of the often courageous efforts of such prominent earlier figures as "Āe'isha al-Taymūriyya (1840–1902), Hudā Sha 'rāwī (1879–1947), and Nabawiyya Mūsā (1890–1951).

Poetry

In 1908 Khalīl Mutrān (1872–1949), known as the "poet of the two countries" (Lebanon and Egypt), published a collection of poetry, *Dīwān al-Khalīl* (the diwan of al-Khalīl) with an important introduction, in which he stated that the poet should be able to express his own feelings and urged poets to devote more attention to the unity of their compositions. While some of his poems show signs of such precepts of romanticism, the bulk of Mutrān's poetry was as occasional as that of Ahmad Shawqī and Hāfiz Ibrāhīm. The real motivating force toward romanticism was the émigré school in the Americas, where a group of poets experimented with form, language, and mood in surroundings essentially detached from the forces of conservatism that were so strong in the Middle East. In Egypt the advocacy of romanticism fell to the so-called "Diwan" school of poets, 'Abbās Mahmūd al-'Aqqād (1889–1964), Ibrāhīm al-Māzinī (1890–1949), and 'Abd al-Rahmān Shukrī (1886–1958), all of whom were strongly influenced by the English romantic poets and critics such as William Hazlitt (1778–1830). Of the three, Shukrī was the greatest poet, while the other two had more influence at the time through their critical writings, which appeared in a volume called *Al-Dīwān* (1921; the diwan). This work contained iconoclastic attacks on Shawqī for his occasional versifying and on al-Manfalūtī for his morbid sentimentality, but more vicious and destructive was al-Māzinī's attack on Shukrī himself, something that had a profound effect on the poet.

In the 1930s a new school of romantic poets emerged who took their name from the magazine *Apollo*, published under the aegis of Ahmad Zakī Abū Shādī (1892–1955). He and other poets like Ibrāhīm Nājī (1893–1953) and 'Alī Mahmūd Tāhā (1902–1949) introduced poetry of a new sensibility to Egypt, particularly during the 1930s. While Abū Shādī wrote a vast amount of poetry and Nājī also wrote a great deal, mainly about unrequited love, Tāhā is probably the most enduring poet of the group.

In a collection called *Plutoland* (1947; Plutoland) the litterateur and critic Lewis 'Awad (1915–1990), who terms the poetry of the romantics "*mal de siècle* poetry," made what some critics consider to be the first attempts at writing free verse; the earliest poem dates from the late 1930s. If this is so, he predates by almost a decade the efforts of Nāzik al-Malā'ika (b. 1923) and Badr Shākir AL-SAYYĀB in Iraq. At any rate, Egyptian poets have, since the end of World

War II, joined their colleagues in other Arab countries in writing poetry outside the dictates of the classical metrical system, ranging from poems using some of the traditional feet in different combinations, to free verse and the prose poem.

The most famous of these poets is Salāh 'ABD AL-SABŪR; his first collection, *Al-Nāsu fī bilādī* (1957; the people in my country), displays considerable commitment to the ideals of the emerging revolutionary society, with its realistic descriptions of life (as in the title poem). During the 1960s this vigorous posture changed to a more personal, melancholy vision. One of 'Abd al-Sabūr's most successful works is the verse play *Ma'sāt al-Hallāj* (1964; *Murder in Baghdad*, 1972), which recounts the story of the crucifixion of a medieval Islamic mystic with considerable skill and impact and with a not too covert contemporary import. Other poets have also made contributions to this genre: the yet more committed 'Abd al-Rahmān al-Sharqāwī (b. 1920), with such plays as *Ma'sāt Jamīla* (1962; the tragedy of Jamīla) and *Tha'r Allāh* (1969; God's revenge); and the very Brechtian contributions of Najīb Surūr (1932–1978) in the form of elongated poetic tableaux drawing their inspiration from popular tales of Egypt, such as *Yāsīn wa Bahiyya* (1963; Yāsīn and Bahiyya). Another Egyptian poet whose writings continue to capture the imagination of readers throughout the Arab world is Ahmad 'ABD AL-MU'TĪ HIJĀZĪ, who, having come to the modern metropolis after a village childhood, depicted the depersonalization and crushing anonymity of the big city, as, for example, in *Madīna bilā qalb* (1959; heartless city). Thereafter, his poetry became more concerned with the cause of commitment to the Egyptian revolution and its leader, Jamāl 'Abd al-Nāsir (Gamal Abdel Nasser).

While Egyptian poetry has tended to stand apart from the more conspicuous attempts at innovation, such as those of ADŪNĪS in Lebanon, in recent times a small group of younger poets in Egypt has been experimenting with new forms and new language; among these we should mention are Amal DUNQUL and Muhammad Abū Sinna (b. 1937). It remains generally true, however, that, in the Egypt of the early 1980s, poetry no longer commands the public attention it has traditionally held since the beginnings of Arabic literature. Its position as the preeminent genre has been taken over by fiction, particularly short fiction.

A number of Egyptian poets continue to retain a position of prominence throughout the Arab world: Ahmad 'Abd al-Mu'tī Hijāzī, Muhammad 'Afūfā Matar (b. 1939), Mahmūd ibrāhīm Ibrāhīm Abū Sinna (b. 1937), Fārūq Shūsha (dates n.a.), and Ahmad Suwaylim (b. 1942). The tragically early death of Amal Dunqul deprived the Egyptian and broader Arabic poetic tradition of one of its most effective and beloved voices, as seen in such collections as *Ta'līq 'alī mā hadath* (1971; commentary on what happened), *Al-Bukā bayna yaday Zarqā al-Yamāma* (1973; lament before Zarqā' al-Yamāma), and *Maqtal al-qamar* (1974; slaughter of the moon). Ahmad Fu'ād Nigm (b. 1929) has earned a wide following in the realm of colloquial poetry with collections such as *Bilādā wa-habābatā* (1973; my country and beloved) and *Ishā yā Misr* (1979; wake up, Egypt), as has 'Abd al-Rahmān al-Abnūdī (b. 1938), who is also a prominent scholar in the field of Egyptian folklore.

A good deal of poetry by younger writers is published in Egypt, normally in one of the many literary periodicals. These outlets, however, offer only ephemeral recognition, and, while a number of collections in book form continue to be published, no figures from this new generation of poets have thus far emerged to a sufficient degree to merit placement alongside the more prominent names mentioned above. The normal difficulties of obtaining public

recognition must be added the fact that in Egypt, poetry no longer seems to command the degree of public attention that it has traditionally done since the beginnings of Arabic literature. A number of possible factors are habitually cited to explain this situation; the popularity of short fiction and the close links between it and the popular media certainly appear to be among the most cogent.

Fiction

The most significant among early works of Egyptian fiction that had any pretensions of depicting contemporary reality was the novel *Zaynab* (1913; Zaynab) by Muhammad Husayn Haykal (1888–1956), written in France and published under a pseudonym. By the time of the second edition of this work (1929), a whole school of Egyptian writers had begun producing short stories. It was between 1910 and 1920 that attempts had first been made to emulate the European short story, and especially those of France and Russia. The early efforts of Muhammad Taymūr (1892–1921) were followed by stories by his brother Mahmūd TAYMŪR, by one of Egypt's major contributors to this genre, Mahmūd Tāhir Lāshīn (1894–1954), by Yahyā HAQQĪ, and by others. The efforts of this "new school" during the 1920s, as well as the great impact of the first volume of Tāhā HUSAYN'S *Al-Ayyām* (3 vols., 1925, 1939, 1967; *An Egyptian Childhood*, 1932; *The Stream of Days*, 1948; *A Passage to France*, 1976), fostered an increasing interest in fiction.

The 1930s saw tremendous activity in this genre. It began with a competition in novel writing, which was won by Ibrāhīm al-Māzinī with *Ibrāhīm al-kātib* (1931; *Ibrahim the Author*, 1976), which, in spite of the author's denials, seems to be an autobiographical piece. A major advance in the use of dialogue in the novel was achieved by Tawfīq AL-HAKĪM is his *'Awdat al-rūh* (1933; the return of the spirit), the first part of which gives a lively portrayal of a group of Egyptian characters within a limited environment. The psychological dimension is investigated by 'Abbās Mahmūd al-'Aqqād in his *Sāra* (1938; *Sara*, 1978) to a degree which robs it of some of its artistic appeal but which was to serve as a model for later novelists. These and other experiments served to develop the different facets of this complex genre; the writers of the next generation were able to proceed on the basis of the successes and failures of their predecessors.

At the end of the 1930s there emerged the figure who has dominated Egyptian fiction for the last two decades, Najīb MAHFŪZ. With his series of novels set in the old quarters of Cairo, written in the 1940s and early 1950s, the Egyptian novel may be said to have achieved its full maturity. To a tremendous skill in construction is added great attention to detail, a clear, straightforward style typical of a well-read civil servant (his career until his retirement in 1971), and an underlying social-realist purpose of showing the gradual breakdown of the societal fabric in Egypt as mirrored in the antagonisms and violence preceding the revolution of 1952. By April of that year, he had completed his monumental *Al-Thulāthiyya* (1956–57; the trilogy), a trilogy tracing an Egyptian family through three generations, with a sweep worthy of a GALSWORTHY. During the 1960s, Mahfūz produced a further set of novels of which *Al-Liss wa al-kilāb* (1961; the thief and the dogs) and *Tharthara fawq al-Nīl* (1966; chatter on the Nile) are probably the best. These concentrate more than his earlier works on the individual within society and his sense of alienation. After the debacle of the Six Day War in June 1967, he expressed his views in lengthy short stories and even a few plays, before returning to the novel during the 1970s.

In the realm of the short story, Yūsuf IDRĪS has shown a particular talent. His works not only display a clear development in technique and themes, but also an adventurous attitude toward the use of language. Mahfūz's language tends to be relatively uncomplicated, even to the point of being occasionally colorless. Idrīs, on the other hand, sprinkles his style with colloquialisms and unorthodox syntax, which lend to his stories an attractive element of liveliness and innovation.

While Mahfūz and Idrīs have dominated Egyptian fiction, there are a number of other excellent writers of their generation. The novels of al-Sharqāwī, especially *Al-Ard* (1954; *Egyptian Earth*, 1962), present a realistic and obviously committed view of the Egyptian peasant. Fathī Ghānim (b. 1924) has written several fine novels such as *Al-Rajul alladhī faqada zillahu* (1960; *The Man Who Lost His Shadow*, 1962) and *Al-Jabal* (1957; the mountain). In the realm of the short story, Edwar AL-KHARRĀT and Yūsuf al-Shārūnī (b. 1924) both write with intense meticulousness.

Egyptian writers reacted with varying degrees of fury, sorrow, and contemplation to the events of June 1967. A younger generation of writers, who emerged in the 1960s, expressed these feelings with particular clarity. These younger writers have in many ways found their path blocked, not only by the tremendous popularity of the writers of older generations, who, with a few exceptions, have kept a hold on most of the positions of influence within the cultural sector, but also as a result of the cultural policies of the Sādāt government, which tended to offer publication opportunities in Egypt only to writers who were prepared to tolerate—or, at least, not express opposition to—the political and social status quo. Writing fiction has never been a full-time occupation in Egypt, and that is certainly more true today than ever before. Many of the younger authors do their writing in their spare time, and, with this in mind, the quality of work produced by such short-story writers as Majīd Tūbiyā (b. 1938) and Yahyā al-Tāhir 'Abdallāh (1942–1980) and novelists like 'Abd al-Hakīm Qāsim (1935–1990) and Jamāl AL-GHĪTĀNĪ is remarkable. The late 1970s offered signs of the revival of a vigorous fictional tradition.

In recent years the world of Egyptian fiction has been dominated by the award of the Nobel Prize in literature in 1988 to the country's most illustrious novelist, Najīb Mahfūz, an event that has brought his works in translation to the attention of a wider audience than has been the case with any other Arab author. Both the award itself and Western and Arab reaction to it have been the occasion for much debate concerning the role of fiction in the Arab world in general and in Egypt in particular, and the relative merits of the Arabic and Western novelistic traditions. The Nobel citation itself makes it clear that the award was granted on the basis of works that Mahfūz published before the June War of 1967, a period concerning which it can be said without exaggeration that he laid the groundwork for the development of an Arabic novel tradition upon which many others have been able to build. With regard to Mahfūz's own writing in recent times, he has produced a large number of works in both novel and short-story form. However, their appeal has not been as broad as was the case with his earlier works; the primary focus has been on local Egyptian issues, and he has often resorted to fictional techniques first essayed in novels written in previous decades. Among his most notable novels from this period are *Malhamat al-Harāfish* (1976; epic of the riffraff) and *Rihlat Ibn Fattūma* (1982; Ibn Fattūma's travels).

Among a younger generation there are a number of writers who have made significant contributions to the novel genre. Pride of place for originality must go to Jamāl al-Ghītānī, who in a series of works has used the styles and structures of earlier types of Arabic narrative as a framework for fictions that discuss the dilemmas of the present; worthy of particular mention are *Al-Zayni Barakat* (1974; *Al-Zayni Barakat*, 1988), *Waqā'i' hārat al-Za'farānī* (1976; *Incidents in Zafrany Alley*, 1986); and *Kitāb al-tajalliyyāt* (3 vols., 1983–1987; book of revelations). The prominent Egyptian feminist writer and physician Nawāl AL-SA'DĀWĪ; has written several novels that portray the status of women in Egyptian society in a graphic and often strident fashion that seems to diminish the gap between author and narrator; among her most famous works are *Mudhakkirāt tabība* (wr. 1959; *Memoirs of a Female Physician*, 1988), *Imra'a 'inda nuqtat al-sifr* (1977; *Woman at Point Zero*, 1983), and *Suqūt al-Imām* (1987; *The Fall of the Imam*, 1988). Only slightly less prolific than these writers are Sun'allāh Ibrāhīm (b. 1937), whose troubled career, emblematic of the issues of writers' freedom in the region, is reflected in the incidents recorded in his works of fiction such as *Tilka al-Rā'iha* (ca. 1960s; *The Smell of It*, 1971) and *Al-Lajna* (ca. 1970s; the committee); 'Abd al-Hakīm Qāsim (1935–1991), whose first novel, *Ayyām al-insān al-sab'a* (1969; *The Seven Days of Man*, 1989) was instantly recognized as a major contribution to the Arabic novel genre and who, after his return from a lengthy period in East Berlin, produced a steady stream of fictional works; and Muhammad Yūsuf al-Qu'ayyid (b. 1944), whose works have moved from an early realism in describing events in the Egyptian countryside of his own childhood to a more symbolic approach, thus from *Akhbār 'izbat al-Minīsī* (1971; *News from the Meneisi Farm*, 1987) to *Shakāwā al-Misrī al-fasīh* (1983; complaints of the eloquent Egyptian). Among other contributors to the Egyptian novel in recent decades, mention should be made of Abū al-Ma'ātī Abū al-Najā (b. 1932), Ibrāhīm Aslān (b. 1939), Hudā Jād (b. 1923), Edwar al-Kharrāt, Sabrī Mūsā (b. 1932), and Bahā' Tāhir (b. 1935).

Almost all the writers just mentioned have also made contributions to the short story. In more recent decades Yūsuf Idrīs, the acknowledged master of the genre in previous decades, made occasional contributions, but few, if any, of them managed to match the artistry and innovative quality to be found in examples from his earlier collections. He himself tended to concentrate much of his attention on short articles for the Cairo daily newspaper *Al-Ahrām*, many of which were collected in volumes such as *Shāhid 'asrihi* (1982; witness of his age).

Even if Idrīs's mastery of the short story is generally acknowledged, there is no shortage of other distinguished contributors to the genre. Edwar al-Kharrāt has written many stories marked by a symbolic and allusive language that seems at times more akin to that of poetry, while an equally careful craftsman and critic, Yūsuf al-Shārūnī (b. 1924) has contributed a smaller but valuable selection of realistic and symbolic stories. In addition to these two author-critics, a whole generation of younger authors has struggled in generally unfavorable political and economic circumstances to eke out some kind of career as creative writers; in addition to names already mentioned in connection with the novel, we may cite *Yahyā al-Tāhir 'Abdallāh* (1942–1980), 'Abd al-'Āl al-Hamamsī (b. 1932), Diyā' al-Sharqāwī (1938–1977), and Majīd Tūbiyā (b. 1938). Another distinctive voice that has emerged during the 1980s has been that of Alīfa Rif'at (b. 1930) who, like Nawāl al-Sa'dāwī, has been concerned with reflecting women's issues in her stories; while the tone of the narrative in Rif'at's fictions may be more muted, it is no less effective.

The popularity of the short story as a literary genre has led to the publication of a large number of individual stories and collections, although it has to be acknowledged that a great deal of the production is of purely ephemeral merit. Among emerging writers whose works seem destined to endure, Salwā Bakr (dates n.a.), Jār al-Nabī alHilw (b. 1945), Muhammad al-Makhzanjī (b. 1950), Munā Rajab (b. 1953), and Mahmūd al-Wardānī (b. 1950) show considerable promise.

Drama

The dramatic tradition in Egypt traces its origins back to the 19th c., although some critics find precedents of one kind or another in still earlier works of belles lettres or folk literature. The popular theater began with the works of Ya'qūb Sanu' and was carried on into this century by Najīb al-Rīhānī. This tradition has continued with undiminished vigor to the present day, and its success can be attributed not only to the popular predilection for farce but also to its unabashed use of the colloquial language, which appeals to the broadest spectrum of society.

The development of "literary" or "serious" drama has been dogged by two issues. The first is the initial association of the genre with music and singing; the historical verse dramas of Ahmad Shawqī, which contain much fine poetry, have been preserved and even revived on the basis of certain songs that were made extremely popular by famous singers. The second issue is the much discussed question of language: particularly to conservative critics, anything not composed in the written language was not literature, whereas to practitioners of the drama, plays not in the spoken language were restricted in their possible themes and extremely difficult to act. It was the great contribution of Tawfīq al-Hakīm to raise the status of the genre and provide it with plays of more stimulating intellectual content. To critics like Tāhā Husayn, al-Hakīm's first lengthy play, *Ahl al-kahf* (1933; *The People of the Cave*, 1971) is a major monument in the history of Arabic literature. Al-Hakīm has followed it with a whole series of similar intellectual plays, among the latest of which is *Al-Sultān al-hā'ir* (1960; *The Sultan's Dilemma*, 1973). All these plays have proved difficult, if not impossible, to stage effectively, a fact that has led several commentators, al-Hakīm included, to retreat to a position that claimed them as "plays to be read." Al-Hakīm has produced a huge number of short plays, on social and political issues.

The revolution of 1952 saw the beginning of the two most productive decades in the history of Egyptian drama. A new generation of playwrights emerged who made significant innovations in both language and form. In a whole series of works, Nu'mān 'Āshūr (1918–1987) brilliantly captured the combination of dynamism and uncertainty following the revolution at all levels of society within the new political structure and exposed many of the inherent problems by showing the clash of generations. In the 1960s Sa'd al-dīn Wahba (b. 1925) began by describing society in realistic terms, although he concentrated initially on the countryside. Later, in plays such as *Kubrī al-nāmūs* (1964; mosquito bridge) and *Sikkat al-salāma* (1965; road to safety), a more symbolic trend can be seen. In two of his most recent works, *Al-Masāmīr* (1967; the nails) and *Sab' sawāqī* (1969; seven waterwheels), he discusses the implications of 1967 with a bitter frankness that led to the banning of the latter play.

Alfred FARAJ drew the inspiration for his comments on the present from history and the folktale; his plays on historical subjects include *Sulaymān al-Halabī* (1964; Sulaymān from Aleppo) and *Al-Zīr Sālim* (1967; Prince Salim). From the famous *1001 Nights,* Faraj took themes for two of his best and most popular works, *Hallāq Baghdād* (1964; the barber of Baghdad) and *'Alī*

Janāh al-Tibrīzi wa tābi'uhu Quffa (1969; *'Alī Janāh from Tabriz and Quffa his henchman*). Among the most important of Faraj's contributions is the use of the literary language in a way that permitted effective stage productions.

A number of other plays were performed with great success in the 1960s: Mahmūd Diyāb's (b. 1932) *Al-Zawba'a* (1964; *The Storm*, 1967); Rashād Rushdī's (b. 1915) *Rihla khārij al-sūr* (1963; *Journey outside the Wall*, 1974), with its heavy symbolism; Yūsuf Idrīs's *Al-Farāfīr* (1964; *The Farfoors*, 1974; also tr. as *Flipflap and His Master*, 1977), with its combination of folklore, slapstick, and the absurd.

During the 1970s and into the 1980s the drama, being the most public of all genres was particularly subject to the vicissitudes of politics and cultural policy. The term "theater crisis" has become a stock phrase of the majority of commentators on the drama, and the forced or unforced absence from the country of a number of critics and directors, and the reticence of several prominent dramatists mentioned above suggests that the present cultural milieu will need to change before we may see a revival of the dynamic tradition of earlier decades.

The problems inherent in the production of Arabic drama on stage—the question of the appropriate level of dramatic language, the debates over public and private financing of production, issues of censorship or "reading committees," the competence and training of actors and directors, the overall political and cultural situation—all of these factors have conspired to pull the Egyptian dramatic tradition in a variety of directions; some might say that the result has been to pull it apart. Since the drama is the most public of all literary genres, it is perhaps hardly surprising that similar difficulties are being encountered in almost all the countries of the Middle East region. In the particular case of Egypt, theater seasons in recent times tend to be divided between productions of a seemingly endless stream of domestic farces—which, it has to be acknowledged, have been a staple of the Egyptian drama tradition from the outset—and adaptations or translations of works culled from the world tradition of drama.

As a consequence of the varying combinations of the above factors at different periods, most critics and dramatists look back on the era of the 1950s and 1960s, for all its political difficulties, as a golden age in Egyptian drama.

Criticism

As is the case with the literature itself, the early criticism of the modern period harks back to the classical ideals, as is clearly seen in the writing of Husayn al-Marsafī (?–1889) and the celebrated criticism on the poet Ahmad Shawqī written by Muhammad al-Muwaylihī in 1898. The first signs of change can be seen in the writings of the Dīwān school. Al-'Aqqād, the most prominent critic in the group, was one of a select number of writers who contributed to the development of literary sensibilities and critical taste in Egypt during the first half of this century. Particular mention should be made of Tāhā Husayn, whose iconoclastic work *Fī al-shi'r al-jāhilī* (1926; on pre-Islamic poetry) was among the first to apply the objective principles of literary criticism to the earliest examples of Arabic literature; Muhammad Husayn Haykal, whose advocacy of objectivity in criticism and of the concept of national literature did much to foster a particularly Egyptian identity during the 1920s and 1930s; and Muhammad Mandūr (1907–1965), a disciple of Tāhā Husayn, whose brilliant studies of both literature and literary criticism were to lay the foundation for the emergence of a number of critics still writing today.

In the aftermath of World War II, 'Abd al-'Azīm Anīs (b. 1922) and Mahmūd Amīn al-'ālim (dates n.a.) produced a famous work of criticism, *Fī al-thaqāfa al-Misriyya* (1955; on Egyptian culture), in which they advocated the need for commitment in literature. This book started a fierce debate among literary scholars, including Tāhā Husayn, who vigorously opposed this notion. During the 1950s and into the 1960s al-'ālim remained a very prominent figure in Egyptian criticism along with Lewis 'Awad, the cultural editor of *Al-Ahrām*. Other writers tended to concentrate on one particular aspect of literature: 'Alī al-Rā'ī (dates n.a.), Rajā' al-Naqqāsh (dates n.a.), and Bahā' Tāhir (b. 1935), for example, tended to deal with the theater, 'Abd al-Muhsin Tāhā Badr (dates n.a.) and Sabrī Hāfiz (b. 1941?) concentrated more on fiction, and 'Izz al-dīn Ismā'īl (dates n.a.) turned his attention to a number of studies on literary theory from a variety of viewpoints.

The political uncertainties that accompanied the period both before and after the June War of 1967 have been particularly reflected in the realm of criticism. Several critics left Egypt or remained in exile for many years, among them Mahmūd Amīn al-'Ālim, 'Alī al-Rā'i, Ghālī Shukrī, and Sabrī Hāfiz (dates n.a.). In recent years the cultural environment has stabilized to a considerable degree, and many critics have felt able to return to their homeland and publish their views in the plethora of cultural journals that are available. There they have joined colleagues from various generations in forging a newly enlivened critical environment. A representative list of significant critics would include, in addition to those mentioned above, 'Abd al-Qādir al-Qitt, Rajā' al-Naqqāsh, Jābir 'Asfūr, Mahmūd al-Rabī'ī, Tāhā Wādī, and Muhammad al-'Inānī (dates n.a.). The status of literary criticism has also been bolstered by the publication of two excellent journals specializing in criticism, *Fusūl*, edited by one of Egypt's most accomplished literary critics, 'Izz aldīn Ismā'īl, and *Alif*, edited by Ceza Qāsim (Kassem) (dates n.a.). These publications and a continuing series of conferences at which critics from Egypt, the Arab world, Europe, and the Americas meet to discuss issues of literary history, criticism, and theory are providing a solid basis for the fostering and development of a diverse and probing critical tradition in Egypt and continuation of the lively literary community that is its focus.

BIBLIOGRAPHY: Sakkut, H., *The Egyptian Novel and Its Main Trends 1913–1952* (1971); Kilpatrick, H., *The Modern Egyptian Novel* (1974); Semah, D., *Four Egyptian Literary Critics* (1974); Awad, L., "Problems of the Egyptian Theatre," in R. C. Ostle, ed., *Studies in Modern Arabic Literature* (1975): 179–93; Badawi, M., *A Critical Introduction to Modern Arabic Poetry* (1975), passim; Hafiz, S., "Innovation in the Egyptian Short Story," in Ostle, R. C., ed., *Studies in Modern Arabic Literature* (1975): 99–113; Hafiz, S., "The Egyptian Novel in the Sixties," *JArabL*, 7 (1976), 68–84; Allen, R., "Egyptian Drama and Fiction in the 1970s," *Edebiyat*, 1 (1976), 219–33; al-Jayyusi, S., *Trends and Movements in Modern Arabic Poetry* (1977), passim; Allen, R., "Egyptian Drama after the Revolution," *Edebiyat*, 4 (1979): 97–134; Jād, A. B., *Form and Technique in the Egyptian Novel 1912–1971* (1983); Brugman, J., *An Introduction to the History of Modern Arabic Literature in Egypt* (1984); Allen, R., ed., *Modern Arabic Literature* (1987); Badawi, M. M., *Modern Arabic Drama in Egypt* (1987); Badran, M. and M. Cooke, eds., *Opening the Gates: A Century of Arab Feminist Writing* (1990); Booth, M., comp., *My Grandmother's Cactus: Stories by Egyptian Women* (1991)

—ROGER ALLEN

EHRENBURG, Ilya Grigorevich

Russian novelist, memoirist, journalist, and poet, b. 27 Jan. 1891, Kiev, Ukraine; d. 1 Sept. 1967, Moscow

E. was born in Kiev, but when he was five his parents moved to Moscow, where he grew up and received his secondary education. He was active in the 1905 revolution, was imprisoned, and then from 1909 to 1917 lived abroad, writing poetry. In 1914 he became war correspondent for a major St. Petersburg newspaper and, in the wake of the February 1917 revolution, returned to Russia. Four years later he left the U.S.S.R. once more, spending much of the 1920s and 1930s in Belgium, France, and Germany. He covered the Spanish Civil War, and in 1941 settled for good in Russia, traveling abroad after that only for visits or on official assignments. During World War II he reported from the eastern front. Having survived the "black years" of the Stalinist period, he heralded the new, more open mood of Soviet society with a novel, *Ottepel* (1956; *A Change of Season*, 1962).

E.'s writing during the 1920s reflected the approach then in vogue, of ridiculing the rhetoric and pretensions of both the capitalist and the communist systems. *Neobyknovennye pokhozhdenia Khulio Khurenito* (1922; *The Extraordinary Adventures of Julio Jurenito and His Disciples*, 1930; later tr. under same title, 1963), a remarkable grotesquerie and probably E.'s best work of fiction, dates from this period. *Burnaya zhizn Lazika Roytshvantsa* (1928; *The Stormy Life of Lasik Roitschwantz*, 1960), describing the "magnificent absurdity" of the revolution, is a Soviet version of Jaroslav HAŠEK'S *The Good Soldier Svejk*. Of his work of the mid-1930s two novels stand out: *Den vtoroy* (1933; *Out of Chaos*, 1934) and *Ne perevodya dykhania* (1935; without pausing for a breath). *Den vtoroy* is a vulgar apologia for SOCIALIST REALISM; *Ne perevodya dykhania* shows E.'s acceptance of official governmental policy in economic and political matters.

E. was one of the most popular and widely read writers of World War II, his searing, indignant reportage serving as a catalytic inspiration to the Red Army, then beleaguered by the invasion of Nazi forces. His *Padenie Parizha* (1941; *The Fall of Paris*, 1943), a crushing indictment of Nazism, earned him his first Stalin Prize; *Burya* (1949; *The Storm*, 1949), his second. These two books, together with *Devyaty val* (2 vols., 1952; *The Ninth Wave*, 1955), make up an engrossing if manipulative historical series, set in France and Russia.

During the more repressive early postwar years E. was, predictably, attacked for his "cosmopolitanism," his Jewish parentage, and his positive assessment of the cultural and intellectual give-and-take of the 1920s in Russia. (E. described himself as a "Soviet citizen of Jewish nationality," and in another place wrote, "I belong to those whom it is proper to persecute.") Having survived against considerable odds the treacherous zigzags of the Stalinist era—among other ways, by discreet reticence, by aiding in the purge of Soviet Jewish intellectuals and writers, and by ridiculing the newly established State of Israel—E. was, after Stalin's death in March

1953, among those who championed intellectual liberation, freer artistic expression, and the dismantling of the reigning political mythology. While not an enduring work of art, his *Ottepel* was a harbinger of the fundamental shifts to come and was emblematic of the transition from Stalinist terrorism to the next stages of Soviet history.

The last years of E.'s life were given over to promoting "rehabilitated" writers and to writing six books of valuable memoirs, an occupation which he shared with other Soviet literati of the 1960s such as Valentin KATAEV, Konstantin PAUSTOVSKY, Korney Chukovsky (1882–1969), Samuil Marshak (1887–1964), and Viktor Shklovsky (b. 1893). These volumes—*Lyudi, gody, zhizn* (1961–66; *People and Life, 1891–1921*, 1962; *Memoirs: 1921–1941*, 1964; *The War, 1941–1945*, 1964; *Post-War Years, 1945–1954*, 1966)— constitute a historical panorama, describing from a sophisticated and refined perspective the writers and artists E. had known and the political movements, gatherings of the intelligentsia, and artistic schools he had observed or participated in.

History will record that E.'s prolific output enjoyed wide popularity during his lifetime. Finally, however, his political adaptability, mordant cynicism, and cautious ideological aggressiveness—punctuated by recantations—had the impact of trivializing his talent, too often pushing him in the direction of opportunism and compromise and raising serious questions about how enduring his place in literature will be. The recipient of two Stalin Prizes for literature, the Lenin Peace Prize, and the Order of Lenin, E. was a paradigm of survival in the Soviet context: negotiating the shoals of Party-line shifts, retreating, advancing, retracting, and then adopting an apparently bold public stand. His silence about the destruction of Soviet Jewish intellectuals in August 1952 was the moral nadir of his career. He seems to have attempted to atone for this during the last years of his life by a concerted campaign to have published works by writers who had earlier been politically condemned by the regime; and by advocating the value of artistic innovation, individual creativity, and personal integrity.

FURTHER WORKS: *Stikhi* (1910); *Ya zhivu* (1911); *Oduvanchiki* (1912); *Budni* (1913); *Poety Frantsii, 1870–1913: Perevody* (1914); *Detskoe* (1914); *Povest o zhizni nekoy Nadenki i o veshchikh znameniyakh, yavlennykh ey* (1916); *O zhilete Semyona Drozda* (1917); *Molitva o Rossii* (1918); *Ogon* (1919); *V zvezdakh* (1919); *Lik voyny: Vo Frantsii* (1920); *Razdumya* (1921); *Kanuny: Stikhi 1915–1921* (1921); *Portrety russkikh poetov* (1922); *Zarubezhnye razdumya* (1922); *Zolotoe serdtse, misteria* (1922); *Veter, tragedia* (1922); *Moskovskie razdumya* (1922); *Opustoshayushchaya lyubov* (1922); *A vsyo-taki ona vertitsya* (1922); *Chetyre povesti o lyogkikh kontsakh* (1923); *Otrechennye* (1923); *Zverinoe teplo* (1923); *Trinadtsat trubok* (1923); *Trest D. E.* (1923); *Zhizn i gibel Nikolaya Kurbova* (1923); *Lyubov Zhanny Ney* (1924; *The Love of Jeanne Ney*, 1930); *Trubka* (1924); *Rvach* (1925); *Nepravdopodobnye istorii* (1925); *Leto 1925 goda* (1926); *Uslovnye stradania zavsegdataya kafe* (1926); *V Protochnom pereulke* (1927; *A Street in Moscow*, 1932); *Bely ugol; ili, Slyozy Vertera* (1928); *Zagovor ravnykh* (1928); *Viza vremeni* (1929); *10 l. s.: Khronika nashego vremeni* (1929; *The Life of the Automobile*, 1976); *Ediny front* (1930); *My i oni* (1931); *Fabrika snov: Khronika nashego vremeni* (1931); *Ispania* (1933); *Moskva slyozam ne verit* (1933); *Moy Parizh* (1933); *Zatyanuvshayasya razvyazka* (1934); *Khronika nashikh dney* (1935); *Kniga dlya vzroslykh* (1936); *Chetyre trubki* (1936); *Granitsy nochi* (1936); *Chto cheloveku nado* (1937); *No*

Ilya Grigorevich Ehrenburg

parasan (1937); *Vne peremiria: Sbornik rasskazov* (1937); *Ispanski zakal: Fevral-iyul 1937* (1938); *Beshenye volki* (1941); *Fashistskie mrakobesy* (1941); *Vernost, stikhi* (1941); *Za zhizn* (1942); *Ozhestochenie* (1942); *Solntsevorot* (1942); *Svoboda, poemy* (1943); *Stikhi o voyne* (1943); *Padenie duche* (1943); *Voyna, iyul 1941–aprel 1942* (1943; *Russia at War*, 1943); *Rasskazy etikh let* (1944); *Derevo, stikhi, 1938–1945 gg.* (1946); *Dorogi Evropy* (1946; *European Crossroad*, 1947); *Lev na ploshchadi, komedia* (1947); *Za mir* (1950); *Nadezhda mira* (1950); *Sochinenia* (5 vols., 1952–54); *Lyudi khotyat zhit* (1953); *Volya narodov* (1953); *O rabote pisatelya* (1954; *The Writer and His Craft*, 1954); *Sovest narodov* (1956); *Frederik Zholio-Kyuri* (1958); *Frantsuzskie tetradi* (1958); *Indiyskie vpechatlenia, yaponskie zametki, razmyshlenia v Gretsii* (1958); *Stikhi, 1938–1958* (1959); *Karel Purkine* (1960); *Perechityvaya Chekhova* (1960; *Chekhov, Stendhal, and Other Essays*, 1962); *Sobranie sochineny* (9 vols., 1962–1967); *Ya zhivu, stikhi* (1971); *Stikhotvorenia* (1972); *Letopis muzhestva: Publitsisticheskie stati voennykh let* (1974)

BIBLIOGRAPHY: Slonim, M., *Modern Russian Literature: From Chekhov to the Present* (1953): 375–79; Ehrlich, V., "The Metamorphoses of I. E.," *Problems of Communism*, 12, 4 (1963): 12–24; Alexandrova, V., *A History of Soviet Literature* (1964): 127–42; Slonim, M., *Soviet Russian Literature: Writers and Problems* (1964): 208–17; Friedberg, M., "I. G. E.," in Simmonds, W. G., ed., *Soviet Leaders* (1967): 272–81; Brown, E., *Russian Literature since the Revolution*, 2nd ed. (1969): 247–57; Hingley, R., *Russian*

Writers and Soviet Society 1917–1978 (1979): 110, 116, 223–24, 233–34

—THOMAS E. BIRD

EICH, Günter

German poet and radio dramatist, b. 1 Feb. 1907, Lebus an der Oder; d. 20 Dec. 1972, Gross-Gmain, Austria

E. studied law and sinology in Leipzig, Berlin, and Paris, but in 1932 he began devoting himself exclusively to writing. During World War II he served in the German army, was captured by the Americans, and held as a prisoner of war until 1946. After the war he became one of the founding members of Group 47. In 1953 he married the Austrian writer Ilse AICHINGER. Until 1963 he lived in Lenggries, Bavaria, and afterward in Gross-Gmain, Austria, where he died.

It was not until after World War II, when he published the poetry collections *Abgelegene Gehöfte* (1948; remote farmsteads) and *Untergrundbahn* (1949; subway), in which he gave a sober lyrical assessment of life in troubled times, that E. won fame and recognition as one of the foremost contemporary German poets. His matter-of-fact poem "Inventur" (1948; "Inventory," 1976), which takes stock of the possessions of a prisoner of war, became the most frequently quoted poem in postwar German literature.

The collection of poems *Botschaften des Regens* (1955; messages of the rain) marks the high point of his lyrical achievement. E.'s poems derive their substance directly from nature or everyday experience and thereby open up a feeling for the mystery of life in a seemingly inconspicuous way. Truth may be found in a feather that a bird lost in front of the house, or in the sound of falling rain, or in an unexpected instance where the ultimate inadequacy of "normal" perception becomes shockingly clear. E.'s images tend to turn this shock into a warning against complacency, in keeping with his often quoted statement that the writer should be gravel rather than grease in the workings of the world.

The enormous success of E.'s radio play *Träume* (1953; dreams) contributed to establishing the genre as a dominant one in Germany. In extending the radio play's poetic expression, E. offered glimpses into the mystery of reality, a technique that also forms the basis of his poems. One of his principal contributions was to oppose, in his quiet but effective way, the forgetfulness of the German people after World War II. His best radio play, *Die Mädchen aus Viterbo* (1960; the girls from Viterbo) presents the fate of two Jews awaiting arrest by the Gestapo in a Berlin hiding place.

In later years, E.'s works showed an increasing impatience with "poetic" messages, and evidenced an abbreviation, almost a fragmentation of lyrical forms and a pattern of rebellion against the established order that corresponded to the protests of the younger generation in the late 1960s.

FURTHER WORKS: *Gedichte* (1930); *Katharina* (1936); *Zu den Akten* (1964); *Fünfzehn Hörspiele* (1966); *Anlässe und Steingärten* (1966); *Kulka, Hilpert, Elefanten* (1968); *Maulwürfe* (1968); *Ein Tibeter in meinem Büro* (1970); *Nach Seumes Papieren* (1972); *Gesammelte Werke* (1973). FURTHER WORKS IN ENGLISH: *Journeys* (1968); *Selected Poems* (1971)

BIBLIOGRAPHY: Enzensberger, H. M., "In Search of the Lost Language," *Encounter*, 30, 3 (1963), 44–51; Fowler, F. M., "G. E.," in Keith-Smith, B., ed., *German Men of Letters* (1966), Vol. IV: 89–107; Müller-Hanpft, S. ed., *Über G. E.* (1970); Krispyn, E., *G. E.* (1971); Unseld, E. ed., *G. E. zum Gedächtnis* (1973); Schafroth, H. F., *G. E.* (1976)

—FRANK TROMMLER

EIDEM, Odd

Norwegian essayist, dramatist, and theater critic, b. 23 Oct. 1913, Oslo; d. 10 June 1988, Oslo

E. has been the most distinctive critic in Norway in modern times, not only of the theater, but also of nations, politics, religion, manners, and individual personalities. He took a master's degree in literary history in 1938, and since then has been a critic for *Tidens tegn, Verdens gang*, and *Aftenposten*.

E.'s distinctive qualities are his clear, highly readable style, his light touch, his satirical yet loving attitude toward life, and, above all, his close, seemingly naïve relationship to the reader. He can and does talk about himself a great deal without revealing too much, obtruding himself on the subject at hand, or seeming to be arrogant or sentimental. Thus, he woos the reader, draws him in, and shares experiences with him. The result has been great success and popularity.

As a theater critic, E. is both feared and respected. He has a wide knowledge of all phases of the theater, including actors, acting, rehearsals, staging, and audiences. His great desire for excellence in Norwegian theater has led him to reject everything mediocre and to call for a concentration of talent in the National Theater in Oslo.

Although he dismisses his own dramas modestly, the comedy *MIN kvinne!* (1956; MY wife!), was quite a success, as was one he wrote together with André BJERKE, *Videnskap og lidenskap* (1951; science and passion).

An active socialist when he was young, E. later adopted a more aesthetic, detached view of life. This attitude comes to the fore in his highly popular, clever, subtle, and mischievous *flanerier* ("strolls"), as he calls them, or books that contain leisurely observations of life in the form of essays or short stories, always told from a personal viewpoint. Whether he is describing the way Norwegians eat, drink, and make love, Disneyland's complete lack of exhibits using live animals, Sonny Liston's attitude toward boxing, or a cremation in India, E. is always lively and interesting, and he always has a point to make that is both witty and revealing. In the fall of 1978, four of these sketches were dramatized, filmed, and broadcast on Norwegian television.

In a recent semiautobiographical novel, *Pieter og jeg* (1979; Pieter and I), E. revisits Holland, where he had lived when he was twenty, meets a young socialist, Pieter, relives his own socialist past, and compares his experiences to Pieter's—a well-done, serious, fast-moving, absorbing story.

FURTHER WORKS: *Diktere i landflyktighet* (1937); *Uten fane* (1939); *Segersted* (1946); *Varm aske* (1947); *Spillet om Bly-Petter* (1947); *Vinden blåser fra nord* (1948); *Fuglen som aldri sang* (1949); *Det norske språk fra uke til uke* (1949); *Fire glass konjakk* (1950); *Frank visitt i Sovjet* (1952); *Den bakvendte familieboken* (1955, with André Bjerke); *Kefir og chiante* (1958); *Guds gjøglere* (1960); *Sett fra Sirius* (1963); *Sett fra min plass* (1965); *Zikzak*

(1967); *Jeppe Jansens giraff* (1969); *Det fjerde øye* (1971); *Kala* (1971); *Flaskepost* (1973); *Karjol* (1975); *Tilskueren* (1976); *Goddag og adjø til nitten herrer* (1977); *Fløyten og orgelet* (1978); *Cruise* (1978)

—WALTER D. MORRIS

EKELÖF, Gunnar

Swedish poet and essayist, b. 15 Sept. 1907, Stockholm; d. 16 March 1968, Sigtuna

Born into a wealthy family, E. had a disturbed childhood because of his father's mental illness. Considering himself an "outsider," as a college student he studied music and Oriental culture in London, Uppsala, and Paris. He returned from Paris with his first collection of poems, *Sent på jorden* (1932; late on the earth), influenced by Stravinsky's music and reflecting E.'s own suicidal crisis. At the time of its publication, no one realized that *Sent på jorden* would eventually be considered one of the first truly MODERNIST collections of poetry to appear in Sweden. With his free-form poetry, apparent spontaneity, and dreamlike intensity, E. was hailed in the journal *Spektrum* as Sweden's first "SURREAL-IST". He accepted the title unwillingly, since he admired the SYMBOLISTS Rimbaud and Mallarmé, and only one surrealist, Robert DESNOS.

E.'s next two volumes continued his musical, neoromantic exploration of dreams, but in *Köp den blindes sång* (1938; buy the blind man's song), E. refers to Hitler's rise to power in Germany and ponders man's paradoxical nature. *Non serviam* (1945; Latin: I will not serve) contrasts the intellectual and the mystical, and concludes with one of the finest Swedish poems of this century: "Absentia animi" (Latin: absence of mind) literally turns words into music, yet manages to pose the relation between absence and presence, nearness and farness in vivid, resonating imagery.

Om hösten (1951; in the autumn) reaffirmed E.'s searchingly sad brilliance as a poet of the world around him and the subconscious life within him. In this volume the poem "Röster under jorden" (voices under the ground) portrays E.'s sense of the closeness of the past to the present, the voices of the dead, the bodies and lives of the past that live within us as we, too, blend into the single liquid substance of time. In 1955 he published *Strountes* (nonsense), a volume that plays with the ambiguous and trivial in order to approach ironically the meaninglessness of the universe. This "antipoetic" volume served as a major influence on the next generation of Swedish poets. In *Opus incertum* (1959; Latin: uncertain work) and in *En natt i Otočac* (1961; a night in Otočac) E. continued to employ the antithetical and antipoetic to pursue, occasionally in burlesque fashion, the problems of death and meaninglessness. During these years he also wrote the long allusive and autobiographical poem *En Mölna-elegi* (1960; *A Mölna Elegy*, 1979).

Throughout his career E. wrote several collections of critical and autobiographical essays. These prose works provided additional insight into the sources of E.'s inspiration. Although already established as the major Swedish poet of the 20th c., E. reached the peak of his career with a trilogy of poems based upon a personal mystical experience: *Dīwān över Fursten av Emgión* (1965; divan

of the Prince of Emgion), *Sagan om Fatumeh* (1966; the saga of Fatumeh), and *Vägvisare till underjorden* (1967; *Guide to the Underworld*, 1980). In the trilogy, E. identifies himself with an exiled and tortured Byzantine prince. A young prostitute, Fatumeh, who serves as guide, mistress, and archetypal woman to the blinded prince, functions as the second narrator of the trilogy. As a whole, the three volumes explore the range of human experience from the agonies of a torturous physical life to the ecstasies of the mystical, the archetypal life which usually lies hidden within man but which can appear in moments of brilliant illumination.

E. is one of the truly original Swedish poets of the 20th c. Diverse, personal, intimate, obscure, profound, mystical, he dominated the craft of poetry and throughout his life played with his craft like a master weaving new tapestries. For a poet of such depth and complexity, perhaps the finest tribute to be paid to him is the Swedish people's acceptance of him as their own national *skald*, or bard. The recipient of every major literary prize awarded in Scandinavia, E. received an honorary doctorate from the University of Uppsala and became a member of the Swedish Royal Academy in 1958. His writings, from his earliest to his last works, continue to be translated and admired throughout the world.

FURTHER WORKS: *Dedikation* (1934); *Sorgen och stjärnan* (1936); *Promenader* (1941); *Utflykter* (1947); *Dikter* (1949); *Dikter 1932–1951* (1956); *Blandade kort* (1957); *Verklighetsfykt* (1958); *Valfrändskaper* (1960); *Sent på jorden, med Appendix 1962, och En natt vid horisonten* (1962); *Lägga patience* (1969); *Partitur* (1969); *G. E.: En självbiografi* (1970); *En röst* (1973). FURTHER WORKS IN ENGLISH: *Selected Poems* (1967); *I Do Best Alone at Night* (1968); *Selected Poems* (1971); *Friends, You Drank Some Darkness* (1975)

BIBLIOGRAPHY: Sjöberg, L., *A Reader's Guide to G. E.'s "A Mölna Elegy"* (1973); Shideler, R., *Voices under the Ground: Themes and Images in the Poetry of G. E.* (1973); Perner, C., *G. E.'s "Nacht am Horizont" und seine Begegnung mit Stéphane Mallarmé* (1974); Sjöberg, L., "Translating with W. H. Auden: G. E.'s Last Poems," *CCrit* 1 (1979): 185–97; Sjöberg, L., "G. E.'s *A Mölna Elegy*: The Attempted Reconstruction of a Moment," *CCrit*, 1 (1979): 199–214

—ROSS P. SHIDELER

EKELUND, Vilhelm

Swedish poet and essayist, b. 14 Oct. 1880, Stehag; d. 3 Sept. 1949, Saltsjöbaden

When E. was fourteen, his family moved from the country village of Stehag to the university town of Lund (both in the southern Swedish district of Skåne). Later E. attended Lund University, without, however, taking a degree (in 1937 he received an honorary doctorate from Lund University). He spent the years 1908–12 in Germany and the following nine years in Denmark, returning to live in Sweden in 1921.

E.'s first seven books were volumes of poetry, including *Melodier i skymning* (1902; melodies at dusk) and *Dityramber i aftonglans* (1906; dithyrambs in evening light). Most of the poems in the early collections, including *Melodier i skymning*, are in rhymed verse; later collections are written in masterful, highly sophisticated free verse. Many of the early lyric poems (examples are the much admired "Kastanjeträden trötta luta" [tired the chestnuts lean] and "Då voro bokarna ljusa" [then the beeches were light], both from *Melodier i skymning*) use the southern Swedish settings of E.'s childhood to explore subjective moods. There is, in E.'s poetry, a continuous struggle between the lyric and romantic on the one hand, and the severe and classical on the other. The latter predominates in *Dityramber i aftonglans*; E.'s next work, *Grekisk bukett* (1906; Greek bouquet), is a collection of translations from Greek poetry in classical meters.

Beginning with *Antikt ideal* (1909; antique ideal), E. abandoned poetry in favor of essays, and, more frequently, aphorisms. Later books, especially *Metron* (1918; Greek: measure) and *Attiskt i fågelperspektiv* (1919; Attic thoughts from a bird's-eye view), are reflections on the works of great writers and thinkers. The classical influence reached E. both directly from Greek writers, especially Plato and Pindar, and by way of German writers who had themselves been influenced by the classics: Goethe, Nietzsche, and August von Platen (1796–1835). E.'s admiration for Nietzsche contributed to both the form and the content of *Dityramber i aftonglans*; Goethe and Nietzsche are the informing spirits of *Antikt ideal*.

Later, E. had some reservations about Nietzsche's prophetic stance. E. himself moved further toward the classical ideal of balance and the golden mean, as exemplified in *Metron* and *Nordiskt and klassiskt* (1914; Nordic and classical). Emerson, whose idealism and humility E. admired, was also an important later influence. *Tyska utsikter* (1913; German views) has the subtitle *Nytt och gammalt om Emerson m.m.* (new and old on Emerson, etc.). Emerson, like Plato and Goethe, remained a literary hero to E. for the rest of his life. *Veri similia* (2 vols., 1915–16; verisimilitudes) includes a short essay on Carlyle and Emerson; more importantly, Emerson's thought pervades the two books.

E.'s prose, like his poetry, evinces a search for beauty in the Platonic sense and for greatness of soul. This search is connected with the necessity, as E. sees it, for the individual to define his own values and to live his life according to the insights he has garnered. In *Plus salis* (1945; Latin: salt added) E. stresses the desirability of a confluence of theory and practice, thought and life. While E. will never be a popular writer—he did not wish to be—his highly wrought and deeply considered poetry and prose continue to win the admiration of discerning readers.

FURTHER WORKS: *Vårbris* (1900); *Syner* (1901); *Elegier* (1903); *In Candidum* (1905); *Havets stjärna* (1906); *Böcker och vandringar* (1910); *Båge och lyra* (1912); *Valda dikter* (1913); *Sak och sken* (1922); *På hafsstranden* (1922); *Levnadsstämning* (1925); *Väst-Östligt* (1925); *Passioner emellan* (1927); *Lyra och Hades* (1930); *Spå och tecken* (1930); *Det andra ljuset* (1935); *Elpidi* (1939); *Concordia animi* (1942); *Atticism-humanism* (1943); *Dikter* (1951); *Prosa* (2 vols., 1952); *Nya vakten* (1953); *Ars magna* (1955); *Saltet och Helichrysus* (1956); *In Silvis cum libro* (1957); *Skoltal* (1961); *Själens tillflykt* (1962); *Campus et dies* (1963); *Brev* (2 vols., 1968, 1970); *Hjärtats vaggvisor* (1970); *Hemkomst och flykt* (1972). FURTHER WORKS IN ENGLISH: *Agenda* (1976)

BIBLIOGRAPHY: Gustafson, A., "Two Early Fröding Imitations: V. E.'s 'Skördefest' and 'I pilhäcken,' (1901)," *JEGP*, 35 (1936):

566–80; Shideler, R., "'The Glassclear Eye of Dreams' in Twentieth-Century Swedish Poetry," *WLT*, 51 (1977): 530–34; Gustafsson, L., *Forays into Swedish Poetry* (1978): 65–71

—YVONNE L. SANDSTROEM

EKMAN, Kerstin

Swedish novelist, b. 27 Aug. 1933, Risinge

Before she became a full-time author, E. was a teacher and literary critic and also active in the film and television industry. She began her writing career as the author of popular detective novels. One of them, *Tre små mästare* (1961; three little masters), earned her the prize for that year's best Swedish detective story. In *Dödsklockan* (1963; the death knell) the traditional elements of a detective story are still in evidence, although E. now places greater emphasis on psychological complications and on the way characters interact as a group. The author also gives particular attention to the description of milieu: The autumnal landscape and the details surrounding a moose hunt are based on exact observation and evoked with remarkable concreteness. Such realism became her hallmark when she left detective fiction and in subsequent works established herself as a leading novelist.

With *Menedarna* (1970; the perjurers) E. made her contribution to the "documentary genre" of the period by turning to a historical event, the execution in Utah of the Swedish labor agitator and songwriter Joe Hill in the early years of the IWW (Industrial Workers of the World). The novel attempts to separate the man from the myth and the legend and presents the protagonist as a victim of both hostile authorities and of "friendly" socialist organizations that wish to make use of Hill's innocence and martyrdom for political purposes. In *Mörker och blåbärsris* (1972; darkness and blueberry scrub), E. presents a tale about life in a remote village in northern Sweden. The erotic triangle drama involving seemingly insignificant characters is described with humor and moving pathos and without a trace of condescension.

The novel *Häxringarna* (1974; the witches' circles) is the first volume in a tetralogy that includes the volumes *Springkällan* (1976; the spring), *Änglahuset* (1979; house of angels), and *En stad av ljus* (1983; a town of light). In this series, her to date most ambitious undertaking, E. follows the example of a number of Swedish writers of the period, Sven DELBLANC and Sara LIDMAN (qq.v.) among them, in tracing the recent history and development of a region. E.'s focus is the town of Katrineholm, south of Stockholm, and its growth from a modest trading place in the 1870s to a modern industrial town. The changing face of the town forms the backdrop for a line of fictional characters, mainly women, beginning with the indomitable Sara Sabina Lans. The novels raise a monument to the toil and hardships of the women of past generations and depict the material progress of the emerging welfare state. But people's easier lot through improved social conditions has been achieved at a price, and the title of the last novel in the series, *En stad av ljus*, is largely ironic; E. manages to convey a sense of loss and alienation in the depiction of this modern town, its neon lights, concrete, and supermarkets. What emerges is a society in which both the older and the younger generations have lost their roots in exchange for economic security.

In her later works, the novel *Rövarna i Skuleskogen* (1988; the robbers in Skule forest) and the verse epic *Knivkastarens kvinna*

(1990; the knife thrower's woman), E. experiments with a mixture of myth, dream, and realism. Her criticism of our technocratic world is here balanced by an exploration of the mystical correspondences between humans and nature.

E.'s reputation rests mainly on her strength as a realistic writer with an uncompromising respect for authenticity and minute observation. Her novels are the result of painstaking research and gathering of details and significant facts, which are elegantly incorporated in her art and frequently jolt the reader with shocks of recognition. With her tetralogy about the small Swedish town she has contributed to the renewal of Swedish historical fiction. As a writer about women and their world she has few equals in contemporary Swedish literature.

In 1978 E. was elected to the Swedish Academy. In 1989 she left her seat in the Academy as a protest against the Academy's unwillingness to take a forceful stand in the Salman RUSHDIE case. Also in 1989 she received the prestigious Selma Lagerlöf Prize.

FURTHER WORKS: *30 meter mord* (1959); *Han rör på sig* (1960); *Kalla famnen* (1960); *Den brinnande ugnen* (1962); *Pukehornet* (1967); *Hunden* (1986); *Mine Herrar . . .*(1986)

BIBLIOGRAPHY: Forsås-Scott, H., "Women's Worlds," *Swedish Books*, 2 (1979): 8–16; Wright, R., "K. E.: Voice of the Vulnerable," *WLT*, 55, 2 (Spring 1981): 204–9; Wright, R., "K. E.'s Crime Fiction, and the 'Crime' of Fiction: The Devil's Horn," *SBR*, 2 (1984): 13–16; Wright, R., "Theme, Imagery, and Narrative Perspective in K. E.'s *En stad av ljus*," *SS*, 59, 1 (Winter 1987): 1–27; Algulin, I., *A History of Swedish Literature* (1989), 272; Zuck, V., ed., *Dictionary of Scandinavian Literature* (1990): 139–40; Wright, R., "Narration as Transformative Power: K. E.'s *The Robbers of Skule Forest*," *SBR*, 1 (1991): 11–12

—LARS G. WARME

EKWENSI, Cyprian

Nigerian novelist and short-story writer (writing in English), b. 26 Sept. 1921, Minna

E. studied at Achimota College, near Accra, Ghana, and obtained a degree in pharmacy at the University of London. On his return to Nigeria, he taught science at colleges in Lagos and in Yaba. He joined the staff of the Nigerian Broadcasting Corporation in Lagos in 1951, later serving as director of information in the federal ministry of information in Lagos. In 1966 E., an Ibo, resigned his position to move to Biafra. When the Nigerian-Biafran conflict (1967-70) ended, he proclaimed that he was "happy to be a Nigerian again." E. is now a practicing pharmacist.

E.'s first two novels show his ambivalence to the city. The first, *People of the City* (1954; rev. ed., 1963), is an episodic work in which a newspaperman, Amusa Sango, serves as commentator on life in Lagos. E.'s view of Lagos is both grim and fascinating. Several of his characters are overwhelmed by the city, turning to prostitution and thievery or committing suicide. Amusa, the protagonist, must work through the "hell" of Lagos (E. uses Dantesque imagery) in order to gain a mastery of life. The destructiveness of the city is strongly presented in E.'s portrait of a beautiful woman, Beatrice the First, who comes to the city, has several lovers (in a descending order of wealth and status), dies unattended and loveless, and is buried in a pauper's grave. Amusa's salvation comes through another Beatrice—Beatrice the Second—who, in her quiet, simple way, provides stability for him.

E.'s second novel, probably his best-known and most influential work, *Jagua Nana* (1961), shows E.'s continuing fascination with the city and its women. A series of events, particularly a romance with a young political idealist, leads Jagua Nana, a sleek, beautiful prostitute, to a new awareness. Her road to understanding, however, is strewn with twists of fate. Unable to bear children for many years, the one thing Jagua wants desperately is a child. Finally, at forty-five, she does give birth, but the child dies two days later. Jagua overcomes her sense of loss and sets off for a new life in a small country town.

E.'s first two novels have been criticized for sentimentality, romanticism, and journalistic exploitation of sensational events. Yet, even his detractors admit the vitality of his characterizations and his broad canvas of urban events. Some critics see in his work a Dickensian sense of comedy and a talent for reportage and the picaresque similar to that of Defoe. E. himself has said that he is less interested in literary style than in getting to the "heart of the truth which the man in the street can recognize." E. calls himself a "writer for the masses," and he prefers to "go down to the people." His stated allegiance to the masses and his fear of literary pretentiousness provide some of the reasons he regards Georges SIMENON and Edgar Wallace (1875–1932) as two great influences on his work. Both Simenon and Wallace wrote their novels quickly, disdaining any pretensions of precious writing.

E.'s third novel, *Burning Grass* (1962), was written before his two earlier published novels. It reveals his deep commitment to the countryside as a source of respite for the battered soul. In *Burning Grass*, the action of which takes place in the northern Fulani countryside, the sense of an older way of life that is passing is conveyed against the ominous undertones of an encroaching city life. In *Beautiful Feathers* (1963), E. shifted the setting to the city again and explored the life of a young, earnest, respected politician, Wilson Iyari, cuckolded by his wife.

E.'s later work shows an increasing concern with style and less reliance on the episodic and sensational. *Iska* (1966)—the title is the name given to the wind that blows through the countryside—is the story of a young girl tragically blown about by the inevitable raging winds of tribal conflicts.

E. is also a prolific writer of short stories and juvenile literature. His best-known collection of stories is *Lokotown* (1966). In a recent collection, *Restless City and Christmas Gold* (1975), E. utilizes sketches of modern conflict—the sophisticated "been-to" bored with his white wife; the innocent girl corrupted by jaded pleasure seekers; the pettiness of industrial society. Much of his children's literature utilizes the motif of a young wanderer through strange lands and forests, settings inspired by his own experience in the forestry service.

E.'s work, various in its moods, style, and genres, centers on the individual act of choice. Far from bearing only simple messages and moralisms. E.'s work suggests unending ambiguities in man. His conclusions are pat, but his people are real and complex.

FURTHER WORKS: *When Love Whispers* (1947); *The Leopard's Claw* (1947); *The Dummer Boy* (1960); *Passport of Mallam Ilia* (1960); *An African Night's Entertainment* (1962); *Rainmaker* (1965); *Juju Rock* (1966)

BIBLIOGRAPHY: Mphahele, E., *The African Image* (1962): 276–78; Gleason, J., *This Africa* (1965): 118–30; Tucker, M., *Africa in Modern Literature* (1967): 73–82; Laurence, M., *Long Drums and Cannons* (1968): 148–69; Cartey, W., *Whispers from a Continent* (1969): 147–73: 193–95; Pieterse, C., and Deurden, D., eds., "Interview with E.," *African Writers Talking* (1972): 77–83; Emenyou, E., *C. E.* (1974)

—MARTIN TUCKER

EL SALVADOR LITERATURE

See Central American Literature

ELIADE, Mircea

Romanian novelist, essayist, historian of religions, and Orientalist (writing also in French and English), b. 9 March 1907, Bucharest; d. 23 April 1986, Chicago, Ill.

E. studied philosophy in Bucharest and, between 1928 and 1931, in Calcutta, India, under Surendranath Dasgupta (1885–1952). He taught at the University of Bucharest between 1933 and 1939 and during the next several years served as his country's cultural attaché in London, and after 1941, in Lisbon. An émigré after World War II, he lived in Paris from 1945 to 1956, taught for a while at the École des Hautes Études, and established himself as one of the foremost contemporary scholars of myth and religion. After 1956 he taught at the University of Chicago.

The unifying element of E.'s early fiction is a strong, immediately recognizable autobiographical bent. Some of his most characteristic works of this period are actually direct outgrowths of his journal, conceived (as he later reveals) as a "storehouse" of reflections, recollections, intimate experiences, intellectual discoveries, and even imaginative experiments. From the existential-sexual obsessions straight-forwardly presented in *Isabel si apele diavolului* (1930; Isabel and the devil's waters) to the thinly disguised love affair between a European man and an Indian girl, poetically recounted in *Maitreyi* (1933; Maitreyi), to the unconcealed use of his Indian diary in *Șantier* (1935; work in progress), E.'s early novels are clearly derived from the personal experiences of a young intellectual torn between his Western urge for "modernity" and his fascination with the Eastern negation of time. Even E.'s fiction on Romanian themes, as exemplified by *Intoarcerea din rai* (1934; the return from paradise) and *Huliganii* (1935; the hooligans), shares in the general autobiographical quality of his early writing, although here the author goes beyond his personal self and tries to embrace the "collective self" of his generation of metaphysical "hooligans" (20th-c. reincarnations of the older "nihilists"), intent on rejecting their society and culture in the name of a feverishly expected revolutionary apocalypse.

The most forward-looking of E.'s early works is, curiously, the one that was received least favorably, *Lumina ce se stinge* (1934; the light that fails), an experimental novel using a Joycean stream-of-consciousness technique, which represents E.'s first encounter with the "fantastic" and anticipates his growing interest in tracing the ways in which the "supernatural" both hides and reveals itself in

the world of everyday "reality." This trend is increasingly visible in the works published during the second half of the 1930s, in the "tale of terror" *Domnișoara Christina* (1936; Mademoiselle Christina); in *Sarpele* (1937; the snake), a short novel that starts realistically and ends "mythically" with a vision of sexuality as a cosmologic force and a manifestation of the sacred; and, most explicitly, in the two tales of the occult included in *Secretul Doctorului Honigberger* (1940; *Two Tales of the Occult*, 1972).

With the exception of the great symbolic novel of initiatory quest, *La forêt interdite* (1955; *The Forbidden Forest*, 1978)—written in Romanian but first published in French translation; published in Romanian in Paris as *Noaptea de Sânziene* (2 vols., 1971; midsummer night)—a synthesis of all the major tendencies of E.'s creative activity, in the postwar years E.'s literary production has consisted of novellas and stories of the fantastic, in which the finest narrative qualities of his writing are most effectively realized. *Pe Strada Mântuleasa* (1968; *The Old Man and the Bureaucrats*, 1979), *La țigănci, și alte povestiri* (1969; with the gypsy girls, and other stories), *Die Pelerine* (1976; the cloak; written in Romanian but published only in German translation), or *In curte la Dionis* (1977; at Dionysus's court) are independent fictional explorations of the problems and paradoxes involved in the dialectic of the sacred and the profane, and are an original literary complement to E.'s theoretical and scholarly works, from *Le mythe de l'éternel retour* (1949; *The Myth of the Eternal Return*, 1954) and *Traité d'histoire des religions* (1949; *Patterns in Comparative Religion*, 1958) to his projected four-volume *History of Religious Ideas*, of which two volumes have appeared (1976, 1978).

The more recent literary productions of E. stand, in many respects, in stark contrast to his early personal-fictional works. They display a more objective fantasy (and a richer one, for that matter); their deep themes are more authentically philosophical; and they are, unlike the rather loosely structured early works, artful and powerful narratives. Between *Isabel și apele diavolului* and the postwar novellas, E. has gone all the way from the modernist obsession with self and existential immediacy to the timeless and serenely impersonal art of story-telling.

FURTHER WORKS: *Soliloquii* (1932); *Intr-o mănăstire din Himalaya* (1932); *Oceanografie* (1934); *India* (1934); *Alchimia asiatică* (1934); *Yoga: Essai sur les origines de la mystique indienne* (1936); *Cosmologie și alchimie babiloniană* (1937); *Nunta în cer* (1938); *Fragmentarium* (1939); *Mitul reintegrării* (1942); *Salazar și revoluția în Portugalia* (1942); *Comentarii la legenda Meșterului Manole* (1943); *Insula lui Euthanasius* (1943); *Techniques du yoga* (1948); *Le chamanisme* (1951; *Shamanism*, 1964); *Iphigenia* (1951); *Images et symboles* (1952; *Images and Symbols*, 1961); *Le yoga: Immortalité et liberté* (1952; *Yoga, Immortality and Freedom*, 1958); *Forgerons et alchimistes* (1956; *The Forge and the Crucible*, 1962); *Mythes, rêves et mystères* (1957; *Myths, Dreams, and Mysteries*, 1960); *The Sacred and the Profane* (1959); *Naissances mystiques* (1959; *Birth and Rebirth*, 1958); *Méphistophélès et l'androgyne* (1962; *The Two and the One*, 1965); *Patanjali et la yoga* (1962; *Patanjali and Yoga*, 1969); *Nuvele* (1963); *Aspects du mythe* (1963; *Myth and Reality*, 1964); *Amintiri: I, Mansarda* (1966); *From Primitives to Zen* (1967); *The Quest: History and Meaning in Religion* (1969); *De Zalmoxis à Gengis-Khan* (1970; *Zalmoxis, the Vanishing God*, 1972); *Australian Religions* (1973); *Fragments d'un journal* (1973; *No Souvenirs*, 1977); *Occultism, Witchcraft, and Cultural Fashions* (1976); *Histoire des croyances et des idées religieuses*, Vol. I (1976; *A History of Religious Ideas*,

1978); *Histoire des croyances et des idées religieuses*, Vol. II (1978); *Mémoires (1907–1937)* (1980; *Autobiography: Volume I, 1907–1937*, 1981)

BIBLIOGRAPHY: Altizer, T. J. J., *M. E. and the Dialectic of the Sacred* (1963); Kitagawa, J. K., and C. Long, eds., *Myths & Symbols: Studies in Honor of M. E.* (1969); Allen, D., *Structure and Creativity in Religion: M. E.'s Phenomenology and New Directions* (1977); Calinescu, M., "Imagination and Meaning: Aesthetic Attitudes and Ideas in M. E.'s Thought," *Journal of Religion*, 57, 1 (1977): 1–15; Calinescu, M., "The Disguises of Miracle: Notes on M. E.'s Fiction," *WLT*, 52 (1978): 558–64; Tacou, C., ed., *L'Herne: Cahier M. E.* (1978); Marino, A., *L'herméneutique de M. E.* (1981)

—MATEI CALINESCU

ELIN PELIN

(pseud. of Dimitur Ivanov Stoyanov) Bulgarian short-story and novella writer, b. 18 July 1877, Baylovo; d. 3 Dec. 1949, Sofia

Brought up in the *shopp* (that is, western Bulgarian) country-side, where he taught school for a brief time, E. resided in Sofia from 1899 on. Originally he wanted to be a painter, but he turned instead to writing and published his *narodnik* (populist) magazine *Selska razgovorka* (1902–3). He was employed by the University Library in 1903, and in 1906 was sent for a year to Paris at state expense to broaden his literary horizons. He was appointed to a position at the National Library in 1908, and in 1926 he became the Ivan Vazov Museum's first curator (he retired in 1944). E. worked on various periodicals, notably *Bulgaran* and *Razvigor*.

Chronically impecunious himself, E. began by depicting the hardships of early 20th-c. Bulgarian village life and *narodnik* teachers' efforts to ameliorate these conditions. But local resilience is the theme of his still famous "Andreshko" (1903; Andreshko), in which a magistrate-bailiff is left stranded in the mud by his not so dumb *shopp* driver. E.'s popularity rests solidly in his gallery of *shopp* portraits in *Razkazi* (2 vols., 1904, 1911; stories). His village tragedies, *Geratsite* (1911; the Gerak family), *Zemya* (1922; land), and *Nechista sila* (1909; unclean power), are novellas; the longer form was less congenial to him.

The Orthodox clergy of village church and monastery also figure in E.'s stories: he considered his best work to be his cycle of such tales about the clergy entitled *Pod manastriskata loza* (1936; under the monastery vine). On the other hand, he considered to be of slight literary value his feuilletons, collected in *Az, ti, toy* (1936; I, thou, he). The latter epitomize E.'s *bêtes noires*, such as the bureaucracy, the former his warm antipuritanical morality, pungently put in the proverb "Too saintly can be too much, even for God."

E. has been represented variously as a dialect and genre writer, a *narodnik*, a "critical realist," an anticlerical writer, and a pessimist. Yet, his dialect sketches *Pizho i Pendo* (1917; Pizho and Pendo) excepted, standard Bulgarian is his language even for dialogue. As with his lyrical landscapes, local color is the setting for his microcosm of humanity, not an end in itself. E. was concerned with his former fellow-villagers' suffering, but also with their joys and dreams. As early as "Kosachi" (1903; mowers) everyday "reality"

is rejected; it is no match for E.'s *istina*, the reality of the creative imagination. His clergymen are not so much evil as inevitably human. So it is more as an idealist, even a romantic, that E. emerged in, for example, "Mechtateli" (1910; dreamers) and "Imyanari" (1921; treasure hunters), which stresses the beneficent power of illusion and poetic imagination. The latter is a prose-poem that later appeared in *Cherni rozi* (1928; black roses). These miniatures, along with E.'s many verse fantasies for children, fill four of the ten volumes of his collected works.

Lionized after World War II as a "living classic," E. wrote a final story, "Vrabchetata na strina Doyna" (1948; Auntie Doyna's wee sparrows), which views the new youth movement through a peasant woman's eyes as "bustling little sparrows." In "Kak pisha" (1949; how I write) he urged colleagues to transfer their attention from tractors to the men upon them, that is, to the inner world of the inhabitant of Bulgaria's rural regions, which was E.'s own consuming interest.

FURTHER WORKS: *Pepel ot tsigarite mi* (1905); *Ot prozoretsa* (1906); *Kitka za yunaka* (1907); *Gori tilileyski* (1919); *Tsar Shishko* (1925); *Yan Bibiyan* (1934); *Yan Bibiyan na lunata* (1934); *Subrani suchineniya* (10 vols., 1958–1959)

BIBLIOGRAPHY: Pinto, V., "E. P. (1877–1949): Humanist of Shopsko," *SEER*, 41 (1962): 158–81; Moser, C. A., *A History of Bulgarian Literature: 865–1944* (1972): 185–93

—VIVIAN PINTO

ELIOT, T(homas) S(tearns)

Anglo-American poet, b. 26 Sept. 1888, St. Louis, Mo.; d. 4 Jan. 1965, London, England

A descendant of Sir Thomas Elyot, the 16th-c. author of *The Boke Named the Governour*, and the grandson of William Greenleaf Eliot, the founder of Washington University in St. Louis, E. grew up in a family that prided itself upon its ancestors and took seriously its Unitarian faith. E.'s mother was especially influential upon him: his moral passion can be traced to her, as well as his intellectual energy, his obsession with the loss and restoration of grace, his industry, and even his interest in poetry. E. had difficulty in reconciling his poetic interest with the Eliot family tradition, however, and as a student at Harvard he fretted about the kind of practical career that his family would approve. Because his bachelor's degree in English and his master's degree in philosophy seemed to point toward an academic career, he completed his Ph.D. dissertation, *Experience and Objects of Knowledge in the Philosophy of F. H. Bradley* (published 1964), in 1916 while in residence at Oxford University. But E. chose not to return to Harvard to defend his dissertation: in response to the encouragements of Ezra POUND, he decided to put academic ambitions aside and to concentrate on his poetry.

The family tradition, however, did not admit of E. starving in a garret. Thus, after one unhappy year teaching schoolboys, E. took a clerk's position in Lloyds Bank, a position which he found comfortable but which scandalized the literary world. In 1925 he left the bank and entered the London publishing firm of Faber & Gwyer (later Faber & Faber), where he remained happily until his death,

T. S. Eliot

very much the responsible man of business that his family would have respected, and decorous to a degree that approached self-caricature. Indeed, the Nobel Prize awarded E. in 1948 was probably testament not only to his literary achievement but also to his gentlemanly stance vis-à-vis the literary establishment.

But dramatic rebellions punctured the conformist surface of E.'s life and hint at ferments that the surface concealed. He affected religious skepticism as a young man, a rebellious posture in itself, yet in 1927 he capped years of scrupulosity and religious anguish by requesting baptism into the Anglican communion. Six months later, in an echoic gesture, he exchanged American for British citizenship. The most radical of his rebellions, however, was his sudden marriage in 1914 to the unstable Vivienne Haigh-Wood, a woman his family (and E. himself) thought déclassé. The marriage turned out to be E.'s personal wasteland, and, as such, it was the emotional foundation of his major poetry. He separated from Vivienne in 1933 after nineteen grim years, and she died in a mental institution in 1947.

There were many literary influences on E. Preeminently, there was Ezra Pound, E.'s first sponsor and his poetic tutor. There was also Arthur Symons (1865–1945), whose *The Symbolist Movement in Literature* (1899) E. read in 1918. There was the French poet Jules Laforgue (1860–1887), whose verse showed E. how to play one voice against another with wit and self-mockery. There was Dante, a touchstone of personal success for E., and there were the late-Elizabethan and Jacobean dramatists, from whom he learned how to energize a poetic line. There was the British philosopher

F. H. Bradley (1846–1924), whom E. admired for his ability to accept the disjunction between absolute truth and everyday experience, and there were the Christian mystics—Theresa of Ávila (1515–1582), Julian of Norwich (fl. 1416), Mme. Guyon (1648–1717), John of the Cross (1542–1591), Jakob Böhme (1575–1624), and Bernard of Clairvaux (1091–1153)—who revivified in him his mother's injunctions to spiritual transcendence. And there was the English prelate and scholar Lancelot Andrewes (1555–1626), whose gentle sermons moved him to religious assent.

Implicit in the conjunction of the decorous E. and these heroic influences is the hesitant stance that almost invariably characterizes E.'s poetry, for, in the language of his undergraduate poem "Spleen" (1910), E. tended to see "Life . . . Punctilious of tie and suit . . . On the doorstep of the Absolute." Certainly this stance is at the heart of E.'s first major poem, "The Love Song of J. Alfred Prufrock" (1917), in which the title character is paralyzed by self-consciousness and unable to step off the doorstep to "disturb the universe." Prufrock is not the pale personification of life that we find in "Spleen," however, but a vividly realized consciousness, tormented by the difficulty of articulating his complex feelings, harrowed by juxtapositions of himself with heroic figures, and cognizant that the you/I polarity of the traditional love song has become the ego/id polarity of himself. "Prufrock" is the single masterpiece of *Prufrock, and Other Observations* (1917), although many of the other poems in that first volume are admirable. "Portrait of a Lady" should be remarked for its masterful control of tone and inflection, and "Preludes" for its imagistic rendering of four units of urban experience, the four brought together at the end in a Bradleyan interpenetration of subject and object. "Preludes" should also be noted as an early example of an assemblage—an ingenious combination of fragments into a single poem. E.'s Yankee parsimony found this method of composition congenial, for it enabled him to make use of "found" quotations as well as previously discarded material, and the success he had with this approach in "Preludes" is an important step toward the construction of complex assemblages in his major poems.

The poems of E.'s second volume, *Ara Vos Prec* (1920; published in the U.S. as *Poems*), develop the dry and cynical strain of the *Prufrock* poems rather to excess, for the Sweeney poems and the religious satires in the volume bespeak not only the young poet's cleverness but also his inability to handle emotion in a substantive way. As a result the poems tend to be brittle and affected, and "Gerontion" is the only poem among them that is impressive. "Gerontion" is also the only poem in this collection that is in the mainstream of E.'s development: it anticipates *The Waste Land* (1922) in abandoning the vivid characterizations of the early dramatic monologues in favor of a generalized, abstract persona who functions as a cultural seismograph, and it tends to use allusions with the same density and complexity as the mature poetry.

The Waste Land is E.'s masterpiece; it is also the most celebrated poem of the 20th c., and it is probably the most famous assemblage in literary history as well. Divided into five sections, it is a series of fragmentary dramatic monologues that fade one into another, sometimes abruptly and sometimes imperceptibly. The effect suggests a dense chorus of voices, a kind of atonal polyphony, and that effect is underscored by numerous quotations and allusions. The unity of the poem is in its pervasive themes of sterility and disordered sexuality; the most powerful aspect of the poem, however, is its rendering of a collective consciousness, nominally belonging to Tiresias, that embraces all of the voices and holds them, meditatively, at its anguished core. E. had always an acute sense of the temper of his age and an instinctive knowledge of its proper symbols: he disclaimed any intention to do so, but the poem gave definitive expression to the doubts and uncertainties of the period, and it haunted its age as no other literary text.

In 1971 Valerie Fletcher, E.'s second wife and his former secretary, published a facsimile edition of the first version of *The Waste Land*, making clear the exact role that Ezra Pound had played in the poem's editing. Pound cut the manuscript poem almost in half, canceling great chunks of material (some anti-Semitic and misogynistic lines among them), and criticizing the rhythms and indecisiveness of some passages he retained. E. was unsure of the quality of his poem, and he accepted most of Pound's editing readily, much to the poem's improvement. It should not be assumed, however, that E. thought of the poem as final in the manuscript form he gave to Pound and that he would not himself have improved the poem substantially before publication. Indeed, it has been argued that Pound's greatest contribution to *The Waste Land* may have been his assurance, first to E., and then to the world, that the poem was a masterpiece.

Some overtly religious poems, reflective of E.'s conversion, followed *The Waste Land*; they are written in a less idiosyncratic style than the earlier poems and in a newly personal, almost confessional, tone. Foremost among these poems is "Ash-Wednesday" (1930), which depicts the doorstep stage of religious conversion as filled with difficulties and indecisions. Dantean and liturgical imagery give resonance to the crabbed twistings of the narrator's feelings, and lyrical interjections from the King James Bible and the *Book of Common Prayer* are juxtaposed with passages of tortured analysis in the chiaroscuric manner that is always E.'s best effect. "Journey of the Magi" (1927) and "A Song for Simeon" (1928) are straight-forward dramatic monologues on the same theme of the convert's agony, both moving from realistic details and sentiments to inexplicable visions on the doorstep of the Absolute, and both are distinguished examples of their genre, although they do not rank with "Ash-Wednesday," which is at a point just below the achievement of *The Waste Land*.

The sequence of poems entitled *Four Quartets* (1943) is the great output of E.'s maturity. The sequence is composed of four, quite separate poems, each occasioned by a different landscape, and each poem is a prolonged meditation, alternating abstract, philosophical reflections with moments of lyricism, expressing thereby the hesitant, doorstep mentality that was E.'s essential subject. Uncharacteristically, however, the four meditations of the sequence end with a vision of total synthesis, as if the lifetime that E.'s characters had spent hesitating on the doorstep of the Absolute were finally over. Indeed, *Four Quartets* is in every sense the culmination of E.'s lifetime of work. The interwoven subjects of the meditations are his familiar ones—redemption, time, and history—but they are approached now with a climatic intensity of thought. Finding its architecture in Beethoven's late quartets, the sequence also brings to culmination E.'s long-standing interest in the possibilities of musical form in poetry. The confessional strain that had been in the ascendancy in E.'s poetry since 1930 emerges with unprecedented clarity, and E. seems even to have echoed images and passages from his earlier work, as if through allusion to establish *Four Quartets* as the capstone of his poetic edifice. This deliberate effort to shape and crown the body of his poetry is not surprising on E.'s part, since he had long argued in terms of Dante and Shakespeare that an artist's greatness is measured by the unity

of his lifetime's work. The artistic success of *Four Quartets* is very much disputed, however. For some readers, it is the greatest of E.'s works and one of the great poetic sequences of the 20th c.; for others, it is marred by strain and pretentiousness.

E.'s religious conversion resulted not only in his writing a newly public poetry, but in his writing poetic drama as well. Indeed, he wrote *The Rock* (1934 [the choruses only]) and *Murder in the Cathedral* (1935) at the suggestion of churchmen and for church performance. *The Family Reunion* (1939), *The Cocktail Party* (1950), *The Confidential Clerk* (1954), and *The Elder Statesman* (1959) were written for the commercial theater, but they are concerned, like their churchly predecessors, with the struggle for spiritual fulfillment in a world divided between the natural and the supernatural orders. E.'s theatrical notions were always more sophisticated than his theatrical instincts, however: his dramatic verse became increasingly indistinguishable from prose, and his attempt in his commercial plays to overlay drawing-room comedy with Greek tragedy is generally thought unsuccessful. His one play of genuine merit is the early *Murder in the Cathedral*. Its central situation is compelling; its chorus is used effectively to amplify the spiritual dimensions of the action; and both its poetry and its prose suit the dramatic medium very well. It overshadows all other attempts to write verse drama in English in the 20th c., and it compares favorably with most such attempts since the 17th c.

E. also enjoyed a notable career as a literary critic. As an assistant to the editor of *The Egoist*, as a reviewer for the *Times Literary Supplement*, and as editor of *The Criterion* from 1922 to 1939, he established a critical dictatorship, in fact, equal to that of Matthew Arnold in the 19th c. He employed no systematic critical method, but his magisterial tone, the intensity of his intelligence, the breadth of his standards for comparison and analysis, and his considerable gift for quotation gave weight to his judgments. His revaluations of such writers as Shakespeare, Milton, and Donne affected the mainstream of literary thought, even when his remarks were merely incidental, and his manner of linking cultural survival to literary distinctions gave a considerable urgency and a propagandist edge not only to his own criticism but to critical activity in general. His critical formulae—most notably the "objective correlative" and the "dissociation of sensibility"—have largely disappeared from the critical vocabulary, but his insistence that tradition is a living force in literature is still influential.

E. had a complex career, then, and he made an enduring mark for himself as a poet, as a dramatist, and as a critic. If his influence in the last categories now belongs to literary history, his major poetry remains vital, continuing to speak with eloquence of man hesitating on the doorstep of the Absolute, caught between his will to act and his terror of the abyss, fully knowing his dilemma and fully recognizing his neurosis, and yet unable to take the step that promises life.

FURTHER WORKS: *Poems* (1920); *The Sacred Wood* (1920); *Homage to John Dryden* (1924); *Poems 1909–1925* (1925); *Selected Essays 1917–1932* (1932); *The Use of Poetry and the Use of Criticism* (1933); *After Strange Gods* (1934); *Elizabethan Essays* (1934); *Collected Poems 1909–1935* (1936); *The Idea of a Christian Society* (1939); *Old Possum's Book of Practical Cats* (1939); *Notes towards the Definition of Culture* (1948); *Selected Essays* (1950); *Poetry and Drama* (1951); *The Complete Poems and Plays* (1952; enl. ed., 1962); *On Poetry and Poets* (1957); *Essays on Poetry and Criticism* (1959); *Collected Plays* (1962); *Collected*

Poems 1909–1962 (1963); *To Criticize the Critic and Other Writings* (1965); *Poems Written in Early Youth* (1967)

BIBLIOGRAPHY: Matthiessen, F. O., *The Achievement of T. S. E.* (1935); Drew, E., *T. S. E.: The Design of His Poetry* (1949); Gardner, H., *The Art of T. S. E.* (1950); Maxwell, D. E. S., *The Poetry of T. S. E.* (1952); Smith, G., *T. S. E.'s Poetry and Plays* (1956); Kenner, H., *The Invisible Poet: T. S. E.* (1959); Smith, C. H., *T. S. E.'s Dramatic Theory and Practice* (1963); Howarth, H., *Notes on Some Figures Behind T. S. E.* (1964); Unger, L., *T. S. E.: Moments and Patterns* (1966); Tate, A., ed., *T. S. E.: The Man and His Work* (1967); Martin, G., ed., *E. in Perspective* (1970); Kirk, R., *E. and His Age* (1971); Patterson, G., *T. S. E.: Poems in the Making* (1971); Bergonzi, B., *T. S. E.* (1972); Litz, A. W., ed., *E. in His Time* (1973); Schneider, E., *T. S. E.: The Pattern in the Carpet* (1975); Traversi, D., *T. S. E.: The Longer Poems* (1976); Gordon, L., *E.'s Early Years* (1977); Gardner, H., *The Composition of "Four Quartets"* (1978); Freed, L., *T. S. E.: The Critic as Philosopher* (1979); Ackroyd, P., *T. S. E.: A Life* (1984)

—ROBERT F. KIERNAN

More than one critic has remarked that in E. the over-all organization of the poem as a whole is not lyrical in any recognizable and traditional way; nor is the poem organized in terms of narrative; nor is it dramatic in the literal theatrical sense; and it is certainly not logical, argumentative, or expository. . . . Where poets in the past would have used a logical, emotional, dramatic, or narrative basis for the transition from part to part, E. uses some one of these kinds of transition freely and alternatively and without committing himself to any one of them or to any systematic succession of them; or he omits the connection between one passage and the next, one part and the part which succeeds it. . . . The characteristic over-all organization of the poem—of which "The Waste Land" is the vividest example—can be called, for the lack of a better phrase, that of sibylline (or subliminal) listening.

Delmore Schwartz, "T. S. E.'s Voice and His Voices," *Poetry*, 85 (1955), 236–37

The image of structural unity pervades E.'s social and literary criticism. What of his own poetry? Is he able to reach his goal of organic unity and write poems which live because they share the life of the European mind?

Most of E.'s poems depend on the assumption that the poet can enlarge his private consciousness to coincide with a collective consciousness. This assumption is so easily and persuasively sustained that it is easy to forget what an extraordinary arrogation of power it is. Only a few early poems, such as "Prufrock" or "Portrait of a Lady," are limited to the perspective of a single ego. In most poems the reader is placed within everybody's mind at once. An act of self-surrender has expanded the private mind of the poet into the universal sphere of the mind of Europe. It

may take long years of hard work to assimilate the riches of that mind, but this is now the exploration of an inner space, not the effort to comprehend something other than the self.

J. Hillis Miller, *Poets of Reality* (1965), p. 172

It seems to me that the more we see of the hidden side of E. the more he seems to resemble Milton, though he thought of Milton as a polar opposite. As we look at all the contraries reconciled in E.—his schismatic traditionalism, his romantic classicism, his highly personal impersonality—we are prepared for the surprise (which E. himself seems in some measure to have experienced) of finding in the dissenting Whig regicide a hazy mirror-image of the Anglo-Catholic royalist. Each, having prepared himself carefully for poetry, saw that he must also, living in such times, explore prose, the cooler element. From a consciously archaic standpoint each must characterize the activities of the sons of Belial. Each saw that fidelity to tradition is ensured by revolutionary action. . . . Each knew the difficulty of finding "answerable style" in an age too late. With the Commonwealth an evident failure, Milton wrote one last book to restore it, and as the élites crumbled and reformed E. wrote his *Notes [towards the Definition of Culture]*. If Milton killed a king, E. attacked vulgar democracy and shared with the "men of 1914" and with Yeats some extreme authoritarian opinions.

Frank Kermode, "A Babylonish Dialect," *SR*, 74 (1966), 228–29

It won't be easy to reclaim his work from the conceptual and scholarly currency already invested in it. It will mean forcing ourselves to forget most of what exegesis has burdened us with, and it will mean returning for help to those very few difficult critics I've mentioned [Leavis, Blackmur, Kenner], all of whom have insisted, to almost no effect, on E.'s deliberate irrationality. In trying to release E. from schematizations contrived mostly for the clarification and boredom of undergraduates, these, and a few others, direct us away from the seductions of neatness and into the wonderful mystery at the center of E.'s poetry and criticism. What we find there, if we stay long enough, is that for E. ideas have no more organizational power than do literary allusions and that neither is as preoccupying as are the furtive memories and hallucinations, the sensuous images that stimulate a poem like "Preludes" but which remain at the end as unassimilated to any design as they were at the beginning.

Richard Poirier, "T. S. E. and the Literature of Waste," *NR*, 20 May 1967, 19–20

What set [E.] apart from the hesitant desiccated figure that he drew of [Henry] Adams was precisely the quality of his sensuous perceptions, his awareness of the abyss and the deepest terrors and desires, and his familiarity with the lonely, painful act of creation. As a poet E. was solitary and unaffected by being culturally institutionalized. If he is less significant now as a force for literary orthodoxy, this is irrelevant to his true stature as a poet; when the cultural idol has been displaced the voice of the poet may be heard more clearly. If that voice is to go on being listened to, as I believe it will, the present decline in E.'s reputation may be both inevitable and salutary. Future readers will acknowledge E.'s genius, but they will see different things in him from his first readers, and from ourselves. All of which, we may be sure, he would have calmly understood and welcomed.

Bernard Bergonzi, T. S. E. (1972), p. 192

Prufrock was solitary, knew that he was, accepted essential character as fate, and looked forward in resignation to an unchanging life. The rather more vital man behind Prufrock, instead, ventured out into the world of human beings, of sex, of external insecurity; found it bitter; said so by projections of disgust bordering on horrors, getting back at the human race through the Burbanks and Bleisteins and pimpled adolescents, taking refuge in the exercise of technical skill and ingenuities of mosaic constructions; found refuge and a function for himself in concern with theories of "tradition" and "unity of culture," and satisfaction in the role (even in youth) of society's elder critic; found the darkened spirit could still create by looking outward upon a waste land of moral and emotional distortions, a world of the heartless and the irresponsible, which might—just might—be saved by the cultivation of human decency ("give, sympathize, control"). But this proves after all no solution. . . . A renewed Christianity becomes the one hope: for the world at large a discipline and perhaps a way of devotion; for the solitary self these, and also a human relationship, acceptable perhaps because less individual than institutional, relieving solitude without invading it.

Elisabeth Schneider, T. S. E.: The Pattern in the Carpet (1975), pp. 210–211

At each stage of his career E. defined his identity and measured his distance from enlightenment. There was, in his poetry, a persistent self-portraiture—from the languid, well-dressed gentleman in "Spleen," who waited impatiently on the doorstep of the Absolute, to Prufrock, whose impulse to assault the universe with a prophetic truth beat beneath his anxiously correct façade; and from the phantom pilgrim searching the city for a miraculous cure for depression to the anxious penitent patiently climbing the purgatorial stair. One developing personality redefined, in each poem, the position won in the previous poem. From the start, E. was preoccupied with his own special fate, but he was uncertain how to characterize himself. He sensed his identity as a "shadow of

its own shadows, spectre in its own gloom." E. haunted his poems like an irresolute ghost seeking shape and form and visible role. When at length he was sure of his best self, he suddenly revealed a preacher, his outlines distinct, his feet firmly planted on an Anglican platform.

Lyndall Gordon, E.'s Early Years (1977), p. 138

ELIZONDO, Salvador

Mexican novelist, short-story writer, and essayist, b. 19 Dec. 1932, Mexico City

After having completed his secondary education in Mexico City, E. studied philosophy and literature in France, Germany, Italy, England, Canada, and the U.S. He has produced experimental films and contributed to numerous Mexican journals. He is now professor of literature at the National University in Mexico City.

E. first attracted the attention of a sophisticated reading public with *Farabeuf; o, La crónica de un instante* (1965; *Farabeuf: The Chronicle of on Instant*, 1992). An experiment in narrative technique with virtually no antecedent in Mexican literature, this disconcerting antinovel attempts to capture a climatic moment of orgasm and death. The characters are Dr. Farabeuf (a fictionalized version of a 19th-c. French anatomist) and his mistress, a woman of shifting identities whom we suspect he is preparing to dissect alive. The themes of eroticism and sadism are intensified by a style reminiscent of the French NEW NOVEL, which presents reality not in terms of logical cause-and-effect relationships but rather as fleeting sensations produced by the perception of opaque objects. Repeated in kaleidoscopic patterns, these sharply defined images give the impression of a haunting, surrealistic dream.

El hipogeo secreto (1968; the secret hypogeum) is based on the philosophy of Ludwig Wittgenstein (1889–1951), who states that the limits of language coincide with the limits of the world and, consequently, that language has no meaning when applied to metaphysics. Like *Farabeuf*, this novel relies on the juxtaposition of poetic images to convey a semblance of plot, the essence of which in this case is the psychic tension experienced by an author as he attempts to create his work of art. His failure to reach the ideal city he is seeking implies that both esthetic perfection and absolute truth are unattainable.

Narda; o, El verano (1966; Narda; or, summertime) is a collection of deftly structured tales conveying a wide range of themes and moods. The erotic adventures of amoral youths vacationing on the Italian Riviera are described in the title story, which can be read as a pastiche of "new wave" European films. In "En la playa" (on the beach) the absurd human experience is dramatized by a terrified fat man's flight from an implacable enemy, a symbol of the senseless but inevitable fate threatening all mortals. Philosophical idealism emerges as the basic ingredient of "La historia según Pao Cheng" (history according to Pao Cheng) when the protagonist discovers that his existence depends on being perceived by another.

E. is one of Latin America's talented young writers who have taken their cue from Jorge Luis BORGES. Less interested in politics, social issues, or national identity, S. shares Borges's literary and philosophical concerns. He has nevertheless developed his own distinct mode of expression.

FURTHER WORKS: *Poemas* (1960); *Luchino Visconti* (1963); *Nuevos escritores mexicanos del siglo XX presentados por sí mismos: S. E.* (1966); *El retrato de Zoe, y otras mentiras* (1969); *El grafógrafo* (1972); *Contextos* (1973); *Antología personal* (1974)

BIBLIOGRAPHY: Carballo, E., "Prólogo," *Nuevos escritores mexicanos del siglo XX presentados por sí mismos: S. E.* (1966): 5–12; McMurray, G. R., "S. E.'s *Farabeuf*", *Hispania*, 50 (1967): 596–600; McMurray, G. R., "S. E.'s *El hipogeo secreto*," *Hispania*, 53 (1970): 330–34; Langford, W. M., *The Mexican Novel Comes of Age* (1971): 192–94; Durán, M., *Tríptico mexicano: Juan Rulfo, Carlos Fuentes, S. E.* (1973): 134–73; Foster, D. W., and Foster, V. R., ed., "S. E.," *Modern Latin American Literature* (1975), Vol. I: 320–23; Larson, R., *Fantasy and Imagination in the Mexican Narrative* (1977): 45–49, 70–71, 87–88

—GEORGE R. MCMURRAY

ELKIN, Stanley

American novelist and short-story writer, b. 11 May 1930, New York, New York; d. 31 May 1995, St. Louis, Missouri

E.'s fictions, which can be very funny as well as prurient, do not fall into a familiar generic category, though his work reflects BLACK HUMOR, satire, popular culture, and the adaptation of literary models. In his narratives he resorts to the rhetorical device of the catalog—the heaping up of descriptive terms and substantives—especially when he details the merchandise in a store. Some of his fictions suggest the influence of Walt Whitman—use of the catalog device and concern with a fictive self, and William FAULKNER. E.'s doctoral dissertation was on Faulkner, and he seems to favor Faulkner's long and involved sentence structure. On occasion E. is a parodist, displaying a variety of prose styles from different time periods and different authors, notably the manner of Henry JAMES in "The Making of Ashenden," in the triple-novella collection *Searches and Seizures* (1973). He has been called an original, but that term fits other offbeat, hard-to-classify writers, and it may be best to take him simply on his own terms, looking at what he does with wordplay, images, metaphors, and wildly improbable storylines.

E. also appears to be an associationist who sometimes starts an individual text as a realist with a specific picture and set of ideas in mind, then rapidly moves into fantasy and/or grotesquerie, almost losing sight of the original concept because of his infatuation with words and his wild rush of ideas. As an example, E. in his introduction to *The Best American Short Stories 1980*, which he edited, attempted to tell why he picked his twenty-two selections for the book. They were easily the best published stories during the preceding year, and it was taste, "the buds of judgment"—his taste in particular—that made those stories declare themselves to him. But to account for his taste, E. fired a barrage of wordy references to a series of barely (if at all) connected topics. Some of them were heroes with their deeds versus the rest of the people with their "opinions, judgment calls, the soul's favorite tunes"; hotel guests in the coffee shop eating on credit or doing con jobs; police lineups; a lengthy series of allusions to global geography and politics; American politics; simile-laden definitions of taste—"the luxury of abeyant claims," "an ideal," "the choice we make when we have no choice," "a series of first impressions," "lodestar aesthetics [lasting] a lifetime," "a notion of order"; his mother-in-law's ideas of how to furnish a living room, and her fearful experiences as a little girl in Russia; the fact that taste "comes with the territory" and is one's birthmark; finally, his own childhood experiences and memories of life in New York and Chicago, with summers in a bungalow in New Jersey. Thus E., expressing his personal views, as he might also do in writing an article or an autobiographical story, reveals his mind's wildly associative tendency, whereby his train of thought seems to have little inclination to stay on track.

E., who obtained his bachelor's, master's, and Ph.D. degrees from the University of Illinois, Urbana, and taught for many years at Washington University in St. Louis, in addition to serving as visiting professor at a number of other universities, received numerous awards for his writing, including an Doctor of Humane Letters degree from his alma mater and membership in the American Academy. Yet despite his critical success as an innovative author of short stories, novellas, and novels, and his modest following of aficionados, this creator of numerous obsessive characters—as critics have typed them—has never received the popular success he so strongly desired.

An early story, "Fifty Dollars," in *Southwest Review* (Winter 1962), is a long-drawn-out study of a diffident woman who wins fifty dollars in a supermarket promotional. After endless agonizing over how to spend the award, she finally rejects the sweater that caught her fancy, and decides to save her money. The fifty dollars represents her fate, keeping her from her other one and from ever needing another fate. Here, E. seems to have been influenced by Henry James's story of the big event that never took place, "The Beast in the Jungle." E.'s first novel, *Boswell: A Modern Comedy* (1964), is a takeoff in contemporary terms on the life of the colorful 18th-c. adventurer, James Boswell, companion and biographer of Samuel Johnson.

The short-story collection *Criers and Kibitzers, Kibitzers and Criers* (1966) is reminiscent, in terms of some of its subject matter, of Bernard MALAMUD's offbeat stories of Jewish-immigrant life in an Eastern city. On the other hand, the title story, about a storekeeper grieving for his dead son only to discover that the boy must have been stealing from the family store, evokes Ernest HEMINGWAY's "My Old Man," about a boy whose father has just been killed, whereupon he learns that his father had been a crook. A number of the characters in these stories are losers or marginal types, such as the playground terrorizer in "A Poetics For Bullies," the drug addict who wreaks havoc in his friends' apartment in "The Guest," and the irresponsible, unstable, grown-up orphan in "I Look Out For Ed Wolfe."

In his novel *A Bad Man* (1967) E. imagines a gruesome and intrigue-filled year in prison for a crooked owner of a department store. A more ambitious novel, *The Dick Gibson Show* (1971), is an extended excursion into the life of a radio talk show host, against the background of the powerful influence that the medium of radio has exerted on American life. "The Bailbondsman" and "The Condominium"—two of the three novellas in *Searches and Seizures*—have certain significant elements. E. identified closely with Alexander Main (called "the Phoenician"), the intellectually curious and eagerly hustling protagonist of the former. The protagonist of the latter, Marshall Preminger, lacks the mental resources to cope with his father's legacy of the condo, and with other exigencies of family relations and urban existence, committing suicide as a result: not what one would expect in E.

The Franchiser (1976) depicts another energetic E. protagonist, Ben Flesh, deeply absorbed in furthering his business or private agenda, this time hustling all over the U.S., checking on his numerous franchise operations. Here E. introduces a destructive disorder into the story line of the novel and Ben Flesh's life—multiple sclerosis—just as MS had been introduced into his own life about fifteen years earlier. Perhaps under the influence of his painful and progressive affliction (which did not seem to stop or slow down his extensive writing), E. brought out *The Living End* (1979), a collection of stories mocking conventional notions of Heaven and Hell and attempting to portray God in very contemporary anthropomorphic terms.

Not long before his death from heart failure in 1995 E. brought out his last collection of novellas, *Van Gogh's Room at Arles* (1993). The first, "Her Sense of Timing," features a professor, incapacitated like E. in his last years, but suddenly abandoned by his spouse, who is moving on to a better life, precisely when he is to have his class of lively graduate students come over for a party. The second, "Town Crier Exclusive, Confessions of a Princess Manque: How Royals Found Me 'Unsuitable' to Marry Their Larry," is a lighthearted spoof of British royalty, the Peerage, and the "carries on" of the nobility, as a young Englishwoman working in the U.S. tells about her former relationship with the young prince, and what came of it. Lastly, "Van Gogh's Room at Arles" is an intellectual romp through Van Gogh country with a clutter of Foundation-funded academics off on a spree.

Though E.'s range of subject matter was far and wide, encompassing the sacred and the profane (especially the latter), his approach to the target at hand was seldom subtle and perhaps not always very serious. With multiple salvos of rapid-fire rhetoric laden with amusing puns, ironic twists, synonyms, and idioms, he continued to strive to hit his mark anyway.

FURTHER WORKS: *George Mills* (1982); *The Magic Kingdom* (1985); *The Rabbi of Lud* (1987); *The Macguffin* (1991); *Mrs. Ted Bliss* (1995)

BIBLIOGRAPHY: Bailey, P., *Reading S. E.* (1985); Dougherty, D., *S. E.* (1991); Morace, R., "S. E.," in Mote, D., ed., *Contemporary Popular Writers* (1997): 133-35

—SAMUEL I. BELLMAN

ELLISON, Ralph

American novelist and critic, b. 1 March 1914, Oklahoma, City, Okla.; d. 16 April 1994, New York, NY

Three years after E.'s birth his father died, and thereafter his mother supported herself and her child by working as a domestic. While growing up, E. met and became friendly with a number of jazz musicians playing in Oklahoma City and began to perform on the trumpet while in high school. He studied music at Tuskegee Institute in Alabama from 1933 to 1936, when he dropped out to pursue a career in the visual arts. From Alabama he moved to New York City; there chance meetings with Langston HUGHES, and later with Richard WRIGHT, led to his first attempts at fiction. E. participated in the Federal Writers' Project, and his stories and

Ralph Ellison

essays appeared in *New Masses* and other periodicals. After service in the Merchant Marine (1943–45) he won a Rosenwald Fellowship (1945). After the publication of *Invisible Man* (1952) E. received many honors, including a National Book Award (1953), the National Newspaper Publishers' Award (1954), a fellowship at the American Academy in Rome (1955–57), and the Medal of Freedom (1969). He was appointed to the American Institute of Arts and Letters in 1964, and has been a Consultant in American Letters to the Library of Congress. Since 1970 E. has been Albert Schweitzer Professor in the Humanities at New York University.

E.'s only novel published to date, *Invisible Man*, has become a classic. A *Book Week* poll of artists and critics cited it as "the most significant work of fiction written by an American" between 1945 and 1965. *Invisible Man* tells the story of the adolescent and adult search for identity of a young black man who remains, throughout the novel, nameless. Enduring a series of picaresque adventures—by turns comic, satirical, agonizing, absurd, and deadly—the protagonist discovers emphatically who he is not; he undertakes a progress *away* from all the seductive and false identities offered to him and finds himself ultimately moving away from identity itself. The dramatic episodes that illuminate this unique character development have been chosen with brilliant care: they are a compendium of nearly all the inept, humiliating stereotypes with which American society has saddled black men.

Best known of the scenes from *Invisible Man* is the widely anthologized "Battle Royal," which begins the novel. It shows the young protagonist as one of a dozen half-naked, blind-folded young black men boxing in a ring for the entertainment of a white men's club. Battered, terrified, and degraded at the end of the match, the invisible man is singled out for special attention and rewards, and is asked to give his high school commencement speech about Negro social responsibility. When he slips, substituting the word "equality" for "responsibility," he is momentarily threatened, but avoids punishment by apologizing, with the excuse that he was "swallowing blood." Similarly ironic vignettes and exchanges appear throughout the novel, showing the invisible man as a master of the sly macabre.

At the novel's end its hero makes an absurd, surrealistic, and telling choice for his life: he takes up residence in a cavern beneath the city's surface, a secret hole, which he furnishes with 1,369 light bulbs powered by an illegal tap into the nearby lines of the Monopolated Light and Power Company, and waits to see how he might be reborn.

Shadow and Act (1964) is a work of criticism and an intellectual autobiography; it has been acclaimed almost as universally as *Invisible Man*. Its critical eye ranges over a wide spectrum of literary experience, focusing on what is central to the artistic vision of, among many others, MELVILLE, Mark TWAIN, CONRAD, FAULKNER, and ELIOT. E. invariably sees in the works of masters a profound social and human concern that may be located in, but is never limited to, the metaphor and fact of race. In his criticism, as in his fiction, E. uses racial issues to express something more than social awareness: the particular dilemma of race is an external manifestation of a universal dilemma which is inward, or spiritual, and which is the source of the external problem.

Irving HOWE and other critics have expressed disappointment at E.'s refusal to write works of overt social consciousness and radical protest. He has frequently been called an "Uncle Tom" because of this propensity, and has responded by insisting that the task of becoming fully human—the artist's central task—requires "a discipline far more demanding than loyalty to a racial group."

E. is at work on a second novel, from which many selections have been published as short stories. Although his short stories and criticism are superbly vivid and intelligent, it is finally on *Invisible Man* that E.'s reputation rests. As both artist and critic, E. has successfully avoided the pigeonhole of black writer, a term he sees as laden with condescension far more damaging than the limited aesthetic boundaries it implies. An ironic idealist, able to describe powerfully what should be and what is, and to hold the two in balance, E. has been compared to writers such as Melville and Hawthorne more often than to black American writers. He has identified in the plight of American blacks a universal predicament, a universal alienation transcending petty categories.

FURTHER WORKS: *The Writer's Experience* (1964, with Karl Shapiro)

BIBLIOGRAPHY: Littlejohn, D., *Black on White: A Critical Survey of Writing by American Negroes* (1966): 109–16; Bluestein, G., "The Blues as a Literary Theme," *MR*, 8 (1967): 593–617; special E. issue, *CLAJ*, 13, 3 (1970); Gottesman, R., ed., *Studies in "Invisible Man"* (1971); Covo, J., *The Blinking Eye: R. W. E. and His American, French, German, and Italian Critics, 1952–1971* (1974); Gray, V., *"Invisible Man"'s Literary Heritage: "Benito Cereno" and "Moby-Dick"* (1978); O'Meally, R. G., *The Craft of R. E.* (1980)

—LARRY TEN HARMSEL

ELSSCHOT, Willem

(pseud. of Alphonsus Josephus de Ridder) Belgian novelist (writing in Flemish), b. 7 May 1882, Antwerp; d. 31 May 1960, Antwerp

E. grew up in a middle-class urban environment. After having been expelled from school at the age of sixteen, he worked as an errand boy, but afterward he made up for his lost years and obtained a certificate in business, consular, and colonial science from the Higher Institute of Business Science. He went to Paris, where he was employed by a South American businessman. He subsequently worked in various businesses in the Netherlands, but in 1911 he returned to Belgium, settling in Brussels, where he was a bookkeeper. At the outbreak of World War I, E. fled with his family to Antwerp, where he remained for the rest of his life, earning his living as the owner of a publicity agency.

E. began his literary career in 1900 by writing romantic, idealistic poems. However, his poems were not published in book form until 1934, in *Verzen van vroeger* (poems of long ago). Most probably because of his experiences in Paris and his business involvements in the Netherlands, E. became cynical. He wrote several novels, which were practically ignored by the critics as well as by the public. The first one, *Villa des roses* (written 1910, pub. 1913; villa of the roses), depicts E.'s Paris years. The main subject, the relation between the cynical boarder Grünewald and the naïve chambermaid Louise is drawn against the background of the bleak boardinghouse in which each person feels lonely and depressed.

Een ontgoocheling (written 1914, pub. 1921; a deception) tells the story of a proud father who wants his son to become a lawyer. The boy, however, is not the studious type and must drop out of school. He holds different jobs but is never quite accepted by his colleagues. Still, although the son is not unhappy, the father becomes increasingly depressed. He loses faith not only in his son but also in himself when he is not reelected president of his card club. The story contains many reminiscences of the author's youth.

Lijmen (1924; *Soft Soap*, 1965) presents the characters Boorman and Laarmans, who reappear in several of E.'s later novels. Boorman is the shrewd businessman, hard as nails and seemingly the personification of the crass world of the publicity business. Laarmans is the sensitive type, forced into business in order to make a living. His pity for deceived customers is a business liability. Boorman and Laarmans most likely express the two sides of the author's personality. E. was a tough businessman, but also a sensitive, dreamy poet, who warmly sympathized with those suffering from illness, old age, loneliness, or poverty; he pointed with sarcasm to the weak spots in a capitalistic society, represented by Boorman, for whom money is more important than happiness.

For ten years after *Lijmen* E. did not publish anything. Then he was "discovered" by two young Dutch writers, Jan Greshoff (1888–1971) and Menno ter BRAAK, who published ten of his early poems in their literary journal *Forum*. Their favorable reception encouraged E. to write again, and in hardly a month's time he finished his novel *Kaas* (1933; cheese). In this book Laarmans is talked into entering a wholesale business in cheese, but the enterprise fails. Laarmans is too honest and scrupulous. He ends by returning to the routine of his office job, feeling secure and protected in the midst of his family.

Tsjip (1934; Tsjip) one of his best works, is based on members of his own family. Adèle, the oldest daughter, marries a Polish student and follows him to his native country. Shortly after her baby is born, she leaves her husband and returns home with her son.

When the child is in Poland for a visit, his father does not seem inclined to send him back. But Adèle fetches the boy and takes him home. Here the principal part of the novel begins: the description of the relation between grandfather and grandson and the influence they have on one another.

E.'s last novel, *Het dwaallicht* (1946; *Will-o'-the-Wisp*, 1956), is his masterpiece. This time Laarmans appears without his counterpart Boorman. With three Afghan sailors he looks for a girl, Maria, wandering through Antwerp on a drizzly November night. It is an adventure for him, and for a moment he feels free from all conventional ties. But then he returns to the routine of his family life.

E. is one of the best novelists Flanders has produced. He pictures the average middle-class citizen with his sorrows and his small joys, and pays especial attention to the distress people cause each other. He looks at human life and loneliness with a melancholy smile and expresses himself in extremely clear and matter-of-fact language. His works have been reprinted many times and remain popular today.

FURTHER WORKS: *De verlossing* (1921); *Pensioen* (1937); *Het been* (1938; *The Leg*, 1965); *Het tankschip* (1941); *De leeuwentemmer* (1943); *Verzameld werk*, 2nd ed. (1976); *Zwijgen kan niet verbeterd worden* (1979)

BIBLIOGRAPHY: on *Three Novels: Soft Soap; The Leg; Will-o'-the-Wisp*, *TLS* (3 March 1966): 157 ; Clements, R. J., on *Three Novels*, *SatR* (2 July 1966): 23; Meijer, R. P., *Literature of the Low Countries*, new ed. (1978): 334–36

—JUDICA I. H. MENDELS

ÉLUARD, Paul

(pseud. of Eugène Grindel) French poet, b. 13 Dec. 1895, Saint-Denis; d. 18 Nov. 1952, Charenton-le-Pont

É. came from a lower-middle-class background: his father was a bookkeeper, his mother a dressmaker. In 1908 É. had to interrupt his studies in Paris and spend two years in a Swiss sanitarium for treatment of tuberculosis. During World War I he served in the infantry. Soon after his discharge he met three major DADAISTS: Tristan TZARA, Louis ARAGON, and André BRETON. A founding member of the SURREALIST movement, É. became politically involved in the 1930s, when he joined the Communist Party. During World War II he actively participated in the Resistance. After the war his political activity took on an international flavor, for he participated in several peace conferences, particularly in Communist-bloc countries.

É., considered one of the most eminent of 20th-c. poets, favored the short lyric. In his verse and prose poems, he eschewed grandiloquence, the artifices of rhetoric, traditional prosody, and syntactical complexity. Unlike the other surrealists, he did not break with the lyricism of the past, as evidenced by the title of one of his major volumes, *Poésie ininterrompue* (1946; uninterrupted poetry), where he proclaims his faith in the continuous presence of poetry and in its power to unite what time and space have torn asunder. When the poet, whether by personal recollection or through other texts, rediscovers a state of consciousness belonging to the past, he endeavors to make it present, to rejuvenate it. He aims at a state of Edenic purity capable of shaping a future devoid of oppression. Nonetheless, É. continued to share the surrealist belief in the need for revolution, and identified with their struggle for political, social, and sexual liberation.

According to É., the mission of poetry was to renew language in order to effect radical changes in all areas of existence. He envisioned the writing of poetry as an action capable of arousing awareness in his readers and of leading them to more purposeful activities.

Several chronological phases can be distinguished in É.'s creative activity: (1) a Dadaist phase, characterized by the enigmatic and subversive texts of *Répétitions* (1922; repetitions); (2) a surrealist period, rich in paradoxical imagery and dream exploration, as exemplified in *Capitale de la douleur* (1926; *Capital of Pain*, 1973); (3) an interlude marked by overt political advocacy, as expressed in *Cours naturel* (1936; natural course), about the Spanish Civil War, and *Poésie et vérité 1942* (1942; *Poetry and Truth, 1942*, 1944), about the Resistance; (4) a final development showing a greater awareness of the mysteries of poetic creation, exemplified in *Le phénix* (1952; the phoenix). But these chronological divisions, however convenient, do not go very far, because the fundamental unity and continuity of É.'s poetic output is undeniable.

Indeed, a dominant theme resounds through all his poetry: love in all its universality. Although he may have addressed his poems to specific women—Gala, Nusch, and Dominique—he unhesitantly transcends the particular. This tendency to universalize individual experience or to use it as a bridge to knowledge appears in its most intense form in *La vie immédiate* (1932; immediate existence), where, however idealized, woman becomes a physical presence whose sexuality is fully acknowledged. Her eyes, her lips, her breasts metonymically stand for her mysterious powers where the poet can discover his own true identity. Woman performs as a liberating force, capable of detaching the poet from the false bonds of the everyday world and the irrelevant chains of memory. Thanks to her mediation, he can transgress boundaries, overcome distances, experience communion. Love for É. was indissociably linked to hope and affirmation. Contemplation and gestures become simultaneous, just as the object of love and the lover ultimately become fused. The woman provides the focal point of new, unlimited images, capable of regenerating the world by transcending both time and space. In this new realm, expressed by images of growth and fertility, contradictions become impossible, and innocence is regained. As dream becomes reality, the intense poetic web spreads ever wider. Like other surrealists, É. transforms the world of objects, which by becoming more nebulous and undefinable lend themselves to unexpected associations.

É.'s love lyrics do not separate the lover and his beloved from the rest of the world, for their love provides the best way to reach universal solidarity and to assure humanity's significance in the universe. Similarly, the political poems reiterate a message of peace and hope for all mankind, by calling for brotherhood and relief of suffering.

In É.'s poetry, the ever-present eye encompasses the outer world while giving physical presence to an even more intense inner vision. Not surprisingly, painting, which is both vision and spectacle, stands out as a source of inspiration second only to love. *Donner à voir* (1939; offering to sight) and *Voir* (1948; to see) consist of poetic texts devoted to contemporary painters, particularly Picasso and Max Ernst. By adding word to line and color, by recuperating their vibrations, É. creates a new experience for his readers. At the same time, he affirms his solidarity with other artists. In his monumental *Anthologie des écrits sur l'art* (1952–54; anthology of writings on art) he shows the same uninterrupted continuity in the visual arts that he had found in poetry. É. strove to abolish the barrier between the "seeing" subject and the "perceived" object. In his universe, "to see," "to know," "to be" ultimately become synonymous when the poet tries to reduce to transparency even the most tenacious opaqueness. Painting, like poetry, according to É., was destined to disseminate truth belonging to both the real and the imaginary. É., especially in his later years, saw a political destiny for art, which should be made available and relevant to all.

Throughout his career he had frequently collaborated with painters in the creation of illustrated books. With Man Ray he produced *Facile* (1935; easy), consisting of love poems where text and image combine in the celebration of woman, where the contours of the printed word and the photographs harmonize. With Ernst he created *Les malheurs des immortals* (1922; *Misfortunes of the Immortals*, 1943). There, the satirical verbal collages, in which both the poet and the painter collaborated, constantly interfere with their plastic collages so as to produce simultaneous movements of attraction and repulsion.

É., eager to suppress the barriers between individual consciousnesses, collaborated with André Breton in writing *L'Immaculée Conception* (1930; *The Immaculate Conception*, 1990) and in composing with René CHAR and Breton *Ralentir travaux* (1930; *Slow Under Construction*, 1990).

É.'s most remarkable achievement would seem to consist in his repeated efforts to eliminate the barriers between intimacy and the problems of the community, between the outside world and inner visions, between verbal and plastic art, efforts that have resulted in an eternal poetry whose appeal will never be lost.

FURTHER WORKS: *Premiers poèmes* (1913); *Dialogues des inutiles* (1914); *Le devoir* (1916); *Le devoir et l'inquiétude* (1917); *Poèmes pour la paix* (1918); *Les animaux et leurs hommes, les hommes et leurs animaux* (1920); *Les nécessités de la vie et les conséquences des rêves* (1921); *Mourir de ne pas mourir* (1924); *152 proverbes mis au goût du jour* (1925); *Au défaut du silence* (1925); *Les dessus d'une vie; ou, La pyramide humaine* (1926); *Défense de savoir* (1928); *L'amour la poésie* (1929); *A toute épreuve* (1930); *Dors* (1931); *Certificat* (1932); *Comme deux gouttes d'eau* (1933); *La rose publique* (1934); *Nuits partagées* (1935); *Le front couvert* (1936); *Notes sur la poésie* (1936, with André Breton); *La barre d'appui* (1936); *Les yeux fertiles* (1936); *L'evidence poétique* (1937); *Avenir de la poésie* (1937); *Premiéres vues anciennes* (1937); *Les mains libres* (1937); *Appliquée* (1937); *Quelquesuns des mots qui jusqu'ici m'étaient mystérieusement interdits* (1937); *Dictionnaire abrégé du surréalisme* (1938, with André Breton); *Solidarité* (1938); *Facile proie* (1938); *Ode à Salvador Dali* (1938); *Chanson complète* (1939); *Médieuses* (1939); *Charles Baudelaire* (1939); *Jeux vagues la poupée* (1939); *Le livre ouvert I* (1940); *Blason des fleurs et des fruits* (1940); *Divers poèmes du livre ouvert* (1941); *Moralité du sommeil* (1941); *Choix de poèmes* (1941); *Sur les pentes inférieures* (1941); *Le livre ouvert II* (1942); *La dernière nuit* (1942); *Poésie involontaire et poésie intentionnelle* (1942); *Les sept poèmes d'amour en guerre* (1943); *Pour vivre ici* (1944); *Le lit la table* (1944); *Les armes de la douleur* (1944); *Dignes de vivre* (1944); *Quelques mots rassemblés pour Monsieur Dubuffet* (1944); *Liberté* (1944); *Au rendez-vous allemand* (1944); *À Pablo Picasso* (1944); *Pablo Picasso*, 1947); *En avril 1944: Paris respirait encore!* (1945); *Doubles d'ombre* (1945); *Lingères légères* (1945); *Une longue réflexion amoureuse* (1945); *Le vœu* (1945); *Souvenirs de la maison des fous* (1946); *Le dur désir de durer* (1946); *Figure humaine* (1946); *Objet des mots et des images* (1947); *Elle se fit élever un palais* (1947); *Le temps déborde* (1947); *Marc Chagall* (1947); *Corps mémorable* (1947); *Deux poètes d'aujourd'hui* (1947); *Le meilleur choix de poèmes est celui que l'on fait pour soi* (1947); *À l'intérieur de la vue* (1948); *Gabriel Péri* (1948); *Premiers poèmes* (1948); *Poèmes politiques* (1948); *Le bestiaire* (1948); *Perspectives* (1949); *Léda* (1949); *La saison des amours* (1949); *Grèce ma rose de raison* (1949); *Je l'aime, elle m'aimait* (1949); *Une leçon de morale* (1949); *Hommage aux martyrs et aux combattants du ghetto de Varsovie* (1950); *Pouvoir tout dire* (1951); *Un poème* (1951); *Première anthologie vivante de la poésie du passé* (1951); *La jarre peut-elle être plus belle que l'eau?* (1951); *Le visage de la paix* (1951); *Grain-d'aile* (1951); *Picasso, dessins* (1952); *Marines* (1952); *Les sentiers et les routes de la poésie* (1952); *Poèmes pour tous* (1952); *Œuvres complètes* (2 vols. plus *Album É.,* 1968). **FURTHER WORKS IN ENGLISH:** *Thorns of Thunder* (1936); *Selected Writings* (1951); *Last Love Poems of P. É.* (1980; bilingual ed.)

BIBLIOGRAPHY: Balakian, A., "The Post-Surrealism of Aragon and É.," *YFS*, 2 (1948), 93–102; Poulet, G., *Études sur le temps humain* (1964), Vol. 3: 126–60; Richard, J. P., *Onze études sur la poésie moderne* (1964): 105–39; Jean, R., *P. É. par lui-même* (1968); Wake, C. H., "É.: 'L'extase,'" in Nurse, P., ed., *The Art of Criticism* (1969): 287–99; Vernier, R., *"Poésie ininterrompue" et la poétique de P. É.* (1971); Greet, A. H., "P. É.'s Early Poems for Painters," *FMLS*, 9 (1973), 86–102; Hubert, R. R., "Ernst and É., a Model of Surrealist Collaboration," *KRQ*, 21 (1974), 113–21; Nugent, R., *P. É.* (1974); Bowie, M., "P. É.," in Cardinal, R., ed., *Sensibility and Creation* (1977): 149–67

—RENÉE RIESE HUBERT

ELYTIS, Odysseus

(pseud. of Odysseus Alepoudhelis) Greek poet and art critic, b. 2 Nov. 1911, Heraklion, Crete; d. 18 Mar. 1996, Athens

Although E. was born on Crete, his parents and ancestors came from the island of Lesbos, with which he feels close emotional and cultural ties. His family settled in Athens in 1914; in his youth E. studied law at the University of Athens, but never graduated. In 1929 his reading of the poetry of Paul ÉLUARD initiated his decisive commitment to SURREALISM, which was further stimulated by his friendship with the Greek poet Andreas Embirikos (1901–1975), who introduced surrealism to Greek poetry. E. made his first appearance in the periodical *Nea grammata*, the harbinger of the Greek poetic renaissance, in 1936. To the tragic conscience of modern Greece as then projected by the poetry of George SEFERIS, E.'s extraordinary lyrical gifts were to counterpose that country's eternal youthfulness and natural and spiritual beauty, and would exert a salutary and liberating influence upon a literature that had long stagnated in postsymbolist decadence and despair.

In 1940–41, to defend his country from the attack of Italian Fascism, he served as second lieutenant on the Albanian front. In 1945–46 and again in 1953–54 he was director of broadcasting and programming for the National Broadcasting Institute in Athens.

From 1948 to 1952 he studied literature at the Sorbonne in Paris, traveled in Europe, and became friends with André BRETON, Tristan TZARA, René CHAR, Pierre Jean JOUVE, Henri MICHAUX, Giuseppe UNGARETTI, Éluard, Matisse, Picasso, and other outstanding modernists in literature and art. An art critic and a painter himself, he has produced illustrations of his poetic world in gouaches and collages. From 1953 to 1958 he served as member of the Greek critical and prize-awarding Group of the Twelve, and as president and governing-board member of Karolos Koun's Art Theater and of the Greek Ballet. In 1960 he was awarded the First National Prize for Poetry, and from 1965 to 1968 he served as a member of the administrative board of the Greek National Theater. In 1962 the Greek Government made him Commander of the Order of the Phoenix. During the regime of the military junta in his country he settled once again in France, from 1969 to 1971. He won the Nobel Prize for literature in 1979, and has been awarded a number of honorary degrees.

Widely known and popular since his early verse as the "poet of the Aegean," E. has been the dominant lyrical voice of that sunlit realm—with its sea and islands under a pure blue sky—where he was born, grew up, and still spends most of his summers. "Adapting surrealism to Greek reality" (E.'s own words) through submitting the liberating force in that movement to the high discipline of a constantly experimenting, exploring, and developing art, he has mostly created in his verse a world of lucidity, purity, balance, beauty, newness, youth, and love as inspired and inspirited by, as E. has said, the "sanctity of the perceiving senses" and that of the natural world itself. His primary concern for the Greek language as it has developed since Homer's time led to his expressive richness, while the scintillating freshness of his imagery is drawn from the ancient birth-place of the Ionian-Greek culture, where the sun, as life-giving sovereign, reigns supreme, penetrating and revealing with its light the physical yet mystical essence of life: man is inseparable from nature, since in both of them the eternal processes of Eros as inspired by beauty are carried on. A feast of the senses, his early poetry as gathered in his first collection, *Prosanatolizmi* (1939; *Orientations*, 1974), has careless young boys and girls initiated into and communing with the power of love in nature's eternal elements and processes.

The war brought a cloud of painful awareness, of maturity, into his sunlit realm, as seen in his collection *Ilios of Protos, mazi me tis parallayies se mian ahtidha* (1943; *Sun the First, together with Variations of a Sunbeam*, 1974). But the war experience found its outstanding expression in *Azma iroiko ke penthimo yia ton hameno anthipolohagho tis Alvanias* (1945; *Heroic and Elegiac Song for the Lost Second Lieutenant of the Albanian Campaign*, 1965), in which the youthful hero killed on the battlefield, the embodiment of the perennial youthful victim of the world's evils, is miraculously resurrected through his youth and heroism to become a symbol and promise of life itself in its eternity.

Fourteen years of apparent silence, devoted by the poet to other intellectual and artistic activities, including his four years of study in Paris, were in fact years of gestation that resulted in the publication of his masterpiece, *To Axion Esti* (1959; *The Axion Esti*, 1974). (The title means "worthy it is," a quotation from the Byzantine laudations to Christ and the Virgin Mary.) It was soon followed by *Exi ke mia tipsis yia ton ourano* (1960; *Six and One Remorses for the Sky*, 1974), considered its contemplative companion piece.

To Axion Esti is a large unity wonderfully constructed out of an immense variety of language, meter, manner, and tone, built with

Odysseus Elytis

mathematical accuracy and ranging from epic to song, and intended to be the "Aegean" equivalent of a Byzantine mass. In its three sections, "I Ghenesis" ("The Genesis"), "Ta Pathi" ("The Passion"), and "To Dhoxastikon" ("The Gloria"), the poet identifies himself in his life experience with the sun, with his race, and with his country since its physical and spiritual creation from the initial light, then passes through the sufferings of the war decade, which he equates with Christ's Passion, and eventually emerges into the glory of a resurrection in the rebuilding of an earthly yet spiritual paradise of justice, freedom, love, and beauty. To the grimness of our postwar reality E. thus counterposed a bright promise for the future of humankind.

The historical and moral awareness that characterizes *To Axion Esti* was to yield, in the "third stage" of his development as inaugurated by *Exi ke mia tipsis yia ton ourano*, to what he has called his "solar metaphysics," best expressed in *To fotodhentro ke i dhekati tetarti omorfia* (1971; *The Light Tree and the Fourteenth Beauty*, 1974), in which a series of "instantaneous," "ascending," "meteoric," and deeply revealing solar and lunar epiphanies unfold the mystery of the Greek light in its search for and creation of a paradise as incorporated in our own world.

His most recent collection, *Maria Nefeli* (1978; *Maria Nephele*, 1981), received with great enthusiasm, in parallel monologues by a "hippie" girl and by the poet as the "counter-speaker" gives an account of the discrepancies, the alienation, the confusing and disheartening absurdity of our modern times, and shows the poet's effort to discover and appreciate in that reality the positive and eternal elements that would support his convictions and beliefs about the meaning and worth of poetry and life.

FURTHER WORKS: *O ilios o iliatoras* (1971); *To monoghramma* (1971; *The Monogram*, 1974); *Ta ro tou erota* (1972); *Ta eterothali* (1974); *Anihta hartia* (1974); *I mayiia tou Papadhiamandi* (1974). **FURTHER WORKS IN ENGLISH:** *The Sovereign Sun: Selected Poems of E.* (1974); *O. E.: Analogies of Light* (1981); *O. E.: Selected Poems* (1981)

BIBLIOGRAPHY: Friar, K., ed., "A Critical Mosaic," *The Charioteer*, 1, 2 (1960): 20–24; Friar, K., *Modern Greek Poetry: From Cavafis to E.* (1973): 82–88: 695–700; Friar, K., Introduction, notes, and bibliography to *The Sovereign Sun: Selected Poems of E.* (1974): 3–44: 179–95; Keeley, E., and Savidis, G. Preface and notes to *The Axion Esti* (1974): xiii–xv: 151–58; Ivask, I., ed., *O. E.: Analogies of Light* (1981)

—ANDONIS DECAVALLES

EMECHETA, Buchi

Nigerian novelist and juvenile fiction writer (writing in English) b. July 1944, Lagos

E. was born and grew up in Lagos, speaking both Ibo and Yoruba. Her Ibo parents died when she was quite young. To her village, Ibusa, and to her father's sister, "Big Mother," she attributes her own desire to write, to tell stories of her own family history and traditions. Although her mother wished E. to be engaged at age eleven, E. insisted on studying at Methodist Girls' High School in Lagos on scholarship until she was sixteen, when she married. After the birth of her first baby, she followed her student husband to London. To support her growing family, she took various odd jobs at places like a library and a home for underprivileged youth. She separated from her abusive and indolent husband. Working, writing at odd hours, she also studied sociology at the University of London. E. obtained her bachelor's degree in 1974. She has won several awards: Daughter of Mark Twain (1975), Afro-Caribbean Post's Golden Sunrise Award (1978), Jock Campbell-New Statesman Award (1977), Best Third World Writer for 1976–1979 Award (1979), and Best Black Writer in Britain Award (1980). Her success and international reputation enabled her to devote her time to lecturing and writing, in Africa, in Europe, and in the U.S. She founded her own publishing house named Ogwugwu Afo for an Ibo goddess. She currently makes her home in London.

"Keeping her head above water" as a single parent, a second-class citizen, poor, black, and foreign in an alien world, she calls a miracle. Most of her works reflect her own experiences as an immigrant Nigerian working woman in London, or those of her relatives in the Nigerian colonial setting of World War II or of the Biafran War (1967–1970). E. first published a column of "Observations of the London Poor" in the *New Statesman*. She later consolidated these and other anecdotes of her own life on the dole in her novel, *In the Ditch* (1972). In 1974 she published *Second-Class Citizen*, her story of her struggle for independence from her husband and from penury. The two were published together as

Adah's Story (1983). She could afford to move with her five children from county council housing to her own home in North London. Her next two novels, *The Bride Price* (1976), based on traditional Ibo marriage customs, and *The Slave Girl* (1977), modeled somewhat on her own mother's experience in Nigeria a generation ago, required sociological research as well as family oral histories. In her ironic novel *The Joys of Motherhood* (1979) she draws her main character from her own mother-in-law, a woman obedient to traditional values of fecundity in a changing world of urbanization and Western belief systems. In *Destination Biafra* (1981) her protagonist, a female military attaché, witnesses the devastation and atrocities of Nigeria's civil war, in which many of E.'s relatives suffered and died. Although she herself was in England at that time, she used eyewitness testimonies and letters to substantiate her war account.

E.'s juvenile fiction follows the course of her adult novels. *Nowhere to Play* (1980) mirrors the lives of her own children at the London housing project. *Titch the Cat* (1979) refers to their first pet in their own home. *The Moonlight Bride* (1980) describes a Nigerian village marriage custom. *The Wrestling Match* (1980) urges postwar youth against conflict and violence. *Niara Power* (1982) exposes faults of current, materialistic African society.

E. turned later to fiction not so literally based on her own experience. The novel *Double Yoke* (1982) is set at the University of Calabar where E. was a guest lecturer, but presents a student view of harassment and chicanery in academia. E.'s science-fiction novel *The Rape of Shavi* (1983) takes place in Europe and Africa, and pleads for world peace. In *Gwendolyn* (1990; pub. in the U.S. as *The Family*, 1990) E. uses a West Indian girl, sexually abused, as her protagonist, who grows up in Jamaica but moves to England and London's immigrant district. Thwarted in her hopes for schooling and security, she survives her hostile family environments and hopes that her daughter, with maternal support, will prosper. In *Kehinde* (1994) E. again exploits her theme of cross-cultural assimilation but reverses her protagonist's journey. Here Kehinde, after establishing a successful life in England for eighteen years, returns to Nigeria, only to lose status and power. Her husband has taken a second wife and sired a new family. Kehinde, disillusioned and disgruntled, chooses to return to expatriate life in England. In E.'s autobiography, *Head above Water* (1986), E. recounts her own first forty years of endurance, hardship, and persistence. She includes some description of her television and radio work. She is justly proud that she has achieved stability for her family, security for herself, and the satisfaction of what had seemed an impossible goal: success as an author, a woman, writing in a "fourth" language in an alien atmosphere.

E.'s strength as a writer relies on the force of her own personality and her clear narrative style. Emulating her "Big Mother's" storytelling power E. succeeds in holding the reader's attention and sympathy. She paints her own adventures with realistic detail, warmth, sympathy, and humor. Her best work is compellingly human, not analytic nor lyric. She feels passionate about woman's position, but is not doctrinaire enough to satisfy all feminists. Her friend, novelist Flora NWAPA, who had written fiction over twenty years and also established a printing company, was a kind of model for E. However, Nwapa remained in West Africa and followed the changing Nigerian scene. E., if she continues to draw her stories from the events of her own life, must turn to England and its multicultural environment for her subjects. Her autobiography reads as easily as her novels, but does not reveal her future plans. She promises to update it from time to time.

BIBLIOGRAPHY: Bray, R., "Nefertiti's New Clothes," *Voice Literary Supplement*, June 1982: 13–14; Bruner, C., and Bruner, D., "B. E. and Maryse Conde," *WLT*, 59, 1 (Winter 1985): 9–13; Bruner, C., "The Other Audience: Children and the Example of B. E.," *AfrSR*, 29, 3 (Sept. 1986): 129–40; Davies, C. B., and Graves, A. A., eds., *Studies of Women in African Literature* (1986): 173–80, 241–56; James, A., ed., *In Their Own Voices* (1990): 34–45; Davies, C. B., "Private Selves and Public Spaces: Autobiography and the African Woman Writer," *Neohelicon*, 17, 2 (1990): 183–210

—CHARLOTTE H. BRUNER

EMMANUEL, Pierre

(pseud. of Noël Mathieu) French poet and essayist, b. 3 May 1916, Gan; d. 22 Sept. 1984, Paris

E. spent his early years in the U.S., where his parents had emigrated, before he was sent to Lyon to study in a Catholic school. There he lived with an uncle who wanted him to become an engineer. But E. was far more interested in philosophy. He became a teacher and started writing poems closely modeled on those of Paul ÉLUARD. The decisive influence on his poetic career proved to be the poetry of Pierre Jean JOUVE, whom he met in 1936. E. has been awarded the Legion of Honor and several honorary doctorates, and was elected to the French Academy in 1968.

Three powerful images of mythic proportions dominate the work of E.: Christ, Orpheus, and, to a lesser degree, the German poet-seer Hölderlin, to whom E. devoted an entire collection of poems, *Le poète fou* (1944; *The Mad Poet*, 1956). E.'s poetic creations are firmly rooted in Christian thought. The figure of Christ, the exemplary innocent victim and implacable witness of human frailty and cruelty, is present throughout his work. E.'s Christ, however, is not the "King of Glory," but the "Man of Sorrow." With *Le poète et son Christ* (1942; the poet and his Christ), he established the image of the suffering Christ between death (Good Friday) and new life (Easter), thus creating a powerful symbol of human anguish that inevitably evokes the gruesome reality of Nazi atrocities. This image of the anguished Christ also permeates his "Resistance" poetry.

The other archetypal figure, Orpheus, appeared for the first time in *Le tombeau d'Orphée* (1941; Orpheus' tomb), the work that brought E. sudden fame. Orpheus here appears as the poet's double who, in search of his lost love, descends into hell, from which he emerges on the third day as "the pure poet born of Christ and his beloved."

With *Jour de colère* (1942; day of wrath), *Combats avec tes défenseurs* (1942; fight with your defenders), and *La liberté guide nos pas* (1945; liberty guides our steps), E. turned away from his own metaphysical quest, taking his inspiration from the immediate historical situation: the German occupation of France and the French Resistance movement. The poems, homages to a tortured nation and its victims, are a horrified indictment of a human race that forsakes the divine image in which it was created.

In spite of his very successful beginnings, E. soon became somewhat disillusioned and turned to himself and his past life. The resulting autobiographical works in prose, *Qui est cet homme?; ou, Le singular universel* (1948; *The Universal Singular*, 1951) and *L'ouvrier de la onzième heure* (1954; the worker of the eleventh hour), deal with the torments, errors, and deceptions—but also with the joys and pleasures—of the writer. During this period of critical self-evaluation, there also appeared his perhaps most ambitious poetic creation, *Babel* (1952; Babel), which reflects the poet's war experience and can be called a meditation on the pernicious hubris of man's boundless desires and misguided ambition. The principal theme deals with the rejection of God and the subsequent rise of a man, readily accepted as a substitute for God by his fellow men, who becomes an ugly tyrant of immense power, only to collapse in the end into nothingness. In *Babel* the demise of God is accompanied by the individuals' loss of their truly human qualities.

Babel did not become a great success, and perhaps did not fulfill the poet's ambition. So, after a rather long unproductive phase, E. tried his hand at a new kind of poetry, that of *Évangéliaire* (1961; evangeliary), a series of short, somewhat naïve poems, whose simplicity is in marked contrast with the difficulty of previous creations. During the 1960s, E. wrote little poetry, but a number of essays, which are very personal meditations on the act of writing itself—*Le goût de l'un* (1963; the taste for unity)—and the fundamental meaning of faith—*La face humaine* (1965; the face of man). But with the poem *Jacob* (1970; Jacob) he returned to the inspiration and style characteristic of *Babel*, which he considers his main work.

A poet of the Resistance and a passionate Christian, E. tried to express the anxiety and frustrations of his generation in poems abounding in Christian symbols and pagan myths. His poems gain in significance from the fact that they are parts of a vast ensemble conceived as the spiritual epic of an era.

In an age in which the distrust of the communicative and evocative aspects of language has become commonplace, E. firmly believes in the creative power of the biblical *logos* to capture the essence of modern man's spiritual crisis. In his poetry, realistic and mystical elements are fused into powerful, suggestive images and intricate metaphors. His versification shows him to be a master of poetic form: free verse, prose poems, alexandrines.

FURTHER WORKS: *Élégies* (1940); *XX Cantos* (1942); *Orphiques* (1942); *La colombe* (1943); *Le je universel dans l'œuvre d'Éluard* (1943); *Prière d'Abraham* (1943); *Cantos* (1944); *Hymne à la France* (1944); *Sodome* (1945); *Tristesse, ô ma patrie* (1946); *Memento des vivants* (1946); *Chansons du dé à coudre* (1947); *Poésie, raison ardente* (1948); *Car enfin je vous aime* (1950); *Visage nuage* (1955); *Versant de l'âge* (1958); *Les jours de la nativité* (1960); *Les jours de la passion* (1962); *La nouvelle naissance* (1963); *Ligne de faîte* (1966); *Baudelaire devant Dieu* (1967); *Le monde est intérieur* (1967); *Notre Père* (1969); *Autobiographies* (1970); *Choses dites* (1970); *Pour une politique de la culture* (1971); *Sophia* (1973); *La révolution parallèle* (1975); *La vie terrestre* (1976); *Tu* (1977)

BIBLIOGRAPHY: Chiari, J., *Contemporary French Poetry* (1952): 95–114; Brereton, G., *An Introduction to the French Poets* (1956): 293–95; Bosquet, A., *P. E.* (1959); Siegrist, S. E., *Pour ou contre Dieu: P. E.; ou, La poésie de l'approche* (1971); Picon, G., *Contemporary French Literature: 1945 and After* (1974): 143–44

—BLANDINE M. RICKERT

EMPSON, William

English literary critic and poet, b. 27 Sept. 1906, Howden; d. 15 April 1984, London

E. received a double degree in English and mathematics from Magdalene College, Cambridge, where he studied with I. A. RICHARDS and absorbed the generalized influence of an intellectual climate fostering the integration of science, literature, and philosophy. He occupied the chair of English literature at Bunrika Daigaku University, Tokyo, from 1931 to 1934, and was professor of English literature at the Peking National University from 1937 to 1939. During World War II he lived in London, serving as BBC Chinese editor. In 1947 he became professor of the Western languages department in Peking and served there for six years, until he was appointed to the chair of English literature at the University of Shefield, where he remained until he retired in 1971.

E.'s *Seven Types of Ambiguity* (1930; rev. ed., 1953), one of the most influential works of modern criticism, grew out of his tutorial with I. A. Richards. Responding to the influence of T. S. ELIOT and the enlightened rationalistic sensibility of the day, E. wished to extend the possibilities of the method of "close reading" invented by Robert GRAVES and Laura Riding (b. 1901) in *A Survey of Modernist Poetry* (1927). Ambiguity, a "phenomenon of compression," was, for E., "any verbal nuance, however slight, which gives room for alternative reactions to the same piece of language." These multiple meanings act to enrich our sense of poetic meaning. The reader often balances several contradictory senses of a word while pondering his own reaction; a reader sorting out the multiple ambiguities has "moving in him . . . the traces of a great part of his past experience and of the structure of his past judgments." The seven particular types are arbitrary, as well: "which class any particular poem belongs to depends in part on your own mental habits and critical opinions." Thus, each individual's interpretation of ambiguous meanings will differ, depending upon the relative circumstances of previous experience and thought. An ambiguous aspect of the work is evident: between its objective appearance as a series of close readings that, when taken together, lead to a heightened understanding of the whole; and its subjective essence as a series of idiosyncratic literary explorations that seeks to establish a communicative situation for "maintaining oneself between contradictions that can't be solved by analysis."

Some Versions of Pastoral (1935) is E.'s most ambitious critical work. In it his sprightly, discursive prose style illuminates his ideas within a historical and generic framework. "Pastoral," for E., recalling his earlier idea of "compression," puts "the complex into the simple." E.'s method is to explore a wide variety of works as they relate to the social implications of pastoral forms. The resulting discussions remain eccentric and personal, yet stylistically compelling as they grapple with moral and philosophical questions from alternatively objective and subjective perspectives. For instance, his statement that "the human creature is essentially out of place in the world and needed no fall in time to make him so" represents his detached, cosmic vantage point; but his suggestion that we, like Alice in Wonderland, should "keep from crying by considering things" underscores his individual tendency toward dexterous, epicurean intellectual investigations. Benevolent rationalistic ideas are held in ephemeral suspension with essentially irreconcilable signals from Einstein's relativistic universe: when E. is successful, we perceive particular truths in a new way; when he is off, we experience a profound tedium.

E.'s later critical work falls short of his earlier achievements. *The Structure of Complex Words* (1951), E.'s most demanding work, presents a machinery of interpretation that never manages to engage the literary examples with the same acuity as his glibly entertaining encompassing discussion. *Milton's God* (1961; rev. ed., 1965) is really a diatribe against religion: the Christian God "is the wickedest thing yet invented by the black heart of man." Milton's accomplishment is the creation of a fictional deity, one considerably more pleasant than E.'s conception of God. E., who once proposed that "the object of life, after all, is not to understand things, but to maintain one's defenses and equilibrium," here sheds his detachment for an accessible (but unpersuasive) literary tirade.

Early in his career, E. produced several volumes of poetry, all assembled in *Collected Poems* (1949; rev. ed., 1961). These recall the work of Eliot and evidence the renewed interest in the metaphysical poets: E.'s conceits are derived from philosophy, physics, and mathematics. At their best, E.'s poems emit a cautious radiance; at their worst, they are cluttered and obscure. Nevertheless, they are important for influencing later poets such as John WAIN, Kingsley AMIS, Philip LARKIN, and Donald Davie (1922-1995).

E.'s critical output, brilliant and flawed, is of inestimable significance for its pervasive effect upon the American New Critics, and for his cultivated attempt at questioning the ambiguities of our modern age.

FURTHER WORKS: *Letter IV* (1929); *Poems* (1935); *Shakespeare Survey* (1937, with George Garrett); *The Gathering Storm* (1940)

BIBLIOGRAPHY: Kenner, H., "Alice in Empsonland," *Gnomon: Essays in Contemporary Literature* (1958): 249–62; Willis, J. H., Jr., *W. E.* (1969); Sale, R., "The Achievement of W. E.," *Modern Heroism* (1973): 107–92; Gill, R., ed., *W. E.: The Man and His Work* (1974); Alpers, P., "E. on Pastoral," *NLH*, 10 (1978): 101–22; Gardner, P., and A. Gardner, *The God Approached: A Commentary on the Poems of W. E.* (1978); Norris, C., *W. E. and the Philosophy of Literary Criticism* (1978)

—GEOFFREY GREEN

ENCHI Fumiko

Japanese novelist and short-story writer, b. 2 Oct. 1905, Tokyo; d. 14 Nov. 1986, Tokyo

E. was the second daughter of the well-known Japanese linguist Ueda Kazutoshi (1867–1937). Sickly and precocious as a child, E. often stayed home from school, and instead read voraciously, thereby familiarizing herself with both modern and classic literary works. This early exposure to literature, plus frequent trips to the Kabuki theater and many hours of listening to tales told by her grandmother, helped forge E.'s own views on love. In her early teens E. was fascinated by the aesthetically sensuous descriptions prevalent in the works of Tanizaki JUN'ICHIRŌ and Nagai KAFŪ. She also enjoyed reading such Western writers as Oscar Wilde and Edgar Allan Poe. Frustrated and unchallenged, she quit high school after the tenth grade and studied English, French, and classical Chinese at home under tutors.

E. began her literary career by publishing a short drama at the age of twenty-one. At twenty-three another of her plays was produced on the stage. After her marriage two years later and the subsequent birth of her only child, E. found that writing plays did not provide her enough freedom to express what was in her mind. Turning to fiction, she attempted to bring out the complexities of human psychology. Her career as a novelist, however, did not have an easy start. Not until twenty years later, at the age of forty-eight, with the publication of her short story "Himojii tsukihi" (1953; the starving years), did E. finally gain recognition. She was awarded the sixth Women's Literary Award for this work in the following year. Her literary activities have been vigorous since then.

Onnazaka (1957; *The Waiting Years*, 1971) is probably the best known of E.'s works. It is also her only novel translated into English so far. Unlike many of her stories, which are admixtures of reality and fantasy, *Onnazaka* is strictly realistic, and has none of E.'s usual "amoral" topics (adultery and seduction). Neither does it deal with eroticism of middle-aged women, E.'s recurrent theme. Instead, Tomo, the stoic heroine, endures long years of humiliation by her lustful husband, who keeps two mistresses—all three women under the same roof. She vents her spite in curt, strikingly revengeful words spoken on her deathbed, which makes a powerfully effective conclusion. The Noma Literary Prize was awarded this work in 1957.

E.'s autobiographical trilogy, *Ake o ubau mono* (1957; one who steals red), *Kizu aru tsubasa* (1962; the injured wing), and *Niji to shura* (1968; rainbow and carnage), is probably more representative of her work. In these novels she depicts a woman's loveless, acrimonious marriage and her relationships with other men. The heroine's intense frustration as a novelist undoubtedly parallels E.'s own experience before she established herself as a writer. She received the fifth Tanizaki Jun'ichirō Award for the trilogy in 1969.

It is in many of her short stories that E. often exhibits her profound knowledge of classical Japanese literature by weaving elements from it into contemporary settings, which become fascinating combinations of reality and fantasy, actuality and apparition. For example, in "Nise no enishi: shūi" (1957; the conjugal ties: gleanings), she borrows the theme of a mysterious tale with the same title by Ueda Akinari (1734–1809), in which a man long dead returns to life, to create a bizarre story about a woman who gives herself over to wild fantasies.

One of E.'s latest accomplishments is the translation into modern Japanese of *The Tale of Genji*, the long 11th-c. tale by the court lady Murasaki Shikibu; E. succeeds well in reproducing the sensitivity of the original.

E. is highly respected by critics for her profound knowledge of classical Japanese literature, her careful choice of words, and her literary versatility. Yet her work is also loved by the general public for being neither overintellectual nor too theoretical.

FURTHER WORKS: *Aki no mezame* (1958); *Onnamen* (1958); *Watashi mo moete iru* (1960); *Aijō no keifu* (1961); *Hanachirusato* (1961); *Minami no hada* (1961); *Onna no mayu* (1962); *Onna obi* (1962); *Tsui no sumika* (1962); *Shishijima kidan* (1963); *Yukimoe* (1964); *Komachi hensō* (1965); *Namamiko Monogatari* (1965); *Azayaka na onna* (1965); *Kakeru mono* (1965); *Senhime shunjūki* (1966); *Saimu* (1976); *Shokutaku no nai ie* (1979)

—YOKO MCCLAIN

ENCKELL, Rabbe

Finnish poet, dramatist, essayist, and critic (writing in Swedish), b. 3 March 1903, Tammela; d. 17 June 1974, Helsinki

E. was a member of a distinguished Finland-Swedish intellectual family: his father was a well-known agronomist, and of his brothers, one, Olof E. (b. 1900) has been a prolific critic and literary scholar, while another, Torger E. (b. 1901), is a painter and etcher with an international reputation. On the surface, E.'s career was notably serene and successful; among the Finland-Swedish MODERNISTS, his verse in particular won early acclaim because of its clarity and precision, and his career was capped, in 1960, by his selection as the resident in the Poet's House at Porvoo, that is, as poet laureate of Swedish Finland. The last decade of his life was darkened, however, by attacks from the political left, which considered him to be an elitist—as he was—in both life and letters.

Even E.'s debut revealed the master; the brief but intense love lyrics of *Dikter* (1923; poems), as free from sentimentality as they were from traditional rhymes and meters, were followed by the epithalamiums of *Flöjtblåsarlycka* (1925; flutist's happiness), directed both to the beloved and to nature. *Vårens cistern* (1931; the spring's cistern) was distinguished by E.'s "matchstick poems," equivalents of the Japanese haiku, in which he apprehended specifically Finnish pastoral scenes.

As a result of a crisis in his personal life, the poetry of the later 1930s changed tone; yet *Tonbrädet* (1935; the sounding board) and *Valvet* (1937; the vault) are not patently confessional, but speak through allusions to classical myth; simultaneously, E.'s sense of form became more conservative, and he sometimes employed regular strophes suggesting those of the Horatian ode. The fascination with antiquity continued into *Lutad över brunnen* (1942; bent over the well), in which the careful reader can find references to the perils then besetting Finland. However, E. was neither an academic poet (although in some ways he resembled his Finland-Swedish predecessor in quasiclassical verse, Emil Zilliacus [1878–1961]) nor a political one; his main poetic concerns now lay with specific literary questions, and in *Andedräkt av koppar* (1947; breath of copper) he analyzed modern poetry itself. It was this collection, and its main poem, "O spång av mellanord" (oh bridge of words between), that firmly established him on the Parnassus of Sweden proper; the major Swedish modernist poet Erik LINDEGREN wrote the introduction to the retrospective selection from E.'s lyrics, *Nike flyr i vindens klädnad* (1947; Nike flees in the wind's raiment), which marks the closing off of the middle phase of E.'s career.

The seven collections of poems that subsequently appeared, from *Sett och återbördat* (1950; seen and restored) to the posthumous *Flyende spegel* (1974; fleeting mirror), might be compared to a long poetic diary, sketches by a skilled hand that had wholly mastered the arts of compression and concision. Of these books, *Det är dags* (1965; it is time), with its sense of leave-taking, its tributes to the towns of E.'s beloved Italy, its self-confessed misanthropy, and its deep-seated cultural pessimism, is the most impressive.

Previously, Greek myth had also informed a series of brief plays on classical themes: *Orpheus och Eurydike* (1938; Orpheus and Eurydice), inspired by the personal crisis and intimate loss that had also given rise to E.'s verse collections of the time; *Iokasta* (1939; Jocasta); the several playlets included in *Lutad över brunnen*; and then *Agamemnon* (1949; Agamemnon); *Hekuba* (1952; Hecuba); *Mordet på Kiron* (1954; the murder of Chiron); and the relatively lighthearted *Alkman* (1959; Alcman). These plays had some success when performed on radio; in the introduction to *Dikt* (1966; poem), where E. reprinted *Iokasta*, together with two new plays (*Laios* [Laius] and *Latona* [Latona]), he conceded that the language of the earlier dramas had been excessively lofty—a fact that may contribute to their neglect in the future. Nonetheless, they are an integral part of E.'s oblique self-revelations.

The prose of E., like his lyrics, shows a mixture of passion and coolness, expressed in a language of quiet elegance. E. analyzed his own personality in *Tillblivelse* (1929; becoming) and *Ljusdunkel* (1930; chiaroscuro), turning then to his first wife in *Ett porträtt* (1931; a portrait); all three of these works could be described as half-narrative, half-essayistic. The reflective novellas *Landskapet med den dubbla skuggan* (1933; the landscape with the double shadow) and *Herrar till natt och dag* (1937; lords of night and day) were artistically less convincing, and he did not try the narrative again. Even in the 1920s, though, he had proved himself to be one of the North's leading critics, and his essays were collected in *Relation i det personliga* (1950; personal report), followed by *Essay om livets framfart* (1961; essay on life's sweep), which contained personal analysis, still more diaristic fragments, poetry, and E.'s portrait of his father. The four later volumes of aphoristic prose (often interlarded with pieces of verse) likewise have the air of being entries in a meditative notebook.

E. is a central figure in Swedish-language poetry of the 20th c. The stamp of a lucid and varied intelligence—one is tempted to use the word "Goethean"—is borne by everything he wrote.

FURTHER WORKS: *Traktat* (1953); *Skuggors lysen* (1953); *Strån över backen* (1957); *Dikter i urval* (1957); *Landskapet med den dubbla skuggan: Ungdomsprosa 1928–1937* (1958); *Kärnor av ögonblick* (1959); *Kalender i fragment* (1962); *Och sanning?* (1966); *Tapetdörren* (1968); *Resonören med fågelfoten* (1971); *Dikter 1923–1937* (1971)

BIBLIOGRAPHY: Schoolfield, G. C., "Canals on Mars: The Recent Scandinavian Lyric, I," *BA*, 36 (1962): 9–19; Schoolfield, G. C., "R. E., *Mot Itaka*," *GN*, 7 (1976): 17–22: 36–39; Petherick, K., "Four Finland-Swedish Prose Modernists: Aspects of the Work of Hagar Olsson, Henry Parland, Elmer Diktonius, and R. E.," *Scan*, 15 (1976): 45–62

—GEORGE C. SCHOOLFIELD

ENDŌ Shūsaku

Japanese novelist, dramatist, and essayist, b. 27 Mar. 1923, Tokyo; d. 29 Sept. 1996, Tokyo

E. lived with his parents in Dalian, China, between the ages of three and ten; when his mother filed for divorce, she returned to Japan with E. and his brother, and there all three became Catholics. E. was eleven at the time of his baptism, and has often described the experience as having a suit of foreign clothing placed on him by his mother. His chief literary task, he has written, has been to retailor those foreign clothes to fit his Japanese body. E. graduated in French literature from Keiō University, and was among the first group of Japanese chosen for overseas study after World War II. In

1950 he sailed to France, where he lived for almost three years, studying Catholic writers at the University of Lyons. A serious lung ailment forced him to return to Japan, where he began publishing essays and fiction. A trip to Europe to study the Marquis de Sade (1740–1814) was cut short by another pulmonary illness, which forced E. into two and a half years of hospitalization and three operations, which resulted in the removal of one entire lung.

After recuperating, E. began writing about the persecution of Japanese Christians in the 17th c. He also undertook management of Kiza, the largest amateur theatrical troupe in Japan, and became editor of the major literary journal *Mita Bungaku*. He was elected to the Japan Academy of Arts in 1981, was voted president of the Japan chapter of P.E.N. in 1985, and was designated a "person of cultural merit" by the Japanese government in 1988.

E.'s earliest works, including the novella *Shiroi hito* (1955; white men) and its companion work, *Kiiroi hito* (1955; Yellow men), and such novels as *Umi to dokuyaku* (1957; *The Sea and Poison*, 1972) and *Kazan* (1959; *Volcano*, 1978) raise large philosophical and moral questions about the differences in spiritual climates between Japan and the West. For the most part they argue, through the presentation of apostate foreign priests and unfeeling Japanese converts, that the sense of guilt and sin that informs the Christian West is absent in Japan. These works are largely pessimistic about the possibility of planting the seeds of Christian moral accountability in Asian soil.

With the publication of the short-story collection *Aika* (1965; elegies), however, and most especially the novel *Chimmoku* (1966; *Silence*, 1969), E. began to suggest the prospect of salvation from the spiritual "mud swamp" of Japan through acts of caring and selfless love on the part of weak, often ineffectual characters. In *Chimmoku*, it is a European priest who cannot stand up to the tortures of Japanese officials in the period of persecution who apostatizes in order to save the lives of innocent Japanese believers. His inverted "conversion" to a more internalized, passive form of worship sets the model for later E. protagonists.

If a highly Japanized version of Christianity emerges victorious in *Chimmoku*, in E.'s next major historical novel, *Samurai* (1980; *The Samurai*, 1982), both the passionately fervent Western priest and the withdrawn, hesitant Japanese samurai convert are allowed to follow their separate visions of Christian devotion. The mode of narration in *Samurai*, shifting between the first-person accounts of the dynamic Spanish priest and the omniscient passages that gently intimate the emotions of the Japanese warrior, allowed E. to affirm both the diversity and the viability of these very disparate approaches to Christ.

In his most recent novel, *Sukyandaru* (1986; *Scandal*, 1988), E. has departed from the historical-fiction genre to examine questions of the nature of evil in the contemporary age, framed in a simple doppelgänger tale. E. parodies his own position as the leading Japanese Christian writer in this work, proposing that the power of wealth and position can bury public scandals, but that scandals of the soul are what canker the individual's relationship with deity.

E. has also written a large number of humorous novels and essays, and in Japan is highly regarded for these lighter works. The entertainment novels include *Obakasan* (1959; *Wonderful Fool*, 1974), which examines the spiritual and cultural gap between Japan and the West from a gentler angle in its portrayal of a bumbling Frenchman loose in modern-day Tokyo; *Watashi ga suteta onna* (1963; the girl I left behind), in which E. presents his view of a contemporary saint in the form of a young woman who sacrifices her own happiness to work at a leper colony; and

Kuchibue o fuku toki (1974; *When I Whistle*, 1979), in which self-centered high achievers of the modern age are contrasted with the bonds of friendship that linked young people during the war years.

E. has cut a unique and original niche for himself in contemporary Japanese fiction, exploring questions of moral responsibility and religious adherence that are largely anathema to his fellow writers. The contrasts between Japan and the West that he explores, the adroit construction of his novels, and the compassionate concern he has for the weak and suffering characters in his stories have made him one of the most controversial and widely read authors of his generation in Japan.

FURTHER WORKS: *Hechimakun* (1961); *Kekkon* (1962); *Tomoshibi no urumu koro* (1964); *Ichi ni san* (1964); *Ryūgaku* (1965; *Foreign Studies*, 1989); *Ōgon no kuni* (1966; *The Golden Country*, 1970); *Kin to gin* (1966); *Kyōsōkyoku* (1966); *Saraba natsu no hikari yo* (1966); *Yami no yobu koe* (1966); *Dokkoisho* (1967); *Kaidanji, kaidanji* (1968); *Kagebōshi* (1968); *Taihen daa* (1969); *Bara no yakata* (1969); *Rakuten taishō* (1969); *Haha naru mono* (1971); *Kurombō* (1971); *Tadaima rōnin* (1972); *Shikai no hotori* (1973); *Menamugawa no Nipponjin* (1973); *Iesu no shōgai* (1973; *A Life of Jesus*, 1978); *Piero no uta* (1974); *Kare no ikikata* (1975); *Minoue sōdan* (1975); *Suna no shiro* (1976); *Tetsu no kubikase* (1977); *Kanashimi no uta* (1977); *Kirisuto no tanjō* (1978); *Jū to jūjika* (1979); *Jūichi no iro garasu* (1979); *Ōhi Marii Antowanetto* (1980); *Mahiru no akuma* (1980); *Chichioya* (1980); *Ōkoku e no michi* (1981); *Tenshi* (1982); *Onna no isshō; Kiku no baai* (1982); *Onna no isshō; Sachiko no baai* (1982); *Shukuteki* (1985); *Waga kou hito wa* (1987); *Hangyaku* (1989). FURTHER WORKS IN ENGLISH: *Stained Glass Elegies: Stories by Shusaku Endo* (1985)

BIBLIOGRAPHY: Uyttendaele, F., "S. E.," *Japan Christian Quarterly*, Fall 1972: 199–205; Mathy, F., "S. E.: The Second Period," *Japan Christian Quarterly*, Fall 1974: 214–20; Woodward, K., "Finding Jesus in Japan," *Newsweek* (1 Dec. 1980): 106; Wills, G., "Embers of Guilt," *NYRB* (19 Feb. 1981): 21–22; Gessel, V. C., "Voices in the Wilderness," *MN*, 37, 4 (Winter 1982): 437–57; Ribeiro, J., "Of Martyrdom and Apostasy," *Asiaweek* (21 Oct. 1983): 63–65; Gessel, V. C., "E. S.," *Encyclopedia of Japan* (1983), Vol. 2, 214; Ribeiro, J., "S. E.; Japanese Catholic Novelist," *America* (2 Feb. 1985): 87–89; Gessel, V. C., *The Sting of Life* (1989): 231–81

—VAN C. GESSEL

ENGLISH LITERATURE

Poetry

In tracing the movements within a poetry so rich and varied as that of England in this century, a cautionary word is in order. Poetic movements are not monolithic. The IMAGISTS, the Georgians, the AUDEN group, the Movement, are motley crews when closely examined—nor do they maintain orderly ranks through time. That they sometimes appear more of a piece than they really are, originates in misconceptions promoted by critics (who may also be writers of poetry) more zealous to establish a pantheon of poets than to examine the variable substance of poetry itself.

English poetry of this century rightly begins with Thomas HARDY. After the adverse critical reception of his last novel, *Jude the Obscure* (1895), Hardy kept to poetry, where he could say, without public censure, what he wanted to about the moral vagaries of human existence and what he took to be cosmic indifference to man's fate. The emphasis in his fiction on dignity, courage, and love is even more evident in the shorter compass and compression of imagery and rhythm in verse.

The integrity with which he maintained his belief that the world could be improved (his "meliorism") in a language of both surface and depth made him attractive to the Georgians, who wanted to anchor their own revulsion against easy moralizing and ornate language in a poetry of nature and an unsentimental view of life. Hardy's influence on individual writers was considerable, appearing in such major poets as Auden and Robert GRAVES.

W.B. YEATS, although Irish of Protestant heritage, lived for some time in England and had close professional relationships with English writers. He, probably more than any other, exemplifies that cultural cross-fertilization within the British Empire and Commonwealth nations, which developed and grew strong even as the Empire was disintegrating. There is a sense in which Yeats's poetry projects a similar inner pressure for renewal. His early poems are vaguely melancholy, as if muted like Ireland itself by North Atlantic mists.

But the maxims of folklore, observation of rural hardships, the struggle for Irish national expression, and most importantly his own profound commitment to the discipline of poetry, toughened the fiber of his verse and brought him to reject "impersonal beauty." These are considerations that in a century of disillusionments made Yeats attractive to the poets who followed.

The association of Yeats with Lady Gregory (1852–1932) in the Irish National Theatre enlarged his outlook and style to accommodate in his poems the frustrations, responsibilities, and bitterness of public affairs. Adjusting to the lead of T. S. ELIOT and Ezra POUND in seeking a more rigorous poetic language, Yeats began to write direct, epigrammatic verse, which incorporated, paradoxically, a symbolic system, described in *A Vision* (1925), based on occultist concepts and automatic writing.

Yeats's poetry illustrates that a poet's world view does not have to be credible to be impressive, even profound. His strength lies in the cadence of day-to-day English enriched by Irish rhythms and subtle echoes of English verse, in the selection of images that induce the intended sensory experience, and in the creation of a poetic world imbued with vitality.

Imagism, reacting against Victorian poeticism, originated in casual meetings of the "Poets Club" at Oxford in 1908, called together by T. E. Hulme (1883–1917). Though of limited achievement, it left a mark on subsequent poetry in rhythm, economy, and in treatment of the subject. Hulme, originally a mathematician and biologist, was one of the first scientific minds in the 20th c. to turn to literature as a way of thought as inevitable as that of science. By early 1909 he had drawn F. S. Flint (1885–1966) into discussions of French, Japanese, and Hebrew poetic practices. The object was to rescue English poetry from the lockstep of iambic meter and to reinvigorate it with fresh images. Hulme's "society" was soon after joined by Ezra Pound, who introduced his own similar ideas into their discussions.

Another American, Hilda DOOLITTLE, along with Richard Aldington (1892–1962), joined the Pound group in 1911. Their practice was formulated in three rules: direct treatment of the thing, economy and precision of language, and composition in the sequence of the musical phrase instead of regular beat. Four annual anthologies followed; the first, *Des Imagistes* (1914), contains poems by the selfstyled imagists—Pound, Doolittle, Aldington, and Flint—as well as verse by James JOYCE, Ford Madox FORD, William Carlos WILLIAMS, Amy LOWELL and others. Before the appearance of *Some Imagist Poets* in 1915, Pound had joined Wyndham LEWIS's Vorticism movement.

The Georgians also reacted against the meretricious moralizing, orotundity, and metaphysical pretentiousness of Victorian poetry at its worst, and against the decadent aestheticism of the 1890s. Their poetry is distinguished by subject matter (English pastoral life and the worlds of children, animals, and dreams) and style (a spare Wordsworthian plainness).

But the Georgian poets could not withstand the trauma of World War I nor compete with the more rigorous theories and practices of Imagism and Vorticism. Although the solidarity of the Georgians could not be maintained, the major principles of their verse and many of their objectives are evident in subsequent writing.

World War I hastened the change in attitude toward subject matter and treatment begun by the Georgians and Imagists. Edward THOMAS, the most accomplished of the Georgians, was killed in 1917. He had earned a living by writing stories for children and travel books, and produced in the last few years of his life a small but distinguished corpus of poetry.

Wilfred OWEN, killed at the war's end, had worked back from his subject to discover the materials and to forge the techniques for expressing in fresh and powerful ways the "pity" of war. The poetry of Isaac ROSENBERG remains the most enigmatic of all those who died in the conflict, leaving unanswered the question of whether his striking, although unfulfilled, originality would have been possible without the pressures of combat and imminent death. The poetic talent of Siegfried SASSOON, one of the survivors, did not last beyond the war. He will be remembered for his help to Robert Graves and Owen, for his bitter, denunciatory poems about combat, and for the single lyric that best expresses the feeling at the armistice: "Suddenly everyone burst out singing" (1918).

The eclecticism that had set in during the last decades of the 19th c. proliferated after the shattering impact of World War I. T. S. Eliot, reacting against the disintegration of standards, worked out an aesthetic based on conservative social, political, and religious principles. His poetry was both admired and condemned for defending the establishment. His program for poetry succeeded in part because it advanced what appeared to be new and exciting solutions to formal problems: the elimination of transitions, and telescoping of images for presenting archetypal ideas.

Beyond new techniques, however, Eliot also proposed several basic principles, which had been prepared for in the work of the 17th-c. metaphysical poets, of Gerard Manley Hopkins, and of the French writer Jules Laforgue (1860–1887). One was the concept of cultural synchronicity, which unified past and present in shared values. The idea that the past had not irrevocably disappeared was welcome in an age when time sped ever faster and when the war had seemed to cut a chasm between this age and what went before.

Another idea ready for its time was the appeal for a "unified sensibility" that would bring together intellect and feeling, sundered, as Eliot theorized, by the first great impact of science in the 17th c. The 20th-c. secular version of the 19th-c. warfare between science and religion was sustained by the ever more startling revelations of science. Humanistic thought, on all fronts vulnerable as a result of

its comparative inactivity, aspired to adopt science and technology as its own. Reconciling thought and feeling was, on this level of insecurity, a consummation to be desired. It was often overlooked that consummation really amounted to capitulation, in which intellect was defined as thinking, and thinking the province of science.

It was Owen who wrote, "true poets must be truthful," a principle that sums up the intent of the Imagists and the Vorticists, and establishes for poets of the two decades between the wars the objective of recalling or discovering what that could mean. Such poets as Pound attempted to catch the truth of translation and the truth of satire; Eliot and Graves would recall it from its classical origins, Yeats would look for it in the rag-and-bone shop of the heart, and Auden and Stephen SPENDER would seek to discover it blossoming out of the dustbins of urban life and industrial ruins, and in the new verities of psychology and communism.

Pound, although American-born, lived in England (1908–20) during the crucial years of change in English poetry. His self-confidence, energy, and commitment to world poetry made his influence irresistible and indelible. In *Hugh Selwyn Mauberly* (1920) Pound satirizes Western culture, that "bitch gone in the teeth." His translations, from Provençal, Italian Renaissance, and Chinese poetry are often small miracles of re-creation. Pound was generous with his help (to Joyce, Wyndham Lewis, and Eliot). His personality and critical theories influenced many others. His own work lacks the amplitude he tried to achieve in the *Cantos* (1917–68) and, except for *Hugh Selwyn Mauberly*, coherence.

The aberrations of his own mind—the discontinuity of both intellectual and imaginative faculties, the intermittently virulent anti-Semitism—are reflected in the *Cantos*, many of the later ones in fragments. Critical opinion remains divided about these "magnificent conversations," unfinished at his death. All that can be said with certainty is that like Joyce's *Finnegans Wake* (1939) and David JONES's *Anathemata* (1952), they represent the attempt to bring literature into a comparable complexity and universality with science and philosophy.

The long perspective distorts. To describe the 1920s and 1930s as dominated by Eliot, the 1940s and 1950s by Auden, largely reflects a predilection for critical theory over the poetry itself, and fails to take into account the richness and variety of poetry written during those decades.

Edwin MUIR was born in the Orkneys and for many years lived in Glasgow. His poetry reflects both these environmental influences—the island's amplitude of nature and the city's feeling of confinement. Rhythmic variety, exciting imagery, music, are not prominent in his poetry. They reflect, nevertheless, the power of his own sweetness of temperament, a mystical insight into the relations of nature and human nature, and an ability to represent the relationship in myths of his own making.

The early poetry of Edith SITWELL continues to be heard in the music of *Façade* by William Walton, and read in those anthologies careful to include the truly experimental. Sitwell's childhood was miserable, dominated by eccentric, rich, and ambitious parents. Attributable to her unhappy early life are the radical syncopation of rhythm, rich color, and surrealistic images, all expressions of a powerful emotional reaction.

Arthur Waley (1889–1966) exercised a strong influence on 20th-c. poetic practice and theory through his translation from the Chinese: *170 Chinese Poems* (1919), *The Book of Songs* (1937), *Chinese Poems* (1946). His own descriptive translations of Chinese ideograms, admired by Pound and Yeats, encouraged a dense imagery and, in subsequent decades, a proliferation of imitators of Chinese and Japanese style and forms.

John MASEFIELD produced several fine narrative poems, the best known being *The Everlasting Mercy* (1911). His attempts at a genuine realism were inhibited by a gentility that he could not shake off.

W. H. DAVIES, tramp-poet of the open road, had little formal education. He wrote a number of fine, simple lyrics among a good many that appear too calculated to impress with their simplicity. Harold Munro (1879–1940), after writing much Georgian verse, expressed a true poetic talent in a few late poems. Herbert READ distinguished as a critic of art and literature, published several volumes of poetry. He influenced the resurgent romanticism of the "New Apocalyptics" in the 1940s.

Another of the war survivors, Wilfred Gibson (1878–1962) left behind his early poetry, Victorian in style and manner, and went on to contribute to the early move in the century toward realistic treatment. His studies of everyday life are brought together in *Collected Poems* (1926). He continued to publish poetry until 1947 (*Cold Knuckles*), including a number of verse dramas.

The best work of Edmund Blunden (1896–1974) is contained in *Poems 1914–1930* (1930). He turned from citing the horrors of war to write a kind of nature poetry that at its best has something of Walter DE LA MARE's magical overtones.

The poetry of Robert Graves is fascinating in part for what lies behind it—vast reading in anthropology and mythology and the poetic schema based on these sources. All mythology, in his view, retains evidence of a matriarchal order found in allegiance to the Triple Goddess, destroyed by invading northern patriarchal forces and replaced by a male sun god. Graves's poetry also retains evidence of its origins in Georgian principles. It is a poetry of nature with correspondences to the muse world elaborated in *The White Goddess* (1945).

The 1920s was a decade of innovative poetry, beginning with the publication of Pound's *Hugh Selwyn Mauberley*. This attempt "to condense the James novel" exhibited the polyglot texture and abrupt transitions that characterize T. S. Eliot's *The Waste Land* (1922). Pound was already at work on the *Cantos*, in which these qualities were dominant.

After World War I journals of small circulation carried writers' work and critical positions to a small, elite readership. This development promoted a sectarian spirit in poetry that polemicists like Pound and Wyndham Lewis were able to exploit in advancing and consolidating their own literary program. Such journals as *Blast* (1914–19) edited by Wyndham Lewis, and *The Criterion* (1922–39), edited by Eliot, encouraged innovative writing and internationalist art. Special forums of this kind advanced the obscurity and elitism so often characteristic of experimental writing from the 1920s through the 1950s. In the 1950s small presses (such as Fulcrum, Migrant, Anvil, and Trigram) performed a signal service in bringing relatively obscure poets into print.

A number of poets were outside the stream of experimentation in the early decades. For example, Ruth PITTER bears some resemblance to Muir in the contemplative intensity of her vision. Her poems, often about nature and domesticity, are Christian in thought and feeling. Although neglected through most of her early and middle life, she received more attention in the 1970s, in part because of the publication of *Collected Poems* in 1969.

There were other poets writing formally traditional verse. Sylvia Townsend WARNER with a well-established following as a novelist, has been underestimated as a poet. Her poems are carefully wrought, succinct, and regular, qualities that may help to explain her neglect by many contemporary readers, who prefer a more robust enthusiasm. The poems of Charlotte Mew (1896–1928) reveal a cool, precise observation, something like that of Hardy (who recognized her talent and encouraged her), but her somber, stoic tone, which matched her way of life, is all her own. Anna Wickham (1884–1947), like Mew, committed suicide. Her poems record a wry disenchantment with the urban scene and its inhabitants.

Apart from the public figures of the 1920s and 1930s was Stevie SMITH; her *Collected Poems* (1976), illustrated by drawings by the poet, reveals a mind of high seriousness that perceives that the comic and the bitter in life are often associated. Also apart from the public involvement of the 1930s generation was Eliot, who, having expressed his sense of the world's fragmentation and emptiness in *The Waste Land* and "The Hollow Men" (1925), joined the Church of England and worked during the 1930s on *The Four Quartets* (1943) in his search for the "still center."

Poetry in the first three decades of the century exhibited the usual opposed tendencies: a "return" to tradition (however identified) and a search for innovation. The Georgians are an example of the first tendency, the Imagists of the second.

Those poets in each movement who had something compelling to say—Graves and Pound, chiefly—went on to other means of poetic formulation. The emphasis of Pound on precision of images and rhythms derived from the subject rather than imposed on it, and Eliot's similar views, especially the importance of finding the just right objects or persons or sensation to represent an emotion (the "objective correlative" for that emotion), had much to do with the kind of poetry written between 1917 ("The Love Song of J. Alfred Prufrock") and 1930 ("Ash-Wednesday")—but not everything.

During these years Graves was staking out his own territory by traditional means in classical form—helped by the example and companionship of Laura Riding (1901–1991)—and beginning to defend it (*A Survey of Modernist Poetry*, 1927, with Riding). Muir was molding the timeless experiences of childhood into poems with archetypal themes of persistent attractiveness.

The personal influence of Pound lessened after he took up residence in Italy, and Eliot, after his public affirmation of royalism and Anglo-Catholicism, was too high above the fray despite the continued respect in which he was held, to make a significant impression on the practice of a new generation of poets. These—the "thirties generation"—found a new leader, a congenial style, and new subject matter, in the person and poetry of W. H. Auden.

Most of the poets of the thirties generation were born too late to participate in the 1914–18 baptism by fire and mud. A sense of guilt and displacement in their time was compounded by the general strike, economic depression, and antiwar movements during the period of their maturation, all of which marked their poetry in subtle ways. Among the representative poets of this generation—Louis MACNEICE, C. DAY LEWIS, Spender—Auden was clearly the dominant figure. The special Auden issue of *New Verse*, brought out in his thirtieth year, 1937, viewed him as possibly a genius, and his poetry likely to develop and endure despite its occasional pedantry and fixation on adolescent gamesmanship. He was, wrote Dylan THOMAS, whose approach to poetry was quite different, "a wide and deep poet."

War and the notion of war spread over the decade. Its vocabulary permeates much of the 1930s poetry. At first the tone was pacifistic, in reaction to the horrors of the past war. But when the

Spanish Civil War began to develop as a symbolic struggle between privilege and socialism, many of the thirties generation felt the need to make a personal commitment.

What they wrote from Spain exhibits the usual complexity of war poetry in its obsession with the senseless acts of brutality and betrayal, and in its meditations on sacrifice, heroism, and loneliness of the spirit. This war, like World War I, took its toll of poets: Julian Bell (1908–1937), Christopher Caudwell (1907–1937), and John Cornford (1915–1936).

Auden appropriated the vocabulary of social struggle and class war (the enemy, armies, frontiers, leaders) and combined it with the concept of "moralized landscape" to construct a poetry of topopsychography, in which the times' guilt, masochism, struggle, and hedonism are displayed in symbolic landscapes.

Poems of the 1930s often preached the doctrines of social solidarity, envisioning an ultimate ideal independence for the individual. Spender's flirtation with communism is characteristic in its search for alleviation of loneliness through the comradeship of those joined in a common enterprise. Spender's life and his writing are characterized by painful self-scrutiny, disarming honesty, and persistent involvement with rebellious youth movements from generation to generation. Following Auden's lead, he attempted to incorporate the imagery of modern technology into his poetry, with only moderate success.

The idealism and reformist zeal of the early 1930s darkened under the events of the middle years. Faith in social action gave way to savage attacks on the system and to a symbolism expressing a more subjective accomodation to an intractable public scene. Poets of this "new generation," George BARKER, Dylan Thomas, Kenneth Allott (b. 1912), David Gascoyne (b. 1916), Roy FULLER Bernard Spencer (1910–1963), and others, found EXPRESSIONISM, SURREALISM, and Romanticism suitable for describing their disintegrating world. It was a poetry suited to an apocalyptic time of genocide, air raids, and the lives of deprivation and restrictions imposed on the population of England.

World War II had a different effect on the imagination from that of the first war with its nightmare of intermittent mass slaughter and persistent misery of the trenches. Sometimes the intervals between military engagements or bombings were more stimulating to the deeper regions of the mind than the trauma of combat. A number of writers developed their talents during time in the Fire Service including Spender and John Lehmann (b. 1907).

In long periods of inactivity during his duty in Kenya, Roy Fuller found himself observing nature intently, and produced poems about animals with profound implications for the meaning of human life (*The Middle of a War*, 1942). For Fuller, as for others, the war had a catastrophic impact on the spirit. Some, broken by the impact, were unable to bring their creative faculties through to a time of relative calm. Others were stimulated by the dangers to which they were exposed to write what they might not otherwise have been able to write. Others scarcely into their careers were killed, notably Alun Lewis (1915–1944) and Keith DOUGLAS. Among the war poets were Henry Reed (b. 1914) and Frank Prince (b. 1912), whose "Naming of Parts" (1948) and "Soldiers Bathing" (1953) capture perfectly two characteristic moments of military service. David Gascoyne survived to continue writing his delicately surrealistic poems.

As the equally freighted rhetoric of Winston Churchill was no longer so moving when the events that provoked it were no more, so the new romantics suffered reaction, the more rapid after Dylan

Thomas's death in 1953. The language and rhythms of Thomas's poems at their best, as in the villanelle "Do Not Go Gentle . . ." (1946) and the meticulous syllabic verse of "Fern Hill" (1946), convey an exciting vitality, especially when read aloud in his own sonorous voice. At their worst, they are turgid, emotionally overstated, and pretentiously cryptic. The successors of the new romantics, the primary reaction, were those poets anthologized in Robert Conquest's (b. 1917) *New Lines* (1955), such as Philip LARKIN, Elizabeth JENNINGS, and D. J. ENRIGHT. They were reacting, in general, to overstatement and lushness, and turning to British ways and scenes in preference to the modernism that was dissolving national cultural boundaries. It was perhaps a return to secure insularity after so much outreach during the war and its drain on feelings and affection.

Larkin's models were Hardy and Edward Thomas, and to the degree that Thomas was one of the Georgian poets and Hardy had been a strong influence, the "New Lines" poets have made a somewhat similar progress, some of them, such as Jennings and Larkin, continuing to write without strong propulsion to say much beyond what they had been saying so well, while others, such as Donald Davie (1922–1995) and Thom Gunn (b. 1929), gravitated toward the international scene under the modernist impulse of Pound.

Basil BUNTING was one of those strongly influenced by Pound who developed a voice of his own—sensuous, musical, and dramatic. His long poem *Briggflatts* (1966) draws on his imprisonment for pacifism during World War I, his years with Pound at Rapallo, and his service with the diplomatic corps in Iran after 1945.

English poetry in the two decades after the war began to show the effects of outside influences, particularly from the Russians PASTERNAK and MAYAKOVSKY and the German TRAKL. The impact on poets of the Surrealist Exhibition (London, 1935), with its collection of works illustrating what was believed to be an ultimately beneficial "derangement" of the senses, was neutralized by the hypersurrealism of World War II, with its spectacular means of destruction and daily atrocities. Surrealism's absurd collocations began to exercise an appeal once more as the gray postwar years of rationing and pedestrian politics wore on, although David Gascoyne, for one, was writing in this mode before, during, and after the war.

Philip Larkin, in his fourth volume of poetry, *High Windows* (1974), expresses the condition of the people with few hopes and attempts to discover in unheroic present a consolation, like the "regenerative union" of the crowd at a fair. His approach to writing poetry has changed little from the beginning. His language is direct, highly wrought, and restrained in feeling. Although aware that his poems have readers, he is, like so many other postwar poets, writing for himself.

Auden's last volume was *Thank You, Fog* (1974), published after his death. His own analysis of his progress over fifty years is given in a poem from this volume, "A Thanksgiving," interesting for the history of poetry, because it represents in a general way its progress during this period. In the late 1920s he "sat at the feet of Hardy, Thomas, and Frost" in a fascination with nature. Then, falling in love, he transferred his poetic admiration to Yeats and Graves. With the economic disasters of the 1930s, he looked to Marxism. At the end of that decade, disillusioned by his experience in Spain during the civil war, and the gathering enormities of Franco, Stalin, and Hitler, his thoughts turned to religion, his guides now Kierkegaard, Charles Williams (1886–1945), and C. S. LEWIS. Toward the end of his life he found his imagination turning more to nature again, this time under the tutelage of Horace and Goethe.

No greater contrast could be made with Auden's poetry than that of Ted HUGHES. "Explosive" is the term often applied to his work. The poetry establishes an elemental relationship between himself and the natural world of animals and weather, especially impressive in his first two volumes, *Hawk in the Rain* (1957) and *Lupercal* (1960). In his later work, from *Crow* (1971) on, the language becomes more expressionistic and the tone more forceful and sometimes forced to the point of stridency.

A somewhat older poet still productive is D. J. Enright, who expresses a distrust of the uses to which language is put. In his long poem *Paradise Illustrated* (1978) he argues, not altogether facetiously, that simile and rhetoric are instruments of Satan: language destroys, but "silences speak for survival."

Clearly, the poetry of the fourth quarter of the century presents a continuing vitality, oscillating as it had throughout the century between the two poles of convention and innovation.

Drama

English drama, which had been in decline for two and half centuries, received new inspiration in the 20th from four external sources. The plays of the Norwegian Ibsen were made available to English readers in William Archer's translations (1906–12). They were publicized by George Bernard SHAW and followed in his practice. Yeats, in Ireland, was experimenting with poetic drama. His plays in verse—from *The Countless Cathleen* (1892) to *Purgatory* (1939)—helped to reestablish poetic drama as a practical option in the English theater. The epic drama of the German Bertolt BRECHT aimed at distancing the incidents and characters of the play from the audience in the interests of intellectual involvement instead of emotional identification, provided an incentive for such writers as Auden, Christopher ISHERWOOD, Eliot, and Christopher FRY to write plays in verse with popular appeal. The contribution to English drama of Samuel BECKETT, Irish-French writer, belongs to the consideration of the THEATER OF THE ABSURD after World War II.

Shaw remains the major figure in 20th-c. English theater. As a Fabian socialist, Shaw was committed to the practicability of social reform. He found Ibesen's drama of social criticism attractive to his beliefs and compelling as dramaturgy. His wit, scandalous subjects (for example, *Mrs. Warren's Profession*, 1898), and provocative ideas helped to generate a new respectability for plays and playgoing. His long prefaces to the printed versions of his plays broadened public knowledge of drama and theatrical technique, and promoted an interest in the theater where it had never existed before.

Despite their unconventional subjects and provocative treatment, Shaw's plays flourished in the context of an established social order. Shaw and other successful playwrights before World War I—John GALSWORTHY, Arthur Wing Pinero (1855–1934), Henry Arthur Jones (1851–1929), W. Somerset MAUGHAM—dramatized themes that belonged properly to a structured society and depended on a public understanding of that structure for their meaning—themes such as ambition, social responsibility, leadership, marriage. Along with these, there were the complementary themes dealing with threats to the established order, like pride, greed, and sensuality.

Yeats wrote in 1904 that "the modern theatre has died away to what it is because the writers have thought of their audiences instead of their subjects." His comment has meaning for the drama of the first two decades. The "problem plays," for instance, of

Pinero were strong for their time but compromised with public taste and intellectual expectations. Shaw's estimate of Pinero's drama is fair, commending his craftsmanship while faulting his weak Ibsenism.

Much the same is true of Henry Arthur Jones, whose social comedies were eclipsed first by Oscar Wilde's and then Somerset Maugham's. Maugham wrote twenty-nine plays during the first three decades of the century, many highly successful, such as *The Circle* (1921) and *The Constant Wife* (1926). The latter, despite its polished wit and high comedy situations (adultery recognized but overlooked in the interests of preserving appearances), has serious implications about the sexual parity of men and women, which might have come straight out of Ibsen.

The episodic, EXPRESSIONIST plays of W. H. Auden in collaboration with Christopher Isherwood reflect pervasive aspects of the 1930s, such as pacifism, political heterodoxy, and anticapitalism. Of their three collaborative efforts, *The Dog beneath the Skin* (1935) evidences the eclecticism of their style and temper, with signs of Gilbert and Sullivan, Brecht, and surrealism.

T.S. Eliot's first verse drama, for which he had made some preparation in the scenic and episodic elements and dramatic monologues of his poetry, was *Murder in the Cathedral* (1935), a religious play for a religious audience. His succeeding plays, from *The Family Reunion* (1939) to *The Elder Statesman* (1959), were religious plays for secular audiences. Thus, Eliot moved from an overt expression of religious themes to a drama of manners in which the moral imperatives of *The Waste Land* (give, be compassionate, control) are only partly concealed by drawing-room comedy, contemporary idiom, and speech rhythms. These changes reduce the elevated tone of his drama. But here, too, Eliot was practicing Old Possum's characteristically sly deception. For in writing his plays for the London theaters, he created a loose, four-stress line which sounds much like prose but which provides the emotional tension and inner rhythmic discipline of poetry.

Christopher Fry, like Eliot, first wrote a religious play, *The Boy with a Cart* (1939), a mode to which he returned at the end of his career. But his reputation as a neo-Elizabethan came with *A Phoenix Too Frequent* (1946) and *The Lady's Not for Burning* (1949). These are scintillating verse dramas, in which highly comic situations and exchanges of wit nearly conceal underlying serious themes, which are not, however, directed toward discernible resolutions.

Drama after World War II developed in several directions, expressing the boredom of a war-weary public, the continuing deprivations, the long-deferred expectations, the accumulated bitterness. Playwrights turned their attention to themes provided by a deteriorating social structure—pointlessness, deformity, ignorance, the fascination with scatology, the failure of belief.

The reaction against traditional ways and values is well reflected in plays of the 1950s and 1960s. Playwrights experimented with the stage, lighting, costumes, dramatic structure, language, and the audience itself. They took their cues from the surrealists, the expressionist film directors, composers such as Schoenberg, Stravinsky, and Bartók, and partly from the EXISTENTIALIST writers who were formulating the pervasive sense of alienation, futility, and anger left over from the preceding decades, exacerbated by postwar dislocations and the psychological impact of the new apocalyptic threat, the atomic bomb.

The most accomplished literary technician of the innovators was Samuel Beckett. The rising internationalism in the arts generally and his English-speaking Irish origin made his *Waiting for Godot* (French 1952; English 1954), although originally written in

French, a power in shaping the concern for basic human predicaments that characterizes the new drama. The dramaturgy of *Waiting for Godot*, with its "Nothing happens, nobody comes, nobody goes," epitomizes the Theater of the Absurd. Beckett's unsequential dialogue and pointless action expose the universal despair afflicting individuals who can then, conscious of their plight, face it without illusion, with courage, and possibly the grace of humor.

There is no doubt a certain fashionable chic in such movements as the absurd, promoted in self-interest by critics and producers. John Whiting's (1917–1963) *Saint's Day* (1951), which savages the pretensions and self-destructive tendencies of artists and intellectuals, fared badly at the hands of critics, in part because of its animus directed against the intellectual establishment.

It took John OSBORNE's *Look Back in Anger* (1956), with its broader base in society, to create an explosive mixture out of antiestablishment slogans, invective, and uncompromising misanthropy. It set the tone for the "angry young men" to follow.

Arnold WESKER and Bernard Kops (b. 1926) modified the "angry" mode of Osborne with plays reminiscent of those of Israel Zangwill (1864–1926) from the early years of the century, in their attacks on religious hypocrisy, war, and social evils. Wesker's trilogy, *Chicken Soup with Barley* (1958), *Roots* (1959), and *I'm Talking about Jerusalem* (1960), exhibit the postwar mood of "anger" with conditions in a Jewish working-class neighborhood in London's East End. *The Friends* (1972) continues the theme of working-class aspiration and defeat.

Kops, like Wesker, exploits the symbolic weight of a Jewish milieu and characters, with more comedy and Brechtian music-hall routines, thereby encountering less audience resistance to his underlying attacks on the human wastefulness of a technological culture.

Harold PINTER's "comedy of menace" derives its impact from several sources: KAFKA's timeless and mysterious situations, PIRANDELLO's disillusionment, Beckett's cosmic despair, and Hollywood gangster films. In *The Dumb Waiter* (1959) the two hired killers waiting in a basement kitchen for orders gradually realize how little knowledge they have on which to act. The dumbwaiter signifies the forces beyond their understanding that govern them. The outraged attempts of the two men to relate cause and effect on the basis of their insufficient knowledge points to the similar state in large of human affairs and suggests the importance we attach to those means of search for understanding, one of which is literature. *No Man's Land* (1975) emphasizes the constriction that ignorance imposes on the human situation. Its "inaction" is clearly related to Beckett's *Endgame* and Eliot's "Prufrock," in their depiction of a moribund world. Pinter's play is, in effect, *about* stasis. The characters are fearful of change, of the unknown. They cherish an immobility that negates the need for decisions or action. The static, centripetal form of the play suggests that its meaning is solely contained in what is seen and heard in the play itself, without reference to a contemporary external society. Pinter's comic situations, saturated with an atmosphere of threat, humiliation, and disorientation, are conveyed by "Pinteresque" effects—broken speech, incoherencies, and expressive silences.

John ARDEN brought a different quality into the new drama—an analytical intelligence like Shaw's in exploring ideas, but without Shaw's certainty of solution. His ambiguities are projected through fascinating plots, situations, and music-hall lyrics that owe something to Brecht.

Edward BOND's plays, from *Saved* (1966) through *Lear* (1972), reveal a controlling thesis that interprets our present society of cruelty and injustice as being the result of humans (and animals)

having to live unnaturally in masses in technological, urban environments. In this state, the older generation imposes its neuroses on the younger. Thus "the fall," Bond's symbolic term for this process, recurs periodically.

Robert BOLT, more traditional, has chosen historical subjects for his two best known dramas, the life (and death) of Thomas More in *A Man for All Seasons* (1960), and the relationship of Elizabeth I and Mary, Queen of Scots in *Vivat, Vivat Regina!* (1970). The steady but impassioned rhetoric of his best scenes demonstrates that "anger" is not the only weapon serviceable in combating the Establishment.

Tom STOPPARD's plays show several points of origin: Shaw, in his enthusiasm for the life of the mind and passion for scintillating dialogue; Wilde and Fry in the play of verbal wit (puns, misnomers, word games); Sophocles, for the play of detection; and the dramatists of the absurd in their collocation of disharmonies and disjunctures. In Stoppard's reflexive drama there is something of Pinter's concern with the theater as a means to explore our understanding of the world. A Stoppard play takes into itself fragments of other plays and investigates the consequences of juxtaposing these fragments.

David STOREY's plays have received unusually diverse critical analysis. They are regarded as naturalism lightened with the poetry of life, or as documentaries thinly disguised as plays, or as celebrations of life. Like Bond, Storey views modern neurosis in long perspective. Western society suffers from the Platonic dualism of body and spirit. A false spirituality revolts against the body. And in the larger context of the city, society does not permit the individual (soul) to rise above the mass (body). The insanity that marks modern society is a consequence of "puritanism" and its associated fear, shame, and loneliness.

Simon GRAY's *Butley*, produced in 1971, was prophetic of what the decade was to be. It is set in a university, where the academic standards are decaying under the guardianship of moral and professional delinquents. Yet through all its painful psychic lacerations (visibly present in the razor cut on Butley's chin) and the quotidian analgesics to ease them (Butley's nursery rhymes and bottle of whiskey) there is a sense of humanity struggling to humanize itself.

Peter SHAFFER, if his subjects were less contemporary, would bear comparison with Robert Bolt in his preference for the conventional well-made plot set in the theater of spectacle. Also like Bolt, he has something large and coherent to say about the quality of modern life. In *The Royal Hunt of the Sun* (1964), *Equus* (1973), and *Shrivings* (reworked in 1974), he uses the middle-aged man linked in various ways to an ancient culture (for example, Dysart's preoccupation in *Equus* with Greece) to point up the inability of religion in Western society to satisfy the human need for ritual worship and faith.

The pattern that emerges from recent English drama is composed of playwrights' response to the contemporary world as artists and as critics of that world. Recurrent armed conflicts, extermination camps, nuclear weapons, and the politics of starvation are dramatized in the observable results on individuals (as in Beckett, Gray, Bolt, Pinter) and indictments made (as Storey, Shaffer, Bond).

Such distinctions of theatrical intent can be drawn too closely, but the vectors are definite enough to indicate that contemporary drama has taken over from the novel part of the function of serving as the conscience of society, without as yet in the 1980s forgoing its aesthetic function to delight and excite in favor of didacticism and propaganda.

The Novel

A survey of the English novel in this century begins with the Irishman George MOORE, an important and often undervalued transitional figure. Although not English, he represents two powerful germinal influences on English writing. His kind of fiction, produced between 1883 and 1930, had one tributary from the Continent and one from Ireland. He modeled his writing on the French naturalistic novel, and in *Esther Waters* (1894) produced a remarkable English version. Esther is an ordinary, credible human being, treated sympathetically but without sentimentality. Viewing the world and people "with the eye of God," Moore's idea of the creative process, can lead in quite the opposite direction—into mysticism, as it does later with L. H. MYERS. But Moore keeps his eye metaphysically impartial and his intentions purely artistic. His work in the 20th c., with its fluent oral tradition derived from Irish folktales, exemplifies his theory of art as rhythmic sequence.

The work of Joseph CONRAD, the transplanted French-speaking Pole, shows influence from within the English tradition. Although the exotic qualities of his fiction owe much to the particularities of his adventurous life—the gun-running and sea duty—he was conscious of Henry JAMES's style and narrative technique and of lasting impressions gained from his early reading in Shakespeare and Dickens. The high seriousness of his themes is implied by such titles as *An Outcast of the Islands* (1896) and "Heart of Darkness" (1902).

Lord Jim (1900) is an example of Conrad's narrative layering. Jim's cowardice, shame, and redemption are recounted from numerous points of view, all controlled by Conrad's master narrator, Marlow. *The Secret Agent* (1907) and *Under Western Eyes* (1911) are the forerunners of innumerable novels of spies and international terrorism, among the best of which are those of Graham GREENE. Conrad's sense of the world's mystery is profound. He was fascinated by moral dilemmas and the struggles of individuals in conflict with the forces of nature.

The contrast between Conrad and his contemporaries, John Galsworthy and Arnold BENNETT, is stark. Galsworthy is best known for his "saga" of the Forsyte family. It has historical interest and certain psychological attraction in the passage of Soames Forsyte, "the man of property," from the Victorian milieu, which is "his," to the modern world, which is not. Two trilogies, published between 1906 and 1922, and later additions, established the Forsyte series as the earliest of many novel sequences to appear during the first three quarters of the century.

The increasing frequency of multivolume panoramic novels indicates a fascination with rapid social and technological changes: the impulse to record the details of a rapidly shifting daily existence, to fix in a pattern of images whatever currents could be discerned in the confusing stream of contemporary life, and to discover a meaning. Thus, Ford Madox Ford called his tetralogy *Parade's End* (1924–28), Anthony POWELL titled his multivolume sequence *A Dance to the Music of Time* (1951–75), and C. P. Snow his sequence *Strangers and Brothers* (1940–70). These reflect preoccupations in the modern world with the menace of armed conflict, with the permutations of time, and with the syndrome of power, alienation, and betrayal.

Ford Madox Ford had a powerful influence on other writers both as a personality and as an artist. His early historical novels, the Tudor Trilogy—*Fifth Queen* (1906), *Privy Seal* (1907), *The Fifth Queen Crowned* (1908)—fascinating and circumstantially persuasive as they are, do not measure up to his novels on contemporary subjects. The first of these, *The Good Soldier* (1915), influenced by the French realistic novel, anticipates by a decade the stylistically

level rendering of moral inertia in postwar fiction. It exemplifies the narrative technique (worked out in association with Joseph Conrad) of "progression d'effet," the selection of event and word to carry a story forward with gathering "rendering" instead of narrating, had a marked effect on the work of such diverse writers as Pound, Joyce, and HEMINGWAY. Ford's masterpiece, and one of the great novels of the century, is the Tietjens Tetralogy, published in America as *Parade's End: Some Do Not* (1924), *No More Parades* (1925), *A Man Could Stand Up* (1926), *The Last Post* (1928). Through Christopher Tietjens, Ford reiterates the value of loyalty to a personal creed rooted in established codes of conduct.

Arnold Bennett, like Moore, worked in the French tradition, which enabled him to treat the unlovely setting of Staffordshire pottery towns in such a way as to establish the appeal of life lovingly described. He records, in cumulative detail, provincial places and people undergoing slow change. But even his first novel, *Anna of the Five Towns* (1902), reveals more than a concern for surfaces in its sympathetic rendering of Anna. Caught in the conflicts generated by religious zeal and commercial greed, she remains true to self even through the consequences of her own bad judgment.

In later novels of the century fidelity to self and principles becomes more and more problematical. The tension between social or political necessity and a personal ideal creates ironic changes in self-evaluation (much as in *Gulliver's Travels*) for many midcentury fictional characters such as these delineated in Angus WILSON'S *The Old Men at the Zoo* (1961).

Bennett's representational mode at its best was consolidated in *Clayhanger* (1910), an autobiographical novel, and *The Old Wives' Tale* (1908). Bennett's quotidian view of time and the amassing of external details were to draw the ire of Virginia WOOLF, who used Bennett, along with Galsworthy and H. G. WELLS, as examples of old-fashioned novel writing. The conventional novel, which had been tested by generations of novelists, survived the theories and experimentation of the decades between the wars by assimilating the experiments. It showed new strength in work by diverse writers like Elizabeth BOWEN, William GOLDING, Olivia MANNING, Margaret DRABBLE, C. P. Snow, and Pamela Hansford Johnson (1912–1981).

Rudyard KIPLING brought the meaning of Empire back to the homeland at a time just before that meaning was to be gradually eroded by rising nationalism in the colonies. Although he attempted several novels, one of which is the memorable *Kim* (1901), Kipling worked more easily in shorter fiction.

H. G. Wells was a complex figure, interesting enough to attract the attention of Henry James, with whom he argued the relative merits of art and journalism. James was right: Wells worked too exclusively with ideas, with social reform achieved through scientific advance, and with types instead of individuals. The argument between James and Wells opened a debate that continued in various modified forms into the 1980s. Prominent among them was the "two cultures" controversy initiated by C. P. Snow.

Virginia Woolf's case against Galsworthy, Bennett, and Wells, "Mr. Bennett and Mrs. Brown" (1924), captures the difference between the old novel and the new. Her analysis of the difference is striking, if oversimplified. Wells, she conjectures, looking at the elderly, threadbare Mrs. Brown seated across from him in a railway compartment, would imagine a utopian world in which no Mrs. Browns existed. Galsworthy, looking at her, would seethe with indignation at social injustice. Bennett would really look at Mrs. Brown, then neglect her in noting all the details of dress and the furnishings of the compartment. All three writers, she insists, laid too much stress on "the fabric of things," losing sight of Mrs. Brown's personality and uniqueness.

Woolf was one of several writers with a new approach to narration and characterization. The psychological novel developed in a variety of directions with Joyce, Dorothy Richardson (1872–1957), Woolf, and D. H. LAWRENCE, but all in reaction against a descriptive representational realism. In place of the surface complexity of the realistic novel they offered the psychological complexities of the mind.

Richardson's contributions to the stream-of-consciousness technique, although substantial (*Pilgrimage* came out between 1914 and 1938 in twelve volumes), are far less engaging than Woolf's multiplicity of techniques and Joyce's more rigorous formal and linguistic exploitation of the mode.

The contributions of Virginia Woolf to the novel emerged from her upbringing in a literary family, from her association with the Bloomsbury group, and from her lifelong illness. Her novels have a rarefied atmosphere that from the beginning made them suspect in some quarters as not being in contact with "real life." They have few scenes of passion, little brutality, and a limited social perspective. But they do have power to convince the reader of their beauty, seriousness, and integrity as art.

In "Mr. Bennett and Mrs. Brown" Woolf had contrasted Bennett's preoccupation with representing the literal surface of character and event and her own concern for the ambiguities of the inner life. Such novels as *Jacob's Room* (1922), *Mrs. Dalloway* (1925), and *To the Lighthouse* (1927) utilize the interiors of dwellings as surrogates for the externalized mind, substantive locales in which psychological dramas are acted out. These dramas are depicted, in *The Waves* (1931), *The Years* (1937), and *Between the Acts* (1941), as tragicomedies, in which the dramatis personae are overshadowed by the ceaseless, implacable actions of external nature.

James Joyce's *A Portrait of the Artist as a Young Man* (1916) is one of many novels relating the story of a young man's growth to maturity and self-realization that are descended from Samuel Butler's (1835–1902) *The Way of All Flesh* (written in the 1870s but published in 1903). It depicts the protagonist's growing resistance to being netted and immobilized by family, church, and country. This classic *Künstlerroman* takes the mythological Daedalus, the namesake of its hero, Stephen, as the cue for creating wings of language to fly over the triple nets into the larger domain of art.

Joyce's masterwork, *Ulysses* (1922), is a monumental product of linguistic art that creates the effect of a mind captured in its entirety through the course of a day. *Finnegans Wake* (1939), his intended masterwork, ransacks the resources of myriad languages to give the impression of nonlogical patterns underlying conscious levels of thought. Such a work stands in a reciprocal relationship to several schools of psychology that emerged in the early decades, with critical systems based on them—for example, those influenced by FREUD and JUNG—and with other critical modes such as linguistic, structural, and semiotic. Subsequent writers have found *Ulysses* an almost endless source of formal and linguistic innovation. *Finnegans Wake* has been a more recalcitrant model, and may prove to be either a century ahead of its time or one of literature's dead ends.

D. H. Lawrence's kind of psychological novel could more accurately be called a psychosomatic novel by reason of his insistence on knowledge by intuition as represented by the primacy of blood and the "solar plexus" over the brain and intellect. His ability to uncover and delineate the depths of primitive experience operating at the social level is at its best in *Sons and Lovers* (1913), classic rendition of mother fixation and its consequences for early heterosexual relationships.

Lawrence's influence—through his theory of blood knowledge, and on style in occasional expressionistic passages of great power and beauty about nature—is limited but observable in several subsequent writers, even in some who have established their own kind of novel, such as William Golding, David Storey, and the Australian Patrick WHITE.

In the 1920s and 1930s the novel as satire began to reflect the change in values after 1914. Better than most of the topical satires is Richard HUGHES's exposure of the fragile basis of conventional morality in *The Innocent Voyage* (1928), which returns to a Blakean concept of innocence and experience as belonging not to youth and age but to contrary states of the soul. This novel, with its skillfully objective depiction of children living in their precariously naïve and dogmatic world, anticipates the more pessimistic *Lord of the Flies* (1954) by Golding.

Aldous HUXLEY's social comedies both described and to an extent promoted the fashion of brittle gaiety in the 1920s especially *Crome Yellow* (1921) and *Antic Hay* (1923). Toward the end of the decade, *Point Counter Point* (1928) presented some of Huxley's contemporaries, including Lawrence (and Huxley himself) in a substantial roman à clef. *Brave New World* (1932), more dystopian social satire than novel, has, like Anthony BURGESS's *A Clockwork Orange* (1962), added to the English language terms for new kinds of experience.

Like Huxley, Evelyn WAUGH in his early novels—*Decline and Fall* (1928), *Vile Bodies* (1930), and *A Handful of Dust* (1934)—satirized the upper-class society of the 1920s and 1930s, but with such brittleness that the satire rings hollow, leaving only the meticulously crafted shell of his hatred. It is, however, a fascinating shell, owing something to Ronald FIRBANK. His dehumanizing approach works in *The Loved One* (1948), which displays the California world of morticians who exploit the living through the dead, and in the novel many consider to be his best, *The Ordeal of Gilbert Pinfold* (1957), essentially autobiographical, centered around bouts of hallucination similar to those he suffered himself.

Among the more popular satires, with literary merit of its own kind (although at last it deteriorates into coy sentimentality), is *Cold Comfort Farm* (1932) by Stella Gibbons (b. 1902). Unlike the customary satire of high society in town and country, this is a parody of the popular novel of farm and cottage and of much Georgian poetry such as Lawrence's "Love on the Farm" (1913). Gibbons has something of the flair for names and the light touch of P. G. WODEHOUSE.

Distaste for the constrictions of a class society and ossified institutions, and fear of the trauma of daily aggressions, motivated a variety of escapist literature, most of it transitory. The exceptions, however, are noteworthy. Influenced by Jules Verne and H. G. Wells, David Lindsay (1878–1945) created a serious metaphysical fable in *Voyage to Arcturus* (1920) in which Schopenhauer's "nothing" is identified with the real world. In a more literary tradition, with medieval and classical antecedents, are David Garnett's (1892–1981) *Lady into Fox* (1922) and *A Man in the Zoo* (1924), whose titles convey the singularity of their themes. A favorite, often reissued, is *Mr. Weston's Good Wine* (1927) by T. F. POWYS. Weston's name derives from the World War I expression for dying, "going west." Mr. Weston is thus the "West One," that is, God, and death itself his good wine.

Somewhat later is J. R. R. TOLKIEN's *Lord of the Rings* (3 vols., 1954–55), derived from folklore, legend, fairy tale, and anthropology. A critical industry burgeoned in the wake of the popular fascination with Tolkien's Middle Earth, with its hobbits and elves and other creaturely constructs.

The breakup of the British Empire was a psychological factor that even while predictable, was at work shaping certain aspects of English writing after World War I, when the winds of nationalism began to blow following the territorial realignments of the Versailles Treaty. Social relations between colonials and English were perceived by novelists as symbolic, expressing racial and religious divergencies and political conflicts.

These ruler/ruled relationships had been displayed in Conrad's "Heart of Darkness" suitably modified to fit the political conditions of the Belgian Congo. The classic novel of colonial relations, however, is E. M. FORSTER's *A Passage to India* (1924), in which a careful balance of character, episode, and setting reveals the essential contrasts between the English and the Indian ways. Forster depicts the "muddle" that is India and the orderly dogmatism of English administration. But he also contrasts the Indian sense of cosmic order with the confusion of the English mind confronting an incomprehensible universe.

A decade later George ORWELL, who had served with the Indian Imperial Police in Burma, wrote his novel of the meeting of East and West, *Burmese Days* (1934). Orwell's style, with its debt to the naturalism of Zola, could report with clarity and force situations similar to those in *A Passage to India*, but the novel's characters, in their two-dimensional conflicts, are not Forster's, who have the personal and moral resonance of living people.

On the home front, however, a different kind of opposition was developing within the novel genre itself. Ronald Firbank and Wyndham Lewis represent two poles of creativity developing in England in the 1920s—the aesthetic and the philosophical, although both labels are misleading.

The work of Firbank, underneath a surface exquisiteness, contends with desperations encountered in the more shadowy purlieus of the spirit. Such slight, stylistically elegant novels as *Caprice* (1917) and *Prancing Nigger* (1925) influenced writers such as Waugh, Huxley, Angus Wilson, Iris MURDOCH, and Anthony Powell in the uses of silence, significant ommissions, the emphasis on dialogue, and what Anthony Burgess calls the achievement of "weight through lightness."

Wyndham Lewis is to Firbank as an eagle is to a butterfly. A prolific writer of great power, Lewis was an externalist, as befitted an accomplished painter. His approach to characterization tends to deprive his humans of ordinary motivation, guilt and other psychological qualities, leaving them vulnerable to interpretation as "hallucinated automata" (Eliot's view). But his unfinished tetralogy, *The Human Age*, presents two characters who are specifically and unforgettably ordinary people. This work—*The Childermass* (1928), *Monstre Gai* (1955), *Malign Fiesta* (1955), and *The Trial of Man* (unpublished)—depicts landscapes representing psychological states with stunning visual impact.

Markedly different from either Firbank or Lewis was Henry GREEN. He was unobtrusively symbolist, working in a realist tradition. The Midlands speech of *Living* (1929) is freshly attractive. The Anglo-Saxon overtones and rhythms introduce vitality and strangeness into the drab monotony of the industrial life it depicts. *Party Going* (1939) captures the prewar spiritual stasis, and *Loving* (1945) objectifies the early wartime atmosphere from the distance of its Irish locale.

The novels of L. H. Myers, emphasizing man's essential goodness, attacked the corrupt morals and temper of modern commercial values. He persisted in an extraordinary singleness of purpose—the search for moral sensitivity in human experience. To this end he attempted to minimize the "machinery of a life that is familiar" to his readers. In his tetralogy *The Near and the Far* (1943) he achieved this objective by setting his story in 16th–c. India.

Myers's novels illustrate philosophical and religious themes in the context of Eastern mysticism, an orientation seen also in Aldous Huxley and Christopher Isherwood, and taken up obliquely into science fiction.

A near contemporary of Myers, Joyce CARY, took a more pragmatic approach to the basic questions of existence. Cary wrote first, in *Aissa Saved* (1932), about the effect on a young African woman of being converted to Christianity. Of the three African novels, dealing with now dated situations, *Mister Johnson* (1939) is probably the best. His two trilogies, both major works, brought his classic English protestantism to bear on art.

When we encounter life itself as the subject of satire, instead of institutions or individuals, we are confronting the novels of Ivy COMPTON-BURNETT. Her dislike for the random quality of existence led to intricate plots, witty, urbane dialogue, and balanced titles. *Pastors and Masters* (1925) was the first of seventeen mordant questionings of end-of-the-century life in upper-middle-class families; the last was *A God and His Gifts* (1963).

Two other markedly skeptical views of life appear in the works of Rose MACAULAY and Nigel DENNIS. Rose Macaulay brought out twenty-two novels between 1906 and 1956. Her reservations about the future of civilization after World War I resulted in *Orphan Island* (1924). It is a forerunner of William Golding's *Lord of the Flies* in situation (children marooned on an island), but the tone, as in all her fiction, is comic, an almost absurdly lighthearted coruscation of language and imagery veiling serious themes. Macaulay's last novel, *The Towers of Trebizond* (1956), embodies her personal reactions to adultery and agnosticism. These matters were treated in an earlier novel, *And No Man's Wit* (1940), set in Spain after the war of 1937.

Witty surface and sophistication mark the novels of Nigel Dennis. His second novel, *A Sea Change* (1949), established his reputation for wit and a kind of black comedy. *Cards of Identity* (1955) displays ironically the search for self in a world of psychiatrists, priests, and politicians, all scheming to provide a readymade identity. What Dennis wrote about the images of Beckett and IONESCO, "We are to watch them move in parallel to reality," points to the quality of parable in his fourth novel, *A House in Order* (1966).

The novels of Rebecca WEST, although not skeptical in the metaphysical way of Macaulay or Dennis, manifest a searching quality of their own. Her early feminism obscured for a time the multiplicity of her concerns, especially her preoccupation with the persistence of evil. Her writing has tended to reduce the differences between fiction and nonfiction. The concerns of her early work, *The Judge* (1922) and *The Thinking Reed* (1936) open out into the "nonfiction" of *Black Lamb and Grey Falcon* (1941), the report of a journey through Yugoslavia, and expand into the psychological complexity and historical breadth of *The Birds Fall Down* (1966).

A similarly exploring mind is that of Doris LESSING, whose writing, in her words, examines "individual conscience in its relation with the collective." Her novel sequence *Children of Violence* (1952–69) treats that relationship first in a social and political context (*Martha Quest*, 1952), then in a psychological context in *The Four-Gated City* (1969). *The Golden Notebook* (1962) places the relationship in an aesthetic context, and *The Memoirs of a Survivor* (1974) in a context derived from Sufi mysticism. Lessing's later fiction, to *The Marriages between Zones Three, Four, and Five* (1980), exploits the paraphernalia and cosmic settings of science fiction in the examination of self and other.

Quite different from Lessing in his concern for artistic expression is Lawrence DURRELL, who, in *The Alexandria Quartet* (1957–60) extended to new limits the self-conscious investigation of the storyteller into his own art, and established the "reality of the artificial" (Robert Scholes) in characterization. His later work, from *Tunc* (1968) through *Livia* (1978), has continued to attract the descriptive term "sensuous."

A large body of work, from before the beginning of the century on, describes quite another kind of English life. One of the chief practitioners of the novel of country life was Henry Williamson (1895–1977). Writing for over half a century, he has so far received little critical attention for a sustained chronicle of that time in more than eighteen novels. His subject matter, like that of Hardy and the Georgians, and his traditional novelistic style, have worked against him.

The appearance of Melvyn Bragg (b. 1939), almost two generations younger than Williamson but much in the same tradition, suggests the persistent attraction of the novel of country life. Novels about life on the land have a basic appeal to English experience, perhaps especially in the middle of the 20th c., when that way of living, its manner and conditions, is rapidly disappearing or being reshaped. It is a literature not often of the highest quality but frequently moving and, with the most capable writers, persuading readers that they are in touch with elemental aspects of life.

H. E. BATES, one of the most prolific of writers about the country scene and people, made the distinction between "the earth" and "the land" that is implicitly recognized in this kind of novel: the earth is "vague, primitive, poetic," the land a composite force of living things, fields, and weather, an "opponent" or "master." This distinction applies in an almost pure state to L. A. G. Strong's (1896–1958) tale of the Dartmoor country of southern England, *Dewer Rides* (1929). His novel *The Garden* (1931), set in Ireland, is less rigorously elemental.

Hardy and Lawrence, although going beyond it, were masters of this mode. Another was John Cowper POWYS, whose early novels set in Norfolk, Dorset, and Somerset, relate landscape and human inscape so completely as to make the country and its people a microcosm of the universal human condition. The best-known of these are *Wolf Solent* (1929), *A Glastonbury Romance* (1932), and *Weymouth Sands* (1934).

Graham Greene has been one of the most durable writers of the middle half of the century. Like the poet W. H. Auden, his contemporary, Greene had an uncanny knack for perceiving what were the pressing concerns of each generation—espionage, revolution, finance, evangelism, civil war, gambling, international warfare. These are the subjects in which he displays the conflicts in his characters. Greene's view of life after the mid-1920s, when he became a convert to Roman Catholicism, is tenaciously Christian. But it is a special kind of Christianity which, as Walter Allen points out, gives his work a special quality derived from his fascination with "sanctified sinners." There is a dogmatism that is open only to grace, one that rejects everything else as unworthy.

A gift like that of Henry Green for combining fancy and the matter-of-fact characterizes the writing of Elizabeth Bowen. One of the important literary Anglo-Irish, she brings wartime London and an Irish country house into a symbiotic relationship in *The Heat of the Day* (1949). Setting is important in her work, but no more so than the psychological states that it often clarifies, as in her best novel, *The Death of the Heart* (1938).

One of the most impressive novel sequences for its coverage of both time and events in Anthony Powell's *A Dance to the Music of Time*. Powell has described in great detail upper-class English social life in twelve volumes that begin in the pre-war 1914 years with *A Question of Upbringing* (1951) and delivers its narrator Nicholas Jenkins into the seventh decade of the century in *Hearing Secret Harmonies* (1975). Powell's characters are credible as representative types, and a few are memorable. The sequence, like Snow's *Strangers and Brothers*, with which it can be compared for two quite different kinds of writing, the one aesthetic, the other pragmatic, is instructive as social history and entertaining in its episodes and gallery of reappearing characters. Powell's style verges on the mandarin, but avoids settling there.

C. P. Snow, for so sound a traditional novelist, has been a controversial figure, partly for his criticism, in which he takes a firm stand against modernism, and partly for the kind of fiction he writes, which has been faulted for developing characters who in some essential way do not correspond to the nature of 20th–c. man. Snow's involvement in the scientific bureaucracy before and during World War II gave his novels an air of authenticity, as his university novels have an authority deriving from his experience as a don. But there remains in Snow's fiction a sense that the modern world is being less written about than rewritten.

In the mid-1950s, a writer quite different from Snow appeared, much under the influence of Joyce in the use of language, but uniquely exuberant. Anthony Burgess is highly talented and productive, having published a dozen novels just during his first decade of professional writing. He is not, however, superficial. Burgess writes persuasively about many subjects. His *The Malayan Trilogy* (1956–59; Am., *The Long Day Wanes*, 1965) is an inside look at the declining British power in southeast Asia. In this respect it deserves comparison with *The Raj Quartet* (1966–78) of Paul Scott (1920–1979). The work of Burgess exhibits a broad range of interests and represents a complex reaction to the postwar malaise of spirit. *A Clockwork Orange* (1962) portrays a society degenerating under foreign influences, and his Enderby novels are speculations about the fundamental nature of poetic inspiration and about the poet as an emblem for the individual struggling with meretricious contemporary values.

The "Angry Young Men" of the 1950s brought the accumulated resentment of the between-the-wars generations to a boil, a combined reaction against hypocrisy, deception and phoniness. Something of Virginia Woolf's hatred for "old men in clubs and cabinets," the war mongers, waste makers, destroyers of the young, and the institutions they dominated appears in the novels of John WAIN, Kingsley AMIS, John BRAINE, and Alan SILLITOE. But their attitude is tougher, more surly and rebellious than hers—in part because they sensed that part of the problem was their own inertia. Braine's *Life at the Top* (1962), sequel to *Room at the Top* (1957), displays this form of self-betrayal. In *Lucky Jim* (1954), Amis makes his serious observations of society through comic situations and dialogue. He chose to exploit more oblique forms of satire in the 1960s and 1970s by using the modes of the mystery story—*The*

Riverside Villas Murder (1973)—and the spy thriller—*The Anti-Death League* (1966). This tendency in Amis's work characterizes the movement of the Angry Young Men away from protest in novels of class conflict toward subtler approaches to analysis of a disturbed, complex, and wayward society.

Similar to Murdoch in his preoccupation with love as a mark of social value, and to Burgess in his reaction to the midcentury decline of values, Malcolm LOWRY wrote one impressive novel incorporating these themes: *Under the Volcano* (1947) reveals that Lowry's mentors were Joyce in language, and Conrad AIKEN, the American novelist and poet, in the psychology of isolation and the death wish. Much in the tone ond outlook of this novel is typical of the decade; the volcano itself is an always present reminder of the bomb.

As wide-ranging as Burgess, William Golding claims a large field for his fiction: Neanderthal man (*The Inheritors*, 1955), medieval clergy (*The Spire*, 1964), a variety of modern subjects, leading to *Darkness Visible* (1979), whose protagonist is a burn victim of the fire bombings of London possessed with extraordinary powers.

Muriel SPARK employs a mannered writing that is reminiscent of Sylvia Townsend Warner without Warner's compassion. A convert to Roman Catholicism, she writes, under the aspect of eternity, with an almost medieval clarity and also callousness, as it were. She also writes economically, as if time were of the essence—except in her elaborate and lengthy *The Mandelbaum Gate* (1965), in which both the moment and eternity fail her. While profundity is not her forte, wit and psychological analysis are, as in *The Prime of Miss Jean Brodie* (1961).

Even more astringent than Spark is Angus Wilson, a novelist of powerful satiric effects. They are of a kind usually associated with expressionism, but in Wilson's writings are achieved via a realistic accumulation of details and characterizations. Representing this mode at its most intense is *The Old Men at the Zoo*, with a range of brutal, sanguinary incidents that provide a disturbing significance for elemental human relationships, professional and domestic.

A novelist emergent in the 1950s, whose constant struggles with her own formidable talents gives the appearance of uncertain progress, is Iris Murdoch. Her strength from the beginning (*Under the Net*, 1954) has been her ability to tell an interesting story. But the novels also engage the reader's mind with philosophical ideas and moral concepts. They illustrate her belief that each person represents a uniqueness that is partly defined by social relationships, that uniqueness warrants acceptance, and that love is the relationship which exemplifies acceptance in its most binding form.

By the time of her sixth novel, *The Needle's Eye* (1972), Margaret Drabble had an established critical reputation. But her next novel, *The Realms of Gold* (1975), was received with mixed reviews. Rather than consistently using a first- or third-person narrator, she was now employing a variety of points of view in individual characters, although authorial oversight remains overt in commentary and occasional direct address to the reader. This unexpectedly old-fashioned effect is less a technique than a habit. From her Quaker background Drabble has inherited the practice of self-examination, the results of which are passed on to the reader as admonitions, advice, and moral commentary.

The working-class novels of the 1960s and 1970s are not remarkable for their spirit of rebellion or political doctrine. The novels of Alan Sillitoe, Wain, and others view the conditions of labor and poverty from a safe distance. They are more nostalgic than revolutionary.

David Storey offers both theory and detailed descriptions of laboring families and their children, who find nonlaboring positions for themselves. His theory, however, is more psychological than sociological (about the spirit-body relationship), and the second generation is apt to discover that intellectual work is less "real" than the physical labor of their parents. A concept that Storey labels "puritan" refers to the disinclination of society to allow an individual to rise above the mass, and to an accompanying revulsion against things of the body. From his first novel, *This Sporting Life* (1960), still among his best work, to *Saville* (1976), about Yorkshire working-class life, his style has remained much the same: spare, taut, barren of ornament, and unremittingly serious.

Among many novelists establishing reputations in the 1960s and 1970s is Simon Raven (b. 1927), who in 1976 published *The Survivors*, tenth and last volume in the sequence *Alms for Oblivion*. Beryl BAINBRIDGE's skilled evocations of middle-class behavior and misbehavior have appeared at the rate of almost one a year. Her singular view of life imparts to her descriptions a dreamlike resonance. So idiosyncratic is her style that *Injury Time* (1977) has been taken by some to be a self-parody.

The first novel of John FOWLES, *The Collector* (1963), he has called a parable about the struggle based on inequality between the Few (the prisoner) and the Many (the kidnapper). His favorite book, *The Magus* (1965; rev. ed., 1977), he describes as a "young Man's book for young people." The concerns of subsequent works—the evolution of a moral and intellectual elite, the "defense and illustration of humanism," and the realistic representation of the dilemmas of the middle class in a disintegrating society, as in *The French Lieutenant's Woman* (1969) and *Daniel Martin* (1977)—suggest the reasons for his popularity among readers who look to serious fiction for illumination of historical as well as psychological processes.

Edna O'BRIEN is a novelist of impulse and sensuous delight. In such novels as *A Pagan Place* (1970), eroticism becomes in its variations and variable intensity the true measure of human experience.

A long-established writer, Olivia Manning evoked in a distinguished line of fiction a tragic view of life and suggested the moral courage needed for confronting it.

The psychic scar of colonial status, like the blue birthmark on the face of Flory, the hero of Orwell's *Burmese Days*, persists in the English literary imagination. It is there in the disparaging treatment that is received by Louis in Virginia Woolf's *The Waves* for being Australian, and in the humiliation that Kumar is subjected to in Paul Scott's *The Jewel in the Crown* (1966). The waves of immigration after 1950 from India, the Caribbean, and Africa, caused changes in social relationships marked by various kinds of ostracism and calculated reactions ranging from rudeness to brutality.

In the work of V. S. NAIPAUL, a Trinidad-born writer, many of whose novels have London settings, the birthmark is the dark skin of immigrants. Naipaul's is the substantial beginning for a literature dealing with the racial adjustments of the Passage to England that has yet to find full expression.

A less specific cultural disorientation already had been reflected in the self-conscious treatment of language in a remarkable range of novels, poems, and plays. The best known is probably Orwell's "Newspeak" in *1984* (1949), a basic English shorn of connotations by Big Brother and aimed at suppressing all deviant or emotional responses. The origin of this lobotomized language was Orwell's response to institutionalized propaganda, the verbiage of "public relations," and advertising, which were clearly subverting the honest use of linguistic resources.

If the English novel is indeed dying, as is periodically diagnosed, it is curiously lacking symptoms of serious disease. A certain preoccupation with style may indicate the onset of a silver age, but leaves uncertain whether the golden age has been or is yet to come.

The Short Story

To look at the modern short story is to look at the developing edge of a narrative form thousands of years old. As a literary form, however, it dates from the middle of the 19th c.

In England in the 1890s writers like James and Conrad were producing short fiction of a kind that could not be profitably imitated, as being too long or too special. Others, like Kipling, Robert Louis Stevenson (1850–1894), and George Moore, were writing true short stories in a memorable style or manner. These and others (Wilde, Bennett, Galsworthy, Maugham) were writing well-plotted short stories at a level of aesthetic achievement that would have to be surpassed if the form were to develop and be established alongside the novel and poetry.

Inspiration for the development of a new style in the English story came from abroad and was provided in the main by Maupassant and CHEKHOV. George Moore early introduced Maupassant's naturalism in *The Untilled Field* (1903), which established a pattern of brevity, economy of structure, and simplicity of subject. Moore also learned from his Irish sources how to display the racy idiom and the marvels that make up the attractions of all his short stories from the 1903 volume through *A Storyteller's Holiday* (1918).

One of the English followers of Chekhov (and also of Turgenev) was A. E. COPPARD, who subordinated action to feeling and established mood through a skillful use of setting. His language—precise, allusive, fanciful—has something of the rich ambiguity of the early 17th-c. masters. His best work appears in *Adam and Eve and Pinch Me* (1921) and the other collections through *Silver Circus* (1928) before the influence of Henry James on his style began to outweigh that of Chekhov.

Moore and Coppard had continued the work of James and Conrad in cultivating an audience capable of appreciating effects beyond those of suspense and resolution. Another 20th-c. master educating a readership was H. G. Wells. Trained in science, he was particularly aware of discoveries and innovations of his time.

Rudyard Kipling also aspired to educate as well as entertain his readers. The first of his story collections in this century, *Puck of Pook's Hill* (1906) and *Rewards and Fairies* (1910), have their settings in Anglo-Saxon and Roman Britain. The burden of these stories, as in the many to follow, is the obligation of Englishmen to practice the prime virtues: courage, discipline, obedience. They retain the edifying impulse characteristic of Victorianism.

D. H. Lawrence, in some ways Victorian, most nearly approaches modernism in his short fiction. In the stories of *The Prussian Officer* (1914) the focus is limited to a spare delineation of persons displayed in vividly realized places. The beautiful and the ugly receive equally careful treatment by a highly sensitized imagination that seemed to miss nothing but had the discipline (in the short story) to include only the essential.

Katherine MANSFIELD, who came to England from New Zealand, wrote for only a decade before she died. In that time she extended the influence of Chekhov into a style unmistakably her own. From Chekhov she learned oblique ways of narration, to tell the story through implication rather than statement and by what is left out. She published three volumes in quick succession until the last and best known, *The Garden Party* (1922). The reasons for Mansfield's influence are difficult to assess. Her work did not have time to mature, nor did she create a variety of characters either in depth or range. But the women and children who populate her stories ring true to the parts of her they express.

Mansfield and Virginia Woolf gained from the competition between them. Not satisfied with her first two novels, Woolf had begun to write short, plotless sketches of an intense meditative quality published between 1917 and 1921. Especially notable among these are "Kew Gardens" (1919) and "An Unwritten Novel" (1921). Woolf explored in these sketches approaches to dealing with time as it is experienced by the mind and with the intensity of experience as time's true measure. They are "short stories" of a special kind in that the narrative line is almost nonexistent. They generate an interest as experimental short fictions quite apart from their role in turning conventional fiction toward the state of poetry.

Following after Lawrence in commitment to the integrity of place and persons through the 1930s were such talents as L. A. G. Strong, W. H. Hudson (1841–1922), V. S. PRITCHETT, Elizabeth Bowen, James HANLEY, and L. P. HARTLEY. They brought to the short story lyric intensity together with descriptive and psychological realism.

These qualities dominated, even when the intention was to create fable or allegory, as in Sylvia Townsend Warner, David Garnett, and T. F. Powys. Among these belongs E. M. Forster, whose stories of suppressed sexual ambivalence and of a delicate, Bloomsbury-related idealism began to appear in the second decade. The titles of his story collections—*The Celestial Omnibus* (1911), *The Eternal Moment* (1928)—imply their inclination toward fantasy.

Another external source of lyricism in the English short story was Ireland. In 1914 James Joyce published *Dubliners*. These were highly original in avoiding contrived plots, two-dimensional characters, and a reliance on action. In *Dubliners* Joyce created a realistic narrative style the surface of which is inconspicuous. But throughout there is a skillful use of language in evoking musical effects that induce emotional responses.

From the Aran Islands, Liam O'Flaherty (1896–1984) went to London in the 1920s. He was encouraged by Edward Garnett to return to Ireland to write about what he knew best. When he got in touch with his native materials the result was a vivid reflection of the elemental passions and scenes that he recorded in *Spring Sowing* (1924), *The Tent* (1926), and *The Mountain Tavern* (1929). His "sensuous poetic energy" (H. E. Bates) was different from Joyce's quieter effects, but equally revolutionary in its impact.

Sean O'Faoláin (1900–1991) brought the transparency and evocativeness of Turgenev and the early Moore to his account (in *Midsummer Night Madness*, 1932) of revolutionary ardors displayed against the background of hauntingly beautiful landscapes. Frank O'CONNOR, O'Faoláin's associate in the Irish Rebellion, is less evocative and overtly poetic, more the detached, judicious observer in *Guests of the Nation* (1954) than O'Flaherty and O'Faoláin.

The Irish contribution to English short fiction was to transmit, in rhythms of English as spoken in Ireland, the Russian explorations of life by Turgenev and Chekhov in subtle renditions of the poetry of place and the bittersweet quality of ordinary lives under duress.

At the end of the first decade the 20th–c. the English short story had appeared to be falling into decay as the result of popular magazines vulgarizing the genre. Three decades later, the rise in the popular appeal of articles in magazines again appeared to be responsible for a decline in "worthwhile" short stories. The short story had failed to develop new techniques and fresh attractions while the article had. But these appearances were deceptive, the perspective distorted by proximity to the events observed. The short story could hardly have been more changed than by the innovations of Joyce, Woolf, Mansfield, and others.

In addition, by this time in the 1930s there were changes in the English story resulting from innovations of American writers. Sherwood ANDERSON was proving the value of looking at ordinary people in diverse local settings and describing their situations pictorially without drawing moral conclusions. In the wake of Anderson appeared HEMINGWAY, who had put the language on a diet, reducing its previous bulk (as in James) to the minimal skeleton, nerves, and muscle. He provided the snapshots of scenes with no retouching of metaphor, and a tight-lipped dialogue that is left to speak for itself. These American developments served English writers not as models but as inspiration for making changes in the technique of the story suitable to English scenes and society.

One development, largely unnoticed, was occurring in the fiction of Jean RHYS. Not until 1968 were the stories from *The Left Bank* (1927) brought together with work published in the 1960s to make the volume *Tigers Are Looking Better*. Rhys is concerned to describe mainly the lives of women trying to cope in a man's world. The "respectable" women of the stories (wives, mistresses, and mothers) are even greater threats than the men. Rhys's use of direct narration and compressed imagery suggest an influence from the French, a linguistic adaptation to be observed later also in the prose of Samuel Beckett.

The well-established and popular story of country life, exemplified in the diverse manners of Coppard, De la Mare, and Lawrence, was carried on into midcentury by H. E. Bates. His stories about rural people in *Country Life* (1938) are effective through direct narration of the beauty of the land and of the hard practical life of those who live on it. No morals are pointed, no conclusions imposed on the reader.

A Welsh contribution to the developing English short story was Dylan Thomas's *A Portrait of the Artist as a Young Dog* (1940). His lush and rhythmic prose was an exotic intrusion into the understated narratives of the 1930s. His unfinished novel, *Adventures in the Skin Trade* (1955), did not appear until the postwar reaction against romanticism was well advanced.

Graham Greene's *Collected Stories* (1973), from three previous collections published in the 1960s, often reveal a kind of severe religious orientation that permeates his longer fiction with an emphasis on the centrality of grace and the subordination of other considerations. Greene makes no innovation in the short story form but, as in the novels, maintains the integrity of his subjects through a disciplined style and economical characterization.

World War II was not the great divide that World War I was between one kind of literature and another. The first generated a new consciousness and approach to aesthetics, the second did not. The decay of values and social conventions during and after the war has benefited the short story because, unlike the novel, it can deal successfully with fragments of life.

During the war, William SANSOM was one writer who worked with fragments of an exploding world in his experiments with language and style. After the war his collections *South* (1948) and *The Passionate North* (1950) suggest mosaics constructed out of a shattered Europe.

The intensity of Angus Wilson's satire of contemporary ways, which cannot maintain its bite over the long run of the novel, is particularly suited to the range of short fiction. From his first work, *The Wrong Set* (1949), through his uncollected stories of the 1970s, Wilson has maintained a high level of wry, sometimes wicked revelations of human insufficiency.

One of the more durable writers of short fiction is V. S. Pritchett. His work is uncomplicated and enjoyable at a level that has reduced his professional value among academic critics. He employs a deliberately colorful prose style, full of closely observed detail. The early work, from the 1930s, was marred by exuberant metaphors, which in the later stories have been disciplined. Pritchett can, however, in a more sober fashion, still convey persuasively the subjective character of people through a certain distortion of the external world that is more Dickensian than expressionistic.

Edna O'Brien represents a later stream of the Irish tributary to English short-story writing in subject and style. Rebel from a Catholic background in the West of Ireland, where, as she puts it, there were no books and a lot of barbarity and a certain innocence, she can describe nonintellectual people convincingly. Through her, too, the concern of Tolstoy and Chekhov for ordinary people and the Russian understanding of the restrictions of country life and the longing for adventure come back into the English short story.

Alan Sillitoe, like O'Brien and Pritchett, attempts to describe the feelings of people who are not themselves disposed to do so and, if they were, not capable of doing so. In *Men, Women and Children* (1973), about working-class people in Nottingham, the characters are unsophisticated, have difficulty coping with life, and have little time or energy for anything except work. Their situations, however, in Sillitoe's imagination become those of any human being anywhere. It is this sense of a common, shared humanity that makes his stories attractive. Sillitoe sees the problems of short-story writing as "essentially poetic problems." The result confirms Bowen's view that the story is as much like poetry as the novel. Sillitoe's stories depend on short, quick revelations of consequence or motive and, like the music of some contemporary composers, does not end on the tonic but hangs unresolved, suggesting continuation.

William TREVOR (pseud. of William Trevor Cox), by diminishing authorial presence to objective perception through a style of simplicity and plainness, is able to illustrate ordinary lives in their drabness and stubborn pride without bitterness, irony, or sentimentality. The people in the collection *Lovers of Their Time* (1979) simply are what they are, trapped by the conditions of history and the circumstances of their immediate lives, often driven to the point of madness, yet clinging to a center of integrity.

John Fowles, better known as a novelist, has written in *The Ebony Tower* (1974) stories that are variations on some of the themes of his novels. They embody an ordeal or quest and are reminiscent of medieval romances in the persistent thread of love or eroticism that runs through them. Still, their reference is the modern world, and their central concern is for the spiritual condition of man.

The main body of short fiction in the century exhibits similar themes and concerns. With stimulating innovations from South America (BORGES, CORTÁZAR) to reinforce those from France, Russia, and the U.S. already at work in the native tradition, the short story continues to flourish.

Literary Criticism and the Essay

English criticism in the 20th c. has moved through many phases, answering in a variety of ways to Matthew Arnold's hope for the "right tone and temper of mind" and to his supposition that English critics would have to look abroad in the endeavor "to learn and propagate the best that is known and thought in the world."

Looking abroad, as it turned out, meant looking beyond literature to psychology, anthropology, political economy, the sciences, and arts, although it was also abroad in the national sense, considering the origins of such scientific innovators and theorists as Max Planck, Einstein, and Wittgenstein, political economists such as Marx and Engels, musicians such as Schoenberg and Stravinsky, and painters such as Kandinsky and Klee. These—as well as natives Alfred North Whitehead (1861–1947), Bertrand Russell (1872–1970), and John Maynard Keynes (1883–1946)—provided challenges to the primacy of literary studies as a civilizing force and to its pretensions to being an intellectual discipline.

English criticism did not, however, develop entirely as a response to forces outside literature. The asthetic movement of the *fin de siècle* continued in the work of Arthur Symons (1865–1945), historical criticism in the monumental work of such writers as William Courthope (1842–1917), George Saintsbury (1845–1933), and W. P. Ker (1855–1923), and the mediation between literature and public by such men of letters as Edmund Gosse (1849–1928), Walter Raleigh (1861–1922), Arthur Quiller-Couch (1863–1944), and H. W. Garrod (1878–1960).

But criticism tended to become more theoretical and rigorous. T. E. Hulme's *Speculations* (1924) was an attempt to foster strictness and precision in poetry. His early death in World War I interrupted his critical thinking in a still eclectic phase.

From the U.S. came Ezra Pound and T. S. Eliot to announce and develop an even more rigorous kind of criticism. Eliot's *Selected Essays* (1932) reveal the derivations of his theories: from the English metaphysical poets that intellect and passion must be joined, from the French SYMBOLISTS that images could be both specific and allusive, both theories anchored in the tradition of western Europe that was classical and Christian. He advanced his views as founder and editor of the influential quarterly *Criterion*.

I. A. RICHARDS invoked the aid of psychology and utilitarian theory in *Principles of Literary Criticism* (1924) and *Practical Criticism* (1929) to promote an empirical approach to literary criticism.

Richards influenced a number of critics, some of whom had been his students. Notable among these, William EMPSON, in *Seven Types of Ambiguity* (1930; rev. ed., 1953) analyzes the effects of multiple meanings inherent in words and images on our awareness of pleasure in aesthetic experience. The purpose of art, in his view, is utilitarian, facilitating our power to deal with our problems. Although a Marxist, Christopher Caudwell, who died in 1937 in the Spanish Civil War, had views similar to Empson's in this respect: that criticism evaluates the suitability of art's "mock world" for translation into action, as well as the work's degree of success in achieving the relationship between a work and its time.

F. R. LEAVIS proposed, following I. A. Richards, that the arts are "our storehouse of recorded values." In the periodical *Scrutiny* (1932–53) he advanced the proposition that great artists are important to a culture because they promote awareness of our human place in the world. Q. D. Leavis (1906–81), Leavis's wife and associate, argues in parallel fashion that civilization depends to a high degree on the arts. This emphasis on the importance of art to civilization brought Leavis into conflict with C. P. Snow, who defended (in "The Two Cultures," 1956) what he considered the equal importance of the sciences.

Among those critics attempting to establish for literature a unifying function in a disintegrating world was Owen Barfield

(1898–1997); in *Poetic Diction* (1928) he sees the language of poetry working to restore the original perception of unity between people and nature, of which humanity is the last stage. Barfield's basic optimism is qualified by awareness that humanity may choose instead abstraction and conceptualization "until it withers altogether."

Cyril Connolly (1903–1974), editor of the monthly *Horizon*, in *Enemies of Promise* (1938; rev. ed., 1948) and *The Condemned Playground* (1946) picked up on Barfield's idea that humanity through language and literature is capable of achieving a higher level of awareness.

David Daiches (b. 1912) renews the position of earlier critics such as E. M. Forster, who thought the critic's job is to "civilize the community," Percy Lubbock (1879–1965), whose *Craft of Fiction* (1921) deals with the literary representation of life in an "ideal shape," and Virginia Woolf, whose essays in *The Common Reader* (1925) took up the problems of the ordinary reader. Daiches, in *The Novel and the Modern World* (1939; rev. ed., 1960), developed the view that because literature manifests several kinds of discourse, criticism is obliged to be pluralistic, and the critic's job that of promoting "appreciation."

An influential eclectic critic is Herbert Read, who modernized romantic theory via Jung's psychology. *Selected Writings* (1964) represents his view that education through art is essential for satisfying the "symbolic needs of the unconscious."

Another critic whose personal influence has been extensive is Stephen Spender. The title of *The Struggle of the Modern* (1963) signifies both his sense of the literary scene in the middle decades and of his own commitment to breaking through social and political strictures on literary art. He worked for a time with Cyril Connolly on *Horizon*.

V. S. Pritchett is an autonomous and reliable critic whose observations reflect the clarity and unpretentiousness of his own fictions. In this respect, the novelist Walter Allen (b. 1911) has produced similarly cogent and enlightening commentary in *The English Novel* (1954) and *Tradition and Dream* (1964; Am., *The Modern Novel in Britain and the United States*, 1965).

From *Purity of Diction in English Verse* (1953) to *The Poet in the Imaginary Museum: Essays of Two Decades* (1976), Donald Davie has advocated a new classicism in language and an antiauthoritarian attitude in the poet.

The essay in England, aside from the critical essay, is not amenable to being surveyed. Its character is to be detached, personal, idiosyncratic, especially so in this eclectic, experimental century. The early decades produced the whimsical, charming, and always adroit pieces of Hilaire BELLOC, G. K. CHESTERTON, and Max Beerbohm (1872–1956).

Writing into midcentury were E. M. Forster, George Orwell, Aldous Huxley, and Bertrand Russell, liberal commentators on the social and moral as well as cultural issues. Three collections characterize the midcentury: *Delight* (1949) by J. B. PRIESTLEY, which describes ways of coping with various pressures; *Reflections in a Mirror* (1945), various forays in search of values, by Charles Morgan (1894–1958); and *The Seven Deadly Sins* (1962), Angus Wilson and others, in which notable literary figures write on their "favorite sin."

The apocalyptic mood of the 1960s and 1970s is sounded in *Beyond All This Fiddle* (1968) and *The Savage God* (1971) by A. Alvarez (b. 1929), while W. H. Auden sounded the eclectic international note in *The Dyer's Hand* (1962) and *Forewords and Afterwords* (1973). In his eclecticism, Auden represents the trend in both literary criticism and the essay to assimilate the massive accretions to knowledge and understanding contributed by midcentury scientists and humanists.

BIBLIOGRAPHY: Graves, R., and A. Hodge, *The Long Week-end: A Social History of Great Britain 1918–1939* (1940); Leavis, F. R., *New Bearings in English Poetry* (1950); Tindall, W. Y., *Forces in Modern British Literature* (rev. ed., 1956); Allsop, K., *The Angry Decade* (1958); Alvarez, A., *Stewards of Excellence: Studies in Modern English and American Poets* (1958); Daiches, D., *The Present Age in British Literature* (1958); Gindin, J., *Postwar British Fiction* (1962); Karl, F., *A Reader's Guide to the Contemporary English Novel* (1962); Hall, J., *The Tragic Comedians: Seven Modern British Novelists* (1963); Johnstone, J. K., *The Bloomsbury Group* (1963); O'Connor, F., *The Lonely Voice: A Study of the Short Story* (1963); Stewart, J. I. M., *Eight Modern Writers, The Oxford History of English Literature*, Vol. XII (1963); Ford, B., ed. *The Pelican Guide to English Literature*, Vol. VII: *The Modern Age* (1964); Stead, C. K., *The New Poetic* (1964); Allen, W., *The Modern Novel in Britain and the United States* (1965); Ross, R., *The Georgian Revolt* (1965); Shapiro, C., ed., *Contemporary British Novelists* (1965); Enright, D. J., *Conspirators and Poets* (1966); Rosenthal, M. L., *The New Poets* (1967); Press, J., *Map of Modern English Verse* (1969); Bradbury, M., *The Social Context of Modern English Literature* (1971); Burgess, A., *The Novel Now* (1971); Sisson, C. H., *English Poetry, 1900–1950: An Assessment* (1971); Taylor, J. R., *The Second Wave: British Drama for the Seventies* (1971); Roy, E., *British Drama since Shaw* (1972); Stade, G., ed., *Six Modern British Novelists* (1974); Fussell, P., *The Great War and Modern Memory* (1975); Gillie, C., *Movements in English Literature, 1900–1940* (1975); Kenner, H., *The Pound Era* (1975); Elsom, J., *Post-war British Theatre* (1976); Morris, R. K., ed., *Old Lines, New Forces: Essays on the Contemporary British Novel* (1976); Cavaliero, G., *The Rural Tradition in the English Novel 1900–1939* (1977); Homberger, E., *The Art of the Real: Poetry in England and America since 1939* (1977); Hynes, S., *The Auden Generation* (1977); Kerensky, O., *The New British Drama: Fourteen Playwrights since Osborne and Pinter* (1977); Hayman, R., *British Theatre since 1955: A Reassessment* (1979)

—MANLY JOHNSON

English Literature since 1980

Britain in the 1980s will long be linked with the rise to power of Margaret Thatcher and the Conservative Party. As prime minister, Thatcher presided over a series of highly controversial policies that brought about substantial cuts in government spending for a wide range of social and industrial programs. Thatcher's backers insisted that a return to market economics would enliven an economy that was sluggish throughout the 1970s; and, indeed, throughout the 1980s much of England enjoyed levels of prosperity rarely seen during the postwar era. But as the critics of "Thatcherism" often noted, unemployment in the nation stayed high throughout the decade, particularly in the industrial north, where—more than once—protestors took to the streets.

As the 1960s had revealed, art tends to thrive during periods of new prosperity and wide social debate; and, in fact, the 1980s proved to be a rich decade for British fiction, drama, and poetry.

Much of this vitality has owed to the fact that many older authors have continued to produce works showing little or no diminution in their creative powers. Among younger writers—those born in the 1940s and 1950s—one finds many highly talented voices at work in both traditional and post-modern modes. The increasing cultural diversity of contemporary Britain has also added vigor to its literature. Several of Britain's best new writers have roots outside the European tradition; others have backgrounds in the lower middle class.

Fiction

With the death of Graham GREENE in 1991, the English-speaking world lost one of its finest storytellers, the creator of a distinctive world of intrigue, exoticism, and sin that critics came to call "Greeneland." Beginning with *Doctor Fischer of Geneva: or the Bomb Party* (1980), Greene's novels tended to become leaner, but continued to reveal a penchant for exploring questions related to politics and religion. In the picaresque *Monsignor Quixote* (1982), the best of his final novels, Greene combines his fine comic skills with a continuing interest in Marxism and Christianity—traits that have always marked much of his fiction. *The Captain and the Enemy* (1988), the last novel Greene published in his lifetime, deftly blends politics and suspense as it deals with several ambitious themes, including the meaning of fatherhood and the nature of love.

In 1983 William GOLDING won the Nobel Prize for literature—a decision that surprised many British and American journalists and critics who had come to assume, understandably, that the award would go instead to Greene. In *Darkness Visible* (1979), the most surreal of his more recent novels, Golding weaves a richly textured account of cruelty and social derangement in contemporary Britain, mixing realism and allegory along the way; in *Rites of Passage* (1980), he echoes both Laurence Sterne (1713–1768) and Joseph CONRAD as he constructs a blackly comic account of a 19th-c. sea voyage, which he continues in *Close Quarters* (1987) and *Fire Down Below* (1989). Golding's underrated *The Paper Men* (1984) raises a series of provocative questions about fiction writing—and fame—as it follows the farcical, finally fatal battle between a celebrated English novelist and a crass American academic on his own quest for success.

Although he calls himself "a busy hack," Anthony BURGESS will surely come to be ranked, with Golding and Greene, as one of his generation's leading literary figures. In such novels as *The End of the World News* (1982) and *The Kingdom of the Wicked* (1985) Burgess exhibits his exuberant wit, erudition, and stylistic bravura; in *Earthly Powers* (1980) he creates, in Kenneth Toomey, one of the decade's most fully realized fictional characters, and again explores moral issues in a cosmos he shows to be continually wracked by the struggle between good and evil. The most entertaining of Burgess's later books, however, is his candid and lively autobiography, published in two widely praised volumes, *Little Wilson and Big God* (1987) and *You've Had Your Time* (1990).

Others known for their philosophical fiction continued to publish notable work in the 1980s, among them Iris MURDOCH, Muriel SPARK, and John FOWLES. In novels such as The *Philosopher's Pupil* (1983), *The Good Apprentice* (1985), and *The Message to the Planet* (1989) Murdoch persists in pairing striking characters with complex plots, focusing again on such concerns as power, enchantment, obsession, and chance; although less shapely than her earlier novels, these works remain filled with sparkling wit and intellectual vigor. Spark's more recent novels have also remained satisfying in their darkly comic way; in *A Far Cry from Kensington* (1988), the best of these, she explores with aplomb several of her favorite subjects—including wickedness and deceit—while providing a vivid portrait of the world of British book publishing in the grim postwar years of the early 1950s. Like Murdoch and Spark, John Fowles developed an enormous following in both Europe and America during the 1970s. But with *Mantissa* (1982)—a lively exploration of eros, gender, and creativity that some critics found self-absorbed and contrived—Fowles's reputation and readership began to decline. Convincingly set in 18th-c. Britain, Fowles's *A Maggot* (1985) is even more demanding, balancing several plots while displaying a keen interest—at once playful and serious—in a wide range of linguistic, social, and metaphysical matters.

Doris LESSING and Margaret DRABBLE also continued to publish what might be called "novels of ideas." Lessing has often puzzled critics by declining to be confined to a particular style, voice, or even genre; for example, with *The Sirian Experiments* (1981), *The Making of the Representative for Planet 8* (1982), and *The Sentimental Agents in the Volyen Empire* (1983) she completed a series of five science-fiction novels (collectively entitled *Canopus in Argos: Archives*) that provided her with an unusual—and unusually expansive—canvas for displaying her deep interest in subjects ranging from politics to economics to Sufi thought. In *The Diary of a Good Neighbour* (1983) and *If the Old Could* (1984) Lessing returned to contemporary Britain and a precisely "realistic" style, but published both novels under the pseudonym "Jane Somers" in order to demonstrate the difficulties faced by unknown novelists in need of publicity and support. Although Margaret Drabble—one of Britain's most visible literary figures—is by no means as unpredictable as Lessing, she has now published several novels quite unlike those that first brought her wide notice in the 1960s. *The Middle Ground* (1980) and the trilogy consisting of *The Radiant Way* (1987), *A Natural Curiosity* (1989), and *The Gates of Ivory* (1992), are more ambitiously structured—and generally darker—than *A Summer Bird-Cage* (1962), or *Jerusalem the Golden* (1967). Increasingly, Drabble has produced large, allusive, multilayered, highly self-conscious fictions that tend to show Britons searching for meaning and normality in a world grown increasingly bizarre and bleak.

In various forms, novels belonging to what Malcolm BRADBURY has termed "the socio-moral tradition of fiction" have continued to thrive in Britain, where—as Drabble's own work shows—the presence of such figures as Dickens, Disraeli, and Gaskell remains strong. Although John Mortimer (b. 1923) is probably best known in Britain as the creator of "Rumpole of the Bailey" and as an insightful interviewer skilled at drawing out the diverse likes of John Gielgud and Mick Jagger, he deserves wider fame for such novels as *Paradise Postponed* (1985) and *Titmuss Regained* (1990). Indeed, these works show a certain Victorian fondness for dark secrets and mysterious inheritances, while offering a sharp commentary on Thatcherite conservativism. Like Mortimer, the prolific Fay WELDON has written many plays for both television and the stage; as a novelist, she is known for a distinctive style that blends breezy plotting, dark—often bitter—humor, and an intrusive authorial voice. Weldon's *Darcy's Utopia* (1990) reflects well her continuing interest in political issues; in *Life Force* (1992) she turns again to the blunt treatment of gender issues and sexual themes.

Martin AMIS, another writer much concerned with the state of modern society, first came to wide attention with *The Rachel Papers* (1973), a brash, funny, and wholly convincing account of adolescent romance and self-absorption. But his subsequent works, including the short-story collection *Einstein's Monsters* (1987) and the novel *London Fields* (1989), reveal more fully the fear and despair that often seemed dominant in the decade of Chernobyl, global warming, and AIDS. Understandably, Amis's work has often been criticized for its persistently nasty tone. But his *Money: A Suicide Note* (1984)—often moving, often annoying—is a postmodern masterpiece, the tragicomic account of one man's self-destruction in an era of rampant materialism and greed.

Like Martin Amis, Indian-born Salman RUSHDIE is also an experimental and controversial novelist. Rushdie's earlier fictions, including *Midnight's Children* (1980) and *Shame* (1983), were widely praised for their exuberance, erudition, and imaginative flights; many critics compared them favorably to works by such internationally acclaimed practitioners of MAGIC REALISM as Jorge Luis Borges and Gabriel GARCÍA MÁRQUEZ. But others have found verbosity, tedium, and a kind of adolescent smugness in Rushdie's novels, including *The Satanic Verses* (1988), easily one of the most controversial works in recent literary history; protests over its treatment of certain aspects of Muslim culture and belief grew intense enough to prompt charges of blasphemy and, eventually, death threats that—in 1989—sent Rushdie into prolonged hiding. Rushdie's *Haroun and the Sea of Stories* (1990), written during his confinement, does not deal overtly with political or religious issues, but—in a style designed to appeal to both children and adults—recounts one storyteller's plight and grants him a happy ending.

Rushdie's *Imaginary Homelands* (1991), a collection of essays on culture and literature, was among the first titles published by Granta Books, an offshoot of *Granta* magazine, which emerged during the 1980s as Britain's most influential literary magazine. Artfully packaged and widely distributed through Penguin Books, *Granta* offered stories and essays by a large range of internationally acclaimed authors and often brilliantly chronicled the massive social and political change facing Europe as economic borders fell and communism collapsed. Indeed, few literary publications in recent decades have managed to sustain both quality and influence as well as *Granta*.

Julian BARNES and J. G. BALLARD are also associated with more experimental forms of fiction. Barnes has published several novels using intriguing structural strategies; in *Flaubert's Parrot* (1984), for example, he constructs a largely comic tale of scholarly obsession that sparks various questions about the conventions of both fiction and literary biography; in *Talking It Over* (1991) he employs three narrators to tell a cleverly compelling tale about the pain of love and the comfort of words. Ballard, like Barnes, often bridges the gap between popular and "serious" literature, and eludes easy categorization. Such works as *Crash* (1973), *Vermillion Sands* (1973), and *High Rise* (1975) blend humor and fantasy with apocalyptic tendencies and a touch of the surreal, and are sometimes labeled "science fiction." But as *The Day of Creation* (1987) particularly proves, Ballard's fantasy fiction has many qualities—including stunningly precise descriptions of landscape and place—that are rarely found in genre literature of any kind. He has, moreover, excelled in such "mainstream" fictions as *Empire of the Sun* (1984), which draws upon Ballard's boyhood in China during World War II, and *The Kindness of Women* (1991), another display of fictionalized autobiography.

The prolific Michael Moorcock (b. 1939) is also hard to classify. But fantasy, wit, and a fascination with history and myth continue to combine in his fictions, including *The City in the*

Autumn Stars (1987) and *Mother London* (1989). Robert Nye (b. 1939) displays a similarly lively sensibility; his novels *Faust* (1981), *The Memoirs of Lord Byron* (1989), and *The Life and Death of My Lord Gilles de Rais* (1990) show him successfully drawing inspiration from history and older literary sources.

Like Ballard, Angela Carter (1940–1991) began publishing usually imaginative fiction in the 1960s but only recently came to wide notice; such novels as *Nights at the Circus* (1984) and *Wise Children* (1991)—as well as several of the essays in *Expletives Deleted* (1992)—confirm her place as one of the most distinctive voices of recent years. Another unusual talent, Christine Brooke-Rose (b. 1923), is perhaps as well known for her literary scholarship as her fiction. To be sure, Brooke-Rose's many novels, ranging from *The Dear Deceit* (1961) to *Textermination* (1991) will never be widely popular, but their mix of sophisticated wordplay and rare erudition will undoubtedly attract more critical interest in the years to come.

Among other established British writers, Kingsley AMIS, David STOREY, and Alan SILLITOE, have continued to publish significant fiction in a more traditional vein. Two of Amis's recent novels, *Stanley and the Women* (1984) and *Difficulties with Girls* (1988), were widely praised for their solid plots and strong characterizations, but also drew fire from some critics who found them marred by misogynist overtones. Amis's *The Old Devils* (1986) was, however, more warmly received for its sympathetic—if unsentimental—depiction of a group of friends on the verge of old age. Storey produced, in *Saville* (1976), a lengthy, intricately shaped account of working-class life that won Britain's prestigious Booker Prize; *A Prodigal Child* (1982), and *Present Times* (1984)—as well as *Storey's Lives: Poems 1951–1991* (1992)—have confirmed his status as one of modern Britain's most versatile and accomplished writers. Sillitoe also centered on working-class characters in several works, including *Out of the Whirlpool* (1987), a novella, and *The Open Door* (1989), a strong addition to his series of novels dealing with the Seaton family of Nottingham. Other notable novelists maintain strong reputations with British critics and readers. These include Stanley Middleton (b. 1919), Elizabeth Howard (b. 1923), Keith Waterhouse (b. 1929), Isabel Colegate (b. 1931), David Pownall (b. 1938), and Rose Tremain (b. 1943).

Both Malcolm BRADBURY and David LODGE continued to attract growing audiences outside the United Kingdom. Because both have superb comic skills and have written frequently—and irreverently—of academic life, they are sometimes referred to simultaneously as "Brodge." Bradbury's more recent fictions include *Cuts: A Very Short Novel* (1987), which lampoons British television while capturing the atmosphere of uncertainty that prevailed in the summer of 1986, when layoffs and firings were common in both government and industry, and talk of "privatization" was much in the air. Bradbury's best novel remains *The History Man* (1975), a brilliantly crafted account of moral confusion and radical chic. Lodge's *Changing Places* (1975) and *Small World* (1984), offering exaggerated but insightful depictions of the rivalries and anxieties of academic life, have acquired a kind of cult status among professors on both sides of the Atlantic. Lodge has also examined the role religion plays in modern life; in *How Far Can You Go?* (1980; pub. in the U.S. as *Souls and Bodies*, 1982), for example, he ably portrays a group of characters caught awkwardly between the demands of the church and the temptations of a newly permissive society.

Penelope FITZGERALD, Anita BROOKNER, and Penelope Lively (b. 1933) also earned much critical praise during the 1980s. After establishing herself as a respected writer of literary biographies, Fitzgerald began producing novels that differ impressively in their selection of characters and settings; *Human Voices* (1980), for example, portrays BBC broadcasters at work during the early days of World War II; *Innocence* (1986) is set in Florence in the 1950s; *The Beginning of Spring* (1988) takes place in Moscow just before the Russian Revolution. Brookner's settings and situations are less varied; as *A Start in Life* (1981; pub. in the U.S. as *The Debut*, 1981), *Hotel du Lac* (1984), *A Friend from England* (1987), and the particularly fine *A Closed Eye* (1991) suggest, she has tended to focus on women facing the difficulties and illusions of romantic love. But Brookner is a precise stylist whose keen sense of irony tends to keep her work from becoming predictable or cloying. Penelope Lively published several well-regarded works of fiction for both children and adults in the 1970s, but her reputation and readership rose significantly after *Moon Tiger* (1987), a memorable meditation on time, history, and personal destiny that won the Booker Prize.

A. S. BYATT and Emma TENNANT also found many new readers during the 1980s. Byatt, an astute reviewer and critic, became known as a novelist in North America with *The Virgin in the Garden* (1978); *Possession* (1990), her most successful novel, also shows an ambitious interest in history, myth, mystery, and 19th-c. Literature. Like Byatt, Tennant often makes artful use of older literary sources while maintaining her own highly distinctive voice. In *The Bad Sister* (1978), for example, she adapts James Hogg's (1770–1835) *The Private Memoirs and Confessions of a Justified Sinner* (1824), a vivid account of mayhem and demonic possession. Gothic elements also inform Tennant's *Woman Beware Woman* (1983; pub. in the U.S. as *The Half-Mother*, 1983), perhaps her best novel, a well-told tale of deception and revenge. In *The Adventures of Robina, by Herself* (1985), Tennant updates Daniel DeFoe; in *Faustine* (1992), she effectively recasts the Faust myth in modern guise.

Other novelists of promise emerged during the decade, including William Boyd (b. 1952), Graham Swift (b. 1949), and Kuzuo ISHIGURO. With his first novel, *A Good Man in Africa* (1981), Boyd produced the best English comic novel since Kingsley Amis's *Lucky Jim* (1954); his *Stars and Bars* (1984) is a shrewdly funny commentary on both English reserve and American vulgarity. Boyd's *An Ice-Cream War* (1982) and *The New Confessions* (1987) show strong narrative skills and a discerning use of historical sources; *Brazzaville Beach* (1990), his most impressive work to date, focuses on scientific ethics and the rather exotic subject of chimpanzee research. With *The Sweetshop Owner* (1980) and the short-story collection *Learning To Swim* (1982), Swift was widely hailed as a writer to watch; his novels *Shuttlecock* (1981) and *Waterland* (1983) show well the tensions and terrors that often swirl beneath the surface of family life. The Japanese-born Kazuo Ishiguro came somewhat more slowly to public attention, first publishing two well-crafted but quiet novels, *A Pale View of Hills* (1982) and *An Artist of the Floating World* (1986); his best-seller *The Remains of the Day* (1989) is a butler's tale that reveals overlooked similarities between Asian and English cultures.

During the 1980s, Timothy Mo (b. 1950), A. N. Wilson (b. 1950), Peter Ackroyd (b. 1949), and Bruce CHATWIN also established their careers. Mo, born in Hong Kong, first won wide praise with *The Monkey King* (1978) and *Sour Sweet* (1982), which draw richly on his Chinese background and display a fine comic sensibility; his *An Insular Possession* (1986) tackles Chinese history and proceeds far more ponderously. In *The Sweets of Pimlico* (1977),

Who Was Oswald Fish? (1981), and *Wise Virgin* (1982), Wilson mixes farce, satire, and black comedy in a manner that echoes, but does not surpass, the early Evelyn WAUGH. Wilson's more recent novels, including *Gentlemen in England* (1985) and *Incline Our Hearts* (1988), show a certain maturing in tone and technique; his biographies of *Tolstoy* (1988) and *C. S. Lewis* (1990) won wide acclaim. Like Wilson, Peter Ackroyd has published several ambitious biographies, including *T. S. Eliot* (1984) and *Dickens* (1990); like Robert Nye and Emma Tennant, he is also a novelist skilled at making imaginative use of biographical and historical sources, as such works as *The Great Fire of London* (1982), *The Last Testament of Oscar Wilde* (1983), and *Chatterton* (1987) prove. Bruce Chatwin sparked a wide renewal of interest in travel writing with *In Patagonia* (1977), a vivid account of his journey to the African Sahara. Chatwin's subsequent works—including the novels *On the Black Hill* (1982) and *Utz* (1988) and many of the sketches in *What Am I Doing Here* (1988)—show that he was among the most promising writers of his generation, a superb storyteller often willing to take Flaubertian pains with his prose.

Those publishing notable short fiction in more recent years include V. S. PRITCHETT, Ian McEwan (b. 1948), and Patrick McGrath (b. 1950). Pritchett's career began when H. G. WELLS and Ford Madox FORD were still publishing; his vast *Complete Collected Stories* (1991) includes six decade's worth of expertly crafted, rather Chekhovian stories that tend to cast an unusually clear-eyed look at lower-middle-class life. McEwan's versatile career now includes several superb novels, including *The Comfort of Strangers* (1981)—an unusually haunting account of violence and sexual desire—and *The Innocent* (1990), a gripping tale of cold-war intrigue that compares favorably to the best novels of John le CARRÉ. McEwan also remains well known, however, for the arresting stories contained in *First Love, Last Rites* (1975) and *In Between the Sheets* (1978). Like McEwan, Patrick McGrath clearly knows his craft, and frequently gravitates to grotesque characters and plots, but he is also more overtly whimsical and droll. The stories in *Blood and Water and Other Tales* (1988), for example, show McGrath producing pieces reminiscent of Roald Dahl (1916–1991).

A revival of interest in Dahl's work became evident as the 1980s came to a close; several collections of his previously published stories appeared, among them *The Best of Roald Dahl* (1983) and *Ah, Sweet Mystery of Life* (1989). Even more significant was the publication of *The Collected Stories of Angus Wilson* (1987), which includes titles from earlier volumes like *Such Darling Dodos* (1940) and *A Bit Off the Map* (1957) and proves anew why Wilson stands as one of the finest fiction writers of the past fifty years.

Drama

Theater in Britain has enjoyed some very lively periods in recent years, at least in part because of the rise to prominence of several figures initially called "fringe playwrights" because their early works were often staged in small theaters and routinely expressed far-left views. David Hare (b. 1947), the most prominent member of this group, first acquired wide critical attention in Britain with *Knuckle* (1974), which parodies the Hollywood thriller as it indicts, among other things, the materialism and hypocrisy that pervade modern life; he is probably best known, however, for the particularly powerful *Plenty* (1978), which centers on one woman's search for meaning in a postwar Britain, which Hare

portrays as unmoored and corrupt, unable to face the future or digest the past.

Hare began collaborating with Howard Brenton (b. 1942) in the early 1970s; their *Pravda: A Fleet Street Comedy* (1985) is a satiric, farcical, melodramatic portrayal of contemporary British journalism that features—in the shape of a monstrous press lord called Lambert Le Roux—one of the decade's most memorable stage characters. Brenton has regularly expressed Marxist-radical sympathies, and his own works—with their frequent use of profanity, violence, and explicit sexuality—have often proved highly controversial. In *The Churchill Play* (perf. 1974, pub. 1986), for example, Brenton depicts a fascist takeover of England while savaging the most widely esteemed figure in 20th-c. British history. With *A Short Sharp Shock!* (1981) Brenton began a scathing attack on the Thatcher government, which he would sustain in such plays as *The Romans in Britain* (1982) and *Bloody Poetry* (1987). Because of its scenes of sexual violence and its blunt criticism of Britain's military presence in Northern Ireland, *The Romans in Britain* sparked a particularly intense reaction in the British press; however, a widely publicized attempt to prosecute the play under the Sexual Offenses Act of 1956 proved unsuccessful.

Like Brenton, Howard Barker (b. 1946) often employs satire and shock as a means of emphasizing his attacks on capitalism, militarism, and various forces he finds inimical to the survival of free expression. In *Downchild* (1985) Barker seeks to depict the ineffectiveness of Labour politicians in the postwar era; in *The Castle* (1985) he centers on the eternal battle of the sexes, here played out in the years just after the Crusades. The work of writer-actor Stephen Berkoff (b. 1937) is similarly flamboyant and politically charged. In *East* (1977) Berkoff constructs a ribald and angry "elegy" for the working-class district of London where he was born and reared; in *Decadence* (1982) he savages the "infantilism" he finds rife in Britain's upper class. In *Sink the Belgrano!* (1987) Berkoff attacks Britain's role in the 1982 Falklands War.

Because Brenton, Barker, and Berkoff tend to produce such deliberately provocative material, critical responses to their plays tend to range predictably from utter admiration to complete disgust. Edward BOND, who vigorously defended *The Romans in Britain*, is himself no stranger to controversy; his *Saved* (1966) was widely condemned for its portrayal of infanticide, even as other critics praised its frank rendering of the process of dehumanization that pervades modern society. With their use of parody, fantasy, and sharp irony, Bond's more recent works—including *Restoration* (1981), *Summer* (1982), and *The War Plays: A Trilogy* (1985)—continue to show something of the influence of Bertolt BRECHT as well as an increasingly didactic strain; his *Two Post-Modern Plays* (1990)—*Jackets* and *In the Company of Men*—includes a series of "Notes on Post-Modernism" illuminating many of his aesthetic and philosophical views.

Harold PINTER, Britain's most distinguished living dramatist, has written frequently about power, violence, and victimization, but never so powerfully as in *One for the Road* (1984), a starkly staged one-act play written in support of Amnesty International and conveying the full evil and horror of torture as well as any work of literature in the 20th c. Pinter's *Mountain Language* (1988) also shows his more explicit interest in political issues as it deals with the horrors faced by political protestors and their families in a growing number of tyrannical states.

Tom STOPPARD also remains an impressive force in British theater, winning praise for *The Real Thing* (1982), a study of love and infidelity that won wide praise not only for its wit and verbal dexterity, but its powerful treatment of a wide range of philosophical and aesthetic issues. In *Hapgood* (1988) Stoppard again cleverly parodies a literary convention—in this case the spy thriller—as he constructs an intricate line of action again examining the limits of perception while raising questions regarding, among other things, quantum mechanics and Einsteinian theories of light. *Hapgood* stands as one of Stoppard's most demanding—and rewarding—plays.

Several other prominent British dramatists—including Alan AYCKBOURN, Simon GRAY, and Alan Bennett (b. 1934)—have maintained their flair for comedy with a willingness to address serious artistic concerns. Perhaps because of his insistence on placing himself "slap-bang in the middle of the English theatergoing public," Ayckbourn has often been dismissed as little more than a lively entertainer with dazzling technical skills. But his *A Chorus of Disapproval* (1986) and *Man of the Moment* (1985) offer not only laughs but sharp, subtle, sometimes painful commentaries on contemporary manners and mores. Like Ayckbourn, Gray repeatedly combines wit, intelligence, and West End success; *The Common Pursuit* (1984), his most ambitious work, ably follows the linked lives of several friends over the course of two decades. In *Melon* (1987), Gray again enters Ayckbourn country, tragicomically dealing with, among other things, the strains and disenchantments of middle-class married life. Bennett began his career writing and performing with Peter Cook, Jonathan Miller, and Dudley Moore in the still fresh *Beyond the Fringe* (1963); his more recent plays, including *Kafka's Dick* (1987) and *Single Spies* (1988), display well his always sophisticated use of verbal comedy. Like many of Britain's leading dramatists, Bennett also writes occasionally for television; his *Talking Heads* (1987)—a series of six "monologues" originally aired by the BBC—are especially compelling, offering convincing testimonies from the often overlooked corners of middle-class life.

Caryl CHURCHILL and Pam Gems (b. 1925) are among the most widely recognized of Britain's growing number of prominent women dramatists. Churchill's early plays, including *Owners* (1973), *Vinegar Tom* (1978), and *Cloud Nine* (1979), were among the most spirited and influential Marxist-feminist plays of the 1970s; her inventive *Serious Money* (1987), which consists largely of couplets, is a witty, searing indictment of the rapacious world of high finance. Pam Gems's *Camille* (1984) deals powerfully with the social and sexual exploitation of women; her *Loving Women* (1984) continues her exploration of gender roles.

Hanif Kureishi (b. 1954) is the best known among an increasing number of dramatists focusing on life among Britain's minorities. In *Borderline* (1981), for example, he deals with the reality of racism as faced by members of the nation's Asian immigrant community. A similar concern informs *My Beautiful Laundrette* (1986), one of several acclaimed screenplays included in Kureishi's *London Kills Me* (1992).

Poetry

The most widely discussed poet of the 1980s was very probably Craig Raine (b. 1944), whose first published volume, *The Onion, Memory* (1978), and whose *A Martian Sends a Postcard Home* (1979) displays a striking, punning, flamboyantly metaphorical style. Along with Christopher REID, whose *Arcadia* (1979) and *Pea Soup* (1982) revealed similar stylistic tendencies, Raine's name became synonymous with the much imitated "Martian" school of poetry, so named by James Fenton (b. 1949) because of its attempt to view life from angles fresh enough to appear, at times, alien.

Fenton and Blake MORRISON must also be placed among the more prominent younger poets of the 1980s. Although probably better known as a travel writer and as a drama critic for the *Times* of London, Fenton won wide praise for the poetry he came to collect in *The Memory of War* (1982) and in *Children in Exile* (1983). This volume includes several exceptional poems drawing upon Fenton's experiences in war-torn Cambodia, and another, "A German Requiem," which is an especially notable example of the trend toward narrative forms in contemporary British poetry. In *The Ballad of the Yorkshire Ripper and Other Poems* (1987), Morrison reveals an interest in topical matters, as well as the ability to write convincingly in dialect, as he does in the volume's title poem, a disturbing but memorable monologue dealing with Peter Sutcliffe's ghastly, widely publicized crimes. With poet-critic Andrew Motion (b. 1952), Morrison has also edited *The Penguin Book of Contemporary British Poetry* (1982), helped direct further attention to the work of such poets as Jeffrey Wainwright (b. 1944) and Hugo Williams (b. 1942), both of whom display, in varying ways, the kind of spare, understated approach that—despite the presence of the "Martians"—has tended to prevail in recent British poetry. However, Williams, in such appealing volumes as *Love-Life* (1979) and *Writing Home* (1985), writes in the kind of more bluntly autobiographical style that remains somewhat rare in contemporary British verse.

Of the other English poets featured in the volume, Carol Rumens (b. 1946) and Tony Harrison (b. 1937) are probably best known to American readers. In such volumes as *Unplayed Music* (1981) and *Star Whisper* (1983) Rumens made her mark as a poet of particular clarity and insight; in *Direct Dialing* (1985) and *From Berlin to Heaven* (1989) she shows her continuing interest in eastern Europe and its history. Harrison combines a working-class upbringing in Leeds with degrees in the classics and linguistics. His sensitivity to diction and the subtle rhythms of everyday speech—as well as his willingness to deal bluntly with various class-related issues—are found in several excellent volumes, including *Selected Poems* (1984), which features many of the sonnets in his continuing "The School of Eloquence" sequence, perhaps the most consistently interesting project undertaken in recent British poetry.

Although not included in the Penguin anthology, John Fuller (b. 1937), Michael Hofmann (b. 1957), and Wendy Cope (b. 1945) must also be ranked highly among the more gifted of Britain's contemporary poets. The versatile Fuller produced several of the decade's most original works, including *The Illusionists* (1980), a tale in verse structured in the four-footed iambic of Pushkin's *Eugene Onegin*, and *Partingtime Hall* (1987), an irreverent collaboration with James Fenton. Hofmann is particularly full of promise. In *Acrimony* (1986), for example, he is gloomy and aloof but often compelling, the maker of stark images and well-shaped lines that linger long in the mind. Cope combines intelligence, accessibility, and a delightful wit; her *Making Cocoa for Kingsley Amis* (1986) displays her strong gift of parody, and won wide praise and high sales.

The 1977 appointment of John BETJEMAN as poet laureat surprised no one. Long identified as a somewhat eccentric presence on Britain's cultural scene, Betjeman's latter poems—including those represented in his *Collected Poems* (4th ed., 1979) and his *Uncollected Poems* (1982)—continue to reveal his preoccupation with such subjects as architecture and death, as well as the satirical and accessible style that made him one of Britain's most popular poets. Next to Betjeman, Philip LARKIN was for many years Britain's most popular "serious" poet, as well known for his bookish, rather cranky bachelor persona as for the lucid, witty, and quotable quality of such poems as "High Windows" and "I Remember, I Remember," which both appear in his posthumously published *Collected Poems* (1988).

Stylistically, Ted HUGHES has little in common with either Betjeman or Larkin; in fact, his appointment as poet laureate in 1985 surprised those who were most familiar with Hughes's earlier work, including *Crow* (1970), and who continued to associate him vaguely with violence and misanthropy. Although Hughes is certainly uneven, he is, at his best, a poet of unusual power and lyrical sensitivity; his *Selected Poems (1957–81)* (1982) as well as *River* (1983) and *Wolfwatching* (1989) show his continuing interest in nature and myth and add to a body of work that is, all things considered, unmatched in modern British poetry.

Geoffrey Hill (b. 1932) and Elizabeth Jennings were also among the well-established poets to publish significant volumes in recent years. Hill is a poet with a scholar's interest in language, Christian mysticism, and English history; his verse is allusive, complex, highly self-conscious, and always scrupulously crafted, as such recent volumes as *Tenebrae* (1978) and *The Mystery of the Charity of Charles Péguy* (1983) indicate. Like Hill, Jennings is deeply interested in Christianity, as her prose works—including *Christianity and Poetry* (1965)—reveal. But her varied body of verse is not as immediately formidable as Hill's; indeed, much of the more recent work in Jennings's *Collected Poems* (1986) features the same clarity of expression that helps explain her frequent appearance on the literature syllabi of Britain's secondary schools.

Other poets to publish significant collections during the 1980s include Peter Reading (b. 1946), whose *Essential Reading* (1986) displays well the work of one of Britain's most idiosyncratic poets. Peter Redgrove (b. 1932) is another highly original poet, as his *The Moon Disposes: Poems 1954–1987* (1987) shows. The more orthodox Robert Conquest, well known for his writings on Russian history, also published his *New and Collected Poems* (1988).

During the 1980s, other important poets published significant collections, among them Gavin Ewart (1916–1995), D. J. Enright, and Geoffrey Grigson (1906–1985). Ewart—for five decades an industrious and lively presence in the world of British letters—has continued to publish poems vividly expressive of his social, political, and erotic concerns; his *The Collected Ewart 1933-1980* (1980), *The New Ewart: Poems, 1980-1982* (1982), and *Late Pickings* (1987) show once more his varying tones and his mastery of an unusually wide variety of verse forms. Enright, like Ewart, can be both witty and grim, sometimes simultaneously; his later works, contained in *Collected Poems* (1987) and *Selected Poems* (1990), also show a continued willingness to engage current social issues in a wry, often satiric voice. Like Enright, Geoffrey Grigson also qualifies as a modern "man of letters" who has worked in a variety of modes, often mixing art with literary journalism. While the best of Grigson's verse can be found in his *Collected Poems 1963-80* (1982), a posthumously published volume, *Persephone's Flowers and Other Poems* (1986), is notable for its inclusion of "Entering My Eightieth Year," the finest poem of his final years. Many other younger poets of varying voices and styles attracted wide attention, including Lawrence Sail (b. 1942), David Scott (b. 1947), Jeremy Reed (b. 1951), Sean O'Brien (b. 1952), Fiona Pitt-Kethley (b. 1954), and David Dabydeen (b. 1956).

BIBLIOGRAPHY: Brown, J. R., ed., *Modern British Dramatists: New Perspectives* (1984); Booth, M., *British Poetry, 1964–1984: Driving through the Barricades* (1985); Thwaite, A., *Poetry Today; A Critical Guide to British Poetry 1960–1984* (1985); Haffenden, J., *Novelists in Interview* (1985); Stevenson, R., *The British Novel since the Thirties* (1986); Wandor, M., *Carry on, Understudies* (1986); Bradbury, M., *No, Not Bloomsbury* (1987); Chambers, C., and M. Prior *Playwrights' Progress: Patterns of Postwar British Drama* (1987); McHale, B., *Postmodernist Fiction* (1987); Morrison, B., "The Filial Art: A Reading of Contemporary British Poetry," *YES*, 17 (1987): 179–217; Ritchie, R., ed., *The Joint Stock Book: The Making of a Theatre Collective* (1987); Cave, R. A., *New British Drama in Performance on the London Stage: 1970–1985* (1988); Dipple, E., *The Unresolvable Plot: Reading Contemporary Fiction* (1988); Hassan, S. K., *Philip Larkin and His Contemporaries* (1988); Kenyon, O., *Women Novelists Today* (1988); Robinson, A., *Instabilities in Contemporary British Poetry* (1988); Taylor, D. J., *A Vain Conceit: British Fiction in the 1980's* (1989); Anderson, L., ed. *Plotting Change: Contemporary Women's Fiction* (1990); Massie, A., *The Novel Today: A Critical Guide to the British Novel 1970–1989* (1990); Logan, W., "A Letter from Britain," *Poetry*, 4 (1991): 222–238; Innes, C., *Modern British Drama, 1890–1990* (1992)

—BRIAN MURRAY

ENGLISH-CARIBBEAN LITERATURE

Defining the Caribbean along language lines seems the most useful way of establishing a discourse of framework within which to talk about the literature from that region. But even that simple construction is problematic. West Indian literature has always assumed a first language of English; however, the literature of Martinique, Guadeloupe, St. Lucia, and Belize have often been included in the syllabuses for West Indian literature at the University of the West Indies. The standard construction of the West Indies has always been a political one, one forged by the term British West Indies, which was the name used for the then colonized islands of the Caribbean properly colonized by the British. The definition became solidified after the period of independence by three important phenomena in the Caribbean: the University of the West Indies, the short-lived West Indian Federation, and the West Indies Cricket Team.

Each, in some way, established—at least in the imagination of West Indians—that there existed a link that connected these sometimes disparate societies to each other. Geographically, it is understandable that the islands of the eastern Caribbean would have a great sense of affinity and connection with each other than the larger island of Jamaica or the mainland of Guyana. These institutions helped to connect the islands around the shared British colonial heritage, but the crumbling of the West Indian federation in 1960 demonstrated that the political notion of a united West Indies was not one that had popular sway throughout the larger populace of the region. Many Jamaicans did not meet other island nationals until they attended the University of the West Indies or until they traveled to England during the major migration period precipitated by the landing of the Empire Windrush in England in

1948. Indeed, the conception of a West Indian literature found a national sensibility in England when the BBC embarked on the Caribbean Voices series that hired a cadre of West Indian writers who would become the first major wave of writers to start to define this entity called Caribbean or West Indian literature.

At the same time the West Indies cricket team would help to establish a sense of a West Indian unity among working-class West Indians through their successes and heroics against other nations during the 1950s, 1960s, and the dominant 1970s and 1980s. The West Indies were a cohesive source of imaginative writing outside of the West Indies and since much of the writing, like cricket, represented some kind of response to a history of colonialism and subjugation, the economy of West Indianness became important as a means to define a new movement of literature. West Indian writers were being published in Britain and were being defined by their geographical connection; but they were, in the relatively small confines of England, growing to know more about each other and growing to find some unity in the numbers that existed. West Indianness was that entity that amounted to a strained, complex relationship with Britain, one that was at once resistance to British colonialism and yet equally marked by a sense of affinity to the colonial mother country.

That historically Britain had managed to define the West Indies as a unique economic force particularly during the period of slavery and the ascendancy of the sugar economy, and especially during the period after the American Revolution in 1776, West Indianness became as easily definable from outside as the term Indianness. The West Indians were a useful other, a society of expatriates living among a society of blacks who were former slaves. The West Indies would become a place for the establishment of various other cultures and societies, an unlikely experiment a social engineering that was not repeated in any other part of the world. The influx of Indians, Chinese, Syrian, Portuguese, Arab, and other nationalities into the Caribbean during the latter part of the 19th c. would alter completely the make up of the society and complicate the cultures that were evolved in these societies. Despite this, the most useful means by which West Indianness would be defined was through the growth of this entity called West Indian literature that would take root in the late 1940s and early 1950s.

Tellingly, today, the term West Indian is no longer is such great currency. It has been usurped somewhat by the term Caribbean, or English-speaking Caribbean. The reasons vary but could include the colonial after taste of the term West Indian, which in itself represents a fundamental mistake by Columbus. More influential, however, has been the impact of American politics in the region and the increasing interest among West Indians to make links with other, non-English speaking nations like that between Cuba and Jamaica in the 1970s and 1990s. America's own dialogue with the West Indies would be couched in the Ronald Reagan coinage, "The Caribbean Basin Initiative," which somehow lumped all the islands of the Caribbean into a single operative until somehow regarded as the backyard of American society. In the publishing realm, the term West Indian as a marketing device did not take root but has now been replaced by terms that seek to include non-English speaking nations. A number of West Indian scholars, including George LAMMING, have determined that there are far too many affinities and cultural connections between all the regions of the Caribbean regardless of the language spoken in each territory for the parochial approach to the study of the region to continue. They argue that the shared history of slavery and colonialism and the growing complications of the relationship with America and with issues of labor all

make these countries closely linked. This pattern has proven attractive to publishers who tend to avoid anthologies and literary studies that appear too narrow and specialist. The Heinemann series is called the Caribbean writers series and Faber and Faber's new initiative into this region has been termed the Caribbean series and has included writers from Haiti, Colombia, Cuba, and Trinidad. The academic world has also sought to include what was formerly West Indian writing into the larger world of Commonwealth Writing and the more recent and quite pervasive, postcolonial literature realm. In this final incarnation the terms West Indian seem rather passé and quite difficult to sell in a marketing context. Indeed, the term West Indian is no longer one easily understood by non-West Indians. The strengthening of the cultures and literatures of the Caribbean islands has only complicated this shift in the way that we understand the region. Popular culture in Jamaica has increasingly distinguished itself from the popular culture of Trinidad, Barbados, or St. Lucia, and the differences between these cultures, the differences in language, history and demography have come to characterized the sometimes contentious relationships that have existed between the different islands particularly in centers like New York, Toronto, and London. The fact is that West Indianness is no longer an easily defined entity, and West Indian literature is now becoming increasingly untenable as a term used to describe the new directions in writing that have emerged from the region.

It is estimated that at least half of the population of these islands, Trinidad, Barbados, Jamaica, Antigua, St. Lucia, St. Kitts, Nevis, Monsterrat, Tortolla, Anguilla, and the mainland of Guyana live outside of these countries forming one of the most important sources of foreign capital to these countries. The migration of West Indians to the United Kingdom, and then to Canada and the U.S., has significantly affected the way we regard West Indian literature today. The concept of exile has always been a fascinating subject for West Indian writers and in many ways the development of West Indian literature has been synonymous with the idea of exile from the West Indies. During the first major wave of West Indian writing in the 1940s and 1950s, this theme of exile was characterized by a quality of nationalism—the nationalism forged by an anti-colonial discourse and a desire to find a voice for a pervious "voiceless" West Indian world. Thus, while most of the writers gained their reputations outside of the Caribbean, living for years in England and to some extent Canada and the U.S., they remained wholly identified with the West Indies and not with the culture within which they were writing. Despite living most of his life in England, Andrew SALKEY, for instance, was always associated with the West Indies, and always identified as a West Indian writer. The same can be said for such "cosmopolitan" writers as George Lamming, Edward Kamau BRATHWAITE, Derek WALCOTT, and V. S. NAIPAUL, all of whom spent many years living in "exile" outside of the Caribbean. What distinguished these writers was their almost consistently held agenda of trying to define themselves as West Indians, as individuals emerging from the colonial influence of Britain. However, an entirely new generation of writers has emerged, writers, many of whom were not born in the West Indies or who spent only a few years in the West Indies, and many of whom, while born and reared in the West Indies, have somehow found it unnecessary to embark on the project of "naming the unnamed," which writers like Brathwaite and Walcott saw as crucial to their experience as writers in the 1950s and 1960s. Their West Indianness or their Caribbeanness has to be redefined and has to be understood in conjunction with their relationship with places such as the U.S., Canada, and the United Kingdom. The leading novelists of the Caribbean today are writers who are also embraced as either Canadian, American, or British. These include Neil Bisoondath (dates n.a.), Austin Clarke (b. 1934), Cyril Dabydeen (b. 1945), Dionne Brand (b. 1953), and Cecil Foster (b. 1954) in Canada; Andrea Levy (B. ca. 1952), David Dabydeen (b. 1955), Caryl PHILLIPS, Fred D'AGUIAR in England; and Colin Channer (b. 1964), Opal Adisa Palmer (b. 1954), Kelvin Arthur (dates n.a.), and Jamaica KINCAID in U.S. The list of poets is equally revealing as it includes writers such as Jean Binta Breeze, James Berry, Archie Markham (dates n.a.), John Agard (b. 1950), Grace NICHOLS, and Linton Kwesi JOHNSON in England; Lillian Allen (b. 1951), Ramabai Espinet (dates n.a.), Pam Mordecai (b. 1942), and Olive SENIOR in Canada; and in the U.S., Claudia Rankine, Geoffery Philps, Rohan Preston, and Marcia Douglas (dates n.a.). Many of these are quite clearly leading writers in the Caribbean, but their connection to the Caribbean is complicated making the subject matter of their literature far more complex. It is not simply that the circumstances of these writers have changed over the years, but that many of these other societies have become far more embracing of multicultural notions thus ensuring that these writers are recognized as valid voices within these societies. This development has come through the intense work of many of these writers, but the result has been a generation of writers and a birthing of literature that is far more eclectic politically, and a literature that can no longer be approached along the lines that the literature of the 1950s and 1960s was approached. This is what complicates attempts to try and define the literature of the West Indies along nationalistic lines. However, if we understand that these literatures have been shaped by the peculiar circumstances of the history and politics of the various islands, we may begin to understand something of the eclectic and complex range of literature that has been produced in the West Indies and out of the West Indies in the last hundred years.

Finally, it must always be understood that West Indian literature cannot be observed in isolation of the popular culture that has come to shape the societies from which these literatures have emerged. There is a sense, for instance, that the somewhat slow period of literary production in Jamaica in the 1960s and 1970s coincided too well with the explosive and prolific emergence of reggae music in that country. The creative center of that country has been located in this area of artistic production and the literature is only just beginning to catch up with this phenomenon. Further, Trinidadian literature is literature that has been shaped greatly by calypso as a social phenomenon and as a source of a literary aesthetic. Separate and apart from the aesthetic that constitute a strained dialogue between the colonizer and the colonized, the aesthetics of reggae and calypso have began to offer more complex and intriguing ways of understanding the literature from the region.

Jamaica

In her important anthology of Caribbean poetry , *The Penguin Book of Caribbean Verse* (1986), Paula Burnett attempts to establish a tradition of West Indian verse that extends beyond the period of the publication of a literary body of work. Her anthology includes popular songs, folks songs, proverbs, and sayings that have been passed down through the lively oral tradition in the Caribbean. Archie Markham in his anthology of Caribbean short stories, *The Penguin Book of Caribbean Short Stories* (1996), does

the same thing, including Anancy tales and other folk narratives that belong largely to the oral tradition. The implication is simple: any attempt to discuss West Indian literature must begin with an acknowledgment of the importance of the oral tradition in shaping the current literature. The implication is further that West Indian literature is a literature that emerges out of both a literary tradition, largely derived from Europe, and an oral tradition, derived from the Caribbean and Africa. Consequently, it is important to acknowledge the influence of a folk tradition steeped in the religious beliefs and cosmologies of the working class, nonliterate population—a tradition that would have a telling impact on the writing of people like Claude MCKAY who in the early 20th c. became interested in writing dialect poems that reflected the language of the society. Prior to that many travelers to Jamaica had embarked on the business of collecting folktales and anecdotes from the largely black population in a somewhat anthropological quest to understand the population of this colony of Britain. However, the establishment of something that could be fairly called literature in Jamaica would not take place until the first decades of the 20th c. with the emergence of those who would now be termed the first wave of West Indian writers.

In 1917 H. G. de Lisser (1878-1944) published his first novel, *Triumphant Squalitone*, producing what is arguably one of the earliest examples of West Indian literature. De Lisser would go on to publish nine novels between 1917 and 1958 and in the process provide some of the earliest examples of West Indian literature to emerge during the 20th c. De Lisser's vision, however, was decidedly colonial and conservative and hardly presaged the arrival of the postcolonial vision of authors such as Victor Reid (b. 1913) and Orlando Patterson (dates n.a.), but what de Lisser achieved in his novels was a strong sense of a writer seeking to discover the landscape of his society in a language that represented an articulation of experience where such articulations did not exist. His novel *Jane's Career* (1914), for instance, would remain a unique work of West Indian fiction for its treatment of the role of the black woman in modern West Indian society. His historical novels, *Revenge* (1919), about the Morant Bay rebellion, *The White Witch of Rosehall* (1929), and *Morgan's Daughter* (1953), all sought to explore important moments in Jamaican history through a largely romantic, politically transparent, and sometimes racist conception of history. But his work was consistently rooted in assiduous historical research and constituted a new way to apprehend West Indian society that would, in many ways, influence the work of writers that came after him. A contemporary of de Lisser was the poet and sometimes novelist Claude McKay who began writing in Jamaica prior to moving to New York where he became an important figure in the Harlem Renaissance. Where de Lisser sought to propagate a view of Jamaican society that privileged the elite and upper class, further regarding the British as largely benevolent colonizers, McKay's work explored the world of the working-class people. Both writers, however, shared a desire to describe the Jamaican landscape as an integral part of the plots that they developed. In these early works, including the poems of McKay and Tom Redcam (1879-1933), a process of exploring the world of Jamaican society was embarked on and it would soon give rise to further work from this region. During this period the works of poets Louise BENNETT and later Una Marson (1905-1965) would play an important part in shaping a distinctive literature that could be said to be indigenous to the English-speaking Caribbean.

During a visit to Jamaica in the early 1900s, George Bernard SHAW admonished Jamaican theater practitioners to devote their time to writing plays about Jamaica and from a Jamaican perspective if a true theater would emerge. That such considerations were being explored in a society still trying to develop a greater sense of nationalism was significant and it would lead to a cultural movement in the theater arts and literature that would culminate with the explosion of the arts in the 1950s and 1960s. The march of writers to emerge during the 1930s and 1940s would gradually increase into something of a flood by the 1950s and 1960s. This rise in writing about Jamaican society and experience coincided with the political developments taking place in the country at the time. The year 1938, for instance, was a crucial year for Jamaican society and marked the beginning of a movement towards independence that would take place twenty-four years later. The riots and the cry for adult suffrage in 1938 led to the formation of two political parties and the ascension of two men who would play a pivotal role in the political future of Jamaica, Norman Washington Manley and Alexander Bustamante. During these years writers like Louise Bennett were writing poems in dialect that were published in the daily *Gleaner* on a regular basis and a group of aspiring young writers were meeting with the wife of Norman Manley, Edna Manley, a British-born woman of Jamaican heritage in what was to be called the Focus Group, which published anthologies of literature that would reveal the fledgling efforts of such writers as George Campbell (b. 1916), Basil Macfarlene (b. 1922), Neville Dawes (1926-1981), Dennis SCOTT, and Mervyn MORRIS, among others who would come to represent the foundation of Jamaican and West Indian literature.

The flow of novels begin in 1949 with the publication of Vic Reid's *New Day*, a historical novel that explored the movement of Jamaican society from the period just after slavery to the arrival of independence. Reid's novel was significant because he was willing to use the dialect of Jamaican society to narrate much of the novel. In the next decade novels would begin to appear by a wide cross section of authors. Neville Dawes's *The Last Enchantment* was published in 1958, Roger MAIS would publish three major novels during that decade along with a collection of short stories. *The Hills Were Joyful Together* (1953), *Brother Man* (1954), and *Black Lightning* (1955) have now become important works that explored the experience of working-class urban society in a novelistic fashion. Mais would have been influenced by the writing of such African-American novelists as Richard WRIGHT and the early offerings of Trinidadian writers, notably Alfred Mendes's *Black Fauns* (1935) and C. L. R. James's *Minty Alley* (1936). In Mais's *Brother Man* he would establish a remarkable grasp of the centrality of rastafarian spirituality in the shaping of the Jamaican society that would come to mark the work of later writers and that would ultimately be realized in the rise of reggae music in the 1970s and 1980s. Novelist John HEARNE would publish five novels during the 1950s, the most important of which, *Voices under the Window* (1955), tackled the themes explored by Reid in *New Day* but from a more contemporary perspective. Hearne's vision was always honest in its desire to explore themes that related to the middle-class Jamaican and that individual's quest for a sense of identity and place. Andrew Salkey, another writer who would spend most of his life outside of Jamaica, remains one of the most prolific of Jamaican novelists. His first novel, *A Quality of Violence* (1959), is set in rural Jamaica and is a work that explores the dynamics of class and culture within Jamaican society. Salkey would go on to produce a series of novels for young readers and to develop a veritable industry in the use of the Anancy figure in various fictional constructions.

Most striking in these novels by the Jamaican writers of the period was a tendency for the authors to regard themselves as the voices of the silenced majority. The inclination toward writing the ghetto novel, for instance, which would continue into the 1960s with the sometimes overly sociological and deterministic efforts of Orlando Patterson, constituted a view that these middle-class writers had that their quest for a sense of national identity rested in a study and retrieval of a folk memory that would somehow be definitively Jamaican or West Indian. Thus, as these writers embarked on the mission to recover a sense of the past through an encounter with the folk tradition, they sought to express these ideas in a form that was quite clearly Western. The tension of these two concerns was part of what made the work deeply interesting and, at the same time, quite a curiosity for the Western readership.

Despite suggestions that the fact that most of this writing was being published outside of the Caribbean was affecting in some way the content of the work, this pattern would continue and still operates today. With a very few exceptions, most Jamaican novels have been published by established British or American presses and the complex relationship has always affected the strange dance between a process of explaining experience and landscape and a push toward an anticolonial agenda. During the 1960s the flood of novels from Jamaican novelists began to slow and the appearance of new novelists would be significantly limited. Salkey, Patterson, Reid, and Hearne all produced novels during that period, but it represented a time for the emergence of poetic voices that would remain at the center of literary production in the next decade.

Mervyn Morris, Dennis Scott, and Anthony MacNeill (1941-1996) all began to publish their poems in journals and periodicals during the 1960s. Along with them, several woman writers began to produce work, including Olive SENIOR, Jean DaCosta (dates n.a.), who published several novels for young readers, and Sylvia Wynter (b. 1928). These poets were developing their craft under the already significant shadow of the three central figures of West Indian poetry, Derek Walcott, Kamau Brathwaite, and Martin CARTER. As a result, their work tended to turn away from the epic and nationalistic concerns of these poets to a more lyrical and modernist articulation of experience. It would not be until the 1970s that these writers would publish their first collections of verse. Morris published *The Pond* (1973) and *Shadowboxing* (1979) in that decade while MacNeill published *Hello Ungod* (1971) and *Reels from "The Life-Movie"* (1975) and Dennis Scott published *Dread Walk* (1982) and *Uncle Time* (1973).

But the 1970s were especially dry in the production of novels. Michael Thelwell's (dates n.a.) publication of the novelization of the film *The Harder They Come* (1971) was endemic of the condition of the literary arts in Jamaica in that period. There was a great deal of activity but that activity was devoted to coming to terms with the meaning of Jamaicaness or West Indianness and the evolution of a distinctive and meaningful understanding of aesthetics. *The Harder They Come* was a film made in 1971 by Perry Henzel, which told the story of a young boy who comes to Kingston from the country to try and make a living. He ends up trying to make it as a singer. He makes a record, it does well, but he is exploited by rather oppressive producers. He turns to crime and dies in a tragic but rather futile heroic death. The soundtrack to this film was entirely reggae and this would spur on the international growth of reggae music. In this film and in the work of the NDTC and such visual artists as Karl Parboosingh, Osmond Watson, and Kappo, the culture of reggae and rastafari was beginning to offer ways of viewing the aesthetic realities of Jamaican society. The work of Kamau Brathwaite, who was editor of a journal and publishing enterprise Savacou, would further the investigation into the notion of reggae and folk culture as a reliable aesthetic for writing from that society. A telling result of this work was the emergence of a completely new genre of writing from the region called dub poetry that would come to characterize some of the most interesting writing to emerge from the region for a few years to come. The dub poets who would emerge in the seventies included Mikey Smith (1954-83), Oku Onuora (formerly Orlando Wong, b. 1952), and Mutabaruka (formerly Allan Hope, b. 1952). Significantly, writers based outside of Jamaica but with strong Jamaican connections would adopt this form of literary production. These included the British-based Jamaicans, Linton Kwesi Johnson and Jean Binta Breeze, and the Canadian-based Lillian Allen. Dub poetry became one of the most successful efforts to tap into the aesthetic of reggae music and to determine how they spoke to a literary aesthetic. But dub poetry suffered from a dilemma of categorization. Because of the strong musical element involved in the performance of dub poetry, it was often lumped in with reggae's pop culture and thus suffered from a dearth of critical responses to it. But it is clear that this form of expression would seriously affect the work of more conventional poets in the future. But the production of novels and significant collections of poetry to match the activity of reggae artists or to match the prodigious generation of records in that decade did not materialize.

It would take the next decade and the emergence of the women writers from Jamaica to begin a new wave of productive writing in Jamaica. At the end of the 1970s Erna BRODBER published her first novel, *Jane and Louisa Will Soon Come Home* (1980), which would completely depart from the conventional narrative forms preferred by writers of the earlier decades for a more experimental and magical approach to literary fiction. Further, her interest in folk mythologies and the oral tradition would grant her work a complexity not seen in many of the works that preceded her. Her fiction would be joined by the short stories and poetry of Olive Senior and the poetry of Lorna GOODISON, Velma Pollard (b. 1937), Pam Mordecai, Christine Craig (dates n.a.), and the later work of Louise Bennett. These women would produce works that would simply fill a gap that had existed in Jamaican literature for decades—that of the position of women in the society. The work of these authors would continue to dominate Jamaican writing for the next two decades. Olive Senior has gone on to establish herself as an important prose stylist of the short story from her base in Canada, while Lorna Goodison is often cited, along with Kamau Brathwaite and Walcott, as one of the most important poets to emerge in the West Indies in years. Erna Brodber has produced several new novels that reflect her interest in stretching the form of the novel even as she tries to explore the themes of identify that interest her. However, the more recent novels produced from "Jamaican" novelists have come from writers who are based outside of Jamaica. Writers like Andrea Levy, reared in England, explore issues related to Jamaican society and experience but are deeply inscribed in the quest to understand British identity in the latter part of the 20th c. The same can be said for the young novelist Colin Channer whose base in New York has fed much of his writing. Yet these writers remain somehow inscribed in a Jamaican sensibility.

The wave of writing that coincided with the movement toward independence has not been replicated since that time. Further there is no "school' of dialogue like the percolating world of Britain that

would somehow challenge writers to explore theme and dialogue around themes through the production of writing. Further the interest in literature from outside has somehow been replaced in the U.S. and the United Kingdom by an interest in the multicultural novel or the novel that offers a cosmopolitan sense of the world. These new challenges are not unexpected for they are the challenges that face most art forms in the region today. Without the strong nationalism that surrounded the movement away from colonial control, there is a growing need to evolve a vision of the Jamaican society that is at once profoundly concerned with exploring the meaning of Jamaicanness, and yet speaking with discourse that is relevant to the world at large. The trend is curious and uncertain. More recent novels by Jamaicans show at once an interest in a future vision of cosmopolitan Jamaicans and yet a strange return to a deeply rural sense of society and belonging. Opal Adisa Palmer treats the themes of rural experience in her novel entitled *It Begins with Tears* (1998) and U.S.-based Ifeona Fulani (b. 1958) regards Jamaica as a kind of refuge from the hardships of British society—her Jamaica is rural and quite retrograde. On the other hand, Colin Channer, in his debut novel, *Waiting in Vain* (1998), offers a rather urban vision of Jamaican society that regards it as simply another complex society not unlike that of New York or London. These worlds are part of his artistic palette and he exploits without an strong sense of nationalism. If this is the future of West Indian literature, there is enough evidence to suggest that it is a growing trend among writers linked with other countries, writers such as Caryl Phillips, Fred D'Aguiar, Jamaica Kincaid, Austin Clarke, and Cecil Grey (b. 1954), among others.

Trinidad

Trinidad has produced some of the most varied and influential writing to have emerged from the Caribbean. With its distinctive demographic mix of East Indians, Europeans, and Africans, the Trinidadian population constitutes one of the most varied and multicultural societies in the world. And yet it has evolved a distinctive culture that is rooted in the complexities of colonial experience and a postcolonial dynamic. Trinidadian popular and folk cultures during the last one hundred and fifty years have produced some of the most important and pervasive cultural forces in the Caribbean. The folk culture of Trinidad, caught in the Hindu and Muslim rituals brought over by the large populace of Indian immigrants during the latter part of the 19th c., and the long-standing tradition of carnival and the attendant calypso have for a long time come to be synonymous with West Indian culture and identity. West Indian cricket, for example, has been labeled calypso cricket to reflect the flamboyance and energy of the players. Calypso music was a dominant popular form in Jamaica and the rest of the Caribbean during the 1930s, 1940s, and 1950s until in Jamaica the music was usurped by mento first and then ska music. Further, some of the earliest and innovative cultural activities particularly in dance and the theater arts found expression in Trinidad and that energy was exported to the rest of the Caribbean through the pioneering work of several stalwart artists. One of the longest standing and most respected theater companies to have emerged from the Caribbean, The Workshop Theater led by Derek Walcott, became established in Trinidad in the 1960s and would continue to influence the work of theater practitioners through out the rest of the Caribbean.

Indeed, while H.G. de Lisser and Claude McKay were writing their first novels in Jamaica in the 1920s and 1930s, two important Trinidadians would produce some of the most influential work to emerged in the preindependence period of West Indian society. In 1936 C. L. R. James's first novel *Minty Alley* was published. This work represented the first genuinely working-class novel to be produced in the West Indies. Set in the urban squalor of Port Spain, *Minty Alley* explored the lives of working-class blacks in Trinidad and offered a strong ideological assessment of the destruction of colonial society on the experience of the West Indian. *Minty Alley* would eventually spawn other versions of the same narrative: Orlando Patterson's *The Children of Sisyphus* (1964), and Roger Mais's *The Hills Were Joyful Together*. More contemporary tellings would appear as recently as 1979 with the publication of Earl LOVELACE's novel *The Dragon Can't Dance*, which would significantly update the telling of James and project the idea of the working-class urban novel into an entirely new sphere. But along with James was the novelist Alfred Mendes (dates n.a.), also a Trinidadian who published a year before James, the novel *Black Fauns*. In these works, the authors were deeply interested in exploring the experience of the working-class Trinidadian and in revealing the seriousness of their conditions as poor people in a colonial society. However, there was a greater agenda at work, a deeply anticolonial agenda that sought to give voice to the silenced narratives of the people of Trinidad. James understood the value of such an activity and would devote the rest of his writing life to finding a means to give voice to the voiceless whether through histories, nonfictional texts, or political manifestoes and discussions. James would become one of the most important writers to have been produced by Trinidad and he, along with V. S. Naipaul would represent two distinct but the most influential threads of the West Indian response to colonialism and to the project of literature to emerge in the Caribbean.

Following the first works by James and Mendes, there appeared in Trinidad the fiction of writers like Ralph De Boissiere (dates n.a.) and the work of Seepersad Naipaul (ca. 1880-1953), the father of V. S. Naipaul. The latter's work did not gain a great deal of attention until the 1970s when his son published one of his novels, *The Adventures of Gurudeva* (1976), with a leading press. The work of the older Naipaul was important for its incorporation of the Indian culture into the conceptualization of Trinidadianess.

But the most significant contribution of Trinidadian writers to West Indian literature after C. L. R. James came in the 1950s when two young Trinidadians of East Indian heritage traveled to the United Kingdom where they began to publish. V. S. Naipaul's status as one of the preeminent writers of the West Indians is matched only by the controversy that surrounds his work. But there is no question that his early novels, *The Mystic Masseur* (1957), *Miguel Street* (1959), and *A House for Mr. Biswas* (1961), offer some of the most sensitively articulated insights into Trinidadian society. His later novels remain classics in West Indian literature even despite their deeply pessimistic outlook. These novels include *The Mimic Men* (1967), *The Guerrillas* (1975), which won the Booker Prize for Naipaul, and *A Bend in the River* (1979). Naipaul's nonfiction writing would provide the fodder for some lively debates about postcolonial West Indian society and his vision and the manner of the telling of this vision continues to generate passionate discussions about nationalism, about the moral imperative of the artist, and the meaning of truth in literary life. His view of the Caribbean in the important travel book *The Middle Passage*

(1962) opened the door for his views of other societies outside of the Caribbean in such works as *An Area of Darkness* (1964), *The Overcrowded Baracoon* (1972), and *India: A Wounded Civilization* (1977). Naipaul has lived in the United Kingdom for most of his life and has never returned to live in Trinidad after his departure from that country when he was eighteen to study in England. He is now an important celebrity in England, a knight of the crown, and a writer that is embraced as an English author by the establishment. But Naipaul continues to regard Trinidad as the formative space for him and there is much in his autobiographical articulations that suggests that he still regards himself as one living and writing in exile.

His contemporary, Samuel SELVON traveled to England on the same boat as did George Lamming. Selvon published fiction that explored the details of Trinidadian life without, at any point, deviating form that focus. His novel *A Brighter Sun* (1952) offered some amusing and important insights into the complications of creolization for the West Indian of Indian extraction living in the West Indies. His novel *The Lonely Londoners* (1956) is still regarded in the United Kingdom as one of the first examples of "black British writing"—a writing that explored the experience of the blacks who moved to Britain during the mid-20th c. Selvon would come to be regarded as one of the more important of that generation of writers who ushered in the independence of the various West Indian islands.

While in some ways belonging to that generation, the fourth major Trinidadian novelist, Earl Lovelace, can also be seen as a writer belonging to the postindependence period in West Indian society. His early novels tackled the dynamic of colonialism and its impact on the peasant community of rural Trinidadian society, *The School Master* (1979) and *While the Gods Are Falling* (1965). In his later work published in the 1970s Lovelace would treat postindependence Trinidad, discovering in the folk culture of the Spiritual Baptists and the rituals of calypso and Carnival the source for a poetic that would shape the work that he was producing. The novels *The Dragon Can't Dance* and *The Wine of Astonishment* (1982) were among the most important contemporary visions of West Indian society to have been written. In 1997 he published yet another novel that explores the politics and culture of contemporary Trinidadian society, *Salt*, using a style of writing that eschews the conventions of straight narratives for a more fragmented narrative style.

Trinidad has produced several other important writers whose contribution to West Indian writing is worth noting. Such writers include Michael ANTHONY who published, in 1965, the novel *A Year in San Fernando*. He would follow this work with a series of novels that despite their literary complexity have been treated largely as sophisticated books for young readers. *The Games Were Coming* (1963), *Green Days by the River* (1967), and *Cricket in the Road* (1973) are all works that remain quite popular in school syllabi in the West Indies. The dramatist and theater critic and director Errol Hill (dates n.a.) has published a number of his plays, the most notable being his folk drama, *Man Better Man*. Hill remains one of the most important figures in West Indian drama having worked or years developing the now defunct West Indian drama series administered by the University of the West Indies that published a significant number of new plays by West Indian writers over a too brief period. More recently the novelist Lawrence Scott has emerged to generate some of the most innovative fiction from the region since the work of Wilson HARRIS. Lawrence Scott, who lives in the United Kingdom, published his first novel, *Witchbroom* in 1994. The novel chronicles through a generous employment of Marquesian magic realism the life of a European Trinidadian family and its strange and complete relationship with history and contemporary Trinidadian society. Wayne Brown (dates n.a.), a contemporary of Morris, MacNeill, and Scott from Jamaica, is a poet who while publishing relatively little has established himself as one of the important stylists of West Indian poetry.

Trinidad has also produced a number of writers who now live and work outside of the country but have generated some very important West Indian texts. Most of these writers are based in Canada. Ramabai Espinet (b. 1948) has published a major collection of poems, *Nuclear Season*, and has published several of her short stories in journals in North America. Her editing work has produced the important anthology of Caribbean women's writing, *The CAFRA Book of Caribbean Women's Poetry* (1989). Neil Bisoondath, a nephew of V. S. Naipaul has published three novels and a collection of short stories that have, in some way, dealt with the experience of West Indians in Canada. His vision of Trinidad is pessimistic, convinced as he is that the conditions from Trinidadians of Indian extraction are so bad in India that emigration seems like the only viable alternative. Bisoondath appears to share some of V. S. Naipaul's penchant for the sometimes caustic analysis of West Indian society, but it is clear that Bisoondath's sense of allegiance to the West Indies is not extremely profound. His work contrasts interestingly with the fiction, notably *She Tries Her Tongue* and *The Silence Softly Breaks* (1989), and poetry of Marlene Nourbese Phillips (b. 1947) who is now based in Canada. Her work is deeply feminist and her concerns often revolve around the issues of voice and language for women. Yet her work is strongly shaped by an interest in the history of Caribbean societies. Dionne Brand, also born in Trinidad, can be regarded, along with Bisoondath, as constituting that new generation of writers whose sense of rootedness in a landscape beyond that of the West Indies. Brand, however, has published six volumes of poems that have revealed a continued interest in the Trinidad society and her own place in that society. Yet her work does not smack of the kind of nostalgia that one expects from such work. Her poetry is deeply influenced by the demands of writing in a largely white society and to a largely cosmopolitan audience. Her collections, *Primitive Offensive* (1982), *Chronicles of the Hostile Sun* (1984), *Winter Epigrams and Epigrams to Ernesto Cardenal in Defence of Claudia* (1984), and *No Language is Neutral* (1997) have established her as one of the leading voices in Canadian letters. In 1998 she won the Governor-General's Award for her collection *No Language is Neutral*. Her novel entitled *In Another Place, Not Here* (1997) is set partly in Trinidad and partly in Canada.

Guyana

Some of the most significant writers in West Indian literature have emerged from Guyana. Any listing of the important writers from the West Indies in the last century would reveal a significant representation from Guyana. Guyana has had a lively literary scene that matched the disturbing social and political upheavals that marked the country's development in the second half of the 20th c. Like most other West Indian countries, Guyana's writers have often spent much of their lives living and writing outside of their native country. The concept of exile has been central to the

Guyanese literary community and has played a significant role in shaping the work that has been produced by Guyanese writers over the years.

The first successfully published writer to emerge from Guyana was Eric Walrond (dates n.a.) who left Guyana for New York to become a part of the Harlem Renaissance in the 1920s. Walrond's collection of stories, *Tropic Death* (1926), was one of the first West Indian texts to speak from a somewhat indigenous perspective. The language, in retrospect, is still deeply couched in the language of colonial discourse, yet Walrond was dealing with a landscape that had not been written about with the kind of affinity and intimacy that he did.

It would take the most prolific West Indian writer to date, Edgar MITTLEHOLZER, to establish the power of the Guyanese imagination. Mittleholzer who was born in Guyana and who claimed to come from Swiss-German ancestry would publish twenty-three novels at a remarkable rate. He began writing while living in Guyana (then British Guiana), but he was faced with numerous rejection letters for years. Eventually his first novel was published and it was then followed by a life in the United Kingdom where he continued to write steadily until his suicide in 1965. Mittleholzer's novels range significantly in theme and concern but were always marked by a remarkable capacity to tell a story and to construct a plot. His most important works include *A Morning at the Office* (1950), *Corentyne Thunder* (1941), *Shadows Move among Them* (1951), *The Life and Death of Sylvia* (1953), *My Bone and My Flute* (1955), and *A Swarthy Boy* (1963). His fiction also included the exotic Kaywana trilogy: *Children of Kaywana, Kaywana Stock,* and *Kaywana Blood,* first published together as *The Harrowing of Hubertus* in 1954.

A contemporary to Mittleholzer, Wilson Harris, arguably one of the most innovative writers in West Indian literature and in modern English Literature first published his complex novel, *Palace of the Peacock*, with Faber and Faber in 1960. The novel received favorable reviews and would lead to a series of novels, including *The Secret Ladder* (1963), *The Whole Armour* (1962), and *The Eye of the Scarecrow* (1965), which were all published along with *A Palace of the Peacock* as the *Guyana Quartet*. Harris's production has been prodigious. His other important novels include *The Far Journey of Oudin* (1961), *Heartland* (1964), *The Eye of the Scarecrow* (1964), *The Waiting Room* (1967), *Tumatumari* (1968), *Accent to Omai* (1970), *The Sleepers of Roraima* (1970), *The Age of the Rainmakers* (1971), *Black Marsden* (1972), *Companions of the Day and Night* (1975), *The Carnival Trilogy* (1993), and *Resurrection at Sorrow Hill* (1993). As early as his first novels it was clear that Harris had abandoned the linear social realist approach of his contemporaries in Caribbean writing for something more akin to what would be later termed magical realism. His vision has always been shaped by the complex and magical landscape of Guyana, a landscape that has led him into explorations of myth and the metaphysical that has produced always difficult and compelling fiction. Harris has published some twenty works of fiction and is regarded as one of the most important voices in West Indian fiction today. He has lived in the United Kingdom since the early 1960s.

A novelist equally rooted in the mysticism of the Guyanese landscape is the brilliant storyteller Jan CAREW who has spent most of his life outside of Guyana. Carew's first novel, *Black Midas* was published while he lived in England in 1958. His other novels include *The Wild Coast* (1958), *The Last Barbarian* (1961), and

Moscow Is Not My Mecca (1964), as well as several children's books, and more recently a range of nonfiction texts that deal with politics, racism in America, and class dynamics.

Of all the writers produced by Guyana, Martin Carter remains one of the few that remained in that country and continued to exercise his craft while there. He is often cited as the third most important West Indian poet after Brathwaite and Walcott for his contribution to the genre of the political poem and for his consistent production of poetry over a fifty-year period without a significant amount of international attention of recognition. His collection *Poems of Resistance* (1951) remains one of his best-known collections, but his work has recently been collected in a volume *The Selected Works of Martin Carter*, which was published in 1990. Martin Carter's poetry is still read as part of political events and he is regarded by Guyanese as a poet gifted with the vision and insight to examine the complexities of Guyanese society. Other important Guyanese poets include A. J. Seymour (1914-1989) who is better known for the important work he has done as an editor and a supporter of West Indian writing through the publication of one of the longest-running journals from the West Indies, *Kyk-Over-Al*. Ian McDonald (b. 1933), author of *The Humming Bird Tree* (1969) among other novels and collections of verse is the current editor of *Kyk-Over-Al*, which he revived with Seymour in 1989. These poets, while not establishing significant reputations outside of the West Indies have continued to be influential voices in the development of West Indian poets over several generations.

Guyana has produced other notable names in novel writing, particularly two writers who did not exercise their craft while living in Guyana but gained international reputations while writing outside of that country. Roy A. K. Heath (b. 1926) published his first novel *A Man Come Home* in 1974, more than twenty years after he had arrived in the United kingdom to live. He has since published *The Murderer* (1978), *The Heat of the Day* (1979), *Genetha* (1981), and *The Shadow Bride* (1988), which won the Guyana Prize for 1989. His novels are all set in Guyana and seek to explore the nature of life in Guyanese society. E. R. Brathwaite's (b. 1921) first novel, *To Sir With Love*, was published in 1959 and went on to be produced as a major motion picture in 1966. He has also published several autobiographical works as well as the novel *A Choice of Straws* (1965), which treats the issue of racial discrimination in Britain during the 1960s. Guyana has also produced at least two important dramatists who have evolved a remarkable reputation on the strength of two plays. Errol John's (dates n.a.) play *Moon on a Rainbow Shawl* is one of the most produced plays in the West Indies. It simple narrative of a family faced with the prospect of immigration is a powerful piece of work that continues to resonate, despite its conventional theatrical form and treatment of themes. More innovative and daring is the play *Couvade* by Michael Gilkes (dates n.a.) who is better known for his critical writing on West Indian literature and his directing for television of Derek Walcott's drama. *Couvade* is a complex play of profound magic that explores the fragmented realities of West Indian history and present.

Of the new generation of Guyanese writers writing today the most well known include the poet and novelist Cyril Dabydeen who lives in Canada and has published numerous volumes of poetry and several short-story collections. His writing remains rooted in the Guyanese landscape, but is also deeply influenced by the Canadian landscape. Dabydeen has published ten collections of poetry including *Islands Lovelier Than Vision* (1986), *Goatsong* (1977), and a series of short story-collections, anthologies, and

novels. In England David Dabydeen (b. 1955), a cousin of Cyril Dabydeen, has carved out a strong reputation as a poet and fiction writer and a remarkable critic of West Indian writing and British 19th-c. society. Dabydeen's poetry collections include *Slave Song* (1984), *Coolie Odyssey* (1988), and *Turner: New and Selected Poems* (1996). He has also published three novels, *The Disappearance* (1989), *The Intended* (1990), which won the Guyana Prize for fiction, and *The Counting House* (1997). Dabydeen regards himself as a direct product of the West Indian writers of the first and second wave of West Indian writing and despite his long-term residence in England and sees himself as a writer in exile, a transcultural writer trying to develop a better understanding of the meaning of exile. A similar condition surrounds the work of Fred D'Aguiar who, though born in London, was reared in Guyana and returned to London when he was about twelve years old. D'Aguiar has published four collections of poetry, including *Mama Dot* (1985), *Airy Hall* (1988), and *British Subjects* (1993). His novels include *The Longest Memory* (1996), which won the Whitbread Prize for best first novel, and *Eating the Dead* (1997). D'Aguiar shares much of his vision for his fiction with writers like Caryl Phillips and David Dabydeen, who, while been interested in the experience of West Indian society, feel no compulsion to devote their fiction writing to themes that are directly related to West Indian experience. Indeed, two of D'Aguiar's three novels have no apparent connection to West Indian society, but treat issues of identity and the history of the African diaspora in a language that is markedly free of an strong nationalistic inclinations. The notion of the novel as a social tool for the amelioration of West Indian society which characterized the work of authors like Lamming, does not quite apply with these writers.

There are several other important Guyanese writers who have made the mark outside of Guyana. The novelist N. D. Williams (b. 1942), who lives in Canada, has published several novels including *Ikael Torass* (1976) and *The Silence of Islands* (1994). Grace Nichols, who lives in England, has published several volumes of poetry including *I Is a Long Memoried Woman* (1983) and *Sunris* (1997). She has also published several books for children. John Agard, who also lives in England, has published several collections of poems and numerous books for children. Beryl GILROY moved to England in 1951. She has published several novels including *Frangipani House* (1986) and *Steadman and Joanna: A Love in Bondage* (1997).

Barbados

Despite its relatively small size, Barbados has, in many ways, played a crucial role in the development of Caribbean writing in English. Most significant has been the long-standing journal *BIM*, which served as the first venue for writers like Derek Walcott, George Lamming, Austin Clarke, Kamau Brathwaite, John Hearne, and Edgar Mittleholzer, among many others who came in contact with the Barbadian poet Frank Collymore (1893-1980), a tireless promoter of West Indian writing and an important encouragement for many of the writers who began to work in the 1940s and 1950s. Along with Collymore has been the poet Eric Roach (1915-1974) who, while not publishing a major volume of verse before his death by suicide in 1974, accumulated a remarkable and impressive body of verse, much of it unpublished and some of it published in obscure journals. In 1991 Peepal Tree Books published his collected poems *The Flowering Rock*, and in the process established

Roach as one of the major poets of the West Indies and revealing why he was such an influence to writers like Brathwaite and Walcott.

At center of Barbadian writing however, remain two authors of significant reputations around the world, Kamau Brathwaite and George Lamming. Both writers would spend many years outside of Barbados but maintained a strong tie with the countries. Both writers now spend most their year in Barbados.

George Lamming began writing while in Barbados winning the interest and support of Frank Collymore a teacher in Barbados. Lamming then elected to travel to England where he felt that his chances of succeeding as a novelist would be greater. At the time he was also writing poetry. In England he worked as a broadcaster with the BBC in the *Caribbean Voices* series and would eventually complete the novel *In the Castle of My Skin*, which was published in 1953. For many West Indian writers of his generation, *Castle* was the watershed both because of the daunting challenge that it placed before other aspiring writers and because of its capacity to articulate the experience of the colonized black in the West Indies with narrative innovation and poetic grace. Lamming's novel was well received in the United Kingdom and the U.S. and was seen as an extension (at least in America) of the socially conscious novels of such writers as Richard Wright and Ralph ELLISON. Lamming would go on to publish five other novels, three in quick succession: *The Emigrants* (1954), *Of Age and Innocence* (1958), and *Season of Adventure* (1960). Ten years later he would produce two more novels, *Water With Berries* (1971) and *The Natives of My Person* (1972). He also published the seminal *The Pleasures of Exile*, a travel book in 1960 which outlined some of his own insights into the condition of the West Indian writer as exile. Lamming remains an important authority of West Indian culture and devotes most of time to his work with trade unions throughout the Caribbean.

His contemporary Kamau Braithwaite traveled to England in the 1950s to study history at the University of Cambridge. After his studies he traveled to West Africa where he lived for several years. Brathwaite's first major collection of poems was the first of what would become the important trilogy entitled *The Arrivants* (1973). *Rights of Passage* appeared in 1967 to significant critical praise. It would begin the career of the only poet to seriously challenge the preeminent status of Derek Walcott as the most significant poet in the West Indies. *Masks* (1968), the second part of the trilogy, explored the landscape of Africa and examined a West Indian's return to Africa. Finally, in *Islands* (1968), Brathwaite would deal with the return of the West Indian to the West Indies after a long journey of absence. *The Arrivants* was a remarkable achievement for its use of varied rhythms and language registers that treated the fabric of West Indian society in its varied manifestations to the Eliotesque fragmentation of language and idea. His use of varied and complex formal structures, his constant battle with the iambic, and a quality of experimentation established Brathwaite as an important poet in the Caribbean. Brathwaite, like Walcott, would serve as one of the most telling influences on the poetry generated by poets in Jamaica and the rest of the Caribbean in the 1970s and 1980s. A full debate would surround the relative merits of the work of Brathwaite and Walcott in the West Indies, a debate that was couched around the questions of aesthetics and cultural sensibility. In the rather false paradigms (sometimes perpetuated by the poets themselves), Walcott was perceived as the Eurocentric poet and Brathwaite was seen as the Afro-centric author. Brathwaite would go on to publish several other collections of verse which continued to stretch the limits of poetic conventions . In 1977 he published

Mother Poem which celebrated his maternal connection with Barbados society; in 1982 he published *Sun Poem* and in 1987 he published *X-Self*. He would then publish a series of even less conventional poetic texts and the important *The History of the Voice* which explored issues of language in West Indian society. Brathwaite is most noted for the manner in which he incorporated elements of popular and folk culture into his poetry, to the extent that his verse reflects an imagination rooted in the metaphysical concerns of the folk experience. His evocation of landscape and the history of the West Indies remains one of the most poignant by any writer from the region.

Along with these two writers, several other writers have emerged from Barbados including the novelists Austin Clarke and Paule MARSHALL who have both spent the majority of their years outside of Barbados. Indeed, Paule Marshall was born in Brooklyn to Barbadian parents who migrated to the United states during the First World War is often regarded as a New York writer, a novelist that has explored with great detail the experience of the West Indian immigrant in America. Her novels *Brown Girl, Brownstone* (1959), *The Chosen Place, The Timeless People* (1969) and *Praisesong for the Widow* (1983) all reflect her sense of a West Indian identity never having spent an extend period of her life there. But like other expatriates writers and writers of West Indian heritage like Andrea Levy in England whose parents migrated to England from Jamaica, Marshall's work reflects an understanding of the immigrant experience in America. Austin Clarke moved to Canada in the 1950s and would begin his career as a writer in Toronto. He has published several novels that are generally regarded as some of the most insightful examinations of Toronto society to have been written by any author regardless of origin. He has also tackled West Indian subjects is his hard-hitting examination of political corruption in *The Prime Minister* (1977) and *Proud Empires* (1986). But Clarke has chosen to avoid such subjects regarding himself as far too distant from the West Indies, now. His current enterprise is to explore the condition of the West Indian immigrant in Canada who is seeking to no longer feel like an outsider. His novels include *The Meeting Point* (1967), *Storm of Fortune* (1972), and *The Bigger Light* (1975).

Other more recent authors from Barbados include the novelist Anthony Kellman (dates n.a.) who lives in Georgia. Kellman has published four collections of poetry, *In Depths of Burning Light* (1982), *The Broken Sun* (1984), *Watercourse* (1990), and the Long Gap (1995). He has also published a novel *The Coral Rooms* (1995). Cecil Foster, who now lives in Canada, has published two novels *No Man in the House* (1983) and *Sleep On Beloved* (1995) both of which deal with the experience of West Indians living in Canada. But Foster's vision is marked by strident political intelligence and a strong sense of narrative. He represents one of the more important voices for the future of writing from Barbados.

Antigua

Born in Antigua, Jamaica Kincaid moved to the U.S. as a teenager and has managed to forge a stellar career as a fiction writer of unusual style. Her novels include *At the Bottom of the River* (1983), *Annie John* (1985), and *Lucy* (1991). She also published the nonfiction work *A Small Place* (1988), which offers a disturbing look at Antigua as seen from the perspective of Kincaid returning home. Kincaid is not always identified as a West Indian writer despite the fact that almost all her fiction is rooted in the Caribbean and her own articulations about her sense of place constantly point to her connection with the island of St. Lucia where she remains a citizen despite having lived in the U.S. for most of her life.

St. Lucia

St. Lucia has produced an impressive cadre of important West Indian writers, some of whom have established themselves as influential voices in Caribbean letters. What is clear, however, is that those writers who have remained in St. Lucia have not been able to establish the kind of publishing record as those who left. It is a simple reality of the Caribbean that migration is sometimes an absolute necessity for success as a writer.

The best known West Indian writer, Derek Walcott, was born in St. Lucia. He wrote his first plays and poems while a teenager in St. Lucia and his first collection of poems, *Twenty Five Poems* (1948), was a self-published affair that eventually caught the attention of Frank Collymore in Barbados. Walcott would go on to carve out an impressive career as a poet and a playwright culminating in the Nobel Prize for literature in 1993. Walcott has published sixteen collections of poetry, including his *Collected Poems 1948-1984* (1986) and the long poems *Another Life* (1972) and *Omeros* (1989). His collection *The Bounty* (1996) demonstrates that Walcott has not lost any of his desire to continue to create the perfect poem. His work as a playwright has been equally prolific having published four collections of plays and the play *The Odyssey* (1995). His most important plays *Dream on Monkey Mountain* and *Ti Jean and his Brothers* (1971) had successful runs in the United States (including a stint on Broadway) in the early 1970s. Walcott was the founder of the Trinidad Workshop Theater and this company produced the first stagings of most of his major plays. Walcott's influence as a poet is evident in the number of West Indian poets who have acquired his strong lyrical style and his devotion to the metaphor. Walcott was not always in vogue as West Indian voice because of his devotion to the works of Western writers. Walcott offers some of the most telling explorations of the origins of West Indian society through a facility with technique and irony that is matched by few.

A contemporary of Derek Walcott, Garth St. Omer (b. 1931) has published a number of novels that have explored the experience of the middle-class West Indian through a deeply metaphysical sensibility that involves a strong dialogue with issues of Catholicism. St. Omer's novels include *A Room on the Hill* (1968), *Nor Any Country* (1969), and *J-, Black Bam and The Masqueraders* (1972). St. Omer taught for a few years in Ghana, then moved to the United States in 1970 where he still lives and teaches.

The current generation of St. Lucian writers include the novelist Earl Long (b. c. 1950) who has published two novels *Consolation* (1994) and *Voices from a Drum* (1986), both novels set in a fictitious Caribbean island that explores through myth and folk tales the story of the evolution of contemporary West Indian society. Long, like St. Omer, resides in the United States where he continues to write.

Of the writers who remain in St. Lucia, the most significant are Kendel Hippolyte (b.1952), a poet and playwright, Jane King (b. ?), a poet, and Robert Lee (b. 1948), a poet and short story writer. Hippolyte has published five slim volumes of verse locally, but recently published a collection *Birthright* (1997) which collects some of his earlier poems and some new material. His plays have been staged in St. Lucia and Jamaica and have almost always been deeply political dramas. They have not been published. Jane King has published two collections of poems, *Fellow Traveller* (1994) and *In To The Centre* (1990). Robert Lee has published several collections of poetry including *Dread Season* (1978), *Possessions* (1984), and *Saint Lucian* (1988).

Dominica

Phyllis Shand Alfrey (1908-1986) and Jean RHYS are the two best known authors from Dominica. Phyllis Shand Alfrey is best known for her novel *The Orchid House* (1953), which many argue is the model for Jean Rhys' *Wide Sargasso Sea* (1966) which is the better known of the two works. Alfrey also published *Circles* in 1940 and *Palm and Oak* in 1950. Her work has only recently been getting the kind of attention that is deserves.

Until the publication of *Wide Sargasso Sea*, Rhys' connections to the Caribbean were always somewhat tenuous despite the fact that she was born in Dominica and did grow up there. Her early novels hint at the connection but it is in *Wide Sargasso Sea* that we see Rhys treating the complex realities of women in a multi-racial and deeply volatile society. The novel is now a classic in West Indian literature and opens the way to readings of her other novels *Good Morning, Midnight* (1939), *Voyage in the Dark* (1934), and *After Leaving Mr. McKenzie* (1930).

BIBLIOGRAPHY: Ramchand, K., *An Introduction to the Study of West Literature* (1976); Coulthard, G. R., *Race and Colour in Caribbean Literature* (1962); Harris, W., *Tradition, The Writer and Society* (1967); James, L ., *The Islands In Between: Essays on West Indian Literature* (1968); Griffiths, G., *A Double Exile: African and West Indian Writing Between Two Cultures* (1978); Ramchand K., *The West Indian Novel and Its Background* (1970); King, B., *New English Literatures* (1980); Gilkes, M., *The Development of the West Indian Novel* (1981); Allis, J. B., *West Indian Literature: An Index to Criticism, 1938-1975* (1981); Taylor, P., *The Narrative of Liberation: Perspectives on Afro: Caribbean Literature, Popular Culture and Politics* (1989); Boyce Davies, C., and E. Fido, eds., *Out of the Kumbla: Caribbean Women and Literature* (1990); Dance, D., *New World Adams: Conversations with Contemporary West Indian Writers* (1992); Hill, E., *The Jamaican Stage* 1655-1900 (1992); Chamberlain, J. E., *Come Back to Me My Language: Poetry and the West Indies* (1993); Brathwaite, K., *Roots* (1993); King, B., *Derek Walcott and West Indian Drama* (1995); Torres-Sailant, S., *Caribbean Poetics: Towards An Aesthetic of West Indian Literature* (1997); Dawes, K., *Natural Mysticism: Towards a New Reggae Aesthetic* (1998)

—KWAME DAWES

ENQUIST, Per Olov

Swedish novelist, dramatist, critic, and columnist, b. 23 Sept. 1934, Hjoggböle

Born and raised in northern Sweden, E. left the religious, provincial forest region to study at the University of Uppsala. A highly successful high-jumper as well as an academic, E. completed two degrees while working on his first novel, *Kristallögat* (1961; the crystal eye). With his third novel, *Magnetisörens femte vinter* (1964; the magnetizer's fifth winter), E. received widespread public and critical acclaim. A semidocumentary work, the novel narrates the story of a man resembling the famous experimenter in magnetism F. A. Mesmer. Even in this early work, the relationship between past and present appears as one of E.'s major themes. In *Hess* (1966; Hess) E. experimented with the novel form, developing techniques from the French NEW NOVEL to explore the unanswered questions about Rudolf Hess, who parachuted into England, supposedly on a peace mission, during World War II.

Legionärerna (1968; *The Legionnaires*, 1973) established E. as one of Sweden's most important young writers. In this novel E. attempted to retell the entire story of Sweden's deportation of a number of Baltic soldiers who fled from the German army at the end of World War II. The novel caused extensive debate, and E. was awarded Scandinavia's most important literary prize for it. *Sekonden* (1971; the second) builds on an actual sports event while it weaves together the puzzle of a dishonest athlete and his emotionally paralyzed son. This novel once again takes up E.'s preoccupation with the fraudulent man. As in *Magnetisörens femte vinter* and *Hess*, E. presents and analyzes the motives within those who deceive, as well as the need for deception in the general public. In *Magnetisörens femte vinter* this need derived from people's desire for faith in something, even if it is an illusion. In *Hess* the deception remains unresolved, while in *Sekonden* the deceiver himself is revealed as a victim of society's need for progress, for new records and accomplishments, whether honestly or dishonestly attained. E.'s strong socialist orientation and human compassion pervade *Sekonden*.

A collection of essays, *Katedralen i München* (1972; the cathedral in Munich), resulted from newspaper articles he wrote at the Olympic Games in 1972, and a collection of stories, *Berättelser från de inställda upprorens tid* (1974; stories from the age of suspended revolutions), reflects his six months of lecturing at the University of California, Los Angeles, in 1973. *Tribadernas natt* (1975; *The Night of the Tribades*, 1977), E.'s first play, portrays August STRINDBERG'S marital life in 1889. It attained international success.

E.'s most recent works continue his political concerns while employing documentary or historical techniques to probe the psychological and philosophical problems of modern man. The novel *Musikanternas uttåg* (1978; the exodus of the musicians) vividly describes the lives and working conditions of nonunion laborers in the early 1900s in northern Sweden. A central theme of this book, similar to that of *Tribadernas natt*, is the tragedy of those people who never find a way to make their lives meaningful, who seem to rot from the inside and destroy their own lives because they have no purpose in life. Hailed as a brilliant work and perhaps his finest novel, *Musikanternas uttåg* solidified E.'s position as a leading, albeit controversial, author.

FURTHER WORKS: *Färdvägen* (1963); *Chez nous* (1976, with Anders Ehnmark); *Mannen på trottoaren* (1979, with Anders Ehnmark); *Till Fedra* (1980); *En triptyk* (1981)

BIBLIOGRAPHY: Shideler, R., "The Swedish Short Story: P.O.E.," *SS*, 49 (1977): 241–62; Shideler, R., "Putting Together the Puzzle in P. O. E.'s *Sekonden*," *SS*, 49 (1977): 311–29; Shideler, R., Introduction to *The Night of the Tribades* (1977): vii—xiv; Gill, B., "Fear of Women," *New Yorker*, 24 Oct. 1977: 143–44; Simon, J., "Strindberg Agonistes," *New York*, 31 Oct. 1977: 59; Björksten, I., "The Monumental Seventies," *Sweden Now*, 13, 1 (1979): 48–54; Schideler, R., *P. O. E.: A Critical Study* (1984)

—ROSS P. SHIDELER

ENRIGHT, D(ennis) J(oseph)

English poet, critic, and novelist, b. 11 March 1920, Leamington

E. received his B.A. (with honors) from Downing College, Cambridge, in 1944, and D. Litt. from the University of Alexandria (Egypt) in 1950. An international lecturer for the British Council, he taught at the Free University of West Berlin, the University of Alexandria, Chulalongkorn University in Bangkok, Thailand, and the University of Malaya at Singapore. A series of absurd clashes with regional authorities, beginning with an arrest in 1948 as a Jewish spy in Egypt (occasioned by a description of his religion as "lapsed Wesleyan Methodist," a persuasion that struck the secret police as seditious), early marked E. as "difficult;" his appointments with the British Foreign Service were frequently short-lived. As an independent scholar and lecturer, E. has also resided in Japan, Hong Kong, and London. In 1961 he was elected a Fellow of the Royal Society of Literature; he was coeditor (1972–74) of *Encounter* magazine; he is a director of the London publishing house Chatto and Windus.

E.'s critical interests range widely: he has written about Shakespeare, Goethe, Japanese poetry, travel literature, Third World academia, and Thomas MANN. Although his criticism is not considered the most important aspect of his work, it is persistently learned and humane, "mixing," according to William Walsh, "moral sanity and sensitive charitableness in its judgments." E. dismisses the novels he has written as inconsequential, as "really travel books, I am afraid." *Heaven Knows Where* (1957), a gently satirical utopia, describes the happiness of an English teacher on the mythical Far Eastern island of Velo, where peace reigns supreme, love conquers all, and travel-poster clichés come to life.

E.'s poetry harbors far less coziness than his criticism or fiction, and it is for his poetry that he has achieved literary standing. His brittle, edgy descriptions of the excolonial Third World mock the few remaining nightmares of British Empire and wonder fearfully about the new tyrannies erupting in its place. Despite a preoccupation with formal prosody, the dominant mood of E.'s writing is anything but mannered; it is jagged, tormented, uncomfortably modern. In *The Old Adam* (1965) E.'s most common persona, the unregenerate observer, describes himself: "all my articulations flapping freely,/Free from every prejudice, shaking all over." An instinct for naked nerve endings pervades E.'s small poems and intimate tragedies. He catalogues items of Third World existence that governments tend to ignore (legless beggars, starving prostitutes, blind suicides) and insists on their reality, their need for attention and love. He can be merciless in depicting the idiocy of officialdom while noting parenthetically that poetry, too, lives in a kind of "rotting ivory tower."

E.'s control of the complex tasks he sets for himself is admirable but not always perfect. His penchant for wordplay at times deflates the serious attention his work otherwise seems to demand. A jarring and sometimes unforgiveable cleverness ("Should one enter a caveat/Or a monastery?") drives out false profundity but it also, unfortunately, makes genuine concern difficult.

At his best, however, E. controls his tone carefully and speaks a compelling language. The condition of expatriate suits his subjects well. A perennial outsider, he captures the sense of transience, displacement, and loss that accompanies being foreign; he creates brilliant portraits of people who are homeless in their own land. While disclaiming any political bent, E. nonetheless writes almost exclusively about the wars—cultural, military, economic, and always intensely human—that dominate the political life of our times. The poet he sees as a minor but necessary combatant. His assessment of the role of poetry is modest: it should show the agony of the poor and voiceless in "words blurred by sweat," and work "some mild magic." And finally it should resurrect, from the exotic and extraordinary, a faith in the ordinary life of humankind.

FURTHER WORKS: *A Commentary on Goethe's "Faust"* (1949); *The Laughing Hyena and Other Poems* (1953); *Academic Year* (1955); *The World of Dew: Aspects of Living Japan* (1955); *Literature for Man's Sake* (1955); *Bread Rather than Blossoms* (1956); *The Apothecary Shop* (1957); *Some Men are Brothers* (1960); *Insufficient Poppy* (1960); *Addictions* (1962); *Figures of Speech* (1965); *Conspirators and Poets* (1966); *Unlawful Assembly* (1968); *Selected Poems* (1969); *Memoirs of a Mendicant Professor* (1969); *Shakespeare and the Students* (1970); *The Typewriter Revolution and Other Poems* (1971); *In the Basilica of the Annunciation* (1971); *Daughters of Earth* (1972); *Man Is an Onion: Essays and Reviews* (1972); *Foreign Devils* (1972); *The Terrible Shears: Scenes from a Twenties Childhood* (1973); *Rhymes Times Rhyme* (1974); *The Joke Shop* (1977); *Paradise Illustrated* (1978); *A Faust Book* (1980); *Collected Poems* (1981)

BIBLIOGRAPHY: Rosenthal, M. L., *The New Poets*, rev. ed. (1967): 222–23; Gardner, P., "D. J. E. under the Cherry Tree," *ConL*, 9 (1968): 100–111; Dunn, D., "Underwriter," *NS*, 28 June 1974: 927–28; Walsh, W., *D. J. E.: Poet of Humanism* (1974); Bayley, J., "Word of an Englishman," *Listener*, 20 Nov. 1975: 681–83

—LARRY TEN HARMSEL

ENZENSBERGER, Hans Magnus

West German poet and critic, b. 11 Nov. 1929, Kaufbeuren

E. grew up in Nuremberg, was drafted into the Volkssturm in 1944, and spent the early post-war years interpreting for the Americans and, like many Germans, dealing on the black market. He studied philosophy and literature in Erlangen, Freiburg, Hamburg, and at the Sorbonne in Paris. He later worked as an editor for the radio and for Suhrkamp publishers. After stays in the U.S., Mexico, Cuba, Italy, and Norway, he settled in Munich. He received the Büchner Prize in 1963 and was a member of Group 47.

E.'s first book of poems, *verteidigung der wölfe* (1957; defense of the wolves), immediately established him as Germany's angry young poet—angry not only at the "wolves" but also at the "lambs" who remain passive in the face of the wolves, that is, the establishment, the bureaucracy, advocates of rearmament, and so forth. His

poetry draws on the whole breadth of literary tradition, myth, and folk poetry, as well as on contemporary science, politics, and advertising slogans. He de- and re-forms these materials through montage, pun, and parody, and fuses the heterogeneous elements into a brilliant new diction that gives his satires their richness and bite. But it is their structural clarity that fixes their intellectual impact. Although E. does not use traditional forms, his poems are highly formal, with carefully worked out correspondences and parallels. Within this frame, syntactical ambiguities add surprise and a texture of multiple possibilities.

In *landessprache* (1960; language of the country), he continued in the vein of the first book, while in *blindenschrift* (1964; braille), the virtuosity gives way to a simpler, sparer mode that can be compared with BRECHT's late poems. In *blindenschrift* E. wrote what he himself calls the best kind of political poem: where politics "creeps in, as it were, through cracks between the words." *Mausoleum* (1975; *Mausoleum*, 1976) shows E. at the height of maturity and skill, handling incisively, yet with ease, the ironies and contradictions of progress. He does it in a series of ballads, a portrait gallery of culture heroes, their achievements and disasters, their public and private nightmares.

E.'s literary activity includes editing many anthologies, in particular, *Museum der modernen Poesie* (1960; museum of modern poetry), and translating poets like William Carlos WILLIAMS, César VALLEJO, and Pablo NERUDA. He has from the beginning also written cultural and social criticism.

Einzelheiten (1962; The Consciousness Industry, 1974) contains pieces on contemporary writers and an essay on the poetics of commitment, but it is mostly noted for its sharp and witty analyses of the media—the "consciousness industry"—from newsreel to tourism, from the paperback book industry to the *Frankfurter Allgemeine Zeitung*. As the title (literally "details") announces, these essays criticize details, assumptions underlying common practices, rather than elaborating political theories. They plead for a life in accordance with reason while giving a good demonstration of it.

Politik und Verbrechen (1964; Politics and Crime, 1974) tries, more ambitiously, to reveal the criminal nature of politics by presenting well-documented parallels between the actions and methods of famous gangsters, businessmen, and statesmen. More recently, *Das Verhör von Habana* (1970; the Havana hearings), a dramatic condensation of the Cuban trials after the Bay of Pigs invasion, and *Der kurze Sommer der Anarchie* (1972; the short summer of anarchy), on the life of Buenaventura Durruti, a key figure of the Spanish revolution of 1936, fuse documentation with literary method to hold up a mirror in which we see ourselves and our society with truly double vision. Since 1965 E. has also edited *Kursbuch*, Germany's most important and original progressive journal. Its contributors represent as wide an international scale as the topics, which range from literature to Third World problems.

While E.'s political position took on a pro-revolutionary sharpness in the late 1960s, his refusal to subscribe to any ideology has been attacked by the left as well as the right. In his social criticism he remains eager to find the "right way," but doubtful that *the* right way exists. His particular importance lies in the fusion of high critical intelligence and extraordinary literary gifts. It is likely that his poems will indeed be political by his own definition, that is, by affecting our consciousness.

FURTHER WORKS: *Zupp* (1958); *Gedichte* (1962); *Einzelheiten*, Vol. II (1964); *Deutschland, Deutschland unter anderm* (1967);

Freisprüche (1973); *Der Untergang der Titanic* (1978); *Die Furie des Verschwindens* (1980). **FURTHER WORKS IN ENGLISH:** *Poems* (1966); *Poems for People Who Don't Read Poems* (1968)

BIBLIOGRAPHY: Bridgwater, P., "H. M. E.," in Keith-Smith, B., *Essays on Contemporary German Literature* (1966): 239–58; Bridgwater, P., "The Making of a Poet: H. M. E.," *GL&L,* 21 (1967): 27–44; Gutmann, H., "Die Utopie der reinen Negation: Zur Lyrik H. M. E.'s," *GQ,* 43 (1970): 435–52; Schickel, J., ed., *Über H. M. E.* (1970); Grimm, R., "The Commitment and Contradiction of H. M. E.," *BA,* 47 (1972): 285–98; Lohner, E., "H. M. E.," in Wiese, B. von, ed., *Deutsche Dichter der Gegenwart* (1972): 531–44; Zimmermann, A., *H. M. E.: Die Gedichte und ihre literaturkritische Rezeption* (1976)

—ROSMARIE WALDROP

EQUATO-GUINEAN LITERATURE

Equatorial Guinea was the only Spanish colony in sub-Saharan Africa. Therefore it is the only sub-Saharan country with a literature written Spanish. The former Territorios Españoles del Golfo de Guinea, which later became Guinea Española, was a Spanish colony for nearly two centuries. Equatorial Guinea gained its independence on 12 October 1968.

Equato-Guinean literature can be classified as African literature or Hispanic literature or as Hispanic African literature. The first writings by Guinean authors began to appear in 1947 in the missionary publication *La Guinea Española.* But those writings were mere transcription and translation into Spanish of the traditional narrative of the groups that inhabited Spanish Guinea such as the Fang, the Ndowe, or the Bubi, and were mostly short stories. Their authors were simply intermediaries between the traditional texts of their ethnic group and the Spanish version. Such works as Rafael María Nze's (1924-1991) "El elefante y el camaleon" (1947; The Elephant and the Chameleon), "Biomo y sus hechos" (1948; Biomo and His Deeds), and "El cazador y el antilope" (1947; The Hunter and the Antelope); Marcelo Asistencia Ndong Mba's (dates n.a.) "La madre" (1959; The Mother) and "La avaricia rompe el saco" (1959; Avarice Breaks the Bag); and Constantino Ocha'a Nve's (1943-1991) "Biom ante la manada de elefantes (1959; Biom and the Elephant Herd) and "Biom se dirige hacia un pueblo extraño" (1962; Biom Goes to a Strange Village) fall within this category.

In the early 1960s some of these writers began writing stories that were no longer transcription nor translation of oral texts. Though still seeking inspiration in the traditional literary corpus of their ethnic group, the new texts were more personal and used writing techniques closer to Western models. Esteban Bualo Bokamba's (date n.a.-1996) "Kon (El Blanco)" (1961-62; The White Man), "Le va toco Buwe (Al fin vimos la luz)" (1962; We Saw the Light at Last), and "Mosodue, el solitario" (1965; Mosodue, the Loner); and Marcelo Asistencia Ndong Mba's "Mientras la tumba brama en su selvática canción"(1968; While the Drum is Resounding in the Forest), to mention but a few, must be placed in that context.

The first novel by a Guinean writer is *Cuando los combes luchaban. Novela de costumbres de la Guinea Española* (1953; When the Combes Used to Fight: A Novel of Customs from Spanish Guinea), by Leoncio Evita Enoy (1929-1996). Evita's novel relies heavily on African oral narrative style, but the portrait of the protagonist is more defined and individualized than in the earlier texts. Though the main character is a white Protestant missionary, Evita's novel gives a very detailed description of different aspects of the Combe ethnic group's social organization, rituals, and customs.

Daniel Jones Mathama's (dates n.a.) *Una lanza por el Boabi* (1962; A Spear for the Boabi), the second novel by a Guinean writer, was published nearly a decade later. Unlike in Leoncio Evita's novel, the author in *Una lanza por el Boabi* shows a very good command of Spanish language. The characterization of the protagonists and the writing style is more like that of metropolitan writers. Jones Mathama's novel defends Spanish colonial action in Spanish Guinea while criticizing natives' customs. These first novels appeared during the colonial period and were published in Spain, the former in Madrid and the latter in Barcelona.

By the mid-1960s a new generation of Guinean writers appeared on the literary scene in Spanish Guinea. Unlike the previous authors, most of them are poets. Guinea and Africa are their inspiration and their theme. Texts of this period include Juan Chema Mijero's (b. 1924) "El león de Africa" (1964; The Lion of Africa), Francisco Zamora Segorbe's (b. 1948) "Lamento sobre Annobón, Belleza y Soledad" (1967; Lament for Annobón, Beauty and Solitude), and Ciriaco Bokesa Napo's (b. 1939) "Isla Verde" (1968; Green Island).

In March 1969, five months after the independence of the country, President elect Francisco Macias Nguema suspended the constitution and established a one-party system. The ensuing indiscriminate repression forced one third of the population into exile. Consequently, between 1969 and 1979, not a single work, neither fiction nor nonfiction, was published in Equatorial Guinea. This period was described by different Guinean writers and intellectuals as "*los años del silencio*" (the silent years), "*la generación perdida*" (the lost generation), or "*los años del mutis*" (the mute years).

The very few texts that came out during this period were published in Spain where there was an important Guinean refugee community. Though some members of the Guinean diaspora living in Spain denounced the traumatic experience of the exile in their writings, most of their texts never got published. However, two texts can be mentioned from this period: Raquel Ilonbé's (1939-1992) *Ceiba* (1978; The Ceiba Tree), a collection of poems written between 1968 and 1977, and *Nueva narrativa guineana* (date n.a.; New Guinean Narrative), a collection of four short stories published by the Unión Revolucionaria de Guinea Ecuatorial (U.R.G.E.). The collection includes Donato Ndongo-Bidyogo's (b. 1950) "El sueño" (The Dream), Francisco Abeso Nguema's "La travesía" (The Crossing), Maplal Loboch's (dates n.a.) "La última carta del Padre Fulgencio Abad, C.M.F.," and Francisco Zamora Loboch's (b. 1948) "Bea."

On 3 August 1979 the government of Francisco Macías Nguema was deposed by a coup d'etat led by his nephew Captain Teodoro Obiang Nguema. Since then, there has been a timid but steady renaissance of cultural activities thanks to the creation of the Centro Cultural Hispano-Guineano de Malabo in 1984. The Centro Cultural Hispano-Guineano was created to promote diffusion and dissemination of culture pertaining to Guinea, Africa, and the Hispanidad in Equatorial Guinea and the rest of the world. The

Centro Cultural has its own press, Ediciones del Centro Cultural Hispano-Guineano, and two publications, *Africa 2000* and *El Patio*. The Centro Cultural has sponsored several publications—fiction and nonfiction—dealing with Guinean cultural heritage. It also organizes a variety of activities, offers language courses in Spanish, Bubi, and Fang, and hosts arts exhibits, lectures, and activities for children.

The 1980s was a period of cultural renaissance in Equatorial Guinea as evidenced by the number of publications. The first phase, which began in Spain in the early 1980s, saw the publication of Juan Balboa Boneke's (b. 1938) *O' Boriba (El exilio)* (1981; The Exiled) and *Susurros y pensamientos comentados: desde mi vidriera* (1983; Commented Whispers and Thoughts from my Window), two poetry anthologies dealing with the experience of the exile; Raquel Ilonbe's *Leyendas guineanas* (1981), a collection of short stories for children based on the oral literature of the different ethnic groups of Guinea; and Donato Ndongo-Bidyogo's *Antología de la literatura guineana* (1984; Anthology of Guinean Literature), notable because it includes all prose and poetry by Guinean authors from the colonial period up to 1977. The Spanish phase closes with two novels: María Nsue Angue's (b. 1945) *Ekomo* (1985; Ekomo), the first novel by a Guinean female writer; and Donato Ndongo-Bidyogo's *Las tinieblas de tu memoria negra* (1987; The Darkness of your Black Memory), the first novel of a trilogy on the Guinean experience. Ndongo-Bidyogo's work is the story of a nameless child and narrator growing up during the colonial situation.

The Guinean phase of this process centers on Centro Cultural Hispano-Guineano de Malabo, which sponsored and published most of the works either through Ediciones del Centro Cultural Hispano-Guineano or through the journals *Africa 2000* and *El Patio*. In 1987 Ediciones del Centro Cultural Hispano-Guineano published two poetry anthologies: Juan Balboa Boneke's *Sueños en mi selva* (1987; Dreams from my Forest) and Ciriaco Bokesa Napo's *Voces de espumas* (1987; Voices of Foams). *Africa 2000* published Anacleto Oló Mibuy's (b. 1951) collection of poems "Gritos de libertad y de esperanza" (1987; Screams of Freedom and Hope); Joaquín Mbomio Bacheng's (b. 1956) poetry collection "El retorno" (1987; The Return), "Soledad" (1987; Solitude), "Rostros hermosos" (1987; Beautiful Faces), "Piedad" (1987; Piety), and "Nostalgia" (1987; Nostalgia); and Gerardo Behori Sipi's (dates n.a.) poetry collection "Elegía a Africa" (1989).

Most prose works of this phase are short stories published in *Africa 2000*, and include Antimo Esono Ndongo's (1950-1996) "No encontré flores para mi madre" (1987; I Could not Find Flowers for My Mother), "La última lección del venerable Emaga Ela" (1991; The Last Lesson of the Venerable Emaga Ela), and "Afén, la cabrita reina" (1989; Afén, The Queen Goat). The only novel of this period is Juan Balboa Boneke's *El reencuentro. El retorno del exiliado* (1985; The Return of the Exiled) published by Ediciones Guinea, a state-sponsored publisher.

In the 1990s a new generation of writers began to publish their works in Equatorial Guinea and abroad. Most of them are young authors who did not live through the trauma of Francisco Macias Nguema's dictatorship. Their writings, fiction and poetry, explore contemporary and universal issues. These include Maximiliano Nkogo Esono's (b. 1972) volume of two short stories *Adjá-Adjá y otros relatos* (1994; Adjá-Adjá and Other Stories) and Joaquín Mbomio Bacheng's novel *El párroco de Niefang* (1996; The Priest of Niefang). Both texts explore, from different perspectives, the difficult postcolonial reality in Equatorial Guinea. The most recent

novel of this period is Donato Ndongo-Bidyogo's *Los poderes de la tempestad* (1997; The Powers of the Storm); in this work, the second in his trilogy, the narrator is again nameless as the novel examines the Guinean reality under the dictatorship of Francisco Macías Nguema.

Other prose works of the 1990s are Pedro Cristino Bueriberi Bokesa's (b. 1947) "Boote-Chiba (El gran Chiba)" (1990; The Great Chiba), Ciriaco Bokesa Napo's "Crónica de un viaje singular" (1993; Chronicle of a Peculiar Trip), María Nsue Angüe's "Adugu" (1993; Adugu), Estaban Bualo Bokamba's (dates n.a.) "Kogu, el cazador" (1992; Kogu, the Hunter) and "Unanga" (1996; Unanga), and María Caridad Riloha's (dates n.a.) "Exilio" (1997; Exile) and "Gusano" (1997; Worm). The only two books of poetry published during this period were Jerónimo Rope Bomabá's (b. 1953) *Album Poético* (1994; Poetic Album) and Juan-Tomás Avila Laurel's (b. 1966) *Poemas* (1994; Poems).

BIBLIOGRAPHY: Ndongo-Bidyogo, D., *Historia y tragedia de Guinea Ecuatorial* (1977); Liniger-Goumaz, M., *De la Guinée Equatoriale. Eléments pour le dossier de l'Afro-fascisme* (1983); Ndongo-Bidyogo, D., "La literatura guineana, una realidad emergente," *Mundo Negro*, 274 (February 1985): 22-26; Eworo Micue, A., "El Reencuentro," *Africa 2000*, 2-3 (1987): 42-43; Bokesa, C., "Ekomo, toda una novela," *Africa 2000*, 10-11 (1989): 95-97; Nerin, G., "El aislamiento, una amenaza constante: entrevista a Donato Ndongo," *Quimera*, 112-114 (1992): 51-55; Osubita, Juan B., "Se habla español. Una introducción a la literatura guineana," *Quimera*, 112-114 (1992): 44-50; Esono Ndongo, A., "La poesía en Guinea Ecuatorial," *El Patio*, 25 (June 1993): 20-24; Lopez Hidalgo, J., "La novela en Guinea Ecuatorial," *Africa 2000*, 7, 20 (1993): 42-44; N'gom, M., "La literatura africana de expresión castellana: la creación cultural en Guinea Ecuatorial," *Hispania*, 76 (September 1993): 410-18; Editorial Labrys 54, *Diálogos con Guinea. Panorama de la literatura guineoecuatoriana de expresión castellana a través de sus protagonistas* (1996)

—M'BARE N'GOM

ERDRICH, Louise

American novelist, short-story writer, poet, essayist, writer of children's books, b. 7 June 1954, Little Falls, Minnesota

Understanding E.'s writing requires some knowledge of her background. She grew up in North Dakota, where her German-American father (a teacher) and Chippewa mother both worked for the Bureau of Indian Affairs. After what she has called a wild youth, E. enrolled at Dartmouth College and later the graduate writing program at Johns Hopkins. She and Michael Dorris, director of Dartmouth's Native American Studies program, married in 1981 and went on to form an unusually close and highly rewarding collaborative relationship.

That her first book was a collection of poems is appropriate, for although best known for her novels, E.'s prose style is decidedly poetic. What distinguishes her work from that of other poetic fiction writers is its combination of lyric intensity, comic sensibility, and keen appreciation of all things physical (sex no less than nature). Equally remarkable is the way she has situated herself in relation to both her Native American heritage and largely Euro-American audience. As E. once pointed out, Native American writers have a task quite different from other American writers: "In the face of enormous loss, they must tell the stories of contemporary survivors while protecting and celebrating the cores left in the wake of the catastrophe."

E.'s Native American fiction stresses survival, resilience, and love over acrimony and accusation. Accepting the hybridity of contemporary Native American life, it bridges the divide separating oral and written cultures and styles while simultaneously embodying a preference for communal values and identity over the prevailing American individualism. These preferences are evident in her first novel, *Love Medicine* (1984), winner of a National Book Award. In its intertwining of various narrative strands (some first published or later anthologized as separate short stories), *Love Medicine* suggests Faulkner's influence and even more powerfully the Native American tradition of intricately textured fabric and beadwork. E. expertly weaves together numerous plots and characters across a considerable expanse of time to form a remarkably unified effect, or pattern.

The Beet Queen (1986) covers much the same geographical territory (near the Turtle Mountain Reservation where E.s grandfather had been a tribal elder) but this time with a largely non-Native American cast of characters. Here her brand of feminism (lowkey but decisive) and love of comic grotesquerie are especially apparent. *Tracks* (1988) is a much more somber novel in which the recycling and further developing of characters and plot lines from work to work that has become one of the hallmarks of E's writing plays an especially important role. Revising and expanding her earliest work, she weaves into the fabric of her first two published novels traces of their own narrative and tribal history. *Tracks* comprises alternating stories told in two distinctive voices that embody opposing responses to the encroachments of the white world in general and the Dawes Act in particular (which required that Native Americans buy and own their land individually rather than share it communally). In telling his tale to Lulu, a young deracinated Indian woman, Nanapush, the novel's trickster figure, hopes to explain her to herself, connect her to her tribal past, and ensure the tribe's precarious future. The novel's other narrator, Pauline, rejects everything Nanapush wishes to preserve. Against the intimacy of his telling, her narrative (told, but to nobody) implies a debilitating, typically western psychopathology.

The Bingo Palace (1994) and *Tales of Burning Love* (1997) are much more hopeful works. The hope in the former derives less from the gambling casinos upon which many tribe have staked their futures, than on far less grandiose forms of commitment. This is even more noticeable in *Tales of Burning Love*, a tour de force of communal storytelling (of storytelling as quite literally a way of staying awake and alive amidst the otherwise certain death in a blizzard). Picking up threads left hanging at the end of *The Bingo Palace*, E. weaves together a story of happy endings and new beginnings, of love's permutating possibilities. Its brightness does little to prepare the reader for *The Antelope Wife* (1998). Here the sense of communal wholeness seems much more fragile, the social problems confronting Native Americans, both individually and collectively, more overwhelming. Written after E. and Dorris had separated and published soon after his suicide, it is an altogether darker and more self-consciously wrought work. Whether *The Antelope Wife* signals a new direction in E.'s writing or only a temporary deviation (though hardly a misstep) remains to be seen.

Either way, her fiction has been commercially successful and critically acclaimed both in the popular press and by academic critics for its stylistic flair, narrative innovations, and gently but determinedly feminist and Native American perspectives.

FURTHER WORKS: *Jacklight* (1984); *Baptism of Desire* (1989), *The Crown of Columbus* (with Michael Dorris, 1991); *The Blue Jay's Dance: A Birth Year* (1995); *Grandmother's Pigeon* (1996)

BIBLIOGRAPHY: Rainwater, C., "Reading Between Worlds: Narrativity in the Fiction of L. E.," *AL*, 62 (1990): 405-22; Owens, L., *Other Destinies: Understanding the American Indian Novel* (1992); Lincoln, K., *Indi'n Humor: Bicultural Play in Native America* (1993); Chavkin, A., and N. Chavkin, eds., Conversations with L. E. and Michael Dorris (1994); Burdick, D., "L. E.'s *Love Medicine, The Beet Queen*, and *Tracks*: An Annotated Survey of Criticism through 1994," *AICRJ*, 20 (1996): 137-66

—ROBERT A. MORACE

ESENIN, Sergey
See Yesenin, Sergey

ESKIMO LITERATURE

Among Eskimo communities, with a combined population of less than eighty thousand spread over a vast geographic area from Siberia to Scandinavia and from Greenland to Canada and Alaska, literature has traditionally been oral and unwritten. It consists mainly of poems and tales; fiction and drama are virtually nonexistent except for a few works by some Greenland authors.

One may consider as part of written literature the collecting, writing down, and translating of the oral heritage in the 20th c. Important recent anthologies in English include: *Beyond the High Hills: A Book of Eskimo Poems* (1961), *I Breathe a New Song: Poems of the Eskimo* (1971), *Songs of a Dream People* (1972), and *Eskimo Poems from Greenland and Canada* (1973).

The Eskimo language, which has numerous dialects, is part of the Eskimo-Aleut family, and may be related morphologically to the Turkic and Monogolian languages. Aside from some primitive picture-writing, Eskimo never had its own orthography. Under the influence of Scandinavian and North American missionaries and scholars who have circulated among them, most Eskimo communities, particularly in the 20th c., have adopted the Latin alphabet. But written literature and publication activity remain scarce.

In the latter part of the 20th c. the anonymous oral tradition is still dominant. Although many poets are identified by their names, it is not always certain if the poems attributed to them are their own individual compositions or merely recitations, with perhaps some modifications, of the received tradition as transcribed by Scandinavian and North American researchers. This uncertainty between originality versus restatement of patrimony is compounded by longstanding Eskimo custom whereby when a poet dies, his or her poems or versions become common property with scarcely a reference to the poet's name. It is fair to assume that, although the vast majority of Eskimo poems and tales seem to have been created spontaneously, they conform to rather rigid conventions handed down from generation to generation.

Eskimo history or life has yet to express itself in the form of an encompassing epic, although various communities have engendered many myths, legends, and tales. There have been no novels or short stories in the tradition of European or American fiction, except for a few tentative beginnings among some contemporary Greenland authors raised in the Christian tradition. Perhaps the most important Greenland Eskimo writer employing the Eskimo language was Henrik Lund (?–1948), who composed Christian hymns and published some nonreligious poems. Jonatan Petersen (dates n.a.) is also well known for many refined poems, which exhibit distinct Danish influences.

Autochthonous Eskimo poetry is the direct outcome of an arduous existence in a spare environment. Its aesthetic concerns are related to work, seasonal change, ritual, and daily life. Despite many fine lyrics expressing love of nature, human sentiments, lament, and the simple joys of life, Eskimo creativity is more utilitarian than artistic per se. The Eskimo language, which is rich in vocabulary relating to concrete objects but deficient in abstract terms, has no word meaning "art." Poetic as well as narrative style is spare, with no apparent concern for systematic form. Eskimo works convey images without embellishment, and make their statements in a straightforward manner with few emotive and affective terms.

Eskimo poetics include no set stanzaic forms, no prosody or rhyme patterns. From the outset, the entire poetic output seems to have been in free verse utilizing the natural built—in rhythmic patterns of the agglutinative language and the occasional, probably accidental, rhyming that results from identical or similar suffixes. It is, however, rich in formulaic and vocative expressions, alliterative devices, and frequent refrains, particularly in work songs that require a functional beat.

The typology of Eskimo poetry could be put into five distinct, occasionally overlapping categories, which share the above–mentioned aesthetic and linguistic features:

1. *Lyrics.* Chanted, usually with some musical accompaniment, these poems express human joy or suffering, scenes from nature, simple observations about life and fauna and flora; they include elegies and love poems.

2. *Work poems and functional verses.* These are recited rhythmically by one person or by a group engaged in rowing or hunting. Women's songs while doing the daily chores and lullabies may be included in this category, since they serve specific functions.

3. *Religious verse.* Much of Eskimo poetry is shamanic: the *angakok* (shamanistic priest), often to the accompaniment of drumbeat, presents stereotyped or improvisational poems for the purpose of sorcery, intercession with the spirits on behalf of his community, and thaumaturgy and cure. These magic prayers, incantations and songs probably have the most resourceful verbal imagination and the most compelling dramatic effect of any type of Eskimo poetic experience.

4. *Festive poetry.* In nonritualistic festivities, joyous songs are presented, with musical accompaniment and dances, mimic acts, various simple dramatic representations, etc., purely for entertainment. Children's songs, which exude joy and are usually accompanied by games, are also in this category.

5. *Satirical verse.* Eskimo communities have a long tradition of poetic satire, which ranges from short verses criticizing human foibles to vitriolic insults. Particularly interesting are the contests that pit two men or two women against one another in an exchange

of accusations and contempt. In some Eskimo communities, such encounters take place for juridical purposes, whereby disputes may be settled as a result of poetic superiority.

Most of the myths and tales have interspersed in them a variety of verses, some of which are integral to the storyline and some of which provide lyric interludes.

The evolution of written literature by individual authors and poets will probably gain momentum by the end of the 20th c., and collective creativity will gradually diminish among Eskimo communities. The challenge facing the new generation of Eskimo writers will be to adapt various borrowed genres to their long tradition of oral poetry and narrative.

BIBLIOGRAPHY: Frederiksen, S., *Stylistic Forms in Greenland Eskimo Literature* (1954); Thalbitzer, W., "Eskimo Poetry," in *Encyclopedia of Poetry and Poetics* (1965): 253–55; Carpenter, E., *Eskimo Realities* (1973): 50–57; Rasmussen, K., ed., Introduction to *Eskimo Poems from Canada and Greenland* (1973): xv–xxii; McGrath, R., "Inuit Poetry," in Preminger, A., and T. V. F. Brogan, eds., *The New Princeton Encyclopedia of Poetry and Poetics* (1993): 625–26

—TALAT SAIT HALMAN

ESPRIU, Salvador

Spanish poet, dramatist, and novelist (writing in Catalan), b. 1913, Santa Coloma de Farners (Gerona); d. 22 Feb. 1985, Barcelona

E. is the most famous of Catalan post-Civil War poets. As a student in the vigorous Catalan university during the time of the Spanish Republic, E. received a fine classical formation and developed a keen sense of a Spain whose political organization was based upon mutual knowledge and respect among its linguistically and culturally distinct regions. After the Francoist victory, the attempt was made by central authorities to suppress all public use of the Catalan language among the approximately four million Spanish nationals whose mother tongue it was. Yet in 1946 E. published in Catalan his first book of poetry, *Cementeri de Sinera* (*Sinera Cementery*, 1988). Before the war, he mainly wrote novels; the turn to the lyric signified in part his intent to express himself in his native language in a genre that authorities more or less tolerated only because of its appeal to very small minorities. This first book of poetry evidences an abiding dimension of E.'s production: personal meditations about a lost past and death. Sinera is a town on the Catalan Mediterranean coast, and E., who uses it as the setting for several of his works, succeeds admirably in evoking the sounds, temperatures, sun, and sights that stimulate and accompany his thoughts.

Shortly after the end of the Civil War and the beginning of anti-Catalan measures, E. wrote the play *Primera historia d'Esther* (first history of Esther), but it was published only in 1948 and was first staged in 1957. More than his brooding poetry, this play signaled the public E., the man who became, for practical purposes, the national poet of Catalonia during the last decades of his life. For this play compares symbolically the persecution of the Jews under King Ahasuerus in Persia with that of the Catalans by Franco during and after the Civil War. The use of puppet actors and the metamorphoses of some puppets into people says much about the censorship of the period and the way E. perceived the time.

With his much translated *La pell de brau* (1960; *The Bullhide*, 1977), E. became a national literary figure in Spain. The title refers to all of Spain since the shape of the country on a map is much like that of an extended bullhide. The message of the book written in Catalan is one of national reconciliation, yet with respect for the different cultural-linguistic groups of Spain. E.'s way of putting his art at the service of society in this book made it rapidly a model of the aesthetic of social literature then in vogue among younger Spanish writers.

When E. died, critics, whether their mother tongue was Spanish or Catalan, united in the feeling that the seventy-two-year-old poet had died before his time. In great measure this was because along with his generation, region, and country E. had gone from the despair portrayed in "De tan senzill, no t'agradarà" (1954; "It's So Simple That You Won't Like It," 1975) to the weary acceptance of the national fate described in "Assaig de càntic en el temple" (1954; "Rehearsal of a Canticle in the Temple," 1975) and, most gratifyingly, to the fulfillment and optimism of post-Franco democracy. The poet, who had once merely wanted to die without mourning, was enjoying the new Catalonia in the new Spain, an experience that recalled and culminated the promise of the Republic. Just as his adopted Barcelona opened itself to the world by bidding for and winning the right to hold the 1992 Summer Olympics, the once pessimistic and persecuted E. was busy with the opportunities and challenges of freedom.

FURTHER WORKS: *El Dr. Rip* (1931); *Laia* (1932); *Aspectes* (1934); *Miratge a Citerea* (1934); *Ariadne al laberint grotesc* (1935); *Letízia i altres proses* (1937); *Antígona* (1939); *Les cançons d'Ariadna* (1949): *Obra lírica* (1952); *El caminat i el mur* (1954); *Final del laberint* (1955); *Evocacions de Roselló-Pòrcel i altres notes* (1957); *Obra poètica* (1963); *Narracions* (1965); *Ronda de mort a Sinera* (1966); *Per al llibre de salms d'aquests vells cecs* (1967); *Setmana Santa* (1971); *Formes i paraules: aproximació a l' art d'Apelles Fenosa, en homenatge* (1975); *Una altra Fedra, si us plau* (1978); *Obras completas* (4 vols., 1980–1985); *Les roques i el mar* (1981); *Per a bona gent* (1984). FURTHER WORKS IN ENGLISH: *Lord of the Shadow: Poems* (1975); *Death around Sinera* (1980); *Selected Poems of S. E.* (1989)

BIBLIOGRAPHY: Castellet, J. M., *Iniciaciòn a la poesía de S. E.* (1971); Terry, A., *Catalan Literature* (1972): 114–18;; Rosenthal, D. H., "S. E. and Postwar Catalan Poetry," *Contemporary Poetry*, 5, 1 (1982): 12–23; Cocozzella, P., "*Ronda de mort a Sinera*: An Approach to S. E.'s Aesthetics," in Dura´n, M., et al., eds., *Actes del Segon Colloqui d'Estudis Catalans a Nord-Amèrica* (1979): 307–30; Cocozzella, P., "S. E.'s Idea of a Theater: The *Sotajador* versus the Demiurge," *MD*, 29, 3 (Sept. 1986): 472–89; Cocozzella, P., "S. E.'s Prophetic Mode: The Voice of a Historicist Persona," *RCEH*, 14, 2 (Winter 1990): 209–34

—STEPHEN MILLER

ESTERHÁZY, Pèter

Hungarian novelist, short-story writer, and essayist, b. 14 Apr. 1950, Budapest

Born into the most famous aristocratic family of his country, E. spent much of his childhood in a small village because his family was deported to the countryside by the communist authorities in 1951. After the revolution of October 1956, the Soviet-type dictatorship became somewhat more tolerant, allowing the family to move to Budapest, where E. went to school. At Eötvös University he studied mathematics. In 1974 he got a job in an institute for computer science. In the same year his first writing was published in a periodical. Four years later, he gave up his job and became a freelance writer.

His first volume, *Fancsikó és Pinta* (1976; Fancsikó and Pinta), is an autobiographical sequence of stories. The events are related from the perspective of a young boy. The action has two basic components: On one level the main characters are the hero's parents, but their conflicts are subordinated to and distorted by a world dominated by Fancsikó and Pinta, who exist only in the boy's imagination. This book and its successor, *Pápai vizeken ne kalózkodj!* (1977; don't sail as a pirate through the pope's waters!), a collection of short stories, made an immediate impact on the part of the Hungarian reading public that cared for innovative prose, but the general reader did not recognize E. as a major writer until the publication of *Termelési-regény* (1979; production novel).

This work was published with two bookmarks, one red and the other black, to encourage the public to read the first part, a parody of a genre of SOCIALIST REALISM, simultaneously with the second part, a spiritual autobiography of the author, written in the form of end notes attached to the first part. A superficial reading will disclose no connection whatsoever between the main text and the metafictional notes. On closer consideration, however, the latter create an alternative teleology which contradicts that of the generic parody. The names of the printers working on the book are inserted in the notes, indicating the author's belief in the role of indeterminacy and even chance in creation. Additionally, this second part is also an attempt to abolish the distinction between life and art.

On the basis of the combination of the structural devices of the avant-garde with the techniques of earlier periods, the mixing up of visual effects and texts, this book was associated with postmodern writing by some critics. Similar tendencies are even more apparent in his *Bevezetés a szépirodalomba* (1986; an introduction to literature), a huge work that was originally published in parts, which seems to juxtapose apparently disparate linguistic utterances and let unexpected relationships of incompatible texts emerge. The various sections are meant to explore different possibilities of prose writing. The incessant flow of words characterizing "Füiggõ" (1981; dependent) does not seem to be related to the extremely economical, decidedly artificial syntax of "Fuharosok" (1983; *The Transporters*, 1985), a short text full of quotations from Pascal, the story of a rape that can be read as an allegory of the Soviet occupation of Hungary. "Kis magyar pornográfia" (1984; *A Little Hungarian Pornography*, 1995) is a collection of fragments, some of them ribald or political jokes, whereas "A szív segédigéi" (1985; *Helping Verbs of the Heart*, 1991) is a sublime and even religious testimony to the memory of the author's mother. This final section of the work proceeds on two levels. Each page, bordered in heavy black, carries at the top a narrative, and at the bottom, in capital letters, another text that is often some quotation.

Having completed this long work, E. wrote a short book that can be regarded as a hoax. *Tizenkét hattyúk* (1987; seventeen swans) was published as a work by an author called Lili Csokonai. Mihály Csokonai Vitéz (1773–1805) was a major Hungarian poet. E.'s above-mentioned book was presented as the work of a Hungarian woman who lived in the early 19th c. The imitation of the style of that period was so successful that except for a very few critics, most readers were taken in, until E. admitted his authorship.

From the beginning of his career, E. was a harsh critic of communism, and his works were censored on several occasions. When the totalitarian system crumbled in Hungary in 1988, he turned to essay writing and journalism. Although he decided not to belong to any of the political parties emerging after the fall of communism, his articles published in the monthly *Hitel*, an unofficial organ of the Hungarian Democratic Forum, greatly helped the transformation of his country. When the change of the political system was complete, he continued to write fiction. His novel, *Hrabal könyve* (1990; *The Book of Hrabal*, 1994), is a tribute to the Czech prose writer Bohumil Hrabal (b. 1914), whose works gave him inspiration for his attempt to understand the situation of Eastern Europe, a region ruled by the Soviet Union for more than four decades.

Although E. is still in the middle of his career, his two longest works are regarded by many critics as the most significant contributions to Hungarian fiction since 1945. He has succeeded in changing reading habits by rejecting a fair number of the conventions of narrative prose. His ambition to create a diction that contains the quaint, the rare, the technical, the obsolete, the borrowed, the nonce, the local slang, together with his heavy reliance on puns and intertextuality make his style hardly translatable, yet his books have been published in such languages as German, French, English, Italian, Dutch, Polish, and Slovenian.

FURTHER WORKS: *A kitömött hattyú* (1988); *Biztos kaland* (1989); *Egy nő* (1995); *Egy kék haris* (1996)

BIBLIOGRAPHY: Szegedy-Maszák, M., "Postmodernism in Hungarian Literature," *Zeitschrift für Kulturaustausch* (Stuttgart), 1 (1984): 150–56; Szegedy-Maszák, M., "The Life and Times of the Autobiographical Novel," *Neohelicon*, 13, 1 (1986): 83–104; Szegedy-Maszák, M., "Teleology in Postmodern Fiction," in Calinescu, M., and Fokkema, D., eds., *Exploring Postmodernism* (1987): 41–57; Jastrzebska, J., *Personnages tragiques et grotesques dans la littérature hongroise contemporaine* (1989): 118–76; Sanders, I., "Elusive Author," *HunQ*, 36 (1995): 136-40

—MIHÁLY SZEGEDY-MASZÁK

ESTONIAN LITERATURE

The Estonian language belongs to the western branch of the Finno-Ugric tongues, and its closest lexical affinities are with Finnish. There has been no illiteracy in Estonia since the beginning of the 19th c., a fact that helped to develop a rich body of literature. In proportion to the size of its population, Estonia has published more titles, and printed them in larger editions, than any other nation in Europe except Iceland.

The principal monuments of Estonian literature before the 20th c. are the great number of of folksongs (400,000 for a population of 1,300,000), and the *Kalevipoeg* (Kalev's son), a folk epic that fused into an organic whole the ancient Estonian myths and legends. It was conceived from the 10th to 13th cs., but was written down in the 19th c. and somewhat awkwardly edited by the poet Friedrich Reinhold Kreutzwald (1803–1882)—an English version was published under the title *The Hero of Estonia* (1895). Unfortunately,

the first translations of the Bible (1688, 1715, 1739), all made by German theologians, lacked literary quality and thus could not help to create a national literary language. Estonian literary writing started to develop in the 17th c. but it achieved its first maturity in the spontaneous lyrics of Kristjan Jaak Peterson (1801–1822), Lydia Koidula (1843–1886), Anna Haava (1864–1957), and Juhan LIIV. Although deeply immersed in 19th-c. romantic traditions, Haava and Liiv belong in the greater part of their work to the 20th c., and Liiv, as highly original, passionate inventor of symbols, was the first Estonian poet to achieve true visionary significance.

Compared with Finnish and Scandinavian literatures, the literature of the Estonian people presents a strangely broken and interrupted course. The explanation of this irregularity of development is to be found in Estonia's checkered political history and in the provocative character of the national mind as expressed in literature. The real significance of its 20th-c. intellectual history is outside literature, namely in six forces that changed it: the abortive revolution of 1905 against Russian government and German landlords; the successful war of independence against Russia in 1918–20; the period of modern national sovereignty between 1918 and 1940; the Soviet annexation of Estonia in 1940; the mass exodus in 1943–44 of writers who sought abroad the intellectual freedom that Estonia under German and Soviet occupation withheld from them; and the reachieving of independence in 1991 with the collapse of Soviet communism.

Poetry

The first artistically perfect work of the 20th c. was Villem Ridala's (1885–1942) *Laulud* (1908; songs). It had flowing meter, a breadth of genuine poetic enthusiasm as well as a melancholy not before touched, and a softness of language in the manner of Verlaine that has not been surpassed in Estonian. At the same time, Ridala was the first to establish in literary poetry what has been the austere rhythmical rule of Estonian folk poetry: the exact union of the phonetic duration of a given syllable with the metrical accent, an acoustic method used by Greek and Latin poets. Ridala's ballads lack the needed epic strength, but in his shorter pieces he remains a poet of indubitable mastery. He contributed to the widening of the Estonian imagination by introducing to Estonians remote literary settings, largely under Italian inspiration. He translated Giosuè Carducci (1835–1907) and Benedetto CROCE earlier than anybody else in Europe, believing that the Italian example was needed for the renascence of Estonian culture.

The great stimulus and activity of the period came, however, from Gustav Suits (1883–1956), a poet, critic, journalist, and literary historian. A volume of lyrical, patriotic, and political poems, *Elutuli* (1905; fire of life), written in part in the vein of the Finnish poet Eino LEINO, established his fame, and four collections published in 1913, 1920, 1922, and 1950 contain a number of neosymbolist poems that still hold the Estonian reader. Suits's tragedy is that his influence as a public figure and inspiring intellectual leader, who fought successfully against the provincialism of Estonian culture as the leader of the Young Estonia group, is greater than his importance as a poet. Like the German poet Stefan GEORGE, his mentor (although Suits seldom achieved the latter's monumentality and finished elegance), he, too, wanted to be a modern Dante, an idea that led him to the autocratic dreams of the cult of self, cramping and almost destroying his considerable creative faculties.

The opposite of Suits, the humble poet Liiv, who lived a tragedy-filled life, did not ask for any recognition or esteem, but he is, nonetheless, the only talent of the period who stands above his time. He was followed by the EXPRESSIONIST Jaan Oks (1884–1918), a prose writer and poet of striking intensity, whose stylistic, philosophical, and mystico-pathological originality has not been fully recognized, and yet may in its power be compared to STRINDBERG's.

Other strongly instinctive poetic talents of the period are the very musical, mystically and theosophically inclined SYMBOLIST Ernst Enno (1875–1934); the symbolist-expressionist August Alle (1890–1952), one of the most gifted Estonian poets, whose work sharply declined in quality after he became an offical spokesman for the Soviet regime in 1940; Henrik Visnapuu (1890–1951) and Marie UNDER, the two most important figures of the Siuru group; Hendrik Adamson (1891–1946), a nature poet who used the south-central Estonian dialect called *mulgi* for his poems resembling folk songs; and the master of quantitative Estonian verse, who successfully used both the meter of old Estonian folk songs and the meter of the *Iliad* and the *Odyssey*, August Annist (1899–1972).

Marie Under's greatness lies in a mind remarkable for its intelligent sincerity and independent temper, as well as in the rhythmical urgency, vivid language, and intense fluency of her line. She started as an impressionist of flaming youth. Her book *Sonetid* (1917; sonnets) contained poems of erotic sensibility that shocked and delighted Estonian's Protestant readers. Under the influence of German expressionism she changed drastically in the early 1920s and ventured into verse full of somber and vehement moral and social pronouncements. By 1930, having matured emotionally, she introduced a philosophical tone into her poetry; her whole being now strained toward the hidden mystery of existence. Without losing her poetic power, she continued to produce books of symbolic and metaphysical insight, her acclaimed and also representative titles being *Kivisüdamelt* (1935; the stone off the heart) and *Ääremail* (1963; in the borderlands). Under is today recognized both by the discriminating few and by the mass of readers as Estonia's national poet.

The work of Henrik Visnapuu is somewhat similar to that of the early Under. His first books were masterpieces of mannerist experiment and showed great promise. Mixing the elements of Estonian folksong with the musical devices of the Russian poets Konstantin BALMONT and Igor Severyanin (1887–1941), Visnapuu achieved sensuous splendor rarely exhibited in the Protestant culture of Estonia. The lyrical impulse, exquisite in local color and fidelity to national characteristics, was present in his work until the middle 1930s (when he became an official poet), and was then replaced by a militantly nationalistic, didactic, and even journalistic weariness foreign to his innermost fire of genius.

There are younger poets whose styles are likewise chiefly lyrical, among them Arno Vihalemm (1911–1990), who started in the tradition of the Arbujad, or Soothsayers, movement of the 1930s, and later followed the styles of Liiv and of the Swede Nils FERLIN, incorporating into them elements of "pop" poetry; the intimate pantheist Bernard Kangro (1910–1994); the modernist stylizer of folk song and patriotic poet Kalju Lepik (b. 1920); the surreal visionary Artur Alliksaar (1923–1966); the authentic lyricist Paul-Eerik Rummo (b. 1942), the seemingly simplistic but in fact sophisticated synthesizer of folk material and contemporary aesopiam allegory Hando Runnel (b. 1938); the ironic and rouguish Juhan Viiding, alias Jüri Üdi (1948–1995); the emotionally sensitive Doris Kareva (b. 1958); and a refined mannerist, poet and

prose writer, as well as geologist and hunter, Nikolai Baturin (b. 1936), whose fine, linguistically and metaphorically innovative work is an impressive artistic achievement.

In contrast to the practitioners of emotional verse that had themes relating to the soil, and to the current of arrogant "titanism" that was developing, Estonia also produced several modernist poets. After Suits there was first Valmar Adams (1899–1993), who excelled in melodious, cerebral poems and *vers de société*, being the only master of Estonian light verse. Poet-thinkers and metrists of the first order, the married couple Heiti TALVIK and Betti ALVER, leaders of the Arbujad group, started as distant disciples of Suits but surpassed him in technique and formal elegance, having molded the language into perfect elasticity. They venerated especially the work of Ants Oras (1900–1982), poet-translator and critic-stylist who combined a cosmopolitan polish with a profound insight. Oras, Alver, and Talvik together created a school of intellectual poetry that is still flourishing. Among their important followers are the "unautomatic" SURREALIST Ilmar Laaban (b. 1921), whose every word and image is aesthetically premeditated; the lyrical classicist Harri Asi (b. 1922); a surreal poet of strong psychic tension, who is at the same time a craftsman of closed form, Ivar Grünthal (1924-1996); and two intellectual poets of surgical grace, Ain Kaalep (b. 1926) and Jaan Kaplinski (b. 1941). Uku MASING, who was a member of the original Arbujad group, is an outsider of metaphysical vigor, originality of form, and extraordinary command in the poetical appeal in sound, imagery, and suggestion filled with mysticism and spiritual significance; he has been compared to Gerard Manley HOPKINS and T. S. ELIOT.

Criticism

A collection of Ants Oras's selected essays and studies, published under the title *Laiemasse ringi* (1961; into a wider circle), showed him as an adversary of criticism that emphasized sociological, ethnological, and political factors in literary creation. For him, literature was an expression of spirituality and form, and he elevated aesthetic appreciation to the primary position. Oras's studies manifest the highest scholarly and stylistic values reached in Estonian thought and show him as a man of almost universal attainment, but it is mainly in his verse that he has left his mark on the literature of Estonia. He also brought to Estonia the influence of English and American belles lettres and criticism. With him Estonian thought and literature arrived in the 1930s at that stability in form and ideas essential to a great literary period.

Next to Oras stands Aleksander Aspel (1908–1975), his friend and codefender of the "spirit of lightness" directed against the "spirit of heaviness" of the naturalists. He, too, turned criticism into an expression of learning, intelligence, and refinement, but guided writers and readers toward French literary art. He introduced French modernist writers to Estonian readers; a romanticist and a pupil-associate of the French philosopher and critic Gaston Bachelard (1884–1962), he insisted that vision should not be dominated by reason alone.

In addition to the studies by Oras and Aspel, much research of scholarly value has been done by August Annist, Felix Oinas (b. 1911), Viktor Terras (b. 1921), Viktor Kõressaar (b. 1916), Endel Nirk (b. 1925), Ivar Ivask (1927-1992)—a noted poet as well, who was praised by Boris Pasternak—Jaak Põldmäe (1942–1980), Jaan Puhvel (b. 1931), and Heino Puhvel (b. 1926). Among the intuitive critics, Friedebert Tuglas (1886–1971), Bernard Kangro, Karl Ristikivi (1912–1977), and Ilmar Laaban must be mentioned.

Others, who have published books of criticism are Grabbi (b. 1929), Mardi Valgamäe (b. 1935), Mihkel Mutt (b. 1953), and Hasso Krull (b. 1964).

Fiction

Like Estonian poetry, Estonian fiction, which has not matched the accomplishments of the poetry, is a braid of alien roots. Its development shows Scandinavian, German, French, and Russian influences. In symbolist prose Friedebert Tuglas and especially Aleksander Tassa (1882–1955) manifested skill in short stories. Tuglas's most mature book, *Väike Illimar* (1937; little Illimar), demonstrates, however, the subtle use of descriptive realism. Before Oras, Tuglas was considered the leading Estonian literary critic; he came to the fore under the influence of impressionism and left behind him a vast legacy of novellas, essays, and reviews.

Two of the most esteemed authors of the 1920s and 1930s were August Gailit (1891–1960) and Karl Rumor (pseud. of Karl Ast, 1886–1971). Gailit began as a writer of great promise—his novel *Toomas Nipernaadi* (1928; Toomas Nipernaadi), written in an impressionistic style, is one of the books most beloved by Estonian readers—but his artistic powers later declined. Rumor was an intellectual journalist whose work belongs more to the history of Estonian thought than to literature, although in his old age he produced a powerful novel, *Krutsifiks* (1960; the crucifix), characterized by Ants Oras as a work of "exciting unity of vision and style."

The leading realists were Eduard Vilde (1865–1933) and A. H. TAMMSAARE. Tammsaare is generally acclaimed for his monumental five-volume novel (or, more accurately, lengthy prose drama) *Tõde ja õigus* (1926–33; truth and righteousness). Strong in its first volumes, it becomes very uneven in the later ones and accentuates that tendency toward the formlessness and length that always have been weaknesses of the Estonian novel. Tammsaare's truly consummate craftsmanship is displayed in the grotesque philosophical novel *Põrgupõhja uus vanapagan* (1939; *The Misadventures of the New Satan*, 1978).

Perhaps the purest single example of critical realism is Karl RISTIKIVI's concentrated socioethical novel *Tuli ja raud* (1938; fire and iron). But this remarkable book, which was praised by Tammsaare, stands alone in Ristikivi's work, since he later changed his style to deeply felt philosophical and poetical realism. Among Tammsaare's and Ristikivi's contemporaries were Karl August Hindrey (1875–1947), who used expertly stylized settings and poetic dialogue, and Peet Vallak (1893–1959), in whose colorful work a thematic collision between idealism and naturalism takes place.

Other writers of fiction of distinction have moved into the spotlight in recent decades. They are Bernard Kangro, a lyric fictionalist whose rhapsodic style may be partly compared with Lawrence Durrell's and who claims surreal room for the play of creative imagination; Asta Willmann (1916–1984) who in *Hundisõidul* (1975; tracking down the wolves) unites theater and novel; the subtly ironic and stirring intellectual Enn Vetemaa (b. 1936); Arvo Valton (b. 1935), whose works embrace existentialist and absurdist elements; Mati Unt (b. 1944), a playwright and neo-modernist novelist; Viivi Luik (b. 1946), a poet and polished author of psychologically elusive fiction; and Tõnu Õnnepalu, (alias Emil Tode, b. 1964), a master of postmodernist lyric prose.

Of writers translated into English and other languages, the most noted are the novelists Arved Viirlaid (b. 1922) and Jaan Kross (b.

1920). Viirlaid's *Sadu jõkke* (pub. 1965; *Rain for the River*, 1964) and *Ristideta hauad* (1952; *Graves without Crosses*, 1972), both about Estonia during World War II, are examples of a fundamentally 19th-c. realist tradition. Kross's short fiction (published in part in English as *The Conspiracy and Other Stories*, 1995) and such novels as *Professor martensi ärasõit* (1984; *Professor Martens; Departure*, 1994) and especially *Keisri hull* (1978; *The Czar's Madman*, 1993) focus on historic characters who struggle to preserve their moral or artistic integrity in the fact of overwhelming political tyranny and conformity.

Drama

Drama has not been a preeminent form in Estonian literature. The popular dramatists at the beginning of the century were Eduard Vilde and August Kitzberg (1855–1927). The first independence period produced A. H. Tammsaare's poetic drama *Juudit* (1921; Judith) and *Kuningal on külm* (1936; the king feels cold), a pamphleteering allegory. Among the successful political dramatists were Oskar Luts (1887–1953) and Hugo Raudsepp (1883–1952), who provoked controversy by their insistence on painful social themes. New talents emerged after World War II, both in exile and, after Stalin's death, in Soviet-occupied Estonia. Of these, the most important are Paul-Eerik Rummo, Ain Kaalep, and Artur Alliksaar, and, most recently, Madis Kõiv (b. 1929) in Estonia, as well, as Bernard Kangro, Asta Willmann, Ilmar Külvet (b. 1920), and Elmar Maripuu (b. 1952) in exile. The various experiments with new techniques—primarily THEATER OF THE ABSURD—as a reaction to SOCIALIST REALISM in Estonia proper, and the wish to convey significant symbolic commentaries in plays written abroad, have added new vigor and aesthetic viability to Estonian drama and have led to the staging of English-language versions of the play of Rummo, Unt, and Maripuu in the Off-Off Broadway theatres of New York.

Estonian literature of the post 1991 second independence period is too recent for meaningful generalizations. It appears, however, that it is holding its own in the free market economy and has already produced several new talents. After fifty years of Soviet domination, passive resistance, internal—as well as actual—exile, and playing cat and mouse with the censor, Estonian literature is once again free to chart its own course.

BIBLIOGRAPHY: Harris, E. H., *Literature in Estonia*, 2nd ed. (1947); Kõressaar, V., and A. Rannit, eds., *Estonian Poetry and Language: Studies in Honor of Ants Oras* (1965); Jänes, H., *Geschichte der estnischen Literatur* (1965); Oras, A., *Estonian Literature in Exile: An Essay*, with a bio-bibliographical appendix by B. Kangro (1967); Aspel, A., et al., *The Yale Lectures on Estonian Poetry* (1968); Mägi, A., *Estonian Literature: An Outline* (1968); Nirk, E., *Estonian Literature: Historical Survey with Bio-bibliographical Appendix* (1970); Ziedonis, A., ed. *Baltic Literature and Linguistics* (1973); Ivask, I., "Estonian Literature," in Ivask, I., and G. von Wilpert, eds., *World Literature since 1945* (1973): 168–77; special Estonian section *BA*, 47, 4 (1973): 636–63; Mallene, E., *Estonian Literature in the Early 1970s* (1978); Terras, V., "American-Estonian Poets," *PCLS*, 9 (1978): 175–92; Valgemäe, M., "Estonian Drama," in Straumanis, A., ed., *Baltic Drama* (1981): 1–112; Leitch, B., ed., *The Poetry of Estonia* (1982); Kurman, G., "Estonian Literature," in Parming, T. and E. Järvesoo, eds., *A Case Study of a Soviet Republic: The Estonian SSR* (1978): 247–80; Valgemäe, M., "Drama and the Theatre Arts," in Parming,

T. and E. Järvesoo, eds., *A Case Study of a Soviet Republic: The Estonian SSR* (1978): 281–317

—ALEKSIS RANNIT
Updated by MARDI VALGEMÄE

ETHIOPIAN LITERATURE

Ethiopia possesses a rich and ancient literary tradition, yet only in recent decades has a truly modern Ethiopian literature begun to evolve. This literature, unlike that of most African countries, has emerged under noncolonial conditions, and thus is not a literature of protest against foreign domination. Instead it has drawn heavily upon centuries of religious and moral writings in Ge'ez, the old Ethiopic literary language which still survives as a liturgical language in the Ethiopian Orthodox Church but which is now meaningless to all but a small number of Church-educated Ethiopians.

Ethiopia's official language, Amharic, existed for centuries as a vernacular before finally becoming in the 20th c. an accepted literary language. The early 1900s saw the beginnings of Amharic literature, even though it had to compete initially with Ge'ez. Earliest Amharic writing tended to be infused with stock moral didacticism, and often still is, influenced as it has been by the traditional association of Ge'ez literature with ethical instruction.

The first Amharic novel, *Lebb wallad tarik* (1908; *Tobbya*, 1964), by Afawarq Gabre Yesus (1868–1947), clearly presented its moral purpose with the introductory comment that "much is due to him who is kind to others, much is lost to him who does evil to others." Other early writers, such as Makonnen Endalkachew (1892–1963) and Kebebe Mikael (b. 1915), concentrated on moral edification and glorification of Ethiopia's past in their short fiction and plays.

More recent Amharic writing has frequently remained in line with tradition or else risked government suppression, and as yet consists largely of short pamphlet-novels, some didactic poetry, and short patriotic plays.

Unfortunately, only a handful of non-Ethiopians can read Amharic, with its unique syllabic script, and Ethiopians have felt the same artistic and economic impulses to write in a language of wider currency that have motivated other African authors. After World War II English became the accepted second language of Ethiopia, and English translations of Amharic and Ge'ez works soon became popular. Such translations directly preceded significant creative work in English. In 1964 the *Ethiopia Observer* published in translation *Marriage by Abduction*, a short play, first published in Amharic in 1955, by Menghistu Lemma (1925–1988), and thus brought this notable author to the attention of the English-speaking world.

This play breaks with traditional Ethiopian sermonizing drama by being a comedy of manners based on reconciling tribal marriage customs with modern ones. It sets the tone for a longer and more important play by the same author, first published in Amharic in 1957 and in English as *The Marriage of Unequals* (1970), whose satire focuses on social and economic inequality, highlighted by the main character, Baharu, an Ethiopian version of the "been-to" who instead of using his foreign education to get the usual cushy administrative job in Addis Ababa, goes to live in a remote village, where he starts a school and a number of self-help programs.

Abbe Gubegna (1934–1980) is well known in Ethiopia for his popular moralistic Amharic writing. Unfortunately his *The Savage Girl* (1964), the first Ethiopian play written in English, does not possess the technical qualities of Menghistu Lemma's drama. An allegory based on history, the play teaches the virtues of isolationism and hatred of change; a forest girl living an idyllic natural life—she has a Bible, however, symbolizing Ethiopia's sixteen centuries of Christianity—finds the impact of the outside world to be fatal.

The weaknesses of *The Savage Girl* are not to be found in the drama of Tsegaye Gabre-Medhin (b. 1936), Ethiopia's leading playwright. He has written and directed over twenty Amharic plays dealing with social and historic themes, and has also written some internationally noted English poetry and drama. His short historical play *Tewodros*, first performed in 1963, led to the opening of the Creative Arts Center in Addis Ababa. Emperor Tewodros (fl. 1855–68), a popular figure in Ethiopian literature and art, is here portrayed as a heroic visionary dreaming of a homeland free of factionalism who is prepared to sacrifice all to this end, beset as he is on all sides by foreign intrigue and local warring chieftains.

Tsegaye Gabre-Medhin's more recent play, *Collision of Your Altars* (1977), turns to a more ancient historical period, that of the disintegration of Emperor Kaleb's Axumite Ethiopia (A.D. 587–629), but this author's best-known English work, *Oda-Oak Oracle* (1965), has found its popularity at least partly because of its more universal and archetypal plot, which includes an ancestral command, an obligatory sacrifice, and a tribal "strong son" who has been blessed with a strength that is also a great curse.

In 1961 the *Ethiopia Observer* published "Truth," an English translation of an Amharic short story (1958) by Alamayyawh Mogas (dates n.a.). Although strictly in the moralistic tradition, relating how a successful man rejects true friendship for a false lover, this story was the harbinger of a series of stories soon to be written in English. Unfortunately, few are available outside of Ethiopia, mostly appearing in *Something*, a transitory journal of the English department of what was then Haile Sellassie I University. Most are concerned with moral instruction, although some venture into social criticism—as does Tesfaye Gessesse's (b. 1937) "Ayee My Luck," which attained wider recognition through its publication in *African Arts* (1971).

Amharic poetry has as yet shown only limited development, in the work of Menghistu Lemma and Solomon DERESSA. Deressa's "Legennaat" (1968; childhood) might be considered the beginnings of modern Amharic poetry. Poetry in English ranges from weak, amateurish attempts published locally by their authors to the inspired work of Tsegaye Gabre-Medhin and Solomon Deressa. A weighty awareness of their country's ancient heritage permeates the work in both English and Amharic of Ethiopia's poets; this heritage is frequently judged an albatross to be rid of, as, by implication, are the traditional ideas of Ge'ez and Amharic literature. Fiercely contrasting images depict Ethiopia; it is a nation with a rich and ancient heritage perhaps, yet also a land of hideous poverty, feudal exploitation, and numbing lethargy. Modernism might be shunned, yet like it or not, after centuries of slumber the nation must awaken, no matter how uncertain the world it awakens to might be.

The artistic limitations of didacticism often found in Ge'ez and Amharic writing are also evident in *Confession* (1962), the first English-language novel by an Ethiopian. Yet its author, Ashenafi Kebede (b. 1937), effectively presents a picture of the problems of an Ethiopian student abroad in race-conscious America—a new theme for Ethiopian literature. Another writer, Sahle Sellassie (b. 1936), places his novels only in indigenous settings. After his successful translation (from his Chaha-language original) of *Shinega's Village* (1964), dealing with village life and the inevitable conflicts with modern influences, Sahle Sellassie wrote his next novel, *The Afersata* (1968), in English.

The Afersata suffers from a thin plot resting on the burning of a villager's hut and an ensuing investigation carried out by a local committee, or *afersata*, yet the author achieves an effective feeling for the highly communal and self-sufficient nature of peasant society. In his next novel, *Warrior King* (1974), he turned to the ever-popular Emperor Tewodros and the sense of patriotism and pride evoked by this historical figure.

Any technical shortcomings in these novels are more than compensated for in *The Thirteenth Sun* (1973), written in English by Daniachew Worku (1936–1994), an author who has also written some Amharic plays, short stories, and poems. Taking its title from the Ethiopian calendar, which consists of a thirteen-month year, the novel is set in the present yet is full of an awareness of the past—a past seen with the critical eye of recent poets rather than traditional or patriotic authors. The past is the pollutant of contemporary life. Goytom's pilgrimage up Mount Zekwala to Abbo Shrine with his half-sister and dying father allows to unfold a broad panorama of the brutal realities of present-day Ethiopia, rooted as they are in the medieval nature of that society. Violence and exploitation overwhelm the reader; the Church is the great profiteer of the poor, the sick, and the superstitious. The land, long ravished by an unenlightened peasantry, now enslaves them; their ignorance, poverty, and the feudal system that victimizes them all work to transform them into callous, sullen, and brutish creatures.

It is not yet evident that *The Thirteenth Sun* is the precursor of a new, sophisticated Ethiopian novel aimed at an international audience. Time may prove it to be, but so far it has been succeeded only by Sahle Sellassie's *Warrior King* and by Abbe Gubegna's *Defiance* (1975), two novels primarily concerned with extolling Ethiopia's past. Set in Addis Ababa in 1937 during the Italian occupation, *Defiance* focuses on an old patriot, Fitawrari Abesha, and his family's resistance to their Italian persecutors. It is clear from the handling of his material that the author has matured considerably since the publication of his drama *The Savage Girl* a decade earlier. Some effective description brings to life a Fascist dungeon for Ethiopians, atrocities, and a hillside battle. If *Defiance* is a timely reminder to Ethiopians of hardships suffered once before under an oppressive rule, it is also an indication, along with the best of Sahle Sellassie, Daniachew Worku, Tsegaye Gabre-Medhin, and others, that Ethiopian writers possess the resources and potential for significant contributions to African literature.

BIBLIOGRAPHY: Harden, J. M., *An Introduction to Ethiopic Christian Literature* (1926); Gérard, A. S., *Four African Literatures: Xhosa, Sotho, Zulu, Amharic* (1971): 271–376; Huntsberger, P. E., comp., *Highland Mosaic: A Critical Anthology of Ethiopian Literature in English* (1973): 1–13: 28–47: 72–82: 106–15; Beer, D. F., "Ethiopian Literature and Literary Criticism in English: An Annotated Bibliography," *RAL*, 6 (1975): 44–57; Kane, T. L., *Ethiopian Literature in Amharic* (1975); Beer, D. F., "The Sources and Content of Ethiopian Creative Writing in English," *RAL*, 8 (1977): 99–124; Molvaer, R. K., *Tradition and Change in Ethiopia: Social and Cultural Life as Reflected in Amharic Fictional Literature, ca. 1930–1974* (1980); Adera, T., and A. J. Ahmed, eds.,

Silence Is Not Golden: A Critical Anthology of Ethiopian Literature (1995)

—DAVID F. BEER

EVTUSHENKO, Evgeny

See Yevtushenko, Yevgeny

EXISTENTIALISM

Existentialism became important as a philosophical position in Germany following World War I, and it dominated the philosophical and literary scene in France for twenty years or so beginning in the late 1930s, particularly during the decade following World War II. Existentialist thinkers can hardly be said to have formed a school or even a coherent group, however; rather than being a systematic philosophy, existentialism is a form of the individualistic, antirationalist current that can be traced back to the very beginnings of Western civilization.

Modern existentialism has its origins in the antirationalism of the late 18th and early 19th cs. The romantics' emphasis on individual experience as opposed to the general human values stressed by neoclassicists; their upholding of emotion and instinct over reason; their revolt against and alienation from the dominant bourgeois society; and their anguish in their alienation can be seen in retrospect as an expression of the existentialist point of view. We find these tendencies in varying degrees in Blake, the early Goethe, Hölderlin, and Musset, to mention only a few major writers, as well as in many minor figures less gifted in formulating their anguish in literary terms. These characteristics are even stronger in poets like Baudelaire and Rimbaud, and are present in many early 20th-c. writers.

None of these 19th-c. antecedents could be said to be a conscious source for modern existentialism, however. The one figure to whom all existentialists acknowledge their indebtedness is Søren Kierkegaard (1813–1855), the Danish thinker who was as much a poet as a philosopher. He reacted sharply against established Christianity and the systematic philosophy of Hegel (1770–1831), who defended a rational Christianity and saw human history as God's intelligible plan for mankind. Kierkegaard insisted rather that the individual make an irrational choice between Christ and the world, a "leap of faith," and that he live, that is, take the responsibility for that choice, not merely reason about it. The primacy of existential reality, the necessity of choice, and the anguish in the face of the responsibility the choice imposes are all found in modern existentialist philosophy and literature.

Friedrich Nietzsche (1844–1900), like Kierkegaard a colorful, nonacademic philosopher, is a second major source for modern existentialist thought. He attacked the basic foundations of Christianity and of the decadent rational world he encountered. He insisted that the superior individual strive toward the creation of new values through his power of self-perfection, eventually emerging as a "superman." Whereas Kierkegaard's point of view was theistic (the religious experience was on a higher level than the aesthetic or the ethical), for Nietzsche the historical God was dead, as were all absolutes in which man had traditionally found his values. They were replaced by the power of the new superman, who had to create himself by transcending the nihilism around him.

Along with Kierkegaard, the poet of theological anguish, and Nietzsche, the dramatizer of philosophical nihilism, a third major 19th-c. source for modern existentialism is Fyodor Dostoevsky. Neither a theologian nor a philosopher, he was nonetheless strongly attached to Russian Orthodox Christianity, and his characters suffer the agony of the struggle between the forces of evil and weakness in themselves and the miracle and mystery of redemption. His exploration of the irrational and the depths of human despair has been a major influence on 20th c. thought and fiction, and particularly on existentialism.

The two most important philosophical descendents of Kierkegaard and Nietzsche writing in 20th-c. Germany were Karl Jaspers (1883–1969) and Martin Heidegger (1889–1976). Jasper's *Die geistige Situation der Zeit* (1931; *Man in the Modern Age*, 1933) responded to the crumbling of the German middle class following World War I; he maintained that the historical meaning of existential philosophy is its attempt to awaken in the individual the possibilities for an authentic and genuine life in our highly organized, technological, depersonalizing society. He joined Kierkegaard in rejecting rationalistic systems like Hegel's, but Kierkegaard's Christian perspective became merely a sense that human limitations imply only some source of being beyond man. Gabriel MARCEL in France was also a part of this theistic orientation, but the influence of Henri BERGSON on him was just as important as Kierkegaard's. Existentialist elements are also present in the work of Martin BUBER and of many other modern theologians and philosophers.

Heidegger was a more formal philosopher and a more direct descendent of Nietzsche, in that God is absent from his world. In *Sein und Zeit* (1927; *Being and Time*, 1962) he attempted to revise and complete the history of ontology, the study of Being. Heidegger went beyond his teacher, the phenomenologist Edmund Husserl (1859–1938), for whom philosophy was a description of what is, of things themselves, and maintained that the phenomena of existence would reveal themselves if we did not impose our preconceptions on them. Man is not defined by his thought and its relationship to the physical world, as Descartes (1596–1650), with his *Cogito ergo sum* (I think, therefore I am), and traditional Western thought claimed, but by his being-in-the-world (*Dasein*, being-there), as distinguished from the abstract *Sein* (being) and the concrete *Seiendes* (beings). And only by an existential awareness of our own death (nonbeing or nothingness) as an integral element of our being can we find the authentic existence sought in various ways by Kierkegaard, Nietzsche, Dostoevsky, and Jaspers.

Marcel's *Journal métaphysique* (1927; *Metaphysical Journal*, 1952) was the first specifically existentialist work in France, and he tried later to popularize his search for Christian being in his plays. But Jean-Paul SARTRE, who studied in Germany and knew Husserl's and Heidegger's work well, was by far the most influential existentialist figure in Paris. In his major early philosophical work, *L'être et le néant* (1943; *Being and Nothingness*, 1956), he carried further Heidegger's concept of nonbeing. He divided being into the *en-soi* (being-in-itself), the static being of things, and the *pour-soi* (being-for-itself), the dynamic being of living persons. The *pour-soi* is aware of the nothingness of human existence, the total lack of established principles, and therefore the total freedom and concomitant responsibility to create itself and its own values. But this free *pour-soi* often insists on denying its freedom by becoming an *en-soi*, on adopting set values for its own. By exploring the

conflicts between this bad faith and the authentic action of the *pour-soi*, Sartre developed and gave new meaning to the existential modes of thought characteristic of his predecessors: the primacy of experience or existence over values or essence; the importance of nothingness or nonbeing as an integral part of existence; the sense of anguish and of man's contingency and mortality resulting from this ontological nihilism; the burden of choice and the responsibility imposed on the individual for the creation of new values.

All the existentialist thinkers discussed here were literary stylists as well as philosophers, but Sartre stands out from the others in his ability to convey his philosophy in literary forms that captured the imagination of the general public. He burst on the Paris literary scene in the final year of the German occupation (1943–44) with the production of two plays, *Les mouches* (1943; *The Flies*, 1947) and *Huis clos* (1944; *No Exit*, 1947). Here, and later in *Les mains sales* (1948; *Dirty Hands*, 1949), he presented graphically various aspects of the conflict between *en-soi* and *pour-soi*. The themes of solitude, freedom, alienation, and commitment, seen by audiences needing to take action against the authority of the occupying forces, and after the war wanting to create a new and better society, gave immediate practical meaning to Sartre's philosophy of existence. His plays had a much greater impact than Marcel's, whose characters and situations tended to express too abstractly a philosophical or theological position.

But in his early novel *La nausée* (1938; *Nausea*, 1949), Sartre had already recorded his protagonist's growing consciousness of the gratuitous contingency of his existence, that is, his freedom, producing the anguish of nausea. This reality is contrasted with the inauthenticity of his banal bourgeois surroundings, mercilessly satirized as *en-soi*. And in his trilogy *Les chemins de la liberté* (1945–49; *The Roads to Freedom*, 1947–51) Sartre analyzed the various forms of bad faith that prevent, among a host of characters, a young philosopher from assuming the burden of his freedom until just before his death at the hands of invading Germans in 1940. The most original of these novels is *Le sursis* (1945; *The Reprieve*, 1947), in which, by moving without transition among groups of characters in different parts of the world, Sartre shows that everyone was equally responsible for the appeasement of Hitler by England and France in the 1938 Munich pact. For example, a private citizen in Paris may complete a sentence begun by a public figure negotiating the pact.

Sartre's early literary criticism is also existentialist. In *Baudelaire* (1947; *Baudelaire*, 1949) and *Qu'est-ce que la littérature?* (in *Situations II*, 1948; *What Is Literature?*, 1949), he insisted on the artist's responsibility to be "committed to his time." But this gave way to a recognition of the social and historical conditioning that formed writers like Jean GENET and Flaubert, on whom he wrote exhaustive studies.

This evolution reflects the gradual shift in Sartre's philosophical position away from his early concern with existence and being toward the historical and sociological perspectives of Marxism. *Critique de la raison dialectique, I: Théorie des ensembles pratiques (1960; Critique of Dialectical Reason, I: Theory of Practical Ensembles*, 1976) is an attempt to reconcile existentialism and Marxism.

Just as Sartre's literary works made his philosophy accessible to the general public, many modern writers who have had little or no formal training in philosophy have used existentialist themes and situations in their quest for meaning in a world devoid of values. For example, in *Der Prozeß* (1925; *The Trial*, 1937) and *Das*

Schloß (1926; *The Castle*, 1930), Franz KAFKA shows the anguish of man in his search for meaning in an incomprehensibly absurd world and universe. Yet his style is so vivid and harmonious, so savagely satirical, that his importance remains literary rather than philosophical.

The same can be said of the importance of André MALRAUX in *La condition humaine* (1933; *Man's Fate*, 1934), for example, his novel of violence and heroism in the face of tragic death, and even of Albert CAMUS, who was often linked with the existentialists. Both were atheistic humanists upholding the need for action in the face of the absurd, but for Camus action was less violent, as in his early essay *Le mythe de Sisyphe* (1942; *The Myth of Sisyphus*, 1955) and novel *L'étranger* (1942; *The Stranger*, 1946). *La peste* (1947; *The Plague*, 1948) turns a quarantine city into a Pascalian prison, where death and resistance are again, however, less violent than in Malraux. And as the latter turned to art as an expression of revolt against the absurd, Camus's *L'homme révolté* (1951; *The Rebel*, 1954) traced the history of individual revolt and extolled it against collective revolution. Camus was then not only in direct opposition to Sartre's growing insistence that individual action was always conditioned by history, but both Malraux and Camus rejected the existentialist notion that man, in creating his life, also creates new values.

Of the writers who came into prominence in the 1950s, Samuel BECKETT is perhaps the most obviously indebted to existentialism and the intellectual climate of the 1940s. His play *En attendant Godot* (1952; *Waiting for Godot*, 1954) and his novel *Molloy* (1951; *Molloy*, 1955) explore the depths of man's alienation and despair, as the existentialists did, but they do not allow for the existentialists' creative action and commitment. This is true as well of the THEATER OF THE ABSURD of Jean GENET and Eugène IONESCO, among others. And the NEW NOVEL writers Alain ROBBE—GRILLET, Michel BUTOR, and Nathalie SARRAUTE, for example, also reflect the absence of established principles depicted by the existentialists, but neither do they permit the creation of new values.

Although an existentialist current will probably always be present in Western thought and literature, its importance as a philosophical and literary movement is confined to a relatively short historical period in Germany and France, when the philosophical preoccupations of Jaspers, Heidegger, Marcel, and Sartre in particular, and a host of literary figures, coincided with social, political, and psychological conditions to produce a sense of solitude, anguish, and despair, a void to be filled by individual creative action. But Sartre's position evolved in response to changing political, social, and intellectual conditions, and with his death, following those of his elders, we must conclude that existentialism as a formal philosophical position can no longer be considered a vital force.

BIBLIOGRAPHY: Blackham, H. J., *Six Existentialist Thinkers* (1952); Hubben, W., *Four Prophets of Our Destiny* (1952); Barrett, W., *Irrational Man: A Study of Existential Philosophy* (1958); Heinemann, P. H., *Existentialism and the Modern Predicament* (1958); Schrag, C., *Existence and Freedom* (1961); Breisach, E., *Introduction to Modern Existentialism* (1962); Hanna, T., *The Lyrical Existentialists* (1962); McElroy, D., *Existentialism and Modern Literature* (1963); Borowitz, E., *A Layman's Introduction to Religious Existentialism* (1965); Sanborn, P., *Existentialism* (1968); Luijpen, W., *Existential Phenomenology* (1969); Harper, R., *The Existential Experience* (1972); Macquarrie, J., *Existentialism* (1972); Poster, M., *Existential Marxism in Postwar France: From Sartre to Althusser* (1975); Barnes, H., *Existentialist Ethics* (1978)

—CHARLES G. HILL

EXPRESSIONISM

Expressionism was a cultural revolution that centered around the verbal arts but extended into most areas of artistic, social, and political life. It originated in Germany around 1910 and remained dominant there until 1925. Deriving its name and its emphatic subjectivism from the preceding revolt of the visual arts—pictorial expressionism was initiated by J. A. Hervé in Paris in 1901 and gave rise in Germany to the leagues called The Bridge (1905) and The Blue Rider (1912)—it was the first major trend within the greater framework of international MODERNISM. Based on disparate intellectual impulses ranging from Nietzsche, Dostoevsky, and STRINDBERG to Walt Whitman and MARINETTI's FUTURISM, as well as, more indirectly, French SYMBOLISM, expressionism did not emerge as a unified aesthetic program. The often used term "movement" thus misleadingly suggests a homogeneity that never existed. In its initial phase (1910–14), expressionism erupted as a cry of protest against obsolete artistic and societal norms from a highly diverse generation of authors. All, however, had in common their revolt against an oppressive, moribund caste system, their resultant radically antibourgeois stance, and their denunciation of naturalism as a mere extension of reality. German expressionism, unlike related phenomena abroad, directly mirrored the feeling of impending doom prior to 1914 and remained closely linked to the subsequent historical developments.

In 1911 Kurt Hiller (1885–1972) proclaimed the goals of this new generation: "We are expressionists. Once more, we are concerned about content, willpower, and ethos." From its beginnings, expressionist art was radically antimimetic. Thus, Kasimir Edschmid (1890–1966) postulated: "The world is already here. There is no sense in duplicating it." Expressionism was idea-oriented to the point of abstraction and visionary declamation: "For the expressionist artist, all space becomes vision. . . . There is no longer a chain of facts: factories, houses, illness, whores, shouting, hunger. Now there is only the vision of these" (Edschmid). Its driving force was the artistic rendering of an ethical imperative, shared by hundreds of authors in their plea for mankind's spiritual and societal renewal.

German expressionism gained additional importance as a mainstay of pacifism during World War I. Although defying all attempts at canonization, it nevertheless produced a flood of manifestos, including inane affronts to the bourgeoisie, essays on poetics and language, and political statements. Fluctuating literary circles were formed through the efforts of various periodicals and their editors. Most influential among these were *Der Sturm* (1910–32), edited by Herwarth Walden (1878–1941); *Die Aktion* (1911–32), edited by Franz Pfemfert (1879–1954); and *Die weißen Blätter* (1913–20), edited by Franz Blei (1871–1942) and René Schickele (1883–1940). These publications were primarily responsible for the dissemination of expressionism abroad, especially after 1918. At the apex of the epoch (1916–20), many expressionists turned toward political activism, propagating socialist and revolutionary thought. After the unsuccessful German revolution of 1918–19, the drive for revolt and renewal gradually gave way to the more resigned tone typical for years of decline (1920–25). By this time expressionism had already reached out to England, the U.S., and to eastern and northern Europe. In Germany it was banned by the Nazis in 1933.

The stylistic and formal innovations of expressionism are as manifold as its authors. Expressionist style does away with traditional logic and grammar. It strives toward the essential, the global and visionary statement, often by means of compression and unorthodox imagery. Its most lasting achievement is the creation of a contemporary poetic language fit to juxtapose the most disparate phenomena: the ugly and the beautiful, death and rebirth, the rhythm of the teeming metropolis and religious ecstasy. Most of the early poetry heralding this stylistic revolution portrays disaster and, at the same time, prophesies the dawn of a new age: the flamboyant eschatological imagery of Georg Heym (1887–1912), evoking the specter of big-city life, poverty and disease, and the more subdued premonitions of doom poured into Georg TRAKL's darkly allusive poems. Jakob van Hoddis (1887–1942) and Alfred Lichtenstein (1889–1914) created the techniques of image collage and poetic simultaneity—devices that linked some of the early expressionists to CUBISM, despite the cubists' different artistic goals. August STRAMM, one of the most innovative talents of the epoch, worked with total syntactic fragmentation. (A similar, highly condensed language was later utilized by the DADAISTS, who aimed to evict all "meaning" from poetry and thus initiated a counterrevolt against idea-laden expressionism.) Yvan Goll (1891–1950), Else Lasker-Schüler (1869–1945), and Oskar Loerke (1884–1941) were among the most talented poets; their poetry centered around the intense feelings of the "I" and often carried overtones of religious or erotic ecstasy.

Gottfried BENN's collections *Morgue* (1912; morgue) and *Söhne* (1913; sons) contributed to a new aesthetic concept based on grotesque disillusionment, whereas Ernst Wilhelm Lotz (1890–1914) and Ernst Stadler (1883–1914) sounded the dithyrambic call for awakening and departure to a new millennium. Both the pacifistic poems in Franz WERFEL's *Der Weltfreund* (1911; friend of the world) and the later activist and revolutionary poetry by Johannes R. Becher (1891–1958), Karl Otten (1889–1963), Rudolf Leonhard (1889–1953), and many others share the appeal for the revitalization of humanity characteristic of the epoch.

Of the many anthologies, *Menschheitsdämmerung* (1919; the dawn of mankind), edited by Kurt Pinthus (1886–1975), remains the most impressive document of expressionist poetry. On the international scene, English vorticism and its proponents Wyndham LEWIS and Ezra POUND were stylistically influenced by expressionist poetry, as well as, to a certain extent, the earlier poems of Stephen Spender and T. S. Eliot. The Belgian expressionist Paul van OSTAIJEN virtually shaped the development of modern Flemish literature, whereas in the Netherlands Hendrik MARSMAN and others founded an influential expressionist circle. In America, E. E. CUMMINGS and Williams Carlos WILLIAMS utilized grammatical fragmentation and rapidly changing, contrasting images—devices they owed to expressionism. Some of the expressionist innovations were also absorbed by SURREALISM.

Expressionist drama is considered the most important pioneer movement of the 20th-c. stage. Among its precursors were the 19th-c. dramatists Georg Büchner (1813–1837) and Christian Dietrich Grabbe (1801–1836), and the plays of Frank WEDEKIND, Alfred JARRY, and Paul Scheerbart (1863–1915).

After the first violently antimimetic experiments, mostly in the form of a single scene—for example, *Sphinx und Strohmann* (1907; sphinx and strawman) and *Mörder, Hoffnung der Frauen* (1907; *Murderer the Women's Hope*, 1963) by Oskar Kokoschka (1886–1980) and *Der gelbe Klang* (1910; the yellow sound) by Wassily Kandinsky (1866–1944)—it focused on the motif of spiritual renewal. The stage, having disposed of most naturalistic devices, became a battleground for conflicting ideas represented by typical or symbolical rather than individualized figures. Characteristic of this drama of ideas are an episodic, acausal structure juxtaposing realistic and visionary, dreamlike scenes; the abolition of coherent plots lines in favor of the inner development of the characters; and a highly abstract, declamatory language that might occasionally strike the modern reader as ludicrous. Such plays as Reinhard Johannes Sorge's (1892–1916) *Der Bettler* (1912; *The Beggar*, 1963) and Walter Hasenclever's (1890–1940) *Der Sohn* (1914; the son) and *Die Menschen* (1918; *Humanity*, 1963) are prototypical of the plea for collective rebirth, also present in many of Georg KAISER's plays. Among the outstanding talents of the epoch are Ernst Toller, Ernst BARLACH, and Carl STERNHEIM. The early Bertolt BRECHT, with his plays *Baal* (1918; *Baal*, 1963), *Trommeln in der Nacht* (1918; *Drums in the Night*, 1961), and *Im Dickicht der Städte* (1923; *In the Jungle of Cities*, 1961) was definitely under the spell of expressionism, even though he conceived *Baal* as an antiexpressionist provocation.

Expressionist drama's immediate offshoot was the early cinema, a medium ripe to absorb many of its techniques (see Film and Literature). Its classics include Robert Wiene's *Das Kabinett des Dr. Caligari* (1919; the cabinet of Dr. Caligari), Paul Wegener's two versions of *Der Golem* (1914, 1920; the golem); and Fritz Lang's *Metropolis* (1926). Both expressionist theater and film had a tremendous impact on European and American drama. In the U.S. many structural and dramaturgic devices were adopted by Eugene O'NEILL, Elmer RICE, Thornton WILDER, Archibald MACLEISH, Paul Green (1894–1981), and many others.

In both drama and poetry expressionism had other ramifications. In Scandinavia, it was embraced and modified by Pär LAGERKVIST in Sweden, Sigurd HOEL in Norway, and Emil Bønnelycke (1893–1953) in Denmark. Sean O'CASEY used expressionist devices in a number of his plays. Russian expressionism emerged in 1919 and particularly influenced the dramatic works of Vladimir MAYAKOVSKY.

Expressionist fiction, while less important than poetry and drama, produced highly subjective experimental novels—such as *Bebuquin; oder, Die Dilettanten des Wunders* (1909; Bebuquin; or, miracle's dilettantes) by Carl Einstein (1885–1940) and a multitude of emotionally charged sketches and short stories by BENN, Alfred DÖBLIN, Edschmid, Albert Ehrenstein (1886–1950), and others. Later expressionist prose was often influenced by James JOYCE.

In the 1920s expressionism lost the creative energy once generated by its revolutionary fervor and its attack on reality. Although its emotional intensity and bombast were spent forever, its formal and stylistic innovations had been absorbed internationally. Through its proclamation of man's freedom to revolt against a stifling reality, it not only unleashed a deep cultural shock on the threshold of the 20th c. but also irrevocably established subjectivism as a driving force in modern art and literature.

Thus, directly or indirectly, it inspired the revival of the subjective in the poetry of the 1940s—particularly in the visionary imagery of Dylan THOMAS—and in various postwar literary trends, especially in German and Swiss drama. Most notably under the influence of expressionism have been the playwrights Wolfgang BORCHERT, Friedrich DÜRRENMATT, Max FRISCH, and Fritz

HOCHWÄLDER. In the poetry of Nelly SACHS and Paul CELAN expressionist and symbolist techniques merged to form a contemporary lyrical language. Günter EICH used the nonlinear plot development derived from expressionism in numerous radio plays, whereas Hans Erich NOSSACK and other novelists modified expressionist structural devices. Even the documentary theater of the 1960s and 1970s—represented by Rolf HOCHHUTH, Peter WEISS, and Heinar KIPPHARDT (1919–1992)—makes frequent use of a declamatory language and other elements of stage technique that derive in part from the expressionist heritage.

BIBLIOGRAPHY: Samuel, R., and R. Thomas, *Expressionism in German Life, Literature and the Theater 1910–1924* (1939); Sokel, W., *The Writer in Extremis: Expressionism in Twentieth-Century Literature* (1959); Krispyn, E., *Style and Society in German Literary Expressionism* (1964); Arnold, A., *Die Literatur des Expressionismus: Sprachliche und the matische Quellen* (1966); Rothe, W., ed., *Expressionismus also Literature: Gesammelte Studien* (1969); Willet, J., *Expressionism* (1970); Furness, R., *Expressionism* (1973); Weisstein, U., ed., *Expressionism as an International Literary Phenomenon* (1973); Hamann, R., and J. Hermand, *Expressionismus* (1977); Knapp, G., *Die Literatur des deutschen Expressionismus: Einführung, Bestandsaufnahme, Kritik* (1979); Pickar, G., and E. Webb, *Expressionism Reconsidered* (1979); Paulsen, W., "Form and Content in German Expressionist Literature," *MR*, 21 (1980): 137–56

—GERHARD P. KNAPP

EZEKIEL, Nissim

Indian poet, critic, editor, and dramatist (writing in English), b. 16 Dec. 1924, Bombay

E., one of India's foremost intellectuals, belongs to Bombay's small Marathi-speaking Bene-Israel Jewish community. Educated in English-medium schools, he received his undergraduate degree from Wilson College (Bombay) and his M.A. in English from the University of Bombay in 1947, where he would later return as reader of English and one of its most distinguished faculty members. In 1948 he went to Britain and studied philosophy with C. E. M. Joad (1891–1953) at the University of London, and avidly pursued his other interests: theater, film, art, but especially poetry. Returning to India in 1952, he worked as a journalist, then as an advertising copy editor, and later as a factory manager. In 1959 he started teaching English at various colleges and universities in Bombay. In addition to writing poetry, he regularly contributes book, art, and film reviews, and essays on social commentary to major Indian journals and newspapers. An active member of the Indian chapter of P.E.N., he received the Government of India's Padma Shree Award in 1988.

E.'s first volume of poetry, *A Time to Change* (1952), was published in London and received excellent critical notice. The influence of T. S. ELIOT and W. H. AUDEN is apparent. The second volume, *Sixty Poems* (1953), published in Bombay, contains a number of notable poems whose impact is diluted by the inclusion of some of his earliest poems which, critics generally agree, should not have appeared there. *The Third* (1959) marks a transition from E.'s early period to that of a mature stylist. *The Unfinished Man* (1960) is a collection of poems written in 1959, which he describes

as, literarily, the most fruitful year of his life. This volume contains many of his most lyrical, yet most ironic, works, many of them dealing with marriage.

The Exact Name (1965) includes many of E.'s best-known pieces, including "Night of the Scorpion," often cited as one of the finest modern Indian poems. With large, brilliant images suggesting childhood awe, fear, and confusion, the speaker recalls the rainy monsoon night his/her mother was bitten by a scorpion and the elaborate rites and incantations performed by various people to save her from death. The mother's only comment is a terse thanks to God that the scorpion bit her and not her child. Other notable poems are the much-anthologized "In India" and "Poet, Lover, Birdwatcher."

Some poems in *Hymns in Darkness* (1976) explore the aesthetic possibilities of "Indian" English, the English spoken in urban centers as a second language with Indian-language grammatical patterns, idioms, and intonation patterns bleeding through. Though these poems were misunderstood as merely satirical, for which E. was criticized, the experiment was continued by a number of other poets. Poems of *Latter-Day Psalms* (1982) are modeled on the Book of Psalms, sometimes pleading, sometimes cynical, and often bittersweetly humorous.

As a critic and editor, E. has exerted a powerful influence on India's intellectual life. Before him much of what passed for criticism in India tended to be either lionizing or fault-finding. E. has done much to change this kind of simplistic approach. His criticism is distinguished by its lucidity, judiciousness, and honesty. Contrary to the hierarchical and tradition-bound thinking that prevails in much of Indian society, E. is unafraid to question hallowed assumptions and received wisdom. He does so with a sense of humility, a lack of pretension, and a strong predisposition to irony. His most famous piece is an essay on *An Area of Darkness* (1964), a harsh critique of India and Indians by V. S. NAIPAUL. Entitled "Naipaul's India and Mine" (1965), it asserts with candor and accuracy that while much of what repulses Naipaul about India is valid, such things repulse most Indians as well. Moreover, E. insists, Naipaul is unable to see India beyond his own "temperamental alienation"; thus, he has failed to make the proper commitment to his subject. Many of E.'s best reviews are collected in *Another India* (1990).

Since 1955 E. has also edited a number of important journals. In these he has encouraged individual literary creativity and has urged Indian writers to learn about intellectual trends from other parts of the world. He has also championed the art of literary translation from India's vernacular languages into English as a means of cross-fertilizing the country's many separate literary traditions. Many of E.'s best reviews are collected in *Selected Prose* (1992).

E. is an urban poet, the poet of the city of Bombay. His earlier poems show technical virtuosity and an almost laconic quality; by contrast, many later poems are freer, looser, and more experimental in structure and expression. Predominant themes in the poetry are alienation and marginality, which some suggest are the result of both his Jewishness and elitist Westernization. Another theme is the disharmony and hurt that modern urban culture inflicts on people, and which desensitizes and dehumanizes them. He is also concerned with the lack of certitude and stability in relationships, including romantic ones, but most particularly marriage. One is struck by the hortative quality of many of the poems, and by the preponderance of travel and bird imagery, both of which suggest transience and instability. Many of these themes so thoughtfully and provocatively explored by E. also preoccupy the poetry of the younger generation of poets writing in English and in India's other languages.

FURTHER WORKS: *Three Plays* (1969); *Collected Poems 1952-1988* (1989); *Another India* (1990); *Don't Call It Suicide: A Tragedy* (1993)

BIBLIOGRAPHY: Belliapa, M., and Taranath, R., *The Poetry of N. E.* (1966); Garman, M., "N. E.: Pilgrimage and Myth," in Naik, M. K., et al., eds., *Critical Essays on Indian Writing in English* (1968): 106–21; Verghese, C., "The Poetry of N. E.," *IndL*, 15, 1 (1972): 63–75; Karnani, C., *N. E.: A Study* (1974); Kher, I., "'That Message from Another Shore': The Esthetic Vision of N. E.," *Mahfil, A Quarterly of South Asian Literature*, 8, 4 (1972): 17–28; special E. issue, *JSoAL*, 11, 3–4 (1976); Harrex, S. C., "A Critical Approach to Indo-English Poetry," in Harrex, S. C., and Amirthanayagam, G., eds., *Only Connect: Literary Perspectives East and West* (1981): 148–76; Narula, S. C., "Negative Affirmation in N. E.'s Hymns and Psalms," *ArielE*, 14, 4 (Oct. 1983): 57–71; Birbalsingh, F., Interview with N. E., *JSoAL*, 22, 2 (1987): 130–38; Börner, K. H., "Indian Poetry in English," *A&E*, 33 (1987): 87–100; Sharma, T., *essays on N. E.* (1994); Das, B., *The Horizons of N. E.'s Poetry*

—CARLO COPPOLA

EZERA, Regīna

(pseud. of Regīna Šamreto) Latvian novelist and short-story writer, b. 20 Dec. 1930, Riga

E. belongs to the generation of writers who began their careers in the wake of World War II. In the fall of 1944, as the Soviet armies advanced into Latvia, E. and her parents were evacuated to Germany. With the arrival of American troops in April 1945, the Šamreto family was transferred to Magdeburg, which eventually came under Russian occupation. As a result, the Šamretos were forced to return to Latvia.

E. became an established and popular writer in the 1960s. Her first collection of short stories, *Un ceļš vēl kūp* (And the Road is Still Steaming), appeared in 1961, as well as her first novel, *Zem pavasara debesīm* (Under Spring Skies). These works—together with her second novel, *Viņas bija trīs* (1963, They Were Three Women)—are representative of the influence of SOCIALIST REALISM. They have as their main subject the destinies of people caught in the dramatic events of the war and its aftermath. Standing out already in these early works is a tendency to bring out the psychological dimension of the narrative by emphasizing the subjective side of the characters' experiences. This attention paid to the individual's psyche implied a clear rejection of the officially sanctioned themes of collective destiny and party allegiance. It was a seemingly paradoxical departure from party norms at a time when E. had decided to join the Communist Party. Nevertheless, while she was to remain a member until 1991, the year of Latvia's independence, she consistently avoided the officially sponsored themes and problems in her writing, adopting instead an explicitly democratic and humanistic outlook.

A most important place in E.'s prose is occupied by ethical issues central to a woman's life and destiny. E.'s conceptualization of the role of women was highly innovative in the context of postwar Latvian prose literature. Her female characters neither hold important positions in society nor have dramatic life stories. Their work and occupations are generally de-emphasized in order to bring out the importance of personal experiences and human relations. Yet these ordinary women who people her fictional world with their simple joys and commonplace suffering have also a special attitude toward life. To love, for a woman, as E. shows, means to fully assume the responsibilities of wife, mother, homemaker, and provider—roles that are as important as any a woman might hold. The figure of woman as mother and life-giver appears in numerous variations throughout E.'s oeuvre. These are themes structuring works such as the mosaiclike and meditative *Nakts bez mēnesnīcas* (1971; Moonless Night) and the dramatic love story in her third novel *Aka* (1973; The Well).

The phantasmagoric novel, *Zemdegas* (1977; Underground Fires), is devoted to a study of the human psyche in its subterranean manifestations and represents one of the high points of the author's creativity. Utilizing techniques valorizing the oneiric borrowed from surrealist poets, E. effectively blurs the boundaries separating the real from the unreal, wakefulness from dreams, the past from the present and the actual from the virtual. The effect is to bring out the strangeness of the ordinary, the uniqueness of the individual's psyche, and the relativity of our human potential. The dilemmas of human psychology intensify in the context of family and social relations, as E. shows in *Vartmācība* (1982; Domination), the first volume of her tetralogy entitled *Pati ar savu vēju* (Myself, with My Own Wind). Here, a blind and irrational motherly love turns into a possessive will to dominate others' lives. The second volume, *Nodevība* (Betrayal), examines the subjects of creativity and the writer's mission. It is one of E.'s most markedly autobiographical works, combining documentary evidence with fantasy, the lyrical with the dramatic, and the intimately personal with the socially relevant.

E.'s writing often gives evidence of her special affection for the animals and birds of her native land, for all living creatures—and, in particular, for the dog who is her constant companion. Thus, one of E.'s more original contributions to Latvian literature is the genre of the zoological novel or story. E. believes strongly in a nature in which the human is inseparable from the animal. She therefore stresses the responsibility homo sapiens bear for preserving this all—encompassing environment for all human activities. These are themes developed in such collections as *Cilvēkam vajag suni* (1975; A Human Being Needs a Dog), *Slazds* (1979; The Trap), and *Princeses fenomens* (1985; The Princess Phenomenon). E. is also well known for indulging in a special kind of narrative genre known as her "dullie stāsti" (loony stories), tales written with an expressly ironic or humorous purpose in mind. Lastly she has also written a large number of critiques and review essays over the years—either for publication or for the internal uses of her Press "Liesma." They appear in such anthologies as *Dzīvot uz savas zemes* (1984; To Live in One's Own Land) and *Virtuve bez pavārgrāmatas* (1989; A Kitchen without a Cookbook). These are essays that reveal not only a remarkable aptitude for literary criticism but speak as well of E.'s deeply felt convictions about life and literature.

E.'s literary involvement remained intensive in the 1990s, following Latvia's independence, making her one of the most prominent figures in contemporary Latvian literature. As in her earlier writing, the focus in her most recent publications is on the contradictions of the human psyche and on the experience of its encounter with the world it discloses around itself. Also notable is the elaboration of an increasingly philosophical thought, as well as the polyphonic quality of a narrative that effectively combines dramatic, tragic, and comical narrative strands. Her work has been translated in Russian, Lithuanian, Estonian, German, and other languages.

FURTHER WORKS: *Daugavas stāsti* (1965); *Mežābele* (1966); *Dzilnas sila balāde* (1968); *Aiztek Gaujas ūdeņi, aiztek* (1968); *Saules atspulgs* (1969); *Grieze, trakais putns* (1970); *Pavasara pērkons* (1973); *Vasara bija tikai vienu dienu* (1974); *Baraviku laika dullums* (1978); *Iziase* (1979); *Saulespuķes no pērnās vasaras* (1980); *Visticamāk, ka ne . . .* (1993); *Zvaigžņu, lietus* (1994); *Pūķa ola* (1995); *Varbūt tā nebūs vairs nekad* (1997)

BIBLIOGRAPHY: Mauriņa, M., "R. E.," in *Latvijas PSR Mazi enciklopēdija* (1967), Vol. 1: 491; Poišs, M., "Noklusētā drāma. Ieskats R. E. daiļradē," *Karogs*, 11 (1973): 137-49, 12 (1973): 108-22; Zeile, P., "R. E. prozas pasaulē," *Karogs*, 2 (1979): 133-39, 3 (1979): 145-49; Tabūns, B., *R. E.* (1980); Vite, A., "R. E.," in *Latviešu ralstmoecība biogrāfijās* (1992): 101

—KARLIS RACEVSKIS

F

FADEEV, Alexandr Alexandrovich

Russian novelist and short-story writer, b. 24 Dec. 1901, Kimry; d. 13 May 1956, Moscow

Of peasant origin, F. spent his childhood and was educated in eastern Siberia. He became a member of the Communist Party in 1918, took part in the civil war, and was active as a Party organizer in Siberia and in the Ukraine. He began his literary career as a "proletarian" novelist in the 1920s at the time of the NEP (New Economic Policy). His novels are inspired by Communist ideology and express his faith in and support of the regime.

F.'s first story, "Protiv techenia" (1923; against the current) and his short novel *Razliv* (1924; the flood) were of no special importance, but his next work, *Razgrom* (1927; *The Nineteen*, 1929; also tr. as *The Rout*, 1955), secured for its author a niche in the pantheon of Soviet writers.

During the 1920s, while still displaying a diversity of points of view and varied artistic methods, writers of the Soviet Union all wrote about the revolution. F.'s *Razgrom* became a classic novel on that subject, for it was the story of a small detachment of Red guerrillas fighting in Siberia against the Whites and the Japanese. Its chief protagonist, Commander Levinson, may be taken to represent the perfect Bolshevik, an early "positive hero" of Soviet literature. A minimum of stylization and the psychological verisimilitude of most of the characters in this well-made, distinctly realistic novel show F. to be a follower of Tolstoy's "psychological realism." F.'s Tolstoyan views on "truth-in-art" are contained in a famous 1928 manifesto in which he challenges the doctrine of "factography"—tendentious naturalism and social behaviorism—put forth by adherents of the antipsychological school of Soviet literature in the years 1927–32.

The year 1932 witnessed the creation of the Union of Soviet Writers, with the result that literature became incorporated in the fabric of the state and was subjected to far more thorough controls than before. The literary doctrine known as SOCIALIST REALISM became the only block on which all subsequent Soviet literature was to be built. The early works of F., the supporter of realism in literature and a convinced Communist, predate the actual formulation of Socialist Realism as a doctrine and paved the way for its adoption.

F.'s unfinished novel *Posledny iz Udege* (4 vols., 1929–40; the last of the Udeges) was conceived as a large-scale work dealing with a multitude of characters and a complex idea. The ideal revolutionary, Langovoy, emerges in the novel as the ubiquitous "positive hero" of Socialist Realism, while one of the book's themes deals with the "rehabilitation" of the Udeges—a primitive Siberian tribe—and their incorporation into the collective farm system. F. knew that his capabilities as a writer did not measure up to the complexity of the task, and although it was heralded by the critics as a true work of Socialist Realism, he realized that the novel was not a successful one.

When first published, F.'s *Molodaya gvardia* (1945; *The Young Guard*, 1959) won great critical praise. But two years later, during a period of political and literary reaction, it was denounced for "serious ideological and artistic errors of the writer." In order to conform to the official doctrine, F. was forced to revise his highly popular novel of anti-German resistance fighting among teenagers in Krasnodon. The "corrected" version was published in 1951.

For many years F. had been a high Party functionary—a member of the Central Committee of the Communist Party as well as the powerful and power-hungry secretary general of the Union of Soviet Writers, but the beginning of the de-Stalinization period brought about his downfall. The dictatorial power held by F. the bureaucrat over Soviet letters was denounced in 1956 by Mikhail SHOLOKHOV in a strongly worded speech to the Twentieth Congress of the Communist Party at the height of the "thaw." By then a victim of alcoholism, unable to write a good story, and suspected of having taken part in Stalin's political purges, F. ended his life by suicide.

FURTHER WORKS: *Stolbovaya doroga proletarskoy literatury* (1929); *Partizanskie povesti* (1938); *Literatura i zhizn* (1939); *Leningrad v dni blokady* (1944; *Leningrad in the Days of the Blockade*, 1945); *Chyornaya metallurgia* [chapters from unfinished novel] (1954); *Za tridtsat let* (1957); *Sobranie sochineny* (7 vols., 1969–1971)

BIBLIOGRAPHY: Reavey, G., *Soviet Literature Today* (1947): 82–84; Swayze, H., *Political Control of Literature in the USSR, 1946–1959* (1962), passim; Brown, E. J., *Russian Literature since the Revolution* (1963): 163, 172–79, 216; Brown, E. J., *The Proletarian Episode in Russian Literature, 1928–1932* (1971), passim; Struve, G., *Russian Literature under Lenin and Stalin, 1917–1953* (1971): 134–37, 217–18, 319–20, 332, 354–55; Slonim, M., *Soviet Russian Literature: Writers and Problems, 1917–1967* (1973): 174–79, 287, 299–300; Mathewson, R. W., Jr., *The Positive Hero in Russian Literature* (1975): 191–200, 213–15

—NADJA JERNAKOFF

FAIZ, Faiz Ahmed

(pseud. of Faiz Ahmed) Pakistani poet (writing in Urdu), b. 1912?, Sialkot (then in India); d. 20 Nov. 1984, Lahore

F.'s family were well-to-do landowners, his father a prominent English-educated lawyer. F. received his education at mission schools in Sialkot in the English language and later earned M.A. degrees in both English and Arabic literatures from Punjab University, Lahore. He came under the influence of the Marxist-oriented Progressive Movement in the late 1930s.

When the Islamic Republic of Pakistan was established in 1947, F. was serving as editor of the leftist English-language daily, the *Pakistan Times*, and as managing editor of the Urdu daily *Imroz*. He was also actively involved in organizing trade unions. In 1951 he and a number of army officers were implicated in the so-called Rawalpindi Conspiracy Case in which the government of Pakistan alleged that the accused were planning a coup d'état. Under sentence of death for several years, F. was quietly released from prison in 1955. In 1962 he received the Soviet Lenin Peace Prize and since then has been active in various Pakistani arts and literary organizations. In recent years he has lent his considerable support to a movement among some of the regional languages of Pakistan, notably Punjabi, Sindhi, Balochi, and Pashto, to gain recognition as legitimate vehicles for public instruction, government, the media, and literary expression. In this connection F. has composed some poems in Punjabi, his first language.

F.'s reputation as the foremost Urdu poet since Muhammad IQBAL rests on four slender volumes: *Naqsh-e faryadi* (1943; image of complaint), which drew considerable critical attention because of the author's blend of traditional meters and imagery with nationalist and leftist sentiments; *Dast-e saba* (1952; hand of the wind), and *Zindan namah* (1956; prison narrative), in which he meticulously chronicles his prison experiences in some of his most famous poems; and *Dast-e tah-e sang* (1965; hand beneath the stone), where he reflects upon his extensive travels abroad and his aspirations for a better world.

F.'s poetry is highly introspective and symbolic, yet markedly positive in outlook. He has infused traditional romantic imagery with new meaning, usually tinged with political overtones. For example, in premodern love poetry the poet (lover) and his rival vie for the affection of the cruel and indifferent beloved. In his famous poem "Raqib se" (1943; "To the Rival," 1971) F. asks the rival to join him in putting aside their differences and to work together to overcome the country's enemies. Similarly, in "Mujh se pahli si mahabbat, meri mahbub na mang" (1943; "Do Not Ask Me, My Beloved, Love Like That Former One," 1971) F. indicates to the beloved that he can no longer offer her the kind of love she has enjoyed in the past; he is now preoccupied with the more important issues of human exploitation and suffering.

F. is perhaps the only contemporary Urdu poet to write both political verse and love poetry of a consistently high quality. He is regarded in Pakistan as that country's unofficial poet laureate and is held in equal esteem by Urdu speakers of India.

FURTHER WORKS: *Mizan* (1964); *Harf harf* (1965); *Sar-e vadi-ye sina* (1971); *Rat di rat* (1975); *Sham-e shahri-yaran* (1978); *Mere dil, mere musafir* (1980). FURTHER WORKS IN ENGLISH: *Poems of F.* (1971)

BIBLIOGRAPHY: Ali, M., "The Poetry of F.," *PakR*, 12 (1964): 5–8; Faiz, A., "F.: A Personality Sketch," *JSoAL*, 10, 1 (1974): 123–30; [Jones, A., and Coppola, C.], "Interview with F.," *JSoAL*, 10, 1 (1974): 141–44; Malik, M., "The Pakistan Poet: F.," *LAAW*, 22 (1974): 36–41; Narang, G., "Tradition and Innovation in Urdu Poetry," in *Poetry and Renaissance: Kumaran Asan Birth Centenary Volume* (1974): 415–34; Lall, I. J., "F.: Poet with Vitality," *IndL*, 18, 4 (1975): 58–62

—CARLO COPPOLA

FALKBERGET, Johan

Norwegian novelist and short-story writer, b. 30 Sept. 1879, Rugeldalen; d. 5 April 1967, Rugeldalen

F. grew up in a copper-mining community near Røros and worked in the mines from age eight to twenty-seven. From 1907 on he made his living as journalist, editor, and writer, mainly in the Oslo region, before settling on the family farm in Rugeldalen (1922), where he lived until his death. From 1930 to 1933 he was member of the Norwegian parliament representing the Labor Party.

F.'s first novels were cast in the semiromantic mold of Bjørnstjerne Bjørnson's (1832–1910) peasant tales, but with *Svarte Fjelde* (1907; black mountains) he introduced the mining community, a setting he used in almost all his later novels, into Norwegian literature. The notable exceptions are *Lisbeth på Jarnfjeld* (1915; *Lisbeth of Jarnfjeld*, 1930), a grim psychological study of a marriage, set in a mountain community in 19th-c. Norway, and *Brændoffer* (1917; burnt offering), an equally grim study of human degradation with the advance of urbanization. Set in the early part of the 20th c., this novel depicts how the protagonist and his family move from rural Norway into Christiania (now Oslo) and succumb to boundless physical and spiritual poverty.

In his early years F. was strongly influenced by utopian socialist thought, and his lifelong commitment to the labor movement was marked by his Christian humanistic ethics. He never accepted the dogmas of Marxism, but the despair depicted in *Brændoffer* could not be overcome within his traditional ethical framework, a fact that undoubtedly contributed to his exclusive interest in historical fiction from 1920 on. F.'s concern with new themes is evident in his first great novel, *Den fjerde nattevakt* (1923; *The Fourth Night Watch*, 1968), in which the power of erotic love—a motif in several earlier novels as well—is put within a Christian ethical framework. The newly arrived parish minister falls madly in love with a young married woman of his congregation, and the ensuing struggle between the laws of Christian ethics and the conscience, on the one hand, and the power of *eros*, on the other, is portrayed with great narrative and psychological force. The novel is set in Røros in the early part of the 19th c., and is faithful to the historical setting, but it is in essence a modern psychological novel in which the historical setting serves as background only.

His next work, the trilogy *Christianus Sextus* (1927–35; Christian VI [the title refers to the name of a copper mine]), is considered his best novel by many critics. It portrays the Røros community in the 1720s and combines intimate knowledge of historical details with epic force and psychological and historical insight. *Christianus Sextus* has been referred to as a collective novel: the entire copper-mining community, in a sense, is the center of the narrative. Not one, but many, persons arise from the shadows of history and give life to the novel. It contains one of the most moving portrayals of a child in Norwegian literature—the story of the little Gølin—but also portrayals of the grim fight for survival, against starvation, mining accidents, and madness.

F.'s last great novel is the tetralogy *Nattens brød* (1940–59; bread of night), which depicts life in the community surrounding one of the smelters thirty miles north of the Røros mines during the latter half of the 17th c. Again F. has made every effort to depict accurately the historical setting: the harsh poverty and brutality of a society being devastated by the uncontrolled advance of industrialization and market economics. But more clearly than before the reader sees F.'s defense of humanistic values—of love, tolerance, and compassion—and of the Protestant ethic: honesty, hard work, and the fear of God. An-Magritt, the young woman protagonist, represents the quintessence of F.'s view of life. She is physically strong and conquers all in her relentless struggle to improve the living conditions of herself and her fellow human beings. She is filled with an unyielding belief in the goodness of man, and borders on being an allegorical figure in her almost super-natural achievements.

Although espousing a strongly traditional view of life, F.'s main works are imbued with a poetic force and a mythic quality that continue to fascinate new readers. He remains one of the pivotal figures in 20th-c. Norwegian literature.

FURTHER WORKS: *Mineskud* (1908); *Ved den evige sne* (1908); *Fakkelbrand* (1909); *Urtidsnat* (1909); *Vargfjeldet* (1910); *Nord i haugene: Eventyr* (1910); *Fimbulvinter* (1911); *En finnejentes kjærlighetshistorie* (1912); *Eli Sjursdotter* (1913); *Jutul-historier* (1913); *Av jarleætt* (1914); *Eventyrfjeld: Historier for barn* (1916); *Helleristninger* (1916); *Sol* (1918); *Barkebrødstider* (1919); *Bjørne-Skyttern* (1919); *Vidden* (1919); *Bør Børson Jr.* (1920); *Byd lykken hånden; eller, Da Johannes Mo løste rebusen* (1920); *Naglerne; eller, Jernet fra Norden* (1921); *I nordenvindens land* (1924); *Vers fra Rugelsjøen* (1925); *Den nye Bør Børson* (1927); *Det høie fjeld* (1928); *Solfrid i Bjørnstu og de syv svende* (1928); *Runer på fjeldveggen: Sagn og fortellinger* (1944); *Jeg så dem* (1963)

BIBLIOGRAPHY: Falkberget, J., "Røros: The Copper Town of Norway," *ASR*, 13 (1925): 412–21; Freding, T., "J. F.," *ASR*, 21 (1933): 401–6; Beck, R., "J. F.," *SS*, 16 (1941): 304–16; Beck, R., "J. F.: A Great Social Novelist," *ASR*, 38 (1950): 248–51; Kojen, J., "Grand Old Man of Literature: J. F.," *Norseman*, No. 6 (1962): 10–13; Popperwell, R. G., Introduction to *The Fourth Night Watch* (1968): vii–xviii; Raastad, O., "J. F.: An Appreciation," *ASR*, 58 (1970): 154–56

—KJETIL A. FLATIN

FANGEN, Ronald

Norwegian novelist, dramatist, and essayist, b. 29 April 1895, Kragerø; d. 22 May 1946, Fornebu

F. was the son of a Norwegian mining engineer and his English wife. Raised in Bergen by two aunts after his parents' early divorce, he compensated for his loneliness as a sickly child prodigy who was rather bored with school by voracious solitary reading. At thirteen he published his first critical essay, at fifteen his first poem, both in a Bergen daily. From 1913 on F. engaged in prolific journalistic activities as a reviewer for various newspapers and as editor of literary magazines.

F. was a key figure in Norwegian cultural life during the interwar period. With his intellectual depth, moral fervor, and religious disposition, he became a tireless champion of Christian humanism not only in *Vor verden*, the journal he founded and edited from 1923 to 1930, but also in most of his belletristic writings.

F.'s early plays, *Syndefald* (1920; the fall), *Fienden* (1922; the enemy), and *Den forjættede dag* (1926; the promised day), generated hopes that he would renew the Norwegian drama. The form of his first two plays was influenced by the late works of STRINDBERG and by German EXPRESSIONISM, their themes by Nietzsche; the third is more realistic, and its theme of illusion is Ibsenesque. But in the late 1920s F. returned to fiction, which he had earlier, but not especially successfully, essayed.

Several of F.'s later novels are remarkably good. With Nietzsche yielding to FREUD and Alfred Adler (1870–1937), and German expressionism to the discussion technique of Aldous HUXLEY, F. develops an effective instrument for probing beneath the surfaces of bourgeois culture and personality. At his best, in *Duel* (1932; *Duel*, 1934), *En kvinnes vei* (1933; a woman's way), and *Mannen som elsket rettferdigheten* (1934; the man who loved justice), discussion is less important than reflection and retrospective rumination. Their routine existences shattered by some untoward event, F.'s characters undertake a ruthless self-scrutiny, the result of which is either Christian conversion or disaster, often in the form of suicide. The action occurring chiefly in the characters' minds, the plot consists of the progressive unveiling of the layers of deception that sustain their functional personalities—self-deceptions ingrained by habit, vanity, the power drive, and false philosophy. *Duel*, widely translated, has been F.'s most popular book, but *Mannen som elsket rettferdigheten*, a Norwegian *Michael Kohlhaas* (by Heinrich von Kleist, 1777–1811) or Book of Job, is artistically superior. In this work, theme, setting, characterization, and style are perfectly blended—a rare occurrence in F.'s novels.

After his conversion to Frank Buchman's (1878–1961) Oxford Group movement in 1934, F.'s social consciousness increased, but the quality of his writing deteriorated. In *På bar bunn* (1936; on rock bottom) and *Allerede nu* (1937; already now), the form changed from individual to group novel, better suited to F.'s Christian message. Here plot is superseded by a largely spatial structure of juxtaposed "case histories" presenting representative intellectuals whose painful life experiences lead them inexorably to religious conversion. *Møllen som maler langsomt* (the mill that grinds slowly), a planned trilogy of which only one volume, *Borgerfesten* (1939; civic festival), was finished, is set in the 1880s and 1890s; yet F.'s concern is still with *Weltanschauung*, specifically the characters' religious development.

En lysets engel (1945; *Both Are My Cousins*, 1949), F.'s last novel before his death in an airplane crash, investigates the roots of Nazism by counterpointing the divergent spiritual evolution of two cousins before and during the German occupation of Norway. Nazism and other subjects are also illuminatingly analyzed in F.'s many collections of essays.

F.'s literary affinities range from Dostoevskian psychology to the balanced humanism of Thomas MANN; his religious-philosophical thought is polarized between Nietzschean moral nihilism and Christian personalism. While some of his contemporaries showed greater narrative talent and stylistic flair, F. surpassed most of them by the spiritual passion with which he pursued themes similar to theirs: the disguises and perversions of love, the dark labyrinth of power, the elusiveness of personal identity. A true European by his broad literary and intellectual culture, F. brought to these themes the new knowledge of psychoanalysis as well as the accumulated wisdom of the Christian tradition. This combination invests his novels with an abiding interest.

FURTHER WORKS: *De svake* (1915); *Slægt føder slægt* (1916); *En roman* (1918); *Krise* (1919); *Streiftog i digtning og tænkning* (1919); *Tegn og gjærninger* (1927); *Nogen unge mennesker* (1929); *Erik* (1931); *Dagen og veien* (1934); *Det nye liv* (1934); *En kristen verdensrevolusjon* (1935); *Som det kunde ha gått* (1935); *Paulus og vår egen tid* (1936); *Kristen enhet* (1937); *Kristendommen og vår tid* (1938); *Krig og kristen tro* (1940); *Presten* (1946); *Nåderiket* (1947); *Om frihet, og andre essays* (1947); *Samlede verker* (9 vols., 1948–1949); *Essays* (1965); *I nazistenes fengsel* (1975)

BIBLIOGRAPHY: Strauss, H., on *Duel*, *NYTBR* (17 June 1934): 8; Plomer, W., on *Duel*, *Spectator* (22 June 1934): 978; Quennell, P., on *Duel*, *TLS* (28 June 1934): 458; Beyer, H., *A History of Norwegian Literature* (1956): 321–22; Govig, S. D., "R. F.: A Christian Humanist," *ASR*, 49 (1961): 152–59; Friese, W., *Nordische Literaturen im 20. Jahrhundert* (1971): 171–73

—SVERRE LYNGSTAD

FAQIRI, Amin

Iranian short-story writer, b. 21 Dec. 1944, Shiraz, Iran

Born to a family of scholars and intellectuals, F. is a native of the Fars province. His formal education at the Nemazi Technical Institute gave way to literary studies for which he had had a penchant since childhood. His writing career began as a poet, writing romantic pieces in praise of nature, love, and loyalty. These poems, however, remained in manuscript form; some were enjoyed by a circle of close friends. Then F.'s brother, a short-story writer, folklorist, and radio personality, arranged for one of his stories to appear in a local newspaper. The publication led to a lasting commitment by F. to pursuing a literary career. After graduation in the early 1960s F. joined the Education Corps in a remote village in southeastern Iran. As an exemplary educated Iranian, he was expected to teach, impress, and influence the villagers, and persuade them to transfer their loyalties from the village head to the central administration and the Shah. For two years F. dealt with perennial rural problems like water distribution squabbles, pairing of workers for plowing the fields, improving the villagers' health, and communicating village needs to government authorities in Jiroft and Kerman.

The everyday life of the village fascinated F. and the tangible social, political, and economic upheavals that led to the great dislocation of the peasantry from its traditional home became the staple of his stories. The ills he witnessed, he felt, were rooted in the exploitative programs installed in Iran at the behest of powers greater than either the Shah or the Tehran technocrats. To expose the system in a credible manner, F. devised tangible characters, appropriate settings, and well-defined story lines. He then allowed social developments to assume the steering role. "Ab" (1967; Water) and "Hammam" (1968; The Bathhouse) illustrate his unique brand of realist fiction. In "Ab" a bureaucrat unaware that rice seedlings must be planted in water on a certain day of the year decides to punish the villagers on that day by depriving them of water. In the process, unwittingly, he also deprives them of their rice crop for the coming year. In "Hammam" a greedy mullah takes it upon himself to build the village a new bathhouse. In the process it becomes known that the "descendant of the Prophet" had been bilking the villagers and the provincial government for the ever-increasing expenses of the bathhouse.

F. became so engrossed in the lives of his village charges that he forgot his original mandate of bringing the villagers into the Shah's fold. Instead, the exposition of the exploitative measures of the system became his foremost concern. A dedicated short-story writer, he thought, should present his reader with not only a story line but also a document which can speak to posterity.

F. observed the events in the village carefully, documented linguistic idiosyncrasies, and studied character traits. He took special delight in picking up on the villagers petty squabbles. Their language, he reports, was at once rich, poetic, and fresh. He also examined the villagers' reactions to each other, to himself as a governmental official, and to other governmental officials who, since the inauguration of the "White Revolution" in 1963, had flooded the villages. To present a balanced view of the interaction he recorded the villagers' fear and secret hatred of the officials as well as the officials' determination to impose tested urban means of intimidation and coercion on the villagers.

Each of F.'s stories captures a "moment of transition" in the lives of its major characters. In "Aqaye Saberi" (1967; Mr. Saberi),

for instance, the theme of xenophobia is explored, while "Abi va Ishq-i U" (1967; Blue and Her Love) delves into the most secret recesses of village mentality. "Tars" (1969; Fear) is a delightful story that turns dark and awesome when age-old superstition enters the picture. "Dihkada-i Purmalal" (1965; The Doleful Village) investigates the drawbacks of introducing new technologies among uneducated indigenous people. In the story a child dies simply because the family is not familiar with the toxic nature of pesticides. Ironically, it was the publication of this story in *Ferdowsi* that brought F. to the attention of the country's major critics and writers.

F.'s style is poetic in fluidity, colloquial in delivery, and direct in transferring information. He succeeded in conveying the speeches and thoughts of his characters in their regional vernacular. This use of language, in addition to giving an authentic flavor to the stories, separated F. from the "Weststruck" language of the so-called urban writers. Furthermore, F.'s collections revived interest in the works of Jalal al-e ahmad, Samad Behrangi (1939-1968), and Gholam Hossein sa'edi, authors who had already explored the themes of Iranian village life.

For centuries Persian literature had been the domain of the poets and literary historians who dwelled primarily in the cities and wrote for the courts. When a transition was made into the fiction genre early in the 20th c., the urban aspect and the patronage system for the creation and dissemination of stories remained intact. By writing about rural Iran, especially through the eyes of a realist and a socialist, F. is credited with adding a new, and lasting, dimension to Persian fiction.

FURTHER WORKS: *Kucheh Baghha-i Izterab* (1970); *Kufiyan* (1971); *Qamha-i Kuchek* (1973); *Du Chashm-i Kuchak-i Khandan* (1975)

BIBLIOGRAPHY: Faqiri, A., *Dihkada-i Purmalal* (1969); Dastgheyb, A. A., "F.'s Fiction," *Ferdowsi*, 929 (1970); Qa'id, M., "F.," *Negin*, 50 (1970); Pahlavan, 'Abbas, "Dihkada-i Purmalal," *Ferdowsi* (1971); Green, J., *Iranian Short Story Writers: A Bio-Bibliographic Survey* (1989)

—IRAJ BASHIRI

FARAH, Nuruddin

Somali novelist (writing in English and Somali), b. 24 Nov. 1945, Baidoa

Although F. came to English as a fourth language, his reputation as a writer rests on the novels he has written in English. After studying literature in India at the University of Chandigarh, F. returned to Somalia and taught in Mogadisho, then lived in England for a time; he now resides in Rome. Besides his English-language work, he has also written a novel, plays, and short stories in Somali, and has translated children's stories from Arabic, Italian, French, and English into Somali.

F.'s novels are set in 20th-c. Somalia, with most of the action occurring in the capital, Mogadisho. In *From a Crooked Rib* (1970) Mogadisho becomes the home of Ebla, a nomad girl who flees her family's camp because she has been promised in marriage to an old man. Her pilgrimage from desert to small town and eventually on to the capital teaches her to exploit men as they exploit her. Ebla is inquiring and analytical; in rejecting the traditional role of the Somali woman, she becomes her own person, with a thoroughly existential attitude. The book is a sociological novel and a novel of character, and realistically portrays some grim realities of Somali life.

A Naked Needle (1976) possesses more breadth and depth, is more cosmopolitan, and is also technically more complex. Written in the present tense, its tone is reminiscent of Wole SOYINKA's *The Interpreters*, the favorite novel of F.'s protagonist, Koschin. Koschin, a Mogadisho teacher, while studying overseas had promised to marry an English girl who now, two years later, arrives in Somalia expecting him to keep his promise. A potential situation comedy becomes in F.'s hands an unsettling novel on the sordidness of mid-1970s Somalia. Koschin, like Ebla, is a complex character who reveals himself as he filters his experiences through his consciousness and internally expresses his attitudes toward them.

F.'s most recent novel, *Sweet and Sour Milk* (1979), received the English-Speaking Union Literary Award. The book explores even further the almost unrelieved grimness of Somali life. This time the all-powerful state's license to arrest, imprison without trial, and torture are sharply focused upon. Loyaan's search for the facts behind the sudden death of his twin brother Soyaan, an economic adviser to Somalia's president, is undertaken in an aura of sheer political terror mitigated only by F.'s constraint and his skillful use of interior monologue—a skill already developed in *A Naked Needle*.

F. has a keen eye for physical and psychological details. His use of English is mature, possessing a colloquial flavor that happily blends with an increasingly cosmopolitan stance that retains its authentically Somali subject matter. He is not a self-consciously African writer, but makes the novel form his own, creating an effective bond between mythic and local references and those aspects of his message that have far-reaching human significance.

FURTHER WORKS: *Close Sesame* (1983); *Maps* (1986); *Sweet & Sour Milk* (1992); *Sardines* (1992)

BIBLIOGRAPHY: Beer, D., "Somali Literature in European Languages," *Horn of Africa*, 2, 4 (1979): 27–35; Cochrane, J., "The Theme of Sacrifice in the Novels of N. F.," *WLWE*, 18 (1979): 69–77; Okomilo, I., on *Sweet and Sour Milk, Africa*, No. 101 (1980): 72–73; Imfeld, A., and G. Meuer, "N. F.: A Modern Nomad," *Afrika* (Munich), 21, 9 (1980): 23–25; Wright, D., *The Novels of N. F.* (1994)

—DAVID F. BEER

FARAJ, Alfred

Egyptian dramatist, b. 1929, Alexandria

F. is one of the most prominent of a group of Egyptian dramatists who established a reputation for themselves during the period between the Egyptian revolution of 1952 and the 1967 June War. Born and educated in Alexandria, F. was much influenced by the work of Tawfīq AL-HAKĪM, the great pioneer of modern Arabic drama. F. served as a drama critic for the weekly journal *Rūz al-Yūsuf* and in 1966 accepted a position as adviser to the Egyptian Theatre Administration. By that time, he had established a reputation as a dramatist of great gifts who could compose plays of considerable dramatic impact that made use of the national heritage

to illustrate the issues confronting the emerging postrevolutionary society in Egypt and, by extension, throughout the Arab world.

F.'s first published play was *Suqūt Fir' awn* (1955; fall of the pharaoh), a work that explores the dilemma of the Egyptian Pharaoh Akhenaton, a ruler who is by personal inclination devoted to peace but whose status as ruler requires that he declare war; he resolves the issue by stepping down from power. During the uncertainties of the initial years of the Egyptian revolution and the rise to power of Jamāl 'Abd al-Nāsir (Gamal Abdel Nasser), the possibilities of a more contemporary interpretation of the play's import were not lost on the Egyptian public, turning it into a political and critical cause célèbre. Leaving aside *Sawt Misr* (1956; the voice of Egypt), a rather ephemeral and strident piece celebrating Egypt's role in the Suez invasion of 1956, F. composed another play that derived its context from Egyptian history, *Sulaymān al-Halabī* (1964; Sulayman from Aleppo). Here the historical event in question is more recent, Napoleon's invasion of Egypt in 1798 and in particular the assassination of General Kléber by a Syrian student attending the Al-Azhar mosque-university in Cairo. The play is couched in Brechtian terms, with a chorus and a series of rapidly moving scenes; contemporary accounts of the production of the play make it clear that a good deal of the credit for its popular acclaim belonged to the producer who succeeded in staging such a complicated piece of theater in a convincing and appealing fashion.

Another source of inspiration that F. has utilized in several plays is that of tales culled from the tradition of popular Arabic narrative. One of his most successful comedies, *Hallāq Baghdād* (1963; the barber of Baghdad), makes use of the primary figure of a nosey barber, Abū al-Fudūl, to combine two traditional tales—one culled from *A Thousand and One Nights*, the other from a collection of tales attributed to the famous litterateur al-Jāhiz (d. 869)—in a humorous concoction of stock characters and situations. Less overtly humorous perhaps but more accomplished as contributions to drama in Arabic are *Al-Zīr Sālim* (1967; Prince Sālim) and *'Alī Janāh al-Tabrīzī wa tābi' uhu Quffa* (1968; 'Alī Janāh from Tabrīz and his henchman, Quffa). Similar to *Sulaymān al-Halabī*, these two plays also make use of many of the distancing devices associated with Brechtian theatrical techniques. In *Al-Zīr Sālim* the tale is culled from the pre-Islamic period, as a ruler endeavors to break out of a cycle of blood vengeance between two tribes. *'Alī Janāh al-Tabrīzī* is, like *Hallāq Baghdād*, inspired by tales from *A Thousand and One Nights*, most particularly the elaborate trick of the delayed caravan with fabled riches: The anticipation of profits from its wealth of goods and the promissory notes exchanged before its arrival cause the economy of an entire kingdom to collapse. In this piece the interplay of illusion and reality is explored in a comedy that transfers most successfully to the stage.

Although F. wrote some of his plays in the colloquial dialect, such as *'Askar wa-haramiyya* (1966; cops and robbers)—a rather facile exploration of opportunism in a socialist society—a major contribution that he has made to the development of modern Arabic drama has been in using the standard written language as a dramatic medium. He has been particularly concerned that his plays and, by extension, those of other dramatists composing in the Arab world, should be exportable from one Arab nation to another. He has therefore remained an advocate of the use of the literary level of the Arabic language—the only common means of communication among different dialect areas—as the discourse of dramatic dialogue during a period when many critics and writers, such as the great Egyptian critic Lewis 'Awad (1915–1991), have been vociferously advocating the use of the colloquial as a requirement for a lively and authentic tradition of drama. In F.'s own case, the dialogue in his plays has been composed with the greatest artistry, providing the model for a lucid dramatic style that few other writers of drama have been able to match.

FURTHER WORKS: *Buqbuq al-kaslān, Al-Fakhkh* (1965); *Bi-al-ijmā't wāhid* (1965)

BIBLIOGRAPHY: Allen, R., "Egyptian Drama after the Revolution," *Edebiyat*, 4, 1 (1979): 97–134; Allen, R., ed., *Modern Arabic Literature* (1987): 92–96; Badawi, M. M., *Modern Arabic Drama in Egypt* (1987): 171–82

—ROGER ALLEN

FARGUE, Léon-Paul

French poet and columnist, b. 4 March 1876, Paris; d. 24 Nov. 1947, Paris

As an adolescent, F. made friends in the arts, then dominated by SYMBOLISM and impressionism. Later, in spite of his modest middle-class background and his idiosyncrasies, such as chronic lateness to appointments and absent-mindedness, his intimates included leading French and foreign writers, painters and musicians. His company was sought after in the most elegant salons for his conversation, which was fantastically rich in word and image. His brilliant success in oral improvisation meant that he was not very interested in publishing. All his life F. lived in Paris; he knew the city intimately enough to earn the sobriquet the "Paris stroller," a name he himself used as the title of one of his collections of prose poems, *Le piéton de Paris* (1939).

In spite of F.'s many friends, one of his leitmotifs is loneliness—a mood suggested in his first poems, which were published in the journal *L'art littéraire* (1893). This theme becomes obvious in *Tancrède* (Tancred), published in the review *Pan* (Berlin, 1895); this was the first text he later acknowledged by allowing his friend Valery LARBAUD to publish it privately (1911; republished commercially in 1943). It is a group of overrefined and affected—in a word, *précieux*—poems, in prose or verse, somewhat inspired by Rimbaud.

Ten other prose poems printed privately as *Poème, premier cahier* (1907; poem, first note-book) were to become the nucleus of his first important work, *Poèmes* (1912, 1919, 1931, 1944, 1947 [painstakingly revised each time]; poems). Some of these prose poems, rich in music, imagery, and emotion, are highly lyrical: outstanding and universal are those expressing his despair at the death of his father (1909), who was disappointed by his son's apparent failure. Other themes include separation, nostalgia, absence of loved ones, and unrequited love.

Most of his long prose poems of the 1920s appearing in *Commerce* (of which he was coeditor from 1924 to 1930 with Paul VALÉRY and Larbaud), *Mesures, Mercure de France, Nouvelle revue française, and transition* were published in four books with significant titles: *Banalité* (1928; banality), which takes daily life as its inspiration; *Vulturne* (1928; title, an invented word, untranslatable), which contains fantastic visions comparable to those of the painters Hieronymus Bosch and Odilon Redon;

Épaisseurs (1928; densities), through which his images rise to the surface; and *Suite familière* (1929; familiar suite), which contains his poetic theory. Later collections, *Haute solitude* (1941; high solitude) and *Refuges* (1942; refuges), show his sensitivity to his surroundings in language filled with unusual metaphors and inventive Rabelaisian vocabulary. A stroke he suffered in 1943 gave him illness as an added theme in *Méandres* (1946; meanders).

Financial need forced F. to become a columnist (1930–47); in hundreds of articles, sometimes reprinted in various publications, he re-created his ramblings throughout Paris and wrote about other memories. Lacking the quality of his poetry, these pieces were nevertheless published in a dozen books.

His poems, continually revised in his endless search for perfection, are the true basis of his fame, for they reveal the dazzling inventiveness in word and image of the lyrical creative artist.

FURTHER WORKS: *Pour la musique* (1914); *Ludions* (1930); *D'après Paris* (1931); *Déjeuners de Soleil* (1942); *Lanterne magique* (1944; *The Magic Lantern*, 1946); *Contes fantastiques* (1944); *Composite* (1944, with André Beucler); *Une saison en astrologie* (1945); *Les quat' saisons* (1947); *Portraits de famille* (1947); *Les grandes heures du Louvre* (1948); *Etc.* (1949); *Les XX arrondissements de Paris* (1952); *Pour la peinture* (1955); *Au temps de Paris* (1964); *Correspondance L.-P. F.—Valery Larbaud* (1971)

BIBLIOGRAPHY: special F. issue, *Les feuilles libres*: Nos. 45–46 (1927); Chonez, C., *L.-P. F.* (1950); Beucler, A., *The Last of the Bohemians: Twenty Years with L.-P. F.* (1954); La Rochefoucauld, E. de F. de, *L.-P. F.* (1959); Schub, L. R., *L.-P. F.* (1973)

—LOUISE RYPKO SCHUB

FARIA, Almeida

Portuguese novelist, b. 6 May 1943, Montemoro-Novo, Alentejo

F.'s fiction delves into the origins of the cultural and philosophical stagnancy of the Portuguese mentality in modern times. Raised in the rural Alentejo province, he studied law and philosophy at the University of Lisbon. He became the first president of the Portuguese P.E.N. Club (1978–1988), which had been prohibited under the Salazar-Caetano dictatorship. F. is currently a professor of aesthetics and philosophy at the New University of Lisbon.

F.'s artistic concern is the substance and image of the written word. As he reformulates earlier novelistic structures, such as the epistolary novel and memoirs, or artistic devices, such as the parody, his fiction pursues a philosophical debate on the ethics of existence in the Portuguese context.

F.'s first novel, *Rumor branco* (1962; white noise), published when he was nineteen, was awarded the Portuguese Society of Writers Award (1962) for a first work of fiction. Its content, style, and use of language, directly influenced by the "new novel" then in vogue, was seen as a challenge to the neorealist fiction that had dominated Portuguese prose since the end of World War II.

Four of his novels form the "Lusitanian Tetralogy": *A paixão* (1965; the passion); *Cortes* (1978; cuttings); *Lusitânia* (1980; Lusitania); and *Cavaleiro andante* (1982; knight errant). The series traces the lives of a tradition-laden family of land-holders from the years of the Salazar-Caetano dictatorship through the Portuguese revolution of 1974 and into the postrevolutionary period.

Cortes, written just before the 1974 revolution, which overthrew the Salazar-Caetano dictatorship, views the continuing decadence of the family through telescopic, almost slidelike projections that mix dream and reality within a twenty-four hour period just weeks before the revolution. These flashes are often sarcastic, subtle puns or broad parodies of the classics of Portuguese letters, Portuguese laws, and popular slogans.

Lusitânia launches us into the immediate prerevolutionary period and through the first turbulent year of democracy. The novel's epigraph is from the illustrious Portuguese 19th-c. novelist Eça de Queiroz's (1845–1900) *O crime do Padre Amaro* (1876; *The Sin of Father Amaro*, 1963); it evokes the heavy burden of the past glories (explorations, conquests, colonies), which Eça and his generation (and F.) view as having led to the total stagnation of the nation in modern times. The author rhetorically questions: Is it possible that a nation can eternally live in its supposed past glories in the present? Can the Portuguese "condition" be corrected or reformed? Is there, indeed, a national future? F. uses a parody of the epistolary novel as the structure for this fiction. His characters are located in Venice, Luanda, Angola, and Lisbon and offer multiple points of view about the events. The author textually subverts the national "classics," from Gil Vicente (c. 1465–1536) to Marcelo Caetano (1906–1980), as a form of protest against the weight of this past.

F.'s most recent novel (and his contribution to the ongoing debate) is *O conquistador* (1990; the conqueror). The "conqueror" is a modern-day King Sebastião—quite a radical and polemical one—who has both a natural and (as befits a true descendant of Portuguese mythology) a supernatural birth in 1954. In seven symbolic and ironic chapters, highlighted with drawings by the late Portuguese artist Mário Botas, Sebastião narrates his life—up to 1978—in the form of a memoir, a quasi-bildungsroman. He has inherited some physical characteristics of the earlier Sebastião, but primarily he, like his 16th-c. ancestor, is preoccupied with conquests—which in this case are sexual rather than territorial. His world is one of unending marvels, nightmares, and phantasmagoric games in which myths turn into eternal sensual realities. His "real" life is a comic battle against ingrained Portuguese superstitions and prejudices. By the time he is twenty-four, he withdraws from the natural Portuguese reality to become an emotional expatriate in a state of self-analysis.

Here, as well as in his earlier works, F. weaves a devilish, black comedy of subtle double entendres on philosophical, linguistic, and ideological levels. The fluid, dreamlike atmosphere of this novel and earlier ones is surely a direct reflection of F.'s view of Portuguese existence since the 16th c.: The national inability to resolve the historical dilemma has left Portugal and her people afloat. F.'s grand novels are a biting commentary on this continuing dilemma.

FURTHER WORKS: *Os passeios do sonhador solitário* (1982)

BIBLIOGRAPHY: Listopad, J., "A paixão," *BA*, 41, 4 (1967 Autumn), 198; Stern, I., "Redefining Identity: Uses of Language in Recent Portuguese Fiction," in Nunes, M. L., ed., *Identity in Portuguese and Brazilian Literature* (1982): 34–4

—IRWIN STERN

FARMĀN, Ghā'ib Tu'ma

Iraqi novelist, short-story writer, translator, and journalist, b. 1927(?), Baghdad; d. 18 Aug. 1990, Moscow, U.S.S.R.

F.'s life was his writing, and his life was his exile. He left Iraq as a young man to study at the University of Cairo, from which he graduated in 1954. While in Egypt, he published a number of short stories in some of the most prestigious periodicals. On returning to Iraq, he could not find a job due to his political activities, so he left to work in Syria, Lebanon, and China. He returned to Iraq in 1958, but left after one year, only to resume the life of the wandering intellectual. He spent the last two decades of his life in Moscow, working as a translator and editor, and was responsible for supervising many of the translations into Arabic of some outstanding Russian and Soviet literary works, such as the selected works of Turgenev and collections of short stories by Pushkin, Tolstoy, and Dostoevsky.

Despite his continued exile, his writings were always about his native Iraq, especially Baghdad and its popular quarters. F. started by writing short stories in the 1950s. The two collections *Ḥaṣīd al-raḥā* (1954; millstone harvest) and *Mawlūd ākhar* (1959; another child) show a young writer in search of a path to take. These early stories witness the movement from a "romantic" to a "realistic" attitude. Some of them were, in fact, first encounters with topics and characters that were to be developed later into novels. This was the destiny of the short story "Salīmah al-khabbāzah" (1959; Salimah, the baker), which developed into his first novel, *al-Nakhlah wa-al-Jīrān* (1965; the palm tree and the neighbors). This novel was rightly considered the first Iraqi novel. It traces the lives of a group of poor people in an old quarter in Baghdad in the post-World War II period. F. is able to portray the ordinary, the daily, and the mundane in a way that makes it heroic without exaggeration. The characters are not heroes endowed with extraordinary powers, they are the poorest of the poor and the most ordinary of the ordinary. The collapse of the dreams of those characters and their tragedy are those of Iraq. In his next novel, *Khamsat aswāt* (1967; five voices), the stage is assumed by intellectuals of different convictions and mentalities, searching for ideals, but unable to find paths toward the realization of their dreams. Their estrangement from their society and their virtual collapse is highlighted.

In *al-Makhāḍ* (1974; labor pains) F. traces the developments in Iraqi society after the collapse of the ancien régime in 1958 and the rise of the new revolutionary fervor. He does this through the eyes of an exiled Iraqi who comes back to his homeland searching for the old quarter, only to find it destroyed. Looking for authenticity, he finds the products of false modernization.

The dream of return from exile is again the subject of his novel *Zilāl 'alā al-nāfidhah* (1979; shadows on the window) in which a university graduate returns to Iraq during the 1960s, full of ambitions to serve his country, only to become disillusioned and have his faith in the revolution collapse.

Ālām al-sayyid Ma'rūf (1982; the sorrows of Mr. Ma'ruf) shows very clearly F.'s ability to portray the forgotten and the ordinary human being as a hero. He does it not as much through empathy as through extracting the inner and hidden strength of such characters by tracing their daily struggles to live and survive in a vicious world.

F. was not a technical innovator. He was a writer sensitive to his characters and his people. F. was a committed socialist and member of the Iraqi Communist Party, but despite his own political convictions and the dominant SOCIALIST REALISM during the 1950s and the 1960s among socialist writers, he gave a lot of freedom to his characters. Not only did he let them develop freely, but he always portrayed them in a sympathetic manner, even when they contradicted his own ideological convictions. This applies to his earlier novels more than it does to the later ones, which is possibly the result of the length of his exile and the separation from his beloved city. F.'s achievement in the context of the modern Arabic novel was through the development of what might be termed the aesthetics of simplicity.

FURTHER WORKS: *al-Hukm al-aswad fī al-'Irāq* (1957); *Lā Shīn: 'imlāq al-thaqāfah al-sīnīyah* (1957); *al-Qurbān* (1975); *al-Murtajā wa-al-mu'ajjal* (1986); *al-Markib* (1989)

BIBLIOGRAPHY: Allen, R., *The Arabic Novel* (1982): 75–77; Ali, M. J., "The Socio-Aesthetics of Contemporary Arabic Fiction: An Introduction," *JArabL*, 14 (1983): 70, 80; Allen, R., ed., *Modern Arabic Literature*, 2nd ed. (1994): 82–83

—WALID HAMARNEH

FAROESE LITERATURE

See section under Danish Literature

FARRELL, James T.

American novelist and critic, b. 27 Feb. 1904, Chicago, Ill.; d. 22 Aug. 1979, New York, N.Y.

A second-generation American, F. came from a working-class, Irish-Catholic family of limited means, but when he was three years old he was taken to live with his more prosperous maternal grandparents and their unmarried children. For most of his first twenty-seven years he remained in Chicago, where he went to parochial schools and later worked as a clerk in an express company. He attended the University of Chicago from 1925 to 1929, for him a period of rapid intellectual growth that culminated in his first publication of short stories and criticism. After his marriage and a year in Paris, where he completed and sold his first two novels, in 1932 he took up permanent residence in New York City. There he plunged directly into the city's literary and intellectual life and quickly emerged, during the early Depression years, as a leading spokesman of the anti-Stalinist Left and a champion of oppressed groups. Over the next four decades he remained politically active in a long odyssey that took him from membership in the Trotskyite Socialist Workers Party in the 1930s to vigorous support of liberal Democrats in the 1960s and 1970s. An omnivorous reader with broad international interests, F. occasionally taught in universities; for many years he lectured throughout America and, in 1956, on a world tour.

Most of F.'s energies, however, went into the writing of fiction. His work was significantly influenced by CHEKHOV, DREISER,

James T. Farrell

Sherwood ANDERSON, JOYCE, HEMINGWAY, and the pragmatists George H. Mead (1863–1931) and John Dewey (1859–1952). Firmly rooted in the realistic tradition, but intensely personal in its reflection of his spiritual growth, his fiction explores the realities of lower-class and middle-class American urban culture, especially of the 1920s and 1930s, by following the interweaving careers of hundreds of characters. F.'s most famous work is the Chicago trilogy consisting of *Young Lonigan* (1932), *The Young Manhood of Studs Lonigan* (1934), and *Judgment Day* (1935), subsequently published in one volume as *Studs Lonigan* (1935), which should be considered as a complete and unified whole. This first of three major series he completed powerfully portrays its hero's degradation and death through a fatal susceptibility to inferior values. The Danny O'Neill pentalogy (*A World I Never Made*, 1936; *No Star Is Lost*, 1938; *Father and Son*, 1940; *My Days of Anger*, 1943; *The Face of Time*, 1953), closely following F.'s Chicago experience, is rich in family characterizations and traces the growth of the child Danny into the incipient artist and the social rebel. The Bernard Carr trilogy, consisting of *Bernard Clare* (1946; repub. as *Bernard Carr*), *The Road Between* (1949), and *Yet Other Waters* (1952), completes the story of the artist's emergence, and his fight to maintain his integrity in the face of economic hardship and the pressures of American communists and literary fellow travelers in New York City from 1927 to 1936. In this connection, F.'s *A Note on Literary Criticism* (1936) is a forceful attack on the methods of Marxist literary critics.

F.'s many collections of short stories and other of his novels, especially *Gas-House McGinty* (1933), *Ellen Rogers* (1941), *Boarding House Blues* (1961), and *New Year's Eve/1929* (1967), interlace with his major series and fill out his story of the education of Americans—for life or death. The result is a unified body of work notable for its singleness of vision and the objective validity with which it re-creates an authentic American past.

In 1958 F. began a new fictional cycle collectively titled "A Universe of Time." This work was planned to include at least twenty-five volumes that would interlock with his earlier fiction but would yield a view of experience more panoramic than that of his three earlier series. Its integrating theme, F. wrote, was "man's creativity and his courageous acceptance of impermanence." At his death he had completed ten books in the cycle (most notably *The Silence of History*, 1963; *What Time Collects*, 1964; *Invisible Swords*, 1971; *Judith, and Other Stories*, 1973; *The Dunne Family*, 1976; and *The Death of Nora Ryan*, 1978) and was working on several others. Central to "A Universe of Time" is the autobiographical character Eddie Ryan. Employing F.'s rigorous realism, the incomplete cycle mainly portrays segments of Eddie's personal, family, and professional past, while reaching out to the broader picture of 20th-c. America that F. had planned.

During his lifetime F. published fifty-two books (fifty-three if *Studs Lonigan* is considered a separate work, as it should be), including twenty-five novels and seventeen short-story collections. These establish him as a major figure in American realism. Philosophically F. is a naturalist whose values are strongly humanistic. The constant assumption of his critical realism is man's capacity for reason and dignity. Although in his writing he often dwells upon man's impressionability and pettiness in the face of debasing conditions, more basically he asserts the possibility of progress toward a humane and democratic society, and the individual's power to attain a degree of freedom and self-fulfillment by means of knowledge and a tenacious will. These same values inform F.'s essays of social and literary criticism in *The League of Frightened Philistines* (1945), *Literature and Morality* (1947); *Reflections at Fifty, and Other Essays* (1954), and *Literary Essays 1954–1974* (1976).

FURTHER WORKS: *Calico Shoes, and Other Stories* (1934); *Guillotine Party, and Other Stories* (1935); *Can All This Grandeur Perish?, and Other Stories* (1937); *The Short Stories of J. T. F.* (1937); *Tommy Gallagher's Crusade* (1939); *$1,000 a Week, and Other Stories* (1942); *To Whom It May Concern, and Other Stories* (1944); *When Boyhood Dreams Come True* (1946); *The Life Adventurous, and Other Stories* (1947); *An American Dream Girl* (1950); *The Name Is Fogarty: Private Papers on Public Matters* (1950); *This Man and This Woman* (1951); *French Girls Are Vicious, and Other Stories* (1955); *An Omnibus of Short Stories* (1956); *My Baseball Diary* (1957); *It Has Come to Pass* (1958); *Side Street, and Other Stories* (1961); *Sound of a City* (1967); *Selected Essays* (1964); *The Collected Poems of J. T. F.* (1965); *When Time Was Born* (1966); *Lonely for the Future* (1966); *A Brand New Life* (1968); *Judith* (1969); *Childhood Is Not Forever* (1969); *Olive and Mary Anne* (1977)

BIBLIOGRAPHY: Beach, J. W., *American Fiction, 1920–1940* (1941): 271–305; Gelfant, B. H., *The American City Novel* (1954): 175–227; Grattan, C. H., "J. T. F.: Moralist," *Harper's* (Oct. 1954): 93–94, 96, 98; Gregory, H., "J. T. F.: Beyond the Provinces of Art," *New World Writing*, 5 (1954): 52–65; Branch, E. M., *A Bibliography of J. T. F.'s Writings, 1921–1957* (1959); Branch, E. M., *J. T. F.* (1971); Salzman, J., "J. T. F.: An Essay in Bibliography," *RALS*, 6 (1976): 131–63; Wald, A. M., *J. T. F.: The Revolutionary Socialist Years* (1978)

—EDGAR M. BRANCH

FARROKHZAD, Forugh

Iranian poet, b. Jan. 1935, Tehran; d. 14 Feb. 1967, Tehran

F. went to school in Tehran but did not receive a high-school diploma. At fourteen she began composing poetry in the classical mode. Married unhappily at sixteen, she was soon divorced after giving birth to a son, who was given into the custody of her husband. F.'s trips to Europe in the late 1950s (she learned Italian, German, and English quite well) had a great impact on her poetry. In 1960, after studying in England, she became very active and successful in documentary film making. In 1965 UNESCO produced a half-hour film about her. She was killed in an automobile accident.

F.'s first collection of verse, *Asir* (the captive), was published in 1952. In 1955 a different collection with the same title appeared. This second volume made her the subject of scandal: for the first time in Persian poetry a writer spoke about her love for a man with all the sensuality and frankness of a personal confession. For perceptive critics, however, this volume signaled the appearance of a shining star among the poets of the so-called "new wave."

The four volumes of her poetry provide us with a guide by which to analyze F.'s development until just before her fatal accident. In her simple and clear poetic style, these poems reflect a transition, both personal and artistic; her art was inextricably bound to her personal growth. She gradually moves away from the bonds of tradition to a yearning for an attainment of freedom and ultimately to a new self and a pure art.

The titles of the collections indicate this progression: *Asir; Divar* (1956; the wall); *'Osyan* (1958; the rebellion), and *Tavvalod-e degar* (1964; another birth) reflect a move away from the restrictions of traditional poetry; in this, she was a close follower of the doctrines of Nima Yushij (1895?–1959), the pioneer of Persian free verse. The first two titles represent the poet's understanding and assessment of those bonds; the second two, the struggle against them and the emergence, from their destruction, of a new poetic form.

She did not, however, cut herself off from the literary past. She took many of her best images from the classical mystical repertoire, particularly her use of light versus dark and her concentration on shadows. Her most consistent appeal is to love, love that ranges from the contentment felt among friends to the devotion of religious activity or the passion of human sensuality. On a deeper plane, F.'s poetry represents the struggle of the individual against the power of evil and ugliness, alienation, fear, and frustration. She is rightly acclaimed a master of modern Persian poetry and the second female poet of greatness in the language, after Parvin E'tesami (1906–1941).

BIBLIOGRAPHY: Tikku, G., "F. F.: A New Direction in Persian Poetry," *StIsl*, 26 (1967): 149–73; Hillmann, M. C., "F. F.: Modern

Iranian Poet," in Fernea, E. W., and B. Q. Bezirgan, *Middle Eastern Muslim Women Speak* (1977): 291–317; Hillmann, M. C., "Sexuality in the Poetry of F. F. and the Structuralist View," *Edebiyat*, 3 (1978): 191–211

—PETER J. CHELKOWSKI

FAULKNER, William

American novelist and short-story writer, b. 25 Sept. 1897, New Albany, Miss.; d. 6 July 1962, Oxford, Miss.

In 1902 F.'s father moved the family to Oxford, where, except for a period in the Canadian air force (F. did not serve in France, despite occasional stories to the contrary), a few months in New York City, a half-year stay in New Orleans, stints of script writing in Hollywood, etc., F. spent the major part of his life. His ancestors were hard-working professional men, his great-grandfather having been a popular novelist and an outstanding (even legendary) figure in his region. Most of F.'s short stories and novels are set in the South and owe much of their character to regional color. His southern origin is also responsible for the historical element in F.'s work, as well as for his preoccupation with racial problems and with points of honor. His aptitude for spinning yarns and the highly rhetorical quality of his writings also derive from this Southern association. The South, more than the North, lives with a sense of its past, and this fact probably accounts for much of F.'s awareness of the past living on into the present.

F. did not, however, begin his career with a schematic plan for portraying the history of the South. Sometimes, as in *Light in August* (1932), he is harshly critical of his region, and sometimes, as in *Intruder in the Dust* (1948), he is almost polemical in his defense of it. In an early novel, *Sartoris* (1929), he describes in a rather uncritical manner the hero's preoccupation with the gallant gesture, but in *The Unvanquished* (1938) he depicts Southern bravery as headlong heroics and the region's concern with honor as rationalization for thoughtless and sometimes even vicious conduct. F.'s work expresses a tremendous admiration for selflessness, love, endurance, and human dignity. He sees these as human virtues that transcend race and class. In other words, he does not depict, as has sometimes been maintained, a specific class as the representatives of noble conduct and of a way of life above criticism.

F.'s work may be divided into three major periods, with certain themes, techniques, and mannerisms being common to all of them. Among his writings of the first period, *Soldiers' Pay* (1926), *Mosquitoes* (1927), and some of the stories in the short-story collection *These Thirteen* (1931) share many characteristics. All of them bear witness to F.'s early reading of Keats, Tennyson, Swinburne, and the literature of the 1890s. There is a Victorian air about them, but one that by comparison with Victorian literature is at once more pallid and more flamboyant. Nor does F. belong to the school of "a pure American prose," insofar as that means a strong tendency toward understatement and sentences built on frequent use of the conjunction.

To the second period, when F. comes into his own as an artist, belong *The Sound and the Fury* (1929), *As I Lay Dying* (1930), *Sanctuary* (1931), *Light in August, Doctor Martino, and Other Stories* (1934), *Pylon* (1935), *Absalom, Absalom!* (1936), *The*

William Faulkner

Unvanquished, and *The Wild Palms* (1939). Most of these are stories of terrifying violence, exacerbated humor, and grim dignity. The horrors are steadily kept in the foreground, and sometimes a thin margin of victory is allowed a protagonist. In many, but not all of these volumes, F. is mainly concerned with his own region, and in almost all of them he experiments with methods of narration, drawing the reader into and through the involutions of page-long sentences and forcing him to hold in mind details and phrases that are meaningful only at the end, when the story, in all of its complexity, evolves brilliantly, with fact illuminating fact. No two stories are told in quite the same way. In *The Sound and the Fury* the consciousness of three characters is revealed as though the reader lived successively in each mind, and then the range of consciousness broadens, enlarging in focus, until a history begins to be clear. In *As I Lay Dying* characters develop in terms of their own awareness (all are narrators) and through the way they are seen by the other characters; and all of them are seen in terms of the way they react to their part in the symbolic, yet highly painful, funeral journey. Most of the remaining stories are episodic, but each deploys unique devices: the Gothic framework of *Absalom, Absalom!*, the double plot and analogous actions of *Light in August* (closest of all of his novels to the typical Elizabethan double plot), the foreshortened action of *Pylon* (similar in narrative technique to F. Scott FITZGERALD's *The Great Gatsby*), the sequence of related short stories in *The Unvanquished*, and the largely thematic relationship between the alternating stories of *The Wild Palms*. *Sanctuary* is less experimental in structure, but its careful imagery (there are alternate patterns of overripeness and of the mechanical) and symbolism suggest the conventions of a highly stylized play.

F. is not a realistic writer in the sense of verisimilitude or documenting a region. In fact, it is extremely misleading to read him as a realist. F. is at the same time indebted to the tradition of the modern novel and a contributor to that tradition. Not the least of these contributions is the way in which his language (like that of JOYCE) seems of a piece with his character or subject, evoking each in the appropriate way, then rising as a choral voice, richly rhetorical and hypnotic.

In the third period, beginning with *The Hamlet* (1940), F. offers some hope for the human condition, a promise of release. The hope is explored in *Go Down, Moses* (1942), most significantly in "The Bear" and "Delta Autumn." *Intruder in the Dust, Knight's Gambit* (1949), and *Requiem for a Nun* (1951) attempt to elevate political programs and sermons into art forms. *Go Down, Moses* contains some of F.'s most brilliant and sustained rhetoric. A mythical wilderness is evoked with great power, but unfortunately the dialectic side of the novel is unsatisfactory. *Intruder in the Dust* and in *Knight's Gambit* merge detective-story solutions and regional sociological themes. The former, although it is sectional in the thesis it argues regarding the place of the Negro, is much the more serious novel. *Requiem for a Nun* (a sequel to *Sanctuary*) combines a play and historical documentation, interlarding acts and chapters from the history of Jefferson (F.'s fictional town), and suggesting thereby the judgments the past makes on the actions of Temple Drake, the "heroine." *A Fable* (1954), the most highly stylized and rhetorical of F.'s books, and perhaps so stylized and rhetorical that most of the reality behind it blurs, concerns the failure of a Christlike figure to bring peace to the trenches of the Great War.

In the later years of his life, F. returned to the Snopes saga, with *The Town* (1957) and *The Mansion* (1959). Neither book has the imaginative force of the first book of the trilogy, *The Hamlet*, in which the Snopeses take on mythical proportions. All of the characters are reduced in scale, and only Mink Snopes, in *The Mansion*, embodies the obsessive self-destructive energy of the Snopeses as may be observed in *The Hamlet*. For about two-thirds of the novel, F. is back in his old form.

With *The Reivers* (1962) F. nostalgically revisits his childhood, and also revisits and extends the world of *Sanctuary*. Set early in the 20th c., the novel is both a paean to the preindustrial world, the small-town and agrarian world of F.'s parents, and the newer world of the automobile and the city. As a novel, it is not equal in stature to the books of the middle period, but it has its own quiet comedy and dignity. It also enlarges the Yoknapatawpha world (his mythical county).

F. died a few months after the publication of *The Reivers*, almost exactly one year after HEMINGWAY. The careers of these two writers illuminate each other, and thus invite critical comparison. F. was almost two years older than Hemingway, but his success came more slowly, except that he was awarded the Nobel Prize before Hemingway. F. was sometimes critical of Hemingway, saying he learned at an early stage what he could do, and was satisfied to repeat himself rather than take risks. One book in particular—*The Wild Palms*—shows the nature of F.'s "quarrel" with Hemingway. *The Wild Palms* can be read as a "dialogue," a critique of *A Farewell to Arms* and a questioning of the "Hemingway world." There are many parallels in the actions of the two novels, and the character McCord in *The Wild Palms* is based on Hemingway himself. "The Wild Palms" story, the love story,

parallels *A Farewell to Arms*, while "Old Man," the story of the Tall Convict, the chapters of which are interlarded with "The Wild Palms," is a fundamental criticism of the characters in "The Wild Palms" and therefore of the "Hemingway world."

Hemingway divides society into the "initiates," and the "messy ones," who believe all the slogans about patriotism and accept easy middle-class values. He admires the initiates, who reject the world, except on their own terms. The universe is meaningless, and the sensitive man meets it on his terms—as a good athlete, a courageous soldier, a skilled physician, or a dedicated writer. He lives the physical life to the full, with sex, drinking, and hunting or fishing. The initiate wrests his narrow victory.

The F. "hero" is very different. He learns to accept the world. The Tall Convict, like Byron Bunch in *Light in August*, knows, although he would not know how to say it, that "love no more exists just at one spot and in one moment and in one body out of all the earth and all time . . . than sunlight does." The Hemingway world, with the sleepless man, tricked by the universe, emphasizes defeat and rejection. After his early "lost generation" stance, F. moved toward acceptance.

This contrast between the "F. world" and the "Hemingway world" is of considerable importance. It has something to do with the way both men lived their lives, and a great deal to do with their literary legacies.

The three periods in F.'s career suggest the varieties of attitudes and of themes to be found in his work. Through several of the books, either as major or minor themes, runs his intense dislike of the repressions caused by rigidity of mind. *Light in August* presents outrages done and violences caused by literal-minded pietists. *Absalom, Absalom!* may be interpreted as a story of the violence caused by the literal adherence to a code. And several of the short stories may be read in similar terms. *The Hamlet* is folk comedy, making ample use of the tall tale and farcical situations. Several of the earlier novels present a vision of things not unlike that presented in ELIOT's *The Waste Land*; perhaps the most successful of these is *The Sound and the Fury*.

In reply to a question once put to him by an interviewer, F. said he had read very little about the history of the Civil War and of the South generally. What he knew, he knew by word of mouth, by having assimilated some beliefs and prejudices and rejecting others. Considering that he is commonly looked upon as the "historian" of Yoknapatawpha county, his stories of the 19th c. are relatively few. He is a fiction writer whose mind and imagination are best engaged by certain themes; and he has written about his region in so luminous a fashion that he seems to be telling its historical truth. He is an apologist for the virtues of his region, and a ruthless critic of its vices.

That F. was an original writer probably made it inevitable that his fellow Americans would be a little slow in recognizing his abilities, but he has now been widely recognized, to which his winning of the Nobel Prize (1950) and numerous other awards bears witness. Undoubtedly he belongs to the small group of novelists who both embody and transcend region and country.

FURTHER WORKS: *New Orleans Sketches* (1953); *F. at Nagano* (1956); *F. in the University* (1959); *W. F.: Early Prose and Poetry* (1962); *F. at West Point* (1964); *Essays, Speeches and Public Letters* (1966); *The F.-Cowley File: Letters and Memories 1944–1962* (1968); *Flags in the Dust* (1973); *The Marionettes* (1975); *Mayday* (1977); *Selected Letters of W. F.* (1977); *Uncollected Stories of W. F.* (1979); *Sanctuary: The Original Text* (1981)

BIBLIOGRAPHY: Warren, R. P., *W. F.: His South* (1951); Howe, I., *W. F.: A Critical Study* (1952; 2nd rev. ed., 1962); O'Connor, W. V., *The Tangled Fire of W. F.* (1954); Stein, J., "The Art of Fiction XII: W. F." [interview], *Paris Review*, No. 12 (1956): 28–52; Vickery, O., *The Novels of W. F.* (1959; rev. ed., 1964); Woodworth, S. D., *W. F. en France* (1959); Slatoff, W. J., *Quest for Failure: A Study of W. F.* (1960); Hoffman, F. J., *W. F.* (1961); Meriwether, J. B., *The Literary Career of W. F.* (1961); Beck, W., *Man in Motion: F.'s Trilogy* (1961); Swiggart, P., *The Art of F.'s Novels* (1962); Brooks, C., *W. F.* (1963); Faulkner, J., *My Brother Bill* (1963); Thompson, L. R., *W. F.: An Introduction and Interpretation* (1963); Dain, M. J., *F.'s Country* (1964); Volpe, E. L., *A Reader's Guide to W. F.* (1964); Nilon, C. H., *F. and the Negro* (1965); Blackman, M., *F.: The Major Years* (1966); Millgate, M., *The Achievement of W. F.* (1966); Blotner, J. L., *F.: A Biography* (1974); Bassett, J., ed., *W. F.: The Critical Heritage* (1975); Guerard, A. J., *The Triumph of the Novel: Dickens, Dostoevsky, F.* (1976); Brooks, C., *W. F.: Toward Yoknapatawpha and Beyond* (1978); Minter, D., *W. F.: His Life and Work* (1980); Sundquist, E., *F.: The House Divided* (1983); Friedman, A. W., *W. F.* (1984)

—ALAN W. FRIEDMAN

In addition to being a fatalist, F. is also an idealist, more strongly so than any other American writer of our time. The idealist disguises itself as its own opposite, but that is because he is deeply impressed by and tends to exaggerate the contrast between the life around him and the ideal picture in his mind . . . of how the land and the people should be—a picture of painted, many-windowed houses, fenced fields, overflowing barns, eyes lighting up with recognition . . . And both pictures are not only physical but moral; for always in the background of his novels is a sense of moral standards and a feeling of outrage at their being violated or simply brushed aside. Seeing little hope in the future, he turns to the past, where he hopes to discover a legendary and recurrent pattern that will illuminate and lend dignity to the world about him.

Malcolm Cowley, "W. F.'s Legend of the South,"
in Allen Tate, ed., *A Southern Vanguard* (1947),
pp. 26–27

To speak of greatness with regard to one's contemporaries is dangerous. But if there are any American novels of the present century which may be called great, which bear comparison—serious if not favorable—with the achievements of twentieth-century European literature, then surely *The Sound and the Fury* is among them. It is one of the three or four American works of prose fiction written since the turn of the century in which the impact of tragedy is felt and sustained. Seized by his materials, F. keeps, for once, within his esthetic means, rarely trying to say more than he can or needs to. *The Sound and the Fury* is the one novel in which his vision and technique are almost in complete harmony, and the vision itself whole and major. Whether taken as a study of the potential for human self-destruction, or as a rendering of the social disorder particular to our time, the novel projects a radical image of man against the

wall. Embodied and justified, this is an image of great writing.

Irving Howe, *W. F.* (1952), pp. 126–27

The European reader finds something uniquely American in F., and obviously no European could have written his books; the few European commentators that I have read seem to me to glorify W. F. in a provincial American (or Southern) vacuum. I believe that as his personality fades from view he will be recognized as one of the great craftsmen of the art of fiction which Ford Madox Ford called the Impressionistic Novel. From Stendhal through Flaubert and Joyce there is a direct line to F., and it is not a mere question of influence. F.'s great subject, as it was Flaubert's and Proust's, is passive suffering, the victim being destroyed either by society or by dark forces within himself. F. is one of the great exemplars of the international school of fiction which for more than a century has reversed the Aristotelian doctrine that tragedy is an action, not a quality.

Allen Tate, "W. F., 1897–1962," *SR*, 71
(1963), p. 162

To the neophyte F. reader, the prose may seem a continual flow of words that obscures the story action rather than developing it. The difficulties should not be minimized. The diction, the syntax, seem designed to obfuscate, not communicate. F. sometimes deliberately withholds important details, and the narrators frequently refer to people or events that the reader will not learn about until much later, making the style seem even more opaque than it actually is. And the long sentences are difficult to follow, with clauses that proliferate, developing not from the main subject or verb of the sentence, but growing out of preceding clauses. As a result, the main thought is often lost in the mass of amplifying or qualifying ideas. Antecedents of personal pronouns are frequently not clear. F.'s style does not provide relaxing reading, but forces the reader to participate in the search for understanding and truth. . . . Had F. been a U.S. senator, his speeches would have been squarely in the tradition of Southern oratory. Some of his sentences sound almost like selected passages from a filibuster. Rather than run the risk of interruption and lose the floor, he does not pause; he rolls on, using all the rhetorical devices of the speechmaker: colorful, grandiloquent and emotive words, repetition, parallel structure, a series of negative clauses preceding a positive, delayed climax.

Edmund L. Volpe, *A Reader's Guide to W. F.*
(1963), pp. 38–39

Out of F.'s sharply realized portraits of individual men and women, there gradually emerges a view of man which involves making a crucial distinction between the social and moral definitions of his nature. The former simply places the individual in certain exclusive categories, the latter restores to him his identity with all humanity. The one provides a formula for morality and enforces it with law, the other leaves moral action undefined and therefore unfettered. In short, the social definition of man predetermines the individual's response to experience by creating an expectation of conformity to certain codes which govern the behavior of each social unit. The moral definition forces man to assume responsibility for recognizing and enacting his own moral nature. At the very heart of the Yoknapatawpha novels and *A Fable* is the problem created by the conflict between the inflexible morality of society and the ethics of the individual based on experience, grounded in specific situations, and usually incapable of formulation beyond the simplest of maxims and platitudes. . . .

Since any social system or moral code tends to replace internal morality with external controls, the only healthy relationship between men and their society is one of mutual suspicion and unrelaxed vigilance. Only such an attitude can ensure the continued existence of a critical revaluation of the former's behavior and the latter's conventions. If this balance is destroyed, the result is either anarchy or social and governmental dictatorship. Because it completely obliterates freedom, because it reduces the individual to an unquestioning automaton, the second is more dangerous. F. levels some of his bitterest and most forthright criticism at this accelerating process of regimentation which he describes in almost all of his novels, though it becomes increasingly prominent in the later works, beginning with *Go Down, Moses.*

Olga Vickery, *The Novels of W. F.*, rev. ed.
(1964), pp. 282–83

F.'s achievement can be adequately estimated only by our seeing him as a great novelist in the context not merely of the South, or even of the United States, but of the whole western tradition. His deep identification with his own region is one of his greatest strengths, especially as it emerges in the marvellous sense of place, whether it be the heart of the wilderness or the interior of Miss Reba's brothel, and in the rich evocation of the world of Yoknapatawpha County; and certainly the intensity of his tragic power in novels such as *The Sound and the Fury, Light in August,* and *Absalom, Absalom!* derives both from this profoundly localised sense of social reality and from a poignant awareness of the proud and shameful history of the courageous, careless, gallant and oppressive South. At the same time, to concentrate too exclusively on this aspect of his work is to be in danger of mistaking means for ends and of seeing F. as a lesser figure than he really is. The solidity of F.'s provinciality provides the unshakable foundation for his immensely ambitious exploration of the fundamental human themes with which he is always primarily concerned, and the examples of Hardy and Emily Brontë may suggest that F. is not alone among novelists in pursuing the universal in terms of the

intensely local. But it is Dickens whom F. most resembles, in the passionate humanity of his tragicomic vision, in the range and vitality of his characterisation and the profusion of his social notation, in the structural complexity of his novels and their broad symbolic patterns. It is also Dickens whom F. most resembles in the sheer quantity and sustained quality of his achievement, and it is alongside Dickens, the greatest of the English novelists, that F. must ultimately be ranked.

Michael Millgate, *The Achievement of W. F.*
(1966), p. 292

The issue of millennialism is . . . one that sets F. off from a great many other American writers. He does not, of course, stand alone; yet his more old-fashioned notion of history has disquieted and confused many a twentieth-century literary critic, and it sets him off sharply from such writers as Hart Crane or, to mention one whose talents he greatly admired, Thomas Wolfe. F. is far less visionary than Wolfe, less optimistic, less intoxicated with the greatness of America. By contrast, F.'s view is more "Southern," and though one should not claim him for Christian orthodoxy, much closer to St. Augustine's view of history. . . .

F. did not scorn the American Dream. Rather, he mourned the fact that it had not been fulfilled. He grieved at having to conclude in 1955 that "the American air, which was once the living breath of liberty [has] now become one vast down-crowding pressure to abolish [freedom], by destroying man's individuality . . ." F., however, was skeptical about the full realization of *any* utopian dream, even the noblest. That is to say, he was evidently seriously concerned that his country might be undone by her sometimes overweening faith in the future, by her belief that progress was inevitable, by her confidence that man's happiness would result from sociological know-how and the right set of plans, by her reliance on her technological might, by her incautious trust in her own virtues and good intentions, and, most dangerous of all, by her unprecedented record of military victories. (F. died before Americans went into Vietnam.) Americans could easily get the impression that they, unlike the other nations of the earth, were immune to defeat, loss, and evil. Such innocence might in the end prove disastrous.

Cleanth Brooks, *W. F.: Toward Yoknapatawpha
and Beyond* (1978), pp. 281–82

Early in his life as an artist F. had begun to dread the moment "when not only the ecstasy of writing would be gone, but the unreluctance and the something worth saying too." In part because the division within him ran deep, in part because work was what he did best, and in part because his relation to his art was so intense and satisfying, he came to that moment slowly. Gradually, however, as his confidence in what he had done increased and his confidence in what he was doing slipped away, he began identifying himself with the work he had finished, the selves he had become, as though he knew that what was valuable was what he had already created and so had lost not shabbily. Repeatedly testing the self that remained, he went on waiting for "the moment, instant, night: dark: sleep: when I would put it all away forever that I anguished and sweated over, and it would never trouble me anymore." Having looked at that moment many times, with mixed fear and desire but with defiance, too, he came to it, as he thought Albert Camus had, knowing that he had done all things in his life that he could.

David Minter, *W. F.: His Life and Work* (1980), pp. 250–51

FAYE, Jean-Pierre

French novelist, poet, and literary theoretician, b. 19 July 1925, Paris

After studying law and economics at the Sorbonne and anthropology at the Museum of Man under Claude Lévi-Strauss, F. went to live in the U.S. in 1954–55. Back in France, he started publishing fiction in 1958 and was on the staff of the journal *Tel quel* from 1963 until 1967. From 1959 to 1972 he was a frequent visitor to Germany, collecting documents for his *Les langages totalitaires* (1972; totalitarian languages).

From the start of his career as a writer and a literary theoretician, F. denied any validity to the established categories. He focused instead on experimentation in order to explore how literary forms, historical discourses, and philosophical constructs combine in the very act of narration. F.'s driving idea throughout his work, whether fictional, historical, or political, is that of a universal process of "change" affecting all symbolic forms, languages as well as societies as a whole. Fictions are but the means through which such a process assumes a form significant for the imagination. More recently, F. has found in the linguistic theories of Noam Chomsky (b. 1928) a conceptual basis for his own theory of "transformatism," the generic name he uses to describe his overall vision of things human, a vision shared by a group of writers whose work appears in the journal and the book series *Change*, edited by F. since 1968, after he left *Tel quel*.

The unity of F.'s endeavor appears most clearly in the way he wants his first six novelistic works to be read as a series, retrospectively titled *Hexagramme* (hexagram) by the author. In those works, characters are variables in complex narrative functions that put into play the very structures of narrative: linguistic events, space, time, point of view. All these elements take part in a polyphony designed to create a well-controlled network of meanings against the backdrop of historically and geographically significant settings. In this fashion, F. uses to a considerable extent the characteristics of some almost mythic cities, between which he creates complex fictional resonances: Berlin in *L'écluse* (1964; the lock), Troyes in France and Troy in *Les Troyens* (1970; the Trojans), his two most successful works. Paris, Munich, and Chicago appear in his earlier novels also.

Two more books have been added to this series. *Inferno, versions* (1975; inferno, versions) and *L'ovale, detail* (1975; the

oval, detail), both set in Jerusalem, while complementary to each other, can also be read as a single work belonging to the set of all potential narratives made possible by the "hexagram" structure. The superimposition of the various narratives and their multiplication, and the overlapping of plots and points of view thus appear more and more as F.'s central concerns in his attempt to create new fictional worlds and techniques.

Better known for his important historical essays—such as *Les langages totalitaires*—and his political involvements and writings—such as *Le Portugal d'Otelo* (1976; *Portugal: The Revolution in the Labyrinth*, 1976)—than for his more ambitious fictions, F. nevertheless should appear in the course of time as a gifted creator of intricate, intriguing stories, as an elegant writer, and as the possessor of a complex mind. His qualities as a writer are sometimes obscured, however, by his somewhat excessive penchant for allusions, hyperbole, and all-encompassing generalizations.

FURTHER WORKS: *Entre les rues* (1958); *Fleuve renversé* (1959); *La cassure* (1961); *Battement* (1962); *Analogues* (1965); *Théâtre* (1964); *Couleurs pliées* (1965); *Hypothèses* (1972); *Iskra; Cirque* (1972); *Luttes de classes à Dunkerque* (1972); *Théorie du récit* (1972); *La critique du langage et son économie* (1973); *Migrations du récit sur le peuple juif* (1974); *Langue: Théorie générative étendue* (1977); *Les portes des villes du monde* (1977); *Verres* (1978); *Les minorités dans la pensée* (1979); *Commencement d'une figure en mouvement* (1980); *Syeeda* (1980); *Les grandes journées du Père Duchesne* (1981)

BIBLIOGRAPHY: Boyer, P., "Le grand écart," *Critique*, 27 (1971): 770–82; Pierssens, M., "L'entreprise de *Change*," *Sub-stance*, 4 (1972): 107–16; Teysseire, D., "Mort des mots: Mots de mort," *Critique*, 29 (1973): 1038–45; Pierssens, M., "J.-P. F.: Vers une sémantique de l'Histoire," *ECr*, 14 (1974): 369–75; Ronat, M., *F.* (1980); Partouche, M., *J.-P.F.* (1981)

—M. PIERSSENS

FEDIN, Konstantin Alexandrovich

Russian novelist, short-story writer, and essayist, b. 24 Feb. 1892, Saratov; d. 15 July 1977, Moscow

F. belonged to the group of Russian writers who bridged the events of October 1917 and personified the link between traditional 19th-c. and Soviet literature. Born in the Volga region, F. spent his formative years in the midst of a family belonging to the radical intelligentsia, and he sharpened his literary tastes by reading the great Russian classics. His first literary piece appeared in a St. Petersburg magazine as early as 1913. The outbreak of World War I found him in Germany, where he was interned for the duration of the war. The autobiographical events of those years served as the backdrop for his first full-length novel, *Goroda i gody* (1924; *Cities and Years*, 1962).

Returning to Russia after the revolution, F. joined the Communist Party; while working in Petrograd (formerly St. Petersburg) he met Maxim GORKY and through him made the acquaintance of other Petrograd writers who formed the literary group known as the Serapion Brothers. Under their influence, F.'s muse flourished, and in 1921 he withdrew from the Party.

Clearly influenced by Gogol, Dostoevsky, CHEKHOV, and BUNIN, F. published a collection of seven stories, *Pustyr* (1923; the wasteland), in which he described the world of the past populated by lonely little people.

The main thrust of F.'s first novel, *Goroda i gody*, may be viewed as the tragedy of individualism in the new world created by the Russian Revolution. It is an ambitious attempt to portray within a mixed chronology the lives of its Russian and German protagonists against the background of social and political events in the cities. The protagonist of the novel, Andrey Startsov, is a utopian idealist, repelled by the bloody struggle, who comes face to face with the revolutionary zeal of his German friend, the painter Kurt Wahn. Andrey's incapacity for action and his own sense of futility earmark him for the category of "superfluous men" so prominent in 19th-c. Russian novels.

In his second important novel, *Bratya* (1928; the brothers), F. again drew on his own life and past to create the hero of the story, Nikita Karev, a composer who is almost crushed in his efforts to adjust to the revolutionary present. Despite Nikita's ultimate acceptance of Soviet reality at the conclusion of the novel, F. had posed in it the problem of the artist having to reconcile his vocation with the revolution.

Throughout his life F.'s creative output was strongly influenced by his knowledge of the West and its people. Nowhere was it more apparent than in his novel *Pokhishchenie Evropy* (2 vols., 1933–35; the rape of Europe), which deals with a Dutch family of timber merchants with business ties in Russia during the time of the first Five-Year Plan. The "Russian question," as it was apprehended in Europe in the early 1930s, is at the center of the story. The tone of the novel is decidedly pro-Soviet, and the realism of its scenes is often striking, but the lack of unity of design is its main weakness. With this novel, F. clearly chose the role of a "fellow-traveling" Soviet writer.

F.'s next published work was a short novel, *Sanatory Arktur* (1940; *Sanatorium Arktur*, 1957), which, departing from an autobiographical experience, is a psychological study of an illness containing several excellent characterizations.

In the early 1940s F. became drawn more and more to the socialist present as a political and artistic concept. Yet F. was not spared public condemnation and an official rebuttal in *Pravda* in connection with the second volume of his literary reminiscences, *Gorky sredi nas* (2 vols., 1943–44; Gorky among us), an honest, wise, and objective book in which F.'s own artistic and social views appear to be out of step with the Party line.

F.'s most ambitious and mature work is a trilogy embracing a vast period of Russian life. It was begun during World War II and was prompted, in F.'s own words, by his search "for a great contemporary hero . . . a Communist whose active will was synonymous with victory." Kirill Izvekov is such a hero in *Pervye radosti* (1945; *Early Joys*, 1948), *Neobyknovennoe leto* (1947–48; *No Ordinary Summer*, 1950), and *Koster* (1961–65; *The Conflagration*, 1968).

F. left his mark on Soviet literature as the writer who, after the political and cultural upheaval brought on by the 1917 revolution, initiated a return to the realistic narrative of the 19th-c. Russian novel and began probing the psychological problems of the revolution, rather than merely describing or exalting it. In F.'s works, the characteristic themes are the individual in relationship to his times, the sensitive intellectual faced with the hard choice between the old and the new, and the question of art and its place in contemporary Soviet life. Despite the orthodox Soviet tenor of F.'s fiction, it is

colored by sympathetic understanding of the Russian past and, artistically, his doubting intellectuals are consistently more successful than his idealistic Bolsheviks.

FURTHER WORKS: *Bakunin v Drezdene* (1922); *Transvaal* (1927); *Ya byl akterom* (1937); *Ispytanie chuvstv* (1942); *Neskolko naselennykh punktov* (1943); *Svidanie s Leningradom* (1944); *Pisatel, iskusstvo i vremya* (1957); *Sobranie sochineny* (10 vols., 1969–1973)

BIBLIOGRAPHY: Reavey, G., *Soviet Literature Today* (1947): 93–94, 120–23; Simmons, E. J., *Russian Fiction and Soviet Ideology: Introduction to F., Leonov, and Sholokhov* (1958): 9–87; Simmons, E. J., Introduction to *Early Joys* (1960): vii–xvi; Brown, E. J., *Russian Literature since the Revolution* (1963): 124–31; Blum, J. M., *K. F.: A Descriptive and Analytic Study* (1967); Struve, G., *Russian Literature under Lenin and Stalin, 1917–1953* (1971): 94–98, 289–91, 342–43, 378–80; Holthusen, J., *Twentieth-Century Russian Literature: A Critical Study* (1972): 102–3, 197–200; Slonim, M., *Soviet Russian Literature: Writers and Problems, 1917–1967* (1973): 130–39, 319–20

—NADJA JERNAKOFF

FEMINIST CRITICISM

The term feminist literary criticism is usually understood as designating the body of commentary about the various relations of gender to the written word that has developed in response to the current, post-1968 phase of the women's movement. It embraces both academic and nonacademic approaches, based on a variety of theoretical models that are often given the rough national labels "French" or "Anglo-American." So much attention has been devoted to the distinctions between the different kinds of feminist criticism that there is a tendency to neglect the core of common assumptions and goals that brought into existence the term feminist criticism and the modes of reading it describes.

Although this article concentrates on work published between 1968 and 1991, it would be a mistake to conclude that feminist criticism began only with the feminism of the late 1960s. There has always been an eager and informed audience for those female voices that were raised during the centuries when literature was a male preserve. And there has been at least intermittent recognition that the dominant literature was gendered masculine, representing the perspective of one sex about the nature and relations of both. Ellen Moers (1928–1980) documents the ways in which English-speaking women writers of the 19th c. read, commented on, and were influenced by one another's work, often seeing themselves, across the limits of time and space, as constituting a separate, definable literary tradition.

In the 20th c., a number of the major Western social theorists who considered the status and condition of women either began or ended with discussions of literature. Virginia WOOLF's *A Room of One's Own* (1929) starts as a meditation on the general topic of "Women and Fiction." But, in order to arrive at the famous conclusion that, to write fiction, a woman must have five hundred pounds a year and a room of her own, Woolf pursues her argument through the entire range of women's economic, psychological, sexual, and cultural situation. By contrast, Simone de BEAUVOIR's *Le deuxième sexe* (1949; *The Second Sex*, 1953), whose central thesis is that one is not born a woman, but becomes one, explores the question of "The Woman Writer" and her relation to the written word as one chapter in her overview of female experience. *A Room of One's Own* is sometimes described as the first piece of feminist literary criticism, but it is also a powerful contribution to social theory; *Le deuxième sexe* is commonly regarded as a landmark in the theory of feminism, but it is also a work of literary criticism.

As feminism took on a new momentum in the early 1970s, a great many of the popular books that raised questions about the treatment of women in our society employed the approach of cultural criticism. The key texts of Western culture—not only fictional texts, but religious and psychological literature as well—were scrutinized for their role in helping to shape society's dominant attitudes toward women and even the institutions those attitudes inform. Books like Kate Millett's (b. 1934) *Sexual Politics* (1970), Shulamith Firestone's (dates n.a.) *The Dialectic of Sex* (1970), Eva Figes's (b. 1932) *Patriarchal Attitudes* (1970), Germaine Greer's (b. 1939) *The Female Eunuch* (1970), and Carolyn Heilbrun's (b. 1926) *Toward a Recognition of Androgyny* (1973) all proceed by reading the society and its formative texts as if both had coequal status as literary texts.

Two other phenomena testify to the relationship of women, literature, and criticism in the early years of the revived feminist movement. One is the way that certain works of fiction—from Charlotte Perkins Gilman's (1860–1935) *The Yellow Wallpaper* (1899) to Doris LESSING's *The Golden Notebook* (1962) to Alix Kates Shulman's (b. 1932) *Memoirs of an Ex-Prom Queen* (1972) to Erica Jong's (b. 1942) *Fear of Flying* (1973)—became part of the experience of consciousness-raising, as they crystallized a sense of identification and provided the raw materials for social analysis. As campus women's studies programs began to proliferate, courses on the work of women writers were many women's introduction to the issues of feminism. The feminist movement also gave rise to the emergence, within women's studies, of a criticism that was more directly focused on literary studies than were the popular works of cultural criticism that provide the charter documents of the contemporary women's movement.

In outlining the twenty-year history of the more specifically literary focus within feminist criticism, many commentators tend to apply a kind of biological fallacy to its development. That is, they imply that early approaches and methods were young and crude, essentially stages that more recent work has "outgrown." In making "early" a pejorative term, such an attitude not only displays ignorance of the processes of intellectual history and the way that ideas build upon the work of the past, it also ignores the fact that, rather than being superseded, some of the now unfashionable earlier approaches continue to be used by critics.

One of the earliest feminist approaches was to consider the male-dominated canon of the literary tradition as a source not only of ideology in the larger cultural sense, but also of specific and often stereotypical "images" of women. Sometimes these conventional images were compared and contrasted with those that emerge from study of the smaller number of women writers who have been acknowledged as part of the common Western cultural heritage. Mary Anne Ferguson's (b. 1918) collection *Images of Women in Literature* (1973), which has undergone five revisions in the past two decades, was designed as a textbook anthology of literary sources reflecting some of these images. A similar critical approach is also represented in one of the earliest collections of

feminist critical essays, Susan Koppelman Cornillon's (b. 1941) *Images of Women in Fiction* (1972).

Contrasts between male and female writers, combined with the growing emphasis within many fields of feminist studies on women's "agency," led many feminist critics, from the early 1970s on, to valorize the work of female authors, rediscovering "lost" writers of the past, rereading and reinterpreting the known but undervalued and misunderstood figures, and reconsidering such characteristically "feminine" genres as domestic and sensational fiction. Mid-1970s studies by Moers, Patricia Mayers Spacks (b. 1929), and Elaine Showalter's (b. 1941) laid the groundwork for this approach. Moers and Louise Bernikow (b. 1940) also suggested that women writers constituted a continuous alternative literary tradition, whose thematic and stylistic parallels to and subversions of the dominant tradition are the subject, notably, of such studies as Showalter's *A Literature of Their Own* (1977), Sandra M. Gilbert (b. 1936) and Susan Gubar's (b. 1944) *The Madwoman in the Attic* (1979), Nina Auerbach's (b. 1943) *Communities of Women* (1978), and Judith Newton's (b. 1941) *Women, Power, and Subversion* (1981).

Certain critics throughout the 1970s and 1980s were particularly involved with connecting feminist concerns to a materialist reading of culture, emphasizing that women, as authors, characters, and readers of literature, were also significantly influenced by society's tensions around race, ethnicity, class, and sexual identity. Lillian S. Robinson's (b. 1941) critical writings from 1968 through 1977, collected in *Sex, Class, and Culture* (1978), mark some of the stages of this effort, as do Jane Marcus's (b. 1938) collected essays in *Art and Anger* (1988) and those by various British and American critics anthologized by Newton and Deborah Rosenfelt (b. 1942) in *Feminist Criticism and Social Change* (1985).

Texts of women writers of color were made popularly available in anthologies by Mary Helen Washington (b. 1941) and by Gloria Anzaldua (b. 1942) and Cherrie Moraga (b. 1952), while black women's writing was also discussed by such critics as Washington, Barbara Smith (b. 1946), Barbara Christian (b. 1943), Marjorie Pryse (b. 1948), Hortense Spillers (b. 1942), Deborah McDowell (b. 1951), Joanne Braxton (b. 1950), Hazel Carby (b. 1953), and Cheryl Wall (b. 1954). The lesbian tradition within women's literature and criticism was examined by Smith in *Toward a Black Feminist Criticism* (1980) and also by critics like Jane Rule (b. 1931), Karla Jay (b. 1947), and Bonnie Zimmerman (b. 1947). As outlined in Robinson's "Treason Our Text" (1983), this range of criticism led to an equally wide range of feminist challenges to the literary canon.

Theoretical writing closely related to the socially based mode of reading characterizes the essays in *Sex, Class, and Culture*, as well as those by such feminist writers of poetry and fiction as Tillie OLSEN in *Silences* (1978), Alice WALKER in *In Search of Our Mother's Gardens* (1983), and Adrienne RICH in *On Lies, Secrets, and Silence* (1979). Another application of theory—the version understood by some as constituting the only authentic definition of feminist literary theory—draws from French linguistically and psychoanalytically oriented models, including the work of such male thinkers as Jacques LACAN, Jacques DERRIDA, and Michel FOUCAULT.

The common denominator of French-derived theory is its emphasis on discourse as the basic cause and the measure of social differences. With the notion of discourse as the base, feminist theories like those of Hélène CIXOUS, Julia KRISTEVA, and Luce Irigaray (b. 1939) center on the connection between control of bodily, linguistic, and narrative experiences. The extremely varied critical writings of Gayatri Chakravorty Spivak (b. 1942), Alice Jardine (b. 1951), Elizabeth Meese (b. 1943), and Jane Gallop (b. 1952) suggest some of the breadth of this tendency and also make it abundantly clear that the "French" national label is no longer adequate.

Showalter's terms for the respective tendencies, "gynocriticism" and "gynesis," embody both their commonality in their centering on women, and their differences in their approach to the nature of discourse and its subjects. It may be that, in the long run, the principal difference will be one of interpreting the nature of women's marginalization from the power of discourse—whether that oppression originates in the symbolic system or in the social system that the symbolic system reflects.

BIBLIOGRAPHY: Woolf, V., *A Room of One's Own* (1929); de Beauvoir, S., *Le deuxième sexe* (1949; *The Second Sex*, 1953); Foster, J. H., *Sex Variant Women in Literature* (1956); Ellmann, M., *Thinking about Women* (1968); Millett, K., *Sexual Politics* (1970); Figes, E., *Patriarchal Attitudes* (1970); Firestone, S., *The Dialectic of Sex* (1970); Greer, G., *The Female Eunuch* (1970); Cornillon, S. K., ed., *Images of Women in Fiction* (1972); Heilbrun, C. G., *Toward a Recognition of Androgyny* (1973); Spacks, P. M., *The Female Imagination* (1975); Cixous, H., "Le rire de la Méduse," *L'Arc*, 61 (1975): 39–54; Kolodny, A., *The Lay of the Land* (1975); Rule, J., *Lesbian Images* (1975); Moers, E., *Literary Women* (1976); Showalter, E., *A Literature of Their Own* (1977); Baym, N., *Woman's Fiction* (1978); Olsen, T., *Silences* (1978); Robinson, L. S., *Sex, Class, and Culture* (1978); Auerbach, N., *Communities of Women: An Idea in Fiction* (1978); Gilbert, S. M., and S. Gubar *The Madwoman in the Attic* (1979); Kristeva, J., "Le temps des femmes," 33/44: *Cahiers de recherche de sciences des textes et documents* 5 (Winter 1979): 5–19; Rich, A., *On Lies, Secrets, and Silence* (1979); Christian, B., *Black Women Novelists* (1980); Jehlen, M., "Archimedes and the Parodox of Feminist Criticism," *Signs*, 6, 4 (1981): 575–601; Newton, J. L., *Women, Power, and Subversion* (1981); Abel, E., ed., *Writing and Sexual Difference* (1982); Russ, J., *How To Suppress Women's Writing* (1983); Walker, A., *In Search of Our Mothers' Gardens* (1983); Radway, J. A., *Reading the Romance* (1984); Christian, B., *Black Feminist Criticism* (1985); DuPlessis, R. B., *Writing beyond the Ending* (1985); Greene, G., and C. Kahn, eds., *Making a Difference* (1985); Irigaray, L., *This Sex Which Is Not One* (1985); Newton, J., and D. Rosenfelt, eds., *Feminist Criticism and Social Change* (1985); Showalter, E., ed. *The New Feminist Criticism: Essays on Women, Literature, and Theory* (1985); Jacobus, M., *Reading Woman: Essays in Feminist Criticism* (1986); Kaplan, C., *Sea Changes* (1986); Pryse, M., Spillers, H. J., eds., *Conjuring: Black Women, Fiction, and Literary Tradition* (1986); Benstock, S., ed., *Feminist Issues in Literary Scholarship* (1987); Carby, H. V., *Reconstructing Womanhood: The Emergence of the Afro-American Woman Novelist* (1987); Meese, E. A., *Crossing the Double-Cross* (1987); Spivak, G. C., *In Other Worlds* (1987); Willis, S., *Specifying: Black Women Writing the American Experience* (1987); Bauer, D. M., *Feminist Dialogics* (1988); Marcus, J., *Art and Anger* (1988); Todd, J. M., *Feminist Literary History* (1988); Wall, C. A., ed., *Changing Our Own Words: Essays on Criticism, Theory, and Writing by Black Women* (1989); Braxton, J. M., and A. N. McLaughlin, eds., *Wild Women in the Whirlwind: Afra-American Culture and the Contemporary Literary Renaissance* (1990); Gates, H. L., Jr. *Reading Black, Reading Feminist* (1990); hooks, b., *Race and Gender in the Cultural Marketplace* (1990); Jay, K., and J. Glasgow, eds., *Lesbian Texts and Contexts* (1990); Meese, E. A., *(Ex-)tensions* (1990); Spivak, G. C., *The Post-Colonial Critic* (1990); Zimmerman, B., *The Safe Sea of Women: Lesbian Fiction: 1969–89* (1990); DuPlessis, R. B., *The Pink Guitar* (1990); Warhol, R. R., and D. P. Herndl, eds., *Feminisms: An Anthology of Literary Theory and Criticism* (1991; rev. ed 1997); Hedges, E., and S. K. Fishkin, eds., *Listening to Silences: New Essays in Feminist Criticism* (1994); Allison, D., *Skin: Talking about Sex, Class and Literature* (1994); Robinson, L. S., *In the Canon's Mouth: Dispatches from the Culture Wars* (1997)

—LILLIAN S. ROBINSON

FENOGLIO, Beppe

Italian novelist and short-story writer, b. 1 March 1922, Alba; d. 18 Feb. 1963, Turin

A reserved and introverted person, F. spent most of his life in his native town, where he pursued his major cultural interest—the study and the translation of English literature. As a writer he found the two basic sources of inspiration in his attachment to his native province (Langhe, in Piedmont), and in his experience as a partisan in the Italian Resistance during World War II. The themes of war and peasant life constantly alternate in his literary production, and at times they fuse with one another against the omnipresent and precisely drawn background of Langhe. F.'s love for English literature and the English language was to become an integral part of his fiction. He attributed this interest to several of his characters, and he used his knowledge of the English language for his own linguistic experimentation.

In his first published work, *I ventitrè giorni della città di Alba* (1952; the twenty-three days of the town of Alba), a collection of short stories, F. ordered his own experience as a partisan. Far from posing as the impersonal chronicler of events, F. alternates between a corrosive tragic-comic representation of the historical material—thus distancing and diffusing the horrors of war—and the painful and more realistic description of how war irremediably upsets human relationships even among the partisans, the harbingers of a new message of freedom.

In *Primavera di bellezza* (1959; spring of beauty), another work based on his own wartime experiences, F. vividly portrays the climate of civil and moral disorder in Italy in 1943. His resentment toward Mussolini for not having set up an adequate Italian army, and toward Marshal Badoglio for handing the army over to the Germans, shapes the vitriolic strength of his language, which deforms and caricatures those characters who represent and still defend the collapsed regime. Although F.'s style in this novel has received almost unanimous praise for its artistic and formal maturity, his characterization of Johnny, the young Anglophile who joins the partisans after Mussolini's fall and dies in a German ambush, has been judged in contradictory ways. Some critics view Johnny's enigmatic detachment from military life and from Fascist rhetoric as the ideal means to document the historical and political events leading to the inevitable conclusion of collective tragedy; other critics, however, view Johnny's detachment as the author's inability or unwillingness to express, through his protagonist, his own interpretation of such events.

La malora (1954; *Ruin*, 1992), a short novel set in Langhe, represents one view of the savage and unmerciful world of the agricultural fields and the peasants, where neither political ideology nor unionization can help the protagonist escape his enslaving condition and regain human dignity. On the other hand, the posthumously published short stories in *Un giorno di fuoco* (1963; a day of fire), also set in Langhe, document F.'s attachment to life in the fields and his hope of finding traces there of archaic religiosity, which might function as a substitute for the moral and civil values destroyed by the war. Occasionally, however, F.'s ironic detachment from the barbaric and primitive actions of the protagonists reveals his awareness of the dangers intrinsic in the blind and promordial world of the peasantry.

The publication of *Il partigiano Johnny* (1968; *Johnny the Partisan*, 1995), five years after F.'s death, generated considerable critical interest, which has resulted in an overwhelming positive revaluation of F.'s writings. This unfinished novel, also set in the time of the Resistance, bears witness to the author's relentless attempt to penetrate and to understand the human condition as it is dominated by the tragic necessity for violence, and his exhausting search for artistic and formal maturity.

Early death, so ominously lying in wait for many of F.'s young protagonists, did not rob this remarkable writer of the opportunity to enrich the literature of the Resistance with what Italo CALVINO defined as the "book our generation wanted to write." On the basis of what he did produce, F. is to be ranked among the most perceptive writers on the phenomenon of violence and among the most sensitive observers of a tragic period of Italian history.

FURTHER WORKS: *Frammenti di romanzo* (1963); *La storia di Aloysius Butor* (1964); *Epigrammi* (1974)

BIBLIOGRAPHY: Merry, B., "More on F.: An Unpublished Novel in English and an English Source," *Italica*, 49 (1971): 3–17; Merry, B., "Thomas Hardy and T. E. Lawrence: Two English Sources for B. F.?" *RomN*, 14 (1971): 230–35; Merry, B., "The Thaumaturgy of Violence," *Books*, 12 (Summer 1973): 11–16; Pietrajunga, M., *B. F. and English Literature* (1987)

—MARIOLINA SALVATORI

FERAOUN, Mouloud

Algerian novelist (writing in French), b. 8 March 1913, Tizi-Hibel; d. 15 March 1962, El Biar, Algiers

F., whose parents were poor peasants, was born and raised in the rugged mountains of Kabylia, east of Algiers. After secondary school he attended the teachers' college at Bouzaréah, outside Algiers. He then held a series of teaching and administrative positions in Kabylia and Algiers. In March 1962, three days before the signing of the cease-fire at the Évian negotiations, F. and five colleagues were assassinated in a suburb of Algiers by a terrorist squad of the illegal Secret Army Organization, which was bent on subverting the impending peace between France and Algeria.

From the mid-1930s on F. associated with Albert CAMUS, Emmanuel ROBLÈS, and other writers of the so-called Algiers School. Roblès urged F. to tell the untold story of his own people. Indeed, F.'s major works all focus on himself, the territorial identity so important in Berber tradition, and the alienation of the emigrant worker.

F.'s first novel, *Le fils du pauvre* (1950; the poor man's son), was published at F.'s own expense and republished in 1954 by Éditions du Seuil. It has the distinction of being the first novel in the new wave of Algerian literature in French, which would become more readily identifiable when the first novels by Mohammed DIB and Mouloud MAMMERI appeared in 1952. *Le fils du pauvre*, whose protagonist bears the anagrammatic name Fouroulou Menrad, is an autobiographical novel about F.'s childhood and youth.

F.'s second novel, *La terre et le sang* (1953; earth and blood), explores the social consequences when an émigré returns with a French wife to his village in Kabylia and then falls in love with another woman. The passions, honor code, and sense of the immediacy of the earth are impenetrable to the outsider but have a firm hold on the Berbers of the area.

Les chemins qui montent (1957; the climbing roads) is ostensibly a fateful love story involving a man named Amer, a young orphan girl named Dehbia, and Amer's rival Mokrane; but it, again, examines Kabylian social constraints and the terrain that holds its inhabitants even as it repels them.

The three novels F. completed fall—as do the early novels of Dib, Mammeri, Malek Ouary (b. 1916), and others—into the category of the "ethnographic novel," written largely to explain to European readers the hidden, true side of Algeria. Because of their simple, naturalistic, accessible style, F.'s novels are more widely read in Algeria than are works by some of his more talented compatriots.

F.'s masterpiece, however, is his posthumously published *Journal 1955–1962* (1962; journal 1955–1962), which chronicles the physical horrors and cultural uncertainties of the Algerian war years (1954–62) and displays in its authentic humanity, quiet courage, and tragic dénouement qualities and a tone all too seldom achieved in fiction.

FURTHER WORKS: *Jours de Kabylie* (1954; new ed., 1968); *Les poèmes de Si Mohand* (1960); *Lettres à ses amis* (1969); *L'anniversaire* (1972)

BIBLIOGRAPHY: Khatibi, A., *Le roman maghrébin* (1968): 49–52; Ortzen, L., *North African Writing* (1970): 3–5, 100–111; Déjeux, J., *Littérature maghrébine de langue française* (1973): 114–42; Déjeux, J., *La littérature algérienne contemporaine* (1975): 62–66

—ERIC SELLIN

FERLIN, Nils

Swedish poet, b. 11 Dec. 1898, Karlstad; d. 21 Oct. 1961, Uppsala

F.'s early years were filled with diverse occupations, but centered chiefly around journalism and songwriting. In the 1920s he toured Sweden as an actor, and this experience left clear traces in his poetry. By the 1930s he was living in Stockholm with his mother, whose death in 1936 affected him deeply. For most of the next ten years he led a wandering life in Sweden.

F.'s early poetry largely took the form of popular songs for revues and gramophone recordings, and his ability to deal inventively with strict forms carried over into his first book, *En döddansares visor* (1930; songs of a death-dancer). Generally speaking, the poems in this collection are suffused with a soft melancholy, rather than, as might be expected, showing anger at the hard times. These are in a sense transitional poems; many are ballads very much in the tradition of Gustaf Fröding (1860–1911), but without his bitterness. F.'s poetry is always pervaded by a certain geniality and tolerance of mankind, especially the poor and the suffering.

In *Barfotabarn* (1933; barefoot children) the tone is considerably sharper: there is a satiric bite here not present earlier. There is also further experimentation with form and a new level of abstraction. Here, he also begins to play with larger structures, linking several poems by a word, a character, or an idea. These new techniques were brought to fruition in his third collection, *Goggles* (1938; title in English), in which all his talent seems to come into focus. The tone, so superficially laconic, and the language, so apparently loose, are carefully wed to his always strong sense of rhythm, and the reader/listener is propelled along. F. is one of the most aural of Swedish poets, sitting well in the mainstream of the Swedish troubadour tradition of Lucidor (1638–1674), Carl Michael Bellman (1740–1795), and Birger Sjöberg (1885–1929).

F.'s fourth collection, *Med många kulörta lyktor* (1944; with many Chinese lanterns), does not reveal any technical advances over his earlier work, although the opening "Monolog i månsken" (monologue by moonlight) is an engaging discourse on the poet's view of the world around him. If there is less intensity in his later poetry, there is a reliability to it that is not to be despised. And, as always, there is the musicality that helped make him the most popular poet of his day.

Throughout F.'s poetry there are several recurring images and themes. From his theater days comes the image of the circus and its clowns. From those restless days, too, come the images of impermanence and transitoriness that course through so many of his poems. From his early interest in theosophy come returning considerations of the divine, although F. had no interest in organized religion. Priests were as vulnerable to attack as politicians. In fact, authority of any kind is lampooned. F. called himself a hobo, and in so doing, clearly aligned himself with others, such as Harry MARTINSON, who championed the underdog.

FURTHER WORKS: *Tio stycken splitter nya visor* (1941); *Kanonfotografen* (1943); *Yrkesvisor* (1944); *Får jag lämna några blommor* (1948); *Kejsarens papegoja* (1951); *Auktion: En lantlig komedi* (1954); *Från mitt ekorrhjul* (1957); *En gammal cylinderhatt* (1962)

BIBLIOGRAPHY: Vowles, R., "N. F.: The Poet as Clown and Scapegoat," *The Norseman*, 12 (1954): 424–29; Gustafson, A., *A History of Swedish Literature* (1961): 480–85

—ALAN SWANSON

FERNÁNDEZ CUBAS, Cristina

Spanish short-story writer and novelist, b. 28 May 1945, Arenys de Mar

As a child, F. C. was intrigued by trunks, cupboards, and attics, and this fascination with closed spaces is echoed in her fiction. Her love for narration was first nurtured by a nursemaid, who captivated her with spine-tingling tales, and by an older brother, who told her stories by Edgar Allan Poe (1809-1849), adding his own embellishments. After completing law school, F. C. worked as a journalist in Peru and Barcelona, studied Arabic in Egypt, and spent a year in Germany on a fellowship. Writing, she has declared, permits her to travel on paper, journeying without restrictions and creating new worlds that satisfy her need for self-expression.

The adjectives "unsettling" and "disquieting" are often applied to F. C.'s writing. Although she resists being labeled a Gothic writer, her fiction reflects some of the main preoccupations of Gothic literature, such as an interest in the divided self and in the "unspeakable," a term that encompasses the unreadable, the incomprehensible, and the unknowable. Indecipherability is, in turn, part of a broader concern with boundaries between the objective and the subjective, inside and outside, self and other. Two of the stories in her first collection, *Mi hermana Elba* (1980; My Sister Elba), are particularly noteworthy. "La ventana del jardín" (The Garden Window), with its references to unintelligible language and inexplicable behavior, draws attention to problems of communication and decoding. The narrator consistently misreads events and behavior and, try though he may, is unable to make sense of what occurs around him. Since he is the readers' only source of information, they remain as baffled as he. The action is set on a secluded farm, and the spatial isolation reinforces the impression that the narrator has entered a world that is distinct from that of everyday experience. Problems of identity and doubling are foreground in the first narrative of the volume, "Lúnula y Violeta" (Lunula and Violet), whose titular characters are inverted images of one another, the first woman being a gifted teller of tales and the second a struggling writer. Mirrors and windows, in which they see themselves reflected, appear throughout the story, and its ending dramatizes the paradox of doubling: simultaneous unity and duality.

Identity is also a major theme in the titular story of *Los altillos de Brumal* (1983; The Attics of Brumal), which was made into a film in 1988. Its protagonist's journey back to the remote village where she was born represents a return to her point of origin and enables her to recuperate her former self. The fact that the name by which she is known as an adult, Adriana, is an inversion of her childhood name, Anairda, underscores that the two selves are mirror images of one another. The concluding story of the volume, "La noche de Jezebel" (Jezebel's Night), is simultaneously a ghost story and a parody of that form, as well as a homage to Poe. The boundary between the frame narrative and a series of embedded tales blurs, and contradictory versions of events undercut narrative authority and destabilize the fact/fiction dichotomy. The unspeakable is manifested in various ways, such as allusions to unnameable, hidden forces and a suicide note that is illegible because it is drenched in blood. Problems of meaning are again central in "La Flor de España" (The Flower of Spain), from *El ángulo del horror* (1990; The Angle of Horror). Verbal and nonverbal signs proliferate, and the narrator's attempts to decode them are hindered by the fact that she is in a foreign country whose language she finds unintelligible. The text frustrates acts of interpretation and judgment even as it encourages them.

The title story of F. C.'s of *Con Agatha en Estambul* (1994; With Agatha in Istanbul) is an excellent example of her sense of humor and an affectionate tribute to Agatha Christie (1890-1976). The fog that envelops the Turkish city obscures the protagonist's surroundings and blocks perception, as she wrestles with the secrets of a foreign language and the mystery of what may be going on between her husband and another woman. Ambiguity, enigma, and obscurity also characterize the novel *El año de Gracia* (1985;

The Year of Grace), which is an ironic rereading of a series of texts that include *Robinson Crusoe* by Daniel Defoe and the Bible. The protagonist's experience consistently differs from that of his literary models, and he is blighted rather than enriched by his stay on the island where he is shipwrecked. The novel illustrates a number of the features of F. C.'s fiction: a preference for first-person and frequently unreliable narration, a preoccupation with linguistic and epistemological problems, doubling, intertextuality, and a rhetoric of ambiguity.

F. C.'s work has been translated into eight languages, and she is recognized as one of the most important of the new women writers of Spain. She has contributed to a growing appreciation of the genre of the short story and its merit as a literary form.

FURTHER WORKS: *El vendedor de sombras* (1982); *Cris y Cros, seguido de El vendedor de sombras* (1988); *El columpio* (1995)

BIBLIOGRAPHY: Zatlin, P., "Tales from F. C.: Adventure in the Fantastic," *MRRM*, 3 (1987): 107-18; Bretz, M. L., "C. F. C. and the Recuperation of the Semiotic in *Los altillos de Brumal*," *ALEC*, 13 (1988): 177-88; Rueda, A., "C. F. C.: Una narrativa de voces extinguidas," *MMRM*, 4 (1988): 257-67; Bellver, C. G., "*El año de Gracia* and the Displacement of the Word," *StTCL*, 16 (1992): 221-32; Glenn, K. M., "Gothic Indecipherability and Doubling in the Fiction of C. F. C.," *MRRM*, 8 (1992): 125-41; Margenot, J. B., "Parody and Self-Consciousness in C. F. C.'s *El año de Gracia*," 11 (1993): 71-87; Spires, R. C., *Post-Totalitarian Spanish Fiction* (1996): 156-72; Zatlin, P., "Amnesia, Strangulation, Hallucination and Other Mishaps: The Perils of Being Female in Tales of C. F. C.," *Hispania*, 79 (1996): 36-44; Pérez, J., "C. F. C.: Narrative Unreliability and the Flight from Clarity, or, The Quest for Knowledge in the Fog," *Hispano*, 122 (1998): 29-39

—KATHLEEN M. GLENN

FERRÉ, Rosario

Puerto Rican short-story writer, poet, essayist, and novelist, b. 28 Sept. 1942, Ponce

F. received world recognition as a writer after the publication of her first book, *Papeles de Pandora* (1976: Pandora's papers). Her literary career began in the 1970s, years before she decided to study Spanish literature and received her M. A. from the University of Puerto Rico, and her Ph.D. from the University of Maryland (1987). Her first poems, short stories, and essays were published during 1972–1974 in *Zona de cargery descarga*, a magazine she founded and directed in Puerto Rico. The emergence of this short-lived magazine became a literary manifesto for new writers. It represented for contemporary Puerto Rican literature an opportunity to voice new aesthetic visions that departed from the style of writers of previous generations. It combined aesthetics with politics and with a new and innovative perspective on Puerto Rico's socioeconomic conditions. F.'s main contribution to Puerto Rican and Spanish literature has been an in-depth exploration of feminine themes. F., the daughter of a former governor of Puerto Rico, was raised in a traditional upper-class home with the same cultural myths and taboos typical to all women of her social status in Latin America. It is out of this experience that in her work F. makes a

deliberate effort to explore, unveil, and condemn the restrictive cultural values imposed by the dominating classes on society, especially on women.

F.'s first published collection of poems and short stories in *Papeles de Pandora* portrays a sociopolitical and psychological reality dominated by economic exploitation and racial and sexist prejudice in enigmatic texts that combine different styles, subtle irony, harsh satire, and fantasy. In accordance with the title of the text, these poems and short stories share the underlying idea that language (the word) is like the evils that escaped from Pandora's box, spreading suffering throughout the world. F.'s innovative meditation on the Greek myth proposes a relationship between the social problems that afflict America in general and the language, rhetoric, and discourses of power that control the way individuals interpret themselves in the world. In the enigmatic twists of her stories, hope for change is voiced in F.'s stories by the subversion and rebellion of her female characters.

In her second book, *Maldito amor* (1986; *Sweet Diamond Dust*, 1989), a collection of one novel and three short stories, F. explores the political and economic dichotomy of Puerto Rico in its dependent-independent relationship with U.S. economic interests, as well as in the dynamics of social and psychological relationships between individual persons and social classes. In this novel, F. evokes life in Puerto Rico during the beginning of the 20th c., a period of economic decline on the island, when the old landowners were displaced by new capitalistic classes dominated by North American companies. This is also the theme and setting of her short story "Isolda en el espejo" (isolda in the mirror), where F. juxtaposes the sociohistorical theme with a complex relationship between art, woman, and male fantasy. In most of her work, F. explores the concept of the feminine double. With it, F. reconjugates in its holistic complexities the image of "woman" as an individual deprived of her human potential, fragmented and adulterated by cultural values that stereotype all feminine figures as either good or bad, virgin or whore, nurturing mother or femme fatale. F.'s work condemns such polarizations and seeks to reunite the feminine self. Restricted from exploring their own human potentials, F.'s women characters cannot recognize themselves in the categories imposed on them by society and must break away from such ties in order to find who they really are.

In her novel *La Casa de la laguna* (1995; *The House on the Lagoon*, 1995), a finalist for the National Book Award, F. meditates again on the history of Puerto Rico. *La Casa de la laguna* is a five-generation saga of a family beginning as early as the Spanish Conquest of Puerto Rico. The story is a narrative dance between a wife and husband whose tales interweave facts and fiction, death and passion, and the uncertainties always already present in any historical account.

In F.'s collection of biographical and autobiographical essays, *Sitio a Eros* (1980; Eros besieged), revised in 1986 with the addition of two more essays, "La cocina de la escritura" (the kitchen of writing) and "De la ira a la ironía" (from anger to irony), F. addresses the issue of women as writers, herself included. The text is basically an account of the lives of those women writers like George Sand (1804–1876), Virginia WOOLF, Anaïs NIN, Sylvia PLATH, Julia de Burgos (1917–1953), and others, whom F. considers exemplary feminine models for their aesthetic rigor, their passion, and their imagination. Recently, a number of her writings have been translated and gathered in two different volumes, *Sweet Diamond Dust* (1988) and *The Youngest Doll* (1991).

In much of her work, but especially in *El acomodador. Una lectura fantástica de Felisberto Hernández* (1986; the usher, a fantastic reading of Felisberto Hernández), F. reiterates the very contemporary view that every critical interpretation of any work of fiction is another work of fiction parallel to the one it tries to recapture. Here, as in most of her writings, F. addresses the themes of human loneliness, isolation, and noncommunication. Though F.'s work is a feminine interpretation of society, she rejects the concept of a feminine nature in favor of the idea that women live and share common experiences due to social stereotypes that make women simple creations of fantasy, molded and distorted through history by way of myths, misprojections, and taboos. In most of her work, F. subverts these stereotypes by inverting traditional androcentric points of view. This partly explains F.'s interest in children's stories, and in the incorporation into the structure of her texts of popular anecdotes and themes like "La bella durmiente" (Sleeping Beauty) or the title of a *plena*, a popular regional song and dance from Ponce, in "Cuando las mujeres quieren a los hombres" (when women love men). F.'s texts are charged with multiple and complex metaphoric and symbolic meanings through which women are portrayed as very complex beings. Her women characters resist any binary classifications like those previously presented in Latin America, and, in general, in Western literature. F.'s work, like her poems in *Fábulas de la garza desangrada* (1982; fables of the bled heron), is also a profound meditation on love, its manifestations, and its distortions.

FURTHER WORKS: *El medio pollito. Siete cuentos infantiles* (1976); *La caja de cristal* (1978); *La muñeca menor* (1980); *Los cuentos de Juan Bobo* (1981); *La mona que le pisaron la cola* (1981); *Sonatina* (1989); *Árbol y sus sombras* (1989); *Coloquio de las Perras* (1990); *Dos Venecias* (1992); *Batalla de las virgenes* (1993)

BIBLIOGRAPHY: López, I., "'La muñeca menor': ceremonias y transformaciones en un cuento de R. F.," *ExTL*, 11, 1 (1982–1983): 49–58; Umpierre, L. M., "Un manifiesto literario: *Papeles de Pandora* de R. F.," *BR/RB*, 9, 2 (May–Aug. 1982): 120–26; Fernández-Olmos, M., "Desde una perspectiva femenina: la cuentística de R. F. y Ana Lydia Vega," *Homines*, 8, 2 (June–Jan. 1984–1985): 303–11; Guerra-Cunningham, L., "Tensiones paradójicas de la femineidad en la narrativa de R. F.," *Chasqui*, 13, 2–3 (Feb. 1984): 13–25; Chaves, M. J., "La alegoría como método en los cuentos y ensayos de R. F.," *Third Woman*, 2, 2 (1984): 64–76; Lagos-Pope, M. I., "Sumisión y rebeldía el doble o la representación de la alienación femenina en narraciones de Marta Brunet y R. F.," *RI*, 51: 132–33 (July–Dec. 1985): 731–49; Acosta Cruz, M. I., "Historia, ser e identidad femenina en 'El collar de camandulas' y 'Maldito amor' de R. F.," *Chasqui*, 19, 2 (Nov. 1990): 23–31; Jaffe, J. A., "Translation and Prostitution: R. F.'s *Maldito Amor* and *Sweet Diamond Dust*," *LALR*, 23 (1995): 66-82; Urrea, B., "El cuerpo femenino: Identidad(es) problematizada(s) en dos cuentos de R. F.," *RCLL*, 22 (1996): 279–300; Murphy, M., "R. F. en el espejo: Defiance and Inversions," *HR*, 65, 2 (Spring 1997): 145–57

—JULIA CUERVO HEWITT

FERREIRA DE CASTRO, José Maria

See Castro, José Maria Ferreira de

FERRON, Jacques

Canadian dramatist, novelist, short-story writer, and essayist (writing in French), b. Jan 20,1921 Louiseville, Quebec; d. 22 Apr. 1985, Longueil

F. received his first instruction in his native Louiseville and pursued his studies at the Collège Jean-de-Brébeuf, the Collège Saint-Laurent, and the Collège de l'Assomption, receiving his baccalaureate degree in 1941. In the early 1940s he studied medicine at the Université Laval (M.D. 1945), and then went into the armed forces until 1946, at which time he began to practice medicine, first in the Gaspé peninsula and then in Montreal.

F. had been writing since his early years, but he became particularly involved in it in his early twenties, all the while pursuing his interest in medicine, an activity that provided abundant subject matter and inspiration for his literary pursuits. His first play, *L'ogre* (1949; the ogre), was presented in 1949. It was followed by *Le licou* (1951; the halter), *Le dodu; ou le prix du bonheur* (1956; the plump one or the price of happiness), *Le cheval de Don Juan* (1957; Don Juan's horse), *Les grands soleils* (1958; the great suns), *Cazou; ou le prix de la virginité* (1963; Cazou or the price of virginity), *La tête du roi* (1963; the king's head), and *Le cœoeur d'une mère* (1969; a mother's heart). His theatrical works, which develop, among other subjects, the world of love as well as contemporary issues in Quebec, were well received. The earlier plays show an awareness of Molière's theater, while the later works become more contemporary, more directly Québécois.

It is upon his prose works, however, and his many short stories and novels, that his popularity and fame rest. F. began to move increasingly in this direction in the early 1960s, when his collection of short stories *Contes du pays incertain* (1962; *Tales from the Uncertain Country*, 1984) and the longer work *Cotnoir* (1962; *Dr. Cotnoir*, 1973) appeared, followed by *Contes anglais et autres* (1964; *English Stories and Other Tales*, 1971), *La nuit* (1965; the night), *Papa Boss* (1966; title in English), *Le ciel de Québec* (1969; *The Penniless Redeemer*, 1984), *L'amélanchier* (1970; *The Juneberry Tree*, 1975), and *Les confitures de coings et autres textes* (1972; *Quince Jam*, 1977). In these works, in which whimsy and the world of the fairy tale exist side by side with the "real" world, with all its seriousness, F. shows his preoccupation with problems in contemporary Quebec society, problems of self-identification and of the relationship of the powerful groups with the dispossessed ones—whether these be Anglophones viewing Francophones as living in a world of ignorance and sordidness, or Francophones looking askance at other, different groups.

Throughout his works, F. displays a striking power of invention, of mischievousness, of irony, mixing purely fictitious legend with historical fact as if they were part and parcel of the same world. The reader must be prepared to find, in the everyday world, figures from the Bible or historical figures from other eras as well as heroes of legend and myth. Yet throughout this new world that F. creates there appears a concern for and an involvement in the world of the present; indeed, these contemporary preoccupations led F. to create a political party, the Rhinoceros party, which poked fun at politicians and their solutions and which enjoyed a considerable amount of popularity. F.'s concern was not limited to the parochial; he was very much concerned with problems confronting all of humankind in the 20th-c. Quebec and its concerns were always on his mind, however, and he was always eager to explore all avenues that would allow it to grow politically and spiritually.

The recipient of many awards, among them that of the Governor General (1963), that of France-Amérique (1973), and the David Prize (1977), F. is one of the most important writers of contemporary Quebec.

FURTHER WORKS: *La charrette* (1968; *The Cart*, 1981); *Les roses sauvages, petit roman suivi d'une lettre d'amour soigneusement présentée* (1971; *Wild Roses: A Story Followed by a Love Letter*, 1976); *La Saint-Elias* (1972; *The Saint-Elias*, 1975); *Escarmouches* (1975); *Les lettres aux journaux* (1985); *La conférence inachevée* (1987); *Théâtre, Vol. 1* (1990); *Piéces radiophoniques* (1993). **FURTHER WORKS IN ENGLISH:** *Selected Tales of J. F.* (1984)

BIBLIOGRAPHY: Robidoux, R., and Renaud, A., *Le roman canadien-français du vingtième siècle* (1966): 185–96; Marcel, J., *J. F. malgré lui* (1970); Lemire et al., M., *Dictionnaire des œuvres littéraires du Québec* (1982), Vol. 3: passim; (1984), Vol. 4: passim; (1987), Vol. 5: passim; Cagnon, M., *The French Novel of Quebec* (1986): 84–90; Hamel, R., et al, *Dictionnaire des auteurs de langue française en Amérique du Nord* (1989): 510–14; New, W. H., *A History of Canadian Literature* (1989): 281–82

—PAUL BARRETTE

FEUCHTWANGER, Lion

German novelist and dramatist, b. 7 July 1884, Munich; d. 21 Dec. 1958, Los Angeles, Cal., U.S.A.

F. rebelled early against his wealthy and Orthodox Jewish background. He studied philology and literature in Munich and Berlin. A honeymoon trip that lasted for two years ended with an adventurous escape from French North Africa at the outbreak of war in 1914. F. started publishing as early as 1903, but his first serious writing came during World War I, and he achieved international fame in the mid-1920s. Between 1933 and 1940 he lived in exile in Sanary-sur-Mer in France; in 1936–37 he visited the Soviet Union, had a controversial interview with Stalin, and thereafter was often tagged with the communist label. In 1939 and again in 1940 he was interned by the French as an enemy alien. After another harrowing escape he came to the U.S., where, after 1941, he lived in California.

His wartime dramas—such as *Die Perser des Aischylos* (1914; the Persians of Aeschylus), *Friede* (1917; peace)—both adaptations, the second of the play by Aristophanes—and *Die Kriegsgefangenen* (1918; *Prisoners of War*, 1934)—represented an attack on nationalism and war and also addressed the philosophical polarities represented by Nietzsche and Buddha, that is, of activism versus resignation. His drama *Thomas Wendt* (1918–19; Thomas Wendt; later retitled *1918; 1918*, 1934), may have influenced his friend and protégé Bertolt BRECHT. *Die häßliche Herzogin Margarete Maultasch* (1923; *The Ugly Duchess*, 1928) was his first successful novel, but it was *Jud Süss* (1925; *Power*, 1927) that quickly established him as a writer of international stature. F. had intended the novel (as well as an earlier play by that title) to serve as a further elaboration of the activism-resignation theme, but against the background of mounting anti-Semitism the story of the 18th-c. court Jew was seen in a different light, more specifically as a statement against anti-Semitism.

While F. continued to write plays, his principal contribution lay in the social and political historical novel. His trilogy *Der Wartesaal* (the waiting room)—*Erfolg* (1930; *Success*, 1930); *Die Geschwister Oppenheim* (1933; *The Oppermanns*, 1934), and *Exil* (1939; *Paris Gazette*, 1940)—dealt with different phases of the Nazis' rise to power and their exercise of it. Nazism and various political and economic issues of the 20th c. also form the basis of the Josephus trilogy—*Der jüdische Krieg* (1932; *Josephus*, 1932); *Die Söhne* (1935; *The Jew of Rome*, 1936), and *Der Tag wird kommen* (1945; repub. as *Das gelobte Land*, 1952; *Josephus and the Emperor*, 1942)—the gripping story of the Jewish-Roman historian and perhaps F.'s best work. *Der falsche Nero* (1936; *The Pretender*, 1937) and *Die Brüder Lautensack* (1945; *Double, Double, Toil and Trouble*, 1943), which in historical guise are attacks on the Nazi leadership, are of lesser literary quality.

After 1945 F. delved into the theme of revolution. *Waffen für Amerika* (1946; *Proud Destiny*, 1947) focuses on the efforts of Beaumarchais and Benjamin Franklin to secure weapons for the American revolutionaries; *Goya* (1950; *This Is the Hour*, 1951) follows Goya's career from uninspired court painter to a socially committed artist; and *Narrenweisheit* (1952; *'Tis Folly to Be Wise*, 1952) deals with the impact of Rousseau's writings on the French revolutionaries. *Spanische Ballade* (1955; *Raquel: The Jewess of Toledo*, 1956) seems a reworking of the Jew Süss novel in a medieval Spanish setting. His final novel, *Jefta und seine Tochter* (1957; *Jephta and His Daughter*, 1957) was set in biblical times.

F. used the historical novel less to vivify the past than to present a contemporary issue in a historical setting, thereby gaining distance and detachment. He experimented little with style, but was a compelling storyteller whose leftist sympathies were barely discernible in his work. F. was immensely skilled in portraying politicians, industrialists, upper-class women, and intellectuals; he was less adept in depicting workers or the common man.

FURTHER WORKS: *Die Einsamen* (1903); *Kleine Dramen* (1905–1906); *Der Fetisch* (1907); *Heinrich Heines Fragment "Der Rabbi von Bacharach"* (1907); *Der tönerne Gott* (1910); *Warren Hastings* (1916; reworked in part with Bertolt Brecht and retitled *Kalkutta, 4. Mai*, 1925; *Warren Hastings*, 1928); *Vasantasena* (1916); *Der König und die Tänzerin* (1916–1917); *Der Amerikaner; oder, Die entzauberte Stadt* (1921); *Der Frauenverkäufer* (1923); *Der holländische Kaufmann* (1923; *The Dutch Merchant*, 1934); *Leben Eduards II von England* (1924, with Bertolt Brecht; *Edward II*, 1966); *Drei angelsächsische Stücke* (1927; contains *Die Petroleuminseln* [*The Oil Islands*, 1928]; *Kalkutta, 4. Mai*; *Wird Hill amnestiert?*); *Pep: J. L. Wetcheeks amerikanisches Liederbuch* (1928; *Pep: J. L. Wetcheek's American Song Book*, 1929); *Marianne in Indien* (n.d.; *Marianne in India*, 1935); *Stücke in Prosa* (1936; *Little Tales*, 1935); *Moskau 1937* (1937; *Moscow 1937*, 1937); *Unholdes Frankreich* (1942; *The Devil in France*, 1941); *Venedig/Texas, und vierzehn andere Erzählungen* (1946); *Wahn; oder, Der Teufel in Boston* (1946; *The Devil in Boston*, 1948); *Centum Opuscula* (1956); *Odysseus und die Schweine* (1960; *Odysseus and the Swine*, 1949); *Stücke in Versen* (1954); *Die Witwe Capet* (1956; *The Widow Capet*, 1956); *Das Haus der Desdemona* (1961; *The House of Desdemona*, 1963)

BIBLIOGRAPHY: Yuill, W. E., "L. F.," in Natan, A., ed., *German Men of Letters* (1964), Vol. III: 179–206; Spalek, J., ed., *L. F.: The Man, His Ideas, His Work* (1964); Kahn, L., *Insight and Action: The Life and Work of L. F.* (1975); Pischel, J., *L. F.: Versuch über*

Leben und Werk (1976); Fischer, L. M., *Vernunft und Fortschritt: Geschichte und Fictionalität im historischen Roman L. F.s* (1979)

—LOTHAR KAHN

FEYDEAU, Georges

French dramatist, b. 8 Oct. 1862, Paris; d. 5 June 1921, Paris

The son of Ernest Feydeau (1821–1873), a writer who was best known for realistic fiction, F. began writing monologues and humorous sketches. Until 1886, when his first full-length play was performed, F. was unsure whether to concentrate on writing or acting. The success of *Tailleur pour dames* (perf. 1886, pub. 1888; ladies' tailor), however, determined his vocation. F.'s next few efforts were failures, but the double success in 1892 of *Monsieur chasse* (pub. 1892; the master goes hunting) and *Champignol malgré lui* (pub. 1925; Champignol in spite of himself) established him as the foremost writer of *vaudevilles* in France.

The *vaudeville*, a vastly popular form of theater, combined the rapid movement and minimal psychological development of farce with the elaborate construction of the "well-made play" (a concept of mechanically efficient drama originated by Eugène Scribe, 1791–1861). F. is usually compared to a clockmaker or a mathematician because of the precision with which the elements in his plays fit together and the inevitability of the "equations" that result. Directors have always agreed that it is impossible to cut even a few lines from a play by F. without destroying large sections of the play as a whole. As the critic Francisque Sarcey (1827–1899) once noted, even a minor prop such as a hat placed on a chair will eventually have an importance in the larger scheme of the play. Stage directions are lengthy and elaborate—the famous second act of *La puce à l'oreille* (perf. 1907; pub. 1909; *A Flea in Her Ear*, 1968) begins with three pages of detailed instructions, meticulously explaining such matters as a revolving bed and a reversible costume for an actor who has to play a double role. It is probably physically impossible to stage the act on any set but the one described by F.

F.'s plays begin slowly, partly because so many props have to be planted and so much exposition is necessary, but every play inevitably builds into a crescendo of mistaken identities, rapid entrances at precisely the worst moments, incomprehensible explanations, and hopeless attempts at concealment. The second act of *Occupe-toi d'Amélie* (perf. 1908; pub. 1911; *Keep an Eye on Amélie!*, 1958), for example, begins with two characters in bed together; they never discover how they got there or what (if anything) happened between them the night before. Yet by the time the girl's father, the man's mistress, the girl's lover, a visiting prince, and assorted servants have successively burst into the room, it is as idle to seek a precise explanation as to seek the precise point at which a hurricane begins to spin. Usually when F.'s comedies end, therefore, the characters have hardly had a moment to take a deep breath, much less indulge in sin. Thus, the once notorious "immortality" of F.'s comedies is by current standards mild indeed, a matter of married women out for a fling and cocottes who would not be averse to a wealthy husband.

Attempts have been made recently to discover serious significance in F. His plays certainly show the absurdity of man's condition, and IONESCO has seen a resemblance between the

rhythm and structure of his own plays and those of F. Nevertheless, it is primarily as the master creator of mechanisms for producing laughter that F. is noted. In his final plays, one-act comedies that savagely satirize marriage, and in individual scenes such as the wedding in the town hall in *Occupe-toi d'Amélie*, F. shows great zest in mocking the bourgeois institutions of his day. To the contemporary playgoer, however, F. himself seems to be the great bourgeois institution of his day. In 1900 it was said that visitors to Paris had two essential items on their agenda: the International Exposition and *La dame de chez Maxim* (perf. 1899; pub. 1914; *The Lady from Maxim's*, 1971). Today, F.'s great three-act farces seem the incarnation of the spirit of Paris at the turn of the century.

F.'s plays fell into almost total oblivion in the period between the two world wars. A revival began in the 1940s, gaining impetus with a production of *Occupe-toi d'Amélie* by Jean-Louis Barrault in 1948, and the publication of F.'s complete dramatic works (thirty-nine farces have survived) that began the same year. In his preface to that collection, Marcel Achard (1899–1974) called F. "the greatest French comic dramatist after Molière," and although Achard's statement is sweeping, there is no question that F. is now the most frequently performed French comic dramatist after Molière. England and America, as well as France, have seen many productions of F. in recent years.

FURTHER WORKS: *Un fil à la patte* (perf. 1894, pub. 1899; *Not by Bed Alone*, 1970); *L'hôtel du libre échange* (perf. 1894, pub. 1928; *Hotel Paradiso*, 1959); *Le dindon* (perf. 1896, pub. 1949); *Théâtre complet* (9 vols., 1948–1956). FURTHER WORKS IN ENGLISH: *Four Farces by G. F.* (1970)

BIBLIOGRAPHY: Achard, M., "G. F.," in Bentley, E., ed., *Let's Get a Divorce!, and Other Plays* (1958): 350–64; Shapiro, N. R., Introduction to *Four Farces by G. F.* (1970); Lorcey, J., *G. F.* (1972); Shenkan, A., *G. F.* (1972); Pronko, L. C., *G. F.* (1975)

—MICHAEL POPKIN

FIEDLER, Leslie A.

American critic, novelist, and short-story writer, b. 8 March 1917, Newark, N.J.

Being Busted (1970), F.'s autobiographical meditation on the unending battle between the forces of societal repression and the individual rebel, suggests something of the spirit that has been at the center of F.'s work as a writer and cultural critic. *Being Busted* begins as an account of F.'s arrest on a marijuana charge and ends as a Kafkaesque allegory about the rights of an individual versus the bureaucratic state. It is a saga that begins with his adolescence in Newark—where he was almost arrested for participating in a political rally—and continues through his conventional education at the University of Wisconsin and New York University. With a Ph.D. in hand F. moved west, to a teaching post at the University of Montana, in 1940. In 1963 he joined the faculty of the English Department at the State University of New York at Buffalo, where he now teaches.

In *An End to Innocence* (1955) F. introduced the hard-hitting prose and wide-ranging concerns that were to become his trademarks. The collection is subtitled *Essays on Culture and Politics*.

Topics ranged from the cold war and the Rosenberg trial to a discussion of Mark Twain's classic, *Huckleberry Finn*, the well-known "Come Back to the Raft Ag'in, Huck Honey!"

For F., the mythic patterns found in literature can tell us much about the culture that produced the literature. Although his method is psychologically oriented—drawing on the work of FREUD and JUNG—the result has been a vision uniquely his own. F.'s major works, *Love and Death in the American Novel* (1960) and *No! In Thunder: Essays on Myth and Literature* (1960), portray the American psyche as a continuing fantasy of boyhood innocence, blissful immaturity, and self-styled rebellion. According to F., "the mythic America is boyhood" and the quintessential American hero is the adolescent male in desperate flight from the threats of marriage, domesticity, and eventual fatherhood.

F.'s critical technique is to weave the scattered threads of separate literary works into a tapestry of meaning. In such representative figures as Washington Irving's Rip Van Winkle, James Fenimore Cooper's Natty Bumppo, and Huck Finn, F. sees ingrained fears about heterosexual love and a yearning for less threatening, homoerotic relationships. Thus, the true love of Natty Bumppo is directed toward the Indian Chingachgook; that of Ishmael, in Melville's *Moby Dick*, for a savage Queequeg; that of Huck Finn for Nigger Jim. F. sees this recurring pattern as distinctly American: "The quest which has distinguished our fiction from Brockden Brown and Cooper, through Poe and Melville and Twain, to Faulkner and Hemingway is the search for an innocent substitute for adulterous passion and marriage alike."

For F., it is but a short step from American literature to American life. He moves easily—too easily, his detractors say—from observations on literature to conclusions about American culture. He has been the tireless champion of the youth culture and the editor of an anthology of science fiction entitled *In Dreams Awake* (1976), the defender of the comic book and the soap opera, as well as the author of *Freaks: Myths & Images of the Secret Self* (1978). In this unusual book F. wears a variety of hats—cultural historian, literary critic, psychoanalyst, guru—to investigate our secret-sharing with those who expand, and thereby define, the human possibility: "The true Freak stirs both supernatural terror and natural sympathy [and] . . . challenges the conventional boundaries between male and female, sexed and sexless, animal and human, large and small, self and other, and consequently, between reality and illusion, experience and fantasy, fact and myth."

F.'s fiction has always seemed an extension of his critical vision. In novels such as *The Second Stone* (1963) and *The Last Jew in America* (1966), F.'s cherished theories intrude upon the fictional fabric. When the mode is comic (as it is in *The Last Jew in America*), the result is wryly amusing, if something less than profound. His collection of short stories, *Pull Down Vanity* (1962), contains, however, some finely wrought satirical, roman-à-clef portrayals of the world of academe.

Collected Essays (1971) established F.'s stature as a major critic. These essays range over wide horizons, both literary and cultural. *A F. Reader* (1977) made F.'s work available in an attractively packaged one-volume sampler. It was a sure-fire indicator that the name alone could attract readers.

It is likely that F.'s work will survive the controversy his ideas have generated. His method of applying literary motifs to cultural phenomena looks deceptively easy, and many an imitator has tried to adopt it. F., the unrepentant "bad boy" of American letters, is, however, always his own man, always lighting out for new territories when the threat of civilization seems too near. His

energetic prose style and incisive vision have made a distinctive mark on the way we think about American culture.

FURTHER WORKS: *The Art of the Essay* (1958); *Back to China* (1965); *The Return of the Vanishing American* (1968); *Nude Croquet* (1969); *The Stranger in Shakespeare* (1972); *The Messenger Will Come No More* (1974); *The Inadvertent Epic* (1980)

BIBLIOGRAPHY: Chase, R., "L. F. and American Culture," *ChiR*, 14 (1960): 8–18; Bellman, S., "The Frontiers of L. F.," *SWR*, 48 (1963): 86–89; Davis, R., "L. F.'s Fictions," *Commentary*, Jan. 1967: 73–77; Alter, R., "Jewish Dreams and Nightmares," *Commentary*, Jan. 1968: 48–54; Bluefarb, S., "Pictures of the Anti-Stereotype: L. F.'s Triptych, *The Last Jew in America*," *CLAJ*, 18 (1975): 412–21; Walden, D., "L. F.," *JPC*, 12 (1978): 208–9; Masilamoni, E. H. L., "Fiction of Jewish Americans: An Interview with L. F.," *SWR*, 64 (1979): 44–59; Winchell, M., *L. F.* (1985)

—SANFORD PINSKER

FIGULI, Margita

Slovak novelist and short-story writer, b. 2 Oct. 1909, Vysny Kubin; d. 27 Mar. 1995, Bratislava

F. grew up in the still strongly folkloric area of northern Slovakia in the Tatra mountains shared with Poland. She finished business school and worked in a Bratislava bank for over a decade, while successfully publishing poetry and numerous stories. In 1940 she was dismissed from her job for political reasons but found enough success with further works to live as a writer from then on. In 1974 she was awarded the title of National Artist but wrote little more and died after twenty years of near silence. F.'s first published stories in the 1930s brought critical approval, and she collected them in *Uzlík tepla* (1936; Knot of Warmth) and *Pokušenie* (1937; Temptation). She shared the theme of ecstatic love in conflict against the boundaries of reason and tradition with the naturist works then being defined as "lyrical prose" for their strongly poetic and mythic treatment of human efforts to keep the rhythms and harmony of nature. This Slovak form of expressionism remains a distinctive and critically interesting literary phenomenon. F.'s antiwar short stories "Olovený vták" (1940; The Leaden Bird) and "Tri dni a tri sny" (1940; Three Nights and Three Dreams) about the effect of German Nazism on Slovak society after the Munich diktak, caused her dismissal from her job. But she had already published the immensely popular short novel *Tri gaštonové kone* (1940; Three Chestnut Horses), which was reprinted seven times in the next seven years. Though only a hundred pages, this epic treatment of the love of a rich farmer's daughter and a village tramp is mythicized by three horses symbolizing the strength, beauty, and inherent goodness of nature as well as the standard virtues of love, obedience, and hope in the Christian moral code. With the rich rhythms and imagery of biblical prose, the work masterfully sustains the atmosphere and tone of fated drama without obscuring the detailed description of Tatra mountain forests or the naive optimism of both villagers, who are rewarded in the end for their devotion and self-sacrifice.

A lyrical and highly ornamental style characterized F.'s work from the beginning, and it fit equally well in her *Babylon* (1946;

Babylon), a massive historical novel about the Babylonian kingdom in the 6th c. B.C. and the capture and long exile of the Jews. The exalted style and epic dimensions tell not only the love story of the fictional characters but also the historic rivalries of the Chaldeans and Persians and the philosophical and theological conflicts of Jewish monotheism with paganism. F.'s basic theme of work and suffering to regain the "lost paradise" after expulsion, as well as her subtext of pacifism in all its dynamic historical sweep, is contrasted by the intimate scenes of love and kindness, but the work is held in one monumental piece by the unifying effect of the exalted style.

F.'s talent and interest lay in such epical and idealizing works, but history moved against her, and *Babylon* was published just before the "Iron Curtain" fell on Eastern Europe and the canons of literary criticism narrowed to allow only SOCIALIST REALISM. The obvious pacifist themes construed as criticism of the recent war did not help the work with Stalinist critics who condemned it as escapist and "merely aesthetic." Though it was popular with readers, it was republished only ten years later, in a revised version in 1956 followed by a new "less Christian" version of *Tri gaštonové kone* in 1958.

Abandoning her pacifist views and exalted style in the postwar glorification of the battle against Nazi Germany, F. began a novel about the Slovak National Uprising near the end of World War II, called "Vlci v dolinách" (Wolves in the Valleys), but she couldn't finish it and published only extracts about an upper-class female heroine who attempts to help the working class in *Zuzana* (1949; Susanna). F. wrote pieces for children but they too seem a mixture of pseudo-patriotic socialistic slogans with authentic memories of her own rural childhood. In the period of documentary and exhortative novels showing the enthusiastic construction of factories and collective farms, F. wrote her last novel as a picture of women workers in a northern Slovak factory. *Víchor v nás* (1974; The Windstorm within Us) begins as expressionism with a magical blacksmith and a troubled girl, but the girl's painful hallucinations are explained realistically through her origin in the rape of her mother by a bestial Nazi soldier, and the magic too is abandoned. This confusion of mythic and documentary elements persists until the middle of the novel when the conflict turns into a banal factory problem with a saboteur who is overcome in a cliché illustration of the building of socialism.

F.'s work was uneven, but despite her later failures *Tri gaštonové kone* and *Babylon* remain classics.

FURTHER WORKS: *Sen o živote* (1942); *Rebeka* (1949); *Životopisné legendy* (1969); *Vybrané spisy*, Vol. 1 (1972)

BIBLIOGRAPHY: Fischerová-Šebestová, A., *M. F.* (1970); Števček, J., *Nezbadané prózy* (1971): 75-101; Števček, J., *Lyrizovaná próza* (1973): 151-59; Strmeň, K., "Slovak Literature: Brief History," in Cincura, A., ed., *An Anthology of Slovak Literature* (1976): xix-liv; Čepan, O., *Kontúry naturizmu* (1977); Rudinsky, N. L., "M. F.," in Wilson, K. M., ed., *Encyclopedia of Continental Women Writers* (1991), Vol. 1: 410-11

—NORMA LEIGH RUDINSKY

FIJI LITERATURE

See Pacific Islands Literature

FILM AND LITERATURE

"I'm sure there's a sort of talking-film cinema in our heads," says the Greek peasant Zorba in Nikos KAZANTZAKIS's novel *Zorba the Greek* (1946). In his simple way, Zorba expresses the truth that film is the medium most like the human imagination: the flow of photographically captured images mechanically reproduced can blend dream and reality much as the human mind can. Furthermore Zorba's remark suggests the degree to which cinema has become a part of individual and international social consciousness in the 20th c. The relationship between film and literature is thus one of cross influences in technique and content based on an ever-increasing awareness of the distinct capabilities and limitations of each medium.

In the beginning was the human perception of images. This consciousness found artistic visual expression in work such as the cave paintings of animals "in motion." Language and thus literature evolved as a symbolic and metaphorical representation of images and emotions. The growth of film, which began with the silent flow of images, has seen the incorporation and juxtaposition of the spoken word with the visual image. It is possible to consider film as a further development of a visual and literary process that stretches back to prehistoric times.

Film is a hybrid art form that has borrowed freely and adapted from literature for its effects and subjects. Like poetry it is able to juxtapose and join images to create moods and illustrate ideas; like drama, film employs actors, dialogue, lighting, *mise-en-scène* in general; and as in prose fiction, film is effective as a narrative art that may manipulate time and space at will.

But for all of these similarities, film differs distinctly from literature. The French critic André Bazin (1918–58) once stated that "cinema has not yet been invented." He was alluding to the ability of film because of its photographic base to mechanically reproduce reality. As the technology of cinema improves, so does film more closely re-create the world "in its own image, an image unburdened by the freedom of interpretation of the artist or the irreversibility of time." Film is thus a reproduction of reality *in time*, a fact that differentiates it from pure photography. Literature, on the other hand, is language-based and is a symbolic representation of reality. Thus, the means of perceiving literature and film are opposites. Whereas a reader must transform language into an internal visualization of a character, scene, or emotion, the film viewer must internalize the cinematic images to "read" their meaning.

The acceptance of film as an art form was slow in coming. Thomas Edison, for instance, considered his early experiments with film as a kind of toy until he understood the commercial possibilities of film as a form of mass entertainment. From the first films in the 1890s of Louis Lumière (1864–1948) and Georges Méliès (1861–1938) in France, R. W. Paul (1869–1943) in England, and Edison, the technology and popularity of film rapidly developed. In the U.S. film became cheap entertainment for the millions of immigrant workers with a poor command of English, who could not afford or understand books, poetry, or drama. Until the end of World War II film could claim to have been the major form of popular entertainment in America in the 20th c.

But while film was accepted by the masses, it was often rejected or ignored by those in the literary world. Particularly in America, the gap between the development of art and literature on the one hand and film on the other was great. Hollywood, which was for the most part founded by immigrants such as Adolph Zukor, William

Fox, and Marcus Loew, began and has largely remained dedicated to 19th-c. approaches to plot and character development. Literature, in contrast, experimented with style and content in the "modernist" phase and with social commitment during the 1930s. While Ernest HEMINGWAY was publishing *The Sun Also Rises* in 1926, William S. Hart was still a major box-office star with his simple Western tales about good and evil on the range.

Others were quick to grasp the potential of film. Vachel LINDSAY wrote in *The Art of the Moving Picture* (1922) before the advent of sound that the invention of film was as great a step "as was the beginning of picture writing in the stone age." His judgment was based in large part on the works of D. W. Griffith (1874–1948), that pioneer who not only developed (but did not invent) the basic language of film but who also helped to make film "respectable" with the quality and scale of *The Birth of a Nation* (1915), itself an adaptation of Thomas Dixon's (1864–1946) novel *The Clansman* (1905). Griffith, an indifferent playwright and actor, used poetry, fiction, and drama as source material for his films, adapting works of such diverse writers as Robert Browning (*Pippa Passes*, 1909), Alfred Lord Tennyson (*Enoch Arden*, 1911), Edgar Allan Poe, George Eliot, Frank Norris (*A Corner in Wheat*, 1909), Jack London, Shakespeare, Dickens, Mark Twain, Montaigne, Victor Hugo, Guy de Maupassant, and Tolstoy (*Resurrection*, 1909).

In Russia, Lenin seized on film as the official art form for the revolution and the Russian masses. Sergey Eisenstein (1898–1948) emerged not only as one of the Soviet Union's first important filmmakers, but also as one of the significant film theoreticians yet to appear. Eisenstein was concerned with film as a "language" and with montage (editing) as the most effective tool of cinematic language. But he was perceptive enough to understand that the basis of film language developed by Griffith may actually be found in literature and, more specifically, in the works of Charles Dickens. Crosscutting between scenes and story lines, the characterization of protagonists with objects and animals (kittens with young women, bulldogs with strong men, for instance), close-ups, dissolves, and double-exposure effects are all prefigured in Dickens's fiction. Since Dickens was Griffith's favorite author, the influence of literature on the structure and style of film is plain to see.

Eisenstein also noted the similarity between poetry and film. In its most basic form, montage is the combination of two different images or shots to create an "explosion" or third image in one's mind. The Japanese haiku, he points out in *Film Form* (1949), is constructed the same way for the same effect. Eisenstein, who began his career in theater, discussed such examples as a means to point out the *plastic* ability of film in the hands of the filmmaker to create a poetic quality to his art. And in fact, early critics felt that the silent film was the highest development of film art, which was ruined by the coming of the talkies in the late 1920s. Films such as F. W. Murnau's (1889–1931) *Sunrise* (1927), Carl Dreyer's (1889–1968) *La passion de Jeanne d'Arc* (1928; the passion of Joan of Arc), and the comic surrealism of Charles Chaplin's (1889–1977) *The Gold Rush* (1925) achieved what Susan SONTAG has called " . . . a new language, a way of talking about emotion through the direct experience of the language of faces and gestures." The absence of sound, and the use of black and white, both of which run counter to everyday reality, helped to free early cinema from a literal representation of reality, as the critic Rudolf Arnheim (b. 1904), in *Film as Art* (1957) has made clear. Filmmakers were thus able to make films in the tradition of Méliès and of Luis Buñuel's (1900–1983) *Un chien andalou* (1928; an Andalusian dog) that

suggested dreams and fantasy, or more poetically realistic films such as Dziga Vertov's (1896–1954) *Chelovek s kinoapparatom* (1928; the man with a movie camera).

The similarity and closeness of poetry and cinema is best represented in film by the avant-garde movement. Because of the much greater expenses involved, the division between commercial and "experimental" film is much more strictly drawn in film than in literature. "Avant-garde" is a loose term that has come to be applied to noncommercial filmmakers who work on their own or in small groups on limited budgets to pursue personal interests in producing "new" approaches to film. Growing out of the convergence of literary, art, and film interests in European movements such as DADAISM, EXPRESSIONISM, SURREALISM, and CUBISM in the 1920s that resulted in films by such filmmakers as Buñuel, Man Ray (1890–1976), Marcel Duchamp (1887–1968), Fernand Léger (1881–1955), and Jean Epstein (1897–1953), the avant-garde has most recently come to mean the wide variety of experimental filmmaking primarily in the U.S. Maya Deren (1908–1961), for instance, was one of the first American filmmakers to explore the poetic combination of images to create a form of surrealistic dream in *Meshes of the Afternoon* (1943). In the 1950s and 1960s the avant-garde film came also to be known as the "underground" film. Gregory Markopoulos (1928–1992) with *Psyche* (1948), Kenneth Anger (b. 1932) with *Scorpio Rising* (1962–64), and Jonas Mekas (b. 1922) with his impressionistic "diary" films represent filmmakers who create on film worlds as personal and as intense as those in poetry. Even Andy Warhol (b. 1926), with his extreme documentary approach in a film such as *Sleep* (1963), could be argued to have created a "poetry of the commonplace" by freeing the viewer from all expectation of plot, character, and action and thus involving the viewer in his own fantasies, memories, and images.

If there was a clear split between those in the forefront of film and literature in the U.S., the opposite has quite often been true in Europe. From the beginning of cinema, many European filmmakers were also writers, artists, or intellectuals in touch with the trends and movements in the literature, art, and ideas of their time. The result has been that the cross-influences and parallel development of film, literature, and the arts in Europe have tended to be much closer than in the U.S. Jean Renoir (1894–1979) was certainly influenced by his father's paintings in the composition of his films and in his general vision of humanity as expressed through his acting, writing, directing, and producing of his films. Jean COCTEAU moved easily between poetry, drama, fiction, and film, drawing from all of them as well as from the music and art of the times to produce such poetic myths as *Le sang d'un poète* (1930; script pub. 1948; *The Blood of a Poet*, 1949), *La Belle et la Bête* (1946; script pub. in Eng. as *Beauty and the Beast: Diary of a Film*, 1950), and *Orphée* (1950; screenplay pub. 1951; *Orphée*, 1972).

European filmmakers have learned from their literary traditions to think of themselves as "auteurs" who often work from original filmscripts to write (*écriture*, as Roland BARTHES would call it) their own films in their own style. Although film is a cooperative venture, Europeans have stressed the desirability of the director's being the guiding force in creating and controlling a film. Hollywood, with its emphasis on the studio production line during the 1930s through the 1950s, would seem to be in direct contrast. Yet the New Wave French critics and filmmakers of the late 1950s helped us to see that the security of the studio allowed American directors such as John Ford (1895–1973), Howard Hawks (1896–1977), and Alfred Hitchcock (1899–1980) to develop as *auteurs*, making films that reflect their personal style and vision as clearly as any work of literature expresses its author.

The relationship between film and literature has depended in part on technology. Once sound was introduced there was a mad rush by Hollywood for Broadway. Plays and playwrights were shipped west, but in those early days of sound, seldom were there results that amounted to more than filmed drama captured with a static camera. The development of lightweight "silent" cameras, of new lenses, of color and faster-stock film, of improved sound quality, and of more sophisticated editing techniques has meant that the plasticity of film has increased. Whereas in the early 1930s film was often no more than a cinematic version of a stage production with the "fourth wall" removed, movies now may be as free-wheeling in form and content as experimental prose.

Although film makes use of many forms of literature, it is prose fiction that it has come most closely to resemble. The commercial feature film represents a narrative art form, as does fiction, and both may manipulate time and space at will to present characters in a narration. For this reason popular novels have always been a fertile source for popular films. *Gone with the Wind* (1939) is a prime example of the Hollywood formula: films that Pauline Kael (b. 1919) says are made up of " . . . love and rape and incest and childbirth and storms at sea and battles and fires and epidemics." Such adaptations occasionally improve upon the original, as in the case of Francis Ford Coppola's (b. 1939) *The Godfather*, Parts I and II (1971, 1974) from Mario Puzo's (b. 1920) 1970 novel and George Roy Hill's (b. 1922) *Slaughterhouse Five* (1973) from the novel by Kurt VONNEGUT. In general, however, Hollywood productions tend to make unimaginative use of the film medium to bring popular fiction to the screen, as if films were no more than lifelike picture books. The commercialization of film and literature has more recently been carried to another extreme with the phenomenon of novelizations. This type of book is contracted to an author to be written based on the screenplay (*Saturday Night Fever* [1977], for instance) *before* the film is made, and it is published simultaneously with the release of the film.

But the differences between film and the novel are also significant. Above all else, film is an *immediate* experience: photography directly reproduces images of people and objects as we know them. Literature is language-bound, however, and is limited to expressing only what can be represented in words. This distinction has further implications: while a writer or artist may impose his control and vision over every aspect of his art, the filmmaker, no matter how carefully he controls the *mise-en-scène*, editing, and camera work, can never control every element within the movie frame. Because cinema is based on photography, the filmmaker shares his creation with the reality of the objects that appear *immediately* and *all at once* as soon as the camera lens opens upon them.

More critical attention has been given recently to the creative possibilities of adaptation from literature to film. In the Hollywood tradition, a film such as John Ford's *The Grapes of Wrath* (1939) with a screenplay by Nunnally Johnson (1897–1977) and cinematography by Gregg Toland (1904–1948)—who also shot *Citizen Kane*—was so effective in transferring the novel to the screen that the author, John STEINBECK, claimed the film was more powerful than his book. Not all of the novel could be represented on the screen, however. Steinbeck's juxtaposition of prose *styles* ranging from the omniscient-epic to an impressionistic flow of first-person speeches is lost (although Steinbeck's style could have been approximated on the screen had the producer, Darryl F. Zanuck, chosen to). Furthermore, because a film is commercially limited to a time span of a few hours, adaptation is by necessity an exercise in condensation. But what Ford's film does well is to capture the documentary directness of the migrant workers' experiences combined with an almost expressionistic use of light and shadow to suggest the conflicts and themes of the drama. Critics often point out that we cannot necessarily speak of the film as "better" or "worse" than the novel: they are two different experiences presented by two different media.

Many European directors have tended to adapt lesser-known literary works so that they may feel freer to transform the original material for their own purposes. Directors such as François Truffaut (1932-1984), Jean-Luc Godard (b. 1930), Claude Chabrol (b. 1930), Wim Wenders (b. 1943), and others have, for instance, used American detective fiction as a basis for films set in their own countries reflecting their own times and concerns. Less literal adaptations may take a variety of forms. A filmmaker may simply alter one significant detail: Thomas MANN'S *Death in Venice* (1911) is written as the internal monologue of a famous writer, but because it is difficult to suggest internal states of being on film, Luchino Visconti (1906–1978) transformed the central protagonist into a famous composer so that we can hear his music represent the emotions he experiences in the 1971 film. Similarly, time and place may be switched: Michelangelo Antonioni's (b. 1912) *Blow-Up* (1967) is set in trendy London during the 1960s, although it is based on a short story by Julio CORTÁZAR set in Paris at an undesignated time. And finally, the literary text may be used in such a freewheeling manner that only marginal resemblances remain between the film and the source. Godard's *Masculin-feminin* (1966; masculine-feminine), is "suggested" by two Guy de Maupassant short stories, yet the similarities are more thematic than dramatic and literal.

Since World War II in many countries and since the 1960s with the "new American cinema" in the U.S., the direction and concern of those in the forefront of literature and film have become remarkably similar. Like much of experimental fiction, film has come to reflect ever more complex and challenging states of consciousness. Early examples of such "modern" films would include Orson Welles's (1915–1985) masterpiece *Citizen Kane* (1941) and Akira Kurosawa's (1910–1998) *Rashomon* (1950), both of which experiment with multiple points of view and multiple story lines to suggest the relativity of truth and reality.

Modernist literature and film often suggest a fusion of style and content. There are works such as those mentioned above that employ the fragmentation of narrative to destroy the psychological neatness of Aristotelian character and plot. Godard, influenced by Bertolt BRECHT and his concept of the "alienation effect," has said that he believes in a story having a beginning, a middle, and an end, but not necessarily in that order. Such destruction of traditional modes of style and narration means that there is a much greater level of self-consciousness about writing and filmmaking. The manipulation of language-as-language and convention-as-convention in fiction (as in the fiction of Jorge Luis BORGES, for instance), has its correspondence in the contemporary filmmakers' manipulation, often in a playful spirit, of film-as-film. Ingmar Bergman (b. 1918) "frames" *Persona* (1966) with shots of a movie projector and film running through it, while François Truffaut in *La nuit américaine* (1973; script pub. in Eng. as *Day for Night*, 1975) devotes the entire film to an inside story of filming a film.

Contemporary film, like contemporary literature, has simultaneously become more subjective as it enters the private world of "self" and more socially conscious and *engagé* as it relates that subjectivity to a social realm. South American fiction and film is a prime example. The "MAGIC REALISM" of a novel such as Gabriel García Márquez's *One Hundred Years of Solitude* (1967) consists of the blending of a fertile imagination and fantasy with a strong sense of the social injustice. Similarly, the Brazilian Bruno Barreto's (b. 1946) film *Dona Flor e seus dois maridos* (1976; Dona Flor and her two husbands), based on the novel by Jorge AMADO, seamlessly fuses dream and reality, fantasy and fact in one work that both delineates the limitations of reality and celebrates the triumphant power of the imagination.

It is much easier to document the influence of literature on film than vice versa. Yet clearly, film has had a pervasive influence on literature and the other arts. In drama, for instance, Brecht acknowledged the influence of silent film, and in particular the comic genius of Chaplin, on his development of "epic theater." Even the breaking up of the silent films with title cards became a technique adopted by Brecht to help distance the audience from events on the stage. Critics have pointed to the similarity between poetry and montage and especially to poets such as Walt Whitman, whose flow of disparate images of the American scene suggests a film montage. While Whitman wrote before the development of film, other poets around the world have used film for subject matter (Hart CRANE'S "Chaplinesque"), and technique, consciously attempting to catch in language a *sense* of montage, even though such imitation is always only an approximation.

In a general sense, the influence of film on literature is simply the influence of a lifetime of moviegoing that each writer has experienced. Such an influence is, as critics such as Stanley Cavell (b. 1926) in *The World Viewed* (1971) suggest, tied to our deepest childhood memories and fantasies. But there are specific influences that have been felt in literature, most clearly in fiction. The French novelist, screenwriter, and director Alain ROBBE-GRILLET reflects this influence when he speaks of the NEW NOVEL as depending on the recording of what is visible rather than the creation of internal projections: "the sense of sight remains, in spite of everything, our best weapon, especially if it keeps exclusively to outlines" (*Pour un nouveau roman*, 1963; *For a New Novel*, 1965). Film has, therefore, helped novelists sharpen their ability to capture the visual aspect of their narratives as well as to convey much of their story through dialogue rather than through the lengthy descriptive passages typical of 18th and 19th c. novels. The lean story line and crisp dialogue of Hemingway's work would be an example of fiction that developed at a time, the 1930s, when story and dialogue were at their best in Hollywood.

As has been suggested, film and prose fiction are different media that can never merge totally. But on numerous occasions the two forms have come as close as they can with interesting results. Partially this is so because writers may write with the screen in mind. Arthur MILLER transformed his short story "The Misfits" into what he named a "cine-novel" and then wrote the screenplay for John Huston's (1906–1987) film based on that story. At other times, film technique approximated in prose is an effort to speed up the action while drawing upon the reader's ability to visualize events. Alexandr SOLZHENITSYN wrote the battle scenes in his documentary novel *August 1914* (1971) in screenplay format, complete with camera directions, while John DOS PASSOS interspersed "camera-eye" montages throughout his trilogy *U.S.A.* (1937–38) to add a sense both of documentary and of a larger objective reality to the personal stories related in between. More recently, the Austrian novelist Peter HANDKE lived with filmmaker Wim Wenders while writing his novel *The Goalie's Anxiety at the Penalty Kick* (1970), knowing that it would be made into a film by Wenders. Finally, James JOYCE, who once ran one of the first movie theaters in Dublin for a few years, was strongly influenced by what he termed the "sixty-miles-an-hour pathos of cinematographs" in the writing of *Ulysses* (1922), especially in the surrealistic scenes in the Nighttown sequence, and of *Finnegans Wake* (1939), which becomes a nightmare of images and language as experimental as any avant-garde film.

In less than a century, film has appeared, caught on, and begun to come of age. The sophistication of many contemporary feature films by directors around the world, of experimental avant-garde cinema, and even of the documentary tradition of film is equal to that of literature. Especially since the eclipse of film as the mass-entertainment form by television, such a development of sophistication has meant that much of film has become an elite art form like experimental literature, reaching a relatively small audience. But popular film, like popular literature, remains a medium for expressing the joys and sorrows of the human condition in human terms. The future for both literature and film is uncertain. In many countries the general level of literacy has declined, and the beginning of the video revolution has meant that movies are now on tape and that therefore the living room is fast replacing the cinema. Yet no matter how much television and video have cornered the image market, there seems to be a social and psychological need to share the experience of the large screen in a dark room with other people. Pauline Kael addresses this point when she notes that " . . . unlike books, but like rock music, movies could be experienced tribally, yet they also provide aesthetic experiences of a sensual complexity that it's merely priggish to deny" (*Reeling*, 1976).

The relationship between film and literature is also seen in criticism and theory. In many ways, a film can be discussed and analyzed like a poem, play, novel. Yet film criticism and theory requires in addition an understanding of the technical aspects of cinema as they apply to the aesthetic experiences they create. Because of the complexity of the film medium and because of its relative youth as an art form, film theory and criticism are still very much in their adolescent period. To date there is no consistent and complete theory of film.

Eisenstein represents the single most important attempt to establish a systematic understanding of film aesthetics to date. His concern with montage led him to discuss the "language" of film, often citing examples from literature. The writings of André Bazin and Siegfried Kracauer (1889–1966) opposed Eisenstein's emphasis on editing as a form of manipulating reality. Both critics championed films that were in their view closer to a sense of uninterrupted "reality" as we know it, represented through *mise-en-scène*. The French New Wave critic-filmmakers, along with Andrew Sarris (b. 1928) in the U.S., have put forth the *auteur* theory mentioned earlier, a theory that at its best helps us focus on the organic development of a director's style and themes. By extension, the study of the entire oeuvre of an actor, cinematographer, screenwriter, or even editor can help us better understand his or her individual contributions and the nature of film.

More recently, film criticism has been influenced by anthropological and literary interest in STRUCTURALISM and semiology. The French critic Christian Metz (b. 1931) in *Essais sur la signification au cinéma* (2 vols., 1971–72; *Film Language: A Semiotics of the Cinema*, 1974) and *Language et cinéma* (1971; *Language and Cinema*, 1974), and the Italian critic Emilio Garroni (b. 1925) in *Semiotica ed estetica* (1968; semiotics and aesthetics) go further than Eisenstein in analyzing film and its relationship to language. Pointing out that film duplicates reality while language transforms it into symbol, they suggest that the difficulty in analyzing the "codes" of film is that it is often impossible to distinguish between the "signified" and the "signifier." Metz in particular thus argues against the possibility of speaking of film as a "language" with a grammar similar to written language. Metz's own analysis of films becomes so detailed about a few codes in a film that his approach offers no clear means of grasping the significance and structure of the whole work. A more fruitful approach has been the influence of Roland Barthes's pluralistic vision of literature expressed in *S/Z* (1970; *S/Z*, 1974) and later writings. His feeling that "to interpret a text is not to give it a . . . meaning, but on the contrary to appreciate what *plural* constitutes it," can easily be applied to film as well as literature and the other arts. While much remains to be done in the history and theory of film, it seems certain that such a broad pluralistic approach will be of use in seeing films as individual "texts" and as parts of a medium used around the world.

BIBLIOGRAPHY: Eisenstein, S., *The Film Sense* (1947); Eisenstein, S., *Film Form* (1949); Arnheim, R., *Film as Art* (1957); Bluestone, G., *Novels into Film*, rev. ed. (1966); Bazin, A., *What Is Cinema?* (2 vols., 1967, 1971); Richardson, R., *Literature and Film* (1969); Kawin, B., *Telling It Again and Again: Repetition in Literature and Film* (1972); Maddux, R., et al., *Fiction into Film* (1972); Magny, C.-E., *The Age of the American Novel: The Film Aesthetic of Fiction between the Two Wars* (1972); Murray, E., *The Cinematic Imagination* (1972); Barthes, R., *S/Z* (1974); Fell, J., *Film and the Narrative Tradition* (1974); Metz, C., *Film Language: A Semiotics of the Cinema* (1974); Enser, A. G. S., *Filmed Books and Plays 1928–74*, rev. ed. (1975); Wagner, G., *The Novel and the Cinema* (1975); Armes, R., *The Ambiguous Image* (1976); Spiegel, A., *Fiction and the Camera Eye: Visual Consciousness in Film and the Modern Novel* (1976); Peary, G., and R. Shatzkin, eds., *The Classic American Novel and the Movies* (1977); Kawin, B., *Mindscreen: Bergman, Godard, and First-Person Film* (1978); Peary, G., and R. Shatzkin, eds., *The Modern American Novel and the Movies* (1978); Beja, M., *Film and Literature* (1979); Goodwin, J., "Literature and Film: A Review of Criticism," QRFS, 4 (1979): 227–46; Kittredge, W., and S. M. Krauzer, *Stories into Film* (1979); McConnell, F., *Storytelling and Mythmaking: Images from Film and Literature* (1979); Berger, J., *About Looking* (1980); Henderson, B., *A Critique of Film Theory* (1980); Horton, A. S., and J. Margretta, eds., *Modern European Filmmakers and the Art of Adaptation* (1981)

—ANDREW HORTON

FINNISH LITERATURE

Several external factors helped to shape the development of Finland's literature as the 20th c. began. The country's Swedish-speaking minority, which then stood at about fourteen percent, had realized that its days of cultural hegemony were numbered, while the Finnish majority felt that it had come into its own at last. However, its triumphant sense of youth and of mission was accompanied by an awareness of the brevity and paucity of a genuinely Finnish tradition; after all, modern Finnish-language

literature had begun with the dramas (from the 1860s) and the great novel *Seitsemän veljestä* (1870; *Seven Brothers*, 1923) of Aleksis Kivi (1834–1872). At the same time, both Finland-Swedes and Finns had to confront the sharp Slavophile swerve of tsarist policy; what had generally been a benevolent rule, ever since the country had passed from Swedish to Russian hands in the War of 1808–9, had suddenly turned oppressive. Finland-Swedish authors began to regard themselves, somewhat melodramatically, as doubly lonely sentinels of the West, threatened both by Finnicization and Russification. The Swedish-language lyric of that time is full of symbols of isolation and exhaustion; the tired trees of Mikael Lybeck (1864–1925), the bleak skerries of Arvid Mörne (1876–1946), the "last Germanics" of Bertel Gripenberg (1878–1947), dying at their posts; Richard Malmberg (1877–1944), calling himself "Gustav Alm," talked about dark autumn days and Finnish aggressiveness, and Ture Janson (1886–1954) used the term "the lonely Swedes" as a title, while Runar Schildt (1888–1925), in novellas that have become classics, looked with sad eyes at Finland-Swedish enervation and self-protective arrogance. (Another writer of the period met the predicted onslaught of barbarism in quite a different way, with exceptional wit: Guss Mattsson [1873–1914], the virtuoso of the *causerie*.)

Some Finnish-language authors, anxious to demonstrate that their own literature was capable of taking a part in the European concert, used similar themes of overripeness and decay; nonetheless, such elegant academic poets as Otto Manninen (1872–1950) and V. A. Koskenniemi (1885–1962) were a great deal more positive toward life than were their Finland-Swedish contemporaries. The often cynical eroticism of Maria Jotuni (1880–1943), in her novellas and plays, resembles that of Schildt; L. Onerva (Hilja Onerva Lehtinen-Madetoja, 1882–1972), in her rather bookish affection for the bizarre and the perverse, drew on the same continental sources as Gripenberg. The greatest lyricist of the time, Eino LEINO, could not resist the temptation to weave some motifs of European decadence (the *femme fatale*, the cursed knight, the superman) into the first part of his masterpiece, *Helkavirsiä* (1903; *Whitsongs*, 1978), while in the second part (1916), he wrote about an end of the world. Yet Leino's poem was born, in fact, out of the Finnish national epic, the *Kalevala* (1849), reconstructed by Elias Lönnrot (1802–1884). Yearning for Europe, Finnish literature still wanted to pay homage to the pristine Finnish landscape, the honest Finnish rustic (often seen as a more or less noble savage), the distinctive Finnish past. The national romanticism that informed Sibelius's tone poems on *Kalevala* themes also captured literary men: Leino himself, the poet and dramatist J. H. Erkko (1849–1906) in his *Kalevala* plays, and the lyric poet Larin-Kyösti (pseud. of Karl Gustaf Larson, 1873–1948), who repeatedly used the folklore and landscape of the semi-exotic eastern province of Karelia (traditionally regarded as the *Kalevala's* place of origin) and of his native Häme. Even such a proponent of realism and clarity as Juhani Aho (1861–1921) was caught up in this ethnocentric patriotism, writing his later novels about Finnish heathendom—*Panu* (1897; Panu); about the zealous efforts of Lönnrot and others to conjure up medieval Finland—*Kevät ja takatalvi* (1906; spring and late winter); about a backwoods erotic triangle—*Juha* (1911; Juha). The novelists and playwrights Teuvo Pakkala (1862–1925) and Johannes Linnankoski (pseud. of Juho Vihtori Peltonen, 1869–1913) celebrated a folk hero and free spirit, the Finnish lumberjack, even as Santeri Alkio (1862–1930) and Artturi Järviluoma (1879–1942) gave a literary gloss to the so-called "knife fighters" of their home region of Ostrobothnia. These stalwarts were turned by

Järviluoma, in his play-with-music, *Pohjalaisia* (1914; Ostrobothnians), into freedom fighters against the Russians.

It is quite possible to detect a split in Finnish attitudes of the early 20th c., a split already evident in Lönnrot's *Kalevala* and Kivi's *Seitsemän veljestä*. The literature loves the freedom of the wilderness but feels impelled to teach moral and behavioral standards; indeed, two novelists taken very seriously in their time are not readily swallowed today, because of their urge to edification—the Tolstoyan Arvid Järnefelt (1861–1932) and the schematist of georgic purity and urban rottenness, Maila Talvio (1871–1951). Probably, the rise during the 1960s and 1970s of the critical fortunes of "Maiju Lassila" (the best-known of the several pseudonyms of Algoth Untola, 1868–1918) resulted not only from his having been the leading leftist polemicist in Finland's civil war, but from the zany and quite unedifying humor of some of his novels, particularly *Tulitikkuja lainaamassa* (1910; the match-borrowing expedition), which builds upon still another strain in Kivi, the love for amusing confabulation.

Finland's sudden independence from Russia (December 1917), the White victory over the Reds in a brief but bloody civil war (January-May 1918), and the establishment of the Republic of Finland in 1919 brought about an optimistic (but not unreflective) atmosphere. Shedding much of its negativism, Finland-Swedish literature entered a period of unexpected brilliance; the MODERN-IST poets—Edith SÖDERGRAN, Gunnar BJÖRLING, Elmer DIKTONIUS, and Rabbe ENCKELL—supported and supplemented by the critic, novelist, and playwright Hagar Olsson (1893–1978), created a body of lyrics quite unlike anything the North had seen before; closely attentive to developments from abroad, hoping to reach an international public, Finland-Swedish modernism succeeded at least in changing the character of poetry in the rest of Scandinavia. The linguistic minority, which had played a leading role in the formation of the new country, subsequently met renewed hostility from certain Finnish quarters; but its literature acquired a reputation outside Finland that it had never had before, and not only because of the modernists: the lushly romantic verse of Jarl Hemmer (1893–1944), and Runar Schildt's play *Den stora rollen* (1923; the great role), a Finland-Swedish counterpart to O'CASEY's *Juno and the Paycock*, set in Helsinki during the civil war, also got extensive attention in Sweden and elsewhere.

It has often been argued, incorrectly, that the civil war remained a taboo subject until the middle of the century, or that its portrayal in literature consisted mostly of propaganda for the winning side; yet, just as Finland's government, after initial excesses, adopted an intelligent policy of reconciliation toward the vanquished, in literature there was a repeated effort to get at the causes for the conflict. Both Schildt and Hemmer, although members of the Finland-Swedish patrician class, dealt with the matter frankly, as in Hemmer's novel, *En man och hans samvete* (1931; *A Fool of Faith*, 1935), where he makes no bones about the brutality of the White prison camps. And still another Finland-Swedish novelist, Sigrid Backman (1886–1938), to be sure, from less privileged circumstances, was not afraid to discuss the war from the standpoint of common humanity. Artistically, however, their investigations stand far below the works of three major Finnish-language novelists. Frans Eemil SILLANPÄÄ, Joel LEHTONEN, and Ilmari Kianto (1874–1970)—the last-named with his novel about Finnish backwoods poverty, *Ryysyrannan Jooseppi* (1924; Joseph of Ryysyranta)—looked either at the conflict or its immediate antecedents, giving their attention in particular to the landless countrymen from whom the Reds had recruited many of their followers. (That the trio was

indifferent to the lot of the industrial worker is significant; the literature's tradition, as it had developed out of Kivi, found the "child of nature," for all his wretchedness, more fascinating—and more authentically "Finnish"—than the factory laborer; besides, to their minds, the latter had been tainted by the theories of socialism.)

Thus, some authors tried valiantly to deal with Finland's most recent past, and with the gap between what Lehtonen termed Finland's "aborigines" and its civilized (and perhaps more superficial) citizens; others looked farther back in time. The dramatist Lauri Haarla (1890–1944) examined the civil war in his *Kaksiteräinen miekka* (1932; the two-edged sword), but the best of his work for the stage lay in his expressionistic plays of the 1920s on themes taken from the *Kalevala* and from Finland's 18th-c. history. Aino KALLAS stylized the history and mythology of a related country, likewise recently become independent, in her short and balladlike novels about Estonia. One might propose that the mixture of intense emotionalism and equally intense self-discipline among the poets of the Flame Bearers group sprang from somewhat the same source as Haarla's and Kallas's application of extreme literary artifice to elemental passion. There is a desire to reconcile the irreconcilable, the primitive world and ordered culture, a desire that, in the case of the poets, led to a mystical thanatophilia. Katri Vala (1901–1944), Uuno Kailas (1901–1933), and Kaarlo Sarkia (1902–1945) rejoiced, in fact, in presentiments of early death; their immediate predecessor in the Finnish lyric, Juhani Siljo (1888–1918), had been killed in the civil war, on the White side, and their comrade Yrjö Jylhä (1903–1956) would write the most important book of verse to come out of Finland's 1939–40 Winter War with the U.S.S.R., with duty and death side by side.

At the start of the 1930s, Finland had witnessed an attempt at a fascist coup by Vihtori Kosola (1884–1936), "Finland's Mussolini"; the Winter War came at the decade's end. The temper of literature grew anxious, with a flaring-up of various literary and emotional fads, many of them escapist—the idyll flourished in the last novels of Sillanpää and the poems of the sometime revolutionary, Diktonius; the endangered reaches of Karelia, which the Finns were forced to cede to the U.S.S.R. in 1940, were written about again and again, in the Finnish-language novels of Unto Seppänen (1904–1955) and the Swedish-language novels of Olof Enckell (b. 1900) and Hagar Olsson; a cult of the flesh appeared in the Finnish narratives of Iris Uurto (b. 1905); and the Russian-born Finland-Swede Tito Colliander (1904-1989), fascinated by sex, was still more fascinated by Dostoevskian repentance. (Although overt frictions between Finland's two language groups continued throughout the 1930s, their literatures show a remarkable number of resemblances and parallels.) It was a febrile time, and even an essentially cool-headed observer, the young Mika Waltari (1908–1979), writing in Finnish, found life-ecstasy at work in Helsinki, while a character in Hagar Olsson's *Chitambo* (1933; Chitambo) beholds the angel of death in one of the capital's parks. Direct political statements were made only occasionally, although both Colliander and the brilliant Finnish-language essayist Olavi Paavolainen (1903–1964) visited Hitler's Germany as neutral observers. The Finland-Swede poet Örnulf Tigerstedt (1900–1962) espoused a rhetorical fascism; the Marxist-Leninist left organized itself into the Wedge group, of which Arvo Turtiainen (1904–1980) and Viljo Kajava (b. 1909), both writing in Finnish, were the first lyric stars, producing poetry about the working man reminiscent of that Diktonius and, in Turtiainen's case, of Edgar Lee MASTERS. However, a potentially vigorous voice of the left, the Estonian-born Finnish-language writer Hella Wuolijoki (1886–1954), made a place for herself in the literature of the 1930s—writing under the pseudonym of Juhani Tervapää—with plays about the family of the "Niskavuori estate" that seemed quite unrelated to their author's political convictions. As for Toivo Pekkanen (1902–1957) and his novels in Finnish about the new factory town of Kotka, he was an unimpeachable member of the proletariat, but refused to align himself with any political faction. Pekkanen's presentation of the worker in literature, by the way, was something of a pioneering deed, even in the 1930s. It is noteworthy that the two most advanced structural and stylistic experiments of the decade still deal with characters who, as it were, have not been incorporated in an industrial society. The main figure of Elmer Diktonius's "woodcut in words," *Janne Kubik* (1932; Janne Kubik), is a drifter, the voices in the Finnish-language novelist Volter KILPI's giant *Alastalon salissa* (1933; in the hall of Alastalo) belong to the sailors and farmers of the skerries.

The Winter War has been accepted as a heroic episode in Finland's history; the so-called "Continuation War" of 1941–44, in which the nation was a "cobelligerent" of Nazi Germany, ended with a sense of relief, of exhaustion, and (in the case of the political left) of vindication. Finland lost about an eighth of its area to the Soviet Union, and heavy reparations had to be paid to the victor; no wonder that literary vitality dwindled. Swedish-language literature seemed ready to vanish (the abrupt failure of Diktonius's talent, the early death of the poet Christer Lind [1912–1942], the suicide of diarist Kerstin Söderholm [1897–1943], and the departure for Sweden of the essayist Hans Ruin [1891–1980], are but a few cases in point); and Finnish-language literature was but little better off—Sillanpää shared Diktonius's fate, such distinct lyric poets as Vala and Sarkia died too soon, Mika Waltari entered upon his new career of composing international best sellers. The sort of "end of Finland" at which Paavolainen hinted in his great war journal, *Synkkä yksinpuhelu* (1946; gloomy monologue), seemed to be at hand. Yet the return to poetry of Aaro Hellaakoski (1893–1952), once the Finnish disciple of APOLLINAIRE, was a sign that Finnish lyric was once again about to try to catch up with that of the rest of Europe, and the novelist Pentti HAANPÄÄ showed new life, first with an ironic treatment of the late war, and then with a comical depiction of an earlier catastrophe, the great famine of 1867–68. Patriotic fervor and patriotic pathos were swept away: for the nonce, wry humor took their place.

The 1950s were years of promises fulfilled. Rather abruptly, after the political crisis of 1948 (when it was feared that Finland might go the way of Czechoslovakia), the nation appeared capable of survival. Promising debutants from the late 1930s and 1940s now flowered again; Finland-Swedish literature got attention around the world by means of the children's books of Tove JANSSON, while the warm-hearted and observant lyrics and stories of Solveig von Schoultz (1907–1997), the carefully made elegiac verse of Bo CARPELAN, and the emotionally perceptive dramas of Walentin CHORELL were readily exported to the rest of Scandinavia. It was, to be sure, a literature that traveled easily, having little that was identifiably "Finnish" about it, concerned with the human lot taken large, and excelling at close psychological analysis, a trait that was shared, to a good extent, by some new Finnish-language authors, Juha Mannerkorpi (1915–1980) Eila Pennanen (b. 1916), and Marja-Liisa Vartio (1924–1966). The experiences of the 1930s and 1940s may have fostered such inwardness, or such concern with the problems of everyday life; the complications of Finland's recent reality were too painfully near, and too ambiguous, to contemplate. The sensitivity to emotional states was coupled, in many cases, with the desire (encouraged by Hellaakoski's example) to give the

Finnish-language lyric what Finland-Swedish poetry had long had, as a result of the modernists, a full liberation from the worn-out imagery, rhyme, and rhetoric of the past. In the 1950s, the victory was finally won, by Eeva-Liisa MANNER, Aila Meriluoto (b. 1924), Tuomas Anhava (b. 1927), and, above all, Paavo HAAVIKKO, writers of poetry that is rich in allusion (but not specifically Finnish allusion) and filled with personal rather than national myth—as a myth-maker, Helvi Juvonen (1919–1959) is of particular interest and value.

Nonetheless, the most notable productions of the 1950s may well be those where, again, Finnish problems and the Finnish past are directly addressed. Haavikko himself, early on, thought about the political and geographical situation of Finland in his parabolic plays; a less intellectual and more gripping address to Finland's abiding difficulties—its fateful location, its social extremes—came, as usual, in the Finnish-language novel. Lauri VIITA's broad and tragicomic chronicle of an industrial community, *Moreeni* (1950; the moraine), opened the decade; Väinö LINNA's vastly popular war novel *Tuntematon sotilas* (1954; *The Unknown Soldier*, 1957) marked its middle; and the first two volumes of Linna's trilogy about a tenant farmer's family closed it. Viita and Linna are clearly spokesmen for the Finnish masses, putting themselves inside their characters in a way that, for example, would have been quite impossible for Lehtonen and Kianto in their time. The question of the Finnish "savage" is no longer of the essence; he still appears, but only as a subsidiary figure to, say, Linna's responsible and clear-thinking common soldier and common man. Similarly, Veijo MERI, is on the side of simple folk, in his accounts of the recent war against Russia and the civil war; but his attitude toward his material and his craft is different from Linna's. An heir to Haanpää, he turns national catastrophes into BLACK HUMOR, and, instead of practicing sequential narration, as Linna does—and other such widely read novelists as Veikko Huovinen (b. 1927) and Paavo Rintala (b. 1930)—he constantly toys with narrative forms, although taking care always to entertain his readers. Other prose writers were less careful of their audience, i.e., less aware of their old-fashioned Finnish function as storytellers (and both Haanpää and Meri construct novels that are, in effect, fabrics made up of short stories). Pentti Holappa (b. 1927) with his mazelike novels and Antti Hyry (b. 1931) with his detailed and compressed tales, in their studied objectivity and their concern with the apparently trivial, found themselves regarded as leaders in the "Europeanization" of their literature—Finnish equivalents, say, of Michel BUTOR. It is not difficult, though, to perceive another of Finnish literature's favorite themes in their texts: that of the man quite outside society, without family or friends, the man for whom neither the wilderness nor civilization provides a refuge.

Irony and double-edged humor lost ground to social and political consciousness during the 1960s and the 1970s, in Finland as in the rest of the North, while the nation enjoyed a prosperity it had never known before: there was a nostalgia, almost, for the unhappy past, a bad conscience about the affluent present. A kind of preaching of the benefits of iron social planning (or a dogmatic harping on the faults that result from its absence) entered the work of one author after another. For example, Christer Kihlman (b. 1930) began as an explorer of what he found to be the rottenness of his own group, the Finland-Swedish upper class, and slid slowly—seducing readers with his graceful style—toward suggestions of armed revolution. Hannu SALAMA, writing in Finnish, started with a look at several kinds of Finnish *malaise* (residual Lutheranism, moral hypocrisy, isolation), to move along to a eulogy of Finnish

Communists in the Continuation War. Claes Andersson (b. 1937), in his unadorned Swedish poetry, complained at first about obvious ills (for example, the treatment of the emotionally disturbed), then laid the blame at the feet of an "undirected" society; in his lively Finnish lyric poetry Pentti SAARIKOSKI tried to show his nation its own absurdities by shocking it with linguistic and personal absurdities of his own. Legitimate complaints became, all too easily, tirades against the establishment. The common man was forever good and forever the victim—as in the novels in Finnish of Alpo Ruuth (b. 1943) and Antti TUURI. Finland's literature has always been keenly interested in the nation's past; now, particularly in Finnish-language writing, a ransacking of that past took place, a march through the battlefields and prison camps of the civil war in search of heroes of the defeated side, a reexamination of the fascistic episode of the early 1930s, which became the subject of the great stage success of the 1960s, the *Lapualaisoopera* (1967; the Lappo opera) of Arvo Salo (b. 1932) and the composer Kaj Chydenius (b. 1939). In short, the process of "democratization" of Finland's society that had begun in 1944, in many respects a laudable effort, had given birth to a literary spirit that came close to a monotonous intolerance, and which, in rightly praising the efforts of the Finnish masses to achieve a measure of dignity and freedom, went in the direction of freedom's denial. Authors could find themselves in situations fraught with irony; in his novels, Timo K. Mukka (1944–1973) described and apparently approved of an undisciplined north Finnish society of reindeer herders quite free of any sexual taboos, yet—like so many of his contemporaries—he entertained an admiration for his nation's thoroughly disciplined eastern neighbor, the Soviet Union; the Finland-Swedish autobiographer Henrik Tikkanen (b. 1924) revelled in telling about his blue-blooded family and *its* sexual excesses, as well as his own, meanwhile interjecting appropriate moralizings about capitalist and elitist corruption along the way.

The word "Finlandization," that is, the transformation of an ostensibly neutral country into what is, in effect, a part of Europe's Eastern bloc, has become popular in discussions of international politics. It cannot be denied that a creeping dogmatism—with a goal not unlike that of "Finlandization"—has entered much of Finland's recent literature. And Kivi's ambiguity of stance, his dialogue between the pull of the wilderness and the requirements of civilization, is by no means the only tradition, or habit, to have come down from the 19th c. Among Kivi's contemporaries were men of a much more rigid and self-righteous stripe, for example, Johan Ludvig Runeberg (1804–1877), with his call for stoic patriotism, and Johan Vilhelm Snellman (1806–1881), with his demand that Finland become monolingual in Finnish. Yet the country's culture appears to have gained most from its balancing acts—between disorder and discipline, between languages, between East and West. Happily, in its contemporary literature, Finland possesses central figures who reflect or smile, rather than accuse or denigrate. The Finn Haavikko has spoken more and more directly about the lot of the nation caught in the middle, and the ways it must take to survive; the Finland-Swede Lars HULDÉN has joked about much that was once sacred in Finland, including Runeberg himself: his jokes are penetrating, even serious, but never hateful.

BIBLIOGRAPHY: Hein, M. P., Introduction to *Moderne finnische Lyrik* (1962): 3–16; Laitinen, K., *Finlands moderne Literatur* (1969); Schoolfield, G. C., "The Spirit of Finland's Literature," *BF*, 5, 3 (1972): 7–14; Ahokas, J. A., *A History of Finnish Literature* (1973); Laitinen, K., Introduction to *Modern Nordic Plays: Finland* (1973): 7–16; Ahokas, J. A., Introduction to *Prose finlandaise* (1973): 13–73; Schoolfield, G. C., Introduction to *Swedo-Finnish Short Stories* (1974): 1–17; Hein, M. P., Introduction to *Finnland: Moderne Erzähler der Welt* (1974): 9–42; Dauenhauer, R., and P. Binham, Introductions to *Snow in May: An Anthology of Finnish Writing 1945–1972* (1978): 21–101; Plöger, A., , ed., Afterword to *Neue finnische Prosa* (1979): 255–60; Tiusanen, T., "Introduction to 20th Century Drama in Finland"; Zilliacus, C., "Group Theatre in Finland during the Seventies," Niemi, I., "The Lapua Opera," in Wrede, J., et al., eds., *20th Century Drama in Scandinavia* (1979): 19–25: 79–89: 177–86; special Finland issue, "The Two Literatures of Finland Today," *WLT*, 54, 1 (1980); Lomas, H., Introduction to *Territorial Song: New Writing in Finland* (1981): vii–xx

—GEORGE C. SCHOOLFIELD

FINNO-UGRIC LITERATURES

The Finno-Ugric peoples of the former Soviet Union, arranged in descending order by the numbers of their native speakers, are Estonians, Mordvins, Udmurts (or Votyaks), Maris (or Cheremis), Komis (both Komi-Zyrians and Komi-Permyaks), Hungarians, Karelians (including Olonetsians and Ludes), Finns, Khantys (or Ostyaks), Vepsians, Mańsis (or Voguls), Saams (or Lapps), Ingrians, Livonians, and Votes. Linguistically related to the Finno-Ugrians are the Samoyeds: Nenets (or Yuraks), Selkups (or Ostyak-Samoyeds), Nganasans (or Tavgis), and Enets (or Yenisei-Samoyeds). The Finno-Ugric and Samoyed languages make up the Uralic language family.

The national groups who number only a few hundred or thousand do not have a literature, although the Mańsi Yuvan Shestalov (b. 1937) has published more than ten volumes of poetry and lyrical prose. Khanty literature has developed mainly since the 1960s; one Khanty poet, Mikul (officially Ivan Ivanovich) Shulgin (b. 1940) is a member of the Writers' Union of the U.S.S.R. Karelian has been very little used as a literary language, Finnish being the official language of the Karelian A.S.S.R. (which was temporarily called the Karelo-Finnish S.S.R.). Among those writing in Finnish, Antti Timonen (b. 1915) is best known, especially for his novel *Me karjalaiset* (1971; we, the Karelians). The Hungarians in the Transcarpathian Ukraine have not yet produced an independent literature. (Estonian literature is treated in a separate article.) Thus, the focus here is on the central Finno-Ugric group, consisting of Permic (Komi and Udmurt) and Volga-Finnic (Mari and Mordvin). These are essentially rural peoples, all of them exposed to similar cultural influences, throughout their histories, with Russian now the overwhelming one.

Until the Russian Revolution hardly anything could be published in local minority languages, except translations of religious brochures, some calendars, and other occasional publications. Since the tsarist authorities did not want native secular literatures, the outstanding Komi poet Ivan Kuratov (1839–1875), for instance, could publish only five of his poems, disguised as folk poetry. When the native literatures began to take shape after 1917, there was much enthusiasm. Since there was no agreement about a fixed literary language, more than one dialect was used. To this day only the Udmurts have a unified literary language.

Many of the early writers were elementary-school teachers active in the Communist Party. Nevertheless, they were not spared the persecutions of the 1930s. The writers were accused of "bourgeois nationalism," that is, of giving too much attention to the past and present of their national cultures. Numerous writers were arrested, and some were executed. After the Twentieth Communist Party Congress (in 1956, under Khrushchev) the doomed could be posthumously rehabilitated, but irreparable damage had been done.

Soviet literary historians often distinguish the following periods in the development of young native literatures: one or two periods from 1917 to 1941, one from 1941 to 1945, one from 1945 to 1956 (the year of the Twentieth Party Congress), and one thereafter. It seems simpler to allow for a preparatory period (before 1917) and to count only three periods after that: (1) unfolding and crisis (from 1917 to 1938 or 1941); (2) transition (until 1956); (3) improved continuation (since 1956).

These literatures usually began with relatively short works, expecially poems. If there were enough talented writers, the development of multiple genres was achieved quite early. This was the case with modern Komi literature, whose four founders complemented each other. There was a dramatist, poet, and prose writer, Viktor Savin (pseud.: Ńobdinsa Vittor, 1888–1943); a "romantic" lyric poet and prose writer, Venyamin Chistalev (pseud.: Tima Veń, 1890–1939); an "epic" poet, prose writer, and dramatist, Mikhail Lebedev (1877–1951); and a lyric poet and linguist, Vasily Lytkin (pseud.: Iĺĺa Vaś, b. 1895). The leader of the second generation of Komi Soviet writers is Gennady Fedorov (b. 1909), whose principal work is the historical novel *Kya petigön* (1959–62; it is daybreak). Among those of the third generation, Gennady Yushkov (b. 1932) has written lyric poems, prose works, and dramas.

Udmurt writers displayed high artistry as early as the 1920s. Their leader was Kuźma Chaynikov (pseud.: Gerd Kuzebai, 1898–1937 or 1941), who was an excellent lyric poet, prose writer, folklorist, and author of textbooks. In 1932 he was accused of bourgeois nationalism, arrested, and later executed, and only in 1958 was he posthumously rehabilitated. Another Udmurt writer, the novelist Dmitry Korepanov (pseud.: Kedra Mitrei, 1892–1949) was exiled to Siberia, and was posthumously rehabilitated in 1956. A highly talented woman poet is the Udmurt Lina Vekshina (pseud.: Ashaĺtsi Oki, b. 1898). She too, was accused of nationalism and was forced to give up her literary career. Mikhail Petrov (1905–1955) wrote the best Udmurt historical novel of the postwar period, *Vuzh Multan* (1954; old Multan). Important among the younger generation was the prose writer Gennady Krasiĺnikov (1928–1975). The Udmurts have also produced a genuinely modern poet, Flor Vasilev (b. 1934).

In Mari literature, Sergey Grigoŕev (pseud.: Chavain, 1888–1942) was a leading writer even before 1917, but he, too, became a victim of the "personality cult." The first Mari novelist was Yakov Mayorov (pseud.: M. Shketan, [1898–1937]), who also wrote plays. Nikolay (Miklai) Kazakov (b. 1918) is representative of the older generation of poets, and Valentin Kolumb (b. 1937) of the younger ones. The best-known Mari dramatist is Sergey Nikolaev (b. 1908). Kim Vasin (b. 1924) is very active as a literary historian and as a prose writer.

Modern Mordvin literature started with poetry. To this day there are a great number of poets, among whom two older writers, Nikolay Irkaev (pseud.: Nikul Erkai, b. 1906) and Artur Moro (b. 1909) are predominant. The Mordvin novel was established by Timofey Raptanov (1906–1936). Among modern novelists, Kuźma

Abramov (b. 1914) stands out. Mordvin drama started with the ill-fated Fyodor Chesnokov (1896–1938), who was a victim of the purges and only posthumously rehabilitated. Later, Pyotr Kirillov (1910–1955) was the main contributor to the development of this genre.

Among the Samoyeds, only the Nenets have been able to produce some literature, initiated by Tyko Vylka (1886–1960). There are even a few Nenets writers who are members of the Soviet Writers' Union.

The future of these literatures will depend on the competence of the writers, the reactions of the public, and, most importantly on the regulations of the Communist Party.

BIBLIOGRAPHY: Domokos, P., "Literaturen finnisch-ugrischer und samojedischer Völker in der Sowjetunion," *Nachrichten der Akademie der Wissenschaften in Göttingen*, 1, 2 (1977): 37–64

—ALO RAUN

FIRBANK, Ronald

English novelist, dramatist, and short-story writer, b. 17 Jan. 1886, London; d. 21 May 1926, Rome, Italy

F. came from a conventional, modish, and socially ambitious family whose large fortune had been made by his paternal grandfather, an energetic collier who rose from the Durham pits to become one of England's wealthiest railway contractors. Ineffectually urged by his parents to enter the British Diplomatic Service, F. went to France in 1903, where he studied those French and Belgian writers—Baudelaire, Flaubert, Gautier, Huysmans, and MAETERLINCK—who were to influence profoundly his literary career. His first publication, *La princesse aux soleils* (1904; *La Princesse aux Soleils*, 1974 [bilingual]), written in French, was a prose poem that illustrated his enduring interest in *fin-de-siècle* literature.

Entering Trinity Hall, Cambridge, in 1906, F. led a leisurely existence. He took no examinations, entertained lavishly, and made frequent excursions to the London theater, opera, and ballet. In 1908, following the examples of Oscar Wilde, Ernest Dowson (1867–1900), Aubrey Beardsley (1872–1898), and Frederick Rolfe (Baron Corvo, 1860–1913), F. was received into the Roman Catholic Church. He left Cambridge in 1909 without a degree and planned to enter the Vatican Service. Unable, however, to secure a Vatican post, F. felt the Church had rejected him, an attitude that imbued his fiction.

Though F.'s professional career as a novelist began with the publication of *Vainglory* (1915), he had already written numerous poems, plays, and short stories, many of them still unpublished. He was a superstitious, distrustful aesthete whose dominating ambition was to realize himself as an artist and achieve fame. Between 1915 and 1926 F. published, largely at his own expense and to slight critical acclaim, seven richly comic novels, the best of which are *Valmouth* (1919) and *The Flower beneath the Foot* (1923). Usually exotic, the settings of these books reflect F.'s varied sojourns in Italy, Spain, North Africa, and Cuba, where his eccentricities were less conspicuous perhaps than in England. His central theme is the dilemma of the hypersensitive individual, often a female, who is somehow isolated and destroyed by the futility and depravity of the surrounding world. Creating sympathy for his alienated victims, F. bitterly satirizes the characters and values opposed to them. If his fictional world is one of frivolity, perversion, and decay, he continually redeems it by gaiety, wit, and elegance. The elaborate flippancy of his tone is the flippancy of honest desperation.

While F.'s humor was too idiosyncratic to become a literary force, his technical innovations were employed by Aldous HUXLEY, Evelyn WAUGH, and Anthony POWELL, among others. F.'s best novels, teeming with brilliant dialogue and meticulously patterned prose, offer no explicit messages but much sardonic artistry and a unique vision of the absurd. He used a baroque humor verging upon the freakish to define the fragmented society around him. Distantly related to the DADAISTS, F. anticipates, through his demoralizing comedy, outrageous fantasy, and grotesque pathos, the work of BECKETT, IONESCO, and GENET.

FURTHER WORKS: *Odette d'Antrevernes, and A Study in Temperament* (1905); *The Wavering Disciple* (1906); *A Study in Opal* (1907); *Odette* (1916); *Inclinations* (1916); *Caprice* (1917); *The Princess Zoubaroff* (1920); *Santal* (1921); *Sorrow in Sunlight* (1924; pub. as *Prancing Nigger*, 1925); *Concerning the Eccentricities of Cardinal Pirelli* (1926); *Works* (1928); *The Artificial Princess* (1934); *The Complete R. F.* (1961); *The New Rhythm, and Other Pieces* (1962); *"The Wind the Roses"* (1966); *Far Away* (1966); *An Early Flemish Painter* (1969); *La Princesse aux Soleils, & Harmonie* (1974); *When Widows Love, & A Tragedy in Green: Two Stories* (1980)

BIBLIOGRAPHY: Waugh, E., "R. F.," *Life and Letters, II* (1929): 191–96; Brooke, J., "R. F." (1951); Benkovitz, M., *R. F.: A Bibliography* (1963); Benkovitz, M., *R. F.: A Biography* (1969); Merritt, J. D., *R. F.* (1969); Potoker, E. M., *R. F.* (1970); Horder, M., ed., *R. F.: Memoirs and Critiques* (1977); Benkovitz, M., *Supplement to a Bibliography of R. F.* (1980)

—EDWARD M. POTOKER

FISHTA, Gjergj

Albanian poet, b. 23 Oct. 1871, Fishta; d. 30 Dec. 1940, Shkodra

F. attended Franciscan schools in Troshan and Shkodra. In 1886, when he was fifteen, he was sent by the Order of the Friars Minor to Bosnia, as were many young Albanians destined for the priesthood at the time. In 1894 he was ordained as a priest and admitted to the Franciscan order. By the turn of the century F. had become a leading figure of cultural and public life in northern Albania and in particular in Shkodra. In October 1913 F. founded and began editing the Franciscan monthly periodical *Hylli i Dritës* which was devoted to literature, politics, folklore, and history. Throughout these years F. continued teaching and running the Franciscan school in Shkodra, known from 1921 on as the *Collegium Illyricum*, which had become the leading educational institution of northern Albania. He was by now also an imposing figure of Albanian literature.

In 1921 F. represented Shkodra in the Albanian parliament and was chosen in August of that year as vice president of this assembly. His talent as an orator served him well in his functions both as a political figure and as a man of the cloth. In later years, he attended Balkan conferences in Athens (1930), Sofia (1931), and Bucharest (1932) before withdrawing from public life to devote his remaining years to the Franciscan order and to his writing. From 1935 to 1938 he held the office of provincial of the Albanian Franciscans. These most fruitful years of his life were now spent in the quiet seclusion of the Franciscan monastery of Gjuhadoll in Shkodra with its cloister, church, and rose garden, where F. would sit in the shade and reflect on his verse. As the poet laureate of his generation, F. was honored with various diplomas, awards, and distinctions both at home and abroad. He was awarded the Austro-Hungarian *Ritterkreu* in 1911, decorated by Pope Pius XI with the *Al Merito* award in 1925, given the prestigious *Phoeni* medal of the Greek government, honored with the title *Lector jubilatus honoris causa* by the Franciscan order, and made a regular member of the Italian Academy of Arts and Sciences in 1939.

Although F. is the author of a total of thirty-seven literary publications, his name is indelibly linked to one great work, indeed to one of the most astounding creations in all the history of Albanian literature, *Lahuta e malcís* (1937; The Highland Lute). *Lahuta e malcís* is a 15,613-line historical verse epic focusing on the Albanian struggle for autonomy and independence and, in particular, on events of northern Albanian history from 1858 to 1913. This literary masterpiece, composed primarily between 1902 and 1909, was refined and amended by its author over a thirty-year period and constitutes the first Albanian-language contribution to world literature. F. succeeded masterfully here in his original intention of presenting the life of the northern Albanian tribes and of his people in general in its heroic dimensions.

Although F. is remembered primarily as an epic poet, his achievements are actually no less impressive in other genres, in particular as a lyric and satirical poet. Indeed, his lyric verse is regarded by many scholars as his best. F.'s first collection of original lyric verse was published under the title *Pika voëset* (1909; Dewdrops). It was followed in 1913, at the dawn of Albanian independence, by the first edition of *Mrizi i zâneve* (1913; Noonday Rest of the Zanas), which includes some of the religious verse of *Pika voëset*. The general tone of *Mrizi i zâneve* is, however, much more nationalist than spiritual, the patriotic character of the collection being substantially underlined in the subsequent expanded editions of 1924, 1925, and in the definitive posthumous edition of 1941. With his nationalist verse concentrated in *Mrizi i zâneve*, F. collected his religious poetry in the 235-page edition *Vallja e Parrîzit* (1925; The Dance of Paradise). The verse in this collection constitutes a zenith of Catholic literature in Albania.

F. was also a consummate master of satirical verse, using his wit and sharpened quill to criticize the educational shortcomings and intellectual sloth of his Scutarine compatriots. His was not the benevolent, exhortative irony of Andon Zako Çajupi (1866-1930), but rather biting, pungent satire, often to the point of ruthlessness, the poetic equivalent of the blunt satirical prose of Faik bey Konitza (1875-1942). F. had printed many such poems in the periodical *Albania* using the telling pseudonym "Castigat ridendo." In 1907 he published, anonymously, the sixty-seven-page satirical collection *Anxat e Parnasit* (1907; The Wasps of Parnassus), which laid the foundations for satire as a poetic genre in Albanian literature and which is regarded by many critics as the best poetry he ever produced. *Gomari i Babatasit* (1923; Babatasi's Ass) is another volume of amusing satire, published under the pseudonym Gegë Toska while F. was a member of the Albanian parliament. In this work, which enjoyed great popularity at the time, he rants at false patriots and idlers.

The national literature of Albania had been something of a Tosk (southern Albanian) prerogative until the arrival of F. on the literary scene. He proved that northern Albania could be an equal partner with the more advanced south in the creation of a national culture.

By the outbreak of the World War II, F. had indeed been universally recognized as the "national poet." Austrian Albanologist Maximilian Lambertz (1882-1963) described him as "the most ingenious poet Albania has ever produced" and Italian poet Gabriele D'ANNUNZIO called him "the great poet of the glorious people of Albania." For others he was the "Albanian Homer." After the war, however, F. was attacked and denigrated perhaps more than any other pre-war writer and fell into prompt oblivion. The national poet became an anathema. Yet despite four decades of unrelenting communist party propaganda, the people of northern Albania, and in particular the inhabitants of his native Shkodra, did not forget him. After almost half a century, F. was commemorated openly for the first time on January 5, 1991 in Shkodra. During the first public recital of F.'s works in Albania in forty-five years, an actor at one point hesitated in his lines, and was immediately and spontaneously assisted by members of the audience—who still knew many parts of *Lahuta e malcís* by heart.

FURTHER WORKS: *Sh' Françesku i Asisit, melodram* (1912); *Juda Makabé, botue së dyti* (1923); *Sh. Luigji Gonzaga, melodram* (1927); *Shna Ndou i Padues* (1927); *Jerina ase mbretnesha e luleve. poem dramatik* (1941); *Die Laute des Hochlandes, Lahuta e Malci* (1958); *Il liuto della montagna—Lahuta e malcís* (2 vols., 1968, 1970)

BIBLIOGRAPHY: Çabej, E., "Der albanische Dichter G. F. (1871-1940), Nachruf," *Südost-Forschungen* 6 (1941): 635-47; Ercole, F. "G. F.," *Rivista d'Albania* 2 (1941): 3-18; Stadtmüller, G., "Die 'Berglaute,' das albanische Nationalepos," *Stimmen aus dem Südosten* (1942): 171-80; Lambertz, M., *G. F. und das albanische Heldenepos Lahuta e Malcís, Laute des Hochlandes, eine Einführung in die albanische Sagenwelt* (1949); Schirò, G., *Storia della letteratura albanese* (1959): 165-93; Klissura, A. "Pater F. grand poète national albanais," *Shêjzat*, 5, 11-12 (1961): 490-93; Kolgjini, T., *Shpalime rreth lahutës 'Kemençe'ye dair izahat'. Shpalon disa fjalë shqip të përdoruna në 'Lahuta e Malcís'. 'Dağ kemençesi' nde kullanilan Arnavutça bâzi kelimeleri açiklar* (1969); Nekaj, Z., "Remembering G. F., the Albanian National Poet on the Occasion of his 110th Anniversary," *Albanian Catholic Bulletin*, 2 (1981): 73-79; Duka-Gjini, P., *Jeta dhe veprat e G. F.* (1992); Elsie, R., "G. F., the Voice of the Albanian Nation," *Albanian Catholic Bulletin*, 14 (1993): 104-13; Zamputi, I., *F.: koha, njeriu, vepra* (1993): 104-13; Çapaliku, S., *F. satirik, studi* (1995); Elsie, R., *History of Albanian Literature* (1995): 386-420; Plasari, A., *F. e dashuruari, studim* (1997); Sopi, V., *Kthjellon terrin e mjeruar, At. G. F., antologji* (1997)

—ROBERT ELSIE

FITRAT, Abdalrauf (Abdurauf)

Bukharan dramatist, poet, short-story writer, and literary scholar (writing in Turki and Persian), b. 1886, Bukhara; d. 1937, Tashkent, Uzbekistan

F. was regarded as the most promising student sent by the Bukharan Cultural Society to get advanced education in Istanbul seminaries. He was a leading social thinker in the "Young Bukharan" movement between 1908 and 1920 and wrote for the Jadid (reformist) press. He served in the Afghan consulate in Tashkent in 1918 and held high posts in the government of the Bukhara People's Conciliar Republic between 1921 and 1923. Additionally, he founded the influential Tashkent literary circle called the Chaghatay Conference in 1918 and headed it until it vanished under communist pressure in 1922. After the Soviet partition of central Asia in 1924–25, F. lived and worked in Samarkand and Tashkent, where he taught literary history in higher educational institutions. In the 1930s he was imprisoned for alleged "nationalism" and met his death at the hands of Soviet secret police.

Three of F.'s most widely known works were first issued in Turkey in the Persian language: *Munazara* (1909; the dispute), mainly in prose; *Sayha* (1910; the cry), in verse; and *Bayyanat-e sayyah-e hindi* (1912; tales of a Hindu traveler), in prose. The prose pieces were soon translated into Russian or Turki and republished within central Asia. Like most of his extensive imaginative writing now known, these three were didactic but entertaining, even stirring in their open appeal to the survival instincts of central Asians. Aware of a pressing need to reach the largely uneducated society of the region, F. poured out a series of plays like *Chin sewish* (1919; real love) and *Timurning saghanäsi* (1919; Tamerlane's tomb), both in Turki, mainly historical dramas with patriotic themes.

His most important creative writings of the 1920s were his powerful poems of personal and group identity printed in the anthology *Ozbek yash shairläri* (1922; young Uzbek poets), and his plays *Hind ikhtilalchilari* (1920; pub. 1923; Hindu insurrectionists), written in Turki, and *'Isyan Vose* (1927; Vose's uprising), written in Persian. These dramas achieved their aim of gaining audiences and stirring feeling throughout central Asia with implicit calls for resistance to Russian domination; for the same reasons they attracted unfavorable official attention.

Two of F.'s principal literary studies appeared in the 1920s: *Ädäbiyat qa'adaläri* (1926; theory of literature) and *Persidsky poet Omar Khayyam* (1929; title in Russian: the Persian poet Omar Khayyam). He also edited a number of anthologies, which immediately became controversial because of their non-Marxist content. One of these, *Ozbek ädäbiyati nämunäläri* (1928; specimens of Uzbek literature), is valuable even today in the study of early central Asian literature.

F. was a dominant figure of his time in the literary development and scholarship of central Asia, but only one of his numerous works seems to have been republished in the U.S.S.R. since his death, namely, *Qiyamät* (1923; judgment day), a novelette in Turki, which was rehabilitated, greatly altered, translated into Russian, and reprinted in Uzbek and Tajik, evidently in order to be construed as antireligious propaganda. It is, in fact, a subtle, wildly amusing satire on clericalism told in lively, idiomatic prose.

FURTHER WORKS: *Muqaddas Qan* (1915–17); *Begijan* (1916–17); *Abu Muslim* (1918); *Ulugh Beg* (1919); *Oghuz Khan* (1919–1920); *Bidil* (1923–1924); *Abul Faiz Khan* (1924); *Shäytanning tängrigä 'iysani* (1924); *Arslan* (1927); *Eng eski turk ädäbiyati nämunäläri: Ädäbiyatimizning ta'rikhi ochon mätiriyällär* (1927); *Äruz häqidä* (1936); *Tolkun* (1937)

BIBLIOGRAPHY: Erturk, M. H., "A. F.," *Milli Türkistan*, No. 80/81B (1952): 9–16; Hayit, B., "Die jüngste özbekische Literatur," *CAsJ*, 8 (1962): 119–52; Allworth, E., *Uzbek Literary Politics*

(1964): 53–58, 109–16, 201–8; Carrère-d'Encausse, H., "A. F.," *Encyclopaedia of Islam* (1965), Vol. II: 932–33

—EDWARD ALLWORTH

F. Scott Fitzgerald

FITZGERALD, F(rancis) Scott

American novelist and short-story writer, b. 24 Sept. 1896, St. Paul, Minn.; d. 21 Dec. 1940, Hollywood, Cal.

The son of Edward Fitzgerald, a descendant of Francis Scott Key, the writer of "The Star-Spangled Banner," F. attended Princeton University (1913–17). His involvement in campus theatricals affected his academic standing, and he left Princeton to receive a commission in the U.S. infantry (1917). He married Zelda Sayre in 1920, shortly after the publication of his first novel, *This Side of Paradise* (1920). Their turbulent relationship is portrayed in much of F.'s fiction, with Zelda often serving as the model for his female characters.

The Fitzgeralds lived in Europe for extended periods, joining other prominent expatriates such as Ernest HEMINGWAY and Gerald and Sara Murphy. To support their extravagant life style, F. frequently interrupted his work on his novels to write short stories that brought high fees from the popular magazines.

F.'s financial problems were increased by Zelda's recurrent attacks of mental illness, which began in 1929 and necessitated long periods of hospitalization. In 1935 F.'s chronic tubercular condition was reactivated by his anxiety and guilt over Zelda's now hopeless mental state and by his own excessive drinking. F. spent the last years of his life in Hollywood writing film scripts under a lucrative contract with Metro-Goldwyn-Mayer. He died of a heart attack.

F. became an immediate celebrity at the age of twenty-three with *This Side of Paradise*. The novel was acclaimed by F.'s youthful readers as the story of their generation—a generation shaped by World War I whose coming of age coincided with that unprecedented American phenomenon, the Jazz Age. F. became both spokesman for and typical product of his time. One of the weaknesses of *This Side of Paradise* is indeed the fact that F. is too close in age to his fictional character to evaluate the quality of Amory Blaine's experiences in his quest for selfhood. By the conclusion of the novel, Amory's transformation from an "egotist" to a "personage," we are told, is complete. F. does not, however, reveal by what means Amory has attained the wisdom to justify his final triumphant claim to self-knowledge. The epigraph announces that on "this side of Paradise" one finds "little comfort in the wise." For Amory's rebellious generation, F. suggests, the wisdom of their ancestors, which consists of "old cries" and "old creeds," provides small comfort. Despite its numerous flaws, the novel retains a reading audience because it is a compelling portrayal of an exceptional age in American history.

F.'s second novel, *The Beautiful and Damned* (1922), is his least successful. It explores the personal and social pressures that cause a person's disintegration. The fate of its protagonists, Anthony and Gloria Patch—young, wealthy, self-indulgent—dramatizes the effects of these corrosive pressures. The epigraph, "The victor belongs to the spoils," proclaims the moral lesson of *The Beautiful and Damned*. Although Anthony and Gloria finally acquire the Patch family fortune, the retribution exacted for their egotism and greed is fearful: Gloria, whose self-definition is in terms of her physical appearance, loses her beauty, and Anthony suffers a complete mental collapse.

F. intended the fate of these pitiful people to be an analogue to the moral and cultural debilitation of Western civilization. America, he perceived, was involved in a celebratory spree after World War I that would destroy the idealism of the American spirit of achievement. The very title of the novel is a deliberate perversion of the concept in Plato's *Symposium* of the beautiful and good. Whereas in the *Symposium* the movement is toward transcendence of the purely physical to the ultimate spiritual good, the lives of F.'s characters work downward from a perverted notion of beauty to a degree of debasement that is a travesty of the platonic concept.

The Great Gatsby (1925) is F.'s greatest achievement. Set in Jazz Age New York City and fashionable Long Island, the novel describes the loss of those romantic illusions that beguile with the promise of an "imagined glory." Jay Gatsby's world is sustained by such illusions. His lack of concern with the "true or false" of things has a deeper significance for F. than one man's failure to distinguish between reality and fancy. Defined in the novel by its narrator, Nick Carraway, indifference is a moral failure—a failure of society to recognize the imperatives of truth and justice.

In order to reestablish his romantic association with Daisy Fay, now married to Tom Buchanan, a man of social position and inherited wealth, Gatsby accumulates a fortune through questionable means. He fails in his quixotic quest for the "golden girl" personified in Daisy Fay Buchanan. But Nick Carraway, F.'s moral commentator, proclaims that only Gatsby, despite his shady associations and tainted wealth, has retained a pure conviction in his "incorruptible dream." In the lush last passages of the novel, F. compares Gatsby's dream with the Edenic vision of the New World beheld by the first Dutch settlers. He implies that the American dream of a utopian world was destroyed by materialism after World War I. It is only the Gatsbys who still believe in the wondrous promise of the past. But this is only the illusion, the "imagined glory."

Tender Is the Night (1934), F.'s most ambitious novel, was also his favorite. Although it lacks the technical perfection attributed to *The Great Gatsby*, it contains some of F.'s finest writing, and reveals an extraordinary maturity of perception of the underlying causes of human failure. His protagonist, Dick Diver, possesses exceptional talent and personal charm. F. intended him to be a man of superior potential without, however, the "tensile strength" of the truly great personality. Dick Diver's personal tragedy exemplifies F.'s fascination with the distance between the two worlds of the ideal and the actual. The novel is concerned with Dick's futile attempts to synthesize these two irreconcilable worlds in his personal, social, and professional relationships.

Dick Diver is a brilliant American psychiatrist who falls in love with Nicole Warren, a rich, beautiful mental patient. Yielding to Nicole's wistful offering of herself, Dick marries her in violation of his professional judgment. Under the constant pressure of Nicole's recurring insanity and the insidious presence of the Warren money, Dick's potential for a great career is lost. By the novel's end, Dick, the romantic idealist, is vanquished, forced into emotional bankruptcy; Nicole, the flawed but wealthy pragmatist, having battened on Dick's strength and love for ten years, emerges victorious.

With *Tender Is the Night*, F. hoped to prove, at last, that he was the best of the young American novelists. He was aiming at something radically different in form and structure, something that would provide a model for the contemporary novel. If *Tender Is the Night* does not measure up to his great ambition, it is, nonetheless, an impressive achievement.

F.'s last, unfinished work, *The Last Tycoon*, published posthumously in 1941, might have developed into his best novel. He had written six of the nine chapters projected in his outline when he died. The 1941 version, edited by Edmund WILSON, includes the fragment, F.'s outline for the entire novel, and notes and drafts he was considering for its completion. Wilson notes that the manuscript represents that point where the artist had organized his material with a firm thematic intention that was not yet completely in focus.

Hollywood is the setting of *The Last Tycoon*, before the onslaught of the anarchic labor movements. Its protagonist, Monroe Stahr, is the last of the Hollywood moguls to be invested with unqualified authority. Stahr, F.'s most perceptively conceived male character, rises from the obscurity of a Bronx ghetto with a minimal education. Developing his natural talents of leadership, he becomes at age twenty-three the boy wonder of Hollywood.

There are two women in Stahr's life: Cecilia Brady, his partner's daughter, and his elusive love, the mysterious Kathleen Moore. The dynamic love story that F. had planned is not developed in the five encounters of the lovers in the manuscript. Cecilia serves a dual function as narrator-character through whom are presented the marvelously drawn minor characters who are woven into the backdrop of an ordinary day in a Hollywood studio. Cecilia is the most appealing character in the manuscript; the episodes in which she appears are presented with compelling immediacy. But, in most of the fragment, the narrative perspective is erratic. Even

though F.'s notes indicate that he intended to refine his narrative technique in the final writing, it is improbable—in view of the complicated plans for the development of the several plots—that Cecilia, as narrator, would have achieved the credibility of Nick Carraway in *The Great Gatsby*.

F. is generally acclaimed as one of America's best short-story writers. The stories return the reader to the moral atmosphere of the novels, as F. explores once again his favorite themes.

He wrote parables such as "The Cut-Glass Bowl" (1920), which laments the perishability of physical beauty; "May Day" (1920), which warns against the corrupt social environment that encourages destructive human relationships. Stories like "Winter Dreams" (1922) and "Absolution" (1924) underscore the disenchantment that inevitably follows the pursuit of romantic illusions. "The Rich Boy" (1926), one of F.'s best stories, considers the debilitating influence of inherited money. True to his persistent belief that the very rich are different from the average American, F. frequently attributed failure to achieve selfhood to the possession of unearned wealth.

Hollywood provided some of F.'s themes of the 1930s. The young idealist, like Joel Coles of "Crazy Sunday" (1932), caught up in tawdry Hollywood intrigues, becomes a favorite subject, looking forward to its most extended presentation in *The Last Tycoon*. Emotional bankruptcy is another of F.'s preoccupations of the 1930s. "Family in the Wind" (1932) and "Babylon Revisited" (1931)—his finest short story—are concerned with the depletion of moral or physical energies caused by unrestrained drinking. Both stories also examine the plight of the middle-aged man who seeks to recapture the innocence of youth through his love for a young girl.

Not all the short stories are superior; in fact, many are hack work. But a number of them have the polish of F.'s best fiction, and at least a dozen rank high among the short stories of the 20th c.

F. contended that authors did not write novels with the intention of presenting a complete philosophical system. Yet, viewing F.'s works holistically, one detects an ultimate unity of theme that might be termed a philosophical perspective. F.'s novels are a re-creation of his own world. He admitted that his world view was dichotomous: he was both a romantic and a moralist. On the one hand, he clung to the illusion of life as romantic; on the other, he saw with puritanical clarity that self-indulgence courts self-destruction. F.'s male protagonists, from Amory Blaine to Monroe Stahr, are all projections of this conflict. The odd excitement of F.'s best fiction derives, in fact, from this inner tension.

Despite the structural flaws in his limited novelistic canon, F.'s place in American letters is assured. His fiction was rooted in the 1920s and early 1930s, but the human situations he examined so minutely with his own distinctly American vision defy the limitations of time and space.

FURTHER WORKS: *Flappers and Philosophers* (1920); *Tales of the Jazz Age* (1922); *The Vegetable; or From President to Postman* (1923); *All the Sad Young Men* (1926); *Taps at Reveille* (1935); *The Crack-up* (1945); *The Portable F. S. F.* (1949); *The Stories of F. S. F.* (1951); *Afternoon of an Author* (1958); *The Pat Hobby Stories* (1962); *The F. Reader* (1963); *The Letters of F. S. F.* (1963); *The Apprentice Fiction of F. S. F., 1909–1917* (1965); *Letters to His Daughter* (1965); *Thoughtbook of Francis Scott Key Fitzgerald* (1965); *Dear Scott/Dear Max: The F.-Perkins Correspondence* (1971); *As Ever, Scott Fitz——* (1972); *Correspondence of F. S. F.* (1980); *The Price Was High: The Last Uncollected Stories of F. S. F.* (1981)

BIBLIOGRAPHY: Mizener, A., *The Far Side of Paradise* (1951; rev. ed., 1965); Turnbull, A., *S. F.* (1962); Callaghan, M., *That Summer in Paris* (1963); Eble, K., *F. S. F.* (1963); Miller, J. E., *F. S. F.: His Art and His Technique* (1964); Perosa, S., *The Art of F. S. F.* (1965); Piper, H. D., *F. S. F.: A Critical Portrait* (1965); Cowley, M., and R. Cowley, *F. and the Jazz Age* (1966); Lehan, R. D., *F. S. F. and the Craft of Fiction* (1966); Graham, S., *Beloved Infidel* (1967); Shain, C. E., *F. S. F.* (1967); Sklar, R., *F. S. F.: The Last Laocoon* (1967); Stern, M. R., *The Golden Moment: The Novels of F. S. F.* (1969); Latham, A., *Crazy Sundays: F. S. F. in Hollywood* (1970); Bruccoli, M., and J. R. Bryer, *F. in His Own Time: A Miscellany* (1971); Cross, K. G. W., *S. F.* (1971); Gallo, R. A., *F. S. F.* (1978); Way, B., *F. S. F. and the Art of Social Fiction* (1980); Bruccoli, M. J., *Some Sort of Epic Grandeur: The Life of F. S. F.* (1981); Donaldson, S., *Fool for Love: F. S. F.* (1983)

—ROSE ADRIENNE GALLO

The Last Tycoon is thus, even in its imperfect state, F.'s most mature piece of work. It is marked off also from his other novels by the fact that it is the first to deal seriously with any profession or business. The earlier books of F. had been preoccupied with debutantes and college boys, with the fast lives of the wild spenders of the twenties. The main activities of the people in these stories, the occasions for which they live, are big parties at which they go off like fireworks and which are likely to leave them in pieces. But the parties in *The Last Tycoon* are incidental and unimportant; Monroe Stahr, unlike any other of S. F.'s heroes, is inextricably involved with an industry of which he has been one of the creators, and its fate will be implied by his tragedy. The moving-picture business in America has here been observed at a close range, studied with a careful attention and dramatized with a sharp wit such as are not to be found in combination in any of the other novels on the subject. *The Last Tycoon* is far and away the best novel we have had about Hollywood, and it is the only one which takes us inside.

Edmund Wilson, Foreword to F. S. F., *The Last Tycoon* (1941), p. ix

One of the most remarkable things about S. F. as a writer is the dual character of his self-knowledge, the curious way in which he combined the innocence of complete involvement with an almost scientific coolness of observation, so that he nearly always wrote about deeply felt personal experience, and nearly always as if the important use of personal experience was to illustrate general values. "Begin with an individual," he once wrote, "and before you know it you find you have created a type." As a general proposition, that may be exceedingly questionable, but as a comment on the character of F.'s best work it is very shrewd. This curious sense of experience is everywhere in Fitzgerald's work because it was the permanent foundation of his awareness of experience.

Arthur Mizener, Introduction to F. S. F., *Afternoon of an Author* (1958), pocrit:The legend of F.'s disorderly romantic life answers, and with a better writer,

the intense American need for a mythical artistic hero like Poe. An interest in F.'s work can scarcely escape entanglement in the F. legend. Nevertheless, his work today seems to enjoy great favor, perhaps because he seems less mannered than Hemingway, less tortuous than Faulkner, and less clumsy than any of a dozen novelists in the naturalistic tradition. The excellence of his style tends to hold his reputation high while other reputations tumble. But at least two other matters operate in his favor. The first is the hard core of morality which makes him one with those writers of greatest strength in American fiction: Melville, Hawthorne, and James. Second, unlike a majority of modern American writers, he offers a fiction which is hard to imitate but from which much can be learned.

Kenneth Eble, *F. S. F.* (1963), p. 153

The Great Gatsby's excellence was immediately seen, but soon the carping began. Mencken wrote "a most enthusiastic letter" to F., in which he complained that "the central story was trivial and a sort of anecdote. . . ." In a characteristic blend of modesty, temerity and odd spelling, F. replied: "Without making any invidious comparisons between Class A and Class C, if my novel is an anecdote so is *The Brothers Karamazoff.*"

Nevertheless, F. granted Mencken's point and agreed that it had been a mistake to becloud the relationship between Gatsby and Daisy from the time of their reunion until Gatsby's death. Yet F.'s error was his triumph. Had he dramatized that relationship he would have been validating a sham. There could be no fulfillment of Gatsby's tragic dream. . . .

The theme of F.'s novel is more inclusive and more shocking than we have known. Its subject is atrophy; the wasting away of the self as one grows into the world of sex and money and time; the wasting away of America as it grows from wilderness to civilization, of the universe as it grows by its impossible plan.

Humanly, the novel reflects the disillusionment and the failure of youthful dreams which is so marked a feature of man's lot. Culturally, it dramatizes, perhaps more cogently than any other American novel, the cause and cost of America's identification with eternal beginnings. Cosmically, it suggests the apocalyptic vision with which we have become familiar in our literature, our intellectuals, and our newspapers.

It is the novel's greatest achievement to have painted this bleak picture with the brightest of colors. Never has the dying swan sung so sweetly or so surely. . . .

Finally, there is the incredible tightness in plotting, characterization and detail. In Joyce's sense of the word, *The Great Gatsby* is one of the few novels *written* in our language. In concentration of meaning, nuance, and effect, there are few books in any language with which to compare it.

Charles Thomas Samuels, "The Greatness of Gatsby." *MR*, 7 (1966), pp. 783, 793–94

If critical and popular opinion are to be taken as the criteria, *The Great Gatsby* is one of the few important works to come out of contemporary American literature. Moreover, F.'s third novel is a work of art which, like good wine, seems to get better with age. John Dos Passos has said in his note on F.: "It's the quality of detaching itself from its period that marks a piece of work as good." Judged by this rigorous standard, *The Great Gatsby* is very good indeed.

Reading it over again is both easy and pleasant, because it is one of the most compressed and concise of the great novels in any language. It can be compared in this respect to Turgenev's masterpiece *Fathers and Sons*, with which F.'s book has much in common. Aside from similarity of length, they are both representative of a whole civilization at a critical point in its history.

But the more one looks at the work both as a whole and as a collection of separable elements, the less it seems possible to account for its tremendous effect or to explain the inner mechanism by which this effect is secured.

T. S. Eliot, who read *Gatsby* three times, was never able to send F. the promised analysis to support the observation made in his letter that "this remarkable book . . . seems to me to be the first step that American fiction has taken since Henry James. . . . When I have the time, I should like to write to you more fully and tell you exactly why."

The sheer efficiency with which this little novel works upon the mind of the reader gives rise to the increasing respect it inspires. Within its strict confines, the writer has succeeded in capturing and giving form to his impressions of a vast and chaotic world. One is surprised at this realization, as one is surprised that some ladies' wrist watches, despite their phenomenally compact size, should accurately tell time. No American prose work of the twentieth century better exemplifies the epigram from the Greek Anthology: "Out of the jewel, grass is grown."

Milton Hindus, *F. S. F.: An Introduction and Interpretation* (1968), p. 35

Although in *Tender Is the Night* the psychological analyses of the characters have the upper hand, it is always in action that their true natures are revealed. . . . And if F., when he thought of rearranging *Tender Is the Night*, had a bitter exchange of letters with Thomas Wolfe in which he maintained the validity of the "novel of selected incident," the same concern with selection and structural symmetry was brought to bear in the "final version" as in the two other novels. . . .

In *Tender Is the Night* F.'s language is maturer and more complex, syntactically more elaborate. Less nervous and evocative, less syncopated and colored than in *Gatsby*, it spreads out in descriptions and analyses, in considerations and comments; it is more diffuse and full-bodied in its diction. Its pattern is here given by the long paragraph; its flow is discursive and spreading; it presupposes the "long time"

and the calm development from sentence to sentence, from period to period. It is difficult to give a single specimen of it, because it is the extension of its rhythm, not the intensity of it, that counts.

Sergio Perosa, *The Art of F. S. F.* (1968), p. 129

Shortly before his death, in 1940, F. S. F. had the humiliating experience of walking into a large city bookstore and finding that none of his books were carried in stock and his name had been forgotten. But since then things have changed. The emergence of *The Great Gatsby* from a position of comparative obscurity a generation ago to its present position as a modern classic is one of the most remarkable events in recent American literary history. According to a recent New York *Times* report on paperback sales, more people are buying *The Great Gatsby* today than any novel by any writer of Fitzgerald's generation, including Faulkner and Hemingway. . . .

Few writers of his generation possessed a more passionate sense of time and place than F. . . . *The Great Gatsby* is not an historical novel. F. was writing about the contemporary world of the early Twenties through which he had just lived. But because of the moral understanding he brought to his interpretation of that world, because of the concreteness of his description, we are brought closer to that world in the pages of his novel than in the more factual accounts of many orthodox historians. F.'s rendering of that world of almost fifty years ago is still relevant—to our understanding of the past, and to our understanding of the world today.

Henry Dan Piper, *F.'s "The Great Gatsby": The Novel, The Critics, The Background* (1970), p. 1

Speculation about the unwritten portion of the novel *[The Last Tycoon]* soon becomes futile. Although this problem is extremely interesting, we cannot speak with confidence about it. F.'s undated last outline provides only topics or ideas for the thirteen unwritten episodes. The most useful approach to the study of the novel is in terms of what Fitzgerald accomplished—not of what he was planning. His novel had developed in ways that were significantly different from his other work. Most notably, Monroe Stahr is a hero without a flaw. Unlike Amory Blaine, Anthony Patch, Jay Gatsby, or Dick Diver who are afflicted with character weaknesses, Monroe Stahr is intact up to episode 17, the last episode F. wrote. It is clear that he was to be defeated in the end, but F. plants no seeds of self-destruction in Stahr's character. Although Stahr's defeat is connected with his love for Kathleen, she is not the cause. Stahr's affair with Kathleen only provides Brady with a weapon to use against him.

F. was a life-long hero-worshipper, but he was not able to create an unflawed hero until he himself was in his forties. It is meaningful that Monroe Stahr is the first hero in a F. novel with a successful career;

Amory and Anthony have no occupations; Gatsby's business activities are shadowy; and Dick Diver abandons his promising career. But Stahr is totally committed to his work and the responsibility that goes with it. He is F.'s only complete professional. Moreover, Stahr is immune to the emotional bankruptcy that is epidemic in F.'s work after 1930. A lonely young widower with a pervasive sense of loss, he is nonetheless not broken by loss, and he retains the capacity to love again. Stahr's one terrible mistake comes when he delays the decision to go away with Kathleen by one day—and during that day he loses her. If one is compelled to seek a flaw in Stahr, it is that he has an excess of reason or discipline; but it would be difficult to support this reading. . . .

Matthew J. Bruccoli, *The Last of the Novelists: F. S. F. and "The Last Tycoon"* (1977), p. 4

FITZGERALD, Penelope

English novelist and biographer, b. 17 Dec. 1916, Lincoln

F. published her first novel when she was sixty. Nevertheless, her work is informed by the long foreground of her upbringing in a literary family and by her experiences as a working woman. Her first book was the 1975 biography of pre-Raphaelite artist Edward Burne-Jones (1833-1898), who designed the west window of St. Philip's Church, Birmingham, where her grandfather had once been rector. The life and times of her father, the editor of *Punch* magazine from 1932 to 1949, and his brothers, one a classicist turned cryptographer for both world wars, are recounted in her 1977 group biography, *The Knox Brothers*. Her first novel, *The Golden Child*, published in the same year, is a mystery that involves code-breaking. Another uncle, a monseigneur, was a noted translator of the Bible and a writer of detective stories; an aunt wrote novels all her life, even after a nervous breakdown. F.'s own writing career began only in the 1950s, when she was an assistant editor for *World Review*. After graduating from Somerville College at Oxford University, F. married, in 1941, Desmond Fitzgerald, with whom she raised three children. Her work experiences at the BBC became the fictional basis for her novel *Human Voices* (1980). Her employment in the only bookstore in Suffolk, which she claims to have featured a poltergeist and the Olympia Press edition of *Lolita*, inspired her second novel, *The Bookstore* (1978). Her tenure as an English teacher at a drama school is recollected in the novel *At Freddy's* (1982). It was only when F.'s husband fell seriously ill in the 1970s that she became determined to write fiction: *The Golden Child* was written as "a thriller" meant to entertain him and earn an income. Life with her family aboard a sailing-barge, which twice sank into the Thames, is reworked in the novel *Offshore* (1979). After the early biographies on personal subjects and her six loosely autobiographical novels, F. wrote three historical romances, beginning with *Innocence* (1986). Four times nominated for Britain's Booker Prize (she won in 1979 for *Offshore*), F. became the first non-U.S. citizen to win the National Book Critics Circle Award in fiction in 1998.

The Golden Child establishes F.'s concern with the workaday life of office politics as a model for modern living. The occasion of the story is the organizing of an art exhibition of the Golden Child. But F. takes for her themes the pettiness and the jealousy on display in the departments of the museum, and her murder plot investigates the nature of greed and human weakness. Her second novel, *The Bookshop*, tells the story of Florence Green, a middle-aged widow who takes on the status quo and loses. Florence uses all her resources of finance and courage to open the only bookshop in an out-of-the-way fishing village. She battles the small-mindedness of the locals of all classes, the deplorable condition of her 500-year-old building and the threat of its poltergeist, censorship, and her own lack of know-how only to be undone by a government bill. *Offshore* continues F.'s investigation into the possibilities of finding a place of one's own in contemporary England. This is the story of a clutch of unusual characters who, for their own reasons, have come to dwell on sailing-barges. Nenna James, a thirty-two-year-old separated mother of two, treads water as life continues to throw her further off course. Nenna is a strong woman who, although powerless to correct the drift of her life, manages to survive. The heroine of *Human Voices*, Annie Asra, is described as "the kind of girl to whom people give a job, even when they didn't originally intend to." In half a dozen concise pages, F. differentiates this character, describing how she spent her childhood with her father and suffered through various injustices done to her by boys, before she arrived as a strong, sturdy young woman ready to help at the BBC in the spring and summer of the dark year of the war 1940. The novel features F.'s portraits of the types of fellow workers she herself may have encountered at the BBC, where some do their jobs well, others to the best of their abilities, and others have their work done for them.

The epigraph from Novalis that F. chose for *The Blue Flower* (1996) serves as a gloss for her three latest novels, the historical romances: "Novels arise out of the shortcomings of history." For two years while researching her novel, F. laboriously translated the German of Novalis. But she found that none of Novalis's letters to Sophie von Kuhn have survived, a major shortcoming to reconstructing their love story, so F. was required to make up all the letters she features in her novel. In this story, as it is told from multiple points of view, F.'s argument seems to be that poetry, even the lofty romantic vision we remember Novalis for, begins in the commonplace. Her Novalis is not yet a poet but a would-be lover who must negotiate his proposed marriage into the moneyless aristocracy of 18th-c. Saxony. Her Sophie is not the muse whose death launched the poet into the masterpiece of *Hymns to the Night*, but a rather dull twelve-year-old whom F. presents with little sympathy. F.'s lesson might be learned from the fifth chapter of Novalis's unfinished book, *Henry von Ofterdingen*, and its dialogue on the fictive uses of history. *The Beginning of Spring* (1988) is set in pre-Revolutionary Russia, at the historical moment when the nation was poised to determine the course of its future. With this novel of the English community in Moscow, F. gives the story to a male character, Frank Reid, who, is poised at his own moment of decision. Abandoned by his wife, he eventually arranges to care for his three children while running his printing business. The working title for F.'s novel *The Gate of Angels* (1990) was *Mistakes Made by Scientists*. The novel features another male protagonist who must decide to change his life, the rational-minded Fred Fairly, a junior fellow of the College of St. Angelicus, once again in the years before World War I. This comedy of errors eventuates from Fairly's bicycle accident, which puts him into a sickbed with a woman, Daisy Saunders, mistakenly presumed to be his wife. Daisy proves to be the cause of change in Fairly when he falls irrationally in love with her.

F. creates strong women characters, the kind who courageously open a bookstore in a backward village or raise a family on a river barge. If these women are not ultimately victorious in their stories, they make for themselves memorable lives that beg comparison to those of the female protagonists of her closest contemporaries. Anita BROOKNER also began writing fiction late in life and then became prolific. Her solitary heroines struggle to advance, in the social and professional hierarchies of the modern world, like the shop owner in *The Bookstore*, Florence Green, who believes the world is divided into exterminators and exterminatees. Barbara PYM's hapless spinsters become overwhelmed by their middle-class lives, much like Daisy Saunders who moves from one bad workplace to another. F.'s heroines, after her own life, come into their own in modern England, which won two world wars even as it lost its empire. Theirs is the quiet revolution of women who contributed mightily to the work force during the wars only to assume more important roles in a diminished culture. In terms of form, F. will be remembered as a master of the nouvelle, or the novel designed to be read in one sitting.

FURTHER WORKS: *Charlotte Mew & Her Friends* (1984)

BIBLIOGRAPHY: Hosmer, R. E., "P. F.," in Schlueter, P., and J. Schlueter, eds., *An Encyclopedia of British Women Writers* (1988): 176-78; Hosmer, R. E., "P. F.," in Todd, J., ed., *Dictionary of British Women Writers* (1989): 252-54; Pritchard, W. H., "Tradition and Some Individual Talents," *HudR*, 45, 3 (1992): 481-90; Sudrann, J., "'Magic or Miracles': The Fallen World of P. F.'s Novels," in Hosmer, R. E., ed., *Contemporary British Women Writers: Narrative Strategies* (1993): 105-27; Bawer, B., "A Still, Small Voice: P. F.," in *The Aspect of Eternity: Essays* (1993); Brooker, A., "P. F.," *The Spectator*, 276 (1996)

—JOANN BLEVINS AND RICHARD L. BLEVINS

FLEISSER, Marieluise

German dramatist and short-story writer, b. 23 Nov. 1901, Ingolstadt; d. 2 Feb. 1974, Ingolstadt

F. studied German and theater arts in Munich, where she became acquainted with Lion FEUCHTWANGER and Bertolt BRECHT. From 1926 until she returned for good to Ingolstadt, in 1932, she lived mostly in Berlin. There she was associated for a time with the group around Brecht and Erwin Piscator (1893–1966). During the Third Reich she was forbidden to publish, and her books were burned. After the war F. resumed writing in spite of great personal difficulties. She was awarded several prizes and, in 1965, became a member of the Bavarian Academy of Fine Arts.

F.'s name is closely associated with Ingolstadt, which provides the background for most of her works. Using the old Bavarian town as a prototype for small towns everywhere, she described and analyzed a way of life: the world of petty provincialism, with its narrow-mindedness and bigotry, created by people whose behavior is dictated by their roles in society, their inadequate education, and their inability to express themselves and thereby to get close to each

other. Man's alienation from himself and the world becomes visible through the transparent medium of language.

In her play *Fegefeuer in Ingolstadt* (1926; second version, 1971; purgatory in Ingolstadt) some young people try desperately to break free of the stifling conventions in which they no longer believe. But since they have no positive convictions of their own to pit against those conventions, they find themselves reduced, in order to survive, to playing the callous game of the very society they reject. In a world characterized by the lack of charity, everybody inflicts upon the other what was inflicted on himself.

Pioniere in Ingolstadt (1928; second version, 1929; third version, 1968; pioneers in Ingolstadt) exhibits similar interpersonal patterns and modes of behavior. The play, with its sexual frankness, its depiction of the brutality of military life, and its derision of the bourgeoisie, clearly shows the influence of Brecht, and the Berlin performance of 1929, under the direction of Brecht, provoked quite a scandal, making her name known to a wider public. But it also furnished the Nazis with a reason to condemn her to temporary oblivion.

F.'s writings are lamentations, sad and angry and occasionally even cynical, over man's failure to realize his humanity, reflecting a world in which "the weak are abused." In a sense, her works can be read as documents of a spiritual biography, since her own experiences form the basis of most of her writing. But her dramatic and narrative works project more than just a personal portrait; they reveal the pettiness and cruelty of a deficient world, where man is man's wolf. Her plays seem to be a dramatization of Brecht's dictum: "The meanest thing alive, and the weakest, is man."

F., who characterized her talent as "basically epic," actually made her literary debut with short stories. Her first collection, *Ein Pfund Orangen, und 9 andere Geschichten der M. F. aus Ingolstadt* (1929; a pound of oranges, and 9 other stories by M. F. from Ingolstadt), displays an impressive mastery of narrative prose forms. The short story seems to have been the most appropriate vehicle for her talents. Her protagonists, inconspicuous people with inconspicuous fates, face the gradual disintegration of a meaningful reality with feelings of anguished helplessness. Her stories have justly been called "merciless idylls."

Praised by Walter BENJAMIN and the Berlin critic Alfred Kerr (1867–1948), called Bertolt Brecht's sister by the writer Curt Hohoff (b. 1913), F. stands as a link between BRECHT and Ödön von HORVÁTH.

FURTHER WORKS: *Mehlreisende Frieda Geier: Roman vom Rauchen, Sporteln, Lieben und Verkaufen* (1931); *Andorranische Abenteuer* (1932); *Karl Stuart: Trauerspiel in fünf Akten* (1946); *Avantgarde* (1963); *Abenteuer aus dem Englischen Garten* (1969); *Gesammelte Werke* (3 vols., 1972)

BIBLIOGRAPHY: Rühle, G., ed., *Materialien zum Leben und Schreiben der M. F.* (1973); Dimter, W., "Die ausgestellte Gesellschaft: Zum Volksstück Horváths, der F. und ihrer Nachfolger," in Hein, J., ed., *Theater und Gesellschaft: Das Volksstück im 19. und 20. Jahrhundert* (1973): 219–45; Kässens, W., and Töteberg, M. "'. . . fast schon ein Auftrag von Brecht': M. F.s Drama *Pioniere in Ingolstadt*," *Brecht-Jahrbuch* (1976): 101–19; Sanger, C., "In the Avantgarde of Bertolt Brecht: M. F.'s *Pioniere in Ingolstadt*," in Nelson, C., ed., *Studies in Language and Literature*, Proceedings of the 23rd Mountain Interstate Foreign Language Conference (1976): 517–22; Karasek, H., "Die Erneuerung des Volksstücks: Auf den Spuren M. F.s und Ödön von Horváths," in Arnold, H. L., and T. Buck, eds., *Positionen des Dramas: Analysen und Theorien zur deutschen Gegenwartsliteratur* (1977): 137–69; Lutz, G., *Die Stellung M. F.s in der bayerischen Literatur des 20. Jahrhunderts* (1979); special F. issue, *Tuk* No. 64 (1979)

—FRIEDHELM RICKERT

FLEMISH LITERATURE

See Belgian Literature

FLØGSTAD, Kjartan

Norwegian novelist, poet, short–story writer, and essayist, b. 7 June 1944, Sauda

F. has his origins in the Norwegian working class, having grown up in a small industrial community in western Norway. He also has traveled the world as a seaman in the Norwegian merchant marine, and has lived in the extreme northeastern part of the country. These geographical aspects of F.'s biography have had a marked effect on his work, but so have his wide–ranging ventures in the world of intellect; F. probably has the best background in literature and philosophy of all contemporary Norwegian writers.

F.'s first books were two volumes of modernist poetry, *Valfart* (1968; pilgrimage) and *Seremoniar* (1969; ceremonies). Unlike most other writers of his generation, he displayed no overt political engagement but offered deeply felt experience of both nature and city environments. His next book, a mixture of narrative and essayistic prose entitled *Den hemmelege jubel* (1970; the secret jubilation) showed that he was a widely read, incisive, and engaging man of letters. The short–story collection *Fangliner* (1972; painters) and the novel *Rasmus* (1974; Rasmus) drew on F.'s own experience as a sailor in the merchant marine and as a worker in industry. Unlike some Marxist–Leninist writers, the foremost among them being Dag SOLSTAD—who admitted that his novels about workers from the same period of time were written for members of the intelligentsia and not for the workers themselves— F. offered genuine portraits of daily life in the factory and onboard the merchant ship, and wrote in such a manner that the common person would be able to identify with the stories. Two mystery novels, written in the mid–1970s, can also be regarded as literature for the people.

The foundation of F.'s literary reputation is the novel *Dalen Portland* (1977; *Dollar Road*, 1989), which is also his first foray into POSTMODERNISM and for which he received the Nordic Literary Prize. An account of the changes that were brought about in a small community in western Norway when the area was industrialized, the book is a blending of the realistic and the fantastic. The lives of several members of one family are chronicled, and the author takes his characters to a large number of places at home and abroad. The text contains elements of the picaresque and other popular literary forms. Its self–reflexivity is shown in an otherwise realistic scene where one of the characters encounters a figure who states that his name is Kj. Fløgstad, and that he is knocking on a boiler in a factory because he is listening for hollow ringing sounds in the language. The author's next book, *Fyr og flamme* (1980; fire and flame), went further along the postmodernist road. Subtitled *Av handling* (which can be translated both as "dissertation" and "from action"), it is, in a sense, both a traditional story and a discussion of its subject and, at the same time, neither of the two. A hybrid text difficult to categorize, *Fyr og flamme* encompasses many different discourses. Its central character, Hertigen, is, like the text, also larger than life.

F.'s next book reads more like a traditional novel. *U3* (1983; U3) takes its title from the U2 episode in the middle of the Cold War, and is more overtly political in the traditional sense than either of its two predecessors. The protagonist, Alf Hellot, is an officer in the Norwegian air force, and he becomes the reader's guide to the history of Norwegian defense policy during the postwar era. The story culminates with the news of the downing of the U2 spy plane, after which Hellot, ever loyal to his people, terminates his life while on a mission to warn of what is happening to Norway as a result of her collaboration with the U.S. through NATO. The postmodern aspects of this novel are found primarily in the relationship between the figures and the narrator, who has at his disposal such aids as the fictional *retrospectoscope*, by means of which he is able to gather the information he needs to tell the story.

F.'s most hotly debated book is *Det 7. klima* (1986; the seventh climate), the fictional biography of one Salim Mahmood, a Pakistani immigrant to Norway who becomes a writer and datalinguist. The novel offered the author's view of what was happening to Norwegian cultural and intellectual life at the time, but his views were presented in such a difficult manner that most of the critics reacted with a great deal of frustration and only limited understanding. F.'s contributions to the debate about the book have been collected in the volume *Tyrannosaurus Text* (1988; tyrannosaurus text).

F. is still very much in the middle of his career. He is almost universally recognized as Norway's most important living writer, and his literary reputation seems secure.

FURTHER WORKS: *Døden ikke heller* (1975); *Ein for alle* (1976); *Loven vest for Pecos* (1981); *Ordlyden* (1983); *Portrett av eit magisk liv; Poeten Claes Gill* (1988)

BIBLIOGRAPHY: Garton, J., "New Directions in Norwegian Literature," *RNL*, 12 (1983): 163–84; Stegane, I., "The New Norse Literary Tradition," *RNL*, 12 (1983): 101–22; Rønning, H., "History, Identity, Communication: Trends in Recent Norwegian Fiction," *ScanR*, 76, 2 (1988): 95–102

—JAN I. SJÅVIK

FO, Dario

Italian dramatist, b. 1926, San Giano

F.'s progressive political outlook was shaped by the socioeconomic status of his family—his father was a railroad worker and his mother came from a peasant background—and by a vigorous tradition of working-class struggle in his native Lombardy. He was so determined in his convictions that while still very young he distinguished himself as a writer and actor of plays that expressed

Dario Fo

political commitment. Today he ranks as the leading militant Italian playwright.

F. first attracted the attention of the critics with *Il dito nell'occhio* (1953; a finger in the eye), a loosely structured harlequinade in which he combined the Marxist philosophy of Italy's young intellectual with gags, songs, and other theatrical devices reminiscent of the commedia dell'arte, the *avanspettacolo* (stage shows that used to be performed before movies until the end of World War II), and 19th-c. farce. Most of the works of his early period are one-act farces with complex comic plots full of twists and turns and unexpected reversals, mistaken identities, amorous triangles, family quarrels, and sexual equivocation.

F. spent a brief time as a film actor and set designer before returning to writing for the theater with a series of short plays that were produced in conjunction with La Compagnia Dario Fo—Franca Rame, a company he formed with the assistance of his wife. In the plays written and performed during this period, he increasingly clarified his political intent and directed himself toward specific targets. *La signora è da buttare* (1967; the lady is to be thrown away) remains the best play of this period. Written and staged at the moment when the war in Vietnam emerged as a motivation for mass mobilization and for a militant political campaign in Italy, the play criticizes American society as one manipulated by legalized crime and by prejudice, a society in which warmongering is a warranty of power.

Because of events of the 1960s, F. entirely rejected the principle of artistic creation as a marketable commodity in favor of a concept that views art as an instrument of social and political change. Consequently, he formed a noncommercial theater group and wrote plays for it that were not expressions of mere concern, but of militancy. The most original work of this period, *Mistero buffo* (1969; the comic mystery), consists of a number of monologues taken from medieval religious works and contemporary chronicles. The parts are linked by didactic commentaries to create a continuous dialectical exchange between past and present, culture and politics.

In 1970 F. dissociated himself from the Communist leadership, whose criticism he had begun to attract because of his open attacks on the Party's bureaucracy and its failure to prepare the masses to face cultural and ideological responsibilities. From a dialectical theater, F. moved on to a rhetorical theater, to "collages" hurriedly constructed and staged in response to specific international, national, and local issues, such as the popular revolt in Chile in *Guerra di popolo in Cile* (1973; the people's war in Chile); the Palestinian question in *Fedayn* (1971; fedayeen); and the arrest of two supposedly innocent anarchists in *Morte accidentale di un anarchico* (1970; *Accidental Death of an Anarchist*, 1979). Moving as rapidly as the course of contemporary history, these last theatrical pieces depend upon improvisation and extensive revisions, with spectators becoming directly involved in the process before, during, and after every performance.

By bridging popular culture and radical thought, F. has established himself as a leading figure in the Italian theater of today. In 1997, F. was awarded the Nobel Prize for Literature.

FURTHER WORKS: *Morte e resurrezione di un pupazzo* (1972); *Ballate e canzoni* (1974); *Pum, pum! Chi è? La polizia* (1974); *Il Fanfani rapito* (1975); *Le commedie di D. F.* (5 vols., 1977)

BIBLIOGRAPHY: Sogliuzzo, A. R., "D. F.: Puppets for Proletarian Revolution," *TDR*, 16, 3 (1972): 71–77; Joly, J., "Le théâtre militant de D. F.," *Travail théâtral*, 14 (1974): 14–22; Cowan, S., "The Throw-Away Theatre of D. F.," *TDR*: 19, 2 (1975): 102–13; Cowan, S., "D. F., Politics and Satire: An Introduction to *Accidental Death of an Anarchist*," *Theater*, 10, 2 (1979): 7–11; Hirst, D., *D. F. and Franca Rame* (1989); Mitchell, T., *File on F.* (1989)

—MARIO B. MIGNONE

FOIX, J(osep) V(icenç)

Spanish poet, essayist, journalist, and critic (writing in Catalan), b. 31 Jan. 1893, Sarrià; d. 29 Jan. 1987, Barcelona

F. came from a middle-class family. After graduating from high school, he entered law school, but left after a year. He then worked in the family pastry business and soon became involved in literary and artistic circles. From 1911 to 1920 F. wrote a poetic diary, which he later used as a main source for a number of his major writings. From 1917 on, he contributed to various influential Catalan periodicals.

F., who received the Honor Prize of Catalan Letters of 1973, is, together with Josep Carner (1884–1970) and Carles RIBA, considered one of the best of the "old guard" Catalan poets. He is the SURREALIST—or more precisely, superrealist—poet par excellence of Catalonia. (Whatever the difference between the two designations might be, the term "superrealist" is often used because of his marked leanings toward dreams and the subconscious.) *Desa aquests llibres al calaix de baix* (1964; store those books in the bottom drawer) brings together miscellaneous writings of the period 1921–31; the collection shows F.'s experiments with superrealist automatic writing.

F.'s first published book, *Gertrudis* (1927; Gertrudis), began a connected cycle of poetic prose collections, some of which were written much later. These poetic fragments, linked by the figure of Gertrudis (invented by F.), constitute a magnificent suite of visual images, distorted perceptions of reality. The alienated speaker ultimately destroys Gertrudis.

In *KRTU* (1932; KRTU), also a succession of visionary images, the solitude of the poet-speaker is set against a background of seascapes and cityscapes. The fragments of *Del "Diari 1918"* (1956; from the 1918 diary) approach a true narrative. In *L'estrella d'En Perris* (1963; Perris's star) the isolated poet witnesses mysterious miracles and enchantments taking place in unreal landscapes; Venus, the reassuring guiding star, functions as a kind of reality amid his uncertain, eerie adventures. The inspired surrealistic and nightmarish fragments of *Darrer comunicat* (1970; last communiqué) have political overtones. Basic in *Tocant a mà* (1972; within reach), which teems with dreamlike fantasies, is the mysterious magic wall separating the poet from discovery, from the source of his creative power.

Sol i de dol (1936; alone and mourning), chronologically F.'s third book, was the first of the category of poetry proper. Its seventy sonnets are inspired by Catalan and Italian classics. Here the search for self gives way to a general human yearning to fathom the meaning of existence and to transcend the limits of time.

Les irreals omegues (1951; the unreal omegas), F.'s most complex book, includes long free-verse poems using the decasyllabic line. In *On he deixat les claus . . .?* (1953; where have I left the keys . . .?) he again explores the theme of personal reality and the concomitant alienation from exterior reality. Keys symbolize the poet's identity. *Onze Nadals i un Cap d'Any* (1960; eleven Christmas poems and one for the New Year) is a magnificently stylized reworking of traditional Catalan Christmas poetry.

F.'s essayistic prose—on art, politics, and other subjects—at its best displays a verbal skill unsurpassed in Catalan. And F. the poet's need to experiment brings him directly to one of the central issues of modern art: to rediscover its own essence while probing the meaning of existence. He may be eccentric at times, but his sensitivity and creative power make him one of the leading contributors to the literature of modern Spain.

FURTHER WORKS: *Revolució catalanista* (1934); *Còpia d'una lletra tramesa a Na Madrona Puignau, de Palau ça Verdera* (1951); *Plant d'En Josep-Vicenç* (1957); *Lletra a En Joan Papasseit, i d'altres texts* (1963); *Quatre nus* (1964); *Obres poètiques* (1964); *Escenificació de cinc poemes* (1965); *Catalans de 1918* (1965); *Els lloms transparents* (1965); *La pell de la pell* (1970); *Allò que no diu "La Vanguardia"* (1970); *Mots i maons o a cuascú el seu* (1971); *Els amants* (1973); *J. V. F. en els seus millors escrits* (1973); *Tres cents aforismes sobre les figuracions poncianes* (1974); *Obres completes*, Vol. I (1974)

BIBLIOGRAPHY: Terry, A., "Sobre les *Obres poètiques* de J. V. F.," *Serra d'or*, May 1968: 47–52; Badosa, E., Preface to *Antología de J. V. F.* (1969): 9–44; Teixidor, J., et al., "En el 80 aniversario de J. V. F.," *Destino*, 27 Jan. 1973: 21–25; Manent, A., et al., "J. V. F.," *Serra d'or*, Jan. 1973: 20–51; Boehne, P. J., *J. V. F.* (1980)

—ALBERT M. FORCADAS

FON LITERATURE
See Beninian Literature

FONSECA, Rubem

Brazilian novelist and short–story writer, b. 11 May 1925, Minas Gerais

Born in Minas Gerais to Portuguese parents, F. moved with his family to Rio de Janeiro when he was a child. Having earned degrees in law and public administration, F. has been a criminal lawyer, professor, and researcher at the Getúlio Vargas Foundation, as well as an executive with a multinational company. Retired from corporate life, he now dedicates his time to writing. F. is a city creature, however, and he maintains an apartment in Rio de Janeiro, where he keeps his library, participates in writers organizations, and receives visitors from all over the world. He has been an activist for writers' rights and is committed to giving his time to promote Brazil's cultural development. He served as secretary of culture for the city of Rio de Janeiro from 1980 to 1981. F. has won travel grants to Germany, where he spent several months researching a recent novel that features action in Europe, *Vastas emoções e pensamentos imperfeitos* (1988; vast emotions and imperfect thoughts). His work has been translated into the major languages.

Sex and violence are weapons in F.'s fiction, manipulated to disturb the complacency of Brazil's ruling technocracy to the point that he has been accused of being a pornographer, and his volume of short stories, *Feliz Ano Novo* (1975; happy New Year), was banned by General Ernesto Geisel's administration (1974–1979). Using the format of the American–style detective novel in the tradition of Dashiell HAMMETT, F. insists on the writer's role as the "subversive" to focus on the malaise of the modern human in the urban setting. Firmly placed in the tradition of great city novelists, such as Balzac, Dickens, and Dostoevsky, and with strong links to contemporary North American fiction writers like Donald BARTHELME, John BARTH, and William BURROUGHS, F. is a moralist and moralist of contemporary Brazilian life.

F. has created four particularly noteworthy characters who reappear throughout his work: Mandrake, Vilela, Guedes, and, recently, in *Agosto* (1990; August), Alberto Matos. Mandrake, a lawyer, is present in the short stories and reappears in *A grande arte* (1983; *High Art,* 1986) and has a tough amoral attitude toward life. He is a model for street survival, and yet full of tender brutality. Vilela is the young vice cop in *A coleira do cão* (1965; the dog collar) who reappears in *O caso Morel* (1973; the Morel case) as a free–lance writer and private detective. Guedes, who appears in the title story of *O cobrador* (1979; the avenger) and again in *Bufo & Spallanzani* (1990; *Bufo Spallanzani*, 1990), and Alberto Matos are the good cops, flatfooted and laconic, who cling obstinately to an ethic of morality in the midst of the chaos they doggedly attempt to right. They are cynical, ulcerous, sweaty, and deliberately unexciting. In most of F.'s narratives the poet, the lawman, and the criminal become one.

F. spent twenty years perfecting his short–story style while aspiring to be a serious novelist. His interest in film, clearly evidenced in his narrative style, has led him to write original screenplays, most recently *Stelinha* (1991; Stelinha), based on the title story "Lúcia McCartney," from the collection *Lúcia McCartney* (1967; Lúcia McCartney). His novels develop the themes of his short stories, albeit in some of the recent works the intensity and poignancy of his story art is diverted into a kind of postmodernist slapstick. F. is at his best with his treatment of human sexuality and the social and philosophical issues that sex raises. He forces the reader to face human weakness, anxiety, and vulnerability by creating characters so believable that their drama transcends the boundaries of fiction. The unsettling effect of F.'s narratives is the fishbowl illusion that the reader, indeed, may be the one at risk.

FURTHER WORKS: *Os prisioneiros* (1963); *O homem de fevereiro e Março* (1973); *Romance negro* (1992); *O Selvagem da ópera* (1994); *Contos reunidos* (1994); *Buraco na parede* (1995)

BIBLIOGRAPHY: Coutinho, A., *O erotismo na literatura: o caso R. F.* (1979); Lowe, E., *The City in Brazilian Literature* (1982): 124–34, 136–44, 146–59, 186–91, 214–16; Tolman, J., "The Moral Dimension in R. F.'s Prose," *New World*, 1 (1986): 61–81; Vargas Llosa, M., on *High Art*, NYTBR, 7 Sept. 1986: 7; Stern, I., ed., *Dictionary of Brazilian Literature* (1988): 133–34; Simpson, A. S., *Detective Fiction from Latin America* (1990): 78–79; Vieira, N. H., "'Evil Be Good': Postmodern Heroics in *Billy Bathgate* and *Bufo & Spallanzani*," *CLS*, 28, 4 (1991): 356-78

—ELIZABETH LOWE

FOOTE, Horton

American dramatist, b. 14 Mar. 1916, Wharton, Texas

Born and reared in Texas, where his parents were small shop-keepers, after high school F. went first to the Pasadena Playhouse. He then moved to New York City, where he acted and began writing for the stage. His dramatic work can be divided into two categories: that written for television and film and that written for the theater. During the late 1940s and throughout the 1950s, F. placed many dramas—such as *The Trip to Bountiful* (later a major movie)—on television's "Playhouse 90" and "Kraft Playhouse." He turned to screenwriting, continuing in this genre through the 1970s and early 80s, completing, for instance, Oscar-winning scripts for *To Kill a Mockingbird* (1962) and *Tender Mercies* (1983).

F.'s rich, reiterated question is: "How can human beings stand all that comes to them?" In the space between question and answer—"You just stand it. You keep going."—stands a deeply realized reality where many kinds of relationships are played out. We bear witness as people "stand it" and "keep going," without bombast or self-pity. His scenes generally promote no moral, his characters, no imitation. Interest seems to be rather in the acknowledgement of character and circumstance than in their direct reformation or reconfiguration; or, in reformation by acknowledgement of both others and of situation. F. causes us to look into earlier versions of our culture, of ourselves, so that that past joins our present and becomes again actual. Life can be bleak, but F. provides a strangely inviting comfort.

Awarded the Pulitzer Prize, *The Young Man from Atlanta* (1995) brings some of his characters, such as Will and Lily Dale Kidder, forward in time from the potential of youth and adulthood—as dramatized in the nine-play *Orphans' Home Cycle*—to a point of disordered realization. The play treads slightly on Arthur MILLER's *Death of a Salesman*, treating the disappointment, regret, and anguish of selling—the Will Dale being a hitherto successful wholesale grocer—only to become in the end oneself a commodity. We experience having become a parent of a child inadequately understood and valued. We learn of the extreme difficulty in facing truth before—or after—its time. All events are as usual modest, undramatic, and compelling; all interaction plausible, individual, finished, often surprising.

The setting is 1950 Houston and F. this time repositions, anachronistically, the corrosive domestic effects of certain levels of awareness of homosexuality—the Dale's son had been presumably gay and presumptively a recent suicide. The effects of this manifold awareness run parallel to failing business loyalties and punctured notions of marital fidelity. The playwright unties a knot of often still unacknowledged patterns in which personal, familial, and social relations are implicated: by seeing the strands of the knot we recognize common antecedent probabilities of our own. Immediate post-World War II America, its atmosphere subtly threatening, appears in *The Young Man from Atlanta* under the aspect of a post-Vietnam American ethos: and we revise once again any facile notion of post-war sensibilities we have been entertaining.

In general F.'s dialogue suggests that the speech in regular use is expressive of our condition, which consists precisely of the names and words designating the people we know, the work we do, the place we live. The pathos which ordinary people experience, the intrinsic worth of the despised and the ignored, the humor in unsuspected houses, the pain at unexpected corners, the explosive potential of the taken-for-granted, the high voltage linked up to all families—these constitute his subject. F. must be considered a dramatist of serious ability and accomplishment.

FURTHER WORKS: *Harrison, Texas* (1956); *Tomorrow* (1963); *Three Plays* (1962); *Plays. Selections* (1987); *Collected Plays* (1996)

BIBLIOGRAPHY: Barr, G. T., *The Ordinary World of H. F.*, (1986); Moore, B., and D. G. Yellin, eds., *H. F.'s Three Trips to Bountiful*, (1992); Wood, G. C., ed., *H. F.: A Casebook*, (1998)

—THOMAS T. APPLE

FORD, Ford Madox

(until 1919 Ford Madox Hueffer) English novelist, critic, editor, and poet, b. 17 Dec. 1873, Merton; d. 26 June 1939, Deauville, France

Family background encouraged in F. a cosmopolitan outlook and artistic interests. His grandfather was the Pre-Raphaelite painter Ford Madox Brown, his uncle William Michael Rossetti. Their circle—including Dante Gabriel and Christina Rossetti, Algernon Swinburne, Edward Burne-Jones, and William Morris—formed part of the literary-artistic milieu in which F. grew up, an environment outside the mainstream of English culture. His father, Francis Hueffer, music critic for *The Times*, was a German émigré;

partly because of family connections in Germany and France, F. traveled on the Continent several times as a youth. Eventually he was to live for long periods abroad.

Gravitating toward the vocation of a writer, F. fell under the influence of Henry JAMES, then for several years was the close friend of Joseph CONRAD, with whom he collaborated on two novels. In 1908 he founded the *English Review*, the most important literary magazine of the period, which counted established writers like H. G. WELLS, John GALSWORTHY, and Conrad among its contributors as well as publishing bright new talents like D. H. LAWRENCE, Wyndham LEWIS, and Norman Douglas (1868–1952).

In 1915, at the age of forty-two, F. obtained a commission in the infantry and was sent to France. His military experience adversely affected his view of the English establishment and convinced him that the war had occasioned undesirable cultural changes. Attempting to pick up the emotional and financial pieces of his interrupted life, he spent several years as a cottage farmer in Sussex. Then, after a short stay in the south of France, F. moved with his family to Paris. At this time he changed his surname, in part because the German name had caused him annoyance during the war years, in part because the difficulty associated with his foreign name seemed a liability in selling his work. His founding in 1924 of *transatlantic review*, which published HEMINGWAY, JOYCE, COCTEAU, and writers of similar stature, put him back in the center of the avant-garde literary community. From 1924 until 1930 F.'s career flourished, relatively speaking, due largely to the publication of the four novels making up the *Parade's End* tetralogy (1924–28).

The last decade of F.'s life was divided mainly between the U.S. (where he exerted considerable influence on Southern writers such as Allen TATE, Caroline GORDON, Robert Penn WARREN, and Eudora WELTY) and southern France. In 1937–38 he was visiting lecturer in literature at Olivet College in Michigan. Although his books continued to appear, they sold poorly, and his financial circumstances during these last years were precarious.

F. was a prolific writer. His more than seventy books are characterized by great variety: they include fairy tales, novels, poetry, biography, art and literary criticism, sociological impressionism, propaganda, history, and reminiscence. The breadth of his oeuvre, together with his activity as an editor, compels us to regard him as a complete man of letters. Indeed, he seemed largely unconcerned about the fate of his books individually, while wishing to regard his cumulative activity as a contribution to the advancement of literature.

F.'s poetry reflects his evolving critical standards. His first five volumes were filled with casually written emotional verse derivative of 19th-c. nature poetry. But influenced by French prose writers like Stendhal and Flaubert and stimulated by talks with Ezra POUND, he gradually became convinced that less restricted rhythms and more precise language would vitalize poetry by bringing it closer to real experience. F.'s "On Heaven" (1918), which compares heaven to a lover's meeting at a small café in Provence, illustrates his methods as well as his philosophy. Between 1908 and 1914, his ideas were adopted by the IMAGIST poets, including F. S. Flint (1885–1960), Hilda DOOLITTLE, Richard Aldington (1892–1962), and Pound, and his imagistic poems were praised by Pound and T. S. ELIOT.

It is generally agreed that F.'s finest literary achievements were made as a novelist. Yet this assessment must be qualified, for of the thirty novels he wrote between 1892 and 1936, some were tossed off casually, and while numerous others reveal talent and competence, including historical romances such as *Ladies Whose Bright*

Eyes (1911), *The Young Lovell* (1913), and the Katherine Howard trilogy (*The Fifth Queen* [1906], *Privy Seal* [1907], *The Fifth Queen Crowned* [1908]), only *The Good Soldier* (1915) and the *Parade's End* tetralogy (*Some Do Not* [1924], *No More Parades* [1925], *A Man Could Stand Up* [1926], *The Last Post* [1928]) are regarded as major contributions to the genre.

F.'s novels include historical romances, farces, comedies of manners, and studies of contemporary political and social life. But in spite of their great diversity, they are broadly linked by a dilemma common to their protagonists: an inability or refusal to come to terms with the society in which they live. Usually these protagonists espouse values from an earlier time, and thus are in conflict with their age. Often they are creatures of honor—compassionate, altruistic, self-effacing, instinctively responsible to their class or nation, exemplary in their contemporary wrongheadedness. Notwithstanding his sympathy toward them, F. shows the quixotic side of this stance and the harm it can cause. Underlying these situations is F.'s concern with the evolution of social forces and values.

In the dedicatory letter that introduces *The Good Soldier*, F. wrote that his previous novels, produced desultorily, were more or less pastiches, that not until *The Good Soldier* had he tried to put into a novel "all I knew about writing." His mature novelistic credo, which he detailed in *Joseph Conrad: A Personal Remembrance* (1924), had been forged gradually with particular debts to Continental writers like Flaubert, Maupassant, and Turgenev. They convinced him that style and technique were crucially important in artistic fiction, that the author must suppress himself and strive for objective, impartial realism, that the surface of experience should be rendered as a "succession of tiny unobservable surprises" through selection of *le mot juste*. To Henry James, F. owed a preoccupation with the technical manipulation of point of view, and commitment to dramatization. Of particular importance were the ideas F. had hammered out with Conrad. Straightforward chronological narration was to be rejected in favor of a more complicated but more lifelike "impressionistic" rendering of events. They believed that indirect, interrupted methods of telling are "invaluable for giving a sense of the complexity, the tantilisation, the shimmering, the haze, that life is." To accomplish this, they relied heavily on juxtaposition of event, image, scene, especially through impressionistic time shifts.

Embodying these principles, *The Good Soldier* is a dazzling display of craftsmanship; it is also—on a limited scale—a penetrating examination of Edwardian social morality and values. It deals with two couples who winter yearly at the same German spa, a microcosm of upperclass society. The action centres on the Englishman Ashburnham, a retired officer of solid public character who is privately a sentimental philanderer. When after a series of shallow infatuations he falls tragically in love with his young ward, each member of the foursome is revealed through his or her response to the progression of events.

Although the materials of the story are potentially lurid—adultery and suicide—F. does not exploit them as melodrama. Rather, he tells the story through Dowell, the rich American, whose involved impressionistic account is a pathetic attempt to find some meaning in these complex and disillusioning relationships. The seeming artlessness of Dowell's associative presentation of details has been contrived by F. to emphasize psychological complexity and to effect the most telling juxtaposition of major characters and their values. Meanwhile, the reader's curiosity is piqued by the gradual process of disclosing relevant information, a process that requires the reader to sort out chronological relationships. Marked by controlled comic irony, *The Good Soldier* has been called (originally by F.'s friend, John Rodker) the "finest French novel in the English language."

F.'s persistent concern with the techniques of fiction has received much critical attention; less well understood is his strong conviction that the novelist should be a historian of social forces and cultural shifts, informing and reshaping public attitudes by examining his age against the values of the past. In the *Parade's End* tetralogy F. brought this conception of the novelist's role to an impressive level of realization. The events recounted relate not merely to the fortunes of particular characters; they are interwoven with and symptomatic of the decline of the ruling class and its values—leisure, culture, responsibility, order, tradition—a break-up hastened by the Great War. Technically no less adroit than *The Good Soldier, Parade's End* presents a far broader picture of an age and reveals more powerfully the complexity of F.'s moral vision. Like Thackeray's *Vanity Fair*, with which it has been compared, it is filled with vivid characters whose social and moral behavior is penetratingly delineated in the context of a great historical and cultural watershed, but F.'s use of impressionistic techniques adds a dimension of psychological subtlety and realism not found in Thackeray.

Christopher Tietjens, the central character, is the quintessential F. hero. A paradoxical combination of disengagement and practicality, he is at once an 18th-c. Tory squire, a 20th-c. infantry captain, and a 17th-c. poet and saint. Tormented by an unfaithful wife, betrayed by friends, undermined professionally and socially, Tietjens is vulnerable to abuse because of his high-principled sense of noblesse oblige. Yet he manages to remain on an even keel amid social and moral confusion, imperturbable even in the chaos of trench warfare. He embodies the paradoxes of a good man trying to remain sane when so much conspires against decency and honor.

F. was a sensitive critic of literature, although anything but academic. His randomly dispersed critical statements, usually impressionistic in form, do insist that literature (and the arts) be assessed by intelligible standards. The principles of fiction which he advocated, mentioned earlier, have been widely influential. F. published volumes such as *The Critical Attitude* (1911), *Henry James: A Critical Study* (1914), and *The English Novel* (1929), but more important, his critical sense pervaded his whole effort as a man of letters. It provided a foundation for the best of his own fiction and verse; it was vitally important to his achievement as an editor. This integration of criticism in his literary activity unquestionably extended his influence.

An account of F.'s contribution to letters must acknowledge his role as instigator and fostering spirit in the literary community. Like his friend Ezra Pound, he was not only a shrewd judge of talent but also by temperament inclined to provide encouragement and assistance to struggling writers. In numerous ways he helped create a social and critical climate among writers that he hoped would be conducive to cooperation. The two literary magazines he founded and edited served especially to advance promising new writers and to champion innovation not encouraged by the conservative establishment.

F.'s books of reminiscence, such as *Ancient Lights* (1911), which describes his growing up among the Victorian greats in his grandfather's household, *Joseph Conrad: A Personal Remembrance*, and *It Was the Nightingale* (1933), provide an informal view of great and not so great writers by an insider in the literary community. Impressionistically written, these books reveal F.'s

engaging humor, his eye for detail, and his ability to render vividly the essence of incident and character. He was a great talker, and this form allowed him room to "talk" on paper. Yet he learned to unify the loosely related materials of such books around a central theme. His reminiscences are frequently inaccurate as to facts, as F. admitted, but he insisted that impressionistically they were absolutely true.

F.'s life and career were marked by paradoxes. He was a writer who never won widespread popular or even critical approval, although he exerted considerable influence on a number of important literary artists. It is frequently said of him that he was "a writer's writer": Graham GREENE, William Carlos WILLIAMS, W. H. AUDEN, Allen Tate, and Caroline Gordon, among others, have praised his work. Oddly, he has been more appreciated in the U.S. than in his own country.

Easygoing and somewhat undisciplined in his character, he nevertheless produced a daily flow of prose and verse. Perhaps his greatest problem as a writer was that his facility with words led him to write too easily, too casually, and finally too much. As a consequence, the bulk of his work is uneven. Seldom did he demand fully of himself the discipline and restraint he advocated and which at his best he achieved.

Although *The English Review* and *transatlantic review* exposed F.'s limitations as a business manager and were short-lived, he was according to Graham Greene, the "best literary editor England has ever had." While he wrote few novels of major importance, his contribution to the theory of the novel puts him squarely in the important genealogy that leads from Flaubert through James and Conrad. He was a transitional artist, with a foot in both the 19th and 20th cs. A modernist in form, with his conservative values he seemed born a century—or two or three—too late.

FURTHER WORKS: *The Brown Owl* (1891); *The Feather* (1892); *The Shifting of the Fire* (1892); *The Questions at the Well* (1893, pseud. "Fenil Haig"); *The Queen Who Flew* (1894); *Ford Madox Brown* (1896); *Poems for Pictures* (1900); *The Cinque Ports* (1900); *The Inheritors* (1901, with Joseph Conrad); *Rossetti* (1902); *Romance* (1903, with Joseph Conrad); *The Face of the Night* (1904); *The Benefactor* (1905); *Hans Holbein the Younger* (1905); *The Soul of London* (1905); *Christina's Fairy Book* (1906); *The Heart of the Country* (1906); *An English Girl* (1907); *From Inland* (1907); *The Spirit of the People* (1907); *The Pre-Raphaelite Brotherhood* (1907); *Mr. Apollo* (1908); *The "Half Moon"* (1909); *A Call* (1910); *The Portrait* (1910); *Songs from London* (1910); *The Simple Life Limited* (1911, pseud. "Daniel Chaucer"); *High Germany* (1912); *The New Humpty-Dumpty* (1912, pseud. "Daniel Chaucer"); *The Panel* (1912); *The Desirable Alien* (1913), with Violet Hunt); *Mr. Fleight* (1913); *Collected Poems* (1913); *Antwerp* (1915); *When Blood Is Their Argument* (1915); *Between St. Dennis and St. George* (1915); *Zeppelin Nights* (1915, with Violet Hunt); *The Trail of the Barbarians* (1917); *A House* (1921); *Thus to Revisit* (1921); *The Marsden Case* (1923); *Women and Men* (1923); *Mister Bosphorous and the Muses* (1923); *The Nature of a Crime* (1924); *A Mirror to France* (1926); *New Poems* (1927); *New York Essays* (1927); *New York Is Not America* (1927); *A Little Less Than Gods* (1928); *No Enemy* (1929); *When the Wicked Man* (1931); *Return to Yesterday* (1931); *The Rash Act* (1933); *Henry for Hugh* (1934); *Provence* (1935); *Vive le Roy* (1936); *Collected Poems* (1936); *The Great Trade Route* (1937); *Mightier Than the Sword* (1938; Am., *Portraits from Life*); *The March of Literature* (1938); *The Bodley Head F. M. F.* (1962)

BIBLIOGRAPHY: Hunt, V., *I Have This to Say* (1926); Bowen, S., *Drawn from Life* (1941); *New Directions: Number Seven* (1942); Goldring, D., *South Lodge: Reminiscences of Violet Hunt, F. M. F. and the English Review Circle* (1942); Cassell, R. A., *F. M. F.: A Study of His Novels* (1961); Meixner, J. A., *F. M. F.'s Novels: A Critical Study* (1961); Wiley, P. L., *Novelist of Three Worlds: F. M. F.* (1962); special F. issue, *MFS*, 9, 1 (1963); Gordon, C., *A Good Soldier: A Key to the Novels of F. M. F.* (1963); Lid, R. W., *F. M. F.: The Essence of His Art* (1964); Ohmann, C., *F. M. F.: From Apprentice to Craftsman* (1964); MacShane, F., *The Life and Work of F. M. F.* (1965); special F. issue, *SR*, 74, 4 (1966); Hoffmann, C. G., *F. M. F.* (1967); Huntley, H. R., *The Alien Protagonist of F. M. F.* (1970); Mizener, A., *The Saddest Story: A Biography of F. M. F.* (1971); Stang, S. J., *F. M. F.* (1977); Stang, S. J., ed., *The Presence of F. M. F.: A Memorial Volume of Essays, Poems, and Memoirs* (1981); Moser, T. C., *The Life in Fiction of F. M. F.* (1981); Cassell, R. A., ed., *Critical Essays on F. M. F.* (1987); Judd, A., *F. M. F.* (1991)

—H. WAYNE SCHOW

When one finds Mr. F. M. F., the most able living novelist, devising a technique more complicated than Conrad's to disguise the same time-problem, one begins to wonder whether any novelist has found it possible to express the passage of time directly. . . . Mr. F.'s novels are novels of dramatic situations, situations of often wildly complicated irony. . . . Indeed the reviewers of the Sunday Press have frequently criticized Mr. F.'s method for what they consider its unnecessary complexity. They grant him vividness in his "big scenes"; they cannot understand that the vividness owes everything to the method. Mr. F. is unable to write narrative; he is conscious of his inability to write, as it were, along the line of time. How slipshod and perfunctory the joins between his dramatic scenes would seem if they were not put into the minds of the characters and their perfunctory nature "naturalized." The memory *is* perfunctory: you do not lose verisimilitude by such a bare record as this if you are looking back to events which have become history. . . . Mr. F. does not simply leave out; he puts in the links in his own good time, but they are properly subordinated to what he can do supremely well, dialogue and the dramatic scene.

Graham Greene, "The Dark Backward: A
Footnote," *London Mercury*, Oct. 1935,
pp. 564–65

I call him Ford Madox Hueffer because that is the name he bore in the days of *The English Review*. He later changed his name to Ford Madox Ford; and under that name indefatigably continued to publish his oddly uneven work in considerable quantity and to give rise in the literary world to innumerable rumours. Hueffer is to me one of the enigmas of current literature. He had great talent, and much taste, to which he added considerable coarseness of spirit and a carelessness of statement which constantly spoil a reader's enjoyment of his work. He wrote

much remarkable poetry, some historical romances which just missed being excellent, many novels on modern themes and situations which with much skill and passages beyond the reach of most living authors combined the coldness of the mortuary, criticism which for a paragraph here and there seems very like revealed truth and then drifts off into perversity, and memoirs of his own life and the lives of others which seem all the time to be boasting of his own unpleasantness.

He was editor of what was without doubt the most interesting periodical of our time, *The English Review*, in which were published . . . specimens of the work of almost all the established and arriving writers to 1908–11 (*The English Review* continued its work under another editor after the first glad Huefferian dawn), and in which living literature for the first time in English history was treated as quite important and quite exciting—much more important and much more exciting than students of English literature could imagine, and even more exciting than the contests of politicians or sportsmen. Books such as *The Fifth Queen* and *The Good Soldier* should be familiar to every investigator of what has been written in this century.

Frank Swinnerton, *The Georgian Literary Scene*
(1935), pp. 195–96

He has been called a writer's writer; he had a deep insight into the techniques of composition, and his views influenced men so widely separated by time and nature as Ezra Pound and Joseph Conrad, and, at the other end of his life Ernest Hemingway, Allen Tate and Robie Macaulay. But the solid and subtle construction of his best books makes them fresh and attractive also to the general reader when many better-known works by F.'s contemporaries begin to seem dated and stale.

. . . Above all, F. makes us see. We are never in doubt as to where the characters are, where the light comes from, what they can see through the window, where at a critical moment their hands are, what lies beyond the door. Sometimes their very movements of joint or neck are noted. They are seen as though on a stage; it is interesting to note that about this time James was telling himself in his notebooks that he should visualize the action of his novels as though it were taking place on a stage-set.

Kenneth Young, *F. M. F.* (1956), pp. 7, 24

Hueffer realized that he was not a gentleman, but it gave him no particular pleasure; there were too many gentlemen and too few writers. Professionals, this was what writing needed; James and Conrad (with whom Hueffer had worked) were both professionals, and Hueffer gave the valuable hint that they had not even been read properly yet. The status of the writer in England was summed up for Hueffer during the demobilization of the army after the war, when the last of the eighteen categories to be released contained: "Travelling salesmen, circus performers, all writers not regularly employed on newspapers, tramps, pedlars. . . ." And like Pound, and for much the same reasons (Hueffer added the reason that Regent Street had been pulled down) Hueffer finally left London for Paris. The opening world had opened and closed again.

Hueffer's work both as novelist and critic still goes unrecognized, here if not in America, and this is a pity. The comments made above on the serious nature of Hueffer's critical concerns should suggest why at least some of his novels are interesting, not only for their great technical interest and skill, their sense of "form," and rendering, but also, to put it briefly, for their sense both of the constructive and destructive nature of a society so concerned with manners at a time when those manners are breaking up and throwing the individual upon his resources. In America his reputation has risen and the Tietjens novels have been reissued there.

Certainly he should serve as a model for editors of literary periodicals; his respect for the artist, the creative being, and his determination to nourish genius made him an invaluable figure.

Malcolm Bradbury. *"The English Review."*
London Magazine, Aug. 1958, pp. 56–57

Parade's End has never yet been a popular success and few critics, I believe, have paid much attention to it. This neglect passes my comprehension. Of the various demands one can make of a novelist, that he show us the way in which a society works, that he show an understanding of the human heart, that he create characters in whose reality we believe and for whose fate we care, that he describe things and people so that we feel their physical presence, that he illuminate our moral consciousness, that he make us laugh and cry, that he delight us by his craftsmanship, there is not one, it seems to me, that F. does not completely satisfy. There are not many English novels which deserve to be called great: *Parade's End* is one of them.

W. H. Auden, "Il Faut Payer," *Mid-Century*, No. 22 (1961), p. 10

F.'s glory and mastery are in two or three of his novels. . . . He himself wrote poetry with his left hand—casually and even contemptuously. He gives sound and intense advice to a beginning poet: "Forget about Piers Plowman, forget about Shakespeare, Keats, Yeats, Morris, the English Bible, and remember only that you live in our terrific, untidy, indifferent empirical age, where not a single problem is solved and not a single Accepted Idea from the poet has any more magic. . . ." Yet he himself as a poet was incurably of the nineteenth century he detested, and to the end had an incurable love for some of its most irritating and overpoetic conventions. . . .

F. had no gift like Yeats for combining a conversational prose idiom with the grand style. I think he must often have felt the mortification of seeing the shining abundance of his novels dwindle away in his poetry to something tame, absentminded, and cautious. He must have found it hard to get rid of his jingling, hard to charge his lines, hard to find true subjects, and harder still to stick to them when found. Even such an original and personal poem as "On Heaven" is forever being beguiled from the road. Yet a magnificence and an Albigensian brightness hover over these rambling steps: F. and Pound were companions on the great road from twelfth-century Toulouse to twentieth-century London.

Buckshee is F., the poet, at his best. It too is uneven and rambling—uneven, rambling, intimate, and wonderful. . . . *Buckshee* coughs and blunders a bit in getting off, but in "Champetre," "Temps de Secheresse," and "Coda," F. finds the unpredictable waver of his true inspiration. In these reveries, he has at last managed to work his speaking voice, and something more than his speaking voice, into poems—the inner voice of the tireless old man, the old master still in harness, confiding, tolerant, Bohemian, newly married, and in France.

Robert Lowell, Foreword to F. M. F., *Buckshee* (1966), pp. xii–xv

FORD, Richard

American novelist and short-story writer, b. 16 Feb. 1944, Jackson, Mississippi

After earning his undergraduate degree and his M.F.A., F. had teaching stints in the 1970s, and has published two collections of stories and five novels. F. is best known for his two award-winning novels, *The Sportswriter* (1986) and *Independence Day* (1995), which feature Frank Bascombe, reminiscent of both John UPDIKE's Harry "Rabbit" Angstrom and Philip ROTH's Nathan Zuckerman.

F.'s first novel, *A Piece of My Heart* (1976), is a Southern Gothic about a law student returning to Mississippi, a drifter, and an old estate. His second, *The Ultimate Good Luck* (1981), follows a Vietnam veteran's attempts to win back an old girlfriend by rescuing her brother from a Mexican jail. With *The Sportswriter* and the subsequent *Rock Springs: Stories* (1987) and *Wildlife* (1990), F. turned to less dramatic and far-flung situations, preferring instead to chronicle the everyday lives of working men and women; this turn, in addition to his spare, cool style, earned comparisons to the minimalist writers of the late 1970s and 1980s such as Raymond CARVER and Ann BEATTIE. As he has continued to write and publish, and as the minimalist label has come to carry less weight, F. has come to be thought of less through these comparisons and more as a stylist of the quotidian in his own right.

Readers first heard Frank Bascombe's distinctive voice in *The Sportswriter*, the book that brought F. wider attention. Living in the New Jersey suburbs and writing for a well-known sports magazine in New York, Frank is a former fiction writer, a former husband, and former father of a son who died young. His ex-wife, charmingly referred to as "X" throughout the novel, lives nearby with their two remaining children, as does his younger Texas-born girlfriend. Somewhat detached from life, Frank is an observer—his traveling sportswriter life, his membership in the Divorced Men's Club, and his shell-shocked reserve keep him at a distance from life and allow him to report upon it with sharp but not entirely cynical commentary.

Independence Day picks up with Frank six years later. He is selling real estate and dealing with his troubled son Paul, his new girlfriend Sally, and his now-named ex-wife Ann. Still half-hoping to reconcile with Ann, thinking Paul's problems might be solved if he were to come live with him, and at the same time half-hoping things with Sally would get more serious, Frank finds himself again in a similar in-between place, but he is more in the fray, trying to reintegrate himself into the rhythms and relationships of life, and so, he feels, in greater danger of losing his independence. And again, as in *The Sportswriter*, Frank's professional situation and personal life afford him the opportunity to see life as participant-observer, as anthropologist of contemporary culture who lives among the natives but, by temperament as much as anything, is not quite of them.

In *Women with Men* (1997) F. attempts the revision of Ernest HEMINGWAY indicated by the title. The influence of Hemingway's *Men without Women* (1927) and of other works such as *In Our Time* (1925) and *The Sun Also Rises* (1926) is apparent in F.'s attention to the struggle to be a man in a changing world, as well as in the Hemingway sentence, in its Flaubertian exactness and its Steinian repetition. The importance of the *bon mot* and the well-lived life has been a constant in F.'s work; also constant has been his characters' attempts to work out their relationships with women in a way different from that chosen by Hemingway protagonists Nick Adams or Jake Barnes. In *Women with Men* F. takes a new angle on these constants by setting the first and last of the three stories among Americans in Paris, and by telling their stories in the third person. The similarity between these two stories, in their relation of attempts by men to deal or to not deal, through affairs, with disintegrating or disintegrated marriages back home, highlight the differences and make of them a greater whole than their separate parts. The insertion of a shorter Montana story, in his customary first-person narration adds a counterpoint in style as well as subject, but contributes to a thematic unity that itself contributes further to F.'s considerable literary reputation.

BIBLIOGRAPHY: DuPuy, E., "The Confessions of an Ex-Suicide: Relenting and Recovering in R. F.'s *The Sportswriter*," *SLJ*, 23 (1990): 93-103; Shelton, F. W., "R. F.," in Flora, J. M., and R. Bain, eds., *Contemporary Fiction Writers of the South: A Bio-Bibliographical Sourcebook* (1993): 147-55; Trussler, M., "'Famous Times': Historicity in the Short Fiction of R. F. and Raymond Carver," *WascanaR*, 28 (1994): 35-53; Crouse, D., "Resisting Reduction: Closure in R. F.'s *Rock Springs* and Alice Munro's *Friend of My Youth*," *CanL*, 146 (1995): 51-64

—SAM COHEN

FORSSELL, Lars

Swedish poet, dramatist, and critic, b. 14 Jan. 1928, Stockholm

F. was born into an upper-middle-class family. As a young man he lived and studied in the U.S. and France, experiences that did much to shape his literary tastes and preferences. His study of English evoked an admiration for Anglo-Saxon poetry, and in France he cultivated a love for the theater and cabaret entertainment. Although it was primarily for his poetry that F. was elected to the Swedish Academy in 1971, he has earned distinction writing plays, popular songs, film scripts, and essays on politics, art, literature, films, and sports.

F.'s second volume of poetry, *Narren* (1952; the fool), established him as the master of lyric poetry of his generation. Equally adept at rhythmic, regular verse and irregular conversational verse, F. has shown a sensitive feel for blending expressively such contrasting elements and themes as tenderness, prankish humor, and existential fear.

In subsequent collections—*Telegram* (1957; telegram), *En kärleksdikt* (1960; a love poem), and *Röster* (1964; voice)—F. moved away from his earlier elaborate style, heavy with classical allusions, toward simplicity of form, improvisatory effects, and colloquial diction. The virtuoso precision of these volumes led one critic to call him a "sniper with words."

In the middle and late 1960s, a growing political consciousness in F.'s works made him one of the most controversial public figures in Sweden. Some of his critics see a conflict between his socialist sympathies and his failure to repudiate his upper-middle-class background. To charges that he is naïve in matters of ideology, he has replied that one has a duty to betray ideology in times when ideology has so consistently betrayed mankind.

Despite his reputation as a poet, F. thinks of himself primarily as a dramatist, and since 1953 more than a dozen of his plays have been performed in Sweden, Denmark, Norway, West Germany, England, Scotland, Ireland, and the U.S. In fact, his first collection of poetry, *Ryttaren* (1949; the equestrain), contained a short commedia dell'arte-style play on the theme of fear and death, *Narren som tillhörde sina bjällror* (the fool attached to his bells).

Like his early verse, F.'s first full-length play, *Kröningen* (1956; *The Coronation*, 1963), is on a classical theme: Euripides' Admetus is transformed into an absurd antihero, unable to deal with the demands of either life or death.

Antiheroes are also the central characters of F.'s next three plays. *Charlie McDeath* (1961; *Charlie McDeath*, 1965-66), a play in one act, is about a ventriloquist who exchanges places with his dummy. *Mary Lou* (1962; Mary Lou) is a long one-acter about an American female traitor who broadcasts for Hitler and lures a GI to his death. The antihero in the thoughtful comedy *Söndagspromenaden* (1963; *The Sunday Promenade*, 1968) is Justus Coriander, a fantast who tries to escape the bonds and demands of reality by leading his family off to imaginary places on weekly picnic strolls around their dining-room table. Set in turn-of-the-century Sweden, *Söndagspromenaden* is F.'s best-represented play in foreign productions.

Political themes are important in F.'s later plays. *Galenpannan* (1964; *The Madcap*, 1973) and *Christina Alexandra* (1968; Christina Alexandra) have as their central characters the Swedish monarchs King Gustavus IV (1778-1837) and Queen Christina (1626-1689), respectively. Each protagonist tries unsuccessfully to assert personal moral values in a world corrupted by power politics.

Show (1971; show), staged in a distinguished production by Ingmar Bergman, is another drama about a social and political outsider, a Lenny Bruce-like entertainer who offends radicals and conservatives alike.

Haren och vråken (1978; the hare and the buzzard), a popular play throughout Scandinavia in the late 1970s, is an adaptation of Lope de Vega's (1562-1635) *Fuente ovejuna*, relocated to Stockholm in the revolutionary period on the eve of the assassination at a masked ball of King Gustavus III (1746-1792).

F.'s eminence as a poet-commentator is due in part to the ease and authority with which he moves through an astonishing range of genres—from passionate, lyrical poetry to stinging satirical songs to crisp, acerbic journalism—and in part to his ability to involve his audience in an intensely personal experience by confessing the world's fear, cruelty, and loneliness as his own.

FURTHER WORKS: *25 dikter* (trans. of Ezra Pound poems, 1953); *Chaplin* (1953); *F. C. Tietjens* (1954); *Cattus* (1955); *Snurra min jord* (1958); *Cantos I–XVII* (translation of Ezra Pound cantos, 1959); *Don Quixotes drömmar: Dikter 1949–1959* (1960); *Prototyper* (1961); *Torsten Andersson* (1963); *Det enda vi har är varandra: Dikter i urval* (1964); *Jack Uppskäraren och andra visor tryckta i år* (1966); *Samtal vid Ganges* (1967); *Upptåg: Flickan i Montréal, Drömmar i Omsk, Borgerlighetens fars* (1967); *Ändå* (1968); *Nedslag* (1969); *Borgaren och Marx* (1970); *Solen lyser på havet blå: Barnvisor* (1971); *Sigfrid Siwertz* (1971); *Oktoberdikter* (1971); *Försök* (1972); *Det möjliga* (1974); *Dikter (Den svenska lyriken)* (1975); *En bok för alla människor* (1975); *De rika* (1976); *Teater* (2 vols., 1977); *Jag står här på ett torg* (1979); *Stenar* (1980); *Brokigheten* (1980)

BIBLIOGRAPHY: Carlson, H. G., "The AntiHero in the Plays of L. F.," *Players*, 40, 2 (1963): 38–40; Carlson, H. G., "L. F.—Poet in the Theater," *SS*, 37 (1965): 31–57

—HARRY G. CARLSON

FORSTER, E(dward) M(organ)

English novelist, essayist, and critic, b. 1 Jan. 1879, London; d. 17 June 1970, Coventry

F.'s architect father died when he was a baby and he was raised by his mother, grandmother, and paternal great-aunt Marianne Thornton, descendant of the Clapham Sect of evangelists and reformers, whose legacy later gave him the freedom to travel and to write. F. read at age four, composed stories at five, educated the maids at six; but, self-possessed in intellectual matters, he was delicate in constitution and sensitive to teasing. A lost lease to the family's country home occasioned F.'s move to Tonbridge ("Sawston" in the novels), where he experienced great unhappiness as a day student at the private school. F. found a new home at King's College, Cambridge, which he entered in 1897 with vague thoughts of becoming a schoolmaster. In the atmosphere of Cambridge skepticism (this was the era of Sir James Frazer [1854–1941] and *The Golden Bough* [1890]), and under the influence of his dons—especially the fiercely antiauthoritarian Nathaniel Wedd (1862–1940) and the philosophical Goldsworthy Lowes Dickinson (1862–1932)—F. shed his not very deep Christian faith and adopted in its stead a creed of personal relationships and appreciation of the arts. This creed, deriving from the philosophy of G. E. Moore (1873–1958), was reinforced by F.'s like-minded friends in the Society of Apostles and his later associates in the Bloomsbury group.

After completing his studies in the classics, F. struck out for Italy and Greece; there, his imagination stimulated, he decided to be a writer by profession. He interspersed work on his fiction with lecturing, tutoring, and editing; with contributions to the new liberal monthly *The Independent Review*; and with what became a twenty-year stint at the Working Men's College in London. F.'s tutoring of an Indian student led, in 1912, to his first "passage to India." Although F. had already published four novels in five years, he now became so haunted by his homosexual tendencies that he was able to produce only several unpublishable erotic stories (which he later destroyed) and the post humously published novel *Maurice* (1971). During World War I, F. temporarily abandoned fiction and spent three years in Egypt with the Red Cross. After the war, a second trip to India as private secretary to the Maharajah of Dewas resulted in F.'s final completed novel: from 1924 until his death almost a half century later, he published no further major fiction. F. was well known for his defense of civil liberties in journals, on international councils, at obscenity trials, and over the airwaves, and was made a lifetime Honorary Fellow at Cambridge in 1946.

F.'s fictional works are moral guidebooks that juxtapose classes or cultures in order to enlarge perspective and achieve liberation from rigid social and national distinctions. In many of the short stories collected in *The Celestial Omnibus* (1911), *The Eternal Moment* (1928), *Collected Short Stories* (1947), and the posthumous *The Life to Come, and Other Stories* (1972), a pedant, aesthete, or snob meets a primitive, earthy, often lower-class individual. The crisis in these stories (most of them fantasies) comes at the moment a choice must be made between accepting the pagan, "foreign" element and thereby transfiguring one's existence or retreating into customary, stultifying modes of behavior.

These motifs figure more successfully in F.'s novels. *Where Angels Fear to Tread* (1905) revolves about the attempts of an Englishwoman's family at rescuing her from her marriage to an Italian and then, after her death in childbirth, at stealing her baby from its father. But it is the main character, Philip Herriton, who needs rescuing: from his snobbery and provincialism as well as from his resistance to active involvement in life. The novel contrasts the Sawston view of Italy, with its Authorized Sights, to the true vision that comes only off the beaten track, without the Baedeker. The guide to this vision is the baby's father, Gino Carrella, who offers Philip brotherhood and hence salvation. F. does not glorify Gino, nor does he gloss over the social and cultural impediments to a relationship. Nevertheless, F.'s sympathies clearly lie with instinct over etiquette, with native wisdom over acquired culture. Although Philip Herriton ultimately fails to connect, he at least has had a glimpse of the possibilities for heroic commitment to a less respectable but richer life.

The highly autobiographical *The Longest Journey* (1907) continues to ask the questions, What is our true home? What values should guide us? Contrasted homes and the values that they represent structure this tripartite book: Cambridge, Sawston, Wiltshire. The dedication to the novel is *Fratribus*, and the work hymns the brotherhood that F. knew with the Apostles; the problem for the main character, Rickie Elliot, as for Philip Herriton, lies in recognizing and acknowledging his true brother. Rickie, an artist who writes of getting in touch with nature but cannot do so himself, is F.'s most ambitious portrait of the aesthete. He marries disastrously, in part because he wants a home to take the place of Cambridge, in part because he transforms his wife, as he had his mother before her, into an ideal of womanhood. The relationship that could save him from his wife's deathly Sawston mentality—smugness, materialism, orderliness, conventionality—is offered by Rickie's illegitimate half-brother, a Pan-like creature of the Wiltshire downs. But Rickie idealizes him, too, and therefore loses his chance at connection. Throughout, F. deals in ethical terms with G. E. Moore's refutation of Idealism. If facing reality is the test that Rickie Elliot takes and fails in this book about educational systems, the novel itself is realistic about the forces of darkness in 20th-c. society and optimistic about the possibilities for their defeat.

A Room with a View (1908) is F.'s second "Italian" novel and his sunniest: the Comic Muse presides, permitting no brutal fights or sudden deaths. The image of windows, important in the first two novels, receives primary emphasis here, as Lucy Honeychurch searches for her room with a view. Having lost her Baedeker and her very proper chaperone in Florence, Lucy finds new guides, the most notable being Mr. Emerson, whose original opinions throw open the windows on art and on love. His flouting of social, religious, and aesthetic conventions threatens the cultivated English society that F. targets here as elsewhere; and, after a few false "rescues" from Emerson's value system, and a few muddles (a favorite Forsterian word) that result from her lies and foolish proprieties, Lucy learns to trust her instincts for right and good. The forces of darkness are kept at bay in this novel by what F. believes to be the true marks of civilization: love and respect for otherness, open channels of communication (truth telling), and faith in humankind's inherent nobility.

F. examines the havoc that creeping urbanization and materialism wreak on the sense of connection to the land and people in such fiction as *The Longest Journey* and "The Machine Stops" (1909), his science-fiction rebuttal to H. G. WELLS. He explores the theme more fully in *Howards End* (1910), the work that established his reputation. In this novel about the making and valuing of money, and the substitution of the cash nexus for human bonds, the fate of the Wilcox country house symbolizes the direction that England will take. The marriage of Margaret Schlegel to a businessman, and Margaret's inheriting of Howards End, indicate F.'s belief that connection can be made between poetry and prose, between idealism and pragmatism, between England's past and her future. Margaret is the New Woman, Lucy Honeychurch one step down the road: outspoken, aggressive, and free, reconciling within herself the "masculine" and "feminine." The humanistic credo of the novel, "only connect," remains a wistful hope, its tentativeness underscored by the unconvincing love relationship between Margaret and her husband; by the extreme spirituality—indeed, the ghostliness—of the guide to action, Ruth Wilcox; and by the disturbingly lower-class characters hovering on the fringes. In response to his growing fear of disorder in the very fabric of life, F. triumphantly expresses order and control in this novel's complex system of leitmotifs and the determined lightness of its tone.

F.'s tone darkens considerably in *A Passage to India* (1924), which, unlike other contemporary works on the same subject, is highly critical of British imperialism. Although it has been faulted for its many inaccurate details, partly attributable to the decade that elapsed between drafts of the novel, its basic truth about Anglo-Indian relations is undeniable. The petty proprieties of class and country that proved dangerous to individual growth in F.'s earlier fiction are here writ large, in the policies of one nation toward another. Even more, by suggesting nature's indifference or even hostility toward man, F. raises unsettling questions about the efficacy of the good will and personal relations that constitute his creed of liberal humanism.

F.'s novels move gradually into silence. In his most lighthearted novel, *A Room with a View*, F. had drawn on his personal experiences at Cambridge to write of good friends engaging in lively conversation about noble ideals; but in *Howards End* the formerly talkative and witty heroine becomes ever less inclined to speak. *A Passage to India*, F.'s final novel, implies that human intercourse may be impossible and language in vain: the echo in the Marabar Caves reduces all sounds to one meaningless noise; and in these caves a misunderstanding between two people of different sex, religion, class, and nation has grave ramifications for the whole notion of human compatibility. F.'s love for the natural and primitive—in landscape and the psyche—is tempered here by a feeling of incomprehension approaching (but stopping short of) despair. *A Passage to India* simultaneously recognizes the limitations of the humanistic creed, insists that the creed must nevertheless operate if we are to make any social and political progress, and hints at mysteries, both marvelous and frightening, lying beyond rational understanding. Because of its grand themes and its artistic unity and complexity, this novel is commonly regarded as F.'s finest work.

In *Maurice* and several of the stories in *The Life to Come* (1972), the "primitive" element that confronts F.'s protagonists is homosexuality. *Maurice* is a comparative failure: self-indulgent and thin, without F.'s saving irony, it is of interest mainly as a picture of British attitudes not long after Wilde; as a partial explanation of F.'s inability to draw convincing heterosexual relationships in his fiction; and as one reason for his eventual abandonment of that fiction. The erotic stories, like F.'s short stories in general, are successful only when they combine gentleness of touch with seriousness of theme.

Much of F.'s nonfiction has proven to be lasting and influential. *Aspects of the Novel* (1927), originally presented as lectures at Cambridge, is an idiosyncratic and engaging discussion of the novel as art form. Its distinctions between story and plot, pattern and rhythm, and "flat" and "round" characters have become commonplaces in literary criticism, and the book is an invaluable guide to F.'s own novels. The collections of his essays, book reviews, and radio braodcasts—*Abinger Harvest* (1936) and *Two Cheers for Democracy* (1951)—are unified stylistically by F.'s detached yet sympathetic tone and thematically by his preoccupation with rescuing the English character, and all of modern society, from its "Sawston" ways. In the second volume especially, F. speaks out against bullying institutions of any persuasion and for art as the only true ordering principle.

The Forsterian voice ensures F.'s place in literary history: at once casual and contentious, soft and strong, it argues without pomposity. In his reverence for instinct and nature, F. is a romantic; in his moralistic attention to man in society, a Victorian; in his skepticism, detachment, and reverence for art, a modern. F.'s beliefs are philosophic, not programmatic, and his "impracticality" has come to be valued as a testament to freedom from narrow systems. Although the fiction occasionally suffers from melodramatic plots, sentimentalized characters, archness of tone, and moralistic heavy-handedness, its strengths are numerous and their combination unique: a conversational, often playful style; the ability to surprise; the puncturing of cant and hypocrisy; a this-world spirituality; and a meticulous attention to craftsmanship.

FURTHER WORKS: *The Government of Egypt* (1920); *Alexandria: A History and a Guide* (1922); *Pharos and Pharillon* (1923); *Goldsworthy Lowes Dickinson* (1934); *Billy Budd* (1951; co-librettist for Britten's opera); *The Hill of Devi* (1953); *Marianne Thornton* (1956)

BIBLIOGRAPHY: McConkey, J., *The Novels of E. M. F.* (1957); Beer, J., *The Achievement of E. M. F.* (1962); Crews, F., *E. M. F.: The Perils of Humanism* (1962); Gransden, K. W., *E. M. F.* (1962);

Wilde, A., *Art and Order: A Study of E. M. F.* (1964); Natwar-Singh, K., ed., *E. M. F.: A Tribute* (1964); Stone, W., *The Cave and the Mountain: A Study of E. M. F.* (1966); Thomson, G., *The Fiction of E. M. F.* (1967); McDowell, F. P. W., *E. M. F.* (1969); Stallybrass, O. ed., *Aspects of E. M. F.* (1969); Parry, B., *Delusions and Discoveries: Studies on India in the British Imagination 1880–1930* (1972): 260–320; Gardner, P., ed., *E. M. F.: The Critical Heritage* (1973); Colmer, J., *E. M. F.: The Personal Voice* (1975); Rosenbaum, S. P., *The Bloomsbury Group: A Collection of Memoirs, Commentary and Criticism* (1975): 24–26, 163–69, and passim; McDowell, F. P. W., *E. M. F.: An Annotated Bibliography of Writings about Him* (1976); Das, G. K., *E. M. F.'s India* (1977); Furbank, P. N., *E. M. F.: A Life* (1978); Das, G. K., and J. Beer, eds., *E. M. F.: A Human Exploration* (1979)

—JUDITH RUDERMAN

No one seizes more deftly the shades and shadows of the social comedy; no one more amusingly hits off the comedy of luncheon and tea party and a game of tennis at the rectory. His old maids, his clergy, are the most lifelike we have had since Jane Austen laid down the pen. But he has into the bargain what Jane Austen had not—the impulses of a poet. . . . At certain moments on the Arno, in Hertfordshire, in Surrey, beauty leaps from the scabbard, the fire of truth flames through the crusted earth; we must see the red brick villa in the suburbs of London lit up. But it is in these great scenes which are the justification of the huge elaboration of the realistic novel that we are most aware of failure. For it is here that Mr. F. makes the change from realism to symbolism; here that the object which has been so uncompromisingly solid becomes, or should become, luminously transparent. He fails, one is tempted to think, chiefly because that admirable gift of his for observation has served him too well. He has recorded too much and too literally. He has given us an almost photographic picture on one side of the page; on the other he asks us to see the same view transformed and radiant with eternal fires. . . . [I]nstead of seeing . . . one single whole we see two separate parts. [1927]

Virginia Woolf, in Philip Gardner, ed., *E. M. F.: The Critical Heritage* (1973), pp. 321–24

[T]here is a good deal of attention to plot in the novels: but it is evidently not aimed at creating the normal relationship between author and reader. An author whose main concern is to entertain his audience will sometimes surprise them—but he will also take care not to jar them. At the point of surprise, the reader will begin to recognize that preceding events contained the seeds of the surprise. F.'s surprises, on the other hand, do sometimes jar—particularly those irruptions of death or violence which break suddenly into a prevailing atmosphere of domestic comedy. On examining the context of such passages, indeed, one sometimes discovers that F. has been deliberately leading his readers in a different direction: that the irruption of violence has actually been preceded by a

letting down of tension in the narrative. The result is that sudden death enters the novel with the jarring quality that it has in real life. The harmonic pattern within which we are comfortably established suddenly gives way. There is a moment of unreality which we then recognize to be in point of fact a moment of reality—but the reality of everyday life, not of art. Such intrusions of an unartistic "reality" should in themselves convince the reader that this is no ordinary storyteller.

John Beer, *The Achievement of E. M. F.* (1962), pp. 11–12

The opening line of *Howards End*—"One may as well begin with Helen's letter to her sister"—is a perfect example of what one of Christopher Isherwood's characters refers to as F.'s tea-tabling. The remark is so casual and understated, the tone so relaxed and personal; here we are, almost before we know it, in the complicated world of the Schlegels and the Wilcoxes. Or the beginning of "Anonymity: An Enquiry," . . . : "Do you like to know who's a book by?" Do we? How flattering it is to have our opinion asked . . . and here we are again, this time in F.'s own world, involved in the process of discovery, sharing the sense of intimacy it is F.'s particular gift to create. This is the voice with which F. has spoken out over several decades for the importance of the individual . . . ; the voice also with which he has attacked, wherever he found them, the abuses of authority and the perils of what he has called, in describing the English. "the undeveloped heart." And we are tempted, in an age of propaganda and advertisement, to listen to someone who refuses to speak in loud and commanding tones, who is hesitant, cautious, acutely aware, even self-conscious, who is—like ourselves.

Alan Wilde, *Art and Order: A Study of E. M. F.* (1964), pp. 1–2

Though F. and [D. H.] Lawrence differ extremely in superficial ways, the kinship between them is profound. They are both prophetic vitalists, hating the machine civilization that has cut men off from their roots, and revering what Aldous Huxley (like F. one of the few Bloomsburians on Lawrence's side) has called "the dark presence of otherness that lies beyond man's conscious mind." Perhaps only Conrad, Hardy, and—at a stretch—Meredith could share with F. and Lawrence what we might call the vision of the cave, the encounter with the chthonic underworld of human experience. . . . [I]t's too easy to think of F. only as the liberal humanist and forget his prophetic vision, the voice that gave heat and light to his humanity. . . . Lawrence is a Stephen to F.'s Rickie, his half-brother, and the prophet of that same "forgotten wisdom" which F. evokes with his Pans and Italians, caves and echoes. Their social criticism, too, stems from the same discontent. And nothing more clearly demonstrates F.'s independence from Bloomsbury, or any party line, than his frank and honest championing of a misunderstood and undervalued author.

Wilfred Stone, *The Cave and the Mountain: A Study of E. M. F.* (1966), pp. 381, 386–87

The assertion that F.'s people are either saved or damned, are either capable or not capable of vision, is true. The implication that this attitude points to hardness of heart and a kind of arrogance is false. . . . We may note that when F. comes forward as social philosopher or commentator in his nonfictional writing his vision of a sheep-or-goat humanity is severely modified; he is well aware of the dangers of arrogance. But in his fiction the drastic separation of good and evil is essential to the romance tradition in which he works. . . . To complain that he is unjust to the Anglo-Indians, unfair to the Wilcoxes (in fact he tries too hard to give them their due), and overly obvious in the short stories is to condemn an essential characteristic of the romance tradition and to ignore the fact that the conventions taken over from realistic fiction are being used for other than realistic ends.

George Thomson, *The Fiction of E. M. F.* (1967), pp. 48–49

. . . E. M. F. is our most musical novelist. And I don't mean that he just likes music or likes going to concerts and operas, or plays the piano neatly and efficiently (all of which he does), but that he really understands music and uses music in his novels, and fairly frequently. The musical *locus classicus* is, of course, *Howards End* . . . where a number of characters are presented in a tiny musical vignette—each of them reacting in a different way to a performance of Beethoven's Fifth Symphony. . . . The whole remarkable passage shows a most sensitive reaction to music, and allows the novelist to make some perceptive observations on Beethoven. . . . [T]he construction of F.'s novels often resembles that of the "classical" opera (Mozart-Weber-Verdi) where recitatives (the deliberately un-lyrical passages by which the action is advanced) separate arias or ensembles (big, self-contained set pieces of high comedy or great emotional tension). As examples of the latter, think of the bathing episode in *A Room with a View*, the Sunday school dinner at which Ansell confronts Rickie in *The Longest Journey*, and, perhaps greatest of all, the trial in *A Passage to India*.

Benjamin Britten, "Some Notes on F. and Music," in Oliver Stallybrass, ed., *Aspects of E. M. F.* (1969), pp. 81–83

F. once told us that he belongs to "the fag-end of Victorian liberalism," and the phrase is often taken with complete literalism and applied against him. As a result his intellectual and his literary destiny has been too readily linked with that strange death of liberal England which historians have dated around 1914, when the equation of economic individualism

with social progress lost political force. . . . In this century critics have increasingly accepted modernist norms for the judgement of literature, even though, of course, many of our writers have not been modernists in the strict sense. F. is a paradox here; he is, and he is not. There is in his work the appeal to art as transcendence, art as the one orderly product, a view that makes for modernism; and there is the view of art as a responsible power, a force for belief, a means of judgement, an impulse to spiritual control as well as spiritual curiosity. The point perhaps is that F. is not, in the conventional sense, a modernist, but rather a central figure of the transition into modernism. . . . He is, indeed, to a remarkable degree, the representative of two kinds of mind, two versions of literary possibility, and of the tensions of consciousness that exist between them.

Malcolm Bradbury, "Two Passages to India: F. as Victorian and Modern," in Oliver Stallybrass, ed., *Aspects of E. M. F.* (1969), pp. 124–25

FOUCAULT, Michel

French philosopher, b. 15 Oct. 1926, Poitiers; d. 25 June 1984, Paris

Next to Jean-Paul SARTRE, F. is often considered the most influential and fecund French philosopher of the century. Born to a provincial family of doctors, he studied philosophy at the École Normale Supérieure and later earned a degree in psychology (1952). F.'s family background explains to some degree his lifelong interest in the history of medicine and psychiatry, along with philosophy, history, and literature. Among his numerous works, *Les mots et les choses; Une archéologie des sciences humaines* (1966; *The Order of Things: An Archeology of the Human Sciences*, 1971) represents a turning point in his oeuvre. Another significant break marks the eight–year gap that separates the publication of volume one of his *Histoire de la sexualité: La volonté de savoir* (1976; *The History of Sexuality I: An Introduction*, 1978) from volumes two and three: *L'usage des plaisirs* (1984; *The Use of Pleasure*, 1985) and *Le souci de soi* (1984; *The Care of the Self*, 1986). During his later years, he came to be associated with such causes as prisoners' rights, the problems of the boat people, and gay rights. After having taught at the universities of Lille, Uppsala, Warsaw, Clermont–Ferrand, and Vincennes, F. held a chair at the prestigious Collège de France when he died in 1984.

The early F. produced a series of illuminating studies devoted to the emergence of the concept of mental illness, culminating with his monumental *Histoire de la folie à l'âge classique* (1961; *Madness and Civilization*, 1965). F.'s aim was to demonstrate that the generalized practice of institutionalizing people considered to be mad is relatively recent, as can be seen by the systematic roundups of beggars, petty criminals, and prostitutes that took place in the 17th c. under absolute monarchy. In the 18th c. madness was criminalized through a series of legal moves and was reinforced by the creation of a uniform network of prisons that F. would later describe in his *Surveiller et punir: Naissance de la prison* (1975; *Discipline and Punish: The Birth of the Prison*,

1977). The hallmark of F.'s early work is to have shown that reason as defined by Descartes could only exist in its relation to madness, the latter being a defining other that is both fascinating and repressed. F.'s *Histoire de la folie à l'âge classique* is also an account of the birth of the modern state and its repressive and disciplinarian apparatuses, which a F. critic has labeled "the rise of unfreedom." It should be pointed out that F. himself acknowledged that his early work contained phenomenological residues and displayed a somewhat romanticized vision of madness.

F.'s next major project, *Les mots et les choses*, was an ambitious reconstruction of the history of human sciences and proffered the much debated concept of *episteme* that did away with the concept of a linear history. It also closed on the no less famous, if often misunderstood, statement that "Man is dead." Focusing on the evolution of sciences, F. isolated three moments in the modern ages when knowledge and representation seem to rely on different foundations. In each of these periods a trilogy of sciences—natural history/analysis of wealth/general grammar, biology/economics/philology, and psychology/sociology/linguistics—appears to be organized according to common patterns ignored by these sciences. For F. this hidden structuring of knowledge, which he called *episteme*, gives each of these periods its intellectual identity; some of F.'s critics have claimed that he was never able to account for change from one *episteme* to another. Finally, by stating that "Man is dead" F. meant that the concept of humankind was a very recent one, as a product of history, and that it might very well disappear.

His next major work, *Surveiller et punir*, addressed the traditional view of power based on force and coercion. According to F., power should be analyzed from the point of view of a "microphysics" (of power) that would take into account, among other things, the body as a fragmented area permeated by thousands of unconscious procedures of discipline. In F.'s eyes, the history of prisons in Europe and the U.S. along with legal literature provided the ideal research material for investigating the constitution and rise of "modern" power. His approach to these various issues caused him to be more or less ambiguously associated with the so-called structuralist generation, that is, with Louis Althusser (1918–1990), Roland BARTHES, and Claude LÉVI-STRAUSS.

What critics have labeled "the final Foucault" is associated with the published volumes of his *Histoire de la sexualité*. In the first volume, F., who had earlier welcomed and praised the advent of psychoanalysis as a liberating technique, turned against it, claiming that it reproduced in a new guise the urge to confess inherited from Christian thought. In subsequent volumes, F. departed from his original stated project and turned his attention to ancient Greece as the producer of the very subjectivity Christian thought was to erase. F. was trying to contribute to what subjectivity and ethics could be and mean in a post-Christian era. Thus, the very philosopher who in the 1960s and the 1970s had delivered a devastating blow to the concept of the subject was reinstating it through his studies of ancient texts dealing with happiness, diet, sexual habits, and personal ethics. At the time of his premature death, F. was devoting his Collège de France lectures to the concept of *gouvernementalité* or "governmentality."

As a philosopher F. remained close to Nietzsche and Heidegger. His relativism and deep distrust of morality, which in the first part of his career he considered a power play always won by the rulers, is reminiscent of Nietzsche's *Genealogy of Morals* (1887). But the manner in which F. also conceived of the limited possibilities that are offered the human mind by each historical horizon, as well as his early rejection of subjectivity, evokes Heidegger.

It is the fate of works of this amplitude that have revolutionized fields including philosophy, psychiatry, history, and legal studies, to be submitted to intense critical scrutiny. Up to *Surveiller et punir* F. was often charged with accounting for the totalitarian world of the modern state without offering the alternatives he clearly endorsed as a left–wing political activist. After volume two of *Histoire de la sexualité* he was perceived by some as a newborn elitist who had dropped all social concerns. And, like Sartre's work, F.'s does not register the existence of other cultures and non–Europocentric experiences of life. This will not prevent F. from being regarded in the future as one of the most influential thinkers of the 20th c., after whom entire sectors of human knowledge will never again be the same.

FURTHER WORKS: *Maladie mentale et personnalité* (1954); *Maladie mentale et psychologie* (1962); *Naissance de la clinique: Une archéologie du regard médical* (1963; *The Birth of the Clinic: An Archeology of the Medical Perception*, 1973); *Raymond Roussel* (1963; *Death and the Labyrinth: The World of Raymond Roussel*, 1986); *L'archéologie du savoir* (1969; *The Archeology of Knowledge*, 1976); *L'ordre du discours* (1971; *Orders of Discourse*, 1971); *Résumés des cours au Collège de France* (1989). FURTHER WORKS IN ENGLISH: *Language, Counter–Memory, Practice: Selected Essays and Interviews* (1977); *Power/Knowledge: Selected Interviews and Other Writings* (1980); *The F. Reader* (1983); *M. F.:Politics, Philosophy, Culture: Interviews and Other Writings* (1988)

BIBLIOGRAPHY: Baudrillard, J., *Oublier F.* (1977); Dreyfus, H. L., and Rabinow, P., *M. F.: Beyond Structuralism and Hermeneutics* (1982); Racevskis, K., *M. F. and the Subversion of Intellect* (1983); Poster, M., *F., Marxism and History: Mode of Production versus Mode of Information* (1984); Rajchman, J., *M. F.: The Freedom of Philosophy* (1985); Deleuze, G., *F.* (1986); Arac, J., ed., *After F.: Humanistic Knowledge, Postmodern Challenges* (1988); Bernauer, J., and Rasmussen, D., eds., *The Final F.* (1988); Canguilhem, G., ed., *M. F. philosophe: Rencontre internationale, Paris 9, 10, 11 janvier 1988* (1989); Fraser, N., *Unruly Practices: Power, Discourse and Gender in Contemporary Social Theory* (1989): 17–66

—JEAN–FRANÇOIS FOURNY

FOWLES, John

English novelist, b. 31 March 1926, Leigh-on-Sea

F. attended an English public school, where he excelled both as scholar and athlete and eventually became head boy. "At the age of eighteen," he later confessed, "I had the power to judge and punish six hundred to eight hundred other boys, and this gave me a distaste for power that has grown and grown." A lieutenancy in the British marines not only confirmed this distaste, but turned him into "a sort of anarchist" and away from the Establishment path.

F.'s intellectual liberation, however, really began at Oxford. Here, reading philosophy and French EXISTENTIALISM and those of the pre-Socratic Greek philosopher Heraclitus. After receiving his degree in 1950, F. spent the next thirteen years teaching in France, Greece, and England, and writing novels.

The Collector (1963), the first novel F. submitted to a publisher, caused only a minor stir in England but became both a critical and popular success in America. Its filming, two years later, brought F. international fame.

While the plot of *The Collector*—that of an artistic girl being imprisoned and wasting away in the home of a dreary, mean-spirited clerk and amateur lepidopterist—was partially inspired by a newspaper account of the 1950s, its principal theme goes back some 2,500 years. More than a psychological thriller or a study in class conflict, *The Collector* is a parable of the tension between the Few (*áristoi*, the good ones and intellectual elite) and the Many (*hoi polloi*, the unthinking, conforming masses). The novel questions whether the Many (like Clegg, the collector), who now seem to dominate society, will allow the Few (Miranda Grey) to live, in F.'s words, "authentically"; or whether the many will suffocate them. By living authentically, F. means (as do the French existentialists) not succumbing to anxieties but overcoming them, not running away from life but engaging it. The novel ties up this theme with that of free will, for the authentic character is one who, after self-discovery and acceptance of the past, believes in free will and achieves it. Miranda, through these psychological processes, becomes the novel's existential heroine, although she never escapes from Clegg.

F. enumerates his existential theories in *The Aristos: A Self-Portrait in Ideas* (1964, rev. ed. 1968). Cast as "one side of a dialogue," these somewhat eccentric notations touch on myth, philosophy, aesthetics, psychology, and history to generalize about our "universal situation": that is, where and what are we? F.'s conclusion to *The Aristos*—"to accept limited freedom . . . one's isolation . . . responsibility . . . to learn one's particular powers, and then with them to humanize the whole"—became the text for his two following novels.

The first of these, *The Magus* (1965), concerns Nicholas Urfe, who, uncertain of who he is or what he wishes to be, takes a teaching post on a remote Greek island, only to be drawn into a strange quest. The magus of the title, Maurice Conchis, engineers elaborate scenarios, masques, and psychological experiments to confuse Urfe's sense of appearance and reality. Urfe is finally led to the moment when he must choose whether or not to become a responsible person. F.'s skilled interweaving of mythic and literary allusion, his symbolic use of the tarot cards, his many fine descriptions, his proper balance between realism and fantasy, and his incredible turns of plot, make the novel a brilliant technical achievement. F. published a considerably revised version of *The Magus* in 1977.

From the point of thematic and technical interplay, however, *The French Lieutenant's Woman* (1969) is the most fascinating of F.'s works. Set in the 1860s, it ostensibly parodies one of the large canvases of Thomas HARDY or George Eliot by incorporating authorial digressions, gratuitous turns of plot, sexual innuendo, and contradictions between morals and manners. On the surface the novel tells a banal story: the thwarted love of a genteel, intelligent "evolutionist," Charles Smithson, for Sarah Woodruff, a passionate and imaginative governess whose affair with a French naval lieutenant has ostracized her from society. Yet this is all about the book that is banal. Because he is writing from a contemporary perspective, with all the devices of the modern novel at his command, F. is able to freely juggle time and space to create patterns of truth and ambiguity about Victorian life. Combining fiction, criticism, and history, F. manipulates anachronisms, sociological reports, factual footnotes, quotations from Darwin, Marx,

and the great Victorian poets, so that past and present ideologies are deftly juxtaposed. Still obsessed with the problem of freedom and authenticity, for his characters as well as for the novelist, F. provides two traditional endings for the novel—endings of which any Victorian might have approved—and then supplies modern denouements, less conclusive but more realistic. In *The French Lieutenant's Woman*, F. captures the sensibilities of the past, as well as subtly telling us a great deal about our present.

F.'s "variations on themes" and his theme of "variation" are further displayed in his curious fourth book, *The Ebony Tower* (1974). Neither a collection of stories nor a novel, this work is a forest of five intertwining fictions, where the quest to define one's freedom and existence becomes entangled with the bolder question of whether the modern writer—having descended from the ivory tower and now residing in an ebony one—is capable any longer of making such quests meaningful. Once again, the book is about Art and Life, but F. has partially lopped off the capitals to make both seem more graspable than they were in *The Magus* and *The French Lieutenant's Woman*, and certainly less hermetic, fantastic, gimmicky, and recondite.

F.'s place as one of the greatest of contemporary novelists was secured at last by *Daniel Martin* (1977), his most thoughtful and formidable novel to date, one that uses art to tell us everything F. knows of life. Indeed, Martin's life emerges as the challenging and dominant theme itself. Detained in England for an inquest after a friend's suicide, Martin is thrown together with people he has not seen for years, led to places he has hoped to avoid. Confronting these, he is also forced to face the past: his boyhood in Dorset; his university days; his sexual initiations and transgressions; his marriage and adulteries; his promise as a playwright and his "selling out" to Hollywood. No mere flashbacks, but considered images that impinge on Martin's mind so that he is able to make of them flashforwards, these events and memories become tiny but significant illuminations that guide him toward rectifying his mistakes, "reifying" the abstraction that has been Daniel Martin. Added to this masterful unfolding of character, and the humane revelation of what direction life must take for authenticity and freedom, are F.'s familiar excursions into a wealth of ideas, each of which has pertinence to modern existence, all of which taken together add layer upon layer to the composite that is the hero/narrator. By the end of the novel's six hundred pages, nothing less emerges than a full-blown portrait of fine, earnest, humanistic sensibilities struggling to make themselves whole in an age of complexity and confusion.

F.'s intent as a writer of fiction has always been to strike the sane balance between art and life, at a time when both seem vulnerable to excess, and neither seems susceptible to control. His fictional works, very different in texture and technique from each other—and one a supreme achievement—are all concerned with man's potential to discover and fulfill himself.

FURTHER WORKS: *Poems* (1973); *Cinderella* (1976); *Shipwreck* (1976); *Islands* (1979); *The Enigma of Stonehenge* (1980); *Mantissa* (1982); *A Maggot* (1985)

BIBLIOGRAPHY: Churchill, T., "Waterhouse, Storey and F.: Which Way Out of the Room," *Crit*, 10, 3 (1968): 72–87; Allen, W., "The Achievement of J. F.," *Encounter*, Aug. 1970: 64–67; Karl, F., "Two New Novelists," *A Reader's Guide to the Contemporary English Novel* (1972): 355–60; Palmer, W. J., *The Fiction of J. F.* (1974); Wolfe, P., *J. F.: Magus and Moralist* (1976); Myers, K. M., "J. F.: An Annotated Bibliography, 1963–76," *BB*, 33 (1976):

162–69; Magalaner, M., "The Fool's Journey: J. F.'s *The Magus*," in Morris, R. K., ed., *Old Lines, New Forces: Essays on the Contemporary British Novel 1960–1970* (1976): 81–92; McSweeney, K., "Withering into the Truth: J. F. and *Daniel Martin*," *CritQ*, 20, 4 (1978): 31–38; Huffaker, R., *J. F.* (1980); Foster, T. C., *Understanding J. F.* (1994)

—ROBERT K. MORRIS

FRAME, Janet

New Zealand novelist, short-story writer, and poet, b. 23 Aug. 1924, Dunedin

F. was brought up in a provincial society, that of Otago, a province in the south of New Zealand. Her family was poor and lived on the outskirts of Oamaru; this small town became the "Waimaru" of her novel *Owls Do Cry* (1957), which contains many autobiographical elements. In the 1940s she studied at the University of Otago in Dunedin. One critic, R. T. Robertson, has remarked that "the cultural milieu of New Zealand obeys what Northrop Frye has called Emerson's law, namely, that in a provincial society it is extremely easy to reach the highest level in cultivation, extremely difficult to take one step beyond that." It was F.'s attempt to take that step that led to the crises in her life between 1945 and 1955 and provided material for *Faces in the Water* (1961).

Although F. has written several volumes of short stories and one of poetry, she is best known as a novelist. She has said that she considers the best thing she ever wrote to be a fable written as a child entitled "Bird, Hawk, Bogie" (published in *Landfall*, 19 [1965], 40–47). This fable, in which the bird (inspiration and imagination) is eaten by the powerful, predatory hawk (materialistic, conformist society), which in turn is eaten by the bogie (repressed imagination and individualism, which must eventually and inevitably return to avenge itself), provides the recurrent symbolism for all her work.

F. has one essential concern: the plight of the individual in a conformist society, a concern she shares with two other major Commonwealth writers, Doris LESSING and Patrick WHITE. What characterizes the excolonial, provincial society for all three writers are an exaltation of the average and a fear of the nonconformist, of the imaginative, of what F. calls "open spaces of the mind."

From an early age F. was conscious of a division of society in which the imaginative people, the visionaries, the inhabitants of what she called "that" world were both feared and ostracized by the inhabitants of "this" world, a world of sterility, conformism, and materialism. Life/death, false/real, seeing/blind, sane/insane, treasure/rubbish are dichotomies recurring in all her work.

In her first novel, possibly her best, *Owls Do Cry*, she presents the two worlds, the movement of one person from the world of conformist society to the lonely world of the isolated individual, and the usual—perhaps inevitable—reaction on the part of the conformist society: to commit the nonconformist to a psychiatric hospital. F. consciously chose to become a citizen of "that" world, and it is a world in which she has remained up to the present day. The cost is high, as she shows in *Owls Do Cry* and even more in *Faces in the Water*. Over a certain period of time F. had repeated nervous breakdowns, caused essentially by her initial endeavors to conform, and these meant stays in psychiatric hospitals. *Faces in the Water* is a semi-autobiographical account of such a hospital and

the people who live in it, both patients and staff. It is a frightening indictment of such places, but it is much more than that, for it presents F.'s feeling that schizophrenia is not madness but an attempt on that part of the "ill" person to free the self from an oppressive society. Madness is a central metaphor in her work, and she can be considered one of the major novelists concerned with the knowledge–through–madness theme.

F. has widened her scope in her later novels to include both England and America, thereby showing that the malaise affecting 20th-c. man is not confined to New Zealand. She has always shown a keen social as well as psychological awareness and has recognized the role society plays in creating certain states of mind in its individual members. She may have rejected "this" world but not the people who inhabit it, for she sees them as victims, automatons robbed of their inner selves, prey to the forces of capitalism, reduced to producing-consuming machines. She reveals this social concern in *Intensive Care* (1970), an antiutopian novel describing a society after a nuclear World War III ruled by supertechnocrats whose "final solution" is the Human Delineation Act, designed, through computerized selection, to rid the world of its misfits. It is a horrifying vision made even more so by the reader's awareness of its real possibility.

F. is a difficult novelist. Rarely does she employ straightforward narrative or conventional characterization. Her language also presents problems, for in her endeavor to convey the at times almost unconveyable, she dislocates both syntax and words. But if she is difficult, she is also disturbing, for she possesses a more acute vision than most other 20th-c. writers of an utterly destitute world.

FURTHER WORKS: *The Lagoon* (1951); *The Edge of the Alphabet* (1962); *Scented Gardens for the Blind* (1963); *Snowman Snowman* (1963); *The Reservoir* (1963); *The Adaptable Man* (1965); *A State of Siege* (1966); *The Rainbirds* (1967; Am., *Yellow Flowers in the Antipodean Room*, 1969); *The Pocket Mirror* (1967); *Mona Minim and the Smell of the Sun* (1969); *Intensive Care* (1970); *Daughter Buffalo* (1972); *Living in Maniototo* (1980); *To the Is-Land* (1982); *An Angel at My Table* (1984); *The Carpathians* (1989)

BIBLIOGRAPHY: Evans, P., "Alienation and Death: The Novels of J. F.," *Meanjin*, 32 (1973): 294–303; Delbaere, J., "Daphne's Metamorphoses in J. F.'s Early Novels," *ArielE*, 6 (1975): 23–37; New, W. H., *Among Worlds* (1975): 149–54; Rutherford, A., "J. F.'s Divided and Distinguished Worlds," *WLWE*, 14 (1975): 51–68; Alcock, P., "On the Edge: New Zealanders as Displaced Persons," *WLWE*, 16 (1977): 127–42; Evans, P., *J. F.* (1977); Delbaere, J., ed., *Bird, Hawk, Bogie: Essays on J. F.* (1978); Mercer, F., *J. F.: Subversive Fictions* (1994)

—ANNA RUTHERFORD

FRANCE, Anatole

(pseud. of Jacques-Anatole-François Thibault) French novelist, short-story writer, essayist, poet, and critic, b. 16 April 1844, Paris; d. 13 Oct. 1924, Tours

F. was born on Quai Malaquais (Paris) above the bookshop owned by his father, François-Noël Thibault, who used "France," the Angevin diminutive of François, as the name of his bookstore and then as his own surname, dropping Thibault. F. had a voracious appetite for books and was always involved with them, as critic, librarian, and eventually author of more than sixty volumes.

For the first half of his life, F. was a conservative, denouncing the government of the Paris Commune (spring 1871) in his novel *Les désirs de Jean Servien* (1882; *The Aspirations of Jean Servien*, 1912) as both evil and ridiculous, and favoring the return of order, which to him meant government by the elite. Although F. evolved politically toward socialism, his abhorrence of violence, even as a means of achieving a desirable end, never changed.

The Dreyfus affair forced F. to abandon his safe position as skeptical observer and openly take sides. He joined Émile Zola and socialist leader Jean Jaurès in coming to the defense of Captain Alfred Dreyfus, who was falsely convicted of espionage. F. incorporated elements of the Dreyfus affair in *L'anneau d'améthyste* (1899; *The Amethyst Ring*, 1919) and in *Monsieur Bergeret à Paris* (1901; *Monsieur Bergeret in Paris*, 1921), the third and fourth novels of his four-volume *Histoire contemporaine* (contemporary history)—the first and second volumes are *L'orme du mail* (1897; *The Elm Tree on the Mall*, 1910) and *Le mannequin d'osier* (1897; *The Wicker Work Woman*, 1910). In the last two novels of the tetralogy he exposed the basic anti-Semitism that lay behind the condemnation of Dreyfus, the only Jew on the French General Staff, and revealed the manner in which Dreyfus's supporters were persecuted.

Although F. had a wife and daughter, the most important woman in his life was Mme. Léontine Arman de Caillavet, a wealthy Jewish-born woman who ran a literary salon in Paris and who encouraged and prodded F. to write. F. lived openly with Mme. de Caillavet from the time of his divorce in 1893 until her death in 1910; the years they spent together were the most productive in F.'s career. Their stormy love affair, tormented by jealousy and possessiveness, is the source of F.'s most romantic novel, *Le lys rouge* (1894; *The Red Lily*, 1898). F. was elected to the French Academy in 1896 and won the Nobel Prize for literature in 1921. A national funeral was held upon his death in 1924.

F. began his career as a critic with *Alfred de Vigny* (1868), a study of the great writer (1797–1863), and as a poet with a collection of philosophical poems, *Les poèmes dorés* (1873; golden poems), dedicated to the Parnassian poet Leconte de Lisle (1818–1894). But it was not until the age of thirty-seven that F. gained wide recognition with the charming tale *Le crime de Sylvestre Bonnard* (1881; *The Crime of Sylvester Bonnard*, 1890). F. was immediately identified with its protagonist, the wise and tender skeptic, just as he would subsequently be identified with the young schoolboy Pierre Nozière, the protagonist of the autobiographical novels *Le livre de mon ami* (1885; *My Friend's Book*, 1913) and of *Pierre Nozière* (1899; *Pierre Nozière*, 1916), later with the good-natured, anarchistic Abbé Jérôme Coignard, the title character of *Les opinions de Jérôme Coignard* (1893; *The Opinions of Jérôme Coignard*, 1913), and finally with Monsieur Bergeret, the skeptical university professor in *Histoire contemporaine*. F. and his protagonists share an underlying pessimism tinged with a kindly indulgence toward human folly. F.'s superior, compassionate smile irritated extremists on the right and on the left, who sought to abolish the existing social order and establish a more perfect, "virtuous" society.

In the second half of his life, F. became a crusader much as Voltaire had been in the 18th-c. Like Voltaire, F. was an Epicurean, a seeker of intellectual and sensual pleasures, who delighted in beautiful works of art, fine furniture, the luxuries of modern times as well as the treasures of antiquity. In their satirical works, such as

Anatole France

Voltaire's *Candide* and F.'s mock history of the French people, *L'île des pingouins* (1907; *Penguin Island*, 1909), both writers used broad Gallic wit and ribald Rabelaisian humor to poke fun at romantic notions of love and to deflate the pretensions of egotistical authorities of church and state. Mysticism was just as incomprehensible to F. as it had been to Voltaire. F.'s *Thaïs* (1890; *Thaïs*, 1892) and *Vie de Jeanne d'Arc* (2 vols., 1908; *The Life of Joan of Arc*, 1908) both deal with Christian themes in an antimystical manner. In *La révolte des anges* (1914; *The Revolt of the Angels*, 1914) F. portrays Satan in a sympathetic light as a Promethean hero.

Probably the most enduring works of F.'s maturity are the story "L'affaire Crainquebille" (1901; "Crainquebille," 1915) and the epic novel *Les dieux ont soif* (1912; *The Gods Are Athirst*, 1913). The short story was the ideal medium for F. since it obliged him to control his tendency toward lengthy digressions. "L'affaire Crainquebille"—which F. later made into a play, *Crainquebille* (1905; *Crainquebille*, 1915)—is the touching story of a poor pushcart peddler, unjustly accused of insulting a policeman, whose downfall is so pathetic that after his release from prison he intentionally shouts insults at a policeman in the hopes of being sent back to prison for food and shelter. The story of Crainquebille is symbolic of the persecution of Captain Dreyfus. By depicting society's need for a sacrificial victim and illustrating the injustice committed against the defenseless poor, F. clearly plants himself alongside the socialists as champion of the masses.

Yet this defender of the common people still had reservations about giving them power. In *Les dieux ont soif* F. exposed the corrupting influence of power, specifically as exercised during the French Revolution. The protagonist, Évariste Gamelin, a pure but overly zealous revolutionary, becomes a judge during the Reign of Terror. F. depicts the way in which this formerly gentle, sensitive intellectual, a painter by profession, is won over by the fanaticism of Robespierre and willingly sentences friends and relatives to death. For F., revolutions inevitably result in tyrannies just as oppressive as those they sought to displace.

The moral of F.'s works is one of tolerance and moderation. After his death, F. became unfashionable, especially from the viewpoint of the SURREALISTS. F.'s humanism, his irony, and even his pity did not appeal to a generation seeking a total break with classical style and culture. Outside France, however, F. has always been regarded as a model of French literary style, exemplifying clarity, irony, and sensitivity, the best characteristics of French wit.

FURTHER WORKS: *La légende de Sainte Radegonde, reine de France* (1859); *Jean Racine* (1874); *Racine et Nicole* (1875); *Les noces corinthiennes* (1876; *The Bride of Corinth*, 1920); *Idylles et légendes* (1876; *Golden Tales of A. F.*, 1926); *Jocaste et le chat maigre* (1879; *Jocasta and the Famished Cat*, 1912); *Abeille* (1883; *Honey-Bee*, 1911); *Marguerite* (1886; *Marguerite*, 1921); *La vie littéraire* (4 vols., 1888–1892; *On Life and Letters*, 4 vols., 1911–1914); *Balthasar* (1889; *Balthasar*, 1909); *L'étui de nacre* (1892; *Tales from a Mother of Pearl Casket*, 1896); *Aphorismes* (1893; *Epigrams on Life, Love, and Laughter*, 1924); *La rôtisserie de la Reine Pédauque* (1893; *At the Sign of the Reine Pédauque*, 1912); *Le jardin d'Épicure* (1894; *The Garden of Epicurus*, 1908); *Le puits de Sainte-Claire* (1895; *The Well of Saint Clare*, 1909); *Poésies; Les poèmes dorés; Idylles et légendes; Les noces corinthiennes* (1896); *Au petit bonheur* (1898; *One Can But Try*, 1925); *Clio* (1889; *Clio*, 1922); *Filles et garçons* (1900; *Child Life in Town and Country*, 1910); *Opinions sociales* (2 vols., 1902); *Funérailles d'Émile Zola* (1902); *Sur la tombe de Zola* (1902); *Histoire comique* (1903; *A Mummer's Tale*, 1908); *L'Église et la république* (1904); *Crainquebille, Putois, Riquet, et plusieurs autres récits profitable* (1904; *Crainquebille, Putois, Riquet, and Other Profitable Tales*, 1915); *Sur la pierre blanche* (1905; *The White Stone*, 1910); *Vers les temps meilleurs* (1906; *The Unrisen Dawn: Speeches and Addresses*, 1928); *Le tombeau de Molière* (1908); *Les contes de Jacques Tournebroche* (1908; *The Merrie Tales of Jacques Tournebroche*, 1909); *Les sept femmes de Barbe-Bleue* (1909; *The Seven Wives of Bluebeard*, 1920); *Les poèmes du souvenir* (1911); *La comédie de celui qui épousa une femme muette* (1912; *The Man Who Married a Dumb Wife*, 1915); *Le génie latin* (1913; *The Latin Genius*, 1924); *Sur la voie glorieuse* (1915; *The Path of Glory*, 1916); *Ce que disent nos morts* (1916); *Le petit Pierre* (1918; *Little Pierre*, 1920); *Stendhal* (1920; *Stendhal*, 1926); *Pensées philosophiques* (1920); *Mémoires d'un volontaire* (1921); *Les matinées de la villa Saïd* (1921); *La vie en fleur* (1922; *The Bloom of Life*, 1923); *Dernières pages inédites* (1925); *Œuvres complètes* (26 vols., 1925–1937); *La vie littéraire*, Vol. 5 (1949). FURTHER WORKS IN ENGLISH: *The Complete Works* (21 vols., 1908–1928); *Great Novels of A. F.* (1914); *The Bride of Corinth and Other Poems and Plays* (1920); *Golden Tales of A. F.* (1926); *The Six Greatest Novels of A. F.* (1936); *The Plays* (1925); *Under the Rose* (1926); *Prefaces, Introductions and Other Uncollected Papers* (1927)

BIBLIOGRAPHY: Maurras, C., "A. F.," *RH*, 18 (1893): 564–91; Brandes, G., *A. F.* (1908); Chesterton, G. K., "The Maid of Orleans," *All Things Considered* (1908): 267–73; Guérard, A. L., *Five Masters of French Romance* (1916): 39–134; Brousson, J. J., *A. F. Himself* (1925); Valéry, P., "In Praise of A. F.," *The Dial*, Nov. 1927: 61–79; Chevalier, H. M., *The Ironic Temper: A. F. and His Time* (1932); Axelrad, J., *A. F.: A Life without Illusions* (1944); Tylden-Wright, D., "A. F.," *The Image of France* (1957): 28–39; Sareil, J., *A. F. et Voltaire* (1961); Bancquart, M. C., *A. F. polémiste* (1962); Jefferson, C., *A. F.: The Politics of Skepticism* (1965); Maurois, A., "Réhabilitons A. F.," *NL*, 26 May 1966, 1, 11; Bresky, D., *The Art of A. F.* (1969)

—DEBRA POPKIN

FRANK, Bruno

German novelist, dramatist, and poet, b. 13 June 1887, Stuttgart; d. 20 June 1945, Beverly Hills, Cal., U.S.A.

F. first embarked upon the study of law before switching to the field of German language and literature, in which he took his Ph.D. in 1912. He subsequently traveled extensively in France and the Mediterranean countries. During World War I he served in Flanders and Poland. In 1924 he settled in Munich, where he enjoyed the life of a successful writer, being one of the more prominent figures in the city's cultural life. He left Germany in 1933, on the day following the burning of the Reichstag. He lived in exile in Austria, England, France, and Switzerland before finally coming to the U.S. in 1937.

Although a respected lyric poet before World War I, a very successful playwright until he joined the exodus of German writers, and, at all times, a novelist and short-story writer recognized at home and abroad, F. has not yet received the serious critical attention his work deserves. With his first publication, *Aus der goldenen Schale* (1905; from the golden bowl), he established himself as a precocious lyric poet. The poems, modeled on those of RILKE, are predominantly intellectual and display an astonishing mastery of form. A more personal, often melancholy tone pervades the later collection *Die Schatten der Dinge* (1912; the shadow of things) and his *Requiem* (1913; requiem).

F.'s best-known dramas are *Zwölftausend* (1927; *Twelve Thousand*, 1928), a historical drama dealing with the recruiting of German mercenaries by the British for their fight against the rebellious American colonies; and *Sturm im Wasserglas* (1930; *Tempest in a Teapot*, 1936), a comedy in the tradition of the folk play, satirizing bureaucracy and politics in a small-town setting. F.'s plays are good theater, eschewing the intellectual agonizing of much of modern drama.

But F.'s favorite medium was fiction. His novels and stories are well written, exciting, and full of action. Their smooth and effective style shows a cultured and sensitive writer of considerable talent at work. F.'s subtle character studies reveal the compassion and understanding of a true humanist who, to quote W. Somerset Maugham, "was more apt to see the good than the evil in his fellow creatures." F. is at his best when dealing with the fates of historical characters. *Tage des Königs* (1924; *The Days of the King*, 1927) consists of three novellas about Frederick the Great, masterpieces in the historical genre that capture the lonely greatness and suffering of the man behind the legend. Far from being a chauvinistic portrayal, *Tage des Königs* represents a truly human picture of the king, a man of "humaneness, genius, and strength."

F.'s insights into the precarious political and cultural situation of his own time are reflected in his *Politische Novelle* (1928; *The Persians Are Coming*, 1937). It is the appeal of a man with a truly European outlook not to forsake the common cultural heritage of Europe and a warning against the threats posed by fascism, the soul-killing materialism of the West, and the collective uniformity of the East. Thomas MANN, a good friend of F.'s, called it "just as ethically courageous and clear-sighted as it is poetic."

All of F.'s work reflects the profound unity of the man and the artist. He never followed any of the "isms" so typical of German intellectual life before 1933. His literary models were Turgenev, Flaubert, and Thomas Mann; his ideal was the type of the "humane gentleman." As an accomplished writer in the tradition of the great 19th-c. novelists, F. holds his own among the writers of the first half of our century.

FURTHER WORKS: *Im dunkeln Zimmer* (1906); *Gedichte* (1907); *Die Nachtwache* (1909); *Das Konzert* (1910); *Flüchtlinge* (1911); *Strophen im Krieg* (1915); *Die Fürstin* (1915); *Die treue Magd* (1916); *Der Himmel der Enttäuschten* (1916); *Bibikoff* (1918); *Die Schwestern und die Fremde* (1918); *Die Trösterin* (1919); *Die Kelter* (1919); *Gesichter* (1920); *Der Goldene* (1920); *Bigram* (1921); *Das Weib auf dem Tiere* (1921); *Leidenschaften* (1921); *Trenck* (1926; *Trenck*, 1928); *Erzählungen* (1926); *Perlenkomödie* (1928); *Der Magier* (1929; *The Magician, and Other Stories*, 1946); *Nina* (1931); *Der General und das Gold* (1932); *Cervantes* (1934; *A Man Called Cervantes*, 1934); *Die Monduhr* (1935); *Der Reisepaß* (1937; *The Lost Heritage*, 1937); *Aus vielen Jahren* (1937); *Die junge Frau Conti* (1938; *Young Madame Conti*, 1938); *Die Tochter* (1943; *One Fair Daughter*, 1943); *Sechzehntausend Francs* (1943); *Ehre Vater und Mutter* (1944; *Honor Thy Father and Mother*, 1943); *Die verbotene Stadt* (1951); *Gesammelte Werke* (1957)

BIBLIOGRAPHY: Poore, C. G., on *A Man Called Cervantes*, *NYTBR* (3 March 1935): 2; Cort, J. C., on *One Fair Daughter*, *Commonweal* (10 Dec. 1943): 211; Hofe, H., von, "German Literature in Exile: B. F.," *GQ*, 18 (1945): 89–92; Weiskopf, F. C., on *The Magician*, *SatR* (14 Dec. 1946): 27; Grimm, R., ed., B. F., Gentlemanschriftsteller," in *Views and Reviews of Modern German Literature* (1974): 121–32; Kamla, T. A., "B. F.'s *Der Reisepaß*: The Exile as an Aristocrat of Humanity," *Monatshefte*, 67 (1975): 37–47

—FRIEDHELM RICKERT

FRANKO, Ivan

Ukrainian poet, novelist, dramatist, critic, scholar, translator, and journalist (also writing in Polish and German), b. 27 Aug. 1856, Nahuyevychi, Galicia (then Austro-Hungarian Empire); d. 28 May 1916, Lvov (Lviv)

Son of a village blacksmith, F. began to write imaginative works while still in school and made his debut as a poet in the journal *Druh* in 1874. Upon completing his secondary education, F. enrolled at the University of Lviv in 1875 and soon became a student activist advocating more social and political freedom for the Ukrainians in Galicia, then part of the Austro-Hungarian Empire. F.'s life was fraught with tragedy and misfortune: clashes

with the Austrian authorities that led to his repeated arrest, unrequited love affairs, an unhappy marriage, continual conflicts with various circles of the Ukrainian and Polish intelligentsia, frustrated political and academic ambitions, poverty, and ill health—all left an indelible imprint on his work, both in terms of quantity and quality. F. responded to adversity by writing indefatigably not only to make a living but also to come to terms with his personal dilemmas. Like Goethe, whose writings have been called "fragments of a great confession," he reacted to life's vicissitudes by transforming experience into art, but unlike the great German, he never had the time to subject his writings to a thorough editing. Thus, some of his works (notably his prose) reveal a hastiness of thought and a lack of polish that contrast sharply with his consummate poetic masterpieces such as *Moysey* (1905; *Moses*, 1938) or *Ivan Vyshensky* (1898; *Ivan Vyshensky*, 1981).

The voluminousness of F.'s work and its rich thematic and stylistic diversity preclude any clear-cut categorization of his literary output. Nonetheless, for the sake of clarity, his literary career may be divided into four periods. The first was one of patriotic romanticism (until 1876), and includes such early dramatic efforts as *Try knyazi na odyn prestol* (three princes for one throne) and *Slavoy i Khrudosh* (Slavoy and Khrudosh), written in 1874 and 1875 respectively and published posthumously in 1956. The dominant theme of these works is the quest for unity of the Kievan Rus pursued by strong, noble warriors who, as dramatis personae, display a spiritual kinship to the warriors in old Ukrainian literature and the heroic individuals of the German *Sturm und Drang* age. F.'s greatest historical drama is the more mature but still highly romantic *Son knyazya Svyatoslava* (1895; Prince Svyatoslav's dream). To this period also belongs F.'s first full-length novel, *Petryi i Dovbushchuky* (1875; the Petry and Dovbushchuk families), a tale from the life of Carpathian brigands, in which the influence of E. T. A. Hoffmann (1776–1822) is evident.

The second period of F.'s career, one of revolutionary realism, primarily comprises biting social satire and political poetry, influenced by the ideas of Mykhaylo Drahomaniv (1841–1895), a trenchant social and political thinker, as well as leading Western European authors. The latter part of this period coincides with F.'s "Polish decade" (1887–97), during which he worked for various Polish publications and wrote largely in the Polish language. Among the works of that period on social and revolutionary themes are poems "Kamenyari" (1878; "The Pioneers," 1948), "Hymn" (1882; "Hymn," 1963), the tale "Boa Constriktor" (1878; "Boa Constrictor," 1957), and *Panski zharty* (1887; *The Master's Jests*, 1979), a novella in poetic form dealing with the passing of serfdom in the Ukraine. This period, however, also includes such patriotic verse as "Ne pora" (1887; "National Hymn," 1963); the novel *Zakhar Berkut* (1883; *Zakhar Berkut*, 1944), a romantic synthesis of socialism and patriotism; and the collection of Decadent love poetry *Zivyale lystya* (1891; withered leaves). Also of importance are F.'s fairy tales, both original works and adaptations. Among the latter, the long narrative poem *Lys Mykyta* (1890; *Fox Mykyta*, 1978), read by children as a fairy tale and by adults as a biting satire, is an especially brilliant work.

The years 1898–1907, his third period, constitute what may be termed as F.'s period of symbolic realism; this marks the zenith of F.'s career as a poet and a scholar. Its more famous achievements are *My izmarahd* (1898; my emerald), a volume of moral and philosophical verse; *Semper tiro* (1906; Latin: always a beginner), a collection of poetry dealing with fundamental social and humanistic questions; *Ivan Vyshensky*, the poetic account of the tragedy of the Ukrainian religious leader (c. 1550–c. 1625) caught between asceticism and social activism; and his unquestioned masterpiece, the symbolic poem *Moysey*, built around the conflict between the leader and the masses he must lead. During this time, too, F. withdrew from political life, giving up his membership in the Rusin-Ukrainian Radical Party, which he had confounded in 1892. He also severely limited his journalistic activities, especially his commitment to the Viennese paper *Die Zeit*, to which he had contributed both fiction and nonfiction since 1895, and devoted himself fully to Ukrainian letters.

The last period (1908–16) was marked by the tragic decline of F.'s powers as a writer and poet, brought about by a progressive paralysis that affected his mental state. He continued to work intermittently, mostly for the Shevchenko Scientific Society, in which he had been active since 1897, translating works from foreign literatures into Ukrainian, revising and editing his manuscripts, and doing some writing. Nonetheless, before his death, F. had some satisfaction in seeing himself acclaimed as *the* Ukrainian writer of his time and the mentor of a new generation of his people.

FURTHER WORKS: *Boryslav smietsya* (1882); *Z vershyn i nyzyn* (1887); *Smert Kayina* (1889); *V poti chola* (1890); *Ukradene shchastya* (1894); *Poemy* (1899); *Iz dniv zhurby* (1900); *Budka ch. 27* (1902); *Mayster Chyrnyak* (1902); *Zbirnyk tvoriv* (3 vols., 1903–1905); *Tvory* (30 vols., 1924–1929); *Vybrani tvory* (1930); *Tvory* (5 vols., 1930–1932); *Vybrani tvory* (2 vols., 1934); *Vybrani tvory* (5 vols., 1935–1936); *Vybrani opovidannya* (1947); *Vybir iz tvoriv* (1956); *Tvory* (20 vols., 1950–1956); *Vybrani tvory* (1957); *Literaturna spadshchyna* (4 vols., 1956–1967); *Tvory* (20 vols., 1956–1962); *Beiträge zur Geschichte und Kultur der Ukraine* (1963); *Zibrannya tvoriv* (50 vols., 1976) ff. FURTHER WORKS IN ENGLISH: *Selected Poems* (1948); *Poems and Stories* (1956); *Boa Constrictor, and Other Stories* (1957); *Stories* (1972); *Moses, and Other Poems* (1973)

BIBLIOGRAPHY: Manning, C. A., *Ukrainian Literature: Studies of the Leading Authors* (1944): 76–88; Doroshenko, V., "I. F. as a Scholar," *UQ*, 12 (1956): 144–51; Rudnytzky, L. D., "I. F.—A Translator of German Literature," *Annals of the Ukrainian Academy of Arts and Sciences in the United States*, 12 (1969–72): 143–50; Čyževs'kyj, D., *A History of Ukrainian Literature* (1975): 603–7; Mihailovich, V. D., et al., eds., *Modern Slavic Literatures* (1976), Vol. II: 462–67; Kipa, A. A., "I. F.'s View of Gerhart Hauptmann," Sokel, W. H., et al., eds., *Probleme der Komparatisik und Interpretation: Festschrift für André von Gronicka* (1978): 136–41; Rudnytzky, L. D., Introduction to I. F., *The Master's Jests* (1979): 9–13

—LEONID RUDNYTZKY

FRENCH LITERATURE

The 20th c. has been a period of swift and radical change, which for the French nation has proved violent and costly. In the fifty or so years that elapsed between the national turmoil generated by the Dreyfus affair (1894–1906) and the establishment of the Fifth Republic (1958), which coincided with a bitter reassessment of France's international position in the nuclear age, French civilization was shaken to its foundations. In the 1960s the France which

emerged from the shock of two world wars and from the syndromes that accompanied decolonialization, and which had to adapt to modern technology, and begin to integrate itself into a planned supranational European economy, seemed to have little in common with the France of the early 1900s. By 1980 France was a prosperous nation, one of the leaders, along with West Germany, in the slowly emerging Western European alliance.

The worldwide revolutionary character of the times was not manifest at the century's inception. In 1900, leaving behind it the critical phase of the Dreyfus controversy, France entered so marked a period of prosperity and equilibrium that it is still known as "*la belle époque*." The distinctive dynamism of the century—disintegrating traditional structures, fostering the emergence of uncertain new ones—was discernible in France at the time only in the first achievements of technology—films, the telephone, the automobile, the airplane—and in the arts. Mathematicians and researchers in French laboratories and clinics participated in the new scientific discoveries, whose impact, with that of Einstein and FREUD, was ultimately to be great; but these had not yet reached the general public.

By contrast, art had already, before World War I, made its own spectacular revolutionary leap—toward abstraction—and Paris, cosmopolitan and urbane, became the center of the art world, the chosen home, at one time or another, of Picasso, Juan Gris, Kandinsky, Chagall, Modigliani, De Chirico, Soutine, Brancusi. Painting moved rapidly by way of EXPRESSIONISM, primitivism, and simultanism, from Fauvism (1905) to cubism (1907), to a short-lived FUTURISM, toward its two-pronged postwar development—SURREALISM and the diverse forms of nonfigurative art. In architecture, the simple lines of functional building were being developed. Sculptors, influenced by the African mask, were on the path to the creation of autonomous volumes and mobiles. And composers like Satie and Stravinsky were making way for the postwar experiments with atonal, dodecaphonic, and finally concrete music. Visible everywhere, the "modern spirit" in the arts, scandalous to the bourgeois spirit of conservatism, was creative, adventurous, and exhilarating. It dominated the pre-World War I years and sealed an alliance between all the arts, including literature and the nascent cinema.

World War I inaugurated a phase of almost unbroken political revolution and international conflict. In the early 1900s, the French proletariat had shown signs of restlessness, but in a country still predominantly agricultural—in spite of a new wave of industrialization—the situation did not appear critical. It was in the realm of ideas, a bourgeois realm, that the future was adumbrated in ideologies which had crystallized early around the Dreyfus case and which seemed, at first, designed merely to counterbalance one another. France in those years of prosperity could accommodate, although uneasily, the socialism of Jean Jaurès (1859–1914), founder of the new unified French Socialist Party, and the doctrinaire "integral nationalism" of Charles Maurras (1868–1952), leader of the reactionary rightist Action Française, and it could ignore Georges Sorel's (1847–1922) theory of revolution, based on the manipulation of the masses and the seizure by force of the controls of power, presented in *Réflexions sur la violence* (1908; *Reflections on Violence*, 1912). But between 1914 and 1950 ideological conflicts, international in character, compounded the difficulties of France's struggle for survival. France sometimes seemed close to civil war; was barely victorious, and at too great cost, in World War I; was defeated, occupied, and deeply humiliated in World War II. The exhilaration of *la belle époque* gave way to a growing anxiety. The rapid deterioration of social and political institutions, the exhaustion attendant upon what turned out to be thirty years of almost unbroken warfare, the atomic explosion at Hiroshima, which left the French with a feeling of horror and insecurity and the sense that they had fallen far behind in the fields of scientific and technological research—all contributed to an intellectual climate of serious, somewhat desperate, questioning. It lasted well into the 1960s, as the costly wars of decolonization in southeast Asia and Algeria compounded the violence of ideological controversy in France itself. The student revolt in 1968 brought the social unrest to a climax and inaugurated a new phase of economic and social planning in an effort to adapt obsolete socioeconomic and institutional structures to the realities of the modern world. In the dialogue between old and new, the women's liberation movement since 1970 has been the most prominent factor in political and cultural change.

Throughout the century, French literature, making of the process of creativity and change one of its major themes, mirrored in its diversity the broad spectrum of collective concerns and individual reactions. At the highest level of achievement, it drew from the writers' efforts at elucidation a validity and capacity for renewal that were to make the century one of the richest in its history. Among minor works, the rapid changes, the excessive tendentiousness, the ruptures and experiments created a bewildering sense of anarchy and confusion.

The French literary language, already enriched and made more flexible by the SYMBOLISTS, benefited greatly during those years, enlarging its vocabulary by the massive inclusion of new terms and, experimenting with a syntax that it disrupted, by the integration of forms prevalent in current French speech. It tended to narrow the gap between the spoken and the literary, the popular and the educated forms of language, while, by experiments in form, it emphasized the distance that separates literary expression from the proliferation of commercialized writing: journalism and popular fiction. Breaking down the barriers between the genres, transforming the traditional genres themselves beyond recognition, literary expression, often to the scandal or confusion of the reading public, became infinitely diversified if not fragmented. Yet perhaps because with the new organization of French education undertaken at the turn of the century, literature had become an honored institution, it is in literature that both the continuity of French tradition and its metamorphosis in the 20th c. can be discerned most clearly. In literature, as in the other arts, the concept of an "avant-garde," opening up the way to new forms of expression, became commonplace in the 1900s. But literary avant-garde movements, with the exception of the iconoclasm of DADAISM, always referred back to literary sponsors chosen among writers of the past, creating for themselves a tradition while enriching the literary history of France, a task in which they were helped by an alert criticism.

In spite of the apparent confusion and fragmentation, the major literary achievements of the 20th c. first evolved from a carefully sought equilibrium between innovation and a recourse to the great masters of the past. Few writers of stature were not also critics. In a fast-changing country, literature tended to be a normative and stabilizing force, whose continuity was emphasized by the living presence throughout the first fifty years of the century of a few great figures born around 1870: Paul CLAUDEL, COLETTE, André GIDE, and Paul VALÉRY.

Writing, in the first half of the century, tended increasingly to involve the writer's whole person, to become the statement of a total outlook, an act that engaged the writer's responsibility. More

than ever in the past, French readers looked to the writer for guidance, while the writer himself questioned the validity of his own occupation, examined the nature and genesis of literary creation and, ever more critically, its social role and function. But the status of literature itself, traditionally considered in France as the highest expression of its culture, became a more and more hotly debated issue after World War II. Within the Marxist perspective adopted by a majority of leftist intellectuals in the aftermath of the French defeat, it seemed urgent to replace established "bourgeois" norms by "new" or "revolutionary" texts. Not continuity but change—in fact rupture—became the leitmotif of those years. The French writer, in strong contrast to the inspired bard of romantic myth, became a conscious, indeed a self-conscious creator who called into question every facet of his craft, including his material, language itself. Writers thus unleashed what has been called a "terrorism" in literature, making of writing a complex and sometimes sibylline form of questioning.

Modern French literature does not always yield easily to classification by schools or movements. Although there was an ephemeral rash of "isms" in the early 1900s—synthetism, integralism, unanimism, Orphism, futurism, simultanism—only two movements, not exclusively French, nor exclusively literary, and never entirely in command, left their imprint on French letters: surrealism in the mid-1920s, and EXISTENTIALISM in the 1940s. Nor does the concept of generations greatly clarify the picture, the two world wars disrupting the orderly succession of generations, destroying or delaying certain talents while precociously fostering others. The history of literature is the history of the major writers, whose itinerary sometimes espouses the brusque oscillations of the time, sometimes not. One may, for the sake of convenience, distinguish three periods in the general evolution of French literature: the "modernist" period, which affected all the arts of the Western world from the early 1900s to the early 1930s; the metaphysical and social current, born of the turmoil of the 1930s; finally, during the 1950s, the upsurge of a critical and "scientific" mentality that heralded a postmodernist period as yet undefined.

The End of the Belle Époque

In the 1880s, the Decadents—to the confusion of the naturalists and to the consternation of the bourgeoisie—had invented a mythical "fin de siècle," a languorous twilight of the gods. The real mood of the fin de siècle, which began to crystallize in the 1890s, was more reassuring. Recovering, in 1900, from the more violent phase of the Dreyfus affair, an urbane, cosmopolitan society seemed ready to open its doors to the writers who, whether for or against Dreyfus, had shared and voiced its alarms. One by one a generation of great writers had disappeared: Hippolyte Taine (1828–1893) and Ernest Renan (1823–1892), the ideological masters of two generations; the poets Jules Laforgue (1860–1887), Arthur Rimbaud (1845–1891), Paul Verlaine (1844–1896), and Stéphane Mallarmé (1842–1898); the fiction writers Guy de Maupassant (1850–1893), Émile Zola (1840–1902), and Alphonse Daudet (1840–1897). Restraint, intelligence, clarity, common sense, and good manners seemed to be criteria common to good writing and good society. Reconciled with society, literature voiced the theme of "return": return to the classics, to nature, to tradition, to humanism, to ethics, to the Church. In fact, beneath a deceptively brilliant and complacent surface, it was undergoing a great change.

Poetry

Poetry, still under the shadow of the great poets, was the most ubiquitous of genres. Between 1900 and 1914 innumerable poets, grouped in small coteries, launched more than two hundred little magazines. Some, like *Vers et prose, La phalange,* and *Le divan,* prolonged the symbolist trend. Refining on symbolist theory, René Ghil (1862–1925) and Gustave Kahn (1859–1936), among others, developed its more superficial mannerisms—the disruption of syntax, the complex intellectualization of the form, the esoteric theme, the rare vocabulary—while, in complete solitude, Saint-Pol-Roux (pseud. of Paul Roux, 1861–1940) evolved his concept of poetry as "ideorealism," a theory that to some degree anticipated surrealism, in *Les reposoirs de la procession* (3 vols., 1893–1907; stations of the procession). Henri de Régnier (1864–1936), after his symbolist beginnings, turned to earlier poets like Ronsard for his models. Elsewhere, the reaction started by Jean Moréas (pseud. of Yannis Papadiamantopoulous, 1856–1910)—whose École Romane, a group founded in 1891, advocated a return to classical sources and forms—was gaining momentum, but not unity. Saint Georges de Bouhélier's (pseud. of Stéphane Georges de Bouhélier-Lepelletier, 1889–1942) "*naturisme*" advocated a return to simple universal emotions—love of nature and mankind—and free lyrical expression; Fernand Gregh (1873–1960) advocated a new humanism. Whatever the theory, simpler forms of lyricism prevailed. Francis JAMMES's intimate verse, in works such as *De l'angélus de l'aube à l'angélus du soir* (1898; from the morning prayer to the evening prayer) and *Les géorgiques chrétiennes* (1912; Christian georgics), expressed in studiedly naïve terms the sane emotions of peasant life. Paul Fort (1872–1960)—in close to forty volumes of *Ballades françaises* (French ballads), published between 1896 and 1958—adapted to his neoromantic fancy popular ballad forms and themes, experimenting with the potentialities of the prose-poem; while Anna de Noailles (1876–1933), the most adulated of a group of women poets, sang easily, in works such as *Le cœur innombrable* (1901; the numberless heart) of love, death, and nature in cadences, stanzas, and rhetoric reminiscent of Victor Hugo. Derivative or esoteric, poetry had become a minor genre.

Drama

In the last years of the 19th c. naturalists and symbolists alike had taken the theater to task—whether the commercial boulevard theater or the state-subsidized Comédie Française—for its old-fashioned techniques, and, in the case of the boulevard, its stereotyped plays. Two little theaters had appeared: André Antoine's naturalistic Théâtre Libre and, successor to Paul Fort's Théâtre d'Art, Lugné-Poë's Théâtre de l'Œuvre. With the introduction of new dramatists—STRINDBERG, HAUPTMANN, MAETERLINCK, and of course Ibsen—the theater seemed to be stirring. By 1900 both the Théâtre Libre and the Théâtre de l'Œuvre had closed down, although only temporarily. The boulevard theater reigned unchallenged, content to live on the formulae that had made French theater famous since the 1850s. The boulevard conceived of theater as pure entertainment. It favored the *vaudeville,* which Georges FEYDEAU raised to the level of an art—light comedy, with its standard stock-in-trade intrigues, quick repartee, and indulgent social satire, whose practitioners also included Tristan Bernard (1866–1947), Robert de Flers (1872–1927), and Robert de Caillavet (1869–1915)—and the Molièresque farces, bordering on the comedy of manners, of Georges Courteline (1858–1929) that exploited the foibles of bureaucracy, more particularly the military.

Serious theater continued to take the form of the well-made "problem play": Eugène Brieux (1858–1932) discussed motherhood, family life, or, as in *La robe rouge* (1900; *The Red Robe,* 1915), the corruption of justice; while François de Curel (1854–1928) dramatized newer problems—the conflict of industrial workers and plant owners in *Le repas du lion* (1897; the lion's meal) and of science and religion in *La nouvelle idole* (1899; the new idol). Elevated in tone, moral in intent, socially acceptable in its solutions, the problem play moved along the well-oiled grooves of a set dramatic pattern. More popular, a so-called "theater of passion"—Georges de Porto-Riche (1849–1930), Félix Bataille (1872–1922), Henry Bernstein (1876–1953)—in an equally set mold, dramatized the conflicts between the passions—love, almost exclusively—and the rules of society. It was in fact not far removed from the *vaudeville,* dealing with the same themes: adultery, respectability, class taboos. To this theater Edmond Rostand (1868–1918), with his enthusiastically acclaimed *Cyrano de Bergerac* (1897; *Cyrano de Bergerac,* 1898) and *L'aiglon* (1900; *L'Aiglon,* 1927), neoromantic historical verse plays, brought a brief new luster and the only drama that survived, but added one more still-born type of play to the roster. While elsewhere in Europe—in Russia, Germany, England—the fin-de-siècle movement of renovation was gaining momentum, the French theater remained what it had been: a brilliant, ritualized, and commercially rewarding social function organized for the entertainment of an elite and the greater glory of the star, the *monstre sacré* that the name of Sarah Bernhardt best exemplifies.

The Novel

The proliferation of novelists was as great as the proliferation of poets, all in some form or other inheritors of the great past. Bolstered by the establishment in 1903 of the Goncourt Prize, varieties of the realistic novel inherited from Flaubert, rather than from Zola, prevailed: historical or social frescoes, by Lucien Descaves (1861–1949), the Margueritte brothers, Paul (1860–1918) and Victor (1867–1942), Paul Adam (1862–1920), and the Rosny brothers, Rosny aîné (pseud. of Joseph-Henry Boëx, 1856–1940) and Rosny jeune (pseud. of Justin Boëx, 1859–1948); case histories, by Octave Mirbeau (1850–1917), Marguerite Audoux (1863–1937), and Charles-Louis Philippe (1874–1909); and innumerable novels of provincial life, by René Bazin (1853–1932) and Henry Bordeaux (1870–1963). But the masters of the younger generation introduced other overtones: a neoromantic exoticism and melancholy, inspired by Pierre Loti (pseud. of Louis Marie Julien Viaud, 1850–1923), was perpetuated by Claude Farrère (pseud. of Charles Bargonne, 1876–1957), the Tharaud brothers, Jérôme (1874–1953) and Jean (1877–1952), and Louis Bertrand (1866–1941). More influential, Paul Bourget (1852–1935) had revived the novel of psychological analysis in a mood of moral righteousness eminently suited to a large bourgeois public. It proliferated to the point that it became synonymous with the term "French novel," a genre which, cultivated by Abel Hermant (1862–1950), Édouard Estaunié (1862–1942), René Boylesve (pseud. of René Tardivaux, 1867–1926), and Edmond Jaloux (1878–1949), reached a wide reading public.

More seminal was the transformation of the social-fresco novel in the hands of both Émile Zola at the end of his career, and of Maurice Barrès (1862–1923) into a vehicle for the dissemination of political doctrine—socialistic with Zola, nationalistic with Barrès. What distinguished the more vigorous, currently read novels of the period, the only ones that have survived, is their undisguised politicization and open didacticism. If Barrès's nationalistic trilogy *Le roman de l'énergie nationale* (1897–1902; the novel of national energy), Anatole FRANCE's socialistically slanted fictions, and Romain ROLLAND's vast ten-volume fresco, *Jean-Christophe* (1904–12; *Jean-Christophe*, 1910–13), have survived, it is as vehicles of thought rather than as novels.

Only one purely literary writer of stature, Colette, seems to have succeeded in truly reflecting the mood of the early 1900s. Free of ideology and didacticism, impressionistic in her style, rich in perception, Colette, after she abandoned the artificial perversity of her first novels, drew upon all that was best in the times: sophistication; a free sensuality; fascination with the joys, dangers, and complexities of sex; a taste for directness and intimacy. To these she brought a sensitivity to the world of sensation—light, color, smell, touch—that bound her closely to a quotidian universe in which she took keen delight. Her fame, slow to establish itself but unquestioned, rests on her command of a precise and fluid prose, an instrument exactly adapted to the expression of her limited and yet inexhaustible world.

Expository Prose

The fin de siècle had witnessed a complex and confused reaction against "scientism" and the methods and tenets of positivism, which had dominated the mid-19th c. Henri BERGSON's critique of intelligence, his rehabilitation of intuition, and his emphasis on a measure of indetermination, hence of creative freedom in the shaping of the future; Nietzsche's exaltation of action and energy; and, among scientists, the critique of the scientific method itself—exemplified by Henri Poincaré's (1856–1912) *La science et l'hypothèse* (1902; *Science and Hypothesis*, 1905)—gave a new impetus to ideological discussion and to the resurgence of various forms of mysticism and religious conversion. A vigorous literature of debate was carried into every realm of thought. With the Dreyfus affair it took on dogmatic political overtones. Deplorable where national issues were at stake, it brought new ideas into circulation and reinvigorated a rather anemic prose. A generation of polemicists and essayists opened the way to the renascence of all forms of expository prose: Bergson, Charles Maurras (1868–1952), Léon Daudet (1867–1942), Charles PÉGUY, Romain Rolland, André Gide, André Suarès (1868–1948), and Julien Benda (1867–1956) were the master-writers of a period that was no longer satisfied to accept the outmoded style, both abstract and ornate, of such pontifical critics as Ferdinand Brunetière (1849–1906), Jules Lemaître (1853–1914), and Remy de Gourmont (1858–1915).

New Orientations: The Prewar Years

Between 1905 and 1910, literature began to take on a new appearance; it was vigorous, deliberately modern, adventurous, ready to proclaim the advent of a new aesthetic attuned to the vast possibilities opening up in art as in the modern world. In the theater, the first real intimation of things to come hit the "tout-Paris" in 1909–10 with Diaghilev's Russian ballets starring Nijinsky and Pavlova, with the sumptuous stage sets and costumes of Léon Bakst. With *L'art théâtral moderne* (1910; modern theatrical art), Jacques Rouché (1862–1957), director of the Théâtre des Arts (1911–13), gave the first coherent survey of the theories and innovations of Konstantin Stanislavsky, Edward Gordon Craig, Adolphe Appia, and Max Reinhardt, and in 1913, Jacques Copeau,

declaring open warfare on the boulevard, announced the opening of the Théâtre du Vieux Colombier, which, in the post-World War I years presided over the renovation of French theater. At Créteil, near Paris, a young group of writers and artists, the "Groupe de l'Abbaye," Tolstoyan in its inspiration, declared their intention of renovating art by going back to its source, the living community of men; while, in 1909, in close connection with them, Jules ROMAINS launched his own program, "unanimism," the discovery, expression, and ultimately the guidance of the collective emotions and forces abroad in the exhilarating urban setting of modern life, born of Walt Whitman, Émile VERHAEREN, Zola, Tolstoy, and the sociologist Émile Durkheim (1858–1917). From Montmartre first, then from Montparnasse, CUBISM—creative, scandalous, sure of itself, and incarnate in the tall figure of the irrepressible poet Guillaume APOLLINAIRE—brought a bevy of irreverent poets; while in his *Cahiers de la quinzaine*, stubborn, dogged, and obscure, Péguy was struggling toward a religious and patriotic commitment as far removed as was possible from the elegant dilettantism of Barrès, accumulating meanwhile a poetic work of considerable dimension, new in all its aspects. In 1906 there began to appear, in a Rouen paper, short chronicles signed "Alain." The *propos* (brief aphoristic pieces) of ALAIN proposing a method of thought, a discipline of free examination rather than a system, exercised a deflationary influence on the rhetorical prose of the warring dogmatisms. At the center of the movement was the young *Nouvelle revue française*, liberal and cosmopolitan in outlook, free from political commitment, and with the high standards of the literary tradition that had passed from Flaubert to Mallarmé. It brought to the fore, along with Gide, two writers whose work had slowly matured in relative obscurity—Paul CLAUDEL, and later Valéry—and sponsored the beginnings of a new generation of writers remarkable in their variety: Roger MARTIN DU GARD, François MAURIAC, Jean GIRAUDOUX, Saint-John PERSE, and Romains.

With the opening of the Vieux Colombier in 1913, the almost simultaneous publication of Apollinaire's *Alcools* (1913; *Alcohols*, 1964), Claudel's *Corona benignitatis anni Dei* (1915; *Coronal*, 1943), following upon the first production of his play *L'annonce faite à Marie* (1912; *The Tidings Brought to Mary*, 1916), Gide's *Les caves du Vatican* (1914; *Lafcadio's Adventures*, 1928), Martin du Gard's *Jean Barois* (1913; *Jean Barois*, 1949), ALAIN-FOURNIER's *Le Grand Meaulnes* (1913; *The Wanderer*, 1928), and, coming unexpectedly from another quarter, Marcel PROUST's *Du côté de chez Swann* (1913; *Swann's Way*, 1922), it seemed that a new literary era had dawned, confident in its powers, undogmatic, eclectic, disciplined, rooted in the most solid of traditions, and at the same time open to all forms of innovation. When, in the *NRF*, its editor, Jacques Rivière (1886–1925), in an all-out attack on the ubiquitous novel of psychological analysis, called for a "novel of adventure," he was voicing the watchword of the day; adventure was in the air.

The Masters

Born around 1870, Gide, Claudel, Proust, and Valéry had started precocious literary careers in the hothouse atmosphere of the symbolist salons. From their early contact with a literary figure of the stature of Mallarmé, Gide, Claudel, and Valéry drew the sense of the nobility of the writer's calling that Proust shared. By the turn of the century all four men were aware that symbolism had outlived its creative potentialities, as had also the summary aesthetic of the naturalists. All four separately and in different ways worked over the years in relative obscurity and solitude, to develop their own aesthetic and forge their own idiom. By 1914, in their mid-forties, they had reached maturity. World War I, although it touched them deeply, did not affect their work. Each had created a style and universe specifically his own.

From his conversion to Catholicism Claudel drew a Thomist vision of a theocentric universe that gave his writings—essays and spiritual meditations, lyrical poetry and drama—their cosmic grandeur, authority, and vast sweep of language.

A close friend and disciple of Mallarmé, Valéry withdrew from literary life to observe and study the creative interplay of mind and language. To the postwar years he brought the lucid prose of his essays; the critical acuity of a mind trained in mathematical speculation; a theory of poetic creation; and a small number of quasi-perfect poems renewing the forms of classical prosody, embodying in their imagery and verbal harmonies the dynamic movement of the creative act.

Proust's vast novel *À la recherche du temps perdu* (7 vols., 1913–27; *Remembrance of Things Past*, 7 vols., 1922–32) is perhaps the greatest novelistic achievement of the 20th c., and its very dimensions for a time somewhat obscured its fundamental creative originality. It brought, besides new techniques that evolved from a new understanding of the working of the human mind, of the powers of memory and sensibility and the relations they establish with the outer world, a vision of literature as the highest form of knowledge, the only complete testimony as to the nature of human experience, an activity so imperious as to subordinate to its needs the very life of the writer.

The real master of the 1920s, however, was Gide, less perhaps for the skilled and subtle narrative forms with which since the turn of the century he had been experimenting, transforming the novel structure more radically even than Proust, but rather for what was called "Gidism"—his appeal to throw off outworn conventions, to become a responsible, authentic individual; his vision, foreshadowing the existentialist, of the human being's contingency in a purposeless universe; and his ethic of disciplined and rational freedom. A great and controversial figure, Gide dominated his time.

In the 1920s the young men who emerged from four years of war, with scant respect for the civilization that had organized and tolerated the hecatomb, with scanter respect for the feverish, cynical postwar Europe, could turn to these men with confidence. In the general collapse of all accepted values, literature as represented by them had stature, significance, and dignity. They had renovated all the traditional genres: the novel, drama, poetry, the essay. In their hands literary expression had acquired new dimensions, metaphysical, intellectual, ethical—incorporated into the work itself, determining its structure, not rhetorically inserted and imposed, and they used language with confidence and mastery.

The Innovators

It was not the literary masters, however, but the artists who gave the most fertile and characteristic impetus to literature. Their sense of art as a form of adventure, born of the unexpected potentialities of the medium itself, of art as the generator of its own language, was a new concept in the 1910s. Among the poets, a group called the "Fantaisistes"—Francis Carco (pseud. of François Carcopino-Tusoli, 1886–1958), Paul Jean Toulet (1867–1920)—was cultivating a light, often humorous, form of verse, drawing its effects from the free and unexpected play of imagery and word, compounded, in the work of Valery LARBAUD, an indefatigable client of the luxury

express train, by the foreshortening of time and space, and in the writings of Blaise CENDRARS by the violence of perceptions rolled in the flux of a dynamic stream-of-consciousness, perpetually renewed, perpetually in the process of creation. But it was the group of poets in close contact with the cubist painters—André Salmon (1881–1969), Max Jacob, Pierre Reverdy, Léon-Paul Fargue—and more especially Apollinaire, the impresario of the cubists—who most nearly incarnate the creative versatility of the period, its dynamic itinerary from symbolism to new open forms of expression, its love of mystification, its commitment to art as a way of life, its superb and unself-conscious disregard of, rather than revolt against, society. Apollinaire, rather than Valéry, Claudel, or Péguy, was the great innovator of the period.

Renewal and Revolt: The Early 1920s

World War I favored the diffusion of a pious literature of social conformism, latent in a good deal of the writing that had predominated since the turn of the century. It survived for some time in the euphoria of victory, but by the early 1920s it had been driven from the boisterous center of the literary scene. The death of Barrès, France, and Loti, the rising influence of Gide, Claudel, Proust, and Valéry, the sensationalism, literary inflation, and anarchy of the time hastened its demise. It had been challenged early. In 1916 the production in Rome of *Parade*, a ballet in which the composer Erik Satie, Picasso, and Diaghilev had collaborated with Jean COCTEAU, and in 1917 the almost simultaneous production in Paris of *Parade* and *Les mamelles de Tirésias* (1917; *The Breasts of Tiresias*, 1961) were launched in open protest against the pall of conformism.

But the aestheticism of the protest was to be overshadowed when, in 1920, Dadaism, with Tristan TZARA as its leading spirit, moved to Paris from Zurich and started systematically to organize and exploit the joys of openly baiting and scandalizing the public. Among its precursors, Dada could recognize Alfred JARRY, whose farce *Ubu roi* (1896; *Ubu Roi*, 1951), a deliberate assault on the sense of propriety of the audience, had created a scandal, which, by his way of life, Jarry had prolonged. Dada was, in a sense, openly miming the senseless violence camouflaged under the noble cadences of official speeches, tearing down false façades in a first upsurge of shock at the brutality of modern war, and countering by its violence the nihilism latent in a confrontation with what was later to be called the "absurd." Dada's assault on all the existing structures—political, social, religious, intellectual, cultural, aesthetic—used as one among its weapons a disruption of language that made the experiments of Apollinaire and Cocteau seem circumspect. It challenged the legitimacy of literature, denounced its fictitious character and the nonauthenticity of language itself. It was Dada that unleashed terrorism in the world of letters, and although by 1922 its energies had spent themselves, its effects on French literature were deep and lasting.

By 1922, under the aegis of André BRETON and Louis ARAGON, surrealism was channeling the inventive impetus of the new spirit in an entirely new direction, while attaching it to a recognizable tradition: William Blake, Gérard de Nerval (1808–1855), Lautréamont (1846–1870), Rimbaud, Raymond ROUSSEL. Language, for the surrealists, when freed from the constraints of logic, became an instrument, a tool for the uncovering of "surreality," the network of relations linking human beings to one another and to the world. The mind, a vehicle of the unknown, appeared to the surrealists as an immense and barely explored realm. Putting to work Freudian concepts, the surrealists plunged into a systematic observation and stimulation of the subconscious working of their own minds. Their experiments with automatic writing and dreams, their cultivation of irrational states, affected the entire range of literary expression: the tenor, rhythms, and syntax of the language, as well as the methods of composition—alogical dream sequences, bizarre combinations of words, the symbolic use of objects, incongruous juxtapositions of images—processes that had been latent in the work of Jacob and Jarry. They massively injected into French literature, with an obscurity that official prewar literature had singularly lacked, an eerie form of black humor and the ability to treat all words—sexual, psychotic, ordinary—with sovereign equanimity. With Freud, they greatly contributed to opening wide to literature a subjective inner realism that had been approached heretofore more surreptitiously. By their severe contempt for commercial success and public opinion, by their insistence on living according to their concepts, by their combativeness, the surrealists served as a kind of counterpoint to the feverish, turbulent, inflated literary activity of the 1920s.

Versatile and restlessly inventive, a poet, dramatist, novelist, essayist, scenarist, actor, distinguished besides in the art of drawing, Jean Cocteau seems the veritable incarnation of the postwar period. From his scandalous beginnings with the ballet *Parade*, to his election to the French Academy, he lived the adventure of the iconoclastic art at whose genesis he had presided. Committed utterly to his work as artist, he made of artistic creation a discipline and a way of life, keeping his freedom intact. His is an independent figure that evades classification.

From Anarchy to Ideology

By the end of the decade, the surrealist group was disintegrating under the impact of new social pressures. Between 1926, when in *La tentation de L'Occident (The Temptation of the West*, 1961) André MALRAUX raised the question of the fate of Western civilization, and 1932, the date of Louis-Ferdinand CÉLINE's *Voyage au bout de la nuit (Journey to the End of Night*, 1934) and Jean Prevost's (1901–1944) *Histoire de France depuis la guerre* (history of France since the war), the intellectual mood in France changed. Political tensions, the economic depression triggered by the Wall Street crash (1929), the rise of fascism, and the increasingly powerful influence of the successful Marxist revolution in Russia created a climate of tension immediately discernible in literature. "Return to order" was the leitmotif of Cocteau in these years, and of *L'ordre* (1929; order), the title of a novel by Marcel Arland (1899–1986) that launched a two-pronged attack on false order and false anarchy, echoed by Pierre Bost's (b. 1901) *Le scandale*; (1931; scandal). Robert Brasillach (1908–1945) announced the end of the postwar years, a formula echoed by Arland in the NRF in November 1931.

In 1929–30 "populism," a short-lived movement launched by Léon Lemonnier (1890–1953) and André Thérive (1891–1967), emphasized a growing preoccupation with social problems and an upsurge of neorealism. In 1930 the surrealists finally split along political lines, Aragon, and with him the bulk of the group, adhering to Marxism. In a climate of increasing anxiety, the emphasis moved from the aesthetic to the social; European civilization, and more particularly bourgeois democracy, were pitilessly scrutinized—by Jean Guéhenno (1890–1978) in *Caliban parle* (1928; Caliban speaks), Emmanuel Berl (1892–1976) in *Mort de la pensée bourgeoise* (1929; death of bourgeois thought), Julien Benda in *La trahison des clercs* (1927; *The Treason of the*

Intellectuals, 1928). Intransigent and aggressive, the embattled ideologies confronted each other, permeating the intellectual life of France once again, as at the time of the Dreyfus affair, but more sharply, more deeply fragmenting it. In this tense atmosphere, a few solid and viable literary works emerged from the froth and confusion of the 1920s. More than either poetry or drama, the novel and essay reflected the change in mood of the post-World War I years.

Poetry

Surrealism, as much perhaps through painters (Max Ernst, Francis Picabia, Fernand Léger, Joan Miró) and filmmakers (Luis Buñuel, Cocteau) as through its verbal experiments, renewed the modes of visual perception, the apprehension of an inner oneiric space in which objects were juxtaposed and organized in new ways. It led to a vigorous expansion of poetic expression and inspiration. From within the surrealist ranks came Robert DESNOS, Paul ÉLUARD, and Aragon. But the major poets of the time, while integrating into their works some of the devices and discoveries of surrealism, developed independently. Pierre Jean JOUVE, Henri MICHAUX, Jules SUPERVIELLE, René CHAR, Pierre Reverdy, and Saint John Perse, each intensely personal, carried poetry to heights seldom attained since the romantic era. But it was not until the 1940s that the extent of depth of the poetic renascence was recognized.

Drama

In 1920 the Vieux Colombier reopened its doors. Within a couple of years, four outstanding directors followed suit: Charles Dullin, Louis Jouvet, Gaston Baty, and Georges Pitoëff. In turn they formed a bevy of young successors: Jean-Louis Barrault, Jean Vilar, André Barsacq. By the mid-1930s the reform of the stage had been accomplished, reaching the boulevard and the Comédie Française; theater was reinstated as a major art, and the actor's function was defined as a noble and selfless devotion to that art. The success of these theater people in turn inspired an opposition, new ideas, new procedures tried out in small avant-garde theaters, challenging the former experiments as soon as they tended to become stereotyped. French theater was so intensely alive by the mid&-1930s that its impetus was not slowed down by the disaster of World War II.

In the euphoria of the 1920s, the boulevard revived a tradition that the sparkling egotistic wit of Sacha Guitry (1885–1957) and the broad humor of Marcel PAGNOL refurbished. Despite the efforts of the new directors, drama in the early 1920s made a slow start, timidly trying out new themes in old molds; plays based on Freudian psychology (HenriRené Lenormand, 1882–1951); intimate dramas of emotion and irony (Marcel Achard, 1899–1974; Charles Vildrac, 1882–1971); dramas of melancholy sentiment and cynicism (Stève Passeur, 1889–1966); or with Jean-Jacques Bernard's (1888–1972) "theater of silence," plays of unspoken emotional intensity, belying an almost inarticulate dialogue. The farce, with Fernand Crommelynck's *Le cocu magnifique* (1921; *The Magnificent Cuckold*, 1966) and Jules Romains's *Knock; ou, Le triomphe de la médecine* (1924; *Doctor Knock*, 1925), made a vigorous reappearance, but was overshadowed by the influence on the French stage of Luigi PIRANDELLO, whose *Six Characters in Search of an Author*, marked an epoch but also inspired a rash of "Pirandellism."

It was not until 1928, with the production by Jouvet of Jean Giraudoux's first play, *Siegfried* (1928; *Siegfried*, 1930), that French drama broke away from the past. The renascence was brilliant. Breaking with the realistic conventions of drama, Giraudoux conceived of theater as a celebration, a festival of the senses and the mind, appealing through both spectacle and language to the sensibilities and imagination of the audience. With him a poetic theater, dealing in large human dilemmas and clothed in the colors of myth, took over the stage and prepared the way for other creative dramatists. While carrying through a series of experiments in dramatic form, Cocteau kept the stage open to new ideas and themes. Taking full advantage of the new freedom in technique, Armand SALACROU and Jean ANOUILH transferred to the stage, in the 1930s, the growing mood of anxiety of the hour; less successfully, Gabriel MARCEL, renewing the problem play, dramatized the intellectual and metaphysical problems besetting the modern mind. Along with the work of the major dramatists, a proliferation of minor plays by dramatists like Jacques AUDIBERTI, the Belgian Michel de GHELDERODE, Jules Supervielle, and Georges Neveux (b. 1900), brought to the stage both quality and excitement, developing a poetic theater of great diversity. The French stage, immensely enriched in its range of expression and its scope, became a vital center of aesthetic expression.

The Novel

The immediate postwar years favored an inflationary trend in the novel, due both to its prestige—Proust's immense novel continued to come out in successive installments between 1918 and 1927, while Gide published *Les faux-monnayeurs* (1926; *The Counterfeiters*, 1927)—and to its immense salability. Heralded by the success of the adolescent Raymond RADIGUET's *Le diable au corps* (1923; *The Devil in the Flesh*, 1932) and *Le bal du comte d'Orgel* (1924; *Ball at Count d'Orgel's*, 1929), the novel continued its reign. Novels of travel, such as those by Paul MORAND, or of adventure, whether in exotic settings—Pierre Benoit (1886–1962), Henri Fauconnier (1879–1955)—in the stadium or arena—Henry de MONTHERLANT—or in the underworld of Paris—Pierre Mac Orlan (pseud. of Pierre Dumarchey, 1882–1970), Francis Carco; novels of fantasy—Giraudoux; novels of childhood and adolescence—Cocteau's *Thomas l'imposteur* (1923; *Thomas the Imposter*, 1925) and *Les enfants terribles* (1929; *Enfants Terribles*, 1930); traditional novels of psychological analysis—Jacques Chardonne (pseud. of Jacques Boutelleau, 1884–1968), Marcel Arland, Jacques de Lacretelle (b. 1888); Catholic novels of psychological problems and spiritual anguish—Julien GREEN, Georges BERNANOS, François Mauriac; novels of provincial life—Jean GIONO, Marcel JOUHANDEAU, André Chamson (b. 1900), Henri Bosco (1888–1976). Georges DUHAMEL's five-volume *Vie et aventures de Salavin* (1920–32; *Salavin*, 1936), a semiepic, semirealistic allegory, traced the itinerary of a quixotic petit-bourgeois "stranger," attempting to give significance to a meaningless life in an indifferent world by trying out one by one and discarding the various traditional solutions open to him: friendship, religion, adventure, and finally saintliness. In *Les Thibault* (8 vols., 1922–40; *The Thibaults*, 1939; *Summer 1914* 1941), Martin du Gard began to describe the prewar social history of a class through the evolution of two bourgeois families. The avalanche of novels—carefully written ones, brilliantly improvised impressionistic ones, exploratory novels charting the new psychoanalytical approaches to dreams, sexuality, and psychosesreceded in the tense political climate of the 1930s.

A renaissance of the neorealistic novel in the 1930s produced many minor writers—Eugène Dabit (1898–1936), Guy Mazeline

(b. 1900), Philippe Hériat (pseud. of Raymond Gérard Payelle, 1898–1971), Maxence Van der Meersch (1907–1951), and Elsa Triolet (1896–1970)—and one major one, Louis Aragon. The novels that have survived from the abundant production of the period are either characteristically imaginative individual works, each enclosed in its own sphere, each reflecting a unity of vision and consequently an ethic—the works of Mauriac, Bosco, Giono, Jouhandeau; the satirical fantasies of Marcel AYMÉ ; and, although less resilient, the multivolume sociohistorical fresco novels, which predominated in the 1930s: Romains's twenty-seven-volume *Les hommes de bonne volonté* (1932–46; *Men of Good Will*, 1933–46); Martin du Gard's seven-part *Les Thibault*; Duhamel's ten-volume *La chronique des Pasquier* (1933–45; *The Pasquier Chronicles*, 1938; *Cécile Pasquier*, 1940; *Two Novels from the Pasquier Chronicles*, 1949); and Aragon's panoramas of life before World War I that were to lead to his attempt at a "heroic and epic" novel of the proletariat, *Les Communistes* (6 vols., 1949–1951; the Communists). Mirroring the concerns of the times, these novels used traditional structure to interpret the recent historical past of the French nation: in humanitarian or ethical terms with Duhamel; in an optimistic and "unanimistic" perspective with Romains. Socialistic with Martin du Gard, Marxist with Aragon, these novels express the main trends of thought among the traditionally leftist "intellectuals"; fiction once again tended to be subordinated to ideology.

Expository Prose

In all the realms of French cultural life, in the 1920s and 1930s criticism abounded. The period could count the *Propos* of Alain, Valéry's *Variété* (5 vols., 1924–44; *Variety*, 2 vols., 1927, 1938); Claudel's *Positions et propositions* (1927, 1934; *Ways and Crossways*, 1933), Gide's articles, the *Approximations* (1926–37; approximations) of Charles Du Bos (1882–1939), the doctrinaire *Jugements* (2 vols., 1923–24; Judgments) of Henri Massis (1886–1970), and, in the NRF, the chronicles of the solid and subtle literary critic Albert Thibaudet (1874–1936). Countering the dogmatism of Massis, Jacques Maritain's (1882–1973) intelligent neo-Thomism and Henri Bremond's (1865–1933) generous mysticism kept alive the dialogue between Christians and rationalists that had opened with the century, in the courteous, dispassionate tone adopted by the NRF group for speculative thought.

With the upsurge of Marxism and fascism, political issues displaced more general ones, positions stiffened to the right and to the left, antagonisms erupted, and even the politically uncommitted *NRF* took political stands. The wide-ranging essay of the 1920s became more specialized: political, philosophical, or literary. Ranging from the fascist propaganda pamphlets of Pierre DRIEU LA ROCHELLE and Robert Brasillach to the communist propaganda essays of Paul Vaillant-Couturier (1892–1937) and Louis Aragon, the political essay accommodated all shades of opinion and was produced by writers like Jean-Richard Bloch (1884–1947), Paul NIZAN, Benjamin Crémieux (1888–1944), Jean Guéhenno, Emmanuel Berl, Thierry Maulnier (b. 1909), Romains, Bernard Groethuysen (1880–1946), Bernanos, and Montherlant. The more traditional literary criticism, influenced by Thibaudet, produced a solid and brilliant group of essayists: Ramon Fernandez (1894–1944), Robert Kemp (1885–1959), Émile Henriot (pseud. of Émile Maignot, 1889–1961), André Rousseaux (b. 1896), René Lalou (1889–1960), and André MAUROIS.

But more significant was the diffusion of the philosophical essay at the hands of the liberal Catholics—Maritain, Marcel, and Emmanuel Mounier (1905–1950)—attempting to counter a dominant Marxism through the diffusion of modern forms of Christian philosphy.

The Metaphysical Midcentury: 1930s to 1950s

Céline's *Voyage au bout de la nuit* is a landmark in the history of the French novel. Its narrative technique—a first-person epic narrative based on the rhythms and patterns of oral language—heralded the massive flow into French literature of new influences: JOYCE, whose *Ulysses* (1922) was translated in 1929; the American "behaviorists," DOS PASSOS, HEMINGWAY, STEINBECK, and FAULKNER. It is also a landmark in the history of French literature. Céline's desperate nihilism inspired his visionary description, on a world-wide scale, of the individual's existence as "absurd"—that is, as derisively insignificant and cruel in an indifferent, purposeless, social and natural world. The writers familiar to the reading public in the 1930s either offered forms of a humanistic ethic based on traditional values (Alain, Gide, Giono, Giraudoux, Duhamel, Romains, Martin de Gard) or like Maritain and François Mauriac, a Christian framework of reference; and with Aragon, a Marxist. But in the novels of Bernanos and Julien Green, both Catholic writers, or of Louis GUILLOUX, in a non-Christian, anarchist-socialistic tradition—*Le sang noir* (1935; *Bitter Victory*, 1936)—a new and urgent note of anxious questioning had prevailed that by the 1940s became dominant. Literature became involved in a tense debate on the nature of man's fate seen in the light of history. The philosphies of history—Hegelian, Marxist, Spenglerian, and Christian—slowly took precedence over merely political ideology. The growing influence of Dostoevsky and Péguy stressed the mataphysical concern of the times.

As the 1930s moved inexorably toward disaster, the sense of the "absurd" began to pervade French letters: KAFKA became widely known. The surrealists' literary experiments, based on a sense of the disparity between the real nature of the individual's relation to the world and its logical representations, had already disrupted traditional literary habits in syntax, composition, and psychological motivation. In the 1930s and 1940s, a heightened awareness of the "absurd" favored the systematic use of some of their techniques. An apparently purely descriptive literature transmitted with cold objectivity an incoherent, alogical image of human life, an image ferocious in Marcel Aymé's mechanically impeccable, arbitrary world; poetically gratuitous in Raymond QUENEAU's "antinovels"; emotionally charged with humor in Henri Michaux's poems; and tragic in those of René Char. But it was André Malraux who gave the literature of the period its prevailing style, its somber character, and its tense overtones, while Jean-Paul SARTRE, Simone de BEAUVOIR, and Albert CAMUS furnished its vocabulary (anguish, gratuitousness, freedom, the "absurd"), its method (phenomenological, existential description) and its ethic, an ethic of choice, commitment, and responsibility, which the life and testimony of Antoine de SAINT-EXUPÉRY seemed to exemplify. The obsessive dominant theme of the period is the tragic dilemma and solitude of individual consciousness confronting an incomprehensible universe, and the means whereby the dilemma can be transcended. Hence the metaphysical overtones of literature and the preponderance of the philosophical and critical essay over creative writing.

The defeat and occupation of France in 1940 dispersed French writers—by exile or deportation or to prisoner-of-war camps—and split the intellectuals into two groups: a minority committed to collaboration with the Germans, a majority to more or less active resistance. The dispersal of the writers favored the creation of a number of new reviews, some of which proved ephemeral although they played a major role at the time: *Poésie, Confluences, Fontaine, L'arche,* and *Les chroniques de minuit.* Others prospered, and became influential: *La Nef, Les temps modernes, La table ronde, La revue française, Preuves.* After a short period of indecision at the time of the Liberation in 1944, a solid core of prewar reviews remained: the *NRF, Mercure de France, La revue de Paris, La revue des deux mondes, Études, Esprit, Europe,* and *Cahiers du Sud.* With the notable exception of the *NRF* and *Cahiers du Sud,* almost all those reviews reflected a social, political, or religious point of view. The fragmentation of the literary milieu was characteristic of the period, as was also, in the light of circumstances, the brusque decline, after 1944, of the influence of certain collaborationists, such as Charles Maurras, and the devaluation of their work (Drieu la Rochelle, Brasillach). Devaluations, independently of any political connotations, affected a whole series of authors who wrote in the 1930s, with the exception of the more urgently questioning Salacrou, Anouilh, Aragon, Bernanos, Michaux, Malraux, and Char. The disappearance of the great figures of the past—Giraudoux, Valéry, Gide, Claudel, and Colette—and the premature disappearance of younger men like Saint-Exupéry and Bernanos, created a vacuum that was filled by two men, Sartre and Camus.

Poetry

Under the double impact of Marxist aesthetics and a real and deep sense of collective suffering, poets, during the Occupation, moving away from the more esoteric themes and forms of the surrealist era, developed a poetry of circumstance, social and political in theme, and greatly simplified in form, a type that had begun to reappear in the late 1930s. Aragon, in *Le crève-cœur* (1941; heartbreak), revived traditional lyrical forms; Éluard in *Le livre ouvert* (2 vols., 1940–42; the open book) and *Poésie et vérité 1942* (1942; *Poetry and Truth, 1942,* 1944) and Char in *Feuillets d'Hypnos* (1946; *Leaves of Hypnos,* 1973) greatly simplified their idiom, Jouve in *La vierge de Paris* (1944; the virgin of Paris) his tormented mysticism. A new generation of younger poets, such as Pierre EMMANUEL and Jean CAYROL, made of poetry the vehicle for a fervent expression of the collective national distress. The unity of mood did not outlast the 1940s, which recognized four new masters: Francis PONGE, Jacques PRÉVERT, Saint-John Perse, and Char. Ponge's *Le parti pris des choses* (1942, taking the side of things), a collection of prose-poems, describing with meticulous care and a subterranean form of fabulating humor, objects—natural and man-made—in the quotidian world, was admittedly an effort at bringing poetry away from its metaphysical speculations and back to the concrete. Ponge's method and approach dominated a current of what might be called phenomenological (descriptive) poetry, another of whose practitioners was Eugène Guillevic (b. 1907). Continuing the political-surrealist trend, Prévert exploited all the surrealistic devices—puns, incongruous juxtapositions of words, unexpected images—in satirical poems, often based on the well-known rhythms of popular, sentimental or nursery songs, politically slanted against all aspects of the Establishment, an attitude that reached its culmination with the quasi-Dadaistic revolt of Henri Pichette's (b. 1924) *Apoèmes* (1948; apoems). In exile in America,

Saint-John Perse, silent since 1924, published one after another great epic poem, developing in ample stanzas, concerned with the eternal question of mankind's destiny in the cosmos. Char, in terse, contracted forms tending toward aphorism, expressed a new humanistic ethic, the concern too of Pierre Seghers (b. 1906), Jean Rousselot (b. 1913), and René-Guy Cadou (1920–1951). Whether politically, socially or humanistically oriented, or turned toward the non-anthropocentric world of things, poetry, in a number of individual idioms, tended to reestablish the continuity of rhythm, the organized sequence of words, and the organic unity of the poem that the surrealists had drastically rejected.

Drama

The theater, dependent upon stable social conditions, suffered attrition. In Paris a premium was put by the occupying forces on the boulevard theater of entertainment. The "cartel" of the four great directors was disrupted; Jouvet toured abroad; Pitoëff died in 1939; Baty concentrated on marionettes; Dullin struggled to keep his theater alive in the face of insuperable financial difficulties, and, at the Comédie Française, Jean-Louis Barrault succeeded in giving a few fine performances, producing, notably, Claudel's *Le soulier de satin* (pub. 1930; *The Satin Slipper*, 1931). In 1945 a major reorganization of the state-subsidized theaters started a new period of expansion. The theater was decentralized, with government-subsidized dramatic centers in the provinces; young troupes were encouraged and support given the Théâtre National Populaire directed by Jean Vilar. With the inauguration of the Festival of Avignon, Vilar started a movement toward outdoor, summer festivals: at Nîmes, Arras, Angers, etc. In Paris innumerable "little theaters," most of them temporary, gave a growing number of directors their chance: André Barsacq, Michel Saint-Denis, Jean Dasté, Georges Vitaly, and Roger Planchon.

After 1942 the decade produced three new dramatists of stature: Montherlant, Sartre, and Camus. Abandoning the novel, Montherlant made his debut with *La reine morte* (1942; *Queen after Death*, 1951), which was followed by Sartre's *Les mouches* (1943; *The Flies*, 1947), Camus's *Le malentendu* (1943; *Cross Purposes*, 1946), and Simone de Beauvoir's *Les bouches inutiles* (1945; useless mouths). Reaching against the poetic, nonrealistic drama of Giraudoux, Montherlant returned to psychological drama, creating stage characters, whether historical or modern, motivated by his own aristocratic, nihilist ethic and in conflict with their entourage. Sartre, brilliant and versatile, eschewing psychological drama, proposed an existential theater of "extreme" situations, in which characters, trapped as it were, must make a choice, commit themselves, act, and so determine their "becoming" while revealing their inner orientation. In keeping with his own theory of literature, Sartre proposed an "efficient theater," directed at the spectators, with the aim of revealing to them the nature of their own situation. Increasingly political in its orientation, Sartre's theater tended toward a neorealism, counterbalanced by a somewhat profuse rhetorical eloquence. Camus's plays centered on the conflicts created by the tragic and insoluble paradoxes inherent in his conception of "absurd" man. Drama became charged with philosophical, often tragic themes, and somber overtones, but did not basically alter in structure. At the turn of the midcentury, the French stage seemed particularly vigorous, simultaneously presenting plays by Claudel, Giraudoux (posthumously), Cocteau, Anouilh, Salacrou, Montherlant, Sartre, Camus, and Marcel.

The Novel

It was Malraux who, in the late 1920s, set the novel on a new course with *Les conquérants* (1928; *The Conquerers*, 1929). He chose for his novels a background of revolutionary action in the immediate present, whether in Indochina, China, Germany, or Spain, and treated it with journalistic intensity and from the point of view of the revolutionary forces with whom he had worked closely. In the foreground a handful of characters, the heroes, engage in tense elliptical dialogues elucidating the reasons that threw them into action: they face prison, torture, and violent death. The human condition is the theme of their desperate meditations—and the title of the most influential of these novels, *La condition humaine* (1933; *Man's Fate*, 1934). Revolt and heroic action in Malraux's world are the answer to the indignity of man's fate in a purposeless universe. With *Courrier Sud* (1929; *Southern Mail*, 1933) and *Vol de nuit* (1931; *Night Flight*, 1932), Saint-Exupéry, in a more humanistic vein, brought fiction close to personal testimony, describing the heroism of the men who established the first commercial airlines. In both works fiction was a pretext rather than a purpose, used as a means to transmit the quality of a personal experience based on a total commitment.

In a different mood and setting, Sartre's *La nausée* (1938; *Nausea*, 1949) and collection of short stories, *Le mur* (1939; *The Wall, and Other Stories*, 1948), and Camus's *L'étranger* (1942; *The Stranger*, 1946) created fictional situations fashioned by an intellectual view of life; their heroes incarnate attitudes latent in the uneasiness of mind of a whole generation, which both writers sought to explore. *La nausée* and *L'étranger* are tales, told in the first person, of a metaphysical adventure.

But the "metaphysical novel" did not last through the 1950s. Malraux abandoned the novel after *Les noyers de l'Altenburg* (1943; *The Walnut Trees of Altenburg*, 1952); Sartre did not finish the fourth volume of *Les chemins de la liberté* (1945–49; *The Roads to Freedom*, 1947–51). After Simone de Beauvoir's *Les mandarins* (1954; *The Mandarins*, 1956) the metaphysical novel gave way to works of direct testimony, of which her four volumes of memoirs, published between 1958 and 1972, and Sartre's *Les mots* (1964; *The Words*, 1964) are outstanding examples. Camus, with *La peste* (1947; *The Plague*, 1948), *La chute* (1956; *The Fall*, 1957), and a collection of short stories, *L'exil et le royaume* (1957; *Exile and the Kingdom*, 1958), and Maurice BLANCHOT in his more obscure esoteric tales, carried on the mode of metaphysical fiction for a time.

Expository Prose

Most characteristic of the period is the literature of philosophical disquisition and debate centered on the Marxist-existentialist conflict, dominated by Sartre's *L'être et le néant* (1943; *Being and Nothingness*, 1956), and fortified by his numerous essays. Beauvoir and Camus also gave new impetus to the philosophical essay. Marxist philosophers—Henri Lefebvre (b. 1910). Georges Politzer (1903–1943); existentialist philosophers—Sartre, Beauvoir, and Maurice Merleau-Ponty (1906–1961) among the atheistic, Gabriel Marcel among the Christian existentialists; Christian "personalists"—Emmanuel Mounier; and independent thinkers—Simone WEIL, Camus—kept up controversies, sometimes violent, that reached a climax with the publication of Camus's *L'homme révolté* (1951; *The Rebel*, 1954), one of many works that presented a critique of Marxism. Among these the most influential were Raymond Aron's (1905–1983) *Le grand schisme* (1948; the great schism) and

L'opium des intellectuels (1955; *The Opium of the Intellectuals*, 1957), and Merleau-Ponty's *Les adventures de la dialectique* (1955; *Adventures of the Dialectic*, 1973). Literary criticism produced important works, characterized by a metaphysical emphasis: *De Baudelaire au surréalisme* (1933; *From Baudelaire to Surrealism*, 1949) by Marcel Raymond (1897–1957) and *L'âme romantique et le rêve* (1939; the romantic soul and the dream) by Albert Béguin (1901–1957). In *Baudelaire* (1947; *Baudelaire*, 1949) Sartre proposed a new biographical approach based on the dialectics of existential psychoanalysis. The criticism of Maurice Blanchot and the speculations of Jean PAULHAN on language and rhetoric, opened the way for a philosophical approach to literary criticism, which a lively debate on the nature of poetry, sparked by the militant poetic theories of the surrealists, emphasized; this approach can be seen in *L'expérience poétique* (1938; the poetic experience) by André Rolland de Renéville (1903-1962); *Clef de la poésie* (1944; key to poetry) by Paulhan; *La poésie moderne et le sacré* (1945; modern poetry and the holy) by Jules Monnerot (b. 1908); *Les impostures de la poésie* (1943; the deceptions of poetry) by Roger Caillois (1913–1978).

But it was in the 1950s that, with Malraux's controversial but eloquent attempt to create a metaphysics of art—*Les voix du silence* (1951; *The Voices of Silence*, 1953), *La métamorphose des dieux* (1957; *The Metamorphosis of the Gods*, 1960)—the trend reached its climax, orienting criticism toward what has been called "metacriticism," a metaphysics of the creative process as such.

From the 1950s to the 1980s: A Rapidly Shifting Stage

The 1950s, with the emergence of a new generation, seem clearly to mark a turning point, a reorientation of literary currents. Both novel and drama broke away from the themes and forms of politically or philosophically committed literature; poetry showed a number of widely divergent trends, and nonfiction prose took on a literary rather than a philosophical coloring.

Narrative Modes

Novels of every type now flooded the market: historical, picaresque, erotic, sentimental. Among hundreds of names, only a few stood out: VERCORS, Pierre Gascar, Françoise MALLET-JORIS, Jean Cayrol. In reaction to the overabundant novelistic production, a publisher, Jérôme Lindon, selected for his Éditions de Minuit (midnight editions) a few original new writers. These "antinovelists," or "midnight," "new," or "experimental" novelists as they were called, did not constitute a school. They were in agreement on a certain number of points: the novel, in order to subsist, should incorporate further experimentations with technical innovations. Plot, character, psychological analysis, description, as traditionally practiced, would have to go. The novel should be politically "uncommitted," free of philosophical concerns extraneous to its purpose. Beyond this, those novelists shared no program, each exploring new forms and possibilities of narrative technique. Samuel BECKETT, Alain ROBBE-GRILLET, Michel BUTOR, Nathalie SARRAUTE, Claude SIMON, Raymond PINGET, Claude OLLIER, and Marguerite DURAS, besides producing novels both varied and challenging to the reader, created around the novel—the NEW NOVEL—a flurry of criticism, and seemed to be preparing the way for new developments in the genre.

As the 1950s wore on, the novelists' concern with theories of narrative structure and semiology led to complex experiments in the production of abstract and arbitrary patterns, antirealistic and antianthropocentric in intent. "New" and "new, new" novels had a greater impact on literary criticism than on narrative fiction as such and never reached a broad reading public, which turned to science fiction, detective novels, history, and biography. One outstanding exception—a serious but widely read novelist—is Michel TOURNIER.

In the late 1940s and into the 1950s autobiography emerged as a major narrative genre: Michel LEIRIS, who had previously published *L'âge d'homme* (1939; *Manhood*, 1963), began his four-volume *La règle du jeu* (1948–1976; the rules of the game), and Sartre, Beauvoir, and Jean GENET all published important autobiographical works.

Drama

More immediately widely acclaimed was the appearance in the 1950s of what has been called "antitheater" or THEATER OF THE ABSURD, a form of drama that drew some of its technique from a theoretician of the stage, Antonin ARTAUD, a former actor and surrealist poet. Influenced by the Oriental stage, Artaud developed his ideas in a series of essays called *Le théâtre et son double* (1938; *The Theater and Its Double*, 1958), advocating a "theater of cruelty," whose aim should be to disrupt the composure of the audience, unleashing collective primitive emotions, thus releasing and exorcising those dark forces of life which, Artaud felt, were dangerously repressed by Europeans: eroticism, cruelty, terror, etc. It was more Artaud's dramaturgy than his ideas that influenced the antitheater of the 1950s: he advocated puppetlike actors, miming a violent action, using a stage "sign" language—where props, dance, and sound counted more than the words themselves. Samuel Beckett, and in their first works, Eugène IONESCO and Arthur ADAMOV, stripping the play down to its bare essentials, drew for their characters on the circus, mime, and the puppet show, and did away with plot, characterization, and rhetoric, developing a tragicomic drama of pattern and repetition. Jean Genet, in contrast, using a flow of language rich in imagery, developed a theater of ceremonial and ritual, based on mask and masquerade, while Georges Schehadé (b. 1910) continued the tradition of the poetic theater. By the 1960s, under the influence of Bertolt BRECHT, Adamov had developed toward a form of "epic theater"; Beckett, continually reducing his stage, was not renewing his themes. In spite of the success of Genet and Ionesco, the French stage was in search of new orientations, experimenting with various new forms of theater, radio plays (Robert Pinget), and chamber plays (Jean TARDIEU).

The most original of the later playwrights is Fernando ARRABAL, a Spaniard residing in France, whose violently baroque and erotic plays from *Pique-nique en campagne* (1961; *Picnic on the Battlefield*, 1967) to *La tour de Babel* (1976; the tower of Babel) escape classification. Two women writers, both novelists, Marguerite Duras and Nathalie Sarraute, have produced some of the more quietly innovative plays of the period. French conceptions of theater changed in the 1960s and 1970s. Moving away from Paris, to summer festivals in centers such as Nancy and Avignon, and international in scope, theater freed itself from the restraints of the conventional stage and the expectations of an urban audience. For the forty or so companies that, in summer, play to some 150,000 spectators, theater is no longer wedded to a literary text. What counts is the quality and audacity of the stage productions. This may account for a certain dearth of playwrights.

Poetry

Postwar France showed an upsurge of lyrical talent, heralded in the 1940s by Pierre Emmanuel, undoubtedly the outstanding figure of his generation. The new poets—Yves BONNEFOY, Alain Bosquet (1919–1998), André du Bouchet (b. 1924), Philippe Jacottet (b. 1925), André Marissel (b. 1928), Claude Vigée (b. 1921), Jean-Claude Renard (b. 1922), Robert Sabatier (b. 1923), Pierre Oster (b. 1933), Marc Alyn (b. 1937), and Edmond JABÈS—reflect a wide diversity of tendencies and techniques. With the exception of Bouchet, influenced by Char, they all tend to use simpler, more direct forms of poetic expression and more traditional forms of prosody than their predecessors. Although no single trend predominates, the central concern of this poetry, born in the aftermath of war, is to probe the relation of the poet to a world under the shadow of destruction. The sense of peril and of beauty induced an elegiac and neoromantic mood, which is emphasized in many poets by a deliberate use of the rhythmical organization and rhetorical flow of the romantic poets, Victor Hugo most particularly. All have developed their own idioms, the most powerfully original being that of Edmond Jabès.

Two main tendencies mark the poetry of the 1960s and 1970s: the drive to renew the language and themes of French poetry without breaking with traditional rules of prosody; and experimentation with new forms, sometimes borrowed from other cultures (the Japanese tanka and haiku) or produced by the permutation of "generic" elements somewhat akin to the techniques of serial music, as seen in the works of Jacques Roubaud (b. 1932), Denis Roche (b. 1937), and the "antipoet" Marcelin Pleynet (b. 1933). Among the many poets untroubled by theory, Andrée CHÉDID, author of *Textes pour un poème* (1950; texts for a poem) has steadily published poems that place her among the two or three outstanding poets of the period.

Expository Prose

The turn of the midcentury showed a characteristic swing away from metaphysical and philosophical speculation toward literary criticism, and, with E. M. CIORAN, found a successor to the great essay writer of the 1920s, Valéry. It has rightly been called an era of criticism.

Drawing on every other discipline—psychoanalysis, whether Freudian—Charles Mauron (1899–1966)—or Sartrian; on Marxist sociology and aesthetics as developed by György LUKÁCS—Lucien Goldmann (1913–1970), Roland BARTHES ; on anthropology—Georges BATAILLE, and Roger Caillois—and structural anthropology and STRUCTURALISM—Claude LÉVI-STRAUSS; on scientific phenomenological studies of the imagination—Gaston Bachelard (1884–1962)—criticism became "metacriticism," a phenomenology of the creative process, a heuristic—Gaëtan Picon (1915–1976); R.-M. Albérès (1920-1982); also important are the "thematic" critics Georges Poulet (1902–1992), Jean Pierre Richard (b. 1922), and Jean Starobinski (b. 1920). Problems of method predominated in university essays and discussions. Poets—Bosquet, Vigée, Bonnefoy, Emmanuel—reexamined the problem of the nature of poetry, its significance and function in the modern world. The New Novelists—Sarraute in *L'ère du soupçon* (1956; *The Age of Suspicion*, 1964), Butor in *Répertoire I* (1960; inventory I), Robbe-Grillet in *Pour un nouveau roman* (1963; *For a New Novel*,

1965)—and the dramatists—Ionesco, for instance, in *Notes et contre notes* (1962; *Notes and Counter Notes*, 1964), also discussed methods and aims. In the early 1960s there were signs that, leaving aside some of its metaphysical ambitions, and less marked by political bias, French criticism, remarkably enriched, was beginning to move away from the turmoil and confusion of the preceding years. A good example of the shift in approach is Jean Rousset's (b. 1910) *Forme et signification: Essais sur les structures littéraires de Corneille à Claudel* (1962; form and signification: essays on literary structures from Corneille to Claudel).

The second half of the 20th c. may well be known, like the 18th c., for its *philosophes*—writers drawn from many disciplines—Claude Lévi-Strauss, anthropology; Jean-Paul Sartre, philosophy; Jacques LACAN, psychoanalysis; Emmanuel LeRoy Ladurie (b. 1929), history; Michel FOUCAULT, sociology. These intellectuals set the ideological stage of the time, its moods, and themes.

Conclusion

In 1980, the French Academy made a momentous if belated decision: it elected its first woman writer, Marguerite YOURCENAR novelist, essayist, playwright, and autobiographer. The election was a tribute to her and to the single most dynamic movement of the 1970s—social and literary—the women's liberation movement. Articulate, involved in passionate debate concerning the modalities of "women's writing," launching its often ephemeral reviews, running its own publishing house, Les Éditions des Femmes, it has made its presence felt in every facet of the intellectual and literary life of France. Since 1970 three generations of women, from different strata of society, whose work is characterized by its diversity and originality, have held the center of attention in literary Paris: Yourcenar, Sarraute, Beauvoir, Duras, Christiane Rochefort (b. 1917), Monique WITTIG, and Hélène CIXOUS. To a certain extent they have filled the void left in the 1960s by Camus' death, Sartre's involvement in politics, and Malraux's withdrawal from the literary scene and his subsequent death, a void that in spite of their success the "new philosophes" of the late 1970s—Bernard Henri Lévy (b. 1948), André Glucksman (b. 1937)—have not filled. As one moves into the 1980s, literary activity in France continues at a hectic pace; furthermore, never have so many of the great and lesser works of the past been available to younger readers; likewise, never have they had such quick access to contemporary world literature, put rapidly into circulation through translations. But, in this open, cosmopolitan world, except for the women, a younger generation was finding it difficult to fashion its own idiom.

A self-styled "avant-garde" grouped around new reviews (*Tel Quel; Change*), basing its activity on concepts and methodologies borrowed from other disciplines, more especially linguistics (see Linguistics and Literature) and psychoanalysis, sought to reorient, simultaneously, both the literary forms and the traditional concepts concerning the nature of literature implicit in critical analysis and interpretation. Accepting as their point of departure the axiom that a text is a "production," a nonreferential structure of words, refusing to privilege either content, "subject," or genre, moving from the analysis of linguistic codes to theories of textual production, they radically affected the vocabulary and goals of academic criticism. The theoretical and applied critical work by Julia KRISTEVA, the "deconstructive" criticism of Jacques DERRIDA, and the highly original texts produced by Philippe SOLLERS exemplify the tight coordination between theory, criticism, and production in

155

the activities of the movement. In the 1970s one could sense a violent reaction against the abstractions and constraints of theoretical discourse, the recourse to a free flow of uncensored language that allegedly emanated directly from the unconscious—Pierre Guyotat's (b. 1940) *Éden, Éden, Éden* (1971; Eden, Eden, Eden) and Hélène Cixous's *Le troisième corps* (1970; the third body) and *Les commencements* (1970; the beginnings).

The most influential intellectual of the 1960s and 1970s, the mentor of this avant-garde, was Roland Barthes, a subtle essayist and critic, whose critical career embraced the successive theories of his time, applied, then transcended them. With *Plaisir du texte* (1973; *The Pleasure of the Text*, 1976), he abandoned the search for a scientifically based critical methodology. His later texts—*Roland Barthes par Roland Barthes* (1975; *Roland Barthes by Roland Barthes*, 1977), *Fragments d'un discours amoureux* (1977; *A Lover's Discourse: Fragments*, 1979)—place him in the tradition of French essayists inaugurated by Montaigne. It seemed plausible to conclude that the period of exacerbated literary experimentation was drawing to its end, while a new synthesis was in the making.

BIBLIOGRAPHY: Magny, C. -E, *Histoire du roman français depuis 1918* (1950); Chiari, J., *Contemporary French Poetry* (1952); Peyre, H., *The Contemporary French Novel* (1955); Brée, G., and M. Guiton, *An Age of Fiction: The French Novel from Gide to Camus* (1957); Grossvogel, D. I., *The Self-Conscious Stage in Modern French Drama* (1958); Chiari, J., *The Contemporary French Theatre* (1959); Mauriac, C., *The New Literature* (1959); Turnell, M., *The Art of French Fiction* (1959); Albérès, R. -M, *Histoire du roman moderne* (1962); Cruikshank, J. ed., *The Novelist as Philosopher: Studies in French Fiction* (1962); Pronko, L. C., *Avant-Garde: The Experimental Theater in France* (1962); Robbe-Grillet, A., *For a New Novel* (1965); Maurois, A., *From Proust to Camus* (1966); Moore, H. T., *Twentieth-Century French Literature* (2 vols., 1966); Fowlie, W., *Climate of Violence: The French Literary Tradition from Baudelaire to the Present* (1967); Guicharnaud, J., *The Modern French Theatre: From Giraudoux to Genet*, rev. ed. (2 vols., 1967); Nadeau, M., *The French Novel since the War* (1967); O'Brien, J., *The French Literary Horizon* (1967); Peyre, H., *French Novelists of Today* (1967); Sturrock, J., *The French New Novel* (1969); Bersani, L., *Balzac to Beckett* (1970); Mercier, V., *A Reader's Guide to the New Novel* (1971); Caws, M. A., *The Inner Theatre of Recent French Poetry* (1972); Fletcher, J., ed., *Forces in Modern French Drama* (1972); Roudiez, L. S., *French Fiction Today* (1972); Simon, J. K. ed., *Modern French Criticism* (1972); Brée, G., *Women Writers in France* (1973); Doubrovsky, S., *The New Criticism in France* (1973); O'Flaherty, K., *The Novel in France 1945–1965: A General Survey* (1973); Picon, G., *Contemporary French Literature: 1945 and After* (1974); Walzer, P. O, *Littérature française: Le XXme siècle I: 1896–1920* (1975); Popkin, D., and M. Popkin, eds., *Modern French Literature* (2 vols., 1977); Brée, G., *Littérature française: Le XXme siècle II: 1920–1970* (1978); Brooks, R. A. ed., *A Critical Bibliography of French Literature: The Twentieth Century* (1979); Flower, J. E., *Literature and the Left in France* (1979)

—GERMAINE BRÉE

French Literature since 1980

With a second millennium in the offing, the last quarter of the 20th c. witnesses the distinctive dynamism that has marked the century. The social and political upheavals of the late 1960s and 1970s, catalyzed by the death throes of the colonial empire and the student revolt of 1968, have continued to work, as noted by Germaine Brée, toward "disintegrating traditional structures [and] fostering the emergence of uncertain new ones."

The structuralist theorists and critics of the 1960s and 1970s, maligned for their formalism, nonetheless have left their stamp on the remarkable varieties of literary exploration following in their wake: semiotics as well as POSTSTRUCTURALISM, POSTMODERNISM—whose bewildering profusion of ideas has heralded a shift in the way we view the world and ourselves. Concepts that had come to be held as invariable truths little by little became open to question: subject, presence, origin, representation. As the end of the 19th c. witnessed a narrowing of the gap between the popular and the learned, the spoken and the written, so literature in the last two decades has increasingly sought to break down the barriers between genres. STRUCTURALISM's devalorization of the canonical great work has furthered this tendency to blend the educated and literary with the popular and commercial.

With the deaths in the late 1970s and the 1980s of many of the writers and thinkers instrumental in fashioning modern literature and literary thought—in 1976 André Malraux and Raymond Queneau, the year following Jacques Prévert, in 1980 Jean-Paul Sartre and Roland Barthes, in 1981 Jacques Lacan, in 1982 Louis Aragon and Georges Perec, in 1984 Michel Foucault and Henri Michaux, in 1986 Simone de Beauvoir and Jean Genet, in 1987 Marguerite Yourcenar and Jean Anouilh, in 1988 René Char, in 1989 Samuel Beckett, in 1991 Edmond Jabés, in 1993 André Frénaud, in 1995 Gilles Deleuze, in 1996 Marguerite Duras, and in 1998 Jean-François Lyotard—one has the impression that an age has passed. With the crisis in French theater in recent years and the increasing alienation of the poet from the public, with the concern about the continued weakening of the reading habits of the French, and with the renewed debate over the mongrelization of the French language through the depredations of English (in 1988 the French Academy opened a "museum of [linguistic] horrors"), doomsayers have sketched scenarios forecasting the decline of literature as a central force of stabilization and innovation upon which French society paces itself.

Many events speak otherwise: the rich pluralism and experimental bent of modern literature and literary theory; the opening of the Centre Pompidou at Beaubourg (1977); the creation of the "Maison de la Poésie" by the City of Paris in 1983 and the "High Committee for Poetry and the French Language" by the French government in 1987 to safeguard "the role of dream and escape" among young people; the creation of "Les Éditions des Femmes" devoted to reediting women's writings of the past (1979); the appearance in 1987 of volume 1 of the first reedition in 50 years of the *Dictionnaire de l'Académie Française*; the election of two women (Marguerite Yourcenar in 1980 and Jacqueline de Romilly in 1989) to the august inner circle of the French Academy; and the opening in 1995 of a new National Library, more vast than the present one, in the suburb of Tolbiac—point to literary renewal and new and inviting byways for cultural expression.

French literature since the 1970s continues the tradition of such illustrious forebears as Paul Valéry, Marcel Proust, and Paul Claudel, who have left rich commentary on the act of writing. The contemporary writer has often pushed this metalinguistic dimension to its ultimate, blurring the line between fiction and criticism, making narrative a critique of itself. Yet another characteristic of recent writing is its sociopolitical involvement. Perhaps more than at any time in the past, the writer and critic begin to conceive of the inseparability of the literary work and the culture that engenders it.

Since the mid-1970s three significant reorientations have distinguished contemporary literary endeavor: writing by women, postcolonial or migrant literature, and what has been called postmodernist literature. These modes, for all the diversity of their approaches, share certain characteristics: that of speaking from the margin, the recognition of the irreducible character of "reality," and oppositionality.

Fiction

Since the mid-1970s the French literary world has been the scene of a remarkable flourishing of fictional narratives in an astounding diversity of modes. The arrival of the autumn literary season (the "rentrée") has come regularly to herald the appearance of more than 200 novels, in time for the literary prizes of November and December. Many of the experimental novelists who attained reputations in the 1950s and 1960s—the so-called new or new-new novelists such as Alain ROBBE-GRILLET, Michel BUTOR, Marguerite DURAS, Jean CAYROL, Nathalie SARRAUTE, Robert PINGET, and Claude SIMON—continue to create important innovative works. Among them are Robbe-Grillet's *Djinn* (1981; *Djinn,* 1982) to *Les derniers jours de Corinthe* (1994; the last days of Corinth), Simon's *Géorgiques* (1981; *Georgics,* 1989) and *L'acacia* (1989; *The Acacia,* 1991), Duras's *L'amant* (1984; *The Lover,* 1985), and Sarraute's *Ici* (1995; here). Novels of Philippe SOLLERS follow one another at a prodigious rate, from *Paradis* (1981; paradise) to *La fête à Venise* (1991; celebration in Venice), as do those of Michel TOURNIER, from *Gaspar, Melchior et Balthazar* (1980; *The Four Wise Men,* 1982) to *Le médianoche amoureux* (1989; *The Midnight Love Feast,* 1991), which explore myths of all ages and realms. Moreover, Elie WIESEL has persevered in his dedicated vigil over the unforgotten past of the Holocaust in works like *Le cinquième fils* (1983; *The Fifth Son,* 1985). The Nobel committee awarded him the peace prize in 1986. These writers, in their characteristic unprogrammatic way, manifest an ever-renewed push to reform writing, to challenge traditional narrative and conventional ordering structures of plot, character, and story. Fittingly, the Nobel Prize for literature went to one of them in 1985—Claude Simon.

Despite their diversity, many present-day fictional narratives share common features inherited from the New Novel; exploded narrative that dissolves the order and linearity of the conventional story line, the calling into question of subject (narrator/character) identity, *mise en abyme* (textural part mirroring the textural whole), ambiguity, plural voices, even contradiction, that result in a multiplicity of viewpoints, of possible interpretations. Moreover, writers have persisted in eroding barriers between genres. *La vie, mode d'emploi* (1978; *Life: A User's Manual,* 1987), the masterpiece of Georges PEREC, presents a mixture of the detective story, history, biography, scientific writing, journalism, and popular literature.

The autobiographical genre has loomed more in evidence. Since 1975, an entire generation seems to be drawing back and looking over its past. Memoirs of Sartre, Beauvoir, Genet, Yourcenar, and Philippe SOUPAULT have appeared, as well as of the generation following, of Robbe–Grillet and Sarraute. Autobiographical writing, owing to its immediacy and call to personal experience and authority, has become the instrument of predilection for many authors, particularly women, and more particularly women born in French–speaking areas outside France: Marguerite Duras and Assia DJEBAR stand out as examples.

After the purism of the "new novelists" and the belief of the writer of the 1960s and 1970s in "uncommitted" writing, the narrative since the late 1970s has tended to manifest political and social commitment, even while conveying that commitment very often through a nonmimetic style and experimental language that create the type of specific (ir)reality we observe in the work of Georges Perec and Maurice BLANCHOT. The narratives of Patrick MODIANO return to the Occupation years to resuscitate the past through the collective memory of the French people—from his film script *Lacombe, Lucien* (1974; *Lacombe, Lucien,* 1975) to *Fleurs de ruine* (1991; flowers in the ruins). Duras, while repudiating the label of feminist, has explored the timbres of the feminine voice in a social context in a way few authors preceding her have. Her work attained worldwide recognition in the 1980s. Hélène CIXOUS and Monique WITTIG, on the other hand, though differing in crucial respects, have both engaged with undisguised fervor the question of woman's sexuality, as have Luce Irigaray (b. 1939), Annie Leclerc (b. 1940), and Julia KRISTEVA. The migrant narratives of *beur* writers (Writers of North African extraction born in France) such as Leïla SEBBAR, Mehdi Charef (b. 1952), Azouz Begag (b. 1957), Farida Belghoul (b. 1958), and Arriz Tamza (pseud. of Maya Bousselmania, b. 1957), and writers born in French-speaking countries outside the metropole, such as Edouard GLISSANT, Abdelkebir KHATIBI, Tahar BEN JELLOUN, Maryse CONDÉ, Sony Labou TANSI, Daniel MAXIMIN, Patrick CHAMOISEAU, Calixthe BEYALA, Rachid MIMOUNI, WEREWERE LIKING, Amin Maalouf (b. 1949), Raphaël Constant (b. 1951), and Nina Bouraoui (dates n.a.).

Several venerable authors continue to compose important works: Julien GREEN caps his career at the age of eighty-five with the 900-page novel *Les pays lointains* (1987; *The Distant Lands,* 1990), judged by some critics to be his masterpiece; André PIEYRE DE MANDIARGUES in his late seventies continues to publish works such as *Tout disparaître* (1987; let everything disappear), as does Christiane Rochefort (b. 1917) whose *La porte du fond* (1988; door at the rear) received the Medecis Prize in 1988. Along with established writers such as Lucien Bodard (b. 1914), Jacques Laurent (b. 1919), Maurice ROCHE, Jean D'Ormesson (b. 1925), Raymond Jean (b. 1925), Françoise Mallet-Joris (b. 1930), Pierre-Jean Rémy (b. 1937), and J.-M. G. Le CLÉZIO, who are still active, a battery of new and talented writers, many of the post-World War II generation, has emerged: Serge Doubrovsky (b. 1928), Jean Vautrin (b. 1933), René-Victor Pilhes (b. 1934), Danièle Sallenave (b. 1940), François Weyergans (b. 1941), Jean-Marie Rouart (b. 1943), Alain Gerber (b. 1943), Patrick Grainville (b. 1947), Georges-Olivier Châteaureynaud (b. 1947), Erik Orsenna (b. 1947), Bernard-Marie Koltès (b. 1948), Jean Echenoz (b. 1948), Yann Queffélec (b. 1949), Marc Cholodenko (b. 1950), Jacques Almira (b. 1950), Raphaële Billetdoux (b. 1951), Muriel Cerf (b. 1951), Jean Rouard (b. 1952), Patrick Thévenon, Yves Berger, Michel Rio, Antoine Volodine, Richard Millet, and Luc Dessignes (pseud. of Pierre Combescot). Their narratives vary radically, from rather traditional forms to bold experimentation in such a narrative as that of Weyergans where a fetus narrates the story in *Vie d'un bébé* (1986; the life of a baby); from metanovels (novels about novel writing)—Almira's *Le voyage à Naucratis* (1975; voyage to Naucratis) or Weyergans's *Je suis écrivain* (1989; I'm a novelist)—autofiction/ autobiography such as Doubrovsky's *Le livre brisé* (1989; the sundered book) or Orsenna's *L' exposition coloniale* (1988; *Love and Empire,* 1991), and works of postmodern myth and allegory such as Grainville's *La caverne céleste* (1984; *The Cave of Heaven,* 1990) or Wittig's *Virgile, non* (1985; *Across the Acheron,* 1987) to novels of social-political orientation—Grainville's *Les flamboyants* (1976; the flamboyants), which treats Africa and revolution; Pilhes's *L'imprécateur* (1974; *The Provocateur*, 1977), which takes as subject the failure of a multinational corporation; Ormesson's *Le bonheur à San Miniato* (1987; happiness at San Miniato), set in the days of fascism and Stalinism of World War II; novels that take up the theme of the Nazi occupation and the Holocaust—Châteaureynaud's *Le verger* (1978; the orchard) tells the story of a child in a death camp; Bertrand Poirot-Delpeche's (b. 1929) *L'été 36* (1984; summer '36) evokes the violence of the 1930s; Jorge Semprun (b. 1923), in *L'ecriture ou la vie* (1995; writing or life), gives us a personal account of life in a concentration camp, reminiscent of Primo LEVI; the work of Edith Thomas (1909-1970), *Le témoin compromis* (written 1952, pub. 1995; the compromised witness), relates her engagement in the resistance and violent break with the Communist Party; finally, the moving novel of Sarah Kofman (1934-1994), *Rue Ordener rue Labat* (Ordener and Labat streets), appearing the same year as her suicide, renders the distressing suffering of a Jewish child during the occupation.

Feminist writing has assumed special importance in the work of Benoîte Groult (b. 1920), Catherine Clément (b. 1939), Annie Ernaux (b. 1940), Hèléne Cixous, as well as in the work of younger women such as Ernaux's sister, Emmanuelle Bernheim, Michèle Fitoussi, Christiane Baroche, Pascale Roze, Camille Laurens, Béatrix Beck, Paule Constant, and Marie Darrieussecq (dates n.a.). Outside of France, several francophone authors have privileged feminist subjects: Condé, Beyala, and particularly Assia Djebar in *L'amour la fantasia* (1985; *Fantasia: An Algerian Calvacade*, 1993). Gay and lesbian themes inform *L'étoile rose* (1978; the pink star) and *Dans la main de l'ange* (1982; in the hand of the angel) by Dominique Fernandez (b. 1929), *Le jardin d'acclimatation* (1980; *Cronus' Children*, 1986) by Yves Navarre (b. 1940), and the postmodern *Virgile, non* by Monique Wittig. In *Les quartiers d'hiver* (1990; winter quarters), Jean-Noël Pancrazi (b. 1949) treats the scourge of AIDS threatening the gay community.

The genre of the detective novel was marked by the death in 1989 of the Belgian Georges SIMENON, whose prolific pen had authored over 300 novels, and by the appearance in the "Série Noire" in 1985 of the 2000th detective novel—a measure of the genre's increasing respectability. San Antonio (pseud. of Frédéric Dard, b. 1921) continues to produce his unique brand of mystery thriller. The "new" mystery flourishing since the early 1970s displaces the mystery intrigue through a metaliterary movement, as in René Belletto's (b. 1945) *L'enfer* (1986; hell), often subordinating it to a radical social and literary reevaluation and contestation: Jean Vautrin's (b. 1933) *Canicule* (1982; dog days) and Joseph Bialot's (dates n.a.) *Babelville* (1979; Babel city), which depict the racism and violence of materialistic society; the writings of A. D. G. (pseud. of Alain Camille, b. 1947) and Jean–Patrick Manchette (b. 1942), which excoriate society from their respective positions of right– and left–wing militancy. The espionage novel maintains its rank as the best-selling genre in France (20 million copies yearly), including among its legion of practitioners (many of inferior talent), the ubiquitous Vladimir Volkoff (b. 1932), awarded the French Academy's Grand Prize for the novel in 1982, for *Le montage* (1982; the setting).

Drama

The last echoes of the THEATER OF THE ABSURD resounded in theater corridors in the mid 1970s and early 1980s, with new plays by Samuel Beckett and Eugène IONESCO, restagings of these dramatists and of Arthur ADAMOV, Fernando ARRABAL, and Georges Shehadé (b. 1910), and new productions by their followers—Robert PINGET, Jean TARDIEU, and René de Olbadia (b. 1918). New plays by Jean Anouilh appeared, the latest of which was the farce *Le nombril* (belly button) in 1981. But since the 1970s, critics like Alfred Simon have emphasized the artistic and economic impoverishment of French theater, the disappearance of major dramatists and actors, the tendency of directors to "dust off" the classics, their failure to encourage young authors, and, consequently, the diminishment of theatergoers to serious theater.

Other tendencies contributing to the changes wrought in theater include the numerous productions of foreign dramatists and directors and the influence of television, film, and radio. Since the 1970s theatrical fare has consisted primarily of popular theater (the boulevard theater and the *caféstheâtres*) and restagings and revivals of time-honored plays. Moreover, a collective theater (*création collective*), in which authors, actors, directors, and even the public merge, arose in the 1970s in the stagings of Ariane Mnouchkine (b. 1939) of the spectacles or historical frescoes of *1798, 1793*, and *L'âge d'or* (the golden age) at the Théâtre du Soleil. The spectacles of Robert Hossein (b. 1927)—*Danton et Robespierre* (perf. 1979), *Les misérables* (perf. 1980), and *Un homme nommé Jésus* (perf. 1983)—have attracted theatergoers by elaborate staging and hundreds of actors. Finally, numerous private theaters failed, and the absorption of the Odeon by the Comédie Française marked the close of a famed state theater.

The decentralization of theater encouraged by the ministry of culture, viewed by many critics negatively, has accounted for a dramatic increase in regional theaters (Lyons, Strasbourg, Marseille, and Grenoble) and summer companies playing in provincial festival centers like Avignon and Nice. These events signal, first, a move of theater out of the dominant Parisian theatrical milieu, secondly, a strengthening of the tendency of theater to free itself from the restraints of the written script and conventional staging. Hence, despite its seeming impoverishment, profound changes in process, which account for the shift from the individual dramatist to the production, invest theater with a new dynamism.

Another notable exception to the sense of general impoverishment lies in the striking productivity of women dramatists such as Duras, Sarraute, Cixous, Wittig, Djebar, and Sylvia Montfort (dates n.a.). Wittig's and Cixous's work, like Montfort's, fastens on contemporary sociopolitical issues. Cixous's *L'histoire terrible mais inachevée de Norodom Sihanouk, roi du Cambodge* (1985; the terrible and unfinished story of Norodom Sihanouk, king of Cambodia) and *L'Indiade* (1988; the Indiad) take as subjects the Cambodian tragedy, Gandhi, and Indian independence. Far from being mere historical accounts, her plays depict the enigmatic contrarieties of historical personages. Outstanding among dramatists of the last two decades is Duras, whose plays like *L'Edencinéma* (1977; Eden-cinema) and *Savannah Bay* (1982; title in English) convey a style founded on absence and silence, which eloquently depicts the anguish of her characters.

The work of the accomplished dramatists François Billetdoux (b. 1927)—*Réveille-toi Philadelphie!* (1989; wake up Philadelphia!)—the *boulevardier* Jean Poiret (1927–1992)—*Les clients* (1987; the clients)—the author-director Roger Planchon (b. 1931), and Jacques Sternberg (b. 1923) have also helped to keep theater alive. New writers of promise include Loleh Bellon (b. 1925), a latecomer to play writing, whose intimate dramas between women have met with deserved success (*Absence*, 1988; absence);

Jean–Claude Grumberg (b. 1939), whose work handles serious social and artistic questions through the medium of humor (*L'Indien sous Babylone*, 1985; the Indian under Babylon); Jean-Claude Brisville (b. 1922), who presents the painful, human confrontation of two famous viewpoints, one anguished, the other reasoned, in *L'entretien de M. Descartes avec M. Pascal le jeune* (1986; conversation of Descartes and young Pascal); the bold theater of Michel Vinaver (b. 1927), which in such plays as *Les travaux et les jours* (1979; works and days) or *L'ordinaire* (1983; the ordinary), depicts modern humankind as in perfect communion with the very system that crushes it; the brilliant and impassioned theater of Copi (1939–1987), whose early death cut short a promising career, and whose last play, *Une visite inopportune* (1988; an inopportune visit), stages a character dying of AIDS; finally, the gifted and prolific Bernard-Marie Koltès (b. 1948), whose *Dans la solitude des champs de coton* (1986; in the solitude of the cotton fields) puts into words a stark dialogue between an addict and a dealer. The work of certain dramatists, including Vinaver, the Belgian René Kalisky (b. 1936), author of *Aida vaincue* (1990; Aida vanquished), and Michel Deutsch (b. 1928), was dubbed *le théâtre du quotidien* (the theater of daily life) for its treatment of the fragmented reality of contemporary life. (For example, Deutsch's *Partage*, "sharing," deals with the tortured portraits of two of Charles Manson's women followers trying to make sense of their complicity in the murder of Sharon Tate.) Other dramatists whose work manifests talent and force include Edouardo Manet (b. 1927), Françoise Dorin (b. 1928, Jacques-Pierre Amette (b. 1943), Yasmina Réza (b. 1955), Agnès Jaoui, Xavier Durringer (dates n.a.), and the Quebecer Michel TREMBLAY. Other francophone authors of note include the Senegalese Souleymane Cissé, the Moroccan Tayeb Saddiki, the Algerians M'Hamed Benguettaf and Fatima Gallaire (dates n.a.), and Werewere Liking from the Cameroons.

Poetry

In the last few years the voices of several major poets have fallen silent: Saint-John PERSE, Pierre Jean JOUVE, Jacques PRÉVERT, Henri MICHAUX, Pierre EMMANUEL, Francis PONGE, and René CHAR. But these years have also witnessed astounding poetic activity—a flowering of festivals, gatherings, and readings devoted to poetry, and the resounding success of the Maison de la Poésie in bringing poetry to the literary public. They have also seen a proliferation of reviews consecrating the work of established and new poets alike: *Poètes Présents, Poésie Présente, Po&sie, Poémonde, Poésie*, launched by the Maison de la Poésie in 1984, and the influential *Argile*, which unhappily folded in 1981 after seven years of outstanding publication. The firm of Seghers continued as the major publisher of poetry, even after the death of the venerable Pierre Seghers in 1987. Finally, poetry collections sprout everywhere—in 1988 alone more than 300 received partial subventions from the Centre National des Lettres.

Poets of earlier generations have continued to affirm their poetic presence: esteemed talents like Eugène Guillevic (b. 1907), Edmond JABÈS, and Alain Bosquet (b. 1919), and the generation of the 1920s and early 1930s of Jean–Claude Renard (b. 1922), Yves BONNEFOY, André du Bouchet (b. 1924), the Swiss Philippe Jaccottet (b. 1925), Jacques Dupin (b. 1927), Michel Deguy (b. 1930), and Pierre Oster Soussouev (b. 1933). The poetry of these latter is a poetry of silence and loss, dealing more with the allegorical figuration of absence than the concreteness of material

existence, poetry stripped to the essentials of being, often conveyed in hermetic language.

Another trend marking contemporary poetry stems from agonistic modes of the 1960s and 1970s seeking to demystify poetry, often framed by a movement or evolving around a journal: *lettrism* under Isadore Isou (b. 1925) that sought to rehabilitate poetic language; the *Tel Quel* group with its political program set forth by Marcelin Pleynet (b. 1933) and Denis Roche (b. 1937) that challenged the generic bases of poetry; the revolutionary poetics of *Change* under Jean-Pierre FAYE, Jacques Roubaud (b. 1932), and Jacques Réda (b. 1929); and the Oulipian wild bunch and its triad of Roubaud, François Le Lionnais (1901–1984), and Jean Lescure (b. 1912), whose ludic experimentation with the help of mathematics and the computer transformed traditional poetic forms.

Some of the most accomplished poetry of the last two decades has come from poets born abroad: Andrée CHEDID (Egyptian of Lebanese origin), Mohammed DIB (Algeria), Edouard Glissant (Martinique), Gaston Miron (b. 1928, Quebec), Salah Stétié (b. 1929, Lebanon), Edouard Maunick (b. 1931, Mauritius), Jacques Izoard (b. 1926, Belgium), Hédi Bouraoui (b. 1932; a Tunisian poet living in exile in Canada), Claude Beausoleil (dates n.a., Quebec), and Tahar Ben Jelloun (Morocco), who read his latest work, a 600–verse poem honoring the unknown Arab soldier killed in the Persian Gulf War at the Capri Festival in June 1991. Younger poets of notable talent include Bernard Noël (b. 1930), Claude-Michel Cluny (b. 1930), Jude Stéfan (b. 1930), Jean Pérol (b. 1932), Marie-Claire Bancquart (b. 1932), Pierre Dalle Nogare (b. 1934), Yves Martin (b. 1936), Jean Joubert (b. 1938), Jean Orizet (b. 1937), James Sacré (b. 1939), Daniel Biga (b. 1940), Jean-Pierre Lemaire (b. 1948), Marc Cholodenko (b. 1950), Pierre Garnier, Vénus Khoury-Ghata, Jean-Claude Schneider, Jeannine Baude, Anne de Staël, Anne Portugal, Jean-Charles Vegliante, Anne-Marie Albiach, Esther Tellermann, Richard Rognet, and Hédi Kaddour (dates n.a.).

The new poetry has been described by many critics as "exploded"—shattering into a multitude of fragments replete with powerful imagery, provocative rhythms, jarring disharmonies. Multiple currents have arisen, ranging from the lyrical, the search for the secular sacred and fascination with nature (Orizet), the corporeal (Noël) and the metaphysical (Dalle Nogare)—on the one hand—to a realistic vein—on the other hand—inspired in part by the events of 1968, that fastens on the urban setting with its pop artifacts, blaring noise, glaring lights, graffiti, and violence (Biga, Martin, Réda).

Theory and Criticism

With theory and criticism as with theater, critics have spoken of crisis and impoverishment without a sense of the rich dynamics of change postwar thought has wrought in seeking to free itself from the procrustean restraints of reductive, doctrinaire thinking that played a part in the political and social debacles of the 1930s, the events of World War II, and the Cold War. Recent years have seen literature and literary theory inflected by theorists from varied disciplines: philosophy, psychoanalysis, anthropology, sociology, and linguistics. The type of critical thought that compartmentalizes knowledge, that ceases to be critical and reproduces rather than renews the status quo has been challenged by the French poststructuralists Jacques DERRIDA, Jean-François LYOTARD, Roland BARTHES, and Michel FOUCAULT. Their works constitute the most innovative development in contemporary French thought—from Derrida's *Éperons* (1978; *Spurs*, 1979) to *La carte postale* (1980; *The Post Card*, 1987) and the autobiographical work

Jacques Derrida par Geoffrey Bennington et Jacques Derrida (1991; *Jacques Derrida by Geoffrey Bennington and Jacques Derrida*), from Lyotard's *Économie libidinale* (1974; libidinal economy) to *Le différend* (1984; *The Different: Phrases in Dispute*, 1988) and *L'inhumain* (1988; *The Inhuman*, 1992), and from Barthes's, *Barthes par Barthes* (1975; *Roland Barthes by Roland Barthes*, 1977) to his posthumous works such as *Le grain de la voix* (1981; *The Grain of the Voice*, 1985). They mutually undertake an adversarial counteraction against absolutist systems, against narratives of the legitimation of knowledge, against the terror of technology in the informational age; they share a belief in the irreducible character of human and cultural phenomena in the face of representational systems; they open to question assumptions and constructs of traditional thought: the notion of a stable subject, of the act of writing (*écriture*) as predetermined by a logo-centered bias; finally, they examine at length the complex questions of "alterity" and "marginality."

These propositions sound strong refrains among other contemporary critics and theorists: Blanchot's writings of the 1980s (*L'écriture du désastre*, 1980; *The Writing of the Disaster*, 1986, and *Le dernier à parler*, 1985; the last to speak); Julia Kristeva's *Pouvoirs de l'horreur* (1980; *Powers of Horror*, 1982) and *Soleil noir: Dépression et mélancolie* (1987; *Black Sun: Depression and Melancholia*, 1989), which views language as originating in loss; Paul de Man's *Blindness and Insight* (1985), which posits language as in constant pursuit of naming what is missing; Michel Serres's (b. 1930) *Le parasite* (1980; *The Parasite*, 1982); Michel de Certeau's (b. 1925) *Heterologies: Discourse on the Other* (1986); and Pierre Bourdieu's (b. 1930) *Ce que parler veut dire* (1982; what speaking means).

In the arena of contestation, these years saw numerous debates on sexuality, beginning with Marc Oraison's *La question homosexuelle* (1976; *The Homosexual Question*, 1977) and including Foucault's three-volume *Histoire de la sexualité* (1976–1984; *The History of Sexuality*, 1978–1986). But by far the most significant event was the proliferation of feminist theory and criticism: Hélène Cixous and Catherine Clément, *La jeune née* (1975; *The Newly Born Woman*, 1986); Benoîte Groult (b. 1920), *Ainsi soit-elle* (1975; thus it/she be); Wittig, *Le corps lesbien* (1973; *The Lesbian Body*, 1975); Irigaray, *Ce sexe qui n'en est pas un* (1977; *This Sex Which Is Not One*, 1985); Sarah Kofman (b. 1934), *L'énigme de la femme* (1980; *The Enigma of Woman*, 1985); and Kristeva, *Au commencement était l'amour* (1985; *In the Beginning Was Love*, 1987).

The work of theorists in other disciplines has impacted significantly on literary study. The influential *Séminaire* of Jacques Lacan continues to appear posthumously (vols. 8 and 17 in 1991). 1985 saw the publication of an important work by Claude LÉVI–STRAUSS, *La potière jalouse* (*The Jealous Potter*, 1988). The rich collaborative series of Gilles Deleuze (b. 1925) and Félix Guattari (b. 1930) entitled *Capitalisme et schizophrénie*, of which the last of two volumes, *Mille Plateaux*, appeared in 1980 (*A Thousand Plateaus: Capitalism and Schizophrenia*, 1988), radically revises the notions of schizophrenia and desire. From *Rhizome* (1976; *On the Line*, 1983) to *Le pli* (1988; the fold) Deleuze pursues his conception of the book and film as sites of "multiplicity," of interchange of diverse theories, genres, concepts, and desires. A. J. Greimas (b. 1917) presses his distinction between the concepts of semantic and semiotic, from the series of writings carrying the title *Du sens* (1970–1983; *On Meaning: Selected Writings*, 1987) to his collaborative work with Jacques Fontanille, *Sémiotique des passions* (1991; semiotics of passion), which

proposes a semiotic description of the universe of passion and emotion. Jean Baudrillard (b. 1929) pursues his study of contemporary society in such works as *Les stratégies fatales* (1983; *Fatal Strategies*, 1990). René Girard (b. 1923), whose writing represents a renaissance of religious thought, investigates violence, desire, and the sacred in works like *Le bouc émissaire* (1982; *The Scapegoat*, 1986). The influential Marxist theorist Henri Lefebvre (b. 1901) was still publishing in the 1980s, along with Louis Althusser (1918–1990), and Cornelius Castoriadis (b. 1922). The psychoanalytic writings of Jean Bellemin–Noël (dates n.a.) have strongly influenced literary study. In *Interlignes: Essais de Textanalyse* (1988; intersections, essays on textanalysis), he rejects, as Barthes before him, the notion of an absolute reality underlying the text, seeking rather to seize how a text "constitutes" itself, what it reveals of the operation of the unconscious. Many other theorists and critics continued to produce works that have strongly influenced the direction of contemporary literary thought: Abdelkebir Khatibi, Vincent Descombes (dates n.a.), Lucette Finas (b. 1921), Gérard Genette (b. 1930), Philippe Lacoue–Labarthe (b. 1940), Jean–Luc Nancy (b. 1940), Michael Riffaterre (b. 1924), and Tzvetan Todorov (b. 1939), to mention only a few.

Conclusion

The years from the mid–1970s to the early 1990s witness a literature in turmoil. Contemporary writers have boldly forged alternate passages, peopled the landscape of modern thought with strange and often bizarre forms, and expanded the perimeters of our thinking to express a changing world. These efforts have often left in their train cries of condemnation and predictions of a dire future for literature. But final judgment must be left to posterity as to whether the brilliant flourishes of these years toll the decadence of a society that has misplaced its values or the birth throes of an exciting era opening before our mind and senses.

BIBLIOGRAPHY: Descombes, V., *Modern French Philosophy* (1980); Culler, J., *The Pursuit of Signs: Semiotics, Literature, Deconstruction* (1981); Bersani, J., and J. Lecarme, comps., *Littérature en France depuis 1968* (1982); Culler, J., *On Deconstruction: Theory and Criticism after Structuralism* (1982); Brée, G., *Twentieth–Century French Literature* (1983); Eagleton, T., *Literary Theory: An Introduction* (1983); Hamon, P., *Texte et idéologie* (1984); Bradby, D., *Modern French Drama 1940–1980* (1984); Bishop, M., *The Contemporary Poetry of France: Eight Studies* (1985); Boisdeffre, P. de, *Histoire de la littérature française des années 1930 aux années 1980* (2 vols., 1985); Caws, M. A., *Reading Frames in Modern Fiction* (1985); Todorov, T., *Literature and Its Theorists: A Personal View of Twentieth–Century Criticism* (1987); Duchen, C., ed., *French Connections: Voices from the Women's Movement in France* (1987); Lecherbonnier, B., D. Rincé, P. Brunel, and C. Moatti, eds., *Littérature: Textes et documents. XXe siècle* (1989); special new French fiction issue, *RCF*, 9, 1 (1989); Atack, M., and P. Powrie, eds., *Contemporary French Fiction by Women* (1990); Suleiman, S., *Subversive Intent: Gender, Politics, and the Avant–Garde* (1990); Jameson, F., *Postmodernism or, The Cultural Logic of Late Capitalism* (1990); Stamelman, R. H., *Lost beyond Telling: Representations of Death and Absence in Modern French Poetry* (1990); Chambers, R., *Room for Maneuver; Reading (the) Oppositional (in) Narrative* (1991); Natoli, J., and Hutcheon, L., *A Postmodern Reader* (1993); Bishop, M., *Contemporary French Women Poets*, 2 vols. (1995); Bancquart, M.-C., *La poésie en France du surréalisme à nos jours* (1996)

—JOHN D. ERICKSON

Basque Literature

Until very recently the Basque language in France (spoken in the western Pyrenees region) was kept alive by the Catholic Church, which had created and sustained its literature. Most of the major authors belonged to religious orders and wrote in the vernacular.

Jean Hiriart-Urruty (1859–1915) was the mentor of the modern generation of French-Basque writers. In 1887 he founded the weekly review *Eskualduna*, which he directed for thirty years and to which he contributed many articles. In a very rich but popular style he attacked the republican, anticlerical ideas of his time. His articles have recently been collected in two volumes: *Mintzaira, aurpegia: Gizon* (1971; tongue; face: man) and *Zezenak errepublikan* (1972; the bulls in the republic).

Among the early modern French-Basque writers, one of the best and most prolific was Jean Barbier (1875–1931), whose novel *Piarres* (2 vols., 1926, 1929; Piarres) is especially worth mentioning. The true protagonist is the Basque way of life of the early 20th c. The novel describes family life, work in the fields, holidays, games, death, and war.

Much of the most important French-Basque writing of the first half of the 20th c. was journalistic. Jean Etchepare (1877–1935) published frequently in the magazines *Eskualduna* and *Gure herria*. In addition he wrote two books: *Buruchkak* (1910; ears of wheat) and *Berebilez* (1931; by car). *Buruchkak* is a collection of articles in which he discusses religious education and morality from a viewpoint not well accepted by traditional Catholics. *Berebilez* narrates his travels in the Spanish Basque country. Etchepare was an outstanding stylist, employing, for the first time, the Basse-Navarre Basque dialect as a literary medium.

Bishop Jean Saint-Pierre (1884–1951) published impressions taken from the battlefields of World War I in *Eskualduna*. His style is direct and easily understandable. In 1921 he cofounded the magazine *Gure herria* and a year later received the "Kirikiño" literary award from the Academy of Basque Language for his efforts. His best articles were published together under the title *Les meilleures pages de Mgr. Saint-Pierre* (1952; the best pages of Monsignor Saint-Pierre).

Jules Moulier (pseud.: Oxobi, 1888–1958) is primarily known for his book *Alegiak* (1926; fables), a collection of fables written in verse. His humor is often bitter.

Later writers continued the journalistic tradition of their predecessors. The prolific writings of Pierre Lafitte (b. 1901) are devoted to the defense of Basque culture and the unification of the various Basque dialects. He has contributed extensively to *Eskualduna, Gure herria*, and *Herria* (which he founded).

More recent French-Basque writing has included some noteworthy drama and poetry. Pierre Larzabal (b. 1915) and Telesforo Monzón (1904–1981) are playwrights concerned with cultural, social, and political problems in the Basque country. Larzabal assisted Basque refugees from Franco's Spain, while Monzón, who had been a member of the Basque government in Spain before the civil war, lived the life of a political exile in the French Basque country. Both depict their experiences in their works. Larzabal has written about a hundred plays, most of which remain unpublished.

The best-known are *Etchahun* (1953; good house), *Bordaxuri* (1962; the white hut), *Hiru ziren* (1962; they were three), *Senperen gertatua* (1964; what happened in Senpere), and *Hila esposatu* (1965; the dead married). His spare style reflects the austerity of the Basque character. Monzón is also a poet and musician, and thus his theater is rather lyrical. *Menditarrak* (1957; the mountaineers) and *Zurgin zaharra* (1956; the old carpenter) are two of his best plays.

The poet Jean Diharce (pseud.: Xabier Iratzeder, b. 1920) is abbot of the Benedictine monastery of Belloc; his translations of the biblical Psalms into Basque—*Salmoak* (1963; psalms)—have been used in the mass and religious songs. Of a totally different style are the works of the Paris-born Basque poet Jean Mirande (1925–1972), which reflect a lack of respect for reforms and conventions alike as the enemies of Basque culture. For him it is more important that poetry be aesthetically and stylistically elegant than that it address social and cultural issues.

Although it is difficult to foresee the future of French-Basque literature, it will most likely be of a political nature because of the Basque revival of the past twenty-five years.

BIBLIOGRAPHY: Lafitte, P., *Le basque et la littérature d'expression basque en Labourd, Basse-Navarre et Soule* (1941); Michelena, L., *Historia de la literatura vasca* (1960); Villasante, L., *Historia de la literatura vasca* (1961); Lecuona, Manuel de, *Literatura oral vasca* (1965); Cortázar, N. de, *Cien autores vascos* (1966); *Enciclopedia general illustrada del país vasco* (1966); Sarasola, I., *Historia social de literatura vasca* (1976); Mujika, L. M., *Historia de la literatura euskerika* (1979)

—GORKA AULESTIA

Breton Literature

The Breton language, like Cornish and Welsh, is a Brythonic language derived from Celtic. In spite of centuries of French oppression, it is spoken by the inhabitants of western Brittany, whose ancestors emigrated from southwest Britain between the 4th and 6th cs.

The publication of the momentous and controversial *Barzaz breiz* (1839; Breton anthology), purported to be folk songs collected by Théodore Hersart de la Villemarqué (1815–1895), has had dramatic influence to this day in activating Breton authors, by kindling in them a sense of pride in their national and Celtic heritage.

A solitary Tangi Malmanche (1875–1953), forerunner of the Breton movement—which strives for cultural freedom and autonomy—and the greatest Breton playwright, writing in seclusion in Paris, reverted to the tales and traditions of Brittany for inspiration. His *Marvailh an ene naonek* (1900; the tale of the hungry soul), among others, was based on a single tradition, but most of his plays are interweavings of intricate patterns of beliefs and customs. All are composed in an excitingly innovative and virile style. In *Gurvan* (1923; Gurvan) there is a strong feeling of national consciousness arising from the hero's battles against the oppression of his cunning and ruthless Frankish neighbor, which loudly echoes the sentiments expressed in de la Villemarqué's collection, in which Malmanche was well versed.

Revolutionary enthusiasm, when it fails to move the masses, often transmutes itself into disillusionment—particularly evident in Malmanche's plays and later in the poetry of Roparz Hemon (1900–1978).

Most 20th-c. Breton writers of note are inextricably associated with the Breton movement. *Gwalarn*, founded in 1925—the first literary magazine—was originally a supplement to the political periodical *Breiz atao*, whose title means "Brittany forever." Its aim, under the guidance of Roparz Hemon, was to produce works of distinction far superior to the sadly decadent peasant literature, and free from French influence. Instead of escaping from their cares to the land of fairies, *Gwalarn* writers found solace in prose portraiture of contemporary society, as in the short stories of Jakez Riou (1899–1937) and Roparz Hemon, and in Hemon's novel *Nenn Jani* (1974; Nenn Jani).

The influence of Irish and Welsh literatures is all-pervading. Plays by Hemon and by Fant Rozenn Meavenn (b. 1911) have been influenced by the Dublin Abbey Theatre Group, while poets such as Hemon and Gwilherm Berthou Kerverzioù (1908–1951) treat themes from Irish mythology. Welsh short-story writers influenced Fanch Elies (1896–1963), and later Ronan Huon (b. 1922), of the new school of the journal *Al liamm*, founded in 1949, which continued the work of *Gwalarn*, suppressed after World War II by the French authorities.

Today, although preoccupation with worldwide contemporary moral and social injustices is increasingly noticeable in the works of the new generation, the strong sense of identity is as tenacious as ever.

BIBLIOGRAPHY: D'Erm, C. Le Mercier, *Les bardes et poètes nationaux de la Bretagne armoricaine* (1919); Gourvil, F., *Langue et littérature bretonnes* (1952); Piette, J. R. F., "Modern Breton Poetry," *Poetry Wales*, 3, 1 (1967): 3–10, and 3, 3 (1967): 25–32; Denez, P., "Notes on Modern Literature in Breton," *AWR*, 19 (1971): 19–33; Piriou, Y. -B., *Défense de cracher par terre et de parler breton* (1971); Denez, P., "Modern Breton Literature," in J. E. Williams, *Literature in Celtic Countries* (1971); Durand, P., ed., *Breizh hiziv: Anthologie de la chanson en Bretagne* (1976)

—RITA WILLIAMS

Occitan Literature

Occitan (frequently, but not accurately, referred to as Provençal outside France, and also known as *langue d'oc*) is a language of southern France comprising a number of dialects, including Provençal (in the restricted sense of the dialect of Provence). A great body of troubadour poetry was written during the Middle Ages in this language, but following a decree of Francis I in 1539 making French the language of his kingdom, Occitan was suppressed and produced few literary works until the 19th c., when the Félibrige revival movement, led by Joseph Roumanille (1818–1891), was founded in 1854.

The Félibrige movement, the fruit of a moral, aesthetic, and political retreat to the countryside, resulted in some major literary successes, but it did not lead to a general revival of the language. The Avignon School, the first incarnation of the Félibrige movement, produced an artist of noble ambitions in Théodore Aubanel (1829–1886), who sensitively expressed the clash between strict Catholicism and a pagan exaltation of the flesh. Above all, the Félibrige movement brought Frédéric Mistral (1830–1914) to world literature. This epic poet, with *Mirèio* (1859; *Mirèio*, 1872), *Calendau* (1867; Calendau), and *Lou pouèmo dóu Rose* (1896; *Anglore: The Song of the Rhone*, 1937), succeeded in revitalizing

for the modern world the rhythms, the splendor, and the spirit of the poetry of old. Mistral, called a "new Homer" after *Mirèio* and recipient of the Nobel Prize in 1905, came to symbolize an unfortunately illusory redemption of the condemned language.

The Félibrige, however, continued in its efforts to reawaken all the regions in which the *langue d'oc* was spoken. Among dozens of talented writers the best were the Gascon Michel Camélat (1871–1962), a wonderfully rough epic poet of the Pyrenees; the Provençal Joseph d'Arbaud (1872–1950), who developed an incantatory prose for Occitan; and Antonin Perbosc (1861–1944) from Quercy, who gave a new impetus to impersonal lyricism.

By around 1930 the Félibrige had outlived its effectiveness. It was at that time that a modern Occitan literature was founded on the pursuit of three fundamental and complementary goals: the perfection of a written language freed from French dominance; the elaboration (under Catalan influence) of the reasons for the demand for autonomy; and the desire for literary MODERNISM. The Society for Occitan Studies, which became the Institute for Occitan Studies in 1945, addressed itself to the first and third of these aims. Among prominent writers of this generation, Renat Nelli (b. 1906), a scholar of the Middle Ages and a poet of great strength influenced by Paul VALÉRY, in *Arma de vertat* (1952; soul of truth) presented the experience of love with philosophical anxiety. Very different is Max Rouquette (b. 1908), a lyrical poet and a prose writer who with wonder but also sorrow vividly portrays Mediterranean Languedoc. Joan Mouzat (b. 1905) of Limousin is a learned poet, like the dazzling Paul-Louis Grenier (1879–1954), but Mouzat sometimes leaps into the realm of the fantastic. Léon Cordes's (b. 1913) poetry, fiction, and drama are firmly planted in his time and land.

The writers who came to prominence after World War II added to these achievements a strong desire to standardize the Occitan language, to treat the most varied subjects, and to turn their backs on regionalism. It is not for the author of this article (Robert Lafont, b. 1923) to discuss his own poems, plays, novels, and essays. Among the other postwar writers, Henri Espieux (1923–1971) wrote poetry of a somber glow. The mystical, violent poet Bernard Manciet (b. 1923) moved from modernist, cosmopolitan odes to the mysterious prose of his novels of the Landes soil, such as *Lo gojat de novémer* (1954; the young man of November). Pierre Bec (b. 1921), whose poetry is very dense, has recently turned to dreamlike or realistic fiction, as in *Contes de l'unic* (1977; tales of the unique). The most important writer of this generation is Joan Boudou (1920–1975). Starting with folkloric prose, in the manner of the Félibrige, he was able, without abandoning regional subjects, to introduce into Occitan literature the great themes of the contemporary era: the loneliness of man at war; the dizzying gaze at the emptiness of destiny; the constant anguish over the absurd. He essayed the fantastic novel—*La santa Estela del centenari* (1960; the hundredth anniversary of Saint Estelle's Day); the historical novel—*La quimèra* (1974; the chimera); and the rural chronicle—*Lo libre de Catòia* (1966; the book of Catòia).

A very different group of writers appeared after 1956. Among its members is the poet Serge Bec (b. 1933), who denounced colonial wars in *Memòria de la carn* (1960; memory of the flesh). The novelist Pierre Pessemesse (b. 1931), who began with a chronicle of Provençal boyhood, *Nhòcas e bachòcas* (1957; wounds and bruises), portrayed an entire era in *De fuòc amb de cendre* (3 vols., 1973–78; fire and ashes). The poets Yves Rouquette (b. 1936) and Jean Larzac (b. 1937) moved from personal to political works. Christian Rapin (b. 1931) is a very accomplished poet, while Robert Allan's (b. 1927) verse is spontaneous and whimsical.

In 1968, a year of political and social turmoil in France, there was an upheaval in Occitan culture. The modern Occitan ballad—at the same time lyrical and aggressive—came into being through dozens of songwriter-singers; a new, militant drama stirred audiences, and formal experiments in other literary genres proliferated. Among writers who came to the fore, outstanding are Roland Pécout (b. 1948), at first a poet, then a writer of fiction portraying the modern world adrift; Roselyne Roche (b. 1946), whose poems chronicle the life of a woman; Florian Vernet (b. 1941), writer of absurdist works of fiction and drama; Jan dau Melhau (b. 1948), a rough novelist from Limousin; and the poet Joël Meffre (b. 1951).

Modern Occitan literature, now robust, is built on the very paradox of the mortal dangers threatening its language. These very dangers have led to an awakening: the need for the survival of Occitan language and culture has now penetrated the public consciousness.

BIBLIOGRAPHY: Camproux, C., *Histoire de la littérature occitane* (1953); Rouquette, J., *La littérature d'oc* (1968); Lafont, R., and C. Anatole, *Nouvelle histoire de la littérature occitane* (1971); Lafont, R., *Clefs pour l'Occitanie* (1971): 131–51; Nelli, R., *La poésie d'oc* (1972); Armengaud, A., and R. Lafont, eds., *Histoire d'Occitanie* (1979), passim

—ROBERT LAFONT

FRENCH CARIBBEAN LITERATURE

When they arrived during the early 17th c., French settlers on the Caribbean islands of Haiti, Martinique, Guadeloupe, and later in French Guiana on the South American mainland, brought to their New World plantations the institutions and cultural norms of their homeland. The African slaves who were forcibly transported to these places maintained certain aspects of their ancestral cultures, while creating new forms in the context of plantation society. The literature of the French-speaking Caribbean therefore reflects the political problems, cultural ambiguities, and aesthetic challenges and achievements resulting from this encounter between varying traditions and systems of values.

Haiti. The uniqueness of Haiti's history is reflected in its literature. Haiti was the first black republic, created by the only successful slave revolt in history. But slavery and racism left Haitian culture with an inferiority complex. The first writers wrote not about Haiti, but in imitation of the French romantics, Parnassians, and symbolists. Haiti's journalists were more original; they influenced the essayist of the end of the 19th c. who responded to Joseph Arthur de Gobineau's (1816-1882) *Essai sur l'inégalité des races* (1853; Essay on the Inequalities of Races). The early Haitian works of contemporary significance are Louis Janvier's (1855-1911) *L'égalité des races* (1884; The Equality of Race), Antenor Firmin's (1850-1911) *De l'égalité des races* (1885; On the Equality of Races), and Hannibal Price's *De la réhabilitation de la race noire* (1900; On the Rehabilitation of the Black Race).

The first timid steps toward exploring the unique originality of Haitian culture in fiction were taken early in the 20th c. The

American occupation beginning in 1915 caused Haitian intellectuals to examine their history and social situation more closely. Jean Price-Mars (1876-1969) published *Ainsi parla l'oncle* in 1928 (Thus Spoke the Uncle, 1987), a landmark in Haiti's self-awareness. Instead of eschewing the folklore of the Creole language, Price-Mars proclaimed its value. In 1927 *La revue indigène* was founded to assert a Haitian identity rooted in Creole culture. Jacques ROUMAIN, political leader and writer, was central to the development of the Indigenist movement and probably Haiti's most important 20th-c. writer. The founder of the Haitian Communist Party may be viewed as the first to conceptualize what we now label the "Third World" with his phrase "the wretched of the earth" from the poem "Sales nègres" (Dirty Negroes). In his early works, during the 1930s, Roumain depicted the Haitian peasants, their Vaudou religion, and the sociopolitical dynamics of his country. His two masterpieces were published after his premature death: *Gouverneurs de la rosée* (1944; Masters of the Dew, 1947) and the collected poetry, *Bois d'ébène* (1945; Ebony Wood, 1972). The other major name of the Ecole indigéniste, Carl Brouard (1902-1965), is known for his dramatic poetry. His poems "Nous" (Us) and "Vous" (You) are still quite alive. Two contemporaries of Roumain left their mark: Phillippe THOBY-MARCELIN, the author of *La bête de Musseau* (1946; The Beast of the Haitian Hills, 1946), and Jean-Fernand Briere (b. 1909), known for plays, poetry, and a single novel, who spent most of his life in exile in Senegal.

Beside Roumain, the two Haitian writers best known outside Haiti are René DEPESTRE and Jacques-Stephen Aléxis (1922-1961), both disciples of Roumain who used their magazine *La Ruche* to produce the coup in 1946. Unfortunately, the victory of the revolt forced them into lives of exile. Despestre was only nineteen when his *Étincelles* (1945; Sparks) made him one of Haiti's leading poets. Of his many volumes of poetry, *Un arc-en-ciel pour l'occident chrétien* (1967; A Rainbow for the Christian West, 1972) and *Poète à Cuba* (1976; Poet in Cuba) received most attention. He later turned to stories, *Alléluia por une femme-jardin* (1981; Halleluia for a Woman-Garden), and novels, notably *Hadriana dans tous mes rêves* (1988; Hadriana in All My Dreams), which won the Prix Renaudot.

Aléxis published three novels and one volume of tales in the late 1950s before becoming a martyr in the struggle against Papa Doc Duvalier. *Compère Général Soleil* (1955; Comrad General Sun) recounts the effort to politicize Haitian peasants and their massacre as migrant workers in the Dominican Republic under Trujillo. *Les arbres musiciens* (1957; The Musician Trees) describes the attack on the practitioners of Vaudou in the early 1940s by the Catholic church backed by American rubber planters.

Duvalierism forced most Haitian writers into exile after 1957. Roger Dorsinville (1911-1992) was prolific, but his "African" novel, *Kimby ou la loi de Niang* (1973; Kimby or the Law of Niang) is best known. Franck Etienne (b. 1936) shook Haitian literature by writing the first novel in Creole, *Dezafi* (1975; Disaffection), translated into French as *Les affres d'un défi* (1979; The Pangs of a Challenge). Marie Vieux CHAUVET is the most well-known Haitian woman writer, primarily for her trilogy entitled *Amour, colère, folie* (1968; Love, Anger and Madness, 1980).

A number of Haitians have settled in Quebec, especially in Montreal. Among the Canadian Haitians are Anthony PHELPS, best known for his novel *Moins l'infini* (1972; Minus the Infinite); Gérard Etienne (b. 1936), author of *Le nègre crucifié* (1974; The Crucified Negro); Dany Laferrière (b. 1953), author of *Comment faire l'amour avec un nègre sans se fatiguer* (1985; How to Make Love with a Negro without Tiring); Emile Ollivier (b. 1940), with novels such as *Mère solitude* (1983; Mother Solitude) and *Passages* (1994; Passages); and Max Dorsinville (b. 1938), author of *James Wait et les lunettes noires* (1995; James Wait and the Black Glasses).

Two writers who continue to describe the life of Haitian peasants are Pierre Clitandre (b. 1954) and Jean-Claude Fignolé (b. 1942) with their respective novels *Cathédrale du mois d'août* (1980; Cathedral of the Month of August) and *Les Possédés de la pleine lune* (1987; The Possessed of the Full Moon).

Martinique. The struggle for independence in the 18th c. having been ruthlessly repressed, Martinique, Guadeloupe and French Guyana remain French possessions. The literature of these territories has been closely related to that of France. The Martiniquais René MARAN served for many years as a colonial administrator in French Africa, where he collected the information he put into Goncourt Prize-winning novel *Batouala, véritable roman nègre* (1921; *Batouala: A Negro Novel*, 1922), one of the first depictions of colonialism. Maran went on to write many other volumes, including *Un homme pareil aux autres* (1947; A Man Like the Others), dealing with subtle aspects of racism.

Aimé CÉSAIRE, who is given credit for the first published use of the word "NÉGRITUDE" in his *Cahier d'un retour au pays natal* (1939; Memorandum on My Martinique, 1947), was influenced by the work of students slightly older than himself during his studies in Paris in the 1930s. There he met Léopold Sédar SENGHOR from Senegal and Léon-Gontran DAMAS from French Guyana; the three created their theory of a new pride and bold defense of the black race by 1937 when Damas published *Pigments* (Pigments), a volume of polemical poetry in jazz-influenced style. In 1938 Césaire published the first edition of his *Cahier d'un retour au pays natal*, a long poem in essay form, with dramatic stories encapsulated, in which he combined psychology, philosophy, and politics in his manifesto of Négritude. Césaire went on to combine his political work as Député-Maire with a rich literary career. After writing several volumes of rather surrealistic poetry, now available in *The Complete Poetry* (1983), a bilingual edition, he turned to theater to better communicate his ideas to common people, presenting *La tragédie du roi Christophe* (1963; The Tradegy of King Christophe, 1969), about the revolutionary king of Haiti, and *Une saison au Congo* (1967; A Season in the Congo, 1969) about the assassination of Patrice Lumumba. His biography of *Toussaint Louverture* (1961), the leader of the slave revolt in Haiti, is an effort to pursue Roumain's theories of decolonization.

The novels of Mayotte CAPÉCIA, *Je suis Martiniquaise* (1946; I Am a Woman from Martinique) and *La négresse blanche* (1950; The White Negress), may be viewed as antithetical to Négritude in using fiction to describe the existential situation of women and those of mixed race. She drew the ire of Frantz Fanon (1925-1961) who used her novels as examples of the complex he documented in *Peau noire, masques blancs* (1952; *Black Skin, White Masks*, 1967). After receiving his doctorate in psychiatry in France, Fanon was sent to administer the French mental hospital at Blida in Algeria, where he joined the Front de Libération Nationale fighting to end French rule. After describing the political, psychological, and cultural aspects of the war of liberation in two volumes of essays, he produced his sweeping study of the disappointments of "independence," *Les damnés de la terre* (1961; *The Wretched of the Earth*, 1965), which documented the structures of "decolonization."

His four volumes may be considered an extension and modification of Négritude using professional psychological and sociological methods.

Joseph Zobel (b. 1915) produced many volumes of short stories and novels using social realism to show the limits of Négritude theory, but his novel *La rue cases-nègres* (1950; *Black Shack Alley*, 1980) is best known. It inspired a very young filmmaker from Martinique, Euzham Palcy (b. 1957), to transform the story of the love between a young boy and his grandmother into a touching film, *Sugar Cane Alley* (1983).

Literary theoretician, poet, and novelist Edouard GLISSANT invented the theory of "Antillanité" to replace Négritude, emphasizing historical milieu over race. His novel, *La lézarde* (1958; *The Ripening*, 1959), has been followed by many historical novels. His *Le discours antillais* (1981; *Caribbean Discourse*, 1989) inspired his followers to develop their theory of *créolité*.

A maverick not associated with identity theories, Daniel MAXIMIN, the young shooting star of Caribbean literature, explored the cultural ties that unite the islands and France, especially for the younger generation, in his novels *L'isolé soleil* (1981; *Lone Sun*, 1989) and *Souffrières* (1987; Souffrières).

In 1989 Jean Bernabé (dates n.a.), Patrick CHAMOISEAU, and Raphael Confiant (b. 1951) published *Eloge de la créolité. Créolité* immediately swept aside Négritude and Antillanité. The many works of Chamoiseau and Confiant, and also of Ernest Pépin (dates n.a.) present their island and its culture as a rather quaint folkloric place peopled by colorful characters drawn from recent legend. Chamoiseau's *Texaco* (1992; *Texaco*, 1997) won the Goncourt Prize. Confiant wrote several novels in Creole before switching to French. His *Le nègre et l'amiral* (1988; The Negro and the Admiral) and *Eau de café* (1991; Coffee Water) are best known.

Ina Césaire (dates n.a.) has made a name for herself by also writing in both Creole and French. Her most important work to date is a play, *Mémoires d'Isles, Maman N. et Maman F.* (1983; Memoirs of Islands, Mama N. and Mama F.).

Guadeloupe. Martinique's sister island, Guadeloupe, is more rural and agricultural; women writers have dominated its literary development. Simone SCHWARZ-BART was the first Francophone black woman from either the Caribbean or Africa to publish an important work. Her novel, *Pluie et vent sur Télumée Miracle* (1972; *The Bridge of Beyond*, 1974), opened the third wave of black Francophone writing (after Négritude and the novel), which is characterized by women writers and feminist themes. Her other important novel is *Ti-Jean l'Horizon* (1979; *Between Two Worlds*, 1981).

Novelist, professor, playwright, and world traveler Maryse CONDÉ is more prolific. Her *Hérémakhonon* (1976; *Heremakhonon*, 1982) was a surprising best-seller. The novel was later revised in French and republished with the title *En attendant le bonheur* (1988; While Waiting for Happiness). Her two-volume novel, *Ségou: les murailles de terre* (1984; *Segu*, 1987) and *Ségou: la terre en miettes* (1985; *The Children of Segu*, 1989), narrated the epic panorama of West African history. The shorter novel, *Moi, Tituba, sorcière . . . noire de Salem* (1986; *I, Tituba, Black Witch of Salem*, 1992), is the only important work set primarily on her native island.

Gisèle PINEAU leads the younger generation of women writers, her *Papillon dans la cité* (1992; Butterfly in the City) takes her protagonist from the islands to public housing in the Parisian suburbs.

Before the dominance of women writers, Guy Tirolien (b. 1917) put his island on the literary map with his poetry, *Balles d'or* (1961; Golden Balls), while Jean-Louis Baghio'o (b. 1915) had received recognition for his novels, especially *Le flamboyant à fleurs bleues* (1973; The Flame Tree with Blue Flowers).

French Guyana. This small territory, with an even smaller population, has suffered a long histroy of colonial neglect. Léon-Gontran Damas, one of the fathers of Négritude as we have seen, documented and protested this negligence in his *Retour de Guyane* (1938; Return to Guyana). The most important writer since Damas has been Bertène Juminer (b. 1927), who has written four novels, all exploring the psychological alienations produced by the rigorous French policy of assimilation. The two best known are *Les bâtards* (1961; *The Bastards*, 1989) and *Le revanche de Bozambo* (1968; *Bozambo's Revenge: or, Colonialism Inside Out*, 1976). *Les bâtards* describes the wrenching return of three medical students from France to Guyana, while *Le revanche de Bozambo* is a satire imagining a world of cultural reversal in which the colonized are European. The most prominent contemporary poet is Elie Stephenson (b. 1944), the author of several noteworthy collections, including his major contribution entitled *Terres mêlées* (1984; Struggle for the Land).

BIBLIOGRAPHY: Fowler, C., *A Knot in the Thread: The Life and Works of Jacques Roumain* (1978); Herdeck, D., *Caribbean Writers: A Bio-Biographical-Critical Encyclopedia* (1979); Depestre, R., *Bonjour et adieu à la négritude* (1980); Arnold, A. J., *Modernism and Négritude: The Poetry and Poetics of Aimé Césaire* (1981); Chamoiseau, P., and Confiant, R., *Lettres créoles Tracées antillaises et continentales de la littérature 1635-1975* (1981); Glissant, E., *Le discours antillais* (1981); Hoffmann, L. F., *Le roman haitein: idéologie et structure* (1982); Séonnet, M., *J-S Akexus ou "le voyage vers la lune de la belle amour humaine"* (1983); Ormerod, B., *Introduction to the French Caribbean Novel* (1985); Antoine, R., *La litérature franco-antillaise* (1993)

—HAL WYLIE

FRENCH GUIANA LITERATURE
See French-Caribbean Literature

FREUD, Sigmund

Austrian neurologist, founder of psychoanalysis, b. 6 May 1856, Freiberg (now Přibor), Moravia; d. 23 Sept. 1939, London, England

F.'s impact on writers and critics in the 20th c. is incalculable. This is so for various reasons: F. was a systematic, and at the same time complex, thinker, but he did not create a static psychological or sociological system; within his work there are numerous inconsistencies, some of them resulting from the evolution of his views between 1900 and 1938 on psychic structure, anxiety, and the vicissitudes of human instincts; his work has been distorted and over-simplified in translation and summary, and the "Freud" of one writer or critic is often far different from the "Freud" of another. F. was not merely a revolutionary psychological thinker; he created a movement that evolved differently in different countries, even during his lifetime, and his own work cannot be considered coterminous with psychoanalysis as a historical phenomenon. F.'s

own thinking exhibits the flexibility, restlessness, dogmatism, and openness of a man in search of inclusive laws of human psychological functioning. He cannot be justly summarized, and the history of his impact on writers and critics, mediated as it is by textual, personal, and national differences, is yet to be written.

Nevertheless, major aspects of F.'s thinking that have been widely influential in the literary world can be defined. These include (1) his theory of the essence and functions of dreams; (2) his ideas on symbolism; (3) his views on language; (4) his ideas on play, art, and the artist; (5) his specific views on various literary works and authors; and (6) his ideological bias. In these areas F.'s work exhibits a mixture of traditional philosophical, aesthetic, and scientific assumptions with radically challenging insights into the dynamic functions of psychic activity. While he accepted a naïve realism that regarded the external world as essentially indifferent to human desires, he also demonstrated the extensive role of "psychic reality" in determining the forms of experience and conflict. While he accepted the romantic idea that the function of art was self-expression, he also demonstrated that the strategies of art were the strategies of the human mind. And while he accepted and built on the language of 19th-c. science, with its metaphors of mechanisms, hydraulics, and impersonal forces, he also developed a language of explanation, interpretation, and meaning that is wholly psychological in its aims and methods.

Dreams

F. regarded *The Interpretation of Dreams* (1900) as his most important work, and he continued to revise it until his death. "The interpretation of dreams is the royal road to a knowledge of the unconscious activities of the mind," he declared, yet he also wrote that dreams are "nothing other than a particular form of thinking, made possible by the conditions of the state of sleep." Dreams, then, provided F. with normal examples of psychic activity that also displayed itself in waking life, pathological symptoms, and creative works. He distinguished dreams from other mental activity by their primary function, which, he argued, is to preserve the sleeping state by transforming residual memories of daily experiences into compromise formations that fulfill unconscious wishes. Unconscious wishes are the motives for the dream, and the form of the dream, F. showed, can be explained as a set of defensive transformations that reveal the wish even as they disguise it. Dreams are, in short, meaningful symbolic expressions.

F.'s "formula" for defining the nature of dreams shows his characteristic way of thinking about mental life in general: "A dream is a (disguised) fulfillment of a (suppressed or repressed) wish." The dream is thought of as a substitute for the wish the dream reveals. Being resolutely dualistic in his thinking, F. divided the dream into manifest content and latent dream thoughts. The manifest dream is the dream as it is retained in conscious memory, and the latent dream thoughts are the unfulfilled unconscious wishes. F. assumed that the meaning of the dream as a symbolic expression could only be determined by a technique of interpretation that decomposes the manifest dream. The manifest dream is a paratactical structure and the process of interpretation uses the free associations of the dreamer to each element in this structure to translate it into a syntactic structure. Interpretation is required because the process of dream formation (the dream work) leaves protective gaps in the memory of the dreamer. The interpretation seeks to approach, but can never completely provide, a continuous "history" of the dreamer. F. decomposed the dream in order to recompose the unconscious continuity of the dreamer's psychic life. His method rests on the assumption that the wish transformed by the dream work can only be revealed in censored form because it represents or derives from erotic or aggressive impulses too extreme to tolerate, often left over from infancy. The manifest dream is a disguised synthesis of the dreamer's present experience and his infantile experience. Interpretation seeks to disclose this synthesis by deviously stripping the dream of its disguise.

F.'s interpretative aim was genetic, locating the essential meaning of the dream in its origin, the unconscious wish, but he also developed a structural theory by describing the techniques of the defensive process, the dream work. Dreams, he argues, are formed by a primary-process mode of thinking. This process is characterized by condensation, displacement, symbolism, and other techniques of distortion such as reversal of affect and splitting of representations united in the dream thoughts. The primary process disregards the material limits of reality in favor of the omnipotence of thoughts, and all the techniques of the dream work are forms of (disguised) affirmation, there being no negation in unconscious thought processes.

The process of interpretation translates primary-process ideation into secondary process, discursive language. The secondary-process mode is grammatical and rational, and takes considerations of external reality into account. F. considered the secondary process superior to the primary process because it recognizes the differences between fantasy and reality, thought and action, omnipotence and the limitations of the mind and body. He thought dreams delusional and regressive departures from the rational, however meaningful they are as symbolic expressions of unconscious wishes.

F. set no limits on the process of interpretation, because he recognized that each element of the manifest dream was potentially overdetermined. That is, one manifest dream image may be the condensed expression of many latent dream thoughts, and any one latent dream thought may manifest itself in many images. Any element in the dream may serve multiple functions. Although he compared the dream to a rebus and a hieroglyphic, F. did not advocate a one-to-one translation of manifest into latent contents, except in the case of certain symbols he regarded as universal, symbols of the parts of the human body, intimate personal relations, and ultimate human concerns, such as birth, death, and exposure. The dreamer, being an "entrepreneur," could use such symbols to invest his thought, but the meaning of his dream could not be limited to them.

Symbolism

Although F. treated dreams and other psychic expressions as symbolic activity, he reserved the name of symbolism for a special class of substitutive images or words. In this restricted usage a symbol is an unconscious identification of an image or word with a repressed idea of the body or of intimate bodily relationships or of instinctual fears and desires. A symbol is a distortion of the real, caused by intrapsychic conflict. Without such conflict there would be no need for the mislocation of affects involved in symbol formation, and hence no symbols in the strictly Freudian sense. If a spear is a phallic symbol, this is so because the affect associated with the phallus is only acceptable to consciousness in disguised form.

F. regarded symbolism from a rationalist point of view, as a residue of primitive thinking. A phylogenetic mode of identifying words and things, especially sexual things, was, he believed,

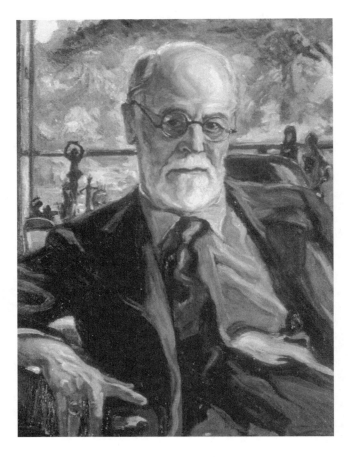

Sigmund Freud

recapitulated in human ontogeny and retained in unconscious, primary-process thinking. His aim was to demythologize this primitive mode of thought in the interest of scientific progress. All symbols are illusions that require interpretation to break the link between words, things, and images, and the unconscious objects, wishes, or fears with which they are confused. For F., all symbols are to be interpreted "downward," toward the bodily and archaic roots from which they arise. Money, for example, is never in this strictly Freudian sense a symbol of wealth, but can be a symbol of feces. A ring does not symbolize marriage, but can symbolize the female genitals.

For F., the study of symbolism was an important link between psychoanalysis and other fields, such as philology, folklore, and the study of religion. He returned frequently to the study of symbols, in *Introductory Lectures on Psycho-Analysis* (1916–17), *New Introductory Lectures on Psycho-Analysis* (1933), and elsewhere, never abandoning his "downward" reading. In fact, he accumulated quite a number of "dream-book" symbolic translations, which he warned against being used as a substitute for free associations. Since F., the theory of symbolism has become the most widely known, used, and misused aspect of his thought, although many subsequent Freudians have expanded and revised the theory. Ernest Jones (1916) and Sandor Ferenczi (1912) stated the orthodox theory, and it has been reinterpreted and transformed by Melanie Klein (1930), Marion Milner (1952), Charles Rycroft (1956), Hannah Segal (1957), Jean Piaget (1951), Ernst Kris (1952), Norman O. Brown (1959), and others.

Language

F.'s emphasis was on language as an expressive phenomenon. He did not develop a theory of language as a symbolic system. Nevertheless, in interpreting dreams and free associations he made psychoanalysis into an almost purely verbal psychology. The subject of analysis is the precise language of the analysand, and the "peculiar plasticity of the psychical material" is revealed by the plasticity of language itself. F. compared the dream works to writing a poem: he saw in both processes the aim of formulating an unconscious fantasy in disguise. "There is no need to be astonished at the part played by words in dream formation," he wrote. "Words, since they are nodal points of numerous ideas, may be regarded as predestined to ambiguity; and the neurosis (e.g., in framing obsessions and phobias), no less than dreams, make [sic] unashamed use of the advantages thus offered by words for purposes of condensation and disguise." Words, like clothes, take the shape of what they hide, and F. regarded them as the primary medium of unconscious disclosure.

One reason for F.'s emphasis on words was his assumption that they originate in images and that they can represent more primitive modes of expression and relationship. "Things that are symbolically connected today were probably united in prehistoric times by conceptual and linguistic identity," he wrote in *The Interpretation of Dreams.* In primary-process ideation, words assumed their "original" concrete functions, and F. showed how word representations could act like thing representations in widely disparate contexts, from delusions and dreams to jokes, poems, and ordinary social discourse. In *The Antithetical Sense of Primal Words* (1910), F. linked the strategies of reversal and antithetical meaning in ancient languages with the strategies of unconscious thinking in general, and he said that "we should understand the language of dreams better and translate it more easily if we knew more about the development of language." This is F. at his most "original." He believed that the unconscious wishes and strategies revealed in and by linguistic structures could be reduced to their beginning in some actual social situation, a prehistoric world in which symbolic events were literally acted out.

Such a belief is not required for us to recognize F.'s immense contribution to the understanding of literary forms and meanings. In *Jokes and Their Relation to the Unconscious* (1905) he investigated the techniques of the joking process, and he showed how jokes and the comic share the strategies of dreams and use condensation, displacement, and other transformations to encourage social identifications between tellers and auditors. In jokes the dream work becomes art work, sharable symbolic communication that uses the devices of literary form: puns, composite words, allusions, double entendre, metaphorical and literal meanings, synecdoche. The informing principle of the joke, he showed, is a sharable economy of psychic expenditure, and jokes thus depend as much for their effects on timing, rhythm, and tone as they do on choice of words. Jokes make language a medium of catharsis and a form of gratifying erotic and aggressive wishes. In short, the joke as F. analyzed it comprises a prototypical example of the strategies of literature in general and offers a way of relating these strategies to their social context.

After 1905 F. continued to explore the linguistic expression of psychic dynamics, and almost all of his works contain instances of verbal play in normal and pathological contexts. In "The Uncanny" (1919) he approached his subject through its linguistic expressions, showing how *unheimlich,* or unfamiliar and strange sensations, are rooted in the *heimlich,* or familiar and homelike. An analysis of "The Sandman" by E. T. A. Hoffmann (1776–1822) provided his central example of the aesthetics of the uncanny, but he also related it to Shakespeare, Sophocles, Heine, Schiller, and other writers. In *Humour* (1927) he returned to the subject of the comic, distinguishing humor from other comic expressions by its alliance with the parental consolations of the superego. In general, although F. offered no theory of language as a symbolic system, he showed many parallels between the structure of language and the structure of the mind.

Play, Art, and the Artist

Much of F.'s analysis of linguistic strategies in dreams, jokes, and literary works implicitly considers language a form of play. He showed how the human mind is inherently playful. "The opposite of play is not what is serious but what is real," he wrote in "Creative Writers and Day-Dreaming" (1908). F.'s most important discussion of play, in *Beyond the Pleasure Principle* (1920), presents the example of a child's game in which his absent mother is represented by small objects that are hidden and retrieved in a symbolic expression of the mother's loss and recovery. The child in play turns a passively experienced loss into an active repetition of the painful experience. F. interpreted the game as an act of symbolic mastery that reveals its origins even as it announces the renunciation of the instinctual satisfaction associated with the actual presence of the mother. The game has an economic motive; it provides pleasure in mastery where there was pain in loss, and it is also a substitute for the lost relationship. F. calls the child's game a "great cultural achievement" because it marks the transition from biological to symbolic expression, from instinct to ego control.

In "Creative Writers and Day-Dreaming" F. views the literary work as "a continuation of and a substitute for what was once the play of childhood." Art is thus a substitute for a substitute, and it is a continuation of play because it shares the aim of the child, which is to manipulate a symbolic medium to disguise and disclose unconscious erotic and aggressive wishes and conflicts. Art is at once a regressive activity and a way for the artist to transform past experiences into a present, though illusory, reality. In "The Claims of Psycho-Analysis to Scientific Interest" (1913) F. wrote: "Art is a conventionally accepted reality in which, thanks to artistic illusion, symbols and substitutes are able to provoke real emotions. Thus art constitutes a region halfway between a reality which frustrates wishes and the wish-fulfilling world of the imagination—a region in which, as it were, primitive man's strivings for omnipotence are still in full force."

F. saw three special aspects of the artist's personality: (1) the laxity of repression; (2) unusually strong instinctual drives; and (3) extraordinary capacity for sublimation. The artist needs and is able to use past, usually infantile, wishes provoked by occasions in the present to create "a picture of the future." Art is thus a synthetic as well as a regressive activity, and although the artist is like the child at play, he is also, for F., a person to be envied for his access to unconscious knowledge. "Creative writers are valuable allies," F. wrote in his study (1907) of Wilhelm Jensen's (1837–1911) "Gradiva," "and their evidence is to be prized highly, for they are apt to know a whole host of things between heaven and earth of which our philosophy has not yet let us dream."

F. believed that the power of the artist over his audience consisted in his ability to provoke and manipulate shared unconscious desires over which the artist had an extraordinary control that matched his extraordinary psychic conflict. The privacy of dreams and daydreams becomes in artistic productions a higher form of wishfulfilling confession, precisely because the confession can be shared and, in some mysterious way, must be shared by the audience. Although F. did begin to develop a theory that could account for this confessional bond in his book on jokes (his explication of the role of identification), he did not expand on it systematically in later works. He regarded all his writings on the nature of the artist and his power as mere beginnings, tentative explorations of an area he thought psychoanalysis could not conquer for science. "Unfortunately, before the problem of the creative artist, analysis must lay down its arms," he wrote in "Dostoevsky and Parricide" (1928).

Specific Works and Authors

Although F. renounced the hope of completely divulging the artist's secret powers, he did not hesitate to write both casual and extensive interpretations of specific works and writers. As early as 1897 he announced, in a letter to Wilhelm Fliess, the relationship between his discovery of the Oedipus complex and the unconscious appeal of *Oedipus Rex* and *Hamlet*. In *The Interpretation of Dreams* he repeated his conviction that these works anticipated and confirmed his most important discovery, the son's ambivalent relation to the father and his desire to possess the mother sexually.

Fuller interpretations followed. In "Psychopathic Characters on the Stage" (written 1905–6, pub. 1942), he discussed the cathartic power of dramatic illusions, using *Hamlet* again as an example. The play, he argued, offers us "forepleasures" that divert our attention from the real sources of its emotional power, repressed impulses we share with the hero. In 1906 F. wrote his most elaborate literary interpretation, *Delusions and Dreams in Jensen's "Gradiva"* (1907). Treating the protagonist as an actual person, F. constructed interpretations of his dreams, offering associations that Jensen did not offer. He described the parallels between the cure for delusions in the story and the analytic method he developed with Josef Breuer. He demonstrated that the delusion of the protagonist of "Gradiva" was a transformation of a repressed incestuous relationship between a brother and sister in their childhood.

The study of Jensen's "Gradiva" was followed by "Some Character Types Met within Psycho-Analytic Work" (1916) and studies of Leonardo da Vinci (1910), Michelangelo's "Moses" (1914), Goethe (1917), and Dostoevsky (1928). In "Some Character Types" F. used characters from Shakespeare and Ibsen to illustrate forms of pathological character structure. His aim was to show the "complete agreement" between some literary characters and personalities encountered in clinical experience. He also explored the mechanisms by which the dramatist is able to "overwhelm us by his art and paralyze our powers of reflection." F. asserted that the "laws of poetical economy" are designed to overcome our resistance to the deeper motives of the work by providing superficial motives derived from them.

In each of the works on individual authors F. read visual or verbal expressions of the artist back into his unconscious or childhood biography, and the psychoanalytic method becomes a way of discovering the intention of the artist's work or life in its origin, a procedure that duplicates the interpretation of dreams. Leonardo is shown to have embodied the details of his childhood experience in the enigmatic figures of the "Mona Lisa" and the "Saint Anne"; Michelangelo, F. speculated, embodied an intense ambivalence in his "Moses," who seems frozen between rage and renunciation; Goethe revealed his childhood desire to eliminate a

sibling rival in his "screen memory" of throwing crockery out of a window; and F. read Dostoevsky's posthumous papers, his epilepsy, and his gambling, each as an expression of his Oedipal struggle with his father.

F. was aware of the incompleteness of these works. Nevertheless, he believed throughout his life and artists shared the insights of psychoanalysis and that an essential part of his work was to translate their work into scientific explanation.

F.'s Ideological Bias

F. viewed the development of the individual in society as a process of restriction and renunciation of instinctual desires. His emphasis is almost always on the ways paternal social authority enforces the repression of childhood wishes. In describing the development of the individual and his relation to the cultural world, F.'s language is almost always that of battle, power, victory, and defeat. He compared character development to the progress of an army that leaves troops behind at points of potential conflict (fixation points), and he regarded these defensive maneuvers as the minimal price civilization claimed of the individual in exchange for participation in an order maintained by the power of the group. In *Civilization and Its Discontents* (1930), F. wrote: "Human life in common is only made possible when a majority comes together which is stronger than any separate individual and which remains united against all separate individuals." Human beings, he thought, are primarily hostile to one another. Pathological symptoms are the result of conflicts between the demands of civilization and the instinctual impulses too extreme for the individual to tolerate consciously, and, as such, they are only quantitatively different from the normal order of things.

F. derived his anti-instinctual view of civilization from the innate ambivalence of human beings. The child's conflict between love and hate for the father could only be resolved, he thought, by the child's internalization of the father's threats of reprisal against forbidden actions. The child identifies with the feared aggressor and becomes civilized because he represses both his own desires and the memory of the conflict with the father's authority. The internalization of the father's authority is seen as an essential step in the acceptance of reality. It marks the transition from the pleasure principle to the reality principle, which teaches the child to seek gratifications in accord with the demands of the external world.

F.'s tendency to equate the demands of reality with the demands of the father derives from his Oedipal model of development. That is, although F. saw an explanation of the hostility and defiance of individuals towards society in the son's Oedipal struggle with paternal authority, his Oedipal theory actually determines his view of this antagonism. By viewing reality through the eyes of the son and the father, F. projected this antagonism onto society as a whole, and then explained social relations by recourse to their origins in father-son conflict. Then, society is seen as creating, in turn, the conditions for father-son conflict.

Another consequence of his emphasis on the father-son relationship is F.'s almost complete neglect of the role of the mother in the development of the child. His views are one-sided, and his relative neglect of the pre-oedipal phases of the boy's development leaves him unable to account for the important phases of the girl's development that parallel the boy's. Hence, he had no context in which to describe the way children take in and integrate the anatomical difference between the sexes, only the limited concept of penis envy. In general, F.'s patriarchal bias led him to overemphasize the power of the Oedipus complex to account for both individual and social relationships.

He did, however, refer in late writings to the "oceanic" importance of the early mother-child relationship, and a major achievement of post-Freudian psychoanalysis has been the study and understanding of the formative role of pre-Oedipal development.

F.'s Influence on Writers

The impact of Freudian ideas has been felt by every major writer of the 20th c. Especially in America, "Freudianism" had become part of intellectual discourse and popular culture by the 1920s. In both Europe and America, however, F.'s influence varied immensely, depending on the particular writer's knowledge of F.'s works and judgment of their significance. F.'s ideas were assimilated to the interests of the century, and writers shared his focus on the inner life, the plasticity of language, the crises of Western society, and the meaning of civilization. "One could be influenced in this sphere," Thomas MANN wrote, "without any direct contact with his work, because for a long time the air had been filled with the thoughts and results of the psychoanalytic school."

Franz KAFKA knew F.'s theories in detail, and his work comprises a profound exploration of the father-son relationship and the meaning of the law in society. Yet he regarded F.'s ideas as approximations of the truth, and he thought that biographical explanations of his work were "too facile." He had not faith in psychoanalysis as a therapy and distrusted F.'s rationalist bias. For Kafka, religion was not an illusion but a reality; for F. religion was to be overcome by scientific knowledge. Kafka and F., although they had much in common, adhered to profoundly different world views.

Thomas Mann, however, felt deep sympathy with F.'s thinking. He defended psychoanalysis as a legitimate scientific comprehension of the demonic aspect of the psyche, and he agreed with F.'s view that psychoanalysis was a work of ego-strengthening, "a reclamation work," as F. said, "like the draining of the Zuyder Zee." For Mann, F. had established the ground for "the building of a new anthropology . . . which shall be the future dwelling of a wiser and freer humanity." Mann also shared F.'s ideas about the links betwween ontogeny and phylogeny; he saw the timeless life of dreams as a link between the primitive and the mythical. History, for Mann, is shaped by mythical recurrence. In *Joseph and His Brothers* Mann embodied this view of history and dreams, and he openly acknowledged his affinity with F. in *F. and the Future*. F. stood for the heroic powers of the intellect in its struggle against the irrational forces devastating the West in these years.

Among writers in English, F.'s stature varied widely. James JOYCE undoubtedly absorbed psychoanalytic ideas in his later linguistic polymorphousness, and there are many references, ironic and skeptical, to psychoanalysis in *Ulysses* and *Finnegans Wake*. Joyce's relation to F., however, is, like his relation to many other writers, incorporative rather than submissive, and his development of interior monologue and dream language reflects his own psyche more than the writings of psychoanalysts.

It was D. H. LAWRENCE who responded most extensively to F.'s theories. In *Psychoanalysis and the Unconscious* and *Fantasia of the Unconscious*, Lawrence attacked the intellectual, "cerebral" aspect of psychoanalysis. He thought that psychoanalysis was a fad, that F. advocated the removal of sexual inhibitions, and he rejected the theory of infantile sexuality. Lawrence advocated

intuitive, vitalistic, spontaneous "blood" knowledge, as opposed to F.'s cognitive approach. He thought that the moral function of art was to express a passionate, undidactic appeal to bodily consciousness. Lawrence's attitudes reveal a profound rejection of F.'s scientific approach and an ambivalent attitude toward F.'s discoveries.

Other writers reveal a wide spectrum of responses to F. Dylan THOMAS studied F.'s works and thought that "poetry must drag further into the clean nakedness of light more even of the hidden causes than F. could realize." W. H. AUDEN's *In Memory of S. F.* acknowledges the profound impact of F. on this century. Conrad AIKEN studied F. as early as 1909 and realized that aesthetics had its source in the emotional life F. revealed. André BRETON and the SURREALISTS saw in F.'s new access to the dream world an ultimate ground of reality, and referred often to F.'s ideas. In his forewords Vladimir NABOKOV unflaggingly addresses sarcastic "words of encouragement to the Viennese delegation" that would read biographical interpretations into literary works and sees the "little Freudian" as a "sleuth" who invades his privacy. Among poets, H. D. (Hilda DOOLITTLE) is unique, in that she was analyzed by F. *Tribute to F.* records her analysis and her ambivalent respect for F.'s thought. Henry MILLER saw psychoanalysis as a liberating force, but objected to its scientific focus. William FAULKNER's style of representing the flow of consciousness undoubtedly owes much to the impact of psychoanalysis. Eugene O'NEILL's dramatizations of the family reveal a deep affinity with F.'s thinking. Among contemporary Americans, Saul BELLOW and Philip ROTH reveal personal acquaintance with psychoanalysis in their portrayals of Jewish character.

The continuing profound impact of F.'s personality and thought is best illustrated in D. M. Thomas's (b. 1935) *The White Hotel* (1981), a brilliant novel that includes F. as a character as it explores a woman's life and sensibility in the traumatic years of European crisis between 1909 and 1941. Thomas's imagination shows how Freudian influence transcends allegiance to F.'s particular theoretical views.

In general, F.'s influence, although pervasive, derives from the identification of his thought with the main currents of literary experiment, especially focus on dreams, the associative representation of consciousness, and confessional modes of writing. His influence on writers has derived, as he foresaw, more from shared concern with human character than from detailed study of his works, and, where he is rejected, more from antithetical styles of thinking than from rational counterargument.

F.'s Influence on Critics

From within the psychoanalytic movement and outside of it Freudian literary criticism has paralleled the development of psychoanalytic theory. F. and many of his followers turned to literature to explicate the unconscious dynamics of writers' and characters' minds. Of all writers, Shakespeare has received the most attention, and a very large body of psychoanalytic commentary has grown around his works. Ernest Jones's studies of *Hamlet* began appearing in 1910, and by 1949, when Jones's *Hamlet and Oedipus* was published, the impact of Freudian thought had produced major works on creative writers by analysts and literary critics.

Early psychoanalytic criticism focused almost exclusively on unconscious motivation, and on such motifs as incestuous desires, Oedipal rivalry, and childhood fixations in the lives and works of artists. Albert Mordell's *Erotic Motive in Literature* (1919) represents this emphasis. Although shunned as "reductive" by most literary critics, this style of criticism continued to be written by analysts, and the works of Sandor Ferenczi, for example, contain many references to and interpretations of literary themes. Otto Rank's studies of the incest motif in myth and literature and *The Myth of the Birth of the Hero* (1909) explore creative and pathological expressions of childhood fantasies and their cultural derivatives. In the 1930s Marie Bonaparte's *Psychoanalytic Interpretations of Stories of Edgar Allan Poe* (1933) was representative of the focus on symbolic decoding prevalent in Freudian interpretation.

The 1930s also saw the development of psychoanalytic ego psychology and serious discussion of Freudian aesthetics by major literary critics. Kenneth BURKE's essay "F. and the Analysis of Poetry" (1939) explored F.'s interpretive strategies that treat the poem as a dream and concluded that they must be supplemented by mapping the literary work also as a "prayer" and a "chart" of associations, and by adding an interpretation of "matriarchal symbolizations" to F.'s patriarchal ones. Burke found F. "not dialectical enough," but has, for almost forty years, produced major criticism that is often markedly psychoanalytic. The criticism of William EMPSON, especially *Seven Types of Ambiguity* (1931), also shows the extensive influence of psychoanalysis in its interpretations of the linguistic designs of poetry.

Lionel Trilling's essay "F. and Literature" (1947) is perhaps the most positive affirmation of F.'s relevance for criticism written by a literary critic before 1950. "The Freudian psychology," Trilling wrote, "is the only systematic account of the human mind which, in point of subtlety and complexity, of interest and tragic power, deserves to stand beside the chaotic mass of psychological insights which literature has accumulated through the centuries." Trilling recognized that "the Freudian psychology is the one which makes poetry indigenous to the very constitution of the mind." Trilling's work has been a major force in American criticism, and through him informed psychoanalytic interpretation has reached a wide audience.

In the 1940s and 1950s Freudian criticism appeared at an accelerating pace. Frederick J. Hoffman's *Freudianism and the Literary Mind* (1945) chronicled the influence of F. on major writers. Edmund Bergler's *The Writer and Psychoanalysis* (1950) probed the infantile origins of the writer's fantasy life. In 1952 Ernst Kris's important book *Psychoanalytic Explorations in Art* greatly expanded the range of psychoanalytic theory in relation to painting and poetry and made extensive use of ego psychology as opposed to early focus on id psychology. In 1957 Simon O. Lesser's comprehensive psychoanalytic view of literature, *Fiction and the Unconscious*, appeared. Many Freudian studies, such as Phyllis Greenacre's *Swift and Carroll* (1955), applied contemporary theories to their subjects. In 1957 William Phillips collected major psychoanalytic statements in *Art and Psychoanalysis*. Although still not widely accepted, psychoanalytic criticism had become recognized as an academic reality in England and America.

In the 1960s the influence of psychoanalysis on critics continued to expand. Biographical studies—*Goethe: A Psychoanalytic Study, 1775–1786* (2 vols., 1963) by Kurt R. Eissler and *Joseph Conrad: A Psychoanalytic Biography* (1967) by Bernard C. Meyer—were published, and critical studies such as *Sins of the Fathers: Hawthorne's Psychological Themes* (1966) by Frederick C. Crews and *Allegory: The Theory of a Symbolic Mode* (1964) by Angus Fletcher represent the range of Freudian influence. In 1968 Norman N. Holland published *The Dynamics of Literary Response*, a systematically developed model of psychoanalytic interpretation. This book and Holland's *Psychoanalysis and Shakespeare* (1966)

made him the foremost psychoanalytic literary critic in America. The 1960s also saw the publication of psychoanalytic criticism dealing with aesthetics, the problems of interpretation, and applied studies of individual writers in numerous anthologies.

Contemporary Freudian criticism draws largely on post-Freudian theories of pre-Oedipal development and on the view that literature is a complex, overdetermined phenomenon. Although F.'s views of art and the artist are influential, they have been supplemented by the reorientations of theory since his death. This combination of older and newer Freudianism can be seen in recent criticism, such as *Psychoanalysis and Literary Process*, edited by Frederick Crews (1970), Norman N. Holland's *Poems in Persons* (1973), and Mark Shechner's *Joyce in Nighttown* (1974). In Europe and America reinterpretations of F. continue to yield a wide range of critical styles. The influence of theorists like Erik Erikson, D. W. Winnicott, and Margaret Mahler can be seen in such works as *Representing Shakespeare: New Psychoanalytic Essays* (1980), edited by Murray M. Schwartz and Coppélia Kahn, Richard Wheeler's *Shakespeare's Development and the Problem Comedies* (1981) and Coppélia Kahn's *Man's Estate: Masculine Identity in Shakespeare* (1980)—to take only examples of Shakespearean criticism. Other works, such as Diana George's *Blake and Freud* (1980), interpret F. and poetic visions in relation to one another. A French style of Freudian interpretation has developed around the theories of Jacques Lacan, and it is producing new critical works, such as *The Fictional Father: Lacanian Readings of the Text* (1981), edited by Robert Con Davis. Prominent journals, such as *New Literary History, Diacritics*, and *Critical Inquiry* often feature Freudian interpretation. In its various forms, Freudian criticism remains very alive in intellectual discourse.

See also Psychology and Literature

FURTHER WORKS: *Gesammelte Schriften* (12 vols., 1924–1934; *Collected Papers of S. F.*, 5 vols., 1959); *Gesammelte Werke* (18 vols., 1952 ff.); *Briefe* (1960; *Letters of S. F.*, 1960); *S. F. und C. G. Jung: Briefwechsel* (1974; *The F.-Jung Letters*, 1974). FURTHER WORKS IN ENGLISH: *Complete Psychological Works: Standard Edition* (24 vols., 1953–1966)

BIBLIOGRAPHY: Phillips, W., ed., *Art and Psychoanalysis* (1957); Fraiberg, L., *Psychoanalysis and American Literary Criticism* (1960); Ruitenbeek, H., ed., *Psychoanalysis and Literature* (1964); Malin, I., ed., *Psychoanalysis and American Fiction* (1964); Ruitenbeek, H., ed., *Literary Imagination: Psychoanalysis and the Genius of the Writer* (1965); Manheim, L. and E., eds., *Hidden Patterns* (1966); Kaplan, M., and Kloss, R., *The Unspoken Motive: A Guide to Psychoanalytic Literary Criticism* (1973); Crews, F., *Out of My System: Psychoanalysis, Ideology, and Critical Method* (1975); Holland, N. N., *5 Readers Reading* (1975); Bersani, L., *A Future for Astyanax: Character and Desire in Literature* (1976); Gordon, D. J., *Literary Art and the Unconscious* (1976); Roazen, P., *F. and His Followers* (1976); Tennenhouse, L., ed., *The Practice of Psychoanalytic Criticism* (1976); Timpanaro, S., *The Freudian Slip: Psychoanalysis and Textual Criticism* (1976); Gay, P., *F., Jews, and Other Germans: Masters and Victims in Modernist Culture* (1978); Sherman, M. H., ed., *Psychoanalysis and Old Vienna: F., Reik, Schnitzler, Kraus* (1978); Brivic, S. R., *Joyce between F. and Jung* (1979); Orlando, F., *Toward a Freudian Theory of Literature* (1979); Sulloway, F. J., *F.: Biologist of the Mind* (1979); Kaufman, W., *Discovering the Mind, Vol. 3: F.*

versus Adler and Jung (1981); Meisel, P., ed., *F.: A Collection of Critical Essays* (1981)

—MURRAY M. SCHWARTZ

FREYRE, Gilberto

Brazilian anthropologist, social historian, essayist, and novelist (writing in Portuguese and English), b. 15 March 1900, Recife; d. 18 July 1987, Recife

Son of an educator and judge, F. completed his elementary and secondary studies at an American Protestant school in Recife, chosen by his father against the wishes of the Catholic family. He went to the U.S. to study at Baylor University in Texas and at Columbia University. His thesis, "Social Life in Brazil in the Middle of the 19th Century," is evidence of his early interest in Brazil's social history and especially the life of the slave. After travel and further study in Europe, he returned to Brazil. After that, in addition to occasional lectures at a number of universities, he devoted most of his time to writing.

F. is best known for his books on Brazilian patriarchal society—*Casa grande e senzala* (1933; *The Masters and the Slaves*, 1946) and *Sobrados e mucambos* (1936; *The Mansions and the Shanties*, 1963). These two volumes, considered national classics, can be read as sociology, anthropology, social history, and social psychology; but they are also great works of literature, written in a conversational style. In the first volume he analyzed the complex, often violent Brazilian family life of the colonial period (1500–1822). He examined the three main ethnic groups—the native Indian, the Portuguese colonizer, and the African slave—in the hybrid, almost feudal, agrarian society that existed in Brazil for about 300 years. His detailed descriptions of every aspect of life, including customs, health habits, clothing, cooking, evoke in the reader a sense of the culture as a whole. We are shown every member of this society in his or her role—the white master, his wife, his concubines, the children, the black slaves, the nomadic Indians—and their relationships with each other.

F.'s ultimate theme in *Casa grande e senzala* is the exploration of the question that haunted Brazilians: Had miscegenation damaged and debased their country? F.'s unorthodox conclusion was that the mixed racial heritage of the people of Brazil was not a liability, but in fact a great asset; it enriched Brazilian culture. From both biologial and cultural points of view, Brazilians could be proud of their ethnic multiplicity.

Sobrados e mucambos focused on the decline of the all-powerful rural patriarch and the development of urban society from the late 1700s to the late 1800s, including the years 1822–89, when Brazil was an independent empire ruled by a monarchy. Here too F. treated in intimate detail the facts of everyday life. He traced the transition of power from the country to the city and the rise of mulattoes to positions of authority.

Brazil: An Interpretation (1945; written in English, and expanded in 1959 as *New World in the Tropics*) is an introductory manual to F.'s sociological ideas about Brazil. It is a synthesis of F.'s main theories about Brazil's unique tropical culture. He stressed Brazil's achievements: an integration of the races and regional diversity within political unity.

Dona Sinhá e o filho padre (1964; *Mother and Son*, 1967), which the author calls a "semi-novel," marked F.'s debut in fiction. It is of importance on two accounts. First, with its intersection of psychological planes and its use of actual newspaper clippings interspersed with the fictional narrative, it is structurally innovative. Second, through sociological knowledge and poetic insight, it deals humanely and objectively with male homosexuality, a subject not previously treated in such a manner in the Brazilian novel.

F.'s later published works reveal his expanded horizons. *O outro amor do Dr. Paulo* (1977; the other love of Dr. Paulo), his second semi-novel, is a combination of an exposé of Brazilians living in exile in late 19th-c. Paris, a narrative of their travels through Europe and their return to Brazil, and a slowly developing love story with a tragic ending. To move back in time and place, to impart veracity to characters, and to permit the inclusion of discussions and interpretations, F. utilized the technique of an informant, an elderly Brazilian exile who told the story of his friend in 1937 to F., who many years later puts it into book form. One suspects this work reveals much of F. himself as a writer and Brazilian.

Through his writings, F. has inspired Brazilians to reassess their history and culture and to change their attitude from self-disparagement to national pride. Although some have criticized his methods, ideas, and style, it cannot be denied that his works are statements of central importance about Brazil. He has been duly credited for his extraordinary contribution to Brazil's new pride in its racial mixture.

FURTHER WORKS: *Apologia pro generatione sua* (1924); *A propósito de Dom Pedro II* (1925); *Bahia de todos os Santos e de quase todos os pecados* (1926); *O estudo das ciências sociais nas universidades americanas* (1934); *Guia prático, histórico e sentimental da cidade do Recife* (1934); *Artigos de jornal* (1935); *Mucambos do Nordeste* (1937); *Nordeste* (1937); *Conferências na Europa* (1938); *Açúcar* (1939); *Olinda: 2.° guia prático, histórico e sentimental de cidade brasileira* (1939); *Uma cultura ameaçada: A luso-brasileira* (1940); *Um engenheiro francês no Brasil* (1940); *O mundo que o Português criou* (1940); *Atualidade de Euclydes da Cunha* (1941); *Região e tradição* (1941); *Ingleses* (1942); *Continente e ilha* (1943); *Problemas brasileiros de antropologia* (1943); *Na Bahia em 1943* (1944); *Perfil de Euclydes e outros perfis* (1944); *Sociologia, I* (1945); *Ulisses* (1945); *Modernidade e modernismo na arte política* (1946); *Ordem, liberdade, mineiridade* (1946); *Ingleses no Brasil* (1948); *Joaquim Nabuco* (1948); *O camarada Whitman* (1948); *Guerra, paz e ciência* (1948); *Nação e exército* (1949); *Quase política* (1950); *José de Alencar* (1952); *Manifesto regionalista de 1926* (1952); *Aventura e rotina* (1953); *Um Brasileiro em terras portuguesas* (1953); *Um estudo do Prof. Aderbal Jurema* (1954); *Assombrações do Recife velho* (1955); *Reinterpretando José de Alencar* (1955); *Sugestões para uma nova política no Brasil: A urbana* (1956); *Integração portuguesa nas trópicos* (1958; *Portuguese Integration in the Tropics*, 1961); *Sugestões em torno de uma nova orientação para as relações internacionais no Brasil* (1958); *A propósito de frades* (1959); *A propósito de mourão, rosa e pimenta: Sugestões em torno de uma possível hispanotropicologia* (1959); *Em torno de alguns túmulos afrocristãos de uma área africana contagiada pela cultura brasileira* (1959); *Ordem e progresso* (1959; abridged, *Order and Progress*, 1970); *Brasis, Brasil e Brasília* (1960); *Uma política transnacional de cultura paro o Brasil de hoje* (1960); *Sugestões de um novo contato com universidades europeias* (1961); *O Luso e o trópico*

(1961); *The Portuguese and the Tropics*, 1961); *Arte, ciência e trópico* (1962); *O Brasil em face das Áfricas negras e mestiças* (1962); *Homem, cultura e trópico* (1962); *Talvez poesia* (1962); *Vida, forma e cor* 1962); *Brazil* (1963); *O escravo nos anúncios de jornais brasileiros do século XIX* (1963); *A Amazônia brasileira e uma possível lusotropicologia* (1964); *O estado de Pernambuco e sua expressão no poder nacional* (1964); *Retalhos de jornais velhos* (1964); *Forças armadas e outras forças* (1965); *Seis conferências em busca de um leitor* (1965); *The Racial Factor in Contemporary Politics* (1966); *O Recife, sim!: Recife, não* (1967); *Sociologia da medicina* (1967); *Como e porque sou e não sou sociólogo* (1968); *Contribuição para uma sociologia da biografia* (1968); *Oliveira Lima, Dom Quixote gordo* (1968); *A casa brasileira* (1971); *Nós e a Europa germânica* (1971); *Seleta para jovens* (1971; *The G. F. Reader*, 1974); *A condição humana e outros temas* (1972); *Pernambuco sim* (1972); *Estácio Coimbra, homem representativo do seu meio e do seu tempo* (1973); *Além do apenas moderno* (1973); *O brasileiro entre os outros hispanos* (1975); *A presença do açúcar na formação brasileira* (1975); *Tempo morto e outros tempos* (1975); *Obra escolhida* (1977); *Alhos & bugalhos* (1978); *Cartas do próprio punho* (1978); *Prefácios desgarrados* (1978); *Heróis e vilões no romance brasileiro* (1979); *O de casa!* (1979); *Tempo de aprendiz* (1979)

BIBLIOGRAPHY: Hanke, L., "G. F., Brazilian Social Historian," *Quarterly Journal of Inter-American Relations*, 1 (July 1939): 24–44; Stein, S. J., "F.'s Brazil Revisited," *HAHR*, 41 (1961): 111–13; Tannenbaum, F., Introduction to *The Mansions and the Shanties* (1963): vii–xii; Mazzara, R. A., "G. F. and José Honório Rodrigues: Old and New Horizons for Brazil," *Hispania*, 47 (1964): 316–25; Skidmore, T., "G. F. and the Early Brazilian Republic: Some Notes on Methodology," *Comparative Studies in Sociology and History*, 6 (1964): 490–505; Loos, D. S., "G. F. as a Literary Figure: An Introductory Study," *RHM*, 34 (1968): 714–20; Martins, W., *The Modernist Idea* (1970): 204–6, 294–99; Holloway, T. H., on *The G. F. Reader, Historian*, 38 (1976): 353–54

—ELIZABETH R. SUTER

FRIEDELL, Egon

Austrian critic, essayist, and dramatist, b. 21 Jan. 1878, Vienna; d. 16 March 1938, Vienna

F. was the youngest son of Moriz Friedmann, a Jewish cloth manufacturer. Shortly after his birth his mother deserted her husband and three children. After the death of F.'s father in 1891 his governess took care of him, keeping house for him until her death in 1917. F. continued his education in Frankfurt, Baden near Vienna, Berlin, and Heidelberg, and after several unsuccessful attempts he finally graduated from secondary school at Bad Hersfeld in 1899.

Having left the Jewish fold in 1897, F. converted to Protestantism two years later. He studied German literature and philosophy at the University of Heidelberg, where he received the degree Doctor of Philosophy in 1904 on the basis of a dissertation on Novalis, the philosophic poet of early German romanticism. This degree qualified F., as he put it, to become artistic director of the Vienna cabaret

Fledermaus (from 1905 to 1910). During those years he wrote several comedies, farces, and parodies in collaboration with Alfred POLGAR, including *Goethe* (or *Goethe im Examen*, 1908; Goethe taking a test), a witty sketch satirizing professorial pedantry in which F., also an actor, frequently played the title role over a period of three decades.

Until the outbreak of World War I, F. was codirector of the avant-garde Intimes Theater in Vienna. Between 1906 and 1924 he also produced translations or editions of Emerson, Hebbel, Georg Christoph Lichtenberg (1742–1799), Carlyle, Hans Christian Andersen, and Macaulay, as well as writings in the fields of literary history and drama criticism. In 1914 F. volunteered for military service but was rejected for physical reasons.

From 1924 on he was associated with Max Reinhardt, appearing in a variety of roles in Reinhardt's theaters in Vienna and Berlin. A few days after the Anschluss, F., who was about to be arrested by two SA men, committed suicide by jumping from a window of his bachelor apartment in Vienna, in which he had lived since 1900.

F.'s very versatility—he was a historian, a philosopher, a critic, an aphorist, an actor, a cabaret wit, a Falstaffian raconteur, a bohemian, and a dilettante in the grand manner—makes his stature somewhat difficult to assess. His first published work was his study *Novalis als Philosoph* (1904; Novalis as philosopher); it bore the name Friedell, though the name change did not become official until 1916. In 1912 F. published *Ecce Poeta*, a study of his friend Peter Altenberg (1859–1919), to whom F.'s collection of writings by and about him, *Das Altenbergbuch* (1922; the Altenberg book), is also devoted. F.'s unconventional five-act play *Die Judastragödie* (1920; the Judas tragedy), performed at the Vienna *Burgtheater* in 1923, portrays Judas as a tragic hero; it was followed in 1921 by an essayistic prose pendant entitled *Das Jesusproblem* (the Jesus problem). F.'s aphorisms appeared in 1922 as *Steinbruch* (quarry), and in the same year F. demonstrated his kinship with Johann Nestroy (1801–1862) by editing *Das ist klassisch!* (that's a classic!), a collection of the satirical dramatist's wit and wisdom.

F.'s magnum opus is *Kulturgeschichte der Neuzeit* (3 vols., 1927–31; *A Cultural History of the Modern Age*, 3 vols., 1930–32), a highly original, brilliant, aphoristic, stylistically notable intellectual and cultural history ranging from the Renaissance to World War I. It bears the subtitle "Die Krisis der europäischen Seele von der Schwarzen Pest bis zum Weltkrieg" ("The Crisis of the European Soul from the Black Death to World War I"). An equally ambitious two-volume *Kulturgeschichte des Altertums* (a cultural history of antiquity), on which F. started working in 1933, remained incomplete: *Ägypten und Vorderasien* (Egypt and the Near East) appeared in 1936 (and was reissued in 1947 as *Kulturgeschichte Ägyptens und des alten Orients* [a cultural history of Egypt and the ancient Orient]); *Kulturgeschichte Griechenlands* (a cultural history of Greece) was issued posthumously in 1940 and 1949.

FURTHER WORKS: *Der Petroleumkönig; oder, Donauzauber* (1908, with A. Polgar); *Soldatenleben im Frieden* (1910, with A. Polgar); *Von Dante zu D'Annunzio* (1915); *Kleine Philosophie* (1930); *Die Reise mit der Zeitmaschine* (1946; repr. as *Die Rückkehr der Zeitmaschine*, 1974); *F.-Brevier* (1947); *Das Altertum war nicht antik* (1950); *Kleine Portraitgalerie* (1953); *Aphorismen zur Geschichte* (1955); *Briefe* (1959); *Ist die Erde bewohnt?* (1961); *Aphorismen und Briefe* (1961); *Wozu das Theater?* (1965); *E. F.s Konversationslexikon* (1974); *abschaffung des Genies. Essays bis*

1918 (1982); *Stelbstanzeige Essays ab 1918* (1983); *Steinbruch. Kleine Philosophie* (1991)

BIBLIOGRAPHY: Polgar, A., "A Great Dilettante," *AR*, 10 (1950): 232–46; Haage, P., *Der Partylöwe, der nur Bücher fraß* (1971); Dencker, K. P., *Der junge F.* (1977)

—HARRY ZOHN

FRIEL, Brian

Irish dramatist and short–story writer, b. 9 Jan. 1929, Derry

F. grew up in the Irish province of Ulster, living in County Tyrone in Northern Ireland but spending extensive vacations in his mother's native County Donegal in the Irish Republic. F. was educated primarily in Derry, Northern Ireland's second largest city, where his father was born and worked as a teacher. At St. Patrick's College, Maynooth, the national seminary of the Republic, F. studied for the priesthood, but took a B.A. instead and taught for a decade in Derry. He currently lives in rural Donegal, and has earned an international reputation as Ireland's finest living dramatist.

Critics tend to categorize F.'s career: In its first phase he writes short fiction and tentatively tries theatrical form; F. then bursts upon Broadway and the world stage as a mature dramatist of character–based drama; that drama then develops a political–critical perspective and ensemble–acting style to accommodate historical fact and its cultural context; and in its current phase his plays identify and focus on language as the structural agency of both the ideological and dramatic dialectic. While within and across these categories doublings and larger groupings by theme and device proliferate, the basic taxonomy discovers a development in the writing of the plays and rediscovers the process of reading–seeing them by progressive contextualizing.

F.'s fiction, published regularly in the late 1950s and early 1960s in American magazines, rests firmly in the tradition of the great Irish short–story writers. Following the dictum and practice of Frank O'CONNOR, the stories collected in *A Saucer of Larks* (1962) and *The Gold in the Sea* (1966) reveal the lives of an intimately observed subculture, the residents, mostly poor and working class, of the border territory and towns of Ulster. The epiphanies, or telling lack of them, that characterize James JOYCE'S short fiction appear in F.'s, with pronounced ambivalence. The charge that F. ignores the border and its political significance can be countered by claims that his work represents and demonstrates the stultifying, fallow politics of Northern Ireland, that the recurrent appearance in the stories of an outsider thematically implies a border, and that epiphanies map experiential and spiritual borders by transcending them.

The characters and their struggles and the mature, complex tone of the stories are also the strengths of F.'s early drama. After having several plays produced on radio and one on the stage, F. retired as a teacher and turned his talent toward the theater. In 1962 the Abbey Theatre produced *The Enemy Within* (1975), considered F.'s first successful play, a historical drama of St. Columba in exile on Iona, an island off western Scotland. Columba, who would become the patron saint of Derry, is tested, his blood ties to his troubled family set against his monastic vows and responsibilities, presenting in a dramatic character the borderland of conscience and how conflicting demands make exile, no matter what the choice, inevitable.

The second stage of F.'s career as a writer begins with a trip to Minneapolis in 1963 to study dramaturgy with the famous director Tyrone Guthrie. This commitment to drama resulted in *Philadelphia, Here I Come* (1965), which premiered at the Dublin Theatre Festival in 1964 and went on to become an international hit in New York on Broadway and in the West End in London. The play details the themes from *The Enemy Within* of exile and paralyzing ambivalence effected by conflicting desires and claims on the conscience; it also shows a new confidence in F.'s handling of dramatic form, incorporating flashbacks and the innovation of dramatizing the interior life and divided nature of the main character, Gar O'Donnell, by portraying him with two personae, Public Gar, who interacts with the other characters, and Private Gar, the embodied inner monologue of the thoughtful, willful, desperate, lonely protagonist. A less novel though more enduring invention is the town of Ballybeg (from *baile beag*, Irish for "small town"), the setting for *Philadelphia, Here I Come* and a number of other F. plays. Northern, dreary, socially stratified, with a church, a school, an aristocratic big house, and fields and forest and an army base hard by, Ballybeg provides ample ground for every conflict of class and creed, age and youth, desire and responsibility.

F.'s character–based drama continued with *The Loves of Cass Maguire* (1966), about a feisty, vibrant exile returned to Ireland to live out her days in a retirement home and slowly succumb to stagnant though sweet illusion, and *Lovers* (perf. 1967, pub. 1969), a pairing of two one–acts, *Winners*, an ironically titled tale of young love and hopes annihilated, and *Losers*, based on one of F.'s short stories about a man who gets his hoped–for love and whose life is diminished as a result. The experiments in dramatic form continue, too, with direct address to the audience, rhapsodic passages, and dramatic irony proceeding from manipulation of narrative. None are outright innovations, but their use demonstrates F.'s displacement of the conventions of his realistic fiction within the expressionistic poetic tradition of the drama of W. B. YEATS, John Millington SYNGE, Sean O'CASEY, and Samuel BECKETT. *Crystal and Fox* (perf. 1968, pub. 1970) opens with a play within the play and proceeds to reckon the withering effects of an itinerant performer's efforts to shed the artifice from his life; in *The Gentle Island* (perf. 1971, pub. 1973) the focus shifts from the traveling troupe of outsiders in the previous play to a family in sole possession of an island, Inishkeen, off Donegal, their sterile, stony existence, and the impact of visitors on the layered narratives of illusion and repressed truth.

Chronologically aberrant in this categorization is *The Mundy Scheme* (perf. 1969, pub. 1970), a farcical satire on the venality of Irish politics. Slight in the virtues of the serious drama from the same period, the work is less concerned with depth of character than it is with the shallow soundings of public life. Seriousness came with Bloody Sunday, 30 January 1972, when a civil rights march in Derry ended with the deaths of thirteen protesters (a fourteenth died months later) shot by the British army. F.'s response, *The Freedom of the City* (perf. 1973, pub. 1974), fictionally posits similar events, delves into their meaning for the doomed participants, and comments upon them in diverse discourses, both partisan and ostensibly objective, resulting in various "official" versions. Some critical opinion maintains that *The Gentle Island* has historical themes in a symbolic mode, Inishkeen, hardscrabble and abandoned, its society/family repressed and violent, standing for Ireland, but *The Freedom of the City* (another bitterly ironic title) is overtly, if equivocally, concerned with historical fact and how it is determined. *Volunteers* (perf. 1975, pub. 1979) returns to the theme of *The Mundy Scheme*, the state–abetted mortgaging of Ireland's heritage in the name of economic development. F.'s genius for dramatic compression is evident in the setting, the pit of an archaeological dig in Dublin soon to be the site of a hotel; the action is contained in claustrophobic quarters, while the whole history of the island is laid bare in the exposed earth.

The plays based on conflicts in the life of a single central figure—Columba, Gar, Cass—have given way to a drama of ensemble playing in which the conflict is among a social set of well–wrought characters; any historical truth can only be the sum total of their understanding. The return to Ballybeg in F.'s next two productions, *Living Quarters* (perf. 1977, pub. 1978) and *Aristocrats* (perf. 1979, pub. 1980, based on one of F.'s stories, "Foundry House"), domesticates this theme. Both works bring families together in reunions; in the former, a narrator represents the factual history to which the surviving characters return in memory; in the latter, an outsider helps salvage the remnants of a family falling from ascendancy. The settings suggest borders, real and symbolic: the detached living quarters of a military man, where heroism and suicide define the limits of public and private struggle; and Ballybeg Hall, on the outskirts of town, the scene of shifting perspectives caused by slippage in the socioeconomic strata.

The Faith Healer (perf. 1979, pub. 1980) carries the theme of the cumulative, relative nature of truth to its logical formal conclusion. The drama is fractured into four monologues by three characters covering the same events. The characters do not, cannot, communicate with one another, and the audience must make a whole of the narrative. The breakdown of the ensemble indicates the reduction of the sociopolitical element in F.'s work to its deconstructed ground, the *logos* of the monologue, the word, speech, language. Voices, internal and official, accents, jargon, rhetoric, quotation, and song have filled F.'s oeuvre from the first radio plays, but in this next phase of his career, language moves from prominence to primacy as means and theme. The metaphor of the faith healer as artist does not exhaust the primal, visionary substance of the drama, but it does initiate a new perspective in F.'s writing from which to reconsider his craft to that point. His next effort, *Translations* (perf. 1980, pub. 1981), was the maiden production of the Field Day Theatre Company, of which F. was a founder. With its openly political agenda, Field Day found in this historical drama—set in an outdoor school outside Ballybeg in 1833, on the theme and occasion of the remapping of Ireland by the British army, symbolic of the indigenous population's disenfranchisement—an apt inauguration. But as the title implies, *Translations* most significantly concerns communication, education, the facility and futility of language when vernacular is outlawed and the idiom of conquest dominates even the illegal education of the peasantry hidden behind hedges and hay sheds. *The Communication Cord* (perf. 1982, pub. 1983) updates the theme and academic context, though ironically the setting is a gentrified peasant cottage near Ballybeg. Employing farcical situations with satirical significance, F. mines the comic potential in dislocations similar to those that result in more dire consequences in *Translations*. Still, language fails, history is trivialized, and education is by accident. Some comedy.

F.'s preoccupation with character, language, and ambivalence led him in 1981 to translate Anton CHEKHOV'S *Three Sisters* into

an Anglo–Irish idiom (this is the play he saw rehearsed during his apprenticeship at the Guthrie Theater). The fit is natural; a Chekhovian sensibility is apparent in a number of F.'s works, most notably *Aristocrats*, which has been called "The Potato Orchard." In 1987 *Fathers and Sons*, F.'s dramatization of Turgenev's novel, premiered. Its conflict of academic theory and frustrating nature, of language and action, of naming and being, defines behavioral borders of lethal subtlety.

F.'s latest plays pair off to demonstrate his range, reiterate his themes, and further develop his formal dexterity. *Making History* (1988) dramatizes the events surrounding the Battle of Kinsale, which resulted in the Flight of the Earls, the first important emigration of native Irish, and the subsequent plantation of Protestant loyalists on their property, laying the foundation for the partition of Ulster in the 20th c. Astride this historical border at the turn of the 16th into the 17th c. stands the figure of Hugh O'Neill, Earl of Tyrone, heroic in accounts by Catholic partisans of the Counter–Reformation, by his own account compromised. The dialectic of events and accounts makes history; in *Dancing at Lughnasa* (1990) the terms of the dialectic are reduced to inaction and silence. Still, when circumstance and language fail the five Mundy sisters of Ballybeg, they find refuge and expression in music and dancing. Their brother, a failed missionary, reprises with characteristically pregnant pathos a character from F.'s 1963 stage and radio play *The Blind Mice*; the unsentimental narration that cuts hope off short and spares no innocent is classic F. The rituals that sustain culture and incarnate desire give *Dancing at Lughnasa* resources of nonverbal knowledge and communication that tap the motive powers and inspiration of drama itself. It seems that F.'s work is broaching another category of radical dramatic techniques and effects. The Broadway production won the 1992 Tony Award for best play.

A list of the salient features of F.'s drama makes apparent his talents: the vocal variety, including numerous tonalities of soliloquizing; the strategies and degrees of dramatic irony; the concentration of philosophical and sociopolitical significance in theatrical, often novel, modes of narrative representation; and his generous, ambivalent characterizations eroded by the entropic effects of circumstance and sentiment. F.'s plays are intelligent and incisive, complex and uncompromising, unsettling yet satisfying. Their parochialism is so finely realized that it achieves a universal expressiveness; their pathos is authentic, immediate, communal; their craft is polished and innovative; their author, nominated to the Irish senate in 1986, the only Irish writer since Yeats to serve in such a capacity, is the leading living Irish dramatist on both sides of the island's bloody border.

FURTHER WORKS: *A Sort of Freedom* (perf. 1958); *To This Hard House* (perf. 1958); *A Doubtful Paradise* (perf. 1960); *The Founder Members* (perf. 1964); *Farewell to Ardstraw* (perf. 1976, with David Hammond); *Selected Stories* (1979); *American Welcome* (1981); *The Diviner* (1983); *Selected Plays* (1984); *Wonderful Tennessee* (1993)

BIBLIOGRAPHY: Maxwell, D., *B. F.* (1973); Johnston, D., "B. F. and Modern Irish Drama," *Hibernia*, 7 Mar. 1975: 22; Murray, C., "Irish Drama in Transition 1966–1978," *EI*, 4 (1979): 187–308; Schleuter, J., "B. F.," in Weintraub, S., ed. *DLB: British Dramatists since World War II*, Part 1 (1982): 179–85; Kearney, R., "Language Play: B. F. and Ireland's Verbal Theatre," *Studies*, 72

(1983): 20–56; Deane, S., Introduction to *Selected Plays* (1984): 11–22; Dantanus, U., *B. F.: The Growth of an Irish Dramatist* (1984); Kiberd, D., "B. F.'s *Faith Healer*," in Sekine, M., ed., *Irish Writers and Society at Large* (1985): 106–22; Bertha, C., "Tragedies of National Fate: A Comparison between B. F.'s *Translations* and its Hungarian Counterpart, Andràs Sutö's *A Szuzai menyegaö*," *IUR*, 17, 2 (Autumn 1987): 207–22; Grene, N., "Distancing Drama: Sean O'Casey to B. F.," in Sekine, M., ed., *Irish Writers and the Theatre* (1987): 47–70; O'Brien, G., *B. F.* (1990)

—DENNIS PAOLI

FRIGGIERI, Oliver

Maltese novelist, short-story writer, translator, poet, critic, essayist, and lexicographer, b. 27 Mar. 1947, Floriana

F. studied at the Archbishop's Seminary in Floriana and at the University of Malta, where he obtained his B.A. (1968) in Maltese, Italian, and philosophy, and then his M.A. (1975) and Ph.D. (1978) with his specialization on the influence of Italian culture on Maltese literature. For a brief time he studied for the priesthood but abandoned the idea and got married. He taught Maltese and philosophy in state schools from 1968 to 1975, and then he became an assistant lecturer at the University of Malta. In 1990 he became a full professor of Maltese at the same university. He was a founding member of the Movement for the Promotion of Literature that revolutionized Maltese literature during the second half of the 1960s. He also became the editor of the *Journal of Maltese Studies*.

F. is the author of the first oratorio in Maltese, *Pawlu ta' Malta* (1985; Malta's Paul), and also the author of the first cantata in Maltese, *L-Ghanja ta' Malta* (1989; Malta's song). F. has also established a reputation as the most prominent critic and historian of Maltese literature. He has created an extensive body of works dealing with literary theory, critical studies, stylistic analysis, and literary biographies that discussed literature sociologically, philosophically, and historically apart from the literary themes it presented and the structures it outlined. In his descriptive criticism, often judgmental by implication, he examines literature in the light of its dynamic relations that make up the literary process to discover the nation's history. His *Dizzjunarju ta' Termini Letterarji* (1996; A Dictionary of Literary Terms) is the first full-scale dictionary of literary terms in Maltese. It serves as a handbook of Maltese literature as key terms, taken from across the whole range of literary and philosophical thought, are defined in their intellectual, historical, and literary context with carefully selected illustrations.

In his poetry F. treats life's tribulations and man's relation with God. But he also sees his mission as a continuation of Carmelo PSALIA's; so he treats national themes such as religion and history to consolidate Malta's identity. This is most evident in his poetic drama, *Rewwixta* (1990; Rebellion), which depicts the Franco-Maltese conflict between 1798 and 1800. The humiliation of a small nation trodden by the boot of a powerful military force is superseded by the collective determination to achieve a real democratic order. F. moves from a national episode, which reflects the true conscience and identity of the Maltese, to a more universal dimension as the play becomes symbolical of a small nation that maintains an iron will in the face of oppression.

In his creative prose F. uses the story to illustrate his idea, but his themes (often treated philosophically) are largely social and psychological. Consequently, his style is characterized by logic and rationality. The dynamism of F.'s prose fiction lies in its claim of taking the place once occupied by religion and ethics. Although he is still respectful of tradition, F. is often confrontational, utilizing his fiction to shock society into realization. His task is not merely to encourage people to hope for a better environment but to encourage them to face reality and to steel their soul to bear evils and shortcomings with fortitude and determination, as illustrated in the novels *Il-Gidba* (1977; The Lie), *L-Istramb* (1980; A Turn of the Wheel*, 1986), and *Fil-Parlament Ma Jikbrux Fjuri* (1986; Flowers Don't Grow in Parliament). In a world where inequity and folly are often successful, to take a stand against a maelstrom of troubles is rather heroic but in the process human beings endow their frail lives with significance. The prose fiction of F.'s novels tends to be more for the moralist than for the storyteller. It creates a character who searches for wisdom to assist the reader in increasing his understanding of life and sharpening his sensibility and honesty. Despite its pessimism, it enhances the Maltese person's interest in living a life that seems bristling with hostility and unprotected by providence. Similar to the American writer Lionel Trilling (1905-1975), F. believes that the novel is an agent of the moral imagination, but to fulfill such a purpose it is essential to muster a structure that can accommodate the complexity that morality begets.

BIBLIOGRAPHY: Ebejer, F., Introduction to Azzopardi, M., ed., *Malta: The New Poetry* (1971): 4-13; Massa, D., "Contemporary Maltese Literature," *ComQ*, 2, 7 (1978): 11-26; Serracino Inglott, P., Introduction to Masa, D., ed., *Limestone 84: Poems from Malta* (1978): 1-9; Briffa, C., "The Voice of a Nation's Conscience: O. F.'s Fiction in Recent Maltese Literature," *WLT*, 71 (Summer 1997): 495-504

—CHARLES BRIFFA

FRISCH, Max

Swiss novelist and dramatist (writing in German), b. 15 May 1911, Zürich; d. 4 April 1991, Zürich

After secondary school F. briefly studied German literature and art history at the University of Zurich. Following the death of his father he supported himself as a journalist for several years, during which he traveled extensively in Europe and the Balkans and completed his first novel. Temporarily giving up his literary pursuits, he studied architecture and received his diploma in 1941. For more than a decade he combined the tasks of an architect with a renewed commitment to literature, alternating intense periods of work at home in Zurich with frequent travel, especially to the U.S., Mexico, and Greece. He turned to writing full-time after the success of his novel *Stiller* (1954; *I'm Not Stiller*, 1958). Leaving Zurich, he lived in various rural communities and then in Rome before eventually settling in Berzona, in the Swiss canton of Ticino.

Even in his earliest works of fiction, which show indebtedness to his compatriots Gottfried Keller (1819–1890) and Albin Zollinger (1895–1941), F. revealed preoccupations that place him in the tradition of 20th-c. novelists concerned with the disintegration of the self, such as JOYCE, KAFKA, SARTRE, and MUSIL. His first published novel, *Jürg Reinhart* (1934; Jürg Reinhart), and particularly its more successful later adaptation, newly titled *J'adore ce qui me brûle; oder, Die Schwierigen* (1943; I adore what burns me; or, the difficult ones; the second version of 1957 reverses the title to *Die Schwierigen; oder, J'adore ce qui me brûle*), already introduce the major themes in his fiction: the need to transcend (Swiss) provincialism, the difficulty of maintaining human individuality in the modern world, the problems of alienation resulting from the collapse of traditional values and the revolution in technology, and the psychological bonds imposed by time. In *Die Schwierigen*, a *Bildungsroman*, the artist-protagonist Reinhart searches in vain for self-fulfillment; denied satisfaction in his own lifetime even after several fresh starts, he attains suprapersonal fulfillment when his son follows in his footsteps and reenacts the search. By emphasizing that single moments in time repeat themselves within the life of an individual as well as from generation to generation, F. shows that sequential events can be perceived as simultaneous in the human imagination.

The urge to seek out a life beyond the confines of place and time becomes the dominant propelling force for the protagonist of F.'s next novel, *Stiller*. Considered by many critics to be the author's most successful work of fiction, it combines the story of an artist in search of his authentic self with an almost Strindbergian portrayal of a marriage that is torturously destructive because husband and wife make absolute demands on each other. The sculptor Anatol Ludwig Stiller, frustrated by the narrow-mindedness and sterility of Swiss society and by his own artistic and marital inadequacies, escapes to the freedom of the U.S. and then attempts to preserve this freedom when he returns home after seven years by assuming a new identity as a "Mr. White." He is recognized at the border and arrested because of his fake passport, but he adamantly denies that he is Stiller. While in prison, he is asked to write down the objective "truth" about himself for the public prosecutor. During this attempt he gradually comes to terms with his past, realizing that his effort to liberate himself from the finished image (*Bildnis*) so insistently imposed on him by other people, including his wife, can succeed only by accepting and transforming it. By means of an ingenious narrative device F. skillfully captures Stiller's ambivalence about his identity, his experiences and failures, and his ability to communicate them: the novel begins with the first-person narrator "Mr. White" already in prison, writing about Stiller as a third person. Passages in the narrative present time by the obviously unreliable narrator alternate with third-person passages reconstructing the past. After "Mr. White" and Stiller merge at the end of Part I, a "Postscript by the Public Prosecutor" lends a further, equally subjective perspective. Ironic juxtaposition of conflicting details injects touches of humor in this narrative texture of great depth and complexity.

The novel *Homo Faber* (1957; *Homo Faber*, 1959) has a similarly multilayered structure, but conveys the ambiguities and difficulties of self-definition quite differently. Another first-person narrator, the fifty-year-old UNESCO engineer Walter Faber, writes a chronological record of his present activities—constant travel in the U.S., Mexico, Central and South America, and Europe—interspersed with numerous flashbacks to incidents in his past, particularly during a period twenty-one years before when he was in love with an archaeologist named Hanna. Self-deceiving like Stiller, Faber has always defined himself in exclusively rational, scientific terms and is reassured by exactly those dimensions of

existence that Stiller rebelled against: repetition, routine, predictability. Utterly lacking in spontaneity, he believes he can achieve absolute control over his life through sober, calculated analysis. Paradoxically enough, the very incalculable forces that Faber challenges or ignores eventually destroy him, just as he is beginning to appreciate them. His rigid preconceptions are undermined as he endures a series of catastrophic and shocking events, including an emergency airplane landing in a Mexican desert, an inadvertently incestuous affair with the daughter he didn't know he had, and an encounter with a horribly emaciated former professor. It is only after his daughter dies in a tragic accident and he learns he has stomach cancer that he finally realizes his blindness and even experiences a euphoric moment of insight: to be human means to be involved, emotionally as well as intellectually, in all facets of life, from love to hate, from bliss to terror. But change occurs too late; as he is wheeled into the operating room at the end of the novel, he senses he will not survive. Throughout the narrative F. endows Faber's report with a remarkable consistency of viewpoint, vividly evoking the defensiveness of a narrow technological mind threatened by an incomprehensible fate. The gradual evolution in style from laconic utterances fraught with scientific and technical vocabulary to artistic expansiveness convincingly reflects the engineer's increasing sensibility.

F.'s ability to reproduce varying psychological states of mind is displayed with almost manneristic virtuosity in the experimental novel *Mein Name sei Gantenbein* (1964; *A Wilderness of Mirrors*, 1966). In a narrative structure reminiscent of the French NEW NOVEL, the first-person narrator-protagonist seeks to prove the idea that every "I" can create his own role in life and thereby preserve absolute freedom. In the course of the virtually plotless novel, the narrative "I" invents a number of identities, including the intellectual, somewhat stuffy Enderlin, the architect Svoboda, and, his favorite, a man called Gantenbein who pretends to be blind in order to see how people really are. He discards or alters these identities at will, relentlessly exploring the possibilities of escaping from a finished, and therefore rigid, image of himself into all the fictions he is capable of imagining. As he repeatedly states, he tries on stories like clothes. While definite patterns of experience emerge, the narrator never quite grows into a character since he avoids commitment to any final role. Highly entertaining and humorous, the open-ended novel confirms in theme and structure, if only playfully, that the feared restrictions of identity and chronology can be overcome.

Montauk (1975; *Montauk*, 1976), a more conventional novel and F.'s most personal work of fiction, recounts a weekend spent by the first-person narrator Max, a sixty-four-year-old writer, with Lynn, a young American friend. Although he attempts to live purely for the moment during this weekend among the sand dunes of Long Island, Max cannot avoid interrupting the narrative present with the memories that constantly intrude on his consciousness and remind him of lost opportunities and the irrevocable passage of time. Because of the intimate style of much of this diarylike chronicle and numerous recognizably autobiographical elements, *Montauk* has often been read as pure autobiography, in spite of its structural and thematic similarities to earlier novels and the absence of any truly confessional passages. Autobiographical elements are characteristic for all of F.'s fiction, however. Indeed, his other novels can also be given the generic designation "diary novel" (*Tagebuchroman*, or "fictitious diary"). It must be emphasized that the first-person narrators in F.'s fiction, including the

Max of *Montauk*, are without exception coherent, stylized characters. The author's real personal diaries—the military diary *Blätter aus dem Brotsack* (1940; leaves from my knapsack) and the two sets of journals, *Tagebuch 1946–1949* (1950; *Sketchbook 1946–1949*, 1977) and *Tagebuch 1966–1971* (1972; *Sketchbook 1966–1971*, 1974)—make fascinating reading, but lack the stylization and artistic unity of his novels.

F.'s fiction tends to focus so exclusively on private, existential concerns that his plays, which treat both public and private issues, seem to many critics to be the work of an entirely different man. While the dramatist F. obviously learned much from Bertolt BRECHT, whom he actually worked with in Zurich, he is hardly a political revolutionary. Even his avowedly political parable plays explore general philosophical questions rather than specific political problems, and in ideology come closer to the works of PIRANDELLO, in structure to those of Thornton WILDER.

Die chinesische Mauer (1947; rev. version, 1955; *The Chinese Wall*, 1961), *Biedermann und die Brandstifter* (1958; *The Firebugs*, 1959) and *Andorra* (1961; *Andorra*, 1962) are F.'s most important plays about political issues. *Die chinesische Mauer* seeks to define a concept of morality transcending the merely aesthetic culture characteristic of today's intellectuals. Set in China to achieve a kind of Brechtian alienation, the action concerns the collapse of Emperor Hwang Ti's vast political power, resulting from the emperor's resistance to change and his deafness to the "voice of the people." At a festive party celebrating the victory of his "Great Order," which is attended by various famous historical figures such as Columbus, Napoleon, and Philip II of Spain, an intellectual named the Man of Today criticizes absolute power, albeit in very theoretical terms, and warns about the dangers threatening mankind. But the intellectual cannot change anything with abstract pronouncements, no matter how articulate, and he consistently fails to act on his convictions. The play intends to expose the fatal tendency of history to repeat itself and the dichotomy of knowing and acting, but it lacks structural coherence, and its message disappears beneath its farcical surface.

In terms of theatrical effectiveness, both *Biedermann und die Brandstifter* and *Andorra* are far more successful. *Biedermann und die Brandstifter* presents a tightly constructed parable about the resistible rise of coercion and terror. The central figure, a bourgeois Mr. Regular Guy, does not oppose the arsonists who cunningly force their way into his house and set up gasoline barrels in his attic. In his cowardice and self-satisfied complacency, Biedermann foolishly rationalizes away all doubts about his visitors. When the inevitable catastrophe happens, he even praises the fire, for the destroyed building can be rebuilt with more comfort and superior materials. With much black humor a chorus of firemen parodying the verses of Greek tragedy comments on the action throughout.

The central theme of the more serious *Andorra* is racial prejudice, particularly anti-Semitism, but the drama obscures the true issues by overemphasizing the problem of self-image. The protagonist Andri is not Jewish at all, but actually the illegitimate son of a woman from the other side of the border and the Andorran schoolteacher who has "adopted" him. His cowardly father has passed him off as a Jew rescued from persecution abroad. Initially accepted by the Andorrans but then disparaged for being "different" when the country is threatened by foreign invasion, Andri gradually assumes the negative character traits people expect from him. His father tries in vain to tell him the truth, but he has become obsessed with his supposed Jewishness. When the foreign invaders

take him away after a grotesque "Jew-inspection," his father, the real tragic figure of the play, hangs himself.

F.'s political parables remain curiously naïve and abstract because they fail to differentiate personal questions of self and image from issues of broader public relevance. More convincing are the plays restricted to private concerns, particularly the parodistic comedy *Don Juan; oder, Die Liebe zur Geometrie* (1953; *Don Juan; or, The Love of Geometry*, 1967), which illustrates how spontaneity may be killed by the images people create. F.'s Don Juan feels trapped in his own myth—he actually finds women tedious and much prefers the analytical purity of geometry. Although he occasionally succumbs to the women who pursue him, he arranges to stage publicly his descent into hell so that he can disappear and study geometry in peace. Ironically, at his place of refuge he falls in love and even fathers a child; the vitality of life has triumphed over geometrical abstractions.

The play *Biografie: Ein Spiel* (1967; *Biography: A Game*, 1969) again treats the theme of freedom of choice. The protagonist, Professor Kürmann (the name means "man who has a choice"), is given the opportunity by a figure called the Recorder of turning back his life to any point and effecting any changes he desires. Provided with an empty stage, actors, and props, Kürmann finds that he cannot alter the pattern of his experience, even by taking the radical step of joining the Communist Party; no matter how he begins and what revisions he makes, the scenes he stages inevitably turn out to reproduce his life.

In spite of his strong commitment to public concerns, then, F. is essentially an author of private sensibilities. With compassion and great subtlety he probes existential anxieties, repeatedly displaying an acute awareness of human transience and of the problematic nature of experience in a world that seems to have lost its axis. In the variety and stylistic originality of his works, in their elegance of form and humanity of substance, he proves himself to be a writer of major stature.

FURTHER WORKS: *Antwort aus der Stille* (1937); *Bin; oder, Die Reise nach Peking* (1945); *Nun singen sie wieder* (1946); *Santa Cruz* (1947); *Tagebuch mit Marion* (1947); *Als der Krieg zu Ende war* (1949; *When the War Was Over*, 1967); *Graf Öderland* (1951; *Count Oederland*, 1962); *Rip van Winkle* (1953); *Der Laie und die Architektur* (1954); *Herr Quixote* (1955); *Die groß Wut des Philipp Hotz,* (1958; *The Great Rage of Philip Hotz,* (1967); *Schniz* (1959); *Ausgewählte Prosa* (1961); *Stücke* (2 vols., 1962); *Zürich-Transit: Skizze eines Films* (1966); *Öffentlichkeit als Partner* (1967); *Erinnerungen an Brecht* (1968); *Dramaturgisches* (1969); *Wilhelm Tell für die Schule* (1971); *Dienstbüchlein* (1974); *Frühe Stücke* (1975); *Der Traum des Apothekers von Locarno* (1978); *Triptychon* (1978; *Triptych*, 1981); *Der Mensch erscheint im Holozän* (1979; *Man in the Holocene*, 1980)

BIBLIOGRAPHY: Stäuble, E., *M. F.* (1957; 3rd. ed., 1967); Bänziger, H., *F. und Dürrenmatt* (1960); Wellwarth, G., *The Theater of Protest and Paradox* (1964): 161–83; Bradley, B., "M. F.'s *Homo Faber*: Theme and Structural Devices," *GR*, 41 (1966): 279–90; Hoffmann, C. W., "The Search for Self, Inner Freedom, and Relatedness in the Novels of M. F.," in Heitner, R. H., ed., *The Contemporary Novel in German* (1967): 91–113; Weisstein, U., *M. F.* (1967); Demetz, P., *Postwar German Literature* (1970): 112–25; Durzak, M., *Dürrenmatt, F., Weiss: Deutsches Drama der Gegenwart zwischen Kritik und Utopie* (1972); Kieser, R., "Man as

His Own Novel: M. F. and the Literary Diary," *GR*, 47 (1972): 109–17; Marchand, W. R., "M. F.," in Wiese, B. von, ed., *Deutsche Dichter der Gegenwart* (1973): 231–49; Pickar, G. B., "The Narrative Time Sense in the Dramatic Works of M. F.," *GL&L*, 28 (1974–75): 1–14; Grimm, R., and C. Wellauer, "M. F.: Mosaik eines Statikers," in Wagener, H., ed., *Zeitkritische Romane des 20. Jahrhunderts* (1975): 278-300; Butler, M., *The Novels of M. F.* (1976); Knapp, G. P., ed., *M. F.: Aspekte des Prosawerks* (1978); Petersen, J. H., *M. F.* (1978); Kieser, R., "Taking on Aristotle and Brecht: M. F. and His Dramaturgy of Permutation," in Haymes, E. R., ed., *Theatrum Mundi: Essays on German Drama and German Literature* (1980): 185–97

—HELENE SCHER

F. experiences with great intensity the necessity to be his brother's keeper. The feeling of being a part of an indivisible world is present, though it is perhaps not as natural here as it is with Thornton Wilder. To the Swiss author, the family of man is not something to be taken for granted but something to be achieved. F.'s personal resiliency always brings him back to his fellow men—at times only to his fellow men in the halls of power—or, again, back to nature.

...F.... measures, so to speak, very much in spatial terms. The world at large enters the field of vision of Stiller, a quiet man caught up in small matters. He learns to accept his world with humility. The promises of the great are a snare and a delusion.

Hans Bänziger, *F. und Dürrenmatt* (1960),
pp. 204–5

The psychological problem which fascinates F. is the inability of man to stand by himself, wholly independent of all other human beings. Man always strives to *be himself*. But, like Peer Gynt, he can do this only in his dreams. Man in search of himself is constantly either *dreaming* of running away to some idyllic paradise where he can live his own life away from all encumbrances and responsibilities, or he actually *is* running away. In either case he is invariably disillusioned, whether by awakening from the futile dream or by coming to the harsh reality of the wished-for paradise.

George E. Wellwarth, *The Theater of Protest and Paradox* (1964), p. 163

What F. has written here [in *Biedermann und die Brandstifter*] is not a propaganda piece against totalitarianism. The book searches more deeply. It "teaches" that we must resist at the very beginnings. But to tell the truth, its lesson comes really somewhat late, at least for Mr. Biedermann—and for Mr. Benes, Mr. Chamberlain, and Mr. Hindenburg.... Biedermann ultimately proves to be his own arsonist, setting fire to his own existence, but we recognize him as such only when we find him, a charred corpse, lying amid the ruins of his house.... Here too, then, as in his

other pieces, the author does not offer us a ready-made solution to the problem he has raised. He merely confronts the public with the disturbing question, which ought not to leave us ever again—unless we are irredeemable Biedermanns—a question to which each of us can answer only with his life, a life in which word and world are one, a "true life."

Eduard Stäuble, *M. F.*, 3rd. ed. (1967), p. 121

In *Stiller, Homo Faber,* und *Mein Name sei Gantenbein* [F.] has created three of the most important novels of the past decade. Taken together, these books are perhaps the most meaningful recent German writing in their particular genre: the psychological novel.

Their significance does not lie so much in F.'s narrative technique. The structure and the plot development in *Stiller* and *Homo faber* are essentially traditional, and only in *Gantenbein* does F. move onto experimental, new narrative ground. He has developed a keenly sensitive and often highly imaginative style for illuminating the anguished consciousness of the contemporary intellectual in particular and of contemporary man in general. But while this brilliant style is evident in many single episodes and scenes of each novel, it is not employed consistently in any of the three. The significance of the works lies, rather, in the astonishing accuracy and depth of psychological insight with which the experiences of his typically modern heroes are viewed and presented. His characters are engaged—often against their will and rarely successfully—in what F. considers to be the most urgent concerns of living. And while these "urgent concerns" are not profound new discoveries, the psychological understanding that F. has for what motivates his characters is rare, indeed. Finally, since most of us can see ourselves in the central figures, the importance of the novels lies also in what they can help us to recognize about our own inner selves.

Charles W. Hoffmann, "The Search for Self, Inner Freedom, and Relatedness in the Novels of M. F.,"
in Robert H. Heitner, ed., *The Contemporary Novel in German* (1967), p. 94

There is something constantly alive and open about M. F.'s mind and work, and after more than thirty years of writing he continues to convey a distinct feeling of youthful energy, endless sympathy, and occasional naïveté. F. strikes me as a writer of renewed beginnings rather than of radical change: he does not sacrifice his interests easily, preferring rather to explore a few questions (involved with the essentials of modern human consciousness) in changing moods, figures, and genres; and if he does discover an answer, he is apt to reject it quickly in order to push his explorations still further. Much of his achievement consists of the revised and the tentative; fascinated by the vagaries of human life ... he will often pursue an analogous theme in a diary note, a story, a novel, or a play. His individual works are imperfect, but individual imperfections are less important than the intense continuity of his search.

Peter Demetz, *Postwar German Literature* (1970), p. 112

The diary-writer's situation is basically and inevitably existentialist. By interpreting and analysing his daily experiences he is forced to reflect on the circumstances of his existence. It is not coincidental that all great theoreticians and philosophers of modern Existentialism were also authors of diaries. Yet while such writers as Kierkegaard, Bernanos, Sartre or Camus based their literary work on a philosophical theory we find in F.'s case a vehement refusal of "abstractions." The existentialist situation for F. becomes doubtful at the moment of the famous leap into the unknown: for this would presuppose the existence of an absolute truth. It is not the existentialist problem of nothingness which bothers F. His deepest concern, his obsession, is the question of truthfulness (*Wahrhaftigkeit*). There is probably no other contemporary non-religious writer whose entire work has been devoted to a similar degree to the subject-matter of truthfulness.

F.'s approach begins with the acknowledgment that there are truths but not truth. Instead he accepts the existence of a *Bewusstseinsschwerpunkt*, a centre of gravity which changes with the variable consciousness of man within the totality of time.

Rolf Kieser, "Man as His Own Novel: M. F. and the Literary Diary," *GR*, 47 (1972), p. 112

While by no means shirking *engagement*, F. has always been preoccupied with issues concerning the individual, primarily the painful problem of identity (which lies at the heart of his novel *Stiller*) and questions of human psychology. Beginning with *Mein Name sei Gantenbein*, he takes a keen interest in biography, which he regards as a cloak thrown around the psyche, changing its color, shape, and size according to the "will" of the subconscious. As F. expressed his thoughts in an imaginary interview with himself: what we commonly take to be the true *Geschichte* (history) of our lives is actually a body of *Geschichten* (stories) conforming to an *Erlebnismuster* (experiential pattern). This pattern, F. maintains, is the only source of stability in the individual; it is all that remains of what used to be called Self, character, or personality. As a logical consequence, then, a biography is little more than the offshoot of a fictive existence (*der Ausläufer einer fiktiven Existenz*).

Ulrich Weisstein, Introduction to *Biografie: Ein Spiel*, text ed. (1972), p. v

But the sense of lost centricity . . . affects, in one way or another, all the characters who people F.'s narrative world. For they are eccentric individuals in that they are shown as living at odds with an environment which, far from exerting any central stabilising power, has itself a void at its core. The frightening nature of this void is disguised from the apparently centric majority only by habit and the repetitive shape of everyday routine. F.'s characters, indeed, are embedded . . . in the well-defined context of a modern bourgeois society which is depicted as deeply flawed. For by the conformity which it demands of its members, the roles which it expects them to perform, and the pressures to which it subjects them, this society is shown to be indifferent, if not inimical, to the maintenance and development of personal integrity. The linchpin of this social system is marriage, and F. uses the institution as a microcosm of the larger community beyond. It is not therefore surprising that marriage—and in particular the problematical nature of its supposed centripetence—is the fundamental experience to which all F.'s protagonists are exposed.

Michael Butler, *The Novels of M. F.* (1976), p. 10

FRISIAN LITERATURE
See section under Netherlands Literature

FROST, Robert
American poet, b. 26 March 1874, San Francisco, Cal.; d. 29 Jan. 1963, Boston, Mass.

F.'s life divides sharply into the thirty-nine years that preceded the appearance of his first book of poetry and the following half-century in which he became one of the most widely known poets of his time. Although indelibly identified with rural New England, F. was reared in California until he was eleven, when he returned to his father's native region. Not until his mid-twenties, when he took up poultry farming in Derry, New Hampshire, did he receive his first real exposure to country life. By then, he had attended Dartmouth and Harvard, although he never completed college, and had worked at various jobs, including teaching school, an occupation he returned to when his farming venture failed. In 1912 F. sailed for England, where he made friends with Ezra POUND and the Georgian poets and published his first two books. The years following his return to America in 1915 brought both serious critical acclaim and popular appeal. His many accolades included four Pulitzer Prizes; academic appointments at Amherst, Michigan, Harvard, and Dartmouth, and countless lectures on other campuses; honorary degrees from Oxford and Cambridge; government-sponsored visits to other nations, and in 1961 an invitation to read "The Gift Outright" (1942) at the inauguration of President John F. Kennedy. F. cultivated the public image of the plain-speaking farmer-poet that endeared him to many, but behind this figure his biography reveals a complicated man haunted by self-doubt and familial conflicts.

F.'s first two books established his two major poetic genres. *A Boy's Will* (1913) introduces his lyric voice in a sequence of introspective poems loosely linked by the quest of the poet for his vocation. Although the style bears traces of conventional 19th-c. poetic diction, poems like "Mowing" and "Storm Fear" show F. discovering his distinctive idiom. *North of Boston* (1914), unquestionably his most distinguished single volume, reveals a masterful dramatic poet. Its dialogues, monologues, and dramatic narratives display his mature style; in "The Pasture" and "Mending Wall" one meets F.'s familiar Yankee persona, inclined toward understatement, mischievous humor, and a sly matter-of-factness. *Mountain Interval* (1916), *New Hampshire* (1923), and *West-Running Brook* (1928) contain fewer strictly dramatic works, but the dramatic element strongly colors both the longer narrative and philosophical poems and the enlarged lyric strain. *A Further Range* (1936), *A Witness Tree* (1942), *Steeple Bush* (1947), and *In the Clearing* (1962) fall short of the earlier volumes, but they contain some superb individual poems. The most comprehensive collection of his work is *The Poems of Robert Frost* (1969).

F.'s poetry transforms the country "North of Boston" into his personal imaginative territory, like FAULKNER'S Yoknapatawpha County. The merging of poet and place occurs not only in F.'s evocation of the landscape and the people, but most tellingly in the Yankee manner he adopts as his favorite way of seeing and speaking. The regional focus does not circumscribe his vision; from this vantage point, he looks outward on modern life and universal human experience. He is, in one guise, a modern pastoralist juxtaposing the declining New England rural order against that of an urban, technological, and cosmopolitan age, either directly— "New Hampshire" (1923)—or indirectly—"A Hundred Collars" (1913), "An Old Man's Winter Night" (1916). Yet F.'s multifaceted sensibility includes as well the nature poet, the speculative poet, and the tragic and the comic observer of the human situation.

Few modern poets have written so often and well about the natural world. From first to last, F. contemplates natural things and processes, and examines the equivocal human relationship to them. Human beings and nature act in harmony in many poems, and their nearness in a rural environment yields a sense of kinship, as in "The Tuft of Flowers" (1906), "Putting in the Seed" (1914), "Two Look at Two" (1923). The feeling of loss that attaches itself to the perpetual running down of things in the physical world is a recurrent theme in poems such as "Nothing Gold Can Stay" (1923), "The Oven Bird" (1916), and "Hyla Brook" (1916). But nature is not for F., as it was for Wordsworth or Emerson, the visible sign of a transcendent spiritual principle that unites the human and nonhuman realms; his outlook more closely resembles Melville's or Dickinson's. Whatever meaning people find in nature is the product of human consciousness; whatever moments of intimacy their relationship offers, nature is essentially indifferent to human-kind. F. insists that human yearnings cannot obscure the hard truth of nature's otherness, even though this recognition may be desolating—"The Need of Being Versed in Country Things" (1920), "Bereft" (1927), "Neither Out Far nor In Deep" (1934). F.'s more typical stance, however, is nowhere better dramatized than in "The Wood-Pile" (1914), where a lone figure walking in a frozen swamp discovers only the abandoned handiwork of another person: the effort to locate oneself leads not to any communion with nature, but to what human beings make of the world through their individual actions.

F. spoke of four beliefs which he knew more intimately from living with poetry: "the self-belief," "the love-belief," "the art-belief," and "the God-belief." All four shape his view of humanity. The first two generate much of his poetry, finding expression both

Robert Frost

in his compassionate portrayals of personal conflict and suffering, and in his celebration of the courage, resiliency, and integrity of the human spirit. F.'s best-known lyric, "Stopping by Woods on a Snowy Evening" (1923), beautifully encapsulates the dialectic between solitary contemplation and the bond with others, which runs through his work from *A Boy's Will* forward. He believes, like so many American writers, that to discover the self, the individual must stand apart; the gesture of turning away is simultaneously a turning within. One continually encounters in his poems a fondness for solitude, the desire to strike out on one's own, and the value he places on independence and self-sufficiency. But the isolation of the self carries with it the burdens of loneliness and fear. In some of F.'s most moving lyric and dramatic poems—for example, "A Servant to Servants" (1914), "The Hill Wife" (1916), "Desert Places" (1934), and "Acquainted with the Night" (1928)—turning inward discloses the chaotic regions of the psyche.

If the solitary questing self, whether drawn to the woods or on imaginative flights out among the stars, is an essential human attribute, so, too, is love, which draws individuals back to familiar earthly things and into communion with someone besides themselves. F. relies less on a social bond among people in general than on the love between two persons, especially a man and a woman. The fulfillment that their mutual affection makes possible, both at its inception and as it endures, renews and sustains life—"The Generations of Men" (1914), "In the Home Stretch" (1916). The darker side of F.'s vision sees the failures of love when it is thwarted by emotional barriers that frustrate communication and empathy—"Home Burial" (1914), "The Subverted Flower" (1942). The themes of selfhood and love reach a culmination of sorts in F.'s late masterpiece, "Directive" (1946). The speaker provides directions back to a brook near a place where human activity and love once flourished but are no more; here, he says, one may "drink and be whole again beyond confusion." The poem invites any reader to set out imaginatively on this journey of self-recovery and self-possession; it must be undertaken alone, but the invitation is a gesture of love.

F. is hardly a religious poet in the usual sense. Nevertheless, the God-belief hovers in the background of several poems and occasionally occupies the foreground, as in his two late verse plays, *A Masque of Reason* (1945) and *A Masque of Mercy* (1947). F. is reticent and enigmatic when he approaches the question of God. He depicts God, by turns, as a distant and uncaring presence, as a well-intentioned human type, as the designer of a brutal universe, as a cosmic joker, and as a conventional afterthought. His intimations of the divine are hedged by a pervasive skepticism toward anything beyond the material cosmos, though the mysteries discerned there by science suggest analogues to the mysteries of religion—"For Once, Then, Something" (1920), "Sitting by a Bush in Broad Sunlight" (1928), "All Revelation" (1938). Even the masques, which, taken together, argue for a faith in a merciful Christian God, dramatize more forcefully the problematic nature of that faith. The foremost impression one gets from F. is that God is largely unknowable, and that perhaps He is whatever man makes of Him. "West-Running Brook" (1928) puts forward the idea that the source of all things is a spiritual reality to which the resistance to the deathward flow of time and change found in both nature and human beings bears witness. But, since the poem is a dialogue between a man and wife, this affirmation is firmly embedded in the immediate experience of their love and their imaginative contemplation of the brook.

What F. finds crucial is the ceaseless searching of the human mind, which is expressed in the God-belief and which is central to his belief in poetry. The human capacity to dream is the subject of two of his best-known poems, "After Apple-Picking" (1914) and "Birches" (1915). Here, as elsewhere, F. recognizes the human importance of the impulse to dream as it pushes against the limitations of finite existence. Yet the ideal or dream world is not a place apart; it closely adheres to the ordinary business of living— the labors of the apple harvest, the boyhood pleasure of swinging on birch trees. This outlook on human experience applies as well to the making of poetry. Where fact and dream converge is not only the point at which some of F.'s finest poems cohere, it is, for him, fundamental to the "literary belief" that brings a poem into being. The other questions of belief depend finally on the clarification of life that poetry makes possible. Every good poem creates "a momentary stay against confusion" that is simultaneously the significance of the poetic act and the act of living.

Writing in the period of modernist experimentation, F. stuck with conventional metrics and verse forms. He is a modern master of blank verse and the sonnet. An innovator in his own right, he fashioned within the framework of traditional forms a uniquely contemporary idiom that, without simply imitating the vernacular, is controlled by the rhythms and phrasings of ordinary speech and the shadings of voice tones. The style created through this medium is a highly flexible and sensitive register of the nuances of human experience, thought, and feeling. Its deceptive simplicity belies the complex range of meaning it expresses, largely through the subtle

overtones of implication that emanate from the common things of rural life. Some, like houses, brooks, woods, and stars, take on symbolic weight through repeated use. This kind of suggestivity, however, seldom obtrudes upon the literal particularity of the represented experience. The same holds true for F. as a thinker. Although his tendency to deal more directly with ideas in his later verse has been frequently noted, he never systematically elaborates a philosophical position. He proceeds rather by certain ingrained habits of mind and ways of seeing life: his preoccupation with contraries in both nature and human nature, his abiding concern with boundaries and limits, his opposing inclinations toward clarifying himself and holding something back. All of these various traits, the formal reflection of F.'s belief that poetry should hew closely to immediate and tangible realities, contribute to a deeply personal but nonetheless distinctly modern style.

Unlike his American contemporaries T. S. ELIOT, William Carlos WILLIAMS, Wallace STEVENS, and POUND, F. is not a primary shaper of modern poetry and poetics, yet he is a major poet of our time. Both his admirers and detractors have sometimes underrated his achievement. He has been applauded simply as the poet of traditional American virtues and verities, and he has been accused of skirting present-day dilemmas by retreating to a bygone vantage point. Undeniably, he at times dismisses serious questions lightly, especially political and social ones, and the playful sententiousness of the later F. is frequently offputting. Yet F.'s best poetry seriously engages the predicaments of modern life and testifies to the value of the ongoing effort to discover what it means to be human.

FURTHER WORKS: *The Letters of R. F. to Louis Untermeyer* (1963); *R. F.: Farm-Poultryman* (1963); *Selected Letters* (1964); *Selected Prose* (1966); *Family Letters of R. and Elinor F.* (1972)

BIBLIOGRAPHY: Thompson, L., *Fire and Ice: The Art and Thought of R. F.* (1942); Lynen, J. F., *The Pastoral Art of R. F.* (1960); Nitchie, G. W., *Human Values in the Poetry of R. F.: A Study of a Poet's Convictions* (1960); Sergeant, E. S., *R. F.: The Trial by Existence* (1960); Cox, J. M., ed., *R. F.: A Collection of Critical Essays* (1962); Brower, R. A., *The Poetry of R. F.: Constellations of Intention* (1963); Squires, R., *Major Themes of R. F.* (1963); Jennings, E., *F.* (1966); Thompson, L., *R. F.: The Early Years, 1874–1915* (1966); Gerber, P. L., *R. F.* (1967); Thompson, L., *R. F.: The Years of Triumph, 1915–1938* (1970); Barry, E., *R. F.* (1973); Thompson, L., *R. F.: A Living Voice* (1974); Greiner, D. J., *R. F.: The Poet and His Critics* (1974); Lentricchia, F., *R. F.: Modern Poetics and the Landscapes of Self* (1975); Thompson, L., and Winnick, R. H., *R. F.: The Later Years, 1938–1963* (1976); Poirier, R., *R. F.: The Work of Knowing* (1977); Wagner, L. W., *R. F.: The Critical Reception* (1977); Borroff, M., *Language and the Poet: Verbal Artistry in F., Stevens, and Moore* (1979): 23–40; Kemp, J. C., *R. F. and New England: The Poet as Regionalist* (1979); Harris, K. G., ed., *R. F.: Studies of the Poetry* (1979)

—PETER W. DOWELL

I conceive that R. F. is doing in his poems what Lawrence says the great writers of the classic American tradition did. That enterprise of theirs was of an ultimate radicalism. It consisted, Lawrence says, of two things: a disintegration and sloughing off of the old consciousness, by which Lawrence means the old European consciousness, and the forming of a new consciousness underneath.

So radical a work, I need scarcely say, is not carried out by reassurance, nor by the affirmation of old virtues and pieties. It is carried out by the representation of the terrible actualities of life in a new way. I think of R. F. as a terrifying poet. Call him, if it makes things any easier, a tragic poet, but it might be useful every now and then to come out from under the shelter of that literary word. The universe that he conceives is a terrifying universe. Read the poem called "Design" and see if you sleep the better for it. Read "Neither Out Far nor In Deep," which often seems to me the most perfect poem of our time, and see if you are warmed by anything in it except the energy with which emptiness is perceived.

Lionel Trilling, "A Speech on R. F.: A Cultural Episode," *PR*, 26 (1959), p. 451

The vagueness and casual quality of the colloquialisms enables F. to hint at the underlying significance in just the right way. He does not wish to make his symbolism flatly mechanical, because the meaning will only be convincing if it grows naturally out of the realistic details of the scene. . . . Hence the importance of the speaker. He tells us of his own experience, and in experience one does not read the meanings of things like neatly written labels, but rather the significance glows dimly beneath the surface. F. is able to portray the speaker in the very act of seeing, because he presents the poem ["The Grindstone"] as a tentative exploration, an awareness of the hidden depths and dark areas of uncertainty. Ironically, the qualities which make colloquial idiom seem unsuited for serious literature are for F. the very means of showing the speaker's superior perceptiveness. The vagueness of the idiom serves as a way of subtly indicating the complications of what he sees. The casual attitude it suggests expresses the careful restraint of one who will not let his feelings confuse him in his cautious searching of reality.

John F. Lynen, *The Pastoral Art of R. F.* (1960), pp. 97–98

The figure the poems make is the figure of R. F. in a New England landscape. The figure and the scene are finally identical, for the poet's language *personifies* his region, making it an extension of himself and converting what was mere geographical space to personal property. F.'s New England is not the alien virgin wilderness occupied by savages and subdued by Puritans; instead it is second growth timber come back to claim land which has been lived over and left behind within the memory of living men; it is thus a grand metaphor for all the past which man throws aside as being at once unpromising and unprofitable. The poet literally enters this abandoned human landscape—human because it has been not only explored but also experienced, still retaining the domestic scars beneath its wilderness—and reclaims it for us all. The result of this imaginative enterprise which converts space to property is a relentless self-possession, bringing into the full range of consciousness as much of that half-remembered life as possible.

James M. Cox, Introduction to James M. Cox, ed., *R. F.: A Collection of Critical Essays* (1962), pp. 2–3

One finds it easy to suppose that R. F. has always been able to make the kind of poem for which he has been readily admired: the horse, the snow, the dark woods—all in a clear congruency, yet squeezed like clay until allegories of grief and joy spread from between the fingers. To do this is to contain and transform the environment, to make a permanent predicate of what merely happens. It is, ultimately, to conquer nature in the formalities of a drama where man faces some manner of temptation: he is tempted to disappear in the dark woods; he is tempted to climb to heaven. In effect, the temptation is only mildly perverse, mildly self-destructive. The resistance to the temptation is, however, of some intensity, and the triumph lies in refusing to give up any degree of being human in order to become more natural. There is something odd in the triumph, for the conqueror and the conquered, man and nature, are assumed to be conspirators. They have an agreement. They mirror each other.

Radcliffe Squires, *The Major Themes of R. F.* (1963), p. 21

There is something pleasant about the solitude of the Wordsworthian speaker, connected it may be with the "pleasing" retirement of the eighteenth century, but more importantly with Wordsworth's sense that the deeper value of his experience depends on his separation from the world of men. Wordsworthian moments of solitude are positively thrilling, as when the mountain rises up "huge and black," or when it magically rolls by in earth's "diurnal round," or when the boy is clinging perilously to a cliff in a tremendous blast of wind. For this solitary voice—as the context usually makes clear—is never quite alone: it feels presences and powers, or hears other voices, admonishing or consoling—the many expressions of ministering nature. F.'s speaker, by being so surely fixed in the physical world, the neutralized nature of the late nineteenth and twentieth century, is much more surely alone. His matter-of-fact tone is based on matters of fact: thrushes sing deep in the woods at evening, the oven bird's "teacher-teacher" is heard in midsummer. The "call to lament" in "Come In" therefore reminds him that there is no one to lament with. For the traveler in "Stopping by Woods" to say he is "between the woods and frozen lake" is to say also how far he is from home.

Reuben A. Brower, *The Poetry of R. F.: Constellations of Intention* (1963), pp. 76–77

This pilgrim's-progress pattern became a matrix. It was used with conscious variations in most of F.'s books, all the way from *A Boy's Will* to *In the Clearing*. In this pattern there is the subtle suggestion that for F. the central problem of his life—artistic and non-artistic—was to find orderly ways of dealing with dangerous conflicts he found operative within himself or between himself and others. It was part of his delight to discover many different processes for dealing with these conflicts; but he liked to give his lyrics a surface effect of playful ease and serenity even when some of them dramatized his deepest uneasiness. Sometimes the effect of serenity was achieved, in his poems of escape, by his representing his own idealized attitude as being real, no matter how blatantly the biographical facts contradicted the poetry. Most of the time, however, he used his poems either as tools or as weapons for actually trying to bring under control and resolve those conflicts which he viewed as being so dangerous that they might otherwise engulf and destroy him.

Lawrance Thompson, *R. F.: The Early Years, 1874–1915* (1966), p. xxii

We come closest to the spirit of F.'s work whenever as readers we get into the action, the performance of the poem, joining him especially in those movements by which he keeps a poem from "tightening up." There are disclaimers embedded in assertions ("For once, then, something"); conciliating understatements that call for correction ("And to do that to birds was why she came," he says of Eve in "Never Again Would Birds' Song Be the Same"); evasive tactics in the use of words like "almost" and "somehow," of "unless" and especially "as if" ("As if the earth in one unlooked for favor/Had made them certain earth returned their love," in "Two Look at Two"); predilections for negatives which evoke the reality being denied ("Not bluebells gracing a tunnel mouth—/Not lupine living on sand and drouth" in "A Passing Glimpse"); ascriptions of perception or capacity where none exist ("The aim was song—the wind could see" in "The Aim Was Song"); open-ended endings ("If design govern in a thing so small," "Design"). He is wonderfully exciting in the daring with which he chooses to show that a poem is "less than everything" because, given the nature of things and language, it is difficult enough to be "more than nothing."

Richard Poirier, *R. F.: The Work of Knowing* (1977), pp. 26–27

The characteristic diction of "Mending Wall" and other similar poems is one important aspect of a seemingly realistic style in which features of syntax, word order, and sentence structure drawn mainly from the common level also play their parts. In this style, too, the meanings of words and the content of successive statements are readily intelligible, even though the thematic interrelationships and implications of the statements may be subject to dispute. Nothing on the verbal surface is eccentric, illogical, or cryptic; there are no difficult metaphors or sophisticated plays on words: the references to stones as *loaves* and *balls* and the metonymy "He is all pine and I am apple orchard" are immediately understood because they are the sort of figures of speech we ourselves might use in conversation. All these aspects of style combine in an artful simulation of straightforward thought or speech which has at the same time a preternatural lucidity.

Marie Borroff, *Language and the Poet* (1979), p. 30

FRY, Christopher

(born Arthur Hammond Harris) English dramatist, translator, and screenwriter, b. 18 Dec. 1907, Bristol

F.'s home environment and early schooling exposed him to music and literature, and as a boy he frequently wrote short plays, poems, and farces. His first play to be produced, *Youth and the Peregrines*, was written when he was eighteen. F. was involved in theatrical activity in England during the 1930s, principally as an actor and director. After World War II he turned to playwriting and has had some two dozen plays produced on stage, film, and television.

F. has been instrumental in the movement to restore verse drama to the modern theater. Among his influences are the Bible, Shakespeare, and T. S. ELIOT, to whom he is often compared. His major plays, written in irregular blank verse, are set in remote periods and places, indicating his belief in the universality of his characters' concerns and in the unchanging nature of the human condition. Although some are called comedies, they all evidence a free mixing of the comic, the tragic, and the religious. All the plays reveal a distinctly Christian outlook; F. himself has divided them into the two categories of the secular and the religious, the latter group intended for staging in a church.

The best of his four religious dramas is *A Sleep of Prisoners* (1951), a long one-act play in which four soldiers, imprisoned in a church, fall asleep and enact biblical stories in their dreams. In each soldier's dream, the other three play out the Biblical roles in ways that profoundly affect the lives of all four after they awaken. Complex in structure, *A Sleep of Prisoners* is a highly theatrical and affecting drama.

F. created the genre of "seasonal comedy," in which the "scene, the season and the characters are bound together in one climate." By stressing the physical details of setting—the weather, the vegetation, the animal life—F. created action that is dominated by the mood and tone of the season in which it takes place. The four seasonal comedies—for spring, autumn, winter, and summer, respectively—are *The Lady's Not for Burning* (1949), *Venus Observed* (1950), *The Dark Is Light Enough* (1954), and *A Yard of Sun* (1970). The best known is *The Lady's Not for Burning*. It concerns a misanthropic soldier in the 15th c. who rescues a young girl accused of witchcraft from burning at the stake. Its witty dialogue is often brilliant and its characterizations are among the strongest in F.'s work.

Generally considered F.'s finest play, *A Phoenix Too Frequent* (1946) is a long one-act comedy based upon the "widow of Ephesus" legend, a narrative popular with writers from the time of Petronius. This play is F.'s most successful statement of a theme that dominates his works: self-realization and redemption through love. It exemplifies his finest work as a dramatic poet; its dialogue, rich in metaphor and imagery, is eminently stageworthy and fully revealing of character.

F.'s sole tragedy is *Curtmantle* (1961), one of three major modern plays recounting the story of Henry II and Thomas à Becket. Unlike the versions by Eliot and Jean ANOUILH, F.'s tragedy focuses on the English king as tragic protagonist and treats the martyr Becket as a secondary figure. *Curtmantle* is not among F.'s better plays.

F.'s translations of the plays of Anouilh and Jean GIRAUDOUX are highly regarded and have done much to enhance the appreciation of those two French dramatists by English-speaking audiences and readers. Since the 1950s, F. has enjoyed some success as a writer for film and television, penning screenplays for the biblical epics *Ben Hur* (1959), *Barabbas* (1962), and *The Bible* (1966) and contributing to television such well-regarded scripts as *The Brontës of Haworth* (1975).

F.'s efforts to restore verse drama to the modern theater have frequently been coolly received and his own verse criticized for its linguistic excesses. He has been accused of superficiality, derivativeness, and verbosity. In his best plays, however, F. has created dramatic verse which is fully expressive of action and character and which is frequently dazzling in its imagery.

FURTHER WORKS: *The Boy with a Cart* (1939); *The Firstborn* (1946); *Thor, with Angels* (1949); *An Experience of Critics* (1952); *The Queen Is Crowned* (1953); *Sister Dora* (1977); *The Best of Enemies* (1977); *Can You Find Me* (1978)

BIBLIOGRAPHY: Spender, S., "C. F.," *Spectator*, 24 March 1950: 364; Stanford, D., *C. F.: An Appreciation* (1951); Schear, B., and E. Prater, "A Bibliography on C. F.," *TDR*, 4, 3 (1960); Kerr, W., "C. F.," in Freedman, M., ed., *Essays in the Modern Drama* (1964): 294–99; Roy, E., *C. F.* (1968); Wiersma, S. M., *C. F.* (1970)

—JACK A. VAUGHN

FRYE, Northrop

Canadian literary theorist and critic, b. 14 July 1912, Sherbrooke, Que.; d. 23 Jan. 1991, Toronto

F. received his B.A. from the University of Toronto in 1933, was ordained in the United Church of Canada in 1936, and took his M.A. at Merton College, Oxford, in 1940. He has taught English at Victoria College, Toronto, since 1939 and served as principal of the college from 1959 to 1966. Holder of numerous honorary degrees, in 1958 he was awarded the Lorne Pierce Medal for distinguished service to Canadian letters.

F.'s first book, *Fearful Symmetry: A Study of William Blake* (1947), was a major reinterpretation of the whole corpus of Blake's writing and exerted an enormous influence over all subsequent Blake criticism. Coming from a background of theological as well as literary training, F. saw Blake as a "poet of the Bible" and interpreted his works as in a tradition that included Spenser and

Milton. F.'s major interest was in the symbolic and archetypal structure of Blake's work, or what has been called Blake's "mythology." Contrary to most previous critics, however, F. saw Blake's mythology not as private, but as a consciously constructed encyclopedic effort to contain within itself the tradition of poetic prophecy.

Between 1947 and 1957 F. published numerous essays in the process of creating his extraordinarily influential *Anatomy of Criticism* (1957). If the book on Blake became the seed of many subsequent works of practical criticism in the archetypal mode, the *Anatomy of Criticism* has had a similar influence in the area of literary theory, seeking to organize the whole study of literary criticism according to an elaborate scheme that includes a place for historical, ethical, archetypal, and rhetorical modes. Some commentators have claimed that F.'s book marks a definite, indeed a total, break with the main movement of Anglo-American critical theory as it expressed itself in the works of the New Critics (*see* LITERARY CRITICISM); others have seen it as an attempt to synthesize the various divergent schools of modern criticism; still others have thought F.'s work represents the culmination of a critical movement begun in romanticism.

The major influence on *Anatomy of Criticism* and all of F.'s subsequent theorizing is, however, William Blake, to whom F. returns for the fundamental symbols of his own thought. Central to *Anatomy of Criticism* is a theory that describes the literary symbol as existing on a scale between a "descriptive" extreme, where the symbol points outward to a referent, and a "literal" extreme, where the symbol is purely self-intentive, or "centripetal." A major part of the book presents an elaborate theory of archetypes, or myths. F.'s theory of archetypes brings in neither Plato nor JUNG, but declares an archetype (for his purposes) to be a repeated symbol that, appearing in different works, unifies our literary experience and makes a theory of *literature* thinkable. In F.'s theory of genres, there is an effort to establish grounds for the criticism of types of literature—the romance, for instance—that in previous criticism had been given relatively little systematic attention. One type of work that F. identifies and describes is the anatomy; thus he ironically includes his own book within the range of literature that it analyzes.

F.'s later work has developed ideas offered in *Anatomy of Criticism*, such as his view that "every deliberately constructed hierarchy of values in literature known to me is based on a concealed social, moral, or intellectual analogy," and that criticism should have to do with recognition, not evaluation. He has argued the usefulness of his "archetypal" criticism to the teaching of literature at all levels, and he has extended theory to practice, as in two short books on Shakespeare—*A Natural Perspective* (1965) and *Fools of Time* (1967); and one on Milton—*The Return of Eden* (1965).

More recently F. has explicitly brought his literary concerns into studies of what might be called the mythical structure of society (implicit in his earlier work). His theory of the competing cultural myths of "concern" and "freedom," developed in *The Modern Century* (1967) and *The Critical Path* (1971), leads to his advocacy of the notion of "open mythology," which for him would allow a culture to escape the stultification of a fixed mythic structure.

FURTHER WORKS: *Fables of Identity* (1963); *T. S. Eliot* (1963); *The Well-Tempered Critic* (1963); *The Educated Imagination* (1967); *A Study of English Romanticism* (1968); *The Stubborn Structure* (1971); *The Secular Scripture* (1976); *N. F. on Culture*

and Literature: A Collection of Review Essays (1978); *The Great Code: The Bible and Literature* (1981)

BIBLIOGRAPHY: Kermode, F., "N. F.," *Puzzles and Epiphanies* (1962); Krieger, M., ed., *N. F. in Modern Criticism* (1966); Krieger, M., "The Critical Legacy of Matthew Arnold . . . ," *SoR*, 5 (1969): 457–74; Denham, R. D., "Science, Criticism, and F.'s Metaphysical Universe," *SCR*, 7, 2 (1975): 3–18; Fisher, M. R., "The Imagination as a Sanction of Value," *CentR*, 21 (1977): 105–17; Fletcher, A., "N. F.: The Critical Passion," *CritI*, 1 (1975): 741–56; Adamson, J., *N. F.: A Visionary Life* (1993)

—HAZARD ADAMS

FUENTES, Carlos

Mexican novelist, short-story writer, critic, and dramatist (writing in Spanish and English), b. 11 Nov. 1928, Panama City, Panama

F.'s father was a Mexican career diplomat, Rafael Fuentes Boettiger; during his early years he lived with his family in various capitals in the western hemisphere. He later attended the prestigious Colegio de México in Mexico City and graduated with a law degree from the National University of Mexico. Another year was spent in Geneva, studying economics at the Institute of Higher International Studies. F. has held a number of positions in the Mexican government. During his university years he became a Marxist and since then has gained renown as an influential writer of the left in Latin America. In 1959 F. married the famous Mexican actress Rita Macedo.

F. began his writing career in the late 1940s but did not become well known until 1954 with the publication of a collection of short stories, *Los días enmascarados* (the masked days), told in the vein of fantasy and satire. F.'s first novel, *La región más transparente* (1958; *Where the Air Is Clear*, 1960), created a sensation with its experimental techniques. It was an attempt to do for Mexico City what John DOS PASSOS had done for New York City in *Manhattan Transfer*. The novel was also viewed as a *roman à clef*, exposing the foibles of the upper class, a group to which F. and his family belonged. *La muerte de Artemio Cruz* (1962; *The Death of Artemio Cruz*, 1964), a brilliant tour de force told in the first, second, and third person, is probably F.'s best novel to date. In it, he follows the rise of a peon during the Mexican revolution to his eventual position as a captain of industry and the influential owner of a newspaper chain.

A third major novel, *Cambio de piel* (1967; *A Change of Skin*, 1968), won a prestigious prize in Barcelona, Spain, but censors would not allow its publication in that country. The most universal of F.'s novels, it treats such diverse topics as German guilt over World War II atrocities, the Jewish community in New York City, and the frustrated artist in Mexico.

More recent novels include *Terra nostra* (1975; *Terra Nostra*, 1976), a fanciful compendium of Spanish and Mexican history covering events from Roman times until the end of the world, in 1999, and *La cabeza de la Hidra* (1978; *The Hydra Head*, 1978), an espionage novel revolving around Jewish, Arab, and North American intrigues involving Mexico's newly discovered oil fields.

F.'s work in other genres consists of two plays and four volumes of collected essays. Although F. turned to theater relatively late in his writing career, he had previously produced numerous film scripts, and his novels have always been characterized by their sparkling dialogue. *Todos los gatos son pardos* (1970; all the cats are dark) is a mythical play re-creating the confrontation between Montezuma (1480?–1520) and Cortes (1485–1547) during the conquest of Mexico. *El tuerto es rey* (1970; the one-eyed man is king) is essentially a dialogue between two blind individuals, neither of whom realizes that the other cannot see, but each of whom is in desperate need for support from the other. The play can best be related to the BECKETT school of contemporary theater.

During his first two decades of writing, F. published numerous articles in diverse foreign journals, as well as regular columns in two leftist magazines in Mexico, *Siempre* and *Política*. A sampling of his political essays can be found in *La revolución de mayo* (1968; the May revolution) and in *Tiempo mexicano* (1971; Mexican time), an interpretation of key events and personalities in recent Mexican history.

La nueva novela hispanoamericana (1969; the new novel in hispanic America) is a seminal work interpreting the rise of the Latin American "new novel." As a participant as well as a thoughtful critic, F. offers valuable insights into one of the most flourishing areas of 20th-c. fiction. His fourth volume of essays, *Casa con dos puertos* (1970; the house with two doors), is of more general cultural orientation and underlines F.'s vast intellectual background.

During the 1980s, C. continued to enhance his literary reputation with *Gringo viejo* (1985; *The Old Gringo*, 1985) and *Critóbal nonato* (1987; *Christopher Unborn*, 1989). In 1990, he published a series of novellas entitled *Contancia y otras novelas para vírgenes*

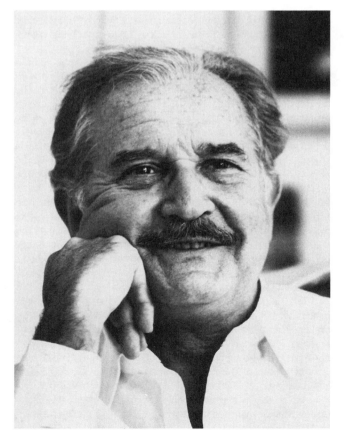

Carlos Fuentes

(*Constancia and Other Stories For Virgins*, 1990) and *La campana* (1990; *The Campaign*, 1991).

F. represents a unique link between the Latin American and the North American novel. He is at home equally in English and Spanish. He has read North American writers in depth and enjoys personal contact with William STYRON, Norman MAILER, and Arthur MILLER. In his writings perhaps his most valuable contribution has been twofold: to introduce innovative techniques into mainstream Latin American fiction and to define the Mexican national character, both in terms of its struggle with its inferiority complex as well as in the more universal terms of the 20th-c. existentialist hero. He, Juan RULFO, and Agustín YÁÑEZ are generally considered the three major novelists of contemporary Mexico.

FURTHER WORKS: *Las buenas conciencias* (1959; *The Good Conscience*, 1961); *Aura* (1962; *Aura*, 1965); *Whither Latin America?* (1963); *Cantar de ciegos* (1964); *Zona sagrada* (1967; *Holy Place*, in *Triple Cross*, 1972); *Cumpleaños* (1969); *Los reinos imaginarios* (1971); *Cuerpos y ofrendas* (1972); *Una familia lejana* (1980; *Distant Relations*, 1981). FURTHER WORKS IN ENGLISH: *Burnt Water: Stories* (1980)

BIBLIOGRAPHY: Mead, R. G., Jr., "C. F.: Mexico's Angry Novelist," *BA*, 38 (1964): 380–82; Harss, L., and Dohmann, B., *Into the Mainstream* (1967): 276–309; Sommers, J., *After the Storm* (1968): 95–164; Reeve, R. M., "An Annotated Bibliography on C. F.: 1949–1969," *Hispania*, 53 (1970): 595–652; Guzman, D. de, *C. F.* (1972); Giacomán, H., ed., *Homenaje a C. F.* (1972); Faris, W. B., *C. F.* (1983)

—RICHARD M. REEVE

FUGARD, Athol

South African dramatist (writing in English), b. 11 June 1932, Middleburg

F., of mixed Afrikaner and English parentage, grew up in Port Elizabeth. He first became involved in the theater in 1957, when he organized an experimental group in Cape Town. A year later his experience as a clerk in the Native Commissioner's Court in Johannesburg, dealing with "pass law" violations, led him to write plays based on the unhappy circumstances of Africans whom he met in the court.

The first works by F. to achieve international recognition were his "Port Elizabeth plays": *The Blood Knot* (perf. 1961, pub. 1963), *Hello and Goodbye* (perf. 1965, pub. 1966), and *Boesman and Lena* (perf. and pub. 1969). *Hello and Goodbye* and *Boesman and Lena* were written for the Serpent Players, a drama group that some hopeful black actors in Port Elizabeth's "township" asked him to organize in 1963. The casts of these plays are small: two or three characters confront each other in tense, painful moments which reveal a humanity that cannot be completely overmastered by an antihuman racial milieu. *The Blood Knot* deals with two half brothers, sons of the same mother, who work to save for a farm where they can be free. Zachariah, the darker brother, learns that the "pen pal" he has discovered in a newspaper advertisement is the sister of a white policeman, and Morris, who is light-skinned enough to "pass" for white, realizes that the dream of the farm is

hopeless but that the blood that links him to Zachariah is less of a "knot" than their love. *Hello and Goodbye*, the most despairing of the three plays, concerns a brother and sister waiting for their father to die so that they can claim an inheritance which, in fact, does not exist. *Boesman and Lena* are a "Coloured" husband and wife, homeless because "progress" has bulldozed their shanty-town; they camp by a roadside and berate each other until Lena finds a release in her pity for an old African who has been dumped in a field to die.

In 1967, influenced by the theories of the Polish experimental theater director Jerzy Grotowski (b. 1933), F. and his black actors began to experiment with improvisational theater. While F. provided the starting point for the two resulting plays and directed the process by which John Kani and Winston Ntshoni improvised the dialogue, the plays' texture and force emerged from the inner experiences of the actors; F. credited them as fellow "devisers" of the plays, *Sizwe Bansi Is Dead* (perf. 1972, pub. 1974) and *The Island* (perf. 1973, pub. 1974). These works avoid the pitfalls of didacticism, a real danger because of their subject matter (the "pass" law and the political prison on Robben Island, respectively), by transforming the real social ordeal of the doubly real people—the actors *and* their roles—into artistic and therefore meaningful structures.

Fugard's international reputation was assured with *"Master Harold" . . . and the Boys* (perf. and pub. 1982), a painful autobiographical work which, after great inner turmoil and pangs of conscience, he was able to write about an episode of his childhood which he has always considered the most shameful moment of his life—spitting into the face of an African friend. For Fugard this lapse apparently defined the exact nature of the veils of apartheid, and his work as a whole perhaps may be said to have emerged from that haunting memory.

Two other major works reflect the political and moral conflicts of apartheid in its final collapsing state. In *My Children! My Africa!* (perf. and pub. 1989) a conservative African schoolmaster who dreams of the reconciliation of all South Africans coaches a white girl and an African boy, his prize student, as a team in an interschool English literature quiz. But he is accused of being a police informer, a mob of his own students kill him, and the African student abandons his education for the sake of political activism. *A Lesson from Aloes* (perf. 1978, pub. 1981) is concerned with a black activist who is preparing to flee the country, his Afrikaner friend, whom he is tempted to suspect was the informer who betrayed him, and the friend's wife, who has not been able to recover from the symbolic rape of having her most personal diaries confiscated and read by the police. One of her lines sums up the point of the play and may serve as a statement of a primary theme that Fugard has served throughout his career: "Politics and black skins don't make the only victims in this country."

Tsotsi, a powerful short novel written in 1959–60, was published in 1979. It is concerned with a Sophia Town thug who is orphaned as a child, survives by crimes ranging from theft to murder, and, before his violent death, begins to discover his humanity when he happens to find an abandoned baby. The novel is stark in its realism, the social conditions it describes are appalling, and the mastery of fictional techniques makes clear that if F. had not chosen the theater he probably would have had an equally distinguished career as a novelist.

F.'s career reveals a great courage to experiment, a willingness to take artistic risks, a remarkable capacity for avoiding mere didacticism, and profound sympathy for his human subjects. His ability to transform local South African conflicts into universal human predicaments suggests that his future career will continue the steady growth he has already demonstrated.

FURTHER WORKS: *People Are Living There* (1970); *The Coat* (1971); *Statements after an Arrest under the Immorality Act* (1974); *Dimetos and Two Early Plays* (1977); *The Guest* (1977); *A Lesson from Aloes* (1978); *Marigolds in August* (1982); *Notebooks: 1960-1977* (1983); *The Road to Mecca* (1985); *A Place with the Pigs* (1988); *Playland* (1993); *Cousins: A Memoir* (1994); *Valley Song* (1996); *My Life* (1996)

BIBLIOGRAPHY: Berner, R. L., "A. F. And the Theatre of Improvisation," *BA*, 50 (1976): 81-84; Tucker, A. C., "A. F. Interviewed," *Transatlantic*, Nos. 53–54 (1976): 87–90; Green, R. J., "Politics and Literature in Africa: The Drama of A. F.," in Hayward, C., ed., *Aspects of South African Literature* (1976): 163-73; Benson, M., "Keeping an Appointment with the Future: The Theatre of A. F.," *TheatreQ*, 28 (1977-78): 77-83; "F. on Acting: Actors on F.," *TheatreQ* 28 (1977–78): 83–87; O'Sheel, P., "A. F.'s 'Poor Theatre,' " *JCL*, 12, 3 (1978): 67–77; Gussow, M., "Witness," *New Yorker* 20 Dec. 1982:47-94; Gray, Stephen, ed., *A. F.* (1982); Vandenbroucke, R., *Truths the Hands Can Touch: The Theatre of A. F.* (1985); Walder, D., *A. F.* (1985)

—ROBERT L. BERNER

FUKS, Ladislav

Czechoslovak novelist and short-story writer (writing in Czech), b. 24 Sept. 1923, Prague; d. 19 Aug. 1994, Prague

F. studied philosophy and psychology at the Charles University in Prague and in 1949 received his doctorate. For some time he worked in various nonliterary professions, but since 1960 he has devoted himself entirely to literature.

F. is one of the most significant of contemporary Czech writers of fiction; he has experimented with highly inventive and original ways of expressing the problems, formal and semantic, that preoccupy contemporary literature. His first novel, *Pan Theodor Mundstock* (1963; *Mr. Theodore Mundstock*, 1968), is set in Prague during the German occupation. It is an ironic treatment of tragedy with strong mythic overtones, and, like so many of F.'s works, it focuses on the inner life of the hero. A Prague Jew, a little man without particular attributes, awaits arrest and transportation to a concentration camp. While waiting, he attempts to prepare himself to withstand the cruelties of the camp by training himself for the rigors he expects. But he is run over by a German military truck on his way to the collection point for the transport.

Mí černovlasí bratři (1964; my dark-haired brothers) is a series of short stories all told in the first person by a young secondary-school student. They take place in the early years of the German occupation and depict the plight of the Jewish fellow students of the narrator, who are tormented by a cruel geography teacher.

F.'s second novel, *Variace na temnou strunu* (1966; variations for a dark string), continues the basic theme of *Pan Theodor Mundstock* and *Mé černovlasí bratři*, that of the threat of the German occupiers. The novel, about the psychological maturing of a boy from the ages of six through fourteen, is dominated by

paradox and a sense of the absurd and is infused with strong SURREALIST and cubo-futurist (see FUTURISM) elements. Multiple temporal perspectives coexist in a complex system in which linearity is intertwined with simultaneity.

F.'s third novel, *Spalovač mrtvol* (1967; *The Cremator*, 1984), which was subsequently made into a film, is cast as a modern horror story whose antihero is a crematorium official, Kopferkringl, who professes kindliness but is in fact a murderer. Again, the novel focuses upon a paradox: the protagonist does not appear to be an evil man; he seems to be harmless and obedient to law and order, and upholds all the normative platitudes, such as that man should not have to suffer. Yet he commits ghastly murders—not out of hate but because the circumstances of his time lead him to crime. He begins by killing his part-Jewish wife and children and ends by putting his crematorium experience to work in the gas chambers of the Nazi concentration camps. The repetitions of key episodes and phrases account for both a fragmentation of traditional reality and an intensification of the internal structure of the work.

F.'s most significant short stories are found in the collection *Smrt morčete* (1969; the death of the guinea pig); they are again set in the time of the German occupation. The longest and most significant story, "Cesta do zaslíbené země" (the trip to the promised land), is based on a biblical myth, which is grotesquely set against the reality of German-occupied Europe.

In the novel *Myši Natalie Mooshabrové* (1970; Natalia Mooshaber's mice) there is a striking culmination of the trends begun in F.'s earlier work. It is a synthesis of various modes of modern literature: the grotesque gothic horror story set in a Kafkaesque dream world; science fiction; and the NEW NOVEL; these elements are, in turn, juxtaposed with the fairy tale and with archetypal myths. In this work, F. amalgamates the most variegated traditional genres into a new stylistic whole, freed from the conventions of both realistic and surrealistic texts.

F. is preoccupied with the fate of the Jews in German-occupied Europe. But he uses his subjects as a point of departure, for the Jews represent the human condition, and their fate is that of all mankind. Furthermore, the Nazi occupation must be seen as a metaphor for any oppressive system. For F. is concerned with the individual living in the alienated world of today, a world of violence and injustice.

Ater the Warsaw Pact invasion of 1968, F. wrote three novels in which he tried to assimilate the demands of official communist propaganda. He returned to authentic writing in an extensive historical novel *Vévodkyně a kuchařka* (1983; a duchess and a cook), a vivid evocation of life in Vienna shortly before the disintegration of Austria-Hungary.

FURTHER WORKS: *Příběh kriminálního rady* (1971); *Oslovení z tmy* (1972); *Návrat z žitného pole* (1974); *Pasáček z doliny* (1977); *Křišťalový pantoflíček: Příběh z dětství Juliusa Fučíka* (1978)

BIBLIOGRAPHY: Elman, R., on *Mr. Theodore Mundstock*, *NYTBR*, 28 Jan. 1968: 5; Winner, T. G., "Some Remarks on the Art of L. F.," *RSI*, 17–19 (1970–72): 587–99; Winner, T. G., "Mystic and Modern Elements in the Art of L. F.: *Natalia Mooshaber's Mice*," in Birnbaum, H., and T. Eekman, eds., *Fiction and Drama in Eastern and Southerneastern Europe* (1980): 443-61; Kanikova, S. I., "The Jews in the Works of L. F.," in Maxwell, E., et al., eds., *Remembering for the Future*, 3 (1989): 2946-57

—THOMAS G. WINNER

FULANI LITERATURE
See Mali Literature

FULLER, Charles H., Jr.

American playwright, b. 5 Mar. 1939, Philadelphia, Pennsylvania

Gaining experience as the cofounder and codirector of the Afro-American Arts Theatre in Philadelphia (1967-71), F. became known for plays that questioned basic assumptions of the civil rights movement. As an African-American, his themes caused some controversy, particularly within the black community. *The Village: A Party* (1968) concerns the social tension that develops when a black member of an imaginary community of black and white couples falls in love with another black member. The play suggests that integration does not solve all racial problems. Coming at a time when the original optimistic perspective of the civil rights struggle was yielding to particular economic and social concerns, *The Village* captured critical attention and some notoriety. F.'s realistic dialogue and developed characterization was praised, but certain critics revealed either relief that integration wouldn't work, or their resentment that F's theme expressed a retrograde viewpoint at a time when civil rights activism was still necessary.

F.'s army experience (1959-62) inspired two of his major plays, *The Brownsville Raid* (perf. 1976) and *A Soldier's Play* (perf. 1981, pub. 1982; adapted for the screen as *A Soldier's Story*, 1984). Both have quite similar themes: racial double standards in the 20th-c. U.S. military. *The Brownsville Raid* began F.'s important association with New York's Negro Ensemble Company. It concerns a true incident in 1906 when all 167 African-American soldiers of a segregated regiment refused to confess to inciting a riot in the largely white Brownsville, Texas. Despite sketchy and contradictory evidence, all members of the regiment were dishonorably discharged, their names not cleared by the army until 1972. Critics praised F.'s realistic characterization and historical accuracy, pointing out that the play went beyond its political tract to represent fully developed black soldiers who are not politically aware ahead of their time.

Zooman and the Sign (perf. 1980, pub. 1982), also first produced at the Negro Ensemble Company (1979), is set in a poor Philadelphia neighborhood. Its characters, victims of urban renewal and neglect, reveal their ambivalence towards the murder of a young neighborhood girl. Ideals of justice and equality seem distant from such a setting, but F. succeeds in presenting a thoughtful, if not fully explored, expression of poverty's despondency. The play won an Obie Award in 1981. *A Soldier's Play*, another Negro Ensemble Company production, won the Obie in 1981 for Best Playwright, the Pulitzer Prize for Drama (1982), the Best American Play Award from the New York Critics (1982), and the Outer Circle Critics Award for Best Play (1982). It concerns an African American army sergeant who has been killed by other soldiers. The black army lawyer sent to investigate the murder is regarded with pride by the black enlisted men, who have never seen a black officer before, but with hostility and suspicion by the white officers. Presented in a series of flashbacks, the murdered sergeant is perhaps F.'s most successfully developed character. Placed between the army's white command staff, who exclude him socially, and the black enlisted men, who regard him with fear and

dislike, Sergeant Waters is a study in self-hatred and sadism. Compelled to harass and eventually destroy soldiers under his command, he loathes a type of black soldier who fits white conceptions of the carefree, uneducated African American. Waters humiliates and frames one such soldier, then reveals to him his own personal history of rejection and humiliation as a black man in the army since World War I. F.'s plot shows obvious parallels with Melville's novella *Billy Budd*, where a noncommissioned officer also develops a hatred for an enlisted man. However, whereas Melville's Claggart hates Billy because of his goodness and popularity, Waters's hatred springs from racial self-hatred, brought on by his own rejection by a military to which he has devoted his life. Despite his villainous behavior, Waters is presented with compassion, as one who has been morally perverted by a racist system that uses him without recognition.

As a playwright F. presents a rare combination of political ideology and psychological exposition. Often critical of the shallowness of the politically correct, he demonstrates the perplexities of social issues, careful to situate his characters within their historical context.

FURTHER WORKS: *In My Many Names and Days* (perf. 1972); *The Candidate* (perf. 1974); *In the Deepest Part of Sleep* (perf. 1974); *First Love* (perf. 1974); *The Lay Out Letter* (perf. 1975); *Sparrow in Flight* (perf. 1978); *A Gathering of Old Men* (1987); *Sally* (1988); *Prince* (1988); *We* (1989); *Sonnyboy* (1993); *Miles* (1994); *Zooman* (1995); *The Badge* (1995)

BIBLIOGRAPHY: White, F., "Pushing Beyond the Pulitzer," *Ebony*, 38 (Mar. 1983): 116-18; Baraka, A., "The Descent of C. F. into Pulitzerland and the Need for African-American Institutions," *Black-American Literature Forum*, 17 (Summer 1983): 51-54; Demastes, W. W., "C. F. and *A Soldier's Play*: Attacking Prejudice, Challenging Form," *Studies in American Drama*, 2 (1987): 43-56; Harriott, E., *American Voices: Five Contemporary Playwrights in Essays and Interviews* (1988); Neal. L., *Visions of a Liberated Future: Black Arts Movement Writings* (1989)

—WILLIAM OVER

FULLER, Roy

English poet and novelist, b. 11 Feb. 1912, Failsworth; d. 27 Sept. 1991, London

F. was born and raised in a provincial, lower-middle-class milieu in Lancashire. When he was eight years old his father died, and two years later the family moved to Blackpool, where he was educated in the local high school. F. was anxious to escape to London, and at the age of sixteen he left school and was articled to a solicitor. Five years later he qualified as a lawyer and from 1933 to 1968 he followed both a legal and literary career.

The poetry that he has always chosen to write is to a large degree socially and politically motivated, and indeed the subject matter and the style of his work may reflect his dual commitment to both verbal and legal matters. In 1968 F. retired as a solicitor and was elected to a five-year term as a professor of poetry at Oxford. After that he kept up a steady stream of poems, reviews, essays, lectures, and novels. The consistency that marks the thirteen books of poems, three children's books, eight novels, and two collections of essays that he published attest to his steadiness and productivity as a writer.

F. was the only English writer affiliated with and influenced by both the political writers of the 1930s (W. H. AUDEN, Stephen SPENDER, and C. Day LEWIS) and the "Movement" writers of the 1950s (Philip LARKIN, John WAIN, and Donald Davie [b. 1922]). He writes a poetry of high civility and intelligibility, and he most often speaks in his poems as a private man registering his response to public events. Auden has been the most important influence on F.'s development, affecting the style, the tone, and the subject matter of his work. As an essentially social poet, F. matured rapidly during World War II, and indeed the war marks the great watershed in his work, separating his first three books—*Poems* (1939), *The Middle of a War* (1942), and *A Lost Season* (1944)—from those that followed. Some of the early poems note the fears and forebodings of the ordinary citizen; others are soliloquies and epitaphs for the war dead. It is in this context that one poem announces, "Life at last I know is terrible . . ." ("What Is Terrible," 1944).

But F. survived the war, and after two books of juvenile fiction—*Savage Gold* (1946) and *With My Little Eye* (1948)—he turned his new poetry to civilian affairs. The voice that animates the postwar poems is still skillful, witty, and formal, still thoroughly political. The majority of F.'s work takes the stance of a middle-aged suburban man addressing in quiet, autobiographical tones the public life of his times. The central political ideology behind F.'s work is Marxist socialism, and the materialist conception of history infuses and informs both his poems and his novels. His imaginative concerns are essentially civic, and he has never swerved from the central Wordsworthian ideal that the poet is a man speaking to other men. But F.'s sensibility is more Augustan than romantic, more rational than emotive, and it is fair to say that his first concern is our shared social life. He has perhaps put his own case best in "Obituary for R. Fuller" (1949) when he writes: "If any bit of him survives/It will be that verse which contrives/To speak in private symbols for/The peaceful caught in public war." One of the major strengths of F.'s work is the way in which his private symbols do in fact reflect the life of a representative man inevitably implicated in the extraordinary events of his own time.

F.'s calm and thoughtful life's work addresses itself to a series of tumultuous events and ongoing social wars. He is one of our minor masters of the public mode.

FURTHER WORKS: *Epitaphs and Occasions* (1949); *The Second Curtain* (1953); *Fantasy and Fugue* (1954); *Counterparts* (1954); *Image of a Society* (1956); *Brutus's Orchard* (1957); *The Ruined Boys* (1959); *The Father's Comedy* (1961); *Collected Poems* (1962); *The Perfect Fool* (1963); *My Child, My Sister* (1965); *Buff* (1965); *Catspaw* (1966); *New Poems* (1968); *The Carnal Island* (1970); *Owls and Artificers: Oxford Lectures on Poetry* (1971); *Professors and Gods* (1973); *Tiny Tears* (1973); *An Old War* (1974); *From the Joke Shop* (1975); *The Joke Shop Annexe* (1975); *Poor Roy* (1977)

BIBLIOGRAPHY: Hamilton, I., "Professor of Poetry," *Listener*, 5 (1968): 761–62; Woodcock, G., "Private Images of Public Ills: The Poetry of R. F.," *WascanaR*, 4, 2 (1969): 21–34; Garfitt, R., "Intimate Anxieties," *London*, Dec.-Jan. 1975–76: 102–9; Austin, A., *R. F.* (1979)

—EDWARD HIRSCH

FURPHY, Joseph

(pseud.: Tom Collins) Australian novelist and short-story writer, b. 26 Sept. 1843, Yering (now Yarra Glen); d. 13 Sept. 1912, Claremont

Except for a short period of formal schooling, F. was educated at home. Subsequently, he found employment in a variety of rural occupations. Drought forced him to take up more reliable work in his brother's foundry in Shepparton. It was during this period, and at the age of fifty, that F. began to write a novel based on his bush experiences.

Such Is Life: Being Certain Extracts from the Life of Tom Collins, described by its author as being of a "temper democratic; bias, offensively Australian," first confronted a bewildered reading public in 1903. It purports to be a plotless, realistic chronicle. However, its narrator, Tom Collins, because of his insensitivity and his fondness for philosophizing, fails to discern the lineaments of a romance between a jilted woman (whose face has been grotesquely disfigured by a fall from a horse) and her remorseful, melancholy, misogynistic lover. Unwittingly, Tom provides inaccurate information, which could reunite the lovers. So elaborate and subtly disguised is this submerged plot that many first-time readers of the novel fail to recognize it, as indeed did many of its early critics. It is not merely the comic potential of this hidden plot that F. exploits; rather, he uses his self-consciously literary narrator to explore the nature of fictional narrative, rejecting unequivocally the romance genre employed in such novels of Australian life as the English writer Henry Kingsley's (1803–1876) *Recollections of Geoffrey Hamlyn* (1859). *Such Is Life* also raises, in a piquantly ironic form, the philosophical question of why events occur. Tom contructs a theory (the "one-controlling alternative" theory), which is finally deterministic, but purports to be a compromise between predestination and free will; the events of the novel ironically undermine the theory, and suggest that the author believes that the moral man is the one who takes responsibility for his own actions.

The Buln-Buln and the Brolga (published posthumously in 1948), nominally a series of bush men's yarns and tall stories, further explores the relationship between fact and fiction. It poses the question of whether artistic reshaping of the facts distorts reality and is therefore morally culpable, or whether it imaginatively enhances reality. Tom, as unreliable narrator, favors the former viewpoint, but finds himself humiliated and outnumbered by exponents of the latter view. F. continually presents him as clownish, as incapable of morally evaluating his own actions, and as continually evading reality and intimacy by escapes into theory and literature.

Rigby's Romance: A "Made in Australia" Novel (first published in serial form in *The Barrier Truth* in 1905–6, and in novel form in 1946) belongs to the genre of argumentative utopian novels. F. uses the character of Jeff Rigby to expound on a subject close to F.'s heart: the Christian socialist state. Like the other novels, this one has an ironic framing narrative, involving another hopeless romance between the stump orator and his lovelorn American woman. In this novel, however, the narrative is secondary to F.'s didactic purposes.

Together with Henry Lawson (1867–1922), F. has been regarded as one of the chief exemplars of the tradition of bush nationalism in Australian literary history. However, because of his erudition (used invariably for ironic ends), his consciousness of belonging to the wider European literary tradition, his concern with moral and social issues and with philosophical and literary questions, his significance is more than merely regional. F. undoubtedly overestimates the patience and perceptiveness of the average reader to penetrate the extraordinarily comic and ironic personae of Tom Collins. Those readers prepared to engage in the intellectual gymnastics involved in reading *Such Is Life* may find that it resembles Laurence Sterne's *Tristram Shandy* in being comic in sensibility and ironic and jocular in mode of narration. But the novel is *sui generis*: it is a witty, daring, and literate novel, an unusual product of a raw colonial culture.

FURTHER WORKS: *The Poems of J. F.* (1916)

BIBLIOGRAPHY: Phillips, A. A., "The Australian Image: (2) The Literary Heritage Re-assessed," *Meanjin*, 21 (1962): 172–80; Barnes, J., *J. F.* (1963); Kiernan, B., "Society and Nature in *Such Is Life,*" *ALS*, 1 (1963): 75–88; McKenzie, K. A., "J. F., Jacobean," *ALS*, 2 (1966): 266–77; Knight, N., "F. and Romance in *Such Is Life,*" *Southerly*, 29 (1969): 243–55

—FRANCES DEVLIN GLASS

FURUI Yoshikichi

Japanese novelist, short-story writer, and essayist, b. 19 Nov. 1937, Tokyo

F. graduated from the German literature department of Tokyo University in 1960 and stayed on to complete his master's degree in 1962. He then took a post as a German literature instructor at Kanazawa University and later at Rikkyō University in Tokyo. During his years as an academic, he published translations of the works of Hermann BROCH and Robert MUSIL. F.'s involvement with German literature in his early career is reflected in the style and themes of his later stories and novels, particularly in his concern with the fragmentation and disorientation of the self in modern society.

In 1966 F. joined the literary coterie *Hakubyō no kai* (plain sketch club), and his first original short story, "Mokuyōbi ni" (on Thursday), was published in its magazine in 1968. Soon his stories began to appear in a wide variety of literary magazines, and F. resigned his teaching position to devote himself to writing on a full-time basis. His career as a writer was assured when he received the prestigious Akutagawa Prize for his novella *Yōko* (1970; Yoko) in 1971.

The title character in *Yōko*, a beautiful schizophrenic young woman, is one of many characters in F.'s works who experience the world from a distorted, but ultimately more discerning, perspective. Through a painstakingly detailed portrayal of the thoughts and perceptions of a human being under the duress of mental or physical illness or exhaustion, F. delves beneath the façade of everyday life in contemporary Japan to reveal the irrational forces lurking within. Subtle shifts in self-awareness rather than broad drama characterize his plots. Another early work, "Tsumagomi" (1971; "Wedlock," 1977), a glimpse into a day in the life of a young married couple living in a newly developed Tokyo suburb, illustrates a setting typical of F.'s works: that of the spatial borderland between virgin wilderness and urban sprawl that serves as a metaphor for the spiritual one between folk traditions and the

Joseph Furphy

monotonous, impersonal existence of the city dweller. The protagonist's brief illness and a chance meeting with an old woman who mistakes him for one of her converts to a new religion disrupt his complacent routine. F.'s protagonists, passive but unusually perceptive observers of life, often find themselves in the wryly humorous situation of being mistaken for someone else by strangers or inexplicably unrecognizable to friends, underlining the instability of human identity.

F.'s scrutiny of the inner experience of ordinary life marks a departure from the politically conscious writers of the 1960s. He and several other writers—among them Kuroi Senji (b. 1932), Abe Akira (b. 1934), Gotō Meisei (b. 1932), Ogawa Kunio (b. 1927), and Kashiwabara Hyozō (1933–1972)—making their debuts in the early 1970s, came to be grouped together as the *naikō no sedai* (introverted generation), a term that has gradually lost its original derogatory slant. F. is generally regarded as the most representative of the group and is noted for the dense texture of his prose and his inaccessibility to the average reader. However, his works are not without implicit social commentary concerning the role of the individual in modern urban society and the pathogenic nature of society itself. Cancer, the metaphorical disease of modern life, frequently appears in F.'s stories.

The novel *Hijiri* (1976; a sage) further explores the power of the ambiguous realm where the Japanese past and present collide. An injured mountain climber temporarily takes on the role of the holy man who disposes of the dead in a remote village and finds himself drawn into rituals of defilement and purification which hearken back to Japan's most ancient myths. The Japanese classics and elements of folk culture play a surprisingly central and evocative role in F.'s portrayals of contemporary life.

More recent works show a greater emphasis on the subject of coming to terms with aging and death, beginning as early as the short-story collection *Aihara* (1977; plain of sorrow). These later collections have a more flexible, flowing structure reminiscent of the traditional Japanese essay. In *Yoru wa ima* (1987; now is night) F. expresses his perennial subjects of the nature of consciousness and the flux of identity in a stylistically complex shift between narrative and personal meditation. *Kari ōjō denshibun* (1989; a tentative attempt at a tale of salvation) juxtaposes elaborated versions of stories from the Heian Period of the death and rebirth of Buddhist monks in paradise, with vignettes of modern life that reveal "the hysteria lurking quietly in everyday life."

F. has also increasingly turned his attention to the Japanese essay proper as is the case with most established writers in Japan. His essays echo the concerns and themes of his novels and stories: the illusive nature of reality and the fluid boundaries of human identity.

F. may well be remembered as one of the definitive writers of his generation, a time when Japan was beginning to become aware of the clash between modern and traditional values and the problem of defining the individual subject in a mass society. His stories and essays show a deep sensitivity to the mystery and the dark humor inherent in the everyday life of ordinary people.

FURTHER WORKS: *Enjin o kumu onnatachi* (1970); *Otokotachi no madoi* (1970); *Yukigakure* (1972); *Mizu* (1973); *Kushi no hi* (1974); *Onnatachi no ie* (1977); *Yoru no kaori* (1978); *Sumika* (1979); *F. Y. zen essei* (1980); *Mukudori* (1980); *Oya* (1980); *Sansōfu* (1982); *F. Y. sakuhin* (1982–1983); *Asagao* (1983); *Shōkon no sasayaki* (1984); *Ake no akauma* (1985); *Biu* (1986); *Rara chūki* (1986); *Hi ya getsu ya* (1988); *Musil no kannen no eros* (1988); *Nagai machi no nemuri* (1990)

BIBLIOGRAPHY: Iwamoto, Y., "F.: Exemplar of the 'Introverted Generation,'" *WLT*, 62, 3 (Summer 1988): 385–90

—DONNA GEORGE STOREY

FUTABATEI Shimei

(pseud. of Hasegawa Tatsunosuke) Japanese novelist and translator, b. 4 April 1864, Tokyo; d. 10 May 1909, on shipboard in the Bay of Bengal

Born into the samurai class, F. entered the Russian division of the Tokyo School of Foreign Languages in 1881 and fell passionately in love with Russian literature. He made his reputation early with translations of stories by Turgenev and with *Ukigumo* (1887–89; *Ukigumo*, 1967), Japan's first modern novel. Despairing of surviving as a professional writer, he entered the government bureaucracy in 1889. He was also subsequently employed as a teacher and journalist. He resumed publication of translations in 1897, and two final works of fiction appeared early in the 20th c.: *Sono omokage* (1906; *An Adopted Husband*, 1919) and *Heibon* (1907; *Mediocrity*, 1927). He died on shipboard of an illness while returning home from Russia.

In constructing *Ukigumo* (whose title literally means "drifting clouds"), F. introduced limitations of time, space, and character

previously unknown in Japanese fiction. Confining his novel to a detailed study of four characters within a two-week period, and limiting the action to a minute geographical area, he concentrated on probing into his characters' lives with an intensity generally absent in earlier fiction. Their problems are such as might be shared by any of his contemporaries, and the language they speak in internalized comments and to each other is the language of his time. Readers were able to approach F.'s narrative without the special knowledge required for much of the earlier fiction of Japan, and they responded eagerly to this new accessibility. It was a novel for and about the emerging, more egalitarian Japan, and it provided a model for subsequent generations.

Sono omokage deals with the agonies of an intellectual adopted into his wife's family, and *Heibon* is actually a series of short sketches—seemingly autobiographical—reflecting the weary and frustrated tone of the Japanese naturalist school.

In all of his fiction F. maintained an attractive balance between bittersweet humor and pathos. There are no major tragedies nor is there sustained slapstick. The reader finds instead a sense of appropriateness. Emotions are confined within plausible boundaries, and actions are no more or less than his contemporaries are likely to have experienced.

The language in which F. wrote his translations and fiction is remarkably vibrant and contributed significantly to the development of modern Japanese prose. Just as F.'s Russian models portrayed their own class and society—with all its limitations—so F. sought to hold the mirror of fiction up to his compatriots in Japan.

FURTHER WORKS: *Zenshū* (16 vols., 1953–54)

BIBLIOGRAPHY: Ryan, M. G., *"Ukigumo": Japan's First Modern Novel* (1967); Ryan, M. G., *The Development of Realism in the Fiction of Tsubouchi Shōyō* (1975)

—MARLEIGH GRAYER RYAN

FUTURISM

Italian Futurism

Initially an Italian literary movement, futurism was founded by Filippo Tommaso MARINETTI in February 1909 when he published, in French, his "Manifeste du Futurisme" ("The Founding and Manifesto of Futurism," 1971) in *Le Figaro* of Paris. Marinetti asserted that civilization was on the threshold of a new historical epoch, and he advocated the absolute rejection of the past with all its museums, libraries, and academies. The essential elements of poetry would henceforth be "courage, audacity, and rebellion"; its new aesthetic criteria were to be speed and aggression, concretized in automobiles, airplanes, and war. The "Manifesto technico della letteratura futurista" ("Technical Manifesto of Futurist Literature," 1971), published in May 1912, specified the means by which writers could achieve this revolution: adjectives, adverbs, punctuation, and syntax were proscribed. In their place, the writer would use substantives, verbs in the infinitive mood, and mathematical symbols; analogy would supplant syntax. Words would thus be freed (*parole in libertà*) from their historical and logical functions. Repudiating the psychological foundations of previous literature,

Marinetti proposed concentrating on the physical—noise, weight, and smells—in order to realize a spontaneous, dynamic, and concrete poetry.

Futurism's emphasis on the sensuous and the dynamic appealed to painters, sculptors, and performing artists. Futurist manifestos, some by Marinetti, some by others, soon appeared on music, theater, and film. Indeed, even the literature of futurism had its theatrical aspect; as the critic Luigi Russo (1892–1961) noted, Marinetti's temperament was not that of a poet: he was an actor whose works must be declaimed rather than read.

The period 1909–15 was the heyday of futurism. It attracted, however briefly, some of Italy's finest writers: Corrado Govoni (1884–1965), Aldo PALAZZESCHI, Giovanni Papini (1881–1956), and Ardengo Soffici (1879–1964). It also spawned or influenced similar movements in other European countries. The roots of English Vorticism, founded in 1914 by Percy Wyndham LEWIS, are embedded in Italian soil. Russian futurism, although in many respects an autonomous phenomenon, was influenced by Marinetti's movement and perhaps by Marinetti himself: he appears to have visited Russia as early as 1910. Unlike the Italian movement, however, Russian futurism produced a significant body of literature.

Although futurism can be said to have disappeared only with Marinetti's death in 1944, its influence declined rapidly after Italy's intervention in World War I. The futurists had long and loudly proclaimed war to be the "hygiene of the world," but their bellicose attitude was not universally popular in Italy. Moreover, in 1914 Marinetti had become friends with Benito Mussolini, and the association between Fascism and futurism alienated many active and potential supporters of the movement. Futurist activities in the 1920s focused on the theater, film, and radio; the last performance took place on radio in 1933.

The significance of Italian futurism does not lie in its literary masterpieces—there are none. Yet its achievements are considerable. It freed Italian poetry definitively from its traditional language and its postromantic themes, thus opening the way for modern poets like Giuseppe UNGARETTI and Eugenio MONTALE. Painting and sculpture of futurist inspiration fared much better: Umberto Boccioni (1882–1916), Giacomo Balla (1871–1958), Carlo Carrà (1881–1966), Gino Severini (1883–1966), and Luigi Russolo (1885–1947) all created distinguished works of art. The futurist music produced by mechanical "noise-intoners" presaged synthetic electronic music, while the futurist theater directly influenced Luigi PIRANDELLO and Thornton WILDER. Although futurism has to a large extent been overshadowed by other avant-garde literary movements in Europe, there can be no doubt that it anticipated and made important contributions to DADAISM, SURREALISM, EXPRESSIONISM, and the THEATER OF THE ABSURD.

BIBLIOGRAPHY: Kirby, M., *Futurist Performance* (1971); Marinetti, F. T., *Selected Writings* (1971); Rye, J., *Futurism* (1972); Apollonio, U., ed., *Futurist Manifestos* (1973); Andreoli-De Villers, J.-P., *Futurism and the Arts: A Bibliography*: 1959–73 (1975); Tindall, C., and A. Bozzolla, *Futurism* (1978)

—LOUIS KIBLER

Russian Futurism

Russian futurism arose after the dissolution of Russian SYMBOLISM around 1910. It represents one of the major Russian contributions to the international avant-garde movement in art and literature. There were four main groups: Hylaea, also known as cubo-futurism, whose earliest activities date back to 1908–9; ego-futurism, organized in Petersburg in 1911 by the popular poet Igor Severyanin (1887–1941); The "Mezzanine of Poetry," a Moscow group initiated in 1913 by Vadim Shershenevich (1893–1942); and Centrifuge, started in 1913 in Moscow and including the poets Boris PASTERNAK and Nikolay Assev (1889–1963).

By far the most important group was the cubo-futurists, organized by the poet and painter David Burlyuk (1882–1967), and including two of the greatest Russian poets of the 20th c., Velemir KHLEBNIKOV and Vladimir MAYAKOVSKY, as well as Alexey Kruchonykh (1886–1968), Vasily Kamensky (1884–1961), and Benedikt Livshits (1887–1939). Livshits later wrote his memoirs, which contain a history of the movement: *Polutoraglazy strelets* (1933; *The One-and-a-Half-Eyed Archer*, 1978). The group's famous manifesto "Poshchyochina obshchestvennomu vkusu" (1912; "A Slap in the Face of Public Taste," 1980), an attack on bourgeois aesthetics and a call for revolution in the arts, set the tempo for its "militant year," 1913–14, which saw a stormy and provocational tour of seventeen provincial Russian cities and the presentation in St. Petersburg's Luna Park in December 1913 of two key futurist works: Kruchonykh's opera *Pobeda nad solntsem* (1913; *Victory over the Sun*, 1971), with backdrops and costumes designed by Kazimir Malevich, and Mayakovsky's extraordinary verse drama *Vladimir Mayakovsky: Tragedia* (1913; *Vladimir Mayakovsky: A Tragedy*, 1968). The cubo-futurists were unanimous in disclaiming the influence of Italian futurism, rejecting its militarism and its emphasis on new content rather than formal innovation, and gave MARINETTI a chilly, at times scandalous, reception when he visited Russia in 1914.

Cubo-futurist aesthetics emphasized the form of poetic language rather than its objective reference or ideational content, and wide-ranging verbal experimentation was its distinguishing characteristic. The futurists' debt to CUBISM is apparent in their call for "rough" poetic texture; their insistence on the break with realism and on the independence of art from reality (Khlebnikov's theory of the *samovitoe slovo*, "selfsome" or "self-oriented word"); their use of "shifts" or "dislocations" (*sdvigi*) on the metrical, semantic, and plot levels; and also their predilection for fragmentary composition. They advocated a new poetic language written "beyond the mind," or *zaum* ("transrational" or "supraconscious" language). For Kruchonykh this concept meant a type of glossolalia, meaningless but expressive sequences of sounds, while for Khlebnikov it entailed the restructuring of the semantics of the language through the revival of dead etymological connections and the creation of new kinships between words based on the similarities in their sound, in particular the "poetic valency" or associative potential of their first consonant. Cubo-futurism was noted for the creation of neologisms and the deformation of existing words through the addition of unusual prefixes and suffixes, the mixing of lexical and stylistic levels, and the cultivation of a generally "antiaesthetic" stance as regards both thematics and the poetic persona.

The futurists failed in their attempt to gain official recognition after the Russian Revolution, although their influence in the 1920s was considerable, as is reflected in the journals Mayakovsky edited, *Lef* (1921–23) and *Novy Lef* (1927–28). Their impact on the development of Russian poetry to the present day has been considerable, and the works of Khlebnikov and Mayakovsky, in particular, remain exemplary for Russian writers of an avant-garde persuasion.

BIBLIOGRAPHY: Markov, V., *Russian Futurism: A History* (1968); Barooshian, V., *Russian Cubo-Futurism* 1910–1930 (1974); Jangfeldt, B., *Majakovskij and Futurism* (1976): 1917–1921; Barron, S., and M. Tuchman, eds., *The Avant-Garde in Russia* 1910–1930: *New Perspectives* (1980); Proffer, C., and E. Proffer, eds., *The Ardis Anthology of Russian Futurism* (1980)

—STEPHEN RUDY

G

GADDA, Carlo Emilio
Italian novelist, short-story writer, and essayist, b. 14 Nov. 1893, Milan; d. 21 May 1973, Rome

G. was born into a family of the well-to-do upper middle class, but because the family lost most of its money and G.'s father died when G. was a child, he was brought up by a mother who tried to keep up appearances and lived beyond her means. G. fought in World War I and in 1917 was taken prisoner by the Germans. In 1920 he received a degree in engineering, and until 1935 he worked at his profession in various countries. In 1926 he began the association with the Florentine review *Solaria* that marked his early career. Between 1950 and 1955 G. worked in Rome for RAI, the Italian radio and television network. He was awarded the Formentor Prize in 1957 and the International Prize for Literature in 1963.

For years G.'s fame as a writer remained confined within the circles of the literati who appreciated his refined belles lettres, memory pieces, and short stories collected in such volumes as *La Madonna dei filosofi* (1931; the philosophers' Madonna), *Il castello di Udine* (1934; the castle of Udine), *L'Adalgisa: Disegni milanesi* (1944; Adalgisa: Milanese drawings), *Novelle dal ducato in fiamme* (1953; tales of the burning duchy), and *Accoppiamenti giudiziosi* (1963; judicious couplings). Yet even in these works there are the qualities to be found in G.'s major books: a keen observation of human behavior and a tormented and merciless introspection (both conducted through psychoanalytic processes), interest in sociological and linguistic subjects (different social classes, various dialects, and technical jargon), and a masterful manipulation of literary style.

These qualities began to be appreciated by a wider public with the first publication in full of *Giornale di guerra e di prigionia* (1955; war and prison journal), a record of his World War I experiences, and above all of his two major novels, written much earlier and previously issued only in installments in literary journals, in 1946 and 1938 respectively: *Quer pasticciaccio brutto de via Merulana* (1957; *That Awful Mess on Via Merulana*, 1965) and *La cognizione del dolore* (1963; definitive ed., 1970; *Acquainted with Grief*, 1969).

Quer pasticciaccio brutto de via Merulana is a "detective novel," in the sense that a Poe or a BORGES used the genre. The protagonist is a police commissioner in Fascist Rome who has to disentangle a murder and a jewel robbery. The mass of external facts, clues, and witnesses corresponds to the inner tangle of the commissioner's thoughts, motivations, emotions, and sentiments, and to the interrelationships between these and the corresponding ones of a dozen or so secondary characters from various Italian regions—with their related dialectal inflections.

La cognizione del dolore is the tragic story of Gonzalo's neurosis—the obscure resentment of and love/hate for his parents and their country estate, reminiscent of G.'s own family villa and a symbol of the bourgeoisie—coupled with the mysterious murder of his mother (for which he feels a terrible sense of guilt), and set against an imaginary South American landscape, which is nothing but a linguistic as well as geographic distortion of the Brianza region north of Milan.

Both novels are based on philosophical presuppositions that can be best ascertained in G.'s treatise *Meditazione milanese* (1974; Milanese meditation), in which the author, starting from Leibniz and Spinoza, explains his concept of reality as a tangle of relationships and his belief in literature as knowledge. Another important work for the understanding of G.'s sociopolitical and moral views is *Eros e Priapo: Da furore a cenere* (1967; Eros and Priapus: from fury to ashes); it starts off as a powerful satire and indictment of Mussolini and Fascism, considered as the result of the degeneration of bourgeois values, and ends up as both a disguised autobiography and an "erotic history of mankind." The posthumous publication of five volumes of G.'s *Opere* (1988-93, complete works), including poetry, theater, essays, and correspondence, has added greatly to his reputation and established him as one of the major figures of high modernism in Italy.

G. is an extremely difficult author, and in fact, the American translator of his two novels, William Weaver, should be commended for the splendid job he did in rendering the originals. G.'s grotesque expressionism is his stylistic (that is, personal) response to the crisis of a world that appears chaotic, "baroque," and dehumanized; it is the vehicle of his moral indignation against, and disillusionment with, the worst aspects of our society—vulgarity, violence, hypocrisy, greed, fascism. That is why G.'s best works, like those of his European counterparts, are so strong yet tender, so ferocious yet melancholic.

FURTHER WORKS: *Le meraviglie d'Italia* (1939); *Gli anni* (1943); *Il primo libro delle favole* (1952); *I sogni e la folgore* (1955); *I viaggi la morte* (1958); *Verso la Certosa* (1961); *I Luigi di Francia* (1964); *Il guerriero, l'amazzone, lo spirito della poesia nel verso immortale del Foscolo* (1967); *La meccanica* (1970); *Novella seconda* (1971); *Le bizze del capitano in congedo* (1981); *Il palazzo degli ori* (1983); *Racconto italiano di ignoto del novecento* (1983); *Azoto e altri scritti di divulgazione scientifica* (1986); *Taccuino di Caporetto: Diario di guerra e di prigionia (ottobre 1917-aprile 1918)* (1991)

BIBLIOGRAPHY: Pucci, P., "The Obscure Sickness," *IQ*, 11, 42 (1967): 43–62; Ragusa, O., "G., Pasolini, and Experimentalism: Form or Ideology?" in Pacifici, S., ed., *From Verismo to Experimentalism* (1969): 239–69; Risset, J., "C. E. G.; ou, La philosophie à l'envers," *Critique* (Paris), No. 282 (1970): 944–51; Dombroski, R. S., "The Meaning of G.'s War Diary," *Italica*, 47 (1970): 373–86; Biasin, G.-P., "The Pen, the Mother," *Literary Diseases: Theme and Metaphor in the Italian Novel* (1975): 127–55; Biasin, G.-P., "The Cornucopia of the World," in *The Flavors of Modernity: Food and the Novel* (1995): 78-96; Sbragia, A., *C. E. G. and the Modern Macaronic* (1996); Bertone, M., and R. S. Dombroski, eds., *C. E. G.: Contemporary Perspectives* (1997)

—GIAN-PAOLO BIASIN

GADDIS, William

American novelist, b. 29 Dec. 1922, New York, N.Y.

Although neither of his two novels has been a commercial sucess, G. has long been involved with commercial writing. After attending Harvard from 1941 to 1945, he was for two years a staff researcher for *The New Yorker*, and, after five subsequent years of world travel, he settled down to a career of writing speeches for corporation executives and of scripting industrial films, with occasional stints of teaching and public relations work. His first novel, *The Recognitions* (1955), was written largely during his years of travel, and grants from the National Institute of Arts and Letters, the Rockefeller Foundation, and the National Endowment for the Arts gave him sufficient leisure to complete his second novel, *JR* (1975). Little is known of G.'s life beyond these simple facts, however, for he is an intensely private person and avoids all publicity.

The Recognitions is an encyclopedic, thousand-page novel that depicts a world of elaborately compounded fictions—art and religion most notable among them. Indeed, the central character, Wyatt Gwyon, abandons thoughts of the priesthood to become an accomplished forger of Flemish old masters in a quest for authentic experience, and at the end of the novel he retreats to a Spanish monastery to scrape old masterworks down to the canvas in an effort to reach the tabula rasa beyond all fictions. Every character in the novel is a counterfeiter of some sort, and there is every kind of forgery in the book, suggesting that Wyatt's quest is manic and that man can know only an irreducible complex of fictions. Freighted with esoterica and with formidable difficulties for the casual reader, the novel has enjoyed only a cult following and the praise of a few major critics, but it continues to stake its claim as a major work of art, and it may yet be recognized as such.

JR is a slightly smaller and more accessible novel that chronicles the rise and fall of J. R. Vansant, a sixth-grader who parlays his way, seriocomically, to implausible eminence in the world of high finance. The satiric illuminations of the novel are many, but its focus is the detritus of contemporary language: G.'s characters bombard the reader, with jargon, clichés, and barbarisms of all kinds, and their elephantine dialogues virtually swamp the narrative line. Unlike *The Recognitions*, which asks serious, metaphysical questions under the surface of its madcap humor, *JR* stupefies the reader with its impenetrable linguistic surface, and the agonized questions of the first novel seem to be replaced in the second with a settled pessimism about man's ability even to ask a metaphysical question.

G.'s reputation is a limited one, since he is largely unread. Nonetheless, his novels are serious works in the modernist tradition, offering the compensation of their aesthetic order for the disorder that is their subject; they bear comparison with Thomas PYNCHON's *Gravity's Rainbow* and Joseph HELLER's *Something Happened*, and even with such a classic text of modernism as James JOYCE's *Ulysses*.

FURTHER WORKS: *Carpenter's Gothic* (1985); *A Frolic of His Own* (1994)

BIBLIOGRAPHY: Benstock, B., "On W. G.: In *Recognition* of James Joyce," *WSCL*, 6 (1965): 177–89; Madden, D., "W G.'s *The Recognitions*," in Madden, D., ed., *Rediscoveries* (1971): 291–304; Tanner, T., *City of Words* (1971): 393–400; Koenig, P. W., "Recognizing G.'s *Recognitions*," *ConL*, 16 (1975): 61–72; Salemi, J. S., "To Soar in Atonement: Art as Expiation in G.'s *The Recognitions*," *Novel*, 10 (1977): 127–36; Stark, J., "W. G.: Just Recognition," *HC*, 14 (1977): 1–12; Klemtner, S. S., "'For a Very Small Audience': The Fiction of W. G.," *Crit*, 19 (1978): 61–73

—ROBERT F. KIERNAN

GAELIC LITERATURE
See Irish Literature and Scottish Literature

GAINES, Ernest J.

American novelist and short-story writer, b. 15 Jan. 1933, Oscar, La.

Born and raised on a plantation in Louisiana, G. may claim an intimate knowledge of the folkways of black Americans in the rural South and of the complexities of relationship between black and white in that region. Not surprisingly, this knowledge has been the source of much of his best fiction. But G., who graduated from San Francisco State College (now University) and who studied creative writing under Walter Van Tilburg Clark (1909–1971) at Stanford, has created work that reflects as well a highly sophisticated literary culture, which has made it possible for him to absorb and transform the influence, not only of such Americans as Ernest HEMINGWAY

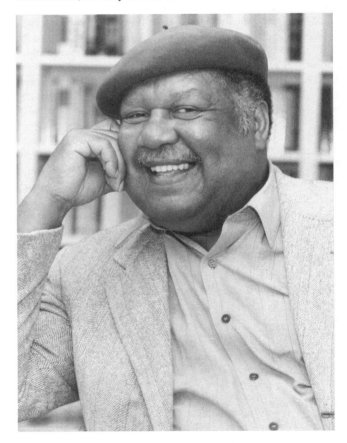

Ernest J. Gaines

and William FAULKNER, but, perhaps with even greater consequences for G.'s work, the great Russian authors Gogol, Turgenev, and Tolstoy. Characteristically, G.'s work involves a high-level literary treatment of an intimately, and often lovingly, observed folk culture.

G. is best known as the author of *The Autobiography of Miss Jane Pittman* (1971), which has acquired the status of a classroom classic; the novel has been adapted as a film that, although not entirely faithful to the text, is effective on its own terms and has had widespread exposure. Unfortunately, this kind of success does not always best serve a writer's critical reputation. Not only may the one text overshadow the writer's other work, thus creating a distorted image of the whole career, but the writer must often contend with the elitist suspicion that anything so widely and quickly popular cannot be very good. Any attempt to do justice to the art of G. must therefore involve both taking a new look at *The Autobiography of Miss Jane Pittman* and looking beyond it to the riches of G.'s work as a whole.

Like other Southern writers, G. is always aware of the presence of the past, and the relation of the individual and the community to the past is one of the major themes of his work. The past is our history, shaping our identity in the present and providing us with strength and perspective. Yet the past also has a destructive potential, as it may take the form of patterns of repetition that entrap the individual and condemn the community to stagnation. How to draw on the past without being trapped by it is a question implicit in much of what G. has written.

Some of G.'s characters seek merely to reject the past. Jackson Guerin, in G.'s first novel, *Catherine Carmier* (1964), tries to follow this course, intending to find his destiny far from the rural community of his origins; the effort is unsuccessful, as Jackson finds he must confront communal and paternal forces, and on their terms, not his. Others are locked into rigid patterns established years before; Raoul Carmier in the same novel exemplifies the destructive consequences of such rigidity. A third way is to acquiesce in established patterns, while maintaining an inner ironic distance; this is the way, ultimately an unsatisfying one, of Kelly, the narrator of G.'s second novel, *Of Love and Dust* (1967). In the course of this novel, Kelly comes to feel a grudging respect for Marcus, a younger black man who represents still another way: outright rebellion against the rules, customs, and tacit understandings established before he was born. Marcus's rebellion, however, although not without heroic resonance, moves inevitably toward a tragic resolution.

And tragedy, as Miss Jane Pittman knows, is not the goal. Miss Jane, over one hundred years old when we meet her, must be coaxed, by the young black historian whose inquiries motivate the narrative, to turn back to the past for her story—a story, we come to realize, as much communal as individual. And that story is a story of moving on. We are made, as we follow Miss Jane's narrative, to understand her (the) past, to value it (not to reject, not to forget, it) and to move beyond it. The last words of the novel are, "I went by him." "He" is the white plantation owner, and he symbolizes that version of the past—the past as repetition, stasis, stagnation—that must be transcended. Miss Jane herself may be said to represent another version of the past—the past as source and resource—on which the generations of the present and future may confidently draw.

Miss Jane is clearly offered as a representative character. Thoroughly individualized, she also embodies the forces that have brought her community out of slavery and toward freedom. The relation of individual to community is a further informing theme of G.'s fiction. In *The Autobiography of Miss Jane Pittman* the theme is reflected, not only in the representative qualities of Miss Jane herself, but in the search for "the One" that is a recurrent motif in the novel. In G.'s *In My Father's House* (1983), the relation of the civil-rights leader Phillip Martin to the community he has represented is troubled both by the inevitability of change and by the reappearance of a figure out of Martin's past: the son he had abandoned years before. Thus the themes of self and community and of past and present are made to converge. And the troubled relation here of father and son points to yet another recurrent theme of G.'s work.

A Gathering of Old Men (1984) embodies in a richly textured and complex narrative many of the themes of G.'s earlier work. Once again, patterns of conduct and attitude formed in a racist past work destructively in the present. At the same time, the "Old Men" of the title find in a renewed understanding of their individual and communal past, of the dynamics of that past, the strength to unite in the present crisis. But G. is not concerned, here, with the black community, alone; he also offers an unsentimental but not unsympathetic portrayal of the Cajun community, which has in the past exercised dominance over the black. He shows us in both communities the tension between the desire to hold on and the need to move on. Both communities are forced to realize that they are affected by changes they have hardly acknowledged. And in the Cajun community another of the intergenerational clashes with which G. has often concerned himself works itself out.

G.'s novels are of considerable thematic interest, and they will no doubt be read by many for the insights they offer into relationships between the races and relationships within the black community. But, as was suggested above, G. is a sophisticated literary artist as well as a concerned and provocative observer of and commentator on the issues of his time. The blending in *A Gathering of Old Men* of a number of individual stories to form one communal story is an impressive formal accomplishment. The interplay, common in his work, of a multitude of voices, old and young, male and female, white and black, each with its own identity and rhythm, lends to his fiction a notable complexity and delicacy of tone. He is consistently assured in his choice of narrative viewpoint. And his exploitation of the possibilities of narrative voice—Kelly in *Of Love and Dust*, Miss Jane, a series of voices in the remarkable short story "Just Like a Tree" in his collection *Bloodline* (1968)—link his literary narratives to an oral folk culture that is G.'s proper heritage. G.'s is a self-effacing art—he scarcely strikes one on first reading as a formal or stylistic innovator—but it is art, and of a high order. G. deserves to be recognized as one of the important American novelists of his generation.

BIBLIOGRAPHY: Stoelting, W., "Human Dignity and Pride in the Novels of E. G.," *CLAJ*, 14 (1970): 340–58; Gayle, A., Jr., *The Way of the New World: The Black Novel in America* (1975): 288–302; Macdonald, W., "You Not a Bum, You a Man: E. J. G.'s *Bloodline*," *Negro American Literature Forum*, 9 (1975): 47–49; Shelton, F., "Ambiguous Manhood in E. J. G.'s *Bloodline*," *CLAJ*, 19 (1975): 200–9; Burke, W., "*Bloodline*: A Black Man's South," *CLAJ*, 19 (1976): 545–58; Andrews, W., "'We Ain't Going Back There': The Idea of Progress in *The Autobiography of Miss Jane Pittman*," *BALF*, 11 (1977): 146–49; Hicks, J., "To Make These Bones Live: History and Community in E. G.'s Fiction," *BALF*, 11 (1977): 9–19; Puschmann-Nalenz, B., "E.J.G.: 'A Long Day in November,'" in Bruck, P., ed., *The Black American Short Story in the 20th Century: A Collection of Critical Essays* (1977): 157–67; special

G. issue, *Callaloo*, 1, 3 (1978); Wertheimer, A., "Journey to Freedom: E. G.'s *The Autobiography of Miss Jane Pittman*," in Bruck, B. and Karrer, W., eds., *The Afro-American Novel since 1960* (1982): 219–36; Byerman, K. E., *Fingering the Jagged Grain: Tradition and Form in Recent Black Fiction* (1985): 67–103; Bell, B. W., *The Afro-American Novel and Its Tradition* (1987): 290–95; Callahan, J. F., *In the African-American Grain: The Pursuit of Voice in Twentieth-Century Black Fiction* (1988): 189–216; Foster, M., "G.'s Louisiana Blues," *MAWAR*, 3, 1 (June 1988): 10–14; Jones, K., "God and Religion in *Of Love and Dust*," *MAWAR*, 4, 1 (June 1989): 4–9; Gaudet, M., and Wooton, C., *Porch Talk with E. G.: Conversations on the Writer's Craft* (1990)

—W. P. KENNEY

GAITÁN DURÁN, Jorge

Colombian poet, essayist, dramatist, short-story writer, and journalist, b. 12 Feb. 1924, Pamplona, Santander; d. 22 June 1962, Pointe-a-Pitre, Guadeloupe, Antillas

G. D. studied philosophy and at an early age traveled to Paris, where he stayed for several years. Along with the Colombian poet Hernando Valencia Goekel (dates n.a.), he founded in 1955 the cultural periodical *Mito*, which became a highly significant Colombian journal dedicated to translating foreign writers, to promoting diverse editorial enterprises, and to inspiring a spirit of agitation among young writers. Between 1955 and 1962, when G. D. died in an airplane crash and *Mito* was dissolved, the journal published modern writers such as Jean-Paul SARTRE, Alain ROBBE-GRILLET, Henry MILLER, Vicente ALEIXANDRE, Jorge Luis BORGES, Alfonso REYES, and Octavio PAZ. To many Colombian intellectuals, *Mito* represented an important link to significant movements and writers in Europe and North America; for young writers *Mito* offered the chance to publish for the first time; and for sociologists and politicians it meant the opportunity to analyze national dilemmas through polemic articles, essays, and scholarly studies.

G. D. belonged to the literary generation that came after the era of the poetic group *Piedra y Cielo* (Stone and Sky). G. D. and his fellow writers shared the intent to endow Colombian poetry with greater intellectual depth while emphasizing contemporary forms and themes. The poets of *Mito* constantly fought for density of the content in their works as opposed to mere formal intensity, while pursuing the discovery of new dimensions of imagination.

G. D.'s literary style is limpid, sometimes surrealistic, sometimes serving to convey social messages. He expressed his preoccupation with his people's political and social destiny through essays published in *Mito* as well as in occasional articles published in newspapers and political gazettes. Among his essays revealing an unusual perspicacity is "La revolución invisible" (1959; the invisible revolution). To G. D. society should be structured according to ethical standards, which, however, when pursued in isolation and without a sense of balance and proportion, diminish our true creative potential. G. D. also sees the need to participate in the aspirations of his people, a conviction that coincided with the political turmoil in Colombia since the "Bogotazo" (The Bogotá Event). This nationwide rebellion in 1949 against the régime in power extended from the capital to the most remote towns of the country, and the bloodshed lasted for the next twenty years. It was

Jorge Gaitán Durán

G. D.'s hope to commemorate this national tragedy by serving as an example of courage and solidarity for his country's ongoing struggles.

G. D. left a series of works that are intensive and rich without being remote. These include poetic prose, short stories, critical commentaries on art and film, political and literary essays, translations, and several volumes of poetry that place him among the greatest lyric poets of his country. As a poet G. D. explored the dimension of such states as death, passion, indifference, anguish, voluptuousness, and beauty. His poetry is flashing and thought-provoking. In *Asombro* (1951; amazement) the poet intensively ponders eroticism and attributes part of human anguish to our obedience to the instincts. In *Amantes* (1959; lovers) G. D. showed beautifully how eroticism is the culmination of all human lives and hopes. In his most important work, *Si mañana despierto* (1961; if tomorrow I wake up), eroticism is transcended to a spiritual love that elevates the ethical being of humans to a higher level.

As an intellectual G. D. fought vigorously against rhetoric, dogmatism, sectarianism, prejudice, and anything that degrades the human condition. Like his fellow contributors to *Mito*, G. D. proposed to use high culture as a means for political and social change. His poetry displays a sense of commitment to himself and to others, with a clear awareness of the precariousness of human destiny.

FURTHER WORKS: *Insistencia en la tristeza* (1946); *Presencia del hombre* (1947); *El libertino* (1954); *La revolución invisible* (1959); *Los hampones* (1961); *China* (1962)

BIBLIOGRAPHY: Núñez Segura, A. S. J., *Literatura colombiana* (1967), 461; Liscano, J., "G. D.: entre el erotismo y la pulsión de muerte," *Eco*, 223 (1980): 17–38; Romero, A., "Los poetas de *Mito*," *RI*: 128–29 (July–Dec. 1984): 689–755; Lara F. Charry, *Poesí y poetas colombianos* (1985): 121–22: 130–41; Cote-Baraibar, R., "Los últimos veinte años en la poesía colombiana," *Ínsula*, 44: 512–13 (Aug.–Sept. 1989): 43–44; Williams, R. L., *The Colombian Novel, 1844–1987* (1991), 77

—VIRGINIA SHEN

GAŁCZYŃSKI, Konstanty Ildefons

Polish poet and satirist, b. 23 Jan. 1905, Warsaw; d. 6 Dec. 1953, Warsaw

Born into a solid urban working-class family, G. never evinced clear-cut political or class affiliations. As a young writer in newly reconstituted Poland after World War I, he worked for journals of both the left and right; indeed, even anti-Semitic papers were not unacceptable to him. He was associated for a while during the 1920s with "Quadriga," a leftist writers' group. In the 1930s he abandoned his former bohemian ways to become a professional poet and family man. During World War II he was a prisoner of war and did forced labor in a German factory. After he was liberated by the American forces he went briefly into exile in the West, but in 1946, homesick for his native land and language, he returned to Poland and his wife and daughter (who had given him up for dead). With typical flexibility, he maneuvered successfully through the thickets of Stalinist literary politics, achieving, despite some criticism from Party hacks and émigrés alike, a large measure of recognition and popularity before a heart attack ended his career prematurely.

G. boasted that he was the "Bacchus of democracy," and indeed, his poetry includes many popular elements, from street speech to commercial jargon. Above all, his writing is characterized by trenchant satirical thrusts at a great range of popular targets—intellectuals, other writers, occasionally politicians—all skewered in the name of the simple outsider. Yet G. did not condescend to his audience: his style is replete with classical imagery, literary allusions, foreign words and phrases (in the best Polish "macaronic" tradition), and complex metaphors. He did not hesitate to use even the grotesque, the macabre, or the absurd to make his poetic points. In his prewar poetry, *Koniec świata: Wizje świętego Ildefonsa; czyli, Satyra na wszechświat* (1929; the end of the world: visions of St. Ildefonso; or, satire on the universe), *Bal u Salomona* (1933; party at Solomon's), and *Zabawa ludowa* (1934; popular pastime), G. dwelt largely on the theme of an impending disastrous conflict in Europe (a point of view known as "catastrophism" in Poland). For a number of years after the war his theatrical fragments called "Teatrzyk 'Zielona geś'" (the minitheater "Green Goose") and his feuilletons, which appeared under the title "Listy z fiołkiem" (letters with a violet), published in the satirical journal *Przekrój*, mocked the false "humanism" so popular at the time. Although topical, G.'s satires are still widely read for the vigor of their wit and playful use of language.

G. also wrote in a lyric vein quite distinct from his satirical pieces. Particularly noteworthy in this regard are his *Noctes aninenses* (1939; nights at Anin); two poems written during the war, "Pieśń o żołnierzach z Westerplatte" (1939; song about the soldiers from the Westerplatte) and "Matka Boska stalagów" (1944; Our Lady of the stalags); *Zaczarowana dorożka* (1948; the magic carriage); and *Pieśni* (1953; songs). Although humor and contemporary concerns figure in these works, too, they differ from G.'s other writings in their calm simplicity and tenderness and their exhibition of G.'s love for man and appreciation of life.

In both lyric and satiric modes G. was a poet with a highly individualized voice. He has some stylistic affinities with the Polish poets of the premodern period, yet in many senses he is sui generis within the literary tradition of his language in the 20th c.

FURTHER WORKS: *Porfirion Osiełek; czyli, Klub świętokradców* (1926); *Utwory poetyckie* (1937); *Wiersze* (1946); *Niobe* (1951); *Wit Stwosz* (1952); *Wiersze liryczne* (1952); *Chryzostoma Bulwiecia podróż do Ciemnogrodu* (1954); *Satyra, groteska, żart liryczny* (1955); *Dzieła* (5 vols., 1957–1960)

BIBLIOGRAPHY: Herman, M., *Histoire de la littérature polonaise* (1963): 625–26; Miłosz, C., *The History of Polish Literature* (1969): 409–11; Krzyżanowski, J., *A History of Polish Literature* (1978): 603–4

—R. HENRY COOPER, JR.

GALICIAN LITERATURE
See section under Spanish Literature

GALLANT, Mavis

Canadian short-story writer and novelist, b. 11 Aug. 1922, Montreal

G.'s short stories are acclaimed throughout the English-speaking world for their explorations of postwar alienation and dispossession in the West. Although she was born in Montreal, where she began her education, G. went to a large number of schools in Ontario and the U.S., only returning to Montreal at the age of eighteen. She worked there for six years as a columnist for the *Montreal Standard*. Determined to make writing her life, G. left for Europe in 1950, settling eventually in Paris, where she has lived for the last thirty-five years.

Before G. left Montreal, she had published a few short stories in Canadian literary periodicals like *Preview*, but her longstanding connection with the *New Yorker*—she has been one of its steadiest contributors of short fiction over the last four decades:—began in 1951 with the publication of "Madeline's Birthday, " a typical G. story in its depiction of a family's misapprehensions of an isolated adolescent's unhappiness. The trials of children at the hands of adults who are lost in their own disordered or deluded worlds often merge in G.'s stories with the cultural displacements suffered by characters lost in the postwar period, or with the shallow, romanticized sense of European history that G.'s North American characters bring with them to a postwar landscape suddenly transformed. The title piece of G.'s first book of stories, *The Other Paris* (1956), is typical in its evocation of a young and naive North American woman's engagement in Paris to her American boss, a narrative traced against the backdrop of her romantic notions of Paris and of love. This story also demonstrates how G. has developed the

Jamesian presentation of the American abroad, although G.'s style, with its spare and incisive irony and wit, is altogether different from the rhythms of Henry JAMES's writing.

Although G. has published two very well received novels, *Green Water, Green Sky* (1959) and *A Fairly Good Time* (1970), she is best known for her eight books of stories. G.'s stories often close, not with the epiphany associated with the stories of writers like James JOYCE, but with a moment of misperception, with an opportunity for insight nearly apprehended, but then lost. This is the ironic rhythm informing Carol Frazier's perception at the end of "The Other Paris" that, happily married in North America, she will be able to look back on her European engagement and remember it as it never was. Memory's distortions and recreations of the past play a crucial role throughout G.'s fiction, particularly when characters' memories are shown to be at odds with the larger historical forces that G. evokes. In *The Pegnitz Junction: A Novella and Five Short Stories* (1973) this theme finds its most powerful expression as G. explores the culture of postwar Germany, where the recent past, never fully understood, always threatens to intrude into the present. In the celebrated title novella, an arduous train ride from France into Germany acquires several layers of metaphorical and allegorical meaning as the passengers traverse geographical and psychic landscapes that resonate with dimly perceived portents of the past.

From the Fifteenth District: A Novella and Eight Short Stories (1979) is G.'s finest work. Several of the stories in this collection are set in Liguria, a region on the Mediterranean coast of northern Italy where national borders have often shifted in the 20th c., providing G. with an apt setting for her explorations of the effects that cultural and historical fragmentation have on the lives and relationships of her characters. In this collection as in much of her fiction, many of G.'s most powerful portraits are of female characters who are revealed as complex, oppressed figures, beset by contradictory demands and impulses that all too often render them indecisive, at once determined to win their independence and tied to their past by the bonds of memory, like Netta Asher, the central character in "The Moslem Wife."

As its title suggests, *Home Truths Selected Canadian Stories* (1981), for which G. was awarded the Governor General's Award for fiction (1982), focuse more specifically on Canadian characters and settings than any other of G.'s works, although several of the stories present Canadian characters adrift in Europe. In *Overhead in a Balloon: Stories of Paris* (1985) G. returns to her adopted city, which she knows intimately, for her deftly comic treatment of Parisian foibles and sensibilities.

G. has continued to write fine nonfiction throughout her career. Many of her best pieces—among them, her two-part diary of the May 1968 student uprising in Paris and her famous essay on the Gabrielle Russier case (1971), in which a young French school-teacher was driven to suicide over her affair with a student—reveal G.'s thoroughgoing familiarity with French institutions and social codes. But her short stories and novellas remain her most enduring contribution to contemporary writing. In depth and breadth, G.'s vision of postwar Europe is one of the fullest and most searching fictional representations of recent history; given G.'s preference for the short story, with its stringent demands for economy and precision, her achievement is all the more remarkable.

FURTHER WORKS: *My Heart Is Broken: Eight Stories and a Short Novel* (1964); *The End of the World and Other Stories* (1974); *What Is To Be Done?* (1983); *Paris Notebooks: Essays and Reviews* (1986); *In Transit* (1988); *Across the Bridge* (1993); *The Selected Stories of M. G.* (1996)

BIBLIOGRAPHY: Stevens, P., "Perils of Compassion," *CanL*, 56 (1973): 61—70; Merler, G., *M.G.: Narrative Patterns and Devices* (1978); special G. issue, *CFM*, 28 (1978); Jewison, D. B, "Speaking of Mirrors: Imagery and Narration in Two Novellas by M. G.," *SCL*, 10: 1–2 (1985): 94–109; Besner, N. K., *The Light of Imagination: M. G.'s Fiction* (1988); Keefer, J. K., *Reading M. G.* (1989); Grant, J. Skelton, "M. G.," in Lecker, R., David, J., and Quigley, E., eds., *Canadian Writers and Their Works: Fiction Series* (1989), Vol. 8: 23–80; special G. issue, *ECW*, 42 (1990); Schaub, D., *Fictional Worlds of Disintegration: M. G.'s Short Stories* (1996)

—NEIL K. BESNER

GALLEGOS, Rómulo

Venezuelan novelist and short-story writer, b. 2 Aug. 1884, Caracas; d. 4 April 1969, Caracas

G. was a schoolteacher for seventeen years. He began his literary career in 1909 as a cofounder of the review *La alborada*, which sponsored debates on themes of social protest. From 1913 on he published naturalistic fiction, and in his short novel *La rebelión* (1922; the rebellion) he took up specifically Venezuelan themes and motifs that he would never abandon. In the novel *La trepadora*

Rómulo Gallegos

(1925; the climber), which revealed the maturing of his narrative art, he defended the cause of the mulattoes in his country and endeavored to show the values of mestization (mixing of the races). In 1929 G. published *Doña Bárbara* (*Doña Bárbara*, 1931), his most important work. The Venezuelan dictator Vicente Gómez felt so threatened by this vibrant, reformist novel that G. had to go into exile. In Spain he wrote *Cantaclaro* (1934; a name meaning "a minstrel of the plains") and *Canaima* (1935; *Canaima*, 1988), both describing the epic struggle of the Venezuelan against nature as well as against other men.

After Gómez's death, G. returned to Venezuela and was appointed minister of education, a post he did not keep for long because of conservative opposition. In 1937 he published *Pobre negro* (poor black man), again defending a dispossessed race in his country. In 1941 he founded and began to lead the Democratic Action Party, while continuing to write novels of social protest. *Sobre la misma tierra* (1944; upon this very earth) exposed the oppression of the Indians living in the oil-rich region of Zulia. In 1947 he was elected president of his country, with eighty percent of the votes, but a right-wing coup d'état forced him into exile once again. While in Cuba he wrote *La brizna de paja en el viento* (1952; the piece of straw in the wind), which deals with opposition in Cuba to dictatorships; in Mexico he conceived what was to be his last, posthumously published, novel, *Pies sobre la tierra* (1971; feet upon the earth), which, using the example of Mexico, depicts agrarian reforms triumphant and the coming of a revolutionary constitutionalism to Latin America. He also made several visits to the U.S., especially to the University of Oklahoma. He returned to his home country upon the advent of democracy in 1958 and lived there until his death.

G.'s fame still rests on *Doña Bárbara*. This novel came at the most opportune moment, when the peoples of Latin America were beginning to search for their identity, when nativism, a blend of local color with social and political protest, was triumphing, and when intellectuals, labor leaders, and revolutionaries kept ideological issues alive. *Doña Bárbara* depicts a double conflict: the struggle of man to tame a violent nature, and the epic efforts of civilizers bent on eliminating human barbarism. G. intelligently used all the resources of realism and nativism at his disposal. Thus, the novel simultaneously depicts a distinctly Venezuelan and a broader Latin American cosmos: customs, superstitions, epic hunts in the rivers, taming of wild horses, and political conflicts. But in spite of its many characters and massive structure, its plot is rather simple: it is basically about the clash of two wills, that of Doña Bárbara, a despotic feudal mistress (drawn from actual life), and that of Santos Luzardo, the civilizer. Underlying the plot is the universal theme of good versus evil and the permanent dilemma as to whether violence in the name of a good cause can be justified. The upright hero Luzardo solves the issue by first gaining popular support and then answering violence with violence, thus overcoming barbarism—a thesis that has haunted dictators ever since.

Doña Bárbara gained high praise everywhere, but it has also been criticized. The overemphasis on the ideal qualities of its hero has been the main weakness noted. But its message is powerfully presented, and that is what G. aimed for. Moreover, G. showed elsewhere that he could also conceive more realistic protagonists. The title character in *Cantaclaro* is a wandering minstrel endowed with warm humor who fights for social justice. And the novel is also a treasure trove of local lore.

G.'s literary production is pedagogical and it must be evaluated as such. By means of his art he sought to promote needed reforms,

and this he did achieve. He died generally admired both in his homeland and throughout South America.

FURTHER WORKS: *Los aventureros* (1913); *El último Solar* (1920); *La coronela* (1928); *El forastero* (1942); *Obras completas* (1949); *Novelas escogidas* (1951); *Obras selectas* (1959)

BIBLIOGRAPHY: Spell, J. F., *Contemporary Spanish American Fiction* (1944): 205–38, 266–86; Torres-Rioseco, A., *Grandes novelistas de la América hispana*, Vol. 1 (1949): 43–77; Leo, U., *R. G.: Estudios sobre el arte de novelar* (1954); Dunham, L., *R. G.: Vida y obra* (1957); Chapman, A. G., "The Barefoot Galateas of Bret Harte and R. G.," *Symposium* 18 (1964): 332–41; Araujo, O., *Narrativa venezolana contemporánea* (1972): 157–203; Dunham, L., *R. G.: An Oklahoma Encounter and the Writing of the Last Novel* (1974)

—EVELIO ECHEVARRÍA

GALLEGOS LARA, Joaquín

Ecuadorean novelist and short-story writer, b. 9 Apr. 1911, Guayaquil; d. 16 Nov. 1947, Guayaquil

G. L. was a key figure in the literary circle known as the Group of Guayaquil, a company of writers that included Enrique Gil Gilbert (1912–1973), José de la Cuadra (1903–1941), Demetrio AGUILERA MALTA, and Alfredo PAREJA DIEZCANSECO. A self-taught individual, G. L. suffered physical ailments most of his life. He worked as a journalist because, like most Ecuadorean literary figures, he was unable to earn a living as a creative writer. Well versed in European and North American literature, he was also a student of classical Greco-Roman civilization.

The three original members of the Group of Guayaquil—G. L., Aguilera Malta, and Gil Gilbert—combined to produce a revolutionary collection of twenty-four short stories that altered the course of fiction writing in Spanish America. This volume, *Los que se van* (1930; those who leave), created a stir in Ecuadorean letters, shocking readers with its scenes of brutality and raw language. Unlike anything written previously, the book came under much harsh criticism, but it was well received by one noted Ecuadorean intellectual, Benjamín Carrión (1897–1979). The stories focus on life among the lower-class citizens living in the tropical coastal region of Ecuador, specifically the *cholos* (the indigenous inhabitants) and the *montuvios* (those of mixed black, white, and Indian ancestry). *Los que se van* may be considered a forerunner of *indigenismo*, although it contains less explicit protest and denunciation than many of the later works in this vein.

Violence, exploitation, and crude language are essential ingredients in G. L.'s fiction. His is a literature of protest against the injustices of the Ecuadorean social and political system. In denouncing these abuses he refuses to shy away from the sordid and unpleasant aspects of the oppressive social environment. For example, in the short story "¡Era la mamá!" (she was his mother) he creates scenes of graphic violence and sexual innuendo in which the black characters undergo physical and emotional suffering. The story relies heavily on dialogue stocked with G. L.'s faithful transcription of rural, uneducated speech.

After *Los que se van*, G. L. published only one book of fiction, the proletarian novel *Cruces sobre el agua* (1946; crosses on the water). This work deals with the 15 November 1922 strike in Guayaquil during which government troops massacred hundreds of workers. The novel's protagonist, a black man, is a popular hero who was one of those killed in the slaughter. The crosses in the title refer to the observance of the anniversary of this tragic event, an occasion marked by the placing of candles on rafts that float across the waters where the bodies of the victims were thrown. G. L. wrote two other novels, neither of which was published during his lifetime: *La bruja* (the sorceress), also known as *Cacao*, concerned with life on the cacao haciendas, and *Los guandos* (1982, with Nela Martínez; the stretchers), which portrays the indigenous litter bearers of the sierra.

The Group of Guayaquil was composed of young, politically committed writers who mixed regionalism with themes of protest in an attempt to interpret contemporary Ecuadorean reality. Of the group, G. L. was the most politically oriented and the most revolutionary. Although not prolific, he was influential in raising the level of social consciousness by helping to introduce social realism into Ecuadorean literature. His writings were an early indication that a new literary aesthetic was evolving, one in which art would once again come to be viewed as an appropriate and effective vehicle for protest. This outlook would exercise a considerable influence on Spanish American literature in the second half of the 20th c.

BIBLIOGRAPHY: Rojas, A. F., *La novela ecuatoriana* (1948): 180–84; Menton, S., *El cuento hispanoamericano* (1964), Vol. 1, 273: 279–80; Schwartz, K., *A New History of Spanish American Fiction* (1972), Vol. 2, 21: 42–43; Jackson, R. L., *The Black Image in Latin American Literature* (1976): 84–86; McMurray, G. R., *Spanish American Writing since* 1941: *A Critical Survey* (1987): 114–17; Diescanseco, A. Pareja, "Los narradores de la generacón del Treinta: El Grupo de Guayaquil," *RI*, 54: 144–45 (July–Dec. 1988): 691–707

—MELVIN S. ARRINGTON, JR.

GALSWORTHY, John

(pseuds.: John Sinjohn; A.R.P.-M.) English novelist, short-story writer, dramatist, essayist, and critic, b. 14 Aug. 1867, Kingston Hill, Surrey; d. 31 Jan. 1933, London

G. was born to wealth; his father was a successful London solicitor and director of companies. G. was educated at Harrow and then at Oxford, where he dutifully read law (although called to the bar, his interest in law was slight), lived the life of a wealthy young man in London, and traveled extensively. A crisis occurred when in 1895 he and Ada, his cousin's wife, became lovers. With her encouragement (after her divorce, G. and Ada married in 1905), he decided to become a writer.

Influenced by Turgenev, Maupassant, and Tolstoy, G. spent the years 1897–1901 learning his craft, and in the process produced two volumes of short stories and two novels. His third novel, *The Island Pharisees* (1904), was, despite weaknesses, a work of significant achievement. In 1906 G. established his importance beyond any doubt with *The Man of Property*, an acknowledged masterpiece and his first full-length treatment of the Forsytes, and with *The Silver Box* (also 1906) he began a distinguished career as a dramatist.

John Galsworthy

He returned to what would become his most famous subject—the Forsytes—in 1918 and earned an international reputation with his two Forsyte trilogies: *The Forsyte Saga*—consisting of *The Man of Property, In Chancery* (1920), and *To Let* (1921) plus two lyric interludes, "Indian Summer of a Forsyte" (1918) and "Awakening" (1920), all published together in 1922—and *A Modern Comedy*, consisting of *The White Monkey* (1924), *The Silver Spoon* (1926), and *Swan Song* (1928) plus two stories, "A Silent Wooing" (1927) and "Passers By" (1927). These works tell of the never-ending struggle between those who judge everything in terms of its material worth and those who know that there are intangible values that cannot be owned. The comfortable, ordered world of the Forsytes is not secure from the incursions of the unorthodox and of passion.

Further evidence of G.'s creative abilities is to be found in his seven non-Forsyte novels, his more than two dozen dramas, and his many short stories and essays. One of his finest non-Forsyte novels was *Fraternity* (1909). Exploring the interrelationships between the impotent world of well-intentioned intellectuals, the Dallisons, and the helpless world of the poor, the novel dramatizes the search for a better world; for some, better plumbing would free the poor and thereby save the world; for the senile Mr. Stone who is its prophet, Universal Brotherhood is the answer. *Strife* (produced 1909), *Justice* (produced 1910), and *Loyalties* (produced 1922) are three of his most compelling dramas. G. almost always created drama out of the mundane and ordinary: the theft of a cigarette box dramatizes that the law for the poor is not the same as the law for the rich (*The Silver Box*). Probably G.'s most famous scene is the one in *Justice* that without any dialogue shows Falder breaking down under the strain of solitary confinement.

After refusing a knighthood in 1918, G. accepted the Order of Merit in 1929 and the Nobel Prize for literature in 1932. Much of his fame rested on the mistaken belief that he was a sociological writer whose satiric analyses of man and society were photographically lifelike. Although this belief still prevails, present-day critical evaluation of his work displays a very different viewpoint: since the society he chronicled and the causes he espoused are now past history, G. is often dismissed as an out-of-date social historian. If, however, the emphasis on the sociological aspects of his writing is a mistaken one, it is evident that G.'s work should be examined anew and on its own terms as literature. His achievement is clearly greater than his present reputation would allow; indeed, he may justly be considered the last great Victorian novelist.

An important statement of G.'s artistic creed is "A Novelist's Allegory" (1909), which tells of an old man, Cethru, who as a nightwatchman aids passers-by as they traverse dark streets. Because the light from his lantern shone on some unpleasant scenes, Cethru is accused of criminal intent. In his defense the point is made that the lantern impartially reveals both good and evil and shows the true proportion of things to one another. In G.'s view the artist is important because he is the discoverer of truth or spiritual proportion. Beauty and art (profound embodiments of the spiritual, the humane, and the civilizing) are the cornerstones of his humanitarianism.

FURTHER WORKS: *From the Four Winds* (1897); *Jocelyn* (1898); *Villa Rubein* (1900); *A Man of Devon* (1901); *The Country House* (1907); *A Commentary* (1908); *A Justification of the Censorship of Plays* (1909); *A Motley* (1910); *The Spirit of Punishment* (1910); *Joy* (1910); *The Little Dream* (1911); *The Patrician* (1911); *The Inn of Tranquillity* (1912); *The Eldest Son* (1912); *The Pigeon* (1912); *Moods, Songs and Doggerels* (1912); *For the Love of Beasts* (1912); *The Dark Flower* (1913); *The Slaughter of Animals for Food* (1913); *The Fugitive* (1913); *The Mob* (1914); *The Army Veterinary Corps* (1915); *The Little Man and Other Satires* (1915); *The Freelands* (1915); *A Bit o' Love* (1915); *A Sheaf* (1916); *Your Christmas Dinner Is Served* (1916); *Beyond* (1917); *Five Tales* (1918); *The Children's Jewel Fund* (1918); *The Land: A Plea* (1918); *Five Poems* (1919); *The Burning Spear* (1919); *Saint's Progress* (1919); *Addresses in America* (1919); *Another Sheaf* (1919); *Tatterdemalion* (1920); *The Foundations* (1920); *The Skin Game* (1920); *The Bells of Peace* (1921); *Six Short Plays* (1921); *A Family Man* (1922); *Windows* (1922); *Captures* (1923); *International Thought* (1923); *Works* (30 vols., 1923–1936); *Memorable Days* (1924); *On Expression* (1924); *Abracadabra and Other Satires* (1924); *The Forest* (1924); *Old English* (1924); *Caravan* (1925); *Is England Done For?* (1925); *The Show* (1925); *Escape* (1926); *Verses New and Old* (1926); *A Talk on Playing the Game with Animals and Birds* (1926); *Two Forsyte Interludes* (1927); *The Way to Prepare Peace* (1927); *Castles in Spain and Other Screeds* (1927); *Mr. G.'s Appeal for the Miners* (1928); *Exiled* (1929); *The Roof* (1929); *A Rambling Discourse* (1929); *On Forsyte 'Change* (1930); *Two Essays on Conrad* (1930); *Maid in Waiting* (1931); *The Creation of Character in Literature* (1931); *Literature and Life* (1931); *Candelabra* (1932); *Flowering Wilderness* (1932); *Forsytes, Pendyces and Others* (1933); *Over the River* (1933; Am., *One More River*); *Autobiographical Letters of J. G.: A*

Correspondence with Frank Harris (1933); *Author and Critic* (1933); *End of the Chapter* (1934); *Collected Poems* (1934); *Letters from J. G. 1900–1932* (1934); *The Winter Garden* (1935); *Glimpses and Reflections* (1937); *J. G.'s Letters to Leon Lion* (1968)

BIBLIOGRAPHY: Chevrillon, A., *Three Studies in English Literature: Kipling, G., Shakespeare* (1923): 153–219; Marrot, H. V., *The Life and Letters of J. G.* (1935); Ross, W. O., "J. G.: Aspects of an Attitude," in Wallace, A. D., and W. O. Ross, eds., *Studies in Honor of John Wilcox* (1958): 195–208; Eaker, J. G., "G. as Thinker in *The Forsyte Saga*," *Phi Kappa Phi Journal*, 51 (1971): 10–20; Gindin, J., "Ethical Structures in J. G., Elizabeth Bowen, and Iris Murdoch," in Friedman, A. W., ed., *Forms of Modern British Fiction* (1975): 15-41 and passim; Stevens, H. R., "G.'s *Fraternity*: The Closed Door and the Paralyzed Society," *ELT*, 19 (1976): 283–98; Stevens, E. E., and H. R. Stevens, eds., *J. G.: An Annotated Bibliography of Writings about Him* (1980); Sternlicht, S., *J. G.* (1987)

—EARL E. STEVENS

GÁLVEZ, Manuel

Argentine novelist and essayist, b. 18 July 1882, Paraná; d. 14 Nov. 1962, Buenos Aires

G. received early religious training and was throughout his life an unswerving defender of Catholicism. He took his degree in law and, interested in social questions, he wrote his thesis on the problem of white slavery. He traveled extensively in his early years and was particularly impressed by Spain and its culture; one of his first works, *El solar de la raza* (1913; the roots of the race), stressed the significance of the Spanish heritage that Argentines enjoyed. In 1906 G. was named inspector of secondary schools, a post that he held for some twenty-five years. One of the most prolific Argentine writers of this century, G. dealt in a forthright way with a number of controversial subjects and is considered one of the most important realistic-naturalistic authors of his time.

G. began his writing career as a poet and dramatist, went on to journalism—producing countless magazine and newspaper articles—and was intermittently involved in a number of publishing enterprises designed to bring deserving writers into prominence. He was perhaps more interested than anyone else of his time in examining the role of the writer in his society.

As a young man, G. devised a plan to document, much in the manner of the Spanish novelist Benito PÉREZ GALDÓS, the society and customs of his age. Argentina was his subject, and in the more than fifty years of his writing career he explored many aspects of Argentine history and culture.

His first novel, *La maestra normal* (1914; the normal-school teacher), re-creates the stifling, conservative atmosphere of Argentine provincial life and offers a deterministic account of a casual love affair and its consequences. G.'s explicit description of the romance between a convalescing Buenos Aires government employee and a small-town school-teacher attracted a wide audience and was the first of his many commercially successful works. The novel remains engrossing and eminently readable.

203

El mal metafísico (1916; the metaphysical illness) is a roman à clef that treats Buenos Aires literary life and portrays, with very little disguise, a number of prominent personalities of the day. *Nacha Regules* (1919; Nacha Regules), which G. himself adapted for the theater, is another stark portrait of Buenos Aires society which, curiously, unlike most naturalistic writing, does not shun sentimentality and which adopts a surprisingly moralistic tone.

G.'s preoccupation with spiritual and carnal conflicts was displayed in a series of novels, of which perhaps the best-known is *Miércoles Santo* (1930; *Holy Wednesday*, 1934). G.'s interest in history is shown in two groupings of novels that are fictional treatments of the events of the disastrous Paraguayan War (1865–70) and of the turbulent regime of the 19th-c. Argentine dictator Juan Manuel de Rosas. The Paraguayan debacle is documented in three novels: *Los caminos de la muerte* (1928; the roads of death), *Humaitá* (1929; Humaitá), and *Jornadas de agonía* (1929; days of agony). Between 1931 and 1954 G. wrote eight novels about the Rosas dictatorship.

In all of his novels G. wrote a straightforward and unadorned naturalistic prose, uniform in distinctive stylistic features. There is a dynamic intensity to his novels that commands the reader's attention.

G. was a fervent nationalist, an attitude that is clearly evident in the subjects he chose for his novels and biographies, and that (since nationalism and fascism were closely linked in Argentina in the 1940s) also found expression in the sympathies he professed for the Axis, during World War II. G. remained active up to the end of his life. At the time of his death he was perhaps underrated or even rejected by some critics. But the merit of his work and the ceaseless dedication to his art he manifested during his long career cannot be dismissed.

FURTHER WORKS: *El enigma interior* (1907); *El sendero de humildad* (1909); *El diario de Gabriel Quiroga* (1910); *La inseguridad de la vida obrera; La vida múltiple* (1916); *La sombra del convento* (1917); *Luna de miel, y otras narraciones* (1920); *Tragedia de un hombre fuerte* (1922); *Historia de arrabal* (1922); *El cántico espiritual* (1923); *El espíritu de aristocracia, y otros ensayos* (1924); *La pampa y su pasión* (1926); *Una mujer muy moderna* (1927); *El hombre de los ojos azules* (1928); *El gaucho de los Cerillos* (1931); *El General Quiroga* (1932); *Vida de Fray Mamerto Esquiú* (1933); *Este pueblo necesita* (1934); *La Argentina en nuestros libros* (1935); *Cautiverio* (1935); *La noche toca a su fin* (1935); *Hombres en soledad* (1938); *Vida de Hipólito Yrigoyen* (1939); *Vida de don Juan Manuel de Rosas* (1940); *Vida de don Gabriel García Moreno* (1941); *Vida de Aparicio Saravia* (1942); *Calibán* (1943); *Vida de Sarmiento* (1944); *Amigos y maestros de mi juventud* (1944); *España y algunos españoles* (1945); *José Hernández* (1945); *Don Francisco de Miranda* (1947); *El santito de la toldería* (1947); *La ciudad pintada de rojo* (1948); *La muerte en las calles* (1949); *Tiempo de odio y angustia* (1951); *Han tocado a degüello* (1951); *Bajo la garra anglo-francesa* (1953); *Y así cayó don Juan Manuel* (1954); *Las dos vidas del pobre Napoleón* (1954); *El uno y la multitud* (1955); *Tránsito Guzmán* (1956); *Poemas para la recién-llegada* (1957); *Perdido en su noche* (1958); *Recuerdos de la vida literaria* (1961); *Me mataron entre todos* (1962)

BIBLIOGRAPHY: Torres-Rioseco, A., *Grandes novelistas de la América hispana* (1943): 137–60; Spell, J. R., *Contemporary Spanish-American Fiction* (1944): 15–63; Lichtblau, M., "The Recent Novels of M. G.," *Hispania*, 42 (1959): 502–5; Anzoátegui, I. B., *M. G.* (1961); Lichtblau, M., *M. G.* (1972); special G. issue, *Symposium*, 36 (Winter 1982–83)

—DONALD A. YATES

GAMBARO, Griselda

Argentine dramatist and novelist, b. 28 July 1928, Buenos Aires

Born to working-class, first-generation Argentines whose family originated from Italy, G. first started working in a business office until she began to win the prizes and awards that have enabled her to devote all her time to writing: G. started writing at an early age and has continued to produce steadily despite economic and political obstacles.

G. was among the Argentine dramatists closely associated with the experimental Buenos Aires art group at the Instituto Di Tella, an avant-garde foundation formed in 1958 to combine sociological investigations with the patronage of the fine arts, where a number of G.'s plays were produced and published, before the institute was forced to close in 1971.

At first G. developed her dramas at the same time that she worked on prose pieces; *Las paredes* (1964; the walls) and *El desatino* (1965; the blunder) are prize-winning plays as well as narratives. She continued this practice until 1972, after publishing *Nada que ver con otra historia* (1972; nothing to do with another story) and the play version *Nada que ver* (1972; nothing to see), both of which are parodies of the Frankenstein story placed in modern Argentina. These early works share a common preoccupation with ordinary people involved in unequal relationships of power, where the victim is usually too passive to fight against his oppressor, who is usually a member of his family or a supposed friend. Plays like *El desatino, El campo* (1965; *The Camp*, 1971), and *Los siameses* (1967; the Siamese twins) make good use of violent physical images to explore the ambiguities and cruelty of existence.

The early plays are divided into two acts and present generic characters involved in a series of situations rather than the developmental plot associated with conventional dramas. Since G. also avoided dialogue using the distinctive accent or nationalist motifs that would situate the plays within a specific Argentine context, critics easily associated these plays with the THEATER OF THE ABSURD. G.'s work, however, is no mere imitation of European absurdists; rather, the elements of the grotesque and BLACK HUMOR are related more to the early-20th-c. Argentine popular theater form called "grotesco-criollo." Moreover, an allegorical reading of the plays reveals that they do relate to the real sociopolitical events of Argentina. G. may use general metaphors, such as the absurd Kafkaesque world that marks *Las paredes*, or the concentration camp in *El campo*, or Frankenstein's monster in *Nada que ver*, yet the kidnapings, mental abuse, and physical torture undergone by her characters parallel real acts perpetrated by the Argentine military beginning in the 1960s and during the so-called Dirty War that ended in 1983.

Although her work was always subtly critical of the repressive Argentine military régimes, she fell into official disfavor in 1977. G. and her family moved to Barcelona, where they stayed for three years. Upon her return she participated in Teatro Abierto (open theater), a vanguardist movement of dramatists, directors, and actors who joined together in 1981 to present a cycle of three one-act plays a day for seven different programs. The majority of the plays, like G.'s *Decir sí* (1981; to say yes), were political in nature and constituted an attack both on the commercialization of Argentine theater and on the military government, which at that time proved too ineffectual to prevent the festival's existence.

As *Información para extranjeros* (perf. 1972, pub. 1987; information for foreigners) shows, G.'s skillful use of gestures and movements along with her manipulation of the space of the stage illustrate her development of theatrical ideas that coincide with Antonin ARTAUD's concept of "total theater." The stage directions call for a house in which the spectators are led by a guide who interacts with them as they wander through rooms in which some actors commit violent acts (kidnapings, torture, murders) and others engage in children's games. When the actor-guide insists that the spectators comment on their surroundings, they are soon forced to become more than passive witnesses to the scenes, and the boundary between stage and life becomes blurred. G.'s understanding of theatrical spectacle is joined by a knowledge of social ills, so that the play forces the spectators to recognize their general inaction and pliability and requires them to question and respond more fully to the nature of events in their environment. G. was not able to publish *Información para extranjeros* until 1987 because of its obvious political commentary.

Instead of remaining silent in the face of censorship, G. employed displacement techniques to veil her criticism and still transform the passivity of the Argentine public. *La malasangre* (1982; *Bitter Blood*, 1988), set in the 1840s during the period of the Rosas dictatorship, ostensibly develops a naturalistic plot that involves a love story. On the allegorical level it describes the awakening of the Argentine public from its passive state to a new consciousness about its oppressive government. *Del sol naciente* (1984; the rising sun) is set in Japan, yet its samurai warrior and geisha maiden are involved in a power relationship that is kindred to the military's treatment of the Argentine people during the Falklands crisis.

Although her fame rests on her plays, her narrative pieces reflect the same interest in Black Humor, parodic techniques, and striking visual images. In *Dios no nos quiere contentos* (1979; God doesn't want us content) the main character works in a second-rate circus where she is always exploited by the bosses. As a trapeze artist who is also a contortionist, her experiences of trying to maintain her equilibrium in an oppressive world serve as a metaphor for our lives today, as we are often tied up in knots and unbalanced by the pressures and ills of modern life. In a lighter vein, the tour de force *Lo impenetrable* (1984; *The Impenetrable Madam X*, 1991) reveals G.'s sarcasm and irony with regard to relations between the sexes. While Madam X eagerly awaits an erotic encounter with the young man who has declared his undying love, she allows herself to be distracted by the sexual play of a varied lot, including her maid, the coachman, and another mysterious stranger. This woman is clearly different from the victimized aging actress in the play *El despojamiento* (1981; the striptease), whose servile demeanor recalls early characters—like Emma of *El campo*.

G. represents one of a number of Latin American women who are successful dramatists. Although her early plays did not reflect the specific problems of women in authoritarian societies, her work in general is recognized for its representation of metaphysical issues relating to the human condition as well as to the specific Argentine sociopolitical problems of the abuses of power. G.

showed her gift of foresight in the way the physical and psychological torture experienced by her characters anticipated the institutional sadism prevalent during the Argentine Dirty War. An acknowledged master in the manipulation of verbal and nonverbal signs, her work continues to be highly regarded for its exciting physical images on stage and for the richness of her dramatic metaphors.

FURTHER WORKS: *Madrigal en ciudad* (1963); *Una felicidad con menos pena* (1968); *Sólo un aspecto* (1973); *Ganarse la muerte* (1976); *La cola mágica* (1976); *Conversación con chicos* (1976); *Teatro. Nada que ver. Sucede lo que pasa* (1983); *Teatro I. Real envido. La malasangre. Del sol naciente* (1984); *Teatro II. Dar la vuelta. Información para extranjeros. Puesta en claro* (1987)

BIBLIOGRAPHY: Holzapfel, T., "G. G.'s Theatre of the Absurd," *LATR*, 4, 1 (1970): 5–12; Cypess, S. M., "Physical Imagery in the Plays of G. G.," *MD*, 18 (1975): 357–64; Cypess, S. M., "The Plays of G. G.," in Lyday, L. F., and Woodyard, G.M., eds., *Dramatists in Revolt* (1976): 95–109; Gerdes, D., "Recent Argentine Vanguard Theatre: G.'s *Información para extranjeros,*" *LATR*, 11, 2 (Spring 1978): 11–16; Foster, D. W., "The Texture of Dramatic Action in the Plays of G. G.," *HisJ*, 1, 2 (1979): 57–66; Garfield, E. P., "Una dulce bondad que atempera las crueldades: *El campo* de G. G.," *LATR*, 13, 2 (Summer 1980): 95–102; Podol, P. L., "Reality Perception and Stage Setting in G. G.'s *Las paredes* and Antonio Buero Vallejo's *La fundación,*" *MD*, 24, 1 (March 1981): 44–53; Méndez-Faith, T., "Sobre el uso y abuso de poder en la producción dramática de G. G.," *RI*, 51: 132–33 (July–Dec. 1985): 831–41; Nigro, K., "G. G. vista desde lejos: Primeros textos y contextos culturales," in Pelletieri, O., comp., *Teatro argentino de los '60* (1990): 169–81; Cypess, S. M., "Frankenstein's Monster in Argentina: G.'s Two Versions," *RCEH*, 14, 2 (Winter 1990): 349–61

—SANDRA MESSINGER CYPESS

GAMBIAN LITERATURE

Gambia is Africa's smallest country, situated along the banks of the Gambia River. A classic illustration of colonial indifference to natural boundaries, it is totally surrounded by its larger and wealthier French-speaking neighbor, Senegal. Having few resources, it is developing into a Caribbean-type winter resort for Scandinavians.

There is here only minimal basis for any identifiable or sustained national literature. Nevertheless it has, surprisingly, produced two major writers: William Conton (b. 1925) and Lenrie PETERS. Conton has lived long enough in Sierra Leone to have rather a marginal residual allegiance, and the themes of both writers are as much contemporary West African as definably Gambian.

William Conton made his name through one influential novel, *The African* (1960); its early date makes him a pioneer in contemporary African literature. The novel proffers a rather awkward mixture. It opens with a conventional portrayal of an African coping with the problems of being educated in Britain, includes several amusing, probably autobiographical, anecdotal incidents to give it reality, and concludes with events after the hero's return when, having achieved political success, he makes a curiously symbolic voyage to a mythic country, presumably South Africa. The novel cannot be critically admired for its technical qualities, but its influence has been considerable. Its fame is apparent from its translation into Arabic, Russian, and Hungarian. It is less regularly read at present, but it is so well known that it has encouraged several African writers to attempt similar exercises.

Lenrie Peters is a doctor by profession and spent many years away from Gambia earning degrees at Cambridge and the University of London. He is a far more subtle and sophisticated writer than Conton. His first novel, *The Second Round* (1965), is set in Sierra Leone, but it could be equally appropriately located in either country, having the common semiautobiographical plot. It details the difficulties, both social and personal, that confront the well-educated doctor on his return to his traditional life at home. Peters's handling of this idea is more sensitive to the psychological complexities of the protagonist's dilemma than is usual in African fiction. Most African novelists choose to blame the external social pressures for their hero's difficulties.

This topic of the anxiety and alienation of the returnee is a regular theme in Peters's volume of poetry, *Satellites* (1967). His verse is highly sophisticated and urbane, sometimes appearing only minimally African. It remains always keenly aware of the core of the African cultural dualism.

Gambia suffers, like all small countries, from the dispersal of its more able people to other places offering more rewarding opportunities. For this reason its literature is for some time likely to appear only as the works of isolated, if individually impressive, writers—too isolated and exceptional to form any markedly national tradition.

BIBLIOGRAPHY: Cartey, W., *Whispers from a Continent* (1969), passim; Dathorne, O. R., *The Black Mind* (1974), passim

—JOHN POVEY

GAMSAKHURDIA, Konstantine

Georgian novelist, short-story writer, and poet, b. 15 May 1891, Abasha; d. 17 July 1975, Tbilisi

G. was born into a family of the Georgian nobility. In 1911, upon completing his schooling in Kutaisi, he traveled to Germany and entered the University of Königsberg. He transferred to the University of Munich in 1913 and finally to the University of Berlin, where, in 1919, he received his doctorate. G. returned to Georgia in the same year.

G.'s first work in his native language was published in 1914; the strong influences of Nietzsche, the individualist anarchism of Max Stirner (1808–1856), and the philosophy of Henri BERGSON are evident in his early novellas, essays, and poetry. A period of impressionist writing followed, primarily novellas, and lasted until the Soviet invasion of Georgia in 1921. Choosing to remain in his native country despite the Communist takeover, G. was obliged to change his style once more, to suit the political climate: a collection of short stories in the realist manner appeared in 1924.

In 1925 G. published his first novel, *Dionisis ghimili* (Dionysus' smile), which reflected once again the early intellectual influences of his formative period in Europe. This book was unacceptable in the Soviet context of the time, and, in order to redeem himself ideologically, he wrote a three-volume novel, *Mtvaris motatseba* (1935–36; the theft of the moon), which described the conflicts between traditional Georgian society and the new Communist order during the bloody and tortured period of collectivization.

G. may be said to have created the school of historical fiction in Georgian literature. His books in this style are unparalleled in the Georgian language and rank with the best serious novels of this type in European and American literature as well. His first work in this genre was *Didostatis mardjvena* (1939; the right hand of the master). It describes the confrontation of the medieval King Giorgi with his nobles over questions of governmental authority, but includes a wealth of information regarding the culture and customs of the period. It also demonstrates a fine degree of psychological perception in the limning of the characters and their individual worlds.

G.'s tetralogy, *Davit Aghmashenebeli* (David the Builder) appeared from 1946 to 1954. This extraordinary novel is unquestionably the crowning achievement of G.'s creative life. Set in the 11th c., it builds an immense panorama around the struggles of the Georgian people and their king, David—called the Builder—to achieve national independence. Against this background, G. recreates the complete cosmos of medieval Georgia, replete with totally convincing characterizations of great depth.

While unable to avoid in his art a certain pandering to the political requirements of life under a Soviet regime, G. nevertheless remains an author of huge stature and the greatest novelist of the 20th c. writing in Georgian. His work has been translated into all the major languages of the Soviet Union, as well as into other languages.

FURTHER WORKS: *Vazis qvaviloba* (1956)

—LEONARD FOX

GANDA LITERATURE

See Ugandan Literature

GARCÍA, Cristina

American novelist and short-story writer, b. 4 July 1958, Havana, Cuba

Born in Havana, Cuba, G. emigrated to the U.S. with her parents when she was two years old as a result of Fidel Castro's revolution of 1959. G. was reared in Queens and Brooklyn Heights, New York. After receiving her undergraduate training at Barnard College, she enrolled at Johns Hopkins University, where she earned a master's degree in international studies. Following her educational training, G. began a career as a journalist, accepting a position with *Time* magazine as a correspondent and, eventually, as a bureau chief, covering primarily Latin American issues.

Drawn to the poetry of Octavio PAZ, Pablo NERUDA, and Federico GARCÍA LORCA, G. was inspired to write fiction in her thirties. Unlike many Latino/a writers who find support for their art predominantly among small, academic presses, G. gained almost immediate recognition from the New York publishing house Knopf. G.'s first novel, *Dreaming in Cuban* (1992), a National Book Award nominee, was critically well received. Consequently, G. has been awarded several prominent writing prizes—a Guggenheim Fellowship, a Hodder Fellowship at Princeton University, and a Whiting Writers' Award, among others.

What is perhaps most unique about G. is her undeniably modern Cuban-American sensibilities, a hybrid between her homeland and her adopted nation. There is no idealization of Cuba in G.'s fiction.

Instead, G. offers her readers a fully-fleshed glimpse into the lives of Cuban and Cuban-American characters. Her interpretation of history is fundamentally agnostic. As such, what is at the heart of G.'s fiction is a deep exploration of the "modern Cuban-American" identity. This quest for self is made clear in G.'s first novel *Dreaming in Cuban* through Pilar Puente, the novel's protagonist and author's alter ego. In essence, like G. herself, Pilar's identity is a product of the Cuban and the American. While she yearns to return to her beloved grandmother (Celia del Pino), Pilar comes to realize that her rightful place is in the U.S. instead of in Cuba. It is Pilar's embrace of America that is so especially removed from the literature by the "Cuban exile" writers, an early ethnic American body of literature marked by its indulgent, romantic nostalgia for the homeland. G.'s fiction, however, is balanced, showcasing the possibilities and freedoms enjoyed by Cubans in the U.S. while also revealing the limitations of the American dream.

At times lyrical and mystical, *Dreaming in Cuban*—an eclectic fusion of journal entries, letters, monologues, and even advertisements blended with conventional narratives—explores the sundry issues circumscribing the plight of Cubans and Cuban-Americans in the U.S. as well as on the island. More specifically, the novel explores issues of politics, gender, and identity—culture, in essence. Through her characters, G. presents her readers with the divergent perspectives that have politically, and subsequently culturally, polarized Cuban and Cuban-American people. The family matriarch, Celia del Pino, for example, is a fervent supporter of El Líder (Castro) and his "social experiment," while Lourdes Puente, Celia's daughter, harboring deep resentment for a nation and political regime she holds responsible for her miscarriage, embraces everything American and dreams of owning a chain of her Yankee Doodle bakeries across the U.S. Between these two women stands Pilar, Lourdes's daughter, who yearns for the Cuban homeland she was forced to abandon as a young child. Nevertheless, G.'s fiction is balanced, offering her readers a critical lens of perception with which to view Castro's failing military state. Through Felicia Villaverde, who has remained in Cuba with her mother, we realize Castro's ridiculous attempt to construct patriotic *compañeros y compañeras* through mandated military boot camps led, for example, by the zealous Lieutenant Rojas.

G. continued her treatment of the "Cuban Condition" in her second novel, *The Agüero Sisters* (1997). Here, G. delves into the lives of Constancia and Reina Agüero, half-sisters who struggle to come to terms with their relationship, their past, and their history. Through metaphor, G. questions the designs of the individual, of culture, and of history itself—a full examination of the intricacies that construct a Cuban diasporic reality. The novel points to the imminent responsibility Cuban-Americans have to deconstruct the myths handed down to them about their histories, both familial and national. It is then, after careful and balanced scrutiny, that Cuban-Americans, like Pilar Puente in *Dreaming* and Constancia and Reina in *The Agüero Sisters*, can begin to reckon with the possibility of a truly bicultural identity that privileges both the American and Cuban strands of the self.

Other topics addressed in G.'s works are the destruction of Cuba's natural landscape and the prevalence of the Afro-Cuban religion *santería* among Cubans and Cuban-Americans. In *The Agüero Sisters* Ignacio Agüero, a naturalist by profession, describes the deterioration and exploitation of Cuba's fauna and flora by continual industrialization and supposed modernization in his journal entries, which are scattered throughout the novel. This theme is apparent also in G.'s first novel, *Dreaming*. Similarly, G.

explores the practice of *santería* among both Cubans and Cuban-Americans, describing various spiritual rites and religious performances. As such, G. brings to the forefront what has historically been referred to as Cuba's other religion.

In her thus short career, G. has firmly established herself as one of the most promising Cuban-American fiction writers of the late-twentieth century. She has made colossal strides from her Cuban forebearers who nearly four decades earlier grappled with their own personal and social constructions that were predicated by a sudden political, and cultural, dislocation that made them residents of the U.S. Like them, through her novels and short stories, G. continues to question the role politics and history play in the lives of individuals, families, and communities.

BIBLIOGRAPHY: Vorda, A., *Face to Face: Interviews with Contemporary Novelists* (1993); Lopez, I., "'... And There Is Only My Imagination Where Our History Should Be': An Interview with C. G.," *MQR*, 33 (Summer 1994): 604-17; Vasquez, M. S., "Cuba as Text and Context in C. G.'s *Dreaming in Cuban*" *Bilingual Review*, 20 (1995): 22-27; Kanellos, N., ed., *The Hispanic Literary Companion* (1997); Luis, W., *Dance Between Two Cultures: Latino Caribbean Literature Written in the United States* (1998)

—JOSEPH M. VIERA

GARCÍA LORCA, Federico

Spanish poet and dramatist, b. 5 June 1898, Fuentevaqueros; d. 19 Aug. 1936, Viznar

G. L. was raised in the Moorish city of Granada, whose pageantry and people he would later celebrate in poetry and drama. Even as a child he was intrigued by puppets, toy theaters, and all sorts of dramatic situations that often became material for impromptu performances. He was a talented musician, taught by his mother and later by the composer Manuel de Falla, with whom he eventually collaborated. He also was an artist of wit and delicacy, qualities that would also mark his poetry and plays.

G. L. attended the University of Granada, where he earned a degree in law in 1923 after an interruption of several years, which he advantageously used by writing and living in Madrid's intellectual and creative hotbed, the Residencia de Estudiantes. There he met the best minds of his generation: Pedro SALINAS, Jorge GUILLÉN, Juan Ramón JIMÉNEZ, among writers; and the painter Salvador Dalí, with whom he had an intimate and stormy friendship.

When G. L. left Spain for a spell, he went to New York, where he lived on the campus of Columbia University in 1929–30. *Poeta en Nueva York* (1940; *The Poet in New York*, 1940; also tr. as *Poet in New York*, 1955) was the fruit of that trip.

After a short visit to Cuba, he returned to Spain and soon became the head of a traveling theatrical company, La Barraca, established by the government of the Second Republic, which brought classical plays and other worthy dramas to the provinces. In 1936, during the first weeks of the civil war, G. L. was killed by partisans of Franco. The circumstances of his death are still shrouded in mystery.

G. L.'s heinous murder angered not only the international literary community but also the world at large, for it robbed them of one of Spain's greatest talents. G. L. was a brilliant poet and dramatist, who not unlike Dylan THOMAS, used words magically. With the sheer musicality of a language that flowed spontaneously, he cast an unforgettable spell. His art was one of prophetic beauty.

In both his drama and poetry G. L. created a delicate balance between the traditional and the modern, between Spanish sensibility and mainstream European ideas, between folk mythologies and high culture. His work was fashioned with a new and daring imagery that was intended, oddly enough, for simple people, with whom he had always chosen to identify.

Although G. L.'s literary production was quite varied, his themes remained constant. His poetry and drama attested to a tacit anxiety about obtaining what seemed to be unobtainable. With primitive passion, G. L. wrote about a lost Eden, frustrated sexuality, the tragedy of ubiquitous death, and the necessity for individual freedom. His work, in short, was a working through of his own personal, literary, and social dilemmas.

G. L.'s first book of poetry, *Libro de poemas* (1921; book of poems) shows wit, daring, and impudence as it mocks the adult world with fablelike poems that are populated by animals. Although clearly a book of apprenticeship, it reveals the poet's promising talent and introduces many of the themes that he continued to develop. *Canciones* (1927; *Songs*, 1976), written between 1921 and 1924, is also ironic and sarcastic in tone. The poems are highly inventive and delicate and have echoes of Antonio MACHADO and Juan Ramón Jiménez.

The publication of *Poema del cante jondo* (1931; *Deep Song*, 1980), written in 1921, and *Primer romancero gitano (1924–1927)* (1928; *The Gypsy Ballads of G. L.*, 1953) firmly established the reputation of G. L. and made him *the* poet of Andalusia. The "deep song" of the title of *Poema del cante jondo* refers to the music and culture of the gypsies, which serve as a backdrop to the poems. G. L. openly accepts the spirit of folk ballads with which he writes sinister poems that sing of death and irretrievable loss. However, amid all this sinister tone and all the lost horsemen of these poems who never return from their journeys, there exist a lightness and playfulness characteristic of much of G. L.'s poetry.

In *Primer romancero gitano* G. L. strikes the perfect balance between the traditional and the modern. Again by using gypsy culture and mythology as a point of departure to express his tragic vision of life, G. L. avails himself of the standard meter and verse form of the Spanish ballad, which he fills with new and exciting metaphors reminiscent of the European vanguard.

Poeta en Nueva York, written 1929–30, marked a departure in G. L.'s poetry, which at first upset some of his admirers. It eschewed traditionally Spanish material, embracing motifs that were more mythical and at the same time more intimate. It is also G. L.'s great virtuoso performance in SURREALISM. With shocking and at times grotesque imagery, G. L. undertakes a psychic journey that goes from personal chaos and alienation, caused by the decadent mores of a dehumanized metropolis, to a point of reintegration with the natural world. In this surrealistic journey of horror, anguish, and hope, G. L. praises Walt Whitman and a homosexuality based on true love and affection; he celebrates the black man, who, like the gypsy, although poor and suffering, has not lost his vitality or his roots in "primitive" culture. *Poeta en Neuva York*, in short, is an Orphic book of painful beauty.

Llanto por Ignacio Sánchez Mejías (1935; *Lament for the Death of a Bullfighter*, 1937), the moving and dramatic four-part elegy for the death of one of G. L.'s close friends, marked another high point in the poet's career. Sánchez Mejías is a symbol of vitality and man's tragic encounter with death. The poem begins on a note of

Federico García Lorca

anguish and pain, which the poet underscores by using shocking surrealistic images and plaintive repetitions. It ends quietly with mellifluous verses of resignation and acceptance.

That G. L. had a flair for drama could be detected easily by an examination of his poetry. For G. L., poetry and drama were not separate. He believed that the theater should offer a complete spectacle, and in this sense, G. L. rebelled against the realistic theater of the middle class. He attempted to infuse the moribund Spanish theater of the 1920s with imagination, poetic vision, and folk speech. His undertaking was enormous, and initially he did not succeed with the general public, who at first misunderstood his work and did not appreciate his elegiac manner.

G. L.'s first play, *El maleficio de la mariposa* (pub. 1954; *The Butterfly's Evil Spell*, 1963), first performed in 1920, was too delicate and precious for Spanish audiences. It is an allegory in which a poet-cockroach falls in love with a wounded butterfly, who ultimately rejects the lowly insect. The love-struck cockroach thus fails to obtain his dream.

Nor were audiences in 1927 prepared for *Mariana Pineda* (pub. 1928; *Mariana Pineda*, 1962), G. L.'s only historical drama, which is set in Granada around 1830. This romantic play is like a faded print of lyric beauty, but lacks dramatic action. Mariana Pineda, a woman who is tragically in love and cries out for freedom, finally decides that it is better to die for a noble cause than to denounce her lover, Don Pedro Sotomayor, a leader of a liberal uprising. Against this historical background, G. L. explores the problems of liberty and repression that were so important to him.

G. L.'s experiments in the theater also involved puppet plays, of which he had been so fond as a child. *Títeres de Cachiporra: La tragicomedia de don Cristóbal y la señá Rosita* (pub. 1949; *The Tragicomedy of Don Cristóbal and Doña Rosita*, 1955), performed in 1931, and *El retablillo de don Cristóbal* (pub. 1938; *In the Frame of Don Cristobal*, 1944), written in 1931, are attempts to escape from the clichés of realism and excessive lyricism. They represent a turn toward a primitive, more action-filled theater.

G. L.'s principal surrealist dramas, *El público* (fragments pub. 1934; *The Audience*, 1958), written in 1933 and only published in its entirety in 1974, and *Así que pasen cinco años* (1937; *If Five Years Pass*, 1941), also written in 1933, further showed the complexity of his theatrical sensibility. *El público* is an outrageous attack not only on commercial theater and its self-satisfied audiences but also on the entire social order. In his play, which his family and intimates begged him to destroy, G. L. publicly aired his problems with his own homosexuality. *Así que pasen cinco años* is an inordinately difficult but delightful play that uses a panoply of surrealist devices. It is an allegory of lost time in which life is seen as a cruel mockery, as are death and sexual frustration. Life is portrayed as being absurd and inharmonious, and man as its half-comprehending victim.

In spite of all his considerable previous achievements in the theater, G. L. is best known by most audiences, and solely by some, for his thematically linked trilogy of rural tragedies, beginning with the hauntingly poetic *Bodas de sangre* (pub. 1935; *Blood Wedding*, 1939), first performed in 1933. The play, which closely resembles a classical Greek tragedy, is a blend of drama and poetry, reality and unreality, played out against the elemental passions of Andalusian peasants. The perennial love triangle is given new urgency and dynamism. It is a gripping theatrical spectacle that transforms G. L.'s previous concerns with repressed vital passions and sexuality, omnipresent death, and the relationship between tradition and modernism into a satisfying and coherent dramatic unity.

Yerma (pub. 1937; *Yerma*, 1941), performed in 1934, the second play in the trilogy, is the tense drama of a man and woman whose marriage is barren, as suggested by the title of the play (*yerma* means "barren" in Spanish). The barrenness can be seen on several levels. Yerma's consuming desire but inability to have a child is echoed by her desire to have her indifferent husband love her. Her dual search leads only to frustration, which then leads to brutal violence—Yerma's murder of her husband.

La casa de Bernarda Alba (pub. 1945; *The House of Bernarda Alba*, 1947), written just before G. L.'s death, is the final play of the trilogy. It focuses on Bernarda and on her five daughters, who, while they hunger for freedom and an opportunity to express their own sexuality, are tyranically imprisoned by their mother. The lack of freedom and the closed system that Bernarda creates immediately bring to mind fascistic societies. G. L. starkly dramatizes the conflict and passions that the one available male, Pepe el Romano, stirs up. Although Pepe is never seen, his presence is always felt. In fact, so skillfully does G. L. create this effect that some critics have called the play a homosexual reverie. The youngest, most sexual and rebellious daughter, who is having an affair with Pepe, although he is dutifully engaged to her oldest sister, commits suicide when she is made to believe that her mother has killed Pepe. It is a tragic but ironic ending to a drama that has been played out in stark simplicity.

Although cut down at the height of his career, G. L. is a writer of great stature. He reached far down into his own being, into man's innermost recesses. He identified with the downtrodden and the alienated, but his work was never meant as a consolation to them or to any other person; his work intensifies fears, scrapes the viscera, gnaws at the soul.

FURTHER WORKS: *Impresiones y paisajes* (1918); *La doncella, el marinero y el estudiante* (1928; *The Virgin, the Sailor and the Student*, 1957); *El paseo de Buster Keaton* (1928; *Buster Keaton's Promenade*, 1957); *Seis poemas gallegos* (1935); *Primeras canciones* (1936); *El amor de don Perlimplín con Belisa en su jardín* (1938; *The Love of Don Perlimplín for Belisa in His Garden*, 1941); *La zapatera prodigiosa* (1938; *The Shoemaker's Prodigious Wife*, 1941); *Doña Rosita la soltera* (1938; *Doña Rosita, the Spinster* (1941); *El diván del Tamarit* (1940; *Divan*, 1974); *Químera* (1957; *Chimera*, 1944); *Obras completas* (1971). **FURTHER WORKS IN ENGLISH:** *Lament for the Death of a Bullfighter and Other Poems* (1937); *Poems* (1939); *The Poet in New York and Other Poems* (1940); *Selected Poems* (1941); *Selected Poems* (1943); *F. G. L.: Some of His Shorter Poems* (1955); *The Selected Poems of G. L.* (1955); *After L.* (1957); *L. (Selected Poems)* (1960); *Five Plays* (1963); *G. L. and John of the Cross* (1968); *Tree of Song* (1971); *L. and Jiménez: Selected Poems* (1973); *Divan and Other Writings* (1974); *The Cricket Sings* (1980; bilingual); *Deep Song and Other Prose* (1980); *Selected Letters* (1984); *Impressions and Landscapes* (1987); *Ode to Walt Whitman and Other Plays* (1988); *Once Five Years Pass and Other Dramatic Works* (1989); *F. G. L.'s Poetry in Word and Image* (1992); *Selected Poems* (1992); *Selected Verse* (1995)

BIBLIOGRAPHY: Honig, E., *G. L.* (1944); Crow, J. A., *F. G. L.* (1945); Barea, A., *L.: The Poet and His People* (1949); Bowra, C. M., *The Creative Experiment* (1949): 189–253; Campbell, R., *L.: An Appreciation of His Poetry* (1952); Trend, J. B., *L. and the Spanish Poetic Tradition* (1956); Durán, M., ed., *L.: A Collection of Critical Essays* (1962); Lima, R., *The Theatre of G. L.* (1963); Young, H. T., *The Victorious Expression: A Study of Four Contemporary Spanish Poets* (1964): 139–216; Freedman, M., *The Moral Impulse* (1967): 89–98; Umbral, F., *L.: Poeta maldito* (1968); Allen, R., *The Symbolic World of F. G. L.* (1972); Higginbotham, V., *The Comic Spirit of F. G. L.* (1976); Craige, B. J., *L.'s "Poet in New York": The Fall into Consciousness* (1977); Predmore, R. L., *L.'s New York Poetry: Social Injustice, Dark Love, Lost Faith* (1980); Edwards, G., *L.: The Theatre beneath the Sand* (1980); Cao, A. T., *F. G. L. y las vanguardias: Hacia el teatro* (1984); Anderson, A. A., *L.'s Late Poetry: A Critical Study* (1990); Soufas, C. C., *Audience and Authority in the Modernist Theater of F. G. L.* (1996)

—MARSHALL J. SCHNEIDER

With each fresh addition to our knowledge of F. G. L., the poet's genius becomes more impressive. That extraordinary brilliance which struck one at once, in the first few of his poems to be translated, has turned out by no means to be an intermittent or accidental thing—it was sustained. Brilliance came as naturally to him, in fact, as dullness or preciosity to others; it was simply his speech. Nothing could be more remarkable, in this new collection, *Poet in New York*, than the apparently inexhaustible fertility of G. L.'s imagination. It was everywhere at once, it was prodigal, it was fantastic—the subjective and objective worlds rolled up and ignited in a single ball—the quotidian married singularly to the classic, the folksong crossed with the baroque. To call him a surrealist is a mistake, for to be a surrealist is to be something else than a poet, something less than a poet: surrealism is perhaps one of many names, merely, for the substratum out of which poetry is made. G. L. devoured all the properties of surrealism, stuffed his cheeks with them, like a conjuror, blew them out of his mouth again as poems—but so he did with everything else that he fed on. The papery guitars, the ingeniously misplaced eyes, the little traplike mouths cropping out of the sides of heads, and all the rest of that slightly sinister and somehow iodine-tinctured phantasmagoria of the followers of Loplop and synesthesia, these are certainly here, in the New York poems, but they have been made into poetry. [1940]

Conrad Aiken, "F. G. L.," *A Reviewer's ABC* (1958), pp. 276–77

With Synge, L. shares the creative mission of returning poetry to its basic dramatic function on the stage. In L.'s work it is impossible to speak of a consistently upheld view of life. His drama celebrates the life of instinct; which is to say, it does not come bearing a message. It comes in the ancient spirit of the magician and soothsayer—to astound; to entertain, and to mystify; it also comes in the spirit of the jongleur, to invent a world and people with whose pathetically valorous lives the audience is quick to identify itself. But it has no hidden didactic motives.

Synge's work is also notable for its artistic selfsufficiency, its renewal of the rich poetic language of the fold, and its re-creation of the primitive drama of feeling.... [Synge and L.] have alike the spontaneity of speech and poetic imagination which grows out of the heart of a fold untouched by the perversities of city life; with whom it is still possible to express pathos and tragedy in terms of the most elemental passions. When drama reaches behind the improvised curtain of middle-class Christian morality to the lives of such people and into their wild old pagan heritage, one comes upon the springs of a new classicism in the theatre, which Synge and L. exemplify. But the difference is that Synge, writing in prose, accepts the conventions of the tight coils of traditional stage techniques. L., on the other hand, a poetic dramatist reviving particular Spanish conventions on the stage and adding techniques of his own, shifts the stylistic emphasis very often from the prose speech of the characters to the verse and bright design of spectacle and musical conception.

Edwin Honig, *G. L.* (1944), pp. 214–15

The final value of Federico's theatre, and the one which most characterizes it, is this fundamental attitude of an author who likes to live; that is to say, to suffer and enjoy life's course as an inevitable universal drama. It seems as though in Federico, both in his life and in his writing, the man was not alive except in his moments of laughter and tears, in his extreme moments of joy and sorrow. Other times are entr'actes....

Laughter and tears, tears above all, run through all his poetry. Federico is fundamentally an elegiac poet. And laughter and tears are the two poles of his theatre. This explains why all his work courses between tragedy and farce. His literary creatures, always poetic embodiments, are conceived either in a tragic sense or with the wry grimace of guignol characters. Poetry, laughter and tears are the ingredients of his dramatic invention.

Francisco García Lorca, Preface to *Three Tragedies of F. G. L.* (1947), pp. 2–3

G. L., a conscious artist despite his seeming spontaneity, imperiously felt the need to give his art, with its deep roots in the past, complete contemporary validity. He was and he wanted to be a man of his period, but without renouncing an atom of himself, in whom there were many links with the past which made him incompatible with the transitory fashions of the moment. He wished to avoid both the applause of the hide-bound majorities and the criticism of the ultramodern minorities, both of which only partially understood him, and find his own path in a harmony between the new and the age-old native qualities that were fused in him. This was what he did in his poetry and it is this that gave him a place that is in a sense unique among contemporary Spanish poets....

G. L. may be regarded as the most purely and essentially Spanish writer of our day and, consequently, the one hardest to translate and understand. Spanish through and through, his art resides in the words and not in the ideas; in the music, the gesture, the physical sensations and the irrational emotions, in a play of forms, rhythms and images which conceal beneath them the mystery of life and of death. It demands an effort on our part to understand him as he was, and to see his work as a poetic creation of pure art in which we find anew, stripped of history, of picturesque romanticism and genre realism, a clear, profound vision of the eternal Spain.

Federico de Onís, "F. G. L.," in A. M. I. Fiskin, ed., *Writers of Our Years* (1950), pp. 30, 35

Being a poet, he did not analyze or describe, he *felt*—and his feeling took the form of thematic images. There are a few which appear very soon, in the first poems [of *Poet in New York*], and are constantly repeated until they become leitmotifs: "things without roots," "flight and dissolution of forms," "forgetfulness of heaven," "lack of outlet," "struggle," and especially "emptiness," "vacuity," "hollowness," "void."

But perhaps more revealing than these recurrent themes and images, is the fact that all the elements of the book's style are organized in a dynamic and at the same time dialectic tension, as a result of seeing the world of reality torn by a permanent duality and conflict. This takes many forms: natural, religious, or conceptual: birth and death, heaven and earth, sin and redemption, geometry and anguish, spirit and passion, man in his constant clash with matter. All are related to a single all-embracing idea: the return to primitive, destructive instincts and passions let loose by a mechanical civilization, deprived of Grace, or, as it were, in rebellion against the spirit. The contrast is one between the primitiveness of human appetites without moral restraints, and of the perfection of technology: man, emptied of his spiritual content in a mechanized world, returns to barbarity. The result is a self-destructive confusion, as if the crumbling of this man-created chaos is necessary for the rising of a new life in which nature and the spirit will find harmony. The book is not so much an impression of New York as an indictment of modern civilization.

> Ángel del Río, Introduction to F. G. L., *Poet in New York* (1955), pp. xxviii–xxix

The inspiration [for *Gypsy Ballads*] derives in part from G. L.'s lively compassion for the gypsies, who in his time were much tormented by the Civil Guard, a green-uniformed police with patent leather tricornered hats. In the celebrated "Ballad of the Civil Guard," these implacable guardians of law and order, their souls as black as their hats and their heads full of a vague "pistol astronomy," wreak brutal havoc upon a gypsy fiesta. To the bourgeoisie of G. L.'s time, as now, the gypsies seemed a useless, inferior, good-for-nothing lot. But G. L. saw in them the elements of poetry and recognized in their disheveled, passionate state a childlike quality. His insight is vindicated by the emotional response we still make to his gypsies, elevated from rags and misery to "bronze and dreams."

G. L. was able to raise the gypsies to the level of poetry by, as he put it, inventing a mythology for them. Unlike the sophisticated Greek and Roman myths, the tradition spun by G. L.'s fancy remained close to primitive roots.

> Howard T. Young, *The Victorious Expression: A Study of Four Contemporary Spanish Poets* (1964), p. 165

While L.'s comic spirit is present in *Blood Wedding* and *Yerma*, his grim humor becomes increasingly critical in his last two more socially oriented plays. No longer engaged in purely personal conflict the heroines of *Doña Rosita, the Spinster* and *[The House of] Bernarda Alba* now struggle against a decadent morality that imprisons them in a tight cocoon. Doña Rosita becomes a passive member of a society of fools, while Adela [*Bernarda Alba*] and her sisters [in *The House of Bernarda Alba*] lose an emotional and psychological combat with the ferocious bully who is their mother. The highly wrought tension between humor and anguish in these two plays is too incongruous to be described by the rather nondescript term "tragicomedy." At the same time amusing and terrifying, *Doña Rosita, the Spinster* and *Bernarda Alba*

recall L.'s puppet plays and the tragic farce *Perlimplín*. Like *Perlimplín*, these last two plays seem best described as, to borrow a phrase from Tennessee Williams, "slapstick tragedy."

L. is horrified by the hypocrisy and cruelty of established morality and expresses his dismay not only by creating rigid, one-dimensional characters, but also by adapting scenes and gestures from ancient farce for the purpose of serious criticism. Although not a polemical dramatist, L. never ceases to rebel against the web of social injustice, hurling satirical barbs at what he considers outmoded social attitudes that might be changed. His outlook on life, however, is darkly pessimistic. Using grim humor to depict social paralysis and decay, he joins other modern playwrights in suggesting that anguish in a morally bankrupt culture is absurd and meaningless.

> Virginia Higginbotham, *The Comic Spirit of F. G. L.* (1976), p. 120

GARCÍA MÁRQUEZ, Gabriel

Colombian novelist and short-story writer, b. 6 March 1928, Aracataca

G. M. spent the first eight years of his life in Aracataca, near the Atlantic coast, in the home of his grandparents, whose store of myths, legends, and superstitions had a profound influence on him. After studying law at the University of Bogotá, he worked in several Colombian cities as a journalist, in Europe as a correspondent for the Bogotá daily *El espectador*, and in New York City for the Cuban news agency Prensa Latina. During most of the 1960s he lived in Mexico, where he wrote film scripts as well as his most famous book, *Cien años de soledad* (1967; *One Hundred Years of Solitude*, 1970). From 1967 until 1975 he resided in Barcelona, Spain, and in recent years he has spent considerable time in Mexico and Colombia.

The setting of many of G. M.'s works is Macondo, a small town modeled after Aracataca. His first novel, *La hojarasca* (1955; *Leaf Storm*, 1972), depicts life in Macondo during the first three decades of the 20th c., a period covering the town's founding by refugees from the Colombian civil wars (1899–1903), its economic boom brought on by the banana industry, and its subsequent decline. The interwoven plots and subplots are narrated in the form of monologues by three characters, all of whom are attending a wake following the suicide of the town's doctor. A man of mysterious origin and questionable character, the deceased appears to embody the forces of guilt and evil threatening the community. *La hojarasca* suffers from monotony and flatness because its three narrative voices lack individuality, but it does succeed in evoking an oppressive, fatalistic atmosphere of moral decay and physical stagnation.

Set against the backdrop of Colombia's civil strife during the 1950s, *El coronel no tiene quien le escriba* (1961; *No One Writes to the Colonel*, 1968) is a masterfully written novella about a retired colonel (inspired by G. M.'s grandfather) who waits in vain for his government pension. Impoverished and ailing, he falls victim to illusion when he inherits a gamecock from his recently slain son and decides to enter it in a contest with a bird from a neighboring

community. The contrast between the naïve, good-natured protagonist and his skeptical, embittered wife provides a vein of
humor that highlights the poignancy of the old man's plight. His
unflagging determination in the face of adversity, moreover, characterizes him as an absurd hero whose valor is symbolically
illuminated by the gamecock. This work's combination of stylistic
precision, verbal economy, and psychological insight has rarely, if
ever, been surpassed in Latin American fiction.

The civil conflict of the 1950s plays a more important role in *La
mala hora* (1962; *In Evil Hour*, 1979), in which the citizens of "el
pueblo," already nervous because of political tensions, find themselves on the verge of panic when slanderous posters of unknown
origin begin to appear in their midst. Ensuing events unveil a
society of morally corrupt citizens whose irrational impulses and
collective guilt find expression in the posters. The novel's spare,
elliptical prose and disjointed montage structure serve to intensify
the atmosphere of uncertainty and fear enveloping the community.

In his first collection of short stories, *Los funerales de la Mamá
Grande* (1962; in *No One Writes to the Colonel and Other Stories*,
1968), G. M. resumed his realistic sketches of Macondo, often
leaving the details of his protagonist's interior drama to the reader's
imagination, as, for example, in "La siesta del martes" ("Tuesday
Siesta"), the tale of a courageous woman who stoically confronts
the hostile curiosity of an entire town. Objective reality is abandoned, however, in the title story ("Big Mama's Funeral"), which
makes use of myth, fantasy, and hyperbole to describe the death
and fabulous funeral of an unforgettable ninety-two-year-old matriarch.

The shift to a more subjective plane of vision becomes increasingly evident in *Cien años de soledad*, a recapitulation of all
G. M.'s previous works. This exceptionally fine novel, which has
been acclaimed as a masterpiece by critics and reading public alike
throughout Latin America, Europe, and the United States, relates
the founding of Macondo by José Arcadio Buendía, the adventures
of six generations of his descendants, and, ultimately, the town's
destruction. It also presents a vast synthesis of social, economic,
and political evils plaguing much of Latin America. Even more
important from a literary point of view is its aesthetic representation of a world in microcosm, that is, a complete history, from Eden
to Apocalypse, of a world in which miracles such as people riding
on flying carpets and a dead man returning to life tend to erase the
thin line between objective and subjective realities. The resultant
impression of totality is further strengthened by the novel's ingeniously conceived spiral structure as well as by its narrative technique. In the final pages the narrator turns out to be not an
omniscient author viewing the action from afar, as the reader has
been led to believe, but one of the characters (the old gypsy
Melquíades), whose manuscript and the fictional universe therein
are obliterated by the hurricane "full of voices from the past." The
illusion is thus conveyed of an all-encompassing novelistic world,
both engendered and consumed from within.

The title—*Cien años de soledad*—alludes to the mental state of
the characters, whose irrational single-mindedness and intense
struggles against a hostile natural and social milieu leave them
frustrated, alienated, and, as in the case of the last two adult
Buendías, condemned to engender a baby with a pig's tail. Nevertheless, *Cien años de soledad* is not primarily a novel of social
protest. Rather it is a poetic depiction of man's solitude in a
labyrinthine universe he can never understand or dominate. G. M.
takes his cue from the Argentine Jorge Luis BORGES, who stresses
the fictive nature of literature because language reflects only the

Gabriel García Márquez

mind of the author, not objective reality. Thus the obliteration of
Macondo in the final lines of the novel could be read as a sleight-of-
hand disappearance of a purely imaginary world that ceases to exist
when it is no longer perceived by the reader.

The fantasy so characteristic of *Cien años de soledad* is even
more prevalent in *La increíble y triste historia de la cándida
Eréndira y su abuela desalmada* (1972; *Innocent Eréndira and
Other Stories*, 1979), a collection of seven delightful tales, several
of which were written for children. "Un señor muy viejo con unas
alas enormes" ("A Very Old Man with Enormous Wings") describes an amusing sequence of events unleashed by an aging
winged creature's fall to earth in a seaside village, but on a more
intellectual level it assails capitalistic exploitation, parodies religion, and suggests the demise of innocence. The collection's title
story displays themes, characters, and an organizational framework
strongly reminiscent of Grimm's fairy tales.

El otoño del patriarca (1975; *The Autumn of the Patriarch*,
1976) is a highly sophisticated novel about an unnamed dictator
(the patriarch), who, at the time of his death, is somewhere between
107 and 232 years of age. The patriarch embodies the archetypal
evils of despotism, but even more significant is his extreme, and
often pathetic, solitude, which becomes increasingly evident with
his advancing age and which emerges as the principal theme.
Despite its political and psychological overtones, *El otoño del
patriarca* can best be described as a lyrical novel, whose plot and
character development are subordinate to formal design and symbolic imagery. The work's narrative content is conveyed by a wide

variety of rhetorical devices, including its figurative language, rambling syntax, and constantly shifting point of view. In addition, frequent infusions of fantasy, hyperbole, and grotesque absurdities further enrich its texture and elicit reader reactions ranging from hilarity to horror. Hailed as a masterpiece by many critics, this brilliantly stylized portrait of solitude resulting from tyranny stands out as an ingenious experiment in fiction.

In 1982 G. M. became Spanish America's fourth Nobel Laureate in literature. His most important novels since *El otoño del patriarca* are *El amor en los tiempos del cólera* (1985; *Love in the Time of Cholera*, 1988), a moving love story inspired by the author's parents, and *El general en su laberinto* (1989; *The General in His Labyrinth*, 1990), which dramatizes the last months of Simón Bolívar's life.

Although G. M. has expressed an avid interest in a multitude of writers, the most important influences on his works are probably HEMINGWAY and FAULKNER, the former for his detached, succinct mode of expression, and the latter for his creation of a single microcosmic universe populated by human failures.

G. M. is presently Latin America's most widely known and admired novelist. In its totality his fiction imparts not only the stark reality of an emerging, strife-torn continent but, through the humanistic and universalizing elements of myth, imagination, and aesthetic perception, an original vision of man and his world.

FURTHER WORKS: *Tres cuentos colombianos* (1954, with Guillermo Ruiz Rivas and Carlos Arturo Truque); *Isabel viendo llover en Macondo* (1967); *La novela en América Latina: Diálogo* (1968, with Mario Vargas Llosa); *Relato de un náufrago* (1970; *The Story of a Shipwrecked Sailor*, 1986); *Ojos de perro azul* (1972); *Cuando era feliz e indocumentado* (1973); *El negro que hizo esperar a los ángeles* (1973); *Chile, el golpe y los gringos* (1974); *Cuatro cuentos* (1974); *Todos los cuentos de G. G. M. (1947–1972)* (1975); *Crónicas y reportajes* (1976); *Operación Carlota* (1977); *Periodismo militante* (1978); *Crónica de una muerte anunciada* (1981; *Chronicle of a Death Foretold*, 1982); *La aventura de Miguel Littín, clandestino en Chile* (1986; *The Adventures of Miguel Littín*, 1987); *Del amor y otros demonios* (1994; *Of Love and Other Demons*, 1995); *Cuentos: 1947-1992* (1996); *Noticia de un secuestro* (1996; *News of a Kidnapping*, 1997). **FURTHER WORKS IN ENGLISH:** *Leaf Storm and Other Stories* (1972); *Collected Stories* (1984); *Collected Novellas* (1990); *Strange Pilgrims* (1993)

BIBLIOGRAPHY: Harss, L., and B. Dohmann, "G. G. M., or the Lost Chord," *Into the Mainstream* (1966): 310–41; Peel, R. M., "The Short Stories of G. G. M.," *SSF*, 8 (1971): 159–68; Rodríguez Monegal, E., "A Writer's Feat," *Review 70* (1971): 122–28; Vargas Llosa, M., "G. M.: From Aracataca to Macondo," *Review 70* (1971): 129–42; Vargas Llosa, M., *G. M.: Historia de un deicidio* (1971); Goetzinger, J. A., "The Emergence of a Folk Myth in *Los funerales de la Mamá Grande*," *REH*, 6 (1972): 237–48; Shorris, E., "G. G. M.: The Alchemy of History," *Harper's*, Feb. 1972: 98–102; Dauster, F., "The Short Stories of G. M.," *BA*, 47 (1973): 466–70; Gallagher, D. P., "G. G. M.," *Modern Latin American Literature* (1973): 144–63; Guibert, R., *Seven Voices* (1973): 303–37; Hall, L. B., "Labyrinthine Solitude: The Impact of G. M.," *SWR*, 58 (1973): 253–63; Luchting, W. A., "Lampooning Literature: *La mala hora*," *BA*, 47 (1973): 471–78; Coover, R., "The Master's Voice," *Amer. Review* (Bantam Books), No. 26 (1977): 361–88; Lipski, J. M., "Embedded Dialogue in *El otoño del patriarca*," *TAH*, 2, 14 (1977): 9–12; McMurray, G. R., *G. G. M.* (1977); Williams, R. L., "The Dynamic Structure of G. M.'s *El otoño del patriarca*," *Symposium*, 32 (1978): 56–75; Zamora, L. P., "The Myth of Apocalypse and Human Temporality in G. M.'s *Cien años de soledad* and *El otoño del patriarca*," *Symposium*, 32 (1978): 341–55

—GEORGE R. MCMURRAY

How he came by his meticulous purity of style is something of a mystery. Perhaps, one may think, he found a precedent in Colombian purism, which may have a positive side, after all. He denies it. His language is not Colombia, he says simply, but his grandmother. She was a great story teller. "She spoke this way." Her voice can often be heard like a whisper in the background, reminding G. M. of the magic childhood world he grew up in, which infests so many of his best pages. There are scenes, gestures, phrases, situations that recur with obsessive regularity in his work. There are sudden beams of blinding light that create a sort of magnetic field around them, charged with unfathomable implications. Their meaning remains deliberately enigmatic. "What gives literary value is mystery," says G. M., who always tries to tap "the magic in commonplace events." In everything he writes there is this "lost chord," as he calls it. It may be a cryptic hint, a glimpse of something caught in flight, undecipherable as a dream lost on waking. Whatever its origin or appearance, it alludes to a private mythology that inhabits him like a message from the deep.

Luis Harss and Barbara Dohmann, *Into the Mainstream* (1966), pp. 336–37

Rather than attempting to recapture the actual world of his childhood in every petty detail, G. M. has created a new world that bears comparison to Faulkner's Yoknapatawpha County; G. M. calls it Macondo. . . . G. M., like the French genius Marcel Proust, recalls the past not by massive conventional realism, but in terms of exquisitely selective insights into remembered characters, situations, and anecdotes. From this welter of odd bits from the past, an image of a whole society's past comes forth. G. M.'s vision is like that of a child, endowed with the magical coherence that only a child can project onto the chaos of reality. Macondo is pure myth filtered out of reality, an enclosed yet living world in fiction.

Alexander Coleman, *Cinco maestros: Cuentos modernos de Hispanoamérica* (1969), pp. 223–24

Anybody who has been enchanted by *The Arabian Nights*, as a child or adult, who has laughed with Rabelais, who has read Faulkner, will find his experiences revived and blooming in the pages of *Cien años de soledad*. Does it surprise, then, that despite so much having been written about the novel, despite the seminars, papers, discussions, etc., nobody so far seems really to have come to grips with it? Whatever one reads or hears about it reveals, I believe, an underlying helplessness in face of this intensely alive work, a kind of embarrassed, secret admission of critical arms thrown away, and of an at first hesitant, then joyful abandon to the seductive powers of the novel. And I by no means wish to claim my own words here to be an exception to this process, or myself to have kept my critical "cool." I doubt if anyone can keep it when reading *Cien años.*

Wolfgang A. Luchting, "G. G. M.: The Boom and the Whimper," *BA*, 44 (1970), pp. 26–27

One Hundred Years of Solitude is about the Buendías and their descendants in much the same way that the Bible is about Adam and Eve and their descendants.

Macondo is a world, a place of greater possibility than the imaginary county of Faulkner, by whom G. M. has surely been influenced. The family of the Buendías . . . is the family of man, the first family, the people of Eden, Canaan, and the world. . . . In *One Hundred Years of Solitude* G. M. has produced a novel that twice delights us, a joy to the senses and the mind, a myth made of unforgettable irony.

It is also necessary to consider G. M. as a moralist, a political man; for myth, though it negates history by making circles of time and events, relates to the way we live; it is not made in a vacuum, but in the deeps of experience. G. M. writes of exploitation, colonialism, and revolution from the point of view of a man who was influenced in his childhood by a grandfather who lived out his days as one of the leavings of a revolution in a town called Aracataca, which was exploited and then abandoned by banana barons from the United States.

Earl Shorris, *Harper's*, Feb. 1972, p. 100

G. M. is one of those writers who enchants us as he deals with those perennial forces that rule our lives and cast us hither and thither. He also represents a highly encouraging phenomenon in world literature, which has been designated as the South American boom in literature. In an age when more and more often we hear that the novel is dying or dead, . . . it is worthwhile, I feel, to find such a countercurrent of fantasy and to bewingedly reflect thus upon the human lot awhile, and refreshed, thence to renew our efforts and even gingerly resume taking arms against a sea of troubles. . . .

It seems to me that G. M. marries realism and objectivity with a most singular sense of the fantastic and delicious fabulating gifts, often employing surrealistic clairvoyance to paint frescoes full of moral indignation and anger protesting against oppression and violence, degradation and deceit. Extolling pride, he clearly depicts certain ludicrous, even grotesque aspects, such as quixotic bravery and intransigent single-mindedness of purpose. It is a joy to encounter a poet who revels in his seductive powers as G. M. does. And yet he is so exact in his formulation and precise in his composition. In juxtaposing

the twin elements of humor and tragedy G. M. often achieves contrapuntal heights where language and image are thoroughly fused.

Thor Vilhjálmsson, "Presentation of G. G. M.," *BA*, 47 (1973), pp. 10–11

Cien años de soledad is a very Latin American *reading* of Borges, for it discovers Borges's relevance to Latin American—the relevance of his cyclical vision of time to the cyclical nature of Latin American history, the relevance of his sense that life is a dream, a fiction, to the dreamlike nature of Latin American politics, the relevance of his sense that the past is inseparable from the fictive words that narrate it to the tragic fact that Latin America's past is inseparable from the deliberately distorted words that have claimed to record it, the relevance, finally of Borges's demonstrations that our perceptions of things depend on our previous assumptions about them to the fact that in a continent shared by so many cultures there can be no common continental perception of anything.

D. P. Gallagher, *Modern Latin American Literature* (1973), p. 163

It is evident that *El otoño del patriarca* is not written in any conventional novelistic mode: with its grotesque extremes, its outlandish images, its exaggerated horrors, it is in fact a caricature of conventional fiction, presenting comic distortions and fantastic perversions of normal novelistic material. The social setting and plot of *Cien años de soledad* is abandoned. Patterns of poetic association, images which project mental realities, fears, dreams, nightmares, and suggestive gestures replace the discursive movement of Melquíades' manuscript. Of course, *Cien años de soledad* is also a poetic novel, but the imagery is used less to project mental realities than to create a novelistic ambience suggestive of man's prodigious capacities for both good *and* evil, love *and* hatred. . . . Like the apocalyptists, G. M. seems to feel that only through grotesquely exaggerated and fantastical imagery can the political evils of his time be fully apprehended.

Lois P. Zamora, "The Myth of Apocalypse and Human Temporality in G. M.'s *Cien años de soledad* and *El otoño del patriarca*," *Symposium*, 32 (1978), pp. 350–51

GARDNER, John

American novelist, short-story writer, librettist, essayist, and author of children's books, b. 21 July 1933, Batavia, New York; d. 14 Sept. 1982, Susquehanna, Pennsylvania

The death of his younger brother in a farm accident for which he believed himself responsible greatly affected G. and his deeply religious parents and appears to have led to his becoming the kind of writer he did: protean, prolific, preoccupied with questions of guilt, redemption, faith, and heroic acts in a world "decayed to ambiguity."

His first two novels attracted little attention but did help establish his reputation as a self-styled philosophical novelist. *Resurrection* (1966) concerns a dying philosophy professor who returns to his—and G.'s—hometown, Batavia, New York, seeking to understand the relationships between art and life, self and other, present and past while trying to die the good death—as father, husband, son, and philosopher. The *Wreckage of Agathon* (1970) is a more exuberant work that, even though set in ancient Greece, stylistically and thematically captures the zeitgeist of G.'s own iconoclastic times. In *Grendel* (1971), his first illustrated novel, G. couched his career-long quarrel with Sartrean EXISTENTIALISM in the form of a postmodern parody of the Anglo-Saxon epic *Beowulf* as told from the monster's point of view. *Grendel*'s popularity helped make his next novel, the huge and intricately structured yet strangely accessible and deeply affecting *Sunlight Dialogues* (1972), a commercial and critical success. Also set in Batavia, the novel combines numerous literary references as well as references to members of G.'s family to form one of the masterworks of contemporary American fiction. It is a novel that manages to be jokey yet deadly serious in its treatment of big ideas: faith and doubt, head versus heart, law and order versus revolution, the intensely personal and the abstractly philosophical. If, as many claim, G. never wrote quite so well again, one reason is his having in *Grendel* and *The Sunlight Dialogues* set himself so high a standard.

Another reason is the unevenness and unpredictability of his output. After the enormous success of *The Sunlight Dialogues* came *Jason and Medeia* (1973), G.'s third retelling of ancient materials from a modern perspective (this time in epic verse) and his first "full-scale literary disaster." The combination of "resonant rural realism" and comic grotesquerie that contributed to the success of *The Sunlight Dialogues* helped make *Nickel Mountain* (1974) G.'s second bestseller, in which he continued his exploration of ways of affirming life by recycling some of his earliest stories into novelistic form. In *The King's Indian: Stories and Tales* (1975) he pursues the same quest in a more self-consciously literary, metafictional way. His parodic retellings of John UPDIKE, Poe, Melville, Kafka, and others do not so much support the view of John BARTH's "literature of exhaustion" thesis (as it was commonly misunderstood) as pave the way for Barth's later celebration of "the literature of replenishment" and more specifically G.'s growing concern about the relationships between literature and individual readers on the one hand, the larger society on the other. This concern is evident in *October Light* (1976), a comic bicentennial novel about the civil war between a cantankerous, variously constipated New England farmer and his more politically liberal sister, reader of a jokey pulp novel inserted into the larger narrative. In *On Moral Fiction* (1978) G. explores literature's effect on readers in a much more polemical, even reactionary manner, arguing for a life affirming "true art" and against much of contemporary American fiction which he judged too cynical and self-indulgent to be morally and socially useful.

The moral fiction debate that was for a time vociferously argued and widely reported played a major role in changing the direction of American fiction away from the innovations of the 1960s and 1970s to the more conservative aesthetics (as well as politics) of the 1980s and 1990s. However, *On Moral Fiction* did G.'s reputation, and some would say his art, irreparable harm. The later fiction—*Freddy's Book* (1980), *The Art of Living and Other Stories* (1981),

and *Mickelsson's Ghosts* (1982)—was read and reviewed in *On Moral Fiction*'s shadow and found wanting. He died in a motorcycle accident before he could reclaim his place in postwar American literature but not before completing *On Becoming a Novelist* (1983) and *The Art of Fiction* (1984), in which he directed his moral fiction argument at young writers, trying to demonstrate, less pugnaciously though no less messianically than in *On Moral Fiction*, that "true art" is a matter of craftsmanship in the service of life-affirming vision.

FURTHER WORKS: *The Construction of the Wakefield Cycle* (1974); *The Construction of Christian Poetry in Old English* (1975); *Dragon, Dragon and Other Tales* (1975); *Gudgekin the Thistle Girl and Other Tales* (1976); *The King of the Hummingbirds and Other Tales* (1977); *The Poetry of Chaucer* (1977); *The Life & Times of Chaucer* (1977); *A Child's Bestiary* (1977); *In the Suicide Mountains* (1977); *Poems* (1978); *Rumpelstiltskin* (1978); *Frankenstein* (1979); *William Wilson* (1979); *The Temptation Game* (1980); *"Stillness" and "Shadows"* (1986); *On Writers & Writing* (1994)

BIBLIOGRAPHY: Cowart, D., *Arches & Light: The Fiction of J. G.* (1983); Morace, R. A., *J. G.: An Annotated Secondary Bibliography* (1984); McWilliams, D., *J. G.* (1990); Chavkin, A., *Conversations with J. G.* (1991); Howell, J., *Understanding J. G.* (1993)

—ROBERT A. MORACE

GARRO, Elena

Mexican novelist, dramatist, journalist, and short-story writer, b. 15 Dec. 1920, Puebla; d. 22 Aug. 1998, Cuernavaca

G.'s plays, novels, and short stories are a complex blend of allegorical symbols, fantasy, and autobiography. The theme of power in its many sociopolitical and psychological manifestations permeates all of G.'s work and is reiterated in various forms always in close relationship with G.'s perception of the situation of women in society and her own experiences as a woman. Her constant fascination with the issues of power, violence, and history can be related to the fact that G. was born only ten years after the beginning of the Mexican Revolution, one of the most violent and historically important revolutions in Latin America, and raised during the difficult period of power struggles and political reorganization that followed the postrevolutionary years.

G.'s career as a writer began while she was still a student at the National Autonomous University of Mexico. Soon after her marriage in 1937 to the Mexican poet and essayist Octavio PAZ, G. began to write for the Mexican journal *Así*. As a reporter, she was bold and daring. On one occasion, in order to complete an article, she had herself locked up as a common prisoner in the Federal District's women's jail for three weeks, and her story, once published, caused the discharge of the director of the prison. It was this boldness that made her an aggressive social activist years later, a boldness that she also transfers to the characters in her writings. Later, in 1948, while traveling back to Mexico from California, she was denied entrance to her country for being the daughter of a Spaniard. G., in spite of the fact that her mother was Mexican and that she had been born and raised in Mexico, had to go through the process of naturalization, was treated as a foreigner, was given a three-month visa, and was forced to leave the country after that time. This experience of feeling like a foreigner in her own country, isolated and marginalized, would also be recaptured in different ways in her work in the life of several of her feminine characters.

In 1954 G. began to write for films, and also wrote her first play, *Felipe Angeles* (1967; Felipe Angeles). By 1958 she had achieved fame as a dramatist. Her first three plays were aired in the same season in "Poesía en voz alta" (spoken poetry) and later published along with several one-act plays in a single volume she entitled *Un hogar sólido y otras piezas en un acto* (1957; a solid house and other one-act plays; repub. as *Un hogar sólido*, 1986). She was also successful with the films *Sólo de noche vienes* (you only come at night) and *Las señoritas Vivanco* (the Vivanco ladies). During this time, G. became involved in the problem of peasants evicted from their land in Ahuatepec, Morelos. The urgent sense of justice that has always accompanied G. made her join in the fight in their favor. She succeeded in helping the workers regain their land and founded a weekly magazine, *Presente*, to voice a defense on behalf of the peasants. The magazine disappeared after several issues, but she became so well known that the peasants of Madera, Chihuahua, called on her for her support on similar demands. G. was then a journalist for *Sucesos*, and she worked together with Gabriel GARCÍA MÁRQUEZ and other well-known writers on these peasants' behalf.

Years before the publication of her first plays, G. became ill while she and Paz were living in Berne. During her convalescence she wrote her first novel, *Los recuerdos del porvenir* (1966; *Recollections of Things To Come*, 1969), a manuscript she put away in a trunk until it was rescued by Paz years later and published. The novel, the winner of the Xavier Villaurrutia Prize in 1984, recaptures the actions occuring in the Mexico of the 1920s in the small town of Ixtepec during the cruel days of the Cristero rebellion, a violent movement in favor of the Church, which emerged as an aftermath of the revolution. In G.'s novel, the town tells its own story against a background of political change, religious persecution, and social unrest. Here, as in her play *Felipe Angeles*, G. portrays the image of a revolution that, like all revolutions, ended up devouring itself.

Mexico's dual heritage, Spanish and Indian, became an important theme in all of G.'s work, especially in the first period of her production when she was fascinated by the ancient Mexican concept of a reality that simultaneously accommodates different levels. Against a background of violence with its many manifestations, G. experimented in her work with the presence of the past in the present, with the concept of an eternal present, and with the idea that women, in spite of having extraordinary potential as human beings, are usually not recognized in a male-oriented culture. In the first period of G.'s production, which also includes the collection of short stories *La semana de colores* (1964; week of colors), where G. again proved her versatility and ingenuity as a writer of fiction, she created a magical world where time can stand still to allow lovers to escape, and where past and present can flow intermittently into each other. In the work of this period, G. also explores the feminine pattern of the Malinche as a Mexican cultural and psychological model in the conceptualization of Mexican women, as seen in her most anthologized short story, "La culpa es de los Tlaxcaltecas" (it's the fault of the Tlaxcaltecas). G.'s perception of the role of women in Mexico, her preoccupation with the pervasive presence of the past in the present, and her view of an eternal reduplication of performance can be seen in her work in the characterization of generations that follow each other, each one repeating the same acts and gestures as those that preceded it. Following this impressive first period of G.'s work, there came fifteen years of silence, which coincided with her divorce, and a self-exile caused by illness and financial hardships. Other incidents were to mark the second period of her production. After the government's massacre of the students in Tlatelolco in 1968, G. was wrongly accused of being an instigator. To escape from the difficult situation of being watched by some and threatened by others, G. fled to the U.S. and then to Spain where she had to become a Spanish citizen since her Mexican passport was confiscated by the Mexican government.

In her earlier writings, G. created characters who existed in two different but parallel and simultaneous times, and through them she explored the traditional myth of female behavior and subverted traditional views in favor of new models in society. In the work of G.'s second period, these characters are superseded by an angry voice exposing injustices committed by society on its weak members, especially women. Perhaps based on her own experiences in 1968 G.'s work deconstructs reality and portrays truth as that which is hidden by the collective imaginary, a construct often dominated by power. To this period belongs her second collection of short stories, *Andamos huyendo Lola* (1980; We are fleeing Lola), and her last novels: *Y Matarazo no llamó...* (And Matarazo didn't call...), written in 1960 but not published until 1989, *Testimonios sobre Mariana* (1981; testimonies about Mariana), *Reencuentro de personajes* (1982; reencounter of characters), and *La casa junto al rio* (1983; the house by the river). This latter work involves a magical encounter of the living with the dead, through a death that is seen not as an end but as a beginning, and as a return to a comforting past where the main character, a girl harassed by the townspeople, is able to reunite with her dead relatives as she crosses from one reality into another. The themes of violence and cruelty, which permeate all of G.'s work, are intensified in this novel, and presented now as a psychic and psychopathological phenomenon. Other changes are also noticeable. G.'s strong and individual woman in her first plays and novel becomes a heroine that falls into passivity and oppression. The heroine in G.'s *La casa junto al rio* is, like the traditional hero in a quest, a woman who must confront the absurd and struggle with solitude, isolation, marginality, and the constant fear of rejection and death in search of identity, knowledge, and meaning. The highly allegorical figure of Consuelo in this novel dies a victim of the townspeople who have kept her from knowing the facts of her family's disappearance. Yet her death is not defeat. It is the encounter with a new model outside of a present decadent order of things, and the reunion with her relatives is the encounter with the long-sought Paradise denied to her in the world of the living.

In G.'s work, death is the other side of one and the same reality, and the antithesis of cruelty is not kindness, but freedom. G.'s skillful control of narrative structure, style, and theme allows her to play successfully with a magical fictional world where history and time, as in the Aztec tradition, possess neither a past nor a future. Through myth and magic, G.'s work has addressed many important issues of 20th–c. Latin America, especially those pertaining to violence and power. Her mastery of action, timelessness, poetry in prose, narrative structure, dramatic intensity and suspense, vivid impressions, and characters drawn with bold strokes allow her to paint the passionate and secret lives of women characters in a constant search for themselves, marginalized, oppressed, rejected, and at times driven to suicide, which for G. is also a form of freedom.

FURTHER WORKS: *La señora en su balcón. Tercera antología de obras en un acto* (1960); *La dama boba: pieza en tres actos* (1963); *Corazón en un bote de basura* (1996); *Inés* (1996); *Buscami esquela primer amor* (1996); *Traje rojo para un duelo* (1996); *Revolucionarios mexicanos* (1997)

BIBLIOGRAPHY: Rosser, H. E., "Form and Content in E. G.'s *Los recuerdos del porvenir,*" *RCEH*, 2, 3 (Spring 1978): 282–94; Candelaria, C., "La Malinche, Feminist Prototype," *Frontiers*, 5 (1980): 1–6; Johnson, H., "E. G.'s Attitudes towards Mexican Society," *South Central Bulletin*, 40, 4 (Winter 1980): 150–52; Mora, G., "Rebeldes fracasadas: una lectura feminista de *Andarse por las ramas y la señora en su balcón,*" *Plaza*: 5–6 (Fall–Spring 1981–1982): 115–31; Mora, G., "*La dama boba de* E. G.: Verdad y ficción, teatro y metateatro," *LATR*, 16, 2 (Spring 1983): 15–22; Leal, L., "Female Archetypes in Mexican Literature," in Miller, B., ed., *Women in Hispanic Literature: Icons and Fallen Idols* (1983): 227–42; Duncan, C., "'La culpa es de los Tlaxcaltecas': A Reevaluation of Mexico's Past through Myth," *CH*, 7, 2 (1985): 105–20; Rodena, A. Mendez, "Tiempo femenino, tiempo ficticio: *Los recuerdos del porvenir* de E. G.," *RI*, 51: 132–33 (July–Dec. 1985): 843–51; Anderson, R. K., "Myth and Archetype in *Recollections of Things To Come,*" *StTCL*, 9, 2 (Spring 1985): 213–27; Larson, C., "Recollections of Plays To Come: Time in the Theater of E. G.," *LATR*, 22, 2 (Spring 1989): 5–17; Stoll, A. K., ed., *A Different Reality: Studies on the Work of E. G.* (1990)

—JULIA CUERVO HEWITT

GASCAR, Pierre

(pseud. of Pierre Fournier) French novelist, short-story writer, and essayist, b. 13 March 1916, Paris

G. spent his childhood in a village in southwestern France. He served eight years in the army, five of them as a prisoner of war in Germany and in the Nazi-occupied Ukraine during World War II. A journalist after the war, he has traveled extensively: to China and, while working with the World Health Organization, to southeast Asia and Africa. He has written for radio and television and has been a literary critic and lecturer.

The short stories of *Les bêtes* (1953, pub. in one vol. with *Les temps des morts; Beasts and Men*, 1956), written when G. was a prisoner of war, depict the atavistic cruelty of men and animals in the suffering of a world at war; both realistic and fantastic, they are rich in SURREALIST, mythic images of the mental darkness in which each man struggles against despair and resignation. In these, and in the other stories of this dark concentration-camp world, including those in the collection *Les femmes* (1955; in *Women and the Sun*, 1965) and the novel *Le fugitif* (1961; *The Fugitive*, 1964), G. affirms his hope of an evolutionary metamorphosis of man.

Other early autobiographical works, *La graine* (1955; *The Seed*, 1959) and *L'herbe des rues* (1956; the grass of the streets) are lyric novels of a tightly controlled rythmic style. They are unsentimental accounts of rural life; the solitary child can "believe in stones," in the natural world, even in this loveless, indifferent milieu.

In his later works, G. abandoned fiction for the personal *récit* and the philosophical essay. His travels in the Third World, his reading in history, and his interest in psychology and the natural sciences provided material for these speculative works. In all of them, the material world and the dreams hidden behind it fascinate G.: the dream imagery of salt, blood, and monstrous grafted plants in *Chimères* (1969; chimeras), lichen in *Le présage* (1972; presage). In these works, G. elaborates his dominant themes: the future evolution of the natural world, man's need for natural forms, the destructive effects of science and of our false cult of rationality. In *Les sources* (1975; the springs), a commentary on the works of a French Renaissance philosopher-naturalist, Bernard Palissy (c. 1510–1589), G. finds the hope of the future world in the rediscovery of the primitive unity of the Whole, the harmony of all form and matter.

Although G. has not created imaginative fiction of wide scope, he excels as the "witness" and "dreamer" of our present and future world. He is both an exact observer and analyst and a disciplined poet of the subconscious and of nature.

FURTHER WORKS: *Les meubles* (1949); *Le visage clos* (1951); *Chine ouverte* (1955); *Les pas perdus* (1957); *Voyage chez les vivants* (1958); *La barre de corail* (1958; *The Coral Barrier*, 1961); *Soleils* (1960; in *Women and the Sun*, 1965); *Le feu mal éteint* (1961); *Camile Hilaire* (1961); *Chambord* (1962; *Chambord*, 1964); *Vertiges du présent* (1962); *Les moutons du feu* (1963; *Lambs of Fire*, 1965); *Le meilleur de la vie* (1964; *The Best Years*, 1967); *Les charmes* (1965); *Histoire de la captivité des Français en Allemagne* (1967); *Auto* (1967); *L'arche* (1971); *Rimbaud et la commune* (1971); *Quartier Latin* (1973); *Les bouchers* (1973); *L'homme et l'animal* (1974)

BIBLIOGRAPHY: Borbas, L., "Man and Beast in G.'s Tales," *KFLQ*, 6 (1959): 1–5; Obuchowski, C. W., "The Concentrationary World of P. G.," *FR*, 34 (1961): 327–35; Radke, J. J., "The Metamorphosis of Animals and Men in G.'s *Les bêtes*," *FR*, 39 (1965): 85–91; Chalfin, D. E., "*Women and the Sun*, by P. G.," *SSF*, 3 (1966): 266–67; Fabre-Luce, A., "L'incidence de l'imaginaire dans les nouvelles de P. G.," *FR*, 41 (1968): 839–48; Lorent, L. E., "P. G.: Charmes et chimères," *La revue nouvelle*, 51 (1970): 204–7; Albérès, R. M., "Le réalisme onirique de P. G.," *Littérature, horizon 2000* (1974): 235–53

—JUDITH RADKE

GASS, William H.

American novelist, short-story writer, and essayist, b. 30 July 1924, Fargo, N.D.

When G. was six months old his family moved to industrial Warren, Ohio, where he grew up, returning to rural North Dakota only for summer visits to relatives. G. received a B.A. from Kenyon College (Ohio) and a Ph.D. in philosophy from Cornell University. Beginning in 1955 he taught philosophy at Purdue University for several years and now teaches at Washington University in St. Louis, Missouri.

G. prefers to balance the contradictory impulses in art, which are to communicate and to make an artifact out of the medium. Both impulses are apparent in G.'s first novel, *Omensetter's Luck* (1966). But the simple story of Brackett Omensetter, the happy man, who does what he does because it feels good, becomes too complex in G.'s straining for language and narrative technique.

G.'s short fiction, which had appeared in little magazines since 1958, was published as *In the Heart of the Heart of the Country* (1968). Each story in this collection presents a mind walled up in its loneliness, desperately producing fantasies to take the place of love and to avert madness. The title story orients the whole collection to G.'s view of the relationship between art and life. It begins with a misquotation from William Butler YEATS's "Sailing to Byzantium," which juxtaposes G.'s midwestern town of "B" and Yeats's mythical city. But the country that in Yeats's poem is not for old men is also, in G.'s story, not for the young. What we think of as childhood, states his aging narrator, is a lie created by poetry. And where Yeats's man forswears bodily existence, G.'s man asserts that body equals being.

This assertion of the primacy of life over art is restated in *Willie Masters' Lonesome Wife* (1968). A sixty-page parody composed of footnotes, distortion of typefaces, and arty photographs, it satirizes the idea of art for art's sake and concludes by admonishing the reader: "You have fallen into art—return to life."

G.'s essays on language, philosophy, and literature, however, collected as *Fiction and the Figures of Life* (1971), argue the case for art. If all were to practice the artist's virtues, a richer state of being for humanity might be possible. But this G. regards as highly unlikely, a dim view of human possibility that runs through his work as an undercurrent of personal despair. Countering it is a delight in recording sensuous experience and a restless inquiry into the human condition. The essays develop G.'s belief that the novelist does not render the world; he creates one from the medium of which he is master—language. G. observes this creativity in the best contemporary writers and evaluates their achievement in making new orders of the world ("figured histories") for their readers. His judgment is divided. BECKETT, BORGES, and BARTH, although they resist literal interpretation, are not merely puzzling but profound. Yet G. believes that these writers' "fear of feeling" inhibits their appeal to a reader's sensibilities. G. finds this fear also in HAWKES, NABOKOV, BARTHELME, and Robert Coover (b. 1932). On the other hand, FAULKNER, LOWRY, LAWRENCE, BELLOW, and Stanley ELKIN command a reader's emotional as well as intellectual involvement.

G. has continued to publish more essays than fiction. His ability to translate the philosopher's concerns for the problems of language and being into the stuff of imagination is inhibited by a conflict in even his best work between medium as a means and medium as an end. This conflict qualifies the achievement of much mid-century American writing and accounts for the many writers who are interested in G. as a theorist-practitioner.

Yet G. at his best, *On Being Blue* (1976), an essay on the semantic and imaginative implications of blueness, leaves no doubt about wherein his strength lies: it is in direct statements one after another, driven by high voltage intellectual energy, and kept in motion by a curious mind that is sometimes reminiscent of Robert GRAVES, although with an unmistakable American toughness of language and attitude.

FURTHER WORKS: *The World within the Word* (1978)

BIBLIOGRAPHY: Kane, P., "The Sun Burned on the Snow: G.'s 'The Pedersen Kid,'" *Crit*, 14, 2 (1972): 89–96; special G. issue, *Crit*, 18, 1 (1976); Merrill, R. B., "The Grotesque as Structure: *Willie Masters' Lonesome Wife*," *Criticism*, 18 (1976): 305–16; Rueckert, W., "Love Lavished on Speech," *ChiR*, 29, 4 (1978):

William H. Gass

53–59; Waxman, R. E., "Things in the Saddle: W. G.'s 'Icicles' and 'Orders of Insects,'" *RS*, 46 (1978): 215–22; Janssens, G. A. M., "An Interview with W. G.," *DQR*, 9 (1979): 242–59; McCaffery, L., "The G.-Gardner Debate: Showdown on Main Street," *LitR*, 23 (1979): 134–44

—MANLY JOHNSON

GATES, Henry Louis, Jr.

American scholar, critic, essayist, cultural theorist, b. 16 Sept. 1950, Keyser, West Virginia

G. may well be the most important late 20th-c. scholar of African-American literature. For his research and writing on a diverse range of topics from ethnicity to anti-Semitism he has received numerous honors, including the MacArthur award, and has been named to the Pulitzer committee. G.'s greatest contribution to scholarship has been his unending quest to see the rewriting of the American literature canon to include a fair percentage of works by African-American authors. He made his name in the field of literary scholarship by "rediscovering" works by 19th-c. African-Americans—most notably Harriet Wilson's *Our Nig* (1859), the earliest known novel by a black author. G. has also brought women's slave narratives to the attention of the literary community.

His first book, *The Signifying Monkey* (1988), is a study of black literature in the context of its linguistic heritage and won him the American Book Award. He coined the term "Signifyin" to denote a crossroad where two languages meet, be they an African language and English or even "the black vernacular and standard English." G. sees a dialogue between African and African-American literature and looks at many black writers with that assumption in mind.

In 1994, G. published a memoir entitled *Colored People* about his hometown, Piedmont, West Virginia, where he took part in the struggle to end legal segregation. There are tensions in the book related to race, family issues, class, education, and an interesting tension between G.'s identity as a black American with all its heritage and importance and his need "to experience a humanity that is neither colorless nor reducible to color." Despite the fact that this is a memoir, G. manages to raise issues that are forward-looking and relevant to his children and their peers and descendants. His greatest piece of advice seems to be that people retain their sense of humor, that they enjoy life despite its struggles and trials.

G.'s next book, *Thirteen Ways of Looking at a Black Man* (1997), considers how definitions of race influence how whites think of blacks and how blacks perceive themselves. He does this through profiles of thirteen black men who have held important positions in the African-American community and in American society as a whole. The point of these profiles is to show the men as regular people whose lives were shaped by their individual experiences and the choices they made. Also in 1997, as general editors, G. and Nellie McKay brought out a seminal work, the *Norton Anthology of African American Literature*. Of this collection of poems, stories, novels, and essays that brings together works that span 250 years of African-American history, G. can rightly say that it "represents . . . a first attempt to draw a line between Phyllis Wheatley and Toni Morrison."

G.'s place in literary and cultural history is firmly set. His writings, lectures, and media appearances all showcase his talent and his relentless pursuit to define a place for African-Americans within the larger context of American literature and culture.

FURTHER WORKS: *Black Literature and Literary Theory* (1984); *"Race," Writing, and Difference* (1986); *The Classic Slave Narratives* (1987); *Figures in Black: Words, Signs, and the "Racial" Self* (1987); *Reading Black, Reading Feminist: A Critical Anthology* (1990); *Bearing Witness: Selections from African-American Autobiography in the Twentieth Century* (1991); *Loose Canons: Notes on the Culture Wars* (1992); *Langston Hughes: Critical Perspectives Past and Present* (1993, with K. A. Appiah); *Zora Neale Hurston: Critical Perspectives Past and Present* (1993, with K. A. Appiah); *Toni Morrison: Critical Perspectives Past and Present* (1993, with K. A. Appiah); *Gloria Naylor: Critical Perspectives Past and Present* (1993, with K. A. Appiah); *Alice Walker: Critical Perspectives Past and Present* (1993, with K. A. Appiah); *Richard Wright: Critical Perspectives Past and Present* (1993, with K. A. Appiah); *Speaking of Race, Speaking of Sex: Hate Speech, Civil Rights, and Civil Liberties* (1994, with others); *The Future of the Race* (1996, with Cornell West)

BIBLIOGRAPHY: Lubiano, W., "H. L. G., Jr. and African American Literary Discourse," *NEQ*, 62 (1989): 561-72; Bucknell, B., "H. L. G., Jr. and the Theory of 'Signifyin(g)'," *Ariel*, 21 (1990): 65-84; Rowell, C. H., "Interview with H. L. G., Jr.," *Callaloo*, 14 (1991): 444-63; Ward, J. W., Jr., "Interview with H. L. G., Jr.," *NLH*, 22 (1991): 927-35

—MARCY TANTER

GATTO, Alfonso

Italian poet and journalist, b. 17 July 1909, Salerno; d. 8 March 1976, Rome

Born to a family of sailors and small shipbuilders, G. did not finish his university studies. In his youth he worked as a bookseller, school-teacher, proofreader, and journalist. In 1933 he moved to Milan, where he wrote articles on literature, architecture, and interior decoration. Jailed as an anti-Fascist in 1936, he became a Communist and joined the resistance in 1943. Like many other intellectuals, he eventually left the Communist Party, in 1951. Married to a painter, he spent the postwar years in Rome, working for various papers as journalist and editor until his death.

Like other writers of his generation, G. contributed to the best periodicals of the 1930s. He wrote for *Circoli* and *Letteratura*, and in 1938 he and Vasco PRATOLINI founded *Campo di Marte* to educate all classes in the appreciation of contemporary arts.

G.'s early poetry, written under Fascism, is influenced by HERMETICISM but does not completely belong to that school: critics have called it SURREALIST and even "neocubist." Other elements in his style are its typically southern musicality, imagery that is both three-dimensional and pliant, and a very cultivated intellectualism alternating with a certain amount of pathos.

G.'s early work is included in *Poesie* (1941; poems), which contains all the poetry he had published since 1932.

Political circumstances and the war caused his work to become more realistic and socially committed, as is evidenced in the war poems of *Il capo sulla neve* (1949; head on the snow). *La madre e la morte* (1960; mother and death), however, reflects a more personal and existential focus. His later books show a continuing preoccupation with social and ethical problems, a controlled sentimentality, and constant stylistic experimentation. The characteristics of his early poetry are slightly modified, being used now to give glimpses of the subconscious world in contrast to everyday reality. The result is a "magic" feeling unique to G.'s poetry.

G.'s best-known collections are *Osteria flegrea* (1962; Phlegraean inn), whose main theme is death, and *La storia delle vittime* (1966; history of the victims), which won the Viareggio prize. *Rime di viaggio per la terra dipinta* (1969; rhymes of travel through the painted earth) is noteworthy for its exceptionally skillful use of formal poetic techniques.

G.'s collected poetry has appeared in the prestigious *Lo Specchio* series. He has also written children's verse, the most important volume of which is *Carlomagno nella grotta* (1962; Charlemagne in the grotto). G. was one of the best and most passionately committed of the formerly hermetic poets; his work has earned him a secure niche in the history of 20th-c. Italian literature.

FURTHER WORKS: *Isola* (1932); *Atanasio Soldati pittore* (1934); *Morto ai paesi* (1937); *Poesie* (1939); *Disegni di Rosai* (1939);

Luigi Broggini scultore (1940); *Ottone Rosai* (1941); *L'allodola* (1943); *Virgilio Guidi pittore* (1943); *La sposa bambina* (1943); *Amore della vita* (1944); *La spiaggia dei poveri* (1944); *Il duello* (1944); *Il sigaro de fuoco* (1945); *Il vaporetto* (1963); *Poesie d'amore* (1973); *Desinenze* (1976)

—JOY M. POTTER

GEE, Maurice

New Zealand novelist, short-story writer, and writer of children's books, b. 22 Aug. 1931, Whakatane

G. grew up in Henderson, west Auckland, a setting that he returns to in his writing. G.'s family background was modest but intellectually supportive, with a strong tradition of social activism. His grandfather, James Chapple, a pacifist, had been imprisoned for sedition in World War I. G. went to university, worked as a librarian, but from 1976 has been a full-time writer.

G. occupies a distinct position in New Zealand writing, sharing many of the characteristic features of novelists of his generation, while extending and intensifying their range and style. His early novels, such as *The Big Season* (1962), develop the agenda set by Frank SARGESON: a distinctly New Zealand rhetoric and subject matter that offer a critique of a culture represented as puritanical and flat. Small town society, repressive family life, and the attempts of the largely inarticulate main character to see beyond such boundaries form the basis of this school of writing.

G. has made this scenario more complex and sophisticated rather than moving on from it. His narrators are from the place but not of it, reticent and unemotional, but apprehending personal and social complexities with an increasing sophistication, which could be said to mirror that of New Zealand writing. As Noel says in "Joker and Wife" (1986), "growing up in my family in our town, I had come to know very well that conflict and ambiguity were the rule, and 'oneness' a room that could not be lived in."

Several aspects of G.'s style contribute to this development. He is more interested in the moral status, challenges, and ambiguities of his characters than this rather laconic and objective style has allowed. Large moral problems, as well as the minor negotiations of daily life, are often his focus. *Plumb* (1978), based on the life of his Chapple grandfather, and *Live Bodies* (1997), an account of wartime internment, are concerned with the moral issues of war and conscientious objection. *In My Father's Den* (1972) and *Crime Story* (1994) deal with murder and its investigation.

His novels and short stories are grounded in a sense of community, even if they concern themselves with the criminal and the delinquent as much as with the upright citizen. G. tends to understand society in terms of its treatment of the outsider, those with special understanding, those who are in some way damaged and those without normal moral boundaries. His narrators and central characters tend to be the socially marginalized, the physically wounded, the unconventional, the alien, and the old. G. writes powerfully about old age, from the eponymous George Plumb to Mr. Pitt-Rimmer in "A Glorious Morning, Comrade" (1975), who attempts an escape from his controlling daughters. Despite the prosaic nature of his narratives, he works through these characters

towards a sense of some central, undisclosed mystery, which the banalities of ordinary life cannot quite penetrate.

G.'s style has been from the outset a form of intense realism, in which actual places—west Auckland, central Wellington, and, in particular Nelson ("Saxton")—all appear in minutely observed detail, a kind of literary topography. In this, he is a provincial writer, affirming, and cautiously celebrating the local. But he refuses to deal in the large gestures, abstractions, or implied insecurities of nationalism. Though landscape is precisely represented, it is rarely given any aesthetic or symbolic value, and he rarely moves outside a lower-middle-class European range of characters. He shows a consciousness of the New Zealand European past, but uses it not as celebration, but as the source of painful wisdom.

G. employs and matures the "suburban gothic" style of New Zealand writers like Janet FRAME, albeit without their formal experimentation. His realism and rationally controlled plotting contains, disconcertingly, the grotesque and the bizarre. *The Burning Boy* (1990), for example, centers on Duncan, a fifteen-year-old boy hideously disfigured by a fire in which his friend died, and the effect this event has on family and community.

G.'s first children's novel, *Under the Mountain*, appeared in 1979, and he has written seven more. In writing for children, the tendency towards the gothic, carefully controlled in his adult fiction, is given range and force, while his habits of realism serve as a springboard into the bizarre. The ordinary coexists with, and is contaminated by, the extraordinary. In *Under the Mountain* the extinct volcanoes of Auckland hide alien beings, the Wilberforces, "people of the mud who conquer and multiply." In the "O" trilogy, *The Halfmen of O* (1982), *The Priests of Ferris* (1984), and *Motherstone* (1985), he invents a universe in which the lost balance between good and evil must be restored by the child, Susan. Though the texture of G.'s children's novels may differ from his adult novels, there are themes common to both—the outsider who possesses special and significant knowledge, the sense of a Manichean world in which good may not necessarily have the upper hand, and the disabling effects of intolerance.

FURTHER WORKS: *A Special Flower* (1965); *A Glorious Morning, Comrade: Stories* (1975; rev. ed., *Collected Stories*, 1986); *Games of Choice* (1976); *The World around the Corner* (1980); *Meg* (1981); *Sole Survivor* (1983); *The Fire Raisers* (1986); *Prowlers* (1987); *The Champion* (1989); *Going West* (1992); *The Fat Man* (1994); *The Plumb Trilogy* (1995); *Loving Ways* (1996)

BIBLIOGRAPHY: Boyd, B, "M. G.: Ironies of Growth and Judgement," *Islands*, 8, 3 (Oct. 1980): 268-81; 8, 4-9 (June 1981): 136-60; Hill, D, *Introducing M. G.* (1981); Manhire, B., *M. G.* (1986); Giffuni, C., "M. G., a Bibliography," *ANZSC*, 3 (1990): 36-43; Reilly, C, "An Interview with M. G.," *Sport*, 5 (Spring 1990): 80-86; Williams, M., *Leaving the Highway: Six Contemporary New Zealand Novelists* (1990)

—MARK SULLIVAN

GE'EZ LITERATURE

See Ethiopian Literature

Jean Genet

GENET, Jean

French novelist, dramatist, and poet, b. 19 Dec. 1910, Paris; d. 15 April 1986, Paris

Of all the writers of France, G. is the most disquieting. The appalling string of descriptive categories with which he is always introduced—illegitimate child, thief, beggar, male prostitute, pornographer, and convict—seems to bear no relationship to his achievement, which in addition to a handful of poems includes five prose works and five plays that hold a central position in modern literature. And yet G.'s life is the ostensible subject of his prose works and implicit even in his plays. While other writers, particularly modern ones, have blurred the boundaries between literature and autobiography, only G. has created a mythic version of his life that has completely replaced whatever that life may have been in reality. Because G. spent so many years either incarcerated or wandering through the lowest strata of European society, and because he has provided so little new information in the rare interviews he has granted, a biography dealing in detail with the first half of his life is not likely to be written. The only accounts of G.'s unique transformation from hardened criminal to major writer would then remain his own and that of Jean-Paul SARTRE, whose EXISTENTIALIST interpretation of G.'s life, *Saint Genet: Comédien et martyr* (1952; *Saint Genet: Actor and Martyr*, 1963), is almost identical to G.'s own, and (appropriately enough) was published as the first volume of G.'s complete works.

Somehow the supposedly self-educated G. became one of the most elegant prose stylists in all of French literature. His first book, *Notre-Dame-des-Fleurs* (1944; rev. ed., 1951; *Our Lady of the Flowers*, 1963), begins in a prison cell, which G. has decorated with pictures of notorious criminals, and the narrative constantly returns to that cell, as G. awaits a hearing that may set him free. In his imagination, however, he is already free, as he weaves stories around the Parisian homosexuals and petty criminals who are the focus of his yearning and admiration. *Miracle de la rose* (1946; rev. ed., 1951; *Miracle of the Rose*, 1965) is a meditation on the meaning of imprisonment, on the reformatory where G. spent his adolescence, and especially on a convict named Harcamone, who like G. has moved from reformatory to prison but by committing murder has surpassed G. and moved even higher—to the scaffold. The "miracle" of the title is the transformation of Harcamone's chains to a garland of flowers, and by an equally miraculous imaginative process G. leaves his own body and ascends to paradise in the body of Harcamone at the moment of the murderer's execution. While in these two works fiction can be said to be blended with autobiography, the distinction between those two forms has vanished in *Pompes funèbres* (1948; rev. ed., 1953; *Funeral Rites*, 1969). As in his other works, G. alternates between a (real?) present and a fantasized past, but in this case his own identity is so tenuous that he moves as well from third to first person, sometimes in the middle of a sentence, and remains aware, even when he has "assumed the form of Erik . . . of the sharp, luminous presence within me of J. G."

In *Querelle de Brest* (1949; rev. ed., 1953; *Querelle*, 1974), G. does not appear as a character at all; in *Journal du voleur* (1949; *The Thief's Journal*, 1964) G. seems to move from fiction to autobiography—yet Richard N. Coe has turned up fragmentary evidence suggesting that even in G.'s memoirs the element of fiction should not be totally discounted. In any case, G. produced a "novel" and an "autobiography" only after showing in three other books that the two forms were in his case virtually identical. Not only does G. thus emphasize the fictional element in his own identity, but his prose works can be viewed as a series of attempts to destroy the whole notion of human identity. (Even *Querelle de Brest*, which is a relatively straightforward novel, deals with doubles and multiple personalities.) When the threat of prison no longer hung over him, G. moved on to the one form of literature in which an individual identity is absolutely essential—the drama— in order to abolish identity even there.

In between G.'s prose works and his full-length plays, however, came Sartre's massive psychoanalytical study *Saint Genet: Actor and Martyr*, which in addition to being one of the greatest critical studies of the century has a certain claim to being another work generated by G. himself, since virtually the only references in it are to G.'s works and to G. in conversation. Whether G. was the best possible example of Sartre's philosophy, because of the way he consciously chose to become what he already was in the eyes of others, or whether Sartre is simply so brilliant that it is impossible to read G. without borrowing Sartre's viewpoint, every subsequent writer on G. has followed in Sartre's footsteps, and written what is at times more a commentary upon Sartre than upon G. One critic has speculated that because Sartre's study is so overwhelming, its publication made G. himself incapable of writing any more prose of his own, but by 1952 G. had already written two short plays and had embarked upon yet another transformation—from novelist to dramatist.

Haute surveillance (1949; *Deathwatch*, 1954) takes place in a prison cell, and its theme is the inability of minor criminals to attain the exalted position of murderers, since murder is a grace given by destiny and not available to the unworthy. *Les bonnes* (1954; *The Maids*, 1954) deals on one level with the relationships between masters and servants, but, as Sartre has shown, G.'s two early plays are really variations of the same basic situation, both dealing with ritualized attempts to gain power—attempts that are ultimately unavailing.

Le balcon (1956; rev. ed., 1960; *The Balcony*, 1957) is set in a brothel where clients who play at being powerful figures have the opportunity to live out their fantasies of power in real life as the result of an abortive revolution. In this play G. uses the house of illusions as a metaphor for the world as a whole, where revolutionaries fail because they are unaware that rituals are more important than ideals.

Les nègres (1958; *The Blacks*, 1960) carries the notion of a play within a play one step further: the blacks onstage perform a play for an audience of black actors wearing white masks, but the "real" white audience in the theater is all the while being entertained by this spectacle in order to be kept ignorant of the "real" black revolution taking place outside the theater.

Les paravents (1961; *The Screens*, 1962) takes place during the Algerian revolution, although the play seems with the passing years to have so little to do with that specific historical reality that the scandal occasioned by its first performances in France (1966) seems almost irrelevant to the play's content. At the end of the play its major characters have burst through the screens on stage to reach a realm where every distinction between individuals has been abolished. In G.'s prose works extremes are reconciled—a Nazi makes love to a Frenchman and a murderer embraces a detective. In *Les paravents* extremes cannot be said to be reconciled because by the end of the play they no longer even exist, and characters who were on opposite sides while they lived sit together chuckling gently, with no bodies, no beliefs, no personalities at all.

G. claims to have been particularly impressed by the novels of Dostoevsky and PROUST, and indeed, their influence is apparent in his prose works, although the childhood paradise he recalls with longing is a reformatory and the Siberia toward which he yearns is a penal colony in French Guiana, where he hopes not to be regenerated but rather to be confirmed in criminality. The influences usually cited among dramatists are ARTAUD and PIRANDELLO. G. shares with Artaud a contempt for the theatrical experience as it has become fossilized and meaningless in the Western world, and like Pirandello he constantly juggles with illusion and reality. As influences on G., however, these writers are problematic. G. is less a product of influences than a seminal figure who sums up in his work the major literary tendencies of his age. This is not to deny the scandal inherent in a figure whose three cardinal virtues are theft, homosexuality, and treason, and whose ten major works constitute a modern antidecalogue whose inverted values contain something to offend almost any reader. Although the thrust of G.'s work may be overwhelmingly destructive, however, his great merit is to have elevated nihilism to an ethical imperative. G. has written of the time a plaster bust in his home "miraculously broke, and I saw the bust was hollow. I had had to leap into the void in order to see it." That leap into the void is both the subject and method of G.'s works, and his pervasive image of that void is as an endless hall of mirrors, where it is impossible to distinguish essence from reflection. Under these circumstances his battle plan, like that of the lieutenant who leads his men in an attack upon an Algerian village in *Les paravents*, is to open fire first upon the mirrors.

FURTHER WORKS: *Poèmes* (1948); *Œuvres complètes* (1951 ff.); *Lettres à Roger Blin* (1966; *Letters to Roger Blin*, 1969). **FURTHER WORKS IN ENGLISH:** *Treasures of the Night: The Collected Poems of J. G.* (1980)

BIBLIOGRAPHY: Sartre, J.-P., *Saint Genet: Actor and Martyr* (1963); McMahon, J. H., *The Imagination of J. G.* (1963); Brustein, R., *The Theater of Revolt* (1964): 361–411; Driver, T. F., *J. G.* (1966); Coe, R. N., *The Vision of J. G.* (1968); Knapp, B. L., *J. G.* (1968); Thody, P., *J. G.* (1968); Coe, R. N., ed., *The Theater of J. G.* (1970); Cetta, L. T., *Profane Play, Ritual, and J. G.: A Study of His Drama* (1974); Choukri, M., *J. G. in Tangier* (1974); Naish, C., *A Genetic Approach to Structures in the Work of J. G.* (1978); Brooks, P., and J. Halpern, eds., *G.: A Collection of Critical Essays* (1979); Oswald, L., *J. G. and the Semiotics of Performance* (1989); White, E., *G.: A Biography* (1993)

—MICHAEL POPKIN

From a literary point of view, it is essentially irrelevant whether a writer indulges in this vice or that, or even whether or not he has been a common criminal. What matters is that, starting out from this or that given vice, or from whatever may have been the singular accidents of his life, his work open out upon the general experience of Man. If Proust had never depicted anything save the scene of M. de Charlus being whipped in a brothel, he would be no more significant than is M. J. G. himself: a highly specialized writer who places a great deal of talent in the exclusive service of his specialty. Proust painted *the* world, not simply *a* world. . . . Whereas M. J. G., himself no less than the heroes of *Deathwatch*, goes around and around in circles like a squirrel in a cage, imprisoned in the dungeon of a vice from which he cannot escape, even through the process of literary creation, since he can conceive of nothing outside the barbed-wire perimeter of his own tiny private hell. [1949]

François Mauriac, "The Case of J. G.," in Richard N. Coe, ed., *The Theater of J. G.* (1970), p. 77

The general impression of him, such as it is, seems to leave out the heart of the matter, which is that however repellent his preoccupations, and however childish the philosophical equipment that he shares with many of his betters in that line, he is with little question one of the most gifted French prose writers of this generation, and the only one to have created a world nearly comparable in compulsion if not in scope to that of Proust or Céline. He is successor to both of them, and their only one, though he has a closer ancestry among the poets of the nineteenth century.

Unfortunately, public prudery being what it is, it will probably be a long time before his reputation will be based on much more than hearsay in this country. It is hard to see how the books could be made generally available here except in mutilated form, or even how they could be mutilated, since G.'s sexual candor, to put it mildly, is not eruptive as in Sartre but entirely of the grain; to doctor his writing for commercial purposes would be to operate on every line.

Eleanor Clark, "The World of J. G.," *PR*, April 1949, pp. 443–44

Since the pariah and God are alike external to nature, it will suffice for the pariah, in his cell, to dare invent being: he will be God. G. creates in order to enjoy his infinite power. . . .

Now that his dreams are written down, he is no longer either God or man, and he has no other way of regaining his lost divinity than to manifest himself to men. These fictions will assume a new objectivity for him if he obliges others to believe in them. And at the core of all his characters is the same categorical imperative: "Since you don't have faith enough to believe in us, you must at least make others adopt us and must convince them that we exist." In writing out, for his pleasure, the incommunicable dreams of his particularity, G. has transformed them into exigencies of communication. There was no invocation, no call. Nor was there that aching need for self-expression that writers have invented for the needs of personal publicity. You will not find in G. the "fateful gift" and "imperiousness of talent" about which the high-minded are in the habit of sounding off. To cultivated young men who go in for literature, the craft of writing appears first as a means of communication. But G. began to write in order to affirm his solitude, to be self-sufficient, and it was the writing itself that, by its problems, gradually led him to seek readers. [1952]

Jean-Paul Sartre, *Saint Genet: Actor and Martyr* (1963), pp. 479, 481–82

What strikes us in *The Blacks* is the great freedom and lightness of the invention, compared with the obsessive and claustrophobic heaviness of G.'s novels. It is as if the theater were the agency through which the damned G. obtains his redemption.

Redemption from what? From the muck of reality, from the obsession with everyday experience, from the insolence of the reprobate enclosed in his autobiography, determined to batten on the reproof of others without being able to answer them except by repeating to himself that he is a criminal and a pervert, segregated in Evil, and therefore inaccessible to the judgment of others. But simply by advancing onto the stage, by playing the game of the theater, there appears, instead, the possibility of a judgment that is not accompanied by condemnation and that is objective because it is purely intellectual; thus the imagination is liberated from autobiographical determinism. The novel was a prison that enclosed G. in his narcissistic obsession. The theater provided an opening onto the world and the love of others. [1966]

Nicola Chiaromonte, "The Ceremonial Theater of J. G.," *The Worm of Consciousness, and Other Essays* (1976), p. 180

Some of the decisive experiences of the European Left have been incorporated into [*The Screens*]. First of all: the possibility of a successful revolt in Algeria, and in other countries throughout the world as well. Then: victory alone will not guarantee men happiness and freedom, nor secure a place within the new order for those values which, as Ommu says, are not to be realized in action but are to become song. The play's three social orders correspond to three basic concepts of European socialist thought: the class society based on oppression; the society born of the successful revolt which does away with oppression but is still rooted in constraint; and the vision of a classless society with no restraints. This last serves the same need for socialist thought as the Kingdom of Heaven does in Christian eschatology.

Saïd and through him G. refuse to participate in these three orders. There is another path which must be followed if we wish to remain men. *The Screens* is the first French theater work to describe the possibilities that men still have intact and—paradoxical as this may sound—to put on stage a hero who, in and through his negativity, is ultimately positive. [1966]

Lucien Goldmann, "The Theatre of G.: A Sociological Study," in Kelly Morris, ed., *G./ Ionesco: The Theatre of the Double* (1969), pp. 105–6

I sit and read *Miracle of the Rose* again. Fever, palpitations, shivers, just the way it was when I read it first, nineteen years ago. I was an adolescent of thirty-eight. I was discovering the happiness of adoration, the joy of admiration. Now I am an adolescent of fifty-seven, I am discovering the happiness of adoration, the joy of admiration. For whom had I caught that fever? For whom was I in a swoon? For Harcamone, the convict condemned to death. I reread G. and my heart beat faster. . . . I can open G. anywhere. The griefs and agonies in G. are my litanies. I am raised up like Harcamone; see how I hover over his majestic misfortunes, his sumptuous experiences, his rituals, his carnivals, his metempsychoses, and G.'s ultimate alchemy when he transforms imprisoning chains to flowering bracelets. . . . Every book he writes is a commemoration of transfigured sufferings. At his high mass I hurry to be early, to get a seat in the front row. [1970]

Violette Leduc, *Mad in Pursuit* (1971), pp. 73–74

I remember Ruth Benedict's remarking that, among the Zuñi Indians of the Southwest, almost every act, every moment of the day, was invested with some sort of ritual significance. This is what it is like in *Querelle*. Each character spends most of his time and energy on his "interior theatricals," obsessively measuring his "power" and "beauty" against those of everyone else.

I suspect that G. is popular simply because he coincides with current fashion. His best literary passages are too complex to win him a wide audience, but he has erected a paradoxical metaphysics around an extremely anti-Establishment position, and this alone is enough to win him a reputation. Add to that his "profound" obscurity and you have the formula for "genius."

Anatole Broyard, "Murder and Mimosas," *NYT*, 6 Sept. 1974, p. 31

For all that has been written about G. the man, he remains a figure of mystery: his truth—including the facts of his biography—seems inextricably interwoven with his fictionalized self-images. He clearly wishes to remain protean, ungraspable. And it is difficult to know what surprises he may yet produce as an artist—if any. His recent creative activity seems to have principally taken the form of political articles and the production of a film. It has been more than a decade since his last major work—*The Screens*—and it may be that his *opus* is substantially complete, ready for overall critical estimate. But it will be a long time before we arrive at a cool, "objective" verdict on G. He continues to be an unsettling force in culture, difficult to assimilate and to make peace with.

Peter Brooks and Joseph Halpern, eds., Introduction to *G: A Collection of Critical Essays* (1979), p. 6

GEORGE, Stefan

German poet, b. 12 July 1868, Büdesheim; d. 4 Dec. 1933, Minusio, Switzerland

G.'s life was peripatetic. After graduating from secondary school he traveled extensively (1888–92). He was often in Paris where he met leading French SYMBOLIST poets, especially Mallarmé and Verlaine. G. never married, but close friendships with congenial poets and scholars were central to his life and work, and there was a large circle of young people who regarded G. as their artistic and ethical model. G.'s crucial personal relationships were those with Ida Coblenz (1870–1942), who later married the poet and playwright Richard Dehmel (1864–1920), and with Maximilian Kronberger (1888–1904), named "Maximin" by G., who saw in the youth's physical and spiritual beauty an incarnation of mythic divinity.

From its outset, G.'s approach to poetry displayed two aspects: as a means of personal expression, and as a medium for cultural and ethical reform. His poetic ideals were exemplified in his translations (1891) of Baudelaire's *Flowers of Evil*, of works by other poets—published in *Zeitgenössische Dichter* (2 vols., 1905; contemporary poets)—mainly French symbolists but also including Dante Gabriel Rossetti, Swinburne, the Danish writer J. P. Jacobsen (1847–1885), and D'ANNUNZIO, of Shakespeare's sonnets (1909), and of parts of Dante's *Divine Comedy* (1912). The journal of the arts, *Blätter für die Kunst*, published from 1892 to 1919, which G. edited and contributed to, and in which many of Hugo von HOFMANNSTHAL's and G.'s poems were first published, reflects the evolution of his thinking about art and culture.

G.'s first three volumes of poetry, *Hymnen* (1890; *Odes*, 1949), *Pilgerfahrten* (1891; *Pilgrimages*, 1949), and *Algabal* (1892;

Algabal, 1949), later always printed together, share the theme of the artist's isolation from nature and society. In the symbolist manner, using a variety of lyrical forms, the poet condenses and manipulates experience into vivid artifacts of the poetic imagination. Artistic alienation and uncertainty about the primacy of the objective versus the subjective world are a source of torment. In *Algabal*, however, the persona of the Roman emperor Heliogabalus transforms his barbarous imaginings into an empirical reality of life as a work of art; perversely sumptuous subterranean chambers and gardens, untrammeled voluptuousness, and murders of exquisite aesthetic brutality characterize his existence. By denying the limits of nature and the validity of a reality outside himself, Algabal falls prey to the suicidal despair of solipsism. *Algabal* represents an artistic experiment, a venture into total subjectivity, a possibility that G. ultimately rejected.

The books that gained G. his widest public acceptance were *Die Bücher der Hirten- und Preisgedichte, der Sagen und Sänge und der hängenden Gärten* (1895; *The Books of Eclogues and Eulogies, of Legends and Lays, and of the Hanging Gardens*, 1949) and *Das Jahr der Seele* (1897; *The Year of the Soul*, 1949). In the earlier work, the universality and timelessness of human feeling are evoked by the retrospective projection of the poet's present experience into Arcadian antiquity, into a medieval world strongly colored by romanticism, and into a legendary realm in Persia. The poems are by turns lyrical, elegiac, and balladesque, recalling but never imitating characteristic forms of each time and place. In their intensity and compression, the love poems of *Das Buch der hängenden Gärten* are especially distinctive. *Das Jahr der Seele*, G.'s most popular collection, contains poems inspired by his unhappy relationship with Ida Coblenz, but transposed onto an apparently impersonal plane of artistic stylization. Characterized by fastidious formal craftsmanship, these verses express profound melancholy through motifs of landscape that are both immediate and transcendently symbolic. The dilemmas of the artist's relationship to experience as well as to form and of his mission in the world are also to be felt deeply here.

Around the turn of the century a significant change in the direction of G.'s thinking and efforts took place, which is most clearly perceptible in *Der Teppich des Lebens und die Lieder von Traum und Tod mit einem Vorspiel* (1899; *The Tapestry of Life and the Songs of Dream and Death with a Prelude*, 1949) and *Der Siebente Ring* (1907; *The Seventh Ring*, 1949). Here G. abandoned his subjective concerns in favor of a didactic, indeed prophetic function. *Der Teppich des Lebens* celebrates the powers of a heroically conceived mankind that have created the vitality and beauty of human culture. In *Der Siebente Ring* the stance becomes more aggressive. The section called "Zeitgedichte" ("Poems of Our Times") bitterly reproaches modern man for not acknowledging his sublime potential to grow beyond the conditions of necessity and for failing to recognize harbingers of a higher destiny, such as Dante, Goethe, and Nietzsche, culminating in dire warnings of what will come if men remain blind to the life of the spirit, to their own innate divinity. For G., the life and death of "Maximin," celebrated in the central section of *Der Siebente Ring*, were exemplary proofs of the spiritual and corporeal perfection of which humanity is capable.

Der Stern des Bundes (1913; *The Star of the Covenant*, 1949) combines scathing condemnation of modern culture and thought with apodictic precepts for an elect brotherhood of the best of the nation's youth who are to propagate and realize in their time the ideal, which G. saw embodied in "Maximin." The prophetic role of the poet, much like Nietzsche's Zarathustra, is definitively elaborated in G.'s last collection, *Das Neue Reich* (1928; *The Kingdom Come*, 1949), in such major poems as "Der Krieg" ("The War"), "Der Dichter in Zeiten der Wirren" ("The Poet in Times of Confusion"), and "Geheimes Deutschland" ("Secret Germany"). The closing section of the volume is notable for lyrics of gnomic profundity and an arrestingly simple beauty.

As the proponent of the formal and ideological values of symbolism in Germany, G., despite his esotericism and exclusivity, was an influential and controversial personality. A dedicated opponent of dehumanizing materialism in culture, of epigonism and naturalism in art, he strove to keep alive the classical ideals of the supremacy of spirit over matter, of form over feeling. The forceful compression of G.'s style left a lasting mark on German lyric poetry, especially among the EXPRESSIONISTS. The rigorous and absolute standards for ethical conduct that G. set in his life and works are best exemplified by the fact that his close friend Count Claus Schenk von Stauffenberg (1907–1944) sacrificed his life as a conspirator in the plot to assassinate Adolf Hitler on July 20, 1944, a deed that has been described by Claude David as "*the* gesture that puts G.'s thought into perspective."

FURTHER WORKS: *Die Fibel* (1901; *The Primer*, 1974); *Tage und Taten* (1903); *Schlußband* (1934); *Briefwechsel zwischen G. und Hofmannsthal* (1938); *S. G.-Friedrich Gundolf Briefwechsel* (1962). FURTHER WORKS IN ENGLISH: *The Works of S. G.* (1949; 2nd rev. and enl. ed., 1974); *S. G. in fremden Sprachen* (1973; contains English translations)

BIBLIOGRAPHY: Gundolf, F., *G.* (1920); David, C., *S. G.: Son œuvre poétique* (1952); Boehringer, R., *Mein Bild von S. G.* (1953); Goldsmith, U. K., *S. G.: A Study of His Early Work* (1959); Landmann, G. P., *S. G. und sein Kreis: Eine Bibliographie* (1960; 2nd rev. and enl. ed., 1976); Morwitz, E., *Kommentar zu dem Werk S. G.s* (1960); Landmann, E., *Gespräche mit S. G.* (1963); Schultz, H. S., *Studien zur Dichtung S. G.s* (1967); Winkler, M., *S. G.* (1970); Metzger, M. M. and E. A., *S. G.* (1972)

—ERIKA A. METZGER

GEORGIAN LITERATURE

Three main trends may be distinguished in Georgian literature during the 19th c.: romanticism (with the concomitant expressions of longing for individual and national freedom), best exemplified by the poet Nikoloz Baratashvili (1817–1845); nationalist realism, represented by numerous writers, most notably Ilia Chavchavadze (1837–1907) and Akaki Tsereteli (1840–1915); and a genre unparalleled in most European literatures with the exception of Albanian, namely, an idealized evocation of the traditional values of isolated mountain tribes, combined with elements of folklore and customary law. The two foremost writers in this genre were Alexander Qazbegi (1848–1893) and Vazha Pshavela (1861–1915). Pshavela's work in particular shows great depth of psychological insight and the endeavor to come to grips with philosophical and ethical problems in a manner not to be found in Georgian literature up to his time.

At the beginning of the 20th c., until about 1914, social concerns make up the primary thematic material of the school of

"democratic poets," especially Irodion Evdoshvili (1873–1916). During World War I a group of young poets organized under the name Blue Horns produced work of fine sensitivity influenced by the ideas and style of French SYMBOLISM. Their movement was a reaction to the realism that had dominated Georgian literature during the several preceding decades. The leading writer of this group was Galaktion TABIDZE, while the outstanding writer and philosopher Grigol ROBAKIDSE acted as its guiding spirit. Other noted poets who belonged to the Blue Horns—and who were later to adapt to the demands of the Soviet regime—included Valerian Gaprindashvili (1889–1941), Titsian Tabidze (1895–1937), Giorgi Leonidze (1899–1966), and Paolo Iashvili (1895–1937). They and their fellow writers published extensively in the Blue Horn journals *Bakhtriani* and *Barikadebi*.

Georgia, which had been under Russian domination since 1801, declared its independence at the beginning of 1918, following the 1917 Russian Revolution. The new state and its social-democratic government were recognized *de jure* and *de facto* by most of the nations of the world, including Soviet Russia, and the next three years were extremely fruitful ones for young Georgian authors of all literary schools and persuasions. Impetus was given to artistic development by the foundation of a university in the capital, Tbilisi, and the official policies of freedom of press, speech, and expression, as guaranteed by the Georgian constitution, were utilized to advantage, resulting in a spate of literary creativity in all genres. The proliferation of literary and political journals and newspapers provided ample outlets for poets, prose writers, and dramatists. Much new and interesting work was also in evidence within the fields of children's literature, humor, and satire.

This remarkable burgeoning of creative expression in diverse modes was abruptly halted by the Soviet Russian invasion of Georgia in February 1921. The assault by the Red Army came despite mutual nonaggression treaties and other legal instruments signed by Lenin himself, which guaranteed the independence and sovereignty of Georgia. The newly established Soviet regime rapidly imposed the precepts of SOCIALIST REALISM on all genres of Georgian literature and put an end to experimentation. Coincident with the Russian invasion and lasting for a brief time into the 1920s was a FUTURIST movement in Georgian literature. Similar in precepts to the Russian futurists, the Georgian group called for the destruction of classical forms and the propagation of a special type of language based on arbitrary usage and invented words having no objective reference. Authors who were later to become well known for more staid literary productions, such as Simone Chikovani (1903–1966) and Demna Shengelaia (b. 1896) were members of this movement, and their work was published in the journals H2SO4 and *Memartskheneoba*.

Soon after the consolidation of Soviet power in Georgia, the leading poets and novelists of the country were constrained to come to terms with the new political exigencies. Galaktion Tabidze, the greatest poet of his generation remaining in Georgia, was obliged to turn from symbolism and lyricism to the production of such poems as "Revolutsionuri Sakartvelo" (1931; revolutionary Georgia) and the cycles "Epoka" (1930; the epoch) and "Patsipizmi" (1930; pacifism), which embodied the Party line at the expense of individual creativity. Other members of the Blue Horn movement, such as the sensitive lyricist Paolo Iashvili, as well as Titsian Tabidze, Giorgi Leonidze, and Valerian Gaprindashvili, were pressed into service to the state and forced to produce propagandistic trivia. Not only were the extent of their subject matter and variety of style reduced to the barest minimum, but their earlier work was forbidden to be reprinted. For some, conditions of literary existence became too suffocating. Iashvili, for example, committed suicide in 1937 at the age of forty-two; Titsian Tabidze died in the same year and at the same age under mysterious circumstances; and in 1959 Galaktion Tabidze—according to popular report—committed suicide, although the authorities simply reported that he had fallen out of a window.

The only way around Party dogmatics after 1921 in Georgian literature lay in the utilization of historical themes and in the heroic folk genre of Vazha Pshavela. Of ideological necessity, certain "messages" had to be conveyed in this type of writing also, in particular the supposedly exploitative nature of the feudal system in medieval Georgia and the ever-present "class struggle." Despite these constraints, however, a number of well-written and interesting works, primarily novels, began to appear in the 1930s. The acknowledged master of the historical novel was Konstantine GAMSAKHURDIA, whose massive work *Didostatis mardjvena* (1939; the right hand of the master), re-creating the life of Georgia in the 10th and 11th cs., established the genre on a firm footing; indeed, it remains one of the best examples of this type of writing in Georgian.

The official Party line on history and social development was promulgated during the 1930s by a large number of novels, such as Leo Kiacheli's (1884–1963) *Gvadi Bigva* (1938; Gvadi Bigva), a humorous work about peasant life; Alexandre Kutateli's (b. 1897) *Pirispir* (1933–43; face to face), a four-volume work woven of completely and deliberately falsified historical "facts" regarding the 1921 Soviet invasion of Georgia, its prelude, and its aftermath; and Ilia Lisashvili's (b. 1897) *Ketskhoveli* (1941; Ketskhoveli), about the origins and subsequent organization of the Communist movement in Georgia.

The dramatic arts during this period were represented by such playwrights as Polikarp Kakabadze (1895–1972), whose comedy on social themes, *Qvarqvare Tutaberi* (1928; Qvarqvare Tutaberi) was widely performed and remains in the repertory of the Georgian theater; I. Vakeli (b. 1900), a "proletarian" author specializing in themes dealing with the lives of Georgian workers following the Communist takeover, but also treating historical subjects, as in his *Shamil* (1935; Shamil); and the Georgian-Jewish writer Hertsel Baazov (1904–1937), known for his play *Itska Rizhinashvili* (c. 1935; Itska Rizhinashvili), among others, and for his novel—unique in Georgian literature—*Petkhain* (1935; Petkhain), which depicted the life of the Jewish quarter of Tbilisi and gave an acute, if necessarily slanted insight into the conflicts between the traditional values and religious life of the Georgian Jews and the new realities imposed upon them by the Soviet regime. Baazov himself died in prison, victimized because of his father's open and avowed Zionism. Many other plays were written and produced in the 1930s, but few were marked by anything more than a slavish adherence to standard Communist ideology. Just like the other arts, drama was used simply as a vehicle to further the propagandizing of the Party line.

World War II created a need for highly patriotic and antifascist literature. As in the other republics of the Soviet Union, so in Georgia writers had to serve the country's requirements. Aside from the more usual displays of patriotic fervor in verse, fiction, and drama, several works of a more nationalistic and historical character appeared. (Indeed the two are inseparable in a Soviet context: nationalism may only be expressed in a historical framework as synonymous with antimonarchism or antifeudalism; its expression in a contemporary framework, that is, as related to conditions within the Soviet Union, is a punishable crime.) Such

were an epic poem about the 18th-c. poet Davit Guramishvili (1705–1792) by Simone Chikovani (b. 1903) and a poem on the medieval Georgian king David the Builder by L. Gotua (b. 1905), who also wrote a historical play, *Mepe Irakli* (1944; King Irakli).

The years immediately following World War II saw relatively little change in the tenor of Georgian literature. While there was less conspicuously antifascist work produced, novels, as well as stories and poems with war themes continued unabated. Hymns and odes to Stalin were also composed in incredible numbers, as were other works incorporating the usual Party dogmatics. Once again, only literature utilizing historical motifs as a mode of expressing both creativity and national pride could be considered worthy of notice, such as M. Mrevlishvili's (b. 1904) play, *Nikoloz Baratashvili* (c. 1950; Nikoloz Baratashvili) about the great 19th-c. Georgian romantic poet who was called the "Byron of Georgia," and I. Vakeli's play, *Mepe Tamara* (c. 1950; Queen Tamara).

After Stalin's death and the subsequent, if temporary, relaxation of certain ideological restrictions under Khrushchev, Georgian literature exhibited an expansion of thematic material. Historical novels still remained the most important genre, little troubled by overt ideological considerations. Foremost among these is the remarkable tetralogy *Davit Aghmashenebeli* (1946–54; David the Builder) by Konstantine Gamsakhurdia, which re-creates the life and times of the greatest king of Georgia during the country's golden age in the early medieval period. Also worthy of mention are Grigol Abashidze's (b. 1914) *Lasharela* (1957; Lasharela) and *Grdzeli ghame* (1963; the long night), which describes the sufferings and heroism of the Georgians during successive invasions by the Persians and Mongols.

Among the first prose works to appear in Georgia that dealt with contemporary life and yet had no overbearing political message to impart were three novels by Nodar Dumbadze (b. 1928): *Me, babia, Iliko da Ilarioni* (1958; I, grandmother, Iliko, and Ilarion), *Me vkhedav mzes* (1962; *I See the Sun*, 1968) and *Mziani ghame* (1967; *The Sunny Night*, 1968). Although of slight literary stature, these short humorous works dealing with student life in present-day Tbilisi show a refreshing departure from ideological concerns and are meant quite simply to entertain—a consideration that had not concerned publishing in Georgia since 1921.

Georgian poetry also began to show signs of renewed vigor in the later 1950s, a trend that continues, although some constraints have become evident in recent years. Themes of Georgian, as opposed to Soviet, nationalism have become more marked and more open, for example, Irakli Abashidze's (b. 1909) cycles "Rustavelis nakvalebze" (c. 1960–66; on the traces of Rustaveli) and "Palestina, Palestina" (c. 1960–66; Palestine, Palestine). Among the younger generation of poets, perhaps the most important in terms of both literary expression and freedom of thematic material is Ana Kalandadze (b. 1924). Her work evokes nature in all its manifestations, as well as the more personal world of the experiences of love.

Dramatic writing in Georgia has remained the weakest literary form. Vakeli, Mrevlishvili, and others have continued to add to the repertory, but it is indicative of the state of the art that Robert Sturua, director of the prestigious and internationally acclaimed Rustaveli Theater of Tbilisi, stated in a 1980 interview with a Georgian newspaper that the standard of Georgian drama is such that he prefers to stage Shakespeare and BRECHT. Sturua did not mention the fact that the greatest play in Georgian, *Lamara* (c. 1925; Lamara) by Grigol Robakidse, produced to outstanding acclaim in the early 1920s, is still banned in Georgia, together with all other works by this extraordinary writer, despite the fact that *Lamara* is based on elements of Georgian folk tradition and contains nothing that could be considered subversive to the Soviet regime.

An extremely successful and well-produced television drama was given in Georgia in the late 1970s based on the novel *Data Tutashkhia* (1973–75; Data Tutashkhia) by the talented author Chabua Amiredjibi (b. 1921). Drawing upon historical material, the novel and play tell the story of an early-19th-c. folk hero who, like Robin Hood, fought the forces of oppression in Georgia together with a band of devoted confederates.

Despite the extraordinary ideological constraints placed upon Georgian authors since the advent of Soviet rule in 1921, two forces have continued to play a major role in tempering the character of Georgian literature: intense nationalism and the fiercely independent nature of the Georgian people. Working within the imposed framework of Communist literary norms, Georgian authors have found ways of enlarging the scope of their creative work by relying on these forces and imbuing their work with them. In the area of unofficial writing, comparatively little Georgian *samizdat* has reached the West, most of it in the photocopied journal *Sakartvelos moambe*. Although the contributions in this journal are not primarily literary in nature, being concerned with human rights particularly, the same two forces of nationalism and independence are very much in evidence. This unwavering tenacity of the Georgians to stress continually their cultural and historical uniqueness continues to find eloquent expression in the best work of their prose writers and poets.

—LEONARD FOX

Georgian Literature since World War II

The year 1956 marked a turning point in Georgian as well as Soviet literature in general. A ten year period, aptly named the Thaw, that started after the 20th Party congress and denunciation of Stalin's cult, promoted a more liberal atmosphere invigorating every sphere of cultural life. It was poetry, traditionally the most developed and important literary form in Georgian culture, that heralded the new era. Lyric poetry in particular, hitherto maligned as "bourgeois individualism," became the genre most favored by the generation of poets who published their first verses still restricted by the ideological demands of Socialist Realism and were especially appreciative of the newly acquired freedom. The uncontested leader among them was Ana Kalandadze, who has since become a renowned master of classic Georgian verse. From her first lyrical stanzas that appeared in 1948 to the recently published collection of verses, *Ortomeuli* (2 vols., 1996; Works) her poetry has been loved and admired by critics and readers alike. In her poetry folk motives are transcribed with force and ardor in the sophisticated language of high literary style and visions of the past reverberate in the images of modern day Georgia. Murman Lebanidze (b. 1922) and Shota Nishnianidze (b. 1929) are the poets who, like Kalandadze, continue and develop the best traditions of 19th-c. Georgian literature. The poems published in the latest editions of their collected works, *Rcheuli lirika* (1991; Selected Lyrics) and *Asi leksi* (1996; Hundred Poems) respectively, reaffirmed their status of classic poets of contemporary Georgian literature.

Mukhran Machavariani (b. 1929) is an innovator of Georgian versification; he experimented boldly with rhyme and meter, giving fresh voice and verve to traditional themes and images. The often colloquial, almost conversational tone and syntax of his verses transform the ordinary and mundane events of daily life into a unique poetic experience. His collection entitled *Gikvirs?!—nu gikvirs!* (1995; Are You Surprised?—Don't Be!) is permeated with biting satire and vitriole, reflecting the poet's attitude to the radical changes taking place in present-day Georgian culture. Tariel Chanturia (b. 1932) pushed the daring experimentation of Machavariani even farther. The exuberance of his strikingly fresh images and style, bold rhymes, and hitherto impermissible poetic vocabulary earned him the name of a Georgian Mayakovsky. In his recent volume of verses, *Guli marjvniv* (1995; Heart on the Right), Chanturia continues to fascinate the reader with the originality of his flamboyant imagination and novel poetic forms. Among the next generation of poets, Lia Sturua (b.1939) and Besik Xaranauli (b.1939) attracted the attention of readers by introducing rhymeless free verse, a genre as yet adopted by few in Georgia.

In the the 1950s and 1960s Georgian prose was still represented to significant extent by the works of renowned masters such as Konstantine Gamsakhurdia, Mikheil DJAVAKHISHVILI, and Levan Gothua, among others. However, a new generation of prose writers began to occupy a more prominent place in the literary life of the country. Nodar Dumbadze's young, rebellious and often vulnerable heroes offered role models with which contemporary Georgian youth could identify themselves, and the light humor of his easily readable novels appealed to young and old alike. The far more talented and deeply philosophical novels of Otar Chkheidze (b. 1920) remained accessible, and until recently appreciated by only a few dedicated connoisseurs. In their short stories and novels Revaz Inanishvili (1926-1991), Archil Sulakauri (b. 1927), Rezo Cheishvili (b. 1933), Guram Gegeshidze (b. 1934), Guram Panjikidze (1934-1997), and Revaz Mishveladze (b.1940) created the world of urban dwellers, a relative novelty in Georgian literature until recently dominated by rural themes or topics related to the tragic and glorious events of Georgia's past. Works of these writers often touched upon previously forbidden social and moral issues. Cheishvili became particularly popular as the author of several original scripts that were made into films in the 1970s and 1980s. One of them, a satirical comedy *Tsispheri mtebi anu daujerebeli ambavi* (1984; Blue Mountains or an Unbelievable Story), directed by Eldar Shengelaya, was awarded several international prizes. In 1991 Cheishvili published a devastating biography of Sergo Orjonikidze, the head of the Georgian government in the 1920s. The author's witty and acrimonious narrative presented a pathetically insecure image of the once celebrated Communist leader. Chabua Amirejibi, the creator of the popular hero Data Tutashkhia, a Robin Hood of the early-20th-c. Georgia, published a semibiographical novel entitled *Gora mborgali* (1996; Gora Mborgali) about a victim of political purges during the Stalin era.

One of the highlights of post-Stalinist Soviet literary life was the availability of works by Western writers such as James JOYCE, Ernest HEMINGWAY, William FAULKNER, Thomas MANN, Gabriel GARCÍA MÁRQUEZ, among others. Their influence is most prominent in works of Otar Chiladze (b. 1933). He and his brother, Tamaz Chiladze (b. 1931), gained popularity first as the authors of subtle lyrical verses, but in the late 1970s they both shifted to prose. Tamaz Chiladze wrote mostly short stories and plays, and Otar Chiladze turned to epic narrative. His novels, often dominated by the stream-of-consciousness style of the narrative recount dramatic moments from Georgia's past, both remote and recent. They present history through the prism of myths that transform reality into images of grandiose proportions and deep philosophical meaning. Thus, his first novel, *Gzaze erti katsi midioda* (1873; A Man Was Walking down the Road), brings to life the heroes of legendary Colchis, king Aeetis, his daughter Medea and the leader of the Argonauts, Jason, who came to the shores of this ancient land to find and steal the Golden Fleece. Chiladze's later novels, such as *Qovelman chemman mpovnelman* (1976; Each One Who Finds Me), *Rkinis theatri* (1981; The Iron Theater) and *Avelumi* (1995; Avelum, a Citizen) established him as one of the preeminent Georgian writers of the century.

Guram Dochanashvili (b. 1939) is another writer for whom myth and fantasy became a vehicle for exploring contemporary problems. His highly acclaimed novels are *Samoseli pirveli* (1974; Garment Number One) and *Khorumi, kartuli tsekva* (1989; Khorumi, a Georgian Dance). In his short stories the intensity of his satirical verve transforms the contemporary reality into almost grotesque images.

In spite of numerous political and economic difficulties that have plagued the country since the dissolution of the Soviet Union, creative energy of Georgian people has not been diminished. Yearly publications of talented works by younger generation of poets and writers promise to keep alive the literary traditions that go back to the 5th c.

See also North Caucasian Literatures

—DODONA KIZIRIA

GERMAN LITERATURE

The Political and Literary Background

The political configuration of the world and the social conditions of the human race changed radically during the century preceding World War II. The changes were more frequent and more abrupt in Germany than in any other Western country. Germany's unification and its victory in the Franco-Prussian War (1870–71) were followed by two decades of peace, prosperity, and increasing national pride under Bismarck, a trend that continued until World War I. The defeat of 1918 shattered the nation's political and economic stability. The founding of Germany's first democratic government, the Weimar Republic (1919), restored a semblance of order, but resentment over the terms of the Treaty of Versailles, as well as the economic chaos of the postwar years, undermined the stability of the republic and contributed to the growth of the Nazi and Marxist movements. The impact of the Great Depression was later added to these phenomena. The German republic died when Hitler assumed power in 1933. The state of the economy improved and by the end of the decade Hitler enjoyed the support of most Germans who had not fled the country or been imprisoned. The effects of the military collapse and unconditional surrender in 1945 greatly surpassed those of 1918. Now Germany faced not only economic privation and the loss of territory, but also national shame, as details of the Nazi policy of genocide became known. The division into eastern and western occupation zones widened into a gulf, and in 1949 two separate German states were founded, the capitalist German Federal Republic and the communist German Democratic Republic (both at the time still closely regulated by the Western Allies and the Soviets, respectively).

The volatile political situation strongly influenced the development of 20th-c. German literature. The years preceding World War I witnessed an increasing tension between writers of conservative, nationalistic persuasion and a smaller but ultimately more significant group of progressives and socialists. The war produced both visionaries and authors with realistic perspectives, although there was little unity or consistency within either group. During the 1930s most writers of the first rank emigrated. Moscow, Los Angeles, and New York became the new centers of German literature, and small groups or isolated individuals sought safety throughout the world, from New Zealand to Brazil. With very few exceptions, the works written in exile were a direct reflection of the political situation, although the points of view and emphases differ according to the individual author's reason for leaving Germany (most were communists or Jews; some were anti-Nazi humanists). Even much contemporary literature constitutes a reaction to Germany's past history or current political situation. And finally, many promising young German writers met violent deaths, while serving in the armed forces in both world wars, or as victims of the Nazis. Especially significant was the loss, during World War I, of a number of writers who later could have been counted on to provide artistic leadership and continuity.

The political birth of the German nation in 1870 coincided with a literary nadir. A score of major authors were born during the first two decades of the 19th c., but few remained active in the 1870s, and only one, Theodor Fontane (1819–1898), lived past 1890. No writers who today enjoy widespread recognition were born between 1830 and 1860, with the exception of Friedrich Nietzsche (1844–1900), known primarily as a philosopher, and Wilhelm Raabe (1831–1910) and Detlev von Liliencron (1844–1909), whose claim to "major" status is dubious at best. The resulting literary vacuum was first filled by two very different writers born in the 1860s, Gerhart HAUPTMANN and Stefan GEORGE.

Hauptmann's *Vor Sonnenaufgang* (1889; *Before Dawn*, 1909) created a sensation. To be sure, this play was indebted to German as well as foreign sources. Yet, given the weak position of German literature in the 1870s and 1880s, it is understandable that inspiration and direction were sought abroad, and during the 1880s several minor writers attempted to introduce French naturalism in Germany—the novels of Émile Zola were especially admired and imitated. Henrik Ibsen exerted a strong influence on the development of the drama. In addition, the theories of Charles Darwin were rapidly gaining attention. *Vor Sonnenaufgang*, the first major work of German naturalism, established a pattern for many dramas of the 1890s, in its careful attention to realistic detail, concern with the lower and middle classes, and portrayal of the disintegration of a family, with emphasis on the negative effects of heredity. The principal theoretician of German naturalism, Arno Holz (1863–1929), attempted to reduce art to an exact reproduction of life, as in the formula "art = nature — x," in which x is the inevitable subjective factor occasioned by the participation of the artist. Hauptmann produced, in addition to several minor naturalist dramas, two great ones, the historical tragedy *Die Weber* (1892; *The Weavers*, 1899) and the comedy *Der Biberpelz* (1893; *The Beaver Coat*, 1912). Otherwise, naturalism is only of historical interest, as a transitional stage between the vacuum of the preceding decades and the realistic, socially critical literature of the 20th c.

Simultaneous with Hauptmann's promulgation of a socially conscious literature written in the naturalist style were the radically different innovations of Stefan George. An avowed disciple of the French SYMBOLISTS, George had no precursors in Germany. In 1890 he published his first collection of verse, *Hymnen* (*Odes*, 1949), and by the end of the decade was recognized by a small and elite, but nonetheless important group as Germany's leading poet. His direct influence was limited, and his austere, finely chiseled verse found few imitators beyond his own circle. But his admiration for the symbolists and for Nietzsche came to be shared, at least to some extent, by many German writers of the 20th c. George's circle of intimates included several of Germany's leading intellectuals, including the literary critics Friedrich Gundolf (1880–1931) and Max Kommerell (1902–1944).

1900–20: From Impressionism to Expressionism

Much of the literature of the first two decades of the century constitutes a revolt against the premises, attitudes, and intellectual background of naturalism. Nietzsche replaced Darwin as the most important mentor for German writers. The terms impressionism, neoromanticism, symbolism, neoclassicism, and EXPRESSIONISM are often used to categorize various authors who participated in the revolt against the naturalists' emphasis on the ugly side of human nature and modern life. All are useful, although only expressionism, which dominated the 1910s, represents a coherent literary movement.

Poetry

Detlev von Liliencron, who established his reputation in the 1880s and continued to write into the 20th c., was the most accomplished of the impressionist poets. His poems, not unlike impressionist paintings, capture the essence of a scene. Sound and image are carefully integrated in his precisely wrought verse. The poetry of Richard Dehmel (1863–1920), who was originally sympathetic to both Nietzsche and the naturalists, combined social consciousness and eros, nature and spirit, an awareness of the ugly, chaotic aspects of life and the belief that art is capable of providing refinement and order. The irrationalistic impulse is even stronger in other poets, including Else Lasker-Schüler (1869–1945), a forerunner of expressionism, whose first collection, *Styx* (Styx), was published in 1902. Her poems are alternately whimsical and visionary; individual images assume an increasing degree of autonomy, and free verse tends to replace traditional forms. Other visionary poets of the period were Max Dauthendey (1867–1918), whose sensual poetry is rich in imagery; Theodor Däubler (1876–1934), best known for *Das Nordlicht* (1910; the northern lights), a lyrical epic poem of some thirty thousand lines; Alfred Mombert (1872–1942), the author of *Der himmlische Zecher* (1909; the heavenly carouser) and other collections of ecstatic verse; and Christian MORGENSTERN, remembered today almost exclusively for his *Galgenlieder* (1905; *The Gallows Songs*, 1964), which are in turn whimsical, grotesque, and parodistic.

Toward the end of the first decade of the century, the beginnings of the expressionist movement began to take shape. MARINETTI's FUTURISM influenced its development, as did the numerous works of aesthetic theory defending visionary "expressive" art over mimetic art. The journals *Der Sturm* (founded in 1910) and *Die Aktion* (founded in 1911), edited by Herwarth Walden (1878–1941) and Franz Pfemfert (1879–1959), respectively, were immediately recognized as the voices of modernist aesthetics. Among the first expressionist poets published in them were Jakob van Hoddis (1887–1942) and Alfred Lichtenstein (1889–1914). Georg Heym (1887–1912), Ernst Stadler (1883–1914), and the Austrian Georg TRAKL were the most accomplished expressionist poets.

Their early deaths—Heym's accidental, Stadler's and Trakl's in the war—had a profound detrimental effect on the development of the German lyric. Heym's verse, collected in *Der ewige Tag* (1911; the eternal day) and *Umbra vitae* (1912; Latin: shadow of life), utilizes strikingly original images to express a dark vision of impending cataclysm. The growth—and evils—of the city, and modern man's loss of substance are common themes. Heym's traditional meter and rhyme stand in sharp contrast to modernist images and content. Stadler's verse is no more mimetic than Heym's, but his vision is less pessimistic, and the effect of his long dithyrambic lines, which are reminiscent of Walt Whitman's, is not as dependent on the presence of autonomous images. Another important early expressionist was the physician Gottfried BENN, now better known for his later works, whose first poems, *Morgue* (1912; morgue), created a sensation because of their morbid subject matter.

Soon after the beginning of the war one branch of expressionism turned to sociopolitical problems. The ecstatic verse of these poets expressed pacifist and socialist sentiments. One, Johannes R. Becher (1891–1958), was later to become president of the Academy of the Arts in East Germany. A smaller group moved in the opposite direction, toward linguistic experimentation. From the terse, ejaculatory style of August STRAMM it is but a small step to the nonsensical antiart of the DADAISM of Hans Arp (1887–1966), Richard Huelsenbeck (1892–1974), and others. The diversity of the expressionist movement is illustrated by Kurt Pinthus's (1886–1975) anthology *Menschheitsdämmerung* (1919; dawn of mankind), in which twenty-three poets, from Däubler and Lasker-Schüler to Becher and Stramm, are represented.

The conservative tradition in poetry was very much alive during the first two decades of the century, although its representatives are today overshadowed by the progressive and avant-garde writers discussed above. Rudolf Alexander Schröder (1878–1962), who published religious and patriotic verse and translations of classical authors, was one of the most prolific and highly respected of these writers. The ballad, which was popular during the age of Goethe, enjoyed a renascence in the early 20th c. Börries von Münchhausen (1874–1945) and Lulu von Strauss und Torney (1873–1948) wrote some of the finest examples of this form.

Drama

At the beginning of the century the drama of Austria—Hugo von HOFMANNSTHAL, Arthur SCHNITZLER—overshadowed that of Germany. With the exception of Hauptmann, who remained a prolific and respected playwright, most German dramatists of the period—impressionists and neoclassicists—are largely forgotten today. One exception is Frank WEDEKIND, an irreverent social critic whose scathing attacks against middle-class morality made him a hero of many progressives, especially those of the younger generation, as well as a favorite target of government censors. During the 1910s Germany (and especially Berlin) assumed a position of international prominence in the theater. The formal and stylistic innovations of the expressionist dramatists and the imaginative direction and stage craft of Max Reinhardt (1873–1943), an Austrian active in Berlin, and, some time later, Erwin Piscator (1893–1966), gained worldwide recognition. The plays of Carl STERNHEIM constitute a transition from impressionism to expressionism. A modern Molière, Sternheim mercilessly lampooned the German middle class. Materialistic values and narrow-mindedness are the hallmarks of the bourgeois heroes of *Die Hose* (1911; *A Pair of Drawers*, 1927; new tr., *The Underpants*, 1960) and other popular plays.

The drama of expressionism, which was indebted to Wedekind and the Swedish August STRINDBERG as well as to Sternheim, leaves realism behind. The language is highly charged—an ejaculatory "telegram style" replaces realistic dialogue—and the structure is loose, as a series of "stations" replace traditional acts and scenes. Furthermore, the characters are not individuals but types. One of the dramas most representative of the movement is Reinhard Sorge's (1892–1916) *Der Bettler* (1912; *The Beggar*, 1963), in which the protagonist (identified only as "the poet" and "the son") attempts, unsuccessfully, to establish a new artistic and social order. Similar in many respects, although more traditionally structured, is Walter Hasenclever's (1890–1940) *Der Sohn* (1914; the son).

The call for a rebirth of mankind, sounded in Sorge and Hasenclever, remains important in later expressionist drama. A strong religious element is present in the plays of Ernst BARLACH. Georg KAISER, the leading dramatist of the era, typically retained the vision of the "new man" while utilizing a more traditional structure. Later expressionist dramas often added a political dimension to calls for moral rebirth. The most significant of these works is *Masse Mensch* (1921; *Masses and Man*, 1923) by Ernst TOLLER, which portrays, in a highly expressionist style, the conflict between the necessity of revolution and the legitimate rights of the individual.

By the mid-1920s, expressionist drama had ceased to be a major force in German literature. Its influence, however, was immense; among the many major dramatists who later utilized and refined expressionist techniques are Bertolt BRECHT, Thornton WILDER, Eugène IONESCO, Samuel BECKETT, Max FRISCH, and Friedrich DÜRRENMATT.

Fiction

The development of poetry and drama from an ill-defined impressionist idiom to an exuberant expressionist style during the second decade of the century, was not paralleled in fiction. The expressionists generally found prose less suited to their purposes than poetry and drama (indeed, it has been said that expressionist prose is almost a contradiction in terms). Furthermore, Theodor Fontane provided a viable model for young novelists, a model that poets and dramatists did not have. The most important work to spring from this background was Thomas MANN'S *Buddenbrooks* (1901; *Buddenbrooks*, 1924), a novel of truly epic proportions that traces four generations of a north-German family in a style that is realistic in detail but not without impressionist elements. Mann's novellas, including the six stories of *Tristan* (1903; Tristan) and *Der Tod in Venedig* (1913; *Death in Venice*, 1925), offer subtle studies of the conflict between the artistic and bourgeois worlds. These works represent the culmination of the impressionist tradition in Germany. Friedrich Huch (1873–1913) also wrote several successful novels in this style. Eduard Graf Keyserling (1855–1918) is perhaps the best known of the many other authors influenced by Fontane. His impressionistic novels and stories, set in northeastern Germany and dealing with tragic love relationships, enjoyed considerable popularity at the time.

Many novelists aligned themselves with neoromanticism. Typical of these writers is an interest in German history, Germanic mythology, and the supernatural; a favorite theme is the struggle of the individual, often an artist, for self-fulfillment. The foremost

representative of this group is Ricarda HUCH, whose works include several historical novels; the novel *Vita somnium breve* (1903; Latin: life is a short dream), in which a young man is torn between his sense of responsibility to his family and his yearning for freedom and beauty; and an outstanding two-volume scholarly study, *Die Romantik* (1899, 1902; romanticism). The early works of Hermann HESSE are likewise firmly rooted in the neoromantic tradition. The novels of Jakob WASSERMANN, which are rich in psychological insight, contain neoromantic elements.

This period also witnessed the rise of the novel of social and political commitment. Heinrich MANN, the brother of Thomas, achieved his first success with a satirical attack against the bourgeoisie, *Professor Unrat* (1905; *Small Town Tyrant*, 1944) and later wrote directly political novels portraying, from a leftist perspective, the conflicts of Wilhelmine Germany.

For the most part the expressionists eschewed prose fiction. Notable exceptions are two collections of novellas (as they are inappropriately labeled in the subtitles) written in an expressionistic style by authors known primarily as lyric poets, Heym's *Der Dieb* (1913; the thief) and Benn's *Gehirne* (1916; brains).

1920–45: Weimar and Hitler

In spite of the economic and political instability, a rich and diverse German literature flourished in the Weimar Republic. As the vision of the expressionists began to fade in the mid-1920s, many authors turned to the realistic style of *Neue Sachlichkeit* (new factualism); but literary pluralism reigned, and Marxists, centrists, and members of the non-Nazi right alike produced memorable works. Upon Hitler's assumption of power in 1933 internal opposition to the Nazis ceased. The writers forced into exile ranged from apolitical assimilated Jews to active Marxists, who in many cases had previously had nothing in common. To be sure, they were not transformed into a homogeneous group upon leaving Germany. But as exiles they virtually all shared financial insecurity, a keen awareness of the significance of politics, and the sense of alienation and rootlessness brought about by being suddenly thrust into a foreign culture. Furthermore, as writers they suffered greatly from the loss of daily contact with the German language. All of these factors are consistently reflected, directly or indirectly, in their works.

Within Germany, only two kinds of literature were sanctioned: that which directly supported Nazi policies, and apolitical works. Enormous quantities of political literature were published, including fiction by Hans Grimm (1875–1959) and Hans Blunck (1888–1961), dramas by Hans Johst (1890–1978) and Hans Rehberg (1901–1963), and poetry by Will Vesper (1882–1962) and Baldur von Schirach (1907–1974) extolling the virtues of the German people and nation or excoriating the Jews and Marxists. Nazi writers produced nothing of lasting value, and they are now of interest only to literary sociologists.

Many accomplished writers remained in Germany. A few, notably Gottfried BENN and Ernst JÜNGER, were at first favorably disposed toward the Nazis, but the majority stayed for a variety of other reasons. Those who did not emigrate but were unsympathetic to Hitler came to be referred to, collectively, as the "inner emigration." Most wrote apolitical works, traditional in style and form (primarily religious poetry and historical novels with neutral settings). Some clandestinely composed anti-Nazi works that remained unpublished until after the war. Occasionally a concealed attack against the regime slipped by the censors and appeared in print, such as Jünger's *Auf den Marmorklippen* (1939; *On the Marble Cliffs*, 1947) and portions of Hauptmann's House of Atreus tetralogy (1941–48).

Poetry

Little poetry of lasting significance was published in the Weimar Republic. Rudolf Alexander Schröder, Ina Seidel (1885–1974), Gertrud von Le Fort (1876–1971), and others, continued to write traditional, often religious verse. Konrad Weiss (1880–1940) and Oskar Loerke (1884–1941) penned some outstanding nature poetry. Among the works by younger writers, Brecht's *Hauspostille* (1927; *Manual of Piety*, 1966), a collection of satirical social criticism, stands out, along with the chansons of the talented and versatile Kurt TUCHOLSKY. The lyric did, on the other hand, prove to be an appropriate vehicle for many of the exiles, including the Jewish authors Else Lasker-Schüler, Karl Wolfskehl (1869–1948), and Yvan Goll (1891–1950). Among the members of the inner emigration who turned to the lyric were the religious poets Reinhold Schneider (1903–1958) and Albrecht GOES, and Wilhelm Lehmann (1882–1968), whose mystical nature poetry received critical acclaim only after the war. Friedrich Georg Jünger (1908–1977), the brother of Ernst, wrote tightly structured verse based on classical models. The Jewish Gertrud KOLMAR, one of the outstanding poets of her generation, remained in Germany and continued to write until she was taken to a concentration camp. Most of her work was published posthumously.

Drama

The German theater maintained its dynamism and diversity during the short life of the Weimar Republic, as Kaiser, Toller, and others continued to write expressionist dramas into the 1920s, and Hauptmann's more traditional plays were enthusiastically received. The first important new face to emerge was Brecht. *Baal* (1918; *Baal*, 1963) and *Trommeln in der Nacht* (1918; *Drums in the Night*, 1961) contained expressionist elements, but Brecht soon abandoned this style in favor of a more directly political drama. *Die Dreigroschenoper* (1928; *The Threepenny Opera*, 1955) and *Aufstieg und Fall der Stadt Mahagonny* (1929; *The Rise and Fall of the City of Mahagonny*, 1976), anticapitalistic works set to music by Kurt Weill (1900–1950), and several short didactic plays with a specifically Marxist slant were produced between 1928 and 1933. *Die Matrosen von Cattaro* (1930; *Sailors of Cattaro*, 1935) by Friedrich WOLF is the most significant of the numerous other dramas of the period reflecting a leftist position. Carl ZUCKMAYER enjoyed a reputation equal to Brecht's during the final years of the Weimar Republic. In the comedies *Der fröhliche Weinberg* (1925; the joyful vineyard) and *Der Hauptmann von Köpenick* (1931; *The Captain of Köpenick*, 1932) a realistic portrayal of simple people is combined with effective satire against nationalism and militarism.

Little noteworthy drama was written during the Hitler years. The theater in Germany was highly political, and the inner emigrants accordingly turned to other genres. The exiles, too, preferred other forms, the one significant exception being Brecht. In several major dramas written in exile, including *Mutter Courage und ihre Kinder* (1939; *Mother Courage and Her Children*, 1941) and *Der gute Mensch von Sezuan* (1938–41; *The Good Woman of Setzuan*, 1948), Brecht developed his concept of the anti-illusionary drama.

Fiction

During the 1920s several established authors rose to new heights. Thomas Mann turned to the novel of ideas in *Der Zauberberg* (1924; *The Magic Mountain*, 1927), and Hermann Hesse, now under the influence of NIETZSCHE and C. G. JUNG, received critical and public acclaim for *Demian* (1919; *Demian*, 1923) and the novels that followed. Simultaneously, a new generation of novelists appeared who abandoned realistic chronological narration. This movement, to some extent influenced by such writers as James JOYCE and John DOS PASSOS and to some extent a parallel development, was stronger in Austria than in Germany. Major German examples include *Berlin Alexanderplatz* (1929; *Alexanderplatz, Berlin*, 1931) by Alfred DÖBLIN, and Hans Henny JAHNN'S *Perrudja* (1929; Perrudja).

The realistic political and social novel was especially vigorous during the last years of the Weimar Republic. Erich Maria Remarque's *Im Westen nichts Neues* (1929; *All Quiet on the Western Front*, 1929) had no rivals as the most significant of the innumerable war (or antiwar) novels. Equally successful in Germany, if not internationally, was Hans Fallada's (1893–1947) *Kleiner Mann—was nun?* (1932; *Little Man, What Now?*, 1933), in which the life of average people during the inflationary period of the early 1920s is portrayed. A Marxist position is taken in Arnold ZWEIG'S *Der Streit um den Sergeanten Grischa* (1927; *The Case of Sergeant Grischa*, 1928), Ludwig Renn's (1889–1979) *Krieg* (1928; *War*, 1929), and Anna SEGHERS'S *Aufstand der Fischer von St. Barbara* (1928; *The Revolt of the Fishermen*, 1929). These three continued to write in exile and later assumed positions of leadership in the literary circles of the GDR. Seghers's concentration camp novel *Das siebte Kreuz* (1942; *The Seventh Cross*, 1942), her best-known work, was written and published in exile. Another important writer of the political left was Lion FEUCHTWANGER, many of whose historical novels treat Jewish themes. Bruno FRANK, Oskar Maria GRAF, and Annette KOLB, all established authors prior to Hitler's assumption of power, continued to write in exile.

Ernst Jünger stands out among the conservative, nationalistic novelists of the 1920s. Others who were popular at the time and who, unlike Jünger, continued to write nationalistic works under Hitler, include Edwin Erich Dwinger (b. 1898) and Erwin Guido Kolbenheyer (1878–1962), a native of Budapest. Erich KÄSTNER, Walter BAUER, Stefan ANDRES, Ernst WIECHERT, and Werner Bergengruen (1892–1963) are important authors of the inner emigration.

1945–80: New Directions

The military defeat of 1945 was followed by four years of political, economic, and artistic upheaval. Much that had been accepted under Hitler, from the currency and the form of government to philosophy and aesthetics, was banned by the allied occupational authorities. Even the German language itself seemed tainted to many, especially the exiles and members of the younger generation. The political situation in the Federal Republic stabilized in the early 1950s, as a strong democracy emerged under the leadership of Konrad Adenauer and the nation moved from destitution to prosperity—the so-called *Wirtschaftswunder* (economic miracle). The economy in Walter Ulbricht's GDR did not improve significantly until after the erection of the Berlin Wall in 1961.

Pro-Nazi writers were banned, but otherwise there was little cohesion in the West German literature of the late 1940s. Some critics referred to a *Nullpunkt* (zero point) of German literature in

1945 and advocated a *Kahlschlag* (clearing the thickets), a purification of the language and the concomitant rejection of the idealistic tradition. The former term is an expressive, but at best inadequate image; the latter captures the mood of one group of young writers but likewise fails to present a true picture of the complex West German literary scene. Traditional authors of the inner emigration continued to publish. Some of their works were apolitical, but others represented reactions to the German defeat and addressed the hotly debated subject of collective guilt. For the most part, only religious authors were able to find cause for optimism. A significant new dimension was added as the works of the exiles—Thomas Mann, Brecht, Zuckmayer, and others—began to appear in Germany for the first time since 1933. Almost immediately the influence of foreign writers banned under Hitler was felt, as such figures as Albert CAMUS, William FAULKNER, Ernest HEMINGWAY, and the French SURREALISTS found admirers and imitators.

A new generation of writers soon made its presence felt. A leadership role was assumed by Hans Werner Richter (b. 1908). Together with Alfred ANDERSCH, Richter edited *Der Ruf* (1946–47), a liberal sociopolitical journal that served as the voice of Germany's disillusioned youth. When the occupational authorities revoked the journal's license, Richter called together several of his friends and colleagues. At the meeting, held in September 1947, the invited guests read from unpublished manuscripts and discussion followed. This marked the birth of the "Gruppe 47" (Group 47), which, under Richter's guidance, continued to meet once or twice a year until 1967 and during that time dominated the West German literary scene. Initially the group was a rather homogeneous collection of writers who shared Richter's preference for a realistic literature reflecting a socialist, but democratic, point of view. Frank discussion invariably prevailed, and even established members were not spared. As the prestige of the group increased in the 1950s, so did the number of participants and the diversity of the works read at the meetings. By 1960 diversity had become the hallmark of the group, and the older writers who had been the angry young men of the 1940s came to be regarded as the "establishment" by some young participants.

Indeed, much had changed in West Germany during this time. The economic miracle was accompanied by an increasingly materialistic orientation and a sense of complacency in society at large. Many writers expressed first alarm and then disillusionment over the developments and began to attack the bourgeoisie with growing intensity. Few, however, turned to Marxism, for the Stalinist regime in the GDR did not seem to offer a viable alternative. Simultaneously, some authors began to experiment with the new modes of expression offered by concrete poetry, an international movement in which the importance of content, or plot, is greatly reduced and the sound and visual appearance of individual words assume a considerable degree of autonomy.

West German literature of the late 1950s and early 1960s was rich and pluralistic. Several new faces appeared who had little in common except their considerable talent and the speed with which they developed international reputations: Günter GRASS, Uwe JOHNSON, Peter WEISS, Hans Magnus ENZENSBERGER, and the cosmopolitan East Germans Johannes BOBROWSKI, Peter HUCHEL, and Christa WOLF. In the mid-1960s a new trend became noticeable. As a result of several factors, especially the hostility of students and intellectuals to the conservative university system, increasing concern over the Vietnam War, and a waxing sympathy to Marxism, many writers—young and old alike—began to espouse a revolutionary position in their works. Herbert Marcuse

(1898–1979) was the idol of the younger generation, and the writings of Walter BENJAMIN and Theodor ADORNO exerted a strong influence, especially on intellectuals. In the 1970s a growing feminist movement also became a significant force.

From about 1965 on, the attention of many writers and critics turned to "realism," although there was (and is) little agreement on the nature of realist literature. Some proponents of a new realism understood the term in its popular meaning and utilized simple language and readily accessible themes in poetry, drama, and fiction alike. Walter Kempowski (b. 1929), for example, enjoyed several commercial and critical successes with his series of realistic autobiographical family novels. Dieter Wellershoff (b. 1925), Günter Herburger (1932–1992), and other members of the "Cologne School of New Realism" looked to the French NEW NOVEL, while still others, taking a position from the debates of the 1930s in which BRECHT and György LUKÁCS were prominently involved, maintained that the complexities of the modern world can be adequately (and, hence, realistically) treated only by eschewing superficially realistic plots and style.

The development of the literature of East Germany was quite different. For a brief period after the end of the war, a degree of artistic freedom was allowed by the authorities, but after the founding of the GDR, writers were generally required to conform to Marxist ideals and aesthetic theories. Older, established figures dominated the scene: Arnold Zweig, Anna Seghers, Johannes R. Becher, and the maverick Bertolt Brecht, whose stature enabled him to maintain a modicum of independence. The situation changed somewhat in 1956, as the effects of the post-Stalin "thaw" were felt. Since that time, brief periods of tolerance on the part of the government have alternated with times of heavy-handed repression. Many of the best writers of the GDR were subjected to harassment, in spite of their professed allegiance to Marxism, and by the late 1970s a significant number, including Wolf BIERMANN, Reiner KUNZE, and Sara Kirsch (b. 1935), had emigrated to the West.

Poetry

Many of the first poets published in the West were older traditionalists, a majority of whom could be described as Christian humanists. With the horrors of the immediate past reflected in the elegiac tone of their verse, these poets faced the future with the muted hope of a moral rebirth of mankind. Important representatives of this group include Werner Bergengruen—*Dies irae* (1945; Latin: day of wrath)—Hans CAROSSA, the younger Rudolf Hagelstange (1912–1984)—*Venezianisches Credo* (1945; Venetian credo)—and Hans Egon Holthusen (b. 1913), also a leading literary critic. Poetry of this kind soon lost favor, although it continued to be written well into the 1950s. A second type of lyric that was popular during the immediate postwar years was mystical nature poetry. The oldest and most influential member of this group, Wilhelm Lehmann, is a respected figure whose work seems destined to survive, although it is viewed as "escapist" by some critics. On the other hand, the works of many of his imitators lack substance and they are now rightly forgotten. Karl KROLOW, who later became one of Germany's most highly regarded literary figures, was one of the few younger poets of stature influenced by Lehmann.

There was little poetry that dealt in a direct and undisguised manner with the Nazi period during the years 1945–48. The first important exception is *Moabiter Sonette* (1946; *Moabit Sonnets*,

1978) by Albrecht Haushofer (1903–1945). Written in the Moabit prison in Berlin shortly before Haushofer's execution by the Nazis, these sonnets vividly convey the terrors of the time from the perspective of a political prisoner. The first postwar work of Nelly SACHS, who barely managed to escape from Germany in 1940, is even more important. *In den Wohnungen des Todes* (1947; in the habitations of death) is a highly emotional reaction to the Holocaust from a Jewish perspective. Sachs continued to write until her death, and although her works became increasingly complex and mystical, the later poetry consistently reflects the themes present in her first poems. Günter EICH was another prominent poet of the period. Some of his poems deal directly with his experiences as a soldier and prisoner-of-war. His later work went through many phases, culminating in the short experimental prose poems, or texts, of *Maulwürfe* (1968; moles) and its sequel, *Ein Tibeter in meinem Büro: 49 Maulwürfe* (1970; a Tibetan in my office: 49 moles)

It would be difficult to overestimate the importance of the year 1948, when the first postwar books of several major figures appeared, including *Statische Gedichte* (static poems) by Gottfried Benn. Younger poets, fascinated by Benn's masterful use of language and poetic form, for the most part ignored the intellectual content of his work and began to imitate the form and language, with unfortunate results. Several of these poets gained brief fame during the 1950s, but practically all are forgotten today. Benn published several volumes of poetry in the following years and his influence grew rapidly. His essay *Probleme der Lyrik* (1951; problems of poetry) was the most significant theoretical document of the decade.

The years 1952–53 marked the debut of a group of important new poets, including Walter HÖLLERER, Heinz PIONTEK, Peter Härtling (b. 1933), and Johannes Poethen (b. 1928), and three who are not, strictly speaking, West Germans, but who are in no sense regional authors: Paul CELAN, a native of Romania, Ingeborg BACHMANN, an Austrian, and Eugen GOMRINGER, a truly international figure who was born in Bolivia. Poethen and others, including Ernst Meister (1911–1979) and Max Hölzer (b. 1915), are generally classified, for lack of a better term, as "surrealist" poets. While they clearly do not follow rigidly the theories of the French surrealists, the work of the two groups does have much in common, most notably the use of metaphors and the dreamlike quality of the poems. Höllerer, Piontek, Walter Helmut Fritz (b. 1929), Hans-Jürgen Heise (b. 1930), Hilde DOMIN, Christoph MECKEL, and many other poets of this talented generation sought a personal idiom, free of rigid philosophical, literary, or political dogma; their work is modern, but not avant-garde. Meckel, a prolific as well as accomplished writer, is also a graphic artist who has illustrated many of his collections of prose and poetry.

Eugen Gomringer, one of the founders of concrete poetry, has been an influential figure. His own poems are among the most significant of their kind, and he has also written several important essays on experimental literature. The effect of his works, as well as those of his followers, is primarily the result of visual and acoustical elements. Franz MON, the editor of the anthology *Movens* (1960; moving), stands close to Gomringer. Max Bense (b. 1910) is a leading theoretician of the avant-garde movement. Helmut HEISSENBÜTTEL also belongs in the group of concrete poets, although his "texts" and "combinations" are quite different in style and effect from Gomringer's work.

The late 1950s witnessed a significant development in the lyric: the emergence of the political poem. To be sure, Wolfgang Weyrauch (1907–1980) and others had written poems dealing with

political questions soon after the war. But with few exceptions these poems expressed little more than the horror of the immediate past and a vague hope for the future. The younger generation of writers, however, began to examine their society in a very critical manner. At first these writers frequently utilized irony, and many poems tended strongly toward the grotesque. Grass and Enzensberger are the most important of this generation of political poets, whose numbers also include Wolfdietrich SCHNURRE (b. 1920), Peter Rühmkorf (b. 1929), Horst Bingel (b. 1933), and Horst Bienek (1930–1990). Recent political poetry has tended to be more direct and vitriolic, beginning with the increasing student activism and general leftward drift of the mid-1960s and culminating in the vehement reaction against the Vietnam War.

If the political poem is one manifestation of many young writers' interest in realism, another can be seen in a new subjectivism similar to the prose of the Cologne school—Herburger, Nicolas Born (1937–1979), and Rolf Dieter BRINKMANN have written this kind of verse. An interesting recent development is the "poetry of facts" of Arno Reinfrank (b. 1934), which attempts to integrate science and literature.

In East German poetry two themes emerged in the first postwar years: the evils of the Nazi past and the prospect of a bright future in a Marxist Germany. Initially, examples of the latter took the form of hymns of praise to Communist leaders and odes to the joys of work and productivity. The traditional verse of J. R. Becher was held up as a model for younger writers. Poets who were unable or unwilling to conform either fell silent, like Peter Huchel, or, like Stephan HERMLIN, turned to other genres. Soon the permissible subject matter was broadened to include more personal themes, such as love and nature, as they relate to human life in a social context. By the late 1950s some poets, emulating the laconic style of Brecht, were beginning to question the shortcomings and repressive policies of the government. Their number increased in the 1960s. The most prominent was Wolf Biermann, whose direct attacks against the regime contributed substantially to the imposition of stricter censorship. Others who to some extent shared Biermann's concerns, but expressed them in more subdued language, include Reiner KUNZE, Günter KUNERT, and Rainer Kirsch (b. 1934). Volker BRAUN and Karl Mickel (b. 1935) attempted, with some success, to reconcile the demands of society with the concerns of the individual. Wulf Kirsten (b. 1934), whose poetry is reminiscent of Bobrowski's, is one of the few poets of stature to have emerged in the GDR during the 1970s.

Drama

The West German drama was slow to recover from the devastating effects of the Nazi years. The only exile to make a significant contribution to the West German stage was Carl Zuckmayer, whose first postwar work was *Des Teufels General* (1946; *The Devil's General*, 1962), a gripping tragedy based on the life of Ernst Udet, an anti-Nazi general in Hitler's air force who ultimately committed suicide in 1941. The inner emigrants wrote few plays, and the younger authors similarly preferred other literary forms. Nonetheless, *Draußen vor der Tür* (1947; *The Man Outside*, 1952), Wolfgang BORCHERT's only drama, proved to be the most successful and sensational single work produced by anyone of his generation during the immediate postwar years. This expressionistic play about the despair of a returning soldier, for all its popularity, found no imitators, and Zuckmayer's later works were clearly inferior to *Des Teufels General*.

Despite the moderately successful attempts of several younger playwrights—Karl Wittlinger (b. 1922), Leopold Ahlsen (b. 1927), Wolfgang Altendorf (b. 1921)—and a few older ones—Hans Henny JAHNN, Ferdinand BRUCKNER—the West German drama of the 1950s in no way compares with that of Austria, Switzerland, or the GDR. The best plays of the 1950s were not written for the stage, but for the radio. The *Hörspiel* (radio play) attracted the attention of many talented playwrights, including Marie Luise KASCHNITZ, Wolfgang HILDESHEIMER, Günter Eich, Erwin Wickert (b. 1915), Ernst Schnabel (b. 1913), and Fred von Hoerschelmann (1901–1976).

Toward the end of the 1950s, the drama began to show signs of a revival. Hildesheimer became the leading German proponent of the THEATER OF THE ABSURD with the three plays of *Spiele, in denen es dunkel wird* (1958; plays in which darkness falls). Two authors better known for their fiction, Siegfried LENZ and Günter GRASS, wrote realistic and absurdist plays, respectively. In 1960 the first of Tankred Dorst's (b. 1925) many successful dramas was produced: *Die Kurve* (*The Curve*, 1968), a "farce" in the absurdist tradition. But not until 1963 did a West German drama become an international success, when Rolf HOCHHUTH'S *Der Stellvertreter* (*The Deputy*, 1964), a polemical attack on the behavior of Pope Pius XII during the war, delighted (or shocked) audiences throughout the world. Hochhuth's reliance on documentary material set a trend that was to dominate the stage for the remainder of the decade. Heinar Zipphardt's (1922–1982) *In der Sache J. Robert Oppenheimer* (1964; *In the Matter of J. Robert Oppenheimer*, 1968) utilized a courtroom setting. After the brilliant tour de force *Marat/Sade* (1964; *Marat/Sade*, 1965), Peter Weiss similarly turned to the documentary drama with a courtroom setting in *Die Ermittlung* (1965; *The Investigation*, 1966), which has the trials of Nazi war criminals as its theme. Hochhuth and Weiss continued to write documentary dramas, and other authors, including Dorst and Enzensberger, were also attracted to this form.

Before the enthusiasm for the documentary theater had waned, several young playwrights became interested in a new kind of drama, one treating everyday life in a matter compatible with the new realism. These plays are indebted to the earlier *Volksstück* (folk play) of Marieluise FLEISSER and the Austrian Ödön von HORVÁTH, and, in many cases, to the American Edward ALBEE. Domestic settings, realistic dialogue, and situations ranging from banal to grotesque are characteristics of the dramas of Jochen Ziem (b. 1932), Martin Sperr (b. 1944), Botho Strauss (b. 1944), and F. X. KROETZ. They are related to the films of Rainer Werner Fassbinder (1946–1982), who also wrote works for the stage. The most successful of these plays was *Die Zimmerschlacht* (1967; *Home Front*, 1972), by the versatile Martin WALSER.

The East German drama had a more auspicious beginning, due to the presence of Brecht. The master of his own theater, the Berliner Ensemble, he offered outstanding productions of works by German and foreign playwrights, as well as his own dramas. Erwin STRITTMATTER'S *Katzgraben* (1954; Katzgraben) was the best of the many early plays that adhered closely to SOCIALIST REALISM. Somewhat later two great talents appeared, Peter HACKS and Heiner MÜLLER. Hacks wrote excellent comedies, and both attempted serious plays set in the GDR before running afoul of the authorities. Later they turned to safer subjects, especially the reworking of classical themes. Other noteworthy East German plays are *Frau Flinz* (1962), a comedy by Helmut Baierl (b. 1926), and *Die Kipper* (1972; the dumpers), a realistic drama by Volker Braun.

Fiction

In the immediate postwar years a plethora of novels by exiles and inner emigrants were published in Germany. For all their differences, virtually all dealt, directly or indirectly, with the Hitler years. In *Stalingrad* (1945; *Stalingrad*, 1948) Theodor Plievier (1892–1955) portrayed the horrors of battle with grim realism, and Ernst Wiechert's *Der Totenwald* (1946; *The Forest of the Dead*, 1947) is realistic both in its portrayal of life in a concentration camp and in the narrator's admission that a factual account cannot capture the essence of the experience. The terrors of the Third Reich are suggested symbolically in the negative utopias of *Heliopolis* (1949; Heliopolis) by Ernst Jünger and *Die Stadt hinter dem Strom* (1949; *City beyond the River*, 1953) by Hermann Kasack (1896–1966), as well as in the most ambitious novel of the age, Thomas Mann's *Doktor Faustus* (1947; *Doctor Faustus*, 1948). A less pessimistic view is offered in *Das unauslöschliche Siegel* (1946; the indelible seal) and *Märkische Argonautenfahrt* (1950; *The Quest*, 1953), by the Christian writer Elisabeth Langgässer (1899–1950). Several older authors began to write in the nonrealistic style of William FAULKNER, Joyce, and Dos Passos that had become popular in the free world during the 1930s. Among these are Langässer, Ernst Kreuder (1903–1972), Wolfgang KOEPPEN, and Hans Erich NOSSACK. Whereas Kreuder never again equaled the success of his first postwar novel, *Die Gesellschaft vom Dachboden* (1946; *The Attic Pretenders*, 1948), Nossack and Koeppen each published several major works.

Younger authors for the most part preferred shorter fiction to the novel. The stories of Wolfgang Borchert, in which the anguish of his generation received poignant expression, were scarcely less popular than his drama. Most younger writers, on the other hand, developed a realistic style in the manner of Ernest HEMINGWAY. Heinrich BÖLL, Wolfdietrich Schnurre, and Hans Bender (b. 1919) were concerned with the fate of individuals—soldiers, POWs, and civilians—caught up in the war and its aftermath. This group of short-story writers shared a leftist, but usually not Marxist perspective, a sense of revulsion over Germany's militaristic history, and a strong desire to prevent a recurrence of the evils of the past. In the 1950s they began to attack bourgeois materialism and complacency.

Conservative voices were not lacking. These writers represented a variety of positions, but in general shared a dislike of contemporary society. Instead of looking forward to increasing socialism as a solution, they stressed the importance of the individual and looked back to religious or philosophical values of the past. In *Der Fragebogen* (1951; *The Questionnaire*, 1955) Ernst von Salomon (1902–1972) offered an account of his life, from his devotion to the German cause in World War I to his internment by the Americans following World War II, in which he bitterly satirized the allies' denazification program. Albrecht Goes, a Protestant minister also known as a poet and essayist, produced two realistic novellas, *Unruhige Nacht* (1949; *Arrow to the Heart*, 1951) and *Das Brandopfer* (1954; *The Burnt Offering*, 1956), set during the Nazi period, in which the author's faith in God and, ultimately, human nature, shines through. The novels and short fiction of Heinz Risse (b. 1898) and Gerd Gaiser (1908–1976) reflect the authors' distrust of modern civilization, Risse from a humanistic Christian perspective and Gaiser from that of a neoromantic youth movement of the 1920s. Gaiser's *Die sterbende Jagd* (1953; *The Last Squadron*, 1959), one of the most important German war novels, consists of a multitude of vignettes focusing on different members of the Luftwaffe squadron in Norway at the turning point of the air war with England. Many attitudes toward the war and the German cause are represented, and the single unifying thread is the pervasive feeling of nostalgia as the fighter pilot, the last of those warriors for whom battle is a ritual with a code of honor, loses his unique position and becomes just another instrument of mechanized modern warfare. Rudolf Krämer-Badoni (b. 1913) is another leading conservative novelist and critic.

The late 1950s and early 1960s witnessed the rise of a number of important writers whose novels are progressive in both form and content, but vary greatly in execution and intent. The first of these was Heinrich Schirmbeck's (b. 1915) *Ärgert dich dein rechtes Aug* (1957; *If Thine Eye Offend Thee*, 1960), a philosophical work of considerable thematic complexity in which the protagonist, a cyberneticist, struggles to reconcile the search for scientific truth with the dangers posed to civilization by the rapid advances of technology. The appearance of *Die Blechtrommel* (1959; *The Tin Drum*, 1962) made an international celebrity of its author, Günter Grass. This picaresque novel, which narrates the improbable adventures of a dwarf during the war and postwar years, is the very antithesis of Uwe Johnson's sober and reflective first novel, *Mutmaßungen über Jakob* (1959; *Speculations about Jakob*, 1963). Johnson, an immigrant from the GDR, indirectly explores—speculates about—the relationship between East and West, as his figures consider the enigmas that surrounded the life and death of the title character, Jakob Abs. Martin Walser should also be mentioned in this context, as should Heinrich Böll, who developed from the promising young author of realistic war stories of the late 1940s to the author of *Billard um halbzehn* (1959; *Billiards at Half Past Nine*, 1962) and *Ansichten eines Clowns* (1963; *The Clown*, 1965), novels of artistic maturity as well as social commitment. With the exception of Schirmbeck, who later turned primarily to theoretical essays on the relationship between science, literature, and society, these novelists have continued to produce works that have received both critical and popular acclaim. Another major figure who emerged at that time was Siegfried Lenz, whose works are somewhat more traditional.

It had long been a cliché in certain critical circles that traditional fiction—novels and stories with a protagonist and recognizable linear plot—was experiencing a "crisis." This was evident in some German writers of the 1950s, most notably Arno SCHMIDT and Helmut Heissenbüttel, but only in the 1960s did avant-garde prose forms become widespread. The writers who were involved, for all their differences, shared a distrust of traditional forms and values, and their works display an attention to minute detail and an awareness of the banality of language. The novelists Dieter Wellershoff and Günter Herburger, and Jürgen Becker (b. 1932), the author of *Felder* (1964; fields) and *Ränder* (1968; margins), collections of short prose texts, soon came to be recognized as the leading representatives of this school. Hubert Fichte (1935–1986), a "German Jack Kerouac" wrote disjointed novels set in the youthful subculture, as did Peter Chotjewitz (b. 1934), one of the most versatile of the experimental prose writers. *Don Quichotte in Köln* (1968; Don Quixote in Cologne) by Paul SCHALLÜCK, is nontraditional, if less radical than the works of Fichte and Chotjewitz. In Gabriele WOHMANN's fiction an attention to the minutiae of daily life is combined with keen psychological insights into the difficulty of achieving satisfying human relationships. Many writers, including Alfred Andersch and Dieter Kühn (b. 1935), turned to a semi-documentary style in which factual material alternates with a connecting fictional narrative.

In the GDR, most fiction written during the 1950s was rather sterile Socialist Realism. The work of Anna Seghers is noteworthy, as is *Nackt unter Wölfen* (1958; *Naked among Wolves*, 1960) by Bruno Apitz (1900–1979), which is set in a concentration camp in 1945. At about the same time the traditional novel of Socialist Realism reached a pinnacle in *Ole Bienkopp* (1963; *Ole Bienkopp*, 1966) by Erwin Strittmatter, a new kind of prose fiction began to appear in the GDR. Beginning with Christa Wolf's *Der geteilte Himmel* (1963; *Divided Heaven*, 1970), East German writers started to examine their society more closely and more critically, discussing the relationship between social theory and practice, as well as that between the individual and society. The expansion of thematic scope was accompanied by a gradual departure from the rigid stylistic and structural requirements of doctrinaire Socialist Realism. *Die Aula* (1965; the auditorium) by Hermann KANT and Christa Wolf's controversial *Nachdenken über Christa T.* (1969; *The Quest for Christa T.,* 1970)—especially the latter—are among the most significant East German novels of the 1960s. Also important are works by Rolf Schneider (b. 1932), Jurek BECKER, Günter de Bruyn (b. 1926), Manfred Bieler (b. 1934), Günter Kunert, and Ulrich Plenzdorf (b. 1934), whose *Die neuen Leiden des jungen W.* (1973; *The New Sufferings of Young W.*, 1979), set in the GDR but based on a sustained allusion to Goethe's *The Sufferings of Young Werther*, was the literary sensation of the 1970s. The prose of Johannes Bobrowski, like his poetry, stands apart from the mainstream of East German literature.

BIBLIOGRAPHY: Eloesser, A., *Modern German Literature* (1933); Lange, V., *Modern German Literature, 1870–1940* (1945); Bithell, J., *Modern German Literature, 1880–1950*, 3rd ed. (1957); Waidson, H., *The Modern German Novel* (1959); Sokel, W., *The Writer in Extremis: Expressionism in 20th-Century German Literature* (1959); Garten, H., *Modern German Drama* (1959); Soergel, A. and C. Hohoff, *Dichtung und Dichter der Zeit* (2 vols., 1961–1963); Hoffmann, C., *Opposition Poetry in Nazi Germany* (1962); Schwitzke, H., *Das Hörspiel: Dramaturgie und Geschichte* (1963); Gray, R., *The German Tradition in Literature* (1965); Hamburger, M., *From Prophecy to Exorcism: The Premises of Modern German Literature* (1966); Hatfield, H., *Modern German Literature* (1969); Hatfield, H., *Crisis and Continuity in Modern German Fiction* (1969); Demetz, P., *Postwar German Literature* (1970); Flores, J., *Poetry in East Germany* (1971); Durzak, M., ed. *Die deutsche Literatur der Gegenwart: Aspekte und Tendenzen* (1971); Koebner, T., ed., *Tendenzen der deutschen Literatur seit 1945* (1971); Domandi, A. K., ed., *Modern German Literature* (2 vols., 1972); Thomas, R., and K. Bullivant, *Literature in Upheaval: West German Writers and the Challenge of the 1960s* (1974); Gumpel, L., *"Concrete" Poetry from East and West Germany* (1976); Patterson, M., *German Theatre Today* (1976); Hutchinson, P., *Literary Presentations of Divided Germany* (1977); Willett, J., *"The New Sobriety": Art and Politics in the Weimar Period* (1978); Krispyn, E., *Anti-Nazi Writers in Exile* (1978); Huettich, H., *Theater in a Planned Society: Contemporary Drama in the GDR* (1978); Van, K. D'Elden, ed., *West German Poets on Society and Politics* (1979); Bosmajian, H., *Metaphors of Evil: Contemporary German Literature and the Shadow of Nazism* (1979); Innes, C., *Modern German Drama* (1979); Taylor, R., *Literature and Society in Germany 1918–1945* (1980)

—JERRY GLENN

German Literature since 1980

In many respects the years between 1984 and 1995 mark a drastic change in German-language literature, for it was a period of monumental endings and beginnings. On the one hand, several of the authors who profoundly influenced postwar literature passed away. They include: Uwe Johnson, Heinrich Böll, the Austrian Thomas BERNHARD, the Swiss Friedrich DÜRRENMATT, the Swiss Max FRISCH, Rudolf Hagelstange, Ingeborg Drewitz (1923–1986), Hubert Fichte, the Austrian Erich Fried (1921–1988), the Swiss Hermann Burger (1942–1989), Horst Bienek (1930–1990), and Austrian Hilde Spiel (1911–1990), and the Austrian Nobel Lauriate Elias CANETTI. The death of these respected authors spelled a deep loss for German belles lettres. In the same vein, the opening of the Berlin Wall on 9 November 1989 and the subsequent rapid unification of Germany on 3 October 1990 meant an end to East German literature as we knew it. Writers from the East, who had previously enjoyed a wide readership since they offered alternative information and an oppositional voice to the dictates of the party, were suddenly subjected to the same market conditions as their western counterparts. Some were criticized in the West for their supposed compromising positions with the G.D.R. regime. A case in point is Christa WOLF, whose *Was bleibt* (1989; *What Remains and Other Stories*, 1995) describes how she continued to live and work in the East even though she realized she was subjected to surveillance by the state security system (the Stasi). Others, who opposed the total abandonment of socialism and were thus against becoming a part of West Germany, like Stefan HEYM, were left rather isolated. It remains to be seen if such authors will be able to integrate themselves into the new German state. On the other hand, a unified Germany, together with the changing structure of Europe, with all its problems and accomplishments, should provide a fertile ground for older and newer authors alike to express their creative talents.

The 1980s saw a continuation of the debate as to whether one or several German literatures exist. While the question of a distinct East German literature will only be of historical interest, controversies still remain about the relative independence of Austrian and Swiss-German letters. Some see the literatures of these two countries as distinct entities, for their authors examine primarily the nature of Austrian and Swiss experiences and identities respectively. Others point out that since many of these authors are published in Germany and since they all share a common language, they all partake in a common "German-language literature." A few want to blur all distinctions and speak only of a world literature. While the debate will probably not be settled soon, Austrian and Swiss authors have been included in this essay if they have made a significant impact in Germany or if they have been expropriated by German readers and critics.

It is difficult to distinguish many trends, movements or groupings for German literature in the past few years. One exception might be what is alternately called guest workers', foreigners', or migrants' literature. This is the writing of non-Germans living in Germany and publishing in German. Authors like Aras Ören (b. 1929), Rafik Schami (b. 1949), and TORKAN (b. 1941, pseud. of Torkan Daneshfar-Pätzoldt) write about the problems that foreigners face in Germany, such as prejudice and the lack of understanding between different cultures. Their professed purpose is to reduce friction, increase awareness, and contribute to a more harmonious integration of various parts of society. The only difficulty that these authors face is that their works, often published in anthologies, remain out of the mainstream and are overlooked by the reading public.

Apart from this one group it is impossible to find any convenient nomenclature for the other 13,000 to 15,000 literary works that appear annually on the German market. Some have applied the term postmodern to the 1980s, and this characterization certainly holds true in some cases. Authors such as Botho Strauss, in several of his prose works like *Der junge Mann* (1984; the young man) or *Niemand anders* (1987; no one else) and in his plays like *Besucher* (1988; visitors), or Peter HANDKE, in his prose such as *Die Wiederholung* (1986; the repetition) or *Nachmittag eines Schriftstellers* (1987; afternoon of a writer), or Patrick Süskind (b. 1949), in his popular best-seller *Das Parfum* (1985; *Perfume*, 1986), tend to display many of the characteristics associated with this movement. They mix a variety of styles that can appeal to different groups of readers simultaneously, they use a complicated if not ornate language, they call their own profession or the literary forms they are using into question (often through parody), and they show an interest in history and biography. One author, Marianne Fritz (b. 1948), carries this trend to an absurd degree. In her monumental novel *Dessen Sprache du nicht verstehst* (1985; whose language you do not understand), which is over three thousand pages long, she purposely leaves out words, places false punctuation within the sentences, and collects over one thousand characters, often under varying names, to tell the history of a German family during the early part of this century.

Other authors, however, have merely prolonged trends begun earlier, yet in many instances they still managed to produce significant works of art. The realm of poetry was perhaps the least productive in this regard, for it has been highly derivative and repetitive. Nevertheless, a few new poets, like Ulla Hahn (b. 1945), were able to find a fairly wide readership, and a few established poets, like Heinz Czechowski (b. 1939), continued to impress the critics. In both cases one admired the timeliness of their messages and the powerful scope of their language. The world of the drama was more exciting, although it was dominated by two authors, Botho Strauss and the Austrian Thomas Bernhard. The latter's *Heldenplatz* (1988; heroes square) caused a major scandal and was also an overnight success due to the hyperbole of its criticism of contemporary Austrian society and the parallels it draws with the events of 1938. The neorealist Bavarian Franz Xaver Kroetz continued to write plays at a furious rate, and most of them, like *Furcht und Hoffnung der BRD* (1984; fear and hope of the FRG), centered on the theme of unemployment, often with surrealist overtones. The newcomer Friederike Roth (b. 1948) won considerable respect for her radio play *Nachtschatten* (1984; night shadows), which is a feminist reflection on the concept of happiness.

Prose continued to be the most popular genre, and committed works that examined societal issues garnered the most notoriety. Günter Walraff (b. 1942) disguised himself as a Turkish worker and documents the horrible prejudices and maltreatment to which he was subjected on and off the workplace in *Ganz unten* (1985; down at the bottom). The book became a scandalous success. The famous Günter GRASS uses an atomic disaster in *Die Rättin* (1986; *The Rat*, 1987) as a pretext to tell a story set in the future, but which has connections to his earlier Danzig trilogy. Jurek BECKER examines contemporary generational conflicts caused by the Nazi years in *Bronsteins Kinder* (1986; *Bronstein's Children*, 1988). Martin WALSER employs the framework of a spy novel to investigate the division of Germany in *Dorle und Wolf* (1987; *No Man's Land*, 1988). Rainald Goetz (b. 1954) shocked the public with his account of the Red Army Faction in 1977 in his book *Kontrolliert* (1988; checked over).

Other prose authors treated more personal issues. Brigitte Kronauer (b. 1940), after a series of books about female emancipation, describes the self-realization of a male protagonist in *Berittener Bogenschütze* (1986; mounted archer). Hermann Burger tries to overcome the spectre of death and depression in *Brenners Leben* (1989; Brenner's life). Christoph Ransmayr (b. 1954), in one of the most critically acclaimed works of the decade, *Die letzte Welt* (1988; *The Last World*, 1990), sends his main character in search of the Roman poet Ovid. He never reaches his goal, but his journey results in a new relationship with nature and the world, which ends in madness. In all three works the reader is confronted with linguistic perfection and the deep inner worlds of the soul.

The tumultuous and partially unforeseen social and economic upheavals that unification brought about have left many writers at a literal loss for words—they seem to be searching for appropriate topics and means of expression in a world suddenly grown extremely complex and unfamiliar. Several, particularly those from the east, feel that they have lost their credibility and relevance, since they did not participate directly in the events leading to the demise of the G.D.R., and have thus ceased writing completely. A number of publishing houses in eastern Germany have collapsed, because the reading public there has neither the money nor the time for literature: they prefer instead travel information, how-to books, or practical advice guides. Of the many authors who left the East for the West during the 1970s and 1980s, only two have returned: Erich Loest (b. 1926) to Leipzig and Joachim Seyppel (b. 1919) to East Berlin.

As might be expected, the problematics of a divided Germany and its subsequent unification has emerged as an important theme in German literature of the 1990s. Some authors, like the former head of the East German Writers' Association, Hermann KANT, in his book *Abspann: Erinnerungen* (1991; end of the film: recollections), have tried to justify their role in the G.D.R. and have earned few complimentary comments for their efforts. Others, like Loest, in such books as *Der Zorn des Schafes* (1990; the anger of the sheep), in which he describes his encounters with the Stasi, or *Katerfrühstück* (1992; hangover breakfast), in which he tries to show how the two former Germanies had grown psychologically far apart, have gained praise and admiration. Still other authors approach this topic on a personal and intimate basis. The heroine of Monika Maron's (b. 1941) novel *Stille Zeile sechs* (1991; *Silent Close No. 6*, 1993) experiences firsthand the collapse of East Germany with a concomitant range of emotions. The individuals in Gabriele Goettle's (b. 1947) four-hundred-page reportage *Deutsche Sitten: Erkundungen in Ost und West* (1991; German customs: research in east and west) present an image of a united Germany in dark and somber tones. The protagonist of Martin Walser's much acclaimed novel *Die Verteidung der Kindheit* (1991; the defense of childhood) experiences great internal suffering during the years of German division. More recent works confront some of the current problems still facing a united Germany. Rolf Hochhath's play *Wessis in Weimar* (1993; Westerners in Weimar) examines the relationships between the western and eastern parts of the country, Wolfgang Hilbig's (b. 1941) novel *Ich* (1993; I) looks at the connection between the Stasi and authors in the former East Germany, and Brigitte Burmeister's (b. 1941) novel *Unter dem Namen Norma* (1994; under the name Nora) paints a broad panorama of the contemporary difficulties facing the people in the East. Such works will no doubt serve as models for literary creations in the coming years.

BIBLIOGRAPHY: Hage, V., ed., *Deutsche Literatur: Jahresüberblick* (1984 ff.—annual survey); Schöne, A., ed., "Vier deutsche Literaturen?," *Kontroversen, alte and neue: Akten des VII. Internationalen Germanisten—Kongresses Göttingen 1985* (1986, Vol. 10); Demetz, P., *After the Fires: Recent Writing in the Germanies, Austria, and Switzerland* (1986); Acker, R., and Burkhard, M., eds., *Blick auf die Schweiz: Zur Frage der Eligenständigkeit der Schweizer Literatur seit 1970* (1987); Arnold, H. L., ed., *Bestandsaufnahme Gegenwartsliteratur: Bundesrepublick Deutschland, Deutsche Demokratische Republik, Österreich, Schweiz* (1988); Suhr, H., "Minority Literature in the Federal Republic of Germany," *NGC*, 46 (1989): 71–103; Winkels, H., "Im Schatten des Lebens: eine Antwort an die Verächter und die Verteidiger der Gegenwartsliteratur," *Die Zeit*, overseas edition (9 Mar. 1990): 15; Baumgart, R., "Boulevard—was sonst?" *Die Zeit*, overseas edition (13 Apr. 1990): 25; special issue on literature of the 1980s, *GQ*, 63: 3–4 (1990)

—ROBERT ACKER

GHALLĀB, Abd al-Karim

Moroccan novelist, short-story writer, and journalist, b. 1919, Fes

G. attended the Qarawiyyin college in Morocco and obtained his B.A. in Arabic literature from Cairo University. While in Egypt, he militated through various Maghrebi organizations for the independence of Morocco, Algeria, and Tunisia. Upon his return to Morocco in 1948, he worked as a journalist and a teacher. He was appointed editor in chief of the weekly magazine *Risālat Al-Maghrib* and contributed to the daily newspaper *Al-'Alam*. He became its editor in chief after his country's independence and is presently its editor and director.

G. militated assiduously for his national cause and was arrested and imprisoned more than once. He related his experience in prison in his largely autobiographical novel *Sab'at Abwāb* (1965; seven gates). He was appointed a plenipotentiary minister for the Middle East from 1956 to 1959. G. then returned to journalism and writing, interrupting his work a second time from 1983 to 1985 upon his appointment as minister in the Moroccan government. G. is a prominent member of the Istiqlal party. He is a devout and dedicated nationalist and a committed writer. His prolific production reflects his deep patriotism and his belief in Arab nationalism and the need for Arab unity. A versatile writer, whose books cover such fields as literary criticism and political and historical analysis, G. is also a novelist and short-story writer and an active member of various writers and journalists associations.

His idealistic concepts of Arab unity were first voiced in his book *Nabadāt fikr* (1961; the beat of a thinking mind). They were the leitmotiv of three other books that followed and dealt with similar topics: *Risālat fikr* (1968; the message of a thinking mind), *Al-thaqāfah wa-al-fikr fī muwājahat al-tahaddī* (1976; culture and thought in the face of challenge), and *Al-fikr al-'Arabī bayna al-istilāb wa ta'kīd al-dhāt* (1977; Arab thought between spoliation and confirmation of the self). In the novel *Al-Mu'allim 'Alī* (1971; master Ali) the national awakening and the political maturity of factory workers are achieved only through the guidance of an intellectual Imam. The choice of an Imam is not a total coincidence as G. is a firm believer in God and is highly critical of the atheists who see in their attitude an exercise of the freedom of expression.

While advocating MODERNISM, G. neither wants a blind imitation of the West nor the loss of his country's individuality and Arab-Islamic character. It is clear in his essays and his fiction that he is weary of the widespread use of French language by the Moroccan people and Moroccan intellectuals. He deplores the limited impact of his writings and those of his colleagues because of the high rate of illiteracy in his country and the lack of circulation of Arabic-written books outside Morocco's borders. He concluded his book *Nabadāt fikr* wondering whether anyone would ever read it. G. considers the poor reading habits of the Arabs as a whole as one of the causes of their cultural disarray. The great loser in literature is the theater, which lowered its standards to cater to an audience interested only in amusement. Its dependence on the spoken word is another threat to its survival as the written text, maintains G., prevails over the spoken word because of the greater depth and value it carries.

G.'s assessment of the decade of the 1960s presented in his book *Risālat fikr* is dictated by his conservative and rather puritan judgment on life. The world according to him turned mad, and materialism overcame spiritualism. He did not react favorably to the liberalism of the 1960s and expressed the need for a cultural revolution to improve the situation. G.'s idealism and deep sense of right and wrong dictated his dislike for the various phenomena of the modern times, although he is a modernist in his own way. He manifests an almost obsessive concern for freedom and considers it a necessity for the development of any culture, a concept that is strongly expressed in two of his main books, *Risālat fikr* and *Al thaqāfah wa-al-fikr fī muwājahat al-tahaddī*. He believes that intellectual backwardness can be remedied through education, training of personnel, development of public opinion, and moral reformation, and that backwardness is not due only to a weak economy.

Although about fifteen years separate *Nabadāt fikr* from *Al-fikr al-'Arabī bayna al-istilāb wa ta'kīd al-dhāt*, G.'s concepts of Arab unity and the role of Arab intellectuals in cementing it did not change in any noticeable way. G. is critical of superficial writers and particularly of poets who depend solely on inspiration to write poetry. He stresses the need for study and research as well as the necessity for constructive criticism to improve the standard of Arabic poetry, particularly in the 1960s. His preference for rhymed poetry over free verse reveals a rather conservative view in art, a position clearly reflected in his fiction works and Arabic style. Moreover, G. believes that good fiction can only derive from personal experience. Some of his assessments of Arabic literature are outdated, but they form part of the trend that characterized the Arabic literary scene, in the Maghreb in particular, during the 1960s, opposing the old and the new schools of thought.

The concepts expressed in *Risālat fikr* served as the basis for G.'s novels and short stories. His collections *Al-ard habū* (1971; the land is my beloved) and *Wa akhrajahā min al-jannah* (1977; he led her out of paradise) can be classified as realistic works, highly descriptive and extremely detailed, with an obvious desire to inform the reader of Morocco's customs and traditions. Both collections reveal the writer's deep nationalism and his love for the land. The importance of holding to one's land at any price and resisting tempting offers to sell it is also one of the messages of *Al-Mu'allīm 'Alī* where the villagers are described as lacking national consciousness. Some of these works are highly autobiographical, a good example being his novel *Sab'at Abwāb* in which G. relates the

arrest and imprisonment of a Moroccan political activist. The insertion of such an experience in the frame of a novel has given the author more immediacy to praise the courage, patience, and patriotism of the characters, especially that of the hero and his wife. G. describes life in the prison at length, stressing the bonding that develops between political prisoners. The same patriotic feeling is at the basis of another novel, *Dafannā al-mādī* (1966; we buried the past), which raises the question of the conflict of civilizations as well as the colonial policy in Morocco, particularly the Arab-Berber relations and the efforts of the French at dividing the Moroccans along these lines. While this novel ends with the independence of Morocco and the return of the king to the country, another novel, *Sabā wa yazhaf al-layl* (1984; morning followed by the night), takes the action to the postindependence period. It tackles the traumatic impact of the French colonial policy and the francophone tendencies of some Moroccans. G. points out the negative effect of such a policy on Islam and on society as a whole through the life of a French-educated young man who resists his wife's efforts to convert him to Moroccan traditional ways. The confrontation between the young couple is an opportunity for the novelist to voice his opinion on Western culture. G. adopts his usual didactic and moralizing approach to condemn the Westernized young man and his peers.

G.'s fiction is burdened by a tendency to give lengthy accounts of events and detailed descriptions of places. Moreover, his style borrows heavily from traditional classical Arabic. His writings sound like a lone voice on the Moroccan literary scene, conservative and even old-fashioned, at a time when Arabic is undergoing a revolutionary rejuvenation. Also, his moral message is too blunt and obvious for the taste of the modern reader who is used to hints and allusions.

It is safe to say that G.'s greatest contributions to the cultural scene in Morocco and the Arab world are in the field of journalism, in the political essay, and to a lesser extent in literary criticism. His writings are in step with Morocco's political evolution as is obvious from works such as *Tārīkh al-harakah al-wataniyyah bi-al-Maghrib* (1988; the history of the national movement in Morocco), *Ma'a al-sha'b fi al-barlamān* (1984; with the people in the parliament), and *Sultat al-mu'assassāt* (1987; the power of the institutions). His interest extends to all Arab causes, particularly the Palestinian problem and the Zionist policy to which he dedicates a whole work entitled *Ma'rakatunā al'Arabiyyah fi muwājahat al isti'mār wa-al-Sahyūniyyah* (1967; our Arab battle with colonialism and Zionism). The Lebanese civil war caught also his attention and is the subject of his latest publication entitled *Bayrūt* (1991; Beirut). He has also published two books on his experience as a journalist, *Sahafī fi Amrīkā* (1963; a journalist in America) and *Min Makkah ilā Mūskū* (1971; from Mekka to Moscow). G.'s long list of publications in the 1980s and the early 1990s reveals a concentrated interest in political analysis, with little contribution to fiction.

One of G.'s merits is his ability to remain open to change in spite of his deeply rooted conservatism. He remains a monument on the cultural scene and a productive mind whose ability to write seems endless.

FURTHER WORKS: *Al-istiqlāliyyah* (1960); *Fī alislāah al-qarawī* (1961); *Hadhā huwa al-dustūr* (1962); *Fi al-thaqāfa wa-al-adab* (1964); *Māta qarīr al'ayn* (1964); *Difā' un'an al-dīmūqratiyyah* (1966); *Difā' 'anfann al-qawl* (1972); *Sirā madhhab waal-'aqīdah fi al-Qur'ān* (1973); *Ma'a al-adab waal-udabā* (1974); *Al-fikr al taqaddumī fi al-īdiyulujiyyah al-ta'āduliyyah* (1979); *Mujtama' almu'minīn* (n.d.); *'Ālam shā'ir al-Hamrā* (1982); *Wa-'āda al-zawraq ilā al-nab'* (1985?); *Al-Ta-tawwur al-dustūrī wa-al-niyābī bi-al-Maghrib min sanat 1908 ilāsanat 1978* (2 vols., 1988); *Limādhā inhārat al-shuyū'iyyah?* (1990)

BIBLIOGRAPHY: Tovimi, B. M., Khatibi, A., and Kably, M., *Écrivains marocains du protectorat à 1965, Anthologie* (1974): 81–93

—AIDA A. BAMIA

GHANAIAN LITERATURE

Ghana's independence on March 6, 1957 marked the first victory of the continent-wide movement to regain self-rule from colonial domination. Although English is the official language, Ghana is a multilingual society, and its current population of 18 million comprises Akan, Mole Dagbani, Ewe, Ga-Adangbe, and numerous other languages and dialects. Any study of Ghanaian literature must recognize not only its cultural and linguistic plurality, but also its diverse artistic modes. This approach fosters a perspective that is capable of accounting for the intricate aspects of the full creative web, and avoids the limitation of defining Ghanaian literature solely on the basis of the contributions of such major writers as Ama Ata AIDOO, Ayi Kwei ARMAH, Kofi AWOONOR, and Efua SUTHERLAND. This method also advances the investigation of the historical evolution, and the connections between the different modes of literature in Ghana.

Oral art is the earliest and the primary creative mode of expression in Ghana. It constitutes the first and sometimes the only experience of literature for most Ghanaians. Oral artists express themselves through both verbal and nonverbal symbolic languages that embody systems of aesthetics and beliefs that are meaningful within the traditions in which they are produced. The structure and social context of oral art reveal a number of identifiable genres: poetry (epic, panegyric, elegy; special purpose poems: war, hunting, and political song); prose (myths, historical narratives, legends, folktales, riddles, and proverbs); drama; drum language, and pseudo-literary nonverbal art forms (adinkra and kente designs).

Orality, much like writing, is amenable to fulfill various artistic functions: to embellish, to obscure, to create ambiguity and general aesthetic effect, and to communicate. Oral artists, like writers, learn complex techniques in order to be successful. They use formulaic expressions and other conventions for oral renditions. Its unique feature of deriving existence through performance, however, distinguishes oral from written literature. Any written version of an oral art pales when compared to an actual performance, which is often vivacious. At the same time, though, its inability to exist outside of performance raises challenges about the dissemination and, consequently, the authenticity of oral literature, causing some critics to dismiss it as a nonviable art form.

Kofi ANYIDLOHO and J. H. Kwabena Nketia (b. 1921), among others, have cautioned against giving cursory treatment to oral literature. In *Funeral Dirges of the Akan People* (1965) Nketia establishes that Akan dirges have structural regularity and formulaic expressions, though variations can occur depending on the social context. He found that the dirge singers take great care to maintain the conventions of the songs, to achieve the right tone, and to express messages as befitting the status of the deceased. The singing of dirges is combined with the social practices of exchange of greetings with the bereaved family, the pouring of libation, the required period of fasting, etc. Such contextual factors make the dirge part of the living traditions of the Akans.

Kofi Awoonor's *Guardians of the Sacred Word* (1974) is a transcription and translation of the Ewe traditional song of abuse, *halo*, which originated as a competition between rival songsters or *henowo* for supremacy in singing abusive songs. The poet or *heno* also uses gestures, voice modulation, and dance in synchrony with drum-beat. *Halo* competitions are usually staged in the village public square. The climax of the halo repertoire is *hatsatsia* or recitation or song chain. The *heno* consciously sets out to goad his opponent to anger and also to draw admiration from the audience. Awoonor's collection includes the works Komi Ekpa (dates n.a.) and Amega Dunya (dates n.a.), both of Tsiame, Volta region, two remarkable traditional poets.

Oral and nonverbal art forms are valued not only for their aesthetic qualities, but also as repositories of traditional knowledge. Moreover, the edifice of much of written literature in Ghana is based on the oral tradition. The oral tradition constitutes the staple and the source of inspiration for several Ghanaian writers. Awoonor's and Anyidoho's poetry is a harmonious blending of oral poetic ingredients within written forms. Atukwei Okai (b. 1941) has also attempted to structure his written poetry in the mode of orature so as to enhance its oral performance. Efua Sutherland harnesses the vital elements of the indigenous tradition for her creative writing. In *The Marriage of Anansewa* (1975) Sutherland relies on the paradigmatic trickster figure, Ananse, whose fertile imagination and roguish behavior create intrigue and ensure a storytelling atmosphere. A similar case can be made about the works of Armah and Aidoo which constitute a syncretism of oral and written forms. Thus, for its vitality as an expression of aesthetics within the traditional society, and as a reservoir for written literature, orature is a legitimate part of the literary system of Ghana.

Perhaps the earliest written works about Ghana were by Europeans such as Aphra Behn (1640-1689), notably in *Oronoko* (1688), who provided imprecise images of the African as existing within a "natural" state, thereby cultivating a myth of the black person as a "noble savage." Brandrand's *Annamaboe, Prince of the Royal Africa* (1720) reinforces European expectations about the primitive African. By the late 18th c., however, much Ghanaian writing came from a small group of educated Ghanaians living in Europe, mostly ex-slaves who wrote to galvanize the antislavery movement, to refute aspersions about blacks, and to protest the colonization of Africa. Anton Wilhem Amo's (1703-1754) *De Jure Maurorum* (1729) is a defense of the humanity and the intellectual capacity of the African, while Ottobah Cugoano's *Thoughts and Sentiments on the Evil and Wicked Traffic of the Slavery and Commerce of the Human Species* (1787) is a passionate indictment of the slavery system, and a bold denunciation of spurious arguments about the inferiority of black people. Amo and Cugoano inaugurate a protest tradition in Ghanaian literature.

From a historical point of view, writing on Ghana from within Ghana began in the 19th c. in the wake of colonial, Christian missionary, and Islamic influences. There are four main strands of such writing: translations of biblical works into local languages along with books on grammar and folklore, such as J. Zimmerman's *The Bible Translated into Ga* (1866) and J. G. Christaller's (1827-1895) *Grammar and Dictionary of the Asante and Fanti Language Called Tschi* (1875); travel literature by colonial officers, such as George Ekem Ferguson's *Report of a Mission to the Interior* (1892); journalistic and constitutional writing and occasional creative writing by early Ghanaian intellectuals, most notably Adelaide Casey-Hayford's (1868-1959) *Gold Coast Native Institutions* (1903); and writing in Arabic and *Ajami* (the use of Arabic alphabet for Hausa and other non-Arabic languages), which increasingly became important by the early decades of the 20th c.

Islamic writing is antecedent to the colonial and Christian missionary literacy programs. Thomas Hodgkins and Albert Gerard observe that by the last decade of the 18th c., writing in Arabic and *ajami* was common in northern Ghana. In *Mission From Cape Coast to Ashantee* (1819) T. E. Bowdich, a British colonial officer, reported that Asante rulers employed Moslem clerics. By the end of the 19th c. Salaga, Kete Krachi, and Wa had become important centers of Islamic learning. Among the major writers of that era were Sheik Umar Bamma who wrote a collection of poems in praise of Mohammed in 1863 and Malam al-Hasam who wrote a narrative poem about the Sudanese empires. But by far the most important Ghanaian Islamic writer was Al- Hajj Umar ibn al-Kanawi (1858-1934) of Kete Krachi whose career spanned from 1877 to 1930, and his writing was known in the entire Islamic world. Umar wrote over 1,200 poems including ''Mashra ma al-khabar li-warid washra bi l'nazar'' (1901), a protest poem against colonialism and Christian missions, and ''Suad Aw Asthma Aw dadow Hausa'' (1918), in praise of the people of Yendi. Umar deserves recognition as a major Ghanaian and West African writer.

Islamic learning was not widely disseminated in Ghana because it was practically restricted to religious leaders, and there was no concerted effort to educate ordinary believers. In contrast, the Christian missionaries who launched their activities in the 19th c. promoted literacy on a large scale. They adopted the Roman alphabet for writing in local languages, and provided support for the translations of the Bible into indigenous languages, and the transcriptions of orature. Moreover, the missions established schools, printing presses, and book depots, thereby laying foundations for the production, distribution, and, ultimately, the development of written literature in Ghana. Perhaps more than any other group, the missionaries provided the impetus for the emergency of Ghanaian literature.

The variations in the educational programs of the missions had some impact on Ghanaian writing. For example, the Wesleyans (from Britain) who settled in Cape Coast had less enthusiasm to learn and teach Fante compared to the Basel (Switzerland) and Bremane (Germany) who produced numerous educational materials and church literature in Akan-Akwapim and Ewe, respectively. In general, the missions created the appropriate environment for the growth of Ghanaian literature. With their involvement in developing writing, training readers and potential writers, and in providing facilities for the production of books, the Christian missions made a lasting contribution to Ghanaian literature.

Ironically, however, the first Ghanaian intellectuals to challenge colonial rule were educated under the auspices of the church. Discontent with some missionary teaching merged with general protest against colonial rule, especially the arbitrary appropriation of native land by Europeans. The leaders of the protest had access to newspapers such as the *West African Herald* and the *Gold Coast Times*, which became platforms for propagating nationalist sentiments, and which served as outlets for occasional creative works. The social and political discontent publicized by these early newspapers helped to shape the sensibilities of the writers of the day. To understand the course of Ghanaian literature, it is necessary to give consideration to these early newspapers. The era produced two highly stylized fictional works, Joseph E. Casely-Hayford's *Ethiopia Unbound* (1911) and Kobina Sekyi's (1892-1956) *The Blinkards* (1914). Casely-Hayford and Sekyi satirized educated Ghanaians who wear a veneer of Western culture. Both authors affirm indigenous values and race pride, a trend that connects them with early writers and later ones such as Armah and Awoonor.

It took nearly four decades before another fictional work in English of literary value, R. E. Obengs's *Eighteenpence* (1943) was produced. However, this period was dominated by writing in Ghanaian languages, mostly edifying works written under the auspices of missionaries. But there were occasional fictional works some of which won critical acclaim or attracted a large readership. For example, Kwasi Fiawoo's *Toko Atolia* (1937; The Fifth Landing-Stage) won the International Institute Award, London in 1937, and Sam Obianim's (b. 1920?) *Amegheto alo Agbezuge fe Natinya* (1949; Man or The Story of Agbezuge) has become a common reader in schools. Other notable publications include J. J. Addaye's *Bere Adu* (1913; The Hour Has Struck), a collection of short stories; Joseph Boakye Danquah's *Nyanonsem* (1941; Fables of the Celestial); and I. K. Hoh's *Sagbadre* (1940; The Swallow). Literature in Ghanaian languages received a tremendous boost from Kwame Nkrumah's government, which established the Bureau of Ghana Languages, which remains the major publisher of Ghanaian language writing. Since the 1960s, publication of Ghanaian language literatures has continued at a steady pace and would compare favorably in output and, in some instances, quality with Ghanaian literature in English.

The post-World War II period witnessed the emergence of popular literature whose subject and style have been designed for mass consumption. Its sensational subjects of crime and love, and predictable plot denouement appeal to a large readership. The successful purveyors of popular literature, for example, J. Benibengor Blay (b. 1915), author of such works as *Emelia's Promise* (1944) and *Love in a Clinic* (1957), and E. K. Mickison (dates n.a.), author of *When the Heart Decides* (1966), are entrepreneurs who write, publish, and market their own works.

The climate of general optimism which characterized the independence period was expressed through the publications of such works as *Voices of Ghana* (1958), edited by Henry Swanza and the journal, *Okyeame*. These works, as well as those of main writers like Michael Dei- Anang's (1909-1978) *Okomfo Anokye's Golden Stool* (1959), and R. E. G. Armattoe's (1913-1953) *Between The Forest and The Sea* (1950), are artistic expressions of a national cultural awakening.

Voices of Ghana and *Okyeame* introduced the early works of a number of writers who would establish their own voices in the 1960s. Since then Ghanaian literature has not only increased in output and quality, but it has also shown identifiable themes and styles. Besides the pseudo-autobiographies or bildungsromans, notably Joseph Abruquah's (b. 1921) *The Catchiest* (1965) and Francis Selormey's (b. 1927) *The Narrow Path* (1966), Ghanaian writers explored familiar themes with complexity. The ''Been-to'' syndrome theme in Sekyi's *The Blinkards* and Bidi Setsoafia's *Mede Ablotsidela* (1956; I Married a ''Been-To'') received fresh artistic explorations in Ama Ata Aidoo's *Dilemna of A Ghost* (1965) and Armah's *Fragment* (1971). Ghanaian writing in the mid-1960s was distinctively marked by feelings of cynicism and angst, reflecting the corruption in the post-Independence era. The malaise and disenchantment pervade such works as Camaron Doudu's (dates n.a.) *The Gab Boys* (1967) and Aidoo's *No Sweetness Here* (1970) and even in popular literature. But perhaps the most eloquent renditions of this mood are Armah's *The Beautiful Ones Are Not Yet Born* (1969) and Awoonor's *This Earth, My Brother* (1972).

Since the 1970s, an increasing number of Ghanaian writers have grafted the elements of oral and written literature. Other writers such as Sutherland and Meshack Asare have won acclaim for children's literature. Also, the issue of pan-Africanism, which is at the heart of Casely-Hayford's *Ethiopia Unbound*, has been given a complex treatment in Armah's *Two Thousand Seasons* and Kwabena Eyi Acquah's (dates n.a.) *Music For A Dream Dance* (1989). Armah's *Osiris Rising* (1995), and Awoonor's *Comes The Voyager At Last* (1992) are latest additions that explore the subject of the quest for meaning and coherence in global black experience. The growth in the economy and political stability since the mid-1980s have provided an impetus for Ghanaian literature, which has garnered momentum with the combined energy of the established voices of Armah, Awoonor and Anyidoho, for example, and new voices such as Kojo LAING, who experiments with the polyphonic novel, as in *Search Sweet Country* (1986) and *Major Gentl and The Achimota Wars* (1992).

BIBLIOGRAPHY: Priebe, R. K., *Ghanaian Literatures* (1988); Angmor, C., *Contemporary Literature in Ghana 1911-1978: A Critical Evaluation* (1996)

—CHRIS AWUYA

GHELDERODE, Michel de

(born Adhémar-Adolphe-Louis Martens) Belgian dramatist (writing in French), b. 3 April 1898, Ixelles; d. 1 April 1962, Schaerbeek

What little is known about G.'s biography can be found in *Les entretiens d'Ostende* (1956; partial tr., "The Ostend Interviews,") in *Seven Plays*, Vols. 1 and 2, 1960, 1964), radio interviews in which G. also discussed his dramatic theories and practices. G.'s father was principal clerk of the Archives Générales and wanted his son to enter the civil service too. G. did earn his living for some twenty years as an archivist, but he also had a second life in the "realm of dreams," in his words. At sixteen, during his convalescence from a near-fatal illness, he wrote his first poems, and as a youth he haunted the marionette theaters of Brussels; these puppet performances were to influence his work profoundly. In 1918 he wrote his first play, *La mort regarde à la fenêtre* (death looks in at the window), in the manner of Poe, for a literary group to which he belonged. In it one can see the characteristics of G.'s later theater: tension caused by hyperbolic plotting; blatant visual antitheses used as a foreshadowing technique; and a strange morality.

G.'s first substantial play was *La mort du Docteur Faust* (1926; *The Death of Doctor Faust*, 1964). In 1926 the director of the Flemish Popular Theater commissioned a play, *Saint François*

d'*Assise* (1927; Saint Francis of Assisi) from G. Adapting techniques from the popular arts, G. told his story not only through dialogue but through pantomime, dance, and acrobatics. The work was the beginning of a brief but fruitful association with this theater, in which his plays were performed in Flemish translation.

One of G.'s finest works, *Pantagleize* (written 1929, pub. 1934; *Pantagleize*, 1960), a "farce to make you sad," is a product of this period. It is about a Chaplinesque Everyman who, by his innocent remark "What a lovely day!", unwittingly triggers a series of events that lead to a revolution and his own death. It is a modern morality play, exploring man's predicament in an indifferent universe.

Two historical dramas from this period are among his most successful works. *Christophe Colomb* (1928; *Christopher Columbus*, 1964), somewhat EXPRESSIONIST, is a "dramatic fairy tale" that amusingly recounts, with many anachronisms, the adventures of Columbus in America. *Escurial* (1928; *Escurial*, 1957), set in 16th-c. Spain, deals with the rivalry of a king and his jester. Similar settings and characters, and indeed, the macabre ambience of the play, were to appear many more times in G.'s work.

A number of plays written for the Flemish Popular Theater were vehicles for the actor Renat Verheyen. When he died young in 1930, G. wrote *Sortie de l'acteur* (written 1930, pub. 1942; actor's exit) as a tribute; the "exit" of the actor is death, and the play is about the nature and mystery of theater itself.

Although G. wrote in French (and changed his name legally in 1929), he was of Flemish origin, and his spirit is distinctly Flemish. His inspirations were, along with the Elizabethan and Jacobean dramatists, the Flemish masters Breughel and Bosch, and the modern Belgian painter James Ensor, whose visions of masks and carnivals had a strong influence on G.'s work. A number of G.'s plays are based directly on Breughel's paintings, including *Les aveugles* (written 1933, pub. 1936; *The Blind Men*, 1960).

What he derived from this Flemish sensibility, particularly in his many plays set in medieval or Renaissance Flanders, was a sense of the grotesque, the macabre, and the satanic. A baroque, hallucinatory atmosphere pervades the plays, which are populated by dwarfs, hunch-backs, resurrected corpses, and devils. Sympathies are paradoxically elicited for unlikable figures. Horror, murder, decay, carnality, scatology, and death are all trademarks of G.'s theater. It could be called a theater of cruelty, although G.'s earlier works antedate the theoretical writings of Antonin ARTAUD. In *L'école des bouffons* (written 1937, pub. 1942; the school for buffoons) Folial, the jester of *Escurial*, reappears and suggests that the source of all true creativity is cruelty.

A prime example of G.'s violent, demonic spectacles is *Fastes d'enfer* (written 1929, pub. 1943; *Chronicles of Hell*, 1960), set in a decaying episcopal palace in medieval Flanders. A bishop, murdered by one of his unspeakably corrupt priests, returns from the dead, unable to rest until he has spat out the Host, which has been choking him. The play, palpitating with evil and cruelty, shocked Paris when it was produced at the Théâtre Marigny in 1949 by Jean-Louis Barrault, and a scandal ensued in which G. was accused of blasphemy and any number of other crimes, including lycanthropy. Other important plays in this mode are *Magie rouge* (written 1931, pub. 1935; *Red Magic*, 1964) and *Hop, Signor!* (written 1935, pub. 1938; *Hop, Signor!*, 1964).

G.'s dramas were almost unknown outside Belgium until 1947, when La Compagnie du Myrmidon presented *Hop, Signor!* in Paris. His fame increased with the *succès de scandale* of *Fastes d'enfer*, and G., who had been hitherto neglected, came to be recognized as a key figure in the avant-garde theater. Although by the late 1940s he was in bad health, he lived to see himself acknowledged as a forerunner of the THEATER OF THE ABSURD and as a playwright who particularly influenced the "cruel" theater of Jean Genet and Fernando Arrabal.

G. has great strengths but also some gaping flaws; at times his grotesqueries pall, the horror is exaggerated, and coarseness overtakes ribaldry. Yet his universe is unmistakably gripping. In G., the macabre is surrounded by true poetry.

FURTHER WORKS: *Le repas des fauves* (1918); *Piet Bouteille* (written 1918, pub. 1925; *Piet Bouteille*, 1964); *Le club des menteurs* (written c. 1920, pub. 1943); *Un soir de pitié* (written 1921, pub. 1929; *A Night of Pity*, 1964); *L'histoire comique de Keizer Karel* (1922); *La halte catholique* (1922); *Têtes de bois* (1924); *La farce de la mort qui faillit trépasser* (1925); *Les vieillards* (1925); *Le mystère de la Passion de Notre Seigneur Jésus-Christ* (1925); *Kwiebe-Kwiebus* (1925); *La corne d'abondance* (1925); *L'homme sous l'uniforme* (1925); *La tentation de Saint Antoine* (written 1925, pub. 1929); *Le massacre des innocents* (written 1926, pub. 1929); *Vénus* (1926); *Trois acteurs, un drame* (written 1926, pub. 1929; *Three Actors and Their Drama*, 1960); *La vie publique de Pantagleize* (1926); *Barabbas* (written 1928, pub. 1932; *Barabbas*, 1960); *Don Juan; ou, Les amants chimériques* (1928); *Les femmes au tombeau* (written 1928, pub. 1934; *The Women at the Tomb*, 1960); *Ixelles, mes amours* (1928); *La transfiguration dans le cirque* (1928); *Noyade des songes* (1928); *Duveloor; ou, La farce du diable vieux* (1931); *Arc-en-ciel* (1933); *Le chagrin d'Hamlet* (1933); *Chronique de Noël* (1934); *Les treize chansons de Pilou, chien* (1934); *D'un diable qui prêcha merveilles* (written 1934, pub. 1942); *Mademoiselle Jaïre* (written 1934, pub. 1942; *Miss Jairus*, 1964); *Sire Halewijn* (written 1934, pub. 1943; *Lord Halewyn*, 1960); *Le ménage de Caroline* (1935); *Le singulier trépas de Messire Ulenspiegel* (written 1935, pub. 1951); *La balade du Grande Macabre* (1935); *Masques ostendais* (1935); *Adrian et Jusemina* (1935); *La farce des ténébreux* (written 1936, pub. 1942); *La pie sur le gibet* (1938); *Le cavalier bizarre* (1938); *Sortilèges* (1941); *Le soleil se couche* (1942); *L'hôtel de Ruescas* (1943); *Mes statues* (1943); *Choses et gens de chez nous* (1943); *Voyage autour de ma Flandre* (1947); *Théâtre complet* (5 vols., 1950–1957); *Théâtre d'écoute* (1951); *Le perroquet de Charles Quint* (1951); *La folie d'Hugo Van der Goes* (1951); *La Flandre est un songe* (1953); *Marie la misérable* (1955); *La grande tentation de Saint Antoine* (1958); *Secret: Poèmes* (1960); *Sortilèges, et autres contes crépusculaires* (1962); *Lettres à Catherine Toth et André Reybaz, René Dupuy, Roger Iglésis, Jean Le Poulain, Marcel Lupovici, Gilles Chancrin, Georges Goubert* (1962); *M. de G. et Henri Vandeputte, correspondance: Autour d'une amitié naissante* (1964); *Le sommeil de la raison* (1967)

BIBLIOGRAPHY: Grossvogel, D. I., *20th Century French Drama* (1961): 254–310; special G. section, *TDR*, 8, 1 (1963): 11–71; Pronko, L. C., *Avant-Garde: The Experimental Theater in France* (1963): 165–80; Vandromme, P., *M. de G.* (1963); Francis, J., *L'éternel aujourd'hui de M. de G.: Spectographie d'un auteur* (1968); DeCock, J., *Le théâtre de M. de G.: Une dramaturgie de l'anti-théâtre et de la cruauté* (1969); Wellwarth, G. E., *The Theater of Protest and Paradox*, rev. ed. (1971): 111–26; Beyen, R., *G.* (1974); Parsell, D. B., *M. de G.* (1993)

—KENNETH S. WHITE

al-GHĪTĀNĪ, Jamāl

Egyptian novelist, short-story writer, and journalist, b. 9 May 1945, Juhaynah, Sūhāj Province

G. grew up in old Cairo. He was trained as a carpet designer and worked in this profession from 1962 to 1968. Since then he has been a full-time journalist with the daily *Akhbār al-Yawm*. Both carpet design, as an intricate and complex activity, and journalism have had an impact on the way he structures his novels and on their smooth style.

G. started publishing short stories in 1963. His first collection, *Awrāq shābb 'āsha mundhu alf 'ām* (1969; the papers of a young man who lived one thousand years ago), already showed a number of aspects that will characterize his later, more mature writings. This and the other short stories that he wrote and published can be seen as preliminary exercises in the process of writing his first novel, *Al-Zaynī Barakāt* (1974; *Al-Zayni Barakat*, 1988). This novel has been rightly considered one of the most interesting and important literary achievements of the post-Mahfūz generation of Egyptian writers. G.'s narrative strategy of juxtaposing many different narrative modes was a breakthrough within the context of the Arabic novel. He made use of the Mahfūzian realistic mode and that of reports of travelers, especially Europeans who visited the Middle East during the 18th and 19th cs. Yet the important addition was using the narrative mode of the late medieval Egyptian historian Ibn Iyās. With this G. opened new venues for the blending of the indigenous narrative traditions with those of the Western novel. The intricate structuring of the novel—the novel takes place during the first two decades of the 16th c., around the time of the Ottoman invasion of Egypt—with its different narrators and characters, coupled with the many analogies to the situation in Egypt during Nasser's reign and the War of 1967, and the successful use of native narrative modes, immediately turned this novel into an event in modern Arabic literature.

With the publication of his next novel, *Waqā'i' hārat al-Za'farānī* (1976; *Incidents in Zafrany Alley*, 1986), G. was still probing the different ways of using the native historical narrative modes, especially those of official reports and cumulative or incremental repetition. He developed a new and interesting literary language that blends the journalistic with the popular and the old classical Arabic. All these devices are used in portraying what happens in one of the quarters of Cairo during the first years of the reign of Sadat (1971–1972). In *Khitat al-Ghītānī* (1980; Ghitani's khitat)—the title refers to those writings in Egypt called *khitat*: encyclopedic descriptions rich with historical, social, and geographical information about the country—the influence of the popular linguistic modes was manifest. But G.'s other discovery was the language of the Muslim sufis—the medieval Muslim mystics. This is most manifest in his three-volume novel *Kitāb al-tajalliyyāt* (1983–1987; the book of revelations). The richness of the sufi linguistic and literary traditions is further explored in *Risālah fī al-sabābah wa-al-wajd* (1987; epistle on passion and ecstasy) and *Risālat al-basā'ir fī al-masā'ir* (1989; epistle of insights into destinies). Among G.'s other writings are collections of short stories and book-length interviews with literary and cultural figures like Najīb MAHFŪZ. He has also written much about the historical geography of Cairo, rendering masterfully the flavor of the old city. G. also wrote journalistic reports as a war correspondent, *al-Misriyyūn wal-al-harb* (1974; Egyptians and war) and *Hurrās al-bawwābah al-sharqīyyah* (1975; guards of the eastern gate), of high literary value, going well beyond mere journalistic descriptions of war heroism—comparable to his early collection of short stories, entitled *Ard . . . ard* (1972; surface to surface).

Despite the large amount of writing that G. has produced over two decades, he has generally been able to preserve the high quality that characterized his works since the beginning of his career. G.'s success has been the result of his ability to introduce formal innovations into the modern Arabic novel, especially through creative use of medieval Arabic prose traditions, without neglecting the traditions of Western realistic writing. His sense of history and place infuses his writings with a unique flavor. The enthusiastic reception of his works, especially the earlier novels, in Europe, and more recently in North America, is further proof that some of his works may become classics of Third World literature.

FURTHER WORKS: *al-zuwayl* (1975); *al-hisār min thalāth jihāt* (1975); *Hikāyāt al-gharīb* (1976); *alrifā'ī* (1978); *Dhikr mā jarā* (1978); *Najīb Mahfūz yatadhakkar* (1980); *Mustafā Amīn yatadhakkar* (1983); *Malāmih al-Qāhirah fī alf 'ām* (1983); *Asbilat al-Qāhira* (1984); *lthāf al-zamān bihikāyat Jalabī al-sultān* (1984); *Ahrāsh al-madīnah* (1984); *Thimār al-waqt* (1989); *Shath al-madīnah* (1990); *Yawmiyyātī al-mu'lanah* (1992); *Hātif al-maghīb* (1992); *Asfār al-mushtāq* (1992); *Min daftar al-'ishq wa-al-ghurbah* (1993); *Nafthat masdūr* (1993); *Mutūn al-Ahrām* (1994)

BIBLIOGRAPHY: Hegazy, S., *Littérature et société en Égypte* (1979): 71–72, 108–11; Ballas, S., *La littérature arabe et le conftit au proche-orient (1948–1973)* (1980): 150–51, 185–86; Tomiche, N., *Histoire de la littérature romanesque de Égypte moderne* (1981): 163–64, 197–200; Draz, C. K, "In Quest of New Narrative Forms," *JArabL*, 12 (1981): 140–44; Mehrez, S., *"Al-Zayni Barakat* Narrative As Strategy," *Arab Studies Quarterly*, 8, 2 (1986): 120–42; Allen, R., ed., *Modern Arabic Literature* (1987): 100–104; Hamarneh, W., "How To Tell a Story in Arabic: Some Narrative Modes in the Contemporary Arabic Novel," *Mundus Arabicus*, 5 (1992); Mehrez, S., "Alternative Fictional Histories: The Case of *Khitat al-Ghitani,"* *Mundus Arabicus*, 5 (1992)

—WALID HAMARNEH

GHOSE, Aurobindo

Indian poet, dramatist, and philosopher (writing in English and Bengali), b. 15 Aug. 1872, Calcutta; d. 5 Dec. 1950, Pondicherry

Educated in English-speaking schools in India and an honors graduate of Cambridge, A. was fluent not only in English and Bengali, but in Greek, Latin, Sanskrit, French, German, and Italian as well. His literary career divides roughly into two periods. The first is from 1893 to 1910, during which time he returned to India, taught in colleges in Baroda and Calcutta, and wrote numerous political and literary pieces for several English- and Bengali-language newspapers and journals. His first major collection of lyric poems, *Songs to Myrtilla*, appeared in 1895, followed by a number of other important works, including the narrative poem *Love and Death* (1921), several blank-verse plays, notably *Perseus the Deliverer* (1907), and the first draft of his magnum opus, *Savitri: A Legend and a Symbol*, published in its final form in 1950–51.

At this time A. came under the influence of the well-known Yogi Lele and started to practice yoga. An ardent nationalist, A. was implicated in a bomb-throwing incident in 1908, for which he was jailed. While awaiting trial he underwent a profound mystical experience in which he said he witnessed the presence of God (Narayana). As a result, he underwent a major personality change. Acquitted of terrorist charges, A. was released, but due to harassment by the British authorities, he retired to the French mandate of Pondichéry (now Pondicherry) in 1910, established an ashram, or spiritual retreat, and remained there for the rest of his life.

At Pondicherry A. completed many of his best-known works, including *The Ideal of Human Unity* (1919), *The Renaissance in India* (1920), *The Life Divine* (1940), *Collective* [sic] *Poems and Plays* (1942), *The Synthesis of Yoga* (1948), *Heraclitus* (1949), *The Human Cycle* (1949), and *Essays on the Gita* (1950). Numerous other works, while completed at various times in his life, were published long after they were written, many posthumously. In 1920 Madame Mirra Richard, subsequently known as "The Mother," joined the settlement, and in 1926, after A. underwent another profound mystical experience—a vision of the god Krishna—she took complete charge of the ashram. For the next twelve years A. went into virtual isolation but kept close contact with disciples through letters. Toward the end of his life he appeared before his devotees on special viewing, or *darshan*, days and continued to write prolifically and to translate Sanskrit works.

While his writings are in the main philosophical, A.'s literary pieces can be looked upon as extensions or elaborations of this larger philosophical view. Essentially A. views the cosmos as having undergone a process of devolution from the pure stage of Absolute Spirit (*sacchidanand*, or "existence-consciousness-bliss") to supermind, mind, and matter, where it languishes at present. According to A., the time has come for the cosmos to evolve once again to that original pristine state of deathlessness, perfection, and infinity. In this process man will become a God-man, possessing not only physical but spiritual superpowers. Ultimately, man as well as the cosmos will achieve perfection.

Opinions vary widely as to the quality of A.'s writings. Some critics, many of them his devotees, contend that he is a sublime literary artist who matches, or even surpasses, Dante and Milton. Others submit that his writings are abstruse, muddled, and have received attention not because of any inherent literary merit, but rather because of the enthusiasm of A.'s zealous followers. Such judgments aside, A. has exercised a considerable influence on a large number of creative writers in both Indian vernacular literatures and in English literature written by Indians.

FURTHER WORKS: *Urvasie* (c. 1896); *Two Lectures* (1908); *An Open Letter to His Countrymen* (1909); *Ahana and Other Poems* (1915); *The Ideal Karmayogin* (1919); *Uttapara Speech* (1919); *Dayananda: The Man and His Work* (1920); *Evolution* (1920); *Ideals and Progress* (1920); *War and Self-Determination* (1920); *The Age of Kalidasa* (1921); *The Brain of India* (1921); *A System of National Education* (1921); *The Yoga and Its Object* (1921); *Baji Prabhou* (1922); *Man: Slave or Free?* (1922); *The National Value of Art* (1922); *Speeches* (1922); *The Need in Nationalism and Other Essays* (1923); *Rishi Bunkim Chandra* (1923); *The Mother* (1928); *Kalidasa* (1929); *The Riddle of This World* (1933); *Six Poems* (1934); *Lights on Yoga* (1935); *Bases of Yoga* (1936); *Sri A.: A Life* (1937); *Swami Dayanand Saraswati* (1939); *Bankim—Tilak— Dayananda* (1940); *Poems, Views and Reviews* (1941); *On Quantitative Metre* (c. 1942); *On the War* (1944); *Poems: Past and*

Present (1946); *Words from Long Ago: The Mother* (1946); *Letters of Sri A.* (First Series, 1947; Second and Third Series, 1949; Fourth Series, 1951); *The Significance of Indian Art* (1947); *The Spirit and Form of Indian Polity* (1947); *The Doctrine of Passive Resistance* (1948); *More Lights on Yoga* (1948); *After the War* (1949); *Chitrangada* (1949); *Conversations of the Dead* (1951); *Letters of Sri A. on The Mother* (1951); *The Phantom Hour* (1951); *Science and Culture* (1951); *Last Poems* (1952); *Life—Literature—Yoga* (1952); *The Problem of Rebirth* (1952); *Sayings of Sri A. and The Mother* (1952); *The Supramental Manifestation upon Earth* (1952); *Elements of Yoga* (1953); *The Foundations of Indian Culture* (1953); *The Future Poetry* (1953); *The Mind of Light* (1953); *Sri A. on Himself and on The Mother* (1953); *Bankim Chandra Chatterji* (1954); *Correspondence with Sri A.* (1954); *Kalidasa* (Second Series, 1954); *Views on National Problems* (First and Second Series, 1954); *On the Veda* (1956); *Vyasa and Valmiki* (1956); *Illion: An Epic in Quantitative Hexametres* (1957); *More Poems* (1957); *Vasavadutta* (1957); *On Yoga* (Second Series, 1958); *Thoughts and Aphorisms* (1958); *The Hour of God* (1959); *The Viziers of Bassora* (1959); *Eric: A Dramatic Romance* (1960); *On Nationalism* (1965); *Sri Aravinder mul bangla racavali* (1969); *Bande Mataram: Early Political Writings* (1972); *The Chariot of Jagganath* (1972); *Light to Superlight* (1972); *New Lamps for Old* (1974)

BIBLIOGRAPHY: Roy, A., *Sri A. and the New Age* (1940); Mitra, S., *Sri A. and Indian Freedom* (1948); Langly, G. H., *Sri A.: Poet, Philosopher and Mystic* (1949); Srinivasa Iyengar, K. R., *Sri A.: A Biography* (1950); Diwakar, R. R., *Mahayogi: Life, Sadhana and Teachings of A.* (1954)

—CARLO COPPOLA

GHOSE, Zulfikar

Indo-Pakistani-American novelist, poet, short-story writer, and essayist, b. 13 Mar. 1935, Sialkot, India (now Pakistan)

G. and his oeuvre defy categorization by nationality. Born in a city that was in India until 1947, and thereafter in Pakistan, he moved with his Punjabi-speaking family to Bombay in 1942, where he, a Muslim, was educated in an English-medium school run by Italian priests. He immigrated to England in 1952, graduating from the University of Keele in 1959 with a degree in philosophy. A journalist for the *Observer*, G. revisited India and Pakistan for the first time in 1965. He married the Brazilian painter Helena de la Fontaine, and in 1966 traveled extensively for the first time throughout Brazil, later the setting for six of his nine novels. In 1969 he joined the faculty of the University of Texas at Austin, where he teaches English literature and creative writing. His works are variously categorized as British, American, Indian, Pakistani, Commonwealth, and even Brazilian or Latin American.

G. made his literary debut as a poet with *The Loss of India* (1964), many poems of which nostalgically recall his Indian boyhood and treat the persistent themes of rootlessness and alienness, which are found throughout much of his writing. These same themes dominate both his autobiography, *Confessions of a Native-Alien* (1965), and his second volume of poems, *Jets from Orange* (1967). In *The Violent West* (1972) the landscape of his poems

shifts dramatically from the Indian subcontinent and Britain, and becomes distinctively American.

His first novel, *The Contradictions* (1966), is set partly in India during the Raj, partly in the Hampshire countryside. Many critics remarked on the elegant, concise, chiseled quality of the prose. G. has said that he deliberately set his second novel, *The Murder of Aziz Khan* (1967), in Pakistan to prove that he could, in fact, write such a piece. A classic case study of the violent confrontation of rural and urban, tradition and modernity, the story of the novel could be told about any Third World country. Critically acclaimed, the book is written in a prose that is often elevated to poetry.

G.'s next novels form a massive trilogy, *The Incredible Brazilian The Native* (1972), *The Beautiful Empire* (1975), and *A Different World* (1978). Set in Brazil, these works follow their picaresque hero, Gregório Peixoto de Silva Xavier, through three reincarnations, each in a different critical period of Brazil's history: the 17th, the 19th, and the 20th cs. respectively. Blending MAGIC REALISM, ultra-Byronic exploits, and sex, these works are considered G.'s finest to date.

His next two novels, set in Britain and the U.S. respectively, show a number of affinities: scathing indictments of contemporary Western civilization, a postmodern manipulation of the novel form, and a virtuosic handling of the English language. *Crump's Terms* (1976) presents the stream-of-consciousness cerebrations of the Middlesex schoolmaster Crump, a masterful punster and manipulator of quotes, who feels that Western civilization, especially that of Britain (which he abhors) and of France (which he adores), is rapidly decaying. Futility, in Crump's view, is the "final" human condition. The metafictionally dense *Hulme's Investigations into the Bogart Script* (1981) is a tabulation of nine separate scripts that often blend with and sometimes contradict one another as they excoriate contemporary American life.

For his remaining novels, all prodigally imbued with magical realism, G. returns to a South American setting. *A New History of Torments* (1982) is the story of Martin Kessel, an idealist gone awry in his unbridled pursuit of money and power. *Don Bueno* (1984) recalls many features of the trilogy, with Don Bueno as the sobriquet of one Calderón, who is then reincarnated as three different men, each living out a different, yet the same, destiny. Dreams are a major feature of *Figures of Enchantment* (1986), in which Gamboa, a government statistician, dreams of winning the lottery and retiring to an island; after his arrest at a political demonstration, Gamboa's dream is fulfilled, for he is banished to one.

In his writings G. seems to be obsessed with Brazil. It has been suggested that Brazil is, in fact, G.'s substitution in local for South Asia. He readily admits that Rio de Janeiro put him in mind of 1940s Bombay, and that one could easily substitute a large Bombay or Hyderabadi family for that of *The Incredible Brazilian*. Because he defies a facile national categorization as a writer, G. might be called multicultural, a label he would probably deny, preferring instead to be called British.

In spite of publication by the best presses, consistently excellent reviews, and translation into the major European languages, G.'s works have not received extensive critical treatment, very likely because scholars have been unable to pigeonhole him by nationality. Recently, however, this situation has begun to change, in part thanks to South-Asian literary specialists who, in addition to admiring the structural sophistication and linguistic brilliance of his novels, view G.'s Brazil as both a substitute India or Pakistan and as Anywhere. These scholars have been instrumental in bringing G. to the attention of the larger academic community and in giving his works well-deserved critical attention.

FURTHER WORKS: *Statement against Corpses* (1964, with B. S. Johnson); *Hamlet, Prufrock and Language* (1978); *The Fiction of Reality* (1983); *A Memory of Asia:* New and Selected Poems (1984); *The Deccan Queen* (1987); *Selected Poems* (1991); *The Art of Creating Fiction* (1991); *The Triple Mirror of Self* (1992); *Shakespeare's Mortal Knowledge* (1993)

BIBLIOGRAPHY: Mukherjee, M., "G., Z.," *Contemporary Poets* (1975): 541–43; New, W., "G., Z.," *Contemporary Novelists* (1976): 511–13; Kohli, D., "Landscape and Poetry," *JCL*, 13, 3 (April 1979): 54–70; Hobsbaum, P, "G., Z.," *Contemporary Poets* (1980): 644–46; Hashmi, A., "Tickling and Being Tickled à la Z. G.," *CNIE*, 1, 2 (1982): 32–38; Kanaganayakam, C., "Z. G.: An Interview," *TCL*, 32, 2 (Summer 1986): 169–86; Vassanji, M., "A Conversation with Z. G.," *Toronto South Asian Review*, 4, 2 (1986): 14–21; Stoerck, B., "New Fiction by Z. G.," *Pakistan Literature: The Contemporary English Writers*, 2nd ed. (1987): 97–104; special G. section, *RCF*, 9, 2 (1989): 103–237; Hashmi, A., "A Stylized Motif of Eagle Wings Woven," *WLT*, 66 (Winter 1992): 66–69; Kanaganayakam, C., *Structures of Negation: The Works of Z. G.* (1993)

—CARLO COPPOLA

GIARDINELLI, Mempo

Argentine novelist, short-story writer, essayist, and journalist, b. 2 Aug. 1947, Resistencia

G. was born and raised in the northern province of Chaco in Argentina, and this rich landscape bordering Paraguay provides the foundation for his narrative production. From 1969 until 1976 he developed his career as a journalist in Buenos Aires, which is the cultural hub of Argentina, and remained there until the military dictatorship, which instituted a period of bloody repression and state-imposed violence, caused him to leave his country for exile. G. spent 1976-85 in Mexico, where he lived an extremely productive life as a writer, editor, publisher, and professor at the Universidad Iberoamericana. In the short period of 1980-84, G. published his first four novels, one volume of stories, and a collection of essays on the *noir* genre—all originally published outside his native Argentina. The linguistic, geographic, and social displacements occasioned by his exile from Argentina are a central issue in his writing, and, as with others from his generation, they directly inform his literary output. G. has been a visiting professor at several U.S. universities, including Wellesley College, University of Virginia, and University of Louisville, and he regularly speaks throughout the U.S. at different universities. In 1985, after the restoration of democracy in his country, G. settled in Buenos Aires. In 1994 he returned to reside in the northern area of his country, where he became an honorary professor of the Universidad Nacional del Nordeste, although he still spends time both in Buenos Aires and the U.S.

G.'s earliest literary production establishes his native Chaco province as the narrative space of telling. *La revolución en bicicleta* (1980; The Revolution on a Bicycle), for instance, recaptures the historic moment of the 1947 Paraguayan civil war through the story of a retired Paraguayan army officer who waits for the call to revolution. This move from the geographically central to the periphery is significant not only because it represents a break with the literary domination of the urban setting (Buenos Aires) in Argentine literature, but also because G. does not simply revert to the "social realism" style of the regional novel from earlier in the 20th-c. with its Manichean oversimplifications and moral commentary. Rather, G. develops a hybrid display of linguistic innovation, humor, parodic wit, and fast-paced dialogue, all features of the so-called post-boom literary movement in Latin America, to which G.'s writing is often linked.

G.'s three middle novels, written while in exile in Mexico, are clear products of the dictatorship years of Argentine literary production. All three explore the effects of exile and the resultant displacements of national identity. The texts explore not Argentine "identity" per se, but rather set up and recreate an Argentina turned inside out and filtered through geographic transference. Thus, the texts contemplate the burdens of history and issues of collusion, guilt and accountability with the history-makers and political figures of society. Both *El cielo en las manos* (1981; Heaven in One's Hands) and *Luna caliente* (1983; Hot Moon), which won the Mexican Premio Nacional de Novela, consider relations of power and identity through erotic themes: in this way, G. explores the intimate connections of public and private forms of power and aggression. One can perceive their roots in the tango and Argentine popular culture, with "transcultural" elements grafted from the Mexican culture, such as binational speech patterns and Rulfo-like ghostly images. Both *Luna caliente*—which also was made into a film in 1985—and his next novel, *Qué solos se quedan los muertos* (1985; How Lonely Are the Dead) adopt features of the hard-boiled detective novel. The protagonists are "ordinary" individuals sucked into extraordinary situations that force them to make difficult choices. The narrative styles are fast-paced and colloquial, full of violent allusions that are both condemnatory while also, perhaps, offering the reader a chance to work through the violence of Argentina's recent history.

In his next work G. contemplates the following dilemma: how does one reconstruct a cultural tradition in the wake of a national tragedy of staggering proportions? G.'s 1991 magnum opus, *Santo oficio de la memoria* (1991; The Holy Office of Memory), which in 1993 won one of the most prestigious awards given in Hispanic letters, the Rómulo Gallegos, is clearly a product of post-dictatorship and of post-exile. This polyphonic text with multiple narrators is the family saga of the Domeniconelle family, and spans almost one hundred years of Argentine history and international cultural production. It attempts to write back through Argentina's past to trace a multiple but simultaneously collective genealogy of Argentine culture. There is no omniscient voice of truth, but rather, in the accumulation of multiple voices, cultural traces, and the recuperation of lost stories, the reader is urged to reconstruct and recollect a heterogeneous while simultaneously collective memory base. G.'s novel, *Imposible equilibrio* (1995; Impossible Balance), returns to a more local and popular literary form: the adventure novel. A humorous, ironic, and parodic novel with possible allegorical overtones, it builds on a rather extravagant story line: the importation of African hippopotamuses, in order to restore safe water conditions to the waters of the Chaco province, and the ensuing abduction of the animals. It seems to fall within the scope of fiction of the 1990s in much of Latin America: the restless search for narrative meaning and solutions in an age of cultural insecurity.

While his novels are often ambitious and grand in scope and innovative in style, it is in G.'s short stories where one can truly admire the work of a well-crafted literary text. G. was founder and director from 1986 to 1992 of the literary magazine *Puro Cuento*, has written a book on the genre, *Así se escribe un cuento* (1992; This Is How One Writes a Story), and has published numerous anthologies of stories, both his own and thematic collections including various writers. Critically, G. is perhaps Argentina's leading "expert" on the short story, and he joins a long line of famous short-story writers, including the names of Jorge Luis BORGES, Julio CORTÁZAR, and Roberto ARLT, among many others.

FURTHER WORKS: *Vidas ejemplares* (1982); *¿Por qué prohibieron al circo?* (1983); *La entrevista* (1986); *Antologiía personal* (1987); *Luli la viajera* (1988); *El castigo de Dios* (1993)

BIBLIOGRAPHY: Marcos, J., "M. G. in the Wake of Utopia," *Hispania,* 70 (1987): 240-49; O'Connell, P., "Individual and Collective Identity through Memory in Three Novels of Argentina's 'El Proceso,'" *Hispania,* 81 (1988): 31-41; Kohut, K., ed., *Un universo cargado de violencia. Presentación, aproximación y documentación de la obra de M. G.* (1990); Stone, K., "M. G. and the Anxiety of Borges's Influence," *Chasqui,* 23 (1994): 83-90; Pellón, G., "Ideology and Structure in G.'s *Santo oficio de la memoria*," *SETCL,* 19 (1995): 81-99

—LORI HOPKINS

GIBRAN, Kahlil

(also known as Jubrān Khalīl Jubrān) Lebanese-American mystic poet, short-story writer, and artist (writing in Arabic and English), b. 6 Jan. 1883, Bsharri, Lebanon; d. 10 Apr. 1931, New York, N.Y., U.S.A.

Born in Lebanon, G. emigrated at twelve to the U.S. to settle first in Boston, then in New York. He returned to Beirut (1897–1901) to study Arabic at al-Hikma College, after which he spent two years in Paris (1908–1910) studying art at the expense of Mary Haskell, his lifelong friend and benefactress. Upon his death, his body was shipped back to his hometown in Lebanon, where alongside his tomb the G. Museum was later established.

G. began his literary career writing Arabic and contributing to journals published by the Lebanese and Arab communities in the U.S. He became the founding president of the Society of the Pen, a literary association of Arab-Americans whose aim was to revolutionize the classically conservative Arabic literature at home.

G.'s first work, *al-Mūsīqā* (1905; music), a short panegyric on music, displays in rudimentary form the basic elements that were to characterize his future writings: a resonant flowery language with a prophetic biblical tone and a deep sense of solitude coupled with nostalgia for a platonic homeland. Next followed two collections of short stories, *'Arā'is al-murūj* (1906; *Nymphs of the Valley*, 1949) and *al-Arwāh al-mutamarridah* (1908; *Spirits Rebellious*, 1949), and a novelette, *al-Ajnihah al-mutakassirah* (1912; *The Broken Wings*, 1957). These works, though hailed in their time as pioneer works of Arabic fiction, were actually no more than literary devices for G. to elaborate his ideas. The principal characters are made to

Kahlil Gibran

denounce with prophetic authority the evils that disfigure the image of the cherished Lebanese homeland: a church order portrayed as the antagonist of Christ, allied with a despotic oligarchy. Typical is the protagonist of "Khalīl al-Kāfir" ("Khalil the Heretic") in *al-Arwāh al-mutamarridah*, who, in a kind of a Socratic apology in the village square, rallies all the villagers behind him and puts the priest and the landlord, his accusers, to flight.

As G.'s homeland becomes increasingly platonic, his prophetic attack in subsequent collections, particularly in *al-'Awāsif* (1920; the tempests), broadens to include humankind at large. Humans are depicted in their terrestrial existence to be living as apes, heedless of their transcendental origin. Yūsuf al-Fakhrī in the title story finds it below his dignity to associate with humankind. His prototype in "Haffār al-Qubūr" (the grave digger) finds society stinking for lack of sufficient graves.

As English started to replace Arabic in G.'s works beginning with *The Madman* (1918), and as his audience became international, his rebellion became artistically more convincing. In this collection, the crude story form, hitherto rhetorical and didactic, gives way to the mystically impregnated parable, prose poem, and allegory in which G.'s poetic genius found its best expression.

Reassured by the immediate recognition brought him by *The Madman*, G. the rebel becomes more conciliatory in his second collection of parables, *The Forerunner* (1920). It was not until his main work, *The Prophet* (1923), however, that his rather biblical theme of prophet/condemner finally develops into the prophet/ guide and redeemer. Almustapha breaks his twelve years of mystic silence among the people of Orphalese, presumably his and everybody's country of "exile," to answer their queries before he is divinely rehabilitated. The resulting twenty-six sermons are meant as passageways between humans in bondage and humans emancipated. A masterly blend in a biblical style of the poetic, the mystical, and the allegorical, *The Prophet*, for several years a bestseller in the U.S., remains G.'s masterpiece. Patterned after Almustapha in an attempt to give him a more masculine image, Jesus in *Jesus the Son of Man* (1928), proves too biblically exacting to be as freely molded as his prototype, and too poeticized to be historically convincing.

Published two weeks before his death, *The Earth Gods* (1931) is G.'s attempt at approaching *The Prophet* in poetic excellence. A dialogue in free verse between three titans on the human destiny, the book betrays the three mental states now struggling in G. for final supremacy: the rebel/nihilist, the prophet/redeemer, and a third who is disenchanted with both and ends up supreme in the dialogue. Standing for sheer human love, in preference to the divine, this third titan is indicative of a budding but short-lived new state in G.'s writing. Of the two posthumous works, *The Wanderer* (1932), a collection of parables, belongs to an earlier date, while *The Garden of the Prophet* (1933) is partly apocryphal.

This tendency toward the human in G.'s work, which only came to be stresed in his later writings, was always detectable in his art. Though concerned with the transcendental, his drawings and paintings are steeped with a human intimacy of exceptional tenderness. Naked human bodies of both sexes, painfully supple and tenderly intertwined, form the basic language of G.'s art as well as its distinctive feature.

A bilingual writer, G. has managed to excel in both languages. In his country of origin, he is associated with the literary revival that ushered Arabic literature out of its medievalism into the 20th c. Orientally prophetic in expression, style, and spiritual content, his English works, on the other hand, especially *The Prophet*, address Western readers, and have succeeded in exercising on them an effect akin to the biblical. G., it would seem, is one of those few writers in modern times in whose works East and West do actually meet.

FURTHER WORKS: *Dam'ah wa ibtisāmah* (1914; *A Tear and a Smile*, 1950); *al-Mawākib* (1919; *The Procession*, 1958); *al-Badā'i' wa-al-tarā'if* (1923). FURTHER WORKS IN ENGLISH: *Twenty Drawings* (1919); *Sand and Foam* (1926); *Prose Poems* (1934); *Secrets of the Heart* (1947); *A Treasury of K. G.* (1951); *Thoughts and Meditations* (1961); *A Second Treasury of K. G.* (1962); *The Voice of the Master* (1963); *Mirrors of the Soul* (1965); *The Wisdom of G.: Aphorisms and Maxims* (1966); *Spiritual Sayings* (1970); *Prophesies of Love* (1971); *Lazarus and His Beloved* (1973); *K. G.: Paintings and Drawings* 1905–1930 (1989)

BIBLIOGRAPHY: Bragdon, C. F., *Merely Players* (1939): 139–47.; Young, B., *This Man from Lebanon* (1945); Naimy, M., *K. G.:His Life and His Work* (1950); Otto, A. S., *The Parables of K. G.: An Interpretation of his Writings and His Art* (1963); Hawi, K. S., *K. G.: His Background, Character, and Works* (1963); Gibran, J., and K. Gibran, *K. G., His Life and World* (1974); Bushrui, S. B., and P., Gotch, eds., *G. of Lebanon: New Papers* (1975); Naimy, N., *The Lebanese Prophets of New York* (1985): 35–56; Shehadi, W., *K. G.: A Prophet in the Making* (1991)

—NADEEM NAIMY

GIDE, André

French novelist, essayist, and dramatist, b. 22 Nov. 1869, Paris; d. 19 Feb. 1951, Paris

Born into a Protestant family with a Catholic branch, with relatives in both Provence and Normandy, G. insisted that his divided nature could be harmonized only through literary expression. After his father's premature death, he was raised by his Calvinist mother, whose influence was harshly repressive. His cousin and childhood confidant Madeleine Rondeaux, whom he married in 1895, shortly after his mother's death, replaced her psychologically, and G.'s love for her always remained idealized and asexual. His marriage also followed two trips to North Africa, where he had discovered the sensual delights of a primitive, "pagan" society and had been introduced to pederasty by Oscar Wilde. The dichotomy between sexual pleasure and the secularized Calvinism his pure love of "Em" (as he referred to his wife) represented, and G.'s effort to harmonize the two, is the subject of his best work.

His earliest works show the influence of Schopenhauer and of Mallarmé, to whose SYMBOLIST literary circle G. belonged. By the late 1890s the influences of Nietzsche and Goethe had helped liberate him from his early aestheticism. For the next twenty years he attempted in his writing to balance this liberating force with the severe restraints which were an integral part of his being and which gave his work a classical purity of form. G. had been one of the founders of the influential *Nouvelle revue française* in 1909, but he gained celebrity as a writer only in the early 1920s, with the publication of *Pages choisies* (1921; selected pages) from his earlier works and the open avowal of his homosexuality in *Corydon* (1924 [privately pub. 1911]; *Corydon*, 1950). *Voyage au Congo* (1927; *To the Congo*, in *Travels in the Congo*, 1929) and *Le retour du Tchad* (1928; *Back from the Chad*, in *Travels in the Congo*, 1929), where he exposed deplorable treatment of the natives and colonial corruption in French Equatorial Africa, launched a decade of involvement with social and political causes, including a brief, regretted flirtation with communism in the mid-1930s. G.'s creative writing continued, however, and he was awarded the Nobel Prize for literature in 1947.

G.'s earliest work, *Les cahiers d'André Walter* (1891; *The Notebooks of André Walter*, 1968), expresses the fundamental conflict between the "angel" and the "beast" within him. His fictional André, as G. himself did, preserves the purity of his love for "Emmanuèle" by renouncing it (the symbolist ideal), then fails, after her death, to maintain it against the demands of the flesh. Besides stating explicitly his erotic dichotomy, G. already uses here the narcissistic device of a hero trying unsuccessfully to finish a book on the same subject as G.'s book.

Paludes (1895; *Marshlands*, 1953) satirizes the stifling atmosphere of the symbolist literary salons G. had frequented before his liberating trips to North Africa. The protagonist sees the hollowness of this life where no one is capable of an original thought, or even of expanding his physical horizons (and writing a book about it), but he cannot break its grip. G., having broken its grip, can return to it only with a satirical perspective.

G.'s real liberation, however, is expressed in *Les nourritures terrestres* (1897; *Fruits of the Earth*, in *Fruits of the Earth*, 1949), in which the angelic and the demonic are not in conflict, but are harmonized. Love of life, spontaneity, desire, pleasure, and freedom are interwoven with the themes of fervor, of the stripping away of acquired culture, and of the purity of the present moment. The longings of the body and the aspirations of the spirit have the same object: the concrete, immediate reality of God. G. unites eroticism and evangelism against the restrictions of conventional morality. His spontaneous, direct poetic rhetoric is an expression of revolt against form as well. This text, which contains the essential of G.'s "doctrine," went largely unnoticed, however, until World War I had effectively destroyed the basis for traditional morality and the withdrawal from society implicit in the symbolist attitude.

The play *Saül* (1897; *Saul*, 1952) was a kind of antidote to *Les nourritures terrestres* as *Paludes* had been to *Les cahiers d'André Walter*. It depicts the undermining of the power and authority of the biblical king by the "demons" of his own sensual weakness, and thereby warns of the dangers inherent in the complete individual freedom extolled in *Les nourritures terrestres*. G.'s Saul is a tragic figure dominated by erotic and religious drives similar to his creator's, which he cannot control and which destroy him and those he loves.

L'immoraliste (1902; *The Immoralist*, 1930), G.'s first *récit*, or short psychological novel, presents a subtler, less tragic hero, Michel, whom he could have become, as he said later, if he had not become himself. Michel discovers the value of life, as G. had, through convalescence from tuberculosis in North Africa. He successfully reconciles this new dimension with his traditional, civilized career as a scholar, at least for a time. His return to the stuffy Paris literary salons and his wife's illness and subsequent miscarriage, which occurs while he is being convinced of the necessity of choice by an old acquaintance resembling Oscar Wilde, force Michel, however, to recognize the fragility of the equilibrium he has established. Eventually Michel chooses a self-cultivation which is destructive of all that represents the traditional side of his character, including his wife (hence the title). Again G. attacks the traditional European bourgeois society, but also the unrestrained destructive freedom Michel claims for himself.

La porte étroite (1909; *Strait Is the Gate*, 1924) served as a counterweight to *L'immoraliste*. In this novel, which also contains many autobiographical elements, G. explored the consequences of excessive and misunderstood Calvinist piety, which cuts the youthful Jérôme and Alissa off from social and sexual reality and eventually destroys Alissa. Although *La porte étroite* was received more favorably than *L'immoraliste* in traditional social and literary circles, the book also criticizes the arranged marriage. More importantly, it presents us, like *L'immoraliste*, with a possible resolution, also rejected by G., of his moral-sexual dilemma, his need to separate totally spiritualized love and hedonistic sensuality.

In *La symphonie pastorale* (1919; *The Pastoral Symphony*, 1931), the last of G.'s *récits*, a Protestant minister who awakens to life a blind, deaf-mute adolescent girl, but who teaches her only the gospel of love, is unaware of his own motives, the sexual nature of his attraction to her, and of the effect of his actions on his family. When she regains her sight and becomes aware of her mentor's unwitting evil, of evil in the world in general, and of the sorrow she has caused, she commits suicide. The novel is a direct statement of some of G.'s religious meditations during World War I, but it is also a veiled allusion to his first "real" infidelity to his wife and an admission of the impossibility of maintaining a separation and balance between pure love and sensual pleasure.

There is much self-irony here, as there had been in *Les caves du Vatican* (1914; *Lafcadio's Adventures*, 1928). G. called this work a *sotie*, after the late medieval satirical farces, which presented

André Gide

exaggerated parodies of Church ceremonies and of other institutions, and it is structurally and psychologically more complex than the three *récits*. Here we meet Lafcadio, young and ostensibly rootless (no father or nationality)—G. as he (perhaps) would like to have been—and without responsibility. He discovers, however, first family relationships and then that his "gratuitous act" of throwing an unknown man from a railroad carriage does in fact entail responsibilities he could not have foreseen. Through the device of a supposed impostor in the Vatican and Lafcadio's interaction with three very different, but very bourgeois brothers-in-law (one of whom, it turns out, is his new-found half-brother and another the man he gratuitously pushed off the train), G. treats the problem of human potential, freedom, and responsibility in a more openly satirical manner than in the novels previously discussed. The three brothers-in-law each glimpse a potential freedom, then reject it, and Lafcadio's encounter with responsibility is left inconclusive.

In 1908 G. had discovered Dostoevsky, whose spirit may be glimpsed in *Les caves du Vatican*, and in 1922 he delivered a series of public lectures on the Russian novelist, while composing his most ambitious novel, *Les faux-monnayeurs* (1926; *The Counterfeiters*, 1927). G. recapitulates here and deepens the themes treated in his earlier novels: individual freedom and restraint, authenticity (all individuals and groups in the novel are to some extent counterfeiters), social and religious criticism, and the nature of literary expression (the protagonist is also writing a novel entitled *Les faux-monnayeurs*). As suggested in *Les caves du Vatican*, and partly because of his further study of Dostoevsky, G. now saw the novel as an organic development rather than as the means for analyzing a limited problem. Édouard, a middle-aged novelist, is related to or becomes involved with all the social groups and forces G. introduces: the diabolical Strouvilhou and his band of young adolescents distributing counterfeit coins; the morally repressive and religiously hypocritical Azaïs-Vedel clan; and their materialistic counterparts, the Profitendieu and Molinier families—all of whom are driving their children away from the values they claim to uphold; the girl Bronja, whose death is the destruction of purity; and the younger Boris, for whose suicide Édouard is at least partly responsible. Édouard, who cannot complete his novel because of his unwillingness to deal with concrete reality, has abandoned his fiancée, and young Bernard Profitendieu and Oliver Molinier, Édouard's nephew, become the focal points of his life. Bernard is a more refined Lafcadio, who will maintain his freedom "provided this leads him upward," and through Édouard and Olivier G. explicitly exalts pederasty for the first time in his fiction. All heterosexual relationships, from Bronja's and Boris's to that of his grandparents', are also in the process of dissolution. The growth and dissolution of relationships is well defined, but G. indicates at the end that his long "organic" novel is not necessarily complete, that it could be continued.

Besides breaking out of the limitations of the *récit*, G. has in effect largely resolved the personal problems explored in his earlier shorter fiction and sees them in a wider social context here. His espousal of social and political causes is explained in part by this recognition that the freedom-restraint conflict had become more social than individual. There was a concomitant decline in G.'s creative power, which was renewed, however, in *Thésée* (1946; *Theseus*, 1950), which he considered his literary testament. Here the symbolist sterility of André Walter, the destructive individuality of Michel, Alissa, and Lafcadio are replaced by Theseus' commitment to freedom and human progress. While G.'s sociopolitical program is unoriginal, Theseus retains much of his earlier heroes' spontaneous creative energy and uses it for the benefit of society. Theseus' encounter with the guilty, introspective Oedipus is a constructive confrontation between the two essential aspects of G.'s character. His positive creative energy must still overcome the sense of guilt at having betrayed his ideal of purity. The victory leaves Theseus serene, and in this sense the novel is a fitting capstone to G.'s long career.

Throughout his life, G. maintained a journal of his thoughts, readings, and literary activities and relationships, which were later published: *Journal 1889–1939, Pages de journal 1939–42, Journal 1939–49* (1939, 1944, 1950; *The Journals of A. G.*, 4 vols., 1947–51), as polished a literary work as any of his creative writings. His published correspondence with other writers, such as Francis JAMMES, Paul CLAUDEL, Paul VALÉRY, and Roger Martin du GARD, to mention only the most important, also reveals many of G.'s literary and psychological attitudes.

G.'s greatness lies in part in his liberating influence, especially through *Les nourritures terrestres*, on the generation reaching maturity during or immediately following World War I, including writers such as ARAGON, MONTHERLANT, SAINT-EXUPÉRY, MALRAUX, SARTRE, and CAMUS. The Calvinist primacy of the individual conscience was here in concert with the liberation of body and spirit from the dying 19th-c. morality. But his greatness lies as much, if not more, in his ability to express his dilemmas, conflicts, and complications in a style and tone that rendered them typical of this generation, and to a great extent of any generation. His writings are not simply the cries of anguish of an individual and (because of

his peculiar Calvinist-homosexual conflict) atypical tortured soul. This is particularly true of *L'immoraliste* and *La porte étroite*, which are perhaps his most successful creations, where the tensions created in the protagonists are conveyed in a tone substantially different from G.'s own, since he had resolved the conflicts differently. In the last analysis, his greatest strength is his literary artistry, although the moral force and influence of his writings is more immediately evident.

FURTHER WORKS: *Le traité du Narcisse* (1891; *Narcissus*, 1953); *Les poésies d'André Walter* (1892); *Le tentative amoureuse* (1893; *The Lover's Attempt*, 1953); *Le voyage d'Urien* (1893; *Urien's Travels*, 1952); *El Hadj* (1899; *El Hadj*, 1953); *Le Prométhée mal enchaîné* (1899; *Prometheus Misbound*, 1953); *Philoctète* (1899; *Philoctetes*, 1952); *Le roi Candaule* (1901; *King Candaules*, 1952); *Prétextes* (1903); *Amyntas* (1906; *Amyntas*, 1958); *Le retour de l'enfant prodigue* (1907; *The Return of the Prodigal*, 1953); *Oscar Wilde* (1910; *Oscar Wilde*, 1949); *Isabelle* (1911; *Isabelle*, 1931); *Nouveaux prétextes* (1911); *Bethsabé* (1912; *Bathsheba*, 1952); *Souvenirs de la cour d'assises* (1914; *Recollections of the Assize Court*, 1941); *Dostoïevsky* (1923; *Dostoevsky*, 1925); *Incidences* (1924); *Si le grain ne meurt . . .* (1926; *If It Die . . .*, 1957); *Le journal des Faux-monnayeurs* (1926; *The Journal of the Counterfeiters*, 1927); *Numquid et tu . . .?* (1926; *Numquid et Tu . . .?*, in *The Journals of A. G.*, 1947–1951, Vol. II); *Essai sur Montaigne* (1929; *Montaigne*, 1929); *L'école des femmes* (1929; *The School for Wives*, 1929); *Robert* (1930; *Robert*, 1950); *La séquestrée de Poitiers* (1930); *Œdipe* (1931; *Oedipus*, 1950); *Divers* (1931); *Perséphone* (1934; *Persephone*, 1952); *Les nouvelles nourritures* (1935; *The New Fruits*, in *Fruits of the Earth*, 1949); *Geneviève* (1936; *Genevieve*, 1950); *Retour de l'URSS* 1936; *Return from the U.S.S.R.*, 1937); *Retouches à mon "Retour de l'URSS"* (1937; *After thoughts on the U.S.S.R.*, 1938); *Le treizième arbre* (1942); *Attendu que* (1943); *Interviews imaginaires* (1943); *Deux interviews imaginaires, suivis de Feuillets* (1946); *Francis Jammes et A. G.: Correspondance 1898–1938* (1948); *Préfaces* (1948); *Notes sur Chopin* (1948; *Notes on Chopin*, 1949); *Robert; ou, L'interêt général* (1949); *Paul Claudel et A. G.: Correspondance 1899–1926* (1949); *Feuillets d'automne, précédés de quelques récents écrits* (1949; *Autumn Leaves*, 1950); *Littérature engagée* (1950); *Lettres de Charles Du Bos et réponses d'A. G.* (1950); *Et nunc manet in te, suivi de Journal intime* (1951; *Madeleine*, 1952); *Ainsi soit-il; ou, Les jeux sont faits* (1952; *So Be It; or, The Chips Are Down*, 1959); *Correspondance avec Rainer Maria Rilke* (1952); *A. G.—Paul Valéry: Correspondance 1890–1942* (1955); *The Correspondence of A. G. and Edmund Gosse 1904–1928* (1959); *Correspondance d'A. G. à Henri de Régnier* (1963); *Correspondance A. G.—Arnold Bennett* (1964); *Correspondance d'A. G. et d'André Rouveyre* (1967); *A. G.—Roger Martin du Gard: Correspondance* (1968); *Correspondance A. G.—François Mauriac* (1971); *Correspondance avec Albert Mockel* (1975); *Correspondance Henri Ghéon et A. G.* (1976); *Correspondance A. G.—Jules Romains* (1976); *Correspondance A. G.—Jacques Émile Blanche* (1979); *Correspondance A. G.—Dorothy Bussy* (2 vols., 1979–1980). FURTHER WORKS IN ENGLISH: *Imaginary Interviews* (1944); *Pretexts* (1959)

BIBLIOGRAPHY: Thomas, L., *A. G.: The Ethic of the Artist* (1950); Pierre-Quint, L., *A. G.: Sa vie, son œuvre* (1952); March, H., *G. and the Hound of Heaven* (1952); McClaren, J. C., *The Theater of A. G.: The Evolution of a Moral Philosopher* (1953); O'Brien, J., *Portrait* of A. G. (1953); Lafille, P., A. G. romancier (1954); Mallet, R., Une mort ambiguë (1955); Schlumberger, J., Madeleine et A. G. (1956); Brachfeld, G., A. G. and the Communist Temptation (1959); Hytier, J., A. G. (1962); Brée, G., G. (1963); Delay, J., The Youth of A. G. (1963); Fowlie, W., A. G.: His Life and Art (1965); Watson-Williams, H., A. G. and the Greek Myth (1967); Cordle, T., A. G. (1969); Guérard, A., A. G. (1969); Ireland, G. W., A. G.: A Study of His Creative Writings (1970)

—CHARLES G. HILL

[G.'s] *récits* have often been misunderstood, primarily because they have been taken for more or less fictionalized confessions, secondly because they have been read without being "placed" in the ensemble of G.'s works, and finally because their hidden irony has not been discerned. G. explicitly states in one of his *Feuillets:* "With the single exception of my *Nourritures,* all my books are *ironic* works; *they are books of criticism.* La porte étroite is the criticism of a certain form of romantic imagination; *La symphonie pastorale,* of a form of lying to oneself; *L'immoraliste* of a form of individualism."

The *récits* therefore constitute a part of the same series of tendentious works to which the *soties* belonged. They too are satires, although G. has hedged a bit here ("'Criticism' doesn't mean the same thing as 'satire'"), but of a special nature: they are serious and indirect satires. We all know that a portrait painted with great fidelity and complete submission to the model can be infinitely more cruel than caricature, especially since, being truthful, it leaves no margin for the illusion of a systematic distortion against which the model could protest. G.'s *récits* are like those implacable portraits in which the painter's very love for his subject serves only to reinforce—emotionally—the severity of his vision by a deliberate accuracy. [1938]

Jean Hytier, *A. G.* (1962), pp. 120–21

G. is a stimulant, a dynamic, hence a potential poison: the invigoration of his doctrine consists in a muscular acceptance of the burden of a temperament, a valiant acquiescence in what is for the sensitive soul more difficult to tolerate than the blows of external fortune—the inward fatality, the thorn in the heart, the original sin: it precognises courage as the highest of the virtues, without particular regard for the ruthlessness it implies, and the human intellect and spirit, unsustained by any such notion as transcendental grace, as adequate sources of strength and instruments of progress. Courage is the insistent thread that connects the Dionysiac assertions of *Les nourritures terrestres, via* the intoxicated heroisms of a Michel, an Alissa, with the lucid, inflexible sobriety of a Thésée. That courage, without constituting greatness, is an ingredient in it, as stimulation is in nourishment, cannot be denied, and only priggish insensitiveness could emerge from immersion in G. without having felt the penetration of an intrepid spirit, the tonic of a rare intellect, without having received the heightened

clarity of vision that comes from contact with an intense sensibility.

Lawrence Thomas, *A. G.: The Ethic of an Artist* (1950), pp. 258–59

As the creative fervor ebbed, as the communist venture proved illusory, as he began to feel tired and discouraged, he turned back to view his life and to attempt to discover its significance. Perhaps he was not after all so much of an innovator as he had thought. He had been, it was true, quickly sensitive to changes of literary climate. He had been one of the first to break with the abstractions of Symbolism and to proclaim the necessity for turning back to the "fruits of the earth." He had recognized that the suavely beautiful style, which charmed the esthetes of the late nineteenth and early twentieth centuries and which found its supreme exemplar in Anatole France, needed reinvigoration, and in *Les caves du Vatican* he had written a book which a postwar generation could embrace as its own. If, like many others, he had been deluded about communism, he was one of the first to confess his disillusionment. And he had said things about God and man that anticipated the Existentialists.

Harold March, *G. and the Hound of Heaven* (1952), pp. 386–87

The complexity of A. G.'s character and writings has long been legendary. He himself frequently wondered at it, and almost all his commentators, according to their views, have admired or deplored his abundant or devious, but ever surprising, resources. To some the epitome of French classicism, to others an outstanding example of current Alexandrianism, he has variously appeared as a profound religious thinker and a devil's henchman, an apostle of sincerity and a crafty purveyor of guile, a broad humanist and an egocentric introvert, a moral teacher and a calculating perverter of youth. His old friend, Charles Du Bos, who felt after years of subtle converse with G. that he had penetrated the secret, characterized him as a "lattice-work labyrinth."

Indeed, G.'s dynamic equilibrium—this is a word he uses with particular and frequent affection—rests upon a number of familiar antinomies, such as the soul and the flesh, life and art, ethics and aesthetics, ardor and austerity, expression and restraint, the individual and society, classicism and romanticism, Christ and Christianity, God and the devil.

Justin O'Brien, *Portrait of A. G.* (1953), pp. 10–11

G.'s personal ease and fine sense of balance, quite rare in the often crass brutality of our own time, may temporarily, perhaps, hide the firmness and integrity of his critical approach and its value as example and discipline. In the long run it will emerge as the very foundation of his reputation. From *Fruits of the Earth* to *New Fruits of the Earth,* G. eliminated all direct messages from his work. His extraordinary ability as author was to probe and reveal indirectly the devious ways of human consciousness in relation to everyday existence. And in this chosen realm G. concentrated upon a topic of no small consequence: the struggle of human beings with truths compulsively followed.

Germaine Brée, *G.* (1963), p. 3

Indeed, it was the Christian significance of Madeleine's presence that made André Gide exclude her from the atheistic universe of *Les Faux-Monnayeurs.* He wrote it at the time when the future of their relationship seemed conclusively compromised by his mad escapade with M[arc] A[llégret], the time at which he thought he had "lost" the "game" he could have "won only with her." And yet the mystical image had such force that, even in such a godless world, he embodied it in the figure of the angelic Bronja, whose death took away little Boris' only hope for salvation: "Without her how could he believe in the angels . . .? Even heaven was now empty. Boris went back to the classroom as one might plunge into hell." More than a fictional episode, it was, at the heart of the book, the representation on a childish level of the drama that the fifty-year-old man was experiencing on an adult level.

Jean Delay, *The Youth of A. G..* (1963), p. 456

G.'s strength was in the "logic" of his nature, in that vital dialectic of desire and restraint, of instinct and culture, that marked the progress of his life from neurotic childhood to the stormy conflicts of his late years. His power as an artist began with his intense preoccupation with himself, with his search for that "superior, secret reason for living" that each man bears hidden within his being.

For every impulse he found an equally authentic counterimpulse. The search for love led him to the delight of the senses *and* to the passionate refusal of the sensual. His Christian education implanted in him the seeds of an ascetic moralist and a lyrical enthusiast. He could renounce neither, and therefore became both. He touched the extremes of his culture and experienced in the most intimate and positive way its tensions and contradictions. It was his recognition of the *typicalness* latent in his "complication" that completed his artistic power and assured his genius of its grasp on the minds of men. That, plus the determination reached at the time of *André Walter* to reveal his personality in all its complexity, to hold back nothing, and to make his work coextensive with his being; to make it the consciousness of his life and the validation of his hesitancies as well as of his desires.

Thomas Cordle, *A. G.* (1969), p. 165

[The value of G.'s novels lies in] their psychological interest and accuracy. Like Conrad, the young G. did not read Freud or his disciples. He nevertheless dramatized the unending buried struggle between

conscious intention and unconscious need, the forms which uncalculated self-destructiveness may take, the minute workings of repression and sublimation, the "gratuitous acts" of unconscious identification. Intuitive knowledge and successful introspection served G. better than close study served others—as the wearied reader of Lawrence's *The Fox* or Huxley's *Point Counter Point* may verify. The largely fictitious psychology of Faulkner (which posits not merely a collective unconscious memory but a collective unconscious foreknowledge) is more amusing and dramatically perhaps more serviceable. And the old-fashioned introspections and associations of Proust certainly lend themselves better to poetic effect. But G.'s "humane nature" is the one with which we must live. He never consciously explored the unconscious, as a few of his contemporaries did. No doubt this is another limitation. But his intuitive psychology has been discredited at not a single point.

Albert Guérard *A. G.* (1969), p. 180

GIJSEN, Marnix

(pseud. of Jan-Albert Goris) Belgian novelist and essayist (writing in Flemish, French, and English), b. 20 Oct. 1899, Antwerp; d. 30 Sept. 1984, Pelenberg

G. received a strict Catholic education, first in a school run by nuns, about which he wrote in *Allengs, gelijk de spin* (1962; gradually, like a spider), later in a Jesuit college, depicted in *De man van overmorgen* (1949; the man of the day after tomorrow). Toward the end of World War I he worked as a journalist with strong anti-Walloon opinions. In the early 1920s, after serving in the army, he began his studies at the University of Louvain. After having finished his dissertation, *Étude sur les colonies marchandes méridionales à Anvers de 1488 à 1567* (1925; a study on settlements of merchants from the south in Antwerp, 1488–1567), G. traveled on a study grant to London, Paris, and Seattle. During these years his love for a young woman sustained him; she died in 1927. His memorial to her, *Klaaglied om Agnes* (1951; *Lament for Agnes*, 1975), is one of the most touching ones in Netherlandic literature. Here G. dropped his sarcasm, behind which, in most of his works, he tried to hide his vulnerability. After holding several diplomatic positions, G. was appointed assistant director of the Belgian Pavilion at the 1939 World's Fair in New York, where he was stranded at the outbreak of World War II. In 1940 he accepted the post of director of the Belgian Information Center in New York. After serving as general commissioner of the Belgian Pavilion at Expo'67 in Montreal, G. retired in 1968 and returned to Belgium.

G. began as a religious writer; in his nonfiction work *Loflitanie van den H. Franciscus van Assisi* (1920; litany of praise for St. Francis of Assisi) he defended Christian morality against the inroads of an immoral literature. But in his early forties he broke radically with the Catholic Church and became a convinced and stoic agnostic. In a much later nonfiction book, *Biecht van een heiden* (1971; confession of a pagan), G. lists among the causes of his apostasy what he saw as the intolerance of the Church toward other religions, and above all the incomprehensibility of the suffering of so many innocent creatures. Like Pushkin, whom he admired, G. has a keen sympathy for the downtrodden, who cannot free themselves from misery and suffering.

G.'s novels, the first of which did not appear until 1947—*Het boek van Joachim van Babylon* (*The Book of Joachim of Babylon*, 1951)—often center on the themes of love and death. In several of them he focuses on the contrast between the Old and New Worlds. Although G. lived in the U.S. for more than twenty years, he never became more than a European observer of American life and the American way of thinking. This attitude is seen not only in G.'s first novel set in America, *Goed en kwaad* (1950; good and evil), but as well in his later works, like *Harmàgeddon* (1965; Armageddon). Yet G. pictures life in the U.S. and especially the life of European immigrants in a vividly realistic way.

In other novels and short stories the setting is Flanders, and the narrative incorporates many reminiscences of the author's childhood and youth—for example, *Telemachus in het dorp* (1948; Telemachus in the village).

The main characters of G.'s novels are seen in their relation to society, to the opposite sex, and to themselves. Most of them are lonely outsiders for whom neither life nor the world has meaning. They seek forgetfulness in drink or study. They are portrayed without sentimentality, but so vividly that the reader feels as much sympathy for them as if he knew them personally. Most of G.'s novels are in the first person, and most contain autobiographical details, since he likes to write about himself, as in *Zelfportret, gevleid natuurlijk* (1965; self-portrait, flattering of course) and *De leerjaren van Jan-Albert Goris* (1975; Jan-Albert Goris's years of apprenticeship). It is his belief that the writer must be honest with himself and that every book should bear testimony. Hence, all of G.'s works establish a close relationship between author and reader.

G. has also written poems. In fact, before 1947 he had published only essayistic works and a collection of poems, *Het huis* (1925; the house), which was later followed by the collection *The House by the Leaning Tree* (1963; title in English). In his poetry G. is less hesitant than in his novels to show his feelings and proves to be a master in evoking specific atmospheres.

G.'s two plays, *Helena op Ithaka* (1967; Helen on Ithaca) and the one-act *Een gezellige avond* (1970; a pleasant evening), have not been very successful, probably because of their lack of action.

G. is considered to be the single most important modern writer in the Netherlandic language. His works, in which the mother, the child, the innocently oppressed, play an important role, show a moralistic bent. The main figures are independent individuals who differ from their fellow men and who adjust to society only with great effort. G.'s greatest merit, besides his mastery of the language, is the warmth and tenderness that lie behind a mask of irony and bitterness.

FURTHER WORKS: *De XII sonnetten van de schoonheydt van Brederoo* (1919); *Karel van de Woestijne* (1920); *Breeroo's lyriek* (1922); *Karel van Mander* (1922); *Ontdek Amerika* (1927); *Odysseus achterna* (1930); *Antwerpen* (1930); *Ons volkskarakter* (1932); *Le cœur des États-Unis* (1933); *Lierre* (1935); *Breviarium der Vlaamsche lyriek* (1937); *Josef Cantré, houtsnijder* (1937); *Albert Dürer: Journal de voyage dans les Pays-Bas* (1937; with G. Marlier); *Hans Memling te Brugge* (1939); *De literatuur in Zuid-Nederland sedert 1830* (1940); *Lof van Antwerpen* (1940); *Peripatetisch onderricht* (1940–1942); *Belgium in Bondage* (1943); *Du génie flamand* (1943); *Vlaamsche lyriek* (1944); *The Miracle of Beatrice* (1944); *Strangers Should Not Whisper* (1945); *The Liberation of Belgium* (1945); *Rubens in America* (1945, with J. Held);

The Growth of the Belgian Nation (1946); *Belgian Letters* (1946); *Modern Sculpture in Belgium* (1948); *Modern Belgian Wood Engravers* (1949); *Portraits by Flemish Masters in American Collections* (1949); *Drawings by Modern Belgian Artists* (1951); *De vleespotten van Egypte* (1952); *De kat in de boom* (1953); *Van een wolf, die vreemde talen sprak* (1953); *De lange nacht* (1954); *Wat de dag meebrengt* (1954); *De oudste zoon* (1955); *Some Scholarly Comments on the Saying of the Dutch Poet Leo Vroman "Liever heimwee dan Holland"* (1955); *Er gebeurt nooit iets* (1956); *Marie-ama van Antwerpen* (1957); *De stem uit Amerika* (1957); *Ter wille van Leentje* (1957); *Karel van den Oever* (1958); *Mijn vriend de moordenaar* (1958); *Lucinda en de lotoseter* (1959); *De school van Fontainebleau* (1959); *De diaspora* (1961); *Onze zuster Alice* (1961); *Van een kat die te veel pretentie had* (1963); *Kaddish voor Sam Cohn* (1964); *Candid Opinions on Sundry Subjects* (1964); *Karel Jonckheere* (1964); *Scripta manent* (1965); *De kroniek der poezie* (1965); *De parel der diplomatie* (1966); *Het paard Ugo* (1968); *August van Cauwelaert* (1968); *Het dier en wij* (1968); *Marie Gevers* (1969); *Del val van Zijne Excellentie Minister Plas* (1969); *Jacqueline en ik* (1970); *Gezegden* (1970); *De afvallige* (1971); *Een stad van heren* (1971); *Mi chiamano Mimi* (1971); *Weer thuis* (1972); *De grote God Pan* (1973); *Orpheus* (1973); *De kroeg van groot verdriet* (1974); *Terug van weggeweest* (1975); *Van een wolf, een kat en een paling* (1976); *Uit het Brussels Getto* (1978); *Overkomst dringend gewenst* (1978); *Verzamelde werken* (1978)

BIBLIOGRAPHY: Hermanowski, G., *Die Stimme des schwarzen Löwen* (1961): 83–87; Meijer, R. P., *Literature of the Low Countries*, new ed. (1978): 361–62

—JUDICA I.H. MENDELS

GILCHRIST, Ellen

American short-story writer, novelist, and poet, b. 20 Feb. 1935, Vicksburg, Mississippi

G. was born in the Mississippi River city of Vicksburg, and after spending her early years in Mississippi, her family moved from state to state like the river itself. But no matter where the family was then living—Illinois, Indiana, Kentucky—G. called home the Hopeton Plantation in Issaquena County, Mississippi, her maternal grandparent's land. An avid reader and nature enthusiast since her youth, G. did not begin her writing career until she was forty. She attended Vanderbilt University after high school, but left to marry. After spending a decade in New Orleans raising her children, she returned to college and in 1967 received her B.A. in philosophy at Millsaps College, where she studied creative writing with Eudora WELTY. She continued writing in New Orleans, and in 1976 studied at the graduate level at the University of Arkansas, where her work first began to appear in magazines. In 1979 she won a NEA Fellowship in fiction. In that same year she published a collection of poems, *The Land Surveyor's Daughter* (1979), followed by a collection of stories, *The Land of Dreamy Dreams* (1981). Gaining rave reviews and strong sales with her story collection, G. quickly built up a national audience for her fiction and is now one of the most widely read contemporary Southern authors.

With *The Land of Dreamy Dreams* G. established herself in the literary world on the strength of her thoroughly original female characters. Twelve of the fourteen stories have female protagonists, and in each case the women/girls try to escape from their tightly bound lives to personal freedom. Images of death, nightmares, dreams, and fantasy pervade the stories, creating a surreal undercurrent to the stark realism of the text. The finest stories in the collection focus on Nora Jane Whittington and Rhoda Manning, characters that G. returns to in several other collections and novels, much like Ernest HEMINGWAY did with his character Nick Adams. And just as Hemingway has been criticized for his one-dimensional women characters, so has G. been criticized for her underdeveloped male characters. While there is truth to the charges against both authors, G.'s men have a lesser impact because they are rarely the focal point. G.'s greatest literary contribution is the creation of explosive female characters who fight for independence from unfaithful husbands, patriarchal customs, and the perceived emotional bankruptcy of affluent Southern society.

Her first novel, *The Annunciation* (1983), was poorly received because of its unevenness. The novel's narrative virtues rest in the cutting depiction of New Orleans high society—a topic also explored in the first section of *The Land of Dreamy Dreams*. After this setback, G. returned to the popular (and autobiographical) character Rhoda Manning in the story collection *Victory over Japan* (1984), which won the American Book Award and international acclaim. G.'s quick-moving, almost breezy writing style and her fine ear for dialogue are naturally suited to short fiction, and she proved with her Rhoda stories that she could also deliver convincing adolescent characters. *Rhoda: A Life in Stories* (1995) gathers all of the Rhoda stories published over a span of fifteen years. *Net of Jewels* (1992), her most critically successful novel, also centers on the Manning family, and in particular Rhoda.

In *Falling through Space: The Journals of E. G.* (1988), a nonfiction selection from her speeches, journalism, and radio commentaries, G. relates the importance of the pastoral Hopeton Plantation to her artistic development and discusses her long apprenticeship as a budding writer. The book also explores with frankness the conflict between the art of writing and the business of writing, particularly the siren call of Hollywood screenwriting that she has answered intermittently. The journal is striking because of the similarity of G's philosophy and life to that of her most prominent characters, but the close identification of the two is a double-edged sword. Readers and newspaper reviewers have tended to praise the Nora Jane/Rhoda works, including those named above and also *Drunk with Love* (1986) and *Light Can Be Both Particle and Wave* (1989), but have largely rejected departures into works set outside of the contemporary South, such as *Anabasis: A Journey to the Interior* (1994), which is set in ancient Greece . But G. continues to publish works drawing on old and new settings, proving she has neither exhausted the old nor hesitates to explore the new.

Like Eudora Welty and Katherine Anne PORTER before her, G. has created a wealth of Southern women characters unlike those that existed in fiction before her work. Though her fiction has not drawn much scholarly attention, it has had a significant impact on American publishing and international readers by its own right and by opening the door for other women writers to share their literary visions.

FURTHER WORKS: *Riding Out the Tropical Depression: Selected Poems, 1975-1985* (1986); *The Anna Papers* (1988); *I Can't Get Close Enough: Three Novellas* (1990); *StarCarbon* (1994); *The Age of Miracles* (1995); *The Courts of Love* (1996); *Sarah Conley* (1997)

BIBLIOGRAPHY: Crace, J., "The Cold-Eyed Terrors," *TLS*, 15 October 1982: 1142; Thompson, J., and A. M. Garner, "The Miracle of Realism: The Bid for Self-Knowledge in the Fiction of E. G.," *SoQ*, 22 (Fall 1983): 101-14; Lowry, B., "Redheaded Hellions in the Crepe Myrtle," *NYTBR*, 23 September 1984: 18; Hoffman, R., "Smart Enough for their Own Good," *NYTBR*, 22 October 1989: 12; McCay, M., *E. G.* (1997)

—JON PARRISH PEEDE

GILROY, Beryl A.

Guyanese-English novelist and writer of children's books, b. 30 Aug. 1924, British Guiana, West Indies (now Guyana)

Born Beryl Alnwich, G. was reared in a small village in British Guiana with some thirty cousins under the care of her grandmother. She did not attend school on a regular basis until the age of twelve. G. resisted formal education with such a vengeance that her aunt, who was also a teacher, was compelled to teach her at home. Yet she loved to read and write, and at the age of five, she won a creative writing competition and received a much valued prize—a genuine silver sixpence.

G. earned her First Class Teachers Diploma in Guyana in 1945 and an advanced diploma in child development psychology in 1954. She later earned an academic diploma from the University of London. In 1980 she earned an M.A. in education with distinction from Sussex University, and in 1987 she completed a Ph.D. in counselling psychology from Century University.

G.'s jobs have been numerous and varied—class teacher, head teacher, educational counselor, parent development specialist, and lecturer. From 1946 to 1951 she worked as a lecturer at a training college for UNICEF. In 1953 G. made history by becoming the first black female teacher in England. In July 1995 the Vice Chancellor and Chief Executive of the University of North London wrote to G. to invite her to accept an honorary degree. He explained that the award is offered in recognition of the major contributions she has made to education.

Additionally, G. has received the Inner London Ethnic Minorities Prize (1983), the GLC Black Literature Competition Prize for *Frangipani House* (1985), and the Guyana Historical Fiction Prize (1992) for *Stedman and Joanna: A Love in Bondage*, among numerous other awards. The honorary doctorate, like the myriad other honors she has received over the years, is testament to the life of an amazing woman who in her writings and daily work posits education as central to her existence.

G.'s writing career is as large and diverse as her educational career. She has to her credit a number of educational and children's books including *Carnival of Dreams* (1970) and *Nippers and Little Nippers* (1970). These books she wrote because of a lack of diversity in the texts of the London classrooms. With the emergence of former colonized peoples' emigration to England, a mechanism for recognizing their humanity (for mainstream students and teachers) as well as an agent for validation had need of being designed. She answered the calls with her children's books. The books explore differences and commonalities among children and the situations they find themselves in.

Additionally, she has to her credit seven fictional works and a volume of poetry. In 1976 she published the autobiographical work *Black Teacher,* which chronicles her experiences as Britain's first black, female teacher. *Black Teacher* was republished in 1995 to wide acclaim. A collection of short stories, *In for a Penny,* was published in 1980, and her much-celebrated *Frangipani House* was published in 1986. Perhaps her best-known work, *Frangipani House* speaks to the condition of the young leaving the Caribbean and their children under the care of mothers and grandmothers in order to eke out a more comfortable existence abroad. In the character Mama King, the archetype of the aged heroine is created.

Frangipani House was followed by *Boy Sandwich* in 1989 and *Stedman and Joanna* in 1992. C. published her first volume of poetry, *Echoes and Voices,* in 1990. In 1992 she published *Sunlight and Sweetwater* and *Gather the Faces. In Praise of Love and Children, Inkle and Yarico* and *Gather the Faces* were published in 1996.

A writer, teacher, and clinical psychologist, G. is the most prolific female writer of the Anglophone Caribbean. Her works have been translated into German, Danish, and French. She describes her writing as "fact-fiction," drawing a picture of contemporary reality through her characters. Critic Joan Anim-Addo contends that G. portrays women from the perspectives of authorial intent, historical context, and intertextual relationships. G.'s fictional women resist stereotypes as they assume the subscribed roles available to them.

BIBLIOGRAPHY: Wilson, L., "Aging and Ageism in *Praisesong for the Widow* and *Frangipani House,*" *JCSt,* 7 (Winter 1989): 189-99; Paravisini-Gebert, L., and O. Torres-Seda, eds., *Caribbean Women Novelists: An Annotated Critical Bibliography* (1993): 147-49; Traver, A., "*Frangipani House:* G.'s *Praise Song* for Grandmothers," in Newson, A., and L. Strong-Leek, eds., *Winds of Change* (1998): 127-30; Amin-Addo, J., "Anguish and the Absurd: 'Key Moments,' Re-created Lives, and the Emergence of New Figure of Black Womanhood in the Narrative Works of B. G.," in Newson, A., and L. Strong-Leek, eds., *Winds of Change: The Transforming Voices of Caribbean Women Writers and Scholars* (1998): 131-43

—ADELE S. NEWSON

GINSBERG, Allen

American poet, b. 3 June 1926, Newark, N.J.; d. 5 April 1997, New York, N.Y.

G. received his B. A. from Columbia University in 1949, after a period of academic probation due to mental instability. Later, he suffered relapses and at one point had himself committed. During the 1940s he formed friendships with the founders of the beat movement, among them William S. BURROUGHS, Jack KEROUAC, and Neal Cassady (1926–1968). They greatly influenced his work, particularly Kerouac's notion of "spontaneous poetics." G. has also traveled widely, and his journeys within the U.S., to South America, Asia, eastern Europe, and the Arctic Circle, have found their way into his poetry.

Although G. first became known as a beat, the label limits him (as it does others) too much, and he underwent a long apprenticeship in traditional forms. Son of poet Louis Ginsberg (1895–1976),

he began with rhymed and metered lyrics, published many years later as *The Gates of Wrath* (1973). While obviously derivative (the best influence is Blake's lyrics), the poems reveal a sharply accurate imitative ear, and many are accomplished, if not remarkable, in their own right.

At the same time, G. wrote free verse, based on William Carlos WILLIAMS's short line of American colloquial speech and published a decade later with an admiring introduction by Williams as *Empty Mirror* (1961). Here, many of G.'s characteristic preoccupations first appear: madness, the journey metaphor, the world not as the veil of divine eternity but as eternity itself, and the notion of poetry as recording. *Empty Mirror,* far more assured and original than *Gates of Wrath,* shows G. as a solid practitioner of the Williams lyric, but with a nightmarish quality of his own.

The appearance of *Howl, and Other Poems* (1956), which led to a well-publicized obscenity trial, turned G. into the biggest American poetic celebrity since Robert FROST. Since then G. has seldom been out of the public eye. His participation in various movements—from the 1950s and 1960s drug counterculture to the Vietnam war protests—have been thoroughly documented by the popular press. Unfortunately, G.'s public persona has interfered with critical appreciation of his work. Critics tend to praise or condemn the poems as expressions of an attitude or political stand and have seldom analyzed G.'s craft. The most detailed examination of "Howl," one of the strongest postwar American poems, remains G.'s own *To Eberhart from G.* (1976).

Williams ended his introduction to *Howl, and Other Poems* by saying: "Hold back the edges of your gowns, Ladies, we are going through hell." The nightmare of *Empty Mirror* has intensified. With such literary ancestors as Christopher Smart (1722–1771), Walt Whitman, the prophetic Blake, and, through the last, Jeremiah and Revelations, "Howl" is essentially a series of lengthy catalogues held together by what G. calls a "fixed base." a phrase or syntactic unit repeated with each line. The first part presents an apocalyptic vision of "the best minds of my generation" destroyed by the horrors of contemporary life. The second part names the catastrophic cause, Moloch, identified with big money and Blake's destroying angel of reason, Urizen. The third part, however, affirms that redemptive human love is possible, even in hell—here, G.'s friendship with Carl Solomon, a fellow inmate in the Rockland mental hospital. The final part, "Footnote to Howl," is a hymn of praise, a true kaddish: because of human love, the world is holy, despite the nightmare.

Kaddish, and Other Poems (1961) contains fewer interesting poems than *Howl.* The title poem, however—on the poet's mother, her madness and death—is unsurpassed in G.'s work and represents and advance on "Howl" in its greater complexity of idea and feeling and subtler use of the "fixed base" "Kaddish" begins with G.'s sense of loss and moves on to document his mother's life and death. The second part ends with a "Hymmnn" to the blessedness of the universe, which includes death. The last three sections meditate on death's meaning but end with the sense of something great and unknowable, as opposed to the definite affirmation of "Howl."

G.'s later work can generally be divided into three types: prophecy, vision, and elegy. The influence of Blake, Whitman, Hart CRANE, and, marginally, Hindu vedas becomes more pronounced. Prophecy in G. is not so much prediction as a call to righteousness. Often it manifests itself in poems on political subjects, mainly in *Planet News* (1968) and *The Fall of America: Poems of These States* (1972). Yet G. is more an ethical or religious poet than a political one. The quality of these prophecies varies greatly. They seem best when most unresolved politically: "Kral Majales" (1965), "Wichita Vortex Sutra" (1966), and the magnificent "Ecologue" (1970) on the spiritual malaise of the times. The visionary poems—from those in *Kaddish* and *Reality Sandwiches* (1963) to those in *Mind Breaths* (1978)—at their best record not only the details of mystical experiences but the poet's sense of their all-importance and his simultaneous inability to articulate their meaning.

Probably influenced by Asian thought, G.'s anger—which lay behind many of his early poems—diminished, and he had to find some other means of sustaining interest, particularly in long works. His experimentation was only partially successful. G. also became interested in music-poetry, particularly blues, but the results were poetically and musically amateurish and without the quirkiness of a genuine primitive. Lacking the early impulse, many of his long poems are "loose, baggy monsters," merely recording phenomena. The visionary poems can become exercises in Hindu deity name-dropping. While G. may admire Eastern philosophies, he often seems not to believe them; in the most moving of his visions, Orientalia play a minor, scenic role.

G. has outlived many friends, and the elegy becomes increasingly important for him. "Don't Grow Old" (1976), on his father's death, suffers when compared to "Kaddish." "Back on Times Square, Dreaming of Times Square" (1958), "Elegy for Neal Cassady" (1968), and the beautiful "On Neal's Ashes" (1968), however, demonstrate mastery of this form and also G.'s continued ability in the short lyric.

FURTHER WORKS: *The Yage Letters* (1963, with William Burroughs); *Ankor Wat* (1968); *Airplane Dreams* (1968); *Indian Journals* (1970); *Improvised Poetics* (1971); *Iron Horse* (1974); *Gay Sunshine Interview* (1974); *Allen Verbatim: Lectures on Poetry, Politics, Consciousness* (1974); *The Visions of the Great Rememberer* (1974); *First Blues* (1975); *Sad Dust Glories* (1975); *Chicago Trial Testimony* (1975); *Journals: Early Fifties, Early Sixties* (1977); *As Ever: The Collected Correspondence of A. G. and Neal Cassady* (1977); *Poems All over the Place, Mostly 'Seventies* (1978)

BIBLIOGRAPHY: Ferlinghetti, L., "Horn on *Howl*," *Evergreen*, 1, 4 (1957): 145–58; Ammons, A. R., "G.'s New Poems," *Poetry*, 104 (1964): 186–87; Kramer, J., *A. G. in America* (1969); Merrill, T. F., *A. G.* (1969); Tytell, J., *Naked Angels: The Lives and Literature of the Beat Generation* (1976)

—STEVEN SCHWARTZ

GINZBURG, Natalia

Italian novelist, short-story writer, essayist, dramatist, and translator, b. 14 July 1916, Palermo; d. 7 Oct. 1991, Rome

Born of a Catholic mother and a Jewish father, G. grew up with no religious training or affiliation. This was an important cause, she has said, of her lifelong sense of social isolation. She spent her childhood and adolescence in Turin (where her father was a professor of biology) until her marriage in 1938 to editor and political activist Leone Ginzburg, who died in 1944 while imprisoned by the Germans in Rome. After his death she worked as an editorial consultant for Einaudi publishers in order to help support her three children. In 1950 she married Gabriele Baldini, a professor of English literature at the University of Rome; he died in 1969. She has been awarded numerous literary prizes.

According to G., her first "real" story was "Un'assenza" (an absence), written at age seventeen and published in the Florence magazine *Solaria*. Like all of her later short stories, it has an intimate family setting and centers on an unhappy, anguished individual who is plagued by boredom. The subject here, as in G.'s other works, is the quiet tragedy of the failure of human relationships and, more specifically of the relationship of a couple.

Using a sparse, everyday vocabulary, G. has created a deceptively simple style. Most of her profoundly moving tales are constructed almost entirely of dialogue; frequently they are devoid of action. She excels in reproducing speech patterns and in creating characters through a few of their revealing phrases. What seems at first glance to be a mere recounting of the intimate trivia of daily life becomes, upon reflection, a deep probing of human psychology.

G.'s fiction is avowedly a mixture of reminiscence, observation, and invention. Much of it is written in the first person. In the preface to a 1964 edition of *Cinque romanzi brevi* (five short novels [also contains four short stories]), G. explains that in her first stories she had tried to avoid autobiographical writing. But soon she discovered the "pleasure of first person narrative" and then realized that unconsciously she had been inserting herself into her characters from the very beginning.

A young woman narrator who is disappointed and betrayed in her search for love and understanding figures prominently in three of G.'s best-known works: *La strada che va in città* (1942; *The Road to the City*, 1952), *È stato così* (1947; *The Dry Heart*, 1952), and *Le voci della sera* (1961; *Voices in the Evening*, 1963). The young woman finally reaches a point of quiet desperation that will continue throughout her life.

G.'s longest novel, *Tutti i nostri ieri* (1952; *A Light for Fools*, 1956, repub. as *All Our Yesterdays*, 1985), is centered on the life of a family during World War II. At the same time, it is the story of a generation that lived through Fascism, war, the German invasion, the Italian resistance, and finally the liberation.

Lessico famigliare (1963; *Family Sayings*, 1967; rev. ed., 1989), G.'s autobiographical novel, is the book in which she feels she attained her greatest freedom as a writer. As the title suggests, it is through the repeated words and phrases of the various members of her family that the recollections of her childhood, adolescence, and early adulthood are presented. But it is more than just the story of her family; it is also that of Italian society between the wars.

With the remarkable subtlety and economy that have prompted critics to compare her with CHEKHOV, G. evokes most penetratingly in *Caro Michele* (1973; *No Way*, 1974) the loneliness and sadness of her characters, who, however, still yearn for happiness. Her most recent book, *Famiglia* (1977; *Family*, 1988), is a volume of two novellas whose titles, *Famiglia* and *Borghesia* (bourgeoisie), suggest the two main themes of G.'s works. They are the stories of two middle-aged characters whose lives, hopes, and ambitions disintegrate and melt away before our eyes. Finally, both die of illness, and all traces of their lives soon disappear.

Three volumes of G.'s essays and articles have been published: *Le piccole virtù* (1962; *The Little Virtues*, 1985), *Mai devi domandarmi* (1970; *Never Must You Ask Me*, 1973), *Vita immaginaria* (1974; imaginary life). As an essayist, she comments on all manner of subjects, ranging from current movies, books, and art to pedagogy and morals. Her observations are penetrating and stimulating; above all, they are humane.

FURTHER WORKS: *Valentino* (1951); *Sagittario* (1957); *L'inserzione* (1965; *The Advertisement*, 1969); *Fragola e panna* (1966); *La segretaria* (1967); *Ti ho sposato per allegria* (1968); *Paese di mare, e altre commedie* (1973)

BIBLIOGRAPHY: Pacifici, S., *A Guide to Contemporary Italian Literature* (1962): 135–43; "Un-Italian Activities," *TLS*, 23 Feb. 1967: 149; Heiney, D., "N. G.: The Fabric of Voices," *IowaR*, 1, 4 (1970): 87–93; "The Unenchanted," *TLS*, 15 June 1973: 661; Quigly, I., "The Low in Spirit," *TLS*, 2 June 1978: 607; Piclardi, R. D., "Forms and Figures in the Novels of N. G.," *WLT*, 53 (1979): 585–89

—JANE E. COTTRELL

GIONO, Jean

French novelist, dramatist, and essayist, b. 30 March 1895, Manosque; d. 8 Oct. 1970, Manosque

Born into a poor family—his father was a shoemaker, his mother operated a laundry—G. left school one year before graduation to accept a job as a bank clerk, so he could help support his family. To find relief from the tedium of his job, G. immersed himself in the literature of classical Greece and Rome. The horrors of World War I turned G. into a passionate and uncompromising pacifist. After the war, he returned to his bank job and also began to write. Success came to him in the late 1920s, enabling him to devote all of his time to his writing career. Because of his pacifist activities, G. was twice imprisoned, once at the outbreak of World War II, and again in 1944, when he was accused of collaboration with the Nazis. He was also blacklisted by the French Liberationist writers, and it took the intervention of André GIDE to rehabilitate him. When G. finally made a successful comeback, he was a different writer, since his encounter with the Nazi version of "blood and soil" mythology had led him to a reevaluation of his own earlier attitudes. In 1954 he was elected to the Goncourt Academy.

When *Colline* (1929; *Hill of Destiny*, 1929) was published in book form, G. was hailed by Gide as the new "Vergil from Provence". It was the first work of the "Pan trilogy," which also includes *Un de Baumugnes* (1929; *Lovers Are Never Losers*, 1932) and *Regain* (1930; *Harvest*, 1939). These short novels are regionalist and unabashedly anti-intellectual. G. celebrates the simple, even primitive but noble people of the countryside in their intricate interrelationship with a nature both hostile and benevolent. The books can be seen as the protest of an extremely sensitive man against the artificiality of modern industrial civilization, with its barren city scapes. G.'s Rousseauesque tendencies became even more dominant in his subsequent works: *Le chant du monde* (1934; *The Song of the World*, 1938), *Que ma joie demeure* (1935; *Joy of Man's Desiring*, 1949), and *Batailles dans la montagne* (1937; battles in the mountain). These works, considerably larger in scope, have been called epic novels. They take their inspiration from a kind of prophetic vision, which reflects the writer's quest for the ideal of a harmonious blending of man with nature.

G.'s idea of a simple life close to nature appealed to many people, and his house in Manosque became a place of pilgrimage. The annual meetings at his farm on the Contadour plateau between master and disciples began in 1935 and ended in 1939. During this Contadour period G. was more of a preacher than a writer. He was deeply disturbed by the growing tyranny of Mussolini, Hitler, and Stalin, and aggressively denounced all political ideologies in Europe. From an artistic viewpoint, however, this period of social involvement resulted in his weakest works.

After the war G. emerged with a new style, which in part can be attributed to his admiration for Stendhal and Machiavelli. In his "chroniques" (chronicles), as G. liked to call them, the effusive poetic descriptions of nature, so prevalent in his previous novels, are subordinated to a more objective depiction of characters. The events are related from the limited perspective of the first-person narrators, who are usually not the protagonists. This seemingly objective detachment on the part of the author himself constitutes an innovation in technique; it owed much to FAULKNER and the American novel, with which G. was familiar, and paved the way for the NEW NOVEL. The style of such "chronicles" as *Un roi sans divertissement* (1947; a lonely king)—film version, 1963—*Les âmes fortes* (1949; strong souls), and *Le moulin de Pologne* (1952; *The Malediction*, 1955) is simple and concise, concentrating on storytelling. Dialogue becomes an important aspect of this new style. The colorful, rather unusual and picturesque adjectives of his early works all but disappeared. The stories are a mixture of minute realism and fantastic adventures.

Probably the most famous of G.'s postwar novels is *Le hussard sur le toit* (1951; *The Horseman on the Roof*, 1954), the picaresque story of Angelo and his efforts to help combat a cholera epidemic and to alleviate the pains of its victims. It is part of the Angelo cycle, whose main characters are largely inspired by G.'s father, mother, and grandfather.

Besides his numerous novels, some youthful poetry, and many provocative essays, G. also wrote several plays, among them the well-known *La femme du boulanger* (1943; the baker's wife) and *Le voyage en calèche* (1947; traveling by calash). In both the much admired poetic spontaneity of his first period and the more spartan style of his later works, G. was a storyteller of extraordinary talent.

FURTHER WORKS: *Accompagnés de la flûte* (1924); *Présentation de Pan* (1930); *Manosque des plateaux* (1930); *Solitude de la pitié* (1930); *Naissance de l'Odyssée* (1930); *Églogues* (1931); *Le grand troupeau* (1931; *To the Slaughterhouse*, 1969); *Jean le bleu* (1932; *Blue Boy*, 1949); *Solitude la pitié* (1932); *Le serpent d'étoiles* (1933); *Les vraies richesses* (1936); *Rondeur des jours* (1936); *Le bout de la route* (1937); *Refus d'obéissance* (1937); *Le poids du ciel* (1938); *Lettre aux paysans sur la pauvreté et la paix* (1938); *Entrée du printemps; Mort du blé* (1938); *Précisions* (1938); *Provence* (1939); *Pour saluer Melville* (1941); *Triomphe de la vie* (1941); *L'eau vive* (1943); *Théâtre* (1943); *Les pages immortelles de Virgile* (1947); *Noé* (1947); *Fragments d'un déluge* (1948); *Fragments d'un paradis* (1948); *Mort d'un personnage* (1949); *Village* (1950); *Les grands chemins* (1951); *Arcadie, Arcadie!* (1953); *Voyage en Italie* (1953); *L'Écossais; ou, La fin des héros* (1955); *Une aventure; ou, La foudre et le sommet* (1955); *Notes sur l'affaire Dominici* (1955; *The Dominici Affair*, 1956); *La pierre* (1955); *Lucien Jacques* (1956); *Bernard Buffet* (1956); *Le bonheur fou* (1957; *The Straw Man*, 1959); *Provence* (1957); *Angelo* (1958; *Angelo*, 1960); *Domitien, suivi de Joseph à Dothan* (1959); *Sur les oliviers morts* (1959); *Chroniques romanesques* (1962); *Le désastre de Pavie* (1963; *The Battle of Pavia*, 1965); *Deux cavaliers de l'orage* (1965; *Two Riders of the Storm*, 1967); *Provence perdue* (1968); *Ennemonde; ou, Autres caractères* (1968; *Ennemonde*, 1970); *Une histoire d'amour* (1969); *L'Iris de Suze* (1970); *Les récits de la demi-brigade* (1972); *Le déserteur, et autres récits* (1973)

BIBLIOGRAPHY: Chonez, C., *G. par lui-même* (1956); Robert, P. R., *J. G. et les techniques du roman* (1961); Brée, G., and Guiton, M., *The French Novel from Gide to Camus* (1962): 107–13; Ullmann, S., *Style in the French Novel* (1964): 217–31; Smith, M. A., *J. G.* (1966); Redfern, W. D., *The Private World of J. G.* (1967); Peyre, H., *French Novelists of Today*, rev. ed. (1967): 123–54; Goodrich, N. L., *G.: Master of Fictional Modes* (1973)

—BLANDINE M. RICKERT

GIOVANNI, Nikki

American poet and recording artist, b. 7 June 1943, Knoxville, Tennessee

G. cannot be pigeonholed into a single career. She began her working life as an artist, creating poems as part of a black arts movement while also becoming involved in the civil rights movement of the 1960s. Her first book, *Black Feeling, Black Talk* (1968), established her as a poetic force and as an advocate for equality. The black arts movement was especially important because G. and others would go out into the community and read their work in cafes, libraries, and churches as a form of outreach. She organized the first Cincinnati Black Arts Festival and became the managing editor of *Conversation*. G. developed a reputation as a radical because of her views advocating violent resistance to white oppression of blacks. She produced two further books of poetry and by 1970, hers was a recognizable name in black homes. She published a volume of poems in 1972 entitled *My House*, which has the distinction of being one of the most banned books of the early 1990s.

G.'s work of the mid-1970s reflects her recognition of the importance of the legacies of women in her past. Representative is *My House*, her tribute to mothers and grandmothers. Written during a difficult time in American race-relations, the work defied the then trend in African-American works of focusing on contemporary political issues. This work was followed in 1975 by *The Women Gather*.

G.'s career quickly expanded to include children's books, conversations with other important black artists, recordings of poetry and song, honorary degrees, awards, and academia. Her concern about the future of the black community and striving to provide a voice for African-American women is reflected in her 1994 publication *Grand Mothers: Poems, Reminiscences, and Short Stories About the Keepers of Our Traditions*. Her work with members of a retirement community, aimed at helping them to write and express themselves, resulted in the formation of the "Warm Hearth" group, which published a book in 1990 under G.'s guidance.

G. is a unique voice in American literary history and in American and African-American culture. She believes her teaching is among her most important work and continues to nurture new writers, young and old, to help them be strong enough to write what they feel and to make their lives significant to themselves.

FURTHER WORKS: *Black Judgement* (1968); *Night Comes Softly* (1970); *Poem of Angela Yvonne Davis* (1970); *Re: Creation* (1970); *Gemini: An Extended Autobiographical Statement on My*

First Twenty-Five Years of Being a Black Poet (1971); *Spin a Soft Black Song: Poems for Children* (1971); *In My House* (1972); *Dialogue* (1973); *My House, Ego-Tripping and Other Poems for Young People* (1973); *A Poetic Equation: Conversations between N. G. and Margaret Walker* (1974, with Margaret Walker); *The Women and the Men* (1975); *Cotton Candy on a Rainy Day* (1978); *Black Feeling, Black Talk, Black Judgement* (1979); *Vacation Time: Poems for Children* (1980); *Those Who Ride the Night Winds* (1983); *Sacred Cows and Other Edibles* (1988); *Knoxville, Tennessee* (1994); *Racism 101* (1994); *The Genie in the Jar* (1996); *Shimmy Shimmy Like My Sister Kate: Looking at the Harlem Renaissance through Poems* (1996); *The Selected Poems of N. G.* (1996); *The Sun is So Quiet: Poems* (1996); *Love Poems* (1997)

BIBLIOGRAPHY: Harris, S., "N. G.," *Virginia Tech Magazine*, 12 (1990); Fowler, V. C., *Conversations with N. G.* (1992); Fowler, V. C., *N. G.* (1992)

—MARCY TANTER

GIPPIUS, Zinaida

See Hippius, Zinaida

GIRAUDOUX, Jean

French dramatist, novelist, and essayist, b. 29 Oct. 1882, Bellac; d. 31 Jan. 1944, Paris

G. was born in a small provincial town in the Limousin region of central France, which was to be the setting of his plays *Intermezzo* (1933; *The Enchanted*, 1950) and the posthumously published *L'Apollon de Bellac* (1946; *The Apollo of Bellac*, 1954) as well as several of his novels. A brilliant student, G. loved the classics of Greek and Roman literature and of 17th-c. France; after secondary school he went on to specialize in German literature, winning a scholarship to continue his German studies in Munich. G. visited the U.S. twice, first as a teaching assistant in the French Department at Harvard University (1906–7), and later during World War I, when, having been wounded at the front and decorated, he was sent by his government as an instructor of military tactics. He recorded his impressions of the U.S. in the essay collection *Amica America* (1918; America my friend).

G. pursued a double career as writer and diplomat. At the age of twenty-seven he entered the foreign service and was assigned to the press bureau. Twenty years later G. became Chief of Press in the Foreign Ministry under Premier Poincaré. He incorporated his impressions of France's leading political figures in his novels: In *Bella* (1926; *Bella*, 1927), G.'s friend Philippe Berthelot, the Secretary General for Foreign Affairs, is the inspiration for the character Dubardeau, while Raymond Poincaré is portrayed in an unfavorable light as the character Rebendart. In *Combat avec l'ange* (1934; struggle with the angel) G. depicts an idealized Aristide Briand in the character Brossard.

In 1939 G. was appointed Minister of Information in the Daladier cabinet, a position in which he felt extremely uncomfortable. Nevertheless, G.'s sense of duty prevailed and he remained in this post until the German Occupation, at which point he resigned, totally discouraged and disillusioned. He died shortly before the Liberation.

As novelist, essayist, and short-story writer, G. was highly regarded by the literary elite. But G.'s early fictional works were too sophisticated to appeal to the general public. His style is highly impressionistic, with plot and character analysis practically eliminated. His protagonists are young, highly cultured intellectuals, usually adolescent girls on the threshold of adulthood. They desire one last chance to escape the humdrum reality of everyday life before they make any permanent commitments. Typical of G.'s early fiction are the novels *Suzanne et le Pacifique* (1921; *Suzanne and the Pacific*, 1923) and *Juliette au pays des hommes* (1924; Juliette in the land of men). *Suzanne et le Pacifique* is set in 1914 at the start of World War I. Suzanne, who comes from G.'s native town of Bellac, is shipwrecked on a desert island in the Pacific, where dead bodies of German and British sailors are washed ashore. G. provides a happy ending for Suzanne when she finds her Prince Charming in the person of the Supervisor of Weights and Measures, a character partially inspired by G.'s own father, a tax collector. A similar character appeared thirteen years later to provide a happy ending for Isabelle in *Intermezzo*. In *Juliette au pays des hommes* the heroine visits several interesting men and explores the various possible existences she might lead before returning to marry her loyal fiancé Gérard. Like several other writers of his time, especially GIDE and COCTEAU, G. felt a special nostalgia for childhood and adolescence. The young and uncommitted are endowed with intuitive powers, beauty, and grace, while the middle-aged characters are generally stereotyped as dull, pretentious, and corrupt.

In addition to its importance as a prefiguration of *Intermezzo*, *Juliette au pays des hommes* is noteworthy for G.'s famous ironic definition of preciosity: "an evil that consists of treating objects like human beings, human beings as if they were chaste gods, and gods as if they were cats or weasels." This definition of preciosity is precisely G.'s technique in his novels and plays. He elevates the status of everyday objects and ordinary human beings while mocking the gods—Jehovah as well as Jupiter.

It was not until he reached the age of forty-six that G. began to write for the theater. In collaboration with the actor-director Louis Jouvet, G. adapted his novel *Siegfried et le Limousin* (1922; *My Friend from Limousin*, 1923) for the stage under the title *Siegfried* (1928; *Siegfried*, 1930). In reworking his novel for the stage, G. was forced to tighten the structure of his work and eliminate the lengthy digressions that tended to make all his novels rather diffuse.

The story of Siegfried, a French amnesia victim who is nursed back to health and given a new identity by the Germans, is G.'s idealistic plea for Franco-German friendship and understanding. When Siegfried renounces the political power he could have enjoyed as a German and decides to resume his French identity and return to France as Jacques Forestier, Geneviève, the Frenchwoman he had loved, cries out, "Siegfried!"—indicating that she now loves the German in him. G. himself loved both France and Germany. His most cherished hope was for a reconciliation between those two great cultures. From G.'s point of view, France represented clarity, order, logic, and the great classics of Molière, Racine, and La Fontaine. G. considered Germany as representing the heroic, the rebellious, the unknowable, and the romantic, as best exemplified in the masterpieces of German music. In 1928 G. was still optimistic enough to believe that the two countries could live in harmony. Through human fraternity, G. thought, it would be possible to blend the best elements of both cultures.

The opening of G.'s drama *Siegfried* was the major theatrical event of the decade; critics hailed the play as marking the return of dramatic "literature" to the stage. It was praised for its verbal inventiveness and its poetic vision. Before the opening of *Siegfried*, the French naturalistic theater was at a low ebb, and the public was ready to turn to poetry and fantasy, which it found in abundance in G.

G.'s second play, the light comedy *Amphitryon 38* (1929; *Amphitryon 38*, 1939) was both a critical and popular success. Supposedly the thirty-eighth version of the classical legend of Jupiter's seduction of the faithful Alcmena, when he visits her disguised as her husband Amphitryon, this play combines bedroom farce with serious discussions about human destiny. In a verbal battle of wits, G.'s Alcmena clearly outsmarts the foolish, egotistical ruler of the universe, Jupiter. She finds nothing especially impressive about Jupiter's performance in bed and characterizes their night of lovemaking as merely pleasant, remembering other more exciting nights spent in the arms of her husband. Irony and paradoxes abound when Jupiter is tricked by his own disguise into feeling totally human—yet feeling more powerful in that form than he had felt as a god.

The failure of *Judith* (1931; *Judith*, 1955), G.'s third play and the only drama he labeled a "tragedy," left him bitter and apprehensive. Just as *Amphitryon 38* poked fun at the gods of antiquity, so *Judith*, a modern version of the killing of Holofernes by the Hebrew maiden Judith, mocks the story of purity and self-sacrifice in the Old Testament. For his next play, G. returned to familiar ground, to Bellac, for the setting of his comedy-fantasy *Intermezzo*, in which the heroine Isabelle must choose between a Ghost, who promises to initiate her into the secrets of the kingdom of the dead, and the more down-to-earth Supervisor of Weights and Measures, who promises to help Isabelle find beauty and poetry in everyday provincial life.

G.'s most important success, both in France and in the U.S., was the antiwar drama *La guerre de Troie n'aura pas lieu* (1935; *Tiger at the Gates*, 1955). At the peak of his creative powers, G. drew upon his own background not only as a scholar of the classics but also as a war veteran and as a diplomat experienced in the subtleties of peace negotiations. G.'s play focuses on the events leading up to the Trojan War and on the desperate efforts of the Trojan general Hector to avert a catastrophe. G.'s ironic theme here, as in his other serious dramas, is that despite their best efforts, human beings are powerless to control their destiny. The Trojan War will take place because it was preordained by the gods. Yet Hector's oration for the war dead, a brilliant and ironic indictment of war for depriving men of the joys of life, is more memorable than any other lines in the play.

During the 1930s G. became increasingly bitter and pessimistic. As his hopes for a reconciliation between France and Germany grew dimmer, the mood of his plays grew darker. *Électre* (1937; *Electra*, 1952) illustrates the devastation brought about by those who seek absolute justice and refuse to compromise. Electra, like Judith, young, pure, self-righteous and unyielding, refuses to forgive the now repentant Aegisthus for the murder of her father Agamemnon, although she realizes that Aegisthus' death will cause the destruction of the city of Argos and the slaughter of thousands of innocent victims who played no part in her father's assassination. The search for the absolute, the refusal to compromise and to accept life's imperfections, leads inevitably to death and destruction.

The same moral can be found in G.'s most delightful fantasy, *Ondine* (1939; *Ondine*, 1954). Based on a German legend popularized by Friedrich de la Motte-Fouqué (1777–1843), *Ondine* deals with man's quest for a perfect love and his failure to achieve a perfect union with his beloved. Much of the character of Ondine, the water sprite, was already sketched out in the chapter entitled "Stephy" (1929), which was incorporated into G.'s novel *Les aventures de Jérôme Bardini* (1930; the adventures of Jérôme Bardini). Ondine, a child of nature, eternally young, sincere, and beautiful, courts and woos the knight-errant Hans von Wittenstein, who is initially bedazzled by her charms. The failure of their love to survive in the artificial society of the royal court, and Hans's failure to appreciate the true value of Ondine's honesty and purity give the play its tragic overtones. Yet here, as in his other works, when a dramatic situation becomes too painful to bear, G. provides escape through comedy and fantasy, with secondary characters supplying humorous interludes.

G.'s most popular success came posthumously when Louis Jouvet directed G.'s *La folle de Chaillot* (1945; *The Madwoman of Chaillot*, 1947). In this farce a delightfully zany old lady and her equally nonconformist accomplices, all of whom are outcasts from society, take on the military-industrial establishment of Paris and actually win, saving the beautiful city from the threat of being torn apart and drilled for oil. The play is a scathing indictment of the greed, materialism, and mechanization of modern society. It is also a hymn to the beauties of everyday life. When Aurélie, the Madwoman of Chaillot, expresses her love for life to Pierre, the young man who has just been rescued from an attempt at suicide, the audience cannot help but be moved. If this destitute old woman can find joy in her meager existence, how much more joy there must be for those more fortunate than she! G.'s zest for life is contagious. According to him, all the living are lucky—lucky to be alive. Beauty and poetry exist. Modern man should not be too sophisticated to appreciate the simple pleasures of being alive.

An early environmentalist, G. awakens us to the beauties of our surroundings and to the need to preserve our towns from the onslaught of modern technology. In the one-act play *L'impromptu de Paris* (1937; the rehearsal in Paris), a theoretical discussion on the theater inspired by Molière's *L'impromptu de Versailles*, G. has Louis Jouvet and his troupe of actors express his own noble ambitions for the theater. As G.'s principal spokesman, Jouvet explains the way in which a good play can touch and transform the viewer, awakening his latent sensitivities. Before the viewer can understand and intellectualize, the play must appeal to his emotions and his imagination. In order for this quasi-mystical experience to take place, the play must move the viewer through its extraordinary style.

Throughout his career, G. was, above all, a great stylist. His elegant language and sparkling wit are the products of a man who, according to his friend the novelist Paul MORAND, never uttered a vulgar word in his life. His writings contain enough stylistic devices (metaphors, similes, litotes, parallels, and antitheses) to illustrate an entire manual of rhetoric, yet his style is very personal. Even today, G.'s verbal technique remains unequaled. It is especially for his style that he is regarded as the outstanding French playwright of the period between the two world wars, and one of the greatest dramatists of the 20th c.

FURTHER WORKS: *Provinciales* (1909); *L'école des indifférents* (1910); *Lectures pour une ombre* (1917; *Campaigns and Intervals*, 1918); *Simon le pathétique* (1918); *Adieu à la guerre* (1919); *Elpénor* (1919; *Elpenor*, 1958); *Adorable Clio* (1920); *La Pharmacienne* (1922); *La prière sur la Tour Eiffel* (1923); *Visite chez le Prince* (1924); *Hélène et Touglas; ou, Les joies de Paris* (1925); *Premier rêve signé* (1925); *Le cerf* (1926); *Les hommes tigres* (1926); *Églantine* (1927); *La grande bourgeoise; ou, Toute femme a la vocation* (1928); *Marche vers Clermont* (1928); *Le sport* (1928); *Divertissement de Siegfried* (1928); *Le signe* (1929); *Racine* (1930; *Racine*, 1938); *Fugues sur Siegfried* (1930); *Mirage des Bessines* (1931); *Je présente Bellita* (1931); *Berlin* (1932); *La France sentimentale* (1932); *Fin de Siegfried* (1934); *Tessa* (1934); *Supplément au voyage de Cook* (1937; *The Virtuous Island*, 1956); *Et moi aussi, j'ai été un petit Meaulnes* (1937); *Les cinq tentations de La Fontaine* (1938); *Cantique des cantiques* (1938; *Song of Songs*, 1961); *Choix des élues* (1938); *Pleins pouvoirs* (1939); *Le futur armistice* (1940); *Pour l'avenir français* (1940; *The France of Tomorrow*, 1940); *Littérature* (1941); *L'Apollon de Marsac* (1942); *Le film de la duchesse de Langeais* (1942); *Sodome et Gomorrhe* (1943; *Sodom and Gomorrah*, 1961); *Le film de Béthanie: Texte de "Les anges du péché"* (1944, with Raymond Léopold Bruckberger and Robert Bresson); *Écrit dans l'ombre* (1944); *Armistice à Bordeaux* (1945); *Théâtre complet* (15 vols., 1945–54); *Sans pouvoirs* (1946); *Pour une politique urbaine* (1947); *Visitations* (1947); *Variantes* (3 vols., 1947–48); *De pleins pouvoirs à sans pouvoirs* (1950); *La Française et la France* (1951); *Pour Lucrèce* (1951; *Duel of Angels*, 1958); *Les contes d'un matin* (1952); *Œuvre romanesque* (2 vols., 1955); *Œuvres littéraires diverses* (1958); *La menteuse* [fragments] (1958); *Un prince* (1962); *Or dans la nuit: Chroniques et préfaces littéraires, 1910–1943* (1969); *La menteuse* [complete text] (1969; *Lying Woman*, 1972)

BIBLIOGRAPHY: Brasillach, R., "Le théâtre de J. G.," *Portraits* (1935): 123–63; Rousseaux, A., "G.; ou, L'éternel printemps," *Âmes et visages du XXme siècle* (1936): 109–56; Sartre, J.-P., "M. J. G. et la philosophie d'Aristote: À propos de *Choix des élues*," *NRF*, 54 (1940): 339–54; Magny, C.-E, *Précieux G.* (1945); Morand, P., *G.: Souvenirs de notre jeunesse* (1948); Sørensen, H., *J. G.: Technique et style* (1950); Jouvet, L., *Témoignages sur le théâtre* (1952): 148–56, 185–213; May, G., "Marriage vs. Love in the World of J. G.," *YFS*, 11 (1953): 106–15; Mercier-Campiche, M., *Le théâtre de G. et la condition humaine* (1954); Albérès, R.-M, *Esthétique et morale chez J. G.* (1957); Inskip, D., *J. G.: The Making of a Dramatist* (1958); Debidour, V. H., *J. G.* (1958); Le Sage, L., *J. G.: His Life and His Works* (1959); Cohen, R., *G.: Three Faces of Destiny* (1968); Lemaitre, G., *J. G.: The Writer and His Work* (1971); Body, J., *J. G.: The Legend and the Secret* (1991)

—DEBRA POPKIN

M. G. is a man of fancy, fantasy and humor. His aesthetic is built upon unexpectedness and disproportion, and leaves us with the minor feeling Poe noted—a sense of difficulties happily surmounted. It moves in the direction of romanticism, not realism, of entertainment, not experience. The heart of his mental machinery is contained in the following sentence: his whole book is a dilation of that heart. "I tasted large scarlet mushrooms: in France I would have had spotted fever, numb fingers, twitching eyelids; but solitude vaccinated me against all these ills." One who believes that the function of literary art is to give a proportioned heightened representation of the actual cannot follow in the direction of M. G.

But to such a one the principal overtone of *Suzanne and the Pacific* may be valuable. Suzanne is adorably attached to modern civilization. Pitched on a desert island, she hunts for rice powders, perfumes, tobacco, feather dresses: she yearns for railway stations, daily newspapers, moving-pictures, metropolitan crowds; she finally makes her island a fragment of France. . .M. G. is adept at turning the texture of modern sensations into literature, and in the exploitation of these new undigested materials, he is a comrade of the dadaists.

Gorham B. Munson, "A Specimen of Demi-Dadaisme," *New Republic*, 18 April 1923, p. 220

G. restores freedom to the French stage [in *Siegfried*]. He demands nothing either of the ballet, the cinema, or the music-hall. He asks everything of words, style, expression. His theater is a literary theater, a poetic theater, a return to dramatic literature; in the very heart of dramatic literature, he succeeds in asserting his originality. . . .

Siegfried marks a date, a point of departure, a new hope. It marks the theater's escape from naturalism, from too much psychology, through poetry (not expressionism or futurism). It marks the renaissance of style in the theater, the resurrection of drama in which each character has the right to finish his sentences, to utter monologues or even long declamations, the resurrection of theater from which intellectual ideology, verbal magic have not been banished, theater which allows ecstasy, expansiveness, enthusiasm, theater big enough to house the world, great enough to contain the struggle between modern consciences and the most burning questions.

Since Musset, no French author has approached the stage with so much ease and grace. With fewer paradoxes and less vehemence, the *Siegfried* of G. introduces into our theater the freedom and diversity which the English stage owes to Bernard Shaw. [1928]

Benjamin Crémieux, "J. G.'s *Siegfried*," in Justin O'Brien, ed., *From the N. R. F.* (1958), pp. 167–68

The role in J. G.'s universe delegated to Isabelle [in *Intermezzo*] is the one that the entire Middle Ages delegated to the young girl, that of the interpreter of the supernatural world. It is she who is tempted to exceed the limits of the earth—but not to betray the world. What she desires is not so much to die as to annex a new kingdom for life—and this kingdom happens to be the kingdom of the dead. . . Although the wise supervisor reprimands her, dangerous tasks are always undertaken by young girls, and it is right that they should: thanks to these young girls, our vision is expanded, our dreams find some foundation, and the most ambitious extravagances acquire some sort of real substance. Are the dead not ready to reenter the world of the living?. . .

Only young girls can suppose so, and perhaps they can even find proof. Isabelle is our Parsifal, declares the sentimental yet ironic supervisor. But as soon as a potential husband appears for Isabelle, the whole beautiful supernatural world she has seen will disappear. . . . She will be converted to the limited wisdom of the supervisor, and since she will no longer be able to know anything else, she will finally consent, with courageous calm, to turn her back upon the charms of ghosts and gods in order to rejoin humanity. It is a shame, no doubt—but that is the price of living.

Robert Brasillach, *Portraits* (1935), pp. 145–47

In order to enter fully into the universe of *Choice of the Elect*, we must first forget the world in which we live. I therefore pretended that I knew nothing at all about this soft, pasty substance traversed by waves whose cause and purpose are exterior to themselves, this world without a future, in which things are always meeting, in which the present creeps up like a thief, in which events have a natural resistance to thought and language, this world in which individuals are accidents, mere pebbles, for which the mind subsequently fabricates general categories. . . .

It would be a mistake, however, to regard M. G. as a Platonist. His forms are not in the heaven of ideas, but among us, inseparable from the matter whose movements they govern. They are stamped on our skin like seals in glass. Nor are they to be confused with simple concepts. A concept contains barely more than a handful of the traits common to all the individuals of a given group. Actually, M. G.'s forms contain no more, but the features that compose them are all perfect. They are norms and canons rather than general ideas. [1940]

Jean-Paul Sartre, *Literary and Philosophical Essays* (1955), pp. 43–44

As with *Siegfried*, the broad political panorama prevents [*The Trojan War Will Not Take Place*] from wallowing in seriousness. G. delighted in wit, word-play, and theatrical legerdemain as before—concluding the play with an extraordinary device in which the curtain begins to fall and then rises again. The theatricalism enforces an objectivity over the crucial issue of war, and prevents the play from rigidly taking a side and becoming propagandistic instead of analytic, which it remains. . . .

The Trojan War [*Will Not Take Place*] is a play about war and against it. It is not mere pacifism—an oversimplification which G. would have abhorred, and it is far from one-sided. But the message is clear, and when the brilliance of the dialogue, the theatricalism of the setting, and the complex progression of the plot have receded in our minds, the bitterness at war's irrationality remains. Easily comprehensible in its major theme, *The Trojan War* [*Will Not Take Place*] is G.'s final despairing cry for peace, and it has become one of the rare masterpieces of the century.

Robert Cohen, *G.: Three Faces of Destiny* (1968), pp. 103–4

As G. advanced in age, his characters seemed to acquire more and more the value of pure symbols. . . .

This progressive degradation of the characters representing passionate reality seems to parallel the change for the worse that took place in G.'s personal views of the real itself. In the last years of his life G. was evidently overwhelmed by a feeling of disgust for the world in which we live. Although he fought as best as he could against that feeling in such works as *L'Apollon de Bellac* and *La folle de Chaillot*, his final outlook remained grim. A few of the "elect"—of whom Lucile is the last example in his plays—may be personally exempt from the taint of almost universal corruption, but they can escape defilement at the contact of the world and retain their essence of purity only by moving out of this world altogether.

During his youth, a happy G. had fondly believed that the ideal and reality could meet. In his mature age, he had toyed with the hundred possibilities of interplay between them. When he grew old, he reached the disconsolate conclusion that they are incompatible. Rather than debase the ideal, rather than submit to the loathsome claims of reality, he chose to retain the ideal intact—in death. This is the fundamental meaning of *Pour Lucrèce* and the last message of G. himself before his own end.

> Georges Lemaitre, *J. G.: The Writer and His Work* (1971), p. 145

GIRONELLA, José María

Spanish novelist, essayist, and critic, b. 31 Dec. 1917, Darnius, Spain

G. grew up in a small village near Gerona in Catalonia, where he has lived most of his life. He never received any formal education and in his youth worked at a variety of odd jobs ranging from factory apprentice to bank clerk; he had ambitions to become a priest but abandoned this idea. At the outbreak of the civil war in 1936 he joined the Nationalist army; during the war he wrote many letters and love poetry. In 1940, after the end of the war, he returned to Gerona and became a newspaper reporter; he also was a correspondent for *Informazione* in Rome. In 1947 G. and his wife left Spain illegally and traveled extensively. He suffered a nervous breakdown in 1951 while in Paris and sought cures at clinics in Vienna and Helsinki; he described his illness in *Los fantasmas de mi cerebro* (1958; in *Phantoms and Fugitives*, 1964). G. returned to Spain in 1952 but has continued to travel abroad periodically.

G.'s first novel, *Un hombre* (1946; *Where the Soil Was Shallow*, 1957), won the Nadal Prize. Somewhat autobiographical, it is an improbable circus tale that displays all the romantic zeal of a young writer trying to discover himself and his métier through literature. *La marea* (1949; the tide) is an "experimental" novel in which he successfully integrated history with a highly unlikely love story among Nazis set in Germany during World War II. It was virtually unnoticed by critics.

G.'s most famous work is *Los cipreses creen en Dios* (1953; *The Cypresses Believe in God*, 1955), which won the National Prize for Literature. It is a long novel of great scope. G. is a master storyteller, and as this novel shows, his forte lies in graphically

explicating the panorama of the Spanish Civil War. *Los cipreses creen en Dios* and two sequels—*Un millón de muertos* (1961; *One Million Dead*, 1963) and *Ha estallado la paz* (1966; *Peace after War*, 1969), both of which are of lesser importance than the first book—trace the vicissitudes of the Alvear family from the period before the civil war to its aftermath. The Alvears are very much individuals, but their struggles also represent the struggles of all Spanish families who shared in the making of history during the civil war, and the characters take on a universal significance.

G. has written, among other things, several travel books on Japan, China, and Israel; a highly praised collection of short stories and essays entitled *Todos somos fugitivos* (1961; in *Phantoms and Fugitives*, 1964), whose central theme is escape—from reality, loneliness, death; and a best-selling novel in two volumes, *Condenados a vivir* (1971; condemned to live), which continues the Alvear family saga, tracing the lives of the characters through the decade of the 1940s. Yet nothing has equaled the quality and success of *Los cipreses creen en Dios*. Nevertheless, he is very prominent on the Spanish literary scene. He spearheaded efforts against government censorship of literature in the early 1950s and is also one of the first Catalan writers still residing in Spain to approach straightforwardly the "forbidden" subject of the civil war. He is also indisputably the first novelist to publish an explanation of the civil war generally acceptable to Spaniards.

FURTHER WORKS: *Ha llegado el invierno y tú no estás aquí* (1945); *El novelista ante el mundo* (1954); *Muerte y juicio de Giovanni Papini* (1959); *Mujer, levántate y anda* (1962); *Personas, ideas y mares* (1963; partial tr., *On China and Cuba*, 1963); *El Japón y su duende* (1964); *China, lágrima innumerable* (1965); *Gritos del mar* (1967); *En Asia se muere bajo las estrellas* (1968); *Conversaciones con Don Juan de Borbón* (1968); *Cien españoles y Dios* (1969); *Gritos de la tierra* (1970); *Los hombres lloran solos* (1971); *El escándalo de Tierra Santa* (1977); *Carta a mi padre muerto* (1978)

BIBLIOGRAPHY: Boyle, K., "Spain Divided," *Nation* (11 June 1955): 506–7; Kerrigan, A., "J. M. G. and the Black Legend of Spain," *Books on Trial*, 14 (1956): 343–45; Devlin, J. J., "Arturo Barea and J. M. G.: Two Interpreters of the Spanish Labyrinth," *Hispania*, 41 (1958), 143–48; Urbanski, E. S., "Revolutionary Novels of G. and Pasternak," *Hispania*, 43 (1960): 191–97; Payne, R., on *Peace after War*, SatR (17 May 1969): 49; Schwartz, R., *J. M. G.* (1972); Schwartz, R., *Spain's New Wave Novelists, 1950–1974: Studies in Spanish Realism* (1976): 50–65

—RONALD SCHWARTZ

GIRRI, Alberto

Argentine poet and translator, b. 27 Nov. 1919, Buenos Aires

Except for occasional trips abroad, G. has lived his entire life in Buenos Aires. He attended the University of Buenos Aires, graduating in 1946. A prolific poet and translator, he has also contributed frequently to important magazines such as *Sur* and the literary supplement of *La Nación*. He has received numerous prizes within Argentina, including the First National Prize for Poetry (1967), as well as foreign honors such as a Guggenheim Foundation fellow-ship (1964 and 1977) and a Gold Medal from the Italian Government (1962).

Although his poetry owes little allegiance to any movement or school, G. began to publish contemporaneously with the Argentine "Generation of 1940," a group of poets who distanced themselves from the avant-garde poetics practiced in the 1920s and 1930s. According to critic Saúl Yurkievich, G. shares with many poets of the "Generation of 1940" a return to the cultural cosmopolitanism of the earlier "modernista" tradition. That is, in opposition to the regional poetry of the Argentine avant-garde, G. opted for an overt universalism, crossing geographic and historical boundaries. This international orientation is nowhere more evident than in G.'s work as a translator, which spans the tradition of poetry in English from John Donne to Robert LOWELL and beyond, as well as including Italian and Japanese poetry.

From his first book of poems, *Playa sola* (1946; deserted beach), G.'s poetry showed great range in terms of its cultural illusions, and this characteristic has not changed over time. His style, however, developed in the opposite direction, becoming progressively more spare over the next decade. This economy of means, now a signature feature of G.'s work, frequently carries the poems to laconic or aphoristic extremes. G. summed up this attitude in a book of metapoetic prose fragments titled *El motivo es el poema* (1976; the motive is the poem) when he said: "Conscious-ness of limitations: consciousness of lucidity. Make do with very little."

According to critic Guillermo Sucre, this lucidity is the central characteristic of G.'s poetry. For Sucre this poetry reveals an intelligence that is supremely self-critical, and critical of literature as well. G. sees language and poetry as inherently separated from reality. The poem cannot create or recreate the world; it can only provide a way of seeing it, of organizing it, and of filling it with meaning. In his poetics the world is silent, and the poem is directed toward that silence with the understanding that it can never reach it. This idea reveals G.'s philosophical debt to Taoism, expressed most noticeably in his collection *El ojo* (1964; the eye). For G. silence is a version of the void, which in Taoism is the origin and end of all life. Poetry, in his view, brings poet and reader close to this void, although one may never reach it. Inherent to his poetics is an insistence on the negation of the self and the creation of an impersonal and anonymous poetry. A similar philosophy was espoused by T. S. ELIOT, whom G. has translated extensively. G. also approaches Eliot in his embracing of the poetic tradition and enthusiasm for intertextual play. This play, and the underlying idea of literature as a shared venture, is openly alluded to by the title of one of G.'s recent collections, *Lo propio, lo de todos* (1980; one's own, that which belongs to all).

The objects of much of G.'s poetry are philosophical issues such as time, the self, and the nature and purpose of art. This last theme is especially important, and it has overflowed into a number of prose efforts which are crucial to an understanding of his poetics. These include *El motivo es el poem, Diario de un libro* (1972; subsidiary of a book), and *Notas sobre la experiencia poética* (1983; notes on the experience of poetry).

G. is an extremely prolific poet known for his bare style and his penetrating explorations of difficult philosophical issues. His works, both poetry and prose, constitute a sustained meditation on the nature of poetry. G. is highly conscious of the limitations of all art, its inability ever to bridge the gap between the world and one's idea of the world. Nevertheless, poetry is seen as a way of approaching

that point at which self disappears, language falls silent, and reality is experienced directly and authentically.

FURTHER WORKS: *Crónica del héroe* (1946); *Coronacíon de la espera* (1947); *Trece poemas* (1949); *El tiempo que destruye* (1951); *Escándalo y soledades* (1952); *Línea de la vida* (1955); *Examen de nuestra causa* (1956); *La penitencia y el mérito* (1957); *Propiedades de la magia* (1959); *La condición necesaria* (1960); *Elegías italianas* (1962); *Poemas elegidos* (1965); *Un brazo de Dios* (1966); *Envíos* (1967); *Casa de la mente* (1968); *Antología temática* (1969); *Valores diarios* (1970); *En la letra, ambigua selva* (1972); *Poesía de observación* (1973); *Quien habla no está muerto* (1975); *Galería personal* (1975); *Bestiario* (1976); *Obra poética I* (1977); *Prosas* (1977); *Árbol de la estirpe humana* (1978); *Obra poética II* (1978); *Obra poética III* (1980); *Homenaje a W. C. Williams* (1981); *Poemas* (1982); *Borradores* (1982); *Lírica de percepciones* (1983); *Páginas de A. G. selecctionadas por el autor* (1983); *Monodias* (1985); *Existenciales* (1986); *Noventa y nueve poemas* (1988)

BIBLIOGRAPHY: Vitale, I., "A. G., poeta de lo real," *Sin Nombre*, 5 (1975): 65–69; Torres Fierro, D., "A. G.: Repaso a una obsesión," *Plural*, 58 (1976): 48–51; Yurkievich, S., "A. G.: Fases de su creciente," *Hispam*, 10, 29 (Aug. 1981): 99–105; Borinsky, A., "Interlocución y aporía: notas a propósito de A. G. y Juan Gelman," *RI*, 49, 125 (Oct.–Dec. 1983): 879–87; Sucre, G., *La máscara, la transparencia: Ensayos sobre poesía hispanoamericana*, 2nd ed. (1985): 345–49; Pascoe, M. S., *La poesía de A. G.* (1986)

—BEN A. HELLER

GLADKOV, Fyodor Vasilievich

Russian novelist and short-story writer, b. 21 June 1883, Chernavka; d. 20 Dec. 1958, Moscow

G. was born into an impoverished peasant family of Old Believers (a sect of Russian schismatics). In his youth, he held various jobs before becoming a teacher in 1902. Except for his exile to Siberia (1906–9) for pro-Bolshevik activity, he taught until 1918. Following the October revolution he fought for the Bolshe-viks and joined the Communist Party in 1920. In 1921 he turned to literature full time.

G. first began to publish as early as 1900. His initial formative period was influenced by Maxim GORKY's sympathetic depiction of rebellious tramps, and by SYMBOLISM—especially its cult of suffering and morbid eroticism. Both influences are seen in *Izgoi* (written 1909–11, pub. 1922; the outcasts), a collection of narra-tives that portray a socially variegated group of political exiles in Siberia. As would prove characteristic of G., authorial sympathies favored the steadfast workers over the seriously flawed intellectuals.

After the revolution, his proletarian orientation notwithstand-ing, G.'s prose reflected ORNAMENTALISM, an essentially nonproletarian, experimentalist trend begun by Andrey BELY, and adopted by many aspiring Soviet authors. Ornamentalism in-creased the expressive potential of prose through metaphoric density, rhythmic and sound devices proper to poetry, and esoteric vocabulary. Ornamentalism was prominent in G.'s tale *Ognenny kon* (1923; the fiery steed), which also reflected a common view (later heretical) that the Russian Revolution was a national, organic event beyond the control of individuals or parties. G. would ultimately renounce *Ognenny kon.*

In 1923 G. joined The Forge, a group of writers who extolled the proletariat and burgeoning technology. The group's principles, together with ornamentalism, would be prominent in G.'s most famous work, the novel *Tsement* (1925; *Cement*, 1929), which focuses upon the efforts of a Communist, Gleb Chumalov, to resume production in a cement factory that closed during the civil war. Gleb overcomes worker apathy and hostility, red tape, sabotage, and various technical problems, but his social victories are offset on a personal level by the death of his daughter and estrangement from his wife Dasha, who, during Gleb's military service, changed from a dutiful housewife to a fully emancipated woman and promiscuous social activist. Through Gleb and Dasha, G. raised, but did not resolve, the question of emancipation for Soviet women and its implications for the family. The same holds true for G.'s handling of the plight of Soviet intellectuals; the problem of maintaining revolutionary fervor in the face of concessions to free enterprise under the NEP (New Economic Policy); and internal Party justice (the purge scenes and the "personality cult" surrounding Badin, a ruthless Party leader).

Tsement became popular, not just because it was topical and proletarian, but also because its stylistic richness and racy characters were interesting. From the later 1920s until his death, however, G. repeatedly weakened *Tsement* by revising it to reflect Socialist REALIST principles of stylistic neutrality, maximal clarity, puritanism, and Party loyalty. Similarly questionable, if less extensive, revisions affected most of G.'s other works, including his unfinished, serially published construction novel *Energia* (1932–38; energy).

The most interesting of G.'s later works is his autobiographical cycle: *Povest o detstve* (1949; a tale of childhood); *Volnitsa* (1950; a free gang); *Likhaya godina* (1954; a woeful year), and the unfinished *Myatezhnaya yunost* (1956; *Restless Youth*, 1958). The cycle is thoroughly Socialist Realist in that it shows the prerevolutionary order as inhumane, corrupt, and historically doomed, while amid religious bigotry and oppression, Russian toilers show promise of revolt in the name of truth, freedom, and social justice. While character and social relationships are basically pat, G. often makes his narratives engrossing through the immediacy of dramatic episodes, colorful language, and the beauty of the natural world.

The retrospective incursion of Socialist Realist criteria into so much of G.'s corpus makes the assessment of his legacy highly problematical. Talented enough to earn the esteem of both Gorky and Bely, he was representative of many Soviet artists of the 1920s who tried to combine a sincere commitment to revolutionary ideals with the search for artistic originality. When political criteria became paramount in Soviet literature from the late 1920s onward, he gradually and dutifully accommodated them with dire effect upon the intrinsic interest of his works. Nevertheless, G.'s *Tsement*, a Soviet classic, many of whose themes, while tempered by revisions, are still relevant in the Soviet Union, has been translated into all major languages of the world, and represents its author's main continuing claim to international renown.

FURTHER WORKS: *Staraya sekretnaya* (1926); *Malenkaya trilogia* (1927); *Novaya zemlya* (1931); *Pyanoe solntse* (1932); *Beryozovaya roshcha* (1940); *Klyatva* (1944); *Sobranie sochineny* (8 vols., 1958); *Myatezhnaya yunost, ocherki, stati, vospominania* (1961)

BIBLIOGRAPHY: Brown, E. J., *Russian Literature since the Revolution* (1963): 162–71; Struve, G., *Russian Literature under Lenin and Stalin, 1917–1953* (1971): 132–34; Busch, R. L., "G.'s *Cement*: The Making of a Soviet Classic," *SEEJ*, 22 (1978): 348–61; Vavra, E., Afterword to *Cement* (1980): 313–25

—ROBERT L. BUSCH

GLATSTEIN, Jacob

(Glatshteyn, Yankev) Yiddish poet, critic and essayist, b. 20 Aug. 1896, Lublin, Poland; d. 19 Nov. 1971, New York, N.Y., U.S.A.

G. received a sound traditional Jewish religious education as well as instruction in secular subjects. As a child he was first exposed to the writings of the Yiddish classics by his father, whose decisive influence G. acknowledged in later life. He began to write at an early age. At thirteen he traveled to Warsaw, like many other aspiring Yiddish writers of the day, to show his work to Yitskhok Leybush Peretz (1852–1915).

In 1914, in response to mounting anti-Semitism, G. emigrated to the U.S., arriving in New York, the city that became his permanent home. That same year he published his first piece, a short story. G. experienced a difficult period of adaptation to his new environment and ceased writing Yiddish for a time. In 1918, while studying law, influenced by the works of Rabindranath TAGORE and Kahlil GIBRAN (1883–1931), he began to write poetry in English. A young Yiddish poet, Nokhem Borekh Minkoff (1893–1958), introduced G. to the then-flourishing Yiddish literary community, which prompted his return to writing Yiddish. The outstanding Yiddish poets Moyshe Leyb HALPERN and H. Leivick (1886–1962) encouraged him. In 1919 G. made his poetic debut. Together with Aron Glants-Leyeles (1889–1966) and N. B. Minkoff, he launched the "Inzikh," or introspective movement in American Yiddish poetry—the name derived from the group's journal, *In zikh* (inside the self).

To insure his livelihood, G. turned to journalism, an occupation he had previously shunned as unfit for a poet. He began a long and respected career as a columnist, commenting on most significant events in Jewish literary and cultural life as well as on world literature.

In 1934 G. returned to Poland to visit his dying mother in Lublin. This journey resulted in two autobiographical travel narratives, *Ven yash iz geforn* (1938; *Homeward Bound*, 1969) and *Ven yash iz gekumen* (1940; *Homecoming at Twilight*, 1962), notable for their innovative poetic prose permeated by a sense of impending doom.

G. is recognized first and foremost for his poetic achievement. At the outset of his career a principal theorist of the introspectivist group, G. was influenced by Ezra Pound and T. S. ELIOT and by IMAGISM. The Inzikh program emphasized the concrete image and preferred association and suggestion to direct statement and logical development. G. helped introduce free verse into Yiddish poetry in order to capture the rhythms of everyday speech and to convey the sounds of the modern metropolis. In his first two volumes, *Yankev Glatshteyn* (1921; Jacob Glatstein) and *Fraye ferzn* (1926; free verse), he asserted his personality and the principles of the Inzikh program.

G. did not remain bound to introspectivist theory or to any literary dogma, but his penchant for the rhythms of the spoken language, his bold imagery, his use of association and suggestion, and his gift for irony are continuing elements that characterize his entire poetic oeuvre.

From the beginning of his career as a poet, G. was in love with the vitality of language and particularly with his medium, the Yiddish language. His brilliant word play, his invention of nonce words and neologisms, although more evident in the earlier stage of his career, persist as striking features of his poetry.

The Holocaust transformed G. into one of the great elegists of eastern European Jewry. He treasured and memorialized the goodness and justness of its life and the humanism of its culture. Yet, significant strains of G.'s post-Holocaust poetry remain personal and private. When G. accepted the burden to bear witness to the Holocaust, in his *Gedenklider* (1943; memorial poems), *Shtralndike Yidn* (1946, radiant Jews), and *Dem tatns shotn* (1953; my father's shadow), previously unsympathetic critics who mistrusted the rebellious individualist now embraced G. as the spokesman of a national culture.

FURTHER WORKS: *Kredos* (1929); *Yidishtayshn* (1937); *Emil un Karl* (1940); *Yosl Loksh fun Khelm* (1944); *In tokh genumen* (1947); *Fun mayn gantser mi* (1956); *In tokh genumen* (1956); *In tokh genumen* (2 vols., 1960); *Di freyd fun yidishn vort* (1961); *Mit mayne fartogbikher* (1963); *A yid fun Lublin* (1966); *Af greyte temes* (1967); *Kh'tu dermonen* (1967); *Gezangen fun rekhts tsu links* (1971); *In der velt mit yidish* (1972); *Prost un poshet* (1978). FURTHER WORKS IN ENGLISH: *Poems* (1970); *The Selected Poems of J. G.* (1972); *I Keep Recalling: The Holocaust Poems of J. G.* (1993)

BIBLIOGRAPHY: Faerstein, C., "J. G.: The Literary Uses of Yiddish," *Judaism*, 14 (1965): 414–31; Howe, I., "Journey of a Poet," *Commentary*, Jan. 1972: 75–77; Lapin, S., "J. G.: Poetry and Peoplehood," *American Jewish Yearbook*, 73 (1972): 611–17; Tabatshnik, A., "A Conversation with J. G.," *Yiddish*, 1 (1973): 40–53; Hadda, J. R., *Yankev Glatshteyn* (1980)

—EUGENE ORENSTEIN

Edouard Glissant

GLISSANT, Edouard

Martinican poet, novelist, and essayist, b. 21 Sept. 1928, Sainte-Marie

Though almost exclusively informed by the Caribbean island of Martinique, G.'s oeuvre extends its relevance far beyond the region. Born in the highlands in the commune of Sainte-Marie, where Creole is the language of the people, G. attended Lycée Schoelcher in Fort-de-France, the capital of Martinique. His teacher was Aimé CÉSAIRE, one of the founders of the NÉGRITUDE movement. In 1946 G. went to the Sorbonne in Paris, where he first studied history, and later philosophy, in addition to ethnology. He befriended many African and Caribbean intellectuals, among them his compatriot Frantz Fanon (1927–1962), the famous psychiatrist and political activist for decolonization. Following his formal studies, G. worked as an editor and wrote critical reviews and essays on the arts and literature. His early poetry and essays reveal his preoccupations with the ambiguities of his personal situation as an Antillean immersed in French culture, a thematic strand that weaves through his work. In 1956 he also published a long epic poem, *Les Indes* (the Indies), which retraces Columbus's voyage to America and poses questions on the destinies of the New World. Two years later, G. published his first novel, *La Lézarde* (1956; The

Ripening, 1959), an exploration of Martinican time and space, which was awarded, not without controversy, the prestigious Renaudot Prize. During the 1950s, G. turned to politics and, together with other writers and intellectuals, founded a political group, the Front Antillo-Guyanais, which, among other things, called for the decolonization of the French overseas departments. Because of his political activities, G. was kept under virtual house arrest, and the Front was banned in 1961. G. resumed his creative work, published a play, *Monsieur Toussaint* (1961; *Monsieur Toussaint*, 1981), dealing with the tragedy of Toussaint Louverture, the leader of Haitian independence, and finished his second novel, *Le Quatrième siècle* (1964; the fourth century), which retraces, through chronologically disrupted sequences, the destinies of two families, the Longoués, the fugitive slaves, and the Belouses, the assimilable plantation slaves, whose descendants reappear in virtually all of G.'s novels. Permitted to return to Martinique in 1967, G. founded his own Institut Martiniquais d'Études, which offered educational programs as well as sponsored research and other cultural activities relevant to Martinican culture. In 1971 G. founded a journal, *Acoma*, dedicated to the study of Martinican society and culture. In 1975 he published his third novel, *Malemort* (foul death), which evokes, in moods of wry humor and a poignant sense of helplessness, scenes of the early days of slavery and contemporary Martinique, corrupt and culturally inauthentic. In 1980 G. returned to Paris to assume editorship of UNESCO publications. While in Paris G. published two novels and a collection of essays and poetry each. In 1988 he accepted a distinguished lectureship position at Louisiana State University. In 1989 G. published another collection of essays, *La Poétique de la relation* (cross-cultural poetics), which pursues his favorite topics of Europocentric cultural imperialism and the dynamics and dilemmas of intercultural relations.

Informed by Martinique and its people, G.'s oeuvre is reaching out to articulate global concerns and intone themes that deal with universal issues. His first novels focus primarily on a search for Martinican identity that necessitates the recovery of the lost past of the Afro-Caribbean, who, traumatized by slavery, the plantation system, and colonization in the past, is today victim of cultural assimilation and socioeconomic exploitation. To recover the authentic past, ignored or distorted by European historiography, G. probes folkloric materials, stories, and legends, which are, for G., the depositories of the untapped collective unconscious. G. is particularly interested in the rehabilitation of the maroon, the fugitive slave, the first authentic hero. This search for the past becomes an urgency as the present-day Martinicans have lost their identity under the impact of urbanization and tourism promoted by metropolitan interests.

G.'s later works, particularly the novel *Mahagony* (1987; Mahogany) and two collections of essays, *Le discours antillais* (1981; *Caribbean Discourse*, 1989) and *La Poétique de la relation*, reject the notion of cultural hierarchies and stress the urgent need to recognize the coexistence of different cultures. These ideas and other topics of universal import, particularly cultural diversity and chaos, are elaborated in his massive subsequent work, *Tout-Monde* (1993; universe), where G. pursues the life stories of his characters from previous novels in settings temporal and geographic that encompass almost the entire world. Similarly his *Faulkner, Mississippi* (1996) ranges far beyond the life and work of the American author and the imaginary Yoknapatawpha county. It offers analyses and meditations on cultures of the South and North, European and Creole. G.'s arguments are complex, predicated on the experience of the Afro-Caribbean who has suffered a series of discontinuities. Thus, the texture of G.'s writing is challenging to the reader who expects causality and chronology as the mainstays of writing. G.'s narratives are polymorphic, sometimes with changing perspectives and contrasting stylistic devices, including peculiar Creole speech patterns. Although G. has commented on many aspects of contemporary culture, his starting point is almost invariably his native land, the little island of Martinique, which can be seen as a microcosm in the image of the macrocosm. G. calls for the acceptance of what is called *créolité*, a cultural state that recognizes the inevitable intercontamination of cultures and languages. With the passing of Négritude as a viable cultural notion, G.'s ideas have given rise to a new generation of writers and intellectuals who call themselves Créolistes. The recognition of G. as perhaps the most visible-intellectual figure in the francophone Caribbean and beyond is incontestable.

FURTHER WORKS: *Un champs d'îles* (1953); *La terre inquiète* (1955); *Soleil de la conscience* (1956); *Le sel noir* (1960); *L'intention poétique* (1969); *La case du commandeur* (1981); *Pays rêvé, pays réel* (1985); *Fastes* (1991); *Introduction à une poétique du divers* (1996); *Traité du Tout-monde* (1997)

BIBLIOGRAPHY: Boisdeffre, P. de, "L'épopée d'E. G." *Une anthologie vivante de la littérature d'aujourd'hui* (1966): 745–49; Silenieks, J., "Deux pièces antillaises: du témoignage local vers une tragédie moderne," *KRQ*, 15, 3 (1968): 245–54; Case, F. I., "The Novels of E. G.," *BlackI* (1973): 3–12; Baudot, A., "D'un pays (re)possé dé," *EF* (1974): 359–73; Roget, W., "The Image of Africa in the Writings of E. G.," *CLAJ* (1978): 390–99; Ormerod, B., "Discourse and Dispossession: E. G.'s Image of Contemporary Martinique," *CarQ*, 27, 4 (Oct. 1981): 1–12; Radford, D., E. G. (1982); special G. issue, *CARE* (1983); Cailler, B., *Conquérants de la nuit nue: E. G. et l'H(h)istorie antillaise* (1988); special G. Issue, *WLT*, 63, 4 (Autumn 1989); Baudot, A., *Bibliographie Annotée d'E. G.* (1993)

—JURIS SILENIEKS

GODBOUT, Jacques

Canadian novelist, screenwriter, and poet (writing in French), b. 27 Nov. 1933, Montreal

After receiving a classical education with the Jesuits, G. pursued his studies at the University of Montreal, where he received his B.A. in 1953 and his M.A. in 1954. He then taught in Addis Ababa for three years. Upon his return to Canada, he worked in film for the government.

G.'s novels and films reflect the political events and important changes taking place in Quebec during the last three decades and explore the role of the individual, especially the writer, within this culture and, beyond the borders of Quebec, within the North American context, English Canadian and American as well. Various ways are explored to achieve happiness within a clearly defined cultural context. One's identity is often best defined, according to G., through the act of writing.

G.'s literary career began with the publication of several collections of poems: *Carton pâte* (1956; papier-mâché), *Les pavés secs* (1958; dry paving stones), and *C'est la chaude loi des hommes* (1960; it is the hot law of men). After this, his principal effort turned to the novel and to film. *L'aquarium* (1962; the aquarium) is set in Ethiopia during the monsoon season and explores the lives and relationships of a group of foreigners waiting for the moment of change when they will leave the country. During this time, revolution is brewing in the land. The parallels to Quebec society are obvious: the long period of isolation, the otherness of the principal characters, outsiders in this land, waiting for change to come, yet often sinking into personal trivialities, uninterested for the most part in becoming involved in the political changes, some preferring simply to take the money and run. In *Le couteau sur la table* (1965; *Knife on the Table*, 1968) the action is closer to home, in both English-and French-speaking Canada, between a francophone hero and his anglophone significant other, Patricia, each one eventually acquiring a homolingual consort. The new anglophone couple fails; the francophone couple fares better, but the ties are cruelly broken when Madeleine dies in a motorcycle accident. The hero will then direct his energies to dealing with Patricia with the knife on the table. Although the hero is from a modest background and is clearly interested in the wealth and power associated with the English-speaking world, it is with his own people, committed to transforming their world into a better one, that he will group; however, though the Anglo world and Patricia are rejected, the knife remains on the table, still not used against her.

G.'s third novel, *Salut Galarneau!* (1967; *Hail Galarneau!*, 1970), was a resounding success. The hero, François Galarneau, tricked into getting married and, after freeing himself from his marital prison, betrayed by his new woman friend Marise, who prefers his brother to him, withdraws from the world, walling himself up and writing in order to better understand himself and to recover from his pain. His freedom, his being, will be achieved and found through this creativity. The work is sprinkled throughout with the realities of everyday Quebec, where the popular language is riddled with Anglicisms, where the ordinary young man dreams of making it in the North American world of commercial enterprise—François dreams of becoming the King of the Hot Dog through a chain of stands he will create. François mother leaves for the U.S., as did so many of her compatriots in the last century and a half, and François will also head in that direction. Not only does G.'s language reflect contemporary middle-class usage, but the story line in part reflects social realities, where from a period of licking his wounds the hero will make his way, through his creativity, in the new world, as a new man. G. continued to explore some of these interests in his next novels and films: *Kid Sentiment* (1967; title in English), a film about francophone youths in an anglophone world; the film *IXE-13* (1971; IXE-13); the novels *D'amour, P.Q.* (1972; Thomas d'Amour, P.Q.), which redirects our attention to involvement in Quebec's political world, and *L'îsle au dragon* (1976; *Dragon Island*, 1978), with its capitalist American invader; the film *Distortions* (1981; distortions), which explores the world of Africans and their relationships to the international press; and *Comme en Californie* (1983; as in California), presenting the "new age" and its influence on Quebec.

Une histoire américaine (1986; *An American Story*, 1988) finds its hero, Gregory Francoeur, spending time to begin his life anew in the new center of the universe, the Bay Area, exploring, as a university researcher, studying happiness, but becoming an unwilling participant in a detective thriller, and seeking refuge, after his arrest, in the writing of his story. As a native outsider in the North American experience, associated with other "outsiders," the protagonist learns to evaluate himself through the ties that bind him to North America in general, and to Quebec in particular. The film *Alias Will James* (1988; title in English) tells of the experience of Ernest Dufault, a Quebecer who transformed himself into a writer, Will James, of stories about cowboys and who succeeded in passing himself off as one of them, with an "Indian" accent. G. explores the attractions of the U.S. for the residents of Quebec.

In addition to his creative works, G. is important for having founded and being president (1977–1978) of the Union of Quebec Writers. He has been the recipient of numerous awards, both from Canadian and French groups, and a number of his works have been published in France.

FURTHER WORKS: *La grande muraille de Chine* (1969); *Le réformiste. Textes tranquilles* (1975); *Les têtes à Papineau* (1981): *Le murmure marchand 1976–1984* (1984); *Souvenir shop. Poèmes et proses* (1984); *Le temps des Galarneau* (1993)

BIBLIOGRAPHY: Bellemare, Y., *J. G. romancier* (1984); Lemire, M., et al., *Dictionnaire des œuvres littéraires du Québec* (1982), Vol. 3: passim; (1984), Vol. 4: passim; (1987), Vol. 5: passim; Cagnon, M., *The French Novel of Quebec* (1986): 74–84; Coulombe, M., and Jean, M. *Le dictionnaire du cinéma québécois* (1988): 203–4; Hamel, R., et al., *Dictionnaire des auteurs de langue française en Amerique du Nord* (1989): 612–14

—PAUL BARRETTE

GOES, Albrecht

German narrative writer, poet, and critic, b. 22 March 1908, Langenbeutingen

A Lutheran pastor, son and grandson of Swabian ministers, G. resigned from the ministry in 1953 to devote most of his time to writing, except for a few regularly delivered sermons. He has written poetry and symbolic plays since about 1930. During World War II he served as an army chaplain. Two of his prose narratives are direct echoes of his war-time experience; *Unruhige Nacht* (1949; *Arrow to the Heart*, 1951) and *Das Löffelchen* (1965; the little spoon). In *Unruhige Nacht* G. displayed great gifts for the dispassionate evocation of stark reality coupled with compassion and a deep sense of humanity. *Das Löffelchen*, although written in the same terse, lean prose, is much more passionate and becomes an outcry against barbarity; G.'s sense of the tragic imbues the vivid scenes, painted even more forcefully than in the earlier work. The novella *Das Brandopfer* (1954; *The Burnt Offering*, 1956) is the moving yet sparely told story of a German butcher's wife who feels compulsion to atone for the Nazis' treatment of the Jews; she experiences that "love that contains the world."

G.'s interests are manifold. He is a precise and knowledgeable literary and music critic and art lover, and an able guide to archaeological treasures, his disclaimer of competence outside a few limited areas notwithstanding. Above all, his ethics are a model of unpretentious, straightforward development of essential themes both in religion and in civil life. His role as a mediator between East and West Germany should not be underestimated—above politics, he is universally respected in both Germanys. G. often expresses the voice of German conscience much in the way critics have found VERCORS to incarnate French conscience. His stature stems from reflection and from quiet strength in confused times. G. received thousands of letters from radio listeners to his oft-repeated exhortation to all Germans during the 1950s and 1960s, reminding them of their duties to those wronged under the Hitler regime. Whereas some of these letters initially took issue with G.'s urging that the guilt must not be forgotten, over the years practically unanimous approval of his viewpoint prevailed. Never raising his voice, either in his writings or his radio addresses and sermons, G. thus got his message across to young Germans. Hence he has an unusual position, above politics but within the mainstream of democratic life.

Some of his shorter writings have been incorporated in two substantial volumes containing poems, solemn addresses, literary criticism, musical analysis, and musings of an exquisite connoisseur. The first, *Aber im Winde das Wort* (1963; words in the wind) represents twenty years of writing; it also contains the two earliest stories. Its dominant note is the fine-grained humanistic tradition that G. knows how to rekindle, bridging the painful "hiatus" of the years of dictatorship. Some of the reminiscences are humorous, others on the sentimental side; others again are timeless testimony to the highest values of culture and ethics. In *Tagwerk* (1976; daily task) G. once again felicitously blends personal impressions of some of the world's great thinkers and artists with incisive views on Mozart, Martin BUBER, and many others whom he revered and whose influence he readily acknowledges.

Perhaps the most striking of all his published works is an imaginary obituary of himself (in *Tagwerk*), in which he squarely faces his responsibility as both a writer and a minister, never equivocating when challenged to state his position as either. The good citizen, the solid thinker, in all his genuine modesty, finds vigorous ways to declare his unorthodox views of religion and art and relates his poetic and fictional work to the spiritual activity quite simply and beautifully. Another fine illustration of his art is also to be found in *Tagwerk* in "Lautloser Dialog" (silent dialogue), an unfictionalized account of a dramatic episode from the war concerning army nurses, a chaplain (the narrator), and the narrator's father.

G. maintains a sober yet noble tone of fine, subtle, and tactful simplicity. But it is the refined simplicity of a virtuoso of word and thought, whose message is as intellectually convincing as it is gripping and enlightening.

FURTHER WORKS: *Verse* (1932); *Die Hirtin* (1934); *Der Hirte* (1934); *Heimat ist gut* (1935); *Lob des Lebens* (1936); *Die Roggenfuhre* (1936); *Vergebung* (1937); *Der Zaungast* (1938); *Mörike* (1938); *Über das Gespräch* (1938; rev. ed. 1957); *Begegnungen* (1939); *Leuchter und Laterne* (1939); *Der Nachbar* (1940); *Die guten Gefährten* (1942); *Die Begegnung* (1944); *Ein erster Schritt* (1945); *Der Weg zum Stall* (1946); *Auf der Flucht* (1946); *Schwäbische Herzensreise* (1947); *Da rang ein Mann mit ihm* (1947); *Die Herberge* (1947); *Der Mensch von unterwegs* (1948); *Die fröhliche Christtagslitanei* (1949); *Von Mensch zu Mensch* (1949); *Gedichte 1930–1950* (1950); *Unsere letzte Stunde* (1951); *Christtag* (1951); *Freude am Gedicht* (1952); *Vertrauen in das Wort* (1953); *Krankenvisite* (1953); *Heilige Unruhe* (1954); *Worte zum Sonntag* (1955); *Erfüllter Augenblick* (1955); *Ruf und Echo* (1956); *Das dreifache Ja* (1956); *Der Neckar* (1957); *Hagar am Brunnen* (1958); *Der Gastfreund* (1958); *Wort zum Fest* (1959); *Stunden mit Bach* (1959); *Wagnis der Versöhnung* (1959); *Das St. Galler Spiel von der Kindheit Jesu* (1959); *Die Gabe und der Auftrag* (1962); *Die Weihnacht der Bedrängten* (1962); *Alle unsere Tage* (1963, with Waldemar Austiny); *Im Weitergehen* (1965); *Erkennst du deinen Bruder nicht?* (1965); *Dichter und Gedicht* (1966); *Nachtgespräche* (1967); *Der Knecht macht keinen Lärm* (1968); *Ein Winter mit Paul Gerhardt* (1973); *Dunkler Tag, heller Tag* (1977); *Lichtschatten du* (1978)

BIBLIOGRAPHY: Lehmann, W., *A. G., Träger des Lessingpreises der Freien Hansestadt Hamburg* (1953); Janzen, W., *A. G. zu seinem 60. Geburtstag* (1961); Rollins, E. W., and H. Zohn, eds., *Men of Dialogue: Martin Buber and A. G.* (1969); McInnes, E., "Abandonment and Renewal: Reflections on the Novellas of A. G.," *FMLS*, 7 (1971): 183–96; Robinson, A. R., "An Approach to A. G.," *ML*, 52 (1971): 161–66; Klein, U., "A. G.," *Bibliographische Kalenderblätter*, 3 (1973): 42–46

—KONRAD BIEBER

GOETEL, Ferdynand

Polish novelist, journalist, and dramatist, b. 15 May 1890, Sucha, Austro-Hungarian Empire; d. 24 Nov. 1960, London, England

G.'s father, a train conductor, died when G. was six, and his widowed mother had to rely on relatives' help in raising her two boys. G. drifted from school to school in Cracow and Lvov, studied architecture in Vienna, then moved to Warsaw in 1912 and tried his hand—at first unsuccessfully—at literature while earning his living by tutoring. At the outbreak of World War I in 1914, as an Austrian citizen in Russian-ruled Warsaw, he was deported by the Russians to Tashkent, where he was employed at building bridges, until the revolution, when he was drafted into the Red Army; during the civil war he served in the Caucasus. He returned to Poland, via Persia and India, in 1921.

In 1945, after the defeat of the Germans in Poland, G. left the country for Italy, where he joined the Polish army, and then went to England. He spent the last years of his life in London, fighting advancing blindness, and earning his living by writing for émigré papers.

G.'s war experiences and his later travels to Egypt, Iceland, and India between 1926 and 1932 served as background for his best-known works: *Kar Chat* (1923; *Messenger of the Snow*, 1930), *Serce lodów* (1930; *The Heart of the Ice*, 1931), and *Z dnia na dzień* (1926; *From Day to Day*, 1931). The last, an experimental novel, is written in the form of a double diary. Its entries alternate between the present—the everyday life in Cracow of a successful writer, returned from the wars to his wife and little daughter—and the past—the story of his love affair with an orphaned Polish girl, owner of a farm to which, as a prisoner of war in Asia, he was assigned as a laborer by Russian military authorities.

G.'s work has lyric, epic, and dramatic elements, although he wrote only one play, a tragedy, *Samuel Zborowski* (1929; Samuel Zborowski), based on the stormy career and death of a 16th-c. Polish nobleman. His lyricism is evinced in the ill-starred love stories of his plots. The epic element is seen in G.'s male protagonists, whose strenuous adventures are sharply etched against a backdrop of political upheaval—war and revolution in *Kar Chat* and *Z dnia no dzień*—or inclement nature, as in *Serce lodów*.

G.'s style, like his heroes, is robust and realistic. He tends to present the complexities of life in simple terms, avoiding psychologizing and detailed descriptions of either events or his protagonists' states of mind. He feels nature deeply—especially its exotic grandeur in central Asia, the Caucasus, and Iceland, as well as the effect it has on men subjected to its cruelty and indifference. This feature of G.'s talent has led some critics to suggest the influence on his work of Joseph CONRAD and the Scandinavian writers, just as the "novel within the novel" form of *Z dnia na dzień* was said to be inspired by André GIDE'S *The Counterfeiters*. Yet G. is an innovator in his own right who has left his mark on the Polish literature of the interwar period.

FURTHER WORKS: *Przez płonący Wschód* (1921); *Pątnik Karapeta* (1923); *Egipt* (1927); *Humoreski* (1927); *Wyspa na chmurnej północy* (1928); *Ludzkość* (1930); *Podróż do Indii* (1933); *Pod znakiem faszyzmu* (1939); *Cyklon* (1939); *Kapitan Luna* (1947); *Tatry* (1953); *Nie warto być małym* (1959); *Anakonda* (1964)

BIBLIOGRAPHY: Galsworthy, J., Foreword to *From Day to Day* (1931): v–vi; Zaleski, Z. L., *Attitudes et destinées* (1932): 342–44; Lorentowicz, J., "Polens literarische Staatspreisträger," *Slavische Rundschau*, No.1 (1938): 19–21; Coleman, A. P., "F.G. Today," *BA*, 12 (1939): 420–23; Kridl, M., *A Survey of Polish Literature and Culture* (1956): 497; Milosz, C., *The History of Polish Literature* (1969): 423; Krzyżanowski, J., *A History of Polish Literature* (1978): 622–23

—XENIA GASIOROWSKA

GOGA, Octavian

Romanian poet and essayist, b. 1 Apr. 1881, Răşinari, Hungary (now Romania); d. 7 May 1938, Ciucea

Trilingual from an early age, G. studied philosophy at the University of Budapest where he became involved in the Transylvanian Liberation Movement and a crusader against the oppression of Romanian minorities in Transylvania and as well established himself as a prolific poet. His first work, *Poezii* (1905; poems), generally considered his best, reflected this nationalistic awareness and his sorrow over Romanians under foreign rule. A second work, *Ně cheamă pământul* (1907; the land calls me), about the Romanian village—its inhabitants, traditions, and customs—was more topical. A later work, *Din umbra zidu-rilor* (1913; from the shadows of the walls), was a melancholy picture of the rootless city. G. published a play *Domnul Notar* (Mr. Notary) in 1914 followed by *Strigăte în pustiu* (1915; cries in the desert) and *Cîntece fără ţară* (1916; songs without a country), both collections of poetry.

Exiled to Iaşi in Moldavia for his nationalistic activities, G. in 1917 with eleven other Romanian-Transylvanian exiles organized the National Committee of Romanian Emigrants from Austria-Hungary that signed a declaration of war against the Austro-Hungarian monarchy. In 1920 a provisional Romanian National Council was set up in Paris, with G. among its members, recognized by France, Great Britain, Italy, and the U.S., but later that year G. left the Council to join the so-called People's Party, which dominated the parliamentary elections that year.

Following the ceding of Transylvania to Romania after World War I, G. embarked upon a political career, and was elected to the Romanian Parliament. In 1930 a faction of the People's Party led by G. formed the National Agrarian Party with a right-wing orientation. In 1935, with A. C. Cuza, he organized the Christian National Party, and then in 1937 reorganized it as the National Christian Party, which formed a government with G. very briefly as prime minister.

In the meantime he periodically returned to his literary career, notably with *Poesie alese* (1924; poems), *Mustul care fierbe* (1927; seething wine), *Mesterul Manole* (1928; retelling of a folk myth), *Fragmente autobiografice* (1934), *O seamă de cuvinte* (1936; words to ponder), *Din Larg* (1939), and *Poezii* (1943; Poems). He was elected to the Romanian Academy and awarded the National Prize for Poetry. His poetry had a popular appeal, but G. was a serious poet committed to the idea of a national tradition as the special source of true literary inspiration. Much of his poetry deals with patriotic events usually taking place in a village (sometimes mythical), events involving social and national struggles. His poetry is among the best of this kind in Romanian literature, prophetic in tone with a messianic vision of his country's future, sensitive to the sufferings of his people and to the providence of God. He identifies the individual and national psyche with nature and the cosmos, a religious participation dating from Dacian times. His poetry has much of the music of the Romanian folk ballads, which carries over into his many excellent translations.

BIBLIOGRAPHY: Papadima, O., *Neam, sat şi oraş în poezia lui O. G.* (1943); Seicaru, P., *Poezia şi politica, O. G.* (1956); Balan, I. D., *O. G.* (1970); Popa, M., *O. G.: între colectivitate şi solitudine* (1981); Gutan, I., *O. G., argumentul operei* (1987); Goga, M., *Lexicul şi structura stilului în poezia lui O. G.* (1989); Fatu, M., *Cu pumnii strînsi: O. G. în viaţa politica a României* (1993)

—THOMAS AMHERST PERRY

GOLDEMBERG, Isaac

Peruvian novelist and poet, b. 15 Nov. 1945, Chepén

G., born in the small town of Chepén to a Jewish father and a European-Quechua mother, moved in 1953 to Lima, where, as he has said, "my father [was] waiting for me and 5,700 years of Judaism rain[ed] on my head." His crisis of identity as Jew, Peruvian-European, and Quechua began in earnest at this point; he entered a school for Jewish boys and was shocked to see Hebrew, which he could not read and did not speak, written on the board. He began to become involved in the activities of the Jewish colony in Lima and to identify more and more with his Jewish roots. G. places his initiation as a writer in 1957, when he moved to a new house with his father and discovered in the library there, left by the former tenant who was a friend of his father's, European and North American literature, and especially the works of Sholem Aleichem (pseud. of Solomon Rabinowitz, 1859–1916).

G. began to write in 1958 and was heavily influenced by the work of two Peruvian authors: César VALLEJO and Ciro ALEGRÍA. The poetry of Vallejo influenced G. because it struck in him sympathetic chords by its emphasis on family and identity; and the novel *El mundo es ancho y ajeno* (1941; *Broad and Alien Is the World*, 1941) by Alegría, which dealt with the Indian experience, was important to him because of the analogies between the Indian and Jewish predicaments in a European world. G. traveled to Israel and to Spain between 1962 and 1964, returning to Peru at the death of his father. After moving to New York, he pursued university studies and published his first book of poems, *Tiempo de silencio* (1970; time of silence). He continues to live in New York, where he is the codirector of the Latin American Writers' Institute at City College and of the Latin American Book Fair. He is currently working on an anthology of Latin American Jewish writers and on a novel, tentatively titled "En la puerta del horno" (in the door of the oven [on the brink]), which concerns Chepén but will eschew concentration on Jewish thematics.

G. first came to critical attention in a rather unusual manner: with the publication of his first novel in an English translation. The novel, *La vida a plazos de don Jacobo Lerner* (1980; first pub. in English as *The Fragmented Life of Don Jacobo Lerner*, 1976), received critical acclaim for its complex narrative, which both tragically and comically portrays the career of its protagonist, a man alienated not only from his adopted country of Peru but also from the Ashkenazi Jewish immigrant community of which he originally formed an active part. The ironic collage of entries from the cultural organ of that community, *Alma hebrea* (Hebrew soul), as well as the *Citizen Kane*-like reminiscences and evaluations of the late Jacobo by his erstwhile friends, acquaintances, relatives, and lovers, realize, as commentators such as Judith M. Schneider have noted, a powerful textual representation of the absence of the immigrant Jew from participation in Peruvian society.

G. has worked both in narrative and poetry, publishing an early collection of poems, *De Chepén a La Habana* (1973; from Chepén to Havana), which combines his work and pieces by Cuban exile poet José Kozer (b. 1940). Many of G.'s poems from the 1973 collection have appeared in revised form in *Hombre de paso/Just Passing Through* (1981), in which the poems are published with parallel translations. The poems of *Hombre de paso* deal with themes similar to those in the fiction of G.: the alienation experienced by the ethnic outsider, the specific concerns of growing up Jewish, and the general existential position of modern consciousness. But the poems, while keenly aware of the difficult position of Jews in a Christianized society, avoid extreme militant stances that would preclude the integration of ethnic experiences into larger cultural participation. The search for meaning in one's past experiences is strongly emphasized.

G. has more recently published a novel, *Tiempo al tiempo* (1984; *play by play*, 1985), which continues his probing of the Jewish experience in Peru, in a manner even more uncompromising than in his first work of fiction. One critic has pointed out that the protagonist Marcos is the "spiritual son" of Jacobo in the first novel and thus represents what Efraín (the illegitimate, mad son of Jacobo) might have become had he lived. The novel departs from the moment of the circumcision of Marcos, which metaphorically encapsulates his initition into Jewish society as well as his alienation from the larger Peruvian culture. The story of Marcos is told by using parallel narrative techniques, which include the treatment of his life story as a soccer game narrated by a rather frantic sportscaster. Within the soccer sections, an interesting technique of fragmented contrapuntal narrative offers commentary on the narration by the sportscaster: a "newsreel" or ticker tape, generally consisting of pieces about the founding of Israel or about biblical history, runs along the bottom of the page and appears to have allusive connections with the larger narration.

G. is consistently a writer unwilling to adhere exclusively either to more traditional narrative technique or to stylistic forms developed in his first novel. His poetry is sometimes accessible and sometimes strikingly private. His voice, both in poetry and in fiction, is an important part of the Latin American literary experience, since it has helped to foreground the largely neglected consciousness of marginalized groups such as the Jews of Peru.

FURTHER WORKS: *La vida a contado* (1992)

BIBLIOGRAPHY: Goldman, M., on *Hombre de paso/Just Passing Through, LALR*, 11, 22 (Spring—Summer 1983): 114–16; Lindstrom, N., on *Hombre de paso / Just Passing Through, RIB*, 49, (1983): 659–60; Roses, L., "El lector como jurado: el monólogo interior en *La vida aplazos de don Jacobo Lerner,*" *DLit*, 2, 1 (1984): 225–32; Tittler, J., *Narrative Irony in the Contemporary Spanish-American Novel* (1984): 172–85; Goldemberg, I., "Crónicas / genealogías / cronologías," *Hispam*, 14, 42 (Oct. 1985): 73–78; Stavans, I., "Judaísmo y letras latinoamericanas: entrevista a I. G.," *Folio*, 17 (1987): 141–50; Schneider, J. M., "Cultural Meanings in I. G.'s Fiction," *Folio*, 17 (1987): 128–40; Rosser, H. L., "Being and Time in *La vida a plazos de don Jacobo Lerner,*" *Chasqui*, 17, 1 (May 1988): 43–49; Gazarian-Gautier, M.-L, *Interviews with Latin American Writers* (1989): 129–54; Mosier, P., in Kanellós, N., ed., *Biographical Dictionary of Hispanic Literature in the United States: The Literature of Puerto Ricans, Cuban Americans, and Other Hispanic Writers* (1989): 115–21

—KENNETH E. HALL

GOLDING, William

English novelist, b. 19 Sept. 1911, St. Columb Minor; d. 19 June 1993; Perranarworthal

While still an Oxford undergraduate, G. published a volume of poetry; it was not until twenty years later, however, that his first novel appeared. In the meantime he had spent four years working in a small London theater, had served five years in the Royal Navy, and had become a schoolmaster (he continued to be one until 1961).

G. has compared himself to an archaeologist: as the latter explores the dark places under the earth, he explores the dark places of the human soul. He is not simply describing the human tragedy but looking for its source—in that human nature of which modern man is appallingly ignorant. His response to liberal and optimistic interpretations of the human condition is to parody them. In *Lord of the Flies* (1954) he takes a schoolboy classic, R.M. Ballantyne's (1825–1894) *Coral Island*, (1857) and reverses what happens in it; his group of boys on a desert island does not live in harmony and happiness but degenerates into savagery. A gripping story whose meaning is debatable, *Lord of the Flies* had an enormous success both in England and the U.S. G.'s characters remain within the world of childhood, yet they suggest or foreshadow a range of adult roles—from Ralph, who tries to create and maintain order, to Jack, who surrenders to a compulsion to hunt and kill. "I should have thought that a pack of British boys . . . would have been able to put up a better show than that," says the naval officer who rescues them; but his rebuke is full of unconscious irony, given the adult world G. has him represent—a world devastated by nuclear war. The Lord of the Flies is Beelzebub, Prince of Devils, the source of evil outside oneself; through his Swiftian parable G. shows that man is a fallen being, with a propensity to worship the wrong gods.

Similarly, in *The Inheritors* (1955) G. overturns H.G. WELLS'S *Outline of History* (1920), "the rationalist gospel *in excelsis*." For Wells, Neanderthal man was a gorillalike monster, possibly cannibalistic; G. shows him as innocent and kindly, so that it is with the coming of Homo sapiens that the fall into complexity, ambiguity, and self-division occurs. In *Pincher Martin* (1956; Am., *The Two Deaths of Christopher Martin*) the central character, a sailor, is a parody Prometheus, a parody Robinson Crusoe, a parody Lear (in the critic Samuel Hynes's view), who loves no one but himself but seems the indomitable individualist, the archetypal survivor—until we suddenly learn that he has been dead all the way through the book. In *The Spire* (1964) the dean of a medieval cathedral has a Promethean ambition: to crown his cathedral with a four-hundred-foot spire. In spite of weak foundations, tainted money, human suffering, and his own suspicion that his motives are corrupt, he succeeds in building a beautiful spire that seems to reach to infinity.

Only in *Free Fall* (1959) did G. deal with an ordinary man, not a Promethean, in an ordinary social situation. Still, out of this situation mythic dimensions emerge, since his hero is looking back over his past to find "the beginning of responsibility, the beginning of darkness, the point where I began." The title suggests both a fall in space and a fall from grace, a scientific and a religious approach to existence; the question the hero must ultimately face is whether there is any pattern to existence at all. Interior darkness is also the theme of *Darkness Visible* (1979), G.'s first full-length novel in twelve years. The beginning is extraordinary: out of fire raging during the London blitz a boy comes walking, his face hideously burned; "a maimed creature whose mind has touched for once on the nature of things," he puts his ability to recognize the darkness in the souls of others to forceful use.

Rites of Passage (1980) portrays, with astonishing realism, life aboard an ancient ship of the line at the end of the Napoleonic Wars, but again, the main interest of the novel is in the interior world. It shows once again that past, present, and future serve G. equally well in his exploration of the dark places of the human heart.

Martin Green has written that G. is not importantly original in thought or feeling because his handling is too predictable and too exaggerated. This is one of the possible criticisms; but nothing could be farther from the truth. If G. deals with age-old moral, religious, and metaphysical questions, he devises very imaginative and original fictional situations by which to examine them. And the answers are never easy; as his best critics have shown, the reader who thinks that a G. novel can be summed up in a simple moral maxim has not begun to understand him. One of his main strengths is his ability to enter into a character, to see him from the inside, as it were—with the objective view probably being given only at the end, and the reader suddenly realizing that he has been accepting the character's perspective all the way through. G. is undoubtedly one of the most interesting, and demanding, of contemporary novelists.

FURTHER WORKS: *Poems* (1934); *Envoy Extraordinary*, in *Sometime, Never: Three Tales of Imagination* (1956); *The Brass Butterfly* (1956); *The Hot Gates* (1965); *The Pyramid* (1967); *The Scorpion God* (1971)

BIBLIOGRAPHY: Hynes, S., *W. G.* (1964); Oldsey, B. S., and S. Weintraub, *The Art of W. G.* (1965); Kinkead-Weekes, M., and I. Gregor, *W. G.: A Critical Study* (1967); Babb, H. S., *The Novels of W. G.* (1970); Tiger, V., *W. G.: The Dark Fields of Discovery* (1974); Medcalf, S., *W. G.* (1975); Biles, J. I., and R. D. Evans, eds., *W. G.: Some Critical Considerations* (1978)

—D. J. DOOLEY

GOMBROWICZ, Witold

Polish novelist and dramatist, b. 4 Aug. 1904, Maloszyce; d. 24 July 1969, Vence, France

G. was born into a landowning family. From 1923 to 1926 he studied law at the University of Warsaw. In August 1939 G. took a pleasure trip to Argentina, but he remained there for twenty-four years owing to the outbreak of World War II and the postwar developments in eastern Europe. He returned to Europe in 1963, and after spending a year in Berlin he settled in Vence.

Two key words for understanding G.'s works are "immaturity" and "form," both repeatedly used by G. The short stories in *Pamiętnik z okresu dojrzewania* (1933; memoir from adolescence) and his first novel, *Ferdydurke* (1937; *Ferdydurke*, 1961) are devoted to the definition and investigation of what G. perceived as perpetual and inevitable human immaturity. In his view, human beings incessantly engage in the game of hiding their own lack of a full understanding of the world while exposing this lack in others. G.'s short stories sketch out instances of that struggle: the hobo against the miser, the misfit against the well-adjusted person, the innocent debutante against her worldly-wise fiancé. *Ferdydurke* begins as a story of a thirty-year-old writer who has been patronized and patted on the head by the "cultural aunts and uncles" (that

William Golding

is, so-called guardians of culture) until he lost his resistance and allowed others to overwhelm him with their claim to know everything better. Eventually he rebels against his captors and exposes the flimsy foundations of their alleged superiority.

Ferdydurke introduces the concept of form and the formal impulse. The latter is an impulse all human beings have to create a communicative network among themselves and to structure the reality around them. The form thus produced both structures the reality and distorts it; it also separates one person from another. People are entrapped by, and hide behind, the form they have produced. G.'s intuitions about form resemble what the French psychologist Jacques Lacan has observed about the distortion of the "I," communication, and language.

The sadomasochistic dependence of one man on another is the ultimate concern of G.'s novels and plays. They contain portraits of people who at first seem to have achieved a certain degree of autonomy and rationality but on second look turn out to be ridiculously dependent on the existence and opinions of others. They are incapable of thinking thoughts and desiring things that others had not thought and desired. They hate others and themselves for that and their actions are motivated by this hate.

Ferdydurke first identified the phenomenon of immaturity and interdependence masquerading as maturity and independence. G.'s next novel, *Trans-Atlantyk* (1953; *Trans-Atlantyk*, 1994), written in Argentina, pokes fun at the ridiculous lengths to which people go to emphasize their separateness and superior knowledge. The two branches of the Polish émigré community in Argentina—the aristocratic and the proletarian—do everything in their power to discredit the other in the eyes of the outsiders and of other Poles. *Pornografia* (1960; *Pornografia*, 1965) explores sexual dependency and the lying associated with it. In this novel, two eldely gentlemen arrange a sexual encounter between two teenagers, and eventually cement with a murder the teenagers' lascivious friendship and their own, too. In *Kosmos* (1965; *Cosmos*, 1966), for which he was awarded the International Publishers' Prize in 1967, Leo Wojtys lives a seemingly independent life amid his family and friends. Like the heroes of *Pornografia*, he is a lecher and a voyeur, and his secret enjoyments depend on the presence of others.

G.'s plays likewise expose man's cruelty to himself and others. In *Iwona, księżniczka Burgunda* (1938; *Ivona, Princess of Burgundia*, 1969), the presence at the royal court of the ugly and awkward girl Ivona makes everyone so self-conscious and uneasy that eventually Ivona has to be murdered so that the comfortable harmony of royal society can be restored. The theme of *Slub* (1953; *The Marriage*, 1969) is a gradual discovery by the Polish soldier Henryk, who fights the Nazis in France during World War II, of the pressure of others on what people think about themselves. Henryk tries to rid himself and his family of this pressure but eventually he submits to it. In *Operetka* (1966; *Operetta*, 1971) the concern with human immaturity and interdependence takes a different form. An uneducated shopkeeper's daughter, Albertine, saves the society depicted in the drama from despair and disintegration by the vigor of her youth and beauty. *Operetka* contains a suggestion that in man's immature drives and desires there is hidden an ability stubbornly to seek after knowledge, wisdom, and joy.

G.'s MODERNISTIC novels and plays share several structural features. The novels use the first-person narrator, who in turn is usually overshadowed by the "stage director," a character who surpasses the narrator in mental acumen and experience. The novels' plots are centered around a sadomasochistic contest between the narrator and the stage producer, and between these two and other characters in the novel. The omnipresence of the sadomasochistic feelings in G.'s novels accounts in large measure for the eccentricities of his plots and the ensuing difficulty of summarizing them. While the action of G.'s novels takes place in an everyday world, in the plays we encounter the world of royalty and aristocracy. Members of this supposedly highly refined society use vulgarisms and dialect words unsuitable to people of their station. The device of mismatching a character with his speech contributes to the parodic atmosphere of G.'s plays.

Several intellectual traditions can be discerned in G.'s writings. From Nietzsche he derives his preoccupation with the individual's desire for self-assertion. His early Catholic training contributed to his perception of human beings as irrevocably deprived of self-sufficiency. His absurdist plots bespeak an awareness of existential philosophy and of post-Freudian psychology. His sadomasochism brings him close to the writings of the Marquis de Sade and to the novels of his countryman Jerzy KOSINSKI. On the other hand, his belief in the capacity of human beings for joy and development makes his fictional world different from the humorless French NEW NOVEL and from the THEATER OF THE ABSURD.

In many ways, G.'s works stand in opposition to the Polish literary tradition, which has favored gentility rather than parody and noble ideas rather than sadomasochism. G. belongs to that tradition, however, in that all his works respond in some way to a specific work of the past, or a specific tendency of Polish literature. G. saw himself as a voice of negation indispensable for the dialectic of literary development. In that, his own views and those of his

critics have often coincided. In Soviet-occupied Poland and in post-communist Poland, G. became the darling of literary critics who found in his sarcasm and skepticism an accurate reflection of Polish reality.

FURTHER WORKS: *Opętani* (1939; *Possessed, or the Secret of Myslotch*, 1981); *Dziennik* (3 vols., 1957, 1962, 1966; *Diary*, 2 vols., 1988-89); *Dziennik* (3 vols., 1962, 1966, 1971); *Rozmowy z G.* (1969; *A Kind of Testament*, 1973); *Varia* (1973); *Wspomnienia polskie; Wędrówki po Argentynie* (1977); *Possessed of the Secret of Myslotch*, 1981); *Jerzy Giedroyc i W. G.: Listy* (1993)

BIBLIOGRAPHY: Roux, D. de., *G.* (1971); Jelenski, C., and D. de Roux, eds., *G.* (1971); Volle, J., *G.: Bourreau-martyr* (1972); Schmidt, K., *Der Stil von W. G.s "Trans-Atlantyk" und sein Verhältnis zur polnischen literarischen Tradition* (1974); Bondy, F., and C. Jelenski, *W. G.* (1978); Thompson, E., *W.G.* (1979); Berressem, H., *Lines of Desire: Reading G.'s Fiction with Lacan* (1998); Ziarek, E. P., ed., *G.'s Grimaces: Modernism, Gender, Nationality* (1998)

—EWA M. THOMPSON

GOMEZ DE LA SERNA, Ramón

Spanish novelist, biographer, essayist, humorist, and dramatist, b. 3 July 1888, Madrid; d. 12 Jan. 1963, Buenos Aires, Argentina

A highly experimental writer, greatly esteemed by members of avant-garde literary groups from the end of World War I to the beginning of the Spanish Civil War, G. published more than one hundred volumes of travel books, short stories, novels, plays, impressions, and humorous essays, and thousands of articles. He excelled at experimentation in what he defined as a world of disintegrating conventionalisms, especially in his *greguerías*, short semiaphoristic statements.

An early interest in art led him to write biographies of Goya, El Greco, Velázquez, and other painters, but he also published many other biographies and literary portraits. Beginning in 1911, he developed a special style, intuitive, often penetrating, and poetic, involving description of personal gestures, physical movements, and anecdotal material. G. stressed special traits in each of his subjects, such as Oscar Wilde's outrageous impudence or George Bernard SHAW's vegetarianism. He also utilized expanded metaphorical constructions, "to pierce the outer layer of reality and to probe into a deeper, more intimate reality." Among his best biographies are *Goya* (1928), an intuitive interpretation of the works of an artist in whose *Caprichos* G. saw a relationship to his own *greguerías; Azorín* (1930), in which he imitated AZORÍN's style to show that author's place in history together with that of the famous Generation of '98; and *Ramón María del Valle-Inclán* (1944), about the Spanish writer VALLE-INCLÁN, with whose extravagant and volatile personality G. could easily identify.

G. wrote several autobiographies, the best of which is *Automoribundia* (1948; autodeathography), which relates his birth, hungers, frustrations, triumphs, defeats, and disappointments, and whose title he explained as "how a man progresses toward death," a subject that always fascinated him.

His novels, quite often filled with sensual and bohemian types, reveal an unreal, absurd, and often humorous world. *El doctor inverosímil* (1921; the unlikely doctor), based on an earlier short story of the same name, depicts a doctor who fancies himself a medical Sherlock Holmes and uses psychiatric techniques to discover the reason for his patients' allergies. Humorous but perceptive, the novel reflects G.'s fascination with human illness and pathology. *El torero Caracho* (1926; the bullfighter Caracho), one of his most popular novels, relates the rise from poverty of Caracho, his rivalry with another bullfighter, Cairel, and their brutal, if heroic deaths, in defense of some spectators. *Cinelandia* (1923; *Movieland*, 1930) penetrates the reality behind Hollywood as it explores its promiscuity, parties, thrill seekers, and stars.

G. also experimented with a series of novels he labeled "nebulous." *El incongruente* (1922; the incongruent one) is an innovative, surrealistic novel of the absurd about a man who lets life live him instead of living life, set in a fantasy world without real time or space. *¡Rebeca!* (1936; Rebeca!), a fragmented, dehumanized novel, treats of an erotic odyssey in search of the ideal woman, whom the protagonist himself has invented. Realizing that reality is more productive, he marries a Jewish lady, an autobiographical re-creation of G.'s own life. These novels, as well as his many novelettes and short stories, quite often deal with the morbid, grotesque, and fantastic and include murder, adultery, and a variety of sexual obsessions.

G. is most famous for his *greguerías*, a word he coined in 1909, short and pithy rearrangements of reality that try to define the incongruities and trivialities of life. At times shocking, they capture fugitive impressions and sensations and express subconscious associations involving God, time, nature, and death. In some twenty volumes written between 1914 and 1960 he indulged in a kind of humorous, lyrical, magic anticreation. He defined these brief insights as "what beings shout confusedly from their subconscious," stating that in these ephemeral fusions of extremes he was trying to define the indefinable: "Thunder, a trunk falling down the stairway of heaven"; "In her wristwatch the time was so small she never had enough of it for anything."

G. created an endless variety of almost unclassifiable, humorous, and lyrical works that broke all the taboos of his day. He attempted aesthetic and verbal games, showing great facility as one of the early experimenters with SURREALISM and the absurd, and he influenced the development of Spanish literature and its 20th-c. literary genres.

FURTHER WORKS: *Entrando en fuego* (1905); *Morbideces* (1908); *El drama del palacio deshabitado* (1909); *Utopía* (1909); *El laberinto* (1910); *El teatro en soledad* (1912); *Ex-votos* (1912); *El lunático* (1912); *El Rastro* (1915); *La viuda blanca y negra* (1917); *El circo* (1917); *Senos* (1917); *Pombo* (1918); *Muestrarios* (1918); *El alba y otras cosas* (1918); *Variaciones* (1920); *Virguerías* (1920); *Libro nuevo* (1920); *Disparates* (1921); *La tormenta* (1921); *Leopoldo y Teresa* (1921); *El miedo al mar* (1921); *El secreto del acueducto* (1922); *La hija del verano* (1922); *El olor de las mimosas* (1922); *La gangosa* (1922); *El gran hotel* (1922); *Ramonismo* (1923); *La quinta de Palmyra* (1923); *El novelista* (1923); *El chalet de las rosas* (1923); *La malicia y las acacias* (1923); *La sagrada cripta del Pombo* (1924); *Por los tejados* (1924); *En el bazar más suntuoso del mundo* (1924); *Aquella novela* (1924); *Caprichos* (1925); *La fúnebre falsa* (1925); *Hay que matar el Morse* (1925); *Gollerías* (1926); *La mujer de ámbar* (1927); *Seis falsas novelas* (1927); *El hijo del millonario* (1927); *El caballero del hongo gris* (1928); *El dueño del átomo* (1928); *La hiperestésica* (1928); *Efigies* (1929); *Los medios seres* (1929); *La*

nardo (1930); *Ismos* (1931); *Elucidario de Madrid* (1931); *Policéfalo y señora* (1932); *Flor de greguerías* (1933); *Siluetas y sombras* (1934); *El Greco* (1935); *Las escaleras* (1935); *Los muertos y las muertas, y otras fantasmagorias* (1935); *El cólera azul* (1937); *Mi tía Carolina Coronado* (1940); *Retratos contemporáneos* (1941); *Lo cursi, y otros ensayos* (1943); *Ruskin, el apasionado* (1943); *Don Diego de Velázquez* (1943); *José Gutiérrez Solana* (1944); *Doña Juana la Loca* (1944); *Oscar Wilde* (1944); *Lope de Vega* (1944); *Nuevos retratos contemporáneos* (1945); *Ventura García Calderón* (1946); *El hombre perdido* (1947); *Trampantojos* (1947); *Cuentos del fin del año* (1947); *Explicación de Buenos Aires* (1948); *Cartas a las golondrinas* (1949); *Las tres gracias* (1949); *Interpretación del tango* (1949); *Quevedo* (1953); *Greguerías completas* (1953); *Edgar Poe, el genio de América* (1953); *Lope viviente* (1954); *Nostalgias de Madrid* (1956); *Cartas a mí mismo* (1956); *Obras completas* (2 vols., 1956, 1957); *Nuevas páginas de mi vida* (1957); *Biografías completas* (1959); *Piso bajo* (1961); *Retratos completos* (1961); *Total de greguerías* (1961); *Guía del Rastro* (1961); *Diario póstumo* (1972). FURTHER WORKS IN ENGLISH: *Some Greguerías* (1944)

BIBLIOGRAPHY: Cardona, R., *Ramón: A Study of G. and His Works* (1957); Gómez de la Serna, G., *Ramón: Vida y obra* (1963); Mazzetti, R., "Some Comments on the Biographical Sketches of R. G." *KRQ*, 17 (1960): 275–86; Mazzetti, R., "The Use of Imagery in the Works of R. G.," *Hispania*, 54 (1971): 80–90; Camon Aznar, J., *R. G. en sus obras* (1972); Mazzetti, R., *R. G.* (1974); Jackson, R., "The Status of the Greguería of R. G.," *MFS*, 22 (1976–77): 237–42; Dennis, N., ed., *Studies on R. G.* (1988)

—KESSEL SCHWARTZ

GOMRINGER, Eugen

Swiss poet (writing in German), b. 20 Jan. 1925, Cachuela Esperanza, Bolivia

G. is considered to be the founder of concrete poetry. He grew up with his grandparents in Switzerland and studied art history and economics in Bern and in Rome between 1946 and 1950. He is a graphic designer by profession. In 1952 he was the cofounder of the magazine *Spirale*, which was devoted to concrete art. From 1954 to 1958 he served as secretary to the artist Max Bill, who was the director of the Hochschule für Gestaltung in Ulm, Germany. In 1959 he founded his own short-lived publishing house. Between 1962 and 1967 he was the business manager for the Schweizer Werkbund in Zurich. Between 1967 and 1985 he was the artistic advisor to the Rosenthal concern. Since 1976 he has served as a professor for aesthetic theory at the Art Academy in Düsseldorf. He now lives in Rehau-Wurlitz in Germany.

G. published his first poems in 1953 in *Spirale* and thus became the initiator of the concrete movement, whose influence was felt throughout Europe and the U.S., but particularly in Germany and Austria, where G. found many admires. He terms his poetry concrete because it ignores conventional syntax, description, and metaphor and instead places individual words in a visual arrangement on the page. The poem is thus not "about" something but forms its own concrete reality using words as the building blocks. The poem becomes a real object and not an abstraction. G. calls these concrete poems "constellations," since meaning arises through the special relationships the words form with each other, as groups of stars may tend to form pictures in the sky.

G.'s best-known books are *das stundenbuch* (1965; *The Book of Hours and Constellations*, 1968) and *wrote sind schaften: die konstellationen 1951–1968* (1969; words are shadows: the constellations 1951–1968). From these works we can discern that his poems fall into four distinct categories: purely visual constellations, visual-audio constellations that can also be read aloud, constellations in languages other than German, and constellations in book form, which develop a sequence of images over several pages, much like the individual frames of a film. In each of these categories a minimum of language is used, and there are usually a great number of combinations and permutations. As an example we can take his perhaps most famous poem "schweigen" (1954; silence). The word "schweigen" is printed fourteen times to form a rectangle on the page—there is an empty hole in the middle, which is the "silence" of the poem.

G. also wrote theoretical tracts to explain his poetry and to argue for its efficacy. The most important are *manifeste und darstellungen der konkreten poesie 1954–1966* (1966; manifestos and representation of concrete poetry 1954–1966) and *poesie als mittel der umweltgestaltung* (1969; poetry as a means for structuring the environment). Here he argues that the modern technological world needs a new, simple, direct, and universal language devoid of any irrationality. Poetry should help develop models for this new language and test them on global readers. If the author is successful, the readers should be able to understand immediately the models presented. Through this process readers can thus gain a heightened relationship to the objects of the real world, which are reflected in the language of this new poetry.

G.'s influence was strong, but short-lived. He helped a postwar generation in German-speaking countries question and examine the linguistic medium, and thereby initiated a whole range of linguistic experimentation. After about 1972, interest in this movement waned, and G. ceased writing poetry; he turned instead to writing monographs on artists and collaborating on art books. Critics began to realize that G.'s approach was too simplistic. His poems only required his readers to project their own knowledge onto the poem, and thus his poetry was unable to provide the hoped-for "new" information. In addition, the lack of any social or political parameters tended to confirm the status quo rather than suggest change.

FURTHER WORKS: *konstellationen* (1953); *5 mal 1 konstellation* (1960); *33 konstellationen* (1960); *die konstellationen* (1963); *15 konstellationen* (1965); *einsam gemeinsam* (1971); *lieb* (1971); *der pfeil* (1972); *1970–1972* (1973); *Richard Paul Lohse* (1973); *konkretes von Anton Stankowski* (1974); *wie weiß ist wissen die weisen* (1975); *konstellationen, ideogramme, studenbuch* (1977); *kein fehler im system* (1978); *Distanzsignale* (1980); *Gucken* (1980); *Identitäten* (1981); *Himmel, erde, frankenland* (1981); *Gewebte bilder* (1984); *wir verschweben—wir verschwinden* (1985); *Helle räume* (1987); *Inversion & öffnung* (1988); *Zur sache der konkreten* (1988)

BIBLIOGRAPHY: Bornscheuer, L., "E. G.s 'Konstellationen': konkrete Poesie als universale Sprachgestaltung unserer Zeit," *DU* 1 (1970): 59–78; Schnauber, C., ed. *Deine Träume—mein Gedicht: E. G. und die Konkrete Poesie* (1980); Demetz, P., "E. G. und die Entwicklung der konkreten Poesie," in Weissenberger, K., ed., *Die deutsche Lyrik 1945–1975* (1981): 277–86; Zeller, M., *Gedichte haben Zeit. Aufriß einer zeitgenössischen Poetik* (1982): 47–85; Solt, M. E., "Charles Sanders Pierce and E. G.: The Concrete Poem As Sign," *PoT*, 3, 3 (Summer 1982): 197-209

—ROBERT ACKER

GONÇALVES, Olga

Portuguese novelist, short-story writer, and poet, b. 12 Apr. 1929, Luanda, Angola

G.'s fiction has vibrantly documented the social changes wrought on Portuguese life during the post-1974 revolutionary period. C. spent her childhood in Angola. She later studied at King's College, London, and has worked as an English teacher. Although G.'s literary career began with lyric poetry in the 1960s, which she continues to write, she has distinguished herself as a novelist.

G.'s fiction may have been inspired by the testimonial literature form. It shows direct influence of the NEW NOVEL's concern with detail. Using what appears to be the interview format, her characters narrate their personal situations and beliefs about the events of the revolution and beyond.

In *A floresta em Bremerhaven* (1975; the forest in Bremerhaven), awarded the Ricardo Malheiros Prize of the Lisbon Academy of Sciences (1975), the postrevolutionary turmoil is viewed through the eyes, ideas, and reactions of a family of Portuguese immigrants to Germany recently returned home. Their experiences abroad had opened their mind to concepts of freedom of expression and justice, neither of which they had enjoyed in dictatorial Portugal. They returned with money to purchase the land where they once had been sharecroppers and to open a guest house on the property. The "author" is present at the guest house and becomes a "sounding board" for these newborn Portuguese citizens.

Este verão o emigrante là-bas (1980; the emigrants down home this summer) presents the Portuguese immigrants to France who had remained in Paris and return *là-bas* (down there, that is, Portugal) only during their August vacations. G.'s characters offer testimonies about their clandestine emigration and life in France. The "interviews" make clear that these people had traveled from one set of repressions in Portugal (social abuse, rural poverty) to another set in France (discrimination based on "race," urban poverty). Their attempts to maintain Portuguese heritage are stymied. The key words of daily existence only have significance for them in French. The volume has a poetic, impressionistic leitmotiv: the immigrants' difficulties are compared to the hardships of Claude Monet's life.

G.'s *Ora esguardae* (1982; hark ye, now!) is a mural of Portuguese life of the early 1980s. She invokes the medieval chronicler Fernão Lopes (ca. 1380-ca. 1460) through the voices and complaints of the Portuguese *povo*, the common people, who had defiantly supported the nation's existence since medieval times. Linguistic subversion (present in the earlier works) assumes greater importance here. For example, the *retornados*, returnees from the old Portuguese African colonies, have brought with them a new register of speech; the political opening has given new connotations to old words; and the now popular Brazilian soap operas reveal new social and linguistic possibilities. This novel possesses an optimistic tone about Portugal's future. G. suggests that the young postrevolutionary generation will "cleanse" the language of its past linguistic and cultural dilemmas.

G.'s fiction has also expressed a special interest in women's situations. Her *Mandei-lhe uma boca* (1978; smarty-pants) describes the change taking place in the cultural situation of Portuguese teenagers. Sara, the protagonist, is revisited, eight years later, in *Sara* (1986; Sara), upon obtaining her M.A. in philosophy. She is still confronting the changes in Portuguese women's lives. G.'s *Armandina e Luciano, o traficante de canários* (1988; Armandina e Luciano, the "canary" trafficker) is a striking STREAM-OF-CONSCIOUSNESS monologue-testimonial novel in which the voice belongs to a young ex-prostitute (often relapsing), Carla Cristina. Carla narrates her own and her family's background in the slums around Lisbon. She is an astute observer of the Lisbon underground—pimps, thieves, smugglers, drug traffickers, and bizarre bohemian spirits—about whom she can casually but earnestly reveal positive qualities. She views the woman's situation, racism, sexual perversion, abuse, and even incest without resentment. Once again, the literary level of the novel invokes the traditional literary concern of the Iberian peninsula with the *povo*, the people, and the picaresque.

G.'s fiction has earned for her the title of portraitist of the sociocultural reality of today's Portugal, in particular the urban existence of Lisbon.

FURTHER WORKS: *Movimento* (1972); *25 composições e 11 provas de artista* (1973); *Só de amor* (1975); *Três poetas* (1981); *Caixa inglesa* (1983); *O livro de Olotolilisobi* (1983); *Rudolfo* (1985); *Contar de subversão* (1990)

BIBLIOGRAPHY: Stern, I., on *Este verão o emigrante là-bas*, *WLT*, 53, 4 (Autumn 1979): 659; Stern, I., "Redefining Identity: Uses of Language in Recent Portuguese Fiction," in Nunes, M. L., ed., *Identity in Portuguese and Brazilian Literature* (1982): 34–42

—IRWIN STERN

GONZALEZ, N(estor) V(icente) M(adali)

Philippine novelist, short-story writer, and poet (writing in English) b. 8 Sept. 1915, Romblon

As a child, G. was taken by his father, who was a teacher, to pioneer Mindoro Island, whose farmers and fishermen have dominated his fiction ever since his autobiographical novel, *The Winds of April* (1940), won a prize in the Commonwealth Literary Contest in 1940. After a Rockefeller-funded postwar visit to U.S. writing centers, G. returned to teach creative writing at the University of the Philippines.

For his defense of traditional Philippine values, G. received the Republic Award of Merit (1954), the Republic Cultural Heritage Award (1960), and the Rizal Pro Patria Award (1961). Since 1969 G. has taught Third World literature at the University of California, Hayward, and in several essays he has offered lessons learned from other developing nations as advisories to his countrymen.

Social change, in G.'s fiction, tends to be subtle to the point of near invisibility, because his frontiersmen take their tempo from natural cycles. Yet although there is a seemingly static quality to the folk life represented in *Seven Hills Away* (1947), a pattern of slow change and movement toward new horizons emerges from these sketches. Women and children are often the narrators in his fiction. G.'s deceptively simple style not only authenticates the quiet manner of ordinary folk but makes their daily encounters with birth and death seem less staggering to the reader.

But while the poor are admired for their honesty and resilience, G. also reveals the destructiveness of their slash-and-burn method of farming, which makes hard field work still harder. Still, their family closeness protects them from the loneliness of those—in the second half of *Look, Stranger, on This Island Now* (1969)—who leave the land entirely and are corrupted in the mainland metropolis. Not only the greedy merchant but also the self-styled intellectual are criticized for the increasing separation between themselves and the peasantry. Ernie Rama, antihero of *The Bamboo Dancers* (1959), is portrayed as a wandering Fisher King whose apathy is both his wound and the symptom of the modern wasteland, which is contrasted to the values of communitarian responsibility indigenous to the Philippines' traditional agrarian culture.

FURTHER WORKS: *Children of the Ash-Covered Loam* (1954); *A Season of Grace* (1956); *Selected Stories* (1964); *Mindoro and Beyond* (1979); *The Bread of Salt and Other Stories* (1993)

BIBLIOGRAPHY: Casper, L., *New Writing from the Philippines* (1966): 42–55; Galdon, J., ed., *Philippine Fiction* (1972): 153–59; Galdon, J., *Essays on the Philippine Novel in English* (1979): 108–24

—LEONARD CASPER

GONZÁLEZ MARTÍNEZ, Enrique

Mexican poet, b. 13 April 1871, Guadalajara; d. 19 Feb. 1952, Mexico City

G. M. began his literary career at the age of fourteen with a translation of Milton's sonnet on his blindness, for which he was awarded a prize. In 1886 he enrolled in medical school at the University of Guadalajara and graduated in 1893. In 1895 he moved with his family to the state of Sinaloa, where his father became director of a school in Culiacán. While practicing medicine, G. M. also contributed to a number of provincial literary magazines. His first collection of poetry, *Preludios* (1903; preludes), was warmly received. In 1907, in collaboration with Sixto Osuna (dates n.a.), he published *Lirismos* (lyrical poems) and founded the journal *Arte*. In 1911 G. M. moved to Mexico City to embark on a university and diplomatic career, became a member of the Mexican Academy, and joined the influential "Atheneum of Youth," a group of young writers and intellectuals responsible for the rebirth of humanism and the break with positivist thought in early-20th-c. Mexican literature. At various points in his life he represented Mexico as ambassador to Spain, Argentina, and Chile. He was also instrumental in the founding of the prestigious National College in 1943 and was awarded the Manuel Ávila Camacho Prize in 1944.

Although literary historians have found it difficult to classify the work of G. M. because of the poet's ambivalent relationship to Spanish American MODERNISM, the American Hispanist John Brushwood has divided G. M.'s work into three main periods. To the early period (1895–1920), which marks the time of his discovery of himself as a poet and is characterized by an emerging awareness of his relationship to the universe, belong *Silénter* (1909; silently), *Los senderos ocultos* (1911; the hidden paths), *La muerte del cisne* (1915; the death of the swan), and *Jardines de Francia* (1915; gardens of France).

"Tuércele el cuello al cisne" ("Wring the Neck of the Swan," 1958); published in *Los senderos ocultos*, is perhaps G. M.'s best-known poem and is characteristic of his preoccupation with the importance of poetry during this period. In this sonnet G. M. replaced the elegant swan, the symbol of modernist extravagance, with the figure of the pensive owl. Many critics consider the poem to signal the end of the modernist period in Spanish American letters.

G. M.'s second period, which runs from about 1921 to 1934, corresponds to the period of his work in the diplomatic corps and shows a subtle change in direction. His two principal books from this time, *El romero alucinado* (1923; the bedazzled pilgrim) and *Las señales furtivas* (1925; the subtle tokens), evince a certain indebtedness to vanguard thought seen in his experimentation with new poetic forms and his use of images related to the modern world. In the last stage of G. M.'s career (1935–52) he returned to the themes and techniques of his first period. These late poems are marked by a pervasive sadness and melancholy and considerable restraint in form and technique. The most important collection of this period is *Poemas truncos* (1935; unfinished poems).

Serving as a transition between modernism and postmodernism, G. M. was a major figure in the history of Mexican literature. It was not innovation but rather constancy, universality, and fidelity to his art that best characterize the work of G. M., who exerted an important stabilizing influence on poetry in Mexico throughout the first half of the 20th c. He also played an important role as a model to the members of the renowned "Contemporaries," the generation of the late 1920s who strived to express Mexican themes within a framework of cultural universality.

FURTHER WORKS: *La hora inútil* (1916); *El libro de la fuerza, de la bondad y del ensueño* (1917); *Parabolas* (1918); *Poemas de ayer y de hoy* (1918); *La palabra del viento* (1921); *Poesía 1909–1929* (1929); *Ausencia y canto* (1937); *El diluvio de fuego* (1938); *Poemas 1938–1940* (1940); *Bajo el signo mortal* (1942); *Poesías completas* (1944); *El hombre del buho* (1944); *Segundo despertar* (1945); *Villano al viento* (1948); *Babel* (1949); *La apacible locura* (1951); *Narciso* (1952); *Cuentos y otras páginas* (1955)

BIBLIOGRAPHY: Goldberg, I., *Studies in Spanish American Literature* (1920): 82–92; Avrett, R., "E. G. M., Philosopher and Mystic," *Hispania*, 14 (1931): 183–92; Paz, O., *An Anthology of Mexican Literature* (1958): 34–35; Topete, J. M., *El mundo poético de E. G. M.* (1967); Brushwood, J., *E. G. M.* (1969)

—EDWARD MULLEN

GONZÁLEZ PRADA, Manuel

Peruvian essayist and poet, b. 5 Jan. 1844, Lima; d. 22 July 1918, Lima

Born into an aristocratic family, G. P. displayed a rebellious spirit at an early age. Against parental opposition he planned to study engineering in Europe; thwarted in this desire, however, he remained in Lima and attended San Marcos University, where he devoted himself to literature. Peru's disastrous defeat by Chile in

the War of the Pacific (1879–83), in which G. P. participated, played a decisive role in arousing his concern for the problems underlying his country's weaknesses.

The fruit of these concerns was a series of highly charged speeches and essays, later published in *Pájinas libres* (1894; free pages). G. P.'s residence in Europe (1885–91) brought him in contact with the latest radical thinkers and movements of the Old World, and influenced the essays of *Horas de lucha* (1908; hours of struggle) as well as subsequent works. While never directly involved in politics, G. P. soon became a mentor of Peru's growing group of young revolutionaries. In his later years, especially between 1912 and 1918, when he held the seemingly innocuous post of Director of the National Library, his office became a gathering place for a group of firebrands that included such future leaders as Victor Raúl Haya de la Torre (1895–1979) and José Carlos Mariátegui (1895–1930).

In *Pájinas libres* G. P. undertook a merciless diagnosis of his country's ills. Peru's military collapse, its corruption, its lack of national will, and the obscurantism of its intellectuals is traced to the negative influence of the army, the Church, and the governing elite. Since Spain, the mother country, determined the character of these institutions, the Hispanic legacy becomes the ultimate target of G.P.'s attacks. By contrast, he repeatedly asserts that Peru's Indian masses, often accused of being lazy, dullwitted, irresponsible—in a word, "inferior"—are simply the victims of exploitation. Once given opportunities to develop and improve their condition the Indians, he believed, could well become the force for a totally regenerated nation.

In his second collection, *Horas de lucha*, G. P. continued to press for the reform of Peruvian society and for the redress of injustices done to the Indian. But he also explored Latin American problems in the broader context of the intellectual currents to which he had been exposed during his European travels. Among these ideologies, anarchism gradually assumed increasing importance in his thinking; and, in his posthumously published collection *Anarquía* (1936; anarchy), it became a central theme.

In addition to his political essays, G.P.'s contributions to Spanish American poetry are substantial. Like his prose, his verse was innovative and individualistic. His introduction of little-used French and German metrical forms links him to the work of the MODERNIST poets, yet unlike this group he shunned the ivory tower and often dealt with social issues. The poetry of his mature years is especially interesting: it reveals G.P.'s deep frustrations, bitterness, and nihilism.

On balance, G. P.'s diagnoses of sociopolitical ills is much more specific than the remedies he suggests. It is clear that he had a strong positivistic faith in science and technology; it is also apparent that he desired the separation of church and state, the redemption of the Indian, and a more equitable distribution of wealth. He was certainly a precursor of 20th-c. Latin American radicalism, especially of *Aprismo* (derived from the acronym APRA, which stands for Alianza Popular Revolucionaria Americana), an indigenous-oriented political movement that gained considerable power in the Andean region during the late 1920s and 1930s. Despite his leftist orientation, G. P. had a fine understanding of the way in which revolutionary ideals age, become rigid, and eventually die: as he observed in *Horas de lucha*, "Every triumphant revolutionary degenerates into a conservative."

FURTHER WORKS: *Minúsculas* (1901); *Presbiterianas* (1909); *Exóticas* (1911); *Baladas peruanas* (1915); *Grafitos* (1917); *Trozos de vida* (1918); *Bajo el oprobio* (1933); *Obras* (8 vols., 1933–40); *Nuevas páginas libres* (1937); *Figuras y figurones* (1938); *Libertarias* (1938); *Baladas* (1939); *Propaganda y ataque* (1939); *Antología poética* (1940); *Prose menuda* (1941); *El tonel de Diógenes* (1945); *Florilegio: Poesía, ensayo, crítica* (1948)

BIBLIOGRAPHY: Sánchez, L. A., *Don Manuel* (1930); González Prada, A., *Mi Manuel* (1947); Mead, R. G., "G. P., Peruvian Judge of Spain," *PMLA*, 68 (1953): 696–715; Zum Felde, A., *Indice crítico de la literatura hispanoamericana: El ensayo y la crítica* (1954): 271–88; Chang Rodríguez, E., *La literatura política de G. P., Mariátegui, y Haya de la Torre* (1957); Davis, H. E., *Latin American Thought* (1972): 117–19; Sánchez, L. A., *Mito y realidad de G. P.* (1976)

—MARTIN S. STABB

GOODISON, Lorna

Jamaican poet, b. 1 Aug. 1946, Kingston

Born and reared in Jamaica, G. studied at the University of Iowa and was a Bunting Fellow at Radcliffe College. She cites the Jamaican use of "double language" as the main influence on her work as a poet and "sometime short-story writer." G. began her career as a visual artist and has had exhibits in Jamaica and Guyana, and she has illustrated her own volume, *Tamarind Season* (1980), and Mervyn MORRIS's work, *On Holy Week* (1975), among others. Yet she is best known as a poet. She has been widely recognized in this genre, having received numerous awards including the Bronze Musgrave Medal and the Centenary Medal from the Institute of Jamaica in 1981; the Commonwealth Poetry Prize in 1986; a nomination for a Pushcart Prize in 1989; and the Nimrod International Award in 1992. Her poems have been translated into French, Hebrew, German, and Spanish.

To date G. has four volumes of poetry to her credit. Her first volume of poetry, *Tamarind Season*, she described as a "crying out" of ideas she had contained since her late teenage years. *I Am Becoming My Mother* (1986) explores more adult themes such as relationships, gender roles, and the economics of society. Her third volume, *Heartease* (1988), she describes as having had the effect of stretching her as a poet. The poems are about "the internal journeying to a place where the heart can find a measure of ease." Her *Selected Poems* (1995) celebrates the best as well as the breadth of her poetry. In this volume she gives voice to those assumed to lack it, reality to those who live without reflection, a sense of place that is distinctively Caribbean, and she creates space for those in exile.

The genius of G. rests with her versatility of language. Velma Pollard asserts that G. is able to manipulate the different grammars of Jamaica in her poetry without losing intelligibility to the English-reading public. She likens G.'s language ability to that of the water colorist. Her poetry illuminates the light and the dark, via language, both metaphorically and linguistically.

FURTHER WORKS: *To Us All Flowers Are Roses*

BIBLIOGRAPHY: Burnett, P., *The Penguin Book of Caribbean Verse in English* (1986): 337-39; Pollard, V., "Mother Tongue: Voices in the Writing of Olive Senior and L. G.," in Nasta, S., ed., *Motherlands: Black Woman's Writing from Africa, the Caribbean, and South Asia* (1982): 240; Pollard, V., "Language and Identity: The Use of Different Codes in Jamaican Poetry," in Newson, A., and L. Strong-Leek, eds., *Winds of Change: The Transforming Voices of Caribbean Women Writers and Scholars* (1998): 31-36

—ADELE S. NEWSON

GORAN, Abdulla

(born Abdulla Sulayman) Kurdish poet and essayist, b. Sept. 1904, Halabja, Ottoman Empire (now Iraq); d. 18 Nov. 1962, Sulaimaniya, Iraq

G. is the outstanding Kurdish poet of the 20th c. He combined the rich heritage of classical and folk poetry with the spirit and techniques of modern lyricism to endow Kurdish poetry with new forms and expanded subject matter. His creative powers evolved continuously from his earliest poems of the 1920s to his mature work of the 1950s as his knowledge of Kurdish society, especially the hard existence and the aspirations of ordinary people, deepened. At first, his poems were suffused with the romantic atmosphere and motifs characteristic of traditional and of much contemporary Kurdish verse, but after World War II his poetic vision was, in a sense, socialized, and he came to be recognized as one of the founders of Kurdish realism. Yet, for him, the boundaries between romanticism and realism were never rigid.

G. was born in the city of Halabja, in presentday northeastern Iraq, the son of a petty functionary. After attending the pedagogical institute at Kirkuk, he taught elementary school in his native city between 1925 and 1937. During this period he studied foreign languages and read widely in modern Turkish and western European literatures, explorations that profoundly influenced his later literary work and philosophical outlook. In the latter 1930s, while employed in the Iraqi ministry of communications, he found time at last to work systematically at his poetic craft. But he also accepted his responsibility as an artist to combat social injustice, and during the next two decades he joined reformers in their efforts to bring about fundamental political and economic change. In the early 1950s he achieved prominence as the editor of *Jin*, a weekly, which he transformed from a purely cultural journal into a militant voice of the poor and dispossessed of Kurdish society. But he paid a heavy price for his commitment to such causes: He was dismissed from his editorship and was repeatedly arrested and jailed. The revolution that overthrew the Iraqi monarchy in 1958 freed him from prison, and until his death he continued to write poetry that reflected undiminished support for long-cherished social causes.

As a conscious poetic craftsman G. set for himself the task of revealing the inherent artistic and expressive capabilities of the Kurdish language. In the process he brought a new vigor and freshness to Kurdish poetry by introducing the prose poem, blank verse, and a syllabic rhythm close to the rhythm of Kurdish folk poetry. In "Awati duri" (1950; distant longing), for example, he abandoned the traditional *aruz* or quantitative meter altogether, turning instead to a prosody that allowed him to vary the number of syllables in each line and to introduce new rhyme schemes. He also experimented with a variety of forms. He was fond of verse dramas, which seemed especially suited to his lyrical temperament. All his poetry is written in a remarkably pure, flowing language, and, because of its simple, easy rhythms, many pieces were put to music.

G.'s early poetry, of the 1920s and 1930s, was unabashedly romantic and brought him recognition as the head of the romantic current in Kurdish poetry. His favorite themes were nature and love. Two longer poems—"Gesht le Hewraman" (journey to Hewraman) and "Gesht le Keredag" (journey to Keredag), both of which appeared in the collection *Behesht u yadgar* (1950; paradise and remembrance)—reveal his skill as a painter of native landscapes. In the former tableaux of nature predominate, whereas the later abounds in descriptions of the rites and traditions of everyday life, thereby suggesting his growing predilection for realistic detail. At the center of his love poetry is woman, portrayed as the source of all that was beautiful and good. But even his most idyllic poetry showed traces of the later, predominant realism, for he curbed the hyperbole of classical Kurdish verse and sought to move the reader by genuineness and depth of feeling. In his "romantic period" G. was animated by strong ethnic feelings. In "Demi raperine" (1943; the voice awakens), for example, he expressed his ardent love of country (Kurdistan) and his yearning for its liberation, and in "Derwêsh Ebdulla" (1950; Dervish Abdulla) he urged the famous Kurdish balladeer to assuage his melancholy by singing pure Kurdish melodies.

The romantic element was rarely absent from G.'s later, realistic poetry. In the lament "Awabunek" (1960; sunset), which he composed on the death of the Kurdish literary scholar Rafik Hilmi (dates n.a.), he interweaves the sorrow of immediate loss with the hope that Hilmi's "star in the heavens" will never cease to inspire Kurdish patriots. More decidedly realistic, despite their preoccupation with romantic love, were G.'s dramas in verse, a new genre in Kurdish literature, which matured between the 1920s and 1940s. They gave him freedom to express his growing civic sense by allowing him to confront contemporary social issues more directly than the traditional genres. Perhaps the most popular of these dramas was "Guli hiwênawi" (1950; the bloody rose), the story of tragic love in an unjust world, which became a modern Kurdish classic. An equally powerful piece, "Bûkêki nakam" (1950; an unhappy bride), emphasizes social themes as two lovers from different classes try to overcome deeply rooted family prejudices.

G. was an accomplished prose writer and translator. He wrote numerous sketches on a variety of themes, and in 1953 he published *Helbijarde* (selections), a volume of his translations of short stories by English and French writers. He was also a prolific essayist. Among his passions was the creation of a single Kurdish literary language, which, he was certain, would enable writers to express the true essence of the Kurdish genius and way of life. He thought that the two main dialects—Kûrmanjî, used in Turkey, Syria, Iran, and northwest Iraq, and Sorânî, the literary language of the Kurds of Iraq, which G. himself used—were gradually coming together, and he railed against "extremists" who would interfere with the process by removing all Arabic and Persian elements and replacing them with "dead" words and "false" neologisms.

G.'s innovative use of language and meter, his introduction of new themes, and his harmonious blending of form and subject, especially in his social poetry, constitute a watershed in the development of modern Kurdish poetry. The generation that followed him no longer composed in accordance with the classical canon and continued to assimilate the experience of everyday life and to seek new means of expression. The evaluation of G.'s work has been aided by the appearance of the first critical edition of his poetry by Muhammadi Mela Karim (dates n.a.), *Dîwanî Goran* (1980; collected poems of G.), which includes G.'s translations

from Persian, Turkish, English, and Arabic poetry. The same editor has promised similar volumes of G.'s prose, which is not as well known as his poetry, and of critical articles about him.

FURTHER WORKS: *Firmêsk a hûner* (1950); *Sirûsht u derûn* (1968); *Lawuk a peyman* (1969)

—KEITH HITCHINS

GORDIMER, Nadine

South African novelist (writing in English), b. 20 Nov. 1923, Springs

G. was educated in the Transvaal and attended the University of the Witwatersrand in Johannesburg. Her home is in Johannesburg, the setting of most of her fiction. Although she has not lived outside South Africa for any extended period, she has traveled extensively in Africa, Europe, and North America, and has made many appearances as a lecturer abroad, particularly in the U.S.

G.'s writing career extends over thirty years of political turbulence in her native country. Her novels and short stories are predominantly concerned with the effects on individual lives and sensibilities of the political situation in southern Africa. "In South Africa, society *is* the political situation," she stated in an interview with Alan Ross in *London Magazine* (May 1965).

Her fiction reflects the changes in the life of the region since 1949, when her first collection of stories, *Face to Face*, was published. She shows a startling clarity of perception as she chronicles the corrosive effects of life in authoritarian, segregated South Africa, with its taboos, restrictions, and intricate apparatus of police power. The world she knows intimately is that of the white, English-speaking middle class. In describing the strange reality of comfortable, isolated white society she usually links closely observed details with overriding emotional effects: aridity, a sense of fear or powerlessness, distrust, lost spontaneity.

Her short stories have changed as the situation in South Africa has deteriorated. In *The Soft Voice of the Serpent* (1952) and *Six Feet of the Country* (1956) many tales reveal injustices caused by white supremacy. "Decent" and "humane" whites are shown to be themselves emotional casualties of the discriminatory system in which they are involuntarily involved. The later collections, *Not for Publication* (1965) and *Livingstone's Companions* (1971), depict the growing powerlessness of opposition to the tentacular police state. As effective political action from both whites and blacks is crushed, opportunistic political gesturing takes its place. Not all the stories carry political overtones, however. Several are short, closely focused evocations of moods, attitudes, or moments in the emotional lives of their protagonists.

G.'s novels show a similar development. *The Lying Days* (1953) is a *Bildungsroman*. Its protagonist is a young woman who decides to remain in South Africa in spite of her sense of guilt and foreboding after the Afrikaner Nationalists come to power in 1948. The novel has many beautifully observed descriptions of the decorum-ridden mining community in which the heroine grows up. The stresses of life in a segregated society are depicted in both *A World of Strangers* (1958) and *Occasion for Loving* (1963). In the former an Englishman finds himself unable to maintain friendships with both middle-class Johannesburg whites and a black acquaintance from the "townships." In the latter an illicit love affair between a black man and a white woman ends bitterly for all those involved.

Political events themselves inform *The Late Bourgeois World* (1966). The central character is a young white divorcee who is asked for help by a friend in the black underground. Her fear at his request and her memory of the futile sabotage attempts of her ex-husband provide constant tension and menace while she goes about her bland daily round in white Johannesburg.

G. maintains an interest in politics in *A Guest of Honour* (1970). Its setting is not, however, South Africa, but a newly independent African country whose problems are revealed through the experiences of a former English official, returned as a guest of the new government.

Two recent novels are again set in South Africa. *The Conservationist* (1974) has at its center a successful industrialist. His sense of possession is troubled by memories of unsuccessful personal relations and by the obtrusive presence of blacks on his weekend farm. They have a more natural claim on the land and community than he. *Burger's Daughter* (1979) is a poignant account of the unsuccessful attempt by the daughter of a renowned Afrikaans Communist to live an apolitical life after her father's death in prison.

Burger's Daughter, dealing with the Soweto riots of 1976 and black-power rejection of all white assistance and good faith, encapsulates the intractability of the tainted society described by G. with haunting clarity throughout her creative life.

In the 1990s G. enhanced her literary reputation with such works as *Crimes of Conscience* (1991), *Jump and Other Stories* (1991), *Writing and Being* (1996), and *The House Gun* (1998). In 1991 G. was awarded the Nobel Prize for literature.

FURTHER WORKS: *Friday's Footprint and Other Stories* (1960); *The Black Interpreters* (1973); *Selected Stories* (1975); *Some Monday for Sure* (1976); *A Soldier's Embrace* (1980); *July's People* (1981); *Something Out There* (1984); *Sport of Nature* (1987)

BIBLIOGRAPHY: Haugh, R. S., *N. G.* (1974); Hope, C., "Out of the Picture: The Novels of N. G.," *London*, 15, 1 (1975): 49–55; Smith, R., "The Johannesburg Genre," in Smith, R., ed., *Exile and Tradition* (1976): 116–31; Green, R. J., "N. G.: The Politics of Race," *WLWE*, 16 (1977): 256–62; Parker, K., "N. G. and the Pitfalls of Liberalism," in Parker, K., ed., *The South African Novel in English* (1978): 114–30; Smith, R., ed., *Critical Essays on N. G.* (1990); King, B., ed., *The Later Fiction of N. G.* (1993); Head, D., *N. G.* (1994)

—ROWLAND SMITH

GORDON, Caroline

American novelist and short-story writer, b. 6 Oct. 1895, Todd County, Ky.; d. 11 April 1981, Chiapas, Mexico

G. graduated from Bethany College in West Virginia in 1916. After newspaper work she married the poet Allen TATE in 1924 (they were divorced in 1959). She won the O. Henry Prize in 1934,

Nadine Gordimer

and at various times lectured on creative writing at Columbia and Purdue and the universities of North Carolina, Washington, Kansas, and California at Davis. She spent the last years of her life in Mexico.

G.'s fictional techniques are derived from the tradition of Gustave Flaubert and of Henry JAMES, Ford Madox FORD, and Joseph CONRAD, and are reflected in her theories about writing, which inform her critical study, *How to Read a Novel* (1957). Her interest in narrative point of view, particularly the Jamesian central intelligence, is revealed continually in her stories and novels, which possess carefully balanced structures, consistent narrators, unified tones, and concrete exactitude in diction. The clarity and order of her language and the coherence of her structure represent her idea that the artist must perceive a unified pattern within the apparent flux of a chaotic reality.

From the beginning of her career G. argued for the importance of order, authority, tradition, and myth. She told largely the same story many times in her works: the destruction of the old South necessitated an ordering myth of salvation, not one that advocated the material values of progress and commerce but one that revitalized the agrarian ethic of the past. Her first novel, *Penhally* (1931), studies the Southern family unit at a time of cultural crisis; Chance Llewellyn, a hero of agrarianism, kills his materialistic brother, an advocate of the new South of progress and change.

Nature is a source of knowledge for man in many of her novels and stories, but it is often antagonistic as well as benevolent. The characters of *Green Centuries* (1941), in their westward migration

Caroline Gordon

Ford (1963); *Old Red, and Other Stories* (1963); *The Glory of Hera* (1972); *Collected Stories* (1981)

BIBLIOGRAPHY: Cowan, L., "Nature and Grace in C. G.," *Crit*, 1 (1956): 11–27; Thorp, W., "The Way Back and the Way Up: The Novels of C. G.," *BuR*, 6 (1956): 1–15; McDowell, F. P. W., *C. G.* (1966); Rocks, J. E., "The Mind and Art of C. G.," *MissQ*, 21 (1967–68): 1–16; Brown, A., "The Achievement of C. G.," *SHR*, 2 (1968): 279–90; Landess, T. H., ed., *The Short Fiction of C. G.* (1972); Stuckey, W. J., *C. G.* (1972); Makowsky, V. A., *C. G.* (1989); Jonza, N. N., *The Underground Stream: The Life and Art of C. G.* (1995)

—JAMES E. ROCKS

GORKY, Maxim

(pseud. of Alexey Maximovich Peshkov) Russian novelist, dramatist, and essayist, b. 28 March 1868, Nizhny Novgorod; d. 18 June 1936, Gorky (near Moscow)

G., hailed as Russia's first proletarian writer, was not of proletarian origin but of the lower middle class. Orphaned at an early age—he lost his father when he was four and his mother at ten—he was sent out into the world by his impoverished grandfather while still a youth. With little formal education G. found various odd jobs: as a servant, a cobbler's apprentice, an errand boy in an icon shop, among others. He also wandered around Russia. Endowed with an astonishing memory and great concentration, G. acquired a very broad education on his own, but he never lost a feeling of inadequacy as a result of his lack of formal training. He became involved in clandestine revolutionary activity beginning with the *narodniki* (populist) circles of Kazan in the 1880s, later moving close to the Russian Socialist Democratic Labor Party (RSDLP), which benefited from his financial assistance and literary contributions.

G. (his pseudonym means "Maxim the Bitter") became famous practically overnight after the publication of *Ocherki i rasskazy* (sketches and stories) in 1898. By 1902 his name was well known both at home and abroad. In that year he became director of the publishing house Znanie and in that position was able to assist many young Russian writers. He took an active part in the 1905 revolution and was imprisoned. Following his release and the suppression of the Moscow uprising in December 1905, G. left Russia for western Europe and the U.S. His task was to propagandize for the revolutionary cause and to collect money for the RSDLP. But he failed in his mission and in 1906 settled on the island of Capri, Italy, where he remained until 1913.

For G., the Capri years were important to both his political and literary work. He became more deeply involved in the affairs of the RSDLP, attended the Fifth Party Congress in London, wrote for the Party's publications, and began an extensive correspondence with Lenin, who admired G.'s literary talents and valued the writer's support but was critical of his political vacillations. In 1913 the two men broke over G.'s preaching the doctrine of "god-building," which was an attempt to graft a religious superstructure onto Marxist ideology. The strain between Lenin and G. was compounded by G.'s joining the Vperyod (Forward) group, which had broken away from Lenin's Bolshevik faction in 1909.

as pioneers, suffer for their pursuit of the unknown and their escape from the past and themselves. Likewise, the 20th-c. families of *The Garden of Adonis* (1937) and *The Women on the Porch* (1944) fight hard to defend a past way of life, but their rootlessness turns their love into lust. This carnality figures in many of G.'s novels; her men, even those who strive for tradition and order, frequently fail to turn to the women who might focus their vision on the love that engenders charity, compassion, and understanding. Aleck Maury, the hero of many of her stories and her second work, *Aleck Maury, Sportsman* (1934), can find salvation only tentatively in the agrarian life style. There is a higher morality in G.'s fiction, the consequence of her own conversion in 1947 to Roman Catholicism, which offers the order and authority of a traditional religious ethic as a prop against the disorder of modern man's fragmented sensibility. *The Strange Children* (1951) and *The Malefactors* (1956) portray G.'s idea that the religious myth is the source of man's salvation.

G.'s work gives evidence of skillful narrative technique and a constant search for a meaningful ethic in a world that has lost its traditional values. Unlike her stories, her novels sometimes fail to cohere into something larger than the sum of their parts, because her craftsmanship is overly conscientious. Yet her work has achieved great success and recognition as part of the Southern renaissance for its intelligence, integrity, and scope.

FURTHER WORKS: *None Shall Look Back* (1937); *The Forest of the South* (1945); *A Good Soldier: A Key to the Novels of Ford Madox*

A tsarist amnesty proclaimed on the three-hundredth anniversary of Romanov rule permitted G. to return to Russia. There he founded the publishing house Parus and the political-literary journal *Letopis*. In 1914 he took a stand against Russia's participation in World War I on pacifist grounds. G.'s attitude toward the February 1917 revolution was one of confusion followed by fear of chaos, anarchy, and disorder. In April he founded the daily *Novaya zhizn* and in a series of articles entitled "Nesvoevremennye mysli" (untimely thoughts) he criticized the Bolshevik party and Lenin for attempting to bring about a socialist revolution in backward Russia.

By 1918 G. had come to an accommodation with the new regime and, as head of numerous societies and associations, assumed the role of curator of Russia's cultural heritage and protector of artists and intellectuals. At Lenin's behest G. left the Soviet state in 1921, settling first near Berlin and later in Sorrento, Italy. He visited the Soviet Union in 1928 and then intermittently until 1933, when he moved back permanently.

Stalin exploited G.'s popularity and used him to rubber-stamp his activities; G. became editor of numerous publications and wrote articles praising Soviet achievements. In 1934 he was chosen chairman of the first All Union Congress of Soviet Writers and is credited with formulating the literary doctrine known as SOCIALIST REALISM. G. died while Stalin was initiating the policy of large-scale purges. The causes of G.'s death are still a matter of controversy.

G. the writer emerged on the literary scene at a crucial period in Russian history. His career spanned the prelude and postlude of the revolution. He believed that literature had to have social significance, that it had to teach and guide; hence the didactic features present in the majority of his works.

In G.'s early works, mainly stories and tales, he sought his heroes among the gypsy nomads of the Black Sea area, fishermen and peasants on the loose, all living outside the society they felt alienated from. The romantic protagonists of the steppes in "Makar Chudra" (1892; "Makar Chudra," 1901) and "Starukha Izergil" (1895; "The Old Woman Izergil," 1905) were, however, soon replaced by characters inhabiting damp cellars, outskirts of cities, ports, and flophouses. "Chelkash" (1895; "Chelkash," 1902), while still in the romantic mode, portrays a drunken harbor thief. "Byvshye lyudi" (1897; "Creatures That Once Were Men," 1906) was G.'s first story in a more realistic style.

G. knew his characters well from his observations during his travels through Russia. He captured their speech, the local slang. The realistic portrayal of the poverty, ignorance, and suffering of the lower strata was novel and attracted wide audiences.

While presenting misery and violence in a harshly realistic manner, G. also wrote of humaneness and beauty. He saw evil as resulting from social injustice and from the general backwardness of Russia. His tramp-heroes, striving for freedom and liberty, are filled with warmth and compassion, regardless of the sordidness of the milieu. Such characters appear in his most famous play, *Na dne* (1902; *The Lower Depths*, 1912), first performed at the Moscow Art Theater in a production directed by Konstantin Stanislavsky. Living in a flophouse, the characters are trodden down by life—and by society. Totally degraded, they drink, gamble, fight, and despair. The central conflict of the play is between the need for messages of hope and consoling illusion, which are dispensed by the pilgrim Luka, and the need to face the truth without comforting lies, the choice offered by the eloquent thief Satin.

G.'s other plays before the revolution focus on the bourgeoisie rather than on the lower levels of society. In *Meshchane* (1902; *The Smug Citizen*, 1906) G. ridicules greed, pettiness, and the tedious

Maxim Gorky

existence of the petite bourgeoisie and would-be intelligentsia. In *Dachniki* (1905; *Summer Folk*, 1905), *Deti solntsa* (1905; *Children of the Sun*, 1912), *Varvary* (1906; *Barbarians*, 1945), *Vragi* (1906; *Enemies*, 1945), *Vassa Zheleznova* (1910; *Vassa Zheleznova*, 1945), *Zykovy* (1913; *The Zykovs*, 1945), and others, G. portrays self-made and ambitious but crude, ruthless, and materialistic middle-class people who exploit workers and peasants, and effete intellectuals who are cut off from the masses. G. sees hope in the rise of the new intellectual, dedicated to helping the proletariat and to effecting a revolution, hope in the struggle of the proletariat itself against its masters.

In G.'s early novels, *Foma Gordeev* (1899; *Foma Gordeyev*, 1901) and *Troe* (1900; *Three of Them*, 1902), portraying the nascent merchant class, G. excels in characterization on a larger scale than in his earlier fiction. But these novels suffer from too much detail, loose structure, and didacticism.

G.'s most celebrated novel, *Mat* (1907; *Mother*, 1907), is regarded as a classic in Russian revolutionary literature; it became a model for many Soviet novelists. It depicts a woman who, as she becomes involved in the revolutionary cause her son serves, loses her timidity and becomes a fulfilled person. Although not of the highest literary merit, *Mat* is important because of its message and its having introduced the new class of industrial worker as a character in Russian literature.

G. came to maturity as a writer during his Capri years. Of the novels composed there, *Ispoved* (1908; *A Confession*, 1909) is particularly interesting. Written in a biblical style, it is full of folkloric touches and poetic images. The main theme is religious faith: its distortion by the established church and its deep roots in the people. The people become the "god" of the new religion and also the "god-builder." Among other important works written on Capri were the novella *Gorodok Okurov* (1909; the town Okurov) and the novel *Zhizn Matveya Kozhemyakina* (1910; *The Life of Matvei Kozhemyakin*, 1959). In both works G. depicted the life he knew well—that of the Russian lower-middle class at the turn of the century—and continued the sociological and psychological analysis of that class, which he had begun in *Foma Gordeev*.

In 1913 the first volume of his autobiographical trilogy, *Detstvo* (*My Childhood*, 1914), appeared, and it was soon hailed as a masterpiece. The second and third volumes, *V lyudyakh* (1914; *In the World*, 1917) and *Moi universitety* (1922; *My University Days*, 1923), were also greeted with acclaim. In many ways G. surpassed his fictional works in this three-volume autobiography. Many of the same themes appear: human cruelty, the need for action, the backwardness of Russia. But, ironically, he is more objective here, with his material under greater control, than in his novels written before it. While writing about himself, G. wrote about things universal: love, compassion, violence, and hatred. In spite of his gloomy childhood and adolescence, G. does not lose sight of the bright and beautiful that existed alongside cruelty and ugliness. The autobiography is rich in the variety of its characterizations; and it is not devoid of humor.

G.'s reminiscences of his fellow writers—CHEKHOV, ANDREEV, BLOK, Vladimir Korolenko (1853–1921)—added to the literary reputation secured by his autobiography. Although he had written literary portraits early in his career, the later ones—especially *Vospominania o Lve Nikolaeviche Tolstom* (1919; *Reminiscences of Leo Nikolaevich Tolstoy*, 1920), perhaps the best portrait of Tolstoy written by any of his contemporaries—complement his autobiography in their great vividness. G. provided insights into giants of Russian literature that no biographer could, for he knew and understood them better. To these memoirs should also be added G.'s portraits of Lenin. The book-length essay *V. I. Lenin* (1924; *Days with Lenin*, 1932), although G. had to revise it several times following its initial publication, remains a fascinating portrait of the revolutionary leader written shortly after his death.

G. was often reproached for failing to depict life in postrevolutionary Russia. And indeed, only his propagandistic works address themselves to the Soviet period. In his major works written after 1917 he again turned to the period leading up to the revolution. In his late plays—*Yegor Bulychov i drugie* (1932; *Yegor Bulichov and Others*, 1937), set immediately before the revolution; and its sequel, *Dostigaev i drugie* (1933; *Dostigayev and Others*, 1937), set during the revolution—G. portrays the decline and fall of a wealthy family. In the novel *Delo Artamonovykh* (1925; *Decadence*, 1927; later tr., *The Artamonov Business*, 1948), which shows a control over structure lacking in his earlier novels, three generations of a merchant family symbolize the corrupt Russian bourgeoisie. *Zhizn Klima Samgina* (4 vols., 1927–36; *The Life of Klim Samgin: The Bystander*, 1930; *The Magnet*, 1931; *Other Fires*, 1933; *The Spectre*, 1938)—which remained unfinished at G.'s death in 1936—is more ambitious but less artistically successful than *Delo Artamonovykh*. It chronicles the period from 1870 through the revolution, focusing on the failings of the intelligentsia.

G.'s significance as a writer and his place in world literature lie in his ability to combine the great Russian literary tradition of the 19th c. with the spirit of the 20th. Although he cannot be ranked as an artist with such writers as Pushkin, TOLSTOY, Dostoevsky, or Turgenev, he was an important innovator as well as a synthesizer. His mode could be called "synthetic realism," combining as it does romantic and naturalistic elements. His great gifts are characterization and the ability to convey through his art important ideas about society and people's personal lives. Finally, G. had an immense influence on an entire generation of Soviet writers.

FURTHER WORKS: *Goremyka Pavel* (1894; *Orphan Paul*, 1946); *Zhizn nenuzhnogo cheloveka* (1908; *The Spy: The Story of a Superfluous Man*, 1908); *Poslednie* (1908); *Leto* (1909; *Summer*, 1909); *Chudaki* (1910); *Skazki ob Italii* (1911–1913; *Tales of Italy*, 195?); *Po Rusi* (1915; *Through Russia*, 1921); *Stati za 1905–1916 g.* (1918); *Revolyutsia i kultura: Stati za 1917 god* (1920); *Starik* (1921; *The Judge*, 1924); *Sobranie sochineny* (21 vols., 1923–1928); *Zametki iz dnevnika: Vospominania* (1924); *O literature: Stati i rechi* (1933; *On Literature*, 1960); *Sobranie sochineny* (25 vols., 1933–1934); *O religii* (1937); *Istoria russkoy literatury* (1939); *Arkhiv G.* (14 vols., 1939–1973); *Sobranie sochineny* (30 vols., 1949–1955); *Literaturnye portrety* (1959; *Literary Portraits*, n.d. [1960?]); *Sobranie sochineny* (18 vols., 1960–1963); *O pechati* (1962); *Polnoe sobranie sochineny* (1968 ff.). FURTHER WORKS IN ENGLISH: *Malva and Other Tales* (1901); *The Outcasts and Other Stories* (1902); *Twenty-six Men and a Girl and Other Stories* (1902); *Tales from G.* (1902); *Creatures That Once Were Men* (1908); *Orloff and His Wife: Tales of the Barefoot Brigade* (1909); *Tales of Two Countries* (1914); *Chelkash and Other Stories* (1915); *Stories of the Steppe* (1918); *Tales* (1923); *Fragments from My Diary* (1924); *The Story of a Novel and Other Stories* (1925); *On Guard for the Soviet Union* (1933); *The Last Plays of M. G.* (1937); *Culture and the People* (1939); *A Book of Short Stories* (1939); *Seven Plays by M. G.* (1945); *Reminiscences* (1946); *Literature and Life: A Selection from the Writings of M. G.* (1946); *The History of the Civil War in the USSR* (1946); *Unrequited Love and Other Stories* (1949); *Articles and Pamphlets* (1951); *Letters of G. and Andreev, 1899–1912* (1958); *A Sky-Blue Life and Selected Stories* (1964); *Untimely Thoughts: Essays on Revolution, Culture, and the Bolsheviks, 1917–1918* (1968)

BIBLIOGRAPHY: Dillon, E. T., *M. G.: His Life and Writing* (1902); Voguë, E. de, *M. G.: L'œuvre et l'homme* (1905); Kaun, A., *M. G. and His Russia* (1931); Roskin, A., *From the Banks of the Volga: The Life of M. G.* (1946); Holtzman, F., *The Young M. G.: 1868–1902* (1948); Alexinsky, G., *La vie amère de M. G.* (1950); Wolf, F., *M. G.* (1953); Pozner, V., *Erinnerungen an G.* (1959); Gourfinkel, N., *G.* (1960); Muchnic, H., *From G. to Pasternak* (1961): 29–103; Hare, R., *M. G.: Romantic Realist and Conservative Revolutionary* (1962); Levin, D., *Stormy Petrel: The Life and Work of M. G.* (1965); Weil, I., *G.: His Literary Development and Influence on Soviet Intellectual Life* (1966); Borras, F. M., *M. G. the Writer: An Interpretation* (1967); Wolfe, B. D., *The Bridge and the Abyss: The Troubled Friendship of M. G. and V. I. Lenin* (1967); special G. issue, *Y/T*, 2 (1976); Scherr, B. P., *M. G.* (1988)

—TOVA YEDLIN

G. must be taken, for better or for worse, as a didactic writer. He is always imbued with a social idea, which he is anxious to convey to his readers, and his literary output may be approached with regard to the proportion and intensity of the message preached in each individual work. It hardly need be suggested that the quality of his work is in inverse proportion to the degree and obviousness of its didacticism. Yet one should remember that it was this latter trait that enhanced his value in the eyes of the masses and their fighting vanguard, and lent him the public significance which cannot be discounted by any purely aesthetic considerations.

Alexander Kaun, *M. G. and His Russia* (1931), p. 553

G. is truly a great landscape painter and, more important, a passionate landscape lover. He finds it difficult to approach a person, to begin a story of a chapter of a novel without first glancing at the sky to see what the sun, the moon, the stars and the ineffable palette of the heavens with the everchanging magic of the clouds are doing.

In G. we find so much of the sea, the mountains, forests and steppes, so many little gardens and hidden nooks of Nature! What unusual words he invents to describe it! He works at it as an objective artist: now as Monet, breaking down its colours for you with his amazing analytical eye and what is probably the most extensive vocabulary in our literature, now, on the contrary, as a syntheticist who produces a general outline and with one hammered phrase can describe an entire panorama. But he is not merely an artist. His approach to Nature is that of a poet. . . .

In order to create Nature's majestic and beautiful orchestrations for his human dramas, G. uses most skilfully the frailest similarities and contrasts between human emotions and Nature, which at times are barely discernible. [1932]

Anatoli Lunacharski, *On Literature and Art* (1965), pp. 222–23

He preferred to praise rather than pity, and to speak of man's conquests of, rather than his submission to, Nature. Impatient with theory, complexity, "psychologizing," he saw existence in the light of his unambiguous dogma. and, like the solicitous father of very small children, told lies to bolster their morale. All men appeared to him in the guise of the snake and falcon of his fable; he wanted all of them to be falcons, never doubted that they could be, and toward the end of his life had the joy of seeing them so transformed, as he thought. It was an ardent zeal, a generous humanistic faith that, to his mind, was more "loving" than Tolstoy's egotistic passion. . . . He was "engaged" in life, in the French sense of *engagé*; as a writer his business was to "serve," to rouse, to work for improvement, to be actively involved in the moment; unlike Tolstoy, he did not look upon human beings as moral entities but only as social organisms: they either destroyed or built communities, and their role in society determined their value as men.

Helen Muchnic, *From G. to Pasternak* (1961), pp. 98–99

He concentrated on the sordid details, primarily those of a physical nature: hunger, drunkenness, pain, filth, the lack of all physical essentials. With the exception of Dostoevsky. there is no other Russian writer of the nineteenth century who dealt as much as G. did with physical violence and murder. Whatever the psychological explanation may be in terms of G.'s personality, it would be next to impossible to detect any grin of sadistic pleasure in his gruesome descriptions of wives mangled by their husbands, of vagabonds beaten up by police. From his early childhood he had been deeply affected by all the excesses of violence around him: the fury of blows, the floggings, the madness of drunken brawls. He had become aware of physical violence as a main feature of Russian life, and its exposé remained one of his principal objectives; he denounced it not only as an Asiatic heritage, a survival of the Tartar yoke, but also as a result of ignorance and oppression: the cruelty of the common people was bred by their misery and was a release as well as a compensation for their slavery.

Marc Slonim, *From Chekhov to the Revolution* (1962), p. 136

His best earlier stories had thrown a highlight on strong and self-reliant characters at loggerheads with their drab environment, by no means only tramps, but also princes, landowners, and legendary figures. . . . While he had neither morally whitewashed nor tried to rationalize their unpredictable, impulsive conduct, he was clearly fascinated by their integrity, by their refusal to be dragged down by convention-bound society. After all these glowing pictures of buoyant energetic men and women, G. changed over paradoxically to an apologia for weak or broken individuals. Sometimes they are the same people as before, seen at the later stage of life. The characters in *The Lower Depths* have all started boldly, and then been broken on the wheel. But G. could more easily start to justify sympathetic but defeated people, because some of his favourite heroes had been men of quite ordinary capacities, struggling to play gigantic roles beyond their strength. It was inevitable that many of his defiant tramps and ultra-individual misfits, if they could not die bravely before their youthful vigour was exhausted, should sink into the dull abasement of the dosshouse.

Richard Hare, *M. G.* (1962), pp. 60–61

G. was always prepared to rework his plays to modify or clarify their meaning (notably *Enemies* to which he gave a significantly different political slant for its Soviet revival in 1933), but he never returned to *The Lower Depths* and it remains as it was originally written—ambiguous and inconclusive. When he wrote it in 1902 he had no choice: the conflict between truth and compassion, between harsh facts and the beautiful lie was within himself. Soon he sought to resolve it by embracing the activist cause of

Marxism and by pursuing the truth in a series of socially committed works of which *Enemies* is perhaps the least compromising. Yet his characters remained . . . "facts of life," complex human beings who transcend dogmatic schematization. In *Enemies* even the unscrupulous factory boss, Mikhail Skrobotov, is treated with a compassion that G. manages still to reconcile with the inescapable social truth of the play.

If *The Lower Depths* is G.'s most humane, hence most inconclusive play, it is by no means a play apart: like all his work it proceeds from the man himself, reflecting his own complexity and his own honest doubt. About one thing only G. was never in doubt: as Satin says "Man! There's the truth for you! What is man? It isn't me—or you—or them . . . no! It's you and me and them and the old man and Mahomet . . . all rolled into one." To that extent he was a political writer. [1972]

Edward Braun, Introduction to M. G., *The Lower Depths* (1973), p. xiv

GOROSTIZA, José

Mexican poet, b. 10 Nov. 1901, Villahermosa (Tabasco); d. 16 Mar. 1973, Mexico City

G., a member of the Mexican Academy of the Language and winner of the 1968 National Literary Prize, came from a family that had strong ties to literature. One of his ancestors was the dramatist Manuel Eduardo de Gorostiza (1789–1851), author of the well-known play *Contigo, pan y cebolla* (1833; bread and onions with you). G.'s brother Celestino (1904–1967) also earned recognition as a dramatist, with several plays to his credit, among them the highly acclaimed *El color de nuestra piel* (1952; the color of our skin). G. spent much of his life in the Mexican diplomatic service. These assignments took him to various locales around the world, including London, Copenhagen, Rome, Guatemala, Havana, Bogotá, Rio de Janeiro, Florence, Paris, Holland, and Greece. In addition to assignments abroad, he also held numerous government posts at home, and in 1964 he was named minister of foreign affairs.

G. belonged to an influential generation of vanguard writers who contributed regularly to the seminal Mexican literary magazine *Contemporáneos* (1928–1931). International in its scope, this review published numerous translations of contemporary poets such as T. S. ELIOT. Among the most prominent members of the *contemporáneos* group were Xavier VILLAURRUTIA, Carlos Pel LICER, Jaime Torres BODET, Salvador NOVO, Bernardo Ortiz de Montellano (1899–1949), and Gilberto Owen (1905–1952). Inspired by European and North American models, they maintained a cosmopolitan attitude toward literature and fostered universal themes rather than purely regional or national ones in their writings.

As a poet G. produced only two books. His initial volume, *Canciones para cantar en las barcas* (1925; boat songs), was characterized by an abundance of sea imagery and a fascination with traditional verse patterns of Spanish popular poetry as well as a nonnative form, the haiku. His renowned masterpiece, *Muerte sin fin* (1939; *Death without End*, 1969), has been called one of the most accomplished extended poems in 20th-c. Spanish American literature. Highly intellectual in content, it is a philosophical composition dealing with the search for meaning in life. The poem's origins can be traced to G.'s reading of metaphysical poetry while living in London in 1927. Both of these works were reissued, along with previously unpublished poems, in a single volume entitled *Poesía* (1964; poetry).

In *Muerte sin fin* the object of the poet's meditation, a glass of water, leads him to the realization that God molds the spirit just as a glass gives water an identifiable form. Despite this discovery the poet wrestles with doubt concerning the existence of the eternal and expresses his existential anguish over the eventual dissolution of form into nothingness. *Muerte sin fin* is a quest for permanence, illustrating the conflict between order and chaos, form and substance, the intellect and irrationality. In its focus on death it is at once universal yet firmly rooted in the Mexican tradition.

Mexican vanguard writers in the 1920s and 1930s were typically linked to either the *estridentistas* (those inspired by Italian futurism and Spanish ultraism) or the *contemporáneos* (who, much like the *modernistas* before them, avoided social issues in order to focus on aesthetic matters). Rejecting nationalistic themes and eschewing politically engaged poetry, the *contemporáneos* concerned themselves instead with archetypal themes and the subconscious. Theirs was an avant-garde poetry intended for a select audience rather than the common reader. G. and the other *contemporáneos* were somewhat aloof, favoring a more intellectual brand of poetry. In many respects they anticipated the achievement of Mexican Nobel laureate Octavio PAZ. G.'s verse deals with metaphysical concerns and treats such eternal subjects as love, life, solitude, death, and God. His lyricism is complex, profound, and transcendent. The significance of G. and the *contemporáneos* lies in their search for the universal, their efforts to link Mexican writing to international literary currents, and their emphasis on the aesthetic function of art rather than simple didacticism.

FURTHER WORKS: *Prosa* (1969)

BIBLIOGRAPHY: Paz, O., *Las peras del olmo* (1957): 105–14; Gómez-Gil, O., *Historia crítica de la literatura hispanoamericana* (1968): 532–35; Franco, J., *Spanish American Literature since Independence* (1973): 180–84; Franco, J., *An Introduction to Spanish-American Literature* (1975): 263–66; Rodríguez Monegal, E., ed. *The Borzoi Anthology of Latin American Literature* (1977), Vol. 2: 600–1; McMurray, G. R., *Spanish American Writing since 1941: A Critical Survey* (1987): 165–66; Pacheco, J. E., "J. G.," in Solé, C. A., ed., *Latin American Writers* (1989), Vol. 2: 923–31

—MELVIN S. ARRINGTON, JR.

GOYEN, William

American novelist and short-story writer, b. 24 Apr. 1915, Trinity, Texas; d. 30 Aug. 1983, Los Angeles, California

Born in rural east Texas, G. received his B.A. in 1932 and his M.A. in comparative literature in 1939 from Rice University. He served in the U.S. Navy from 1940 to 1944 aboard an aircraft carrier in the South Pacific. During this period he wrote of his wartime experiences and found publication in the *Southwest Review*. Having received a grant from the review in 1948, G. soon published the lyrical novel *House of Breath* (1950), which brought him several literary awards. In the 1950s G. received two Guggenheim Fellowships and moved to New York City where he set his second masterpiece, *In a Farther Country: A Romance* (1955). Over the next thirty years, he taught at several Ivy League universities and wrote novels, short-story collections, and plays, as well as nonfiction, poetry, song lyrics, and television scripts.

Among Europeans, G. is recognized as one of the finest American short-story writers of the postwar period. Indeed, his work is much better known in France and Germany than in his native America. Though his lasting contribution to literature may be his short stories, most American critics and readers know G. for his first two novels, *The House of Breath* and *In a Farther Country*, both of which have been popular enough at home and abroad to merit repeated reissuings. These novels, as with all of G.'s novels except *The Fair Sister* (1963), are episodically structured; they are built upon interconnecting stories and thematic tales rather than linear, plot-progressing chapters. In his writing G. explored the traditions of MAGIC REALISM, SURREALISM, and the Southern grotesque while maintaining a highly stylized modernist approach best exemplified in T. S. ELIOT, James JOYCE, and particularly D. H. LAWRENCE.

The foundation of his prolific career, *The House of Breath* is a bittersweet autobiographical remembrance of family and childhood that recalls the works of fellow Southerners Thomas WOLFE and James AGEE. The novel evokes a sense of infinite longing for a simpler time, for an illusionary inner peace somehow lost. Rich in poetic imagery, it lacks plot and character development in the traditional sense; rather, life in rural Charity, Texas, unfolds through many Joycean "voices," including that of the wind and the river. The focus of the novel is the leaving and returning of the self-exiled "children" of Charity—the interrelatedness of people and place. No less original than his first novel, the surrealistic *In a Farther Country* is more straightforward and dramatic in its writing style. The well-received novel focuses on Marietta, a Spanish-American who longs for the glorious rise of her native land in the modern world. The isolated individuals Marietta meets in the course of her life also share their own dreams of resurrection. This image of the disconnected journeyer is repeated throughout G.'s novels and short stories in original, creative ways that clearly delineate his work from that of his contemporaries.

G.'s later novels—and for some critics his early ones too—are known for their incantatory passages, their fragmented brilliance, but not their seamless design. For many American critics, his novels are often too unstructured, and for popular audiences they are too cerebral. Hard to catagorize as a writer, G.'s American neglect is unfortunate but understandable. He was not a novelist at heart, but a storyteller. *Faces of Blood Kindred* (1960) and *Collected Stories of W. G.* (1975) solidified his position as a master storyteller, and showed his ability to tightly control his narratives when he desired such a style.

Written by a fine craftsman with a unique narrative voice, G.'s *House of Breath*, *In a Farther Country*, and *If I Had a Hundred Mouths: New & Selected Stories, 1947-1983* (1985) shall long resonate with international readers.

FURTHER WORKS: *Ghost and Flesh* (1952); *The Bite of the Diamond Rattler* (1960); *The House of Breath Black/White* (1972); *A Book of Jesus* (1973); *Aimée* (1974); *Come the Restorer* (1974); *Selected Writings of W. G.* (1974); *Arcadia* (1983); *Correspondence: Selections* (1995)

BIBLIOGRAPHY: Gossett, L., *Violence in the Recent Southern Fiction* (1965); Phillips, R. S., *W. G.* (1979); Phillips, R. L., "The Mythopoeic Imagination of W. G.," *SoR*, 15, 1 (1979): 234-37

—JON PARRISH PEEDE

GOYTISOLO, Juan

Spanish novelist, essayist, and critic, b. 5 Jan. 1931, Barcelona

Early in his childhood, G. experienced the horrors of the Spanish Civil War. His mother was killed in 1938 during a Nationalist bombardment of Barcelona, and the family was forced to abandon the city and take refuge in a small village in Catalonia until the war was over, when they returned to Barcelona, where G. continued his formal education. Between 1950 and 1953 G. studied law in Barcelona and Madrid and began testing his narrative skills. During this time he founded the "Turia" literary group with the distinguished novelist Ana Marí MATUTE and others, and wrote three short stories, a novelette, and his first full-length novel, *Juegos de manos* (1954; *The Young Assassins*, 1959). The publication of this work marked his first formal step into the world of the novel and the end of his aspirations to practice law.

Before leaving Spain to establish permanent residence in Paris in 1957, he published *Duelo en le paraíso* (1955; *Children of Chaos*, 1959), wrote *El circo* (1957; the circus) and *Fiestas* (1958; *Fiestas*, 1960), enhancing his reputation, at home and abroad, as one of the most talented novelists in 20th-c. Spain.

Stylistically, G.'s novelistic output shows two distinctive phases. The first, which includes the novels mentioned above, plus *La resaca* (1958; the undertow) and *La isla* (1961; *Island of Women*, 1962), is characterized by rather traditional construction, manipulation of time and space, and portrayal of character. Detailed, objective descriptions and dialogue are used to capture the moral and physical reality of Spain immediately before, during, and after the Spanish Civil War, which in these novels becomes the cause for the characters' moral degradation and the vivid evidence of a fanatical society where there is no room for justice or tolerance. Most of the characters are children and adolescents who, following their parents' behavior, resort to deception and murder as the only choices in order for them to survive. Although objective depiction of events is prevalent in this phase, there is also lyricism, used especially to embody the dreams of those striving to escape the cruelty of the world in which they are trapped.

In the mid-1960s G.'s initial objective realism, evident also in most of the writings of other authors of his literary generation, began to move in a new direction, toward more imaginative technical experimentation. Three major works belong to this new phase: *Señas de identidad* (1966; *Marks of Identity*, 1969), *Reivindicación del Conde don Julián* (1970; *Count Julian*, 1974) and *Juan sin tierra* (1975; *Juan the Landless*, 1977). They are the product of a mature novelist whose primary commitment is to his genre, the novel, more than simply to society, as seen in his earlier works. In these three later novels G. progressively creates a more ambitious and challenging world where language becomes the central force for poetic experimentation in point of view, time, space, character development, and structural design. As fragmentation leads to ambiguity, ambiguity leads to reader participation in the creation of the work whose open structure turns it into a never-ending source of meanings. More than novels of traditional form, they are malleable texts wherein the three protagonists search for new identities while destroying their present ones. To do this they must attack everything that is held sacred by Spaniards and Westerners: religion, social institutions, conventional morality, and so on, and irony, parody, and sarcasm become the main weapons. Nothing is left intact in this process of annihilation.

Even though these works form a three-part unity of self-discovery, each maintains its distinctive individuality of form and content.

Álvaro Mendiola, in *Señas de identidad*, while listening to Mozart's *Requiem* in his family's home near Barcelona, looks through some old family albums, letters, and newspaper clippings that had been kept for a long time in drawers and forgotten and that now are about to take him back to his personal past, and to the past of his country. At first, this rummaging appears to be only a trivial pastime, but later it turns into an obsessive exploratory journey whereby the character—in a series of interior monologues, intense, fragmented recollections, and collages, with the author using multiple narrative points of view—brings to light the horrors of Spanish Civil War, including his recent and bitter experiences of his self-imposed exile in Paris between 1952 and 1953, when the opposition forces to the Franco regime began to disintegrate for lack of internal unity. Even though the exploratory journey into Álvaro's past leads him nowhere, except to more anguish and deeper alienation, the sincerity of his efforts, to strip himself of the identity imposed on him by the society he criticizes, becomes the redeeming trait of the character.

In *Reivindicación del Conde don Julián* G. intensified his attacks on the system. This time he utilizes as the central force of the novel the legend of Don Julián, who is said to have allied himself with the Arabs, in the invasion of Spain in 711, in retaliation to his daughter's seduction by Roderick, the last Gothic king of Spain. The protagonist is a lonely Spaniard, exiled in Tangiers, who having transformed himself into a Moor and with the inspiration of Count Julián's rebellious spirit and treason, in an interior monologue that lasts twenty-four hours, in his imagination invades Spain and systematically destroys its religious, political, and literary institutions. This symbolic destruction is also the destruction of his present identity, which enables him in turn to create a new one and redefine his individuality. Under the guidance of the Marquis de Sade, Lautréamont, and Jean GENET, and with skillful manipulations of intricate imagery and surreal fragmentations of plot, time, and space, he commits a variety of atrocities: he rapes Queen Isabella I, embarks on a surreal trip through her vagina, sodomizes a child (representing the protagonist's own past), and breaks all rules of decency. He assaults every political and religious institution, and, as if that were not enough, finishes off, one by one, with all the literary classics of Spanish literature, including Lope de Vega, Calderón de la Barca, Miguel de UNAMUNO, and most of the writers of the so-called Generation of '98. Cervantes and Luis de Góngora are among the few masters he shows respect for and saves from his literary massacre. Furthermore, he honors them by following their example in developing an autonomous, highly metaphoric, complex text wherein the destruction of an entire literary corpus (as in *Don Quixote*) becomes the subject and the method of literary creation.

Unlike the two previous novels, in *Juan sin tierra* the protagonist, transformed into a modern wandering Jew (hence the title), through a complex succession of dreams contained in numerous narrative units, systematically attacks not only Spain, but also all the commonly held sacred values of Western civilization: family,

religion, social institutions. By engaging in this violent attack, which is conceived and executed within a general framework of vengeance, hatred, and perversion, the character, once again, seeks to annihilate his present self and replace it with another, free of guilt and shame. His guiding principle for self-realization is clear: the more he destroys society's values (and thus his present self) the more he develops his new identity. And the more he vilifies himself, the more effective the destruction becomes. In time and space the novel reaches apocalyptic proportions. His self-destruction extends not only to his childhood but all the way to the moment he was conceived by his mother. And the more he travels in terms of space the more complete and satisfying his aggression becomes.

Juan sin tierra is the culmination of G.'s thematic aggression and artistic experimentation. It is perhaps one of the most powerful texts in 20th-c. literature. Compared to this work, *Makbara* (1979; *Makbara*, 1981) is wanting in stylistic power and imagination. G.'s attack on modern capitalist society in *Makbara* lacks the intensity and the artistic subtlety of the three preceding novels.

G. has also written literary theory and criticism. In three critical works—*Problemas de la novela* (1959; problems of the novel), *El furgón de cola* (1967; the caboose), and *Disidencias* (1977; dissidences)—G. develops perceptive and controversial commentaries on the novel in general and on specific literary works written by old and new, Spanish and foreign, authors.

G.'s novelistic art, especially that of his second phase, has placed him among the most innovative Hispanic authors of this century. His rich poetic imagination and his daring manipulation of language is comparable only to those of such Spanish American writers as Guillermo CABRERA INFANTE, Carlos FUENTES, and Mario VARGAS LLOSA.

FURTHER WORKS: *Campos de Níjar* (1959); *Para vivir aquí* (1960); *Fin de fiesta* (1962; *The Party's Over*, 1967); *La chanca* (1962); *Pueblo en marcha* (1963); *El problema del Sahara* (1979)

BIBLIOGRAPHY: Schwartz, K., *J. G.* (1970); Sobejano, G., *Novela española de nuestro tiempo* (1970): 260–92; special G. issues, *Norte*, Nos. 4–6 (1972); Ortega, J., *J. G.: Alienación y agresión en "Señas de identidad" y "Reivindicación del Conde don Julián"* (1972); Romero, H., "Los mitos de la España sagrada en *Reivindicación del Conde don Julián*," *JSSTC*, 1 (1973): 169–85; Ríos, J. ed., *J. G.* (1975); Levine, L. G., *J. G.: La destrucción creadora* (1976); Cabrera, V., "Movilidad y repetición narrativas en *Juan sin tierra*," *TAH*, 1,9 (1976): 7–9; Spires, R., "La autodestrucción creativa en *Reivindicación del Conde don Julián*," *JSSTC*, 4 (1976): 191–202; Ríos, J., *Juan sin tierra* (1977); Robatto, M. A., *La creación literaria de J. G.* (1977); Pérez, G., *Formalist Elements in the Novels of J. G.* (1979)

—VICENTE CABRERA

Signs of Identity, G.'s most outspoken attack on the Franco regime, presents biographies of birth and death, suffering and sorrow in the Spanish police state where, during twenty-five years of "peace," man had beaten, arrested, and killed defenseless fellow citizens for the crime of having defended their legal government, the Republic. No progress, says G., will be able to wipe away the humiliations, the injustices, the persecution, the destroyed lives, of those years.

G. examines Spanish history from the 1930's on, the days of José Antonio Primo de Rivera, Ledesma, and others, recalling the public works programs, the depression, the Popular Front, the violence and unrest among starving peasants and their battles with the Civil Guard; he more forcefully condemns Franco for the spiritual and physical murder of his countrymen who are born, multiply, and die in silent resignation. Andalusia recalls a cemetery to him in its eternal misery: "A woman in mourning carried a jug on her head and even the mangy dog swatting flies with his tail seemed an exact replica of others seen a thousand times in a Southern town."

Kessel Schwartz, *J. G.* (1970), pp. 98–99

With Count Julian, J. G. has succeeded in giving us a meticulous and clear-minded account, both brilliant and full of salutary laughter, of a first voyage into the interior of a volcano. . . . It is a thorough, lyrical, passionate account of a task of systematic destruction. . . . Without doubt—and there has been no lack of those who have said it—Count Julian follows a typically Spanish tradition because of the haughtiness of its excess and the corrosive bite of its humor. It is almost a century since Valle-Inclán cried: "Poets, guillotine your swans," and since he promised to work relentlessy "to dig the grave in which to bury the hollow and pompous Spanish prose which can no longer be ours. . . . " The anonymous character who haunts the last novel of J. G. re-creates, in effect, this situation of exile and marginality of the writer in Spanish society, who is obliged, generation after generation, to wage the same struggle, to renew the same subversion of values.

Jorge Semprum, on *Reivindicación del Conde don Julián, L'express,* 26 July-1 Aug. 1971, pp. 67–68

Señas de identidad is the detailed and intimate, yet broad and panoramic exploration of a personal crisis. Álvaro Mendiola, the author and protagonist . . . portrays his own experience as a member of a specific generation of young Spaniards who were born during the thirties, and for whom the Civil War is one of their childhood memories. He is the descendant of a tradition-bound family of industrialists and landowners whose values he despises. But it is not until he is a young man struggling to orient himself ideally and intellectually to the causes of social and economic justice for Spain's working classes at home and in exile that he becomes aware of the extent to which he is cast in the mold of the social class he is opposing. It is not a question of his intellect or even his moral values resembling those of his family, for he appears to have set himself fiercely against everything they stand for in those respects. There is something deeper and far subtler that he has inherited from his elders that seems in spite of everything to determine his consciousness at the deepest level: it is a sense of life, a mythology, a "Weltanschauung" which he can

scarcely identify rationally that has brought him to this critical impasse.

Reed Anderson, "*Señas de identidad*: Chronicle of Rebellion," *JSSTC*, 2 (1974), p. 3

Count Julian represents for Spain what a combined critical consciousness of black, Indian, Chicano, Women's Liberation and Gay Power attitudes would represent in the United States. There is a difference, however. The contesting minorities in the United States have questioned a success story. G. is questioning a failure. The risks he takes are proportionately greater. . . . Count Julian is the most terrible attack against the oppressive forces of a nation that I have ever read. Nothing that black has written against white, or woman against man, or poor against rich, or son against father, reaches quite the peak of intense hatred and horror that G. achieves in this novel. That he does it with magnificent beauty and perfect craftsmanship only adds to the power of his invective against his "harsh homeland." It is quite a feat, and quite a risk, for the novelist works with words, yet he is conscious that "violence is mute."

Carlos Fuentes, on *Count Julian, NYTBR,* 5 May 1974, pp. 6–7

Juan sin tierra is inspired by one of the most difficult concepts in literature—irony—by that "perception of life in terms of incongruities occurring between appearances and reality," even though "reality" here must be used in quotation marks. Sometimes the ironic undertone seems to be mere humor, but if one is to read a few more lines apparently in the same vein, irony stands out to the point that it overwhelms the entire book. Much more compact than *Conde Don Julián* (I use this name instead of the complete title because of the joy the English translation, *Count Julián* produces in me), more open than *Señas de identidad, Juan sin tierra* is perhaps J. G.'s best book. No critical analysis could ever supplant the pleasure of its reading, which, as in any good table, forces us to forget reading its maxim; yet there is no other book that is so Spanish, so relevant to the Spaniard and, at the same time, so irreverent to Spain. The book's only heroine is the Spanish language— but do I have to remind anyone that "heroine" (in Spanish) means both heroine and heroin?

Guillermo Cabrera Infante, "El fin como principio," in Julián Rios, ed., *Juan sin tierra* (1975), pp. 228–29

Because of its radical difference not only to novels in general but to G.'s previous works, *Juan sin tierra* could be classified as an entirely new genre in the vein of *Finnegans Wake.* Samuel Beckett's comment about Joyce's magnum opus is pertinent: "It [the novel] is not to be read—or rather it is not only to be read. It is also to be looked at and listened to. His writing is not about something; it is that something itself." G.'s work had elements of a travelogue, a book of memoirs, and even a diary "to see clearly," as Roquetin said in [Sartre's] *La nausée.* The intentions of the author appear to be that of engaging the reader in a voyage of self-discovery in which fact and fiction, the present, the past, and the future are intermingled. Furthermore, the frequent use of the second-person singular point of view contributes, as in *Don Julián,* to the amalgamation of the protagonist and the reader. Unlike *Don Julián,* however, the author, who shows himself in the act of writing, indicates that he is the narrator-protagonist and fuses himself with the protagonist and reader.

Genaro J. Pérez, "Form in J. G.'s *Juan sin tierra,*"
JSSTC, 5 (1977), pp. 137–38

GOZZANO, Guido

Italian poet, b. 19 Dec. 1883, Turin; d. 9 Aug. 1916, Agliè Canavese

From an upper-middle-class family, G. received a traditional education and lived most of his life in his native region of Piedmont, alternating between Turin and his country estate in Agliè. He studied law but followed his natural bent for journalism and literature. His collections of poems *La via del rifugio* (1907; the road to shelter) and *I Colloqui* (1911; *The Colloquies,* 1981) were favorably received and established him, in his twenties, as one of the authentic voices in Italian poetry of the early 20th c.

His short life was marked by a long fight against tuberculosis, an illness that resisted years of medical care and may have been partially responsible for the melancholy and disillusioned outlook that characterizes G. as a representative of the *Crepuscolari,* the poets of the "twilight" school.

In 1912 G. undertook a long voyage to India and Ceylon, hoping to regain his health. His impressions of that venture were published as letters in the Turin newspaper *La stampa* and later collected in *Verso la cuna del mondo* (1917; toward the cradle of the world) with a preface by the critic Giuseppe Antonio Borgese (1882–1952). G. also left an unfinished poem on butterflies, one of his favorite subjects of study and naturalistic observation, in which he treats a traditionally didactic genre with a fundamentally lyrical inspiration. Of considerable value for the understanding of his life and work is his correspondence with Amalia Guglielminetti, with whom he had a difficult relationship.

G.'s disenchantment with reality and often also with literature made him yearn for the simple values and bourgeois settings of past years. In poems such as "Paolo e Virginia" (1910; Paolo and Virginia) and "La signorina Felicita" (1909; Miss Felicity) he expressed emotions and insights in a freshly colloquial style whose natural fluency succeeded in opening new paths beyond D'ANNUNZIO'S high diction and refined style. But it is the ironic self-awareness of his style that distinguishes G. from all the poets of his time, including the *Crepuscolari,* whose world he contemplates and cherishes while implicity confessing and regretting the impossibility of a full acceptance of it beyond a carefully modulated and balanced compromise between detachment and sympathy, melancholy and cheerfulness, participation and irony.

G. also wrote fables, tales, and verse for children, as well as an outline for a film on St. Francis of Assisi that bespeaks an uncommon gift for visual imagery.

FURTHER WORKS: *I tre talismani* (1941); *La principessa si sposa* (1917); *L'altare del passato* (1918); *L'ultima traccia* (1919); *Lettere d'amore di G. G. e A. Guglielminetti* (1951); *Poesie e prose* (1961). FURTHER WORKS IN ENGLISH: *The Man I Pretend to Be: "The Colloquies" and Selected Poems* (1981, bilingual)

BIBLIOGRAPHY: Bracegirdle, M., "D'Annunzio and G.," *IRLI,* 6 (1977): 95–103; Williamson, E., Introduction and Biographical Note, in Lind, R. F., ed., *Twentieth Century Italian Poetry* (1974): 34–69: 367–88

—A. ILLIANO

GRACE, Patricia

New Zealand novelist, short-story writer, and writer of children's books, b. 17 Aug. 1937, Wellington

G. grew up with two cultures, from a Maori father and European mother, but with English as her language. When young she spent holidays with her father's family, and now lives within their tribal territory, by the sea near Wellington. After attending Roman Catholic schools, G. trained as a teacher and taught, often in the country, until becoming a full-time writer in 1985. Those experiences and her marriage and seven children explain prevalent themes in her work of family and community, and of Maori determination to retain their heritage in a predominantly European New Zealand.

G. began writing short stories in the 1960s. Acknowledging renowned predecessors such as Katherine MANSFIELD and Frank SARGESON, she has yet acquired her own reputation for this genre. Her first collection, *Waiariki* (1975; Waiariki), is representative of a preference for vignettes of ordinary, domestic life, and for characters (most are Maori) who are at some disadvantage. A persistent strain in her social realism is the dislocation of Maori tribal communities, as intimated in titles: *Waiariki* is the ancestral home, but *Electric City* (1987) is where "you always have to pay." Such gravity, however, is balanced by humorous and lyrical celebration of life, and by the metaphysical. Her fourth collection, *The Sky People* (1994), reaches into this realm by title and an ironic rewriting of a cosmological myth. Other stories return to earth but many have metaphorical allusion to Maori tradition complicating a seeming simplicity.

G. is a storyteller. The maxim that recurs about her work, "Stories who tell us who we are," derives from her explicit aims to write about being Maori as a distinctive voice in New Zealand literature. It also reveals G.'s appreciation of the rhetorical and conciliatory power of speech, and her tendency to raise social issues through what her characters have to say. This is notable in her novels. *Mutuwhenua* (1978; The Moon Sleeps) contemplates Maori-European relations through a young girl's adjustment to her Maori upbringing and marriage to a European. Various viewpoints of family members in *Potiki* (1986; The Youngest) illuminate the values that inform a Maori community's challenge to European entrepreneurs. Intimate chronicles of the lives of three women in

Cousins (1992) mirror the fragmentation of Maori society over their generations.

G.'s fiction encompasses a small world. Maori rural or coastal communities are common settings and often opposed to urban, European life. The political edge of this opposition is moderated by an implicit recognition of the need for justice for all people. Human relationships, especially within families, provide impetus and focus for G.'s writing, and in exploring them she artfully transfigures the introspective, memoried, and imaginary worlds of children, the young, elders, and ancestors. The centrality of past and present generations in community brings a coherence and timelessness to her narration, which is reminiscent of Maori oral tradition. In part homage to that tradition, the oral quality and concision of her language claim attention. By select use of Maori and the idioms of Maori-English, G. strives for ways in which English can signify what Maori want to tell.

G.'s work has a conservative, national focus. But, in the way of other Maori writers, such as Witi Ihimaera (b. 1944), it also challenges by experimenting with the conventions and language of English literature. Her success in this is preeminent. G. is a conscientious writer, an acclaimed author of children's books, her work translated and included in teaching curricula in Europe; she also takes a prominent public role in support of readings and encouragement of writers, especially young Maori. Her distinguished contribution to New Zealand literature, which is sure to continue, has been acknowledged by writing fellowships, book awards, and an honorary doctorate.

FURTHER WORKS: *The Dream Sleepers and Other Stories* (1980); *Wahine Toa* (1984, with Robyn Kahukiwa); *Selected Stories* (1991); *Collected Stories* (1995)

BIBLIOGRAPHY: Simms, N., "A Maori Literature in English: Prose Fiction—P.G.," *PQM*, 3 (1978): 186-99; Pearson, B., "Witi Ihimaera and P. G.," in Hankin, C., ed., *Critical Essays on the New Zealand Short Story* (1982): 166-84; New, W. H., *Dreams of Speech and Violence* (1987); Bardolph, J., "'A Way of Talking': A Way of Seeing: The Short Stories of P. G.," *CE&S*, 12 (1990): 23-39; Arvidson, K., "Aspects of Contemporary Māori Writing in English," in McGregor, G., and M. Williams, eds., *Dirty Silence* (1991): 117-28; Robinson, R., "The Strands of Life and Self: The Oral Prose of P. G.," *CRNLE Reviews Journal*, 1 (1993): 13-27

—JANE MCRAE

GRACQ, Julien

(pseud. of Louis Poirier) French novelist and essayist, b. 27 July 1910, Saint-Florent-le-Vieil

G. studied in Paris at the École Normale Supérieure and the École des Sciences Politiques, receiving his degree in history in 1934. He then taught history at various secondary schools throughout France and, from 1947 to his retirement in 1970, at the Lycée Claude Bernard in Paris. During World War II he served in the French army. He now lives in Paris.

A disciple of André BRETON, whom he admired and on whom he wrote a study, G. was deeply influenced by SURREALISM. His novels could be called vast prose poems exploring the strangely mysterious, giving new life to old myths in stories abounding in quaint enchanted castles with secret passages, desolate shores, and dense impenetrable forests. Although written in a surrealistic vein, these novels show no trace of "automatic writing." On the contrary, G.'s style is sumptuous, with a rich and suggestive vocabulary. His elegant prose, characterized by slow-moving, long, involved sentences, seems to delay forever the coming of the enigmatic "Event."

Unlike the surrealists, G.'s foremost preoccupation is with destiny and the tragic sense of life. In *Au château d'Argol* (1938; *The Castle of Argol*, 1951), three exceptional characters (all strangely beautiful, all educated on Hegel and able to comprehend life's deepest intricacies) live an intense spiritual adventure in a remote enchanted castle in Brittany. The themes and scenery were undoubtedly inspired by Wagner's *Parsifal*. In fact, G. himself conceives of his narrative as a "demonic version" of the Grail legend. But other myths—man's fall and the Faust legend—also play a significant part in the intricately woven fabric of the novel, which explores the dialectical nature of good and evil, spirit and flesh.

G.'s most famous novel, *Le rivage des Syrtes* (1951; *The Opposing Shore*, 1986), won the Goncourt Prize, which G., however, refused. The book is another interesting interpretation of the Grail myth, and shows affinities with Ernst JÜNGER'S *On the Marble Cliffs*, of which G. said he would have enjoyed claiming authorship. Like Jünger's "Marina," G.'s imaginary "Orsenna" is a highly civilized state, whose inner decay, nevertheless, is unmistakable. Yet, in spite of the prevailing "indecent affirmation of life" characteristic of the people of Orsenna, "who were never given to value the tragic," there exists at the same time a secret desire for the possibly redeeming catastrophe. Also, G.'s protagonist, is aware of this undercurrent and, seized by an irresistible inner urge, becomes the traitor or redeemer of Orsenna by provoking fate. He deliberately crosses the line of demarcation between Orsenna and its enemy of three hundred years, uncivilized Farghestan, thus bringing about a resumption of hostilities, which could very well lead to Orsenna's annihilation. But it is neither pure lust for adventure nor simply a destructive instinct that drives him to his act; they are only part of a more encompassing desire to experience life once more to its fullest, even though it may be for the last time. The thirst for purification and the desire for redemption are inextricably fused with any death wish.

G.'s literary production is not limited to novels. It includes short stories, prose poems, a play, and several volumes of critical essays. But his reputation is based above all on his novelistic work. His novels are long meditations on man's fate, revealing a strong and disturbing obsession with death, reminiscent of classical tragedy. The traditional concept of characters and plot has been shattered. In each novel a multitude of dark forces are at play; little by little they seem to converge and intensify until the final catastrophe, which more often than not remains only suggested. The main characters are "marked" beings who act as catalysts to those forces, bringing with them inevitable disaster.

G.'s work stands decidedly apart from the main currents of contemporary French literature. It is characterized especially by those traits that link surrealism with romanticism—German romanticism and Hegelian idealism in particular.

FURTHER WORKS: *Un beau ténébreux* (1945; *A Dark Stranger*, 1951); *Liberté grande* (1947); *André Breton: Quelques aspects de l'écrivain* (1948); *Le roi pêcheur* (1948); *La littérature à l'estomac* (1950); *La terre habitable* (1951); *Prose pour l'étrangère* (1952); *Un balcon en forêt* (1958; *Balcony in the Forest*, 1959); *Préférences*

(1961); *Lettrines* (1967); *La presqu'île* (1970); *Les eaux étroites* (1977); *Lettrines* 2 (1978)

BIBLIOGRAPHY: Leutrat, J. -L., *J. G.* (1967); Matthews, J. H., "J. G. and the Theme of the Grail in Surrealism", *RR*, 58 (1968): 95–108; Dobbs, A. -C., *Dramaturgie et liturgie dans l'œuvre de J. G.* (1972); Peyronie, A., *La pierre de scandale du "Château d'Argol" de J. G.* (1972); Gaudon, S., "J. G.'s *Un balcon en forêt*: The Ambiguities of Initiation," *RR*, 67 (1976): 132–46; Denis, A., *J. G.* (1978); Francis, M., *Forme et signification de l'attente dans l'œuvre romanesque de J. G.* (1979); Murphy, C. J., *The Allegorical Impulse in the Works of J. G.* (1995)

—BLANDINE M. RICKERT

GRADE, Chaim

Yiddish poet, novelist, and memoirist, b. 5 April 1910, Vilna, Lithuania; d. 26 June 1982, New York, N.Y.

Son of a Hebrew teacher and grandson of a grenadier in Napoleon's invading army of 1812, G. was raised in a household devoted to the observance of traditional Judaism as well as the acquisition of secular knowledge. But he abandoned Orthodoxy in his early manhood. In the face of the Nazi onslaught, he took with him only a Hebrew Bible and a German translation of Dante's *Divine Comedy* and fled first to Vilna, the Jerusalem of Lithuania, from Russia, where he was living, and later to Soviet Central Asia. In Lithuania he emerged as a leader of the "Young Vilna" group of Yiddish writers. This self-assertive and eager pleiad of young literati shunned the accepted rules of writing, denounced the common wisdom about the essence and purposes of literature— preferring introspection and the pursuit of idiosyncrasy—and refused to assume the mantle of "professional writers."

After World War II G. left the Soviet Union, sojourned briefly in Paris, and in 1950 settled in the U.S. He established himself in the canon of modern Yiddish literature by the quality of his narrative skill, both puissant and gentle; by his relentless perception of the human psyche when it is faced with philosophical dilemmas; and by the tender sensitivity he exhibits for the millennial treasure of his beloved language. He was the only Yiddish poet invited to read at the literary festival held in the White House in January 1980.

In post-World War II Yiddish belles lettres, G. and Avrom SUTZKEVER stand as the two contemporary bards of the Holocaust, which truncated their people and brought their language to the threshold of annihilation. The national motif undergirds much of G.'s elegiac poetry. He summons the Jewish people, as a latter-day prophet "tossed between oblivion and life," to awaken, live, and continue.

The second national (and personal) trauma that enflames his creative imagination is the destruction in the early 1950s of the flower of Yiddish literati in Moscow. G. has immortalized these writers in his "Elegiye of di sovetish-Yidishe shrayber" (1962, "Elegy for the Soviet Yiddish Writers", 1969), already recognized as a classic in the repertory of modern Yiddish poetry.

The Musar, or Moral Discipline, movement was initiated in 19th-c. Lithuania by Rabbi Israel Salanter, who preached the need for higher Jewish learning to bring about moral perfection. G.'s epic poem *Musarnikes* (1939; the ethical ones) chronicles life in a yeshiva of this type, tracing the way a young Orthodox Jew gropes among the perplexities of faith, only to emerge as a determined humanist and affirmer of life.

G.'s writing is haunted by three figures from his youth: his father, his mother, and his mentor, Rabbi Chazon Ish. These three personages, together with the author himself, appear and reappear in various guises in his major works, *Tsemakh Atlas* (2 vols., 1967–68; *The Yeshivah*, 2 vols., 1976–77); *Di agune* (1961; *The Agunah*, 1974); and his novelette, *Der brunem* (1958; *The Well*, 1967). These works demonstrate a zest for subtle characterization and an impressive architectonic skill that limns the ethical, philosophical, and theological currents that have percolated through Lithuanian Jewry for the past two hundred years.

Inspired by an abiding affection for the centuries-old way of life of East European Jewry, G. lays open with a surgeon's skill the strengths and weaknesses of both the sages and the pious ordinary folk of this now vanished world. In a series of remarkable panoramas, he fills out their biographies, finding the merit and salvation of these lives in their quest for the spiritual and in their self-oblation.

Only in the 1960s did G. allow his works to be translated. Since then critical interest and appreciation of his talent have grown and his reputation has become international. He has received the Bimko Prize for *Di mames tsuve* (1949; partial tr., *The Seven Little Lanes*, 1972); and the Lamed Prize for his volume of short stories, *Di mames shabeysim* (1955; my mother's Sabbaths), his first volume of prose.

A man of East and West, possessed of cosmopolitan sophistication, he is at the same time the leading student of the Torah among today's writers in Yiddish. Reworking the themes of shtetl life, Talmudic and biblical riches, Hasidic and Musarnik lore, his oeuvre constitutes an ongoing dialogue between the Jew who believes despite the Holocaust and the poet, seeking faith and understanding. G. illustrates, in the words of one critic, the Pauline principle by which the spiritual man slays the carnal.

FURTHER WORKS: *Yo* (1937); *Has: Lider un poemen* (1943); *Doyres* (1945); *Oyf di khurbes* (1947); *Farvaksene vegn: Lider un poemes* (1947); *Pleytim* (1947); *Der shulhoyf* (1958); *Der mentsh fun fayer* (1962); *Yerushalayim shel mayle un Yerushalayim shel mate* (1965); *Parmetene erd* (1968); *Mayn krig mit Hersh Raseyner* (1969); *Oyf mayn veg tsu dir* (1969); *Di kloyz un di gas* (1974); *Der shtumer minyen* (1976)

BIBLIOGRAPHY: Madison, C., *Yiddish Literature* (1968): 315, 325; Biletzky, I. C., *Essays on Yiddish Poetry and Prose Writers of the Twentieth Century* (1969): 233–42; Liptzin, S., *The Maturing of Yiddish Literature* (1970): 261–67; Hecker, I., "C. G.: The Challenge to God" and "C. G.: A Portrait of the Man", *Judaica Book News* (1979): 15–22; Slotnick, S. A., "C. G.'s Central Concern", *Jewish Book Annual*, 37 (1979–80): 106–115

—THOMAS E. BIRD

GRAF, Oskar Maria

German novelist and short-story writer, b. 22 July 1894, Berg, on Lake Starnberg; d. 28 June 1967, New York, U.S.A.

The son of a village baker and a farmer's daughter, G. first learned his father's trade; but at age sixteen he went to Munich, where he began to write and participated in the anarchist movement. During World War I he was drafted and, after he had refused to carry out an unreasonable command, was thrown into prison. He pretended to be insane and was committed to an asylum. After his release, he worked at a number of odd jobs in Munich and took part in the revolution of 1918–19.

G.'s literary career in Germany coincided with the fate of the Weimar Republic. After Hitler's rise to power he went into voluntary exile, first to Vienna (until 1934), then to Brno, Czechoslovakia (until 1938—his stay was interrupted by an extended trip to the Soviet Union in 1934), and finally New York. After World War II, he wanted to visit Germany again, but not until he had become an American citizen. Because he refused to sign the clause that would require a person to bear arms on behalf of the U.S., his process of naturalization was not completed until 1958.

Although his first publications were poetry, G. is now primarily known as a prose writer. *Frühzeit* (1922; early youth), the first part of his autobiography, while it received little notice in Germany, was published in two Russian editions in 1925. G.'s reputation was established when he added a second part of this work and published both parts together under the title *Wir sind Gefangene* (1927; *Prisoners All*, 1929). As an open confession of the author's personal past and of his having witnessed the historical events leading up to the Munich revolution, the work self-critically examines the role of a confused German intellectual during the time of political and social crisis. G. took a firm stand against war in *Einer gegen alle* (1932; *The Wolf*, 1934), a novel about a German soldier who cannot adapt to a peacetime society. In another novel, *Bolwieser* (1931; *The Station Master*, 1933), G. showed how a self-indulgent German petit bourgeois becomes the victim of his own weakness.

During his exile G. depicted a number of characters who either directly or indirectly aided Hitler in his usurpation of power. The novel *Anton Sittinger* (1937; Anton Sittinger), for example, centers around a retired postal employee who has always voted for the party that happened to be in power; after the Nazi victory, the protagonist almost finds himself on the wrong side, but he has been saved once more by his shrewd, opportunistic wife, who has secretly enrolled him in Hitler's party. The tragic consequences of an apolitical position are depicted in the novel *Unruhe um einen Fried-fertigen* (1947; agitation around a peaceful man). Here the main character is a German Jew who has tried to make himself secure by skillfully concealing his background; but he is brutally killed by the Nazis when his identity is revealed in connection with an unforeseen inheritance.

The personal and the historical aspects of G.'s oeuvre achieved their highest degree of artistic integration in the biographical novel *Das Leben meiner Mutter* (1946; published first in English as *The Life of My Mother*, 1940), in which Germany's history from the time of Bismarck until the beginning of the Hitler tyranny is reflected in the story of a simple Bavarian woman and her (G.'s) family. Another work in which autobiographical elements are depicted against the background of a historical situation is *Die Flucht ins Mittelmäßige: Ein New Yorker Roman* (1959; escape into an average life: a New York novel). The plot centers around refugees from the Third Reich whose exile has become a permanent state after the war.

In Germany G.'s reputation rests perhaps more on his short stories than on his longer prose works. His frequently reprinted collection of Bavarian peasant stories, *Das bayrische Dekameron* (1928; the Bavarian Decameron) abounds in earthy, humorous, and erotic situations reflecting the cultural and linguistic milieu of the author's upbringing. In the *Kalendergeschichten* (1929; calendar tales) G. made a lasting contribution to a specifically German form of the short story that can be traced back to the 19th-c. authors Johann Peter Hebel (1760–1826) and Jeremias Gotthelf (1797–1854). Like his literary ancestors, G. wrote about the day-to-day problems of simple people, but he revealed his more modern position by letting his characters become the victims of an unjust political system and frequently of their own greed and social ignorance.

G.'s active social conscience and his personal integrity of character are the ever-present elements in all of his works. The strongest of his works are those in which he depicted people's lack of social maturity and political justice; he was less successful as a writer when he tried to show how human and social conditions should be improved. With his partly autobiographical, partly fictitious political novels and short stories, he has become a part of the best tradition of European realistic literature.

FURTHER WORKS: *Die Revolutionäre* (1918); *Amen und Anfang* (1919); *Ua-Pua . . .!* (1921); *Maria Uhden* (1921); *Zur freundlichen Erinnerung* (1922); *Georg Schrimpf* (1923); *Bayrisches Lesebücherl* (1924); *Die Traumdeuter* (1924); *Die Chronik von Flechting* (1925); *Die Heimsuchung* (1925); *Finsternis* (1926); *Licht und Schatten* (1927); *Wunderbare Menschen* (1927); *Im Winkel des Lebens* (1927); *Dorfbanditen* (1932); *Notizbuch des Provinzschriftstellers O. M. G. 1932* (1932); *Der harte Handel* (1935); *Der Abgrund* (1936); *Der Quasterl* (1938); *Der Quasterl, und andere Erzählungen* (1945); *Das Aderlassen* (1947); *Die Eroberung der Welt* (1949); *Mitmenschen* (1950); *Menschen aus meiner Jugend auf dem Dorfe* (1953); *Der ewige Kalender* (1954); *An manchen Tagen: Reden, Gedanken und Zeitbetrachtungen* (1961); *Der große Bauernspiegel* (1962); *Altmodische Gedichte eines Dutzendmenschen* (1962; *Old-Fashioned Poems of an Ordinary Man*, 1967); *Größtenteils schimpflich* (1962); *Er nannte sich Banscho* (1964); *Gelächter von Außen* (1966); *O. M. G.: Beschreibung eines Volksschriftstellers* (1974); *Reise in die Sowjetunion 1934* (1974)

BIBLIOGRAPHY: Genschmer, F., "O. M. G. since World War I", *GQ*, 20 (1947): 57–61; Heydt, A. von der, "O. M. G.", *GQ*, 41 (1968): 401–12; Recknagel, R., *Ein Bayer in Amerika: O. M. G. Leben und Werk* (1974); Pfanner, H. F., *O. M. G.: Eine kritische Bibliographie* (1976); Johnson, S. K., *O. M. G.: The Critical Reception of His Prose Fiction* (1979); Pfanner, H. F., "O. M. G.: Exile in Permanence," in Spalek, J. M., and R. F. Bell, eds., *Exile: The Writer's Experience* (1981)

—H. F. PFANNER

GRAHAM, Jorie

American poet, b. 9 May 1951, New York, New York

G. was born in New York, the daughter of a former *Newsweek* correspondent and a well-known sculptor and socialite. Raised in the south of France and Rome, she attended the Sorbonne in Paris before enrolling in New York University's film school, where instead of film she fell in love with poetry. In 1976 she enrolled in the University of Iowa's Writers' Workshop, where she received an M.F.A. in 1978. After teaching at Murray State University in Kentucky and Humboldt State University in California, she returned to teach in the Writers' Workshop in 1983.

G.'s first book, *Hybrids of Plants and Ghosts*, appeared in 1980. She was already publishing regularly in literary journals such as the *Iowa Review* and *American Poetry Review* as well as high profile magazines like the *New Yorker*. Her work was immediately acclaimed in the poetry world: she received the American Academy of Poets Prize from the University of Iowa, the American Poetry Review Prize in 1982, and Pushcart Prizes in 1980, 1981, and 1983.

Like the poets she admires, including William Butler YEATS, Emily Dickinson, and Wallace STEVENS, G.'s poetry is often difficult, tackling weighty philosophical issues. The title for her first book was taken from a quote by Friedrich Nietzsche. Although there is a profusion of natural imagery in the poems, it leads to abstract speculations and flights of language. G., reviewer William Logan remarked in *Parnassus*, "thinks before she feels." While most critics admired her intelligence and ambition, some criticized the poems as obscure or emotionally distant.

G.'s second book, *Erosion* (1983), elicited an even stronger response. Taking up painful subjects—death, murder, blindness, atrocities such as extermination camps, torture, castration and rape—the poet explored the issues of beauty, morality, and accountability. While some critics were offended by her contemplation of the interrelationship between beauty and horror, most felt that *Erosion* improved on her first collection, and was both less obscure and more confident.

The End of Beauty (1987) did not continue to make G. more accessible. Here G. deployed originary myths to frame the contemporary world, and characters to refract an image of the self. Even more difficult and cerebral than her earlier books, *The End of Beauty* included many poems with blank spaces and mathematical variables that challenged the idea of the poem as a finished, static object. The many section divisions interrupting the flow of the language questioned the notion of the poem as a teleological process, a series of small resolutions leading to a final conclusive thought.

Regions of Unlikeness (1992) was similarly difficult and flamboyant. G. continued to take on the cultural and historical heritage of Western culture, grappling with metaphysical issues in the process. *Materialism* (1994) drew attention to the poet's feminine perspective as it took up a favorite dichotomy, that of flesh and the spirit, arguing that "there are, there really are,/ things in the world." In 1996 G. published a volume of collected poems entitled *The Dream of the Unified Field* that won the Pulitzer Prize. A volume of new poems, *The Errancy*, published in 1997, was well received.

Throughout her career G. has been a somewhat controversial figure, accused of obscurantism and gothic grandiosity by her detractors, designated by her champions one of the few inheritors of the American tradition of boldly intellectual poetry.

FURTHER WORKS: *Photographs & Poems* (1998, with Jeannette Montgomery Barron)

BIBLIOGRAPHY: Jarman, M., "The Grammar of Glamour: The Poetry of J. G.," *NER*, 14 (1992): 251-61; Costello, B., "J. G.: Art and Erosion," *ConL*, 33 (1992): 373-95; Gardner, T., "An Interview with J. G.," *DenQ*, 26, 4 (1992): 79-104; Isaacson, L., "Ad Interim 2000—A Delayed Reading Lightly Attended," *DenQ*, 28, 4 (1994): 136-41; Vendler, H., *The Breaking of Style: Hopkins, Heaney, G.* (1995); Vendler, H., *The Given and the Made: Strategies of Poetic Definition* (1995)

—ANNE-LISE FRANÇOIS

GRASS, Günter

German novelist, dramatist, and poet, b. 16 Oct. 1927, Danzig (now Gdańsk, Poland)

G. came from an ethnically mixed, lower-middle-class background in the (former) Free City of Danzig—an ancestry and environment that finds extensive direct reflection in his writing. His father owned a grocery store. His mother was of Kashubian origin (the Kashubians are a Slavic people indigenous to the rural area around Danzig, quite distinct from the Poles both as to language and culture). G. was five years old when the Nazis seized power in Germany. While a student in the Danzig schools, he was a member of Hitler youth groups. He left school in 1943 to do paramilitary duty. He was drafted into the army in 1944 and was wounded in April 1945. While recovering from his wounds he was captured by the Americans.

Freed in 1946, G. supported himself for the next two or three years by working on farms, in a potash mine, and as a stonemason's apprentice, until he enrolled as a student of painting and sculpture in the Düsseldorf Academy of Art. In 1952 he moved to West Berlin to continue his art studies. In both Düsseldorf and Berlin he also wrote lyric poetry, some of which he read before Group 47, an influential group of writers. He moved temporarily to Paris in 1956, where he wrote his hugely successful first novel, *Die Blechtrommel* (1959; *The Tin Drum*, 1962). At about the same time and shortly afterward he wrote several dramas, which, like his verse, achieved only modest public acclaim. After establishing his fame with the "Danzig Trilogy," of which *Die Blechtrommel* was the first part, G. became active in politics, championing the cause of Willy Brandt and the Social Democrats, and inveighing—as in his writing—against the prominence and influence of former Nazis and against the state of mind in West Germany that preferred the delights of conspicuous consumption to the agonizing acceptance of responsibility for Nazi crimes. In G.'s view, Nazism is to be equated absolutely with the German petite bourgeoisie.

By 1977, after a decade of political activism and world travels, both substantially incorporated into his writing, G. was beginning again to accord a primacy to more purely literary work, although his political tenets and his literary creations remain very closely connected.

Die Blechtrommel, awarded the distinguished Group 47 Prize before it was published, was an instant critical and commercial success. It thrust G. into a worldwide prominence that has scarcely diminished to the present. Like G.'s subsequent works, *Die Blechtrommel* resists facile interpretation, and indeed G. regards interpretation, especially the academic variety, as superfluous. Critics nonetheless have offered quite elaborate explications, worked out, for example, on the basis of myth, or the picaro tradition, or the New Testament. These perspectives, as well as that of psychology, are not without advantage in providing insights into the novel. More recent criticism, however, aided by an increasing G. oeuvre, inclines to regard the novel as primarily historical or even—with certain reservations—as realistic. G. himself calls it a "realistic novel."

The history under consideration, the realism, including generous autobiographical detail reinforced by later personal reconnaissance, is the history and realism of Danzig at the beginning of and during the Nazi terror and that of West Germany during the Adenauer years—the latter of which G. also finds little reason to be sanguine about. Thus, Oskar Matzerath, the owner of the tin drum, a present on his third birthday, wills his own stunted stature, that of a three-year-old, as a protest against the misery of his human existence. The drum and drumming are consonant with, among other things—for example, sex—the military tenor of the Nazi years, and at least to this extent we are to regard Oskar as a petit-bourgeois representative of Nazism. With the capitulation of the Nazis in May 1945, Oskar resumes growing. He develops a hunchback, however, a deformity that may signal Oskar's warning response to the questionable direction of the Adenauer regime, with its rehabilitated Nazis and its turn to the prosperous consumer society. In postwar West Germany, Oskar's feeling of guilt—the guilt of the petit bourgeois about Nazism—is such as to make him an outsider, to a pathological degree. For as we know from the start, he is writing his memoirs, with their sweep of revelation, while in an insane asylum, perhaps not permanently, but confined for observation. His memoirs constitute one level of straightforward, if amazing chronological. The relationship of time levels and of the narrator to the author will become more complex in the later G.

G. wrote the second part of the Danzig Trilogy, the novella *Katz und Maus* (1961; *Cat and Mouse*, 1963), after he made what he later regarded as a false start on the third part, the novel *Hundejahre* (1963; *Dog Years*, 1965). *Katz und Maus* dwells on the experiences and adventures of lower-middle-class youth in Danzig from 1939 to 1944, related by one of their number, Pilenz. More specifically, it is Pilenz's story of Mahlke, whose status as an outsider is emphasized from the beginning by his overdeveloped Adam's apple, that is, "Maus." Mahlke's career parallels the Nazi effort in World War II—launching, successes, and collapse. Like Oskar Matzerath, Mahlke is later afflicted with guilt. His more youthful days were characterized by a fierce devotion to the Virgin Mary and by swimming out to a sunken Polish minesweeper in the bay and making himself at home—quite literally—there. Mahlke's end consists in humiliation at his former school in being refused a forum, even as a wearer of the Iron Cross; and finally, in a trip to the familiar minesweeper, from which, for whatever reason, he does not emerge.

The long novel *Hundejahre* amplifies and focuses more sharply the concerns of G. that found voice in the earlier parts of the Danzig Trilogy: the Nazi crimes and the postwar prosperity and acceptability of former Nazis. The crimes against the Jews are focused in the love-hate relationship between Walter Matern and the half-Jew, Eduard Amsel, also known as Brauxel (spelled variously). This relationship is one of the two chief subjects. The second is suggested by the title of the novel: it is, in fact, Hitler's own dog, the ancestry of this dog, and the dog's seeking, in May 1945—and finding—his fortune west of the Elbe, that is, in West Germany. The plight of Walter Matern in the West as a former Nazi and present guilty outsider resembles that of Oskar Matzerath. G. names former Nazis and Nazi apologists evidently less encumbered by guilt than the fictional Matern, who in the 1950s are doing quite well in Adenauer's Germany.

The great diversity and idiosyncratic sweep of *Hundejahre* is emphasized structurally by G.'s device of attributing committee authorship to the novel. Early episodes in the 1930s, celebrating the childhood friendship of Amsel and Matern, are narrated by an

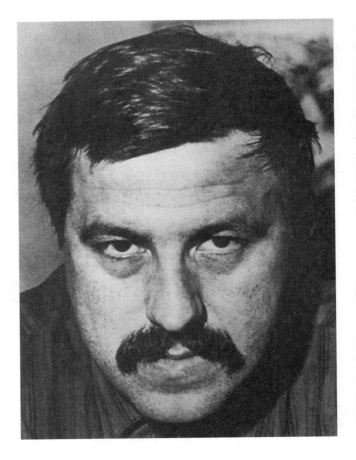

Günter Grass

omniscient author, Brauxel-Amsel; the second part is carried forward by means of love letters from their friend Harry Liebenau to his cousin Tulla Pokriefke (a network of identical characters inhabit the component works of the Danzig Trilogy); the narrative point of view of the postwar episodes is that of Walter Matern. All three fictive writers bring their completed and frequently shocking segments together in 1962, thus replicating the compositional efforts of G. himself.

In the play *Die Plebejer proben den Aufstand* (1966; *The Plebeians Rehearse the Uprising*, 1967) G. turned from the familiar prewar Danzig and postwar West Germany to the Berlin of the 1950s, where he himself was by then living. Bertolt BRECHT appears in the play as the Boss—an art-oriented Boss who declines to leave his theatrical preoccupations to support the East Berlin workers' uprising. The uprising is not, however, aimed at revolution, but reform. Berlin is likewise the scene, and reform the theme, of a drama *Davor* (1969; *Max: A Play*, 1972) and an intrinsically related novel, *Örtlich betäubt* (1969; *Local Anaesthetic*, 1969), which G. wrote simultaneously; the play is an expansion of the central portion of the novel. On a historical canvas not unlike that of the Danzig Trilogy, G. has superimposed a new historical picture, that of the disenchanted student radicals of the mid-1960s. Abandoning the grand sweep of the trilogy, G. presents a tightly controlled, highly dialectical argument, with little action. In fact, the dilutionary effect of objectification on potential action is an important theme, which stands in a dialectical relationship to the principal theme: that revolution dialectically induces inaction and failure, and that reform is thus to be preferred. Failure to perceive that this conclusion does not stand in exclusive relation to the above line of reasoning, but relates as well to G.'s passionate denunciation of the complacent consuming, gadget-worshiping society, may account for the otherwise curious fact that *Örtlich betäubt* achieved greater success in the U. S. than any of G.'s other works.

In *Aus dem Tagebuch einer Schnecke* (1972; *From the Diary of a Snail*, 1973) G. for the first time revealed himself completely in his writing. He did so by using the device of a fictive colloquy with his children, a "diary" of his travels and involvement—and commitment—as a campaigner for the Social Democrats and Willy Brandt in the 1969 election. Interwoven with this account of G., the campaigning reformer, is a story by G., the writer, based on the history of the Danzig Jews in the Nazi era, vignettes from the life of one Hermann Ott, also called Doubt. Doubt collects snails and as a non-Jewish friend and supporter of Jews takes refuge from the Nazis with a Kashubian who wants to become a German. The snail metaphor, developed with astounding virtuosity, pervades, and is central to, the fictional history. It represents G.'s political philosophy and his notion of the only possible way toward progress: "being a little quicker than the snail. . . ." The slow, unaggressive snail is the symbol of peaceful evolution working out its path between the violent and aggressive extremes of Communism and Fascism. The recommended attitude of skepticism and the character, Doubt—into whose role G. sometimes steps—even challenge G.'s self-acknowledged lapses into political partisanship, the latter fueled by his contemplation of ex-Nazis in high places to the accompaniment of public insouciance. In this novel G. the father, the fiction writer, and the political reformer successfully inform a single written work.

The lengthy novel *Der Butt* (1977; *The Flounder*, 1978) marked the return of G. to primarily literary endeavor after a decade in which politics and literature were symbiotic. As to authorial approach, however, *Der Butt* has much in common with *Aus dem Tagebuch einer Schnecke*. The narrator and the author are to a great extent identical. And that narrating author illustrates—to adults as well as children—what he has on his mind that he wants to communicate. Such illustration in *Der Butt* is, however, complex and elaborate.

G. elevates to thematic significance his long interest in cooking, research into which brings him up against—or to awareness of—the historical role of cooks, who turn out to be women cooks. A series of nine such cooks, each representing one month of the term of pregnancy, from in and around Danzig, and from different eras, and the men with whom history associates them, illustrates the sexual role conflicts besetting the narrator and his consort through the ages, Ilsebill. Another arena of conflict based on the sex role is composed of the tribunal of—taken as a group, less than admirable—feminists in Berlin who are sitting in judgment on the talking flounder caught by three of their number. The flounder, here confined to a tank as a prisoner, is based on the flounder in the Grimms' fairy tale "The Fisherman and His Wife," in which a fisherman is granted favors for his wife by a talking flounder, who is actually an enchanted prince. G. develops the flounder as the initiator of, and eloquent spokesman for, the male-dominated society that millennia ago succeeded the society in which women were dominant. G.'s flounder, in accord with G.'s political principle of reform (or at least, change), is however, far from rigid and ultimately declares himself ready to champion the feminists' cause.

The novel has three endings, coinciding with possible live birth at seven or eight months, as well as at nine months. The first two endings, with man resigned, or with woman replicating the errors of man, are followed by an open ending, a birth. Not necessarily a happy ending—there are disquieting signs—but an ending with dialectical possibilities: there may be a third way. G. still seems concerned about reform, but his area of concern has transcended politics.

In 1961 G., who had made his literary debut some years earlier as a poet, explained that his poetry and plays, as well as his fiction, were built on dialogue. No doubt his concept of the underlying role of dialogue facilitated his transition to plays and fiction, in both of which genres is to be found the elaboration of originally poetic pictures and metaphors. G.'s verse is itself occasional—as he insisted—object-oriented metaphors, the objects often being removed from their conventional context and aligned with other objects so as to produce unconventional and striking relationships. G.'s later verse approaches SURREALISM. He has no use for the poetry of abstraction and individual lament, nor for that of didacticism. As with his politics and his novels and plays, G. eschews the antagonism of the extremes.

G. declared that his "master" was Alfred DÖBLIN, but it is more appropriate to give credit to G.'s own literary originality, power, and versatility. It may be that Döblin foreshadowed some of the devices G. used in *Die Blechtrommel*, but it is difficult to speak of any continuing literary influence. More to the point, in the longer run, is Döblin's preceptoral role as a writer-politician. Certainly G. has pursued both those careers vigorously; despite objections by purists, his literary work is not lessened thereby. G. is something of a latter-day Renaissance man: novelist, poet, dramatist, sculptor, politician, illustrator, book designer. G.'s politics have exposed him to a special intensity and variety of criticism, both of his art and of the politics (and social credos) that he does not hesitate to couch in his art. Preferring moderate reform, he offers an easy target to the extremes. From both the artistic and political point of view, he not only faced down old Nazis when that was perhaps not so difficult to do, but faced up to the excesses of the new left when for an artist that was a rather lonely office.

FURTHER WORKS: *Die Vorzüge der Windhühner* (1956); *Beritten hin und zurück* (1958; *Rocking Back and Forth*, 1967); *Noch zehn Minuten bis Buffalo* (1958; *Only Ten Minutes to Buffalo*, 1967); *Hochwasser* (1960; *Flood*, 1967); *Gleisdreieck* (1960); *Die bösen Köche* (1961; *The Wicked Cooks*, 1964); *Die Ballerina* (1963); *POUM; oder, Die Vergangenheit fliegt mit* (1965); *Onkel, Onkel* (1965; *Mister, Mister*, 1967); *Ausgefragt* (1967; *New Poems*, 1968); *Über das Selbstverständliche: Reden, Aufsätze, Offene Briefe, Kommentare* (1968; *Speak Out!: Speeches, Open Letters, Commentaries*, 1969); *Briefe über die Grenze* (1968, with Pavel Kohout); *Tschechoslowakei 1968* (1968); *Über meinen Lehrer Döblin, und andere Vorträge* (1968); *Gesammelte Gedichte* (1971); *G. G.: Dokumente zur politischen Wirkung* (1971); *Mariazuehren* (1973; *Inmarypraise*, 1974); *Liebe geprüft* (1974); *Der Bürger und seine Stimme: Reden, Aufsätze, Kommentare* (1974); *Denkzettel: Politische Reden und Aufsätze 1965–1976* (1978); *Das Treffen in Telgte* (1979; *The Meeting at Telgte*, 1981); *"Die Blechtrommel" als Film* (1979, with Volker Schlöndorff); *Kopfgeburten; oder, Die Deutschen sterben aus* (1980); *Aufsätze zur Literatur* (1981); *Die Rattin* (1986; *The Rat*, 1987); *Zunge zeigen* (1988; *Show Your Tongue*, 1989). FURTHER WORKS IN ENGLISH: *Selected Poems* (1966); *Four Plays* (1967); *Poems of G. G.* (1969); *In the Egg and Other Poems* (1977); *Novemberland: Selected Poems, 1956-1993* (1996)

BIBLIOGRAPHY: Cunliffe, W. G., *G. G.* (1969); Tank, K. L., *G. G.* (1969); Willson, A. L., *A. G. G. Symposium* (1971); Woods, J. M., "G. G.: A Selected Bibliography," *WCR*, 5, 3 (1971): 52–56, and 6, 1 (1971): 31–40; Diller, E., *A. Mythic Journey: G. G.'s "Tin Drum"* (1974); Everett, G. A., Jr., *A Select Bibliography of G. G. (From 1956 to 1973)* (1974); Leonard, I., *G. G.* (1974); Mason, A. L., *The Skeptical Muse: A Study of G. G.'s Conception of the Artist* (1974); Miles, K., *G. G.* (1975); Reddick, J., *The "Danzig Trilogy" of G. G.* (1975); O'Neill, P., *G. G.: A Bibliography, 1955–1975* (1976); Rothenberg, J., *G. G.: Zeitgeschichte im Prosawerk* (1976); Rölleke, H., *Der wahre Butt* (1978); Brode, H., *G. G.* (1979); Neuhaus, V., *G. G.* (1979); O'Neill, P., ed., *Critical Essays on G. G.* (1987); Keele, A. F., *Understanding G. G.* (1988)

—RICHARD H. LAWSON

Every myth takes place within a given culture, at some point in history, but then, as in a literary work such as *The Tin Drum*, myth is posited as an attempt to transcend history by shifting focus from measurable time and specific events to paradigmatic ritualized forms of a timeless order. It is precisely here, in the conjunction and pressure of mythogenesis colliding with secular reality, that the author of *The Tin Drum* most fully exercises his genius. The historical context of *The Tin Drum* is of course obvious and should not be ignored, for that is *the* significant moment of time which is to be transcended by sacred repetition and purpose. But our concern here is with the embracing sweep of the novel, the attempt to reconceive and experience myth as divine history and witness its triumphs and failures in relationship to profane history, to the "powerhouse of change."

Edward Diller, *A Mythic Journey: G. G.'s "Tin Drum"* (1974), pp. 3–4

[G.] has worked to become a major novelist in the German tradition; he has come to grips with both German literary tradition and German history, having seen how changed historical circumstance has profoundly disrupted, but not wholly destroyed that tradition. Out of this awareness, he has realized in his early novels a wealth of comic fantasy that is quite distinctive for German literature; he has created narrators who are acutely conscious of their art of storytelling and who use all the tricks of that art with remarkable energy and inventiveness. Recently, he has worked towards an art which more sharply criticizes itself; correspondingly, his artist-heroes and narrators have been more conspicuously portrayed as failures, juxtaposed with a social reality they have difficulty understanding or accepting.

Ann L. Mason, *The Skeptical Muse: A Study of G. G.'s Conception of the Artist* (1974), p. 128

Dialectical thinking constitutes the most striking structural element in G.'s compositions. In *The Tin Drum* it extends to the individual images as well as to their overall pattern. The drum has its dialectical opposite in the Black Witch. Oskar's drumming is an attempt to synthesise the two extremes of morality and amorality, of construction and destruction. This general duality also governs the details of the novel, down to its smallest episodes. The drum itself is made up of contradictions, for it can be put to good and bad purpose, radiate love as well as hatred, even if its primary function is positive. The negative aspect of Oskar's gifts, the purely destructive impulses, are symbolised by his glass-shattering voice. Such polarity between light and dark is followed through in juxtaposing Goethe and Rasputin, Apollo and Dionysus, Jesus and Satan, and is further evoked in the colour symbolism of white and black.

Irène Leonard, *G. G.* (1974), p. 84

In his novel *From the Diary of a Snail* G. describes how Hermann Ott, confined to a cellar for the duration of the war, entertains his hosts by solo performances of classic dramas of the German theatre. To differentiate between characters, he employs a series of old hats, making discarded headgear the basis of his art. G.'s poetry anticipates Ott's cellar presentations. Like Ott the snail-collector, G. the poet wears a variety of hats; he takes on the roles of lyric poet, educationist, jester, moralist, realist, surrealist, traditionalist, experimentalist. His poems can evoke the light-heartedness and delicacy of a Paul Klee or the nightmarishness and abrasiveness of a Georg Heym. They can be playful celebrations of innocence or grim reflections of experience. They can reproduce the exterior world or exist in a realm of their own. Where G.'s art is more subtle than that of Ott is in his ability to wear all the hats at the same time, to fuse the disparate personalities into one. The artist does not vanish when the political activist speaks: the jester does not disappear in the presence of the moralist. It is the characteristic feature of G.'s poetry that it finds a way to make each cap, separately and simultaneously, fit.

Keith Miles, *G. G.* (1975), pp. 25–26

In G. G.'s work the lyric forms a universal constant. Not only is the lyric—together with sculpture and graphics—G.'s earliest form of artistic expression, but right up to the many poems in *The Flounder* he has never given it up. His lyrical oeuvre is correspondingly extensive. At the same time, the lyric is the genre with which he has the most intimate connection. It is the germ cell of his dramatic and narrative works.

Volker Neuhaus, *G. G.* (1979), p. 158

Central to the novel *[The Flounder]* is the question of the disturbed role-relationships between the sexes. To that extent the book is historically and directly allied to the questions—much discussed in the western world in the mid-seventies—of female emancipation and the related shock to male self-perception. Ilsebill and the narrator are profoundly disturbed at their insight that the traditional rules of conduct are now obsolete; the well-indoctrinated role-stereotypes no longer function. The male illusion of superiority is at the brink of collapse—and on a global scale, because the planning rationale as well as the exploitive appropriation of the world are leading to political and ecological catastrophe. For her part, woman on the way to emancipation has not yet progressed beyond shaking the foundations of her previous understanding of herself and her role. On both sides, there are no new, substantial positions in sight.

Hanspeter Brode, *G. G.* (1979), p. 180

GRAU (DELGADO), Jacinto

Spanish dramatist and essayist, b. 1877, Barcelona; d. 14 Aug. 1958, Buenos Aires, Argentina

G. was a singular writer. Much of his life was spent out of Spain in other European countries and, after the Francoist victory in the Civil War, in Argentina. Although G. was a contemporary of the great figures of the Spanish Generations of 1898 and 1914, the so-called "problem of Spain"—its national identity and position in the world—is distant from the center of his production. He is a classicist in the sense that he sees life in terms of the basic paradigms of biblical, classical, and national myths. Hence his dramas center on figures such as the prodigal son, Judas, Pygmalion, and Don Juan. In another sense he is a modernist because he views true art, especially in the theater, as diametrically opposed to the "industrialized" art favored by the businessmen of culture (theater owners and impresarios), the vitiated public, and, most tellingly, the bourgeois capitalists who run the society.

As did José ORTEGA Y GASSET, G. disdained realist-naturalist art. Both considered the best art to be a creation rather than a recreation. In order to foster such art, G. favored constant artistic innovation and experiment. Repeating a not always justified commonplace among Spanish writers of the 19th and 20th cs., G. felt there was no literary-theatrical criticism worthy of the name in his country. So he followed the example of George Bernard SHAW and came to write prologues (albeit much shorter than Shaw's) for his dramatic works. Forty years before the widespread currency of the idea, G. proposed the function of the reader and critic was to use the work of art, be it famous or not, as the stimulus to a personal creation. The prefaces would presumably help to guide the process.

As might be expected, G. was by no means a popular dramatist in Spain. His prologues, dedications of his works, and record of successes show that G.'s own frame of reference was much more European than peninsular. His greatest work in this regard may have been *El señor Pigmalión* (1923; Mr. Pygmalion). Karel ČAPEK, director of the Prague City Theater and artistic director of National Art Theater, heard about the play and eventually had it translated and staged in Prague. Čapek, as author of *R.U.R.* (1920), was most interested in G.'s robot play. For G.'s Pygmalion is a Spaniard who emigrated to the U.S. where he learned the necessary technology to create the humanoid machines. As opposed to Čapek's work-oriented robots, G.'s are actors for whom his Pygmalion has created a repertory of some two hundred farces. Although this Pygmalion's dream is to use his increasing knowledge of robotics to create a better world for human-kind, one of his female creations is so attractive that Pygmalion wavers in his purpose and other men are driven nearly crazy with desire for her.

In the end, Pygmalion is killed by others of his robots in their bid for freedom from their creator.

While G. is not a very nationally oriented writer, his Spanish origins probably suggest a special place in his production for his two very different versions of the myth of Don Juan. While the titular protagonist of *Don Juan de Carillana* (1913; *Don Juan of Carillana*) is more of a man who has loved many women, the one of *El burlador que no se burla* (1930; the trickster who doesn't play) is defined by his incessant seductions and his murder of the men who object. This second Don Juan is credited with reinvigorating the myth by bringing it closer to its origins in Tirso de Molina's creation, and then adding new dimensions to it.

G. is a significant author whose work has become poorly known. In addition to the titles already mentioned, *El hijo pródigo* (1918; the prodigal son), for example, can be easily read today as a meditation on the responsibilities society has for the homeless. And in a number of plays he gives his own version of the Nietzschean Superman. As a European-class intellectual and artist G. was very familiar with the cultural life of his time. His works reveal this knowledge and add to the body of texts that must be known by anyone who wishes to understand the period during which G. was active.

FURTHER WORKS: *Trasuntos* (1899); *Las bodas de Camacho* (1903); *El tercer demonio* (1908); *Entre llamas* (1915); *Cervantes y Shakespeare* (1916); *El conde Alarcos* (1917); *En Ildaria* (1917); *Conseja galante, La redención de Judas, Sortilegio, Horas de vida* (1919); *El rey Candaules* (1920); *El mismo daño* (1921); *El caballero Varona* (1929); *La señora guapa* (1930); *Los tres locos del mundo* (1930); *Unamuno y la angustia de su tiempo* (1943); *Don Juan en el drama* (1944); *Teatro* (1954)

BIBLIOGRAPHY: Giulano, W., "A Spanish Version of the Authentic Don Juan," *Hispania*, 34 (1951): 256–60; Torrente Ballester, G., *Panorama de la literatura española contemporánea*, 3rd ed. (1965): 254–57, 597; Rodríguez Salcedo, G., "Introducción al teatro de J. G.," *Papeles de San Armadans*, 42 (1966): 13–42; Torrente Ballester, G., *Teatro español contemporáneo*, 2nd ed. (1968): 288–95; Navascues, M., *El teatro de J. G.: estudio de sus obras principales* (1975); Navascues, M., "Fantasy and the View of Destiny in the Theater of J. G.," *REH*, 11 (1977): 265–85; Dougherty, D., "The Semiosis of Stage Decor in J. G.'s *El señor de Pigmalión*," *Hispania*, 67, 3 (Sept. 1984): 351–57

—STEPHEN MILLER

GRAVES, Robert

English poet, novelist, critic, essayist, biographer, translator, and mythographer, b. 26 July 1895, London; d. 7 Dec. 1985, Mallorca, Spain

G.'s father, Alfred Percival Graves, was a Gaelic scholar and an inspector of schools; his mother, Amalie von Ranke Graves, was related to the German historian Leopold von Ranke (1795–1886). G.'s education, therefore, began early in his parents' excellent library. His formal education included attendance at Charterhouse and at Oxford University. As an officer in the Royal Welsh Fusiliers, G. was seriously wounded in France during World War I. He taught one year at the University of Cairo, and lectured at Oxford and elsewhere in Europe and in the U.S. With the American poet Laura Riding (b. 1901) he established the Seizin Press (1928) and published the critical magazine *Epilogue* (1929). He was married twice, has eight children, and lived most of his life since 1929 in Majorca, except when lecturing or when political upheavals required evacuation of British citizens.

G. considered himself primarily a poet. His earliest adolescent poems were heavily freighted with 19th-c. romantic diction and gothic subject matter. He quickly became his own best critic, however, and continually refined his craftsmanship. His early poems were first published during World War I in *Over the Brazier* (1916), *Goliath and David* (1916), and *Fairies and Fusiliers* (1917).

The horrors of trench warfare had a profound effect upon his poetry for the next ten years. He, like other poets in this situation, such as his friend Siegfried SASSOON suffered from serious neuroses connected with their war experience. Dr. W. H. R. Rivers, a Freudian psychologist and a specialist in war neurasthenia, influenced G.'s theory of poetry during this period. G. agreed with Rivers that poems deal symbolically with emotional conflicts and can help to achieve a resolution of such conflicts, both for the writer and for the reader who has similar difficulties. G. later discarded the idea of poetry as therapy, but during the period immediately following the war his poetry was often haunted by images of guilt and fear. He seldom wrote about war experience itself, but often translated his emotional turmoil into more traditional gothic imagery. Some of the most representative poetry of this kind is in *The Pier-Glass* (1921). The title poem, for instance, uses a haunted-house ambience; "The Castle" re-creates the sensations of nightmare and entrapment in a medieval setting. One of the best poems of this period, "Down," also in this collection, achieves a striking combination of associations—the mythical geography of the underworld, the childhood experience of dropping a stone down an abandoned well, the subconscious mind, madness, and death.

After 1929, when he published his autobiography, *Goodbye to All That*, one of the best descriptions of trench warfare to come out of World War I, G. turned his back upon his past in more ways than one. His poetry gradually became more objective, more devoted to exploring philosophical ideas, the complexities of love, and the ambiguous qualities of language itself, as a means of both striving for truth and disguising reality. "The Cool Web" (1927), for instance, suggests that language is a way of mitigating the intensity of raw experience.

G.'s later poetry, stemming from his brilliant, though idiosyncratic, combination of literary and mythological research in *The White Goddess* (1945), deals mainly with the experience of love, expressed within the mythological framework he discovered both in archaic poetry and in ancient fertility religions. He became the oracle of the Goddess, who is both the artist's Muse and the Triple Goddess of moon, earth, and underworld who controls birth, love, and death. G. experienced a burst of poetic power that resulted in some of the best love lyrics written in this century. Including periodic collections of those poems he wished to preserve, G. has published forty-seven volumes of poetry. About two thirds of these followed the publication of *The White Goddess* and are, in some measure, influenced by the Goddess mythology.

G.'s interest in ancient myth was not confined to poetry, but led to the writing of several prose works displaying an impressive knowledge of ancient lore combined with an imaginative flair for comparative and causal analysis. His mode of explaining origins of myth in his two-volume study, *The Greek Myths* (1955), is quite eclectic. He admits sources, for instance, in both religious ritual and historical event (two views of myth origin that are sometimes

Robert Graves

thought to be mutually exclusive). He consistently avoids psychological explanations of either the Freudian or Jungian schools. In general terms, he attributes the famous myths of the Olympian gods to the process of changing from the worship of goddesses (variations of the Triple Goddess noted above) to the cult of masculine deities introduced by invading patriarchal tribesmen from the north. Thus, the notorious rapes and seductions attributed to the Achaean sky god Zeus establish his superiority over the resident female dieties of Greece. And the all-powerful goddesses became wives, mistresses, or daughters to Father Zeus.

Critics often find fault with G.'s methodology in these books. G. was influenced by a number of 19th-and early-20th-c. anthropologists, such as Sir James Frazer (1854–1941), Robert Briffault (1876–1948), J. J. Bachofen (1815–1887), Jane Harrison (1850–1928), and Margaret Murray (1863–1963). G.'s theory that not only religion, but society itself, was originally matriarchal in structure seemed the revival of supposedly outmoded theories explored in 1861 in Bachofen's *Mother Right*. Yet the primacy of matriarchy or, at least, the early dominance of the female principle in religion, has received renewed attention since G. proposed it. Part of this response may be attributable to the recent rise of feminist critics, some to post-Jungian psychologists like Erich Neumann (1905–1960), author of *The Great Mother* (1955), some to new archeological evidence, such as that put forth in *The Cult of the Mother Goddess* (1959) by E. O. James (1888–1972). Academic scholars hesitate to acknowledge indebtedness to G. because of his tendency to fill in the gaps of historical fact with generous dollops of intuition. Yet his widespread impact on general interest in mythology and matriarchal values seems undeniable.

G. collaborated with Joshua Podro (dates n.a.) on *The Nazarene Gospel Restored* (1953) and with the Jewish scholar Raphael Patai (b. 1910) to produce *The Hebrew Myths: The Book of Genesis* (1964). The former brought shocked responses from some biblical scholars, but one prominent theologian, Reinhold Niebuhr (1892–1971), praised the volume as a "work of careful scholarship."

G. is probably best known to the general public for his novels based on history or myth. He received both the Hawthornden Prize and the James Tait Black Memorial Prize for *I, Claudius* and *Claudius the God* (both 1934). These studies in the dynamics of power in ancient Rome enjoyed a resurgence of public interest in the 1970s through an engrossing television series based on them, produced by the BBC. His subjects for historical novels are extremely varied: the career of a Byzantine general (*Count Belisarius*, 1938), the American Revolution from the point of view of a British soldier (*Sergeant Lamb of the Ninth*, 1940), John Milton as a bigoted and tyrannical husband (*The Story of Marie Powell, Wife to Mr. Milton*, 1943), a 16th-c. expedition to colonize the Solomon Islands (*The Islands of Unwisdom*, 1949). G. also wrote novels based on myth, such as *The Golden Fleece* (1944) and *Homer's Daughter* (1955). His most striking and original vehicles for myth are *King Jesus* (1946) and an entertaining futuristic fantasy, *Seven Days in New Crete* (1949). *King Jesus* fuses the Goddess mythology with Hebrew legend to create a new myth about Jesus. G.'s novels will not stand among the world's great literature, but his best, such as *I, Claudius, King Jesus*, and perhaps *Count Belisarius*, will surely retain their fascination for a long time to come.

G.'s reputation will probably come to rest most surely on his poetry, some of which is among the best written in the 20th c. He has always disdained fashionable literary movements and demonstrated again and again how every true poem is original not imitative, each poem determining its own diction, rhythm, and form. The impact of his voluminous prose, both fiction and nonfiction, is considerable, not just for itself alone, but for the example of an erudite, rebellious, original thinker who has revitalized our appreciation of the past.

FURTHER WORKS: *Country Sentiment* (1922); *On English Poetry* (1922); *Whipperginny* (1922); *The Meaning of Dreams* (1924); *Poetic Unreason and Other Studies* (1925); *Poems 1914–1926* (1926); *Poems 1914–1927* (1927); *A Survey of Modernist Poetry* (1927, with Laura Riding); *The English Ballad: A Short Critical Survey* (1927); *Lawrence and the Arabs* (1927); *Mrs. Fisher; or, The Future of Humour* (1928); *Poems 1926–1930* (1931); *But It Still Goes On* (1931); *Poems 1930–1933* (1933); *The Real David Copperfield* (1933); *Antigua, Penny Puce* (1936); *Collected Poems* (1938); *No More Ghosts* (1940); *The Long Week-end: A Social History of Britain 1918–1939* (1940, with Alan Hodge); *Proceed, Sergeant Lamb* (1941); *The Reader Over Your Shoulder* (1943, with Alan Hodge); *Poems 1938–1945* (1945); *Collected Poems 1914–1947* (1948); *The Common Asphodel* (1949); *Occupation: Writer* (1950); *Poems and Satires* (1951); *Poems* (1953); *Adam's Rib* (1955); *Collected Poems* (1955); *Catacrok!* (1956); *English and Scottish Ballads* (1957); *Jesus in Rome: A Conjecture* (1957, with Joshua Podro); *They Hanged My Saintly Billy* (1957); *5 Pens in Hand* (1958); *Steps* (1958); *Collected Poems* (1959); *Food for Centaurs* (1960); *Collected Poems* (1961); *More Poems* (1961); *Selected Poetry and Prose* (1961); *New Poems* (1962); *The Big Green Book* (1962); *The Siege and Fall of Troy* (1962); *Nine Hundred Iron Chariots* (1963); *Man Does, Woman Is* (1964); *Mammon* (1964); *Collected Short Stories* (1964); *Majorca Observed* (1965); *Mammon and the Black Goddess* (1965); *Love Respelt* (1965); *Collected Poems* (1965); *The Crane Bag* (1969); *The Green-sailed Vessel* (1971); *Poems 1968–1970* (1970); *Difficult Questions Easy Answers* (1973); *New Collected Poems* (1977)

BIBLIOGRAPHY: Seymour-Smith, M., *R. G.* (1956); Cohen, J. M., *R. G.* (1960); Day, Douglas, *Swifter than Reason* (1963); Higginson, F. H., *A Bibliography of the Works of R. G.* (1946); Hoffman, D., *Barbarous Knowledge: Myth in the Poetry of Yeats, G., and Muir* (1967): 129–222; Stade, G., *R. G.* (1967); Kirkham, M., *The Poetry of R. G.* (1969); Mason, E., *Focus on R. G.*, No. 1 (Jan. 1972); Vickery, J. B., *R. G. and "The White Goddess"* (1972); Fussell, P., *The Great War and Modern Memory* (1975): passim; Matthews, T. S., *Jacks or Better* (1977): passim; Snipes, K., *R. G.* (1979)

—KATHERINE SNIPES

GRAY, Simon

English dramatist and novelist, b. 21 Oct. 1936, Hayling Island, Hampshire

G.'s best plays are about academia and, except for an early period of dramas featuring farcical situations with colloquial dialogue, his stagecraft reflects the life of British intellectuals through verbal wit, literary allusion, and complex character study. G. has spent most of his adult life in university settings. During World War II he was sent to Canada by his father, a first-generation Canadian. G. returned to England after the war, attended Westminster School in London, then returned to Canada in 1954 to study English at Dalhousie University. In 1958 he was lecturer at the University of Clermont-Ferrand, France, but began a second degree in English at Cambridge University in 1959. Among a close group of writers and satirists at Cambridge, G. published his first satirical novel, *Colmain* (1963), while there. In 1964 he moved to Canada a third time to lecture in English at the University of British Columbia. G. became a supervisor in English at Trinity College, Cambridge, until 1966, when he began as lecturer in English at Queen Mary College, London University, where he remained until 1985. Since the production of his first play in 1967, G. has spent most of his time on the teaching faculty while writing for stage, film, and television.

Two plays, *Wise Child* (1968) and *Dutch Uncle* (1969), received some critical attention, often being compared to the comedies of Joe Orton (1933–1967), but *Butley* (1971) became G.'s first popular and critical success. Wit is central to the style of this play, its characters using idiosyncratic phrases, rhetorical questions, literary allusion, and pithy remarks about themselves and others. Butley, a university English teacher, shares an office and home with a man whose presence so perturbs Butley that he hazes and misleads him about his promotion. There is some enjoyment of the stage villain here, and of the way Butley treats people. The most distinctive aspect of character in this dark comedy involves the interest the protagonist has in keeping others at a distance and protecting himself from not fully realized terrors. Butley's personal problems occur within a professional and institutional context, a feature of the play that might account for its popularity. Butley is alone at the end, but his isolation is self-induced, since he has estranged everyone around him. Reality remains unpleasant, and Butley's attempts to achieve freedom from others through avoidance and verbal aggression results in a kind of self-imprisonment. Not simply a victim, Butley seems to become what he is through his own actions. Butley's failed attempts to extricate himself from his entanglements is a clear ironic reversal. This hints at Sophoclean tragedy; in fact, the classical unities of action, place, and time are almost fully obeyed, as the plot consists of a succession of characters who enter Butley's office, confront him, then leave. G.'s earlier emphasis on physical action and convolutions of plot are replaced in *Butley* by psychological character study and the power of language both to deny and deceive.

Part of G.'s box office appeal is doubtless drawn from the fortunate collaboration of Harold PINTER's stage direction and Alan Bates's acting in the leading roles for most of the major plays. *Otherwise Engaged* (1976) won both the New York Drama Critics Circle Award and the Evening Standard Award for best play. As in *Butley*, the protagonist, Simon Hench, shows brilliance in keeping his significant others at arms length through the use of critical humor, an agnostic type of questioning that undermines the intentions of his listeners, and a uniquely low-key emotionality. Only at the end, as in *Butley*, is there a realization of how destructive such denial can be. G. seems to leave his audiences with a disturbing sense of the helplessness of modern intentionality. No one is able to break through the barriers of Simon's material preoccupation and self-centered insouciance (while others plead with him for his attention, Simon only wants to play *Parsifal* on his stereo). The adeptness of this isolating behavior is a characteristic quality of many of G.'s protagonists.

Quartermaine's Terms (1981), another play about academe, is rife with bright dialogue, topical allusion, and humor derived from confrontational language. However, unlike G.'s previous plays about university teachers, a deep sadness pervades this dark comedy, a feeling derived perhaps from the barely disguised loneliness of the characters. Quartermaine is a teacher of foreign students at a language school in Cambridge. He is taken for granted by the other teachers, who follow lives of not-so-quiet desperation. Failing marriages, vocational disappointments, and the realization of artistic mediocrity all appear to preoccupy the people around Quartermaine. Although he remains the only stable person in the play, he is taken advantage of perhaps because of his stability. In the end he is fired from the school, ostensibly for budgetary reasons, in fact because it is assumed he is incompetent. The play is unique for G. in that the feeling of pathos is overwhelming, the comedy of manners style being overcast by the sense of injustice and a sympathy for the protagonist.

The Common Pursuit (1984) and *Melon* (1987) both demonstrate G.'s ability to recreate the educated dialogue of the Oxbridge world, but also reveal a fatalistic note, as the characters gradually lose their ideals and self-confidence to become glib and mannered.

G. builds his dramas around a sense of isolation and noncommunication inherent in both professional and private life; his best plays evoke strong fears that seem to result from the demands and hidden agendas of close relationships. Although some of G.'s plots leave the protagonist with at least a partial perception of his life, notably *Butley* and *Quartermaine's Terms*, the overriding effect, even in these plays, is one of spiritual resignation and emotional surrender, if not despair. What saves these dramas as performance pieces is particularly clever dialogue used in familiar social and professional situations, and the thematic connection between the ambiguities of conversational language and the denial of true communication and connectedness.

FURTHER WORKS: *Simple People* (1965); *Little Portia* (1967); *Sleeping Dog* (1968); *A Comeback for Stark* (1969); *Spoiled* (1971); *The Idiot* (1972); *Two Sundays* (1976); *Plaintiffs and Defendants* (1976); *Dog Days* (1977); *The Rear Column* (1978); *Molly* (1978); *Man in a Side Car* (1978); *Pig in a Poke* (1979); *Close of Play* (1979); *Stage Struck* (1979); *Tartuffe* (1982); *Chapter 17* (1982); *An Unnatural Pursuit and Other Pieces* (1985); *After Pilkington* (1987); *A Month in the Country* (1987); *How's That for Telling 'Em, Fat Lady* (1988); *Old Flames* (1990); *Hidden Laughter* (1991); *The Holy Terror* (1993); *Fat Chance* (1995); *Simply Disconnected* (1996)

BIBLIOGRAPHY: Taylor, J. R., *The Second Wave* (1971): 169–71; Blaydes, S. B., "Literary Allusion As Satire in S. G.'s *Butley*," *MQ*, 18 (1977): 374–91; Hamilton, J., *The New Review*, 3 (1977): 39–46; Kerensky, O., *The New British Drama: Fourteen Playwrights since Osborne and Pinter* (1977): 132–44; Shaw, P., on *Otherwise Engaged, Commentary*, 65 (1978): 88–90; Jones, J. B., "The Wit and the Wardrobe: S. G.'s Tragic(?) Comedies," *WVUPP*, 25 (1979): 78–85; Shafer, Y., on *Quartermaine's Terms, TJ*, 34, 4 (Oct. 1982): 532; Gordon, G., "Person to Person," *The Spectator*, 14 July 1984: 33–34; Hodgson, M., on *The Common Pursuit, The Nation*, 243 (1986): 617

—WILLIAM OVER

GREEK LITERATURE

Greek literature has the longest and the most persistent tradition in the Western world, one that sweeps over three millennia and embraces every form of literature known to man, many of these forms having been invented by the ancient Greeks themselves. There is a continuity in the history of Greek literature, as there are elements of discontinuity, but the modern author is aware of a weighty tradition, which he may accept or reject, but he more often than not reacts to his Greek tradition in some way, using it to compose his own work in a way that will be meaningful to him and his times. The Greek tradition is, of course, not limited to the classical but includes the Byzantine (one must remember that the Byzantine Empire, which was culturally Greek, lasted for eleven hundred years and was a world-state) and the period of the Turkish domination (1453–1821), and shows definite Western influence from various European sources and the Greek War of Independence.

In connection with the development of modern Greek literature it must be pointed out that with the birth of the modern Greek nation there arose in sharply defined terms the question of the use of language. It was only natural that with political freedom there would be some effort to return to the classical heritage, and the easiest way to do this practically (or so it seemed) was to return to the classical language (albeit with some modifications). The modern classical language, or *katharevousa*, was an important factor in the development of modern Greek literature. It came into direct conflict with the popular language, or *dhimotiki* (demotic), which owed much to the Greek folk song and which contained a good number of foreign elements. Opponents of *dhimotiki* pointed out that this "vulgar" language was not fit to express Greek literature. The "language problem" plagued Greek writers and readers for some time, even resulting in riots when the New Testament appeared in the demotic language in 1901. Two years later other riots broke out because the *Oresteia* of Aeschylus was translated into the vernacular and so presented. But in the recent past there has not been the violent quarreling over what language the literature of modern Greece should employ. The demotic has won the day because it has developed naturally and has shown beyond any reasonable doubt that it can express great ideas, great thoughts, and even the Greek tradition.

Poetry

Two literary schools should be noted before proceeding to 20th-c. writers. The Old School of Athens (flourished 1821–49), whose head and founder was Alexandros Soutsos (1803–1863), generally employed *katharevousa* and was characterized by an excessive romanticism. The greatest representative of the second half of this period was Achilles Paraschos (1838–1895), whose themes were patriotism, love, and death.

The greatest figure of the Ionian School (flourished 1850–1880) is a man who was basically bilingual (Italian and Greek) and who became the national poet of modern Greece, Dionysios Solomos (1798–1857). Solomos is significant for many reasons in the history of modern Greek literature, but it cannot be overlooked that his choice of the *dhimotiki* as his linguistic vehicle of expression was a major breakthrough whose impact would be felt for generations to come and would make really creative poetry possible. Solomos combined the classical and romantic spirit and demonstrated that he was no mere verse technician but a poet who had succeeded in bringing Greek literature into the mainstream of European literature.

In 1880 the New Poetic School of Athens was founded. Often called the Greek Parnassians, these men reacted against romanticism and were encouraged by *To taxidhi* (1888; the voyage) of Ioannis Psykharis (1854–1929), which, although ostensibly a travel book, actually promoted the cause for *dhimotiki*, as did the work of the great folklorist Nikolaos Politis (1852–1921), who gathered together the folk songs of the Greek people in a monumental enterprise that was to have repercussions far beyond his own field of research. The New School of Athens, among whose members were Kostis PALAMAS, Yorghos Dhrossinis (1859–1949), Ioannis Polemis (1862–1925), Nikolaos Kambas (1857–1932), and Yorghos Straitigis (1860–1938), gave ample evidence that the tide was turning in favor of demotic.

Yorghos Dhrossinis devoted his entire life to poetry. His verse is distinguished by great dignity but is at times too detailed and superficial. His poems are really poetical sketches with a simple idea made into a poem marked by fineness and delicacy. Ioannis Polemis cultivated a rather facile poetry. Sometimes, however, he produced poems of tender simplicity. Writing in *katharevousa* and demotic, Nilolaos Kambas did not express violent passions but rather emotions concerned with the small pains and joys of everyday life. Unpretentious, his poetry is said to have murmured with a soft smile. Yorghos Straitigis wrote in *katharevousa* and demotic. His later collections seem pallid and weak in inspiration and form.

The most important figure of this new school was Kostis Palamas, who was twice nominated for a Nobel Prize. He was knowledgeable in mythology, history, poetry, and philosophy, and

aware of the social and spiritual problems of his own and previous generations, and in his poetry revealed both European and Eastern influences. His most famous and most important work is probably also his most obscure, the epic-lyric poem *O dhodhekaloghos tou ghiftou* (1907; *The Twelve Words of the Gypsy*, 1964), in which the gypsy musician, initially presented as a symbol of freedom and art, slowly becomes the Greek patriot, and finally becomes the cosmopolitan Hellene, the citizen of the world. *I floghera toy vasilya* (1910; *The King's Flute*, 1967) is a historical epic in Byzantine dress that celebrates the continuity of Hellenism from the medieval Christian and ancient pagan traditions. His collection *I asalefti zoi* (1904; *Life Immutable*, 1919) shows French influences.

The importance for modern Greek literature of Palamas must not be underestimated. He exerted his influence not only on his contemporaries but on practically all of Greek poetry that has followed. Ioannis Ghryparis (1872–1942), Konstantinos Hatzopoulos (1871–1920), Miltiadis Malakasis (1869–1943), Lambros Porfyras (1879–1932), Zakharias Papandoniou (1877–1938), and Kostas KARYOTAKIS all show that Palamas was important in their development and expression, for it was with this group that German and French SYMBOLISM made its impact felt; even free verse was introduced into modern Greek literature.

Ghryparis knew the language of the people well, and he was able to make good use of popular medieval literature, while absorbing the influence of French Parnassianism. Later he turned to the symbolists, and his verse became freer and more musical, his images more suggestive. Influenced by German literature and life, Hatzopoulos attached himself to the German social movement, which he attempted to propagate in Greece by connecting social ideology with the innovative trends of demoticism. Following the teaching of the symbolists, he produced a musically charming verse that is a vague, elegiac reverie lacking concrete detail. The verse of Malakasis has great robustness but lacks lyric depth. Porfyras, a few of whose poems are symbolist, possesses a delicacy of feeling and tender sympathetic melancholy, although his powers of expression are not as great as those of Hatzopoulos. A learned man, Papandoniou was first of all a stylist, prolific in poetical production but careless in thought and expression; he wrote essays, biographies, travel literature, and criticism. Still, he has a sympathetic comprehension of life and nature. Often called the most representative writer of his generation, Karyotakis wrote serious poetry expressing an intense desire for a fulfilled life and a total consciousness of reality. His verse also shows a pervading feeling of futility and loss, which became starker and starker and led to his suicide.

Although the 20th c. is marked by the triumph of the *dhimotiki* in poetry, one of the greatest Greek and also European poets of the early 20th c., an inhabitant not of Greece but of Alexandria, Egypt, did not employ the demotic tongue but rather a modified form of *katharevousa*. C. P. CAVAFY, looked back at the decadent Hellenistic world in which he found the landscape, so to speak, through which he could express himself and depict the decadent individual behind many masks, the human condition as it appeared to him. In no other Greek poet are the tragic aspects of life so sensually expressed or sensuality so tragically depicted. Out of touch with the mainstream of Greek literature, Cavafy ironically recorded high and low life in ancient or modern Alexandria and in the medieval world of the Byzantine Empire.

Another major poet was the flamboyant Angelos SIKELIANOS who together with his American wife reintroduced the Delphic idea by establishing the Delphic Festivals of 1927–30. Described by some as a poet of pantheism; clearly marked by Dionysiac mysticism; philosophic in his approach to nature, tradition, and history; beautiful, rich, incisive, and lucid in his use of language and vocabulary—Sikelianos created some of the finest poetry ever composed in Greek. Two aspects have been observed in the poetry of Sikelianos: the lyrical positing of the natural world with the human body as a part of it, and the knowledge that the natural world is replete with tragedy and suffering, with the essence of man's real life to be found elsewhere.

The modern Greek author who is perhaps better known throughout the Western world than any other is Nikos KAZANTZAKIS. His *Odyssia* (1938; *The Odyssey: A Modern Sequel*, 1958) had tremendous impact on other literatures through its many translations. With the English translation of this poem in 1958 by Kimon Friar the literary world was made aware of Kazantzakis's bold attempt to restore epic poetry as a legitimate and meaningful form in modern literature. The poem is drenched in sex, violence—and philosophy. The poetry ranges from the nauseatingly vulgar to the ethereally sublime. It is a search for an answer to the eternal question of "Who am I and what am I doing here?" in which Kazantzakis attempts to find order in a world infested with so much disorder and violence.

A contemporary of Kazantzakis, the poet Kostas VARNALIS, wrote originally in *katharevousa* but after returning from Paris dedicated himself to writing only in demotic. The author of the first completely leftist poem in Greek literature, he became Greece's greatest socialist poet. He praises the "kingdom of work," hates war, and protests against slavery and fascism. Initially influenced by the Parnassians and symbolists, his later poetry is marked by a strong Dionysiac flavor and a deep sense of music. Playful and humorous, he can also be satirical and even savage.

Greece's first Nobel Prize winner was George SEFERIS, considered by many Greece's leading modern poet. The actual number of his poems is small, but they are extremely significant. When the Swedish Academy awarded him the 1963 Nobel Prize for literature, it acknowledged one whose lyric poetry combined the best in the Greek and Western traditions. It transcends the particular, the ephemeral, and attains the universal, the permanent. Seferis is acutely aware of the triumphs and tragedies of both ancient and modern Greece, and of his own roots in Asia Minor. The musicality of Seferis's poetry, and his deep insight into the human predicament have given modern Greek poetry and literature the international recognition that it has long deserved.

The award of the Nobel Prize to Odysseus ELYTIS in 1979 marked the second time in sixteen years that a Greek poet received this honor. The Swedish Academy praised his "poetry, which, against the background of Greek tradition, depicts with sensuous strength and intellectual clearsightedness modern man's struggle for freedom and creativeness," and also noted that "sensuality and light irradiate Elytis's poetry. The perceptible world is vividly present and overwhelming in its wealth of freshness and astonishing experiences." Elytis himself regards "poetry as the only thing that can preserve man's spiritual integrity."

In *To Axion Esti* (1959; *The Axion Esti*, 1974) Elytis attempts to set a new moral order in a complex tapestry of prose, liturgical forms, odes, and his pattern of rhyme and strict syllabic stress. Elytis, the poet of the sun, sea, earth, youth, and the beauty of nature, believes that it is the poet's duty to cast drops of light into darkness. This he has done and continues to do.

Yannis RITSOS, the author of seventy-seven volumes of poetry, as well as plays, essays, and translations, has been translated into forty-four languages. He is probably Greece's major poet of the left. A sense of dislocation, inertia, and silence pervade much of Ritsos's landscape. Tyranny, oppression, torture, and degradation are reflected in the nightmarish imagery and absurdities of his poetry. Pain is everywhere; humanity is debased. Ritsos intensely feels the tragedy of mankind. A poet of the Greek people, he is also a poet of all.

Nikiforos Vrettakos (1911–1991), another prolific poet, hates injustice and believes that art must be the expression of love and goodness. Christian and democratic, he tends to moralize at times. Nikos Gatsos (1915–1992), the author of only a single long poem, *Amorghos* (1943; *Amorgos*, 1961), exerted great influence on the writers of his generation. In his poetry, SURREALISM, the Bible, and the tradition of Greek folk songs are combined in an elegiac way. The poet Takis Sinopoulos (1917–1981), trained as a physician, was also a painter, translator, and critic. His poetry reinterprets ancient Greek themes and evokes, perhaps more than any other contemporary author, the horrors of life during the 1940s—both the Nazi occupation and the civil war. For Sinopoulos, the world is a ravaged land of black trees, inhabited by the wandering dead, where the sunlight is blinding, destructive, and merciless.

Fiction

Much of contemporary Greek fiction has been concerned with the relation of the individual to society. It critically and often satirically questions the very basis of that society. The Asia Minor disaster, World War II and the Nazi occupation, and the civil war after World War II had a strong impact on writers. Man's inhumanity to man—be it of the Turks, the Nazis, or the Greeks themselves, of either the right or left—frequently occurs in the fiction of modern Greece.

Gregorios XENOPOULOS was the most distinguished Greek novelist of the early modern generation. His realistic novels, set in his own time, skillfully blend a fine narrative technique with sharpness of observation. Alexandros PAPADIAMANTIS, also of the older generation, is still considered Greece's best short-story writer. Papadiamantis vividly portrayed the life, and problems, of the simple people of his native island of Skiathos before the turn of the century and that of the lower-class Athenians. He had a profound Christian faith, a love of nature, and a sympathy for the downtrodden. He created many memorable characters and sought to penetrate the cosmic mystery that encases the tragic human condition.

The novels of Nikos Kazantzakis have excited a great deal of attention in literary circles. *O telefteos pirasmos* (1955; *The Last Temptation of Christ*, 1960) is a novel of great intensity and power; it was condemned by the Greek Orthodox Church. It re-creates the figure of Christ as a man. For Kazantzakis, Christ is the prototype of the free man who by force of will transmutes matter into spirit. His Christ is a personal experience that has no connection with any ecclesiastical tradition.

In *O Kapetan Mihalis* (1953; *Freedom or Death*, 1956) Kazantzakis concentrates on the background and character of the Cretan rebellion of 1889, which was directed against the Turkish overlords—a rebellion that ended unsuccessfully for the Greeks. But more than this, Kazantzakis gives a detailed characterization of the people who make up the various racial and religious elements of the population living in and about the city of Megalokastro (where half the action of the novel takes place)—a picture of both oppressors and oppressed, of Turks, Greeks, Armenians, and Jews.

The title character of *Vios kai politia toy Alexi Zorba* (1946; *Zorba the Greek*, 1953) has been described as a kind of subconscious or alter Kazantzakis. Zorba is undoubtedly a primitive, sensual man, but the important thing to note is that he does not survive in the novel. Only the artist, the analytical Kazantzakis, survives.

O Hristos xanastavronete (1954; *The Greek Passion*, 1953) is a magnificent and powerful novel. Through the Christian Passion story, Kazantzakis examines good and evil in the world; through vividly depicted characters he presents the reader with a concretization of the philosophical and theological problems of good and evil.

Stratis MYRIVILIS, author of *I panaghia i ghorghona* (1949; *The Mermaid Madonna*, 1959), is one of the most highly respected literary figures. His powerful war novel *I zoi en tafo* (1914; rev. ed., 1930; *Life in the Tomb*, 1977), written in the form of a journal of a sergeant in the trenches, is probably the most widely read work of fiction in Greece.

Fotis Kontoglou (1897–1965), better known as an icon painter, made a stirring debut as a writer with *Pedro Cazas* (1913; Pedro Cazas), the story of a Spanish corsair drawn from popular sources and written with unusual force and a tense, vibrant language.

Pandelis G. PREVELAKIS, one of the leading contemporary novelists, also ranks high as an art critic. In the tradition of his fellow Cretan Kazantzakis, Prevelakis uses the Cretan theme in novels such as *To hroniko mias politias* (1938; *The Tale of a Town*, 1976).

Significant attention has recently been given to the novels of Anghelos TERZAKIS. He is representative of Greek fiction after Kazantzakis. As one critic has recently put it, Terzakis, who is much interested in the uncertain aspects of life between the two world wars, probes into the social and psychological characteristics of the modern family, its problems and tribulations. Terzakis concentrates on the microcosm of the family or a certain number of characteristic individuals who cannot successfully cope with the world about them. By dealing with the specific and concrete, Terzakis uncovers the souls of his characters, revealing their desperation and failure.

Elias VENEZIS, awarded the Greek National Prize for Literature in 1939, has written travel impressions and histories as well as novels and short stories. A depth of perception and feeling for events of everyday life and a dreamlike atmosphere characterize his works, and symbolism, lyricism, and a deep love of humanity mark his novels. Rooted in the soil, charming, nostalgic, his novels are often loosely structured and at times emotionally overloaded.

Yorghos THEOTOKAS, a lawyer by profession, was dedicated to literature and also to the theater. He was much concerned with the sociological problems of the middle class and the anxieties and ideological conflicts of the youth of the post-World War II generation. In his novels he searches for the inner man and shows his acute awareness of the critical times in which he lived.

I. M. PANAYOTOPOULOS, a prolific writer who together with George Seferis was awarded the Palamas Prize in 1947, has written more than thirty volumes, including novels, poetry, literary and art criticism, essays, and travel literature. His early poetry was characterized by neoromanticism and symbolism; his later poems express a burning desire for newer, more personal expression. In his novels and short stories he evinces an introspective response to life that gives meaning and depth to the present but does not look to the future, which contains only old age and decay.

Stratis TSIRKAS, born in Cairo, Egypt, is the author of the trilogy *Akyvernites politeies* (cities adrift)—*O kyklos* (1960; the circle),

Ariagne (1962; Ariagne), *Nykteridha* (1965; the bat)—which deals with World War II in the Middle East, and especially with the mutinies of the Greek expeditionary forces. Called the Greek FAULKNER, Tsirkas concerns himself with the ambiguity of historical destiny and with political drama, the concept of freedom, and man's inherent contradictions. A contemporary of Tsirkas, Petros HARIS, is essentially a short-story writer and essayist. The editor of the most important literary magazine in Greece, *Nea Estia*, his fiction is marked by warm lyrical impressions of life and by sympathetic reminiscences. He probes the inner world of his characters for the special moment of painful discovery.

Takis Doxas (1913–1976) writes novels and short stories depicting life in the Greek provinces. His characters consist of the oppressed peasants and provincials for whom life holds little or no hope, and who symbolize the spiritual agony of contemporary man.

Two outstanding writers of fiction of more recent times are Andonis SAMARAKIS and Vassilis VASSILIKOS. In simple, direct prose, Samarakis writes about the common city dweller for whom the boredom of contemporary life alternates with the increasing threat of totalitarianism. His protagonists are often frustrated middle-aged men who take political stands in antiheroic ways. Using flashback and detective-fiction techniques, Samarakis always speaks out for the humanity of mankind. Vassilikos, internationally known as the author of *Z* (1966; *Z*, 1968), is one of Greece's most prolific and most outspoken novelists, the author of more than fifty books that have been translated into twenty languages. In his work one can trace the development of his own psyche and the conflicts and contradictions of his nation and his age.

Drama

Modern Greek drama is much concerned with the relation of the individual to society. It is critical and satirical, often in a highly metaphorical way.

Spyros Melas (1883–1966), one of the older established playwrights, was a very prolific writer and a demoticist par excellence. He wrote social and historical dramas influenced by Ibsen, as well as satirical comedies.

The plays of Anghelos Terzakis have had considerable success, and two of them have been performed by university groups in the U.S. Since 1937 he has served the National Theater of Greece as secretary, director, instructor, and general manager. At the center of his plays are investigations about the difficulties and tormenting doubts of contemporary man.

Iakovos KAMBANELLIS satirizes contemporary social and political life. He is very much in the tradition of American realist drama of the 1930s through the 1950s, while producing a form of impressionistic celebration of Greek folk traditions. In a rich demotic Greek, Kambanellis manages to capture the life and spirit of the Greek people and show Greek history as cyclical—alternating between tyranny and revolution, idealism and selfishness.

Kostas Mourselas (b. 1934), a quiet man whose satires are fierce, cries out against man's capacity for depravity in contemporary urban existence. Blending tragicomedy and satire, and proceeding from simple and often humorous situations to increasingly complicated and serious dilemmas, Mourselas is concerned with humanistic values. He has been a leading figure in resuscitating the Greek theater through his interest in the individual and his relation to contemporary society. In Mourselas the tragic becomes comic.

Yorghos Kampanellis (b. 1922) presents Greek history as a ritual repetition of a modern myth showing internecine strife, revolt, and betrayal. Myth and history become a cyclical nightmare of glory destroyed by treachery and ending in defeat and subjugation. Kampanellis's use of myth has strong political implications.

Yorghos Skourtis (b. 1940), using the popular folk art of the shadow theater, utilizes these caricatures of human personalities as the archetypes of the Greek experience.

Modern Greek literature was in a real sense reborn around 1930. It could be said that Greek literature came of age then and caught up with Western Europe. Greek literature in the 20th c. has shown itself to be a living literature with a living tradition, aware of the glorious Greek past but not its slavish imitator. Rather, modern Greek writers are striking out on their own with vigor, originality, and a full awareness of the world and the times in which they live.

Modern Greek Literature

In a late 1990s perspective, mention must be made of the character and social foibles comedies produced by the humorist Dimitris Psathas (1907–1979) which provided numerous lasting scenarios for motion pictures still appealing to the populace and surpassing in popularity the serious dramas of Theotokas, Terzakis, Prevelakis, and the older master Xenopoulos.

After the restoration of Democracy in 1974 a new bunch of dramatists gained recognition mostly through deft adaptations of mildly absurdist techniques grafted into local-interest or situation plots. Among the most popular are Manolis Korres (b. 1920), Vassilis Ziogas (b. 1925), Pavlos Matessis (b. 1929), Dimitris Kehaidis (b. 1940), and Yoryos Maniotis (b. 1949), plus the only female playwright of importance Loula Anagnostaki (b. 1933). The already mentioned Mourselas had some English translations of his plays published: *To afti tou Alexandhrou* (1970; *The Ear of Alexander*, 1975), *Monoprakta* (1970–73; *Selected Short Plays*, 1975), and *Vamena kokkina mallia* (1989; *Red Dyed Hair*, 1992).

In the post-1974 years a number of women writers emerged, enjoying their recently earned freedom to speak about their special problems from a feminine perspective and in an innovative manner. In fiction profundity was achieved by Maro Dhouka (b. 1947), narrative inventiveness by Eleni Ladhia (b. 1946), avant-garde popularity by Kostoula Mitropoulou (b. 1927). In poetry Katerina Anghelaki-Rouk (b. 1939) and Nana Issaia (b. 1934) joined the veteran Zoe Karelli (b. 1901) plus the men G. Th. Vafopoulos (b. 1903), Takis Varvitsiotis (b. 1916), Dinos Christianopoulos (b. 1931), and Titos Patrikios (b. 1928) as aspiring successors to Ritsos, Seferis, Sinopoulos, Vrettakos, and the belatedly recognized Tassos Livadhitis (1921-1988).

Another salutary development was the translation into English and publication in 1991 of a series of representative modernist novels. With the exception of Dido Sotiriou's (b. 1909) *Matomena Homata* (*Farewell Anatolia*), written in 1962, all others air issues and psychological or sociopolitical problems characterizing the last twenty-five years. These are the late Alexander Kotzias's (1926-1992) *O Iayouaros* (1986; *The Jaguar*), the popular Menis Koumandareas's (b. 1931) *Kyria Koula* (1978; *Koula*), the innovator Yoryos Heimonas's (b. 1938) *I chtistes* (1979; *The Builders*, Petros Abatzoglou's (b. 1931) *Ti theli i kyria Friman* (1989; *What Does Mrs. Freeman Want*), Eugenia Fakinou's (b. 1945) strange *Astradheni* (1989; *Astradeni*), Maro Dhouka's (b. 1947) very

popular *I archea skouria* (1979; *Fool's Gold*), and Alki Zei's (b. 1925) celebrated tour-de-force *I arravoniastikia tou Achillea* (1987; *Achilles's Fiancée*), the last two plus *Kyria Koula* having also become television serials of quality.

Literary criticism also achieved international levels of professionalism as newer commentators are mostly university-trained theorists and critics rather than empirical readers writing impressionistic and author-oriented critiques.

See also Cypriot Literature

BIBLIOGRAPHY: Trypanis, C., *Medieval and Modern Greek Poetry* (1951); Sherrard, P., *The Modern Greek Threshing Floor* (1956); Keeley, E., and P. Sherrard, Introduction to *Six Poets of Modern Greece* (1961): 3–27; Gianos, M. P., *Introduction to Modern Greek Literature* (1969); Bien, P., and E. Keeley, eds. *Modern Greek Writers* (1972); Bien, P., *Kazantzakis and the Linguistic Revolution in Greek Literature* (1972); Dimaras, C. T., *A History of Modern Greek Literature* (1972); Friar, K., *Modern Greek Poetry: From Cavafis to Elytis* (1973); Politis, L., *A History of Modern Greek Literature* (1973); Mackridge, P., "Greece: The Modern Voice," special issue, *RNL*, 5, 2 (1974); Doulis, T., *Disaster and Fiction: The Impact of the Asia Minor Disaster of 1922 on Modern Greek Fiction* (1977); Sherrard, P., *The Wound of Greece: Studies in Neo-Hellenism* (1979); Raizis, M. B., *Essays and Studies from Professional Journals* (1980); Lorenzatos, Z., *The Lost Center and Other Essays in Greek Poetry* (1980); Beaton, R., ed., *The Greek Novel A.D. 1-1985* (1988); Vassilis, L., *Literature as National Institution: Studies in the Politics of Modern Greek Criticism* (1988); Philippidis, D. M. L., *Census of Modern Greek Literature: Checklist of English Language Sources Useful in the Study of Modern Greek Literature* (1990); Jusdanis, G., *Belated Modernity and Aesthetic Culture: Inventing National Literature* (1991)

—JOHN E. REXINE; UPDATED BY M. BYRON RAIZIS

GREEN, Henry

(pseud. of Henry Vincent Yorke) English novelist, b. 29 Oct. 1905, Tewkesbury; d. 15 Dec. 1973, London

After Eton, G. went to Oxford, where he wrote a novel, *Blindness* (1926), astonishingly sophisticated for an undergraduate. The theme expands from the accidental blinding of a sensitive young man somewhat like James JOYCE's Stephen Dedalus to the discovery that blindness is universal in this wasteland world. As Angus WILSON has said, G. had discovered a theme that obsessed him: the disintegration of old ways of living. "The truth is," G. himself wrote, "these times are an absolute gift to the writer. Everything is breaking up." His response was not to retreat into aestheticism like Joyce and Virginia WOOLF, but to leave Oxford and go to work in his father's foundry in Birmingham, "with my wet podgy hands." Out of his life as a shop apprentice came his second novel, *Living* (1929). Christopher ISHERWOOD described it as the best proletarian novel ever written; amused, G. said that he just wrote what he heard and saw. Although he eventually became managing director of the family firm, he remained much more sympathetic in his novels to ordinary working people than to members of his own class. He was aware of the drabness of ordinary lives, yet he described them with humor and without either condescension or political bias.

G. specialized in claustrophobic situations, emotional Black Holes of Calcutta. In *Party Going* (1939) the setting is a London railway hotel in which a group of idle rich young people is marooned. In *Caught* (1943) it is London before and during the blitz; his own experiences with the Auxiliary Fire Service enabled him to explore the tensions in a group of people, chiefly of the lower class, thrown together because of the war. In *Concluding* (1948) it is a training institute for young girls in some future welfare state, where individuality is dangerous deviationism.

In G.'s masterpiece, *Loving* (1945), it is a country house in Ireland during World War II; the novel begins with "Once upon a day" and ends with "Over in England they married and lived happily ever after," but the fairy-tale framework provides scope for comic juxtapositions and ironic reversals. Ogres figure prominently—they are the I.R.A.; a ring that is lost and found, as in many a fairy tale, brings trouble rather than gifts and blessings; peacocks and doves lend enchantment to the scene but, as the critic Edward Stokes writes, they become complex symbols of pride, vanity, beauty, sex and greed. The King of the Castle is missing; the Queen, Mrs. Tennant, is fearful of the Germans, the Irish, and her own servants; and a Prince Charming, Captain Davenport, comes riding on a bicycle to commit adultery with the golden-haired princess, whose husband is away on active service. If the morals of the upper class are no better than they should be, the servants below stairs are capable of surprising us. When the butler Raunce falls in love with the housemaid Edie, he changes from a lecherous and conniving person to a moral, responsible, and conventional one. Loving may mean romantic enchantment, as in Raunce's vision of his beautiful fiancée at the end; most of the time and for most of the characters, however, it means thralldom rather than happiness.

If Evelyn WAUGH was the satirist of his generation and Graham GREENE the moralist, it has been said, G. was the artist. He described his writing as an advanced attempt to break up the old-fashioned type of novel; he kept himself out of his books, and, as his one-word titles show, he pared things down to essentials, even leaving out definite and indefinite articles. In his first eight novels, the dialogue was economical and pointed; nevertheless there were enough poetic descriptive passages and dense symbolism to remind readers of Virginia Woolf. Some critics thought that in *Back* (1946) and *Concluding* poetry had taken over, to the exclusion of everything else. As if in reaction, in his last two novels, *Nothing* (1950) and *Doting* (1952), he left out almost all description and made dialogue carry the whole burden of narration and character portrayal. Brilliant experiments though these novels were, he had squeezed out the poetry, and squeezed out too much of life.

The rest was silence. Perhaps he felt like a modernist betrayed, when the traditional novel form was revived in the 1950s. Perhaps he had nothing to say to the world of the Angry Young Men. Or perhaps, like many a humorist, he walked on thin ice; John UPDIKE speculated that he had made a "personal withdrawal into the despair that always fringed his pellucid world." Whatever the reason, he published no novels at all during the last twenty years of his life. Nevertheless, in spite of his withdrawal and the temporary eclipse of his reputation, he remains one of the few important English novelists of his time.

FURTHER WORKS: *Pack My Bag* (1940)

BIBLIOGRAPHY: Dennis, N., "The Double Life of H. G.," *Life*, 4 Aug. 1952: 83–94; Stokes, E., *The Novels of H. G.* (1959); Russell, J., *H. G.: Nine Novels and an Unpacked Bag* (1960); Weatherhead, A. K., *A Reading of H. G.* (1961); Bassoff, B., *Toward Loving: The Poetics of the Novel and the Practice of H. G.* (1975); Ryf, R. S., *H. G.* (1967); Odom, K. E., *H. G.* (1978)

—D. J. DOOLEY

GREEN, Julien

American novelist, diarist, and dramatist (usually writing in French), b. 6 Sept. 1900, Paris, France; d. 13 Aug. 1998, Paris

Youngest child of American Southerners living in Paris, G. experienced expatriate isolation from birth. The only native French speaker in his English-speaking family and the only boy in a household of Southern belles, he created his own private world. Into this world he brought his beloved mother's horror of sex and her love of religion (both associated with English) and his own passionate nature (safely expressed only in French). After his mother's death in 1914, he followed his father into the Catholic Church. This religion, however, did not accommodate his sensuality, for he had discovered another cause for isolation—homosexuality. It added to his alienation while studying at the University of Virginia in the early 1920s. Unwilling to risk sacrificing his homosexuality, he became a lapsed Catholic in the Paris literary scene of the 1920s and 1930s. However, he reconverted to Catholicism in 1939. Exiled to the U.S. during World War II, he returned to Paris in 1945. Yet he has maintained his American citizenship and in 1971 became the first American elected to the French Academy. Despite his unhappiness with Vatican II for eliminating the Latin liturgy, which had protected him from the language of sin (French) and guilt (English), he now seems serene with the realities of his riven self.

From these polarities initially caused by an accident of birth and an atypical childhood, G. has transformed his private fantasy world into a special fictional one. His protagonists, whether American or French, male or female, adolescent or middle-aged, are exiles. They never find their true homeland, never find anyone who speaks their true language. Their sensuality, whether expressed overtly as sexual aggression or covertly as religious fanaticism, never finds satisfaction. With their life the battleground of flesh and spirit, they seek death. Only Denis, the young hero who relates his homosexual awakening in *L'autre sommeil* (1930; the other sleep), is willing to accept mere intimations of immortality. Directly autobiographical, *L'autre sommeil* combines experiences G. had in both the U.S. and France. More typical of G.'s formula are his two best novels, *Moïra* (1950; *Moïra*, 1951) and *Chaque homme dans sa nuit* (1960; *Each in His Darkness*, 1961). Here the autobiographical heroes in heterosexual disguise play out their compulsions of eroticism and mysticism in the South Atlantic seaboard settings that were G.'s when he was expatriated to his official fatherland. G. punishes Joseph of *Moïra* by sending him to the police; he raped and killed Moïra (a word meaning fate in Greek, and Mary—or salvation—in Gaelic). G. punishes Wilfrid of *Chaque homme dans sa nuit* by having him shot by the young man whose overtures he had rebuffed. These "translated" heroes are not so credible as G.'s self-characterization in his *Journal*, which covers the years 1928–70 (9 vols., 198–72; selections in *Personal Record* [1939,] and *Diary* [1964]) seven autobiographies (five written in French, two in English). Here his authenticity and sincerity put him in the moralist tradition of his friends and mentors, André GIDE, François MAURIAC, and Jacques Maritain (1882–1967). The diary and autobiographies, valuable to cultural historians, are even more interesting to linguists, since Green, sometime translator and foreign-language scholar, is acutely aware of how the language he uses influences what he says and who he is.

G.'s plays, coming midway in his career, owed their limited success to his reputation in other genres. *Sud* (1953; *South*, 1955) takes place the weekend before the start of the U.S. Civil War and features a triangle of a transcendentalist girl, the Yankee lieutenant she loves, and the Confederate officer he loves. The dialogue, a direct transcription of American Southern speech, is only of linguistic interest.

As a foreign writer of French, G. is very conservative in style and content. His distraught characters think in impeccable French. Their reprehensible conduct is off-camera. The apparent strangeness comes from G.'s literal translation of American diction and idiom and from his assimilation of the Anglo-American literary tradition. Like Poe and Hawthorne, he connects physical darkness with spiritual blindness. Like the Brontës, he blurs the distinction between fictional reality and dream. Like Dickens, he uses the consciousnesses of characters too young or too disturbed for a balanced perspective. Like many Anglo-American writers down through his generation, he finds his chief symbols and motifs in the King James Version of the Bible—in his case, translated. In short, his work, like his life, has been productively poised between two major cultures, making him one of the foremost bilingual authors of his generation.

FURTHER WORKS: *Pamphlet contre les catholiques de France* (1924); *Mont-Cinère* (1926; *Avarice House*, 1927); *Le voyageur sur la terre* (1926; *Christine and Other Stories*, 1930); *Adrienne Mesurat* (1927; *The Closed Garden*, 1928); *Suite anglaise* (1927); *Un puritain homme de lettres* (1928); *Léviathan* (1929; *The Dark Journey*, 1929); *Épaves* (1932; *The Strange River*, 1932); *Le visionnaire* (1934; *The Dreamer*, 1934); *Minuit* (1936; *Midnight*, 1936); *Varouna* (1940; *Then Shall the Dust Return*, 1941); *Memories of Happy Days* (1942); *Si j'étais vous . . .* (1947; *If I Were You*, 1949); *L'ennemi* (1954); *Le malfaiteur* (1955; *The Transgressor*, 1957); *L'ombre* (1956); *Le bel aujour-d'hui* (1958); *Partir avant le jour* (1963; *To Leave before Dawn*, 1967); *Mille chemins ouverts* (1964); *Terre lointaine* (1966); *Les années faciles* (1970); *L'autre* (1971; *The Other One*, 1973); *Qui sommes-nous* (1972); *Ce qui reste du jour* (1972 [Vol. 9 of *Journal*]); *Jeunesse* (1974); *La liberté* (1974); *La nuit des fantômes* (1976); *Memories of Evil Days* (1976); *Le mauvais lieu* (1977); *Ce qu'il faut d'amour à l'homme* (1978); *Dans la gueule du temps* (1979)

BIBLIOGRAPHY: Saint-Jean, R. de, *J. G. par luimême* (1967); Rose, M. G., *J. G.: Gallic-American Novelist* (1971); Burne, G. S., *J. G.* (1972); Kostis, N., *The Exorcism of Sex and Death in J. G.'s Novels* (1973); Piriou, J.-P. J., *Sexualité, religion et art chez J. G.* (1976); Dunaway, J. M., *The Metamorphoses of the Self in the Works of J. G.* (1978); Piriou, J.-P. J., ed., *Une grande amitié: Correspondance de J. G. et Jacques Maritain* (1979)

—MARILYN GADDIS ROSE

GREENBERG, Uri Zvi

Israeli poet (writing in Hebrew and Yiddish), b. 22 Sept. 1896, Bilikamin, Austro-Hungarian Empire; d. 8 May 1981, Tel Aviv

Born in Galicia and descended from a line of rabbis, G. began his career as a bilingual poet in Lvov (then Lemberg) and associated with such Yiddish writers as Perets MARKISH and Melikh Ravitsh (b. 1893). His earliest poems were published in 1912, the first in Yiddish, the second in Hebrew; in them he already articulated a sense of special mission. He was one of the founders of a Jewish literary EXPRESSIONISM, which in his case was to become more specifically nationalistic. His World War I experiences are echoed in his first volume of poems (in Yiddish), *Ergits oyf felder* (1915; somewhere in the fields), and later, after he had moved to Warsaw in 1921, in such poetic works as *Mefista* (1921; Mephisto) and in pieces in the new journals *Kaliastre* and *Albatross*. He advocated the impregnation of contemporary literature with contemporary reality: "Therefore there should be cruelty in the song." Poetry (including and especially Jewish poetry) must come down to earth and address men's immediate concerns in contemporary language. Expressionism broke with the traditional subject matter of Yiddish verse, as well as with its cadences, rhythms, and diction.

G., unlike many of his fellow Yiddishists, saw Zionism as the only salve to the ills of the Jewish people; after spending a year in Berlin, he emigrated to Palestine in 1924, at the end of the third *aliyah* (wave of immigration). This move signaled, too, his almost exclusive adoption of Hebrew as a literary language. The Yiddishists, in G.'s words, sought out the Gentile *emes* (Yiddish for "truth") in association with the revolution, whereas he went to the Jewish *emet* (Hebrew for "truth") in Erets Yisrael. He "expressed" and represented "Hebrew man" in his first volume of Hebrew verse, *Emah gdolah veyareach* (1924; great dread and a moon), as worker and prophet in the recreated homeland. From an early stage, G. adopted a politically maximalist stance (that is, he supported the demand for a Jewish state to be established on both sides of the Jordan River). He moved toward a total identification with the so-called Revisionists, the political party formed in the mid-1930s to work for immediate Jewish statehood. This point of view is a major theme in his poetry.

In addition to the dozen or so volumes of Hebrew verse, the works in Yiddish (now collected in two volumes) and the programmatic material (that stating his ideological position and his view of the direction of Hebrew literature), a great deal of G.'s writing remains as yet unpublished, a situation of his own volition. He always saw himself as out of step with the contemporary literary scene in Israel, which he regarded as a trivial marketplace, not truly representing the historical moment. All phases of G.'s work attempt to express the story of our times, the Holocaust, the Jewish nation, and his own particular mission in their regard. Thus, he was sui generis, the paramount Jewish expressionist.

FURTHER WORKS: *Hagavrut haolah* (1926); *Klape tishim vetishah* (1927); *Chazon achad haligyonot* (1928); *Anakreon al kotev haitsavon* (1928); *Kelev bayit* (1929); *Ezor magen unum ben hadam* (1930); *Sefer hakitrug vehaemunah* (1937); *Min hachachlil umin hakahol* (1950); *Mitoch sefer haigul* (1951); *Rechovot hanahar* (1951); *Minofim rechoke mahut* (2 vols., 1952–1953); *Lisif sela etam* (2 vols., 1967–1968); *Gezamelte verk* (2 vols., 1979)

BIBLIOGRAPHY: Alter, R., "A Poet of the Holocaust," *Commentary* (Nov. 1973): 57–63; Arnson, C., "U. Z. G.: The Early Years,"

MHL, 1 (1975): 4–7; Yudkin, L. I., *U. Z. G.: On the Anvil of Hebrew Poetry* (1980)

—LEON I. YUDKIN

GREENE, Graham

English novelist, short-story writer, journalist, and essayist, b. 2 Oct. 1904, Berkhamsted; d. 3 April 1991, Vevey, Switzerland

G. was educated at Berkhamsted School, where his father was headmaster, and at Balliol College, Oxford. After graduation he worked as an assistant editor for the London *Times* until the publication of his first novel, *The Man Within* (1929). Two unsuccessful novels in the style of Joseph CONRAD followed, and G. was about to abandon writing when, as a last try, he changed his style and produced a fast-paced thriller, *Stamboul Train* (1932; Am., *Orient Express*), which gave him a new impetus and direction. His fiction thereafter alternated between "entertainments," as he called them, and more serious novels which reflect the influence of Ford Madox FORD and Henry JAMES, and which, although cast in the mold of pursuit fiction, deal seriously with social issues. G. converted to Roman Catholicism in 1926, and Catholic themes mark the four novels that made him famous: *Brighton Rock* (1938), *The Power and the Glory* (1940), *The Heart of the Matter* (1948), and *The End of the Affair* (1951).

Graham Greene

Throughout his life G. had been a great traveler. A trek across northern Liberia is reported in *Journey without Maps* (1936), and he investigated religious persecution in Mexico in *The Lawless Roads* (1939; Am., *Another Mexico*). From 1941 to 1943 he served with the British Secret Service in Sierra Leone. After the war, as an independent journalist, he visited political hot spots throughout the world which provided background for most of his subsequent novels: Indochina for *The Quiet American* (1955), the Congo for *A Burnt-Out Case* (1961), Haiti for *The Comedians* (1966), Paraguay for *The Honorary Consul* (1973).

A humorous vein surfaced in *Our Man in Havana* (1958) and reached its apogee in *Travels with My Aunt* (1967). In *The Human Factor* (1978) he remained true to the thriller genre he has perfected, but as a traveler returned full circle, to his native Berkhamsted, where much of this spy novel is set.

G. was a prolific writer. Besides novels he published several volumes of short stories, most included in *Collected Stories* (1973). He wrote five plays and the screenplays of several of the many films based on his novels. In the 1930s and early 1940s he wrote over five hundred reviews of books, films, and plays, mainly for *The Spectator*. A selection of his literary essays appears in *Collected Essays* (1969) and of his film criticism in *The Pleasure Dome* (1972; Am., *The Collected Film Criticism of G. G.*). Autobiographical writings, besides his travel books, include *In Search of a Character* (1961), *A Sort of Life* (1971), and *Ways of Escape* (1980).

In a modern idiom G. continues the tradition of Robert Louis Stevenson, a distant relative. The strange, the dangerous, and often the uncivilized and subtropical have always fascinated him; when his scene is urban, it is most often the shifty, seedy world of the petty criminal and the hunted spy, a setting critics have labeled "Greeneland." Superficially, his novels are suspense fiction, treating contemporary subjects from a melodramatic angle with techniques close to those of film. But although the early novels may be read as an alarmed commentary on social decadence as Europe lurched toward war, they already bear the stamp of the special perspective G. was to cultivate throughout his fiction. He always took the side of the underdog, the unregenerate, the eccentric, the individual. His pursuit fiction was criminal-centered; his Catholic novels skirted heresy; his journalism espoused unpopular causes; his comedies were sad, and his politics paradoxical.

What G. developed in his novels was a consistent view of the human condition. He gave it aphoristic expression in several places. Describing the impulse that drove him to write, he said that he discovered very young that "human nature is not black and white but black and grey." He praised the "virtue of disloyalty" as freeing the novelist from accepted opinions and giving him the "extra dimension of understanding." Recalling Browning's Bishop Blougram's chessboard, he said that one must be able to write "from the point of view of the black square as well as of the white." He takes as perhaps the only sign of a Christian civilization "the divided mind, the uneasy conscience, the sense of personal failure." And as the epigraph he would choose for his complete work, he again cites Bishop Blougram: "Our interest's on the dangerous edge of things."

This controversial attitude is embodied in all G.'s writing, early and late. The title of his first novel is taken from Sir Thomas Browne's (1605–1682) "There's another man within me that's angry with me." Heroes of the novels of the 1930s, like remittance man Minty in *England Made Me* (1935; Am., *The Shipwrecked*), the hired killer Raven in *A Gun for Sale* (1936; Am., *This Gun for Hire*), and the adolescent gang leader Pinkie in *Brighton Rock*, are social outcasts whom G. follows with sharp psychological penetration and deep sympathy. The corruption that these characters are tainted with is extra-personal; the world they live in is so much more corrupt than they. Minty's spoiled youth, Raven's harelip and institutional childhood, Pinkie's slum upbringing are all crippling handicaps, like social or physical equivalents of original sin. The violence of these characters is just the excrescence of a larger international, not to say universal, violence. If they are doomed or damned, the responsibility is widely shared. G. challenges his reader to withhold quick judgment, to take the comprehensive view, to allow that "between the stirrup and the ground" there remains a possibility of understanding and pardoning these dark wayward heroes.

G.'s saints are just as complex and contradictory as his sinners. In fact, the two categories are barely distinguishable. The whiskey priest, hero of *The Power and the Glory*, is a drunkard, father of an illegitimate child, a wanted man in the eyes of the state, in his own eyes a failure. His heroism consists mainly in his flight from the police, in his tired persistence in continuing surreptitiously to administer the sacraments, in exposing others to the danger of protecting him. His sanctity lies in his sense of his own unworthiness, in the office he so humbly and badly fills, and in his martyr's death. G. strips conventional notions of sainthood of their usual connotations and illustrates Charles PÉGUY's statement that the sinner is at the heart of Christianity.

This thesis is taken as epigraph for *The Heart of the Matter*. Scobie, Assistant Police Commissioner in Sierra Leone during World War II, is a just man, a devout Catholic, a devoted husband. But his justice is corrupted by pity, and he is led inexorably to a triple betrayal of trust: as a police officer, as a husband, and as a Catholic—falling successively into corruption, adultery, and suicide.

A simplistic view of G.'s "Catholic" novels of the late 1930s and 1940s (and one that G. had aired on occasion himself) is that Pinkie is slated for Hell, the whiskey priest for Heaven, and Scobie for Purgatory. But such classifications belie G.'s compassionate concern for all his characters and his ultimate appeal to the "appalling strangeness of the mercy of God."

In the 1950s G.'s emphasis switched from religion to politics. *The End of the Affair* and his first play, *The Living Room* (1953), are his last "Catholic" works, the novel bright, the play dark in tone. Thereafter the religious concerns of his characters take second place to political preoccupations. Yet there is a continuity to G.'s vision, for whether he is investigating in his fiction Papa Doc Duvalier's repressive rule in Haiti (*The Comedians*), American involvement in Indochina (*The Quiet American*), a hostage drama in Paraguay (*The Honorary Consul*), or Communist counterespionage in Britain (*The Human Factor*), his main concern has always been the problem of faith, religious or political, in an increasingly complex and faithless world. The intention G. attributes to *A Burnt-Out Case*, "to describe various types of belief, half-belief and nonbelief," might be taken as the broad canvas for all his work, if one remembers not to narrow the definition to religious belief alone.

Whatever the political scene and whatever the dialectics of political choice involved, G. also remains true to his earliest commitment as a novelist. His loyalty always goes to the individual ahead of the state, the party, the cult. Querry in *A Burnt-Out Case* fights against the stereotype others would make of him as a famous Catholic architect. Wormold in *Our Man in Havana*, because he is an eccentric individual, not a cipher in a system, turns his secret-service mission into farce. Although defeated by Duvalier's nightmarish police, the unimportant and slightly ridiculous characters in *The Comedians* triumph in human terms. Castle, hero of *The Human Factor*, becomes involved as a double agent on personal rather than ideological grounds; this novel, unlike most spy novels, focuses on the humdrum, unsensational aspects of life as a spy, and the drama results from the conflict between the impersonal intricacies of superstate politics and private loyalties.

The frontier land of G.'s fiction is a place of contradictory responsibilities, of dangerous choices, and of constant revision of judgments and attitudes. It is not just Greeneland but a place very like the difficult world we live in. The virtues his characters bring to cope with it, sometimes successfully in comedy, sometimes unsuccessfully in tragedy, are not heroic ones but are those of tolerance, humor, and intense personal loyalties.

G.'s reputation as a novelist is secure. His fiction meets T. S. ELIOT's criteria for greatness; "variety, abundance and complete technical competence." To this one might add "poetic quality" in the sense Ford Madox Ford defines it: "not the power melodiously to arrange words, but the power to suggest human values." This accomplishment is backed by outstanding contributions in many fields. He was one of the most brilliant film critics of the 1930s. He is the most-filmed British novelist of his generation. As a director of the publishing houses Eyre & Spottiswoode (1944–48) and The Bodley Head (1958–68), as well as in a personal way, he was very generous with his help to younger writers. His literary criticism has been described as a dark lantern throwing intense light from a particular angle on the subjects it focuses on. His plays are interesting corollaries to his fiction, his journalism is daring, and his political commitments are provocative. Over a long career G. has given vivid dramatic expression to universal concerns, presenting them in a popular, entertaining, yet always intellectually stimulating way and in a style that has shed its early melodramatic excesses to become classically simple, dense, and direct.

FURTHER WORKS: *Babbling April* (1925); *The Name of Action* (1930); *Rumour at Nightfall* (1931); *It's a Battlefield* (1934); *The Basement Room and Other Stories* (1935); *The Confidential Agent* (1939); *British Dramatists* (1942); *The Ministry of Fear* (1943); *Nineteen Stories* (1947); *Why Do I Write?* (1948); *The Third Man* (1950); *The Lost Childhood and Other Essays* (1951); *Essais catholiques* (1953); *Twenty-One Stories* (1954); *Loser Takes All* (1955); *The Potting Shed* (1957); *The Complaisant Lover* (1961); *A Sense of Reality* (1963); *Carving a Statue* (1964); *May We Borrow Your Husband?* (1967); *Lord Rochester's Monkey* (1974); *The Return of A. J. Raffles* (1975); *Doctor Fischer of Geneva; or, The Bomb Party* (1980)

BIBLIOGRAPHY: Rostenne, P., *G. G.: Témoin des temps tragiques* (1949); Madaule, J., *G. G.* (1949); Mauriac, F., *Mes grands hommes* (1951): 245–53; Rischik, J., *G. G. und sein Werk* (1951); Allott, K., and M. Farris, *The Art of G. G.* (1951); de Pange, V., *G. G.* (1953); Mesnet, M. -B, *G. G. and the Heart of the Matter* (1954); Wyndham, F., *G. G.* (1955); O'Faolain, S., *The Vanishing Hero* (1956): 71–97; Atkins, J., *G. G.* (1957); Zabel, M. D., *Craft and Character* (1957): 276–96; Matthews, R., *Mon ami G. G.* (1957); Kunkel, F. L., *The Labyrinthine Ways of G. G.* (1959); Lewis, R. B. W., *The Picaresque Saint* (1961): 220–74; Pryce-Jones, D., *G. G.* (1963); Evans, R. O., ed., *G. G.: Some Critical Considerations* (1963); De Vitis, A. A., *G. G.* (1964); Stratford, P., *Faith and Fiction: Creative Process in G. and Mauriac* (1964);

Lodge, D., *G. G.* (1966); Turnell, M., *G. G.* (1967); Cargas, H., *G. G.* (1969); Vann, J. D., *G. G.: A Checklist of Criticism* (1970); Boardman, G. R., *G. G.: The Aesthetics of Exploration* (1971); Wolfe, P., *G. G. the Entertainer* (1972); Phillips, G. D., *G. G.: The Films of His Fiction* (1974); Veitch, D. W., *Lawrence, G., and Lowry: The Fictional Landscape of Mexico* (1978); Bloom, H., ed., *G. G.: Modern Critical Views* (1987)

—PHILIP STRATFORD

"Novels" and "Entertainments" are both written in the same grim style, both deal mainly with charmless characters, both have a structure of sound, exciting plot. You cannot tell from the skeleton whether the man was baptized or not. And that is the difference; the "Novels" have been baptized, held deep under in the waters of life. The author has said: "These characters are not my creation but God's. They have an eternal destiny. They are not merely playing a part for the reader's amusement. They are souls whom Christ died to save." This, I think, explains his preoccupation with the charmless. The children of Adam are not a race of noble savages who need only a divine spark to perfect them. They are aboriginally corrupt. Their tiny relative advantages of intelligence and taste and good looks and good manners are quite insignificant. The compassion and condescension of the Word becoming flesh are glorified in the depths.

Evelyn Waugh, "Felix Culpa?" *The Tablet*, 5 June 1948, p. 352

He appears to share the idea, which has been floating around ever since Baudelaire, that there is something rather *distingué* in being damned; Hell is a sort of high-class night club, entry to which is reserved for Catholics only, since the others, the non-Catholics, are too ignorant to be held guilty, like the beasts that perish. We are carefully informed that Catholics are no better than anybody else; they even, perhaps, have a tendency to be worse, since their temptations are greater . . . But all the while—drunken, lecherous, criminal, or damned outright—the Catholics retain their superiority since they alone know the meaning of good and evil. . . .

This cult of the sanctified sinner seems to me to be frivolous, and underneath it there probably lies a weakening of belief, for when people really believed in Hell, they were not so fond of striking graceful attitudes on its brink.

George Orwell, on *The Heart of the Matter, New Yorker*, 17 July 1948, p. 66

G. G., then, employs a distinctive form: he also exhibits a distinctive concern. Just as Balzac came back again to avarice and Stendhal to ambition, so, in book after book, G. G. analyses the vice of pity, that corrupt parody of love and compassion which is so insidious and deadly for sensitive natures.

. . .Behind pity for another lies self-pity, and behind self-pity lies cruelty.

To feel compassion for someone is to make oneself their equal; to pity them is to regard oneself as their superior and from that eminence the step to the torture chamber and the corrective labour camp is shorter than one thinks.

For providing us with such exciting reading and at the same time exposing so clearly a great and typical heresy of our time, G. G. deserves our lasting gratitude.

W. H. Auden, "The Heresy of Our Time," *Renascence*, 1 (Spring 1949), p. 24

This hidden presence of God in an atheistic world, this subterranean circulation of grace, fascinates G. G. far more than the majestic façades that the temporal Church still raises up above the people. If there exists a Christian who would not be troubled by the collapse of the visible Church, he is certainly . . . G. G. . . .

[The Power and the Glory] providentially addresses itself to the generation that the absurdity of a mad world has seized by the throat. To the young contemporaries of Camus, and Sartre, desperate prey of a mocking liberty, G. will perhaps reveal that this absurdity is in truth that of a boundless love.

François Mauriac, *Mes grands hommes* (1951), pp. 250–51

There is a sentence by Gauguin, quoted approvingly by G., that comes near to expressing his main obsessional outlook: "Life being what it is, one dreams of revenge." A terror of life, a terror of what experience can do to the individual, a terror at a predetermined corruption, is the motive force that drives G. as a novelist. With different degrees of plausibility in his various books G. is continually saying that happiness is unusual and anxious routine nearer the disappointing 'natural' state of man, that experience saddens, that we must bear rather than rejoice because, in Matthew Arnold's words, of a "something that infects the world." Failure, ugliness, the primitive are in some sense truer than success, beauty and civilization with their deceptive gloss.

Kenneth Allott and Miriam Farris, *The Art of G. G.* (1951), pp. 15–16

All G. G.'s best work can only be read as "a sort of poem," an exciting blend of realism as to its detail and poetry as to its conception. It is not only the brainless and predestined quality of his characters that makes them move so fast: they have been conceived under the emotional pressure of poetic inspiration which flies them as high as maddened kites. In this sense, G.'s characters really are hunted men, the hounds of heaven at their heels. It is one significant reason why they are least interesting when they pause. Then they come down to earth, to common life, and common life is a range of experience beyond G.'s powers, since it is outside his interest.

Sean O'Faolain, *The Vanishing Hero* (1956),
pp. 93–94

He would have made an admirable Pierrot in the eighteenth-century Commedia dell' Arte, concealing under his rather woebegone mask a great capacity for cynical humour. He was often exuberant: he could be positively blithe. Nor have the exuberance and the blitheness vanished. And even at the present period, when I reread his books—those sombre chronicles of sin and suffering, where every form of pleasure is naturally suspect, every love-affair inescapably doomed, and a breath of Evil mixes with the fog that swirls the lonely street lamps—I sometimes feel that I am confronting the spirited schoolboy in a more accomplished and more portentous guise. I cannot resist the suspicion that he gets a good deal of fun—lighthearted schoolboyish fun—from causing his own and his reader's flesh to creep, and that he half enjoys the sensations of disgust and horror that he arouses with such unusual terror.

Peter Quennell, *The Sign of The Fish* (1960), p. 64

G. often turns away from the relatively civilized to inspect human life in its cruder and more exposed conditions: in a dark corner of Brighton, the jungles and prisons of Tabasco, the coast of West Africa—all places where, as Scobie tells himself in *The Heart of the Matter*, "human nature hasn't had time to disguise itself"; places where there openly flourished "the injustices, the cruelties, the meanness that elsewhere people so cleverly hushed up." In these primitive scenes we encounter the *dramatis personae* of G.'s recurring drama and of his troubled universe: the murderer, the priest, and the policeman, . . . they tend more and more to resemble each other. The murderer Pinkie is knowingly a hideously inverted priest; the policeman Scobie becomes involved with crime and criminals; the lieutenant in *The Power and the Glory* has "something of a priest in his intent observant walk," while the priest in turn has queer points of resemblance with the Yankee killer whose photograph faces his in the police station. The three figures represent, of course, the shifting and interwoven attributes of the Greenean man: a being capable of imitating both Christ and Judas; a person who is at once the pursuer and the man pursued; a creature with the splendid potentiality either of damnation or salvation.

R. W. B. Lewis, *The Picaresque Saint* (1961),
pp. 241–42

GREENLAND LITERATURE
See Eskimo Literature

GRIEG, Nordahl

Norwegian poet, novelist, dramatist, and journalist, b. 1 Nov. 1902, Bergen; d. 2 Dec. 1943, Berlin, Germany?

G. provides a severe test of the tenet that a writer's works should be judged independently of the individual who wrote them. It is likely that G.'s works have been both overly praised and unfairly deprecated in reaction to the man, a man truly of large and varied dimensions. He was, at the same time, an ardent patriot, a dedicated communist, a concerned pacifist, a solider, and ultimately a military martyr.

To the extent that Norway has a patrician class, G. may be said to be of that stock. G.'s given names—Johan Nordahl Brun—were those of a forebear who was an eminent 18th-c. cleric and writer. G.'s surname derives from lineage with the great composer. G.'s father held a university position as a teacher of music while his mother was of a politically active family.

At the age of seventeen, G. went to sea, and began a hectic career of adventure, travel, writing, and political action. The first literary result of his stint as a seaman was *Rundt Kap det gode Håp* (1922; *Around the Cape of Good Hope*, 1979), a book of sea poems with the flavor, the style, and the popularity of John MASEFIELD and Rudyard KIPLING.

A counterpoint to the general romanticism of the sea poems was struck by the explicit realism of the quasi-autobiographical novel he published two years later, *Skibet går videre* (1924; *The Ship Sails On*, 1927). This book has been translated into at least nine languages and was the precipitating event leading to the worldwide campaign by the International Red Cross against the venereal disease problem in port cities.

G.'s first important political statement was *Barrabas* [sic] (1927; Barabbas), a play in which he presented the choice of pacifism or violence, the cross or the sword, in the struggle for freedom. It was a hastily constructed but daringly experimental work that presented Barabbas as a violent rebel against Roman rule who was needed more than was Jesus in the grand strategy of the Pharisees.

The play *Vår ære og vår makt* (1935; *Our Power and Our Glory*, 1971) is a flawed but powerful indictment of war and war profiteers. It deals with the corrosive forces eating at Norway as a "neutral" country during World War I. The theatrical techniques and stage effects drew heavily on the experience G. gained during his two-year stay in Russia (1932–34).

G.'s most successful play is *Nederlaget* (1936; *Defeat*, 1944), a depiction of the Commune revolution in Paris in 1871. Without equivocation the play makes clear that freedom must be won through struggle. The theatrical technique represents a maturation of that employed in *Vår ære og vår makt*; additionally, *Nederlaget* is less stylized, has a sharper dramatic development, and depicts people more realistically.

With the Nazi invasion of Norway, all pacifistic doubts were resolved. G. joined the military service and participated in the dramatic removal of Norway's gold reserves to England. Above all, he wrote and read over Radio Free Norway resistance poetry that played a vital role in strengthening the common purpose and the common will to survive during the dark days of the Occupation. The war poetry was published in a number of books after his death. G. was killed when the bomber on which he was an observer did not return from an attack on Berlin.

For all his enduring popularity in Norway, G. is little known outside of Scandinavia. However, the continued republication of his works attests to the fact that he will remain read and respected in his native land, which he loved so well.

FURTHER WORKS: *Stene i strømmen* (1925); *Kinesiske dage* (1927); *En ung mands Kjærlighet* (1927); *Norge i våre hjerter* (1929); *De unge døde* (1932); *Atlanterhavet* (1932); *Men imorgen* (1936); *Spansk sommer* (1937); *Ung må verden ennu være* (1938); *Dikt i utvalg* (1944); *Flagget* (1945); *Friheten* (1945); *Håbet* (1946); *Veien frem* (1947); *Samlede verker* (7 vols., 1947); *Samlede dikt* (1948); *Længselen* (1957); *Langveisfra* (1964); *Morgen over Finnmarksvidden* (1967); *Skuespill/ N. G.* (1975); *Norge, og andre dikt* (1976). FURTHER WORKS IN ENGLISH: *War Poems of N. G.* (1944)

BIBLIOGRAPHY: Barrett, K., "Between Curtains," *TA*, 22 (1938): 384–86; Lescoffier, J., "N. G.," *Mercure de France*, 291 (1939): 721–23; Koht, H., "N. G.," *ASR*, 30 (1942): 32–40; special G. issue, *WZUG*, 12 (1963); Dahlie, H., "Lowry's Debt to N. G.," *CanL*, 64 (1975): 41–51

—HAROLD P. HANSON

GRÍMSSON, Stefán Hördur

Icelandic poet, b. 31 March 1919, Hafnarfjörður

G. is self-educated and well read in literature and philosophy. He belongs to the group of writers and artists who finally brought MODERNISM to Iceland during World War II.

G.'s first volume, *Glugginn snýr í norður* (1946; window to the north), showed a clear connection with the traditional poetry of the 1930s, both in form and content. Many of the poems have fragments of narration and deal with social criticism as well as with love. Their style is often heavy and ornamental. There are, however, some poems that are predominantly modernistic and free in form.

In his second volume, *Svartálfadans* (1951; dance of the black fairies), G. completely broke with the past and found his own personal expression through modernistic poetic imagery. Gone are the narrative fragments; instead, the poems contain concentrated imagery, and are simple and concise. Images of nature are often used to express the poet's sensitivity and personal philosophy. There is less direct social criticism than in his first book, and what there is is often symbolically veiled or hidden in philosophical speculation on human nature.

Hliðin á sléttunni (1970; the gates [or side] of the plain) is a logical continuation of *Svartálfadans*. The poetic quality has increased, the style is simpler and more transparent; at the same time the thought is more profound and more complicated. The images, at first glance, seem clear and even ordinary; but they usually are laden with complex symbols and allusions. The poems in this slim volume are largely expressions of a deeply felt personal philosophy, but some also contain sharp social criticism and reveal G.'s fear for the future of mankind.

G. is not a prolific poet. In the three volumes published together in 1979 under the title *Ljóð* (poems) there are only sixty-six poems. But he is undoubtedly one of the most accomplished poets of contemporary Iceland. His development has been toward an even simpler form, and he has succeeded in deepening his poetic vision and giving it mythical dimensions.

—NJÖRÐUR P. NJARÐVÍK

GROSSMAN, David

Israeli novelist, short-story writer, journalist, and dramatist, b. 25 Jan. 1954, Jerusalem

After studying philosophy and theater at Hebrew University, Jerusalem, G. quickly established himself as one of the leading innovators in the Israeli fiction of the 1980s. His first collection of stories, *Ratz* (1983; jogging), developed a plastic prose, adopting rhythms of thought waves and vernacular in STREAM-OF-CONSCIOUSNESS writing. Even here, as for example in the title story, the narrator enters extreme situations of stress, in this case, that of a runner attempting to transcend the limitations of the body and to carry on running. The rhythm, vocabulary, and syntax match up with the situation.

G.'s writing welds the political and personal. Both in his fictional and in his journalistic work, the personal situation meets the national, political point of crisis. *Hiyukh hagdiy* (1983; *The Smile of the Lamb*, 1990) is a fictional representation of life in the West Bank under Israeli occupation, a story told by the protagonists, Jews and Arabs, governors and governed, where the personal lives and conflicts of the characters intersect with the political nexus, creating a tapestry of mixed motives and surprising resolutions. *Hazman hatsahov* (1987; *Yellow Wind*, 1988) is the sort of reportage made familiar by Amos OZ in *Po vesham beerets yisrael* (1983; *In the Land of Israel*, 1983), a piece of "straight" reporting, based on interviews and impressions of the material and the situation. But whereas Oz deliberately contrived a multifaceted composite of different views, so as to offer the reader a notion of the complexity of Israeli opinion across the political spectrum, G.'s material is worked to present a specific point of view, arguing the case against Israeli military presence and control and in favor of Arab self-determination. This is a prophecy of doom and a plea for disengagement. *Hiyukh hagdiy*, although an earlier work, can be seen as a fictional equivalent of the piece of reporting, deconstructing the coherent, assured writing set up in the journalistic account, mixing up the motives, casting doubt on readers' certainties and presumptions. The good guy turns out to be ineffective, the bad guy resilient, and all positive thrust questionable. It does, however, make for confusion.

The later work reinforces this direction, where stories are told in a multiplicity of modes and voices. *Ayen erekh ahavah* (1986; *See Under Love*, 1990) is a "novel," not only told in four parts through four different voices, but in four different modes, only tangentially related to each other. The first section, "Momik," establishes the subject, the Holocaust as reconstructed by a nine-year-old child, through his survivor relative, and his child's imagination. The next three sections are not chronologically sequential but, rather, parallel and alternative attempts at understanding through fantasy— Bruno Schulz's only apparent death and the song of the sea— through the grotesque vision of the relative, Anshel Wasserman, in Auschwitz, who was unable to die, and, finally, through the encyclopedic series of definitions to concepts raised by the novel as a whole. Indubitably experimental, this work enthusiastically challenges traditional narrative standpoint and chronology, so as to offer a full-blooded, linguistically exuberant, and imaginatively penetrative account of how reality might be grasped afresh and then conveyed.

The way to see the world anew in G.'s terms can be to enter the world of the child. This is carried out with rigid purity in the play *Gan riki* (1988; Riki's kindergarten), entirely set in a kindergarten where the sole participants are young children, and where there exists no mediating adult presence. Thus, the world of the child becomes self-authenticating, not seen as subsidiary or as a stage on the way to adulthood. A further step in this direction is made by the novel *Sefer hadiqduq hapnimiy* (1991; book of internal grammar).

G.'s work, while it attaches itself to objective political and national reality, moves freely into the consciousnesses of the characters in narrative. It particularly enters the mind of the child, tracing the contours of child thought from within, and thus renders a fresh view of the world.

FURTHER WORKS: *Sefer hadiqduq hapnimi* (1991; *The Book of Intimate Grammar*, 1994); *Nokhahim nifqadim* (1992; *Sleeping on a Wire: Conversations with Palestinians in Israel*, 1993); *Yesh yeladim zigzag* (1994; *The Zigzag Kid*, 1997)

BIBLIOGRAPHY: Yudkin, L. I., "Victims and Oppressors in the Writing of D. G.," *Remembering the Future* (1988), Theme 2: 1649–54; Ramras-Rauch, G., on *See Under: Love, WLT*, 64, 1 (Winter 1990): 189; Mazor, Y., on *The Smile of the Lamb, WLT*, 65, 4 (Autumn 1991): 762

—LEON I. YUDKIN

GRUŠAS, Juozas

Lithuanian dramatist, short-story writer, and novelist, b. 16 Nov. 1901, Žadžiunai; d. 21 May 1986, Lithuania

G., from a family of small farmers, graduated from the University of Kaunas in 1931. From 1928 to 1939 he earned his living as a teacher, and for a time he also edited a weekly Christian newspaper. In 1940–41 he was the editor of the state publishing company of Lithuania. After the second Soviet occupation of Lithuania he worked as a literary consultant for the theater of Šiauliai. Since 1944 he has lived in Kaunas, engaged solely in creative writing.

In all of G.'s writing, from traditional, realistic short stories to modern, psychological plays to surrealistic prose sketches, two themes remain constant. The first is life seen as a constant struggle between the inhibitions of an ethical conscience and the destructiveness of uncontrolled passions; the second is his pity for the weak and downtrodden.

In his short stories G. deals with variations on the theme of the psychology of a victim. In the stories in two of his best collections, *Rūstybés šviesa* (1969; the light of anger) and *Laimingasis—tai aš* (1973; the luckiest of all—myself), the main characters are the victims of society and circumstances—the humiliated poor, the cripples leading a marginal life among the normal people, those who live in the shadows and are often brutalized by those who cannot stand their suffering. The stories also portray emotionally starved and weak characters who are victimized by the passions of others. In both cases G. is interested not so much in the social structures that isolate the victim as in the relationship between the aggressor and the victim. Additionally, G. often analyzes the

character who lives in a world of illusion and is considered mad by the standard of sanity in the "normal" world; the madman is his archetypal victim. The real enemy of humanity is the intolerance of those who refuse to see the truth beyond logic.

G. is known in Lithuania above all as a dramatist. His plays fall roughly into three categories. The first group are realistic plays that deal with moral dilemmas. The central conflict of these plays is the difficult choice: between family loyalty and social responsibility, as in *Tévas* (1942; father); between a scientist's duty to scientific progress and the possible consequences of scientific advances on future generations, as in *Profesorius Markas Vidinas* (1963; Professor Markas Vidinas); between the integrity of an individual and the revelation to his son of a truth that will destroy the son's beliefs, as in *Adomo Brunzos paslaptis* (1967; the secret of Adomas Brunza).

The second type of play is a mixture of moralistic allegory and THEATER OF THE ABSURD. In *Meilé, džiazas ir velnias* (1967; love, jazz, and the devil) a group of young people, rejecting the values of their parents, search for self-definition. To achieve this they try to impose their will on the outside world, but the result is only a series of pointless, brutal actions that result in the destruction of the only character they respect.

The plays in the third category are large-scale historical dramas. *Herkus Mantas* (1957; Herkus Mantas), *Barbora Radvilaité* (1971; Barbora Radvilaité), *Švitrigaila* (1976; Švitrigaila), and *Rekvijum bajorams* (1978; a requiem for the nobles) all deal with the theme of the tragedy of historical characters who must reconcile public and personal levels of existence. The moral problem they confront is often that they desire noble ends while being fully aware of the bloody means they demand.

The psychological realism of G.'s works has never wavered from its original premise—to see human destiny in a scheme of moral imperatives. His knowledge of the human soul has always revealed to the reader his greatest moral imperatives: vivid indignation in the face of injustice and great respect for its victims.

FURTHER WORKS: *Ponia Bertulienė* (1928); *Karjeristai* (1935); *Sunki ranka* (1937); *Nenuorama žmona* (1955); *Dūmai* (1956); *Gintarinė vila* (1979)

—ILONA GRAŽYTŽ-MAZILIAUSKAS

GUADELOUPE LITERATURE

See French-Caribbean Literature

GUARE, John

American dramatist and screenwriter, b. 5 Feb. 1938, New York City

At the age of eleven G. wrote and directed his first plays in a neighbor's garage, and his parents supported him in his vocational choice from the start, giving him a typewriter for his twelfth birthday, and taking him to see plays on Broadway. Early on, he developed an enthusiasm for musical comedies, as well as the plays of Shakespeare, Anton CHEKHOV, and August STRINDBERG, while simultaneously developing an aversion to American stage realism, as manifested in the domestic dramas of William INGE. To this day, G.'s plays remain outside the realistic mainstream of American drama. They are boldly theatrical, rupturing the fourth wall with songs, monologues, and other presentational devices. Avoiding sentimentality, these complexly plotted plays boldly juxtapose poetic lyricism and wisecracks, social commentary and surrealistic fantasy, farce and despair.

G.'s first full-length play, *The House of Blue Leaves* (1972), is not completely unrelated to the American tradition of realistic drama, and its first Broadway production largely presented it in those terms. From this perspective, it is a variation on Tennessee WILLIAMS's *The Glass Menagerie*, with its domestic setting and dreamy, alienated eccentrics. In G.'s play the Pope's visit to New York City offers hopes of an epiphany equal to the coming of Laura Wingfield's "Gentleman Caller." But the desires of G.'s characters are more fiercely obsessive than Williams's and lead to outbursts of cruelty; the Pope's visit leaves terrorism and murder in its wake. Described by its author as the offspring of a liaison between Strindberg and Georges Feydeau (1862-1921), *The House of Blue Leaves* does not offer sympathetic figures for spectatorial identification, but an attack on American dreams of celebrity and success.

G.'s early work Off-Broadway in the late 1960s revealed him to be a satirist of New Leftist convictions, opposing sexual repression, big business, and the military-industrial complex. In these plays idealistic impulses are perverted and betrayed by Establishment values. In *Cop-Out* (1968) we see the destructive effects of mass culture, as we see the supervirile, B-movie fantasies of a policeman, and his tortured affair with an antiwar protester, which ends with him shooting her. Argue, the protagonist of *Muzeeka* (1968), hopes to launch a Dionysian transformation of the U.S. by infiltrating the country's leading piped-music company, and subverting it. He quickly, however, falls victim to its banality, and is found stealthily resisting a prostitute in Greenwich Village while his wife is in labor. When he is drafted, Argue finds himself in a media event, with various patrols under exclusive contact to NBC or CBS. This commodification of identity is taken a step further in G.'s theatrical satire, *Rich and Famous* (1977), where Hollywood star Tybalt Dunleavy is persuaded that his brilliant career can only become legendary if he commits suicide. Throughout G.'s work the false values of a celebrity culture imperil those of humanism.

G.'s earlier work held out very little hope for human beings. In them not only is the system a powerful, monolithic structure, but individuals are obsessively narcissistic. In a typical Guarean bout of narcissism, Elliot in *Marco Polo Sings a Solo* (1977) becomes a transsexual, and then impregnates herself with sperm that he left in storage before the operations. The emotional exhibitionists of *Bosoms and Neglect* (1980) squabble over which one of them their therapist finds more interesting. Later works offer more hope. G.'s screenplay for Louis Malle's *Atlantic City* (1980) shows characters who are able to forge some supportive and mutually rewarding relationships, however idiosyncratic. *Six Degrees of Separation* (1990) was warmed by the presence of G.'s most compassionate protagonist, the wife of an art dealer who is stimulated when an eloquent, small-time, confidence man enters her hitherto superficial life. G.'s most impressive investigation of American values can be found in his "Lydie Breeze" tetralogy, composed of *Women and Water* (1990), *Gardenia* (1982), *Lydie Breeze* (1982), and *Bullfinch's Mythology* (1998). Here G. abandons the contemporary scene in favor of a broader historical perspective. He traces the history of a utopian experiment from its origins in the carnage of the Civil War, its collapse, and the repercussions for the offspring of that experiment. The tetralogy is both a postmortem of the failed utopianism of the 1960s and an examination of larger tensions between idealism and possessiveness that have run throughout

American culture. G. worked to give these plays both the narrative complexity and richness of detail found in the 19th-c. novel, and the slower overall tempo throughout the tetralogy allows it to attain a deeper thoughtfulness than his earlier plays.

G's work has rarely been given its due by reviewers and prizegivers; his vision is often too tough-minded, his disinterest in well-made dramaturgy too pronounced, and his juxtapositions too jarring. Yet, as our awareness of a postmodern aesthetic of fragmentation develops, G's vigorously theatrical experiments appear not self-indulgent and clumsy, but trailblazing and visionary.

FURTHER WORKS: *Something I'll Tell You Thursday* (1967); *The Loveliest Afternoon of the Year* (1967); *Home Fires* (1970); *Kissing Sweet* (1971); *A Day for Surprises* (1971); *Taking Off* (1971, with Milos Forman) *Two Gentlemen of Verona* (1973, with Mel Shapiro); *Landscape of the Body* (1978); *In Fireworks Lie Secret Codes* (1981); *Four Baboons Adoring the Sun* (1993); *Moon Under Miami* (1996); *Chuck Close: Life and Work, 1988-1995* (1995)

BIBLIOGRAPHY: Harrop, J., "'Ibsen Translated by Lewis Carroll': The Theatre of J. G.," *NTQ*, 10 (1987): 150-54; Gross, R., "Life in a Silken Net: Mourning the Beloved Monstrous in Lydie Breeze," *JDTC*, 9 (Fall 1994): 21-42; Roman, D., "Fierce Love and Fierce Response: Intervening in the Cultural Politics of Race, Sexuality and AIDS," in Nelson, E. S., ed., *Critical Essays: Gay and Lesbians Writers of Color* (1993): 195-219

—ROBERT F. GROSS

GUATEMALAN LITERATURE
See Central American Literature

GUÐMUNDSSON, Tómas

Icelandic essayist and poet, b. 6 Jan. 1901, Grímsnes; d. 20 Nov. 1983, Reykjavík

Already as a high-school student in Reykjavík G. attracted notice for poems he had written. He earned a law degree from the University of Iceland in 1926, and then practiced law in Reykjavík. He also worked for the Bureau of Statistics for a time, but after 1943 dedicated himself wholly to writing. He edited the literary magazine *Helgafell* from 1942 to 1955 and another magazine, *Nýtt Helgafell*, from 1956 to 1959. He has translated several books into Icelandic including works by Giuseppe TOMASI DI LAMPEDUSA and Erich Maria REMARQUE.

G.'s first volume of verse, *Við sundin blá* (1925; beside the blue channels), has the markings of the new romantic life-worship introduced into Icelandic poetry around 1920 through the works of Stefán frá Hvítadal (1887–1933) and Davíð Stefánsson (1895–1964). Most of the poems in this book concern the pleasures of youthful love, although there is often an undercurrent of nostalgia for the past—a tone of sadness that grew in intensity in G.'s later verse. On the whole, these early poems have a thoughtful and intellectual quality, while the romantic sentiment tends to be somewhat detached. The intellectual humor that was to play such a prominent role in his later poetry can hardly be detected in this first volume.

With *Fagra veröld* (1933; beautiful world), G. established himself as a mature poet. The book was a tour de force that gained him immense popularity, among other reasons because many of the poems were about Reykjavík, Iceland's still young capital, and life there—a subject largely ignored by poets up to that time. G. opened the eyes of Reykjavík residents to the beauty of their own town. *Fagra veröld* at the same time shows a make-believe world far from the reality of economic depression and class conflicts that dominated the headlines when the book appeared. As a reward for singing its praise, the city of Reykjavík gave the poet a stipend that enabled him to travel in southern Europe, and some of the poems in his next volume, *Stjörnur vorsins* (1940; the stars of springtime), evolved from the experiences of that trip. Although this book has more pure lyricism in it than any of G.'s other works, it also contains poems on social concerns such as race bigotry and the rise of Nazism in the 1930s. The terrors of World War II, however, affected him more profoundly than any other political events, as is clearly seen in *Fljótið helga* (1950; the sacred river), the most pessimistic, philosophical, and religious book of verse that G. wrote.

His latest collection of verse, *Heim til pín, Island* (1977; return to Iceland), largely contains poems dedicated to various festive occasions—reflecting his status as Icelandic poet laureate. Also in this volume are several personal poems, expressing concern over approaching death along with nostalgia for a vanished youth, and disappointment with life's limitations.

G.'s poetry has in many respects a classical quality, yet it is shot through with romantic worship of beauty and nostalgic longing. His poetic forms are varied, but long lines of colloquial diction are typical of much of his work. His fondness for paradox gives his humor an intellectual cast, but his greatest achievement is perhaps that he was the first mature poetic spokesman for Icelandic city dwellers; he adapted the traditional diction of verse to suit emerging life styles by using an idiom close to the rhythms of colloquial speech.

—SVEINN SKORRI HÖSKULDSSON

GUIDO, Beatriz

Argentine novelist, short-story writer, and screenwriter, b. 13 Dec. 1925, Rosario; d. 4 Mar. 1988, Madrid, Spain

G. was born and raised in the interior city of Rosario amidst a stimulating intellectual atmosphere provided by her parents. She traveled extensively in Argentina and Europe with her father, a successful architect, and developed an early interest in philosophy. She spent three years at the University of Buenos Aires and then continued her studies in Rome, Naples, and Paris in 1948. Following her return to Argentina, she gravitated to Buenos Aires, wrote her first novel, *La casa del ángel* (1954; *The House of the Angel*, 1957), and met Argentine film director Leopoldo Torre Nilsson, whom she later married, and with whom she would collaborate on a score of full-length films, half of which were based on her own narratives.

From the outset, her novels and stories stressed psychological introspection and focused on adolescence and its conflicts. This is particularly noted in *La caída* (1956; the fall), her most autobiographical novel. In subsequent works she revealed a critical view of her society and a growing political awareness, as exemplified in *Fin de fiesta* (1958; party's end). The latter work evoked in realistic terms the grim political circumstances—torture, assassination, electoral fraud—of an earlier period, that of the decline of Argentina's last conservative government. But following the publication of a collection of short stories, *La mano en la trampa* (1961; the hand in the trap), she wrote a novel that dealt directly with the Peronist years, *El incendio y las vísperas* (1964; *End of a Day*, 1966). The novel covers the period from October 1952 to April 1953, which serves as historical backdrop for the account of the personal crisis of a wealthy Argentine landowner, Alejandro Pradere, morally compromised by his passive collaboration with the Peronist régime. G. thus joined the ranks of the numerous River Plate writers who, in the 1960s, undertook an examination and an evaluation of the economic, social, and spiritual deterioration of the decade (1945–1955) under Perón.

G.'s style during this period had gradually begun to incorporate a number of narrative techniques that could be ascribed to her intimate familiarity with cinematic devices, such as flashbacks and flashforwards and experiments in reproducing film's continuous present with almost exclusively present-tense verbs. These stylistic features culminate in her most original and ambitious novel, *Escándalos y soledades* (1970; scandals and solitudes).

G.'s subsequent work consists mainly of testimonials, reminiscences, personal essays, short fiction, and extensive interviews concerning her writing. The new democratic government in Argentina named her, now widowed, to a diplomatic post in Madrid, and it was there she died in 1988, tireless to the end in her pursuit of the appropriate images with which to convey a sense of her understanding of her life and times.

FURTHER WORKS: *Regreso a los hilos* (1947); *Estar en el mundo* (1950); *El único ojo de la ballena* (1971); *Una madre* (1973); *Los insomnes* (1974); *Piedra libre* (1976); *¿Quién le teme a mis temas?* (1977); *La invitación* (1979); *Apasionados* (1983); *Rojo sobre rojo* (1987)

BIBLIOGRAPHY: Yates, D. A., on *End of a Day, SatR* (4 June 1966): 53; Imbert, E. Anderson, *Spanish-American Literature*, 2nd ed. (1969), Vol. 2, 739; Orgambide, P. G., and Yahni, R., eds., *Enciclopedia de la literatura argentina* (1970): 305–6; Brushwood, J. S., *The Spanish American Novel* (1975), 192: 229–30

—DONALD A. YATES

GUILLÉN, Jorge

Spanish poet and critic, b. 18 Jan. 1893, Valladolid; d. 8 Feb. 1984, Málaga

After receiving his secondary education at the Institute of Valladolid, G. studied at the Maison Perreyve of the French Fathers of the Oratory in Fribourg, and at the universities of Madrid and Granada. In 1917 he began at the Sorbonne a long academic career that took him to Murcia, Oxford, Seville, Middlebury College in Vermont (after 1938, when he became a voluntary exile from war-torn Spain), McGill University in Montreal, and finally, Wellesley College in Massachusetts (1940–57). Since 1947 he has also been a visiting professor at various universities in North and South America, having delivered the Charles Eliot Norton Lectures in Poetry at

Harvard in 1957 and 1958. He received the first Cervantes Prize in 1976, the most important Hispanic literary prize, after being nominated for it by both Spanish and Argentine academies. He now lives in Málaga.

On his seventy-fifth birthday, the collected poems of G. up to that time were published as *Aire nuestro* (1968; our air). In this volume of 1700 pages the poetry written during forty-seven years is gathered into one carefully planned composition. *Aire nuestro* is made up of the following books published earlier: *Cántico: Fe de vida* (1928, 1936, 1945; 1st complete ed., 1950; canticle: certificate of life); the three-volume *Clamor: Tiempo de historia* (clamor: time of history)—Vol. I, *Maremágnum* (1957; pandemonium), Vol. II, . . . *Que van a dar en la mar* (1960; . . . that flow down to the sea), Vol. III, *A la altura de las circunstancias* (1963; rising to the occasion); and *Homenaje: Reunión de vidas* (1967; homage: a reunion of lives).

For many years G. was known as the author of one book, *Cántico*, which grew and was perfected from one edition to another. "It has an overall architectural design like Baudelaire's *Les fleurs du mal*, with a mathematically conceived order of Dantean severity" (Hugo Friedrich). "In Spanish poetry there is probably no creation more austere than *Cántico*, or any work more simple, dedicated to one single theme. . . . The composition of *Cántico* is that of a rose" (Joaquín Casalduero). What these critics say about *Cántico* can also be said about *Aire nuestro*, an even more amazing achievement of organic growth and architectural planning.

G. has inherited something of the dynamic fervor of Saint John of the Cross (1542–1591) and the classical clarity of Fray Luis de León (1527–1591). Yet G.'s *Cántico* is dedicated to the celebration of this world and its real wonders. As a matter of fact, the spiritual beyond is right here, according to "Más allá" ("Beyond," 1965), the opening poem in *Cántico*. Air is celebrated all through these poems as the giver of life, light, happiness. Air reveals to us what is real while being the perfect symbol of spirituality, even of eternity itself. G.'s technique owes much to the French poets from Baudelaire to VALÉRY, but he has infused their approach with a spirit all his own. In its *élan vital*, G.'s poetry has more affinities with Gerard Manley Hopkins and with Boris PASTERNAK than with the masters of French SYMBOLISM.

Because of G.'s highly concentrated style, one that is often even elliptical and that forgoes nonessentials, he may seem difficult. Brief questions, abrupt answers, ecstatic exclamations mark his style; nouns are given preference over verbs, and the present is the preferred tense. These features of G.'s poetry have led to charges of abstraction, intellectualism, and hermeticism by critics who were unable to penetrate the style to discover the meaning. G.'s form is as disciplined as his style. He moves with masterful assurance from *décimas* (stanzas of ten octosyllabic lines) to romances, from sonnets to poems in free verse, and summarizes his main themes in contrapuntally built longer poems such as "Más allá," "Anillo" ("Ring," 1965), and "Vida extrema" (extreme life), all in *Cántico*.

Cántico embodies G.'s vision in its most original form. It presents the reader with, in G.'s words, an "affirmation of being and living." Chance, chaos, evil, suffering, death are held in the background in order to voice more effectively G.'s "jubilant existentialism" (Eugenio Frutos), which celebrates the elemental life of childhood, youth, adulthood transfixed in an eternal present.

Cántico exhibits a spiritual discipline that does not surrender to anxiety, despair, or negation in contemplating reality in all its aspects. It strives for a vital equilibrium and hence does not overlook joy and hope as fundamentals of human existence. *Cántico* is one of the rare books of consolation in modern poetry. Yet there is nothing facile about G.'s luminous affirmation, which has to be wrested again and again from the encroaching shadows of absurdity, ever present and threatening.

The emergence of *Clamor* in no way annulled the faith in life proclaimed by G.'s *Cántico*. Many of the poems in *Clamor* are continuations of poems in *Cántico*. Thus, *Clamor* acts as a clarification of and a complement to *Cántico*, one in which the negative aspects of life are brought to the fore. G., now older, evinces a natural gift for the elegy. The "In Memoriam" of *Clamor* moves one as strongly by its restrained but intense evocation of lost love as one is moved by the cycle "Salvación de la primavera" ("A Springtime Salvation," 1965) in *Cántico*, which has been described as Spanish love poetry at its most ecstatic.

Clamor in general is immersed in time and the present age through references to places, autobiographical episodes, facts, and anecdotes. Satire, epigrams, narrative, and politically engaged poems, such as "Potencia de Pérez" ("The Powers of Pérez," 1979) are new departures in G.'s work. Almost a book within a book is formed by the many *tréboles*—the three-to-four-line "cloverleaves" that distill the themes of *Clamor* with haiku-like lyricism or nail them down with epigrammatic force.

Homenaje constitutes the cornerstone of the structure of *Aire nuestro*. New facets enter into G.'s poetry, while the main preoccupations of the previous two works are woven together. The central section of *Homenaje* is titled precisely "El centro" (the center) and contains the third great cycle of G.'s love poems, dedicated to his second wife, which reveals a Goethean ability to be renewed in love. This love poetry is deceptively simple, yet full of freely given love, of grace, and of human dignity.

In other poems in *Homenaje* G. looks back upon a lifetime of friendships with poets and years of reading and teaching literature. The section called "Al margen" (in the margin) is made up of poems of homage (or protest) written in response to various works—from Genesis to his own *Cántico*. "Atenciones" (attentions) are verse portraits of writers, among whom are Juan Ruiz (1283?–1350?) and G.'s friends Pedro SALINAS and GARCÍA LORCA. "Variaciones" (variations) is a section made up of translations/imitations from Tasso and Shakespeare to VALÉRY and YEATS.

Homenaje reflects not only G. the voracious reader but also the exile and traveler who literally made the world his home. France, Italy, Greece, Portugal, and North and South America are celebrated in occasional verse. Indeed, in this volume G. proves himself to be a major writer of minor poems, one who equals the artistry and wit of a Mallarmé in this demanding genre.

Y otros poemas (1973; rev. and expanded, 1979; and other poems) gathers verse from 1966–75 in a volume the size of one of the three preceding books of *Aire nuestro* and further enriches the three modes embodied in them. *Final* (1981) is the concluding book of the monumental design of *Aire nuestro*.

Although *Aire nuestro*, through a web of mottoes, references, and quotations, belongs at the heart of the Spanish literary tradition, it is just as aware of the great European poetry, past and present. Ingratitude does not mar G.'s generous humanism, nor does admiration for other poets handicap his originality. Perhaps only the poet who is completely assured of his own vision of the world can be so open to the achievement of others.

The richness of variations that makes up *Aire nuestro* springs from the one fundamental intuition that sees human life as a constant impulse toward form, as an appeal to human inventiveness to create and re-create order out of absurdity. It is not any extraordinary order that G. has in mind. The "energy of normality" that enables us to perceive the "minimal miracles" in everyday living, the only one we have, will do. A secular mystic, G. has realized in his *Aire nuestro* that *ars vivendi* for which he praises the city of Paris, because "ceaselessly inventing itself, it inheres in its being."

FURTHER WORKS: *La poética de Bécquer* (1943); *Federico en persona* (1959); *El argumento de la obra* (1961; "Introduction," in *Affirmation*, 1968); *Lenguaje y poesía* (1962; *Language and Poetry*, 1961); *En torno a Gabriel Miró* (1970); *Hacia "Cántico": Escritos de los años* 20 (1980). FURTHER WORKS IN ENGLISH: *Cántico: A Selection* (1965; undated ed., 1977); *Affirmation: A Bilingual Anthology 1919–1966* (1968); *G. on G.: The Poetry and the Poet* (1979)

BIBLIOGRAPHY: Pleak, F. A., *The Poetry of J. G.* (1942); Casalduero, J., *J. G.: Cántico* (1946; rev. and expanded eds., 1953, 1974); Gullón, R., and Blecua, J. M., *La poesía de J. G.* (1949); Darmangeat, P., *J. G.; ou, Le cantique émerveillé* (1958); Muela, J. G., *La realidad de J. G.* (1962); Ivask, I., and Marichal, J., eds., *Luminous Reality: The Poetry of J. G.* (1969); Dehennin, E., *Cántico de J. G.* (1969); Ciplijauskaité, B., *Deber de plenitud* (1973); Debicki, A. P., *La poesía de J. G.* (1973); Ruiz de Conde, J., *El "Cántico" americano de J. G.* (1974); Prat, I., *"Aire nuestro" de J. G.* (1974); Yudin, F. L., *The Vibrant Silence in J. G.'s "Aire nuestro"* (1974); Ciplijauskaité, B., *J. G.* (1975); Macrí, O., *La obra poética de J. G.* (1976); [Wellesley College], *Homenaje a J. G.* (1978); MacCurdy, G., *J. G.* (1982)

—IVAR IVASK

In spite of what some people said, and even still say today, regarding influences and preferences, it became sharply clear in this book [*Cántico*] that the poetry of J. G. was undoubtedly the most personal and highly individualized poetic statement that had ever been made by any Spanish poet. Regardless of the opinion of many critics, this was poetry which was sparklingly clear, optimistic and jubilant like the circumference of a circle drawn without lifting the hand—exultant, vivid and admirable. Some apparently found it difficult to understand its formal content. Not everyone understands the beauty of a circle when it is not formed by a compass but by a trembling hand which is able to trace it with complete perfection and with one stroke of the pen. This was not prefabricated poetry, as Juan Ramón [Jiménez] sarcastically suggested in his attack. It was poetry that grew directly from the objects it described in a dynamic ecstasy before the world; a transparent world in which even the shadows were clearly outlined and bathed in light. A poet who is eternally young, elastic and forever confident, G. has been nourished by his canticle which has continued to surge upward until today. From its zenith, it can capture better than any other Spanish poetry the realities of the earth and also the very special and terrible reality of Spain. [1959]

Rafael Alberti, *The Lost Grove* (1976), pp. 266–67

Such is the spectacle that G.'s poetry offers. From the outset, perfection is attained, and from the outset too, it is revealed. Here, there is therefore neither progress, nor opposition, nothing but the recording of objective splendor. From this point of view, G.'s poetry separates itself distinctly from the rest of European poetry. It does not begin from the interior but from the exterior. It places that which is, not in the central hollow of the consciousness, but in the peripheral manifestation of a tangible reality. Everything is there, and everything begins from there. It is nevertheless true that the exterior perfection of the being having been immediately verified, the poet runs the risk of having nothing left to say. Everything has been said once, and for all. But G.'s attitude is not to be confounded with that of the Eleatics. It is not satisfied to recognize the splendor of the external being. It seizes and describes its efficacy. Yes, without a doubt the being is that which is placed outside. It develops itself on all sides in curves which close in on themselves; but, in closing, these curves enclose the point at which their action converges. The perfection is not static. It is an organization of the cosmos directed toward a center. . . .

A singular relationship which seems to reverse the habitual direction of thought. What? Everything no longer springs forth from the interior? What? It is no longer *from the center* that life is born and is propagated? Coming from within the soul, as with Rilke, or from the divine center, as with Eliot, will not a whole series of rays or of eccentric circles issue forth and cover space? On the contrary, with G., it is concentrically that space is traversed and that the beneficent forces converge to pour out their influence on the object on which their rays finally meet and coincide. So G., counter to all the poetry preceding him, rediscovers not only the sense of ambient fecundity, of the cosmic generosity, but, also, by a corollary movement, the feeling of the receptivity, the happy humility of the being which finds itself overwhelmed by a luminous and dispensing nature. To the simple presentation of an objective center there is now substituted the revelation of a median consciousness. Not a flower, a tree, a town, but myself. Myself at the center of the world, I who receive all from the world.

Georges Poulet, *The Metamorphoses of the Circle* (1966), pp. 348–49

G. occupies a central place in modern Spanish poetry. It is central in a paradoxical way; his work is an island, yet at the same time it is the bridge uniting the survivors of Modernism and the Generation of '98 to the Generation of 1925. . . . He is the least intellectual poet of his generation, by which I do not mean that he is the least intelligent. Perhaps just the opposite: he exercises his intelligence in his poems, not outside them. Like all intelligence, his is critical; like all creative criticism, it is invisible: it is not in what he says but in how he says it and above all in what he does not say. Silence is part of language and an authentic poet is distinguished more by the temper of his silences than by the sonority of his words. G.'s intelligence is not speculative; it is knowledge in action, a sentient wisdom; a feeling for weight and heat, the color and meaning of words, not excluding the almost incorporeal monosyllable. . . . G.'s transparency reflects the world, and his word is perpetual will for embodiment. Seldom has the Castilian language achieved such corporeal and spiritual plenitude. Totality of the word. G. has been called the poet of being. That is precise, on the condition that being is conceived of, not as idea or essence, but as presence. In *Cántico* being actually *appears*. It is the world, the reality of this world. Multiple and unique presence, a thousand adorable or terrible appearances resolved into one powerful affirmation of pleasure. Joy is power, not dominion. It is the great Yes with which being celebrates itself and sings of itself. [1966]

> Octavio Paz, *The Siren and the Seashell* (1976), pp. 153, 155–57

J. G., who is beyond dispute the greatest living Spanish poet, seems at first sight to stand definitely outside the literary tradition of Spain. He never strives after local color as so many . . . of his countrymen do; he is not self-consciously Spanish. Gradually, one begins to realize that he harks back to a tradition that came before Gongorism or Euphuism, the Platonic tradition of Fray Luis. . . . Literature in our time is only too full of dark mazes and of harrowing involutions; the poems of J. G., though signally and splendidly modern, breathe a serenity and a tenderness that have something of the godlike about them. Precision and infinitude, as of music, are their constant gift to the reader.

> Jorge Luis Borges, in J. G., *Affirmation* (1968)

Although in "La salida" G. celebrated "the joyful accuracy of the sudden muscles of instinct," he never allowed his instinct or his senses to accelerate into a feverish pose or distort his vision of the universe as a compact and marvellously normal sphere encircling a man humbly grateful to be inside it. In *Cántico*, as G. himself has pointed out, there is "No fusion, no magic," only "the enrichment of him who lives by exalting his life." What *Cántico* offers is poise, control, harmony and a classic simplicity of form, feeling and diction. It is no accident that in describing G.'s poetry as precise, intact, sparse, incisive and balanced, one is using some of the words G. himself favoured as he tried constantly to achieve the aim expressed in the final dedication to the 1950 edition of *Cántico*: "to consummate the fullness of being in the faithful fullness of words." The timeless dignity and measured eloquence of his tribute to the gift of life make *Cántico* transcend the age in which it was written.

> C. B. Morris, *A Generation of Spanish Poets 1920–1936* (1969), p. 142

The tone of serene contemplation in many of G.'s poems results, in fact, from the effort of achieving a vital contact and integration with the world, a sometimes hard-won meshing of observer and observed. G.'s restrained fervor is never passive, for his work as a whole pursues a difficult goal: to embrace and comprehend all human activity.

. . . We do not have to look far for analogues in other languages and other eras. Whether it be Coleridge's concrete universal, Eliot's objective correlative, or William Carlos Williams' mere things, this sense of poetry is not unfamiliar. The rigorous intellectual attention that G. brings to sensual experience, however, distinguishes him among modern poets. To some small degree it is the Spanish literary tradition that allows him to unite the humble table and the abstract notion of "reality" so gracefully and so immediately; but by the same token, the Anglo-American literary tradition may hinder the English-speaker's appreciation of G.'s dexterity and seriousness in doing this.

Thus we do well to look to the formal texture of G.'s poetry for the sense of physical presence which is so vital and impressive in his work. G.'s mastery of exacting metrical forms, predominant especially in his early work, and his acute sense of formal effects at the most minute level of sound and sense, dignify those commonplace things and events that hold for him the values of vitality and coherence. He perceives experience as a kind of radiance of these values, and fixes them in poems whose metrical and musical shape expresses a contained ecstasy. If the phrase seems a paradox, let it then suggest the tension between the form and matter characteristic of many poems in *Aire nuestro*.

. . . He uses metaphor not to mystify the reader, ;but rather to assess the just proportions of precise observation. Though often a poet of things, he is also interested explicitly in ideas and emotions. His metaphors, then, frequently yoke not two disparate objects, but a level of emotional intensity with an essential perception. . . . In some of his later poetry G. can very nearly dispense with metaphor entirely.

> Reginald Gibbons and Anthony L. Geist, trs., Preface to *G on G: The Poetry and the Poet* (1979), pp. 6–9

GUILLÉN, Nicolás

Cuban poet, b. 10 July 1902, Camagüey; d. 16 July 1989, Havana

G., a mulatto, used NEGRITUDE and left-wing ideology to forge a distinctive poetry that is a blend of AFRO-CUBANISM and social consciousness. His early verse was in the romantic-modernist vein, but he first came to the attention of the poetic world with *Motivos de son* (1930; *son* [a Cuban dance] motifs), eight poems based on an Afro-Cuban dance form and filled with primitive rhythms, dialect, humor, and black sensuality.

In *Sóngoro Cosongo* (1931; Sóngoro Cosongo), whose title comes from a verse in *Motivos de son*, G. stresses the mulatto

aspects of Cuba. Continuing his series of satirical Cuban caricatures, he portrays the pimp, the street vendor, the boxer, and so
forth, in verse imbued with black music and sensuality; but he also
portrays black tragedy and superstition. In his first two volumes,
then, he created a magical, ironic atmosphere and interpreted both
the joys and sorrows of his compatriots.

In his next collection, *West Indies Ltd.* (1934; title in English),
G. intensified his portrait of the black as a social victim, although
he did not completely abandon his folkloric vision of the world.
Here he explores relationships between the races and in revolutionary terms attacks the political situation and the exploitation of all
Cubans. As he expresses his hatred, pain, and outrage at U.S.
imperialism in ironic, sarcastic, and even violent imagery, at the
same time he engages in a revolutionary search for human identity.
In this and later collections he tries to destroy, in his petrified
society, the very stereotypes that he had previously helped create
by concentrating on Cubans as social beings exploited by
foreign capitalism.

In the antimilitaristic *Cantos para soldados y sones para
turistas* (1937; songs for soldiers and dances for tourists) G. sees
the soldier as a pawn of imperialistic forces, one victim among
many. He contrasts the poverty of blacks with the wealth of
American tourists, whose gambling, drunkenness, and sexuality
he mocks.

Having been exiled and having suffered because of his political
beliefs, G. produced his most virulent social poetry in *La paloma de
vuelo popular* (1958; the dove of popular flight) whose themes
include prison, slavery, racism, the integration troubles in Little
Rock, Arkansas, the activities of Senator Joseph McCarthy, and
proletarian solidarity.

In his *Elegías* (1958; elegies), some of which have an epic
quality, G. recalls his youth in Camagüey and writes of his Cuban
heritage and of actual victims of racism. He employs striking color
imagery to add intensity to his human sentiment and search
for idealism.

Tengo (1964; *Tengo*, 1974) celebrates his pride at the triumph
of the Castro revolution. Along with themes of national independence, revolutionary passion, and hatred of the past, he includes a
note of tenderness for his country and people.

In *El gran zoo* (1967; *Patria o Muerte!: The Great Zoo, and
Other Poems*, 1972) G. softens propaganda about exploitation and
racial prejudice to produce an antirhetorical, playful, and almost
whimsical symbolic tour of a stylized Cuban zoo. A kind of fable of
human behavior as seen through the eyes of animals, from crabs to
tigers, the collection stresses lighthearted fantasy.

G., perhaps Cuba's greatest living poet, whatever his political
proclivities, has attempted to serve his artistic conscience. Master
of avant-garde techniques and startling imagery, he tempers them
with a simplicity that furthers his political passions and social
purposes as he identifies his black and Cuban roots.

FURTHER WORKS: *Cerebro y corazón* (1922); *España: Poema en
cuatro angustias y una esperanza* (1937); *El son entero: Suma
poética* (1947; partial tr.: *Cuba Libre*, 1948); *Balada* (1962);
Antología mayor (1964); *Poemas de amor* (1964); *La rueda
dentada* (1972); *El diario que a diario* (1972); *Prosa de prisa* (3
vols., 1975); *El corazón que vive* (1975); *Poemas manuables*
(1975); *Antología mayor* (1978). FURTHER WORKS IN ENGLISH:
Selected Poems (1946); *Man-Making Words: Selected Poems*
(1972)

BIBLIOGRAPHY: Augier, A., *G.: Notas para un estudio biográfico
crítico* (1965); Cartey, W. G., *Three Antillean Poets: Emilio
Ballagas, Luis Palés Matos, and N. G.* (1965); Tous, A., *La poesía
de N. G.* (1971); Márquez, R., Introduction to *patria o Muerte!: The
Great Zoo, and Other Poems* (1972): 1–29; Bario, C. Sparrow de
García, *The Black in Cuban Literature and the Poetry of N. G.*
(1975); Davis, S., *Development of Poetic Techniques in the Works
of N. G.* (1977); Johnson, H., "N. G.'s Portraits of Blacks in Cuban
Society," in Chang-Rodríguez, R., and Yates, D. A., eds., *Homage
to Irving A. Leonard: Essays on Hispanic Art, History and Literature* (1977): 197–207; special G. issue, *Callaloo*, 10 (Spring 1987)

—KESSEL SCHWARTZ

GUILLOUX, Louis

French novelist and essayist, b. 15 Jan. 1899, Saint-Brieuc

Born in Brittany, the son of a cobbler, G. studied philosophy
and also medicine before starting out as a journalist. His first novel,
La maison du peuple (1927; the house of the people), shows him as
a keen, yet warmhearted observer, capable of evoking human
drama against the background of social struggle. A sense of
mystery pervades the clipped and powerful prose of *Dossier
confidentiel* (1928; confidential file), the narrative of the boyhood
and slow but determined self-assertion of a lonely individual.

His most accomplished work, *Le sang noir* (1935; rev. ed. 1964;
Bitter Victory, 1936) is rated one of the great French novels of this
century, along with MALRAUX's *Man's Fate* and SARTRE's *Nausea*. It is the story of a philosophy teacher at a lycée in western
France whom his students derisively called "Cripure"—a pun on
his pet subject, Kant's *Critique of Pure Reason*—who has failed
dismally, intellectually and also in life. He is "stuck" with a woman
well beneath his station; he braves society on her account but is
spineless on more important, ethical matters concerning his students' lives. The novel portrays the atmosphere of a town in France
during World War I, with its smug, conformist society. There are
glimpses of human passion, of genuine and of mock devotion to
causes, and of monsters engendered by the hero's imagination—to
wit, the famous theme of the "cloporte" (inadequately translatable
as "wood louse," because it is quite akin to KAFKA's unhappy
creature in *Metamorphosis*). Cripure is duty-bound to shoulder
responsibilities toward his young charges that are more than merely
educational; he must advise them in an exceptionally critical time.
At times ruthless when asked what a young man should do about
his obligations in wartime, he is nevertheless torn between an easy
answer—"Go and fight"—and his deeper understanding of the
situation, which has made him a pacifist. When it comes to
speaking up against the draft, he throws up his arms in despair. G.
adapted the plot of the novel as a play, *Cripure* (1962), maintaining
the essential preoccupation with ideals betrayed through everyday
compromise, and putting the monsters into a ballet.

Le pain des rêves (1942; the bread of dreams) deals with the
hardships of a family poor in worldly goods but rich in perception
and affection. *Le jeu de patience* (1949; the jigsaw puzzle) is a vast
panorama of G.'s hometown as it goes through the two worlds wars
and many social upheavals. Again G. sketches a gripping indictment of social injustices, enlivened by the colorful portrayal of
Frenchmen of all classes and numerous waves of refugees from all
parts of Europe. The title is amply justified by the clever use of

flashbacks and of glimpses into the future, yet the frequent shifting from one set of historical and political circumstances to another never becomes confusing.

Les batailles perdues (1960; lost battles), perhaps G.'s most ambitious endeavor, is disappointing in its verbose and sometimes repetitious development of characters. *La confrontation* (1967; the confrontation) is noteworthy, however, for its complete change of pace and style. Even though it uses techniques decidedly unoriginal, strongly reminiscent of CAMUS's *The Fall*, it achieves an artistic success of sorts by deemphasizing plot to the benefit of a dreamlike vision. While the novel's mystery—which involves the search for an elusive heir to a treasure—is never completely solved, the quest is worthwhile because its results in the discovery of the self for several of the characters. The almost compulsive soliloquy of the narrator, less tortuous but also less compelling than in Camus's book, leads to a liberation of the individual that opens vistas of universal happiness through contemplation.

G. has also distinguished himself as a translator and, lately, as an essayist on literary and artistic subjects. His stature is growing, although few of his works have yet been translated.

FURTHER WORKS: *Compagnons* (1930); *Hyménée* (1932); *Le lecteur écrit* (1933); *Angelina* (1934; new ed., 1950); *Histoires de brigands* (1936); *Souvenirs sur Georges Palante* (1939); *Absent de Paris* (1952); *Parpagnacco; ou, La conjuration* (1954); *Le muet mélodieux* (1957); *Merveilles des Châteaux de Bretagne et de Vendée* (1970; with Claude Fregnac); *Salido* (1976, with O. Joël); *Carnets 1921–1944* (1978)

BIBLIOGRAPHY: "Interview avec L. G.," *NL*, 17 Dec. 1935: 1; Clark, E., "Death of a Thinker: A Note on the French Novel, 1925–1940," *KR*, 3 (1941): 322–34; "The World of L. G.," *TLS*, 26 March 1954: xii; Brombert, V., *The Intellectual Hero: Studies in the French Novel, 1886–1955* (1961): 119–33; Braudeau, M., "L.G., témoin discret," *L'express*, 4 Nov. 1978: 28–29

—KONRAD BIEBER

GUIMARÃES ROSA, João

See Rosa, João Guimarãs

GUINEA-BISSAU LITERATURE

The tiny west African country of Guinea-Bissau lags far behind other Portuguese-speaking African nations in imaginative writing. In colonial times the small enclave was little more than a neglected trading outpost of the far-flung Portuguese empire. The absence of anything approaching the indigenous bourgeoisie that in other lusophone African colonies gave rise to small but significant elites of black and mixed-race intellectuals explains why little Portuguese-language and creole writing emerged in preindependence Guinea-Bissau.

Not to be discounted, of course, is the rich oral expression in indigenous languages and in the region's Portuguese-based creole. But what little Portuguese-language writing did appear in colonial times was chiefly quasi-ethnographic and mainly produced by Europeans and Cape Verdeans.

In 1974 Guinea-Bissau gained its hard-fought independence amidst a surge of cultural and literary activity. A prime mover was Mário de Andrade (1928-1990), a distinguished Angolan intellectual and writer who was eventually appointed Guinea-Bissau's Minister of Culture. Andrade played an important role in the publication of *Mantenhas para quem luta!* (1977; hail to those who struggle!), a landmark anthology of poems in Portuguese by fourteen Guineans, most in their twenties. This historically important collection was followed by *Antologia dos jovens poetas* (1978; the young poets' anthology), comprising thirty-eight poems, almost equally divided between those in Portuguese and those in creole.

With independence, the creole lingua franca came to play a major role in literacy campaigns and primary education. Moreover, a project aimed at collecting creole oral traditions resulted in *'N sta li 'n sta la* (1979; I'm everywhere) and *Junbai* (1979; togetherness), both attractively illustrated, bilingual (Portuguese/creole) collections of traditional riddles and stories.

In November of 1980 the cultural-literary impetus suffered a setback when the government was overthrown. The cultural leadership of Andrade ended, and several promising writers fled into exile.

The publication of *Antologia poética da Guiné-Bissau* (1990; Anthology of Poetry of Guinea-Bissau) ushered in a decade of considerable literary activity and productivity. Foremost among several coordinated efforts was the founding, in 1994, of GREC (the Portuguese acronym for Cultural Expression Group), an initiative of young Guinean writers, artists, and researchers. In that same year, GREC published the first issue of *Tcholona* (a creole term meaning, roughly, "heralding a new beginning"), the group's journal of "letters, art, and culture."

Another important literary event was the publication of *A escola* (1993; The School), a collection of three short stories. Not only is *A escola* the first postcolonial work of Guinean prose fiction, but the author, Domingas Samy (b. 1955), is the first native-born Guinean woman to publish a book of short stories in Portuguese.

Yet another historic event was the publication, in 1994, of *Eterna paixão* (Everlasting Passion) by Abdulai Sila (b. 1958). This work has the distinction of being the first novel by a native-born Guinean ever to appear in print. In the late 1970s, while a student in the former East Germany, Sila wrote *A última tragédia* (1995; The Ultimate Tragedy), Guinea-Bissau's second novel to appear in print. *Mistida* (1996; a creole term meaning "taking care of business"), Sila's third published novel, was launched in Bissau as part of a two-week long celebration of Guinean culture. *Ku Si Mon*, Guinea-Bissau's first privately-owned publishing house, co-sponsored the two-week festival.

Abdulai Sila is the editor of *Ku Si Mon*, which he, along with two associates, founded and whose name derives from the first syllable of each of the three partners' surnames (i.e., Kudawo, Sila, Montenegro). Moreover, in keeping with Sila's and his associates' entrepreneurial spirit, *Ku Si Mon* is a creole phrase meaning "with their own hands." By 1996 *Ku Si Mon* had issued ten titles, including Sila's three novels.

In the capital city of Bissau literary activities did indeed begin to flourish in the 1990s, as evidenced by the establishment of a literary series called the *Kebur* (creole for "harvest") Collection as part of the publications of the National Institute for Study and Research (INEP), which previously had issued only non-fiction works about Guinea-Bissau. Among the inaugural publications in the literary series is *Kebur: Barkafon di poesia na kriol* (1996; Harvest: An Anthology of Poetry in Creole), in which appears the work of thirteen poets. This anthology, as well as *Entre o ser e o amar* (1996; Between Being and Loving), a bilingual (creole-Portuguese) collection of poems by Odete Costa Semedo (b. 1959), suggest that Guinea-Bissau's vernacular is becoming an accepted language of literary expression.

By the mid-1990s, Tony Tcheka, pen name of António Soares Lopes Júnior (b. 1951), had become one of Guinea-Bissau's most distinguished writers of "art" poetry in both creole and Portuguese. Tcheka's *Noites de insónia na terra adormecida* (1996; Sleepless Nights in the Slumbering Land) also appeared as one of the first *Kebur* collection publications.

As literature and the arts, including music, painting, and sculpture, flourished in Guinea-Bissau in the 1990s, a home-grown literary and cultural criticism emerged. This criticism, much of which appears in the pages of the aforementioned *Tcholona*, helps validate what can be termed a cultural renaissance in that small West African nation.

BIBLIOGRAPHY: Bull, B. P., *Le Créole de la Guiné-Bissau* (1975); Hamilton, R. G., *Voices from an Empire: A History of Afro-Portuguese Literature* (1975): 358–62; Moser, G. M., on *'N sta li 'n sta la, RAL,* 11 (1980): 402–3; Hamilton, R. G., "Portuguese-Language Literature," in Owomoyela, O., ed., *A History of Twenti-eth-Century African Literatures* (1993): 240-84

—RUSSELL G. HAMILTON

GUINEAN LITERATURE

Although Guinea, which achieved independence from France in 1958, consists of twenty-four ethnic groups, three predominate: the Malinké in Upper Guinea, the Peul in Middle Guinea, the Soussou in Lower Guinea. With this mosaic of ethnic diversity, Guinea acknowledges eight national languages: Poular, Soussou, Malinké, Kissi, Guerzé, Coniagui, Toma, and Bassari. A program initiated in 1962 encourages Guineans to learn to read and write in their national tongues, using a modified Latin alphabet for transcribing their oral languages. Devoutly Muslim, the Peuls have used Arabic script to translate the Koran into Poular and to write religious poetry and prose. French, the legacy of colonialism, is the tool of communication for all administrative, commercial, and technical tasks, and, as the lingua franca of educated Guineans, is the official language. Yet it is understood by barely one fifth of the population.

The first modern Guinean literary works appeared in the 1950s, all of them in French, with the exception of the writings of Modupe Paris (b. 1901), a Guinean who studied in the U.S. and published his autobiography, *I Was a Savage* (1957), in English.

Guinean literature bears the stamp of history, both modern and traditional. Mamadou Traoré's (b. 1916) *Vers la liberté* (1961; toward liberty) and Sadan-Moussa Touré's (b. 1932) *Les premières guinéades: Contres, légendes de chez nous* (1961; the first Guineads: stories, legends of our homeland) celebrate Guinean independence in verse. Condetto Nenekhaly-Camara's (1930–1972) two plays, *Continent-Afrique* (African continent) and *Amazoulou* (Amazulu), published in one volume in 1970, present historical figures; the first play portrays Antar, a 6th-c. Arab warrior, and the second, Chaka, the 19th-c. Zulu king. Alpha Sow (b. 1935) has published an

anthology of Peul folklore, *Chroniques et récits du Fouta Djalon* (1968; chronicles and tales of the Fouta Djallon mountains).

The Guinean literary scene has been largely dominated by Camara LAYE, whose first novel, *L'enfant noir* (1953; *The Dark Child,* 1954), was awarded the Charles Veillon Prize in 1954 and brought international recognition to its author. This work, profoundly poetic, recounts the life of a boy growing up in an African village, learning about his ancestors, appreciating his father's skills as a goldsmith. Camara's next novel, *Le regard du roi* (1954; *The Radiance of the King,* 1956), highly symbolic, presents a French protagonist unequipped for life in black Africa. Political difficulties with President Sekou Touré sent Camara into exile from 1965 until his death in 1980, first to Ivory Coast, then to Senegal, an exile made all the more painful when Sekou Touré detained Camara's wife in Guinea for several years. After leaving Guinea, Camara published *Dramouss* (1966; *A Dream of Africa,* 1968), a novel highly critical of Guinea's present political regime. Shortly before his death, he published an ethnographic work, *Le maître de la parole* (1978; the wordmaster), a transcription in French of the Malinké epic recounting the legend of Soundiata.

Djibril Tamsir Niane (b. 1932) had also published a version of this epic, entitled *Soudjata; ou, L'épopée mandingue* (1960; *Sundiata: An Epic of Old Mali,* 1965), in which he relates the tales of the crippled boy who grew up to rule the Mali empire (1230–55). Although the two versions are similar, Niane and Camara had based their work upon the accounts of different *griots,* or Malinké oral historians. In his introduction, Niane defines the role of the griot: "In the very hierarchical society of Africa before colonization, where everyone found his place, the griot appears as one of the most important men in this society, because it is he who, for want of archives, records the customs, traditions, and governmental principles of kings." Niane, who has griot ancestors, has also collaborated with the French historian Jean Suret-Canale (b. 1921) on an illustrated history of West Africa, *Histoire de l'Afrique occidentale* (1960; history of West Africa), and written two plays, *Sikasso* (1971; Sikasso) and *Chaka* (1971; Chaka), both with historical subjects.

As interested in Malinké history and tradition as Niane, but choosing a different vehicle of expression, Fodéba Keita (1921–1969), also of griot background, has composed music, poetry, and dance based on traditional sources. Keita's Ballets Africains, the Guinean national dance troupe, toured the globe in the early 1960s. After serving in the government from 1968 to 1971, Keita was imprisoned and disappeared. He is presumed dead.

One can only hope that Guineans in the future will have greater freedom of expression—both artistic and political—than they do at present, and that their rich oral tradition will continue to provide inspiration. It is unfortunate that talented artists such as Camara and Keita fell victim to repression. It is everyone's loss that their talents were not nurtured in their homeland.

BIBLIOGRAPHY: Gleason, J., *This Africa: Novels by West Africans in English and French* (1965); Brench, A. C., *The Novelists' Inheritance in French Africa: Writers from Senegal to Cameroon* (1967); Larson, C., *The Emergence of African Fiction* (1972); Olney, J., *Tell Me Africa: An Approach to African Literature* (1973); Blair, D., S., *African Literature in French* (1976); Cook, D., *African Literature: A Critical View* (1977); Owomoyela, O., *African Literatures: An Introduction* (1979)

—MILDRED MORTIMER

GÜIRALDES, Ricardo

Argentine novelist, short-story writer, and poet, b. 13 Feb. 1886, Buenos Aires; d. 8 Oct. 1927, Paris, France

G. belonged to a wealthy family of landowners, and was thus acquainted with Argentine country life. In Paris, which he visited many times and where he died, he became acquainted with avant-garde writers, who had a decisive influence on his literary career. In Buenos Aires and in Montevideo, Uruguay, he was befriended by postmodernist Latin American poets: Conrado Nalé Roxlo (b. 1898), Raúl González Tuñón (b. 1905), Leopoldo Marechal, and Jorge Luis BORGES.

G.'s first work, the collection of poems *El cencerro de cristal* (1915; the crystal bell), placed him at the forefront of avant-garde writers in Latin America. The same year he published a book of short stories, *Cuentos de muerte y de sangre* (1915; tales of blood and death), basically romantic. Although outright failures with the reading public, both works showed G. to be a master of language. *Raucho* (1917; Raucho), a semiautobiographical novel, followed and then *Rosaura* (1922; Rosaura) and *Xaimaca* (1923; Xaimaca). The latter two works, sentimental and melancholy, also showed G. as an innovator in language, since he experimented constantly with the techniques initiated by the postmodernist and by the European and Spanish American avant-garde movements. In 1923, with Jorge Luis Borges and Pablo Rojas (1896–1956), G. founded the review *Proa*, which encouraged the presentation of themes drawn from Argentine life but expressed by means of "all the technical discoveries of postwar Paris." But G. soon retired to his estate to write a novel he had begun to conceive around 1919. This was *Don Segundo Sombra* (1926; *Don Segundo Sombra: Shadows on the Pampas*, 1935), his last work.

As is the case with many Spanish American writers, G.'s fame rests on a single work. *Don Segundo Sombra* brought its author instant success. It tells the story of an orphan who follows Don Segundo Sombra, an old gaucho, who initiates him into the life of the roaming cowboys of the pampas at the time of their imminent disappearance, since progress was destroying their precious freedom and forcing them to become farmhands. The novel is, then, the portrait of a virile frontier life about to recede into the past, and the scenes it contains thus have the feeling of a fond farewell: encounters at a country store, dances, folkloric tales, cock fights, long herding cavalcades, stampedes, and knife duels. G.'s style, polished to perfection, is a harmonious blend of avant-garde metaphoric elegance and gaucho popular language. The novel can be classified as a *Bildungsroman* describing the upbringing of a lad under the guidance of a wise elder; it has been said that it reveals the influence of Cervantes's *Don Quixote*, Mark TWAIN's *Adventures of Huckleberry Finn*, and Rudyard KIPLING's *Kim*.

The genesis of this novel must ultimately be found in Domingo Faustino Sarmiento's (1811–1888) essay *Facundo: Civilization and Barbarism* (1845), in which the gaucho, the savage master of the plains, is portrayed in his hour of triumph. A sequel to the biography of the pampas is José Hernández's (1834–1886) *Martín Fierro* (1872, 1879), the Argentine epic poem that describes the gaucho when, defeated by progress, he has to submit to assimilating to a life on the farms or in the cities. The freedom-loving cowboy thus dies, and G.'s novel met the need to portray this type when he was becoming nothing but a mere shadow of an epic past. But *Don Segundo Sombra* is a quite complex novel, since it also afforded a glimpse into the future. G. published it when Latin Americans had begun the quest for their identity. And *Don Segundo Sombra* made clear that a firm identity rested only on the bonds between man and the land. This novel thus buries the world of a breed of men who had had such an identity and foreshadows the advent of another, the world of the alienated man of today.

FURTHER WORKS: *Poemas místicos* (1928); *Poemas solitarios* (1921–27); *Seis relatos* (1929); *Pampa: Poemas inéditos* (1954) *Sonat* (1929)

BIBLIOGRAPHY: Chapman, A. G., "Pampas and Big Woods: Heroic Initiation in G. and Faulkner," *CL*, 11 (1959): 61–77; Weiss, G. H., "Technique in the Works of R. G.," *Hispania*, 43 (1960): 353–58; Previtali, G., *R. G. and "Don Segundo Sombra": Life and Works* (1963); Ghiano, J. C., *Introducción a R. G.*(1967); Beardsell, P. R., "French Influences on G.," *BHS*, 46 (1968): 511–44; Saz, S. M. de, "G. and Rudyard Kipling," *Neophil*, 55 (1971): 270–84; Echevarría, E., "Nuevo acercamiento a la estructura de *Don Segundo Sombra*," *RI*, 40 (1974): 629–37; Alonso, C. J., *The Spanish American Regional Novel* (1990)

—LARS G. WARME

GUJARATI LITERATURE

See Indian Literature

GULLBERG, Hjalmar

Swedish poet, b. 30 May 1898, Malmö; d. 19 July 1961, Bökebergsslätt

G., born out of wedlock, was left by his mother in the care of foster parents, whose name he adopted. In 1927 he received an advanced degree in literature from the University of Lund, which awarded him an honorary doctorate in 1944. From 1936 on G. was program director for drama of the Swedish National Broadcasting Corporation. In 1940 he became a member of the Swedish Academy.

In his very first collection of poetry, *I en främmande stad* (1927; in a strange city), G. displayed a very personal style, which harked back to the high-spirited, witty rhymings of his student days. He borrowed his means of expression from a variety of sources ranging from religious hymns to contemporary journalistic jargon and gave his poems an elegant, at times flippant form through unconventional rhymes, deliberate anachronisms, and startling contrasts by mingling the sublime and the trivial. Although aware of the danger of this style's becoming a mannerism, G. never completely abandoned his fondness for ironic juxtapositions in form and content. Behind his attitude of a detached and skeptical observer and a cosmopolitan tourist in life, G. expressed religious and metaphysical concerns and a sense of his poetic calling. *Andliga övningar* (1932; spiritual exercises) and *Att övervinna världen* (1937; to conquer the world) abound in Christian symbols, from Bethlehem to Golgotha, and show a leaning toward mysticism and a wish to escape from the world in self-effacement and death.

In *Kärlek i tjugonde seklet* (1933; love in the twentieth century) G. caught the modern erotic sensibility in a series of love poems in which a sober medical or psychoanalytical terminology alternates with expressions of sensuous exultation, melancholy reflections on partings, and bitter regrets.

The previously mentioned *Att övervinna världen*, as well as *Fem kornbröd och två fiskar* (1942; five loaves and two fishes) show an increased awareness of the political situation in Europe. G., who had been staying in Berlin at the time of Hitler's takeover, displays an unremitting opposition to the fascist ideologies of violence.

After an unproductive period during the 1940s G. returned with *Dödsmask och lustgård* (1952; death mask and garden of delights). G.'s fascination with ancient Greece and his familiarity with its myths and literature (as a translator he brought a number of classical Greek dramas to the Swedish public) had always been evident in his poetry. In contrast to the earlier sun-drenched Apollonian visions of Hellas, the later collections emphasize the dark, tragic aspects of Greek antiquity, and the figures of Dionysus, Orpheus, and Christ merge into one embodiment of the timeless sufferings of man and his gods.

G.'s last collection of poetry, *Ögon, läppar* (1959; eyes, lips), marks a high point in his production. Written during his agonizingly protracted illness, the poems are whittled down to a naked simplicity and stripped of illusions in the face of death. The collection contains some of G.'s most moving love poems dedicated to the woman who had been his companion during his last years.

Except for some early experimentations in free verse, G. remained within the discipline of established verse forms. His poetry derives its strength from the tensions between a modern skeptical sensibility, a classical traditionalism, and a yearning for religious commitment.

FURTHER WORKS: *Sonat* (1929); *Ensamstående bildad herre* (1935); *Terziner i okonstens tid* (1958). **FURTHER WORKS IN ENGLISH:** *"Gentleman, Single, Refined,"* and *Selected Poems, 1937–1959* (1979)

BIBLIOGRAPHY: Vowles, R. B., "H. G., An Ancient and a Modern," *SS*, 24 (1952): 111–18; Sjöberg, L., Foreword to *"Gentleman, Single, Refined,"* and *Selected Poems, 1937–1959* (1979): xi–xvii

—LARS G. WARME

GUMILYOV, Nikolay Stepanovich

Russian poet, literary theorist, and dramatist, b. 3 April 1886, Krostadt (now Kronshlot); d. Aug. 1921, Petrograd? (now St. Petersburg)

G.'s father was a doctor in the Russian navy. G. was educated at the Imperial Lyceum at Tsarskoe Selo (now Pushkin) and in St. Petersburg. While at school he met the future poet Anna AKHMATOVA, whom he married in 1910. After finishing secondary school in Russia, he enrolled at the Sorbonne in 1906 or 1907. In 1907 G. made his first of several trips to Africa. The subject of Africa was to remain important throughout his creative work.

Before the revolution G. played a central role in the literary life of St. Petersburg as one of the chief theorists and proponents of the Acmeist school of poetry. During the first years of World War I G. saw action in Prussia and Poland. Between the March and October 1917 revolutions he traveled as a lieutenant to Paris, where he

stayed for six months, then went to London for three months. He returned to Petrograd in May 1918.

On August 3, 1921, G. was arrested by the Petrograd Secret Police for alleged involvement in a counter revolutionary conspiracy. His execution was announced on September 1, 1921, about one week after it had taken place. His burial place remains unknown.

G.'s first three books of poems—*Put konkvistadorov* (1905; path of the conquistadors), *Romanticheskie tsvety* (1908; romantic flowers), and *Zhemchuga* (1910; pearls)—contain, at least in germinal form, all the major themes that were to occupy G.'s more mature work: the search for an ideal love, the conflict between earthly passion and spirituality, the theme of adventure, including wandering, conquest, and battle. All three books were written under the heavy influence of the major writers of Russian Decadence, Bryusov, Bely, and Balmont. They have been criticized for their overabundance of exotic colors, decorative imagery, and bombastic tone.

Chuzhoe nebo (1912; foreign skies) marked the end of G.'s apprenticeship to Bryusov and the other Decadents. It was the culmination of his participation in the Poets' Guild and the Acmeist school. The tenets of Acmeism included balance, precision, clarity, craftsmanship, respect for tradition, and restraint. The movement opposed the dominant though declining school of Russian SYMBOLISM, an opposition articulated by G. and Sergey Mitrofanovich Gorodetsky (1884–1967) in articles about the nature of the word in poetry. Acmeism did not deny the appropriateness of spiritual themes for poetry. It defended, however, the place of *this* world, with its own colors, forms, weight, and time, in modern poetry. It argued for the direct, clear, referential properties of language.

With its almost complete lack of fantasy, with its more direct expression of personal lyricism, with its simple and more straightforward style, *Chuzhoe nebo* is G.'s most Acmeist work. It is significant that G. included five of his translations of Théophile Gautier in this book of poems. That spiritual themes are not excluded from the Acmeist canon is demonstrated by the central place religious impulses occupy in this book. Yet even here the accent is on earthly experience and the poet's struggle to reconcile his quest for spiritual purity with his belief in the transcendent value of intense physical experience.

Kolchan (1916; the quiver) and *Shatyor* (1921; the tent) develop a tendency in G.'s work toward a more strongly expressed subjective artistic personality. The themes of love, battle, exotic travels, and religion, all important in *Kolchan*, are found in its central autobiographical poem "Pyatistopnye yamby" (1913; iambic pentameters). G.'s attraction to Africa, expressed in *Shatyor*, complements his own deeply felt attraction to extreme situations that tested and provoked elemental human drives: poetry, war, kingly rule, and erotic passions.

G.'s last two books, *Kostyor* (1918; the pyre) and *Ognenny stolp* (1921; the fiery pillar), are concerned with the fantastic, with the ineffable, and with ideal love. They are, in a sense, a return to the metaphysical concerns of symbolism. The romantic conception of love as a link between the earthly and the ideal runs throughout G.'s work, but it becomes central to the love lyrics of *Kostyor*. The experience of love becomes a way of access to the world of the ideal, but the beloved remains the remote "blue star," a shadowy female presence, always ultimately unattainable, always the source of erotic frustration.

The appearance of Russia as a theme is connected with the increasing interpenetration of the lyrical world of the poet with the world around him. This process reaches a climax in two fantastic poems from his last books: "Muzhik" ("The Muzhik," 1972) in *Kostyor* and "Zabludivshysya tramvay" ("The Lost Tram," 1972) in *Ognenny stolp.* "Muzhik" is a vision of half-pagan peasants marching out of primeval Russian bogs and forests against an alien urban civilization imposed by St. Petersburg. "Zabludivshysya tramvay" concerns itself with the fate of Russia and the Orthodox religion and with the poet's own personal concern for his love.

G. also wrote six dramatic works, three of them little more than one-act sketches. Only *Otravlennaya tunika* (written 1917–18, pub. 1952; *The Poisoned Tunic*, 1972), a tragedy, can be considered a true, full-length play, and it stands comparison with his better lyric and narrative poetry.

G.'s work occupies a significant place in the history of modern Russian poetry. Although he has never been extensively published in Soviet Russia, he continues to be a significant presence for Russian poets both within the U.S.S.R. and in the emigration.

FURTHER WORKS: *Akteon* (1913); *Gondla* (1917); *Ditya Allakha* (1917); *Farforovy pavilon* (1918); *Mik: Afrikanskaya poema* (1918); *Ten ot palmy* (1922); *Pisma o russkoy poezii* (1923); *Sobranie sochineny* (4 vols., 1962–68). FURTHER WORKS IN ENGLISH: *The Abinger Garland* (1945); *Selected Works* (1972); *N. G. on Russian Poetry* (1977)

BIBLIOGRAPHY: Strakhovsky, L., *Three Poets of Modern Russia* (1949): 5–52; Maline, M., *N. G., poète et critique acméiste* (1964); Monas, S., "G.: Âkme and Adam in St. Petersburg," in *N. G., Selected Works* (1972): 3–26; Sampson, E. D., *N. G.* (1979)

—GERALD PIROG

GUNNARSSON, Gunnar

Icelandic poet, dramatist, essayist, and novelist (writing in Danish and Icelandic), b. 18 May 1889, Fljótsdalur parish; d. 21 Nov. 1975, Reykjavík

G.'s father was a farmer. The early death of his mother left deep psychological scars on him, as many passages in his writings clearly suggest. His father was poor, so the boy received little formal education.

G. made his literary debut with two collections of verse: *Vorljóð* (1906; spring poems) and *Móðurminning* (1906; remembering mother). In order to get some education and to establish himself as a writer, he went to Denmark in 1907, enrolling there at the folk high school of Askov, where he studied until 1909. He lived in Denmark until 1939, when he returned to Iceland.

As a writer in Danish, G. first published a volume of poems entitled *Digte* (1911; poems), but his breakthrough work was the tetralogy of novels *Borgslægtens historie* (4 vols., 1912–14; abridged tr., *Guest the One-Eyed*, 1920)—consisting of *Ormarr Ørlygsson* (1912; Ormarr Ørlygsson), *Den danske frue på Hof* (1913; the Danish lady at Hof), *Gæst den enøjede* (1913; Guest the one-eyed), and *Den unge ørn* (1914; the young eagle). This "history of the family at Borg" is a neoromantic family chronicle set in Iceland for which G. created a special character type that was to recur frequently in his subsequent fiction: the solid and dependable Icelandic farmer. In this case, however, the farmer's two sons belong to different worlds; one is a dreamer and a nobleminded artist, torn between the call of his art and the call of the soil where

he has his roots, while his brother is a demonic evildoer whose misdeeds stem from blind instinct. The conflicts in the story grow out of the tension between these two polarities—a dualism that was to become one of the prime characteristics of G.'s fiction.

World War I was a severe blow for G., demolishing, as he saw it, his ideological world view, and the next phase of his literary career evinces deep pessimism as well as a struggle with psychological and ethical problems. Thus, his novel *Livets strand* (1915; the shore of life) focuses on the tragic life of a clergyman caught in a bind between the principle of human reason and his faith in divine providence. *Varg i veum* (1916; wolf in sacred places) concerns the ruin of a young man who has rebelled against bourgeois standards of decency. *Salige er enfoldige* (1920; *Seven Days' Darkness*, 1930) takes place in Reykjavík in seven days while the Spanish flu is raging—against a backdrop of a volcanic eruption.

Departing after 1920 from the pessimistic psychological tack, G. returned to material from his youth and place of origin, with his five-volume fictionalized autobiography *Kirken på bjerget* (1923–28; the church on the mountain; tr. of Vols. I–III, *Ships in the Sky*, 1938, and *The Night and the Dream*, 1938). *Kirken på bjerget* is at once the story of the maturing of a young writer and a significant contribution to cultural history, since it is also an account of rural life in Iceland at the turn of the century.

In the period 1920–40 G. was also a very productive essayist. He lectured extensively in the Nordic countries, and also in Germany, where he won acceptance and became a significant influence as a writer. The unification of the Nordic countries is a central concept in his essays, while they deal, broadly speaking, with Icelandic culture and Icelandic problems. A selection was published as *Det nordiske rige* (1927; the Nordic state).

G. supplemented the thoroughgoing self-examination of *Kirken på bjerget* by charting in a similar way the nature and fate of the Icelandic nation—a work he envisioned as a twelve-volume series of historical novels, although he never completed it. The first was *Edbrødre* (1918; *The Sworn Brothers*, 1920), about the first two settlers in Iceland. In *Jord* (1933; earth), G. moved on to the establishment of an organized state in the early history of the nation; this book contains a strong element of religious mysticism, with ancient Nordic paganism shown as being typified by a reverence for life, simple worship, and belief in fate. A similar mystical feeling also runs deep in *Hvide Krist* (1934; white Christ), which focuses on events leading to Iceland's conversion to Christianity around the year 1000. *Gråmand* (1936; the man in gray) treats of the incipient dissolution of the Icelandic Commonwealth during the 13th c., while *Jón Arason* (1930; Jón Arason) is both the story of the last Catholic bishop in Iceland and a survey of the nation's transition to a new religious order during the Reformation (the first half of the 16th c.).

Not all of G.'s works are so concerned with Icelandic history. *Svartfugl* (1939; *The Black Cliffs*, 1967), for example, which is based on a murder case in about 1800, is a novel shot through with religious mysticism, but also a psychological probing of the evil in human nature. Another novel, *Vikivaki* (1932; folk dance), G.'s most enigmatic work of fiction, is an absurdist fantasy about the responsibility of a writer toward his art and toward humanity.

After his return to Iceland, G. wrote and published his books in his native language. While he had projected a five-volume series of novels on life and social developments in Iceland during the first half of the 20th c., he completed only two: *Heiðaharmur* (1940; grief in the mountains) and *Sálumessa* (1952; requiem). His last work was *Brimhenda* (1954; the sonata of the sea), a short novel.

The hallmarks of G.'s fiction are strong individualism, psychological insight, and religious mysticism—as well as creation of characters of an unusual range. Although the bulk of his literary output is the work of an expatriate, G. derived his subject matter exclusively from his native soil, and his descriptions of life in Iceland have great immediacy, at the same time viewing what is characteristically Icelandic from an artistic distance.

FURTHER WORKS: *Sögur* (1912); *Små historier* (1916); *Små skuespil* (1917); *Drengen* (1917); *Små historier II* (1918); *Ringen* (1921); *Dyret med glorien* (1922); *Den glade gård, og andre historier* (1923); *Island* (1929); *En dag til overs, og andre historier* (1929); *Rævepelsene* (1930); *Verdens glæder* (1931); *De blindes hus* (1933); *Sagaøen* (1935); *Advent* (1937; *Advent*, 1939 [repub. as *The Good Shepherd*, 1940]); *Das Rätsel um Didrik Pining* (1939); *Trylle og andet småkram* (1939; *Trylle and Other Small Fry*, 1947); *Siðmenning og siðspilling* (1943); *Árbók 45* (1945); *Árbók 46–47* (1948); *Vestræn menning og kommúnismi* (1954); *Rit* (21 vols., 1941–63); *Skáldverk* (19 vols., 1960–63)

BIBLIOGRAPHY: Einarsson, S., *A History of Icelandic Literature* (1957): 285–87

—SVEINN SKORRI HÖSKULDSSON

GURNAH, Abdulrazak

Tanzanian-English novelist, short-story writer, and critic, b. 1948, Zanzibar

G. was educated in Zanzibar and in England, where he has lived since 1968. He is on the faculty of the University of Kent, in Canterbury, specializing in postcolonial literature. G. began publishing short fiction in the Nigerian journal, *Okike*, in the late 1970s. Since then, he has published five novels, and has edited a two-volume critical collection, *Essays on African Writing: A Reevaluation* (1993), to which he contributed the introduction and an essay on NGUGI WA THIONG'O. G. has also served as the editor of the journal *Wasifiri*, and has published book reviews in the *Times Literary Supplement* and the *Guardian*.

Memory of Departure (1987), G.'s first novel, is a critical look at the East Africa he left, in the form of a coming-of-age tale set in 1968. Hassan Omar, the narrator, is saved from his hometown—the squalid, Zanzibar-like seaport of Kenge, with its endless cycles of physical, moral, and political abuse and corruption—by an invitation to join his wealthy uncle Ahmed in neighboring Kenya. There, Hassan discovers, on one level, that the materialism of Nairobi is as spiritually degrading as the socialism back home; on another, he meets Salma and experiences a short-lived sense of the personal fulfillment that comes with love. The same two themes, first explored in *Memory of Departure*, are consistent features of G.'s later fiction: the clash of two worlds in which the alienated protagonist lives, and that protagonist's need to find emotional fulfillment.

In his next two novels G. located that clash along racial lines in Britain. In *Pilgrims Way* (1988) the novel's main character, the East African Daud, comes to England and finds work as a hospital orderly, as G. himself did on first arriving. The depressing conditions of his life, and the senselessness of the racism he encounters, is offset to some degree by Daud's wit and optimism. G.'s third

novel, *Dottie* (1990), an almost allegorical treatment of British racism as the result of imperialism, concerns the children of a prostitute of mixed colonized antecedents. The youngest, Hudson, is given to juvenile delinquency, while the middle child, Sophie, is given to the self-indulgent romanticization of everything from sex to religion. The household is held together, in the face of poverty and racism, by the title character, whose name, Dottie Badoura Fatma Balfour, like her parentage, makes G.'s postcolonial point.

G.'s fourth novel, *Paradise* (1994), marks a return to an East African setting. Perhaps following up on a reference to Joseph CONRAD's *Lord Jim* at the end of *Memory of Departure*, *Paradise* seems to be inspired by Conrad's *Heart of Darkness*, and shares much of that novel's lyrical voice and mythic vision. The story takes place in the years before World War I and, like Conrad's West African tale, involves trade between the colonized coast and the "dark" interior—the two worlds of this novel. The protagonist, Yusuf, is a boy of twelve when he is sold as an indentured servant, as his biblical namesake Joseph was sold into slavery, and he comes of age in this servitude to an Arab merchant as his country enters the long bondage of European colonialism. *Paradise* was shortlisted for the Booker Prize, an achievement unfortunately overshadowed by the controversy that surrounded the prize in 1994.

The two worlds of G.'s *Admiring Silence* (1996) reflect the inner tension of the author's own cultural and emotional allegiances. As did G. himself, the narrator of *Admiring Silence* leaves Zanzibar in the 1960s, determined to receive an education at an English university, and meanwhile falling in love with Emma, an English woman. Though he ends up a schoolteacher and has a daughter with Emma, the narrator is never really reconciled to English society, the racism of which is personified by Emma's parents, among others. Nor has he come to terms with his Zanzibar past, as becomes clear when the narrator takes advantage of an opportunity to visit his family there after a twenty-year absence. Instead, he has suffered in the "silence" of the title both the racism of England and the opportunism of Zanzibar, the victim of a colonized identity that has left "his generation with the despising anxiety of frightened men."

Like the narrator in *Admiring Silence* G. also returned for a visit to Zanzibar, made feasible by changes in the Tanzanian government, before he wrote *Paradise* and *Admiring Silence*. The accomplishment of the two fictions published subsequent to that trip has confirmed G. as an important East African writer in self-imposed exile, eclipsing the immigrant British novelist he sometimes appeared to be in his earlier works.

BIBLIOGRAPHY: Bace, M., "Question Marks over the Empire's Decision," *The Independent*, 10 Sept. 1994: 26; Jaggi, M., "Glimpses of Paradise Lost," *The Guardian*, 24 Sept. 1994: 31; Phillips, C., on *Admiring Silence*, *Financial Times*, 30 Nov. 1996: 17

—DAVID MESHER

GURNEY, A(lbert) R(amsdell)

American dramatist and novelist, b. 1 Nov. 1930, Buffalo, New York

Throughout his career G. has focused his attention on the manners and mores of affluent WASPs living on the Eastern coast of the U.S. during the second half of the 20th c.—people who inhabit a world of dancing classes, prep schools, private colleges, country clubs, and cocktail parties. A graduate of St. Paul's School, Williams College, and the Yale School of Drama, G. writes about the WASP milieu as an insider, though far from a complaisant one. Beneath the deceptive ease and good-humored repartee of a G. play lies a poignant, and even angry awareness of the limitations this society imposes on its members. Sometimes the individual is limited by unthinking adherence to WASP values; Sam in *The Old Boy* (1992) is haunted by the painful knowledge that he helped destroy a gay schoolmate by forcing him to submit to the heterosexist expectations of their world. *Richard Cory* (1985) is drawn to a sacrificial suicide by his awareness of his social advantages and the economic injustice upon which they rest. Revolt against established values can, however, prove to be illusory; Barney in *The Middle Ages* (perf. 1977, pub. 1982), stages decades of rebellion, only to admit that he wanted his conservative father's attention. Often working in the tradition of such masters of American high comedy as Philip BARRY and S. N. BEHRMAN, G. not only shares their ability to fuse witty invention with realistic observation, but also their fascination with the pathos and frustration that underlie lives of privilege. Only in a few sprightly and more farcical comedies, most notably *The Perfect Party* (1986) and *The Fourth Wall* (1994), are his protagonists able to break through to a larger and more joyous sense of community.

G.'s early dramatic experiments occasionally show the influence of absurdism, most notably in *The Problem*, but more often recall Jean ANOUILH's jaded reworkings of classic myths. *The Comeback* (1967) takes a satiric point of view toward Odysseus's return to Ithaca, while *The Golden Fleece* (1970) transplants Medea to suburban America. Although his later work has grown more realistic, G. has continued to draw on both myths and literature. *Another Antigone* (1988) recasts Sophocles's tragedy as a struggle between a classics professor and a rebellious student; *The Golden Age* (perf. 1981; pub. 1985), revisits Henry JAMES's *The Aspern Papers* with a young scholar fascinated with American artistic life in the 1920s, and *Overtime* (1995) spins contemporary variations on Shakespeare's *The Merchant of Venice*.

G. gained wider attention in 1970 when *Scenes from American Life* (1991) was produced by the Repertory Theatre of Lincoln Center. A highly episodic and satiric drama, it provides vignettes of WASP life from 1930 into a future dystopia vision of middle-class privilege in an authoritarian state. *The Dining Room* (1983) manifests the same episodic structure and multi-generational sweep, as well as some of the same satiric points, but with a less trenchant tone. With its combination of nostalgia and gently comic social criticism, *The Dining Room* has become G.'s most popular play, both in regional theaters across America, and abroad.

Despite their historical breadth, both *Scenes from American Life* and *The Dining Room* devote scant attention to socioeconomic forces. Indeed, G.'s characters usually lack any articulate understanding of how these forces shape their lives; they feel an anomie which they can rarely account for in any but the most personal terms. In this sense, they tend to resemble the adolescents in *What I Did Last Summer* (1983), who suffer from the absence of their father in World War II, while immersed in the more immediate dilemmas of their daily lives. In the absence of demystifying analysis, G.'s characters are often prone to nostalgia. In *The Snow Ball*, published first as a novel in 1985 and then as a play in 1992, the protagonist, confused in the contemporary world, becomes immersed in his attempt to recreate a treasured past moment.

G.'s most formally inventive and probing work to date is the performance piece *Love Letters* (1990). Presented as a reading by two actors who do not even look at each other until the work's final moments, it presents the correspondence of two unlikely friends, from childhood, through adulthood, romance and estrangement, to death. G. skillfully dramatizes the volatile relationship between an emotionally repressed politician, who can find release only through writing, and a deeply troubled artist, who distrusts language, and their inevitable misunderstandings.

G's plays are highly stageworthy, and their small casts and simple scenic requirements have made them standard fare for regional, college, and community theaters, despite the fact that they usually require accomplished actors. Despite his wide popularity, however, G. has yet to attract much respect or attention from scholars; his conservatism in both form and subject matter has led him to be overlooked. This is unfortunate, since his delicate observations and assured dramatic craftsmanship may well lead his plays to survive far longer than more experimental contemporary fare. In his keen observation of WASP destinies, G. has not only served as a social historian of a class, but has created deft, comic meditations on the tension between the needs of the individual and the constraints of society.

FURTHER WORKS: *The Gospel According to Joe* (1974); *Children* (1975); *Who Killed Richard Cory?* (1976); *Entertaining Strangers* (1977); *The Wayside Motor Inn* (1978); *Sweet Sue* (1987); *The Cocktail Hour* (1989); *Public Affairs* (1992); *Later Life* (1994); *A Cheever Evening* (1995); *Nine Early Plays: 1961-1973* (1995); *Sylvia* (1996)

BIBLIOGRAPHY: Levett, K., "A. R. G., Jr., American Original," *Drama*, 149 (Autumn 1983): 6-7; DiGaetani, J. L., *A Search for Postmodern Theater* (1991): 114-20; Laing, J. M., "Missed Connections in A. R. G.'s Love Letters," *NConL*, 25 (Mar. 1995): 3-4; McConachie, B. A., " *The Dining Room*: A Tocquevillian Take on the Decline of WASP Culture," *JADT*, 10 (Winter 1998): 39-50

—ROBERT F. GROSS

GUSTAFSSON, Lars

Swedish poet, novelist, dramatist, essayist, and critic, b. 17 May 1936, Västerås

G. spent his childhood in Västmanland, mostly in the city of Västerås but also in the country district of northern Västmanland: both locales recur frequently in his works. G. studied philosophy at Uppsala University, receiving a "fil. lic." (doctorate) degree in 1961 and a Ph.D. in 1978. G. edited the influential *Bonniers litterära magasin* from 1961 to 1972. He was elected to the Academy of Art, West Berlin, in 1974. G.'s world travels are reflected in many of his works, such as *Världsdelar* (1975; continents), *Kinesisk höst* (1978; Chinese fall), and *Afrikanskt försök* (1980; African attempt). G.'s several extended visits to the U.S. have inspired poems in *Bröderna Wright uppsöker Kitty Hawk* (1968; the Wright brothers visit Kitty Hawk), and the novella *Tennisspelarna* (1977; the tennis players), set at the University of Texas in Austin, where G. taught in 1976 and again in 1979.

G.'s fusion of international and home-district backgrounds in his works makes him at once cosmopolitan and regional, a combination used to masterly effect in *Kärleksförklaring till en sefardisk dam* (1970; declaration of love to a Sephardic lady), a long poem that ranges from Västmanland to Berlin to the Sinai desert. G.'s early reputation was mainly that of a lyric poet. *Sonetter* (1977; sonnets) marked G.'s return to poetry after almost a decade of writing prose. The fixed-from poetry of *Sonetter*, skillful and intricate sonnets and sestinas, are departures from G.'s earlier free verse. However, the melancholy theme of homelessness in the world again dominates. In *Artesiska brunnar cartesiska drömmar* (1980; artesian wells Cartesian dreams) G. uses strongly rhythmic free verse in poems that pose philosophical riddles or explore the theses of philosophers such as Descartes and Kant.

G.'s play *Den nattliga hyllningen* (homage at night), published in *Två maktspel* (1970; two power plays), received particularly favorable attention in Germany and Switzerland. Although set in 19th-c. Västerås, the play deals with contemporary misuses of power.

G.'s doctoral thesis, *Språk och lögn* (1978; language and lies), and his more popularly written *Filosofier* (1979; philosophies) evidence an interest in semantic problems like those explored by Ludwig Wittgenstein (1889–1951) and Noam Chomsky (b. 1928), an interest that found earlier expression in his essays, especially those in *Utopier* (1969; utopias).

G.'s greatest achievement to date is a series of five novels with the overall title *Sprickorna i muren* (1971–78; the cracks in the wall): *Herr Gustafsson själv* (1971; Mr. Gustafsson himself) is an autobiographical novel dealing with G.'s time as an editor and with a prolonged stay in West Berlin. *Yllet* (1973; wool) focuses on problems of depopulation and dehumanization in rural Västmanland. *Familjefesten* (1975; the family party) is concerned with political power and corruption in Swedish society. *Sigismund* (1976; Sigismund) develops the themes of the power of the subconscious and of science-fiction fantasy first introduced in *Yllet*. After the inferno and purgatory of the first four novels, *En biodlares död* (1978; *Death of a Beekeeper*, 1981) supposedly takes us to paradise, which turns out to be absence of pain as experienced by the dying protagonist; true paradise can only be shown in fantasy, in a science-fiction section entitled "När Gud vaknade" (when God awoke).

G. is one of the most productive and versatile of contemporary Swedish writers, and because his works address problems common to all Western societies, he is also one of the Swedish writers of his generation best known outside his country.

FURTHER WORKS: *Vägvila* (1957); *Poeten Brumbergs sista dagar och dod* (1959); *Bröderna* (1960); *Nio brev om romanen* (1961, with Lars Bäckström); *Följeslagarna* (1962); *Ballongfararna* (1962); *Enförmiddagi Sverge* (1963); *The Public Dialogue in Sweden* (1964); *En resa till jordens medelpunkt och andra dikter* (1966); *Den egentliga berättelsen om herr Arenander* (1966); *Förberedelser till flykt, och andra berättelser* (1967); *Utopier* (1969); *Konsten att segla med drakar* (1969); *Varma rum och kalla* (1972); *Kommentarer* (1972); *Den onödiga samtiden* (1974, with Jan Myrdal); *Strandhugg i svensk poesi* (1976; *Forays into Swedish Poetry*, 1978); *Den lilla världen* (1977); *Konfrontationer* (1979); *I mikroskopet* (1979); *För liberlismen* (1981); *Lyckliga människor* (1981). FURTHER WORKS IN ENGLISH: *Selected Poems* (1972); *Warm Rooms and Cold* (1975)

BIBLIOGRAPHY: Höllerer, W., "L. G.," *Ein Gedicht und sein Autor: Lyrik und Essay* (1967): 7–35; Sjögren, L., "Eine Seltsame Landschaft: Über die Lyrik L. G.s," *Akzente*, 17 (1969): 424–35; Sandstroem, Y., "The Machine Theme in Some Poems by L. G." *SS*, 44 (1972): 210–23; Sandstroem, Y., "Three Poems from the New World: Translation and Commentary," *The American—Swedish '72*: 31–36; Rovinsky, R., "'The Machines': Translation and Commentary," *American Review*, 21 (1974): 116–25; Mortensson, J., "G.'s Bee-Keeper," *Swedish Books*, 2 (1979): 6–7

—YVONNE L. SANDSTROEM

GÜTERSLOH, Albert Paris

(pseud. of Albert Konrad Kiehtreiber) Austrian novelist and poet, b. 5 Feb. 1887, Vienna; d. 16 May 1973, Baden

Educated for the priesthood, G. refused to take the vows; instead he studied painting (with Gustav Klimt) and acting; in 1907 he went to Berlin, where he worked with Max Reinhardt as a stage designer and director. There he wrote his first novel, *Die tanzende Törin* (1911; shortened version, 1913; the dancing fool), an early example of EXPRESSIONIST prose. In 1929 he was appointed professor at the Vienna School for Applied Arts. After the Anschluss in 1938 he was forced to resign his professorship and to do factory and office work. In 1945 he became a professor at the Vienna Academy of Fine Arts; he served as its rector from 1954 to 1955. In 1952 he was awarded the Austrian State Prize for painting; in 1961 he received the same award for literature.

Although G.'s early prose works are significant contributions to the development of expressionism, his writing cannot be explained in terms of any particular modern school or literary movement. His art is the result of his unusual life and his diverse talents. A strong inclination toward theological—philosophical speculation is equaled by the painter's sensuous delight in surfaces and textures. By means of his humor G. overcame dialectically the tensions between his talents and interests, the spiritual and the sensual, the divine and the human. His writing also reflects a love of the baroque—its vitality, exaggeration, obscurity, and lucidity, and its view of the world as a stage. In this preference G. is profoundly Austrian.

G.'s very unusual autobiography, *Bekenntnisse eines modernen Malers: Quasi un'allegoria* (1926; confessions of a modern painter: almost an allegory), can serve as an introduction to his life's work. *Kain und Abel* (1924; Cain and Abel) is called a legend, but *Die Vision vom Alten und vom Neuen* (1921; the vision of the old and the new) and *Innozenz; oder, Sinn und Fluch der Unschuld* (1922; Innozenz; or, the meaning and curse of innocence) are also closer to allegory and legend than to realism.

The subtitle of the last mentioned—the meaning and curse of innocence (which could also be translated as "purity")—characterizes well the central preoccupation of these shorter works as well as an important theme of the novels *Die tanzende Törin, Der Lügner unter Bürgern* (1922; *The Fraud*, 1965), and *Eine sagenhafte Figur* (1946; a legendary figure). These three works focus on the theme of the fate of spiritual purity in an impure, material world. The stories of *Die Fabeln vom Eros* (1947; the fables of Eros) actually move more and more out of the realm of allegory, legend, and fable and into that of realistic narrative.

G. is most accessible to the reader in his late collection of stories *Laßt uns den Menschen machen* (1962; let us create man) and the major novel *Sonne und Mond: Ein historischer Roman aus der Gegenwart* (written 1935–62, pub. 1962; sun and moon: a historical novel from the present). It is one of the great original novels of Austrian self-interpretation. The story is centered upon Austria, yet manages easily to soar almost everywhere in time and space; it is a delightful pretext for the author to give us the sum total of his wisdom and insight gathered in a lifetime of seventy-five years. Count Lunarin has inherited a ramshackle castle near the village of "Recklingen." No sooner has Lunarin, the "moon" of the novel, arrived in the village than he meets a former love of his and takes off again, yet not without first selecting a caretaker for his castle during his absence of just three days. The three days, however, stretch into a full year and the manager, a rich and capable farmer named Till Adelseher, is simply forced—and tempted—to rebuild the run-down castle from his own funds. Till's "sunlike" conscientiousness exceeds by far the rights bestowed upon him by his absent master. After a year the count returns and makes a present of the refurbished castle to his eager manager, but takes from him the woman Till loves.

On one level of meaning, the novel can be read as an allegory of Austria between 1913 and 1938, on another as being about the idea of kingship and the question of succession; birth stands against virtue, ontological man is played against logical man. But these are only a few of the subtle implications of this major work. G.'s humor and wit, his linguistic and metaphoric inventiveness all come to his aid in building a baroque castle that is the very opposite of KAFKA's abstractly constructed *The Castle*.

FURTHER WORKS: *Egon Schiele* (1911); *Die Rede über Franz Blei; oder, der Schriftsteller in der Katholizität* (1922); *Der Maler Alexander Gartenberg* (1928); *Musik zu einem Lebenslauf* (1957); *Gewaltig staunt der Mensch* (1963); *Zur Situation der modernen Kunst* (1963); *Der innere Erdteil* (1966); *Zwischen den Zeiten* (1967); *Die Fabel von der Freundschaft* (1969); *Miniaturen zur Schöpfung* (1970); *Paradiese der Liebe* (1972); *Treppe ohne Haus* (1974); *Beispiele* (1977); *Briefe an Milena 1932–1970* (1980)

BIBLIOGRAPHY: Doderer, H. von, *Der Fall G.: Ein Schicksal und seine Deutung* (1930); Blei, F., *Schriften in Auswahl, Nachwort von A. P. G.* (1960): 288–94; *A. P. G.: Autor und Werk* (1962); Basil, O., Eisenreich, H., and Ivask, I., *Das große Erbe: Aufsätze zur österreichischen Literatur* (1962): passim; Ivask, I., "Sonne und Mond," *BA*, 37 (1963): 304–5; Thurner, F., *A. P. G. Studien zu seinem Romanwerk* (1970); Prokop, H. F., "A. P. G.: Bibliographie," *Luk*, 68 (1972): 483–92; Hutter, H., *A. P. G. Beispiele: Schriften zur Kunst/Bilder/Werkverzeichnis* (1977)

—IVAR IVASK

GUYANESE LITERATURE
See English-Caribbean Literature

GUZMÁN, Martín Luis
Mexican novelist, essayist, journalist, and editor, b. 6 Oct. 1887, Chihuahua; d. 22 Dec. 1976, Mexico City

G. spent his childhood in Mexico City and Veracruz. At the age of fifteen he enrolled in the National Preparatory School, famous for its programs in mathematics and the sciences. He received a degree in jurisprudence from the National University of Mexico in 1913.

The life, literary work, and journalistic career of G. parallel and reflect the beginning, consummation, and consolidation of events of the Mexican Revolution in successive stages of its trajectory. He was a member of the Atheneum of Youth, a firm supporter of the political leader Francisco Madero, and a partisan and adviser of General Francisco (Pancho) Villa. For political and ideological reasons he spent the years 1915–20 and 1924–36 in exile, principally in Spain but also in the U.S. In Spain he edited the periodicals *El sol* and *La voz* and wrote and also published two of his most famous works: *El águila y la serpiente* (1928; *The Eagle and the Serpent*, 1930) and *La sombra del caudillo* (1929; in the leader's shadow). *La sombra del caudillo*, an authentic story of intrigue and violence set in the 1920s in the period of political dominance in Mexico of Álvaro Obregón, is probably Spanish America's best political novel.

Back in Mexico City to stay in 1936, G. founded the review *Romance* (1940–41) and in 1942 *Tiempo*, which ranks as Spanish America's most prestigious news weekly. He was elected to the Mexican Academy in 1954. In 1958 he received the National Prize for Literature. As a politician he served in both houses of the Mexican legislature.

In the years following his return to Mexico G. wrote and published a five–volume work titled *Memorias de Pancho Villa* (1938–51; *Memoirs of Pancho Villa*, 1965), employing the style in which Villa talked. While some critics consider this work to be his masterpiece, most G. scholars assign this distinction to *El águila y la serpiente*. G.'s contrast of the eagle, representing "idealism," with the serpent, representing "Calibanism," provides a graphic and universal image of the polarities involved in the experience of the Mexican Revolution.

Contrasts constitute basic and unifying structural components of G.'s major works. Images of light and shadow are used in the presentation of characters and situations: Pancho Villa is portrayed as having a flawed personality but as being well motivated in intent and potentially a serviceable idealist; the Mexican Revolution is seen as a dynamic aspiration and hope culminating in a truncated opportunity and result; postrevolution politics is depicted as a viscous web of venal interests and violence undermining the thrust for national regeneration and reconstruction.

Because of his distinctive style and his insights into recent historical events and personalities, G. is considered one of the best prose writers in Spanish of the 20th c.

FURTHER WORKS: *La querella de México* (1915); *A orillas del Hudson* (1917); *Mina el mozo: Héroe de Navarra* (1932); *Filadelfia, paraíso de conspiradores* (1933); *Kinchil* (1946); *El liberalismo mexicano en pensamiento y acción* (15 vols., 1947–1950); *Apunte sobre una personalidad* (1954); *Islas Marías, novela y drama* (1959); *Obras completas* (2 vols., 1961)

BIBLIOGRAPHY: Morton, F. R., *Los novelistas de la revolución mexicana* (1949): 115–40; Carballo, E., *Diecinueve protagonistas de la literatura mexicana del siglo XX* (1965): 61–99; Carter, B. G., "El contraste como eje literario de *El águila y la serpiente,*" *Revista mexicana de cultura*, 28 Feb. 1965: 1–2; Brushwood, J. S., *Mexico in Its Novel* (1970): 200–203; Ocampo de Gómez, A., and Prado Velázquez, E., *Diccionario de escritores mexicanos* (1967): 166–68; Langford, W. M., *The Mexican Novel Comes of Age*

(1971): 39–42; Alegría, F., *Historia de la novela hispanoamericana* (1974): 146–49

—BOYD G. CARTER

GUZMÁN, Nicomedes

(born Oscar Nicomedes Vásquez Guzmán) Chilean novelist and editor, b. 25 June 1914, Santiago; d. 26 June 1964, Santiago.

Because his family was very poor, G., to be able to attend school, worked outside of the home even as a young boy. Principally self-taught, he wrote novels and short stories that depicted the plight of the poor in the slums of Santiago. In the little that he wrote about his own life, he stated that he was his own worst enemy mostly because of a drinking problem. He eventually destroyed his first marriage with an affair that produced an illegitimate child, but then he continued living with both families for the next twenty years. To support his families, he worked at many different jobs: He was a newspaper journalist; he held positions in different branches of the government where he promoted proletarian literature and culture; he sold his books as he traveled around Chile giving lectures; and at one time he resorted to selling women's lingerie from office to office.

Though G.'s first book was a collection of poems, *La ceniza y el sueño* (1938; ashes and dreams), it was his novel *Los hombres obscuros* (1939; the obscure men) that caught the attention of the public. It has the innovation of four narrators, telling the tale in a present-tense, first-person point of view. Each narrator is a different voice of Pablo the shoeshine-boy protagonist, and the reader can identify the different voices because each has different punctuation.

La sangre y la esperanza (1943; blood and hope) is considered G.'s masterpiece, and it is required reading in Chilean high schools. It was awarded the Santiago Municipal Prize for Fiction (1943) and has gone through numerous editions and printings. Even in its antithetical title, the novel is an excellent example of neobaroque style, which became the trademark of the group G. belonged to, the Generation of 1938.

Many of G's chapters are interspersed with a prose-poem frame called a "stamp" in Chile. A metaphor of the slum environment in terms of beauty, not degradation, the sandwich-like stamp often appears at the beginning and ending of chapters or subchapters. This use of stamps was also a characteristic of the Generation of 1938.

Even though G.'s works can be classified as proletarian novels, they are currently praised as important works of testimonial literature, because they depict, as if they were autobiographies, the difficulties that the poor, hard-working Chileans have living in the slums. G.'s family considered *La sangre y la esperanza* to be a true autobiography, but besides obvious influence from Chilean works it shows influences of Michael Gold (1894–1967) of the U.S., Georg Fink (b. 1903) of Germany, Maxim GORKY of Russia, as well as other international proletarian writers of SOCIALIST REALISM.

G. was a leader of the Generation of 1938, which helped establish through the authors' writings Marxist governments in 1938 and 1970. As an editor, G. published an anthology of his generation, *Nuevos cuentistas chilenos* (1941; new Chilean short-story writers), one of the group's main documents. He also edited and published novels and other writings of his colleagues, as well as anthologies of several important Chilean novelists.

An author with an ability to show human tenderness, a common motif in G.'s stories, as well as a brutal side to humanity, G. has created a poetic prose that has made an impact both in Chile and abroad.

FURTHER WORKS: *Donde nace el alba* (1944); *La carne iluminada* (1945); *La luz viene del mar* (1951); *Una moneda al río y otros cuentos* (1954); *Autorretrato de Chile* (1957); *El pan bajo la bota* (1960)

BIBLIOGRAPHY: Zenteno, L. González, "N. G., figura representativa de la generación del 38," *Atenea*, 392 (1961): 116–27; special G. issue, *Cultura: Revista de educación*, 96 (1964); Dyson, J., "Los cuentos de N. G.," *Atenea*, 404 (1964): 228–49; Ojeda, J. Promis, "El sentido de la existencia en *La sangre y la esperanza* de N. G.," *AUC*, 145 (1968): 58–68; Pearson, L., *N. G., Proletarian Author in Chile's Literary Generation of* 1938 (1976); Ferrero, M., *N. G. y la generación del* 38: *Antología mínima* (1982)

—LON PEARSON

GYLLENSTEN, Lars

Swedish novelist and essayist, b. 12 Nov. 1921, Stockholm

Concurrently with his literary work, G. has pursued a medical career. He received his medical degree in 1948 and then resumed research in histology at Caroline Institute, the famous teaching hospital in Stockholm, where he worked as a teacher and researcher after 1953. He left this post in 1973 to devote himself completely to writing. G. was elected to the Swedish Academy in 1966 and has been its permanent secretary since 1977.

G.'s first published work was a parody of 1940s' surrealist poetry, *Camera obscura* (1946; Latin: dark room, punning on "obscure"), written with his friend Torgny Greitz (b. 1913) and published under the pseudonym Jan Wictor. *Camera obscura* received a great deal of attention—it did not altogether come across as the hoax it was intended to be—but it remains G.'s only excursion into poetry.

In his novels G. is a consistent experimenter, both in form and in the attitude toward life displayed in the different works. The role of the narrator in particular has been interesting to G., some of whose earlier novels, in particular *Barnabok* (1952; child book) can be seen as a reaction to the "absent author" device (whose most renowned exponent is James JOYCE) characteristic of many Swedish novels of the 1940s and 1950s. G. instead stresses the novel as art form, as conscious manipulation of and experimentation with several possible realities, rather than as a "slice of life" representing this reality. G.'s technical experiments also take the form of so–called collage novels, in G.'s case a collection of texts not assembled from different quarters, but written and arranged by the author himself. The most typical and most fragmented of these collage novels is *Juvenilia* (1965; Latin: writings of/about youth). His nonfiction prose, as well, for example, *Diarium spirituale* (1968; Latin: spiritual diary) and *Lapptäcken—Livstecken* (1976; patchwork guilts—signs of life), consisting of G.'s own work notes, comments, and reflections, make a collage impression.

Like Ibsen and Kierkegaard (the latter profoundly influenced G.), G. often explores a particular personality type and attitude toward life to plumb its opposite in a following work. Thus, in

Barnabok an essentially infantile reaction to life is presented, while *Senilia* (1956; Latin: writings of/about old age) exhibits a more mature personality type but with a distancing attitude toward life that brings its own difficulties. Several critics have seen *Barnabok* and *Senilia* as thesis and antithesis, with *Juvenilia* as synthesis, an attempt to reconcile the opposing attitudes of the two earlier novels.

Like many modern authors, such as Thomas MANN and Joyce, both of whom influenced his work, G. often uses myth. Thus the Jonah myth serves as a frame of reference in *Barnabok*, the Pasiphaë myth in *Senatorn* (1958; the senator). In later works myth is used for a deeper purpose, as revealing permanent truth about the human condition. *Palatset i parken* (1970; the palace in the park) uses the Orpheus myth as its thematic basis.

G.'s realization that, as he says in *Lapptäcken—Livstecken*, his exploration of humanity can provide neither final answers nor final victory has resulted in his consistently questioning stance and also contributed to the difficulty of his novels, for the problems he deals with admit neither easy answers nor easy treatment. G. is one of the most important and influential of contemporary Swedish novelists, as well as one of the most rewarding.

FURTHER WORKS: *Moderna myter* (1949); *Blå skeppet* (1950); *Carnivora* (1953); *Sokrates död* (1960); *Desperados* (1962); *Kains memoarer* (1963; *The Testament of Cain*, 1967); *Nihilistiskt credo* (1964); *Lotus i Hades* (1966); *Ur min offentliga sektor* (1971); *Mänskan, djuren, all naturen* (1971); *Grottan i öknen* (1973); *I skuggan av Don Juan* (1975)

BIBLIOGRAPHY: Sjöberg, L., "L. G.: Master of Arts and Science," *ASR*, 55 (1967): 158–62; Isaksson, H., *L. G.* (1978); Warme, L., "L. G.'s *Diarium spirituale* The Creative Process as a Novel," *Scan*, 19 (1980): 165–80

—YVONNE L. SANDSTROEM

H

HAANPÄÄ, Pentti

Finnish novelist and short—story writer, b. 14 Oct. 1905, Piippola;
d. 1 Oct. 1955, Piippola

During his lifetime H. was the object of several persistent
misconceptions: that he held communist sympathies; and that he
was a kind of natural genius—a writer who came by his talent
without the help of family background, training, or wide reading. In
fact, both his grandfather and father were published authors, and H.
himself conscientiously prepared for a literary career by wide
reading, even in the English language. As to his communist
sympathies, these were in large part attributed to him by a populace
made conservative by the Finnish civil war of 1918, during which
communist revolutionary activities were seen as a threat to Finnish
independence. Except for brief travels, he lived quietly and simply
in Piippola, a town in northern Finland. He is presumed to have
died by suicide.

The predominant tone of H.'s writing is one of disillusion. He
subjects life to rational scrutiny and finds no reliable source of
happiness. Human relations, in his view, both private and social,
produce only frustration. H.'s one comfort is in nature; he finds
something approaching joy in its peace, beauty, and steadfastness.
Consequently H.'s favorite character is the lumberjack, whose life
is free and who is attuned to the seasons and the forces of nature.

The destruction of this natural freedom is the theme of most of
H.'s writings. In his most controversial work, the collection of
short stories *Kenttä ja kasarmi* (1928; the field and the garrison), H.
criticized the peacetime military for moral decay. The book aroused
such a violent outcry that no publisher would publish H.'s works
for the next seven years. In the enthusiastic promilitary atmosphere
of Finland in the 1920s, any criticism of the army, the instrument
and symbol of national independence, was interpreted as socialism
or communism. Seen from today, these stories seem to address only
H.'s constant subject: the violation of human liberty by social institutions.

H. depicted the military in several other works, notably the
novels *Vääpeli Sadon tapaus* (written 1935, pub. 1956; the case of
Sergeant Major Sato), *Korpisotaa* (1940; war in the wilderness),
and *Yhdeksän miehen saappaat* (1945; the boots of nine men).
These works all have a war setting, but in them the author
condemns war itself.

In 1931, while under the publishing boycott, H. wrote his best
novel, the posthumously published *Noitaympyrä* (1956; the vicious
circle). It is about a lumberjack who, in spite of his misgivings
about society, gets a job, advances to foreman, but quits in protest
against company pressures. He experiences the hardships of unemployment and poverty. He then meets an unusual and well–educated man from the south and spends a summer of freedom with him in
remote Lapland. The companion, however, has an automobile
accident and ultimately commits suicide. The protagonist, left
alone, makes a quick decision: he walks over the border to the
Soviet Union and disappears. His act is presented not as a solution
but as an act of despair.

H.'s reputation rests chiefly on his short stories, of which he
published twelve collections. He is a true master of short fiction,
many of his novels being in effect only series of short episodes. His
stories, with their colorful and expressive language, are written in a
style that gives the reader a feeling of actually listening to a master
teller of tales. In fact, H. is said to have used the largest vocabulary
of any Finnish author. It is clear, however, that H. is not just a great
storyteller; he is also very conscious of literary technique. If one
were to single out one collection above the others, it would
probably be *Jutut* (1946; stories).

With his skeptical, appraising pessimism, H. viewed injustice
and oppression as ills for which no remedy can exist. Social
arrangements cannot accommodate human individuality. With his
monumental pessimism, relieved typically by a harsh humor, and
his focus on simple people, H. is the last of Finland's peasant writers.

FURTHER WORKS: *Maantietä pitkin* (1925); *Kolmen Torapään
tarina* (1927); *Tuuli käy heidän ylitseen* (1927); *Hota-Leenan
poika* (1929); *Karavaani* (1930); *Isännät ja isäntien varjot* (1935);
Lauma (1937); *Syntyykö uusi suku* (1937); *Taivalvaaran näyttelijä*
(1938); *Ihmiselon karvas ihanuus* (1939); *Nykyaikaa* (1942); *Heta
Rahko korkeassa iässä* (1947); *Jauhot* (1949); *Atomintutkija* (1950);
Iisakki Vähäpuheinen (1953); *Kiinalaiset jutut* (1954); *Akkuna ja
maantie* (1956)

BIBLIOGRAPHY: Ahokas, J., *A History of Finnish Literature* (1973):
228–34

—K. BÖRJE VÄHÄMÄKI

HAASSE, Hella

Dutch novelist, b. 2 Feb. 1918, Batavia, Indonesia

Born Hélène Serafia Haasse, H. spent the first twenty years of
her life alternately in Indonesia and the Netherlands and also went
to school in both countries. After high school, she studied Scandinavian languages and Dutch literature in the Netherlands, where
she also attended a school for dramatic art. Among the Dutch poets
to whom she felt particularly attracted were Jan Jacob SLAUERHOFF
and Adriaan Roland Holst (1888-1976). In their predominantly
lyrical poetry both these poets tend to be preoccupied with a quest
into the meaning of life, also the leading theme in H.'s works.

H. made her debut in 1938 with the publication of a number of
poems in the periodical *Werk*. Her first novel, *Oeroeg* (1948;
Oeroeg), was published ten years later. This short novel deals with
the doomed friendship between the son of a Dutch administrator
and a young Indonesian native. Their gradual, painful alienation
and eventual final separation was caused by the friction between
Dutch colonialism and the ambition of the Indonesians for independence. The relationship between the two boys and the course it took
serves to demonstrate the difficulty of establishing satisfying
relationships between people in general. With *Oeroeg* H. established her name in the history of Dutch literature and she has
remained one of the most respected contemporary Dutch authors.

Alienation and estrangement have remained the central theme
in H's work throughout her long career. *Het woud der verwachting*
(1949; *In a Dark Wood Wandering*, 1989) has received high praise

abroad, particularly in the U.S. It describes in great detail the hectic and agitated life of the medieval poet-king Charles d'Orleans of France. His inability to harmonize and coordinate his personal ambitions with the stark reality of court life in the Middle Ages and his romantic tendency to reflect on the meaning of life, specifically his own, is a quality he shares with most of H.'s main characters. In this novel as well as in the other early novels, such as *De scharlaken stad* (1952; The Scarlet City), H. does not deviate far from the style and general composition of the historical novel as conceived by Sir Walter Scott in the 19th c.

During the five years that separate the publication of *De scharlaken stad* from *Het woud der verwachting* the first signs of an interesting development are noticeable. In spite of impressive authenticity concerning historical data and great accuracy in their description, H. has removed herself to a considerable extent from the practice of Scott as well as her well-known 19th-c. compatriot Bosboom-Toussaint (1812-1868) and, later, Louis COUPERUS, both very prominent authors in their own time. At this point she still supplies the facts as they have come to us in history books but refrains from fantasizing about interpreting them; she presents the fragmented information, full of blanks, and allows several narrators, such as Michelangelo, Vittoria Colonna, Machiavelli, and Pietro Aretino to give their opinions on incidents, thus forcing the fragments to be formed into a sensible whole. In other words the perspective of the narrator has changed. H. still projects her thinking on her characters though, her alter ego in this novel being Giovanni Borgia, member of the famous family that during the Renaissance produced several prominent religious and political leaders. With him and via him she searches for his, and indirectly her own, identity.

De tuinen van Bomarzo (1968; The Gardens of Bomarzo) constitutes a crucial point not only in the development of H.'s work but also in the development of Dutch fiction. In a certain sense it can be regarded as one of the first Dutch novels consciously written in a POSTMODERNIST style. It is not possible for the spectator to understand the meaning of the monsters in the garden of Bomarzo; likewise, it is not possible for people anywhere to understand the labyrinth which this world is. Thus this book, more than her earlier works, ends with more questions than solutions to problems relative to history and the world.

In her so-called Bentinck novels—*Mevrouw Bentinck of Onverenigbaarheid van karakter* (1978; Mrs. Bentinck or the Incompatibility of Character) and *De groten der aarde of Bentinck tegen Bentinck* (1981; The Great of the Earth or Bentinck versus Bentinck)—H. is less concerned with historical data and local color. Instead, she restricts herself to arranging the documents at her disposal and allows those to tell the story of the predicaments of marriage and the gradual emancipation of 18th c. women: in this way she demonstrates that historical truth is, like so many things, primarily in the eye of the beholder.

In addition to her historical novels, H. wrote autobiographical works and essays and was active in writing for Dutch television. H. is the recipient of a large number of literary awards; for her contribution to Dutch culture in general she received the prestigious Golden Medal of Honor for Art and Science. With contemporary Harry MULISCH she is probably the strongest candidate for a Nobel Prize in literature the Netherlands has ever produced.

FURTHER WORKS: *De verborgen bron* (1950); *Zelfportret als legkaart* (1954); *De ingewijden* (1957); *Cider voor arme mensen* (1960); *De meermin* (1962); *Een nieuwer testament* (1966);

Persoonsbewijs (1967); *Krassen op een rots. Notities bij een reis op Java* (1970); *Huurders en onderhuurders* (1971); *Een gevaarlijke verhouding* of *Daal-en-Bergse brieven* (1976); De wegen der verbeelding (1983); *Berichten van het Blauwe Huis* (1986); *Schaduwbeeld of Het geheim van Appeltern* (1989); *Heren van de thee* (1992); *Een handvol achtergrond. Parang Sawat* (1993); *Transit* (1994); *Ogenblikken in Valois* (1996); *Uitgesproken opgeschreven. Essays over achttiende-eeuwse vrouwen, een bosgezicht, verlichte geesten, vorstenlot, satire, de pers en Vestdijks avondrood* (1996); *Zwanen schieten* (1997)

BIBLIOGRAPHY: Anbeek, T., *Geschiedenis van de Nederlandse literatuur 1885-1985* (1990); Blok, A., ed. *De historische roman* (1988); Drop, W., *Verbeelding en historie, Verschijningsvormen van de Nederlandse historische roman in de negentiende eeuw* (1958); Kralt, P., *De toverbron, S. Vestdijk en de geschiedenis* (1988); Schenkeveld-Van der Dussen, A., *Nederlandse literatuur, Een geschiedenis* (1993)

—MARTINUS A. BAKKER

HAAVIKKO, Paavo

Finnish poet, dramatist, novelist, and short-story writer, b. 25 Jan. 1931, Helsinki

H.'s father was a Helsinki businessman, and he himself has managed to combine a career in publishing with that of a writer. After spending some time in the real estate business, H. joined one of the major Finnish publishing companies, Otava. He became a member of the board at the age of thirty-seven, soon after his appointment as literary editor, a post he still holds. He is also a director of Yhtyneet Kuvalehdet Oy (United Illustrated Magazines). His business experience is reflected in the themes of money and power in his work. H. married Marja-Liisa Vartio (1924–1966), a prominent Finnish writer, in 1955. He is now married to Ritva Rainio (b. 1929), who is also well known in literary circles. H. did not attend a university, but he received an honorary Doctor of Philosophy degree from Helsinki University in 1969.

H. appeared as a full-fledged modernist with his first collection of poems, *Tiet etäisyyksiin* (1951; ways to faraway), setting the pace for a whole generation of young writers and helping decisively to bring Finnish poetry up to date. Highly individual in thought and language, he has been prolific both as a poet and a writer of prose.

The themes of his poetry are language and poetry itself, love and death, and—especially more recently—history and power. These themes are brought together in *Talvipalatsi* (1959; The Winter Palace, 1968), a long poem that has been said to have had an impact on contemporary Finnish poetry comparable to that of T. S. ELIOT'S *The Waste Land* on English and American poetry.

H. has said that everything is history. The world of Rome or Byzantium is where man's destiny was worked out; man made blind mistakes at these moments, and he is repeating them today. But he may blend myth with history, as in the long narrative poem *Kaksikymmentä ja yksi* (1974; twenty and one), which draws heavily on the Finnish folk epic *Kalevala* for both style and theme. In history, as in H.'s poetry, permanence is an illusion. Life slips by without our noticing it. Speech flows in a flowing world. But man is not aware of this impermanence, nor is he aware that each historical event is unique. He believes in his own power. H. often chooses people of high rank as the symbols of impermanent power—kings, statesmen, wealthy merchants, the Empress Zoe in her Byzantine court.

H.'s poetry is characterized by a free, strong, rhythmic line, with the impact and flexibility of speech. He makes surprising connections, and his poems often operate on several levels simultaneously.

In his numerous stage and radio plays H. continues the theme of power, often with a historical setting. His early works are close to those of the THEATER OF THE ABSURD. There are strong elements of grotesque, black comedy in *Ylilääkäri* (1968; *The Superintendent*, 1978), where a Freud-like father figure, superintendent of a hospital in 1906, plays sadistic games with his subordinates and his wife's relations. In what is perhaps his best play, *Agricola ja kettu* (1968; Agricola and the fox), Finland is caught between Sweden and Russia, between King Gustavus Vasa and Ivan the Terrible (the two rulers are played by the same actor). In the libretto of an opera, *Ratsumies* (1974; *The Horseman*, 1974), with music by the Finnish composer Aulis Sallinen, H. returns to a similar theme.

During the 1960s, H. wrote several novels. They are objective, spare, along the lines of the French NEW NOVEL. In "Lumeton aika" (snowless time), the most important story in the collection called *Lasi Claudius Civiliksen salaliittolaisten pöydällä* (1964; a glass at the table of Claudius Civilis' conspirators), H. sets the scene in a Finland of 1963 in which he imagines the Communists have taken over fifteen years previously. The story deals with the relation between man's public role and his private self. His latest examination of Finland is a historical "comment on the unknown history of an unknown nation 1904–1975" called *Kansakunnan linja* (1977; national line), which has aroused considerable discussion. H. sees the nation as a business enterprise, struggling to keep ahead in the world. He differs from "official" historians in suggesting that Finland got through World War II successfully because unlike many other small countries she preserved her freedom to make decisions according to the situation.

From his wide production over almost thirty years, H. emerges as a complex, deep-reaching poet with a superb command of language. He has been accused of cynicism (which he strongly denies), ambiguity, and a certain coldness. But he is generally recognized as an important and stimulating thinker and as the leading living Finnish poet today.

FURTHER WORKS: *Tuuliöinä* (1953); *Synnyinmaa* (1955); *Lehdet lehtiä* (1958); *Münchausen* (1960); *Yksityisiä asioita* (1960); *Toinen taivas ja maa* (1961); *Vuodet* (1962); *Runot 1951–1961*(1962); *Puut, kaikki heidän vihreytensä* (1966); *Puhua, vastata, opettaa* (1972); *Neljätoista hallitsijaa* (1970); *Runoja matkalta salmen ylitse* (1973); *Sulka* (1973); *Harald Pitkäikäinen* (1974); *Kuningas lähtee Ranskaan* (1974); *Runot 1949–1974* (1975); *Runoelmat* (1975); *Viiniä, kirjoitusta* (1976); *Ihmisen ääni* (1977); *Näytelmät* (1978); *Soitannollinen ilta Viipurissa 1918* (1978); *Viisi pientä draamallista tekstiä* (1981). FURTHER WORKS IN ENGLISH: *Selected Poems* (1968)

BIBLIOGRAPHY: Hollo, A., Introduction to H. P., *Selected Poems* (1968); Laitinen, K., "How Things Are: P. H. and His Poetry," *BA*, 43 (1969): 41–46; Binham, P., "Dreams Each within Each: The Finnish Poet P. H.," *BA*, 50 (1976): 337–41; Dauenhauer, R., "The View from the Aspen Grove: P. H. in National and International Context," in Dauenhauer, R., and P. Binham, eds., *Snow in May: An Anthology of Finnish Writing 1945–1972* (1978): 67–97; Binham, P., "Poet's Playground: The Collected Plays of P. H.," *WLT*, 53 (1979): 244–45

—PHILIP BINHAM

HABĪBĪ, Emile

Palestinian novelist, short-story writer, and essayist, b. 28 Aug. 1921, Haifa, Palestine (now Israel); d. 2 May 1996, Nazareth, Israel

Until the publication of his collection of short stories *Sudāsiyyat al-ayyām al-sittah* (1968; sextet of the six days), H. was better known as a political activist and commentator than as a writer of imaginative fiction. For decades before that event, he was a prominent member of the Israeli Communist Party, which he joined in the early 1940s, when it was still the Palestinian Communist Party. He represented the party in the Knesset between 1951 and 1971 and served for many years as editor of its biweekly *al-Ittihād* and its other political and literary periodicals. His regular weekly column, published under different pen names, was a mainstay of this Arabic newspaper.

Sudāsiyyat al-ayyām al-sittah first appeared serialized in the Party's monthly *al-Ghadd*, under H.'s pen name Abū Salām. It immediately attracted wide attention for its originality and was successively reprinted in several Arab periodicals before it appeared in book form (with other stories) in 1969.

Still more momentous was the publication of H.'s masterpiece *Al-waqāi' al-gharībah fī ikhtifā' sa'īd abī al-nahs al-mutashā'il* (1974; *The Secret Life of Saeed, the Ill-Fated Pessoptimist*, 1982). This book has since been published independently by several publishing houses inside Israel and in the Arab world, and has appeared in a number of printings. It has also been translated into several languages, including English, French, Russian, and Hebrew and was staged in both Arabic and Hebrew in Israel. H.'s subsequent three works, though not without literary and artistic merit, appear anticlimactic when compared with this outstanding work.

H. views his fiction writing in strictly political terms. He defines himself primarily as a political activist, and only secondarily as a fiction writer. Moreover, he insists that an intrinsic connection binds the two fields to which he has devoted the larger part of his life. His stories initially drew attention in the Arab world for their unique blend of savvy political acumen and consummate artistic quality. They were immediately viewed in the Arab world as part of what came to be known as "the literature of the Palestinian resistance" or "the literature of the occupied land."

H.'s fiction deals exclusively with the concerns and experiences of the Palestinian Arab minority living in Israel. References and allusions to the peculiar rules and conditions that govern daily life in this community permeate these works to such an extent that annotation is virtually necessary if the works are to be fully grasped by the outsider. Thus, the thematic thread that binds the six tableaux of *Sudāsiyyat al-ayyām al-sittah* is the renewed contact between Palestinians from within Israel and fellow Palestinians from the newly occupied territories of the West Bank and Gaza.

Although hardly the circumstances under which they had hoped to be reunited after nearly twenty years of forced separation, both parts of the Palestinian people derive some solace from their awkward reunion. This is particularly true of the Palestinians of Israel who were left behind and felt abandoned. The six episodes of the collection dramatize the healing effect of this reunion on individuals whose lives had suffered from a fundamental lack. In all cases, the wounds are psychological in nature. They range in severity from the schizophrenic condition of a man who could not remember that he was the hero of a love story that haunts him, "Wa-akhīran nawwar al-lawz" (and finally the almond trees blossomed), to that of a boy whose stunted growth and inferiority complex are cured by the discovery that he has an extended family in the West Bank. The stories occupy a dramatic space between the political imperative that requires an Israeli withdrawal from the occupied territories, to which both the author and his fictional characters subscribe, and the need to spare the Palestinian individual the psychological trauma of a renewed separation from the collective body.

The generic status of *Sudāsiyyat al-ayyām al-sitta*, that is, the question whether it is a novel or a collection of short stories, is somewhat problematic. The six parts of which it is comprised are discrete enough to stand independently of each other. But they are also bound by lines of continuity that give the whole a distinct sense of unity, though perhaps not quite that of a tightly structured novel.

Daring experimentation with narrative form is one of several features that make H.'s *Al-waqā'i' al-gharībah fī ikhtifā sa'īd abī al-nahs al-mutashā'il* unique in the annals of the Arabic novel. Here H. utilizes the rich rhetorical and stylistic tradition of the classical Arabic genre of *maqāma* to depict the predicament of the Arabs in Israel. His treatment of this grave subject, however, is shot through with irony and humor. In large measure, the novelty resides in the choice of a singularly unheroic Palestinian, Sa'īd, as the protagonist of this work. For Sa'īd is at once a willing collaborator with the Israeli authorities against other fellow Palestinians and a victim of the general conditions that govern the daily life of all Arabs in Israel. In a series of loosely connected episodes reminiscent of the picaresque novel H. parades Sa'īd through the labyrinth of Israeli officialdom, only to discover that it leads absolutely nowhere. H. takes these spatial terms quite seriously. Most of the movement in this novel occurs on a vertical, not a horizontal, axis. The novel begins with a series of letters that Sa'īd addresses to the author, presumably from outer space whither he had been conducted by his extraterrestrial rescuers, and ends with him practically impaled on a high post from which he is unable to descend. The fact that the Sa'īd letters originate in Acre, which in contemporary Arabic and Hebrew vernacular stands metonymically for the mental asylum in it, imparts to the whole story a fantastic and comic quality that relieves much of the tension inherent in the serious subject matter.

Much of the satirical humor is directed against the vagaries of the Israeli political establishment. But the inept Arab regimes and the backward Arab condition in general also come under H.'s scathing satire. The satire is all the more biting because it is couched in a high form of classical Arabic that deliberately evokes past Arab glory only to contrast it with the dismal condition of contemporary Arab life. Nor is the humor exclusively political. The novel literally bristles with linguistic and rhetorical puns that proclaim its literary status. In this respect, it is among a handful of serious Arab novels that consciously flaunt their literary artifice and technical virtuosity.

H.'s subsequent works carry experimentation a significant step farther. In one of them H. mixes the generic features of novel and play so thoroughly that the hybrid is neither. H. calls it *misriwāyah*, which is an acronym made up of parts of the words of "play" and "novel." On the whole, the literary value of these latter works may reside primarily in their experimental nature as they constantly press against the contours of established genres and redefine the norms of modern Arabic narrative.

FURTHER WORKS: *Luka' ibn Luka'* (1980); *Ikhtayye* (1985); *Sarāyā bint al-ghūl* (1991)

BIBLIOGRAPHY: Gassick, T. Le, "The Luckless Palestinian," *MEJ*, 34, 2 (1980): 215–23; Jayyusi, S. K., Introduction to *The Secret Life of Saeed, the Ill-Fated Pessoptimist* (1982): 7–20; Mehrez, S., "Irony in Joyce's Ulysses and H.'s Pessoptimist," *Journal of Comparative Poetics*, 4 (1984): 33–54; Tamari, S., "Saeed, the Ill-Fated Pessoptimist," *Merip Reports* (Oct.-Dec. 1985): 53–55; Allen, R., ed., *Modern Arabic Literature* (1987): 104–9; Boullata, I. J., "Symbol and Reality in the Writings of E. H.," *Islamic Cultures*, 62: 2–3 (1988): 9–21

—MUHAMMAD SIDDIQ

HACKS, Peter

German dramatist, poet, and essayist, b. 21 March 1928, Breslau (now Wroclaw, Poland)

H. spent his youth in Silesia, a part of Germany that was annexed by Poland following World War II. After the war, H. studied sociology, philosophy, modern literature and theater in Munich, where he received a doctorate in 1951 for a dissertation on drama of the Biedermeier period (c. 1815–48). He was active in West German theater and radio until 1955, then moved to East Germany for political reasons. In the late 1950s he was associated with the Berliner Ensemble, and from 1960 to 1963 he worked as a dramatist for the Deutsches Theater. He was actively involved in the East German Academy of Performing Arts and the presiding council of the East German branch of the international PEN Club until 1991 when he withdrew from both organizations during conflicts regarding their reformation. Following the reunification of Germany, his involvement in serious artistic endeavor declined, and he devoted himself primarily to the writing of children's literature, essays, and some poetry.

H. was influenced by models as diverse as Shakespeare, Aristophanes, and the modern agitprop tradition. He learned much from Bertolt BRECHT and has further developed the historical and folk-drama forms that are characteristic of Brecht's works. Especially visible in H.'s dramas is the use of Brecht's techniques of employing songs to replace monologues, to explain attitudes, and to connect ideas. The resulting product is an oeuvre of realistic drama comprising comedies that achieve their effect through masterful construction and didactic plays that convince through artfully employed naïveté.

In his early works, H. contrasted a Marxist view of history with myths and legends of bourgeois tradition. His first successful play, *Eröffnung des indischen Zeitalters* (1954; opening of the Indian era; repub. as *Columbus; oder, Die Weltidee zu Schiffe*, 1970; Columbus; or, the world idea aboard ship), presented Columbus as a leader into a new age of scientific reason and introduced him into East German literature as a symbol for man on his way to the new society. Among other important early works are *Die Schlacht bei Lobositz* (1956; the battle at Lobositz), a satire of Prussian militarism intended as an attack against West German remilitarization;

and *Der Müller von Sanssouci* (1957; the miller of Sanssouci), a satirical assault on the legend of Frederick the Great, in which H. introduced for the first time his concept of the "giant" as a key historical figure.

Near the end of the 1950s H. turned away from historically remote materials and focused directly upon specific problems in the evolution of East German society. The ensuing plays became extremely controversial and were rejected by Marxist critics as lacking a properly positive sense of reality. Enormous tension arose because H.'s portrayals were uncomfortably realistic, his criticisms of the society were valid, and his attitude was nonsubmissive.

The best drama of this period is *Moritz Tassow* (1961; Moritz Tassow), a realistic, dialectically argumentative verse comedy about a revolutionary swineherd, in which H. attacked the state's insensitivity to individual needs. With its blatant detail and colorful secondary characters, *Moritz Tassow* significantly elevated the quality of the East German peasant drama while satirizing such postwar developments as the land reform and the farm commune. The play also contains an innovation of special importance for East German drama: the introduction of an antihero in the figure of the ideal socialist Mattukat.

In the late 1960s H. responded to sharp criticism against his direct portrayals of East German reality by returning to politically safer substance from history and mythology. Typical of works created since 1965 are *Omphale* (1970; Omphale), in which a Hercules legend becomes a vehicle for exploring the problem of male and female social roles, and *Adam and Eva* (1973; Adam and Eve), an interpretation of the biblical account of the fall of Adam employed as a poetic allegory for the dialectic self-determination of man.

Among plays written after 1975, *Ein Gespräcg im Hause Stein über den abwesenden Herrn von Goethe* (1976; A Conversation in the Stein Hom about the Absent Mr. Goethe), a hilarious satirical comedy about the relationship between Geothe and Charlotte von Stein, must be regarded as one of his best works. It clearly reemphasizes the fact that H.'s dramatic strength lay in his ability to employ theatrical devices to shatter illusions and compel his audience toward personal introspection.

Later dramas were much less successful. Although *Fredefunde* (1984), a formally classical five-act that seems quite modern in its focus on the role of women in history, offers a finely woven play of intrigues that illuminate the problem of the need for a compelling rational force in human progress, it is relatively unconvincing because of its anacreontic trappings. H.'s attempt to deal with the problems encountered by Germans from East and West in the aftermath of reunification in the comedy *Fafner, die Bisam-Maus* (1992; Fafner, the Musk-Mouse), was resoundingly panned by critics as a trivial kitchen-sink farce that based its effect on cheap jokes and prejudices. These later failures give mute testimony that his voluntary withdrawal from the mainstream of post-reunification Germany literary life effectively ended the productive theatrical career of a man who was in his prime the most important dramatist in the German Democratic Republic.

FURTHER WORKS: *Das Volksbuch vom Herzog Ernst; oder, Der Held und sein Gefolge* (1953); *Der gestohlene Ton* (1953); *Das Fell der Zeit* (1954); *Das Windloch* (1956); *Geschichte eines alten Wittibers im Jahre 1673* (1956); *Theaterstücke* (1957); *Die Kindermörderin* (1957); *Die unadlige Gräfin* (1958); *Literatur im Zeitalter der Wissenschaften* (1960); *Die Sorgen und die Macht* (1960); *Falsche Bärte und Nasen* (1961); *Frieden* (1962); *Das Turmverlies* (1962); *Die Form ist das Politikum* (1962); *Zwei Bearbeitungen* (1963); *Die schöne Helene* (1964); *Stücke nach Stücken: Bearbeitungen 2* (1965); *Der Flohmarkt: Gedichte für Kinder* (1965); *Polly; oder, Die Bataille am Bluewater Creek* (1965); *Der Schuhu und die fliegende Prinzessin* (1965); *Fünf Stücke* (1965); *Lieder zu Stücken* (1967); *Kasimir der Kinderdieb* (1967); *Margarete in Aix* (1967); *Amphytrion* (1968); *Vier Komödien* (1971); *Nocheinen Löffel Gift, Liebling?* (1972); *Die Katze wäscht den Omnibus* (1972); *Das Poetische* (1972); *Der Bär auf dem Försterball* (1972; *The Bear at the Hunter's Ball*, 1976); *Gedichte* (1972); *Ausgewählte Dramen* (2 vols., 1972, 1976); *Kathrinchen ging spazieren* (1973); *Lieder, Briefe, Gedichte* (1974); *Die Dinge in Buta* (1974); *Die Sonne* (1974); *Meta Morfoß* (1975); *Das Pflaumenhuhn* (1975); *Oper* (1976); *Das Jahrmarktsfest zu Plundersweilern* (1975); *Das Jahrmarktsfest zu Plundersweilern; Rosie träumt* (1976); *Die Maßgaben der Kunst* (1977); *Das musikalische Nashorn* (1978); *Sechs Dramen* (1978); *Stücke* (1978); *Armer Ritter* (1981); *Pandora* (1981); *Jules Ratte; oder, Selber lernen macht schlau* (1981); *Essais* (1983); *Zwei Märchen* (1985); *Historien und Romanzen. Urpoesie; oder, Das scheintote Kind* (1985); *Die Binsen. Fredegunde* (1985); *Schöne Wirtschaft* (1988); *Die Gedichte* (1988); *Kinder kurz weil* (1988); *Jona* (1989); *Die last mit der Lust. Von der rechten Art mit Pornographie umzugehen* (1990); *Ascher gegen Jahn: Ein Freiheitskrieg* (1991); *Die Erzählungen* (1994); *Lebrecht am schiefen Fenster* (1994); *Kathrinchen ging spazieren* (1996); *Liebkind im Vogelnest* (1996); *Prinz Telemach und sein Lehrer Mentor* (1997); *Der Hof zieht um* (1998)

BIBLIOGRAPHY: Glenn, J., "Hofmannsthal, H., and Hildesheimer: Helen in the Twentieth Century," *Seminar*, 5 (1969): 1–20; Laube, H., *P. H.* (1972); Schleyer, W., *Die Stücke von P. H.* (1976); Schütze, P. F., *P. H.* (1976); Scheid, J. R.,, *"Enfant Terrible" of Contemporary East German Drama: P. H. in His Role as Adaptor and Innovator* (1977); Gerber, M., "After the Revolution–What Then? P. H.'s Theory of a Socialist Classicism," *UDR*, 13, 2 (1978): 3–11; Trilse, C., *P. H.* (1980); Heitz, R., *P. H.* (1984); Jäger, A., *Der Dramatiker P. H.* (1986); Di Napoli, T., *The Children's Literature of P. H.* (1987); Bosker, M. R., *Sechs Stücke nach Stücken* (1994)

—LOWELL A. BANGERTER

HAGIWARA Sakutarō

Japanese poet, essayist, and literary theorist, b. 1. Nov. 1886, Maebashi; d. 11 May 1942, Tokyo

The son of wealthy parents, H. was able even as a young man to devote himself full time to writing poetry. He never finished college, but studied Western authors on his own and was especially attracted to Poe, Nietzsche, Schopenhauer, and Dostoevsky. His first collection of poems, *Tsuki ni hoeru* (1917; *Howling at the Moon*, 1978), immediately established him as a highly imaginative poet. During the next twenty-five years he published five volumes of poetry, eight collections of essays, four books of aphorisms, one novelette, and three treatises on poetry. He also helped to found several literary magazines, and taught at Meiji University in Tokyo from 1934 until the year of his death.

Tsuki ni hoeru gained lavish critical acclaim because it represented the first successful attempt to give, in colloquial Japanese, a poetic form to existential anxiety. The poems skillfully articulated what H. called a "physiological fear," a fear that, lying deep in man's physical existence, ceaselessly threatens his mental well-being. A modern man afflicted with this fear feels something rotten in the core of his being and vainly looks up toward the sky for salvation. In H.'s metaphor man is a dog fearful of his own shadow and forever howling at the moon.

In H.'s second collection of poems, *Aoneko* (1923; *Blue Cat*, 1978), this anxiety gives way to ennui, gloom, and despair. The central image of the book is a tired, melancholy cat sitting lazily and indulging in fantasies. Man, having lost all hope in life, no longer howls at the dream world; he is completely within it. The nihilism pervading the book was partly derived from Schopenhauer, but in giving verbal expression to it H. made masterful use of a dull rhythm characteristic of colloquial Japanese.

Hyōtō (1934; the iceland), H.'s last major book of poetry, marks a return from the dream world to the realities of daily life. The predominant tone of these poems is neither fear nor melancholy; it is the anger of a man ostracized by contemporary society because of his extrasensitivity as a poet. For H., this anger was too intense to express in colloquial Japanese. Making effective use of sonorous literary Japanese, he vented his rage at the people who failed to understand him. Modern Japan seemed like an iceland.

As he grew older, H. turned increasingly to prose. In *Nekomachi* (1935; *The Cat Town*, 1948) he tried to bridge the gap between poetry and prose; in his words, he created a novelette "in the form of a prose poem." The experiment, however, was not entirely successful. Describing a journey into an imaginary land, the book is much like *Aoneko*, but without its evocative power.

H. fared better in writing aphorisms and critical essays. An avid reader of classical poetry, he compiled the anthology *Ren'ai meika shū* (1931; a treasury of love poems), in which he provided his own interpretive analysis of each poem. The analysis was most successful in dealing with poems that sang of longing for a remote, metaphysical lover. His study of an 18th-c. haiku poet, *Kyōshū no shijin Yosa Buson* (1936; Yosa Buson, the poet of nostalgia), likewise is a personal interpretation of poems of longing and nostalgia.

H.'s talent for literary theory found its best expression in *Shi no genri* (1928; principles of poetry). "Through a uniquely dreamlike method," he wrote, "poetry articulates the essence of the self that looms in the twilight zone of consciousness." "A uniquely dreamlike method" meant symbolic representation ("imagerization" was H.'s equivalent for it), and H. considered the Japanese language as lending itself especially well to the symbolist mode, because it was imagistic by nature. On the other hand, he lamented the paucity of musical qualities in modern Japanese.

H. made two major contributions to modern Japanese poetry. First, with his consummate skill with words he demonstrated that vernacular Japanese could be used in an artistically satisfying way. Other poets before him had made use of the vernacular in their works, yet their diction was essentially little different from everyday speech. With H., modern Japanese became a *poetic* language for the first time. Second, he was the first Japanese author who successfully created poetry out of the existential anxiety typical of a modern intellectual. Nietzsche and Schopenhauer had been known in Japan before his time, but no one else had taken their pessimism so much to heart as H. did. For better or for worse, Japanese poetry has come markedly closer to that of Europe through H.'s effort.

FURTHER WORKS: *Atarashiki yokujō* (1922); *Chō o yumemu* (1923); *Junjō shōkoyoku shū* (1925); *Shiron to kansō* (1928); *Kyomō no seigi* (1929); *Junsei shi ron* (1935); *Zetsubō no tōsō* (1935); *Rōka to shitsubō* (1936); *Shijin no shimei* (1937); *Mu kara no kōsō* (1937); *Nippon e no kaiki* (1938); *Shukumei* (1939); *Kikyōsha* (1940); *Minato nite* (1940); *Atai* (1940). FURTHER WORKS IN ENGLISH: *Face at the Bottom of the World and Other Poems* (1969)

BIBLIOGRAPHY: Piper, A., "Das Shi als Ausdruck des japanischen Lebensgefühls in der Taishōzeit: H. S. und Takamura Kōtarō," *Nachrichten der Gesellschaft für Natur- und Völkerkunde Ostasiens*, 77, 79–80 (1955–56): 8–21, 110–30; Wilson, G., Introduction to *Face at the Bottom of the World and Other Poems* (1969): 11–32; Tsukimura, R., "H. and the Japanese Lyric Tradition," *JATJ*, 11 (1976): 47–63; Sato, H., Introduction to *Howling at the Moon* (1978): 11–26

—MAKOTO UEDA

HAITIAN LITERATURE

See French-Caribbean Literature

al-HĀJJ, Unsī Lūwīs

Lebanese poet, critic, and translator, b. 1937, Kaitouli

Born in the south of Lebanon, H. studied at a French lycée, the Collège de la Sagesse in Beirut. As a journalist he contributed to the dailies *al-Hayāt* and *al-Nahār* and became director of the weekly literary supplement of this journal. As a young poet he was associated with the avant-garde review *Shi'r* from 1957 to 1964 and again from 1967 to 1969, in which he published his prose poetry. He translated poetic works of Antonin ARTAUD, André BRETON, and Jacques PRÉVERT and also translated plays from Shakespeare, as well as Eugène IONESCO, Friedrich DÜRRENMATT, Albert CAMUS, and Bertolt BRECHT

In the spirit of *Shi'r* he published in 1959 his first collection of prose poems, *Qasā'id al-nathr* (poems in prose), also entitled *Lan* (never). Later followed *al-Ra's al maqtū'* (1963; the severed head) and *Mādī al-ayyām al-ātiya* (1965; the past of the days to come). In his poetry one notes a surrealistic tendency and estrangement from the conventional poetic language. *Qasā'id al-nathr* should be in his eyes the framework for what is deepest and most genuine in poetry. Density, compactness, and organic unity are essential in this most liberal form of poetry. Together with ADŪNĪS he made himself the enthusiastic defender of this new poetic genre. In their hands prose poetry, which existed since Amīn al-Rayhānī (1876–1940) and Kahlil GIBRAN wrote their *shi'r manthūr* in the beginning of the century, became an instrument of revolutionary poetic experiments and a revolt against all the existing metrical tradition. H. made himself the most extreme exponent of the exclusive use of prose as the poetic medium. Others reproached him that he demonstrated a conscious quest for originality and a desire to shock. Certainly he is the most outspoken representative of those who have been called *alshu'arā' al-ghādibūn al-rāfidūn* or "the angry refusing poets."

In fact, H.'s work shows a resemblance to the history of the American English verse and the role of Walt Whitman (1819–1892) in it. In his evolution to prose poems H. was certainly influenced by the Lebanese poet of prose poetry Fu'ād Sulaymān (1912–1951), himself a great admirer of Gibran.

FURTHER WORKS: *Mādhā sana't bi-l-dhahab mādhā fa'alt bi-l-warda* (1970); *al-Rasūla bi-sha'rihā al-tawīl hattā l-yanābî* (1975)

BIBLIOGRAPHY: Moreh, S., *Modern Arabic Poetry*, 1800–1970 (1976): 306–7; Boullata, I. J., *Edebiyat*, 1, 2 (1967): 133–35; Jayyusi, S. K., *Trends and Movements in Modern Arabic Poetry* (1977), Vol. 2: 632–38; Beik, K. Kheir, *Le mouvement moderniste de la poésie arabe contemporaine* (1978), passim; Jayyusi, S. K., ed., *Modern Arabic Poetry: An Anthology* (1987): 247–51

—ED C. M. DE MOOR

al-HAKĪM, Tawfīq

Egyptian dramatist, novelist, and short-story writer, b. 9 Oct. 1898 (or 1902?), Alexandria; d. 26 July 1987, Cairo

After graduating as a lawyer in Cairo, H. was sent by his father to Paris in 1925 to continue his legal studies and submit a doctoral thesis. Instead of devoting his energies to his studies, however, he was strongly attracted to the theater and deeply influenced by SHAW, PIRANDELLO, and Ibsen, whose plays he read or saw. In 1928 he returned to Egypt without a doctorate, but with the skill and inspiration of a promising writer.

Although he had written some music-hall plays before leaving for France, H. came into prominence only after publishing his first novel, *'Awdat al-rūh* (1933; *The Return of the Consciousness*, 1985), in which he tried to describe and account for the sudden awakening of nationalist feelings that led to the 1919 revolution. In this novel, which is in part based on H.'s own experiences, a symbolic layer is superimposed on the essentially realistic, day-to-day story. *'Awdat al-rūh* was meant to be a literary expression of the then-popular notion according to which Egypt has always retained a distinctive national and cultural identity.

Yawmiyyāt nā'ib fī al-aryāf (1937; *The Maze of Justice*, 1947) is a distinctive novel written in the form of diary and draws on H.'s personal experience as a public prosecutor in provincial towns. Autobiographical material is also found in his novel *'Usfūr min al-sharq* (1938; *A Bird from the East*, 1966), which depicts the emotional and intellectual reactions of an Easterner in his first encounter with the West. In spite of the personal material in these three novels, however, H. has repeatedly warned literary critics not to take them as autobiographical documents. Like all novels, he insists, they are fictional works of art and should, therefore, be read as such.

His fame as a novelist notwithstanding, it is in the realm of drama that H.'s talent is best manifested. He wrote scores of social plays and playlets in which the dialogue, often in colloquial Arabic, is full of wit and dramatic tension. But H. is at his best in intellectual plays, which he introduced into Arabic literature. As dramas of ideas, they ought to be considered in the light of H.'s world outlook. Man, he believes, is constantly at war with forces stronger than himself. In his perseverance lurk the secret of his greatness and the source of his tragedy. The heroes of *Ahl al-kahf* (1933; *The People of the Cave*, 1971), which is based on the Koranic version of the Christian legend of the Seven Sleepers of Ephesus, are engaged in a hopeless struggle against time, whereas Shahriyār, the hero of his *Shahrazād* (1934; *Scheherazade*) aspires to free himself from the confinements of space.

H.'s tragic heroes are also subject to an inner conflict between various dualisms, such as life and art, as in his play *Pygmalion* (1942; Pygmalion), or strength and wisdom, as in *Sulaymān al-hakīm* (1943; Solomon the wise).

H. also wrote a number of experimental plays. In *Yā tāli' al-shajara* (1962; *The Tree-Climber*, 1966), he borrows some of the devices employed by the dramatists of the THEATER OF THE ABSURD, although he does not share their sense of loss and despair: he still has faith in a meaningful and well-ordered universe. A play within a play is found in *Al-Ta'ām li-kull fam* (1963; food for every mouth), in which the characters in the outer play undergo exhilarating experiences under the impact of what happens in the inner one. In *Bank al-qalaq* (1967; the bank of anxiety), which is set against the political background of 1960s Egypt, the dramatic episodes are interspersed with narrative ones.

Although H. is often referred to as an artist shut up in his ivory tower, his literary production displays an acute awareness of Egypt's cultural and social problems, as well as deep concern over the present situation of mankind.

FURTHER WORKS: *Ahl al-Fann* (1934); *Muhammad* (1936); *Masrahiyyāt T. al-H.* (1937); *Al-Qasr al-mashūr* (1937); *Taht shams al-fikr* (1938); *'Ahd al-Shaytān* (1938); *Ash'ab* (1938); *Prāxā* (1939); *Rāqisat al-ma'bad* (1939); *Nashīd al-anshād* (1940); *Himār al-H.* (1940); *Sultān al-zalām* (1941); *Min al-burj al-'ājī* (1941); *Taht almisbāh al-akhdar* (1942); *Zahrat al-'umr* (1943); *Al-Ribāt al-muqaddas* (1944); *Shajarat al-hukm* (1945); *Himārī qāla lī* (1945); *Qisas T. al-H.* (1949); *Al-Malik ūdūb* (1949); *Masrah al-mujtama'* (1950); *Fann al-adab* (1952); *'Adāla wa fann* (1953); *Arinī al-Lāh* (1953); *'Asā al-H.* (1954); *Ta'ammulāt fī al-Siyāsa* (1954); *Al-Aydī al-nā'ima* (1954); *Al-Ta'āduliyya* (1955); *Īzīs* (1955); *Al-Safqa* (1956); *Al-Masrah al-munawwa'* (1956); *Lu'bat al-mawt* (1957); *Ashwāk al-salām* (1957); *Rihla ilā al-ghad* (1957); *Adab al-hayāt* (1959); *Al-Sultān al-hā'ir* (1960; *The Sultan's Dilemma*, 1973); *Sijn al-'umr* (1964); *Rihlat al-rabī' wa al-Kharīf* (1964); *Shams al-nahār* (1965); *Laylat al-zifāf* (1966); *Masīr sarsār* (1966); *Al-Warta* (1966); *Qālabunā al-masrahī* (1967); *Qultu dhāt yawm* (1970); *Ahādīth ma'a T. al-H.* (1971); *T. al-H. yatahaddath* (1971); *Majlis al-'adl* (1972); *Thawrat al-shabāb* (1972); *Rāhib bayn nisā'* (1972); *Hadīth ma'a al-Kawkab* (1974); *Al-Dunyā riwāya hazliyya* (1974); *'Awdat al-wa'y* (1974); *Al-Hamīr* (1975); *Wathā'iq fī tarīq 'Awdat al-wa'y* (1975); *Safahāt min al-tārīkh al-adabī* (1975); *Mukhtār tafsīr al-Qurtubī* (1977); *Bayn al-fikr wa al-Fann* (n.d.). FURTHER WORKS IN ENGLISH: *Plays, Prefaces, & Postscripts of T. al-H.*, Vol. I (1981)

BIBLIOGRAPHY: Landau, J. M., *Studies in the Arab Theater and Cinema* (1958): 138–47; Long, C. W. R., "T. al-H. and the Arabic Theatre," *MES*, 5, 2 (1969): 69–74; Haywood, J., *Modern Arabic Literature* (1971): 197–204, 219–34; Starkey, P., "Philosophical Themes in T. al-H.'s Drama," *JArabL*, 8 (1977): 136–52; Fontaine, J., *Mort—Résurrection: Une lecture de T. al-H.* (1978); Long, R., *T. al-H.: Playwright of Egypt* (1979)

—DAVID SEMAH

HAĽAMOVÁ, Maša

Slovak poet, b. 28 Aug. 1908, Blatnica; d. 17 Aug. 1995, Bratislava

H. was born and started school in central Slovakia, but after her mother's death during World War I she was sent to live with family friends in Serbia until Czechoslovakia was established in 1918. She finished business school in Bratislava, published her first verses in 1926, studied for a year in Paris, married, and lived in the Tatra mountains for the next thirty years. This natural environment became essential to her poetry. In 1983 H. was awarded the title of National Artist.

Immediately striking are the tiny quantity of H.'s work, scarcely a hundred published verses, and its profoundly lyrical simplicity. In both respects she continues the legacy of the symbolist and modernist Ivan KRASKO. Unlike many of her contemporaries, H. never attempted to accommodate her poetry to the paradigms of SOCIALIST REALISM, and her subjects remained the intimate personal events of everyday life with very subtly nuanced social concerns. After publishing in literary magazines, she had her first collection of poems, *Dar* (1928; Gift), at the age of twenty, and it showed none of the poses and overstatement of many beginners. With a fairly free melodic meter and expressively clear diction, these poems, at times almost frail and ethereal, express the dualities of hope and disappointment, happiness and sorrow. Appreciating folk forms as well as formal versification, H. wrote several ballads and songs among her best pieces.

Her second collection, *Červený mak* (1932; Red Poppy), continued the intimate revelation of her daily life amid the extraordinary beauty of the Tatra mountains, their vistas and flowers. Her new happy life of love and marriage is apparent, but she also widened her social scope with memories of her own orphanhood after her late mother's death, and with concern for poverty among the mountain folk. Symbolically, eyes and hands carry major themes of her works. Both collections were well received critically and achieved a steady appreciative readership.

After a near silence of over thirty years, upon the death of her husband H. published her finest collection, *Smrt ťvoju žijem* (1966; I Am Living through Your Death). Divided into two parts, the first, entitled "September," gathered love poems recently published in periodicals, but the second part, entitled "Bez teba" (Without You), was her elegy with reflections, meditations, monologues, and even dialogues with her late husband. H. still occasionally published poems, which were gathered into the several editions of her works. Her last work was a short memoir, *Vyznania* (1988; Confession), which approaches prose poetry.

The word "fragile" is often used for H., but she is also known as a poet "of the heart." She generalized her intimate, private experiences through their clarity and intensity. She achieved her status as the most admired woman poet of her generation with a tiny body of poems and without any political attachment in the highly politicized world of eastern Europe during the socialist period.

FURTHER WORKS: *Básne* (1955); *Komu dám svoju nehu* (1968); *Básne* (1972); *Básne* (1978)

BIBLIOGRAPHY: Tomčík, M., *Básnicke retrospektivy* (1974): 215-20; Strmen, K., "Slovak Literature: A Brief History," in Cincura, A., ed., *An Anthology of Slovak Literature* (1976): xlviii; Šmatlák, S., *Dve storočia slovenskej lyriky* (1979): 339-49; Pišút, M., "Lyrický triptych M. H.," *SlovP*, 94 (1978): 8, 4-9; Barto, M.,

Poézia prostoty: Esej o diele M. H. (1983); Rudinsky, N. L., "M. H.," in Wilson, K. M., ed., *Encyclopedia of Continental Women Writers*(1991): 525-26

—NORMA LEIGH RUDINSKY

HALAS, František

Czechoslovak poet, essayist, and translator (writing in Czech), b. 3 Oct. 1901, Brno; d. 27 Oct. 1949, Prague

H.'s father, a textile worker, was a repeatedly jailed left-wing radical. H. himself was active in the Communist Party from his early youth. He worked in a Prague publishing house and was coeditor of various left-wing avant-garde journals. During the Nazi occupation he was involved in the Resistance. After the war H. became a high official at the Ministry of Information, head of the Writers' Syndicate, and member of the National Assembly. Not long after the Communist takeover of 1948 he died in angry despair at what he called his "whored-up dreams."

H.'s first book of verse, *Sépie* (1927; sepia), loosely associated him with the then-leading Czech avant-garde group of poets, who were influenced by French DADAISM and SURREALISM. H.'s serious concerns and his unique style, however, soon excluded him from a movement chiefly distinguished by brilliant verbal gamesmanship.

Nevertheless, this early alliance marked H.'s later work with an enduring love of metaphor and of the densely charged image. His painstaking quest for the potent word, combined with his continuous striving for simplicity, ultimately resulted in verses in which bare nouns are gathered together and juxtaposed not only with each other but also with the all-meaningful bare spaces between the words, the white silences, containing all colors. Often he mates words in violent conjunctions, reminiscent of the 17th-c. metaphysical "conceit." His mixture of colloquialisms, neologisms, and folk and archaic terms is also typically baroque, as is his use of assonance and dissonance in preference to rhyme. Against the songlike, fluid quality of mainstream Czech poetry, H. built rocklike, static, harsh, gratingly rhythmic lines. Although he could, and occasionally did, write melodious stanzas—notably in his collections *Tvář* (1931; face) and *Hořec* (1933; gentian) and in some of his best translations, such as those of the Polish poets Adam Mickiewicz (1798–1855) and Juliusz Słowacki (1808–1849)—most of his work is constructed from monumental, majestic blocks of verse.

After the Munich betrayal of Czechoslovakia in 1938 H. discarded his private voice to become the voice of the silenced land, of its fierce yet tenuous hopes, its anxieties, its anger. His forceful *Torzo naděje* (1938; torso of hope) was read, memorized, and repeated throughout the period of the Nazi occupation, and again during the 1968 invasion of Czechoslovakia by the Warsaw Pact armies.

Even after his death H. continued to serve his country. He became the pivot of the Czech writers' rebellion against Stalinist dogma. The prolonged battle over H. started during the Writers' Congress of 1956, where voices were raised in his defense, and continued until the explosive Writers' Congress of 1967, the eloquent harbinger of the Prague Spring. The controversy was, above all, over H.'s undoubted preoccupation with darkness and death, so irritating to the mindless optimism of the official culture.

H.'s work was repeatedly assailed as "morbid" and "macabre" and as exhibiting "desolate nihilism," "sickly pessimism," and "blackest despair." Yet the darkness that fascinated H. is the life-giving darkness of the earth, "where the stream of primeval life trembles and quickens the rhythm of life, of faith, of memories"—a line from the posthumously published *Magická moc poesie* (1958; magical might of poetry). In these essays particularly, H. made clear that he was speaking of the seed that must be plunged into the dark in order to live and of "the roots that grope in the darkness of the earth for life-saving nourishment."

Like his style, H.'s vision of death-in-life and life-in-death is reminiscent of 17th-c. baroque poetry. The fateful, the unavoidable fusion of life and death is what concerns H. This is no nihilism, but precisely the opposite. The strength and energy animating his verse are built on his refusal to evade the eternal presence of death in life.

Despair appeared only at the end, over-whelming H.'s last poems, written in secret, at a time when the political system he had helped to bring to power dropped its mask, revealing its inhuman face. In his posthumously published verse—for instance, in *A co?* (1957; so what?)—he seems literally to be gasping for air.

H. is one of the giants of modern Czech poetry. His passionate honesty and his dogged search for truth made his poetry a battlefield between hope and mounting disillusionment. It also reflects the tragic destiny of his native land.

FURTHER WORKS: *Kohout plaší smrt* (1930); *Tiše* (1932); *Staré ženy* (1935; *Old Women*, 1947); *Dokořán* (1936); *Časy* (1939); *Naše paní Božena Němcová* (1940; *Our Lady Božena Němcová*, 1944); *Ladění* (1942); *V řadě* (1948); *Počítadlo* (1948); *Halas dětem* (1954; *A Garland of Children's Verse*, 1968); *Potopa* (1956); *Básně* (1957); *Potopa; Hlad* (1965); *Hlad* (1966); *Obrazy* (1968)

BIBLIOGRAPHY: Otruba, M., and Z. Pešat, eds., *The Linden Tree: An Anthology of Czech and Slovak Literature* (1962): 180; French, A., *The Poets of Prague* (1969), passim; Blackwell, V., "The Rock and the Roots," *BA*, 43 (1969): 13–17; Novák, A., *Czech Literature* (1976): 321–22; Kundera, L., "F. H. (1901-1949)," *Cross Currents*, 11 (1992): 65–69

—VERA BLACKWELL

HALPERN, Moyshe Leyb

Yiddish poet, b. 2 Jan. 1886, Zloczów, Austro-Hungarian Empire; d. 31 Aug. 1932, New York, N.Y., U.S.A.

Born in eastern Galicia, H. attended both the traditional Jewish religious elementary school and a modern Polish-Jewish school. At age twelve he was sent to Vienna to study applied art. During a nine-year sojourn in the Hapsburg capital, H. familiarized himself with modern German literature and began to write verse in German. Returning to Zloczów in 1907, he was persuaded by the young Yiddish poets Samuel Jacob Imber (1889–1942) and Jacob Mestel (1884–1958) to write in his mother tongue. At this time H. published his first Yiddish poems in the Galician Yiddish press.

In 1908 H. immigrated to New York. His arrival coincided with the debut of The Young, the insurgent literary group that first gave a distinctively modern voice to American Yiddish literature. H. contributed to the group's publications and was acclaimed as its most forceful and daring poet. His first collection of poems, *In Nyu-York* (1919; *In New York*, 1982), assured him recognition as a major Yiddish poet. Its subject matter and imagery are permeated by his sense of alienation in the modern metropolis, and the plight of modern man is brought into sharp focus through the eyes of the immigrant.

H. became a regular contributor to the Yiddish communist daily *Frayheyt* from its inception in 1922. After a brief period of popularity in radical circles, unable to submit to restraints or party discipline, H. terminated his association with *Frayheyt* in 1924. That same year his second book of verse, *Di goldene pave* (1924; the golden peacock), appeared.

Although originally associated with The Young, H. departed on his own, violently rejecting the self-conscious aestheticism characteristic of this group. He is considered the enfant terrible of modern Yiddish literature. His is a poetry of the grotesque, of disjunctive rhythms, coarse idioms, bold-faced images, and imprecations. Yet H. loved to cavort and clown in his poems. Nevertheless, the lyric voice is not lost in his tempestuous poetry. H. created the persona of "the rascal Moyshe Leyb," which achieved broad recognition and an almost autonomous existence, even during his own lifetime.

FURTHER WORKS: *Lider* (2 vols., 1934)

BIBLIOGRAPHY: Liptzin, S., *The Flowering of Yiddish Literature* (1963): 216–18; Madison, C. A., *Yiddish Literature: Its Scope and Major Writers* (1968): 302–5; Howe, I., and E. Greenberg, eds., *A Treasury of Yiddish Poetry* (1969): 34–36; Wisse, R., "A Yiddish Poet in America," *Commentary*, July 1980: 35–41

—EUGENE ORENSTEIN

HAMMETT, Dashiell

American novelist, short-story writer, and screen-writer, b. 27 May 1894, St. Mary's County, MD.; d. 10 Jan. 1961, New York, N.Y.

Before embarking on a literary career, H. had worked at a number of jobs, had served in the U.S. Army during World War I, and had spent some time in hospitals, undergoing treatment for tuberculosis. One looks in vain for early signs of literary genius, but one is intrigued by the fact that the creator of at least two of American literature's most memorable private detectives was for several years an operative of the Pinkerton Detective Agency.

Although H. lived to 1961, his claim to our attention as an important American writer is based almost completely on work that he produced between 1922 and 1934—barely over a decade. In that time, H. was, by critical consensus, the most important and influential participant in the development of what came to be called hard-boiled detective fiction, contributing to the establishment of a distinctly American idiom within a major popular genre. Moreover, H. developed and defined possibilities for authenticity and art within hard-boiled detective fiction itself, thus raising the standard by which work in this subgenre might be judged, and toward which later writers would aspire. Finally, H.'s work at its best goes beyond narrow considerations of genre, blurring the distinction between the popular and the serious.

Among the activities that involved H. after 1934 were some screenwriting, writing continuity for a comic strip, a good deal of drinking, service with the U.S. Army in the Aleutians during World War II (H. was forty-eight years old when he enlisted), and political activism that led to his spending six months in jail for contempt of court in 1951. During this period he was also involved as an advisor in the work of his longtime companion, the American dramatist Lillian HELLMAN; and he worked sporadically on a novel he would never finish.

H. first made his mark as a writer in the so-called "pulp" magazines that flourished in the 1920s. Aimed at a male mass audience, the pulps specialized in fiction that stressed action and adventure. Most of H.'s best short stories appeared initially between 1923 and 1929 in *Black Mask*, the most respected of the pulps, and most of them follow pretty closely the formula of hard-boiled detective fiction. But H.'s stories are distinguished from those of his contemporaries by qualities of craftsmanship and style. Carroll John Daly (1889–1958) is today often recognized as the first of the hard-boiled detective writers; his "Knights of the Open Palm" appeared in *Black Mask* in June 1923, some four months before the publication in the same magazine of H.'s "Arson Plus," the first of H.'s "Continental Op" stories. Daly's hero, Race Williams, is swaggering, callous, brutal. He is as overstated as the events in which he becomes involved and the style in which, as first-person narrator, he recounts those events to us. The events in the stories H. devotes to the exploits of the Continental Op are often as extravagant as those in Daly's yarns; certainly the action is as fast, the violence as wild. But the Continental Op (H. doesn't give him a proper name) doesn't swagger, isn't brutal or callous; he is tough. And the ability to establish and maintain the distinction between toughness and its counterfeits is one measure of H.'s art.

Red Harvest (1929), H.'s first published novel, in many ways marks the culmination of the Op saga. The character himself is fully realized, and the novel's portrayal of corruption and violence in a western American city is a compelling achievement. The action was apparently inspired in part by H.'s experiences as a Pinkerton man. That H. had actually been a private detective no doubt contributes to the special quality of his fiction, especially of the Continental Op stories, but the result of that experience is hardly "realism" in any of the more restricted senses of that word; rather, it's a matter of the air of authenticity H. can sustain, however extravagant the material he exploits.

The Dain Curse (1929), the second of the Continental Op novels and the last narrative in which that character appears, is a lesser work, although certainly not a dull one. Instead of the narrative drive one finds in his best work, H. here offers mechanical elaboration of plot. And there are hints of a dangerous softening in H.'s portrayal of his protagonist; H.'s decision to abandon the Op at this point seems well advised.

Certainly no one can regret a change of direction that produced a novel as fine as *The Maltese Falcon* (1930). H. replaces the first-person narration of the Op stories with a rigorously objective point of view. We are always "with" Sam Spade, H.'s detective protagonist—the book contains no scene at which he is not present—but H. never admits us directly to Spade's thoughts and feelings. He is viewed, as are all the other characters, from the outside. This technique, combined with an air of moral ambiguity ("Don't be too sure I'm as crooked as I'm supposed to be," Spade says at one point), generates a detective story in which the most mysterious character is the detective.

Not that Spade is the only memorable character in the novel. The conspirators, the police, the women in Spade's life, his mediocre partner, are all vividly, economically, and unforgettably

Dashiell Hammett

drawn. And the falcon itself is one of H.'s most impressive creations: jewel-encrusted object of fabulous history and wild imaginings, worthy goal of an endless quest; worthless leaden fake, reducing romantic quest to parody; in any event "the stuff that dreams are made of."

The Glass Key (1931) was apparently H.'s favorite among his novels and certainly represents a serious effort at the detective novel as literature. More than any other novel by H., this one tends to divide his critics and admirers. The stylistic objectivity that is a major strength of *The Maltese Falcon* strikes some readers as an annoyance in the later novel: an obstinate and perverse refusal, some argue, to satisfy the reader's desire, motivated by other qualities in the text, to go below the surface. Yet there is no denying the work's formal integrity—perverse or not, H. doesn't compromise. And there are many critics for whom *The Glass Key* is H.'s most impressive achievement.

The Thin Man (1934) was H.'s last novel. It was also his most successful in commercial terms and, perhaps, his least successful in critical terms. It is by no means without merit, but it is a novel of parts, of witty or otherwise arresting passages that never cohere to form a satisfying whole. It is perhaps symptomatic of where H. was at this point in his career that much of what is best in *The Thin Man* is peripheral to the detective interest, an observation one could not have made of *The Glass Key*. It had begun to seem that, in order to grow as an artist, H. would have to move beyond detective fiction.

This is the move he was never able to make. One may look to biographers—H. has already had several—for theories that might explain his silence. Personal problems, including alcoholism, may certainly have contributed. But it seems that H.'s problem as an artist was his recognition that he had reached that point in his development at which he had to find his material within himself, without the disguise and protection that generic conventions, even when employed as creatively as in H.'s work, could provide. And he found that he could not take off the mask.

H.'s reputation seems secure. Indeed, it may well ascend, as POSTMODERNISM, whatever its sins, properly encourages us to question such limiting oppositions as serious versus popular. Certainly H. deserves our lasting respect as one who achieved excellence in the world of pulp/pop fiction, a world in which, according to long-standing academic prejudice, excellence isn't supposed to matter.

FURTHER WORKS: *$106,000 Blood Money* (1943); *The Adventures of Sam Spade and Other Stories* (1944); *The Continental Op* (1945); *The Return of the Continental OP* (1945); *Hammett Homicides* (1946); *Dead Yellow Women* (1947); *Nightmare Town* (1948); *The Creeping Siamese* (1950); *The Woman in the Dark* (1951); *A Man Named Thin and Other Stories* (1962); *The Big Knockover* (1966); *The Continental Op* (1974)

BIBLIOGRAPHY: Chandler, R., "The Simple Art of Murder," *Atlantic Monthly* (Dec. 1944): 53–9; Bazelon, D., "D. H.'s Private Eye: No Loyalty Beyond the Job," *Commentary*, 7 (1949): 467–72; Blair, W., "D.H., Themes and Techniques," in Ghodes, C., ed., *Essays on American Literature in Honor of Jay B. Hubbell* (1967): 295–306; Edenbaum, R., "The Poetics of the Private Eye: The Novels of D. H.," in Madden, D., ed., *Tough Guy Writers of the Thirties* (1968): 80–103; Malin, I., "Focus on *The Maltese Falcon*," in Madden, D., ed., *Tough Guy Writers of the Thirties* (1968): 104–9; Nolan, W. F., *D. H.: A Casebook* (1969); Wolfe, P., *Beams Falling: The Art of D. H.* (1980); Layman, R., *Shadow Man: The Life of D. H.* (1981); Porter, D., *The Pursuit of Crime: Art and Ideology in Detective Fiction* (1981): 130–45; Margolies, E., *Which Way Did He Go?: The Private Eye in D. H., Raymond Chandler, Chester Himes, and Ross Macdonald* (1982): 17–31; Johnson, D., *D. H.: A Life* (1983); Nakjavani, E., "The Red Harvest: An Archipelago of Micro-Powers," *Clues: A Journal of Detection*, 4, 1 (Spring-Summer 1983): 105–13; Naremore, J., "D. H. and the Poetics of Hard-Boiled Fiction," in Benstock, B., ed., *Art in Crime Writing* (1983): 49–72; Symons, J., *D. H.* (1985); Lehman, D., *The Perfect Murder* (1989): 126–30, 147–67;

—W. P. KENNEY

HAMSUN, Knut

(pseud. of Knud Pedersen) Norwegian novelist, dramatist, and poet, b. 4 Aug. 1859, Lom; d. 19 Feb. 1952, Nørholm

H. is generally recognized as Norway's greatest novelist, and, after Ibsen, the nation's second most important literary figure. Although H. was born in Gudbrandsdal, the fertile valley that runs through the spine of south-central Norway, his family moved when H. was three years old to Hamarøy in Nordland. Here his father, an itinerant tailor and sometime farmer, worked the farm called Hamsund, which H.'s maternal uncle had purchased. In these northern reaches, where nature was most harsh and demanding, H. developed his love of the earth by observing the rush of the Arctic seasons and the grandeur of the mountains and forests.

At the age of nine, H. was sent to the uncle to live and work in the store, where he was cruelly disciplined. It seems likely that this experience developed the feeling of defiance and bitterness that permeates his writings, and also his distrust of older people and age itself. After unsuccessful efforts to run away, H. succeeded eventually and returned to Gudbrandsdal for his confirmation; but when he had this certification of his maturity and independence, he returned to Hamarøy to work at a wide variety of odd jobs.

At the age of eighteen, he published his first book under the name of Knut Pedersen, and two more books the following year under the name of Knut Pedersen Hamsund. A printer's error later on dropped the final *d* on Hamsund, and H. accepted this as a felicitous accident. Although he published various newspaper articles, he was not to be accepted by a major publishing house until another grueling and frustrating decade had elapsed. In the meantime he worked at more trades in Norway and was in the U.S. twice for two-year periods.

In 1888 H. returned to Europe with a manuscript entitled *Fra det moderne Amerikas åndsliv* (1889; *The Intellectual Life of Modern America*, 1969). In this bitingly witty work he excoriated the shallowness and materialism of the U.S. He viewed it and Britain as the least cultured nations of the world because of the industrial mechanization that had left the two countries without meaning, without purpose, and without souls.

H.'s first masterpiece was *Sult* (1890; *Hunger*, 1899). It is a completely egocentric book, largely autobiographical. Detailing the kaleidoscopic and often nearly delirious perceptions of a homeless man close to starvation, the novel is a piece of pure art without any hint of social message. While it is realistic enough as to subject, namely indigence and loneliness in the big city, its technique is unalloyed impressionism. In many ways it is stream-of-consciousness prose, antedating JOYCE and later writers, but the spirit is Dostoevskian.

H. then embarked on a widely discussed lecture tour in which he attacked the Brahmins of Norwegian literature, most notably Ibsen, for preoccupation with utilitarian literature written for a social purpose. While the lectures were not met with universal approval, it is impossible to overestimate the impact that *Sult* and the lecture series had on Norwegian belles lettres.

Consistent with his lectures and with the literary thrust he had initiated in *Sult*, H. published the enigmatic *Mysterier* (1892; *Mysteries*, 1927). H.'s primary motif of the erratic wanderer, who makes no appeal for sympathy or even understanding, propels the novel. Perhaps more than any of his other writings, *Mysterier* allowed H. to display his contempt for politicians, his antipathy toward the old, his exaltation of the individual, and his admiration of the Nietzschean superman.

Many critics consider *Pan* (1894; *Pan*, 1920) to represent H.'s most magnificent writing. The leading character is akin with other wandering strangers in H.'s work, but he is a stronger, more primordial force. However, what truly distinguishes *Pan* is the lyrical description of the magic beauty of the Norwegian north country. Perhaps nowhere in literature has H.'s description of the colors, the lights, and the vastness of the sub-Arctic in the summer-time been matched. H. expresses an urgent longing for the melding of man and nature, for a return to a more elemental, meaningful life.

The other side of the same coin is expressed in the two coupled novels *Børn av tiden* (1913; *Children of the Age*, 1924) and *Segelfoss by* (1915; *Segelfoss Town*, 1925). The books are social satires depicting the evolution of a patriarchal farming community into a capitalistic town. The societal development is portrayed with far less of the subjective lyrical style that H. employed in his other works. Nevertheless, the two novels constitute a witty, savagely ironic contribution to literary art. In their realism they reveal a deep pessimism about a society that apparently belongs to self-centered men of no imagination and no horizons.

Markens grøde (1917; *Growth of the Soil*, 1920), which led to his being awarded the Nobel Prize in 1920, is his most widely read and universally acclaimed work. Just as H. distrusted and disapproved of modern civilization, which he regarded as a sickness of mankind, he honored the individual farmer-pioneer who extracted both his physical and his psychological nourishment from the soil. Writing with a powerful lyric style reminiscent of the Bible, H. created an indelible picture of the persevering and uncomplaining farmer for whom the soil is sufficient reason for being. H. himself farmed, and he, like Robert FROST, chose to regard himself as a farmer as much as a writer.

Because of the intrinsic difficulty of translating poetry, and because of the small corpus of poems that H. permitted to be published (he tells of two major burnings), he is little known as a writer of poetry to the non-Nordic world. Nevertheless he must be ranked among Norway's finest poets.

His one major poetic contribution is *Det vilde kor* (1904; the wild choir), which with a few additions and changes was published again in *Samlede verker* (1916; collected works). H. was a craftsman of language, and while he was uncharacteristically modest about his poetic ability ("I am no Robert Burns," he confessed), his poetry was on an artistic level with his prose. The lyric quality that pervades *Markens grøde* is magnified in *Det vilde kor*. The mad humor and passionate recklessness of *Sult* are distilled and condensed in his poetry. All the arrogance, tenderness, and sardonic sense of humor that appear in H.'s novels are paralleled in his poems.

H.'s last years were tragic, although it is not likely that he regarded them as such. His support of Nazi Germany during World War II was unfortunate but not surprising. He hated the British (he was merely contemptuous of Americans), and he had favored the German cause in World War I. H.'s basic philosophy was Nietzschean, and his vision of the solitary independent wanderer was warped somehow into its direct antithesis, the Nazi ideal. Most of H.'s wartime writings consisted of political polemics and appeals to Norwegians to accept and even support the Germans.

After World War II, H. was arrested and tried as a traitor. He could have easily had his case passed over had he been willing to live with the widely held view that he was senile. Instead he goaded and prodded the government, and displayed little sign either of senility or contriteness. After he was convicted and fined, he published *På gjengrodde stier* (1949; *On Overgrown Paths*, 1967), a journal of his thoughts from the time of his initial arrest to his conviction and sentencing. It is a poignant, rueful, but in no way pathetic statement.

In 1952, at the age of ninety-two, H. died. He departed with wit and wits intact. During his life span he had seen the establishment of an independent Norway, two world wars, and a great depression. He had received adulation, and had been condemned as a traitor and renegade. Had he merely lived his biblically allotted three

Knut Hamsun

score and ten, instead of more than four score and ten, he would have died completely honored and revered. But whatever judgments are made of his politics, as a writer he was a towering figure who made a magnificent contribution not only to Norwegian literature, but to the world.

FURTHER WORKS: *Den gådefulde* (1877); *Et gjensyn* (1878); *Bjørger* (1878); *Lars Oftedal* (1889); *Redaktor Lynge* (1893); *Ny jord* (1893; *Shallow Soil*, 1914); *Ved rigets port* (1895); *Livets spil* (1896); *Siesta* (1897); *Aftenrøde* (1898); *Victoria* (1898); *Munken Vendt* (1902); *I æventyrland* (1903); *Dronning Tamara* (1903); *Kratskog* (1903); *Sværmere* (1904; *Dreamers*, 1921); *Stridende liv* (1905); *Under høststjærnen* (1906; *Under the Autumn Star*, 1922); *Benoni* (1908; *Benoni*, 1925); *Rosa* (1908; *Rosa*, 1926); *En vandrer spiller med sordin* (1909; *A Wanderer Plays on Muted Strings*, 1922); *Livet ivold* (1910; *In the Grip of Life*, 1924); *Den sidste glæde* (1912; *Look Back on Happiness*, 1940); *Konerne ved vandposten* (1920; *The Women at the Pump*, 1928); *Dikte* (1921); *Sidste kapitel* (1923; *Chapter the Last*, 1929); *Landstrykere* (1927; *Vagabonds*, 1930; new tr., *Wayfarers*, 1981); *August* (1930; *August*, 1931); *Men livet lever* (1933; *The Road Leads On*, 1934); *Ringen sluttet* (1936; *The Ring Is Closed*, 1937); *Samlede verker* (17 vols., 1936)

BIBLIOGRAPHY: Larsen, H. A., *K. H.* (1922); Wiehr, J., *K. H., Smith College Studies in Modern Languages*, 3, 1–2 (1921–22); Gustafson, A., *Six Scandinavian Novelists* (1940): 226–85; Hamsun,

T., *Mein Vater* (1940); Mendelssohn, P. de, *Der Geist in der Despotie* (1953); Hamsun, M., *Der Regenbogen* (1954); McFarlane, J. W., "The Whisper of the Blood," *PMLA*, 71 (1956): 563–94; Lowenthal, L., *Literature and the Image of Man* (1957): 190–220; Naess, H., "The Three H.s: The Changing Attitude in Recent Criticism," *SS*, 32 (1960): 129–39; Naess, H., "H. and America," *SS*, 39 (1967): 305–28; Ferguson, R., *Enigma: The Life of K. H.* (1987)

—HAROLD P. HANSON

HANDKE, Peter

Austrian novelist, dramatist, poet, and essayist, b. 6 Dec. 1942, Griffen

H.'s work first appeared while he was studying law at Graz (1961–65), where a group of like-minded coevals, including the playwright Wolfgang BAUER and the novelist Gerhard Roth (b. 1942) staged plays and literary events and contributed to the magazine *manuskripte*. In the mid-1960s H. moved to Frankfurt-am-Main, West Germany, where his first play was performed and his first novel published (both in 1966). With a move to Paris in 1969 and another one back to Frankfurt in 1971 came a greater concentration on writing fiction; by the end of the 1970s, having returned to his native Austria (Salzburg), he had eight novels to his credit but had apparently stopped writing for the theater—although

Peter Handke

he was writing (and directing) more for the screen. He was awarded the German Academy's prestigious Büchner Prize in 1973.

H. has essayed most forms of writing, but it was as an anticonventional playwright (coupled with a provocative public persona) that he made his initial impact. In his first play, *Publikumsbeschimpfung* (1966; *Offending the Audience*, 1969), four actors inform the audience that what they are watching is not a play but simply a stage with four people on it; they then alternately insult the audience and compliment them on their "performance," a strategy that often provoked extreme audience reaction. There followed three less outrageous plays—*Selbstbezichtigung* (1966; *Self-Accusation*, 1969), *Weissagung* (1966; prophecy), and *Hilferufe* (1967; *Calling for Help*, 1971)—which nonetheless shared with *Publikumsbeschimpfung* a lack of plot, character, and dramatic construction. The aim of these plays, said H., was not to "revolutionize, but to make [the audience] aware"—of themselves and of certain realities.

This was also the aim of *Kaspar* (1968; *Kaspar*, 1969), H.'s first—and probably best—full-length play, and the first to feature a dramatic character. Using as a model the real-life Kaspar Hauser, who mysteriously turned up in Nuremburg in 1828 at the age of sixteen, but with the mind of a child, H. created an abstract parable to "make audiences aware" of how accepted modes of expression are imposed on an individual, thus circumscribing his originality. Kaspar, a speechless innocent, is indoctrinated into becoming an orderly, articulate member of society. But his final lapse into incoherence indicates a Wittgensteinian realization that, in learning a language, one has to accept the values implicit in it, and that it is therefore impossible to form thoughts independent of that value system.

After *Das Mündel will Vormund sein* (1969; *My Foot My Tutor*, 1971), a compelling one-act scenario in which two half-masked men perform odd rituals of domination and subservience, H. explored an idea suggested by a ballad about a horseman who rides unsuspectingly across a thinly frozen lake only to die of fright when subsequently told of the danger he had been in. The characters in *Der Ritt über den Bodensee* (1971; *The Ride across Lake Constance*, 1972) are all skating on the thin ice of "normal" behavior, which H. depicts as a random collection of stock theatrical speeches and gestures. The tension arises from the fact that these mechanical figures are constantly on the brink of breaking through the clichés to something unknown and untried but, H. implies, more exciting than stale normality.

This uncompromising piece was followed by H.'s most conventional play—apparently his last—*Die Unvernünftigen sterben aus* (1974; *They Are Dying Out*, 1975), about a consumer-goods capitalist who cannot reconcile his emotional sensitivity with the demands of business life. The treatment is fresh, but the theme is well tried, and the dramatic conventions are clumsily handled. H. had seemed surer on less familiar terrain.

Just as Wittgenstein haunts Handke's plays, his influence is also present in H.'s novels, most noticeably in their tendency to approach a phenomenon over and over again from different angles in search of its absolute reality (a preoccupation, along with a rejection of conventional character and plot, that H. shares with Alain ROBBE-GRILLET and other New Novelists). As with the plays, the initial critical reaction was hostile, but H.'s deadpan, ultraobjective accounts of characters in extreme states of mind moving through "normal" yet alien landscapes have won increasing acclaim—and numbers of readers.

In *Die Angst des Tormanns beim Elfmeter* (1970; *The Goalie's Anxiety at the Penalty Kick*, 1972) a murderer—the goalkeeper of the title—is on the run from a pointless, spur-of-the-moment killing. *Der kurze Brief zum langen Abschied* (1972; *Short Letter, Long Farewell*, 1974) is the first-person account of a young Austrian writer's picaresque journey across the U.S. in search of his estranged wife, a journey that allows H. to interlard lengthy quotations from books, plays, films, dreams, memories, and the surface phenomena of American life, thus paying homage to a number of his literary heroes, among them William FAULKNER, Raymond Chandler (1888–1959), and Patricia Highsmith (b. 1921).

Die Stunde der wahren Empfindungen (1975; *A Moment of True Feeling*, 1977) concerns another murderer, a press attaché at the Austrian embassy in Paris, but despite nods in the direction of KAFKA the careful depiction of tedium becomes itself dangerously tedious. In *Die linkshändige Frau* (1976; *The Left-handed Woman*, 1978), based on an original screenplay that Handke himself had filmed, an apparently happily married young mother, having suddenly asked her husband to leave her, has to cope both with her newfound independence and with a sense of disorientation, which is described in a style exactly matching the dispassionate eye of a camera.

In the middle of this sequence of novels, spurred by his mother's suicide, H. wrote an unsentimental yet affecting memoir of her life—not unlike that of his fictional characters. Called a "story," *Wunschloses Unglück* (1972; *A Sorrow beyond Dreams*, 1974) is told with beguiling simplicity but nonetheless embraces a complex interplay between factual content and fictional conventions. It represents H.'s technique at its best.

H. has also published poetry, essays, short stories, radio dramas, a television play, and a long journal of the eighteen months of his domicile in Paris, *Das Gewicht der Welt* (1978; *Fantasies and Prejudices*, 1979). Whatever the medium, however, H.'s concern is to demonstrate that experience is a succession of ready-made, preordained components, whose deadening effect must be painstakingly countered. Hence the persistent dialectic in his work between conventional and unconventional forms. Although his work can be difficult, in the breadth and variety of his experimentation and the uniqueness of his best fiction and drama, H. is one of the most exciting and original of the postwar generation of European writers.

FURTHER WORKS: *Die Hornissen* (1966); *Der Hausierer* (1967); *Begrüßung des Aufsichtsrat* (1967); *Die Innenwelt der Außenwelt der Innenwelt* (1969); *Deutsche Gedichte* (1969); *Wind und Meer* (1970); *Quodlibet* (1970); *Chronik der laufenden Ereignisse* (1971); *Ich bin ein Bewohner des Elfenbeinturms* (1972); *Als das Wünschen noch geholfen hat* (1974; *Nonsense and Happiness*, 1976); *Langsame Heimkehr* (1979); *Die Lehre der Sainte-Victoire* (1980); *Kindergeschichte* (1981); *Über die Dörfer* (1981)

BIBLIOGRAPHY: special H. issue, *TuK*, No. 24 (1969; 2nd ed., 1971); Heintz, G., *P. H.* (1971); Hern, N., *P. H.* (1972); Rischbieter, H., *P. H.* (1972); Scharang, M., ed., *Über P. H.* (1972); Gilman, R., *The Making of Modern Drama* (1974): 267–88; Mixner, M., *P. H.* (1977); Taëni, R., "On Thin Ice: P. H.'s Studies in Alienation," *Meanjin*, 36 (1977): 315–25; Nägele, R., and Voris, R., *P. H.* (1978); Klinkowitz, J., "Aspects of H.: The Fiction," *PR*, 45 (1978): 416–24; Jurgensen, M., ed., *H.: Ansätze, Analysen, Anmerkungen* (1979); Schlueter, J., *The Plays and Novels of P. H.* (1981); Malkin, J. R., *Verbal Violence in Contemporary Drama: From H. to Shepard* (1992); Firda, R. A., *P. H.* (1993)

—NICHOLAS HERN

HANLEY, James

Anglo-Irish novelist, dramatist, essayist, biographer, and poet, b. 3 Sept. 1901, Dublin, Ireland; d. 11 Nov. 1985, London

H., a very prolific author, was born into a poor Irish family. He left school when he was thirteen but educated himself by voracious reading and extensive travels by shipping out to sea for ten years. He worked at a variety of jobs: as a journalist, a railway porter, and race-course cashier. He lived in Wales for a number of years but the last part of his life was spent in London.

Two themes dominate H.'s writings: men in ships at sea, and men and women self-imprisoned in their private worlds of dreams and despair. H.'s world is crowded with marginal people, outcasts, loners, and strangers. In portraying their broken business of living, H. relentlessly conducts a complex but compassionate investigation to reveal the rugged individuality of their lives, whether they are adrift at sea, trapped in a Welsh rooming house, or frightened and huddling in a damp cellar in a London blitz.

Boy (1931), H.'s first novel of the sea, is an angry, realistic novel about the brutalization of an adolescent on a merchant steamer. It stirred a literary and social controversy, was suppressed under the British obscenity laws, and became a cause célèbre.

H.'s magnum opus is *The Furys Chronicle*—a five-volume family saga consisting of *The Furys* (1935), *The Secret Journey* (1936), *Our Time Is Gone* (1940), *Winter Song* (1950), and *An End and a Beginning* (1958)—about the fortunes of a lower-class Liverpool-Irish family. H.'s social concerns, his theme of men at sea, and his uncompromising realism in the portrayal of a people and a place are all harmoniously orchestrated in this work. Fanny Fury is one of the most fully realized women in contemporary fiction, while the portrait of John Kilkey is an impressive study of a pacifist.

Hollow Sea (1938), one of H.'s personal favorites, is an intense study of men under personal and professional pressure while involved in a secret wartime mission on a ship. *The Ocean* (1941) tells the story of six sailors in a lifeboat after their ship has been torpedoed by a German submarine. Through a series of flashbacks, H. tells the grim tale of survival at sea. *Sailor's Song* (1947) is the story of a wounded and delirious sailor afloat on a raft. His remembrance of things past before he drifts into death is narrated in a spare, poetic style. In *The Closed Harbour* (1953), set in Marseille, an outcast sailor has lost his honor and his ship: without his ship he disintegrates, and H. analyzes the strange umbilical relationship that exists between a sailor and his ship. *Levine* (1956) is a tale of two human wrecks, Felix and Grace, and their stormy relationship. Felix is a fascinating study of a man without a country and with no identity except in his memory.

After *Say Nothing* (1962), a novel about a man who takes up lodging with a strange couple that in its depiction of noncommunication and its imagery drawn from prison portrays what life is like for the totally damned, H. did not write fiction for ten years. But he took up playwriting for radio, television, and the stage. His plays indicate a temperamental affinity with STRINDBERG, BECKETT, and PINTER.

H.'s recent novels, *A Woman in the Sky* (1973), *A Dream Journey* (1976), and *A Kingdom* (1978), reveal an artist at the height of his powers. In these works H. uses a plain but chiseled prose and much dialogue. Thus, the novels read like plays.

Although H. has been admired by many leading writers and has consistently received good reviews, he has had only a small cultish audience. Of his own writing H. has said, "It's like a prisoner, being a writer." As for the writing of a novel, he has said that it is "a series of blind gropings in a dark tunnel."

FURTHER WORKS: *Drift* (1930); *The Last Voyage: A Tale* (1931); *Men in Darkness: Five Stories* (1931); *Ebb and Flood* (1932); *Stoker Haslett: A Tale* (1932); *Aria and Finale and Other Stories* (1932); *Captain Bottell* (1933); *Quartermaster Clausen* (1934); *At Bay* (1935); *Stoker Bush* (1935); *Half an Eye: Sea Stories* (1937); *Broken Water: An Autobiographical Excursion* (1937); *Grey Children: A Study in Humbug and Misery* (1937); *People Are Curious* (1938); *Between the Tides* (1939); *No Directions* (1943); *Sailor's Song* (1943); *At Bay and Other Stories* (1944); *Crilley and Other Stories* (1945); *What Farrar Saw* (1946); *Emily* (1948); *Towards Horizons* (1949); *A Walk in the Wilderness* (1950); *The House in the Valley* (1951); *Collected Stories* (1953); *Don Quixote Drowned* (1953); *The Welsh Sonata: Variations on a Theme* (1954); *Chaliapin* (1967); *John Cowper Powys: A Man in the Corner* (1969); *The Face of Winter* (1969); *Herman Melville: A Man in the Customs House* (1971); *Another World* (1972); *The Darkness* (1973); *Against the Stream* (1981)

BIBLIOGRAPHY: Stokes, E., *The Novels of J. H.* (1964); "A Novelist in Neglect: The Case for J.H.," *TLS*, 11 June 1971: 675–76; Morris, R. K., "Saved and Damned by Imagination," *Nation*, 11 May 1974: 601–2; Howe, I., "An Original and Abrasive Novelist," *NYTBR*, 19 Dec. 1976: 1, 26; Mathewson, R., "H.'s Palimpsest," *New Leader*, 2 Jan. 1977: 17–18; Gibbs, L., *J. H.: A Bibliography*

—K. BHASKARA RAO

HANSBERRY, Lorraine

American dramatist, b. 19 May 1930, Chicago, Ill.; d. 12 Jan. 1965, New York, N.Y.

H. developed as a writer during the 1950s and early 1960s, a period of racial tension and the nonviolent civil rights movement, both of which influenced her work. Although born to a prosperous black Chicago family, of which she was the youngest child, she could not ignore racism. After two years at the University of Wisconsin she moved in 1950 to New York City and settled in Greenwich Village, where a small group of dedicated friends encouraged her playwriting.

In 1959 H.'s first play, *A Raisin in the Sun*, opened on Broadway to rave reviews. The first black woman to have a play produced on Broadway, H. was also the first Afro-American whose work won the New York Critics' Circle Award for the best play of the year. The popularity of the play is quite understandable.

Timely, moving, well crafted, it exposes the consequences of racism while generally avoiding platitudes, slogans, and one-dimensional characters. H. can sketch a white racist with understanding and treat her black protagonists, the Younger family, critically as well as sympathetically. Based on an actual incident when the Hansberrys moved into a white neighborhood, *A Raisin in the Sun* pits Lena, the strong matriarch, against Walter Lee, her weak, self-indulgent son who "comes into manhood" when he refuses the white community's bribe to leave. His pan-Africanist sister, Beneatha, and her Nigerian boyfriend, Asagai, reinforce the importance of black pride and unity. Although the characters are black, the subjects—cultural pride, family responsibility, individual honor, and self-respect—are universal. Translated into over thirty languages, performed throughout America and Europe, adapted as a film and in 1973 as the successful musical *Raisin, A Raisin in the Sun* has gained international recognition as a major American drama.

H.'s versatility is evident in her second play, *The Sign in Sidney Brustein's Window* (1965), completed shortly before her death. Set in Greenwich Village, the play focuses on Sidney Brustein, a frustrated Jewish intellectual, and on his neurotic family and his friends. With the exception of Alton Scales, a black engaged to Sidney's sister-in-law, the characters are all white; the problems are human, only peripherally racial. By testing her characters' commitment and decency, H. shatters common stereotypes. Thus, a black can be bigoted, a racist tolerant, and a reform politician corrupt. The play touches on homosexuality and prostitution, but centers on Sidney Brustein, who, like Walter Lee Younger, matures and accepts responsibility for people and principles. In contrast to *A Raisin in the Sun*, *The Sign in Sidney Brustein's Window* was not initially well received. Criticized for its didacticism, slow pace, and flat characters, the play nearly closed after opening night, but the devoted producers, cast, and theater lovers kept it on Broadway until H. died, of cancer, three months later.

After her death, Robert Nemiroff, H.'s former husband (they had been secretly divorced), edited and published her unfinished manuscripts. *Les Blancs* (1972), the play H. was working on when she died, reflects her continued support for African nationalism. Consistently realistic, she recognized the problems confronting new nations and leaders, but believed in the struggle for independence. Her protagonist, Tshembe Matoseh, a British-educated African married to a white woman, symbolizes the complexities of race relations and the conflict between personal and communal obligations. His insights, growth, and commitment to freedom reflect H.'s values and life. In *To Be Young, Gifted and Black* (1969), autobiographical dramatized readings compiled by Nemiroff from her speeches, letters, journals, and plays, H. emerges as an intelligent, witty, courageous woman who dedicated her talent to the furthering of justice.

Although she completed only two plays, H. created memorable characters who defy stereotypes and transcend limited environments. Her treatment of racism, African nationalism, and social change foreshadowed the turbulent late 1960s and its protest movement.

FURTHER WORKS: *The Drinking Gourd* (1960); *The Movement: A Documentary of a Struggle for Equality* (1964)

BIBLIOGRAPHY: Davis, O., "The Significance of L. H.," *Freedomways*, 5 (1966): 396–402; Baldwin, J., Preface to *To Be Young, Gifted and*

Black (1969): xi–xv; Miller, J., "L. H.," in Bigsby, C. W. E., ed., *The Black American Writer* (1969), Vol. II: 157–70; Weales, G., "Losing the Playwright," *Commonweal*, 5 Sept. 1969: 542–53; Farrison, W. E., "L. H.'s Last Dramas," *CLAJ*, 16 (1972): 188–97; Brown, L. W., "L. H. as Ironist: A Reappraisal of *A Raisin in the Sun*," *JBIS*, 4 (1974): 237–47; special H. issue, *Freedomways*, 19, 4 (1979)

—EVELYN AVERY

Lorraine Hansberry

HANSEN, Martin A.

Danish novelist, short-story writer, and essayist, b. 20 Aug. 1909, Strøby; d. 27 June 1955, Copenhagen

Born into a family of religious small farmers, H. was deeply influenced in his youth by the blend of simple Christian and traditional rural values that characterized the last vestiges of the dying peasant culture in Denmark. In the late 1920s and the early 1930s, while a student and subsequently as a young teacher in Copenhagen, he turned away intellectually from his religious, social, and political roots, espousing atheism and Darwinism and becoming a communist sympathizer. But by the 1940s, he had gradually become convinced of the inadequacy of the ideologies he had accepted. World War II in particular shattered his faith in rationalism, disclosing, it seemed to him, the lack of an all-embracing meaning in life.

Paradoxically, most of H.'s best fiction was written between 1939 and 1947, as he struggled to cope with Europe's external chaos and his own disillusionment. The conflict between his nihilistic perception of reality and the values of his rural-Christian past became the dialectical basis for his mature fiction. His personal response to that conflict, best described as existential, would provide the passionate, humanly engaged perspective that informs his work. This perspective is seen in the dialectical structures of *Jonatans rejse* (1941; Jonathan's travels), a satiric picaresque novel in which a smith, having captured the devil in a bottle, sets out to bring him to the king, and of *Lykkelige Kristoffer* (1945; *Lucky Kristoffer*, 1974), perhaps H.'s finest novel, which describes the episodic quest of an idealistic, impoverished young nobleman who leaves his provincial home and journeys to Copenhagen during the religious wars of the Reformation. In both novels the protagonists are naïve and either intuitive or idealistic, creatures of heart, faith, and simple virtues. Both protagonists have as foils companions committed to reason, intellect, science, atheism, men whose more sophisticated vision weakens their moral fiber.

This intense period of creativity climaxed with the publication of three novellas in the volume entitled *Tornebusken* (1946; the thorn bush), and with *Agerhønen* (1947; the partridge), a collection of short stories. While greatly varied in style, setting, and point of view, these stories repeatedly present people in complex existential situations, people who are in the process of examining their lives, making choices, and wrestling with the burdens of moral awareness.

After the war, H. gave up teaching and supported himself and his family exclusively with writing. In the widespread ideological debate that flourished in postwar Denmark, his was an influential voice seeking to define those aspects of the cultural tradition that

were still vital and steadying in the chaos of modernity. This effort reached a high point with the publication of *Orm og tyr* (1952; serpent and bull), an impressive cultural history that examines the complementary relationships of pagan and Christian religions in Scandinavia. Yet his best known and most widely translated novel, *Løgneren* (1950; *The Liar*, 1954), harked back to the intense existential ambiguities of his earlier work. Originally a radio narrative, *Løgneren* is a compelling psychological revelation of its protagonist-narrator; it delineates the complex ethical struggle of a sensitive schoolmaster on a small ice-locked island as he vacillates between demonic self-indulgence and disciplined self-denial; it demonstrates H.'s mastery of lyrical and symbolic form.

With few exceptions, H.'s fiction vividly depicts the milieu in which he grew up, the farms and villages of rural Denmark. His characters' lives are linked to birds and seasons, fields and plants, water and weather. His fiction implies the need for a natural religiousness, suggesting the value of being in touch with natural cycles, with the land, with animals, and with people at a level more profound than mere rational awareness. Yet he does not show rural life as simply idyllic.

H.'s fiction is characterized by disarmingly simple, unpretentious language. Its rhythms are typically those of oral storytelling. A rich vein of humor, often warmly playful, occasionally grimly ironic, pervades his work. The impression of simplicity is also conveyed by H.'s vigorous narration; he is a natural storyteller who engrosses readers quickly and sustains their interest at a high level until he reaches often startling conclusions. Yet readers caught in the web of H.'s engaging narrative surface gradually become aware that his fictions are far more subtle than they at first seem. This paradoxical yoking of simplicity and complexity in characterization, moral vision, and artistic form is one of the most striking features of his work.

In his twenty years as a writer, H. produced a substantial body of work. Now generally acknowledged as the foremost Danish writer of his generation and among the greatest Danish writers of this century, H. focused in a spiritually troubled time the cultural, ethical, and existential concerns of his countrymen in such a way as to appeal widely to both sophisticated readers and the more general public alike. His work has significantly influenced modern Danish literature. The gradual growth of his reputation outside Denmark since his premature death is evidence that his best fiction transcends his own time and place.

FURTHER WORKS: *Nu opgiver han* (1935); *Kolonien* (1937); *Tanker i en skorsteen* (1948); *Leviathan* (1950); *Dansk vejr* (1953); *Kringen* (1953); *Paradisæblerne, og andre historier* (1953); *Rejse på Island* (1954); *Konkyljen* (1955); *Midsommerkrans* (1956); *Efterslæt* (1959). FURTHER WORKS IN ENGLISH: *Against the Wind* (1979)

BIBLIOGRAPHY: Vowles, R. B., "M. A. H. and the Uses of the Past," *ASR*, 46 (1958): 33–40; Printz-Påhlson, G., *"The Liar*: The Paradox of Fictional Communication in M. A. H.," *SS*, 36 (1964): 263–80; Schow, H. W., "Kierkegaardian Perspectives in M. A. H.'s *The Liar,*" *Crit*, 15, 3 (1974): 53–65; Ingwersen, N., Introduction to *Lucky Kristoffer* (1974): 5–22; Ingwersen, F., and N. Ingwersen, *M. A. H.* (1976); Schow, H. W., Introduction to *Against the Wind* (1979): 1–12

—H. WAYNE SCHOW

HANSEN, Thorkild

Danish documentary novelist and critic, b. 9 Jan. 1927, Copenhagen; d. 4 Feb. 1989, Guadeloupe

Following studies in literature at Copenhagen University, a literary debut in 1947, and a stay in Paris from 1947 to 1952, H. worked as a journalist and literary critic on several Copenhagen newspapers. His deep interest in history and archeology led to his participation in archeological expeditions to Kuwait (1960), Sudan (1961), Hudson Bay, Canada (1964), and Guinea (1965). These expeditions laid the foundation for his literary production.

H. had his artistic breakthrough with *Pausesignaler* (1959; interval signals), a collection of travel notes and philosophical reflections, in which he rejects all ideological standpoints in favor of factual, undogmatic reporting of concrete reality. Drawing the full consequence of his demand for factual as opposed to fictitious narration, H. embraces a new genre in Danish literature—the documentary novel—in *Det lykkelige Arabien* (1962; *Arabia Felix*, 1964), which tells of a Danish expedition to Arabia during the 18th c. Through on-the-spot studies, archival research, and the use of diaries kept by the expedition leader, H. was able to draw a personal

portrait of the explorer set against a geographical background with an exceedingly vivid atmosphere. In *Jens Munk* (1965; *The Way to Hudson Bay*, 1970), which deals with a Danish admiral and seafarer who in the 17th c. unsuccessfully sought the Northwest passage, H. likewise combined precise documentation with his personal narrative technique, utilizing comedy, satire, and pathos. H.'s next published work, a three-volume study of the Danish slave trade between the Gold Coast and the sugar plantations of the West Indies, *Slavernes kyst* (1967; the slave coast), *Slavernes skibe* (1968; the slave ships), and *Slavernes øer* (1970; the slave islands), combines characteristics of the epic novel, the essay, and historical writing.

Another form of achieving closeness to reality is found in *De søde piger* (1974; the sweet girls)—the first in a projected ten-volume series. It consists of H.'s own diary entries from the years 1943–47. Although structured as a novel, the book gives a documentary close-up of a past era as well as providing background to the development of H.'s literary career. H. himself has labeled the book a documentary *Entwicklungsroman* (novel of development). His latest work, *Processen mod Hamsun* (1978; the trial of Hamsun), published simultaneously in the three Scandinavian countries, is a piece of historical documentation with the Norwegian author Knut HAMSUN as the main character and hero. It has been criticized for its subjectivity and its defense of a man who collaborated with the Nazis during the occupation of Norway (1940–45). The underlying tenet is, however, a probing of the incompatibility of art and politics, and the rejection of the political man makes it a highly provocative work in our time.

In Danish literature H. stands outside modernism, and on the border between history and fiction. His use of the documentary novel, a genre that builds on authentic material from reality in contrast to the subjectivity of most modern novels, has given H. international fame. His success is also due to his exceptional ability to live up to the epic demand—his knack for telling a plain, unvarnished tale.

FURTHER WORKS: *Minder svøbt i vejr* (1947); *Resten er stilhed* (1953); *Syv seglsten* (1960); *En kvinde ved en flod* (1961); *Jens Munks minde-ekspedition* (1965, with Peter Seeberg); *Vinterhavn* (1972)

—MARIANNE FORSSBLAD

HAQQĪ, Yahyā

Egyptian short-story and novella writer, literary critic, and essayist, b. 7 Jan. 1905, Cairo

Born into a highly educated family, H. was brought up in a popular area of Cairo. In 1925 he graduated from the Sultaniya Law School. After practicing law for two years, he gained employment with the government, which sent him as a legal inspector to Upper Egypt. The two years he spent there had a profound impact on his literary career. The five short stories that he wrote there dwell on a topos addressed by many 20th-c. writers: the barriers that confront outsiders, particularly officials, as they try to penetrate the worlds of closed, traditional communities. In 1929 he joined the Egyptian foreign service and was sent to Jeddah. Subsequent posts were in Istanbul, Rome, Paris, Ankara, and finally Tripoli in 1953. From the foreign service he moved to the department of fine arts, and his last employment was as editor-in-chief of the literary magazine *Al-Majallah*. Although he officially retired in 1970, he continued to be active on the literary scene. His autobiography, entitled *Khallīhā 'alā Allāh* (1959; leave it to God), gives a lively account of the highs and lows of his career.

H. is best known for his first collection of short stories, *Qindīl Umm Hāshim* (1944; *The Saint's Lamp*, 1976). The story that gave the book its title tells of an individual's reconciliation between Eastern and Western cultural values that until then had been portrayed as mutually exclusive. The plot may seem hackneyed today, but at the time of its publication it caused a stir. Although the protagonist clearly navigates between two cultures that have both good and evil in them, critics, including the Muslim fundamentalist Sayyid Qutb (1903–1966), hailed what they claimed to be the story's advocacy of Islamic values. H.'s other novella, *Sahh al-nawm* (1955; *Good Morning!*, 1987), schematically compares the lives of some villagers before and after the return of one of their members from studying in the capital. The analogy with Nasser was inevitable since it came out only three years after the Free Officers' Revolution. H.'s sharply etched vignettes of the village-tavern habitués take the reader into the heart of a society in transition. In the same year that *Sahh al-nawm* came out he published two collections of short stories, *Umm al-'awajiz* (1955; mother of miracles) and *Dimā' wa-tīn* (1955; blood and mud). Rural and urban subjects mix to tell the multiple stories of 20th-c. Egyptians of the less-privileged classes.

H. is esteemed for his literary criticism. His first collection of literary articles, which he had published in journals and newspapers from the late 1920s until the 1950s, was *Fajr al-qissa al-misriyyah* (1960; dawn of the Egyptian story). These essays deal with Egyptian fiction from 1914 until 1934. He subsequently published literary articles in three more collections: *Khutuwāt fī al-naqd* (1961; stages of criticism), which includes also articles written about non-Egyptian writers; *ltr al-ahbāb* (1971; the scent of loved ones), whose articles are more in the form of literary reminiscences than of criticism; and *Unshūda li-al-basāta* (1972; an anthem to simplicity), whose message is simplification of language so as to assure communication. H. was also prolific as an essayist. His four collections of wry commentaries on life in the Cairo street, such as *Nās fī al-zill* (1971; people in the shadows), or on his numerous travels, such as *Haqībah fī yad musāfir* (1969; a suitcase in a traveler's hand), represent only a small fraction of the essays that lie scattered among dozens of newspapers, magazines, and journals.

H.'s lucid, elegant style has won him the esteem of the leading literary figures in the Arab world. He has won several prizes and has played an important role in promoting young writers.

FURTHER WORKS: *'Antar wa Jūliyāt* (1960); *Dam'ah fa-ibtisāmah* (1965); *Ta'ālama 'ī ilā al-kūnsīr* (1969); *Yā layl yā 'ayn* (1972)

BIBLIOGRAPHY: Jomier, J., "Deux extraits des souvenirs de M. Y. H.," *Mélanges: Institut Dominicain des Études Orientales*, (1960) 325–30; Vial, C., "Y. H. Humoriste," *Annales Islamologiques*, 11 (1972) 351–65; Cooke, M., *The Anatomy of an Egyptian Intellectual, Y. H.* (1984); Allen, R., ed., *Modern Arabic Literature* (1987): 124–29; Layoun, M. N., *Travels of a Genre: The Modern Novel and Ideology* (1990): 56–105

—MIRIAM COOKE

HARDY, Thomas

English poet and novelist, b. 6 June 1840, Higher Bockhampton; d. 11 Jan. 1928, Dorchester

H.'s long life extended from the early years of Queen Victoria's reign to the restless period between this century's two world wars. He was writing fiction during the time of Dickens, Trollope, and George Eliot, and he published poetry in the decade of T. S. ELIOT's *The Waste Land* and HEMINGWAY's *The Sun Also Rises*.

From his family and his early surroundings H. gained a deep perspective on the past. He was born in the thatched cottage of the family's lifehold estate in Dorset, near a wild waste that H. would celebrate as the timeless Egdon Heath. He grew up in a region bristling with Roman rings and still more ancient tumuli; when he returned to his native section as a successful novelist, he built his home within sight of an early burial mound.

At the time of H.'s birth, the family fortunes had declined somewhat from a long tradition of gentility. His father, a master mason and building contractor, was also a church musician, and

Thomas Hardy

from him H. learned the trade of stonecutting and a love of music. The rich folkloric materials that were to permeate his writings were absorbed from the live traditions of ballads and tunes, mummers' spectacles, local superstitions, and tales told by his elders, particularly his paternal grandmother.

H.'s mother, whose tastes included Latin poets and French romances, provided for his education. Although H.'s formal schooling ended when he was fifteen, he continued the study of languages on his own, and eventually was able to read the *Iliad* and the New Testament in Greek. At fifteen, H. began teaching Sunday school in the Stinsford Parish Church, and for a time it seemed possible that he would go to a university and prepare for holy orders; but instead he was apprenticed for a period of six years to a Dorchester architect, John Hicks. Next door to Hicks's office was a school kept by William Barnes, a poet who taught H. the value of local dialect. Both Hicks and Barnes drew around them a circle of young men of intellectual promise; association with these and with Horace Moule, of Queen's College, Cambridge, did much to stimulate H.'s critical powers and to awaken his literary ambition.

Still, it seemed that H. was settled for life in a provincial career of restoring churches, when in 1862 he traveled from the rural isolation of Dorset to London, there to work as an assistant in the architectural firm of Arthur Blomfield. Although he applied himself enough to win two architectural prizes, the next five years also included visiting art galleries, attending Dickens's public readings, and enjoying Shakespeare and opera. During these years he was reading Charles Darwin, Herbert Spencer, T. H. Huxley, and John Stuart Mill, whose positivism moved him to a reluctant agnosticism. He attended evening classes in French at King's College; he read Greek drama, the Elizabethan and romantic poets, and Tennyson and Swinburne, and gave informal lectures on poetry to Blomfield's staff; and he wrote poems, many of them grim, all of them rejected by editors. Most of these poems would appear years later in successive volumes of verse. His only published work at this time was a piece of prose fiction, "How I Built Myself a House," in *Chambers's Journal* (March 18, 1865).

In July 1867 H. left London for the family home in Dorset, and resumed work briefly with Hicks in Dorchester. It was at this time that H. entered into a temporary engagement with Tryphena Sparks, a sixteen-year-old relative on his mother's side. The relationship, which was long concealed from the public, deeply affected H. and formed an emotional base for much of the content of his fiction and poetry, although he mentioned her by name in only one poem.

In July 1868 H. sent the manuscript of a novel, *The Poor Man and the Lady*, to Alexander Macmillan, who rejected its social satire as excessive. The next March he visited George Meredith, then a reader for Chapman and Hall, who persuaded H. to suppress the work and instead to try a novel "with more plot." The result was *Desperate Remedies* (1871), published anonymously at H.'s expense. An extravagant blend of romance and crime, the book was a failure.

Meanwhile, H. had been working at church renovation with G. R. Crickmay of Weymouth, and while on an assignment in St. Juliot, Cornwall, had met Emma Lavinia Gifford. A young woman with social aspirations, and some literary skill herself, she encouraged H. to consider literature as his "true vocation." Although he continued his architectural work, including another stint in London, he moved doggedly toward a professional writing career.

In 1872 appeared *Under the Greenwood Tree*, also anonymously. A slight work, whose idyllic scenes and rustic humor are unclouded by calamitous events, this novel was nevertheless an early example of H.'s eventual achievement in depicting the "emotional history" of the region he called Wessex (after the ancient kingdom of Alfred the Great).

About this time Emma Gifford was assisting H. in the preparation of the manuscript of *A Pair of Blue Eyes*, which ran serially in *Tinsley's Magazine* and was published in book form in 1873. The serial publication, in Leslie Stephens's *Cornhill Magazine*, of *Far from the Madding Crowd* (1874) and its favorable reception in book form insured H.'s exchange of architecture for a career as a writer. The same year he and Emma Gifford traveled to London where they were married, over the objection of her father.

H. wrote *The Hand of Ethelberta* (1876) during a period when the couple lived in London and traveled on the Continent. At this time H. began making notes for a treatment of the Napoleonic wars as "grand drama."

During 1877, while residing in a cottage overlooking Dorset's River Stour, H. wrote *The Return of the Native* (1878). This novel was a masterful creation of classic austerity, presenting willful human beings who struggle against themselves and against an indifferent fate that dooms them through chance combinations of their own impulses and the witless whims of external nature.

By 1885 the couple had settled near Dorchester at Max Gate, a house designed by H. and built by his brother, Henry. With the exception of seasonal stays in London and occasional excursions abroad, this was H.'s home for the rest of his life.

The product of H.'s pen in the 1880s was uneven. *The Trumpet-Major* (1880), reflecting his persistent interest in the story of England's struggle with Napoleon, was followed by his weakest novel, *The Laodicean* (1881), and by *Two on a Tower* (1882). These were succeeded by a masterpiece, *The Mayor of Casterbridge* (1886), the study of a "man of character" whose fate evolves along Sophoclean lines, whose psychology H. plumbed to its unconscious depths before the world had been supplied with the convenient charts of Sigmund FREUD.

The Woodlanders (1887) showed the influence of H.'s recent reading of Schopenhauer's *The World as Will and Idea*, although the novel's plot emphasis is upon social tragedy arising from class discrimination and unjust divorce laws.

Another masterpiece, *Tess of the D'Urbervilles*, which ran serially in a bowdlerized form before its publication in 1891, seemed to confirm H.'s claim to reader affection and critical esteem—in spite of the fact that he had presented his heroine as "a pure woman" destroyed by Victorian prudery, hypocrisy, and intolerance. Another novel, *The Well-Beloved* (not published in book form until 1897) was running serially; the author and his wife were reveling in London invitations to "crushes, luncheons, and dinners"; and H. was collecting his third volume of short stories, *Life's Little Ironies* (1894). Then in 1895, the storm broke, following publication of *Jude the Obscure*.

This book, like *Tess of the D'Urbervilles* a consequence of H.'s exploration of a dark side of his family connections in Berkshire, set forth the gloomy tale of a stonemason whose tangled sexual relationships in and out of marriage wreck his scholarly ambitions and eventually drive him to a miserable death. The novel was met with public outrage, and critics on both sides of the Atlantic abused the author as degenerate, called the work itself disgusting, impious, obscene. H.'s wife, who hitherto had helped in the preparation of his novel manuscripts, had bitterly opposed the project, and their own marriage, already in difficulty, suffered from the fallout.

The uproar over *Jude the Obscure* so offended H. that he never wrote another novel. Instead he turned to his first love, poetry, and before the century was over he had published *Wessex Poems* (1898). He acknowledged in a brief preface that many of the fifty-one poems had been written "long before"—only four had been previously published; some had been revised or reclaimed from the prose of the novels. Notable inclusions were the early poems "Hap," lamenting that the world seems ruled by two "purblind Doomsters," Casualty and Time; and "Neutral Tones," an etching in words expressing despair at extinct love.

Reception of this first volume of verse was inconclusive, but H. persevered, and *Poems of the Past and the Present*, issued late in 1901, was an immediate success. The book's ninety-nine poems included early ballads and love poems as before; but there were also more recent pieces: the "In Tenebris" trio, "I Have Lived with Shades," "The Darkling Thrush," "The Subalterns," and a sampling of poems reflecting H.'s opposition to the South African war. The transformation of the artist from novelist to poet was assured; in the next three decades H. would establish himself as one of the most productive poets of the 20th c.

In 1902 H. began work on his long-meditated "epic-drama of the War with Napoleon," *The Dynasts.* As early as 1875 he had conceived the idea of a succession of ballads treating episodes in the career of Bonaparte. Five of these ballads were printed in *Wessex Poems.* Now, working intensely over the next five years, H. produced a massive poem in three parts, nineteen acts, and 130 scenes. The three parts were published, successively, in 1904, 1906, and 1908. This "spectacular poem," H. himself admitted, was more epic than drama. Its blank-verse passages are generally undistinguished, the dialogue and diction are too often leaden. But the prose speeches of the common folk, the songs and other lyrical transitions, including, for example, the Trafalgar chorus, are impressive.

The scope of H.'s epic intention is equally impressive. Part I opens in 1805 with the English in high and low places discussing the threat of a French invasion of southern England, describes Napoleon's coronation, the battle of Austerlitz, and Nelson's triumph at Trafalgar and his death (in the arms of Captain Sir Thomas Hardy, H.'s ancestor), and concludes with the death of Pitt. Part II presents the defeat of the Prussians at Jena, the meeting of Napoleon and Czar Alexander at Tilsit, the war in Spain, Napoleon's abandonment of Josephine, and his marriage to Maria Louisa. Part III presents his Russian disaster in 1812, his multiplying defeats and his abdication, Elba, and Waterloo.

Perhaps H.'s most original conception was an adaptation of traditional epic machinery: the creation of "supernatural spectators of the terrestrial action," including the Spirit of the Years, the Spirit of the Pities, and the Spirits Sinister and Ironic, together with their choruses and other Intelligences. Unlike divinities in classical epics, these "impersonal abstractions" are detached from active involvement in human affairs. But like mortals, they are subordinate to the Immanent Will, the unconscious force that moves the world. The running comment of the Intelligences, delivered from their vantage point in the Overworld, adds a cosmic dimension to the work, providing a series of choral interpretations of the action and, at the same time, paradoxically reducing Napoleon and the other "dynasts" from the rank of heroes and, by implication, diminishing the significance of all human endeavor.

Now approaching seventy years of age, H. busied himself with the preparation of *Time's Laughingstocks, and Other Verses* (1909), a collection of ninety-six poems, some still dating back more than forty years, more composed in the new century: "The Revisitation," "A Trampwoman's Tragedy"; a number of love lyrics and country songs; "Panthera," based on an apocryphal story of Jesus' parentage and death; and a powerful antiwar poem, "The Man He Killed."

Honors were beginning to come to H. On the death of his friend George Meredith in 1909, he succeeded to the presidency of the Society of Authors. In 1910 King George V conferred on him the Order of Merit. YEATS was among those who journeyed to Max Gate in 1912 to present him with the gold medal of the Royal Society of Literature.

Then, in November 1912, H. was shaken by Emma Hardy's sudden death. *Satires of Circumstance, Lyrics and Reveries* (1914) contains "Veteris vestigia flammae," a group of twenty-one poems—some of H.'s very finest lyrics—that reveal H.'s retrospective view of their early love and the gradual deterioration of the marriage; and more than a hundred poems in later volumes continue themes relating to this complex relationship. *Satires of Circumstance* also contains "The Convergence of the Twain," an ironic elegy on the sinking of the *Titanic*; "Channel Firing," a prophetic piece printed just three months before the outbreak of World War I; and bleak philosophic meditations like "A Plaint to Man."

H. had married his secretary, Florence Emily Dugdale, early in 1914. The remaining fourteen years of his life were lived in relative serenity. His productivity continued at an astonishing rate. *Moments of Vision and Miscellaneous Verses* (1917) and *Late Lyrics and Earlier* (1922) each contained more than 150 poems, among them "In Time of 'The Breaking of Nations'" and "And There was a Great Calm." The latter volume was prefaced by a lengthy "Apology" in which H. defends himself against the repeated charge of pessimism and states a provisional faith in "evolutionary meliorism," bolstered by the frail hope that "the human and kindred animal races" may keep pain to a minimum "by loving-kindness operating through scientific knowledge, and actuated by the modicum of free will conjecturally possessed by organic life when the mighty necessitating forces—unconscious or other . . . happen to be in equilibrium."

From about 1920 through 1927 H. was working on his autobiography, which was disguised as the work of Florence Hardy, published in two volumes (1928 and 1930), later as the one-volume *Life of T. H.: 1840–1928* (1962).

Human Shows, Far Phantasies, Songs and Trifles (1925) was the last book of poems published in H.'s lifetime. *Winter Words in Various Moods and Metres* (1928) was ready for the press when he died. In all, H. had written close to a thousand poems, not counting *The Dynasts* or his verse drama *The Famous Tragedy of the Queen of Cornwall*, which he wrote and saw produced in 1923 when he was eighty-three years old.

Following H.'s death in his eighty-eighth year, his heart was buried in Stinsford churchyard and his ashes were buried in Westminster Abbey. His pallbearers included, besides the Prime Minister, Rudyard KIPLING, Bernard SHAW, J. M. BARRIE, John GALSWORTHY, A. E. HOUSMAN and Edmund Gosse (1849–1928).

H.'s position as a novelist of the first rank seems secure; his place among 20th-c. poets, while undergoing reassessment, seems a permanent one. The poet Philip LARKIN allotted more pages and many more poems to H. than to any other poet in the 1973 *Oxford Book of Twentieth Century English Verse*.

In the light of the midcentury onslaught on realism, H.'s long-dispraised stress on accident and coincidence may be seen as his strategy for depicting the absurd. The Wessex of the novels and the poetry, like FAULKNER's Yoknapatawpha, may be understood as a region in which the artist explores, in metaphor and symbol, the geography of the human mind.

The measure of H.'s influence on both fiction and poetry has been debated. H. G. WELLS as a youthful writer derived ideas for one of his social comedies from the serial version of *Jude the Obscure*. The same novel fascinated D. H. LAWRENCE who drew upon it and other Wessex novels in his treatment of character and locale, and in "A Study of Thomas Hardy" (*Phoenix*, 1936) revealed how much H. occupied his thoughts at the time he was writing *The White Peacock* and *The Rainbow*. Ezra POUND, who praised H.'s poetry for its clarity of expression, sent the older poet copies of his own verse for criticism. W. H. AUDEN confessed that he was under the spell of H.'s poetry for a period, and acknowledged that he owed H. an important debt of technical instruction. John Crowe RANSOM, calling H. a "late Victorian" poet, remarked on his closeness to the succeeding generation "by reason of his naturalism and rebellion against the dogma."

Television adaptations of H.'s short stories and recent films based on *Far from the Madding Crowd* and *Tess of the D'Urbervilles* have helped to keep H.'s name before the public. Those who read the books themselves are thereby engaged with a world that was already disappearing in H.'s day, and also with an artistic temperament and a noble intelligence that have added luster to the human spirit.

FURTHER WORKS: *Wessex Tales* (1888); *A Group of Noble Dames* (1891); *A Changed Man and Other Tales* (1913); *The Play of St. George* (1921); *Life and Art: Essays, Notes and Letters* (1925); *An Indiscretion in the Life of an Heiress* (1934); *The Letters of T. H* (1954); *T. H.'s Notebooks and Some Letters from Julia Augusta Martin* (1955); *"Dearest Emmie": T. H.'s Letters to His First Wife* (1963); *The Architectural Notebooks of T. H.* (1966); *T. H.'s Personal Writings: Prefaces, Literary Opinions, Reminiscences* (1966); *One Rare Fair Woman: T. H.'s Letters to Florence Henniker, 1893–1922* (1972); *The Literary Notes of T. H.* (1974); *The Complete Poems of T. H.* (1976); *The New Wessex Edition of the Stories of T. H., Including Hitherto Uncollected Stories* (3 vols., 1977); *The Collected Letters of T. H., Vol. 1, 1840–1892* (1978); *The Personal Notebooks of T. H., with an Appendix including the Unpublished Passages in the Original Typescript of "The Life of T. H."* (1979); *From H. at Max Gate: A Series of Letters* (1979); *The Variorum Edition of The Complete Poems of T. H.* (1979); *The Collected Letters of T. H., Vol. 2, 1893–1901* (1980)

BIBLIOGRAPHY: Weber, C. J., *H. of Wessex: His Life and Career* (1940; 2nd ed., 1965); Guerard, A. J., *T. H.* (1949; rev. ed., 1964); Brown, D., *T. H.* (1954; rev. ed., 1961); Hardy, E., *T. H.: A Critical Biography* (1954); Purdy, R. L., *T. H.: A Bibliographical Study* (1954); Hynes, S. L., *The Pattern of H.'s Poetry* (1961); Orel, H., *T. H.'s Epic Drama: A Study of "The Dynasts"* (1963); Wing, G., *H.* (1963); Carpenter, R. C., *T. H.* (1964); Howe, I., *T. H.* (1967); Wright, W. F., *The Shaping of "The Dynasts": A Study in T. H.* (1967); Pinion, F. B., *A. H. Companion: A Guide to the Works of T.* H. *and Their Background* (1968); Marsden, K., *The Poems of T. H.: A Critical Introduction* (1969); Bailey, J. O., *The Poetry of T. H.: A Handbook and Commentary* (1970); Miller, J. H., *T. H.: Distance and Desire* (1970); Brooks, J. R., *T. H.: The Poetic Structure* (1971); Millgate, M, *T. H.: His Career as a Novelist* (1971); Stewart, J. I. M., *T. H.: A Critical Biography* (1971); Davie, D., *T. H. and British Poetry* (1973); Gerber, H. E., and Davis, W. E., *T. H.: An Annotated Bibliography of Writings about Him* (1973); Gittings, R., *Young T. H.* (1975); Hawkins, D., *H.: Novelist and Poet* (1976); Orel, H., *The Final Years of T. H., 1912–1928* (1976); Page, N., *T. H.* (1977); Gittings, R., *T. H.'s Later Years* (1978); Wright, T. R., *H. and the Erotic* (1989); Morgan, R., *Cancelled Words: Rediscovering T. H.* (1992); Taylor, D., *H.'s Literary Language and Victorian Philology* (1994); Langbaum, R. W., *T. H. in Our Time* (1995); Pettit, C. P., *Celebrating T. H.: Insights and Appreciations* (1996); Turner, P. D. L., *The Life of T. H.: A Critical Biography* (1998)

—CARL D. BENNETT

The Wessex novels . . . cover an immense stretch; inevitably they are full of imperfections—some are failures, and others exhibit only the wrong side of their maker's genius. But undoubtedly, when we have submitted ourselves fully to them, when we come to take stock of our impression of the whole, the effect is commanding and satisfactory. We have been freed from the cramp and pettiness imposed by life. Our imaginations have been stretched and heightened; our humour has been made to laugh out; we have drunk deep of the beauty of the earth. Also we have been made to enter the shade of a sorrowful and brooding spirit which, even in its saddest mood, bore itself with a grave uprightness and never, even when most moved to anger, lost its deep compassion for the sufferings of men and women. Thus it is no mere transcript of life at a certain time and place that H. has given us. It is a vision of the world and of man's lot as they revealed themselves to a powerful imagination, a profound and poetic genius, a gentle and humane soul.

Virginia Woolf, "The Novels of T. H.," *The Second Common Reader* (1932), p. 257

H.'s characters are full of moral conflicts and of decisions arrived at by mental processes. Certainly, Jude, Gabriel Oak, Clem Yeobright, above all, Henchard, are men who have decisions to make, and if they do not make them entirely on the plane of reason, it is because H. was interested most in that hairline dividing the rational from the instinctive, the opposition, we might call it, between nature, and second nature; that is, between instinct and the habits of thought fixed upon the individual by his education and his environment. Such characters of his as are led by their emotions come to tragedy; he seems to say that following the emotions blindly leads to disaster. Romantic miscalculation of the possibilities of life, of love, of the situation; of refusing to reason their way out of their predicament; these are the causes of disaster in H.'s novels. Angel Clare is a man of the highest principle, trained in belief, religion, observance of moral law. His failure to understand the real nature of Christianity makes a monster of him at the great crisis of his life. The Mayor of Casterbridge spends the balance of his life in atonement and reparation for a brutal wrong committed in drunkenness and anger; his past overtakes and destroys him. H. had an observing eye, a remembering mind; he did not need the Greeks to teach him that the Furies do arrive punctually, and that neither act, nor will, nor intention will serve to deflect a man's destiny from him, once he has taken the step which decides it.

Katherine Anne Porter, "Notes on a Criticism of T. H.," *SoR*, 6 (1940), 159–60

One by one the striking things about H.'s art as a story-teller fall naturally into place as functions of balladry. There is the reliance, especially at the outset, upon the sharp definition of scene and background. There is the easy alliance of the grotesque and disproportionate with the substantial and natural, and the unselfconscious boldness with which they are offered. There are the slighter rhythms and movements of the story suggesting that the sung stanza is never far behind. There are the neat, rounded, and intertwining groups of events, the simple and decisive balancing of characters. There is the vivid sense of the meaning of scenery, the human and the natural involving one another. There is the narrative method whereby encounter (whether of person with person, or person with Fate) is the life of the tale. The ballad situations and the ballad coincidences are carried off partly by boldness and verve; partly by an art which holds all spare attention concentrated upon the vividness of the presentation itself.

Douglas Brown, *T. H.* (1961), p. 111

As a writer of novels T. H. was endowed with a precious gift: he liked women. There are not, when one comes to think of it, quite so many other nineteenth-century novelists about whom as much can be said. With some, the need to keep returning in their fiction to the disheveled quarters of domesticity causes a sigh of weariness, even at times a suppressed snarl of discontent; for, by a certain measure, it must seem incongruous that writers intent on a fundamental criticism of human existence should be sentenced to indefinite commerce with sex, courtship, adultery and family quarrels. H., by contrast, felt no such impatience with the usual materials of the novel. Though quite capable of releasing animus toward his women characters and casting them as figures of destruction, he could not imagine a universe without an active, even an intruding, feminine principle. The sexual exclusiveness of nineteenth-century American writing would have been beyond his comprehension, though probably not beyond his sympathy.

Throughout his years as a novelist H. found steadily interesting the conceits and playfulness of women, the elaborate complex of stratagems in which the sexual relationship appears both as struggle and game. He liked the changefulness, sometimes even the caprice, of feminine personality; he marveled at the seemingly innate capacity of young girls to glide into easy adaptations and tactical charms. And he had a strong appreciation of the manipulative and malicious powers that might be gathered beneath a surface of delight. Except perhaps with Sue Bridehead, he was seldom inclined to plunge into the analytic depths which mark the treatment of feminine character in George Eliot's later novels; but if he did not look as deeply as she did into the motivations of feminine character, he was remarkably keen at apprehending feminine behavior. He had observed and had watched, with uneasy alertness. The range of virtuosity which other writers had believed possible only in a stylized high society or sophisticated court, H., in his plain and homely way, found among the country girls of southwest England.

Irving Howe, *T. H.* (1967), pp. 108–9

H.'s multiple vision of experience brings him close to the modern Absurdist form of tragi-comedy or comi-tragedy. . . . The Kafka-like distortions of figure or scene . . . stress the ironic deflation of romance, heroism, and tragedy by the objective incursion of absurdity; without, however, denigrating the value of romance, heroism, and suffering. . . . In all his work H.'s personal voice, with its humane values, its Gothic irregularities, its human contradictions and rough edges, its commonness and uncommonness, strains against the rigidities of traditional patterns and expectations. The first two paragraphs of *The Mayor of Casterbridge*, for example, can provide the mixture to be found in all the other novels, *The Dynasts*, and most of the poems—the amalgam of homely simplicity, awkward periphrasis, triteness, and sharp sensuous vision that invests an ordinary scene with the significance of myth and Sophoclean grandeur. The dissonance of the multiple vision dramatically enacts H.'s metaphysic of man's predicament as a striving, sensitive, imperfect individual in a rigid, nonsentient, absurd cosmos, which rewards him only with eternal death.

Jean R. Brooks, *T. H.: The Poetic Structure* (1971), pp. 13–14

H.'s poetry, with its tentative contexts and interrupted perspectives, invites condescension, in the neutral sense of the word. H. seldom writes with the authority of Yeats, or even Browning. He does not manhandle his reader, but instead asks him (politely) to excuse the potentially inexcusable, to tolerate or to ignore entirely whatever seems too jagged or wayward. . . . He is beset by omens and haunted relentlessly, and it is remarkable that these visitations should be so empty of any suggestion of guilt. H., for all his obsessions, is a healing poet. He forgets heroically and loses cleanly. . . . Regret is no stranger to him, but his regret is not for what he has done or left undone but for the passing of what was good and beautiful. His only sadness is that life, though it must be loved as all we have, is, after all, too small for us. In saying these things, we excuse his faults, for we have found in him a great and difficult sanity.

James Richardson, *T. H.: The Poetry of Necessity* (1975), pp. 77–78, 131–32

His novels, although so little concerned to cheer us up, are not in their total effect dispiriting—as is today so much of the literature of despair and of the absurd. We see man as a minute "vitalization" amid the dust of the stars, and individuals as crawling specks on a Roman road, an immemorial heath, a brutal terrain of hacked turnips. . . . H. himself offered as his ultimate apologia the proposition that if a way to the better there be it exacts a full look at the worst. He often provides us with the worst in a distillation so extreme as to strain our sense of the verisimilar, but the proposition itself does speak to our condition. . . . In part it is a psychological statement, affirming the classical theory of catharsis. The confronting of spectacles of pity and terror is purgative, so that we *feel* better . . . provided the personages we are invited to contemplate are moral beings much like ourselves. . . . His people are moral agents, constantly aware of the paradox that, in a neutral universe, significance and dignity are theirs because they see good and evil around them and own a duty to conduct their lives, however senselessly tormented, in terms of that perception.

J. I. M. Stewart, "The Major Novels," in Margaret Drabble, ed., *The Genius of T. H.* (1976), pp. 65–66

What defeats the attempt to discriminate the better from the worse among H.'s poems is not just the great number of the poems, and their variousness. It is not even the impossibility, for the most part, of categorizing the poems as "early" or "late"; nor the almost equal difficulty of categorizing them according to genre, except in the broadest and most impressionistic way. These impediments to taking H. the poet as a whole, the good with the bad, do not come about by accident. Behind them is the curious paradox that H., who imposes himself on imperiously upon his medium, imposes himself on his reader hardly at all. On every page, "Take it or leave it," he seems to say; or, even more permissively, "Take what you want, and leave the rest."

This consciousness of having imposed on his reader so little is what lies behind H.'s insistence that what he offers is only a series of disconnected observations, and behind his resentment that he should be taken as having a pessimistic design upon his reader, when in fact he so sedulously respects the reader's privilege not to be interested, not to be persuaded. It is on this basis—his respect of the reader's rights to be attentive or inattentive as he pleases—that one rests the claim for H. as perhaps the first and last "liberal"

in modern poetry. And it is because we are so unused to liberalism as a consistent attitude in a poet, that we have so much difficulty with the poetry of H.

But the outcome is that every new reader of H.'s poetry finds there what he wants to find. And in the event this means, for the most part, that each reader finds in the poems what he brings to them; what he finds there is his own pattern of preoccupations and preferences. If this is true of every poet to some degree, of H. it is exceptionally true.

Donald Davie, *T. H. and British Poetry* (1972), pp. 28–29

HARIS, Petros

(pseud. of Yiannis Marmariadis) Greek short-story writer, critic, essayist, poet, and editor, b. 26 Aug. 1902, Athens

A versatile man of letters, H. has for more than two generations been at the literary and cultural center of Greece. He studied law at the University of Athens but made literature his lifelong career. Among his many posts, H. served on the board of the National Theater, as president of its Committee on Artistic Affairs, and on the National Board of Literature. As editor of *Nea Estia* from 1933 on H. exerted widespread influence and provided a regular forum for the finest Greek writers. The many honors he received culminated in his election to the Athens Academy in 1946. His travel book *Politeies kai thalasses* (1955; cities and seas) won the annual First National Award.

In *Nea Estia* and elsewhere H. published many essays on literary subjects. However, he is primarily noted for short stories that range from reminiscences of the past to revelations of character during moments of self-discovery. H. published six volumes of short fiction, beginning with *Teleftaia nichta tis yis* (1924; last night on earth). Along with other demotic writers he departed in his stories from the traditional "heroic style" in favor of a new realism. Both by precept in his essays and by example in his fiction H. helped to set high standards for the genre.

The title story of *Phota sto pelagos* (1958; lights on the sea) is set on a tiny island during the German Occupation. H. personifies freedom as a phantom ship that appears at night and is seen first by Vangelis, a retarded youth, who is not believed. He awakens the islanders by ringing the church bell. Then others who are more reliable also see the ship, and they also ring the bell. The ship of freedom can be glimpsed by individuals, but not by groups—not until liberation. And so the islanders ring the bell, and wait.

As a poet H. coauthored *Dialogoi kai poeimata* (1926; dialogues and poems) with I. M. PANAYOTOPOULOS. He published travel articles in *Nea Estia*, as well as books on his travels, which took him as far as China. He also translated into Greek works such as *The Red and the Black* by Stendhal and *The Blue Bird* by MAETERLINCK. As an essayist commenting on literature, art, and life, H. wrote six volumes; the last of these books was *E zoe kai e techni* (1963; life and art).

As editor of *Nea Estia*, the most prestigious Greek journal, he maintained the high standards that helped to spark a literary renascence in modern Greece.

His best critical work is the six-volume series on Greek prose writers entitled *Hellenes pezographoi* (1953-82) while his only novel, *Imeres oryis: Delemvris 1944* (1979; Days of wrath: December 1944), considered the best work of fiction on the communist insurrection in Athens in 1944, was widely acclaimed and turned into a fine television series.

FURTHER WORKS: *K. G. Kariotakis* (1943); *Makrinos kosmos* (1944); *Krisimis oras* (1944); *Otan e zoe yinete oneiro* (1945, 1947); *Eleftheroi pnevmatikoi anthropoi* (1947); *Ellenes pezographoi* (1953); *Paleoi kai neoi dromi* (1956); *E Kina exo apo ta teichi* (1961); *Metapolemikos kosmos* (1962); *Dromos ekato metron* (1962); *Otan oi agioi katevainon sti yi* (1965); *E magali nichta* (1969, *The Longest Night: Chronicle of a Dead City*, 1985)

BIBLIOGRAPHY: Gianos, M. P., *Introduction to Modern Greek Literature* (1969): 22, 222

—ALEXANDER KARANIKAS

HARJO, Joy

American poet, scriptwriter, and editor, b. 9 May, 1951, Tulsa, Oklahoma

Born into a family of Muscogee Creek artists, H. was enrolled as a full member of the tribe. Reared in Oklahoma, H. moved to Sante Fe, New Mexico to study theater and painting at the Institute of American Indian Arts, an Indian boarding school. After changing her major from art to poetry, H. received her B.A. in poetry in 1976 from the University of New Mexico; she received her M.F.A. in 1978 from the University of Iowa. H. has taught at a number of institutions, including the Institute of American Indian Arts, the University of Colorado, the University of Arizona, and most recently, the University of New Mexico. She has won numerous awards, including a Lifetime Achievement Award from the Native Writers Circle of the Americas, the New Mexico Governor's Award for Excellence in the Arts, the Bravo Award from the Albuquerque Arts Alliance, the Oklahoma Book Arts Award, the American Book Award from the Before Columbus Foundation, and the William Carlos Williams Award from the Poetry Society of America for the best book of poetry in 1991. H.'s wide-ranging artistic interests also include playing saxophone and giving poetry readings with her band, Poetic Justice.

H.'s poetry has from the first reflected a Native American heritage, feminist consciousness, and a desire to test the boundaries of language. She uses an autobiographical and mythical focus to explore not only the political but the transcendent. H. established herself as a major contemporary American artist with two highly acclaimed, full-length collections, *Secrets from the Center of the World* (1989) and *In Mad Love and War* (1990). H. worked with photographer Stephen Strom in *Secrets from the Center of the World* to integrate language with tableau, the visual with the poetic; the collection combines prose poems with photographic, colored visions of the American Southwest to achieve its artistic impact. Critics have noted that in H.'s poetry, the American landscape is alive, sentient—imbued with both identity and intelligence. Strom's photographs, situated in a perfect balance with her poetry in this collection, help to foreground this aspect of H.'s work.

H.'s most celebrated work, *In Mad Love and War*, also demonstrates a bifurcated structure. In this case the collection is divided into two sections, "The Wars" and "Mad Love," through which H. explores the somewhat tangled path to resolution. The "war" poems of the first section are often overtly political, probing subjects like the story of the martyred Native American Anna Mae Pictou Aquash (1945-1976) and the Nicaraguan conflict. H. also examines in this first section politically charged linguistic boundaries—in particular, the inadequacy of Anglo-American language as a means of expressing the realms of myth: "In this language there are no words for how the real world collapses." "Transformations," one of the "love" poems of the second section, represents a pivotal moment in H.'s search for resolution, and thus illuminates transformation itself as a central theme in this work. H. has commented that the poem is "about turning someone else's hatred into love," and indeed, such a transformation is enacted in the poem itself, as the poetic speaker finds resolution by returning hatred as love. Critics have noted that in this work, H.'s landscapes, often cold and forbidding, are yet focused through a Native American sensibility, presenting ultimately a positive and transformative vision that can recapture what is lost.

FURTHER WORKS: *The Last Song* (1975); *What Moon Drove Me to This?* (1979); *She Had Some Horses* (1983); *Origin of Apache Crown Dance* (1985); *The Woman Who Fell from the Sky* (1994); *The Spiral of Memory: Interviews* (1996); *Reinventing the Enemy's Language: Contemporary Native Women's Writings of North America* (1997, with Gloria Bird)

BIBLIOGRAPHY: Smith, P. C., and P. G. Allen, "Earthy Relations, Carnal Knowledge: Southwestern American Indian Women Writers and Landscapes," in Norwood, V., and J. Monk, eds., *The Desert Is No Lady: Southwestern Landscapes in Women's Writing and Art* (1987): 174-96; Scarry, J., "Representing Real Worlds: The Evolving Poetry of J. H.," *WLT*, 46 (Spring 1992): 286-91; Goodman, J., "Politics and Personal Lyric in the Poetry of J. H.," *MELUS*, 19 (1994): 35-56; Holmes, K., "This Woman Can Cross Any Line," *SAIL*, 7 (1995): 45-63

—MARSHA WATSON

HARRIS, Wilson

Guyanese novelist, critic, and poet, b. 24 March 1921, New Amsterdam

The originality and maturity of H.'s first novel, *Palace of the Peacock* (1960), and his consistent exploration and expansion of his themes in the novels he has produced since can be explained by the fact that that novel did not appear until he was thirty-nine and had put in a long apprenticeship. Before he went to England, H. worked as a surveyor in the 1940s and 1950s, becoming intimate with the peoples, rivers, and forests of his native Guyana. His speculations about the relationship of man to his landscape no doubt began then. During that time H. contributed poems and stories regularly to the Guyanese journal *Kyk-Over-Al*, in which his fascination with the bonds between myth and history and with the remarkable connections between the mythologies of different cultures can be observed. These early interests, experiences, and perceptions recur in his fiction, and many of his characters are autobiographical. Fenwick of *The Secret Ladder* (1963) and Wellington of *Genesis of the Clowns* (1977) are both Guyanese surveyors; and Da Silva of *Da Silva da Silva's Cultivated Wilderness* (1977) is, like H., a South American artist of mixed radical background working in London.

H. himself has described his work as "groping towards something . . . within a deepening cycle of exploration." It is possible to see this process beginning in *Palace of the Peacock* and continuing throughout his fiction. The journey the characters in that novel undertake to the heart of the South American continent is reminiscent of the one in CONRAD's *Heart of Darkness* and is symbolic of a journey into their own histories and mythologies, a step necessary for self-awareness, which in turn will permit them to identify with life everywhere and throughout time.

In the early novels the jungles of South America are symbolic of the eternal present, the context in which man must learn to see himself. In later novels the art of painting is used to suggest this sense of eternity. H. attempts to encourage his readers to abandon their preconceptions, and to see the entirety and complexity of life afresh. He keeps reminding man that he possesses a "living closed spiritual eye" whose perceptions are more trustworthy than those of his "dead seeing material eye." Such juxtaposition of apparently incongruous ideas is one of the main devices H. uses to urge modern man to look at life constructively. This vision and the technique intrinsic to it is H.'s contribution to contemporary fiction.

FURTHER WORKS: *Fetish* (1951); *The Well and the Land* (1952); *Eternity to Season* (1954; new ed., 1978); *Far Journey of Oudin* (1961); *The Whole Armour* (1962); *Heartland* (1964); *The Eye of the Scarecrow* (1965); *The Waiting Room* (1967); *Tradition, the Writer and Society* (1967); *Tumatumari* (1968); *Ascent to Omai* (1970); *The Sleepers of Roraima* (1970); *History, Fable and Myth in the Caribbean and Guianas* (1970); *The Age of Rainmakers* (1971); *Black Marsden* (1972); *Fossil and Psyche* (1974); *Companions of the Day and Night* (1975); *The Tree of the Sun* (1978)

BIBLIOGRAPHY: James, C. L. R., *W. H.: A Philosophical Approach* (1965); Hearne, J., "The Fugitive in the Forest," in James, L., ed., *The Islands in Between* (1968): 140–54; Sparer, J. L., "The Art of W. H.," in La Rose, J., ed., *New Beacon Reviews* (1968): 22–30; Ramchand, K., *The West Indian Novel and Its Background* (1970): 164–74; Gilkes, M., *W. H. and the Caribbean Novel* (1975); Maes-Jelinek, H., *The Naked Design: A Reading of "Palace of the Peacock"* (1976); Maes-Jelinek, H., "'Inimitable Painting': New Developments in W. H.'s Latest Fiction," *ArielE*, 8, 3 (1977): 63–80

—ANTHONY BOXILL

HARTLEY, L(eslie) P(oles)

English novelist, short-story writer, and critic, b. 30 Dec. 1895, Whittlesea; d. 13 Dec. 1972, London

H. assumed his rank as a distinguished novelist rather late in life, after early successes in short stories and book reviewing. His first full-length novel, *The Shrimp and the Anemone* (1944), the initial volume of his later acclaimed trilogy, comprising also *The Sixth Heaven* (1946) and *Eustace and Hilda* (1947) (the latter title standing for the trilogy), appeared when H. was forty-nine years old. Thereafter, H.'s career developed with remarkable smoothness, and his literary output achieved near prolificacy, with an

especially large number of novels appearing in the last five years of his life.

Educated at Harrow and Oxford, and blessed with a considerable family fortune, H. lived the existence of a gentleman writer, concentrating in his fiction on upper-middle-class gentility with delicate, yet precise, psychological and moral delineations. A lifelong bachelor, H. often peopled his novels and short stories with slightly sinister, ambiguous servants who were necessary adjuncts for such a single man's domestic arrangements. H. invested many of his characters with his own moral concerns, his passion for Venice and for rowing, his somewhat diffident Christianity, and often something of his own charm, wit, and style.

H.'s fiction represents a distinctive synthesis of a dual tradition in the novel: romance derived from his much-beloved Nathaniel Hawthorne and realism indebted to Henry JAMES, with nods in the direction of some English favorites like the Brontës and Jane Austen. Much of H.'s best work features a rich symbolic structure that hints at fable and allegory behind his plausible and generally realistic narratives. For example, in the *Eustace and Hilda* trilogy H. shows how a brother and sister fulfill the destructive relationship, despite their genuine love for each other, of the shrimp and the anemone, into whose world the siblings as children intrude in the first scene of the initial volume.

H. often sought spiritual and metaphysical meanings besides clarification of social and psychological details, thereby suggesting metaphors for the condition of life in the 20th c. His most successful and best-known novel, *The Go-Between* (1953), offers a double perspective on the century as an aged narrator looks back from midcentury at events from his boyhood. Victim of his own distorting fantasy, like numerous protagonists in H.'s fiction, Leo Colston suffers permanent emotional damage when reality overtakes him and his grandiose conception of the inhabitants of a grand country house where for a short time one summer he, the usual outsider, felt himself to be the charmed insider.

A similar traumatized character whose adolescent vulnerability in the face of premature initiation into adult life has serious consequences is the protagonist of *The Brickfield* (1964). Like Elizabeth BOWEN, H. displayed special sensitivity in his portrayal of adolescents whose innocence becomes corrupted by the mature world.

H.'s pathos of misapprehended motives and situations on the part of children and adolescents frequently yielded to comedy of manners when adult protagonists pursue willful fantasies rather than face reality. The prototype was *The Boat* (1949), wherein a middle-aged bachelor novelist devoted to sculling brings his own war in the midst of World War II to a quiet English village in which the gentry had reserved the neighboring waters for fishing.

One of the most moving, although neglected, novels in the H. canon is *The Hireling* (1957). Here H. reveals an increasingly Lawrentian element in his figure of the attractive working-class male who obliquely woos the widow Lady Franklin.

H. turned to political satire and cautionary fable, criticizing the modern welfare state and celebrating individuality, in his dystopian novel *Facial Justice* (1960). Similarly, H. treated recent social experiments in modern Britain with irony and comic outrage in *The Betrayal* (1966) and *The Collections* (1972). As an old man, H. produced novels of a somewhat lighter tone and less symbolic structure. In subject matter, however, H. became more daring, with the introduction of incest and homosexuality as subjects in later novels.

Few 20th-c. English novelists can match H.'s portrayals of the romantic temperament caught in the cross-fire of the Edwardian past and the complex, equivocal present, or his humor and compassion in his deft exploration of the English class system, especially in his studies of masters and servants. H. remains an attractive minor master of a distinctly English restrictiveness, one of those rare artists who has something to say about culture and civilization and who can express sensibility and insight with ingratiating humor, well-turned style, and moral energy.

FURTHER WORKS: *Night Fears, and Other Stories* (1924); *Simonetta Perkins* (1925); *The Killing Bottle* (1932); *The Traveling Grave, and Other Stories* (1948); *My Fellow Devils* (1951); *The White Wand, and Other Stories* (1954); *A Perfect Woman* (1955); *Two for the River* (1961); *The Novelist's Responsibility: Lectures and Essays* (1967); *The Collected Short Stories* (1968); *Poor Clare* (1968); *The Love-Adept* (1969); *My Sisters' Keeper* (1970); *The Harness Room* (1971); *Mrs. Carteret Receives, and Other Stories* (1971); *The Will and the Way* (1973); *The Complete Short Stories* (1973)

BIBLIOGRAPHY: Melchiori, G., "The English Novelist and the American Tradition," *SR*, 18 (1960): 502–15; Bien, P., *L. P. H.* (1963); Hall, J., "Games of Apprehension: L. P. H.," *The Tragic Comedians: Seven Modern British Novelists* (1963): 111–28; Bloomfield, P., *L. P. H.* (1970); Webster, H. C., "L. P. H.: Diffident Christian," *After the Trauma: Representative British Novelists since 1920* (1970): 152–67; Mulkeen, A., *Wild Thyme, Winter Lightning: The Symbolic Novels of L. P. H.* (1974); Jones, E. T., *L. P. H.* (1978)

—EDWARD T. JONES

HAŠEK, Jaroslav

Czechoslovak poet and novelist (writing in Czech), b. 30 April 1883, Prague; d. 3 Jan. 1923, Lipnice

H.'s father, a rather unsuccessful teacher and later an office clerk, died when H. was thirteen. Although intelligent, H. did not exert himself at school and became a pharmacist's assistant for a while; better results from his studies at a commercial school in Prague brought him a job in a bank, but he could not keep it because of his often irresistible wanderlust. Walking penniless through large areas of central and southeastern Europe, H. gained some valuable experience. His World War I record is marred by his changing allegiance; he first worked as a patriotic journalist with Czech troops stationed in Russia, but later he collaborated on Communist propaganda as a member of the Bolshevik Party. After the war, when he returned to Prague to work as a professional writer, he was not very welcome, and even less so when he had to answer a charge of bigamy (which was true).

H. was a gifted writer and a very colorful character, who loved hoaxes and horseplay; convivial and anarchistic as he was, and an excellent raconteur, he could entertain his friends for hours. Yet, the coarseness of his humor and his total irreverence caused embarrassment to Czech literary critics who made an effort to appreciate his work, and it was instead foreigners who first called attention to the special quality of his greatest creation, the good soldier Švejk.

In his early amusing stories H. explored the character of simple folk; this subject matter eventually led him to develop the type of a lower-class man defying his oppressors by simple cunning. The good soldier Švejk appears in stories published as early as 1912—*Dobrý voják Švejk, a jiné podivné historky* (the good soldier Švejk, and other strange tales). There he is a grotesque dog dealer, doing his national service and ridiculing the Hapsburg military bureaucracy by his pretended mental deficiency, which brings about his desired release from the army. This, however, is the prewar Švejk. Not even the Švejk in *Dobrý voják Švejk v zajetí* (1917; the good soldier Švejk in captivity) is the fully crystallized Švejk of H.'s masterpiece, *Osudy dobrého vojáka Švejka za světové války* (4 vols., 1921–23; *The Good Soldier Švejk and His Fortunes in the World War*, 1973). H. himself had to experience war in order to endow his great character with such cynicism and grotesqueness; his creation attests to H.'s strong disapproval of war.

Švejk is no fighter; in fact, his feigned obedience and eagerness to carry out orders only show up their absurdity and result in highly comic situations. Fully aware of his superiors' weaknesses, Švejk uses his boundless imagination to exploit them for his own benefit; his innocent smile and his good humor even in the most precarious situations infuriate his superiors, and in the long run, slowly but steadily, he undermines the whole bureaucratic system. This method of passive resistance stems from the subjugated position of the small Czech nation within the Austro-Hungarian Empire: noncooperation and sabotage were the only means of defense against oppression. Although the term "Švejkism" was later used to connote the Czechs' passive resistance in general, Švejk is not really a typical Czech; rather, he resembles "any 'little man' who gets caught up in the wheels of a big bureaucratic machine" (C. Parrott). As a comic character, Švejk embodies the wide range of H.'s humor: high comedy, sarcasm, satire, and irony, as well as simple folk wisdom. For these H. must be given credit, even if his Rabelaisian humor and the irresponsibility of the "hero" provoked objections on moral grounds from some critics. As a novel, the work is rather loose and episodic in structure, as is natural for H.'s gift as a raconteur; yet, the hero is a clearly delineated and very unusual protagonist.

H.'s other works also reveal his exuberant imagination, his wit, and his love of hoax; if he had, in real life, no misgivings about confounding the public by selling dogs with dyed furs and forged pedigrees, or advertising the sale of "two thoroughbred werewolves"—hoaxes he actually perpetrated—he could go even further in his fiction, as in *Můj obchod se psy* (1915; my dog business), *Průvodčí cizinců, a jiné satiry z cest i domova* (1913; *The Tourist Guide*, 1961), and *Tři muži se žralokem, a jiné poučné historky* (1921; three men with a shark, and other instructive stories).

However objectionable H.'s famous character and his own real-life behavior may have been, as a writer H. had a genius of a special kind; Švejk deserves a place in the gallery of great characters of world literature. Under the coarse surface, H.'s humor brings home quite subtly some very serious truths about human nature.

FURTHER WORKS: *Májové výkřiky* (1903, with L. H. Domažlický); *Trampoty pana Tenkráta* (1912); *Kalamajka* (1913); *Dva tucty povídek* (1920); *Pepíček Nový, a jiné povídky* (1921); *Dobrý voják Švejk před válkou, a jiné podivné historky* (1922); *Mírová konference, a jiné humoresky* (1922); *Paměti úctyhodné rodiny* (1925); *Šťastný domov* (1925); *Zaválky i za sovětů v Rusku* (1925); *Zpověď starého mládence* (1925); *Ze staré drogerie* (1926); *Všivá historie* (1926); *Podivuhodná dobrodružství kocoura Markuse* (1927); *Když kvetou třešně* (1927); *Můj přítel Hanuška* (1928); *Fialový hrom* (1958); *Zrádce národa v Chotěboři* (1962); *Dějiny strany mírného pokroku v mezích zákona* (1963). **FURTHER WORKS IN ENGLISH:** *The Red Commissar* (1981); *Little Stories by a Great Master* (1984)

BIBLIOGRAPHY: "The King of Bohemia," *TLS*, 7 Sept. 1962: 665–66; Peter, P., *H.'s "Schweik" in Deutschland* (1963); Vlach, R., "Gogol and H.: Two Masters of 'Poshlost,'" *Études slaves et est-européennes*, 7 (1963): 239–42; Frynta, E., *H., the Creator of Schweik* (1965); Procházka, W., *Satire in H.'s Novel "The Good Soldier Schweik"* (1966); Enright, D. J., "The Survival of Švejk," *Listener*, 30 Aug. 1973: 284–85; "The Art of Survival," *TLS*, 21 Sept. 1973: 1083–84; Parrott, C., *The Bad Bohemian* (1978)

—B. R. BRADBROOK

HASS, Robert

American poet, translator, and essayist, b. 1 Mar. 1941, San Francisco, California

Born in San Francisco, H. has spent most of his life in the San Francisco Bay Area. After earning a bachelor's degree from St. Mary's College in California and a master's degree and Ph.D. from Stanford, H. taught at State University of New York at Buffalo; St. Mary's College; University of Virginia; Goddard College; Columbia University; and University of California at Berkeley, where he is currently a professor of English. Twice awarded the National Book Critics Circle Award (1984, 1997), H. also won the Yale Series of Younger Poets in 1973 for his first book, *Field Guide*, the MacArthur Fellowship, and has served two terms as Poet Laureate of the U.S. (1996-97). As Poet Laureate, H. battled American illiteracy, speaking frequently to small civic groups as well as making several appearances on television and radio. Actively committed to environmental issues, in 1997 H. was chosen as Educator of the Year by the North American Association on Environmental Education. Though primarily a poet, H. has also translated several books by the Nobel Prize-winning Polish poet Czeslaw MILOSZ, as well as edited *Selected Poems: 1954-1986 by Thomas Transtromer* and *The Essential Haiku: Versions of Basho, Buson, and Issa*.

Extremely well-read, H. easily traverses the territories of the natural sciences and history, all the while ruminating on Plato, LACAN, Hobbes, and DERRIDA in a plain, though ever-so-slightly elevated conversational style—in both his poetry and his essays. His meditative lyrics appear intimate yet detached simultaneously, as though he is close and watching from a distance. Given the frailty and beauty of relationships with other people, with nature, and with language itself, and given the impossibility of ever fulfilling our desires, H. explores and affirms alternate ways of living a life—fully involved in or detached from the world—in what most critics consider beautiful, simple, everyday meditations of enormous intellect and breadth. Though quite aware of inexplicable and purposeless suffering, overall he finds the world brimming with pleasure.

In *Field Guide*, his debut book of poetry, H. displays wit, curiosity, and brilliant perceptions about the body and its place in nature, and about the separation between naming and that which is named. In self-assured, often compressed lines he admires both the

peacefulness of Eastern asceticism and the engagement of the West. His next book of poetry, *Praise* (1979), is slightly looser in form but continues to concentrate on the natural world and humanity, all the while remaining phenomenological. Words, the poet's most obvious tools, are abstractions, and though "a word is elegy to what it signifies" and we are surrounded by loss, H. finds pleasure in his art and life. His poems carry a pleasant, conversational music with them, and perhaps it is this music and its bodily connection which ultimately lead H. away from the nihilistic despair so popular among many of his contemporaries.

In *Human Wishes* (1989) and *Sun Under Wood* (1997), his third and fourth books of poetry, H. includes prose poems, some fairly conventional stylistically, some more akin to compressed short stories. There is more darkness in these books than displayed in his earlier ones, but the focus on desire and its center in the body continues. H. looks more directly at human relationships—women's and men's relations, having children, losing a wife to divorce, his alcoholic mother—and also at the self-indulgence of self-expression. In these books loosened by longer lines and juxtaposed prose H. demonstrates once more his dual roles of participant and onlooker; of naturalist and metaphysician.

Twentieth Century Pleasures (1984), H.'s book of essays, perhaps provides the clearest view of H.'s aesthetics. In this collection of essays and reviews H.'s tone is once again meditative and intimate at the same time. Interspersed with meditations on imagery, rhythm, and form, we find stories of his childhood and early adulthood; this book of essays on poetry ends by optimistically affirming "the fullness and emptiness of being."

H.'s contribution to poetry is to make it as human as possible and at the same time philosophical—everyone in conversation has his philosophies, explicit or not. Instead of East versus West, one comes away reading H.'s poetry believing the two can find, at times, the same melody. Knowing fully well of the tragedy of pain without purpose, of desire that goes unfulfilled, of bodies that give out too soon or too late, the people of this world still talk to one another, and H. finds enough pleasure to make living more a gift than a burden. Instead of ignoring the bleaker facts of life—or worse yet becoming infatuated with them—H. writes beautifully about the histories of words and the places and people which gave birth to them—of both the darkness and lightness of being expressed—and all in all he leaves the reader feeling glad to be with him in this world of ours. H. keeps reminding us of the enjoyment we find in naming and talking and listening—in the useful pleasure of language that succeeds often enough to make us happy.

BIBLIOGRAPHY: Ford, Mark, "Reality Bites," *NewR*, 31 Oct. 1994, 48-51; Perry, T., "Poetry Man," *LA Times*, 31 Oct. 1996, E1; Davison, Peter, "The Laureate As Onlooker," *Atlantic Monthly*, March 1997, 100-102

—MICHAEL GUISTA

HAUGE, Olav H.

Norwegian poet, b. 18. Aug. 1908, Ulvik

H. has spent most of his life on his father's smallholding in Ulvik in the Hardanger district of western Norway, where he has made his living tending a small apple orchard. A trained orchardist,

H. has reaped both tangible fruit and a harvest of poetic inspiration from this activity; his literary work is firmly rooted in his native soil. But H. is no country bumpkin: he has received inspiration from a variety of poetic traditions and styles, including Japanese Haiku poetry, and has translated verse from German, French, and English.

H. was close to forty at the time of his literary debut. *Glør i oska* (1946; embers in the ashes) was considerably indebted to the works of two earlier poets, namely Olav Aukrust (1883–1929) and Olav Nygard (1884–1924), who, like H., had strong ties to their native soil and wrote in *nynorsk* (New Norwegian). His second volume of poetry, *Under bergfallet* (1951; beneath the crag), however, showed that H. was in the process of finding his own voice as a poet. He abandoned the abstractions and the romanticism of his predecessors and turned to physical nature for inspiration. *Seint rodnar skog i djuvet* (1956; slowly the woods redden in the gorge) and *På Ørnetuva* (1961; on the eagle's tussock) testify to years of laborious striving for a clarity of vision. His style was now further simplified and his images became increasingly powerful. *Dropar i austavind* (1966; drops in the east wind) and *Spør vinden* (1971; ask the wind) represented a further turning toward concrete, everyday subjects.

H. is extremely well informed about both the literature of his native land and world letters, having taught himself several foreign languages. Like the earliest poets in the *nynorsk* tradition, Ivar Aasen (1813–1896), A. O. Vinje (1818–1870), and Arne Garborg (1851–1924), and like his contemporary Tarjei Vesaas (1897–1970), H. has remained within a fixed native sphere and yet transcended it through his wide-ranging intellect. H. stands as one of the foremost modernists in postwar Norwegian poetry, and as one of the greatest poets in Norwegian literature. He is also one of Norway's most outward-directed writers, and has continued writing poetry into advanced age. The most recent edition of his works, *Dikt i samling* (1980; collected poems), contains a number of new poems under the common title *Janglestrå* (a few blades of grass), in which the poet comments on his experience of growing old.

FURTHER WORKS: *Utanlandske dikt* (1967). **FURTHER WORKS IN ENGLISH:** *Don't Give Me the Whole Truth* (1985); *Trusting Your Life to Water and Eternity* (1987)

BIBLIOGRAPHY: Fulton, R., Introduction to *Don't Give Me the Whole Truth* (1985): 9–15; Stegane, I., "The New Norse Literary Tradition," *RNL*, 12 (1983): 101–22

—JAN I. SJÅVIK

HAUPTMANN, Gerhart

German dramatist and novelist, b. 15 Nov. 1862, Obersalzbrunn; d. 6 June 1946, Agnetendorf

H.'s ancestors had lived in Silesia since 1600, where many of them had been weavers, but his father owned a resort hotel. His school years were unhappy and unsuccessful; he spent 1878–79 working on his uncle's farm, where the pietism of his relatives heightened a natural leaning toward mysticism. He turned to sculpturing, and spent two years at the Art Academy in Breslau and another year of desultory study at the University of Jena before

Gerhart Hauptmann

setting up a sculptor's studio in Rome. Typhoid fever forced him to return home. At Jena he had listened to lectures on philosophy, archaeology, and literature. Through his brother, who was a student in the natural sciences, H. came under the influence of the German exponent of Darwinism, the popular lecturer Ernest Haeckel. The scientific determinism of the age, combined with a youthful zeal for social reform, challenged the religious orthodoxy of his boyhood. This unresolved conflict helps to explain the polarity of his literary work.

H.'s engagement to the wealthy Marie Thienemann in 1881 and his marriage in 1885 provided the financial support that made his literary career possible. His earliest poetic efforts are now available in a facsimile printing *Früheste Dichtungen* (1962; earliest poetry), but his serious concern with literature began after an unsystematic study of Greek literature, history, and philosophy and wide reading in the German classics and modern authors. After his marriage he lived first in Berlin and then in its suburb Erkner. He established contacts with the leaders of naturalism. Performances of Ibsen's *Ghosts* and Tolstoy's *The Power of Darkness* made him study the dialogue and the effectiveness of these dramas. At his own expense he published *Promethidenlos* (1885; the Promethean's fate), a Byronic epic, and a collection of lyrics, *Das bunte Buch* (1888; the many-colored book), and contributed to magazines two realistic stories, "Fasching" (1887; carnival), and "Bahnwärter Thiel" (1888; "Flagman Thiel," 1933).

The success of his first drama, *Vor Sonnenaufgang* (1889; *Before Dawn*, 1909), signaled the beginning of a new era for the

German theater. It was performed by the Freie Bühne, the German equivalent of Antoine's Théâtre Libre in Paris, where Ibsen's social dramas had already avoided official censorship. The shocking details of the life of a dissolute peasant family, presented with grim realism, aroused the audience. Indignant protests against the revolting presentation of a sordid environment and the vicious consequences of hereditary alcoholism mingled with vociferous acclaim for the courageous young dramatist. The ponderous style of the day was suddenly swept away and a painstakingly accurate reproduction of the speech and mannerisms of every character introduced a new technique to the drama.

More plays followed in rapid succession: *Das Friedensfest* (1890; *The Coming of Peace*, 1900) and *Einsame Menschen* (1891; *Lonely Lives*, 1898), both family tragedies; and *Die Weber* (1892; *The Weavers*, 1899), the masterpiece of German naturalism, in which the historic uprising of 1844, a protest against the mechanical looms that destroyed the simple livelihood of Silesian weavers, is vividly recreated. In *Die Weber* five seemingly independent acts form a crescendo in dramatic action in which the numerous characters are carefully individualized but in their totality become the tragic protagonists of the suffering masses. Despite H.'s objective presentation of the misery and wretchedness that he had witnessed in visiting some areas of his province, he was accused of tendentious writing by the imperial government, which tried unsuccessfully to prevent public performances.

Der Biberpelz (1893; *The Beaver Coat*, 1912), using similar dramatic techniques and realistic characterizations, is a social satire and ranks high as a comedy. *Florian Geyer* (1895; *Florian Geyer*, 1929), a drama of the Peasant War, attempted to present the social, cultural, and linguistic background of the 16th c. with such an abundance of characters and epic breadth that the audience was overwhelmed. A complete failure at its first performance, it won understanding and appreciation after the collapse of Germany at the end of World War I, when the tragedy of political disunity had become meaningful.

A year earlier, in *Hanneles Himmelfahrt* (1894; *Hannele*, 1894), H. had combined the sordid atmosphere of the village poor house with a sensitive, psychological analysis of the bruised and tortured spirit of an adolescent girl who finds solace in a sensuous dream world of religious symbolism. The neoromantic aspects surprised the critics, who had called H. a "naturalist," but gave further proof that H.'s art transcended all labels. An almost complete surrender to romanticism is reflected in *Die versunkene Glocke* (1897; *The Sunken Bell*, 1898), his most popular dramatic success. Its folklore and fairy-tale elements, combined with the sentimental love story of a struggling artist, delighted an audience surfeited with drab realism, but its fame was ephemeral.

More permanent, perhaps even the most enduring of the tragedies depicting the brutality of life that destroys the individual, are *Fuhrmann Henschel* (1899; *Drayman Henschel*, 1913), *Rose Bernd* (1903; *Rose Bernd*, 1913), and *Michael Kramer* (1900; *Michael Kramer*, 1914), which might be grouped together as tragedies of isolation. Henschel and Rose Bernd are simple peasant types who are goaded and hounded to death. They are guided by instinct rather than reason, and in despair become the victims of their loneliness. H.'s sympathetic understanding of these characters, whose inevitable destruction is presented with restraint and artistic veracity, is unmatched in modern drama. In *Michael Kramer* the tragedy is transferred to an artist's family, where the son possesses the divine spark but lacks moral fiber, and the father has artistic integrity but limited talent. The son yearns in vain for a love that might redeem his soul and restore him to society. Despair drives him to self-destruction. *Der arme Heinrich* (1902; *Henry of Aue*, 1914) reveals the only solution: redemption through love. This drama contains some of H.'s finest poetry and psychologizes this miraculous legend of Middle High German literature.

H. continued to return to older themes in literature, which he reinterpreted with a sympathetic understanding of the demonic conflicts of the soul: *Elga* (1905; *Elga*, 1906), *Kaiser Karls Geisel* (1908; *Charlemagne's Hostage*, 1915), *Griselda* (1909; *Griselda*, 1909), *Der Bogen des Odysseus* (1914; *The Bow of Odysseus*, 1917), *Winterballade* (1917; *A Winter Ballad*, 1924), and *Veland* (1925; *Veland*, 1929). Despite its realistic background, *Und Pippa tanzt!* (1906; *And Pippa Dances*, 1907) is perhaps the finest expression of H.'s yearning for beauty, symbolized by this fragile, exotic creature pursued by all men.

After years of marital difficulties H. was divorced in 1904 and married Margarete Marschalk, a gifted young violinist. A journey to Greece three years later yielded not mere travel impressions in *Griechischer Frühling* (1908; Greek spring) but a profound appreciation of the Dionysian spirit of the Hellenic world, in which human sacrifice is the bloody root of tragedy. Henceforth H.'s dramatic work freed itself more and more of the artifice of the modern theater and its popular realism. He attempted to recapture the essence of what he called *das Urdrama*, the simplest and yet most dramatic conflict of the individual, split and torn asunder by antagonistic facets of his own personality.

H.'s narrative work, though secondary in importance, gives further proof of the breadth and scope of his literary genius. The novel *Der Narr in Christo Emanuel Quint* (1910; *The Fool in Christ, Emanuel Quint*, 1911) chronicles the life of a simple peasant who literally relives the experiences of the historical Jesus. H.'s deeply religious nature comes to grips with modern scientific skepticism and his own anticlerical leanings. The religious ecstasy of a modern mystic, combined with asceticism and naïve faith, reflect H.'s own feeling for a religious experience almost incompatible with the temper of modern society. The profound sympathy and psychological insight of the narrative are tempered with a faint irony that suggests the inadequacy of both mysticism and rationalism. Diametrically opposed in spirit is *Der Ketzer von Soana* (1918; *The Heretic of Soana*, 1923), a Rousseauan paean of praise to the goodness and fullness of life governed by natural instincts. The sensuous beauty of the landscape of Ticino and the pagan assertion of the senses make it a hymn to Eros. Stylistically and structurally it is H.'s most perfect narrative work.

Public recognition came soon after the first theater successes. The Imperial Academy in Vienna gave H. its highest award, the Grillparzer Prize, three times (1896, 1899, 1905) for *Hanneles Himmelfahrt*, *Fuhrmann Henschel*, and *Der arme Heinrich*. Only the personal antagonism of the emperor prevented his receiving the German drama award, the Schiller Prize, for which he was repeatedly recommended. In 1905 Oxford University bestowed on him the honorary degree of doctor of letters; other honorary degrees followed from the universities of Leipzig (1909) and Prague (1921), and from Columbia University (1932). Most important of all was the international recognition that came with the Nobel Prize (1912). The Weimar Republic gave him its highest decoration and celebrated his sixtieth birthday as a national event. The Third Reich ignored him, but his dramas continued to be performed. After World War I H. published the dramas *Der weiße Heiland* (1920; *The White Saviour*, 1924) and *Indipohdi* (1920; *Indipohdi*, 1924), which represent something of a flight from reality into an exotic world of fantasy. *Der weiße Heiland* depicts the cruel conquest of Mexico and the tragedy of the guileless and trusting Montezuma, who falls victim to the avarice of the Christian invaders. *Indipohdi* reflects H.'s disillusionment and despair during the war years; inspired and suggested by Shakespeare's *The Tempest*, it was meant as H.'s farewell to the world of the drama. The epic *Till Eulenspiegel* (1928; Till Eulenspiegel), written in hexameters, tells the adventures of a former aviator who wanders in despair through postwar Germany in the guise of the legendary prankster of German folk literature. H. not only portrays the chaotic conditions of his fatherland but takes his hero back through history in a series of visionary episodes that include a blissful existence in the realm of ancient Greece before his return to the chaotic real world, where he plunges to his death in the Swiss Alps.

After years of preoccupation with the study of Shakespeare and the "Hamlet problem," H. published a revision of the text, wrote the drama *Hamlet in Wittenberg* (1935; Hamlet at Wittenberg), and a novel, *Im Wirbel der Berufung* (1936; in the turmoil of the vocation), concerned with the theater and the staging of *Hamlet*. *Das Buch der Leidenschaft* (1930; the book of passion), a novel in diary form, is a veiled confession of the emotional stress occasioned by his divorce and remarriage; *Das Abenteuer meiner Jugend* (1937; the adventure of my youth) is a detailed autobiographical account of his formative years and early literary struggles. The story "Das Meerwunder" (1934; the chimera) moves far beyond the realm of reality, and its almost surrealistic style reflects H.'s despair at man's inhumanity and betrayal of the brotherhood of man. The tortured cry "I don't want to be a part of the human race," which becomes the watchword of the protagonist, symbolizes H.'s repugnance at the Hitler era. Written during the war years, the epic *Der große Traum* (1942; the great dream) depicts a series of grandiose visions of the eternal conflict between the forces of darkness and light. Again H.'s speculative thinking, tinged with the philosophy of the gnostics, attempts to transcend human limitations. The tragedy of medieval witchcraft and the Inquisition, *Magnus Garbe* (1942; Magnus Garbe), had its origin in H.'s interest in the age of the Reformation and the Anabaptists, and was completed by 1915; but its unmitigated gloom, the "bitterest tragedy of mankind," as the poet called it, made him postpone its publication until the end of his lfe. The House of Atreus tetralogy, the tragedy of Agamemnon and his family, consists of the concluding drama *Iphigenie in Delphi* (1941; Iphigenia in Delphi), the opening drama *Iphigenie in Aulis* (1944; Iphigenia in Aulis), and the connecting one-act dramas *Agamemnons Tod* (1948; Agamemnon's death) and *Elektra* (1947; Electra), the last two published after H.'s death. All the horror and despair that the war years had aroused find full expression in this cycle of crime, passion, and bloodshed. The curse of Tantalus and his race endangers and destroys humanity. Mankind longs helplessly for salvation. Only human sacrifice makes any sort of atonement possible.

H.'s last work, the unfinished novel *Der neue Christophorus* (1943; the new Christopher), is again the story of suffering humanity, to be redeemed by Erdmann, who represents the eternal rebirth of mankind. Shortly after the end of World War II and the occupation of Silesia by the Russians, who showed respect and friendship for the aged poet and protected him and his property against the indignities of Polish looting, H. died—at the very moment when orders were given for the mass evacuation of all Germans from that province. H., whose greatest fear at the end of his life had been the threat of deportation, virtually died with the anxious words "Am I still in my house?" on his lips.

His versatile talent in creating real human beings, his subtle exposition of milieu, and his lifelike dialogue gave his work a dominant place in German literature for fifty years after his sensational success in 1889, and made H. the representative figure of that epoch. Despite excessive adulation or temporary neglect, his work is firmly established and reflects the complexity, doubts, uncertainties, and relativism of our time. It represents the highest artistic expression of what may eventually be regarded as a transitional age. The contradictions and irrational forces of human nature are revealed sympathetically and understandingly. The simplicity and yet the universality of his work, the sympathetic understanding of suffering humanity, received high recognition and praise from his greatest contemporaries, RILKE and Thomas MANN.

FURTHER WORKS: *Schluck und Jau* (1900; *Schluck and Jau*, 1915); *Der rote Hahn* (1901); *Das Hirtenlied* (1904; *Pastoral*, 1917); *Die Jungfern vom Bischofsberg* (1907; *The Maidens of the Mount*, 1915); *Die Ratten* (1911; *The Rats*, 1913); *Gabriel Schillings Flucht* (1912; *Gabriel Schilling's Flight*, 1915); *Atlantis* (1912; *Atlantis*, 1912); *Festspiel in deutschen Reimen* (1913; *Commemoration Masque*, 1917); *Lohengrin* (1913); *Parsival* (1914); *Peter Brauer* (1921); *Anna* (1921); *Phantom* (1922; *Phantom*, 1922); *Ausblicke* (1922); *Die blaue Blume* (1924); *Die Insel der großen Mutter* (1924; *The Island of the Great Mother*, 1925); *Dorothea Angermann* (1926); *Wanda* (1928); *Spuk* (1930); *Um Volk und Geist: Ansprachen* (1932); *Die goldene Harfe* (1934); *Die Tochter der Kathedrale* (1939); *Ulrich von Lichtenstein* (1939); *Mignon* (1947); *Die Finsternisse* (1947); *Die großen Beichten* (1966); *Gesammelte Werke* (6 vols., 1906); *Gesammelte Werke* (6 vols., 1912); *Gesammelte Werke* (12 vols., 1922); *Gesammelte Werke; Ausgabe letzter Hand* (17 vols., 1942); *Sämtliche Werke* (11 vols., 1962–1974). FURTHER WORKS IN ENGLISH: *The Dramatic Works* (9 vols., 1912–1929)

BIBLIOGRAPHY: Holl, K., *G. H.: His Life and His Work* (1913); Fechter, P., *G. H.* (1922); Schlenther, P. and A. Eloesser, *G. H.* (1922); A., Reichart W., "Fifty Years of H. Study in America (1894–1944): A Bibliography," *Monatshefte*, 37 (1945): 2–28; Muller, S., *G. H. and Goethe* (1949); Weisert, J. J., *The Dream in G. H.* (1949); Garten, H. F., *G. H.* (1954); Behl, C. F. W., *G. H.: His Life and Work* (1956); Sinden, H., *G. H.: The Prose Plays* (1957); Shaw, L. R., *Witness of Deceit: G. H. as Critic of Society* (1958); Grueneberg, E., *Demon and Eros in Some Plays of G. H.* (1960); Michaelis, R., *Der schwarze Zeus* (1962); Reichart, W. A., "H. Study in America: A Continuation Bibliography," *Monatshefte*, 54 (1962): 298–309; Knight, K. G., and F. Norman, eds., *H. Centenary Lectures* (1964); Guthke, K. S., "Nihilism and Modern Literature: The Case of G. H.," *Forum* (Houston), 5, 1 (1967): 4–13; Usmiani, R., "Towards an Interpretation of H.'s *House of Atreus*," *MD*, 12 (1969): 286–97; Tschörtner, H. D., *G. H. Bibliographie* (1971); Lea, H. A., "The Specter of Romanticism: H.'s Use of Quotations," *GR*, 49 (1974): 267–83; Mellen, P. A., *G. H. and Utopia* (1976); Gousie, L., "G. H. and German Surrealism," *GR*, 53 (1978): 156–65; Dussère, C. T., *The Image of the Primitive Giant in the Works of G. H.* (1979); Ley, R., et al., eds., "The Shattering of the Construct: G. H. And His Ketzer," *Perspectives and Personalities: Studies in Modern German Literature Honoring Claude Hill* (1978): 238-60; Webb, K. E., "Islands, Maidens, and the Life Force: G. H.'s Literary Fugendstil," *Theatrum Mundi: Essays on German Drama and German Literature* (1980): 109-24; Guthke, K., "The King of the Weimar Republic: G. H.'s

Role in Political Life, 1919-1933," *Probleme der Moderne: Studien zur Deutschen Literatur von Nietzsche bis Brecht* (1983): 369-87; Mellen, P., *G. H.: Religious Syncreticism and Eastern Religions* (1984); Cowen, R. C., "*Die Ratten* and G. H.'s Troubled Social Conscience," *Imperial Germany* (1985); Lewis, W. B., "O'Neill and H: A Study in Mutual Admiration," *Comparative Literature Studies*, 22.2 (1985): 231-43; Lehman, R. H., "A New Look at Victimization in H.'s *Before Dawn*," *Within the Dramatic Spectrum* (1986): 139-50; Crosby, D., "Nature's Nightmare: The Inner World of H.'s 'Flagman Thiel'," *Journal of the Fantastic in the Arts,*, 1.2 (1988): 25-33; Wynn, D. D., "H. and Böcklin: an Artistik and Historical Synthesis in Michael Kramer," *The Germanic Review*, 64.2 (1989): 67-72; Hodge, J., "How H. Solved the 'Agamemnon Problem'," *Classical and Modern Literature: A Quarterly*, 12.1 (1991): 15-27; Good, C. F., *Domination, Dependence, Denial and Despair: Father-Daughter Relationships in Grillparzer, Hebbel and H.* (1993); Whitinger, R., "Rethinking Anna Mahr: Reflections on the Characterization and Function of the Emancipated Woman in G. H.'s *Einsame Menschen*," *Seminar: A Journal of Gemanic Studies*, 29.3 (1993): 233-52

—WALTER REICHART
updated by FRIEDHELM RICKERT

G. H . . . has not only a true tone, but also true courage and true *artistic skill* to match this courage. It is foolish to assume that naturalistic coarseness is always tantamount to artlessness. On the contrary, if properly employed . . . it attests to the highest artistry. . . .

He altogether appears to me as the fulfillment of Ibsen. All I had been admiring in Ibsen for years, the "reach into life, it is a teeming ocean," the novelty and the boldness of the problems, the ingenious simplicity of the language, the talent for characterization, together with the most rigorous organization of the action and the elimination of anything not directly related to the plot itself—all of this I also found in H. Moreover, all the things I disliked about Ibsen . . . I did *not* find in H. He is not a realist who sporadically suffers from whimsical fits of philosophical romanticizing but a realist in good style, which is to say that from beginning to end he is always the same. [1889]

Theodor Fontane, *Sämtliche Werke* (1969), Vol. II, pp. 819–20

G. H. was a great man, one of the greatest—and G. H. was a weak man who failed in the decisive hour of the German genius, at a moment, when it became the duty of the great spiritual leaders to make their decision known. When, in 1933, darkness descended upon Germany, G. H. remained silent. . . . No, there is no excuse for his silence; and indeed, we would do neither him nor ourselves any favor whatsoever, if we were to attempt, by way of embellishing touches, to brighten up the distressing image presented by the aged G. H. He was no equal to the greatness of his task; he chose to remain a bystander at a loathsome spectacle from which to emphatically turn away would have been his duty, even though it is true—and it is true a thousand times—that he himself remained

the same, and that no inner ties bound him to the barbarians among whom he lived.

Oskar Seidlin, *Monatshefte*, 38 (1946), 332

H. lacks an essential ingredient: an awareness of evil, of man's productive demonism. Thus he is not truly and essentially a psychologist, that is, a discoverer and portrayer of areas of the soul hitherto unexplored and often characteristic of a specific period, in the exact and decisive sense in which, for instance, Shakespeare and some of his contemporaries and, later, Stendhal and Strindberg were psychologists. He is not so much an explorer of the soul as an apologist for it. . . . In H. there is none of the splendid—so to speak, total—harmony and unity, the dialectical and contrapuntal fugal treatment of all themes, that appears in its full glory in the drama of Schiller, Kleist, and Racine. This is undoubtedly connected with the fact that this genius who makes no assumptions has absolutely no relationship to history. For him all history finally becomes happening.

Hans Hennecke, *Dichtung und Dasein* (1950), p. 129

Although H., particularly in the latter part of his life, contributed to every genre of literature, he will always be known first and foremost as a dramatist. It was in drama that his greatest faculty, the creation of live characters, found its fullest scope. . . . H. sees drama in all human existence; life, for him, is in its essence an unceasing strife—a strife that rends the heart of man from the first moment of his conscious existence. . . . Hence genuine drama is for H. in the first place a drama of the mind, of character, and not of action. . . .

This basic conception of drama partly explains why H.'s principal characters are throughout passive. They do not act; things happen to them. Their tragedy springs not so much from an excess of action, or of passion, as from an insufficiency, an incapacity to cope with the exigencies of life. Their keynote is suffering. However, H.'s intrinsic philosophy is not one of fatalism. His central theme, shaped in countless variations, is redemption through suffering. In the end, when tragedy has taken its course, the victim, though felled by the force of circumstances, emerges as the true conqueror.

Hugh F. Garten, *G. H.* (1954), pp. 12–13

The earlier plays . . . remain his finest single accomplishment, and if there have been frequent references to Ibsen and Shaw in these pages it is because he has no other rivals in modern literature in the field of realistic prose drama. . . . H.'s work has breadth, a unique power of creating men and environment, and an attitude which makes it as progressive as that of his often more argumentative contemporaries. His first service to his own and succeeding generations is his ability to paint human beings from many spheres of society, from the lower classes as well as the middle, and with equal understanding and concern for both. But his second service is that, though his plays lack the intellectual quality of those of Ibsen or Shaw, he touches in his own way on just as wide a range of problems, social and economic, religious and political. And his whole attitude implies a desire for reform wherever it appears to him that the society of his day has become rigid in its ideals, careless of the lives of its individual members, or blind to the inevitability of change.

Margaret Sinden, *G. H.* (1957), pp. 230–31

H. shared the slogans and arguments employed by most writers of his time and, in particular, . . . he participated in their attack on the so-called *Kulturlüge*, or Lie of modern society.

H.'s action against the cultural lie was motivated by the two-fold conviction that man's problems lie within society and that an accurate representation of social conditions would lead almost of itself to an improvement of the situation. One needed only to inform the ignorant about abuses they had not yet become aware of, and appeal to the conscience of those who were still using social instruments for their own gain. In spite of this basic assumption, however, . . . H. had little confidence in direct reform. Even when the reformer appears as protagonist . . . he does so only to reveal the wrongs which H. wished to condemn and to serve as an example of the futility or impracticability of his particular way of reform. Each of these reformers represents a point of view which H. had already rejected for himself.

Leroy R. Shaw, *Witness of Deceit* (1958), p. 97

H.'s dramatic work, various and abundant (he has written more than forty dramas), is not without consistency. The tetralogy of the last decade is not too far removed from the early plays that he wrote in the 1890's. H. has simply advanced from the immediate—although no less universal—problems of individuals and their environment to broader issues of mankind, irrespective of time and place. However, the deep compassion and feeling for humanity have remained the same. This is indeed the distinguishing mark of H.'s dramatic work: social sympathy, social pity, social compassion. His social feeling is not intellectual; it is intuitive. Thanks to this elemental feeling for his fellow men, H. has remained the foremost social poet of Germany. And thanks to this deep feeling for humanity he is counted among those modern dramatists who, like Ibsen, Strindberg, and Shaw, have outlasted the changes of time and fashion.

Horst Frenz, Introduction to G. H., *Three Plays* (1977), pp. xiii-xiv

HAUSA LITERATURE

See Nigerian Literature

HAVEL, Václav

Czechoslovak dramatist, essayist, and poet (writing in Czech), b. 5 Oct. 1936, Prague

In accordance with the Communist regime's guidelines during the 1950s for suppressing all bourgeois elements, H., the son of a wealthy property owner and thus a member of the bourgeoise, was refused acceptance to any institution of higher learning. After his military service he found employment in Prague theaters, first as a stagehand. Later he became the dramatic consultant of the theater Na Zábradlí, which in 1963 staged his first play, *Zahradní slavnost* (1964; *The Garden Party*, 1969). Also in 1963, at the age of twenty-seven, he was accepted as a student at the Academy of Dramatic Arts in Prague, from which he graduated in 1967. In 1968 H. was involved in the Czechoslovak reform movement. His work has been under complete ban since the reimposition of strict controls in 1969. H. took part in various civic initiatives protesting against the infringement of human rights in Czechoslovakia in the 1970s. Throughout this period he was subjected to police harassment and arrests. In October 1979 he was sentenced to four and a half years' imprisonment for his activities as a member of the Committee for the Defense of Unjustly Prosecuted Persons (VONS). In the 1980s, H. became the undisputed unofficial leader of the Czechoslovak human rights movement. Between January and May 1989, he was imprisoned. In June 1989, H. and other human rights activists drafted a general human rights petition, "Just a Few Sentences." Several tens of thousands of Czechoslovak citizens signed this petition before the fall of communism in November 1989.

On December 27, 1989 and again on July 5, 1990 (after the first free general elections in Czechoslovakia) H. was elected Czechoslovak President. After the division of Czechoslovakia, H. became President of the Czech Republic in February 1993. His role as a public figure has now somewhat overshadowed H.'s record as a playwright, dissident and political essayist.

In *Zahradní slavnost* H. adopted some of the devices of the THEATER OF THE ABSURD to satirize modern bureaucratic routines and their dehumanizing tendencies, as well as some features of the Czech national character, namely the unprincipled adaptability to circumstances shown by the middle classes. The play was an immediate success both at home and abroad.

In his next play, *Vyrozumění* (1966; *The Memorandum*, 1967), staged two years later by the same theater that did *Zahradní slavnost*, he examined in a more complex way the effect that patterns imposed by the mechanics of bureaucracy have on society and on the individual mind. The plot turns around the introduction of an artificial language that is supposed to allow for greater precision in communication. H. uses this absurd idea to expose the emptiness of established clichés devoid of any real meaning. As no one can understand the monstrous new language, the ridiculous attempt to improve efficiency results in a complete breakdown of human relationships. It is finally rejected, only to be replaced by another, equally incomprehensible system, but fostered by people who see in it a means to advance their careers. The play also contains an implied criticism of the weakness and ineffectuality of certain liberal humanist attitudes, as represented by one of the main characters.

The theme was taken even further in *Zitížená možnost soustředění* (1968; *The Increased Difficulty of Concentration*, 1972), produced again by the theater Na Zábradlí. This time it is mainly the language and postures of the modern social sciences that come under attack.

In the course of the play, the protagonist, a man who appears quite unable to cope with the problems of his marriage and his love affairs, dictates a radio lecture that discusses the complexity of contemporary life and uses fashionable sociological terminology. The gradually revealed failings of his personality, his inability to resolve anything, and his degeneration into an intellectual and psychological automaton, are reflected in a computer used by a farcical research team observing him.

The plays written in the 1970s, *Spiklenci* (1970; the conspirators), *Horský hotel* (1976; mountain hotel), and *Žebrácká opera* (1976), an adaptation of John Gay's (1685–1732) *The Beggar's Opera*, were widely produced outside Czechoslovakia, but did not achieve the same degree of success as his earlier work. He was more successful when he turned for his subjects to the greatly changed conditions of life in his country in a series of one-act plays: *Audience* (1975; *Audience*, 1978), *Vernisáž* (1975; *Private View*, 1978), and *Protest* (1978?; *Protest*, 1980). The three are connected by the character of a dissident playwright in trouble with the authorities, whose principled stand provokes hostile reactions from others, who had adapted to the prevailing circumstances. In the first, the playwright, now working as a laborer in a brewery, is asked by the head maltster to provide written reports on himself, which the maltster could pass on to the secret police. His refusal to comply results in an outburst of pent-up frustrations from the maltster. In *Vernisáž*, his mere presence lays bare the shallowness of the good life enjoyed by a couple who had sacrificed their conscience in favor of material advantages. A fellow writer, who has managed to do well under the new regime, is similarly exposed in *Protest*. In these plays the microcosm of an individual situation reflects the larger problem of moral corruption under pressures imposed by a totalitarian state.

In the 1980s, H. wrote three full-length plays which mark a new stage in the development of his dramatic art. The hero of *Largo desolatio* (1985), a dissident deeply traumatized by the police, finds it very difficult to deal with the burdens imposed on him by both his enemies and by his friends. *Pokoušení* (1986; Temptation) is a modern re-working of Faust, a morality, in which H. warns against game playing. By pretending to cooperate with all sides in a conflict, at the same time deceiving all of them, one loses one's integrity and identity. In *Asanance* (1988; Redevelopment) H. parodies attempts at reforming communism.

H. was the most original dramatist to appear in Czechoslovakia in the 1960s, and during the following decade his work was among the most interesting to come from eastern Europe. Although the 1960s plays were evidently inspired by a peculiarly Czech brand of bureaucratic absurdity, the social evils and individual follies that they exposed are universal.

In the 1970s and the 1980s, as a dissident and a major figure in the Czechoslovak human rights movement, H. gradually came to prominence as an author of political essays ("The Power of the Powerless," "Politics and Conscience," "The Anatomy of a Reticence") in which he analyzes the essence of Czechoslovak communism after 1968. *Dopisy Olze* (1985; *Letters to Olga*, 1988) which H. sent to his wife from prison in 1979-1982, consist of psychological and philosophical observations, which eventually develop into an essay of transcendence in human life.

FURTHER WORKS: *Autostop* (1961, with Ivan Vyskočil); *Nejlepší rocky paní Hermanové* (1962, with Miloš Macourek); *Protokoly* (1966). FURTHER WORKS IN ENGLISH: *Three V. plays* (1990); *Disturbing the Peace: A Conversation with Karel Hvížďala* (1990);

Open Letters: Selected Writings, 1965-1990 (1991); *Selected Plays, 1963-1983* (1991); *Summer Meditations* (1992); *Fragments of Memory* (1992); *Selected Plays, 1984-1987* (1994); *Literature and Tolerance* (1995)

BIBLIOGRAPHY: Blackwell, V., "The New Czech Drama," *Listener*, 5 Jan. 1967: 10–12; Grossman, J., "A Preface to H.," *TDR*, 11, 3 (1967): 117–20; Mihailovich, V. D., et al., eds., *Modern Slavic Literatures* (1976), Vol. II: 91–96; Tynan, K., "Withdrawing with Style from the Chaos," *New Yorker*, 19 Dec. 1977: 41-111; Trensky, P. I., *Czech Drama since World War II* (1978): 104–24 and passim; Goetz-Stankiewicz, M., *The Silenced Theatre: Czech Playwrights without a Stage* (1979): 45–87 and passim; Keane, J., ed., *The Power of the Powerless: Citizen against the State in Central-Eastern Europe* (1985); Kundera, M., "A Life Like a Work of Art," *NR*, 29 Jan. 1990: 16-17; Baranczak, S., "All the President's Plays," *NR*, 23 July 1990: 27-32; Kriseova, E., *V. H.* (1993); Thomas, A., "Philosophy and Politics in V. H.'s *Largo Desolato*," in *The Labyrinth of the World* (1995): 144-57

—IGOR HÁJEK

HĀWĪ, Khalīl

Lebanese poet and critic, b. 1 Jan. 1925, Shwayr

H.'s early education was in Christian missionary schools, where he learned French and English and began an ambitious reading program in Western literature. He studied Arabic literature and philosophy at the American University of Beirut (1947–52) and in 1959 received a doctorate in Arabic literature from Cambridge University. While at Cambridge, he came under the influence of F. R. LEAVIS, who introduced him to the major schools and techniques of Western literary criticism.

In 1940 H. published his first poems in the Lebanese dialect, but he soon abandoned the use of dialect in favor of Modern Standard Arabic. H.'s first poem in Modern Standard, "Ilāh" (1947; a god), elicited favorable critical response.

H.'s fine master's thesis, *Al-'Aql wa al-īmān bayn al-Ghazzālī wa Ibn Rushd* (1952; reason and faith: between al-Ghazzālī and Averroes), and his highly acclaimed *Kahlil Gibran: His Background, Character, and Works* (1963), written in English, mark the consummation of his education in philosophy and literary criticism.

To date, H. has published five volumes of poetry—*Nahr al-ramād* (1957; the river of ashes), *Al-Nāy wa al-rīh* (1960; the wind and the flute), *Bayādir al-jū'* (1965; the threshing-floors of hunger), *Al Ra'd al-jarīh* (1979; the wounded thunder), and *Min jahīm al-kūmīdya* (1979; from comedy's inferno)—as well as numerous long poems and critical essays on Arabic, French, and English poetry. He is also the editor of the *Encyclopedia of Arabic Poetry*, of which four volumes appeared in 1974.

H.'s poetry represents something new in Arabic literature in both form and content. Writing in *al-shi'r al-hurr* (mistakenly referred to as "free verse"), a form of verse that substitutes the unity of foot to the unity of meter, H. successfully exploits those meters that are used in folk songs and are most familiar to people's ears. This metrical quality, along with his fresh, simple diction, has had great influence on his contemporaries. Moreover, H. succeeds, where other poets before him failed, in eliminating narration from

his poetry by transforming legends and folktales into fundamental symbols that simultaneously evoke intellectual and
emotional associations.

His poetry is a universal in that it addresses the existential
questions and the problems of the present-day Arab world within a
universal and philosophical context, striking a happy balance
between the intellectual and the emotional. Some critics note his
tendency toward pessimism and his profuse use of dark and violent
images, but others attribute this quality to his unwavering engagement with the problems of his world and his commitment to the
truthfulness of his visions.

BIBLIOGRAPHY: Badawī, M., *A Critical Introduction to Modern
Arabic Poetry* (1975): 245–50; Haydar, A., and M. Beard, "Two
Interpretations of H.'s 'The Cave,'" *Edebiyat*, 3, 2 (1978): 57–71;
Jabra, J. I., "The Rebels, the Committed and Others," *MEF*, 1
(1967): 19–32; Jayyūsī, S., *Trends and Movements in Modern
Arabic Poetry* (1977), passim

—ADNAN HAYDAR

HAWKES, John

American novelist, b. 17 Aug. 1925, Stamford, Conn.

H.'s childhood and adolescence were spent in such widely
dispersed parts of the U.S. as New York City and Juneau, Alaska.
After serving as an American Field Service ambulance driver in
Italy and Germany during World War II, he attended Harvard,
where he studied creative writing under Albert J. Guerard (b. 1914)
and completed his first two novels, *The Cannibal* (1949) and
Charivari (1949). Since 1958 he has been a professor of English at
Brown University.

H.'s vision of life is one of the bleakest among contemporary
American novelists. His fictional practice has been to portray
individuals acting out their obsessions in a hallucinatory landscape,
living with terrifying vividness their libidinal dreams of self-
fulfillment and self-destruction. Employing surrealistically the
subterranean fears and fantasies of human nature, he strips life of
the illusions used as insulation from the reality of self and the
horrors of history. Only the saving graces of a richly poetic prose
and of a comic inventiveness make his sadomasochistic exposures
of human desire acceptable, and sympathetic.

Uncompromisingly experimental, he parallels a narrative concentration on random violence and sexual grotesquerie with
disjunctions of time and space and violations of verisimilitude. His
rebellious originality, rejecting traditional fictional forms, has
produced unconventional, even ferocious, parodies of the western—*The Beetle Leg* (1951)—the picaresque tale—*The Goose on
the Grave* (pub. in one vol. with *The Owl*, 1954)—and the detective
thriller—*The Lime Twig* (1961). And his effort to thwart conventional thematic response to narrative realism has led him to create
landscapes of the mind, fictive settings ostensibly signifying Renaissance Italy, postwar Germany, contemporary France, postwar
England, the American West, and mythical lands and islands in the
Mediterranean and Caribbean, which are disconcertingly familiar
and yet bewilderingly strange, tantalizingly resistant to recognition
as places. Significant in this regard has been his shift to the first
person, whereby his protagonist-narrator has become his own
mythographer. With *The Lime Twig* and *Second Skin* (1964) H. has

gradually modulated these surrealistic extremes in favor, relatively
speaking, of a more realistic surface and of a more dramatic and
narrative coherence. Still, H.'s difficultness prevails, and the
severity of his imagination has tended to restrict readers to a small
but admiring group of writers and academics.

In *The Blood Oranges* (1971), *Death, Sleep & the Traveler*
(1974), *Travesty* (1976), and *The Passion Artist* (1979), H. has
increasingly concentrated his attention on the entangling relationship in the human psyche of love and death, sexuality and imagination, impotence and sterility. An allied leitmotif is the relationship
of victim and victimizer, who act out their dark terrors of the
psyche against a background of society's normal comings and
goings. With his moral passion for exposing the destructive instincts in the night journey of the human soul, H. is the Savonarola
of American novelists. He has called himself a New England
puritan in rebellion against the puritanical version of life with its
law, dictum, and insistence on human perversity. His "sex-singers"
and "passion artists" are a rebellious expression of his contrary
lyrical espousal of Eros; but the havoc he imagines them causing,
and even courting for themselves—Eros locked in wedlock with
Thanatos—reflects an equally stubborn residual survival in H.,
despite his extreme maintenance of icy authorial detachment, of the
puritanical moral code.

There has always been criticism of the excesses of H.'s style,
with its overwritten and overblown language, and objection to his
reduction of narrative to brilliant but isolated and unassimilated
events. As if deaf to such carping, H. has gone his independent
original way; and as novel has followed novel, he is hailed ever
more justifiably by a growing number of readers as a major
contemporary novelist.

FURTHER WORKS: *The Innocent Party: Four Short Plays* (1966);
Lunar Landscapes: Stories & Short Novels 1949–1963 (1969)

BIBLIOGRAPHY: special H. and John Barth issue, *Crit*, 6, 2 (1963);
Graham, J., ed., *Studies in "Second Skin"* (1973); Busch, F., *H.: A
Guide to His Fictions* (1973); Greiner, D., *Comic Terror: The
Novels of J. H.* (1973; rev. ed., 1978); Greiner, D., *Comic Terror:
The Novels of J. H.* (1973); Kuehl, J., *J. H. and the Craft of Conflict*
(1975); Santore, A. C., and Pocalyko, M., eds., *A J. H. Symposium*
(1977); Hryciw, C. A., *J. H.: An Annotated Bibliography, with
Four Introductions by J. H.* (1977)

—MAX F. SCHULZ

HAYASHI Fumiko

Japanese novelist, short-story writer, and poet, b. 31 Dec. 1904,
Shimonoseki; d. 2 June 1951, Tokyo

Daughter of an itinerant peddler, H. spent most of her childhood
traveling from town to town, living always in flea-ridden inns.
What she remembered most vividly about those days was perpetual
hunger. She found solace, however, in writing poetry and reading.
H. managed to put herself through high school by working as a
factory hand and as a maid. Upon graduating, she went to Tokyo,
only to experience the most bitter hardships of her life. Since
childhood, roving had become almost second nature; she never
settled in one place and constantly switched jobs (waitress, clerk,
peddler, maid). She changed lovers just as swiftly.

Between her jobs and love affairs she found time to write poetry and children's stories. She also kept a diary, excerpts of which were serialized in the women's literary magazine *Nyonin geijutsu*, in 1928, under the title *Hōrōki* (journal of a vagabond). When *Hōrōki* was published in book form in 1930 it immediately attained tremendous popularity. It depicts a young heroine who manages to live with impressive honesty and cheerfulness in the lowest stratum of society. It is candidly narrated, devoid of pessimism and sentimentality. The montage-like sequence of diary entries creates a natural time flow of events, and H.'s style is compellingly vivid and intensely lyrical.

The success of *Hōrōki* put an end to H.'s precarious mode of life; she was able to travel to China and, in 1931, to Europe. She spent much time in Paris frequenting museums, concert halls, and theaters. Returning home in 1932, she wrote a number of short stories that gradually established her place in literary circles.

In 1935 H. wrote her first successful novel, *Inazuma* (lightning), whose characters were modeled on the members of her own family. During the Second Sino-Japanese War (1937–45), she was dispatched to China as a special correspondent by the newspaper *Mainichi*. She also served as a member of the Japanese wartime press corps in the South Pacific in 1942. These experiences gave further scope and depth to her later writings. During the remainder of the war she lived in the country and concentrated on writing children's stories.

In 1948 H. published one of her finest stories, "Bangiku" ("Late Chrysanthemum," 1960). It delineates with consummate skill the subtle, shifting moods of a retired geisha who is visited by a former lover. But on arrival the man confides that the purpose of his visit is to solicit financial assistance. Struggling to hold onto her receding romance, she receives a second blow on learning that the money is for extricating him from a tangled affair with a young woman.

Ukigumo (1951; *Floating Cloud*, 1957) was acclaimed as H.'s major work. The heroine Yukiko leaves for Indochina, trying to forget a rape incident. There she falls in love with Tomioka, and together they return to Japan. Spurned by him, she vainly tries to revive Tomioka's affection and gradually degenerates to the point of prostitution. Tomioka, having failed in business, leaves for Yaku Island. Enfeebled with tuberculosis, Yukiko follows him to the island only to die while he is away in the mountains. Just before her death Yukiko abandons herself to beautiful memories of their days in Indochina. A dark pessimism prevails in this work, but H.'s controlled detachment and penetrating insight into the fallen, wandering Yukiko generate a genuine pathos and an added dimension to the world of H.'s hobo protagonists.

Few of her contemporaries can rival H.'s skill in vividly evoking a particular atmosphere. Perhaps more important, she felt and understood the loneliness of displaced women, creating female characters, alienated but always alive, who speak with a universal voice that transcends their milieu and their homeland.

FURTHER WORKS: *Hatō* (1939); *Shitamachi* (1948; *Tokyo*, 1957); *Chairo no me* (1949); *Meshi* (1951); *H. F. zenshū* (23 vols., 1951–1952)

BIBLIOGRAPHY: Morris, I., ed., *Modern Japanese Stories* (1962): 349–50; Janeria, A. M., *Japanese and Western Literature: A Comparative Study* (1970): 172–74; Johnson, E. W., "Modern Japanese Women Writers," *LE&W*, 18 (1974): 98–99

—KINYA TSURUTA

HAYDEN, Robert

(born Asa Bundy Sheffey) American poet, b. 4 Aug. 1913, Detroit, Mich.; d. 2 Feb. 1980, Ann Arbor, Mich.

Given the name by which we know him by his foster parents, William and Sue Hayden, H. made the traumatic discovery late in life that his name had never been legally changed; before the law, he was still Asa Bundy Sheffey, and he now had to effect the legal change himself, no easy task for an intensely sensitive man whose relationships with foster parents, stepfather, and, above all, natural mother were already sufficiently complicated. He could at any rate now claim as his own the name under which he had received his B.A., from Detroit City College (now Wayne State University) in 1936, and his M.A. from the University of Michigan in 1944. It was also the name under which he had written some of the finest poems yet produced by an African-American poet of any generation.

Writing in 1972 the editors of a comprehensive anthology of African-American literature could note that, although H. had "sustain[ed] a high quality of writing over the years," his poetry had "received little published critical attention." The relative neglect up to that time of a body of work that, while not large, was highly impressive both in quality and in variety, may be attributed to two causes. The first was the indifference to African-American poets on the part of a white-dominated literary establishment; it was not until 1966 that a book of poems by H. was published by a "mainstream" publisher, although H.'s first book had appeared as early as 1940. Second, and probably more painful to this sensitive black American, was the hostility toward him, his work, and what that work was taken to represent, by the mostly younger African-American writers and critics who, during the 1960s and 1970s, espoused the causes of Black Nationalism, Black Art, and the Black Aesthetic. The implication was that H. was not "black" enough. Ironically, the widespread renewal and awakening of interest in African-American art during the 1960s and 1970s did not lead directly to the discovery of H. and his recognition as an important American poet.

Although long deferred, the recognition has come, and with it honors that gave H. a sense, if any was needed, of vindication. In 1966 H. was the recipient of the Grand Prix de la Poesie conferred by the First World Festival of Negro Arts, held in Dakar, Senegal; Langston HUGHES chaired the committee that made the selection. In 1969 the National Institute of Arts and Letters granted H. its Russell Loines Award for distinguished poetic achievement. In the same year, H. was offered, but felt unable to accept, appointment as consultant to the Library of Congress; offered a similar position in 1975, he did accept it, becoming the first African-American to be so honored. Also in 1975, he was appointed a fellow of the Academy of American Poets. In the last years of his life, H. was awarded a number of honorary doctorates, signifying the belated recognition of his achievement by the academic community. Finally, in February of 1980, the Center for African-American and African Studies at the University of Michigan, whose department of English H. had joined in 1969, spent a day in tribute to R. H. Unfortunately illness made it impossible for H. to attend; he died the following day.

H.'s earlier poems tend to be dominated by the influence of the poets of the Harlem Renaissance of the 1920s and are more frequently in the mode of social protest than would be true of his mature work. In fact, H. would later all but disown the poems of his first collection, *Heart-Shape in the Dust* (1940), which he came to regard as apprentice work. As H. found his own voice, the inheritance of African-American folk culture and the traditions of African-American poetry, including that of the Harlem Renaissance, entered into a creative tension with the MODERNISM of poets like T. S. ELIOT and W. H. AUDEN. Thus a poem like "Middle Passage," in *A Ballad of Remembrance* (1962), deals with the experience of slavery (the "middle passage" is the sea voyage of the slaves from Africa) and affirms the exploits of Joseph Cinquez, whose leadership of a slave uprising aboard the ship *Armistad* has made him one of the heroes of black history and legend. But the formal strategies (montage, irony, allusion, indirection) are those of literary modernism. "Runagate Runagate," in *Selected Poems* (1966), brings the same modernist sensibility to bear on the Underground Railway and the work of Harriet Tubman.

African-American history, then, provided H. with material for some of his most powerful poems, and the modernist idiom provided him with strategies for the artistic realization of that material. But H. also found inspiration in black popular culture, in black religion, and in the folkways of the black community, especially in the urban setting he knew from his childhood. And in dealing with these varied materials, H. demonstrated mastery of a range of formal strategies, consistently finding the formal correlative to the thematic drive of the poems. The controlled elevation of rhetoric in his sonnet "Frederick Douglass," the blues feeling of "Homage to the Empress of the Blues," the echoes of Gospel in "Mourning Poem for the Queen of Sunday," the baroque elaboration of "A Ballad of Remembrance" and of "Witch Doctor," or the approach to unadorned statement in "Those Winter Sundays" can only begin to suggest the range and variety of H.'s achievement, an achievement that fully justifies the observation by the younger African-American poet Michael S. Harper (b. 1938) that H. is a poet of perfect pitch.

When one takes into account as well that, in poems like "The Diver" and the sequence "An Inference of Mexico," H. establishes that he is not limited to racial themes (not that those themes were in any way limiting for H.); it is all the more remarkable that in reading H.'s work one is always aware of the overall coherence, the "presence" of the poet. No doubt a major contribution to that coherence was made by H.'s profound commitment to the faith of Baha'i, to which he was converted, having been raised a Baptist, in 1942. The tenets of Baha'i certainly bear on the note of hope one finds even in those poems that confront most directly the tragic history of race relations in America: "Middle Passage," for instance, is a poem that affirms "The deep immortal human wish."

Some have noted an irony in the questioning of H.'s "blackness." At least one critic has wondered why H. was so adamant in rejecting the category "black poet," since much of H.'s best work deals with the black experience. But, for H., any category narrower than "human" was unacceptable. At the same time, no one knew better than H. that to be human is to be rooted in time, place, and history. It is in this spirit that, in his own words, H. "reaffirm[s] the Negro struggle as part of the long human struggle toward freedom."

FURTHER WORKS: *The Lion and the Archer* (1948); *Figure of Time: Poems* (1955); *Words in the Mourning Time* (1970); *The Night-Blooming Cereus* (1972); *Angle of Ascent* (1975); *American Journal* (1978; rev. ed., 1982); *Collected Prose* (1984); *Collected Poems* (1985)

BIBLIOGRAPHY: Davis, C., "R. H.'s Use of History," in Gibson, D. B., ed., *Modern Black Poets: A Collection of Critical Essays* (1973): 96–111; Stepto, R., "After Modernism, after Hibernation: Michael Harper, R. H., and Jay Wright," in Harper, M. S., and Stepto, R. B., eds., *Chant of Saints: A Gathering of Afro-American Literature, Art, and Scholarship* (1979): 66–84; Wright, J., "Homage to a Mystery Boy," *GaR*, 36 (1981): 904–11; Cooke, M. G., *Afro-American Literature in the Twentieth Century: The Achievement of Intimacy* (1984): 133–57; Fetrow, F. M., *R. H.* (1984); Hatcher, J., *From the Auroral Darkness: The Life and Poetry of R. H.* (1984); Fetrow, F., "Portraits and Personae: Characterization in the Poetry of R. H.," in Baxter, R. Miller, ed., *Black American Poets Between Worlds, 1940–1960* (1986): 43–76; Kutzinski, V. M., "Changing Permanences: Historical and Literary Revisionism in R. H.'s 'Middle Passage,'" *Callaloo*, 9, 1 (Winter 1986): 171–83; Williams, P. T., *R. H.: A Critical Analysis of His Poetry* (1987)

—W. P. KENNEY

HEAD, Bessie

South African novelist, short-story writer, and historian (writing in English), b. 6 July 1937, Pietermaritzburg; d. 17 April 1986, Serowe, Botswana

H. is South Africa's best-known black woman writer. She has written novels, short stories, and a history of the royal Khama family of Botswana. She has also been a teacher and journalist.

Bessie Head

Born in a Pietermaritzburg asylum to a white mother and a black stable worker, she left South Africa for Botswana after having to contend for years with racism and discrimination. Before she left South Africa, H. had completed her teacher's diploma and taught school for a short while. Not satisfied with teaching, she became a journalist and lived in cities such as Johannesburg, Port Elizabeth, and Cape Town. She began to write seriously in Botswana.

All of H.'s novels, *When Rain Clouds Gather* (1969), *Maru* (1971), *A Question of Power* (1974), and *A Bewitched Crossroad: An African Saga* (1984), and her collections of short stories, *The Collector of Treasures and Other Botswana Village Tales* (1977) and *Tales of Tenderness and Power* (1989), deal extensively with the questions of racial discrimination, exile, the ill-treatment of women, and insanity. In so many ways, the themes are related to H.'s own life. A mixed-race person discriminated against by both the white minority and black majority of South Africa, she finds little peace in Botswana because the black majority dislikes her. The female characters in her novels and stories must all suffer, and freedom is an illusion; H. writes feelingly and powerfully about the pain her characters and herself must experience in Botswana. In *A Question of Power*, truly a landmark novel, she explores in detail the question of insanity and male domination. Using her own birth in an asylum as the focus for her study, H. examines in deep and painful detail the viciousness of these phenomena. In the process, she creates characters and situations that seem to emanate from hell.

Yet H.'s work has a healing quality. In both of her early novels and her collection of stories, she introduces the simple and kind people of Botswana. In a largely rural country H. learns to appreciate human compassion. Also when looking at the history of the Khama family, we learn about the kind people of this country. Though H. died prematurely when she was at the height of her creativity, in her short span of life she left both for Africa and the world a valuable creative legacy.

FURTHER WORKS: *Serowe: Village of the Wind* (1981); *A Woman Alone: Autobiographical Writings* (1990)

BIBLIOGRAPHY: Taiwo, O., *Female Novelists of Modern Africa* (1985): 185–214; Katrak, K. H., "From Pauline to Dikeledi: The Philosophical and Political Vision of B. H.'s Protagonists," *Ba Shiru: A Journal of African Languages and Literature*, 12, 2 (1985): 26–35; Eko, E., "Beyond the Myth of Confrontation: A Comparative Study of African and African-American Female Protagonists," *ArielE*, 17, 4 (Oct. 1986): 139–52; Geurts, K., "Personal Politics in the Novels of B. H.," *PA*, 140 (1986): 47–74; Ola, V. U., "Women's Role in B. H.'s Ideal World," *ArielE*, 17, 4 (Oct. 1986): 39–47; Chetin, S., "Myth, Exile, and the Female Condition: B. H.'s *The Collector of Treasures*," *JCL*, 24, 1 (1989): 114–37; MacKenzie, C., *B. H.: An Introduction* (1989); Abrahams, C. A., ed., *The Tragic Life: B. H. and Literature in Southern Africa* (1990)

—CECIL A. ABRAHAMS

B. H.'s reputation as a writer rests on three novels, a collection of stories and a book on Serowe village. The three novels—*When Rain Clouds Gather, Maru* and *A Question of Power*—form something like a trilogy. In each of them the novelist exhibits strong disapproval for the misuse of power by any individual or group. This dislike is evident in the way she dramatises the process of the abdication of power which gets more complex from the first novel to the last. By the time the reader gets to the end of the third novel the novelist's message is clear: the naked display of power by the racists in South Africa or any other bigots elsewhere can only lead to disaster. There is no way of avoiding the rewards of oppression whether it is of blacks by whites, whites by blacks, whites by fellow whites or blacks by fellow blacks. The wise thing to do is to conceive of power in a progressive evolutionary manner. But, given man's insatiable lust for power, this is hardly possible. The novelist considers at length the psychological basis of power and finds that this has been largely eroded in a world dominated by conflict and the desire for political ascendancy. It is because of this stated position that B. H. is, for example, said to express "an indiscriminate repugnance for *all* political aspirations in *all* races."

The collection of stories *The Collector of Treasures* affords the author a chance to display her mastery of the art of storytelling. She understandably concentrates on the position of women and takes every opportunity to project a feminist point of view. She needs all the artistic talents displayed in her previous works to succeed with *Serowe: Village of the Rain Wind*. Here she combines imaginative writing with the fruits of a year's research study to produce work of great distinction. She succeeds magnificently in her reconstruction of the village life of Serowe. The daily occupations, hopes and fears of the ordinary people of the village come alive in the reader's mind mainly because of the opportunity given the inhabitants to tell their own stories. The conception of history here is edifying—history is made out of the preoccupations of the common man, not out of the lofty ideals, cruelty or benevolence of the wealthy and powerful. This reflects the concern for the under-privileged and oppressed masses of the people which is easily discernible in B. H.'s writings.

Oladele Taiwo, *Female Novelists of Modern Africa* (1984), pp. 185–86.

B. H. is a crusader for sexual and social justice for all men and women. Her favourite theme is the drama of interpersonal relationships and their possibility for individual growth and regeneration. She explores not only social harmony but also what is unique in each individual who contributes to it. In the realization of this task she employs an imaginative power and an original grasp of style which match her forceful moral vision. In all this, the woman's identity is fundamental; for it is still easy to encapsulate the central issues of all H.'s novels into the vital issues of power and identity. . . . She truly approaches her characters as individuals and, with her usual sensitivity and thoroughness, journeys through the innermost recesses of their lives. The product of this exploration is the emergence of that uniqueness which makes each of them special. To B. H., South Africa typifies power in its ugliest form, and the revulsion with which she views such a moral wasteland has aroused in her a special reverence for human life and dignity.

Virginia U. Ola, "Women's Role in B. H.'s Ideal World," *ArielE*, 17, 4 (Oct. 1986), p. 39

B. H. has created some powerful and unusual characters in the work she has so far produced. We have seen that they strive to treat people equally in both interpersonal and community relations. Then, through their struggles as expatriates, or leading their lives in exile, they dissolve feelings of alienation and work toward a firmer and deeper commitment to their friends and lovers and humanity on a global scale.

For her characters, this commitment is not abstract. We see it tangibly enacted in their efforts to share responsibilities, decision making, power and profits. But we also see their mental and spiritual process of reconnecting to the horrors of political oppression, especially in South Africa. Each character has personal experience with sexual inequality, caste discrimination, political oppression by white and black rulers alike, etc., etc. For them, "politics" (in the form of power relations and issues of social injustice) has always impinged upon their own personal lives. Each character, however, reaches a point where the pain he or she experience through having such a lucid consciousness (about the connection between personal and political problems) makes it impossible for them to go on. Some of the characters run away and deny that they care about anyone or anything; others have mental breakdowns but all find or choose some path through which they begin to dissolve their feelings of alienation and begin to reconnect with humanity. In fact, their "connection" far exceeds what we might expect. Their concerns do not remain selfish or even simply geared toward their local community. Rather, we see each character express his/her vision of the soul of Africa rising and transferring this power into a global unity and peace through the *brotherhood of man."* . . .

H., herself, is very idealistic. She creates characters who have an incredible drive to "right the wrongs" of their local communities and who dream about such change for all of Africa and even the entire world. We come to respect her characters as admirable and ethical people. Her own hope that "those who rule" or "the powers that be" will also develop the kind of idealism her characters embody is certainly a dream with a political base. She is hoping for a better balance of power in society, a more egalitarian world where women and Masarwa people are not subordinate. She brings this dream to reality in the world of her fiction. She provides us with models or prescriptions for how such idealistic goals can actually be achieved. B. H.'s faith and her belief in the strength of common people shines through the thoughts and action, the spirit and commitment of the characters she creates.

Kathryn Geurts, "Personal Politics in the Novels of B. H.," *PA*, 140 (1986), pp. 72–73

B. H.'s background has obviously influenced the way she perceives the narrative tradition of oral storytelling and the myths that have informed it. Born of mixed parentage in South Africa, raised primarily by white missionaries and self-exiled to Botswana, H. had no particular sense of belonging to a particular tribe or ethnic group. As a result, she is not only aware of her "outsider" status but self-consciously exploits this position in her art by deliberately distancing herself from the community whose tales she narrates so that her stories reveal a distinctly ambiguous, unresolved tone. Her intention is to reinforce not only her own outsider status but also her literate audience's "unknowingness," an audience who is forced to search for a way to enlarge their vision of a world from which they are exiled. H. uses for her point of departure the framework of the traditional dilemma tale in which the audience is expected to debate the moral questions raised by the storyteller, but she not only involves the real audience but also a fictive or "knowing" audience who are part of the communal structure of her stories. Unlike other storytellers who do not openly acknowledge the fictive audience but allude to it by subtly pretending to remind their listeners of half-forgotten historical events, H. frequently fills in the gaps by giving some kind of historical comment so that the "unknowing" reader may situate the stories within a specific cultural context, thereby acknowledging their realistic viability. Yet this structural tension becomes even more complex when in some of H.'s stories her own voice completely disappears or when she disconcertingly shifts her tone and narrative persona within the same story so that the "outsider" voice can no longer be heard. At times H. appears to purposely dissolve her own structural function and become part of the excluded audience, all the more aware of its limited vision. In the process, H. subtly leads her audience into the realm of myth where her characters become so stylized that no reader is allowed to identify with them—or even accept them as plausible—but must use his/her own imagination, as H. has done, to translate historical experiences into a larger symbolic context that questions the universal nature of existence. We must not only read her stories to learn about the experiences of her Botswana villagers and how their history has shaped their consciousness, but must also learn to use the mythic imagination to shape our own moral vision of a future where we will no longer remain "outsiders," exiled from ourselves and each other.

Sara Chetin, "Myth, Exile, and the Female Condition: B. H.'s *The Collector of Treasures*," *JCL*, 24, 1 (1989), 114–15

The title *A Question of Power* clarifies further what this novel is about. To B. H. whose daily life was shaped by the racist practices of South Africa and the sexist attitudes of the men she lived with, the question of who has the power is indeed important. Like Virginia Woolf, Zora Neale Hurston, and Doris Lessing, B. H. views the need of the male to see himself twice as big as he really is as one of the chief causes of unjust, undemocratic, and unkind behavior. In *A Question of Power* the male need to dominate and feel superior to others is represented by two men, Sello and Dan. They come to life and into power through the mad imaginings of Elizabeth. They are so real to her that she talks with them and feels her life literally threatened by them. It is because Sello and Dan use every power they have to try to destroy Elizabeth psychologically that she is mad. To regain her sanity, she must defeat them. . . .

B. H. chooses to focus on sexism rather than racism in *A Question of Power*. This forces her African readers, more familiar with racism, to see the similarities between the two and their common root in the philosophy of domination. Men degrade, manipulate, and abuse women in Elizabeth's nightmare, basically because they fail to perceive sacredness in them. Elizabeth advocates a philosophy that insists upon the sacredness of all life because of her subjection to this patriarchal behavior. This is typical of the evolution of feminist thought. That is why feminists speak of ecological and peace issues as well as equal rights; and that is why they speak of equal rights not only for women but also for the poor, the handicapped, and the racially oppressed.

Nancy Topping Bazin, "Venturing into Feminist Consciousness," in Cecil Abrahams, ed., *The Tragic Life: B. H. and Literature in Southern Africa* (1990), pp. 51–56

HEANEY, Seamus

Irish poet, b. 13 April 1939, County Derry, Northern Ireland

H. was born and raised on a farm in Northern Ireland. He moved to Belfast in 1957, took his B.A. in English at Queen's University (1961), taught in local Belfast schools and colleges (1962–66), and then returned as a lecturer to Queen's University (1966–72). He has been a guest lecturer in the U.S. at both Berkeley and Harvard, but since 1972 he has lived primarily in the Republic of Ireland, first in County Wicklow and then in Dublin. Nevertheless, he remains a Northern writer, and his work is firmly rooted in the rural, Catholic, County Derry soil of his boyhood. Inevitably, he also continues to remember and brood upon the political troubles of a strife-torn Northern Ireland.

H.'s early collections of poetry include five books of poetry to date: *Death of a Naturalist* (1966), *Door into the Dark* (1969), *Wintering Out* (1972), *North* (1975), and *Field Work* (1979). "Digging," the first poem in H.'s first book, established both the ground and the artistic mode of operation for his future work. Almost all of his books echo with deep personal memories of a grandfather cutting turf, a father digging his spade into gravelly ground. This patient hard-working digging becomes a metaphor for the literary process itself: "Between my fingers and my thumb/The squat pen rests./I'll dig with it." By reading poets like Patrick KAVANAGH, Robert FROST, and Ted HUGHES, H. learned to trust his rural background and to believe that it is possible to write of local things without being restricted by them. Thus, the language of

his finest poems attends closely to the traditional life of thatcher and farmer. He is a poet who meditates often on the depth and elemental force of the green world.

But H.'s digging also goes beyond the merely provincial. As his work has progressed, he has dug deeper and deeper into Ireland's past, trying to find the linguistic and archeological roots of an older northern world, a common Irish heritage. The central symbol in H.'s work is the bog, the wide unfenced country of rural Ireland that reaches back millions of years. It is in the bog, whose "wet centre is everywhere" ("Bogland," 1969), that he seeks to find the different layers of the Irish past, the material and cultural remains of an ancient race, the older Norse and Viking worlds. H.'s difficult task is to find the archetypal center of the Irish world.

Each of H.'s books has marked his quiet but steady poetic development. H. has emerged as one of the most indispensable contemporary Irish poets. In 1995 H. was awarded the Nobel Prize for literature.

FURTHER WORKS: *Poems: 1965–1975* (1980); *Preoccupations: Selected Prose, 1968–1978* (1980)

BIBLIOGRAPHY: Press, J., "Ted Walker, S. H., and Kenneth White: Three New Poets," *SoR*, 5 (1969): 673–88; Kiely, B., "A Raid into Dark Corners: The Poems of S. H.," *HC*, 7, 4 (1970): 1–12; Buttel, R., *S. H.* (1975); McGuiness, A., "'Hoarder of Common Ground': Tradition and Ritual in S. H.'s Poetry," *Éire*, 13, 2 (1978): 71-92; Zoutenbier, R., "The Matter of Ireland and the Poetry of S. H.," *DQR*, 9 (1979): 4–23; Druce, R., "A Raindrop on a Thorn: An Interview with S. H.," *DQR*, 9 (1979): 24–37; Bloom, H., ed., *S. H.* (1986); Curtis, T., ed., *The Art of S. H.* (1994); McGuiness, A. E., *S. H.: Poet and Critic* (1994)

—EDWARD HIRSCH

HEARNE, John

Jamaican novelist and essayist, b. 4 Feb. 1926, Montreal, Canada; d. 12 Dec. 1995, Kingston

Born to Jamaican parents in Montreal, Canada, H. returned to Jamaica at the age of two and there attended the elite Jamaica College. Much of H.'s family background is marked by privilege. H. volunteered for war service overseas at the outbreak of World War II, and served in the RAF as a gunner. After the war he attended Edinburgh University where he studied history. He then divided his time between 1950 and 1962 between Jamaica and England, spending the bulk of that time teaching in England. He would eventually return to Jamaica and spend the rest of his life working as an arts administrator at the Creative Arts Center at the University of the West Indies and during the 1970s as a senior adviser to then Prime Minister Michael Manley. During that period H. worked as a journalist regularly producing pieces on politics, history, and economic issues in Jamaican society.

H. published six novels during his life—all of them providing insight into a part of West Indian society that was largely ignored by the wave of anticolonial writers that emerged in postwar West Indian literature. His first five novels appeared in a flurry of novel-writing activity that led Faber and Faber to publish a novel a year between 1955, when his first novel *Voices under the Window* was published, and 1961, when he published *Land of the Living*. There would then be a twenty-two-year hiatus before he produced his final novel, *A Sure Salvation* (1983).

H.'s work distinguished itself by both the tidy and even writing style that he would perfect, which would stand in stark contrast to the magical leaps of Wilson HARRIS and the formal experimentations of George LAMMING. H.'s first novel, *Voices under the Window*, studied with care, and with not a smattering of personal angst, the politics of belonging among the privileged brown-skinned Jamaicans that were forming the leadership core of the new Jamaican society. Set during the troubling days of riots and social unrest of the late 1930s, the novel chronicles the journey of a mixed-raced Jamaican, Mark Lattimer, through a sometimes violent encounter with the working class world of Jamaican society. Mortally wounded by a rioting black man's machete, Lattimer remembers his past and traces his life's journey to this pivotal period in his life. Lattimer is never comfortable with his role as a leader of the black masses, but he assumes the role as if it is a birthright. H.'s ambivalence about the value of working-class culture and the role of the middle and upper classes in effecting change in Jamaican society is what distinguishes this work from much of what was being published by other writers at the time.

In his second novel, *Stranger at the Gate* (1956), H. introduces the fictional setting of Cayuna, a setting that will be repeated in the rest of his novels. In this novel his character remains a middle-class, light-skinned man struggling with questions of commitment to party, people, and country. In this novel as in many of his later novels H.'s characters become increasingly preoccupied with romantic issues—themes of the meaning of love and the way that love can be integrated into the politics of everyday living. Ultimately, however, H.'s sense of the possibility of social integration across the lines of race and class is decidedly pessimistic. With *A Sure Salvation* (1983), he will abandon any effort to celebrate the middle-class, light-skinned Jamaican as a heroic rescuer of the masses.

The promise that in H. we would find a writer who would be willing to tackle the complicated politics of West Indian society through sophisticated fiction is eroded by the shift in vision for H. from a belief in the role of political action and individual involvement in political action to effect change to the almost lyrical importance of discovering love and developing intimate relationships among social equals in the quest for a place of belonging and home. H.'s third novel, *Faces of Love* (1957), is entirely romantic, and the problems of Cayunan society fade into the background—a pattern that continues in his fourth novel, *The Autumn Equinox* (1959). Yet even as he shifts his political ideas, there is a stronger articulation of a less revolutionary ethic in his work suggesting a disillusionment with the revolutionary politics of the late 1950s that amounted to a cult of personality more than anything else. In *The Autumn Equinox* H. expounds on his deep distrust of political power. His main character, Jim Divers, like many of H.'s characters, moves from a strong sense of political commitment toward a distinctive sense of disillusionment, finding comfort and rootedness in the interpersonal relationships that he develops.

In *Land of the Living*, H.'s last novel before the long silence of ten years, he explores a theme that fascinated almost every major West Indian novelist of his generation—the question of the relationship between the working-class black masses of West Indian society and Africa. Like Andrew SALKEY after him, and Roger MAIS and Jan CAREW before him, H. examines the themes of pan-Africanism epitomized in the urban folk religion of Rastafarianism. Through this work he is able to tackle questions of home and

rootedness that recur in all his novels. H.'s view, however, is ultimately conservative. The idea of repatriation to Africa would constitute a denial of his own place in Jamaican society as a mixed-raced individual. His black character, Heneky, who has devoted himself to the almost Garveyite project of leading blacks back to Africa, fails violently and tragically. In this moment a certain West Indian nationalism takes root, a nationalism forged in the long-established middle classes of West Indian society—that West Indians must not look to Africa for a sense of self and belonging, but must simply turn to the brief but defining history of West Indian existence for that sense of self. In the end rootedness comes from a willingness to accept the West Indies as a place that contains its own meaning, its own value. Yet H.'s vision is largely optimistic. His characters do find some comfort, some sense of peace in their relationships and ultimately are at peace with their West Indianness.

Twenty-two years later H. would tackle the Middle Passage and in the process articulate a somewhat pessimistic vision of West Indian society. There is no certain salvation in this novel. In its setting on a slave ship traversing the middle passage, the novel examines closely the relationship between Hogarth and Alex, who begin the novel divided by race and end the novel further divided by race. H.'s usual trope of allowing interpersonal relationships to resolve these complex divides is not employed here. Instead his characters are shown to have no points of intersection and optimistic coexistence.

H.'s importance lies specifically in the quality of his vision and his willingness to articulate sometimes disturbing views of West Indian society that ultimately are not handled by other writers more preoccupied with the nationalistic issues of postcolonialism. Yet as a novelist H. is deeply conservative in his style and his use of form and language. There is a constant interest in the psychological workings and instincts of his characters. H. is an important West Indian writer largely because he offers us interesting ways to read later writers such as Lawrence SCOTT and Fred D'AGUIAR who tackle similar themes as H.

BIBLIOGRAPHY: Davies, B., "The Seekers: The Novels of J. H.," in James, L., ed., *The Islands in Between* (1968): 109-20; Cartey, W., "The Novels of J. H.," *CarQ*, 16 (1969): 45-58; Wynter, S., "We Must Learn to Sit Down Together and Talk about a Little Culture: Reflections on West Indian Writing and Criticism, Part 2," *Jamaica Journal*, 5 (1969): 27-42; Birbalsingh, F. M., "Escapism in the Novels of J. H.," *CarQ*, 16 (1970): 28-38; Morris, M., "Pattern and Meaning in *Voices under the Window*," *Jamaica Journal*, 5 (1971): 53-56; Baugh, E., "Men Acting as Men: J. H.'s *The Sure Salvation*," *Jamaica Journal*, 16 (1983): 61-63; Samad, D. R., "In Search of the Chrysalis of the Voice: The Language of the Slaves in J. H.'s *The Sure Salvation*," *WLWE*, 30, (1990): 11-16

—KWAME DAWES

HÉBERT, Anne

Canadian poet, novelist, and dramatist (writing in French), b. 1 Aug. 1916, Sainte-Catherine de Fossambault, Que.

Daughter of the influential critic Maurice Hébert (1888–1960), and cousin of the poet Hector de Saint-Denys Garneau (1912–1943), H. grew up in a home where literature was important. She has been awarded major literary prizes, both Canadian and French, and in 1960 became a member of the Royal Society of Canada. She has worked for Radio Canada (1950–53) and the National Film Board (1953–60). Since 1954 she has spent increasing amounts of time in France, where since 1958 her works have mainly been published.

Although H. has written short stories, film scripts, novels, and plays for the stage, television, and radio, she is known primarily as a poet. Her first volume of poetry was *Les songes en équilibre* (1942; dreams in equilibrium), but her best work is *Poèmes* (1960; poems), which contains the previously published *Le tombeau des rois* (1953; *The Tomb of the Kings*, 1967) as well as "Mystère de la parole" (mystery of the word). The latter is prefaced by an essay, "Poésie, solitude rompue" (poetry, a broken solitude), from which it becomes apparent that H. sees herself as having the mission to offer her readers a new reality, one that will feed them like bread and wine. In practice, in her austerity, which is sometimes mistaken for simplicity (although her verse is by no means simple), she frequently offers water rather than wine, and the water is that of tears. In distress and deprivation there is communion. She writes in free verse, using dense, closely packed images, achieving an almost surrealistic effect. Her main themes are sorrow and joy, love, solitude, and death. The image of water predominates, recurring as rain, tears, the sea, and rivers.

Next in importance to her poems are the title story in her collection of short stories, *Le torrent* (1950; *The Torrent*, 1972), and her novels, *Les chambres de bois* (1958; *The Silent Rooms*, 1974) and *Kamouraska* (1970; *Kamouraska*, 1973). In "Le torrent," a story about a young man's alienation owing to his mother's determination to make him atone for the sin she committed in bearing him, she castigates the morbid sense of sin that is a product of the old traditions of Quebec. Added to this is another French-Canadian phenomenon, the feeling of the weight of the past, inhibiting freedom of action in the present and the future. *Le tombeau des rois* and *Les chambres de bois*, about a young woman who ultimately escapes from a husband who has a horror of sex, offer the hope that the weight of the past may be lifted.

In *Kamouraska*, the story of a woman who conspires with her lover to murder her husband, this hope offers little promise. In a quiet frenzy, the protagonist struggles with her memories of a past that she has done her best to negate, in the name of respectability, but whose truth refuses to be suppressed. She is a symbol of alienation, passionately desiring a fulfillment that cannot be achieved by a woman in 19th-c. Canada.

Les enfants du sabbat (1975; *Children of the Black Sabbath*, 1977), a tale of witchcraft, incest, and intercourse with the devil, set in a French-Canadian convent, was poorly received in Quebec, where it seemed out of touch with present-day preoccupations. The novel *Héloïse* (1980; Héloïse) is the story of a young couple living in Paris who are destroyed by two vampires, male and female. Set in the period around 1900, it is her only fictional work to date that does not deal with Quebec.

Recent studies on H. focus on her poetry, and it is for her poetic qualities that she is chiefly respected.

FURTHER WORKS: *Théâtre: Le temps sauvage; La mercière assassinée; Les invités auprocès* (1967); *Dialogue sur la traduction* (1970, with Frank Scott). FURTHER WORKS IN ENGLISH: *Saint-Denys Garneau and A. H.* (1962; bilingual)

BIBLIOGRAPHY: Collin, W. E., "Letters in Canada, 1953," *UTQ*, 23 (1954): 325–26; Purcell, P., "The Agonizing Solitude: The Poetry of A. H.," *CanL*, 10 (1961): 51–61; Pagé, P., *A. H.* (1965); Grand, A. Le, *A. H., de l'exil au royaume* (1967); Lacôte, R., *A. H.* (1969); Major, J. L., *A. H. et le miracle de la parole* (1976); Bouchard, D., *Une lecture d'A. H.: La recherche d'une mythologie* (1977); Lemieux, P. H., *Entre songe et parole: Structure du "Tombeau des rois" d'A. H.* (1978)

—BARBARA J. BUCKNALL

HEBREW LITERATURE
See Israeli Literature

HECHT, Anthony
American poet, critic, and translator, b. 16 Jan. 1923, New York, New York

H. is a New Yorker by birth, part of a generation whose youth was beset by world war, a generation that has produced several of America's finest poets. H. holds degrees from Bard College and Columbia University, and honorary degrees from Bard and Georgetown University. He has taught at several institutions, including Kenyon College and Harvard, Yale, and Georgetown Universities, among others. He holds a plethora of awards and honors, some of which are the Pulitzer Prize, the Bollingen Prize in Poetry, and the Librex-Guggenheim Eugenio Montale Award.

H.'s poetry is ordered and formal. He eschews free verse, but is adventurous in the use of many forms—blank verse, sonnet, prose poem, ode, and others, including rhymed structures of his own devising. He believes that the laws governing poetry echo the laws governing the universe, and that the poet, imposing a proper order upon his poem, seeks through such discipline a deep experience of the true nature of things. H. shows a strong influence of John Crowe RANSOM, with whom he studied at Kenyon College in 1946. Like Ransom (also a formalist), H. specializes in character studies and narrative; and he sometimes uses the technique, perfected by Ransom, of using obsolete words in the context of a comment on modern situations. H.'s poetry is learned and allusive, drawing freely upon biblical, mythological, and literary lore.

H. shares with other poets of his time a keen awareness of tragedy, which manifests itself not only in his long poems, but in shorter, more frequently anthologized works, as well. One popular example is "The Dover Bitch," a seemingly light-hearted parody of Matthew Arnold (1822-1888). But the poem is more dark than light. The Victorian speaker in Arnold's poem knows that the world has neither love, nor joy, nor peace; nevertheless, he believes that if lovers are faithful to each other they can somehow make a safe harbor for themselves in such a world. The message of H.'s poem is that a lover's plea for faithfulness is bound to fall on deaf ears; the Dover bitch is just that after all. "The End of the Weekend" takes as its setting a deserted lakeside cabin where a young couple have planned a weekend tryst, apparently without the knowledge of his father, who owns the cottage. Expecting privacy and romance, they encounter instead a gruesome reminder that the wages of sin is death. The twin images of a graveyard across the lake, visible from the window, and a pile of scattered skeletons of mice in the attic, provide an eerie stageset for the "great black presence" that suddenly obtrudes itself on the would-be lovers. There is in the poem, however, an irony that undermines any neat moral message: the graveyard holds the bones not only of those who have sinned, but also of those who have not.

In "Jason," a joyful ode celebrating the birth of his son, the poet plays with the connotations offered by allusions to the mythical adventurer; he invites dreams of the triumph of a little boy with a wooden sword and a shield made of the lid of a garbage can, in a field of marigolds. This delightful image, however, is followed in due time by the dark implications in "It Out-Herods Herod. I Pray You, Avoid It." In this poem the narrator watches his children as they watch television heroes defeat all bad guys, realizing that the children believe implicitly that their father could do the same. He knows the truth, however: that he could not even have saved them from the gas chambers. Perhaps the best known of H.'s poems is "More Light! More Light!" The title alludes to the last words of Johann Wolfgang von Goethe (1749-1832), who had such faith in human nature that he believed in a period of enlightenment to come, when mankind would be truly good. The poem is horrific. It begins with a vignette of a religious martyr being burned at the stake at some unspecified time in the past; then the narrative switches to a German wood during World War II, where two Jews and a Pole are being tortured by German soldiers. Juxtaposing the two scenes, the poet demonstrates that the modern situation is the worse: at least the martyr burned at the stake is allowed his dignity, while the last bit of humanity is ruthlessly stripped from the modern victims.

H. writes as an American, as a highly learned man, and as a Jew who saw action in World War II. While his poetry in its formal orderliness claims affinity with a cosmic order overarching human experience, his themes are typical of the 20th c.: disorder, alienation, the tragedy inherent in our condition and our time. His work will continue to be read for both of these reasons; each poem is a virtuoso performance.

FURTHER WORKS: *A Summoning of Stones* (1954); *The Hard Hours* (1967); *Millions of Strange Shadows* (1977); *The Venetian Vespers* (1979); *Jiggery-Pokery* (1983, with John Hollander); *The Pathetic Fallacy* (1985); *Obbligati* (1986); *Collected Earlier Poems* (1990); *The Transparent Man* (1990); *The Hidden Law* (1993); *On the Laws of Poetic Art* (1995); *Flight Among the Tombs* (1996)

BIBLIOGRAPHY: Howard, R., *Alone With America: Essays on the Art of Poetry in the United States Since 1950* (1969): 164-173; Brown, A., "The Poetry of A. H.," *Ploughshares*, 4 (1978): 9-24; Sydney, L., ed., *The Burdens of Formality: Essays on the Poetry of A. H.* (1989); German, N., *A. H.* (1989); Bayley, J., "Living Ghosts," *NYRB*, 27 Mar. 1997: 18

—CECELIA LAMPP LINTON

HEDAYAT, Sadeq

Iranian short-story writer, novelist, and essayist, b. 17 Feb. 1903, Tehran; d. 9 April 1951, Paris, France

H. was born into a family of landowners; among his ancestors were many prominent statesmen and men of letters. In his twenties he was sent to Belgium and France to study. After having considered numerous scientific and academic professions, he committed himself to writing.

On returning to Iran, H. published his first collection of short stories, *Zendeh be-gur* (1930; buried alive). He joined a group of progressive intellectuals, but instead of mingling with friends he immersed himself in the study of Iran's history, folklore, and traditional beliefs, and in writing about them. This search into the past led him to study Zoroastrian, Hindu, and Buddhist philosophy and to travel to India in the 1930s.

Very little is known about H. as an individual; he preferred to live modestly and in solitude. However, it is known that he cared for the underprivileged and the humble people of his country and that he was an ardent patriot. At the same time he was obsessed with isolation, alienation, dead ends, barriers, walls, prisons, madhouses, and the idea of self-destruction—obsessions that led eventually to his suicide. These themes are well reflected in his second and third collections of stories: *Seh qatreh khun* (1932; three drops of blood) and *Sayeh rowshan* (1933; chiaroscuro).

Despite his preoccupation with Iran at this stage, it is abundantly clear that H. had not ceased being involved in the artistic realities of Europe and America. The prose works of Stefan ZWEIG, CHEKHOV, Poe, and Maupassant, and the writings of contemporary philosophers were still stirring his imagination. Having the sensitivities of Iranian art as a heritage, and having adopted the EXISTENTIALIST convictions of SARTRE and of KAFKA, the latter of whose "In the Penal Colony" he translated into Persian with extensive notes, H. was confronted with existential torment.

The thread of H.'s obsessions with man's veiled search, culminating in his despair at his unfulfilled yearnings in the face of an absurd universe, can be followed throughout his work. The subverting of temporal and spatial concepts in the plot of his masterpiece, *Buf-e kur* (1937; *The Blind Owl*, 1957; new tr., 1974), creates a surreal atmosphere in which the allegorically unenlightened, unseeing owl (an animal possessing human wisdom in Persian tradition) searches, questions, and entreats, only to discover terror and frenzy in the realization that he will find only silence. In *Buf-e kur* one can trace the predominant influence of RILKE, FREUD, Poe, and Kafka on H.'s own personality. Like his contemporary Western writers, H. is concerned with the psychological implications of man's existence and of his interaction with his fellows. He constantly probes into the uneven forces that govern life's unrelieved misery, irrespective of social class, but he writes mostly about the little people, with their problems, sorrows, hates, and weaknesses—sympathetic yet repulsive. His characters include the slang-speaking mule attendant, the laborer who is a local hero among the poor by virtue of his bullish strength, the brooding scullery maid, and the sullen streetwalker to whom the measure of a man's love is the stoutness of the blows with which he pummels her.

The satirical tone in some of his short stories is an indirect criticism of a society that obstructs the education and advancement of the masses. H. is particularly sympathetic toward the backward condition of women. His love for Iran and for its heritage is an important element in his work. We are constantly confronted with the displaced Iranian, adrift in the West, as an allegory of the eternal conflict of East and West, a conflict to which he was also subject.

Despite the unevenness of H.'s work he has compelled Iranian authors to look further than politics and sociology, without abandoning them. Through his pioneering position and literary distinction he has exerted an extraordinary influence on Iranian writers, especially since World War II. The work of H. signaled the victory of prose in the face of serious claims that the Persian language had no merit when used to adorn nonpoetic expression. And that is probably why he has acquired a status as the most important Persian author of the 20th c. With H., Persian prose at last earned a place in the body of world literature.

FURTHER WORKS: '*Alaviyeh Khanom* (1933); *Vagh Vagh Sahab*' (1933); *Sag-e velgard* (1942); *Haji Aqa* (1945; *Hāji Āghā*, 1979). FURTHER WORKS IN ENGLISH: *S. H.: An Anthology* (1979)

BIBLIOGRAPHY: Kamshad, H., *Modern Persian Prose Literature* (1966): 137–208; Kubičkova, V., "Persian Literature of the 20th Century," in Rypka, J., et al., *History of Iranian Literature* (1968): 410–12; Bashiri, I., *H.'s Ivory Tower* (1974); Katouzian, H., "S. H.'s 'The Man Who Killed His Passionate Self': A Critical Exposition," *IranS*, 10, 3 (1977): 196–206; Hillmann, M. C., ed., *H.'s "The Blind Owl" Forty Years After* (1978); Yarshater, E., Introduction to *S. H.: An Anthology* (1979): vii—xiv

—PETER J. CHELKOWSKI

HEIJERMANS, Herman

Dutch dramatist, novelist, and journalist, b. 3 Dec. 1864, Rotterdam; d. 22 Nov. 1924, Zandvoort

H. is the Netherlands' most important modern playwright, and the only Dutch dramatist since Joost van den Vondel (1587–1679) to win international renown. Born into a Jewish family and son of a journalist, he took up journalism and playwriting at the age of twenty-eight, after twice failing in business ventures. These early days of his literary career in bohemian Amsterdam are recounted with folksy candor in his autobiographical novel *Kamertjeszonde* (1898; sin in rented rooms). He joined the Socialist Party in 1896, embarking on a lifelong commitment to assailing the social ills of the age, especially the exploitation of the poor. A prolific writer of newspaper sketches, comedies, and naturalistic dramas in the vein of HAUPTMANN and Ibsen, H. achieved his greatest international triumph with the play *Op hoop van zegen* (1901; *The Good Hope*, 1928), a moving portrayal of North Sea fisher folk overwhelmed by powers beyond their control or understanding. Its impact in the Netherlands was such that a new law for the protection of sailors and their dependents was enacted.

H.'s plays of the 1890s reveal a grim world of religious persecution and intolerance. More than the loosely woven plots, it was H.'s characters that held audiences spellbound: a pious Russian Jew caught in the horror of a pogrom—*Ahasverus* (1893; *Ahasverus*, 1929); a Jewish rag merchant eager to sell into marriage a son who is alienated from his corrupting environment—*Ghetto* (1899; ghetto).

At the turn of the century H. wrote a series of short, unmistakably socialist plays. *De machien* (1899; the machine) focuses on a factory owner forced by the industrial revolution to invest in machinery, and on his hapless workers who must toss a coin to determine who will be laid off. He also addressed domestic problems, notably the double standard in sexual mores among the affluent bourgeoisie, and parent-offspring relationships. In *Het zevende gebod* (1900; the seventh commandment) a tubercular

student is disowned by his self-righteous father because of an unacceptable liaison. *Schakels* (1903; *Links*, 1927) features an old-fashioned industrialist beleaguered by his rapacious children.

While H. was a harried manager-producer-director of a theatrical company from 1912 to 1922, his output diminished, and what did appear was often written in a lighter vein, such as the satire *De wijze kater* (1918; the wise tomcat).

In his minor works H. succumbed to the Dutch penchant for realistic visual details and thereby created a kind of genre tableau. In his finest plays he showed a gift for indignation, for humor, and for delineating character. The people of his dramatic world move in authentic milieus. Their speech, often a rough-hewn, comic jargon, reflects all the nuances of their background. No mere representatives of their class, they are imbued with individual vitality.

FURTHER WORKS: *Dora Kremer* (1893); *Trinette* (1893); *Interieurs* (1897); *Nummer tachtig* (1898); *Puntje* (1889); *Het antwoord* (1899); *De onbekende* (1899); *Toneel en maatschappij* (1899); *Een Mei* (1900); *Het pantser* (1902); *Ora et labora* (1903); *Het kind* (1903); *Het kamerschut* (1903); *Sabbath* (1903); *In de Jonge Jan* (1903); *Diamanstad* (1904); *Buren* (1904); *Saltimbank* (1904); *Kleine verschrikkingen* (1904); *Bloeimaand* (1905); *Allerzielen* (1905); *Gevleugelde daden* (1905); *Feest* (1906; *Jubilee*, 1923); *Biecht eener schuldige* (1906); *Berlinger Skizzenbuch* (1908); *De grote vlucht* (1908); *Een wereldstad* (1908); *Wat niet kon* (1908); *Vreemde jacht* (1909); *Uitkomst* (1909); *Drijvende Klompjes* (1909); *Joeps wonderlijke avonturen* (1909); *Beschuit met muisjes* (1910); *Vierundzwanzig Stunden in der Irrenanstalt* (1910); *De schone slaapster* (1911); *De opgaande zon* (1911; *The Rising Sun*, 1926); *Glück auf* (1911); *De roode flibustier* (1911); *De meid* (1911); *Robert, Bertram & Comp.* (1914); *Eva Bonheur* (1919); *De vliegende Hollander; of, De grote weddenschap* (1920); *De dageraad* (1921); *Brief in schemer* (1921); *De buikspreker* (1921); *Een heerenhuis te koop* (1921); *Droompaard* (1923); *Van ouds "De Morgenster"* (1924); *Droomkoninkje* (1924); *De moord in de trein* (1925); *Vuurvlindertje* (1925); *Duczika* (1926)

BIBLIOGRAPHY: Panter, P. [Kurt Tucholsky], "H. H.," *Die Weltbühne*, 20, 49 (1924): 849–51; Engel, F., "H. H.," *Berliner Tageblatt* (24 Nov. 1924): 2; Raché, P., "H.'s Leben und Werk," *Berliner Tageblatt* (24 Nov. 1924): 2; Barnouw, A. J., "H. H.," *Theatre Arts* (Feb. 1925): 109–12; Flaxman, S. L., *H. H. and His Dramas* (1954); Jong, E. de, *H. en de vernieuwing van het Europese drama* [summary in English] (1967)

—PETER BRUNING

HEISSENBÜTTEL, Helmut

West German literary critic and author of avant-garde texts, b. 21 June 1921, Rüstringen bei Wilhelmshaven; d. 19 Sept. 1996, Glückstadt

Following active service in World War II, H. studied literature, architecture, and art. He became a publisher's reader and in 1959 assumed the directorship of the radio essay department of South German Radio. He was awarded several literary prizes, including the Büchner Prize (1969).

H.'s belletristic works are often discussed under the rubric "concrete poetry," although they defy categorization, and even description. His first books, *Kombinationen* (1954; combinations) and *Typographien* (1956; typographies), belong in the tradition of DADAISM and such modernist writers as APOLLINAIRE and Gertrude STEIN, and are characterized by a reduction of normal grammatical patterns, which leads to striking ambiguities. A primary concern with language itself remains central to the six volumes bearing the title *Textbuch* (1960–67; textbook). Some of these texts are called prose and others poetry, but virtually all are suggestive rather than discursive and lack traditional form and content.

H.'s next literary works are called "projects": Project 1, *D'Alemberts Ende* (1970; D'Alembert's end), an avant-garde novel, and Project 2, *Das Durchhauen des Kohlhaupts* (1974; chopping through the cabbage head), a collection of texts and radio plays. *D'Alemberts Ende* narrates a brief period at the end of the life of the fictitious critic D'Alembert; facts, episodic elements of plot, and commentary are juxtaposed and blended. In *Das Durchhauen des Kohlhaupts* language per se is of somewhat less importance than in the works of the 1960s; content and plot lines are more recognizable and the comments on contemporary social problems less ambiguous.

H. is considered by many to be among Germany's leading postwar literary critics and theoreticians. In *Über Literatur* (1966; on literature) and *Briefwechsel über Literatur* (1969; correspondence about literature), the latter coauthored with the like-minded critic Heinrich Vormweg (b. 1928), H. stresses the primacy of language over emotion, the necessity of breaking with the romantic tradition, and the role of the contemporary writer as a resister, an irritant, in a regulated society.

H. is one of contemporary Germany's most controversial literary figures. His insistence, in belletristic and essayistic works alike, on the necessity of making a complete break with the tradition, has been received with lavish praise, bewilderment, and scornful derision. Nonetheless, his position as one of the avant-garde's leading spokesmen is secure.

FURTHER WORKS: *Ohne weiteres bekannt* (1958); *Texte ohne Komma* (1960); *Mary McCarthy: Versuch eines Autorenportraits* (1964); *Was its das Konkrete an einem Gedicht?* (1969); *Memorabiler Lochtext* (1970); *Das Texbuch* (1970); *Die Freuden des Alterns* (1971); *Zur Tradition der Moderne* (1972); *Ruprecht Geiger* (1972); *Gelegenheitsgedichte und Klappentexte* (1973); *Der fliegende Frosch und das unverhoffte Krokodil* (1976); *Mümmelmann oder die Hasendämmerung* (1978); *Eichendorffs Untergang und andere Märchen* (1978); *Wenn Adolf Hitler den Krieg nicht gewonnen hätte* (1979); *Die goldene Kuppel des Comes Arbogast; oder, Lichtenberg in Hamburg fast eine Geschichte* (1980); *Das Ende der Alternative* (1980). FURTHER WORKS IN ENGLISH: *Texts* (1977)

BIBLIOGRAPHY: Döhl, R., "H. H.," in Weber, D., *Deutsche Literatur seit 1945* (1968): 546–76; Bezzel, C., "A Grammar of Modern German Poetry," *Foundations of Language*, 5 (1969): 470–87; Waldrop, R., "H. H., Poet of Contexts," *GR*, 44 (1969): 132–42; Demetz, P., *Postwar German Literature* (1970): 84–88; Endres, E., "H. H.," in Wiese, B. von, ed., *Deutsche Dichter der Gegenwart* (1973): 469–80; Burns, R., *Commitment, Language, and Reality: An Introduction to the Work of H. H.* (1975); special H. issue, *Tuk*, No. 69/70 (1981)

—JERRY GLENN

HELLER, Joseph

American novelist and dramatist, b. 1 May 1923, Brooklyn, N. Y.

After serving as a bombardier in the U.S. Army Air Corps stationed in Corsica during World War II, H. returned home, enrolled at New York University, and began writing short stories, some of which were published in *Esquire* and *The Atlantic* (1947–48). He took an M.A. at Columbia University and was a Fulbright scholar at Oxford in 1949–50. After teaching English for a few years, he worked in advertising and promotion at a number of major magazines, until the tremendous success of *Catch-22* (1961), which he had written in his spare time, enabled him to quit his job. (The original opening chapter of the novel appeared under the title "Catch-18" in *New World Writing*, No. 7, in 1955.)

Catch-22 is a novel based in part on H.'s war experiences. The protagonist, a life-loving, comic, rebellious bombardier named Yossarian, will do almost anything to avoid being killed in the war and by those who are running it: the officer who, hoping for promotion, keeps raising the number of missions the men must fly, and Milo Minderbinder, who will do anything (including bombing his own squadron) to save from ruin the financial empire he has built from his blackmarket business. Yossarian's struggle to survive amid such forces represents the individual's predicament in a world whose systems of order have turned destructive. H.'s satire shows how those in power put their own ends above the value of human life. H.'s criticism thus is aimed less at war itself than at those who subvert our institutions to their own advantage.

To capture the absurdity and chaos produced by this subversion, H. employs a disordered narrative chronology, and to suggest Yossarian's entrapment in this chaos H. uses repetition of scenes: the men seem caught up in a pattern of destruction that negates both life and individuality. It is therefore not surprising that most of the characters are flat, comic, and cartoon-like, rather than fully developed personalities. The large number of characters (over forty), the war setting, and the rapid changes of scene and sequence give *Catch-22* an epic sweep, while the novel's humor adds emotional force to H.'s attack on the society he portrays. This BLACK HUMOR is increasingly blended with horror and death, until it becomes grotesque comedy, evoking pain rather than laughter.

Yossarian eventually escapes this insane world epitomized by the military regulation "Catch-22," which forces him to fly the bombing missions if he is sane, but defines "sanity" as the healthy desire not to fly them. The phrase "catch-22" has entered the English language to signify an individual's entrapment in a no-win situation, particularly one created by an institutional regulation.

In *Something Happened* (1974) H. attacks the corporate bureaucracies of American business. But the protagonist does not share Yossarian's zest for life or his energetic protest against a dehumanizing system; instead, Bob Slocum, a weary, middle-aged executive, cynically resigns himself to a success he secretly despises. His high salary, social status, and material acquisitions have brought not satisfaction but unhappiness, which is shared by his family. Slocum's monologue attempts to discover how such unhappiness "happened." Although *Something Happened* satirizes the corporate hierarchy, its deepest concern is with what "happens" to the person who internalizes the corporation's ideals and demands so completely that they usurp his individual identity and humanity.

After exploring the unhappy life and consciousness of an upper-management executive within the power structure of American finance, H. turned in *Good as Gold* (1979) to a discontented outsider. Bruce Gold, a cynical college professor who plans to write a book on the American Jewish experience, feels outside the mainstream of American political and social power because he is Jewish. As a result, he jumps at the sudden promise of a high government appointment in Washington, even if it means divorcing his wife to marry the daughter of an influential gentile millionaire. By alternating family scenes with Gold's experience in Washington, H. satirizes American political power and portrays his protagonist's behavior as neither better nor worse than that of Everyman, who under the same circumstances would probably act as "good" as Gold.

H.'s play *We Bombed in New Haven* (1968) was written in part to express his protest against the American role in the Vietnam war. But in this play-within-a-play, where the actors self-consciously explain that they are only "acting" the part of soldiers in a play about war, the focus is not a specific war but instead the denial that makes war possible—the denial of death.

Although *We Bombed in New Haven* attests to H.'s versatility, his strength lies in his novels' depiction of the interplay between the individual and the institutional systems wielding power in America: the military, the corporations, and the federal government. H.'s work exhibits an increasing pessimism about what any individual can do about society's drift toward corruption and decay—besides retreating to a private safety. H.'s contribution to the novel lies in his innovative combination of elements in *Catch-22*—humor and horror, repetition, fragmented chronology, and a multiplicity of bizarre characters—to achieve a form expressive of chaos and absurdity.

FURTHER WORKS: *Catch-22: A Dramatization* (1971); *Clevinger's Trial* (1973); *A Critical Edition of "Catch-22"* (1973); *Closing Time* (1994); *Now and Then: From Coney Island to Here* (1998)

BIBLIOGRAPHY: Tanner, T., "A Mode of Motion," *City of Words* (1971): 72–84; Kiley, F., and McDonald, W., eds., *A "Catch-22" Casebook* (1973); Nagel, J., ed., *Critical Essays on "Catch-22"* (1974); Aldridge, J., on *Something Happened*, SatR, 19 Oct. 1974: 18–21; Plimpton, G., "The Craft of Fiction, LI: J. H.," *Paris Review*, No. 60 (1974): 126–47; Dickstein, M., "Black Humor and History: The Early Sixties," *Gates of Eden* (1977): 91–127; Aldridge, J., on *Good as Gold, Harper's*, Mar. 1979: 115–18; Merrill, R., *J. H.* (1987); Pinsker, S., *Understanding J. H.* (1991); Sorkin, A. J., ed., *Conversations with J. H.* (1993)

—MELANIE YOUNG

HELLMAN, Lillian

American dramatist and memoirist, b. 20 June 1905, New Orleans, La.; d. 30 June 1984, Martha's Vineyard, Mass.

H. moved to New York City with her family when still a child, although her frequent visits to relatives in New Orleans would later provide her with much literary material. She attended New York University but left before graduating and in 1924–25 was a manuscript reader for the publishing firm of Horace Liveright, where she was introduced to the literary world. In 1925 H. married humorist and playwright Arthur Kober (1900–1975), and began to write, and later went with him to Hollywood, where she was a scenario reader while continuing to write stories, articles, and

reviews. (H. wrote several screenplays later in her career.) They were divorced in 1932; previously she had met the mystery writer Dashiell Hammett (1894–1961), with whom she formed an intimate attachment that lasted until his death.

H. achieved immediate success with her first play, *The Children's Hour* (1934), which introduces the recurring theme in her work—that of the pressures of a corrupt and hypocritical society on its "good" victims. Two young women who run a small girls' school are destroyed by malicious rumors of "unnatural" affection, although the subject of lesbianism is treated very gingerly.

H.'s most important play, *The Little Foxes* (1939), brilliantly develops the conflict between good and evil, greed and love, against a background of Southern society in the process of industrialization. The predatory Hubbard family, especially Regina, are the "eaters of the earth," the "little foxes who spoil the vines" in their ruthless pursuit of money and power. Although in 1939 the play was interpreted as a specific attack on capitalism, it has come to be regarded as a condemnation of avarice and lust for power in general. In *Another Part of the Forest* (1947) H. takes the Hubbard family back to twenty years before the events of *The Little Foxes* and presents them as they were then—consumed by hatred and selfishness.

Watch on the Rhine (1941) depicts an American family that is suddenly shaken out of isolation and indifference to the war in Europe when the daughter arrives with her German refugee husband and children. H. here attacked the complacency of those who allow evil to flourish and tried to awaken the American conscience to the European tragedy.

Among H.'s later plays, *Toys in the Attic* (1960) is most notable. Set in the South and reminiscent at times of Tennessee WILLIAMS, it is less involved with social issues than her other plays. Rather, it is a perceptive psychological study of a weak and irresponsible man dependent on two older spinster sisters who try to survive on dreams doomed to remain unfulfilled.

Years after she stopped writing plays H. has emerged in a new role as the author of several highly acclaimed volumes of memoirs, which are not only autobiographical narratives but also explorations of her emotions and moral perceptions vis-à-vis her family and her relationships with her friends and colleagues. *An Unfinished Woman* (1969) proceeds more or less chronologically and includes moving portraits of Hammett and her friend Dorothy Parker (1893–1967). *Pentimento* (1973) presents reminiscences and more portraits (including the famous "Julia") unified by the theme of, in H.'s words, "seeing and then seeing again. . . . I wanted to see what was there for me once, what is there for me now." The controversial *Scoundrel Time* (1976) is an account of her experiences during the investigations of the House Un-American Activities Committee in the late 1940s and early 1950s.

H.'s political liberalism is reflected in her plays and her memoirs, but her ability to focus on subjects other than social evils saves her from being an agitprop writer. In most of her work she depicts personal lives being worked out against a backdrop of social change or historical crisis. Although H. the dramatist has often been accused of overusing the machinery of melodrama and the well-made play, in her best work the contrivance is expert and efficient. Her total moral commitment, as well as her skill at psychological characterization, makes her a major figure in the realistic mode of modern American drama.

FURTHER WORKS: *Days to Come* (1936); *Four Plays* (1942); *The North Star: A Motion Picture about Some Russian People* (1943);

The Searching Wind (1944); *Montserrat* (adaptation of Roblès's *Montserrat*; 1950); *The Autumn Garden* (1951); *The Lark* (adaptation of Anouilh's *L'alouette*; 1956); *Candide* (libretto for operetta based on Voltaire's *Candide*; 1957); *Six Plays* (1960); *My Mother, My Father and Me* (1963); *The Collected Plays* (1972); *Three* (1979); *Maybe: A Story* (1980)

BIBLIOGRAPHY: Clark, B. H., "L. H.," *CE*, 6, 3 (1944): 127–33; Phillips, J., and A. Hollander, "The Art of the Theater—L. H.: An Interview," *Paris Review* 33 (1965): 65–95; Gould, J., *Modern American Playwrights* (1966): 168–85; Adler, J., *L. H.* (1969); Moody, R., *L. H.: Playwright* (1972); Falk, D. V., *L. H.* (1978); Lederer, K., *L. H.* (1980)

—RITA STEIN

HEMINGWAY, Ernest

American novelist, short-story writer, and journalist, b. 21 July 1899, Oak Park, Ill.; d. 2 July 1961, Ketchum, Idaho

In his youth H. had already begun the travels which are reflected in his work and which also shaped it to suggest an allegorical pilgrimage of a modern Odysseus. From the American youth Nick Adams, protagonist of many early short stories, to the Cuban Santiago of the late novel *The Old Man and the Sea* (1952), H.'s protagonists share a concern with performing well under the mental and physical stresses of richly varied lives. From his family's summer home in northern Michigan, where H. began to learn the skills of hunting and fishing from his physician father, to France, Spain, Italy, East Africa, and the Gulf of Mexico, where he and his heroes savored life and experienced death, H. made both a personal and literary pilgrimage.

H. came of age at the historical watershed of World War I, when a new literature began confronting new psychological and philosophical problems. While the subtle conflicts within his own family may have exerted long-lasting influence, he was unquestionably a child of the 20th c. At eighteen he was already a newspaper reporter for the prestigious Kansas City *Star*, covering a tough city beat, and as a volunteer in a Red Cross ambulance unit in Italy in 1918 he received his violent initiation to life "in our time" when he was blown up by an Austrian mortar shell and narrowly escaped death. While this traumatic event may not have been essential and critical to his artistic development, it does provide a metaphor for much of his subsequent work. In his fiction, many of his protagonists are the wounded, sometimes sacrificed heroes, not simply of a historical world in crisis, but of a mythic world emotionally felt by a wide-ranging audience that has crossed intellectual as well as national boundaries. Those of H.'s heroes who survive become, as he put it, "strong at the broken places," but the first reaction of the maimed body and sensibility was a withdrawal from life and then a gradual return to it as a sensitive observer of life. Like many of his heroes, H. was a wanderer on the face of the earth, an outsider with a keen eye for what places and feelings were really like. Strictly speaking he was not an intellectual who valued ideas in and of themselves. In the tradition of American pragmatism, the true or moral was what worked. ". . . I know only that what is moral is what you feel good after . . ." (*Death in the Afternoon*, 1932). While he could be a courageous

Lillian Hellman

supporter of a political cause (such as the Loyalists' in the Spanish Civil War or the incarcerated Ezra POUND), more often than not his best work was that of the skeptical critical pragmatist attacking the entrenched, the self-satisfied, the hypocritical.

As far as he had abstract values, they seem to have been fairly traditional. In spite of his position as an innovative stylist, there is an important truth in Gertrude STEIN's observation (recorded in her *Autobiography of Alice B. Toklas*) that " . . . after all, you are ninety percent Rotarian. Can't you, he said, make it eighty percent." For instance, although married four times, he seems to have had a strong and conventional sense of the values of marriage and family. As for his craft of writing, he regarded it as seriously as the great craftsmen Gustave Flaubert and Henry JAMES of an earlier generation, and he could be a hard taskmaster in the tradition of the Protestant work ethic. He was stoical and skeptical but enduring as long as the power of his art of writing provided the necessary articulation of his experience and imagination that were also suggestive of the common lot of mankind.

After the war H. returned to journalism but also began his career in creative writing. While he was European correspondent for the Toronto *Star*, virtually unknown and newly a husband and father, he quit his job and devoted himself to his creative writing until he had achieved professional skill and status.

H.'s first two slender books, *Three Stories and Ten Poems* (1923) and *in our time* (1924), were both published in Paris in very small editions for very few readers, but his readers and counselors were of the most influential and helpful sort, including Gertrude

Ernest Hemingway

Stein, Ezra POUND, Sherwood ANDERSON, and F. Scott FITZGERALD. In 1925 the expanded *In Our Time* was published in the U.S. and signaled the beginning of a successful and illustrious career. But as his literary reputation grew, so did his personal fame as a sportsman and bon vivant. Many of the stories spread about his life were apocryphal, but some of them were credible enough to make the man himself as widely discussed as his work. Unfortunately for the sake of accuracy, much of his fiction was read as autobiography; and unfortunately for the sake of the seriously conceived and carefully written fiction, it was often read as hard-boiled adventure and enjoyed or depreciated on this ground alone. In fact, far from being a largely autobiographical writer celebrating the cult of experience, H. was a dedicated craftsman who read omnivorously and intelligently, so that he had the rare combination of being a writer of wide and often dramatic experience who was also a sensitive aesthete. Gertrude Stein, an early mentor, perceived that "... he looks like a modern and he smells of the museums" (*Autobiography of Alice B. Toklas*).

Some initial reactions to his first serious novel, *The Sun Also Rises* (1926), illustrate the problem. It was read as a roman à clef and a collective biography of the post-World War I "lost generation," the disillusioned, suffering, yet attractive young men and women whose values and faiths, like some of their very bodies, were also blown up in the war. H. denied that he or his sexually incapacitated hero Jake Barnes was "lost," but many readers submerged or overlooked the traditional values like love and courage that H. championed; glamorous nihilism and toughness were more the vogue of the 1920s, and the timeless theme keynoted by the epigraph from Ecclesiastes, the theme of the abiding earth and the indifference of life, the *élan vital*, to self-pitying romantics, was perhaps lost on many readers until the corpus of his work grew and revealed the underlying existential strength of his perceptions. Beyond them was the style that married so well to the bittersweet themes.

Jaded, disoriented, valueless, the characters hear neither drums nor prayers, but those like the narrator Jake Barnes and his hard-living lover *manqué* Lady Brett Ashley have a certain awareness and generosity of spirit that makes them superior to the other pitiful expatriates who are the "lost generation." By the assertion of love and courage and with a protective irony and humor, the admirable characters survive with dignity if not with victory. The novel affirms that "the earth abideth forever," but for the humans who inhabit it, life can seem chaotic and brutal, stupid and comical. In the closing lines, the antiheroine slips into self-pity: "'Oh, Jake,' Brett said, 'we could have had such a damned good time together,'" and the antihero, the man who does not act so much as react, the man to whom things are done, replies, "'Yes. . . . Isn't it pretty to think so'"?

This novel and the next, *A Farewell to Arms* (1929), were written in an understated, informal, but carefully controlled and objective or closely dramatic prose style, even though both novels are first-person narrations. Along with the bulk of the short stories, this early work best exemplifies the style that was of great influence in shaping modern prose fiction. The early H. distrusted abstract terms, but still this style was rich in imagery and symbolic action that suggested a tentative ethic or moral code. Certain character types suggested implicit principles: on one hand was the so-called "code hero" who denied or ignored traditional faiths or found them inadequate in coping with a meaningless world. This recurrent character type turned to self-imposed and often stringent rituals that obviated metaphysics or faith. On the other hand were either the careless and undisciplined men with no ritual controls or men living by corrupted beliefs, such as chauvinism or romanticism, that were irrelevant to H.'s efforts to give shape to those values a violent world and careless people had mutilated. Between these extremes, both rather simplistic and naïve, stood the H. protagonist who was drawn to the admirable and controlled life of the code hero but who was also too complex and sensitive to accept the planned discipline of, for example, a matador's or professional hunter's life.

By making his "separate peace" in a senseless world at mad war, Lt. Frederic Henry in *A Farewell to Arms* briefly enjoys an idyllic love affair, but inexorable fate destroys the committed and uncommitted alike; there is no escape. The protagonist has volunteered for ambulance service with the Italian army in World War I, but, typically, he has no particular commitment to any political cause: "I was always embarrassed by the words sacred, glorious, and sacrifice and the expression in vain. . . . There were many words that you could not stand to hear and finally only the names of places had dignity. . . . Abstract words such as glory, honor, courage, or hallow were obscene beside the concrete names of villages, the numbers of roads, the names of rivers, the numbers of regiments and the dates." This reduction is an extreme reaction to the general and the abstract, which are the bane of the artist trying to re-create beauty as well as the thinker trying to rediscover truth.

Thus, while the narrator studiously avoids such abhorred abstractions and rarely interrupts his description and narration with exposition, the discourse is always heavy with meaning. The brilliant description of the military action in the brief first chapter foreshadows the doom of the conclusion in which the lovers have deserted the war and its dangers only to find death and grief in the supposed haven of each other's, not the military's, arms. The narrator does, however, learn from his defeats, and he does dryly pontificate: "If people bring so much courage to this world the world has to kill them to break them, so of course it kills them. The world breaks every one and afterward many are strong at the broken places. But those that will not break it kills. It kills the very good and the very gentle and the very brave impartially. If you are none of these you can be sure it will kill you too but there will be no special hurry." Abstract words like *good* and *brave* have a simple dignity that has not been debased, and they are current in the H. vocabulary.

The style of H.'s later work changed somewhat to a prose more loosely structured and yet more complex than before. This change has been variously judged by his critics. Similarly, his subjects and themes evolved into socially and politically conscious contemporary problems. At the time of the swing to the political left by many writers in the U.S. during the 1930s, H. was widely applauded for his championing of the economic "have-nots" and his apparent loss of detachment in *To Have and Have Not* (1937). But this novel was one of his weakest in its stylistic achievement; its experimental techniques were not fully realized, partly because the novel as planned was radically changed in the editorial process to avoid potentially libelous passages. (H. frequently used real names and people in his fictions.)

For Whom the Bell Tolls (1940) also aligned the wandering H. hero—this time in civil-war Spain–with the left, but H.'s liberalism was far from orthodox. His conclusion in this novel, his most ambitious and judged by some critics as his best, was that neither political programs nor action on their behalf offered a substitute for the individual's need to obtain salvation for himself through tragedy, love, and self-knowledge. The hero, Robert Jordan, fights for the Spanish Loyalists against the Fascists; but this widely acclaimed novel was for many years not published in the Soviet Union, although H.'s other work had been given a sympathetic audience there.

H. wrote in a different mode in this long novel that has epic characteristics. The author who was stereotyped as writing a clipped "hard-boiled" prose became expansive in the story of the last few days of an American's life, but typically the hero dies in a futile ironic effort to aid in the larger war. His sacrifice is meaningful only in personal terms: he has been true to himself, he has demonstrated his courage ("grace under pressure"), and he has loved "truly and well." Far from glorifying war or political action, H. again underlines their awful ambiguities. Isolated on a mountainside with a band of guerrillas who form a microcosm, the hero suffers and dies for them, morally ambiguous real people, neither his compatriots nor uniformly laudable but nevertheless part of mankind: "any mans *death* diminishes *me*, because I am involved in *Mankind*; And therefore never send to know for whom the *bell* tolls; It tolls for *thee*" (from John Donne; epigraph to the novel).

H. participated in World War II, first as a modern privateer on antisubmarine duty in the Caribbean and then as a European war correspondent and sometime leader of an irregular armed patrol during the liberation of France. His next novel, *Across the River and into the Trees* (1950), was partly based on his World War II experiences and had for its hero an aging U.S. Army colonel who was having an affair with a young Italian countess in Venice. The story lacks the drama of H.'s previous work, and its critical reception was generally unsympathetic, it being read as a discursive apologia and an embarrassing self-parody of his successful style of the 1920s and 1930s. While it lacked the force of earlier work, it, too, has interesting thematic dimensions and perhaps was misunderstood because it was a shift in mood and subject of a still developing, exploring author moving into an unexpected region and upsetting some critical preconceptions.

The Old Man and the Sea was even more radically different from his preceding work; but this deceptively simple, short fable of the courage, faith, love, and endurance of a poor Cuban fisherman was widely acclaimed. It both won H. a Pulitzer Prize and helped win him the Nobel Prize for literature in 1954. Although he had conceived other ambitious projects, this novella was to be his last book published in his lifetime.

After months of failure fishing in the Gulf Stream, a culmination of the losses of an ordinary yet dignified life, the fisherman finally hooks a huge marlin and fights it heroically for three days until in the majesty of the beautiful, dreadful sea, the hunter and hunted merge, tied together by the fishing line. But as if in a paradigm of man's fate, the victorious Santiago has his prize fish taken from him by rapacious sharks who mutilate and then devour the marlin, leaving the exhausted fisherman with nothing but a skeleton to show for his epic struggle. Yet he has survived, endured, and enlarged the feelings of true heroism. The gaunt, ascetic, isolated, beset man living in harmony with an indifferent environment again suggests how existential struggle can ennoble.

H.'s short stories are not numerous, but a significant number are of the highest quality, and a few critics think his short stories are more important than his novels. They are sometimes little more than tightly written sketches, sometimes nothing less than complex and infinitely rewarding narratives like "The Short Happy Life of Francis Macomber" (1936), "The Snows of Kilimanjaro" (1936), "Big Two-Hearted River" (1925), "In Another Country" (1926), "The Undefeated" (1926), "Soldier's Home" (1925), and "A Clean Well-Lighted Place" (1933). His gifts for the telling image, economy of plot, and brilliant dialogue are sometimes best seen in short stories like these.

H.'s nonfiction is of widely varying quality and seriousness, but it includes some of his best work: *Death in the Afternoon* (1932), an unsurpassed book on bullfighting, also contains important statements on his aesthetics; *Green Hills of Africa* (1935) is a novelistic but factual narrative of his hunt for big game on safari in East Africa, it too contains important commentary on the art of writing; *A Moveable Feast* (1964), his posthumously published reminiscences, mainly set in Paris in the 1920s, includes sketches of Ezra Pound, Gertrude Stein, and F. Scott Fitzgerald written in an extremely lively and insightful if sometimes subjective style. His other posthumously published work—a novel, *Islands in the Stream* (1970) and *The Nick Adams Stories* (1972), containing some previously unpublished fiction—were neither edited, completed, nor authorized by H. and have value mainly to the literary mortician, although the former contains some exciting and beautifully written passages.

The publication of *Selected Letters, 1917–1961* (1981), letters he himself never wanted published, rekindled the sport of H.-baiting among readers and reviewers who have new "evidence" to cloud the perception of the fiction by the smoke of the personality who was at turns loving and kind, egomaniacal and hateful, creative and imaginative, contradictory and ultimately self-destructive. With the powers of body and mind waning, the self-made hero chose suicide, but the continuing stream of posthumous works and publications about him keep his ghost ever present.

Along with William FAULKNER, H. is often considered the major writer of fiction in American literature of the 20th c. For some readers, H.'s value stops at a grudging appreciation of his style and at a belief that he is anti-intellectual and even adolescent. But as the exact quality of that style comes to be better understood and is seen as an organic medium for the expression of symbolic meaning and human understanding, his reputation grows.

FURTHER WORKS: *The Torrents of Spring* (1926); *Men without Women* (1927); *Winner Take Nothing* (1933); *The Spanish Earth* (1938); *The Fifth Column and the First Forty-nine Stories* (1938); *Complete Stories* (1954); *By-Line: E. H.* (1967) *E. H.: Eighty-eight Poems* (1979)

BIBLIOGRAPHY: Baker, C., *H.: The Writer as Artist* (1952; 4th ed., 1972); Young, P., *E. H.* (1952; rev. ed., 1966); Fenton, C. A., *The Apprenticeship of E. H.: The Early Years* (1954); Baker, C., ed., *H. and His Critics: An International Anthology* (1961); DeFalco, J., *The Hero in H.'s Short Stories* (1963); Rovit, E., *E. H.* (1963); Asselineau, R., ed., *The Literary Reputation of H. in Europe* (1965); Lewis, R. W., *H. on Love* (1965; new ed., 1973); Baker, S., *E. H.: An Introduction and Interpretation* (1967); Hanneman, A., *E. H.: A Comprehensive Bibliography* (1967; *Supplement*, 1975); Hovey, R. B., *H.: The Inward Terrain* (1968); Stephens, R. O., *H.'s Nonfiction: The Public Voice* (1968); Bruccoli, M. J., ed., *The Fitzgerald/H. Annual* (1969 ff.); Baker, C., *E. H.: A Life Story* (1969); Benson, J. J., *H.: The Writer's Art of Self-Defense* (1969); Wylder, D. E., *H.'s Heroes* (1969); Watts, E. S., *E. H. and the Arts* (1971); Grebstein, S. N., *H.'s Craft* (1973); Astro, R., and Benson, J. J., eds., *H. in Our Time* (1974); Benson, J. J., ed., *The Short Stories of E. H.* (1975); Hemingway, M., *How It Was* (1976); Reynolds, M. S., *H.'s First War: The Making of "A Farewell to Arms"* (1976); Donaldson, S., *By Force of Will: The Life and Art of E. H.* (1977); Oldsey, B., *H.'s Hidden Craft: The Writing of "A Farewell to Arms"* (1979)

—ROBERT W. LEWIS

Not that life isn't enjoyable. Talking and drinking with one's friends is great fun; fishing in Big Two-Hearted River is a tranquil exhilaration. But the brutality of life is always there, and it is somehow bound up with the enjoyment. Bullfights are especially enjoyable. It is even exhilarating to build a simply priceless barricade and pot the enemy as they are trying to get over it. The condition of life is pain; and the joys of the most innocent surface are somehow tied to its stifled pangs.

The resolution of this dissonance in art made the beauty of H.'s stories. He had in the process tuned a marvelous prose. Out of the colloquial American speech, with its simple declarative sentences and its strings of Nordic monosyllables, he got effects of the utmost subtlety. F. M. Ford has found the perfect simile for the impression produced by this writing: "H.'s words strike you, each one, as if they were pebbles fetched fresh from a brook. They live and shine, each in its place. So one of his pages has the effect of a brook-bottom into which you look down through the flowing water. The words form a tessellation, each in order beside the other."

Edmund Wilson, *The Wound and the Bow* (1947), pp. 215–16

. . . His writing career argues cogently that whatever philosophical validity the H. code may have possessed, its pragmatic functioning for him was cardinal and irrefutable. It enabled him to take over the role of what we might call "*jongleur* of pain" that he imagined so poignantly in his description of Belmonte in the Pamplona bull ring. He exhausted himself beyond his natural means, but he maintained that "grace under pressure," which, for him, was one of the conditions from which immortality might come.

But rather than end on such a subdued note, let us remember that if his range was narrow, it was not shallow. Art is long and it is large and it can also be deep; and if the sum of H.'s achievement was to project in compelling symbols his own human situation, his popularity attests to the fact that his was not a unique human condition. Too fragmented to make a rebellious vain rush against life and too proud to accept the inevitability of defeat and resignation, H. found in himself and communicated to countless readers a stance of heroism—positive, unillusioned, and defiantly humanistic.

Earl Rovit, *E. H.* (1963), pp. 172–73

Things like the "H. style," the "H. hero," the "manner" and "attitude" of H. are very widely recognized. Back in the minds of all literate Americans there is a place where this man etched a few lines. He is a part of our reading past, and the cleavage between what has happened to us directly, and what has happened to us in books, is not so deep as some think.

H. made a difference. There are people who do not admire his work, but even these are perfectly ready to admit—if only that they may deplore the fact—that he is "important." It is hard to think of a contemporary American who had more influence on modern writing, or on whom both general readers and literary critics are more likely to agree that the experience of his fiction is worth having, or, in his own time, of a writer more widely publicized. And yet despite all the attention, H.'s work, which is what we should ultimately remember him for, is still by no means as well understood as it might be.

Philip Young, *E. H.: A Reconsideration* (1966), pp. vii–viii

What carried H. along his path was a total dedication to art and an unrelenting will to make his writing true. Perhaps his range of vision can be seen in some respects as limited, but his aim was penetration, not comprehensiveness. H., unlike many of his contemporaries, was there during the wars, the evacuations, the social convulsions. Despite the attempt by many to minimize the importance of such direct experience with most of the major events of his time, and despite the exhibitionism that often colored H.'s attempts to expose himself to danger, this effort to sense the actual event and to reproduce its emotional effect artistically as precisely as possible is exactly what we need in an age when even war itself has become a spectator sport and our sensitivity to the suffering of others has dimmed.

The emotional intensity which led H. into his excesses also led him to his victories and fostered those qualities of character that made his victories possible: self-discipline, self-honesty, and a very real courage. He was locked in mortal combat all his life with an opponent, art, which grants no quarter and never allows total victory. The artist can be, will be, and must be destroyed by such a conflict, but he need not be defeated.

Jackson J. Benson, *H.: The Writer's Art of Self-Defense* (1969), p. 191

So much has been written on the H. "hero" that it might seem unproductive to undertake another examination of this literary phenomenon. But I believe that one of the longstanding problems of H. criticism has been the failure to disentangle the H. personality, as evidenced in his life and in his nonfictional statements, from the characters that he has created for his novels. Coupled with this tendency to link H. with his protagonists, despite his own often vehement objections, has been an equal proclivity to view the H. protagonist as a recurring hero in a progression of novels so that the critical treatment of the H. hero has become almost an exercise in fictional biography. Nick Adams grows into Jake Barnes into Frederic Henry into Robert Jordan into Richard Cantwell; all are considered to be one character at different ages. The result, unfortunately, has been that the recurring biographical hero has provided almost the sole critical focus for the interpretation of separate novels which are unique artistic creations, distinctive not only in the concept of the hero and his environments but in artistic techniques as well. That critical focus, it seems to me, has frequently forced a preconceived and rigid pattern upon the interpretation of some of H.'s novels. This is particularly unfortunate, for such a view does not allow a demonstration of H.'s artistic versatility, his experimentation, and his increasing skill as a writer.

Delbert E. Wylder, *H.'s Heroes* (1969), pp. 3–4

The primary intent of his writing, from first to last, was to seize and project for the reader what he often called "the way it was." This is a characteristically simple phrase for a concept of extraordinary complexity, and H.'s conception of its meaning subtly changed several times in the course of his career—always in the direction of greater complexity. At the core of the concept, however, one can invariably discern the operation of three esthetic instruments:

the sense of place, the sense of fact, and the sense of scene.

The first of these, obviously a strong passion with H., is the sense of place. "Unless you have geography, background," he once told George Antheil, "you have nothing." You have, that is to say, a dramatic vacuum. Few writers have been more place–conscious. Few have so carefully charted out the geographical groundwork of their novels while managing to keep background so conspicuously unobtrusive.

Carlos Baker, *H.: The Writer as Artist,* 4th ed. (1972), pp. 48–49

His image as an anti-intellectual was one that H. himself encouraged through his rugged appearance, his adventurous outdoor life, and his open contempt for any language that smacked of the pretentious. A writer, he believed, always got in trouble when he started thinking on the page, and in Big Trouble when he went in for Big Thinking. "The essential of big writing," he commented in 1930, "is to use words like the West, the East, Civilization, etc." He'd discovered, to bring the abstractions down to earth, that "when you stand with your nose toward the north, if your head is held still, what is on your right will be east and what is on your left will be west," and though you could write "very big" putting those words in capitals, it was "very liable not to mean anything."

The easy mistake to make about H., and about his writing, is to take both at surface value alone. Margaret Anderson, who knew Ernest during his expatriate days in Paris, concluded that the one adjective to describe him was "simple." Malcolm Cowley, on the other hand, chose "complicated" as the one word which best summed him up, and Cowley, who knew Ernest for many years, came far nearer the mark, for H. was a complicated man, with a difficult, a quirky, and frequently a contradictory mind.

Scott Donaldson, *By Force of Will: The Life and Art of E. H.* (1977), pp. xii–xiii

HEPPENSTALL, Rayner

English novelist, critic, and translator, b. 27 July 1911, Huddersfield

H. was educated in his native Yorkshire and was graduated from the University of Leeds in 1932 after attending the University of Strasbourg, France, in 1931. The towns of his boyhood are described in detail in his novel *The Woodshed* (1962), Strasbourg and its cathedral in the novel *The Connecting Door* (1962). In *The Greater Infortune* (1960) H. described life in London immediately preceding World War II, interweaving the chronology of events in the life of his protagonist and the chronology of political events; in the earlier *The Lesser Infortune* (1953) he described his army life.

H. was a producer for BBC Radio in London from 1945 to 1967. In this position, as well as in his freelance writing, he has been in contact with many key figures in arts and letters, and he writes with expertise on various arts.

His knowledge of French literature and his interest in France are predominant in his work. He has translated or adapted works from French and treats French culture in several of his books. He has had a long friendship with J. I. M. Stewart (the mystery writer Michael Innes, b. 1906) since his student days at Leeds, and he has himself written several books on crime in France and in England. His most recent novel, *The Shearers* (1969), is a fictionalization of an actual French murder trial, transplanted to England.

H. is a cultural historian in his emphasis on events preceding and during World War II, in his literary histories, his crime histories, and his reminiscences of such figures as George OR-WELL. He often uses first-person narration to link events in the manner of a diarist. In both his fictional and his nonfictional works, H. emphasizes the process of dating events and verifying these dates. Yet his concern with the chronology of events is rather for its surface pattern than for any inherent or constructed drama.

The keynote of H.'s fictional style is his presentation of sensual detail. In his first novel, *The Blaze of Noon* (1939), the protagonist is blind. The preface points to the direct influence of MONTHERLANT's novel series, *The Girls*, and indeed, H.'s subject is not the disability of blindness but the experience of physical love. He expresses a free sexuality which, although hedonistic, is not libertine. His protagonists commit adultery without guilt, but they do not seduce. His novels reject conventional moral judgment and advocate, at least by implication, dismissal of both sentimentalism and vulgarity.

H.'s work as a whole is a significant contribution to 20th-c. letters. What has not been recognized yet is his important achievement in novelistic technique. He is an originator and transmitter of innovations in construction and style in his method of treating levels of reality and time in *The Connecting Door* and in his handling of stream-of-consciousness and interior monologue, especially in *The Shearers*. He translated work by and wrote two studies of Raymond ROUSSEL, who is only now beginning to attract attention as a forerunner of the NEW NOVEL and its descriptive technique, which H. uses in his presentation of rooms and streets in *The Woodshed* and again in *The Connecting Door*. The latter, furthermore, is important as an antinovel. Even in his earliest fiction, H. was influenced by French writers, and he realized in the English language technical novelistic achievements that were in part the results of French literary influence and in part new developments. H. was disposing of conventional plot and characterization before such writers as ROBBE-GRILLET were doing so; in his later fiction, he not only transmitted but contributed to technical advances made by French writers. H.'s work is unlike that of any of his English contemporaries, although his literary criticism shows his understanding of English literary trends. He is particularly interesting as a recorder of English life and as a channel by which French style comes into the English world of letters.

FURTHER WORKS: *Middleton Murry: A Study in Excellent Normality* (1934); *First Poems* (1935); *Apology for Dancing* (1936); *Sebastian* (1937); *Blind Men's Flowers Are Green* (1940); *Saturnine* (1943; revised and expanded as *The Greater Infortune*); *Poems 1933–45* (1946); *The Double Image: Mutations of Christian Mythology in the Work of Four French Catholic Writers of To-day and Yesterday* (1947); *Léon Bloy* (1954); *Four Absentees* (1960); *The Fourfold Tradition: Notes on the French and English Literatures, with Some Ethnological and Historical Asides* (1961); *The Intellectual Part* (1963); *Raymond Roussel: A Critical Guide* (1966); *Raymond Roussel: A Critical Study* (1967); *A Little Pattern of French Crime* (1969); *Portrait of the Artist as a Professional Man* (1969); *French Crime in the Romantic Age* (1970); *Bluebeard and After: Three Decades of Murder in France* (1972); *The Sex War and Others: A Survey of Recent Murder, Principally in France* (1973); *Reflections on the Newgate Calendar* (1975)

BIBLIOGRAPHY: Bowen, E., "The Blaze of Noon" (1939), *Collected Impressions* (1950): 53–55; Monod, S., "R. H. and the *Nouveau Roman*", in Mack, M., and I, Gregor, eds., *Imagined Worlds* (1968): 461–75; Nye, R., "R. H.," in Vinson, J., ed., *Contemporary Novelists*, 2nd ed. (1976): 625-28

—JUDITH LEIBOWITZ

HERBERT, Xavier

(pseud. of Alfred Herbert; pseud.: Herbert Astor, E. Norden) Australian novelist and short-story writer, b. 15 May 1901, Geraldton; d. 10 Nov. 1984, Alice Springs

Born in Western Australia, H. graduated from Perth Technical College in 1922 with a diploma of pharmaceutical chemistry. In 1935–1936 H. was the superintendent of Aborigines in Darwin, which contributed to the experience he would draw on for his first novel, *Capricornia* (1938). Throughout an illustrious literary career that also included a three-year stint (1942–1944) with the Australian Imperial Force, H. received numerous awards and honors, including the Commonwealth Sesqui-Centenary Literary Prize (1938), the Australian Literary Society's Gold Medal (1940), and doctors of letters from the Universities of Newcastle (1975) and Queensland (1976), among others.

H. is most famous for his controversial classic novel of protest against racism, *Capricornia*, and for his monumental *cri de cœur, Poor Fellow My Country* (1975)—the first and last novels of his literary career. *Capricornia* grew directly from H.'s realization that there was widespread ignorance in Australia of the continuing sexual exploitation of Aboriginal women that he had seen as a boy on the northern frontier of Western Australia. But it depended upon its author gaining a good deal more nonliterary experience than he had before he felt equipped to write it: frontier experience in the Northern Territory, as a swagman, drover, railway fettler, and pearl diver. *Capricornia* is shocking in its angry depiction of the treatment of Aborigines in the (thinly veiled) Territory. Yet its real focus is on the tragedy of the (then rapidly expanding) Creole population, and despite its social concern it is at least equally and imaginatively interested in the plight of a white society that H. believed has so alienated itself from its conquered environment that its only hope of spiritual survival is to connect with Aboriginality, through blood identification with mixed-race offspring. This, he claims, is why he made his main characters "half-caste," and it gives his fiction much in common with the Jindyworobak movement of the 1930s (one of the major principles of which was "to join" on to Aboriginal culture as a way of bringing Australian literature into contact with its proper environmental values). This explains also, at least in part, the deeply personal theme of psychological relationship between fathers and sons that runs throughout much of H.'s oeuvre.

After twenty years of self-imposed isolation, self-analysis, and literary struggle, during which he made substantial progress on several novels only to abandon one after another in a continuing crisis of confidence, H. burst into print again with *Seven Emus*

(1959), publishing four books in four years. In fact, *Seven Emus* had been completed much earlier, while H. was serving in the bush commando North Australia observer unit during World War II, but had escaped serious notice because it had been serialized in the popular-fiction magazine *The Australian Journal*, where most of his early short stories had also first appeared. A slim novella with a quirky style of punctuation, developed, according to its author, in order to discover and liberate "style," *Seven Emus* offers a satirical and cynical critique of the anthropological exploration of Aboriginal sacred sites in Northern Australia. As a type of modern culture hero, the anthropologist is caricatured as an exploitative and self-serving bully and thief who thus has much in common with the original European settler-invader of Australia. *Soldiers' Women* (1961) purports to be a study of women unfettered by moral convention and liberated by the absence of husbands and boy-friends fighting in World War II. Often defended by the author as his personal favorite, for in it he developed his highly idiosyncratic theory of sexuality, it is nevertheless the least critically popular of his works. The detailed description of women's clothing seems not only fetishist but an indication of the author's unwillingness to observe more deeply than external appearances allow, while the focus on feminine desire is obviously masculine and, for most readers, distorted.

The bread and butter of H.'s writing had always been his short stories. *South of Capricornia: Short Stories by X. H., 1925–34* (1990) collects the earliest of his writings in order to trace his literary career up to the writing of *Capricornia*. Written for the popular-magazine and newspaper market, and initially to romantic-fiction formulae, H.'s stories were often "pipe-openers" for his longer fiction—set pieces in the manner of burlesque, satire, mystery writing, and autobiography—and were recycled in many different shapes and combinations. *Larger Than Life* (1963) is the author's own selection, mostly later works, but still with the emphasis on narrative, for H.'s are obviously "contrived" stories, much in the manner of O. Henry (1862–1910). The subject matter ranges widely, but racial themes and republican sentiments are never far below the surface.

The psychological substructure of much of H.'s writing reveals a more personal dimension, a deep concentration on self-exploration, which often was the author's own acknowledged motive for composition. This makes for more enigmatic subject matter than at first might seem the case, and indeed the fascination of even his first novel lies partly in subtleties of imaginative vision, masked initially by stridency of voice, contrivance of plot, and intrusive polemicism. *Disturbing Element* (1963), H.'s autobiography of his youth to the age of twenty-five, confirms the enigma. Written in the genre of a rake's progress, it nevertheless provides glimpses of many of the myth-making personae that feed not only into his fiction but also into the highly public exercises in self-promotion that, in later life, inevitably accompanied H.'s occasional forays from the isolation of his home in northern Queensland into what he called "civilization," the cities of the South—Sydney and Melbourne.

Poor Fellow My Country, H.'s magnum opus—winner of the Miles Franklin Award (1976), and one of the longest novels written in the English language—marks a final return to the thematic concerns of *Capricornia*, extending the chronology from 1936, when that novel had left off, to 1942. The subtitles of the three "books" (or volumes) tell the story: "Terra Australis—Blackman's Idyll Despoiled by White Australis—Blackman's Idyll Despoiled by White Bullies, Thieves, and Hypocrites"; "Australia Felix—Whiteman's Ideal Sold Out by Rogues and Fools"; "Day of

Shame—A Rabble Fled the Test of Nationhood." The last title refers to the Japanese bombing of Darwin and the infamous evacuation that became known subsequently (after a horse race) as the Adelaide River Stakes. Between 1935 and 1938, and again in 1942, H. had again been in the Territory—as a pharmacist, government medical officer, superintendent of the Aboriginal Compound, gold fossicker, member of the Japan-Australia Society, agitator for the Euraustralian League (fighting for the rights of people of mixed race), union organizer, and finally a sergeant in the armed forces. For *Poor Fellow My Country* he drew upon all of these experiences. He satirized his enemies of old, he revealed the absurdities and injustices of his society, and he dramatized what he regarded as his own personal tragedy—the tragedy of Australia as a nation: failure to connect, to identify, with Aboriginality and the spiritualized Land, and failure to uphold the ideals of the "True Commonwealth" of Australia.

H. did not regard himself as an artist by destiny, but as a social revolutionary by national necessity. His importance to Australian literature lies undoubtedly in his contribution to the continuing debate on race and nation, on land rights, as well as in his mastery of the art of yarn spinning. However, the complexity of H.'s writing goes beyond narrative complication, beyond even the social issues involved, because the other major subject is himself: a social, psychic, sexual, cultural, and national creature of masks, and of monumental mythopoesis.

BIBLIOGRAPHY: Buckley, V., "*Capricornia*," *Meanjin*, 19 (1960): 13–30; Atkinson, A., "Mixed Grill," *Meanjin*, 20 (1961): 237–38; Heseltine, H. P., *X. H.* (1973); Heseltine, H. P., "X. H.'s Magnum Opus," *Meanjin*, 34 (1975): 133–36; McQueen, H., "*Poor Fellow My Country*," *Arena*, 41 (1976): 79–81; Hergenhan, L. P., "An Australian Tragedy: X. H.'s *Poor Fellow My Country*," *Quadrant*, 21, 2 (1977): 62–70; McDougall, R., "*Capricornia*: Recovering the Imaginative Vision of a Polemical Novel," *ALS*, 10, 1 (May 1981): 67–78; McLaren, J., *X. H.'s Capricornia and Poor Fellow My Country* (1981); Clancy, L., *X. H.* (1981)

—RUSSELL MCDOUGALL

HERBERT, Zbigniew

Polish poet, dramatist, and essayist, b. 29 Oct. 1924, Lvov (now in Russia)

H. was an active member of the Polish resistance during the Nazi occupation. After World War II he studied in Cracow at the Academy of Fine Arts and then at the Academy of Commerce, from which he received a master's degree in economics in 1947. In 1950 he earned a law degree from the Nicolas Copernicus University in Toruń and stayed on there for a time to study philosophy. Between 1965 and 1971 he lived abroad.

H.'s poems reflect his war experience, although they seldom deal directly with the tragic scenes he witnessed. His poems began to appear in periodicals in 1950, but H. did not publish his first collection of poetry, *Struna światła* (1956; the chord of light), until the political thaw made greater freedom of expression possible. In a later collection, *Studium przedmiotu* (1961; study of the object), he discreetly refers to this fact in "Szuflada" ("Drawer," 1968). His second collection of poetry, *Hermes, pies i gwiazda* (1957; Hermes, dog and star), had come quickly on the heels of the first one.

H. does not easily fit into any rigid classification. Although usually considered the most classical of his contemporaries, H., like most of them, disdains traditional rhyme and meter (some of his poems are in prose). He has his own brand of classicism, and he has developed to an extraordinary degree the dramatic monologue, which he makes the vehicle for ironic and questioning reflections on the world about him.

H.'s eyes are not closed to the political realities amid which he lives, and much of his poetry has political overtones, but he never deals directly with political events. The tension in his work transcends the political plane; it is a Platonic tension between the ideal and the real that permeates his poetry, which he sees not as an end but as a means in the service of the good. He strives for a world without suffering.

H.'s recent collection of poems, *Pan Cogito* (1974; *Mr. Cogito*, 1993), has already been translated into about fifteen languages. (English translations of most of the poems of this book are included in *Selected Poems*, 1977.) Mr. Cogito, whose name reminds us of the Cartesian point of departure, serves the poet as a device in his search for the identity of the self. H.'s hero is a very ordinary human being rather than a great thinker, and his weaknesses and failures become his greatest assets. In the opening poem, Mr. Cogito observes his face in the mirror; in this and in some other poems, Mr. Cogito asks himself who he is. In *Studium przedmiotu*, it was a pebble that was close to attaining perfection. H. does not attempt to bring "pebbly" qualities to the human world. Instead, feeling the sense of communion with a stone, in "Poczucie tożsamości" ("Sense of Identity," 1977), he humanizes the inanimate objects. The poet's wisdom lies in his ability to accept defeat. As in his earlier poem, "Dojrzałość" (1957; "Maturity," 1968), so in many of the poems in *Pan Cogito* H. tells us without a trace of didacticism that we have to accept reality. He never pontificates. H. sounds most powerful when he does not raise his voice. In *Pan Cogito* H. departs only once from his low-key, subdued tone, in the very last poem, "Przesłanie Pana Cogito" ("The Envoy of Mr. Cogito," 1977). H. calls for courage when reason leaves us, for anger when we hear the voice of the beaten, and for scorn for the informers, executioners, and cowards. The poem ends with a call to march on, faithful to our ideals. Yet even in this departure, H. shows that he is only human and that there is a limit to his anger. Instead of defeating his purpose by breaking away from his tone, H. wins us and scores, in a roundabout way, another victory.

Like Tadeusz RÓŻEWICZ, with whom he is often compared, H. has endeavored to reach a wider audience through the stage. *Drugi pokój* (1958; the other room) exemplifies in a dramatic form his searching analysis of complex human relationships. There is, however, a fundamental difference between Różewicz and H. The former represents the war generation, which had lost the earlier morality and did not replace it with new moral values. H. keenly feels that there is a real need for "tablets of values" (a reference to the tablets of the Ten Commandments) in the contemporary world, and considers nihilism as the most serious menace of our modern culture.

One result of H.'s travels in France, England, Greece, and Italy is *Barbarzyńca w ogrodzie* (1962; *The Barbarian in the Garden*, 1985), a collection of essays examining a variety of aesthetic and historical problems. Coming from eastern Europe, the author plays the role of the "barbarian," while the West is represented by the "garden."

Deeply humanitarian, H. rarely becomes moralistic. His tragic view of life is balanced by his own brand of subtle irony. Highly intellectual, H.'s poetry is always filtered through a lyrical sensibility that transforms ideas into imagery and mood.

It may be premature to designate any contemporary Polish poet as the greatest of his generation; H. is already widely recognized as the most original. The freshness of his approach to classical themes is matched by form that reconciles the traditional and the modern. Czesław MIŁOSZ, in *The History of Polish Literature* (1969), has said of H.'s poetry that it is a distillation of the crushing experiences shared by all Poles during World War II, but that its meaning is universalized into a valid contribution to world poetry in this century.

FURTHER WORKS: *Napis* (1969); *Dramaty* (1970); *Poezje wybrane* (1970); *Wiersze zebrane* (1971). FURTHER WORKS IN ENGLISH: *Selected Poems* (1968); *Selected Poems* (1977)

BIBLIOGRAPHY: Kijowski, A., "Outcast of Obvious Forms," *PolP*, 9 (1966): 34–41; Lieberman, L., "A Confluence of Poets," *Poetry*, 114, 1 (1969): 40–58; Alvarez, A., "Z. H." (1967), *Beyond All This Fiddle: Essays 1955–1967* (1969): 142–47; Miller, S., "The Poetry of Z. H.," in Cheuse, A., and R. Koffler, eds., *The Rarer Action* (1970): 244–57; Piontek, H., "Die Lyrik H.'s," *Männer die Gedichte machen* (1970): 66–77; Matuszewski, R., "Tradition Triumphant," *PolP*, 14 (1971): 25–29; Carpenter, B., and J. Carpenter, "The Recent Poetry of Z. H.," *WLT*, 51 (1977): 210–14

—JERZY J. MACIUSZKO

HERMANS, W(illem) F(rederik)

Dutch novelist, b. 1 Sept. 1921, Amsterdam; d. 27 Apr. 1996, Utrecht

Bitterness, disillusionment, and resentment, apparently adding up to a form of nihilism, the most characteristic of the sentiments expressed in H.'s work, may be a disguise for the disappointments and pain he experienced during his life, more specifically his early adulthood. After completing high school his father made him study sociography; in the same year both his sister and a cousin committed suicide around the time when the Germans invaded the Netherlands. After one year at the unversity H. switched to physical geography and obtained a Ph.D. in 1955. He began teaching at the University of Groningen in 1958 but left in 1973 amidst many disagreements and friction with the authorities and colleagues.

De tranen der acacia's (1948; The Tears of the Acacia's) is an analysis of the identity crisis a young man experiences growing up in World War II. It was not the fact that the protagonist in the book continuously fails in everything he undertakes but rather the cynicism of the description that shocked the reading public. In *Het behouden huis* (1952; The Preserved House) a partizan who hardly seems to know what he is fighting for, discovers a house that seems like an oasis in a desert, but which in the end appears to be no more than what it had in fact always been: "a hollow, dank lump of stone, on the inside full of rubble and filth"—in spite of the angels carved in the ceiling. This book as well as many others that followed has World War II as its background. H. believed that war is the situation in which people feel "at home"; the time between wars is no more than a pause between wars. *De donkere kamer van Damocles* (1958; The Dark Room of Damocles) is H.'s most popular book. It contains elements which can be described as belonging to postmodernist thinking in as far as POSTMODERNISM differs from cynicism with life. The protagonist in this book struggles for years, also after the war, to prove his real personality. The most remarkable element regarding this situation is that the reader at the end knows no more than the secondary characters who the real Osewoudt is: is he a hero, a traitor, a victim, or a psychopath? H. believes that we all possess these qualities and that nobody really knows who or what he or she is and what the sense of it all is. H. attempts to prove in one book after another that there is no system, there is no controlling "higher" force, there are no absolutes in any form.

During the course of his career H. came into conflict with institutions of all sorts and particularly those that, in his view, pretend to know the truth, or "a" truth. Examples of such institutions are the church, described in *Ik heb altijd gelijk* (1951; I Am Always Right), his fellow writers in *Mandarijnen op zwavelzuur* (1964; Mandarins on Sulphuric Acid), the academic world in *Onder Professoren* (1975; Among Professors) and *Uit talloos veel miljoenen* (1981; Out of Numberless Millions), and finally all of Dutch society when he decided to leave the country and settle in Paris. In *Het sadistisch universum* (1964; The Sadistic Universe), a collection of essays, he defines his philosophical and literary principles in clear terms: a novel cannot be a representation of reality, because a novel is a construction for which the author has the neccesary tools. This is not the case with "real life." A novelist should also not attempt or pretend to be realistic, naturalistic, or psychological. A novel is a myth in which the characters represent or parallel certain aspects of lifeand thus are in this respect no more than archetypes.

H. has written essays on a variety of subjects such as literature, art, technology, philosophy, politics, and history. It is difficult to classify H. with any literary group or movement. His themes which in effect deal with the problem of ethics has, in that sense, the most in common with those of romanticism. Although he does not believe that any person or institution ever really puts its principles into practice, he indirectly recognizes their existence.

H.'s characters are personifications of his world view: they are lonely, they cannot relate to their fellow human beings, they never succeed in any meaningful project, and continually fall victim to the deceit and guile of others. Life is a jungle whose natural forces will always foil any attempt at bringing order into its natural state, which is chaos. H.'s repeated refusal of literary awards corresponds with his convictions relative to social and cultural institutions in general.

FURTHER WORKS: *Moedwil en misverstand* (1948); *Paranoia* (1953); *De God Denkbaar, Denkbaar de God*(1956); *Een landingspoging op Newfoundland* (1957); *De woeste wandeling* (1962); *Nooit meer slapen* (1966); *Wittgenstein in de mode* (1967); *Een wonderkind of total loss* (1967); *Overgebleven gedichten* (1968); *Fotobiografie* (1969); *Herinneringen van een engelbewaarder* (1971); *Het evangelie van O. Dapper Dapper* (1973); *De raadselachtige Multatuli* (1976); *Homme's hoest* (1980); *Een heilige van de horlogerie* (1987); *Door gevaarlijke gekken omringd* (1988); *Wittgenstein* (1990); *De laatste roker* (1991); *Ruisend gruis* (1995)

BIBLIOGRAPHY: Janssen, F.A., and Delvigne, R., "Bibliografie van de verspreide publicaties van W.F. Herman," *Raster*, 5, 2 (1971): 133-38; special H. issue *Kritisch Akkoord* (1967); Janssen, F.A., *Over De donkere kamer van Damokles* (1976); Janssen, F.A., *Scheppend nihilisme* (1979); Schenkeveld-Van der Dussen, A, *Nederlandse literatuur, een geschiedenis* (1993)

—MARTINUS A. BAKKER

HERMETICISM

Although hermeticism is often loosely used to describe tendencies in modern poetry in a number of literatures, it properly identifies a fundamental tendency in modern Italian literature, mostly in poetry. The term derives from Hermes Trismegistus (first two centuries B.C. or A.D.), the putative author of occult, mystical writings.

Not a movement but a moment and an atmosphere, hermeticism had no programmatic manifesto, it followed no recognized leader, it formed no homogeneous group. Therefore, the identification of memberships, dates, and evolutionary stages within its history is often problematic. In its most ample scope, hermeticism describes a new manner of considering the function of poetry and its modalities, developed during the period 1915–50, to which a large body of contemporary writers adhered in varying degrees and with different results: Giuseppe UNGARETTI, Eugenio MONTALE, Salvatore QUASIMODO, Alfonso GATTO, Mario LUZI, Carlo BETOCCHI, Piero BIGONGIARI, Leonardo Sinisgalli (1908–1981), and others.

Hermeticism has its roots in the "pure poetry" of French SYMBOLISM, and is related to schools of poetry in France, Germany, Spain, Russia, and the English-speaking world—including imagism and SURREALISM. Yet hermeticism is typically Italian, with its own inner needs and recognizable characteristics. Hermeticism responded to exigencies within its national culture by continuing the process of the renovation of poetry begun by Giovanni PASCOLI, Gabriele D'ANNUNZIO, Benedetto CROCE, the Crepuscolari poets, and FUTURISM.

The fulcrum of hermetic poetry is typically the word—a word that is no longer descriptive, oratorical, representational, but essentially evocative. Its aim is to suggest without naming, to allude without describing. The poetry that results is of lyrical fragments, where brevity and essentialness are defining prerogatives of an almost ascetic utterance. The controlling function of analogy in hermetic poetry, while revealing a crisis of knowledge in the accepted modes of communication, also attests to an effort to recover a lost innocence by an exploration beyond facts and appearances into the innermost recesses of existence and essences. A similar intention is evident in the "poetics of objects," where, with some suggestions from T. S. ELIOT's objective correlative, reality becomes symbolic of a human condition.

In hermeticism the role of the poet is redefined. He operates from a framework of solitude, intended not as the exclusive prerogative of an elitist caste but as a precondition for the chaste inwardness of his exploration. His operation is characterized by a sensitive awareness of the creative act, which results in a meticulous work of poetic elaboration, and by an intensely autobiographical preoccupation, in which poetry, while being a process of inner deciphering, becomes at the same time also a definition of the mood of the time.

It has often been said that hermetic poetry was a political gesture prompted by a refusal to join in the exaltation of the Fascist era, and thus that the choice of autobiographical solitude should be viewed as a sign of protest. The factors, however, that determined its genesis would seem to imply the gratuitousness of such historical interpretation, although for some of these poets their artistic posture provided, after the fact, an aesthetic pretext for their political noninvolvement.

BIBLIOGRAPHY: Williamson, E., "Contemporary Italian Poetry," *Poetry*, 79 (1951–1952): 159–81, 233–44; Ragusa, O., "French Symbolism in Italy," *RR*, 46 (1955): 231–35; Cecchetti, G., "The Poetry of the Past and the Poetry of the Present," *FI*, 10 (1976): 159–77

—ANTONINO MUSUMECI

HERMLIN, Stephan

(pseud. of Rudolf Leder) German poet and short-story writer, b. 13 April 1915, Chemnitz; d. 6 Apr. 1997, Balin

Reared and educated in Berlin, H. joined the Communist Youth League in 1931, then published antifascist propaganda until 1936. After extensive travels he fought with the Loyalists in the Spanish Civil War. During World War II he lived in exile in France and Switzerland. In 1947, following two unhappy years in West Germany, he moved to East Germany, joined the Socialist Unity Party, and was elected vice president of the German Writers' Union. He also worked as an editorial adviser for the monthly periodical *Aufbau*.

In 1961 H. became secretary of the poetic arts division of the East Berlin Academy of Arts, but was relieved of that office in 1963 for supporting young, politically deviant writers. Appropriate penance later enabled him to regain some of his lost stature, but in the late 1970s he again ran afoul of the regime by protesting against the expatriation of Wolf BIERMANN and the expulsion of nine dissidents from the East German Writers' Union.

During the early 1980s, H. endeavored to encourage a relaxing of the arms race between the United States and the Soviet Union and to contribute to a resolution of the relentless struggle for power through political dialogue with other writers and intellectuals. In 1985 he was awarded the Great Star of International Friendship.

H. is unusual among modern East German poets. While important contemporaries sought to divorce themselves from bourgeois tradition, H. studiously became the eclectic's eclectic. The debts owed most especially to the French SURREALISTS Paul ÉLUARD and Louis ARAGON and the German EXPRESSIONIST Georg Heym (1887–1912) cannot be overemphasized. These writers gave him important models for form, syntax, and language, as well as for imagery, mood, and theme. Yet, with all his synthesizing, H. imbued his work with an ideological commitment to communism that thrust him into the mainstream of East German literature and set him apart from his precursors.

H.'s first collection of poems, *Zwölf Balladen von den großen Städten* (1944; twelve ballads of the great cities), contains works that are typical of his oeuvre as a whole and among the best he has written. These ballads anticipate the tone and themes of *Zweiundzwanzig*

Balladen (1947; twenty-two ballads), for which H. received the (West German) Heinrich Heine Prize in 1948. They are marked by bold, often harsh imagery, conscious stylization, and the use of an elaborate esoteric and technical vocabulary. The focus is the urban world as a demonic setting for nightmares of universal destruction and collapse. And yet the poems are not pessimistic. They feature a peculiar duality between awareness of impending disaster and hope for regeneration. Each poem ends projecting a feeling of community and faith in the future.

The vitality and virtuosity of the poems of the 1940s are painfully lacking in the propagandistic *Mansfelder Oratorium* (1950; Mansfeld oratorio) and *Der Flug der Taube* (1952; the flight of the dove). *Mansfelder Oratorium*, however, was so politically successful that it became required reading in East German schools.

Although H. is primarily a poet, he has written some of the best fiction that has come from East Germany. The surrealistic dreams and illusions of the novella *Der Leutnant Yorck von Wartenburg* (1946; Lieutenant Yorck of Wartenburg), for example, reflect great narrative skill and psychological insight.

During his later years, H. no longer wrote the vivid, sophisticated literature for which he had once been known. *Abendlicht* (1979; *Evening Light*, 1983), a collection of melancholy personal reminiscences, and *Bestimmungsorte* (1985; Destinations), an anthology of short prose texts, reflect both his interest in reducing political tensions and his continuing effort to come to grips with the past, but they are only an echo of what was once one of the most important voices in modern political literature.

FURTHER WORKS: *Wir verstummen nicht* (1945, with Jo Mihaly and Lajser Ajchenrand); *Die Straßen der Furcht* (1946); *Ansichten über einige neue Schriftsteller und Bücher* (1947, with Hans Mayer); *Reise eines Malers in Paris* (1947); *Russische Eindrücke* (1948); *Die Zeit der Gemeinsamkeit* (1950); *Die Zeit der Einsamkeit* (1950); *Die erste Reihe* (1951); *Die Sache des Friedens* (1953); *Ferne Nähe* (1954); *Beethoven* (1954); *Dichtungen* (1956); *Nachdichtungen* (1957); *Begegnungen 1954–1959* (1960); *Gedichte* (1963); *Gedichte und Prosa* (1965); *Die Städte* (1966); *Die Zeit der Gemeinsamkeit; In einer dunklen Welt* (1966); *Erzählungen* (1970); *Scardanelli* (1970); *Lektüre 1960–1971* (1973); *Poesiealbum* (1973); *Die Argonauten* (1974); *Städteballaden* (1975); *Gesammelte Gedichte* (1979); *Aufsätze-Reportagen-Reden-Interviews* (1980); *Lebensfrist* (1980); *Äußerungen 1944-1982* (1983); *Traum der Gemeinsamkeit* (1985); *Nachdichtungen* (1987); *Drei Erzählungen* (1990); *Entscheidungen* (1995); *In den Kämpfen dieser Zeit* (1995); *Lektüre* (1997)

BIBLIOGRAPHY: Reich-Ranicki, M., "S. H., der Poet," *Deutsche Literatur in West und Ost* (1963): 386–410; Huebener, T., *The Literature of East Germany* (1970): 98–105; Flores, J., "S. H.: 'Volkstümlichkeit' and the Banality of Language," *Poetry in East Germany* (1971): 27–71; Anderle, H. P., "S. H.," in Wiese, B. von, *Deutsche Dichter der Gegenwart* (1973): 384–94; Ertl, W., "*Der Flug der Taube:* S. H.'s Attempts to Adjust to the Cultural-Political Demands in the GDR in the Early Fifties," *UDR* 13, 2 (1977): 49–62; Ertl, W., *S. H. und die Tradition* (1977); Schlenstedt, S., *S. H.* (1985); Witt, H., *S. H.* (1985); Rost, M. and R. Geist, *S. H. Bibliographie* (1985); Corino, K., *Außen Marmor, innen Gips* (1996)

—LOWELL A. BANGERTER

HERNÁNDEZ, Felisberto

Uruguayan short-story writer, b. 20 Oct. 1902, Montevideo; d. 13 Jan. 1964, Montevideo

In spite of the loyal support of some of his contemporaries, and the recognition of a handful of critics, H. did not achieve a well-deserved reputation as a major Latin American writer until after his death. His childhood in Montevideo left quite an impact on his writings, most of which can be considered autobiographical. He was not a gifted student, and had serious problems with conventional institutions of learning. In fact, he barely made it through elementary school, and never completed his secondary education. He was, however, obsessively interested in music, and started playing the piano at an early age. Very enterprising as a young man, at age sixteen he started his own music conservatory and became a piano instructor. Around that time he was working in local movie houses, providing the musical background to silent films. He continued perfecting his technique, enhancing his knowledge of theory, and developing his musicianship. A few years later, he was known as a concert pianist, and that prompted Arturo Sergio Visca (b. 1917) to assert that "actually one doesn't know if he was a pianist who became a writer or a writer who during many years swerved away from his vocation as a narrator channeling it into that of a concert pianist." It is safe to say, however, that nobody would remember H. today as a pianist of any note. He was to become a writer, and that is exactly what he wanted to be, against all odds, and in spite of the fact that at the end of his life he was planning a comeback piano recital that never materialized.

His literary career was irregular. H. started writing in his early twenties, but there were significant lapses throughout his production. José Pedro Díaz (b. 1921) suggests a division of H.'s works in three periods or stages of development. Between 1925 and 1931 he published very short texts, which—though they might be considered somewhat experimental, or perhaps even tentative—prefigure much of his later works. These editions, poor, limited, and self-published, were distributed among friends, who constantly encouraged the young author to continue writing. Over a decade later, a group of those loyal friends published, at their expense, a novella titled *Por los tiempos de Clemente Colling* (1942; in the times of Clemente Colling) immediately followed by *El caballo perdido* (1943; the lost horse), also a novella. A third and relatively long text, *Tierras de la memoria* (1965; lands of memory), was written in that same period, but was not published with the exception of a fragment that appeared in *El Plata*, a local newspaper. It came out shortly after H.'s death.

His second period is marked by an intense preoccupation with the remembrance of things past. (It is common among critics to consider these texts a Proustian trilogy.) After another hiatus of more than a decade, H. came up with a collection of short stories that Editorial Sudamericana published in Buenos Aires under the title *Nadie encendía las lámparas* (1947; nobody turned on the lamps), a rather successful book, followed by the publication in newspapers and magazines of some very interesting short stories, notably "Las Hortensias" (1949; the hydrangeas) and "El cocodrilo" (1949; the crocodile). This last phase showed a preference for texts that did not rely so much on the memory of actual events as it incorporated an abundance of purely imaginative circumstances. It must be said, however, that some of the most successful stories of this third period were written in the first person, and were still based upon the author's biography, but the deformation of the

material is much more deliberate, and they often enter the realm of the fantastic.

H.'s texts are often hard to follow and abound in irregularities of style that might startle some readers. He was well aware of what he himself termed "ugliness" in his prose, but defended it, and indeed cultivated it, as something that endowed his work with a special character, a personality of its own. That prompted noted author and critic Italo CALVINO to affirm that H. was "a writer unlike any other, European or Latin American; . . . an 'irregular' who [could] not be classified or categorized, but revealed to us his uniqueness in every page."

H.'s most significant contribution to the literature of our times was his persistent inquiry into the mechanisms of memory and the processes of writing. His stories are constantly intertwined with metatextual considerations that ultimately become the most important elements of his work. He was in many ways a forerunner of the narrative of the "post-boom" in Latin America, and that might account for the abundant and enthusiastic criticism that his work has generated in recent years.

FURTHER WORKS: *Fulano de tal* (1925); *Libro sin tapas* (1929); *La cara de Ana* (1930); *La casa inundada* (1960); *Obras completas* (4 vols., 1967–1983); *F. H. y yo* (1974, with Paulina Medeiros)

BIBLIOGRAPHY: Giraldi de Dei Cas, N., *F. H.: del creador al hombre* (1975); Sicard, A., ed., *F. H.: ante la crítica actual* (1977); Rela, W., *F. H.: bibliografía anotada* (1979); Lasarte, F., *F. H. y la escritura de "lo otro"* (1981); Echavarren Welker, R., *El espacio de la verdad: práctica del texto en F. H.* (1981); special H. issue, *Escritura*, 7, 13–14 (1982); Pallares, R., and Reyes, R., *¿Otro Felisberto?* (1983); Antúnez, R., *El discurso inundado* (1985); Xaubet, H., *Desde el fondo de un espejo: autobiografía y (meta) ficción en tres relatos de F. H.* (1995); Graziano, F., *The Lust of Seeing: Themes of the Gaze and Sexual Rituals in the Fiction of F. H.* (1997)

—HORACIO XAUBET

HERNÁNDEZ, Luisa Josefina

Mexican dramatist and novelist, b. 2 Nov. 1928, Mexico City

Prolific and successful author of more than thirty plays and thirteen novels during the past thirty-five years, H. grew up in Mexico City, an avid early reader of literature and history. She has translated many English, French, and German plays and prose works into Spanish, and her own novels and dramatic works reflect her wide readings. She wrote her first play when she was twenty-two and studied drama with Rodolfo USIGLI, one of the foremost dramatists of modern Mexico. H. succeeded Usigli as a professor of dramatic composition at the National Autonomous University of Mexico, and has been teaching there for more than thirty years. Beginning in 1951, when she won the first prize at the Spring Festival for her play *Aguardiente de caña* (1951; sugarcane alcohol), H. has been very active as a dramatist and has won many prizes and competitions, even though her topics are often controversial.

H. writes out of anger and indignation. Most of her plays and novels decry the abuse suffered by her characters, most of whom are women. She writes about problems of individuals and also about social conflicts. Many of her plays about individuals deal with self-realization, identity, and the ability or inability of individuals to act effectively. Other plays consider the topic of social justice: the marginalization of certain groups, the relationship of authority to justice, and the equity of marriage and divorce practices.

Among the plays that center upon the individual, *Los frutos caídos* (1957; the fallen fruit) explores the frustrations of a divorced woman who feels stifled by social conventions. In *La hija del rey* (1959; the king's daughter), the main character's identity derives from how others see her. Many other plays also focus on identity crises and inhibited sexuality: *Los huéspedes reales* (1958; the real guests), *El ambiente jurídico* (1950; judicial surroundings), *Botica modelo* (1953; corner pharmacy), and *Los sordomudos* (1953; the deaf-mutes) are some of these. H.'s novel *El lugar donde crece la hierba* (1959; the place where grass grows) also focuses on a woman's identity crisis. Many plays dramatize the perils and problems of male-female relationships, where one partner may destroy the other's sense of identity. This is a central theme of such plays as *Agonía* (1951; agony) and *Los duendes* (1960; the elves), a farce, as well as novels such as *Los palacios desiertos* (1963; the deserted palaces) and *La cólera secreta* (1964; the secret wrath).

Plays that dramatize the failure to act or the heroism of those who do struggle to effect change include *Afuera llueve* (1952; it is raining outside), *Los frutos caídos*, *La hija del rey*, and *La corona del ángel* (1951; the angel's crown). The novel *La memoria de Amadís* (1967; the memory of Amadís) is also based on the tensions between a weak-willed husband and a stronger wife.

Social justice is the theme of most of H.'s strongest works, such as *Botica modelo*, *La paz fecticia* (1960; fictitious peace), and *Historia de un anillo* (1961; the story of a ring), about the massacre of a town that believes in justice. *La fiesta del mulato* (1979; first pub. in English as *The Mulatto's Orgy*, 1971) is a complex and multilayered play that analyzes legal and ecclesiastical justice and questions of private and public identity: the extent to which women wear many masks and how these are viewed by society. It is one of many of H.'s works that effectively dramatize periods of Mexican history and the ideological issues of those times, as well as ours. H.'s novel *La primera batalla* (1965; the first battle) discusses the ideals of the Mexican Revolution compared with those of the Cuban revolution.

The mystical transcendence of anger and injustice is a theme of many of H.'s plays and novels from the 1960s on. Mysticism is a central concern of the two versions of *Apostasía* (1974; rev. ed., 1978; apostasy), *Las fuentes ocultas* (1980; the hidden fountains), and *Apocalipsis cum figuris* (1982; apocalypse with figures). The mystical experience enables people to endure and transcend their immediate circumstances and confirms their faith in a higher and more meaningful spirit of humanity.

H. is widely recognized as a major contemporary dramatist and as one of the important Mexican novelists of the 20th c.

FURTHER WORKS: *La Plaza de Puerto Santo* (1961); *La calle de la gran ocasión* (1962); *Arpas blancas, conejos dorados* (1963); *Clemencia* (1963); *La noche exquisita* (1965); *El valle que elegimos* (1965); *Popol-vuh* (1966); *Quetzalcóatl* (1968); *Nostalgia de Troya* (1970); *Los trovadores* (1973); *Danza del Urogallo múltiple* (1974); *La Pavana de Aranzazú* (1975); *Hecube* (1976); *Apocrypha* (1978); *Caprichos y disparates de Francisco Goya* (1979); *Carta de navegaciones submarinas* (1987); *La Cabalgata* (1988); *Almeida: danzón* (1989)

BIBLIOGRAPHY: Pacheco, C., "Con L. J. H.: La misoginia no existe," *Siempre*, 1321 (1978): 41–3; Miller, B., and A. González, "L. J. H.," *Veintiséis autoras del México actual* (1978): 239–51; Fox-Lockert, L., "L. J. H.," *Women Novelists in Spain and Spanish America* (1979): 241–59; Knowles, J. K., *L. J. H.: Teoría y pr´ctica del drama* (1980); Toro, F. de, "*La paz fecticia* de L. J. H.," *Brecht en el teatro hispanoamericano contemporáneo* (1984): 122–34; Valdés, M. E., de "L. J. H.," in Marting, D. E., ed., *Spanish American Women Writers* (1990): 241–53; Knowles, J. K., *L. J. H.: teoría y práctica del drama*

—MARY G. BERG

HERNÁNDEZ, Miguel

Spanish poet and dramatist, b. 30 Oct. 1910, Orihuela; d. 28 March 1942, Alicante

Born into a poor peasant and laboring family, H. worked as a goatherd and at other farm tasks, a country life that was essential to his poetic development. During the Spanish Civil War he fought for the Republic. Imprisoned and for a time condemned to death, he suffered unbearably from hunger, cold, tuberculosis, and pulmonary complications, from which he died.

H. wrote several dramas, among them a neo-Catholic morality play, *Quien te ha visto y quien te ve y sombra de lo que eras* (1934; he who has seen thee and he who sees thee and the shadow of what you were), which treats innocence and guilt, desire and the flesh, grace, and redemption and pardon through Christ. Following his pastoral orientation, H. exhibits in his religious feeling a natural sensuality that verges on the mystic.

H. combined the popular, classical, and traditional, the physical and the temporal in his poetry. In his dramatic and pantheistic *Perito en lunas* (1933; moon connoisseur), written in ottava rima, H., undoubtedly influenced by some of the poets of the Generation of 1927, employed hermetic, dehumanized, and artificially elaborate metaphorical constructions. At the same time he stressed the ambivalent role of nature, whatever its violent or chaotic aspects, depicting Mother Earth as something that both destroys and engenders.

In *El rayo que no cesa* (1936; rev. eds., 1942, 1949; *Unceasing Lightning*, 1986), consisting of twenty-seven sonnets and three long poems, H. emphasized more human and personal themes, especially those of love and death. Pantheistic and existential, these poems, which utilize symbols such as the bull and the orange, also show his sensuality, frustration, sadness, sorrow, and anguish and horror at the thought of his own death and man's tragic destiny. Included in this volume is H.'s moving elegy to his intimate friend, Ramón Sijé, who died in 1935.

In his next collection, *Viento del pueblo* (1937; winds of the people), more realistic than metaphysical, H. exalted heroes in epic song but also dwelled on the horrors of war. Patriotic and passionate, social and sarcastic, these poems, which won H. a share of the National Prize for Poetry, paint a picture of poverty and sorrow, although the poet, compassionate and tender, refuses to despair. This collection has an immediacy and honesty far removed from the baroque aesthetics of his first collection, as religiosity yields to revolutionary fervor.

El hombre acecha (1939; man in ambush), in press but never published in book form during his lifetime, painfully reflects on wounded war victims and Spain's tragedy. H. laments the blood and sacrifice caused by war, but he also proclaims his proletarian solidarity. Spontaneous and socialistic, these poems show us man, stripped of his pretensions and cultural veneer, and prey to his brutish instincts as he ambushes his fellow man.

Cancionero y romancero de ausencias (wr. 1938–41, pub. 1958; *Songbook of Absences*, 1972), poetry written in jail, contains H.'s most personally moving traditional and popular poetry. He muses on the paradox of temporal existence, expresses undying love for his family, and shares with others his memories and belief in brotherhood, freedom, peace, and truth. Despairing at imminent death, H. denounces war as a solution for human problems, but to the very end uses symbols of forest, sun, and wheat, extolling physical existence close to the earth he loved.

For all his culture and utopian idealism, H. was essentially a deeply telluric and autobiographical poet who sang of love, both sexual and spiritual, fulfilled and unrequited, and nature, almost with mystical fervor. His is a personal, almost confessional, poetry filled with sadness and solitude, light and color, wind and shadow, sun and earth, blood and death, renunciation and purification. He eventually abandoned his religious faith but never his belief in humanity; and his poetic gifts, had he lived, would have placed him among the greatest names in Spanish literature.

FURTHER WORKS: *El silbo vulnerado* (1934); *Teatro en la guerra* (1937); *El labrador de más aire* (1937); *El pastor de la muerte* (1938); *Sino sangriento* (1939); *Los mejores versos de M. H.* (1954); *Dentro de luz, y otras prosas* (1957); *Los hijos de la piedra* (1959); *Obras completas* (1960); *Poemas de amor* (1969); *Obras completas* (1973); *Obra poética completa* (1976). FURTHER WORKS IN ENGLISH: *M. H. and Blas de Otero: Selected Poems* (1972)

BIBLIOGRAPHY: Zardoya, C., *M. H.: Vida y obra* (1955); Ballesta, J. Cano, *La poesía de M. H.* (1962); Puccini, D., *M. H.: Vida y poesía* (1970); Berns, G., "Familiar and Natural Violence in the Early Poetry of M. H.," *HR*, 38 (1970): 386–404; Ifach, M. de G., *M. H.* (1975); Nichols, G., *M. H.* (1978)

—KESSEL SCHWARTZ

HERRERA Y REISSIG, Julio

Uruguayan poet, b. 1 Aug. 1875, Montevideo; d. 18 March 1910, Montevideo

Although H. journeyed to countless faraway regions in his imagination, he spent his entire life in Montevideo except for a brief interlude in neighboring Buenos Aires, Argentina. From childhood he was immersed in a world of refinement, for his patrician family gave him wealth and rich surroundings. Unfortunately, he was also afflicted from birth with a heart condition, which killed him at the age of thirty-four.

H. stands out as one of the most original of the group of MODERNIST poets who flourished in Latin America at the beginning of the 20th c. His earliest poems (1897–99), immature and romantic, nonetheless attest to an incipient verbal gift. In his second transitional stage—in *Las pascuas del tiempo* (1900; the feasts of time) and *Los maitines de la noche* (1902; the matins of night)—H. discovered modernism and plunged wholeheartedly into this new modality, absorbing the French influences in vogue,

chiefly the SYMBOLISTS and Decadents, and also Rubén DARÍO's *Prosas profanas* (1896). His final, mature period of poetic productions displays a true brilliance. *Los éxtasis de la montaña* (2 vols., 1904, 1910; ecstasies of the mountain), *Los parques abandonados* (1908; the abandoned parks), *La torre de las esfinges* (1909; the tower of the sphinxes), and *Las clepsidras* (1910; the water clocks) reflect much of the taste and tenor of the modernist movement: a striving and straining for originality of expression; an emphasis on vivid colors, plasticity of form, and musicality of verse; voluptuous, frivolous, and hedonistic tones, and a delight in the exotic.

The ivory-tower poet par excellence, H. actually spent much of his time from 1902 to 1908 in a real tower he had constructed atop his house, where he wrote and received his friends to read poetry and discuss aesthetics. There he escaped from a hostile bourgeois society into his own reality, turning to exotic sources for much of his inspiration—the opulent, sensual world of classical mythology, the dark, satanic spheres of the French Decadent poets—shunning the facile and obvious, and seeking out the subtle and bizarre. Like a glittering dragonfly, he went skimming over the modernist garden, flashing and iridescent at times, but also elusive. His extraordinary imagination loved to heap metaphor upon metaphor, often producing a dazzling kaleidoscope of images.

But all is not exquisite refinement in his verse. The Uruguayan countryside, for example, with its atmosphere of simple domestic life, serves as a setting for a large number of his poems. H., the urbanite, takes solace in a pastoral, rural vision. Nonetheless, he is well aware of the uglier aspects of country life and is capable of presenting them in scenes of sharply drawn, grotesque imagery, as in his poem "La cena" (1910; the supper).

H. handled various metrical forms and both long and short poems with grace and ease, but he had a particular gift for the sonnet. In addition to his several well-known volumes consisting entirely of verse in that form, he translated Albert Samain's (1858–1900) collection *Aux flancs du vase* (1898) from the French.

Faithful to the modernist cult of beauty, H.'s poetry continues to impress with its predominately aesthetic qualities. Despite certain Parnassian excesses, his poems still command attention and admiration for their exquisite lyricism, verbal richness, and originality.

FURTHER WORKS: *La vida* (1900); *Ciles alucinada* (1903); *Sonetos vascos* (1906); *Berceuse blanca* (1910); *Obras completas* (5 vols., 1911–1913); *Prosas* (1918); *Poesías completas* (1941)

BIBLIOGRAPHY: Torre, G., de, Introduction to *Poesías completas* (1941): 7–35; Píriz, R. Bula, *H. y R.: Vida y obra; Bibliografía; Antología* (1952); Gicovate, B., *J. H. and the Symbolists* (1956); Seluja, A., M. Olivieri, and D. Pérez Pintos, *Homenaje a J. H. y R.* (1963); Miraz, R., *H. y R.: Antología, estudio crítico y notas* (1975)

—GEORGE D. SCHADE

HESSE, Hermann

German novelist, short-story writer, poet, and essayist, b. 2 July 1877, Calw; d. 9 Aug. 1962, Montagnola, Switzerland

The son of devout parents, H. was exposed from childhood to a broad range of religious and philosophical doctrines. The early models that eventually became important for the world view reflected in his writings range from elements of his immediate Pietistic heritage to the various directions of Eastern thought with which his parents had become familiar while in India. In preparation for a career as a theologian, H. was sent to the Latin Grammar School in Göppingen, and then to the Protestant seminary at Maulbronn. His antipathy for the seminary was so great, however, that he ran away in the spring of 1892. Nor did he subsequently adapt any more readily to secular schools. Following abortive mechanic's and shopkeeper's apprenticeships, H. successfully completed a training program in the book trade. From 1899 to 1903 he worked as a bookdealer in Basel, Switzerland. When his first novel, *Peter Camenzind* (1904; *Peter Camenzind*, 1961), brought him success as an author, H. settled in Gaienhofen on Lake Constance. A journey to India in 1911 was the first in a series of important, if disappointing and even painful, personal experiences that shaped H.'s creative life during and after the years of World War I. The war itself was especially odious to H., although during that time he worked with German prisoners and edited a newspaper for them, the *Deutsche Internierten-Zeitung*. Under the pressures of the prolonged illness of his oldest son and the mental illness of his wife, H. suffered a nervous breakdown. In 1916 he began a two-year period of psychoanalytic therapy administered by a disciple of C. G. JUNG, an experience that had significance for his subsequent literary works. When his unhappy marriage ended in divorce in 1919, H. moved to Montagnola, becoming a Swiss citizen in 1923. Among the honors H. received for his writings were the Goethe Prize of the City of Frankfurt and the Nobel Prize, in 1946, and the Peace Prize of the German Bookdealers' Association, in 1955.

Viewed as a whole, H.'s fiction and poetry are most accurately described as literature of experience. They document H.'s belief that the role of the writer is neither to explain his age, nor to better it, nor even to teach, but rather to employ the revelation of the author's own sufferings and dreams in opening to the reader the world of images, of the soul, of experience. Accordingly, the course of H.'s literary development was shaped, modified, determined by the areas of personal confrontation and involvement that impressed themselves most deeply upon his day-to-day existence. The abiding influence of his parents, their ideas and attitudes, called forth in H.'s works repeated expression of reverence for tradition, for middle-class values, for order. The most significant literary focus of his preoccupation with tradition is the realm of personal religious and spiritual experience. H.'s deep love of nature also influenced his writings in several ways. It contributed to a consistent effectiveness and beauty of landscape description that paralleled his considerable achievements in landscape painting. Moreover, it allowed literary models created by earlier nature-oriented writers—among them, Gottfried Keller (1819–1890)—to provide positive stimulus for the development of his own descriptive technique. On a third level, his feeling for nature led him to seek an appropriate philosophical relationship to it. As a result, he was drawn very early to the writings of Friedrich Hölderlin (1770–1843), Eduard Mörike (1804–1874), and the German romantic poets. The influence of romanticism lent to H.'s works the flavor of a search for a universality that comprehends and resolves the manifold and contradicting aspects of the human spirit. Unlike the romantics, however, who sought to define the problems of man's existence in terms of man's spiritual unity—or lack thereof—with the rest of the universe, H. directed his literary attention toward the more basic problem of man's internal nature. For the works written after 1916, his encounter with Jungian psychoanalysis gave more precise direction to H.'s quest for man's identity. His mature narratives reflect especially an interest in Jung's ideas about introversion versus extroversion, the collective unconscious, idealism, specific symbols, and the fundamental duality of man. Application of Jung's theories enabled H. to explore the traditional problem of Faustian man in much greater depth than had Goethe or subsequent German writers. Under Jung's influence, H. began to view all of the tragedy of human existence as a product of man's fragmented spiritual nature. Because of H.'s profound skepticism with respect to contemporary life—induced in part by his view of World War I and its aftermath—his characters only rarely achieve the goal of their individual struggles for self-realization: harmonious inner unity.

H. began his literary career as a lyric poet. His *Romantische Lieder* (1899; romantic poems) and subsequent collections of verse exhibit many qualities that also characterize his stories and novels. Strongly influenced by romanticism and the folk-poetry tradition, H.'s lyric creations are sensitive, pensive, and melodic. Although their language is simple and unassuming, the poems have a power of expression seldom equaled in 20th-c. German poetry. In what they convey to the reader, H.'s lyrics are an important complement to his narrative prose through their projection and realization of the goals toward which his characters strive. Perhaps no other modern German poet has so forcefully achieved in his work a productively positive, unclouded resolution of the tension between idealistic striving and the narrow limits of reality. The concept of love is the creative unifying principle upon which this poetic harmony is based. It is an immortal love that appears behind the afflictions and trials of life as a deeply elemental quality of existence itself. The element of love, viewed as true reality buried beneath the façade of appearances, is H.'s personal guide to the secret wellspring of life, his poetic path to inner unity and to God.

Like Goethe, H. saw himself as a wanderer and seeker. He projected that view of his own nature into his major literary figures. All of H.'s novels feature variations on the theme of the quest for personal fulfillment and self-realization. Peter Camenzind, the restless, insatiable wanderer of H.'s first novel, is a sensitive man whose consciousness seeks to assert and articulate itself in the feeling of a precarious connection to the world. Camenzind is the prototype of what later became a relatively standard character in H.'s works: the struggling artist who finds fulfillment in the experience of life rather than in his art. The conflicts of H.'s own childhood and youth in provincial Swabia inform much of Camenzind's relationship to the world of his encounters. And yet it is not the psychological penetration of the central character that gives this particular work its artistic power. Rather, it is the intensely personal, vibrantly captivating portraits of nature that draw the reader into the work with irresistible force. The visible dominance of nature throughout the work demands that H.'s hero experience fulfillment only in his ultimate return to the natural state symbolized in his final role as a farmer.

The positive, healthy state of nature is contrasted sharply with the destructive influence of civilized culture in H.'s novel *Unterm Rad* (1906; *The Prodigy*, 1957). A literary examination of H.'s Maulbronn experience, which reflects his disgust with the constrictions of traditional education, *Unterm Rad* was the first of H.'s novels to analyze the tensions between the spiritual-intellectual side of the artistic individual and the paralyzing institutions of bourgeois society. In his portrayal of conflicting components of human personality in the contrasting figures of Giebenrath and Heilner, H. established problem and character patterns that are central to subsequent novels. Certain polarities that H. identified as contending aspects of his own nature generate the story's tension, for example, in *Gertrud* (1910; *Gertrude and I*, 1915) and *Roßhalde* (1914; *Rosshalde*, 1970), two novels in which H. depicted conflicts between life in art and the demands of marriage.

With the remarkable novel *Demian* (1919; *Demian*, 1923), for which he received—and returned—the Fontane Prize, H. began a series of works that document his so-called "inward journey," a deeply psychological literary reaction to the negative stimuli of the war years. Under the influence of Jung, for whom the only true reality is within the self, H. came to regard the external social and political chaos of his time as a mirror of his own internal confusion. Accordingly, in *Demian* and subsequent works, H. sought to penetrate to his own identity in a process of psychological sorting and discovery. The results are the most powerful of H.'s novels.

The overwhelming strength of *Demian* lies in its portrayal of the semimystical dreamworld experience of the demonic abysses of the human soul. The life of the first-person narrator, Emil Sinclair, which H. intended as a protracted symbol for the uncertainty of the era, is visibly Faustian. Sinclair lives a fear-filled existence, torn between the clarity and purity of the morally ordered world of his bourgeois home and the darkly sinful, sensually seductive realm of the servant girls and workers. The process of his internal struggle is one of self-judgment leading to a cathartic rebirth. Demian, the shadowy alter ego of Sinclair's dreams, enables Sinclair to find himself by teaching him to unite the opposing aspects of existence into a harmonious whole. The strong influence of Goethe's *Faust* upon the resolution of the central problem is especially apparent in Sinclair's association with Demian's mother, an embodiment of Sinclair's dream ideal of love who is symbolically related to the "mother" archetypes of the second part of *Faust*.

In its conception and approach, *Demian* is H.'s most important preliminary study for the internationally popular novel *Der Steppenwolf* (1972; *Steppenwolf*, 1929), in which the author carried the Faustian problem of man's fragmented nature to the extreme. One of H.'s most inventive and complex novels, *Der Steppenwolf* represents a further development of the narrative style employed by Thomas MANN in *The Magic Mountain*. *Der Steppenwolf* describes the "inward journey" of Harry Haller, a man in whom are combined the dilemmas of Faustian duality multiplied a hundredfold and the timeless situation of the suffering outsider in search of a place for himself within a society to which he does not belong. In numerous respects Haller is a composite of earlier H. figures, and as such a many-sided symbol for H. himself. Nevertheless, unlike predecessors such as Emil Sinclair, Haller only glimpses the end of his quest—symbolized here in the "immortals," another variation on Goethe's ideal archetypes. In the magical theater sequence, in which truth emerges from illusion, Haller's belief in the immortals enables him temporarily to transcend the limitations of time and to scan the hidden corners of his own soul. Yet the inability to assimilate the entire world into his being causes him to fall short of permanent internal harmony. In the psychological and expressionistic imagery employed to underscore the workings of opposing civilized and animalistic tendencies in Harry Haller's character, H. exposed the neuroses of his entire generation.

Der Steppenwolf exhibits literary power and depth unequaled in H.'s other major "inward journey" novels of the period: *Siddhartha* (1923; *Siddhartha*, 1951), a lyric novel set in the time of Buddha that describes the path to internal harmony via asceticism—a major literary fruit of H.'s journey to India in 1911; *Narziß und Goldmund* (1930; *Death and the Lover*, 1932; new tr., *Narcissus and Goldmund*, 1968), H.'s most balanced novel, featuring attempted resolution of the polarities of existence in Goldmund's lifelong quest for the archetypal "mother"; and *Die Morgenlandfahrt* (1932; *The Journey to the East*, 1957), a narrative that reworks themes from *Der Steppenwolf* in its portrayal of the figurative pilgrimage to the East of a timeless brotherhood of individuals in search of the light of truth.

Just as H.'s novels document the progress of the author's own search for identity, inner unity, and self-understanding, so they also present the course of his attempts to arrive at an ultimate symbolic representation of the real nature and destiny of man. Both of those strivings found their culmination in the symbolism of the futuristic utopia portayed in H.'s final masterpiece, *Das Glasperlenspiel* (1943; *Magister Ludi*, 1949; new tr., *The Glass Bead Game*, 1969). In the symbol of the Castalian Order bead game of the early twenty-third century, a transcendent form of spiritual and intellectual discipline and meditation featuring a synthesis of universal values from all the arts and sciences, H. described his vision of a possible state of culturally ordered existence based upon self-denying spiritual austerity that might evolve in the ashes of a civilization destroyed by irresponsible mass production, narrow nationalism, and militarism. The major literary themes and problems of H.'s novels and stories are examined once more in an analysis and criticism of culture that is generated around the bead-game symbol, and in what is actually a discussion of the possibility and the desirability of Castalia's eventual existence. With grand irony, H. employed the account of Josef Knecht's life—his early studies, introduction to the bead game, entry into the Castalian Order, final mastery of the game, withdrawal from the Order in search of active rather than contemplative humanism—to reveal the incompatibility of a static cultural ideal with the creative vitality of the individual, thereby proclaiming his own true identity and defining the real values toward which his search for self-understanding had led him.

In the framework of his oeuvre as a whole, H.'s shorter fiction can be viewed as minor experiments with variations on the "inward journey" concept. Some of them are closely related to the author's nonliterary activities. In "Klingsors letzter Sommer" (1920; "Klingsor's Last Summer," 1970), for example, H. employed the style of his own painting to reveal how the artist Klingsor produces with Van Gogh-like passion and color an expressionistic panorama of his personal inner landscape. Other short works explore themes treated more successfully in H.'s novels. "Klein und Wagner" (1920; Klein and Wagner) carries the problem of psychological polarity to a destructive extreme in the tale of a man who lives a Jekyll and Hyde existence as a conscientious official/unscrupulous murderer. "Kinderseele" (1920; the soul of a child) is an additional document of H.'s early preoccupation with the problems of the adolescent who is torn between middle-class morality and sin. With only one or two exceptions, H.'s short stories are artistically less satisfying than his novels.

Many qualities of H.'s creations cause him to stand out among German writers of the 20th c. Despite his obvious reliance upon elements of tradition and his literary kinship to other important modern novelists, especially Thomas Mann, the lyrical quality of his prose and the vitality and color of his nature studies set him apart from other authors. At the same time, the intense psychological penetration of his characters and the originality with which he approached traditional themes and the timeless problems of his own era combine to make him an important spokesman not only for his own "lost generation" but also for future generations that must still make their own journey to individual and social fulfillment.

FURTHER WORKS: *Eine Stunde hinter Mitternacht* (1899); *Die hinterlassenen Schriften und Gedichte von Hermann Lauscher* (1902); *Gedichte* (1902); *Boccaccio* (1904); *Franz von Assisi* (1904); *Diesseits* (1907); *Nachbarn* (1908); *Unterwegs* (1911); *Umwege* (1912); *Aus Indien* (1913); *In der alten Sonne* (1914; *In the Old Sun*, 1914); *Knulp* (1915; *Knulp*, 1971); *Musik der Einsamen* (1915); *Am Weg* (1915); *Brief ins Feld* (1916); *Schön ist die Jugend* (1916; *Youth, Beautiful Youth*, 1955); *Kleiner Garten* (1919); *Märchen* (1919; *Strange News from Another Star and Other Tales*, 1972); *Zarathustras Wiederkehr* (1919); *Gedichte des Malers* (1920); *Wanderung* (1920; *Wandering*, 1972); *Blick ins Chaos* (1921); *Ausgewählte Gedichte* (1921); *Italien* (1923); *Sinclairs Notizbuch* (1923); *Psychologia Balnearia; oder, Glossen eines Badener Kurgastes* (1924; repub. as *Der Kurgast*, 1925); *Kurzgefaßter Lebenslauf* (1925); *Prosa* (1925); *Piktors Verwandlungen* (1925); *Bilderbuch* (1926); *Die Nürnberger Reise* (1927); *Betrachtungen* (1928; *Reflections*, 1974); *Krisis* (1928; *Crisis*, 1975); *Eine Bibliothek der Weltliteratur* (1929); *Trost der Nacht* (1929); *Der Weg nach Innen* (1931); *Kleine Welt* (1933); *Fabulierbuch* (1935); *Das Haus der Träume* (1936); *Stunden im Garten* (1936); *Gedenkblätter* (1937); *Neue Gedichte* (1937); *Orgelspiel* (1937); *Die Gedichte* (1942); *Berthold* (1945); *Der Pfirsichbaum* (1945); *Traumfährte* (1945); *Der Europäer* (1946); *Krieg und Frieden* (1946; *If the War Goes On*, 1971); *Frühe Prosa* (1948); *Briefe* (1951); *Späte Prosa* (1951); *Gesammelte Dichtungen* (6 vols., 1952); *Zwei Idyllen* (1952); *Engadiner Erlebnisse* (1953); *Beschwörungen* (1955); *Gesammelte Schriften* (7 vols., 1957); *Bericht an die Freunde* (1961); *Traktat vom Steppenwolf* (1961; *Treatise on the Steppenwolf*, 1975); *Cavaliere Huscher und andere Erzählungen* (1963); *Ein Blatt von meinem Baum* (1964); *H. H.—Thomas Mann: Briefwechsel* (1968; *The H./Mann Letters*, 1975); *Mein Glaube* (1971; *My Belief*, 1974); *Gesammelte Briefe* (1973). **FURTHER WORKS IN ENGLISH:** *Poems* (1970); *Autobiographical Writings* (1972); *Stories of Five Decades* (1972); *Tales of Student Life* (1976); *Pictor's Metamorphoses and Other Fantasies* (1982)

BIBLIOGRAPHY: Ball, H., *H. H.* (1947); Schmid, M., *H. H.* (1947); Brunner, J. W., *H. H.: The Man and His World as Revealed in His Works* (1957); Mileck, J., *H. H. and His Critics* (1958); Rose, E., *Faith from the Abyss: H. H.'s Way from Romanticism to Modernity* (1965); Ziolkowski, T., *The Novels of H. H.* (1965); Ziolkowski, T., *H. H.* (1966); Serrano, M., *C. G. Jung and H. H.* (1966); Boulby, M., *H. H., His Mind and Art* (1967); Baumer, F., *H. H.* (1969); Field, G. W., *H. H.* (1970); Zeller, B., *Portrait of H.* (1971); Reichert, H. W., *The Impact of Nietzsche on H. H.* (1972); Ziolkowski, T., ed., *H.: A Collection of Critical Essays* (1973); Norton, R. C., *H. H.'s Futuristic Idealism* (1973); Glenn, J., *H. H.'s Short Fiction* (1974); Sorell, W., *H. H.* (1974); Casebeer, E. F., *H. H.* (1976); Mileck, J., *H. H.: Biography, Bibliography* (1977); Mileck, J., *H. H.: Life and Art* (1978); Liebmann, J., ed., *H. H.: A Collection of Criticism* (1978); Freedman, R., *H. H.* (1978); Fickert, K. J., *H. H.'s Quest* (1978); Stelzig, E. L., *H. H.'s Fictions of the Self* (1988)

—LOWELL A. BANGERTER

The secret of H.'s work lies in the creative power of his poetic similes, in the "magic theater" of the panoramas of the soul that he conjures up before the eyes and ears of the world. It lies in the identity of idea and appearances that, to be sure, his work—like any work of human hands—can do no more than suggest. But in H.'s work the asymptotic approximation reaches a point that few beside him can claim to have reached. In suggesting this identity H. H. becomes the mediator of what cannot be said, the prophet of what remains silent, and time and again his creative spontaneity vanquishes the arbitrariness of existence through his "ability to live by the strength of a faith."

Hugo Ball, *H. H.* (1947), p. 271

His struggle with the basic problems of his life, with the dichotomy of mind and soul, thus leads the poet toward a biocentric world view instead of the logocentrism that has dominated the attitudes of modern European man since the time of the Renaissance.

In the narrative *Die Morgenlandfahrt . . .* there is evidence of an impending change in H.'s attitudes, and in the poem "Besinnung" that change is first given a conceptually clear formulation. Meditation becomes H. H.'s major concern. It assures him the harmonious style of the life of reason imbued with a vital warmth, whose major stress, however, undergoes in *Glasperlenspiel* a progressively apparent shift from the element of warmth to that of reason. The world view of the aging poet, whose power of imagination revolves around the central harmony, becomes progressively logocentric. The Castalian harmony is not—as Goethe's was—an organic growth. It is the fruit of self-discipline, forced into being by a strict monastic code, by meditation, by ascetic self-control exercised under the rules and regulations of sober vigilance, and by the most meticulous exclusion of all external influences from the inner core of the soul. This Castalian harmony is a mask that conceals the face of the wolf of the steppe.

The romanticist H. has thus a classicist H. as his next-door neighbor, and the more the poet approaches the classical ideal of harmony, the more logocentric his world view becomes.

Max Schmid, *H. H.* (1947), p. 223

The extraordinary consistency of his opposition to the political course of his country from 1914 until 1945—in which the *total* attitude is not gradually evolved but stands there clear and whole from the outset—is an impressive (and rare enough) phenomenon in German intellectual life of this period. But always the message is in fact that of *Demian*. The tract *Zarathustra's Return* (1919), for instance, which tries and inevitably fails to recapture the authentic Nietzschean note, preaches the attainment of individuality and freedom through the acceptance of fate, exhorts German youth to eschew self-pity, and requires them to seek their god not in external slogans but in their own hearts.

Within the heart, however, lies chaos—especially the dissolution of every pseudo-objective moral canon; and the acceptance of chaos is combined with the exercise of a most sensitive conscience—this is the antinomy on which thenceforward H.'s moral out-look is based. The process which he calls "Erwachen" (awakening) shatters the shell of convention and opens the Way Within (*Weg nach Innen*); and this Way, ambiguously and profoundly, leads at one and the same time to the stringency of extreme responsibility and to anarchic freedom of the self.

Mark Boulby, *H. H.* (1967), p. 83

When considered as an ensemble, the novels from *Demian* to *Journey to the East*, with their various emphasized antinomies, bear a more balanced and less contradictory relationship with each other than one might otherwise expect. Many of the critical controversies concerning them have stemmed from the fact that commentators have tended to look upon each as a separate and final utterance rather than as the illumination of this or that facet of an interconnected and developing complex of ideas and problems. In regard to H.'s ideas on the future it can similarly be said that within an intriguing and sometimes bewildering melange of overlapping and intertwining concepts having to do with times and states to come, one can distinguish basic common directions.

A primary time-related characteristic shared by all of these novels is their renunciation of stasis, which evidences itself in the concept of dynamic, sequential occurrence as the chief impulse of both the plots and, particularly, of their open endings. As the product, so to speak, of this sequentiality the future stands in a sense as a goal in itself—a goal in no place clearly defined, and yet as palpable as any higher spiritual ideal can be.

Roger C. Norton, *H. H.'s Futuristic Idealism* (1973), p. 69

The Steppenwolf, one of H.'s most popular novels, . . . is as disconcerting as it is powerful in its structure and in the strength with which it indicts an era of jazz and loud-mouthed lies, a sham world in which the sensibilities of man are tested and crucified. Like H., the Steppenwolf is an outsider living on the edge of reality. Wrestling with his despair, groping for his innocence and his beliefs in a life of lost values, he seeks to find himself. His bearings are those of a bourgeois, but the stamp of his soul spells the anathema of the outsider. The city in which the novel's hero, Harry Haller, seems to be lost, is a symbol of unrelatedness. Someone puts a pamphlet into his hand, "The Treatise on the Steppenwolf," in which he finds the analysis of himself. There is his split nature, being man and wolf, kind and wild, full of love and tenderness as much as baring his wickedness and savagery. God and the Devil are in these people, "the capacity for happiness and the capacity for suffering; and in just such a state of enmity and entanglement were the wolf and man in Harry."

Walter Sorell, *H. H.* (1974), pp. 45–46

H.'s attachment to nature was intimate and long. Nature was his childhood wonderland and his boyhood playground; she became for him the refuge she is for his Peter Camenzind, and the source of solace and spiritual rejuvenation she is for his St. Francis of Assisi; her ephemeral beauty was a poignant reminder of man's mortality, and her authenticity exemplified H.'s conception of self-will . . . and his associated ideal of self-living. Nature was also a lasting creative inspiration, remained a common theme in H.'s writing and painting, and became his most characteristic backdrop and metaphor. Water is primordial matter, rivers are life in all its flux, and fish a prehuman stage of evolution; forests are preculture and the roving wolf is man's instinctual self; gardens are a paradise, flowers and butterflies epitomize life's lasting beauty and its evanescence, and birds are associated with the soul; nature's seasons are man's stages of life and night is the mother—and day the father—principle; trees are life's stoic outsiders, mountains its imperturbable observers, and clouds are the blue flower of H.'s early romanticism, a symbol of man's eternal longing and of his soul's endless quest for a *Heimat* home.

Joseph Mileck, *H. H.* (1978), p. 121

H.'s inner landscape had become the arena of his life, the stage on which his anxieties were directly exposed. He molded a form that he thought commensurate with this condition and found an adequate symbol in the modern city.

Steppenwolf was the first and actually the only work by H. in which the entire action takes place in a contemporary metropolis. In almost all of his other work the scene was nature or the Middle Ages or a symbolic Orient. For this choice of the city he was to be attacked by many of his followers, but it agreed with his experience. The combination of Zurich and Basel that he used to develop his symbolic city was designed to expose the individual and collective neuroses H. viewed as symptomatic of his time. Its dehumanized mass culture he had already condemned in his travelogue *Journey to Nuremberg* . . . in which he had assailed the degradation of ancient Nuremberg by commerce and industry. The tone of the city is set by the . . . "music of doom." Among its tenements, in its boulevards lit up by electric lights, its automobiles and clanging streetcars, its modish shops and bars, H. sensed the temptation to which sensual man is subject, as well as the premonition of his anonymous death.

Ralph Freedman, *H. H.* (1978), pp. 277–78

HEYM, Stefan

(pseud. of Helmut Flieg) German novelist and short-story writer (writing in German and English), b. 10 Apr. 1913, Chemnitz

After being expelled from school for publishing an antimilitaristic poem, H. eventually studied Germanic philology in Berlin. He emigrated to the U.S. in 1935, where he received his M.A. from the University of Chicago and then became editor of the weekly newspaper *Deutsches Volksecho* in New York. During the 1940s he joined the U.S. Army, became a specialist in psychological warfare, participated in the Normandy invasion, and worked as a newspaper editor in Munich during the early occupation period. After his return to the U.S. he began writing again, but his political attitudes caused him to return his Army medals in protest against McCarthyism and the Korean War. In 1953 he moved to the German Democratic Republic, where he remained active as a writer and journalist. Repeated conflicts with the communist regime eventually led to his expulsion from the East German Writers' Union and to his active participation in the protest actions that preceded the collapse of the government in 1989. In 1994 he was elected to the Bundestag as a member of the new Democratic Socialist Party, and when the legislature convened, he presided at its opening session as its oldest member. A year later, however, he gave up his seat in protest against a proposed constitutional amendment that later failed. Among the awards that he has received for his writing are the Heinrich Mann Prize (1953), the East German National Prize for Art and Literature (1959), and the Chemnitzer Ernst Art and Culture Prize.

H.'s novels and short stories, which exhibit the influence of American realism, are flavored by personal experience and marked by negative political and social criticism. They reflect his journalistic orientation toward the experiences of both everyday life and history. Among the most important features of his best narratives are skillfully crafted absorbing plots, the successful combination of documentary and fictional elements, dramatically pointed dialogues, and the effective use of irony and satire.

Compelling development of characters is one of the most consistent strengths of H.'s works. Although an obvious lack of accurate knowledge concerning the workings of the Gestapo diminishes the realistic effect of H.'s first novel, *Hostages* (1942), that weakness is offset by powerful psychological penetration of the characters in the portrayal of a hostage situation set within the context of the Czechoslovakian resistance to Nazi terror. Mastery of the psychological element is also a significant strength of *The Crusaders* (1948), the most successful of his early novels. In *The Crusaders*, H. employs the American march from France into Germany and scenes from the first year of the occupation as a backdrop for the depiction of human conflicts, behaviors, corruption, and vice that result from individual failure to grasp the meaning of World War II. The struggle of individual conscience against corruption is again a central theme in *Goldsborough* (1953), H.'s response to the experience of a miners' strike in Pennsylvania.

The more interesting works of H.'s middle period are engaging historical novels that use settings and situations from the past as frameworks for the critical examination of modern problems. *Die Papiere des Andreas Lenz* (1963; *The Lenz Papers*, 1964) is a colorful treatment of the contradiction between dictatorship and freedom, presented in the trappings of the Baden revolution of 1949, while the biographical novel *Uncertain Friend* (1969) explores the relationship between revolution and liberty through illumination of the unhappy life of Ferdinand Lassalle (1825–1864).

From the literary standpoint, the best of H.'s historical creations are the novellas *Die Schmähschrift; oder, Königin gegen Defoe* (1970; *The Queen against Defoe*, 1974) and *Der König-David-Bericht* (1972; *The King David Report*, 1973). In a style reminiscent of the early 18th c., *Die Schmähschrift* focuses on the career of

Daniel Defoe and presents an interesting treatment of the relationship between literature and its audience, while *Der König-David-Bericht* employs a new version of the biblical King David's life as a vehicle for examining the abuses of Stalinism.

H. reached the peak of his literary development with *Ahasver* (1981; *The Wandering Jew*, 1984). The title figure is the author's projection of the archetypal revolutionary intellectual who, at critical junctures in world history, stands in conflict with reactionary forces personified in the figure of Satan. To some extent the Wandering Jew also represents H.'s perception of his own role as a writer with the responsibility to speak out on contemporary issues such as the threat of nuclear destruction and the dangers of bureaucratic stagnation, and to be active in furthering the cause of true democracy. His attempt to carry out those obligations in *Schwarzenberg* (1984; Schwarzenberg), a rather naive political fairy tale about an ideal democratic republic in postwar Germany, lacks the artistic quality and depth that he achieved in *Ahasver*.

In the late historical-biographical novel *Radek* (1995) H. returned to the theme of the Wandering Jew in describing the life of the revolutionary title figure from the time of his expulsion from the Social Democratic Party in 1912 to his mysterious death in 1937. Unfortunately, however, the work does not recapture the vitality of *Ahasver*, and its glorification of the revolutionary process comes across as out of date.

Although less well-known than his novels, H.'s short stories are significant reflections of his personal literary style and clear demonstrations of his ability to present barbed social criticism effectively in compact narrative form. The most representative collection of his short fiction is *Schatten und Licht* (1960; *Shadows and Lights*, 1963), with its sometimes humorous but penetrating examination of specific problems of divided Germany and life in the German Democratic Republic during the reconstruction era.

Unlike most writers who reached the peak of their careers in East German semi-isolation, H. must be credited with producing literary works that combine substantial artistic mastery and intellectual depth with qualities that also give them an unusually broad international appeal in the English-speaking world.

FURTHER WORKS: *Die Hinrichtung* (1935); *Tom Sawyers großes Abenteuer* (1952, with Hanus Burger); *Die Kannibalen, und andere Erzählungen* (1953; *The Cannibals, and Other Stories*, 1957); *So liegen die Dinge* (1953); *Forschungsreise ins Herz der deutschen Arbeiterklasse* (1953); *Im Kopf sauber* (1954); *Reise ins Land der unbegrenzten Möglichkeiten* (1954); *Offen gesagt* (1957); *Casimir und Cymbelinchen* (1966); *5 Tage im Juni* (1974; *Five Days in June*, 1977); *Cymbelinchen; oder, Das Ernst des Lebens* (1975); *Das Wachsmuth-Syndrom* (1975); *Erzählungen* (1976); *Die richtige Einstellung, und andere Erzählungen* (1977); *Erich Hückniesel und das fortgesetzte Rotkäppchen* (1977); *Collin* (1979; *Collin*, 1980); *Wege und Umwege* (1980); *Atta Troll: Versuch einer Analyse* (1983); *Märchen für kluge Kinder* (1984); *Gesammelte Erzählungen* (1984); *Reden an den Feind* (1986); *Nachruf* (1988); *Meine Cousine, die Hexe, und weitere Märchen für kluge Kinder* (1989); *Der bittere Lorbeer* (1989); *Auf Sand gebaut* (1990); *Einmischung* (1990); *Auferstanden aus den Nischen: Dokumente einer revolution* (1990); *Stalin verläßt den Raum: Politische Publizistik* (1990); *Der fall Glasenapp* (1991); *Filz* (1992); *Der Winter unseres Mißvergnügens* (1996); *Immer sind die Weiber weg* (1997); *Die großen Romane* (1998). FURTHER WORKS IN ENGLISH: *Nazis in U.S.A.* (1938); *Of Smiling Peace* (1944); *The Eyes of*

Reason (1951); *The Cosmic Age* (1959); *The Queen against Defoe and Other Stories* (1974)

BIBLIOGRAPHY: Moskin, R., "The Creator and the Commissars: An Encounter with S.H.," in *The Queen against Defoe, and Other Stories* (1974): 115–26; Petr, P., "S. H. and the Concept of Misunderstanding," *AUMLA*, 48 (1977): 212–21; Dorman, M., "The State versus the Writer: Recent Developments in S. H.'s Struggle against the GDR's *Kulturpolitik*," *ML*, 62, 3 (Sept. 1981): 144–52; Zachau, R., *S. H.* (1982); Lauckner, N. A., "S. H.'s Revolutionary Wandering Jew: A Warning and a Hope for the Future," in Gerber, M., ed., *Studies in GDR Culture and Society* (1984), Vol. 4: 65–78; Ecker, H. P., *Poetisierung als Kritik* (1987); Hutchinson, P., "Problems of Socialist Historiography: The Example of S. H.'s *The King David Report*," *MLR*, 81, 1 (Jan. 1986): 131–38; Graves, P. J., "Authority, the State, and the Individual: S. H.'s Novel *Collin FMLS*," 23, 4 (Oct. 1987): 341–50; Ecker, H. P., *Poetisierung als Kritik* (1987); Hutchinson, P., *S. H.: The Perpetual Dissident* (1992); General, R., and Sabath, W., eds., *S. H.* (1994)

—LOWELL A. BANGERTER

HIENG, Andrej

Slovene novelist, short-story writer, and dramatist, b. 17 Feb. 1925, Ljubljana

H. graduated from the Academy of Dramatic Art in Ljubljana. His first literary text, *Študije o nenavadnih znaèajah* (Studies of Unusual Characters), appeared in the mid-1950s, outlining his later literary interests and main preoccupations. He was primarily interested in "unusual characters," people standing out from the average and from the expected social attitude and individual gesture. A markedly modern writer, orientated towards the experience of the European postwar novel, H. attracted critical attention with his collections of stories, *Usodni rob* (1957; The Fatal Brink), and *Planota* (1961; The Plateau), and novels *Gozd in pečina* (1966; The Forest and the Cave) and *Orfeum* (1972; Orpheus).

H.'s prose focuses on the theme of man's impossibility of breaking down the walls of isolation and the impossibility of communication. H's characters are stigmatized and neurotic (weak, ill, or criminals), burdened by fear and the feeling of guilt. H. is not interested in the story itself; to him, the real event never happened, he is primarily interested in conditions resulting from some previous event. The traditional structure of the text collapses, and the world is presented in fragments. H. starts from the belief that man's destiny, the essence of which is death, is random and accidental, and that everything happening in the world is coordinated from some higher center. Man is only a victim of unexpected and unpredictable forces. H. therefore devotes most of his attention to the subconscious, to which he subordinates the logic of the narrative, as in *San o razbijenom autobusu* (1995; The Dream of a Wrecked Bus). With its isolated traumas, neuroses, dreams, and instincts, it links H. with the experience of FAULKNER's writing.

In the collections of stories *Usodni rob* and *Planota* the content is accompanied by two formal characteristics, first of a neoromantic heritage, putting emphasis on the atmosphere created by sensuous mental images and moods (picturesque descriptions, nature), and the other from the modern narrative procedure, consisting of the immediate introduction of the idea into the story, which marks H.'s prose as rationally cold, typified and stylized.

Gozd i pečina, written in the form of a novel, is composed of loosely connected self-contained stories connected with parts of Croatia (Karlovac, Osijek, and Zagreb). The stories are held together by the unity of the character. They focus on the relationship of a composer Leban and a girl Ana, who are, unsuccessfully of course, trying to get together. In dealing with existential and moral questions H. focuses on the tragic isolation which, regardless of all efforts, can not be overcome. In the forest of life's dangers, one can only climb up the cliff of realization that everything ends in nothingness.

His dramatic writing is, in critical opinion, characterized by an aestheticism that is sometimes its own end. In *Cortesova vrnitev* (1969; The Return of Cortes), thematizing the split between the "historic" and "normal" time, the hero realizes that life is governed by chaos, but still believes in the possibility of fulfilling the ideals created by human efforts. *Burleska o Grku* (A Burlesque of a Greek) and *Gluhi mož na meji* (1969; A Deaf Man at the Border) direct the attention away from the problems of humanity to the problems of art. Here the relationship between the socio-political and human power is analysed, as well as moral impulses and intentions of the individual human act and the biological and physical determination of human existence. The heroes of the first two plays accept the burden of reality, whereas the hero of the third play takes the responsibility for his destiny into his own hands and lives life to the full. With this, a new phase in H's writing is foreshadowed.

A play from this new phase is *Osvajalec* (1971; The Conqueror), dealing with the problem of revolutionary activism. The author analyses social action in two historical periods (father and son), and finds arguments for their justification in the time they belong to.

H. published several plays in the 1970s: *Osvajalec*; *Lažna Ivana* (1973; False Ivana); *Izgubljeni sin* (1976; The Lost Son); *Nori malar*, (1979; A Mad Painter); *Večer Ženinov* (1979; A Dinner at Ženinovs'); *Može na meji* (1980; Men at the Border).

FURTHER WORKS: *Novele* (1954, with others); *Čarodej* (1976); *Obnebje metuljev* (1980)

BIBLIOGRAPHY: Pogačnik, J. and F. Zadravec, *Istorija slovenačke književnosti* (1973); Pavletić, V., ed., *100 romana jugoslavenskih književnosti* (1982)

—IRENA LUKSIC

HIJAZI, Ahmad 'Abd al-Mu'tī

Egyptian poet, b. 1935

Born in a village of Lower Egypt, H. moved to Cairo after his elementary schooling and spent seven years studying Arabic at the Teachers' Training College. He then went to France for graduate work, having spent some time in Cairo as a journalist. In 1987 he took a position in Arabic studies at the University of Paris.

H. was a leading poet of the late 1950s, 1960s, and 1970s. He has also edited collections of poetry by Ibrāhīm Nājī (1898–1953) and Khalīl Mutrān (1872–1949) and written critical works. H. had begun writing while still in his village, but the move to the metropolis had a profound effect on him. His first collection,

Madīnah bi-lā qalb (1959; heartless city), was immediately praised, and is the one for which H. is best known. It is a contemplation of the city, and although H. does not pioneer the treatment of this theme—he is preceded by the Iraqi Badr al-Shākir AL-SAYYĀB, for example—it is his own move from village to city that remains an enduring theme throughout his œuvre.

Madīnah bi-lā qalb reflects H.'s feelings of bewilderment and anguish: the poetry is for the most part plaintive, a search for meaning in the urban morass. Alienation, loneliness, and anonymity all find expression in writing that is beginning to show signs of the socialism and Nasserism that was later to emerge in his work. He is exemplary of a generation whose social realism was a reaction against the romanticism of its predecessors.

In three subsequent collections, *Lam yabqā illā al-i'tirāf* (1965; there remained only confession), *Marthiyyat al-'umr al-jamīl* (1973; elegy on the handsome life), and *Ka'ināt mamlakat al-layl* (1978; creatures of the night kingdom), the predicament faced by the estranged inhabitants of the city (now including Paris) is still a concern, but the initial bewilderment is replaced by feelings of unavoidable vulnerability: the citizen is like a "naked corpse devoured by buzzards." Nasser, about whom the poet has already written in earlier works, is also the object of considerable attention. "lb-tada'at al-rihlah" (1971; the journey's begun) from *Marthiyyat al-'umr al-jamīl*, is an elegy, to Nasser or, in H.'s words, "not elegy, but a page in the history of revolution and poetry." It first appeared in a collection edited by H. entitled *Kitabā 'alā qabr 'Abd al-Nāsir* (1971; writings upon the grave of Nasser), which includes poems by other prominent poets including the Syro-Lebanese ADŪNĪS. The influence of the latter's concern with the mythic Near Eastern past, song, and Western (especially American, French, and Spanish) cultural icons is unmistakable.

In the introduction to *Ūrās* (1959; Aurès), a collection of five poems devoted to the Algerian revolution, H. writes that his search for Arab unity found an exemplary prototype in a group of three writers he encountered, which included the contemporary Saudi novelist 'Abd al-Rahmān MUNĪF. The second poem, "Ilā al-ustādh al-'Aqqād" (1960; to Professor 'Aqqād), is a response to that critic's attack on socialism and accusation that poets of the new generation were unaware of the roots of their poetic tradition. It is written on the classical model (hemistich, mono-end rhyme) and mockingly includes several lines consisting entirely of a classical metrical paradigm.

Ashjār al-ismant (1989; trees of cement) is H.'s most recent work. The search for Arab unity and authenticity begun in Cairo and continued in the streets of Paris in *Ka'ināt mamlakat al-layl* remains important, but the poet's attention has turned to the intellectual and personal influences upon him. *Ashjār al-ismant*, which includes a poem dedicated to Munīf, is an introspective collection whose unifying theme is the use and treatment of Time.

Throughout his career, H. has written in a free verse style all his own. It is exemplified by repetition and reiteration of opening phrases and by an erratic metrical and rhyme scheme. His early poetry, that of the newcomer to the city who is startled by its soullessness, is now the poetry of one who has become somewhat inured to its victimization and who has turned inward. His language has become more fractured, and the logic of his metaphors more obscure. Although his collections are not of equal merit, all include examples of the intense, unpredictable, and sustained writing for which he became justly popular. Regrettably, none of his collections exist in translation, but selected poems are anthologized in English and in French.

FURTHER WORKS: *Dīwān* (1973); *Ru'ya hadāriyyah tabaqiyyah li-'urūbat Misr: dirāsah wa-wathā'iq* (1979); *al-Shi'r rafīqī* (1988); *Hadīth al-thalāthah* (1988); *Qasīdat lā: qirā'ah fī shi'r al-tamarrud wa-al-khurūj* (1989); *Ahmad Shawqī* (1992); *As'ilat al-shi'r* (1992)

BIBLIOGRAPHY: Badawi, M. M., *A Critical Introduction to Modern Arabic Poetry* (1975): 218–19; Moreh, S., *Modern Arabic Poetry 1800–1970* (1976): 216–88; Jayyusi, S. K., *Trends and Movements in Modern Arabic Poetry* (1977), Vol. 2: 605–25, 640–57, 709–19; Bencheikh, J., ed., *Terre émeraude: poémes* (1980); Enani, M., ed., *An Anthology of the New Arabic Poetry in Egypt* (1986): 20–25; Allen, R., ed. *Modern Arabic Literature* (1987): 143–46; Jayyusi, S. K., ed., *Modern Arabic Poetry: An Anthology* (1987): 32–33: 261–68; Al-Bazei, S., "Realms of the Wasteland: H. and the Metropolis," *WLT*, 67 (Spring 1993): 306-9

—SHAWKAT M. TOORAWA

HİKMET, Nazım

Turkish poet, dramatist, and novelist, b. 1902, Salonika (now Thessaloniki, Greece); d. 3 June 1963, Moscow, U.S.S.R.

H. studied briefly at the French-language Galatasaray Lycée (Istanbul) and at the Turkish naval academy (Istanbul), which he left because of poor health. From 1922 to 1924 he studied economics and sociology at the Oriental University in Moscow. There he came under the influence of YESENIN, MAYAKOVSKY, and the constructivists.

In 1928, by then a member of the Turkish Communist Party, H. returned to Turkey, where he worked on a newspaper and at various other jobs. In 1938 he was arrested on charges of sedition, convicted by a military tribunal, and sentenced to a prison term of twenty-eight years. After extensive pressure on the Turkish government from intellectuals in Turkey and abroad, he was released in 1950. In 1951 he returned to the Soviet Union. He lived there and in other socialist countries until his death.

In 1950 H. shared the Soviet Union's International Peace Prize with Pablo NERUDA. Since then, his poetry has been translated into many languages. The only complete edition of his poems came out in Bulgaria in the 1960s. The multivolume complete works project, started in Turkey in 1968, remained incomplete by the early 1980s. His plays have enjoyed success in the Soviet Union and other communist countries, and, although those of his plays that were published and produced in Turkey in the 1960s were received with little critical enthusiasm, his earlier plays, of the 1930s, were more popular there. In France and Greece, his poetry and plays enjoy wide popularity. In the 1970s H. received critical praise from some prominent American poets. In Turkey vast numbers of books and articles about H. and his work were published in the late 1970s and early 1980s.

H. was the dominant force in the evolution of socially engaged poetry since the early 1920s in Turkey. He introduced free verse to Turkish poetry; his work merges lyrical, dramatic, and rhetorical elements. Essentially Turkish, yet also universal, he is a romantic as well as a rationalist.

H.'s revolutionary poems first appeared in a variety of periodicals in the 1920s. Soon, volume after volume was appearing rapidly. The last of these before his imprisonment, *Şeyh Bedrettin destani* (1936; *The Epic of Sheik Bedreddin*, 1977), narrates the actions of an early–15th–c. Anatolian religious sect. Committed to ideas of communal ownership, equality, and the brotherhood of man, the group took up arms against the Ottoman sultan, but was defeated by the sultan's armies. The volume is the high point of H.'s achievement and perhaps the best long poem written in Turkish in the 20th c.

The five-volume *Memleketimden insan manzaraları* (1966–67; humanscapes from my country), a sprawling episodic saga of the 20th c. in twenty thousand lines, was to be his magnum opus. Many of the sections and passages in this ambitious work are representative of the best in H.'s art, although the work as a whole did not score an impressive success.

As a playwright, H. made a strong impact with his innovative play *Kafatası* (1932; the skull) and consolidated his reputation with *Unutulan adam* (1935; the forsaken man), which demonstrates the dubiousness of fame and the frequent discrepancy between one's success in the world and one's unhappiness in private life. Applying the techniques of BRECHT's epic theater, H. created characters that are vehicles for his ideology rather than persons of psychological and emotional depth. The actors create their parts on the stage, directed by the author, whose voice cuts into the action.

H.'s satirical comedy *Ivan Ivanovič var miydi yok muydu* (1956; has Ivan Ivanovich lived at all?) enjoyed popularity when it was performed in Moscow in 1956. It has been compared, by Tristan TZARA, to Mayakovsky's *The Bedbug*. Written shortly after Stalin's death, in the de-Stalinization period, it is a virulent attack on the cult of personality, on bureaucracy, and on the new hierarchy that replaced the old. The play lampoons in particular the prevailing official literary criticism in the Soviet Union. If H. took issue with the deficiencies of the Soviet system, he did so out of concern about the dangers by which he saw the cause of communism threatened.

H.'s novels do not compare in quality to his poetry and plays. But his collection of tales, *Sevdalı bulut* (1968; the cloud in love), and his anthology of newspaper columns, *İt ürür kervan yürür* (1965; the dog barks, the caravan moves on), include many effective pieces. His three volumes of collected letters, posthumously published, are not to be overlooked; he emerges in them as a master letter writer.

H. proclaimed in the early 1930s that "the artist is the engineer of the human soul." Although he claimed that he was "only concerned with the literary aspects of Marxism and communism," it was his poetry that is to be credited with inspiring an ever-growing number of communist activists in Turkey. Few poets in the long history of Turkish literature have had a political or literary influence comparable to that of H., internationally the best known of Turkey's poets.

FURTHER WORKS: *Jokond ile si-ya-u* (1929); *835 satır* (1929); *Varan 3* (1930); *1 + 1 = 1* (1930); *Sesini kaybeden şehir* (1931); *Bir ölü evi* (1932); *Benerci kendini niçn öldürdü* (1932); *Gece gelen telgraf* (1932); *Portreler* (1935); *Taranta babu'ya mektuplar* (1935); *Kurtuluş savaşı destanı* (1965); rev. ed., *Kuvâyı milliye*, 1968); *Şu 1941 yılında* (1965); *Saat 21–22 Şiirleri* (1965); *Kan Konuşmaz* (1965); *Yeşil elmalar* (1965); *Ferhad ile Şirin* (1965); *Sabahat* (1965); *İnek* (1965); *Dört hapishaneden* (1966); *Yeni şiirler* (1966); *Rubailer* (1966); *Ocak başında—yolcu* (1966); *Yusuf ile Menofis* (1967); *Yaşamak güzel sey be kardeşim* (1967); *Kemal Tahir'e mahpusaneden mektuplar* (1968); *Oğlum, canim evladim, memedim* (1968); *Son şiirleri* (1970); *Va-Nu'lara mektuplar* (1970); *Henüz vakit varken gülüm* (1976); *Türkiye işçi sınıfına selâm* (1978). FURTHER WORKS IN ENGLISH: *Poems by N. H.* (1954); *Selected Poems* (1967); *The Moscow Symphony and Other Poems* (1970); *The Day before Tomorrow* (1972); *Things I Didn't Know I Loved: Selected Poems of N. H.* (1975); *The Epic of Sheik Bedreddin and Other Poems* (1977)

BIBLIOGRAPHY: Halman, T. S., "N. H.: Lyricist as Iconoclast," *BA*, 43 (1969): 59–64; Baybars, T., translator's notes to "N. H.: Poems," *Delos*, 4 (1970): 192–97; special H. issue, *Europe*, Nos. 547–48 (1974); Dohan, M., "The Poetry of N. H.," *LAAW*, 26 (1975): 24–35; Pres, T. Des, "Poetry and Politics: The Example of N. H.," *Parnassus*, 6, 2 (1978): 7–25

—TALAT SAIT HALMAN

HILDESHEIMER, Wolfgang

German dramatist, novelist, and short-story writer, b. 9 Dec. 1916, Hamburg; d. 21 Aug. 1991

H. spent his formative years in many places: a German-born Jew, he was educated in Holland, England, Palestine (Jerusalem), and Austria, as well as Germany, and worked as a carpenter, scenic designer, painter, and graphic artist. From 1939 to 1945 he worked for the British as an intelligence officer in Palestine; from 1946 to 1949 he served as interpreter at the Nuremberg war crimes trials. Coming late to a literary career, he began to write in Germany in 1950. Since 1957 he has lived in Poschiavo, Switzerland. Along with many of the older postwar German writers, such as Heinrich BÖLL and Günter GRASS, he was a member of Group 47. In addition to other honors, he received the prestigious Georg Büchner Prize in 1966.

H. achieved renown as a prose stylist with his volume of short stories, *Lieblose Legenden* (1952; loveless legends). Characterized by a surrealist sense of the ridiculous and an original droll wit, the collection satirizes cultural pretensions and other absurdities of everyday life and language: in a café, a simple man casually purchases a locomotive; another man brings live owls to Athens, the German equivalent of bringing coals to Newcastle. By taking an improbable premise to its final consequences with unremitting logic, H. creates a world in which familiar habits and norms suddenly become precarious.

H. turned primarily to dramatic works in 1953. His initial success was with the radio play, *Prinzessin Turandot* (1953; Princess Turandot), a reworking of the legend already treated by Gozzi and Schiller. It was adapted for a full stage production by the noted director Gustaf Gründgens, and premiered as *Der Drachenthron* (1955; the dragon throne). In his collection of short plays, *Spiele, in denen es dunkel wird* (1958; plays in which darkness falls), word play and visual gags—which bespeak the influence of IONESCO—form parables to convey the disconnectedness of life. Through a professor's confrontation with a hypothesized primeval bird, H.'s best-received play, *Die Verspätung* (1961; the delay) tests the limits of human imagination, a theme reminiscent of PIRANDELLO. H. is considered Germany's foremost representative of the THEATER OF THE ABSURD.

H. achieved international acclaim with his novel *Tynset* (1965; Tynset). During a sleepless night, the first-person narrator reads a Norwegian train schedule. The name of one town, Tynset, becomes a kind of refrain in his interior accounting, a series of meditations and memories that revolve around the themes of murder and religious faith, and include his experience of the Nazi period. Ultimately, the troubled insomniac has no hope, and no recourse outside of his own mind and its activity in isolation.

As an essayist, H. has written on BECKETT and the Theater of the Absurd, and on JOYCE and Büchner in *Interpretationen* (1969; interpretations). This essayistic bent culminated in his massive and controversial biography *Mozart* (1977; *Mozart*, 1981). Challenging the clichés of Mozart scholarship, he advances his own, psychoanalytically founded analysis of the great genius. A fresh, vivid picture emerges, governed in each detail by H.'s unsentimental intelligence. No carefree darling of the muses, H.'s Mozart is a dark, eccentric figure, one who ultimately eludes understanding.

H. has also distinguished himself as a translator (of Djuna BARNES's *Nightwood*, plays by Sheridan), opera librettist (*Das Ende einer Welt* [1953; the end of a world], music by Heinz Werner Henze), and drama critic.

More than anything else, it is his diversity as an artist that distinguishes H. Aside from literature, the scope of his expertise includes music, theater, and the visual arts. In this sense he is a consummate man of culture, a connoisseur. In all the forms of his artistic activity his work is informed by an intellectual clarity. The occasional murkiness of his prose style is lightened by his flashing wit. This honed edge of his intelligence can be pixieish, somber, or forcefully analytical, depending on the context. His detached cleverness sometimes leads to facile conclusions in his earlier works; in his later works, it is in the service of a greater depth and personal involvement.

FURTHER WORKS: *Das Ende kommt nie* (1952); *Aktion Dschungel* (1952); *Paradies der falschen Vögel* (1953); *An den Ufern der Plotinitza* (1954); *Das Atelierfest* (1955); *Ich heiße Robert Guiscard* (1955); *Ich trage eine Eule nach Athen* (1956); *Begegnung im Balkanexpreß* (1956); *Die Bartschel-Idee* (1957); *Der schiefe Turm von Pisa* (1959); *Nocturno im Grand-Hotel* (1959); *Herrn Walsers Raben* (1960); *Unter der Erde* (1962); *Quo vadis?* (1962); *Nachtstück* (1963); *Vergebliche Aufzeichnungen* (1963); *Betrachtungen über Mozart* (1963); *Monolog* (1964); *Das Opfer Helena* (1965); *Mary Stuart* (1971); *Zeiten in Cornwall* (1971); *Masante* (1973); *Hauskauf* (1974); *Biosphärenklänge* (1977); *Exerzitien mit Papst Johannes* (1979)

BIBLIOGRAPHY: Esslin, M., "W. H.," *The Theater of the Absurd* (1969): 224–26; Glenn, J., "Hofmannsthal, Hacks and H.: Helen in the 20th Century," *Seminar*, 5 (1969): 1–20; Rodewald, D. von, *Über W. H.* (1971); Parkes, S., "West German Drama since the War," in Hayman, R., ed., *The German Theater* (1975): 129–51; Faber, M., "W. H.'s *Mozart* as Meta-Biography," *Biography*, 3 (1980): 201–8

—MARION FABER

HILL, Geoffrey

English poet, b. 18 June 1932, Bromsgrove

H. must have had what one of his poems (hymn V in *Mercian Hymns*, 1971) calls a "rich and desolate childhood" in the English West Midlands. The same poem speaks of his being taken as "a king of some kind, a prodigy, a maimed one." This sense of both rapture and despair animates and informs his first apprentice

pamphlet, *Poems* (1952), published while he was still a student at Keble College, Oxford. These poems showed him to be an audacious new English talent. Through the years H. has won a number of prizes for his small canon of painstaking and well-shaped poems, including the Gregory Award (1961), the Hawthornden Prize (1969), and the Heinemann Award (1972). For some years he has been a senior lecturer in English at the University of Leeds.

H. has published four full-length collections of poetry to date: *For the Unfallen* (1959), *King Log* (1968), *Mercian Hymns*, and *Tenebrae* (1979). He is a bleak, skillful, and profoundly religious poet, one of the few writers of his generation who is heir to a Christian visionary tradition that extends from John Donne's *Holy Sonnets* and Christopher Smart's "Jubilate Agno" through T. S. ELIOT's *Four Quartets* and Allen TATE's *Sonnets at Christmas*. The first poem in *For the Unfallen*, "Genesis," announces that "there is no bloodless myth will hold," and thereafter H.'s fierce, compressed lyrics continually reenact the painful sacrifice of Christ. But most often in H.'s work men are not set free by that sacrifice: the Deity is terse, distant, difficult, and unappeasable, and the various personae of the poems are bewildered survivors. Thus, they witness their own abandonment, forced to watch what often appears as meaningless sacrifice, themselves untransfigured. For H. is a martyrologist. His first subject is human violence and pain, and he discovers the reenactment of sacrifice in the atrocities of war: the Wars of the Roses, the American Civil War, the two world wars. The argument of his poems is that the 26,000 who died in the Battle of Towton in 1461 (see "Funeral Music," 1968) and the 23,000 buried at Shiloh Church in 1862 (see "Locust Songs," 1968), command our belated witness. The grim music of H.'s poetry vigilantly remembers the long suffering and torment of the dead. He is one of the sublime poetic excavators of our unbearable holocausts.

At the center of H.'s work is the sense of a responsibility to a shared human past. The poems invoke the blood-bespattered muse of history. But the poems also know the irony of their own helplessness, their commitment to a reality that evades language. The poet labors at speech in a world where the Logos has lost its meaning, and his laborious task, however difficult and doomed to failure, is to reinfuse meaning into the discredited Word. The task is Promethean, but H. faces it squarely, questioning his own enterprise, but mustering great strength in the process. At the same time, the poems consider their own motives, accusing their maker of voyeurism, of being too in love with the sublime appeal of sacrifice. Finally, however, H.'s poems transcend their own reflexivity. The real quest is to establish "true sequences of pain," and indeed, it is "proper to find value/In a bleak skill, as in the thing restored" ("The Songbook of Sebastian Arruz," 1968). All of H.'s complex subjects are transfigured and illuminated by the intense light of his "bleak skill."

H. is one of the most important poets of his generation. He is also one of the few poets of a presiding Christian imagination still writing poetry of the highest order. He is a religious poet of great intensity, and his rich and desolate poems command our full attention.

FURTHER WORKS: *Somewhere Is Such a Kingdom: Poems 1952–1971* (1975)

BIBLIOGRAPHY: Ricks, C., "Cliché as 'Responsible Speech': G. H.," *London*, Nov. 1964: 96–101; Martin, W., "Beyond Modernism: Christopher Middleton and G. H.," *ConL*, 12 (1971): 420–36; Bloom, H., "Introduction: The Survival of Strong Poetry," in

Somewhere Is Such a Kingdom (1975): xiii—xxv; Hirsch, E., "Flesh and Blood," *SR*, 85 (1976): xcvi–xcviii; special H. issue, *Agenda*, 17, 1 (1979); Brown, M., "Flesh of Abnegation: The Poems of G. H.," *SoR*, 15 (1979): 64–77; Robinson, P., ed., *G. H.: Essays on His Work* (1985)

—EDWARD HIRSCH

HIMES, Chester

American novelist and short-story writer, b. 29 July 1909, Jefferson City, Mo.; d. 12 Nov. 1984, Morava, Spain

H.'s father taught industrial skills at southern black colleges. The family later moved to Cleveland, and H. entered Ohio State University in 1926 with the intention of studying medicine. He did not do well: he turned to sex, liquor, gambling, and crime. In November 1928 H. was arrested for armed robbery, and in 1929, at the age of nineteen, was sent to the Ohio State Penitentiary. While in prison, he began to write short stories about crime, criminals, and life in prison. *Esquire* published the first of several in 1934. After his release in 1936, H. wrote for the Federal Writers' Project and sold more stories to *Esquire* and *Coronet*.

H.'s early novels—*If He Hollers Let Him Go* (1945), *Lonely Crusade* (1947), and *The Third Generation* (1954)—treat the themes of black bourgeois life, interracial sex, and the psychological importance of the degree of blackness—that is, the darkness or lightness of skin; in the first two novels he also deals with the American labor movement. Using this subject matter, he emphasized the bitterness in the efforts of blacks to come to terms with their roots and their environment, especially in *The Third Generation*, which is autobiographical.

Seventeen years after his release from prison, H. wrote a novel based on his seven years there—*Cast the First Stone* (1953). *The Primitive* (1955), a very autobiographical work, H. considers his best novel. It relates the drunken interracial love affair of a black failed author and a white woman executive.

H. moved to Paris in 1953 and later to the south of Spain. His critical and popular acceptance was far greater in France than in America. The French translation (1958) of *For Love of Imabelle* (1957) won a prize in France. This was the first of a string of detective stories, and H. was, in fact, known in France primarily as a detective-story writer. The series featured two black detectives assigned to Harlem, Grave Digger Jones and Coffin Ed Johnson. The best known of this series in America is *Cotton Comes to Harlem* (1965; first pub. in French translation 1964): thieves steal from thieves as everyone scrambles for $87,000 hidden in a bale of cotton. This novel was made into a Hollywood film (1970), the success of which rekindled some American interest in H.'s work in general.

Blind Man with a Pistol (1969; retitled *Hot Day, Hot Night*), H.'s eighth detective novel, picks up the trail of the same detectives but turns to harsher tones, and the mood is in many ways reminiscent of H.'s earliest novels. H. handles the violence of frustrated, angry people and the cast of shadowy Harlem characters with skillful surrealism comparable to sections of Ralph ELLISON's *Invisible Man*.

An atypical novel, *Pinktoes* (1961), shows H.'s ability to write satire, and to be more hilarious than harsh. It is a farcical portrayal of Harlem street life, a catalogue of the exploiters and the exploited. Harlem's hustlers, pimps, prostitutes, gamblers, and store-front preachers—its flamboyant characters—are brought together with downtown whites by a fat, loveable, black party-giver who believes that the best way to better interracial understanding is for people to know each other sexually.

During much of the 1970s H. was ill, living in Spain. This decade saw the publication of his two-volume autobiography, *The Quality of Hurt* (1973) and *My Life of Absurdity* (1976). His reputation has been made in France and rests on his series of detective novels; in his native U.S. he unfortunately remains largely unread.

FURTHER WORKS: *The Crazy Kill* (1959); *The Real Cool Killers* (1959); *All Shot Up* (1960); *The Big Gold Dream* (1960); *Une affair de viol* (1963); *The Heat's On* (1966); *Run Man Run* (1966); *Black on Black: Baby Sister and Selected Writings* (1973)

BIBLIOGRAPHY: Micha, R., "Les paroissiens de C. H.," *TM*, 20 (1965): 1507–23; Margolies, E., "Race and Sex: The Novels of C. H.," *Native Sons: A Critical Study of Twentieth-Century Negro American Authors* (1968): 87–101; Margolies, E., "The Thrillers of C. H.," *SBL*, 1, 2 (1970): 1–11; special H. issue, *Black World*, Mar. 1972; Nelson, R., "Domestic Harlem: The Detective Fiction of C. H.," *VQR*, 48 (1972): 260–76; Lundquist, J., *C. H.* (1976); Milliken, S., *C. H.: A Critical Appraisal* (1976); Muller, G. H., *C. H.* (1989)

—DAVID BAKISH

HINDE, Thomas

(pseud. of Sir Thomas Willes Chitty) English novelist, b. 2 March 1926, Felixstowe

Son of the headmaster of a boys' school, H. went to Winchester, served three years in the Royal Navy, and then read modern history at Oxford. After a variety of jobs—including a brief period operating the Big Dipper at Batter-sea Fun Fair and seven years as a public relations officer for Shell Oil—he settled into a writing career, with intervals of university lecturing. He inherited his title on the death of his father in 1971.

His first novel, *Mr. Nicholas* (1952), employed the bitter conflicts within one family to epitomize the social changes going on all over England. The domineering father, Mr. Nicholas, expects his son Peter, an Oxford undergraduate, to be interested in cricket and the Conservative Party; the conflict between them brings out the fading nature of middle-class ideals of gentility, and the strong resentment of the younger generation against anything that appears bogus. H. sounded a new note with this novel, a note soon to be taken up by Kingsley AMIS, John WAIN, and the other "Angry Young Men"; he himself, however, was not angry but cool, detached, and observant.

As one critic has said, *Mr. Nicholas* was so good that its very excellence seemed to put a curse on H.'s career. His greatest gift has been described as an ability to suggest emptiness. Even Samuel BECKETT cannot make such a theme consistently interesting. The difficulties H. had with it became apparent in his second novel, *Happy as Larry*. Larry Vincent, a typical antihero of the 1950s, drinks heavily, drifts from job to job, and is aimless and irresponsible; he can find no values in society worth upholding, and none even worth attacking. As a consequence, he is not sufficiently important or engaging to make the novel seem worthwhile.

H. has extended his range beyond the rural England he knows best to African and American settings; *High* (1968) and *Generally a Virgin* (1972) both deal with campus life in American universities. Yet he is more interested in states of mind than in setting and plotting; his plots are sometimes thin and obvious. Remaining detached and impersonal, he concentrates on the job at hand, often the depiction of the mind of a first-person narrator who is warped and limited. In *The Day the Call Came* (1964), for example, the contemporary popularity of spy stories provides a background; this call comes to and is the product of a disturbed mind, but the point apparently being made is that the only call a modern man can receive and acknowledge is a call to murder someone, without a reason why. The closest H. can come to a major theme is perhaps to parody it.

Despite his intelligence and his disciplined approach to the novelist's art, familiar criticisms continue to be made—that his central characters are shadowy figures, that he takes a theme on the grand scale and underplays it to a whisper, and that he has not found the major subject for which his talents fit him. In a sense, he has not gone beyond *Mr. Nicholas*; at his best he gave a brilliant rendering of life in the 1950s.

FURTHER WORKS: *For the Good of the Company* (1961); *A Place Like Home* (1962); *The Cage* (1962); *Ninety Double Martinis* (1963); *Spain* (1963); *Games of Chance* (1965); *The Village* (1966); *Bird* (1970); *Agent* (1974); *Our Father* (1975); *On Next to Nothing: A Guide to Survival Today* (1976, with Susan Hinde); *The Great Donkey Walk* (1977, with Susan Hinde); *Daymare* (1980); *Sir Henry and Sons* (1980)

BIBLIOGRAPHY: Allsop, K., *The Angry Decade* (1958): 69–73; Podhoretz, N., *Doings and Undoings* (1958): 171–73; Gindin, J., *Postwar British Fiction* (1962): 94–95; Allen, W., *Tradition and Dream* (1964): 278–79; "Forms of Insanity," *TLS* (27 Oct. 1966): 973; "Sherry Pie," *TLS* (9 June 1972): 649

—D. J. DOOLEY

HINDI LITERATURE

See Indian Literature and Pacific Islands Literature

HINDKO LITERATURE

See Pakistani Literature

HINOJOSA-SMITH, Rolando

American novelist, essayist, and poet, b. 21 Jan. 1929, Mercedes, Texas

Although a native-born American, H.-S. was raised a few miles north of the Mexican-U.S. border in an area that is more Mexican than American in its outlook and customs. From his earliest days, H.-S., whose mother's family were Anglos transplanted from Illinois, was bilingual in English and Spanish. H.-S. attended private schools, where Spanish was the language of instruction. Following two years of military service, H.-S. attended the University of Texas but was soon recalled by the army to serve in the Korean War. Upon discharge, he again attended the University of Texas, receiving a bachelor's degree in Spanish in 1953. He taught on the high school level, after which he worked for four years as a laborer before returning to secondary school teaching. In 1963 he received a master's degree in Spanish from New Mexico Highlands University, then entered the University of Illinois at Urbana-Champaign, where he received a Ph.D. in Spanish in 1969. He taught at San Antonio's Trinity University, where novelist Tómas Rivera (1935-1984) encouraged his writing. H.-S. taught and was an administrator at Texas A&M University for six years, becoming vice president for academic affairs in 1976. In 1977 he became chair of the Chicano Studies Program at the University of Texas at Austin.

The "Klail City Death Trip" series, begun in 1973 with the publication of *Estampas del valle y otras obras: Sketches of the Valley and Other Works*—published in an English revision as *The Valley* (1983)—is a large, still unfinished work reminiscent of Marcel PROUST's *Remembrance of Things Past*, a huge literary work that consists of seven novels, all parts of the whole. H.-S. has completed eight discrete smaller works, parts of the larger work as he conceives it. Some of the total work is in Spanish, some in English. Although most of these works can be broadly designated novels, one important section, *Korean Love Songs from Klail City Death Trip* (1980), consists largely of poetry.

The first two major works of the series, *Estampas del valle y otras obras* and *Klail City y sus alrededores* (1976; *Klail City: A Novel*, 1987), were written in Spanish and translated into English. Inasmuch as the third contribution to the larger work, *Korean Love Songs*, was set in Asia but was populated largely by people from Klail City, H.-S. chose to write it in English. However, his next contribution to the larger work, *Mi Querido Rafa* (1981; *Dear Rafe*, 1985), set around H.-S.'s native Mercedes, was written in Spanish with H.-S. himself doing the English translation. His *Rites and Witnesses* (1982) and *Partners in Crime: A Rafe Buenrostro Mystery* (1985) are both set in H.-S.'s fictional Belken County and are both written in English, whereas his *Claros varones de Belken: Fair Gentlemen of Belken County* (1986) is written in both English and Spanish, with Spanish on one page and English on the facing page. This intermixture of Spanish and English throughout H.-S.'s work is significant because it reflects the linguistic intermixture within the community he focuses upon.

Throughout his career, H.-S.'s vision has focused on understanding society, notably the Hispanic-American community from which he comes, through understanding its common people. He is overwhelmingly concerned with depicting community, using characters always to contribute to a broad understanding of the community. Through his characters, one gains insight into what it meant to be a Mexican-American in South Texas in the last half of the 20th c. Like William FAULKNER's fictional Yoknapatawpha County in Mississippi, H.-S.'s Belken County provides the microcosm in which the author achieves his overall end of portraying a community through its people. In order to emphasize community over individuals, however, H.-S. often intentionally blurs relationships among characters to strengthen the overall impression of the community of Klail City.

H.-S. often uses a loose interview style in his writing, showing his characters in different lights as various people—in *Becky and Her Friends* (1990), for example, some twenty-seven individuals—offer their insights into a character's personality. Inconsistencies occur in the telling of H.-S.'s tales, which the author freely acknowledges, explaining that he is unwilling to manipulate his characters in order to give them greater consistency. Because most of his sketches are brief, H.-S.'s readers never gain a deep psychological understanding of his major characters. Despite this, anyone who has read his books develops a strong sense of the Tex-Mex community, which is his intended focus overall. The voices that inform H.-S.'s writing are often contrapuntal, but out of this counterpoint emerges a dramatic tension that sustains his work.

FURTHER WORKS: *Generaciones, Notas, y Brechas/Generations, Notes and Trails* (1978); *Agricultural Workers of the Rio Grande and Rio Bravo Valleys* (1984); *The Useless Servants* (1993); *El Condado de Belken-Klail City* (1994)

BIBLIOGRAPHY: Tatum, C. M., *Chicano Literature* (1982): 120-24; Saldívar, J. D., ed., *The R. H. Reader: Essays Historical and Critical* (1985)

—R. BAIRD SHUMAN

HIPPIUS, Zinaida

(also spelled Gippius) Russian poet, short-story writer, dramatist, and critic (also writing in French), b. 20 Nov. 1869, Belev; d. 9 Sept. 1945, Paris, France

Born into a cultured family of Western European stock, H. received a broad education from private tutors. Vivacious and beautiful, she married Dmitry MEREZHKOVSKY, a prominent SYMBOLIST theorist, novelist, and poet. From 1905 to 1917 their apartment in St. Petersburg was a mecca for like-minded poets and philosophers.

Greatly concerned with the Orthodox church, which they believed had allied itself with the earthly forces of autocracy and hypocrisy, H. and her husband founded a new faith. Universal love in Christ was to be the ruling principle, and the members wrote the liturgies and prayers for the services, which were patterned after the love feasts of the early Christians. These religious activities, described in their writings and memoirs, were continued in Paris, where the Merezhkovskys emigrated in 1919. Despite their great dedication, the church attracted few followers and did not survive their deaths.

H. subscribed to the symbolist creed that the purpose of art, particularly poetry, is to fuse the material and otherworldly spheres and so to lead man to a higher level of awareness. H. suffered great anguish when mystical ecstasy gave way to despair at the impossibility of union with God; many of her finest poems are distillations of those moments of agony, when isolation and self-disgust overwhelmed her. Because of this poetry, in which she describes her soul as "shameless, base, and sluggish," H. has sometimes been labeled a Decadent. Beside these poems, however, are to be found startling, vivid lyrics composed at the height of divine guidance and religious ecstasy. This dichotomy is basic to H.'s *Weltanschauung* and characteristic of the figures in her narratives and in her lyrical persona.

H.'s striving for otherworldliness and for a universal religion is the underlying theme of all her work. Her early poems—for example, "Belaya odezhda" (1904; "A White Garment," 1978)—are structurally and thematically like prayers, owing a great deal to the Orthodox liturgy. "Svet" (1922; "The Light," 1978), with its repeated long, dark vowels and its mood of prostrate supplication, is a litany of her unworthiness and failure to attain Christian simplicity and purity of heart.

H.'s technical skill was prodigious, and her daring yet polished lines contributed much to the liberation of Russian poetry from traditional prosody. To suggest the structure of a prayer, song, or verbal exchange, or to enhance the emotive force of her lyrics, she freely combined different rhythms or rhyme schemes.

Allegorical imagery is central to much of her poetry. In "O drugom" (1904; about something else) she offers herself as a candle before God. The poem itself as it is laid out on the printed page resembles a candle burning in a holder.

H.'s prose writings are primarily short stories. Although they are not on a level with her poetry, they too are spiritual and philosophical. The stories in such collections as *Novye lyudi: Rasskazy, pervaya kniga* (1894; new people: stories, first book) and *Zerkala: Vtoraya kniga rasskazov* (1898; mirrors: second book of stories) show characters struggling to free themselves from mundane concerns, petty pursuits, and loneliness, and to attain a synthesis of the intellectual, artistic, and spiritual spheres of life. The Dostoevskian dilemma—how to reconcile God's perfect wisdom and mercy with the evil in the world—persists in her stories as in her poems. Not surprisingly, H.'s characters often seem rather abstract, and some stories lapse into tendentiousness.

Under the pseudonym Anton Krayny, among others, H. wrote highly personal, trenchant, and perspicacious reminiscences of literary acquaintances. In one such sketch, "Moy lunny drug" (1925; my moonlight friend), she recalls her friendship with Alexandr BLOK and their common efforts to attain spiritual fulfillment through poetry.

Although H. considered her religious activities the most worthwhile accomplishment of her life, she is better recognized for her highly innovative, polished, passionate lyrics and for her imaginative handling of age-old philosophical questions.

FURTHER WORKS: *Pobediteli* (1898); *Svyataya krov* (1902); *Tretya kniga rasskazov* (1902); *Sobranie stikhov: 1889–1903* (1904); *Aly mech: Rasskazy: Chetvyortaya kniga* (1906); *Chyornoe po belomu: Pyataya kniga rasskazov* (1908); *Le tsar et la révolution* (1908); *Literaturny dnevnik, 1899–1907* (1908); *Makov tsvet* (1908); *Sobranie stikhov: Kniga vtoraya, 1908–1909* (1910); *Chyortova kukla: Zhizneopisanie v 33–kh glavakh* (1911); *Literaturny dnevnik* (1911); *Lunnye muravi: Shestaya kniga rasskazov* (1912); *Roman-Tsarevich* (1913); *Kak my voinam pisali i chto oni nam otvechali* (1915); *Zelyonoe koltso* (1916; *The Green Ring*, 1920); *Poslednie stikhi: 1914–1918* (1918); *Dnevnik Z. N. G.* (1921); *Nebesnye slova i drugie rasskazy* (1921); *Tsarstvo Anti-Khrista* (1921); *Varshavsky dnevnik* (1921); *Stikhi: Dnevnik, 1911–1921* (1922); *Zhivye litsa* (1925); *Sinyaya kniga: Peterburgsky dnevnik 1914–18* (1929); *Chto delat russkoy emigratsii* (1930); *Siania* (1938); *Dmitry Merezhkovsky* (1951); *Dnevnik 1933 goda* (1968); *Epokha Mira Iskusstva* (1968); *Posledny krug* (1968); *Contes d'amour, 1893–1904* (1969); *Korichnevaya tetrad* (1970); *O byvshem* (1970); *Vybor?* (1970); *Zhenshchiny i zhenskoe* (1970); *Reklama: Otryvok s romana* (1971); *Stikhotvorenia i poemy* (1972); *Pisma k Berberovoy i Khodasevichu* (1978). FURTHER WORKS IN ENGLISH: *Selected*

Works of Z. H. (1972); *Intellect and Ideas in Action: Selected Correspondence of Z. H.* (1972); *Between Paris and St. Petersburg: Selected Diaries of Z. H.* (1975)

BIBLIOGRAPHY: Maslenikov, O., *The Frenzied Poets: Andrey Biely and the Russian Symbolists* (1952): 128–45; Pachmuss, T., *Z. H.: An Intellectual Profile* (1971); Matich, O., *Paradox in the Religious Poetry of Z. G.* (1972); Zlobin, V., *A Difficult Soul: Z. G.* (1980)

—MARY CARROLL SMITH

HISTORICISM

Broadly defined, historicism can refer to any method whereby we seek to understand the artifacts and traces of the past and our relationship to that past. According to a prominent figure of the so-called new historicism, Stephen Greenblatt (b. 1943), it begins "with a desire to speak with the dead." As recently as the mid-1970s, historicism occupied, under the rubric "historical criticism," the place of a neutral-seeming adjective, one of many possible modifiers for the activity called literary criticism. In the early 1980s, the response of various literary historians to literary theory led not only to historical criticism's acquisition of its new, more polemical suffix—historicism—but also to its splitting into two basic kinds: new and old.

Because the terms new and old historicism are now in common parlance, and because they do offer convenient labels for some differing critical assumptions, they seem to be worth using, but only with the understanding that their use encourages biases of the kind that the new historicists themselves struggle to make us see. Just as the concept "Renaissance" necessitated the envisioning of a preceding period, the Middle Ages, which it could claim to revise, the new historicism was obliged to create its own ugly sister, old historicism. New historicists campaign against their inheritance of such notions of progress, but at the same time tolerate and even enjoy the irony of being called new. In any case, practitioners of the new historicism would agree that the labeling process erroneously suggests a unified school of thought, a doctrine, where, instead, we have only a related set of themes, attitudes, and preoccupations—various historicisms.

A good way to think of the new historicism is as a common label for the renewed interest of literary critics in history. This is to suggest, of course, that literary critics have gone through an essentially antihistorical phase. Thus, to understand historicism, new or old, one needs to be aware of the New Critics' and other formalists' (structuralism) case against historical approaches to literary analysis, and of the poststructuralist argument against the concept of history itself.

What explains the renewed interest of literary critics during the last decade or so in historical analysis? What caused that interest to decline in the first place? And how and who did historicism change in its process of restoration after the New Critical and structuralist interregnum? The last question is the sort new historicists tend not to ask. A striking tendency in their practice is the avoidance of both causal analysis and the positing of linear sequences of development. New historicists don't so much deny the value of studying change as they defend their wish to see some things that the conception of history as progress seems to them to obscure.

A new historicist conviction that encourages this essentially synchronic as opposed to diachronic approach to history is that aesthetic representations (texts) should be read not only in relation to each other but to nonliterary and nondiscursive texts (events) as well. The method of the new historicist is thus what has been called cultural montage. Carefully avoiding words implying causal relationships, new historicists speak of reading texts "against" or "with" other "cultural practices," a term taken from anthropology, specifically from the work of Clifford Geertz (b. 1926), who, along with Michel FOUCAULT, has had a major impact on new historicist thinking.

The kind of overlapping that the new historicist tends to find between an event in the culture and a text can tend toward the bizarre—for example, the trial of hermaphrodites read against Shakespeare's *Twelfth Night*; anti-Semitic charges of kidnappings and forced circumcisions by Jews in Renaissance England read against the pound of flesh in *The Merchant of Venice*; accounts of Queen Elizabeth's private showings of her collection of miniatures read with the English sonnet. This kind of new historicist method aims at seeing things in cross section; like Geertz's "thick description," it captures a given moment in spatial rather than in linear terms. Some scholars have noted in this respect that new historicism models itself not on the forward momentum of narrative, like traditional history, but on the vertical organization of the lyric poem.

Thick description represents a reaction against the fairly simple reflectionist model of the historical criticism that the New Critical movement of the 1930s worked to supplant. In this historical model, the critic would point, for example, to instances of anti-Semitism in the culture and use these to "explain" *The Merchant of Venice* as a reflection of a cultural reality. Literature, in this model, mirrored and imitated life. And so it followed that to understand literature one needed to get out of the text into its context—that is, the relevant "facts" about the culture revealed to us through historical research.

By contrast the new historicism posits a more complex relationship between literary texts and history, one in which neither is simply a mirror or background for the other. The new historicists argue that literary representations don't simply spring from what is happening in the culture, but that texts also make things happen because they shape human consciousness. Consequently, history is not used only in the service of interpreting the text, nor is the text "used" to explain history. Instead, both a particular cultural phenomenon (for instance, the trial of hermaphrodites) and particular kinds of literature (gender benders like *Twelfth Night* or *A Midsummer Night's Dream*) together illuminate the complex relationship a text has to other processes in the culture. So, for example, Roy Strong's (b. 1935) influential study *The Cult of Elizabeth* (1977) attempts to show how court pageantry and literature functioned similarly to enhance the power of the queen.

Historical approaches to literature like Greenblatt's or Strong's suggest that a direction of the new historicism is not only to move away from a simple reflectionist model, but to overhaul the entire text/context model so as to break down the traditional distinguishing of literary text and history as foreground and background. Yet, as recently as 1975, handbooks of literary terms defined historical criticism as having two largely unquestioned aims, both rooted in a reflectionist way of reading the relationship between text and context: to locate the meaning of a work of literature in terms of the social and historical context in which it was produced and, further, to recreate for readers the meaning and value the work may have possessed for its own time. The slightly but tellingly revised version of these two objectives in new historicist terminology is: refiguring the sociocultural field in which texts were originally produced, and studying the uses to which the present has put its version of the past.

The new historicist critique of traditional historicist aims is not entirely new. However, the New Critics, who in the 1930s attacked traditional literary historical objectives, did so, they thought, in order to free the text by explaining it in isolation from historical, biographical or other contexts. Alienated by what seemed to them a deforming pressure to place literature at the service of ethical and political contexts—from seeing Dickens, for example, as an exhibitor of manly virtues or Balzac as representative of a decadent bourgeoisie—the New Critics proposed seeing a work of literature in its own terms, as a more or less self-contained entity operating according to its own rules. Although new historicists tend to deride New Criticism for its supposedly "empty" formalism, New Criticism interestingly anticipates certain new historicist strategies, and is thus worth looking at. New historicism, much more than the New Criticism, stresses the importance of historicizing, but like New Criticism, it rejects the traditional serial, progression-oriented notion of history and the idea of a simple relationship between historical facts and the meaning of literary texts.

The differing orientations of historical criticism and New Criticism are evident if one compares a classic from each, for example, E. M. W. Tillyard's (1889–1962) *The Elizabethan World Picture* (1944), a classic work of older historical criticism, with William Empson's (b. 1906) basically New Critical study, *Seven Types of Ambiguity* (1930; rev. 2nd ed., 1947; rev. 3rd ed., 1953). Tillyard seeks to explain central features of English Renaissance literature by relating them to a specific cultural context—in this case, Elizabethan cosmology and the essentially hierarchical views that it seemed to Tillyard to have engendered. So, for example, when Hamlet complains to Ophelia about man's awkward placement between two realms or ways of being ("What should such fellows as I do crawling between heaven and earth?"), Tillyard would point to the elaborate ranking of angel, human, animal, vegetable, mineral, etc. to be found in Elizabethan philosophy, science, and natural history (the Great Chain of Being) and assert the explanatory power of this context. Readers are thus enjoined, though indirectly, from making any "ahistorical" associations with Hamlet's phrase, for example, a Freudian one. (Freudian readings of literature, like structuralist readings, tend to be ahistorical, as their concern is with common features of the human psyche throughout time. Although historical critics readily allowed that the psychic structures Freud described didn't need the advent of Freud to exert their pressure on literature, historicist critics stress that modern notions of the meaning and importance of Freudian psychology are not readily transferable to the 16th c., and can, in fact, prevent us from seeing another century's values and ways of thinking.)

The New Critic's primary objection to Tillyard's and others' recourse to history as explanatory key is that such an interpretation too quickly focuses attention on information outside the text, with the result that the text's actual language—Hamlet's speech—is inadequately mined for meaning. To the New Critic, historical criticism at its worst replaced a rich and complex reading experience with a facile and ultimately rather arbitrary "answer."

The title alone of Empson's *Seven Types of Ambiguity* suggests its New Critical difference from Tillyard's traditional historicism. A typical new historicist title is Stephen Greenblatt's (b. 1943) *Shakespearean Negotiations: The Circulation of Social Energy in Renaissance England* (1988). Tillyard's title, *The Elizabethan World Picture*, names not a tendency of a literary text, but a broad cultural phenomenon. In fact, it posits with striking confidence its author's ability to name *the* worldview of an entire culture. As we shall see, this is the new historicist's primary objection to uses of history like Tillyard's—that they create too homogeneous and thus too exclusive a picture, a tendency new historicists call "totalizing." New historicists prefer the analysis of local conflicts over an attempt to construct any holistic account of the elements directing a whole society. Empson's typically New Critical title does not aim, as does Tillyard's, at establishing a broad definition of a culture. Rather, the book applies the same basic method of analysis to works from many different historical periods, thus demoting the importance of historical contextualizing.

In its focus on categorizing and on a feature of language rather than a philosophical system, Empson's title announces an apparently more limited aim than Tillyard's. Interestingly, however, Empson's title reveals only slightly less confidence in its author's authority than Tillyard's, despite the reduced area of analysis Empson claims as his own—a tendency of literary texts rather than an all-encompassing worldview. Lack of a definite article before the Seven in Empson's title, for example, acknowledges that the author may have missed a few types; and yet the title's assertion that its author can comfortably reduce literary complexity to seven manageable categories remains. In fact, Empson's book, which virtually defines literature in terms of its deliberate exploitation of ambiguity as a means of positing the irreducible complexity of human and aesthetic experience, goes well beyond an exposition of technique into a worldview of its own, though Empson doesn't name it as such, nor does he historicize it in terms of his own century's experience.

Predictably, the penchant of New Criticism and related critical orientations—formalism, structuralism, and deconstruction—for formal analysis and for the elevation of literary texts over other kinds of discourse and cultural practices impelled succeeding generations to examine the very thing that the New Critics marginalized—the connection between literature and culture. To clarify this progression, it may be helpful to offer a new historicist critique of the preceding analysis. The explanation I have provided of Tillyard's and Empson's book titles is essentially New Critical in technique. I try to draw my conclusions from the language itself. I supply no biographical information about Tillyard or Empson, nor do I look for other events and practices in their culture that might help to explain the attitudes they assume. In other words, I choose not to historicize Tillyard and Empson's critical practice. My formalist orientation moves toward a deconstruction formalism when I note that Empson's insistence on categorizing and labeling contradicts (deconstructs) his claim for the value and inescapability of a complex (ambiguous) approach to experience. As New Critic in technique and old historicist in purpose (that being to explain the evolution of the term "historicism"), I walk around but carefully avoid most of the issues that the new historicists invoke in their critique of both New Criticism and the older kind of literary historicism.

Summed up concisely, albeit somewhat reductively, the new historicist claims against the New Criticism and ensuing formalisms are that these critical practices are apolitical, sexist, elitist, and hermetic. New historicists argue that neither literature nor the act of studying it can be separated from ideology. The challenge of the new historicism to the political detachment of the New Critics draws on Foucault in its insistence that a work of literature survives not because of its supposed universality, but because it continues to serve powerful interests. In this respect the guilding philosophical light of the new historicism moves from the humanist's choice—Locke—to Hobbes, for whom everything could be revealed as a sign of power.

Another blow to the claims of New Criticism is the current insistence of historicism on the historical positioning not only of the text, but of the critic herself. An implicit assumption of traditional historicism is that historians could arrive at similar and demonstrably true readings of texts and of the past regardless of their own experiences. In line with the new historicist argument that all claims to objectivity are inevitably illusory, women, for example, have questioned the categories of both literary and social history, and the notions of progress and periodizing that an older historicism put in place. Joan Kelly-Gadol (b. 1928) has thus invited a rethinking of traditional literary historical categories by suggesting that there was, in a sense, no Renaissance for women.

A good example of a basically new historicist, as well as feminist critique of old historicist premises can be seen in Toril Moi's (dates n.a.) attack on reflectionist readings of the literature of courtly love. Old historicists C. S. LEWIS and D. W. Robertson (b. 1914), among others, approached medieval and Renaissance courtly-love poetry largely by attempting to discover whether or not courts of love existed, that is, as historical "facts." Each of these scholars then analyzed courtly-love literature in morally evaluative terms by trying to decide to what extent courtly love was bad (or good) for the culture and for the literature that presumably reflected it. Moi asserts that it doesn't matter whether or not courts of love existed. Instead, she directs readers to consider other questions. Why, she asks, would someone want to invent a literature of this sort? Who benefited from it and why? What system of power relationships did the literature of courtly love negotiate, for example, the struggle of the Norman aristocracy to assert its cultural superiority over the rising English middle class, and/or the struggle of one gender, men, to define themselves by inscribing feared traits onto a distanced other—the alternately loved and loathed courtly love lady? Moi's new historicist position thus insinuates that literary texts produce at least as much as they reflect culture.

An argument like Moi's challenges not only the aims and methods of traditional literary historians but the discipline of history itself. First, she discounts the value of a long-standing (basically reflective) means of arriving at an understanding of older texts. Then, further, by pointing to the difficulty of locating a boundary between fact and representation, she questions the value of traditional kinds of historical evidence, and even the historian's claim to the discovery of facts. In her argument, Moi pursues another key new historicist strategy—she historicizes the critical engagement itself, questioning the possibility that critics can climb out of their own historical positions to arrive at an objective depiction of reality.

In this vein, other obvious influences away from the New Criticism and toward the assumptions of new historicist practice emerge in the related trends of multiculturalism and the reader-response school of criticism, both of which aim to diversify literary interpretation in the academy. Obviously, the multicultural perspective creates formidable challenges to modes of criticism that assume there is some ideal reading to be gleaned from literary texts and that meaning finally inheres in the object (the text) and not also in its readers.

One charge provoked by new historicist challenges like Moi's, along with other destabilizing trends in contemporary theory, is that they are so obsessively antiauthoritarian that they celebrate

anarchy in the name of freedom. To E. D. Hirsch (b. 1928), for example, the insistence of some theorists on the idea that meaning is always historical opens the door to complete relativism from which historical reconstruction of authors' intended meanings is one of the only antidotes. Thus, for Hirsch, the older historicism's pressure on readers to construe meaning in accordance with a text's probable authorial intentions is an admittedly arbitrary but defensible tactic. Hirsch argues that without such an interpretive "norm" we are doomed to critical anarchy. New historicists and other contemporary theorists counter that reconstruction of an author's probable intention goes on within the critic's own historically and linguistically conditioned frames of perception so that the traditional historian's humanist goal of arriving at an unchanging, universal, and sublimely disinterested reading of a text is impossible. Multicultural and reader-response schools of criticism are as interested as Hirsch in the limits and validity of interpretation, but they argue from the opposite point of view—that relativity breeds complexity, not chaos.

The new historicism has its critics on the left as well as the right. Scholars whose orientation directs them to the study of cultural change and its causes—feminists, for example—take issue with the new historicism's lack of attention to the possibility and means of changing the status quo. This criticism in particular promises continued negotiation between the perspectives of the older historicism and the new.

In sum, approaches to literature that are threatening or inhibiting to some readers are revelatory and liberating to others. Such is the case, for example, with contemporary theory's assertion that selves and texts are not autonomous, but are instead, at least in part, created by both overt and obscure cultural forces. The new historicism accepts the implications of this view when it argues against literary interpretation as a means of accessing unchanging truths and acknowledges that literary historical critiques of cultural and textual practices are neither objective nor free from the conditions they describe. If, as Greenblatt observed, historicism begins "with a desire to speak with the dead," its results may be less a revivification of those voices from the past than a clearer hearing of ourselves in the present.

BIBLIOGRAPHY: Hirsch, E. D., Jr., *The Aims of Interpretation* (1976); Barthes, R., *Image-Music-Text* (1977); Bridenthal, R. and C. Koonz, eds., *Becoming Visible: Women in European History* (1977); Strong, R. C., *The Cult of Elizabeth* (1977); Iser, W., *The Act of Reading: A Theory of Aesthetic Response* (1978); Fish, S. E., *Is There a Text in This Class?* (1980); Greenblatt, S. J., *Renaissance Self-Fashioning, From More to Shakespeare* (1980); Lentricchia, F., *After the New Criticism* (1980); Tompkins, J., ed., *Reader Response Criticism: From Formalism to Post-Structuralism* (1980); Eagleton, T., *Literary Theory: An Introduction* (1983); Geertz, C., *Local Knowledge* (1983); Selden, R., *A Reader's Guide to Contemporary Literary Theory* (1985); Aers, D., ed., *Medieval Literature: Criticism, Ideology, and History* (1986); Ferguson, M. W., et al., eds., *Rewriting the Renaissance: The Discourses of Sexual Difference in Early Modern Europe* (1986); Dubrow, H., and R. Strier, eds., *The Historical Renaissance: New Essays on Tudor and Stuart Literature and Culture* (1988); Lodge, D., ed., *Modern Criticism and Theory, a Reader* (1988); Summers, C. J., and T. L. Pebworth, eds., "Historicism, New and Old: Excerpts from a Panel Discussion," *"The Muse's Common-Weale": Poetry and Politics in the Seventeenth Century* (1988): 207–17; Liu, A., "The Power of

Formalism," *ELH*, 56, 4 (Winter 1989): 721–71; Veeser, H. A., ed., *The New Historicism* (1989)

—JILL STEPHEN

HJARTARSON, Snorri

Icelandic poet, b. 22 April 1906, Hvanneyri; d. 27 Dec. 1980, Reykjavík

H.'s father was the principal of a school, and H. grew up in a prosperous and cultured home. He enrolled in secondary school in Reykjavík, but contracted tuberculosis and never completed the course of study. After spending some time in Danish sanatoriums recuperating, H. studied to be a painter in Copenhagen and later in Oslo in 1931–32.

H.'s first published work was a novel in Norwegian, *Høit flyvver ravnen* (1934; high flies the raven), which dealt with a young Icelandic artist and his struggle in choosing between dedicating his life to art and following an ordinary profession. Although this novel won favorable notices, H. was to write no other work of fiction; he returned to Iceland and became a librarian in Reykjavík, a position he held from 1939 to 1966.

Despite his limited output of verse—only four books: *Kvæði* (1944; poems), *Á Gnitaheiði* (1952; on Gnita Heath), *Lauf og stjörnur* (1966; leaves and stars), and *Hauströkkrið yfir mer* (1979; autumn twilight)—H. has been a leading voice in Icelandic poetry since World War II. When the modernist school burst upon the scene in Iceland in the 1940s with free forms and complex symbolism, he struck a compromise between old tradition and new style. Thus he uses conventional rhyme schemes but varies them at times. His imagery is modernistic, and shows influences from his background in painting. By reconciling Icelandic tradition in poetry and modernism, he set an example followed by many other contemporary poets in Iceland, of whom Hannes Pétursson (b. 1931) is the best known. H.'s own development, however, has been such that his last poems show the greatest concentration of images and the highest degree of freedom in form of all his works.

Icelandic history and the nature of the country are central motifs in many of H.'s poems, especially those contained in the first two collections. His descriptions of nature are rich in color and of exalted tone; the landscapes often serve to communicate a state of mind. Such pictures, however, are less pronounced in his two last books, where they function more like a backdrop or as a means of underscoring thoughts or sentiments. Longing and the search for happiness are recurring themes in H.'s poetry, but as he sees it, happiness can be achieved only by undergoing severe trials.

Á Gnitaheiði, the least introspective of H.'s books of verse, is a good example of the worry and uncertainty that prevailed during the Cold War period. In the face of the concerns that confront him, the poet celebrates Icelandic national cultural values. *Lauf og stjörnur*, on the other hand, is the most private of his verse collections, characterized by pessimism and disillusionment. Still, art and other achievements of the human spirit are seen here as affording a measure of relief. Many of the poems in this book deal with time and the transitory nature of life, but the poet can accept the prospect of approaching death as long as he can savor the pleasures that art and nature's beauty can afford him.

In his latest book of verse, *Hauströkkrið yfir mér*, H. reconciled himself to the human condition, replacing his prior sense of futility

with basic acceptance. The language in this collection is his most direct. H. was awarded the Nordic Council's literary prize in 1981 for this volume of poetry.

—SVEINN SKORRI HÖSKULDSSON

HŁASKO, Marek

Polish novelist and short-story writer, b. 14 Jan. 1934, Warsaw; d. 14 June 1969, Wiesbaden, West Germany

Born into a middle-class family, H. spent his childhood in Warsaw, but World War II prevented him from receiving a regular education. After the war he attended secondary school and worked as a truck driver. Encouraged by friends, he submitted his first short story in a contest for new talent and saw it published. The start of his literary career coincided with the beginnings of the Polish "thaw" in the mid-1950s, and by 1957 he had achieved immense popularity as the spokesman for the disenchanted younger generation. He ran afoul of the censorship and defected in 1958 while traveling in western Europe, moving first to Israel (although he was not Jewish), and, after a few years, to the U.S. But after settling in the U.S., he ceased writing. Later he moved to West Germany, where he committed suicide in a state of deep depression.

H.'s favorite motif is that of love destroyed by the shabbiness of the characters' physical surroundings and by the cynicism and brutality of the world. It is most brilliantly developed in the novel *Ósmy dzień tygodnia* (1956; *The Eighth Day of the Week*, 1958), which deals with the plight of a young couple who cannot consummate their love because of lack of privacy in war-ravaged Warsaw. In the novel *Cmentarze* (1958; *The Graveyard*, 1959), published in Paris after his defection, H. depicts the corruption of ideals and human relationships in Stalinist Poland, skillfully combining nightmarish and humorous elements in an excellent example of sustained grotesquery that is perhaps his finest artistic achievement.

Another novel, *Następny do raju* (1958; *Next Stop—Paradise*, 1960), exemplifies H.'s preoccupation with violence as a major factor in life. Set in the mountains of southwestern Poland, this story of a group of truck drivers working under the most inhumane conditions emphasizes the contrast between the brutal truth of their daily struggle for survival and the falseness of official slogans with which the Communist Party tries to embellish their work. One by one the drivers are killed in unnecessary accidents while the Party boasts about their alleged contribution to the welfare of society. Such ironic contrasts also underly most of H.'s stories dealing with the living conditions in the postwar period, and led to the ban imposed on the publication of his work for almost twenty years in Poland.

In a series of novels and short stories written in Israel H. developed the theme of alienation combined with a gradual erosion of traditional values such as faith and love. In these works his world has become even more brutal and merciless. In a short autobiographical account, *Piękni dwudziestoletni* (1966; the handsome young men of twenty), H. explored the roots of his new philosophy, tracing them to his experiences in the socialist system, which has corrupted his generation back in Poland.

H.'s novels show the influence of KAFKA; elsewhere, however, HEMINGWAY's example is supreme. H. cultivates an extreme economy of style and infuses his stark naturalism with a strain of lyricism. H. has made a lasting impact on the entire generation of young Polish writers of the 1960s.

FURTHER WORKS: *Pierwszy krok w chmurach* (1956); *Opowiadania* (1963); *Wszyscy byli odwróceni; Brudne czyny* (1964); *Nawrócony w Jaffie; Opowiem wam o Esther* (1966); *Sowa, córka piekarza* (1968); *Opowiadania* (1976)

BIBLIOGRAPHY: Anon., "Notes about the Author," *East Europe*, 2, 9 (1957): 11; Kryński, M. J., "M. H.—the Lyrical Naturalist," *PolR*, 6, 4 (1961): 11–21; Blöcker, G., *Kritisches Lesebuch* (1962): 63–87

—JERZY R. KRYŻANOWSKI

HO Ch'i-fang

Chinese poet, journalist, critic, and essayist, b. 1912, Wanhsien, Szechwan Province; d. 24 July 1977, Peking

Destined to become one of the more influential cultural figures in the People's Republic of China, H. began his literary career as a holdout among his youthful peers who advocated increased social involvement. Born into a wealthy Szechwan family at a time when warlords and bandits were ravaging the country, he developed an intense abhorrence of war and a keen distrust of political authority. His taste in poetry, which tended toward romanticism, was nurtured during his studies at Peking University (1931–35), when he came under the influence of the work of French SYMBOLIST Paul VALÉRY. H.'s earliest poems were published in the literary quarterly *Wen-hsüeh chik'an* and subsequently included in a volume by him and two of his schoolmates, entitled *Hanyüan chi* (1936; the garden of Han). His first individual volume, a collection of essays entitled *Hua-meng lu* (1936; record of painted dreams), won the prestigious Ta Kung Pao literary award, not because of the themes of romantic love and the musings of a young artist but because of the poet's polished diction and vivid imagery. He then embarked on an often agonizing journey from noninvolvement and individualism to ardent patriotism and eventually to socialism. Falling under the influence of Romain ROLLAND, H. began to use poetry as a weapon of political struggle; in 1937 he traveled to Yenan, where he soon became a dedicated Marxist. Up until his death in 1977, just as the Cultural Revolution was ending, he remained an unwavering supporter of Mao's literary policy and, as such, an influential member of the cultural hierarchy.

Although primarily remembered as a poet, H. also made his mark as a journalist during the Sino-Japanese War (1937–45), when he spent much time traveling with and observing Communist troops. His philosophical convictions spawned a succession of polemical works, satirical essays, and propaganda pieces that placed him firmly among the upholders of Maoist literary theories.

Owing to his fine traditional training in Chinese literature, a keen eye for nature, and an early appreciation of Western romanticism, H. wrote highly refined poetry. A deft application of symbols and rich imagery characterized his verse, particularly that of his university days. Although it occasionally lapses into sentimentality, his early verse is appealing in its sparseness of language and the captured essence of natural beauty. Following his conversion to Marxism, H. published a volume of poems, *Yeh-ko* (1945; nocturnal songs), that focused on his new experiences among the soldiers

and villagers and reflected his newly acquired outlook on the role of the writer. He soon renounced this attempt as too feeble, however, sensing that his poetic language was still mired in his intellectual, romantic past. Over the next decade he wrote no poetry, immersing himself instead in a study of the people of New China and of their folk songs. His reemergence in the mid-1950s was accompanied by active participation in public debates over literary orthodoxy and by a corpus of poems in praise of socialism.

FURTHER WORKS: *K'o-yi chi* (1938); *Huanhsing jih-chi* (1939); *Yü-yen* (1945); *Hsing huo chi* (1945); *Wu Yü-chang t'ung-chih koming ku-shih* (1949); *Hsing huo hsin-chi* (1949); *Kuan-yü hsien-shih chu-yi* (1950); *Hsi-yüan chi* (1952); *Kuan-yü hsieh-shih ho tu shu* (1956); *San-wen hsüan-chi* (1957); *Mei-yu p'i-p'ing chiu pu-neng ch'ien-chin* (1958); *Lun "Hung lou meng"* (1958); *Ch'ihmu te hua* (1961); *Shih-ko hsin-chang* (1962); *Wen-hsüeh yi-shu te ch'un-t'ien* (1964); *Huang-hun* (1970). FURTHER WORKS IN ENGLISH: *Paths in Dreams: Selected Prose and Poetry of H. C.* (1976)

BIBLIOGRAPHY: Goldman, M., *Literary Dissent in Communist China* (1967): xii, 30–32, and passim; Boorman, H. L., and R. C. Howard, *Biographical Dictionary of Republican China* 2 (1971): 58–60; Průšek, J., *Dictionary of Oriental Literature* (1974), Vol. I: 49; Gálik, M., "Early Poems and Essays of H. C.," *AAS*, 15 (1979): 31–64

—HOWARD GOLDBLATT

HOCHHUTH, Rolf

West German dramatist and essayist, b. 1 April 1931, Eschwege

Brought up in a middle-class Protestant family, H. did not finish secondary school, preferring to work as a clerk in a bookstore while pursuing his interest in literature and history by voracious reading. He later worked as an editor for a publishing house until the success of his first play.

H. became famous overnight when his first play, *Der Stellvertreter* (1963; *The Deputy*, 1964), provoked a storm of controversy. In this play H. accuses Pope Pius XII of partial responsibility for the deaths of European Jews during World War II because he did not publicly protest the Nazi persecutions. The vehement international response to H.'s accusation—an open letter from the Vatican, demonstrations at performances in Basel and New York, and a spate of articles and books arguing pro and con—focused primarily on historical questions and tended to obscure considerations of literary merit.

In *Der Stellvertreter* H. contrasts Pope Pius XII with a fictitious protagonist, the idealistic young Jesuit Riccardo Fontana. Upon learning about the mass exterminations in the concentration camps, Riccardo attacks the politically circumspect but morally dubious nonintervention policy of the Vatican. In a climactic scene he confronts the Pope with the demand for a politically effective protest to Hitler. The Pope responds with a coldly analytical discussion of political and economic considerations, and then issues an elegantly stylized statement devoid of any concrete position. Riccardo accuses him of inhumanity and decides to take upon himself the role of Christ's deputy among the suffering: he pins the yellow Star of David on his cassock and joins a transport to

Auschwitz. Desperately trying to help the victims, Riccardo repeatedly challenges the satanic camp administrator and eventually dies a martyr's death.

Written in free verse, which is often rhythmically tortuous or overly grandiloquent, *Der Stellvertreter* presents its controversial theme in the traditional framework of a classical five-act drama. Brutally realistic scenes alternate with lofty moral disputations, and fictitious characters and situations are combined with carefully selected historical data, the latter meticulously documented in over fifty pages of printed text. Unlike the documentary theater of Heinar KIPPHARDT and others, however, the scholarship of this background material is only instrumental to H.'s objective—that of expressing his intensely felt moral outrage. Essentially a modern morality play with a historical core, *Der Stellvertreter* suffers from its divergent ideological and documentary intentions. Black-and-white, unconvincing characterizations and polemical confrontations tending toward sensationalism or cheap melodrama undermine the author's insistent claim for historical objectivity.

In the drama *Soldaten: Nekrolog auf Genf* (1967; *Soldiers: An Obituary for Geneva*, 1968), H. examines another controversial issue from World War II—Winston Churchill's role in the Allied decision to fire-bomb German cities. While the author expressly states that the play was written to demonstrate the need for a new international convention to regulate aerial warfare, it has been misunderstood as a vicious attack on Churchill and was even banned in England for a time. Structurally, *Soldaten* encloses a three-act, realistic inner play entitled "The Little London Theater of the World" within a morality-play frame dominated by the modern Everyman Peter Dorland. Dorland, a guilt-ridden former bomber pilot in the RAF who was involved in the devastation of Dresden, struggles to come to terms with his own moral responsibility by staging a play about Churchill, rehearsed before the ruins of Coventry on Cathedral. In this central play Dorland insists on Churchill's fundamental moral culpability not only for the politically expedient saturation bombing of noncombatants in German cities, but also for the similarly motivated prearranged death of General Sikorski (1881–1943), premier of the Polish government in exile.

While H. again offers much documentary evidence, here in the form of extensive (and often superfluous) stage directions, the frame play of *Soldaten* motivates the controversial attitudes expressed in the inner play by identifying them as Dorland's personal interpretation of historical events. Churchill emerges as a powerful and complex man who realizes that political circumstances have forced him into an insoluble moral dilemma; he grows into an almost tragic figure as a he accepts his agonizing responsibilities. *Soldaten* has stylistic and structural flaws, yet its more sophisticated understanding of the political pressures of a historical situation and its moving and skillful characterization of Churchill make it dramatically more successful than *Der Stellvertreter*.

H.'s subsequent dramas—*Guerillas* (1970; guerrillas); the comedies *Die Hebamme* (1971; the midwife) and *Lysistrate und die NATO* (1973; Lysistrata and NATO); and *Die Juristen* (1980; the legal profession)—do not achieve even the limited literary persuasiveness of his first two plays. In these later works, which display a simplistic understanding of current events, H. extrapolates conceivable although utopian developments from actual contemporary situations. In *Guerillas* U.S. Senator Nicolson makes an abortive attempt to instigate a social revolution from within the American political establishment; in *Die Hebamme* the midwife Sophie outwits bureaucracy to help the homeless social outcasts of

West Germany; in *Lysistrate und die NATO* women on a Greek island employ the ancient antiwar method recommended by Aristophanes to keep their husbands from leasing their land for use as a U.S. military base; and in *Die Juristen* a powerful judge is forced to confront his dishonorable past (long forgotten summary sentences passed in Nazi courts), and his exposure helps to effect reforms in the present-day West German judicial system. All these situations present ideas that are curiously naïve and characters that are one-dimensional. H. nevertheless continues to draw large audiences and provoke debate with his plays, and his impact on public opinion remains so significant that the publication in the weekly newspaper *Die Zeit* of an excerpt from a novel based on his *Juristen* material (*Eine Liebe in Deutschland* [1978; *A German Love Story*, 1980]) contributed directly to the resignation of a prominent West German politician.

The flaws of H.'s work should not detract from his achievements as a public figure and moral conscience. With *Der Stellvertreter* and *Soldaten* he provoked many writers into active political involvement and initiated the important literary trend of the documentary theater (Kipphardt, Peter WEISS, and others). Whatever the literary qualities of his plays and frequent journalistic essays, H. possesses an almost uncanny knack for uncovering fraud and hypocrisy. His courage to deal publicly with controversial moral and political issues has had a profound impact on postwar German cultural life.

FURTHER WORKS: *Die Berliner Antigone* (1964); *Die Hebamme, Erzählungen, Gedichte, Essays* (1971); *Krieg und Klassenkrieg: Studien* (1971); *Zwischenspiel in Baden-Baden* (1974); *Tod eines Jägers* (1976)

BIBLIOGRAPHY: Raddatz, F. J., ed., *Summa iniuria; oder, Durfte der Papst schweigen: H.'s "Stellvertreter" in der öffentlichen Kritik* (1963); Bentley, E., ed., *The Storm over "The Deputy"* (1964); Schmidt, D. B., and E. R. Schmidt, eds., *The "Deputy" Reader: Studies in Moral Responsibility* (1965); Zipes, J., "Documentary Drama in Germany: Mending the Circuit", *GR*, 42 (1967): 49–62; Thompson, C., *The Assassination of Winston Churchill* (1969); Demetz, P., *Postwar German Literature* (1970): 137–46; Zipes, J., "The Aesthetic Dimensions of the German Documentary Drama," *GL&L*, 24 (1970–1971): 346–57; Taëni, R., *R. H.* (1977); Ward, M. E., *R. H.* (1977); special H. issue, *TuK*, No. 58 (1978)

—HELENE SCHER

HOCHWÄLDER, Fritz

Austrian dramatist, b. 28 May 1911, Vienna; d. 20 Oct. 1986, Zürich, Switzerland

H. first worked as a craftsman in wood and leather; he was a skilled cabinetmaker and upholsterer, largely self-educated. When Hitler occupied Austria in the spring of 1938 his political convictions and his "non-Aryan" origin drove him into exile. He succeeded in getting into Switzerland. Here he met the great German EXPRESSIONIST playwright Georg KAISER, a fellow exile in Zurich who exercised a decisive influence on his work. And it was here in Switzerland that H. wrote his first important play, *Esther* (1940; Esther), a satirically updated version of the biblical story with obvious references to Hitler in the character of Haman.

H.'s breakthrough came with *Das heilige Experiment* (perf. 1943, pub. 1947; *The Strong Are Lonely*, 1954); it was first performed in Biel, Switzerland, and went on to achieve considerable international success. This play, freely based on actual historical events, deals with the fate of the Jesuit state in Paraguay, that fascinating attempt to create a perfect theocratic society, a Christian-communist state in the virgin territories of 18th-c. South America. The "holy experiment" is a success—so much so that the Indians, exploited and oppressed by the Spanish colonial settlers, flock to it. The settlers have denounced the Jesuit fathers at the court of the king of Spain for all sorts of malpractices; the play opens with the arrival of the king's investigator. The subsequent trial is a masterly discussion about the nature of society. The Jesuits are proved innocent of all accusations, but, in a brilliant dramatic turn, it is for that very reason that the ecclesiastical authorities order them to dismantle their new state, for all social experiments based on a theory, and rigidly organized accordingly, contain the seeds of totalitarianism and tyranny. *Das heilige Experiment* thus deals with a highly topical subject in a manner that lifts it out of its immediate context and gives it lasting validity. It also displayed to the best advantage H.'s peculiar talent of combining intellectual depth with supreme theatrical craftsmanship, a brilliantly original use of the technique of the well-made play.

H.'s subsequent successes showed this talent in a variety of original variations. *Der öffentliche Ankläger* (1947; *The Public Prosecutor*, 1958) is a prime example of H.'s sheer technical ingenuity. Here he solves the problem of how to construct a plot about a public prosecutor who prepares and argues a convincing case against a criminal only to discover at the end of the trial that the defendant he has doomed to the guillotine is himself. This variation of the age-old Oedipus theme seems almost impossible to bring off. Yet H.—by making ingenious use of the historical situation and character of Fouquier-Tinville, the hated prosecutor of the Terror of the French Revolution—accomplishes this feat: Fouquier-Tinville has so often coached and prepared false witnesses that he quite willingly obeys Tallien, a member of the Directoire, who asks him to prepare such a case against a personality so powerful that any inkling of his being under accusation would entail his striking first.

In *Donadieu* (1953; Donadieu) the problem of forgiveness of political crimes and atrocities, so burningly real in post-World War II Europe, is tackled with ingenuity and deep humanity in presenting an incident from the wars between Catholics and Huguenots in 17th-c. France. Donadieu recognizes the man who slaughtered his family, but ultimately renounces the opportunity of avenging himself on him.

H. returned to the Oedipus theme, which exercises an immense fascination on him, in a play, originally written for television but subsequently also staged, *Der Befehl* (1967; *The Order*, 1970), in which an Austrian policeman ordered to investigate a wartime crime committed by the Germans in Holland ultimately discovered that it was he himself who killed the Dutch child in the course of an operation that was such a routine event in the occupation duties of Gestapo men that he had completely forgotten it.

In a completely different vein H. explored the possibilities of creating a modern equivalent to the medieval mystery play: in *Donnerstag* (1959; Thursday) he attempted to put a modern individual, a product of our industrialized and overmechanized society, into the situation of Faust, who is tempted to sell his soul to the devil.

H. has also written a number of successful comedies and farces, notably his bitterly satirical re-creation of Gogol's *The Government Inspector* transferred to a post-Nazi Austria, *Der Himbeerpflücker* (1965; *The Raspberry Picker*, 1970). Here Gogol's original situation is ingeniously varied and updated. The citizens of the small Russian town of Gogol's play mistake a petty gambler for a government inspector and heap favors on him to bribe him to overlook their corruption. In H.'s play a petty criminal is taken by the citizens of a small Austrian community to be a major war criminal, whom they, as ex-Nazis to whom the Hitler years were the happiest of their lives, want to pamper and revere, only to discover to their horror that he is anything but the admired concentration camp butcher—he is just a petty thief, and Jewish to boot.

H.'s mastery of traditional dramatic techniques may have made him seem, in the 1960s and 1970s, less experimental and avant-gardist, and more conventional than many of the playwrights then fashionable. But in fact, it may well be that his constant attempts to solve ever more difficult problems of the technique of drama in ever more daring and ingenious ways will reveal him, in a longer perspective, to have been more advanced and experimental than many of his contemporaries. Even more impressive in H.'s dramatic oeuvre is his uncompromising moral integrity, his commitment to the highest values of humanity, decency, and civilized standards of conduct. There are few playwrights of H.'s generation of whom that can be said with such complete conviction.

FURTHER WORKS: *Jehr* (1932); *Die unziemliche Neugier* (1934); *Liebe in Florenz* (1936); *Hôtel du Commerce* (written 1944, pub. 1954); *Der Flüchtling* (1945); *Meier Helmbrecht* (written 1946, pub. 1956); *Die verschleierte Frau* (1946); *Der Unschuldige* (1949; rev. 1958); *Virginia* (1951); *Die Herberge* (1956); *1003* (1964); *Lazaretti; oder, Der Säbeltiger* (1975; *Lazaretti; or, The Saber-Toothed Tiger*, 1980); *Dramen* (3 vols., 1975–1979); *Im Wechsel der Zeit: Autobiographische Skizzen und Essays* (1980). FURTHER WORKS IN ENGLISH: *The Public Prosecutor and Other Plays* (1980)

BIBLIOGRAPHY: Garten, H. F., *Modern German Drama* (1959): 244–46; Loram, I., "F. H.," *Monatshefte*, 57 (1965): 8–16; Wellwarth, G. E., *The Theater of Protest and Paradox*, rev. ed. (1971): 207–21; Harper, A. J., "Tradition and Experiment in the Work of F. H.," *NGS*, 5 (1977): 49–57; Schmitt, J., "The Theater of F. H.: Its Background and Development," followed by "F. H. Bibliography," *MAL* 11, 1 (1978): 49–73; Innes, C., *Modern German Drama* (1979): 213–15; Esslin, M., "Introduction: H., Mastercraftsman of Ideas," in F. H., *The Public Prosecutor and Other Plays* (1980): vii–xix

—MARTIN ESSLIN

HODGE, Merle

Trinidadian novelist and short-story writer, b. 1944, Curepe

H. was reared in Trinidad and won the Trinidad and Tobago Girls Island Scholarship in 1962, which enabled her to study at the University College of London where she pursued studies in French. She earned her B.A. in 1965 and her M.A. degree in 1967. She has traveled widely throughout Europe, the Caribbean, and the U.S.

After 1970 she began postgraduate work in Francophone Caribbean and African literatures. In 1979 H. went to Grenada where she was appointed director of the development of curriculum. She left Grenada in 1983 because of the assassination of Prime Minister Maurice Bishop and the resulting U.S. invasion of the country. She currently works at the University of the West Indies in Trinidad.

To date H. has written two novels *Crick Crack, Monkey* (1981) and *For the Life of Laetitia* (1993). She has also written numerous articles and essays, including works on Léon-Gontran DAMAS, male and female relationships in the Caribbean, as well as perspectives on Grenada. She has also written a children's book and a volume of poems as yet unpublished.

With the publication of *Crick Crack, Monkey*, H. was assured a place in the annals of Caribbean writing. A bildungsroman, *Crick Crack, Monkey* offers a perspective on the Afro-Caribbean girl's passage into adulthood against a backdrop of influences (both traditional and colonial) that arrest her development. Debate on the novel centers around the central character's choice of flight (her decision to join her father in London) as opposed to remaining in the Caribbean. The novel suggests that there is no one way for the Caribbean child to be in the western world.

For the Life of Laetitia is considered a young adult book. It features a twelve-year-old village girl's foray into city life as a result of passing her exams for secondary school. Again the traditional versus the cosmopolitan is brought to the fore in this novel as the title character leaves her traditionally "grounded" grandparents to live in the city with her pompous father. Issues of class, alienation, woman's roles, and education are reflected in this novel of island life.

H. posits the reconstruction of an African heritage, traditional values, resistance to colonial ideas of decorum, and the woman's way of being in the world as central to her fiction. Additionally, her language (both standard English and Nation language) is central to the identification of the collective Caribbean experience.

BIBLIOGRAPHY: Balutansy, K. M., "We Are All Activists: In Interview with M. H.," *Callaloo*, 12 (Fall 1989): 651-62; Lawrence, L. S., "M. H.," in Dance, D. C., ed., *Fifty Caribbean Writers* (1986): 2242-328; Le Seur, G., "One Mother, Two Daughters: The Afro-American and the Afro-Caribbean Female Bildungsroman," *Black Scholar*, 17 (March-April 1986): 26-33; Paravisini-Gebert, L., and O. Torres-Seda, *Caribbean Women Novelists: An Annotated Critical Bibliography* (1993): 165-68

—ADELE S. NEWSON

HØECK, Klaus

Danish poet, b. 27 Nov. 1938, Copenhagen

H. has his origins in the Danish middle-class and the postwar society. He graduated from the University of Copenhagen, but gave up a promising academic career at the Department for Philosophy to concentrate on writing poetry. To provide for himself he took a job as a postman and chose to live in an old working-class district of Copenhagen. He made his debut as a poet in 1966 with a small collection of poems *Yggdrasil* (Yggdrasil).

H. was soon recognized as a leading poet by a young generation of Danish poets and critics who introduced new postmodernist concepts of poetry that became inspiring to Danish literature in the last decades of the 20th c.

The title of H.'s first collection of poems refers to the tree of life in Nordic mythology, Yggdrasil, and the poems combine a deep knowledge of ancient mythology with modern cybernetic theories of language. In following collections H. often refers to Yggdrasil as a metaphor of his poetry and a mythological and philosophical awareness characterizes his experiments with still more comprehensive poetic forms.

Yggdrasil became the opening of a cycle of poems entitled *Rejse* (5 vols., 1971-73; Journey). The topic of *Rejse* is the longing of man to explore nature and space and to control his surroundings. Though the poems praise the great explorers from Christopher Columbus to Robert Edwin Peary and Neil Armstrong, a critical awareness as well as a linguistic ecology becomes the result of the poem's expedition into the structures and networks of language.

H.'s major works include *Projekt Perseus* (1977; Project Perseus), *Canzone* (1981; Canzone), *Metamorphoses* (1983; Metamorphoses), and *Lukas O'Kech* (1988; Lukas O'Kech). *Projekt Perseus* consists of cyberspace poems, partly written in English, and describes a linguistic odyssey in space. In *Canzone* sonnets and canzones describe everyday life at Nørrebro, the old Copenhagen working-class district, during the economic crisis of the 1970s. The poems follow strictly elaborated cybernetic rules and the traditional metres of the sonnet and the canzone. The poet wanders the polluted streets of the district and his poems demonstrate a different ecological practice using and reusing the linguistic material of the poems and of the poetic tradition.

Hjem (1985; Home) forms a large cycle of poems following three tracks: the track of nature, the track of culture, and the track of the spirit. The cycle's linguistic material is elaborated from the chemical formulas of the elements of Denmark's subsoil and from quotations from the Bible, and the poems tell a story of the poet's love and faith. *Heptameron* (1989; Heptameron) is inspired by the old European tradition of poems on Genesis, and the poems reflect the shape of the DNA-molecule. In *Eventyr* (1992; Fairy Tales; pub. in part as *The Woods*, 1998) the poet faces taking leave of his dying mother and as in the fairy tale it is the three little stones representing faith, hope, and charity that show the poet the way to his farewell, but also the way back to life. Inspired by Søren Kierkegaard's philosophy, *Eventyr* emphasizes the fact that man cannot arrive at any exhaustive understanding of the living, concrete totality of existence, however many bits and pieces he finds on which to form his interpretation. Man cannot place the last piece in this jigsaw puzzle and view the whole, for he himself is part of the living totality that he thereby seeks to understand and interpret. Humanity is confronted with the paradoxical situation that we know something that we cannot understand or explain. It is the task of the fairy tale and the poem to demonstrate the condition of our existence and to point to the great fairy tale that is our life.

It is typical of H.'s poems that the philosophical and epistemological themes arise from the concrete reality of everyday life and from the reflections on the masterpieces of music, literature, and painting. His poems refer to romantic poets such as Hölderlin, Novalis, Shelley, Keats, and Byron; to such contemporary musicians and poets as Bob Dylan, Brian Eno, and David Bowie; and to such modern writers as Ezra POUND and Federico GARCÍA LORCA. There are always several poetic topics in H.'s poems that correspond or form counterpoints in a kind of fugue. H.'s collections of poems are often framed as narratives and they include the greatest as well as the smallest. Deep experiences of love, sorrow, and faith alternate with descriptions of everyday activities like listening to music, watching television, drinking a cup of coffee, or doing the laundry. *1001 digt* (1995; 1001 Poems) praises everyday life in both traditional and modern innovative lyrical forms using fourfold Japanese haikus, and the collection is formed as an almanac following for four years in four different tracks. The reader himself has to decide on which page to begin his reading of the cycle.

H.'s poetical expression ranges freely within the tight framework of his complex poems with a combination of discipline and innovation that makes his poetry surprising and original. The content becomes the form's account of itself, while the form denotes the content's account. His poems are characterized by an astonishing beauty of the poetic imagery and by intense philosophical reflections.

FURTHER WORKS: *Mitr-enf-snee* (1967); *Transformations* (1974); *Pentagram* (1976); *Ulrike Marie Meinhof* (1977); *Topia* (1978); *Skygger* (1978); *Dylan Forever* (1979); *Winterreise* (1979); *Sorte sonetter* (1981); *International Klein Bleu* (1984); *Marienbad* (1984); *Blackberry Winter* (1987); *Salme* (1991); *Hommage* (1995); *Honey Moon* (1997)

BIBLIOGRAPHY: Schnack, A., and J. G. Brandt, *80 moderne danske digtere* (1988): 99-104; Bagge Pedersen, C., "Men alt kan jo ikke være suppe—om K. H. Canzone," in Mai, A. M., ed., *Digtning fra 80'erne til 90'erne* (1993): 63-78; Sørensen, S., and A. M. Mai, "Freedom of the Frame," *Danish Literary Magazine*, 5 (1993): 17-18; Sørensen, S., *Den ottende dag* (1994); Andersen, F., *Realismens metode* (1994): 295-324; Conrad, N. A., "Portraits of Danish Poets," *Danish Literary Magazine*, 12 (1997): 12-13

—ANNE-MARIE MAI

HØEG, Peter

Danish novelist and short-story writer, b. 17 May 1957, Copenhagen

Earning a degree in comparative literature from the University of Copenhagen in 1984, H. has been a professional dancer, an actor, a sailor, a fencer, and a mountaineer. He has authored five books of fiction, and his literary debut was in 1988, only five years before his international breakthrough with the best-selling novel *Frøken Smillas fornemmelse for sne* (1992; *Smilla's Sense of Snow*, 1993), which director Bille August later filmed for his first U.S. release.

After his first novel, *Forestilling om det tyvende århundrede* (1988; *The History of Danish Dreams*, 1995), H. published *Fortællinger om natten* (1990; Tales of the Night) and has since issued two more novels, *De måske egnede* (1993; *Borderliners*, 1994) and *Kvinden og aben* (1996; *The Woman and the Ape*, 1996). Notwithstanding striking differences in terms of subject matter, plot development, and style, his books share many thematics and existential concerns.

As intimated by the title of his first novel, H.'s writings take place at the intersection of time and dream. While the former alludes to cosmos, the latter, like chaos, tends to defy all structure and order, and the tension between the two marks the mode of his writing. And while the English translation of the debut title focuses on dreams within an expressly national but otherwise unspecified

historical genre, the original Danish title speaks more broadly and fictitiously of notions devoid of national specifications but narrowly confined to the 20th c.

The dichotomy is indicative of efforts to reconcile the mind with an omnipresent conventional time. But expressions of the unpredictable do not conform easily to clockwork. Characters attempting to run away from time get run down by it, and only rarely do they get a sense of freedom without constant reminders of the hours. As time comes apart, day and night, summer and winter, past and present, collapse into new formations while powerful men who believe they know how to capture the present get disappointed. H. is at once obsessed with the merciless reality of measurable time and the utopian liberty inherent in its timeless alternatives.

In *Fortællinger om natten* he briefly explains that each of its nine nocturnal tales is about love and takes place on the night of March 19, 1929. Once again he confronts the strictures of times and systems as bright as day with the less regimented and more clandestine qualities of life he associates with females or children, subjectivity or openness. His tales have been called neo-Gothic pastiches in the spirit of Isak DINESEN, but while their basic dichotomies are quite familiar, the collection as a whole affords an impressive stylistic variation on the central theme. Like H.'s first book, his second spreads its insights onto intertextual patterns and two-dimensional characters. Its storytelling belongs to the postmodern tradition of calling attention to its own craft.

In *Frøken Smillas fornemmelse for sne* the same fault lines extend through the title character, who is half Greenlander, of seal-hunter stock, and half Danish, of upper-middle-class extraction. Part of her is rooted in a male-oriented culture of technological supremacy, driven by progress and profit, while her other part is female-oriented, giving allegiance to an exploited Inuit culture aligned with feelings for nature at large and within. Smilla's sense of snow is a synthesis of her double nature and conflict-ridden complexity.

Challenged by a six-year-old Inuit boy and his mysterious fall from a Copenhagen rooftop, her dual personality engages in a two-fold quest. She boards a ship to Arctic regions on a secret mission, and she journeys inwardly through the dubious cultural and mental landscape of hegemonic Denmark in the 1990s. Frightened by the subterranean connections between the two worlds, her otherwise disillusioned humor and realism serves as a shelter for dreams of life and love. The struggles between divisive and harmonious forces in the world around her resonate with her inner conflicts, and her humanistic worldview is both frail and inconclusive. Yet, as a central character she combines her author's postcolonial sentiments and postmodern fiction with more traditional epic virtues and novelistic schemes, which makes the novel that bears her name the most central in H.'s production.

Not that its successor, *De måske egnede*, lacks plot or narrative passion as it reveals the plight of three young children in a Danish reform school in the 1970s; in fact, a certain autobiographical background for the horrors it describes is unmistakable. But still, the characters and their destinies remain secondary to the art of storytelling and its extensive essayistic passages on education and philosophy about time.

The purely linear time of school indoctrination represents a mathematical abstraction from the vagaries of life in dreams and visions and from the promises of cyclical and existential time. While one child is silenced and crushed by this conflict, the narrator, with the authorial name Peter, makes a virtue out of necessity by telling his story of the borderline kids and by arguing that only they can perceive the evils of an integrationist culture and society.

Like Smilla, Peter favors a world in balance but entirely within the realm of human sensations and fellowship. The implied message is for people to be true to their nature and god-given imperfections and to leave it to the future to decide the future. The verdict teeters between thought-provoking criticism of a well-intended progressiveness gone haywire and simple fixation with a few bad apples among school reformers.

In *Kvinden og aben* H. takes his implicit criticism of Western culture to an explicit, satirical extreme by having the allegedly lower nature of an ape conquer the allegedly higher nature of an upper-middle-class woman. Yet the woman is a caricature from the beginning, and while their budding romance is ingeniously contrived, it reflects an authorial bent for good environmental causes along with a tendency toward political correctness and essayistic doctrine, which is even more clearly pronounced here than it was in H.'s previous books.

That said, his erudition and experimental skills have endowed his limited oeuvre with a sense and sensiblity that is both wide-ranging and timely, both natural and cultural, both Danish and international.

BIBLIOGRAPHY: Jensen, R. H., "Om Høeg-debatten," *Synsvinkler*, 8 (1994): 119-26; Larsen, A. G., "Indblik i et øjeblik: Om P. H. *De måske egnede*," *Synsvinkler*, 8 (1994): 40-63; Schou, S., "Kompleksitet og forkyndelse hos P. H.," *Kritik*, 107 (1994): 1-8; Enander, C., *Relief: Författerporträtt* (1995): 181-202; Hesselaa, B., "En utopi søger sin form," *Pinkerton* 61 (1996): 3-15; Møller, H. H., "P. H. or the Sense of Writing," *Scan*, 69 (1997): 29-51; Norseng, M. K., "A House of Mourning: *Frøken Smillas fornemmelse for sne*," *Scan*, 69 (1997): 52-83

—POUL HOUE

HOEL, Sigurd

Norwegian novelist, essayist, and critic, b. 14 Dec. 1890, Odal; d. 14 Oct. 1960, Oslo

The son of an elementary-school teacher in eastern Norway, H. showed an early aptitude for mathematics and natural science, and from 1909 to 1912 distinguished himself as a brilliant student at the University of Oslo. Until 1918 he taught at a high school in Oslo, and from 1919 to 1924 served as secretary of the Oslo Academy of Science. In 1931 and 1932, while living in Berlin during the time his wife was studying there to become an analyst, H. gained firsthand acquaintance with what Nazism stood for. A decade later he was forced to take refuge in Sweden, where he continued to work in secret for the Norwegian cause and to prepare notes and manuscripts for subsequent publication.

Apart from his own masterful writings, H. has made two other great contributions to the literary life of Norway: his many years of service to Gyldendal Publishing House as chief literary adviser and his twenty-two years of editorship of *Den gule serie* (the yellow series). As early as 1929 his interest in contemporary authors of other countries prompted him to introduce Norwegian readers to the translated works of such writers as FAULKNER, HEMINGWAY, STEINBECK, WILDER, and others. The series quickly won enduring popularity.

With his first collection of short stories, *Veien vi gaar* (1922; the road we take), H. was nationally acclaimed as one of Norway's most promising young writers. His real breakthrough, however, came with the publication of *Syndere i sommersol* (1927; *Sinners in Summertime*, 1930), a witty, satirical story of postwar youth, who while accusing their elders of self-deception, themselves fall victim to their own duplicity.

Infidelity in marriage, one of H.'s frequent themes, is the focus of the boldly experimental novel *En dag i oktober* (1931; *One Day in October*, 1932). Set in Oslo, it exposes unfaithfulness in a number of bourgeois families. In spite of detailed analysis of emotional dispositions and behavioral reactions, here, as in some of H.'s other writings, the reader is left to draw his own conclusions about the characters' guilt or innocence.

Although most of H.'s books deal with urban life, he also wrote sensitive and convincing stories of childhood. *Veien til verdens ende* (1933; the road to the end of the world) is at once simple and profound. In following the joys and disappointments of Anders, a young farm boy, from the ages of three to fifteen, the author reveals memories of his own early years with warmth and intimacy.

A major psychological novel of the interwar years is *Fjorten dager før frostnettene* (1934; fourteen days before the frosty nights). The influence of FREUD is clearly reflected in this novel as well as in many of H.'s narratives and essays, in which he shows that the feelings of lack of fulfillment in adults are traceable to fear- and anxiety-ridden years of childhood.

Møte ved milepelen (1947; *Meeting at the Milestone*, 1951), a distinctly psychological novel, is designed to throw light on the nature of Nazism, the contention being that Nazism is not merely a political phenomenon of a particular country at a particular period in history. It is a certain type of mentality, a tyrannical temperament extant in many people at all times, which under special circumstances may be stimulated to action, thereby bringing about catastrophic consequences. H. went so far as to propose that Nazi tendencies may be attributed to a highly authoritarian education smothering a child's impulses and claims to freedom and equity. He also analyzes the personal and sociological conditions that may have inclined some Norwegians to embrace Nazi ideology and turn traitors.

A collection of speeches and essays from the 1933–45 period, *Tanker i mørketid* (1945; thoughts in the time of darkness), deals with various subjects, such as the persecution of the Jews, the propaganda of Goebbels, and Norwegian literary output during the Occupation. These discourses give a critical, realistic picture of the structure of a society that cripples and corrupts spiritually and morally, thereby making people easy prey to the dictatorship of bigots.

H.'s deep understanding of human foibles, and his empathy with people engaged in soul-searching trials have placed him in a central position in the history of Norwegian literature.

FURTHER WORKS: *Syvstjernen* (1924); *Ingenting* (1929); *Don Juan* (1930); *Mot muren* (1930); *Sesam, sesam* (1938); *Om flyktningen* (1939); *Prinsessen på glassberget* (1939); *Arvestålet* (1941); *Tanker fra mange tider* (1948); *Samlede romaner og fortellinger* (1950); *Jeg er blitt glad i en annen* (1951); *Tanker mellem barken og veden* (1952); *Stevnemøte med glemte år* (1954);

Trollringen (1958); *Tanker om norsk diktning* (1955); *Ved foten av Babels tårn* (1956); *Essays i utvalg* (1962)

BIBLIOGRAPHY: Jorgenson, T., *History of Norwegian Literature* (1933): 534–35; Kielland, E., "The Literary Scene in Norway (S. H.)," *ASR*, 39 (1951), 42; Grunt, O. P., "S. H.," *ASR*, 41 (1953): 31–38; Beyer, H., *History of Norwegian Literature* (1956): 317–19

—AMANDA LANGEMO

HOFMANN, Gert

German novelist, b. 29 Jan. 1932, Limbach

H. initially studied sociology, French, and German at the universities of Leipzig, Freiburg, and Paris, and then taught German and comparative literature for many years in Klagenfurt, Austria. He first became known as a prolific author of radio plays, and he has published all of his prose works in the relatively short time since 1979 until the present. Recurrent themes in his work are the indictment of hypocrisy and bigotry in hierarchically structured communities, people put under extreme pressures by a hostile state or bureaucracy, the marginalized and social outcasts. While H. criticizes such closed societies, he does not offer a solution or a redemptive vision. The tenor of his works is one of apocalyptic pessimism and a melancholy that is characteristic of many postwar German writers insofar as it reflects their attitudes to Germany's Nazi past and its reverberations in the present.

H.'s first novel, *Die Denunziation* (1979; the denunciation), traces the impact of a Nazi crime on the lives of twin brothers who victimized their parents and their neighbors, a Jewish couple. While one brother remains in Germany and leads an unexamined bourgeois existence, the other emigrates to America after the war and is driven nearly insane by his memories of the war crimes and his feelings of guilt. *Die Fistelstimme* (1980; the small hoarse voice) describes the conflicts between a German university lecturer and the Yugoslavian institution at which he is employed to teach German. The protagonist's increasing paranoia leads him to believe that others are copies of real people and that he himself is in danger of being replaced. He is then exposed as a fraud and forced to return home where he blames his domineering mother for his failures and kills her. H. criticizes the dehumanizing influence of bureaucracies and exposes the attempt to colonize other countries through the imposition of the German language. *Gespräch über Balzacs Pferd* (1981; *Balzac's Horse and Other Stories*, 1988) continues the investigation of authoritarian structures in society that prevent the individual from being fully realized, by examining family relationships in different historical epochs—ranging from an imaginary encounter between the old Casanova and his mother to the German poet Siegfried LENZ and his unsupportive father, Balzac's manipulation of his audience through a theater of cruelty to the contemporary poet Robert WALSER and a literary club that sponsors him. *Der Turm* (1984; *The Spectacle at the Tower*, 1985) exposes the cruelty of small-village society in Sicily, which reflects the sadistic power games the narrator plays with his wife, both of whom are German tourists stranded in the village. *Der Blindensturz* (1985; *The Parable of the Blind*, 1986) is set in 16th-c. Holland and details that society's inhuman treatment of a band of old men who

have been blinded for various misdemeanors and who are now objects of horror who will be painted by a famous artist. One of H.'s best novels is the recent *Veilchenfeld* (1986; Veilchenfeld), which once again takes up the theme of scapegoating the other by chronicling the persecution of a Jewish philosopher by "ordinary" small-town Nazis, and is told from a child's perspective.

H. has established himself as one of the most incisive critics of postwar German society, his prolific writings describing Kafka-esque social structures that maim or deform the individual trapped in them.

FURTHER WORKS: *Die Überflutung: Vier Hörspiele* (1981); *Unsere Eroberung* (1984; *Our Conquest*, 1985); *Die Weltmaschine* (1986); *Unsere Vergeßlichkeit* (1987); *Vor der Regenzeit* (1988; *Before the Rainy Season*, 1991); *Das allmähliche Verstummen des Kinoerzählers* (1990; *The Film Explainer*, 1996)

BIBLIOGRAPHY: Schwartz, L., "Korrekte Verzweiflung. Zu G. H.'s Romanen und Novellen," *Merkur*, 1 (1983): 108–12; Painter, K., "Writer Lives in Imagination," *The Oberlin Review*, 20 Apr. 1984: 6; Lützeler, P., "Der verstoßene Sohn," *Die Zeit*, 4 July 1986: 14; Pulver, E., "Die Zerstörung der Überwelt," *Schweizer Monatshefte* (1986): 527–29; Kosler, H. C., *G. H.: Auskunft für Leser* (1987)

—HELGA DRUXES

HOFMANNSTHAL, Hugo von

Austrian poet, dramatist, essayist, and novelist, b. 1 Feb. 1874, Vienna; d. 15 July 1929, Rodaun

H. became involved in the cultural life of Vienna at an early age. While attending secondary school he published poetry and essays in Austrian and German periodicals. The artistic maturity of his earliest writings won him immediate literary acclaim. In 1891 he began a stormy fifteen-year friendship with the German poet Stefan GEORGE, and between 1892 and 1906 many of H.'s poetic works appeared in George's journal *Blätter für die Kunst*.

In 1892 H. entered the University of Vienna. An unsatisfying encounter with law school was followed in 1894 by a brief period of military service. H. returned to the university in 1895, and four years later he received a doctorate in Romance philology. After his marriage in 1901 he settled in Rodaun, near Vienna. Rodaun remained his home for the rest of his life, although frequent travels abroad had important impact on his literary creations. Italy became his second home, and there he wrote several important early works.

Two artistic friendships were extremely significant for H.'s creative development after the turn of the century. In 1903 he met Max Reinhardt, who became instrumental in H.'s increased involvement in the theater. Reinhardt's production of H.'s *Elektra* (1904; *Electra*, 1908), a free rendition of Sophocles's play, gave H. his first taste of popular success with drama and paved the way for the productive collaboration with Richard Strauss that began in 1906. A revised *Elektra* was the first of six librettos that H. wrote for Strauss's operas.

During the years of World War I. H. served briefly in the Austrian army and then in the Austrian War Ministry. Deeply moved by the collapse of the monarchy, he then involved himself with the preservation and restoration of German and Austrian culture. In 1917 he helped found the Salzburg Festival, and during the 1920s he edited collections of writings by earlier German-language authors in an effort to reintroduce them to the reading public. Until his death H. remained completely committed to the whole spectrum of creative art that informed the cultural heritage he loved so much.

H.'s lyric poems attracted wide attention as products of supreme mastery of poetic technique. Although his verse depended on ideas and prosody from a broad range of models and traditions, he is best classified as an impressionist. His most important poems deal with incidentals, with transitoriness, with the unique spiritual state in all its finest differentiations, nuances, halftones, and hues. Visual themes are treated most effectively. Special emphasis is given to perfecting and purifying literary language and form of expression.

During his "lyric decade" (1890–1900) H. contributed to Austrian literature poems of lasting beauty that outshine the total oeuvre of many poets, and capsulized in verse the major aspects of his approach to life. His poems are a combination of vision and interpretation of the world and its phenomena.

Central to the worldview presented in H.'s poetry is the concept of "preexistence." Preexistence is man's state outside mortal life: before birth, after death, when he is temporarily apart from life in dreams. In the framework of absolute existence, mortality is a transitory condition that is meaningless without reference to preexistence. H.'s poetic treatment of death, for example, merges present, past, and future into and eternal "now." Man follows a course from mortality to preexistence and back again, passing through a sequence of life forms in a never-ending process of purification.

In defining in his poetry the essence of mortality, H. employed three major metaphors for life: the dream, the game, the drama. In his dream imagery, H. explored life as a creative process within people. The drama metaphor reveals life as a set of roles played and interpreted within the absolute framework of preexistence. One important variation of life-as-drama occurs in H.'s elegies that treat the actor as symbolic man and dwell on the actor's power to give life to his roles. H. used the game metaphor to focus on strengths and weaknesses of man as an individual. Life is presented as a gamble that man often loses, and the game becomes a symbol for unfulfilled life. H.'s three metaphors are extremely important for his perception of the nature of the poet. He viewed the poet as a synthesis of man the dreamer, man the actor, and man the game-player: the ultimate creator who causes others to create by finding what is within themselves.

The most important goal of H.'s writing was the explanation and the education of the self. Nowhere is that more evident than in his many essays. H. cultivated the essay as a literary form throughout his life, examining a broad spectrum of topics ranging from Beethoven to Eugene O'NEILL, from Czechoslovakia to Africa, from classical antiquity to Buddhism, and treating each subject with remarkably careful attention.

The essays vary considerably in form. Some are even written as dialogues, others as letters. In each instance H. chose a style suited to the content. Most of the essays are creative rather than analytical. They are rich in imagery and feature language that is often poetic, even rhythmic, full of color and nuance.

H.'s most famous essays, "Ein Brief" (1902; "The Letter of Lord Chandos," 1952), is a fictitious letter of Phillip Lord Chandos (an imaginary person) to Sir Francis Bacon. It examines the plight of the poet who has lost the facility to express himself coherently, because he can no longer cope at all with language. The letter describes a process of psychological fragmentation, in which language disintegrates into incohesive, meaningless parts, thereby eroding all possibility of being understood. "Ein Brief" is commonly interpreted as H.'s attempt to cope with a crisis in his own literary productivity. Yet the essay does nothing to suggest that H. was experiencing the same problems as the fictional Chandos. Its images are bright, colorful, and vibrant. The selection of words and organization of ideas are flawless. Each sentence, each phrase is constructed with care and precision and is impregnated with life and meaning. Its impeccable style and its deep insight into problems of creativity and of effective use of language make the Chandos letter a landmark of the modern European essay.

Among H.'s most interesting creations are a few masterfully executed works of narrative prose. Offering deep psychological insight into the human situations, these stories focus on engaging variations on the themes of the search for personal identity and the confrontation with self.

"Das Märchen der 672. Nacht," (1895; "Tale of the Merchant's Son and His Servants," 1969) is a rather cold, uncomfortable, although highly polished and poetic tale. In exploring the problem of a young man who tries to withdraw from society and ultimately causes his own destruction, H. created a horror story reminiscent of the narratives of Franz KAFKA. The account is a dreamlike portrayal of a psychological real sitation in which the protagonist is forced to face a reality from which he cannot escape.

The better-known *Reitergeschichte* (1908; *Cavalry Patrol*, 1939) is set in historically real circumstances: the war waged by the Austrians in 1848 against the Italian liberation army. The description of events leading to the execution of Anton Lerch for insubordination is a starkly brilliant psychological analysis of the emergence of the baser self. Like "Das Märchen der 672. Nacht," *Reitergeschichte* takes the form of an eerie nightmare in which a symbolic confrontation with self proves fatal.

H.'s unfinished novel, *Andreas; oder, Die Vereinigten* (1932; *Andreas; or, The United*, 1936), portrays coming to grips with one's self as a constructive process. Openly patterned after Goethe's *Wilhelm Meister, Andreas* equates the search for identity with the general process of maturation. The novel describes an educational journey from Vienna to Venice in 1778. In the course of his development, the protagonist must cope with love, negative aspects of life, and art. Andreas encounters life as an array of fragments, and his major task is to integrate its elements into a harmonious whole. He gains insight into himself and his relationship to others by freely assuming identities related to H.'s poetic metaphors for life. The resulting experiences expand both the world within him and his external sphere of influence. Unfinished portions of the novel suggest that H. also intended to explore sophisticated psychological problems, such as schizophrenia, while portraying Andreas's development.

Theatrical works are H.'s most well-remembered contribution to modern Austrian literature. To H., theater was life as he experienced it. *Der Tor und der Tod* (1894; *Death and the Fool*, 1913), his best-known and best-loved short lyric play; *Das kleine Welttheater* (1897; *The Little Theater of the World*, 1961); and *Jedermann* (1911; *The Play of Everyman*, 1917), based on the old English morality play, belong to a series of dramas that focus on H.'s stage metaphor for life. The most important drama in this group is *Das Salzburger große Welttheater* (1922; *The Salzburg Great Theater of the World*, 1963), which borrowed its central metaphor from Calderón's *The Great Theater of the World*. The scheme of Calderón's drama was especially attractive to H. because it allowed him to develop his notion of "preexistence" more clearly than he had done in the opera *Die Frau ohne Schatten* (1916; prose narrative, 1920; *The Woman without a Shadow*, 1957).

A major component of H.'s life-is-theater dramas is social criticism. His comedies are especially forceful in that respect. *Der Schwierige* (1921; *The Difficult Man*, 1963) and *Arabella* (1933; *Arabella*, 1955), for example, convey strong criticism of Viennese society while developing the idea that man as an actor plays his best and happiest role when playing himself.

Variations of H.'s game-player metaphor received significant elaboration in a group of plays that includes *Gestern* (1891; yesterday), *Der Abenteurer und die Sängerin* (1909; the adventurer and the singer), and *Christinas Heimreise* (1910; *Cristina's Journey Home*, 1916). The respective protagonists of these dramas are Casanova types. *Der Abenteurer und die Sängerin*, H.'s first major dramatic expansion of the game-player metaphor *per se*, presents a precise picture of the adventurer as a basic human type.

Later variations on the game-player theme employ specific games to make statements about man's nature. In *Der Unbestechliche* (first act only, 1923; complete play, 1933; the incorruptible man) the main character views life as a game of billiards. The success of his approach makes him a symbol for the man who understands life for what it is and plays the game accordingly. For other, more tragic H. heroes, life is a gamble that cannot be won.

Dramas in which H. developed his life-is-a-dream metaphor explore the idea that the dreamer is a creator of an alternate reality. The most important of these plays, *Der Turm* (1925; 2nd version, 1927; *The Tower*, 1963), is an outgrowth of many years' work with material from Calderón's *Life Is a Dream*. It became H.'s final major tragedy. With pessimistic overtones arising from H.'s experience of World War I, *Der Turm* portrays life as a nightmare, examining the problem of the innocent individual in a chaotic world that has forsaken all spiritual values. It is a symbolic representation of H.'s own "prophetic dream" of the future of his own society.

For H., the main task of the modern writer was to provide the reader with access to all of human experience. Through his poetry, essays, dramas, and narratives, by editing collections of earlier writings, and in his commitment to the cultural life of the German-speaking countries, H. accomplished much toward the achievement of that goal, thereby earning a place among the most significant literary figures in Austrian history.

FURTHER WORKS: *Die Hochzeit der Sobeide* (1899; *The Marriage of Sobeide*, 1920); *Theater in Versen* (1899); *Der Kaiser und die Hexe* (1900; *The Emperor and the Witch*, 1961); *Studie über die Entwicklung des Dichters Victor Hugo* (1901); *Der Schüler* (1902); *Ausgewählte Gedichte* (1903); *Unterhaltungen über literarische Gegenstände* (1904); *Das gerettete Venedig* (1905; *Venice Preserved*, 1915); *Das Märchen der 672. Nacht, und andere Erzählungen* (1905); *Kleine Dramen* (1906); *Oedipus und die Sphinx* (1906; *Oedipus and the Sphinx*, 1968); *Der weiße Fächer* (1907; *The White Fan*, 1909); *Die gesammelten Gedichte* (1907); *Die prosaischen Schriften* (3 vols., 1907, 1917); *Vorspiele* (1908); *Die Frau im Fenster* (1909; *Madonna Dianora*, 1925); *König Oedipus* (1910); *Alkestis* (1911); *Der Rosenkavalier* (1911; *The Rose-Bearer*, 1912);

Ariadne auf Naxos (1912; *Ariadne on Naxos*, 1922); *Der Bürger als Edelmann* (1912); *Deutsche Erzähler* (4 vols., 1912); *Josephslegende* (1914; *The Legend of Joseph*, 1914); *Österreichischer Almanach auf das Jahr 1916* (1916); *Dame Kobold* (1920); *Reden und Aufsätze* (1921); *Buch der Freunde* (1922); *Deutsches Lesebuch* (2 vols., 1922–1923); *Die grüne Flöte* (1923); *Florindo* (1923); *Prima Ballerina* (1923); *Deutsche Epigramme* (1923); *Augenblicke in Griechenland* (1924; *Moments in Greece*, 1952); *Achilles auf Skyros* (1925); *Die Ruinen von Athen* (1925); *Früheste Prosastücke* (1926); *Schillers Selbstcharakteristik* (1926); *Drei Erzählungen* (1927); *Wert und Ehre deutscher Sprache* (1927); *Der Tod des Tizian* (1928 [written 1892]; *The Death of Titian*, 1914); *Die ägyptische Helene* (1928; *Helen in Egypt*, 1928); *Ad me ipsum* (1930); *Loris* (1930); *Die Berührung der Sphären* (1931); *Wege und Begegnungen* (1931); *Das Bergwerk zu Falun* (1933; *The Mine at Falun*, 1961); *Nachlese der Gedichte* (1934); *Briefe 1890–1901* (1935); *Der Briefwechsel H.-Wildgans* (1935); *Dramatische Entwürfe* (1936); *Briefe 1900–1909* (1937); *Das Leben ein Traum* (1937); *Festspiele in Salzburg* (1938); *Briefwechsel zwischen George und H.* (1938); *Gesammelte Werke in Einzelausgaben* (15 vols., 1945 ff.); *Erlebnis des Marschalls von Bassompierre, und andere Erzählungen* (1950); *Richard Strauss und H. v. H. Briefwechsel* (1952; *Correspondence between Richard Strauss and H. v. H.*, 1927); *H. v. H. und Eberhard von Bodenhausen: Briefe der Freundschaft* (1953); *H. v. H. und Rudolf Borchardt Briefwechsel* (1954); *H. v. H. und Carl J. Burckhardt Briefwechsel* (1956); *Sylvia im "Stern"* (1959); *H. v. H. und Arthur Schnitzler Briefwechsel* (1964); *H. v. H. und Helene von Nostitz-Wallwitz Briefwechsel* (1965); *Die Lästigen* (1965); *H. v. H. und Edgar Karg von Bebenburg Briefwechsel* (1966); *Briefe an Marie Herzfeld* (1967); *H. v. H. und Leopold von Andrian Briefwechsel* (1968); *H. v. H. und Willy Haas: Ein Briefwechsel* (1968); *H. v. H. und Harry Graf Kessler Briefwechsel 1898–1929* (1968); *Reitergeschichte: Erzählungen und Aufsätze* (1969); *H. v. H. und Josef Redlich Briefwechsel* (1971); *H. v. H. und Richard Beer-Hofmann Briefwechsel* (1972); *H. v. H. und Ottonie von Degenfeld Briefwechsel* (1974); *Komödien* (1974); *Sämtliche Werke* (1975 ff.); *H. v. H. und Rainer Maria Rilke Briefwechsel* (1978); *Gesammelte Werke in zehn Einzelbänden* (10 vols., 1979 ff.); *Briefwechsel H. v. H. und Paul Zifferer* (1983); *Briefwechsel mit Ottomie Gräfin Degenfeld und Julie Freifrau von Wendelstedt* (1986); *Briefwechsel 1907-1926: H. v. H. und Rudolf Pannwitz* (1993). FURTHER WORKS IN ENGLISH: *The Lyrical Poems of H. v. H.* (1918); *Selected Prose* (1952); *Poems and Verse Plays* (1961); *Selected Plays and Libretti* (1963); *Three Plays* (1966); *Four Stories* (1968)

BIBLIOGRAPHY: Schaeder, G., *H. v. H.* (1933); Naef, K. J., *H. v. H.'s Wesen und Werk* (1938); Hammelmann, H., *H. v. H.* (1957); Hederer, E., *H. v. H.* (1960); Fiechtner, H. A., ed., *H. v. H.* (1963); Norman, F., ed., *H* (1963); Coghlan, B. L., *H.'s Festival Dramas* (1964); Burckhardt, C. J., *Erinnerungen an H.* (1964); Wunberg, G., *Der frühe H.* (1965); Weber, H., *H. v. H. Bibliographie des Schrifttums 1892–1963* (1966); Ritter, F., *H. v. H. und Österreich* (1967); Alewyn, R., *Über H. v. H.* (1967); Pickerodt, G., *H.'s Dramen* (1968); Goldschmit, R., *H.* (1968); Bauer, S., ed., *H. v. H.* (1968); Kobel, E., *H. v. H.* (1970); Bangerter, L. A., *Schiller and H.* (1974); Mauser, W., *H. v. H.* (1977); Bangerter, L. A., *H. v. H.* (1977); Kovach, T. A., *H. and Symbolism* (1985); Frink, H., *Animal Symbolism in H.'s Works* (1987); Bennett, B., *H. v. H.: The Theaters of Consciousness* (1988); Koch, H.-A., *H. v. H.* (1989);

Del Caro, A., *H. v. H.: Poets and the Language of Life* (1993); Mayer, M., *H. v. H.* (1993); Bottenberg, J., *Shared Creation* (1996); LeRider, J., *H. v. H.* (1997)

—LOWELL A. BANGERTER

In all the facets of his thoughts on poetics the same underlying trend can be observed, a trend toward a fuller engagement with reality, noticeable in the demand for . . . harmony, order and plasticity. . . . However, these imaginary conversations and letters do more than elucidate some basic problems of aesthetics . . . in their essence they constitute an act of self-clarification. It is nothing less than the quintessence of H.'s experience, as we know it from his early lyric period, now reviewed and revised. It is the old problem of personality, its identity and continuity that occupies him throughout these essays.

The receptivity of the young poet who surrendered to the impressions and experiences of the moment was such that at times he was threatened with a loss of any sense that he himself was a continuous entity in time, capable of enduring and assimilating these experiences . . . . This is the poet of *Gestern* who expresses by the very title of his playlet that that residue of personality beyond the immediate here and now of experience is felt as an obsolete remnant, an appendage that cannot be removed from the consciousness but which does not truly belong there.

Mary E. Gilbert, "H.'s Essays 1900–1910: A Poet
in Transition," in Frederick Norman, ed., *H.*
(1963), pp. 44–45

Time is the measure of mutability; and nothing is more patent than H.'s oppressive awareness of the transience of earthly things. . . . His very first playlet, *Gestern*, is an ironic comment upon the failure of his hero to come to terms with this basic fact. The awareness of time is a threat at all . . . levels. . . . For the neoplatonic mystic whose gaze is fixed on the eternal and unchanging essences, it is a confirmation that he is right in turning away from a world of shadows; there is an echo of this in the text from St. Gregory of Nyssa with which H. prefaced *Ad me Ipsum*. . . . An experience of time is one thing, an acceptance of its implications is another. To accept is to bind oneself, to have a fate; and this, for the lyric poet, can lead to crisis. . . . H.'s life was an endeavor to come to terms with the problems of time and eternity. The corrosive effect of time was a permanent threat; it was the meaning and possibility of eternity which had first to be thrashed out, starting with that painful process which led from the testing and rejection of a false notion of eternity as time open at both ends to that transcendence of change which can be achieved by the acceptance of a fate and metamorphosis through love.

John Bednall, "From High Language to Dialect: A
Study in H.'s Change of Medium," in Frederick
Norman, ed., *H.* (1963), pp. 101–2

He had much of that cosmopolitanism of outlook, both political and cultural, which has for long been a distinguishing feature of Vienna, standing from Roman times at a crossroads in Europe, the gateway to the Balkans, to the Slavonic East and the Near East, to the Germanic North and to the Mediterranean South.

Sensitive to currents flowing into Vienna from all directions, H. presents a finely balanced dualism, for this supranational side of his intellectual character appears with equal strength alongside his abiding love for simple rural custom, folk language and traditions, which are depicted in his work with marked sympathy. This dualism . . . was with time to become a dominating characteristic. . . .

The young H. was . . . one of those phenomena which an old civilization brings forth without effort from time to time. H., even more perhaps than Mozart or Richard Strauss, sprang fully armed at all points into the intellectual world. . . . At the age of seventeen, while still a schoolboy, H. was using the German language with an ease, a coruscating magic and wealth of overtone and suggestion whose like had not been experienced since the death of Goethe.

Brian Coghlan, *H.'s Festival Dramas* (1964),
pp. 7–8

In terms of plot, then, *Andreas* appears to be just one more historical novel of picaresque adventures set in foreign lands. Yet what a plot summary conceals are the work's two most singular aspects: its extraordinarily modern, spatial structure and its highly symbolic mode of narration. Fully half of the eighty completed pages of the fragment deal, in the form of a flashback, with Andreas' adventures in the Alps; the episodes with Romana and Gotthilff, in other words, are given to us through the internal focus of Andreas' memory, as he sits musing for an hour or so in his room in Venice. In the Venetian scenes, on the other hand, style and narrative standpoint strike the reader as disturbingly modern and surrealistic, for the technique employed is very similar to that of both E. T. A. Hoffmann and Kafka, and the themes involved are those of reality-confusion, projected psychological disturbances and split personality. . . . Through its symbolic form and style, the action throughout the novel is thus effectively shifted from the outer landscape of epic narrative . . . to the complex inscape of twentieth century fiction. . . . Andrea's development does not press ever outward toward a Goethean fulfillment of the total personality, but rather inward . . . to an ultimate renewal and reassertion of the self.

David H. Miles, *H.'s Novel "Andreas"* (1972),
pp. 109–10

Many of these early works of H. were illustrated with Jugendstil nature scenes. In these intricate and elaborate designs a natural world was depicted in which each separate organism is organically connected with some other entity, a plant stalk joins up with the tail of a peacock, a brook becomes the leaf of a tree. It is a vision of the universe as a magically harmonious dream garden, beyond the divisive power of time. Precisely this is however the incomprehensible—for events do pass by, the present does not remain present, an organic part of our own being has gone through the process of being forgotten. The writer realizes that the single body of himself, his childhood, and his ancestors is made possible only through the liquid flow of time, the gliding motion which causes present to become past, and the ancestors to die physically only to remain alive in the body of the children. H. cannot rid his magic garden of the process of history. He feels in the identification of himself with the bodies of the past the drive of time: it is a realization he is reluctant to come to, but it occurs over and over in his struggle to draw some conclusion regarding his magic lyric powers.

> Peter A. Stenberg, "*Der Rosenkavalier*: H.'s Märchen of Time," *GL&L*, 26 (1972), p. 25

When H. no longer needed to explore and define the shifting transitional stages of his inner maturation, and when his concern with more general themes had reached a degree of complexity that burst the bounds of the lyric genre, he had little left to say that could best be said in the medium of poetry. The later poem "Reiselied" (1898) shows that technically speaking he could still write poetry very well indeed, but it is a poem without human complexities, a symbolic summing up of his own poetic ideal of Arcadian serenity and gentle beauty. . . . If we posit the view that by the end of his lyric phase poetry had outlived its usefulness for H., we have a more convincing answer to the question of why he stopped writing in the genre than the answer most frequently given, namely that he lost faith in the power of language to do justice to experience. . . . The preeminence given to the "language crisis" has of course been largely based on the questionable . . . assumption that the famous "Chandos Letter" was an autobiographical utterance. If H. did suffer a "Sprachkrise" this did not prevent him from giving consummate linguistic expression to that very crisis, nor did it impair his powers of language in any of his contemporary or subsequent writings.

> David E. Jenkinson, "The Poetry of Transition: Some Aspects of the Interpretation of H.'s Lyrics," *GL&L*, 27 (1974), p. 301

HØJHOLT, Per

Danish poet, b. 22 July 1928, Esbjerg, Jutland

Born in the western Danish province of Jutland, H. trained as a librarian and worked at various libraries in Copenhagen (and, for a time, Norway) until the mid-1960s, when a combination of state financial support and freelance work allowed him to devote himself full-time to writing. At that time he and his wife returned to live in Jutland, making their home in a renovated stable near the town of Silkeborg.

H.'s early work, published in periodicals and in his first two collections, *Solen og hesten* (1949; The Sun and the Horse) and *Skrift på vind og vand* (1956; Writing on Wind and Water), shows an affinity with the group of writers associated with the literary journal *Heretica*, proponents of international literary MODERNISM in Denmark. His real breakthrough, however, came with *Poetens hoved* (1963; The Poet's Head). Many of these radically depersonalized poems explore the poet's relationship to nature. A theoretical essay, *Cézannes metode* (1967; Cézanne's Method), complements H.'s work from this period. Of central importance is the concept of the "formless" (from the Greek "apeiron") to which poetry ultimately refers, and H.'s view of poetry as the experience of an interval of time.

A new phase of H.'s production begins with *Show* (1966; Show), where the poems often verge on the nonsensical in their play with linguistic situations. *Turbo* (1968; Turbo) is a long poem in the form of a letter (later released as a recording in a somewhat revised form). *Turbo* is, as the title implies, a dynamic mass of language and associations, considered one of the milestones of Danish poetry of the 1960s. *Punkter* (1971; Points), on the other hand, is more contemplative, originally published in a ring binding, with the poems in sequence but without a fixed starting or ending point. H.'s method in this phase of his production, including the idea of "show" and the poem as mask or grimace, is discussed in a second theoretical collection of essays, *Intethedens grimasser* (1972; The Grimaces of Nothingness).

H.'s later work has been published in a numbered series of chapbook-sized volumes under the common title "Praksis" (Practice). The poems in *Praksis, 1: Revolver* (1977; Revolver) and *Praksis, 2: Groteskens område* (1978; The Region of the Grotesque) both reprise various aspects of the poet's work since *Poetens hoved* and suggest new directions. In the latter category are a series of poems about a comic book superhero. Several sections of *Groteskens område*, including the title poem, contemplate the role of the artist.

H. has also published a number of experimental prose works. *6512* (1969), for example, is an experimental novel, or antinovel. In a parody of the diary novel, an unnamed narrator makes daily entries, never more than a page long, in a notebook. These entries are, however, arranged alphabetically rather than chronologically. The result is an often comic depiction of a group of characters living on the margins of small-town Danish society.

Praksis, 3: Det fireogtresindstyvende frokost i det grønne (1979; The 64th Lunch in the Open) is a prose work with an unusual form. Sixty-three short sections (each about a paragraph in length) present four different narratives, at times reminiscent of *6512*. Midway in the book a discussion of Manet's famous painting, *Déjeuner sur l'Herbe* (and multiple reproductions of it), appears as a footnote that takes up more and more space on successive pages. The work as a whole can be read as a meditation on the place of human activity (including art) in nature.

In three volumes of the *Praksis* series, *Lynmuseet* (1982; The Lightning Museum), *Salamandaren* (1986; The Salamander), and *Hundekunsteren* (1988; The Dog Artist), H. developed a genre of short, fantastic tales which he calls "blindgyder" ("blind alleys" or "dead ends"). These tales show an acknowledged debt to Edgar Allan Poe, Jorge Luis BORGES, and Isak DINESEN, and are written in a sober, "classical" style at deliberate odds with the fantastic elements.

H. has also written and performed a number of experimental pieces for radio broadcast. In 1979 he began publishing and performing occasional poems for radio collected in *Kvababbelser* (1985; Kvababbelser). Many of these pieces deal with current events in an oblique, humorous fashion. About the same time H. created the character of "Gitte," a young, married woman from Jutland who takes on diverse subjects—gardening, Mont Blanc, social democracy—in the extremely popular series, *Gittes monologer* (1984; Gitte's Monologues). H.'s performances of these pieces around Denmark made him a well-known figure in the late 1970s and 1980s.

Consistently experimental and an inspiration for several generations of younger writers, H. is clearly one of the most important writers of the postwar generation in Denmark.

FURTHER WORKS: *Provinser* (1964); *Min hånd 66* (1966); *+1* (1969); *Volumen* (1974); *Smerteskolen og andre digte* (1979); *Digte 1963-79* (1982); *Praksis 5: Nuet drunknet i latter* (1984); *Praksis, 8: Album, tumult* (1989); *Praksis, 9: Det gentagnes musik* (1989); *Praksis, 10: Manøvrer* (1993); *Stenvaskeriet og andre stykker* (1994); *Praksis, 11: Lynskud* (1995); *Praksis, 12: Anekdoter* (1996)

BIBLIOGRAPHY: Egebak, N., *H.'s metode* (1974); Jørgensen, B., "Opspring fra nulhuller," *Danske digtere i det 20 århundrede. Bind 4* (1982): 169-83; Holk, I., ed., *Natur/retur* (1984); Jørgensen, B., *Primitivitetens paradoksale kostume—om P. H.'s forfatterskab* (1986); Jörgensen, B., ed., *Rocky Mountains* (1988)

—PAUL NORLEN

HOLAN, Vladimir

Czechoslovak poet and translator (writing in Czech), b. 16 Sept. 1905, Prague; d. 31 May 1980, Prague

H.'s highly complex poetic work is considered to be one of the most important achievements of modern Czech literature. He dedicated to it the greater part of his life almost exclusively. Having completed his education at a *gymnasium*, H. was employed from 1927 as a clerk, but poor health made him retire in 1935. The rest of his years were largely spent in contemplative solitude. He withdrew into almost complete seclusion in the early 1950s after he had fallen into official disfavor with communist ideologists. The significance of his writing could be fully acknowledged only in the more liberal 1960s.

In the 1930s H. began to publish intellectually demanding hermetic poetry in collections such as *Vanutí* (1932; wafting) and *Oblouk* (1934; the arc). Multiplicity of meaning was couched in a style rich in imagery and permeated by paradoxes, inversions, misshapen words, and neologisms. It was in this type of poetry, reminiscent of Rainer Maria RILKE or Stéphane Mallarmé (1842–1898), that H. established his own poetic realm in which different modes of vision conflicted with each other. His imagination, bizarre yet based in reality, was shaped by this clash. H.'s meditations, his favorite means of approaching a subject, were filled with a dramatic tension emanating from the poet's essential metaphysical dualism, viewing the world as ever oscillating between good and evil, being and nothingness, the moment of time and eternity.

The national tragedy caused by the Munich Agreement about the dismemberment of Czechoslovakia in September 1938 and by German occupation six months later brought about a period of committed poetry: H.'s verse acquired an emotional and forcefully critical tone directed against the perpetrators of the country's betrayal. He conceived the political realities of the time as being part of a wider schism, and saw Nazism as a physical manifestation of the timeless evil. The tendency toward a simpler, down-to-earth style, reflected in particular in the use of a proselike free verse, culminated in H.'s postwar collections *Panychida* (1945; the wake) and *Tobě* (1947; to you), in which he celebrated the nation's regained freedom.

During the period of increased social and patriotic concern (1938–1947), H. also wrote *Terezka Planetová* (1943; Theresa Planet), the first of his poetic stories. These long poems, inspired by real-life events, are endowed with a strong epic sense. Each of the stories is presented as a symbol of the universal human condition and thus attains the quality of myth. Outstanding among them are *Příběhy* (1963; histories) and *Noc s Hamletem* (1964; A Night with Hamlet, 1980). The latter, a philosophical meditation in verse, contains the sum of H.'s thought on humans and the world, on existence, and on creativity and art.

Along with this narrative poetry H. kept up his output of lyric verse, which was collected in several volumes. In it he mainly attempted to transcend the world of the senses into a sphere of philosophical reflection.

The last four books of H.'s poetry represent the closing chapter of his creative development and are joined in an ideational and structural unity. They give the impression of a poetic diary in which he abandons the metaphor and reduces his style to gnomic terseness.

A considerable amount of H.'s effort was dedicated to the translation of poetry. Rilke, Charles Baudelaire (1821–1867), Luis de Gongóra y Argote (1561–1627), Charles Vildrac (1882–1971), Jean de La Fontaine (1621–1695), Pierre Ronsard (1524–1585), Adam Mickiewicz (1798–1855), and others found a kindred spirit in H., whose sympathetic interpretation assured them a permanent place in the wider context of Czech literature.

Although all of H.'s work was marked by contemplation, the angle from which he perceived the world changed with time. While in the 1930s his metaphysical dualism often assumed the manner of cold rationalistic construction, in the 1960s and 1970s his lyric poetry was inspired by a compassionate Christian understanding for the mysterious imperfection of human life. Posing oneself ever new questions about the fundamental aspects of existence was regarded by H. as the very purpose of writing poetry.

FURTHER WORKS: *Blouznivý vějíř* (1926); *Triumf smrti* (1930); *Kolury* (1932); *Torzo* (1933); *Kameni, přicházíš . . .* (1937); *Září 1938* (1938); *Sen* (1939); *Lemuria* (1940); *První testament* (1940); *Záhřmotí* (1940); *Chór* (1941); *Cesta mraku* (1945); *Dík Sovětskému svazu* (1945); *Zpěv tříkrálový* (1947); *Rudoarmějci* (1947); *Prostě* (1954); *Bajaja* (1955); *Tři* (1957); *Mozartiana* (1963); *Bez názvu* (1963); *Dvě jezera* (1963); *Na postupu* (1964); *Trialog* (1964); *Bolest* (1965); *Dva světy* (1966); *Na sotnách* (1967); *Asklépiovi kohouta* (1970); *Noc s Ofélií* (1973); *Sebrané spisy V. H.* (11 vols., 1965–1988); *Když růže přestaly chrlit krev* (1990). FURTHER WORKS IN ENGLISH: *Selected Poems* (1971); *Mirroring* (1983)

BIBLIOGRAPHY: Milner, I., Introduction to *Selected Poems* (1971): 9–15; Mihailovich, V. D., et al., eds., *Modern Slavic Literatures*

(1976), Vol. 2: 98–103; special H. issue, *La Revue de Belles-Lettres* 1–2 (1991)

—JAROSLAV MED

K. H., ed., *West German Poets on Society and Politics* (1979): 141–61

—JERRY GLENN

HÖLLERER, Walter

German poet, novelist, critic, and editor, b. 19 Dec. 1922, Sulzbach-Rosenberg

After service on the Mediterranean front during World War II, H. earned his doctorate in comparative literature and became a professor in Frankfurt and, later, Berlin. In the 1970s he taught at the University of Illinois.

The poems of H.'s first book, *Der andrere Gast* (1952; the other guest) reveal the author's familiarity with the literary tradition. Although many poems are rhymed and some are written in classical meters, his voice is strikingly original, especially in the use of images. The Mediterranean landscape often appears, in reference to antiquity as well as to the war. H.'s next three volumes of poetry, *Gedichte; Wie entsteht ein Gedicht* (1964; poems; how does a poem originate), *Außerhalb der Saison* (1967; off season), and *Systeme* (1969; systems), move further and further away from traditional forms, and *Systeme*, in appearance, although not in content, resembles concrete poetry.

If the early poems capture the essence of a single mood or scene, the later ones reflect H.'s growing interest in the complexities of contemporary society and his desire to address them in his works. Each of H.'s collections is progressive but not avant-garde, in relation to other verse written at the same time.

The novel *Die Elephantenuhr* (1973; the elephant clock) is a long, complicated work in which H.'s conception of the chaos and fragmentation of the contemporary world is reflected in the apparently chaotic style, structure, and plot. The protagonist is ultimately confined in a mental institution, where the manuscript is ostensibly written.

Few people have made a greater overall contribution to the contemporary German literary scene than H., who has also been active as a scholar, critic, editor, and literary theorist. One of the founding editors of *Akzente* in 1954, he remained a coeditor of this important periodical until 1967. In 1956 he edited *Transit*, one of the most significant anthologies of modern German poetry, and five years later became one of the founding editors of the journal *Sprache im technischen Zeitalter*. In his theoretical essays H. consistently takes a progressive position, but demands a solid intellectual basis and an understanding of different national literary traditions.

FURTHER WORKS: *Zwischen Klassik und Moderne* (1958); *Modernes Theater auf kleinen Bühnen* (1965); *Alle Vögel alle* (1978)

BIBLIOGRAPHY: Leonhard, K., "W. H.," in Nonnemann, K., ed., *Schriftsteller der Gegenwart* (1963): 157–62; Heselhaus, C., "Völlig versteckt im Frühwind (3)," in Domin, H., ed., *Doppelinterpretationen* (1966): 221–32; Lorbe, R., "W. H.: Schneeblauer Wind," *Lyrische Standpunkte* (1968): 135–42; Hinck, W., "Ein Boot ist immer versteckt," *Frankfurter Anthologie*, 3 (1978), 223–25; Van D'Elden,

HOLT, Kåre

Norwegian novelist, b. 27 Oct. 1917, Våle

The son of a railroad worker, and coming of age in the economically depressed 1930s, H. early became actively involved in the labor movement and worked as a journalist in the labor press. Eventually he was able to earn his living as a freelance writer and novelist. H.'s novels center, on the one hand, on a social theme—the struggle between the haves and the have-nots—and, on the other, on an existential one—at what point does man cease to be a product of heredity and environment and begin to be able to exert free will and assume responsibility for his actions.

H.'s artistic breakthrough was *Det store veiskillet* (1949; at the crossroads). On the eve of the Nazi invasion of Norway a young man is cornered in a desperate situation, and on the basis of the ensuing choice of action H. develops three different life stories for the boy. The novel is a psychological study of the collaborator, the traitor, and the hero, but above all H. treats the problem of choice and, as he sees it, man's ethical responsibility for his actions.

H.'s next important work was a thoroughly researched historical trilogy depicting the rise of the labor movement: *Det stolte nederlag* (1956; the proud defeat), *Storm under morgenstjerne* (1958; storm under morning star), and *Opprørere ved havet* (1960; rebels by the sea). The three novels are written with great poetic force and superb craftsmanship. *Kongen* (1965–69; the king) H.'s next novel, also a trilogy, portrays the medieval Norwegian king Sverre, a legendary rebel and impostor whose rise from poverty to power in H.'s view does not lead to the democratic revolution that King Sverre claimed in his own official saga. *Kongen* is a major novel in postwar Norwegian fiction, it is rich in historical detail and powerful in its psychological portrayal of human loneliness and the corruption of power. *Kappløpet* (1974; *The Race*, 1975) emphasizes the less heroic aspects of the life and psyche of the Norwegian national hero, the polar explorer Roald Amundsen, and caused a great stir among patriotic readers. H.'s thorough research, his great narrative talent, and his claim to poetic license, however, soon silenced his critics.

Similar debates (with similar results) occurred after his novels on the 18th-c. admiral Tordenskiold and the 17th-c. missionary to Greenland, Hans Egede, *Sjøhelten* (1975; hero of the sea) and *Sønn av jord og himmel* (1978; son of earth and heaven), respectively. These books strip the glamour from their protagonists, emphasizing human tragedy and human folly. H.'s studies of historical personages are at the same time critical and compassionate. They demonstrate his deep-seated suspicion of the corrupting influence of power as well as his fundamental belief in humanistic values.

FURTHER WORKS: *Tore kramkar* (1939); *Tore finner vei* (1940); *Spillemann og kjøgemester* (1941); *Hurra for han som innstifta da'n* (1945); *Udåden* (1945); *Demring* (1946); *Cleng Peerson og Nils med luggen* (1948); *Nattegjester* (1948); *Brødre* (1951); *Hevnen hører meg til* (1953); *Mennesker ved en grense* (1954); *Rømlingen Oskar og Maria fra Hulesjøen* (1959); *Den gamle veien til Kjerlighed* (1961); *Perlefiskeren* (1963); *Oppstandelsen* (1971);

Kristine av Tunsberg (1971); *Ansikter i sagaens halvlys* (1971); *Farvel til en kvinne* (1972); *Folket ved Svansjøen* (1973); *De lange mil til Paradiset* (1977); *Gjester fra det ukjente* (1980); *Mørke smil* (1981); *Biter av et bilde* (1981)

—KJETIL A. FLATIN

HOLUB, Miroslav

Czechoslovak poet, essayist, and translator (writing in Czech), b. 3 Sept. 1923, Plzeň; d. 14 July 1998, Prague

Having completed his secondary education at a *gymnasium* during the German occupation in 1942, H. worked on the railways and could resume his studies only after the war. He obtained an M.D. from Charles University in Prague in 1953 and a Ph.D. in immunology in 1958. He worked as a research scientist in various institutes in Czechoslovakia and abroad, including the Public Health Research Institute in New York (1965–1967) and the Max Planck Institute in Freiburg (1968–1969). He is the author of well over a hundred scientific papers and monographs in his field.

H.'s first poem came out in print in 1947, but he did not attract serious attention until he joined, in the mid-1950s, a group of younger writers associated with the literary magazine *Květen*, who were challenging the pompous, bloated, and sham heroic clichés of SOCIALIST REALISM. With his sober lyricism supported by intellectual analysis rather than spontaneity and instinct, H. was soon recognized as the foremost representative of this school referred to as "Poetry of Everyday Life." Conditions were not yet ready for a program of this kind, and after a brush with the political authorities, the magazine was closed down. However, many of the names that first appeared in its pages were later to reemerge as those of the best-known Czech poets and novelists.

H.'s first collection, *Denní služba* (1958; day duty), was followed two years later by *Achilles a želva* (1960; Achilles and the tortoise), and by 1970 he had produced another eight volumes of poetry. They met with almost unanimous praise from the critics, but the reception by the Czech public was more reserved. H.'s apparent trust in the near omnipotence of science and the emphasis he placed on a conscious human effort to improve the world seemed to be suspiciously close to official Marxist ideology. Moreover, the altogether cerebral nature of his verse was outside the traditional perception of poetry as experienced by his compatriots. Many of them had been nurtured on the romantic, emotional lyricism, the mellifluous language, and the dazzlingly beautiful imagery of earlier Czech poets, and found these qualities missing in H.

On the other hand, he was accorded the respect and admiration due to a major poet as soon as his work began to be published in the West. It was particularly well received in the U. S. and Britain, where in the 1960s an intellectualized conception of poetry was already well established through the efforts of William Carlos WILLIAMS and Lawrence Ferlinghetti (b. 1919), among others. It seemed that both in spirit and in style H.'s poetry was ideally suited for translation into English; in fact, some of it may read better in English than in the original Czech.

While he was steadily growing in stature abroad, at home H.'s scientific and poetic careers both suffered setbacks caused by the political repression that followed the Soviet invasion in 1968. In 1973 H. issued a statement in which he revoked his previously held "incorrect" views and which in effect contradicted the ethos of all his work. Afterward, he could publish and attend poetry festivals in the West, yet had to wait nine years to see a new collection of his verse appear in Czechoslovakia. When at long last *Naopak* (1982; *On the Contrary*, 1984) was published, it could not escape notice that a new note of skepticism had entered H.'s world of irrefragable scientific certainties and unrelenting rational progress, perhaps as a consequence of the recognition that reason need not always prevail. More questions were being asked than answers offered, but the mood was far from gloomy. Some poems, most notably "Sny" ("Dreams"), interpreted usually as alluding to the dismal situation in Czechoslovakia, in fact expressed hope of future change. A similar shift in attitude was noted in that part of H.'s work that up to 1982 had been known only in the West, such as *Notes of a Clay Pigeon* (1977 [*holub* means pigeon in Czech]), *Sagitální řez* (1988; *Sagittal Section*, 1980), and *Interferon čili o divadle* (1986; first pub. in English as *Interferon or On the Theater*, 1982).

As well as poetry, H. published a number of witty travelogues and several collections of refined essays in which his point of view advocating the necessity of a constant struggle to expand the realm of knowledge was applied to the discussion of aspects of contemporary life.

With a force stemming from the combination of art and science, H.'s poetry offers a terse comment on the state of humankind in the second half of the 20th c. It reflects the self-confidence of the first part of this period as well as the increasing doubt about the rationality of individual and social behavior as the end of the century approaches. Nonetheless, the essential message of H.'s work remains one of moderate encouragement and hope for the advance of scientific humanism. Many critics and fellow poets regard H. as one of the dozen greatest living poets. The clinical precision of his style and the compact imagery of his verse has such a direct appeal that the reader may forget that the original had been written in Czech. It could be argued, however, whether H.'s poetry would have been as universally effective had it not been supported by the poet's unique east European experience.

FURTHER WORKS: *Slabikář* (1961); *Jdi a otevři dveře* (1962); *Anděl na kolečkách* (1963); *Kam teče krev* (1963); *Zcela nesoustavná zoologie* (1963); *Tak zvané srdce* (1963); *Anamnéza* (1964); *Tři kroky po zemi* (1965); *Žít v New Yorku* (1969); *Ačkoli* (1969); *Beton* (1970); *Události* (1971); *K principu rolničky* (1987; *The Jingle Bell Principle*, 1991); *Maxwellův démon čili o tvořivosti* (1988); *nePATRNĚne* (1989); *Syndrom mizející plíce* (1990; *Vanishing Lung Syndrome*, 1990); *Skrytá zášť věku* (1991); *O příčinách porušení a zkázy těl lidských* (1992); *Ono se letělo*. FURTHER WORKS IN ENGLISH: *Selected Poems* (1967); *The Fly and Other Poems* (1987); *Poems Before and After* (1990); *The Dimension of the Present Moment and Other Essays* (1990); *Supposed to Fly* (1996); *Intensive Care* (1996)

BIBLIOGRAPHY: Alvarez, A., Introduction to *Selected Poems* (1967): 9–17; Mihailovich, V. D., et al., eds., *Modern Slavic Literatures* (1976), Vol. 2: 103–6; Schechter, B., "A Man for Two Cultures," *Discover*, May 1982: 60–64; Young, D., Introduction to *Interferon or On the Theater* (1982): 9–22; Heaney, S., *The Government of the Tongue* (1989): 45–53; Milner, I., Foreword to *Poems Before and After* (1990): 13–16; Reynolds, O., "A Voice for the Mute," *TLS*,

4–10 May 1990: 467–68; Crawford, R., "The Transnationality of the Czech Immunologist," *PoetryR*, 80, 2 (Summer 1990): 8–10

—IGOR HÁJEK

HONCHAR, Oles

Ukrainian novelist and short-story writer, b. 3 April 1918, Sukha

H. was born into a family of farm workers. In 1937 he completed his studies in journalism in Kharkov, and, following a brief career in journalism, he enrolled (in 1938) at Kharkov University. He served during World War II with distinction. In 1946 he entered the University of Dnepropetrovsk, where he studied literature and philology. The recipient of several major literary awards, he served (1958–66) as the chairman of the Writer's Union of the Ukrainian S.S.R., then as its first secretary (1966–69).

H.'s artistic development has paralleled a growth in national self-awareness. Despite his status as a pillar of Communist society he has dealt in a forthright manner with moral dilemmas in his wartime and war-focused pieces, and with the question of cultural vandalism by unsympathetic bureaucrats in his postwar writing.

Several novels concern the moral and ethical dilemmas posed by war. His trilogy *Praporonostsi* (2 vols., 1947–48; *The Standard Bearers*, 2 vols., 1948–50), deals with the officially promulgated messianic notion that informed the Soviet Union's postwar policies in Europe. It chronicles the pursuit of the defeated Wehrmacht to Prague by the Soviet army, following the Battle of Stalingrad. *Tavria* (1952; Tauris) describes the growth of class consciousness among the Ukrainian proletariat. The novel is directed against the "bourgeois nationalists" and their sympathizers. *Perekop* (1957; *Perekop*, 1958) gives a panorama of the postrevolution civil war in the Ukraine. The novel ends with the fall of Perekop into the hands of the Bolsheviks.

In sharp contrast to these works are H.'s shorter novels, *Shchob svityvsya vohnyk* (1955; so the fire may gleam) and *Masha z Verkhovyny* (1959; Masha from the Highlands), both essentially love stories, Soviet-style, that is, sad and tender in tone, with no attempt to include the physical side of love.

H.'s writing during the 1960s demonstrates more self-assertiveness and awareness of Ukrainian traditions. In *Tronka* (1963; *The Sheep Bell*, 1964), a "novel in twelve novellas," H. portrays contemporary people attempting to achieve a viable synthesis of earlier life styles with today's, contrasting the old shepherd and his way of life with that of the narrator, a pilot. He praises Soviet man, but also critically examines some negative traits of life under socialism.

The novel that has come to be recognized as his masterpiece, *Sobor* (1968; the cathedral), is an indictment of the Russian authorities and their Ukrainian minions who are oblivious to the values of the Ukrainian past and ruthless in uprooting them. *Sobor*, although initially praised by the literary establishment, came under scrutiny and was eventually banned and its author censured.

Tsyklon (1970; *Cyclone*, 1972) glorifies the Party and served to rehabilitate H., reestablishing his credentials with the Soviet authorities. The title has a double meaning: the storm of Nazism and the natural flood disaster that moves in from the Atlantic. These themes provide the basis for a philosophical discussion of the destructive forces in man and nature.

No writer publishing in the Ukraine today demonstrates a keener or more subtle awareness of man's dependence on the past and his responsibility to the future than H., who is, moreover, a continuer of the Ukrainian classical literary heritage. Whole passages in his recent writing appear to derive directly from the work of the great poet Taras Shevchenko (1814–1861).

H. has taken as his civic and literary task a serious, long-term, unrelenting assessment of his nation's present and past, distinguishing the healthy impulses from the pernicious, and postulating spiritual absolutes as the inescapable answer to current problems.

FURTHER WORKS: *Alpy* (1947); *Zemlya hude* (1947); *Holubay Dunay* (1948); *Modry kamen* (1948; *The Wise Stone*, 1955); *Novely* (1949); *Zlata Praha* (1949); *Mykyta Bratus* (1951; *Mykyta Bratus*, 1955); *Pivden* (1951; *The South*, 1955); *Doroha za khmary* (1953; *The Road to the Mountains*, 1953); *Partyzanska iskra* (1956); *Tvory* (4 vols., 1956–60); *Chary-Komyshi* (1958; *The Magic Reeds*, 1955); *Lyudyna i zbroya* (1960; *Man and Arms*, 1961); *Zirnytsi* (1960); *Yaponski etyudy* (1961); *Ilonka* (1972); *Pro nashe pismenstvo* (1972); *Bryhantyna* (1973); *Bereh lyubovi* (1976). FURTHER VOLUME IN ENGLISH: *Short Stories* (1955)

BIBLIOGRAPHY: Shabliovsky, Y., *Ukrainian Literature through the Ages* (1970): 216; Mihailovich, V. D. et al., *Modern Slavic Literatures* (1976), Vol. II: 467–69; A Note on O. H.," *Journal of Graduate Ukrainian Studies*,1, 1 (1976); Sverstiuk, Y., "A Cathedral in Scaffolding," in Luckyj, G. S. N., ed., *Clandestine Essays* (1976): 17–68; Rudnytzky, L., "O. H.'s *Cathedral*," *Mitteilungen: Arbeits- und Förderungsgemeinschaft der ukrainischen Wissenschaften*, 15 (1978): 96–125

—THOMAS E. BIRD

HONDURAN LITERATURE
See Central American Literature

HONGO, Garrett Kaoru

American poet, b. 30 May 1951, Volcano, Hawaii

Born in the village of Volcano, Hawaii and then later raised in a working-class neighborhood in Los Angeles, California, H. has written poetry and prose that memorialize these rediscovered places and people. In 1973 H., a Yonsei (fourth-generation Japanese American), received his B.A. from Pomona College in Claremont, California. He first achieved success as a writer while the founder and artistic director (1975-77) of the Asian Exclusion Act theater group in Seattle, Washington. After receiving his M.F.A. at the University of California, Irvine in 1980, he achieved prominence with his noted volumes, *Yellow Light* (1982) and *The River of Heaven* (1988). The latter received a Lamont Poetry Prize and a Pulitzer Prize nomination in poetry. H. has twice won the National Endowment for the Arts Fellowships in poetry; he also received a Guggenheim Fellowship, the Hopwood Prize for Poetry from the University of Michigan, and a Thomas J. Watson Fellowship to travel and write in Japan. His eminent status as a American poet and professor of creative writing at the University of Oregon has been augmented by his published prose work, *Volcano: A Memoir of Hawai'i* (1995).

Stylistically, H.'s Whitmanesque use of parallel phrasing, where he layers carefully words and images, creates a nexus of visual and sensate details. In addition, he uses animal imagery as well as Hawaiian legend to inform his poetic impressions. These cultural and organic memories reverberate with profound resonance. Contextually, H.'s poetry and prose are expansive, for they touch upon the personal, social, historical, and philosophical. In fact, many of his poems contain poignant examinations of people, places, nature, heritage, and history. *Yellow Light*, H.'s first poetic collection, offers tender homages to Japanese American history and the working class. Mainly, H. writes about the laborer, venerating his own grandfather and father and those in poor neighborhoods who struggle daily to maintain dignity. He also records history through illuminating and bracing personal points of views. In "Stepchild" H. highlights how Japanese American historical exclusion from school textbooks and discussions demonstrates a cruel erasure from history and society because America as a whole has not acknowledged them as Americans. Also forgotten are the Asian laborers, many of whom were used and then ousted from the country when no longer needed. In other poems H. explores our need not only to discern our own essences but also to generate a depth of feeling for humanity. The poem "Roots" encourages the location of the deeper self, the dedication to its discovery, and the knowledge that there is a unique signature to all things animate and inanimate.

The River of Heaven explores themes carried over from *Yellow Light*. H. emphasizes the importance of shared common experiences and the need for dignity and escape from ridicule. In many of his poems, H. invokes memories by reconstructing the past through a variety of perspectives. On the one hand, he wants to commune with departed elders, memorializing those gone by inhabiting specific people and characters in order to tell their stories. Consequently, he documents their lives so that they may continue to live. "The Pier" speaks to the "splendor" H.'s father and many immigrants imagine for themselves in the day-to-day world where they experience often pain, humiliation, and ridicule. On the other hand, "96 Tears" reveals how the disparity in language use in America becomes hierarchicalized, but that those who choose to act, to verbalize, can define themselves, even if their language abilities are not considered acceptable. Largely, this poem specifies how this urban, multiclass, multicultural high school yields hybrid portraits of complex and romantic Asian American males, where the mood and tenor enacted by these young men are creatively informed by the music and fashion of that time.

H.'s inspiration to write *Volcano: a Memoir of Hawai'i* (1995) stems in part from reading "natural history writers" such as Herman Melville, Ralph Waldo Emerson, and Henry David Thoreau. Rather than the high seas or Walden Pond, however, H. shows reverence for Hawaii, a place he considers his "center" to which "the roots" of his soul should remain loyal. Yet, rather than a call for a nostalgic imagining of a homeland, H. pays mindful consideration to the inextricable historical, cultural, and personal ties of people, land, and culture. Through description and storytelling, H. displays that a quest for meaning and placement ultimately aids knowing self. H.'s memoir carefully renders the multilayered aspect of life and identity as he explores places of origin and influence in his life.

At this point in his career, H.'s work emphasizes the need to recognize the complexity of human and natural existence and to reexamine our detachment from ourselves, from our spirits, from each other. His poetry and prose ask that we open our minds and souls to the magnanimous formulations regarding the preciousness of humanity and nature. Moreover, H. emphasizes that we must make part of our life's goals to find the "unique signatures" within ourselves.

FURTHER WORKS: *Nisei Bar and Grill* (1976); *The Buddha Bandits Down Highway 99* (1978, with Alan Chong Lau and Lawson Fusao Inada)

BIBLIOGRAPHY: Uba, G., " *Yellow Light*," *JEthS*, 12, 4 (1985): 123-25; Schultz, R., "Passionate Virtuosity," *HudR*, 17 (Spring 1989): 149-57; Evans, A., "A Vicious Kind of Tenderness: An Interview with G. H.," *P&W*, 20 (Sept.-Oct.1992): 36-46; Filipelli, L., *G. H.* (1997)

—SUZANNE K. ARAKAWA

HOPE, A(lec) D(erwent)

Australian poet and literary critic, b. 21 July 1907, Cooma

After graduating from the universities of Sydney (1928) and Oxford (1930), where he read philology, H. taught in Sydney and lectured at Sydney Teachers' College and Melbourne University. In 1951 he was appointed professor of English at Canberra University College (later the Australian National University), where he remained until his retirement in 1968. From 1969 to 1972 he was a Library Fellow at A.N.U. and in 1972 was awarded an O.B.E.

Although H. published in journals, his was a coterie audience until his first book, *The Wandering Islands* (1955). This collection, which received wide acclaim and immediately placed him in the vanguard of contemporary Australian poetry, is notable for its formalism, its satire of modern mass culture, and its themes of isolation, anxiety, and guilt. Subsequent volumes, *Poems* (1960), *New Poems* 1965–1969 (1969), and *A Late Picking: Poems 1965–1974* (1975), continue themes and formal preoccupations set down in *The Wandering Islands*, but from *New Poems* on, a depth and range of feeling was realized that was only hinted at in the first volume: the demonic pride gives way to a communal poetry of humility and love. *A Late Picking* draws imagery from astronomy and physics, further exploring the efficacy of journeying into the unknown, a central concern of H.'s poetry from the outset. His *Dunciad Minor: An Heroick Poem* (1970) takes for its target an Australian critic, but its broad references to modern critics and criticism leads it beyond the local to an indictment of what H. takes to be an accelerating loss of faith in reason and a corresponding erosion of a uniform theological and intellectual (poetic and critical) tradition.

H. also wrote numerous essays on poetry and on literature in general, in which he elaborated his formalism, fitted Australian writing into a larger pattern of writing in English, and asserted the function of the poet "to participate in and support the order of the world." H. also wrote monographs on Australian literary history and on Australian writers, and published a long study of the Scottish poet William Dunbar (1460?–1520?), *A Midsummer Eve's Dream: Variations on a Theme by William Dunbar* (1970). Dunbar's greatness, H. argues with relevance to his own work, lies in his "amplitude of reference to great issues in human life and human history."

Central to H.'s poetry is a tension between his "classical" concern for form and a late romantic view of man and the poet, recognizing questions of isolation and guilt and positing the artist as a synthesizer struggling to find order and relation, to restore connections to personal and social life. What appeared at first to be savage and ironic in his poetry, can, in the context of his later work, be seen as more truly celebratory, "even when what is asserted is itself a tragic or a terrifying truth." H. turns to the cultural reservoir of European literature for his sources, speaking in a public voice the "great commonplaces"; thus, his narratives, landscapes, and characters carry analogical significance beyond the particular case.

H. has established himself as one of the most significant poets in Australian literature, noted for his eloquence and candor. His formalism never falters, but, like his themes, speaks of his MODERNISM, for in it we sense the need to impose order on chaos.

FURTHER WORKS: *Australian Poets Series—A. D. H.: Selected Poems* (1963); *Australian Literature 1950–1962* (1963); *The Cave and the Spring: Essays on Poetry* (1965); *The Literary Influence of Academies* (1970); *Henry Kendall: A Dialogue with the Past* (1971); *Collected Poems 1930–1970* (1972); *Selected Poems* (1973); *Native Companions: Essays and Comments on Australian Literature 1936–1966* (1974); *Judith Wright* (1975); *A Book of Answers* (1978); *The Pack of Autolycus* (1978); *The Drifting Continent and Other Poems* (1979); *The New Cratylus: Notes on the Craft of Poetry* (1979)

BIBLIOGRAPHY: Goldberg, S. L., "The Poet as Hero: A. D. H.'s *The Wandering Islands*," *Meanjin*, 16 (1957): 127–39; Wright, J., "A. D. H.," *Preoccupations in Australian Poetry* (1965): 181–92; Heseltine, H. P., "Paradise Within: A. D. H.'s *New Poems*," *Meanjin*, 29 (1970): 405–20; Brissenden, R. F., "Art and the Academy: The Achievement of A. D. H.," in Dutton, G., ed., *The Literature of Australia* (1976): 406–26; Kramer, L., *A. D. H.* (1979); Hooton, J., *A. D. H.: A Bibliography* (1979)

—JAMES WIELAND

HORA, Josef

Czechoslovak poet (writing in Czech), b. 8 July 1891, Dobříň u Roudnice; d. 21 June 1945, Prague

Following his parents' separation, H. was raised by his mother's family. Having graduated from law school in 1916, H. moved to Prague, where he joined the staff of *Právo lidu*. When the Communist Party was founded, he joined and transferred to its organ, *Rudé právo*, which he left in 1929, disappointed with the leadership. Next he joined *České slovo*, the organ of the Czechoslovak Socialist Party. From 1929 to 1932 H. published *Plán*, a journal of literature, art, and science, and, in 1935, he founded a series of monographs called *Postavy a dílo* (men and creative work), to which he contributed a monograph (1935) on Karel Toman (pseud.

of Antonín Bernášek, 1877–1946), a Czech poet and translator. When war was imminent, he became one of the organizers of the antifascist movement in Czechoslovakia. The last years of his life H. spent seriously ill in his Prague apartment, where he died shortly after the liberation.

H.'s first collection of poetry, *Básně* (1915; poems), shows the influence of prewar SYMBOLISTS, but it already reveals H.'s creative program, namely, the reflection of the world and himself in a subjective record. Vitalism, characterized by an enthusiasm for the joy and beauty of life, the trend prevalent at the time, found expression here and in H.'s next collection, *Strom v květu* (1920; a tree in bloom). But in the second book, vitalism is combined with admiration for civilization. The motifs of nature and civilization intertwine, as do the personal and the social tones of these poems.

H.'s concern with social themes grew, and *Pracující den* (1920; the working day), one of H.'s greatest literary achievements, can best be described as proletarian poetry. Here his description of social wrongs and poverty attained a level of hymnic celebration of work and became a call for justice. The belief in justice and the dualism of the intimate and the social is also the theme of *Srdce a vřava světa* (1922; the heart and the turmoil of the world). H's next volume, *Bouřlivé jaro* (1923; the tempestuous spring), gives evidence of a crisis of creativity: the poems, decrying the abuses of technological civilization and the ambivalence of justice, have neither the intensity of experience nor the daring imagery of his earlier work.

Itálie (1924; Italy) and *Struny ve větru* (1927; strings in the wind) were inspired by H.'s visits to Italy and the Soviet Union, respectively. The former volume represents the peak of vitalist lyricism not only in H.'s works, but also in Czech poetry as a whole. Impressionistic images and poetic fancy blend in superb melody. The latter collection marks a new period in H.'s work. Whereas in *Itálie* the objective and the subjective elements are still in balance, in *Struny ve větru* there is greater subjectivity: the poet is now disgusted with social reality, and as a means of escape he tends to use an inner, more spiritual lyricism and to stop and ponder over "time and silence"—the time of the painful crisis of the 1930s and the silence of nature in his own countryside.

H.'s leaning toward metaphysics gained momentum, and in collections like *Tonoucí stíny* (1923; drowning shadows); *Dvě minuty ticha* (1934; two minutes of silence), and *Tiché poselství* (1936; a silent message) H. demonstrated a melancholy about the futility of life and an inconsolable fear of transitoriness. These feelings brought him to the romantic pessimism of the Czech poet Karel Hynek Mácha (1810–1836), whom he acknowledged as his master in *Máchovské variace* (1936; Mácha variations). Eventually, under pressure of the impending Nazi occupation, H. paradoxically regained some of his faith in life. His *Jan houslista* (1939; Jan the violinist) clearly shows H.'s ardent love for his homeland. This work is strongly influenced by Pushkin's *Eugene Onegin*, which H. masterfully translated.

Although H. also wrote essays and criticism, his main achievement lies in his poetry, and as the foremost of the Czech lyric poets writing after World War I, he had a tremendous influence on the young generation of the period from the 1930s to the end of World War II.

FURTHER WORKS: *Socialistická naděje* (1922); *Hliněný babylón* (1922); *Z politické svatyně* (1924); *Probuzení* (1925); *Hladový rok* (1926); *Mít Křídla* (1928); *Smrt manželů Pivodových* (1928); *Deset let* (1929); *Tvůj hlas* (1930); *Chvíle v Estonsku* (1932); *Popelec*

(1934); *Domov* (1938); *Dech na skle* (1938); *Zahrada Popelčina* (1940); *Život a dílo básníka Aneliho* (1945); *Zápisky z nemoci* (1945); *Proud* (1946) *Pokušení* (1946); *Pozdravy* (1949); *Dílo J. H.* (1927–40); *Dílo J. H.* (1950–61)

BIBLIOGRAPHY: French, A., *The Poets of Prague* (1969), passim; Harkins, W. E., Supplement, in Novák, A., *Czech Literature* (1976): 316–18

—PETER Z. SCHUBERT

HORVÁTH, Ödön von

Austrian dramatist and novelist, b. 9 Dec. 1901, Fiume (now Rijeka, Croatia); d. 1 June 1938, Paris, France

The son of a Hungarian diplomat, H. moved frequently during his youth, living in a number of cities of the Austro-Hungarian Empire. His mother tongue was German, but from his exposure to the other languages of the monarchy, he developed a sharp ear for usage and for the mixtures of idioms characteristic of that part of the world.

After desultory studies at the University of Munich, H. turned to writing. *Buch der Tänze* (1922; book of dances) was a commissioned project, a series of poetic texts to serve as the basis for pantomime performances. Dissatisfied with the florid style, H. later borrowed money to buy up all remaining copies and have them destroyed.

In 1924 H. moved to Berlin, where he participated in the exciting cultural life of the city and achieved considerable renown as a playwright. On the recommendation of Carl ZUCKMAYER, he was awarded the prestigious Kleist Prize for young dramatists in 1931. In 1933, after the Nazi takeover, he left for Vienna, returning to Berlin briefly in 1934 to work on film scripts and study the phenomenon of Nazism firsthand. During the next four years, which H. spent in Vienna, he continued to write plays but found it increasingly difficult to get them performed. The German annexation of Austria in 1938 forced H. to flee. He was killed on the Champs Élysées in Paris in a freak accident: a tree limb fell on him during a storm. In addition to *Buch der Tänze*, H. left eighteen completed plays, three novels, a number of short prose works, and numerous fragments; most of these works were not published during his lifetime.

H. designated his first notable play, *Revolte auf Côte 3018* (1927; rebellion on slope 3018), which was revised as *Die Bergbahn* (1927; the mountain railway), a *Volksstück*, or "play for and about the common folk"; H. here drew upon the conventions of a traditional genre, but revised the content, language, and dramaturgy to reflect how the character and situation of the *Volk* had changed since the genre's heyday in the 19th c. The play centers around a group of workmen constructing a mountain railway in the Bavarian Alps. Under pressure from the financial backers, the engineer in charge insists that work continue despite a winter storm. An accident results, providing the catalyst for a revolt by the workers. This early play, ideologically closer to Marxism than any of H.'s subsequent works, show a certain stylistic affinity to EXPRESSIONISM in the staging devices. But H.'s chief concern is language. All the characters, including the uneducated construction workers, have been infected by *Bildungsjargon*, the pretentious jargon shot through with advertising and propaganda clichés, which H. regards as both a symptom and a cause of the modern moral and political crisis.

With *Italienische Nacht* (1931; Italian night), his first play to attract great attention, H. continued his revision of the *Volksstück*. It depicts a confrontation between a small-town Social Democratic club and the local fascist group. Political obtuseness and cowardice are conveyed through language or through the juxtaposition of speech and action. The one Marxist character spouts theory without following it up in practice, and the Social Democrats hide behind phrases to avoid acknowledging the real menace to democracy posed by the fascists. Berlin audiences loved the play, which they mistook for a harmless comedy.

In his masterpiece, *Geschichten aus dem Wiener Wald* (1931; *Tales of the Vienna Woods*, 1977), H. used a large cast of Viennese to show various aspects of the petit-bourgeois mentality, which he saw as characteristic of his times. The characters cherish sentimental delusions about themselves but are actually motivated by resentment and aggression, the result of political and economic impotence. Through a deft combination of language, visual imagery, music, and action, H. stripped away the clichés that make up the popular image of Vienna. The city becomes a symbol of a moribund society, the waltz a dance of death that determines the structure of the play.

Two more *Volksstücke*, written just before Hitler came to power, reflect the economic misery caused by the Depression and the concomitant breakdown in human solidarity and compassion. In *Kasimir und Karoline* (1932; Kasimir and Karoline) H. used the backdrop of the Munich *Oktoberfest* to highlight the ugly desperation of the chauffeur Kasimir, whose girlfriend Karoline deserts him when he loses his job. As Kasimir and Karoline roam through the fair, hoping for new connections that will improve their prospects, they reveal the moral bankruptcy and the social alienation that helped prepare the way for Hitler, with his message of German race pride and his promise of economic recovery. *Glaube Liebe Hoffnung* (1932; faith hope love) illustrates the destruction of an individual by a judicial system biased against the unfortunate. Elisabeth, having been fined for peddling without a license, finds herself driven from one minor deception to another. When her new lover, a policeman, learns of her "past," he drops her, out of fear of jeopardizing his career. Her suicide makes plain the absence of faith, hope, and love in a society whose institutions are as rotten as its foundations.

After several years of writing plays that no major theater dared perform, H. turned to the novel, writing two in rapid succession: *Jugend ohne Gott* (1938; *The Age of the Fish*, 1939) and *Ein Kind unserer Zeit* (1938; *A Child of Our Time*, 1939). In a plain, sometimes rhythmic prose that combines elements of *Bildungsjargon* with streaks of uncritical sentimentality, these novels portray the effects of totalitarianism and its roots in the individual. The narrator of the first novel is a schoolteacher who witnesses the spread of corruption among his pupils. The second novel presents the interior monologue of a young man who finds pride and identity in becoming a soldier. Both works may be seen as psychological analyses of the fascist mentality. In addition, the two novels, like most of the plays written after 1933, display a distinctly religious cast. Fascism, whose psychological and economic origins H.

perceived with remarkable accuracy, appears in his later works as an overwhelming manifestation of evil, in the face of which the remaining good folk must go into hiding, like the early Christians in the catacombs. Divine grace, not an improvement in economic conditions, becomes the prerequisite for salvation.

Because of his untimely death and the Nazi ban on publication and performance of his works, H. was nearly forgotten. In the 1960s, however, a few television performances of his plays in West Germany awakened interest in H., not only for his acute observation of pre-Hitler social conditions but also for his precise recording of linguistic alienation and its relationship to political manipulation. Within the space of a few years, H. became a modern classic, performed throughout the German-speaking countries and ranked by a number of critics with Bertolt BRECHT.

Although the plots and linguistic references of H.'s works grow out of the specific atmosphere of the 1920s and 1930s, H.'s writings are better understood today than when they first appeared. Abuse of language by the Nazis and by subsequent political movements on both the right and the left has recently come under increasing scrutiny. H.'s recognition of the phenomenon of prefabricated speech links him with several of his contemporaries, who are likewise only now receiving the recognition they deserve: Karl KRAUS, Kurt TUCHOLSKY, and Marieluise FLEISSER. In the English-speaking world, George ORWELL's examination of language abuse is closely related to H.'s concerns. H.'s influence on such young playwrights as Peter HANDKE, Franz Xaver KROETZ, Wolfgang Bauer (b. 1941), and Martin Sperr (b. 1944) and the filmmaker Rainer Werner Fassbinder (b. 1946) is unmistakable.

In his choice of unheroic, ordinary people as characters, H. holds up a mirror to modern mass society. His works provide a powerful warning against jargon of all kinds, and against the mentality that seeks refuge from thought in clichés. His masterful, provocative portrayal of the verbal and characterological deformities typical of the modern industrial age makes H. a significant figure in 20th-c. literature.

FURTHER WORKS: *Mord in der Mohrengasse* (written c. 1923, pub. 1970); *Sportmärchen* (1924–1926); *Zur schönen Aussicht* (1927); *Sladek; oder, Die schwarze Armee* (1928; rev. as *Sladek der schwarze Reichswehrmann*, 1929); *Der ewige Spießer* (1930); *Die Unbekannte aus der Seine* (written 1933, pub. 1961); *Hin und Her* (written 1933, pub. 1969); *Himmelwärts* (1934); *Mit dem Kopf durch die Wand* (1935); *Der jüngste Tag* (1937); *Figaro läßt sich scheiden* (written 1936, pub. 1961); *Don Juan kommt aus dem Krieg* (1937); *Ein Dorf ohne Männer* (1937); *Pompeji, Komödie eines Erdbebens* (1937); *Gesammelte Werke* (4 vols., 1970–1971)

BIBLIOGRAPHY: Weisstein, U., "Ö. v. H.: A Child of Our Time," *Monatshefte*, 52 (1960): 343–52; Strelka, J., *Brecht—H.—Dürrenmatt: Wege und Abwege des modernen Dramas* (1962); Kahl, K., *Ö. v. H.* (1966); Loram, I., "Ö. v. H.: An Appraisal," *Monatshefte*, 59 (1967): 19–34; Hildebrandt, D., "Der Jargon der Uneigentlichkeit: Zur Sprache Ö. v. H.s," *Akzente*, 19 (1972): 109–23; Jarka, H., "Sprachliche Strukturelemente in Ö. v. H.'s Volksstücken," *CollG*, 4 (1973): 317–39; Kurzenberger, H., *H.'s Volksstücke: Beschreibung eines politischen Verfahrens* (1974); Winston, K., *H. Studies: Close Readings of Six Plays* (1977); Winston, K., "Ö v. H.: A Man for This Season", *MR*, 19 (1978): 169–80; Krischke, T., *Ö. v. H.: Ein Kind seiner Zeit* (1980)

—KRISHNA WINSTON

HOSTOVSKÝ, Egon

Czechoslovak novelist (writing in Czech), b. 23 April 1908, Hronov; d. 7 May 1973, Millburn, N.J., U.S.A.

After studying philosophy at the universities of Prague and Vienna, H. worked as an editor in various publishing houses. In 1937 he became an official in the Czechoslovak diplomatic service. During World War II he was assigned to Paris and later New York. In 1949, following the Communist takeover of the previous year, he resigned in protest from his position as chargé d'affaires at the Czech embassy in Oslo; from then on he lived in the U. S., earning his living as a scriptwriter for Radio Free Europe.

H.'s books written before and during the war deal with alienation, loneliness, guilt—real or imagined—fear of life, and the inability of their heroes, many of them Jewish like H. himself, to communicate. The problem of Jewish assimilation in the Czech milieu, the motif of the Dostoevskian double, the theme of "the insulted and the humiliated" all play important parts in his works. Many of his writings imply or reflect the struggle of good and evil forces both within and among men. A typical H. hero, clumsy, well-meaning, frustrated, can be found in his novel *Případ profesora Körnera* (1932; the case of Professor Körner). The author shows here an unusual ability to analyze the thinking and emotions of a Jewish intellectual, who is tormented by an inferiority complex and by the problem of assimilation and reacts by escaping into a world of dreams and illusions. In the novel *Žhář* (1935; the arsonist), for which H. received the prestigious State Prize for Literature, a triple arson in a small town is conceived as a symbol of the common danger and uncertainty threatening the world in the prewar period. The chaos of Europe in the late 1930s is mirrored in the novel *Sedmkrát v hlavní úloze* (1942; *Seven Times the Leading Man*, 1945), a tale, partly realistic, partly fantastic, concerned with the acceptance or rejection of Nazism by a group of intellectuals in Prague just before the fall of Czechoslovakia.

In his writings after 1948 H. added political events and espionage to his earlier subject matter, very likely as reflections of the Cold War. These new themes can be seen as a possible parallel to the works of Graham GREENE, whose influence (unlike that of DOSTOEVSKY and KAFKA), H. was willing to admit. The first book of this period was *Nezvěstný* (1955; *Missing*, 1952), whose protagonist, a Czech diplomat, finds himself in the center of interest of both Western and Eastern intelligence services during the 1948 Communist takeover in Prague. The autobiographical elements in this novel, as in many others, are rather obvious. Another "espionage" novel, *Půlnoční pacient* (1959; *The Midnight Patient*, 1954) is set in New York, as is *Dobročinný večírek* (1958; *The Charity Ball*, 1957), a satire peopled with refugees from east-central Europe and having a dubious "charity" as its central feature.

H.'s most significant work is *Všeobecné spiknutí* (1969; *The Plot*, 1961). It is a first-rate narrative, a brilliantly executed psychological tale in which fantasy, adventure, and philosophy are mingled in a nearly surrealistic and yet credible way. It was unfortunately ignored by most American critics, probably owing to a poor translation. Again, it is partly autobiographical, the hero being a former Czech diplomat and writer long resident in the U. S.

In the memoirs *Literární dobrodružství českého spisovatele v cizině aneb o ctihodném povolání kouzla zbaveném* (1966; literary adventures of a Czech writer abroad, or about an honorable profession deprived of charm), H. wrote with unusual frankness and often with painful self-irony about his parents, siblings, and himself living in the Czech countryside, and his failure to achieve world success as a writer. His only dramatic work, *Osvoboditel se vrací* (1972; the liberator is coming back), was never produced on stage. It portrays a fictitious land, probably Czechoslovakia, where a civil war has just ended and everyone crossed over to the victorious rebels who now expect their leader, the "liberator," to return from abroad, not knowing that he is bringing but another tyranny to his country and his family alike.

H.'s probing of subconscious drives, the sensitivity with which he treats his heroes, his rich inventiveness, and his craftsmanship remain unsurpassed in Czech literature. Next to Karel ČAPEK he is the best-known Czech writer outside Czechoslovakia.

FURTHER WORKS: *Zavřené dveře* (1926); *Stezka podél cesty* (1928); *Ghetto v nich* (1928); *Danajský dar* (1930); *Ztracený stín* (1932); *Černá tlupa* (1933; *The Black Band*, 1950); *Cesty k pokladům* (1934); *Dům bez pána* (1937); *Tři starci* (1938); *Kruh spravedlivých* (1938); *Listy z vyhnanství* (1941; *Letters from Exile*, 1942); *Úkryt* (1943; *The Hideout*, 1945); *Cizinec hledá byt* (1947); *Osaměli buřiči* (1948; *The Lonely Rebels*, 1951); *Tři noci* (1964; *Three Nights*, 1964); *Epidemie* (1972)

BIBLIOGRAPHY: Prescott, O., on *The Plot, NYT* (3 Feb. 1961): 23; Sturm, R., ed., *E. H.: Vzpomínky, studie a dokumenty o jeho díle a osudu* (1974, multilingual); Kunstmann, H., *Tschechische Erzählkunst im 20. Jahrhundert* (1974): 129–42

—RUDOLF STURM

A. E. Housman

HOUSMAN, A(lfred) E(dward)

English poet and classical scholar, b. 26 March 1859, Fockbury; d. 20 April 1936, Cambridge

From his birthplace H. could see to the northwest the hills of Shropshire for which his celebrated book of sixty-three lyrics, *A Shropshire Lad* (1896), is named. The eldest son of a Victorian middle-class family, H. was fondly devoted to his mother, whose death on his twelfth birthday had a considerable effect on him. After attending Bromsgrove School and, as he tells us in an autobiographical sketch, becoming attached to paganism by reading John Lemprière's (1765?–1824) *Classical Dictionary* (1788), he matriculated in 1877 at St. John's College, Oxford, where he met Moses J. Jackson. There is good reason to believe that his strong homosexual affection for Jackson was instrumental in his failure of the Greats at Oxford in 1881, since he was distracted from his studies. Disappointed, he went from Oxford to the menial drudgery of a clerk in the Patent Office in London. For the next ten years he spent his evenings in the British Museum perfecting scholarly papers on Aeschylus, Sophocles, Ovid, and other classical writers. These pursuits led in part to his appointment as Professor of Latin, University College, London, in 1892. Meanwhile, his work on Manilius and Juvenal began to appear, and in 1911 he was made Kennedy Professor of Latin at Cambridge and held the position until his death.

H.'s poetic output was meager, his reputation resting primarily on *A Shropshire Lad* and two other thin volumes, *Last Poems* (1922), and *More Poems* (1936). His reputation as a classical scholar is based primarily on his edition of Manilius's *Astronomica* (Books I–V, 1912–30), but also on his editions of Juvenal's *Satires*

(1905), and of Lucan (1926). H. was a conservative textual scholar, his reviews of other scholars were caustic and often narrow, characteristic of the emphasis placed on the importance of textual studies (as opposed to literature and history) in England and Germany. Monastic, eccentric, austere, H. withdrew into his rarefied world of intellectual arrogance, to pursue his work with zealous passion.

But during his London years H. experienced the "continuous excitement" that culminated in *A Shropshire Lad*, one of the great lyric achievements of the 19th c. The bittersweet quality of the lyricism reflects the trauma of H.'s personal disappointments, his repressive withdrawal, and his stoic commitment to textual scholarship.

In *Last Poems* and *More Poems* H. continued his melancholic lament, the emphasis remaining on regret and loss. Often sentimental, the lyrics are nonetheless remarkably controlled, an attempt by H. to make his poetry essentially classical. Yet in trying to capture in English the brevity of such Latin masters as Horace and Juvenal, Housman overemphasized control. It is not unusual, therefore, in a lyric of H.'s for technique (the liberal use of the monosyllable, for example) to be the essence of the poem, narrowly reducing the poet's potential ability to deal with the ambiguous and complex.

Despite his many followers, H.'s poetry has often been labeled as adolescent, simplistic (in theme as well as form), pessimistic, banal, self-indulgent, and antiintellectual. As summed up by Ezra POUND, his message was one of woe. But more recently Housman has attracted the sharper eye of the newer critics and other admirers who praise his metrical skill, his subtle tonality, his classical symmetry, his consummate craft, his skillful use of irony, and his theme of courage and stoic endurance.

Like Blake in his *Songs*, Housman has suffered from being too easily accessible. His clipped, colloquial speech patterns, incisiveness and felicity of phrasing, often too palatable to cursory readers, obscure the elegance and grace of his language and his masterful use of literary convention.

FURTHER WORKS: *Collected Poems* (1939); *Manuscript Poems* (1955); *Selected Prose* (1961); *Collected Letters* (1971)

BIBLIOGRAPHY: Housman, L., *A. E. H.* (1937); Richards, G., *H.: 1897–1936* (1941); Watson, G. L., *A. E. H.: A Divided Life* (1957); Marlow, N., *A. E. H.: Scholar and Poet* (1958); Ricks, C., ed., *A. E. H.: A Collection of Critical Essays* (1968); Leggett, B. J., *The Poetic Art of A. E. H.* (1977); Graves, R. P., *A. E. H.: The Scholar Poet* (1980)

—JULES SEIGEL

HOVEYDA, Fereydoun

Iranian novelist, essayist, and film critic (writing in French), b. 21 Sept. 1924, Damascus, Syria

H. was born in Syria, the son of an Iranian diplomat. He was educated in Beirut, Lebanon, and obtained a doctorate in law from the Sorbonne in Paris in 1948. H. joined the Iranian foreign service and was press attaché at the embassy in Paris from 1947 to 1951. He joined UNESCO in 1952 as a mass-communications specialist, but returned to Iran in 1965 to serve as undersecretary for international organizations in the foreign ministry. He was the Iranian ambassador to the United Nations from 1971 to 1978. H. now lives in the U. S. and paints, lectures, and writes books and articles, all on a range of political and literary subjects.

As an artist H. in his many shows in the U. S. developed a new technique of "papiers collés," leaving a very narrow white space between papers. In the words of Andy Warhol, H. "combines his literary sensitivity, his cinematic instinct, and his international experience, to create images that are beautiful, perceptive, and funny."

His first book, *Histoire du roman policier* (1956; history of the detective novel), was given a preface by Jean COCTEAU. H. became a regular contributor to *Mystère-Magazine*, the French counterpart of Ellery Queen's magazine *Fiction*, a science-fiction monthly, and to the celebrated *Les cahiers du cinéma* that in the early 1960s launched what was to be known as the "new wave" of film directors. H. is represented in two volumes of *Les cahiers du cinéma*, on the 1950s and 1960s respectively, which were published by Harvard University in 1985–1986 in an English translation.

H. published his first novel, *Les quarantaines* (1962; a many-faceted word whose possible meanings include medical quarantines and the state of being forty years old). Its plot was of a French-educated Arab living in France during the Algerian war, caught between his traditional Arab culture and his Western education. Using cinematic and psychoanalytic techniques, H. describes accurately and vividly the emotions of the growing group of multicultured Middle-Eastern people and their problems. The novel succumbed to polemics in the heat of the Algerian war, but was eventually honored as a "healer" between Western and Eastern cultures. H.'s

second novel, *L'aerogare* (1965; the airport), recounted the production of a script, in two weeks, by a Paris-born American film director. In the course of his writing, many questions concerning the coming of the "age of image" and the relationship between cinema, literature, and metaphysics are illuminated for the filmmaker.

H.'s third novel, *Dans une terre étrange* (1968; in a strange land), is the story of a child who feels cheated by his own parents. In this novel H. applied to literature the techniques of comic books to underline the distance between the worlds of adults and children. A year later, he wrote *Le losange* (1969; the lozenge), a collection of science-fiction stories.

His next novel concerned a French-born American writer drifting toward alcoholism, *Les neiges du Sinai* (1973; the snows of the Sinai). It opens with the protagonist reading the Sunday edition of the *New York Times*. In this work H. used in many ways the techniques of the STREAM-OF-CONSCIOUSNESS novel, introducing "sounds" and "images" in combination with words. The book won the Leopold Senghor Prize for foreigners writing in French.

When the Iranian revolution was victorious and Khomeini returned to Iran after fourteen years of living in exile, H. published in English *The Fall of the Shah* (1979; pub. in French as *La chute du Shah*, 1980), a personal account of the events that led to the tragic death of his brother, the longtime prime minister of Iran.

H. wrote an autobiographical piece, *Les nuits féodales* (1983; the feudal nights), and his first historical novel, *Le glaive de l'Islam* (1985; the sword of Islam), treating the rise of Islam in the 7th c. and its first sixty years. H.'s essays on the Middle East are *Que veulent les Arabes* (1991; What Do the Arabs Want?) and *L'Islam Bloqué* (1993). In this volume of essays H. compares the Islamic world at the end of the first Christian millenium with that at the end of the second millenium. The book in English entitled *The Broken Crescent* (1998) deals with the threat of militant Islamic Fundamentalism. The hero of *Les mirroirs de Mollah* (1992; The Mullah's Mirrors) is Mollah Nassreddin, a comic folk personality known to the Muslim peoples for centuries.

H.'s novels concentrate on characters pertaining to two or more cultures simultaneously. Even in *Dans une terre étrange*, although the story is about the French, his young character is caught between childhood and adulthood, which in the view of H. are two completely separate "cultures." In *Le glaive de l'Islam* the hero, an Arab general, is influenced by the cultures of the conquered nations: Persia, Syria, Egypt, and North Africa. In all his works, H. searches for the ultimate unity of all human cultures.

As a writer, H. argues that the cultures, civilizations, political and religious systems complement each other rather than merge together. The vision of the world in his writings is strongly reflected in his collages and "papiers collés," where there is a sharp edge between colors and sometimes even a space between them, while their totality creates a pattern in which color and shape are complementary.

—PETER J. CHELKOWSKI

HOWE, Irving

American literary critic, cultural historian, and social commentator, b. 11 June 1920, New York, N.Y.; d. 5 May 1993, New York, N.Y.

H. attended New York City public schools and from an early age adopted the attitudes of the socialist movement: thirst for change, skepticism about the dominant culture, and a taste for polemic. He studied at City College in New York, received a B. S. in 1940, and did graduate work for a short time at Brooklyn College. After a stint in the army, he took up an academic career and taught at Brandeis, Stanford, and Princeton universities. He became a professor of English at the City University of New York in 1963 and continued his work as editor of the socialist magazine *Dissent*; the latter position, which he has held since the 1950s, has contributed to his authority and influence in the world of letters as well as in contemporary political discourse.

Passionate about ideas, steeped in a tradition of dialectic, literary without being ivory-towered, H. is a representative leader of the New York intellectuals. In his words, this means being "an anti-specialist . . . a *Luftmensh* of the mind, a roamer among theories." H.'s style—the "thrust and parry" of debate—is pungent, often ironic, and sometimes blunt. His essays frequently display the "brilliance" he describes as a hallmark of New York critics: "free-lance dash, peacock strut, daring hypothesis, knockabout thrust."

As a literary critic, H. is concerned with the social and political problems of a text, its informing conceptions, and its place within a culture. *Politics and the Novel* (1957) is a unified study of ideology and the artist: it traces the emergence of the political novel and sees it as postdating 19th-c. stable conceptions of society. The political novelist explores disorder and the modern tension between ideas and personal emotions. He must "melt" political ideas into the behavior of characters and function as a "nimble dialectician" in dealing with abstractions and people.

The troubled, ambivalent modern consciousness emerges as a theme in this book and becomes a central concern in *Decline of the New* (1970); here H. ranges over many works, examining the origins and breakup of the modernist literary tradition. Modern literature, arising as a rebellious response to 19th-c. progress and positivism, has been institutionalized in our time. Its restlessness and protest are now cultural clichés. H. therefore wants the modern temper to be scrutinized and its worn-out ideas retired. At the same time he is concerned about what comes next. Will postmodernist literature find arresting subjects and a way to express them? Or will the literary mind become "a docile attendant to an automated civilization"?

The burden of such questions informs *The Critical Point* (1973). H. typically measures the modernist vision—especially its irrationality and glorification of the sick self—and proposes that we look beyond it. As a socialist he seeks the "City of the Just"; as a literary critic he reminds us that at least one 20th-c. writer, James JOYCE, had a humane and skeptical vision that transcended the nihilism of his age. H.'s pursuit of de-alienation continues in *Celebrations and Attacks* (1979), a volume of reviews written over a period of thirty years. Here he begins by explaining Jewish immigrants' struggle for a relationship with American literary tradition; he then measures a variety of contemporary authors by using his criteria of artistic complexity and social responsibility.

This latter standard is the theme of *Steady Work* (1966), a collection of social and political essays from the 1950s and 1960s. He focused on threats to democratic radicalism—whether the ease of "welfarism" or the arrogance of the New Left. H. is especially disturbed by mass society—a passive, consumer-oriented, infinitely assimilative society that could dull men's devotion to change. In seeking "secular transcendence," H. champions the ideals of pluralism and autonomy. *World of Our Fathers* (1976) is written from the same perspective: this massive, richly textured account of Jewish emigration from Europe, the new life and culture created in America, and the struggle to preserve identity is presented as a kind of secular transcendence. At once a sociologist, literary historian, and chronicler of individual lives and movements within the Jewish community, H. demonstrates his range, feeling, and stylistic expansiveness as he deals with a part of his own past.

In an age inundated by bizarre theories of literature and society, H.'s unusual directness makes him especially valuable. His place among the New York intellectuals has been especially important, but not without its qualifying circumstances. As a literary critic he is less subtle and elegant than Lionel TRILLING; his political commitments sometimes give an edge to his analysis of a work. He has little of the juicy, heart-on-sleeve quality that makes Alfred Kazin (b. 1915) a poetic and highly personal recorder of American Jewish life. And his ideas are less startling and original than those of Leslie FIEDLER on literature or Paul Goodman (1911–1972) on society. Nevertheless, H. remains a stimulating, sane, and lucid witness to the spectacle of modern literature and the politics of change.

FURTHER WORKS: *The U. A. W. and Walter Reuther* (1949, with B.J.Widick); *Sherwood Anderson* (1951); *William Faulkner* (1952; 3rd ed., 1973); *The American Communist Party* (1958, with Lewis Coser); *A World More Attractive* (1963); *Thomas Hardy* (1967); *Trotsky* (1978)

BIBLIOGRAPHY: Adler, R., on *A World More Attractive, New Yorker* (4 July 1964): 60; Capouya, E., on *Steady Work, Commonweal* (9 Dec. 1966): 295; Solotaroff, T., "I. H. and the Socialist Imagination," *The Red Hot Vacuum* (1970): 133–41; Wood, M., on *Celebrations and Attacks, NYRB* (8 Nov. 1979): 34; Donoghue, D., on *Celebrations and Attacks, NYTBR* (8 Nov. 1979): 9

—DAVID CASTRONOVO

HRABAL, Bohumil

Czechoslovak short-story writer, novelist, and poet (writing in Czech), b. 28 March 1914, Brno; d. 3 Feb. 1997, Prague

H. spent his childhood in Nymburk, where his father was the manager of a brewery. It was also there that he experienced the influence of his eccentric uncle Pepin, an incessant talker, who came for a two-week visit and stayed on for forty years. Just before World War II H. began to study law in Prague, but when Czech universities were closed by the Nazis, he took up various jobs, starting in the Nymburk brewery and ending as dispatcher in a small railway station. Although he completed his law studies after the war, he chose to work as a commercial and insurance agent rather than a lawyer. Later he worked in a steel mill, in a scrap-paper warehouse, and as a stagehand in a Prague theater. Since 1963 he has been a full-time writer.

H. had to wait long to see his first book published. In 1958 a volume of short stories was at the printer, but as a result of the ideological tightening-up following the publication of Josef ŠKVORECKÝ's *The Cowards*, H.'s book was not printed. The author was just a year short of fifty when the volume, *Perlička na dně* (1963; the pearl in the deep), finally appeared to critical acclaim. By this time, non-ideological writing was no longer taboo, but the main novelty of H.'s short stories was the author's peculiar, often grotesque vision. Far from being exemplary, the characters presented in H.'s stories are people from the lower social strata, who compensate for the triviality of their lives by embellishing banal incidents with humorous exaggeration and transforming them into brilliantly unique experiences. Often these tall tales are both inspired by and told over a mug of beer. The atmosphere is reminiscent of early silent movies and the method used by the author is purely anecdotal, as he places in his tales the momentous side by side with the commonplace in a montage without a hint of hierarchical order.

The same zany lust for life, reflected in an eccentric, hyperbolical mirror, has characterized all H.'s writing. *Perlička na dně* was followed by another volume of short stories, *Pábitelé* (1964; the palaverers), and then *Taneční hodiny pro starší a pokročilé* (1964; *Dancing Lessons for Advanced Pupils*, 1995), an old man's life story told in a single unfinished sentence.

H. had by now acquired many enthusiastic admirers, but his unselective approach to the realities of life had also offended some more conservative members of the reading public. Even in his next book, *Ostře sledované vlaky* (1965; *Closely Watched Trains*, 1968)—the most conventional of H.'s works and the closest to the traditional novel in form—the heroism of a young man's deed during World War II is preceded and deflated by a discussion of his intimate problems. This short novel was made into a very successful film (the screenplay, written by H. and Jiří Menzel, was published in English as *Closely Watched Trains*, 1971).

In the aftermath of the suppression of the 1968 reform movement, two complete editions of H.'s books, *Domácí úkoly* (home works) and *Poupata* (buds), both printed in 1970, were destroyed. After having publicly expressed support for the new authorities, however, the author was later allowed to publish again, but only the more conventional of his works, which have hardly added to his previous achievement. In *Postřižiny* (1976; the haircutting) he draws in a series of scenes and in the usual grotesque fashion a lovable portrait of an early emancipated woman, and both *Slavnosti sněženek* (1978; celebration of snowdrops) and *Krasosmutnění* (1979; beautiful mourning) turn to the past for most of their subjects.

Some of H.'s books that could not be published in Czechoslovakia until the fall of communism in 1989 circulated in the West as duplicated manuscripts or as private editions. These works, such as *Obsluhoval jsem anglického krále* (MS. 1971; *I Served the King of England*, 1989) and *Příliš hlučná samota* (MS. 1976; *Too Loud a Solitude*, 1990), are definitely superior to H.'s works officially published in Czechoslovakia in the 1970s and 1980s. In an interview in 1990, H. admitted that he had rewritten his works "to give them the kind of form that would be publishable."

However, returning to his earlier texts and rewriting them is for H. a basic working method. H.'s literary poetics is based on the principle of reiteration and variation. H. strives for perfection by constantly reworking his texts.

The novel *Obsluhoval jsem anglického krále* tells the story of a waiter who is trying, unsuccessfully, to ingratiate himself with the various regimes that he lives through during his lifetime. *Příliš hlučná samota* is a monologue by a self-educated workman, who operates a hydraulic press at a wastepaper collection plant. There he witnesses the wholesale destruction of libraries of unorthodox books in the early years of Communist rule. He compacts the books

into bales together with other kinds of wastepaper, including blood-spattered, fly-infested paper from the butcher's. He drinks beer while working and in the most authentic version of the work, his semi-alcoholic monologue culminates in an apocalyptic vision in which the whole world is compacted into a giant cube.

A three-volume autobiography—*Svatvy v domě* (1987; weddings in the house), *Vita nuova* (1987), *Proluky* (1987; vacant sites)—narrated by H.'s wife Eliška, forms a single structure, although, as is the case with most texts by H., it is a conglomerate of short, at first sight free-standing stories and anecdotes, a rough-hewn structure of miscellaneous elements held together by the author's immense creative energy. Perhaps the most important theme of H.'s autobiography is the relation between the Czechs and the Germans, German fanaticism and barbarity during the Second World War, and the cruel Czech retribution after the war.

Since the end of the 1980s H. has been writing essayistic letters in which he comments on his recent experiences and the political developments in his country: *Listopadový uragan* (1990; the november hurricane), *Kpouzelná flétna* (1990; the magic flute), *Ponomé říčky* (1990; underground rivers), *Růžový kavalir* (1991; the pink cavalier), *Aurora na mělčině* (1992; the aurora grounded), *Večerníčky pro Cassia* (1993; evening for Cassius).

H. has become one of the best-known modern Czech writers, and his comic texts of urban folklore, which he claims only to have recorded in a surrealistic collage, have been enjoyed throughout the world. But there is a great amount of literary sophistication behind the façade of tavern bragging, and the naïveté is often as deceitful as that of the primitive painters whose imagination H. in many respects shares. What impresses most is H.'s fresh and striking vision, which creatively transforms triteness into a miracle of the everyday.

FURTHER WORKS: *Inzerát na dům, ve kterém již nechci bydlet* (1965); *Automat Svět* (1966); *Toto město je ve společné péči obyvatel* (1967); *Morytáty a legendy* (1968); *Městečko, kde se zastavil čas* (MS. 1978); *Každý den zázrak* (1979). FURTHER WORKS IN ENGLISH: *The Death of Mr. Baltisberger* (1975); *I Served the King of England* (1989); *Cutting It Short and the Little Town Where Time Stood Still* (1993)

BIBLIOGRAPHY: Mihailovich, V., et al., eds., *Modern Slavic Literatures* (1976), Vol. II: 113–17; Gibian, G., "*The Haircutting* and *I Waited on the King of England*: Two Recent Works by B. H.," in Harkins, W. E. and P. I. Trensky, eds., *Czech Literature since 1956: A Symposium* (1980): 74-90; Gibian, G., "Forward movement through backward glances: Soviet Russian and Czech Fiction (H., Syomin, Granin)," in Birnbaum, H., and T. Eekman, eds., *Fiction and Drama in Eastern and Southeastern Europe* (1980): 161-75; Heim, M., "H.'s aesthetic of the powerful experience," in Birnbaum, H. and T. Eekman, eds., *Fiction and Drama in Eastern and Southeastern Europe* (1980): 201-06; Škvorecký, J., "American motifs in the work of B. H.," in *Cross Currents*, 1 (1982): 207-18; Roth, S., *Laute Einsamkeit und bitteres Glueck* (1986); Čulik, J., "B. H. Interviewed in Scotland," *Scottish Slavonic Review*, 16 (Spring 1991): 18-21; Roth, S., "The Reception of B. H. in Czechoslovakia and in the 'West'," *Czechoslovak and Central European Journal*, 11 (Summer 1992): 66-72

—IGOR HÁJEK

HRONSKÝ, Jozef Cíger

(pseudonym of Jozef Cíger) Slovak novelist, b. 23 Feb. 1896, Zvolen; d. 13 July 1960, Lujan, Argentina

Born in central Slovakia, H. became a teacher of painting in local schools, but was taken into the Austro-Hungarian infantry and fought on the bloody Italian front. This war experience appears in certain works. He returned to teaching for several years, then became a secretary at Matica slovenská, the Slovak foundation and national library. As director he showed great administrative ability and enlarged the foundation while at his most creative literary peak from 1933 to 1944. As World War II ended, though H. had not been active politically, he joined the exile groups leaving Slovakia and lived in Italy before moving to Argentina. He returned to his love of painting, worked in commercial and church window design, and wrote one novel. He died in Argentina, but his body was returned to the national cemetery in 1993. His works had already been republished since the political thaw of the 1960s.

H.'s first stories about village life followed the sympathetic and humorous realist tradition of Martin KUKUČÍN. They were collected in *U nás* (1923; At Our Place), *Domov* (1925; Going Home), and *Medové srdce* (1929; Gingerbread Heart). The increasing complexity of H.'s villagers and plots was accompanied by experiments with urban settings and intellectual artistic characters, as in the novel *Proroctvo doktora Stankovského* (1930; The Prophecy of Dr. Stankovský). The complicated but basically optimistic *Podpolianske rozprávky* (1932; Tales from the Foot of Mt. Polana) was followed by contrasting village and urban moralities in the expressionistic *Tomčíkovci* (1933; The Tomčík Family) and the melancholy impressionistic *Sedem sŕdc* (1934; Seven [Female] Hearts).

H.'s four greatest novels, though not a quartet, range philosophically and aesthetically over the actual Slovak village, the metaphorical villager as Everyman, the modernist alienated loner, and the transcendant Christian mystic. Strikingly varied narrative modes with suggestively nuanced lyrical personae are among H.'s innovations. *Chlieb* (1931; Bread) is a multilevel wide-lens picture of a famine-stricken village, its many characters forming a collective consciousness that is itself the main character along with the land providing bread as the essential food of humanity. Another expressionist village novel soon followed, *Jozef Mak* (1933; *Jozef Mak*, 1992), which intensifies the stolid inarticulate hero into an unlucky Everyman, as common as poppyseed (= *mak*) but as resilient as grass and more enduring than stone. This is generally considered H.'s chief masterpiece. *Pisár Gráč* (1940; Gráč the Clerk) gives an alienated protagonist, an embittered survivor of World War I who carries on long dialogues with his late employer in the grave. These grotesque scenes are interrupted by nonchronological flashbacks and episodes revealing Gráč's love for a young widow who eventually heals his alienation. A different kind of transcendant salvation is achieved by the protagonist in *Andreas Búr Majster* (1948; Master Andreas Búr), an enigmatic outcast who is feared and eventually killed by uncomprehending villagers.

In Italy H. had published a brief novella about ancient Rome, *Predavač talizmanov* (1947; *Seller of Talismans*, 1978). His last novel, *Svet na trasovisku* (1960; The World in a Quagmire/The World of the Village Trasovisko), probably written earlier in Italy, returns somewhat to his early realism in its depiction of the Slovak Uprising against fascism and the end of the wartime independent Slovakia, which H. regarded as tragic. Full interpretation of the novel requires the earlier, little noticed *Šmákova mucha* (1944; The Filthy Fly), H.'s *roman-à-clef* about domestic and wartime politics.

Extraordinarily prolific, H. is considered the only Slovak novelist whose great novels number more than two or three. His expressionist lyrical prose widely influenced postwar novelists who slipped away from SOCIALIST REALISM, and his grotesque *Pisár Gráč* provided a model for later analytical novels. Throughout his career H. also wrote cultivated and sensitive children's literature that was widely beloved. He set a standard of originality, variety, and profundity that no other Slovak writer has yet met.

FURTHER WORKS: *Žltý dom v Klokoči* (1927); *Jarný vietor a iné rozprávky* (1938); *Cesta slovenskou Amerikou (1940)*; *Zobrané spisy J. C. H. pre mláádež* (1937-42); *Na Bukvovom dvore* (1944); *Zobrané spisy J. C. H.* (1938-44); *Pohár z brúseného skla* (1964); *Na križných cestách* (1966); *Dielo* (1993)

BIBLIOGRAPHY: Matuška, A., *J. C. H.* (1970); "Hronského *Pisár Gráč* a slovenská próza" [symposium], *SlovP*, 86, 3 (1970): 30-43; Števček, J., *Lyrizovaná próza* (1973): 92-131; Strmeň, K., "Slovak Literature: A Brief History," in Cincura, A., ed., *An Anthology of Slovak Literature* (1976): xlv-xlvi; Rudinsky, N. L., "J. C. H: Chronology and Partial Bibliography," *Slovakia*, 30 (1982-83): 128-41; Petro, P., *History of Slovak Literature* (1995): 132-37; special H. issue, *Biografické štúdie*, 19 (1992)

—NORMA LEIGH RUDINSKY

HSÜ Chih-mo

Chinese poet, diarist, essayist, and translator, b. 15 Jan. 1897, Hsia-shih, Chekiang Province; d. 19 Nov. 1931, Tsinan, Shantung Province

In his own lifetime the fame of H. as a poet rested as much on his life, which epitomized a fearless attack on conventions and a relentless pursuit of freedom, love, and beauty, as on his work. The son of a wealthy banker, he first sought reform in China through a study of law and politics at Peiyang University (later known as Peking University), of banking and sociology at Clark University in Massachusetts (1918–19), and of political science at Columbia University, where he obtained a master's degree in 1920. As early as 1915 he had come under the strong influence of the most liberal reformist thinker of his time, Liang Ch'ich'ao (1873–1929). He left the U.S. for England, and it was at King's College, Cambridge, that H. discovered his affinity with literature and began to write poetry.

At this time he also discovered love. Before leaving China, H. had been married to an educated, modern girl from a prominent family, and the young bride had followed him to Cambridge. But H. carried on a secret love affair with Lin Hui-yin, the seventeen-year-old daughter of a friend. He clamored for a divorce which was granted in 1922, but because of objections of family and friends, he did not marry Miss Lin.

For several years following his return to China in 1922, H. wrote and taught; he was rocketed to national fame when he became the interpreter for the Indian poet Rabindranath TAGORE on his 1924 tour of China. At about the same time, he became the center of a cause célèbre by falling in love with yet another prominent woman, the wife of a young Chinese military officer. To cure himself of this attachment and to allay gossip, H. took a trip through Europe in 1925; but he returned to Peking to insist upon his right to marry the woman he loved, which he did in 1926. These several episodes of his love life found curious parallels in the life of the English poet he admired most, Shelley; and they accomplished as much in shocking the traditional Chinese society and tearing down the old conventions as did his bold and lyrical treatment of his experience in his writings.

In 1925, the year his first volume of poetry, *Chih-mo ti shih* (poems of Chih-mo), was published, H. became the editor of the literary supplement of the newspaper *Ch'en pao*. For this magazine, a year later, he started the now famous poetry journal *Shih-k'an*, which ran for eleven issues. (It resumed publication in 1931 as an independent journal with the aid of WEN I-To.) Also for the pages of *Ch'en pao*, to introduce Western-style plays to China, he started a drama section. Together with Wen I-to, H. became the founder in 1928 of the monthly *Hsin-yüeh*, or *Crescent*. In the manifesto of the new journal H. called for a union of music (rhythm), painting (color), and architecture (form and structure) as the sine qua non of *pai-hua* (vernacular) poetry. The *Crescent* poets countered the popularity of the Whitmanesque free verse by insisting upon the supremacy of form and the fusing of classical diction with colloquial speech. With unerring sensitivity to the rhythm of spoken Chinese, H. successfully experimented with metrics, producing a poetry that is simple, direct, and never bookish. One particularly famous poem, "Ai ti lin-kan" (love's inspiration), included in the posthumously published collection *Yün-yu* (1932; wandering in the clouds), a dramatic monologue of over four hundred unrhymed lines that effectively rely upon enjambment and the natural rhythm of vernacular speech, became a classic of the new poetry. His imagery is highly visual and often ethereal, again bespeaking a kinship with Shelley. While some of his early poems were mildly satiric, most of his works reflect the basic romantic attitude concerning the attainability of a dream or an ideal in an imperfect, transitory world. Some of the poems written during the last two years of his life, however, are imbued with a deep sense of despair. "Huo-ch'ê ch'in chu kuei" (night train)—included in *Yün-yu*—a poem in sixteen stanzas with two decasyllabic lines in each, and designed to appear in print like parallel railroad tracks, is H.'s most philosophical—and most pessimistic—work.

During the last years of his life H. held teaching posts at several universities in Shanghai, Nanking, and Peking. He was killed in a plane crash. Like Shelley, whose life was also cut short, H. seems for modern Chinese poetry the "beautiful angel" whose "luminous wings" symbolize a poet's constant search for order and cadence, for beauty and truth.

FURTHER WORKS: *Lo-yeh* (1926); *Fei-leng ts'ui ti i-yeh* (1927); *Pa-li ti lin-chua* (1928); *Tzup'ou wen-chi* (1928); *Pien-k'un Kang* (1928, with Lu Hsiao-man); *Meng-hu chi* (1929); *Lung-p'an hsiao-shuo chi* (1929); *Ch'iu* (1931); *Ai-mei hsiao-cha* (1947, with Lu Hsiao-man)

BIBLIOGRAPHY: Birch, C., "English and Chinese Meters in H. C.'s Poetry," *Asia Major*, New Series, 7 (1959): 258–93; Lin, J. C., *Modern Chinese Poetry: An Introduction* (1972): 100–132; Lee, L. O., *The Romantic Generation of Modern Chinese Writers* (1973): 124–74

—IRVING YUCHENG LO

HU Shih

(birth-name: Hu Hung-hsing) Chinese poet, literary reformer, and scholar (writing in Chinese and English), b. 17 Dec. 1891, Shanghai; d. 24 Feb. 1962, Taipei, Taiwan

H. changed his name to mean "to fit into" after being inspired by T. H. Huxley's (1825–1895) *Evolution and Ethics*. He studied under the American philosopher John Dewey (1859–1952) at Columbia University, from which he received a doctorate in philosophy in 1917. He then taught at Peking University and other colleges. H. lectured extensively in Europe and the U.S.—he received numerous honorary degrees—and was the Chinese ambassador to the U.S. from 1938 to 1942. He returned to China in 1946 but came back to the U.S. in 1948 and worked as a librarian at Princeton University. During the 1950s he was condemned by the Communist Chinese government as a lackey of U.S. imperialism. In 1958 H. became president of the Academia Sinica in Taiwan.

In the field of literature, H. is better known for advocating reforms and for his scholarship in vernacular literature, than he is for his creative writing. A skeptic and critic of traditional Chinese mores, he wrote a story entitled "Chen-ju tao" (1906; the surrealist isle) in which Chinese superstitious practices were attacked. Another short story, "I-ko wen-t'i" (1919; a problem), and the play *Chung-shen ta-shih* (1919; marriage), a farce, were both quite superficial in dealing with social issues.

In his youth, H. called for the reform of the literary tradition. In essays like "Wen-hsüeh kai-liang ch'u-i" (1917; a modest proposal for literary reform), he declared basically that the *wen-yen* (literary written language) should be abolished and that the practical *pai-hua* (spoken language) should be adopted for all writing, and he published *Ch'ang shih chi* (1919; the experiment), a collection of poems written in the vernacular. The work itself was very immature, as H. admitted; nonetheless, its publication signified the quest and victory of the *pai-hua* literary movement over the time-honored *wen-yen* literary tradition.

H.'s contribution to the new literature movement also lies in his scholarship. His *Pai-hua wen-hsüeh shih* (1928; history of vernacular literature) proved the existence of a vernacular tradition in Chinese literature. Unfortunately, the book's contents ended prematurely with the 9th c. In addition, H. published numerous research studies that dealt with matters of the authorship and textual and historical significances, as well as the literary merits of almost all the well-known Chinese vernacular fictional works. Until very recently, for example, his research on *Dream of the Red Chamber*, which linked it to the family history of its author, Ts'ao Hsüeh-ch'in (1717–1764), dominated all studies on the novel. The fact that vernacular fiction is now respected in Chinese literature is due mainly to H.'s efforts.

H. also promoted the writing of *chuan-chi wen-hsüeh* (biographical literature), claiming that China has yet to produce an interesting and readable biography. He tried writing some himself, including one of his mother, and an autobiography.

As a believer in reforming China through "wholesale Westernization" and "wholehearted modernization," H. is admired and condemned for the destruction of the Chinese literary tradition and for his pro-Western outlook. Nevertheless, his importance in modern Chinese literature is undeniable: known as the "father of the literary revolution," H. was a pioneer in the dawning of a new era of literary expression in China.

FURTHER WORKS: *Chung-kuo che-hsüeh shih ta-kang, shang p'ien* (1919; *The Development of the Logical Method in Ancient China*, 1922); *China's Own Critics: A Selection of Essays* (1931); *The Chinese Renaissance* (1934); *H. S. yen-lun chi* (2 vols., 1953–1955); *H. S. liu-hsüeh-jih-chi* (1959); *H. S. wen ts'un* (rev. ed., 1961)

BIBLIOGRAPHY: Forster, L., *The New Culture in China* (1936): 221–34; Chow, T., *The May Fourth Movement* (1960): 271–79; Shih, V., "A Talk with H. S.," *ChinaQ*, 10 (1962): 149–65; Grieder, J., *H. S. and the Chinese Renaissance: Liberalism in the Chinese Revolution, 1917–1937* (1970)

—MARLON K. HOM

HUANG Chun-ming

Taiwanese short-story writer, folklorist, and writer of children's books, b. 1939, I-lan

A native of I-lan, a small coastal town in northeastern Taiwan, H. lost his mother early in his life and had trouble adjusting to changes in his family situation, for he was a runaway at an early age. His higher education in Taiwan's normal colleges was chaotic and undistinguished: beginning in Taipei, his performance resulted in one move after another, until he received his bachelor's degree from Pingtung Normal College, the southernmost of all Taiwan campuses. He spent a year in the U.S. in the late 1970s, gathering material for works he has yet to write.

H. has held a number of jobs and was the reigning "free spirit" among Taiwan writers of his generation. A man of diverse interests and talents, he has published a collection of Taiwanese folk songs, produced two film documentaries of Taiwan festivals, and worked with children's television. He has also published half a dozen volumes of short stories and a variety of children's books, illustrated by the author.

H. first came to public notice in the late 1960s, when he began publishing stories of rural Taiwan and the effects of industrialization and modernization on Taiwan's traditional, conservative, primarily agricultural society. His writings, and those of a small number of like-minded native Taiwanese, signalled a turn away from the "elitist," modernist fiction and poetry written almost exclusively by mainland China-born intellectuals, and set the stage for a prolonged debate in the highly dichotomized literary circles. H. quickly became a "nativist" hero and the most popular writer of fiction in Taiwan of that time. The works comprising his early period are involved with issues of identity, dignity, and adaptability among the economically disadvantaged, often illiterate or semiliterate, and generally law-abiding, decent common folk of Taiwan. He is, essentially, a storyteller, a humanist, and, at his best, a writer of superb comic satire. While not an experimentalist—hard-core realism informs most of his fictional creations—H. frequently includes local dialect in his characters' dialogue, endearing him to Taiwanese readers and alienating those who emigrated from the Chinese mainland following the establishment of the People's Republic of China in 1949.

Representative of H.'s early stories are "Ni-szu i-chih lao-mao" (The Drowning of an Old Cat) and "Lo" (The Gong). In the former

the land itself stands in the way of progress and must be sacrificed to the god of modernization. The planned construction of a swimming pool in the most hallowed spot of Uncle Ah-sheng's (the "old cat") village, affords one man an ill-fated but spectacular opportunity to transcend his humble origins and become a leader of men. When asked why he so strongly opposes the "desecration" of his land, he replied, "Because I love this piece of land and everything on it"—so simple, so direct, so revealing, and so futile. Just before the inevitable construction is completed, Uncle Ah-sheng drowns himself in the pool, and is quickly forgotten. In this, as in most of stories from this period, H. is seen as a social pathologist, one who deals with the diagnostic rather than the prescriptive or the remedial. That will change in his later works. In the second story a town crier has been rendered superfluous by a loudspeaker-equipped pedicab. He too represents the inexorable march of "progress" and its bleak consequences in Taiwan's rural society. Yet even here, foolish decisions and human frailties participate in the crushing defeats of H.'s "tragic heroes."

After 1972, the year that Taiwan was kicked out of the United Nations and Taiwan's urbanization project was all but a fait accompli, H. turned his attention to more narrow national concerns, in particular, Taiwan and its relations with the outside world. Joining the chorus of compatriots who inveighed against the forces of economic and cultural "imperialism," he began to write more openly ideological stories, employing a biting satirical style to mock both the "imperialists" and those who, wittingly or not, fell under their influence.

H.'s best-known story—translated into many languages in Asia and in the West—is "Sha-you-na-la tsai-chien" (Sayonara, Tsai-chien), a savage, yet brilliantly structured attack on Japanese male sexual predators who roam the Asian world on sex tours, and their big-city hosts, who pander to their visitors' loathsome tastes as they themselves wrestle with feelings of guilt, shame, and prurience. Ultimately, the first-person narrator, the self-lacerating local tour guide, gains a moral victory, however shallow, by taking advantage of a chance encounter between the Japanese tourists and a sycophantic young Taiwanese to humiliate both and salve his own conscience.

H.'s legacy in Taiwan, where he continues to be active in a variety of creative endeavors, is both artistic and moralistic. As one of the earliest post-World War II "nativist" writers to experiment with local dialect and comic satire, he continues to be a model for writers of later generations. And his humanistic concern for the "little man" struggling to survive in an increasingly depersonalized world has earned him a reputation of one of Taiwan's most popular cultural figures of recent decades.

FURTHER WORKS: *Er-tzu ti ta wan-ou* (n.d.); *Lo* (1974); *Sha-yo-na-la tsai-chien* (1974); *Hsiao kua-fu* (1975); *Ch'ing-fan Kung ti ku-shih* (1985). **FURTHER WORKS IN ENGLISH:** *The Drowning of an Old Cat and Other Stories* (1980)

BIBLIOGRAPHY: Goldblatt, H., "The Rural Stories of H.," in Faurot, J., ed., *Chinese Fiction from Taiwan: Critical Perspectives* (1980): 110-33; Chang, S., *Modernism and the Nativist Resistance* (1993); Haddon, R., ed., *Oxcart: Nativist Stories from Taiwan, 1934-1977* (1996)

—HOWARD GOLDBLATT

HUCH, Ricarda

(pseuds. in first works: Richard Hugo, R. I. Carda) German poet, novelist, short-story writer, critic, essayist, and historian, b. 18 July 1864, Braunschweig; d. 17 Nov. 1947, Kronberg

H. came from a merchant family with strong artistic inclinations. Her brother Rudolf (1862–1943) and her cousins Felix (1880–1952) and Friedrich (1873–1913) Huch were writers. H. had to move to Zurich, Switzerland, to obtain her high school certificate and her Ph. D. in history at the university, since women were not yet admitted as regular students in Germany. After working as a librarian and a high school teacher in Zurich and Bremen she married an Italian dentist, Ermanno Ceconi, and lived with him in Trieste and Munich. After an amicable divorce, she married her lifelong love, her cousin Richard Huch, but the marriage ended in complete failure. In her later years, H. lived with her daughter's family and followed her to Berlin, Heidelberg, Freiburg, and Jena. She died near Frankfurt shortly after her move to the Western-occupied zones.

H. received the Goethe Prize of the city of Frankfurt (1931) and was the first woman to be elected to the Prussian Academy of the Arts (1927), a position she courageously resigned in 1933, protesting the expulsion of writers such as Heinrich MANN and Alfred DÖBLIN by the Nazi regime. Having been close to the Lutheran opposition and the anti-Hitler conspirators of July 20, 1944, she planned a collection of biographies of German Resistance fighters, a project completed after her death by Günther Weisenborn (*Der lautlose Aufstand* [1953; the silent rebellion]).

A contemporary of the major naturalist writers—Gerhart HAUPTMANN, Frank WEDEKIND, Arno Holz (1863–1929)—H. was independent of, even opposed to, this movement. She is generally classified as a leading writer of neoromanticism, but she herself rejected that label. A kinship with the flowery, manneristic style of writing called *Jugendstil* is evident in her early works. Later, she strove for a blending of the tradition of Goethe and Gottfried Keller (1819–1890) with modern sensitivity.

After a number of early publications, H. became known to a wider audience through her first novel, *Erinnerungen von Ludolf Ursleu dem Jüngeren* (1893; *Unconquered Love*, 1931). Against a Hanseatic-merchant background similar to that of Thomas MANN's *Buddenbrooks*, this work traces the demise of a family succumbing to the fatal, overwhelming passion of love. H.'s tragic characters try to follow their inner calling in an unsympathetic world of rigid conventionality and decadence. In her next novel, *Aus der Triumphgasse* (1902; from Triumphal Lane), it is poverty—encountered by H. herself in Trieste, where the story is set—that prevents the characters from fulfilling themselves. *Vita somnium breve* (1903; Latin: life is a short dream; 4th ed., 1909, retitled *Michael Unger*) returns to H.'s native milieu. The same basic conflict is treated in a more fairy-tale-like manner in *Von den Königen und der Krone* (1904; of kings and crown), where the descendants of a supposedly royal family prove unable to protect and preserve the legendary crown in the era of modern capitalism, reaching out in vain for a future ideal. While failing, H.'s heroes gain an awareness of themselves, of their time, tradition, and potential, and ultimately of God. With a pessimistic view of the present age, H. combines a faith in the vital forces of humanity in a more Christian than Nietzschean sense.

A major work of this early period is H.'s study of German romanticism, *Die Romantik* (2 vols., 1899, 1902; romanticism). In opposition to the then dominant school of positivism, H. tried to express the essence and meaning of the romantic movement, concentrating on the romantics' ways of life, religion, and modes of expression, and presenting a series of model biographies. *Die Romantik* was received as a manifesto of neoromanticism, but it contains as much criticism as praise.

During the second phase of her work, H. turned mainly to history, writing both historical novels and essays. Her interest in the Italian unification movement of the 19th c. resulted in the novels *Die Geschichten von Garibaldi* (2 vols., 1906–7 [a projected third part was never written]; *Garibaldi and the New Italy*, 1928–29); *Das Leben des Grafen Federigo Confalonieri* (1910; the life of Count Federigo Confalonieri), considered by many critics to be her best novel; and the essay *Das Risorgimento*, later retitled *Menschen und Schicksale aus dem Risorgimento* (1908; men and destinies of the Risorgimento).

Her chief interest remained the history of the Holy Roman Empire, whose social structures—such as local self-government, social and political action on a personal, not a bureaucratic or abstract level, a stable yet flexible class system—she preferred to modern government, in its various democratic, socialist, or dictatorial forms. The ultimate breakdown of the Holy Roman Empire during the Thirty Years' War (1618–48) was described by H. in her most ambitious novel, *Der große Krieg in Deutschland* (3 vols., 1912–14; the great war in Germany; later retitled *Der Dreißigjährige Krieg* [the Thirty Years' War]). For H., Freiherr vom Stein, the Prussian reformer of 1807, about whom she wrote in *Stein* (1925; Stein), wanted to restore the old Empire in a new form, but his heritage lost out against mechanistic capitalism and liberalism from 1848 on, a view she propounded in *Alte und neue Götter: Die Revolution des 19. Jahrhunderts in Deutschland* (1930; old and new gods: the revolution of the 19th century in Germany). Her three-volume history of Germany, *Deutsche Geschichte* (1934, 1937, 1949; German history), synthesized this view of history. H.'s clear opposition to the Nazi view of history prevented the publication of the last volume until after World War II.

During H.'s third and last period of creativity, historical writings alternated with essays conveying her *Weltanschauung*. The roots of her conception of humanity and human history can be found in early German romanticism and the works of C. G. Carus (1789–1869). In *Entpersönlichung* (1921; depersonalization) she described how human development from a preconscious harmony with the environment leads to states of consciousness and self-consciousness involving an unavoidable alienation of the individual from the environment and a breaking-up of the whole personality, although in different forms for men and women, because of their essentially different characters. H. called for a return to life forces as found in the writings of Martin Luther—*Luthers Glaube: Briefe an einen Freund* (1916; Luther's faith: letters to a friend); the Bible—*Der Sinn der Heiligen Schrift* (1919; the meaning of the Bible); and the writings of Goethe.

H. remained a poet all her life and also wrote a large number of stories. Her detective novel *Der Fall Deruga* (1917; *The Deruga Trial*, 1927), although written for money, is one of the most valuable examples of the genre. *Der wiederkehrende Christ Christus* (1926; Christ returning) exemplified H.'s criticism of her age in a less convincing satirical manner.

H.'s strong personality has elicited a number of biographies. Most criticism so far has focused on the relationship between her life and her work. A critical assessment of H.'s ideas and achievement and of her place in German literary history is urgently needed.

FURTHER WORKS: *Gedichte* (1891); *Die Hugenottin* (1892); *Evoë* (1892); *Der Mondreigen von Schlaraffis* (1896); *Drei Erzählungen* (1897); *Fra Celeste* (1899); *Gottfried Keller* (1904); *Seifenblasen* (1905); *Neue Gedichte* (1907); *Der Hahn von Quakenbrück* (1910); *Der letzte Sommer* (1910); *Natur und Geist als die Wurzel des Lebens und der Kunst* (1914); *Wallenstein* (1915); *Jeremias Gotthelfs Weltanschauung* (1917); *Michael Bakunin und die Anarchie* (1923); *Graf Mark und die Prinzessin von Nassau-Usingen* (1925); *Im alten Reich: Lebensbilder deutscher Städte* (1927–1929); *Frühling in der Schweiz* (1938); *Weiße Nächte* (1943); *Herbstfeuer* (1944); *Urphänomene* (1946); *Der falsche Großvater* (1947); *Briefe an die Freunde* (1960); *Gesammelte Erzählungen* (1962); *Gesammelte Werke* (11 vols., 1966–1974)

BIBLIOGRAPHY: Hoppe, E., *R. H.* (1936; rev. ed., 1951); Flandreau, A., *R. H.'s Weltanschauung as Expressed in Her Philosophical Works and in Her Novels* (1948); Baum, M., *Leuchtende Spur* (1950); Leopold, K., *R. H.'s "Der letzte Sommer": An Example of Epistolary Fiction in the Twentieth Century* (1962); Baumgarten, H., *R. H.: Von ihrem Leben und Schaffen* (1964); Emrich, W., Foreword to *Gesammelte Werke*, Vol. I (1966): 9–130; Kappel, H.-H., *Epische Gestaltung bei R. H.* (1976)

—WULF KOEPKE

HUCHEL, Peter

German poet and editor, b. 3 April 1903, Berlin; d. 30 April 1981, Staufen

H., who grew up in Mark Brandenburg, studied literature and philosophy in Berlin, Freiburg, and Vienna. In the mid-1920s he began to publish poetry in periodicals and in 1932 received the literary prize of the leftist journal *Die Kolonne*. H. voluntarily cancelled the planned publication of a collection of poetry in 1933 as a protest against the Nazi regime. Following military service during the war he worked for the East German radio. In 1949 he became editor-in-chief of *Sinn und Form*, which soon came to be recognized as the most liberal journal in East Germany, and one of the outstanding literary periodicals in Europe. His refusal to adapt his editorial policy to the principles of SOCIALIST REALISM led to his dismissal in 1962, following which he lived in Potsdam in virtual isolation. He was allowed to emigrate in 1971, settling eventually in West Germany. He received numerous literary prizes in the GDR in the early 1950s and in the West in the 1960s and 1970s.

H.'s poetry is firmly rooted in the world of nature. He has often been compared with Oskar Loerke (1884–1941) and Wilhelm Lehmann (1882–1968), and some of his early poems, collected in *Gedichte* (1948; poems) and *Die Sternenreuse* (1967; the star basket), do in fact have much in common with the writers of the "nature-magical school": The mysteries and majesty of a landscape are celebrated, as a scene is described in minute detail, often with little or no reference to human beings. Other early poems, however, reveal the poet's sense of social consciousness. Nature is again used as a setting, and description is not lacking, but here the emphasis is placed upon the people who are surrounded by nature, especially children, and servants and other representatives of the lower classes. The mood is frequently idyllic, but occasionally elegiac. H. is often praised by critics for his effective use of rhyme, meter, assonance, and alliteration in these early poems.

Never a prolific poet, H. wrote very little verse during the Nazi years, and some of these poems were lost during the war. Nature continued to play an important role in the extant works of H.'s second period. The tone, however, is quite different. Images of snow and ice replace the summer and autumn imagery of the earlier poetry. The feeling of desolation is underscored by a decrease in the regularity of rhyme and meter. H. enthusiastically welcomed the early postwar reforms of the East German government, and much of his poetry from the years 1945 to 1952 reflects his support of the government and his hope for the future. The Land Reform Law of 1945, which dissolved the large estates and distributed the land among the lower classes, was celebrated in "Das Gesetz" (1950; the law), which, like a few other works of this period, closely corresponds to the criteria of Socialist Realism.

Soon, however, H. lost faith in the policies of the regime, primarily because of the failure of the lot of the working class to improve and the government's lack of tolerance for artistic experimentation. The poetry of the 1950s and early 1960s, collected in *Chausseen Chausseen* (1963; highways highways), became increasingly hermetic and melancholic, reflecting the poet's growing sense of isolation and resignation. Rhyme and regular meter virtually disappeared, and, as in the poetry of the war years, snow and ice are among the most common images. The poems of *Gezählte Tage* (1972; counted days), written during H.'s period of isolation, are even more pessimistic. Veiled references to the political situation of the GDR and to the author's position as an exile in his own country are frequent. *Die neunte Stunde* (1979; the ninth hour), which contains poems written after H.'s emigration, is dominated by the presence of death. The tone, however, is now one of stoical resignation, as is reflected in the controlled use of language and images.

Although he published relatively little, H. remained until his death one of Germany's foremost literary figures, admired for his personal integrity no less than for his literary achievements. In recent years many critics have come to consider him the most important German-language poet of his time.

FURTHER WORKS: *Gedichte* (1973). FURTHER WORKS IN ENGLISH: *Selected Poems* (1974)

BIBLIOGRAPHY: Flores, J., *Poetry in East Germany* (1971): 119–204; Mayer, H., ed., *Über P. H.* (1973); Scher, H., "Silence in the Poetry of P. H.," *GR*, 51 (1976): 52–61; Vieregg, A., *Die Lyrik P. H.'s* (1976)

—JERRY GLENN

HUGHES, Langston

American poet, novelist, short-story writer, dramatist, anthologist, translator, and editor, b. 1 Feb. 1902, Joplin, Mo.; d. 22 May 1967, New York, N. Y.

When he was very young H.'s parents separated, eventually to be divorced. Until his thirteenth year he lived largely in Lawrence, Kansas. He spent his high-school years in Cleveland, Ohio. After graduation he sojourned for a year in Mexico with his father, who had found in Mexico a release from American racism. But H.'s

Langston Hughes

father also worshiped moneymaking. He wanted H. to be an engineer. From his father's bounty H. did accept a year at Columbia. At the end of the year, however, breaking permanently with his father, H. subsisted in, and around, New York on his own for another year, then went to sea. Successive jobs as a waiter and doorman supported him for a season in Paris. Having worked his way home on a ship and already recognized as a poetic luminary of the Harlem Renaissance, he matriculated at Lincoln University in Pennsylvania, which granted him a bachelor's degree in 1929. During the early 1930s he traveled widely in America and Russia and saw the Far East. An assignment as a war correspondent took him to Spain during the civil war. But New York City was his home for virtually the last thirty years of his life.

In *The Confident Years* (1953) Van Wyck Brooks calls H. the "most adventurous and versatile of Negro authors." A quarter of a century has produced nothing to contradict Brooks's judgment. It was H.'s poetry that first brought him fame. His "The Negro Speaks of Rivers" written on a train taking him to Mexico, may be the most quoted of all poems by black poets. The poetry of *The Weary Blues* (1926) assimilated techniques associated with the secular music of black folk to the medium of verse even while its content reflected the lives of that same folk, especially in terms of how those lives were adjusting their Southern agrarianism to the alien environment of the urban North. *Fine Clothes to the Jew* (1927), more poetry, followed. But then came the novel *Not without Laughter* (1930). Starting with *The Ways of White Folks* (1934), H. was to publish three collections of the sixty-six short

stories he wrote, preeminently in the 1930s and exclusive of his Simple tales.

As an adolescent in Cleveland he had participated enthusiastically in every phase of the activity of the celebrated, though nonprofessional, Karamu Players. The first play of his to be published was *The Gold Piece* (1921). His *Mulatto*, revised without his knowledge and decidedly not to his liking, ran on Broadway in 1935. In the 1930s and early 1940s he founded Negro little theaters in Harlem, Los Angeles, and Chicago. And he wrote more than twenty plays, musicals, and hybridizations of plays and musicals, as well as a special kind of play, of his own invention, which he called the gospel song-play.

His autobiography of his youth, *The Big Sea* (1940) is indispensable for students of the Harlem Renaissance. It is supplemented by *I Wonder as I Wander* (1956). He translated a novel by the Haitian writer Jacques ROUMAIN and poetry by Nicolás GUILLÉN, Federico GARCÍA LORCA, and the Nobel laureate Gabriela MISTRAL. For juveniles he did a series of "Famous" biographies, beginning with *Famous American Negroes* (1954) and the "First Book" histories, starting with *The First Book of Negroes* (1952). He turned out a steady stream of articles on many subjects, wrote, with the actor Clarence Muse (1889–1979), the screenplay for the Hollywood film *Way Down South* (1942) and, by himself, the lyrics for the musical version of Elmer RICE's *Street Scene*. He also wrote radio scripts, a television script, and the lyrics for at least forty popular songs.

H. may have crowned his career with the character Simple, whom he created in 1942 for his column in the *Chicago Defender*. Simple grew, in effect, into every black person's Everyman; the Simple stories are now most conveniently available in five collections garnered from the more than fifteen years of columns H. wrote.

H.'s poetry and prose both tend to impress a reader with their apparent simplicity. Both for the most part, read easily. Moreover, both never seem to center on epic figures or to attempt epic themes or epic manners—and certainly both never extend to epic lengths. Yet neither in poetry nor prose does H. ever seem to be inconsequential either as an artist or as a critic of society. His apparent simplicity is therefore much more apparent than real, and betokens a genuine and tremendous effort on his part not to be obscure or grandiose or to pretend to profundities for which he feels he should not try to stake a claim. On the other hand, it does not indicate a want of aesthetic discipline or the absence of a respectable addiction to contemplative thought. One has but to recognize the formal accuracy of H.'s blues or to be made aware of the intense study he gave to models of the short story to guess the truth, that he was a conscientious artist who worked hard at achieving his passionate desire, forms of expression palatable to ordinary people, yet serious and significant as commentaries on the life of man. He has been rightly called an authentic voice, probably without a peer, of, and for, the Negro folk.

He once testified unequivocally to a very inquisitive Senate committee that he was not, and never had been, a Communist. Even so, he was sometimes, also, an ardent voice of sociopolitical protest. He affected an avoidance of the complex, the difficult, the unpleasant, and the unpopular only in the manner of his art. In its substance—or, at least, in what he wanted that substance to communicate—he often did precisely the opposite. There, upon numerous occasions, he did come to grips with troublesome issues, helped by his rich sense of humor and, not too infrequently, by ingenious resorts to irony.

FURTHER WORKS: *Dear Lovely Death* (1931); *The Negro Mother* (1931); *The Dream Keeper and Other Poems* (1932); *Scottsboro Limited* (1932); *Popo and Fifina: Children of Haiti* (1932, with Arna Bontemps); *A New Song* (1938); *Shakespeare in Harlem* (1942); *Freedom's Plow* (1943); *Jim Crow's Last Stand* (1943); *Lament for Dark Peoples, and Other Poems* (1944); *Fields of Wonder* (1947); *One-Way Ticket* (1949); *Simple Speaks His Mind* (1950); *Montage of a Dream Deferred* (1951); *Laughing to Keep from Crying* (1952); *Simple Takes a Wife* (1953); *The First Book of Rhythms* (1954); *Famous Negro Music Makers* (1955); *The First Book of Jazz* (1955); *The Sweet Fly-paper of Life* (1955, with Roy DeCarava); *The First Book of the West Indies* (1956); *A Pictorial History of the Negro in America* (1956, with Milton Meltzer); *Simple Stakes a Claim* (1957); *Famous Negro Heroes of America* (1958); *The L. H. Reader* (1958); *Tambourines to Glory* (1958); *Selected Poems* (1959); *The First Book of Africa* (1960); *Ask Your Mama: 12 Moods for Jazz* (1961); *The Best of Simple* (1961); *Fight for Freedom: The Story of the NAACP* (1962); *Something in Common, and Other Stories* (1963); *Simple's Uncle Sam* (1965); *Black Magic: A Pictorial History of the Negro in American Entertainment* (1967, with Milton Meltzer); *The Panther and the Lash: Poems of Our Times* (1967); *Black Misery* (1969)

BIBLIOGRAPHY: Redding, S., *To Make a Poet Black* (1939): 113–17; Emanuel, J., *L. H.* (1967); O'Daniel, T., ed., *L. H., Black Genius: A Critical Evaluation* (1971); Dickinson, D. C., *A Biobibliography of L. H., 1902–1967* (1972); Wagner, J., *Black Poets of the United States* (1973): 385–474; Jackson, B., and L. Rubin, *Black Poetry in America* (1974): 51-58; Barksdale, R. K., *L. H.: The Poet and His Critics* (1977)

—BLYDEN JACKSON

HUGHES, Richard

Anglo-Welsh novelist and dramatist, b. 19 April 1900, Weybridge; d. 28 April 1976, Bangor, Wales

Born in England of Welsh parentage, H. went to Charterhouse and Oxford. While still an undergraduate, he had a volume of poems published and a play produced on the London stage. Nevertheless in his early twenties he did write other plays (including the first "listening play," or play for radio), together with stories collected in *A Moment of Time* (1926) and poems collected in *Confession Juvenis* (1926). Then he began writing the novel that made his name. It appeared first in the U.S. as *The Innocent Voyage* (1928), and then in England under its more familiar title, *A High Wind in Jamaica* (1929).

A gripping story, this novel contains extraordinary evocations of life in Jamaica and aboard a sailing ship in the middle of the 19th c. After a hurricane has destroyed their home, the Bas-Thorntons decide to send their five children home to school in England. But the ship is captured by pirates, and the children spend weeks on a schooner sailing the Spanish Main. Most of the story is told from the children's perspective, particularly that of ten-year-old Emily; as H. himself said, he tried to get two kinds of thinking into the novel, the adult's and the child's. They are often in ironic contrast; the children miss connections, but the adults' expectations of the children are often wildly wrong. The rescue of the children leads to

a deceptively conventional "happy ending" in which, because of the way in which Emily's evidence is misinterpreted by a judge and jury, the pirate leaders are hanged for a murder they did not commit. Suspense and melodrama, humor and horror, are completely at the narrator's command, to summon up as he wishes; but what stands out particularly is his portrayal of the minds of children at various stages of maturity.

H.'s next novel did not appear for almost another decade; once again it was a striking success. *In Hazard* (1938) is a tense story about a ship caught in a tropical hurricane. Easily and confidently, H. explains at the beginning how modern technology has taken away the terrors of the sea. Then, having established this atmosphere of confidence and security, H. destroys it; nature plays games with the ship, toying with it for six days and blowing the funnel clean away. For the crew it is a learning and a testing experience. As in CONRAD, the focus is on the moral qualities that the sea—and life—demands, that is, on virtuous behavior in extreme conditions.

H. published no more novels for twenty-three years. During World War II he held an important position in the British Admiralty; later he collaborated with the historian J. D. Scott (b. 1917) on a section of the Official History of the War dealing with war production (1955). Not until 1956 did he begin writing *The Human Predicament*, an ambitious fictional chronicle of his own times planned to be in four volumes. The first, *A Fox in the Attic*, came out in 1961. It begins with Augustine Penry-Herbert carrying a drowned girl out of a marsh in Wales; because of the suspicion surrounding her death he is forced to leave his home and visit relatives in Germany. So he begins on what amounts to a personal quest, and H. on an examination of why the world is heading for catastrophe and barbarism. The novel contains an effective mingling of real and imaginary people and events; in particular, it shows how patterns of events that people cannot see penetrate deeply into their own psyches. Nevertheless, Augustine is far too passive and uncomprehending to serve as a focus; for example, he understands nothing of the political machinations leading to Hitler's abortive Munich beer hall *putsch*.

In the only other part of his saga H. completed, *The Wooden Shepherdess* (1973), he brings in the American scene as well as the English and the German; he is not entirely successful with the American setting and characters. He also finds it more difficult to assimilate and convey the necessary background information in this novel, even though there are gripping and convincing episodes such as the account of the Night of the Long Knives in Germany. Since *The Human Predicament* is unfinished, and since it is not easy to see how H. could have brought it to a successful conclusion, especially in view of the inadequacies of his central character, it must be judged an ambitious failure.

H. wrote only four novels in a long lifetime. The last two are difficult to evaluate, since they are parts of an incomplete chronicle. The first two, however, are masterpieces of their kind, and because of them he will not soon be forgotten.

FURTHER WORKS: *Gipsy Night and Other Poems* (1922); *Lines Written upon First Observing an Elephant Devoured by a Roc* (1922); *The Sisters' Tragedy* (1922); *Meditative Ode on Vision* (1923); *The Sisters' Tragedy and Other Plays* (1924); *Ecstatic Ode on Vision* (1925); *R. H.: An Omnibus* (1931); *The Spider's Palace* (1931); *Don't Blame Me!* (1940); *Liturgical Language Today* (1962); *Gertrude's Child* (1966); *Gertrude and the Mermaid* (1968); *The Wonder-dog: The Collected Children's Stories of R. H..* (1977); *In the Lap of Atlas* (1979)

BIBLIOGRAPHY: Symons, J., "Politics and the Novel," *Twentieth Century*, 170 (1962): 147–54; Bosano, J., "R. H.," *EA*, 16 (1963): 58–62; Henighan, T. J., "Nature and Convention in *A High Wind in Jamaica*," *Crit*, 9 (1966): 5–18; Thomas, P., "The Early Writings of R. H.," *AWR*, 20 (1971): 36–57; Swinden, P., *Unofficial Selves: Character in the Novel from Dickens to the Present* (1973): 181–202; Thomas, P., *R. H.* (1973)

—D. J. DOOLEY

HUGHES, Ted

English poet, dramatist, critic, and short-story writer, b. 17 Aug. 1930, Mytholmroyd; d. 28 Oct. 1998, Devon

The youngest son of a carpenter, H. spent his early youth among the Yorkshire moors and mountains, which later provided both subject and background for much of his poetry. From 1950 to 1954 he attended Cambridge on scholarship, studying anthropology and archaeology. In 1956 H. married the American poet Sylvia PLATH.

In his first book of verse, *The Hawk in the Rain* (1957), H. offered a sardonic appraisal of man's function in the universal scheme. Deceptive, helpless, frustrated human beings are measured against predatory beasts, whom H. sees as their counterparts. The natural manifestations of power and ferocity of the beast evoke the admiration of the poet, whereas he has only contempt for the

Ted Hughes

studied violence of man. *The Hawk in the Rain* was immediately recognized as the work of a potential genius, even though the poems are flawed by some straining for effect, and by forced diction and imagery.

Lupercal (1960) is concerned primarily with history, both religious and political, and with myth and ritual. H. limns human transience against the indestructible continuity of history. The volume contains three of H.'s finest poems, "Hawk Roosting," "Thrushes," and "Pike." Each exalts the ruthless efficiency with which the subject performs what is, according to its kind, a demonstration of its natural propensities. Throughout *Lupercal* H. catalogues the intransigent nonhuman energies that overmaster man's pitiable pretensions to historical continuity or personal immortality.

Wodwo (1967) is a collection of poems, stories, and a play intended "to be read together, as parts of a single work." The epigraph from *Sir Gawayne and the Green Knight* identifies the wodwo as a wood dweller and suggests the quest, initiation, and metamorphosis motifs developed in the volume. Hallucinatory and deathly images contrast oddly with the wistful figure of the wood sprite. Organic nature is called upon to suffer tortures as the dismembering force of Death rends its victims into sacrificial bits.

In the short stories of *Wodwo*, such as "The Rain Horse," "The Harvesting," and "Sunday," man is seen in curious relationship to the animals who are mastered. At the climactic moment man becomes one with his victim, tasting its anguish. The animals are exquisitely rendered, both in their struggle and defeat. In each case man is diminished in stature, checked in his attempt to establish control.

Crow (1971) presents a mordant view of civilization trapped in "the war between vitality and death." The very choice of protagonist—Crow—expresses a desperate and frenetic vitality that is generated and sustained only by an irrational determination to survive. In the H. world, anguish creates. Birth is a sundering experience with Death, its concomitant, stalking at the womb's door. Crow challenges the supremacy of Death, and the battle is on between the horrific vitality of Crow and the excruciating mutilations that Death can effect. Like Crow emerging from his progenitor Scream, the volume's energy derives from the presence of sound. This emphasis points toward the stylistic development that H.'s work was undergoing. His dramatic experiment, *Orghast* (performed 1971), goes after nothing less than a new language whose meaning emerges entirely from sound.

With *Season Songs* (1975), H. moved from the relentless nihilism of *Crow* to participate in the revivifying rhythms of the changing seasons. Birth and death, fruition and decomposition, in this collection are but recurrent processes in nature's continuing impulse toward a unified state of being. Intended at first for "young readers," the seasonal songs express the simple wonder of the perennial youth whose perception is profound in its childlike directness.

Gaudete (1977) has been heralded as one of the major innovative poetic accomplishments of the decade. Once again H. pushes language beyond its traditional limits as he plunges now into the phantasmagorical world of the psyche. Reverend Lumb is spirited away from his small, puritanical parish to minister to the deformed goddess of a mythical world. Meanwhile, a changeling Lumb, placed on earth to perform the clergyman's duties, seduces—in direct contrast to his celibate alter ego—his women parishioners by promising that one of them will give birth to a messiah fathered by him. Reverend Lumb, after a series of mutilating initiation rites, experiences his renascence into the world of the body and of elemental nature, even in its most unlovely forms. After the annihilation of the promiscuous changeling, the transformed Reverend Lumb returns to earth and in the role of priest-poet composes verses of praise to the goddess of nature. *Gaudete* suggests that the "loyalty of heart" divided between the flesh and the spirit is harmful.

Cave Birds: An Alchemical Cave Drama (1978) was inspired by a set of bird drawings by Leonard Baskin. Envisioning the birds as characters, H. wrote individual poems for each drawing and incorporated them into a poetic drama. He added to the bird poems another series of verses in which the same story is presented with a human protagonist. The work is a formidable attempt to synthesize the visual and verbal arts.

Moortown (1979) consists of four different sequences. The "Prometheus on the Crag" section was written at the same time as *Orghast*, which is also based on the Prometheus myth. Chained to his crag, Prometheus represents man trapped in the "numbness of his humanity"; Prometheus endures his mutilation and is reborn. Another sequence, "Earth-Numb," describes the futility of striving for fulfillment. In "Adam and the Sacred Nine" the nine muses assuming different bird forms finally succeed in reviving Adam after his Fall. With the coming of the ninth bird, the Phoenix, Adam rises. The title sequence "Moortown," which is the center of the collection, dwells on the brutal aspects of farm life. With relentless realism, H. focuses on "fox corpses . . . beaten to their bare bones," on cattle suffering the pitiless process of dehorning with "mouth drooling, the eye/Like a live eye caught in a pan, like the eye of a fish imprisoned in air." The unceasing gore underscores the indomitable will to endure, for in the H. universe the act of survival becomes the supreme challenge and justification.

Throughout his work, H. brilliantly objectifies the tumultuous quality of nonhuman forces. He is not a romantic nature lover even though his favorite protagonists and personae are animals. H. is well aware of the rapacious urges that quicken all forms of existence. His particular genius lies in the ability to apprehend and to convey the sentient qualities of being itself. For H., the writing of poetry demands the experiential involvement of the total person. Each word possesses a sensory life of its own that must be felt and controlled by the poet. H. believes that poems, like animals, are each one "an assembly of living parts, moved by a single spirit." An extraordinarily versatile craftsman, H. charges traditional poetic forms and devices with compelling energies. Not always successful in controlling his tempestuous imagination, H. still manages in his best work to shape style and subject into tangible forms of meaning.

FURTHER WORKS: *Meet My Folks!* (1961); *Selected Poems* (1962, with Thom Gunn); *The Earth Owl and Other Moon People* (1963); *How the Whale Became* (1963); *Nessie, the Mannerless Monster* (1963); *The Burning of the Brothel* (1966); *Recklings* (1966); *Scapegoats and Rabies: A Poem in Five Parts* (1967); *Animal Poems* (1967); *Poetry in the Making: An Anthology of Poems and Programmes from "Listening and Writing"* (1967; Am., *Poetry Is*, 1970); *Five Autumn Songs for Children's Voices* (1968); *The Iron Man: A Story in Five Nights* (1968); *Poems* (1968, with Gavin Robbins); *Seneca's Oedipus* (1969); *The Coming of the King and Other Plays* (1970; Am., *The Tiger's Bones and Other Plays for Children*, 1974); *A Crow Hymn* (1970); *A Few Crows* (1970); *The Martyrdom of Bishop Farrar* (1970); *Crow Wakes* (1971); *Poems* (1971, with Ruth Fainlight and Alan Sillitoe); *Eat Crow* (1971); *Shakespeare's Poem* (1971); *In the Little Girl's Angel Gaze* (1972); *Selected Poems 1957–1967* (1972); *Eclipse* (1976);

Chiasmadon (1977); *Sunstruck* (1977); *Moon-Bells* (1978); *Orts* (1978); *Calder Valley Poems* (1978); *Under the North Star* (1981)

BIBLIOGRAPHY: Rosenthal, M. L., *The New Poets: American and British Poetry since World War II* (1967): 224–33; May, D., "T. H.," in Dodsworth, M., ed., *The Survival of Poetry* (1970): 133–63; Lodge, D., "*Crow* and the Cartoons," *CritQ*, 13 (1971): 37–42, 68; Bauson, J., "A Reading of T. H.'s *Crow*," *CP*, 7 (1974): 21–32; Bedient, C., *Eight Contemporary Poets* (1974): 95–118; Hahn, C., "*Crow* and the Biblical Creation Narratives," *CritQ*, 19 (1977): 43–52; Heaney, S., "Now, and in England," *Critl*, 3 (1977): 471–88; Sagar, K., *The Art of T. H.* (1978); Faas, E., *T. H.: The Unaccommodated Universe* (1980); Hirschberg, S., *Myth in the Poetry of T. H.* (1981); Gifford, T., and Roberts, N., *T. H.: A Critical Study* (1981)

—ROSE ADRIENNE GALLO

HUGO, Richard

American poet and essayist, b. 21 Dec. 1923, Seattle, Washington; d. 22 Oct. 1982, Seattle, Washington

H. is usually described regionally, as a poet of the Northwest. He spent his early life in Seattle and served in World War II flying bombing runs in the Mediterranean theater, for which he was awarded the Distinguished Flying Cross. After the war H. studied at the University of Washington under Theodore ROETHKE, receiving his M.A. in 1952. After working twelve years for the Boeing Company in Seattle and publishing his first book of poems, *A Run of Jacks* (1961), he went, with much trepidation, to teach at the University of Montana, where he became director of the creative writing program and made Missoula a beacon of influence to writers of the Northwest as well as elsewhere. H. founded *Poetry Northwest* and, in 1977, became editor of the Yale Younger Poets Series. He published eight volumes of poetry before his death in 1982, as well as several lesser-known novels, a prodigious output for a relatively short creative life. H.'s name is the first that comes to mind whenever the poetry of the Northwest is discussed. Although he cannot be separated from his region, his legacy extends beyond his landscapes: Washington, Montana, and the often hopeless, workaday failures, the gradations of gray, and the stony-hard reality he typically portrays.

If H. has a signature, it is an ambidextrous one, to wrest the metaphor. His first volume, *A Run of Jacks*, makes this clear. His is the voice of nature rawly observed, as well as the voice of failure and defeat, which he addresses head-on and all but nurtures. If H. is a pessimist, he is one who wishes better for all, who humanizes by seeing, analyzing the rusts and weeds of the past, and testifying always as a witness for the defense in what is to him a consistently harsh world. The origins of these feelings are clear in his autobiography, *The Real West Marginal Way* (1986), a work essential to a full appreciation of H.'s aesthetic. Likewise, his *The Triggering Town: Lectures and Essays on Poetry and Writing* (1979), a collection of essays about how to write poems, admittedly, how to write as H. writes, stakes out the parameters of his creative methods, or, some have worried, its limits, and his form—itself troublesome to many.

Following the generally well-received first book came *The Death of the Kapowsin Tavern* (1965), *Good Luck in Cracked Italian* (1969), and *The Lady in Kicking Horse Reservoir* (1973), each dividing critics rather similarly, yet each yielding more in the direction of gentleness and self-analytical use of his materials, always an ulterior progression with H. By the time of the latter book, James WRIGHT could find H.'s work "all of a piece," like Thomas HARDY's, like George ORWELL, "a man with whom he has deeper and truer spiritual affinity than any man I know." One gets "the sense of the man" from reading the poems. Dick Allen writes: "we are forever at the side of the poet: having fun, fishing, driving through Montana, constantly participating in the life about which he writes." Those elements, as H. admits in *The Triggering Town*, may have been fabrications, for, to H., truth is caught in essences and you do what you have to apprehend them. His country is the projection of his vision, as Marjorie G. Perloff writes, "the paradigm for the starkest, barest, existential reality." His values appear among losses, griefs, and defeat. He is one who waves from the passing ship.

According to Bob Group, H.'s form reached perfection in his fifth volume of poems, *What Thou Lovest Well Remains American* (1975), then *31 Letters and 13 Dreams* (1977) marked his "masterpiece" to date: "Here the reader finds not the abstract posturing and uncertain humanistic focus that sometimes dilute his previous work." But other critics, such as William H. Pritchard, charge H. with a lack of sufficient form. His poems are commonly in blank verse, with sentences often stopped and begun in mid-line. To Alan Helms, he tends to move "in starts and stops, dispersing energy, and scattering attention, twisting truth." But in the same year as *Selected Poems* (1979) came the aforementioned *The Triggering Town*, which, read with H.'s posthumously published autobiography, *The Real West Marginal Way*, offers valuable insight into the poet's origins, intents, and methods. Though H. is often seen as hardboiled, it is clear that he was no more a "tough guy" than Robert FROST was a farmer. To Tom Simmons, "one of his greatest strengths is his willingness to examine the backs of things, the remnants, the junkyards of society." H. is the essential literary democrat "who found a good bar better company than a university . . . and those dreary committees / where people actually say 'considering the lateness / of the hour.'" To read H. is to explore one's own hungers and rejections. He is as a friend to his reader. Let form bury its dead.

It offends fairness not to acknowledge that H. wrote his way out of the mildly hardboiled persona of the earlier works. His art was for him curative, which is anomalous among a generation of confessionalist suicides who so often wrote themselves into emotional difficulties. H. was one of the tenderest and most honest of men. His last two books of poetry make this clear: *White Center* (1980), about the community near Seattle where he grew up, and *The Right Madness on Skye* (1980), drawn from experiences in Scotland. The two works move further toward control of form and lyricism, as if he would prove his mastery of craft, along with his discovery that, at least on the Isle of Skye, one chose one's proper madness. A fitting close for so astute an observer.

FURTHER WORKS: *Death and the Good Life* (1981); *The Hitler Diaries* (1983); *Sea Lanes Out* (1983)

BIBLIOGRAPHY: Pritchard, W. H., "Poetry Matters," *HudR*, 26 (1973): 584-85; Wright, J. H., "H.: Secrets of the Inner Landscape," *APR* (May-June 1973): 13; Helms, A., "Writing Hurt: The Poetry of R. H.," *MPS*, 9 (1978): 107-8; Group, B., "R. H.," in Greiner, D., ed., *DLB*, 5 (1980): 369-74

—BOB GASKIN

HUIDOBRO, Vicente

Chilean poet, essayist, novelist, and dramatist (writing in Spanish and French) b. 10 Jan. 1893, Santiago; d. 2 Jan. 1948, Cartagena

H. was born into a wealthy upper-class family and educated by the Jesuits. As a young man, H. suffered a spiritual crisis that had a profound effect on his development as a poet as well as on his political beliefs. His revolt against his aristocratic Catholic upbringing led to a break with his family. When he left for Paris in 1916, H. had already published six books of poetry and had begun to reveal the tenets of a new poetic aesthetic that he and the French poet Pierre REVERDY would call "creationism." In Paris H. began to contribute to avant-garde literary magazines such as *Sic*. He was a cofounder with Reverdy and Guillaume APOLLINAIRE of the famous magazine *Nord-Sud*. During his first two years in France he published six books of poetry, including three written in French. On a trip to Madrid in 1918, he encouraged experimentation by other Hispanic poets: Gerardo Diego (b. 1896), Juan Larrea (b. 1895), and Jorge Luis BORGES. And as a result, the Hispanic vanguard poetry—called ULTRAISM because of its attempt to expand metaphor to its ultimate limits—was born. Thus, H. played a role similar to that of Rubén DARÍO for Spanish American MODERNISM, as the principal propagator of avant-garde ideas and techniques throughout Latin America. He returned to Chile for one year in 1925 and became the editor of a short-lived newspaper as well as a presidential candidate sponsored by the Chilean Federation of Students in the national elections (he did not win). H. then returned to France and diversified his literary output to include several unconventional novels with innovative language and form. He also wrote two short plays. In 1936 H. participated in the Spanish Civil War on the side of the Republic. As the Republic's fall became imminent, H. returned, in 1938, to Chile, where his most important novel, *Sátiro; o, El poder de las palabras* (1939; Satyr; or, the power of words), was published. At the outbreak of World War II H. enlisted in the French army. He performed heroically and received a serious head wound that eventually led to his death. His last poems were collected and published posthumously by his daughter under the title *Ultimos poemas* (1948; last poems).

Although H.'s early poetry was mainly modernist in technique and modeled on the works of Darío and Ramón del VALLE-INCLÁN, he had already begun his search for new poetic forms and language. After H. lost his Christian faith, his search for an artistic revolution included a metaphysical quest to satisfy a spiritual yearning that tormented him throughout the rest of his life. *Canciones en la noche* (1913; songs in the night), contained the first Spanish-language *caligrammes*, in which the spatial configuration of the words on a page converted the poem into a veritable pictograph. The most important books of H.'s early poetry were *Adán* (1916; Adam) and *El espejo de agua* (1916; the mirror of water) because they constitute the first application of creationist theory to H.'s own poetry. *Adán* is a harbinger of H.'s mature poetry and is structured on the archetypal image of the fallen man who is also, like the poet, the originator of a new language that describes the world he inhabits. *El espejo de agua* is famous especially for the poem "Arte poética" (poetic art), in which H. likens the poet to a "small god" who creates his own realities and discerns the occult relationships between disparate objects. The poem represents a manifesto of all the essential principles of creationism.

H. had written an earlier literary manifesto in prose called *Non serviam* (1914; Latin: I shall not be a slave), in which he boldly asserted the idea that the poetic creator should not be the slavish imitator of the products of natural creation but should emulate the creative act itself and give birth to truly original creations. Inspired in part by Emerson's notion that poetic creation need not be constrained by adherence to preconceived rules and conventions, H. viewed the poem as an autonomous reality and generator of its own forms of expression. H. also attempted to redefine "poetry" according to the original Greek meaning of the word, which means "to create." Creation would be the poet's sole objective.

Creationism flourishes in *Poemas árticos* (1918; *Arctic Poems*, 1974) and *Ecuatorial* (1918; equatorial); each book corresponds to one of the two most pervasive tendencies in his work. The former emphasizes the tendency toward experimentation and a break with poetic tradition, while the latter reveals a more personal side of H.'s poetry and also a marked social concern for the plight of man in war-ravaged Europe. *Poemas árticos*, a book of forty-four poems, is particularly noteworthy for its radical treatment of the perennial themes of poetry through a rupture with punctuation and the conventional stanzaic form of the poem. The entire poem, not only individual verses, affects the reader's sensitivity through the spatial representation of words in columns with capitalization of some of the words, reiteration, and the inclusion of futuristic elements of the modern technological world (such as airplanes, steamships, cigarettes), which are used as poetic images or symbols for the first time. The reader was forced to view the poem as an artistic whole and as a unique visual design that underlines its full significance. Both the verbal and spatial impact of the whole poem determines its essential meaning.

Altazor: El viaje en paracaídas (1931; Altazor: the trip in a parachute) is H.'s masterpiece. This long poem joins the poet's intimate quest for personal salvation through the religion of poetry to his search for a new poetic language. As a consequence of this literary and personal inquiry, words are stripped of conventional meaning and morphologically transformed into a series of nonsense syllables, which produce a new language. This new, created language is recondite for the reader but charged with emotive significance for its creator. As Altazor, the poet's alter ego, plummets to earth aware of his inevitable confrontation with death, he dramatizes one of the universal literary themes of the 20th c.: the existential predicament of an alienated and anguished soul in search of self-identity and fulfillment. The poem is structured on the archetype of the Fall and is divided into seven cantos in which Altazor retells his life, relates the importance of woman in creation, and becomes a word magician who dismantles conventional language and syntax. Altazor's tragic spiritual disintegration and vulnerability are shown to stem from personal disillusionment and an awareness that he cannot totally free himself from a dependence on the traditional word. In this poem, as in most of H.'s poetry, the pictorial aspect stands out, along with plays on words and concepts, onomatopoeia, paradox, and the "created word" that results from the transposition of halves of old words fused together to form new ones.

The poet's last two major poetic words, *Ver y palpar* (1941; seeing and touching) and *El ciudadano del olvido* (1941; the citizen

of oblivion), are intensely personal and contain autobiographical elements. H.'s reiterative technique to heighten emotional effects is the most salient stylistic feature of both books. In both there is also less word play and emphasis on the graphic and spatial dimensions of the poem as a verbal design with underlying symbolic meaning than in H.'s earlier works.

Most critics now rank H., the Peruvian César VALLEJO, and H.'s fellow Chilean, Pablo NERUDA, as the most important and influential voices of the 20th-c. Spanish American poetry. H. was undoubtedly Latin America's first avant-garde poet and boldly removed the last obstacles to freedom of expression in poetry. H. also transformed the genre into a truly spatial and pictorial art form akin to painting.

FURTHER WORKS: *Ecos del alma* (1911); *La gruta del silencio* (1913); *Pasando y pasando* (1914); *Las pagodas ocultas* (1914); *Horizon carré* (1917); *Tour Eiffel* (1918); *Hallali* (1918); *Saisons choisies* (1921); *Finis Britanniae* (1923); *Automne régulière* (1925); *Tout à coup* (1925); *Manifestes* (1925); *Vientos contrarios* (1926); *Mío Cid Campeador* (1929; *Portrait of a Paladin*, 1931); *Temblor de cielo* (1931); *Tres novelas ejemplares* (1931); *Gilles de Raíz* (1932); *En la luna* (1934); *La próxima* (1934); *Papá; o, El diario de Alicia Mir* (1934); *Cagliostro, novela—film* (1934; *Mirror of a Mage*, 1931); *Obras completas* (2 vols., 1964). FURTHER WORKS IN ENGLISH: *Selected Poetry* (bilingual, 1981)

BIBLIOGRAPHY: Holmes, H. A., *V. H. and Creationism* (1934); Forster, M. H., "V. H.'s *Altazor*: A Reevaluation," *KRQ*, 17 (1970): 297–307; Goiç, C., *La poesía de V. H.*, 2nd ed. (1974); Caracciolo Trejo, E., *La poesía de V. H.* (1974); De Costa, R., ed., *V. H. y el creacionismo* (1975); Wood, C. G., *The Creacionismo of V. H.* (1978); special H. issue, *RI*, 45 (1979): 106–7

—JAMES J. ALSTRUM

HULDÉN, Lars

Finnish poet (writing in Swedish), b. 5 Feb. 1926, Jakobstad (Pietarsaari)

H. has described as a formative poetic influence the verbal games he played by himself and with other youths of his native region Österbotten (Pohjanmaa). The games, quests for the perfect expression in a given situation, were no doubt reinforced in H.'s home, with its literary tradition. His father, Evert, was a noted poet. But H.'s preoccupation with the verbal led most immediately to an academic career; he currently occupies a chair in Nordic languages at the University of Helsinki. In this position he has contributed to scholarship on C. M. Bellman (1740–1795) and J. L. Runeberg, (1804–1877), two influential poets whose spirits can be observed in H.'s own works.

Österbotten has always been a primary source for H.'s inspiration. His first book, *Dräpa näcken* (1958; kill the kelpie [water sprite]), and those immediately following blend nostalgia and a nearly burlesque narration of the lore and the customs of that region. His style is mundane, reflecting his down-to-earth subjects, and can be seen as a position taken against a trend in Finno-Swedish poetry toward increasingly abstract themes. H. is a versatile writer who has also produced songs and dramatic works; the short-story collection *Hus* (1979; houses), marked his debut as a prose writer. But poetry forms the bulk of his production, and it is as a poet that he occupies the prestigious Poet's Residence in Borgå (Porvoo).

Much of H.'s production is lyrical, expressed in numerous forms, athough narrative poems and 2-line units of verse dominate. Its mark is a perception of specific events as a microcosm mirroring an irrational world where irony and compassion must stand guard. While the early works have frivolous overtones, H.'s later poetry, beginning with *Herr Varg!* (1969; Mr. Wolf!), often takes somber turns, even morbid ones, as in the collection of epitaphs, *Läsning för vandrare* (1974; reading for wanderers). An equilibrium is reached in *Herdedikter* (1973; shepherd songs), where H. alternates lyrical poems and terse commentary verses, the former epigrammatic, the latter objective as footnotes. A deceivingly simple style depends on unobtrusive metaphorical imagery, yielding poetry of incisiveness and surprising sublimity.

Expressions from H.'s native dialect frequently appear in his works suggesting a dilemma vis-à-vis dialect and standard Swedish. In *Heim/Hem* (1977; home), the obstacle, if it is one, is removed as H. presents a bilingual collection. In these compassionate poems dialect poetry reaches new heights in Finno-Swedish literature. It is too early to tell whether *Heim* represents a threshold in H.'s development, but the next collection, *J. L. Runeberg och hans vänner* (1978; J. L. Runeberg and his friends), in standard Swedish, approaches the elegance of *Heim*. In *J. L. Runeberg och hans vänner* H.'s refined talent for adopting the spirit of poetry other than his own is most fully developed; it is as if the two poets from Österbotten, both transplanted to Borgå, though in different ages, were performing a preordained duet.

Because H.'s poetry seems so effortless, it may give an impression of being hasty, or tied to seemingly insignificant phenomena, but the simplicity masks irony, sophistication, and a deep concern for the fate of mankind. In Swedish Finland, where a long tradition of MODERNISM may have run its course, H.'s poetry gives a fresh alternative through a concrete vision.

FURTHER WORKS: *Speletuss* (1961); *Spöfågel* (1964); *Enrönnen* (1966); *Två raseborgasspel* (1974); *Island i december* (1976); *Visbok* (1976); *Dikter vid särskilda tillfällen* (1979)

BIBLIOGRAPHY: Jones, W. G., "L. H.," *BF*, 11 (1977): 140–45

—KIM NILSSON

HULME, Keri

New Zealand poet, short-story writer, and novelist, b. 9 Mar. 1947, Christchurch

H. is of Maori (Kai Tahu), Orkney, Scots, and English descent. After a year at Canterbury University, she worked in a range of jobs, and now describes herself as a "whitebaiter" and writer. The wild and isolated environment surrounding the small town of Okarito on the West Coast of New Zealand's South Island, where she now lives, has an obvious impact on the settings and tone of her published work.

Previously known only for occasional short stories and the sequence of poems *The Silences Between* (1982), H. came rapidly to prominence with the publication of her novel, *The Bone People* (1984). It immediately won both the New Zealand Book Award for

Fiction and the Mobil Pegasus Award for Maori Literature; in 1985 it won the Booker McConnell Prize. H. has since published a brief narrative fiction, *Lost Possessions* (1985); a short-story collection, *Te Kaihau:/The Windeater* (1986); and another volume of poems, *Strands* (1992).

H.'s poems combine sensuality and earthiness, often celebrating an almost animistic conjunction between the human and natural worlds—an emphasis not uncommon in Maori poetry. Her short fiction ranges in style but frequently deploys elements of the fantastic or the macabre. Both poems and stories display a taste for idiosyncratic imagery and flamboyant word-play, an oblique suspicion of conventional sexuality, and a preoccupation with the voracious and destructive aspects of human intercourse. All these features coalesce in H.'s most substantial work, *The Bone People*, upon which her controversial place in the New Zealand literary canon currently rests.

The novel employs a flexible interior monologue, shifting between three protagonists. Kerewin Holmes, the primary character, estranged from her family and embittered by the dormancy of her artistic ability, has withdrawn into a reclusive domain of fetishized treasures collected in a tower-shaped house. She encounters a child, Simon—or, in the Maori transliteration preferred by the characters, Haimona—Gillayley, who also occupies a private world, signified by his muteness. Kerewin then meets Simon/Haimona's adoptive father, Joe, whose violent outbreaks relate to a puritanical upbringing, grief at the deaths of his infant son and his wife Hana, and a degree of alienation from his Maori ancestry and kin. The conflicts and rapprochements ensuing from the developing intimacy between these three socially autistic protagonists reflect the potential for various kinds of segregation or mutuality within the wider society of New Zealand/Aotearoa.

The Bone People was at first widely acclaimed, but critical and popular opinion soon began to polarize; reactions to the novel still manifest considerable levels of either enthusiasm or hostility. The negative criticism takes a variety of forms. Some readers find H.'s self-consciously allusive and punning style to be obscurantist, pretentious, or incompetent. Objections have also been made to the novel's representation of child abuse; in particular, it has been suggested that the narrative invites an identification by the reader with Joe and Kerewin that is inappropriate, given their mutual complicity in the final beating of Simon/Haimona. Others see H.'s use of Maori myth and symbolism as artificial; or, alternatively, as an overprivileging and mystification of non-European cultural signifiers: for instance, in the section where Joe, after his imprisonment, meets a kaumatua (elder) who entrusts him with the guardianship of a mauri (talisman) that preserves the threatened life force of the whole land of Aotearoa. Finally, many see the end of the novel, with its representation of familial and cultural reconciliation—between Kerewin, Joe, Simon/Haimona, and their families (and perhaps by implication, between Maori and non-Maori as well)—in a spiral house built from the ruins of Kerewin's tower, as an indulgent wish-fulfilment, a moment of escapism that does no justice to the problems raised by the narrative situation.

Despite these and other criticisms, it is clear that H. has produced something quite distinct from any other New Zealand novel before or since. While the combination of graphic naturalism, modernist narrative technique, and a certain kind of magic realist sensibility does at times pose difficulties for readers, the novel nevertheless stands as an innovative experiment in the rapidly expanding field of Maori writing in English, and as a significant contribution to postcolonial writing in general. Its eschewal of gendered or racial stereotyping gives the characterization a marked vitality; in particular, by blocking the (hetero)sexualization of the relationship between the protagonists, H. avoids romanticizing or sentimentalizing the novel's intervention into areas of vital concern for New Zealand as for other postcolonial societies: familial violence, cultural alienation and hybridity, materialism, the relationship between humans and the environment, and the development of localized notions of subjectivity.

In the context of the critical debate so far, it seems clear that the work's imagistic economy, and especially its final vision of bicultural reconciliation—or in H.'s idiom, "commensalism"—remain more suggestive than many would allow; but the disputed state of bicultural politics in New Zealand/Aotearoa renders any interpretation or assessment of such aspects of the novel, for the present time, highly provisional.

FURTHER WORKS: *Homeplaces: Three Coasts of the South Island of New Zealand* (1989, with Robin Morrison)

BIBLIOGRAPHY: Smith, S., "K. H.: Breaking Ground," *Untold*, 2 (1984): 44-49; Stead, C. K., "K. H.'s *The Bone People* and the Pegasus Award for Maori Literature," *Ariel*, 16, 4 (1985): 101-8; Prentice, C., "Rewriting their Stories: Postcolonialism and Feminism in the Fictions of K. H. and Audrey Thomas," *Span*, 23 (Sept. 1986): 68-80; Fee, M., "Why C. K. Stead Didn't Like *The Bone People*: Who Can Write As Other?," *ANZSC*, 1 (1989): 11-32; Smith, A., "K. H. and 'Love's Wounded Beings'," in Williams, M., and M. Leggott, eds., *Opening the Book: New Essays on New Zealand Writing* (1995): 140-61

—PHILIP ARMSTRONG

HULTBERG, Peer

Danish novelist and short-story writer, b. 8 Nov. 1935, Vangede

An academic specializing in psychoanalysis and Polish literature and an author in voluntary exile, H. is one of the most widely traveled and internationally experienced authors of modern Danish literature. His doctoral dissertation is on Waclaw Berent's (1873–1940) symbolistic authorship, and he has taught Polish at the universities of London and Copenhagen. Formerly a student in eastern Europe, he has since the late 1950s lived in Switzerland, West Germany, and London.

Mythical themes and musical tones are discernible throughout H.'s work. In his recent texts the myth has submerged beneath a realistic, almost minimalistic, surface from where it continues to offset a musical style. In his debut, the novel *Mytologisk landskab med Daphnes forvandling* (1966; mythological landscape with the transformation of Daphne), this interest in minute details is more maniacal and appears to reflect a neurotic suppression of essential concerns. Transformation of major frustrations into small activities breaks the deadlock, and diabolic short-circuits between separate levels of meaning deny the grand narrative a free-wheeling show-off. Whether exposed directly as a grand illusion or subjected to less direct romantic irony, it signifies a depersonalized and fragmented world in which any existential situation dissolves into possible or probable, but ultimately undecidable, alternatives.

With no certainty at hand, dialogues and plots either run parallel or collide; an erotic triangle is typically devoid of meaningful encounters. Human identities elude clarification, and stylistic repetitions only testify to the permanence of confusion. With barely visible borders between narration and dialogue, the distinctions between first- and third-person narratives become precariously fickle and beholden to the narrative viewpoint. No wonder that even H. used different pronouns synonymously or with ambiguous reference. Pros and cons are intertwined.

In H.'s principal work, *Requiem* (1985; requiem), the musical score has been elevated to a mass for the repose of the dead, and yet this formidable choir of 537 independent voices, or texts, is the epitome of situational representation, verisimilitude, and everydayness. H. has accepted that his discourse be called stream-of-unconsciousness and merely added that his book is 537 snapshots of anonymous individuals' minds in the moment before they each formulate their sentiments to other people. Merciless hatred and obscure sexuality blend with projected despair and self-contempt, and petty vindictiveness teams with studied generosity. These are the moments when people say "yes" but mean "no," and when conscious self-censorship is most ineffectual. While intended to set matters straight and right, this state of mind is held hostage by duplicity and self-righteousness. Insight in self-deception only serves to refute it, modesty is pride in disguise, openness a calculated risk, and confidence the last resort of the powerless.

The sounding board for these pessimistic tones is the classical rift between spirit and matter. It is a neurotic or psychotic frustration, but at least it is dynamic and live. The alternative resolution is dead and soulless, and to discharge the split, one must dispense with life itself—or at least with male supremacy. The narrative voices are mostly male, and there is an indirect feminism and a humanistic sense of balance involved in H.'s modern orchestration of classical European dilemmas in this vital and viable requiem.

In part one of *Slagne veje* (1988; beaten tracks) the scene has changed to the U.S. and the key to forty short narratives or verbal stills of modern Americans and their mores and ways. Whether successful or not in their particular endeavors, theirs are stories about human vanity—a patchwork of alarming uniformity.

Part two consists of six longer and more intimate monologues or streams-of-unconsciousness. Although "personalities" are conspicuous by their absence throughout his universe, H.'s characters experience circumstances so turbulent as to occasion unforeseen angles of incidence on their traumatic patterns of life. The narrative subtly escapes the confines of the narrated—leaving the reader with a sense of catharsis.

The title of the novel *Præludier* (1989; preludes) suggests a preliminary mode of fiction marked by improvising and by free and poetic movements, and the novel does indeed exude some refined naive insight into the childhood and adolescent years of Frédéric Chopin. Again, H.'s "prelinguistic" licentia poetica provides a blend of character and characterizer, of narrative segments and lyrical poems, and of French and Polish idioms—on the background of the protagonist's fear of death and deadly parental discipline. A conflict-ridden process of human maturation springs from the process of mature writing.

Because of H.'s all-European orientation, combined with his attempts at stylistic innovation, it took about two decades for his art and audience to meet and for critics and others to appreciate his artistic powers. When it finally happened—in *Requiem*—the occasion was commonly celebrated as a rare event, and his subsequent books seem to confirm that H. is a migratory bird whose literary offspring has come to stay.

The proof is most evident in *Byen og verden* (1992; The City and the World), where the exile has actually found his inner home. Subtitled *Roman i hundrede tekster* (Novel in a Hundred Texts), the interwoven stories speak the minds of characters who live within familiar city limits. Yet as part of the novel composition, all the voices echo the voice of the city itself and its conflicting norms. As so many dialogues unfold within one restricted code, they subtly display both quotidian drama and comedy.

Kronologi (1995; Chronology) consists of short prose texts from H.'s whole writing career. In its preface the author reviews not only the pieces at hand but his entire oeuvre as one developmental novel informed by international themes and artistic concerns. It was thus thanks to Proust and his lost Parisian metropolis that H. recreated his Danish provincial point of departure. Although it too is now lost, it is, like other postmodern states of mind, a city to be found all over the world.

FURTHER WORKS: *Desmond* (1968); *Fjerut fra Viborg* (1990)

—POUL HOUE

HUMBERT, Marie-Thérèse

French novelist and essayist, b. 1940, Mauritius

Residing in France since 1959, H. is a mother of five and a professor of literature. Her work is marked both by her early proximity to the sea and by the infinite gradations of color prejudice on her native island which, British since 1810, nevertheless preserves a sizable Francophone minority.

Her first published novel, *A l'autre bout de moi* (1979; At the Other End of Myself), satirizes the color prejudice that afflicts a mixed-race family in an intensely hierarchical society. It is told as an autobiographical confession by Anne, a proper, prejudiced young woman obsessed with her color. She admires and envies her liberated, life-affirming twin Nadège, who has taken a young Indian politician as a lover. The stresses of puberty, the imperative to "marry up" with a white person, and Anne's intensely incestuous feelings for her father create a claustrophobic atmosphere. After the death of Nadège and her parents, Anne takes Nadège's lover Gopaul for herself, hoping to find an identity through him.

H.'s next two novels, *Le volkameria* (1984; The Clerodendron) and *Une robe d'écume et de vent* (1989; A Dress of Foam and Wind), tell of a lonely childhood on the imaginary island of Le Ligoualan near Bermuda. The evocation of the windswept seascape and its fishermen recalls Victor Hugo's regional novel, *Les travailleurs de la mer* (1866; Toilers of the Sea, 1866). The first novel is told by Christophe, a boy trying to learn about his mysterious father, a Finnish architect. A wise ambulant peddler Maxime befriends and guides him. He loves Ilse, whom he thinks is his cousin, and must watch in agony for years while other friendships engulf her. She tells the second novel from a strikingly different point of view, which shifts every ten pages from her adult life in Europe to her island childhood. Her mother Helga had her by an unknown father during World War II, and went mad when Christophe's father Erwin rejected her for not waiting for him. She is being reared by him as his own daughter. She tries to win her mother back to sanity and free her from her delusional relationship with Erwin's brother Marc. Toward the conclusion, Helga's memories of her flight from wartime Berlin blend with Ilse's memories of

her journey to Hanoi during the Vietnam War. Ilse's identity then blurs into that of the implied author.

Un fils d'orage (1992; A Child of the Storm) is a noteworthy regional novel of La Camargue, the salt marshes east of Marseilles, where bulls are bred. Here the author's narrative experiments become even bolder, and she alternates without warning between the viewpoints of grandmother, mother, and granddaughter, all proudly independent women in another acutely dysfunctional family. The granddaughter learns that all freedom can be had only at the cost of loneliness. She resolves to buy back the farm and raise bulls as her grandmother has done.

La montagne des signaux(1994; Signal Mountain) returns to Mauritius and the motif of rivalry between two sisters, carried on through two generations of self-destructive behavior. The younger, Cecilia, hates April, a famous cardiologist who has returned for their mother Dolly's funeral after an absence of twenty years. Racial prejudice against Indians has prevented Dolly's happy remarriage with a fine man. During the reunion Cecilia learns to understand and pity her sister's ineradicable loneliness, and to accept her own past decision to remain on Mauritius.

H. is a gifted psychological analyst, lyric stylist, innovative narrator, and important regional novelist. Despite her achievements, the republication of three of her novels in the popular Livre de Poche series, and her literary prizes, she has not yet attracted the attention she deserves. She is not militantly feminist, and the racial prejudice she satirizes is not a variety familiar to most Western readers; however, her depiction of doomed love relationships and sisters' rivalry is intense and memorable.

FURTHER WORKS: *Balzac: Saché, ou le nid de coucou* (1991); *Le Chant du seringat la nuit* (1997); *Tombeau du coeur de François II* (1997)

BIBLIOGRAPHY: Lionnet, F., " *Métissage*, Emancipation, and Female Textuality in Two Francophone Writers," in DeJean, J., and N. K. Miller, eds., *Displacements: Women, Tradition, Literatures in French* (1991): 254-74

—LAURENCE M. PORTER

HUNGARIAN LITERATURE

The classic-romantic populist movement that began with a bang in the 1840s, when the reform generation burst on the literary scene, ended with a whimper amid the placid artificiality of the century's end. The reform generation fought for political emancipation as well as for the revitalization of Hungarian literature. At the end of the century its political and, particularly, its literary programs were hopelessly outdated. The lull caused by the gradual exhaustion of traditional literary form was, however, of short duration. In the first years of the 20th c. the creative forces of the rising generation regained sufficient momentum to give entirely new dimensions to Hungarian literature.

The process of revitalization was triggered mainly by poets. This was hardly surprising since poetry, particularly lyrical poetry, was the traditional genre in which the literary genius of Hungary usually manifested itself. As in the age of enlightenment and in the reform period, poetry thus provided the most effective means through which the hopes and aspirations of the new generation were to be expressed.

The group formed around the periodical *Nyugat*, founded in 1908 by the critics Ignotus (pseud. of Hugo Veigelsberg, 1869–1950) and Ernő Osvát (1877–1929), did not, of course, consist entirely of poets. But although the group included fine writers such as Zsigmond Móricz, Margit KAFFKA, and Frigyes KARINTHY, it was chiefly through *Nyugat* poets, headed by Endre ADY, that the movement exerted the galvanizing effect that was to result within the next decades in the radical transformations of the literary scene. This was due, in addition to the traditional response to poetry, to Ady's almost demoniacal ability to present in strikingly new forms the revolutionary message that was to change—so he hoped, at least—the spiritual and political physiognomy of the "vast fallow lands of Hungary."

When *Nyugat* was founded, Ady had already published two volumes—*Uj versek* (1906; new poems) and *Vér és arany* (1907; blood and gold)—containing some of his major poems (many of these have been translated by Anton N. Nyerges in *Poems of Endre Ady*, 1969). The influence of French SYMBOLISM—Ady had spent some time in Parisis evident, particularly in his early poems. Nevertheless, Ady was too individualistic and too original to be classified as the representative of any one literary school. While he preferred to express himself by means of symbolist techniques, as shown by his famous poems "Az ős kaján" (1907; "The Demon Guile," 1969) and "A fekete zongora" (1907; "The Black Piano," 1969), biblical and folkloric influences are also clearly discernible in the sometimes moody, sometimes apocalyptic lines in which he described the tragic search of an oversensitive but dedicated man for truth, justice, love, faith, and inner peace. His poems, abounding in an overpowering imagery, melodious resonance, and almost ballad-like density, represented the quintessence of the "new songs of new times," which the members of the *Nyugat* group were singing while setting out to give a new form and concept to Hungarian literature.

In contrast to Ady's tumultuous individualism, Mihály BABITS, the second most influential poet of the *Nyugat* group, displayed a classic discipline that brought fully into relief the immaculate perfection of his artistry. Dezső KOSZTOLÁNYI expressed, with the self-assurance, and often with the audacity of the virtuoso, the changing moods of his generation. Erudition, refinement, and an impressive faculty to translate into poetical terms the sensitivities of a lonely soul were the hallmarks of Árpád TÓTH's poetry. Regardless of their allegiance to various schools, ranging from Parnassianism to symbolism, from Pre-Raphaelitism to early FUTURISM, all the poets of the *Nyugat* group, such as Gyula JUHÁSZ, Oszkár Gellért (1882–1967), Milán Füst (1888–1967), Simon Kemény (1883–1945), Anna Leszani (1885–1966), and Ernő Szép (1884–1953), united originality of expression with astounding versatility in their search for new poetical forms and techniques.

One of the great accomplishments of the group was the widening of literary horizons through close contacts with Western European and American literature. Most poets gathering around *Nyugat*, particularly Babits, Kosztolányi, Tóth, and later Lőrinc SZABÓ, were exceptionally gifted translators whose masterly renderings of YEATS, JAMMES, VERHAEREN, RILKE, GEORGE, Wilde, Byron, Keats, Shelley, Rossetti, Baudelaire, Verlaine, Rimbaud, Mallarmé, Poe, and Whitman contributed considerably to refining literary tastes and adding further momentum to the great literary renaissance.

Social protest, so strongly expressed in Ady's revolutionary poetry as well as in the lyrical output of poets such as Tóth and Juhász, provided the main theme for the novelists who appeared on the literary scene in the decade preceding World War I. The social, economic, and psychological plight of the peasantry was described with forceful realism by Móricz, considered the most significant Hungarian prose writer of the 20th c. While village life—*Sárarany* (1910; golden mud); "Hét krajcár" (1910; "Seven Pennies," 1962)—the Hungarian past—*Tündérkert* (1922; fairy garden)—and the eccentricities of the country squires—*Úri muri* (1928; squirish feast)—provided the raw material for Móricz's penetrating sociopsychological analyses, the drab monotony of petit-bourgeois existence, and the sullen hopelessness of the proletariat inspired the caustic protests voiced in the novels and short stories of Lajos NAGY. In Karinthy's books of imaginary travels—*Utazás Faremidóba* (1916) and *Capillária* (1921)—translated together as *Voyage to Faremidóba* (1965)—the fantastic, interwoven with the absurd, became the vehicle for witty social satire, while his collection of parodies—*Így írtok ti* (1912; so you write)—concealed highly spirited literary criticism under a façade of whimsical playfulness.

It is fairly safe to say that the *Nyugat* group represented, in both a political and a literary sense, leftist-radical tendencies (radicalism in the European sense, that is, moderates on the left-center). To the right of the radical opposition stood the proponents of 19th-c. liberalism, such as the poet József Kiss (1843–1921), the novelist and playwright Sándor BRÓDY, and the highly versatile Jenő Heltai (1871–1957). Kiss, whose literary weekly *A Hét* has paved the way for *Nyugat*, showed great skill and sincerity in broadening the poetic scope of classic-romantic traditions. Bródy contributed considerably to the development of a new literary idiom marked by strong naturalistic tendencies, as seen in *A tanitónő* (1908; the schoolmistress). Heltai, who began his career as the author of song-like poems and amusing novelettes, acquired, after World War I, solid literary stature with his psychological novel *Álmokháza* (1929; house of dreams) and the play *A néma levente* (1936; the mute knight). Géza Gárdonyi's (1863–1922) impressive historical frescos, *Isten rabjai* (1908; slaves of God) and *Egri csillagok* (1901; stars of Eger), were highly appreciated by critics as well as the public.

In the period 1908–18 the increasing activities of the literary avant-garde did not fail to call forth a vigorous reaction from conservative nationalists, headed by the influential Jenő Rákosi (1842–1929). The polemics between defenders of literary orthodoxy and their progressive opponents, such as the critics Zoltán AMBRUS, Aladár Schöpflin (1872–1950), and György LUKÁCS, created an exceptionally tense literary atmosphere in which the clash of ideological and particularly aesthetic currents added further stimulus to the creative processes. In the conservative camp the leading literary figure was Ferenc Herczeg (1863–1954), a novelist—and outstanding work is *Pogányok* (1902; pagans)—and playwright—*Bizánc* (1904; Byzantium)—whose psychological insight, stylistic skill, and highly developed sense for both humor and drama commanded the respect even of his most resolute opponents.

Curiously, the playwrights who succeeded about this time in putting Budapest on the theatrical map took little or no part in the momentous debates. The reason for this was that essentially they had no program to defend, no ideology to propagate, no message to deliver. Dezső Szomory (1869–1944), from a literary point of view perhaps the most interesting figure in this group, dedicated all his talents to the search for artistic perfection, which he sought to attain by projecting the opaque elements of the subconscious through the medium of a highly colored, impressionistic imagery, as in, for example *II. József* (1918; Joseph II). Ferenc MOLNÁR was at his best when describing the secret tragedies of metropolitan life, for instance, in his novel *A Pál-utcai fiúk* (1907; *The Paul Street Boys*, 1927), and plays like *Széntolvajok* (1918; coal thieves) and *Liliom* (1909; *Liliom*, 1921). Sincere, moving, and abounding in poetic tenderness, these masterly reconstructions of the world of children, vagabonds, and thieves provide far better evidence of Molnár's exceptional literary talents than his technically flawless comedies like *Játék a kastélyban* (1926; *The Play's the Thing*, 1927) and *Az ördög* (1907; *The Devil*, 1908). A very similar technical virtuosity and dramatic flair contributed to making Menyhért Lengyel's (1880–1974) *Tájfun* (1907; *Typhoon*, 1911) a great success.

By the early 1920s the literary revolution triggered by the *Nyugat* group had run its course. But while humanistic-cosmopolitan ideas propagated by the periodical lost much of their significance as a result of the social and intellectual upheavals that followed World War I, the revolutionary-populist content of Ady's and Móricz's writings provided a rich source of inspiration for younger poets and novelists. The most original representative of the revolutionary-populist mystique was Dezső Szabó (1879–1945), whose torrential style and polemical zest in such works as *Az elsodort falu* (1919; the swept-away village) and *Segítség* (1925; help) added an entirely new and powerful note to Hungarian prose. The tendency to consider the peasantry as the main source of national regeneration was clearly reflected in the novels of János Kodolányi (1899–1969) and Pál Szabó (1893–1970). The leading figure in this group was Gyula ILLYÉS, who succeeded in lending both persuasiveness and originality to all genres—poetry, drama, fiction, and journalism—to which he dedicated his impressive talents.

While the interest of writers gathering around the so-called village sociographers (*falukutatók*) remained focused on rural life, particularly on the plight of the agrarian proletariat, other novelists chose different terrains for their psychological and social explorations. Gyula KRÚDY, who belonged to the first *Nyugat* generation, used almost SURREALIST techniques in evoking with nostalgic tenderness the moods of the past and in recalling dreamlike episodes in the lives of strange, lonely men and women as in *A vörös postakocsi* (1914; *The Crimson Coach*, 1967). In contrast to Krúdy's delicately emotional approach, Sándor Márai (1900–1988) followed a rigorous intellectual method in his brilliant analyses of the bourgeoisie in *Idegen emberek* (1930; foreign people) and *Vendégjáték Bolzanóban* (1940; guest performance in Bolzano). Mihály Földi (1894–1943), a physician by profession, used Freudian techniques to depict intricate psychological problems in *Sötétség* (1918; darkness) and *Szahara* (1920; Sahara). Ferenc Móra's (1894–1934) tender and amusing character sketches revealed great literary skill joined with a genuinely humanistic outlook in *Ének a búzamezőkről* (1927; *Song of the Wheatfields*, 1930). Lajos ZILAHY's well-constructed plays, like *Süt a nap* (1927; the sun shines) and novels like *Két fogoly* (1927; *Two Prisoners*, 1931) and *Ararát* (1947; *The Dukays*, 1949) reflected an intense awareness of the social and psychological developments that preceded the moral and political disintegration of central and eastern Europe.

The remarkable autobiography, *Egy ember élete* (8 vols, 1928–39; the life of a man), of Lajos KASSÁK, the first Hungarian poet of stature to experiment with futurist and EXPRESSIONIST techniques, provided in highly articulate literary terms a valuable human document on the corrosive processes that were threatening 20th-c. Hungarian society. The critic, novelist, and playwright László

NÉMETH adopted the technique of the great Western realists to offer in a highly individualistic style a critical analysis of Hungary's political and social institutions. His novels—such as *Iszony* (1947; *Revulsion*, 1965) and *Égető Eszter* (1956; Eszter Égető)—his plays—such as the historical drama *Galilei* (1956; Galileo)—and his essays abound in original, although often confusing ideas expressed with great verbal artistry.

The same extraordinary diversity that distinguished Hungarian poetry in the beginning of the century remained the characteristic feature of the new literary era. Gyula Illyés, József Erdélyi (1896–1979), and Ferenc Juhász (b. 1928) represented the populist trend; Lőrinc Szabó, Miklós RADNÓTI, and Sándor WEÖRES followed in the footsteps of the first *Nyugat* generation by seeking to broaden in a highly individualistic manner the classic-romantic forms of poetical expression. Catholic poets such as László Mécs (1895–1979) and Sándor Sík (1889–1963) successfully translated into lyrical terms their spiritual yearnings and experiences. Unconnected with any group or literary school, Attila JÓZSEF emerged as the greatest poet of this period. Uniting a moving, almost naïve sensitivity and an inexhaustible artistic imagination with a melodious flexibility of expression and a passionate commitment to human dignity and justice, József succeeded in expressing with equal ease and credibility moods and attitudes ranging from serene introspection and quiet nostalgia to indignant social protest.

Social criticism, which had been one of the leitmotifs of 20th-c. Hungarian literature, was turned into parodistic farce by the Party hacks who dominated literature in the years following the establishment of the Communist regime in Hungary. Curiously enough, the intellectual terror that lasted from 1948 to 1956 provided the best evidence of the resilience of Hungarian writers, who succeeded in preserving the traditional vigor of their creative powers even in the literary Sahara of the era of compulsory SOCIALIST REALISM. In fact, writers, led by Gyula Illyés, in the postwar era the dean of modern Hungarian letters, played a leading role in preparing the intellectual climate for the uprising of 1956. Having hailed the advent of "redemptory socialism," most prominent poets of that era took considerable risks, both before and after the Russian intervention, by denouncing the despotic measures the regime had taken in trying to conceal the glaring defects of the Stalinist system.

The inner conflict triggered by a clash between socialist ideals and harsh realities colors the poems of László BENJÁMIN written in the mid–1950s. After experimenting with expressionist techniques, Zoltán Zelk (b. 1906) returned to more traditional poetic forms to reaffirm with great sensitivity his commitment to affirm with great sensitivity his commitment to an undogmatic world view, seen in the collections *Tűzből mentett hegedű* (1963; violin saved from fire) and *Zuzmara a rózsafán* (1964; hoarfrost on the rose tree). Uniting sensuous originality with great artistic virtuosity, György Faludy (b. 1913), in *őszi harmat után* (1947; after the autumn dew) and *Emlékkönyv a rőt Bizáncról* (1961; memorial volume of red Byzantium), succeeded in keeping alive the traditions of the first *Nyugat* generation. Gyula Illyés's poem "Egy mondat a zsarnokságról" (1956; "One Sentence on Tyranny," 1968) galvanized public opinion on its publication and is now considered a lasting monument of modern Hungarian poetry.

The role played by writers and poets such as Illyés and Faludy in the 1956 events added considerable momentum to the literary revival that took place in the following decade. The revival was most noticeable in lyric poetry, which has always been the literary genre in which Hungary's national genius expressed itself most eloquently and convincingly. Moreover, in the 1960s and 1970s, poetry left wider room for subjectivity and experimentation than other literary genres. No less important was the country's emergence from almost complete cultural isolation. The works of YEATS, POUND, ELIOT, and Dylan THOMAS became available, and some of their poems were even published in translation. The effects of that cultural cross-fertilization are clearly discernible in the works of the younger poets.

The public, long subjected to the cultural devastation of Socialist Realism, responded enthusiastically to the poetic revival. According to official statistics, between 1957 and 1972, 804 volumes of poetry by then living poets was published in addition to 57 anthologies.

The spiritual, moral, and intellectual tensions of the post-Stalinist period are clearly reflected by the efforts of most contemporary Hungarian poets to bring into accord conflicting moods and orientations. Their deep disappointment over the defects of the socialist experiment has been gradually mitigated by hope for a better future, while commitment to collectivity became sufficiently flexible to leave room for subjective concerns and inclinations. The search for a middle ground on which the conflicting ideological, social, and psychological trends could be successfully reconciled is manifest in the works of Ferenc Juhász, whose over-powering imagery, abounding in folkloristic and mythical elements, evident in *Harc a fehér báránnyal* (1965; struggle with the white lamb) and *A Szent Tűzözön regéi* (1969; the tales of the Sacred Fire-Flood), expresses the individual's fears and perplexities in a dangerously restless world. Inspired by Christian ethics, János PILINSZKY voiced with disciplined artistry his protest against war and oppression in *Nagyvárosi ikonok* (1970; big-city icons) and *Szálkák* (1972; splinters).

Distinguished by fascinating virtuosity, the poems of Sándor Weöres reflect the whole gamut of human emotions, ranging from playful insouciance to a soberly sympathetic understanding of man's existential problems. In the poems of István Vas (b. 1910) a rationalist-humanist philosophy in the Greco-Roman tradition irradiates the melancholy themes of senescence and death. Like Babits, Tóth, and Kosztolányi, Vas too has greatly enriched Hungarian literature with masterly translations ranging from the tragedies of Shakespeare, Racine, and O'NEILL to MAETERLINCK's and APOLLINAIRE's works. In contrast to Vas's elegiac mood, Mihály Váci (1924–1968) gave free rein to revolutionary passions in asserting his faith in the prophetic vocations of poets in his collections *Kelet felől* (1965; from the East) and the posthumously published *Sokaság fia* (1970; son of multitude). László Nagy (b. 1925), one of the most impressive poets of his generation, experimented with various techniques, including surrealism, before fashioning the highly original style in which he expresses moods ranging from subdued pessimism to a rapturous celebration of the joys of life, as in *Himnusz minden időben* (1965; hymn in all times).

The evolution of modern Hungarian prose writing reflects the same tensions that characterized the poetic revival. Prose writers, however, faced difficulties greater than poets did in trying to overcome the limitations imposed on them by Party ideologists, who continue to consider Socialist Realism as the norm of literary acceptability. The difficulties were partly overcome by trying to reinterpret the meaning of realism. Thus, a new trend emerged that is often described as "new realism"—an amalgam of "traditional" and "popular" realism. Popular realism is distinguished from traditional realism by its preoccupation with sociopolitical problems affecting the working classes.

Whatever the label attached to their style, most Hungarian writers continue to focus their attention on one or another of the great issues that came to the fore amid the radical changes that took place in Hungary after World War II. Tibor DÉRY's novel *Feletet* (2 vols., 1950–52; answer) triggered a long and impassioned ideological debate because of the author's allegedly "subjective" views on the evolution of the worker's movement in Hungary. Before defecting to the West, Tamás Aczél (b. 1921) published several novels—*A szabadság árnyékában* (1948; in the shadow of freedom), *Vihar és napsütés* (1949; storm and sunshine)—which were well received by critics as well as the public. The playwright Gyula Háy (b. 1900), a veteran Communist who was to take an active part in the 1956 freedom uprising, showed great skill in using the stage for sustaining the Marxist view of history in such plays as *Isten, császár, paraszt* (1946; God, emperor, and peasant), which had first been produced in Germany in 1932.

József Lengyel (b. 1896), another veteran Communist who had spent long years in Stalin's prison camps, described with documentary-like precision the crimes and aberrations of the Stalin era in his short stories and in such novels as *Igéző* (1961; *The Spell*, 1968) and *Elévült tartozás* (1964; prescribed debt). József Darvas (b. 1912), had revived his childhood memories in portraying village life—in *A legnagyobb magyar falu* (1937; the greatest Hungarian village); in his later works he explored the psychological and social significance of individual responsibility in works such as *Részeg eső* (1963; drunken rain). The impact of historical upheavals on individual morality is the main theme of Ferenc Sánta's (b. 1927) writings, which are inspired by a deep-rooted humanism; two of his best works are *Az ötödik pecsét* (1963; the fifth seal) and *20 óra* (1964; 20 hours). The life of "small people" living on the peripheries of the big cities, and their inability to adapt themselves to social and economic progress, is critically analyzed by Endre Fejes (b. 1923) in his novel *Rozsdatemető* (1962; *Generation of Rust*, 1970), which triggered an animated literary debate. So did György KONRÁD's novel *A látogató* (1969; *The Caseworker*, 1974), which underscored the difficulty of solving ethical problems by sociological means.

In spite of the dominant trends that called for investing every literary work with social significance, many writers sought to add new dimensions to "realism" by infusing into it psychological and even allegorical elements. In analyzing the existential problems of individuals as they try to find their place in successive Hungarian societies, Magda Szabó (b. 1917) uses with great skill modern literary devices, including the interior monologue in such novels as *Freskó* (1958; fresco) and *Az őz* (1959; the deer). György Moldova (b. 1934) portrays with sympathy, flavored with a touch of bitter humor, the solitary eccentrics who appear in works like *Az idegen bajnok* (1963; the foreign champion) and *A sötét angyal* (1964; the dark angel). In his novels, short stories, and plays inspired by a cool but imaginative rationalism, István Örkény (b. 1912) seeks to reveal a reality that remains hidden behind the grotesque or even absurd façade of everyday life: *Házastársak* (1951; spouses), *Jeruzsálem hercegnője* (1966; the princess of Jerusalem), and *Egyperces novellák* (1968; one-minute short stories) are among his best works of fiction.

Literary debates on important subjects such as the nature of realism or socialist aesthetics are greatly stimulated by the publication of several literary periodicals of outstanding quality: *Kortárs, Nagyvilág, Alföld, Jelenkor*. In addition to contributing to the clarification of aesthetic and other theoretical issues, these debates attest to the continuing vitality of Hungarian letters in spite of the ideological restrictions to which all creative endeavors are subjected.

See also sections on Hungarian writing in the articles on Czechoslovak, Romanian, and Yugoslav literatures.

BIBLIOGRAPHY: von Farkas J., *Die Entwicklung der ungarischen Literatur* (1934); Gömöri, G., *The Hungarian Literary Scene, 1957–1959* (1959); Cushing, G. F., Introduction to *Hungarian Prose and Verse: A Selection with an Introductory Essay* (1956): xi–xxxv; Fenyő, M., "The *Nyugat* Literary Magazine and Modern Hungarian Literature," *NHQ*, 3 (1962): 3–4, 7–19; Sivirsky, A., *Die ungarische Literatur der Gegenwart* (1962); Klaniczay, T., et al., *History of Hungarian Literature* (1964); Reményi, J., *Hungarian Writers and Literature* (1964); Gömöri, G., "Hungarian Literature," in Ivask, I., and G. von Wilpert, eds., *World Literature Since 1945* (1973): 357–71

—ANN DEMAITRE

Hungarian Literature since 1980

Hungarian literature, whose development and very character had been shaped traditionally by poets, has become considerably more prose-oriented in the past two decades. Several writers of fiction who remained on the sideline of literary life for much of their careers, either for political reasons or because they never met the litmus test for social relevance in art, have seen their reputation grow in recent years. Géza Ottlik (1912–1990) was one such loner. His *Iskola a határon* (1959; *School at the Frontier*, 1966), now recognized as one of the most significant Hungarian novels of the post-1956 period, focuses on the recollections of a group of former cadets in an old-style central European military academy, though the novel is just as concerned with the process of fiction itself, with the difficulties of conventional narration, the inconclusiveness of memory, and, in a larger sense, with the impossibility of truly objectifying reality. Miklós MÉSZÖLY is another more or less experimental writer, who in sparse and precise narratives—*Az atléta halála* (1966; the death of an athlete), *Saulus* (1968; Saulus), and *Film* (1976; film) are his most important fictions—offers bleak and open-ended studies of solitary individuals in the throes of excruciating though never fully comprehended spiritual crises. Mészöly's best short stories—"Jelentés öt egérről" (1958; "Report on Five Mice," 1982) and "Ló-regény" (1982; "A Tale of Horses," 1986)—which also revolve around dimly perceived existential dilemmas and struggles, are somewhat more accessible, and his essays contain even more forthright discussions of specifically east European political and cultural issues.

Both Ottlik and Mészöly used to be classified by Marxist critics as alienated, "existentialist" writers, yet they had a strong impact on a generation of younger prose writers who appeared on the literary scene in the 1970s, and whose allusive, self-reflective and parodistic fiction exudes a post-modern sensibility. Writers like Péter ESTERHÁZY, Péter NÁDAS, Ferenc Temesi (b. 1949), Péter Lengyel (b. 1939), and others clearly admire their masters' moral and artistic integrity, but their rejection of literary forms sanctioned by ideology or tradition led them away from Ottlik's painstaking, irreproachable fictional reconstructions or Mészöly's stark moral fables to a skeptically playful, stylistically far more exuberant and inventive treatment of personal and communal history. In the process they often revisit, always with satiric intent, traditional

anecdotal realism and embrace other classical, popular, once-obligatory genres. For example, Péter Esterházy's first long work of fiction, *Termelési-regény* (1979; production novel), is a takeoff on the SOCIALIST REALIST "production novels" of the 1950s, and his *Kis magyar pornográfia* (1984; *A Little Hungarian Pornography*, 1995), rooted also in the totalitarian experience, is a compendium of lusty anecdotes and vignettes about the political perversions of recent and not-so-recent Hungarian history. Péter Nádas is another self-consciously literary writer. His magnum opus *Az emlékiratok könyve* (1986; book of memoirs), first strikes the reader as a confessional *je roman* in the grandly modernist manner, replete with Proustian and Mannian echoes, but what it really is is an endlessly refined and modified postmodern reprise of the European psychological novel. Ferenc Temesi has chosen yet another unusual narrative device. His two-volume *Por A-Zs* (1986–1987; dust A-Z) is a novel in encyclopedic form, in which alphabetical entries do coalesce into a narrative of sorts, though the author's real aim is to present an in-depth portrait of a single Hungarian town: its past and present, its official and underground history, including tantalizing local legends, scandals, and villains. Similarly, Péter Lengyel's *Macskak* (1988; cobblestone), subtitled a "detective story," uses the formulas and clichés of this particular genre to explore the urban folklore of his native Budapest, focusing on the period of the turn of the century when the city was young and vital and its underworld, too, was enviably resourceful and robust. Both Temesi and Lengyel are in some ways indebted to another "old master," Iván Mándy (1918-1995), who in his impressionistic stories and sketches also evokes the lore and romance of old Budapest.

There are even more radical experimenters among the younger Hungarian prose writers, and they, too, have attracted critical attention of late. László Márton (b. 1959), for example, a Germanist and translator by profession, favors linguistic parodies of old literary texts, whereas László Krasznahorkai (b. 1954) describes a timeless world of utter desolation and hopelessness with curiously suggestive and lively language. Krasznahorkai's remarkable first novel, *Sátántangó* (1985; satan-tango), dealing nominally with a group of isolated and sullen peasants deceived by a would-be savior, becomes an unnerving depiction of spatial-temporal immobility.

In general, one could say that the innovative prose writers who revolutionized Hungarian fiction are obsessed with form and language. In various ways they all engage in subtle culture criticism, which includes conspicuous linguistic criticism. Behind their parodies and pastiches there is the recognition that in a society where public discourse is warped, language itself is hopelessly compromised. POSTMODERNISM, then, in the Hungarian context, is not simply a new way of telling old stories but an attempt to make language relevant again, to purge it of cant without being solemn about it. Approaches vary, of course. Péter Esterházy and Péter Nádas, by far the most versatile and accomplished members of this group, have opted for markedly different stylistic solutions. Esterházy fights off linguistic corruptions by producing some of his own. His texts are riddled with untranslatable puns, wordplays, and distorted literary allusions. Nádas, on the other hand, protects his work from the debased political and intellectual jargon of the day by creating a highly intricate, rarefied, and classically serene literary language.

Naturally, not all contemporary Hungarian novelists are quite this form-conscious, or are followers of experimental, postmodernist trends. A number of important recent Hungarian novels have closer ties with the still flourishing realist school of fiction. For example, György Spiró's (b. 1946) widely acclaimed *Az ikszek* (1981; the X's) is a fiction set in 18th-c. partitioned Poland. Concerned exclusively with the inbred world of Polish theatrical people of the time, this intriguingly modern-toned historical novel reveals a great deal about conflicts and compromises characteristic of all occupied east European societies. A lesser-known figure, Imre Kertész (b. 1929), achieved belated fame only recently with his novel *Sorstalanság* (1975; *Fateless*, 1992), a detailed and dispassionate account of a fourteen-year-old Jewish boy's ordeal in wartime concentration camps.

Actually, Kertész is one of many Hungarian writers whose prominence has been more clearly acknowledged since the historic "quiet revolution" of 1989. While quite a few previously active, popular, even stylish writers—Ferenc Karinthy (1921–1992), György Moldova (b. 1934), László Gyurkó (b. 1934), Gyula Hernádi (b. 1924)—have been eclipsed by these changes, others came to the fore since the fall of Hungary's communist régime. These latter artists had either been under publication bans before, or they simply did not want to subject their works even to mild forms of censorship. It is true enough that the cultural policies of the pre-1989 Kádáar régime were much more liberal than those of other east European communist governments, and the number of taboo subjects in literature remained relatively small, but in the past several years the country's unfettered media made it amply clear that the manipulation of the arts, though subtle, had been nevertheless pervasive even during the latter phase of one-party rule. Writers who once again became full-fledged members of the Hungarian literary community include the poet and publicist István Eörsi (b. 1931), the documentarist Zsolt Csalog (b. 1935), the satirist György Dalos (b. 1943), and the poet György Petri (b. 1943).

But the best-known author to have reentered literary life in the late 1980s, and one of the few Hungarian writers who established an international reputation in the past two decades, is George (György) KONRÁD. His masterful first novel, *A látogató* (1969; *The Case Worker*, 1974), a devastating, sociologically revealing depiction of Budapest lowlife was brought out in a modest edition in 1969. A slightly censored version of his second, more abstract, experimental fiction, *A városalapító* (1977; *The City Builder*, 1977), could still be published in Hungary, but after that Konrád became an internal exile, and his writings could be read inside the country only in the underground *samizdat* press. His third novel, *A cinkos* (1978; *The Loser*, 1982), is a more traditional, loosely episodic narrative concerned with the checkered life history of a disenchanted modern revolutionary, and his latest, *Kerti mulatság* (1989; *Feast in the Garden*, 1992), is an even more diffuse, essayistic examination of the life and hard times of a present-day Hungarian intellectual.

The publication, or republication, of George Konrád's works were among the first sensations of the new democratic era. The reappearance in print of actual émigrés—the seminal modernist Gyõzõ Határ (b. 1914), the popular lyricist György Faludy (b. 1910), the excommunist novelist Tamás Aczél (1921-1994), and above all the doyen of Hungarian literary exiles, Sándor Márai—was likewise greeted with lively interest. Yet, ironically, the political changes also created an air of crisis in literature. To be sure, the proliferation of new, uncensored publications and private publishing ventures stirred great initial excitement, but as a result of slashed government subsidies and other reforms, serious literature has fallen on hard times—and this in spite of the fact that a number of well-known writers, journalists, and historians are members of the democratically elected government, including the president of the Hungarian Republic, Árpád Göncz (b. 1922), a noted translator of American literature.

The freewheeling and combative new political atmosphere favors literary journalism and the political essay, and it seems to have diminished the importance of imaginative literature. Moreover, some of the long-standing divisions in Hungarian cultural life—the antagonism between "populist" and "urban" writers—have also resurfaced and led to several acrimonious public debates, with undercurrents of intolerant nationalism and anti-Semitism.

With the death of Gyula ILLYÉS in 1983, the mantle of national poet passed to Sándor CSOÓRI, the most prominent and influential populist literary figure. In his recent volumes of poetry and prose—*Kezemben a zöld ág* (1985; green twig in my hand); *Készülõdé a számadásra* (1987; preparing for the reckoning); and *A világ emlékmûvei* (1989; memorials of the world)—Csoóri continues to focus on such themes as the erosion of Hungarian national values, the decline of rural life, and the fate of the Hungarian minorities in neighboring east European countries. Another populist, the playwright István Csurka (b. 1934), has become better known in recent years as a controversial political figure. The finest "urban" poets of the day—Dezsõ Tandori (b. 1938), Agnes Gergely (b. 1933), Szabolcs Várady (b. 1943), Péter Kántor (b. 1949), Zsuzsa Rakovszky (b. 1950)—tend to be less visible. Influenced by the understated intellectualism of István Vas (1910–1991) and the objective lyricism of Ágnes Nemes Nagy (1922–1991)—and reacting against the overwrought wordiness of much Hungarian poetry—these poets write sparingly, and with ironic detachment, about recent upheavals. The one possible exception is the former dissident György Petri (b. 1943), whose forceful and explicit political poetry effectively fuses public and private traumas. With his first collected edition of his verses, *Petri György versei* (1991; the poetry of György Petri), the once-banned poet gained a wider readership. The poems of Dezsõ Tandori cannot be said to have broad popular appeal: The minimalism of his early poetry yielded to a more obsessive privatization of experience in his later work; yet Tandori is a formidable talent, and not only as a poet but as a prose writer, critic, and translator as well—his quiet virtuosity is evident in all of these areas. (A selection of Tandori's poems, *Birds and Other Relations*, was published in English in 1986.) Though a more traditional poet drawn to somber moods and wistful insights, Ágnes Gergely is equally versatile, and Szabolcs Várady was hailed, already at the beginning of his career, as a "complete" poet. Indeed, what Tandori, Gergely, and Várady share with other "urbanists" is unobtrusive formal sophistication, polish, and reticence. Like the new fictionists, they distrust words, but they prefer to use fewer rather than more words to express this distrust.

Hungarian drama, always more conservative and convention-bound, produced fewer surprises in the 1970s and 1980s. Among the younger playwrights Mihály Kornis (b. 1949) stands out as the most original. Kornis's affinity for symbolist and absurdist modes lends his down-to-earth, zany, and very Hungarian plays, notably *Halleluja* (1980; hallelujah) and *Kozma* (1981; *Kozma*, 1991), an air of universality. György Spiró achieves a similar effect by turning to historical subjects. His *Az imposztor* (1982; the imposter) is a highly successful adaptation of a section of his novel *Azikszek*. In a more recent play, *Csirkefej* (1985; *Chicken Head*, 1991), Spiró uses the stylized naturalism preferred by some contemporary American playwrights to portray the crude and cruel world of Budapest slum dwellers. The more traditional historical dramas of the Transylvanian Hungarian writer András Sütõ (b. 1927) have also received memorable productions in Budapest in the past decade. The frequent performances of Sütõ's dramas *Csillag a máglyán* (1975; star at the stake) and *Egy lócsiszár virágvasárnapja*

(1978; *The Palm Sunday of a Horse Dealer*, 1991) attest to the renewed literary and political interest in the works of Hungarian writers living beyond the country's borders. Some of these authors—Lajos Grendel (b. 1948) in Slovakia, Nándor Gion (b. 1941) in Yugoslavia, Ádám Bodor (b. 1936), formerly of Romania—are very much in the mainstream of Hungarian literature, though their writings often reflect the double isolation of minority nationals in repressive or aggressively nationalistic east European societies.

Since the 1989–1990 watershed, as might be expected, the tone-setting, ideologically committed analysts of Hungarian literature have lost much of their power and influence. Literary criticism, too, has become more variegated, more relevant. In this field two new personalities emerged: the erudite Sándor Radnóti (b. 1946), whose training in philosophy and formal aesthetics enables him to view literary developments from a broader perspective, and Péter Balassa (b. 1947), who is particularly in tune with the world of the innovative prose writers of the 1970s and 1980s. The dramatic political changes also affected, inevitably, the institutions and organizational structure of cultural life. Even under new leadership, the large state publishing houses and theaters are struggling to stay solvent. Similarly, the established literary journals such as *Kortárs, Új Írás, Élet és Irodalom,* and *Nagyvilág* have lost much ground—they now have to compete with a plethora of new publications of varying quality. Of the newly founded literary periodicals, the most significant appear to be *Holmi, 2000,* the populist-oriented *Hitel,* and *Budapesti Könyvszemle* (The Budapest Review of Books), modeled after its sister publication in New York.

Hungarian literary life in the early 1990s is clearly in a state of flux. The excitement over new freedoms and opportunities has given way to concern that the commercial spirit of the new age may lead to the further marginalization of literature. Yet, since this is a society where the printed word still matters, the desire to see thoroughgoing literary treatments of the most recent turn of events—and in general, to see the literary validation of the nation's historical experience—remains strong.

BIBLIOGRAPHY: Vajda, M.,ed., *Modern Hungarian Poetry* (1977); Klaniczay, T., ed., *A History of Hungarian Literature* (1982); Czigány, L., *The Oxford History of Hungarian Literature* (1984); Balassa, P., "On Recent Hungarian Prose: A Survey and Introduction," *Formations*, 3 (1986): 153–56; Sanders, I., "Budapest Letter: New Themes, New Writers," *NYTBR* (10 Apr. 1988): 1; Brogyányi, E., ed., *DramaContemporary: Hungary* (1992)

—IVAN SANDERS

HURSTON, Zora Neale

American novelist, short-story writer, folklorist, and essayist, b. 7 Jan. 1901 (?), Eatonville, Fla.; d. 28 Jan. 1960, Fort Pierce, Fla.

Raised in an all-black Southern town, one of eight children, H. attended Howard University for two years, where she learned short-story writing, then graduated from Barnard College in 1928. While at Barnard H. journeyed to Alabama to interview the ex-slave Cudjo Lewis, then published the result in 1927. With a Rosenwald Fellowship she attended Columbia University Graduate School to study anthropology under Franz Boas. She returned to her home state to record black folklore from 1928 to 1932, which produced the collection *Mules and Men* (1935). H.'s first published novel, *Jonah's Gourd Vine* (1934), was praised for its authentic use of folklore but criticized for ignoring the influence of racism. From 1935 to 1937 she studied voodoo practices in Haiti and Jamaica under a Guggenheim fellowship, which produced *Tell My Horse* (1938; repub. as *Voodoo Gods: An Inquiry into Native Myths and Magic in Jamaica and Haiti*, 1939), a folklore collection. *Their Eyes Were Watching God* (1937), regarded as her best novel, was a response to an experience of unrequited love. H. continued collecting folklore in Florida for the WPA (1938–1939).

Her autobiography, *Dust Tracks on a Road* (1942), became her most popular work, wherein she stated that the race question always left her unmoved. H. spent years raising funds to study black folklore in Honduras, traveling there in 1947. Her final decade was beset with financial problems, failing health, isolation from family and old friends, and destitution, punctuated by a few freelance writing assignments, 1950–1956, as well as sundry part-time jobs as a librarian, maid, and school teacher.

H. gained early experience writing short fiction in college, contributing stories to the Howard literary magazine *Stylus*, and to the black journal *Opportunity*, whose editor, Charles S. Johnson, encouraged her to go to New York to broaden her literary development. During this formative period she began folkloric study from a scientific perspective, encouraged by Boas to combine empathic interviewing techniques with anthropological disinterest. She was known to stop Harlemites on the street to measure the shape of their heads. This combination of distance and empathy would characterize H.'s literary style throughout her life. To some extent the distancing devices in her work were a response to a felt need. "It was only when I was off in college, away from my native surroundings, that I could see myself like somebody else and stand off and look at my garment. Then I had to have the spyglass of anthropology to look through at that." Her first folklore collection, *Mules and Men*, reflected both the intimacy and the distance of her writer's point of view. H. always included herself as part of the culture she represented, even at times appearing as her own character Zora to record folktales and humor on the front porches of the homes she visited. Then her role was that of an eccentric woman taken to writing down the "lies" of the townsfolk while they "killed groceries" and drank freely. Later H. was accused by some critics of making her fiction and plays mere recordings of what other people told her.

H.'s sharp ear for the sounds of spoken English was reflected in *Jonah's Gourd Vine*, which was loosely based on her father's career as a minister, the personality of her mother, and her hometown milieu of an all-black township. Throughout this novel H. alternates between elevated prose and the figurative language of rural dialect as she examines the inner lives and hidden emotions of her characters. The critical success of *Jonah's Gourd Vine* brought H. literary recognition and commissions for magazine stories and articles.

Although *Their Eyes Were Watching God* (1937) has been criticized for lacking suitable political orientation and literary theme, Richard WRIGHT calling it "counterrevolutionary," it is now generally considered her greatest work. Written over an eight-week period in Haiti, the plot concerns Janie Crawford, whose self-awareness develops as a result of her experience with three successive husbands. Disappointed in love with her first husband, unable to endure the strictures of social propriety in her second marriage, Janie finally finds love and a measure of equality in her third marriage. However, she must kill her demented husband in self-defense when he threatens her life as a result of his hydrophobia brought about by a rabid dog's bite. Read from a feminist perspective, Janie's marital histories show a progression from conventional submissiveness to middle-class restrictiveness and finally to a kind of freedom with equality, resulting from a marriage based on mutual sharing instead of status and material worth. The "counterrevolutionary" climax is Janie's acquittal of her husband's murder by an all-white jury. As she returns to her all-black town, Janie is condemned by her black neighbors, who reject her self-defense motive, interpreting the killing as a willful act against her husband: "No nigger woman ain't never been treated no better." Rather than a condemnation of black society, or "a lack of bitterness towards whites," as one early reviewer saw it, H.'s novel seems to describe the social, economic, and patriarchal dominance that crosses over both black and white worlds.

Dust Tracks on a Road reveals signs of H.'s defensiveness toward the growing criticism of her novels and folklore collections. While the accounts of her childhood and parents seem straightforward, disclosure about important aspects of her adult life is lacking. Though Alice WALKER called the autobiography's tendency to circumvent self-analysis "oddly false-sounding," H.'s ruminations on life's difficulties are often subtle and revealing in their own right.

A member of the Harlem Renaissance, H. intended to write about the black experience in its full humanity, with stories "incisive and intimate . . . from the inside." Her fiction abandons what she has called "the reversion to type," by which she meant the persistent reluctance of writers and critics to transcend traditional stereotyping and simplistic psychology when depicting black life in America. H. juxtaposed the cadences of folk dialect with an eloquent prose style that explored the inner world of black Americans. She sought realistic situations and dialogue conveyed through a sensitive prose narrative that at times approached the Homeric. H.'s ear for folk dialect and stories was so keen and her understanding of black life so integrated with her own personality that her fiction was often attacked as mere novelized folklore. Her works integrated so fully social environment with the inner lives of her characters that such misinterpretations might have been inevitable.

FURTHER WORKS: *Mule Bone: A Comedy of Negro Life in Three Acts* (1931, with Langston Hughes); *Fast and Furious* (1932, with Clinton Fletcher and Tim Moore); *Moses, Man of the Mountain* (1939; repub. as *The Man of the Mountain*, 1941); *Seraph on the Suwanee* (1948); *I Love Myself When I Am Laughing . . . And Then Again When I Am Looking Mean and Impressive: A Z. N. H. Reader* (1979); *The Sanctified Church* (1981); *Spunk: The Selected Short Stories of Z. N. H.* (1985)

BIBLIOGRAPHY: Turner, D. T., *In a Minor Chord: Three Afro-American Writers and Their Search for Identity* (1971): 89–120; Davis, A. P., *From the Dark Tower: Afro-American Writers (1900–1960)* (1974): 113–20; Hemenway, R. E., *Z. N. H.* (1977); Newson, A. S., *Z. N. H.: A Reference Guide* (1980); Howard, L. P., *Z. N. H.* (1980); Bloom, H., ed., *Z. N. H.* (1986); Washington, M. H., ed., *Invented Lives: Narratives of Black Women, 1860–1960* (1987): 237–54; Krasner, J., "The Life of Women: Z. N. H. and Female Autobiography," *BALF*, 23, 1 (Spring 1989): 113–26; Wall, C. A., "Mules and Men and Women: Z. N. H.'s Strategies of Narration and Visions of Female Empowerment," *BALF*, 23, 4 (Winter

Zora Neale Hurston

1989): 661–80; Nathiri, N. Y., ed., *Zora! Z. N. H., A Woman and Her Community* (1991)

—WILLIAM OVER

HUSAYN, Tāhā

Egyptian novelist, short-story writer, critic, literary historian, and educator, b. 14 Nov. 1889, Maghāgha; d. 28 Oct. 1973, Cairo

H.'s loss of sight at a very early age had a deep effect on his life and his writing. In 1902 he went to Cairo and became a student at al-Azhar, Egypt's venerable institute of religious studies, but his disappointment with the traditional system of education brought him into conflict with his conservative teachers. At the newly established Egyptian University H. made his first acquaintance with modern scholarship. His thesis on the famous Arab poet Abī al-'Alā' al-Ma'arrī (973–1057), *Dhīkrā Abī al-'Alā'* (1915; the memory of Abī al-'Alā') earned him the first Ph.D. to be granted in Egypt. In France H. obtained from the Sorbonne his second Ph.D. for a dissertation on Ibn Khaldūn (d. 1406), the great Arab philosopher of history. Back home in 1919, he embarked on a university teaching career, and from 1950 to 1952 he was Minister of Education. He received honorary degrees from several European universities.

The publication of H.'s defiant book *Fī al-shi'r al-jāhilī* (1926; on pre-Islamic poetry), in which he claimed that the poetry attributed to the pre-Islamic period was forged in a later period and questioned some religious beliefs, placed him in the center of a public storm, and the teachers of al-Azhar accused him of heresy and tried to have him prosecuted. In retrospect, it is the intellectual courage displayed in his critical approach, rather than his actual conclusions, that earned H.'s study its prominent place in Arabic scholarship.

H. was a prolific writer whose output consists of six novels, as well as short stories, epigrams, and artistic paraphrasing of ancient Arabic poems. He also wrote books on Islamic history and Arabic literature, critical essays, translations of classical Greek and French plays, and innumerable journalistic articles on social and political topics.

H.'s autobiography, *Al-Ayyām* (3 vols., 1929, 1939, 1967; *An Egyptian Childhood*, 1932; *The Stream of Days*, 1943; *A Passage to France*, 1976), may be considered one of the finest works in modern Arabic literature. In addition to the insight it provides into the inner world of the blind youth, it sheds valuable light on Egyptian social and cultural life. The idiosyncratic style, which makes full use of the resources of the Arabic language, is extremely evocative. Its imagery shows that H.'s attitude toward people and things is determined by his reaction to the sounds they make rather than their appearance. This book, with its emotional appeal, helped mold the sensibilities of two generations of readers.

H.'s novel *Shajarat al-bu's* (1944; the tree of misery) depicts the life of a traditional family with great sympathy, whereas the short stories in *Al-Mu'adhdhabūn fī al-ard* (1949; the sufferers on earth) are symptomatic of growing resentment against social injustice prior to the 1952 revolution.

In his work as a literary historian and critic, a certain line of evolution is discernible. H. came to believe that criticism is an art, not a science. His book on the poet al-Mutanabbī (d. 965), *Ma'a al-Mutanabbī* (1936; with al-Mutanabbī), in which he laid greater emphasis on his personal taste, contrasts sharply with his earlier book on al-Ma'arrī, in which he tried to apply a rigid scientific method.

Although the Arabic cultural heritage ranked high in his esteem, H. was an admirer of Western civilization, and of French culture in particular. These meant for him not only material prosperity and scientific achievements, but also freedom of thought and respect for human rights. In his famous *Mustaqbal al-thaqāfa fī Misr* (1938; *The Future of Culture in Egypt*, 1954) he reiterated his adherence to the cause of Westernization, and exhorted the Egyptians to adapt themselves to the requirements of modern life.

An ardent lover of freedom, H. was opposed to a politically committed literature. His own writing, however, was motivated by a deep sense of mission and responsibility. His contribution, therefore, cannot be evaluated merely in terms of aesthetic excellence; it should also be taken in the context of the role he played in the emergence of a new culture. During his lifetime H. gained general recognition as the most outstanding figure in modern Arabic literature.

FURTHER WORKS: *Étude analytique et critique de la philosophie sociale d'Ibn Khaldun* (1917); *Qādat al-fikr* (1925); *Hadīth al-arbi'ā'* (3 vols., 1925, 1926, 1945); *Fī al-Adab al-jāhilī* (1927); *Ma'a Abī al-'Alā' fī sijnihi* (1930); *Fī al-sayf* (1933); *Hāfiz wa Shawqī* (1933); *'Alā hāmish al-sīra* (3 vols., 1933, 1939, 1943); *Du'ā' al-karawān* (1934); *Adīb* (1935); *Min ba'īd* (1935); *Min hadīth al-shi'r wa al-nathr* (1936); *Al-Qasr al-mashūr* (1937); *Al-Hubb al-dā'i'* (1942); *Ahlām Shahrazād* (1943); *Sawt Abī al-'Alā'*

(1944); *Fusūl fī al-adab wa al-naqd* (1945); *Jannat al-shawk* (1945); *'Uthmān* (1947); *Rihlat al-rabi'* (1948); *Mir'āt al-damīr al-hadīth* (1949); *Al-Wa'd al-haqq* (1950); *Jannat al-hayawān* (1950); *Alwān* (1952); *Bayn bayn* (1952); *'Alī wa banūhu* (1953); *Khisām wa naqd* (1955); *Naqd wa islāh* (1956); *Ahādīth* (1957); *Min adabinā al-mu'āsir* (1958); *Mir'at al-Islām* (1959); *Min laghw al-sayf* (1959); *Al-Shaykhān* (1960); *Min laghw al-Sayf ilā jidd al-shitā'* (1961); *Khawātir* (1967); *Kalimāt* (1967)

BIBLIOGRAPHY: Cachia, P., *T.H.: His Place in the Egyptian Literary Renaissance* (1956); Hourani, A., *Arabic Thought in the Liberal Age*, 1798–1939 (1962): 324–40; Semah, D., *Four Egyptian Literary Critics* (1974): 109–50

—DAVID SEMAH

HUXLEY, Aldous

English novelist, essayist, and critic, b. 26 July 1894, Godalming; d. 22 Nov. 1963, Los Angeles, Cal.

H. was born into an eminent British family of letters and science. His grandfather was the renowned biologist Thomas Henry Huxley, who popularized Darwinism; his granduncle was the poet-essayist Matthew Arnold, and his grandaunt was the novelist Mrs. Humphrey Ward; his father, Leonard, was an essayist and the editor of *Cornhill* magazine; his brother, Sir Julian, a noted biologist; and his half brother, Andrew Huxley, won the Nobel Prize for physiology in 1963. H. maintained an interest in science throughout his life, and indeed he first decided on a career in medicine, but a serious eye affliction that nearly blinded him forced him to abandon his medical studies and instead turn to the study of literature. He published his first two books of poetry, *The Burning Wheel* (1916) and *The Defeat of Youth* (1918), while still a student at Oxford. It was during this time that he met D.H. LAWRENCE, with whom he had a lifelong friendship and who influenced his early philosophy. He married Maria Nys in 1919 while on the editorial staff of *The Athenaeum*, and in 1920 published a volume of short stories, *Limbo*, and a third volume of poetry, *Leda*. In 1921 he published his first novel, *Crome Yellow*, and his literary career was well launched.

H. wrote numerous volumes of nonfiction, ranging from the early travel book *Jesting Pilate* (1926), in which he examines the cultures of the East, to biographies such as *Grey Eminence* (1941), a study of Cardinal Richelieu's assistant François Leclerc in which H. indicates his dissatisfaction with orthodox Christianity, and *The Devils of Loudun* (1952), in which he explores the psychological and spiritual implications of nuns seemingly possessed by devils; and to philosophical essays such as *Ends and Means* (1937), in which he views the inadequacies of modern Western civilization, and *The Perennial Philosophy* (1945), in which he suggests personal mysticism as the means of salvation for modern man, and *The Doors of Perception* (1954) and *Heaven and Hell* (1956), which analyze his experiences under the influence of mescaline (he believed that the heightened perceptions induced by this hallucinatory drug lead to visionary revelations, either mystical or artistic). Yet H.'s literary reputation is mainly that of a novelist. However, there is a continuity and an interrelationship between H.'s fiction and his nonfiction in the development of his philosophy and his art.

H. once described himself as an essayist who sometimes wrote novels: there is an essential truth in this remark made somewhat facetiously late in his career when he was writing more nonfiction than fiction: all of H.'s novels are novels of ideas, a genre that derives its form in part from the dramatic essay in which a symposium of ideas is presented; thus, for example, ideas and attitudes on politics, religion, and education expressed in the essays in *Proper Studies* (1927) are dramatized in the novel *Point Counter Point* (1928). H., through his character Philip Quarles, defines the novel of ideas also in relation to allegory: "The character of each personage must be implied, as far as possible, in the ideas of which he is the mouthpiece. Insofar as theories are rationalizations of sentiments, instincts, dispositions of soul, this is feasible." In his early novels (through *Brave New World*, 1932) H. maintains a philosophical skepticism about the differing ideas and attitudes, and he achieves the necessary artistic balance through satire, using the technique of counterpoint to play one idea or attitude against another. In his later novels, beginning with *Eyeless in Gaza* (1936), H. is no longer skeptical, and characters such as Miller and Beavis in *Eyeless in Gaza*, Propter in *After Many a Summer Dies the Swan* (1939), and Barnack and Rontini in *Time Must Have a Stop* (1944) become mouthpieces for H.'s mysticism.

Crome Yellow (1921), *Antic Hay* (1923), and *Those Barren Leaves* (1925), his first three novels, of which *Antic Hay* is the best, form a continuity of characterization, ideas, and situations found in *Point Counter Point*; together they are a satiric portrait of the 1920s with that decade's skepticism, hedonism, and clash of ideas and values. Gumbril, Jr., and Mrs. Viveash in *Antic Hay* are the earlier counterparts of Walter Bidlake and Lucy Tantamount in *Point Counter Point*, sophisticated young men and women of the 1920s, hedonistic, certain that the old values of the prewar generation died in the war but uncertain of anything else beyond pleasure-seeking and personal freedom; Coleman the cynic and Shearwater the scientist but incomplete man are prototypes of Spandrell and Lord Edward Tantamount. The changing patterns of the characters' relationships, suggested by the title (a rustic dance in which the partners weave in and out), is the same technique of counterpoint used to dramatize the conflict of ideas or the instability of human relationships in a world where intellectual values themselves are unstable. In *Point Counter Point* H. provides a norm (the artist Mark Rampion) against which the lives and ideas of the other characters are counter-pointed, whereas in *Antic Hay* no single view point dominates. Rampion, who expounds Lawrentian ideas in *Point Counter Point*, is happily married, the only character in the novel who has a satisfactory love relationship; thus his naturalistic philosophy of life and his criticism of modern science and industrialism and of orthodox Christianity for creating incompleteness and disharmony in modern life and human relationships are given added credence. Burlap represents the perversion of spirituality in the modern world, and Illidge and Webley represent the perversion of political action; even Philip Quarles, who essentially agrees with Rampion, is satirized for his over-intellectualism. Yet in the end H. withholds from Rampion in his debate with Spandrell the ultimate answer to the meaning of life. Thus H. remains sufficiently detached from even the Lawrentian philosophy of life, which he obviously admired at this time, by not presenting it as a final solution and means of human salvation; for while it may work as a practical solution to the problem of living in the modern world, it does deny the soul. Inherent in the inadequacy of Rampion's philosophy of life to explain the soul is the clue to H.'s later adoption of mysticism as a way out of the modern wasteland.

Brave New World (1932), an antiutopian novel, is the last of H.'s novels in which his philosophical skepticism balances opposing ways of life; Mustapha Mond's controlled society, with its modern technological advances utilized solely for the purpose of achieving material happiness, and John Savage's "primitive" belief in the tragic condition of man are both equally untenable ways of life. Although the former eliminates war, disease, and suffering, it creates a monstrously hedonistic society devoid of humanistic and spiritual values; it is the direction in which modern society is moving, provided mankind does not annihilate itself in atomic warfare, H. indicates in the foreword he wrote to the 1946 American edition of the novel, a theme he expands upon in the volume of essays *Brave New World Revisited* (1958). While John Savage's world of traditional values, the world of Shakespeare's plays from which the ironic title of this novel is taken, has its poetry, spiritual visions, and deeper human relationships, it also has its wars, poverty, suffering, and unhappiness because the artistic and spiritual vision and the significant human relationship are dependent on man's acceptance of his tragic condition. Nowhere is H.'s changed philosophical viewpoint better illustrated than in his fictional "brave new world revisited," *Island* (1962), a utopian novel in which an isolated island of sanity exists in this still wasteland world, an island where the people devote their lives to the contemplative life, utilizing such scientific knowledge as necessary to the good life, such as hallucinatory drugs to induce or intensify spiritual and creative visions.

In 1932 H. met the English theologian and mystic Gerald Heard (1889–1971), who had an important influence on his acceptance of mysticism, but H. was not suddenly converted to mysticism by his association with Heard; the whole direction and development of his thought, as it was for T.S. ELIOT, was a quest for certainty, and behind the urbane, sophisticated mask of intellectual wit and satire was the moralistic indignation of an Old Testament prophet. All of H.'s later works of fiction, from *Eyeless in Gaza* to *Island*, are dramatic essays expounding his own personal philosophy; H. is no longer the detached, skeptical novelist but an explicit philosopher, a partisan rather than an observer in the drama of ideas. Thus H.'s later novels are less satisfactory artistically because in writing them H. the philosophic essayist overshadows H. the satiric novelist.

H.'s mystical philosophy as developed in these later novels and in his volumes of essays, particularly *The Perennial Philosophy*, is a search for what Heard called "the eternal gospel," the essential truths that are found in all great religions. As Anthony Beavis in *Eyeless in Gaza* states, everything that causes separation and division is evil, whether it be of the body, mind, or soul; everything that creates unity and harmony is good. Since the human condition of modern man is divisive and separatist in all aspects of human endeavor—social, political, religious, and psychological—the individual must seek to achieve inner peace by transcending time through the contemplative life. Time, which is associated with the ego, must have a stop. This is the realization Sebastian Barnack comes to in *Time Must Have a Stop*. "It is axiomatic," H. stated explicitly the following year in *The Perennial Philosophy* "that the end of human life is contemplation, or the direct and intuitive awareness of God." Modern man, however, beset by a confusion of moral standards, by a standardization of material life, and by social and political regimentation, is lost in the wasteland of technology, totalitarianism, and militant religious orthodoxy. He follows the ape of bodily passions, not the essence of being, which is the spirit, H. shows in *Ape and Essence* (1948); he worships the genius of science, not the goddess of love, H. suggests as his allegorical theme in *The Genius and the Goddess* (1955). It is the mission of what Heard called "men of the margin," modern prophets, to act as voices in the wilderness pointing the way to the promised land of spiritual fulfillment and happiness, the "island" of inner peace. Thus in his later novels H., through his characters who act as spokesmen for his philosophy, assumes the role of such a prophet.

FURTHER WORKS: *Chapbook* (1920, with T. S. Eliot); *Mortal Coils* (1922); *On the Margin* (1923); *Little Mexican* (1924); *The Gioconda Smile: A Play* (1924); *Along the Road* (1925); *Selected Poems* (1925); *Two or Three Graces* (1926); *Essays, New and Old* (1926); *Arabia Infelix* (1929); *Do What You Will* (1929); *Holy Face* (1929); *Vulgarity in Literature* (1930); *Brief Candles* (1930); *The Cicadas* (1931); *Music at Night* (1931); *The World of Light* (1931); *Texts and Pretexts* (1932); *Beyond the Mexique Bay* (1934); *The Olive Tree* (1936); *Stories, Essays, and Poems* (1937); *The Art of Seeing* (1942); *Verses and Comedy* (1946); *Science, Liberty, and Peace* (1946); *Collected Edition* (1947); *Themes and Variations* (1950); *Joyce, the Artificer* (1952, with Stuart Gilbert); *Adonis and the Alphabet* (1956; Am., *Tomorrow and Tomorrow and Tomorrow*); *Collected Short Stories* (1957); *Collected Essays* (1959); *On Art and Artists* (1960); *Literature and Science* (1963); *The Crows of Pearblossom* (1968); *Letters of A.H.* (1969); *Collected Poetry* (1971); *Moksha: Writings on Psychedelics and the Visionary Experience, 1953–1963* (1977)

BIBLIOGRAPHY: Atkins, J. A, *A.H.: A Literary Study* (1956); Ghose, A., *A. H.: A Cynical Salvationist* (1962); Huxley, J., ed., *A.H., 1894–1963* (1965); Huxley, L. A., *This Timeless Moment: A Personal View of A. H.* (1968); Bowering, P., *A. H.: A Study of the Major Novels* (1969); Meckier, J., *A. H.: Satire and Structure* (1969); Watts, H. H., *A. H.* (1969); Brander, L., *A. H.: A Critical Study* (1970); Holmes, C. M, *A.H. and the Way to Reality* (1970); Birnbaum, M., *A. H.'s Quest for Value* (1971); Firchow, P., *A. H., Satirist and Novelist* (1972); May, K., *A. H.* (1972); Bedford, S., *A. H.: A Biography* (1974); Kuehn, R. E., ed., *A. H.: A Collection of Critical Essays* (1974)

—CHARLES G. HOFFMANN

The search for "a more desirable way of life," what H. has called a philosophy based on "all the facts of human experience," is the underlying motif of all the major novels. The very meaninglessness of the life he saw about him was in itself a challenge; and it is not without significance that *Eyeless in Gaza*, H.'s single complete expression of the conversion theme, his first novel to restore the meaning, stands central to his work as a whole. Everything he wrote earlier is in a sense preparatory, everything subsequent a tailing off, except for the final utopian vision of *Island*. After *Crome Yellow* the theme of moral regeneration, leading to Anthony Beavis's conversion, is latent in all the novels of the nineteen twenties. . . . After *Eyeless in Gaza*, the exemplary characters, the "virtuous, adultly non-attached personages," hold the centre of the Huxleyean stage.

Peter Bowering, *A. H.: A Study of the Major Novels* (1968), pp. 19–20

H.'s major achievement, especially when compared with that of previous discussion novelists such as Thomas Love Peacock and W. H. Mallock, consists in the development of a structure for his novels that in itself carries out and supports his satire. The structural technique he prefers continually exposes the egotism of his characters. It satirizes their fragmentary existence while also suggesting they are parts of a recoverable whole. By structure this essay means the planned framework of a novel, the overall arrangement of the entire work or of a particular scene and, finally, the technical method by which the structure is attained. In *Point Counter Point*, the format is supposedly a musical one but the characters or instruments that come together in the discussion scenes fail to produce anything but discord. . .

In effect [in *Point Counter Point*], theme has become structure. What is being satirized and what makes the novel go are one and the same: the eccentricity of its characters. What the novel is about and the way it is put together have merged.

Jerome Meckier, *A. H.: Satire and Structure* (1969), pp. 41–42

For the H. of *After Many a Summer Dies the Swan* and *Time Must Have a Stop*, the persons who achieve superior existence are those who have gone beyond the trammels of personality, the fear of death, and the constriction of being this man or that man at a particular time and place. All who plunge into the great sea of being, who merge with primal unity, have only one way to swim. Furthermore, in contrast with the graceful and easy motion that this sea makes possible, the ordinary movements of man must seem a floundering. And the depiction of such floundering—in novels and in essays that make an analysis of human behavior—is marked, in H., by a kind of impatient reportage, lively when the sheer grotesqueness of human folly amuses the writer and dull when the writer is oppressed by the basic tediousness of human behavior.

It may be added that H.'s insight into man—that he is the creature who must supplement or fulfill his animal and rational natures by some sort of vision that is the same for all who enjoy it—is peculiarly limiting to a novelist.

Harold H. Watts, *A. H.* (1969), p. 149

To one school of ontology the world as a whole is unintelligible, whatever order we may discern in its parts. . . From *Eyeless in Gaza* on, H. assumes the opposite. He takes it on faith that there is a Nature, an Order of Things, which we must both assume and within our limits try to grasp. We can confirm this immanence in our day-to-day existence if we are willing to use all our available resources, and subject all but the basic assumption to a pragmatic, existential test. *Island* is H.'s equivalent to Yeats' *Vision*. Both writers began as divided men, and poets; both were alert to contraries for most of their lives; both were ultimately reconciled to them; both were able to make final assertions of joy. *A Vision*, however, is a more symbolic work, *Island* a far more literal one. Both symbolize a belief in ultimate order, but *Island* offers a human order here and now. Contraries are resolved on the plane of the divine, yet the divine resolution can be—it really is—immanent in our lives.

Charles M. Holmes, *A. H. and the Way to Reality* (1970), p. 199

Wherein then lies the value in giving serious consideration to H.? Precisely in his being able to articulate the intellectual and moral conflicts being fought in the collective soul of the twentieth century. D. H. Lawrence would express his reactions viscerally but failed to look through a microscope, as H. reminds us. James Joyce could disentangle himself from the nets in which he felt caught, but he did not seem aware of the oases to be found in Eastern meditative systems. E. M. Forster knew of passages to other cultures but preferred to regard art as self-sufficient rather than as catalytic. Virginia Woolf knew the agony of private torment but did not realize the healing that can emerge from societal involvement. It was H. of all these twentieth-century English writers who best reflected and coordinated the divisions of the modern world; he best expressed its *Weltanschauung* in its most universal sense. Thomas Henry Huxley. A. H.'s grandfather, was called "Darwin's bulldog" because he so tenaciously clung to and advocated Darwin's theories; similarly, A. H. may become best known for being both an observer of and a contributor to the shifting values of our world.

Milton Birnbaum, *A. H.'s Quest for Values* (1971), p.4

In the useful terminology employed by Erich Auerbach in *Mimesis*, H. is a hypertactic writer, Lawrence a paratactic one; H. is the Hellene who must see and elaborate all the connections which go to make up an experience, Lawrence the Hebrew who intimates and suggests rather than states; H. is the Platonic rationalist who finally prefers history to fiction, Lawrence the Aristotelian who knows that art can be truer than life.

Not that the one is wrong and the other right. They are merely different, with each having his particular virtues and concomitant vices. And surely it is good that it should be so, that there should be many great traditions and not merely a single exclusive (not to say, narrow-minded) one. If the bent of the modern mind is still more toward an appreciation of the paratactic or "congenital" type of novelist, this should not mean that its sympathies might not extend occasionally to writers of the opposite kind.

Peter Firchow, *A. H., Satirist and Novelist* (1972), p. 8

[H.] was a religious man who felt twentieth-century problems in the quick of his being long before many people became fashionably and often rather spectatorially aware of them. I doubt if it is possible to think of one contemporary spiritual or social crux which H. was not urgently concerning himself with forty years ago. The general assumption that his answer after the mid-thirties was mystical is true, though it may give rise to misunderstandings. He never became a fully fledged mystic, but remained a professional writer (the two vocations probably are incompatible). His profound interest in the mystical, continually reinforced or modified by the most up-to-date finding of psychologists (for, unlike most literary men, he was not content with smatterings of Freud, Jung and Adler) did not force out enthusiasm for the reform of institutions. He was what many aspire to be, the complete liberal, being the embodiment, except in physical capacities, of his grandfather's famous definition of a liberal education.

Keith M. May, *A. H.* (1972), p. 226

HYDER, Qurratulain

Indian novelist and short-story writer (writing in Urdu), b. 1927, Aligarh

H., the Urdu-speaking world's most famous novelist, has also made a mark as a short-story writer and a journalist. She was born in Aligarh, where her father, Sajjad Hyder Yildirim (1880–1942), also a short-story writer and prose stylist, was at that time registrar of the Muslim University. Her mother, Nazr Sajjad Hyder (1894–1967) was also a well-known Urdu writer of her times who played a leading role in Muslim social reform. H. received her M.A. in English from the University of Lucknow, studied Urdu and Persian at home, and learned classical Indian and Western music and painting. She migrated to Pakistan in 1947 and worked for the Ministry of Information and at the Pakistan High Commission in London. On her return to India, she edited a literary magazine, *Imprint*, became a member of the editorial board of *The Illustrated Weekly of India*, served as advisor to the chairman of the Board of Film Censors, and was invited as visiting professor by the Aligarh Muslim University and the Jamia Millia Islamia, Delhi. As the most celebrated author in Urdu, she received the Indian Academy of Letters Award (1967), the Soviet Land-Nehru Award (1969), the Government of India's Civilian Honour (1984), the Ghalib Award (1985), the Iqbal Award (1987), and the Altar of Knowledge Award (1989).

The predicament of the modern human being, confronted with cruel and formidable forces, finds powerful expression in her novels and short stories. Her writings also reflect her preoccupation with India's cultural heritage and its relevance to modern civilization. The trauma of the partition of India on the basis of religion, the miseries that came in its wake, the divided loyalties and bruised psyches it created, and a sense of longing for the positive values of the feudal and aristocratic way of life are the prime concerns in her early novels, like *Mere bhi sanamkhane* (1949; my temples too) and *Safina-e-gham-e-dil* (1952; the barge of heart's sorrows), and also in all her major works.

Aag ka darya (1959; the river of fire), her most significant novel, is spread over three thousand years of India's rich and turbulent history. The Hindu, Muslim, British, and the modern periods of the country's history are depicted in different episodes, held together by a single cord of prototype protagonists. These characters, in spite of their creative powers and indomitable spirits, ultimately fall victim to the vicissitudes of the forces of history. In this voluminous novel, H. tries to reinterpret history, and while doing so unravels interesting and thought-provoking facts. Political upheavals, more often than not, result in bloodshed, destruction, and misery for the common person who stoically suffers and undergoes exploitation. The horrors of war especially are graphically depicted. H.'s concerns with the plight of humans are not confined to her compatriots; her heart goes out to all the oppressed and the wronged—be they the victims of the Korean War, the dwellers on either side of the Berlin Wall, the Muslim and Hindu refugees in Pakistan and India respectively, the American blacks, or the German Jews. Nearer home, her heart bleeds for the division of India, an event she views as a deathblow to the composite cultural heritage that took centuries to evolve. The question of Hindu and Muslim identities is also examined minutely. Apart from its intellectual and philosophical overtones, the novel stands out as a great tribute to Indian civilization. *Aag ka darya* has been translated into fourteen languages and remains the most talked-about novel in both India and Pakistan.

Aakhir-e-shab ke humsafar (1979; travelers at the end of night) deals with revolutionary movements in politically sensitive Bengal. This novel satirizes the pseudointellectuals, armchair politicians, and half-hearted revolutionaries who in India have invariably ended up becoming part of the establishment. Though largely political in content, the novel shows rare finesse in painting picturesque scenes of idyllic Bengal, its flora and fauna, its land and people, its culture and tradition.

Kar-e-jahan daraz hai (2 vols., 1978, 1979; the task of the world is unending), a family saga, which H. has chosen to designate as an autobiographical novel, again travels far and wide in time and space. Its tentacles are spread over eight hundred years of political, social, and cultural history. Even while H. recounts the lives and times of her own ancestors, there is never a dull moment. The reader breaks away from the shackles of the present and is taken on a conducted tour of bygone eras. The journey is crowded with people and events, and at times the scenario is resonant and throbbing, at others tragic and melancholic.

Gardish-e-rang-chaman (1987; changing hues of the garden) shows H.'s prowess as a master storyteller. The semidocumentary novel, spread over a century and a half, has a very poignant tale and in-depth characterization. H. speaks of the insignificance of the human individual and our destiny in the cosmic scheme of things. Her characters put up a valiant fight, but in vain—they are mauled by the forces of history. A male protagonist, however, finds salvation in the mystical powers of the East.

Like H.'s novels, her short stories and novelettes unfold themselves not only on the narrative level but also on the philosophical and metaphorical plane. Her female characters have almost heroic dimensions, particularly in the novelettes.

H.'s creative process is highly personal. Her imagination is boundless. She does not follow any set pattern of thought and ideology. Her writings, though steeped in a particular social and cultural milieu, are a picture of common human experience. Plots, settings, and characters keep changing, but her sensibility and vision remain steadfast.

FURTHER WORKS: *Sitaron se aage* (1947); *Shishe ke ghar* (1952); *Patjhar ki awaz* (1967); *Roshni ki raftar* (1982); *Char novelettes* (1982); *Chandni begam* (1990. FURTHER WORKS IN ENGLISH: *Ghalib's Prose and Poetry* (1968, with Sardar Jafri); *Selected Indian Stories* (1970, with Khushwant Singh); *A Woman's Life* (1979)

—HUMAYUN ZAFAR ZAIDI

I

IBARGÜENGOITIA, Jorge

Mexican novelist, dramatist, and short-story writer, b. 22 Jan. 1928, Guanajuato; d. 27 Nov. 1983, Madrid, Spain

I. graduated from Mexico's National University with a degree in engineering in 1949 and two years later returned to the same institution to study dramatic art under Rodolfo USIGLI, one of Mexico's best-known playwrights. In 1955 he received a fellowship from the Rockefeller Foundation to study theater in New York. After writing more than a dozen plays, many of which were never performed or published, he abandoned the theater for prose fiction, the field for which he is best known. I. has published many articles in Mexican journals, including *Excélsior, Siempre, Vuelta,* and *Revista de la Universidad de México.* He lectured at several universities in the U.S. and was residing in Paris when he was killed in an airplane crash.

I. is best known for his humorous satires of Mexican life, both present and past. His most highly regarded play, which in 1963 won the Casa de las Américas Prize in Cuba, is *El atentado* (1978; the attempted murder). A farce with elements of the absurd, this tragicomedy depicts the assassination of president-elect Alvaro Obregón in 1928 by a Catholic fanatic, José de León Toral. The play dramatizes the return of ex-President Obregón to the political scene after his first term of office (1920–1924), the assassination of two of his rivals, the election campaign, and the trial and execution of the culprit, whose accomplice was a nun, la madre Conchita. The influences of German dramatist Bertolt BRECHT on this work are particularly evident: the rapid changes in scenes, the use of signs instead of stage sets, and, most important, the distancing effects designed to alienate characters from spectators and thus allow the didactic message to have its maximum impact. I.'s criticism is also conveyed by absurd episodes, ludicrous characters, and ironic juxtapositions, which elicit guffaws from the audience despite the appearance of many acts of violence.

For decades after the Revolution of 1910, numerous novels and an occasional volume of memoirs depicted the upheaval in tragic and heroic tones. Realizing that the ideals motivating the civil conflict had been betrayed from the beginning, I. wrote his first novel, *Los relámpagos de agosto* (1964; *The Lightning of August,* 1986) to discredit those who led the struggle and/or profited from it. The narrator and antihero is retired General José Guadalupe Arroyo, a stupid, amoral incompetent who pens his memoirs to disprove the "slanderous" statements made about him in the memoirs of other military hacks. The period referred to is 1928–1929, when President Plutarco Elías Calles was ending his term of office and President-elect Obregón was assassinated. Having been named the private secretary of the president-elect just before the latter's untimely death (from apoplexy in the novel), Arroyo is left to fend for himself in the political arena. He participates in battles between ambitious generals, all of whom lie and change allegiance according to the dictates of raw power or financial gain. Skirmishes are won by luck and lost through bungling. In the final pages Arroyo is captured and sentenced to death, but the general in charge of the execution allows him to escape to the U.S., meanwhile

having another man shot to prove that the order was carried out. Replete with grotesque humor and irony (the unreliable narrator unwittingly exposes his ignorance and hypocrisy), *Los relámpagos de agosto* is a hilarious parody of the volumes written about the Mexican Revolution before 1964. Its reexamination of the past exposes the beginnings of a bankrupt political system that has lasted for seven decades.

I.'s second novel, *Maten al león* (1969; kill the lion), is almost as funny as his first. It too is set in the 1920s, but instead of in Mexico, its action takes place on a fictitious Caribbean island (Arepa), governed by a ruthless dictator (the lion) who is ultimately assassinated. The history of Arepa is compressed into the life span of the director (Belaunzarán), who rids the island of the Spaniards but then proceeds to torture, murder, and execute his enemies. (I. stated that Belaunzarán was patterned after Obregón, but that the former was disguised as a Caribbean strongman to avoid problems with zealous government censors.) Virtually all the characters are caricatures whose words and actions border on the absurd. Belaunzarán is celebrated as a national hero, even though his exploits to defeat the Spaniards were anything but heroic—he attacked and killed everyone in the enemy stronghold after the Spaniards had left. The nation's greedy landholders oppose him only because they seek power, not social reform. When the carefully planned attempt to eliminate him fails, he is accidently murdered by an impoverished musician. And when he finally dies, he is replaced by his handpicked successor, Cardona, meaning that nothing will change. The novel's proper names also have a humorous ring, a case in point being Arepa (pancake in Spanish), which ridicules the size and importance of the island nation.

In the late 1970s I. published two murder mysteries, both of which parody the popular genre. *Las muertas* (1977; *The Dead Girls,* 1983) is based on a criminal case that made sensational headlines in 1964 when two brothel owners in a small Mexican community allegedly kidnaped and murdered dozens of prostitutes. In the course of his investigation I. discovered that Serafina and Arcángela Baladro, the fictional names of the accused sisters, while not free of guilt, had been forced to pay bribes to corrupt politicians, police officers, and court officials. I. reveals, moreover, that the alleged crimes were greatly exaggerated, the number of dead totaling only six, four of whom died from natural causes. The novel desensationalizes the entire case by discrediting the news media and placing much of the blame on corrupt government authorities.

Dos crímenes (1979; *Two Crimes,* 1984), I.'s other murder mystery, is a humorous and erotic tale, also set in a provincial town. Marcos González, the protagonist and narrator of the first half of the novel, escapes from Mexico City to the home of his wealthy Uncle Ramón after having been unjustly accused of arson. While staying with his uncle, he tries with some success to obtain money from the crusty old man by claiming to have knowledge of a mine he would like to exploit for considerable gain. He also has sexual encounters with his cousin Amalia and his niece Lucero. After both Ramón and Lucero are murdered by mistake (both murderers intended to kill Marcos), the local pharmacist Don Pepe Lara narrates his investigation of the case, leading up to the suspenseful denouement. *Dos crímenes* is a tightly structured detective story sprinkled with allusions to social and political impropriety. But I.'s main thrusts are his ingenious structuring of plot and his ironic treatment—through narrative distancing—of character and social customs.

I.'s last novel, *Los pasos de López* (1981; López's footsteps; also published as *Los conspiradores*, 1981; the conspirators), dramatizes the beginnings of the War of Independence (1810) between Mexico and Spain. Because of his position as an army officer, the first-person narrator, Matías Chandón, has been chosen by a group of conspirators to direct military operations against the Spaniards. Mainly *criollos* (people of Spanish parents born in the New World), the conspirators are inspired by Don Periñón (historically Father Miguel Hidalgo), whose name derives from a kind of champagne (Dom Perignon), and thus refers obliquely to Father Hidalgo's wine-making enterprise. Although sincere, Periñón and his followers are portrayed by Chandón as bunglers, as are the inept Spanish authorities, who are told of the impending revolt but refuse to believe their informants. The climactic capture and execution of Don Periñón are foreshadowed by a drama the conspirators rehearse just before the uprising begins, a drama in which Don Periñón plays the role of the eponymous conspirator López. Although it describes events a century earlier, *Los pasos de López* has been compared to *Los relámpagos de agosto*, both serving to demythicize heroic moments of the Mexican past. I.'s later novel, however, portrays a more human side of its protagonist.

In their entirety I.'s works lampoon Mexico's most revered institutions, utilizing as weapons caricature, satire, irony, and parody. I. is an important man of letters not only because of his unique views of Mexican society, but also because of his accessibility to a large portion of the reading public. An enemy of hypocrisy and amorality, he revised both past and present in order to spark badly needed change.

FURTHER WORKS: *Susana y los jóvenes* (1958); *Ante varias esfinges* (1960); *El loco amor viene* (1960); *Clotilde, El viaje, y El pájaro* (1964); *La ley de Herodes* (1967); *Viajes en la América ignota* (1972); *Estas ruinas que ves* (1975); *Sálvese quien pueda* (1975); *Autopsias rópidas* (1988); *Obras completas* (1989); *Piezas y cuentos para niños* (1989)

BIBLIOGRAPHY: Acevedo, Escobedo A., *Los narradores ante el público* (1967): 125–34; Langford, W. M., *The Mexican Novel Comes of Age* (1971): 190–92; Bruce-Novoa, J., and D., Valentín, "Violating the Image of Violence: I.'s *El atentado,*" *LATR*, 12, 2 (Spring 1979): 13–21; Rama, A., *Novísimos narradores hispanoamericanos en marcha, 1964–1980* (1981), 195; Azuela, A., "J. I.: Múltiples espejos de utopías gastadas," *CA*, 4, 255 (July-Aug. 1984): 75–79; Ugalde, S. K., "Beyond Satire: I.'s *Maten al león,*" *DLit*, 1, 2 (Spring 1984): 217–29; McMurray, G. R., *Spanish American Writing since 1941: A Critical Survey* (1987): 88–89, 251–52; Corral, I. del, "Humor: When Do We Lose It?" *TRev*, 27 (1988): 25–27; Campbell, F., "I.: La sátira históricopolítica," *RI*, 55 (July-Dec. 1989): 1047–55; Leñero, V., *Los pasos de Jorge* (1989); González, A., "J. I.: The Mexican Mock Heroic," *Euphoria and the Crisis: Essays on the Contemporary Mexican Novel* (1990): 52–63; Sklodowska, E., "I. y Giardinelli: Reconocimiento y cuestionamiento de la novela negra," *La parodia en la nueva novela hispanoamericana (1960–1985)* (1991): 120–27

—GEORGE R. MCMURRAY

IBN HADŪQA, ʿAbd al-Hamīd

Algerian novelist, short-story writer, and dramatist, b. 9 Jan. 1925, Al-Mansurah

I. H. contributed the first significant Arabic novel in Algeria. He also wrote short stories and radio and television plays in colloquial Algerian. He studied in Algeria, Tunisia, and France. He received a solid education in Arabic at the hands of his father, a teacher of Arabic and Islamic thought. He pursued his education at the al-Hamlāwī Institute in Algeria, an affiliate of ibn al-Hamlāwī's *zāwiyah*. I. H. went to Tunisia for his secondary and higher education and joined al-Zaitunah Mosque College where he graduated from its Arabic literature section. While in Tunis, he completed four years of study at the Arab Drama Institute. Back in Algeria, he spent two years at the faculty of law at the University of Algiers. He studied French at school while pursuing his education at a Koranic school. In France he shifted his education toward technology, spending three and a half years in Marseille and Paris studying plastic transformation.

I. H. worked both as a journalist and as a producer of radio plays during the colonial period. After the independence of his country in 1962, he occupied various positions in the Algerian broadcasting service up to the time he was nominated cultural adviser at the general administration for radio and television. In 1987 he retired but was soon recalled to be appointed first as director general of the National Book Foundation, then president of the National Council for Culture, a position he holds to the present day.

I. H. began his writing activities with a collection of short stories entitled *Zilāl Jazāʾiriyyah* (1960; Algerian shades). It was soon followed by a second collection, *al-Ashiʿah al-Sabʿah* (1962; the seven rays). Though published during the years of the war of independence, his two collections were generally removed from patriotic topics. Whenever the events of a story touched on the subject of the war, the primary concern of the author was the human dimension of the characters depicted in unusual situations. I. H. seems intent on proving the humane nature of a soldier through his story "al-jundī wa-al-layl" (1960; the soldier and the night), in which a *mujāhid* is seen reflecting on his emotions and the attraction that an unsuspecting young woman exercised on him. Writing at a time of profound nationalism, when the freedom fighter was glorified and endowed with superhuman power, I. H. was more interested in pointing out his humanity.

Love is central to many of I. H.'s fiction works. He examines it in its various kinds and forms, conjugal, filial, paternal and maternal, as well as the love between a man and a woman; he does not indulge, however, in any detailed description of sexual relations. His story "Zaytūnat al-hubb" (1960; the olive tree of love) typifies his tendency to maintain love on a platonic level, as the two teenagers in love are fully satisfied with their mere meetings under an olive tree and take pleasure in inscribing their names on its trunk.

I. H.'s attitude in his writings is generally that of a compassionate man, concerned for the fate of the meek and the wronged members of society, eager to see justice established wherever fairness has been trampled. A clear preoccupation with fairness is obvious in his novel *Nihāyat al-ams* (1975; the end of yesterday) for the wife of a *harkī* (an unpatriotic Algerian serving in the hated French military) and generally for women who did not receive their fair share from society. Most of I. H.'s novels and to a lesser degree his short stories reveal a deep affection and respect for women, though at times maladroitly expressed in the form of either a failed effort at emancipation as in *Rīh al-janūb* (1971; the southern wind), or a trial-and-failure effort as in *Bāna al-subh* (1980; the morning appeared). The best and most successful portrayal of a feminine character is that of Jāziyah in *al-Jāziyah wa-al-darāwīsh* (1983; Jāziyah and the dervishes), projecting a clear message of change in the status of women within the boundaries of the cultural entity of the country. This latter attitude reinforces both I. H.'s nationalist position as well as his deep appreciation for Algerian folklore.

I. H. clearly wishes to see his society advance on the path of affection and mutual understanding, away from the hindering action of some outdated and useless traditions. He refutes the restrictions imposed by parents on their daughters' emancipation, the imposition of exorbitant dowries that either delay marriages or force young men to emigrate to France in search of high-paying jobs. Whether referring to the negative impact of traditions or expressing compassion for the unfortunate and wronged members of society, I. H. reverts to dramatic situations and tragic ends. His tone is often moralizing and didactic, reinforcing the concept of the writer as his society's guide. The short story "Thaman al-mahr" (1962; the price of the dowry) ends with the death of the protagonist, who reached his goal that consisted in saving enough money to pay the requested dowry but died of tuberculosis. *Rīh al-janūb* presents also a tragic conclusion to a courageous story of elopement as the enraged father of the heroine charges against a man he accuses arbitrarily of dishonoring him: blinded by his anger, he does not even try to understand the situation before attacking the innocent shepherd.

The interest that I. H. manifested in the human experience throughout his fiction works stems from his socialist ideology and a particular concern for the human spirit and its capacity to face life's difficulties and injustices. The historical periods and the geographical settings designated in his books serve as a frame for the study of human behavior. The dire circumstances of the war of independence described in both *Rīh al-janūb* and *Nihāyat al-ams*, through the device of flashbacks, reveal the exploitative nature of Ibn al-Sakhrī and Ibn al-Qādī, two men who pursued their material gains at the cost of their fellow men. The author's preoccupation with the greedy nature of people in power extends to the postindependence period as he reveals the wide-spread hypocrisy that dictates human actions. I. H. seems to abhor those whose actions are in total contradiction to their words. He preached honesty in a world and time when opportunism prevailed.

I. H. promotes a number of specific topics, foremost among them is the emancipation of women. A devout admirer of country life, he seems to find it more virtuous and amenable to positive changes. The action in most of his fiction works takes place in rural settings, with the exception of *Bāna al-subh*, located in Algiers. The corrupt and hypocritical life of the characters, mainly from the Algerian bourgeoisie, stands in sharp contrast to the simpler and healthier world of the country. Another issue dear to I. H. is folk culture, which he revives in his novels in various ways, mainly through descriptions of pottery work and design. He also uses folk characters, the most famous being al-Jāziyah, whose name is given to the heroine of the novel *al-Jāziyah wa-al-darāwīsh*. The personality of al-Jāziyah is central to a very popular love story in Algeria. I. H. successfully uses the symbol as a reward for a returning

migrant young man in search of his identity. This dependence on folklore among postindependence writers is a reflection of a recovered pride in their national entity.

I. H.'s main contribution has been in the field of fiction writing—in short stories and novels as well as plays—mainly in Algerian dialect for radio broadcasting. He translated stories from foreign literature and wrote poetry, which he published in a collection entitled *al-arwāh al-shāghira* (1967; the free souls.)

Although I. H. holds some noticeably modernist positions in relation to various aspects of life in his society, he is rather a conservative in other areas. An example is his deep respect for the Arabic language; he maintains that its sanctity does not allow him to use it to tackle certain topics that he deems unworthy of its holy nature. This outlook explains his reluctance to describe in Arabic what he terms "the immorality of the Arab society."

I. H. remains one of the pioneers of Arabic fiction in Algeria with a slow but steady production. There is an obvious progress and mastery of both the style and the artistic concept of the novel from the first book he published to the latest one. I. H. relies on a simple style and a direct approach in most of his early fiction, with an obvious tendency toward symbolism and a greater sophistication in his later works such as his novel *al-Jāziyah wa-al-darāwīsh*. He makes heavy use of STREAM-OF-CONSCIOUSNESS and flashback, particularly in relating the events of the war of independence, which he recalls often to assess a character's behavior or justify a judgment or a condemnation.

Continuing a trend initiated in his first novel *Rīh al-janūb*, I. H. pursues the theme of confrontation between the village and the city. *Ghadan Yawmun Jadīd* (1993; tomorrow is a new day) opposes the purity of rural life to the corruption of urban life. The narrator is a peasant woman, relating her life story in the form of a public confession. The historical framework is Algeria's modern history, between 1930 marking the celebration of the centennial of the French occupation and the early 1990s, as the violence was tearing the country apart. While harshly critical of the colonizer and the Algerian collaborators for their role in suppressing the people, I. H. is not kind to the Algerians either. His position is summarized in these words uttered by the Mas'ūda, the narrator in his novel: "Fear during the revolution united us, and freedom divided us." It is clear throughout the novel that I. H. is weary of the disturbances and disapproves of the events. He also reveals his opposition to the Gulf War. In spite of an optimistic title, the novel can't be qualified as one that promotes hopes. It rather oscillates between hope and despair.

FURTHER WORKS: *Al-Jazā'ir bayna al-ams wa-al-yawm* (1959); *Al-kātib wa-qisas ukhrā* (1972); *Qisas min al-adab al-'ālamī* (1983); *Al-nisr wa-al-'iqāb* (1985); *Difā' 'an Fidā'in* (n.d.); *Amthāl Jazā'iriyyah* (1992)

BIBLIOGRAPHY: Makarius, R., and Makarius, L., *Anthologie de la littérature arabe contemporaine* (1964): 356–62; Dejeux, J., *La littérature algérienne contemporaine* (1975): 113–15; Bamia, A. A., "La littérature algérienne de langue arabe," *Europe*: 567–68 (July–Aug. 1976): 38–48; Bamia, A. A., "Le roman algérien de langue arabe depuis L'Indépendance," *Annuaire de L'Afrique du Nord*, 19 (1980): 1127–33; Bonn, C., *Anthologie de la littérature algérienne* (1990): 150–51

—AIDA A. BAMIA

IBUSE Masuji

Japanese novelist, short-story writer, essayist, and poet, b. 15 Feb. 1898, Kamo; d. Dec. 1993, Tokyo

Born into an old family of independent farmers, I. spent his childhood in the country. In 1917 he moved to Tokyo and for several years studied literature and painting. Although he specialized in French literature, he became interested in Russian writers, chiefly in Tolstoy and CHEKHOV.

In 1923 I. published his first successful story, "Yūhei" (confinement). The story, a satirical allegory of intellectual and artistic pretense, is better known by its revised title, "Sanshōuo" ("Salamander," 1971). In another early story, "Yofuke to ume no hana" (1925; "Plum Blossom at Night," 1971), I. blended a self-mocking humor with a dreamy, symbolist mood.

The allegorical or symbolist overtones of these early works suggest Western influences, but in 1926, with "Koi" ("Carp," 1971), I. turned to the more traditional techniques of his homeland. Using the highly subjective Japanese "I-novel" mode, in which narrator and author are one, he interwove fiction and reality, literary symbols and actuality. In sharp contrast, however, with other I-novelists who concentrate solely on expressing their own feelings, he used the techniques as a means of restraining the emotion-filled memories precipitated by a friend's death.

During the 1930s, I.'s thematic interest shifted to the rustic countryside of southern Japan where he was born. A painstaking craftsman, he had always spent more time revising and polishing his stories than taking sides in ideological polemics.

The symbolic return to his native soil inspired some of I.'s best stories and novellas, such as "Tangeshitei" (1931; "Life at Mr. Tange's," 1971), a loving, humorous evocation of two colorful rustics, master and servant, in a remote mountain valley.

In these works, I.'s expression acquired its full, mature flavor. Skillful use of dialect, subtle contrasts in dialogue, nuances of mood and setting, a wry humor and sparse characterization through gesture and manner of speech, are the distinguishing traits of this style.

As the military clique rose to power and Japan was moving toward World War II, I. steadily worked on the most remarkable of his works on historical themes, *Sazanami gunki* (1930–38; a war diary). The historical background of the novella is the actual escape and the final defeat of the Heike clan in the 12th c.; the story itself portrays the initiation of a sensitive young Heike samurai into a brutal world.

I.'s last major prewar work, the novella *Tajinko mura* (1939; "Tajinko Village," 1971), presents a broad portrayal of the life of a village; it is also a fond farewell to a gentler way of life that cannot last.

I. did not write much during the war; his unwilling induction into the army as a war correspondent probably inspired his biting satire of the debilitating influence of army drills in "Yōhai taichō" (1950; "Lieutenant Lookeast," 1971).

Although I. returned to publishing short stories and novellas in the years following World War II, he was preparing for his longest and most important novel, *Kuroi ame* (1966; *Black Rain*, 1969), which deals with the atomic ordeal of Hiroshima. A quiet elegy for a city and its population, *Kuroi ame* emerges as a significant work of art distinct from the many sentimental or political accounts of the bombing.

I. avoided portraying the disaster in its totality, but rather set the beauty of the southern landscape, the ancient customs of the people, their colorful foibles, the little, everyday details of their lives, against the absurd brutality of the atomic holocaust. All his previous techniques and thematic interests served him well here. He needed not only his characteristic sympathy for the simple life and an intimate knowledge of popular lore, but also the calm tone and detached poise of a chronicler that he had acquired in his earlier historical writings. He also needed the skill to handle a vast documentary montage of eyewitness accounts and authentic journals.

Using the rich resources of his literary tradition, I. cautiously experimented with a number of prose techniques and styles, trying to expand the limits of the novel. He enlivened the conventional I-novel, grafted onto the ancient stock of romantic nature-lyricism a robust, epic quality, and introduced a dry, original humor into the often too serious and sometimes too sentimental art of modern Japanese prose writing.

FURTHER WORKS: *Shigotobeya* (1931); *Kawa* (1932); *Zuihitsu* (1933); *Keirokushū* (1936); *Shūkin ryokō* (1937); *John Manjirō hyōryūki* (1937); *John Manjiro: The Cast-Away, His Life and Adventures*, 1940); *Shiguretō jokei* (1941); *I. M. zuihitsu zenshū* (3 vols., 1941); *Chūshū meigetsu* (1942); *Gojinka* (1944); *Wabisuke* (1946); *Magemono* (1946); *Oihagi no hanashi* (1947); *I. M. senshū* (9 vols., 1948); *Honjitsu kyūshin* (1950); *Kawatsuri* (1952); *I. M. sakuhinshū* (5 vols., 1953); *Hyōmin Nanakamado* (1955); *Usaburō* (1956); *Kanreki no koi* (1957); *Ekimae ryokan* (1957); *Nanatsu no kaidō* (1957); *Chinpindo shujin* (1959); *Tsurishi, Tsuriba* (1960); *Kinō no kai* (1961); *Shuzai ryokō* (1961); *Bushū hachigatajō* (1963); *Mushinjō* (1963); *I. M. zenshū* (12 vols., 1964); *Gendai bungaku taikei* (1966); *Shinchō nihon bungaku* (1970); *Tsuribito* (1970); *I. M. zenshū* (14 vols., 1975). FURTHER WORKS IN ENGLISH: *Lieutenant Lookeast, and Other Stories* (1971)

BIBLIOGRAPHY: Lifton, R., "*Black Rain," Death in Life* (1967): 543–55; Kimball, A., "After the Bomb," *Crisis in Identity and Contemporary Japanese Novels* (1973): 43–59; Liman, A. V., "I.'s *Black Rain*," in Tsuruta, K., and Swann, T., *Approaches to the Modern Japanese Novel* (1976): 45–72; Treat, J. W., *Pools of Water, Pillars of Fire: The Literature of I. M.* (1988)

—ANTHONY V. LIMAN

ICAZA, Jorge

Ecuadorian novelist and dramatist, b. 10 July 1906, Quito; d. 26 May 1978, Quito

I. worked for a time as a government employee, bookseller, and director of the National Library. Beginning his literary career as a dramatist, he was wrote seven plays, of which the most challenging was *Flagelo* (1936; flogging), a revolutionary literary manifesto written in colloquial language, utilizing sexual symbolism, and depicting and attacking the degradation of the Indians by the whites.

Barro de la sierra (1933; mountain clay), I.'s first short-story collection, displayed most of the themes and concepts that were to appear in later works. The stories dwell on the defects of the *latifundio* system (of great landed estates) and the evils of Church and State; his indignation over social injustice is supported by Freudian analysis. One of his subjects is the fate of an Indian village deprived of water by a greedy landowner and the relationship of mestizo half-brothers. In later story collections, I. also fused MAGIC REALISM with folklore elements.

Huasipungo (1934; *The Villagers*, 1964) may well be the most brutal portrayal of Indian misery ever written. In a series of indicting incidents I. portrays the plight of the suffering Indians as he dissects their unhappy existence. Deprived of their *huasipungos*, or inherited land, by those in power, the Indians can neither fathom white psychology nor plan resistance. With the aid of the priest and the local political boss, the landlord, Alfonso Pereira, forces the Indians to build a highway. When they revolt, the police kill all those who stay to fight. I. thus depicts the Ecuadorian government's complete disregard for human life and dignity. Although laced with local color, Indian traditions, and Quechua vocabulary, the novel, perhaps impressionistically exaggerated, conveys an appalling picture of human degradation. With good reason it has been called the "*Tobacco Road* of the Ecuadorian highlands."

Cholos (1938; half-breeds) concentrates on caste distinctions and social barriers. A more complex and poetic and more structured novel than *Huasipungo*, it concerns three half brothers: one white, one of mixed blood, and one Indian. I. examines the complicated caste relationships and racist impulses of those who hate both the Indians and their white masters, whom they nonetheless envy and try to emulate. I. uses the same amalgam of social problems, traditions, and customs as before, but here he emphasizes individual guilt over political degradation. He combines the complicated psychology of the protagonist Alberto Montoya and his attempt to climb the social ladder with a visionary prophecy of racial union as the hope for the future. In spite of its cloying symbolism, the novel is a very persuasive portrayal of Ecuadorian society.

El chulla Romero y Flores (1958; the upstart Romero y Flores) concentrates on the city mestizo. I. depicts a city filled with beggars, crooks, drunks, and prostitutes and examines Romero's attempt to escape both his bloodlines and poverty. I. vividly exposes Romero's inner conflicts and his resolution of them against a background of sexuality, religious bigotry, discrimination, exploitation, and political corruption. Romero, a naïve but roguish small-time bureaucrat, tormented by his inability to accept what he is, finally acknowledges his heritage and seeks salvation through moral regeneration.

Los atrapados (1972; the trapped) consists of three volumes: *El juramento* (the oath), *En la ficción* (in fiction), and *En la realidad* (in reality). In this novel I. employs dream, hallucination, and free association to reinforce his mixture of autobiography and fiction. A pastiche of previous works, with less inflammatory anger, it deals with racial prejudice and social change. As I. becomes aware of his literary abilities, he decides to use them for his people, especially the Indians with whom he had always felt attuned. He attempts to fulfill his vow, but his characters, who in a sense have free will and who fear for their own identity, impede his psychological and literary objectives. I. attempts to discover the total reality of his country's problems and to penetrate Ecuadorian masks, but he finds that reality a mutable and essentially iniquitous entity.

I., considered Ecuador's greatest novelist, portrayed shocking scenes of human degradation; he offered symbolic union of classes (the three brothers of *Cholos* walking arm in arm toward the rising sun, for example) and the elimination of landed estates as solutions to problems that appear to have none, given the human depravity he seems to accept as the norm. In this sense, his social realism, even allowing for his occasional probing study of the individual citizen, fails to convince or arouse empathy. From I.'s pessimistic point of view, the common man, obviously, will never control his destiny, nor will the exploitation I. depicts appreciably change. Although his conclusions are not cogent because his totally black and bleak portrayal of human brutishness fails to convince readers, I. nevertheless manages to move us by his conviction and by the vividness of his documentation of man's inhumanity to man.

FURTHER WORKS: *El intruso* (1928); *Comedia sin nombre* (1929); *Por el viejo* (1929); *Como ellos quieren* (1931); *Cuál es* (1931); *Sin sentido* (1932); *En las calles* (1935); *Media vida deslumbrados* (1942); *Huairapamushcas* (1948); *Seis relatos* (1952); *Seis veces la muerte* (1953); *Viejos cuentos* (1960); *Obras escogidas* (1961); *Relatos* (1969)

BIBLIOGRAPHY: Dulsey, B., "J. I. and His Ecuador," *Hispania*, 44 (1961): 99–102; Ferrandiz Alborz, F., "El novelista ecuatoriano J. I.," in J. I., *Obras escogidas* (1961): 9–71; Vetrano, A. J., *The Ecuadorian Indian "Cholo" in the Novels of J. I.: Their Lot and Language* (1966); Sacoto, A., *The Indian in the Ecuadorian Novel* (1967): 129–228; Cueva, A., *J. I.* (1968); Vetrano, A. J., "Imagery in Two of J. I.'s Novels, *Huasipungo* and *Huairapamushcas*," *REH*, 6 (1972): 293–301; Sackett, T., *El arte novelística de I.* (1974)

—KESSEL SCHWARTZ

ICELANDIC LITERATURE

At the beginning of the century Icelandic literature, after a short period of realism, took a turn to neoromanticism, which became more or less a dominant factor for about three decades, especially in poetry. Icelandic society was changing from a completely rural one to a more urban one based on a small-scale fishing industry. This change can clearly be seen in the works of two pioneers of the Icelandic novel. Jón Trausti (1873–1918) was still preoccupied with the life of the farmer, while Einar H. Kvaran (1859–1938) dealt with the way of life in the small capital of Reykjavík. In many ways Kvaran can be regarded as a typical Icelandic writer of the turn of the century. He was one of the leaders of the realistic movement in Iceland, but he soon turned against it to a kind of progressive romanticism. He later came under the influence of spiritualism, and after that his writing mostly concerned the Christian duty of forgiving and the immortality of the soul.

The term "progressive romanticism" implies optimism, which characterized the first quarter of the century. In 1918 Icelanders won their independence after ages of Danish colonial rule, and both in the last phase of the struggle for independence and in the first years afterward they had a feeling of bold self-assurance and great expectations for a bright future of technological wonders. World War I did not change this feeling, since it had very little impact in Iceland. This optimism was strongly expressed by the poet Einar Benediktsson (1864–1940), one of the two most important poets of the neoromantic school. In flamboyant, rhetorical poems, in which nature imagery and the portrayal of human situations are used as entries into philosophical or metaphysical discussions, often of a slightly didactic nature, Benediktsson pointed out the limitless possibilities of a newly freed nation on the road to technological and industrial progress based on the great Icelandic sources of energy, above all hydroelectric power. His grand visions, mixed with a kind of pantheism, have made him one of the most popular poets of the century in Iceland. The other great neoromantic poet, Jóhann SIGURJÓNSSON, was quite different. In his short, concentrated poems the images speak for themselves. His dense imagery was something completely new, and he stands out as perhaps the most important shaper of modern Icelandic poetry. Immensely popular during the 1920s were Stefán frá Hvítadal (1887–1933) and Davíð Stefánsson (1895–1964). Their main contribution was to write poetry in an easygoing style, close to everyday language, although their work sometimes had the tendency to sink into sentimentality.

In his time, around the turn of the century, Jóhann Sigurjónsson was not only one of Iceland's most important poets, he was also the most important playwright and a leading figure among the group of Icelandic poets and writers who moved to Denmark, started writing in Danish in order to make a living, and for a while became important to Danish literary life. For the most part they wrote about life in Iceland, a fact that seems to have given their work an exotic flavor in the eyes of Continental readers. Jóhann Sigurjónsson was the first Icelandic writer in modern times to gain a European audience, especially through his plays, in which he portrayed Icelandic life using themes from folklore and history. The most successful of this group, however, was the novelist Gunnar GUNNARSSON, who won international fame with his writings about Iceland past and present; his autobiographical novel *Kirken påbjerget* (5 vols., 1923–28; the church on the mountain; tr. of Vols. I–III, *Ships in the Sky*, 1938, and *The Night and the Dream*, 1938) is his most outstanding achievement. A third important writer of this group is the playwright and novelist Guðmundur Kamban (1888–1945), whose characters, unlike those of his colleagues, were not necessarily Icelandic. Most of Kamban's writings deal with either of two subjects: marriage, and criminals and their punishment. He was extremely critical of the institution of marriage, and he also wrote extensively about what makes a man become a criminal and about the inhumane penal system.

Since World War I had very little effect in Iceland, a so-called postwar literature hardly exists. Important literary movements like expressionism, SURREALISM, and FUTURISM were represented only sporadically in individual works. Thus, the latter half of the 1920s could be called a period of hesitation, when a recently freed people groped for a new form of expression, a time when neoromanticism was still dominant but drawing toward a close.

During the 1930s Icelandic literature steered a much clearer course. The world economic depression hit Iceland hard and caused profound changes in the structure of its society. Since farming was no longer profitable, farmers gave up in great numbers and streamed into fishing villages and towns, where soaring unemployment caused general unrest. The trade unions were greatly radicalized, and there were serious labor conflicts and strikes. These conditions also radicalized literature in Iceland. The socialist literary periodical *Rauðir pennar* became the voice of young radical writers and poets, and the publishing company Mál

of Menning was formed on an idealistic, noncommercial basis to spread radical literature.

Above all, the 1930s were the decade of the Nobel Prize winner Halldór LAXNESS. In three great novel cycles he analyzed different aspects of Icelandic society from a more or less Marxist point of view: he describes the fishing villages, the poor farmers, and the situation and the role of the poet in society. The second most important writer of the 1930s was Þórbergur ÞÓRÐARSON, who made his breakthrough as a major writer with his collection of essays and stories *Bréf til Láru* (1924; a letter to Lára). His most important contribution to a radical literature are two autobiographical works: *Íslenzkur að all* (1938; *In Search of My Beloved*, 1967) and *Ofvitinn* (2 vols., 1940–41; the eccentric), both written with a shrewd, biting humor and irony. Among the emerging writers of fiction of the time, Ólafur Jóhann SIGURÐSSON both in novels and short stories dealt with the hard life of the farmers during the depression, but also excelled in beautiful lyrical descriptions of nature.

Poetry also became radicalized during the 1930s, although not all of it. In the middle of the depression Tómas GUÐMUNDSSON published a collection of poems with the surprising title of *Fagra veröld* (1933; beautiful world), an immensely popular book full of subtle lyricism, occasional mild humor, and nostalgic dreams. Most of the other important poets, however, dealt more directly with the harsh realities of poverty and unemployment. Jóhannes úr KÖTLUM began in the 1920s as a neoromantic, and developed into a revolutionary poet who wrote emotional, rhetorical appeals for immediate action. He later came under the influence of MODERNISM. Steinn STEINARR started off in the early 1930s as a revolutionary poet who used daring and original imagery and a bitter, ironic humor. His political interests, however, gradually gave way to profound skepticism and pessimism, his poetry becoming more and more introverted. His preoccupation with experiments in form made him one of the forerunners of modernism in Iceland. Guðmundur Böðvarsson (1904–1974) was a self-educated farmer who expressed his hopes with the inborn wariness of a farmer. His socialism was often closely related to patriotism, a link that became quite common after Iceland joined NATO. He was more reasoning than rhetorical, and more often warned rather than preached.

World War II changed Iceland completely, although it was not fought there. In 1940 Iceland was occupied by the British, who withdrew, however, the following year and were replaced by American forces. Iceland had suddenly become strategically important. The foreign forces needed a lot of workers, and unemployment vanished overnight. In 1944 the Icelandic Republic was declared. At the end of the war Iceland had become quite rich, the country was industrialized, and the ideological struggle of the 1930s, except in the field of foreign affairs, diminished. Laxness wrote a much debated novel, *Atómstöðin* (1948; *The Atom Station*, 1961), but apart from that, directly political literature was on the decline, and Laxness himself became less and less interested in ideological questions.

The postwar years, with their radical changes and booming economy, provided an ideal ground for modernism, which particularly flourished in poetry. The members of the modernist group published their own literary periodical, *Birtingur*. Icelandic poetry had been very traditional and formally conservative; the modernists, therefore, had to revolutionize form, although they met great resistance from a very conservative public. Although greatly influenced by T. S. ELIOT and Ezra POUND, they still belonged to the political left and wrote extensively against NATO and the American forces in Iceland. They changed Icelandic poetry completely, freed it from formal bonds, and based it on imagery, often combined with complicated use of metaphors, personification, and allusion. Images became the most important element instead of rhymed discussions, which were prevalent in earlier poetry. The modernist poets—Einar Bragi (b. 1921), Hannes Sigússon (1922–1997), Jón Óskar (b. 1921), Sigfús Daðason (1928–1996), and Stefán Hörður GRÍMSON—dominated Icelandic poetry in the 1950s.

Along with the modernists, another group of poets was gaining strength. These were poets who combined certain elements of modernism, above all its stress on imagery, with the more traditional forms of classical Icelandic poetry. They have never completely deserted the rules of rhyme and alliteration, but rather use them in a personal way as a part of their own poetic language. They are bound together not only by this formal element, however; their themes also link them. Very Icelandic in their poems, these poets are preoccupied with Icelandic nature, history, folklore, mythology, and language, and with the struggle of a small cultural unity to survive intact in a world of growing internationalism. To this group belong Snorri HJARTARSON, Hannes Pétursson (b. 1931), and Þorsteinn frá Hamri (b. 1938).

Thor VILHJÁLMSSON is the most important modernist prose writer. His development is based on a revolt against the classical epic tradition of Icelandic prose. In his novels and travel books, written in a style full of complex imagery, the main theme is the modern, alienated European intellectual's search for identity. But Vilhjálmsson stands quite alone among Icelandic novelists. Other important prose writers have mainly dealt with the way of life in Iceland, the forces that have shaped Icelandic society, and what may happen to it. Indriði G. Þorsteinsson (b. 1926), in his most important novels, has described the changes in Icelandic society in the 1930s and during and after World War II. Jakobína Sigurðardóttir (1918–1994) has written political satires of great strength, and Svava Jakobsdóttir (b. 1930) deals mostly with the position of women and the tendency of both individuals and the nation to lean on others instead of going one's own way. Guðbergur BERGSSON has written novels about people of a small village near the American base in Keflavík. In these books, written with subtle humor and an edge of sarcasm, he shows how people slave to keep a standard of living they never have time to enjoy, and presents a consciously distorted picture of a gray and monotonous reality. He has been influenced by Latin American writers, and is a creator of a sort of grotesque realism that shows the Icelandic people a mirror image of themselves that they might not care to see.

Professional theater in Iceland is only thirty years old. Since Icelanders wrote plays in Danish at the beginning of the century, it is only recently that professional playwrights have developed. The most important of them are Jökull Jakobsson (1933–1978) and Guðmundur Steinsson (1925–1996), who have both dealt with various aspects of the modern Icelandic way of life and its problems, although in different ways. Jökull was a literary playwright who stressed the word. Guðmundur, on the other hand, is a very theatrical playwright who stresses action rather than language.

During the second half of the 20th c., some crucial changes have occurred in Icelandic literary production. Icelanders became increasingly international in orientation and education abroad fostered an integration of varied ideas and practices. Aesthetic trends from all over the world entered the artistic life of the country, and in the last two decades of the century, immigration from other cultures into Iceland added even newer dimensions. In particular, the growth of the women's movement had a strong effect on society as a whole, and many more women writers entered what had up to then been a male-dominated practice. Finally, emigration from Iceland added a diasporic dimension previously unseen. Icelandic writers began to live abroad for longer or shorter periods and were greatly influenced by their new environments.

Among emerging women writers in the late 20th c. we include Steinunn Sigurdardottir (b. 1950), whose works have a feminist and domestic orientation. Previously underrated women writers have been rediscovered in later years, such as Asta Sigurdardottir (1930-1972), whose short, difficult life became emblematic of some of the problems women writers faced. Asta Sigurdardottir published only one book of short stories, but the writing shows great sensitivity and attention to detail. The poet Nina Bjork Arnadottir (b. 1941) likewise can be seen as representative of an almost lost women's poetic tradition in Iceland. Arnadottir writes emotionally charged, psychologicaly portraits of pain, much in the vein of her Swedish and Norwegian peers, again showing some neglected dimensions of Icelandic modernism. Vilborg Dagbjartsottir (b. 1930) likewise became a well-known poet just after the mid-century, and continued to write tender, nature-oriented, love poems for several decades.

In later decades there sprang up a more theoritically oriented coterie of writers, mainly from the academy. These were influenced by international theory, which inspired a turn away from more provincial concerns. Of these newer modernist writers, we may include Alfrun Gunnlaugsdottir, Njordur P. Njardvik, Runar Gelgi Vignisson, and Thorarinn Eldjarn, among other.

It may be said that the end of the century shuffles some commonly held notions about Icelandic literature, in light of the opening up of Icelandic aesthetics to the rest of the world. Some writers who have appeared important seem less so at the end of the century, and some underrated trends begin to loom with significance. Both Gudbergur Bergsson and Thor Vilhjalmsson may be reassessed, for example, as the innovators of modern Icelandic fiction they have proved to be. Bergsson's work has become increasingly impoortant and sensitive over the years, while Vilhjalmsson's writing will perhaps appear monotonous, although most innovative in the Icelandic context. Laxness towered above the scene for much of the century, and the exclusion of women from the picture begins to look conspicuous. The prevalence of the romantic in poetry and the epic in fiction is established, but the innovator (such as the "atom poets" of the mid-century, and surrealists like Steinn Steinarr) will also appear more striking with time. Landmark contributions that break the back of established traditions, such as Jon ur Vor's small volume of poetry *Thorpid* (1946), which ushered in free verse and vernacular language and themes, and Steinn Steinarr's *Timinn og vatnid* (1948), which energized the metaphysical and the surreal in the nations's literary life, will no doubt loom large in the history of the nation's changing values.

BIBLIOGRAPHY: Einarsson., S., *History of Icelandic Prose Writers 1800–1940* (1948); Beck, R., *History of Icelandic Poets 1800–1940* (1950); Einarsson, S., *A History of Icelandic Literature* (1957); Carleton, P., *Tradition and Innovation in Twentieth Century Icelandic Poetry* (1967); Jónsson, E., "Icelandic Literature," in

Ivask, I., and G. von Wilpert, *World Literature since 1945* (1973): 372–77

—NJÖRDUR P. NJARDVÍK; UPDATED BY KRISTJANA
GUNNARS

IDRĪS, Yūsuf

Egyptian short-story writer, dramatist, and novelist, b. May 1927, al-Bayrūm; d. 14 August 1991, London

After a childhood spent in the Nile delta, I. came to Cairo to attend university. He studied medicine, and upon graduation (1951) became a medical inspector in the Department of Health. He had already been writing short stories for amusement as a student, and the requirements of his medical position that he visit the poorer quarters of Cairo served to strengthen and expand his innate ability to portray the living conditions of the poor in realistic detail. His first collection of short stories appeared in 1954 and was an instant success; between 1954 and 1958 he published five collections and three plays. His increasing fame as a writer led him to give up his medical career, and he then worked as a full-time creative writer and journalist. During the 1970s and 1980s his creative input in fictional forms diminished. Much of his time was spent on weekly articles for the newspaper *Al-Ahrām*, that were later collected into volumes such as *Shahid 'asrihi* (Witness of His Era, n.d.). These pieces may not contain quite as much of the direct social and political criticism that made I. an enfant terrible earlier in his career and led to his imprisonment on more than one occasion, but they still succeed in penetrating to the core of the Egyptian character and in reflecting the concerns and aspirations of his fellow countrymen of all classes. His final years seemed full of frustrations, personal and political, not least when Najib MAHFUZ was awarded the Nobel Prize in 1988. The award of the Saddam Husayn Prize in Literature that same year did not compensate for his sense of disappointment. He died in a London hospital in 1991.

The short-story collections of the 1950s, beginning with *Arkhas layālī* (1954; the cheapest nights), describe in vivid and often gruesome detail the conditions of Egypt's poorest classes both in the towns and the countryside. In the majority of cases, the reader is introduced to the character within his surroundings and shown the routine of his life; little has changed by the end of the story. The title story of his first collection is typical. A man emerges from evening prayer in the mosque and has to wade through scores of children in order to proceed in any direction. He curses them and the hole in heaven through which they come. His mind is spinning because of a cup of strong tea he has been given. After despairing of finding any of his friends with whom he might spend the evening, he heads for home and makes love to his wife, if only to keep warm. In due time he is being congratulated yet again on the birth of a child. The way in which I., the doctor and short-story writer, projects the overwhelming problem of Egypt's birth rate with such force and clarity is exactly the quality that has made his works at once so popular and so important in the history of this genre.

During the 1960s I. began to write symbolic and surreal tales. Examples of these are "Al-Aurta" ("The Aorta," 1978) from *Lughat al-ay ay* (1965; the language of screams), a horrifying parable concerning the callousness of human beings spurred on by the herd instinct; "Alif al-ahrār" ("The Omitted Letter," 1978) from *Ākhir al-dunyā* (1961; the end of the world), an amusing yet poignant tale of bureaucratic man as victim; and "Mu'jizat al-'asr" (the wonder of the age) from *Al-Naddāha* (1969; the clarion). Another feature of I.'s recent writings has been a concern with the role of sex in society, explored, for example, in "Bayt min lahm" ("House of Flesh," 1978) from the collection *Bayt min lahm* (1971; house of flesh).

I.'s contributions to the novel and drama are also numerous, but, with a few notable exceptions, they tend to show a certain lack of affinity on the writer's part with longer genres. For example, by far his most successful play is *Al-Farāfīr* (1964; *The Farfoors*, 1974; also tr. as *Flipflap and His Master*, 1977), a brilliant attempt at combining elements of Egyptian popular dramatic forms with the modern techniques of the THEATER OF THE ABSURD. Yet, the work suffers from an excess of padding and farce that lessens the total impact. Of I.'s novels, perhaps only *Al-Harām* (1959; the taboo), with its themes of moral hypocrisy among villagers faced with an annual visit of transhumants (people who move seasonally from one area to another in search of pasturage for their animals) avoids this same lack of cohesion or excessive concern with politics.

One of the most interesting aspects of I.'s craft is his style, which has reflected an adventurous spirit of growth during his career. When he began to publish his stories, I.'s language was criticized severely. Far from paying any attention to such views, I. persisted in his distinctive style to such a degree that his latest works were a blend of the written and spoken languages. I. himself admitted that he wrote in an impulsive fashion, and this may well account for his greater success in short stories than in other genres. As a short-story writer and as a brilliant and controversial innovator in language and form, I. is guaranteed a major place in the history of modern Arabic literature.

FURTHER WORKS: *Jumhūriyyat Farahāt* (1956); *Al-Batal* (1957); *A laysa kadhālika?* (1957); *Al-Lahza al-harija* (1957); *Hādithat sharaf* (1958); *Al-'Ayb* (1962); *Al-'Askarī al-aswad* (1962); *Al-Mahzala al-ardiyya* (1966); *Al-Mukhattatīn* (1969); *Al-Baydā'* (1970); *Al-Jins al-thālith* (1971); *Ana sultan qanun al-wujud* (n.d.); *al-Bahlawan* (n.d.); *Al-'atb 'ala al-nazar* (1987). **FURTHER WORKS IN ENGLISH:** *In the Eye of the Beholder: Tales of Egyptian Life from the Writings of Y. I.* (1978); *The Cheapest Nights* (1978)

BIBLIOGRAPHY: Beyerl, J., *The Style of the Modern Arabic Short Story* (1971): passim; Cobham, C., "Sex and Society in Y. I.," *J ArabL*, 6 (1975): 80–88; Somekh, S., "Language and Theme in the Short Stories of Y. I.," *J ArabL*, 6 (1975): 89–100; Allen, R., Introduction to Y. I., *In the Eye of the Beholder* (1978): vii–xxxix; Mikhail, M., *Images of Arab Women* (1979): 77–89: 91–111; Kurpershoek, P. M., *The Short Stories of Y. I.* (1981); Somekh, S., "The Function of Sound in the Stories of Y. I.," *JArabL*, 16 (1985): 95-104; Badawi, M. M., *Modern Arabic Drama in Egypt* (1987): 153-71; Malti-Douglas, F., "Blindness and Sexuality: Traditional Mentalities in Y. I.'s 'House of Flesh'," in *Critical Pilgrimages; Studies in the Arabic Literary tradiion, Literature East and West* (1989): 70-78; Mikhail, M., *Studies in the Short Fiction of Mahfouz and I.* (1989); Somekh, S., "Structure of Silence: a reading of Y. I.'s 'Bayt min lahm'," in Elad, A., ed., *Writer, Culture, Text* (1993): 56-61; Roger, A., ed., *Critical Perspectives on Y. I.* (1994)

—ROGER ALLEN

IGBO LITERATURE

See Nigerian Literature

IGNATOW, David

American poet and editor, b. 7 Feb. 1914, Brooklyn, N.Y.; d. 17 Nov. 1997, East Hampton, N.Y.

I. spent most of his life in New York City, and the influence of the city, especially its dark side, is evident in much of his poetry. He graduated from New Utrecht High School in Brooklyn in 1932 and attended Brooklyn College for a short time. At his family's insistence he left school to work for his father's bindery firm. I. was not happy in business, and although he left the firm two year later, he was never entirely free of its demands until almost thirty years later when he sold the company, in 1962. His harshly negative view of this experience and of American business tactics in general informs much of his early work. In the 1930s and 1940s I. worked at various jobs, from reporter to handyman in a shipyard to night admitting clerk in a hospital. In 1949 he became coeditor of the *Beloit Poetry Journal*, a position he held for ten years. He also worked as poetry editor of the *Nation* from 1962 until 1963.

I.'s teaching career began in 1964 when he became an instructor at the New School for Social Research in New York City. He was visiting lecturer at the University of Kentucky at Lexington (1965–1966), at the University of Kansas at Lawrence (1966–1967), and at Vassar College (1967–1968). In 1969 he became poet-in-residence at York College of the City University of New York and adjunct professor in the writing program of the School of the Arts at Columbia University. I.'s honors and awards include the National Institute of Arts and Letters Award (1964), two Guggenheim fellowships (1965 and 1973), the Shelley Memorial Prize from the Poetry Society of America (1966), a Rockefeller Foundation grant (1968–1969), a National Endowment for the Arts grant (1970), the Bollingen Prize (1977), and the Wallace Stevens Fellowship (1977).

I.'s first volume, *Poems*, was published in 1948. His often matter-of-fact comments on everyday life and his rhetorical style show the influence of Williams Carlos WILLIAMS, whom he greatly admired and who praised and encouraged I. Other influences I. acknowledges as playing major roles in shaping his thinking and writing include Walt Whitman (1819–1892), the great Russian writers, and the Bible. I.'s typical poem is the short lyric, and while his material is strongly autobiographical, he more often than not adopts personae. His simple, straightforward use of the urban American vernacular underscores the horror he sees and feels as he looks at the minute details of both his private and his public life. Although I.'s themes defy easy categorization, it can be said that his unrelenting focus on his personal response—sometimes guilty, sometimes angry, often wryly humorous—gives an overall sense of unity to his work.

His political and social poems reflect his lived experience: the Depression of the 1930s, World War II, Vietnam, the evils of the American lust for money, the pervasive violence and outright insanity that has become a given in late 20th-c. America. His personal poems rely more on his felt experience. These works often contain a tension generated by juxtaposing the difficulties in marital and family relationships with the blighted, crumbling landscapes the speakers of the poems perceive both inside as well as outside their windows. In many of the poems in *The Gentle Weight Lifter* (1955) I. seems to be experimenting with distancing his work from the urban setting and focusing on the isolation and alienation that results from social decay. The settings are biblical, classical, or timeless. It is with these poems that I. begins to work in parable form, and while he does not maintain the impersonal distancing stance (his later work returns to the concrete and specific here and now of his surroundings), much of his work in the early 1960s is parablelike, especially the social poetry. This technique is evident in many of the poems in *Say Pardon* (1961) and *Figures of the Human* (1964). The urban nightmares of violence and corruption are rendered in a slightly surreal manner, and I. often moves away from free verse into the less structured narration of the prose poem.

While *Figures of the Human* has been judged to contain some of I.'s weakest work—short, flat pieces hinting at emotional exhaustion—his next book, *Rescue the Dead* (1968), articulates a personal and, in I.'s case almost necessarily, a poetic rebirth. He presents and recasts the issues he has been dealing with in his earlier work: parents, children, romantic and sexual love, marriage, the violence of American society, and the personal threat the narrator perceives such violence to be. There are also poems that hint at themes that I. will go on to explore more fully—the individual's connection with and relationship to nature. It might be speculated that, as I. started to spend more time living and writing in his home in East Hampton, Long Island, his poetry began to reflect both his physical and his emotional distance from New York City.

Facing the Tree (1975) and *Tread the Dark* (1978) delve into the complexities and contradictions the poet discovers in exploring his place within the natural world. But, paradoxically, the comfort that might be derived from imagining oneself part of a cycle that hints at an eternal return seems to shatter at some point and become instead a longing for the release from time and its evils that death offers. Many of the poems in *Tread the Dark* are concerned with suicide and escape from self. This volume also contains a number of wry poems about poems that often employ the voice of the poem itself as the speaker.

Although I. has sometimes been compared in a negative light to those who have influenced his work, and for many years critical appreciation was slow in coming, his gifts are now well recognized. In his most recent collection, *Shadowing the Ground* (1991), his voice is as authentic as it is individual. The early bitterness has been transmuted into a deeper and more complex moral and intellectual vision full of strongly felt and strongly realized emotions, and I. has achieved the status of an American poet worthy of serious acclaim.

FURTHER WORKS: *Political Poetry* (1960); *Walt Whitman: A Centennial Celebration* (1963); *William Carlos Williams: A Memorial Chapbook* (1963); *Earth Hard: Selected Poems* (1968); *Poems 1934–1969* (1970); *Notebooks* (1973); *Selected Poems* (1975); *The Animal in the Bush* (1977); *Open between Us* (1980); *Whisper to the Earth* (1981); *Leaving the Door Open* (1984); *New and Collected Poems 1970–1985* (1986); *The One in the Many: A Poet's Memoirs* (1988); *Despite the Plainness of the Day: Love Poems* (1991)

BIBLIOGRAPHY: Bly, R., "Some Thoughts on *Rescue the Dead*," *Tennessee Poetry Journal*, 3 (Winter 1970): 17–21; Kazin, A., "The Esthetic of Humility," *APR* (April–May 1974): 14–15; Melange, G., "The Art of Poetry XIII: D. I.," *Paris Review*, 76 (Fall

1979): 55–79; Sjoberg, L., "An Interview with D. I.," *CanL*, 28, 2 (Summer 1987): 143–62

—MARGARET D. SULLIVAN

ILF, Ilya

(pseud. of Ilya Fainzilberg) Russian novelist and essayist, b. 5 Oct. 1897, Odessa, Ukraine; d. 13 April 1937, Moscow

PETROV, Yevgeny

(pseud. of Yevgeny Kataev) Russian novelist and essayist, b. 13 Dec. 1903, Odessa, Ukraine; d. 2 July 1942, near Sevastopol, Ukraine

Both I., the son of a bank clerk, and P., the son of a history teacher and younger brother of Valentin KATAEV, grew up in Odessa. Both began their literary careers as journalists; both moved to Moscow in 1923. They did not, however, become acquainted until 1925, when they were working on the railwaymen's newspaper *Gudok*. In 1927 they formed a literary partnership that was to last until I.'s death.

I. and P.'s first significant joint effort was the hilarious satirical novel *Dvenadtsat stulev* (1928; *Diamonds to Sit On*, 1930). The novel was a great popular success, and a sequel, *Zolotoy telyonok* (1931; *The Little Golden Calf*, 1932), soon followed. In 1935 I. and P. visited the U.S. and made a transcontinental automobile trip. Their impressions of American life are described in their witty, satirical book *Odnoetazhnaya Amerika* (1936; *Little Golden America*, 1937). The two writers also coauthored a large number of satiric stories, sketches, and feuilletons, which appeared in Soviet journals and newspapers under different pseudonyms, most notably "Tolstoyevsky." Grieved by the death from tuberculosis of his close friend and collaborator, P. wrote little fiction in the next few years. In 1940 he became editor of the journal *Ogonyok*. When World War II broke out, he became a war correspondent; his reports from the front were collected and published posthumously under the title *Frontovoy dnevnik* (1942; front-line diary). P. was killed in an airplane crash returning from besieged Sevastopol.

I. and P. are best known for *Dvenadtsat stulev* and *Zolotoy telyonok*, which are perennial favorites with Russian readers. Both novels are picaresque and revolve around the adventures of one Ostap Bender, who longs to become a millionaire in a society where it has become impossible to satisfy such an ambition. Bender, a cunning, imaginative rogue, is one of the most memorable characters in Soviet literature. His audacity and ingenuity continually delight and amuse the reader. In *Dvenadtsat stulev* Bender searches high and low for diamonds that have been hidden in one of a set of twelve chairs. His treasure hunt takes him throughout Russia, and this device allows I. and P. to show us glimpses of provincial towns and large cities and to introduce a wide variety of characters—Soviet bureaucrats, journalists, former noblemen, provincials, Muscovites. *Dvenadtsat stulev* has an appropriate ideological ending: Bender is killed by a diamond-hunting rival; the diamonds are found and sold, and the money is used to build a club for workers. The unforgettable picaro, however, is brought back to life in the sequel, *Zolotoy telyonok*. Here he succeeds in becoming a millionaire but discovers that money in a Communist society brings him no power. Again the hero's adventures are played out against scenes of Soviet life. While equally entertaining, the satire here is more biting. Its target is Soviet bureaucracy, philistinism, and greed.

The wonderful humor in I. and P.'s novels—the absurd comic situations and clever use of language—accounts for their continued popularity. There have been numerous stage and film versions of their books in the Soviet Union and a movie adaptation of *Dvenadtsat stulev* in the U.S. (Mel Brooks's *The Twelve Chairs*, 1970). Although much of I. and P.'s satire is topical, their works contain pithy observations about human foibles that give them universal appeal and meaning. Officially criticized for insufficient ideological militancy, I. and P.'s works express a deeply humane and warm hearted attitude toward life.

FURTHER WORKS: *Svetlaya lichnost* (1928); *1001 den; ili, Novaya Shakherezada* (1929); *Kak sozdavalsya Robinzon* (1933); *Ravnodushie* (1933); *Silnoe chuvstvo* (1933); *Direktivny bantik* (1934); *Bezmyatezhnaya tumba* (1935); *Chuvstvo mery* (1935); *Chudesnye gosti* (1935); *Poezdki i vstrechi* (1936); *Tonya* (1937). I.: *Zapisnye knizhki* (1939); P.: *Radosti Megasa* (1926); *Bez doklada* (1927); *Sluchay s obezyanoy* (1927); *Stsenarii* (1943)

BIBLIOGRAPHY: Zavalishin, V., *Early Soviet Writers* (1958): 342–44; Struve, G., *Russian Literature under Lenin and Stalin, 1917–1953* (1971): 165–67; Wright, J., "Ostap Bender as a Picaroon," *PPNCFL*, 25, Part 1 (1974): 265–68; Friedberg, M., Introduction to I. and P., *The Twelve Chairs* (1961): v–xii

—SONA STEPHAN HOISINGTON

İLHAN, Attilâ

Turkish poet, novelist, and essayist, b. 1925, Menemen

İ. cut his education at the faculty of law at the University of Istanbul short to become a journalist, a career that culminated in his serving as editor in chief of the Izmir daily *Demokrat Izmir* and as a columnist for several leading newspapers and magazines. He first attracted attention in 1946 when he won second prize in a poetry contest, probably the most important contest of that time, organized by the ruling People's Republican Party. In the early 1950s he lived and studied in Paris. He had a short-lived involvement with Marxism-Leninism, which he renounced later in the decade. From 1973 to 1980 he was editorial consultant for Bilgi Yayinevi, a major publishing house. He has also been a prolific writer for film and television.

Starting with his first collection of poems, *Duvar* (1948; the wall), İ. has enjoyed popular and critical acclaim. Many of his early poems exhibit the angst of the turbulent times after World War II. His shorter early verses are marked by their raw emotions and forceful style, and the longer ones by an epic flair. *Sisler bulvari* (1954; boulevard of fogs) and *Yağmur kaçaği* (1955; fugitive from rain) are comprised of poems of unabashed neoromanticism that are remarkable for their lyricism and extravagant vocabulary. In these, İ. made a synthesis of the aesthetic values of Ottoman classical verse, traditional folk poetry, and modern poetics. The two collections, published in quick succession, swiftly endeared İ. to the larger poetry-reading public.

Ben sana mecburum (1960; I am obliged to you) augmented İ.'s reputation as a lyric poet. Here the metaphors are more audacious than ever, passions erupt into a whirlwind, and the style, although hyperbolic at times, is admirably controlled. *Belâ çiçeği* (1962; the flower of turbulence) represents İ.'s attempt to reconcile his Turkish sensibilities with his heightened preoccupation with European culture. The result is a mixed blessing: the innate lyric gifts remain vibrant although the cultural admixture seems to leave a lot to be desired. A cycle of poems glorifying the military coup of 27 May 1960 appended to the collection tends to reduce the level even further. His *Yasak sevişmek* (1968; loving is banned), however, is a powerful combination of love and political oppression. The tragic sense is acute here, with tenderness and anger coalescing into very poignant poetic statements.

1973 saw the publication of *Tutuklunun günlüğü* (diary of a detainee), poems mainly about the suffering of a sensitive man in prison and under interrogation. For this book, which effectively delineates the plight of a public-spirited individual in a harsh oppressive regime, İ. was given the Poetry Award of the Turkish Language Society in 1974.

Elde var hüzün (1984; there remains sorrow) and *Korkunun krallığı* (1987; sovereignty of fear) represent the highlights of İ.'s poetic art. They contain many of his most accomplished poems of private joy and sadness as well as acute social concerns. Both collections possess the wealth of fresh metaphors, lilting rhythms, and the sensuous vocabulary that Turkish poetry lovers have come to cherish. *Ayrilik sevdaya dahil* (1993; separation is part of love) contains many of İ.'s most touching love poems.

İ. enjoys high esteem as an essayist and newspaper columnist as well. His probing short prose pieces are remarkable for their unusual perspectives and insightful analyses of politics, culture, and literature. He has collected these, along with autobiographical essays, in numerous volumes including *Hangi sol* (1970; which left), *Hangi batı* (1972; which west), *Faşizmin ayak sesleri* (1975; fascism's footsteps), *Hangi seks* (1976; which sex), *Hangi sağ* (1980; which right), *Gerçekçilik savaşı* (1980; realism's crusade), *Hangi Atatürk* (1981; which Atatürk), *Batının deli gömleği* (1982; straitjacket of the west), *Hangi laiklik* (1995; which secularism), and other volumes. İ.'s travel pieces, collected in *Abbas yolcu* (1959; must go), earned praise as first-rate specimens of the genre.

İ. showed great promise in fiction when he published *Sokaktaki adam* (1953; the man in the street) and *Zenciler birbirine benzemez* (1957; blacks don't resemble each other), both of them conventional novels whose characters lacked psychological depth, though presented with considerable narrative skill. With his two-volume *Kurtlar sofrası* (1963–1964; a feast for wolves) he established his credentials as a major novelist. This impressive work portrays the vast vista of a society in turmoil—Turkey's middle class and intellectual elite—after World War II. It moves very swiftly, like a film script, through many dramatic episodes that are fragmentary but interrelated. *Kurtlar sofrası* led directly into İ.'s magnum opus, *Aynanın içindekiler* (those in the mirror), a sprawling work consisting of five long novels, each one of which can be read independently. Collectively, this tour de force is a saga of Turkey in the 20th c. caught in political turbulence, spiritual crisis, and private anguish. Many of the characters are from real life, identified by name, although basically the work is a roman à clef. The first novel in İ.'s modern epic, *Bıçağın ucu* (1973; tip of the knife), did not generate much critical enthusiasm. The second, however, *Sırtlan payı* (1974; hyena's share), won the prestigious Yunus Nadi Prize (1974–1975). After the mild success of *Yaraya tuz basmak* (1978;

rubbing salt on the wound), his *Dersaadet'te sabah ezanları* (1981; morning calls to prayer in Istanbul) became a *succès d'estime* with its captivating personae, narrative power, and fascinating plot. *O karanlıkta biz* (1988; we in that darkness), fifth in the series, is a gripping account of political intrigue and foreign interference in the Turkey of World War II.

Fena halde Leman (1980; Leman in a bad way) and *Haco Hanım Vay* (1984; oh Mme. Haco) are two of İ.'s acclaimed novels in which, with an unmistakable poetic touch, the author excelled in depicting the lives and psychological personalities of two vivid woman protagonists.

A versatile and prolific literary figure, İ. has claimed the legacy of classical Ottoman verse, modern lyric poetry, and late Ottoman and contemporary Turkish history as his terra firma, infusing into them brave new forms and interpretations, always putting on them his own stamp of originality.

FURTHER WORKS: *Böyle bir sevmek* (1977); *İkinci yeni savaşı* (1983); *Sağım solum sobe* (1985)

BIBLIOGRAPHY: Halman, T. S., "A. İ. and the Promise of Turkish Poetry," *BA* (Autumn 1963): 403–5

—TALAT SAIT HALMAN

ILLYÉS, Gyula

Hungarian poet, essayist, dramatist, and novelist, b. 2 Nov. 1902, Rácegres-puszta; d. 15 Apr. 1983, Budapest

Born into a mixed marriage—his father was a Catholic, his mother a Calvinist—and amid feudal surroundings (his parents were estate servants), I. was exposed to the best blend of tradition and rebellion. Early in his youth, he joined the revolutionary army; when the short-lived dictatorship of the proletariat in Hungary collapsed (1919) and I. was forced into exile, he was barely seventeen. After short stays in Vienna and Berlin, I. arrived in Paris, where he found a second home. While working as a miner, a bookbinder, and also as a teacher, he studied at the Sorbonne. His exposure to French culture made a deep and lasting impression on him. SURREALISM was the literary fashion of the time, and I.'s first poems, appearing in émigré papers, bore its stamp, with an undertone of revolutionary zeal.

Returning to Hungary in 1926, I. went to work as a clerk, but his driving passion was writing. The grand old man of Hungarian literature, Mihály BABITS, offered him space in the avant-garde monthly *Nyugat*; I.'s poems were received with skeptical interest. Here was a young poet who addressed himself to burning Hungarian problems with a surrealistic style. The country reeked of feudalism: a thousand aristocrats and a dozen bishops owned more than half of the land; the agrarian laborers were semiserfs; and the independent peasantry as well as the industrial workers were in the shackles of the Horthy regime. In his writings I. presented the oppressed life of the peasantry vividly, warmly, and also sarcastically.

In his first work, a collection of poems, *Nehéz föld* (1928; heavy earth), he lamented the plight of the poor peasants and expressed his dismay with the feudal establishment. But he dealt it his strongest blow with the nonfiction prose work *Puszták népe* (1936;

People of the Pusztak, 1967). In this masterfully written book, I. recollected the events of his youth on one of the *pusztas* (feudal hamlets) where the peasants lived in subhuman conditions. This book aroused the national conscience and shattered the romantic belief that the peasantry would regenerate the Hungarian nation. A strong movement was born—populism for radical reform. I. fought so hard for the rights of the peasants to a better life that in 1945 he was elected to the Hungarian Parliament.

After the Communist coup d'état in 1947, I.'s individualistic and anti-Marxist views made him the target of Communist zealots, and he was silenced for a while. But in the mid-1950s, when the writers again appeared on the scene as the stormbirds of the revolution, he courageously declared: "I, who gave voice to the voiceless,/Let me express the mute torment again . . . ." And during the 1956 revolt he published a poem (written in 1951) that is regarded as the Hungarian poem of the century: "Egy mondat a zsarnokságról" ("One Sentence on Tyranny," 1968). It is a majestic indictment of the torture suffered by spirit and intellect in a totalitarian state.

After the uprising was crushed, I. was silenced again and was even investigated by the Hungarian secret police. Yet he was not muted. First he continued to write for his literary drawer; later, in a somewhat more relaxed climate, for the public.

In the third phase of his life, I. perhaps mellowed, but he gave up none of his beliefs. Using the stage for his message, I. exposed man's ambitions. Most of his dramas deal with the Hungarian past. His principal theme is that the cause of all human tragedy is lack of freedom and the misinterpretation of the meaning of liberty.

Haunted and anguished throughout his life by the fate of his people, I. was obsessed with the future of the Hungarian nation. In one of his dramas, *Tiszták* (1969; puritans), set in French Provence, I. worries about the small ethnic groups who are not regarded as important or needed on the world stage. The play is about the Provençals of the Middle Ages who are lectured by a papal visitor for their heretical views and told that they, like many of the ancient nations, could disappear from the face of the earth if they do not give up their stubborn insistence on "freedom."

FURTHER WORKS: *Sarjurendek* (1931); *Három öreg* (1932); *Hősökről beszélek* (1933); *Ifjuság* (1934); *Oroszország* (1934); *Szálló egek alatt* (1935); *Petőfi* (1936; *Sándor Petőfi*, 1973); *Rend a romokban* (1937); *Magyarok* (1938); *Külön világban* (1939); *Ki a magyar?* (1939); *Lélek és kenyér* (1940); *Összegyüjtött versek* (1943); *Csizma az asztalon* (1941); *Mint a darvak* (1942); *Válogatott versek* (1943); *A tű foka* (1944); *Egy év* (1945); *Honfoglalók között* (1945); *Hunok Párizsban* (1946); *Kiáltvány a parasztság művelődése ügyében* (1946); *Szembenézve* (1947); *Tizenkét nap Bulgáriában* (1947); *Összes versei* (1947); *Franciaországi változások* (1947); *A lélekbúvár* (1948); *Két kéz* (1950); *Két férfi* (1950); *Ozorai példa* (1952); *Válogatott versek* (1952); *Tüz-viz* (1952); *Föltámadott a tenger* (1952); *Fáklyaláng* (1953); *Tűvetevők* (1953); *Dózsa György* (1956); *Hetvenhét magyar népmese* (1956); *Három dráma* (1957); *Kézfogások* (1957); *Uj versek* (1961); *Nem volt elég* (1962); *Másokért egyedül* (1963); *Ingyen lakoma* (1964); *Tűz vagyok: Petőfi élete* (1964); *Hajszálgyökerek* (1971); *Iránytüvel* (1975); *Szives kalauz* (1975); *Összegyüjtött versek* (1977); *Összegyüjtött drámák* (1977); *Uj testamentum* (1977); *Az Éden elvesztése* (1978); *Beatrice* (1979); *Homokzsák* (1979). FURTHER WORKS IN ENGLISH: *Once upon a Time: Forty Hungarian Folktales* (1964); *A Tribute to G. I.* (1968); *Selected Poems* (1971)

BIBLIOGRAPHY: Klaniczay, T., et al., *History of Hungarian Literature* (1964): 254–57; Reményi, J., *Hungarian Writers and Literature* (1964): 383–87; Gömöri, G., *Polish and Hungarian Poetry* (1966): 70–75; Follain, J., "The Poetry of G. I.," Tabori, P., "Ten Encounters with G. I.," and Kabdebo, T., "Notes on G. I.," in Kabdebo, T., and Tabori, P., eds., *A Tribute to G. I.* (1968): 7–8, 9–19, 137–45; Beládi, M., "The Seventy Years of G. I.," *NHQ*, 48 (1972): 83–89; Ferenczi, L., "G. I., Poet of a Nation," *NHQ*, No. 68 (1977): 54–65; Nagy, K., "G. I.'s Poetry of Hope" *CARHS*, 5, 2 (1978): 53–61

—IMRE KOVACS

ILOKO LITERATURE
See Philippines Literature

IMAGISM

Imagism began as a literary movement early in the 20th c.; its critical manifesto, "Imagisme" (the final *e* was later dropped) appeared in *Poetry* in 1913. The term was coined by Ezra POUND in part as a counter to the host of literary "ismes" attracting attention on the Continent, but also to distinguish poems written in accordance with a stringent technical criterion and a theory of the image. Pound may have been the foremost publicist and practitioner of imagism, but his ideas were influenced by T. E. Hulme (1883–1917) and Ford Madox FORD, both of whom he met in London in 1909.

The main impetus for the movement was the desire to break free from the current, worn-out poetic modes, to create a poetry independent of the uncritical imitations of late Victorian romanticism. Imagists objected to sentimentality and provincialism, to vague and pretentious language, to commonplace and ill-defined ideas, and to predictable and artificial metrical forms. They advocated (1) direct treatment of the subject, (2) precision and concentration of language, (3) invention of new rhythms, and (4) adherence to a "Doctrine of the Image." Pound found precedents for his aesthetic in such eclectic sources as classical, Oriental, and medieval poetry.

The imagist doctrine was based on a double concept of the image. Not merely a visual sense impression, the image involves the perception of relationships. It forms in the moment of awareness, what Pound called the moment of metamorphosis, when one thing is understood to be like another. Faces in the gloom are perceived as "petals on a wet, black bough." On a more complex level, imagism works by ideogram; concrete particulars are juxtaposed in order to suggest commonality. The imagist avoids abstractions and instead cites specific examples, for instance: cherry, flamingo, rust, and sunset. The reader is left to infer their relationship, in this case, redness. The world is thus viewed as dynamic patterns of correspondences, and the very act of reading imagist poetry mirrors the creative process.

In their determination to reform poetry, the imagists were attempting to meet the challenge posed by science. In a skeptical age, scientific rationalism had claimed that it was the only reliable approach to knowledge, the final arbiter of truth. By combining the scientific methods of accurate observation and precise definition with the traditional poetic methods of analogy and intuition, the imagists sought to restore the credibility of poetry as a significant source of information about human experience.

Hilda DOOLITTLE, Richard Aldington (1892–1962), and F. S. Flint (1885–1960) were founding members of the group. They were represented along with only eight others, including James JOYCE and William Carlos WILLIAMS, in Pound's anthology *Des Imagistes* (1914). Amy LOWELL adopted the term and began publicizing imagism in America. Her three anthologies, *Some Imagist Poets* (1915, 1916, 1917), were limited to the work of three American and three British poets: Hilda Doolittle, John Gould Fletcher (1886–1950), and herself as well as Aldington, Flint, and D. H. LAWRENCE.

Believing that Amy Lowell had misunderstood the doctrine of the image and neglected his critical principles, Pound dissociated himself from her group, calling it "Amygism." In 1914 the poetics of imagism were translated by Pound into vorticism, a new movement emphasizing the dynamic energy of art and including such writers and artists as Wyndham LEWIS and Henri Gaudier-Brzeska (1891–1915). Thus, imagism continued to inform Pound's work and to exert a considerable influence on modern poetry.

BIBLIOGRAPHY: Lowell, A., *Tendencies in Modern American Poetry* (1917); Hughes, G., *Imagism and Imagists* (1931); Coffman, S., *Imagism* (1951); Pound, E., "A Retrospect," *Literary Essays of Ezra Pound* (1954): 3–15; Kenner, H., "Imagism," *The Pound Era* (1972): 173–91

—JO BRANTLEY BERRYMAN

IMBUGA, Francis

Kenyan dramatist and novelist, b. 2 Feb. 1947, Chakavali, North Maragoli

I.'s childhood corresponded with a period of great uncertainty and change in what was then the colony of Kenya. The decade of the 1950s, when he completed his elementary school years, saw increased resistance to British colonial rule in Kenya, eventually leading to political independence in 1963. I. came from a relatively poor, rural family home in the western part of the country; his father had served in the King's African Rifles during World War II and later worked as a security guard in Nairobi. I.'s early academic achievements earned him a place at the selective Alliance High School in Nairobi, where he pursued his secondary education from 1964 to 1969 and where he began to explore his interest in drama. He attended the University of Nairobi in the 1970s, during an era in which that campus was the center for lively debate about the role of literature and art in Kenyan society. He went on to balance an academic career at Kenyatta University (where he served in teaching and administrative roles) with a highly productive writing career. That career has been punctuated by involvement in international theater and writing programs in Britain and the U.S., and by awards and recognition for his work both in Kenya and abroad.

I. first became involved in drama in high school, where he wrote, directed, and acted in Omolo, for which he won the coveted Best Actor's Award in the highly competitive Kenya National Schools' Drama Festival. He deepened his involvement in drama at the University of Nairobi where, in addition to his regular studies,

he wrote, directed, and acted in a variety of plays as well as more than fifty dramatic productions for the African Theatre Series of the Voice of Kenya television station. The well-known Ghanaian playwright Joe de Graft (1924-1978), who was at the time on the University of Nairobi faculty, wrote his most well-known play, *Muntu* (1982), with I. in mind as the lead character.

In content and style I.'s writing is richly informed by his rural roots. In interviews I. cites his family and community (particularly his grandparents) for the ways they influenced his dramatic voice. His plays are populated by lively personalities whose speech is punctuated by vivid parables and concrete metaphors. Like many of his literary colleagues in East Africa, one of I.'s primary thematic concerns is nature of cultural identity in the region, given its heritage of European colonialism and the neocolonial structures that have followed independence. I. is a social critic but, in a country and a time where writers have suffered harassment for being too outspoken in their criticism, that criticism is always couched in humor. I. is a master of what the Ugandan critic and playwright John Ruganda (b. 1941) describes as "indirect criticism."

I.'s first plays, published in the early 1970s when he was still a university student, are largely family dramas dealing with complications in love and marriage relationships, while his later works are more overt in addressing issues in the political realm. *Betrayal in the City* (1976), I.'s most popular play to date, directly addresses the corruption of politics in Africa's postindependence era. Set in the fictional nation of Kafira (an anagram for the Swahili spelling of Africa), the play calls for an honest evaluation of Africa's social ills and encourages ordinary people not to remain silent in the face of them. *Betrayal in the City* was selected by Kenya's Ministry of Education as a set text for the nation's secondary schools and was also sent as Kenya's entry to the second World Black and African Festival of Arts and Culture (FESTAC) in Lagos, Nigeria in 1977.

In the 1990s I. began to experiment with new forms, but still with an emphasis on the problems of forging a cultural identity in a neocolonial setting. It was while he was participating in the University of Iowa's International Writing Program and completing a doctoral degree in English that I. wrote his first novel, *Shrine of Tears* (1993). Though it was his first foray into narrative fiction, the work focuses on the world of Kenyan drama that I. knows so well. The novel examines the role of a fictional nation's National Theater (which is remarkably similar to the same institution in Nairobi). The conflict surrounds who in fact controls what happens at this supposedly "national" institution, in the process drawing a critical eye on the roles of politicians, the police, the national universities, the expatriate community and traditional cultural forms.

I. has been the most prolific and important Kenyan dramatist in the postcolonial era. As a leading member of the second generation of Kenyan writers, he has drawn from and expanded upon the themes laid out by compatriots and predecessors like NGUGI WA THIONG'O, Grace Ogot (b. 1930), and Leonard Kibera (b. 1942). Together with his novel and his children's stories (and more works in these genres may be expected from him), these dramatic writings have made I. one of the most significant voices in East African literature during the latter half of the 20th c.

FURTHER WORKS: *The Fourth Trial* (1972); *Kisses of Fate* (1972); *The Married Bachelor* (1973); *Betrayal in the City* (1976); *Game of Silence* (1977); *The Successor* (1979); *Man of Kafira* (1984); *Imbaalo Ya Vaana Va Magomere* (1986; *Magomere's Children*, 1995); *Aminata* (1988); *The Burning of Rags* (1989); *Shrine of Tears* (1993)

BIBLIOGRAPHY: Arden, R., and A. Bukenya, *F. I.: Betrayal in the City* (1978); Harb, A., "The Aesthetics of F. I.: A Contemporary Kenyan Playwright," *LitR*, 34 (Summer 1991): 571-82; Obyerodhyambo, O., "Of Betrayal in *Betrayal in the City*," *LitR*, 34 (Summer 1991): 583-88; Ruganda, J., *Telling the Truth Laughingly: The Politics of F. I.'s Drama* (1992); Kurtz, J. R., *Postcolonial African Writers: A Bio-Bibliographical Critical Sourcebook* (1998)

—J. ROGER KURTZ

INDIAN LITERATURE

Traditionally, India has been regarded more as a cohesive cultural entity than as a single political one, a "nation of confederate sovereignty"—with the cohesiveness of a "unity in diversity." In the past four centuries two foreign powers invaded India—the Moghuls and the British—established two empires, and left behind their contributions to the composite Indian culture.

Because of the numerous political changes in the Indian subcontinent—the variety of governing authorities in British India, the creation of the independent states of India and Pakistan in 1947, the declaration of Bangladesh as an independent nation in 1971—and the realignment of Indian states along linguistic lines and also across linguistic regions, it is difficult, or rather too early, narrowly to define what is state or national literature.

Dravidian, the oldest language family on the subcontinent, has produced four literary languages in the south: Tamil, the oldest; Kannada; and subsequently Telugu from Kannada, and Malayalam from Tamil. In the north the Dravidian dialects, coalescing with the dialects of Indo-Aryans, contributed to the growth of the language of composite Dravido-Aryan culture and became known as Sanskrit. A great many Dravidian dialects of northern India have survived in limited areas.

Sanskrit, the mother of Indo-Aryan languages, one of the oldest languages belonging to the Indo-European language family, and the classical language of Hinduism, gave rise to a number of dialects, which have become the modern Indo-Aryan languages of north India, viz., Assamese, Bengali, and Oriya in the east; Maithali, Hindi, Nepali, and Marathi in the center; Rajasthani, Gujarati, and Sindhi in the west; and Punjabi and Kashmiri in the north. (A dialect of Oriya transplanted to Sri Lanka became known as Sinhala.)

Sanskrit occupies a unique place in Indian culture because of its pervasive influence on all the Indian religions (including Buddhism, Jainism, Sikhism), and on all the Indian languages, both Indo-Aryan and Dravidian. Sanskrit is recognized as the language of subcontinental cultural unity and also as the source for new creative, critical, and research vocabulary, like Greek and Latin in European culture. Sanskrit, therefore, functions not only as a sacred language of a continuing tradition but also as a secular language of culture. It is being cultivated as a living official language in the form of Modern Sanskrit, like Hebrew in Israel.

When the imperial Moghuls and the imperial British superimposed Persian and English as the languages of the court and administration, Indians acquired proficiency in these studied second languages, first as a means for securing patronage and jobs, and second for producing extraterritorial literature.

Urdu, on the other hand, emerged as a mongrel speech of the soil in the 17th c. in the marketplaces and the military camps around Delhi. Urdu is basically Hindi in structure, Turkish and Persian in vocabulary, written in Arabic script. Because of the script, it is often erroneously identified as a "Muslim language." Urdu became the medium of Indo-Moghul synthesis and was vigorously cultivated for literary expression by 18th-c. Indians regardless of religion. During the freedom movement, however, Urdu became more and more subjected to Persian and Arabic influences by Muslim writers, thus making it less intelligible to non-Muslim Indians. Urdu is one of the official languages of India; it is also the state language of Pakistan.

In terms of languages and literature, the Indian subcontinent may be compared to the European continent. What is national literature in Europe is state literature in India, and what is national literature in India is the literature of the European continent.

Indian literature has been studied in terms of individual languages, and there are as many surveys as there are languages producing literature. In a nation that has eighteen major official languages used for administration as well as for literary writing, about a hundred minor languages, each spoken by over a million people, and two thousand dialects, the question of national literature becomes more of a composite idea than the usual philological approach to language and its literature.

The literary tradition in India has had a three-layered existence: there is regional literature in regional languages; pan-Indian literature in the dominant language of the civilization—Sanskrit, Pali, Tamil, or English—without reference to the regional language; and a continuously flourishing oral literature among the Adivasis, the tribal hill people, which in recent years has been studied as Adivasi literature (the proto-Dravidian, pre-Aryan peoples, scattered throughout the subcontinent, have not only been granted cultural autonomy but have also been encouraged to cultivate their arts and literature).

Among the major influences affecting the mental climate of the Indian subcontinent in the 20th c. are the "English education" and exposure to European culture; the internal movements for reformation and renascence; the impact of Marxist ideas and the Russian Revolution; the freedom movement and the traumatic experiences of Gandhi's nonviolent-resistance doctrine of Satyagraha (Sanskrit: "truth-fire" or "truth-force"), and, in recent decades, UNESCO's "Major Project for the Mutual Appreciation of Cultural Values of East and West."

Among all these movements perhaps no single one has been as overpowering as the "English education." It produced generations of Indians aware of the European tradition and alienated from their own culture. But this education also led to an intense nationalism in the early decades of the century. While English education has been a blessing in making possible instant communication of literary moods, attitudes, techniques, and values from European and American literature, the mental subordination has also prevented Indian creative minds from generating major literary movements of their own. Jawaharlal Nehru, who had the best of English educations, having reeducated himself in the British prisons during nine terms, saw that Indians were so mentally conditioned that they perceived the world with "English eyes and English prejudices." Some writers are now beginning to see that a true renascence can only come to India not through imitation but through assimilation within the consciousness of national tradition.

Rabindranath Tagore

With the award of the Nobel Prize for literature in 1913, the Bengali Rabindranath TAGORE, who also wrote in English, became known internationally as the major literary figure of modern India. He was the first Asian writer to receive that prize.

At the beginning of the 20th c., India produced two outstanding men of striking personalities who resurrected distinct aspects of the Indian culture and ways of life: Gandhi, with his spiritual austerity and renunciation, ventured into social reform and practical action to achieve political independence; while Tagore, asserting the intellectual aristocracy of the Upanishadic tradition, aimed at personal, intellectual, and artistic freedom.

During his long and active life, Tagore was prodigious in his literary creation. In his poems he dramatized man's quest to understand the spirit within and its relation to the Supreme Spirit in the manner of the *rishis*, or sages, of the Upanishads, breathing the mystics' "divine frenzy." The spirit of humanism pervades his plays. His fiction presents conflicts arising from the changing mores within the traditional orthodox society, but he is never without compassion for the individual.

Tagore became an institution in India, like Goethe in Europe. Non-Bengali Indians read Tagore in translation in other Indian languages or in English. Yet there did not emerge a distinct Tagore school in literature. The influence of Tagore lies in his quickening of the literary impulse in other Indian writers, his serving as a catalytic guru who gave others confidence to write about Indian life and portray Indian values and conflicts. Even Indo-English writers who were slavishly copying European authors began to assert their identity, taking cues from Tagore's bold independence. Tagore's romanticism, however, soon gave way to the new wave of social realism that began to affect the literary scene in India in the 1930s, in the form of the Progressive movement.

Poetry

The spirit of nationalism generated in the 19th c. pervaded Indian poetry in the early decades of the 20th. Following Tagore's enlightened nationalism, many poets expressed deeply felt patriotic sentiments and perceptions of national ideals in varying moods and shades. Outstanding among them were Subramania BHARATI, Vallathol Narayana MENON, Sarojini NAIDU, Muhammad IQBAL, and Aurobindo GHOSE.

The Tamil poet Bharati's patriotism merged with his mysticism. In his poetry, he moved freely from the love of Mother India to the worship of the "Mother of Livingkind". Patriotism and freedom became essentially a state of being in a dynamic person, aware of spiritual possibilities. Some of Bharati's lyrics also depict the perennial values of the household, the tender graces of childhood, and the delicate beauty of womanhood.

Vallathol Narayana Menon, Malayalam poet and critic, was a classical scholar steeped in Sanskrit poetry. His patriotic feelings developed into a deep and abiding love for ancient Indian culture and its poetry. It was his mission to make the classical vision part of contemporary consciousness. Along with his associates, Kumaran Asan (1873–1924) and Ullur Parameswara Aiyar (1877–1949), he ushered in the modern era in Malayalam poetry. His poems move from a romantic to a realistic approach to life.

Sarojini Naidu, educated in India and England, was one of the most gifted Indo-English poets India produced in the 20th c. Acquiring felicity of expression in English, her third language, she used it with consummate skill, creating exquisite lyrics marked by haunting rhythms and lilting Oriental melodies. Like her predecessor Toru Dutt (1856–1877), who died before she could fulfill her promise, in her early life Sarojini Naidu demonstrated how a young woman could write poetry with ease and emotion and still be Indian, whereas most Indo-English poets up to her time were simply imitating British poets. Critics found in her early verse poetic qualities in "heaped measure" and praised her poems for enriching the English language. In her last volume, *The Broken Wing* (1917), her lyricism bordered on mystical ecstasy. Although she lived thirty-two years after this volume was published, she did not write verse during the long political struggle of that era, in which she was very active. Apparently she realized that for true poetic creation one needs to write in one's mother tongue.

Muhammad Iqbal, a Muslim poet writing in Urdu and Persian, is regarded by Pakistanis as their national poet. His early poems, written in Urdu, celebrated Indian nationalism and the freedom movement. These poems, written before he left Punjab for England, echo the sentiments and vocabulary of the Persian Sufi mystics and the English romantic poets. Iqbal's European visit restructured his thinking. He discovered that European nationalism resulted in jingoistic adventures into other people's land and that colonialism gave rise to intense economic monopoly and rivalry. Disillusioned, he turned to theological nationalism, claiming that Islam was the answer for the people of southwestern Asia. To make his pan-Islamic dream known to other Muslim countries, he abandoned Urdu and began writing in Persian.

Among 20th-c. Indian poets, Aurobindo Ghose (later Sri Aurobindo) alone is a true Vedic seer-poet; he resurrected a whole way of life from the substratum of Indian culture, a way of life in which literary expression became only incidental to mystic visions and enlightenment. Because he spent his early years in England, insulated from Indian schools, culture, and language, English became, for all practical purposes, his mother tongue.

In the 1890s Ghose felt that the Indian freedom movement was misled by a feeble group of empire-supporting Indian politicians who rather timidly advocated some moderate demands for reform within the colonial system. The British considered all his writings as seditious. During one of his imprisonments, he experienced mystical visions, which completely altered his attitude to life. In French-controlled Pondicherry he became a master yogi and established an ashram. In his writings Sri Aurobindo formulated a metaphysics and a system of spiritual discipline that he called "purna yoga" (integral yoking), or reintegrating experience and human personality.

He also wrote five plays in blank verse, but these are more dramatic poems than plays. In all these works his major theme is that love is divine and has redemptive power, which, he predicts, will one day deliver the world. In his later works Sri Aurobindo developed a technique for his visionary poems, which he discussed in *The Future Poetry* (1953)—something bordering on telepathic communication of meaning through rhythmic sound in concentrated imagery, like the Vedic mantras.

Apart from the major pan-Indian poets, there were many other regional poets, who, absorbing the various influences coming to India in the 1930s, began to express themselves in their own languages in a variety of moods and techniques. Although they are too numerous to cover comprehensively, some significant ones deserve to be singled out.

Early 20th-c. Hindi literature was dominated by the *Chhayavada* movement, or Indian romanticism, with an attitude of wonder at nature and with Vedantic synthesis as a theme. Progressive ideas were ushered in by the *Pragativada* movement, or Indian realism, which pointed to the ruthless amorality of nature and sympathized with the sufferings of the exploited and downtrodden. The pioneers of the *Chhayavada* movement were Suryakant Tripathi (pseud.: Nirala, 1896–1961) and Sumitranand Pant (b. 1900). Although the novelist PREMCHAND gave *Pragati-vada* a progressive, liberal slant, it soon became the closed shop of an explicitly Marxist-oriented group, Yashpal (b. 1904), Nagarjun (b. 1911), and Rameshawar Shukla (pseud.: Anchal, b. 1915) are some of the leading writers of this group.

Mohan Singh's (b. 1905) early poems in Punjabi were considered progressive; his later poetry has a definite Marxist stamp. Amrita Pritam (b. 1919), a successful woman poet, is popular on both sides of the India-Pakistan border in the Punjab. Her works are remarkable for their spontaneity and musicality.

A group of Marathi poets set out to reclaim poetry from the extravagances into which it had fallen and to make it speak to everyday issues. A. R. Deshpande (pseud.: Anil, b. 1901) advocated free verse to liberate Marathi poetry from its stiltedness. B. S. Mardekar (1909–1956), influenced by ELIOT and POUND, wrote sensitive poetry expressing the bleak life of a frustrated man.

In eastern India, the "people's poets" writing in Oriya, Sachidananda Routray (b. 1916) and Anant Patnaik (b. 1913), were mouthpieces of the Progressive Party's attitudes and values. Writing in Bengali, Buddhadev Bose (b. 1908) called for Westernization as a means of modernization, while the more radical Sudhindranath Dutt (1901–1960), who considered himself a "nihilist," advocated free inquiry into all values, traditional or modern. Kazi Nazrul ISLAM began his literary career with short stories, but gained fame with his heroic poems and popular songs glorifying the freedom movement. With his uncompromising opposition to oppression and injustice, he became a "people's poet" in both western and eastern Bengal (now Bangladesh).

The swing to realism in Telugu poetry was led by Srirangam Srinivas Rao (pseud.: Sri Sri, b. 1910). He had no admiration for the Taj Mahal, for instance, but saw it only as a monument to forced labor and exploitation of artists. Dattatreya Ramachandra Bendre (b. 1896), a pioneer in modern Kannada poetry, drew on folklore and traditional ballads in his approach to social realism. In Malayalam, G. Shankar Kurup (b. 1901) combined symbolism with social realism.

Indo-English poets experimented with a variety of techniques taken over from British and American poetry. Outstanding among them are Nissim EZEKIEL and the outspoken woman poet Kamala Das (b. 1934). Most assertive among the champions of Indo-English literature is P. Lal (b. 1928), with his Writers' Workshop in Calcutta.

Modern Sanskrit poetry is showing vitality. Important achievements are Jitendra Nath Bhattacharya's (dates n.a.) two short eulogies on Gandhi and Tagore, G. C. Jhala's (dates n.a.) elegies and descriptive verses, and Mathuranatha Kavi Sastri's (dates n.a.) poems about nature and modern technology. Some Sanskrit poets have revived classical subjects, while others have written on contemporary political events. In *Bharati gita* (19??; song of India) Lady Lakshmi Ammal (dates n.a.) calls on Mother India to energize her children to a fruitful renascence. In *Satyagraha gita* (1932; song of satyagraha) Kshama Rao (dates n.a.) romantically treats political developments in graceful epic measures. What is most significant in these works is that Modern Sanskrit—having achieved a flexibility, a style distinct from classical diction, imagery, and mood—is emerging as a secular language capable of expressing modern aesthetic concerns.

Drama

Modern drama in India has had to compete with regional popular and folk theater. In some states folk theater has an unbroken tradition of dramatizing events from the Indian classics, sacred and secular; these dramatic presentations are like the miracle and mystery plays of medieval Europe. Most often they are unscripted and depend upon the ability of the actors to develop and sustain the well-known story through extemporaneous dialogue. These plays frequently include song, dance, and mime. In Kerala and Karnataka there are traditional dance-dramas, called Kathakali and Yakshagana respectively, with elaborate costuming, skillful dancing, and stylized acting. In states like Mysore and Orissa, where royalty formerly gave patronage to classical learning, many classical plays in the original language or in modern translations appealed to sophisticated audiences.

When the modern Indian theater emerged in the early decades of the 20th c., it evinced a strong passion for nationalism and a still stronger zeal for social reform. Such a transformation was precipitated by the spread of English education, and through it, the study of European drama.

Rabindranath Tagore dominated the Bengali stage early in the century, with comedies, tragedies, farces, symbolic plays, and operalike dance dramas. He also introduced new techniques of acting. The spirit of humanism pervades his plays. The Bengali dramatist Mukunda Das (dates n.a.) introduced the Swadeshi political philosophy, which called for India to produce its own goods rather than being merely a market for industrialized countries, into one of his plays, *Jatra-wala* (1905; pilgrim). Saratchandra CHATTERJI'S dramatizations of some of his novels were popular on the Bengali stage because of their acute social criticism.

The Bengali theater influenced the neighboring Assamese and Oriya stages. Lakshminath Bezbarua (1868–1938), who married into the Tagore family, brought Tagore's innovations to Assamese drama. His romantic plays depict feudal ways of life. Jyoti Prasad Agarwal (dates n.a.) wrote lyrical plays about romantic love, incorporating music and dance. Writing in Oriya, Godavaris Mishra (1888–1956) and Ashwani Kumar Ghosh (dates n.a.) introduced modern techniques and themes. They turned from mythological stories to social, historical, and biographical subjects. Kalicharan Patnaik (b. 1900), a musician and poet, wrote lyrical plays.

In western India, the commercial city of Bombay generated a lively audience, which helped activate the Gujarati and Marathi theaters. A powerful Gujarati dramatist is the prolific Manilal Tribhuvandas (pseud.: Pagal, dates n.a.), who wrote about a hundred plays, dealing mainly with social problems, filled with earthy humor. Umashankar Jethalal Joshi (b. 1911), in a series of one-act plays, depicted the variety of Gujarati village life.

Many successful plays were written by enterprising Marathi dramatists. K. P. Khadilkar (pseud.: Kakasaheb, 1872–1948) established a dramatic society in Poona in 1905, for which he wrote many plays. In *Keechaka-vada* (1910; the slaying of Keechaka) Khadilkar allegorically satirized the Governor-General, Lord Curzon. The play was banned by the British authorities but was revived by the Congress ministry in 1937. Khadilkar's powerful historical plays were eclipsed by the musical plays of Shreepad Krishna Kolhatkar (1871–1934), who combined satirical comedy and romantic tangles with avowed social criticism. The Marathi stage reached maturity in the plays of Bhargavaram Vithal Varerkar (pseud.: Mama Varerkar, 1883–1964). He was a tireless experimenter in theme and technique; he dealt with such diverse topics as politics, the evils of the dowry system, the forced conversion by

Christian missionaries, and the problems of the untouchables. His later plays are in a more realistic mode. Motiram Gajanan Rangnekar (b. 1907) introduced elegant drawing-room comedies to the Marathi stage, with lively dialogue and only a few songs.

Urdu is deficient in drama, since the language was generally a vehicle for Muslim sentiment and there is no Islamic dramatic tradition. After 1930, when Indian dramatists started using social and political themes for plays, Urdu writers saw the potential of the theater. Much Urdu talent, however, was channeled into the more popular and lucrative film and radio industries after the establishment of the broadcasting system in 1935.

In the absence of a vigorous dramatist, the Hindi stage had languished. In the early 20th c. some experiments were made in verse and fantasy plays, but without much success. Among dramatists who later attempted to gain an audience are Upendranath Ask (b. 1910), Ramkumar Varma (b. 1905), Lakshminarayan Mishra (b. 1903), and Bharatabhushan Agarwal (b. 1919). Mohan RAKESH, after publishing a number of novels and short stories, turned to the theater and wrote controversial but innovative plays: *Asadh ka ek din* (1958; *A Day in Ashadh*, 1969) and *Lahon ke rajhans* (1962; *The Swans of the Great Waves*, 1973) treat classical themes, while *Adhe adhure* (1969; *Halfway House*, 1971) portrays the disintegration of traditional Indian family life under the impact of independence and an industrial economy.

T. P. Kailasam (1884–1945) was an innovator on the Kannada stage. He used humor to expose current social prejudices. Kailasam also wrote plays in English, dramatizing events from the epics. Verse plays by the poets D. R. Bendre and Govinda Pai (b. 1883) were enthusiastically produced by amateur dramatic groups. In recent times Girish Ragunath Karnad (b. 1938), a Rhodes scholar at Oxford (1960–63), returned to India to write for the Kannada stage. He has been in the forefront of the New Drama in India. His *Yayati* (1961; Yayati) is an EXISTENTIALIST play retelling an Indian classical legend in terms of contemporary life and dealing with the problem of individual responsibility. *Tughlaq* (1964; Tughlaq) explores the paradox of the idealistic 14th-c. sultan of Delhi, Muhammad bin Tughlaq; his rule in north India became a spectacular failure, but his ideas were nevertheless far in advance of his time. The novelist Kota Shivaram KARANTH has also made important contributions to the Kannada stage.

Sanskrit dramatists were not far behind in presenting contemporary conflicts and concerns. *Manoharam dinam* (1941; lovely day) by A. R. Hebare (dates n.a.) presents school-boys maneuvering to make the principal declare a school holiday. Contemporary women's domestic problems were dramatized in *Aranya-rodana* (1949; forest roaring) by Sita Devi (dates n.a.). Tiru Venkatacharya (dates n.a.) presents the conflict of an irate officer at home and in his office in *Amarsha mahima* (1951; sway of temper). Surendra Mohan Panchatirtha's (dates n.a.) play *Vanik-suta* (1955; merchant's daughter) depicts the wooing of a young rich widow by a Hindu and a Buddhist. The theme of romantic love was used by Sundersena Sarma (dates n.a.) in *Prema vijaya* (1943; triumph of love). C. Venkataramanayya (dates n.a.) composed a long allegorical play *Jiva-sanjivani nataka* (1949; drama of life after life) on the efficacy of Ayurvedic medicine.

There is a paucity of good actable Indo-English plays, although many writers have written English plays in both verse and prose. Harindranath Chattopadhyaya (b. 1898), brother of Sarojini Naidu, wrote a number of plays on contemporary life, collected in *Five Plays* (1937). His *Siddhartha: The Man of Peace* (1956) is a historical drama about the Buddha.

The dancer Bharati Sarabhai's (b. 1912) first play, *The Well of the People* (1943), is a symbolic, poetic pageant. A widow, unable to make a pilgrimage to the holy places in the Himalayas, decides to spend all her savings on a well for the *harijans* (untouchables) in the village. Her second play, *Two Women* (1952), portrays the dual personalities of each woman—what she is and what she would like to become and contrasts the modern and traditional aspects of their lives.

S. Fyzee Rahamin's (dates n.a.) play *Daughter of Ind* (1940) treats the love of an untouchable girl for her master, an idealistic Englishman. Pratap Sharma's (b. 1939) *A Touch of Brightness* (1968) portrays the degradation and corruption in the infamous red-light district in Bombay called "The Cages." Asif Currimbhoy (b. 1928) experimented with a variety of techniques. *The Tourist Mecca* (1961) portrays star-crossed lovers who in the end passively accept separate continued existence. Currimbhoy frequently blends the satirical and the serious.

Fiction

Fiction is the dominant genre in 20th-c. Indian literature. It is also, unlike in Europe, one of the oldest, going back as far as the 4th c. B.C.

With the exposure to European fiction, Indian writers adopted its forms and techniques and produced innumerable volumes of short stories and novels. At the beginning of the 20th c. fiction writers for the most part patronizingly depicted social situations. But in the 1930s, social realism began to take hold, and the majority of Indian writers of fiction may be classified as "social chroniclers," exposing a decadent society emerging from feudalism into the industrial age.

Premchand popularized social realism in India. He wrote in Urdu until 1914, then switched to Hindi. He was at his best in his many short stories. In the novel *Godan* (1936; *The Gift of a Cow*, 1968) he describes the problems of peasant India with striking realism. Premchand is regarded as the GORKY of India because of his reformist zeal.

Kota Shivaram Karanth used social realism to present the life of tribal people in the south-west coastal region of Karnataka; he also wrote many lyrical novels in Kannada.

The fictional representation of tribal life was carried forward by Gopinath MOHANTY. In his novels and short stories in Oriya, he uses a rich and powerful folk idiom to depict the common people against Orissa's picturesque setting.

In Bengal, writers like Saratchandra Chatterji abandoned Tagore's sweet music of humanity to portray realistically urban middle-class characters. Bibhuti-Bhusan BANERJI concentrated his vision on a Bengali rural family in stark poverty in his haunting novel *Pather panchali* (1929; *Pather Panchali: Song of the Road*, 1968). Manik Bandopadhyaya (1908–1956), born in East Bengal (now Bangladesh), presents such nontraditional characters as cheaters and the sexually frustrated. *Putul nacher itikath* (1936; dance of the dolls) depicts characters who are thoroughly disillusioned. *Padma nadir majhi* (1936; *Padma River Boatman*, 1973) portrays the life of boatmen, fishermen, palm-tappers, weavers, and peasants.

The most aggressive champion of social realism is Mulk Raj ANAND, who in his tremendous output of fiction in English has proved himself an indefatigable polemicist. He won early recognition with *Untouchable* (1935) and *Coolie* (1936). Focusing on the destitute and downtrodden, Anand exposes social injustices, and shows great compassion for the unfortunate victims.

Another powerful writer who has achieved international fame is the Malayalam Thakazhi Sivasankara Pillai (b. 1914); with great skill he portrays varied life styles in the state of Kerala. *Tottiyte makan* (1947; *The Scavenger's Son*, 1970) deals with three generations of scavengers, attacking the social degradation to which they have been subjected. *Rantitangazhi* (1949; *Two Measures of Rice*, 1967), which established Pillai as the foremost novelist in Malayalam, presents the struggles and humiliations of members of outcaste communities who work in the rice fields of Kuttanad. In his novels of maturity Pillai abandons the overriding concern with social realism to concentrate on individuals caught in the web of social conflicts. His most outstanding novel, *Chemmeen* (1956; *Chemmeen*, 1962), portrays the love of a daughter of a Hindu fisherman and a son of a Muslim fish merchant. Social realism is tempered by romance and a deeper human interest.

P. Vaithialingam Akilandam (pseud.: Akilon, b. 1923), writing in Tamil, is another prolific writer of both short stories and novels. His novel *Pon malar* (1978; *Flower of Gold*, 1978) tells a touching story of a woman's awesome capacity for self-sacrifice.

Expatriate Indian writers, writing in English, seem to telescope Indian life and its varied conflicts and concerns. Balachandra Rajan (b. 1920), in such novels as *The Dark Dancer* (1958) and *Too Long in the West* (1961), deals mainly with experiences of returning Indians in the process of being reabsorbed into Indian life. John A. Karkala's (b. 1923) *Nightless Nights* (1974) and *Joys of Jayanagara* (1980) are about the problem of rootlessness of Indians living in two worlds. Arthur S. Lall's (b. 1911) *House at Adampur* (1956) and *Seasons of Jupiter* (1958) explore the problem of cultural identity.

A noted writer, G. V. DESANI, displays a quaint sense of humor and even quainter style in *All About H. Hatterr* (1948). His bold experimentation with language, reminiscent of JOYCE, annoyed some and delighted many. Another successful novelist, Kamala MARKANDAYA, has attempted an East-West synthesis in works such as *Nectar in a Sieve* (1954), *Some Inner Fury* (1955), *A Silence of Desire* (1960), and *A Handful of Rice* (1966).

The Gandhian revolution was a traumatic experience on the subcontinent, and no writer was left untouched by it. Although the movement was based on the ideals of nonviolence, it was bedeviled by religious conflict, and the partition in 1947 was accompanied by bloody riots and massacres in which millions were killed and millions more left homeless. Both the idealism of the freedom movement and the passions of partition were portrayed in numerous works of fiction. Anant Gopal Sheorey (b. 1911), writing in Hindi, produced an outstanding novel, *Jwalamukhi* (1956; *Volcano*, 1965), which deals with the convulsions of August 1942 with Gandhi's "Quit India" movement; he movingly depicts the sufferings of a great nation on the verge of freedom. Birendra Kumar Bhattacharya's (b. 1924) *Iyanuingam* (1961; *Iyanuingam*), written in Assamese, presents the volatile situation in eastern India during World War II. Nanak Singh's (b. 1897) Punjabi novel *Ik miyan do talwar* (1961; two swords in one sheath) describes the Ghadar Party, a revolutionary group organized by young Sikhs to throw off the British yoke. The novel re-creates a time when Hindus, Muslims, and Sikhs were united against the common foreign enemy.

The period leading up to and following partition is vividly portrayed in Khushwant SINGH'S novel of horror, written in English, *Mano Majra* (1956; reprinted as *Train to Pakistan*, 1961), Raja RAO'S *Kanthapura* (1938), also written in English, on the other hand, presents a much richer cultural life underneath the sufferings during the nationalist strivings of the 1930s, pointing to the redemptive nature of the suffering. Govind Malhi's (b. 1921)

Sindhi novels, from *Ansoo* (1952; tears) to *Desi sen kajan* (1963; one must marry in one's fold), depict the life of Sindhi refugees after the partition and their attempt to rehabilitate themselves.

One of the most delightful writers among Indian novelists, whose strength lies in his humor, is R. K. NARAYAN, who writes in English. In his short stories and novels he depicts the world of an imaginary south-Indian town, Malgudi. Among his fine later novels are *Waiting for the Mahatma* (1955), *The Guide* (1958), which was also filmed, *The Man-Eater of Malgudi* (1961), *The Sweet-Vendor* (1967), and *A Painter of Signs* (1976).

Shripad Narayan Pendse (b. 1913), a Marathi novelist, portrays the picturesque Konkan coastal region from Bombay to south of Goa and creates memorable comic characters—quarrelsome social misfits who refuse to submit to conventions. Pendse is a feminist; his women demand the right to love and be loved, rather than being mere appendages to their mates. His most popular novel is *Garambicha Bapu* (1952; *Wild Bapu of Garambi*, 1969), dealing with an eccentric old village man.

Ahmed ALI started writing short stories in Urdu but later switched to English for his novels. *Twilight in Delhi* (1940) portrays the decadence and decline of a Muslim aristocratic family in Delhi at the turn of the century. *Ocean of Night* (1964) is a haunting romantic tale, depicting the life and values of the declining wealthy leisure class and the rise of the newly rich, with their lack of culture.

Vishnu Sakharam KHANDEKAR, a Marathi writer, attempts to retell legends of the past in modern terms. His outstanding work of fiction, which powerfully retells an episode from the *Mahabharata*, the ancient Sanskrit epic, is *Yayati* (1959; *Yayati*, 1978).

Raja Rao has achieved honor among Indian novelists for being both profoundly rooted in the Indian tradition and at the same time aware of the cultural springs of the Western tradition. Writing in Kannada, French, and English, he belongs to the intellectual and artistic tradition of the scholar-poet, producing lyrical fiction in the manner of metaphysical fables. *Comrade Kirillov* (1976) is a fine example of his distinctive qualities.

In recent decades many novelists writing in English have produced accomplished work. Manohar MALGONKAR, in portraying Indian feudal aristocracy or former British military officials, shows a nostalgic fondness for the values of the vanishing past. *A Bend in the Ganges* (1964) deals with the idealism of the freedom movement and the tragedy of partition. Bhabani Bhattacharya (b. 1906) has successfully portrayed contemporary social conflicts: *So Many Hungers* (1947) shows the havoc caused by the Bengal famine of 1943–44; *He Who Rides the Tiger* (1954) is a rather vicious satirical portrait of a bogus holy man.

A new trend in Indo-English literature is the rise of women writers. Among the novelists, two are outstanding. Anita DESAI's first novel, *Cry, the Peacock* (1963), presents a young Indian woman of artistic sensibilities in conflict with her older, worldly husband. In *Voices in the City* (1965) she takes up the interior desolation of contemporary Indian youth who are abandoning traditional values. Kamala Das, also a poet, writes in Malayalam as well as in English. *My Story* (1976), her unorthodox autobiography, written in poetic prose, shocked and dazzled the Indian literary world because of its sensuality. It was followed by the novel *Alphabet of Lust* (1976), about the adventures of a married woman poet in the world of politics; it presents uninhibited ideas about male-female relations.

Another woman writer, who during her residence in India created fiction with the felicity of an insider, is Ruth Prawer

JHABVALA. Born in Germany of Jewish parents and raised and educated in England, she lived in India for some time after marrying an Indian architect. In her novels she mirrors Indian life in Delhi, portraying with irony and brilliant satire some of the social conflicts of Indians as well as expatriate British and European characters lingering in India in quixotic dreams. Jhabvala has shown an extraordinary ability to see two worlds from an ambivalent position. Yet because of her background she cannot be regarded as an Indo-Anglian writer. Rather, she is an outstanding contemporary representative of a distinct line of Anglo-Indian writers, including Rudyard KIPLING, E. M. FORSTER, and Paul SCOTT, who wrote of the Indian experience from a non-Indian point of view.

Indian literature in the composite sense is still evolving, mainly because the concept of a truly national literature is yet to develop. The paucity of translations, both within India among the various languages and abroad, has been a hindrance. The Sahitya Akademi (National Academy of Letters) in New Delhi has launched a systematic translation program and has encouraged a comparative approach to the literature of India, and its efforts may produce a more balanced presentation of the major and significant works among the mass of writing that is produced every decade. Additionally, UNESCO's translation program has helped to popularize some of the major authors from the various language regions of India. In view of the complexities of the literary scene, a survey of 20th-c. Indian literature is unavoidably somewhat limited.

BIBLIOGRAPHY: Kumarappan, B., ed., *The Indian Literature of Today: A Symposium* (1947); Publication Division, Government of India, *Indian Drama* (1956); Publication Division, Government of India, *Literature in Modern Indian Languages* (1957); Sahitya Akademi, *Contemporary Indian Literature: A Symposium* (1957; rev. ed., 1959); Kabir, H., *Modern Indian Literature* (1959); Sen, S., *History of Bengali Literature* (1960); Mansinha, M., *History of Oriya Literature* (1962); Srinivasa Iyengar, K. R., *Indian Writing in English* (1962); Chatterji, S., *Languages and Literatures of Modern India*; (1963); Bakhtiyar, I., ed., *The Novel in Modern India* (1964); Barua, B. K., *History of Assamese Literature* (1964); Sadiq, M., *A History of Urdu Literature* (1964); Derrett, M. E., *The Modern Indian Novel* (1966); Dwivedi, R. A., *A Critical History of Hindi Literature* (1966); Kabir, H., *The Bengali Novel* (1968); Kripalani, K., *Modern Indian Literature: A Panoramic Glimpse* (1968); Sitapati, G. V., *History of Telugu Literature* (1968); Clark, T. W., ed., *The Novel in India: Its Birth and Development* (1970); Chaitanya, K., *A History of Malayalam Literature* (1971); Dimock, E. C., Jr., et al., eds., *The Literatures of India: An Introduction* (1974); Machwe, P., and E. Chelishew, eds., *Problems of Modern Indian Literature* (1975); Williams, H. M., *Studies in Modern Indian Fiction in English* (2 vols., 1975); Machwe, P., *Four Decades of Indian Literature* (1976); Machwe, P., *Modernity and Contemporary Indian Literature* (1977); Singh, R. S., *The Indian Novel in English* (1977); Williams, H. M., *Indo-Anglian Literature, 1800–1970: A Survey* (1977); special Indian issue, *RNL*, 10 (1979)

—JOHN B. ALPHONSO-KARKALA

Postcolonial Indian Literature

Not unlike their counterparts in other excolonial, Third World countries, Indian writers have been preoccupied with two major concerns since the country gained freedom in 1947. First is the profound sense of disillusionment in independence, which, many Indians believed, would usher in a halcyon age in which all things would be better than when the British were there. In fact, they have not been. This disappointment, especially among the educated urban classes, has sometimes given way to anger, alienation, despair, and even violence. Second, many writers address the dilemma of modernity versus tradition: What, they ask, should they accept or reject from the modern industrialized West as part of their own value system, and what from their own traditional cultural heritage should they retain or discard? Both themes are found in varying degrees in the dozen major literatures of India and in a number of the minor ones as well.

Fiction

Writers in India's national language, Hindi, such as Mohan RAKESH, Rajendra Yadav (b. 1929), and Kamaleshwar (b. 1932), ushered in the *nai kahani* (new story) movement during the 1950s and 1960s. Influenced by EXISTENTIALISM, it focused in both novels and short stories on urban, middle-class, often educated, characters who experience the world as incomprehensible and meaningless, and whose limited choices invariably turn out to be the wrong ones.

At the other end of the socioeconomic spectrum, village-based regional literature flourishes throughout India. Referred to by various names in different languages, it is called *anchalik* literature (*anchal* is the end of a woman's sari used to cover her head) in North India and concentrates on villagers—peasants and farmers—coping with the encroachments of modern technology, urbanization, and government into their lives. One of its leading exponents is the Hindi novelist Phanishwarnath Renu (b. 1921), whose voluminous *Maila anchal* (1954; soiled anchal) is an outstanding example of this type of writing. A strong anchalik movement is also found in Bengal.

One of the most controversial yet highly acclaimed postindependence novels is U. R. Ananthamurthy's (b. 1932) *Samskara* (1965; *Samskara: A Rite for a Dead Man*, 1976). Written in Kannada and set in a tiny southern Indian village community of highly orthodox Brahmins, it details the morally vacuous religious values and traditions of believers who, in pursuit of the subtle, often arcane, practices of their religion, have lost the true meaning of their faith.

In Tamil fiction T. Janakiraman (b. 1921) is a major figure. He began writing from a Marxist point of view, but rejected this ideology in the early 1960s to embrace a broader humanism. His works deal with themes from everyday middle-class life in small towns in Tamilnadu. He is especially concerned with changing family relationships, particularly between spouses and between parents and children.

Punjabi writer Gulzar Singh Sandhu (b. 1934) has published four major collections of short stories, most recently *Amar katha* (1979; immortal story). Dealing with both urban and rural themes, he depicts the conflicts and divided loyalties that face India's small but economically powerful Sikh community.

Poetry

A number of modernist, antiestablishment movements, often called *akavita* (nonpoetry), have emerged since the 1960s, several of them finding their roots in radical left-wing politics. In 1962

Allen GINSBERG made his first visit to India, which turned out to be important not only to him but to large numbers of young Indian writers as well. In Bengali, fledgling poets embraced his thinking, imitated his poetry, and formed the so-called "Hungry Generation," college-educated but unemployed writers in their twenties whose works reflect a sense of futility, disillusionment, and anger at the political and literary establishments. Five of these poets, notably Shaileshwar Ghose (b. 1938), Subimal Basak (b. 1939), and Malay Roy Choudhury (b. 1939), were arrested and tried on charges of obscenity.

Marathi *dalit* (oppressed) literature is the revolutionary writing of the downtrodden Untouchables. Foremost among this group is the poet Namdeo Dasal (b. 1949), who grew up in a Bombay slum. The title of his major work, *Golpitha* (1973; Golpitha), refers to one of Bombay's red-light districts, famous for its "cages" in which the prostitutes ply their trade. It contains his best-known poems, angry, surrealistic descriptions of the plight of those who live in this area. Other important poets in this movement are Daya Pawar (b. 1935) and Trymbak Sapkale (b. 1930).

Naxalite writers, whose political sympathies support in some degree the terrorist activities of a small, violent group of Maoist communists formed in the Naxalbari district of northern Bengali in 1970, are also found in many of India's languages. Notable among these are the Digambara poets of Telugu. The name of this latter group literally means "sky-clad," a reference to a type of ancient Jain monk who went about naked, having the sky as his clothing. However, the group preferred to translate the term into English as "bare-assed." Politically and literarily iconoclastic, many of these writers were at odds with the law. One of their most radical members, Baddam Bhaskara Reddy (pseud.: Cherabanda Raju, 1939–1982), was hounded by the authorities even as he lay dying of brain cancer. His "Vandemataram" (1970; hail to thee, mother) is a scathing parody of the poem of the same name (1882), India's first nationalist anthem, by Bankimk Chandra Chatterji (1838–1894).

Always quick to react to political events in their country, poets did so vocally when in 1975 Prime Minister Indira Gandhi suspended civil liberties, ushering in the so-called "Emergency" period, which continued until 1977. Perhaps no single event in India's recent history, save the assassination in 1948 of Mohandas Karamchand Gandhi has produced an equivalent literary response. Many of the best poems from the major languages have been collected by American poet John Oliver Perry (b. 1938) in *Voices of Emergency* (1983).

Munibur Rahman (b. 1924) is an outstanding example of a contemporary Urdu poet. Initially influenced by Marxist ideology, his poetry has moved beyond its ideological beginnings and reveals a poet concerned about the large but especially the small anomalies of the human condition. His two collections are *Bazid* (1965, expanded 1988; visitation) and *Shahr-e ghamnam* (1983; the obscure city).

Among India's many English-language poets, Nissim EZEKIEL and Jayanta Mahapatra (b. 1928) are notable. The latter, a college physics teacher by profession, received the English literary prize of India's Sahitya Akademi in 1981 for his long poem *Relationships*. The author of eight collections, he is widely published in both India and in the West. He also edited *Chandrabhaga*, India's most important English-language poetry journal.

Women writers are extensively represented in postindependence Indian literature. Urdu novelist and short-story writer Qurratulain HYDER has long been a major feminist voice in Indian literature. In Gujarati, Pann Naik (b. 1938) has emerged as a major feminist

force in poetry. Writing in Philadelphia, she has produced two major volumes of poems, *Pravesh* (1979; entrance) and *Philadelphia* (1981), which have attracted a great deal of critical attention, some of it negative from a conservative, male-dominated literary establishment.

Expatriate Writers

Living in Great Britain and the U.S., and writing in English, expatriate authors have made major contributions to Indian literature, though some of them would prefer to be treated as British or American. In fiction, Salman RUSHDIE, who lives in Great Britain, is the best known and, in many ways, one of the most innovative and noteworthy writers in this category. Bharati MUKHERJEE has treated the theme of biculturalism and marginality in her novels *The Tiger's Daughter* (1972), *Wife* (1975), and *Jasmine* (1989) and in several short-story collections.

In poetry, University of Chicago professor A. K. Ramanujan (1929-1993), author of three collections, *The Striders* (1966), *Relations* (1971), and *Second Sight* (1986), is known for his highly visual images sculptured with precision and concrete details.

Other notable writers include poet Meena Alexander (b. 1951), whose collections, including *House of a Thousand Doors* (1988), have been critically acclaimed. Vikram Seth's (b. 1952) *The Golden Gate* (1986), "a novel in verse" about California yuppies, cleverly utilizes many traditional English poetic forms. Hanif Kureishi (b. 1954), who lives in London, has written a number of theatrical and screen plays, including *My Beautiful Laundrette* (1985) and *Sammy and Rosie Get Laid* (1987). His novel *The Buddha of Suburbia* (1990), like his plays and film scripts, portrays the expatriate experience with irreverence and honesty. Shashi Tharoor (b. 1956), who works at the United Nations, received the 1990 Commonwealth Writer's Prize for *The Great Indian Novel* (1990), an imaginative and humorous retelling of modern Indian history using some of the style and form of the Indian epic *Mahabharata*.

Scholars frequently debate whether an entity known as "Indian literature" truly exists. Recent political events, which often prefigure much of the country's literary activity, suggest that, instead of developing a single, integrated literary tradition, India is becoming balkanized and, politically and literarily, may end up resembling Europe.

In the past several decades India has undergone several dramatic transformations, a major result of which has been a widespread, rapid accumulation of a great deal of political and a modest amount of economic power by India's lower classes, which are developing into a burgeoning new Indian middle class. This phenomenon, in turn, has fanned a surge in the rise of religious fundamentalism among the country's former privileged elites, especially high-caste Hindus. Additionally, feminism in its multifarious guises has become a distinguishing feature of contemporary Indian life due to various factors, not the least of which were several hundred widely publicized "bride burnings" in which newly married women, whose families could not meet additional after-dowry demands by the groom's family, died "accidentally" when hot cooking oil spilled on them while they prepared a meal, thereby freeing up the husband to marry again after the bride's death. Finally, writing by expatriate Indians from India, but also East and South Africa, and the Caribbean, currently living in Great Britain and North America (both the U.S. and Canada) has increased significantly. While the effects of this type of writing on literature produced in India itself is probably minimal, the perception of India by the rest of the world is drawn heavily from these writers.

Political efforts to raise the status of India's various depressed classes has resulted in major gains for these groups, usually at the expense of upper-class and -caste Indians, many of them professionals who have emigrated from India and other parts of the former British Empire to Great Britain and North America. The rise of these traditionally oppressed groups, some of them former untouchables, has been abetted by a kind of liberation theology, both Hindu and Christian in origin, and by scholars and academics in India and in the West who have translated this literature into English in an effort to disseminate it beyond the confines of just a few Indian languages. The best-known and best-organized of these various groups are the Dalits. Hence, numerous publications devoted to Dalit literature, written in Marathi, have appeared, including no less than four 1992 anthologies, each devoted to a different genre, edited by Ashok Dangale. The International Dalit Support Group has been established, as well as several Dalit international journals and newsletters; Dalit literary conferences are held regularly, and several Dalit web sites are found on the Internet.

Another of India's oppressed groups to receive considerable attention in contemporary literature are its tribal peoples, especially those of Bengal, whose adversity and mistreatment has been featured in the writings of the leftist fiction writer and political activist Mahasweta Devi (b. 1926). Knowledge of the struggle of these tribals has been extended beyond India through the translation, commentary, and analysis of a number of her best short stories by the Indian-American literary critic and polemicist Gayatri Chakravorty Spivak (b. 1941), who discusses the plight of these "marginal subjects," or "subalterns," within the matrix of feminism, neo-Marxism, and postcolonial cultural and literary theory. Spivak provides a chilling interpretation of the manner in which decolonized people oppress their own minorities.

Expatriate Indian writers, some of whom have left India due to what they perceive as lack of opportunity, or privilege, there, have delineated extensively and nostalgically the India of their youth, or a contemporary India that they view through the filter of their current lives in the West. The most noted of these writers is Salman Rushdie, whose best-known and most controversial novel, *The Satanic Verses* (1989), addresses various aspects of the Indian immigrant/expatriate's question: "Where do I belong?" His novel, *The Moor's Last Sigh* (1995), is the bitterly satirical story of the "fall from grace" of an Indian, Moraes (I.e., "Moor") Zogoiby, whose forefathers were Portuguese and Jewish immigrants to India. Narrated with an eye and ear for the sardonic and grotesque, the novel relates the decline of a once-powerful, wealthy, but markedly eccentric family, exacerbated by the brutal excesses and flagrant corruption of right-wing Hindu religious and political groups in contemporary India.

Other expatriate writers have addressed the problems of immigrating to the West and continue to produce a significant body of works that address questions about assimilation, changes and shifts in what were once their solid, unchanging moral and spiritual values, the struggles to achieve success in the West, invariably described as a well-paying job as a professional, and the price to be paid for success, and the dilemma faced by many ethnic groups that have preceded them to the U.S.: whether and how to retain an ethnic identity in the face of a significantly different, racially prejudiced, and often hostile dominant culture. Several anthologies of writings dealing with these topics have appeared, the most notable of them being *Our Feet Walk the Sky* (1993) and *Living in America* (1995).

South Asian women writers, many of them feminists, have offered alternate analyses and points of view to counter the phallocentrism of Indian literature and literary criticism. One important, basic task of these women has been the identification and presentation of writing by Indian women both from the past and from the present in order to show that, indeed, women have been producers of literature in India for over two millenia. In this context, the appearance of the two-volume *Women Writing in India* (1991, 1993) from Feminist Press, New York, is especially important. The first volume includes women writers from 600 B. C. to the early 20th c.; the second is devoted entirely to writing by modern and contemporary authors. Both volumes contain extended introductions by the editors, Susie Tharu and K. Lality, which address, among other topics, the politics of gender in Indian literature, and plead for a more "gynocentric" approach to the criticism of all Indian literature. Various anthologies of fiction and poetry written by Indian women have appeared, in good part through the efforts of several women's publishing cooperatives, the best-known of them being Kali for Women.

The future of Indian literature will be enriched by the addition of new voices, some of them previously muffled, others of them heretofore unheard, which will add original dimensions and novel textures to the already diverse tapestry that constitutes Indian literature.

BIBLIOGRAPHY: Coppola, C., ed., *JSoAL* (1963–present); Mukherjee, M., *The Twice Born Fiction: Themes and Techniques of the Indian Novel in English* (1971); Jussawalla, A., ed., *New Writing in India* (1974); special issue on the Indian novel, *Contributions to Asian Studies*, 6 (1975); Bald, S., *Novels and Political Consciousness: Literary Expression of Indian Nationalism 1919–1947* (1982); special issue on Indian literature, *NewL*, 48: 3–4 (1982); Bharucha, R., *Rehearsals of Revolution: The Political Theater of Bengal* (1983); Schomer, K., *Mahadevi Varma and the Chhayavad Age of Modern Hindi Poetry* (1983); Mukherjee, M., *Realism and Reality: The Novel and Society in India* (1985); Jamal, M., ed., *The Penguin Book of Modern Urdu Poetry* (1986); Coppola, C., ed., *Marxist Influences and South Asian Literature* (1988); Tharu, S., and K. Lalita, eds., *Women Writing in India* (2 vols., 1991); Innaci, C., *Unity and Diversity in Indian Literatures* (1994); Dhawan, R., *Indian Women Novelists* (1995); Soraba, V., *Women Writers in South India* (1995); Krishna Sastry, L., et al., *Indian Writing Today* (1996); Singh, R., *Anger in Action: Explorations in Indian Writing in English* (1996); Zelliott, E., *From Untouchable to Dalit* (1996)

—CARLO COPPOLA

INDONESIAN LITERATURE

In 1928 the Second Congress of Indonesian Youth proclaimed Malay, which had been for centuries the lingua franca of the region, the language of the Indonesian nationalist movement. The language, since known as Indonesian (*Bahasa Indonesia*), is today the republic's official language and the principal vehicle for innovative literary expression.

The history of modern Indonesian literature must be viewed against the traditional literatures in regional languages. Many traditional theatrical genres remain vigorous. Djakartan *lenong* drama and Javanese *ludrug* are predominantly urban and contemporary in character, while Balinese *gong* drama, Javanese *ketoprak*,

Sundanese *gending karesmen*, and Minangkabau *randai* present performances modernized to varying degrees of mainly historical stories.

Attempts at writing modern literature have been made in most of Indonesia's major regional languages, with Javanese and Sundanese exhibiting the greatest fecundity. Writing in these languages differs in some fundamental respects from that in Indonesian. Literature in Indonesian is governed by the values of the urban middle class, is influenced by foreign literatures, appears in expensive, hard-to-get books, and is written in a language most people do not use in their homes and do not learn until they go to school. By contrast, literature in the regional languages tends to deal more with life in rural areas or provincial towns, is stylistically more lively and linguistically more accessible to readers for whom the language concerned is their mother tongue. Regional literatures make more unselfconscious reference to the corpus of symbols, allusions, and literary conventions peculiar to certain regions and already familiar to readers there. Regional literature appears predominantly in magazines, which makes it cheaper and easier to obtain.

In Indonesian

Fiction

Fiction in Indonesian began toward the end of the 19th c. Three main streams contributed to its genesis: popular tales (*penglipur lara*) and narrative verse (*syair*) in Malay, Chinese romances of love and the martial arts, and melodramatic romances in Dutch. Early novels were predominantly romantic melodramas spiced with sensational crimes and supernatural occurrences, but soon a more serious strain of social criticism and nationalist sentiment appeared.

In 1908 the Netherlands Indies government established a state commission for reading matter in vernacular languages, later known as the Balai Pustaka publishing house. In the 1920s and 1930s Balai Pustaka encouraged the writing of fiction, but its editors carefully vetted manuscripts for what they regarded as politically or morally contentious content and insisted on a somewhat pedantic style.

Despite alterations at the insistence of Balai Pustaka, *Salah asuhan* (1928; a wrong upbringing) by nationalist activist Abdoel Moeis (1898–1959) remains the outstanding achievement of early Indonesian fiction. Racism and the question of cultural identity are the themes pursued with fluent passion in this narrative of a Dutch-educated Indonesian whose admiration for European society renders him contemptuous of his own people. The interaction of Indonesian and European value systems is, in fact, a consistent theme in preindependence novels.

In *Layar terkembang* (1936; sails unfurled), Sutan Takdir ALISJAHBANA contrasts two sisters, one independent, earnest, and an activist in the women's welfare movement, the other carefree, dreamy, and feminine in the traditional fashion. Takdir criticizes what he sees as the debilitating tendency of Indonesians to glorify the achievements and institutions of the past. *Belenggu* (1940; shackles) by Armijn Pane (1908–1970) also juxtaposes two women, one Western-educated and busily involved in social welfare work, the other a self-sacrificing prostitute who excels in the domestic arts and in singing traditional songs.

Possibly the most original and brilliantly executed work of preindependence fiction is *Sukreni, gadis Bali* (1936; Sukreni,

virgin of Bali) by Anak Agung Pandji Tisna (1908–1978). Utilizing the symbols and conventions of traditional Balinese theater, Pandji Tisna portrays the destructive effect of contemporary commercial ethics on Balinese society. The fragility of traditional values is also the theme of *Atheis* (1949; *Atheis*, 1972) by Achdiat Karta MIHARDJA, in which a young man from rural west Java finds that his mystically tinged Islamic faith crumbles before the materialism, Marxism, and atheism of urban radicals.

The Japanese occupation (1942–45) and Indonesia's armed struggle for independence from the Netherlands (1945–49) swept away the romanticism and dilettante nationalism of the contributors to the elite literary journal *Pujangga baru*. Disillusionment and a note of tough realism became evident in the fiction of the late 1940s and 1950s. The short-story writer Idrus (1921–1979), together with the novelist and short-story writer Pramoedya Ananta TOER, wrought a revolution in prose style, replacing prewar formality and archness with an expressive but terse and colloquial style.

For both Idrus and Pramoedya, the Japanese occupation and the revolutionary war provided both the setting for their major works and the touchstone against which the characters in these works are tried. Idrus's influential early stories, laced with cynicism and sardonic humor, are collected in *Dari Ave Maria ke jalan lain ke Roma* (1948; from Ave Maria to another road to Rome). Pramoedya's novels are unmatched for their somber exploration of man's alienation and disillusion in the midst of war. *Keluarga gerilya* (1950; guerrilla family) depicts a family that, like Indonesian society, is split geographically and in political allegiance by the revolutionary war. *Bukan pasar malam* (1951; *It's Not an All Night Fair*, 1973) explores the essential loneliness of the human condition, catching the mood of dislocation and dispiritedness that marked the immediate post-revolutionary period.

While the revolutionary war and nationalism remained prominent themes in the fiction of the 1950s, writers increasingly turned their attention to the young republic's burden of social ills. The kaleidoscopic *Senja di Jakarta* (pub. 1964; *Twilight in Jakarta*, 1963) by Mochtar Lubis (b. 1922) is a mosaic of images contrasting Djakarta's corrupt rich with its helpless poor. Achdiat's collection of short stories *Keretakan dan ketegangan* (1956; fissures and tensions) turns a jaundiced eye on the country's hypocritical politicians and nouveaux riches.

From the late 1950s to the mid-1960s literary life was dominated by the conflict between leftist insistence on the social and political utility of art, and liberal insistence on the possibility of divorce between art and organized politics. Before the October 1, 1965 incident (a power grab in which right-wing forces emerged victorious), leftist pressure forced many liberal writers into silence, but after 1965 the tables were turned. A number of writers with leftist sympathies disappeared or were imprisoned and their works banned.

Curiously, the ideological conflict of the 1960s left popular fiction largely untouched. Fueled by newly created mass literacy and accompanied by a decline in the authority of elite literary magazines, popular publishing boomed in the late 1960s and throughout the 1970s. A leading figure in this boom was Motinggo Boesye (b.1937), whose many novels combine a highly readable narrative style with mild sexual titillation and satirical observation of the urban middle class. Fiction by women writers swelled in quantity and quality. *Pada sebuah kapal* (1973; on a ship) by Nh. Dini (b. 1936) chronicles with rare sensitivity a young woman's disengagement from allegiance to traditional social and marital roles.

The question of national identity, hitherto an almost inevitable element in fiction, virtually disappeared in the works of younger writers but remained prominent in those of the older generation. Sutan Takdir Alisjahbana's *Kalah dan menang* (1978; defeat and victory) explores Indonesia's cultural options against the background of Japan's wartime occupation, rejecting fascism and the authoritarianism of tradition for liberal values adopted from Western Europe. In a short novel, *Sri Sumarah* (1975; Sri Sumarah), Umar Kayam (b. 1932) vividly and sympathetically conveys the spirit of traditional Javanese culture and affirms its continuing relevance in the emerging national culture. Alienation attendant upon cultural deracination and urban life styles brought the appearance of absurdist fiction. *Ziarah* (1969; *The Pilgrim*, 1975) by Iwan Simatupang (1928–1970) is a Kafkaesque study of the encounter between the anarchic artist and the social reality of Indonesia.

Following his release from prison in 1979 Pramoedya Ananta Toer published *Bumi manusia* (1980; man's earth), a novel of epic proportions that traces in its central figure the first stirrings of a distinctly modern Indonesian consciousness in the early years of this century. Despite, or perhaps because of, its enthusiastic popular reception, the book was banned by the government in mid-1981.

Poetry

Distinctly innovative poetry began to appear in Indonesia in the 1910s. The European sonnet form was especially popular, but the influence of traditional verse forms remained strong. The poetry of the 1920s and 1930s was marked by an intense and largely reflective romanticism.

Arguably Indonesia's greatest modern poet, and certainly the most prominent figure in preindependence poetry, was Amir Hamzah (1911–1946), whose work is collected in two small volumes, *Nyanyi sunyi* (1937; songs of silence) and *Buah rindu* (1941; fruits of longing). Amir's best poetry expresses the agony of doubt about his Islamic faith.

The iconoclastic verse of Chairil ANWAR released Indonesian poetry from the bonds of traditional forms and literary language, exerting a profound influence on postindependence poetry. His works convey a powerful, vitalistic individualism.

Sitor Situmorang (b. 1923) was strongly influenced by Chairil. A sojourn in Europe inspired his early work, represented most notably in the collection *Surat kertas hijau* (1953; a letter on green paper), which reveals an unquiet personality burdened with moral doubts and guilt, nostalgic for the Indonesian homeland. Like Pramoedya Ananta Toer and a number of other writers, Sitor became attracted to socialism in the late 1950s, and his poetry changed markedly. His *Zaman baru* (1961; new era) records the impact upon him of a visit to China. The anguished subjectivism of his earlier work disappeared, to be replaced with unequivocal praise of socialist ideals and achievements.

Zaman baru typifies the unadorned, politically committed verse of the 1960s. After the demise of the Indonesian Communist Party in 1965, the spare and strident poetry of protest against exploitation of workers and peasants gave way to equally strident protests against the illiberalism, economic bungling, and rhetorical humbug of the preceding years. Much poetry of the 1960s and 1970s was strikingly public in character, and no poet more dominated the public scene in the 1970s than the charismatic Rendra (b. 1935). His collections *Blues untuk Bonnie* (1971; *Indonesian Poet in New York*, 1971) and *Pamflet penyair* (1978; *State of Emergency*, 1980)

are preeminently declamatory. They contain hard-hitting, sometimes crudely worded attacks on misuse of authority and the degradation of the poor at the hands of the rich.

Drama

Most plays of the 1920s and 1930s were ponderous historical dramas or allegories of nationalist struggle and colonial oppression. The Japanese occupation produced an upsurge of interest in more realistic dramas of everyday life, but neither these plays nor those of the prewar period are today of any more than academic interest.

Utuy Tatang Sontani (1920–1979) was the first Indonesian dramatist to gain wide recognition. His early plays, most notably *Bunga rumah makan* (1948; ornament of the restaurant) and *Awal dan Mira* (1952; Awal and Mira), are concerned with the possible avenues for dignified living open to ordinary individuals in the midst of a society obsessed with false and empty values. After aligning himself with the political left Utuy wrote *Si Sapar* (1964; Sapar) and *Si Kampeng* (1964; Kampeng), two short plays that treat class differences and exploitation, employing a style in which caricature is of paramount importance.

Drama in the 1970s was dominated, on the one hand, by the immensely popular satirical plays of Rendra, and, on the other, by the absurdist works of Arifin C. Noer (b. 1941) and Putu Wijaya (b. 1944). Rendra's *Kisah perjuangan suku Naga* (1975; *The Struggle of the Naga Tribe*, 1979) is a brilliantly funny condemnation of the Indonesian elite's economic and cultural dependence on foreigners. The play is thoroughly modern, but it draws upon the conventions of the traditional Javanese shadow play, thereby emphasizing in its form the theme of cultural autonomy that lies at its heart. Arifin C. Noer's *Kapai-kapai* (1970; *Moths*, 1974) is a crazy pastiche of episodes, sometimes macabre and mystical, dramatizing one man's suffering and his escape into unreality.

In Javanese

Fiction in Javanese (the language of central and east Java) is characterized by three somewhat overlapping streams. The *priyayi* (aristocratic and official class) stream is dedicated largely to the defense of aristocratic values and status in the face of social mobility and creeping egalitarianism. It is indebted to the belletristic writing of the Javanese courts and emphasizes refinement, etiquette, mystical knowledge, and mastery of formal Javanese. *Rangsang Tuban* (1913; song of Tuban) by Padmasusastra (1843–1926) is an early masterpiece of this type. Ostensibly a historical novel, it in fact gives complex expression to *kabatinan*, the characteristically Javanese form of mysticism. *Serat Riyanta* (1920; Riyanto's story) by Sulardi (1888–19??), often called the first true novel in Javanese, utilizes the conventional love romance to express aristocratic ideals. In *Ngulandara* (1936; wanderlust), Margana Djajaatmadja (dates n.a.) affirms the superiority of the *priyayi* by fashioning a contemporary transmutation of the traditional Panji romance of courtly love, while *Anteping tekad* (1975; unshakable determination) by Ag. Suharti (b. 1920) defends the *priyayi* ethic in a non-Javanese, postindependence context.

The second stream of writing, the popular, seems to be preoccupied with forging a sense of security and identity in the newly emergent lower middle class. Written, since its rise in the 1930s, at the informal level of Javanese, popular fiction has been much indebted to popular novels in Indonesian, especially those by

Chinese-Indonesian authors. Popular theater, too, has been influential in this stream. The novel *Sala peteng* (1938; darkness in Solo) by Mt. Suphardi (b. 1913) has a plot strikingly similar to those of Javanese *ludrug* stage melodramas. The theme of unwitting incest, common in popular Javanese fiction, suggests that *Sala peteng* and similar novels are appealing for the preservation of the traditional family unit in the midst of fragmenting social change. The prolific giants of the postindependence romance were Any Asmara (b. 1913) and Widi Widajat (b. 1928), both of whose works are highly formulaic and strongly influenced by the conventions of oral narrative and popular theater.

Writers in the third, or "modernist," stream have sought to develop a prose style at once expressively literary yet close to colloquial usage. Unlike *priyayi* and popular writers, they evince strong interest in individualized characterization and taut structure. The romantic but frequently somber short stories of St. (Sulistyoutami) Iesmaniasita (b. 1933), in her collections *Kidung wengi ing gunung gamping* (1958; nocturne in the limestone hills) and *Kalimput ing pedhut* (1976; veiled in mist), are noteworthy for their vivid portraits of village and urban middle-class women. *Lara lapane kaum republik* (1967; agony and sacrifice in the republican cause) by Suparto Brata (b. 1932) is a down-to-earth and wryly humorous story of the revolution. Sudharma K. D. (1934–1980) and Esmiet (b. 1938) address the problem of economic development in the Javanese cultural context. Esmiet's *Tunggaktunggak jati* (1977; trunks of teak) examines the impact upon a rural community of the alliance between an unscrupulous Chinese businessman and corrupt community leaders.

Innovative poetry in Javanese has developed vigorously since Indonesia's independence. It has been dominated by St. Iesmaniasita and by Muryalelana (b. 1932), whose verse is mostly inward-looking. Modern stage drama has not developed significantly in Javanese, but the radio plays of Soemardjono (b. 1925), some of which are adaptatations from European sources and others romances of his own creation, gained a huge following in the 1960s and 1970s.

In Sundanese

Preindependence fiction in Sundanese (the language of inland west Java) is almost synonymous with the name of Mohamad Ambri (1892–1936). His interest in rural life, particularly rural religious practices, is the common thread of his novels. *Ngawadalkeun nyawa* (1932; self-sacrifice) gives an absorbing portrait of life in a rural Islamic academy (*pesantren*), while *Munjung* (1932; homage) demonstrates how Sundanese villagers make sense of cash-based commerce by relating it to the demonic figures of the spirit world.

Mohamad Ambri's prose style has exercised an enormous influence on later writers. Some of his novels consist almost entirely of dialogue, in colloquial, unadorned, yet remarkably expressive language. Among postindependence writers indebted to him is Ki Umbara (pseud. of Wirdja Ranulaksana, b. 1914), whose collection of short stories *Diwadalkeun ka siluman* (1965; sacrificed to demons) explores some of the darker corners of Sundanese folk religion. By contrast, the novel *Manehna* (1965; she) by Sjarif Amin (pseud. of Mohamad Koerdie, b. 1907) is a lyrical, sometimes painfully nostalgic evocation of the Sundanese world of the author's youth.

Haji Hasan Mustapa (1852–1930) wrote poetry in traditional forms, but brought to his work a new spirit of individualism and innovation. Like Mohamad Ambri, he did not hesitate to make creative use of colloquial Sundanese, raising the poetic forms of folk narrative and children's songs to a new level of seriousness. Only in the 1950s did Sundanese poetry directly face contemporary society and achieve release from traditional verse forms. In the work of Sajudi (dates n.a.) Sundanese poetry found a powerful voice. In his collection *Lalaki di tegal pati* (1963; a man on the field of battle) he pays tribute to the heroic spirit of old Sunda, but also writes lyrically of love, patriotism, and the sufferings of the weak in postindependence Indonesian society. Allusions to the Sundanese past and a prominent note of romanticism are evident too in the works of Surachman R. M. (b. 1936) and the prolific Wahyu Wibisana (b. 1935). Wayhu Wibisana, together with Utuy Tatang Sontani and short-story writer Rachmatullah Ading Affandie (usually abbreviated R. A. F., b. 1929), have gained some recognition as playwrights, but by and large modern stage drama in Sundanese has been infertile.

In Minangkabau and Balinese

Of the other regional literatures, west Sumatran Minangkabau and Balinese writing have displayed promising stirrings of innovation. The traditional Minangkabau *kaba*—a romantic narrative in rhythmic prose—has been transformed by a few writers into a popular comic genre making satirical comment on contemporary life. Innovative verse has flourished in the lyrics of popular songs.

In the Balinese language two novels have appeared: *Nemu karma* (1931; punished by fate) by Wayan Gobiah (dates n.a.) and *Mlancaran ka Sasak* (1939; rev. ed. 1978; journey to Lombok) by Gde Srawana (dates n.a.). Both are romances, the former marked by the theme of karmatic retribution, the latter remarkable for its humor and its lively, earthy style. Stimulated by government and privately sponsored competitions, Balinese writers turned their attention to the short story in the late 1960s and 1970s. The stories in the collection *Katemu ring Tampaksiring* (1975; meeting at Tampaksiring) by Made Sanggra (b. 1926) examine the fate of the poor in Bali, but also touch on the persistence of traumatic memories in those who experienced the revolutionary war. In the anthology of poetry *Ganda sari* (1973; scent and blossoms) Made Sanggra and Nyoman Manda (b. 1938) display an idealistic but almost prosaic interest in the impact of economic development on Balinese society.

In Chinese-Indonesian

Chinese have lived in Indonesia from earliest historical times. In the second half of the 19th c. migration from China swelled, and many of the descendants of these migrants adopted the languages and cultures of their new home while still maintaining a distinctly Chinese identity. In the first half of the 20th c. the Chinese dialect of Indonesian became the vehicle for a lively literature.

Toward the end of the 19th c. Chinese-Indonesian writers adopted the traditional Malay *syair* verse form, using it for narratives of contemporary events and for romantic stories. An early and accomplished exponent of the *syair* was Lie Kim-hok (1853–1912), whose *Sair cerita Siti Akbari* (1884; the story of Siti

Akbari), a legendary romance set in India, became the most admired work of the genre. Lie Kim-hok's many detective stories also played a key role in establishing the viability of prose fiction in this dialect. The finest Chinese-Indonesian novelist was Liem King-hoo (dates n.a.); in *Berjuang* (1934; struggle) and *Masyarakat* (1939; community) he analyzes the character and social role of Indonesia's Chinese, urging them to search for a humane, socialistic alternative to capitalism.

Indonesia's independence brought the death of the Chinese-Indonesian dialect as a literary language, but the spirit of Chinese-Indonesian literature lived on in the immensely popular works of Asmaraman Sukowati (previously Kho Ping Hoo, b. 1926) and Marga T. (previously Tjoa Liang Tjoe, b. 1943). Marga's *Gema sebuah hati* (1976; echoes in a heart) is a romantic and melodramatic novel depicting the lives of Chinese-Indonesian students caught in the conflicting loyalties and political turmoil of Djakarta in 1965.

In Dutch

Although Dutch was for hundreds of years the upper-echelon language of administration and commerce in Indonesia, indigenous Indonesians did not find it a congenial vehicle for literary expression. Among the few exceptions was Kartini (1879–1904), whose eloquent letters of protest against colonial paternalism and the feudal oppression of women were collected and published posthumously in *Door duisternis tot licht* (1911; *Letters of a Javanese Princess*, 1921). The most substantial work of fiction in Dutch by an Indonesian author is the novel *Buiten het gareel* (1940; out of harness) by Suwarsih Djojopuspito (1912–1978). It is a sensitive portrayal of day-to-day strains in the marriage and work of an educated woman.

Romance, interest in Oriental exotica, and, most recently, intense nostalgia for the colonial past are the hallmarks of the Indies novel by Dutch writers. A few outstanding works, however, echo the impassioned brilliance of Multatuli's (pseud. of Eduard Douwes Dekker, 1820–1887) *Max Havelaar* (1860; *Max Havelaar*, 1868; new trs., 1927, 1967) and capture the essence of Dutch colonial society with its special Indies character and its ambivalent attitude toward its Indonesian subjects. One such work is the novel *De stille kracht* (1900; *The Hidden Force*, 1922) by Louis COUPERUS, which superbly catches the superciliousness of Dutch officialdom in confrontation with the incomprehensible yet tangible power of Javanese culture. The works of Madelon Hermina Székely-Lulofs (a.k.a. Madelon Lulofs, 1899–1958), among them the popular *Rubber* (1931; *Rubber*, 1933) and *Koelie* (1932; *Coolie*, 1936), attack colonialism, especially as it manifested itself in the exploitative plantation enterprises of North Sumatra. The novel of nostalgia is raised to high art in the works of Maria Dermoût (1888–1962). Her *De tienduizend dingen* (1956; *The Ten Thousand Things*, 1958) is a justly praised evocation of colonial society in a remote corner of eastern Indonesia. The pithy short stories of Vincent Mahieu (a.k.a. Tjalie Robinson, pseuds. of Jan Boon, 1911–1974) are collected in *Tjies* (1954; pea rifle) and *Tjoek* (1960; constriction). Using dialect and the imagery of hunting and boxing, they conjure up the tough world of the Indonesian Eurasian.

The poet Notosoeroto (1888–1951), a Javanese, and Getrudes Johannes Resink (b. 1911), a Eurasian, were influenced by the neoromanticism of late-19th-c. European verse. But Notosoeroto's collection *Wayang-liederen* (1931; songs of the shadow play) and

Resink's *Kreeft en steenbok* (1963; Cancer and Capricorn) both reveal an outlook profoundly colored by Javanese mysticism.

(See also Netherlands Literature.)

BIBLIOGRAPHY: Raffel, B., *The Development of Modern Indonesian Poetry* (1967); Nieuwenhuys, R., *Oost-Indische Spiegel* (1973); Aveling, H., *A Thematic History of Indonesian Poetry: 1920–1974* (1974); Balfas, M., "Modern Indonesian Literature in Brief", in Spuler, B., ed., *Handbuch der Orientalistik*, Vol. 3, Part 1 (1976): 41–116; Freidus, A. J., *Sumatran Contributions to the Development of Indonesian Literature, 1920–1942* (1977); Johns, A. H., *Cultural Options and the Role of Tradition: A Collection of Essays on Modern Indonesian and Malaysian Literature* (1979); Ras, J. J., *Javanese Literature since Independence* (1979); Teeuw, A., *Modern Indonesian Literature* (2 vols., 1979)

—GEORGE QUINN

INGE, William Motter

American dramatist, novelist, and screenwriter, b. 3 May 1913, Independence, Kan.; d. 10 June 1973, Los Angeles, Cal.

I. gained a wide reputation throughout the 1950s for his moving exploration of the fractured lives of ordinary people. The strong sense of spiritual abandonment and loss of values in his Midwestern settings continued through the drama the tradition of alienation developed in the novel by Sinclair LEWIS and Sherwood ANDERSON. As a writer, I. had the ability to build upon simple story lines. All four of his most important plays were expansions of earlier short stories and one-act plays. When *Come Back, Little Sheba* (1949) was revived on Broadway in 1974, critics, while acknowledging a certain superficial resemblance to soap-opera plots, still found I.'s powerful psychological portraits and stifling social settings credible and haunting. Each of his four major plays was successfully translated into Hollywood films, and he learned quickly the exigencies of screenwriting. The original screenplay of *Splendor in the Grass* (1961) won for I. an Academy Award.

Although I. was interested in acting since childhood and active in high-school and college dramatics, financial reasons prevented him from leaving Kansas for New York to study acting. He took sundry stage roles in summer stock and a tent show after his graduation from the University of Kansas (A.B., 1935). While a graduate student at George Peabody College for Teachers (A.M., 1938) in Nashville, Tennessee, he taught high school. Between 1938 and 1943, I. was an instructor at Stephens College, Columbia, Missouri, where he met Maude Adams, his first important mentor. For three years he worked under her in the drama department. With her encouragement he renewed his interest in drama and became a theater and film critic for the *St. Louis Star-Times* (1943–1946). In St. Louis he resumed teaching from 1946 to 1949 at Washington University. A meeting with Tennessee WILLIAMS led to a lifetime friendship and a contract with the Theatre Guild, which presented *Come Back, Little Sheba* in 1949, and its Broadway production in 1950. Throughout the 1950s and most of the 1960s, I. was able to sustain himself completely through his writing. Following his Broadway successes, screenplays and television plays were bought, but he never regained success as an author after *The Stripper*

(1963). In 1969 he taught drama at the University of North Carolina and in 1970 at the University of California, Irvine. His last years saw the publication of a novel, *Good Luck, Miss Wyckoff* (1970), and the largely autobiographical *My Son Is a Splendid Driver* (1971).

I. received the George Jean Nathan Award and the Theatre Time Award in 1950 for *Come Back, Little Sheba*, and the Pulitzer Prize, Outer Circle Award, New York Drama Critics Circle Award, and Donaldson Award (shared with Tennessee Williams) for *Picnic* (1953). I. has been one of the most frequently anthologized American dramatists, and his plays have often been performed in college and community theaters and studied widely on campuses.

Come Back, Little Sheba combines unadorned language, psychoanalytic character study, and tight unity of plot to create a striking example of extreme realism. Considered by many critics his best play, its strengths derive from the ability to dramatize the psychological lives of a childless couple who face middle age without fulfillment. The husband, Doc, a recovering alcoholic, faces remorse for what he has missed in life—true romance and spontaneous pleasure. The wife, Lola, lacking communication and intimacy with her husband, struggles to overcome her compulsive retreats into fantasy and her remorse for the inability to produce children. The adroit use of depth psychology, the typical nature of the characters, and the oppressive influence of their social background combine to create a naturalistic style of stagecraft. However, what saves the play from a cold and clinical tone is the credibility of the husband and wife with Midwestern roots, the accuracy of the colloquial dialogue, and the sympathetic treatment of the characters that avoids sentimentality.

I.'s most acclaimed drama, *Picnic*, retains a Midwest setting, but the locale is a small Kansas town, not an urban environment as in *Come Back, Little Sheba*. The action occurs on Labor Day, the end of summer, which is symbolic of the end of youthful visions, a recurring theme for I., and also indicative of the play's preoccupation with choice of vocations, or life's calling, which challenges the characters in different ways. Hal, a youthful and handsome vagrant, incites the women of the play to reveal well-hidden longings. As a result, the older women are confronted with the vacuity of their emotional and intellectual lives, while the two teenaged daughters come to accept themselves and their own destinies. Wearing veneers of respectability, each major character unleashes an inner world of unfulfilled needs. This occurs during a very short period of time and within a very confined, claustrophobic space. The fact that the theatrical unities of time, place, and action are strictly observed helps intensify the play's overall effect. In this way, I. achieves dramatic intensity in spite of the conformist and complacent attitudes of the small-town characters he portrays.

Critics who dismiss I.'s approach to playwriting as colloquial rather than probing, as avoiding ideas in favor of regional color and character verisimilitude, overlook the thoughtful exploration of human relationships evident in *Bus Stop* (1955). In this expansion of I.'s one-act play *People in the Wind* (1953), its characters confront the question of how love can be sustained. *Bus Stop* departs from I.'s earlier full-length plays in its form, in its romantic comedy, and in its dialogue, which is witty and exuberant. Compared with I.'s other 1950s dramas, *Bus Stop* offers the most hopeful tone, departs most from the psychodynamics of family life, and is only indirectly concerned with Midwestern complacency and repression. I.'s thesis, that love is dependent upon the selfless opening of the heart, works its way through the main characters, who present a spectrum of human desire and loving. *Bus Stop* is

able to dramatize the anatomy of love, in spite of a rather bare story line, through dynamic character relationships and finely crafted dialogue.

I. returned to the inner life of the family and to a more detached, clinical approach to characterization in *The Dark at the Top of the Stairs* (1958). Shrewd dialogue and intriguing situations contributed to the play's Broadway success. Much of the material was autobiographical and supported by Freudian presuppositions. I.'s Hollywood screenplay *Splendor in the Grass* deals with the Wordsworthian theme of the passing glory of youth and offers a particularly compelling treatment of adolescent perspectives. In the early 1970s I. turned to novel writing with mixed critical, and little popular, success. *Good Luck, Miss Wyckoff* (1970) is a return to the plays of the 1950s in both its Midwestern setting and strong character portrayals. I. reveals few new insights in this novel, in spite of attempts at more explicit dialogue and sexuality. His last published work, a novel written as a memoir, *My Son Is a Splendid Driver* (1971), contains many revealing autobiographical elements, yet remains objective and unsentimental in tone. It was, unhappily, ignored by the reading public and did not attract sufficient critical commentary.

FURTHER WORKS: *Farther Off from Heaven* (wr. 1947); *To Bobolink, for Her Spirit* (1950); *Glory in the Flower* (1958); *The Mall* (1959); *A Loss of Roses* (1960); *Summer Brave* (1962); *A Social Event* (1962); *The Tiny Closet* (1962); *Memory of Summer* (1962); *Bus Riley's Back in Town* (1962); *The Rainy Afternoon* (1962); *An Incident at the Standish Arms* (1962); *The Strains of Triumph* (1962); *Natural Affection* (1963); *Where's Daddy?* (1966); *The Call* (1968); *The Disposal* (1968); *A Murder* (1968); *Midwestern Manic* (1969)

BIBLIOGRAPHY: Barko, N., "W. I. Talks about *Picnic*," *Theatre Arts*, 37 (July 1953): 66–67; Weales, G., "The New Pineros," *American Drama since World War II* (1962): 40–56; Newquist, R., "W. I.," *Counterpoint* (1964): 356–63; Lewis, A., "The Emergent Deans: Kimpley, I., and Company," *American Plays and Playwrights of the Contemporary Theatre* (1965): 143–63; Shuman, R. B., *W. I.* (1966); Gould, J., "W. I.," *Modern American Playwrights* (1966): 264–72; Mitchell, M., "Teacher As Outsider in the Works of W. I.," *MQ*, 17 (July 1976): 385–93; Burgess, C. E., "American Experience: W. I. in St. Louis, 1943–49," *Pennsylvania Language and Literature*, 12 (Fall 1976): 438–68; Smotle, G. M., "W. I.: Homosexual Spite in Action," *Like a Brother, Like a Lover* (1978): 121–33; Centola, S. R., "Compromise As Bad Faith: Arthur Miller's *A View from the Bridge* and W. I.'s *Come Back, Little Sheba*," *MQ*, 28, 1 (Autumn 1986): 100–13; Voss, R. F., *A Life of W. I.: The Strains of Triumph* (1989)

—WILLIAM OVER

INGUSH LITERATURE

See North Caucasian Literatures

INNER MONGOLIAN LITERATURE

See Mongolian Literature

INOUE Yasushi

Japanese novelist, short-story writer, essayist, and poet, b. 6 May 1907, Asahigawa; d. 29 Jan. 1991, Tokyo

The son of a military physician who was subject to frequent transfers, I. spent his childhood years apart from his parents in the family's native village of Yugashima, Shizuoka Prefecture, in the care of his grandmother, a fact that may help to account for the themes of loneliness and alienation that appear in most of his works. After having his literary interests aroused by classmates at the Numazu Middle School, he began to write and to publish poetry while attending the Fourth Higher School in Kanazawa. Although he continued this pursuit while a university student, his first works of fiction, mostly winning entries in contests sponsored by popular magazines, also appeared during those years, and he might have begun to write professionally at that time had he wished to. However, after graduating from Kyoto Imperial University in 1936, he chose to become a reporter for the weekly magazine *Sandē Mainichi*, in which some of his stories had been published. It was not until after World War II that he again attempted to write fiction.

Through the good offices of the novelist Satō Haruo (1892–1964), who had recognized his talent, I. was able to publish two short novels, *Ryōjū* (1949; *The Hunting Gun*, 1961) and *Tōgyū* (1949; the bull fight), in the prestigious journal *Bungakkai*; his literary career began in earnest when *Tōgyū* was awarded the Akutagawa Literary Prize in 1950. In 1951 he gave up his position with *Sandē Mainichi* to write full time.

Despite the fact that he became a novelist only after reaching middle age, I. proved to be remarkably prolific. During the next few years he produced a great number of short stories, as well as newspaper and magazine serials, for popular consumption. "Hira no shakunage" (1950; "The Azaleas of Hira," 1955), "Aru gisakka no shōgai" (1951; "The Counterfeiter," 1965), *Ashita kuru hito* (1954; those who come tomorrow), *Michite kuru shio* (1955; rising tide), and *Hyōheki* (1956; wall of ice) may be especially worthy of note, but represent a fraction of his total output during those years.

Stories with a historical setting were included among his early works, but it was not until his career was firmly established that he began to produce the kind of fiction for which he is celebrated—meticulously researched historical tales that ponder the littleness of the human being in the vastness of space, and the brevity of our existence in the flow of eternity. Representative are *Tempyō no iraka* (1957; *The Roof Tile of Tempyō*, 1975), which relates the experiences of Japanese monks studying in 8th-c. China; "Rōran" (1958; "Loulan," 1959), about the rise and fall of a small state in Central Asia; *Tonkō* (1959; *Tun-huang*, 1978), which offers an explanation for the Buddhist writings sealed in the caves at Tun-huang; *Aoki ōkami* (1959; the blue wolf), based on the life of Genghis Khan; and *Fūtō* (1963; *Wind and Waves*, 1989), which examines from the Koreans' point of view the Mongol invasions of Japan in the 13th c.

Although he continued to the end of his career to produce novels and stories about ordinary people in ordinary situations, as he grew older the usual lighthearted tone of such works became muted as he began to treat more seriously questions about the nature of the human spirit, what it means to have lived, social values, and the relationships that drive people apart and bind them together. *Shirobamba* (1960; *Shirobamba*, 1991), a "coming-of-age" novel based on his own childhood experiences, *Kaseki* (1965; fossils),

about a middle-aged man coming to terms with his impending death from cancer, and *Waga haha no ki* (1975; *Chronicle of My Mother*, 1982), actually a series of essays written over a ten-year period portraying his mother in her declining years, were especially successful.

I.'s historical fiction has won such acclaim that many readers associate his name with no other genre, but such stories and novels represent only a small part of his total oeuvre. Indeed, his success and his popularity can only be accounted for by his ability to write prolifically in a variety of genres, and for readers of widely differing tastes and intellectual levels. The lyric style and the tacit affirmation of life that pervades his works contribute to their wide appeal. Although first and foremost a storyteller, I. also produced numerous accounts of his extensive travels, critical essays, personal reminiscences, and a substantial collection of poems.

FURTHER WORKS: *Kuroi ushio* (1950); *Fūrin kazan* (1953); *Asunaro monogatari* (1953); *Kuroi chō* (1955); *Yodo dono nikki* (1955); *Shatei* (1956); *Gake* (1961); *Yōkihi den* (1963); *Go-Shirakawa-In* (1964); *Natsugusa fuyunami* (1964); *Oroshiya-koku suimutan* (1966); *Yoru no koe* (1967); *Nukata no Ōkimi* (1968); *Seiiki monogatari* (1968; *Journey Beyond Samarkand*, 1971); *Kita no umi* (1968); *Keyaki no ki* (1970); *Shikaku na fune* (1970); *Hoshi to matsuri* (1971); *Osanaki hi no koto* (1972); *I. Y. shōsetsu zenshū* (32 vols., 1972–1975); *Utsukushiki mono to no deai* (1973); *Waga ichigo ichie* (1975); *Kadan* (1975); *I. Y. zenshi shū* (1979); *Honkakubō ibun* (1981); *I. Y. rekishi shōsetsu shū* (11 vols., 1981–1982); *Kōshi* (1987); *I. Y. zenshū* (28 vols., 1995–97). FURTHER WORKS IN ENGLISH: *The Counterfeiter and Other Stories* (1965); *Lou-lan and Other Stories* (1979); *Selected Poems of I. Y.* (1979)

—B. M. YOUNG

INTERIOR MONOLOGUE

See Stream of Consciousness

IONESCO, Eugène

French dramatist, essayist, short-story writer, and novelist, b. 13 Nov. 1912, Slatina, Romania; d. 28 March 1994, Paris

Born of a Romanian father and a French mother, I. was a year old when his mother brought him to Paris. His first language was French. When he was nine years old, he and his younger sister were sent by their parents to spend some time in the care of a kind peasant family in the village of La Chapelle-Anthenaise in Mayenne, where he attended the local school. For I. the years at La Chapelle-Anthenaise were Edenic. In the mind of the adolescent, and later of the mature writer, the peaceful hamlet acquired archetypal dimensions.

When I. turned thirteen, the family left France to join his father, an attorney, in Bucharest. Shortly afterward his parents were divorced, but the boy, although he sided with his mother, had to remain with the parent who was able to provide for his life and education. In Romania, I. perfected his knowledge of his father's language, completed his secondary-school training, and entered the University of Bucharest. He began to teach French when he was eighteen and also embarked on his literary career, publishing poetry and essays in various reviews. His first book of essays, *Nu* (no), was published in 1934. As a young man growing up in Romania, I. learned to recognize the signs of political and intellectual fascism; he seemed to develop an immunity to the malady he would later call "rhinoceritis."

In 1936 I. married, and the couple left Romania in 1938 when I. received a government scholarship to study at the Sorbonne, where he was planning to write a thesis on the theme of death in modern poetry, starting with Baudelaire. War broke out and the couple sought refuge in the south of France, living in the country, then in hiding in Marseille. Returning to Paris in 1945, I. worked as a proofreader. This was a period of great financial hardship, and yet also a time when the young married pair felt happy in a world at peace. I. no longer thought of himself as a writer. He was to become a dramatist "by accident," as he himself often says.

In 1948 I. decided to add a third language to the ones he acquired as a child. He embarked on the study of English, using the Assimil conversation method. As I., the would-be student of the English language, began to transcribe the obvious, almost simple-minded sentences into his notebook, he was struck with the fact that things one takes for granted might indeed have a quality of strangeness, that indeed the world, and our being in the world, which we do not question, are phenomena that can fill one with amazement. This realization filled him with metaphysical angst, and he had to lie down. When he returned to his working table he continued to transcribe the Assimil sentences, but now both the characters and the dialogue began to run away with themselves, to acquire a kind of autonomous existence. The result was a neosurrealist comedy, actually "a tragedy of language," as I. states. *La cantatrice chauve* (1949; *The Bald Soprano*, 1958), an "antiplay," was staged by Nicholas Bataille on May 11, 1950, at the Théâtre des Noctambules. It went unnoticed and unattended until some established writers, such as the dramatist Jean ANOUILH and the avant-garde novelist Raymond QUENEAU, supported it, and embarked on a systematic campaign to attract an audience and a number of critics. They succeeded beyond anyone's expectation. It is a classic of the THEATER OF THE ABSURD.

Although I.'s most favorable critics saw the play as a satire on bourgeois society, *La cantatrice chauve* was already a metaphysical farce. Apsychological, derisive, absurdist, it is a celebration of Dionysian rebirth, of the power of language once it has been stripped of its clichés. The Martins and the Smiths may be interchangeable automatons, but the Dionysian couple, the Fireman and the Maid, the latter composing a poem on the power of fire, are savage forces that precipitate the staid and boring world of routine into a frenzy of deconstruction, and of ultimate freedom.

La cantatrice chauve was quickly followed by *La leçon* (1953; *The Lesson*, 1958), *Jacques; ou, La soumission* (1953; *Jack; or, The Submission*, 1958), and *L'avenir est dans les œufs* (1958; *The Future Is in Eggs*, 1960). *La leçon* is a terrifying picture of the erotic thrust of tyrannical power. As in *La cantatrice chauve*, language is here the protagonist and the hero-villain. The Professor will kill the girl student with a knife as word and object. The murder is a rape, and the knife a phallus. The student's preparation for her *"doctorat total"* is a grotesque mating dance. It is the lecture on philology that unleashes the Professor's murderous sexuality. The play has been called a parable of destruction by habit and magic.

I.'s masterpiece of the first period is probably *Les chaises* (1954; *The Chairs*, 1958). In it the real and the imaginary coincide in a single semicircle of proliferating chairs, seats for imaginary

Eugène Ionesco

guests of the old couple. The play reveals the fundamental mechanism of the imagination. It also suggests absence through the presence of the empty chairs, it is a stage poem about the ontological void. Although the Old Man hopes to leave a message after a mock-heroic double suicide with his wife, the Orator turns out to be afflicted with a form of aphasia. There will be no message. The only reality lies in the tenderness of the Old Woman for her husband, and in the Old Man's vision of the Emperor, "the King of Kings," as I. has revealed in private conversation. It is important not to miss the mystical level of *Les chaises*.

A mystico-comical ascension, a liberation from a stultifying marriage, are portrayed in *Amédée; ou, Comment s'en débarrasser* (1954; *Amédée; or, How to Get Rid of It*, 1958). A mysterious corpse, stretched out on the conjugal bed of Amédée and his wife Madeleine, is afflicted with a strange malady, growth. As its legs begin to protrude into the living room, the only room where the married couple lives and works, it is clear that soon it will become uninhabitable. We are never told when, how, or why the cadaver got into the apartment; its presence is a phenomenological evidence. It suggests, however, a stifling atmosphere, the break-up of a marriage. Madeleine urges her weak, passive husband, an unsuccessful playwright—clearly I. is caricaturing himself—to "get rid of it." One detects also a parody of the detective play, one of I.'s cherished Sophoclean devices. As Amédée, the God-be-loved fool, lowers the incriminating, cumbersome body out the window, into the street, then, running out of the house, tries to drag it in the direction of the Seine, the corpse, grown light, floats up, carrying away a delighted runaway husband. The stage is filled with lights, fireworks, the atmosphere of the carnival. Never has the euphoria of freedom regained been more eloquently concretized upon the stage.

A reverse apprehension, that of weightiness and of secret guilt informs *Victimes du devoir* (1954; *Victims of Duty*, 1958). Here a strong Oedipal motif underlies the action as Madeleine (wife/mother) and the Detective (father/analyst/judge/detective) force Choubert, the protagonist, to question his "unfinished symphony" by plumbing his inner depths. The gaps in Choubert's memory are to be filled with the crusts of the stale bread he is forced to chew by the Detective-Executioner. An unexpected guest arrives, the ectoplasmic projection of the wicked parents, Nicolas d'Eu, whose name suggests a regal incognito (Nicolas II). Madeleine, elated, turns into a frantic hostess, balancing a proliferating number of coffee cups. Her frenzied entrances and exits, her juggling act, remind the audience of the whirling dervish dance of the Old Woman in *Les chaises*. Here, what Antonin ARTAUD called the "anarchy of humor" borders on the demonic.

One of I.'s most joyous plays, despite a strong hint of an inevitable apocalypse, is *Le piéton de l'air* (1963; *A Stroll in the Air*, 1968). The protagonist is an astronaut who has no need of spaceships since he can levitate out of pure joy, a shamanic exercise in the powers of the spirit. He rises where world and antiworld interpenetrate, while an inhabitant of this antiworld wanders among earthlings, clearly lost. Unlike Amédée, who is borne aloft by the corpse-balloon, the stroller treads air as we do water. He moves into outer space *under his own power*. The exultant mood of *le piéton* yields to angst once he begins to circle the earth. He sees from above that our planet is the only verdant place in the universe, and that it is surrounded by "deserts of ice, deserts of fire". Man is indeed a creature caught between the infinity of smallness and the other infinity, that of vastness. I.'s protagonist is happy to return to those he loves upon the earth, and to live a little longer in a state of truce.

I. is a libertarian, perhaps even a gentle anarchist. Two plays reveal this aspect of his philosophy: *Tueur sans gages* (1958; *The Killer*, 1960) and *Le rhinocéros* (1959; *Rhinoceros*, 1960). The first of these presents I.'s "hero in spite of himself," Bérenger, the dramatist's Everyman. A timid, honest, secretly lyrical, deeply committed human being, Bérenger wanders by error—taking the wrong tramway—into an ersatz paradise, the "radiant city." This architectural marvel can offer its dwellers no protection against the universal human condition of mortality symbolized by the murderous will of a *tueur sans gages* (killer without wages)—I. invented this term—who, unlike a *tueur à gages* (a hired assassin), kills gratuitously, for no reason of gain or profit—in fact, irrationally. Bérenger is aghast when the killer's existence is revealed to him by the Architect, an efficient technocrat who takes the scandal of mortality and the presence of evil in his stride. At the end of the play I.'s antihero finds himself facing a puny creature; he realizes that this is the Killer. The final scene of the play is a dialogue-monologue in the course of which the murderer never answers; he just snickers. As Bérenger talks on, attempting to fathom the mentality of one who destroys for the sake of annihilation, he finds only arguments for his own demise. To argue with nihilism is to enter the void, to embrace Nothingness. Although Bérenger is armed—he carries old-fashioned pistols—the Killer's short knife and long-lasting determination are bound to triumph. Unable to kill the Killer, even in self-defense, Bérenger seems to accept his fate.

The Bérenger of *Le rhinocéros* is another incarnation of his namesake. The protagonist of the later play may be outwardly a weak man, even a tippler, and a sentimentalist, but he will have the immense courage of retaining his humanity in the face of universal metamorphosis to bestiality and brutality. Rhinoceritis is the disease of conformity. Bérenger seems to be immune, and yet, sadly, he will remain quite alone at the end of the play, the last human being among creatures whose thick green skin and hoarse, bellowing voices he begins to envy. I. has said in conversation: "There was a time when it seemed to me that everyone had become a fascist, all members of my family, my friends, my colleagues. It was somehow up to me, little me, to resist." *Le rhinocéros* is the stage image of this resistance.

I.'s third profoundly political play is *Macbett* (1972; *Macbett*, 1973). This play is a cartoon version of Shakespeare's *Macbeth*, a grotesque rendition of the ways in which absolute power corrupts absolutely.

Death, the process of dying, trying to search for the meaning of life, such are the great universal themes of I.'s most ambitious later works. He wrote *La soif et la faim* (1966; *Hunger and Thirst*, 1968) for performance at the Comédie Française. In this allegorical drama, Jean, the protagonist, deserts his wife and child to go in quest of the ideal. He is mistaken as to the roads he chooses, and even as to his desires. His thirst cannot be slaked, nor his hunger sated. Finally he will reach a dubious inn, run by fake monks. The monastic society smells of the concentration camp. He will be held prisoner for an indeterminate amount of time, and will be condemned to serve at table, dressed in monk's habit. Time is fragmented into infernal minutes, their numbers appearing on illuminated screens. Now, in this Purgatory, Jean understands the mistake he made when he left home to look for a happiness that was there for him to find. It is too late.

The image of the process of dying finds its most eloquent expression in an earlier play, perhaps I.'s masterpiece, *Le roi se meurt* (1963; *Exit the King*, 1965). Here the same Bérenger has become Bérenger I, the sovereign of a decaying country. Early in the play, he is informed by Marguerite, his first wife, that he is to die soon, at the end of the play. The court physician, who is also the astrologer and the executioner, confirms this prognosis. The king at first refuses to believe this, despite the signs of his own decrepitude, and of the disintegration of his country, but after a while it becomes evident that the end is near. The play echoes the lamentations of Job, and of Shakespeare's Richard II. The final monologue of the shrewish Marguerite, who slowly changes into a divinity of death, is based on Plato's account of the end of Socrates, and on *The Tibetan Book of the Dead*. *Le roi se meurt* is a tone poem on the process of dying and a paean to life. The death of Bérenger I is not only that of an individual, but the decline of our civilization, the end of the planet earth. It is a comic apocalypse.

Two dream plays form a diptych: *L'homme aux valises* (1975; *Man with Bags*, 1977), a play in which the voyage becomes an allegory of man's search for his identity, and *Thème et variations; ou, Voyages chez les morts* (1980; *Journey among the Dead*, 1980). The latter is a series of conversations between Jean, the protagonist, and his dead relatives, including his mother and father. Ancient guilts, remorses, and debts are brought up to the surface. I.'s infernal voyage echoes that of Odysseus to the land of the Cimmerians and that of Aeneas and Dante. W. H. AUDEN once said: "Art is breaking bread with the dead". This play shows us that the way is always open for the living to make contact with their ancestors.

Although he is best known as a playwright, the creator of the genre that could be called metaphysical farce, I. is also an important essayist. *Notes et contre notes* (1962; *Notes and Counter Notes*, 1964) is a lucid collection of *pensées* on modern dramaturgy. His other volumes of essays include *Journal en miettes* (1967; *Fragments of a Journal*, 1968); *Présent passé passé présent* (1968; *Present Past Past Present*, 1971), *Antidotes* (1977; antidotes), a collection of essays on politics and philosophy, *Un homme en question* (1979; a man in question), and the earlier *Découvertes* (1970; discoveries), an illustrated volume of childhood remiscences for which I. composed drawings reminiscent of those of Paul Klee. *Découvertes* is one of the most charming and important books by I.; it translates that sense of wonder which is at the basis of his apprehension, and without which there would have been no *La cantatrice chauve*.

The man who became a member of the French Academy in 1971 has remained also a prankster. He likes to say that as a writer he belongs to the "cabaret school of literature". His ancestors are Charlie Chaplin, the Marx Brothers, and Buster Keaton. But this eternal child is a reader of Plato and Plotinus. For him, nothing is actual; one must rend the veil of appearance. It is through language that we get at the truth. I. wishes to invent a language that will translate the original world, the world of "before" which is that of pure thought. To do so the dramatist often deconstructs speech, as at the end of *La cantatrice chauve* and also of *voyages chez les morts*. Not unlike Dante, I. longs for Paradise, where language was never the seed of doubt and misunderstanding because it coincided with Being, with God.

FURTHER WORKS: *Le salon de l'automobile* (1953; *The Motor Show*, 1963); *Théâtre* (7 vols., 1954–1981); *L'impromptu de l'Alma* (1958; *Improvisation; or, The Shepherd's Chameleon*, 1960); *Le nouveau locataire* (1958; *The New Tenant*, 1958); *Le maître* (1958; *The Leader*, 1960); *La vase* (1961; "Slime," 1966); *La photo du colonel: Récits* (1962; *The Colonel's Photograph, and Other Stories*, 1969); *Délire à deux* (1963; *Frenzy for Two or More*, 1968); *Le tableau* (1963; *The Picture*, 1965); *La colère* (1963; *Anger*, 1968); *Scène à quatre* (1963; *Foursome*, 1963); *La lacune* (1966; *The Gap*, 1969); *Entretiens avec Claude Bonnefoy* (1966; *Conversations with E. I.* 1970); *Jeux de massacre* (1970; *Killing Game*, 1974); *Discours de réception d'E. I. à l'Académie Française et réponse de Jean Delay* (1971); *Ce formidable bordel!* (1973; *What a Bloody Circus!*, 1975); *Le solitaire* (1973; *The Hermit*, 1974); *Voyages chez les morts* (1981); *Le blanc et le noir* (1981). **FURTHER WORKS IN ENGLISH:** *The Killer, and Other Plays* (1960); *Hunger and Thirst, and Other Plays* (1969)

BIBLIOGRAPHY: Fowlie, W., *Dionysus in Paris* (1960): 229–37; Pronko, L. C., *Avant-Garde: The Experimental Theatre in France* (1962): 59–111; Sénart, P., *I.* (1964); Pronko, L. C., *E. I.* (1965); Benmussa, S., *I.* (1966); Donnard, J. H., *I. dramaturge; ou, L'artisan et le démon* (1966); Guicharnaud, J., *Modern French Theater from Giraudoux to Beckett*, rev. ed. (1967): 215–29; Jacobsen, J., and Mueller, W. R., *I. and Genet: Playwrights of Silence* (1968); Abastado, C., *I.* (1971); Coe, R. N., *I.: A Study of His Plays*, rev. ed. (1971); Tarrab, G., *I. à cœur ouvert* (1971); Wulbern, J. H., *Brecht and I.* (1971); Vernois, P., *La dynamique théâtrale d'E. I.* (1972); Lamont, R. C., ed., *I. A Collection of Critical Essays* (1973); Saint, T., *E. I.; ou, À la recherche du paradis perdu* (1973); Esslin, M., *The Theater of the Absurd*, rev. ed. (1973): 100–65; Jacquart, E., *Le théâtre de dérision: Beckett, I., Adamov* (1974); Bondy, F., *I.* (1975); Hayman, R., *E. I.* (1976);

Lamont, R. C., and Friedman, M. J., eds., *The Two Faces of I.* (1978)

—ROSETTE C. LAMONT

La cantatrice chauve [*The Bald Soprano*] goes back to 1950, and yet it has managed to remain unaltered through the nine intervening years. The other day, I found it more spare and bare than ever before, and still funnier. This "antiplay" has become a play, as one might have easily predicted, one that makes fun of other dramatists' works, and of itself as well; it constitutes the most burlesque parody of conversation that I have ever been given to encounter, whether in the salon or on the stage, also of "dramatic situations," and, more generally, of the peculiar mania that afflicts one and all, the utter inability to keep quiet.

The thought has crossed my mind—who is not afflicted by occasional doubt?—that if I had had such a good time discovering *The Bald Soprano*, the work of some unknown, presented at the now defunct Théâtre des Noctambules, it might have been due to its novelty and singularity. The production at La Huchette, and frequent rereadings as well, have served to reassure me. In fact I laughed more heartily than on the first day. Nicolas Bataille's staging, inseparable from the play itself, has managed to retain these precious qualities of surprise, of grace in the midst of the absurd, banality within insanity, qualities which had appeared so striking, and had congested the brains of pure Cartesians when the play first opened . . . .

Today, E.I. remains true to himself with an ever increasing discipline, one that does not exclude the aesthetic and the amusing. Neither the overstrung sycophants who attempt to push him in the direction of abstraction and systematization, of "a philosophy of language," nor the detractors who try to bludgeon him as soon as he makes an appearance, have been successful in distracting him from his goal, which is to make the audience laugh at its own intimate void, its own zaniness.

Jacques Lemarchand, "Les débuts de I.," *Cahiers des saisons*, No. 15 (1959), pp. 215, 218

The horror of proliferation—the invasion of the stage by ever-growing masses of people or things—which appears in *The Future Is in Eggs* is one of the most characteristic images we find in I.'s plays. It expresses the individual's horror at being confronted with the overwhelming task of coping with the world, his solitude in the face of its monstrous size and duration.

This is also the theme of *The Chairs* . . . often considered one of I.'s greatest achievements . . . . A play like *The Chairs* is a poetic image brought to life—complex, ambiguous, multi-dimensional. The beauty and depth of the image, as symbol and myth, transcends any search for interpretations. Of course it contains the theme of the incommunicability of a lifetime's experience; of course it dramatizes the futility and failure of human existence, made bearable only by self-delusion and the admiration of a doting, uncritical wife; of course it satirizes the emptiness of polite conversation, the mechanical exchange of platitudes that might as well be spoken into the wind. There is also a strong element of the author's own tragedy in the play—the rows of chairs resemble a theatre; the professional orator who is to deliver the message, dressed in the romantic costume of the mid-nineteenth century, is the interpretative artist who imposes his personality between that of the playwright and the audience. But the message is meaningless, the audience consists of rows of empty chairs—surely this is a powerful image of the absurdity of the artist's, the playwright's, own situation.

Martin Esslin, *The Theatre of the Absurd* (1961), pp. 99–100

The type of theatre against which I. usually inveighs is the ideological theatre which claims social usefulness as its main function. This, he says, is nonsense . . . and it is more illuminating to read a psychological treatise than to visit a psychological theatre, for the latter is insufficiently psychological. . . . I. does not maintain that ideas have no place in the theatre. He draws a line between ideas and ideology . . . . He makes a distinction between ideas which are universal in character and those which are local and specific, such as political ideas.

Bernard F. Dukore, "The Theatre of I.: A Union of Form and Substance," *ETJ*, 13, 3 (1961), pp. 174–75

What was being displayed to those tiny audiences who attended the first performances of *The Bald Soprano* and *The Lesson* was, as Jean Vannier has written, "a drama of language, wherein human speech is put on exhibition." The clichés of the first play, which I. was inspired to write by his dizzying encounter with an English phrase-book, and the deadly logical flights of the second, were the dramas themselves, not simply means of advancing some anteriorly conceived "action" or of illustrating character or even, as the chief dignified misreading of I. would have it, of mocking the orderly process of social existence and celebrating an absurd counterpart . . . .

I., however, had a future, and it was to go beyond the exigencies and fatalities of language, although they were always to remain a condition of his work. His later plays are richer and more complex; in them new lyrical and philosophic modes develop, humor becomes less a matter of linguistic sport than of the tension between appearance and reality, the dramatic consciousness spreads to include fuller states of being and more inclusive attitudes toward the horrifying, the banal, the metaphysically unjustifiable. In his greatest plays—*Amédée, Victims of Duty, Killer without Wages*—I. has written works of the same solidity, fullness and permanence as his predecessors in the

dramatic revolution that began with Ibsen and is still going on. [1963]

Richard Gilman, *Common and Uncommon Masks: Writings on Theatre—1961–1970* (1971), pp. 87–88

I.'s people—unlike Beckett's or Genet's—are lonely where, according to any materialist philosophy, they have no right to be: in a social situation. In their families, their sitting-rooms, their offices, surrounded by relatives, *concierges*, policemen and visitors, they discover willy-nilly an additional dimension to be lonely in. And this brings us back, finally, to I.'s dilemma in relation to the current *avant-garde*—the "Happening" and the drama of participation. For the "enclosed" situation of I.'s heroes (and hence the structure of his plays) has nothing accidental about it; it is essential to the deepest elements in his vision of the world. They are enclosed *in* a society: to escape that prison, there is only one way out—into the solitude of a dimension of which society has no knowledge. Whereas the drama of participation sees the problem exactly in reverse: it is the stage-"character" who is solitary, imprisoned in his theatre, enslaved by the dictatorial will of his dramatist and his producer, locked away inside the dungeon of his individualism and his vain private dreams. His escape is outwards, into the street, into the pub and the park, into the world. For the Living Theatre, society offers the escape from solitude. For I., solitude offers the escape from society. It does not look as though the dilemma has any obvious solution.

Richard N. Coe, *I.: A Study of His Plays*, rev. ed. (1971), p. 164

Critics have attempted to distinguish various periods in I.'s inspiration, and thus varied styles in his dramaturgic writing. In reality, the dramaturgy he espouses issues from a single way of looking at himself, the way in which each human being envisions the existential fact of being alive. The diversification of stage expression flows from the necessity to express varied, though limited, relations created by the interaction of an individual with the ambient universe . . . . These relations with beings and things may be many, but they are all viewed in the light of an archetypal feeling, that of amazement, the astonishment that invades a human consciousness when it grapples with the mystery of its existence. If I. seems to question language, knowledge, society, and death, it is in order to deepen and probe the modes of these relations, and the final relation of all these with nonbeing: in turn, the object, the other, the others, and the beyond. I.'s dramaturgy lays the foundation of the *derisive* genre, an amalgam of the laughable and the bitter. A haunting, obsessive doubt hovers over the public: man and the universe are reduced to a simple, desperate interrogation.

Paul Vernois, *La dynamique théâtrale d'E. I.* (1972), p. 2

I., the absurdist playwright, is like Pär Lagerkvist, the cubist playwright, in that he discovers classicism, with its constants of balance, tension, primitivism, and archetypality, to be the vehicle and not the fellow-traveler of certain modes or genres. Lagerkvist's classicism incorporates cubism and tragedy; I.'s incorporates absurdism and tragicomedy. The two dramatists share an aversion to being classified by critics. In each case the aversion is qualified: Lagerkvist upholds classicism and virtually defines it as cubism; I. is willing to be identified as a classicist. But I. is not willing to be labeled as a dramatist limited to any one of the modes which contribute to his classicism—for example to comedy, tragedy, or absurdism. With proper qualification of the critical terms that bear application to Ionescan drama, it is feasible to conclude that I., well attuned to the absurdity exposed in Aeschylean and Sophoclean tragedy, has transmuted this exposure into true tragicomedy and has become the classic dramatist of the theatre of the absurd.

Roy Arthur Swanson, "I.'s Classical Absurdity,"
in Rosette C. Lamont and Melvin J. Friedman,
eds., *The Two Faces of I.* (1978), p. 147

IQBAL, Muhammad

Indian poet and philosopher (writing in Urdu, Persian, and English), b. 9 Nov. 1877, Sialkot (now in Pakistan); d. 21 April 1938, Lahore (now in Pakistan)

I. started to write poetry seriously while a student at Scotch Mission College, Sialkot, and earned a considerable reputation as a poet in Urdu prior to leaving for England in 1905 to study at Trinity College, Cambridge. He also studied law in London and received a Ph.D. in philosophy from the University of Munich in 1907. Returning to India, he distinguished himself both as a statesman and poet-philosopher, in recognition of which he was knighted in 1922. An activist in the Muslim League, I. articulated in 1930 his famous plea for a separate state for Muslims in northwest India. In 1932 he traveled throughout Europe and met a number of intellectual and political leaders, including Henri BERGSON and Benito Mussolini. I. continued to champion the cause of Muslims in India and to write poetry until his death.

In order to reach a Muslim audience beyond India, I. wrote his first major poem, *Asrar-e khudi* (1915; *The Secrets of the Self*, 1920), in Persian. In this work he enuciated his concept of the self (*khudi*), the living principle of the universe, the foundation of all human endeavor. To I.'s thinking, life is not a static but rather a dynamic, evolutionary process of "becoming." The only way in which one can activate this process is to affirm and enlarge the self. This self, whether of individuals or nations, grows and expands as long as it is held in a state of tension, which, in turn, produces action, adventure, and inquiry. The urge to maintain such a tension is love (*ishq*), a concept that bears a close resemblance to Bergson's *élan vital*. To relax this tension is to create inertia, weakness, a negation of life—in short, evil. Such evil manifests itself in the form of *saval*, or questioning, which appears in various guises, such as borrowing another person's or country's money, ideas, customs, mores, and so forth. By imitating, I. states, one shows a

lack of resourcefulness and of courage to accept the challenge of life and living. His thinking was revolutionary in Muslim intellectual circles, which were dominated by the principles of classical Muslim mysticism and its notions of fatalism and quietism.

In his second collection of Persian poems, *Rumuz-e bekhudi* (1919; *The Mysteries of Selflessness*, 1953), I. counterbalances the sense of egoism and individuality of *Asrar-e khudi* with the ideas of brotherhood and service in Islam. His masterpiece is another Persian poem, *Javid nameh* (1932; *The Pilgrimage of Eternity*, 1961). Modeled on Dante's *Divine Comedy* and Milton's *Paradise Lost*, the work depicts the poet's ascent through the various spheres of heaven until he experiences a vision of the Divine. His guide through this pilgrimage is the 13th-c. Persian mystic-poet, Jalaluddin Rumi.

I.'s first collection of Urdu poems, *Bang-e dara* (1924; call of the highway), contains poems from two distinct periods: those written between 1895 and 1905 in India, which are essentially nationalistic in outlook, and others composed between 1905 and 1908 in Europe, which deal with love themes in various guises. The earlier poems are often couched in lush nature imagery drawn from I.'s Indian surroundings. Among the latter group of poems is the famous "Khizr-e rah" (guide of the road), in which I. warns Indians against being dazzled by Western modes of government and law, especially as vehicles with which to solve the problems of the East.

The second Urdu collection, *Bal-e Jibril* (1936; wing of Gabriel), contains many of I.'s most famous poems, including "Masjid-e Qartabah" (mosque of Cordova), which commemorates his emotional visit to the cathedral of Cordova, Spain, a structure that had been a mosque prior to 1236. Another is "Lenin khuda ke huzur men" (Lenin in the presence of God), a dramatic confrontation between the apostle of Marxism and the Divine.

I.'s major English work is *The Reconstruction of Religious Thought in Islam* (1930), which crystallized his political thinking and articulated the intellectual position of Muslim separatists in their pursuit of a Muslim homeland in India, to be called Pakistan. I. stresses the need for reform in Islam much the same way Christianity required change just prior to the advent of Protestantism. While progressive in advocating change, I. is conservative in expounding methods for the actualization of these reforms.

I. is considered the spiritual father of Pakistan, which was established in 1947. In Persian literature he is accorded a place of honor among modern poets; in Urdu he is revered as the greatest poet of this century by Urdu speakers in both Pakistan and India, where many of his verses have entered the language as adages and sayings. His message of self-reliance and Islamic activism both shaped and reflected the Indian nationalist movement during the 1920s and 1930s, especially for Muslims, who look upon him even today as their leading intellectual figure of the 20th c.

FURTHER WORKS: *The Development of Metaphysics in Iran* (1908); *Payam-e mashreq* (1923; *The Tulip of Sinai*, 1947); *Zabur-e ajam* (1927; *Persian Psalms*, 1948); *Pas che bayad* (1936); *Musafer* (1936); *Zarb-e kalim* (1937); *Armaghan-e hijaz* (1938). FURTHER WORKS IN ENGLISH: *A Voice from the East: The [Urdu] Poetry of I.* (1922); *[Urdu] Poems from I.* (1955)

BIBLIOGRAPHY: Singh, I., *The Ardent Pilgrim* (1951); Bilgrami, H., *Glimpses of I.'s Mind* (1954); Vahid, S., *I.: His Art and Thought* (1959); Dar, M., *Introduction to the Thought of I.* (1961); Schimmel, A., *Gabriel's Wing* (1963); Malik, H., ed., *I.: Poet-Philosopher of*

Pakistan (1971); Memon, M., ed., *I.: Poet and Philosopher between East and West* (1979)

—CARLO COPPOLA

IRANIAN LITERATURE

The thousand-year-old classical Persian literature has been admired not only in countries of western and central Asia and the Indian subcontinent but also in Western Europe, especially during the romantic movement. It was praised and even considered one of the four main bodies of world literature by such writers as Goethe. In the long history of the Iranian people the Persian language and its literary idiom have played a pivotal role around which the nation and the culture have revolved.

The revolt in Iran at the end of the 19th c. and the beginning of the 20th c. finally brought forth the constitution of 1906, which changed the absolute monarchy into a constitutional one. Although the literati of the country actively participated in trying to implement this innovation, it proved to be easier in theory than in practice. This was true also in the application of drastic and decisive reform measures in the establishment of a modern literary idiom in Iran.

During the Pahlavi rule of Iran (1925–79) the constitutional process suffered a setback. Although great strides were made toward the modernization and Westernization of the country, literature was not encouraged unless it served the monarchy. With the steady erosion of political freedom in Iran, literary repression prevailed, but it could not really inhibit the writers.

In the view of the majority of Iranian writers, the imposition on the Iranian nation of the regime of the Islamic Republic, after the revolution brought down the Pahlavis, is a further setback. The goals and workings of the Islamic Republic are in contradiction to the ideas and ideals for which the majority of writers fought since the mid-1950s.

Fiction

Up to the end of the 19th c. stylized prose forms and emphasis on theology, philosophy, and history had long prevailed. There had been no creative fiction. As in poetry, rhetorical considerations had become the object, the goal, rather than the vehicle. Originality was frowned upon, and attempts at writing novels in the Western manner were both unsuccessful and unacceptable.

During the upheaval of the constitutional period the need for a new form of expression became apparent. Even reporting of daily events in the mushrooming press required a new prose style. Translations of Western works were very helpful models. Under the influence of Alexandre Dumas père, Victor Hugo, and Jules Verne, writers of fiction chose the historical novel as the vehicle for their social and political comments.

Hasan Badi's (dates n.a.) *Dastan-e bastan* (1921; an old legend) provided a transition to the more modern approach. Having studied in Western sources the history of the Achaemenids, the first historical Persian dynasty, Badi produced a historical novel that, while dealing with a traditional subject, succeeded in a new way by using fully rounded characters and a unified plot; he also appealed to the current patriotism. By contrast, *Daliran-e Tangestani* (1932–33; the heroes of Tangestan) by Hussein Roknzadeh Adamiyat

(dates n.a.), while by no means a fine creative work, was acclaimed for its anticolonial sentiments.

The short story patterned on Western examples proved to be a more suitable vehicle for Persian prose. *Yeki bud, yeki nabud* (1921; once upon a time) by Mohammad'Ali Jamalzadeh (b. 1896) should be considered not only the literary manifesto of the author but also a Magna Carta for the written word in the Persian language. The volume contains six stories, which represent the first artistically successful attempt at social comment. Jamalzadeh portrayed the signs of a decayed system—corrupt religious and governmental ideologies, the need for social reform—and he condemned the men who perpetuated social ills. His criticism was tempered by his humor, his vivid descriptions, his caricatures of common life, and his lucid language. Although *Yeki bud, yeki nabud* had to overcome opposition from religious and governmental circles, Jamalzadeh's use of the short story as an artistic and effective tool assured his canonization as the guiding spirit for the next generation of Persian writers.

The most outstanding of these was Sadeq HEDAYAT, who epitomized the confluence of post-World War I Western influence and the evolution of Persian fiction. He was concerned with the psychological implications of man's existence and human interactions, and preoccupied with silent and malign unseen forces which seemed predominant and to which he finally succumbed by committing suicide in 1951. In writing about the seamy elements of Iranian street life, he showed omnipresent compassion for the futility and frailty of human life, as in *Buf-e kur* (1937; *The Blind Owl*, 1957; new tr., 1974). His stories are of the gutters and slums as well as of the students and minor officials.

Hedayat was an ardent patriot. His love for Iran and for its heritage is an important element in his work. He was also a great collector of Iranian folk tales, which he often used in his creative writing. Hedayat was probably the most important Persian writer of the 20th c. With him, Persian fiction at last earned a place in the body of world literature. Thirty years after his death his presence is still strongly felt, not only among the literati and the intellectuals but especially among the youth of Iran, for whom Hedayat is an idol.

One of his many followers is Sadeq CHUBAK, although his style differs from that of Hedayat. Chubak, the realist, writes of similar everyday situations of flesh and blood, but without the metaphysical overtones of Hedayat and with an underlying optimism. He, too, reproduces realistic pictures of Iranian locales and people by using their own language with aggressive vigor. His technique is like a snapshot of an event, but it has a distressing emotional and intellectual impact. It proceeds single-mindedly to its climax unencumbered by compound sentences, peripheral descriptions, or inconsequential dialogue. Chubak likes to exploit certain common social stereotypes and colloquial language, triggering predetermined images and emotional reactions that render lengthy exposition unnecessary. A full range of stock characters and behavioral patterns of varying complexity are thus incorporated in a few sentences. His writing is an intricate counterplay between the lyric and the macabre, the poetic and the horrible. Although the literary content, symbolism, and setting of Chubak's short stories and novels are very Iranian, they never lose their universal appeal.

The works of several outstanding writers of fiction, in addition to their literary value, are eternal monuments to the fight for artistic and political freedom, social justice, and tolerance. Buzurg ALAVI is especially noted for short stories vividly portraying oppression, injustice, and suffering. Jalal AL-E AHMAD exposed in his fiction the problems of Iranian society. His social criticism is written in a straightforward, unadorned prose, as in *Modir-e madraseh* (1958; *The School Principal*, 1974). His essays in literary criticism were of great value in introducing that genre to Iran.

Another writer with a very sharp pen who understood his role as artist and social critic was Samad Behrangi (1939–1968). Because of his outspoken political, economic, and social criticism, most of Behrengi's writings were offically banned by the Shah's security police. His short stories are mostly about children and for children. A selection in English translation appeared under the title *The Little Black Fish* (1976). Beh'azin (pseud. of Mahmud Etemadzadeh, b. 1915) also had a great impact on modern Iranian fiction. His masterful short stories mainly portray the humble peasants of his native Caspian province.

In 1961 a very long novel was published by the then-unknown writer 'Ali Mohammad Afghani (b. 1925): *Showhar-e Ahu Khanom* (Ahu Khanom's husband). This event was considered by Iranian literary critics as a turning point in contemporary literature, because of the novel's perceptiveness and penetration.

The period extending from Jamalzadeh and his followers until today has been quite aptly termed the "age of prose." Persian prose has matured in the last six decades. After fighting with poetry for its existence as a valid art form, it has now equaled it in expression and popularity.

Poetry

Poetry, with its elevated position, although very popular among all classes of Iranians, had for a long time become a staid and rigid system. The *'aruz* (classical prosody) acquired a prestige demanding total obedience. Poetic diction also solidified at the expense of ideas.

One of the first great masters who tried to bring poetry into synchronization with the 20th c. was Mohammad Taqi Bahar (1886–1951), known as the "king of poets." He did not try to divorce himself from the style that had been prevalent for centuries but, instead of putting the emphasis upon perfection of form, stressed content and simplicity of language. He was one of the first Persian poets to write about his private life—portraying his family, his work, his associates; and about city life, with its streets, public bathhouses, bazaars, mosques, squares, and especially its people. He was also one of the first to introduce a simplified vocabulary and common expressions into poetry.

However, the appearance of a free-verse poem entitled *Afsaneh* (1921; the legend), by Nima Yushij (pseud. of 'Ali Esfandyari, 1895?–1959), should be thought of as a point of departure from the centuries-old domination and despotic rule of *'aruz* over Persian poetry. Nima Yushij destroyed the strongest and longest-surviving elements of classical poetry—its meter and rhyme. It was a revolution. The country was divided between the *nowparastan*— worshipers of the new—and the *kohneparastan*—worshipers of the old. Although young poets joined forces with Nima Yushij, it took a long time and many battles in the pages of literary journals until the free-verse poets achieved recognition. This recognition was won thanks to such poets as Fereydoun Tavallali (b. 1919), who can still attract more traditional audiences through his mastery of the poetic image.

After World War II the main impulse in poetic creativity became antitraditional in its attitudes toward politics, social life, and literature. Many people could not understand the socio-psychological causes of this revolutionary eruption. From the mid-1950s on, modernist poetry proliferated. Younger poets carried modernism further. But not all of them pursued a headlong course. Some returned to more traditional verse, which obviously could not remain unchanged after such an experience; some were content with what they had gained; and some went to the extreme of the new wave. The extremists insisted that poetry remain free from social, political, and moral commitments, or even a commitment to logic.

In the history of modern Persian poetry, the other end of the spectrum—the lyrical poetry of Nader Naderpour (b. 1929)— should not be neglected, despite his predilection for classical diction. In a sense, he represents an important link to the past, binding modern poetry to its great tradition.

Among the modernists, two early followers of Nima Yushij were Manuchehr Sheybani (b. 1923) and Esmail Shahrudi (b. 1925). With clarity of expression, Sheybani presents the pre-Islamic, Zoroastrian world of light and darkness, truth and falsehood.

According to many critics, Forugh FARROKHZAD is not only the most important poet since Nima Yushij but also Iran's best poet after the great classical period of the 15th c. In her poetry she violates not only the norms of form but also those of expression by freely stating her feelings unencumbered by symbolic representations and metaphor. Her uncensored personal communications are startlingly plain, but in a way innocent. *Tavvalod-e degar* (1964; another birth), the last volume before her untimely death in an automobile accident, is a personal and artistic climax—a victory for a woman who could free herself from the fetters of the alienation and frustration of that male-dominated society and a victory for artistic achievement in modern Persian poetry.

Another leading modern poet of Iran, who like Farrokhzad strove for the Sufi-like integration of man and a transcendent unity of being, was Sohrab Sepehri (1928–1979). His poetry, like his painting (Sepehri was one of the best painters of modern Iran, and exhibited in many countries), is like contemplation and meditation about nature, which is seen by his inner "eye of the heart." While his art is definitely Persian, it never loses its universality; although it is very modern and avant-garde, it is also timeless. The most representative collection of Sepehri's poetry is *Hasht ketab* (1976; eight books).

The living masters who have been most influential on the youngest generation of modern poets of Iran are Ahmad Shamlu (b. 1925) and Mehdi Akhavan-Sales (b. 1928). Shamlu, ceaseless searcher for new means of poetic expression, is like a prestidigitator whose hat is full of ever fresh and extraordinary metrical and verbal resources. But he is not a trickster who tries to impress his audience. On the contrary, he is probably the most honest Iranian poet, the one most committed to the totality of Iran's past, present, and future. At the same time, his innovative lyrics tie modern Persian poetry to that of the rest of the world.

The poetry of Akhavan-Sales has been governed by what may be termed homeostatic dynamics: discarding certain values of the past that were hindering political, social, cultural, and especially literary development, and striving at the same time to preserve some of the old values, and if possible adapt them to the new circumstances of a rapidly changing society. His poetry, although very modern, is nevertheless an exponent of the continuity of the past.

Siavash Kasrai (b. 1927) combines lyricism with an epic breadth. Manuchehr Ateshi (b. 1931) reflects in his poetry the rugged landscape of the desert near the Persian Gulf and the toughness of the nomadic tribes. Mohammad 'Ali Sepanlu (b. 1938), like many contemporary Iranian short-story writers, tries to weave into his poetry the spoken language and everyday situations.

The majority of today's poets, despite all the innovations and experiments, do not forget that poetry has been a point of reference, a mirror of Iran's history and myths and an expression of national identity.

Drama

There has been no established literary corpus of Persian creative drama. On the other hand the only indigenous drama in the world of Islam is Persian *ta'ziyeh*, a ritual theater that derives its form and content from deep-rooted religious traditions. Its genius is that it combines immediacy and flexibility with universality. But since there is no fixed text, it has not been considered literature. There are *ta'ziyeh* manuscripts, but they are mostly written as individual parts for each performing character, and therefore they are not intended to be read separately.

At the end of the 19th c. *ta'ziyeh* was on the brink of giving birth to a secular theater in Iran. Unfortunately, this birth did not occur, since the trend was toward Western-style drama. Until recently, however, all the attempts at imitating Western drama were very poor. The playwrights were not completely aware of the dramatic functions and forces of the play. But since the 1960s literary dramatic activity has flourished. It is probably the fastest-growing literary genre, despite the fact that the political restrictions on freedom of expression have probably hampered drama more than any other form.

There are two main schools of playwriting in Iran. One is familiar with Western drama but borrows very little from it, other than structure. These dramatists turn to Iranian folklore and traditional entertainment, and they employ familiar stock characters. The main representative of this school is Bahram Beyzai (b. 1938).

The other school bases itself to a great extent on Western patterns, especially the work of such post-World War II dramatists as BECKETT and IONESCO. The action is set in predominantly Iranian locales. The best representative of this group is Gowhar Murad (pseud. of Gholam-Hossein SA'EDI. His plays—outstanding among which are *Chub be dasthaye Varazil* (1965; the stickwielders of Varazil) and *Ay ba kulah ay bi kulah* (1968; oh fool, oh fooled)— are marked by political symbolism and allegory.

Like fiction and poetry, modern drama in Iran for the most part takes its subjects from everyday life and employs colloquial speech.

Iranian Literature since 1980

The Islamic revolution of 1978–1979 in Iran, given its magnitude and impact on the life of Iranians, can only be compared to the Soviet Revolution of 1917. In the sphere of literature, however, the comparison does not hold. For the majority of writers who made names for themselves in Iran before the revolution, the goals and accomplishments of the Islamic Republic stand in contradiction to the ideas and ideals for which they had fought with their pens since the 1950s. Those literary men and women were socially committed liberals, if not radical leftists, who applauded the victory of the revolution during the first year after the Shah had left Iran. That year did not produce any literary or artistic masterpieces but allowed the intellectuals, writers, and artists to express themselves without constraint. This permissive atmosphere, however, did not

last long after the introduction by the government of new Islamic codes of life-style and conduct for Iranian citizens. As a result of various strictures, many prose writers, poets, and dramatists emigrated. The execution by firing squad in mid-1981 of a dramatist, Sa'id Soltanpur (dates n.a.), was an ominous signal for those writers who stayed in the country. Only one year before his execution, Soltanpur had won critical acclaim for his play *Abbas Aga, Kargar-e Iran Nasional* (1980; Abbas Aga, a worker at the Iran National Company).

Despite this, the last decade must be seen as a measured success for Iranian literature as a new generation of Iranian writers has appeared on the scene. In these new circumstances, a dramatic shift has occured in literary form and content. It has been a decade of the novel as the predominant literary form, succeeding a thousand-year-old Persian preference and indeed love for poetry. The new crop of novelists in Iran have come into their own without being influenced by their Western counterparts, owing in great part to the relative isolation of Iran from the rest of the world after its revolution. The only foreign influence that can be noticed is that of the contemporary Latin American literature. These writers found the right medium of expression for Iranian readers who had gone through the convulsions of the revolution and eight years of a bloody and heartbreaking war with Iraq. It is interesting to note that not only has the contemporary Persian novel, espousing realism as its vocabulary, surpassed contemporary poetry in popularity, but that foreign novels translated into Persian have experienced the same reception. In the last decade alone more than one-hundred-fifty novels worthy of mention have been written in Iran. The best evidence for the novel's esteem in today's Iran is the fact that 30,000 copies of the longest, ten-part, five-volume novel of some 2,800 pages by Mahmoud Dowlatabadi (b. 1941) entitled *Klidar* (1978–1984; Klidar) were sold as they appeared on bookstore shelves. It is a modern folk epic structured almost entirely in the pattern of the *Shahnameh*, the famous national epic of Ferdowsi of the 11th c. The same epical approach is found in a novel by a woman writer, Moniru Ravanipur (b. 1953), called *Ahl-e qharq* (1990; the drowned). In this novel she creates a mythical atmosphere in a village by the sea where earthly and underwater inhabitants struggle. Their conflict is the millennia-long preoccupation of Iranians with the neverending duel between the forces of light and darkness, between good and evil. This Zoroastrian concept is transposed onto both allegorical and real situations in historical and contemporary times by another woman writer, Shahrnush Parsipur (b. 1946), in her novel *Tuba va Ma'na-ye Shab* (1989; tuba and the meaning of the night). One of the most gifted living writers of fiction is Abbas Ma'rufi (b. 1958); his *Semfoni-ye-mordegan* (1989; symphony of the dead) is just short of a masterpiece. Among established writers Ismail Fasih (b. 1935) should be included for making his readers think as they laugh over situations, others, and themselves. Hushang Golshiri (b. 1937) has contributed penetrating observations about the human condition, while Reza Baraheni (b. 1935) is known for his outspoken insights, in his creative writing as well as in literary criticism, published in 1987 as *Razha-ye sarzamin-e man* (secrets of my land). This two-volume, 1,275-page account of American secret involvements in Iran, especially in Azerbaijan, is a well-informed and acerbically written book. One of the great masters of the short story, Sadeq CHUBAK, seems to have closed his writing pad since he settled in the West fifteen years ago. The short story is still a very popular vehicle for Persian prose but is not being used as much as it was in the 1960s and 1970s. In poetry, under the shadow of two long-established giants of Persian verse, Ahmad Shamlu (b. 1925) and Mehdi Akhavan-Saless (1928–1990), newcomers are not abounding. Shamlu's output during the last decade has been erratic compared with his prerevolutionary production. Nevertheless, most of his poetry is pregnant with the ideas of an intellectual genius and a visionary. Akhavan-Saless's poetry is rooted deeply in Iranian culture and will influence many generations of Persian poets to come. Nader Naderpur (b. 1929), who chose to live in the West, must be seen as a poet that any national literature would like to claim—he is a ship on an even keel, proudly unfurling the sails of Iranian poetic tradition.

On the whole, important poetry and fiction appear to have managed to avoid the pitfalls of censorship, although self-censorship has doubtless deprived us of many creative works. What is even more significant is that the great bulk of poetry and fiction managed to avoid the taint of propaganda. Such has not been the lot of drama, and especially not of children's literature. This last along with young-adult literature in the Islamic Republic of Iran occupies, calculated on the percentage of books published on these lines, second place after religion and before poetry and fiction. The prominence given to children's literature is due to the fact that the Iranian population has been for many years one of the fastest growing in the world, with more than ten million children in primary schools. A youthful population played a very important role in the revolution and especially in the war against Iraq, and the government is intent on making an Islamic revolutionary imprint on its young minds. The content of this literature is further supported by graphic illustrations of great imagination.

Drama has probably been the fastest-growing literary genre since the 1960s. Before the revolution there were two schools of dramatic craftsmanship in Iran. One was structured after the classical and modern Western drama, while the other turned to traditional Iranian performing arts: professional storytelling and religious passion plays. After the revolution the latter school was encouraged by the existing regime to propagate its weltanschauung. However, since a great number of Iranian dramatists, theater, and film directors, and actors left the country as a result of the revolution, drama as a form became politicized and polarized, with many dramatists in Iran and in the diaspora exalting and degrading the same issues. This is most evident in the plays of the greatest Iranian dramatist, Gholam-Hossein SA'EDI, and Hamid Reza A'zam (dates n.a.). Sa'edi died in exile in Paris in 1985. His *Pardedaran-e a'ineh afruz* (1986; the mirror-polishing storytellers) and *Otello dar sarzamin-e ajayeb* (1986; Othello in wonderland), both published posthumously, are a sardonic attack on the governmental enforcement of behavior patterns acceptable to the new, revolutionary standards as well as the conduct of war. A'zam in his *Shegerd-e akhar* (1986; the final art) is apotheosizing a sacred war against Iraq. An interesting aspect is that both playwrights use *naqqals* or storytellers to advance their plots. A'zam uses a famous tea-house storyteller in the national epic *Shahnameh* as a point of departure from praising the heroic deeds of ancient champions to glorify the heroism of Iranian youth in the battlefields of the Iran-Iraq war. Sa'edi's storyteller, on the other hand, uses a traditional backdrop painting (*pardeh*) to show the audience how young men are being used, and die only to bring anguish to their families. With its progression, the play becomes a black comedy. The master of the black comedy is another exiled Iranian man of theater, Parviz Sayyad (b. 1937). His *Samad be jang mirevad* (1984; Samad goes to war) and *Samad az jang barmigerdad* (1988; Samad returns from war) are the most frontal attacks on the Iranian regime and

how Iranian youth was brainwashed by the regime in order to wage war. In *Mohakemeh-ye sinema reks* (1987; the Cinema Rex trial) Sayyad accuses the Islamic regime of starting the fire in Cinema Rex in Abadan in 1978 to gain revolutionary momentum against the Shah. Four hundred people died in that fire. In his *Khar* (1983; jackass), Sayyad mocks the Iranian society, which could so easily be manipulated. Never in the history of Iranian theater have as many spectators attended dramatic performances as they now do in the U.S., Canada, and Europe as Sayyad travels with his theater, making a circuit of Iranian communities on both continents and performing these four plays for them. A new literary form that became prominent in postrevolutionary Iran is *filmnameh*. These are published screenplays. The major proponent of this form is Bahram Beyzai (b. 1938), a famous dramatist.

Iran's greatest success in the literary field during the last decade may be measured by the rapidly growing number of readers. Again probably as the result of the revolutionary conditions in the country, the Iranians now spend more time at home, and have more leisure time to read than before the revolution. The pace of life in Iran before the revolution was very fast, and there was a great variety of available entertainment, drawing potential readers away from serious literature. Today they read more of Persian classics, contemporary Persian literature, and translations from world literature than ever before. One of the factors helping to enlarge general readership is an increase of literacy in Iran by some twenty percent during the last fifteen years, and a vastly increased number of women readers.

For non-Persian writing in Iran, see under Azerbaijani Literature and Kurdish Literature

BIBLIOGRAPHY: Brown, E. G., *Press and Poetry of Modern Persia* (1914); Avery, P., "Developments in Modern Persian Prose," *MW*, 45 (1955): 313–23; Kamshad, H., *Modern Persian Prose Literature* (1966); Kubičkova, V., "Persian Literature of the 20th Century," in Rypka, J., et al., *History of Iranian Literature* (1968): 353–418; Yarshater, E., "The Modern Literary Idiom," in E. Yarshater, ed., *Iran Faces the Seventies* (1971): 284–320; Ricks, T., ed., special Iran issue, *LitR*, 18, 1 (1974); Hillmann M. C., ed., special Iran issue, *LE&W*: 20, 1–4 (1976); Chelkowski, P., "The Literary Genres in Modern Iran," in G. Lenczowski, ed., *Iran under the Pahlavis* (1978): 333–64; Hamalian, L., and J. D. Yohannan, eds., *New Writing from the Middle East* (1978): 271–400; Karimi-Hakkak, A., Critical Introduction to *An Anthology of Modern Persian Poetry* (1978): 1–27; Southgate, M. S., *Modern Persian Short Stories* (1980); Farrukhzad, F., *Another Birth: Selected Poems of Forugh Farrokhzad* (1981); Sa'edi, G.-H., *Dandil: Stories from Iranian Life* (1981); Hillmann, M. C., "Revolution, Islam, and Contemporary Persian Literature," in Jabbari, A. and R. Olson, eds., *Iran: Essays on a Revolution in the Making* (1981): 121–42; Farrokhzad, F., *Bride of Acacias* (1982); Hillmann, M. C., ed., *Iranian Society: An Anthology of Writings by Jalal Al-e Ahmad* (1982); special Iranian literature issue, *IranS*, 15: 1–4 (1982); special Iranian literature issue, *IranS*, 18: 2–4 (1985); Alishan, L. P., "Ahmad Shamlu: The Rebel Poet in Search of an Audience," *IranS*, 18 (1985): 375–422; Fasih, E., "The Status: A Day in the Life of a Contemporary Iranian Writer," *Third World Review*, 9 (1987): 825–47; Hillmann, M. C., "Iranian Nationalism and Modernist Persian Literature," *LE&W*, 23 (1987): 69–89; Kapuscinski, G., *Modern Persian Drama* (1987); Yarshater, E., ed., *Persian Literature* (1988): 291–402, 513–18; Ghanoonparvar, M. R., and J.

Green, *Iranian Drama* (1989); Hillmann, M. C., *Iranian Culture: A Persianist View* (1990)

—PETER J. CHELKOWSKI

IRAQI LITERATURE

On the eve of World War I Iraq had languished in a state of cultural stagnation brought about by centuries of alien rule. During the period of Ottoman Turkish rule of Iraq that lasted from 1534 until 1917 Arabic had been supplanted by Turkish as the official language of the state, the language of rulers, and of the elite. This had the effect of stunting the growth of Arabic literature. The demise of the Ottoman Empire in the aftermath of the war, however, freed Arabic literature and culture from Turkish hegemony and cleared the way for increased cultural contacts with Europe.

Iraq's reluctant encounter with European civilization in the 20th c. unleashed creative energies that lay dormant for centuries and led to a revival (*nahda*) affecting, *inter alia*, literary and cultural production. It is noteworthy that the poetic revival got underway and reached high levels of excellence more quickly than other genres. This is primarily due to the fact that, unlike the novelist or the dramatist, the Iraqi poet had a long and rich poetic tradition to draw on.

Poetry

The first major poet of the 20th c. was Jamīl Sidqī al-Zahāwī (1863-1936). Al-Zahāwī's verse occupies a transitional position between the rigid formalism of the 19th c. and the reformist tendencies of the 20th c. In his poetry and polemic are discernible in embryonic form the notions that would dominate literary and social debate for the rest of the century. In verse as well as in numerous articles al-Zahāwī championed often unpopular social causes—an article in a Baghdad newspaper calling for the emancipation of women led in 1910 to a local riot. In the realm of poetry al-Zahāwī sounded an early call for a poetics that reflected the spirit of the modern age and was the first Arab poet to have experimented in poetic form. His verse, which remained largely conventional, contains some of the earliest attempts to eschew excessive ornamentation in favor of a simpler idiom. This may have been due to his inclination to employ science and philosophy as subject-matter for his poetry.

Al-Zahāwī's contemporary and rival for the mantle of the "Neoclassical school" of poetry in Iraq was Ma'rūf al-Rusāfī (1875-1945). Al-Rusāfī's poetry is staunchly realistic, preoccupied as it is with the portrayal of the ills besetting Iraqi society in the opening decades of the century. Widespread poverty, the inferior status of women, corruption, and colonialism are common themes in his poetry. With al-Rusāfī the concerns of "the common man" become appropriate subject matter for Arabic poetry that had traditionally been oriented toward the upper echelons of society. Much of al-Rusāfī's verse, collected in his *dīwān* (collection of verse), is occasional, didactic, and declamatory as necessitated by the subjects he broached. Like al-Zahāwī he often opts for familiar idiom in preference to the ornamentation that characterized the verse of his predecessors. Here lies his (and al-Zahāwī's) important contribution to the evolution of modern Arabic poetry, in setting in motion a process that would culminate in the rise in Iraq of new modes of poetry more suited to articulating the concerns of the 20th c.

The neoclassical school of Arabic poetry reaches its apogee with Muhammad Mahdī al-Jawāhirī (1900-1997) considered by many to be the most important Arab poet of the 20th c. Since the appearance of his first poem in 1921, al-Jawāhirī had remained an unwavering classicist looking to the great Arab poets of the 'Abbāsid age, especially al-Buhturī and al-Mutanabbī, for his poetic models. His forthright classicism coupled with the somewhat archaic diction of his verse caused that verse to receive little critical attention outside the Arab world.

Al-Jawāhirī was the most politically engaged Arab poet of the 20th c. In his poetry, which he often declaimed to large and enthusiastic audiences, he lashed out at colonialism, political oppression, and social inequality. His championing of national, social, and political causes, which the *qasīdah* form was uniquely equipped to articulate, caused him to spend much of his life in exile in various countries. Al-Jawāhirī's verse is collected in a five-volume *dīwān*: *Dīwān al-Jawāhirī* (1973).

As the first half of the 20th c. drew to a close, a revolution in Arabic poetry was taking place, the most decisive development in the history of Arabic poetry. That revolution ushered in a new poetry that came to be known as "the free verse." Poets such as al-Zahāwī and al-Rusāfī had made important strides toward eliminating excessive artificiality in the language and diction of Arabic poetry. They, however, largely conformed to its metrical conventions, which insisted on the use of a certain number of feet and a single meter throughout the poem. It was widely recognized that such extreme metrical regularity placed inordinate restrictions on a poet's creativity. Yet an effective solution to this problem continued to elude reformers for decades. Some poets, notably the Egyptian Ahmed Zakī Abū Shādī (1892-1955), attempted to introduce variations on the basic Arabic prosodic order such as the use of different meters in the same poem. These experiments, however, were largely unsuccessful, and it was not until the end of the 1940s that two Iraqi poets, Nāzik AL-MALĀ'IKA and Badr Shākir AL-SAYYĀB, were able to devise a solution. Their approach involves a shift from the use of a predetermined number of feet to the use of the single foot as the basic metrical unit. According to this approach, a poet can use as many feet as necessary to meet the needs of his or her creative process. Moreover, the use of the rhyme becomes optional; a poet may choose to use it throughout, sparingly, or he or she may do without it altogether without injury to the integrity of the poem. The implications of this in terms of allowing greater freedom for the creative imagination of the poet have been significant.

The first two poems written in the free verse mode were al-Malā'ika's poem entitled "al-Kolerā" (The Cholera), which appeared in a Beirut review in 1947, and al-Sayyāb's poem, "Hal Kāna Hubban?" (Was it Love?), which was included in his collection of verse, *Azhār Dhābila* (Wilted Flowers) published in that same year. The free verse movement in Arabic poetry was formally launched in 1949 with the publication of al-Malā'ika's volume of verse, *Shazāyā wa Ramād* (Splinters and Ashes). This was followed in 1950 by al-Sayyāb's collection, *Asātīr* (Myths). Each of these two volumes included a number of poems written in the free verse mode. It was largely due to al-Sayyāb's highly sophisticated poems, however, that this new form was widely adopted throughout the Arab world and has become the dominant poetic form in Arabic poetry.

The second significant aspect of the poetic revolution that started in Iraq in the late 1940s involved the content of poetry. The new generation of poets attacked their immediate predecessors, the romantics, on the grounds that their poetry was too sentimental, escapist, and that its practitioners were out of touch with the new realities of Arab life. These new realities included World War II, during which much of the Arab world was transformed into a battleground for the Allies and the Axis powers with heavy political, economic, and social consequences for the Arab people. They also included the 1948 Arab-Jewish War, which ended with the defeat of the Arab armies and the creation of the state of Israel on Arab land.

Badr Shākir al-Sayyāb is one of the most significant figures in modern Arabic poetry. In his short and grief-ridden life he was able to transform both the form and content of Arabic poetry, notably in his poems published in the 1950s that lent credence to the free verse movement and popularized the new mode of writing throughout the Arab World. In addition to launching the revolution in the form of the Arabic qasīdah, al-Sayyāb revolutionized its content. Noteworthy in this respect is his incorporation, under the influence of T. S. ELIOT, of myths and historical archetypes as well as his introduction of new themes in Arabic poetry the most recurrent of which is the theme of the city as a center of oppression and that of the village as symbol of innocence and nurturing.

Al-Sayyāb's most famous poem is "Unshūdat al-Matar" (The Song of the Rain), which first appeared in 1954 and is included in his major volume of the same title. Arguably the most influential poem written in Arabic in the 20th c., "Unshūdat al-Matar" describes the poet's feeling as he watches the rain fall on the Arabian Gulf in Kuwait where he then lived in exile. The poem alludes to the ancient Babylonian myth, the Tammuz fertility myth of resurrection through life-giving rain. Such allusion reflects the poet's faith in the eventual rebirth and regeneration of his nation following long periods of decline.

Al-Sayyāb's poetic corpus is generally divided into three stages. The romantic stage includes the verse he wrote between 1946 and 1950. Much of the poetry of this period is generally deemed unremarkable with the exception of "Hal Kāna Hubban?," which represents an early example of al-Sayyāb's experimentation in form. This second stage includes the poetry he wrote in the 1950s. The poetry of this period can be described as "committed," reflecting the poet's political affiliations first as Communist and later as advocate of Arab nationalism then in its heyday. It is during this decade that he wrote some of his most memorable verse contained in his volume, Unshūdat al-Matar (1960; The Song of the Rain). It is also during this period that al-Sayyāb assimilates influences from Western poetry especially T. S. Eliot's "mythical method."

The third and final stage of al-Sayyāb's poetic development, "the subjective stage," comprises the verse he wrote in the early 1960s contained in such diwans as Al-Ma'bad al-Gharīq (1962; The Drowned Temple) and Manzil al-Aqnān (1963; The House of Slaves). A subdued, introspective mood predominates in the poetry of this period reflecting the poet's growing disillusionment with leftist politics but also his deteriorating health as a result of a degenerative disease that would soon cut short his life.

Al-Sayyāb's rival for the leadership of the free verse movement was the Iraqi poetess Nāzik al-Malā'ika. One of the foremost Arab women poets of the 20th c., al-Malā'ika is the author of seven collections of poetry of which the best known are her first two volumes, 'Āshiqat al-Layl (1947; Lover of the Night) and Shadāyā

wa Ramād (1949; Shrapnel and Ashes). Like al-Sayyāb she began composing poetry in the romantic vein. In this she was influenced by the Egyptian poet 'Alī Mahmūd Tāhā (1901-1949) and also by the English romantic poets such as Keats on whose Hyperion she modeled her own long poem Ma'sāt al-Hayāt wa Ughniya lil Insān (1970; The Tragedy of Life and a Song for Man). Unlike al-Sayyāb, however, the romantic tendency lingers on, coloring much of her poetic corpus. A melancholy note pervades her verse that (at a later stage) intermingles with mystical overtones.

Although al-Malā'ika wrote poems on political themes such as colonialism, Algeria's fight for freedom, and Arab unity, her treatment of these themes remains at a superficial level, lacking the profundity and engagement of al-Sayyāb's. Al-Malā'ika's paramount importance in the history of modern Arabic literature is as critic and theorist of the new school of poetry. In the preface to her volume Shadāyā wa Ramād and in her study Qadāyā al-Shi'r al-Mu'āsir (1962; Issues in Contemporary Poetry) she provides a theoretical underpinning for the free verse mode. Moreover, the publication of Shadāyā wa Ramād, which included a number of poems written in the free verse mode, caused an uproar in the still largely conservative Arab literary circles. This, together with the ensuing controversy with al-Sayyāb over who was the first to "invent" the free verse mode served to draw considerable attention to the new method of writing poetry. It is in these rather than in the poetry per se that al-Malā'ika's important contribution to modern Arabic literature lies.

The social-realist mode of writing found in 'Abdul al-Wahhāb AL-BAYYĀTĪ an ardent proponent. One of the most prolific Arab poets of the 20th c., al-Bayyātī's corpus includes Malā'ika wa Shayātīn (1950; Angels and Devils), Abārīq Muhashshamah (1954; Broken Pitchers), Al-Majd Lil Atfāl wal Zaytūn (1956; Glory Be to Olive Trees and Children), and Sifr al-Faqr wal Thawra (1965; The Book of Poverty and Revolution).

Like al-Sayyāb's, al-Bayyātī's early verse (collected in the volume Malā'ika wa Shayātin) is written in a predominantly romantic vein. Following this romantic phase, al-Bayyātī embraced Marxism, an ideology to which he has remained firmly committed ever since. In verse couched in a phrase that comes close to ordinary speech, al-Bayyātī's ideological commitment finds expression. The dominant themes of his poetry are the poverty of the masses, the suffering of the peasants, political oppression, and the emancipation of the proletariat. Al-Bayyātī has spent much of his life in exile to escape persecution for his dissenting views. Predictably, the themes of exile and alienation recur in many of his poems, as does a melancholy note that almost always mingles with one of hope for ultimate emancipation.

Another Iraqi poet who is often associated with the rise of the free verse movement in Arabic poetry is Buland al-Haydarī (1926-1996). Al-Haydarī's poetic oeuvre includes nine volumes of poetry the best known of which are Aghānī al-Madīnah al-Mayyitah (1951; Songs of the Dead City), Khatawāt fi al-Ghurbah (1965; Steps in Exile), Rihlat al-Hurūf al-Sufr (1968; Journey of the Yellow Letters), and Aghānī al-Hāris al-Mut'ab (1971; Songs of the Weary Guard). In these and other works al-Haydarī's sense of alienation born of prolonged exile from his homeland finds anguished expression. Oppression, whether by an urban environment that obliterates the individual sense of identity or by totalitarian regimes, is another recurrent theme in his poetry. His resistance to the latter form of oppression led to his exile to the relative safety of Beirut where he lived from 1963 until 1976. Following the outbreak of the Civil War in Lebanon in 1975, however, he was forced to seek refuge in London, wherein he decried, in verse drenched with feelings of frustration, sorrow, and despair, the tragic turn of events in Lebanon, the subject of his volume *Ilā Beirut maʿa Tahiyyātī* (1989; To Beirut with My Greetings). Al-Haydarī was among few Arab poets who believed that the language of the age is the language of poetry. His verse is marked by an economy in the use of words freighted with maximum connotative possibilities. In verse whose texture is as elegant as it is acute al-Haydarī brought poetry closer to the spoken idiom. In this his poetry stands in sharp contrast to that of many of his contemporaries.

Fiction

Some literary historians trace the beginnings of the fiction genre in Iraq to 19th-c. attempts by Mahmūd Abū al-Thanāʾ al-Ālūsī (1802-1854) at writing *Maqama*s. It is certain, however, that the novel and short story are 20th-c. introductions made possible by contacts (though belated) with Western modes of narrative writing, at first through translations of European literary works and later through direct encounter with originals. Other factors that contributed to the development of the fiction genre in Iraq were the rise of a middle class that provided not only the fiction writers but also the readership, and accelerated Westernization, involving as it did the spread of education and the subsequent swelling of the numbers of reading public. Mention must also be made of the role played by the increasing number of newspapers and periodicals that provided a venue for publishing (in serial form) numerous fictional works.

It is generally agreed that the first Iraqi novel was *Fī Sabīl al-Zawāj* (1921; For the Sake of Marriage) written by Mahmūd Ahmad Al-Sayyid (1903-1937). As its title suggests, *Fī Sabīl al-Zawāj* deals with the regressive attitudes to marriage in the early 20th c. The work echoes early calls for women's emancipation. Al-Sayyid's second novel, *Masīr al-Duʿafāʾ* (1922; The Fate of the Weak), alludes to the inequities and oppression of Turkish colonial rule of Iraq. *Masīr al-Duʿafāʾ* is regarded as first Iraqi novel written in a social-realist mode. The tendency to write in this mode was made imperative by the then prevalent circumstances of Iraq. Hopes for liberation and independence had been dashed as World War I ended with a mere change of colonizers; the Turkish colonizers were merely replaced by new ones, the British. This tendency was also necessitated by the general backwardness of the country that, in addition to making possible the continued colonization of Iraq by foreign powers, made for a multitude of social and economic illnesses.

Since the appearance of al-Sayyid's two novels, the genre has carved a permanent niche for itself on the literary scene with a large number of writers contributing to it. Abd al-Haqq Fādil (b. 1910) is an early important contributor to the fiction genre in Iraq. His novel *Al-Majnūnān* (1939; Two Mad People), which broaches social issues, represents a noticeable departure from the didacticism of Mahmūd al-Sayyid and achieves a relatively complex treatment of the subject matter. The novel reflects a moderate level of assimilation of Western novelistic techniques derived from the writer's readings of European literary works.

Dhunnūn Ayyūb (1908-1996) is a key figure in the development of the Iraqi novel. A prolific writer, Ayyūb has authored six novels and fifteen collections of short stories. Ayyūb is known chiefly for his first two novels, *Al-Duktor Ibrāhīm* (1939; Doctor Ibrahim) and *Al-Yad wal Ard wal Māʾ* (1948; The Hand, the Land, and the Water). These works are reformist in intent and clearly belong to the category of "committed literature," which in its Iraqi

context amounted to a conscious attempt on the part of the author to chronicle instances of social inequity, oppression, and the exploitation of the masses, and to call for a more equitable social order. *Al-Duktor Ibrāhīm* and *Al-Yad wal Ard wal Māʾ* address, in a style that comes close to being reportage, such themes as they pertain to urban and rural Iraqi society respectively. In numerous instances the works degenerate into outright didacticism, a feature not relieved by the inordinate amount of descriptive detail with which they are encumbered. These shortcomings notwithstanding, the two novels are unmistakably Iraqi in their settings and characterization. They moreover broach themes inspired by a distinctly Iraqi milieu.

The novelist and short-story writer Ghāʾib Tuʿma FARMĀN is another major contributor to the fiction genre in Iraq. The author of ten novels and collections of short stories, Farmān's best-known work is his novel *Al-Nakhlah wal Jīrān* (1965; The Palm Tree and the Neighbors). Set against a backdrop of World War II, the novel chronicles the trials and tribulations of its relatively large number of characters who hail from an impoverished Baghdad quarter, and delineates the impact of that war on the fabric of Iraqi society. *Al-Nakhlah wal Jīrān* is intended as a microcosm of Iraqi society during the war years, a claim supported by the use in the novel of material derived almost exclusively from Iraqi sources and by the extensive use of Iraqi colloquial in the dialogue. This fast-paced work achieves a high level of complexity in the treatment of its locally derived subject matter and character development, and some critics consider it to be the first Iraqi narrative work identifiable as a novel in the strict technical sense of the term.

Of the post-World War II generation of fiction writers ʿAbdul Rahmān Majīd al-Rubayʿī is perhaps the best known. Al-Rubayʿī has published seven novels of which *Al-Washm* (1972; The Tatoo) is his first and most critically acclaimed. *Al-Washm* portrays a stormy period in the modern history of Iraq, the post-Qāsim era. It represents an indictment of the spirit of defeatism and self-centeredness that flourished following the downfall of the Qāsim regime in 1963. With regard to form, the novel represents an important step in the development of this genre in Iraq. The author's use of such modernist techniques as the interior monologue, the flashback, and a generally fractured structure has led to their adoption by a number of younger Iraqi writers.

The fictional works of ʿAbd al-Rahmān MUNĪF, a Saudi-born writer who took up residence in Iraq during the 1970s, represent a significant boost to the genre in Iraq. Munīf is a prolific writer, whose works include *al-Ashjār wa Ightiyāl Marzūq* (1973; The Trees and Marzūq's Assassination), a novel that deals with political oppression in an unnamed Arab county. This theme is further explored in Munīf's second novel, *Sharq al-Mutawassit* (1977; East of the Mediterranean), which represents a powerful indictment of political oppression in the Arab world. Prefacing the novel with excerpts from the Universal Declaration of Human Rights serves to underscore the systematic and widespread violations of those rights in the Arab world. Such violations of human rights are also highlighted through passages that describe in gruesome detail the methods of torture to which dissidents are subjected in an unnamed country that is meant to stand for any Arab country.

The best-known Iraqi short-story writers are ʿAbd al-Malik Nūrī (b. 1921) and Fuʾād al-Takarlī (b. 1927). Nūrī's second collection of short stories entitled *Nashīd al-Ard* (1954; The Song of the Land) has had a major influence on the evolution of the short-story genre in Iraq. Most of the stories of this collection focus on the plight of the downtrodden in society. They draw heavily on material derived for the most part from Iraqi sources and make use of Iraqi colloquialisms. Al-Takarlī's more recent writings include a novel *Al-Raj' al-Ba'īd* (1980; The Improbable Return). It is, however, as a pioneer short-story writer that he is chiefly known. His best-known work in this genre is his long short story "Al-Wajh al-Ākhar" (1960; The Other Face), which, in typical existential fashion, provides vivid portrayal of the inner world of its characters, a world characterized by an overwhelming sense of loss, frustration, and fear.

Drama

The beginnings of drama in Iraq can be dated to the closing decades of the 19th c. Despite this relatively early beginning, drama remains the least developed genre by comparison with the novel and the short story. A number of factors have contributed to this untoward state the most significant of which are the almost total lack of indigenous dramatic tradition on which to anchor the new genre and the dilemma pertaining to the inappropriateness of the use of Iraqi colloquial as opposed to *fushā*, the received form of Arabic.

The first half of the 20th c. saw few Iraqi dramatic works composed and even fewer staged. Most dramatic activity was confined to translations of dramatic works (undertaken mainly in Egypt and Lebanon) and performances by visiting troupes (again mainly Egyptians and Lebanese). This situation, however, began to change towards the mid-20th c. From the 1950s onwards a number of dramatists have appeared on the literary scene and have made some contributions to the development of the genre in Iraq. Jalīl al-Qaysī (b. 1937), also a short-story writer, is one such contributor. His *Jīvārā 'Ād* (1971; Guevara has Returned), a collection of one-act plays, were staged in Baghdad in 1974 to some critical acclaim. Another contributor to the dramatic genre is Shākir Khusbāk (b. 1930) who in 1962 published *Bayt al-Zawjiyyah* (The Matrimonial House), a play of a manifest reformist bent. It was, however, the dramatist and actor Yūsuf al-'Ānī (b. 1927) who has made the most significant contributions to the development of the dramatic genre in Iraq. Al-'Ānī's repertoire includes * Āna Ummak yā Shākir* (I'm Your Mother, O Shākir), a two-act play written in 1955 but not staged until after the 1958 revolution. Like many of his works, this highly acclaimed play addresses overt political and social issues. It is noteworthy for its portrayal of Iraqi women in a positive role. *Al-Miftāh* (The Key) was another acclaimed play by al-'Ānī. The play, which was staged in 1968, is noteworthy for its creative use of Iraqi folk traditions. *Al-Miftāh* was followed by *Al-Kharābah* (The Ruin), a play in two acts that broaches the subject of social exploitation and political hegemony.

Since the 1980s the dramatic genre in Iraq has suffered a steady decline as a result of intensified efforts by the ruling Ba'th regime to use theater to disseminate its political propaganda. The long-term effects of such wholesale state requisition of drama (and of literary production in general) on the evolution of the drama genre in Iraq are uncertain at this juncture. What is certain, however, is that the process of forging new modes of literary production set in motion in the 20th c. will continue in the 21st c. and will result in further works of enduring literary and cultural value.

BIBLIOGRAPHY: Altoma, S. J., *Modern Arabic Literature: A Bibliography of Articles, Books, Dissertations, and Translations in English* (1975); Badawi, M. M., *A Critical Introduction to Modern Arabic Poetry* (1975); Boullata, I., ed., *Critical Perspectives on Modern Arabic Literature* (1980); Badawi, M. M., *A Critical Introduction to Modern Arabic Poetry* (1975); Moreh, S., *Modern Arabic Poetry 1800-1970* (1976); Jayyusi, S. K., *Trends and Movements in Modern Arabic Poetry* (2 vols., 1977); Jayyusi, S. K., ed., *Modern Arabic Poetry: An Anthology* (1987); Badawi, M. M., ed., *Modern Arabic Literature* (1992); Altoma, S. J., *Modern Arabic Poetry in English Translation: A Bibliography* (1993)

—HUSSEIN N. KADHIM

IRISH LITERATURE

Writing in Ireland in the 20th c. is the outgrowth of two cultures and languages: Gaelic and English. Since modern Ireland is a postcolonial culture, the naming of territory and literature is closely bound up with politics and history. Thus, over the past four centuries, literature written in English in Ireland has been referred to as "Anglo-Irish," while "Irish literature" could mean literature written in either Gaelic or English. For the purposes of this article, the term "Irish Literature" is used to refer to literature written in either language.

Beginning in the 17th c. the common use of Gaelic was eroded by wave after wave of cultural attrition by English colonists so that the production of Gaelic literature had dwindled to a trickle by the end of the 19th c. This trend was temporarily reversed with the advent of the Gaelic Revival. The revival was spurred on by a series of important historical events: the land-reform movement, political pressure for Home Rule, and the emergence of a series of heroic political figures who were to influence greatly the course of politics and literature in the 20th c. Probably the most important of these was Charles Stuart Parnell (1846–1891), who waged a vehement political campaign for Home Rule. His rejection by political opponents and the hierarchy of the Catholic church in Ireland and his premature and tragic death after a bitter public scandal over his apparent involvement in an adulterous affair inspired the young William Butler YEATS and others to invest great energy in generating an Irish cultural revival as part of a more militant movement to remove British political and cultural control in Ireland. Parnell, after his death, was inducted into Yeats's heroic pantheon along with Cuchulainn, and thus became another recurring figure in the work of Yeats, James JOYCE, and others.

Yeats felt that the rise of middle-class values in England and the powerful influence of the Catholic church in Ireland were threats to what he saw as the heroic Irish tradition that predated Christianity. In Yeats's opinion, Ireland was one of the strongholds against the "filthy modern tide." He thus led a movement whose purpose was to reinvent an Ireland that had been lost to numerous waves of colonization by Vikings and Normans, but most especially the imperialist English. Yeats's form of nationalism came as a direct response to Ireland's postcolonial history, so he focused his energies at this time on the founding of the National Literary Society (1892), and later the Abbey Theatre (1904). These, along with the founding of the Gaelic League by Douglas Hyde (1860–1949) in 1893, led to widespread renewal of interest not only in the Irish language, but also in ancient Irish myth and folklore. While Irish political and social changes exerted their own forces on the production of literature in Ireland, we cannot dispute the stylistic influence of the continental realists and symbolists. As Yeats himself put it, "Every man everywhere is more of his age than of his nation."

Drama

In 1899, Yeats, along with George Moore (1852–1933), Lady Augusta Gregory (1852–1932), and Edward Martyn (1859–1923), founded the Irish Literary Theatre, later renamed the Irish National Theatre, which in 1904 found its permanent home at the Abbey Theatre. In 1899 the company produced Yeats's second play, *The Countess Cathleen*, which tells of a young countess who sells her soul to the devil to save the lives of a group of famine-stricken Irish. The Irish public, many of whom did not see the play, protested vehemently the play's unorthodox religious implications, and thus began Yeats's often stormy relationship with the Irish public and the inauguration of the Abbey as not only the country's national theater, but, most extraordinarily, a platform for political and social debate. This was one of the first times in modern European history when the staging of plays in a metropolitan theater had the persistent power to provoke riots. Along with Yeats's plays, the drama of John Millington SYNGE and Sean O'CASEY at times verged on the incendiary. After a series of riots over the plays of these three dramatists, the Abbey Theatre was thrust into the international public eye.

Yeats exploited the controversy surrounding *The Countess Cathleen* to produce a play with a similar theme, called *Cathleen ni Houlihan*. In this play, set in the rural west of Ireland during the 1789 uprising, an old woman, who is the embodiment of dispossessed Ireland, asks the young hero to forsake married life to become a martyr for his country. The old woman is magically transformed into a beautiful young maiden as the rejuvenating blood of the young male is spilled. *Cathleen ni Houlihan* came to represent, for all subsequent Irish literature, the bloodthirsty but irresistible spirit of Ireland who would call young men to their deaths. The Irish National Theatre also saw the production of the first play in Irish: Douglas Hyde's *Casadh an Tsugain* (*The Twisting of the Rope*, 1901), which was a remarkable event in that its production came at the twilight of the use of the Gaelic language and the culture that cradled it.

Lady Gregory, Yeats's mentor and collaborator, wrote over forty, mostly one-act, plays, many of which were performed at the Abbey, including *Spreading the Word* (1904), *The Workhouse Ward* (1909), and *The Rising of the Moon* (1910). Synge was "discovered" in Paris by Yeats, who advised him to go to the west of Ireland and write about the people there, to "express a life that had never found expression." In 1903 the Irish National Theatre Society produced Synge's *In the Shadow of the Glen*, one of a series of plays that explore the folkways of a dying rural culture. When his best-known play, *The Playboy of the Western World* (1907), was performed, riots occurred in Dublin because nationalist feeling had reached such a pitch that any perceived insult to the sacred "national character" or the "noble Irish country people" was virtually sacrilegious. Synge's plays are outstanding because he successfully reproduced on stage the authentic dialect of the western Irish: He had ostensibly stripped the English language of its "Englishness." But it was George Bernard SHAW who was to play masterfully with the stereotype of Englishman and Irishman on stage, using as his model the stage-Irishman popularized in the drama of the 19th-c. Irish-American dramatist Dion Boucicault. In the preface to *John Bull's Other Island* (1904), which was expressly written for Yeats's Irish Literary Theatre, Shaw states, "Ireland is the only spot on earth which produces the ideal Englishman of history."

In 1923, after the partition of the island and the formation of the Irish Free State, the Abbey was now state subsidized and ready to resume production after civil conflicts that began with the uprising of 1916. It was the new dramatist O'Casey whose plays were to take the stage at the Abbey by storm, beginning with *The Shadow of a Gunman* (1923), *Juno and the Paycock* (1924), and the notorious *The Plough and the Stars* (1926), the last of which caused riots in the streets of Dublin of the kind that had not been seen since Synge's *Playboy* nineteen years earlier. All three of O'Casey's early plays are set against the background of the political turmoil of 1916, to the war of independence, and the subsequent civil war; however, they are more of a social study of life in the Dublin slums, in which the male characters are music-hall stage-Irish caricatures and the women are rational, tolerant, and heroic in the face of tragedy. O'Casey's later drama tends toward the EXPRESSIONIST. *The Silver Tassie* (1928) was rejected by the Abbey, causing a split between Yeats and O'Casey. The Dublin Gate Theatre took on more experimental works than the Abbey, particularly the work of Denis JOHNSTON and Paul Vincent CARROLL in the late 1920s and the 1930s. Brendan BEHAN's drama is outrageous tragicomedy that contains the autobiographical elements of his involvement with the I.R.A. and subsequent imprisonment in 1939, but unfortunately it verges on self-caricature. *The Quare Fellow* (1954) is set in a prison the night before an execution; and probably his best play, *The Hostage* (1958), looks at the capture of a British soldier in a brothel.

Brian FRIEL is recognized as today's greatest Irish dramatist, whose *Philadelphia, Here I Come* (1964), *The Freedom of the City* (1973), *Aristocrats* (1979), and *Translations* (1981) examine the history and psychopathology of a people suffering from a profound sense of dispossession and failure. His characters are starved of love and filled with worthless fantasies of historical grandeur, but in *Dancing at Lughnasa* (1991) Friel makes a claim for the Dionysiac rituals among the most repressed country people. Thomas Murphy's (b. 1931) *A Crucial Week in the Life of a Grocer's Assistant* (1969) and *The Gigli Concert* (1984) expose the squalor and repressions of provincial small-town life, while Thomas Kilroy's (b. 1934) *The Death and Resurrection of Mr. Roche* (1969) and *Talbot's Box* (1979) focus on the isolation of being an outcast, in this case a homosexual, in Dublin. Frank McGuinness (dates n. a.) moves into the more experimental and challenging territory with *Innocence: The Life and Death of Michelangelo Merici, Caravaggio* (1987) and *Observe the Sons of Ulster Marching to the Somme* (1986), in which we follow the ironic political and tribal allegiances of a group of Irish soldiers on the front during World War I.

Poetry

Yeats dominates the poetic landscape both in Ireland and abroad, for he belongs to both the canons of Irish literature and high MODERNISM. As in his drama, Yeats's early poetry uses Irish myth and folklore as a means of expressing his romantic ideals, and his early style has the elaborate poise of the Pre-Raphaelites. In "The Stolen Child" (1886) we find wistful escapism in enchanting lines like "In pools among the rushes / That scarce could bathe a star." But Yeats also had the remarkable ability to transform himself from an imaginary wanderer in fairyland into a realist who could confront the violence in the streets of Dublin after the uprising of 1916 and the subsequent war of independence, as well as World

War I. In "The Second Coming" (1920) the speaker expresses an overwhelming sense of helplessness in the maelstrom of violence at home and abroad: "The blood-dimmed is loosed, and everywhere / The ceremony of innocence is drowned." This poem also contains Yeats's important theory of the repetitive cycles of history and violence. The legacy that Yeats wanted his poetic inheritors to adopt in "Under Ben Bulben" (1939) was "Irish poets learn your trade, / Sing whatever is well made."

Yeats's death in 1939 left a seemingly unfillable void on the Irish literary scene, particularly in the enveloping dark of the war in Europe in which the Republic chose to be neutral. Austin CLARKE adopted the idea of the poet as social commentator, attacking the powerful influence of the Catholic church. Patrick KAVANAGH, the first father figure of the northern poets, railed against the limitations of rural life, most especially in his great antipastoral masterpiece "The Great Hunger" (1942). He marked a geographical shift in the center of poetic activity from south to north. Louis MACNEICE, while he belonged to a circle of radical English poets of the thirties along with W. H. AUDEN and Stephen SPENDER, was a lyrical poet who elevated the pastoral west of Ireland and criticizes the encroachment of the modern world in urban Belfast, though he is less romantic and more skeptical that Yeats. Thomas KINSELLA is one of a series of poets to look both backward, to Irish mythology, and outside Ireland, especially to Carl Gustav JUNG and Ezra POUND, for poetic models. Richard MURPHY writes on the starkness of life in confrontation with the elements on his native west coast. Probably his greatest poem is the nostalgic "The Battle of Aughrim," which attempts to bridge the gap between history and the self. John MONTAGUE made the north the definitive territory for Irish poetry, territory that had to be recovered from its colonial history, and resituated in mythology. Montague looks to the landscape itself for evidence of ancient history, to the neolithic remains that litter the countryside, especially in *The Rough Field* (1972). Seamus HEANEY began his career by taking Montague's analytical gaze on the landscape a step further, to the point that he approaches the land more like a lover than an archaeologist. Having grown up in rural County Derry and a member of the Catholic nationalist minority in British Northern Ireland, Heaney is keenly aware of the tremendous pressure exerted on him to be a spokesman for the dispossessed nationalist community. He has persistently resisted this role, and has worked, especially in the 1980s, to expand his horizons within an artistically limiting situation. Nevertheless many of his poems tackle the thorny issue of violence in today's Northern Ireland, particularly in *North* (1975), in which the poet struggles to make connections between archaeological evidence of ritual slayings in prehistoric Europe with today's violence. In *Station Island* (1985) Heaney takes a spiritual and artistic pilgrimage to meet the spirits of dead father figures, not to mention Joyce. *The Haw Lantern* (1987) contains a brilliant and moving elegy, "Clearances," to the poet's mother. Derek MAHON much of whose work takes place in the landscape of urban Belfast, is more skeptical about history and politics then Heaney; his loyalties vacillate, for he is less physically attached to the landscape than his fellow northerners, and thus sees it in a different light. John Hewitt (1907–1987) is an important northern pastoral Protestant poet, writing, as it were, from the other side of the barbed wire from Heaney. Paul Muldoon (b. 1951) has been hailed as the leader of the next generation of northern poets, with fine collections such as *Why Brownlee Left* (1980) and *Quoof* (1984), in which he casts a cold eye on the pressure placed on the poet to comment on politics, by painting ever-shifting, often surreal images to reinforce the freedom that he

demands in poetry. Tom Paulin (b. 1949), another important northerner, instead confronts head-on the bigotry in war-torn Ulster in *Strange Museum* (1980) and *The Liberty Tree* (1983) and insists on the poet's role in offering a useful vision to his community. While the north seems to have been the solitary wellspring of poetry for the past twenty years, the south has also produced some important new poets, notably Paul DURCAN, whose easy conversational style contrasts with his acidic but humorous attacks on the conventions of family, the church, and art. North and south, a number of new women poets have emerged whose work proves to be even more diverse, more tangible in its imagery and less abstract than the work of their male counterparts. Medbh MacGuckian's (b. 1950) contemplative pastoral and Irish mythic topics and Eavan Boland's (b. 1944) sharp eye for detail and feeling for place have produced some of the finest nature poetry in the tradition, which in Ireland is rich. Nuala NI DHOMHNAILL, who is one of many poets today writing in Irish, has a unique feeling for the landscape of the coast of her native Kerry. She also resists the traditional projection of feminine imagery onto the landscape by replacing the female figure with a male one. In this case, an ancient tradition—poetry in Irish—has been merged with the modern feminist ideology.

Fiction

The revival of the Irish language, spearheaded by Douglas Hyde, spurred many prose writers to turn away from English and write in Irish. This is true not only of writers from the predominantly Irish-speaking west, but also the urban east. The problem, of course, is that by rejecting the language of the oppressor, one is also greatly narrowing one's audience. Padraic O'Conaire (1883–1928) wrote short fiction about the rebellion against English rule, as did Seamus O'Grianna (1891–1969). Irish-language folk writers in rural and western Ireland wrote stories about a dying culture in its own dying language. Among the notable classics are Muiris O'Suilleabhain's (1904–1950) *Fiche blian ag fas* (*Twenty Years A-Growing*, 1933), and Peig Sayers's (1873–1958) *Peig* (1936).

James STEPHEN's writing gives us a vivid fictionalized account of the Easter 1916 rising in *The Insurrection in Dublin* (1916); and in *The Charwoman's Daughter* (1912) he provides a disturbing picture of squalid poverty in the Dublin of the time. In George Moore's first collection of short stories, *The Untilled Field* (1903), which was originally published in Irish in 1902, we find one of the central theme's of 20th-c. Irish fiction: the necessity of exile from an Ireland that is spiritually stifling. Moore also introduced continental styles to Ireland, notably those of Zola, Flaubert, and Mallarmé. The writing of a collection of thematically related short stories was also taken up by Joyce with *Dubliners* (1914) and by Samuel BECKETT in *More Pricks than Kicks* (1934). Joyce's *A Portrait of the Artist as a Young Man* (1916) is a moral history of the development of the author's semiautobiographical persona, Stephen Dedalus, whose peregrinations we later follow in the modernist masterpiece *Ulysses* (1922). In Joyce's final work, *Finnegans Wake* (1939), the distinction between order and chaos has been removed, so that the reader is locked in a linguistic labyrinth that few have found penetrable. Samuel Beckett, a member of Joyce's literary circle in Paris, helped translate *Finnegans Wake* into French and adopted, or rather distilled, to his own use, many of Joyce's stylistic sleights of hand. His first novel, *Murphy* (1938), tells of the life and death of an Irish immigrant in London. But his later writings, notably the trilogy *Molloy* (1955), *Malone Dies* (1956), and *The Unnamable* (1958) (all of which he translated from the French in which they were first written), reduce plot and character and landscape to an absurd minimalism. Nevertheless, the "Irishness" of character and topography pervades the overwhelming anonymity and bleakness of his work.

Flann O'BRIEN wrote his first classic, *An Beal Bocht* (1941; *The Poor Mouth*, 1961), as a direct satiric attack on attempts to revive and edify the Gaelic language and culture in the west, but in *At-Swim-Two-Birds* (1939) we are delighted by his parody of Celtic mythical figures and the act of writing itself.

The 1930s and 1940s saw the rise of a new group of writers who launched a seemingly concerted attack on the parochialism of the new Irish Free State. Sean O'Faolain (1900–1991) was the central personality in this group. *The Bell*, the group's literary magazine, succeeded in embracing a wide range of regional Irish writers who might otherwise have gone unpublished. O'Faolain's three great novels, *A Nest of Simple Folk* (1934), *Bird Alone* (1936), and *Come Back to Erin* (1940), depict an Ireland that is populated by characters whose nationalist aspirations are doomed, or who yearn for the modern world and its freedoms but who are spiritually anchored in the strictness of Irish Catholicism. Frank O'CONNOR became the master of the Irish short story; his sense of ease with his audience has produced a writer whose warmth with his subject matter surpassed his peers. Liam O'Flaherty (1897–1984) was born on the Aran Islands off the west coast. He is best known for his short stories, many of which tell of life and death from an animal's point of view, such as in "The Cow's Death" (1923) and "The Wounded Cormorant" (1925). His fiction is consciously stripped of sentimentality. Mary Lavin (b. 1912) writes about the young female, who in many cases is forced to cling to love lost in the cold world of modern Ireland in her *Collected Tales* (1971). Much of Elizabeth BOWEN's fiction is centered on the decay of the English ascendancy in her family home in County Cork. *The Death of the Heart* (1938) and *The Heat of the Day* (1949) are her best-known works. Edna O'BRIEN's novels and short stories follow the fortunes of young women who seek to escape rural and restraining Ireland. Her females are abused and self-abusing, while her males are treacherous, as in *The Country Girls* (1960), *Night* (1972), and *Johnny I Hardly Knew You* (1977).

James Plunkett's (b. 1920) *Strumpet City* (1969) fictionalizes the struggle of the labor leader James Larkin, who sought to raise the consciousness of Dublin workers against the opposition of the employers and clergy. Benedict Kiely (b. 1919) examines the violence present in a community that believes firmly in fixed values, as in *Dogs Enjoy the Morning* (1971) and *Nothing Happens in Carrickmacross* (1985). Brian MOORE's unrelentingly bleak vision of life in the north is best crafted in *Judith Hearne* (1955) (repub. as *The Lonely Passion of Judith Hearne*, 1959). His novel *Lies of Silence* (1990) lacks the sharp ironies of his earlier work and verges on moralizing about paramilitary violence in the north. John McGahern's (b. 1934) vision is no less bleak than Moore's, for his characters in their search for love are led into alienation. We find the physical and spiritual illness of a people in *The Dark* (1963) and *The Pornographer* (1979), but in his best novel to date, *Amongst Women* (1990), we find the inevitable demise of a tyrannical father and his effects on his children as they grow up. William TREVOR is a gifted storyteller, which shows in his short fiction, but his novels lack the same finesse, his finest collections being *The News from Ireland* (1986) and *Family Sins* (1990). John Banville (b. 1945) emerged in the early 1970s as an important new novelist, and his *Birchwood* (1973) is hailed as a masterpiece. Set in a background of famine and civil war, the memoirlike narrative is a nightmarish

vision of the decay of the ascendancy and the accompanying social breakdown. Jennifer Johnston's (b. 1930) writing examines the shifting distinctions between social and moral values in the violent north of today. In *Shadows on Our Skin* (1975) a young Catholic woman who dates a British soldier is "tarred-and-feathered" by an outwardly genteel people. Bernard Mac Laverty's (b. 1942) fiction is set in the same tense situation, and his characters are as isolated as Moore's, especially in *Cal* (1983).

BIBLIOGRAPHY: Boyd, E. A., *Ireland's Literary Renaissance* (1922); Corkery, D., *Synge and Anglo-Irish Literature* (1931); Foster, J. W., *Forces and Themes in Ulster Fiction* (1974); Marcus, D., and R. Deutsch, *Northern Ireland 1921–1974, A Select Bibliography* (1975); Brown, T., *Northern Voices: Poets from Ulster* (1975); Hogan, R. G., and J. Kilroy, eds.,*The Modern Irish Drama* (4 vols.: 1975–1979); Rafroidi, R. P., and M. Harmon, eds., *The Irish Novel in Our Time* (1976); Hunt, H., *The Abbey: Ireland's National Theatre, 1904–1978* (1979); Lyons, F. S. L., *Culture and Anarchy in Ireland 1890–1939* (1979); Brown, T., *Ireland: A Social and Cultural History 1922–79* (1981); Kenner, H., *A Colder Eye: The Modern Irish Writers* (1983); Trevor, W., *A Writer's Ireland* (1984); Deane, S., *Celtic Revivals: Essays in Modern Irish Literature 1880–1980* (1985); Hederman, M. P., and R. Kearney, eds., *The Crane Bag Book of Irish Studies* (2 vols.: 1987); Bradley, A., ed., *Contemporary Irish Poetry* (1988); Hildebidle, J., *Five Irish Writers: The Errand of Keeping Alive* (1989); Deane, S., ed. *The Field Day Anthology of Irish Writing* (3 vols.: 1991)

—FERGAL O'DOHERTY

IRVING, John

American novelist, b. 2 Mar. 1942, Exeter, N.H.

I. is an American novelist who has achieved both critical acclaim and widespread popularity. He was educated at Exeter Academy, the University of Pittsburgh, the University of New Hampshire (B.A. 1965), and the University of Iowa Writers Workshop (M.F.A. 1967), where he completed his first novel and later returned as a writer in residence. Between 1963 and 1964 he studied at the University of Vienna, and the city is a recurring setting in his novels.

I.'s first three novels—*Setting Free the Bears* (1969), *The Water-Method Man* (1972), and *The 158-Pound Marriage* (1974)—earned some critical praise but little popular success. All three are experimental in form and blackly humorous; all feature young adult protagonists. In *Setting Free the Bears*, two young men, Siggy and Hannes, take off on a motorcycle from Vienna to the countryside, where Siggy dies bizarrely, trapped under a truck and stung by bees; Hannes returns to Vienna to carry out his friend's plan of freeing the animals in the Vienna Zoo. The novel contains a mixture of narratives: Hannes's narrative of his and Siggy's actions, Siggy's zoo-watch journal, and Siggy's autobiography, the tale of his family's sufferings and persecution at the hands of Yugoslavian factions during World War II. *The Water-Method Man*, the story of a graduate student's successful attempts to turn his life around by finding a cure for a rare urinary-tract disorder, reconciling himself with his father and his former wife, and fully committing himself to marriage and parenthood with his current mistress, also introduces one of I.'s recurrent themes—the relationship between life and art—by using a wild mixture of narratives: present time, flashbacks, excerpts from the Old Norse epic the hero is translating for his dissertation, his tape recordings and letters, and excerpts from a documentary film about him. All come together at the end as the hero achieves personal fulfillment; this is I.'s most sweetly optimistic novel. In contrast, *The 158-Pound Marriage* is a bleak tale of a four-way affair between two married couples that ends up causing all of them pain; this novel also mixes present-time narrative and the past-time stories of how each couple met (in Vienna).

I.'s breakthrough book, in earning not just critical attention but widespread popularity, was *The World According to Garp* (1978). The novel was a best-seller in hardcover and mass-market paperback; one of I.'s phrases, the Under Toad (a child character's mistaken notion of "undertow," which becomes a metaphor for life's uncontrollable sadness and violence), is now listed in some dictionaries. Perhaps because of the topicality of some of its concerns—including feminism, rape, the assassination of public figures—and its mixture of exaggeration, violence, and black humor, the novel was controversial; since then, all of I.'s novels have been best-sellers. In the judgment of most critics, *Garp* was also—and to some it still is—I.'s best book. It tells the life story of T. S. Garp, a wrestler and a writer, from his bizarre conception to his assassination, and conveys a coherent vision of a world where "we are all terminal cases"—readers learn how almost all of the characters die—where violence is random but family patterns recur oddly through generations, a world "rich with lunacy and sorrow" that I. himself described as "an artfully designed soap opera," modeled in part on the great 19th-c. novels, intended to make readers laugh and cry. It also continues I.'s preoccupation with life and art; it contains two of Garp's stories and the opening chapter of one of his novels and descriptions of the other three, all of which bear intriguing resemblances to I.'s own fiction. In fact, the title of the novel Garp is planning to write. *My Father's Illusions*, might well serve as the title of I.'s next book.

The Hotel New Hampshire (1981), which actually outsold *Garp* in hardcover, disappointed many critics. A novel I. described as "fairy-tale-like," *The Hotel New Hampshire* returns to some of *Garp's* settings—New England prep schools and coastal estates, Vienna—and themes: rape, politically motivated violence, revenge, family patterns, oddly recurring events, and the influence of childhood on adult identity. Black humor abounds, but feels more strained, and I. uses, with more frequency and exaggeration, some of the literary techniques of *The World According to Garp*, like different typefaces for emphasis (italics and all caps) and the aphorism ("Sorrow floats"; "Life is serious but art is fun"). Compared with *Garp, The Hotel New Hampshire* is a thinner and more mannered book.

The Cider House Rules (1985) divided critics. It has two heroes. Dr. Wilbur Larch, who heads an orphanage where he also performs abortions on request, and his adopted son Homer Wells, who eventually after some moral struggle follows in his father's footsteps, and thus two major plot threads, and two settings, the orphanage in the Maine interior and an apple orchard on the coast. A few critics saw it as I.'s best work, his most successful in avoiding cuteness and exploring an important public issue—abortion—seriously. Others found it sentimental, dully written, and repulsive in its gynecological detail.

John Irving

A Prayer for Owen Meany (1989) is I.'s soundest artistic, critical, and popular success since *Garp*. Its plot and symbols seem more carefully designed and intertwined; its narrator, John Wheelwright, tells his and Owen's story in retrospect, and Owen's destiny as a Christlike sacrificial figure is both frequently foreshadowed and known to Owen well before it takes place. In fact, John and Owen believe—and the novel seems to endorse them—that Owen's fate is God's plan; John says that he had become a Christian because of Owen. This Christian perspective is a radical departure in the world according to I. From *Setting Free the Bears* on, I. has seen patterns, resemblances between present and past too striking to be entirely coincidental, but he never offered a religious explanation for them, and formal religion never was an issue in his characters' lives. Besides suggesting a change in I.'s world view, *A Prayer for Owen Meany* may also indicate new literary influences: Robertson DAVIES and perhaps Stephen King (b. 1947).

I. has achieved what he said he wanted all along: a wide general audience for his work, a readership like that enjoyed by the great 19th-c. British novelists. Like Dickens and Hardy, I. is first and always a storyteller, a creator of genuinely sympathetic characters to whom terrible things may happen. Critical reaction to his mature work has been mixed—in fact, British reviewers have been particularly unsympathetic—but at least for *The World According to Garp* and *A Prayer For Owen Meany*, far more favorable than unfavorable. I.'s reputation as a serious, if uneven, novelist seems secure. For all his protests that he is an imaginative writer and not a sociologist, I.'s best work reflects the America of the last three decades. Like F. Scott FITZGERALD's, the best of I.'s novels should endure both as representations of their time and as timeless works of art.

FURTHER WORKS: *Three by I.* (1980)

BIBLIOGRAPHY: Drabble, M., "Muck, Memory, and Imagination," *Harper's* (July 1978): 82–84; Tyler, A., "Three by I.," *NewR*, 182 (26 April 1980): 32–33; Wymard, E. B., "New Version of the Midas Touch: *Daniel Martin* and *The World According to Garp*," *MFS*, 27, 1 (Summer 1981): 284–86; Priestley, M., "Structure in the Worlds of J. I.," *Crit*, 23 (1981): 82–96; Epstein, J., "Why J. I. Is So Popular," *Commentary*, 73 (June 1982): 59–63; Hill, J. B., "J. I.'s Aesthetics of Accessibility: Setting Free the Novel," *SCR*, 16 (Fall 1983): 38–44; Adams, R. M., "The Story Isn't Over," *NYRB*, 32 (18 July 1985): 20–23

—SARAH ENGLISH

ISHERWOOD, Christopher

Anglo-American novelist and memoirist, b. 26 Aug. 1904, High Lane, England; d. 5 Jan. 1986, London

Born into the landed gentry in Cheshire, I. was educated at Repton School and Corpus Christi, Cambridge. After leaving

Christopher Isherwood

Cambridge without a degree in 1925, he renewed his friendship with W. H. AUDEN, his former classmate at St. Edmund's preparatory school. He lived in Berlin from 1930 to 1933; there he felt released from the social and sexual inhibitions that stifled his development in England. Disillusioned with left-wing politics and with English insularity, he emigrated to the United States in 1939 and declared himself a pacifist. Settling permanently in Los Angeles, I. began writing film scripts. In 1940 the influence of a Hindu monk and surrogate father, Swami Prabhavananda, prompted his conversion to Vedantism. He became a U.S. citizen in 1946. In 1971 he publicly revealed his homosexuality and became an active participant in the gay liberation movement.

I.'s earliest novels, *All the Conspirators* (1928) and *The Memorial* (1932), depict English middle-class malaise in the 1920s and reveal his mastery of narrative technique and ironic perspective. In the Berlin stories—*Mr. Norris Changes Trains* (1935; Am., *The Last of Mr. Norris*) and *Goodbye to Berlin* (1939)—I. created some of the most memorable characters in modern fiction, perfected his apparently naïve first-person narration, and brilliantly portrayed a city decaying from within. *Goodbye to Berlin* is among the most significant political novels of the 20th c., exploring the Nazi nightmare with startling insight and prophetic accuracy.

I.'s collaboration with Auden on three experimental verse dramas in the 1930s yielded less satisfactory work. The only really distinguished product of the Auden-I. collaboration is *Journey to a War* (1939), a travel book based on their 1938 trip to China.

His later novels, from *Prater Violet* (1945) through *A Meeting by the River* (1967), are enriched by the Vedantic influence. *Down There on a Visit* (1962) is a disturbing study of the Protean self, an unsentimental dissection of the author's past. *A Single Man* (1964), I.'s finest novel, masterfully balances worldly and religious concerns to create a double vision of the mundane and the transcendent. Beautifully written in a style that alternates between poetic intensity and ironic understatement, the book is a technical tour de force in which every nuance is perfectly controlled.

I.'s explicitly autobiographical works—*Lions and Shadows* (1938), *Kathleen and Frank* (1971), *Christopher and His Kind* (1976), and *My Guru and His Disciple* (1980)—succeed largely because of his novelistic gift of portraying his earlier selves as incomplete versions of his current consciousness.

I. may be the most self-absorbed of contemporary writers; yet his novels and autobiographies are never self-indulgent. They confront questions of alienation and isolation, of sexuality and spirituality, of maturity and transcendence. Born of scrupulous self-examination, I.'s penetrating vision illuminates the conflicts of our time.

FURTHER WORKS: *The Dog beneath the Skin* (1935, with W. H. Auden), *The Ascent of F 6* (1936, with Auden), and *On the Frontier* (1938, with Auden); *The Condor and the Cows* (1949); *The World in the Evening* (1954); *An Approach to Vedanta* (1963); *Ramakrishna and His Disciples* (1965); *Exhumations* (1966); *Frankenstein: The True Story* (1973, with Don Bachardy)

BIBLIOGRAPHY: Heilbrun, C. G., *C. I.* (1970); Wilde, A., *C. I.* (1971); Hynes, S. L., *The Auden Generation* (1976); Piazza, P., *C. I.: Myth and Anti-Myth* (1978); Finney, B., *C. I.: A Critical Biography* (1979); Funk, R. W., *C. I.: A Reference Guide* (1979); Summers, C. J., *C. I.* (1980)

—CLAUDE J. SUMMERS

ISHIGURO, Kazuo

Japanese-British novelist, b. 8 Nov. 1954, Nagasaki, Japan

I. grew up mainly in England, but continued to be influenced by the Japanese culture of his parents. The dichotomy of the two societies is evident in his novels, written in English but often describing Japanese society. I.'s novels have been lauded by critics and awarded several prizes, including the Booker Prize. While I. acknowledges the Japanese influence on his early novels, he cites writers such as Anton CHEKHOV and Dostoyevsky as direct influences on his work. He resists being grouped with other British writers who are racially identifiable, preferring instead to be recognized for his writing style and his effort to mythologize the landscapes of his novels.

I.'s first novel, *A Pale View of Hills* (1982), is the story of a woman dealing with her daughter's suicide. I.'s intermingling of past and present distinguish this work, which won I. his first literary prize. With his second novel, *An Artist of the Floating World*, I. proved himself to be a serious contender in the British literary scene as he was shortlisted for the Booker Prize, which he eventually won in 1989 with the highly acclaimed *The Remains of the Day*. In all three of these novels history plays a crucial role. I. parallels the history of individuals with the history of their nations, interweaving those histories to showcase the importance of dealing with the past to move on and create a better future. In *The Remains of the Day*, I. sets out to "subvert . . . the notion of benevolent paternalism . . . both at home and abroad." The political subtexts of the novel are also parallel, highlighting the volatile politics of World War II and the hierarchy of the servant-master relationship. The complexities of the novel attracted Harold PINTER, who bought the rights for a film version that won several Academy Awards. In 1995 he published his next novel, *The Unconsoled*. As in his early novels I.'s protagonist, Ryder, is an artist—in this work a musician—who finds himself thrown into a confusing, surreal situation in which he is expected to sort out everything. Underneath the surreality, however, lies the truth of Ryder's life.

I.'s longevity as a novelist is assured by the warm reception each of his novels has received. He is able to create tales that have cultural importance and also articulate very real human traits of fear, anxiety, confusion, and insecurity. Although he writes in English, he is able to communicate across cultures and through cultures, thus situating himself very firmly into the postmodern, postcolonial era.

BIBLIOGRAPHY: Mason, G., "An Interview with K. I.," *ConL*, 30 (1989): 335-47; Vorda, A., "Stuck on the Margins: An Interview with K. I." in Vorda, A., ed., *Face to Face: Interviews with Contemporary Novelists* (1993)

—MARCY TANTER

ISHIKAWA Jun

(born Shiba Kiyoshi) Japanese novelist and essayist, b. 7 Mar. 1899, Tokyo; d. 29 Dec. 1987, Tokyo

The second son of a local banker and politician in the old downtown quarter of Tokyo known as Asakusa, I. was adopted and raised by his maternal grandparents. The grandfather, Ishikawa Shōsai, had been a samurai and scholar of Chinese and Japanese poetry employed by the last Tokugawa Shogun. As a boy I. received training in classical Chinese texts such as the *Analects*, the repertoire of the Nō theater, and the popular fiction of the Edo period. He was also a fan of MORI Ōgai's translations of modern European literature. Later he studied French at the Tokyo School of Foreign Languages and, coming under the influence of the French symbolists and antinaturalists, numbered among the first to translate into Japanese the works of Andreé GIDE, such as *L'immoraliste* (1902) and *Les caves du Vatican* (1914) in 1924 and 1928, respectively.

After a period of artistic vagabondage and flirtation with anarchist politics, I. began to publish his first novellas or récits. His debut work, "Kajin" (1935; the beauty), is a definitive statement of his antinaturalism as well as a parody of the *shishōsetsu* or "I-novel." Also conceived in a tongue-in-cheek tone, *Fugen* (1936; *The Bodhisattva; or, Samantabhadra*, 1990) is the tale of an improverished novelist who, beset by the quotidian realities of life in Tokyo, is driven by the dream of the millennium. His dream is manifest in writing about Joan of Arc and her chronicler Christine de Pizan, and in his madcap affair to save Yukari, a young woman involved in the Japanese political underground, from falling into the hands of the police. By drawing successive layers of parallels between "dust and flowers"—Japan in the 1930s and France in the 15th c.—the novel comes to the conclusion that there will be no "bodhisattva" to save Japan. The last line of defense for those who oppose the times are "gratuitous" acts of resistance. Awarded the fourth Akutagawa Prize for literature in 1937, this seminal novel is a powerful combination of parody, allegory, and satire that employs both the palimpsest construction of European modernist prose and the mystification style (*tōkai-buri*) of fiction of the Edo period.

I.'s next major sally, "Marusu no uta" (1938; "Mars' Song," 1998), a denunciation of the chorus of jingoism that swept Japan after the invasion of China in 1937, was banned by the authorities. Along with *Fugen*, this work establishes I.'s reputation as one of Japan's few "resistance" writers.

During the war, I. produced largely criticism, especially his famous critique *Mori Ōgai* (1941; Mori Ōgai) that treats Mori Ōgai's late historical novels as precursors of metafiction, and a theory of prose, *Bungaku taigai* (1942; all about literature), which espouses I.'s theory of automatic writing and spiritual vitalism. He wrote only one novel, *Hakubyō* (1939; line drawing), a roman à clef that takes Bruno Taut (1880–1938), the modernist architect who resided briefly in Japan, as its protagonist. During the war I. sought his "inner emigration" in Edo-period literature, especially the *kyōka* or comic verse of the Temmei era (1781–1789), in which he saw the incipience of modernist attitudes in Japanese writing.

In 1945 DAZAI Osamu, Sakaguchi Ango (1906–1955), and I. emerged as the new leaders of the postwar literary scene. They are often treated as members of the so-called "libertine" (*burai*) or "new burlesque" (*shin-gesaku*) school—labels that refer to their iconoclastic attitudes toward traditional values, and their interest in the parody fiction of the Edo period. Couched in Christian analogies instead of Buddhist, I.'s short stories—allegories for the destruction and resurrection of Japan such as "Ōgon densetsu" (1946; "The Legend of Gold," 1998) and "Yakeato no Iesu" (1946, "The Jesus of the Ruins," 1998)—are his best-known works, and his most representative short fiction.

Although I. faded from public attention as of the 1950s, he continued to be touted in Japanese literary circles as a "novelist's novelist" and a *shibui* writer. He divided his energies between his work as an essayist—writing an ongoing series under the name Isai and in the style of the *propos* of the French essayist Alain (pseud. of Émile-Auguste CHARTIER)—and creating what he called *jikken shōsetsu* or experimental novels. Adopting third-person narration and a less-garrulous style, I.'s mature novels are deeper explorations of the terrain of metafiction and social satire: *Taka* (1953; *The Raptor*, 1998) speaks of a mysterious language called futurese; *Aratama* (1963; wild spirit), the story of Sata—embodiment of the darkling forces at the bottom of society—is both a parody of comic-book or *manga* heroes, and a prophesy of the "black mist" or *kuroi kiri* that enveloped Japanese politics in the 1970s. *Shifuku sennen* (1965; the millennium), an imaginary scenario in which bands of hidden Christians attempt to seize control of the city of Edo, is inspired no doubt by Gide's tale of the Vatican cellars, as well as the factionalism endemic to Japan's politics and its new religions.

I. was recipient of the Ministry of Education Prize for literature in 1957 for *Shion monogatari* (1956; *Asters*, 1961), and the Asahi Cultural Prize in 1982 after publication of his longest novel, *Kyōfūki* (1980; record of a mad wind). He was elected to permanent membership in the *Geijutsuin*, Japan Academy of the Arts, in 1963. At the time of his death, he was at work on *Hebi no uta* (1986; song of the snake), a "banquet" of sex, power, and money in contemporary Japan.

Generationally speaking, I. ranks alongside critics and writers such as KOBAYASHI Hideo and Yokomitsu Riichi (1898–1947), who called for an end to naturalist, first-person narration and raised the clarion call for the "pure novel." Clearly he was the first among his generation to advance the cause of MODERNISM and metafiction, and what in the West is called "writing degree zero." Often he has been anthologized with his younger protégés ABE Kōbō and OE Kenzaburō as an "internationalist" because of their shared love of French existentialist literature and desire to wrest the novel in Japan from subjects particular to the culture. Moreover, he is often compared to Jorge Luis BORGES and Vladimir NABOKOV because of his brilliance as a stylist, his mastery of parody, and his advocacy of experimental fiction. At the same time, it must not be forgotten that I. is equally heir to the *bunjin* or literati tradition that, introduced to Japan from China, starts from the *nanga* painters and *kyōka* poets of the Edo period and is transmitted to modern Japanese letters by Mori Ōgai and Nagai Kafū. Thus he has also been hailed as Japan's *saigo no bunjin*, "the last of the literati," and embodies the critical, epicurean, and cosmopolitan spirit of that tradition.

FURTHER WORKS: *Watanabe Kazan* (1941); *Giteiki* (1943); *Isai hitsudan* (1951); *Isai rigen* (1952); *Isai seigen* (1954); *Shokoku kijinden* (1957); *Hakutōin* (1957); *Isai jōzetsu* (1960); *Isai yūgi* (1963); *Zenken yōin* (1975); *Isai Zadan* (1977); *Edo bungaku jōki* (1980); *Shinsaku kojiki* (1983); *Rokudu yugyō* (1983); *I. J. zenshū* (14 vols., 1974–1975; 19 vols., 1989–1991). FURTHER WORKS IN ENGLISH: *The Legend of Gold and Other Stories* (1998)

BIBLIOGRAPHY: Keene, D., *Dawn to the West* (1984), Vol. 1: 1087–102; Tyler, W., "Art and Act of Reflexivity in I. J.'s *The Bodhisattva: or Samantabhadra*" (1990): 139–66; Tyler, W. J., "Critical Essays," in *The Legend of Gold and Other Stories* (1998): 174-294

—WILLIAM J. TYLE

ISHIKAWA Takuboku

Japanese poet, critic, and diarist, b. 20. Feb. 1886, Hinoto village, Iwate perfecture; d. 13 April 1912, Tokyo

The only son of a Zen priest in a rural community in northern Japan, I. developed a strong, individualistic personality. From his student days on, he engaged in literary activity, dropping out of school in 1902 in order to go to Tokyo to become a writer. His first verses, in the form of *tanka* (or *waka*, thirty-one-syllable poems), were published in the influential periodical, *Myōjō*, and I. benefited from the tutelage of the editor, Yosano Tekkan (1873–1935), and his wife, the poet Yosano Akiko (1878–42). In February 1903, I. became ill and was forced to return to his home in northern Japan. From this time until his death from tuberculosis, he struggled against abject poverty and failing health.

I.'s first collection of verse. *Akogare* (1905; longing), demonstrated a strong romantic bent, but thereafter his poetry took on an independent direction. With *Ichiaku no suna* (1910; *A Handful of Sand*, 1934) he established himself as a leading writer of *tanka*, to which hue imparted a new tone of realism. He endeavored to write "poems that are down to earth, poems with feelings unremoved from actual life," and he abhorred all traces of imitativeness. The 551 verses of *Ichiaku no suna* were integrated to form a unified whole, imparting a sense of growth and progression to the collection and giving somewhat the effect of a spiritual autobiography in verse. Through *Ichiaku no suna* and his posthumously published book of verse, *Kanashiki gangu* (1912; sad toys), I. infused a powerful new current of life into the old tradition of *tanka*. His verses continue to be anthologized in Japanese school texts, and later *tanka* poets have accepted his innovations, which changed the very nature of this form of poetry.

In the last years of his life, after the trial behind closed doors and execution (which followed immediately) of the Japanese anarchist philosopher Kōtoku Shūsui (1871–1911), I. was increasingly moved by socialist ideals, as verses such as the following reveal: "Still quite far away/I believed it all to be;/But the terrorists'/Plaintive and heart-rending cry/Day by day now draws nearer." In 1910–12, in association with Toki Zemmaro (1885–1980), *tanka* poet, essayist, and scholar of Japanese literature, I. attempted to publish a socialist literary magazine. The venture failed, but their friendship, ardor for socialism and efforts to establish a proletarian *tanka* group continued undiminished. One week before I.'s death, Toki Zemmaro delivered the manuscript for *Kanashiki gangu* to the publisher and used the twenty-yen advance to buy medicine to comfort his dying friend.

I.'s diaries and miscellaneous writings, as well as his verse, are admired for the stark revelation of his search for love and his struggle against poverty, despair, and death. His *Romaji nikki* (1948–49); partial tr., *The Romaji Diary*, 1956), the especially noteworthy journal that I. kept in the spring of 1909, stands out as one of the memorable works of 20th-c. Japan. It reveals a completely modern three-dimensional man, capable of introspection and displaying fierce, self-destructive honesty.

One of the first modern voices in Japanese poetry, I. is best remembered for the way in which he utilized the traditional *tanka* form to articulate new problems of the modern age. Despite the brevity of his life, I.'s subsequent influence on *tanka* poets such as Saitō Mokichi (1882–1953) Nishimura Yōkichi (1892–1959), and Watanable Junzō (1894–1972) marks him as one of the significant innovators and as one of the enduring voices in 20th-c. Japanese literature. I.'s writings reveal not a tranquil world of soft rain sounds and delicate relations but rather the shrill outcry of a tortured young soul, pouring forth a red-hot stream of uncontrollable passion.

FURTHER WORKS: *Yobiko to kuchibue* (1913); *Takuboku zenshū* (8 vols., 1978). FURTHER WORKS IN ENGLISH: *The Poetry of I. T.* (1959); *Takuboku: Poems to Eat* (1966)

BIBLIOGRAPHY: Takamine, H., *A Sad Toy: A Unique and Popular Poet, Takuboku's Life and His Poems* (1962); Keene, D., *Landscapes and Portraits* (1971): 131–70; Hijiya, Y., *I. T.* (1979)

—LEON M. ZOLBROD

ISKANDER, Fazil Abdulovich

Russian novelist, short-story writer, and poet, b. 6 Mar. 1929, Sukhum, U.S.S.R. (now Abkhazia)

Of mixed Persian and Abkhazian descent, I. was born in Sukhum, the capital of Abkhazia, an autonomous republic in Georgia. I. has written that as a child he witnessed the passing of the patriarchal way of life in Abkhazia, which provides the setting for much of his prose. I. grew up speaking both Abkhazian and Russian, but writes only in Russian. A graduate of the Moscow Gorky Literary Institute (1954), I. for over three decades he has divided his time between Moscow and Abkhazia. In the tradition of such Russian novelists as Gogol, Turgenev, and Vladimir NABOKOV, I. began his literary career as a poet. I. published five volumes of verse between 1957 and 1964 and continues to write poetry to this day. A selection of I.'s poetry from the 1950s through the 1980s appeared under the title *Put* (1987; the path).

While I. is a competent poet, he has made an indelible impression on the Russian novel a short story. In 1962 I.'s short fiction began to appear in the journal *Iunost*, the bastion of the "young prose" movement. The publication of the satirical *Sozvezdie kozlotura* (1966; *The Goatibex Constellation*, 1975) created a sensation and catapulted the young author to prominence. Several collections of I.'s fiction appeared in the late 1960s and 1970s. In 1973 excerpts from I.'s epic novel *Sandro iz Chegema* were published in *Novyi Mir*. The tortured publication history of I.'s masterpiece and one of the landmarks of postwar Russian literature outlines his literary career from the mid-1970s through 1989. The novel was issued as a separate book in 1977, but in a severely abridged form. Unable to publish the uncensored and complete text of *Sandro* in the U.S.S.R., I. resolved on publication in the West, and a full edition in Russian appeared in 1978. The following year saw the publication of the literary almanac *Metropol'* (1979; Metropol, 1982), in which I. figures not only as contributor, but also as one of the editors. I. was severely censured for his role in the *Metropol'* affair, his name disappeared from the pages of literary journals, and the publication of his books in press was halted. In 1981 a volume of additional chapters to *Sandro* was brought out in the West as *Novye glavy: Sandro iz Chegema*, followed the next year by his last major publication abroad, the parable *Kroliki i udavy* (1982; *Rabbits and Boa Constrictors*, 1989). The book *Zashchita Chika* (1983; the defense of Chik) signaled the beginning of I.'s gradual rehabilitation in the U.S.S.R. In 1983 *Sandro iz Chegema* was translated in

part into English as *Sandro of Chegem*; the rest of the novel was translated the following year as *The Gospel According to Chegem*. In the late 1980s, the period of Gorbachev's glasnost, works by I. appeared in all the major journals, but, most important, a complete edition of *Sandro iz Chegema* was published in Moscow (3 vols., 1989). I. currently serves as an adviser to the the editorial board of the journal *Znamia*, he has facilitated the publication of many repressed and forgotten authors, and he continues to add new chapters to his *Sandro*.

Although I. began his career as prose writer in the pages of *Iunost'* and his work had much in common with the young-prose school, there are a number of traits that set his fiction apart. In general, young prose strived for contemporaneity, the setting was usually the city in the 1960s, and the protagonist was a young person embarking on adult life, a new career, or a journey. On the other hand, I.'s short fiction for the most part was set in his native Abkhazia in the 1940s and 1950s, and his first-person narrator was often a child. The fictional world I. has created in Abkhazia with its ever-expanding cast of the narrator's relatives, friends, and eccentrics has its own mythology and history. The comic events are seen from two points of view: through the eyes of the child and those of the adult narrator who is remembering his childhood. I.'s preference for first-person narration gradually gave way to a third-person narrator who chronicles the events of the young Abkhazian boy Chik.

Sozvezdie kozlotura, I.'s lightly veiled satire of journalism and politics in the Khrushchev era, in particular the agricultural "reforms" and Lysenko's pseudogenetics, is narrated in the same unhurried and ambling manner as the Chik stories. As in all of I.'s work, digression is the storyteller's trademark.

I. has written that *Sandro iz Chegema* began as a parody of the picaresque novel. Comprised of a series of loosely related chapters, the novel tells the story of Uncle Sandro from the 1880s to the 1960s, and concurrently offers a microcosm of the history of the Abkhazian people. While part of the fictional world is clearly grounded in reality—the fictional city Mukhus is an anagram of I.'s birthplace Sukhum—other place names and tribes are pure invention, which has prompted critics to see parallels between I.'s method and the magic realism of William FAULKNER and Gabriel GARCÍA MÁRQUEZ. Chronology and plot development are largely ignored, so that Uncle Sandro becomes the only unifying principle in the novel. However, I.'s fondness for digression and framing a story within a story often leaves Sandro on the periphery of the narration. The concepts of family, tradition, honor, courage, and honesty that are central to the Abkhazian way of life have not yet been corrupted by "civilization," although Uncle Sandro will resort to trickery to achieve just ends. I.'s novel is not merely a gentle recreation of village life, but it is also a moral commentary on the contemporary world. The most overtly political chapter, "Piry Baltasara" (Belshazzar's feasts), depicts a banquet given in Stalin's honor. In essence, the banquet scene is a parody of a banquet—the noble traditions of feasting etiquette are completely debased. The story paints a psychological portrait of a tyrant whose paranoia instills fear in the guests. Sandro, who dances for Stalin, escapes unscathed, but without any illusion about his host.

I.'s *Sandro* alternates between comedy and tragedy, but humor largely prevails. Although his portrayal of Abkhazia sometimes borders on the idyllic, there are also stories of injustice and vengeance. The loose organization of the novel has prompted some critics to insist that it is not a novel at all. But it is precisely the open-endedness that allows I. to supplement and modify one of the great novels of 20th-c. Russian literature.

FURTHER WORKS: *Gornye tropy* (1957); *Dobrota zemli* (1959); *Zelenyi dozhd'* (1960); *Deti Chernomor'ia* (1961); *Molodost' moria* (1964); *Zapretnyi plod* (1966); *Trinadtsatyi podvig Gerakla* (1966); *Zori zemli* (1966); *Derevo detstva* (1970); *Pervoe delo* (1972); *Vremia shchastlivykh nakhodok* (1973); *Pod seniu gretskogo orekha* (1979); *Prazdnik ozhidaniia prazdnika* (1986); *Izbrannoe* (1988); *Kroliki i udavy. Proza poslednikh let* (1988); *Stoianka cheloveka* (1990). **FURTHER WORKS IN ENGLISH:** *Forbidden Fruit and Other Stories* (1972); *The Thirteenth Labor of Hercules* (1978); *Chik and His Friends* (1985)

BIBLIOGRAPHY: Babenko, V., "F. I.: An Examination of His Satire," *RLJ*, 106 (1976): 131–42; Burlingame, H., "The Prose of F. I.," *RLT*, 14 (1976): 123–65; Chapple, R., "F. I.'s *Rabbits and Boa Constrictors*: A Soviet Version of George Orwell's *Animal Farm*," *GSlav*, 5, 2 (1985): 33–47; Frank, M., "F. I.'s View of Muslim Caucasia," *WLT*, 60, 2 (Spring 1986): 261–66; Lowe, D. A., *Russian Writing since 1953: A Critical Survey* (1987): 50–51, 91, 99 114–115; Ryan-Hayes, K., "I. and Tolstoj: The Parodical Implications of the Beast Narrator," *SEEJ*, 32, 2 (1988): 225–36

—RONALD MEYER

ISMĀ'ĪL, Ismā'īl Fahd

Kuwaiti novelist, short-story writer, dramatist, and critic, b. 1940, Basrah, Iraq

I. is little known outside the Arab world, although he is a prolific writer and a major contemporary Kuwaiti novelist. He was born and educated in Iraq, and most of the material in his early works is derived from life and society there.

His first published work was a collection of short stories, *al-Buq'ah al-dākinah* (1965; the dark spot), characterized by their experimentation. This was followed by his most celebrated work, a quartet of three short and one longer novel, *Kānat al-sama' zarqā'* (1970; the sky was blue), *al-mustanqa'āt al-daw' īyah* (1971; the light swamps), *al-Habl* (1972; the rope), and *al-difāf al-ukhrā* (1973; the other shores). In this quartet, I. attempts to provide a cross section of the divergent political and social attitudes of different characters that represent the different social groups in Arab society, especially Iraq, during the 1950s and 1960s—a period of significant transformation. What is also important and innovative is the way he juxtaposes dialogue, which dominates the quartet, with interior monologues, thereby weaving dual levels of narrative time, one usually moving very slowly, while the other may cover years or decades. His next novel, *Milaff al-hādithah 67* (1974; the file of incident 67), develops the techniques used in the quartet by adding to dialogues and interior monologues excerpts from radio broadcasts that provide a background for the interrogation that is taking place in the novel. If I.'s earlier novels were about Iraqis, this novel emphasizes the Palestinian who is subjected to the repression of Arab régimes. Shortly after the beginning of the civil war in Lebanon, I. published his novel *al-Shiyyāh* (1976; al-Shiyyāh)—a title that refers to the name of a quarter in Beirut, destroyed in the early stages of the war—which emphasizes the meaninglessness of the war.

It was not until the 1980s that I. shifted his interest toward Egypt and started to develop a new mode of writing. Following the lead of

novelists like Jamāl AL-GHĪTĀNĪ, I. wrote a novel in two parts, entitled *al-Nīl yajrī shamālan: al-bi-dāyāt* (1981; the Nile flows northward: the beginnings) and *al-Nīl yajrī shamālan: al-nawātīr* (1982; the Nile flows northward: the keepers). The novel is about Egypt around the time of Napoleon's invasion of the country. Narrative assumes central position, and is reinforced by the abundant references to historical incidents and persons. Historical writings from that period, especially those by the 18th-19th-c. historian and witness of the Napoleonic escapade al-Jabartī (1754–1822) are also quoted verbatim in the text. But the novel has many references to the more recent history of Egypt.

This chapter of Egyptian history constitutes the subject matter of I.'s latest novel, *al-Nīl: al-ta'm wa-al-rā'ihah* (1988; the Nile: the taste and the smell) which can be read as a continuation of the two earlier Nile novels. If the earlier novels bear the traces of the 1967 defeat of the Arabs, it is the 1973 war and its aftermath that provides the background for the later works.

I.'s fascination with dialogue is not only apparent in his novels, but also in the fact that he has written a play, *al-nass* (1980; the text) and two books of drama criticism, *al-Fi'l wa-al-naqīd fī Ūdīb Sūfūkl* (1980; action and contradiction in Sophocles's Oedipus) and *al-Fi'l fī masrah Sa'd Allāh Wannūs* (1981; action in the theater of Sa'd Allāh Wannūs), the latter referring to the most prominent contemporary Syrian dramatist, Sa'dallāh WANNŪS.

I.'s output has been relatively large, but its quality has not been uniform. He sometimes repeats himself and overuses some literary devices. He also tends to treat some of his characters as mere puppets, especially when attempting to provide an ending that suits his ideological or political purpose. Yet I. remains probably the only Kuwaiti novelist who has been able to achieve a prominent place in the contemporary Arabic novel. This is due to his bold literary experimentation coupled with his rootedness in, and sensitivity to, the cultural and social life of the Arab world.

FURTHER WORKS: *al-Aqfās wa-al-lughah al-mushtarakah* (1974); *al-Qissah al-'Arabiyyah fī al-Kuwayt* (1980); *Khatwah fī al-hulm* (1980); *al-Tuyūr wa-al-asdiqā'* (1980)

BIBLIOGRAPHY: Allen, R., *The Arabic Novel* (1982): 144–56; Allen, R., ed., *Modern Arabic Literature* (1987): 160–64

—WALID HAMARNEH

ISRAELI LITERATURE

Because Israel declared itself an independant state only in 1948, any literature before that date is technically non-Israeli. In practice, however, May 1948 is not a particularly significant literary watershed. The official language of the new state was to be Hebrew, and Israeli literature inherited the long tradition of Hebrew literature, whose origins are biblical and whose written output extended over several millennia and to all those parts of the world where Jewish communities and culture flourished.

More specifically, Israeli literature is in the tradition of the new Hebrew literature of modern times, encapsulating two major trends: (1) the secularizing, although partially national, tendency of the Jewish Enlightenment (late 18th c. and following) and (2) the tendency toward a return to the ancient Palestinian homeland, where the reborn culture could flourish unhampered. The Hebrew

Enlightenment struggled for increased lexical and syntactic scope, and for an extension of literary genres beyond the medieval and traditional bounds. A breakdown of old forms of community and religion in the wake of secularization and social unrest was noted by the greatest of the new Hebrew masters, sometimes with enthusiasm and sometimes with foreboding. In the late 19th c. satirists such as the Yiddish and Hebrew novelist Mendele Mokher Sforim (1836–1917) both attacked characteristic social patterns and mourned the passing of the old. The leading poet of the generation, Chayim Nachman BIALIK, blended his own sense of existential tragedy with a description of the national character of the Jewish people to create the effects of an ineradicable pathos.

Until World War I the chief centers of modern Hebrew creativity were in the Diaspora, particularly in eastern Europe. But the ravages of that war, the Bolshevik revolution, and the Russian civil war effectively destroyed the old-style Pale of Settlement and the *shtetl* within. This process was to be completed during World War II and the Holocaust of European Jewry. Meanwhile, the World War I victory of the British, who had offered the Balfour Declaration of November 1917, stimulated the movement of Jews to Palestine. The wave (now the third such wave) of the period following the war more than doubled existing Jewish settlement, and, in spite of major setbacks, the so-called *yishuv* (Jewish community of Palestine) established itself as a state on the way. The ongoing disaster of European Jewry reinforced this tendency, so that by 1939, a state, now challenged by systematic Arab opposition, could begin to emerge. Other centers of Hebrew creativity were dying in three major areas: (1) in western Europe, where the Holocaust was to trap the Jews, and, of course, their culture; (2) in eastern Europe, where Communism was throttling the "counterrevolutionary" language of Hebrew, together with other independent sources of Jewish expression; and (3) in the U.S.A. (which had become the home of the single largest Jewish population in the world), where cultural and linguistic assimilation was proceeding apace. In the new circumstances, only Palestine/Israel was a possible Hebrew center.

With Israeli independence Hebrew could now flourish not just as a literary language but as a current vernacular and the official medium of expression in the new state. Meanwhile, Hebrew writers of the early part of the century had established themselves in Palestine, so that by the 1920s a self-conscious Palestinian-Hebrew literature had been created. Avaraham Shlonsky (1900–1973), Uri Zvi GREENBERG, and Natan ALTERMAN—all poets nourished in eastern Europe—moved to Palestine in this period with the third wave. S. Y. AGNON returned to Palestine in 1924 after an earlier stay there before World War I. The Oriental Hebrew novelist Yehuda Burla (1887–1969) was Palestinian-born, as was the poet Esther Raab (b. 1899). On the one hand, there was a natural drawing on the local soil by the native writer, and, on the other hand, some of the immigrant writers, in different ways, sought to assume a Palestinian identity by obligerating traces of the Diaspora. The earlier warnings issued by Yosef H. Brenner (1881–1921) against the Palestinian genre as such might have exerted their influence on the writers of the second wave (from 1909 onward—the first was in the early 1880s), but the third wave saw Palestine and a specifically local literature established as a major focus. In "Masada" (1929; Masada), a long poem by Yitzhak Lamdan (1900–1954), the poetic narrator idealized labor in the tones of a Russian revolutionary poet; Greenberg donned prophetic garb; Agnon turned to the Palestinian epic; and Chayim Hazaz (1898–1972) incorporated the Palestinian scene in his narrative subject matter.

In the poet Saul TCHERNICHOWSKY we find an interesting fusion of universalism and nationalism. The poet regarded himself as "a strange plant" among the Jewish people, a rebel renegade admiring Greek and Canaanite strength rather than Jewish weakness. Thus, he argued for a more masculine Jewish assertiveness and nationalism. He emigrated to Palestine in 1931, at a stage where he could still be shaped by the new environment in his creativity. His writing marks out a program for the life of the individual and the nation. Its combination of heresy and ethnicity sat well with the conditions of emergent Israel.

So by 1948, the literary character of the country was established, just as the social and political molds had also settled. Some of the most notable exponents of Israeli literature had begun writing earlier. The Sabra novelist Yizhar Smilansky (b. 1916) began to publish in 1938, seeking a richer lexical and syntactic language for the expressive consciousness of his narrative pivot. However long his story, the plot is always sparse. His central concerns are the landscape, the moral issue, the indecisive hero, and the language itself. But the plot is characteristically unresolved by any action. The poetry of Chayim Guri (b. 1921), which started to appear at the close of the War of Independence, focuses on war, the hero, his beloved, his bloody memories—a very local scene. Many of the heroes in the novels and stories of Moshe Shamir (b. 1921) are not only native-born, but see themselves as a different species from the Diaspora Jew. The new Israeli is characterized as simple, direct, active, healthy, single-minded, and strong, in contrast to the divided, urban, tortured Diaspora Jew. Shamir, like others, set up a small journal, *Yalkut hareim*, and the general description of this writing as "Palmach literature" (named after the striking arm of the Haganah—defense forces) owes its origins to this sense of comradeship and a single, collective purpose. The subject matter for treatment was, in general, emergent Israel: absorption of immigrants, the war, the kibbutz, the issues of the new state. The concerns were practical and ideological, of public polity rather than the individual.

The 1950s witnessed changes on various fronts. Poets became more introspective and skeptical, doubtful of the collective thrust, and began uncertainly to look over their shoulder to their forebears and earlier Jewish existence. Yehuda AMICHAI made much of the contrast between the generations, highlighted by the surprising image become metaphor. Amir Gilboa (b. 1917), whose initial power derived its original expression from the public Jewish situation and Israeli independence, articulated uncertain introspection in his later poetry. Natan Zach (b. 1930) has always been concerned with the private world of the poet and with the delicate structure of interpersonal relationships. Pinchas Sadeh (b. 1929), seeing "life as a parable", started to produce a rather un-Israeli type of confessional prose, whose concerns were the self, truth, and God. Intense religious experience has not been a prominent subject of Israeli authors, although the poet known simply as Zelda (b. 1913) has more recently begun to express an ecstatic certainty of God's presence in the constant face of death. But away from public commitments, the heroes of Israeli novels of the 1950s and 1960s are seen in flight from their official or imagined roles. Shamir's work moved in this direction. The characters of the novelist Aharon Megged (b. 1920) are sometimes disillusioned, making their way from the kibbutz to the city, as in *Chedvah vaani* (1954; Chedvah and I) or away from the enslavement to the national myth, as in *Hachai al hamet* (1965; living on the dead).

Israeli existence was, of course, multitinted. But ideologies had not only been promoted as in conflict, but sometimes as peculiar and exclusive to the new Israel. One such ideology was aired in the periodical *Alef*, which was founded in the 1940s to advocate a sort of Hebrew Semitic Union unconnected with Diaspora Jewry and which continued to press for a secular Middle Eastern state. Another, although less certain, ideology appeared in a forum entitled *Likrat*, distributed from 1952 on—it had neither a leftist nor rightist orientation. These were alternative voices to the predominant public policy of strong Zionism. But these voices were often muted as the literature of the State of Israel in general became less sure of itself and its direction less certain. Israel was and is characterized by division and has become increasingly "normalized", that is, the people are now more concerned with their own personal situation. So too has its literature become less publicly oriented, although the Land of Israel—Erets Yisrael—naturally remains, at least subliminally, its subject—and its object, too, in the sense that the literature expresses ideological aspirations for the country.

One aspect of the revival of Israel in the context of Hebrew literature is the emergence of the Cinderella of literary genres into the limelight. Hebrew drama had always been relatively weak—for lack of a living vernacular, for lack of a stage, and for lack of a tradition in the genre. The two best Israeli dramatists are Nissim ALONI, who is also a short-story writer, and Hanoch Levin (b. 1943). Aloni has written naturalistically of his youth in his fiction, and built poetic fantasies in his plays. Perhaps this removal from current reality illustrates a difficulty of Hebrew drama. Levin, on the other hand, is a satirist, whose low-keyed characters comment on Israeli obsessions and political and social attitudes. At first execrated as unpatriotic, particularly with the staging of *Malkat haambatyah* (1972; queen of the bathtub), Levin is now in the acceptable mainstream of the Israeli stage. His predominant character bases his life on expectation rather than fulfillment, and so illuminates the nature of human aspirations.

More recent years have seen moves backward in time, to earlier history formative of the present, and forward, to a concern with total contemporaneity. Aharon APPELFELD, in fiction such as *Badenhaim ir nofesh* (1975; *Badenheim* 1939, 1980), writes mainly of Israel's prehistory, of a European Jewry in its twilight world, reaching for assimilation on its path to destruction, and of the world of the survivors in Israel rooted in that past. It is both the world of the author's childhood and the public Israeli world of an often unacknowledged infancy. The novelist A. B. YEHOSHUA, author of *Bitchilat kayits 1970* (1971; *Early in the Summer of 1970*, 1977) and *Hamahev* (1977; *The Lover*, 1978), among others, has stated that his object is to render contemporary Israeli man and his paradoxical dilemmas. Amos OZ has sought symbols of the Israeli situation, images of terror and siege that haunt ordinary people, whose interior lives are really quite extraordinary. He, too, has attempted to recover his own childhood world and the pre-1948 Palestinian world in a collection of novellas *Har haetsah haraah* (1976; *The Hill of Evil Counsel*, 1978).

Many of Israel's younger fiction writers, then, view Israel within a larger context: either in its conditions of terror and siege, or in relation to a past, which, although gone, still lives in the present. Israel may be small and isolated, but it is revealed in its literature as relating to history and current politics.

The current scene abounds with experimentation in mimesis. Amalia KAHANA-CARMON has long been writing intensely rendered stream-of-consciousness stories, often as if they were narrated by a child or by an adult with a childlike point of view who is fixated on another individual. Yaakov SHABTAI produced a series

of short narrative extravaganzas, then a long novel written in one paragraph, *Zichron dvarim* (1977; *Past Continuous*, 1983), moving from one death at its opening, to another at its close, the first of Goldmann's father, the second the suicide of the son; it moves as well from the banal to the tragic with apparently effortless control. Shabtai has also contributed to the drama with a political satire based on the biblical story of Ahab and Jezebel called *Ochlim* (1979; eating). Yona Wallach (b. 1935) has attempted to reproduce the effect of trance in her poems, which seek to etch unusual experience; a very frail individual stands at their center. Confessional autobiography of the type of Pinchas Sadeh's, although without Sadeh's religious mysticism, and with a fair admixture of humor, has been produced by Dan Ben-Amots (b. 1923), either directly, reporting his own history and thought à la Henry MILLER, or through someone else, only thinly disguising the authorial voice.

One of the most striking recent achievements of Israeli fiction writers is a reconstruction of the European background told, as it were, by a Berlin-born Israeli narrator: the novel by David SCHÜTZ called *Haesev vehachol* (1978; the grass and the sand). Although the narrator Emmanuel controls the novel, different voices speak within, giving their account of events and the family. It is Emmanuel those initiative it is to return to his "home" and attempt a resolution of his past with his present, of himself with his family and background, with a history going back to the middle Europe of the turn of the century.

A very complex picture emerges in a survey of the Israeli literary scene. By now, the dominant language is Hebrew, although literature in other languages is produced by, for example, long-standing English-speaking expatriates, or by more recent Soviet immigrants. A Hebrew literary tradition has been inherited and modified, sometimes by writers with little knowledge of or sympathy with that tradition. Hebrew is a language rich in traditional and liturgical associations but young as a vernacular. Its writers are of several generations and vastly different cultural and geographical backgrounds. But they jostle together in the turbulent current of Hebrew literature: the young and the old, the Israeli-born and the recent immigrant, the Zionist conservative and the radical, the Oriental and the European Jew, the religious and the secular Jew, the hopeful and the disillusioned.

Israeli Literature since 1980

In the decade of the 1980s, it is fiction that has proved most adventurous and innovative among the genres in Israel. The quantity and variety of types of expression indicate some dissatisfaction with linear narrative, time-bound, place-bound, limited to the traditional restraints of Hebrew grammar and vocabulary. So narrative has been tensed and stretched, mixing the modes and the forms. Chronological moments have been juxtaposed, voices have been transposed, points of view shuffled, time sequences broken, narrative segments highlighted or challenged by alternative versions and statements.

Leading experimenters have included well-established authors. Amos OZ has discovered several ways of handling plot development. In *Qufsah shehorah* (1987; *Black Box*, 1988) he presents a story from different points of view, through an epistolary novel. This form, of its nature, extracts different views of the same objective materials; that is the point of the story. In a later novel, *Ladaat ishah* (1989; *To Know a Woman*, 1991), we have a principal narrative consciousness in the novel's hero, but the different time scales allow another perspective, as well as some skepticism regarding the author's own account. A. B. YEHOSHUA has continued to experiment with narrative technique, particularly in *Mar maniy* (1990; *Mr. Mani*, 1992), where the "telephone" technique is adopted: When we hear someone speaking on the telephone, we not only hear one side of what is a dialogue, we also inevitably construct the other side in our mind. The other technical surprise lies in the reversal of normal expectations. We expect time to move forward, and fiction often explores the results and implications in the seeds of earlier action. Human experience of time is progressive, although memory moves back. But *Mar maniy*, in a series of five episodes, opens with the most recent, in the 1980s, and then moves backward over two centuries in an apparent attempt to explore the nature of the place in history of the Mani line. So Yehoshua has played with various approaches to narrative, including fantasy, surprise, reversal, STREAM-OF-CONSCIOUSNESS, as well as with the traditional type of narrative in *Molkho* (1987; *Five Seasons*, 1989). The reader is involved in the understanding and even in the creation of the narrative.

Fundamental to recent developments has been the contribution of Yaakov SHABTAI to the novel. His two works, *Zikhron dvarim* (1977; *Past Continuous*, 1983) and *Sof davar* (1984; *Past Perfect*, 1987), because of their artistic success, have suggested new ways of representing reality in fiction. The earlier novel is a string of consciousnesses presented from the outside, where time and association link motifs and narrative parts together. Here, time moves on, and the reader has all sorts of markers to facilitate the understanding of the plot. So external reality bears closely on the internal awareness and does much to engender it. On the other hand, the specific shape of the text is created by the individual consciousness, so that there is constant interplay between the inner and outer layers of reality. Although the story is told by the protagonists and seen through their various lenses, the novel as a whole bears the stamp of a unity of vision. Perhaps this is because of the way that these three lives intertwine, particularly over the nine months covered, and within the limited environment of Tel Aviv. The detailed observation, the linguistic precision, the mental associations, the humor, and the imagination have created a unitary text. The posthumous *Sof davar*, in the main, adopts a quite different approach. Here, there is a single focus of consciousness, holding several different approaches to the protagonist's mental state at an especially critical phase in his life. Reality and fantasy, waking and dream world, are molded together, as eventually are present and past. The reader is unsure whether objective reality is being offered or whether it is an alternative version of that reality, with a cocktail of memory and fantasy added.

It is these flexible versions of reality that have done something to shift the vistas of recent Israeli fiction. One of the leading voices of the 1980s, David GROSSMAN, is much concerned with alternative versions of reality, not only within any one particular work, but in his ongoing opus. We can see *Hiyukh hagdiy* (1983; *The Smile of the Lamb*, 1990) and *Hazman hatsahov* (1987; *Yellow Wind*, 1988) as obverse and reverse sides of one coin. Both works purport to describe the situation under Israeli occupation in the West Bank and the course of the Intifada. But whereas the earlier work is a novel, with a complex view of character, time, motivation, and development (this makes it all very hard for the reader), the latter account is journalistic and polemical, tendentious in its straightforward attempt to persuade the reader of a certain view of events. Of course, these works represent different genres. But even so, the genres themselves are deliberately jumbled; there is, for example, a story inserted in *Hazman hatsahov*. Grossman's novel *Ayen erekh*

ahavah (1986; *See Under: Love*, 1990) constitutes a very ambitious effort to see the Holocaust (and reality generally) afresh, this time, through the eyes of a child (the primary account), but also by a variety of narrative devices, including SURREALISM, fantasy, and dictionary definition.

Other novelists who are interested in expanding fictional range through MAGIC REALISM include Itamar Levy (b. 1956). Magic realism is on the one hand anchored to reality and seeks to explore it, but, on the other, it handles it freely, and so can dispense with the laws of fictional gravity. In this case, the limiting determinants are time sequence and place limitation. If time sequences can be shifted, speeded up or slowed down (as has been done in all fiction through the ages), skipped and reversed, if distance can be contracted and places moved, and if the narrative voice can allow itself the freedom to shift in and out of various characters at will and at need, then a kaleidoscope of effects can be achieved. Magic realism is the product of a growing need to absorb larger and more astonishing portions of actuality, to confront the incredible with the surprising, and to provide innovative tools in the search for representation.

Fiction has moved in all sorts of diverse directions, and much Israeli fiction is likewise experimental. As seen, Yehoshua has allowed the reader space in which to create the missing parts of the dialogue in his "telephone" novel. Yoel Hoffman (b. 1932) has his novels printed on one side of the leaf only, so that the reader is confronted by a blank page for every printed page. Is the reader to create his own story, his own counterpoint? He has indeed no alternative but to do this. Yuval Shimoni (b. 1955), in *Meof hayonah* (1990; the flight of the dove), writes two parallel stories on facing pages in different print types, and these stories intersect in time and place. One is the story of an American couple visiting Paris as tourists, and the second is of a lonely woman living there. But sometimes, plot is abandoned altogether, as by Aner Shalev (b. 1958) in *Opus 1* (1988; opus 1), where, as the title implies, narrative, as in Pater's motto, may aspire to the condition of music. Instead of the normal components of narrative, namely, linear time, logical sequence, coherent plot, we have a sort of musical notation—staccato, legato, and so forth. Or we have, as in the novel by Avram Heffner (b. 1935), *Sefer hamforash* (1991; an annotated book), a novel with its own commentary attached to the text. So, in this case, the reader is not left alone to draw his own conclusions, but is bombarded with suggestions, options, and interpretations.

But, of course, literature is not music. It is made of words, and words have meanings, connotations, and implications for external reality. One line of experimentation in fiction can lead to its own demise or silence. Fiction, that is, invention, can invent prodigiously, not only materials, but also ways of looking at materials. Frustration is inevitable in the search for the nugget of truth that is thought to lie at the source, or for the catchall means of grasping that truth. Reality is enormous, and it is the function of the writer to sharpen its outlines and encapsulate it. Just as reality expands in our consciousness and we learn more, so literature has to expand its capacity. This, at any rate, seems to be the impulse behind the ambition.

Nevertheless, literary concerns, in that they are human, remain static, and our consciousness, as well as the means for its representation, limited. We want to know how people understand each other, how people see themselves, others, and their mutual interaction. One of the most notable features of recent Israeli literature is the increased articulateness of the woman writer. Amalia KAHANA-CARMON has long given expression to a specifically female view of interpersonal contact. But now, many others, in prose and poetry, are also presenting an uninhibitedly female view of subjects that often are assumed to be the exclusive male preserve.

Israeli drama has become more adventurous in choice of subjects and in manner of presentation. Yehoshua Sobol (b. 1939) continues to mix document and fantasy in his semihistorical plays, and Hanoch Levin (b. 1943) presents his masochistic figures in grotesque situations, for amusement and distress.

For Yiddish writing in Israel, see Yiddish Literature.

BIBLIOGRAPHY: Klausner, J., *A History of Modern Hebrew Literature* (1932); Ribalow, M., *Modern Hebrew Literature: A Volume of Literary Evaluation* (1959); Epstein, G. L. and Zeldner, M., *Modern Hebrew Literature* (1965); Mintz, R. F. ed., Introduction to *Modern Hebrew Poetry: A Bilingual Anthology* (1968): xxiii–liv; Rabinovich, I., *Major Trends in Modern Hebrew Fiction* (1968); Alter, R., *After the Tradition* (1969): 163–256; Halkin, S., *Modern Hebrew Literature: From the Enlightenment to the Birth of the State of Israel* (1970); Yudkin, L. I., *Escape into Siege: A Survey of Israeli Literature Today* (1974); Sandbank, S., Introduction to Anderson, E., ed., *Contemporary Israeli Literature: An Anthology* (1977): 3–17; Alter, R., "Afterward: A Problem of Horizons", in Anderson, E., ed., *Contemporary Israeli Literature: An Anthology* (1977): 326–38; Hamalian, L., and Yohannan, J.D., "The Israeli Background," *New Writing from the Middle East* (1978): 189–95; Abramson, G., *Modern Hebrew Drama* (1979); Yudkin, L. I., *Jewish Writing and Identity in the Twentieth Century* (1982); Joseph, H. S., ed., *Modern Israeli Drama* (1983); Yudkin, L. I., *1948 and After: Aspects of Israeli Fiction* (1948); Fisch, H., *A Remembered Future* (1984); Fuchs, E., *Israeli Mythogynies* (1987); Yudkin, L. I., *Beyond Sequence: Current Israeli Fiction and Its Context* (1992)

—LEON I. YUDKIN

ITALIAN LITERATURE

A survey of 20th-c. Italian literature must begin with such turn-of-the century writers as Giovanni VERGA, Giovanni PASCOLI, and Gabriele D'ANNUNZIO, whose innovations in technique and content have exerted a vast influence on the writers of our country.

Verga is now considered—especially for the two novels of his maturity, *I Malavoglia* (1881; *The House by the Medlar Tree*, 1890) and *Mastro-don Gesualdo* (1889; *Mastro-Don Gesualdo*, 1893)—one of the greatest masters of modern European literature. He was a practitioner of *versimo* (truthfulness-to-life)—a poetic of the poor and humble—which itself emphasizes impersonality: "The work itself [he wrote] must have the imprint of a real event; the work of art will seem to have been made by itself . . ." In the novels on which his fame rests, Verga succeeded in putting himself "under the skin" of his characters in order to speak with and through their brains, hearts, and language. His Sicilianism is evident throughout—in syntax, rhythm, inflection, words, solecisms, proverbs—because Verga's major goal was to write what he "picked up along the paths of the countryside, almost with the same simple and picturesque words of a popular narration". *I Malavoglia* and *Mastro-don Gesualdo* were the first two books of a projected sequence of five novels—the other three were never written—to be

called *I vinto* (the defeated ones). He wanted to give the reader "the naked and unchanged facts, instead of having him look for them between the lines of a book". Massimo BONTEMPELLI—the writer of MAGIC REALISM—perceptively observed at the centennial of Verga's birth in 1940 that "he opened the doors of the twentieth century years before D'Annunzio closed the doors of the nineteenth".

Pascoli, the father of modern Italian poetry, was another antitraditionalist whose main concern was to re-create the lives, feelings, and language of humble people. Perhaps it is true, as Pier Paolo PASOLINI claimed, that modern Italian poetry is an elaboration of Pascoli. Certainly, we find a complexity of psychological depth and existential predicament in him that we later find in poets from the *Crepuscolari* (twilight poets) to Eugenio MONTALE.

Pascoli works in a manner of deliberate primitivity, and his poetics have been called "pregrammatical" or "biological". His "Il fanciullino" (1897; the little boy) is the basic essay for understanding his work. Although man grows older, he still carries in his heart the simplicity and humility of a little boy who sees everything with innocent awe and astonishment and who speaks in his own infantile language to "animals, trees, stones, and stars". This is not to say that Pascoli is not a poet of considerable consciousness, and Pasolini rightly states that "an irrational power forces Pascoli to a stylistic firmness and to an *intentional* power that lead him to stylistic tendencies very different [from those of his contemporarires]." He was particularly interested in the preservation of dialectal forms, and at the end of his *Canti di Castelvecchio* (1903; songs of Castelvecchio) he printed a dictionary of dialect words. He was a precursor of the national popular literature, which Antonio Gramsci (1891–1937) always advocated, although it must be also said that an autobiographical thread runs through all Pascoli's work: his family, his home, his people, his patriotism, his pessimism, and his obsession with death.

Unlike Verga and Pascoli, D'Annunzio has been an object of both praise and repudiation in Italy and the rest of Europe not only for his writings but also for his audacious military enterprises, his extravagant life, and his support of Fascism (although he later came to reject Mussolini and to write an epigram against Hitler). What looks like the sheerest bombast becomes upon reconsideration a document of an artist's life and work. That he was given to the hyperbole of the superman is true beyond doubt: verse, he wrote, "can represent the superhuman, the supernatural, the superadmirable . . ." But he was not without a certain modesty, and in "Contemplazione della morte" (1912; Contemplation of death), speaking of his last encounter with Pascoli, he candidly admits that "no modern craftsman possessed Pascoli's art . . . Nobody knew better than he [Pascoli] that art is nothing but practical magic. 'Teach me some secret,' I asked him." Montale, not just a great poet but an incisive critic, well knew that D'Annunzio's influence "is present in all [writers] because he experimented or touched all the linguistic and prosodic possibilities of our time. In this sense, not to have learned anything from him is the worst sign".

Verismo-elsewhere called realism or naturalism—is a significant element in many modern Italian writers. Matilde Serao (1850–1927), the Neapolitan "verista," anecdotal and impressionistic in her best novels, explored the poorest, most squalid places in order to portray the tragic existence of a people who have borne the social injustice of centuries. Ada Negri (1870–1945), another analyst of suffering and humiliation, characterized the poor so accurately in her novels because she saw in them her "own suffering and humiliation". Sibilla Aleramo (pseud. of Rina Faccio, 1876–1960), in her largely autobiographical novel *Una donna* (1906; *A Woman at Bay,* 1908), examines the struggle of a woman in a society dominated by men. In her consciousness of the impact of women in social and artistic endeavors, Aleramo was the chief forerunner of Italian feminist literature.

The Nobel Prize-winning Grazia DELEDDA portrays her native Sardinia as an almost mythical country: in the autobiographical *Il paese del vento* (1931; country of the wind) or in that fable of childhood *Cosima* (1937; Cosima), Sardinia emerges as a place of fantastic natural beauty whose people live in subjection to their violent instincts and passions. Salvatore Di GIACOMO, who mostly wrote in Neapolitan dialect, was another brilliant representative of southern *verismo* in his depiction of dirty houses, public dormitories, almshouses, hospitals, prisons, and the underworld of thieves, murderers, and prostitutes. But Di Giacomo's descriptions are compassionate outcries on behalf of human dignity.

Realism assumed new psychological dimensions in the work of Luigi PIRANDELLO, Italo SVEVO, and Federigo TOZZI. Pirandello's representative characters are haunted by their quicksilver powers of reasoning, which at times change them into grotesque clowns in search of a self, in search of a life to be lived, or in search of a demiurge to create for them a play—as the internationally famous *Sei personnaggi in cerca d'autore* (1921; *Six Characters in Search of an Author,* 1922)—that would summon their essence into existence. The Pirandellian self is always on the brink of dissolving into a hundred thousand different entities in a world without secure coordinates; his characters have difficulty differentiating between reality and fiction, between dream and what "perhaps is not" dream. Pirandello is the most important Italian playwright of the century.

Like Pirandello, Svevo rejected a pure *verismo* for a new analysis of interior reality, as in *La coscienza di Zeno* (1923; *The Confessions of Zeno,* 1930). His intent is to scrutinize the unconscious—by using, for example, the technique of the interior monologue—investigating the psyches of his characters and their conflicts in an interplay of past and present. In a kind of psychoanalytic vivisection, Svevo reveals the ineptitude and emptiness of his antiheroes. Although he has been criticized for grammatical and syntactical incertitude, it is precisely his simple, ordinary language, often arid and imperfect, that makes him so modern and fascinating.

In his youth, Tozzi was influenced by D'Annunzio, by the Christian mystics of his native Siena, and then by Verga, although his "defeated ones" are not characterized by "impersonality". In *Tre croci* (1920; *Three Crosses,* 1921) and *Il podere* (1921; the farm), for instance, the critic Gianfranco Contini (b. 1912) observes that there is a "psychopathological analysis" of the solitude of man without any possibility of redemption. Tozzi penetrates his subject with an anguished intuition, his characters (and he himself) oscillating between reason and hallucination. His work is the autobiography of a tormented writer, utopian and inept, wild and doomed, mystical and sinning.

Another writer influenced by Verga was the Sicilian Vitaliano BRANCATI, an accomplished artist who was able to enter the soul of his people, to analyze their suffering and frustrations. He was particularly successful in satirizing the Sicilian *gallismo,* the erotic obsession of the male that makes him a bragging dominator and seducer of women, even when he is impotent and his sexual bravado is entirely faked. Although his subject matter was often crude and gloomy, Brancati, in a brilliant fusion of pessimism and wit, realism and comedy, portrayed his characters forcefully and vividly. Moreover, the satire of male chauvinism is a metaphor of a Fascist regime built on empty words, not on facts.

Francesco JOVINE, a southern writer of fiction, one of the most important later followers of *verismo,* like Iganazio SILONE or Corrado ALVARO, is concerned with the humiliating conditions of the peasants of his Abruzzi province. Their poverty is due not only to the bareness of their land but also to the exploitation by the rich people with whom they try, unsuccessfully, to deal. In his masterpiece, *Le terre del Sacramento (1950; The Estate in Abruzzi,*1952), a novel about the origins of Fascism, he depicts the defeat of the farmers in their struggle with the feudal landlords, the police, and the Fascist soldiers.

Mario SOLDATI is also a committed yet popular novelist. His stylistic simplicity and his study of the human psyche are strictly connected with his concern for the moral welfare of his characters as they wrestle with the deceptions of their society.

At the beginning of the 20th c., creative Italian literature was closely tied to the activity of a new generation of critics, the most important and influential member of which was Benedetto CROCE, whose notions of lyrical intuition and the identification of intuition with expression are argued in many of his books, and in *La critica,* the journal of history, literature, and philosophy he edited (1903–44), and its supplements, *Quaderni della critica,* which played an important role in the intellectual and cultural life of Italy. Croce's criticism of Verga, Pascoli, Pirandello, and other modern writers no longer seems appropriate, but his vision of poetry is as apt as ever: "This is the enchantment of poetry: the unity of tumult and calm, of the passionate impulse of the mind that contains it while contemplating it". Croce must also be praised for his daring anti-Fascist manifesto of 1925.

Giuseppe Prezzolini (b. 1882) founded *La voce* in 1908 with the intention of inspiring a new consciousness in the psychological and moral attitude of the young in regard to contemporary life. Until 1912 *La voce* was primarily a journal of social concern. Afterward it became more literary, and from 1914 to its demise in 1916 it was edited by Giuseppe de Robertis (1888–1963), who gave it real literary merit, welcoming a host of writers who would soon become important, such as Vincenzo CARDARELLI, Umberto SABA, Riccardo BACHELLI, Clemente REBORA, Camillo SBARBARO, Aldo PALAZZESCHI, Dino CAMPANA, Giuseppe UNGARETTI, and Salvatore Di Giacomo.

The first important movement in 20th-c. Italian poetry is called *Crepuscolarismo,* or "twilight poetry," so called by the critic Giuseppe Antonio Borgese (1882–1952), who thought the great 19th-c. sun of Italian poetry had set. The *Crepuscolari* specialized in existential anxiety: the world is empty, the city is made of stones, Sundays are boring. Montale's poem "Non chiederci la parola" (1925; do not ask us for the word) is perhaps the best description of the movement's consciousness: "Do not ask us the word. . ./Do not ask us for the formula that might open worlds . . . /Today we can tell you only this/what we are *not,* what we *do not* want".

The existential predicament is also visible in Guido GOZZANO, Sergio Corazzini (1886–1907)—especially in his famous poem "Desolazione del povero poeta sentimentale" (1906; "Desolation of the Poor Sentimental Poet," 1962)—Corrado Govoni (1884–1965), Aldo Palazzeschi, Dino Campana, Camillo Sbarbaro, Umberto Saba, and Clemente Rebora. Since they opened a new direction (after Pascoli) in Italian poetry, perhaps they should be called the "sunrise poets."

FUTURISM, on the other hand, was devoted not only to poetry, but to painting, sculpture, and theater, as well as to political and social action. The movement was started by Filippo Tommasco MARINETTI, whose first manifesto, which appeared in French in *Le*

Figaro in 1909, exalted speed, danger, rebellion, and war. Marinetti was the herald of Fascism and associated his own movement with it in *Futurismo e Fascismo* (1924; futurism and Fascism). In *Lacerba*, a journal founded by Giovanni Papini (1881–1956) and Ardengo Soffici (1879–1965), Marinetti published such essays as "Parole in libertà" (1913; words set free), which in their grammatical and syntactical license and their typographical oddity sought to violate the logical and sequential representations of literature.

Two journals that took implicit and explicit issue with Fascism were *La ronda* (1919–23) and *Solaria* (1926–36). *La ronda* was edited by Cardarelli, Bacchelli, Emilio Cecchi (1884–1960), and Antonio Baldini (1889–1966); it sought a "pure poetry," cited the virtues of Giacomo Leopardi (1798–1837) and Alessandro Manzoni (1785–1873), and rejected Fascism as an expression of barbarism. *Solaria* affirmed not only such modern European masters as PROUST and JOYCE but such younger Italians as Elio VITTORINI, Cesare PAVESE, Vasco PRATOLINI, Carlo Emilio GADDA, Guido PIOVENE, Saba, and those who would become the exponents of NEOREALISM.

The important school of 20th-c. Italian poetry is doubtless HERMETICISM, a term coined in 1936 by the Crocean critic Francesco Flora (1891–1962) as an expression of polemical disdain. And, in truth, hermeticism is a poetry for the initiated. Silvio Ramat (b. 1939) describes it is an "ideology of the word," which had to be obscure not only in the face of Fascist censorship but in the endless significations of language. "The poet is a partisan of freedom," Ungareti said of APOLLINAIRE; "he nourishes the dream that one day all persons will be free".

Eugenio Montale, a Nobel Prize winner, claimed that nobody writes verses "to be understood". The problem is to make readers "understand that *quid* which words cannot express." In Montale the simple and modest facts of life and poetry assume a symbolic and emblematic function. Against the "laureate poets" in their ivory towers, he creates a literature of pessimism. Gianfranco Contini calls him a "negative" poet, like Leopardi, but one who has made the highest contribution to a new European poetry. Nor has Montale been unaware of his contribution: "I believe that my poetry has been the most musical poetry of my time. . .".

Salvatore QUASIMODO, honored with the Nobel Prize in 1959, is a critic and translator who also started writing poetry in the hermetic climate. But he transcended it for a mythicization of Sicily. There is in him a sense of isolation and a mystery of symbols that pervades his solitude. Diametrically opposed is Carlo BETOCCHI, a poet of humble things, forever faithful to his Christian aspiration, learned in a life that did not spare him long suffering. Betocchi, the holy patriarch of Italian letters, attracts everyone who meets him with a magnetism of peace and light.

The second phase of hermeticism flourished in Florence from about 1930 to 1945. Piero BIGONGIARI, a poet and critic, was and still is the soul of the movement, at once reminiscent of such older poets as Ungaretti and Montale, and prophetic of a new avant-garde. Mario LUZI, moving from his hermetic origins, has investigated the precarious condition of man in our time with the *piety* of a religious sensibility. Alfonso GATTO gravitated toward a poetry of lyrical—yet heart felt—impact with his poems on World War II and the Resistance. Vittorio Sereni (b. 1913), also once hermetic, moved toward a poetry of private sorrow and passivity, of empathy with people exploited by a capitalist society. The early work of a younger poet, Andrea ZANZOTTO, was a continuation of hermeticism. In fact, his masters included Montale, Ungaretti, and Luzi. Later he created a personal and distinctive poetry based on the most daring linguistic innovations, aimed at a "verbalization of the world". Praised by great poets and critics, such as Montale and Contini, Zanzotto, like his hermetic predecessors, has opened the doors to new and audacious trends in poetry.

It was during the twenty years of Fascism and in response to the apparent splendor of that regime that the forerunners of neorealism began to gather force. Among these, Corrado Alvaro, in *Genti in Aspromonte* (1930; *Revolt in Aspromonte*, 1962) dramatized the injustices perpetrated in the south against the poor; Carlo BERNARI, in *Tre operai* (1934; three workers), expressed the fears, discouragement, and suffering of the proletariat; Elio Vittorini, in *Conversazione in Sicilia* (1941; *In Sicily,* 1947); described the misery of Sicilians as the misery of the world; Cesare Pavese, in *Paesi tuoi* (1941; *The Harvesters*, 1961), exposed the countryside as a place of superstitious and savage archaism; Alberto MORAVIA, with the novel *Gli indifferenti* (1929; *The Indifferent Ones,* 1932), portrayed with a crude realism the false values of the bourgeoisie. Later, in *La mascherata* (1941; *The Fancy Dress Party,* 1952), Moravia presented a sarcastic and grotesque depiction of Fascist dictatorship.

Ignazio Silone must be included among the forerunners of neorealism, although his novel *Fontamara* was published in Italy only after the war, in 1947. Written in Italian in 1930 (during Silone's exile in Switzerland), *Fontamara* was first published in German translation in 1933, and in English (as *Fontamara*) in 1934. It achieved an immediate and astounding international success and was translated into twenty-seven languages. Set in Fontamara, an imaginary town in the Abruzzi, the novel is a poignant, realistic picture of the tragic and debased life of the poor, ignorant peasants (*cafoni*) during the Fascist period.

In the aftermath of World War II it was natural, as Italo CALVINO, said, that the passion for literature should have become a passion for the fate of the world. Writers sought in the spheres of words and forms something to equal the force and tragedy of their time; the Resistance became the new myth. It was the first time in Italian history that Catholics and Communists, intellectuals and the poor, women and children fought for the freedom of their country, and mythicizing the Resistance provided the richest ingredient in the new Italian fiction called neorealist.

Neorealism is not a school, but, as Calvino has said, "an epoch, a climate". "The Resistance made us believe in the possibility of an epic literature, charged with an energy at the same time rational and vital, social and existential, collective and autobiographical; *a literature of tension.*" Other critics speak of a literature that, perhaps for the first time in centuries, could have changed the course of the history and civilization of a people.

Such writers as VITTORINI, CALVINO, PRATOLINI, Giuseppe BERTO, and Carlo LEVI portrayed the horrors of war as an insult to human dignity, although even as they condemned the past, they looked toward a better future. "I am sure that a better time will come," an old man tells some adolescents in Berto's novel *Il cielo è rosso* (1947; *The Sky Is Red,* 1948). "I don't know when, but it will come. You have a mission to accomplish in the world, so that men may become better and forget violence and hatred.".

The best novel of the Resistance was *Il partigiano Johnny* (1968; Johnny the partisan) by Beppe FENOGLIO, published posthumously. It dramatizes the life of the partisan in the field, his anguish at the death of his comrades, his solitude, and the desperate conditions of his people. Speaking of Fenoglio, Calvino said: "We now have the book our generation wanted to write; Fenoglio succeeded in writing the novel we all dreamed of writing".

Another important novel of the Resistance is Elio Vittorini's *Uomini e no* (1945; men and not-men), with its background of Nazi-Fascist cruelties. Among other novelists who wrote important works about the Resistance are Carlo CASSOLA, Giorgio BASSANI, Calvino, Pavese, and Moravia, although two of the most instructive anti-Fascist narratives of the Fascist period are Carlo Levi's *Cristo si è fermato a Eboli* (1945; *Christ Stopped at Eboli*, 1947), which relates the author's experience in exile in the primitive town of Gagliano in Lucania, the encounter of a northerner with the immemorial problems of the south; and Vasco Pratolini's *Cronache di poveri amanti* (1947; *A Tale of Poor Lovers*, 1949), in which people are abused and mistreated in the formative days of Fascism. To the many works of fiction describing the horrors of the war must be added the verse of such famous writers as Saba, Govoni, Palazzeschi, Ungaretti, Montale, Quasimodo, Pavese, Gatto, Rebora, and Pasolini, who in their outstanding poems condemned the Nazi-Fascist brutalities.

One of the greatest novelists of the century, another Rabelais or Joyce in his linguistic vitality is Carlo Emilio Gadda, an engineer by profession. His subject is the disorder of modern man in "the forms and cubes of life" in the cement cities no less than in the emergence of Fascism. His best novel is *Quer pasticciaccio brutto de via Merulana* (1959; *That Awful Mess on Via Merulana*, 1965), set in Rome in 1927, with a plot concerning a jewel theft and a murder mystery. But this plot is only a pretext for Gadda, who wants to represent the psychological depth of unrestrained passions during Mussolini's time. Gadda condemns the society of the "Duce" and his regime in this ferocious anti-Fascist novel. Writing, he says, "is often a means of taking revenge, sometimes the only means". Or as Pasolini said of him: "Gadda belongs to a historical time when it was impossible to see the world—this magma of disorder, corruption, hypocrisy, stupidity, and injustice—in a perspective of hope".

Representing a different kind of Roman novel are Pasolini's *Ragazzi di vita* (1955; *The Ragazzi*, 1968) and *Una vita violenta* (1959; *A Violent Life*, 1968). The protagonists are poor boys with an instinct for survival in a world they never made. Pasolini's language of slang, dialect, and vulgarisms grants an immediacy to the instinctual lives of his protagonists. The novels are a document of desperation in the Roman subproletariat. Another sort of desperation animates the workers in Berto's *Il brigante* (1951; *The Brigand*, 1951), a novel of social protest set in the south, in Calabria—which Gramsci called a colony of northern Italy—about feudally exploited and degraded farmers.

There are several other writers of note who are part of the neorealism movement or its aftermath. Michele PRISCO, a Neapolitan, moved from an analysis of "the bourgeois world of my province" to the larger world and the largest questions—the problem of evil and human violence. Domenico REA, another Neapolitan, is at once violent and humorous, cynical and glamorous, "verista" and expressionist. Anna Maria ORTESE, who has been called a Neapolitan writer (although she does not identify herself with Naples) because of her famous book of stories, *Il mare non bagna Napoli* (1953; *The Bay Is Not Naples*, 1955), describes the brutal conditions of that city; her novel *Il porto di Toledo* (1975; the port of Toledo)—Toledo is a metaphor for Naples—is a mythopoeic inquiry into the social, moral, and psychical chaos of our time. Leonardo SCIASCIA'S novels concentrate on Sicilian issues, poverty, ignorance, suffering, and the Mafia, and he later became active in legislative politics in the hope of bringing some "light" into the crisis of our time. Guido Piovene, an observer of the

secret heart, and a severe moralist, momentarily revived the 19th-c. tradition of the epistolary novel with *Lettere di una novizia* (1941; *Confessions of a Novice*, 1950); his posthumously published *Inverno d'un uomo felice* (1977; winter of a happy man), a collection of stories originally published between 1938 and 1959, revealed a genuine interest in the daily life of his subjects. Mario TOBINO'S books document the atrocities of the Nazi-Fascist dictatorship, psychological as well as physical. Elsa MORANTE'S *La storia* (1974; *History: A Novel*, 1977), a powerful indictment of World War II, takes its tone (and its epigraph) from a survivor of Hiroshima: "There is no word in any language that may console the guinea pigs who do not know the reason for their death."

Lucio PICCOLO, the baroque poet whose work is rooted in the southern realism in the manner of Verga, wrote his "past memories" of "baroque churches and old convents, and of souls suited to these places who lived here without leaving a trace". He is able to translate the most complicated subjects into a pure poetry, for he is a poet of extreme musicality. Tommaso LANDOLFI is a writer of marked singularity, comparable only to Gadda, Antonio Pizzuto (1893–1976), and the Florentine hermetics. A writer given as easily to surrealism as modes of verisimilitude, Landolfi is a translator of such diverse writers as Novalis, Gogol, and Tolstoy. Pizzuto is another iconoclast who, as Contini observes, "eliminates the present and perfect tense for the imperfect . . . of a vague temporal duration . . . and ends by using mainly the infinitive". Pizzuto de-creates the representation of reality and re-creates a new and original language in Italian literature.

The novels of Lucio MASTRONARDI, which deal principally with the people of Vigevano, are remarkable for their linguistic innovations in the manner of Gadda. His writings are in the Italo-Pavesian dialect and are major examples of the modern use of vernacular language.

The end of neorealism can be dated to the publication of Pratolini's *Metello* (1955; *Metello*, 1968), a social and historical novel set in Florence at the end of the 19th c. that suggests that a neorealistic literature of "document, memorial, and testimony" is finished. Another modern novel that is also set largely in the 19th c. and that leads us to the same conclusion is Giuseppe Tomasi di LAMPEDUSA'S *Il gatopardo* (1958; *The Leopard*, 1960), which chronicles the political and economic decline of a noble family and the leveling of social classes in a manner reminiscent of Stendhal. And Pasolini, who had been a very active neorealist, proclaimed its death in a poem with that very name, "In morte del realismo" (1960; death of realism).

After the war and throughout the 1950s and early 1960s Italy experienced the so-called "economic miracle". The country was industrialized as never before, and creature comforts became available as never before—but at what price? In his novel *Teorema* (1968; theorem) Pasolini scored the materialism of a big industrial city and the loneliness, emptiness, and boredom of capitalist society. But even worse than the loneliness and boredom of the rich is the alienation of the urban worker in the newly industrialized cities—the man who leaves his home town and works in a factory that does not belong to him, who is regimented in repetitious activity, who barely communicates with his fellows.

The alienation of modern man, his unintegrated relation to the world, is the subject of the novels of Ottiero OTTIERI, who condemns the factory as an instrument of depersonalization. So, too, does Paolo VOLPONI, as in the novel *Memoriale* (1962; *My Troubles Began*, 1964). "The strongest feeling I felt," says the protagonist, "was that I had become factory property". All loneliness and frustration, however, are not associated with socioeconomic conditions. *Il male oscuro* (1964; *Incubus*, 1966), by Giuseppe Berto, is the story of a man who finds in his own conscious and subconscious an explanation of his physical and mental suffering. *Il paradiso* (1970; *Bought and Sold*, 1973) by Alberto Moravia is a collection of short stories in which wealthy women narrate their extramartial affairs and describe their abnormal lives.

Quasimodo wrote of writers in general, young writers in particular: "There does not exist a work of art which is not a protest against the establishment . . . The contemporary work of art, in order to survive, must be a work of protest". Or as Silvio Ramat wrote: "Every authentic writer is authentically experimental". These statements help explain the origins of a new avant-garde literature of dissent. The forerunners are Luciano Anceschi (b. 1911), who in 1956 founded the journal *Il Verri*, which is a mine of experimental writing, and Alfredo Giuliani (b. 1924), who in 1961 published the anthology *I novissimi* (the newest), which contains poetry by himself, Elio Pagliarani (b. 1927), Edoardo SANGUISENTI, Nanni Balestrini (b. 1935), and Antonio Porta (b. 1935). In his introduction, Giuliani remarks: "To understand contemporary poets one must refer not to the memory of past poems but to the physiognomy of today's world." In 1963 a group of writers—among them Anceschi, Luigi MALERBA, Sanguineti, Umberto ECO, and Balestrini—held a glamorous meeting in Palermo, whence issued the volume *Gruppo 63* (group 63), the official document of neo-avant-gardism in Italy. In quest of a language appropriate to a technological society, Sanguineti emphasized the "consciousness of the relation between the intellectual and bourgeois society . . . Any literary work is the expression of an ideology".

From a rather different angle of vision, another member of Group 63, Angelo Guglielmi (b. 1924), wrote: "Up to now language has tried to reflect reality as in a mirror. Henceforth, language must take its place at the very heart of reality". The result is that some experimentalists express their ideas through complicated and often frustrating verbal and typographical approaches: concrete poetry, audiovisual texts, and so forth.

There is, to be sure, a certain amount of social and political rebelliousness among these writers. Lamberto Pignotti (b. 1926), for instance, deplored the "anonymity of mass production in technological civilization". In the journal *Quindici*, Umberto Eco argued that the modern writer "must not make an intellectual, but a practical, discourse", and that he must participate in any "political discourse" protest allows. Walter Pedullà (b. 1930) spoke of the work of art as a "consumer's object" and emphasizes the "social function of poetry". Elio Pagliarani proclaimed an "attitude of protest" against the establishment, while Nanni Balestrini said that language must become a "concrete method of transforming the world". The poet Nelo Risi (b. 1930) wrote that the artist is "up to his neck in history, with his ounce of aspiration for the eternal . . . As long as the artist is conscious of the evils of society, he has to operate beyond personal engagement in the search for a common conscience".

The debasement of language has been examined by Sanguineti in *Il giuoco dell'oca* (1967; the goose game), a game played by casting dice and moving wooden geese from place to place. Sanguineti has made up his own squares—one hundred and eleven vignettes, each with its own illustration: mermaids, monsters, advertisements, the legs of Marilyn Monroe, paintings by Dalí, and so on. This is an example of "open work", a work opened to all meanings, although the goose game is certainly symbolic of life

and death. *Super-Eliogabalo* (1969; super-Heliogabalus) by Alberto Arbasino (b. 1930) is an endless play with words with obscure allusions; it is a satire and a farce involving hundreds of historical characters and institutions, all of which circle about the superstar, super-Heliogabulus. *Non libro* (1970; not a book) by Cesare Zavattini (b. 1902) is a book which says it is not a book and which comes with a record and is written in a phantasmagoric language, using typography that immediately suggests the destruction of reality.

Dino Buzzati (1906–1972), whose early novels established his reputation, may be said to have experimented with the idea of the book in yet another way in *Poema a fumenti* (1969; poem in cartoons,) which he amusingly asserts is a "work a little inferior to *The Divine Comedy* but much superior to *Faust*". Told in large part through comic strips—drawn by him—it is a modern version of the legend of Orpheus and Eurdice—of Orfi, a young rock musician, and Eura. Buzzati recounts the destruction of myth: "And the last kings of the fables started walking toward exile." On the other hand, Italo Calvino returns to myth with his novel *Il castello dei destini incrociati* (1969; *The Castle of Crossed Destinies*, 1977), first published in the elegant book *Tarocchi* (tarot cards), which contains a superb reproduction of the 15th-c. Viscontean tarot cards. The novel is about mute knights who take refuge in a castle, where each one is able to narrate his prodigious adventures with different combinations of the cards. Thus, Calvino finds a support against alienation in the return to myth, legend, and fable. The tarot cards may be endlessly combined; they are a machine for generating meanings and stories. Using the same structural-semiotic approach, Calvino's *Le città invisibili* (1972; *Invisible Cities*, 1974) deals with an imaginary Marco Polo who, not knowing the language of his lord, Kublai Khan, describes to him the fabulous cities he has visited with objects and other signs.

After Pirandello, whose narrative and dramatic works are so closely related, the Italian drama gradually asserted itself as an autonomous genre. In this sense, Ugo BETTI is perhaps the most important Italian playwright of the century. His theater focuses on the plight of the individual who discovers that he is at variance with what he thought he was. Bewildered by his own feelings, thoughts, and acts, he hopes to find wholeness in the hands of a higher being—perhaps the Christian God. Betti's plays usually take the form of a trial or inquest, the purpose of which is not to investigate a person's guilt (which is a given) but its unavoidability. In some of his plays Diego Fabbri (1911–1980) used Pirandellian conventions like the contrast between theatrical fiction and life, although he also worked in a Christian context, sometimes, in the manner of Betti. Fabbri believed that every man, confronted with the choice between good and evil, will become aware of his spiritual restlessness and choose the good. Eduardo De FILIPPO is Italy's most popular playwright, and perhaps the most talented comic actor since the death of Totò. His plays are an inventive fusion of standard Italian and Neapolitan dialect. They concentrate on the tragicomic struggle of the lower-and lower-middle-class man to survive economically and emotionally. Luigi Squarzina (b. 1922) is able to seduce an audience with his re-creation of historical settings in which the conflicted fate of an individual emerges; what results is a painful insight into the stupidity and banality of evil. Dario FO'S intention is to change the stage into a tribunal and to make of the playwright a social gadfly. His irony at the expense of his native land sparkles with delight and originality, since Fo is a great clown-actor and he performs in his own pieces.

The number of authors who wrote poetry, plays, and even narrative works in the native dialect of their region is very great indeed, and the literary use of dialects such as Milanese, Neapolitan, Piedmontese, Sicilian, and Venetian goes back at least several centuries. Nevertheless, only a relatively small minority of the writers who chose a dialect rather than standard Italian as their medium of expression may be objectively regarded as worthy of a permanent place in the history of Italian letters.

Until a few decades ago the main thrust of Italian culture was centripetal: dialect authors represented a deviation from a linguistic norm, that of the common national language, and this deviation was generally regarded with at least a degree of intolerance by literary historians and critics. Thus, even very great dialect poets, such as the Milanese Carlo Porta (1775–1821) and the Roman Giuseppe Gioacchino Belli (1791–1863), were often excluded from anthologies and rarely—if ever—studied in schools or universities. It would be too complex to examine here in depth the reasons for this kind of neglect. Suffice it to say that the aspirations toward national unity of the Risorgimento and the centralizing tendencies of the Fascist regime had much to do with it.

A turning point of decisive importance, however, came not too long after World War II with the rise of neorealism in fiction and cinema, partly as a reaction to the Fascist myth of a country that was supposed to be in every way united and uniform. In reality, linguistic diversity in Italy is of such magnitude that foreigners may have difficulty in comprehending it. Dialects of different regions are generally not even mutually intelligible.

Pier Paolo Pasolini was perhaps the first important author to turn to his mother's native language, Friulian, with his first collection of verse, entitled *Poesie a Casarsa* (1942; Casarsa poems). The case of Friulian is a special one: spoken in the extreme northeastern region of Italy, it has no official status, but is regarded by many scholars—especially non-Italians—as differing so profoundly in matters of phonology, morphology, and lexicon from standard Italian as to constitute a separate language, akin to the Rhaeto-Romance dialects of Switzerland. The question is not an easily settled one, since the difference between a "language" and a "dialect" can rest more on sociological and political grounds than on linguistic ones. In fact, it is enough to consider that any "dialect" could achieve the status of a "language" overnight if, due to political upheavals, it were to be recognized officially by a newly established state.

The postwar decades saw not only the flowering of several important dialect poets, but also a growing scholarly interest in the study and reevaluation of dialect writers from earlier centuries and especially from the first half of the 20th c. Thus, Carlo Porta, Giuseppe, Gioacchino Belli, and the Neapolitan Salvatore Di Giacomo, to mention only a few, were reprinted in modern editions by important publishers and made the object of extensive critical work by leading scholars. At the same time, the works of a number of poets who had appeared in the first half of the century and had been generally ignored in spite of their obvious merit were rediscovered. Among these were the Milanese Delio Tessa (1886–1939), the Abruzzian Cesare de Titta (1862–1933), the Veronese Berto Barbarani (1872–1945), the Neapolitan Ferdinando Russo (1866–1927), the Piedmontese Nino Costa (1886–1945), and the Genoese Edoardo Firpo (1899–1957). A great deal of attention went also to the Roman poets Cesare Pascarella (1858–1940) and Trilussa (pseud. of Carlo Alberto Salustri, 1871–1950), whose easily intelligible dialect made them popular outside of Rome as well.

In 1952 Pasolini and Mario Dell'Arco (b. 1905), himself a poet in the Roman dialect, published an important anthology entitled *Poesia dialettale del Novecento* (dialect poetry of the 20th c.), which did much to call to the attention of both scholars and readers the significance of the contribution made by dialect poets. Pasolini's extensive introduction, which runs to 119 pages, constitutes to this day an essay of fundamental importance for a critical understanding of dialect literature in Italy.

In recent years, the number of publications dealing with dialect works has continued to increase as scholars rediscover, for instance, the wealth of dramatic works in dialects such as Piedmontese, Milanese, Venetian, and Neapolitan, and as dialect authors from earlier centuries are found worthy of critical editions and of a place in both anthologies and histories of Italian literature.

Among the living dialect poets, one of the most highly regarded is undoubtedly Albino Pierro (b. 1916), who started writing in the dialect of his native Tursi, a town in the region of Basilicata, around 1960, when he published his first collection of verse entitled *A terra d'u ricorde* (the land of memories), and whose later works have had the honor of publication by Laterza, one of Italy's most prestigious publishing houses.

BIBLIOGRAPHY: Arrighi, P., *Le vérisme dans la prose narrative italienne* (1937); Brandon-Albini, M., *La culture italienne* (1950); Livingston, A., *Essays on Modern Italian Literature* (1950); Fernandez, D., *Le roman italien et la crise de la conscience moderne* (1958); Vittorini, D., *High Points in the History of Italian Literature* (1958); De Sanctis, F., *History of Italian Literature* (1959); Calvino, I., "Main Currents in Italian Fiction Today," *IQ*, 4: 13–14 (1960): 3–14; Pacifici, S., *A Guide to Contemporary Italian Literature* (1962); Brandon-Albini, M., *Midi vivant* (1963); Heiney, D., *America in Modern Italian Literature* (1964); Donadoni, E., *A History of Italian Literature*, updated by E. Mazzali and R. J. Clements (1969); Pacifici, S., ed., *From, "Versimo" to Experimentalism: Essays on the Modern Italian Novel* (1969); Ballerini, L., ed., *Italian Visual Poetry, 1912–1972* (1973); Molinaro, J. A., ed., *Petrarch to Pirandello* (1973); Wilkins, E. W., *A History of Italian Literature*, updated by T. G. Bergin (1974); Biasin, G. P., *Literary Diseases: Theme and Metaphor in the Italian Novel* (1975); Ragusa, O., *Narrative and Drama: Essays in Modern Italian Literature from Verga to Pasolini* (1976); Gatt-Rutter, J., *Writers and Politics in Modern Italy* (1978); Bondanella, P. and J. C. Bondanella, eds., *Dictionary of Italian Literature* (1979); Perella, N. J., *Midday in Italian Literature: Variations on an Archetypal Theme* (1979); Whitfield, J. H., *A Short History of Italian Literature*, updated by J. R. Woodhouse (1980)

—M. RICCIARDELLI

Italian Literature since 1970

Throughout the 1960s and 1970s established and veteran authors continued to write narratives that, for the most part, were considered traditional in style, structure, and content, and were aimed at a steady number of faithful readers. Publishers on the other hand were competing for prestigious literary prizes such as the "Strega," "Viareggio," and "Campiello" that increased the sales for their authors and also by launching newly discovered or relaunching long forgotten writers such as Antonio Pizzuto, Tommaso Landolfi, Achille Campanile (1900-1977), Salvatore Satta (1908-1975), Guido Morselli (1912-1973), and Gesualdo Bufalino (1920-1996). At the same time readers were facing new styles of writing—often considered much too difficult for average readers—from innovative writers; notable are Edoardo Sanguineti's *Capriccio italiano* (1973; Italian caprice), Roberto Di Marco's (b. 1937) *Telemachia* (1968; Telemachia), Gianni Celati's (b. 1937) *Comiche* (1971; comics) and *Lunario del paradiso* (1978; the almanac of paradise), Giuliano Gramigna's (b. 1920) *Il Gran Trucco* (1978; the big trick), Nanni Balestrini's (b. 1935) collage of fiction and journalistic reportage *Vogliamo tutto* (1971; we want everything), Luigi MALERBA's *La scoperta dell'alfabeto* (1963; the discovery of the alphabet) and *Il Serpente* (1966; *The Serpent*, 1968), Antonio Porta's first novel *Partita* (1967; game) as well as his poetry *Metropolis* (1971; metropolis), and particularly Giorgio Manganelli's (1922-1990) works of verbal and cerebral virtuosities such as *A&B* (1974; A&B) and *Sconclusione* (1975; no conclusion).

Experimental writing styles became more common as writers chose to put into narrative form some of the key theoretical (semiological, structuralist, narratological, and intertextual) notions of 20th-c. aesthetics. For nearly three decades narrators and poets freely underlined the central role of language in their compositions, and thus "corporeal," "visible," and spoken language joined the "explosive chains of signifiers"—as defined by Roland BARTHES's and Jacques DERRIDA's concepts of *écriture*—as literature became more and more clever manifestations of literariness.

After the phase of neorealism came to a close and as Marxist ideology began to lose the support of intellectuals and writers, conservative critics often spoke about the death of the novel even though the vitality and spectrum of Italian fiction was actually growing. Professors including Maria Corti (dates n.a.) and Umberto Eco; critics such as Enzo Siciliano (b. 1934) with *La coppia* (1966; the couple), *La principessa e l'antiquario* (1980; the princess and the antiquarian), *Diamante* (1984; *Diamante*, 1987), and his 1998 Strega Prize-winning *I bei momenti* (beautiful moments), and Roberto Cotroneo (b. 1961) with *Presto con fuoco* (1995; soon with fire) and *Otranto* (1997; Otranto); judges such as Salvatore Satta (1902-1975) with *Il giorno del giudizio* (1979; judgement day) and Dante Troisi (b. 1920) with *Viaggio scomodo di un giudice* (1981; unpleasant journey of a judge), *La sopravvivenza* (1981; the survival), and *La finta notte* (1984; the faked night); doctors such as Giuseppe Bonaviri (b. 1924) and Mario Tobino (b. 1910); journalists like Oriana Fallaci with *Un uomo* (1979; *A Man*, 1980); and factory workers such as Tommaso Di Ciaula, Vincenzo Guerrazzi, and Luigi Davì (dates n.a.) joined new narrators, young and old.

Italian fiction was being infused with new vitality and was experiencing a rediscovery of the historical novel that began with a revival of the Middle Ages as in Giuseppe Pederiali's (b. 1937) *Il tesoro del Bigatto* (1978; the treasure of bigatto), Umberto Eco's *Il nome della rosa* (1980; *The Name of the Rose*, 1983), Laura Mancinelli's (dates n.a.) *I dodici abbati di Challant* (1981; the twelve abbots of Challant), Roberto Vacca's *Dio e il computer* (1984; God and the computer), and Marta Morazzoni's (b. 1950) *L'invenzione della verità* (1988; the invention of truth). The Manzoni historical legacy and the interests in metahistory and new historicism expanded to include a wider range of centuries from the days of Byzantium in Luigi Malerba's *Il Fuoco greco* (1990; the Greek fire), to Rome in the 3rd c. in Carlo Cassola's *Il ribelle* (1980; the rebel), to 15th-c. Turkish invasions in southern Italy in Maria Corti's *L'ora di tutti* (1966; *Otranto*, 1996), to 17th-c. witchcraft in Sebastiano Vassalli's (b. 1941) *La Chimera* (1990; *The Chimera*, 1993), to the years of the ruling Czars in Russia in Roberto PAZZI's *Cercando L'imperatore* (1985; searching for the

emperor) and *La principessa e il drago* (1986; the princess and the dragon), and to 18th- and 19th-c. backgrounds as in Antonio TABUCCHI's Tuscany in *Piazza d'Italia* (1975; Italian piazza) and Vincenzo Consolo's (dates n.a.) tales during the days of the Risorgimento in Sicily in *Il sorriso dell'ignoto marinaio* (1976; *The Smile of the Unknown Mariner*, 1994), to the days preceding Fascism in *Nottetempo casa per casa* (1992; night time, from house to house), Raffaele Nigro's (b. 1947) Basilicata region in *I fuochi del Basento* (1987, the fires of the Basento), several commemorative works celebrating Alessandro Manzoni, such as Natalia GINZBURG's *La famiglia Manzoni* (1983; the Manzoni family), and Mario Pomilio's (dates n.a.) *Il Natale del 1883* (1983; Christmas 1983), and Francesca Sanvitale's (dates n.a.) reconstruction of the post-Napoleonic period in *Il figlio dell'impero* (1993; the son of the empire). History, however, was not being used merely to learn about the past; rather, history provided excellent material for making analogies between past and present.

While a few writers were still revisiting the atrocities suffered by humanity under Fascism and during World War II, for instance Elsa Morante (1912-1985) in *La Storia* (1975; *History*, 1977), many more stories were set against the backdrop of such later political events as the student revolution of 1968 and the terrorist years of the late 1970s, including Alberto Moravia's *La vita interiore* (1978; *Time of Desecration*, 1980), Luce D'Eramo's (b. 1925) *Nucleo Zero* (1981; nucleus zero), Dacia MARAINI's *Il treno per Helsinki* (1984; *The Train*, 1986), L. Ravera's (dates n.a.) *Porci con le ali* (1976; pigs with wings), written in collaboration with Marco Lombardo Radice (dates n.a.), and *Ammazzare il tempo* (1978; to kill time), Luigi Malerba's *Il pianeta azzurro* (1986; the blue planet), Nanni Balestrini's *La violenza illustrata* (1976; illustrated violence) and *Gli invisibili* (1987; the invisible ones), Andrea De Carlo's (1952) *Due di due* (1989; two of two), Sandra Petrignani's (b. 1952) *Come cadono i fulmini* (1991; how lightnings fall), and Bianca Maria Frabotta's (dates n.a.) *Velocità di fuga* (1989; speed of flight), which expresses her disillusionment with both the revolution of 1968 and the militant feminist movement that followed it.

The popularity of Sigmund FREUD and Jacques LACAN in the 1960s and 1970s was in part responsible for the appearance of several psychoanalytical dramas, notably Giuseppe BERTO's *Il male oscuro* (1964; *Incubus*, 1966), most of Ottiero Ottieri's production that follows *Il campo di concentrazione* (1972; the field of concentration), Paolo Volponi's trilogy of *Memoriale* (1963; *The Memorandum*, 1968), *La macchina mondiale* (1963; *The Worldwide Machine*, 1969), and *Corporale* (1975; corporeal), most of Goffredo PARISE's fiction from the 1970s on, Edoardo Sanguineti's *Capriccio italiano* (1963; Italian caprice), and Giuliano Gramigna's (dates n.a.) work from his Proustian novels such as *Marcel ritrovato* (1969; Marcel found) and *L'empio Enea* (1972; ungodly enea) to his Lacanian poetry *Es-O-Es* (1980; S.O.S.) and his Freudian novel *La festa del centenario* (1989; the feast of the centennial). Most interesting was Ferdinando Camon's (dates n.a.) *La malattia chiamata uomo* (1981; *The Sickness Called Man*, 1992) based on the idea that "man is a sickness and that he goes through analysis not to get better but in order to know why he goes through analyses." More psychosocial are the works of Dr. Mario Tobino, who reported his direct experiences with the effects of a law that closed psychiatric hospitals in Italy in such fictional accounts as *Per le antiche scale* (1972; through the old stairway), *La bella degli specchi* (1976; the beauty of the mirror), and *Gli ultimi anni di Magliano* (1982; the last years at Magliano).

The sociopolitical complexities of modern Italy were often illustrated in a variety of intriguing and suspenseful detective stories by Leonardo Sciascia, Umberto Eco, and Luisi Malerba. The conditioning effects of mass media were also attracting more attention. And while very few writers mentioned the role of radio in daily life as Giuseppe Cassieri (b. 1926) did in *L'uomo in cuffia* (1982; the man with earphones), or magazines and journalism as Andrea De Carlo did in *Tecniche di seduzione* (1991; techniques of seduction), several authors such as the writing team of Carlo Fruttero, Franco Lucentini, and Stefano Benni (dates n.a.) and practically all of De Carlo's work illustrated the overall effects of cinema and television on a consumer-oriented society. Quite common became also works that narrated the behind-the-scenes intrigues of the academic world as Maria Corti did in *Il ballo dei sapienti* (1966; the dance of the wise), of literary conventions as Libero Bigiaretti did in *Il congresso* (1976; the congress).

In the early 1970s, as the fears of a possible nuclear war increased, so did the number of narrations treating apocalyptic themes and the horrific scenes of "the day after," as demonstrated by Guido Morselli's (dates n.a.) *Dissipatio HG* (1977; the dissolution of the human race) and Paolo Volponi's *Il pianeta irritabile* (1978; the irritable planet). In both novels we find deserted and haunting scenes after a cataclysm that has practically eliminated all human life.

The post-1968 revolution also brought to the front a variety of erotic novels, notably the fiction of Aldo Busi, A. Bevilaqua (dates n.a.), Pier Paolo Pasolini, Goffredo Parise, and of new women writers such as L. Ravera, whose *Porci con le ali* became a forerunner to several works such as M. Mazzucco's (dates n.a.) *Il bacio della medusa* (1997; the kiss of Medusa), C. Llera Moravia's (b. 1954) *Lola e gli altri* (1989; Lola and the others), and F. Mazzuccaro's (dates n.a.) phone sex story *Hot line* (1998; title in English).

The fast growing market of the novel can be attributed to several economic and cultural factors. During the economic boom years of the late 1950s and 1960s there appeared the first innovations in fiction and poetry from authors associated with the "Neoavanguardia" and the "Gruppo 63," who, for the most part, were reacting against the established bourgeois novel of writers such as Cassola, Moravia, and Giorgio Bassani. Many of their experimental and highly intellectual works were hastily labeled as imported echoes of the French NEW NOVEL and of the Parisian group "Tel Quel." Likewise, the popular translations of the writings of James JOYCE, Jorge Louis BORGES, Mikhail BAKHTIN, and Roland Barthes, the renewed interests in psychoanalysis that accompanied the debates surrounding Jacques Lacan's writings for nearly two decades, and the ideological polemics spurred by the interdisciplinary essays of Theodor ADORNO and the other representatives of the Frankfurt School were all seen as major foreign forces behind the works of the new writers promoted by critics such as Angelo Guglielmi and Renato Barilli (dates n.a.) in *Il Gruppo 63. Critica e teoria* (1976; Gruppo 63: criticism and theory) and in journals such as *Il Verri*, *Quindici*, *Marcatré*, and *Alfabeta*.

On the domestic scene, industrialization and economic growth served as a stimulus in the 1960s to fascinating narratives that contributed to the success of the short-lived trend labeled "letteratura e industria" (literature and industry). The massive changes occurring at all levels of society—at work, at leisure, and within family relationships—were examined by several authors, all very different in their style, language, content, and ideology. Luciano Bianciardi (1922-1971), for example, depicted factory workers in Milan in *La*

vita agra (1962; the bitter life) and wrote about the frustrations of an intellectual trying to integrate himself within the new industry of culture in the essays *L'integrazione* (1957; integration) and *Il lavoro culturale* (1957; the cultural work); Ottiero Ottieri related his experiences with human relations personnel in the process of industrialization in *Donnarumma all'assalto* (1959; *Men at the Gate*, 1962) and *Tempi stretti* (1964; hard times); Lucio Mastronardi (1930-1979) offered some comical but also very ironic portraits of people caught in the follies of commercialism and consumerism that accompany sudden economic success in the trilogy *Gente di Vigevano* (1962-1964; people of Vigevano); Paolo Volponi depicted eccentric characters who become disillusioned after having believed in the potentials of technology in *Memoriale* (1962; Memorial) and *La macchina mondial* (1965; the worldwide machine) up to *Le mosche del capitale* (1989; the flies of capital); Carlo Bernari fused realism, hopes, and nightmarish experiences surrounding the failure of an intellectual who had hoped to bring neocapitalism to the South in *Era l'anno del sole quieto* (1964; it was the year of the quiet sun); and Nanni Balestrini presented his remarkable collage of journalistic reportage, diary, and fiction in *Vogliamo tutto* (1971), which led the way for a myriad of fiction in which collage, linguistic features and open structures prevail; unique also was Goffredo Parise's brilliant ironic depiction of a psychological master-slave relationship between boss and workers in *Il padrone* (1971; *The Boss*, 1966).

These novels encouraged a new wave of writings, the so-called "letteratura selvaggia" (wild literature) of factory workers such as Tommaso Di Ciaula's *Tuta blu* (1970; blue overalls) and Vincenzo Guerrazzi's *La fabbrica dei pazzi* (1979; the factory of the insane). Workers' diaries and first-person accounts offered a direct vision of the alienating aspects of industrialization and technology and of the frustrating experiences of workers coming from what was once a predominantly agrarian society and now facing assembly lines, piece work, overtime, and strikes.

Advertising, television, cinema, comic books, computers, and the domination of media in general became the themes of the technical and experimental "audio-visual" poetry of Elio Pagliarani's *Lezioni di fisica e Fecalaro* (1968; physics lessons), Adriano Spatola's (b. 1941) *Poesia da montare* (1965; poetry to be framed) and *Verso la poesia totale* (1978; towards total poetry), Lamberti Pignotti's *Una forma di lotta* (1967; a form of struggle) and *Albo d'oro. Poesie visive d'amore* (1989; love visual poems), and A. L. Totino's (dates n.a.) *Futura* (1978; future). An excellent overall view of this genre of poetry is presented in Pagliarani's *Manuale di poesia sperimentale* (1966; manual of experimental poetry) and Pignotti's *Zeta* (1986), one of the most comprehensive anthologies of "poesia concreta" (concrete poetry) and "poesia verbo-visiva" (verbal-visual poetry).

Poetry continued to enjoy a traditionally stable market of readers as veteran poets like Andrea Zanzotto, Vittorio Sereni, Mario Luzi, Alfonso Gatto, Attilio Bertolucci (b. 1911), Giorgio Caproni (1912-1990), Sandro Penna (1906-1976), and Franco Fortini (1917-1997) were joined by several new poets like Edoardo Sanguineti, Antonio Porta, Bianca Mario Frabotta, T. Ottonieri (b. 1958), Valerio Magrelli and Dario Bellezza (dates n.a.). The experiments of the new poetry publicized in Alfredo Giuliani's anthology *I novissimi* (1965) continued throughout the 1970s and 1980s and reached a new peak with a new wave of poets labeled "Gruppo 93" and the anthology *Poesia italiana della contraddizione* (1989; Italian poetry of the contradiction), which featured works by nearly fifty experimental poets from the 1960s to the 1990s.

With postmodern pastiches came also a gamut of playful metafictions and examples of pure literariness, antinovels, and theoretical essay-novels. In the early 1980s began the real explosion of postmodern Italian narratives by authors as diverse as Alberto Arbasino (b. 1930), Andrea De Carlo, Pier Vittorio Tondelli, E. Palandri, and Stefano Benni (dates n.a.), as well as new movie directors like Maurizio Nichetti (b. 1948) with films such as *Ratataplan* (1979), *Ladri di saponette* (1989; icicle thief), and *Volere Volare* (1991; wanting to fly).

Stefano Benni is one of the most unconventional, witty, and clever Italian writers to exploit the postmodern technique of combining fiction, science fiction, parodies, super heroes, cinematic effects, and a variety of intertextual echoes coming from cinema, television and cartoons. Benni's style of parody and political satire is most evident in *Comici spaventati guerrieri* (1980; comical and scared warriors) and *Elianto* (1986; Elianto). The plot of *Comici spaventati guerrieri* develops around the homicide of Leo, a young hoodlum. His former teacher, and girlfriend, tries to disentangle the mystery, which involves interconnected prostitutes, drug dealers, and cover ups. At the end everything points to political corruption. Benni's unusual art of mirroring within a fantastic world the real world is demonstrated first in the science fiction *Terra* (1983; Earth) and then in *Elianto*. *Terra* is a humorous postmodern pastiche set in the year 2157 full of pop-culture allusions, especially to all sorts of Hollywood blockbuster science fiction movies like *Star Wars*, *2001 A Space Odyssey* and *Star Trek*. In the more serious *Elianto*, Benni uses the imaginary city of Megalopolis to launch one of his sharpest political satires and a critique of the power of computers, television, and mass media in general. The manipulation of television and corrupt government return in *Baol* (1990). Typical of Benni, the characters in this work are so numerous that it is difficult to keep track of them. This is even more true in *Bar Sport* (1976; title in English) and in its sequel *Bar Sport 2000* (1997; title in English) where Benni is at his best satirizing contemporary Italy in the 1970s and 1990s. Exploiting a city's popular bar as a surreal setting, the author brings together not so much people but caricatures of already bizarre and grotesque people.

1975 was a historic year for the Italian novel. Within a few months there appeared three major works, all exceeding 500 pages, by three outstanding writers: Morante's *La Storia*, Volponi's *Corporale* and S. D'Arrigo's (dates n.a.) *Horcinus Orca*. Leftist critics immediately rejected Morante's fusion of historical and psychological elements that resulted in a bitter condemnation of social injustices and cruelties inflicted on mankind; some suspected a publisher's ploy to create a bestseller, while others felt that Morante's form of neorealism was dead. On the other hand Volponi's masterful narration of a divided self ("Aspri-Murieta") constantly at war with his loved and hated "Other" ("Aspri vs. Overath") and obsessed with the coming of a nuclear war went unnoticed mainly because the majority of reviewers and academic critics were busy praising the linguistic features of D'Arrigo's narrative. Unquestionably it was an exceptional novel, but for the general public *Horcinus Orca* proved to be too difficult mostly because what little plot it contains is overwhelmed by a plurilinguism that includes archaic language, technical terms, and fishing jargon, all masterfully combined to compliment a highly detailed portrait of the ambience, language, and saga of a small Sicilian fishing village near Messina. It was not long before readers and critics recognized both Morante's and Volponi's novels as major works of Italian fiction. On the other hand D'Arrigo joined the company of other excellent Sicilian writers such as Antonio Pizzuto, Leonardo

Sciascia, Gesualdo Bufalino, and Vincenzo Consolo, who were receiving international attention after the translation of their works into several languages.

Bufalino became an instant success with *Diceria dell'untore* (1981). With this debut novel, the sixty-year-old retired teacher won the Campiello prize as well as the heart of many readers. The story is set in 1946 in a sanatorium in Sicily. Tormented characters, including the narrator, converse in the shadow of their imminent death. With clear echoes of Thomas MANN's *The Magic Mountain*, Bufalino treats love, sickness, and death, eros and thanatos, and everyday and philosophical discussions as the narrator falls in love with Marta and at the end follows her to a hotel room where, to satisfy her last wish, they make love for the last time. The narrator, the only survivor, appears like Orpheus to have defeated death, temporarily, with his art. *Argo il cieco ovvero i sogni della memoria* (1984) confirmed the author's exceptional narrative skills. From a lonely hotel room in Rome, the sixty-year-old narrator remembers a year of his life in the town of Modica where he used to teach and relives a memorable summer of passionate loves, sensuality, and overall happiness. In Bufalino's elegant fiction we recognize the eternal Sheharazade, from *1001 Arabian Nights*, who defeats death by narrating. His narratives are also a wonderful demonstration of writing as therapy, as self-reflection, and as a way of understanding one's destiny. Moreover, in his prose one notices the author's predilection for monologues, dreams, memories, and stories as powerful tools for examining one's past, anxieties, and dreams. Memories, nostalgia for the past, and story-telling return in *Le menzogne della notte* (1988), winner of the Strega prize. Here four anarchists, a poet, baron, soldier, and student, spend their last night telling stories while waiting to be executed in the morning. Instead of writing a confession of their guilt, they choose to tell existential narrative lies about the human condition, reducing life to a theatrical performance full of illusions and appearances. *Qui pro quo* (1991) is a light and entertaining mystery story told by the secretary, Agatha Sotheby (an allusion to Agatha Christie), of an editor who invites to his villa relatives, friends, and authors. In the midst of the party the perfect murder occurs. The author offers so many possible solutions that in the end none is the right one and the murder remains unsolved. Also full of suspense is *Tomaso e il fotografo cieco* (1996) in which a journalist with ambitions of becoming a writer becomes a spectator to a series of events that take place daily in an apartment building. When the journalist gives the story to a blind photographer to see if it can be published, the photographer tells him that the story is of no interest because it does not contain history and is mainly filled with daily routines.

Vincenzo Consolo (b. 1931), whose works share the literary characteristics of memory, history, baroque and expressionist linguistic features, and carefully veiled autobiographic dimensions with Bufalino, has yet a more intertextual, metaliterary, and encyclopedic vision of literature than Bufalino. In 1976 Consolo surprised readers with his *Il sorriso dell'ignoto marinaio* (1994; the smile of the unknown mariner). The story is set in Sicily in the days of the Italian Unification, and the title refers to a painting by Antonello da Messina. There are several connections between art and life in this story, just as there are in *Retablo* (1987), an exquisite tale in three parts about a painter who travels to Sicily in search of antiquity and to forget his love, in the company of a monk who in turn falls in love with a mysterious woman. Perhaps one of Consolo's best fusions of historical and invented elements comes through in *Nottetempo casa per casa* (1992). Petro Marano tries to find some comfort among anarchists and socialists while his his father and his two sisters are afflicted by insanity. Nené Cicio on the other hand, a decadent figure who adores Gabriele Dannunzio, joins the satanic cult of Aleister Crowley, mainly as an excuse to satisfy his sexuality. Equally sad is the story of a shepherd who cannot comprehend all the changes that are occurring around him. Set in the 1920s, the novel is a strong criticism of the days that precede fascism, as irrational thinking seems to take over in every corner of Italy. In *L'olivo e l'olivastro* (1994; the olive and the olive drab) we find Consolo's strongest defense of the culture, language and history of his native Sicily. Here the narrator returns home like a modern Ulysses, only to find his land drastically changed.

In the 1980s the overwhelming popularity of fiction writing was such that new narrators appeared literally overnight—many of them trying to repeat the unprecedented success story of Umberto Eco. The polemics surrounding the publications of "i giovani narratori" (the young fiction writers), in particular Andrea De Carlo, Roberto Pazzi, Pier Vittorio Tondelli (1955-1991), G. Del Giudice (b. 1949), Aldo Busi (b. 1948), and Antonio Tabucchi exploded in 1985 when critics like Edoardo Sanguineti labeled their fiction as a "useless elegance." The negative criticism and overall prejudice subsided as even the most conservative critics began to recognize the validity of Tabucchi and of others who after their second or third novels became widely accepted by the public. The great diversity among these writers asserted once again that the Italian novel was not following any particular trend. Moreover, some writers took the initiative to seek fresh new narrative voices. Tondelli started this trend with two anthologies of "under twenty-five writers," *Giovani Blues* (1986; young blues) and *Belli Perversi* (1987; beautiful and perverted). In the 1990s there appeared, as documented by the anthology *Gioventù cannibale* (1996; young cannibals), a new wave of young writers who presented life in a most raw, crude, and unpretentious fashion. In this group stand out G. Culicchia's (dates n.a.) sense of rebellion in *Tutti giù per terra* (1994; we all fall down) and *Bla bla bla* (1997), and the vivacious S. Ballestra (b. 1969) with her humorous stories about university years in *La guerra degli Antó* (1992; the war of the Anthonys), *Gli orsi* (1994; the bears), and *Compleanno dell'iguana* (1991; the birthday of the iguana).

After the wave of experimental novels there began to appear numerous more traditional works written for a larger public of readers. Popular authors of these works include Consolo, Ferdinando Camon, the writing team of Carlo Fruttero and Franco Lucentini, Giuseppe Cassieri, Sebastiano Vassalli, G. Montefoschi (b. 1946), Franco Cordelli (b. 1943), Giuseppe Pontiggia (b. 1934), A. Bevilaqua (b. 1939), Piero Chiara (1913-1987), Ennio Flaiano (1910-1975), Carlo Castellaneta (1931-1998), Fulrio Tomizza (b. 1935), Mario Pomilio (1921-1990), Raffaele La Capria (b. 1922), Luigi Meneghello (b. 1933), N. Orengo (b. 1944), Gianni Celati (b. 1937), Alessandro Baricco (b. 1958), E. Palandri (b. 1956), Susana Tamaro (b. 1957), Francesca Duranti, and Claudio Magris (dates n.a.).

These were also some of the authors who made up the so-called "industry of bestsellers Italian style" as discussed by Gian Carlo Ferretti (dates n.a.) in *Il best seller all'italiana* (1983), A. Cadioli in *La narrativa consumata* (1987; the consumed fiction), and Vittorio Spinazzola in *Dopo l'avanguardia* (1989; after the avant-garde). For the most part it was felt that the boost in popularity of reading fiction was riding on the coattails of Eco's *The Name of the Rose* and that the marketing strategies of major publishers were conditioning the reading habits of Italians. However, it was also recognized that Italy was producing several high quality novels.

From his earliest fiction works *La vita eterna* (1972; the eternal life), *Occidente* (1975; the west), and *Un altare per la madre* (1978, *Memorial*, 1983), the writer and critic Ferdinando Camon continues to write consistently solid social and psychological dramas that please a vast public of readers. In most of his works the author's native region, the Veneto, is the background for both his agrarian and urban settings against which characters experience violence, cruelty and tragedies. *Il canto delle balene* (1989; the song of whales) is a story of secrets, infidelity, marital relationships, trust, and love. Camon likes to write trilogies or sets of novels that deal with cycles in the lives of workers and families. His latest cycle deals with people from the third world who have come to Italy. *La terra è di tutti* (1996; the earth belongs to all) opens with scenes of gratuitous violence, murders, thieving, and occult rituals, witnessed or reported by the main protagonist, the journalist Giovanni. The events are all described as being routine happenings in the life of a frustrated journalist who is waiting for his divorce and for his son's marriage to an Asian woman. Except for Giovanni and his family, all the characters are immigrants to Italy from the third world who have arrived illegally and who seem to be scary, unappealing and untrustworthy at best; the author's irony becomes apparent, however, as we discover Camon's call for compassion and collaboration to ensure the survival of all.

Another important socially committed writer with a large repertoire of topics, characters, historical settings, and narrative strategies is Sebastiano Vassalli. His first success came with *La notte della cometa* (1984; *The Night of the Comet*, 1989), a fictional reconstruction of the life of the poet Dino Campana. Vassalli harshly criticized the deterioration of leftist ideology and the failures of the revolutionary and terrorist years in the late 1970s in *Abitare il vento* (1980; to inhabit the wind) and *Mareblú* (1982; blue sea). He adds humor to his bitter criticism of the mechanisms and traps set up by the culture industry that conditions writers and readers in *L'oro del mondo* (1987). But in general Vassalli is most effective when he is parodic and sarcastic in his *romans philosophiques*, including *3012* (1995)—a cyber-story about politics and religion set in the year 3012. At a time when no one dies as long as one has money to pay for transplants, Anato is kidnapped by people who want to use his body parts. While peace has become a religion, Antalo spreads a new gospel that "war is holy, just, beautiful and necessary." In the novel there appear several masked allusions to contemporary writers and intellectuals such as Eco, Fortini and Barilli. Vassalli is most courageous in examining the touchy issues of the Mafia, honor, silence, and the government's corruption in Sicily in one of his most polemical novels, *Il cigno* (1993; *The Swan*, 1997). Among his most popular bestsellers remains *La Chimera* (1990; *The Chimera*, 1993), set in the 17th c. and mirroring a chaotic modern Italy in a story about witches, plague, floods, atrocities, corruption, the Holy inquisition, and the Counter Reformation.

Carlo Castellaneta was not prolific, but most of his works were widely read. In his first novel *Viaggio con il padre* (1958; traveling with father) and in most of his works one of his trademarks is his love and need to recall personal, intimate, and indelible true-life episodes. The familiar themes of growing up in Milan, the difficult relationship with a father who drinks, gambles, and neglects the family, and the experience of first love return in *L'età del desiderio* (1990; the age of desire), which may be one of the author's most enjoyable nostalgic journeys into his adolescent years. The title is clearly explained toward the end of the novel where the narrator, echoing Lacan, concludes that "to desire is more important than to have." Some of his other popular novels are *Gli incantesimi* (1968; *Until the Next Enchantments*, 1970), *La paloma* (1972; the dove), *Anni beati* (1979; blissful years), *Ombre* (1982; ghosts), and *Passione d'amore* (1987; passion of love).

Elegant in style, humorous in his colorful descriptions, and always ready to offer an entertaining satire of Italian society, N. Orengo was noticed first in the early 1980s and especially after his publication of *Ribes* (1988; ribes), in which he attacks the vulgarity of television and mass media while constructing a mystery story with no victims. The author's talent in entertaining his readers with relatively short, lighthearted narratives that were both witty and intriguing can be appreciated in the surreal love story of Martino for a trout in *Dogana d'amore* (1986; custom house of love). *La guerra del basilico* (1994; the basil war) is set in Orengo's favorite ambience: the land and towns between Turin and the coastal region of Liguria. Here, a hotel located on the Italian side of the border between France and Italy serves as the main stage for a fascinating love story between a marine biologist and private detective who try to solve the mystery of who is poisoning the Mediterranean sea. The plot is enriched by a private war between a cook and a mad woman who tries to kill a giant basil plant and above all by a mystery story that implicates the private life of Grace Kelly. Orengo's 1974 novel *Miramare* (on the sea), a story about rebellion against a father figure, was reprinted in 1989 after critics discovered that the novel contained many of the characteristics of Orengo's later works.

The increase in sales of popular texts sold in supermarkets and newspaper stands received an impetus from the success of writers like Carlo Fruttero and Franco Lucentini, who regularly produced such bestsellers as *La donna della domenica* (1972; *The Sunday Woman*, 1973) and the suspenseful mystery story *A che punto è la notte* (1979; at what stage is the night), which gets mentioned in Eco's *Foucault's Pendulum*. In Fruttero's and Lucentini's novels, characters, events, and places are familiar because they all derive from today's consumeristic world of objects, mass media, and celebrities. The authors' unpretentious style and language appeal to a variety of readers and their plots range from love and mystery stories to a smooth fusion of realism and fantasy. This fusion is brilliantly produced with the help of a television and a remote control that rapidly changes channels between commercials in *Il palio delle contrade morte* (1983; the palio of the dead contrades), where the authors exploit the famous medieval festival setting of the "Palio of Siena" as background and accomplice to a murder.

The overwhelming and unprecedented success of Eco's entertaining and didactic interdisciplinary encyclopedic novels, together with the translations of Italo Calvino's writings that reached international audiences not limited to classrooms, encouraged foreign publishers to look for more translations of new successful writers such as De Carlo, Del Giudice, Tabucchi, Tamaro, and Primo Levi. The 1980s and 1990s also saw a tremendous increase of publications by women writers such as Tamaro, Ravera, Frabotta, Morazzoni, Petrignani, E. Rasy (b. 1947), Paolo Capriolo (b. 1962), Fabrizia Ramondino (b. 1936), and I Avalli (b. 1958), several of whom felt that the fast expanding market of readers had changed and that they finally had a chance to compete in a previously male-dominated publishing industry.

One of the key features of contemporary Italian fiction is an attempt to break away from provincialism and national boundaries, first exemplified in the 1960s in the works of Calvino and with the promoters of the Gruppo 63. Moravia's metafictional antinovel *L'attenzione* (1965; *The Lie*, 1969) was written mainly in response to the criticism of the Gruppo 63 against the bourgeois provincialism that prevailed in Italian fiction. Outstanding among authors interested in a literature that transcends national boundaries is A. Arbasino. From the days of *Parigi o cara* (1960, 1995; dear Paris) and *Certi romanzi* (1967; some novels) he proved a most erudite, witty, and ironic spectator and commentator of contemporary culture. In his work, plot and characters seem less important than the author's elegant use of language and his sharp observations on theater, art, and literature. Arbasino has rewritten some of his main works. One of his masterpieces, *Fratelli d'Italia* (1963; brothers of Italy), a social comedy of the literary Italian scene of the 1960s, grew from the original 500 pages of the first edition to over 1300 pages in the third edition (1997). This postmodern pastiche reads like an inventory of cultural events, facts and personalities of European culture. Reading Arbasino's novels is like being a guest at a literary salon where intellectuals, artists, and writers chat, gossip, comment, recall, and criticize a variety of features of contemporary culture, including fashion, kitsch, mass media, music, and cinema. From his first writings Arbasino was considered one of the leading proponents of a new literature that made culture and literature its main subject. Beginning with his participation in the "Gruppo 63," he remained a key figure at the center of literary polemics, round tables, prizes, and conventions and has kept up his prolific writing of fiction and of stimulating literary essays and provocative journalistic writings. Arbasino has been praised for his linguistic skills—labeled as neo-baroque and representative of Carlo Emilio Gadda's style, so much that he was nicknamed the "nipotino" (little nephew) of Gadda; Arbasino as well as Pizzuto, Pasolini, Manganelli, and Consolo were often compared to Gadda for baroque linguistic features that in the 1960s and 1970s were highly praised by academics. Arbasino was also recognized for his courage in treating homosexual relationships, as in *L'anonimo lombardo* (1959, 1996; the anonymous Lombard), at a time when the subject was still considered an unspoken social taboo, and for opening the doors for other writers such as Tondelli in *Altri libertini* (1980; other libertines) and *Camere separate* (1989; separate rooms) and above all for Aldo Busi.

Pier Vittorio Tondelli and Andrew De Carlo are in many ways the leaders of a youth oriented society. Tondelli affirmed himself as part of the "giovani narratori" with the novel *Pao Pao* (1982; Pao Pao), an account of his experiences during his military service, and *Piccoli equivoci senza importanza* (1985; small misunderstandings of no importance). Tondelli focused on the concerns, actions, sexuality, behavior, and linguistic manifestations (with all its obscenities) of protagonists representing a restless generation of young people always moving, traveling, searching, partying, or discussing, and yet bored with their lives. *Camere separate* (1989) is the love story of two homosexuals in which the protagonist discovers the meanings of love, death, separation, and solitude—some of the major themes of Tondelli. In novels like *Rimini* (1985; Rimini) and *Un weekend postmoderno* (1990; a postmodern weekend) he painted lively and loud images of a 1970s and 1980s pop rock culture with all its jargon, night life, and crowded scenes of disco bars and vacation spots. In 1987, when the author discovered that he had AIDS, he wrote twenty-four brief notes, one for each hour of the day and dedicated to a different friend. *Biglietti agli amici* (1997), published posthumously, is an excellent testimonial of the sensitivity of an author who appeared happy surrounded by music, parties, and friends, but in reality felt deep solitude and abandoned by his friends.

Andrew De Carlo, G. Del Giudice, and Gianni Celati, three of Calvino's favorite new writers, distinguished themselves in the early 1980s with their poetics of "watching." To some extent they echo the French "new novel" trend. De Carlo, a photographer, relies quite heavily on visual effects that magnify his realism. De Carlo had worked with Federico Fellini and in his descriptions the use of light and movement shows his skillful reliance on cinematic, television, painting, and photographic montage techniques. He narrates scenes, or frames, in a way that a camera captures the surface of objects, people, and events. In his debut *Treno di panna* (1981; *The Cream Train*, 1987) and in *Uccelli di gabbia e di voliera* (1982; birds of cage and aviary) Calvino identified the influence of paintings of American hyperrealists. This is not surprising because De Carlo was quite knowledgeable of Jack KEROUAC and the whole Beat Generation of writers, and was also an expert on the rock music, cinema, and pop culture of the 1960s and 1970s and American minimalism of the 1980s. Moreover, California, Los Angeles, Mexico, and New York were places that he knew very well and thus appear authentically and not as artificial settings in his novels. Thus in *Treno di panna* Giovanni, a young photographer, travels to Los Angeles, works at a variety of odd jobs to support himself, is a guest of a movie actress, and all the while searches for friends and for himself. Less successful is *Macno* (1984; *Macno*, 1987), set in an imaginary South American country ruled, with obvious allegorical allusions to the world of politics in Italy, by a dictator who was among other things a journalist and a rock star. *Tecniche di seduzione* (1991) followed *Arcodamore* (1993; the love bow), a disturbing and obsessive love story between a young photographer, Leo, and a harp player, Manuela. With *Due di Due* (1989; two of two) De Carlo writes another generational novel about men, women, parents, and children. Mario's relation of his close friendship with Guido from 1967 to 1987 is constitutes a powerful bildungsroman about friends who drift apart as their ideologies and life styles change.

Del Giudice is not a prolific writer but he is certainly a highly skilled author who, in his interest in the phenomenological and sensorial perception of reality and in a narrative that is essentially a cognitive process, most resembles Calvino. Also like Calvino he prefers short fiction and narration in which science and literature are perfectly fused in precise and technical descriptions of machines, motors, planes, paintings, photographs, and landscapes. His exact language is extremely well-controlled in clear syntax and a prose that relies very little on subjectivity and psychology to convey deeper meanings that emerge from observations of objects, people and dialogues. In his first two novels *Lo stadio di Wimbledon* (1983; Wimbledon stadium) and *Atlante Occidentale* (1985; *Lines of Light*, 1988) he featured novelists and scientists as protagonists. *Atlante occidentale* is mainly about the deep friendship that develops between a young physicist, Pietro Bahe, and an old writer, Ira Epstein, who has come to a place near Geneva to receive the Nobel prize for literature. In their long conversation the two men complement each other with their concerns over creation, vision, precision, and knowledge. Del Giudice's most successful fusion of writing and painting is offered in the short story *Nel museo di Reims* (1988; in the museum of Rheims). In *Staccando l'ombra da terra* (1995; *Take-Off: The Pilot's Lore*, 1996) Del Giudice makes clever links of images and metaphors about flying/writing in eight stories dealing with planes and flying activities. In *Mania* (1997; mania) the author relates six captivating short stories about individual obsessions and again demonstrates that his writing is not about understanding as much as it is about seeing, hearing, and feeling.

Gianni Celati began his narrative career with an experimental short novel, *Comiche* (1971; comics) and light narratives such as *Le avventure di Guizzardi* (1973; the adventures of Guizzardi), *La banda dei sospiri* (1976; the band of sighs), and *Lunario del paradiso* (1978; the almanac of paradise). *Comiche* caught the attention of Calvino and several other critics who appreciated the linguistic and comical effects of the most bizarre story. A man sits in a paper house (a book?) that could be a vacation spot or psychiatric ward in a state of delirium and transcribes what is being dictated by mysterious voices. The language is also bizarre, a delirious prose, not entirely grammatically correct, full of lapses, witty gags, popular speech, and gross corporeal jargon. It is, to quote the author, as if Laurel and Hardy were performing slapstick commedia dell'arte in which the physical expressions are integral parts of communication. After the seven years of silence that followed *Verso la foce* (1989; towards the outlet) Celati published thirty stories that secured his reputation as one of the most respected authors in Italy. *Narratori delle pianure* (1985; *Voices from the Planes*, 1989) are more reflections than stories, and deal with a variety of characters from different socioeconomic backgrounds. Celati is also a fine critic, as demonstrated by his significant literary essays in *Finzioni occidentali* (1975; western fiction).

Also critically well-received, Aldo Busi's earliest novels *Vita standard di un venditore di collant* (1985; *The Standard Life of a Pantyhose Salesman*, 1988), *La delfina Bizantina* (1987; the Byzantine dauphin), and *Seminario sulla gioventù* (1984; *Seminar on Youth*, 1988) were sufficient for critics to identify his special narrative talents and to agree that this new writer could be sincere and provocative at the same time. Neither the explicit sexuality, homosexuality, and prostitution that abound in novels such as *Sodomie in corpo 11* (1988; *Sodomies in Eleven Points*, 1992) or *Cazzi e canguri* (1994; pricks and kangaroos) nor his excessive narcissism, nor his insistence on wanting to be vulgar, irreverent, and transgressive in his work, interviews, journalism, and public appearances detracts from his clear and elegant style in narrating stories filled with human dramas. In *Altri abusi* (1989; *Uses and Abuses: Journeys, Sleepwalking and Fool's Errands*, 1995), with his name clearly present in the title, the author relies on his experiences as journalist and traveler to compose a series of social sketches. After *Pazza* (1990; crazy), *Sentire le donne* (1991; to hear women), *Manuale del perfetto gentiluomo* (1992; manual of the perfect gentleman), *Vendita galline Km. 2* (1993; chickens sold at 2 km.) Busi may have written one of his best novels with *Suicidi dovuti* (1996). Told mainly through monologues, it is a touching story of an alienated sixty-three-year-old man who, afraid of women and having become a voyeur of women and of life in general, ultimately decides to commit suicide.

Among younger writers Alessandro Baricco, author of *Castelli di rabbia* (1991; castles of anger), *Oceano Mare* (1993; sea ocean), and *Seta* (1996; silk) and Marco Lodoli, author of *Diario di un millenio che fugge* (1986; diary of a millennium in flight) and *Il vento* (1996; the wind) have met with strong critical approval. Lodoli's *Il vento* is a most entertaining short metafictional novel about an extraterrestrial that lands in Rome only to live in silence and agony until he is found by Luca, a cab driver who tries to keep him alive. Lodoli appears in his story as a novelist who is asked to rewrite the story in order to save the extraterrestrial.

E. Palandri's postmodern manifesto of the young generation represented by his short stories in *Boccalone* (1979; Boccalone) won the author overwhelming praise that continued with *Le pietre e il sale* (1986; the stones and salt) and *La via del ritorno* (1990; The

Way Back, 1993). In *The Way Back* Davide, an Italian psychiatrist, and his wife Julia return to Rome from London, Davide begins remember with great clarity his childhood, his native land, his generation, and the days of terrorism. In the thirteen stories of *Allegro ma non troppo* (1993) Palandri's style of narration shows a distinct postmodern flavor that often recalls that of Borges and such leading contemporary Italian authors as Calvino, Eco and Malerba. It is difficult to say if Palandri is emulating these models or if he is demonstrating how well he has assimilated characteristics of their styles and language; nonetheless, he is a natural storyteller with a special talent for writing amusing short fiction about unusual situations encountered by common characters. In *Allegro ma non troppo* his narration is so swift and smooth that one hardly notices that he has moved from one story to another. The thirteen captivating stories run the gamut of topics from dreams, the overpowering effects of television, secret doors leading to secret places, a woman who insists on robbing a bank, a man and his shadow, the need of a credit card in order to prove one's existence, and the nightmares of a greedy businessman to a story about the interaction between characters and readers.

Among the post-1950 generation of women writers Paola Capriolo, Susanna Tamaro, and Marta Morazzoni have had the most success with readers. Capriolo had one success after another as critics like Maria Corti praised her for her short stories in *La grande Eulalia* (1988; the great Eulalia) and the short novel *Il nocchiero* (1989; the steersman). In the four stories of *La grande Eulalia* the author makes extensive use of magic, allegory, symbols, and dreams. Echoes of Franz KAFKA, Dino Buzzati and Borges enrich Capriolo's subsequent fiction *Il doppio regno* (1991; the double kingdom), a surreal story narrated by a nameless woman who takes refuge in a hotel-labyrinth where workers move around in perfect silence. *Vissi d'amore* (1992; *Floria Tosca*, 1997), the title of which alludes to Puccini's opera *Tosca*, is a love story of deep emotions and manifestations of evil. *La spettatrice* (1995; the spectator), one of her best examples of metafiction, is filled with outstanding descriptions of movements, light, and sensations. It is the story of an actor, Vulpius, who in the middle of acting on stage falls in love with a woman in the audience who is staring at him. Vulpius feels the gaze of the woman no matter where he goes, and in it he discovers the dark side of his own existence.

Susanna Tamaro's talent was first noticed in *La testa fra le nuvole* (1989; the head among the clouds) and especially in *Per voce sola* (1991, alone by voice)—a collection of five disturbing stories about girls and women who are subjected to physical and mental cruelties such as rape, molestation, and being deprived of their children or belongings. In 1994 her popularity exploded with a bestseller that outsold Eco's *Foucault's Pendulum* for an entire year. *Va dove ti porta il cuore* (1994; *Follow Your Heart*, 1995), simple in style and language, has been translated into several languages. It is a moving story of an adulteress grandmother, Olga, who writes letters to her granddaughter Gelsomina. Deep emotions, nostalgia, the need of freedom, unconditional love, request for forgiveness, and an attempt to close the gap between generations are some of the key elements in this light psychological and confessional epistolary that extends from grandmother to daughter to granddaughter. Olga feels that she has failed as daughter, mother, wife, and now even as grandmother having lost Gelsomina, who has moved out. Her bird, her last companion, dies as a foreshadowing of her own imminent death. Tamaro's second novel is more weighted down by politics and religion. *Anima mundi* (1997) was in fact condemned by critics who saw in the intense

relationship between Walter and the protagonist Andrea a mixture of fascist ideology, Nietzsche's superman and St. John's apocalypse. A much more convincing portrait is of Andrea's father, who has enclosed himself in his own prison of silence and madness for having killed his best friend.

Marta Morazzoni (b. 1950) enjoyed great success with her first novel *La ragazza col turbante* (1986; *Girl with a Turban*, 1988). Equally successful were her subsequent novels *Casa materna* (1992; *His Mother's House*, 1994) and *Invenzione della verità* (1988; *The Invention of Truth*, 1993). In *Invenzione della verità* the author's strong interests in art and literature come through as the story unfolds around a tapestry, a gothic church, and a clever juxtaposition of the present with the Middle Ages. Her latest work *L'estuario* (1996; estuary) focuses on a female character, Margot, who attempts to put some life into three male friends who interact only marginally.

New and even younger women writers like R. Campo (b. 1963), S. Ballestra, and Lara Cardella (b. 1969) continue to attract new readers. Like Ravera's *Porci con le ali* Campo aroused attention with her erotic and comical novel *In principio erano le mutande* (1992; first there was the underwear). S. Ballestra distinguished herself with entertaining, sarcastic stories set for the most part in Bologna. The Sicilian writer Lara Cardella, on the other hand, became famous with her act of rebellion against ultraconservative Sicilian social customs that had penalized women in *Volevo i pantaloni* (1989; *Good Girls Don't Wear Trousers*, 1993). Her sociological and at times psychological portraits continue in *Fedra se ne va* (1992; Phedra goes away), *Intorno a Laura* (1991; about Laura)—a story centered around her young daughter, and *Una ragazza normale* (1994; a normal girl).

The private dimensions of the heart, familial relationships, the process of aging, solitude, the intimate dialogues or heated exchanges between mothers and daughters, or daughters and parents in general are some of the main topics examined extensively in the family centered novels of such new writers as C. Carati (dates n.a.) in *La cattiva figlia* (1990; the bad daughter) and Francesca Sanvitale in *Madre e figlia* (1986; mother and daughter), where the author develops the tense emotional story of Marianna who embodies for the author the condition of every woman as mother and daughter.

Italy has produced far fewer playwrights than novelists at the end of the 20th c. Virtually no contemporary playwright other than Dario Fo, winner of the 1997 Nobel Prize for literature, has won international recognition; while several accomplished novelists have successfully written for the theater, including Enzo Siciliano and Alberto Moravia, none has been recognized primarily as a playwright. Italy's theater has become a director's theater: Giorgio Strehler (1921-1998), Carmelo Bene (b. 1937), and Luca Ronconi (b. 1933) have staged their work throughout the globe and have found international acceptance. Their manipulation of texts is such that their directing is considered authorial; thus their *mises en scènes* are commonly referred to as, for example, "Strehler's *Mountain Giants*," "Bene's *Hamlet*," and "Ronconi's *Orlando*."

Strehler was born in Barcola in the Northeastern province of Trieste. During World War II he founded his first theater company, *Compagnie des Masques*, in Switzerland. His directorial debut *Calligola* was a great success. He and Paolo Grassi (dates n.a.) then founded *Il piccolo teatro di Milano*, which soon became one of Europe's most important theaters. In 1968 Strehler headed the theater group *Teatro-azione* (Action Theater), but returned in 1972 to the *Piccolo teatro* as sole director. He has directed both opera and prose theater. His focus is on two different aspects of theater:

the epic and realistic. The former, influenced greatly by Bertolt BRECHT, produced famous stagings such as *L'opera da tre soldi* (three penny opera), *L'anima buona di Se-zuan* (The Good Soul of Se-zuan) , *Schweyk nella seconda guerra mondiale* (Schweyk in World War II), and *Coriolano* (Coriolanus); *Arlecchino servitore di due padroni* (Arlecchino servant of two masters) and *La trilogia della villeggiatura* (the vacation trilogy) reflect the latter.

Carmelo Bene, Italy's *enfant terrible* of the stage, began his career in the early 1960s. During the 1970s he experimented with cinema but later returned to the theater where his presence was very controversial as he continually attempted to subvert the codes of traditional theatrical conventions. The theatricality of Bene's work is explicitly discursive; his stagings comment upon theater in progress. Although he has used the bombastic models of 19th-c. England, and has appeared in Paris to great acclaim, Bene's reputation has not traveled much beyond Italy where his reputation is that of a great and yet isolated visionary. Most of his productions in the 1970s, including *Omelet for Hamlet* (1987; title in English), were reinterpretations of Shakespeare.

Luca Ronconi, born in Susa, Tunisia, started out as an actor in Italy's most important theater companies working with prominent directors. His performances in two versions of *Tre quarti di luna* (Three quarters of the moon) by Luigi Squarzina, the first directed by the author himself and the second by Strehler, were hugely successful. In 1968 Ronconi's directing of *L'Orlando furioso*, a spectacle written in collaboration with Edoardo Sanguineti and based on Ariosto's 16th-c. epic poem, was an international success. He also directed opera, including *Valchiria* at the prestigious Scala theater in Milan in 1975, Rossini's *Il barbiere di Siviglia* (The barber of Seville) in Paris, and operas by Wagner. Ronconi was appointed director in 1974 to the theater and music section of the Biennale di Venezia, and his theatrical research marked the beginning of a convergence of the diverse theatrical techniques that had swarmed the Italian scene during the preceding ten years.

BIBLIOGRAPHY: Gatt-Rutter, J., *Writers and Politics in Modern Italy* (1978); Smith, L., ed., *The New Italian Poetry: 1945 to the Present* (1981); Caesar, M., and P. Hainsworth, eds., *Writers and Society in Contemporary Italy* (1984); Tani, S., *The Doomed Detective: The Contribution of the Detective Novel in Postmodern American and Italian Fiction* (1984); Lucente, G., *Beautiful Fables: Self-Consciousness in Italian Narrative From Manzoni to Calvino* (1986); Cannon, J. A., *Postmodernism Italian Fiction* (1989); Aricó, S. L., *Contemporary Women Writers in Italy* (1990); Caesar, M., "Italian Fiction of the Eighties," in Smyth, E., ed., *Postmodernism and Contemporary Fiction* (1991): pp. 74-89; Baranski, G., and L. Pertile, eds., *The New Italian Novel* (1993); Russel, R., ed., *Italian Women Writers: A Bibliographical Source Book* (1994)

—ROCCO CAPOZZI

IVANOV, Vyacheslav Ivanovich

Russian poet, essayist, and classical scholar, b. 28 Feb. 1866, Moscow; d. 16 July 1949, Rome, Italy

After attending Moscow University and spending almost twenty years abroad in travel and further study, I. settled in St. Petersburg in 1905 and soon became the leading spokesman of

Russian SYMBOLISM. Until 1912 his apartment (popularly known as "The Tower") was the site of frequent gatherings of the Russian literary and artistic avant-garde, where readings by the most prominent poets of the day were typically followed by I.'s refined commentary. I. later moved to Moscow, and his influence waned rapidly as symbolism lost its literary preeminence. I. welcomed the fall of autocracy in Russia but remained hostile to Bolshevism. From 1920 to 1924 he taught classical philology in Baku. In 1924 he was allowed to depart for Italy, where he lived the last twenty-five years of his life, teaching first in Pavia and later in Rome at the Russicum, the Vatican's institute for the study of Russia and the Eastern Church. I. joined the Roman Catholic Church in 1926, although he did not renounce Eastern Orthodoxy.

I.'s first two volumes of verse, *Kormchie zvyozdy* (1903; pilot stars) and *Prozrachnost* (1904; transparency) exhibit the characteristic features of his poetry: a strong metaphysical orientation, a profusion of references to Western (especially ancient Greek) culture, a special affinity for myth, and a penchant for complex, archaic diction. His next collection, the two-volume *Cor ardens* (1911; Latin: burning heart), is an even more lavish display of erudition and technical virtuosity, and is reminiscent of the ornate, allusion-laden poetry of the Baroque age. Much of *Cor ardens* was written after the death of I.'s beloved wife Lydia, and the victory of love over death is a recurring motif, presented as an ecstatic epiphany that takes its cue from the myth of the "ever-suffering and ever-resurrected" god Dionysus.

I.'s poetic output diminished sharply after around 1915—a reflection of his growing loss of faith in the quasi-religious expectations that had been a central part of his message—but his increasingly rare productions were almost all achievements of a high order. The poetic cycles "Zimnie sonety" (1920; winter sonnets) and "Rimskie sonety" (1924; Roman sonnets) are particularly noteworthy. A final burst of poetic inspiration came in 1944, when I. wrote "Rimsky dnevnik" (Roman diary), a superb cycle that marks a distinct evolution of his style toward simplicity of expression. These late works are included in the posthumously published volume *Svet vecherny* (1962; vespertine light).

Between 1928 and his death, I. worked sporadically on what he referred to as a "novel," *Povest o Svetomire Tsareviche* (account of the Tsarevich Svetomir), which was to be the ultimate statement of his views. This is an allegorical narrative, in rhythmic and heavily archaized prose, which points to a vision of a world finally cleansed of sin. I. did not live to complete this work, which was first published—with the missing half reconstructed by I.'s close companion O. Deschartes (pseud. of Olga Chor, 1894–1978)—in Volume I of his *Sobranie sochineny* (1971; collected works).

I.'s great influence as a critic and literary theorist is only partially suggested by his published essays. A brilliant conversationalist with an unsurpassed ability to make polished and incisive analyses on first acquaintance with a new work, I. probably affected Russian modernism more through personal contact than by his printed works. Nevertheless, the latter are extremely important: I.'s early essays, collected in *Po zvyozdam* (1909; by the stars) and *Borozdy i mezhi* (1916; furrows and boundaries), present most of his theoretical ideas bearing on symbolism. In these and other essays I. articulates his belief in the religious ("theurgic") nature of true art, where the symbol serves as the medium for the revelation of "higher reality."

I. also wrote a great deal of literary criticism; his seminal essays on Dostoevsky (1916–17; uncollected in Russian but available in English as *Freedom and the Tragic Life*, 1952) are the best-known examples. Other writers discussed by I. range from Pindar and Homer to Petrarch, Goethe, and Pushkin. Of I.'s numerous works outside the narrowly literary sphere, the most influential is his eloquent defense of culture in I.'s polemic with Mikhail Gershenzon (1869–1925), *Perepiska iz dvukh uglov* (1921; *Correspondence between Two Corners*, 1948).

I. played a key role in the cultural ferment in Russia at the beginning of the 20th c. But as a poet, he remained an isolated figure whose early verse evoked admiration but little real sympathy, and whose late, and probably best, poetry remained virtually unknown to his contemporaries. Although a scholarly evaluation of his oeuvre is only beginning, I.'s place in the pantheon of Russian literature seems assured.

FURTHER WORKS: *Ellinskaya religia stradayushchego boga* (1904–1905); *Tantal: Tragedia* (1905); *De societatibus vectigalium publicorum populi romani* (1910); *Nezhnaya taina* (1912); *Alkei i Safo: Sobranie pesen i liricheskikh otryvkov* [trans. and introd. by I.] (1914); *Rodnoe i vselenskoe: Statyi* (1917); *Mladenchestvo* (1918); *Prometei: Tragedia* (1919); *Dionis i pradionisiistvo* (1923); *Chelovek* (1939); *Sobranie sochineny* (1971 ff.)

BIBLIOGRAPHY: Deschartes, O., "V. I.," *OSP*, 5 (1954): 41–58; Poggioli, R., "A Correspondence from Opposite Corners," *The Phoenix and the Spider* (1957): 208–28; Poggioli, R., *The Poets of Russia* (1960): 161–70; Stepun, F., *Mystische Weltschau* (1964): 201–78; Stammler, H. A., "V. I.'s Image of Man," *WSJ*, 14 (1967–1968): 128–42; Tschöpl, C., *V. I.: Dichtung and Dichtungstheorie* (1968); West, J., *Russian Symbolism: A Study of V. I. and the Russian Symbolist Aesthetic* (1970); Rannit, A., "V. I. and His Vespertine Light," *RLT*, 4 (1972): 265–68; Davidson, P., *V. I.: A Reference Guide* (1996)

—ALEXIS KLIMOFF

IVORY COAST LITERATURE

The age-old traditional literatures in African languages of the Ivory Coast, indeed of most of sub-Saharan Africa, have been primarily oral. The colonization of this now-independent West African country by France early in this century was accompanied by a forceful imposition of the French language from elementary school on. This, coupled with the presence of multiplicity of African languages (making the choice of any one as a national tongue difficult), has resulted in a written literature that is overwhelmingly in French.

Generally speaking, criticism of colonial excesses, cultural self-assertion, the conflict between tradition and modernism, and, more recently, disenchantment with independence and the new leadership have been the major themes.

Perhaps because of the low literacy rate, it is in the theater—with its roots in traditional spectacle and its ability to reach a broad audience—that the Ivory Coast has shown the most vitality. Born in 1932 in a school setting, dramatic activity was brilliantly fostered through playwriting and the organization of theater troupes by Ivoirian students of the celebrated William-Ponty School and others. The theater was early dominated by three graduates of that school, François-Joseph Amon d'Aby (b. 1913), Germain Coffi

Gadeau (b. 1915), and Bernard Binlin DADIÉ, the last the most outstanding, prolific Ivory Coast writer.

Two tendencies dominate this theater: (1) historical or legendary themes based on the oral tradition, e.g., Dadié's *Assémien Déhylé* (1936; Assémien Déhylé), Amon d'Aby's *L'entrevue de Bondoukou* (1939; the Bondoukou interview), and Gadeau's *Kondé Yao* (1939; Kondé Yao) and (2) more modern preoccupations, to be found in plays dealing with certain social ills inherited from tribal life, or in comedies of manners and political criticism reflecting a widespread disaffection with contemporary abuses, e.g., Amon d'Aby's *Kwao Adjoba* (1953; Kwao Adjoba) or Gadeau's *Nos femmes* (1940; our wives). In this vein, Dadié's very popular *Monsieur Thôgô-gnini* (1970; Mr. Thôgô-gnini) is exemplary.

Many talented younger playwrights have become active, often centering their dramas around great figures of the past. Thus, for example, Charles Nokan (b. 1936) re-creates (taking considerable liberties) the Baoule legend of Queen Pokou in his *Abrah Pokou* (1970; Abrah Pokou), while Bernard Zadi Zaourou (b. 1938) chronicled the career of the 19th-c. Mandingo (Malinké) leader Samori Touré, whose resistance to the French colonial armies has become legendary, in *Les Sofas* (1975; the Sofas [name given to Samori's soldiers]). Here, as elsewhere among dramatists of this generation, historical themes are rarely presented for their own sake, but rather as a reinterpretation of the past in the search for solutions to the problems of newly independent African states.

In keeping with their concern for the continuity of the oral tradition, Dadié and Amon d'Aby have also published collections of legends and tales: *Le pagne noir* (1955; the black loincloth) and *La mare aux crocodiles* (1973; the crocodile pond), respectively. Léon Maurice Anoma Kanié's (b. 1920) *Quand les bêtes parlaient aux hommes* (1974; when animals spoke to men) is a similar venture with a significant addition: the author has appended several of La Fontaine's fables translated into Ivory Coast Creole, a blending of French and local languages.

Although his forte seems clearly to be the theater, Dadié also stands out as the leading poet of the Ivory Coast. His three volumes of poetry reflect his evolving concerns over the years. Among other poets of note there is Joseph Miézan Bognini (b. 1936), whose sensitive exaltation of nature and "controlled fervor" in his collection *Ce dur appel de l'espoir* (1960; this harsh call of hope) make him one of the better Francophone lyric poets. The unclassifiable ("dramatic poem"?) *Le soleil noir point* (1962; the black sun dawns) by Charles Nokan, as well as his poetic "novel" *Violent était le vent* (1966; violent was the wind), both passionate pleas for a true liberation in post-independence Africa, are noteworthy in their sincerity and their formal and stylistic innovations.

Ivoirian writers came rather late to the novel. Their themes tend to parallel those of the dramatists: at the outset, we find a preoccupation with the colonial experience, depiction (and occasionally criticism) of traditional life, and the myriad problems—both individual and societal—implied in the conflict of cultures. This last theme has, of course, carried over into the postindependence period. A common characteristic of many of these novels is their autobiographical nature, following (with variations) a more or less set pattern from village to school, to the big city (African or European), and the final return home. Both Dadié's *Climbié* (1956; *Climbié*, 1971) and Aké Loba's (b. 1927) *Kocoumbo, l'étudiant noir* (1961; Kocoumbo, the black student) are important autobiographical works, the first tracing the moral and political itinerary of its hero during the late colonial period, the second vividly depicting the African student milieu in Paris during the same era.

The confrontation of the old and the new within an African village is the subject of Aké Loba's second novel, *Les fils de Kouretcha* (1970; the sons of Kouretcha), while his *Les dépossédés* (1973; the dispossessed) chronicles the life of a simple peasant and that of his adopted city, Abidjan, during sixty years of colonial rule. New political developments have engendered new themes: disaffection in the wake of independence is at the very core of the most interesting and best written Ivoirian novel to date, Ahmadou KOUROUMA's *Les soleils des indépendances* (1968; the suns of independence). The subject has appeared frequently in recent African fiction, but its treatment here results in a highly successful molding of a Western genre to the realities of African thought and speech. With *Wazzi* (1977; Wazzi) by Jean D. Dodo (b. 1919?) and Tidiane Dem's (date n.a.) *Masseni* (1977; Masseni), women for the first time became the chief protagonists of Ivoirian novels.

BIBLIOGRAPHY: Cornevin, R., *Le théâtre en Afrique noire et Madagascar* (1970): 185–200; Jahn, J., and Dressler, P. D., *Bibliography of Creative African Writing* (1971); Bonneau, R., *Écrivains, cinéastes et artistes ivoiriens, aperçu bio-bibliographique* (1973); Herdeck, D. E., *African Authors* (1973); Blair, D., *African Literature in French* (1976); Baratte-Eno Belinga, T., et al., *Bibliographie des auteurs africains de langue française*, 4th ed. (1979): 74–85

—FREDRIC MICHELMAN

IWANIUK, Wacław

Polish poet, essayist, and translator (also writing in English), b. 4 Dec. 1915, Chełm

I. is one of the most renowned contemporary Polish poets. He has published fifteen volumes of poetry and is translated into numerous languages. Born in Chełm, in eastern Poland, I. studied law and economics at the Free University of Warsaw, specializing in emigration and colonial problems. In 1939, with the help of a state grant, he undertook consular training in Buenos Aires and was offered a further course of studies at the École Coloniale in Paris. At the outbreak of World War II, he joined the Polish army in France. After the capitulation of France, I. attempted to reach England via Spain. Caught by the Spanish police, he was first imprisoned in Figueras and then in the camp in Miranda, from which he escaped and eventually made his way to England. Enlisted in the First Armoured Division, I. fought in Holland, Belgium, France, and Germany, where he remained until 1946. He returned to England to study language, and two years later emigrated to Canada. Despite adverse conditions I. found employment as an official interpreter for the tribunal of the Province of Ontario and settled in Toronto.

I.'s first volume of poems, *Pełnia czerwca* (1936; fullness of June), was welcomed by the critics as a promising debut. There he demonstrates his ability to evoke landscape in combination with rich poetical imagery—qualities that characterize his later writing. Following his second volume, *Dzień apokaliptyczny* (1938; day of the apocalypse), World War II interrupted this auspicious start and provoked his exile from Poland. From that moment, I.'s autobiography becomes pivotal to his output. There is an apparent rift between his pre- and postwar life. The former belongs to the lost paradise of his native country; the latter belongs to Western civilization, which he views with the eye of an outsider who is angry with the present political order. He raises a voice of protest against communism and accuses the West of acquiescence. A tone of disappointment appears alongside the attempts to adapt to the new life and culture. All these elements constitute the core of I.'s postwar volumes of poetry, of which *Ciemny czas* (1968; *Dark Times: Selected Poems of W. I.*, 1979) is the most significant.

I. adds a historical dimension to the everyday life of an émigré. He speaks as a survivor emerging from a monstrous catastrophe. He acts as a guardian of memory to those who perished and as witness of a cruelty that unfortunately may recur. Full of genuine despair over the brutality of humankind, *Ciemny czas* is a pessimistic and revealing volume commemorating the victims of a tragic past.

The mood of catastrophe permeates *Lustro* (1971; mirror) and *Nemezis idzie pustymi drogami* (1978; nemesis walks empty roads). It is intensified by the poet's alienation from society and a sense of ill-adjustment to the world. However, I. expresses a sensitive perception of the world around him through gentle nostalgia, sympathy for human failure, feeling for nature, and an awareness of the expansion of urban civilization.

In 1981, I. published his first volume written in English, *Evenings on Lake Ontario*, where he presents his Canadian ordeal in diary form. Here the clash between the exile from eastern Europe and a nation with few antecedents is most apparent. The "client of war," as he calls himself, encounters people for whom the tragic experience of the other continent remains a "complete mystery." Yet from this encounter emerges a lasting partnership. Canada offers a chance to rebuild his shattered life. It also presents a challenge that enhances creativity. This in turn helps I. to be reconciled with his feelings of estrangement. I. writes about Canada with respect and a quiet touch of admiration.

I. is a veteran of many battles. The longest one was fought with the communist regime in Poland. Labeled like many other uncompromising émigré writers as an enemy of the state, he was consigned at home to oblivion. Yet his continuing involvement with people and occurrences in Poland surfaces in *Nocne rozmowy* (1987; nocturnal conversations). Only recently, after the collapse of the communist regime, has he been rewarded with publication of his works in Poland. The volume, significantly called *Powrót* (1989; return), marks his rightful reinstatement as a Polish poet.

I.'s poetic style derives from observation of everyday life. His use of language is direct, tending to the succinct. He often oscillates between sharp irony and restrained emotion, and perhaps the most striking facet of his writing is an attempt to reconcile extremes in subject matter as well as in form. His art is a blend of involvement in past and contemporary life, while at the same time being detached from it. He has mastered the contemplative attitude to the turmoil of the world and the dramatic condition of an exile. In this way he brings a sense of constancy into the uncertainty of the human predicament. I.'s poetry exemplifies a search for lasting values in the midst of raving confusion.

FURTHER WORKS: *Czas Don Kichota* (1946); *Dni białe i dni czerwone* (1947); *Dziennik z podróży tropikalnej* (1951); *Pieśń nad pieśniami* (1953); *Milczenia* (1959); *Wybór wierszy* (1965); *Podróż do Europy* (1982); *Moje obłąkanie* (1991)

BIBLIOGRAPHY: Grabowsky, Y., "On Lustro," *UTQ*, 4 (Summer 1977): 497–98; Islam, S. M., on *Dark Times: Selected Poems of W. I.*, *The Wig Standard Magazine* (12 July 1980): 21; Colombo, J. R., "I.," in Toye, W., ed., *The Oxford Companion to Canadian*

Literature (1983): 391–92; Miązek, B., *Teksty i komentarze* (1983): 97–113; Cybulska, M. E., *W. I. poeta* (1984); Colombo, J. R., "Our Cosmopolitans: The Ethnic Canadian Writer in a Provincial Society," *CanL*, Supplement I (1987): 90–101

—MAJA E. CYBULSKA

IWASZKIEWICZ, Jarosław

(pseud.: Eleuter) Polish poet, novelist, dramatist, literary and music critic, and translator, b. 20 Feb. 1894, Kalnik, Ukraine; d. 2 March 1980, Warsaw

I. studied law at Kiev University simultaneously with his studies at the musical Conservatory from which he graduated. His literary debut took place in 1915 in a Kievan monthly publication. Three years later he moved to Warsaw, where he was to become an influential member of Skamander, the leading poetic group of the 1920s. From 1920 to 1923 I. was the editor of the literary section of the important daily *Kurier polski*, and then served as a secretary to the marshal of the Polish parliament from 1923 to 1925. During the period 1927–39 he was in the foreign service, living in Copenhagen and Brussels. During World War II, I. was in Warsaw, where he was involved with underground cultural activities. After the war, in 1945, he assumed the editorship of the weekly *Nowiny literackie*, where he remained until 1954, when he became the editor of the most important Polish literary monthly, *Twórczość*, a post he held until his death. Besides his formal duties as an editor, I. was always involved in various cultural and political activities. He was the president of the Polish P.E.N. Club for over twenty years, a member of parliament, and a participant in the International Peace Movement. He was also the recipient of a great many literary awards.

I.'s contributions are indeed of vast importance. During his long literary career, I. published nearly fifty volumes of poetry, novels, plays, essays, and books of memoirs. In addition, there are at least as many volumes of his literary translations. Of his poetry, three volumes deserve special attention: his youthful *Lato* (1932; summer), his mature *Ciemne ścieżki* (1957; dark paths), and the collection *Liryki* (1959; lyrics), which offers an excellent representative selection of all his poems. The common denominator of his poetry is its humanism. I.'s works of fiction are closely linked with his poetry by their striking authenticity and vividness of feelings and their intuitiveness—characteristics that were his trademark. Novels as early as *Księżyc wschodzi* (1925; the moon rises) or as recent as trilogy *Sława i chwała* (1956–62; fame and glory) are prime examples of these traits. In all of I.'s novels and short stories there are autobiographical elements and a great sense of identification with the characters, whose fates are mostly tragic. In *Sława i chwała* I. paints a picture of Polish life in the period during and between the two world wars. The destinies of the characters are determined by the political, social, economic, and cultural changes that Poland underwent during this period. Yet the historical events that determine the lives of I.'s characters by no means apply to the Poles alone or solely to this specific period. I.'s underlying philosophy is universal: history determines the fate of each of us, and the individual with all his complexities can be at the same time both its victim and its conqueror. Of all I.'s short stories, perhaps the most memorable are those contained in the volume *Panny z Wilka* (1933; maidens from Wilk). They are imbued with a sense of things passing and with eroticism—a poetically expressed sensuality that is another one of his characteristics.

I.'s musical training and interests are also evident in his literary works. His fascination with sounds and rhythms results in an unexpected symphony of images and produces a sense of a magic world that one half remembers from one's dreams or from childhood. I. also wrote about music and produced opera librettos, and one of his plays (which in general do not match the excellence of his poetry or prose) is built around the life of Chopin: *Lato w Nohant* (1936; *Summer in Nohant*, 1942).

Of I.'s translations, the most noted are those of Rimbaud's poetry, of CLAUDEL's and GIRAUDOUX's plays, and of work by André GIDE, as well as some of the short stories of Tolstoy and CHEKHOV.

I. was one of the most important Polish writers of the 20th c. His influence on the younger generation of writers and poets has been enormous, but so is his works' impact upon the ordinary reader. The truthfulness of I.'s theme, combined with the authenticity of its expression, accounts for his works' appeal and for his high place in Polish literature.

FURTHER WORKS: *Oktostychy* (1919); *Zenobia Palmura* (1920); *Hilari syn buchaltera* (1923); *Siedem bogatych miast nieśmiertelnego Kościeja* (1924); *Kochankowie z Werony* (1928); *Fryderyk Szopen* (1928; new ed. as *Chopin*, 1966); *Księga dnia i księga nocy* (1929); *Zmowa mężczyzn* (1930); *Powrót do Europy* (1931); *Pasje błędomierskie* (1938); *Maskarada* (1939); *Kongres w Florencji* (1941); *Wiersze wybrane* (1946); *Nowele włoskie* (1947); *Czerwone tarcze* (1949); *Warkocze jesieni* (1955); *Wzlot* (1956); *Proza poetycka* (1958); *Wiersze* (1958); *Dzieła* (4 vols., 1958–1964); *Tatarak* (1960); *Wesele Pana Baltaka* (1960); *Jan Sebastian Bach* (1963); *Opowiadania wybrane* (1964); *Heydenreich* (1964); *Poezje wybrane* (1967); *Wiersze zebrane* (1968); *O psach kotach i diabłach* (1968)

BIBLIOGRAPHY: Kridl, M., *A Survey of Polish Literature and Culture* (1956): 498; Miłosz, C., *Postwar Polish Poetry* (1965): 23–25; Miłosz, C., *The History of Polish Literature* (1969): 389–93

—MALGORZATA PRUSKA-CARROLL

IYAYI, Festus

Nigerian novelist and short-story writer, b. 1947, Benin-City

I. received his education in Nigeria, the U.S.S.R., and the U.K. In the U.S.S.R. he attended the Kiev Institute of National Economy, and in the U.K., Bradford University, where he obtained his Ph.D. with an emphasis on economics and commerce rather than literature and the arts. A Marxist, I.'s left wing politics have led to his imprisonment without trial on a number of occasions, as well as losing his job at the University of Benin, where he had become a lecturer in business administration after leaving the U.K.

In three novels and a collection of stories I. exposes the corruption and greed of the rich and powerful, the oppression, suffering, and dignity of the poor, and the violence and evil of the Nigerian state.

I.'s best-known and most popular novel is his first, *Violence* (1979). Its achievement is its handling of complex issues accessibly, which has enabled it to capture a readership of urban youth with only a basic command of English. What the novel lacks in depth and craft it compensates for with the passion and power of its unambiguous and moving images of the suffering of the poor and the evil dishonesty of the rich. Idemudia, the incorruptible hero, is so poverty stricken that he has to sell his blood to earn money to feed himself and his wife. Figuratively this blood-letting stands for the manner in which the wealthy and privileged drain the flesh and vitality of the poor in order to maintain their own health and swollen bank accounts. Idemudia's life is contrasted with those of the wealthy and vicious Queen and her weak, sexually insatiable husband, Obofun. The novel takes its title from its more central purpose, which is to explain institutionalised violence embedded within the social fabric and thereby to broaden an understanding of violence beyond its personal and individual manifestations. Perhaps the most serious flaw in the novel is that in attempting to reach a more popular audience and in having to compete with the raw sex and violence of much pulp entertainment, *Violence* has recourse at times to the gratingly melodramatic, to the sexually lurid, and to gender stereotypes, such as woman as *femme fatale* or prostitute.

I.'s next novel, *The Contract* (1982), deals with similar themes, though the female character Rose is an extraordinary portrayal of a woman who is independent, intelligent, and brave and who breaks away from the prevailing gender stereotypes. His third novel *Heroes* (1986) is both a continuation of his earlier works and a break from them. Unsurprisingly, his critique of the Biafran war, the theme of this novel, treats the betrayal of the rank and file soldiers by the officers: the struggle is not between Biafra and the Federal troops, but between rich and poor, cutting across both sides. Again, ordinary, decent, and oppressed men are the canon fodder for the elite in the army, government, and business. But this novel signifies a change insofar as the writing is more dense, its techniques more complex, including long passages of internal monologue. While its audience may have been less popular, this novel won the Commonwealth Writers' Prize. I.'s collection of short stories, *Awaiting Court Martial* (1996), retains his sense of social outrage at oppression, his opposition to the war, and his understanding that human relationships are mediated by social forces.

I.'s writing is apparently at a cross-roads. He has not been able to repeat the success of *Violence* as a popular novel that entertains as it teaches. *The Contract* lacks the compelling images and passion of the first novel, while dealing with similar themes. *Heroes* experiments with literary technique in interesting ways, but retains an uneasy and ambiguous status, neither popular nor polished enough to break into the "high" cultural achievements of fellow countrymen, such as Wole SOYINKA or Ben OKRI. However, I.'s sharp, witty, symbolic, and powerful stories show signs of a writer moving to capture a smaller, more educated audience, with all the gains and losses politically and aesthetically that this implies.

BIBLIOGRAPHY: Fatunde, T., "Images of Working People in Two African Novels: Ouloguem and I.," in Gugelberger, G., ed., *Marxism and African Literature* (1986): 110-117; Maja-Pearce, A., "The Trouble with Babangida: Interview with F. I.," *IonC*, 18, 2 (1989): 9-13; Emenyonu, E. N., *Studies on the Nigerian Novel* (1991): 113-115; Cooper, B., *To Lay These Secrets Open* (1992): 165-173; Creachain, F. N., "How the Present Shapes the Past: F. I.'s Heroes—The Nigerian Civil War Revisited," *The Journal of Commonwealth Literature*, 27, 1 (1992): 48-57; Maja-Pearce, A., *A Mask Dancing: Nigerian Novelists of the Eighties* (1992): 74-86; Udenta, O. U., *Revolutionary Aesthetics & The African Literary Process* (1993): 76-89

—BRENDA COOPER

IZUMI Kyōka

(pseud. of Izumi Kyōtarō) Japanese novelist and dramatist, b. 4 Nov. 1873, Kanazawa; d. 7 Sept. 1939, Tokyo

I.'s native city of Kanazawa was one of the great centers for the flourishing arts and crafts of Japan throughout the Edo (1603–1868) period. I.'s family was very much a part of this traditional world; his mother had deep ties with the Nō theater, and his father was a craftsman specializing in metal engraving. This ambience of traditional culture and art proved to be a major source of I.'s literary background. His writing is enriched by the traditions of *gesaku* (popular) fiction, the Kabuki theater, the art of the storytellers, and local legends. Of particular importance were the prose and poetry of the Nō texts.

Like other aspiring writers of the period, he went to Tokyo, where in 1891 he apprenticed himself to Ozaki Kōyō (1867–1903) and began to learn the writer's craft. By 1895 he had achieved a position in the literary establishment, and his first important works began to appear, at the same time as the rise of Japanese romanticism.

Kōya hijiri (1900; *The Kōya Priest*, 1959–60) is I.'s best and most representative work of this period. It displays the full range of his commitment to romanticism, fantasy, and beauty. Central to the story is his depiction of the disturbingly beautiful seductress, a figure who appears in many of his works and whom critics view as a nostalgic evocation of his mother who died when he was nine. The story is replete with the Buddhist notions of sinful passion and salvation by grace, while its style, called *gembun-itchi*, is a mixture of the classical and the colloquial languages, rich with Chinese words, yet supple and musical in its rhythms.

Just as I. reached this peak of literary development, naturalism came to full flower in Japan, and he found himself increasingly isolated within the literary world. He never wavered, however, in his commitment to romantic writing. In an age when other writers were rushing forward to embrace new styles and to use literature as a vehicle for the expression of the "self," I. remained steadfast in his old-fashioned style of writing. At this time he published *Uta andon* (1910; the paper lantern of poetry), one of the masterpieces of his mature period. This work draws significantly on the literary heritage of both the Nō and Kabuki theaters as well as on Edo travel fiction. At one level it can also be seen simply as a celebration of artistic beauty. It is written in the elegant *gembun-itchi* style that immediately sets this story apart from the spare, clinical narratives of the naturalist writers.

I.'s final work, *Rukō shinsō* (1939; a web of crimson thread) appeared a few weeks before his death. This novel combines all the elements for which I.'s work is known: ghosts from the past, the beautiful temptress, the distorting power of passion, and the redeeming power of mercy.

I. has been greatly admired by such modern writers as KAWABATA Yasunari and MISHIMA Yukio. In a literary career of fifty years, I. recognized that the literature of the present is necessarily based on the literature of the past. And so he looked to the old Edo culture and spun his elaborate, dreamlike fantasies, and with this web of dreams he built a link with the past.

FURTHER WORKS: *Yushima mōde* (1899); *Muyūju* (1906); *Nanamotozakura* (1906); *Aika* (1906); *Shikibu kōji* (1907); *Kusa meikyū* (1908); *Onna keizu* (1908); *Shinsaku* (1909); *Koinyōbo* (1913); *Nihonbashi* (1914); *Oshidorichō* (1918); *Yukari no onna kushige shū* (1921); *Rindō to nadeshiko* (1924)

—STEPHEN W. KOHL

J

JABÈS, Edmond

French poet, b. 16 Apr. 1912, Cairo, Egypt; d. 2 Jan. 1991, Paris

J. was part of the French-speaking Jewish community of Egypt. He came from a banking family and managed the family business until the expulsion of the Jews at the time of the Suez crisis. After 1957 he lived in Paris. He received the Critics' Prize in 1970.

J. began with poems in the wake of the SURREALISTS and Max JACOB, which have been collected under the title *Je bâtis ma demeure* (1959; I build my dwelling). His main work, *Le livre des questions*, comprises seven volumes: I, *Le livre des questions* (1963; *The Book of Questions*, 1976); II, *Le livre de Yukel* (1964; *The Book of Yukel*, 1977); III, *Le retour au livre* (1965; *Return to the Book*, 1977); IV, *Yaël* (1967; Yaël); V, *Elya* (1969; *Elya*, 1973); VI, *Aely* (1972; Aely); VII, *El; ou, Le dernier livre* (1973; *The Book of Questions: El; or, The Last Book*, 1984). It is altogether sui generis: an untold story forms both the pretext and the pre-text for a blend of rabbinical commentaries, poems, aphorisms, wordplay with philosophical implications, and reflective and densely metaphorical prose. Shifting voices and constant breaks let silence have its share and allow a fuller meditative field than linear narrative or analysis would. The seven volumes combine into a profound look at the "law of the book," which is also the law of man who questions and defines himself through the word. J. challenges the unifying tendency of our thinking not only by his method of fragmentation and discontinuity, but also by his concentration on man's singularity as exemplified by the otherness of the Jew and in confrontation with the irreducible otherness of the infinite, death, God, silence, the void. The images of the desert, with its inevitable wide dispersion of people, and, on the other hand, the concentration camp, grotesque historical parody of an unreachable ontological center, are perhaps the two focal points of J.'s elliptical thought.

Le livre des ressemblances, with its three volumes—*Le livre des ressemblances* (1976; the book of resemblances), *Le soupçon le desert* (1978; suspicion desert), and *L'ineffaçable, l'inaperçu* (1980; the indelible, the unnoticed)—marks a further turn of involution by using *Le livre des questions* as the basis for its meditations. This "book that resembles a book" probes the nature of analogy, which is at the root of our thought and language yet is a tenuous support for man, who was created in the image of a God who does not exist.

J.'s importance lies in his extraordinary fusion of innovation and tradition. He draws on current linguistic theory as well as on the Cabala for work that defies all classification yet treats the most basic human questions with the greatest intellectual and emotional power. His influence was summed up by Jacques DERRIDA in 1973: "Nothing of interest has been written in France in the last ten years that does not have its precedent somewhere in the texts of J."

FURTHER WORKS: *Ça suit son cours* (1975)

BIBLIOGRAPHY: Blanchot, M., "L'interruption," *NRF*, May 1964: 869–81; Bounoure, G., "E. J.; ou, La guérison par le livre," *Lettres nouvelles*, July-Sept. 1966: 98–115; Derrida, J., "E. J. et la question du livre," *L'écriture et la différence* (1967): 99–116; Waldrop, R., "E. J. and the Impossible Circle," *Sub-stance*: Nos. 5–6 (1973): 183–95; special E. J. issue, *Change*, No. 22 (1975); Guglielmi, J., *La ressemblance impossible* (1978); Zoila, A. F., *Le livre, recherche autre d'E. J.* (1978)

—ROSMARIE WALDROP

JABRĀ, Jabrā Ibrāhīm

Palestinian poet, novelist, translator, and literary critic, b. 28 Aug. 1920, Bethlehem; d. 2 Dec. 1994, Baghdad

J. was one of the leading creative writers of the modern Arab world. Born in Bethlehem, where he grew up as a boy and first went to school, he moved with his family to Jerusalem, where he continued his education and won a fellowship to study English literature in England. He earned his B.A. (1943) and M.A. (1948) at Fitzwilliam House, Cambridge University, and returned to Palestine to teach at the Rashīdiyya College in Jerusalem (1943–1948). At the end of the British Mandate in Palestine in 1948, the hostilities leading to the establishment of Israel forced him into exile. In Iraq he became a lecturer in English literature at the College of Arts of the University of Baghdad (1948–1952), then won a two-year research fellowship in the U.S. at Harvard University (1952–1954). Returning to Iraq, he became head of publications at the Iraq Petroleum Company (1954–1977), then cultural consultant at the Iraqi Ministry of Culture and Information until his retirement (1977–1985). He died on 12 December 1994 in Baghdad.

His autobiography, *al-Bi'r al-ūlā* (1987; *The First Well*, 1995), tells the story of his boyhood in Bethlehem and chronicles his many literary and artistic interests since early age. It is a good introduction to understanding the man he became, with his many talents and achievements, in each of which his modernizing thought, his strong personality, and his liberal values are abundantly clear.

A witness to many political and social upheavals in the Middle East, J. was particularly affected by the loss of Palestine, his homeland. The feeling of being an exile pervades his writings, but he did not permit it to make him bitter and destructive. Nostalgic memories of the homeland abound in his poetry, and fictional characters searching for their identity and roots recur in his novels and short stories. Transcending personal feelings, however, he sought a universal vision of humans in the 20th c. and a deep insight into their condition.

Writing in an age when urban growth has become a pronounced feature of the Arab world, as it is elsewhere, J. focused a great deal of attention on the city, its people, its problems, and its opportunities, as well as its power to crush individuals and values while developing its own urban rules of living. His first collection of poems, *Tammūz fī al-madīnah* (1959; Tammuz in the city), laments the spiritual death that prevails in the city as its people move away from life-giving principles in their search for material gain and power. His second collection, *al-Madār al-mughlaq* (1964; the vicious circle), decries the constraints imposed on people undergoing dramatic change in the city and being forced to lose their natural selves and their real voice. His third collection, *Law'at alshams* (1979; the anguish of the sun), reveals the evils that enslave humans caught in the mesh of city life, from which nothing but love can redeem them. A symbol of modern civilization, the city in his view—like T. S. ELIOT'S "wasteland"—needs a revivifying force to bring back fertility and happiness to it.

J.'s poetry is among that of a very few Arab poets who have daringly discarded the traditional Arab meters and rhymes to create, in prose, a new poetry that has a rhythm of its own, which is not quantitative like traditional Arabic verse, but qualitative in its attempt to capture a new vision of Arab life and generate a new poetic harmony.

J. produced seven works of fiction, including a collection of short stories, a novel written with 'Abd AL-RAHMĀNMUNĪ, and five other novels of varying lengths. His characters are mostly drawn from a rising bourgeoisie and a declining propertied urban class of tribal origins. Their conflicts and their search for identity and stability constitute J.'s major plots, but intellectuals dominate the dialogues as they discuss problems of their society and express aspects of their sense of alienation.

In al-Safīna (1970; The Ship, 1985), the passengers cruising the Mediterranean are escaping their social straits at home only to realize they are carrying them along, ending with the suicide of one character. In al-Bahth 'an Walīd Mas'ūd (1978; search for Walīd Mas'ūd), the characters assembles to discuss the mysterious disappearance of their friend Walīd Mas'ūd, a rich Palestinian in Baghdad, but they embark instead on uncovering their own relations with him and baring their complexities, while it is rumored that he has gone to join the PLO commandos in his occupied homeland. In al-Ghuraf-al-ukhrā (1986; the other rooms), the protagonist is led into a labyrinthian building, where he is brought for a purpose he does not know, accused by mercurial persons of acts he never thought he committed, and then his very identity is put to question to an extent that he begins to doubt who he is. The idea of being besieged is an insistent one in J.'s fiction, and human beings in it try incessantly to break out of their vicious circle.

J.'s works in various genres have contributed in a large measure to the introduction of modern ideas and styles in Arabic letters and the Arab arts, and his name will remain eminently associated with other modernizing influences in the Arab world in the second half of the 20th c.

FURTHER WORKS: Surākh fī layl tawīl (1955); 'Araq wa qisas ukhrā (1956); al-Hurriyyah wa-al-tūfān (1960); al-Rihla al-thāminah (1967); al-Fann al'irāqī al-mu'āsir (1972;Contemporary Iraqui Art, 1972); Sayyādūn fi shāri' dayyiq (1974; first pub. in English as Hunters in a Narrow Street, 1960); Jawād Salām wa-nusb al-hurriyyah (1974); al-Nār wa-al-jawhar (1975); Yanābi' al-ru'yā (1979); 'Ālam bilā Kharā'it (1982 with 'Abd al-Rahmān Munīf); al-Sūnitāt li William Shakespeare (1983); al-Fann wa-al-hulm wa-al-fi'l (1985); Judhār al-fann al-'irāqā (1986; first pub. in English as The Grass Roots of Iraqi Art, 1983); al-Malik al-shams (1986); Baghdād bayn al-ams wa-al-yawm (1987, with Ihsān Fathā); Ayyām al-'uqāb: Khālid wa-ma'rakat al-Yarmūk (1988); Ta'ammulāt fī bunyān marmarī (1989). FURTHER WORKS IN ENGLISH: Art in Iraq Today (1961); A Celebration of Life (1988)

BIBLIOGRAPHY: Barakat, H., Visions of Social Reality in the Contemporary Arab Novel (1977): 21–25; Boullata, I. J., "The Concept of Modernity in the Poetry of J. and Sāyigh," in Boullata, I. J., ed., Critical Perspectives of Modern Arabic Literature (1980): 263–79; Allen, R., The Arabic Novel (1982): 69–71, 138–44;

Haydar, A., and Allen, R., Introduction to The Ship (1985): 3–10; Moosa, M., "J.'s Ship," Gilgamesh, 1 (1988): 77–81

—ISSA J. BOULLATA

JACOB, Max

French poet, prose writer, and art critic, b. 12 July 1876, Quimper; d. 5 March 1944, Drancy concentration camp

J. was at the heart of the intensely creative period in which modern French art and poetry came into being. A Breton of Jewish origin, he arrived in Paris in 1894, met Picasso and APOLLINAIRE several years later, and from 1904 onward immersed himself in the experiments that led to the creation of CUBISM and SURREALISM. As early as 1909, J., drawn both to religion and the bohemian life, experienced a vision of Christ. This mystic encounter led to his conversion to Catholicism (1915) and left an imprint upon his writing, lending it depth, power, and introspection. A forceful but elusive personality, to many of his contemporaries a clown or a mystic, J. did not attain the fame of Picasso or Apollinaire. But he exercised a major influence upon younger writers, serving as their mentor even after his retirement to the semimonastic seclusion of Saint-Benoît-sur-Loire, first from 1921 to 1927 and again in 1936. J. lived there until World War II; in February 1944 he was arrested by the Germans together with other Jews and interned in the concentration camp at Drancy, where he died of pneumonia.

J. united in his work literary and painterly concerns, poetic practice and theory, and he emerged as an important catalyst figure. He helped redefine poetry as a nonmimetic art, expanded lyricism to include humor, parody, wordplay and other devices previously associated with prose, and thought of poetry in terms of means of expression, not message.

The brilliant collection Le cornet à dés (1917; the dice cup) expresses best J.'s bent for innovation and remains his most influential work. It contains prose poems built around dream sequences, puns, hallucinations, satirical sketches, images that modulate one into another and convey an oblique vision of the world in the manner of cubist paintings, sometimes no more than a sense of style or the author's attempt to break down literary conventions. J. brings together prose and poetry, strives for effects of flatness in rhythm and diction, and relies on irony, parody, and pastiche to set off his work against the romantic and SYMBOLIST schools. In Le cornet à dés, a puzzling but fascinating universe that has no easily definable meaning seems to emerge.

In his subsequent collections, the innovative Le laboratoire central (1921; the central laboratory) or the simpler, more introspective Les pénitents en maillots roses (1925; the penitents in pink tights), J. continued to use unorthodox techniques, juxtaposing disparate elements, fragmenting images, disrupting anecdotal and melodic lines. He achieved unity through movement—not linear structures but the sustained verbal play and aggressive rhythms that mirror the poet's creativity and carry value without reference to reality. Autonomy, attentiveness to expression and to linguistic effects, and the desire to divorce the poem from the real form the core of J.'s aesthetic, developed in the preface to Le cornet à dés and two longer works, Art poétique (1922; the art of poetry) and the posthumously published Conseils à un jeune poète, suivis de Conseils à un étudiant (1945; advice to a young poet, followed by advice to a student; first part tr. as *Advice to a Young Poet*, 1976). These treatises equate art and inventiveness and see the poem as a force that solicits, absorbs, and disturbs the reader.

Primarily a poet, J. experimented with biography, art criticism, tales, drama—a bewildering variety of genres and multiform texts characterized by tension between outward-going observation and introspection, fantasy, and spirituality. *Saint Matorel* (1909; Saint Matorel), an unstructured narrative, recounts with ironic compassion the droll and also serious adventures of a Parisian turned abbot. *La défense de Tartufe* (1919; the defense of Tartufe), an anguished record of J.'s conversion to Catholicism, modulates from speculative inquiry, to self-analysis, to humor and the notation of realistic details. J.'s novels, notably *Le roi de Béotie* (1921; the king of Boeotia) and *Le terrain Bouchaballe* (1923; the land of Bouchaballe) paint a vast verbal fresco of Parisian and Breton society. They reveal a sardonic observer, a mime who delights in recording men's words and gestures, a writer with a rich visual memory and the talent to fix in an image settings, objects, faces, and also a fervent but tormented believer who writes in order to surmount inner conflict.

In J.'s last works the pendulum swings toward spirituality. The posthumously published *Derniers poèmes en vers et en prose* (1945; last poems in verse and in prose) and *L'homme de cristal* (1946; the crystal man) express J.'s mystical side and hint at the final reconciliation of extremes that marked his personality, a personality that gave rise to the iconoclastic texts that rank among the most innovative in modern French letters.

FURTHER WORKS: *La côte* (1911); *Les œuvres burlesques et mystiques de Frère Matorel mort au couvent* (1912); *Le siège de Jérusalem: Grande tentation céleste de Saint Matorel* (1914); *Dos d'Harlequin* (1921); *Ne coupez pas, mademoiselle; ou, Les erreurs des P.T.T.* (1921); *Le cabinet noir* (1922); *Filibuth; ou, La montre en or* (1923); *Visions infernales* (1924); *L'homme de chair et l'homme de reflet* (1924); *Fond de l'eau* (1927); *Sacrifice impérial* (1929); *Tableau de la bourgeoisie* (1930); *Rivage* (1931); *Le bal masqué* (1932); *Ballades* (1938); *Méditations religieuses* (1945); *Poèmes de Morven le Gaëlique* (1953); *Correspondance* (2 vols., 1953–1955). FURTHER WORKS IN ENGLISH: *The Dice Cup: Selected Prose Poems* (1980)

BIBLIOGRAPHY: Billy, A., *M. J.* (1945); Belaval, Y., *La rencontre avec M. J.* (1946); Andreu, P., *M. J.* (1962); Kamber, G., *M. J. and the Poetics of Cubism* (1971); Plantier, R., *L'univers poétique de M. J.* (1976); Brownstein, M., Introduction to *The Dice Cup: Selected Prose Poems* (1980): i-v

—VIKTORIA SKRUPSKELIS

JACOBSEN, Rolf

Norwegian poet, b. 8 Mar. 1907, Oslo; d. 20 Feb. 1994, Hamar

J. is one of Norway's most distinguished poets, one of the few to have achieved an international reputation. J. grew up in Oslo, then moved to Hamar, a city about 60 miles north of Oslo, where he earned his living as a journalist.

From his first book of poems, *Jord og jern* (1933; earth and iron), J. wrote modernist free verse distinguished by compelling rhythms and startling images. His strong, strange rapport with both the natural and urban world is conveyed in striking images and in a free verse that convincingly mimed the movements of the poet's feeling; this distinguished J.'s poetry from the start, making it hard to categorize. Because he wrote poems about such things as trains, electrical turbines, office windows, racing cars, and airplanes, he was often taken as a kind of futurist, like Filippo Tommaso MARINETTI, as if modern civilization had found in him another troubadour. But even his first book contained clear signs that J. was not really on the side of the machine.

Two years later, in *Vrimmel* (1935; tumult), a stronger undertone of sadness and compassion entered J.'s poetry. Age, decay, and rust began to evoke a gentle, undismayed sympathy from him. War, business, and industry seemed driven by an indifferent and unstoppable energy. One senses J.'s underlying dismay at the destructiveness inherent in modern civilization, but as an artist he refuses to react conventionally and simplistically to it. His poetry fixes the permanent natural world and the speeded-up world of the modern city in a kind of metaphorical mirror relationship to each other, each commenting on the other, each striving to overcome the other. J.'s sympathies are on the side of nature, but his intuition and long-sighted wisdom seem to suggest to him that even the gasoline-driven cities may simply be nature moving at another tempo, one ultimately indifferent to the fate of humans.

J. is a master poet, so it is difficult to say which are his best books. *Fjerntog* (1951; express train) and *Hemmelig liv* (1954; secret life) are perhaps the collections that display his gifts most abundantly. Many of these poems seem to spring from some passionate sixth sense that allows J. to look to the edge of the thing he is considering and render its aura more powerfully than the thing itself. Within these collections J. has refined his art to the point where it is mystical and realistic all at once. Describing the auras of fountains, the faces of old people, the scent of pine reminiscent of bread, J. celebrates the beauty and mystery of the world at the same time as he conveys a deep, troubled compassion for it.

In J.'s later poetry—*Sommeren i gresset* (1956; summer in the grass), *Stillheten efterpå* (1965; the silence afterwards), *Headlines* (1969; title in English), *Pass for dørene—dørene lukkes* (1972; watch the doors—the doors are closing), *Pusteøvelse* (1975; breathing exercise), and *Tenk på noe annet* (1979; think about something else)—one notices, very generally speaking, that he becomes less "modernistic" as time goes on. He becomes more of an explicit and public poet—not in a pompous way, but from a need to speak clearly and directly about ecological matters, taking the word in its widest and deepest sense.

FURTHER WORKS: *Nattåpent: dikt* (1985). FURTHER WORKS IN ENGLISH: *Twenty Poems/R. J.* (1977); *The Silence Afterwards: Selected Poems of R. J.* (1985)

BIBLIOGRAPHY: Naess, H. S., "The Poetry of R. J.," *American Scandinavian Review* (1962): 265–69; Bly, R., "What Norwegian Poetry Is Like," *The Sixties*, 10 (1968): 37–77; Loanhead, S., *Five Norwegian Poets: Tarjei Vesaas, R. J., Olav Hauge, Gunvor Hofmo, Stein Mehren* (1976); Grinde, O., "R. J.," ScanR, 70, 4 (Dec. 1982): 49–59; Grinde, O., "Interview with R. J.," *SDR* (Spring 1983): 7–13; Hass, R., *Twentieth Century Pleasures: Prose on Poetry* (1984); Gouchet, O., "R. J.: La pierre, la lumière et l'être," *Revue Littéraire Mensuelle* (Mar. 1987): 11–35

—WILLIAM E. MISHLER

JACOBSON, Dan

South African-English novelist and short-story writer, b. 7 Mar. 1929, Johannesburg, South Africa

The child of Baltic Jewish parents, J. grew up in Kimberley in the Cape Province (the model for his fictional Lyndhurst). After taking a degree in English at the University of the Witwatersrand (1948), he spent nine months in a kibbutz in Israel and a year teaching in a Jewish boys' school in London before returning to South Africa in 1951 to work in his family's business and to write his first short stories and his first two novels, *The Trap* (1955) and *A Dance in the Sun* (1956). Before returning to England permanently, he spent a year as a creative-writing fellow at Stanford University, an experience that gave him the material for *No Further West: California Visited* (1959), a brilliant examination of American society and culture that places him among the most significant foreign observers of the U.S. Except for visiting professorships in the U.S. and Australia, he has been since 1975 a professor of English at University College, London.

J.'s career can be sharply divided into two periods. His first five novels and almost all of his short stories, published in *The Zulu and the Zeide* (1959), *Beggar My Neighbour* (1964), and *Through the Wilderness* (1968; pub. in England as *Inklings: Selected Stories*, 1973), have South African settings.

The Trap deals with an essentially decent Afrikaner farmer and his African foreman, who conspires to steal his employer's sheep with a racist white neighbor who is able to betray him because of a social system that finds it easier to believe a white thief than a black one. *A Dance in the Sun* concerns two hitchhiking university students who, taken in for a night by a mad South African English racist and his Afrikaner wife, discover a terrible family secret about the woman's brother, his African mistress, and the African girl's brother, who asks the boys to help him but is primarily concerned to blackmail his employer. These two novels reveal the qualities of method and intention that characterize all of J.'s later works: exact diction, economy of exposition, and a preoccupation with moral concerns that avoids didacticism.

J.'s upbringing was almost entirely secular, and his sense of being Jewish is cultural and historical rather than religious, but he dealt frequently in his early work with Jewish subjects. "The Zulu and the Zeide," probably his most famous story, is a moving portrayal of an old Jew who turns to a Zulu servant for the attention and affection that he cannot get from his materially successful son, who wishes to show him his love but cannot. *The Price of Diamonds* (1957) deals with two Jewish business partners and the crisis that threatens their friendship when a diamond smuggler mistakenly leaves a package of illegal diamonds with one of them. *The Beginners* (1966), a major work of South African fiction, is a long panoramic novel that reveals the influence of the great 19th-c. Russian masters as well as certain similarities to J.'s own family. A chronicle of the descendants of two brothers, Jewish immigrants from Lithuania, and set in South Africa, England, and Israel, it is a social history of South Africa in the first half of this century.

J.'s other South African novel, the less successful *Evidence of Love* (1960), may be regarded as his contribution to what might be called a genre of South African fiction—the story of miscegenation.

A key work for understanding J.'s career and his decision to abandon his South African subject is the story "Fresh Fields," published in *Through the Wilderness*, a story of a young South African's encounter with a famous émigré South African writer who has produced little in recent years and thus advises the young writer to return home to his true subject. When the young man shows him some of his work and the older man plagiarizes it, the young man expresses J.'s own declaration of independence from his South African origins: he will find his subject wherever he happens to be.

The novels J. produced when he abandoned South Africa as a subject are remarkably experimental in their various ways of distancing the reader from their material and drawing attention to their artistry. *The Rape of Tamar* (1970) is based on the biblical story of Tamar and her brother Ammon, Absalom's murder of Ammon and rebellion against King David, and his death in battle, all told in a modern idiom and with frequent anachronisms from the point of view of Yonadab, a manipulator of the emotions of others and a troublemaker who enjoys the confusion he creates. *The Wonder-Worker* (1973) is a remarkable story told by a lunatic in a Swiss sanatorium who, in telling his own story, also tells the story of a young Englishman who possesses the power to transform himself into inert objects. *The Confessions of Josef Baisz* (1977) is a story of conspiracy, set in a fictitious country that resembles South Africa in many ways; its narrator is a police informant in a totalitarian state who practices betrayal in his personal life and achieves power and prestige when he practices it on behalf of the state.

In his later career J. produced less fiction, but except for *Hidden in the Heart* (1991), which is relatively conventional in method, he has maintained his concern for narrative experiment. In an ironic reversal of the roles of East European Jews and Gentiles, *The God-Fearer* (1992), an eloquent indictment of religious bigotry, is narrated by a Jewish scholar who encounters in his nearly senile imagination two ghostly figures who, he comes to realize, are the children never borne to a "Christer" girl whom he betrayed many years before.

In spite of his physical and artistic abandonment of South Africa, J. remains one of the major figures of South African literature in the latter half of the 20th c. Looking at South Africa from the special position of a member of a Jewish minority in an English-speaking minority in a white minority, he was able to see the paradoxes inherent in South African society with an artistic vision that is ironic and skeptical and yet sympathetic with all elements in South Africa's racially complex population. His later novels also reveal this remarkable insight into social relationships, and two of them, *The Rape of Tamar* and *The Confessions of Josef Baisz*, show greater understanding of what motivates people in actual political conflicts—and thus may tell us more about South African reality—than any number of more obviously "socially conscious" works.

FURTHER WORKS: *Time of Arrival* (1962); *The Story of the Stories* (1982); *Time and Time Again: Autobiographies* (1985); *Her Story* (1987); *Adult Pleasures* (1988); *The Electronic Elephant: A Southern African Journey* (1995)

BIBLIOGRAPHY: Hicks, G., "No End to Beginnings," *SatR*, 19 Feb. 1966: 37–38; Wolff, G., "'Such a World, We Have To Live In,'" *NewR*, 9 Apr. 1966: 21–24; Alter, R., "A Long Story," *Commentary*, 42, 2 (Aug. 1966): 64–66; Schneidau, H. N., "Desire and Gratification," *Commentary*, 51, 1 (Jan. 1971): 95–96; Kaplan, J., "On *The Wonder-Worker*," *Commentary*, 57, 6 (June 1974): 94–96;

Wilkinson, D. R. M., "A Comment on Race Relationships: D. J.'s *The Trap* and *A Dance in the Sun*," *DQR*, 5 (1975): 270–81; Baxter, C., "Political Symbolism in *A Dance in the Sun*," *EinA* 5, 2 (1978): 44–50; Roberts, S., *D. J.* (1984); Roberts, S., "Tamar and After: A Glance at D. J.'s Recent Work," in Diamond, M. J., Jacobs, J. U., and Lenta, M., eds., *Momentum: On Recent South African Writing* (1984): 14–46; Solotaroff, T., *A Few Good Voices in My Head* (1987): 22–31; Gready, P., "D. J. as Expatriate Writer," *RAL*, 25, 4 (Winter 1994): 17-32

—ROBERT L. BERNER

JÆGER, Frank

Danish poet, novelist, and short-story writer, b. 19 June 1926, Frederiksberg; d. 4 July 1977, Elsinore

Trained as a librarian, J. was able to earn a living from his writings alone from 1950 on. His critically acclaimed debut as a poet, *Dydige digte* (1948; virtuous poems), is engagingly accessible even on a casual first reading. Its tone ranges from the idyllic, through the humorous and ironic, to the frustrated and the melancholy.

The poems of *Morgenens trompet* (1949; the trumpet of morning) differ both in tone and style from *Dydige digte*. Underlying many of them is a despair occasioned by physical or emotional suffering.

In *De 5 årstider* (1950; the 5 seasons) the poet's earlier optimism and predilection for the idyllic once again predominate. The four seasons are depicted from a variety of standpoints, most of which are life-affirming. The poems of the "fifth" season, however, transcend the limitations of the calendar cycle. In *Tyren* (1953; the bull) J. further restricted his poetic style by rhyme and meter. Increasingly J. is drawn toward such questions as death and rebirth, man's isolation, and the irreconcilability of illusion and reality.

Many of the poems in *Havkarlens sange* (1956; songs of the merman) and *Cinna, og andre digte* (1959; Cinna, and other poems) are more brooding and sensual than is most of J.'s earlier poetry. This inquietude is, however, offset by the mood of the majority of the poems, which stress the idyllic, the romantic, the lighthearted and whimsical, affirming art's place in life. *Idylia* (1967; Greek: collection of small pictures) is, as its title suggests, a volume of essentially idyllic poetry, although in several of the poems J. enters the realm of the surreal.

At first blush, J.'s novel *Iners* (1950; Iners) would seem to reflect the same idyllic bent as most of his early poetry. The protagonist, Iners, initially appears to be a guileless good-for-nothing. But it gradually becomes clear that he is possessed of malevolent subsciousness drives that leave misery and suffering in their wake. Iners slowly isolates himself from the rest of society and is eventually abandoned even by his one true love, the innocent young woman Ene. In the end, Iners disintegrates as a rational human being. Although the conclusion to this short novel is ambiguous, the work as a whole is a disequieting study of man's demonic nature.

In *Hverdagshistorier* (1951; everyday stories) J. imposes a fairy-tale framework on eighteen loosely connected short stories. Ranging from an allegory about the renewal of nature to a parable of the redemptive death to the grotesque fable of human cruelty, the stories in *Hverdagshistorier* probe the surreal and the chimerical with irony, humor, and human sympathy.

J.'s autobiographical fantasy *Den unge Jægers lidelser* (1953; the sufferings of young Jæger) consists of nine prose sketches that proceed from the childhood to the early manhood of the first-person narrator which focus on the coming-of-age of the protagonist. Written in a light-hearted, ironic style, they are grounded in realism but make frequent excursions into the realm of the illusory.

The five stories of *Kapellanen og andre fortællinger* (1957; The curate and other stories) extend the theme of *Dem unge Jægers lidelser* and describe how each of the young male protagonists discovers his true inner self. In "Foraarsaften med Faust" (spring evening with Faust), for instance, the despondent itinerant artist has travelled through provincial Denmark bringing excerpts from Goethe's drama "Faust" before pitifully small audiences. Finally overcome by the combined powers of poetry and the erotic, he flees preciptously to take up life as a worker in his father's window-blind factory.

In like vein, the stories of *Danskere: Tre fortællinger af fædrelandets historie* (1966; Danes: three narratives from the history of the fatherland) question the place of art in life and reveal the potentially destructive forces that slumber in the sensual and erotic.

The protagonist of the psychologically realistic novel *Døden i skoven* (1970; death in the forest) is suddenly banished to an isolated forest house. Unable to adapt to his seclusion, he withdraws inwardly and slowly disintegrates as a human being. J. makes clear that, although the middle-aged Cornelius bears the immediate responsibility for his own downfall, there are forces beyond his control ultimately determining his destiny.

Although J. began his career as an idyllic poet, he ended it as primarily an author of realistic fiction. He was frequently absorbed with the problems of art's relation to reality and man's isolation. Never the social critic and only rarely the conscious purveyor of metaphysical thought, J. nevertheless made his characters, for better or for worse, conform to conventional morality. The fact that much of his fiction ends abruptly and equivocally, often before the work's problem can be resolved, should not be viewed as a flaw; for in forcing readers to draw their own conclusions, J. has made them active rather than merely passive participants in the creative process.

FURTHER WORKS: *Tune* (1951); *19 Jægerviser* (1953); *Didrik* (1955); *Jomfruen fra Orléans, Jeanne d'Arc* (1955); *Til en følsom veninde* (1957); *Kapellanen, og andre fortællinger* (1957); *Velkommen, vinter* (1958); *Hvilket postbud—en Due* (1959); *Pastorale* (1963); *Pelsen* (1964); *Drømmen om en sommerdag* (1965); *Danskere: Tre fortællinger af fædrelandets historie* (1966); *Naive rejser* (1968); *Der er en verden også i Verona* (1969); *Alvilda* (1969); *Den som ingen holder tilbage* (1970); *Essays gennem ti år* (1970); *Provinser* (1972); *J. A. P.* (1973); *S* (1973); *Hvor er Ulla-Katrine?* (1974); *Udsigt til Kronborg* (1976)

BIBLIOGRAPHY: Hugus, F., "The Dilemma of the Artist in Selected Prose Works of F. J.," *SS*, 47 (1975): 52–65; Maelsaeke, D. van, *The Strange Essence of Things* (1977): 142–65, 168–74, 192–201; Hugus, F., "F. J.'s Defeated Protagonists," *SS*, 54 (1982)

—FRANK HUGUS

JAHNN, Hans Henny

German novelist and dramatist, b. 17 Dec. 1894, Hamburg-Stellingen; d. 29 Nov. 1959, Hamburg-Blankenese

Son of a shipbuilder, J. divided his interests among writing, musical theory and composition, and organ building. Opposed to war, he spent the years 1915–18 in Norway. After 1933 he emigrated to Denmark, where he lived with his family, working as a farmer and biologist. He returned to Hamburg in 1950.

Like his literary next-of-kin Alfred DÖBLIN and Hans Erich NOSSACK, J. was a novelist to the extent to which a novel can be regarded as an allegory of human life. Maintaining in his works the precarious utopian balance between art and propaganda so characteristic of EXPRESSIONISM, metaphysical anxiety shaped his message to man fixed in a system with the coordinates *poverty, wealth, man*, and *beast*. The same four concepts emerged as the title of J.'s most significant drama written after his return to postwar Germany, *Armut, Reichtum, Mensch und Tier* (1948; poverty, wealth, man, and beast). In its reduction of the fateful rural existence of a Norwegian farmer to those elemental motives, the play restates J.'s earlier convictions tempered by the harsh events in his own life yet is far removed from any specific intellectual or social cause. Its starkly simple message has the power of early Greek drama, urging mankind to seek salvation in compassionate love—the river unbound uniting all disparate life in deep sympathy (in biological and spiritual symbiosis)—to recapture the lost mythic state of nature.

The earliest examples of this concern are found together with faint narcissistic overtones in the play *Der Arzt, sein Weib, sein Sohn* (1922; the physician, his wife, his son) and the long novel *Perrudja* (1929; Perrudja). *Perrudja* is a work of cascading images and words that articulate the cosmic pathos of an exile from the conventions of society, who is searching, in the Norwegian wilderness, for complete harmony of existence. This cannot be achieved without its measure of evil, as shown in J.'s magnum opus, *Fluß ohne Ufer* (river without banks), a trilogy consisting of *Das Holzschiff* (1949; *The Ship*, 1961), *Die Niederschrift des Gustav Anias Horn* (2 vols., 1949, 1950; Gustav Anias Horn's written narrative), *Epilog* (1961; epilogue). This novel of suspense, at first seemingly concerned with murder and mutiny during a mysterious voyage ending in shipwreck, develops into a retrospective account that analyzes motives and meaning in the lives of two central characters. The novel is finally expanded to proportions of universal principle through the technique of cyclic repetition—another murder is committed, another murderer assumes his share of guilt, which is but transmuted love.

Reflecting the expressionist urge for direct communication, J.'s plays are, for the most part, built on the thesis that man's despair, that is, the curse of evanescent youth, results from his loss of animal innocence, and that this sanctuary of innocence can be recovered only partially through an archetypal love of which the goddess in *Medea* (1926, Medea) becomes a symbol. This theme, first expressed in *Der Arzt, sein Weib, sein Sohn*, persists through the posthumously published *Die Trümmer des Gewissens* (1961; the ruins of conscience), which tries to assess the consequences of man's fall from innocence in a vision of atomic holocaust as proof of scientific and political vanity. Becoming more and more convinced in his last years that the "league of the weak"—men of good faith—had to take political action, and possibly to sacrifice themselves to save mankind from pointless destruction, J. was working on another drama of protest entitled *Die andere Seite greift ein* (the other side intervenes) on the eve of his death.

His creed he had stated long ago, in his essay "Aufgabe des Dichters in dieser Zeit" (1932; the writer's task in these times): "We have witnessed too much; ignorance no longer becomes us. It is not our misfortune but our hope that man's soul has been found inconstant. Let us rebuild it and strengthen it against the tide of rational catastrophes, to reunite it to the harmonious structure of being."

FURTHER WORKS: *Pastor Ephraim Magnus* (1919); *Die Krönung Richards III* (1921); *Hans Heinrich* (1922); *Der gestohlene Gott* (1924); *Neuer Lübecker Totentanz* (1931); *Straßenecke: Ein Ort, eine Handlung* (1931); *Spur des dunklen Engels* (1952); *Thomas Chatterton* (1955); *Die Nacht aus Blei* (1956); *Aufzeichnungen eines Einzelgängers* (1959); *Dramen* (1963); *13 nicht geheure Geschichten* (1963) *Über den Anlaß, und andere Essays* (1964); *Werke und Tagebücher* (7 vols., 1974); *H. H. J.—Peter Huchel: Ein Briefwechsel 1951–1959* (1974)

BIBLIOGRAPHY: Nossack, H. E., "Nachruf auf H. H. J.," *Jahrbuch 1960 der Akademie der Wissenschaften und der Literatur* (1960): 43–48; Muschg, W., *Von Trakl zu Brecht: Dichter des Expressionismus* (1961): 264–334; Marr, W. M., "Compassion and the Outsider: H. H. J.'s *Die Nacht aus Blei*," *GR*, 39 (1964): 201–10; Meyer, J., *Verzeichnis der Schriften von und über H. H. J.* (1967); Jenkinson, D. E., "The Role of Vitalism in the Novels of H. H. J.," *GL&L*, 25 (1972): 359–67; Kobbe, P., *Mythos und Modernität: Eine poetologische und methodenkritische Studie zum Werk H. H. J.s* (1973); Detsch, R., "The Theme of the Black Race in the Works of H. H. J.," *Mosaic* 7, 2 (1973–74), 165–87

—KURT OPITZ

JAIMES FREYRE, Ricardo

Bolivian poet, essayist, and historian, b. 12 May 1868, Tacna, Peru; d. 24 Apr. 1933, Buenos Aires, Argentina

Born to a prominent and intellectual Bolivian family, J. F. was predestined to a promising artistic life, which he fully realized. He became the first Bolivian author to gain an international reputation, a historian of distinction, and a diplomat representing his country abroad. J. F. spent a decisive early life in Buenos Aires and settled there to pursue his literary ambitions. He published there his first and most important work, *Castalia bárbara* (1899; drawn from a barbaric fountain). He then lived in the city of Tucumán in northern Argentina, where he did extensive research on local history. Back in Bolivia in the later part of his life, he was elected a house representative, then appointed ambassador to several countries, including the U.S. (1923–1927). He again settled in Buenos Aires, where he died. His remains were repatriated, and his tomb placed next to his father's in the cathedral of Potosí.

Argentinian Emilio Carilla, J. F.'s main biographer, divided the author's life into three main periods: his early residence in Buenos Aires, his university service in Tucumán, and his diplomatic and public work in Bolivia (almost to the end of his life). J. F.'s literary production can be easily placed within the same divisions.

Critics agree that the first of these three periods is the one that matters most to Spanish American letters. And some have also stated that J. F. was a one-book author and that it is for *Castalia bárbara* that he will be always remembered. At least as a poet he was not a prolific author. In 1888, when the Nicaraguan poet Rubén DARÍO launched his literary school that he himself named *modernismo*, J. F. became his most faithful ally and even economic supporter. They jointly edited *Revista de América*, organ of the new movement, published briefly during 1894. And in 1899 J. F. gave further strength to Modernismo by publishing his *Castalia bárbara*. The major part of the work contains poems that introduced to Latin Americans the exotic world of Norse mythology. Critics are right in mentioning Leconte de Lisle's (1818–1894) *Poèmes barbares* (1862) as the model J. F. followed, but Wagner's operas, then quite fashionable, must have also been an influence. Dexterously combining the subtlety of SYMBOLISM with the perfectionistic obsession of Parnassianism, J. F. created a unique magical, medieval world utterly removed from Latin American reality, thus also meeting one of the main goals of Modernismo—escapism. Faithful to that movement, this work was a purely aesthetic effort.

Leyes de la versificación castellana (laws on Spanish versification) appeared only in 1912, but it was again a solid contribution. J. F. became one of the few Hispanics to set theories for the proper use of meters, melody, and harmony in poetry.

Five years later his second and last poetry work appeared. *Los sueños son vida* (1917; to dream is to live) also follows the changes that Rubén Darío had impressed into his own movement of MODERNISM. Although still pursuing aesthetics, exotic settings tended now to disappear, to be replaced by themes exposing the spiritual problems of human beings and the suffering of the exploited. To this day one of the poems of this second book by J. F. astonishes us: In "Rusia" (Russia), which he wrote in 1905, he predicted the Russian Revolution fully eleven years before it happened. But always a good Parnassian, J. F. continued to uphold stylistic perfection in poetry writing.

In prose this Bolivian did shine, albeit briefly. Two dramas he composed received no attention, but one of his five short stories, like the poem "Rusia," must have again frozen readers. "En las montañas" (1906; in the mountains) is a typical piece of social protest. It seems to have been influenced by J. F.'s famous countryman, the novelist Alcides ARGUEDAS, whose indigenist novel *Wata Wara* (1904; Wata Wara) ended with a massacre of landowners in the hand of rebellious Indians. So does, too, this short story by J. F., whose suffering highlanders cruelly torture the haughty oligarchs and indifferently watch their slow death. Thus, J. F. is also a pioneer of the vigorous literature of social protest that characterizes Bolivian letters.

Thereafter, J. F. spent some twenty years researching the history of Tucumán, in whose university he worked. He produced five valuable books and also founded in 1905 the *Revista de Letras y Ciencias Sociales*. Returning to Bolivia to take up public and diplomatic posts, he was able to travel widely. In the last six years of his life he settled in Buenos Aires. He belongs to Argentina for having efficiently researched its history; to Bolivia, for putting as a modernist his country on the literary map; and to Latin American letters, for pioneering, with Rubén Darío, the free verse and the cosmopolitanism that then began to take hold of the continent.

FURTHER WORKS: *La hija de Jephté* (1899); *Tucumán en 1810* (1909); *Historia de la República de Tucumán* (1911); *El Tucumán del siglo XVI* (1914); *El Tucumán colonial* (1915); *Historia del descubrimiento de Tucumán* (1916); *Los conquistadores* (1928); *Poesías completas* (1944)

BIBLIOGRAPHY: Torres-Rioseco, A., "R. J. F. (1870–1933)," *Hispania*, 16, 4 (Nov.–Dec. 1933): 389–98; Jaimes , Freyre, *Raúl, Anecdotario de R. J. F.* (1953); Carilla, E., "J. F., cuentista y novelista," *Thesaurus*, 16 (1961): 664–98; Carilla, E., *R. J. F.* (1962); Ocampo, E., *Personalidad y obra poética de don R. J. F.* (1968); Cáceres, A., and J. Ortega *Diccionario de la literatura boliviana* (1970): 140–44; Guzmán, et al., A., *R. J. F.: estudios* (1978); Cortés, D., "R. J. F." in Solé, C. A., ed., *Latin American Writers* (1989), Vol. 1: 419–23

—EVELIO ECHEVARRÍA

JAMAICAN LITERATURE
See English-Caribbean Literature

JAMES, Henry

American novelist, short-story writer, dramatist, critic, and essayist, b. 15 April 1843, New York, N.Y.; d. 28 Feb. 1916, London, England

J. is, next to FAULKNER, America's most distinguished prolific novelist. His reputation has waxed and waned since his first story ("A Tragedy of Error") appeared in 1864, but it seems safe to include him among a handful of classic American writers of fiction. During his own last years, and between the 1940s and the mid-1960s, his standing as *the* self-conscious craftsman of prose, the writer's writer, was supreme. Whatever the fluctuations of his reputation, his experiments with limited point of view and unreliable narration provided a generation of modernists with a useful model for breaking out of Victorian conventions of plot, character, and narrative voice. Himself a 19th-c. man in his insistence on the social values of wit, self-possession, and civility, he nevertheless served as a touchstone for several of the more jagged and unsettling voices of the 20th c., notably those of T. S. ELIOT and Ezra POUND.

J. was born into an oppressively distinguished American family. His father, Henry James, Sr., was a Swedenborgian philosopher of note, and a good friend of Emerson and other New England transcendentalists. J.'s older brother William became a professor at Harvard and eventually one of America's foremost philosophers. The three youngest siblings, by contrast, led markedly ineffectual lives, while Henry, in between, perfected the techniques of second sonship: since William was the aggressive doer, preempting the space of active pursuit, Henry became the reflector, requiring only the space of imaginative musing. "There was the difference and the opposition, as I really believe I was already aware," he wrote in *A Small Boy and Others* (1913), "that one way of taking life was to go in for everything and everyone, which kept you abundantly occupied; and the other was to be occupied, quite as occupied, just with the sense and image of it all, and on only a fifth of the actual immersion; a circumstance extremely strange." It is a short step from this autobiographical reflection to the privileged role of consciousness over action that underlies J.'s fictional innovations in plot, character, and narrative technique.

Seeking for his sons "a sensuous education" they were unlikely to obtain in America, Henry James, Sr., took them abroad between 1855 and 1860, arranging tutors and boarding schools in several European countries. They visited myriad churches, but prayed in none. J. developed during these years his "pewless" state, his dislike of ideology, his passion for diverse points of view, and his love for European art and culture. In 1860 he returned to America, where he sat out the Civil War, trying Harvard Law School for a year and champing to return to Europe. After two brief trips abroad in 1869 and 1872 he finally left America for good in 1875, settling first in Paris, and then a year later in London.

The hold of European culture on J.'s imagination cannot be overestimated. His earliest successful story, "A Passionate Pilgrim" (1871), centers on the obsessive yet sinister appeal of the Old World, and in one form or another this theme roused J.'s finest powers, from *Roderick Hudson* (1875) to *The Golden Bowl* (1904). Although *Watch and Ward* (1871) is technically his first novel, *Roderick Hudson* is legitimately viewed as J.'s first characteristic performance. There—in the fable of the talented young American who journeys to Italy to realize his artistic promise and who then comes to ruin in the enterprise—J. sounded his abiding note. Undone by his recklessness and his innocence, Roderick squanders himself, wasting his genius on works he cannot terminate, wasting his feelings on a woman who will betray him. Waste itself emerges as J.'s theme, the waste incurred by an innocent, Emersonian spirit unable to husband its resources or to recognize the tangle of motives lurking both in the self and in others. Already in 1875 the idealistic, journeying spirit has been seen in its American colors; and the cluster of beckoning opportunities, temptations, and traps emerges as experienced, immemorial Europe.

Roderick Hudson metamorphoses into Christopher Newman in J.'s next successful novel, *The American* (1877); this figure achieves its purest form, however, as a woman, Isabel Archer, in J.'s finest early novel, *The Portrait of a Lady* (1881). Even those who dislike J.'s later development agree that *The Portrait of a Lady* is a masterpiece. Isabel's journey from New York to England to Paris and finally to Rome enacts a beautifully modulated passage from youth to maturity, innocence to experience, the illusion of freedom to the awareness of necessity. It is not a bitter novel, however, because the necessity that Isabel discovers is no outward imposition, but rather her own deepest proclivities, as these emerge in the course of her experience. The cast of supporting characters—her charming English cousin Ralph Touchett and his parents, her suitors both American (Caspar Goodwood) and English (Lord Warburton), the accomplished pair who eventually "seduce" her (Madame Merle and Gilbert Osmond)—is fleshed out and nuanced with an authority J. was never to surpass. Capping a group of novels and a host of stories (the well-known "Daisy Miller" [1878] among them) on the "international theme," *The Portrait of a Lady* marks J.'s greatest achievement in the form of the realistic novel. It marks as well the acme of his popularity.

Dickens, Balzac, and Hawthorne were continuous models in J.'s mind; he never ceased to reckon with them. His aesthetic aims, however, may best be described as a midposition between the extremes of George Eliot and Gustave Flaubert. Eliot he saw as the first English novelist to probe moral issues seriously. She alone, in the English tradition, met his standard of *inclusive* treatment of difficult issues. "The essence of moral energy," he wrote in "The Art of Fiction" (1884), "is to survey the whole field." But the problem with Eliot, he later claimed, was her didacticism. Beneath her surfaces he found the limiting insistence on ideology; if you

Henry James

scratched one of her characters you found not flesh and blood but an idea. To free himself from Eliot (more broadly: to free himself from the blinkered innocence of Anglo-American idealism), he turned to Flaubert. During 1875 and 1876 he attended Flaubert's literary Sunday afternoon salons, where he not only met Daudet, Maupassant, and Zola, but also drank in the heady air of free aesthetic inquiry: "It would have been late in the day to propose among them . . . any question as to the degree in which a novel might or might not concern itself with the teaching of a lesson. They had settled these preliminaries long ago" (Leon Edel, *The Life of H. J.*, Vol. II [1962], p. 221).

Yet J. found Flaubert's insistent amorality ultimately as limiting as George Eliot's piety; he began to chafe at Flaubert's rendering "only the visible . . . he [Flaubert] had no faith in the power of the moral to offer a surface . . ." ("Flaubert," 1893). *The power of the moral to offer a surface*: this phrase best captures J.'s own enterprise, his attempt to make visible the drama of the spirit, to follow its movement through the tangle of material objects and obstacles in which it actually, day by day, finds itself. Flaubert's Emma Bovary, J. decided, "is really too small an affair . . . Why did Flaubert choose, as special conduits of the life he proposed to depict, such inferior . . . human specimens?" (a later essay, also titled "Flaubert," 1902). What was missing was not an optimistic ending, but a consciousness capable of extracting the full moral value of the defeat Emma had endured. When J. rewrote Flaubert's novel so as to find the moral in its surface, the novel he achieved was *The Portrait of a Lady*.

During the 1880s J. wrote what his father would have called "interesting failures": three ambitious novels that, drawing on the naturalist vogue of Zola, sought the larger canvas to illuminate social concerns of the day. *The Bostonians* (1885) surveys with knife-edged detachment the struggles and internal contradictions of the feminist movement in Boston. *The Princess Casamassima* (1886), resurrecting two characters from *Roderick Hudson*, centers on violent political disturbances in England. *The Tragic Muse* (1890) explores more blandly some of the inevitable conflicts between political and aesthetic aspirations in the English scene. Of these three novels, the first was attacked in America and praised in England, the second was attacked in England and praised in America, the third elicited neither praise nor blame anywhere. James as a realistic novelist had reached a sort of dead end.

His way out of this dilemma was extraordinary. He began a last-ditch attempt for a large audience, seeking to capture the London stage. The dramas he wrote, however, were based on outdated models of the "well-made play"; and failure, when it came, in 1895, in the form of *Guy Domville*'s opening night fiasco in a London theater, was spectacular. His career as a playwright thus ended, he finally accepted the lyrical inwardness of his imaginative bent, and entered his major phase, writing in the next eight years five remarkable short novels and three full-length masterpieces.

The Spoils of Poynton (1896), *The Other House* (1896), *What Maisie Knew* (1897), *The Awkward Age* (1899), and *The Sacred Fount* (1901) resemble nothing in J.'s oeuvre so much as each other. Drawing creatively on the theater fiasco by fashioning dialogue so self-sufficient that, as on stage, it requires no further explanation, J. structures these novels scenically. In them he moves back and forth between the subjective perceptions of a character and the objective (though mystifying) conversations of a group. No omniscient narrator explains anything. The more limited the center of consciousness—Maisie, Nanda in *The Awkward Age*, the narrator in *The Sacred Fount*—the more interesting the tensions that are generated. He had now created structures that could make the most of the subjective drama of the journeying spirit.

In *The Ambassadors* (1903) J. returned triumphantly to the "international theme." Lambert Strether, middle-aged, well-behaved, and yet secretly hungering for new experiences, is sent by the straitlaced Mrs. Newsome as her special ambassador to France. There he is to retrieve her errant son Chad, who, it is feared, has lost his Puritan bearings while enjoying the pleasures of Parisian society. The ensuing comedy centers irresistibly on Strether's expanding consciousness, as he reluctantly discovers that Chad has, despite his mother's concern, changed for the better. The prose in this novel, as in the two that follow, is of a metaphoric richness and syntactic complexity rarely equaled elsewhere.

The Ambassadors is a comedy, *The Wings of the Dove* (1902) is a tragedy, and *The Golden Bowl* (1904) is something for which we have no adequate categories. In this last completed novel Maggie Verver, the mythically wealthy princess, discovers that her charming Italian husband, Prince Amerigo, has resumed an affair (hitherto unknown) with her closest friend, Charlotte. Since Charlotte has in the meantime, at Maggie's instigation, become married to Maggie's widowed father, Adam Verver, the psychological complications multiply. Moving discreetly among the points of view of the prince, Charlotte, Adam, and their friends the Assinghams, J. focuses the last half of his novel on Maggie's burgeoning consciousness. As she moves from unthinking complicity to full awareness, she enacts the trajectory from innocence to experience that has been J.'s abiding theme ever since *Roderick Hudson*.

Recapturing her husband, mending the marriage between Adam and Charlotte (or apparently doing so: this novel insists on supplying nothing beyond the appearances), managing both of these tasks while outwardly acknowledging neither, Maggie represents J.'s final synthesis of American idealism and European knowingness. The combination is as chilling as it is compelling.

Although J. is primarily a novelist, he also wrote over one hundred impressive short stories. They divide roughly into four categories: stories of the "international theme," of which "Daisy Miller" is the best known; stories of artists and writers—all of these are interesting: perhaps "The Aspern Papers" (1888) and "The Real Thing" (1892) are the finest; ghost stories, of which "The Turn of the Screw" (1898) is the masterpiece, virtually transforming the genre; and stories of "the unlived life," a category all J.'s own, of which "The Beast in the Jungle" (1903) and "The Jolly Corner" (1908) are the most memorable.

J. began his career as a critic, and he maintained that function throughout his life, producing four volumes of essays and numerous uncollected articles. His 1884 piece on "The Art of Fiction" has become a classic statement of the writer's freedom to choose his own form and subject matter: the responsibility of the critic is only to assess what the writer has *done* with his choices. In the same essay J. reveals his own creative principles, defining experience as "an immense sensibility, a kind of huge spider-web of the finest silken threads suspended in the chamber of consciousness, and catching every air-borne particle in its tissue. It is the very atmosphere of the mind . . ." Experience emerges as a function not of objective actions, but of subjective impressions—not the raw materials but what the mind and heart succeed in making of them.

Throughout his life J. was a literary figure among literary figures—meeting Turgenev and the Flaubert circle in the 1870s, becoming a friend and supporter of Ford Madox FORD, Joseph CONRAD, Edith WHARTON, and Stephen Crane in his later years. By the turn of the century he was held in high repute by cognoscenti: they called him—half playfully, half seriously—The Master. After World War I broke out, J. became horrified by the tardiness of America's entry into the war. As a gesture of devotion to his adopted country he renounced his American citizenship and in 1915 became a naturalized British subject. Two months before his death he was awarded the prestigious Order of Merit.

In perhaps the most suggestive statement yet made about J., T. S. Eliot said that "he had mind so fine that no idea could violate it." The statement means not that J. repudiated ideas, but that his fiction revealed them never as abstractions, but as the property of thinking, feeling people. Free of overt ideology, "pewless," J.'s fiction served as an exemplary late-Victorian attempt to escape the emphatic moralizing of his Victorian forebears. It was welcomed on those terms by modernists like Conrad, Ford, and Virginia WOOLF, all of whom found moral issues matters to whisper rather than shout about. In addition, J.'s ceaseless effort to remove himself from his fiction—to let his imaginative world speak in its own voice, not his—acted as a point of reference for the modernist urge away from confession and toward impersonality. To this end J.'s fiction—and perhaps more importantly his prefaces to the New York Edition (1907–17) of his works—meshed smoothly with the nascent New Critical emphasis on showing rather than telling, on responsible craft rather than oracular utterance.

In the last sixty years J. has been subject to a wide range of critical postures: tellingly attacked by E. M. FORSTER in *Aspects of the Novel* (1927) and by Van Wyck Brooks in *The Pilgrimage of H. J.* (1925); neutrally interrogated by Edmund WILSON in *The*

Triple Thinkers (1948) and by F. W. Dupee in *H. J.* (1951); and lavishly praised by Percy Lubbock in *The Art of Fiction* (1921), Laurence Holland in *The Expense of Vision* (1964) and Leon Edel, most extensively in *The Life of H. J.* (5 vols., 1953–72). Since the Vietnam War J.'s reputation has, it seems, been somewhat in eclipse; readers attuned to violence, apocalypse, and the grotesque turn the pages of his novels in bewilderment. But he will endure because, as he wrote to Henry ADAMS on the eve of World War I, he remained, despite all, "that queer monster, the artist, an obstinate finality, an inexhaustible sensibility."

FURTHER WORKS: *A Passionate Pilgrim, and Other Tales* (1875); *Transatlantic Sketches* (1875); *French Poets and Novelists* (1878); *The Europeans* (1878); *The Madonna of the Future, and Other Tales* (1879); *Confidence* (1879); *Hawthorne* (1879); *Washington Square* (1880); *Portraits of Places* (1883); *The Siege of London* (1883); *Tales of Three Cities* (1884); *A Little Tour in France* (1884); *The Author of Beltraffio* (1885); *Stories Revived* (1885); *Partial Portraits* (1888); *The Reverberator* (1888); *The Aspern Papers* (1888); *A London Life* (1889); *The Lesson of the Master* (1892); *The Real Thing, and Other Tales* (1893); *The Private Life* (1893); *Essays in London and Elsewhere* (1893); *The Wheel of Time* (1893); *Theatricals* (1894–95); *Terminations* (1895); *Embarrassments* (1896); *In the Cage* (1898); *The Two Magics* (1898); *The Soft Side* (1900); *The Better Sort* (1903); *William Wetmore Story and His Friends* (1903); *English Hours* (1905); *The Question of Our Speech, and the Lesson of Balzac* (1905); *The American Scene* (1907); *Italian Hours* (1909); *The Finer Grain* (1910); *The Outcry* (1911); *A Small Boy and Others* (1913); *Notes of a Son and Brother* (1914); *Notes on Novelists* (1914); *England at War: An Essay* (1915); *The Question of Mind* (1915); *The Middle Years* (1917); *The Ivory Tower* (1917); *The Sense of the Past* (1917); *Within the Rim, and Other Essays* (1919); *The Letters of H. J.* (2 vols., 1920); *Notes and Reviews* (1921); *The Novels and Stories of H. J.* (35 vols., 1921–23); *The Art of the Novel: Critical Prefaces* (1934); *The Notebooks of H. J.* (1947); *The Scenic Art* (1948); *The Complete Plays of H. J.* (1949); *The Selected Letters of H. J.* (1955); *H. J.: Autobiography* (1956); *The Painter's Eye* (1956); *Parisian Sketches* (1957); *Literary Reviews and Essays* (1957); *The Complete Tales of H. J.* (12 vols., 1962–64); *Letters* (3 vols., 1974–80)

BIBLIOGRAPHY: Beach, J. W., *The Method of H. J.* (1918); Lubbock, P., *The Craft of Fiction* (1921): 142–202; Brooks, V. W., *The Pilgrimage of H. J.* (1925); Matthiessen, F. O., *H. J.: The Major Phase* (1944); Matthiessen, F. O., ed., *The James Family* (1947); Wilson, E., *The Triple Thinkers*, rev. ed. (1948): 88–132; Leavis, F. R., *The Great Tradition* (1948); Dupee, F. W., *H. J.* (1951); Bewley, M., *The Complex Fate* (1952); Edel, L., *The Life of H. J.* (5 vols., 1953–72); Anderson, Q., *The American H. J.* (1957); Wegelin, C., *The Image of Europe in H. J.* (1958); Poirier, R., *The Comic Sense of H. J.* (1960); Cargill, O., *The Novels of H. J.* (1961); Edel, L., and Laurence, D. H., *A Bibliography of H. J.*, 2nd ed. (1961); Krook, D., *The Ordeal of Consciousness in H. J.* (1962); Holland, L., *The Expense of Vision: Essays on the Craft of H. J.* (1964); Lebowitz, N., *The Imagination of Loving: H. J.'s Legacy to the Novel* (1965); Tanner, T., *The Reign of Wonder: Naïveté and Reality in American Literature* (1965): 259–335; Sears, S., *The Negative Imagination: Form and Perception in the Novels of H. J.* (1970); Weinstein, P., *H. J. and the Requirements of the Imagination* (1971); Chatman, S., *The Later Style of H. J.* (1972); Yeazell, R., *Language and Knowledge in the Late Novels of H. J.* (1976); Anderson, C. R., *Person, Place, and Thing in H. J.'s Novels* (1977)

—PHILIP M. WEINSTEIN

J.'s critical genius comes out most tellingly in his mastery over, his baffling escape from, Ideas; a mastery and an escape which are perhaps the last test of a superior intelligence. He had a mind so fine that no idea could violate it . . . . J. in his novels is like the best French critics in maintaining a point of view, a viewpoint untouched by the parasite idea. He is the most intelligent man of his generation. [1918]

T. S. Eliot, "On H. J.," in F. W. Dupee, ed., *The Question of H. J.* (1945), pp. 110–11

He has, in the first place, a very short list of characters . . . . In the second place, the characters, beside being few in number, are constructed on very stingy lines. They are incapable of fun, of rapid motion, of carnality, and of nine-tenths of heroism. Their clothes will not take off, the diseases that ravage them are anonymous, like the sources of their income, their servants are noiseless or resemble themselves, no social explanation of the world we know is possible for them, for there are no stupid people in their world, no barriers of language, and no poor. Even their sensations are limited. They can land in Europe and look at works of art and at each other but that is all. Maimed creatures can alone breathe in H. J.'s pages—maimed yet specialized. They remind one of the exquisite deformities who haunted Egyptian art in the reign of Akhenaton—huge heads and tiny legs, but nevertheless charming. In the following reign they disappear.

E. M. Forster, *Aspects of the Novel* (1927, rpt. 1954), pp. 160–61

Since other novelists have used and misused the J. novel and since by contagion it has modified the actual practice of many novelists who never read J. at all, we had better try to say what the J. novel is. It is consistent to its established variety of skeleton forms; it is faithful to its established method of reporting; and it insists on its chosen center of attraction. To do these things it first of all gets rid of the omniscient author; the author is never allowed to intrude directly or in his own person; the story is always some created person's sense of it, or that of some group of persons, so that we see or feel the coercive restriction of someone's conscious experience of the story as the medium through which we ourselves feel it. Secondly, the J. novel uses device after device, not merely to invite the reader's ordinary attention, but to command his extraordinary attention . . . . The scenes between persons are dramatized as substance, not as ornament; true action is in speech and gesture; and thus the dialogue creates a new form of attention, in which we always sail close-hauled or trembling on the tack. As the the command to attend is obeyed, the reader learns a new game which, as it seems to partake of actual experience, he can take for truth; and which, as it shows a texture of sustained awareness never experienced in life, he knows to be art. To gain that effect, to make art truth, is the whole object of J.'s addiction to the forms of fiction . . . [1947]

R. P. Blackmur, "H. J.," in Robert E. Spiller, et al., eds., *Literary History of the United States*, 3rd ed. rev. (1963), p. 1062

In many of his books—in *The Ambassadors*, for instance—the characters remind one a little of Proust's. But unlike Proust, he wipes the shadows of damnation from under their eyes, and for their sakes he averts his gaze at embarrassing moments. Little Bilham cries out for the Faubourg St. Germain as Proust presented it; but he is safer with J., because J. will never bring age and ruins toppling on his head . . . . The terrorist explosions toward which his tremendous insights would, in any other writer, move, he must at all events avoid, for the fine high windows of the Jamesian villa are no less breakable than they are valuable. He knows that the material conditions for his values are too deeply embedded in the lives of their opposites to destroy the one without endangering the other. Unlike Proust, he will not play Samson and pull the temple down on our guilty heads. In the end he is a kind of Edwardian Atlas holding up the old cracked heavens.

Marius Bewley, *The Complex Fate* (1952), p. 76

The father's desire to surround his boys with "an atmosphere of freedom" was itself surrounded by contradictions . . . . The senior Henry gave him, he felt, no sense of values save to realize the value of *all* life and *all* experience. At one point the novelist likens his brother and himself to Romulus and Remus, disowned by the parent, thrown into the Tiber of Life, left to flounder as best they could and called upon to build Rome—that is to have the right answers to the Divine Truth which the father affirmed was all around them. The novelist reasoned that this free-and-easy mode of education—or absence thereof—was the best thing that could have happened to him: it made him "convert"—everything had to be translated into his own terms and rendered in the light of his own inner resources which in the end helped him to bring order into his world. He had a terrible need for order, for design, for apprehending—and later communicating—the world around him in an elaborately organized fashion. It stemmed undoubtedly from the disordered fashion in which, as a boy, he was asked to cope with it.

Leon Edel, *The Life of H. J.*, Vol. I (1953), pp. 115–16

It is not simply in the organization of character, dialogue, and action that H. J. reveals The Moral Passion, nor is it reflected further only in his treatment of surroundings, but it represents itself and its

ideal in the increasing scrupulosity of the style: precision of definition, respect for nuance, tone, the multiplying presence of enveloping metaphors, the winding around the tender center of ritual lines, like the approach of the devout and worshipful to the altar, these circumlocutions at once protecting the subject and slowing the advance so that the mere utility of the core is despaired of and it is valued solely in the contemplative sight. The value of life lies ultimately in the experienced quality of it, in the integrity of the given not in the usefulness of the taken . . . . He does not find in today only what is needful for tomorrow. His aim is rather to appreciate and to respect the things of his experience and to set them, finally, free.

William Gass, "The High Brutality of Good Intentions," *Accent*, 18 (1958), 71

Art or aesthetic reality was not for J. an order of value to be ranked in relation to others but a process of creation to be engaged in, with a product—the union of form and vision which in the late Prefaces he came to call a *marriage*—to be fashioned and enjoyed. And the process of making his novels is what joined him to the world he knew and rendered in his art and kept him from sorting his characters into categories of good and evil with serenely Olympian assurance and detachment. Neither his criticism nor his fiction makes paramount the rigor of moral judgment . . . . We critics have tended to make J. guilty of the "'flagrant' morality" which his father taught him to disdain. The moral implications of J.'s fiction are to be found not only and not principally in the judgments he passes on his characters but in the fully creative function of J.'s form, whether comic or otherwise. His form often creates the follies it mocks, and on occasion he celebrates them rather than simply evaluating or correcting them. Like gods and other parents, authors not only confront moral problems but create them, and J. constantly confessed this fact in his fiction. One of his chief contributions to the lyric dimension of English fiction is his distinctive fusion of moral and technical concerns, which has the effect of founding his moral vision on the act and form of intimate confession.

Laurence Holland, *The Expense of Vision: Essays on the Craft of H. J.* (1964), pp. ix–x

The human mind is, for J., by definition a haunted mind. The haunting, furthermore, was implicit for him in the nature of consciousness, as the mode by which we both encounter life and are detached from it. For J., "experience" had two meanings, which themselves stand in an analogical relation to this opposition in the make-up of consciousness. On the one hand, experience meant action: the effective imposition of one's will upon the external world, participation, mastery; on the other, it meant *reaction*, a response of the mind, "a mark made on the intelligence," contemplation, passivity.

The first was something J. could not imagine for himself . . . . By a feat of intelligence . . . he transformed the latter definition into the one delineating the superior mode of being. Finally, experience wasn't experience unless it stirred that "vibration," and anything that did so—a mere act of seeing—qualified. But the other notion lingered in his imagination . . . .

His characters repeat the process their author engages in: they construct imaginary worlds with their "visiting" minds, worlds that are the objectification of their desires but that are also unreal and doomed to collapse when brought into conjunction with the "facts." The facts are always that things are different from what a given character had wanted. The basic pattern of J.'s work is the creation and collapse of the fiction, its failure.

> Sallie Sears, *The Negative Imagination: Form and Perception in the Novels of H. J.* (1970), pp. 126–27

JAMMES, Francis

French poet and novelist, b. 2 Dec. 1868, Tournay; d. 1 Nov. 1938, Hasparren

J., educated in Pau and Bordeaux, worked for a while in a law office before deciding to live by his pen. He spent most of his life in his native southwestern part of France, first in Orthez, later in Hasparren, in the Basque country.

J. began to write while still in high school. His literary breakthrough came with the publication of his collection of poetry *De l'angélus de l'aube à l'angélus du soir* (1898; from the morning prayer to the evening prayer), which is among the poet's most important works. It already contained all the themes that J. was to develop further in later volumes, the principal one being that of nature. With a naïveté that at times appears somewhat studied, J. writes about the various aspects of rustic life. He is a keen observer of nature who expresses, with disarming simplicity and sincerity, a love of fields and flowers, of mountains and rivers, a childlike affection for all animals, and a great compassion for the poor and suffering. His very romantic sensibility is conveyed through sometimes strikingly sensuous images.

J. did not pretend to be a profound thinker. His aim was "to tell his truth," that is, his feelings, emotions, and dreams. Such a refreshingly unpretentious look at himself and nature was greeted as a welcome change from the elitist hermeticism of SYMBOLISM. J. did, however, inherit from symbolism the form he used, a kind of free verse consisting of irregular lines of varied length.

In 1905, under the influence of Paul CLAUDEL, and prompted by his own experience of Lourdes as well as his admiration for Saint Francis of Assisi, J. returned to the Catholic faith he had abandoned in his youth. Thereafter, strong religious overtones became characteristic of his writing. In *Les géorgiques chrétiennes* (1912; Christian georgics) he describes the life of a peasant family who, whether they cultivate their fields or feed the animals, or do any other chore, unceasingly praise God's greatness. In keeping with poetic conventions, J. employed the classical alexandrine line.

J. is also well known as a writer of fiction. His early narratives possess great charm; they are natural, romantic, and delightfully old-fashioned. J.'s masterpiece of lyrical prose is perhaps *Le roman du lièvre* (1903; *Romance of the Rabbit*, 1920), the tale of a hare who, having followed Saint Francis to heaven, yearns to escape from the eternal blissfulness of heavenly animal existence to the dangers and excitements of the terrestrial life he had left behind. If most of these fictional works seem to be somewhat too didactic, they are nevertheless remarkable for the wonderful descriptions of nature they contain. J.'s conversion is also noticeable in his fiction; the later works are often colored with overly religious sentimentalism. Although the stories are well told, there is no complicated psychology in J.'s novels. Frequently the characters are too idealized, and they rarely assume a convincing personality of their own, remaining largely types.

J., who has been referred to as a symbolist, neosymbolist, or *naturiste*, never belonged to any systematic school of poetry. He always was only himself, in the process creating *Jammisme*, which embraces but one guiding principle, "the truth that is the praise of God." It is innocence, simplicity, and humility; it extols the beauty of the native soil and the virtues of family life; it is adoration of God and love of all He created. This attitude finds its perfect expression in the poet's totally unpretentious style. His vocabulary is surprisingly simple, at times even childlike, but always very effective when combined with his exceptional gift of observation.

FURTHER WORKS: *Clara d'Ellébeuse* (1899); *Le deuil des primevères* (1901); *Almaïde d'Etremont* (1901); *Le triomphe de la vie* (1902); *Pomme d'Anis* (1904); *Tristesses* (1905); *L'église habillée de feuilles* (1906); *Clairières dans le ciel* (1906); *Ma fille Bernadette* (1910; *My Daughter Bernadette*, 1933); *Cinq prières pour le temps de la guerre* (1916); *Monsieur le curé d'Ozeron* (1918); *La vierge et les sonnets* (1919); *Le poète rustique* (1920); *Cloches pour deux mariages* (1924); *Les Robinsons basques* (1925); *Ma France poétique* (1926); *Basses-Pyrénées: Histoires naturelles et poétiques* (1926); *Le rêve franciscain* (1927); *Champêtreries et méditations* (1930); *L'arc-en-ciel des amours* (1931); *L'école buissonnière; ou, Cours libre de proses choisies* (1930); *L'Antigyde; ou, Élie de Nacre* (1932); *Le crucifix du poète* (1935); *Alouette* (1935); *De tout temps à jamais* (1935); *Le pélerin de Lourdes* (1936); *Sources* (1936); *Sources et feux* (1944); *Solitude peuplée* (1945); *Le patriarche et son troupeau* (1949. FURTHER WORKS IN ENGLISH: *Homer Had a Dog* (1946); *The Early White Narcissi* (1953); *Selected Poems of F. J.* (1976, bilingual)

BIBLIOGRAPHY: Lowell, A., *Six French Poets* (1916): 213–68; Drake, W. A., *Contemporary European Writers* (1928): 243–51; Flory, A., *F. J.* (1941); Soulairol, J., *F. J.* (1941); Inda, J.-P, *Du faune au patriarche* (1952); Mallet, R., *Le Jammisme* (1961); Mallet, R., *F. J., sa vie, son œuvre* (1961); Van der Burght, R., and L., *F. J., le jeune Chrétien* (1961)

—BLANDINE M. RICKERT

JANDL, Ernst

Austrian poet and dramatist, b. 1 Aug. 1925, Vienna

J. served in the army during World War II. After his release from an American POW camp in 1946, he began studying German and English at the University of Vienna, where he earned his doctorate in 1950. He has served on and off as a teacher at various high schools in Vienna. He started writing in 1952. In 1954 he began his lifelong friendship with the Austrian writer Friederike MAYRÖCKER. He has held guest lectureships at several universities in Germany and was a visiting writer at the University of Texas at Austin in 1971. In 1973 he was a cofounder of the Graz Authors Society. He often reads his works in connection with orchestral performances. He has won over fifteen prizes for his work, including the prestigious Büchner Prize in 1984. He still resides in Vienna.

Although J.'s works are usually ascribed to the concrete school, this classification is misleading, for he never expresses a radical mistrust of language, and his works always have some message connected with the outside world. His playful experimentation with the linguistic medium usually has a humorous, didactic, contemplative, or introspective intent, and his poems and plays are never just comments on language alone. J. has developed a whole scale of innovations, which he constantly improves and amplifies. This accounts for his continued popularity with the reading public, who quickly forgot other less versatile experimenters.

J.'s first collection of poems, *andere augen* (1956; other eyes), was fairly traditional, but he soon was to develop his unique style. His most important early collections are *laut und luise* (1966; sound and Luise) and *der künstliche baum* (1970; the artificial tree), both of which reflect his output for the preceding several years. These volumes contain a wide variety: visual poems, texts meant to be read aloud, dialect poems, puns on foreign languages, montages, poems which repeat phonemes, and combinations of all of these. Inevitably the last line shocks, surprises, or bemuses, and drives home the message. Thematically the poems run the gamut of human experience, with a concentration on the earthy and the mundane. Together with the anthology *sprechblasen* (1968; speech bubbles), which contains only acoustic poems, these books made J. extremely popular in Austria and Germany and firmly established him in literary circles. Contributing to his success was the wickedly wry humor of many of the poems as well as J.'s extraordinary ability to perform his work in public.

In the late 1970s and early 1980s, J. entered into a more somber stage of his writing. In a series of poetry volumes, *die bearbeitung der mütze* (1978; the treatment of the cap), *der gelbe hund* (1980; the yellow dog), and *selbstporträt des schachspielers als trinkende uhr* (1983; self portrait of the chess player as a drinking clock), he discusses old age, death, problems with writing, depressions, his uneasy relationship with Mayröcker, and an identity crisis. We see little of his usual caustic wit and instead meet a tortured individual whose writing appears to be his only solace. The language has been likened to guest workers' or children's German in that the structures are simple and verbal infinitives prevail. It is as if J.'s collapsing self-image is reflected in a decaying language. In his most recent volume, *idyllen* (1989; idylls), there is also a somber mood, but there are some indications J. is regaining a more positive outlook on life.

J.'s play *aus der fremde* (1980; from abroad) was extremely popular with audiences and was performed on dozens of German-language stages. It details a little over a day in the life of two writers, a "he" and a "she," who speak to each other in 655 triplets whose verbs are all in the subjunctive. The play is clearly autobiographical, with J.'s creative crisis, his friendship with Mayröcker, and his daily life at the foreground. In spite of the potentially depressing thematics the play is both humorous and fascinating.

J. may be Austria's best-known contemporary poet and one of its best. His works are both entertaining and incisive without being ponderous, and this should ensure him a permanent place in literary history.

FURTHER WORKS: *lange gedichte* (1964); *klare gerührt* (1964); *mai hart lieb zapfen eibe hold* (1965); *Hosi-Anna!* (1965); *no music please* (1967); *flöda und der schwan* (1971); *fünf mann menschen* (1971, with Friederike Mayröcker); *dingfest* (1973); *übung mit buben* (1973); *die männer: ein film* (1973); *serienfuss* (1974); *wischen möchten* (1974); *für alle* (1974); *der versteckte hirte* (1975); *alle freut was alle freut* (1975); *drei schörspiele* (1975, with Friederike Mayröcker); *die schöne kunst des schreibens* (1976); *klatschmohn* (1977); *augenspiel* (1981); *falamaleikum* (1983); *das öffnen und schliessen des mundes* (1985); *gesammelte werke* (1985); *ottos mops hopst* (1988); *das röcheln der mona lisa* (1990)

BIBLIOGRAPHY: Acker, R., "E. J. and Friederike Mayröcker: A Study of Modulation and Crisis," *WLT*, 55, 4 (Autumn 1981): 597–602; Schmidt-Dengler, W., ed., *E. J.: Materialienbuch* (1982); special J. issue *manuskripte*, 88 (1985); König, F., "E. J. and Concrete Poetry," in Daviau, D. G., ed., *Major Figures of Contemporary Austrian Literature* (1987): 265–92; Siblewski, K., ed., *E. J.: Texte, Daten, Bilder* (1990)

—ROBERT ACKER

JANSSON, Tove

Finnish children's book author, short-story writer, and novelist (writing in Swedish), b. 9 Aug. 1914, Helsinki

The daughter of the Finnish sculptor Viktor Jansson (1886–1958), J., too, first began in the field of art. It was the least serious of her artistic endeavors, as an illustrator of children's books, that led her to writing. Today, she is the most widely read of Finland's authors because of her "Moomintrolls." In fact, for a time she reached beyond the world of books, drawing a cartoon series about the trolls that was carried in newspapers around the world (1952–59).

Her debut as a writer came in 1945, with *Småtrollen och den stora översvämningen* (the little trolls and the great flood); out of this rather simple beginning, there developed the realm of the Moomintrolls, with their generosity and tolerance, their inventiveness and powers of imagination (which reflect salient qualities of their creator), their dislike of sternness and pedantic order, and their close if somewhat haphazard family life. As a rule, the Moomintrolls have none of the malice attributed to the trolls of Nordic myth; instead, they resemble cheerful miniature hippopotami who walk, or waddle, upright. They are inveterate if nervous adventurers, but prefer not to wander far from Moominvalley. The canon of the Moomin books consists of *Kometjakten* (1946; *Comet in Moominland*, 1950), *Trollkarlens hatt* (1948; *Finn Family Moomintroll*, 1950); *Muminpappans bravader* (1950; *The Happy Moomin*, 1950), *Farlig midsommar* (1954; *Moominsummer Madness*, 1955), *Trollvinter* (1957; *Moominland Midwinter*, 1958), *Det osynliga barnet och andra berättelser* (1962; *Tales from Moominvalley*, 1963), *Pappan och havet* (1965; *Moominpappa at Sea*, 1966), and *Sent i November* (1970; *Moominvalley in November*, 1971). There are also two shorter tales with extensive illustrations: *Hur gick det sen? Boken om Mymlan, Mumintrollet och lilla My* (1952; *Moomin, Mymble and Little My*, 1953) and *Vem skall trösta Knyttet?* (1960; *Who Will*

Comfort Toffle?, 1960). (Several of the books have been given new titles in subsequent editions.) A darkening is perceptible in the later volumes; the inhabitants' growing fear of natural catastrophe becomes more and more apparent, and an atmosphere of loneliness seems gradually to get the upper hand over the happy spirit of community that had prevailed at the start.

With the Moomin books J. offers an equivalent to the "moral messages" of her distant predecessor in Finland's literature for children, Zachris Topelius (1818–1898), whose tales preached patriotism, a sense of duty, and industry. J., however, inculcates a set of softer virtues, among them kindness, the ability to laugh at one's self, and a love of life's small pleasures.

As the Moomin series was drawing to its close, J. began to write directly for a mature public. She has produced three books of short stories—*Bildhuggarens dotter* (1968; *The Sculptor's Daughter*, 1976), the very title of which gives the collection an air of autobiography; *Lyssnerskan* (1971; the woman who hearkens); and *Dockskåpet, och andra berättelser* (1978; the doll's house, and other stories)—and two novels—*Sommarboken* (1972; *The Summer Book*, 1977), composed of views, happy and sad, of a child and its grandmother in the Finnish skerries, and *Solstaden* (1974; *Sun City*, 1977), an unsentimental description of an old-people's home in St. Petersburg, Florida. In the children's books, the idyll, often threatened, is never destroyed; in the narratives for adults, the idyll is frequently artificial, or it undergoes a terrifying metamorphosis, as in "Ekorren" (the squirrel), the finale of *Lyssnerskan*.

BIBLIOGRAPHY: Fleisher, F. and B., "T. J. and the Moomin Family," *ASR*, 51 (1963): 47–54; Jones, W. G., *T. J.: Pappan och havet, Studies in Swedish Literature*, No. 11 (1979); Jones, W. G., "Studies in Obsession: The New Art of T. J.," *BF*, 14 (1981): 60–62; Jones, W. G., *T. J.* (1984)

—GEORGE C. SCHOOLFIELD

JAPANESE LITERATURE

As the 20th c. began, the chief impetus in Japanese literature involved a concerted effort to break with older Japanese traditions, an impetus that has had both its positive and negative side. On the positive side, Japanese writers embraced Western literary movements and theories and tried to model some works on particular European or American examples. Although the result in many cases was imitative, the impulse to reach out and to adapt Western literature to native needs was basically constructive, with Western modes of literature imparting fresh vitality. On the negative side, writers pointedly rejected traditional Japanese myths, archetypes, and literary conventions, turning away from their own heritage.

But tradition dies hard in Japan, where the conservative impulse is strong. Older forms of prose, poetry, and drama have survived in 20th-c. Japan, albeit undergoing transformation. Even today traditional forms of lyric poetry, such as the thirty-one-syllable *tanka* (or *waka*) and the seventeen-syllable *haiku* (a 20th-c. term for an independent short poem that emerged from the *haikai*) remain popular along with a modern style of free verse inspired by contact with the West. Traditional modes of drama—Nō, Kabuki, and the Bunraku (the Japanese puppet theater)—flourish together with Western-style realistic plays and postmodernist theater.

Likewise, modern fiction, which has emerged as the principal literary genre, after having overshadowed earlier lyrical and dramatic forms, also remains indebted to an indigenous lineage of narrative prose that goes back to chronicles compiled largely in the Chinese language in the 8th c. and to purely fictional narratives written in Japanese that date from the 10th c. This earlier tradition of narrative prose, often interspersed with thirty-one-syllable lyric poems, culminated in *Genji monogatari* (c. early 11th c.; *The Tale of Genji*, 6 vols., 1925–33; new tr., 1976).

During the first three decades of the 20th c. the modern counterpart of older forms of narrative prose proved particularly amenable to expressing the most significant theme in 20th-c. Japanese literature, namely awareness of the self, and Japanese writers began espousing the ideology of individualism. Thus, a characteristically Japanese version of the novel, the *shishōsetsu* (also called *watakushi-shōsetsu*), literally, "I-novel," came into being. Concurrently, Japanese authors capitalized on newly found freedom to deal with topics that suggested social and political awareness. An exemplar of the early 20th-c. *shishōsetsu* is *An'ya kōro* (serial pub., 1921–28; 2 vols., 1938; *A Dark Night's Passing*, 1976), by SHIGA Naoya. An example of an early 20th-c. novel that deals with social and political awareness is *Hakai* (1906; *The Broken Commandment*, 1974), by SHIMAZAKI Tōson. In the words of NATSUME Sōseki, a critic as well as an outstanding and widely translated novelist, *Hakai* was "the first [genuine] novel of the Meiji era [1867–1912]."

At the same time that the *shishōsetsu* deserves to be seen as a manifestation of a new-found sense of individual identity, reflecting the process of Westernization, this species of modern Japanese novel also evinces connections with earlier Japanese literary genres such as the *nikki* ("diary") and the *zuihitsu* ("miscellaneous essay"), two forms that involved a conception of self, as distinct from that of group or corporate self. Certain situations in *An'ya kōro*, moreover, call to mind close parallels with *Genji monogatari*, the outstanding achievement of all ages in Japanese literature. Likewise, the idea of a socially committed literature predates *Hakai*, being found, for instance, in late-18th-and early-19th-c. tales and romances by Ueda Akinari (1734–1809) and Takizawa Bakin (1767–1848), both of whose great moral concern betrays an indebtedness to Chinese literature.

Besides the dichotomies of old and new, native and Western, self and other, which permeate 20th-c. Japanese literature, certain other dualities may also be perceived. One of these is the split between the so-called *jun-bungaku* ("pure literature") and *taishū bungaku* (literally, "mass literature," or by extension, "popular literature"). Unavoidably, these terms imply class differences of high and low, just as in earlier times there existed similar distinctions, such as *gabun* ("elegant writings") and *zokubun* ("common writings"). Likewise, *tanka* on the one hand had its aristocratic origin in salons of court poets, and *haiku* on the other hand derived from plebeian groups of ordinary citizens. Despite the modernization of these forms by MASAOKA Shiki and the composition of thirty-one-syllable *tanka* on everyday topics in a new, modern idiom by poets such as ISHIKAWA Takuboku, the old associations with a particular social class linger. The earlier dramatic forms of Nō and Kabuki also continue to have overtones of social class, the former being thought to belong to an elite level of society, the latter to the ordinary people. One of the 20th-c. authors most adept at creating both "pure" and "popular" literature was MISHIMA Yukio; his *Shiosai* (1954; *The Sound of Waves*, 1956) is representative of the latter category, and *Kinkakuji* (1956; *The Temple of the Golden Pavilion*, 1959) of the former.

Among other general points that deserve attention, several may be singled out. Centralization of Japanese literary activity in the capital city of Tokyo, for instance, has its earlier counterpart in literary history. The names of literary periods (Nara, Heian, Kamakura, Muromachi, Edo) identify literary activity with centers of political administration. In this sense the 20th c. may well be thought of as the Tokyo period. One of the first 20th-c. Japanese authors to exploit the sense of Tokyo as a distinctive place and of its people as being worthy of literary attention was NAGAI Kafū, himself a native of the city and heir to the older traditions of Edo. To an unprecedented degree modern novelists, poets, dramatists, and critics live and work in the city of Tokyo and depend on a system of communications centered in the modern capital of Japan.

Closely related to the concentration of literary activity in Tokyo, newspapers and serials in 20th-c. Japan serve as the primary medium of literary publication, having also absorbed the function of promulgating ephemeral forms of literature such as the *kusazōshi* ("chapbooks") of Japan, popular in the late 18th and early 19th cs. (The importance of seasonal celebrations and the seasonal element in traditional Japanese aesthetics also deserves consideration in any analysis of the function of newspaper and serial literature in Japan.) The book version of a novel, for instance, even today often follows its appearance in the daily, weekly, or monthly press. Moreover, literary men and women are public personalities to a greater degree than in English-speaking countries, a fact that gives authors added reason for living and working in the Tokyo area. IZUMI Kyōka best exemplifies an early-20th-c. Japanese author who began his career and sustained it by writing popular fiction that appeared serially, that exploited traditional aesthetic sensibilities, and that brought him public acclaim.

One other noteworthy characteristic of 20th-c. Japanese literature is the form of language of most literary works. The modern colloquial Japanese language has become established as the preeminent medium for literary expression. Previously, there existed a much larger gap than now between the linguistic forms used in literary texts and ordinary discourse. Although this change has taken place gradually, two stages may be singled out. The first came late in the 19th c., when efforts to find a suitable idiom for translating Western literature into Japanese began in earnest. Most of all, FUTABATEI Shimei deserves to be remembered for his efforts to bring literary composition more closely into line with the idiom of everyday speech. The second stage dates from the period following World War II, when from 1948 to 1952 a number of reforms in language and education took place. All the while there has been a decline in the use of Chinese, the earliest literary language in Japan. Natsume Sōseki, for example, is sometimes called the last important 20th-c. author to have left a body of poetry in Chinese. Meantime, literature in translation has flourished. In the late 1970s, for instance, a specialized monthly journal, *Hon'yaku no sekai*, devoted to the theory and practice of translation, appeared.

Fiction

A new era in Japanese literature following the Russo-Japanese war (1904–5) brought fame and popularity to many young writers, and 20th-c. world literature, with all its complexity, took root in Japan. Writers, several of whom remained active into the 1940s and 1950s, felt a surge of inspiration and confidence after Japan forced Russia to sue for peace.

By 1906 Japanese naturalism began supplanting romanticism. Innovations by an intense group of young writers in their thirties hastened the break with tradition. The naturalistic novel was established by KUNIKIDA Doppo, Shimazaki Tōson, and Tayama Katai (1871–1930), along with Iwano Hōmei (1873–1919) and Tokuda Shūsei (1871–1943), whose common goal was to depict life as it is, not glossing over its seamier side. Chiefly out of their work arose the *shishōsetsu*, oftentimes a type of autobiographical confessional in which a semifictional hero and an actual writer tend to be identified.

In their efforts to oppose naturalism, Natsume Sōseki and MORI Ōgai, both several years older than the above-mentioned writers, rose to prominence. Mori and Natsume still hold a firm place in the Japanese reader's affections. Natsume's crisp conversational style has influenced young writers particularly. In *Kusamakura* (1906; *Unhuman Tour*, 1927; new tr., *Three-Cornered World*, 1965), he taught that the leisure moments one devotes to art and letters offer the sole relief from the unavoidable suffering of existence, an uplifting belief contrary to the naturalists' creed. Natsume's philosophy and theory of literature, in spite of his period of study in England, show an affinity for those of the earlier *haikai* master, Matsuo Bashō (1644–1694). In *Kokoro* (1914; *Kokoro*, 1941; new tr., 1957), written toward the end of his life, he granted man only three equally dreary choices: death, madness, or religion. Natsume's thought therefore combined "art for art's sake" and pronounced Buddhist tenets.

Mori, who began as a romantic, turned to historical fiction and to belief in stoic self-discipline. A prodigious worker, he combined a medical and military career with authorship in the novel, drama, poetry, criticism, translation, scholarship, and philosophy. One edition of his complete works fills fifty-three volumes. During the last decade of his life he devoted his talent to a series of historical stories for which he is best remembered. Many 20th-c. Japanese writers, late in their careers, have similarly immersed themselves in their own national tradition.

Near the end of the Meiji era and into the Taishō era (1912–26), a group of writers who shared their disapproval of the excess of the naturalists published a periodical called *Shirakaba* (1910–23). Humanitarian in outlook and aristocratic in background and temperament, the group's members included Shiga Naoya, Arishima Takeo (1878–1923), Mushakoji Saneatsu (1885–1976), and Satomi Ton (b. 1888). Although the boundary between naturalist and antinaturalist now seems vague, such distinctions at least show how modern writers in Japan have tended to band together into small independent groups. One of the leading writers who first published prior to 1912 is TANIZAKI Jun'ichirō, who explored human life with daring, sensitivity, and psychological acumen. His writing appeals readily to Western readers, and he rates as one of the eminent literary figures of the 20th c.

Taishō literature usually includes several years of Meiji and the early part of the Shōwa era (1926 to the present). Until recently Japanese commentators have criticized Taishō authors for failing to transcend traditional, feudal, or nationalistic concepts. Nevertheless, the authors of the 1910s and 1920s produced delicately wrought detail and displayed acute perception. Some writers, to be sure, shirked social responsibility and feigned moral decadence, but Western readers may readily discover untranslated literary works that are at once original and part of the 20th-c. *Zeitgeist*. Reevaluation of the contribution of Taishō authors to the creation of a distinctly modern sensibility is just getting under way. In the

1910s Dostoevsky, Tolstoy, the German Nobel Prize winner Rudolf C. Eucken (1846–1926), Henri BERGSON, Rabindranath TAGORE, and Maurice MAETERLINCK became known in Japan. The art of Cézanne, Van Gogh, and Rodin attracted attention; the aestheticism of Poe, Wilde, and Baudelaire found numerous emulators.

During and after World War I, Romain ROLLAND, Henri BARBUSSE, and Vicente BLASCO IBÁÑEZ became widely read in Japan. Satō Haruo (1892–1964) and Kikuchi Kan (1888–1948) emerged as part of an avant-garde group that declared that only in society can man achieve individuality. Although the group traced their intellectual origins to Europe, the members never completely abandoned traditional style and sensibility. Kikuchi Kan worked as the iron-handed editor of *Bungei shunjū* (founded 1923), making it a leading Japanese literary monthly.

Other writers, such as AKUTAGAWA Ryūnosuke, Yamamoto Yūzō (1887–1974), and Kume Masao (1891–1952), made their debuts in private periodicals. One of these periodicals, *Shin shichō*, founded in 1907, was associated with Tokyo Imperial University students who had literary aspirations. In 1923 KAWABATA Yasunari revived this periodical. Together with YOKOMITSU Riichi and their followers, in 1924 he was involved in yet another periodical, *Bungei jidai*, which advanced such European causes as FUTURISM, EXPRESSIONISM, and DADAISM. Kawabata's short-lived group, however intuitive, subjective, sensual, and faintly decadent, owed as much to medieval Japanese drama as to modern European "isms." Kawabata was the first Japanese writer to win the Nobel Prize for literature.

For a time in the 1920s it appeared that leftist literature might overshadow the efforts of these avant-garde writers and modernists. Government authorities, however, repressed the proletarian movement, despite the support of many established writers. Two noteworthy leftist authors who failed to survive beyond World War II are Hayama Yoshiki (1894–1945) and Kobayashi Takiji (1903–1933). Leftist writers who lived through government repression and the hardships of war resumed literary activity after Japan's defeat. The most notable of them are Nakano Shigeharu (b. 1902), author of *Muragimo* (1954; nerve), Miyamoto Yuriko (1899–1951), Hirabayashi Taiko (1905–1972), Miyamoto Kenji (b. 1908), and HAYASHI Fumiko. MIYAZAWA Kenji's selfless altruism and his active participation in agricultural reform movements suggest a devotion to humanitarian ends similar to that of the proletarians.

Nonleftist writers active during the 1930s included IBUSE Masuji and Hori Tatsuo (1904–1953). DAZAI Osamu best typified the immediate postwar period, a time of excruciating self-examination and extreme nihilism. His autobiographical narratives in some respects anticipated "beat" literature. Many other writers emerged after World War II, the most notable being Mishima. His spectacular suicide in the conventional manner of the Edo-period samurai in 1970, followed by Kawabata's self-asphyxiation in 1971, startled the world. Other writers representative of the immediate post-World War II years include Inoue Yasushi (1907–1991)—author of *Ryojū* (1949; *The Hunting Gun*, 1961), *Tempyō no iraka* (1957; *The Roof Tile of Tempyō*, 1976), *Tonkō* (1959; *Tun-huang: A Novel*, 1978)—Takeda Taijun (1912–1976), and Noma Hiroshi (1915–1991), who wrote *Shinkū chitai* (1952; *Zone of Emptiness*, 1956).

In the 1960s new writers continued to appear, and certain established authors extended their reputation. The work of ABE Kōbō, for example, which has been widely translated, combines a scrupulous attention to the individual's emotional state (a characteristic of much of the best traditional literature) with a deft

appreciation of the present human predicament. ŌE Kenzaburō, active as author, editor, and critic, has probed into modern youth's confrontation with sex and society. Among older authors, Ibuse Masuji has published *Kuroi ame* (1966; *Black Rain*, 1969), the best novel about the prolonged suffering and the lingering side effects that the atomic bomb can cause.

During the 1970s yet other fresh authors contributed to the vibrant state of Japanese literature. For instance, a fantasy of sex, drugs, and violence by Murakami Ryū (b. 1952), *Kagirinaku tōmei ni chikai burū* (1976; *Almost Transparent Blue*, 1977), won a coveted literary prize and became a spectacular, albeit controversial, best seller. By means of rich imagery and crude bluntness, a repellent and filthy world in an advanced state of disintegration, decay, and corruption is projected. Such works fairly represent one facet of the Japanese literary scene today. Meanwhile, among established authors, ENCHI Fumiko published a well-received and highly praised new translation into modern Japanese of *Genji monogatari* in ten volumes. And Endō Shūsaku (b. 1923), a Catholic novelist, has had several of his works translated into English: *Umi to dokuyaku* (1958; *The Sea and Poison*, 1980), *Chimmoku* (1966; *Silence*, 1969), and *Kuchibue o fuku toki* (1975; *When I Whistle*, 1979).

Poetry

Developments in poetry in Japan during the 20th c. have roughly corresponded to the pattern set by narrative prose. Shimazaki Tōson expressed the exuberant recognition of a fresh age in poetry when he wrote, in 1904, "All seemed intoxicated with light, with new tongues, with new imaginings. . . ." An incipient romantic movement soon gave way to SYMBOLISM in the early 1900s with the appearance of Ueda Bin's (1874–1916) collection of translations, especially from French poetry, *Miotsukushi* (1905; sound of the tide). The sensuous language of Kitahara Hakushū (1885–1942) in, for example, *Jashūmon* (1909; heretical religion), and the taut yet colloquial idiom of HAGIWARA Sakutarō, in *Tsuki ni hoeru* (1917; *Howling at the Moon*, 1978) and his subsequent collections, mark the establishment of modern free verse in 20th-c. Japan. Hagiwara, however, who is probably the most widely translated 20th-c. Japanese poet, went on to write in "Nihon e no kaiki" (1938; return to Japan) of abandoning "the mirage of the West across the sea" and of returning "to our ancient country, with its more than two thousand years of history."

Although older lyrical forms have survived, the charge that they are hardly poetry has persisted. The dynamic young nationalistic *haiku* and *tanka* poet Masaoka Shiki led a revolution in *haikai* by insisting that the seventeen-syllable *haiku* must stand as an independent verse. Hitherto all *haiku* were theoretically written for linked verse (*renku*, or *renga*). Masaoka's followers, Takahama Kyoshi (1874–1959) and Kawahigashi Hekigodō (1873–1937), continued the *haiku* revolution begun by Masaoka. Takahama, remaining narrowly loyal to Masaoka's objectives, helped to institute a new orthodoxy in terms of form and technique. Irrepressibly innovative by temperament, Kawahigashi, however, instituted a free style of *haiku*, in which the traditional syllable count, season word, and seasonal topic were no longer held to be essential. Kawahigashi's idea of *haiku* as a form of lyrical expression of an individual sensibility brought this traditional kind of verse closer to modern European-style poetry. A follower of Kawahigashi, Nakatsukasa Ippekiro (1887–1946), on the one hand, carried the free-meter *haiku* to a creative pinnacle, rejuvenating it as a poetic tool to embody the modern experience. On the other hand, Ogiwara Seisensui (1884–1976), another of Kawahigashi's disciples, argued that even the seasonal element, however much it preserved continuity with the past, might be sacrificed for the sake of self-expression. TANEDA Santōka, who began writing *haiku* as a disciple of Seisensui, also extended the possibilities of free-verse *haiku*. His restless quest for spiritual enlightenment and his search for release from worldly anxiety mark him as kinsman to earlier Japanese poet-monks and followers of Zen Buddhism.

Lest it be thought that the traditionalists were left clinging only to worn-out concepts of an increasingly forgotten past, Takahama Kyoshi's many followers, especially in the periodical *Hototogisu* (founded 1897), argued cogently for an orthodoxy that might be consistent both with modern theories and with the function of literature. A proletarian school of *haiku* also thrived from the 1920s until 1942, when government repression and internal dissension brought the movement to an end. Today, with around one thousand magazines appearing regularly and with a thriving national organization, modern Japanese *haiku* evinces amazing resilience, and a lively international *haiku* movement flourishes outside Japan. No other non-Western literary form has proven as widely influential as the Japanese *haiku*.

Similarly, the thirty-one-syllable *tanka*, prevalent for over twelve hundred years, has retained its supporters and won a growing number of practitioners in the West. During World War II certain extremists urged the exclusion of "decadent" Western poetry in favor of *tanka*. Inspired by the earlier example of Yosano Akiko (1878–1942), Wakayama Bokusui (1885–1928), and Saitō Mokichi (1882–1953), postwar *tanka* poets of various schools have sustained this lyric art. Ishikawa Takuboku, one of the first modern voices in Japanese poetry, is best remembered for his *tanka*.

Drama

Although in fiction new and old have merged to replace premodern forms, in poetry, perhaps because of its closeness to religion, traditional modes persist alongside modern verse. The same holds true in the drama. Some theatergoers prefer modern plays to the Nō, Kabuki, or Bunraku, but not so much that they completely withhold patronage from the traditional forms. Meantime, well-organized groups and associations preserve the traditional theater, its continuity since the Middle Ages unbroken. Because the conventions of these traditional forms of theater are increasingly remote from modern experience, from time to time new productions of a similar sort are offered to the public, including adaptations from the Western drama and opera. For example, a Japanese version of YEATS's poetic drama *At the Hawk's Well*, at first entitled *Taka no izumi* (perf. 1949; hawk's well) and later revised and called *Takahime* (1969; hawk princess), adapted by Yokomichi Mario (b. 1916) and Nomura Man'nojō (b. 1930), has been presented on Nō stages in Tokyo and Kyoto. Among modern playwrights and theater critics, KISHIDA Kunio worked assiduously to establish a form of theater that projects the conditions of actual life with originality and psychological acumen. Yashiro Seiichi (b. 1927) is the most recent example of a modern playwright whose work has been performed in English translation. His play *Hokusai manga* (1973; *Hokusai Sketch-books*, 1979) was staged in Hollywood early in 1981, demonstrating his uninhibited ribaldry drawn straight from Edo culture and portraying the triumphant free expression of a famous creative artist,

Hokusai (1760–1849), whose zest for lif overcame seemingly insurmountable human adversities.

Abe Kōbō, better known for his surrealistic novels, is also one of the most productive play-wrights and imaginative theater directors in Japan. And two of the plays of the prolific Yamazaki Masakazu (b. 1934) have appeared in English translation: *Zeami* (1969; *Zeami*, 1980) and *Sanetomo shuppan* (1973; *Sanetomo*, 1980). Both plays, very much rooted in Japanese culture, deal with the Middle Ages.

Despite the fame of certain modern poets and playwrights, narrative prose writers have probably made Japan's greatest contribution to world literature in the 20th c. Yet, poetry and drama, as well as modern Japanese fiction, command increasing attention from Western readers, not because of their supposedly exotic qualities but because of their literary artistry and attention to problems common to modern life. If some readers may complain of lack of power, others will surely find meaningful comment on human life, death, and love. Nowhere on earth does one encounter a more world-minded literary atmosphere.

The theme that dominates much of modern Japanese literature is the search for the self in society. Toward the end of the Edo era (1603–1867) and in the early Meiji, traditional society collapsed. Old morals, religion, and loyalties proved inadequate. Modern authors, by using all the resources of a rich language with a long literary tradition, have continually groped for solutions to the human predicament. At times some have accepted without question Western ideology, religion, or literary forms, but the best writers have sought original answers to the questions of life, literature, and art. In recent years the search for identity of the self in society continues unabated. Young authors still seek a place for the individual in mass society. They search, so far without success, to find a substitute for the accepted system of duties and obligations that gave structure to traditional society.

Japanese literature reflects the continuing vitality of a prosperous nation of more than a hundred million people. For successful writers the rewards are enormous, both in terms of wealth and public acclaim. Nevertheless, the current educational system places low emphasis on creative writing, which as an occupation is discouraged, making it all the more of a marvel that so much energy and attention is devoted to this particular human activity.

BIBLIOGRAPHY: Kokusai Bunka Shinkōkai, ed., *Introduction to Contemporary Japanese Literature* (3 vols., 1939, 1959, 1972); Keene, D., *Modern Japanese Novels and the West* (1961); Shea, G. T., *Leftwing Literature in Japan: A Brief History of the Proletarian Literary Movement* (1964); Arima, T., *The Failure of Freedom: A Portrait of Modern Japanese Intellectuals* (1969); Keene, D., *Landscapes and Portraits: Appreciations of Japanese Culture* (1971); Japan PEN Club *Studies on Japanese Culture* (1973) Vol. I: 157–557; Kimball, A. G., *Crisis in Identity and Contemporary Japanese Novels* (1973); Harper, J., et al., eds.,*An Invitation to Japan's Literature* (1974): 5–9, 33–40, 96–154; Kijima, H., and R. A. Miller, introductory essays in Kijima, H., ed., *The Poetry of Postwar Japan* (1975): xi–xlix; Tsuruta, K., and T. E. Swann, eds., *Approaches to the Modern Japanese Novel* (1976); Ueda, M., *Modern Japanese Writers and the Nature of Literature* (1976); Ueda, M., Introduction to *Modern Japanese Haiku: An Anthology* (1976): 3–25; Takeda, K., ed., *Essays on Japanese Literature*(1977); Rimer, J. T., *Modern Japanese Fiction and Its Traditions: An Introduction* (1978); Yamanouchi, H., *The Search* for *Authenticity in Modern Japanese Literature* (1978); Bowring, R. J., *Mori Ōgai and the Modernization of Japanese Culture* (1979); Peterson, G. B., *The Moon in the Water: Understanding Tanizaki, Kawabata, and Mishima* (1979); Takaya, T., ed., Introduction to *Modern Japanese Drama: An Anthology* (1979): ix–xxxvii; Walker, J. A., *The Japanese Novel of the Meiji Period and the Idea of Individualism* (1979); Keene, D., tr., Introduction to *The Modern Japanese Prose Poem: An Anthology of Six Poets* (1980): 3–57; Lippit, N. M., *Reality and Fiction in Modern Japanese Literature* (1980)

—LEON M. ZOLBROD

Japanese Literature since 1970

The 1970s began with several significant deaths, which in turn announced a new era of uneasy cultural transition as well as unprecedented economic growth. MISHIMA Yukio committed a ritual suicide (*seppuku*) in 1971. One year after, his mentor, the Nobel Prize laureate KAWABATA Yasunari, took his own life too. There were also many bloody deaths as a result of infighting among factions of leftist students whose dream of revolution was simply gobbled up by the huge machinery of Japan's late capitalism. Literary culture looked threatened to be erased by the plethora of visual media, rock music, and copywriting in a computer-generated information society.

Fiction

The first significant group of writers to emerge in the 1970s promptly received the label of the "introspective generation." This group included FURUI Yoshikichi, ŌBA Minako, Gotō Meisei (b. 1932), Kuroi Senji (b. 1932), and Abe Akira (b. 1934). Many sensed in their works a tendency to turn away from society and politics and to turn inward in the hope of locating one's own place, however powerless it may be. Critics read their works as symptomatic of the general decline in the power of literature to speak to contemporary society.

New writers were of course also emerging. Nakagami Kenji (1946–1992), Murakami Ryū (b. 1952), Mita Masahiro (b. 1948), TSUSHIMA Yūko, and Aono Sō (b. 1943) were among the most prominent, though their works were first greeted with such weary captions as "the generation of blue," or "the generation of emptiness."

Nakagami Kenji stunned the literary world with the inordinate power of his writing when he began publishing short stories in the mid-1970s. His award-winning novel *Misaki* (1976; promontory) evokes a powerful sense of raw physicality through the character of a young day laborer who uncontrollably revolts against the already crumbling family institution in rural Japan. His subsequent works continue to show that he is indeed one of the few writers who can raise literature to a mythological height without being uprooted from his most significant site—his birth place, Kishū, rich with ancient myths that speak of primordial sexuality, violence, and undeniable vitality.

After his sensational debut in 1976 with a novel filled with drugs, sex, and rock music, Murakami Ryū has continued to write provocative works that touch on the most grotesque reality of our contemporary world. His third novel, *Koinrokkā beibīzu* (1980; *Coin-Locker Babies*, 1994), was highly acclaimed for its bold and imaginative treatment of the postmodern world, with its interrelated themes of autistic self, imaginative construction of reality, and the final destruction of all. In his most recent novel, *Kokku sakkā burūsu* (1991; cocksucker blues), he explores the underground sadomasochistic world in Tokyo, linking an unspeakable sexual crime to contemporary Japan's political and economical practices.

The daughter of the famous novelist DAZAI Osamu, Tsushima Yūko, has firmly established her own place in the literary world. Her works often deal with themes that seem to derive from her own life: the absence of father, divorce, single mother, death of her son. However, her work cannot be confined within the convention of the *shishōsetsu* or "I-novel," for it often incorporates surreal situations and appropriates classical literature as its framework. Her ability to produce the unforgettable image of a female physicality that is solitary yet inseparably tied to the flow of all-inclusive life on earth, marks her as one of the major writers of contemporary Japan.

One of the significant changes in contemporary Japanese literature is how foreign countries and cultures function in Japanese texts. Thanks to the strong yen, foreign travels are no longer a remote dream for the Japanese, who have come to be known as the most-traveled people on earth. Correspondingly, there is a noticeable increase of novels staged in foreign countries as some Japanese writers begin to seek, whether voluntarily or not, new situations to write in and about. Writers with foreign locales include the following recipients of the most prestigious award for new writers, the Akutagawa Prize: Ōba Minako in 1968, Ikeda Masuo (b. 1934) in 1977, Takahashi Michitsuna (b. 1948) in 1978, Aono Sō in 1979, Mori Reiko (b. 1928) in 1979, and Kometani Fumiko (b. 1930) in 1986. Ōba writes about her experiences in Alaska. Ikeda, a noted visual artist, wrote his highly erotic novels while living in East Hampton. Takahashi's works reflect his experiences of having been a student in California. Both Mori and Kometani reside in the U.S. and write about being wives to Americans. Aono, the son of an eminent literary critic, began writing fiction during his eleven years of roaming around the globe.

Awarded the Nobel Prize for Literature in 1994, ŌE Kenzaburō, who began his literary career in the late 1950s as the most outrageous innovator of Japanese fiction, continues to be an uncompromising avant-gardist of the field. Going beyond the existential mode of his early works, his later works show his distinctive employment of methodology informed by the writings of Mikhail BAKHTIN as well as a unique appropriation of the style of the "I-novel." He also continues to explore and deepen the two most fundamental themes of his writing: the isolated, forested village of his birthplace in Shikoku, and his relationship with his brain-damaged son. His foreign sojourns in Mexico and at Berkeley, California, also contribute to his vigorous production of new materials.

There have been many talented women writers in modern Japan, though their works are categorized separately from the mainstream "male" literature as *joryū bungaku* (women's literature). Among the established older generation of women writers, two names deserve mention for their lifelong accomplishments: Nogami Yaeko (1885–1985) and Uno Chiyo (1897–1996). Nogami has been known as a steadfast, yet nonactivist liberal throughout her long literary career. At the age of seventy-eight, she received the Women's Literature Prize for her historical novel *Hideyoshi to Rikyū* (1963; Hideyoshi and Rikyū). Uno, as an epitome of "new woman," has led a colorful life, on which many of her works are based. Her best-selling novel, *Irozange* (1935; *Confessions of*

Love, 1989) deftly recounts a story of a failed double suicide, which her then lover, the noted painter Tōgō Seiji, actually had lived through.

As the changes of daily reality brought out by Japan's rapid economic growth took root, it became evident that conventional realism was no longer able to produce the gestalt of the contemporary Japanese woman. With its radical antirealist stance, the appearance of *Parutai* (1960; *Partei*, 1982) by Kurahashi Yumiko (b. 1935) showed the possibility of a new type of women's literature that moved away from the usual convention of sensitively detailing one's own life. Kōno Taeko (b. 1926) also succeeded in presenting the distinctive image of women in her highly conceptual and often fantastic style that explored the depths of human sexuality. She received the Tanizaki Prize for her novel *Ichinen no bokka* (1980; one year's pastoral song). There are also outstanding women writers whose works directly address social issues. ARIYOSHI Sawako dealt with ecological issues as well as the problems of elderly people. After publishing highly literary works, Takenishi Hiroko (b. 1929) began to write about Hiroshima's unhealed wound. Hayashi Kyōko, whose debut work *Matsuri no ba* (1975; "Ritual of Death," 1978) received the Akutagawa Prize, continues to write about her experience as a victim of the atomic bomb dropped in Nagasaki.

No other novel has captured the situation of the postmodern consumer society better than *Nantonaku kurisutaru* (1981; somehow crystal) by Tanaka Yasuo (b. 1956), written while she was still a college student. It depicts the life of a college girl living amidst hundreds of mostly foreign brand names, for which the book provides a parallel text of notes that resemble those in a city guidebook. The city has become a map of consumer signs; and its inhabitants are defined by them. MURAKAMI Haruki's emergence as a major literary figure of the 1980s cannot be explained without an understanding of the cultural and semiotic transformation of city life. Utterly divorced from the longstanding tradition of *jun bungaku* (serious literature), Murakami's works nonetheless seek a new framework to address the emptiness of signs, communication, and self.

Drama

After separating itself from the traditional drama of Kabuki and Nō, *Shingeki* (new drama) firmly established itself after World War II with talented dramatists including KINOSHITA Junji and Mishima Yukio. Toward the end of the 1960s, however, a countermovement to such a modern establishment began to appear. Commonly known as the *angura* (underground) theater, it was led by Kara Jūrō (b. 1940) and Terayama Shūji (1936–1983) who advocated the need to move beyond the modernity represented by *Shingeki* through incorporating more primitive, spontaneous, and immediate aspects of a show-tent atmosphere.

The second generation of the underground movement was led by Tsuka Kōhei (b. 1948) who debuted in the early 1970s with his satirical plays seeped in black humor. While the earlier underground theater carried a politically revolutionary agenda, Tsuka's plays, free from such confrontational approaches, comically depicted grotesque figures trapped in the sameness of daily life. Another new playwright to emerge around this time was Inoue Hisashi (b. 1934), who is now also known as an important novelist. His light comedies, which embraced many aspects of popular culture, heralded the recent ascension of popular culture to the status of high culture.

Poetry

Beginning in the late 19th c. with awkward translations of Western poetry, modern Japanese poets absorbed various modernist schools—ROMANTICISM, SYMBOLISM, DADAISM, SURREALISM—with bewildering speed and produced highly original works of their own.

SHIMAZAKI Tōson, who later became a naturalist novelist, is commonly credited as the creator of modern Japanese poetry. His first collection of poems, *Wakana shū* (1897; seedlings), effectively conveys his romantic lyricism. Kambara Ariake (1876–1947) succeeded in producing his own symbolist poetry, though much inspired by Dante Gabriel Rossetti (1828–1882) and Stéphane Mallarmé (1842–1898). Kitahara Hakushū (1885–1942) was the most talented poet before HAGIWARA Sakutarō who redefined the language of modern Japanese poetry with his use of colloquialism soaked with a modern sense of alienation in *Tsuki ni hoeru* (1917; *Howling at the Moon*, 1978). Hagiwara's contemporary MIYAZAWA Kenji is still revered as a poet-saint who led a life of altruism. The son of a famous sculptor, Takamura Kōtarō is remembered for his direct expressions of love for his mentally ill wife, recorded in *Chieko-shō* (1941; *Chieko and Other Poems*, 1980).

In the 1930s, centering around the modernist poet and scholar NISHIWAKI Junzaburō, some fine modernist poets began to appear: Kitagawa Fuyuhiko (1900–1990); the editor of the important journal *VOU*, Kitasono Katsue (1902–1978); Anzai Fuyue (1898–1965); and surrealist Takiguchi Shūzō (1903–1979). Less-experimental poets gathered around the journal *Shiki*, notably Miyoshi Tatsuji (1900–1964) and Nakahara Chūya (1907–1937). Nakahara, whose work was much inspired by Arthur Rimbaud (1854–1891), still invokes romantic adoration for his intense lyricism as well as for his tragically brief life.

From the ashes of World War II rose many original poetic voices. The vagabond poet Kaneko Mitsuharu (1895–1975) emerged as one of the few who dared to write antiwar texts during the war. The leading figure of *Arechi*, the first poetry journal to appear after the war, was Tamura Ryūichi (b. 1923). Arguably the most important postwar poet, Yoshioka Minoru (1919–1990) wrote distinctively sensual, surreal works. The important poet and critic Ōoka Makoto (b. 1931) began writing under the influence of Paul ÉLUARD; his erudition in classical Japanese literature has allowed him to revive a modern version of *renga* (Japanese linked verse) with foreign poets. The first Japanese "beat" poet, Shiraishi Kazuko (b. 1931), weaves her unabashed expression of sexuality with the pulsating rhythm of jazz. She could be seen as the precursor of the talented young women poets who began to emerge in the 1970s. The most gifted one among them seems to be Itō Hiromi (b. 1955), whose bold experimentation in poetic language and explicit expressions of sexuality exhibit a voice that is at the same time unique and reflecting of our contemporary situation at large.

BIBLIOGRAPHY: Miyoshi, M., *Accomplices of Silence: The Modern Japanese Novel* (1974); Kato, S., *A History of Japanese Literature* (1983), Vol. 3; Ueda, M., *Modern Japanese Poets and the Nature of Literature* (1983); Keene, D., *Dawn to the West: Japanese Literature of the Modern Era* (2 vols., 1984); Marks, A. H., and B. D. Bort, *Guide to Japanese Prose*, 2nd ed. (1984); Pronko, L. C., *Guide to Japanese Drama*, 2nd ed. (1984); Rimer, J. T., and R. E. Morrell, *Guide to Japanese Poetry* (2nd ed., 1984); Rubin, J., *Injurious to Public Morals: Writers and the Meiji State* (1984);

Rimer, J. T., *A Reader's Guide to Japanese Literature* (1988); Fowler, E., *The Rhetoric of Confession: Shishōsetsu in Early Twentieth-Century Japanese Fiction* (1988); Vernon, V. V., *Daughters of the Moon: Wish, Will, and Social Constraint in Fiction by Modern Japanese Women* (1988); Goodman, D. G., ed., *Japanese Drama and Culture in the 1960s: The Return of the Gods* (1988); Gessel, V. C., *The Sting of Life: Four Contemporary Japanese Novelists* (1989); Miyoshi, M., and H. D. Harootunian, eds., *Postmodernism and Japan* (1990); Wolfe, A. S., *Suicidal Narrative in Modern Japan: The Case of Dazai Osamu* (1990); Fujii, J., *Complicit Fictions: The Subject in the Modern Japanese Prose Narrative* (1993); Gessel, V. C., *Three Modern Novelists: Sōseki, Tanizaki, Kawabata* (1993); Karatani, K., *Origins of Modern Japanese Literature* (1993); Washburn, D., *The Dilemma of the Modern in Japanese Fiction* (1995); Suzuki, T., *Narrating the Self: Fictions of Japanese Modernity* (1996)

—HOSEA HIRATA

JARNÉS, Benjamín

Spanish novelist and critic, b. 7 Oct. 1888, Codo; d. 11 Aug. 1949, Madrid

The leading writer of fiction and the stylistic virtuoso of the Spanish vanguard of the 1920s and 1930s, J. belonged to the cosmopolitan group gathered around ORTEGA Y GASSET'S *Revista de Occidente*. His provincial upbringing and his seminary education contrast with the experimental artistic values he embraced later in his search for new forms and his hyperintellectualized treatment of reality. Although he shied away from social or political commitment in writing, he sided with the Republicans and went into exile after the civil war, living in Mexico from 1939 to 1948. He opposed the idea of literary schools and doctrines, although his works typified contemporary movements in their formalism and stylization. His techniques, however, were not aesthetic ends in themselves but vehicles for resolving the problem of commitment to reality even when the artist's work represents an evasion of this reality.

Thus, J.'s novels are a forum for speculating on questions about human destiny, the relationship between realism and myth, and the nature of art and beauty. In his early novels, such as *El profesor inútil* (1926; the useless professor), *El convidado de papel* (1928; the paper guest), and *Paula y Paulita* (1929; Paula and Paulita), innumerable scenes and character studies appear without much narrative action. J. explores the distinction between eroticism and sexuality, studies women as embodying the eternal feminine, and initiates those practices for which he is most famous: mirrored and doubled characters, shifting points of view, a highly imagistic lyricism, irony, wit, and abstraction.

At the same time, J. carried forward his career as a critic of film and literature for various journals. The articles collected in *Ejercicios* (1927; exercises), *Rubricas: Nuevos ejercicios* (1931; flourishes: new exercises), *Feria del libro* (1935; book fair), and *Cita de ensueños: Figuras del cinema* (1936; appointment with dreams: film personalities) attest to his perceptiveness: he called public attention to the rising stock of HUXLEY, GIRAUDOUX, GIDE, JOYCE, and Charlie Chaplin while assimilating their innovations for his own literary gain.

In J.'s greatest novels he invents a new reality whose tension between the conceptual and the concrete remolds the traditional genre. In *Locura y muerte de nadie* (1929; madness and death of nobody) the dominant theme is the search for identity in a depersonalized world. The SURREALIST *Teoría del zumbel* (1930; theory of the string for spinning a top) inaugurates a fairy-tale atmosphere that, in conjunction with dream sequences here, and fable or allegory in works like *Escenas junto a la muerte* (1931; scenes near death), *Viviana y Merlín* (1930; "Vivien and Merlin," 1962), and *Venus dinámica* (1943; dynamic Venus), seek out the mythic eternalness that is immanent in the vital human condition. Both *Locura y muerte de nadie* and *Teoría del zumbel* celebrate beauty as intellectual voluptuousness. They extend J.'s favorite theme of art as being the supreme experience: art blends reason, the senses, and passion into a horizon of truth, and its equilibrium and harmony rest on grace, joy, and plenitude.

Stylistically, however, J.'s mathematical objectivism, CUBIST metaphors, abstract dialogues, and self-referential narrative details make his works seem self-conscious and dehumanized. Yet despite their static quality, the novels are interesting milestones in the genre's history. The way in which the surface properties of reality are defined by sensory and conceptual imagery is a major contribution to Spanish avant-garde creativity.

FURTHER WORKS: *Vida de San Alejo* (1928; "Saint Alexis," 1932); *Salón de estío* (1929); *Sor Patrocinio: La monja de las llagas* (1929); *Zumalacárregui, el caudillo romántico* (1931); *Las siete virtudes* (1931); *Lo rojo y lo azul: Homenaje a Stendhal* (1932); *Fauna contemporánea: Ensayos breves* (1933); *Castelar: Hombre del Sinaí* (1935); *Libro de Esther* (1935); *Doble agonía de Bécquer* (1936); *Don Alvaro; o, La fuerza del tino* (1936); *Cartas al Ebro* (1940); *La novia del viento* (1940); *Manuel Acuña: Poeta de su siglo* (1942); *Orlando el pacífico* (1942); *Don Vasco de Quiroga, obispo de Utopía* (1942); *Escuela de libertad: Siete maestros* (1942); *Stefan Zweig: Cumbre apagada, retrato* (1942); *Españoles en América* (1943); *Cervantes: Bosquejo biográfico* (1944); *Ariel disperso* (1946); *Eufrosina; o, La gracia* (1948)

BIBLIOGRAPHY: Putnam, S., "B. J. y la deshumanización del arte," *RHM*, 2 (1935): 17–21; Ilie, P., "B. J.: Aspects of the Dehumanized Novel," *PMLA*, 76 (1961): 247–53; O'Neill, M. W., "The Role of the Sensual in the Art of B. J.," *MLN* 85, (1970): 262–68; Bernstein, J. S., *B. J.* (1972); Zuleta, E., *Arte y vida en la obra de B. J.* (1977)

—PAUL ILIE

JARRELL, Randall

American poet and critic, b. 6 May 1914, Nashville, Tenn.; d. 14 Oct. 1965, Greensboro, N.C.

Educated at Vanderbilt University, where his teachers Allen TATE and John Crowe RANSOM were formative influences on his craft, J. nevertheless did not align himself with the Fugitive group. An excellent teacher, J. began his career at Kenyon College (1937–39). He held several other positions; as an instructor in the U.S. Army Air Force (1942–46), J. learned much that appeared in his subsequent verse. From 1947 onward, Woman's College of the University of North Carolina (now University of North Carolina at Greensboro) was J.'s home institution. He was consultant in poetry to the Library of Congress from 1956 to 1958.

From *Blood for a Stranger* (1942); to *The Lost World* (1965), J.'s poetry focused in various ways on a sense of loss that he felt in himself and in others, and his favorite mode is the dramatic monologue, frequently in the voice of a child. *Blood for a Stranger* represents the early phase of his development and includes poems about the self and others, who confront a sense of entrapment and reach out futilely to an unresponding world for comfort. J.'s military service, however, provided him a vivid sense and concrete images of the nightmare of the experience of war and of the loss of human value in an inhuman world. *Little Friend, Little Friend* (1945) and *Losses* (1948) contain sharply focused poems founded on these war experiences.

Increasingly for J. in his poetry, dreams or other fictions became the poet's response to the problems of bearing life, meeting adversity, and suffering losses. His child narrators facilitated the development of these poetic constructs, and unsurprisingly J. derived much of his matter from tales of the Brothers Grimm. He turned to the *Märchen*, with its generic emphasis on metamorphosis, in an attempt to recover the principle of change that is natural for a child and inaccessible, he believed, to an adult. Thus the *Märchen* poems frequently gave voice to the profound disillusionment that informs J.'s poetry generally, beginning in *Losses* and continued in *The Seven League Crutches* (1951) and *The Woman at the Washington Zoo* (1960). Although perhaps irrepressibly witty in detail, the main body of J.'s poetry is somberly serious.

J.'s translations of RILKE remind us of the affinity for the sensibilities of children and women that the two poets shared, and for some readers the translations have suggested that J. turned to Rilke for philosophical inspiration, which is progressively evident in *The Seven League Crutches* and *The Lost World*. For J., the world had always been the lost world, which he approached with various poetic stratagems but could not change. In *The Lost World*, however, he shed these fictions, and expressed his vision in deeply personal terms, finally in a profound commitment claiming the lost world as his own.

A Sad Heart at the Supermarket (1962)—essays and fables—continued his complaint against a tawdry, valueless world, especially against the demeaning media-inculcated consumer culture of America. Conversational and idiomatic in style, this volume reveals (as J. does elsewhere) a great range and depth of familiarity with music, art, and other literatures. In *Pictures from an Institution* (1954), his most lighthearted work, J. carved his initials exquisitely on some venerable trunks in the grove of academe.

As acting literary editor of *The Nation*, poetry critic for *Partisan Review* and the *Yale Review*, member of the editorial board of *The American Scholar*, and contributor to *Kenyon Review*, the *New Republic*, the *New York Times Book Review*, and other publications, J. was a prolific and exacting critic. His *Poetry and the Age* (1953) is a selection of his critical articles; others are gathered in *The Third Book of Criticism* (1969). The former volume stands as a minor classic in American criticism and argues that contemporary poetry can only be judged fairly if we do not insist on imposing on it or other contemporary art any single standard or opinion: one simple aspect cannot be made the test of a complicated whole. As a critic, too, J. had severe—some say cruel—standards of excellence. John Crowe Ransom regarded *Poetry and the Age* as "almost

epoch-making in establishing for the first time securely the position which Robert Frost and Walt Whitman occupy in American poetry." Whether cruel judge or king-maker, J. is an eminently readable critic.

In assessing J.'s contributions to literature, one would be negligent to ignore his extraordinary performance as a teacher, an achievement that could all too readily be overshadowed by his own publications and other literary activities. As a poet, J. received mixed reviews, although certainly more favorable than otherwise. While some of his critics applaud his technical virtuosity, others fault him for what they perceive as carelessness and for promising more than he succeeded in delivering. Critics who, for whatever reasons, are more confident than J. himself in their view of the world, find J.'s quest for the lost world unnecessarily prolonged and anxiety-ridden. His poetry, however, and the facts of his life validate the authenticity of his anxiety. Perhaps his vigorous and seminal critical essays will ultimately emerge as J.'s literary monument. Finally, J. is representative of his age, for like many of his contemporaries he was frustrated by a world reality that resists change. Like many of them, J. altered his medium to produce adaptive fictions, but these ultimately proved to be for him inadequate. Shortly after claiming the lost world as irrevocably and inescapably his, J. suffered a nervous breakdown and was subsequently killed by an automobile in an event that is now acknowledged to have been suicide.

FURTHER WORKS: *Selected Poems* (1955); *Uncollected Poems* (1958); *The Gingerbread Rabbit* (1964); *The Bat Poet* (1964); *The Animal Family* (1965); *Complete Poems* (1969); *Kipling, Auden & Co.: Essays and Reviews, 1935–1964* (1981)

BIBLIOGRAPHY: Rideout, W. B., "'To Change, To Change!': The Poetry of R. J." in Hungerford, E., ed., *Poets in Progress: Critical Prefaces to Ten Contemporary Americans* (1962): 156–78; Lowell, R., et al., eds., *R. J., 1914–1965* (1967); Ferguson, S., *The Poetry of R. J.* (1971); Donoghue, D., "The Lost World of R. J.," in Owen, G., ed., *Modern American Poetry: Essays in Criticism* (1972): 205–15; Mazzaro, J., "Between Two Worlds: The Post-Modernism of R. J.," in Boyers, R., ed., *Contemporary Poetry in America* (1974): 78–90; Rosenthal, M. L., "R. J.," in Donoghue, D., ed., *Seven American Poets: From MacLeish to Nemerov—An Introduction* (1975): 132–70; Quinn, M. B., *R. J.* (1981); Meyers, J., *Manic Power: R. J. and His circle* (1987); Pritchard, W. H., *R. J.: A Literary Life* (1990)

—ARTHUR B. COFFIN

JARRY, Alfred

French dramatist, novelist, and essayist, b. 8 Sept. 1873, Laval; d. 1 Nov. 1907, Paris

One of the most celebrated dates in the history of the French theater is 10 December 1896, when *Ubu Roi* (1896; *Ubu Roi*, 1951) was staged by Lugné-Poë at his experimental Théâtre de l'Œuvre. From the first word—a slightly modified obscenity—the battle lines were drawn between the traditionalists and those who saw one of the functions of avant-garde drama as an assault upon the audience.

The protype of *Ubu Roi* was originally composed by J.'s future classmates at the Rennes lycée even before he arrived at the school in 1888, but he immediately entered into the spirit of the play and helped his classmates stage it, using his own marionettes. Although the extent of J.'s revisions is unclear, what began as a collective enterprise had become J.'s own by the time his definitive version of the schoolboy farce was staged in Paris. The principal character, who was originally intended to ridicule an incompetent physics teacher at the school, had become an archetype of all that is basest in mankind: egotism tempered only by cowardice, and unlimited appetite symbolized by his enormous belly. The influence of the play, which in 1896 ran for only two performances, can scarcely be exaggerated: it inspired APOLLINAIRE and through him the SURRE-ALISTS; it inspired COCTEAU and through him ANOUILH; it inspired ARTAUD, who in 1927 named his own company the Théâtre Alfred Jarry, and through Artaud much of what is most characteristic in modern French drama. *Ubu Roi's* power to shock has faded considerably over the years, but several recent productions have demonstrated that the crude vitality and savage humor of the play survive undiminished.

In *Ubu Roi* Father Ubu becomes king of Poland and butchers everyone in his path until a Russian invasion sends him packing, along with Mother Ubu, to France. The complementary play *Ubu enchaîné* (1900; *King Turd Enslaved*, 1953) shows how in France, the country of "free men," Ubu chooses to become a slave in chains. In contrast to the conventions of classical drama, in which a character holds fast to the same identity through all the changes inflicted upon him by destiny, Ubu's values undergo a complete metamorphosis from one play to the next, even though his appearance and idiosyncratic language remain the same. The idea seems to be that modern man has no "essence" at all, an idea also expressed by Ibsen in *Peer Gynt*, another play staged by Lugné-Poë in 1896, and in which J. himself played a minor role. As if to further illustrate this idea, Ubu spilled out into other works by J., both dramatic and fictional, and to a degree that is highly controversial also became part of J.'s own identity.

As many anecdotes demonstrate, J. adopted the staccato speech of his character and was known to fire his revolver with an Ubu-like disdain for proprieties. After one such incident, according to Apollinaire, J. told him in Ubu's voice, "Isn't this as lovely as literature?" André GIDE put J. into an episode of his novel *The Counterfeiters* without even changing his name, presumably because J. was so much a work of fiction in "real life" that there was no need to transform him any further. J.'s more recent critics protest that this emphasis on the way J. abolished the distinction between life and art serves only to denigrate J.'s many fine novels and other works, which have never received as much attention as the Ubu plays. Yet despite the invigorating misogyny of such episodic novels as *L'amour en visites* (1898; love goes visiting), at the center of which Lucien breaks his engagement by biting his fiancée on the lip, and despite the philosophy of Pataphysics (the science of imaginary solutions) elaborated in a famous chapter of *Gestes et opinions du docteur Faustroll, pataphysicien* (1911; *Exploits and Opinions of Doctor Faustroll, Pataphysician*, 1965), Jarry seems destined to remain indissolubly linked to the monstrous yet all too human Ubu.

FURTHER WORKS: *Les minutes de sable mémorial* (1894); *César-Antéchrist* (1895); *Les jours et les nuits* (1897); *L'amour absolu* (1899); *Almanach du Père Ubu* (1899); *Messaline* (1901; *The*

Alfred Jarry

Garden of Priapus, 1936); *Almanach illustré du Père Ubu* (1901); *Le surmâle* (1902; *The Supermale*, 1968); *Par la taille* (1906); *Albert Samain* (1907); *Le moutardier du pape* (1907); *Pantagruel* (1911, with Eugène Demolder); *Gestes* (1921); *La dragonne* (1943); *Ubu cocu* (1944; *Turd Cuckolded*, 1953); *L'autre Alceste* (1947); *La revanche de la nuit* (1949); *L'objet aimé* (1953); *La chandelle verte* (1969); *Le manoir enchanté* (1974). **FURTHER WORKS IN ENGLISH:** *Selected Works* (1965)

BIBLIOGRAPHY: Shattuck, R., *The Banquet Years* (1958): 146–94; Wellwarth, G. E., *The Theater of Protest and Paradox* (1964): 1–14; Arnaud, N., *A. J.* (1974); Bierman, J. H., "The Antichrist Ubu," *CompD*, 9 (1975): 226–47; LaBelle, M. M., *A. J.: Nihilism and the Theater of the Absurd* (1980); Beaumont, K., *A. J.* (1984)

—MICHAEL POPKIN

JASTRUN, Mieczysław

(pseud. of Mieczysław Agatstein) Polish poet, novelist, literary critic, and translator, b. 29 Oct. 1903, Korolówka; d. 22 Feb. 1983, Warsaw

J. received his doctorate from the Cracow Jagielonian University. His literary debut occurred in 1923 while he was close to

Skamander, the important poetic group of the 1920s. His first volume of poetry, *Spotkanie w czasie* (meeting in time) appeared in 1929. From 1928 to 1939, J. was a high school teacher in Cracow. During World War II he lived in Lvov, where he was involved in underground cultural and educational activities. After the war he came to Warsaw and became a coeditor of the journal weekly *Kuźnica*. From 1950 on J. devoted his entire time to literary work, only occasionally serving in official capacities in the Polish P.E.N. Club.

J.'s chief contribution to Polish literature is his poetry, although his work in his favorite genre, the biographical novel, is fascinating and widely read. J.'s poetry demonstrates his rich artistic individuality. He is concerned as much with individual destinies as in the destiny of all mankind, and his preoccupation with eternity adds a definite mystical element to his poetry. J., however, avoids abstract symbolism by identifying individual experiences with those of mankind in general. His symbolism is derived from personal experiences: in a poem to his little son he negates the cruelty of the passage of time and celebrates the continuous process of rebirth. Seen from the historical perspective, this coming to terms with the passage of time and with eternity becomes something more than the resolution of his personal soul searching, and instead becomes a symbol of the spiritual rebirth of an entire generation whose youth was spent during the horrors of World War II.

J.'s poetry is not facile: its formal complexities match the weight of its themes and philosophy. J. is not a "popular" poet; he forces his readers to think and expects from them a certain degree of literary and intellectual sophistication. His subject matter is serious and often topical. *Sezon w Alpach* (1948; a season in the Alps) and *Rok urodzaju* (1950; the year of the harvest) are collections of lyrics that render the Polish and Jewish tragedies during World War II. The volume *Poezja i prawda* (1955; poetry and truth), depicting the everyday heroism of the postwar period, demonstrates J.'s faith in the indestructibility of man.

J.'s biographical novels, *Mickiewicz* (1949; Mickiewicz) and *Poeta i dworzanin: Rzecz o Janie Kochanowskim* (1954; the poet and the courtier: the case of Jan Kochanowski), show J. the humanist looking at the great Polish poets from a contemporary point of view.

J.'s translations of Russian poets such as PUSHKIN and BAGRITSKY and of French poets such as APOLLINAIRE, ÉLUARD, and Rimbaud are important. Especially well known is his anthology of French poetry, *Symboliści francuscy: Od Baudelaire'a do Valéry'ego* (1965; French symbolists: from Baudelaire to Valéry). He is also a noted literary critic and has written numerous essays about Polish, Russian, German, and French poets and writers.

J.'s role in Polish literature today is that of the guardian of the best of European traditions in Polish poetry, and his poems are examples and inspirations for the younger generation of poets.

FURTHER WORKS: *Godzina strzeżona* (1945); *Rzecz ludzka* (1946); *Poezje wybrane* (1948); *Poezje 1944–1954* (1954); *Genezy* (1959); *Większe od życia* (1960); *Między słowem a milczeniem* (1960); *Piękna choroba* (1961); *Intonacje* (1962); *Mit Śródziemnomorski* (1962); *Strefa owoców* (1964); *Poezje i rzeczywistość* (1965); *W biały dzień: Poezje* (1967); *Poezje wybrane* (1969); *Eseje* (1973)

BIBLIOGRAPHY: Herman, M., *Histoire de la littérature polonaise* (1963): 280; Gillon, A., and Krzyżanowski, L., *Introduction to Modern Polish Literature: An Anthology of Fiction and Poetry* (1964): 438; Miłosz, C., *Postwar Polish Poetry* (1965): 47–50; Miłosz, C., *The History of Polish Literature* (1969): 408

—MALGORZATA PRUSKA-CARROLL

JAVANESE LITERATURE
See Indonesian Literature

JEFFERS, Robinson

American poet and dramatist, b. 10 Jan. 1887, Pittsburgh, Pa.; d. 20 Jan. 1962, Carmel, Cal.

J. was once ranked with T. S. ELIOT as a major poet. But his pessimism and unorthodox views are apparently responsible for the decline in his reputation until recently. His work, however, is being read again in this country and in Europe, where his poems have been translated into several Slavic languages. J., whose father was a Presbyterian minister and professor of Old Testament literature, attended European and American schools and studied widely in classical and modern languages, literature, medicine, and forestry. His first two volumes of poems contained traditional lyrics, but the publication of *Tamar, and Other Poems* (1924) marked the beginning of his major work, for which he won international recognition.

J. believed that "poetry is bound to concern itself chiefly with permanent aspects of life." His several long, highly charged narrative poems are explorations of this belief, and his many, often delightful, lyrics are celebrations of permanent things, usually the beauty of nature. Together the narratives form a poetry of ideas that moved toward defining what J. called "inhumanism." J. explains it as a "shifting of emphasis and significance from man to notman; the rejection of human solipsism and recognition of the transhuman magnificence.... It offers a reasonable detachment as rule of conduct, instead of love, hate, and envy." To develop "inhumanism," J. took what he could use from Nietzsche's philosophy, followed classical themes and archetypal myths, drew from the historicism of Vico (1668–1744) and Oswald Spengler (1880–1936) and from the theories of the English Egyptologist Flinders Petrie (1853–1942) about the periodicity of civilizations, and adapted a modified materialism from Lucretius' *De rerum natura*.

Most of J.'s narratives are tales of violence, adultery, and incest, with settings in the Carmel-Big Sur region of California. Characteristically, they describe the conflict of a young rebellious figure, usually a female who cunningly uses sex to win her way, and an older patriarchal figure, who is sternly orthodox or hypocritical or both. With few exceptions, these conflicts move from the individualistic and abortive rebellion in "Tamar" (1924) to those of "Cawdor" (1928), "Thurso's Landing" (1932), and "Give Your Heart to the Hawks" (1933), in which, progressively, the individual's rebellion is compared to the values of society.

Like "Margrave" (1932), "Such Counsels You Gave Me" (1937) introduces into the theme of rebellion a hero modeled after Dostoevsky's Raskolnikov, and in "Hungerfield" (1954) the hero discovers the gross impropriety of his fantastic struggle with death. In many of these poems, J. apparently tested various principles of Nietzsche's philosophy and rejected those that proved untenable.

Because of his explorations of Nietzscheanism, and his restatements of the lesson from Greek tragedy that to learn is to suffer, critics have erroneously charged J. with nihilism.

These critics believe that J.'s "Roan Stallion" (1925), *The Women at Point Sur* (1927), "Dear Judas" (1929), and "The Double Axe" (1948) support their opinions, but in these poems the Nietzschean principles of revaluation of values and of the anti-Christ operate to clear the way for J.'s "inhumanism," which challenges institutionalized Christianity but affirms God the creator. It also holds that "man is no measure of anything," that "the beauty of things is . . . absolute," and that "old violence is not too old to beget new values."

In 1947 J.'s very successful *Medea* (1946), a free adaptation from Euripides, was produced in New York; "Solstice" (1935) was a modernized, nondramatic version of *Medea*. *The Cretan Woman* (1954), a verse drama, was modeled after Euripides' *Hippolytus*, which also provided a theme in "Cawdor." *The Tower beyond Tragedy* (1925), a verse play adaptation of the *Oresteia* of Aeschylus, has also been staged several times. In each instance J. reshaped the classical source to conform to his own ideology.

J.'s troublesome and inferior "political" poems approve of World War II and the Korean War as methods of eliminating undeserving human beings, whose "civilizations" have violated the holy beauty of things. He regarded Hitler, Mussolini, Stalin, and Franklin Roosevelt as helpless but necessary victims of circumstances. Accordingly, metropolitan life is seen as vicious and corrupting, life in the mountains as desirable, clean, and lonely. Borrowing from Lucretius, J. believed that the truly worthy and passionate individual might transcend the "flaming world walls" of his being to attain direct access to the "transhuman magnificence" of things, and that, best of all, he might be comforted by the thought that in death his atoms would mingle again with those of nature.

FURTHER WORKS: *Flagons and Apples* (1912); *Californians* (1916); *Roan Stallion, Tamar, and Other Poems* (1925); *Cawdor, and Other Poems* (1928); *Dear Judas, and Other Poems* (1929); *Descent to the Dead* (1931); *Thurso's Landing, and Other Poems* (1932); *Give Your Heart to the Hawks, and Other Poems* (1933); *Solstice, and Other Poems* (1935); *Such Counsels You Gave to Me, and Other Poems* (1937); *The Selected Poetry of R. J.* (1938); *Be Angry at the Sun* (1941); *The Double Axe, and Other Poems* (1948); *Poetry, Gongorism and a Thousand Years* (1949); *Hungerfield, and Other Poems* (1954); *The Beginning and the End, and Other Poems* (1963); *Not Man Apart* (1965); *Selected Poems* (1965); *Selected Letters of R. J., 1897–1962* (1968); *Cawdor and Medea* (1970); *The Alpine Christ, and Other Poems* (1973); *In This Wild Water: The Suppressed Poems of R. J.* (1976); *The Women at Point Sur* (1977); *Dear Judas* (1977); *The Double Axe* (new enl. ed., 1977)

BIBLIOGRAPHY: Powell, L. C., *R. J.: The Man and His Work* (1940); Squires, L. C., *The Loyalties of R. J.* (1956); Carpenter, F. I., *R. J.* (1962); Coffin, A. B., *R. J.: Poet of Inhumanism* (1971); Vardamis, A. A., *The Critical Reputation of R. J.* (1972); Brophy, R. J., *R. J.: Myth, Ritual, and Symbol in His Narrative* (1973); Nolte, W. H., *Rock and Hawk: R. J. and the Romantic Agony* (1978); Zaller, R., *The Cliffs of Solitude: A Reading of R. J.* (1983); Everson, W., *The Excesses of God: R. J. As a Religious Figure* (1988); Boswell, J., *R. J. and the Critics 1912-1983* (1986); Karman, J., ed., *Critical Essays on R. J.* (1990); Zaller, R., ed., *Centennial Essays for R. J.* (1991); Beers, T., " . . . A thousand

Robinson Jeffers

graceful subtleties": Rhetoric in the Poetry of R. J.* (1995); Brophy, R., ed., *R. J.: The Dimension of a Poet* (1995); Karman, J., *R. J.: Poet of California* (rev. ed., 1995); Thesing, W. B., *R. J. and a Galaxy of Writers: Essays in Honor of William H. Nolte* (1995)

—ARTHUR B. COFFIN

JENNINGS, Elizabeth

English poet, b. 18 July 1926, Boston, Lincolnshire

The daughter of a doctor, J. attended Oxford High School and St. Anne's College, Oxford University, where she read English language and literature. She worked as an assistant in the Oxford City Library (1950–58), and at present lives in Oxford. From 1958 to 1960 she was a reader for the publisher Chatto & Windus, and since then she has earned a living as a writer, composing poems (including two volumes for children), editing anthologies, writing books on poetry and religion, and doing reviews and articles for a variety of newspapers and periodicals.

J. started writing poetry when she was thirteen. She describes this juvenilia as "doggerel, but it had a sense of form." This "sense of form" characterizes all her work. Her first collection, *Poems* (1953), won an Arts Council Prize (1953), and her second, *A Way of Looking* (1955), won the Somerset Maugham Award (1956) and helped her to find the courage to become a freelance writer. There followed four more books of poetry, of which the fourth, *The Mind Has Mountains* (1966), won the Richard Hillary Prize (1966). She also wrote a number of critical works, including a study of the relationship between poetry and religious experience entitled *Every Changing Shape* (1961) and *Christianity and Poetry* (1965). She was sufficiently established by this time that she was able to publish her *Collected Poems* (1967), a volume that includes almost all the poems in her previous books and twelve new poems. Here her major preoccupations can be clearly seen: man's essential loneliness, the fear that this loneliness can generate, and the psychological pain of human relations, as well as her devout Catholicism and love of Italy. Beginning with *Recoveries* (1964) there are many very personal poems about mental illness, based on the experience of her own breakdown.

The work of J. exhibits a remarkable consistency of tone and style; there is not very much development, the early poems resembling the recent ones. There is, however, a deepening and a maturing. Although J. has experimented with prose poems and free verse, most of her poems are in more or less regular forms. They are short, usually less than five stanzas, and the vocabulary is simple. She resists strange and unusual words and proper nouns, and she works for smoothness, evenness, and clarity. Her poems rarely have very detailed settings, even those that are observations of hospital life or descriptions of individual paintings. The attention is always on the inner world, and the purpose is to distinguish nuances of emotion. J.'s tone is one of detached, sober reasonableness, of understatement more often than not. Her effort is always for control.

In a period in which so far there are apparently no major British poets, J., with her honest craftsmanship, works diligently to make accurate, harmonious, and simple statements about friendship, belief, ineffable pain, and beauty. J. has found that as an insecure, solitary writer, poetry can help her relate to the larger world and constitutes a form of prayer; even her celebratory verse reflects her concern with isolation and the effects of the passing of time. Her quiet, mystical poems suggest, in their metrical formality and understated diction, an admittedly subdued voice but one acknowledged for its emotional conviction and spiritual power.

FURTHER WORKS: *A Sense of the World* (1958); *Let's Have Some Poetry* (1960); *Song for a Birth or a Death* (1961); *The Sonnets of Michelangelo* (1961); *Poetry Today 1957–1960* (1961); *Robert Frost* (1964); *The Secret Brother* (1966); *The Animals Arrive* (1969); *Lucidities* (1970); *Relationships* (1972); *Growing Points* (1975); *Seven Men of Vision* (1976); *Consequently I Rejoice* (1977); *After the Ark* (1978); *Moments of Grace: New Poems* (1979); *Selected Poems* (1979); *Winter Wind* (1979); *A Dream of Spring* (1980); *Celebration and Elegies* (1982); *Extending the Territory* (1985); *In Shakespeare's Company* (1985); *Collected Poems, 1953-1985* (1986); *In the Meantime* (1997); *Every Changing Shape: Mystical Experience and the Making of Poems* (1997)

BIBLIOGRAPHY: Thwaite, A., *Contemporary Poets of the English Language* (1970): 559–61; Byers, M., "Cautious Vision: Recent British Poetry by Women," in Schmidt, M., and Lindop, G., eds., *British Poetry since 1960* (1972): 74–84; Hamilton, I., "E. J., Collected Poems," *A Poetry Chronicle* (1973): 170–71; Morrison, B., *The Movement: English Poetry and Fiction of the 1950's* (1980): passim; Oram, C., "A Life in the Day of E. J.," *Sunday Times Magazine* [London], 27 July 1980: 62; Orr, P., ed., *The Poet*

Speaks (1966); Schmidt, M., *An Introduction to 50 Modern British Poets* (1979); Schofield, M. A., *NConL*, 13 (1983): 9-11; Stüzl, E. A., in Hogg, J., *On Poetry and Poets, Fifth Series* (1983); Wheeler, M., *Hopkins Among the Poets: Studies in Modern Responses to Gerard Manley Hopkins* (1985)

—ROBERT M. REHDER

JENSEN, Johannes Vilhelm

Danish novelist, short-story writer, essayist, and poet, b. 20 Jan. 1873, Farsø; d. 25 Nov. 1950, Copenhagen

J. studied medicine at the University of Copenhagen from 1893 to 1898. He traveled to the United States in 1896, around the world in 1902–3, to the Far East in 1912–13, and to Egypt and Palestine in 1925–26. In 1944 J. was awarded the Nobel Prize for literature.

The life and nature of J.'s home region, Himmerland, in North Jutland, remained a focal point in his writing as a longing for a lost paradise, which could only be recaptured through an expansion of the mind in time and space. Through this process he aimed at conquering the modern technological world, the fullest expression of which he found in the pragmatic American way of life. This longing for a reconciliation of the introvert and extrovert, guided by a Darwinist view of man as part of an evolutionary trend, forms the basic theme of J.'s works.

In his first novels, *Danskere* (1896; Danes) and *Einar Elkær* (1898; Einar Elkær), the main characters, obsessed by a paralyzing introspection, which is a dominant feature of Danish literature of the 1890s, are unable to accept an entirely practical, materialistic view of life. The preoccupation with the self is, however, strongly rejected in *Den gotiske Renaissance* (1901; the Gothic renaissance), a collection of travel letters from Spain and the World Exhibition in Paris in 1900, previously published in a newspaper, which glorify the technological, expansive spirit of the Gothic, that is, Anglo-Saxon, race, whose roots J. found in Himmerland.

Its people are portrayed in the realistic short stories in *Himmerlandsfolk* (1898; Himmerland people), and in the two volumes of *Himmerlandshistorier* (1904, 1910; Himmerland stories). The early stories are marked by a preoccupation with the tragic meaninglessness of life and its inevitable end; the later ones are masterful character studies rendered with humor and irony deriving from J.'s awareness of human frailties, as well as from his deep respect for the old peasant traditions. On the other hand, the double novel, comprising *Madame D'Ora* (1904; Madame D'Ora) and *Hjulet* (1905; the wheel), set in the splendidly depicted milieus of New York and Chicago respectively, advocate modern scientific viewpoints. They are, however, marred by lengthy diatribes against metaphysical speculation, by stereotyped suspense effects, and by grotesque character delineation based on J.'s wish to portray not individuals but progressive stages in man's evolution.

J.'s mythical works represent a supreme artistic achievement, in which extrovert and introvert elements are finally brought together. *Kongens fald* (3 vols., 1900–1; *The Fall of the King*, 1933, 1992), regarded as the most significant historical novel in Danish literature, attacks the inability to act perceived by the author as the major component of the Danish mentality. It is exemplified by the Renaissance king, Christian II, and his companion, the mercenary Mikkel Thøgersen. Breaking with the realistic novel, J. blends dream passages of exquisite lyrical beauty with explosive, ruthlessly naturalistic scenes. The result is a magnificent, deeply pessimistic vision of man's inability to reach happiness.

The expansion beyond time and reality is also present in J.'s smaller works, *Myter* (myths), which were published in eleven volumes between 1907 and 1944. In essays and prose sketches describing nature, animals, and journeys J. symbolically presents his basic ideas: a total acceptance of present reality as the final goal of all longing, and a belief in the cyclical eternity of revitalizing nature.

Several of these myths laid the foundation for the six-volume novel *Den lange rejse* (1908–22; *The Long Journey*, 1922–24), which forms an evolutionary history of mankind and a scientific counterpart to the biblical legends set in the primeval rain forests of Jutland. The challenges of nature are seen as the driving force of the progress that brings about the transition from animal to man. According to J., a basic trait of the Nordic people—the "Gothic race"—is the longing for distant places, for warmth and sun. The Viking migrations, he says, were a result of this longing, as was the first voyage of the "Goth" Columbus, which resulted in the discovery of America, of reality.

The contrast between longing and a stubborn belief in the bliss of the present moment also forms the major theme in J.'s first poetry collection, *Digte* (1906; poems; later enlarged eds. 1917, 1921, 1943, 1948), a milestone in the development of Danish lyric poetry. The collection features a number of prose poems modeled after Goethe's, Heine's, and Whitman's free verse but containing the imagery of modern technology and the metropolis. J.'s subsequent poetry volumes are dominated by verse in traditional meter or alliterative poems in the Old Norse style. They are not self-analyzing; rather they praise woman as wife and mother, children, and Danish nature, sometimes in a most grandiose manner, sometimes with the deepest intimacy, melting together observation, vision, and reflection into a perfect artistic whole.

Eventually rejecting poetry and fiction as a means of communication, J. turned to essays, which he wrote in a terse, matter-of-fact style. In them he set out to popularize the Darwinist, evolutionary view of life, although his ideas were often based on dubious anthropological and scientific theories and deductions. Stylistically, however, these prose works are often of high quality.

Although of little significance as a scientist, J. was one of the greatest innovative spirits in Danish cultural life and the writer who has had the greatest impact on Danish literature of the 20th c.: through his vigorous yet often lyrical style, through his extremely precise powers of observation as well as his visionary perspective, through his intense love for the microcosm in nature and his dynamic international orientation, and finally through his ability to connect the present with eternity, reality with dream.

FURTHER WORKS: *Intermezzo* (1899); *Skovene* (1904); *Myter og jagter* (1907); *Den ny verden* (1907); *Singaporenoveller* (1907); *Nye myter* (1908); *Lille Ahasverus* (1909); *Myter* (1910); *Nordisk ånd* (1911); *Myter* (1912); *Rudyard Kipling* (1912); *Olivia Marianne* (1915); *Introduktion til vor tidsalder* (1915); *Årbog* (1916, 1917); *Johannes Larsen og hans billeder* (1920); *Sangerinden* (1921); *Æstetik og udvikling* (1923); *Årstiderne* (1923); *Myter* (1924); *Hamlet* (1924); *Evolution og moral* (1925); *Årets højtider* (1925); *Thorvaldsens portrætbuster* (1926); *Verdens lys* (1926); *Jørgine* (1926); *Dyrenes forvandling* (1927); *Ved livets bred* (1928); *Åndens stadier* (1928); *Retninger i tiden* (1930); *Den jydske blæst* (1931); *Form og sjæl* (1931); *På danske veje* (1931); *Pisangen* (1932); *Kornmarken* (1932); *Sælernes ø* (1934); *Det blivende* (1934); *Dr.*

Renaults fristelser (1935); *Gudrun* (1936); *Darduse* (1937); *Påskebadet* (1937); *Jydske folkelivsmalere* (1937); *Thorvaldsen* (1938); *Nordvejen* (1939); *Fra fristaterne* (1939); *Gutenberg* (1939); *Mariehønen* (1940); *Mindets tavle* (1941); *Vor oprindelse* (1941); *Om sproget og undervisningen* (1942); *Kvinden i sagatiden* (1942); *Folkeslagene i østen* (1943); *Møllen* (1944); *Afrika* (1949); *Swift og Oehlenschläger* (1950); *Tilblivelsen* (1951)

BIBLIOGRAPHY: Marcus, A., "J. V. J.," *ASR*, 20 (1932): 340–47; Toksvig, S., "J. V. J.," *ASR*, 31 (1943): 343–46; Nyholm, J., "The Nobel Prize Goes Nordic," *BA*, 19 (1945): 131–35; Nielsen, M. L., *Denmark's J. V. J.* (1955); Friis, O., "J. V. J.," *Scan*, 1 (1962): 114–23; Ingwersen, N., "America as Setting and Symbol in J. V. J.'s Early Work," *Americana-Norvegica*, 3 (1971): 272–93; Rossel, S. H., *J. J.* (1984)

—SVEN H. ROSSEL

JERSILD, P(er) C(hristian)

Swedish novelist and dramatist, b. 14 March 1935, Katrineholm

J. grew up in a middle-class suburb of Stockholm and attended medical school. He specializes in social medicine and has also been an administrator. His professional experiences are reflected in his fiction, which often satirizes modern man's helplessness against the structures of society.

Notable among J.'s satirical novels about bureaucratic hierarchies are *Grisjakten* (1968; the pig hunt), which portrays the lack of humanity in administrative thinking; and *Djurdoktorn* (1973; *The Animal Doctor*, 1975), which demonstrates how inconvenient humanitarian concerns are nullified in the name of corporate democracy. The protagonist in *Vi ses i Song My* (1970; see you in Song My) believes he can change the system but is instead manipulated by it. In *Babels hus* (1978; the house of Babel) J. explores the impact of huge financial interests on health services in a hospital.

J. does not confine his satires to Sweden. In *Calvinols resa genom världen* (1965; Calvinol's journey through the world) both the Soviet Union and the United States are targets of his wit, while *Drömpojken: En paranoid historia* (1970; the dream boy: a paranoid story) takes place in an America marked by intrigues and conspicuous consumption.

Individual destiny is particularly well portrayed in *Stumpen* (1973; the stump), about an alcoholic bum who thinks he is worthless and should be eliminated by society; and in *Barnens ö* (1976; the children's island), about an eleven-year-old boy who learns about life and evil when he is left alone one summer in Stockholm. In J.'s autobiographical sketches about suburban Stockholm, *Uppror bland marsvinen* (1972; revolt among the guinea pigs) we find the prototype for his heroes in the protagonist who masks his bewilderment with humor and comedy.

J. has also written a few plays, among them a play for television, *Sammanträde pågår* (1967; meeting in session), about man's vulnerability in an impersonal bureaucratic society.

J.'s works are full of grotesque, bizarre, and absurd episodes, an aspect of his interest in the manipulative possibilities of the language. His vivid and dynamic style, combined with his professional insights, through which he often achieves a documentary effect in his social satire, have made him one of the most popular contemporary writers in Sweden.

FURTHER WORKS: *Räknelära* (1960); *Till varmare länder* (1967); *Prins Valiant och Konsum* (1966); *Den elektriska kaninen* (1974); *En levande själ* (1980); *Professionella bekännelser* (1981)

—TORBORG LUNDELL

JHABVALA, Ruth Prawer

Anglo-Indian novelist, short-story writer, and scriptwriter, b. 7 May 1927, Cologne, Germany

Born to Polish-Jewish parents who went as refugees to England in 1939, J. became a British citizen in 1948 and earned an M.A. in English literature from the University of London in 1951. She married a Parsee architect and from 1951 to 1975 she lived in India, where they had three daughters and she began writing her fiction. She has lived much of the time since 1975 in New York City, continuing to produce novels and short stories and also launching into a distinguished career as a writer of screenplays and television scripts.

Soon after settling in New Delhi, J. began drawing upon the rich resources of her European heritage to create an impressive series of works reflecting her experience of India. Her first novel, *To Whom She Will* (1955; pub. in the U.S. as *Amrita*, 1975), which deals with the comic maneuverings within two Indian families, recalls the matrimonial minuets of Jane Austen. The comic strain continues in *The Nature of Passion* (1956) and in *Esmond in India* (1957), but in the latter the irony deepens in its portrait of an unpleasant Englishman and the Indian wife he subjugates.

The Householder (1960) is a delightfully droll story commenting on the irrelevance of ancient customs and the contradictions of new ways. This book and the next, *Get Ready for Battle* (1962), present the funny, sad ironies of failure in human communication particularly between husbands and wives. In her rendering of individuality based not so much on distinctiveness of personality as on mutual inaccessibility, J. recalls the manner of Anton CHEKHOV.

In 1963 appeared J.'s first collection of short stories, *Like Birds, Like Fishes*, and in the same year she began a remarkably productive film collaboration with Ismail Merchant and James Ivory that continues today. She has written scripts based on her own books and has adapted works of Henry JAMES, E. M. FORSTER, and others, so far winning two Academy Awards.

J.'s sixth novel was *A Backward Place* (1966). Into India, still regarded by many Westerners and some Indians as a "backward" nation, she brings three European women, Etta and Clarissa suggesting sterile elements of Western culture in the Indo-European synthesis, and Judy who symbolizes a fruitful blending of Europe and the East: the feminine durability and resilience of India and the resourcefulness and adaptability of the West. Always J.'s keen vision records telling details of Indian locale.

A New Dominion (1973; pub. in the U.S. as *Travelers*), was followed by *Heat and Dust* (1975), which won the prestigious Booker Award. Both these novels show evidence of J.'s affinity with Forster. J.'s "travelers" to India include characters that resemble those who took the earliest "passage" to India. In *Heat and Dust*, anchored half in the 1970s and half in the 1920s, J. employs wit and precision to show the futility of attempts at understanding, not merely between Westerners and Indians, but between the men and women of one time and another.

During the 1970s, while busy with Merchant-Ivory productions, J. was turning out a spate of short fiction. In her fifth volume of stories, *Out of India* (1986), a single remarkable piece, "Rose Petals," conveys J.'s acknowledgement that most people in privileged circumstances find ways to isolate themselves from the poverty and injustice they see on all sides. J.'s characters who retreat from ugly reality are treated with ironic wit and humor, yet they also receive compassionate forgiveness from the author. In the book's introduction, "Myself in India," J. confesses her own inaction as a privileged observer of India, and she adds further hints of complex motivations leading J. to New York City and her experiences of a third continent.

J.'s first novel reflecting life in the U.S., *In Search of Love and Beauty* (1983), introduces European immigrants—specifically Austrian and German refugees—to the New World as they work out their destinies through three generations. The novel has been fairly called Proustian for its treatment of the way the past affects the present in a complicated mix of nationalities, religions, and unique personalities. J.'s mastery of ethnic detail is manifest in the way she marshals styles of food and costumes and even of furniture to support the cultural diversity she envisions.

Three Continents (1987) is J.'s longest novel to date, an ambitious but somehow disappointing study of the moral decline of an American family in a round-the-world search for spiritual security. By means of a naive nineteen-year-old narrator, Harriet Wishwell, J. manages a fiercely unrelenting exposure of a cultic scam known as the Fourth World movement. But what might have been the author's own satiric perspective is suppressed and the reader soon tires of infinite details about the family's decay among assorted international rogues and rascals.

Poet and Dancer (1993), a short work, also set in America deals with the destructive relationship between two women, first cousins within a third-generation German-American family operating behind a Manhattan brownstone front. The pair work out their doom amidst J.'s careful rendering of ethnic and personal complexities she has observed in more than two decades as a resident of the U.S.

J.'s twelfth novel, *Shards of Memory* (1995), is another multigenerational effort, moving from America to London to India and back to America again. A member of the fourth generation traces the family's puzzling history through old documents, "odd shards and fragments of the past." From these bits and pieces of memory readers are able to explore again the fascinating dichotomies of East and West, the divisions between and within personalities.

In most of her work J. has preserved a balance between satire and sympathy for her human creations. Her graceful and economical prose proceeds from an intelligence well served by ear and eye and memory. Her people are contradictory of themselves and of each other, but everything they say is true because—as she learned in India long ago—all things are true of mankind generally.

FURTHER WORKS: *Like Birds, Like Fishes* (1963); *The Householder* (screenplay, 1965); *A Stronger Climate* (1968); *An Experience of India* (1972); *Shakespeare Wallah* (screenplay, 1973, with James Ivory); *Autobiography of a Princess* (screenplay, 1975); *How I Became a Holy Mother, and Other Stories* (1976); *The Bostonians* (screenplay, 1984); *A Room with a View* (screenplay, 1985); *Howard's End* (screenplay, 1992)

BIBLIOGRAPHY: Pritchett, V. S., "Snares and Delusions," *New Yorker*, 16 June 1973: 106–9; Williams, H. M., *The Fiction of R. P. J.* (1973); Bell, P. K., on *Heat and Dust, NYTBR*, 4 April 1976: 7–8; Annan, G., "The Acceptance World," *TLS*, 25 June 1976, 757; Shahane, V. A., *R. P. J.* (1976); Singh, R. S., *The Indian Novel in English: A Critical Study* (1977): 149–63; Souza, E. de, "The Expatriate Experience," in Narasimhaiah, C. D., ed., *Awakened Conscience: Studies in Commonwealth Literature* (1978): 339–45; Rubin, D., "R. J. in India," *MFS*, 30 (Winter 1984): 669-83; Sucher, L., *The Fiction of R .P. J.: The Politics of Passion* (1989); Long, R. E., *The Films of Merchant Ivory* (1991); Bailur, J., *R. P. J.: Fiction and Film* (1992); Crane, R. I., *R. P. J.* (1992); Newman, J., "Postcolonial Gothic: R. P. J. and the Sobhraj Case," *MFS*, 40 (Spring 1994): 85-100; Urstad, T. S., "Protecting One's Inner Self: R. P. J.'s 'Rose Petals,'" *SSF*, 33 (Winter 1996): 43-49

—CARL D. BENNETT

JILEMNICKÝ, Peter

Czechoslovak essayist, journalist, short-story writer, and novelist (writing in Slovak), b. 18 March 1901, Kyšperk (now Letohrad); d. 19 May 1949, Moscow

Although Czech by birth, J. adopted the Slovak language as the medium of his literary work. Having graduated from an agricultural college, he came to Slovakia as a teacher in 1921, did his two years of military service there, and then returned to his teaching profession. The experience of living in and observing some of the poorest and most backward areas of the country had a profound influence both on his political views (he joined the Communist Party in 1922) and on his writing. Equally important was his two-year stay (beginning in 1926) in the Soviet Union, where he was first a teacher and then journalism student in Moscow. After his return, he worked for a short time for the Slovak Communist press, but soon returned to teaching.

Following the dismemberment of Czechoslovakia at Munich, J. was expelled from Slovakia at the beginning of 1939 by the pro-Nazi Slovak authorities, and he settled again in his native eastern Bohemia. In October 1942 he was arrested by the Gestapo and for his association with the underground Communist Party and sentenced to eight years' hard labor by a Nazi court. When he returned after the war from a labor camp in Germany, he at once became very actively engaged in public life; he died while serving as cultural attaché at the Czechoslovak embassy in Moscow.

J.'s first novel, *Víťazný pád* (1929; glorious fall), completed early in 1926, mainly shows the impact on the author of the beauty of mountainous northwest Slovakia. Social problems, although not entirely omitted, were not yet the focus of his interest, and the struggle that he described was rather that of man against nature. Equally strong, but influencing him in a different direction, was the impression made on J. by what he witnessed in the Soviet Union. His novel *Zuniaci krok* (1930; thundering step), which, two years before Sholokhov's *Virgin Soil Upturned*, described the changes in the life of the Soviet village at the beginning of the collectivization, is often considered to be the founding work of SOCIALIST REALISM in Slovak fiction.

Pole neorané (1932; the untilled field) is again set in the mountainous Kysuce region of the first novel, but this time J. concentrated on the chronic poverty, backwardness, economic

emigration, and alcoholism with which it was plagued. The realization that such social evils cannot be cured by mere charity and individual effort but only by a removal of the exploiting class through a radical change of the political system, is hastened in the awareness of the main character by his contact with Communist workers in the nearby industrial town of Ostrava.

A similar process takes place in *Kus cukru* (1934; a piece of sugar), whose story is based on the paradox that workers in the sugar refineries were unable to afford sugar and replaced it with saccharine smuggled from abroad. The urban working class here seeks an alliance with the impoverished farmers. In this novel J. wanted to express his belief that "we are all entitled to a piece of sugar, a piece of the sweetness, glory, and fullness of life." Its construction, however, became too obviously subordinated to his political design.

In *Kompas v nás* (1937; the compass within us), a cycle of long stories set alternately in the Soviet Union and Czechoslovakia, J. explored the question of human happiness. He concluded that it could not be found where greed and egoism reigned. True happiness and security could be achieved only within the collective struggle for social justice and a better life for all. Almost as an afterthought appears the idea that people also need to be rooted in a place they can call their home.

After the war, J. wrote about the Slovak National Uprising of August 1944, in which he himself could not take part. In *Kronika* (1947; chronicle), life in a Slovak village during this crucial period is being described by a gamekeeper to the local teacher who wants to make a record of it. By presenting a personalized view of momentous historical events, J. avoided the danger of producing a pompous heroic epic. In fact, the novel does not have any individual hero, his place being taken by the village collective, although Communists are portrayed as leaders in the anti-Nazi fight.

Most of J.'s works are marked by his compassion for the poor and oppressed, by his enchantment with the simple and natural life as well as by his commitment to the ideals of socialism and communism. He himself characterized his work as "fight and song," the former representing the political, the latter the balladic element in it. J., who worked hard to achieve formal and stylistic perfection, was conscious of the risk associated with this approach. Indeed, he managed to blend the two invisibly only on few occasions; very often the seam shows, and this is considered to be a shortcoming of his work.

FURTHER WORKS: *Devadesát devět koní bílých* (1921); *Dva roky v krajine sovietov* (1929); *Návrat* (1930, 1938)

BIBLIOGRAPHY: Mihailovich, V., et al., eds., *Modern Slavic Literatures* (1976), Vol. II: 124–27; Součková, M., *A Literary Satellite: Czechoslovak-Russian Literary Relations* (1970): 78–81

—IGOR HÁJEK

JIMÉNEZ, Juan Ramón

Spanish poet, essayist, and critic, b. 23 Dec. 1881, Moguer; d. 29 May 1958, San Juan, Puerto Rico

J. left Moguer, where he spent his childhood and adolescence, and which he had so often celebrated in his verse, to study law at the

Juan Ramón Jiménez

University of Seville. There he also showed an interest in painting, but he abandoned law studies and also stopped painting to devote himself entirely to writing poetry and reading the French and German romantics and the French SYMBOLISTS. He also read with great pleasure the 19th-c. Spanish poets Rosalía de Castro (1837–1885) and Gustavo Bécquer (1836–1870).

In April 1900, J. was invited to Madrid by the MODERNIST poets Francisco Villaespesa (1877–1936) and Rubén DARÍO, who were attracted to his verses published in *Vida nueva*, a Madrid review. J. soon became an active member of the modernist literary circles and helped to found two important reviews, *Helios* in 1902 and *Renacimiento* in 1906.

J. returned to Moguer in the summer of 1900. Deeply depressed by his father's sudden death, he was sent to a sanatorium in France to recover from his first bout with mental illness. His depressions, neurasthenia, morbid fear of dying, and penchant for withdrawing from people would remain with him throughout his life, but at no time did his condition diminish his creativity. In fact, it seemed to drive him on.

In 1916, after a decade of intense productivity, J. traveled to New York to marry Zenobia Camprubí, whom he had met while living in Madrid. He collaborated with her on the Spanish translations of the Indian poet Rabindranath TAGORE.

At the outbreak of the civil war in 1936, J. and Zenobia left Spain and returned to America. He lectured and taught at many American universities. In 1951 J. and his wife moved to Puerto Rico, where he lectured and gave classes at the university. In 1956,

a few days before his wife's death, J. was awarded the Nobel Prize for literature.

It is difficult to imagine a poet more dedicated to his craft than was J., who considered poetry a religion, a path to salvation, a mode of preserving values from the ravages of time. A Platonist, he believed in a universal consciousness that existed apart from individual consciousness and felt it was the poet's task to express this concept through symbolism.

J.'s poetic development is emblematic of his struggle to attain full consciousness. He started by capturing fleeting impressions of nature and the sadness inherent in a universe that is transitory. At a later stage he wished to commune with the universe, until at the end of his life he believed he had mystically encountered absolute beauty and eternity on the deepest level of consciousness permitted to him.

J. himself described these three stages of development: he called his first period, up until 1909, an "ecstasy of love"; he called the second stage, from 1910 to 1921, an "avidity for eternity"; after 1921, he said his poetry was marked by the "necessity for inner consciousness."

J.'s earliest books of poems, *Ninfeas* (1900; water lilies) and *Almas de violeta* (1900; violet souls), although derivative and studied in their melancholy tone and sentimentality, show the poet to have had a facility with a variety of meters, especially the eight-syllable line, and an ability to capture lyric beauty and subtle emotions.

His next books—*Rimas* (1902; rhymes), *Arias tristes* (1903; sad airs), *Jardines lejanos* (1904; distant gardens), and *Pastorales* (1905; pastorals)—were still imbued with a fascination for modernism, but they have a stronger, more mature and original voice. They are delightfully lyrical and at times elegantly simple impressionistic studies of nature, filled with musicality and mystery. Also present is a heartsick, fin-de-siècle malaise.

In *Elegías puras* (1908; pure elegies), *Baladas de primavera* (1910; ballads of spring), and *La soledad sonora* (1911; the sonorous solitude), J. continued to experiment with different meters, especially the alexandrine, and his style became more ornate and baroque. In these works he leaves the parks and gardens to contemplate the countryside with vague nostalgia, heightened sensuality, and chromatic richness, communing with the world in graceful tranquillity, but he is still burdened with a recurring anxiety about death.

His trip to New York in 1916 to be married led to the publication of *Diario de un poeta reciéncasado* (1918; diary of a newlywed poet), which represents a major change in J.'s poetic development and in all poetry in Spain. This work, the first important one in Spain in free verse, clearly reveals that J. had moved beyond the confines of modernism into a new creative sphere. Freed from rhyme and meter, J. explores the metaphysical concerns that would interest him for the rest of his life. He uses the newly found rhythms of the sea to contemplate the delicate but precarious balance between the poet's own consciousness and the frightening immensity of the sea, which personifies solitude. At times he feels engulfed by the sea, and at other times it is he who engulfs it—a standoff of two equals.

In *Eternidades* (1918; eternities), J. established a new norm for his poetry, denouncing all of his past verse. In a famous (untitled) poem that begins "Vino, primero pura" (1918; "Poetry," 1942), in which he compares poetry to a woman, he decides to return to the simplicity of his earlier poetry, for he sees his verse as having become overdressed, laden with jewels—and he now rejects this approach. Not unlike Paul Valéry, he seeks "naked poetry," that is, pure poetry purged of everything that is extraneous to its essence. As a result, *Eternidades* is filled with slender, epigrammatic poems that are highly conceptual.

In *Belleza* (1923; beauty) and *Poesía (en verso)* (1923; poetry [in verse]) J. continued to ponder the nature of poetry and the meaning of his own "Work," to which he had begun referring as *Obra*, with a capital *O*. He is also concerned with poetry's relationship to beauty and death: it is through poetry that J. hopes he will be saved.

In the eloquent *La estación total con canciones de nueva luz* (1936; the total season with songs of new light) a full awareness of the beauty and harmony of the world is revealed by the poet. The very title suggests a paradox with which J. has always grappled: "season" implies impermanence and change, while "total" connotes a synthesis, a hard-won eternity. Within the flux, there is the eternal moment where everything fuses.

The height of J.'s deepened consciousness and full integration with the cosmos can be seen in his brilliant last book, *Dios desendo y diseante* (1949; *God Desired and Desiring*, 1987). In it J. created a god, who is fully attuned to the beauty of the universe. It is a song of joy, of mystical union, of the creation of a pantheistic god for all people of all faiths for all ages. It is the testament of his struggle toward perfect consciousness.

It should not be forgotten that J. was also a fine prose writer. Besides having written many essays on the ethics and aesthetics of poetry, he wrote two very important books of prose. One is *Platero y yo* (1914; *Platero and I*, 1956), which consists of short lyrical sketches of the poet and his donkey, set in Moguer. It is J.'s most popular work, and deservedly so, for it portrays in a captivating manner the great theme of death and rebirth. The other is *Españoles de tres mundos* (1942; Spaniards of three worlds), a series of lyrical caricatures written over a period of many years about important literary figures.

Although periodically unbalanced by depression and anxiety, a semirecluse for most of his life and totally self-absorbed, J. gave Spain a body of lyric poetry from which all other 20th-c. Spanish poetry originated. He was a poet's poet, who, in almost complete solitude, portrayed the unending crises of the inner world, passing over the tumult of the outer world; for this he has been criticized. His goal was nothing less than the creation of a system of salvation within the framework of poetry. His work was his life, and his life a search for authentic poetry and metaphysical consciousness.

FURTHER WORKS: *Elegías intermedias* (1909); *Olvidanzas: Las hojas verdes* (1909); *Poemas mágicos y dolientes* (1911); *Melancolía* (1912); *Laberinto* (1913); *Estío* (1915); *Poesías escogidas* (1899–1917) (1917); *Sonetos espirituales* (1917); *Piedra y cielo* (1919); *Segunda antología poética* (1899–1918) (1922); *Unidad* (1925); *Obra en marcha* (1929); *Sucesión* (1932); *Presente* (1934); *I (Hojas nuevas, prosa y verso)* (1935); *Canción* (1936); *Política poética* (1936); *Verso y prosa para niños* (1937); *Ciego ante ciegos* (1938); *Antología poética* (1944); *Voces de mi copla* (1945); *Animal de fundo* (1947); *Diario de poeta y mar* (1948; new version of *Diario de un poeta reciéncasado*); *Romances de Coral Gables* (1939–1942) (1948); *Tercera antología poética* (1957); *El zaratán* (1957); *La corriente infinita* 1903–1954 (1961); *Por el cristal amarillo* 1902–1954 (1961); *El trabajo gustoso* 1948–1954 (1961); *El Modernismo: Notas de un curso* (1962); *Cartas* 1898–1958 (1962); *Primeras prosas* 1890–1954 (1962); *La colina de los chopos* 1913–1928 (1965); *Isla de la simpatía* (1981); *Tiempo y espacio* (1982; *Time and Space: A Poetic Autobiography*, 1988);

La realidad invisible (1917-1920, 1924) (1983; *Invisible Reality [1917-1920, 1924]*, 1987); *Guerra en España, 1936-953*, (1985). **FURTHER WORKS IN ENGLISH:** *Fifty Spanish Poems* (1950); *Selected Writings* (1957); *Three Hundred Poems* 1903–1953 (1962); *Forty Poems* (1967); *Lorca and J.: Selected Poems* (1973); *Light and Shadows: Selected Poems and Prose* (1987); *The Complete Perfectionist: A Poetic of War* (1997)

BIBLIOGRAPHY: Gullón, R., *Estudios sobre J. R. J.* (1960); Schonberg, J.-L, *J. R. J.; ou, Le chant d'Orphée* (1961); Zardoya, C., *Poesía española contemporánea* (1961): 219–40; Young, H. T., *The Victorious Expression: A Study of Four Contemporary Spanish Poets* (1964): 77–137; Predmore, M. P., *La obra en prosa de J.R.J.* (1966); Olson, P., *Circle of Time: Time and Essence in the Poetry of J. R. J.* (1967); Cole, L. R., *The Religious Instinct in the Poetry of J.R.J.*(1967); Palau de Nemes, G., *Vida y obra de J. R. J.* (2 vols.), (1974); Cobb, C. W., *Contemporary Spanish Poetry (1898–1963)* (1976): 49–64; Fogelquist, D. F., *J.R.J.* (1976); Cardwell, Richard, "J. R. J.: An Introduction," *Renaissance and Modern Studies*, 25 (1981): 2-23; Coke-Enguídanos, M., *Word and Work in the Poetry of J. R. J.* (1982); Wilcox, J. C., *Self and Image in J. R. J.: Modern and Post-Modern Studies* (1987); Palau de Nemes, G., in Mujica, B., ed., *Premio Novel: Once grandes escritores del mundo hispánico* (1997)

—MARSHALL J. SCHNEIDER

J.'s work is a sort of *comédie mystique*. Singly, the poems have variety of notes. Yet there is a cryptic quality in them, and a subtle allusiveness to something not explicit, which must repugn the shallow sense, even as it entrances the mind hungry for great vistas. His poems have prosodic value. Yet their chiefest value is that they *create aesthetically* a sense of incompleteness. Aesthetically, they are whole because they contain this *lack*—this positive surge toward an apocalyptic sense which lives in them only by the imprint of its absence. Each of his poems is at once a sensory form, and a spiritual inchoation. . . . One might say that a poem of J. is like an instant in a human life: full-limned, full-equipped with thought, emotion, will; and yet this fullness is but the passing function of an implicit unity which transcends and subscends it.

Waldo Frank, *Virgin Spain* (1926), p. 291

J. R. J. is sometimes described as an apostle of *vers libre*; but if so, he is an apostle who hides his vocation under his mantle. His verse is not printed to look like *vers libre*; and the proportion of lines which will fit into no recognized scheme is not large. The traditions of Castilian verse, which have always permitted assonance as well as rhyme, accentual as well as syllabic metre, give possibilities of which so accomplished a technician is not slow to avail himself. Indeed, it might be said of the Spanish poet, as was said of a French contemporary of his, that he, too, has written free verse, but by some magic his verses always end by being regular. They have, at any rate, the certainty of rhythm and sense of repose which make them convincing as real lines of poetry. . . .

[J. R. J.] found that the poems which he held to be the most simple and spontaneous always proved to be those of the most clean and deliberate workmanship. He cannot share the view that failure and lack of discipline in art is an attitude of any interest, and he does not believe in the existence of finished, popular poetry which is at the same time simple and spontaneous.

> John B. Trend, "J. R. J.," *Alfonso the Sage, and Other Spanish Essays* (1926), p. 150

Platero and I is one of those felicitous works in which the author's most brilliant and solid qualities are responsive to the spirit of the times. Seldom has an Andalusian backdrop been shown with such poetic truth; its expressiveness is the most evocative and perfect that any author of that generation [1898] has been able to realize; the warm, solitary, and human simplicity that makes these pages tremble is the best guarantee that such a book will not diminish in the interest that was present from the very moment of its initial appearance. Its theme is nature, nature that is reflected in the eyes of the poet, and the beauty of this theme has no equal except in the crystalline transparency with which the poet's eyes reflect it, so that as soon as the vision is obscured by some veil, we do not know if it is of mist or of tears.

> Luis Cernuda, "J. R. J.," *BSpS*, 19 (1942), p. 174

Belleza and *Poesía* (1917–1923), twins one might say, were published in 1923 and both accentuate the essential part of the poet's work, that becomes more and more subjective and intimate with light accents of intellectualism and a constant meditation on those very words: poetry and beauty. Together, the two offer the key to J.'s preoccupation. It is not a question of deciding in his works the relationship between poetry and truth, as in Goethe's case; between beauty and truth as in Keats or Emily Dickinson but between beauty and poetry which with love, woman and death form the abiding themes of his life. Death, for example, is constantly present in the poet of Moguer. . . . At times the *death* of Rilke is recalled by J.'s figure of death. This theme becomes almost an obsession, and it can be seen that this preoccupation with the death of others is nothing other than the mirror of his own imaged death, almost a dialogue with it. Now, too, we can appreciate how the total work of the poet of Moguer could be—and in fact is—a triumph, not over the D'Annunzio style of death, but over death itself; the triumph of beauty and of poetry; the ultimate triumph of the permanent over the temporal and perishable.

> Eugenio Florit, Preface to J. R. J., *Selected Writings* (1957), pp. xxii-xxiii

J. reconciles, besides, restraint and intensity: tirelessly sincere, but never given to prattling or gesticulation, he will express moments of plenitude or of rapture while preserving a muted tone, a singular poise and weightlessness. This is especially evident in his folkloric pieces, where colorful effects are shunned. Restraint is also compatible in J. R. J. with the boldness of the experimenter. Here his role as an innovator must be recalled once more, for he never ceased to invent, to search for that straightest line between the emotion and the reader which would be the purest form. He has been, like Gide, always a young poet, for whom every book was a beginning. Hence his considerable variety and—to mention a final wedding of opposition—the fusion of it with a remarkable singleness of intent and style. J. concentrates in each poem on almost a single device, plays but one of the many strings on his instrument at a time. If one virtue or one method may be considered characteristic of his poetry, it is that of concentration above all on the single word, on the force and the magic of which language is capable.

> Claudio Guillen, "The Problem of J. R. J.," *New Republic*, 16 Dec. 1957, 17–18

[J.'s] dialogue with nature, enriching the constant spinning of the creative imagination, was crystalized in that admirable work [*Platero y yo*, 1914], lyrical biography, collection of etchings, Andalusian elegy . . . Yes, Andalusian and universal, as the author wanted it, striving to achieve universality by reaching into his own depth until he could touch the most particular and local, the essential human. He concentrated on the simple incidents of living, in the bare instant, to the point of not dividing his life into days, but his day into lives: "each day, each hour, an entire life." Such concentration gave his poetry density and intensity: in each line we feel him complete, gravitating above it with all the weight of his soul and of his dream—lucid dream of deep realities, penetration into the other face of reality, to the point of converting the temporal into substance of the eternal and the limited into expression of the infinite. To give himself up to poetry was to give himself up to life, to life each day different and the same, like daybreak; to life at its deepest level, with the bird and the rose, the child and the cloud.

> Ricardo Gullón, Introduction to J. R. J., *Three Hundred Poems* (1962), p. xxi

In his completeness J. is almost unrivaled in Spanish poetry. He began as an Adamic poet in a fresh world of inexhaustible beauty, determined to express every nuance, every emotion. He mastered all the forms of Spanish poetry: the song, the ballad, the sonorous Alexandrine, the sonnet form, free verse, and the concentrated free verse of "pure poetry." He developed extensively most of the essential symbols of Western poetry with his own emphasis: the sea, the rose, the sun, the tree, the flower, the bird, the cloud, the diamond, the glowing coal, the circle. Admittedly he failed to exploit the ugly: as a man he suffered the ugly and the confused; as a poet, discipline in the quest for beauty was paramount. J. is an outstanding example of the modern poet: since the time of Poe and

Baudelaire, given the disintegration of the Christian world view, the poet has been cast adrift to create his own metaphysical system of salvation. J. creates such a system, grounded in a fusion of natural religion and aesthetics and employing the modern preoccupation with the extension of time through heightened consciousness. Moreover, his metaphysical system is properly created in a convincing poetic structure. Surely J., a deserving recipient of the Nobel Prize, can be meaningfully compared with major European poets such as Yeats and Rilke. Take him for all in all, J. R. J. may well be the greatest lyric poet in Spanish literature.

Carl W. Cobb, *Contemporary Spanish Poetry (1898–1963)* (1976), pp. 63–64

JIRÁSEK, Alois

Czechoslovak novelist, short-story writer, and dramatist (writing in Czech), b. 23 Aug. 1851, Hronov; d. 12 March 1930, Prague

As a high-school history teacher and researcher in ethnography, J. led an uneventful life, interrupted only by travels during which he studied the locale of his future writings. It was not until World War I that he assumed the role of a spokesman for the Czech people in their efforts to gain national independence; the Manifesto of the Czech Writers of 1917 was connected primarily with his name. From 1918 through 1925, he served in the Czechoslovak parliament as member of the conservative National Democratic Party.

Like the majority of his countrymen, J. considered the 15th-c. Hussite movement as the most glorious epoch in the nation's history and devoted several important works to it. His trilogy *Mezi proudy* (1886–91; between the currents) depicts the events leading to the Hussite revolt. The zenith of the upheaval is the subject of a three-part cycle, *Proti všem* (1894; against the whole world). Another trilogy, *Bratrstvo* (1899–1908; brotherhood), artistically J.'s most mature work, deals with the disintegration of the movement, when the Hussite units transferred to Slovakia. The reign of the "national king" of Bohemia, George of Poděbrady, and the activities of the Czech Brethren are the subjects of J.'s novel *Husitský král* (2 vols., 1921, 1930; the Hussite king), which remained unfinished.

The second most significant period in Czech history for J. was the time of the National Revival, from the 1770s to the mid-19th c. To this era he devoted a monumental five-part chronicle, *F. L. Věk* (1888–1905; F. L. Věk), portraying the national and linguistic reawakening in Prague and in a provincial town; and a four-part cycle, *U nás* (1896–1903; in our country), set in his native eastern Bohemia. The novella *Filosofská historie* (1878; *Gaudeamus Igitur*, 1961) is a charming picture of student life in the pre-1848 decade.

Another period that attracted J.'s interest was the aftermath of the Thirty Years' War, a time of national decline. He described it in somber colors in such books as *Skaláci* (1875; the Skalák family) and *Psohlavci* (1886; the dog-heads), both concerned with uprisings of Czech peasants against their overlords; and *Temno* (1913; the darkness), dealing with the Counter-Reformation. The title of the last-named novel, probably his most popular book, became a household word, designating any dark time in Czech national life. In *Staré pověsti české* (1894; *Stories and Legends of Old Prague*,

1931; new trans., *Legends of Old Bohemia*, 1963) he collected legends and stories from the country's early history.

Especially important among J.'s extensive dramatic works are *Vojnarka* (1891; Vojnarka) and *Otec* (1895; the father), tragic pictures from the life of country people; a Hussite triptych, *Jan Žižka* (1903; Jan Žižka), *Jan Hus* (1911; Jan Hus), and *Jan Roháč* (1914; Jan Roháč); and the fairy-tale allegories with national and social undertones, *Lucerna* (1905; *The Lantern*, 1925) and *Pan Johanes* (1909; Mr. Johanes). Most of these plays achieved great success on the Czech stage.

J. was one of the most effective writers for his nation's struggle against foreign domination and for the independence of his people. In his writings (which are of uneven quality, to be sure), the Czech reader found a source of patriotic inspiration, and the impact of his work, particularly during World War I and again during the German occupation in 1939–45, is undeniable. In world literature he is considered on a par with Henryk SIENKIEWICZ.

FURTHER WORKS: *Slavný den* (1879); *Na dvoře vévodském* (1881); *Ze zlatého věku v Čechách* (1882); *Konec a počátek* (1882); *Obětovaný* (1883); *Ráj světa* (1883); *Sousedé* (1884); *Poklad* (1885); *Pandurek* (1886); *V cizích službách* (1886); *Maryla* (1887); *Zemanka* (1887); *Skály* (1887); *Nevolnice* (1888); *Na ostrově* (1888); *Maloměstské historie* (1890); *Z Čech až na konec světa* (1890); *Sebrané spisy* (45 vols., 1890–1930); *Kolébka* (1892); *Emigrant* (1898); *M. D. Rettigová* (1891; *Dobromila Rettig*, 1920); *Gero* (1894); *Samota* (1908); *Z mých pamětí* (1911–13); *Sebrané spisy* (47 vols., 1927–1934); *Básně A. J.* (1930); *Obnovit pamět' minulých dnů* (1954); *Odkaz národu: Soubor díla* (32 vols., 1954–1958)

BIBLIOGRAPHY: Nejedlý, Z., *A. J.* (1952); Novák, A., *Czech Literature* (1976): 198–200

—RUDOLF STURM

JOAQUIN, Nick

Philippine novelist, poet, short-story writer, dramatist, and essayist (writing in English), b. 3 May 1917, Manila

In 1947 J.'s essay on what was believed to be the miraculous defeat of a Dutch fleet by the Spaniards off the Philippines in 1646 led the Dominicans to offer him a scholarship to study in Hong Kong. But in 1950 he left Hong Kong to write for the *Philippines Free Press*, under the pseudonym "Quijano de Manila" (an anagram of his name). In 1970 he became coeditor of the *Asian-Philippines Leader*, subsequently suspended for its political views when martial law was declared in 1972.

Because of his seminarian training and his antiquarian expertise in Spanish influences on Philippine culture, J. used to be accused of pious nostalgia. More recent critics, however, impressed by J.'s decades of reportage on contemporary issues, both knowledgeable and passionate, have come to understand his sense of the interplay between all periods of history. The struggle for individuality within contesting cultural contexts not only is his recurrent theme but finds expression through the nonchronological structures of such stories as "Guardia de Honor," "May Day Eve," and "The Mass of St. Sylvestre," as well as through fusion of legend, myth, and history in "The Summer Solstice" (all four first published in *Prose and Poems*, 1952) and "The Order of Melkizedek" (first published in *Tropical Gothic*, 1972). Figures representing the voice of conscience and the pressures of the past upon the present dominate his key works: Marasigan, the offstage father in his play *Portrait of the Artist as Filipino* (1952); the elder Monzon in the novel *The Woman Who Had Two Navels* (1961).

His sometimes gemlike style has often been imitated, but rarely with an understanding of its function in his work, which is to suggest with crystalline brilliance the various planes and prismatic angles in human affairs. J. reminds his countrymen of the uneasy coexistence of "primitive" and "civilized" dimensions in all men; the difficulty the moral intelligence has in distinguishing sinner from saint; and the special problem that Filipinos have of reconciling their mixed Asian and Western heritages, and then of shaping the best of these traditions into a continuing, compassionate national identity.

His short stories about these cultural ambiguities having already made him the most anthologized of all Philippine authors, he was declared a National Artist in 1976.

FURTHER WORKS: *Selected Stories* (1962); *A Question of Heroes: Essays in Criticism on Ten Key Figures in Philippine History* (1977); *Reportage on Crime* (1977); *Reportage on Lovers* (1977); *Nora Aunor, and Other Profiles* (1977); *Ronnie Poe, and Other Silhouettes* (1977)

BIBLIOGRAPHY: Furay, H., "The Stories of N. J.," *PSM*, 1 (1953): 144–53; Busuego-Pablo, L., "The Spanish Tradition in N. J.," *PSM*, 3 (1955): 187–207; Constantino, J., "*The Woman Who Had Two Navels*," *PSM*, 9 (1961): 639–50; Casper, L., ed., *Modern Philippine Short Stories* (1962): 21–56; Casper, L., *New Writing from the Philippines* (1966): 137–45; Manuud, A., ed., *Brown Heritage* (1967): 765–92

—LEONARD CASPER

JOENPELTO, Eeva

Finnish novelist, b. 17 June 1921, Sammatti

J. belongs in the front rank of Finnish fiction writers; her work is valued both by a large readership and by critics and scholars alike. She was nearly thirty when she published her first novel, *Kaakerholman kaupunla* (1950; The Town of Kaakerholma), and twenty-six novels later, she was still producing work that rates among the best, as proven by the awarding of the Finlandia Prize to her novel, *Tuomari Müller, hieno mies* (1994; Judge Müller, A Fine Man).

Many consider *Neito kulkee vetten päällä* (1955; The Maiden Walks upon the Water) J.'s breakthrough novel. After experimenting with various approaches and settings, J. had found a new way to describe the unhappy life of a poor farm woman who goes to work in a factory, as well as the hardships of her daughter, whose belief in a brighter future keeps her afloat. J.'s style is crisp and spare. She does not spell things out unnecessarily but trusts the reader to get the point. The sequel, *Kipinöivät vuodet* (1961; The Sparkling Years), continues the daughter's story. The transformation of a formerly rural area into an industrial society serves as the background for these books, but the focus is on the characters and their

lives—the strong women and their inconstant men. Some of J.'s earlier shorter fiction had already used this milieu. The southern Finnish community of Lohja, where J. herself was born and still lives, has provided her with a kaleidoscope of types and fates to use in her stories.

After several more novels, praised for her sharp eye for social and historical detail, J. was ready to start on the four novels referred to as her "Lohja series." *Vetää kaikista ovista* (1974; A Draft from Every Door) begins the story of a family whose members circulate from middle class up and down into other social groups—farmers, left-wing workers, more or less successful businessmen. The time is right after Finland's independence; the bitter scars left by the civil war have not yet healed. In the stagnant closed rural community a draft is beginning to be felt as uninvited guests arrive, and the events of the world outside begin to impact people's lives. J. puts her characters through all the difficulties that the times and their own desires and disappointments inflict upon them. *Kuin kekäle kädessä* (1976; Like Holding a Red Hot Coal in Your Hand) and *Sataa suolaista vettä* (1978; Salty Rain) continue the story, and the series ends in the early 1930s as the Great Depression sets in with *Eteisiin ja kynnyksille* (1980; Into the Hallways and onto the Thresholds). J. lets the reader see the world through her characters. They are as the times allow them to be. Social change tears them up by the roots. Land and property no longer guarantee security. People are elbowed out into the hallways and onto the thresholds of the 1930s, feverishly buying, selling, pawning as the approaching depression is making itself felt on both an individual and a political level. J. creates an uncannily correct picture of the times, precise to the smallest detail.

"Natural and forceful characterization, a plot marked with dramatic climaxes, a historically exact picture of the times"—these are the great merits of J.'s "Lohja" series, writes Kai Laitinen; "but even together they are not sufficient to explain why it seems so significant. It is vivified by a further factor that might be the theme of life, or more precisely, the theme of life's difficulty and unpredictability." This is true of J.'s later production as well. She places her characters in the context of the times and lets them struggle with the hand they have been dealt. Values, decency, morality, and moderation are what counts; some of J.'s characters live up to them, others do not, but even those who do not receive an understanding treatment.

Cross commercialism had been present in J.'s earlier books, but her next work was a brilliant psychological study of a wheeler-dealer woman who, despite life's harsh blows, always lands on her feet: *Elämän Rouva, Rouva Glad* (1982; *The Bride of Life*, 1995). Another look at a businessman's psyche is *Rikas ja kunniallinen* (1984; *Rich and Respected*, 1997), where the main protagonist happens to be a man. "Why would you want to write about a rich man," J. was asked. "There has been too much idealization of poverty in Finland. Writing about poor people is easy," she says; "Money as such isn't evil, but it makes some people behave in disgusting ways." "And the upstarts are the worst," says Eero Kuula, the protagonist. This was one of the first novels in Finland to delve into the world of business, and some found the idea of writing about an *honest* businessman curious. The problem of ethics has always been central in J.'s books.

Perhaps J.'s most intriguing book is *Jottei varjos haalistu* (1986; Lest Your Shadow Fade), which reads almost like a mystery. The time is right after World War II, the late 1940s. The main characters are an aging spinster and her happy-go-lucky veterinarian brother. Interwoven with the "current" action is a horrible story of treachery and neglect of their grandparents, gradually becoming clear as Erika digs into archives and listens to old stories. There is a strong ethical undercurrent here. Old wrongs must not be excused or forgotten, and creative ways are devised to prevent that from happening. Yet, actions can have unexpected consequences. How was Erika to know that insisting on a cousin not being buried in the family grave would lead to her own brother ending up in jail for hiding arms? The petty postwar administrators, the small-minded townspeople, and the Lutheran clergy all receive lashes. J. is a master at ridiculing pretentiousness. But one of the most touching scenes in all of J.'s books is the brother's funeral, the church filled with people from far and wide, who almost all walk out as the preacher keeps reciting the popular veterinarian's "transgressions." Much of the book is based on actual fact. "A hard life is a magnificent life" was J.'s grandfather's observation.

J.'s next book, *Ei ryppyä, ei tahraa* (1989; Not a Wrinkle, Not a Stain), is about the irreparable harm caused to children by the deprivation of love and by insistence on "keeping up appearances." J. is delving into the psyche of her main characters; social description is less present than usually. Two life philosophies and systems of morality are juxtaposed in *Avoin, hellä ja katumaton* (1991; Open, Tender, and Unrepentant). An unscrupulous tinsmith is trying to take advantage of a pair of conservative patriotic siblings. He gets the alcoholic brother to will all his property to the smith's little girl. The sister has survivorship rights and decides to cling to life as long as possible in order to prevent the tinsmith from collecting on the inheritance. Again J. shows that different social strata contain both honest people and crooks. The realistic milieu makes the book come alive for the reader on many levels.

Tuomari Müller, hieno mies is another version of what deprivation of love in childhood can do to a person, and what greed and selfishness lead to. The son of a bootlegger becomes a scrupulously honest bank manager who refuses to play along with crooked local politicians. His widow has herself a dark deed on her conscience, which she sees a way of easing with a game of cat and mouse with the small-town big-wigs who want to buy a plot of land she happens to own in town. Mrs. Müller has a grand old time teasing the local businessmen and showing them their comeuppance. J.'s satire is delicious in describing it all, her style as spare and compact as ever, proving she is still a true master of the narrative style.

Before receiving the Finlandia Prize, J. had won the Government Prize for Literature six times, as well as numerous other awards. Her Lohja series has been adapted for stage and television. *Rikas ja kunniallinen* was also produced on Finnish television. A number of her novels have been translated into some Scandinavian and East European languages. The universal theme of how women and men interact is present in all of J.'s novels, where generally "men make a lot of fuss; the women keep the world going." And J.'s men and women are always memorable, which makes her books fascinating reading. The suffering and loneliness people go through, the vanity and pointlessness of much of life, our inability to get close, are universal themes that transcend the local landscape.

FURTHER WORKS: *Veljen varjo* (1951); *Johannes vain* (1952); *Kivi palaa* (1953); *Missä lintuset laulaa* (1957); *Ralli* (1959); *Syyskesä* (1960); *Naisten kesken* (1962); *Viisaat istuvat varjossa* (1964); *Ritari metsien pimennosta* (1966); *Liian suuria asioita* (1968); *Halusit tai et* (1969); *Vesissä toinen silmä* (1971)

BIBLIOGRAPHY: Koskimies, R., and D. Barrett, "E. J.: An Extract from the Novel *Kuin kekäle kädessä*," *BF*, 11 (1977): 176-78; Laitinen, K., and P. Binham, "Life at the Turning Point: E. J. and Her Lohja Trilogy," *WLT*, 54 (Winter 1980): 33-37; Hämäläinen, R., *Me naiset*, 48 (1984): 53ff; Tarkka, P., *Författare I Finland*, (1980): 60-63

—MARGARETA MARTIN

JOHANIDES, Ján

Slovak novelist and screenwriter, b. 18 Aug. 1934, Dolný Kubín

Born in northern Slovakia, J. started to study art history and aesthetics at the university in Bratislava, but left and worked at widely varied positions before settling down to write seriously. His first magazine stories, collected as *Súkromie* (1963; Privacy), showed his interest in the EXISTENTIALISM of Jean-Paul SARTRE and Albert CAMUS, through the loneliness, anxiety, and fear of the characters. His next collection, *Podstata kameňolomu* (1965; Essence of the Stone Quarry), moved toward the absurd as the characters' anxiety turned into aimlessness and Kierkegaardian amorphous guilt. Upon this philosophical basis J. constructed surrealist and symbolic elements in *Nie* (1966; No). Such experimentalism reflected the liberal political movement that precipitated the Soviet invasion of Czechoslovakia in 1968.

After an extended forced silence, J. resumed his stylistic experiments and intensified his already apparent ecological interests in several stories published in magazines. *Nepriznané vrany* (1976; Unacknowledged Crows) involved the workers in a factory for chemical fertilizer with the tragic and horrible pollution of their land and air. For J., the threat of destroying the earth's ecological balance remains an important theme.

J.'s turn to 16th-c. history in the apocalyptic *Marek koniar a uhorský papež* (1983; Marek the Groom and the Hungarian Pope) changed his personal metaphysics to religious existentialism comparable to that of Mikhail BULGAKOV. The work has been called a polysemantic allegory. *Slony v Mauthausene* (1985; Elephants in Mauthausen) and *Najsmutnešia oravská balada* (1988; The Saddest Orava Ballad) treat Slovak history during World War II and the Holocaust with equal scenes of guilt and suffering.

One of J.'s latest collections, *Krik drozdov pred spanim* (1992; Cry of Thrushes before Sleep), has stories still allowing (but not forcing) metaphorical political interpretation. For example, in "Don Giovanni" (1992; "Memorial to Don Giovanni," 1994) the ultimate egoist can be viewed as pointing to political opportunism and worse, as the opera singer/narrator gets botulism at an artistic cocktail party and dreams of a strangling fit of coughing in a ruined synagogue. His doctor, after a long denial of the illness, advises, not a better diet, but never to sing Giovanni again.

Essential to appreciation of J.'s distinguished reputation is the linguistic virtuosity of his style. The early analytic works are striking for their spareness and laconicism. The historical works are surprisingly rich, expressive, flowing, and sometimes dream-like. Pervasive in all his work is multilevel verbal as well as situational irony.

J. has been called the major living Slovak novelist whose claim to European stature is clear. The prevalence of blood in the symbolism of most of his works can be viewed as a purgative and purifying element through the value of pain and suffering in the late-20th-c. world.

FURTHER WORKS: *Spoznávanie* (1964); *Balada o vkladnej knižke* (1979); *Pochovávanie brata*(1987)

BIBLIOGRAPHY: Felix, J., *Harlekýn skloneny nad vodou* (1965); Mistrík, J., "Kapitoly o štýle mladej prózy (Skica o Johanidesových skiciach)," *SlovP*, 82 (1966): 55-60; Petro, P., "Modern Slovak Fiction: The Sixties, a Decade of Experimentation," *Slovakia*, 30 (1982-83): 153-64; Pynsent, R. B., "J. J.: The Consistency of Blood," in Pynsent, R. B., ed. *Modern Slovak Prose*(1990): 79-107; Rayfield, D., "The Use and Abuse of History in Recent Slovak and Georgian Fiction," in Pynsent, R. B., ed., *Modern Slovak Prose* (1990): 114-24

—NORMA LEIGH RUDINSKY

JÓHANNES ÚR KÖTLUM
(Jónasson)

Icelandic poet and novelist, b. 4 Nov. 1899, Goddastaðir, Dalasýsla; d. 27 April 1972, Reykjavík

J., who for most of his life worked as a teacher and who was widely known for his radical political activity, made his debut as a poet in 1926 under the influence of national romanticism, which dominated Icelandic poetry during the first three decades of the 20th c. It was not until 1932, in his third volume of poetry, *Ég læt sem ég sofi* (I pretend to sleep), that he emerged as a powerful revolutionary poet. In *Hrímhvíta móðir* (1937; frost-white mother) J. interpreted Icelandic history from a Marxist point of view, and a great many of his poems of the 1930s and 1940s are directly rhetorical, political appeals to the working class. But in spite of its obvious political urgency, J.'s poetry is always full of glittering beauty, and his love of nature is often expressed in the most tender and delicate ways.

During World War II J. became more cosmopolitan in his poetry, and in *Sól tér sortna* (1945; the sun turns black) he dealt, among other things, with recent events in Spain, Czechoslovakia, and the Soviet Union. In *Sóleyjarkvæði* (1952; poem of Sóley [Sóley being a symbolic name for Iceland]) J.'s political poetry took a new direction, one that soon became a common theme among leftist Icelandic writers. In 1951, only seven years after Iceland became an independent republic, an American military base was established at Keflavík. In *Sóleyjarkvæði* J. blended citations from old folk poetry with verse expressing his own bitterness, and combined patriotism, love of Icelandic nature, political conviction, and sarcasm in a poetic appeal to his nation.

Sjödægra (1955; book of seven days) was a turning point in J.'s poetic development. Gone were his former rhetorical verses in traditional form. Instead, he now expressed himself through a more modernistic imagery, often laden with metaphor and personification. His former revolutionary optimism had turned into a more somber struggle against what he called the "disgusting resignation" of his own generation, which, he says, has forgotten its ideals in the banality of the so-called welfare society. This tone continued to typify J.'s poetry. In his last volume, *Ný og nið* (1970; waxing moon and waning moon), he finally switched his hopes from his own generation to the youth of Iceland, who he believed would take up the struggle again.

Although J. wrote five novels, the quality of his prose works never equaled that of his poetry, although the themes of his fiction are more or less the same as those of his verse. But in J.'s poetry one can see the development of Icelandic poetry in general during this century: he begins with neoromanticism, goes through the optimistic radical commitment of the 1930s, and adopts modernism after World War II. Throughout his career he was regarded as one of the most important leaders of radical socialism in Iceland, while the quality and the power of his poetry continued to grow to the end of his life.

FURTHER WORKS: *Bí bí og blaka* (1926); *Álftirnar kvaka* (1929); *Og björgin klofnuðu* (1934); *Samt mun ég vaka* (1935); *Hart er í heimi* (1939); *Eilífðar smáblóm* (1940); *Verndarenglarnir* (1943); *Dauðsmannsey* (1949); *Siglingin mikla* (1950); *Frelsisálfan* (1951); *Hlið hins himneska friðar* (1953); *Óljóð* (1962); *Tregaslagur* (1964); *Mannssonurinn* (1966)

—NJÖRÐSWUR P. NJARÐVÍK

JOHNSON, B(ryan) S(tanley)

English novelist, poet, screenwriter, and editor, b. 5 Feb. 1933, London; d. 13 Nov. 1973, London

Born into a working-class family in a class-conscious society, J. persistently used the details of his varied life in his art; spokesman for innovation in the novel in a time of rigorous conservatism, he became a well-regarded if controversial writer. His mother, wife, children, friends, and former lovers appear in his novels (he refused to call them "fictions"). And he himself, both as man and as novelist, becomes a character in his books. Permeated by the fear of loss and betrayal, his works are nonetheless a celebration of life: rich in humor, in inventiveness, in wordplay, and in the willingness to feel and to express emotion. We are often tempted, unwisely, to seek for details of his life in his novels. But the broad connection is clear. J.'s suicide seems in some respects as much an act of his art as of his life.

At a time when most English novelists and critics were deploring the modernists' example, J. was virtually alone in following in their path. He insisted that there was much that his contemporaries could learn still from James JOYCE; he refused to accept for his own work the rubric "experimental"—used as a pejorative by English critics—contending that when he applied some innovative technique in a novel, it was no longer an experiment but that he had already tried it out and knew that it could work. We can learn much about his principles of art and the hostile environment in which he worked from the revealing personal essay included in the volume *Aren't You Rather Young To Be Writing Your Memoirs?* (1973). His novels in this atmosphere are as daring as his public statements. Although in recent years the tide in English fiction has turned away from denial and increasingly in J.'s direction, his own works seem destined to be read by a limited audience only. This is not because they are difficult or unrewarding or even because they sometimes have an unusual physical appearance. J.'s premature death, soon after he had completed his best novel, *See the Old Lady Decently* (1975), in the midst of his most ambitious project, may have cut him off from a potentially larger audience. Yet he remains a figure worthy of consideration, in some respects the most serious novelist of his English generation.

In *Travelling People* (1963), J. employs a different narrative technique in each chapter (following Joyce's example in *Ulysses*), running the range from omniscience to STREAM-OF-CONSCIOUS-NESS. Endeavoring to link form integrally to function, the narrative is at once playful in tone and serious in intent; thus pages turn gray as a character grows ill and blacken as he dies. The central metaphor is traveling, as characters reach out to one another, touch briefly, and then move apart, their emotional rootlessness a factor of modern life. For a first novel, this is quite sophisticated work (it won the Gregory Award for 1963), but J. subsequently refused to allow it to be reprinted, effectively removing it from his canon.

It is in *Albert Angelo* (1964) that J. discovers the pattern that will serve for almost all of his subsequent novels: his own experience transmuted into art, the act of writing about his life becoming a vital part of both the art and the life. The self-reflexive act of writing his life is from now on a constant theme, but there is little of the self-conscious cleverness here that we find in so much contemporary American metafiction. For J., this is but one more way of seeking the truth, one of the oft-stated goals of his novel writing. J. distinguishes between "novel" and "fiction," arguing that it is only in the former that he can achieve "truth." These terms appear repeatedly in his essays and letters and even in his novels.

While *Albert Angelo* builds on J.'s activities as a substitute schoolteacher (his last resort when free-lance writing and film work had totally dried up), these are surely not his own experiences that are detailed here. For Albert Angelo is an architect working as a teacher, and—in a scene undoubtedly imagined by every substitute with a difficult class—he is murdered by his pupils. The funeral of their teacher is seen in the final chapter from the joint point of view of the students, one more of the many narrative possibilities explored in the novel—including elements from outside the text that become part of the text (letters, ads, student essays, excerpts from architectural tomes) and variations in the physical text itself (a shift between roman and italic typefaces for differing perspectives within the classroom, slits in certain of the pages so that the reader can peer into the future). It is in *Albert Angelo* that J. first understands—or so he tells us—what it means for him to be a novelist.

J. would later offer *Trawl* (1966) as illustration of his writer's need for personal experience on which to base his writing. He had the idea for a book set on an oceangoing trawler, and so he went to sea on one. His account of seasickness and lovesickness is the result of that experience. (The latter clearly predates the sea journey; the former is its immediate result.) Everything we see here is presented through the character J.'s interior monologue (which varies, of course, with the degree of his seasickness), yet this remains the most conventional of J.'s novels. It won the Somerset Maugham Award for 1967.

The most unusual of J.'s novels is *The Unfortunates* (1969), issued in a box of separately bound, variously sized folios, of which only the first and the last are labeled. The others can be shuffled and read in any order, however random or carefully arranged, that the reader desires. Based apparently on a newspaper sports story that the freelancer J. was commissioned to write in Nottingham and on the news learned there of the impending death, from cancer, of a dear friend, one of the few who had encouraged the writer early in his career. The line between J. the character and J. the writer seems very thin at this point, and the intimate point of view may induce us to feel his/their emotional dilemma with special urgency. Similarly, the random shuffling of time sequences can be either inconsequential (it hardly matters at what point we hear that the narrator

takes the bus back from the stadium) or powerfully emotive (learning that his friend, Tony, is dying after being told that his cancer has been cured). The fear of loss remains J.'s most persistent theme.

The connection to *House Mother Normal: A Geriatric Comedy* (1971) is not, at first, easy to find; it is more likely in the novel's form than in its content, since its events seem to have little to do with J.'s life. The text consists of nine almost perfectly symmetrical narratives from within the minds of the residents of a nursing home and of their head nurse. Some of the patients are infirm; at least one is senile; only the nurse is aware of her audience. And she reveals herself—her rigidity, her masochism, her strong sexual urges—quite consciously and without hesitation. She also reveals on a final, additional page (a page denied the other consciousnesses)—the one lack of symmetry in the novel—that behind her is an author, controlling all: not quite a Dickensian final page. The work is clever, comic, a playing with form, but it is not meant, perhaps, to be taken with full seriousness. It is one of the few J. novels in which neither J. the character nor any of his surrogates makes an appearance.

Rich in both narrative innovation and emotional content, *See the Old Lady Decently* is the first part of a planned trilogy, to be called The Matrix Trilogy, its combined titles to be read consecutively: *See the Old Lady Decently Buried Although Amongst Those Left Are You*. Although J. makes only, as it were, a cameo appearance, this is the most autobiographical of all his novels, the one that most forcefully relates life to art to the process of converting life to art. Its elaborate system of notations and sources barely disguises its impact. Impelled by the death of his mother, Emily, from cancer, in 1971, J. set out to reconstruct her life and to parallel it with that of modern-day Britain, the Mother Country, her early life at the height of the Empire, her death in the time of its decay. Outside the reconstruction, we learn of J.'s suicide shortly after he completed this novel, the ultimate act, we might say, of life intersecting with art.

FURTHER WORKS: *Christie Malry's Own Double Entry* (1973)

BIBLIOGRAPHY: Levitt, M. P., "The Novels of B. S. J.: Against the War against Joyce,"*MFS*, 27, 4 (Winter 1981–1982): 438–44; Ghose, Z., "Bryan," *RCF*, 5, 2 (1985): 23–34; Levitt, M. P., *Modernist Survivors: The Contemporary Novel in England, the United States, France, and Latin America* (1987): 60–72

—MORTON P. LEVITT

JOHNSON, Eyvind

Swedish novelist, b. 29 July, 1900, Överluleå; d. 26 Aug. 1976, Stockholm

The events of J.'s own time and the fact that he grew up in an isolated rural area stimulated his exploration of the history and culture of a wider European context. Except for a short return to Sweden in 1924, J. spent the 1920s in Berlin and Paris amid the turmoil of postwar depression and the upsurge of strong intellectual and political currents. In Sweden during the 1930s J. worked actively against the onslaught of Nazism. As editor of the magazine *Håndslag* he helped establish a link between Resistance workers in Norway and Sweden. Following World War II J. traveled extensively in Switzerland. Its culture and landscape provided the setting for several of his novels, and its political structure became central in J.'s utopian vision of a federation of European states. Among other literary distinctions, J. was elected a member of the Swedish Academy in 1957, and in 1974 he shared the Nobel Prize with Harry MARTINSON.

J.'s early novels are sociocritical, directed against the complacency and narrow scope of bourgeois society. Among them, *Minnas* (1928; remembering) and *Kommentar till ett stjärnfall* (1929; commentary to a falling star) make use of the interior monologue, which J. is credited with having introduced into Swedish fiction. A dominant theme in these early works is the protagonist's inability to deal effectively with oppressive forces. This Hamlet-like conflict was overtly solved in *Avsked till Hamlet* (1930; farewell to Hamlet), but the question of an individual's right to take aggressive action remains an intermittent theme in later novels.

The 1930s were a time of experimentation with primitivist ideas, as in *Regn i gryningen* (1933; rain at dawn), and with autobiography. J.'s tetralogy about the adolescent Olof—*Nu var det 1914* (1934; *1914*, 1970), *Här har du ditt liv!* (1935; here is your life), *Se dig inte om!* (1936; don't look back), and *Slutspel i ungdomen* (1937; postlude to youth)—was the first work to win immediate recognition; the four parts were later published in one volume as *Romanen om Olof* (1945; the novel about Olof).

J.'s production during World War II may be labeled his military service in words. Most remarkable is the voluminous Krilon trilogy—*Grupp Krilon* (1941; group Krilon), *Krilons resa* (1942; Krilon's journey), and *Krilon själv* (1943; Krilon himself). The work condemns Nazi oppression and explores the controversial policy of Swedish neutrality during the war. On an allegorical level the real-estate agent Krilon and his friends represent European states struggling for humanist ideals against the forces of evil. Abundant digressions suspend narrative action to make room for reflections, dreams, and flashbacks. Fictional, allegorical, and symbolic levels are woven together with an obvious delight in storytelling and a firm belief in the power of words to relieve suffering and to sustain an individual's right to dignity and freedom.

The majority of J.'s later novels are built around mythical and historical subjects, and nearly all centuries from ancient Greece to our own are represented. Foremost among them are *Strändernas svall* (1946; *Return to Ithaca*, 1952), based on the story of Ulysses; *Drömmar om rosor och eld* (1949; dreams of roses and fire), revolving around the power struggle between Catholics and Huguenots in 17th-c. France; *Hans nådes tid* (1960; *The Days of His Grace*, 1968), set in the days of Charlemagne's rise to power; and *Livsdagen lång* (1964; life's long day), an eight-episode chronicle spanning the 9th to 16th cs. The historian and the narrator in these novels—both personae of J. himself—are interrelated for a particular purpose: to make the literary work reflect the interaction of times past and present. J.'s increasingly subtle fusion of time levels emphasizes his cyclical concept of history, the illusion of chronological time and the similarity of man's condition under varying circumstances.

Only a few of J.'s novels have reached widespread popularity. One reason may be that J.'s readers are seldom left alone with the story. The fictional world is continually tested and questioned by the many roles of the storyteller. But this characteristic also constitutes the essence of J.'s greatness as a writer, making him the pioneer of 20th-c. Swedish fiction. As a guide and companion, as a masterful artisan in the literary workshop, J. invites his readers to probe and expand the possibilities of the verbal medium and to experience innumerable facets of fictional reality.

FURTHER WORKS: *De fyra främlingarna* (1924); *Timans och rättfärdigheten* (1925); *Stad i mörker* (1927); *Stad i ljus* (1928); *Bobinack* (1932); *Natten är här* (1932); *Än en gång, Kapten!* (1934); *Nattövning* (1938); *Den trygga världen* (1940); *Soldatens återkomst* (1940); *Pan mot Sparta* (1946); *Strändernas svall: Ett drama* (1948); *Dagbok från Schweiz* (1949); *Valda skrifter* (1950); *Ett vårtal* (1951); *Lägg undan solen* (1951); *Romantisk berättelse* (1953); *Vinterresa i Norrbotten* (1955); *Tidens gång* (1955); *Molnen över Metapontion* (1957); *Vägar över Metaponto: En resedagbok* (1959); *Spår förbi Kolonos* (1961); *Stunder vågor* (1965); *Favel ensam* (1968); *Några steg mot tystnaden* (1973)

BIBLIOGRAPHY: Sjöberg, L., "E. J.," *ASR*, 56 (1968): 369–78; Orton, G., *E. J.*, (1972); Stenström, T., "Summary in English," *Romantikern E. J.* (1978): 277–83; Schwartz, N., "Summary in English," *Hamlet i klasskampen* (1979): 252–58

—MONICA SETTERWALL

JOHNSON, James Weldon

American poet, novelist, and essayist, b. 17 June 1871, Jacksonville, Fla.; d. 26 June 1938, Wiscasset, Maine

J.'s mother, a teacher, was a native of Nassau, Bahamas, his father a black freeman born in Richmond, Virginia. Since there was no high school available to black students in Jacksonville, where J. grew up, he received preparatory and college training at Atlanta University, from which he graduated in 1894. At twenty-three he returned to Jacksonville to become principal of the elementary school he had attended. After instituting a high school and a daily paper, and after studying for and being admitted to the Florida bar, J. left Jacksonville for New York in 1902, to engage in popular songwriting with his brother, J. Rosamond Johnson, and Robert Cole. Republican political activities led him in 1906 and 1908 to appointments as U.S. consul in Venezuela and Nicaragua. In 1916 he became field secretary of the National Association for the Advancement of Colored People, and in 1920 the first black secretary of that interracial activist organization. In 1931 he was appointed to a chair in creative literature at Fisk University in Nashville, Tennessee, a post he held until his death in a car accident in 1938.

J.'s only novel, *The Autobiography of an Ex-Colored Man*, was published anonymously in 1912 and reissued under his name in 1927. J.'s narrator is a black man who can "pass" for white, and who travels through the U.S. and Europe in alternating white and black identities. A consummate musician interested in collecting and transforming black folk music, the narrator is finally dissuaded from his black identity by the sight of a lynching. In his "shame at being identified with a people that could with impunity be treated worse than animals," he takes on white identity permanently, although wondering if he perhaps chose the less worthy option.

In 1917 J.'s poems, dialect verses, and songs were collected as *Fifty Years, and Other Poems*. These works of protest, love, and humor include J.'s well-known poem in praise of the slave creators of the spirituals, "O Black and Unknown Bards." (His prefaces to the two collections of spirituals done with his brother in 1925–26 give an excellent historical analysis of the Negro spirituals.) Many of the poems from the 1917 volume also appear in *Saint Peter Relates an Incident: Selected Poems* (1935). In the latter volume, J.

includes "Lift Every Voice and Sing," written in 1900. Set to music by his brother, this song became the "Negro national anthem."

The most famous and noteworthy of J.'s poems are those collected in *God's Trombones: Seven Negro Sermons* (1927). Based on folk sermons of the "old-time Negro preacher," the collection includes an introductory prayer and seven biblical narrations, such as "The Creation" and "Judgement Day." In these folk poems J. succeeds in creating the kind of black poetry he recommends in his lengthy and thorough preface to *The Book of American Negro Poetry* (1922; rev. ed., 1931). There J. writes that traditional dialect verse must be replaced by symbols that "express the racial spirit . . . from within."

J.'s nonfiction prose works include a history of the Negro in New York City, *Black Manhattan* (1930); his autobiography, *Along This Way* (1933); and a long essay, *Negro Americans, What Now?* (1938). *Black Manhattan* concentrates on black Americans' emergence in sports, music, theater, and literature. In *Negro Americans, What Now?* J. defended the integrationist program of the NAACP as the best solution for America's racial problems.

J.'s contribution to American literature lies in the knowledge and discussion of black literature he promoted through his articles and prefaces, and in the few models of excellence he left in his novel and poems. His learning and artistry, coupled with an active and effective political and civil rights career, made of J. a powerful literary and social model for Americans, black and white.

FURTHER WORKS: *The Changing Status of Negro Labor* (1918); *Africa in the World Democracy* (1919, with Horace Katlen); *The Race Problem and Peace* (1924); *Native African Races and Culture* (1927); *The Shining Life: An Appreciation of Julius Rosenwald* (1932); *John Hope: President, Morehouse College, 1906–1931; President, Atlanta University, 1929–1936*1936)

BIBLIOGRAPHY: Special J. issue *Phylon*, 32, 4 (1971); Levy, E., *J. W. J.: Black Leader, Black Voice* (1973); Wagner, J., *Black Poets of the United States* (1973): 351–84; Baker, H., "Forgotten Prototype: *The Autobiography of an Ex-Colored Man* and *Invisible Man*," *VQR*, 49 (1973): 433–49; Davis, A., *From the Dark Tower: Afro-American Writers 1900–1960* (1974): 25–32; Fleming, R., *J. W. J. and Arna Bontemps: A Reference Guide* (1978): 3–70; O'Sullivan, M., "Of Souls and Pottage: J. W. J.'s *The Autobiography of an Ex-Coloured Man*," *CLAJ*, 23, 1 (1979): 60–70

—CAROLYN WEDIN SYLVANDER

JOHNSON, Linton Kwesi

Jamaican-English poet, b. 24 Aug. 1952, Chapeltown, Jamaica

Born in Jamaica, J. was eleven when he moved with his mother to live in England. J. later attended Goldsmith College where he studied social sciences. He began writing poetry during his high school days, writing pieces to be performed by various voices, backed up by drumming. J.'s inclination toward radical black politics began with his involvement with the British Black Panther organization. He brought to this experience an understanding of the abject abuse of immigrant blacks and the disfranchisement that the parents of British-born blacks faced from a political system that was indifferent to their needs and unwilling to recognize these

James Weldon Johnson

people as part of the British fabric. J. would find himself embroiled in the lively political atmosphere of the 1970s in Britain and would soon become the unparalleled spokesman for a generation. His poetry would describe the brutish behavior of the police force and the British government with wit, irony, and a strident rhetoric that was uncompromising. In many ways this voice of the disfranchised was entirely a reggae voice—a voice that recognized the importance of a vernacular that emerged from the streets and that addressed complex ideological questions in an accessible and poetic manner.

J. has several distinctions as one of the more important late 20th-c. writers to have emerged in the United Kingdom. He was one of the first black British writers to write from a distinctly black British position that challenged the very notions of Britishness. It was J.'s use of both patois and a distinct brand of black British language that introduced a discourse that went beyond the largely immigrant concerns of writers such as Sam SELVON and Edward Kamau BRATHWAITE. J. assumed his Britishness and proceeded to argue that what he wrote about was defined by the British political climate; he was not a West Indian writing in exile, but a Briton claiming a right to be in Britain and to be seen as British. This was both an aesthetic stance and a strongly ideological stance. Moreover J. pioneered a new aesthetic that would give rise to a whole generation of performance poets and dub poets with popular followings, though J.'s influence would go beyond the realm of performance poetry and permeate into the enclaves of more formal poetic practice. J. brought to conventional poetry a new aesthetic in much the same way that Langston HUGHES brought to American poetry the cadences of blues and jazz. J.'s poetry was steeped in reggae music—he was not performing reggae songs, but was in fact creating a distinctive literary style based largely on the fundamental principles of beauty derived from reggae music. J.'s verse would challenge Caribbean writing in the same way that Brathwaite challenged Caribbean poets to look to the popular culture of Caribbean people for models and for literary aesthetics. J. picked up where Brathwaite had left off, and he turned to reggae music. J. in that sense was ahead of his time—in many ways dialogue about the force of a reggae aesthetic is only beginning to emerge in literary circles. J. breathed new life into the idea of the political poem—the poem as protest song, the poem as a chronicler of social history and as an instigator of revolutionary action. Not since Martin CARTER's seminal works of the 1950s and early 1960s had there emerged as clear a political vision contained in the poetry and language of resistance.

J.'s recognition of the importance of performance and the power of the spoken word would change significantly the way poetry was approached in Britain for many writers. It is arguably on the basis of J.'s success as a recorded poet that the idea of performance poetry took strong root in London in the 1980s. Published in 1975, J.'s most important collection entitled *Dread Beat and Blood* was poetry that emerged from the moment of history. Always relevant and always reflective of the social unrest and violence that swept England in the 1970, the poems collected in that volume captured the spirit of anger and impatience among young people of all races. But it represented the language and discourse of the black youth who were finding themselves citizens of a country that was uncertain what to do with them. J.'s experiment with Jamaican dialect and British voices created a lyric that was always complex and evocative of black British experience.

Dread Beat and Blood is not, however, his most accomplished collection. The verse in *Inglan Is a Bitch* (1980) is sometimes far more complex and even truer to the inherent allusiveness of the best of reggae lyrics. The confidence and control in *Tings and Times* (1991) combined with the wisdom of experience and irony make it an excellent example of J.'s craftsmanship as a poet. Indeed, in *Tings and Times* we begin to sense J.'s desire to expand the notion of reggae as an aesthetic as he writes elegies for his father and moving poems about the twisted ironies of political commitment, illustrated in the poem "Nursery Rhyme." His exploration of rhythm is increasingly complex, and his capacity for self-reflection, a shift from the strong polemic of his earlier work, reveals a deeper range in J. and a telling direction in his work.

Since his first volume *Voices of the Living and the Dead* (1974) J. has published three other volumes of poetry, but his most significant and pervasive work has appeared in the form of recordings of his poetry. J. has recorded ten albums, including a live version of his *a capella* rendering of many of his most popular works. In all but one recent recording, J. has teamed with reggae bass guitarist Dennis Bovell and his remarkable Dub Band to create some of the most insightful and complex reggae ever to have been produced. With J.'s calm but deadly serious intonations riding with almost deadpan monotone over the jazz-flecked arrangements of Dennis Bovell, a distinctly new and fascinating brand of performance has emerged.

J. is noted in Britain as a writer who is committed to encouraging younger artists. His legacy will continue through such work, but his most telling legacy rests in his poetry that spoke so directly and convincingly to the emerging black British world. He gave this community a voice that it never had, a voice that would permanently alter the way blackness in Britain would be defined. His work also challenged notions of poetry as belonging entirely to the quirky or the intellectual elite. J.'s poetry celebrates a strong democratic sensibility, and it is the political commitment of writers such as Martin Carter, Octavio PAZ, and Nicholás GUILLÉN that we find fitting parallels.

BIBLIOGRAPHY: Welsh, S. L., "L. K. J., *Tings and Times*; Selected Poems," *BeteN*, 12-13 (Autumn 1991-Spring 1992): 406-24; Caesar, B., "Interview: L. K. J. Talks to Burt Caesar at Parkside Studios, Brixton, London, June 1996," *CritQ*, 38 (1996 Winter): 64-77

—KWAME DAWES

JOHNSON, Uwe

German novelist, b. 20 July 1934, Cammin; d. 12 Feb. 1984, Sheerness, England

J.'s own biography reflects the tumultuous period of German history in which he came to maturity and which finds expression in his novels. Having spent his childhood in the once-German territory of Pomerania, now part of Poland, J. fled with his family to Mecklenburg, a mostly agrarian area in what is now East Germany, in 1945. From 1952 to 1954 he studied at the University of Leipzig. In 1959 he moved to West Berlin so that his first novel, unacceptable in the East, could be published in the West. From 1966 to 1968 he lived on Riverside Drive in New York City like the heroine of his last novel. He won the Berlin Fontane Prize in 1960, the International Publishers' Prize in 1962, and the Büchner Prize in 1971.

J.'s first novel, *Mutmaßungen über Jakob* (1959; *Speculations about Jakob*, 1963), established his reputation as a major postwar German writer and also set forth what were to be the central formal and thematic concerns of J.'s subsequent writing. All of J.'s novels revolve around a major political crisis with which his characters must come to terms but for which they find no easy ethical answer. "Where is the moral Switzerland to which we could emigrate?" asks a character in his latest novel. The structure and language of J.'s works also indicate to readers the difficulty of finding a standpoint from which it is possible for human beings to assess a situation accurately and truthfully. Drawing upon modernist techniques, particularly those of FAULKNER, J.'s complex novels make his readers speculate about how to understand the novel as his characters must speculate about how to understand their world.

Mutmaßungen über Jakob is an avant-garde detective story structured around the attempt of the acquaintances of Jakob Abs, an East German railway worker, to understand why he had been run down by a train: an accident? suicide? Their dialogues, interior monologues, and recollections allow the complicated events leading up to Jakob's death to be told. Jakob had been a dedicated worker for East German socialism until he had to help dispatch troop trains to suppress the Hungarian uprising of 1956. But the West is not any better: the British and French are about to occupy the Suez Canal, to the indignation of Jakob and his childhood friend and present lover, Gesine Cresspahl, who works for NATO in West Germany. Gesine will not go back to the East, and Jakob will not move to the West; in the real world of work and politics, there is no place where lovers can live happily together. The novel's intricate plot, involving an attempt to recruit Gesine as a spy for East Germany and her flight from the secret police when she returns for a clandestine visit to the East, remains shadowy and unclear to readers, like the options available to J.'s characters.

J.'s later works continue his examination of the conflict between East and West and his characters' difficulty in finding an adequate epistemological position between the two. *Das dritte Buch über Achim* (1961; *The Third Book about Achim*, 1967) is subtitled "description of a description." Karsch, a West German journalist, tries to write a biography about Achim, an East German bicycle racer and national hero. The novel takes the form of a long telephone conversation in which Karsch explains why he could not write his book. Like any biographer, Karsch finds it difficult to select appropriate biographical details that pin down Achim's character, and he also discovers that East and West German conceptions of what a biography should contain are not easily united. But when Karsch learns that Achim, the socialist hero, had participated in the East German workers' uprising against the regime in June 1953, the biography becomes impossible, for this image of Achim cannot be reconciled with that of the two earlier East German biographies. To remain the new socialist man, Achim has to deny his own history. Karsch breaks off his book and returns to the West.

J.'s first two novels are formally his most interesting, for in them he pursues seriously his attempt to find a way of seeing that would correspond to the official ideologies of neither East nor West and that would meet human needs more adequately than either system does. As J. seems increasingly to have given up hope for that solution, his works have grown more conventional. In *Zwei Ansichten* (1965; *Two Views*, 1966) J. juxtaposes the perspectives of two lovers separated by the building of the Berlin Wall. Both characters conform to certain stereotypes about their countries: D., the East German, is a self-sacrificing nurse, while B., from the West, is a self-indulgent commercial photographer with a sports car. D. undertakes the risk of a complicated and dangerous escape from the East to rejoin B., but the love affair does not work out; their "two views" can't be reconciled.

J.'s mammoth and uncompleted *Jahrestage* (Vol. I, 1970; II, 1971; III, 1973; *Anniversaries*, 1975) confronts the most difficult dilemmas yet. Gesine Cresspahl of J.'s first novel and her daughter Marie (conceived during Jakob's visit to the West in *Mutmaßungen*) have moved to New York City, where they live through the difficult days from August 21, 1967, to August 20, 1968. Told day-by-day, Gesine's life is framed by excerpts from *The New York Times*, which recount the brutal events of daily life in the city, racial unrest, political assassinations, the Vietnam War, and the protests against it. Counterposed to the present and narrated with 19th-c. omniscience are Gesine's tales from her childhood in Nazi Germany. Although politically tainted, her life then in a small village in Mecklenburg was more comfortable and compatible with human needs than the present allows. Gesine places her hopes for a human future in the liberalization of Czechoslovak socialism, but it seems likely that the final volume of the novel will end on the day of the Russian invasion of Czechoslovakia, which crushed that possibility. The final volume of *Jahrestage*, often announced by J.'s publisher, has not yet appeared. One suspects J. can find no aesthetic solution to the problems of *Jahrestage* because there is no real solution to them.

In *Jahrestage* all the characters from J.'s previous works reappear, and the childhood landscape Gesine recalls was also the setting of *Mutmaßungen*. In this respect J.'s latest novel is a summary of and conclusion to his previous work. Although *Jahrestage* is an impressive achievement, it nonetheless does not fulfill the promise that J.'s earlier works embodied. In form and content, his first two novels struggled for new solutions; *Jahrestage*, looking to a flawed past for its vision of happiness, resigns itself in the present to its disappointment at what now exists.

FURTHER WORKS: *Karsch, und andere Prosa* (1964); *Eine Reise nach Klagenfurt* (1974); *Berliner Sachen* (1975)

BIBLIOGRAPHY: Popp, H., *Einführung in U. J.s Roman "Mutmaßungen über Jakob"* (1967); Baumgart, R., ed., *Über U. J.* (1970); Migner, K., *U. J.: "Das dritte Buch über Achim"* (1970); Schwarz, W. J., *Der Erzähler U. J.* (1970); Durzak, M., *Der deutsche Roman der Gegenwart* (1971): 174–249; Boulby, M., *U. J.* (1974); Post-Adams, R., *U. J.* (1977); Hye, R., *U. J.s "Jahrestage"* (1978); Neumann, B., *Utopie und Mimesis: Zum Verhältnis von Ästhetik, Gesellschafts-philosophie und Politik in den Romanen U. J.s* (1978); Riedel, N., *U. J. Bibliographie* (2 vols., 1976, 1978)

—SARA LENNOX

JOHNSTON, Denis

Irish dramatist, scriptwriter, and biographer, b. 18 June 1901, Dublin; d. 23 Aug. 1984, Dublin

After attending St. Andrew's College, Dublin (1908–15), and Merchiston Castle School, Edinburgh (1915–17), J. received his law degree from Cambridge in 1923. He practiced law in Dublin until 1936, at the same time pursuing activities in the theater under the pseudonym of "E. W. Tocher." J. directed, acted, and wrote for the Abbey and Gate theaters in Dublin throughout the 1920s and 1930s, earning a reputation as a major new force in Irish drama. He was also a scriptwriter for the BBC (1936–38); drama critic for *The Bell* (1941–42); war correspondent for the BBC (1942–45); drama critic for Radio Eireann (1947); and scriptwriter for the NBC Theatre Guild of the Air (1947–49). J. was awarded the Order of the British Empire in 1946, and from 1949 to 1973 he served as visiting professor in various American colleges and universities.

J.'s early plays, highly experimental in form, were influenced by the European avant-garde, especially the EXPRESSIONISTS. His first play, *The Old Lady Says "No!"* (1929), shocked Dublin audiences with its expressionistic theatricality, its frank language, and its satiric thrust. The play is suggestive of STRINDBERG'S *A Dream Play* (1902) in tone and structure, although J. acknowledged George S. Kaufman (1889–1961) and Marc Connelly's (1890–1980) *Beggar on Horseback* (1924) as his model. J.'s play satirizes the failure of the Irish Republic to achieve the goals upon which it was founded. J. criticizes contemporary attitudes and institutions by bringing the Irish patriot Robert Emmet (1778–1803) into 20th-c. Dublin, showing Emmet's despair and frustration at the dismal situation he finds there. In many of his plays, J. similarly debunks the sentimental idealism he feels impedes progress in Irish culture and politics.

J.'s first Abbey play, *The Moon in the Yellow River* (1931), was a popular success, securing him an international reputation. Another of his popular early works was *Blind Man's Buff* (perf. 1936, pub. 1938), based on Ernst TOLLER'S *The Blind Goddess* (1933).

This courtroom "whodunit" explores the weaknesses of the jury system in a conventional well-made-play format, signaling J.'s shift to the more traditional, realistic style of playwriting that is characteristic of his mature work.

Two plays of interest from J.'s middle period are *The Golden Cuckoo* (perf. 1939, pub. 1954) and *The Dreaming Dust* (perf. 1940, pub. 1959). The former is perhaps J.'s funniest and most tender play. Based upon a real event, it chronicles the fate of a singularly unheroic chap who follows his conscience, rebels against authority, and commits an act of civil disobedience. *The Dreaming Dust*, although unsuccessful, is the best of several plays by various dramatists on the subject of Jonathan Swift. J. was fascinated with the enigmatic Swift and wrote as well a fictionalized biography of the writer, *In Search of Swift* (1959). He also published another biography on SYNGE, *John Millington Synge* (1965).

J.'s finest play is his most recent one, *The Scythe and the Sunset* (1958), a drama of the Easter Week rising of 1916. The title parodies Sean O'CASEY's *The Plough and the Stars* (1926), and his avowed purpose was to deromanticize the ugly events that O'Casey had somewhat melodramatically treated in the earlier work. J. calls his play an "antimelodrama." Set in a Dublin cafe during Easter Week, it concerns a dozen characters whose lives are reshaped—in some cases ended—by the bloody battle raging in the street below. The drama is rich in characterization and bitter humor—poetic in the vein of Synge and as volatile as the work of Brendan BEHAN. *The Scythe and the Sunset* is one of the finest Irish history plays.

J.'s nine full-length plays, written over a thirty-year period, display considerable diversity in style and structure, although there is unity in their thematic content. J. was concerned with the nature of evil, and he advocated the responsibility of the individual to recognize it and deal with it. All of the plays attest to the writer's comic sense and his sharp wit, which he frequently employed in the cause of satire. In all his works, J. exhibited a passionate devotion to his homeland, coupled with the desire to force the Irish people to confront themselves honestly, without illusions and romantic ideals.

FURTHER WORKS: *A Bride for the Unicorn* (perf. 1933, pub. 1935); *Storm Song* (perf. 1934, pub. 1935); *A Fourth for Bridge* (1947); *Nine Rivers from Jordan* (1953); *Strange Occurrence on Ireland's Eye* (1956); *Siege at Killyfaddy* (1960); *The Brazen Horn* (1976); *The Dramatic Works of D. J.* (2 vols, 1977–1978); *The Tain: A Pageant* (1979)

BIBLIOGRAPHY: Canfield, C.,, "A Note on the Nature of Expressionism and D. J.'s Plays," *Plays of Changing Ireland* (1936): 25–36; Edwards, H., "D. J.," *The Bell*, 13, 1 (1946): 7–18; Hogan, R., "The Adult Theatre of D. J.," *After the Irish Renaissance* (1967): 133–46; Ferrar, H., *D. J.'s Irish Theatre* (1973); Barnett, G. A., *D. J.* (1978)

—JACK A. VAUGHN

JOLLEY, Elizabeth

Australian novelist and short-story writer, b. 4 June 1923, Birmingham, England

J. came to Perth, Western Australia, where she still lives, with her family in 1959. She grew up in the industrial Midlands in England and was educated at home by her English father, a teacher, then at a Quaker boarding school. J.'s mother was Viennese. J. trained and worked as a nurse during World War II. Writing from an early age, J.'s first public recognition came when a children's story was broadcast on regional radio in England. During many years when her work was regularly rejected for publication, J. had a variety of casual jobs, including work as a geriatric night nurse and a door-to-door salesperson. More recently, J. has taught writing at Perth University and worked with community writing groups. Years of rejection ended when the Western Australian publishers Fremantle Arts Centre Press released a collection of short fiction, *Five Acre Virgin and Other Stories*, in 1976.

The stories in this first collection reveal the preoccupations that characterize J.'s work; an ability to combine a sense of the significance yet absurdity of ordinary lives, an interest in the effects of displacement and exile on those lives, and a deep feeling for place. Recognition of J. as a major Australian writer occurred with the publication in 1983 of *Mr. Scobie's Riddle* and *Miss Peabody's Inheritance*. Nine novels and three further volumes of short stories have now been published, and a number of radio plays have been performed on Australian and British radio. While this output may seem prolific, it derives from writing over the last four or more decades. J. worked on the novel *Milk and Honey* (1984), for instance, at different times from the early 1960s, simultaneously with other manuscripts and ideas for novels and short stories. J.'s work should not be read as a progression, linked in a linear sense, but as a network of influences. Characters, incidents, and motifs or references are often repeated with a difference in a novel, a story, and a radio play; things constantly recur as they do in life, while the characters are used to explore central human problems: the nature of human love and the capacity of human beings for idealism and manipulation.

Growing up in England in a German-speaking household has marked J.'s imagination and her writing, which is highly allusive, drawing on a huge range of reference from major religious and secular texts, both poetry and prose, in the Western cultural tradition. Music occupies an important place in her oeuvre. The cultural differences between life in Australia and Europe are often marked by those characters who are music lovers and others who are indifferent to or scorn music. J.'s prose structures are also often likened to musical forms, where the recurrences inside and among her novels and stories recall the classical musical practice of variation on a theme and counterpoint, or the interplay of independent themes or melodic fragments. The short story is J.'s favorite form, and her novels are episodic, often poetic, and compressed. Formally, J. constructs a recognizably realistic fictional world but one that is constantly interrupted or shifted by bizarre events or the interpolation of fantastic elements. Generic experimentation with modes such as the gothic, the romance, and the thriller is used to interrupt readers' singular generic expectations. These modes are used, too, as ways of exploring women's lives. Relationships between women are a major concern in J.'s writing; they sometimes involve lesbian sexuality and are presented through a range of configurations. Women and their creativity provide a constant theme, and the narratives, in which comedy and irony, the grotesque and the lyric form an unsettling blend, are often deliberately fragmented, fractured by a range of narrative modes and voices.

J. is now regarded as one of Australia's major writers, and her work has been translated into a number of European languages. While the metafictional aspect of her work constantly interrogates the categories of truth and fiction, the values espoused are deeply humanist, with a central belief in the possibility of a moment where truth may be discovered. The question of human responsibility, to oneself and to others, is always present and never lightly dealt with. J.'s depiction of Australian life is sharply idiosyncratic, and her work as a whole provides an unusually close-knit, witty yet compassionate observation of contemporary existence, and a meditation on its momentary joys and major limitations.

FURTHER WORKS: *The Travelling Entertainer and Other Stories* (1979); *The Newspaper of Claremont Street* (1981); *Woman in a Lampshade* (1983); *Stories* (1984); *Foxybaby* (1984); *The Well* (1986); *The Sugar Mother* (1988); *My Father's Moon* (1989); *Cabin Fever* (1990); *The George's Wife* (1993); *The Orchard Thieves* (1995); *Lovesong* (1997)

BIBLIOGRAPHY: Garner, H., "E. J.: An Appreciation," *Meanjin*, 42 (1983): 153–57; Riemer, A. P., "Between Two Worlds—An Approach to E. J.'s Fiction," *Southerly*, 43, 3 (1983): 239–52; Jones, D., "The Goddess, the Artist and the Spinster," *Westerly*, 29, 4 (1984): 77–88; Howells, C. S., "In Search of Lost Mothers: Margaret Laurence's *The Diviners* and E. J.'s *Miss Peabody's Inheritance*," *ArielE*, 19, 1 (1988): 57–70; Daniel, H., *Liars* (1988): 269–300; Trigg, S., "An Interview with E. J.," *Scripsi*, 4, 1 (1988): 244–64; Kavanagh, P., "This Self the Honey of All Beings: A Conversation with E. J.," *Southerly*, 49, 3 (1989): 438–51; Bird, D., and Walker B., eds., *E. J.: New Critical Essays* (1990); Saltzman, P., *E. J.'s Fictions: Helplessly Tangled in Female Arms and Legs* (1993); Turcotte, G., "Sexual Gothic: Marian Engel's *Bear* and E. J.'s *The Well*," *Ariel*, 25 (1995): 65–91; Livett, J., "Two Answers to Every Question: E. J.'s Fictions, Ethics and Criticism," *ALB*, 17 (1996): 10–18

—DELYS M. BIRD

JONES, David (Michael)

Anglo-Welsh poet and essayist, b. 1 Nov. 1895, Brockley, England; d. 28 Oct. 1974, London

J. whose father was a printer by profession, was introduced early to words as a visual experience. Visits to his grandfather, John Jones, confronted him with his Welsh heritage and the rich sounds of the Welsh language. J.'s Cockney mother had had an early aptitude for drawing and properly encouraged her son's preoccupation with that art. From 1909 to 1914, J. studied at Camberwell Art School, where he discovered modern French painting, the Pre-Raphaelites, and 19th-c. English illustrators. When World War I broke into his life, J. enlisted in the Royal Welsh Fusiliers, with whom he served as a private on the Western front from December 1915 until he was invalided home in March 1918. The brutality of trench warfare and the loyalty of his soldier comrades are evoked in J.'s 20th-c. epic, *In Parenthesis* (1937), awarded the Hawthornden Prize in 1938.

In 1919 he went on a government grant to the Westminster School of Art, where he encountered the work of William Blake and other English watercolorists, whom he greatly admired. In 1921 he was received into the Catholic Church, rooted in symbol and ritual as modes of experiencing human thought and history, as are J.'s art and writing. J.'s close friendship with Eric Gill (1882–1940), sculptor and engraver, led in 1922 to his joining the Guild of St. Joseph and St. Dominic, a religious fraternity at Ditchling for

those involved in hand-crafted arts. There he learned engraving on wood and copper, which resulted in some of his finest illustrations for St. Dominic's and the Golden Cockerel Press.

The period from 1926 to 1933 was the most prolific in J.'s life: he produced numerous engravings, as well as watercolors and drawings, and began writing *In Parenthesis*, a creative labor that was to take seven years. A striking fusion of Welsh myth, Christian sacrament, and the shattering personal experience of a soldier confronted with modern warfare, J.'s narrative of the Somme offensive of 1916 is a work of great verbal intensity. Utilizing *anamnesis*, a kind of remembrance in which the individual's private stock of data is linked with the common stock of human memory, J. draws upon ancient and medieval heroic myth to strengthen the ultimate meaning of Private John Ball's experience in battle. Thus through many allusions, this Anglo-Welsh soldier is simultaneously a hero of the *Mabinogion*, the *Chanson de Roland*, and Aneirin's medieval Welsh epic *Y Gododdin*.

The 1940s saw J.'s increasing preoccupation with themes from myth and legend, particularly the Matter of Britain. Two of his Arthurian paintings, the culmination of his visual art, hang in the Tate Gallery. J.'s concern for tradition, and particularly with the concept of sacrament as sign, led him to create *Anathemata* (1952). A monumental vision of Britain as the islands appear through the deposits of many cultural epochs, this long poem is a *universum*, a poetic totality including the whole of British history as an ever-accumulating collage or palimpsest. Calligraphy is an important art form in this work, for it unites J. the painter with J. the poet in celebration of a life-giving mystery.

After *Anathemata* appeared, J. continued work on another book of poetry based on themes evolving from the experience of Roman soldiers in the Near East at the time of Christ. Only fragments, in the form of shorter poems, compact and episodic, have appeared. From 1941 onward, over a period of fifteen years, J. also wrote a number of essays, collected as *Epoch and Artist* (1959). Representing a poet-artist's struggle to express in prose the background and theory of his artistic work, the essays are exploratory in mood and reflect the influence of the Catholic philosopher Jacques Maritain (1883–1972). J.'s most significant essay, "Art and Sacrament" (1955), deals with the gratuitous nature of art, the idea of *sign* and its relation to *sacrament*, and the role of the latter in religion and culture. For J., the whole of life and experience is sacramental, an attitude epitomized in the Christian rite of the Eucharist. Significant for J.'s notions of sign and sacrament was an English *résumé* (1934) of *Mysterium fidei* (written 1915; pub. in 2 vols., 1941, 1950 [in Latin] by a Jesuit scholar, Maurice de Taille).

J. remains a somewhat inaccessible poet, for only intrepid lovers of symbolism and densely worded poetry dare enter the labyrinth of his lines. He speaks a language that has been forgotten in modern times. Questers, however, are richly rewarded in sign and song and rite.

FURTHER WORKS: *The Wall* (1955); *The Tribune's Visitation* (1958); *The Tutelar of the Place* (1961); *The Dream of Private Clitus* (1964); *The Hunt* (1965); *The Fatigue* (1965); *The Sleeping Lord* (1967); *Fragments of an Attempted Autobiographical Writing* (1975)

BIBLIOGRAPHY: Johnston, J. H., *English Poetry of the First World War* (1964): 284–340; Special J. issue, *Agenda*, 5: 1–3 (1967); Blamires, D., *D. J.: Artist and Writer* (1971); Hooker, J., *D. J.: An*

Exploratory Study of His Writings (1975); Mathias, R., ed., *D. J.: Eight Essays on His Work as Writer and Artist* (1976); Hague, R., *A Commentary on the "Anathemata"* (1977); Rees, S., *D. J.: An Annotated Bibliography and Guide to Research* (1977); Corcoran, N., *The Song of Deeds: A Study of the Anathemata of D. J.* (1982); special D. J. issue, *Renascence*, 38 (1986); Dilworth, T., "Remembering D. J.," *JML*, 14 (1988); special D. J. issue, *New Welsh Review*, 2 (1989); Mathias, J., ed., *D. J.: Man & Poet* (n.d.); James, M., *D. J., 1895-1974: A Map of the Artist's Mind* (1995); Miles, J., *D. J.: The Maker Unmade* (1996); Hyne, A., *D. J.: A Fusilier at the Front: His Record of the Great War in Word and Image* (1997); Hills, P., ed., *D. J.: Artist and Poet* (1998)

—JANET POWERS GEMMILL

JONES, James

American novelist, b. 6 Nov. 1921, Robinson, Ill.; d. 9 May 1977, Southampton, N.Y.

Because of the Depression, J.'s education ended with high school. He joined the army and was at Pearl Harbor when the Japanese attacked; he was injured in combat on Guadalcanal, and discharged in 1944. He moved to Paris in 1958, then to Sagaponack, Long Island, 1974. He taught at Florida International University 1974–75.

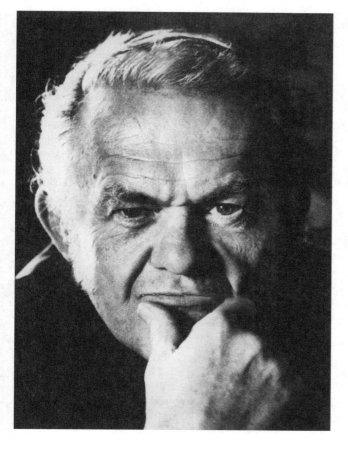

James Jones

J. was preeminently a novelist of war and military life. His major work is a trilogy based on his World War II experiences: *From Here to Eternity* (1951), *The Thin Red Line* (1962), and *Whistle* (1978)), the last published posthumously. The final three chapters of *Whistle* were completed by a friend, the writer Willie Morris (b. 1934), with the aid of J.'s notes and taped conversations.

From Here to Eternity won the National Book Award and became an immediate best seller. It has been described as the "definitive novel of the American peacetime army" by Maxwell Geismar, and, with J.'s other works, has been translated into a number of languages. It is a detailed account of the life of an enlisted man in the pre-World War II army. In the tradition of naturalism (second only to DREISER's *An American Tragedy* as a 20th-c. American naturalistic novel, according to F. L. Gwynn), the book set new limits in realistic description of soldiers' language and sexual behavior. As Richard P. Adams showed, with its presentation of the self-reliant individual struggling against dehumanizing institutions, it is in the Thoreau-Whitman tradition. The novel taps the emotional power of the archetypal American folk hero to give the enlisted man tragic stature.

The Thin Red Line, an account of an infantry company on Guadalcanal, demonstrates J.'s narrative power, his ability to create many individualized characters and dramatic episodes, such as the one of the decaying corpse of the Japanese soldier, dragged out of a mass grave.

Whistle is less successful, perhaps because J. waited so long after his war experiences to write it. The novel describes the hospital experiences of four wounded soldiers. The four characters that appear in this novel are the same personae that appear in *From Here to Eternity* and *The Thin Red Line*; in each novel the men are given different names, but they are used to illustrate the various kinds of tragedy that come to the soldier.

Leonard Kriegel has argued persuasively that American masculinity is J.'s most basic subject, as illustrated both by the war novels and by other novels that critics have generally regarded as of less value. These include *Go to the Widow-Maker* (1967), in which a successful playwright asserts his masculinity by learning scuba diving and by his relationship with various women; *In the Merry Month of May* (1971), based on the student protest movement in Paris, May, 1968, in which J. criticizes student protest movements for their disorderliness, self-indulgence, and hypocrisy; and *A Touch of Danger* (1973), a good example of the American private-detective story.

J. implies that the pressures of this society coerce men to demonstrate their masculinity by the use of violence, by sexual athleticism, by skill in sports, and by the ability to drink heavily and to withstand pain courageously. This bleak view is modified by an Emersonian emphasis on the inner, enduring self. Nevertheless, both in the novels and in his private life, J. valued gentleness highly. In all the novels the male characters seem most fully developed; his women seem wooden and one-dimensional.

J.'s attitude toward war is paradoxical. He wrote that his works are antiwar, that an accurate report of war must show the "regimentation of souls, the systematized reduction of men to animal level, the horror of pointless death, the exhaustion of living in constant fear." A true antiwar work must show that "modern war destroys human character." Moreover, J. intimates in his fiction that the dehumanizing institutions of war symbolize the tendency of all contemporary institutions. However, some later works are less critical of war.

Although J. was not a graceful stylist, his intuitive mastery of the traditional novel form, as John W. Aldridge has observed, gave his best works lasting value. His World War II trilogy seems likely to remain among the four or five most valuable fictional treatments in English of the war.

FURTHER WORKS: *Some Came Running* (1958); *The Pistol* (1959); *The Ice-Cream Headache, and Other Stories* (1968); *Viet Journal* (1974); *World War II* (1975)

BIBLIOGRAPHY: Fielder, L., "J. J.: Dead-End Young Werther: The Bum as American Culture Hero," *Commentary*, Sept. 1951: 252–55; Adams, R. P., "A Second Look at *From Here to Eternity, CE,* 18 (1956): 205–10; Griffith, B. W., "Rear Rank Robin Hood: J. J.'s Folk Hero," *GaR*, 10 (1956): 41–46; Geismar, M., *American Moderns*, (1958): 225–38; Geismar, M., on *The Thin Red Line, NYTBR*, 1 Sept. 1962: 1 ff.; Kriegel, L., on *Whistle, Nation*, 8 Apr. 1978: 406–7; Aldridge, J., on *Whistle, NYTBR*, 5 March 1978: 1 ff.; Giles, J. R., *J. J.* (1981); Garrett, G., *J. J.* (1984); MacShane, F., *Into Eternity: The Life of J. J., American Writer* (1985)

—LEE A. BURRESS

JONES, Marion Patrick

Trinidadian novelist, b. 1934, Woodbrook, Trinidad

J. has had a stimulating and richly intellectual life. She was an outstanding student at Trinidad's St. Joseph's Convent where she won the prestigious Girls Open Island Scholarship in 1950. She also had the distinction of being the first of two women accepted by Trinidad's Imperial College of Tropical Agriculture. Her school days in Woodbrook were crucial in J.'s developing sensibilities. Woodbrook, a Port of Spain suburb where the black middle class, Chinese, Syrians, and fallen white families lived, is both setting and metaphor in her fiction. The men and women of *Pan Beat* (1973) and *J'ouvert Morning* (1976), her two published novels, are composites of the people of Woodbrook, and their values and attitudes fuel much of the dramatic tension in both novels.

J.'s ambivalent relationship with Woodbrook's residents, especially the black middle class, is at the heart of her two uncompromisingly realistic novels. When J.'s mother, a devoted Methodist, married Patrick Jones, a Catholic, trade union activist and calypsonian—a suspect career in the 1930s—the family was boycotted and ostracized by the staid middle class. J. had her first dose of racism at an exclusive Woodbrook elementary school which catered to the white children of French and Spanish creole families, and established and enforced segregated entrances and exits for white and black children. At Tranquility, which she next attended, J. was often physically abused by students who thought she read too much, a traumatic experience later mirrored in Elaine Grant's experiences in *J'ouvert Morning*. Nevertheless, J. succeeded in winning one of the few "Exhibitions," free secondary education awarded to excellent students in the 1930s and 1940s. Her school days at St. Joseph's Convent were also traumatic. Despite its reputation for excellence, the school was racist and catered to white, upper-class families. The school's strict Catholic regimen and the nuns' petty prejudices are transmuted into her fiction and

are noticeable in the brooding bitterness of Earline Hill and Elaine Grant, former students of St. Joseph's, and the obsessed women of *Pan Beat* and *J'ouvert Morning.*

In the mid-1950s J. left Trinidad for New York where she earned a diploma in library science; but it was her years in London and Paris that shaped and consolidated her social, political, and religious ideologies. In London, where she was a graduate student in social anthropology, J. met and worked closely with West Indian intellectuals and political activists such as C. L. R. JAMES, and Andrew SALKEY, the Jamaican novelist. Her years in London and Paris deepened her comprehension of racism, social injustice, and gender discrimination, and her experiences confirmed and strengthened her cynicism about the materialistic middle class. She was involved in the campaign for nuclear disarmament and helped to establish a multiracial movement to counteract Britain's anti-immigration movement then in full swing. She worked for UNESCO in Paris where she was actively involved in the antiapartheid movement. J. now lives in Woodbrook, but her relationship with Trinidad is ambiguous and uneasy. The island's stunning landscape and the steel band's exhilarating music, a strong leitmotif in *Pan Beat*, continue to fascinate her; but she is repelled by the island's moral deterioration, pervasive crime and violence, and the growth of a pernicious drug culture.

The colonial *angst*—a sense of rootlessness and incompleteness—is a prominent theme in J.'s fiction. It is pervasive in *Pan Beat* which is set in the slums and lower and middle-class districts of Port of Spain. Many of her men and women are plagued by the dissatisfaction of an incomplete, largely unfulfilled life. Earline Hill's husband's unfinished novel is a metaphor of the stasis in the lives of J.'s characters. Of these, Earline Hill is the most fully embodied and is one of the most complex females in West Indian fiction. For all her arrogance and jaunty sensuality, she is vulnerable, always close to hysteria, and subconsciously seeking redemption. Haunted by the ghost of unrequited love, she resembles a female Flying Dutchman doomed to chase the phantom of the dead Dave Chow, the lover whose suicide turns her into a vengeful London whore. *Pan Beat* and *J'ouvert Morning* are disquieting explorations of Trinidad society in the pre and postindependence periods, a society skeptical of its value and in search of an identity. Commentators have noticed the strength and courage of J.'s women characters and the quality of her poetic prose. But J.'s social realism, her gritty, candid portrait of Port of Spain, and her depiction of the neurotic Trinidadian hobbled by insularity and claustrophobia are also notable features of her best work.

FURTHER WORKS: *Apartheid: Its Effects on Education, Science, Culture and Information* (1967); *Namibia: The Effects of Apartheid on Culture and Education* (1977); *Southern Rhodesia: The Effects of a Conquest Society on Education, Culture and Information* (1977)

BIBLIOGRAPHY: King, L., "A Call to Two Different Worlds," *Tapia*, 3 (May 1973): 4; Questel, V., " *J'ouvert Morning*: Middle Class Fears," *Caribbean Contact*, 5 (Apr. 1977): 2; Loncke, J., "The Image of the Woman in Caribbean Literature with Special Reference to *Pan Beat* and *Heremakhonon*," *Bim*, 16 (December 1978): 272-81; Barratt, H., "A Shuttered Cleavage: M. J.'s Tormented People," *WLWE*, 19 (Spring 1980): 57-62

—HAROLD BARRATT

JORGE, Lidia

Portuguese novelist, b. 18 June 1946, Boliqueime

J. was born and raised in a rural community in the Algarve and studied at the University of Lisbon where she first became politically conscious. Upon completing her studies, she spent several years as a teacher in the African colonies of Angola and Mozambique. She returned to Lisbon to teach, first at the secondary level and later at the university. She began writing as a child, but it was at the age of thirty-three that she published her first book.

Her first novel, *O dia dos prodígios* (1980; the day of the prodigious events), acclaimed by an eminent Portuguese scholar as one of the key works of the Portuguese revolution of 1974, was an immediate success. It revealed already most of the characteristics that were to define her as a novelist: formal experiment, an idiosyncratic style marked by a pronounced orality, an inclination toward magic REALISM, a fascination with her historical moment. Many novels were written about the 1974 revolution in the years immediately following it, but none of them records its failure as brilliantly as does J.'s. The author figures her commentary in the juxtaposition of two prodigious events: the revolution itself and the sudden appearance and equally sudden disappearance in the rural village of Vilamaninhos of a mysterious winged snake. For the villagers, the former is a remote "prodígio," far less real and far less fascinating than their own prodigious snake. By depicting these villagers as an insular, culturally deprived community, implicitly like many others throughout the country, J. questions the viability of a political program as sophisticated as the one espoused by the makers of the revolution. On a secondary level, the novel is as much about the art of narration as it is about the inability of political reform to penetrate the remote corners of Portugal. Early in the novel, J. reveals an interest in the dynamics of group storytelling. The task she sets for herself is not merely to describe the process but to reproduce it, to transpose the oral experience of simultaneous narration (essentially temporal) to the medium of writing (primarily spatial). For this novel, she won the Ricardo Malheiros Prize (1980).

J.'s second novel, *O cais das merendas* (1982; the snack wharf), is again a response to social change. Here the issue is an insidious colonization: the tourist invasion of the Algarve. The author exposes its devastating consequences for the inhabitants of a small rural village, lured by the perceived sophistication and economic promise of rededicating their lives to service at a thriving resort hotel. The price is the sacrifice of cultural identity and of selfhood in new roles that require J.'s characters to be no longer members of a culturally valid community but simply functionaries in the world of the tourist, a world that appropriates their time and space but systematically excludes them from full participation. J.'s artistic medium is again a brilliant use of language and form: shifting narrators and temporal planes, symbolic and allegorical detail, a touch of magic realism. Most impressive is her depiction of language itself in the process of being colonized, her revelation of the cultural charge that words carry, and the cultural and psychological ramifications of replacing one word with another.

Colonization of a more traditional, though no less devastating, kind is the subject of J.'s fourth novel, *A costa dos murmúrios* (1988; the coast of murmurs). As in the second novel, the setting is a hotel, this time one that houses the wives of military personnel in war-ravaged Mozambique during the final throes of the colonial enterprise. The author's primary intention is to expose the brutality of the war, but, as in the other two novels, there is a secondary, one might say literary, concern as well. This book is in reality two novels in one. The first is an account of a tragic war-related episode that once occurred at the hotel. The second, a telling of the "true story" of that event by a participant who twenty years later has just finished reading the account. The author's intention here is to explore the relationship of truth, reality, and history (history as the way in which reality is interpreted, recorded, and remembered). She intends not simply to question the events and the rationale of the colonial war but to challenge the way contemporary Portuguese society is processing the "memory" of that war. Again the novel is enriched by the oral style, the numerous and varied discourses of that African experience.

While all of these novels have met with a highly favorable reception, there is one group of readers that has been less than enthusiastic about J.'s work: the radical feminists. J. gives a prominent place to women in each of the works, but she does not privilege them, undoubtedly because it was the broader national picture that absorbed her. Her third novel, *Notícia da cidade silvestre* (1984; word from the sylvan city), focuses on two female characters through the first-person confessional narrative of one of them. The narrative appears at first to be the story of women's friendship, but it soon becomes evident that it is something quite different: an examination of the power struggles and the subliminal forces that inform human relationships whether they be with women, with men, or even with children. All are at issue in the novel, which in that sense continues to have a broader social theme. This work breaks with the others not only in dealing with more intimate, subjective material but in doing so in a more straightforward manner, shorn of the allegorical and magic realist cast that characterizes them. Orality alone continues. For this work J. received the City of Lisbon Fiction Award (1984). After these works J. wrote a play dealing with the early-20th-c. feminist and medical doctor Adelaide Cabete; a stage production was soon planned.

In the novels that followed those published in the 1990s, J. moved away, in large measure, from the geographical and temporal specificity of the earlier works and the political and cultural truths of her country's history, towards more "literary" worlds, constructs of imagined spaces and equally imagined lives, characters rooted more in their own passions and aspirations than in an easily identifiable common reality. *A última dona* (1992; the final woman) is an example of this new vein, as is *O jardim sem limites* (1995; the garden without boundaries). J. has also moved in new directions in terms of genre, not only in *A maçon: peça em dois actos* (1997; the mason: a play in two acts) but in *Marido e outros contos* (1998; the husband and other stories). Early on J. attained a prominent position on the Portuguese literary scene and found herself sought after in academic and literary circles in her own country and abroad.

BIBLIOGRAPHY: Sadlier, D. J., *The Question of How: Women Writers and New Portuguese Literature* (1989): 49–73

—ALICE R. CLEMENTE

JOUBERT, Elsa

South African novelist, b. 1922, Cape Province

J. is one of the first Afrikaans authors to write sympathetically about Africa and black Africans as well as to deal with African travels. She has received numerous literary awards, including the Winifred Holtby prize awarded by the British Royal Society, of which she is also a fellow.

J. is most famous for her novel *Die Swerfjare van Poppie Nongena* (1978; *The Long Journey of Poppie Nongena*, 1980; *Poppie*, 1981). This novel is written as the autobiography of a black South African woman, and is based on the actual narrative of a woman—for whom J. employs the pseudonym Poppie Nongena—who came to J.'s house in Cape Town one day to tell her life story to someone who would write it down. Critical reception of the novel has focused on the extent to which J. was merely an amanuensis; J. herself acknowledges that she reworked the narrative as a novelist. The debate surrounding the status of the text and its authorship is illustrative of a trend in South African writing, namely a concern with questions of ventriloquism and representativeness in art and public discourse. Perhaps the most significant effect of J.'s text was due to the facts that it was written in Afrikaans and serialised in the Afrikaans-language Sunday newspaper *The Rapport*, read mainly by conservative Afrikaners: J. was thereby able to make emotionally real and widely-known the experiences of a woman who might otherwise have been invisible to white, Afrikaans-speaking readers. Others of her novels that have been translated into English include J.'s first novel *Ons Wag op die Kaptein* (1963; *To Die at Sunset*, 1982) and her 1983 novel *Die Laaste Sondag* (*The Last Sunday*, 1989).

J.'s later work, like that of many South African writers, turns to topics from the history of South Africa. In her novel *Missionaris* (1988; Missionary) she fictionalizes the experiences of a group of missionaries and their sympathizers on the 19th-c. Cape. In *Die Reise van Isobelle* (1995) (The Journey of Isobelle), which covers the period from 1894 to 1994, she returns to the trope of life as a journey, and reflects on South African history through the narrative of a series of connected women's lives. The text is concerned with issues of cultural adaptation, racial identity, and the changing identities of Afrikaner women.

FURTHER WORKS: *Water en woestyn* (1956); *Die verste reis* (1959); *Suid van die wind* (1962); *Die staf van Monomotapa* (1964); *Swerwer in die herfsland* (1968); *Die Wahlerbrug* (1969); *Bonga* (1971); *Die nuwe Afrikaan* (1974); *Melk* (1980); *Die vier vriende en ander stories uit Afrika* (1985); *Dansmaat* (1993); *Die gordel van smarag: 'n reis met Leipoldt* (1997).

BIBLIOGRAPHY: Carlean, K., "The Narrative Functions of E. J.'s *Poppie Nongena*," *ESA*, 16 (1989); McClintock, A., "The Scandal of Hybridity: Black Women's Resistance and Narrative Ambiguity," in *Imperial Leather: Race, Gender and Sexuality in the Colonial Context* (1995); Schalkwyk, D., "E. J.: Women and Domestic Struggle in *Poppie Nongena*," in Clayton, C., ed., *Women and Writing in South Africa* (1989)

—CARLI COETZEE

JOUHANDEAU, Marcel

French novelist, essayist, and short-story writer, b. 26 July 1888, La Clayette; d. 7 April 1979, Rueil-Malmaison

The son of a butcher in Guéret, J. always felt much closer to his mother, a very pious woman; he first planned to become a priest,

but after completing his studies in Paris, he worked as a schoolteacher there from 1912 until 1949, devoting most of his time to literature. The eccentric woman he married in 1929, the former dancer Caryathis, became one of the main characters in his fiction, under the name of Élise: *Élise* (1933; Élise); *Chroniques maritales* (2 vols., 1935, 1938; chronicles of married life); *Nouvelles chroniques maritales* (1943; new chronicles of married life). Their adopted daughter, Céline, appears also in his novels *L'école des filles* (1961; the education of girls) and *Une adolescence* (1971; an adolescence).

J., who in 1914 had destroyed his first literary writings, was a very prolific writer until the very end of his life: he published more than 150 books. Their three main centers of interest are the people he knew, himself (under various fictitious names: Théophile, Juste Binche, Mr. Godeau), and God. The persons who surrounded him in his childhood and youth became the characters of a series of chronicles, which are a transposition of provincial life in the small town of Guéret, in central France (Chaminadour in J.'s fiction), with its satanic or angelic sides.

J.'s first book, *La jeunesse de Théophile* (1921; Théophile's youth), is the ironic and mystic tale of a young man aspiring to an ideal of beauty and the absolute, but too sensual to be a priest. J. then re-created unforgettable faces and figures from his own youth in *Les Pincengrain* (1924; the Pincengrains), *Prudence Hautechaume* (1927; Prudence Hautechaume), *Chaminadour* (3 vols., 1934, 1936, 1941; Chaminadour), *Les miens* (1942; Uncle Henry), while evoking his own struggle between good and evil in *Monsieur Godeau intime* (1926; Mr. Godeau in his intimacy), *Monsieur Godeau marié* (1933; Mr. Godeau married). A series of realistic portraits and cruel or tender anecdotes resurrect the past in the six volumes of *Mémorial* (recorded memories) published between 1948 and 1958. They are completed and brought to the present by acute observation of daily reality noted in a nervous but elegant style in the twenty-six volumes of the monumental *Journaliers* (1961–78; day-to-day happenings).

In a series of moral essays J. pursued a dialogue with God, even from the depths of sin and often beyond good and evil: *L'algèbre des valeurs morales* (1935; algebra of moral values), *De l'abjection* (1939; on abasement), *L'éloge de la volupté* (1951; in praise of voluptuous pleasure), *Les carnets de l'écrivain* (1957; the writer's notebooks). His scandalous confessions are not a sign of complacency about vice but rather an attempt to transcend it. They reveal a rich inner life, an unshakable optimism, and they affirm the omnipotent freedom of man in his confrontation with God.

The diabolic and visionary aspect of J.'s talent appears at its best in fantastic tales such as *Astaroth* (1929; Ashtaroth) and *Contes d'enfer* (1955; tales from hell).

J. is recognized as one of the greatest writers of fiction in 20th-c. French literature. He has managed to create in his novels and stories a universe of his own through the magic of his style, the acuteness of his observation, and a unique vision in which cynical irony is mixed with an almost sacrilegious belief in the absolute value of man.

FURTHER WORKS: *Les Térébinte* (1926); *Ximénès Malinjoude* (1927); *Opales* (1928); *Le parricide imaginaire* (1930); *Le journal du coiffeur* (1931); *L'amateur d'imprudence* (1932); *Tite-le-Long* (1932); *Veronicana* (1933); *Binche-ana* (1933); *Le saladier* (1936); *Petit bestiaire* (1944); *Essai sur moi-même* (1946); *Carnets de Don Juan* (1947); *Ma classe de sixième* (1949); *Un monde* (1950); *L'imposteur* (1950); *De la grandeur* (1952); *Ana de Madame* d'*Apremont* (1954); *Nouvelles images de Paris* (1956); *Réflexions sur la vieillesse et la mort* (1956); *Saint Philippe Neri* (1957; *St. Philip Neri*, 1960); *Réflexions sur la vie et le bonheur* (1958); *Trois crimes rituels* (1962); *Chronique d'une passion* (1964); *Que la vie est une fête* (1966); *Et nunc dimittis* (1978). FURTHER WORKS IN ENGLISH: *Marcel and Élise* (1953)

BIBLIOGRAPHY: Mauriac, C., *Introduction à une mystique de l'enfer* (1938); Turnell, M., Introduction to *Marcel and Élise* (1953): 7–25; Cabanis, J., *J.* (1959); Gaulmier, J., *L'univers de M. J.* (1959); Heppenstall, R., *The Fourfold Tradition* (1961): 170–77; Rode, H., *J.* (1972)

—FREDERIC J. GROVER

JOUVE, Pierre Jean

French poet, novelist, and music critic, b. 11 Oct. 1887, Arras; d. 8 Jan. 1976, Paris

By his own account, J.'s childhood was not a happy one, marred as it was by a serious operation followed by years of depression and emotional instability. During these years he developed a taste for music, which thereafter always held a special attraction for him and to which he would devote some of his most probing critical writings. He spent both world wars in Switzerland. After returning to France in 1945, J. settled in Paris, where he remained until his death, save for occasional short trips abroad.

J.'s early career was marked by false starts, ambiguous alliances—with the Abbaye group of poets and with Jules ROMAINS and Romain ROLLAND—and unevenness in the quality of his work.

J.'s mature phase as a writer was the product of a period of intense reading and reflection, spanning the years 1922–25. As a result of this crisis, J. boldly repudiated, in his preface to the volume of poetry *Noces* (1928; nuptials), all of his writings prior to 1925. During this period he experienced a "religious conversion" in the broadest sense of the term, to spiritual values inherent in poetry, J. was careful to point out in the autobiographical essay *En miroir* (1954; in the mirror), and not specifically to Catholicism or any other particular faith or dogma, as some critics have claimed. Almost concurrently, J. became interested in Freudian psychoanalysis. The preface to another poetry collection, *Sueur de sang* (1933; sweat of blood), was misinterpreted in some circles as J.'s espousal of a kind of "poeticized psychoanalysis," and not as the poet intended it, namely, of psychoanalysis as a point of departure for artistic creation.

J.'s dramatic gesture of rejection, his repudiation of his early work, announced a new beginning, to which he alluded by choosing the phrase "vita nuova" (new life), the title of Dante's collection of poems, as the epigraph to *Noces*. This was by no means a cry of victory, but rather a statement of hope. For J.'s poetic development was characterized by a relentless search for a singular voice and language, a search that was remarkable in its unity of composition and imagery. His poetry posits a world of seemingly irreconcilable contraries, which the poet seeks to harmonize. These gravitate around two main figures representing two divergent paths of poetic creation: Christ-Apollo, the "Christ of poetry"; and Mnemosyne, goddess of memory and mother of the Muses. While the former embodies an inaccessible artistic originality, pure creation, the Logos, as it were, the latter functions as the only mediating presence available to the poet, the vast but out-worn resources of poetic myths, themes, and language that have inspired the writings of artistic precursors. The struggle between these two opposing forces becomes the focal point of J.'s poetics, and the desire for resolution provides the dialectical nature of the poetry as a whole.

This drama is played out in successive stages. *Noces* and *Sueur de sang* constitute the preliminary "dark phase" of gradual awakening to the reality of opposites in which the female (as memory's surrogate) is the object of mistrust. *Matière céleste* (1937; celestial matter) and *Kyrie* (1938; Kyrie) contain the poet's slow and patient refinement of the feminine figure in its most erotic manifestations; her death makes possible her emergence under the guise of Eurydice, the lost lover. A mystical stage is subsequently inaugurated in *La vierge de Paris* (1944; the virgin of Paris) and *Hymne* (1947; hymn) centering on the higher, sublimated figure of the "vierge noire" (black virgin). Although the general tenor of J.'s poetry is heavily pessimistic and tormented by a pervasive intuition of failure, his later poetry, particularly *Mélodrame* (1957; melodrama) and *Moires* (1962; moirés), gives evidence of a gradual sense of serenity and resignation.

J.'s language is inextricably linked to the development of his poetry. Violence and rebellion prevail in *Noces* and *Sueur de sang*, and the style of these early collections is dry, almost antilyrical, while the thematics rely heavily on the love/death duality. J.'s mystical phase shows a certain release of tension, but his vocabulary is further restricted, displaying skillful variations on key concepts and images, such as death and darkness, silence, emptiness, and nothingness. In his last collections J. wrote with an exalted tone and frequent use of repetition.

J. experimented for some years (1925–35) with the novel and short narratives, which echo many of the themes and preoccupations of his poetry. But his prose remains "poetic" by virtue of its elliptical style and his shunning of conventional techniques of plot and characterization. *Paulina 1880* (1925; *Paulina 1880*, 1973), *Le monde désert* (1927; deserted world), and *Hécate* (1928; Hecate) explore the conflict between human and divine love, purity and guilt.

A "poet-seer" in the tradition of Baudelaire and Rimbaud, J. translated the quest for pure art into the search for an artistic creation that would be free from historical influences and cross-cultural currents by focusing on an "interior continent" revealed by the unconscious. Yet his manifold, and often disguised, references to other poets and artists constitute a dialogue with a revisionist attitude, which seeks to assert the originality of the modern poet vis-à-vis his forerunners. It is in this sense that J.'s poetry transcends the narrow labels that one may be tempted to ascribe to it to reveal the poetic conscience of a tormented age.

FURTHER WORKS: *Le paradis perdu* (1929); *Vagadu* (1931); *Histoires sanglantes* (1932); *La scène capitale* (1935); *Le Don Juan de Mozart* (1942; *Mozart's Don Juan*, 1957); *Tombeau de Baudelaire* (1942); *Aventure de Catherine Crachat* (1947; contains *Hécate* and *Vagadu*); *Diadème* (1949); *Commentaires* (1950); *Ode* (1950); *Langue* (1952); *Wozzeck; ou, Le nouvel opéra* (1953, with M.Fano); *Lyrique* (1956); *Inventions* (1958); *Proses* (1960); *Ténèbres* (1965). FURTHER WORKS IN ENGLISH: *An Idiom of Night* (1968)

BIBLIOGRAPHY: Starobinski, J., and P. Alexandre, and Eigeldinger, M., *P. J. J.: Poète et romancier* (1946); Callander, M., *The Poetry of P. J. J.* (1965); special J. issue, *NRF*, 183 (1968); special J. issue, *L'Herne*, 19 (1972); Sanzenbach, S., *Les romans de P. J. J.: Le romancier en son miroir* (1972); Brosman, C. S., "J.'s Spatial Dialectics in *Les noces* and *Sueur de sang*," *AJFS*, 2 (1973): 164–74; Rivas, D. E., "J.'s *Mnémosyne*: An Alchemical View," *ECr*, 18 (1978): 51–61

—DANIEL E. RIVAS

JOVINE, Francesco

Italian novelist, short-story writer, and journalist, b. 9 Oct. 1902, Guardialfiera; d. 30 April 1950, Rome

From a poor family in the Molise region, J. studied in provincial towns and in 1925 moved to Rome, where he graduated from the university with a degree in philosophy. A teacher by profession, he also became an active anti-Fascist and took part in the Resistance during World War II. After the war J. wrote for several leftist newspapers and periodicals and, in 1948, joined the Communist Party. Although he began his literary career in the late 1920s, his finest creative achievements are concentrated in the ten years before his untimely death.

Un uomo provvisorio (1934; a temporary man), J.'s first and most autobiographical novel, is a psychological study of the alienation and moral uncertainty of a young, introspective doctor who tries to break away from his backward and stifling Molise in the 1920s. J.'s second novel, *Signora Ava* (1942; *Seeds in the Wind*, 1946), derives its title from a mythical folk figure and is set in his native town at the beginning of the unification of Italy. Written during the war, the novel reveals a less private, more ethically and historically inspired narrative manner. Its dominant theme is the author's rediscovery of the Molise region, with overtones of social indignation becoming prominent in the second half of the book.

J.'s posthumously published and stylistically finest novel, *Le terre del Sacramento* (1950; *The Estate in Abruzzi*, 1952), marks a further shift of his narrative in the direction of a more vigorous social protest and greater political commitment. The novel's setting is again the Molise region, and the action unfolds at the time of the rise of Fascism. It is the story of a group of disenfranchised peasants who are persuaded by rich landowners to work on lands confiscated from the Church. Later, when the peasants have occupied these lands, they are driven off by force by the police and the Fascists. Their young leader, Luca Marano, killed in the final confrontation with the Fascist authorities, emerges as the hero who not only represents new social forces but also attempts to bring about historic changes. Generally considered J.'s masterpiece, *Le terre del Sacramento* made his reputation as one of the most original interpreters of postwar Italian NEOREALISM.

In the 1940s, J. also published four collections of short fiction. The settings and themes of these stories, which are often uneven and less satisfactory than longer works, are similar to those of the novels: the probing psychological study of the uprooted provincial intellectual; the careful depiction of southern life; the strong interest in social justice and political issues.

J.'s links with the Italian narrative tradition of the 19th c. and, more precisely, with southern realism, are both evident and natural. His fiction springs from events, usually political ones, yet it always goes beyond them to seek a universal human meaning; it springs from his public interests, yet it is at the same time highly lyric in quality. His basic mode of expression is an intensely personal blend of historical, autobiographical, and ideological elements.

FURTHER WORKS: *Il burattinaio metafisico* (1928); *Berluè* (1929); *Ragazza sola* (1936–1937); *Ladro di galline* (1940); *L'impero in provincia* (1945); *Il pastore sepolto* (1945); *Tutti i miei peccati* (1948); *Giorni che rinasceranno* (1948); *Racconti* (1960); *Viaggio nel Molise* (1967)

BIBLIOGRAPHY: Della Terza, D., "The Neorealists and the Form of the Novel," *IQ*, 10 (1966): 3–20; Moloney, B., "The Novels of F. J.," *IS*, 23 (1968): 138–55; Procaccini, A., "Neorealism: Description/Prescription," *YItS*, 2 (1977): 39–57; Pacifici, S., *The Modern Italian Novel: From Pea to Moravia* (1979): 1–17

—ALBERT N. MANCINI

JOYCE, James

Irish novelist, short-story writer, dramatist, poet, and essayist, b. 2 Feb. 1882, Dublin; d. 13 Jan. 1941, Zurich, Switzerland

Born on Candlemas Day, 1882, in Dublin, J. was the first-born of a solidly Catholic family. His father was a Cork gentleman, but suffered severe economic decline into genteel poverty, a condition

James Joyce

of J.'s childhood he recorded graphically in *A Portrait of the Artist as a Young Man* (1916), as he turned every aspect of his life, his country's history, and his city's topography into literary art. His Ireland was a Catholic nation that had been under centuries of British rule, and J. is distinct in being one of the few Irish artists of his age who did not come from the ruling Anglo-Irish Protestant Ascendancy.

J.'s education was almost exclusively at the colleges of the Jesuits. He began as a boarding student at the prestigious Clongowes Wood College, but financial factors changed him into a day student at Belvedere. His university days at the Catholic University were relatively undistinguished, probably because he already considered himself intellectually superior to and in revolt against his Jesuit mentors. Their pedagogical methods exposed him to selected statements by great writers, a limitation he turned into effect: in formulating asethetic theories based on Aristotle and Aquinas; in writing short lyric poems; in collecting "epiphanies," overheard snippets of conversation or recorded dreams. His early efforts (none published in his life-time) were multidirectional, and included an autobiographical essay, "A Portrait of the Artist" (written 1904); a contemptuous broadside, "The Holy Office" (also written 1904); vignettes for journalistic publication; book reviews; a long (but never completed) novel, *Stephen Hero* (posthumously published in 1944); and presumably two plays influenced by Henrik Ibsen.

Although J. was to abandon drama for fiction, his dedication to Ibsen, as to Aristotle, Aquinas, and Dante, was formative. At seventeen he learned Dano-Norwegian to read Ibsen; he wrote to the master and published an essay on his work, "Ibsen's New Drama," in the *Fortnightly Review* in 1900. Ibsen was both a cause and a *cause célèbre* whom he championed in a paper before the Literary and Historical Society at his university and made the subject of a virulent essay, "The Day of the Rabblement" (privately printed, as a pamphlet, 1901), in which he portrayed him as the leading spirit of European modernism, along with Gerhart HAUPTMANN, and a mysterious "third" waiting in the wings. He translated at least one of Hauptmann's plays and sent his own to Ibsen's English translator for approval, yet the only extant J. drama, *Exiles* (written 1915, published 1918) was more in homage to than imitation of Ibsen.

In dedication to the lonely integrity of the artist, J. renounced both his Catholicism and Irish nationalism, and although a mild socialist generally, he abjured politics in general. In *A Portrait of the Artist as a Young Man* Stephen Dedalus denounces "nationality, language, religion," nets flung at his soul to keep it down, and chooses as his weapons "silence, exile, and cunning." J.'s apostasies were in opposition to all demands that his society made upon him: the parochial character of the Irish Literary Renaissance, the Gaelic language revival, and nationalist politics. Yet he opposed British rule and conceded the efficacy of Sinn Fein. For himself he chose exile on the Continent.

Tentative stays in Paris in 1902–03, ostensibly to study medicine, developed into permanent residence on the Continent. In 1904 he left Dublin with Nora Barnacle, his lifelong companion whom he married in 1931, returning sporadically during the early years but remaining on the Continent from 1912 until his death. His stay in Trieste, employed by Berlitz as an English teacher, came to an end with World War I, and after refuge in Zurich he lived in Paris until World War II returned him to neutral Switzerland. In Europe he felt comfortable with a literary tradition rooted in Homer and Dante, a vestige of medieval Catholicism devoid of the 19th-c. pragmatic, and a modern spirit conducive to his own innovations.

He viewed the Ireland he left as "an afterthought of Europe," a "backwash," preferring the "mainstream" of European culture.

In Trieste he gathered together his thirty-six poems as *Chamber Music*, and when they were published in 1907 in London he already had misgivings about their worth. Fragile and somewhat insubstantial (in *Ulysses* [1922] Stephen is teased about his "capful of light odes"), they are redolent of the Pre-Raphaelite tempered with a pseudo-Elizabethan precision, and probably replete with double entendres. J. later claimed that the title came from hearing the urinary tinkle in a prostitute's chamber pot, an anecdote that points to the dual character of much of J.'s work: the blending of the sacred and profane, the exalted and the mundane. At the same time he augmented his handful of vignettes, from a grouping of ten "epicleti" to the final structure of fifteen stories as *Dubliners* (1914); frustrating delays caused by publishers gave him time to add "The Dead."

Dubliners reveals J.'s ear for naturalistic detail, his sense of short fiction devoid of artificial climaxes and resolutions, his deceptively simple style of "scrupulous meanness," and his contention that in writing a "chapter in the moral history" of Ireland he views Dublin as the "centre of paralysis." The book is carefully structured: the first three stories deal with children, the next four with young adults; then there are four on mature adults and three on "public life," and the book culminates with "The Dead." The milieu is the Dublin of British Ireland; the time, at the turn of the 20th c. The characters are almost exclusively middle-class Catholics, ranging from shopgirls and unemployed ne'er-do-wells to the scion of a wealthy butcher and the survivors of a starch-mill owner, a cross-section of the bourgeoisie who populated J.'s city as he was growing up.

The Trieste years were chaotic, frustrating, intemperate, poverty-stricken, and productive. Several of J.'s siblings joined them, and two children, Giorgio and Lucia, were born. A short stint in Rome as a bank clerk ended in illness, and J. returned to Trieste, at which time he scrapped *Stephen Hero* and rewrote his quasi-autobiographical novel as the concise and modernistically lean *A Portrait of the Artist as a Young Man*. Unconnected segments of Stephen Dedalus's life, from infant impressions to his flight to Paris after leaving the university, are stitched together by a structuring principle; only those factors that contribute to his eventual choice of a vocation as "the priest of eternal imagination" are included. The technique is portraiture; the focus is on the artistic potential; the distancing perspective is on the sensitive but arrogant youth. The five-chapter structure established the governing rhythm of the novel as each chapter ends on a note of triumph (Stephen vindicated after an unfair caning, ecstatic in the arms of a prostitute, exalted in a cleansed state of grace, transported at the sight of his muse, determined as he prepares to depart for France), but each chapter begins again with the commonplace, the mundane, and the depressed.

The narrative stance of *A Portrait of the Artist as a Young Man* employs Stephen as the exclusive source of awareness, yet the third-person narration, although it tracks his consciousness from baby talk to intellectual articulation, remains outside Stephen's mind, an indirection of style that allowed for a degree of irony as well as empathy. The child sees himself as victim; the university student as a "hawklike man"; but the narrative never loses sight of the limitations of youth. Stephen is the total center of *A Portrait of the Artist as a Young Man*, all other characters (parents, teachers, fellow students, his beloved) exist only in relation to him as Stephen moves through the formative events of his early life. And a series of symbolic systems, consisting of birds, eyes, colors, rats, water, provide the texture of the novel, replacing the traditional fleshing out of narrated sequences that J. abandoned. From Gustave Flaubert primarily J. fashioned a style through which the artist remains "within or behind or beyond or above his handiwork," expounding in *A Portrait of the Artist as a Young Man* the credo of the artist rivaling God in creativity.

As *A Portrait of the Artist as a Young Man* established J.'s reputation, *Ulysses* brought him international acclaim and notoriety. Begun in Trieste, continued in Zurich, completed in Paris, *Ulysses* was published in that *annus mirabilis* of modernist literature, 1922, contemporary with T. S. ELIOT's *The Waste Land*. As *A Portrait of the Artist as a Young Man* took its mythic departure from Daedalus and Icarus, *Ulysses* deployed Odysseus, Telemachus, and Penelope, in a complex assortment of parallels, parodies, and pastiches highlighting the events of a single day in Dublin on 16 June 1904. The detailed documentation of an ordinary day was considered the heights and depths of naturalism by early critics, obscene by the authorities of almost every English-speaking country, cloacal by British critics, a libel on Ireland by Irish. For over a half-century *Ulysses* has proven itself to be like the elephant for the blind men in Aesop's fable; Eliot assumed that J., like himself, was comparing the present age unfavorably with classical antiquity. Ezra POUND, J.'s significant early champion, lost interest when he realized that Stephen was being replaced in *Ulysses* by an ordinary citizen, *un homme moyen sensuel*, a Dubliner of Hungarian Jewish ancestry.

Although *Ulysses* finds Stephen back in Ireland, disgruntled, guilt-ridden, haunted by his dead mother, teaching ineffectively in a boy's school, at loose ends trying to write a bit of poetry, formulating theories on Shakespeare, holding forth with arcane anecdotes, drinking excessively, and by the end ready to fly once again into exile, the central focus is on Leopold Bloom, whom J. specifically referred to as a "good man." An outsider in an obliquely hostile environment, disappointed at the loss of his infant son and aware of the impending infidelity of his wife, Bloom is nonetheless prudent, sober, cautious, considerate, a man of unusual equilibrium and equanimity, steering an even course through the obstacles and pitfalls of Dublin. Much has been made of the theme of surrogate fathers and sons groping toward each other, but some have discerned that J. handles it with a light and even comic touch. And at the resolution of the novel there is Molly Bloom, whose unpunctuated night thoughts reveal a complex and contradictory wellspring of womanhood, a faithful/faithless Penelope, a sacred/profane Madonna, a patient/impatient Griselda.

J. constructed his *Ulysses* as a self-generating narrative composed of eighteen chapters, each with a style of its own, the stylistic variations graduating into extremely distinctive entities during the latter portions. Variant interior monologues for each of the major characters (with one chapter featuring interior monologues for several minor ones as well) supplement the narrative, which is augmented by verbal intrusions, polyphonic variations, epic cataloguing, parodies of literary styles, disembodied catechisms, a temporary extrinsic narrator, and other devices that distinguish *Ulysses* as generically unclassifiable. Yet the sum of its parts indicates a tightly controlled narrative, highly mosaic and involuted, a comic, ironic, poetic masterpiece that is multifoliate and kaleidoscopic, revealing new dimensions and proportions with each rereading.

The work on *Finnegans Wake* (1939) occupied J.'s time for the next sixteen years, during difficult periods of eye operations and his daughter's mental illness, and segments of this "Work in Progress" appeared regularly in avant-garde periodicals, particularly in Eugene Jolas's *transition*. Exposing isolated fragments in this manner was essential, as was J.'s willingness to comment and explicate and his marshaling of disciples who published exegeses long before the book was published. For *Finnegans Wake* J. invented a "night language" consisting of the dozens of languages he knew overlaid on an English already embellished by Irish brogues and other dialects. Multiple voices carry the narration, overlapping with each other and running headlong through various simultaneous bits of narrative, and produce what at one instance is called a "continuous present tense integument slowly unfolded all marryvoising moodmoulded cyclewheeling history." Whereas Stephen in *Ulysses* feared history as a "nightmare from which you will never awake," *Finnegans Wake* is a multifaceted dramatization of numerous nightmares of history, wildly comic and confusing and constantly replaying itself into endless variations. One pedestrian point of departure is a music-hall ballad of a drunken hodcarrier, Tim Finnegan, killed when he fell from his ladder but revived by splashing whiskey during a brawl at his wake. A more exalted origin is in the Irish hero Finn MacCool, the buried giant in the Dublin landscape, whose resurrection would revive the Irish nation. And with all mankind postulated in numerous Finnegans, hero and hodcarrier, insect and giant, *Finnegans Wake* records universal history in a Möbius strip of past, present, and future.

Five archetypal characters suggest themselves in *Finnegans Wake*: a husband/father dubbed H. C. Earwicker; a wife/mother, Anna Livia Plurabelle; twin sons, Shem/Jerry and Shaun/Kevin; and a daughter Issy. In the drama of life and the nightmare of history they play all the parts, committing sins and indiscretions, writing letters and testaments, fighting battles and healing wounds, marrying and dying, falling and rearising, living "life unlivable, transaccidentated through the slow fires of consciousness into a dividual chaos, perilous, potent, common to allflesh, human only, mortal." In contradistinction to *Ulysses*, *Finnegans Wake* is timeless, located in space in the Dublin suburb of Chapelizod that is every city and town, and its adjacent Phoenix Park that is every battlefield and every paradise garden.

Finnegans Wake was published just before World War II began, and the J. family once again prepared to take refuge in neutral exile. J. mentioned several new projects but started nothing, perhaps already aware that he was a very sick man. After only a few weeks back in Zurich, he died after an operation three weeks before his fifty-ninth birthday, having established himself in his lifetime as perhaps the most important literary innovator of the 20th c.

FURTHER WORKS: *Collected Poems* (1936); *Letters* (3 vols., 1957, 1966); *Critical Writings* (1959); *Workshop of Daedalus* (1965); *Giacomo Joyce* (1968); *J. J. Archives* (1975–)

BIBLIOGRAPHY: Beckett, S., et al., *Our Exagmination Round His Factifaction for Incamination of Work in Progress* (1929); Gilbert, S., *J. J.'s "Ulysses"* (1930); Budgen, F., *J. J. and The Making of "Ulysses"* (1934); Levin, H., *J. J.* (1941); Campbell, J, and Robinson, H. M., *Skeleton Key to "Finnegans Wake"* (1944); Kain, R. M., *Fabulous Voyager: J. J.'s "Ulysses"* (1947); Tindall, W. Y., *J. J.* (1950); Kenner, H., *Dublin's J.* (1955); Magalaner, M., and Kain, R. M., *J.: The Man, the Work, the Reputation* (1956); Noon, W. T., *J. and Aquinas* (1957); Schutte, W. M., *J. and Shakespeare* (1957); Ellmann, R., *J. J.* (1959); Atherton, J. S., *The Books at the Wake* (1959); Litz, A. W., *The Art of J. J.* (1961); *A Wake Newslitter* (1961–); Adams, R. M., *Surface and Symbol: The*

Consistency of J. J.'s "Ulysses" (1962); Hart, C., *Structure and Motif in "Finnegans Wake"* (1963); *J. J. Quarterly* (1963–); Goldberg, S. L., *Classical Temper: A Study of J. J.'s "Ulysses"* (1963); Benstock, B. J., *J.-again's Wake* (1965); Goldman, A., *The J. Paradox* (1966); Cixous, H., *L'exil de J. J.* (1968); O'Brien, D., *The Conscience of J. J.* (1968); Solomon, M., *Eternal Geomater: The Sexual Universe of "Finnegans Wake"* (1969); Hart, C., ed., *J. J.'s "Dubliners": Critical Essays* (1969); Hayman, D., *"Ulysses": The Mechanics of Meaning* (1970); Epstein, E., *The Ordeal of Stephen Dedalus* (1971); Brandabur, E., *A Scrupulous Meanness: A Study of J.'s Early Work* (1971); Ellmann, R., *Ulysses on the Liffey* (1972); Hart, C., and Hayman, D., eds., *J. J.'s "Ulysses"* (1974); Shechner, M., *J. in Nighttown* (1974); Begnal, M., and Senn, F., eds., *A Conceptual Guide to "Finnegans Wake"* (1976); McHugh, R., *The Sigla of "Finnegans Wake"* (1976); Peake, C. H., *J. J.: The Citizen and the Artist* (1977); Benstock, B., *J. J.: The Undiscover'd Country* (1977); Kenner, H., *J.'s Voices* (1978); Boyle, R. B., *J. J.'s Pauline Vision* (1978)

—BERNARD BENSTOCK

I have read several fragments of *Ulysses* in its serial form. It is a revolting record of a disgusting phase of civilisation; but it is a truthful one; and I should like to put a cordon round Dublin; round up every male person in it between the ages of 15 and 30; force them to read it; and ask them whether on reflection they could see anything amusing in all that foul mouthed, foul minded derision and obscenity. To you, possibly, it may appeal as art . . . but to me it is all hideously real: I have walked those streets and know those shops and have heard and taken part in those conversations. I escaped from them to England at the age of twenty; and forty years later have learnt from the books of Mr. J. that Dublin is still what it is, and young men are still driveling in slackjawed black-guardism just as they were in 1870. It is, however, some consolation to find that at last somebody has felt deeply enough about it to face the horror of writing it all down and using his literary genius to force people to face it. In Ireland they try to make a cat cleanly by rubbing its nose in its own filth. Mr. J. has tried the same treatment on the human subject. [1921]

George Bernard Shaw, in Sylvia Beach, *Shakespeare and Company* (1959), p. 52

The *Portrait of the Artist as a Young Man* is a book of such beauty of writing, such clarity of perception, such a serene love of and interest in life, and such charity that, being the ungenerous creature man is, one was inclined to say: "This surely must be a peak! It is unlikely that this man will climb higher!" But even now that Mr. J. has published *Ulysses*, it is too early to decide upon that. One can't arrive at one's valuation of a volume so loaded as *Ulysses* after a week of reading and two or three weeks of thought about it. Next year, or in twenty years, one may. For it is as if a new continent with new traditions had appeared, and demanded to be run through in a month. *Ulysses* contains the undiscovered mind of man; it is human consciousness analyzed as it has never before been analyzed. Certain books change the world. This, success or failure, *Ulysses* does: for no novelist with serious aims can henceforth set out upon a task of writing before he has at least formed his own private estimate as to the rightness or wrongness of the methods of the author of *Ulysses*. If it does not make an epoch-and it well may!-it will at least mark the ending of a period.

Ford Madox Ford, "A Haughty and Proud Generation," *YR*, 9 (1922), 717

To my knowledge, no writer has ever subordinated his life to his work more completely than did J. At the cost of real suffering, which I witnessed, he accepted a condition of permanent slavery, a slavery of both mind and body, that was complete. I can still see him, during one of the days that I spent with him, tortured by a word, constructing, almost rebelliously, a sort of framework; questioning his characters, turning to music for a more fictitious dream, a more vivid hallucination; and finally dropping exhausted onto a sofa, the better to hear the word about to spring shining into being. Then for an hour or more, there would be a long silence, broken only by laughter (his childlike laughter). . . .

Indeed, the reader is obliged to take this life into account. It requires genuine effort on that part of all who would approach J.'s work. But it also restores to reading the meaning and dignity which are lost when one reads most contemporary novels.

The value of this nearly forty-year-long experiment to the victorious completion of a work which constitutes one of the highest achievements in all literature cannot be sufficiently stressed. [1943]

Philippe Soupault, "Autour de J. J.," *J. J. Yearbook* (1959), 127–28

[*Finnegans Wake*] is controlled by a sharp intellect which filters every detail with great discrimination through the meshes of a Machiavellian alertness. One senses its fullness, the reverberations of the psyche as well as of history and culture even if it is impossible to follow all their implications without sharing J.'s polyhistoric and multilingual knowledge. At the frontier between a passing and a new epoch his language is composed of all languages and all the contemporary slangs in order to make understandable the present, past and future travail of the world in its variegated yet eternal recurrence. J. is the vessel of very old knowledge and very new hunches. One feels behind his work a universal wisdom from which the conscious and subconscious receive their impetus. This two-edged intelligence of J. creates the atmosphere in which the subconscious releases the poetic quality; the bleeding from a thousand wounds followed by a Homeric laughter. . . . He stood for a totality of existence, of sex and spirit, man and woman; for the universal against the specialized; for the union of intellect and emotion; for blending history with forecast, fairytale with science. . . . J. contained multitudes. And with these "multitudes" he paved the way to a related, space-time thinking on a larger scale than any writer had done before.

Laszlo Moholy-Nagy, *Vision in Motion* (1947), pp. 345–46

J.'s development as a writer is characterized by a continuous and rapid movement away from paradigmatic art—the selection and recreation of a typical and powerfully symbolic unit of experience which illuminates things far beyond the bounds of its own context (that is, the technique which he called the "epiphany")—towards the all-inclusive art of *Finnegans Wake* where, instead of choosing the most typical and illuminating example of a theme, he attempted to present every conceivable trope. In his later years J. seems to have adopted as his motto Voltaire's paradox that the superfluous is a very necessary thing. Caution and literary asceticism were abandoned and the utmost richness was allowed to replace the most "scrupulous meanness." If *Finnegans Wake* can be contained within any one artistic mode, it must be the baroque; the great themes of death and resurrection, sin and redemption, are moulded into firm cyclic outlines, while masses of ornate particulars—a closely woven network of motifs and symbols—define, develop and embellish these thematic abstractions.

Clive Hart, *Structure and Motif in "Finnegans Wake"* (1962), p. 24

. . . What J. tried to do: to declare war against the national language. He said he would fight this war until the end. That is, in a way he based his work on a language that had disappeared—Gaelic. He wanted to destroy an official, imposed language—English. Doing that, he wanted to reach all language. Why did he want to achieve his own revolution by using the maximum possible number of languages? To show that the end of nationalities had been decided. And this is a political act which has a very strong impact.

Another aspect is that he wanted to reach the unconscious. So if you remain attached to one national language, in that way you remain in the preconscious. That is why great numbers of people who only speak one language are enclosed and refuse on the one side the unconscious and on the other side internationalism. J. wants to destroy nationalism, but he wants to go further than internationalism. What he is building with his book is trans-nationalism. Because the language spoken by internationalism is also that of dead languages.

What is his real political action? He is going to dismember, analyze, go through, re-articulate, annihilate, the maximum culture, ideological, historical, mythological, linguistic, and religious residues. His most important political act is the way he obstinately tried to analyze religion. If we take religion as, according to Freud, the most important neurotic phenomenon of our civilization, we have to consider that

apart from J., nobody has been able to get out of the religious state. Why did he manage to do that? The reason would be that through his writing he managed to achieve sexual knowledge of our species. J. has the same ambition as Freud: he wants to analyze 2000 years of humanity. . . . *Finnegans Wake* is the most important anti-Fascist book written between the two World Wars, at a time when Fascism was gaining throughout Europe. What a Fascist leader does is destroyed by such writing, because it destroys all ideologies. So this book is the strongest action that has been taken against political paranoia. That's why it's both a very amusing and a very serious book.

Philippe Sollers, in Maria Jolas and Jacques Aubert, eds., *J. & Paris*, Papers from the Fifth International J. J. Symposium (1975), Vol. II, pp. 111–12

JÓZSEF, Attila

Hungarian poet and translator, b. 11 April 1905, Budapest; d. 3 Dec. 1937, Balatonszárszó

Son of a soapmaker—who abandoned his family when J. was three—and a laundress in poor health, J. spent some of his formative years with foster parents. Even when his mother was able to work, the boy helped out by doing odd jobs. In 1919 his mother died of cancer. Although J. was an excellent student, his nerves were already overstrained, and he attempted suicide. By age seventeen he was a published poet, his work appearing in the prestigious *Nyugat*.

A tragic combination of circumstances kept him from ever achieving financial or emotional stability. A clash of ideologies with a professor at the university in Szeged prevented him from attaining a degree; his poetry was published but did not put enough bread on his table; his talents and hard work did not secure him steady employment; his idealism, which made him for a while a member of the underground, illegal Communist Party, brought him nothing but trouble. When he was in love, he was unable to marry, in the beginning for financial reasons, at the end because of his deteriorating mental health. Finally, only his sisters remained; fearful of being a burden to them, he threw himself under a passing freight train. Now statues of him stand in public squares in Hungary, and streets are named after him.

His first volume, *Szépség koldusa* (1922; beauty's beggar), published with the help of Gyula JUHÁSZ, is surprising in its maturity. J. mastered the lessons of his elders and assimilated them, but he did not imitate anyone. There are echoes of Endre ADY'S revolutionary vision and SYMBOLIST techniques; but the voice is that of the young worker, using the first-person plural. The volume also shows that J. had learned from Dezső KOSZTOLÁNYI'S finely wrought, delicate wedding of substance and form.

Three years elapsed before J.'s second volume, *Nem én kiáltok* (1925; it is not I who shouts), appeared. Those years spanned the promising opening and dispirited ending of his academic career. The young man continued to study, often literally starving, at the University of Vienna, at the Sorbonne, and at the University of Budapest, but did not have the financial means to finish the preparation for a degree. While in Vienna and Paris, he formed friendships with avant-garde poets and left-wing radicals, and met his great benefactor, the patron of the arts and man of letters Lajos Hatvany (1880–1961).

J.'s most ambitious poetic undertaking dates from this time: "A kozmosz éneke" (1923; song of the cosmos) is a "sonnet ring," or *sonetti a corona*, a cycle of fourteen sonnets and a "master sonnet" composed of the first lines of the other fourteen. This virtuoso performance, written when he was just eighteen years old, is a testimony to his ability to think out and execute a complex and challenging project. The mood of the poems of this period ranges from the spirituality of "Imádság megfáradtaknak" (1924; prayer for those who are tired) to the revolutionary muscle-flexing of "És keressük az igazságot" (1924; and we are searching for justice). The title poem of *Nem én kiáltok* expresses an idea that remained central to his world view: that his destiny is to become one with the whole world, but—should this prove impossible—he would fight the world's antihuman forces and try to conquer them. The contradictory instincts of self-preservation and yearning to be dissolved in a greater entity were responsible for much of the tension in his poetry. There are similar contradictions in his technique. He is simultaneously a preserver and a destroyer of poetic traditions.

The university years gave him opportunities to experiment with widely differing poetic styles. "Anyám meghalt" (1925; my mother died) and "Beteg vagyok" (1925; I am ill) are EXPRESSIONISTIC, "Egy átlátszó oroszlán" (1926; a transparent lion) SURREALISTIC. The years 1927–29 were critical for J. His health, his marriage plans, his education, his financial situation all failed; even his future as a poet seemed doubtful. After a brief flirtation with the Socialist Workers' Party in 1929 he fell in love with a Communist girl and threw himself into the cause with naïve enthusiasm. He published a revolutionary volume with a punning title, *Döntsd a tőkét, ne siránkozz* (1931; remove the tree stump, don't whine, *or* knock down capital[ism], don't whine).

In a 1937 curriculum vitae he wrote for a job application he summed up the years 1929–37 in the single sentence: "I have supported myself with my pen ever since." Actually, the "support" was never much above starvation level, although his greatest poems were written in these final years. The volumes *Külvárosi éj* (1932; night in the outskirts), *Medvetánc* (1934; bear dance), and *Nagyon fáj* (1936; it hurts very much) show the tragic dilemma of his life: even as his poetic powers were increasing, his isolation as a man and a poet also increased. His schizophrenia is documented with clinical exactness in "Ki-be ugrál" (1936; it keeps jumping in and out) and "Kirakják a fát" (1936; they are unloading the firewood). "Thomas Mann üdvözlése" (1937; greeting Thomas Mann) may be taken as his poetic testament. There was one last, desperate attempt at happiness, immortalized in the Flóra poems, written for his last love, but when that also failed, he wrote the final tragic poems of despair and resignation.

FURTHER WORKS: *Nincsen apám, sem anyám* (1929); *J. A. összes művei* (4 vols., 1952–1967); *Összes versei* (1972). FURTHER WORKS IN ENGLISH: *Poems* (1966); *Selected Poems and Texts* (1973); *Poems of A. J.* (1973)

BIBLIOGRAPHY: Rousselot, J., *A. J. (1905–1937)* (1958); Pődör, L., "A Portrait of A.J. the Poet," *NHQ*, No. 1 (1961): 32–44; Reményi, J., *Hungarian Writers and Literature* (1964): 371–77; Klaniczay, T., et al., *History of Hungarian Literature* (1964): 286–94; Lotz, J., *The Structure of the Sonetti a Corona of A. J.* (1965); Nyerges, A., Introduction to *Poems of A. J.* (1973): 9–12; special J. section, *NHQ*, No. 80(1980): 46–74; Brunauer, D. H., "Parallel Lives: Edgar Allan Poe and A. J.," *Journal of Evolutionary Psychology*, 3, 1 (1982): 1–8

—DALMA H. BRUNAUER

JUHÁSZ, Gyula

Hungarian poet, critic, and journalist, b. 3 April 1883, Szeged; d. 3 April 1937, Szeged

J., descended from shepherds of the Hungarian lowland, served a novitiate with the Piarists but left the teaching order before he was ordained. For some years he taught literature in secondary schools in various provincial cities. Literary critics first took notice of him when his poems appeared in 1908 in an anthology published by the Holnap Literary Society. He was also associated with the writers of the literary review *Nyugat*, a monthly publication that became the nucleus of modern Hungarian literature.

As a young teacher and poet, J. had taken little interest in domestic politics or international affairs. But the inhumanity of World War I aroused him to activism, and he became one of the leaders of the radical party (in Szeged), which called for an early end to the bloodshed. After the collapse of the Austro-Hungarian monarchy in the fall of 1918, J. became the dramatic consultant to the municipal theater of Szeged. Later, during Béla Kun's short-lived Communist regime in 1919, he worked as director of Szeged's National Theater. With the establishment of Horthy's regime, J. lost this position and could not regain a job as a teacher. He withdrew more and more from the world, lived in poverty, and on his fifty-fourth birthday committed suicide.

J. was one of the most erudite of Hungarian poets. In his early years he was strongly under the influence of the Greek and Latin classics, the French poets of the Parnassian and SYMBOLIST schools, and Endre ADY, modern Hungary's preeminent poet. But he soon freed himself from all literary masters. His poetry reflects the burning conflicts in his heart and mind, the deeply felt struggles between his Christian beliefs and his pagan impulses. A critic of political Catholicism, J. extols true Christianity, which means for him unselfish and untiring efforts to obliterate social ills. In a different vein, his poems written to a woman he idolized in his youth and others addressed to a beloved patroness are deeply moving for their expression of unfulfilled cravings.

Noted literary critics contend that his best love poems are the most beautiful, moving poems of their kind in the Hungarian language. Two of his volumes, *Testamentum* (1925; testament) and *Hárfa* (1929; harp) have been particularly singled out as manifestations of J.'s sensitivity and inner need for continual probing for beauty and truth. *Hárfa* reprints some of the best poems he wrote in his youth together with poems he wrote later in life.

Underlying all of his poetry is a tone of pessimism that results from identifying his personal frustrations with the tragedies of his country. His best poems are those in which the voice of the persona becomes that of his ancestors, singing the beauty of the Hungarian lowland and of the banks of the Tisza River with its poplars and acacia trees. J.'s identification with his cultural inheritance is expressed not only in his seven volumes of poetry, but also in his essays, short stories, and three one-act plays.

J., a major modern Hungarian poet, was a master versifier. Whether he worked within traditional prosody or in free verse, his cadences and rhymes always blended with his topics. Yet, his creative spirit, despite his broad cultural background, was limited by a rather narrow horizon. This may account for the fact that his work has not been as widely translated as it deserves to be. Only a few of his poems have been translated into English.

FURTHER WORKS: *Versek* (1907); *Szép csendesen* (1909); *Uj versek* (1914); *Késö szüret* (1918); *Ez as én vérem* (1919); *Nefelejts* (1921); *Szögedi Szinház* (1926); *Holmi* (1929); *Fiatalok, még itt vagyok!* (1935); *Örökség* (2 vols., 1958); *Összes művei* (3 vols., 1961); *J. G. összes mővei* (2 vols., 1980)

BIBLIOGRAPHY: Reményi, J., *Hungarian Writers and Literature* (1964): 279–83; Klaniczay, T., et al., *History of Hungarian Literature* (1964): 208–9

—PAUL NADANYI

JUNG, Carl Gustav

Swiss psychiatrist and psychologist, b. 26 July 1875, Kesswyl; d. 6 June 1961, Küsnacht, Zurich canton

J. was born the third child of a clergyman of the Swiss Reformed Church. The paternal grandfather after whom J. was named had been a highly successful medical doctor in Basel, a rector of the university there, and grand master of the Swiss Freemasons. As a youth this grandfather had been acquainted with German romantic poets; in the course of a full life he wrote scientific treatises, as well as plays, and he founded a home for retarded children. J.'s maternal grandfather was also a remarkable man, a theologian and Hebraist, and president of the company of pastors of the Basel church; he is said to have had visions and to have communed with spirits. J.'s father, Paul, also learned in Hebrew as well as the classical languages, married the daughter of his professor of Hebrew and pursued the life of a modest country parson, also serving as Protestant chaplain of the Friedmatt Mental Hospital in Basel. J. grew up in the parsonage at Klein-Hüningen, then a village of peasants and fishermen, outside Basel, on the bank of the Rhine.

J. studied medicine, specializing in psychiatry, at the University of Basel and completed his studies with a dissertation, *On the Psychology and Pathology of So-Called Occult Phenomena* (*CW*, Vol. 1; *Zur Psychologie und Pathologie sogenannter okkulter Phänomene*, 1902), is the translation of the definitive *Die gesammelten Werke von C. G. J.* (1958 ff.), based on communications of a medium. In 1900 he joined the staff of the Burghölzli Psychiatric Hospital, Zurich, and in time became assistant to its distinguished director, Eugen Bleuler. There J. engaged in extensive research with the word-association experiment (see *CW*, Vol. 2, *Experimental Researches*) and made the first thorough psychological analysis of the psychic products of schizophrenia, then called dementia praecox (see *CW*, Vol. 3, *Psychogenesis of Mental Disease*).

In 1907 J. came into contact with Sigmund FREUD, nineteen years his senior, and collaborated with him until about 1913. With

Carl Jung

Symbols of Transformation (*CW*, Vol. 5; *Wandlungen und Symbole der Libido*, 1912; rev. ed., *Symbole der Wandlung*, 1952), J. established an independent path; this work is crucial to the entire further development of his thought.

In 1913 J. resigned both from his associations with the psychoanalytic movement and from his position at the University of Zurich. Continuing his work with patients but publishing little for the next few years, he devoted himself to an exploration of his own psychic processes, an enterprise comparable to Freud's self-analysis. This self-exploration presents the remarkable phenomenon of a thinker steeped in the values and methods of empirical science adopting the means of the poet and the artist—he drew and painted and gave poetic expression to his fantasies—in his quest for knowledge of the psyche. An important product of the same period of reflection was *Psychological Types* (*Cw*, Vol. 6; *Psychologische Typen*, 1921).

J.'s psychological concerns led him to remarkably wide-ranging studies of non-European cultures, both past and present. In the early 1920s he became acquainted with such ancient Chinese texts as the *I Ching*; he traveled in Africa, visited the Pueblo Indians, and (in 1938) made a trip to India. His ethnological interests were related to his study of alchemy (the quasi-chemical, quasimystical quest that engaged so many fine minds in the Middle Ages), which he regarded as a matter of psychic processes. His research into alchemy is contained mainly in *Psychology and Alchemy* (*CW*, Vol. 12; *Psychologie und Alchemie*, 1944) and in *CW*, Vol. 13, *Alchemical Studies*.

In 1933 J. became president of the International Medical Society for Psychotherapy, an organization consisting of national organizations and individual members. This arrangement, created in response to Nazi pressures on the German Society for Psychotherapy, of which J. had been vice-president, served the purpose of allowing Jewish psychotherapists expelled from the German society to remain in the international organization. Later, in protest to the same pressures, J. resigned the presidency and the editorship of the society's journal.

The writings of J.'s later years were concerned less with personal psychology than with broader issues of civilization, especially as expressed in symbols. *Aion* (*CW*, Vol. 9, Pt. 1; *Aion*, 1951), for example, is largely devoted to the symbolism of the fish in Christianity, gnosticism, and alchemy, and *Mysterium Coniunctionis* (*CW*, Vol. 14; *Mysterium Coniunctionis*, 1955–56) is "an inquiry into the separation and synthesis of psychic opposites in alchemy." But in his later years J. also effected important theoretical refinements and elaborations of earlier ideas. In his later years, too, he wrote, along with his most difficult works, the three books that have been most widely read: *Answer to Job* (in *CW*, Vol. 11; *Antwort auf Hiob*, 1952); an inner biography, *Memories, Dreams, Reflections* (1961; *Erinnerungen, Träume, Gedanken von C. G. J.*, 1961); and a work of popularization, *Man and His Symbols* (1964), written with three collaborators.

In his later life J. was awarded official honors of various kinds in many parts of the world. Indeed by the beginning of the 1930s, he was secure in the fame that caused distinguished figures from all over the world to visit him as "the wise old man of Küsnacht," the town near Zurich where he lived in a magnificent house from 1906 until his death. His influence has grown steadily with the publication of his *Collected Works*.

J.'s early psychiatric work centered upon a careful description of "feeling-toned complexes," which could interfere with such conscious psychic processes as directed memory and thought; his analysis of these complexes provided empirical, and statistically verifiable, evidence for the existence of unconscious psychic processes.

Because of the towering stature of both Freud and J., the relationship between them, and their final parting, has taken on mythological dimensions in the imaginations of many readers. And, indeed, their relationship did in part conform to mythical motifs: the royal father's yearning for a crown prince, the son's rebellion against the father whom he regards as a tyrant. The history of that relationship is recorded in an extraordinary human and historical document, *The Freud—J. Letters* (1974; *Sigmund Freud und C. G. J.: Briefwechsel* 1974), which may be read as a gripping epistolary novel, and which conveys a vivid sense of the intellectual and social setting in which 20th-c. depth psychology developed. (It should be noted, however, that at the time of these letters (1906–13) Freud had already formulated his fundamental ideas, whereas J. was for the most part yet to formulate his.)

The scientific reasons for J.'s divergence from psychoanalysis were first stated in *Symbols of Transformation*, in which he moved toward a conception of libido not as sexual but as qualitatively neutral in the way that the energy of physics is neutral. In this work he developed a new conception of symbols—for example, the events of a hero's life—as transformations of that energy. While being a landmark in the development of psychological theory, the book is also passionate and personal. In his review of the version in the *Collected Works*, R. D. Scott wrote that it is "a most natural expression of life and the life force not surpassed in any other psychological work known to me. This may seem somewhat strange in view of the extreme difficulty the material often presents to ... intellectual comprehension.... It was as J. says ... 'a landslide that cannot be stopped ... the explosion of all those psychic contents which could find no room, no breathing space, in the constricting atmosphere of Freudian psychology and its narrow outlook.' It was a landslide which launched him upon the course of his own development into 'the second half of life,' and which led to his own unique contribution to the understanding of the psyche.... It contains the emotional force of this eruption.... What gives shape and expression to this force is above all poetry, of which the book is full, in the form both of quotations and of the author's expression in the text. The poetic vehicle of feeling is not just a decoration, it is absolutely essential to the finding of one's way among these images. The work is also an intellectual *tour de force* of a very considerable caliber, as witnessed by the extraordinary amount of mythological material put into it, and the extensive research this must have required." (*The Journal of Analytical Psychology*, 2, 2).

Indeed, *Symbols of Transformation* contains a lengthy discussion of Longfellow's *Hiawatha*, which is regarded as a poetic compilation of mythical motifs, including those of the dual mother and dual birth, and of death and rebirth in the form of the sun-hero's battle with a sea monster. Some of J.'s other literary examples in the same work have the effect of suddenly opening vistas. Thus, one discovers Hölderlin and Goethe, for example, thinking in accordance with highly archaic thought forms, such as that in which the sound of speech is associated with the fire of the sun.

Such forms, which J. first called primordial images, or dominants, and later archetypes, express inherited psychic dispositions (as distinct from inherited ideas) to experience the world in certain ways. These forms find their clearest expression in mythology and religion, but they also arise spontaneously in the dreams and fantasies of individuals, and they provide basic themes of art and literature. The archetypes are the structural forms of the collective unconscious, which J. distinguished from the personal unconscious, largely made up of repressed and forgotten psychic material. The more important archetypes include those of the shadow, consisting of contents of the personal unconscious and their personifications, of the anima and animus, or the contrasexual psychic components of the masculine and feminine personalities. They also include the self, which is at the same time the deepest center of the personality, its totality (including consciousness and the unconscious), and its ultimate ordering principle. The self is thus supraordinate to the ego, which is the center of the field of consciousness. The realization of the self—that is, compliance with its demands and the establishment of a harmony between it and the ego—is the chief goal of the process of individuation, which became one of the main subjects of J.'s psychological interest.

By individuation J. meant, negatively, the dissolution of one's identification with internalized parental images and with social roles; he meant, positively, the differentiation and development of the individual personality in its uniqueness but also in its relation to the collective psychic facts of the archetypes. Since the urge to individuation makes itself felt most strongly in the second half of life, J.'s concern with it complements the emphasis of most other forms of depth psychology upon the first half of life and especially on psychic development in infancy and adolescence. These basic ideas of J. are most clearly and succinctly presented in *Two Essays on Analytical Psychology* (*CW*, Vol. 7; *Über die Psychologie des Unbewußten*, 1917; rev. eds., 1926, 1943, and *Die Beziehungen zwischen dem Ich und dem Unbewußten*, 1928).

In later years J. effected important theoretical refinements and elaborations of ideas first adumbrated in *Symbols of Transformation*, for example, establishing an analogy between the archetype and the biological pattern of behavior; coming to see the archetype as "psychoid," occupying an indeterminate status between spirit and matter, and supplementing the customary notions of causality with that of synchronicity, or the meaningful coincidence of causally unrelated events (see *CW*, Vol. 8, *Structure and Dynamics of the Psyche*, and Vol. 9, Pt. 1, *Archetypes and the Collective Unconscious*). And two works of J.'s last years, *Answer to Job*, and *Memories, Dreams, Reflections*, mark an essentially confessional return to the concerns of his self-exploration.

In *Psychological Types* there is an extensive discussion of Schiller's *On the Aesthetic Education of Man*, which J. regarded as a forerunner of his own attempt to create a psychological typology. (J.'s typology describes two main psychological attitudes, those of extroversion, a positive relation to objects, and introversion, a positive relation to inner psychic processes. These terms have entered everyday speech, and the concepts named by them have been used in literary criticism, as, more rarely, have J.'s concepts of the four main functions of consciousness, thinking, feeling, sensation, and intuition.)

In the same work J. also treated the Swiss author Carl Spitteler (1845–1924); Nietzsche, Dante, Hölderlin, and other writers also figure in his description of attitudes and functions, of the progression and regression of libido, and of symbol formation. He also used their works to illustrate his conception of psychic life as being rooted in history, and of history as having an important psychic aspect, which is illuminated by his psychological concepts. Historical periods, for example, display the principles of compensation, of symbol formation, of the differentiation of psychic functions, that he has examined in individual writers. Hence, he regards Schiller's views on poetry, for example, in light of the remnant of archaic man in the modern European, and of psychic trends at the time of the French Revolution.

J. was fascinated by Nietzsche, and J.'s most searching study of a work of literature was presented in a series of seminars (in English) on the "Psychological Analysis of Nietzsche's *Zarathustra*," in the years 1934 through 1939. In these seminars J. analyzed Nietzsche's book as though it were a vision describing a process of initiation, the characters representing part-personalities, based on archetypes, principally those of the wise old man and the self. J. "amplified" every symbolic detail in the text, bringing it into relation with parallel material from myth, legend, folklore, and literature. Showing his astonishing erudition and his imaginative grasp of great sweeps of history, J. viewed *Thus Spake Zarathustra* in the context of late 19th-c. rationalism, positivism, and materialism, and in the larger context of the Christian era, which he in turn regarded as a historical movement formed in compensation to cultural currents that had preceded it. He also viewed *Thus Spake Zarathustra* in light of the development of other cultures. And since it recorded a countermovement to dominant philosophical trends of Nietzsche's time, J. also regarded Nietzsche's book as an attempt to supply the collective consciousness of Nietzsche's time with psychic contents that would balance its one-sidedness.

Apart from the works already mentioned, J.'s writings about literature are confined to three essays (in *CW*, Vol. 15). The volume in which they appear is entitled *The Spirit in Man, Art, and Literature*, which suggests its highly miscellaneous character; and it is, significantly, the slenderest volume in the series. That is to say, J. was in no sense a literary critic, and he only rarely dealt with literature except in connection with larger and basically nonliterary issues. One of these essays, "*Ulysses*: A Monologue" ("*Ulysses*," 1934), is an attempt to come to terms with JOYCE'S *Ulysses* by seeing it as symptomatic of the spiritual condition of modern man, especially the brutalization of his feeling. Admirers of Joyce's book must feel that J. partly missed an important point, which is that it records a descent into the depths of the unconscious of a kind to which J. elsewhere gave much sympathetic attention. (J., incidentally, had been consulted concerning Joyce's psychotic daughter, Lucia, and had given Joyce unwelcome advice concerning the closeness of his relationship with her).

In another of these essays, "On the Relation of Analytical Psychology to Poetry" ("Über die Beziehungen der analytischen Psychologie zum dichterischen Kuntswerk," 1922), J. insists that a work of art must not be analyzed reductively, since "it is a creative reorganization of those very conditions to which a causalistic psychology must always reduce it." In the same essay he makes a distinction between literary works, on the one hand, that accord with the conscious intentions of their authors and that draw upon materials of the personal unconscious, and those "visionary" works, on the other hand, that are direct outpourings of the collective unconscious. As to the much-debated question of the relation of art to neurosis, J. claimed that "the artists's relative lack of adaptation . . . enables him to follow his own yearnings far from the beaten path, and to discover what it is that would meet the unconscious needs of his age. Thus, just as the one-sidedness of the individual's conscious attitude is corrected by reactions from the unconscious, so art represents a process of self regulation in the life of nations and epochs." He further explores the relationship of psychology and literature in "Psychology and Literature" ("Psychologie und Dichtung," 1950). As J.'s emphasis on the visionary suggests, his utterances about art and literature are often very much in the spirit of German romanticism, although such statements often express a very different attitude, one preoccupied with a fear of "aestheticism."

Despite the paucity of J.'s writings about literature as literature, his psychology as a whole does imply an attitude toward literature that can be summarized by means of a few characterizing attributes.

First, J. called attention to the archaic elements in literature, elements also to be found in mythology. These are ultimately psychic, in that they originate in dreams, fantasies, visions, and delusional ideas.

Second, in keeping with J.'s emphasis on the value of introversion, works of literature, like dreams and fantasy, are to be interpreted not only with reference to outer reality but also on the "subjective level," on which the persons and situations represented "refer to subjective factors entirely belonging to the subject's own psyche." Interpretation on the subjective level allows us to take a broader psychological view not only of dreams but also of literary works, in which the individual figures then appear as representatives of relatively autonomous functional complexes in the psyche of the author (*CW*, Vol. 6, *Psychological Types*, pp. 472–73).

Moreover, the subjective level can also apply to literary response, since the work touches complexes and archetypes in the reader. Thus, such common literary motifs as birth, the fight with the dragon, incest, and marriage, may be conceived as representing intrapsychic processes rather than, or in addition to, events between the subject and the object. In this view, birth may, for example, represent the separation of subject and object, the birth of the ego as the center of the field of consciousness. Incest may represent the reunion of the subject with its own unconscious ground, a retrogression of libido, activating unconscious contents, which may then be brought to consciousness. And marriage may be seen under the aspect of the *hieros gamos*, the sacred marriage, symbolic of the unification of isolated parts of the personality and the resolution of what J. called the problem of the opposites, including, for example, those of the ego and the shadow. Equally, literary works are often concerned with the process of individuation, which they present in projected form.

Third, literature is to be viewed in the context of history, which reflects the vicissitudinous development of consciousness, both collective and individual. The role of the literary work in this development is compensatory, reviving contact with those unconscious forces that are needed for a balanced conscious viewpoint. Literature, like dreams, can be regarded prospectively as well as reductively, that is, with respect to antecedent causes.

To these points a fourth must be added: literary works are often merely "aesthetic." This deserves separate mention because there was in J.'s attitude toward literature an odd ambivalence—it sometimes seems a deliberate, even blustering philistinism—that is important to understand. For J., aestheticism "is not fitted to solve the serious and exceedingly difficult task of educating man, for it always presupposes the very thing that it should create—the capacity to love beauty. It actually hinders a deeper investigation . . . because it always averts its face from anything evil, ugly, and difficult, and aims at pleasure, even though it be of an edifying kind" (*CW*, Vol. 6, p. 121).

One might then expect J. to have been sympathetic toward 20th-c. art and literature, much of which is not aesthetic in this sense, but when he talked about such works, he almost always did so in a way that expresses scorn toward them—precisely for being evil, ugly, and difficult. Visionary literature is safely above the accusation of aestheticism, and naïve and trivial literature is safely beneath it. Thus, he often talked at length about H. Rider Haggard's (1856–1925) *She* as an embodiment of the anima, and he admitted: "Indeed, literary products of highly dubious merit are often of the greatest interest to the psychologist" (*CW*, Vol. 15, pp. 87–88).

J.'s distrust of aestheticism and admiration for the visionary colored his judgment of literary works when he did try to judge them. Thus, for example, he claimed that Spitteler's *Prometheus and Epimetheus* has greater truth than Goethe's *Faust* and Nietzsche's *Thus Spake Zarathustra*, although the latter are more satisfying aesthetically. Indeed, in *Psychological Types* he speaks of Nietzsche's "aesthetic defenses" against the true content of his vision.

This ambivalence is illuminated by a passage in a letter (of 28 February 1932) in which, reversing the judgment of *Faust* just given, J. says that it "is the most recent pillar in that bridge of the spirit which spans the morass of world history, beginning with the Gilgamesh epic, the *I Ching*, the Upanishads, the Tao-te-Ching, the fragments of Heraclitus, and continuing in the Gospel of St. John, the letters of St. Paul, in Meister Eckhart and in Dante." In other words, for J. truth was scientific, and it was religious; and despite his own artistic works in drawing, painting, poetry, and sculpture, with part of himself he belonged to the ancient tradition that regarded art as idolatrous, an "aesthetic defense" against the primacy of a certain kind of religious experience.

J.'s views have inspired some notable works of literary criticism, written from a specifically Jungian viewpoint, including Maud Bodkin's *Archetypal Patterns in Poetry* (1934) and Christine Gallant's *Blake and the Assimilation of Chaos* (1978). His influence is indirectly present in a great many works that can be brought under the headings of "myth criticism" and "archetypal criticism." Indeed, J. is the single source of "archetype" as a critical term important to various recent critics, especially Northrop FRYE, although such critics often do not accept unreservedly J.'s concept of the collective unconscious. Hermann HESSE'S stories and novels reflect his experience in Jungian analysis—see the letters between J. and Hesse in J.'s *Letters, Vol. 1: 1906–1950* (1973). (*Vol. 2: 1951–1961* was published in 1975.) Such experience is also directly the subject of a novel, *The Manticore* (1972), by the Canadian writer Robertson Davies (b. 1913).

J.'s influence on literature and on the *Zeitgeist*, including the climate of literary opinion, is more indirect than direct, and that influence is, for various reasons, difficult to isolate, label, and measure. The first is the extreme difficulty of many of J.'s works owing to the complexity of his thought and to the fact that he dealt with such little-known subjects as gnosticism and alchemy. Thus, people may be moved and intellectually stimulated by J.'s writings, without being certain that they have understood them. The second is the currently modest position of J.'s analytical psychology among competing scientific paradigms. The third is that J. was in many ways genuinely prophetic, so that some of his ideas came to have their impact fifty or more years after he first published them, thus obscuring the question of whether late variants of those ideas derive directly from J. or are independent attempts to answer needs that he had foreseen. Thus, many current psychologists, without crediting J. as their source, are concerned with "self-realization," which is essentially J.'s "individuation," fully described several decades earlier. And fourth, J. created his psychology at a time when writers of literature shared some of his interests, and often the similarities between him and them are based on indirect causes rather than being the result of direct influence. Thus, the similarities between the concerns and even the specific ideas of J. and William Butler YEATS are astonishing, yet neither directly influenced the development of the other's thought. And J. was engaging in his mythological researches at a period when a great many writers, including Thomas Mann, Hermann BROCH, and T. S. ELIOT, were concerned with mythological themes. But Eliot, for example, claimed during the Bollingen Prize controversy never to have read J., and J., in a letter at about the same time (1948), admitted that he had never heard of Eliot.

J. has a remarkably wide readership among people whose interest is more in literature than in psychology, and ironically, they read him in part for precisely the reasons that put him so on guard against the dangers of "aestheticism" in literature. The title of a collection of J.'s essays in translation, *Modern Man in Search of a Soul* (1933), helps to explain this.

Modern man lacks a soul in a real and definite sense. Earlier, people assumed that they had souls, souls that were subject to various perils. For most of us, "soul" is a word signifying something we would like to have but fear we lack, or an intellectual hypothetical entity; or a poetic image. For J., on the other hand, the existence of the soul was an absolute, unshakable certainty, not the creation of an act of faith. At the same time he maintained an unswerving allegiance, which he proclaimed again and again, to the values of empirical science. Thus, one of the dilemmas afflicting writers and readers of literature for far more than a century—the dilemma created by the split between the objective world and our less substantial, subjective selves, which make themselves known murkily in our anxieties and neuroses—was for J. resolved from the very outset of his mature work. For him the psyche was objective; and a psychic fact, such as that of a fantasy, was as real as any fact concerning, say, a piece of wood or steel. Moreover, for J. the psyche was of enormous richness, betraying a complex history and marvelous subtleties of organization. In recreating a sense of wonder concerning the psyche, in elaborating a phenomenology of its imaginative forms, in showing the complex life of those forms in the great currents of history, J. has helped modern man to know that he has a soul and to find nourishment for it.

See also Psychology and Literature

BIBLIOGRAPHY: Martin, P. W., *Experiment in Depth: A Study of the Work of J., Eliot, and Toynbee* (1955); Neumann, E., *Amor and Psyche* (1956); Jacobi, J., *Complex, Archetype, Symbol in the Psychology of C. G. J.* (1957); Neumann, E., *The Archetypal World of Henry Moore* (1959); Neumann, E., *Art and the Creative Unconscious* (1959); Bennett, E. A., *C. G. J.* (1961); Fordham, M., ed., *Contact with J.: Essays on the Influence of His Work and Personality* (1964); Jaffé, A., *The Myth of Meaning in the Work of C. G. J.* (1967); Jaffé, A., *From the Life and Work of C. G. J.* (1968); Serrano, N., *C. G. J. and Hermann Hesse: A Record of Two Friendships* (1968); Ellenberger, H. F., *The Discovery of the Unconscious* (1970); Neumann, E., *The Great Mother: An Analysis of the Archetype* (1972); Storr, A., *C. G. J.* (1973); McGuire, W., and Hull, F. R., eds., *C. G. J. Speaking: Interviews and Encounters* (1977); Vincie, J. F. and M., *C. G. J. and Analytical Psychology: A Comprehensive Bibliography* (1977); Brome, V., *J.: Man and Myth* (1978); Edinger, E. F., *Melville's "Moby-Dick": A Jungian Commentary* (1978); Gallant, C., *Blake and the Assimilation of Chaos* (1978); Brivic, S. R., *Joyce between Freud and J.* (1979); Homans, P., *J. in Context: Modernity and the Making of a Psychology* (1979); Jaffé, A., ed., *C. G. J.: Word and Image* (1979); O'Neill, T. R., *The Individuated Hobbit: J., Tolkien, and the Archetypes of Middle-Earth* (1979); Olney, J., *The Rhizome and the Flower: The Perennial Philosophy of Yeats and J.* (1980); Singer, J., *Boundaries of the Soul: The Practice of J.'s Psychology* (1994)

—WILLIAM WILLEFORD

JÜNGER, Ernst

German novelist and essayist, b. 29 March 1895, Heidelberg; d. 17 Feb. 1998, Wiflingen

Even as a boy, J. was at odds with middle-class life and, generally, with the age into which he was born. He joined the rebellious youth movement, than ran away to serve briefly in the French Foreign Legion—see his *Afrikanische Spiele* (1936; *African Diversions*, 1956). In 1914 he enlisted in the army and distinguished himself at the western front. From 1919 to 1923 he served in the army of the Weimar Republic.

J. began his career as a writer by setting down his unusual war experiences. *In Stahlgewittern* (1920: *Storm of Steel*, 1929) recounts the heroic exploits of an infantry soldier and a leader of assault troops; it is also a statement of J.'s conviction that World War I was but the first encounter in a planetary conflict of ever-increasing violence. J. further expounded and explored his war experiences in *Der Kampf als inneres Erlebnis* (1922; fighting as

Ernst Jünger

an inner experience), *Das Wäldchen 125* (1925; *Copse 125*, 1930), and *Feuer und Blut* (1925; fire and blood).

From 1923 to 1925 J. studied philosophy and zoology at the University of Leipzig. Although he did not finish his studies, he developed an abiding and productive interest in entomology, as is seen in *Subtile Jagden* (1967; delicate pursuits). After moving to Berlin in 1927, J. became active in radically nationalistic organizations, serving their journals as contributor and editor. During that time he developed his political philosophy, which he designated as *heroischer Realismus* and which may be characterized as "militant nihilism" or "aggressive totalitarianism." Convinced that the world was engulfed in a fundamental crisis, the ideas and ideals of democratic humanism having lost their cohesive force and motivating power, and that the ultimate struggle for power and world domination was imminent, he called for "total mobilization" in *Die totale Mobilmachung* (1930; total mobilization). In *Der Arbeiter* (1932; the worker) J. describes the emergence of a new type of man who, by virtue of his technical skill and military prowess, is destined to conquer and reorganize a chaotic, strife-torn world. *Der Arbeiter* is J.'s most significant political treatise; it is the only radical, honest, and comprehensive exposition of totalitarianism written in Germany.

Yet J. disdained the Hitler regime; its policies, he felt, could only lead to ultimate disaster. He expressed his misgivings in the novel *Auf den Marmorklippen* (1939; *On the Marble Cliffs*, 1947), a thinly veiled allegory of the heinous practices of totalitarianism (although veiled enough to get by the censor); the book also reaffirms the ideals and values of the humanistic tradition. It thus exemplifies the work of the "inner emigration," of those who were opposed to the Hitler regime but did not go into exile.

At the outbreak of World War II J. was called back into the army. This time around he saw no action, serving with the forces of occupation and as staff officer with the commander-in-chief of occupied France. *Strahlungen* (1942 ff.; radiations) is his diary of the war and the occupation years in Germany until 1948. J. keenly observed the course of the war, never in doubt about its outcome. He had close contact with some of those officers who militantly opposed the regime. *Der Friede* (written 1943, pub. 1947; *The Peace*, 1948), while recognizing Germany's responsibility and guilt, is a plea for a constructive and enduring peace. This pamphlet marks the end of J.'s involvement in politics. He withdrew to the countryside; since 1950 he has lived in Wilflingen, a small village in southern West Germany.

After the war, J. was for a time forbidden to publish in Germany because of his erstwhile identification with the Nazi regime (he could and did publish in the Netherlands and Switzerland, however). *Heliopolis* (1949; Heliopolis) is an anti-utopian novel dealing with the unresolved conflict between liberty and tyranny, between the humanistic tradition and nihilism. *Heliopolis* is also significant as a comprehensive recapitulation of the author's ideas as they had evolved in the course of thirty years.

Although J. continued to write novels—among them *Gläserne Bienen* (1957; *The Glass Bees*, 1961), science fiction with strong political overtones; *Die Zwille* (1973; the sling-shot), primarily an account of the author's boyhood); and *Eumeswil* (1977; Eumeswil), a fantasy of the future—he preferred the genres of the essay and the travel book.

J.'s essays are significant for two reasons: they exhibit wide-ranging concerns, and their style is exemplary. An early but outstanding attempt at nonfiction prose was *Das abenteuerliche Herz* (1929; rev. ed., 1936; the adventurous heart), concise accounts of adventures of the mind and the imagination. *Sgraffiti* (1960; sgraffiti) is its companion volume. The essays of the early 1950s probe issues of nihilism and EXISTENTIALISM: *Über die Linie* (1950; crossing the line), *Der Waldgang* (1951; withdrawing to the woods), and *Der gordische Knoten* (1953; the Gordian knot). *Das Sanduhrbuch* (1954; the book about the hourglass) ponders the problem of time; it is one of J.'s most engaging and convincing accomplishments.

Some of J.'s essays are highly speculative. In *An der Zeitmauer* (1959; at the wall of time) he tries to show that mankind, and, indeed, the cosmos are about to enter upon a new age. Political prospects are the theme of *Der Weltstaat* (1960; the world state). Opposing the widely held belief that the conflict between East and West is irreconcilable, J. holds that the adversaries are the unwitting agents of historical forces aiming at the ultimately constructive reorganization of the planet. This essay complements *Der Arbeiter* as well as *Der Friede*.

Annäherungen (1970; approaches) is J.'s longest and, in many ways, most provocative essay. Actually, it is a collection of essays dealing with drugs—his own experiments supplemented by literary references (De Quincey, Baudelaire, Aldous HUXLEY, and others). In the early 1920s J. used ether, cocaine, and hashish; thirty years later he turned to mescaline, ololuqui, and LSD. His reasons were threefold: to indulge his propensity for adventure, to gain new and deeper metaphysical insights, and to open vistas into what he felt to be a new cosmic age. No book deals as comprehensively and probingly with drugs and drug-taking as does *Annäherungen*.

J. traveled widely and made good use of his experiences. His observations are keen, his perceptions clear. He disdained what he calls "psychological digestive processes"; instead, he recorded what the senses perceive and the mind suggests. J.'s travel books are also stylistically of a high order. They include *Dalmatinischer Aufenthalt* (1934; sojourn in Dalmatia); *Myrdun* (1943; Myrdun), about Norway; *Atlantische Fahrt* (1947; Atlantic voyage), about Brazil and Morocco; *Am Sarazenenturm* (1955; at the Saracen tower), about Sardinia; and *Zwei Inseln: Ceylon und Formosa* (1968; two islands: Ceylon and Formosa).

FURTHER WORKS: *Blätter und Steine* (1934); *Sprache und Körperbau* (1947); *Ein Inselfrühling* (1948); *Besuch auf Godenholm* (1952); *Rivarol* (1956); *Serpentara* (1957); *San Pietro* (1957); *Jahre der Okkupation* (1958); *Ein Vormittag in Antibes* (1960); *Werke* (10 vols., 1961–1965); *Das spanische Mondhorn* (1963); *Typus, Name und Gestalt* (1963); *Sturm* (1963); *Geheimnisse der Sprache* (1963); *Grenzgänge* (1966); *Im Granit* (1967); *Lettern und Ideogramme* (1970); *Ad hoc* (1970); *Zahlen und Götter* (1974); *Sämtliche Werke* (18 vols., 1979 ff.); *Paul Léautaud in memoriam* (1980); *Siebzig Verweht* (1980)

BIBLIOGRAPHY: Brock, E., *Das Weltbild E. J.s* (1945); Martin, A. von, *Der heroische Nihilismus und seine Überwindung: E. J.s Weg durch die Krise* (1948); Stern, J. P., *E. J.: A Writer of Our Times* (1953); Mohler, A., *Die Schleife: Dokumente zu . . . E. J.* (1955); Loose, G., *E. J.: Gestalt und Werk* (1957); Paetel, K. O., *E. J. in Selbstzeugnissen und Bilddokumenten* (1962); Schwarz, H. P., *Der konservative Anarchist: Politik and Zeitkritik E. J.s* (1962); Kranz, G., *E. J.s symbolische Weltschau* (1968); Des Coudres, H. P., *Bibliographie der Werke E. J.s* (1970); Loose, G., *E. J.* (1974); Katzmann, V., *E. J.s magischer Realismus* (1975); Hervier, J., *The Details of Time: Conversations with E. J.* (1995)

—GERHARD LOOSE

JUSTICE, Donald R(odney)

American poet, b. 12 Aug. 1925, Miami, Florida

J. grew up in the Miami of the Depression era—the Miami of fifty-cent piano lessons, "forlorn suburbs," and palmettos—which has provided settings and color for many of his poems and stories. J. studied composition with Carl Ruggles (1876-1971), a precocity in music earning him this chance in his teens. As to music, there have been few performances of his compositions, but J. continues occasionally to write music. J. also paints; the cover illustrations for several recent books, *New and Selected Poems* (1995), *Oblivion: On Writers and Writing* (1998), and *Orpheus Hesitated Beside the Black River* (1998), are samples of his work. He has written two opera librettos, two one-act plays, a collection of essays, and several prize-winning short stories, often treating in a genre other than poetry the same subjects that he is concerned with in the poems.

By college, though, poetry was his central interest, and the restrained and clarified verses that date from his first book publication in 1951 have secured J.'s reputation. Married to the writer Jean Ross Justice (dates n.a.), J. has traveled between the coasts and in Europe and taught writing at several universities, among them the

University of Iowa Writers' Workshop (where in 1954 he received his Ph.D.), Syracuse University, the University of California at Irvine, and the University of Florida, and quietly, almost modestly, written his peerlessly crafted poems.

In 1960 he published *The Summer Anniversaries*, his first full-length collection, which won the Lamont Prize for 1959 and gave first evidence of his uncanny attention to the details of perception, memory, and language. J. is not a poet who writes only what he sees or, more accurately, remembers, but a poet who writes what the reader needs to hear (read) so that the initiating event can be felt and imagined. This requires a disappearance—a kind of magic where syntax, image, voice, and diction relate, but transparently. Indeed, the writer is articulate, but is everywhere absent or nearly so. Even so, when the poems are perhaps most memorable—in a book of many memorable poems—their forms are visible. J.'s skill and forbearance are never limitations, because the moral dream that poetry is is so strong in his work. It isn't that he moralizes, but that the poems present our large and, more often, our small moral dilemmas—less often resolved than clearly noted.

The work since *The Summer Anniversaries* has been characterized by a formal curiosity and restlessness, as in *Departures* (1973), and a deepening sense of the beauty and terror of our lives. There have been European and British literary influences all along—Baudelaire, Rimbaud, Hardy, AUDEN, ALBERTI, and VALLEJO—and American—chiefly William Carlos WILLIAMS, Wallace STEVENS, and Hart CRANE—and the sensual is ever distinct. Childhood, nostalgias, separations, the self both in and outside itself, the possibilities of madness, time and mortality's sting, art and the artistic temperament, "which isolates / And saves," these are his subjects.

Though J. writes often about art's power to represent feelings unnamed and scarcely known and to resist time's sifting sands, his aesthetics, he has said, "in so far as I have any such thing, are not influenced by modern art or any other art so far as I know—except the photographs of the Farm Security Administration from the 1930s by Walker Evans, Ben Shahn, etc." "Mule Team and Poster" in *The Sunset Maker* (1987) describes the scene from one such photograph—by Walker Evans in 1936. There are mules hitched to a flatbed wagon, mud encrusted wheels that resemble crude flowers, a sun just beginning again to shine, and a poster for a traveling show. In it dancing girls, one with a Spanish comb, are caught on the upkick—"Someone's idea of heaven," J. says, having noted the resemblance between the wall that it's posted on and a flap of the brain peeled back. The mules continue eating cornshucks, and a shadow offering the only possibility of a coolness in Alabama, in what must be relentless heat, stretches like a giant scythe. It is this mixture of the shabby and the lovely, the plain and the exotic, and of hopefulness and forbearance and irremediable death that characterizes J.'s imaginative stretch in the later work—a return to, or never-leaving of, his early brushes with art and life.

J.'s realism and clarity rest in a quiet, if uneasy, balance with his romantic spirit. If the past—by fate Southern—is to be honored and sometimes rued, no improvements on the truth need to be made, except in the language. J.'s reputation will continue to grow for his technical brilliance, for the blending of the rhythms of American speech and the formalities, the mixture of high diction with low, the limpidity of the lines, and his elegiac intensity. The careful reader, enjoying these beauties, may look past them to the sympathies and compassion inherent in J.'s treatment of our human frailties and to the trued modulations of feeling—too deeply meant to be carelessly written.

FURTHER WORKS: *The Old Bachelor and Other Poems* (1951); *A Local Storm* (1963); *Night Light* (1967); *Sixteen Poems* (1970); *Selected Poems* (1979); *Platonic Scripts*(1984); *The Death of Lincoln* (1988); *A. D. J. Reader* (1992); *New and Selected Poems* (1995); *Oblivion: On Writers and Writing* (1998); *Orpheus Hesitates Beside the Black River: Selected Poems* (1998)

BIBLIOGRAPHY: Wright, C., "Homage to the Thin Man," *SoR*, 30 (Autumn 1994): 741-44; Gioia, D., "D. J.: An Interview," *APR*, 25 (Jan.-Feb 1996): 37-46; Gioia, D., and W. Logan, *Certain Solitudes* (1997)

—CAROL FROST

K

KABARDIAN LITERATURE
See North Caucasian Literatures

KADARÉ, Ismail

Albanian prose writer and poet, b. 26 Jan. 1936, Gjirokastra

Born in the museum-city of Gjirokastra, K. studied at the Faculty of History and Philology of the University of Tirana and subsequently at the Gorky Institute of World Literature in Moscow until 1960 when relations between Albania and the Soviet Union became tense. He maintained a visible presence as a leading figure of Albanian cultural and public life throughout the next three decades. In October 1990, taking advantage of the collapse of the dictatorship in Albania, K. emigrated to Paris where he has lived with his family ever since.

From 1961 onwards, together with Dritëro AGOLLI and Fatos Arapi (b. 1930), K. set the pace for modern Albanian literature, being groomed by the communist party, perhaps consciously, as an Albanian pendant to the Russian writers Yevgeny YEVTUSHENKO and Andrey VOZNESENSKY.

K.'s first major prose work, still perhaps one of his best, is the novel *Gjenerali i ushtrisë së vdekur* (1963; *The General of the Dead Army*, 1971), the tale of an Italian general on a mission to Albania to recover the remains of his soldiers who had fallen some twenty years earlier. At the time of original publication, many features of the novel made it a clear step forward in Albanian letters. The grey stormclouds, mud, and the humdrum reality of everyday life that it portrayed contrasted sharply with the otherwise obligatory sunshine and blithe victories of SOCIALIST REALISM. So did the Italian general. Here too we find a favorite device of the writer who, more than any other, was to bring his country's literature out of its stylistic and thematic lethargy—that of a remote and haunted Albania as seen through the eyes of the innocent or uncomprehending foreigner.

Kronikë në gur (1971; *Chronicle in Stone*, 1987), a novel in eighteen chapters and an epilogue, is the chronicle of his stunning hometown under occupation during World War II. This work of linguistic finesse and subtle political allusions offers not so much a portrayal of the grim historical events of a city under occupation, but rather a compelling mixture of the childhood observations, impressions, and fantasies of a young Albanian boy.

In *Ura me tri harqe* (1978; *The Three-Arched Bridge*, 1994) K. turned to the mythical origins of Albania's haunted history to bring to life one of the most awesome motifs of Balkan legendry, that of immurement. The legend of a human being walled in during the construction of a bridge or castle is widespread in Albanian oral literature (cf. the tale of Rozafat Castle) and is based no doubt on a reality. Even today, animals are still sacrificed on such occasions in Albania and their blood immured to 'stabilize' the foundations of bridges and homes. Reviving this practice in all its original horror, this novel has been interpreted as an Albanian response to Serbian Nobel Prize-winner Ivo ANDRIĆ's *Na Drini ćuprija* (1945; *The Bridge on the Drina*, 1959). K. is at his best with Balkan themes.

Prilli i thyer (1978; *Broken April*, 1990), published in the volume *Gjakftohtësia* (1980; Cold-Bloodedness), begins with a murder in the 1930s. Gjorg Berisha has accomplished what all his relatives insisted he must do: cleanse his honor by slaying his brother's murderer from the rival Kryeqyqe clan. There was no way out of the bloody rituals of vendetta, anchored in the ancient Code of Lekë Dukagjin. Whole families had been wiped out in the "taking of blood" and now he, too, was obliged to follow suit, only to set himself up as the next victim. This novel is no doubt the finest literary portrayal of the tragically absurd institution of blood-feuding, which has resurfaced in the country with such grim force since the fall of the dictatorship.

Nëpunësi i pallatit të ëndrrave (1981; *The Palace of Dreams*, 1993) is considered one of K.'s masterpieces. It is the world of Franz KAFKA and of George ORWELL's "1984" set in the sybaritic if somewhat torpid atmosphere of the Ottoman Empire. Mark-Alem, scion of a noted family of public servants, is appointed to work at the Tabir Sarrail, the awesome government office responsible for the study of sleep and dreams. It is his duty to analyze and categorize the dreams and nightmares of the Sultan's subjects and interpret them in order to enable the authorities to stifle any incipient rebellions and criminal acts. It is a basically humorous novel, but perhaps not entirely so for those who have lived in a totalitarian state. The analogy for Albanians is more than evident.

K. did his utmost to emancipate Albanian literature in the 1970s and 1980s. On many occasions during the long years of gruesome dictatorship, he courageously voiced criticism of standards in the field of literature and the arts while, at the same time, he gave his unconditional support to the political system from which he himself no doubt suffered. This caused his critics subsequently to refer to him as the "court writer" or the "showpiece of the regime." Be this as it may, there can be no doubt that K. used his relative freedom and his talent under an awesome dictatorship to launch many a subtle attack against the regime in the form of political allegories which occur throughout his works. As the best example of creativity and originality in contemporary Albanian letters and the only Albanian writer to enjoy a broad international reputation, K. brought a breath of fresh air to a suffocating culture.

FURTHER WORKS: *Frymëzimet djaloshare* (1954); *Ëndërrimet* (1957); *Shekulli im* (1961); *Përse mendohen këto male* (1964); *Vjersha dhe poema të zgjedhura* (1966); *Qyteti i jugut* (1967); *Dasma* (1968; *The Wedding*, 1968); *Motive me diell* (1968); *Kështjella* (1970; *The Castle*, 1974); *Autobiografi e popullit në vargje dhe shënime të tjera* (1971); *Dimri i vetmisë së madhe* (1973); *Linja të largëta, shënime udhëtimi* (1973); *Nëntori i një kryeqyteti* (1975); *Poezia shqipe 28*, (1976); *Koha, vjersha dhe poema* (1976); *Emblema e dikurshme, tregime e novela* (1977); *On the lay of the knights* (1979); *Poezi* (1979); *Buzëqeshje mbi botë* (1980); *Autobiografia e popullit në vargje* (1980; *The Autobiography of the People in Verse*, 1987); *Vepra letrare* (12 vols., 1981 ff.); *Koha e shkrimeve: tregime, novela, përshkrime* (1986); *Doruntine: a novel* (1988); *Koncert në fund të dimri* (1988; *The Concert*, 1994); *Dosja H.* (1990; *The File on H.*, 1997); *Eskili, ky humbës i madh* (1990); *Ftesë në studio* (1990); *Migjeni ose uragani i ndërprerë* (1990); *Ardhja e Migjenit në letërsinë shqipe* (1991); *Ëndërr mashtruese: tregime e novela* (1991); *Nga një dhjetor në tjetrin: kronikë, këmbim letrash, persiatje* (1991; *Albanian Spring: The Anatomy of Tyranny*, 1994); *Përbindëshi* (1991); *Pesha e kryqit* (1991); *Oeuvres*(1993 ff.); *Vepra* (1993 ff.); *Noël, une anthologie des plus beaux textes de la littérature mondiale* (1994); *Albanie: visage des Balkans, écrits de lumière* (1995); *Piramida* (1995; *The Pyramid*, 1996); *Dialog me Alain Bosquet* (1996); *Legjenda e legjendave* (1996); *Shkaba* (1996); *Spiritus, roman me kaos, zbulesë dhe çmërs* (1996); *Kushëriri i engjëjve* (1997); *Poèmes, 1957-1997* (1997)

BIBLIOGRAPHY: Byron, J., "Albanian Nationalism and Socialism in the Fiction of I. K.," *WLT*, 53 (Summer 1979): 614-16; Pipa, A., "Subversion gegen Konformismus: das Phänomen Kadare," *Münchner Zeitschrift für Balkankunde*, 5 (1983-84): 165-78; Pipa, A., "Subversion vs. Conformism: The K. Phenomenon," *Telos*, 73 (1987): 47-77; Mitchell, A. M., *Un rhapsode albanais: I. K.* (1990); Beqiri, S., ed., *Sfida e gjeniut: K., Ekzili, Kosova* (1991); Elsie, R., "Evolution and Revolution in Modern Albanian Literature," *WLT*, 65 (Spring 1991): 256-63; Faye, E., *I. K.: entretiens avec éric faye, en lisant en écrivant* (1991); Faye, E., *I. K.: Prométhée porte-feu* (1991); Klosi, A., *Mythologie am Werk: Kazantzakis, Andrić, K., eine vergleichende Untersuchung am besonderen Beispiel des Bauopfermotivs* (1991); Pipa, A., *Contemporary Albanian Literature* (1991): 49-123; Terpan, F., *I. K.* (1992); Çaushi, T., *Universi letrar i Karadesë* (1993); Nauni, E., *Kadareja i panjohur: Laokonti filloi të flasë* (1993); Zamputi, I., *Ekskursion në dy vepra të Kadaresë* (1993); Çaushi, T., *K.: fjalor i personazheve* (1995); Elsie, R., *History of Albanian Literature* (1995): 541-63, 593-96; Elsie, R., *Një fund dhe një fillim* (1995); Elsie, R., *Studies in Modern Albanian Literature and Culture* (1996); Sinani, S., *Pengu i moskuptimit* (1997)

—ROBERT ELSIE

KADEN-BANDROWSKI, Juliusz

Polish novelist and short-story writer, b. 24 Feb. 1885, Rzeszów; d. 8 Aug. 1944, Warsaw

Born to a family of artists and intellectuals, K.-B. initially intended to become a musician; however, because his arm was broken twice in his early childhood, he abandoned these plans and instead turned his attention to literature. Shortly after graduating from secondary school, K.-B. was on his way to the Caucasus, from where he went to Germany and Belgium to study music history and theory. From abroad K.-B. sent accounts of cultural life in the West to Polish newspapers. He returned to Poland in 1913, and when World War I broke out he fought against Russia with the Polish Legion organized by Józef Piłsudski, the leader of the Polish independence movement. Thenceforth, both the literary and the political careers of K.-B. were closely tied to the ideology of Piłsudski.

K.-B.'s first novel, *Niezguła* (1911; dull-witted person) rejected revolutionary ideology as a means of solving social conflicts and questioned the validity of the SYMBOLIST movement, which dominated the Polish literary scene before World War I. Although his early fiction reveals some stylistic affinities to symbolism, K.-B. broke with its essential aesthetic premises: the cult of individual "I," and the belief in the existence of an ideal world of beauty. In his early fiction K.-B. tried to show plain reality, without any embellishment, ugly and devoid of idealism.

During World War I K.-B.'s writings were almost entirely devoted to the struggle of the Polish Legion. One of the most interesting accounts of this period is the novel *Łuk* (1917; the bow), in which he describes the disintegration of traditional social and moral values, psychological perversion, and the decline of human integrity caused by the war. After the war K.-B. participated in numerous cultural and political activities and was one of the founders of the Polish Academy of Literature.

Still, writing remained his greatest passion. In the early 1920s he published a number of prose works devoted to his childhood, but fame came only with the publication of the political trilogy consisting of *Generał Barcz* (1923; General Barcz), *Czarne skrzydła* (2 vols., 1928–29; black wings), and *Mateusz Bigda* (1933; Mateusz Bigda), written in an EXPRESSIONISTIC style. K.-B. was often called the official writer of the new, independent Poland, but his relationship with the state was complex and far from unequivocal. On the one hand, he mocked revolutionary rhetoric and held the parliamentary system in contempt; on the other, he did expose and criticize the weaknesses of the political system established in Poland after Piłsudski's coup d'état of 1926. The trilogy contains a clear message: if you want to save the country, rid yourself of corruption, political dishonesty, and demoralization.

Compelled to go into hiding during World War II, K.-B. continued to write. Unfortunately, almost all his manuscripts from this period have been lost. He died of a wound inflicted by a German shell during the Warsaw uprising.

FURTHER WORKS: *Zawody* (1911); *Proch* (1913); *Zbytki* (1914); *Bitwa pod Konarami* (1915); *Iskry* (1915); *Piłsudczycy* (1915); *Mogiły* (1916); *Spotkanie* (1916); *Wyprawa wileńska* (1919); *Wiosna* (1920); *Podpułkownik Lis-Kula* (1920); *Rubikon* (1921); *Przymierze serc* (1924); *Wakacje moich dzieci* (1924); *Miasto mojej matki* (1925); *W cieniu zapomnianej olszyny* (1926; *Call to the Cuckoo*, 1948); *Europa zbiera siano* (1927); *Nad brzegiem wielkiej rzeki* (1927); *Rzymianie wschodu* (1928); *Na progu* (1928); *Stefan Żeromski, prorok niepodległości* (1930); *Pióro, miłość i kobieta* (1931); *Za stołem i na rynku* (1932); *Aciaki z 1A* (1932); *Pod Belwederem* (1936); *Droga wolności* (1936); *Wspomnienia i nadzieje* (1938); *Życie Chopina* (1938)

BIBLIOGRAPHY: Kridl, M., *A Survey of Polish Literature and Culture* (1956): 501; Krejči, K., *Geschichte der polnischen Literature* (1958): 489–91; Miłosz, C., *The History of Polish Literature* (1969): 425–26; Krzyżanowski, J., *A History of Polish Literature* (1978): 615–20

—EDWARD MOŻEJKO

KAFFKA, Margit

Hungarian novelist, short-story writer, and poet, b. 10 June 1880, Nagykároly; d. 1 Dec. 1918, Budapest

On her mother's side, K. was descended from generations of by then impoverished Hungarian gentry. Her father, a lawyer, died when she was six. She completed her schooling and obtained a teaching certificate, and then earned a higher degree in 1902. For fifteen years she taught school in Miskolc and Budapest. Her poems began to appear in *Magyar géniusz* in 1901, and she began to publish fiction in 1905. She was a contributor to the avant-garde journal *Nyugat* from its founding in 1908. She was married twice. In 1915 K. gave up teaching to devote all her time to writing. Both she and her only son died in the influenza epidemic just as World War I ended.

K., the most outstanding Hungarian woman novelist of the early 20th c., first attracted notice with a spirited essay and some traditional verse. She soon broke with traditional subjects and modes of expression, however. Her contributions to *Nyugat*— daring experiments in free verse and short fiction—outraged conventional sensibilities. She wrote memorable poems about the war, about social injustice, about her own struggles to juggle the duties of a teacher and a mother with those of a writer; she also wrote some of the finest love poems in Hungarian literature (to her second husband).

Her first short-story collection, *A gondolkodók, és egyéb elbeszélések* (1906; the thinkers, and other short stories), is skeptical and disillusioned. The "thinkers" of the title story await their own inevitable disillusionment with cynical detachment. Her other notable collections are *Csendes válságok* (1910; quiet crises), *Csonka regény és novellák* (1911; unfinished novel and short stories), *Süppedő talajon* (1912; on sinking ground), and *Szent Ildefonso bálja* (1914; the ball of St. Ildefonso). With few exceptions, these are stories of two types of women; those who are repressed and those who manage to break out of their bondage. Eventually most of her stories about women were republished in two volumes with the revealing title *Lázadó asszonyok* (1958; women in rebellion).

In longer fiction, she and Zsigmond MÓRICZ represented the breaking-away from 19th-c. models. Móricz received K.'s epoch-making novel *Szinek és évek* (1912; colors and years) with the enthusiasm of a brother and comrade-in-arms. He declared, "A critic of society can draw many more conclusions from it about the workings of society than from life itself." It combines acute insights into the country's changing social structure with authentic psychological portrayals; its daringly innovative, impressionistic style is ideally suited to the topic. The heroine, Madga Pórtelky (modeled after K.'s mother), develops from a callow provincial girl to an enlightened, disillusioned, tough, yet serene woman. Twice widowed, the mother of four, Magda looks with satisfaction at the promise of a new life that is opening for her daughters. K.'s technique involves daring leaps in the plot, which force the reader to assess the nature of each new situation instantly. Magda's development is seen against the backdrop of her class, the provincial gentry, which sinks into oblivion as she rises spiritually.

K.'s next novel, *Mária évei* (1913; Maria's years), is in a sense the antithesis of *Szinek és évek*: Maria, a first-generation career woman, is unable to make a satisfactory adjustment to modern life and is destroyed. By contrast, Éva Rosztoky, in *Állomások* (1917; stations), the novel that followed, succeeds and becomes her own person.

During World War I, K. wrote two pacifist works: the long story "Lírai jegyzetek egy évről" (1915; lyric notes about one year) and the novel *Két nyár* (1917; two summers).

Hangyaboly (1917; ant colony), her last novel, plumbs the depths of myth and archetype in showing the maturing process of a few young women during their senior year in a convent school. At the time of its publication it attracted attention—both favorable and unfavorable—because of its strident anticlerical overtones; today it can be admired for its ripe imagery and its skillful portrayal of the kinds of career choices confronting young women in the early years of the century.

K. is the most significant woman writer of Hungary. Other women of the period either reveled in their dainty femininity or denied it. K. was able to raise the problems confronting women to the level of the universally human, combining the stories of individual women with the history of the disintegrating Hungarian gentry.

FURTHER WORKS: *Versek* (1903); *Levelek a zárdából* (1904); *Nyár* (1905); *Könyve* (1906); *Képzelet-királyfiak* (1909); *Tallózó évek* (1911); *Utólszor a lyrán* (1913); *Azélet útján* (1917); *Kis emberek, barátocskáim* (1918); *A révnél* (1918); *K. M. összes versei* (1961); *K. M. regényei* (1968)

BIBLIOGRAPHY: Reményi, J., *Hungarian Writers and Literature* (1965): 284–91; Brunauer, D. H., "A Woman's Self-Liberation: The Story of M. K. (1880–1918)," *CARHS*, 5, 2 (1978): 31–42; Brunauer, D. H., "The Woman Writer in a Changing Society," *Center for Women's Studies Lectures and Seminars*, Tokyo Women's Christian University (1978): 40–44

—DALMA H. BRUNAUER

KAFKA, Franz

Austrian novelist and short-story writer, b. 3 July 1883, Prague, Austro-Hungarian Empire; d. 3 June 1924, Kierling

K. was the son of a self-made merchant; his mother belonged to one of the leading families in the German-speaking, German-cultured Jewish circles of Prague. He was regarded as a competent student despite his habit of self-disparagement. In 1901 he began studying at the German Karl-Ferdinand University in Prague. Here he met Max BROD, who became his lifelong friend and eventually his literary executor. Acceding to parental pressure, as well as to his own desire to separate completely his inner life from his public life, K. settled on the study of law, and received his degree in 1906. The next year he began work in the office of an insurance company. The atmosphere, reminiscent of that associated with his father at home, was authoritarian. K. established the pattern of enduring the office by day and writing stories by night. In 1908 he moved to the semigovernmental Workers' Accident Insurance Institute, where a more agreeable atmosphere prevailed. Still, he was tormented not only by the disharmony between his civil-service career and his literary endeavors, but also by poor health and indecisiveness about marriage. Tuberculosis manifested itself in 1917. Despite K.'s initial reluctance, he agreed to undergo treatment. By 1922 he was obliged to relinquish his civil-service position completely. In his mature years K. was engaged several times to be married, but all the engagements were broken. He had frequent stays in sanatoriums, and otherwise lived in Prague, Berlin, and Vienna. From 1912 on, K. strengthened his originally very tenuous ties with Judaism. His tuberculosis having run its fatal course, he died after almost seven years of struggle in a sanatorium in Kierling, not far from Vienna.

K. was invariably dissatisfied with his literary efforts. He instructed Brod to destroy after his death his considerable amount of unpublished writing. Instead, Brod edited and published the material. He has been taken to task by critics for presumed errors and arbitrariness in arranging and editing K.'s manuscripts—essentially to accord with Brod's own religious, eschatological propensity. Against this charge, the imputation of willfulness, Brod has defended himself rather convincingly.

K.'s fear and mistrust of his father, his complete incompatibility with his father's domineering nature—the latter manifested in mental abuse, threats, and savage sarcasm directed against his son—found written expression in 1919 in the lengthy, unsent *Brief an den Vater* (1952; *Letter to His Father*, 1953). K.'s unresolved hatred and love for his father, presented here in a way that reveals at once a measure of infantilism as well as a great deal of self-knowledge and psychological awareness, is regarded as an important basis of K.'s literary works. K., according to his own word, wrote to escape his father's heritage, that is, the striving, middle-class world that K. was obliged to labor in. Writing was necessary to his survival. And marriage would threaten his writing and so destroy him.

K.'s first published story of greater than sketch-length was "Das Urteil" (1913; "The Judgment," 1945). It gives an indication of the intensely autobiographical orientation that would characterize K.'s subsequent works, whether their symbolism is to be understood as psychological, religious, metaphysical, or existential—or indeed as all four at once. The judgment in question is the death sentence of the father on the son Georg, who thereupon commits suicide, not perhaps primarily to carry out his father's judgment, but because his father, by exploiting a common bond with Georg's friend, by driving away Georg's bride, by thus expanding his primacy in Georg's life and suffocating all else, has left Georg with nothing but a vision of his father—and that is destroyed by the judgment. In addition to the obvious Freudian relevance of the narrative facts, one may also suggest that Georg's father is the symbol of an Old Testament God, or, alternatively, a God produced by man's inner division.

In "Die Verwandlung" (1915; "The Metamorphosis," 1936) the son Gregor Samsa—the family name is clearly an analogue of the name Kafka—a rising young businessman, awakens one morning to find himself changed into a monstrous bug. The paradoxically realistic and restrained narrative relates the ever more intense suffering of the bug from the progressive alienation of the family for whom he had been the chief support. The nexus of the alienation is the father, whose influence, as in "Das Urteil," expands until he becomes the agent of the bug's willing death. From a short epilogue we gather that with the timely disposal of the bug that was Gregor, the family's respectability and inner harmony, under the father's dominance, may be regained.

Ein Landarzt (1919; *The Country Doctor*, 1940) is a collection of fourteen tales. The theme of the title story is the disruption—finally turned into chaos—of the country doctor's orderly but unperceptive existence by an irrational and oblivious world. Like Parzival before the Grail King, the country doctor fails the test of human sympathy before the boy with a mysterious and repulsive wound. At least at the primary narrative level, K. here departs from his preoccupation with sons and fathers. On the other hand, if we wish to see the country doctor as an unwilling father figure in relation to his young, doomed patient, the broad outlines of the earlier K. topos reemerge.

"In der Strafkolonie" (1919; "In the Penal Colony," 1941) again presents a father figure, or certainly an authority figure, the old commandant of the penal colony. Or rather, it does not present him, for he has died before the story begins; but his cruel heritage,

Franz Kafka

though waning, has not yet been eliminated by his successor. Still devoted to the use of the old commandant's exquisite and horrible execution machine is the officer in whose charge the machine has been put and who is demonstrating it to a visiting explorer, finally indeed placing himself in its bed. While it is easy and tempting to credit K. with a visionary perception of the future horrors of concentration camps and World War II—and particularly the horrors perpetrated on the Jews—probably a critically sounder approach, relating "In der Strafkolonie" more integrally to the body of K.'s writings, would be to regard this tale as a symbolic amplification of K.'s perception of himself as a victim not undeserving of punishment—although for no clear reason—at the hands of the preceding generation, which is naturally equated with authority.

K.'s last four story-length narratives were collected in a group published shortly after his death under the title *Ein Hungerkünstler* (1924; *The Hunger Artist*, 1938). The hero of the title story has chosen his unusual profession because he cannot adapt to the world about him. To be sure, this profession makes its own special demands on him: extreme resignation and passivity, while still not exempting him from the abuse and suspicion of the world. This artist, moreover, confined in a cage while he scorns earthly food, has nothing substantial—at any rate nothing recognized as substantial—to offer his audience. The circus crowds eventually become indifferent to his striving for accomplishments beyond the compass of their own narrow orbits. Desiring admiration, he earns incomprehension, and is left to die unwatched. The crowds gravitate to the cage of a healthy, hungry black panther, who even in his captivity is admirably adapted to the expectations of the world.

The theme of incommensurability between an artist of questionable talent and a world of limited horizon is also developed in another story in the same collection, "Josefine, die Sängerin; order, Das Volk der Mäuse" (1924; "Josephine the Songstress; or, The Mouse Folk," 1942). The creatures designated in the subtitle, perhaps ironically symbolic of the Jews, seem also to be parallels of the uncomprehending crowds who at first throng to, then ultimately desert the hunger artist. Josefine, too, is a mouse. Although she makes much to-do about her supposed talent for singing, and prevails upon her reluctant fellow mice to attend whenever she feels impelled to give a concert, in fact, she is only squeaking, much as any mouse does. But then, K. suggests, developing the paradox with characteristic irony, no harm is done and perhaps there is even some benefit in the mouse folk's subscribing to the delusion foisted on them by Josefine. On the other hand, after Josefine dies, she is in the long run doomed to oblivion, for the mouse folk have no truck with history.

K.'s first novel, *Amerika* (1927; *America*, 1938), was written between 1912 and 1914. The first chapter, called "Der Heizer" (1913; the stoker) had been published separately soon after its completion. K.'s other two novels, which, like the first, were never completed, are *Der Prozeß*, begun in 1914 (1925; *The Trial*, 1937) and *Das Schloß*, begun in 1921 (1926; *The Castle*, 1930). For each of the novels it may well be that K. had in mind a sequence of chapters different from the one that emerged from Brod's hands.

Amerika is exceptional among the novels in that the environment, however strange and inscrutable, is at least not consistently hostile to the hero Karl Rossmann. And, if we take the novel as it stands, it ends atypically on something like a happy note—but also conceivably an ironic note. Karl is neither very intelligent nor very forceful. Or, when forceful, he is misguidedly so, as K. makes clear in the opening chapter; Karl's intercession on behalf of his new friend, the stoker, reflects the naïve idealism that will precipitate him from one scrape to another, as he is subjected to the unpredictabilities of life in the United States.

Karl repeatedly fails to comprehend the gap between myth and reality in America. How can there be such an enormous gulf between the rich and the poor? How can his benign Uncle Jakob condemn him, on account of disobedience, to leave his splendid house and take to the road? (*Amerika* is a road novel as well as, at least to some extent, a *Bildungsroman*.) How much abuse must Karl take before he realizes that his road companion Delamarche (K. appreciated puns), is less than a friend? In the light of Karl's misapprehensions, one is justified in wondering if the "Nature Theater of Oklahoma" in the (presumed) final chapter is going to prove quite as happy as Karl is led to believe: something for everybody, and freedom from bureaucracy.

In *Der Prozeß* the unpredictable counter-force—here more distinctly antagonistic—is a court of dubious legality, the ambiguous minions of which persistently and illogically bedevil the hero Josef K. Hardly less a bumbler than Karl Rossmann, Josef K. does not enlist our sympathy as a victim to the extent the latter does in *Amerika*, for Josef K., though self-confident, is otherwise largely without emotion. The court retains ultimate jurisdiction over his case, but it gives him a certain leeway, which perhaps vitiates any inchoate impulse on Josef K.'s part toward confrontation. In the end, he is executed by strangling and knifing, having refused, with unwonted courage, the opportunity to commit suicide.

The structural center and climax of *Der Prozeß* is a parable, representative of a genre that K. esteemed and cultivated. This particular parable, "Vor dem Gesetz" ("Before the Law"), concerns a man from the country, that is, a simpleton, prevented by a doorkeeper from entering an opening in the wall before him. His timorousness before the threats of the doorkeeper and his desire nonetheless to enter are in enervating balance, the result of which is a life-long torment of inertia before the opening in the wall. As the man from the country is dying, the doorkeeper tells him that the entrance, now to be closed, had been meant for him all along.

To a degree the situation of the man from the country is like that of K.'s country doctor and, again, like that of Parzival. Except that in *Der Prozeß* it is not the suffering of someone else—the young patient, the Grail King—before which the hero falls silent. It is his own suffering, perhaps his own salvation that is at stake. And like Josef K. he lacks the impulse, quite possibly even the requisite sympathy with himself, to take a chance, to break out of his angst and ask what is going on.

In *Das Schloß*, K.'s longest but evidently least complete novel, the adversary consists in a mysterious officialdom in an equally mysterious castle. The castle and its officialdom at once attract, repel, and bemuse the hero, here known simply by the letter K., the ultimate reduction of the author's significantly autobiographical nomenclature. The goal of the fictional K., ostensibly a surveyor summoned to a job by the castle—but this and most other "facts" are ambiguous—is to enter the castle to ascertain the details of his commission so that he may get on with the work. His original purpose, however, suffers a loss of focus in the course of his long and futile, and often indirect, efforts to enter the castle from the dependent village to which he is relegated.

But *Das Schloß* is much more than the mere satire on bureaucracy it might appear to be at first glance. As the inhabitants of the castle are enigmatic and not to be counted on, so the castle itself is an uncertain entity, never seeming to K. to be quite the same thing as it was earlier. Metaphysically as well as physically it is not to be comprehended. Ultimately K., certainly a more forceful quester than Karl Rossmann or Josef K., but maladroit for all that, abets his own failure even when he appears to be on the verge of success. The inaccessible, to state the inevitable conclusion parabolically, remains inaccessible.

The authorial K.'s range of theme is not great, and his world view, intensely autobiographical as it is, is essentially cheerless. Potential danger or catastrophe lie everywhere, apt to descend on the helpless but not guiltless human victim quite unpredictably and illogically. What the victim is guilty of is usually unclear—perhaps simply of existence. And yet K.'s virtuoso development and modulation of his own thematic range—let us grant, moreover, its perfect timeliness—in addition to his uniquely wrought prose style, clear, precise, and to the point, have made him a leading figure, and a leading influence, in 20th-c. literature. Owing but little to his own literary and philosophical models, chiefly Goethe, Dostoevsky, Kleist, Flaubert, Dickens, and Kierkegaard, hardly known beyond a rather narrow circle of friends and enthusiasts during his lifetime, thereafter to be suppressed as a consequence of the racist nonsense of Nazism, K. since World War II has exerted a pervasive and continuing effect not only on the narrative literature but as well on the drama and film of Western Europe and the Americas.

FURTHER WORKS: *Betrachtung* (1913; *Meditation*, 1940); *Beim Bau der chinesischen Mauer: Ungedruckte Prose aus dem Nachlaß* (1931; *The Great Wall of China*, 1933); *Gesammelte Schriften* (6 vols., 1935–1937); *Beschreibung eines Kampfes* (1936; *Description of a Struggle*, 1958); *Gesammelte Werke* (11 vols., 1950–1974); *Tagebücher 1910–23* (1951; *The Diaries of F. K.*, 2 vols., 1948–1949); *Briefe an Milena* (1952; *Letters to Milena*, 1953); *Briefe an Felice Bauer* (1967; *Letters to Felice*, 1973). **FURTHER WORKS IN ENGLISH:** *The Penal Colony: Stories and Short Pieces* (1961); *The Complete Stories* (1971); *I Am a Memory Come Alive: Autobiographical Writings* (1976); *Letters to Friends, Family, and Editors* (1977); *Letters to Ottla and the Family* (1982)

BIBLIOGRAPHY: Brod, M., *F. K.: A Biography* (1947); Wagenbach, K., *F. K.: Eine Biographie seiner Jugend* (1958); Brod, M., *Verzweiflung und Erlösung im Werk F. K.s* (1959); Sokel, W. H., *F. K.: Tragik und Ironie* (1964); Politzer, H., *F. K.: Parable and Paradox* (1966); Foulkes, A. P., *The Reluctant Pessimist: A Study of F. K.* (1967); Emrich, W., *F. K.: A Critical Study of His Writings* (1968); Greenberg, M., *The Terror of Art: K. and Modern Literature* (1968); Urzidil, J., *There Goes K.* (1968); Janouch, G., *Conversations with K.* (1971); Thorlby, A., *K.: A Study* (1972); Gray, R., *F. K.* (1973); Beicken, P. U., *F. K.: Eine kritische Einführung in die Forschung* (1974); Kuna, F., *F. K.: Literature as Corrective Punishment* (1974); Nagel, B., *F. K.: Aspekte zur Interpretation und Wertung* (1974); Rolleston, J., *K.'s Narrative Theater* (1974); Hibberd, J., *K. in Context* (1975); Binder, H., *K. in neuer Sicht* (1976); Flores, A., ed., *The K. Debate* (1977); Robert, M., *Seul, comme F. K.* (1979); Stern, J. P., *The World of F. K.* (1980)

—RICHARD H. LAWSON

While I lay special worth on the hopeful side of K.'s work, which rejoices in activity, that is to say in the fundamental recognition of the fact that man, with his spark of reason, will, and ethical perception is not altogether the plaything of super-mighty powers, who judge according to other laws than his, which he does not understand and never can understand, faced with which he is lost, and only thrown unconditionally on God's mercy—the old problem of Job—while underlining then the position of human freedom in the case of K., I do not of course wish to forget that this attitude of K.'s is only an occasional flash, and that passages which describe man as powerless, crowd in on the reader in an overwhelming majority. But the propositions of freedom and hope *are there, too!*

Max Brod, *F.K.: A. Biography* (1947), p. 171

Any individual work by K. may baffle the reader when considered in isolation. If examined within the context of K.'s other works and personal documents, the nature and meaning of his images become clear. The individual work will then appear as a variation of a single theme—the inner autobiography of the author—and a step in its development. Each work is aesthetically self-sufficient and, if completed and published by K. himself, a complete and satisfying statement of one approach to the master theme.

There is, nevertheless, a difference in the degree of transparency K.'s images possess in different works.

The central images of his long narratives—Gregor Samsa's bug form, the Court in *The Trial*, the Castle in the late novel of that name—are more opaque and denser than the symbols of his shorter pieces. The reason is that the central images of the long works have a variety of functions and meanings. Indeed, they unite mutually contradictory meanings and functions.

Walter H. Sokel, *F.K.* (1966), p. 8

There is not one self-explanatory word in a typical K. narrative. His mature prose shows nothing but a surface spread over happenings that remain profoundly impenetrable. Paradoxically this enables K., the visionary, to furnish his stories amply with realistic detail. Since even the inanimate objects he describes point to an undefined and mysterious background, they no longer relate to one another according to the customs and conventions of reality. Clefts, cracks, and crevices open, revealing the depth behind the realistic detail. The same is true of the figures acting on a stage thus prepared. Ostensibly most of them are well grounded in reality, even in the reality of K.'s own life.

Heinz Politzer, *F. K.: Parable and Paradox* (1966), p. 17

The crucial element . . . in this story ["Der Jäger Gracchus"] as well as in all of K.'s stories—the element, too, that characteristically distinguishes K. from his contemporaries—is the fact that the hunter who moves in this earthly world is a "dead" person who does not belong to this earthly world at all, whom no one understands, and who, by the same token, does not understand any living person.

This "dead" person who is "in a certain sense alive, too," embraces in the midst of the earthly world the duality of death and life. Only now can one understand why this story represents the universal in its universal significance, the totality of all that is, the All-encompassing that has crossed the borders between life and death, that is found both *above* and *within* all that is. In him the mystery of all that is has awakened: everything that all human beings, mountains, and stars, from the beginning of time to the present, have told one another and continue to call out to one another.

A twofold aspect results from this: on the one hand, this dead and, at the same time, living man possesses total perspective, universal knowledge of all that has been and is . . . On the other hand, by reason of this intermediate position of his between life and death, he no longer fits into any fixed earthly or spiritual classification; he sails "without a rudder," completely disoriented upon the earthly waters, and is, therefore, able to reach and comprehend neither the limited world of ideas of the much-occupied living, nor the "gate" of the Hereafter that "shines on high."

Wilhelm Emrich, *F. K.: A Critical Study of His Writings* (1968), p. 10

K. is an extreme instance of a writer who abandoned himself to all the forces that could destroy a man, without trying to put in their way any of the conscious blocks that most of us use . . . to separate ourselves from unacceptable insights. We are likely to go wrong, though, if we try to rule K. out of court because of any objection we have to the defeats his characters suffer. If the comparisons with William Sansom and Poe show nothing else, they show that K. was too scrupulous an artist to be challenged on any grounds except that of the art of novel-writing and story-writing which was his deliberate choice of activity. His lasting quality will be found in a work that grows out of this basic integrity. But to see the work as a whole means taking into account much more than individual passages. The patterns of whole stories and novels go towards making the full picture, and then too the pattern of K.'s whole life as a writer has to be sought.

Ronald Gray, *F. K.* (1973), p. 28

What first impresses itself on the reader of K.'s work is a vision of an incomprehensible world, a mood of total impotence in the face of the unintelligible power of circumstances, as a consequence of which "the inner world of the subject is transformed into a sinister, inexplicable flux" (Georg Lukács) requiring exorcism by the harshest punitive measures. Yet it is equally true that beneath the nightmare a more positive assessment of reality can be detected. Though for the most of the time it was impossible for K. to make such an assessment an integral part of his poetics, he could on occasion intimate that, as he explained to [Gustav] Janouch, reality is also "the strongest force shaping the world and human beings. . . . Dreams are only a way round, at the end of which one always returns to the world of most immediate reality." The final chapter of *The Castle*, for example, describes such a return. One must also understand the therapeutic and utopian quality of K.'s nihilism. If he could not bring himself unambiguously to celebrate the positive aspects of human existence, then he at least indirectly pointed the way, by pushing the nihilistic view of it to its limits.

Franz Kuna, *K.: Literature as Corrective Punishment* (1974), pp. 10–11

Accustomed to an ever-decreasing gap between fiction and "reality," the reader of K.'s time had developed an analytic sense, an insistence on verisimilitude that continually questioned the synthesizing process whereby fictional characters had come into being. K.'s response was to incorporate both reactions of the reader, the synthetic and the analytic, the constructive and the destructive, into an entirely new approach to the notion of character. Virtually all his stories are focused on a single hero: yet nothing is harder than to evolve an image of the "character" of a K. hero, even though he is usually placed very close

to the reader's perspective, makes constant appeals to common sense, and seemingly has nothing to hide.

James Rolleston, *K.'s Narrative Theater* (1974), p. 140

F. K.'s life was a private tragedy mingled with farce, almost as strange and terrible as that of any of his fictional heroes. His biography is a story of mental conflict and torment which he himself recorded in his diaries and letters with the genius of a great writer and the scrupulous accuracy of a hypochondriac and introvert. He paints a compelling self-portrait of a man unfit for life who failed miserably in all his endeavours. The knowledge that his problems arose from his mentality as much as from external circumstances did not help him solve them, for his mind was to him more real than anything else in the world. His searching vision was turned inwards. From the city of Prague he observed, yet apparently all but ignored, the historic events of his time, the Great War, the collapse of the Austro-Hungarian Empire, the birth of Czechoslovakia. He believed that his pronounced individuality, his vocation as a writer and his Jewishness made him an outsider. From a position of isolation he created stories of estrangement for which he has become famous.

John Hibberd, *K. in Context* (1975), p. 7

KAHANA-CARMON, Amalia

Israeli novelist and short-story writer, b. 18 Nov. 1930, Tel Aviv

K.-C.'s first collection of stories, *Bkhfifah ahat* (1966; under one roof), already testified to a literary maturity and decisiveness. Both in theme and in style, these stories deviate from the prevalent norms of Israeli fiction. They relate primarily to feeling, to the individual, and to the contact between individuals, particularly in respect to romantic attraction. This attraction is seen as ungraspable, perhaps irrational and mystical, but more significant than any other human emotion in the writing. The language of the stories is condensed, intricate, and elliptical. The sentences are short, and the phraseology alludes little to classical sources. The narratives here explore the relationships and feelings of narrator or narratee with a growing intensity, often playing off such feelings against external reality. The person to whom such feeling attaches may be totally unaware of what is happening. Such an infatuation is always modified by the narrative irony of an alternative voice. There is a commentator behind or at the side or in the action. The implied questions are posed: What is true reality? Is it the subject's version of the inner event, or is it the observer's or the object's version?

What makes for some difficulty in the reading of K.-C. is the paucity of "stage directions" or manifest context. Although the settings vary from Swiss villages through English country houses to Tel Aviv and Jerusalem, the material is interior. In K.-C.'s subsequent work, the novel, *Veyareah beemeq ayalon* (1971; and moon in the valley of Ayalon), material from the earlier collection, there seen as a story, here becomes part of the extended, ongoing narrative. The third-person account of Mrs. Talmor incorporates now this first-person account from an earlier phase of her life. So we see her both from within and without, sometimes wavering between accounts appropriate to the limited focus of a single character or within the province of the omniscient narrator. The unusual title of the novel is taken from *Joshua* 10:12, and refers to the stopping of the sun and moon in their tracks to give time to the Israelites to overcome the Amorites within one day.

The overall title of the triptych, *Sadot magnetiyim* (1977; magnetic fields), states the author's concern with the attraction between man and woman. The metaphor is suggestive of the fact that this attraction is neither consistent nor predictable. These magnetic fields delimit the range of the two individual paths. As often as not, K.-C. describes the encounter from the male point of view, as in the main unit of the triptych, "sham hadar hahadashot" (the newsroom is over there). In this case, the American girl, Wendy, holds they exist in two separate fields, and so they part.

Themes of attraction, support, and dependence are explored by K.-C. in her later work, *Lemaalah bemontifer* (1984; up in Montifer) and in *Livitiy otah baderekh levetah* (1991; I accompanied her home). In *Lemaalah bemontifer* the main section has a medieval setting, so the archaic style favored by the author seems ever more appropriate. The narrator is a Jewess, subject to the Christian Peter, previously a torture victim, but now ruminating her fate and her relationship to the master who has free access to Montifer. Her own account of the past and present situation is both realistic and masochistic.

K.-C.'s work is unique in Israeli narrative for its close analysis of relationships and for its condensed, yet metaphorical and unusual, language.

FURTHER WORKS: *Kan nagur: 5 novellas* (1996)

BIBLIOGRAPHY: Telpaz, G., *Israeli Childhood Stories of the Sixties* (1983): 121–46; Yudkin, L. I., *1948 and After: Aspects of Israeli Fiction* (1984): 97–111, 164–67; Fuchs, E., *Israeli Mythogynies: Women in Contemporary Hebrew Fiction* (1987): 87–104

—LEON I. YUDKIN

KAISER, Georg

German dramatist and novelist, b. 25 Nov. 1878, Magdeburg; d. 4 June 1945, Ascona, Switzerland

K. quit school at the age of sixteen and, after a short stint in the book trade, served an apprenticeship in an import-export firm. In 1898 he set out for Argentina, earning his passage as a coal trimmer on a freighter. A severe case of malaria forced him to return to Germany in 1901. His great breakthrough as a writer came in 1917, with the spectacularly successful premiere of *Die Bürger von Calais* (pub. 1914; the burghers of Calais). He quickly became the leading playwright of EXPRESSIONISM and the most performed dramatist in Germany after Gerhart HAUPTMANN. When the Nazis came to power, they wasted no time in silencing K., whose antimilitarism and pacifism they loathed. They accused him of "cultural Bolshevism" and "Jewish tendencies," and prohibited the publication and performance of his plays in Germany. He continued to live near Berlin until 1938, when he fled into exile, first to

Amsterdam, then to Switzerland. Attempts by Albert Einstein and Thomas MANN to obtain a U.S. visa for K. failed. Feeling more isolated than ever, K. continued to write until his death from an embolism.

By the time K. made a name for himself, a good third of his total dramatic production had already been written, although not much of it was published. His approximately twenty-five pre-expressionist plays explore the possibilities of tragedy and comedy as well as tragicomedy. They show K. to have been very much under the sway of contemporary literary trends; they also show the effect of an intensive study of Nietzsche and Schopenhauer, whose ideas were to exert a powerful and lasting influence on K. The dilemma posed by the conflict between instinct and intellect, body and mind, the problematic nature of love, the dehumanizing effect of a society clinging to ossified norms and values, man's inhumanity to man, themes that become ever more significant for K.'s later work, are already very much in evidence.

The need for a regeneration of man and the blindness of the masses form the background of one of K.'s earliest plays, the "bloody grotesque" *Schellenkönig* (wr. 1896, pub. 1966; king of diamonds), a one-act play in verse in a neoromantic vein. It unmasks the hollowness and inhumanity of a society living by the grotesquely distorted norms and values of mere form as the measure of all things.

An inquiry into the nature of love is made in *Claudius* (wr. 1911, pub. 1918; Claudius) and *Friedrich und Anna* (wr. 1911, pub. 1918; Friedrich and Anna), presenting two diametrically opposed human responses to the meaning of love. In Claudius, a knight in black armor married to a fair maiden, K. shows us a crass example of love that is utterly confined to the frenzy of blind passion and a murderous drive for the exclusive possession of a prized object. Friedrich's love, on the other hand, is based not selfishly on any property rights but on the unconditional recognition and acceptance of the other, Anna, as a human individual in her own right. K.'s later work would seem to support the idea expressed in these early plays that the problem of love is primarily a question of man's regeneration so that he may transcend the egoistic desire to treat others as manipulable objects of self-gratification.

The antithetical opposition of body and mind is the focus of interest in *Rektor Kleist* (wr. 1903, pub. 1914; principal Kleist), a "tragedy of illness and yearning." Kleist, a sickly hunchback, while strongly believing in the authority of the intellect, nevertheless longs for the vitality of life, from which he feels excluded. He would like to think that his intellectual abilities make up for his physical handicaps, but he becomes responsible for a schoolboy's suicide, thus exemplifying the "uncanny wisdom" of the gym teacher's saying: "In a sick body a sick spirit." Yet the vitalistic gym teacher is shown to be equally guilty. Both the fanatic adherence to vitalistic principles and the self-righteous proclamation of the supremacy of the intellect are proven wrong and dangerous in their one-sidedness.

The revolutionary poetic vision and concomitant new form of expressionism, as well as its messianic call for a spiritual regeneration of mankind, provided a perfect mode for K. In his view, a drama presents not so much a story or a plot as an idea—hence, the necessity of form to establish the inner coherence of the *Denkspiel* (thought-play). The idea not only determines the structural principles of K.'s plays: it also makes the characters into typical exponents of ideas, that is, abstractions, who no longer speak a personal idiom. Language, silence accentuated by gestures and pantomime, symbolism (especially color symbolism), stage setting, decoration, and lighting—all derive their functional meaning from the idea they serve to develop.

In *Von morgens bis mitternachts* (wr. 1912, pub. 1916; *From Morn to Midnight*, 1920), the Cashier awakens from the deadly monotony of his trivial existence and, with embezzled money, sets out in search of passionate life. But he fails in his quest, a victim of his illusion to be able to *buy* a new life. Genuine human values are not to be had for money. The Cashier, himself a prisoner of a perverted value system based on purchasing power, never achieves a spiritual regeneration.

Die Bürger von Calais, a powerful drama of pacifism, celebrates the birth of the "New Man." The destructiveness of traditional heroic patriotism, based on martial ideals only, is overcome by a nonviolent heroism born of humanitarian idealism. K. turns a historical incident into a timeless parable of the true hero who lays down his life for the common good.

The exalted vision of one shepherd (the New Man) and one flock (mankind regenerated) reaches its high point in *Hölle Weg Erde* (1919; hell way earth), K.'s only play depicting the realization of utopia on earth. The optimism of this ecstatic vision, however, amounts to no more than a short-lived flicker of hope. The *Gas* trilogy, written about the same time, projects an utterly pessimistic view for the future of mankind. In the three plays, *Die Koralle* (1917; *The Coral*, 1929), *Gas I* (1918; *Gas I*, 1924), *Gas II* (1919; *Gas II*, 1924), each a complete drama in its own right, K. explores the implications of a technological society in an age of capitalism whose exploitational character reduces human beings to mere exponents of mechanical functions.

The Billionaire, in *Die Koralle*, has tried in vain to rid himself of the haunting memory of an unhappy childhood in abject poverty by a ruthless pursuit of power through wealth. When his children turn against him and espouse the cause of the downtrodden and exploited, he has to face the haunting specter again, but now sees no other salvation than that of self-extinction. In *Gas I* the Billionaire's Son has put his social theories into practice. But it quickly becomes obvious that even revolutionary social measures cannot restore man's dignity and human potential as long as purely materialistic values are the decisive factors determining the lives of the workers. In *Gas II*, the possibility of a totally mechanized world has become reality. Once more the call for regeneration is sounded and goes unheard, resulting in the apocalyptic annihilation of mankind.

In *Der gerettete Alkibiades* (1920; *Alkibiades Saved*, 1963), a masterpiece of dramatic form, K. again turns to the conflict of life and spirit. Because of the excruciating pain caused by a thorn in his foot, Socrates disdains public honor, devises a new theory of art, and invents platonic love. The new spiritual values he promotes all owe their existence to the secret wound of the thorn in the flesh. Yet if the thorn in the flesh gives rise to revolutionary spiritual values, it demonstrates at the same time the ultimate mastery of the body. Only death constitutes a synthesis of sorts.

The plays written in the post-expressionist years, until K.'s flight into exile, range from exclusive "worlds of the mind" to comedies, in a more realistic vein, and musicals that appear to be a concession to the general public's taste for lighter fare. But K. was also very much aware of the growing danger of nationalistic and militaristic sentiment and the threat posed by the rising tide of Nazism.

Die Lederköpfe (1928; the leatherheads) represents K.'s first direct dramatic reaction to the contemporary political scene. An impassioned indictment of war, the play illustrates the degradation of man to an anonymous puppet in the hands of a belligerent dictator. K.'s intent was "to denounce the facelessness of the SA and to encourage antifascist resistance." *Die Ächtung des Kriegers* (1929; outlawing the warrior), a short but brilliant Platonic dialogue, voices K.'s critique of the Kellogg Pact (1928). The fatal flaw, as he points out with Socratic irony, resides in the paradox that "the warrior remains a man of honor but war is a crime." Direct allusions to the political and social situation of the early 1930s are also to be found in *Der Silbersee* (1933; the silver lake), a "winter's tale in three acts," K.'s last play to be performed on a German stage before his works were proscribed by the Nazis.

In exile K. continued to write against the evils and horrors of war. *Der Soldat Tanaka* (1940; *Private Tanaka*, n.d.) and *Napoleon in New Orleans* (1941; *Napoleon in New Orleans*, n.d.) are eloquent protests against the destructive curse of war. His pacifist ideals were voiced, for the last time, in *Zweimal Amphitryon* (1943; twice Amphitryon), the first of three "Greek" dramas in blank verse, in which K. reverted to the classic five-act form. It combines the denunciation of war with the expressionist's vision of a New Man to be born from the union of the divine with the human. Love, the redeeming power, will lead to the salvation of the world.

The remaining two "Greek" dramas, *Pygmalion* (1948; Pygmalion) and *Bellerophon* (1948; Bellerophon), can be viewed as the testament of K. the artist. They deal with the fate of the artist in this world, once more exposing the irreconcilable antagonism between life and art, between a society in need of salvation, in which the spiritual values of the artist count only in so far as they represent a promising investment fund, and the divinely inspired artist and misunderstood savior, scorned and rejected by those for whom he guards the divine spark.

Although K.'s work also comprises two novels, several short stories and essays, as well as poetry, he is first and foremost a playwright. His dramas of ideas combine a strong intellectual impulse with a consummate instinct for theatrical effect. His work, uneven as it may be at times, occupies an important place in the history of German drama and has left its mark on modern theater in general, influencing not only Max FRISCH and Friedrich DÜRRENMATT. but also, among others, American playwrights like Eugene O'NEILL and Elmer RICE. BRECHT, expressing his indebtedness to K., perhaps sums it up best: "In fact, K. already gave a new purpose to theater by making it an intellectual affair. . . . He has made possible the entirely new attitude of the audience of the scientific age."

FURTHER WORKS: *Der Fall des Schülers Vehgesack* (written 1902, pub. 1914) *Die jüdische Witwe* (written 1904, rev. 1909 ff., pub. 1911); *Der Geist der Antike* (other title: *Die Falle*; written 1905, pub. 1923); *Der Präsident* (other titles: *Der Kongreß, Der echte Blanchonnet*; written 1906, pub. 1927); *Margarine* (other titles: *Der Zentaur, Konstantin Strobel*; written 1906, rev. 1914 ff., pub. 1925); *David und Goliath* (other title: *Großbürger Möller*; written 1906, rev. 1914 ff., pub. 1920); *Die Sorina* (1909); *Die Versuchung* (other title: *Die Muttergottes*; written 1910, pub. 1917); *König Hahnrei* (written 1910, pub. 1913); *Ballade vom schönen Mädchen* (written 1910, pub. 1911); *Der mutige Seefahrer* (written 1910, rev. 1911, 1925, pub. 1926); *Hyperion* (1911); *Europa* (1915); *Das Frauenopfer* (written 1916, pub. 1918); *Juana* (1918); *Der Brand in Opernhaus* (1919; *The Fire in the Opera House*, 1927); *Der Protagonist* (1921; *The Protagonist*, 1960); *Noli me tangere* (1922); *Kanzlist Krehler* (1922); *Gilles und*

Jeanne (1923); *Die Flucht nach Venedig* (1923; *The Flight to Venice*, 1923); *Nebeneinander* (1923); *Kolportage* (1924; *Literary Trash*, n.d.); *Gats* (1925); *Zweimal Oliver* (1926; *Two Olivers*, 1927); *Der Zar läßt sich photographieren* (1927); *Papiermühle* (1927); *Oktobertag* (1927; *The Phantom Lover*, 1928); *Hellseherei* (1929); *Mississippi* (1929); *Zwei Krawatten* (1929); *Es ist genug* (1931); *Das Los des Ossian Balvesen* (written 1934, pub. 1972); *Agnete* (written 1935, pub. 1972); *Adrienne Ambrossart* (1935; *Adrienne Ambrossart*, 1935); *Rosamunde Floris* (1937); *Alain und Elise* (written 1937, rev. 1938, pub. 1940); *Vincent verkauft ein Bild* (written 1938, pub. 1972); *Pferdewechsel* (written 1938, pub. 1972); *Der Gärtner von Toulouse* (1938); *Der Schuß in der Öffentlichkeit* (1939); *Villa Aurea* (1939; *Vera*, 1939); *Klawitter* (written 1939–40, pub. 1952); *Der englische Sender* (written 1942, pub. 1972); *Die Spieldose* (1943; *The Musical Box*, n.d.); *Das Floß der Medusa* (1943; *Medusa's Raft*, 1951); *Stücke, Erzählungen, Aufsätze, Gedichte* (1966); *Werke* (6 vols., 1971–1972)

BIBLIOGRAPHY: Kenworthy, B. J., *G. K.* (1957); Paulsen, W., *G. K.* (1960); Shaw, L. R., "G. K.: A Bio-Bibliographical Report," *TSLL*, 3 (1961): 399–408; Kauf, R., "G. K.'s Social Tetralogy and the Social Ideas of Walter Rathenau," *PMLA*, 77 (1962): 311–17; Garten, H. F., "G. K.," in Natan, A., ed., *German Men of Letters* (1964), Vol.II: 157–72; Jones, R. A., "German Drama on the American Stage: The Case of G. K.," *GQ*, 37 (1964): 17–25; Reichert, H., "Nietzsche and G. K.," *SP*, 61 (1964): 85–108; Last, R. W., "Symbol and Struggle in G. K.'s *Die Bürger von Calais*," *GL&L*, 19 (1966): 201–9; Schürer, E., *G. K.* (1971); Garten, H. F., "G. K. Re-examined," in Robson-Scott, W. D., ed., *Essays in German and Dutch Literature* (1973): 132–55; Weimar, K. S., "G. K.—At Last!!!(?)," in Weimar, K. S., ed., *Views and Reviews of Modern German Literature* (1974): 213–30; Turnstall, G. C., "Light Symbolism in G. K.'s *Die Bürger von Calais*," *JEGP*, 78 (1979): 178–92; Davies, P., "The Political and Social Aspects of G. K.'s Dramas in the Context of Expressionism," *Revue Frontenac Review*, 1 (1983): 61-87; Schueler, H. J., "The Symbolism of Paradise in G. K.'s *Von morgens bis mitternachts*," *Neophilologus*, 68, 1 (1984): 98-104; Tunstall, G. C., "Autobiography and Mythogenesis: The Case of G. K. And Nietzsches *Ecce Homo*," *German Life and Letters*, 37, 2 (1984): 105-11; Tyson, P., *The Reception of G. K.* (1984); Buffinga, J. O., "From 'Bockgesand' to 'Ziegenlied': The Transformation of a Myth in G. K.'s *Zweimal Amphiryon*," *German Studies Review*, 9, 3 (1986): 475-95; Williams, R. W., "Culture and Anarchy in K.'s *Von morgens bis mitternachts*," *Modern Language Review*, 83, 2 (1988): 364-74; Diethe, C., *Aspects of Distorted Sexual Attitudes in German Expressionist Drama: With Particular Reference to Wedekind, Kokoschka and K.* (1988); Welliver, E., "G. K.'s *Kolportage*: Commentary on Class in the Weimar Republic," *German Review*, 64, 2 (1989): 73-78

—FRIEDHELM RICKERT

G. K. is probably the greatest dramatic artist of our time writing in the German language. His arrangement of scenes, his dialogue, his skill in construction and development will be a pattern for many others, long after the idea-content of his plays has been exhausted. In almost two score dramas K. has acquired a technique that functions as effortlessly as effectively, and often derives the highest measure of the dramatic from a minor motive. This procedure is, dramatically, highly instructive. . . .

And yet, it is never mere technique that sets K.'s subjects in motion . . . ; undoubtedly, G. K. is born of the spirit—he is not only spirited but also spiritual. His words are always striking (so are his titles), sparks sputter at the poles where sentence and sentence meet in dialogue, yet it is not only words' wit that makes his plays dramatic, but the antithesis of character, the wittiness of situation. And who, after *The Burghers of Calais*, after *From Morn to Midnight*, after *The Sacrifice of a Woman* and *The Fire in the Opera House* would doubt that G. K. is a poet with vision? Only, this poet is never lyric, but always dramatic.

Victor Wittner, "G. K., Playwright," *Theatre Arts*, Oct. 1931, 813–14

K. is considered one of the chief exponents of Expressionism . . . the best known example of which, in his repertoire, is *From Morn to Midnight*, the story of man's futile attempt at realizing his ideals, compressed into the events of a single day. The drama depicts such typical scenes of modern life as a sport palace, a cabaret, a bank, all symbolizing various human activities. Most of the characters are nameless abstractions or types—a bank cashier, a lady, a stout gentleman, a mask. No attempt is made to have us know his characters; their features "are apprehended in the same vivid, perfunctory way that a man in a desperate hurry at a crowded railway station, looking for somebody or something, takes in the faces of other travellers."

K.'s language is factual, concise, at times even brutal, his style laconic, staccato, emphasizing with telegraphic brevity the haste and tempo of the action. As in all his plays, he evinces a deep understanding of theatrical contrasts, stage effects, and dramatic tension. Always an eager student of the scenic and staging techniques of modern stage designers—particularly the stylists and constructionists—he makes extensive use of such striking technical devices as the revolving stage, cyclorama, platforms, and masks.

Horst Frenz, "G. K.," *Poet Lore*, 52 (1946), 363–64

G. K.'s production, viewed as a whole, shows an astounding compass and variety: it ranges from romantic—occasionally even lyrical—plays to carefully contrived dialectical pieces; from the satirical to the ecstatic; from comedy and revue to tragedy. Its material is drawn from such diverse sources as Greek legend, the Platonic Dialogues, the events of history, the problems of the modern industrial world and K.'s own fertile imagination. In the form of his drama there is such variety as to suggest that a resourceful talent was for ever experimenting with new methods of expression, while the language, though it always retains its own distinctive note, catches the raciness of colloquial speech, argues and reasons with cool detachment or explodes in outbursts of emotion. Work follows upon work in a bewildering stream, and with a prolificness that can have few parallels; differing and often contradictory solutions are offered to the same problem, as the approach to it shifts. There appears to be no order, no underlying unity.

B. J. Kenworthy, *G. K.* (1957), p. 198

The kinship between Wedekind, Sternheim, and K. lies in their tendency to unmask "the essence" of social reality not by naturalistic imitation, which would still lull us in illusions, but by crass and shocking formulations. Their drama seeks to demonstrate in pure and, therefore, abstract and distorted conditions (in the experimental laboratory, as it were) the true nature of existential or social problems. . . . In his *Burghers of Calais*, probably his greatest work, K. demonstrates by two highly dramatic surprise effects the true nature of heroism as pacifism and self-sacrifice. In his *Alkibiades Saved* he demonstrates by a highly ironic tour de force the true nature of the intellect as both a wound and a heroic fraud. Here the trick, K.'s basic dramatic form, merges with the dramatic content and idea. . . .

Nietzsche saw the historical Socrates as the initiator of Greek decadence and the pioneer of the Christian "slave revolt"; K. sees in Socrates the fateful innovator who ends the age of naive self-assurance and ushers in a self-conscious, i.e., guilt-ridden, civilization. The mind replaces the muscles. Reflection drives out spontaneity. The cripple wins out over the athlete. But Socrates' revolutionary philosophy does not result from the cripple's resentment of the strong and healthy; it results from his compassion for them.

Walter H. Sokel, *The Writer in Extremis* (1959), pp. 108–9

This central idea, the "renewal of man" . . . links his work closely to the expressionist movement, from which it received its most vital impetus. It gives his writings the moral impulse which is the hallmark of literary Expressionism. But while with most of the other Expressionists the force of this impetus shattered form and reduced language to an inarticulate stammer, K. harnessed it to a rigid, almost classical form. These two principles—the driving force of expressionist zeal, on the one hand, and the rationally constructed, "cubist" form, on the other—actually merge in his plays. This antinomy is reflected in the very language of K.—in the juxtaposition of impassioned, rhetorical outpourings and terse, clipped dialogue. This unique language of K.'s, which he also uses in his narrative writings . . . , is an essential ingredient of his work; it is as far removed from colloquial speech as is verse (to which it finally rose). With its repetitions, its symmetries and climaxes, its precisely calculated dashes and exclamation marks, it has an intensely musical quality. However, it is not a

music of halftones and subtle shades but of glaring, white-hot passion and the violent clash of ideas. K. admits of no distinction between "feeling" and "thinking." For him both are one—merely different degrees of intensity.

H. F. Garten, "G. K.," in Alex Natan, ed., *German Men of Letters* (1963), Vol. II, p. 158

Twice Amphitryon is the first of his three so-called Greek dramas, the other two being *Pygmalion* and *Bellerophon*. In these plays, K. not only reverted to classical themes, but also to the traditional five-act structure and to the blank-verse form. Stylistically, the retreat of the Expressionist had ended in the safe haven of traditional forms, but K.'s message remains the same: the play, inspired by Molière and Kleist, is his final protest against militarism. . . .

In *Twice Amphitryon*, some of K.'s main themes are intertwined: first, his protest against war; second, the salvation of the world by a pure woman; and third, the promised birth of a child as the future redeemer. The curse of war destroys all that is good in man; it can only be overcome if love, as exemplified by Alkmene, rules the world. And a new world can only be created by individuals; therefore it must be started by a single man, the child.

Ernst Schürer, *G. K.* (1971), pp. 170–71

KALLAS, Aino

Finnish short-story writer, dramatist, and poet, b. 2 Aug. 1878, Viipuri; d. 9 Nov. 1956, Helsinki

K. was born into the culturally prominent Krohn family, known for contributions in the arts and sciences. After she married Oskar Kallas, an Estonian folklore scholar, she lived in Tartu, Estonia, until 1918, when that country became independent and her husband joined the diplomatic corps of the young nation. From 1922 to 1934 the couple lived in London. K.'s last years were spent in exile in Sweden and Finland.

K. found an inexhaustible source of literary motifs in the grim history and rich folklore of her new homeland, Estonia. In the two volumes of *Meren takaa* (1904–5; beyond the sea) and the short novel *Ants Raudjalg* (1907; Ants Raudjalg) she vents, in a vein of stark realism, her indignation at the vestiges of the centuries-old serfdom in Estonia under the ethnically German aristocracy and the new threat of Russian nationalism, which was hindering the ascending forces of national identity.

K.'s contact with the intellectually progressive Young Estonia circle and with the aesthetics of impressionism and of SYMBOLISM left its mark on the short stories in *Lähtevien laivojen kaupunki* (1913; the town of departing ships) and *Seitsemän* (1914; seven). Her focus shifted from Estonian social issues to problems of a more universal nature and to the individual psyche. Her full artistic mastery over subject and style, however, came in the 1920s. In *Barbara von Tisenhusen* (1923; *Barbara von Tisenhusen*, 1927), *Reigin pappi* (1926; *The Rector of Reigi*, 1927), and *Sudenmorsian*

(1926; *The Wolf's Bride*, 1930) K. delves, in a strange and archaic language, deep into the mysteries of human emotions. Outwardly faithful to historical facts and folk legends, all three tales recount the awesome power of love. An intriguing tension prevails between the seemingly calm and neutral narrative voice and the explosive and gruesome narrative content. While utilizing unusual linguistic idiom and depicting alien social customs, K. sings the praises of the irrational and celebrates the high mass of love.

K.'s dramatic works, mostly adaptations of earlier short stories, were written mainly in the 1930s, while all of her poetry was produced during periods of crisis and transition in the author's personal and artistic development. K.'s five volumes of diaries are also artistically meritorious and are of permanent documentary value as well.

K. belongs to the classics of Finnish literature. The best of her tales, the meticulously chiseled stories of the 1920s, testify to an unparalled craftsmanship and can stand comparison with those of any European short-story writer. Their setting in this obscure corner of Europe, their timeless themes, and their agelessly antique language guarantee a growing interest in their author.

FURTHER WORKS: *Lauluja ja ballaadeja* (1897); *Kuloa ja kevättä* (1899); *Kirsti* (1902); *Suljettu puutarha* (1915); *Tähdenlento* (1915); *Nuori Viro* (1918); *Musta raita* (1919); *Katinka Rabe* (1920); *Vieras veri* (1921); *Langatonta sähköä* (1928); *Novelleja* (1928); *Pyhän Joen kosto* (1930); *Marokon lumoissa* (1931); *Bathseba Saarenmaalla* (1932); *Mare ja hänen poikansa* (1935); *Talonpojan kunnia* (1936); *Sudenmorsian* (1937); *Valitut teokset* (3 vols., 1938); *Kuoleman joutsen* (1942); *Kuun silta* (1943); *Löytöretkillä Lontoossa* (1944); *Polttoroviolla* (1945); *Mallen tunnustukset* (1945); *Kanssavaeltajia ja ohikulkijoita* (1945); *Uusia kanssavaeltajia ja ohikulkijoita* (1946); *Kolmas saattue* (1947); *Seitsemän neitsyttä* (1948); *Virvatulia* (1949); *Rakkauden vangit* (1951); *Päiväkirja vuosilta 1897–1906* (1952); *Päiväkirja vuosilta 1907–1915* (1953); *Päiväkirja vuosilta 1916–1921* (1954); *Päiväkirja vuosilta 1922– 1926* (1955); *Päiväkirja vuosilta 1927–1931* (1956); *Vaeltava vieraskirja vuosilta 1946–1956* (1956); *Elämäntoveri* (1959); *A. K. kauneimmat runot* (1959). FURTHER WORKS IN ENGLISH: *The White Ship: Estonian Tales* (1924)

BIBLIOGRAPHY: Ahokas, J., *A History of Finnish Literature* (1973): 238–42

—VIRPI ZUCK

KAMBA LITERATURE

See Kenyan Literature

KAMBANELLIS, Iakovos

Greek dramatist and screenwriter, b. 12 Dec. 1922, Naxos

K. studied to be a draftsman in Athens. During 1943–45 he was a prisoner of the SS at Mauthausen concentration camp. He had never considered a career in playwriting until he saw productions of Karolos Koun's Art Theater during the winter of 1945–46.

Impressed by Koun's innovative staging of foreign and Greek drama, he began to write for the theater.

K. has been a major force in modern Greek drama since his first play was produced in 1950. Making his reputation with dramas that reflect a strong sense of Greek social reality much in the tradition of American realist drama of the 1930s through the 1950s (Elmer RICE, Arthur MILLER, and others), he has more recently fused the fragmentation of epic theater to produce a form of impressionistic celebration (*panayeri*) of Greek folk traditions and spirit. At the same time these works satirize contemporary social and political life.

Three of his early plays form a loose trilogy: *Choros pano sta stahna* (1950; dance on the wheat), *Evdomi mera tis dimiourgias* (1955; the seventh day of creation), and *E avli ton thavmation* (1957; the courtyard of miracles) all concern lower-middle-class/ working-class protagonists who end by committing suicide because they are unable to reconcile personal and social realities.

The best of the three, and perhaps K.'s greatest work, is *E avli ton thavmation*. Believing that Greeks express themselves through *groups* rather than as isolated individuals, K. depicts a working-class apartment-house courtyard of Athens during the 1950s. He presents eleven characters, each with his own "miracle" or dream that is expressed but ultimately shattered before the end of the play. In the end the courtyard itself will be torn down to make way for a modern apartment building. Stelios, a gambler and a cuckold, and extremely sensitive, finally commits suicide. The other characters will learn, with deep bitterness, to survive in the new Athens.

K.'s more recent play, *To megalo mas tsirko* (1973; our great circus), suggests a broader thematic and impressionistic approach to drama. Playing off the traditional Greek satirical review (*epitheorisis*), K. uses scenes, songs, and signs to display Greek history as a cycle of alternating tyranny and revolution, a cycle that moves toward idealism and then back again through betrayal and selfishness. The characters and situations are archetypal rather than realistic—hence both Greek and universal. Produced during the dictatorship of 1967–74, this play helped give rise to a group of new plays that were both entertainment and strong satire of the political reality.

K.'s talent lies in his rich demotic language, which captures the life and spirit of the Greek people. He is also able to create dramatic moments that reflect both group life and a vividness of character for each individual. His recent works tend toward impressionism but are not abstract. He rejects psychological development, seeing it as an Aristotelian plot mechanism, and instead favors thematic and chronological "jump cuts."

As a screenwriter, K. helped form the new Greek cinema of the 1950s by writing films such as *Stella* (1955; Stella), and *Drakos* (1956; fiend).

FURTHER WORKS: *E Ilikia tis nichtas* (1958); *O gorillas ka e ortansia* (1959); *Paramithi horis onama* (1959); *Yeitonia ton angelon* (1963); *Viva Aspasia* (1966); *Odissea yirise spiti* (1966); *Apoikia ton timorimenon* (1970); *Aspasia* (1971); *To kouki kai to revithi* (1974); *O echtrhros laos* (1975); *Prosopa yia violi kai orchestra* (1976); *Ta tessera podia tou trapeziou* (1978); *Paterino polemo* (1980)

BIBLIOGRAPHY: Karampetsos, E. D., "Tyranny and Myth in the Plays of Four Contemporary Greek Dramatists," *WLT*, 53 (1979): 210–14

—ANDREW HORTON

KAMPMANN, Christian

Danish novelist and short-story writer, b. 24 July 1939, Gentofte; d. 12 Sept. 1988, Loesø

After finishing secondary school K. passed his university exams, but he decided not to attend the university. He worked as a journalist in Jutland and in New York, where he also attended the Columbia Graduate School of Journalism.

K. is a representative of the so-called neorealistic school in Denmark, which carried on the tradition of the psychological novel of the 1930s. Making his debut with the short-story collection *Blandt venner* (1962; among friends) K. set out to analyze critically middle-class milieus and values. His novels and short stories show the characters to be prisoners of an environment that determines and limits everyday life. Sexual frustrations, dominant themes in K.'s books, are the result of these social conditions and conventions, which pervert man's desire for security and tenderness.

In his second collection of short stories, *Ly* (1965; shelter), K. revealed the hollowness and hypocrisy that lie beneath the surface of an apparently pleasant and unproblematic reality, and in the novel *Sammen* (1967; together) he continued the unmasking of the bourgeoisie.

While K. up to this point had striven for complete objectivity, he began to experiment with the narrative structure in *Nærved og næsten* (1969; near and nearly), which deals with man's loneliness and inability to establish meaningful relationships. This work, together with the novels *"Vi elsker mere"* (1970; "we love more") and *Nok til hele ugen* (1971; enough for the whole week), both of which accuse popular magazines of acting as social tranquilizers, and *En tid alene* (1972; a time alone), a scathing indictment of an uncaring and unfeeling society, can be read as preliminary studies to K.'s major accomplishment, a four-volume series about the greatness and fall of an upper-middle-class family. K. used a classical genre, the traditional family novel, but although the private sphere has a major role, the period background is given a most significant function and reflects the cold war of the 1950s, the prosperity of the 1960s, and the economic crisis of the 1970s. *Visse hensyn* (1973; certain considerations) describes the life of the Gregersen family during the years 1954 to 1957; political, social, and economic consciousness is lacking, and problems are never allowed to be acknowledged. *Faste forhold* (1974; firm relationships) shows the family fifteen years later, when a changing pattern of life emerges, and insecurity and restlessness become increasingly evident. In *Rene linjer* (1975; pure lines) the old life style has definitely broken down, but experiments with new ways of living create complications. In *Andre måder* (1975; other ways) the characters search for alternative life styles such as collective living, liberation from stifling sex roles, and, possibly, another economic system.

Although composed as novels, K.'s two latest books, *Fornemmelser* (1977; feelings) and *Videre trods alt* (1979; continue despite everything), are autobiographical in content. They constitute an attempt by K. to break through fiction in order to tell the truth about himself: his bisexual experiences and the bigotry of a society that places the homosexual in a subjugated position.

K.'s superb character delineations, his faithful rendering of place, and his vivid narrative style have gained him a prominent place among the contemporary realistic authors of Scandinavia.

FURTHER WORKS: *Al den snak om lykke* (1963); *Uden navn* (1969); *Pinde til en til en skønskrivers ligkiste* (1971)

—MARIANNE FORSSBLAD

KANAFĀNĪ, Ghassān

Palestinian novelist, short-story writer, and dramatist, b. 9 Apr. 1936, Acre, Palestine (now Israel); d. 8 July 1972, Beirut, Lebanon

During the 1948 Israeli-Arab war, when K. was twelve years old, his family filed their native city of Acre to Lebanon and thence to Syria, where they settled in a refugee camp near Damascus. After acquiring his secondary-school diploma in 1952, K. enrolled in the department of Arabic literature at the University of Damascus but was expelled for political activity three years later before completing his studies. From Damascus he moved to Kuwait, where he worked in journalism until his permanent relocation to Beirut in 1960. In Beirut K. wrote regularly for several major dailies and rapidly rose to editorial positions in a number of them. In 1969 he became spokesman for the Popular Front for the Liberation of Palestine and chief editor of its publication *al-Hadaf*. He retained both positions until his assassination in a car bomb planted by Israeli agents in Beirut in 1972. In 1975 K. was posthumously awarded the Lotus Prize for literature by the Conference of Afro-Asian Writers.

Although he died at the young age of thirty-six, K.'s relatively short adult life produced an extraordinarily prolific and diverse literary career. In addition to political commentaries, he wrote short stories, novels, plays, literary criticism, and historical expositions. He was also a painter of some standing. His literary fame, however, rests primarily on his fiction.

With a few exceptions, Palestinian concerns furnish the subject matter of K.'s fiction. His intense involvement in Palestinian national affairs gave him a unique vantage point from which he could closely observe the evolution of Palestinian political consciousness during a crucial phase of modern Palestinian history. K.'s short stories and novels preserve an imaginatively rendered record of that consciousness. But K. was no mere observer of the Palestinian scene. As a committed writer, he invariably sought to influence the course of the events he was describing in his fiction. His constant experimentation with narrative possibilities was largely motivated by the desire to make the formal means of fiction yield optimal political results. In response to this clear order of priorities, K.'s fiction grew progressively simpler in form and more direct and discursive in style. Of K.'s four novels, the first two reflect the supremacy of the literary imperative, while the last two reflect its subordination to a strict political agenda.

In theme and outlook K.'s first two novels, *Rijāl fi-al-shams* (1963; *Men in the Sun*, 1978) and *Mā tabaqqā lakum* (1966; *All That's Left to You*, 1990), bear the unmistakable marks of the period in which they were written. Since the Palestinian question was in deep limbo at the time, the outlook of both novels is quite bleak, though the second is far less so than the first. This correspondence between actual events and fiction is built into the plot of both novels. Thus, the three Palestinian refugees of *Rijāl fi-al-shams* perish in an empty water tank in the desert as they are being smuggled by a Palestinian driver into Kuwait in search of an alternative to life in the refugee camps. What makes this gloomy ending even more harrowing is the symbolism with which K. invests the characters. The three men, being of different ages, represent three generations of Palestinians; the driver represents a fourth. But since he is a castrate and no one is left in the novel to perpetuate the Palestinian species, the conclusion virtually spells the physical end of the Palestinian people.

This ending enacts a recurrent pattern in Palestinian fiction, only here it is more graphic and more brutally stark than anywhere else. The outline of this pattern is as follows. Movement in the opposite direction to Palestine invariably leads to death and loss of identity, while movement in the direction of Palestine, even when it ends in physical death or captivity, leads to a symbolic recovery of the self and a reassertion of individual and national will.

Movement in K.'s second novel, *Mā tabaqqā lakum* begins in one direction and ends in the other. The Palestinian protagonist inadvertently encounters an Israeli soldier on his flight route from Gaza to Jordan and is thus forced to eschew his original escape plan and turn to confront his enemy. And even though the novel ends with the two protagonists practically locking horns, for the Palestinian the very act of confronting the enemy constitutes a symbolic victory. This thematic development reflects the change in the general condition after the initiation of the Palestinian armed struggle against Israel a year before the publication of the novel.

In form and narrative technique both of these novels rank among the most complex and experimental in all of Arabic fiction. Under the acknowledged influence of William FAULKNER, K. skillfully uses the techniques of interior monologue, flashback, and fragmentation to depict the psychological effects of dislocation and uprootedness on his characters. The symbolic treatment imparts a universal dimension to the specific Palestinian content of both novels. Artistically, they mark the zenith of K.'s literary achievement.

In the wake of the War of 1967, K.'s fiction underwent a fundamental change. Questions of technical and stylistic virtuosity were no longer relevant; the political imperative of reaching and mobilizing the masses became paramount. Both *Umm Sa'd* (1969; the mother of Sa'd) and *'Ā'id ilā Haifā* (1969; returning to Haifa) reflect this change in K.'s approach to fiction writing. In both novels straightforward narrative and dialogue replace the fragmented narrative and interior monologue of the earlier novels. In place of the tightly structured symbolic plots, episodic structures that K. calls tableaux constitute the "plot" of *Umm Sa'd*. In this novel it is the illiterate working class woman Umm Sa'd who speaks, often in the Palestinian vernacular, while the learned narrator-writer records "verbatim" her artless accounts.

From the posthumously published fragments of the three novels he was working on at the time of his assassination, it appears that K. continued to be preoccupied with the relationship of fiction to history. In one of these fragments he adopts the means and format of scholarly research by appending footnotes to the events of the fictional plot. Anticipating the rise of women in the Palestinian struggle for national liberation, K. entrusts the lead role in this novel to a woman who acts as his own female counterfoil. In this and other fundamental respects, K.'s pioneering contributions to Palestinian literature have remained unsurpassed.

FURTHER WORKS: *Mawt Sarīr Raqm* 12 (1961); *Ard al-burtuqāl al-hazīn* (1963); *al-Bāb* (1964); *'Ālam laysa lanā* (1965); *Adab al-muqāwamah fī filastīn al-muhtalla 1948–1966* (1966); *Fī al-Adab al-sahyūnī* (1967); *al-Adab al-filastīnī al-muqāwim tahta al-ihtilāl: 1948–1968* (1968); *'An al-rijāl wa-al-banādiq* (1968); *al-'Āshiq*

(1972); *al-A'mā wa-al-atrash* (1972); *Barqūq Naysān* (1972); *al-Qubba'ah wa-al-nabī* (1973); *Thawrat 1936–39 fī filastīn* (1974); *Jisr ilā al-abad* (1978); *al-Qamīs al-masrūq wa-qisas ukhrā* (1982)

BIBLIOGRAPHY: Kanafani, A., *G. K.* (1973); Wild, S., *G. K.: The Life of a Palestinian* (1975); Kilpatrick, H., "Tradition and Innovation in the Fiction of G. K.," *JArabL*, 7 (1976): 53–64; Kilpatrick, H., Introduction to *Men in the Sun* (1978): 1–7; Magrath, D. R., "A Study of *Rijāl fil-shams* by G. K.," *JArabL*, 10 (1979): 95–108; Allen, R., *The Arabic Novel* (1982): 108–19; Siddiq, M., *Man Is a Cause: Political Consciousness and the Fiction of G. K.* (1984); Allen, R., ed., *Modern Arabic Literature* (1987): 176–80

—MUHAMMAD SIDDIQ

KANNADA LITERATURE
See Indian Literature

KANT, Hermann

German novelist and short-story writer, b. 14 June 1926, Hamburg

Shortly before the end of World War II, K. completed an electrician's apprenticeship and entered the army. From 1945 to 1949 he was a prisoner of war in Poland, where he became politically active in an antifascist group in a Warsaw labor camp. When he returned to Germany, he entered an experimental preparatory institute for students from working-class and farm families at the Ernst Moritz Arndt University in Greifswald, East Germany. He studied Germanic philology at the Humboldt University in East Berlin from 1952 to 1956, after which he worked as a journalist and newspaper editor until 1962. Since then he has committed himself entirely to his literary career. In 1969 he became a member of the Academy of Arts of the German Democratic Republic, and in 1978 he took the highly controversial office of president of the East German Writers' Union, where he remained until 1989. Since the demise of the German Democratic Republic, K. has found it difficult to become part of the post-reunification literary establishment because of his history as a politically active literary functionary under the East German regime. Among the awards that he has received for his writing are the Heinrich Heine Prize (1963), the Erich Weinert Medal (1966), the Heinrich Mann Prize (1967), and the National Prize of the German Democratic Republic (1973 and 1983).

In K.'s narrative prose, a focus on personal involvement in reality is combined with pointed, sometimes humorous or satirical, sometimes evenly objective but constructive social, cultural, and political criticism. Among the themes and problems that are central to his works are the establishment and justification of individual identity through coming to grips with the past, analysis of specific experiences, such as those of a prisoner of war, as a basis for perceptions of the world, and the contradictions, dilemmas, conflicts, and challenges that are visible on a private level in the process of building a new and different society. The general tone of his writing is optimistic, although in some instances the optimism seems forced and fails to convince the reader. Particularly visible elements of his best work include freshness and vitality of character portrayal, effective development of situational humor, the successful combination of didactic intent and readability, compelling presentation of human interaction, and penetrating interpretation of life in the German Democratic Republic during the reconstruction period.

In his first collection of stories, *Ein bißchen Südsee* (1962; a little South Pacific), with its autobiographical focus on themes such as childhood, first love, war, and confinement, K. presented flashes of the humor and witty satire that became attractive features of his more mature works. Later anthologies, however, including *Eine Übertretung* (1975; a transgression), *Der dritte Nagel* (1982; the third nail), and *Bronzezeit* (1986; Bronze Age), are not uniform in quality or literary effectiveness. In addition to subtle, realistic tales that are both compelling and entertaining, they also contain pieces in which satire and pointed irony lose much of their force because of the author's very visible unwillingness to risk transcending the limits imposed upon him by East German cultural politics. Social and political criticism are promoted and then immediately negated; attention is shifted from significant problems to trivial bureaucratic matters; attempts to reveal truth are reduced to apologies for existing conditions.

K.'s first novel, *Die Aula* (1964; the auditorium), is based in part on his personal experiences at the institute in Greifswald. It has become a classic of East German literature and remains his most important creation. Within the programed cultural context of the time, *Die Aula* is especially remarkable for its fresh, captivating style. A variety of literary devices, including internal monologues, flashbacks, humorous understatement, and reflective analysis are successfully employed in a presentation that examines complex problems of the reconstruction era on multiple narrative levels. An ironic skepticism colors the novel's refusal to justify the failings of the new society, while honest criticism and vibrant, believable characters become effective vehicles for conveying the spirit of the times.

In his subsequent novels, K. failed to maintain the vitality and spontaneity of presentation that set *Die Aula* apart from much of East German reconstruction literature. *Das Impressum* (1972; the journal), with its treatment of the relationship between individual self-realization and political necessity, also gives interesting insights into East German society, but it is more programmatic than the earlier novel, lacks authentic human conflicts, and comes across as a slightly inferior structural and stylistic imitation of *Die Aula*. Although *Der Aufenthalt* (1977; the stay), an autobiographically motivated reflection on the prisoner-of-war experience, did not have the public impact of *Die Aula*, it is a significant document of the subjective current in late-20th-c. German literature that has emphasized grappling with and overcoming the past.

Kormoran (1994; Kormoran), a work that returns to some of the narrative devices that made *Die Aula* successful, but which lacks the vitality of the early book, reflects the author's continuing struggle to come to grips with the past. Although *Kormoran* is somewhat successful in its portrayal of the psychological problems associated with growing old, its more powerful—and perhaps unintended—message is that both the dying title figure and the era and society that he represents have ceased to have measurable impact on the world. And perhaps that is a statement about the author as well.

While K. has not consistently produced narratives of high literary quality, his best writings are certainly among the most significant creations that appeared in the German Democratic Republic during the forty years of its existence. For that reason, he was able to exert a powerful—often sinister—influence upon

cultural policy as it pertained to literature and upon the concrete efforts of other writers. Within that context he is a very important—though politically highly controversial—representative of what was the East German literary establishment.

FURTHER WORKS: *In Stockholm* (1971); *Anrede der Ärztin O. an den Staatsanwalt F. gelegentlich einer Untersuchung* (1978); *Zu den Unterlagen* (1981); *Unterlagen zu Literatur und Politik* (1982); *Schöne Elise* (1983); *Krönungstag* (1986); *Die Summe* (1987); *Abspan: Erinnerungen* (1991); *Escape: Ein Word-Spiel* (1995)

BIBLIOGRAPHY: Herd, E. W., "Narrative Technique in Two Novels by H. K.," in Siefken, H., and Robinson, A., eds., *Erfahrung und Überlieferung* (1974): 185–96; Gerber, M., "Confrontations with Reality in H. K.'s *Die Aula,*" *Monatshefte*, 67 (1975): 173–84; Langenbruch, T., *Dialectical Humor in H. K.'s Novel "Die Aula"* (1975); Holmes, J. E., "An Interview with H. K.," *StTCL*, 4, 1 (Fall 1979): 89–102; Langenbruch, T., "H. K.'s *Die Aula*: Literary References in a Contemporary East German Novel," in Nelson, C., ed., *Studies in Language and Literature* (1976): 325–30; Krenzlin, L., *H. K.* (1980); Ertl, W., "A Poetry Lesson in K.'s *Die Aula*: Notes on the Theme of Socialist Education in the GDR," *Schatzkammer*, 8 (1982): 23–30; Krenzlin, L., "Erzählstruktur und Leserreaktion. H. K.'s Roman *Die Aula* in der zeitgenössischen Rezeption," *WB* (1986): 912–36; Corino, K., ed., *Die Akte K.* (1995)

—LOWELL A. BANGERTER

KAO Hsiao-sheng

(also romanized as Gao Xiaosheng) Chinese short-story writer and essayist, b. 6 July 1928, Tungshu Village, Wu-chin County, Kiangsu

K. was born in a peasant village where many of his fellow villagers were near or distant relatives. His father held the distinction of local intellectual since he had attended a modern-style university established in Shanghai near the end of the last dynasty of imperial China. Despite a young life of field labor, poverty, and only irregular schooling, K. too managed to get into a university in Shanghai, where he was studying economics just before the Communist Party assumed power. The change in government allowed him to abandon these studies and engage in the literary career he had always desired. In 1957, however, he was labeled a rightist for having written a proposal for an independent journal. This forced his return to the harsh peasant life of his village for the next twenty-one years. After the political changes following Mao Tse-tung's death, K. began to write again. He was politically "rehabilitated" along with many other intellectuals in 1979 and allowed to move to the city of Ch'ang-chou, where he resumed his life as a professional writer of fiction.

K. is best known for his "peasant fiction" from the post-Mao period. Since the early 1940s, in accordance with the official political line and requirements of SOCIALIST REALISM, Chinese authors had dutifully portrayed a heroic peasant type who was naturally patriotic and progressive in socialist terms. In "Li Shun-ta tsao-wu" (1979; "Li Shunda Builds a House," 1983) and his series of stories about Ch'en Huan-sheng, K. expressly challenges this mythic figure by replacing it with a peasant who is uneducated, generally unreflective, preoccupied with the need for food and shelter, and conditioned to an attitude of awe toward authority. The stories are a complex mix of humor and satire as the author simultaneously sympathizes with the plight of the peasants and regards with profound concern the political implications of their ignorance and passivity. The object of K.'s satire, however, is not the particularly simpleminded and humble peasant who serves as his protagonist. Li Shun-ta and Ch'en Huan-sheng are both surrounded by a far more reprehensible crowd of greedy, manipulative cadres, friends, and even family, as well as an occasional cynical and powerless intellectual. Higher levels of authority in the stories, like the county party secretary, still retain a glow of socialist purity (necessary undoubtedly because of possible symbolic connection to more powerful figures in the real Chinese political structure). Yet even these characters are depicted as, if nothing else, willing to require sacrifice of their peasant brothers for the sake of that aura of purity.

While the thematic concerns of K.'s peasant fiction secured his most immediate significance in the post-Mao literary scene of China, his other writings may ultimately insure his longer reputation. Among these are a group of stories that critics refer to as K.'s "philosophical tales" or "parables." These are short pieces developed around an extraordinary event and thus reminiscent of the traditional Chinese *chih-jen chih-kuai* (records of men and anomalies). Like the traditional writings, K.'s accounts of odd, even grotesque occurrences offer the reader an exaggerated portrait of more "ordinary" human characteristics or behavior. The complex nature and effects of paranoia, greed, dishonesty, and moral evasiveness serve as focus in such pieces as "Shan-chung" (1981; on the mountain), "Ch'ien-pao" (1980; "The Briefcase," 1980), "Yu tiao" (1980; "Fishing," 1987), or "Sheng-tzu" (1982; the rope). Thematic ties to current political issues in China remain evident if not always immediately obvious in these stories. For instance, one can easily read the excessive timidity and paranoia presented in "Shan-chung" as describing a historically specific habit of mind made prevalent in China by several decades of constant political and physical struggles in the name of socialism. The spareness of historical detail in the story, however, both obscures this level of political satire and enhances interpretive richness. Not only does the traditional form of K.'s philosophical tales encourage reading them as broader cultural explorations, they also stand as more universal reflections on human nature.

Since the mid-1980s, K. has ventured with different degrees of success into new materials. Along with many other middle-aged writers, he has written some "reform literature," basically optimistic stories concerning the effects of recent economic reforms. Several of these have a rather prescriptive tone, recommending less conservative and more scientific methods in such sideline agricultural production as honey or fish. At the same time, K. has written a few works that might loosely be categorized as his "love stories" "Tieh-chiao yin-yüan" (1984; falling into a marriage), "Ts'untzu li te feng-ch'ing" (1990; amorous feelings in a village), and his first novel, *Ch'ing t'ien tzai shang* (1991; blue skies above). The love element of these stories, like K.'s peasants, is not heroic or glorious and, while subjected to scrutiny, not entirely the subject of the pieces. Rather the concern of the texts is the excessive interference at this personal level caused by social attitudes and abuse of power. *Ch'ing t'ien tzai shang* is more complicated, as it is an autobiographical novel about K.'s own first wife, who accompanied him in his exile to the countryside and died there of tuberculosis exacerbated by malnutrition and inadequate medical care. The author's deeply painful experience of loss and grief colors the narrative,

which dwells on the beauty and gentle goodness of the young woman. Nonetheless, the relationship described retains an understated and ordinary dimension, as the novel reveals the devastating effect that the often absurd implementation of the rural policies of the Great Leap Forward had on this insignificant couple.

The satiric tone of K.'s writings, particularly in his depiction of peasants, has caused many critics to compare him to LU HSÜN, a writer generally acclaimed as the father and best author of modern Chinese short stories. Narrative styles differ greatly, though, as K. prefers the voice of an apparently uninhibited storyteller, while Lu Hsün's narrator tends to be tersely omniscient or a self-conscious intellectual, frequently tormented by a sense of moral failure. K.'s storyteller, by contrast, is more openly entertaining. He delights in word play and never hesitates to comment on the characters or events of the story, sometimes in straightforward fashion, sometimes tongue in cheek. A detail of this story may take the narrator off on a tangent, offering, for instance, a diatribe on the Chinese preoccupation with sex or comic reflections on time and space. While this storyteller cast of K.'s style is a strength and major source of the appeal of his works, it arguably neglects the larger elements of narrative structure. The language is delightful but may seem arbitrary, superficially witty, and employed at the expense of the organization and significance of the story. The very pleasure of the text disguises the fundamental intellectual honesty and seriousness of purpose that underlie K.'s works.

FURTHER WORKS: *Chieh yüeh* (1955); *Kao Hsiao-sheng 1979 nien hsiao-shuo chi* (1980); *Kao Hsiao-sheng 1980 nien hsiao-shuo chi* (1981); *Kao Hsiao-sheng hsiao-shuo hsüan* (1983); *Kao Hsiao-sheng 1982 nien hsiao-shuo chi* (1983); *Kao Hsiao-sheng 1983 nien hsiao-shuo chi* (1984); *Sheng-huo, ssuk'ao, ch'uang-tzo* (1986); *Sheng-huo te chiao-liu* (1987). FURTHER WORKS IN ENGLISH: *The Broken Betrothal and Other Stories* (1987)

BIBLIOGRAPHY: Lee, L. O., "The Politics of Technique: Perspectives of Literary Dissidence in Contemporary Chinese Fiction," in Kinkley, J. C., ed., *After Mao: Chinese Literature and Society, 1978–1981* (1985): 159–90; Feuerwerker, Y. M., "An Interview with G. [K.]," *MCL*, 3: 1–2 (1987): 113–35; Wagner, R. G., "Documents Concerning *Tanqiuzhe* [the explorer], an Independent Literary Journal Planned during the Hundred Flowers Period," *MCL*, 3: 1–2 (1987): 137–46; Ye, Z. C., "The String That Will Never Break—Introducing the Writer G. [K.]," *The Broken Betrothal, and Other Stories* (1987): 212–18

—MARGARET H. DECKER

KARAKALPAK LITERATURE
See Uzbek Literature

KARANTH, Kota Shivaram

Indian novelist, dramatist, and essayist (writing in Kannada), b. 1 Oct. 1902, Kota, Karnataka

From his birthplace in a village in the South Canara district in southern India, K. took his first name. Although he has traveled widely, he writes mainly of the rural folk of his native region. Existence is harsh in this rainy land, and K. evokes the life of these simple but rugged people as they pit themselves against a hostile nature to eke out a living. His novel *Bettada jiva* (1947; mountain people) is an excellent example of such a portrait. In his most famous novel, *Marali mannige* (1940; *Back to the Soil* 1950; repub. as *The Whispering Earth*, 1974), K. minutely analyzes the complex relationships of three generations of a rural family and the clash between modern ideas and traditional values.

Chomana dudi (1949; *Choma's Drum*, 1978), which typifies K.'s keen social observation, depicts the struggles and sorrows of an untouchable who tries to free himself from bonded labor and become a farmer. In the novel *Kudiyara kusu* (1951; *The Headman of the Little Hill*, 1979) K. draws on his knowledge of ethnography to portray the Kudibi, a tribal hill people. A more recent novel, *Mukajjiya kanasugalu* (1968; *Mookajji's Visions*, 1979), for which he received India's highest literary award, the Seat of Learning Prize, deals with a woman who, having been widowed at the age of eight, has to live celibate until her death at eighty-five.

K. has written several plays, works of social protest against injustices to the poor and downtrodden. They are reminiscent of the dramas of John GALSWORTHY in their compassionate sociological analysis.

K. also wrote the first Kannada encyclopedia for children and the first Kannada dictionary. He is currently promoting the folk-oriented rural Kannada dance-drama called Yakshagana, directing and touring with groups throughout India and overseas. He has written a study of this folk theater, *Yakshagana bayalata* (1957; *Yaksagana*, 1975).

FURTHER WORKS: *Karnarjuna* (1929); *Hasivu* (1931); *Bharatiya chitrakale* (1930); *Bauddha yatre* (1933); *Chitramaya dakshina kannada* (1934); *Bala prapancha* (1937); *Hegadarenu* (1937); *Sarasammana samadhi* (1937); *Sirigannada arthakosha* (1940); *Cikka doddavaru* (1941); *Halliya hattu samastaru* (1944); *Balveya belaku* (1945); *Gita natakagalu* (1946); *Navina natakagalu* (1946); *Audaryada urulalli* (1947); *Gajaraja* (1947); *Jnana* (1947); *Aidu natakagalu* (1948); *Dehajyotagalu mattu praniprabandhuagalu* (1948); *Mangana maduve* (1948); *Moga padeda mana* (1948); *Sanyasiya baduku* (1948); *Karulina kare* (1949); *Prajaprabhutvannu kuritu* (1949); *Abuvinda baramakke* (1950); *Kaleya darshana* (1950); *Bittida bele* (1951); *Cigurida kanasu* (1951); *Devadutaru* (1952); *Jaruva dariyalli* (1952); *Panjeyavara nenapigagi* (1952); *Apurva pashcima* (1953); *Battada tore* (1953); *Samikshe* (1956); *Vijnana prapancha* (1959); *Jagadoddhara . . . na* (1960); *Maigallana dinacariyinda* (1960); *Ala nirala* (1962); *Huccumanassina hattu mukhagalu* (1965); *Janapada gitegalu* (1966); *Mailikallinodane matukategalu* (1966); *Onti dani* (1966); *Svapnada hole* (1966); *Oda huttidavaru* (1967); *Innonde dari* (1968); *Vicar sahitya nirmana* (1968); *Alida mele* (1969); *Calukya vastu, shilpa* (1969); *Karanta prapancha* (1969); *Mugida yuddha* (1969); *Shanishvarana neralalli* (1969); *Mai mangala sulyalli* (1970); *Ukkide nore* (1970); *Hiriya kiriya hakkigalu* (1971); *Karnatakadalli chitrakale* (1971); *Kevala manushyaru* (1971); *Nambidavara naka, naraka* (1971); *Bidi barahagalu* (1972); *Dharmarayana samsara* (1972); *Hettala tayi* (1973); *Patalakke payana* (1973); *Gondaranya* (1974); *Kanyabali* (1974); *Mujanma* (1974); *Celuvina kannada nadu* (1975); *Ileyemba* (1975); *Karnatakadalli nrtyakala* (1975); *Karnatakadalli shilpa* (1975); *Manodehiyada manava* (1975); *Muktadvara* (1975); *Ade urur, ade mar* (1977)

BIBLIOGRAPHY: Sitaramiah, V., "K. S. K.," *IndL*, 3, 3 (1960): 107–11; Moorthy Rao, A. N., "S. K.'s *Marali mannige,*" *IndL*, 5, 2 (1962): 28–30; Mugali, R. S., *A History of Kannada Literature* (1975): 122–24; Aithal, S. K., "S. K.'s *Ade urur, ade mar,*" *IndL*, 22, 4 (1979): 12–20; Sitaramiah, V., "S. K.: A Multi-faceted Personality," *I&FR*, 16, 4 (1979): 19–20

—K. BHASKARA RAO

KARAOSMANOĞLU, Yakup Kadri

Turkish novelist, short-story writer, essayist, and translator, b. 27 March 1889, Cairo, Egypt; d. 13 Dec. 1974, Ankara

Moving to Istanbul in 1908, K. attended law school at the University of Istanbul. For two years he taught philosophy and literature.

K. joined the nationalist forces in the Turkish war of independence (1919–22), and when the Turkish Republic was inaugurated (1923), he became a member of the Turkish legislature. In the early 1930s, he belonged to the Kadro group, which advocated Marxist ideas in an influential periodical of the same name. From 1934 to 1954 he served as Turkey's ambassador to Albania, Czechoslovakia, the Netherlands, Iran, and Switzerland. From 1961 to 1965, he returned to the Turkish legislature.

Although his fame rests on his novels, K.'s literary career has embraced many other genres—essays, plays, short stories, memoirs, monographs, and prose poems. With the publication of his first book, *Bir serercam* (1913; a happening), a collection of short stories, K. emerged as a masterful stylist and a passionate nonconformist. *Rahmet* (1923; mercy), his second collection of short stories, marks the beginning of his commitment to the literature of social engagement.

Erenlerin bağından (1922; from the garden of the sages) is a cycle of twelve prose poems expressing the joys and agonies of the mystic spirit. This manual for a blessed life ranks as one of the best achievements in the genre in Turkish.

In 1922 K. published the outstanding novels *Kiralık konak* (mansion for rent) and *Nur Baba* (Father Light). *Kiralık konak* tells the tale of the downfall of the imperial Ottoman society as exemplified by the disintegration of one aristocratic family. *Nur Baba* exposes the sybaritic life among the followers of an antiorthodox Islamic sect; spiritual communion with God and brotherly love—once the highest principles of Islamic mysticism—have been reduced in this sect to mere physical love.

Hüküm gecesi (1927; night of the verdict) is a scathing *roman à clef* about the Young Turks and the convulsive politics of the twilight years of the Ottoman Empire. It is a compelling study of ambition and avarice, a tour de force of political fiction. *Sodom ve Gomore* (1928; Sodom and Gomorrah) is a panoramic and poignant study of Istanbul under occupation after World War I. K. painted a powerful picture of the intellectual and spiritual crisis of the East confronted with the West.

K.'s best-known novel is the prize-winning *Yaban* (1932; stranger), which is set in central Anatolia at the time of the war of independence. It is a study of the emergence of the new Anatolian man, torn between nationalism and religion, between the claims of east and west, oppressed by poverty, yet imbued with hope. This novel, which depicts Turkey as an unmerciful wasteland, was the first to expose the wretched conditions of the peasant villagers in republican Turkey. Dominated by the superstitious, fanatically reactionary sheiks and imams, who exploit the ignorance of the people, the peasants, K. believed, had been abandoned by the urban intellectuals, who had turned a cold shoulder to their misery.

K.'s last major novel was *Panorama* (2 vols., 1953–54; panorama), a wide-ranging canvas of Turkish society. K. demonstrated in *Panorama* that the Turkish revolution of the 1920s, like other national revolutions, deteriorated and fell prey to reactionary forces.

Few novelists in the 20th c. have portrayed the Turkish upheavals with the craftsmanship and psychological insight that characterize the novelistic art of K.

FURTHER WORKS: *Ergenekon* (1929); *Ankara* (1934); *Bir sürgün* (1937); *Okun ucundan* (1940); *Alp dağlarından ve miss chalfrin'in albümünden* (1942); *Atatürk* (1946); *Millî savaş hikâveleri* (1947); *Atatürk'ün gerçek siması* (1955); *Zoraki diplomat* (1955); *Hep o sarkı* (1956); *Anamın kitabı* (1957); *Vatan yolunda* (1958); *Politikada 45 yıl* (1968); *Gençlik ve edebiyat hatıraları* (1969)

—TALAT SAIT HALMAN

KARELIAN LITERATURE
See Finno-Ugric Literatures of the Soviet Union

KARINTHY, Frigyes

Hungarian humorist, novelist, dramatist, and poet, b. 24 June 1887, Budapest; d. 29 Aug. 1938, Siófok

The liberal atmosphere of K.'s childhood home, as well as his mother's early death and his experiences as a schoolboy, had a profound effect on his creative life. The young K. was a medical student for a short time, but then he switched to journalism, contributing short, humorous pieces and skits to a number of Budapest newspapers before World War I. He married an actress who fell victim to the influenza epidemic of 1918. His stormy second marriage to Aranka Bőhm is well documented in recent Hungarian literary memoirs. K. had a son from each of his two marriages: Gábor (1914–1974), a reclusive poet, and Ferenc (b. 1921), a well-known contemporary Hungarian writer.

K. was Hungary's first truly urban, cosmopolitan writer. Although his life and work were closely associated with his native Budapest, he, unlike most of his contemporaries, was never attracted to specifically Hungarian issues and problems. His themes were universal, and he approached them with the enlightened rationalism of an 18th-c. *philosophe*. He was also a satirist in the Swiftian manner, and his writings reveal a 19th-c. humanist's faith in—and a 20th-c. man's fear of—modern science.

K. achieved his first major success with a series of literary parodies, *Így írtok ti* (1912; that's how *you* write). In these delightful and trenchant caricatures K. satirized the pet themes and characteristic mannerisms of the popular and influential writers—both Hungarian and foreign—of his time. But K. had always been more than just a humorist; his humor, with its speculative undercurrents, went beyond the conventions of his day and often veered toward the grotesque and the tragic.

K.'s stories and sketches contain a curious mixture of adolescent optimism and jeering pessimism. His evocation, in some of his darkest tales, of a dislocated, nightmarish world is strongly reminiscent of KAFKA—although there is no evidence that he was directly influenced by Kafka. His world view was, however, affected by FREUD's psychoanalytic theories and by August STRINDBERG's paradoxical views on male-female relationships. K. also combined his interest in science fiction (one of his early loves was Jules Verne) with his predilection for satire. His *Utazás Faremidóba* (1916; *Voyage to Faremido*, 1965) and *Capillária* (1921; *Capillaria*, 1965) are modern-day sequels to *Gulliver's Travels*. In both novels he depicts a world in which flesh and spirit, instinct and rationality, are hopelessly disjoined.

One of K.'s most popular works, the semi-autobiographical *Tanár úr kérem* (1916; *Please Sir!*, 1968) presents a gallery of portraits of boys growing up in a very Victorian turn-of-the-century Budapest. Their timidity and repressed grandiosity are revealed in a series of bittersweet sketches that deal with such things as the rigors of school life, the dreadful prospect of failure, and the mystery of awakening sex. His celebrated *Utazás a koponyám körül* (1937; *A Journey round My Skull*, 1939) is also autobiographical; it is an engrossing account of the author's struggle with a developing brain tumor, and of his journey to Stockholm, where he was operated on by a famous Swedish surgeon. In his serious prose as well as in his contemplative dramas and roughhewn, expressionistic poetry, K. often returned to the same themes he treated lightly in his humorous pieces and comic one-acters. As a journalist he was also keenly aware of the absurdities of public and private life.

Some critics feel that K.'s undisciplined life style, as well as the grimly exploitative world in which he lived, prevented him from realizing his creative potential. The author himself often expressed these sentiments. Actually, K.'s intellectual brilliance came mostly in flashes; his wit and satire, in some of the longer works, tends to become repetitive and mechanical. His masterpieces are to be found among the brief sketches and essays that he considered mere trivia.

FURTHER WORKS: *Kötéltánc* (1923); *Mennyei riport* (1937); *A lélek arca* (2 vols., 1957); *Hőköm szinház* (3 vols., 1957); *Számadás a tálentomról* (1957); *Az egész város beszéli* (4 vols., 1958); *Hátrálva a világ körül* (1964); *Naplóm, életem* (1964); *Miniatűrök* (1966); *Összegyűjtött művei* (1975 ff.). FURTHER WORKS IN ENGLISH: *Grave and Gay: Selections from His Work* (1973)

BIBLIOGRAPHY: Vajda, M., "F. K.: Humorist and Thinker," *NHQ*, 2 (1961): 84–99; Reményi, J., *Hungarian Writers and Literature* (1964): 298–305; Tabori, P., Introduction to F. K., *Voyage to Faremido; Capillaria* (1965): vii–xxi; Szalay, K., "F. K.," in *F. K., Grave and Gay: Selections from His Work* (1973): 239–46

—IVAN SANDERS

KARVAŠ, Peter

Czechoslovak dramatist, novelist, and short-story writer (writing in Slovak), b. 25 April 1922, Banská Bystrica

K. completed high school in Slovakia and studied at the universities of Prague and Bratislava. During World War II he worked in radio and took part in the uprising against the Germans of 1944. After 1945 he was dramaturge of the National Theater in Bratislava, cultural attaché in Bucharest, Romania (1949–50), staff member of the Ministry of Culture, and editor of the journal *Kultúrny život*, among other positions. An active member of the Communist Party of Slovakia and of its Central Committee, he received important awards from the state. After the invasion of Czechoslovakia by Warsaw Pact armies in 1968, K. lost his membership in the Communist Party for favoring liberalization and opposing the invasion.

K. is a very prolific writer, and his talent has found expression in short stories, plays, satires, and novels, all written with a keen sentivity for tragic as well as comic social situations and containing rational analyses of people and historical events.

Although K. was acclaimed for some of his EXISTENTIALIST short stories, he established himself as principally an imaginative and influential playwright. The highly praised drama *Meteor* (1945; meteor) analyzed the state of mind of people on the threshold of World War II. Some of K.'s plays have been performed in other European countries, four of them in East Germany, where they are valued for their modern technique, humor, and sober social criticism and concern. He has brought Slovak satire to a high level.

In the 1950s, when SOCIALIST REALISM became the official literary dogma, K. wrote a number of works characterized by staunch loyalty to the prevailing political postulates. In all his works K. dealt with social problems, the horrors and barbarities of war, and the revolt against oppression. He ridiculed human frailties, especially those weaknesses seen in the enemies of progress, lampooning them from a Marxist point of view. His successful, politically motivated collection of stories *S nami a proti nám* (1950; with us and against us), depicts the anti-German uprising in Slovakia with all its horrors, inhumanity, and sacrifices; German soldiers, Slovak and Soviet partisans, village people, heroes and traitors are portrayed in a variety of tragic and tragicomic situations.

His attempts at writing novels were less successful. Of a planned trilogy, in which K. intended to describe the social and political life in Slovakia from 1918 to 1945, with its social and ideological clashes, he completed only the first two volumes: *Toto pokolenie* (1949; this generation) and *Toto pokolenie v útoku* (1952; this generation on attack)

In 1963 K. was among those Slovak literati who exhorted writers to be mindful of their duty to be the "conscience of the nation," and bitterly criticized the period of the cult of personality. He was silenced by the government but was recently "forgiven" his "deviations." Although he is now allowed to work, he has not published anything in the last few years. Nevertheless, he continues to influence younger writers in his yearning for a more humane and just society.

FURTHER WORKS: *Most* (1946); *Niet prístavu* (1946); *Spolok piatich P* (1946); *Hannibal pred bránami* (1946); *Polohlasom* (1947); *Bašta* (1948); *L'udia z našej ulice* (1951); *Čert nespí* (1954); *Srdce plné radosti* (1954); *Diet'a a meč* (1954); *Čertovo kopýtko* (1957); *Zločin Dariny Piovňovej* (1958); *Diplomati* (1958); *Zmŕtvychstanie deduška Kolomana* (1960); *Polnočná omša* (1960); *Antigona a tí druhí* (1962); *Jazva* (1963)

BIBLIOGRAPHY: Noge, J., *An Outline of Slovakian Literature* (1968): 100-01; Richter, L., *Slowakische Literatur* (1979): 177, 192

—JOSEPH M. KIRSCHBAUM

KARYOTAKIS, Kostas

Greek poet, b. 30 Oct. 1896, Tripolis; d. 21 July 1928, Preveza

The greater part of K.'s youth was spent in Hania, Crete, although his father's profession of civil engineer kept the family on the move. After graduating from the law school at the University of Athens in 1917, K. registered at the School of Philology to escape military service, only to be inducted in 1919, the year he was admitted to the bar; he was discharged in 1920. The remainder of K.'s short life was spent in public service. For three years he was a member of the parliament, successively representing a number of different cities. Transferred to the Ministry of Welfare, he traveled extensively, visiting Italy, Germany, Romania, and France. Ultimately, he was assigned to a disappointing post in Patras. Depressed and tired with his life, K. committed suicide at the age of thirty-two.

K. published only three collections of poetry during his lifetime, *O ponos tou anthropou ke ton praghmaton* (1919; the pain of men and things), *Nepenthe* (1921; nepenthe [the name of a pain killer]), and *Eleghia ke satires* (1927; elegies and satires). A few of his early poems and essays were published posthumously. A melancholy young man who considered himself one of life's rejects and relied increasingly on medicine to maintain his health, K. wrote poems that expressed his own sense of disillusionment and futility. His first collection is clearly the effort of a young man; his second shows a growing sureness of hand as it begins to display his tendency to the morbid. The last, a mature expression of the dark themes that haunted his life, is permeated with the spirit of defeat and pessimism for which he became famous. It is in the bitter and mocking phrases of his last poem, "Preveza" (Preveza) that K.'s pessimism finds its strongest expression. In its imagery all is deathlike: Having by now decided to end his own life, he expresses indifference to death, mocking its pretensions.

K. was the most worthy representative in his own country of that French-influenced generation of the 1920s that manifested the anguish of the period between the wars. With language rich in irony and sarcasm, he unashamedly broaches the subject of his suicidal despair in a manner that, while conservative both in its meter and its rhyme, manages to suggest a mind whose occasional lapses into sentimentality could not overshadow its originality and strength.

FURTHER WORKS: *Apanta* (2 vols., 1965–1966)

BIBLIOGRAPHY: Myrsiades, K., "K. K.," *Charioteer*, 14 (1972): 20–25; Friar, K., Introduction to *Modern Greek Poetry* (1973): 44–46

—KOSTAS MYRSIADES

KASCHNITZ, Marie Luise

German poet, essayist, novelist, short-story writer, and radio dramatist, b. 31 Jan. 1901, Karlsruhe; d. 10 Oct. 1974, Rome, Italy

An officer's daughter from an aristocratic family, K. grew up in Potsdam and Berlin. After finishing school, she learned the book trade, whereupon she established herself as a book dealer in Rome.

During the 1930s and 1940s K. lived in a number of German cities where her husband, an archaeologist, held university posts. After World War II she returned to Rome. K. accompanied her husband on numerous trips around the Mediterranean, visiting historical sites that greatly influenced her work. By the end of her career she had received many literary prizes for her work and was one of the most respected writers in contemporary German literature.

Although K. published two novels in the 1930s, *Liebe beginnt* (1933; love begins) and *Elissa* (1937; Elissa), it was not until after 1945 that she began to write extensively. Shocked by the war and its effect on humanity, she expressed in poetic works such as *Totentanz, und Gedichte zur Zeit* (1947; dance of death, and poems of the times) and *Zukunftsmusik* (1950; music of the future) an anguish that is nevertheless tempered by hope and guarded optimism. Her combining of traditional and modern forms, along with her highly original diction, resulted in a distinctive style.

When her husband died in 1958, K.'s world collapsed. In the poetry collection *Dein Schweigen—meine Stimme* (1962; your silence—my voice) she reflects on life and death, living together and living alone, but in her sorrow and despair and her inability to grasp the meaning of existence, she eventually comes to terms with life and learns to deal with her loneliness.

Although K. excelled in poetry, she was a master of prose as well. One of her most interesting novels, *Das Haus der Kindheit* (1956; house of childhood), takes place in a kind of museum where the visitor is confronted with childhood memories through visual images of the past. At first, everything seems remote and unreal to the visitor. Not until the end does the meaning of the visit become clear. In *Wohin denn ich* (1963; whither then I) and *Tage, Tage, Jahre* (1968; days, days, years), written in diary form, K. is able to transform her personal experiences into something that transcends the merely autobiographical. This may also be said of *Beschreibung eines Dorfes* (1966; description of a village), an impressionistic description of the village of Bollschweil K. knew well.

K. characterized her own narrative style as belonging somewhere between poetry and prose. This is especially true of her short stories, which contain many lyrical passages. Man's existential loneliness and sorrow as well as his insistent hopes and ambitions are observed and recorded with poetic sensitivity and insight. Of all her short stories, K. considered "Das dicke Kind" (1951; the fat child) her best work. Through the technique of distancing, she heightens the suspense and resolves it.

The content of K.'s essays ranges from philosophical meditation on everyday occurrences to a deep concern about important scientific issues. *Griechische Mythen* (1946; Greek myths) are very personal interpretations of eternally relevant myths. Her Roman essays, *Engelsbrücke* (1955; bridge of angels), are reflections on literature, art, life, and death. And the collection *Zwischen Immer und Nie* (1971; between always and never) is a perceptive analysis of literary characters and themes.

As a dramatist, K. preferred writing for the radio to writing for the stage, since radio allowed her to use a greater variety of artistic devices. Here again she turned to both mythical and contemporary subjects. Among the latter, two have been especially popular: *Die Kinder der Elisa Rocca* (1962; the children of Elisa Rocca) and *Die Fahrradklingel* (1965; the bicycle bell). Both of these deal with man's inhumanity to man and have a moral tone that is akin to the fable.

K. treated many of the same subjects that occupied other writers of the period, but what made her stand apart was her compassionate point of view and her positive attitude toward life.

FURTHER WORKS: *Menschen und Dinge* (1945); *Gedichte* (1947); *Gustave Courbet: Roman eines Malerlebens* (1949); *Ewige Stadt* (1952); *Neue Gedichte* (1957); *Lange Schatten* (1960; *Long Shadows*, 1966); *Hörspiele* (1962); *Ein Wort weiter* (1965); *Überallnie* (1965); *Ferngespräche* (1966); *Die Wahrheit, nicht der Traum* (1967); *Vogel Rock* (1969); *Steht noch dahin: Neue Prosa* (1970); *Nicht nur von hier und heute* (1971). FURTHER WORKS IN ENGLISH: *Selected Later Poems of M. L. K.* (1980)

BIBLIOGRAPHY: Plant, R., "The Strange Poetic World of M. L. K.," *AGR*, 32 (1966): 15–16; Linpinsel, E., *K.-Bibliographie* (1971); Elliott, J. C., "The Child as Protagonist in Short Stories of M. L. K.," *Faculty Journal*, Tennessee State University (1973–1974): 11–16; Baus, A., *Standortbestimmung als Prozeß: Eine Untersuchung zur Prosa von M. L. K.* (1974); Walter, D. E., "Grundhaltungen in Gedichten der M. L. K.," *Du*, 27 (1976): 108–14

—ANNI WHISSEN

KASHUBIAN LITERATURE

See section under Polish Literature

KASSÁK, Lajos

Hungarian poet, novelist, and editor, b. 21 March 1887, Érsekújvár; d. 22 July 1967, Budapest

K., both as a writer and as a literary organizer, was responsible for creating, in the early decades of the 20th c., a Hungarian avantgarde movement that was at once plebeian and elitist. K.'s own political radicalism and his proletarian background—his father was a pharmacist's assistant; his mother, a washerwoman—did not prevent him from labeling most forms of popular art as kitsch. He was a natural enemy of bourgeois culture, but his unrelenting insistence on his own brand of revolutionary art and his refusal to relinquish his leadership also alienated many sympathetic friends and protégés. In his later years, K. became increasingly isolated and embittered, and during the repressive early 1950s, when his "formalism" was officially condemned, he disappeared completely from the literary scene. It was only toward the end of his life that the historical importance of his work began to be appreciated both at home and abroad.

K. was among the first poets in Hungary to reject traditional poetic forms in favor of free verse. His first collection, *Éposz Wagner maszkjában* (1915; epic in the masque of Wagner), reveals the influence of his early idol, Walt Whitman. Although he was philosophically opposed to artists joining political parties, and had great disdain for writers who did become involved in practical politics, K. was a lifelong socialist, and many of his works deal with the problems and promises of working-class life. However, he could be doctrinaire even without subscribing to official doctrines, and many of his writings are tractlike in their didacticism. His discriminating aesthetic sensibility is in evidence in relatively few works, but these have a sinewy eloquence and stateliness that is quite impressive. For example, his most famous early poem, "Mesteremberek" (1915; "Craftsmen," 1977), is a soaring tribute to the proletariat.

To a large extent K.'s fame rests on his role as an editor and mentor of young modernist poets. During his long career he published a number of periodicals; the most important of these were *Tett* (1915–16), *Ma* (1916–19; 1920–22), and *Munka* (1928–39). *Ma*, which he edited first in Budapest and later in Vienna, was especially significant, since it introduced the latest avant-garde "isms" to Hungarian readers. After the fall of the 1919 Hungarian Commune K. spent six years in exile in Vienna, where he met, and collaborated with, the editors and leading contributors of other influential avant-garde journals.

The 1920s proved to be K.'s most creative period. Inspired by the aesthetics of surrealism, futurism, even DADAISM, he produced many of his most important poems; *Világanyám* (1921; my world-mother) contains his most daringly experimental work. It was also during the 1920s that K. began to paint, using the purely abstract idiom of the constructivists.

While most of K.'s poetry bears the stamp of the various avant-garde trends of his time, as a prose writer he remained a down-to-earth realist. His most important prose work is a voluminous autobiographical narrative, *Egy ember élete* (8 vols., 1928–39; the life of a man); he describes with dispassionate candor his youthful wanderings, his days as a factory worker, his struggles as a budding artist, and his uneasy relationship with fellow writers and public figures. K. was a crusader for avant-garde art all his life. Nevertheless, critics nowadays seem to agree that his most lasting achievements were his realistic autobiographical writings.

FURTHER WORKS: *Misilló királysága* (1918); *Máglyák énekelnek* (1920); *Tisztaság könyve* (1926); *Megnőttek és elindulnak* (1932); *A telep* (1933); *Az utak ismeretlenek* (1934); *Fújjad csak furulyádat* (1939); *Mélyáram* (1962); *Összes versei* (2 vols., 1970); *Az izmusok története* (1972)

BIBLIOGRAPHY: Reményi, J., *Hungarian Writers and Literature* (1964): 388–93

—IVAN SANDERS

KÄSTNER, Erich

West German poet, novelist, journalist, and dramatist, b. 23 Feb. 1899, Dresden; d. 29 July 1974, Munich

After interrupting his education for a year of military service during World War I, K. studied German literature in Rostock, Berlin, and Leipzig. In 1925 he received a doctorate for a dissertation on Frederick II and German literature. When he lost an editorial position in 1927 he went to Berlin and became a free-lance writer. Although the Nazis burned his books in 1933, he remained in Germany during Hitler's rule. At the end of the war he became active as a journalist in Munich, editing *Die neue Zeitung* and the children's periodical *Pinguin* until 1948. During the postwar years he was also an active participant in the Munich cabaret Die Schaubude (after 1951, Die kleine Freiheit). In 1957 K. was awarded the Büchner Prize for literature, and from 1952 to 1962 he was president of the West German chapter of the PEN Club, an international writers' organization.

K. is most widely known for his children's books and popular light novels. Two of them, the famous children's story *Emil und die Detektive* (1928; *Emil and the Detectives*, 1930) and *Drei Männer*

im Schnee (1934; *Three Men in the Snow*, 1935), written for adults, were successfully filmed in the 1930s. In his works written especially for young people, K. successfully combined a lively, warm humor with moralizing didacticism to expose human frailty and folly while attacking social ills. K.'s juvenile novels are particularly significant for their reflection of the author's social optimism, an optimism based upon his deep belief in the regenerative power of the race that is most visible in each new generation of youth.

Of far greater literary moment, however, are K.'s lyric poems. K. is the most important, and perhaps also the only truly successful, poet of the primarily prose-oriented "new factualism" movement that began in Germany in the 1920s. His first four collections of verse—*Herz auf Taille* (1928; heart on the waist), *Lärm im Spiegel* (1928; noise in the mirror), *Ein Mann gibt Auskunft* (1930; a man gives information), and *Gesang zwischen den Stühlen* (1932; singing between the chairs)—established the new approach to poetry that continued to characterize all of his lyric creations. Combining stylistic elements of EXPRESSIONISM with conservative verse forms and his own social philosophy, K. produced a light yet serious poetry, in tone reminiscent of the politically critical works of Heinrich Heine (1797–1856) and similar to the early didactic lyrics of Bertolt BRECHT.

In those first groups of poems, the pedagogue-moralist K. attempted to reach two closely related goals: to lay bare the festering social and political malaise of pre-Hitler Germany; and to use the devices of irony, criticism, mockery, accusation, and laughter to warn of the consequences of social indifference, militarism, and perverted nationalism. The powerful accuracy of K.'s perception of the prewar German situation is well exemplified in the prophetic satirical poem "Kennst du das Land, wo die Kanonen blühen?" (1928; "Knowst Thou the Land Where Only Cannons Grow?" 1963), a parody of a poem by Goethe, in which K. predicted with terrible precision the rise of the Nazis.

The most visible postwar development in K.'s poetry is a strong preference for concise, yet sensitive aphorisms and epigrams. The collection *Kurz und bündig* (1948; short and to the point) remains the best document of his efforts in that direction.

The tragic novel *Fabian* (1931; *Fabian: The Story of a Moralist*, 1932), a mainstream literary work of the "new factualism," is K.'s only major work of fiction that examines prewar moral and social decay and the predicament of Germany's "lost generation." Although it has been criticized as lacking a convincing world view, *Fabian* is witty and clever in its conception. Characterized by precision of language and expression, and resembling many of the early poems in its thrust, the novel successfully penetrates and exposes inhumanity, while justifying morality through its portrayal of immorality.

K.'s dramas are less successful than his fiction and poetry. *Die Schule der Diktatoren* (1949; the school of the dictators), a comedy that unmasks inhumanity once more in a grim portrayal of the human fall foretold by K.'s poetry, is his most significant play, yet its characters lack sufficient graphic power to make the work effective.

The major strength of K.'s writings lies in their universality and timelessness. Although K. wrote of specific problems pertaining to his own society and time, his works still force the reader toward constructive introspection. Therein lies the measure of their absolute worth.

FURTHER WORKS: *Leben in dieser Zeit* (1930); *Pünktchen und Anton* (1931; *Annaluise and Anton*, 1932); *Der 35. Mai; oder,*

Konrad reitet in die Südsee (1931; *The 35th of May; or, Conrad's Ride to the South Seas*, 1933); *Arthur mit dem langen Arm* (1932); *Das verhexte Telefon* (1932); *Das fliegende Klassenzimmer* (1933; *The Flying Classroom*, 1934); *Emil und die drei Zwillinge* (1933; *Emil and the Three Twins*, 1961); *Die verschwundene Miniatur; oder auch, Die Abenteuer eines empfindsamen Fleischermeisters* (1935; *The Missing Miniature; or, The Adventures of a Sensitive Butcher*, 1937); *Doktor E. K.s lyrische Hausapotheke* (1936); *Georg und die Zwischenfälle* (1938; repub. as *Der kleine Grenzverkehr*, 1949; *A Salzburg Comedy*, 1957); *Streiche des Till Eulenspiegel* (1938; *Till Eulenspiegel, the Clown*, 1957); *Bei Durchsicht meiner Bücher* (1946); *Tucholsky* (1946); *Zu treuen Händen* (1948); *Der tägliche Kram* (1949); *Die Konferenz der Tiere* (1949; *The Animals' Conference*, 1949); *Das doppelte Lottchen* (1949; *Lottie and Lisa*, 1950); *Der gestiefelte Kater* (1950; *Puss in Boots*, 1967); *Des Freiherrn von Münchhausen wunderbare Reisen und Abenteuer zu Wasser und zu Lande* (1952); *Die kleine Freiheit* (1952); *Die Schildbürger* (1954); *Die 13 Monate* (1955); *Der Gegenwart ins Gästebuch* (1955); *Eine Auswahl* (1956); *Don Quichotte* (1956; *Don Quixote*, 1957); *Als ich ein kleiner Junge war* (1957; *When I Was a Little Boy*, 1959); *Über das Nichtlesen von Büchern* (1958, with Paul Flora); *Heiterkeit in Dur und Moll* (1959); *Heiterkeit kennt keine Grenzen* (1960); *Notabene 45* (1961); *Gullivers Reisen* (1961); *Heiterkeit braucht keine Worte* (1962); *Das Schwein beim Friseur* (1962); *K. in Probepackung* (1962); *Liebe will gelernt sein* (1962); *Wieso, warum!* (1962); *Von Damen und anderen Weibern* (1963); *Der kleine Mann* (1963; *The Little Man*, 1966); *Der kleine Mann und die kleine Miss* (1967; *The Little Man and the Little Miss*, 1969); *Kennst du das Land, wo die Kanonen blühen?* (1967); *Unter der Zeitlupe* (1967); *Was nicht in euren Lesebüchern steht* (1968); *Da samma wieda* (1969); *Friedrich der Große und die deutsche Literatur* (1972); *Wer nicht hören will, muß lesen* (1972); *Ein Mann, der Ideale hat* (1973); *Der Zauberlehrling* (1974); *Die Zeit fährt Auto* (1974); *Große Zeiten, kleine Auswahl* (1969); *Heiterkeit braucht keine Worte* (1972); *Das große E. K. Buch* (1975); *Briefe aus dem Tessin* (1977); *Gedichte* (1983); *Letzte Kapitel* (1988; *Final Chapters*, 1988); *Gemischte Gefühle* (1989); *Briefe an die Doppelschätze*. FURTHER WORKS IN ENGLISH: *Let's Face It: Selected Poems* (1963)

BIBLIOGRAPHY: Winkelman, J., *Social Criticism in the Early Works of E. K.* (1953); Winkelman, J., *The Poetic Style of E. K.* (1957); Enderle, L., *E. K. in Selbstzeugnissen und Bilddokumenten* (1966); Beutler, K., *E. K.* (1967); Benson, R., *E. K.: Studien zu seinem Werk* (1973); Wagener, H., *E. K.* (1973); Last, R. W., *E. K.* (1974); Kiesel, H., *E. K.* (1981); Schneyder, W., *E. K.* (1982); Wolff, R., ed., *E. K.* (1983); Lämmerzahl-Bensel, U., ed., *E. K.: Eine Personalbibliographie* (1988); Bemmann, H., *E. K.* (1994); Flotnow, M., ed. *E. K.* (1996)

—LOWELL A. BANGERTER

KATAEV, Valentin Petrovich

Russian novelist, dramatist, short-story writer, essayist, and poet, b. 28 Jan. 1897, Odessa; d. 12 Apr. 1986, Moscow

K.'s literary career spans seventy years, beginning in 1910 with the publication of his first poem. K. was born and educated in Odessa; his younger brother Yevgeny was also a writer (see Ilf and Petrov). K. belongs to the southern school of Soviet writers, also known as the Odessa school, whose members were noted for their gift of humor and a certain romantic flavor in their work. By his own admission and as evidenced in his early works, K. greatly admired Ivan BUNIN. Although not one of the Petrograd literary group called the Serapion Brothers himself, K. clearly came under their influence during the 1920s.

K.'s first postrevolutionary work of any consequence was the short story "Otets" (1925; the father), which was followed by his most successful satirical novel, *Rastratchiki* (1926; *The Embezzlers*, 1929). Mixing farce, satire, and realism, *Rastratchiki* is best understood against the background of the NEP (New Economic Policy), that brief period of Soviet history when a certain amount of free enterprise was permitted and in which the heroes of the novel—two drunken officials of a Moscow trust—abscond with a sum of money and go on a merry, if short-lived, adventure.

During the 1930s and 1940s, K.'s writing took a more serious turn and followed the typical pattern of the period: the integration of all aspects of technology into fiction. In *Vremya, vperyod!* (1932; *Time, Forward!*, 1933), a novel about the first Five-Year Plan (1928–32), the satirical element appears deliberately blunted. What sets this work apart from other "industrial" novels is that it is more genuine, concerning itself with the production process itself in the real setting of the huge metallurgical plant at Magnitogorsk. The novel is vivid and dynamic in its depiction of the workers bent on breaking a world record for concrete pouring, and captures some of the genuine excitement of that period. Written in cinematic style, with people and objects shown in constant motion, rapidly changing scenes, flashbacks, and terse dialogue, this novel is stylistically closer to EXPRESSIONISM than to psychological realism.

Beleet parus odinoky (1936; *Lonely White Sail; or, Peace Is Where the Tempests Blow*, 1937) is K.'s most engaging and lyrical work. This semiautobiographical story set in Odessa during the eventful year of 1905 has as its main characters two nine-year-old boys from different backgrounds. Humor, warmth, and spontaneity permeate this novel, in which K. displays a deep insight into child psychology. While *Beleet parus odinoky* was warmly acclaimed as the first part of a tetralogy—the second part was *Khutor v stepi* (1956; *The Cottage in the Steppe*, 1957), the third *Zimny veter* (1960; winter wind)—the book that was destined to become the fourth part, *Za vlast Sovetov* (1949; for the power of the Soviets), a novel describing the wartime underground activities in German-occupied Odessa, came under severe criticism for its failure to portray "correctly" the role of the Communist Party in the resistance movement. K. was obliged to publish a revised version in 1951.

In the post-Stalin years K. has turned to a modified genre of memoirs, in which he combines biography and autobiography, fact, fiction, semifiction, and contemplation. The two best examples of this genre are *Svyatoi kolodets* (1966; *The Holy Well*, 1967), an unusually complex story for Soviet literature, almost surrealistic in style and admittedly cinematic in technique, and *Trava zabvenia* (1967; *Grass of Oblivion*, 1969), a moving, unchronological narrative in which K. attempts to arrest the passage of time and cleverly juxtaposes portraits of MAYAKOVSKY and Bunin, the two mentors of his early literary years.

K. is also well known as a playwright. His remarkable dramatic talent, laced with humor and a penchant for satire, produced a series of farcical plays, of which *Kvadratura kruga* (1928; *Squaring the Circle*, 1934) is the most famous. The problems of everyday Soviet life are the subject of these comedies. K. also successfully adapted several of his novels for the theater.

Throughout his long career K. has exhibited a remarkable power of adaptability in the face of official pressure yet has managed to retain a certain degree of freshness and independence of style. From 1955 to 1961 K. was the editor-in-chief of the literary magazine *Yunost*, in which were published works by younger, less orthodox Soviet writers.

FURTHER WORKS: *Ostrov Ehrendorf* (1924); *Avangard* (1929); *Doroga tsvetov* (1934; *The Path of Flower*, 1935); *Ya syn trudovogo naroda* (1937); *Zhena* (1943; *The Wife*, 1946) *Syn polka* (1945); *Pochti dnevnik* (1962); *Malenkaya zheleznaya dver v stene* (1964); *Kubik* (1968); *Sobranie sochineny* (9 vols., 1968–72); *Razbitaya zhizn; ili, Volshebny rog Oberona* (1972; *A Mosaic of Life; or, The Magic Horn of Oberon: Memoirs of a Russian Childhood*, 1976)

BIBLIOGRAPHY: Borland, H., *Soviet Literary Theory and Practice during the First Five-Year Plan, 1928–1932* (1950): passim; Brown, E. J., Introduction to *Time, Forward!* (1961); Hayward, M., and Shukman, H., Introduction to *The Holy Well* (1967): 9–16; Struve, G., *Russian Literature under Lenin and Stalin, 1917–1953* (1971): passim; Slonim, M., *Soviet Russian Literature: Writers and Problems, 1917–1967* (1973): 237–39, 259, 287; Brown, D., *Soviet Russian Literature since Stalin* (1978): 256; Russell, R., V. K. (1981)

—NADJA JERNAKOFF

KATEB Yacine

Algerian novelist, poet, and dramatist (writing in French and Arabic), b. 6 Aug. 1929, Constantine

The son of Islamic parents, K. was raised on tales of Arab achievement as well as on the legends of the Algerian heroes who had resisted the French invaders from the beginning.

After attending Koranic school (the elementary school of the traditional Arabic world), K. entered the French-language school system. When he was only sixteen years old, he took part in the demonstration in Setif on 8 May 1945, which resulted in the massacre of thousands of demonstrators by the police and the army. K. was jailed and reflected later that this period was crucial in his development, for during his imprisonment he discovered the two things closest to his heart. One was the Algerian struggle for independence from France, which was a struggle by those who had neither rights nor possessions against those who had both. The other was poetry; one of K.'s best-known poems, "La rose de Blida" (1963; the rose of Blida) was written about his mother, who, believing him to have been killed during the demonstration, suffered a mental breakdown. After K.'s release from prison, he embarked on what has since been basically an itinerant life.

The same themes and symbols, the same vision, are the subject of all of K.'s writings before 1970: poems, novels, plays, and criticism. As he himself has said, all of his works "are a single work written in one long breath and still in gestation." The first expression of his lifelong work was the powerful poem "Nedjma; ou, Le poème ou le couteau" (1948; Nedjma; or, the poem or the knife).

The reader is introduced to the figure of Nedjma—the girl-spirit who will move hauntingly through K.'s work—and to the palm trees, the primeval desert, the archetypal ancestor who even in incestuous, moronic decadence contains a certain glory derived from the magnificence of accumulated victories and defiant inviolability.

The publication of the novel *Nedjma* (1956; *Nedjma*, 1961) was to assure K. his place in modern literature. So unusual is the form and structure of *Nedjma* that only an impression of it can be offered. The story involves Nedjma, the four men bonded by friendship and revolutionary ardor who love her, and a gallery of secondary characters of varying importance. The vitality of the work lies not in its narrative content, although it is a highly readable novel, but in the novel's structure, which is best described as radial. The action is not chronological. It moves out from a central point, returning time and again to that point only to move out on another radius. Universality is implied in the center and in the circumference and an infinite variety of shapes and repetitions are suggested by analogy to the arabesques and geometric forms of Islamic art.

Nedjma, the daughter of a French woman and an Arab from the Keblouti clan, becomes mythic through being portrayed in an ethereal way. As the star (*nedjma* in Arabic) she symbolizes the nationalism of the new nation, the importance of the desert in Algerian life, the quest of the unattainable. As a member of the Keblouti clan, she embodies the attachment of traditional Algerians to their clan, the strong emotional ties of those who can trace their kinship back to a legendary ancestor. *Nedjma*, widely considered a masterpiece, is the greatest French-language work to come out of North Africa. In it, the French language and the Arab soul have joined to achieve a new dimension in literature.

The impulsive flow of inspiration that produced *Nedjma* seems to have yielded to a more contrived and facile idiom akin to that of guerrilla street theater and the political cartoon. Representative of this later style is *L'homme aux sandales de caoutchouc* (1970; the man with the rubber sandals), a series of vignettes highlighting the military history of Vietnam and the plight of the transient Algerian labor force in Europe.

Since 1972 K. has lived in Algiers and has renounced French to devote his talents to the production of plays in the local Arabic dialect. Structurally these plays resemble *L'homme aux sandales de caoutchouc*.

K.'s works have been criticized as regressive by some Algerian critics who wish to see their country reject the heritage of the past in order to concentrate on becoming a modern technological nation. Most critics, however, both French and African, agree that K.'s major works masterfully blend past and present and successfully interweave personal vision—even hallucination—and cultural tradition.

FURTHER WORKS: *Soliloques* (1946); *Abdelkader et l'indépendance algérienne* (1948); *Le cercle des représailles* (1959); *La femme sauvage* (perf. 1963); *Le polygone étoilé* (1966); *Les ancêtres redoublent de férocité* (perf. 1967)

BIBLIOGRAPHY: Sellin, E., "Algerian Poetry: Poetic Values, Mohammed Dib, and K. Y.," *JNALA*, Nos. 9–10 (1971): 45–68; Mortimer, M. P., "K. Y. in Search of Algeria: A Study of *Nedjma* and *Le polygone étoilé*," *ECr*, 12 (1972), 274–88; Déjeux, J., *Littérature maghrébine de langue française* (1973): 143–79; Déjeux, J., "Les structures de l'imaginaire dans l'œuvre de K. Y.," *ROMM*, Nos. 13–14 (1973): 267–92; Déjeux, J., "K. Y., romancier, poète et dramaturge algérien," *PFr*, No. 15 (1977): 127–47; Aresu, B.,

"Polygonal and Arithmosophical Motifs, Their Significance in the Fiction of K. Y.," *RAL*, 9 (1978), 143–75

—ERIC SELLIN

KAVANAGH, Patrick

Irish poet, journalist, and novelist, b. 21 Oct. 1904, Inniskeen; d. 30 Nov. 1967, Dublin

K. dropped out of Kednaminsha Grammar School at age twelve and began, despite the limitations of his rural life, to read and write poetry. At twenty-two he had become, like his father, a farmer and cobbler. Keenly aware that his poetic aspirations alienated him from country people, he nevertheless sent poetry to local newspapers and to the *Irish Statesman*, whose editor, AE (George RUSSELL), published some early verse and encouraged the peasant poet. The reception of his first volume, *Ploughman, and Other Poems* (1936), encouraged K. to go to England, where his autobiography *The Green Fool* (1938) was published but withdrawn because Oliver St. John Gogarty (1878–1957)—JOYCE's Buck Mulligan—threatened to sue for libel.

By 1939 K. had moved to Dublin, where his sense of isolation was intensified by his reception by other writers who dismissed him as an uneven, uneducated country poet. In spite of the publication of his tour de force *The Great Hunger* (1942) and of *A Soul for Sale* (1947), which mirrors his frustration and fear of failure, poverty drove him to journalism.

In spring 1955 he survived an operation for lung cancer. Late that summer on the banks of Dublin's Grand Canal he had an epiphany; feeling reborn, he began to write some of his best pastoral poetry. In New York, his brother Peter printed on a hand press what became *Recent Poems* (1958). *Come Dance with Kitty Strobling, and Other Poems* (1960) was a Poetry Book Society's selection. Although in the 1960s his health continued to deteriorate, K. wrote *Self-Portrait* (1962), a corrective of his two earlier portraits of the artist, *The Green Fool* and the autobiographical novel *Tarry Flynn* (1948). Heavy drinking hastened his death.

For K., poetry was the struggle "with the crude ungainly crust of earth and spirit"—himself in and as the clay of County Monaghan and the flowering rubble of Dublin. The ploughman writer bent reality to fit his vision of ordinary life in rural Ireland. At first influenced by English romantics and AE, he discovered *Poetry* magazine and fell under the influence of IMAGISM, learning the value of showing instead of telling. Frank O'CONNOR influenced him to temper romantic subjectivity with new perspectives on rural people and scenes. In K.'s poems nature is almost sacramental: nature is a teacher, the poet both recorder and seer.

The Great Hunger, perhaps his greatest poem, epitomizes K.'s artistic subject and stance. Experiencing the deprivations of Irish life, the farmer Maguire is starved for satisfactions denied him by the land, family, and religion. Skillfully blending flashbacks and dramatic presentation with dialogue, interior monologue, and organic rhythms, K. examines the effect of environment—psychological and physical—upon the Irish Catholic peasant for whom tilling fields does not bring a harvest for spirit or flesh. Body and soul are stunted by the requirements of the agrarian economy, its mores and morality.

Whereas rural Ireland was the stony gray inspiration for the compelling "Great Hunger," Dublin was the "pig-sty" where some literary pigs were more equal than others; when "Paddies" patronized the farmer poet, he struck back with satire. Frustrated in his desire for recognition, irate at what seemed to be Dublin's hypocritical, provincial smugness, K. became the poet-critic exposing cultural and literary fraud. As a journalist he damned whatever and whoever offended him, declaring war on his contemporaries with crusading zeal, disparaging poets who came after YEATS and avowing an almost religious commitment to poetry. During the 1940s he lashed out at the Irish Literary Renaissance, laughed at Anglo-Irish portraits of peasants (by Yeats, Lady Gregory [1852–1932] and SYNGE), and decreed politics an unfit poetic subject. Mocking writers like Austin CLARKE for their interest in the Celtic Twilight, K. attacked the Irish literary and artistic establishment. In his role as bellicose critic and poet-prophet, he became a pariah to his Irish critics.

The late poems, however, witness a change of mood. From the passionate Swiftian denunciations of his middle-period writing, he returned to the simple, common vocabulary of praise and the solaces of the banal beauty of canal water, grass, and passersby. After his "rebirth" he reaffirmed his dedication to poetry as the direct, lyric treatment of nature and ordinary life. His best poems celebrate the homely clay; plain, blunt, conversational, they reject the mythopoeic and symbolic frameworks of Yeats and Joyce, although his spare lyrics owe something to late Yeats, and his ability to document authentic details of country life owes something to Joyce's re-creation of Dublin. Unadorned with complex allusions, unencumbered by a sense of history, his poetry and prose are about the poet's relation to his parochial environment. His poetic assertions of self and soil became a testing ground for younger Irish poets such as Seamus HEANEY. The confessional qualities of his writing—autobiography, *roman à clef*, "pruse" (sic), or poems—mark him as a voice of the new personalism in literature.

FURTHER WORKS: *Collected Poems* (1964); *Collected Pruse* (1967); *Lapped Furrows* (1969); *November Haggard* (1971); *Complete Poems* (1972); *By Night Unstarred* (1978); *Lough Derg* (1978)

BIBLIOGRAPHY: Payne, B., "The Poetry of P. K.," *Studies*, 49 (1960), 279–94; Freyer, G., "P. K.," *Éire*, 3, 4 (1968), 17–23; Kennelly, B., "P. K.," *ArielE*, 1, 3 (1970), 7–28; Kavanagh, P., *The Garden of the Golden Apples* (1972); Warner, A., *Clay Is the Word: P. K., 1904–1967* (1973); O'Brien, D., *P. K.* (1975); special K. issue, *JIL*, 6, 1 (1977); Nemo, J., *P. K.* (1979); Kavanagh, P., *Sacred Keeper* (1979)

—MARTHA FODASKI-BLACK

KAVERIN, Veniamin

(pseud. of Veniamin Zilberg) Russian novelist, short-story writer, and memoirist, b. 19 April 1902, Pskov; d. 5 May 1989

Born into a family of musicians, K. studied the violin until he was fifteen. He attended the University of Petrograd (now Leningrad) and received degrees in Oriental languages (1923) and Russian literature (1924). While at the university he studied under the leading Russian FORMALIST critics, Boris Eikhenbaum (1886–1959) and Yury Tynyanov (1894–1943; later his brother-in-law).

K. began writing fiction in 1920, and in 1921 he joined the Serapion Brotherhood, a group of talented young writers dedicated to defending the autonomy of art. With his close friend Lev Lunts (1902–1924), K. represented the group's Western wing, which sought inspiration from Western writers of fantasy and adventure—Robert Louis Stevenson, Edgar Allan Poe, and E. T. A. Hoffmann. His early stories reveal their influence and also that of the formalists. In them K. plays with literary conventions à la Laurence Sterne (recommended as a model by formalist and fellow Serapion Brother, Viktor Shklovsky [b. 1893]), experiments with plot construction and narrative techniques, refuses to philosophize or to describe reality, and shows little concern for political or social problems.

By 1928, however, K. had become drawn to the problem of the intelligentsia and the revolution: the most famous work of his early period, *Khudozhnik neizvesten* (1931; *The Unknown Artist*, 1947), deals with the dilemma of the artist in a Communist society. The novel, which purports to be a documentary, depicts the struggle between the eccentric painter Arkhimedov, portrayed as a modern Don Quixote, and his engineer friend Shpektorov, the new technocrat who is contemptuous of ethical values and art. In the end Arkhimedov is destroyed, but his art triumphs, for he leaves behind an unsigned painting of exceptional beauty portraying the suicide of his wife.

K. returned to the theme of the artist and his struggle to remain true to his vision in his fine recent novel *Pered zerkalom* (1972; before the mirror). This time his protagonist is a woman painter, Lisa Turaevna. Like the Soviet bacteriologist Tatyana Vlasenkova, heroine of his postwar trilogy *Otkrytaya kniga* (1956; *The Open Book*, 1957), Turaevna struggles against everyday and political pressures and endures to triumph. Both novels cover a wide span of time and chronicle the development of the heroine from girlhood to middle age. *Otkrytaya kniga* is written in the form of a diary and memoirs; *Pered zerkalom* in the form of letters between Turaevna and her lifelong friend Karnovsky. While *Otkrytaya kniga* deals with the period between the revolution and World War II, *Pered zerkalom* focuses on the period 1910–30, with special emphasis on the artistic experience of the 1920s. A desire to preserve the memory of that period for the present generation is also evident in K.'s own recent memoirs, *Sobesednik* (1973; interlocutor) and *Osveshchennye okna* (1978; illuminated windows).

K. has played a part in all of the many and varied phases of Soviet literature from 1922 to the present. In the 1930s he adapted to the demands of SOCIALIST REALISM, but he did not capitulate to it. His novels never ceased to engage and interest readers. In the postwar period he had been outspoken both in his own works and in his defense of the works of other authors. For this he had been censured by the regime more than once.

FURTHER WORKS: *Mastera i podmasterya* (1923); *Konets khazy* (1925); *Devyat desyatykh sudby* (1925); *Bolshaya igra* (1926); *Vorobinaya noch* (1927); *Bubnovaya mast* (1927); *Skandalist; ili, Vechera na Vasilevskom Ostrove* (1928); *Prolog* (1931); *Chernovnik cheloveka* (1931); *Ukroshchenie Robinzona; ili, Poteryanny ray* (1934); *Ispolnenie zhelany* (1937; *The Larger View*, 1938); *Rasskazy* (1942); *Dva kapitana* (1945; *Two Captains*, 1957); *Sem par nechistykh* (1962); *Kosoy dozhd* (1962); *Zdravstvy, brat, pisat ochen trudno* (1965); *Dvoynoy portret* (1966); *Shkolny spektakl* (1968); *Dvukhchasovaya progulka* (1978)

BIBLIOGRAPHY: Piper, D. G., *V. A. K.* (1970); Oulanoff, H., *The Prose Fiction of V. A. K.* (1976); Beaujour, E., "K.'s *Before the Mirror*," *SEEJ*, 24 (1980): 233–44

—SONA STEPHAN HOISINGTON

KAWABATA Yasunari

Japanese novelist, b. 11 June 1899, Osaka; d. 16 April, 1972, Kamakura

K. lost all his closest relatives by the age of fourteen. His diary, virtually his first literary product, published only in 1925 as *Jūrokusai no nikki* (the diary of a sixteen-year-old-boy), records the boy's observation of his dying grandfather (the "sixteen" in the title refers to the old style of reckoning age). As a middle-school student well versed in the Japanese classics, K. chose to become a writer and soon began to contribute short stories to a local paper. In 1924 he became a leading member of the "New Perceptionist" group of young writers interested in the literary and art trends from the West. During this experimental period K.'s works revealed the modernist influence. Soon after his reaffirmation of his inheritance of Japan's literary tradition K. began to publish in serial form the celebrated *Yukiguni* (1935–48; *Snow Country*, 1956); this work was succeeded by numerous serialized novels that appeared after the defeat of Japan. K. was also noted as an acute critic and discoverer of new talents. He won the Nobel Prize for literature in 1968. Four years later he took his own life.

Izu no odoriko (1926; *The Izu Dancer*, 1955) established K.'s reputation. On a journey a young student encounters a fourteen-year-old dancer, a member of a family of traveling entertainers. The youth appreciates their kindness and feels a genuine innocent love for the girl. The autobiographical hero, a receptive observer, foreshadows his fictional successors. This simple story ends with a separation, as in most of K.'s novels.

K. generates a pervasive sadness not with the depiction of catastrophic conflicts, but with great subtlety, as best exemplified in *Yukiguni*, a story about a country geisha, Komako, who falls in love with Shimamura, a dilettante from Tokyo. This novel demonstrates K.'s remarkable style, uniquely his own, and characterized by refined simplicity and evocative images. Lyric descriptions of nature are central to the narrative progression in K.'s novels. Their basically episodic form emerges through the allusive links of successive scenes, not according to a well-defined plot structure. As is often pointed out, this form echoes the Japanese poetic tradition, especially that of *renga*, linked verse.

The traditional Japanese sensibility discerns the quality of evanescence in beautiful objects. The search for and admiration of beauty are dominant Kawabata themes. Beauty in K. is not unattainable absolute beauty; it is manifested in the innocence and purity of a girl or in the warmth of a woman's love, or in a kind of devotion exemplified by the hero in *Meijin* (1954; *The Master of Go*, 1972). Pursuit of such beauty cannot be isolated from an awareness of deprivation or from the encroachment of fatigue, degeneration, and death.

Sembazuru (1952; *Thousand Cranes*, 1959) and *Mizuumi* (1954; *The Lake*, 1974) explore the degradation and guilt into which man is liable to be led through the attraction of beauty. *Sembazuru*, centering on the tea ceremony, recalls the karmic, incestuous relationships in the famous 11th-c. Japanese novel *The Tale of Genji. Mizuumi*, with few references to the tradition, is perhaps the most experimental among K.'s postwar novels. Hallucinations, stream-of-consciousness, and free associations in the complex shifts of time are used to portray an ex-teacher's impelling desire to follow beautiful women. In spite of the character's grotesquely ugly degeneration, this exploration into the dark subconscious is again permeated with lyrical pathos.

Direct human relationships are avoided in *Kinjū* (1933; *Of Birds and Beasts*, 1969), whose hero, rejecting human affection, raises birds and dogs, and in *Nemureru bijo* (1961; *House of Sleeping Beauties*, 1969), a bizarre, but nonetheless masterfully controlled story of an old man who visits an establishment to sleep for a night with drugged girls. This evasion is carried to an extreme in a strange story, *Kataude* (1964; *One Arm*, 1969), in which a human relationship exists only through a severed arm. These works might be read as satires on dehumanizing alienation, but again the lyrical and often reflective note implicitly calls for the recovery of a wholesome communion.

K.'s most important work, *Yama no oto* (1954; *The Sound of the Mountain*, 1970), subtly embodies his profound understanding of human nature and suggests the possible achievement of such a communion. This difficult task is undertaken in the spiritual chaos following Japan's defeat. The aging protagonist, Shingo, is deeply concerned about the marital crises of his two children and tries, as much as he can, to assist. The novel attempts to redeem and reaffirm that traditional Japanese sensibility that enjoys communion with nature and caring human relationships. Stylistically as well, this novel is K.'s finest achievement. The dialogue, which exhibits his accomplished ease in creating scenes from daily life, is skillfully interwoven with the hero's dreams, recollections, and reflections. The poetic descriptions of nature, often consisting of extremely evocative one-sentence paragraphs, are suggestive of the psychological state of the protagonist. At the same time these passages also allow the reader's participation in the hero's communion with nature.

K.'s works represent a rare combination of tradition and modernity. The quiet realism, the seeming formlessness, and above all the poetic intensity in K., while testifying to the tenacious literary legacy of Japan, suggest to the West many innovative possibilities.

FURTHER WORKS: *Kanjō sōshoku* (1926); *Asakusa kurenaidan* (1930); *Hana no warutsu* (1940); *Maihime* (1951); *Hi mo tsuki mo* (1953); *Tokyo no hito* (1955); *Niji ikutabi* (1955); *Onna de aru koto* (1957); *Kaze no aru michi* (1959); *Koto* (1962); *Kawa no aru shitamachi no hanashi* (1962); *Utsukushisa to kanashimi to* (1965; *Beauty and Sadness*, 1975); *Rakka ryūsui* (1966); *Gekka no mon* (1967); *Utsukushii Nihon no watakushi* (1969; *Japan the Beautiful and Myself*, 1969); *Bi no sonzai to hakken* (1969; *The Existence and Discovery of Beauty*, 1969)

BIBLIOGRAPHY: Tsukimura, R., "A Thematic Study of the Works of K. Y.," *JATJ*, 5 (1968): 22–31; Seidensticker, E. G., "K.," *HudR*, 22 (1969): 6–10; Tsukimura, R., "Theme and Technique in *Mizuumi*," in Japan P.E.N. Club, ed., *Studies on Japanese Culture* (1973), Vol. I: 433–39; Miyoshi, M., *Accomplices of Silence: The Modern Japanese Novel* (1974): 95–121; Ueda, M., "The Virgin, the Wife, and the Nun: K.'s *Snow Country*," in Tsuruta, K., and Swann, T. E., eds., *Approaches to the Modern Japanese Novel* (1976): 73–88; Tsuruta, K., "Two Journeys in *The Sound of the Mountain*," in Tsuruta, K., and Swann, T. E., eds., *Approaches to the Modern Japanese Novel* (1976): 89–103; Ueda, M., *Modern Japanese Writers and the Nature of Literature* (1976): 173–218; Tsuruta, K., "The Colour Scheme in *House of the Sleeping Beauties*," in Tsukimura, R., ed., *Life, Death and Age in Modern Japanese Fiction* (1978): 21–34; Tsukimura, R., "The Symbolic Significance of the Old Man in *The Sound of the Mountain*," in Tsukimura, R., ed., *Life, Death and Age in Modern Japanese Fiction* (1978): 45–54; Gessel, V. C., *Three Modern Novelists: Sāseki, Tanizaki, K.* (1993)

—REIKO TSUKIMURA

Yasunari Kawabata

KAZAKH LITERATURE

During the first decade of the 20th c., Kazakh literature departed decisively from a long heritage by shifting abruptly from the famed verbal poetic art of its past while adding imaginative prose and modern drama to its genres. Lyric verse, written very late in the 1880s, still circulated mainly in recitations from memory. Few of the compositions by the popular Ibrahim (Abay) Qŭnanbay-ŭlï (1845–1904), for example, had yet been printed. His first volume, *Qazaq aqïnï Ibrahim Qŭnanbayŭlïnïng ölengderï* (1909; poems by the Kazakh poet Ibrahim Qŭnanbay-ŭlï), significantly, came out in St. Petersburg rather than a Kazakh town.

Longer works of written prose in Kazakh were closely linked with Tatar influence in centers of upper Kazakhstan, like Orenburg and Troitsk. The first edition of a Kazakh novelette, Mir Jaqib DUWLAT-ŬLÏ's 94-page *Baqïtsïz Jamal* (1910; unlucky Jamal), typically appeared in Kazan, the Tatar capital. This story was characteristic of a school of sentimental tragedy, which viewed Kazakh girls as miserable in arranged marriage and polygamy. Duwlat-ŭlï also composed fiery anti-Russian poetry and cooperated with the prominent Kazakh poet and translator Aqmet Baytursin-ŭlï (1873–1937) in editing the early newspapers *Qazaqstan* (1911 and 1913) and *Qazaq* (1913–18, intermittent).

The first published Kazakh drama, *Nadandïq qurbandarï* (1914; victims of ignorance), by Kölbey Toghïs-ŭlï (dates n.a.), was the creation of a reformist author and modernizer. Drama and theater rapidly developed as indoctrination media in the 1920s for the largely illiterate (over 93 percent in 1926) Kazakh population. Controversial plays were offered by Säken Seyfullin (1894–1938): his *Qïzïl sŭngqarlar* (1920, pub. 1922; red falcons); by Mŭkhtar O. Auez-ŭlï (AUEZOV): the tragedy *Änglik-Kebek* (1917, pub. 1922; Änglik and Kebek); and by Duwlat-ŭlï: his *Balqiya* (1922; Balqiya). The three new playwrights underwent scathing ideological criticism after 1917 for these and other writings. Of the three, only Auez-ŭlï survived, by careful accommodation, the Soviet political purges of the 1930s. Many Kazakh writers, including prolific Communist versifiers and prose writers such as Beyimbet Maylin (1894–1938), known widely in Kazakhstan for his novel *Azamat Azamatovich* (1935; Azamat Azamatovich), about nationalism, perished during the purge years. That stifling ideological control over Kazakh letters intensified noticeably from the date the state-run Writers' Union of Kazakhstan was established for supervisory purposes in 1934.

Curiously, the tone of writing in recent decades often resembles the didactic spirit of pre-1917 novelettes such as the short *Qalïng mal* (1914; the bride price), by Ispandiyar Köbeyŭlï (1878–1956), which also condemned the custom of obligatory dowry and arranged marriage. A series of tendentious novels illustrating Soviet slogans came out, for example, under the signature of Writers' Union chief Ghabiden Mŭstafin (b. 1902), starting with his *Ömir ne ölim* (1938; life or death), about mining and industrialization in Kazakhstan. His most widely circulated and translated novel, *Millioner* (1948; millionaire farm), dealing with collectivization of Kazakh agriculture, was followed by the autobiographical *Qaraghandï* (1952; Karaganda), an ideological recasting of his earlier *Ömir ne ölim*.

Communist spokesmen describe the short story as a "militant genre," but the greatest literary success in the new Kazakh prose fell to a long historical novel. *Abay* (2 vols., 1945, 1947; *Abai: A Novel*, n.d.), by Auez-ŭlï, depicts the life and times of the pre-Soviet poet Ibrahim Qŭnanbay-ŭlï, known as Abay. It won the Stalin Prize in 1949 and was translated into many languages, including English.

A new, possibly minor, phase in Kazakh development arrived with a few works from bilingual Kazakh authors writing in Russian (very early in the 20th c., Kazakhs had sometimes composed in Chaghatay or Tatar). Increasingly known for such literature, among others, is Olzhas Omar-ŭlï Suleymanov (b. 1936), educated in Moscow and Alma-Ata, and author of a powerful literary polemic, *Az-i-ia* (1975; Asia) arguing for Asia's cultural influence over

Europe/Russia. He earlier published short volumes of verse in his own Russian, including *Solnechnye nochi* (1962; sunny nights) and *Glinianaya kniga* (1969; the clay book). An interesting inter-ethnic language experiment is the two-act play entitled, in the Russian-language version, *Voskhozhdenie na Fudziamu* (1973; *The Ascent of Mount Fuji*, 1975), by the Kazakh writer Qaltay Mŭkhamedzhanov (b. 1928) and the Kirgiz writer Chïngïz AYTMATOV, which explores guilt and responsibility among creative writers under Stalin's repression.

Drama in Kazakh moved, after the controversies of the early 1920s, into Soviet stylistic and thematic grooves, with establishment playwrights like Ghabit Makhmud-ŭlï Müsrepov (b. 1902). His *Amankeldï* (1936, rev. version 1958; Amankeldï) is considered by Marxists a perfect specimen of SOCIALIST REALISM in its use of stock characters involved in class warfare in Kazakhstan against implacable enemies during the Russian civil war of 1918–21.

Notwithstanding public encouragement given different genres, poetry has continued as before to be the most popular among readers. Kazakh poets incessantly receive exhortations to produce socially and politically useful verse. Nevertheless, a great deal of universal lyric, as well as narrative, poetry appears in print. Younger poets in the 1960s and 1970s also revealed a fascination with the history and significance of their native land for ethnic-group identity and for deep Kazakh attachments. Erkesh Ibrahim (Ebekenov, b. 1930) published five books of poetry before 1969, starting with *Qarlïghash* (1958; the swallow) and including two about Kokchetau, his native locality in northern Kazakhstan. Others, like Sagi Zhienbayev (b. 1934), Qayrat Zhŭmaghaliev (b. 1937), and Dukenbay Doszhanov (b. 1942), took more interest in humanity and nature than in the prescribed topicality reflected so much in the writings of older poets, such as Tayïr Zharokov (1908–1965). Zharokov's many volumes of verse, beginning with *Zhŭldiz zharïghï* (1932; radiance of the star), through *Stalin sŭngqarlarï* (1941; Stalin's falcons), to the several editions of *Qïrda tughan qŭrïsh* (1954 ff.; steel born in the prairie), and others, responded directly to the persistent call for metrical elucidation of the Communist Party outlook.

BIBLIOGRAPHY: Winner, T. G., *The Oral Art and Literature of the Kazakhs of Russian Central Asia* (1958); "La littérature kazakh," *Philologiae Turcicae Fundamenta* (1964): 154–55; Allworth, E., "The Changing Intellectual and Literary Community" and "The Focus of Literature," in Allworth, E., ed., *Central Asia: A Century of Russian Rule* (1967): 349–433

—EDWARD ALLWORTH

KAZAKOV, Yury

Russian short-story writer, b. 8 Aug. 1927, Moscow; d. 29 Nov. 1982

Having begun a career as a jazz musician, K. began to publish short stories in 1952 and then entered the Gorky Institute of World Literature, graduating in 1958. In the 1950s and 1960s K. traveled extensively in northern Russia. These travels generated, among other works, his *Severny dnevnik* (1961; northern diary).

Appearing after twenty years of Stalinist fiction glorifying agricultural and industrial production, K.'s early short stories had a special impact. His return to the lyricism, open-endedness, and the "eternal questions" of pre-Soviet authors, especially CHEKHOV, BUNIN, and the Turgenev of *A Sportsman's Sketches*, seemed a radical step during the period of the so-called first thaw (1953–57). K.'s use of character, plot, setting, and language is antithetical to traditional SOCIALIST REALISM. His characters are seldom heroic. Some are irredeemably negative: the hypocritical mendicant who tries to seduce his hostess's daughter in "Strannik" (1956; "The Mendicant," 1963); peasants grossly insensitive to the women close to them in "V gorod" (1961; "Going to Town," 1963) and "Na polustanke" (1954; "At the Station," 1963); the egotistical artist embittered by professional rejection in "Adam i Eva" (1962; "Adam and Eve," 1963). Other characters are presented ambiguously: Egor in "Trali-vali" (1959; "Silly Billy," 1963) may be lazy but he has moments of inspiration when he sings; a son leaving the village is unduly brusque with his tearful mother because he is afraid of his own emotions. Positive characters are shown not for their personal qualities but as people in the throes of a poignant experience— closeness to a loved one in the wilds in "Osen v dubovykh lesakh" (1963; "Autumn in the Oak Woods," 1963), the passing of first love in "Goluboe i zelyonoe" (1963; "The Blue and the Green," 1963). Plot is reduced to a minimum so that the quality of subtle and complex emotional shifts may dominate.

Central to K.'s work—and this is his most important, if least remarked, departure from Socialist Realism—is the view of man as an integral part of nature, subject to its eternal cycles. Men, women, children, and animals are manifestations of nature, rather than its subjugators, and ultimately must be part of it. The circus bear in "Teddi" (1961; "Teddy," 1963) detaches himself from his unnatural life and returns to the woods; city life distorts the love of man and woman in "Osen v dubovykh lesakh." People divorced from nature are out of touch with their inmost selves: the woman who returns from the city to her village in "Zapakh khleba" (1962; "The Smell of Bread," 1963); the sailors on vacation in "Proklyaty sever" (1964; "The Accursed North," 1963). In "Nikishkiny tayny" (1951; "Nikishka's Secrets," 1970), an eight-year-old boy mutely and vividly communes with the woods in his imagination. The nonverbal nature of his experience is conveyed by a spare narrative that approximates the boy's simple language.

K. was attacked for his atypical stories by some Soviet critics, who found his work pessimistic, overly literary, and not clear enough in its moral position. Similar criticism was later made of the work of many of the new generation of writers. This conflict of views was openly acknowledged in the early 1960s and may be understood as a result of the transition of post-Stalinist society into a more settled and prosperous state after the deprivations of forty years of social upheaval. By the end of the 1950s the model shock-worker (Stakhanovite) hero of earlier Soviet literature was no longer appropriate to the complex life of literate urban readers. K.'s work heralds and reflects this change.

K. was one of the first to write in a fresh, sincere voice about questions of conscience in contemporary life. By setting his stories in the wilderness of northern Russia, K. could present universal moral issues in isolation from their sociopolitical context. This method made him an influential forerunner of the two major types of short story to emerge in the 1960s: Young Prose, which examines the problems faced by the new generation of urban youth—especially the works of Anatoly Gladilin (b. 1935), Vasily AKSYONOV, and Andrey Bitov (b. 1937); and Village Prose, in which personal moral values are restored by a return to the simple,

eternal life of country folk—for example, works by Vasily Belov (b. 1933) and Valentin Rasputin (b. 1937). While K.'s stories are not of the literary quality of the 19th-c. masters he draws upon, they contain some moving vignettes of universal appeal and embody the characteristic artistic and moral integrity of the Russian literary tradition.

FURTHER WORKS: *Pervoe svidanie* (1955); *Manka* (1958); *Na polustanke* (1959); *Po doroge* (1961); *Rasskazy* (1962); *Tropiki na pechke* (1962); *Lyogkaya zhizn* (1963); *Selected Short Stories* [in Russian] (1963); *Dvoe v dekabre* (1966); *Vo sne ty gorko plakal* (1977). FURTHER WORKS IN ENGLISH: *Going to Town, and Other Stories* (1963); *Autumn in the Oak Woods* (1970)

BIBLIOGRAPHY: Gibian, G., Foreword to *Selected Short Stories* (1963): ix–xxv; Whitney, T. P., ed., *The New Writing in Russia* (1964): 97–102; Kramer, K. D., "Jurij K.: The Pleasures of Isolation," *SEEJ*, 10 (1966): 22–31; Collins, C., "Nature and Self in K.," *SEEJ*, 12 (1968): 397–406; Brown, D., *Soviet Russian Literature since Stalin* (1978): 157–61, 218–19

—PRISCILLA MEYER

KAZANTZAKIS, Nikos

Greek novelist, poet, dramatist, essayist, and travel writer, b. 18 Feb. 1883, Heraklion, Crete; d. 26 Oct. 1957, Freiburg, West Germany

The central fact in the life of K. is that it began on Crete in the last generation of that island's centuries-long resistance to foreign domination. Its central symbol is an event that occurred when he was a child, in 1889, during one of the final rebellions against Turkish rule. "My mother, my sister, and I sat glued to one another, barricaded within our house. We heard the frenzied Turks in the street outside, cursing, threatening, breaking down doors, and slaughtering Christians.... My father stood in wait behind the door, his musket loaded. In his hand, I remember, he held an oblong stone which he called a whetstone. He was sharpening a long black-handled knife on it. We waited. 'If the Turks break down the door and enter,' he had told us, 'I plan to slaughter you myself before you fall into their hands.' My mother, sister, and I had all agreed. Now we were waiting." The story is recounted in K.'s posthumously published "spiritual autobiography," *Anafora ston Greko* (1961; *Report to Greco*, 1965), which is not always reliable as literal history. But K. tells it again in the most factual of his novels, *O Kapetan Mihalis* (1953; *Freedom or Death*, 1956)—a likely indication of its historicity and a certain sign of its symbolic significance for the man who would become the greatest and most controversial of modern Greek writers. From so insular a beginning, K., who lost the Nobel Prize by a single vote in 1957, became one of the most universal of writers, at once Greek and more broadly European. That he left Crete as a young man and spent most of his life in the West merely reaffirms his homeland's attraction, for he returns constantly to it in his art, raising such local incidents to the level of universl metaphor. Drawn both to the intellectual constructs of the West (he wrote his dissertation at the University of Athens on Nietzsche and studied with Henri BERGSON at the Collège de France) and to the unique heritage of his native

Crete, K. created a literature expressive of Greek and of modernist culture alike.

One theme that unifies his career—from the early translations, textbooks, verse dramas, and travel books through the fourteen-year enterprise of his *Odyssia* (1938; *The Odyssey: A Modern Sequel*, 1958), to the novels of his final phase—is the fight for linguistic reform. It is difficult for outsiders to comprehend the significance of the language issue in modern Greek culture. There are two separate Greek languages: one, the *demotiki*, the spoken tongue, grafting naturally to ancient Greek the results of centuries of interpenetration with foreigners; the other, the *katharevousa*, an invented language, designed after Greek independence to bypass foreign influence and restore the pristine glories of classical Greek. The latter is an artificial and inflated language, well suited to scholars and bureaucrats; the former is wonderfully adaptable, the language not just of the people but of the poets as well. Yet, for nearly a century, the scholars and bureaucrats (particularly under right-wing regimes) endeavored to impose their language upon the poets.

K. devoted much of his life to this battle; it served to brand him as a radical and affected the reception of even his greatest works within Greece. *Odyssia* has repeatedly been accused of being too revolutionary in vocabulary and diction, and the radicalism of K.'s language has inevitably become associated with the independence of his thought. There was an early move to excommunicate him from the Orthodox Church; *O telefteos pirasmos* (1955; *The Last Temptation of Christ*, 1960) was attacked as heretical (in one case by a critic since proven not to have read the novel); the Archbishop of Athens refused to allow K.'s burial from the cathedral. It is hardly coincidental that K. lived most of his life as an artist outside Greece—except for the years of World War II, which he felt he had to share with his suffering countrymen—or that his reputation for a long time was greater beyond Greece's borders (he has been translated into some forty languages), or even that his grave in his native Heraklion has become something of a shrine.

For his work is inevitably and unmistakably Greek, or, more specifically, Cretan. A second unifying theme of K.'s canon is the metaphor which he labels the "Cretan Glance" and which he defines as that attitude with which man, "without hope yet without fear," acknowledges the limitations and dangers inherent in human life and despite them—because of them even—persists in living fully at the edge of the abyss. "This glance which confronts life and death so bravely, I call Cretan." The metaphor is obviously drawn from the heroic yet futile Cretan resistance to Venetian and then Turkish oppression, and it is at the heart of each of his works of fiction: not merely in *O Kapetan Mihalis*, which is based on the Cretan revolt of 1889, or in *Vios kai politia toy Alexi Zorba* (1946; *Zorba the Greek*, 1953), whose action similarly takes place on Crete; but also in those novels set on the mainland—*I adherfofadhes* (1963; *The Fratricides*, 1964), based on the civil war of 1946–49; or in the Greek lands of Asia Minor—*O Hristos xanastavronete* (1954; *The Greek Passion*, 1953), concerned with the exodus that followed the defeat by Turkey in 1922; or in lands beyond Greece—*O telefteos pirasmos*, set in biblical Galilee and Judea. It informs each of the movements of K.'s Odysseus as he progresses beyond Ithaca to the Mycenaean mainland to Minoan Crete to Egypt and the African interior and finally to the Antarctic seas, a movement as much philosophical as it is historical and geographical. Each of K.'s heroes—he calls each one a "colossus"—is a development from the Cretan *pallikari*, the heroes of the long resistance whose portraits are found even today throughout the island.

But the Kazantzakian colossus has Western roots as well: here his source is the Nietzschean *Übermensch*, that philosophical hero who extends his grasp beyond the normal but who does no more than all men could, as K. views it, were they willing to bear the cost. This union of disparate forces (made still more disparate by a dash of the Bergsonian *élan vital*) is characteristic of K.'s thought; characteristic, too, is the unresolved tension that emerges from such a union. For Kosmas, the artist figure of *O Kapetan Mihalis*, a character derived and extended from K.'s self-image, the tension is between his Western education and a Cretan tradition to which he is impelled but which he knows is archaic; for Jesus in *O telefteos pirasmos* it is between his desire for a simple human life and the impulse toward godhead; for Odysseus, who encapsulates them all, it is between the just and joyful needs of the body and the more imperative demands of the spirit. When Odysseus at the end of his long and challenging journey dissolves, quite literally, into pure spirit, we may assume that his creator has chosen one supreme good over the other; but then we note the vital, even sensuous verse in which this final progression is recorded, and we realize that the conflict has simply been moved to some higher level. In the end, it is the tension itself for which K. strives. The only novel of his in which a full thematic resolution is reached, *O ftohoylis toy Theoy* (1956; *Saint Francis*, 1962), is also, not coincidentally, the least successful of his mature fictions.

The continuity of K.'s imagery and thought is apparent throughout his work, from the early poetic essay called *Salvatores Dei: Asketiki* (1927; *The Saviors of God: Spiritual Exercises*, 1960), where he first elaborated his complex dialectic, to the late novels for which he is best known outside Greece. But it is *Odyssia* which he considered his masterwork and for which he believed he would be remembered. (Had he lived one more year after its appearance in English he would surely have won the Nobel Prize.) K.'s epic poem is a quite conscious challenge to Homer, encompassing all the knowledge of our world as Homer's does of Bronze Age Greece: the poet called it simply *Odyssia*; it was Kimon Friar, with whom he collaborated on the superb English translation, who suggested the subtitle, *A Modern Sequel*. Here we find functioning in concert all those concerns that dominate individual novels: the themes of Cretan and Greek history (*O Kapetan Mihalis*), of radical politics and the need for renewal (*O Hristos xanastavronete*), of spirituality and myth (*O telefteos pirasmos*), of an evolving philosophy of art and humanity (*Vios kai politia toy Alexi Zorba*). *Odyssia* manifests as well a profound sensitivity to ancient civilizations and mythopoesis, a deep knowledge of and insight into modern archaeological and anthropological discoveries, and a moving and convincing statement of humanistic concern.

It is *Odyssia* that leads us to inevitable comparisons to K.'s modernist contemporaries: to the moral sense of Thomas MANN; to the vision of ascendant man, the spirit of place, and the personal travel essay of D. H. LAWRENCE; to the encyclopedic structure and mythic perspective of James JOYCE. But it is the differences between K. and the Western modernists that are most revealing: the conviction and intensity at the heart of the metaphor of the Cretan Glance make Mann's pervasive irony seem out of place; its humane center makes the mystical Lawrence of, say, *The Plumed Serpent*, seem rather jejune; its inherent feeling for the workings of myth makes the Homeric analogue of Joyce's *Ulysses* appear somewhat formal and even superficial. The particular humanistic involvement of K.'s art—Western in its intellectuality, Cretan at its core—distinguishes the artist from all his contemporaries. The strengths and flaws alike of K.'s art are derived from this mixture of Cretan and Western influence. He is representative of the modernist literary experience and, because of this mix, uniquely beyond it.

FURTHER WORKS: *Ti ida sti Rousia* (1928); *Toda-Raba* (1934; *Toda-Raba*, 1964); *Ispania* (1937; *Spain*, 1963); *Iaponia-Kina* (1938; *Japan/China*, 1963); *Anghlia* (1941; *England*, 1965); *Omirou Iliada* (1955); *Theatro* (1955); *Boudhas* (1956); *Epistoles apo ti Galatia* (1958; partial tr. in *The Suffering God: Selected Letters to Galatea and to Papastephanou*, 1979); *Le jardin des rochers* (1959; *The Rock Garden*, 1963); *Tertsines* (1960); *Taxidevontas* (1961; *Journeying: Travels in Italy, Egypt, Sinai, Jerusalem, and Cyprus*, 1975); *O Morias* (1961; *Journey to the Morea*, 1965); *Tetrakosia Grammata toy K. ston Prevelaki* (1965); *Symposion* (1971; *Symposium*, 1975). FURTHER WORKS IN ENGLISH: *Three Plays* (1969); *Alexander the Great* (1981)

BIBLIOGRAPHY: Stanford, W. B., *The Ulysses Theme* (1954): 211–40; Prevelakis, P., *N. K. and His Odyssey* (1961); Izzet, A., *N. K.: Biographie* (1965); Kazantzakis, H., *N. K.: A Biography Based on His Letters* (1968); Janiaud-Lust, C., *N. K.: La vie, son œuvre* (1970); special K. issue, *JML*, 2, 2 (1971–82); Bien, P., *K. and the Linguistic Revolution in Greek Literature* (1972); Bien, P., *N. K.* (1972); special K. bibliographical issue, *Mantatoforos*, No. 5 (1974); McDonough, B. T., *Nietzsche and K.* (1978); Friar, K., ed., *The Spiritual Odyssey of N. K.* (1979); Lea, J. F., *The Politics of Salvation* (1979); Levitt, M. P., *The Cretan Glance: The World and Art of N. K.* (1980); Bien, P., *N. K., Novelist* (1989)

—MORTON P. LEVITT

K. has found many new ways of understanding Ulysses in terms of modern thought. He has devised many new and significant adventures for him. He has presented a fully integrated portrait of the hero—as wanderer and politician, as destroyer and preserver, as sensualist and ascetic, as soldier and philosopher, as pragmatist and mystic, as legislator and humorist. He has combined many scattered elements in the ancient and modern tradition. But the earnestness with which he urges his Cretan view of life must not make us accept his Odysseus as an entirely new conception of the hero. On the contrary this neo-Greek hero is something much more like a "synthesis" of the whole post-Homeric myth. And the prevailing mood is fundamentally that of the Stoics. As one studies K.'s philosophic writings in general one constantly recalls the *Meditations* of Marcus Aurelius.

W. B. Stanford, *The Ulysses Theme* (1954), p. 239

According to K. something of the nature of the divinity is expressed in poetic creation. Amid the general corruption, certain privileged beings are endowed with the capacity to carry on the work of "God." Generally speaking, the action of all rational creatures participates in this mystery. But poetic creation is the God-bearing activity par excellence. The poet's longing for immortality is not only a desire to triumph over the common lot of man. It is the

manifestation of a supernatural reality, of the primordial impulse "penetrating plants, beasts and men." But "God," if He is ever present, is not almighty. Man's dedication to creative activity alone "saves God" (*The Saviors of God*). Beneath this pretense of submission to the spirit of creation smoldered a tyrannical ambition and a haughty faith in the power of man such as had not been seen since the Renaissance. [1958]

Pandhelis Prevelakis, *N. K. and His Odyssey* (1961), p. 27

The Cretan Glance for K., therefore, was an attempted synthesis of those contraries which he believed underline all human and natural endeavor, but a synthesis not so much of permanent as of momentary harmony, which in turn builds into a greater tension and explodes toward a higher and more inclusive synthesis in an ever upward and spiraling onrush, leaving behind it the blood-stained path of man's and nature's endeavors. This may explain much that, from a more restricted point of view, seems contradictory in his life and thought, but which takes on another value when seen as the ever-shifting sections of larger and, in themselves, ever-changing unities . . . It is a double vision between whose dual tensions rises the third inner eye that soars on the balancing wings of good and evil, that no sooner creates a new law than it begins immediately to conceive of an opposed and contrary law with which to knock it down.

Kimon Friar, Introduction to *The Odyssey: A Modern Sequel* (1958), p. xx

K.'s great cohorts, the "bodyguards of the Odyssey" as he called them [Homer, Bergson, Nietzsche, and Zorba], along with a host of secondary, though by no means inferior figures, Christ, Lenin, Dante, Buddha, Greco, Psycharis and others, whom he enshrined in a series of *terza rima* cantos, helped enrich him with the formal means, the discipline, the example . . . for the technical consummation of his creation. But from his dreams and travels he drew the raw material of his work . . .

Each of K.'s works should be viewed as the repetition, elaboration or elucidation of a concept or image from the *Odyssey*. The novels . . . all embody one of the many germs of the Odyssean conception; the travel books to a lesser extent, without the same concentration. Here it is essential to clarify the often overlooked fact that K. was a writer (and a man) of one single, all-encompassing vision: Within the *Odyssey* can be found the points of departure for all his later novels. Through the novels K. sought a level from which he might successfully address himself to a much broader readership than his poetry would have ever permitted . . . The travel books are of a different category: They do not elaborate, they prefigure.

F. A. Reed, "Translator's Note," in N. K., *Journey to the Morea* (1965), pp. 178, 183

I have always nurtured much admiration and . . . a sort of affection for [K.'s] work. I had the pleasure of being able to give public testimony of my admiration in Athens, at a period when official Greece was frowning upon her greatest writer. The welcome given my testimony by my student audience constituted the finest homage [K.'s] work and acts could have been granted. I also do not forget that the very day when I was regretfully receiving a distinction that K. deserved a hundred times more, I got the most generous of telegrams from him. Later on, I discovered with consternation that this message had been drafted a few days before his death. With him, one of our last great artists vanished. I am one of those who feel and will go on feeling the void that he has left. [1959]

Albert Camus, quoted in Helen Kazantzakis,
N. K.: A Biography Based on His Letters (1968),
p. 560

If we study K. apart from demoticism we severely limit our understanding not only of him but of the general conditions of Greek literary life. Linguistic problems have been intimately connected with literary ones in Greece, and with political life as well. . . . It is vital for us to realize that the problem of language obsessed K. from the very start and that this obsession was one of the few constants stretching unchanged throughout all the other permutations of his career. . . . The totality of K.'s work seems to have as its common denominator—perhaps even more than the search for God, even more than political or humanitarian zeal—a determination to mobilize the twenty-four recalcitrant letters of the Greek alphabet and make them express his complicated soul.

Peter Bien, *K. and the Linguistic Revolution in
Greek Literature* (1972), pp. 4–5

When one looks back over K.'s *Odyssey* and recalls its thousands of vivid details as well as its irresistibly forceful major passages . . . one sees that one has had part in what is likely the most remarkable sustained accomplishment in verse that the modern imagination has been privileged to record. When one notes, too, that this huge, questing hymn to daring and fecundity has been written, not at all in a Miltonic striving for "greatness," but in the most intense and personal creative joy, one is but the more impressed, and the more indebted to both poet and translator . . .

The final good of the new *Odyssey*, I suspect, will not be to glorify the Nietzschean hero, or make aesthetically viable the ideas of Bergson, Nietzsche, or Spengler, or even "man's dauntless mind," but to restore the sense of the heedless delight in living to a jaded populace. To poets it is, and it will be a living demonstration of the profound vitality that words may be made to carry by a poet who is himself profoundly vital, and of the human power that makes the best poetry nearly as valuable as life . . . It is this

power which appropriates the forms of writing and uses them to create and explore new realms of the imagination, and ultimately to establish them, so that they may become the most enduring ground of the spirit. In this connection, Odysseus is likely to prove a hero to us in more ways than even his chronicler has envisioned, and K. himself in all ways.

James Dickey, in Kimon Friar, ed., *The Spiritual
Odyssey of N. K.* (1979), p. 49

KAZIN, Alfred

American critic and essayist, b. 5 June 1915, Brooklyn, New York; d. 4 June 1998, New York, New York

K. was born and reared in the Brownsville section of Brooklyn, the son of Jewish immigrants. He received his undergraduate degree from City College of New York, and an M.A. from Columbia University in 1938. At nineteen he began his career as a critic, reviewing books for the *New Republic*, under the tutelage of literary editor Malcolm COWLEY. During this same period he also did occasional reviewing for the *New York Times* and the *New York Herald-Tribune*. Among the earliest influences on both his thinking and writing were the leftist writers associated with Philip Rahv (1908-1973) and the *Partisan Review*. Beginning in 1953, when he accepted a lectureship at Harvard for one year, K. taught at various universities in or near New York City, including Smith, Amherst, New York University, and the New School for Social Research. In 1961 he was the Christian Gauss Lecturer in American Studies at Princeton University, and in 1963 gave the Beckman lectures at the University of California at Berkeley. From 1973 until his retirement in 1985 he was a professor at Hunter College and the Graduate School of the City University of New York.

In 1942 K. published his first book, *On Native Grounds*, a study of modern American Prose from 1890 to 1940. He began the book in 1938 at the suggestion of Carl Van Doren (1885-1950), one of his professors at Columbia, and completed it with the aid of a Guggenheim Fellowship, awarded in 1940. Although it generally avoids poetry and such significant movements as American romanticism, the book was well received critically, and provided the solid foundation for K.'s enduring reputation as an authority on American literature and culture. *On Native Grounds* begins with William Dean Howells and the concept of realism in American fiction, and concludes with the 1930s, a period in which literature was often subsumed by politics and leftist idealism. It was a time with which K., coming of age living and writing in New York during the Great Depression, was intimately acquainted.

K.'s second book, *A Walker in the City* (1951), was the first of an autobiographical trilogy that would eventually include *Starting Out in the Thirties* (1965) and *New York Jew* (1978). These studies of a literary life combine penetrating criticism and analysis of a vital intellectual milieu with a nostalgic regret at the transitions in urban Jewish culture, both social and intellectual, which was so essentially a part of his generation. The optimism that informs the intellectual spirit and energy of *On Native Grounds* is generally balanced in *A Walker in the City* by the sobering awareness of the Holocaust, which had the ironically positive effect of renewing a sense of cultural heritage across the strata of the American Jewish population. K.'s analysis of his formative decade in *Starting Out in the Thirties* is largely a defense of the idealism and confidence among the radicals of the American anti-Stalinist Left. In the 1940s and 1950s that sense of purpose had largely been eclipsed by the rise of Soviet totalitarianism, in particular events such as the purges of dissident Communists conducted under the regime of Joseph Stalin, and the nonagression pact between Stalin and Hitler in 1939.

K. resisted the shift of many of his contemporaries toward the political and cultural conservatism prevalent in the 1950s, and in his essays published in *The Inmost Leaf* (1955) and *Contemporaries* (1962) took issue with the complacency of the American Intellectual community. The rebellious enthusiasm that had energized the quest for a radical socialist democracy of the 1930s had, to his profound regret, given way to the alienation and self-absorbed complacency of what he termed the "Alone Generation." In *Bright Book of Life* (1973) K. surveyed contemporary American fiction from Ernest HEMINGWAY to Norman MAILER, and further lamented the unfulfilled promise of 20th-c. American writing. K. found the works of admittedly talented and celebrated writers such as Truman CAPOTE, Ralph ELLISON, John UPDIKE, and others lacking a comprehensive social and historical substance and solidity. In K.'s view the writers of that time lacked essential social and imaginative vision. There was no one whose work clearly demonstrated that the artist was indeed a force for change in society and history.

With the publication of the essays in *An American Procession* (1984) K. continued his study of the American writer as the artist separated, in the pursuit of a personal freedom, from the forces of change in society. In K.'s view there is a preoccupation with "style," in the form of a subjective view of history that is shaped as a personal defense against the duplicity and prevarication that all too frequently characterize what purport to be forces for change in American society.

It could be cogently argued that *God and the American Writer* (1998), with its emphasis on American letters as a God-infused post-Calvinist literature, is a distinct departure from K.'s best-known work, *On Native Grounds*, which placed its emphasis on realism and the promise of a continuing process that was moving America toward a political and cultural liberation. In *God and the American Writer* K. traces the heritage of Calvinism from the earliest Puritan writers such as Increase Mather and Jonathan Edwards through the modern authors of the American canon. Organized religion may fail or come up short for the writer, but questions of mortality invariably arise and lead back to God as pervasive entity.

K. has always been a staunch defender of the radical-democratic tradition in American literature, with a particular admiration for the writer as a latter-day romantic rebel. As literary fashions and trends changed, he remained consistent, writing with a distinct personal voice and reserving his highest praise for those who wrote with a passion for integrity and broad social vision.

BIBLIOGRAPHY: Cook, R. M., "The Journals of A. K.," *AmLH*, 2 (1990): 242-50; Cowan, M., "Walkers in the Street: American Writers and the Modern City," *Prospects*, 6 (1981) 281-11; Hazlett, J. D., "Repossessing the Past: Discontinuity and History in A. K.'s *A Walker in the City*," *Biography*, 7 (1984): 325-40; Schneider, R., "A. K.: Americanist," *JAC*, 13 (1990): 61-69

—RICHARD KEENAN

KEILLOR, Garrison

(pseud. Gary Edward Keillor) American novelist, humorist, short-story writer, storyteller, poet, essayist, and entertainer, b. 7 August 1942, Anoka, Minnesota

K. was raised in a strict but loving fundamentalist Minnesota home. His fierce sense of independence and talent in writing led him to enter the University of Minnesota, where his poetry for student-run publications was awarded the Academy of American Poets prize. He also worked in college radio, which trained him for his eventual career as the host of the long-running National Public Radio program *A Prairie Home Companion*. The stories narrated on this program by K.—considered one of the foremost storytellers in the U.S. today—have been collected and published in journals and books, and *A Prairie Home Companion* has been inducted into the Radio Hall of Fame.

K.'s first publication was a poem in the *Atlantic* in 1968, entitled "Some Matter Concerning the Occupant." In the following years he began to write articles for the *New Yorker* while continuing to work in radio. By 1980 *A Prairie Home Companion* was broadcasting live shows on a regular basis. K.'s improvisational storytelling is a major portion of the radio show. The stories are focused around the fictional town of Lake Wobegon and end with a subtle moral. By 1982 K. had enough stories to publish his first book, *Happy to Be Here*. The success of the radio show and of his book led to further writings, including *Lake Wobegon Days* (1985), *Leaving Home* (1987), *We Are Still Married* (1989), *WLT: A Radio Romance* (1991), *The Book of Guys* (1993), *Wobegon Boy* (1997), two children's books, *Cat, You Better Come Home* (1995) and *The Old Man Who Loved Cheese* (1996), and pieces for such periodicals as the *Atlantic Monthly* and the *New Yorker*.

K.'s place in American literary history is assured because of his natural ability to weave a story around a simple plot. The characters he creates are realistic, with foibles and talents, and they cope with the daily minutiae of life in ways that K.'s readers would like to, but are often afraid to try. K.'s stories are told in the tradition of the storytellers of yesteryear, gentle tales of everyday life with a moral at the end that the reader can take away and remember.

BIBLIOGRAPHY: Lee, J. Y., *G. K.: A Voice of America* (1991); Scholl, P. A., *G. K.* (1993)

—MARCY TANTER

KELLEY, William Melvin

American novelist and short-story writer, b. 1 Nov. 1937, New York, New York

Having received an education at prestigious private schools—Fieldston School and Harvard University—K. started his career as a writer auspiciously: he received the Dana Reed Price for creative writing in 1960 and fellowships for work on his first novel, which received a Richard and Hinda Rosenthal Foundation Award. In the course of his career he has taught at the State University of New York, Geneseo, at the New School for Social Research, and at the University of Paris, Nanterre. He has lived in Italy and France, where his contact with the expatriate African community had a significant impact on his work, as did his travels in Europe.

His first novel, *A Different Drummer* (1962), precedes those travels and focuses on black-and-white relations in the American South, but it anticipated a theme of his later novels: the significance of African ancestry for African Americans. Tucker Caliban, the descendant of a fiercely resistant African chief brought to the U.S. on a slaveship, after living a quiet life working in the service of a white family who has employed—and previously owned—all of his ancestors, one day decides to end this state of continued servitude and buys a plot of land, destroys all his property, with special destructiveness reserved for those objects reminiscent of slavery, spreads salt on the land, and leaves. The novel implies that Tucker serves as a kind of reincarnation of his African ancestor, and his actions spawn an exodus of all African Americans living in the fictitious Southern state that provides the setting for the plot. The novel is organized into many subsections, all of which explore these events and the history leading up to them from the subjective point of view of the narrator of that subsection. K. thus sympathetically renders the history of an African American leader from the North who has become too bound up with the prestige and power of leadership to be able to lead the folk—only they can lead themselves. Similarly impotent are sympathetic white characters in the novel; they experience the exodus with bafflement, doing nothing to help or stop it. However, as the novel shows, the act of liberation begun by African Americans has liberating effects on some whites as well, since they will no longer be implicated in oppression. The novel skillfully interweaves the perspectives of a host of characters to illustrate how a system of racial oppression leaves no-one untouched, however different the effects—though always negative—of it may be on individuals.

Written while K. spent time in Rome, his second novel, *A Drop of Patience* (1965), focuses on Ludlow Washington, a blind jazz musician. His very blindness becomes a biting metaphor for the absurdities of racism: despite his own inability to perceive color, he must attend a segregated school for the blind. Later, as a jazz musician, he marries his landlord's daughter, has a child with her, and then leaves her. This act is visited upon him when he has an affair with a younger white woman who leaves him once she is pregnant. His career as a musician is revived by a fan—in an approximate parallel to Charlie Parker's life—after he undergoes years of misery in minstrelsy and mental institutions. Similarly to *A Different Drummer*, K.'s second novel emphasizes the need to free oneself psychologically from crippling racism; however, it also cynically comments on the idea of a "colorblind" society.

K.'s third novel, *dem* (1967), is similarly cynical and deals with black-white relations as well. But while *A Different Drummer* still sounds a note of hope, in that the exodus inspired by Tucker Caliban not only frees African Americans but appears to have redemptive potential even for some whites, *dem* sees black-white relations as beyond repair. Tam Mitchell gives birth to twins, one black and one white. When Pierce, her young executive husband, sets out to find Tam's African American lover in Harlem, he needs Carlyle Bedlow and Calvin Coolidge Johnson as guides, because he cannot even understand people in Harlem, a fact that symbolically underlines how far apart K. sees black and white worlds. When Pierce finds out that Calvin Johnson is the father of one of the twins, Johnson refuses to acknowledge his paternity. His act is to be seen as a form of revenge for the legacy of illegitimacy white slaveholders left behind.

Dunford Travels Everywheres (1970) may well be K.'s most ambitious work in terms of experimentation and style. Often compared to James JOYCE's *Finnegan's Wake* in its experimental language, K.'s fourth novel poses a serious challenge for readers. Alternating conventional narrative with sections using a new language based in English but utilizing Harlem street language, Pidgin, and Bantu, as well as innovative spelling in an attempt to create a language of the African Diaspora, *Dunford Travels Everywheres* interweaves the stories of two protagonists. Chig Dunford is an educated African American travelling in Europe while Carlyle Bedlow lives in Harlem with connections to a world of crime. Both move in a netherworld of intricate conspiracies that appears to be surreal, yet they encounter evidence of the reality of this conspiracy, which involves, in one "Chig Dunford episode" in the novel, an oceanliner that carries African slaves on the lower decks. Though from different spheres of life, both characters encounter the continued oppression of peoples of African descent and, in sections that are dream-like and almost defy understanding because of their linguistic difficulties, attempt to grasp the truth behind the surface lives they lead. While this novel is K.'s most ambitious, it has not found a wide readership and a mixed critical reception, largely because of its linguistically difficult passages, which make up about half of the novel.

K. established his reputation as a writer with *A Different Drummer*, which remains his most widely read novel and the one that has remained in print consistently. The reasons for the less enthusiastic reception of his other novels might not be merely artistic; his political vision becomes both more pessimistic and tends to have more separatist leanings. It remains difficult to assess whether this has contributed significantly to their neglect.

FURTHER WORKS: *Dancers on the Shore* (1964)

BIBLIOGRAPHY: Gayle, A., *The Way of the New World: The Black Novel in America* (1975): 367-76; Bell, B., *The Afro-American Novel and Its Tradition* (1987): 295-301; Faulkner, H., "The Uses of Tradition: W. M. K.'s *A Different Drummer*," *MFS*, 21 (1975-76): 535-42; Nadeau, R. L., "Black Jesus: A Study of K.'s *A Different Drummer*," *StBL*, 2 (Summer 1971): 13-15

—MARTIN JAPTOK

KEMAL, Yaşar

(Anglicized as Yashar Kemal, born Yasar Kemal Gökçeli) Turkish novelist, short-story writer, and essayist, b. 1922, Adana

K., Turkey's most famous novelist, frequently mentioned in the Western press as a leading contender for the Nobel Prize for literature, was born in southern Turkey, where he was exposed to the squalor, brutality, and injustices of village life. At five, he saw his father killed while praying at the mosque. During the same incident, K. lost one eye. At nine, he started going to school, walking to a remote village. He never went beyond eighth grade.

In the ensuing years, K. worked at a variety of jobs—cotton-picker, construction foreman, farmhand, clerk, cobbler's helper, petition writer, and substitute teacher—and these youthful experiences brought him closer to both the deprivations and the dauntless spirit of the laboring classes. During this same period he also developed an interest in and acquired a strong knowledge of Turkish folklore.

Among K.'s first publications were some poems and several surveys of Anatolian folklore. His first book, *Ağıtlar* (1943;

laments), was a compilation of folk elegies. In 1950 he was arrested on charges of disseminating Communist propaganda but was acquitted. Moving to Istanbul in 1951, K. joined the staff of the leading Istanbul daily, *Cumhuriyet*, as a roving reporter, later becoming a columnist and special-feature writer. He also wrote screenplays for several successful Turkish films based on Anatolian legends and themes.

K.'s journalistic writing, utilizing a colloquial and lyrical style, set a new trend in reporting. His travelogues, interviews, and feature stories have been collected in a number of volumes. In 1963 K. left *Cumhuriyet* to devote himself to creative writing and to campaign for the leftist Turkish Labor Party. He also published a political weekly, *Ant*.

K. first attracted literary attention with *Sari sicak* (1952; yellow heat), a collection of short stories, and *Teneke* (1955; tin can), a novella, but it was not until the publication of *İnce Memed* (1955; *Memed, My Hawk*, 1960) that he was catapulted to national literary fame. This action-filled novel presents as a folk hero a bandit who—somewhat like Robin Hood—takes up arms against the exploiters of the poor. *İnce Memed*, which has been translated into twenty-five languages, set K. on the road to international renown and remains his all-time popular work.

İnce Memed was followed by *Ortadirek* (1960; *The Wind from the Plain*, 1964), a moving saga of destitute peasants traveling in search of work. This novel, compared by some critics to STEINBECK's *The Grapes of Wrath*, further enhanced K.'s literary reputation as a master of the "village novel," which became a major mode of Turkish fiction from the mid-1950s onward. With two subsequent major novels, *Yer demir gök bakır* (1963; *Iron Earth, Copper Sky*, 1979) and *Ölmez otu* (1968; *The Undying Grass*, 1978), it forms a trilogy about the tragic life of the Anatolian peasant as well as his indomitable spirit in the face of natural disasters and the injustice perpetrated by privileged landowners. The final book of the trilogy is also an interesting novelistic study of myth and fantasy.

İnce Memed II (1969; *They Burn the Thistles*, 1977) is the sequel to his best-known work. Although it continues the story of his original protagonist, it can be read as an independent novel. His huge two-volume novel *Akçasazın ağaları* (the lords of Akchasaz), consisting of *Demirciler çarşısı cinayeti* (1974; *The Lords of Akchasaz: Murder in the Ironsmiths Market*, 1979) and *Yusufcuk Yusuf* (1975; turtledove Yusuf), explores the human drama and the traditional strifes of southern Turkey.

In his fiction, K. delineates the suffering of the underprivileged in the countryside, mainly in and around the Chukurova region. His style is both lyrical and dramatic. Most of his characters are vivid. The narration combines the directness of social realism with techniques reminiscent of STREAM OF CONSCIOUSNESS. His ear perfectly attuned to the vernacular of the peasant, K. excels in dialogue.

K. has made a deliberate attempt to create a modern mythology out of the tales and legends of southern Turkey. His abiding interest in folklore has led him to write new versions of some of Turkey's best-known folk tales: *Üç anadolu efsanesi* (1967; three Anatolian legends); *Ağrıdağı efsanesi* (1970; *The Legend of Ararat*, 1975), a simple and moving story about starcrossed loves in eastern Turkey; *Binboğalar efsanesi* (1971; *The Legend of the Thousand Bulls*, 1976), based on the stories of the Yürük nomadic tribes; and others. In addition to his retelling of this traditional material, K. seems to be striving toward the creation of a mythic world of his own in a manner similar to FAULKNER's Yoknapatawpha.

In the 1970s K. began to explore the city of Istanbul and the coastal towns in his fiction. *Al gözüm seyreyle Salih* (1976; *Seagull*, 1981) is an evocation of a Black Sea fishing town written in a lilting, almost poetic style. *Kuşlar da gitti* (1978; the birds too are gone) is a novella of corruption and pollution in Istanbul. In *Deniz küstü* (1979; the sea is angry) K. paints a gripping panorama of human drama against the backdrop of the sea.

K.'s short stories have been collected in *Bütün hikâyeler* (1967; enlarged ed., 1975; complete stories). His novella *Teneke* was successfully adapted for the stage in 1965. In 1967 the dramatization of his *Yer demir gök bakır* shared first prize at the Nancy (France) International Theater Festival. K. has won numerous awards in Turkey and abroad, the first being the Varlik Prize of 1955 for *İnce Memed*.

K.'s popularity and stature stem from his dynamic plots, a narrative style that blends stark reality with lyricism, a skillful use of myths and local color, and vivid peasant characters of universal interest.

FURTHER WORKS: *Yanan ormanlarda elli gün* (1955); *Çukurova yana yana* (1955); *Peri bacalari* (1957); *Taş çatlasa* (1961); *Bu diyar baştan başa* (1971); *Çakircali efe* (1972); *Bir bulut kayniyor* (1974); *Baldaki tuz* (1974); *Yilani öldürseler* (1977). FURTHER WORKS IN ENGLISH: *Anatolian Tales* (1968)

BIBLIOGRAPHY: Tube, H., on *Anatolian Tales*, *Spectator* (9 Aug. 1968); 198; Blythe, R., on *Iron Earth, Copper Sky*, *Listener* (13 June 1974): 777; Jones, D. A.N., on *The Legend of Ararat*, *TLS* (5 Sept. 1975): 998; Theroux, P., on *They Burn the Thistles*, *NYTBR* (10 July 1977): 11; Pollitt, K., on *The Undying Grass*, *NYTBR* (18 June 1978): 14; special K. issue, *Edebiyat*, 5: 1–2 (1980)

—TALAT SAIT HALMAN

KENAZ, Yehoshua

Israeli novelist, short-story writer, and translator, b. 2 Mar. 1937, Petah Tikva

The semipastoral environment in which K. grew up is reflected in the background of his first novel, *Aharey hahagim* (1964; *After the Holidays*, 1987), an invocation of the life of the veteran Hebrew colony Petah Tikva under the British Mandate. But the calm and order associated with this environment are a veneer over seething turmoil, conflict, and misery.

K.'s narrative is apparently naturalistic, relating to the surfaces of Israeli life, but the underlying currents are tempestuous and cruel. Through the Weiss family, the tensions within the Jewish sector, as well as those between Jews and Arabs, are exposed. Also exposed is the unbearable frustration of the crabbed life, pretending to imperturbable normality amongst the orchards and against the backdrop of the nationalist politics of the emergent *yishuv* (prestate Zionist establishment). The passions seem to be ignited by the heat of the summer, and relief beckons only "after the holidays," in the autumn. Yet there is violence and evil in this apparently placid setting. Limpid, transparent prose presents the narrative simply, so the violence of the emotions stands in stark contrast to the manner of the telling. What seems to be the gratuitous violence of the characters Baruch and Langfuss as well as the more oblique spite of the two Weiss daughters and Masha stem from the ubiquitous sexual frustration that is so rampant in the colony.

The concerns evinced in the first novel reappear in K.'s second, *Haishah hagdoiah min hahalomot* (1973; the great woman of the dreams). This again is a story taken from everyday Israeli life, this time based in Tel Aviv. The characters once more are not notably successful in the management of their business and personal affairs. Once more, we have the eruption of extreme situations within an apparent context of social naturalism. But here there is an explicit movement in the direction of the grotesque and the surrealistic. This is hinted at in the title, so that the reader is unsure whether the subject is waking reality or dream. The characters are inarticulate, either because they lack the vocabulary to put their feelings into words or because the words themselves are trimmed to the social needs of the environment, whereas their feelings are much stronger. For K.'s characters, violence is the normal means of expression. The prose is direct, allowing the action, unfiltered, to indicate the underlying emotions. But even in the case of the pathetic Shmulik, there is a shadow archetype that stands behind and beyond his actual wife, Malka—the great, dark woman who haunts his fantasies. The "great woman" stands on the outside, but it is the "mad dog" within him that does not allow him to sleep. And it is this mad dog that he feels might take its revenge on him at any moment.

If there is one subject that lies at the center of K.'s writing, it is the way in which individual passion accommodates itself within Israeli society. This society is represented by the veteran colony and its new immigrants, by the disadvantaged poor of Tel Aviv, by the child moving into adolescence, and by the new recruits facing their test, their rites of passage, in the Israeli army. The collection of long stories *Moment muziqaliy* (1980; musical moment) revolves around childhood. The title story, referring to Schubert's "Moments Musicaux," recalls the deep impression it made on him.

The theme of life's significant transitions is also handled in K.'s subsequent novel, *Hitganvut yhidim* (1986; infiltration of individuals), which tells of a platoon of new recruits in the Israeli army of the 1950s. The first-person narrative draws a complex, composite picture of different types, facing a grueling and fundamental experience. K. recalls not just his own initiation, but that of a collective within Israeli society, its maturation (reaching its potential) and its loss of previous attachments and old worlds.

FURTHER WORKS: *Baderekh el hahatulim* (1991)

BIBLIOGRAPHY: Yudkin, L. I., on *Moment muziqaliy, MHL*, 6, 1–2 (Summer 1980): 84–85; Ramras-Rauch, G., on *Moment muziqaliy, WLT*, 55, 1 (Winter 1981), 171; Vardi, D., on *Haishah hagdoiah min hahalomot, WLT*, 61, 3 (Summer 1987): 487–88; Mazors, Y., on *After the Holidays, WLT*, 62, 1 (Winter 1988), 174

—LEON I. YUDKIN

KENEALLY, Thomas

Australian novelist and dramatist, b. 7 Oct. 1935, Sydney

K. is one of the most prolific Australian novelists of the 20th c. His work covers a wide range of styles and subject matters, including suspense novels and mysteries, historical fiction, expressionism, and realism. His constant experimentation with literary forms and the consistent, craftsman-like quality of his work have established K. as a major figure in world literature.

K. was brought up in a Catholic family, and Catholicism is a recurring issue in his novels. At St. Patrick's College in New South Wales K. originally studied for the priesthood, and these experiences formed the backdrop of *Three Cheers for the Paraclete* (1968), a novel about a priest who struggles with the "local taboos" of the Australian church. K. received praise for the objective and compassionate portrayals of his principal characters, and this talent for characterization has served him well in his later novels, many of which feature actual historical figures as characters. K.'s early work earned him the Miles Franklin Award in 1967 and 1968 and the Captain Cook Bi-Centenary Prize in 1970.

Following a brief period with the Australian Citizens Military Forces (1968–1970), K. published *A Dutiful Daughter* (1971). This novel, the story of an Australian family of which the parents are half-human and half-bovine, was a departure for K., as he abandoned the realistic plots and characters of his earlier works and experimented with expressionistic techniques. Although he has never duplicated such an extreme departure from realism in any later novel, K. has continued to experiment. *Passenger* (1979), for example, features a narrative written from an unborn child's point of view.

Although several of K.'s early novels deal with his native Australia, he is a truly international writer. *The Chant of Jimmie Blacksmith* (1972) is a compelling story of an aborigine forced into a life of crime. K.'s first historical novel, *Blood Red, Sister Rose* (1974), is a recounting of the story of Joan of Arc, and the highly praised *Gossip from the Forest* (1975) takes place at the signing of the armistice ending World War I. In *Confederates* (1979) K. creates a mosaic of a group of soldiers at the second battle of Antietam, and critics lauded the writer for the accuracy and "American-ness" of his presentation of the American Civil War. One of K.'s best-known books, *Schindler's List* (1982; pub. in U.K. as *Schindler's Ark*, 1982), is the novelization of the real-life story of Oskar Schindler, a German manufacturer who helped European Jews escape the Holocaust. In *A Family Madness* (1985) K. deals with cultural conflicts in Australia. K.'s most recent novel is *Flying Hero Class* (1991).

While primarily regarded as a novelist, K. has established a successful reputation in other genres. His plays include *Halloran's Little Boat* (perf. 1966), *Childermass* (perf. 1968), and *An Awful Rose* (perf. 1972), all of which were produced in Sydney. His 1987 novel *The Playmaker* was adapted by Timberlake Wertenbaker (dates n.a.) as the play *Our Country's Good*, which enjoyed successful runs in both London and New York. He has written teleplays: *Essington* (1974) and *The World's Wrong End* (1981); travel literature: *Outback* (1983); and even a children's book: *Ned Kelley and the City of Bees* (1978).

The critical response to K.'s work has varied. Although generally responding favorably, many critics have been reluctant to accept K. as a true literary artist because of his prolific body of work and his general popularity. The critical debate over whether K. is a major literary figure or a strictly popular writer continues. But due to his consistent creativity and sensitive depiction of internationally accessible plots and characters, K. has established himself as an important figure in modern world literature.

K.'s reputation has continued to grow throughout the 1990s, helped in no small measure by the spectacular success of the film version of *Schindler's List* (Stephen Zaillian screenplay, 1993). K.'s recent literary works include the non-fiction *The Place Where*

Souls Are Born (1992), about his experiences in the American Southwest, as well as the novels *Woman of the Inner Sea* (1993), a picaresque novel about a woman fleeing an abusive husband and encountering adventure in the Australian outback; and *A River Town* (1995), which, like *Schindler's List* and other K. novels, features a reluctant hero in the person of the Irish-immigrant shopkeeper Tim Shea. In addition to literary activities, K. has been active in Australian politics, advocating complete independence for the British commonwealth.

FURTHER WORKS: *The Place at Whitton* (1964); *The Fear* (1965); *Bring Larks and Heroes* (1967); *The Survivor* (1969); *Moses the Lawgiver* (1975); *Season in Purgatory* (1976); *A Victim of the Aurora* (1977); *Bullie's House* (perf. 1980); *The Cut-Rate Kingdom* (1980); *Australia: Beyond the Dream Time* (1987, with Patsy Adam-Smith and Robyn Davidson); *To Asmara* (1989)

BIBLIOGRAPHY: Beston, J. B., "K.'s Violence," *JCL*, 9 (1974): 71–73; Breitinger, E., "T. K.'s Historical Novels," *Commonwealth Newsletter*, 10 (1976): 16–20; Vargo, E. P., "Struggling with a Bugaboo: The Priest Character in Achebe and Greene and K.," in Narasimhaiah, C. D., ed., *Awakened Conscience: Studies in Commonwealth Literature* (1978): 284–93; Brady, V., "The Most Frightening Rebellion: The Recent Novels of T. K.," *Meanjin*, 38 (1979): 74–86; Erhardt, M., "T. K.: A Checklist," *ALS*, 9 (1979): 98–117; McInherny, F., "Woman and Myth in T. K.'s Fiction," *Meanjin*, 40 (1981): 248–58; Hulse, M., "Virtue and the Philosophic Innocent: The British Reception of *Schindler's Ark*," *CritQ*, 25, 4 (1983): 43–52; Goodwin, K., "Political Power and Social Flexibility in African and Australian Novels," *WLWE*, 23 (1984): 96–108; Magill, F. N., ed., *Cyclopedia of World Authors II* (1989), Vol. 3: 824–26; Buckbridge, P., "Gossip and History in the Novels of Brian Penton and T. K.," *ALS*, 14, 4 (Oct. 1990): 436–49

—JASON BERNER

KENNEDY, William

American novelist, b. 16 Jan. 1928, Albany, N.Y.

Few writers have remained so inspired by their place of birth as K. His novels have consistently drawn from the three-hundred-year history of his home city, Albany, New York. He observed, "I write . . . as a person whose imagination has become fused with a single place, and in that place finds all the elements that a man ever needs for the life of the soul." Yet K.'s regard for his roots is complex. As the only child of a working-class couple from the Irish neighborhood of the North End, he admits that he didn't like the Albany of his youth. His restlessness motivated his leave-taking, but he eventually returned to Albany to channel his dissenting views into fiction. K.'s novels seek to reveal both the turpitude and the moral stature of his native characters. His creative focus clearly advanced beyond the depiction of social milieu with *Ironweed* (1983), which continued his exploration of contemporary Albany life, but revealed a more lyrical approach that expressed the interior lives of its characters.

After receiving a B. A. from Siena College, Loudonville, New York, in 1949, K. became an assistant sports editor and columnist

for the *Post Star* in Glen Falls, New York, for one year, then served in the U.S. Army as a sports editor and columnist from 1950 to 1952. Returning to his home town he worked as a reporter for the Albany *Times-Union* between 1952 and 1956, then moved to San Juan, Puerto Rico, to become an assistant managing editor and columnist for the *Puerto Rican World Journal*. In 1957, however, he was in Miami, Florida, as a reporter for the Miami *Herald*, where he received an award from the Puerto Rican Civil Association of Miami for investigative reporting. K. returned to Puerto Rico as a correspondent for Time-Life Publications and Knight newspapers from 1957 to 1959. He helped found the San Juan *Star* and was its managing editor between 1959 and 1961, but spent much of his time writing fiction. Returning to Albany when his father became ill in 1961, he decided to resume work at the Albany *Times-Union*. As a special writer for this newspaper from 1963 to 1970, K. asked to work only part-time so that he could continue his creative writing in earnest. His investigative reporting during this period earned him the Page One Award from the Newspaper Guild and the NAACP Award for responsible reporting. For a series of articles on Albany slums, he received the New York State Publishers Award for Community Service in 1965. That year K. also was nominated for the Pulitzer Prize in reporting.

While an Albany reporter, K. wrote his first novel, *The Ink Truck* (1969), which sold only a few thousand copies and remained underreviewed until its republication. His fellow Albany writer Doris Grumbach (b. 1918) secured him adjunct teaching assignments in creative writing at Empire State College, and he became a lecturer at the State University of New York at Albany from 1974 to 1982. The publication of *Legs* in 1975 began the "Albany cycle" of novels that would include *Billy Phelan's Greatest Game* (1978) and *Ironweed*. Saul BELLOW, who had K. as a writing student at the University of Puerto Rico, approached Viking Press to publish *Ironweed*, remarking on K.'s talent as a writer as evidenced in *Legs* and *Billy Phelan*. Viking agreed, also deciding to republish his previous novels during 1983 and 1984. K. became professor of English and was given tenure at State University of New York, Albany, in 1983 following the critical and popular success of *Ironweed*, which won both the Pulitzer Prize for fiction and the National Book Critics Circle Award in 1984. He was visiting professor at Cornell University during 1982–1983 and founder of the New York State Writers Institute in 1983.

Critics were impressed by the brilliant dialogue and expressive power of language in *The Ink Truck*. Using jargon from the city desk of an urban newspaper, phrases from the police blotter, language from local politicos, and slang from the Albany demimonde, K. sustained interest through sheer verbal energy and the believable eccentricities of his social character types.

Legs, the first novel of a trilogy that chronicled the vibrant past of Albany, featured the legendary 1930s criminal Jack "Legs" Diamond, whose gangster associations touched every class and culture in Albany. The clash of ethnic groups, the mix of gangsters, gamblers, and corrupt politicians, vivified by a narrator who is the gangster's legal advisor, led the reviewer Peter S. Prescott to comment that the novel "translated the career of a gangster into a shimmering witty story that combined fact and myth to prod at our national ambivalence toward celebrity criminals." Other reviewers, while acknowledging K.'s ability to present compelling social types through an accurate historical context, remarked on the lack of moral vision in *Legs*. *Billy Phelan's Greatest Game* continued the history of the Albany underworld with its corrupt politicians and crossover characters. The novel's hyperactive plot structure included numerous flashbacks—some reviewers judged them unnecessary—tangential character disclosures, and abundant subplots. The dialogue is teeming with wit and creative neologisms; the characters are well-oiled and exuberant; and the complicated plot structure is matched by complex character delineations. For most critics, K.'s superb dialogue, idiosyncratic but with the feel of historical authenticity, and his revealing period characters compensated for the novel's unfocused and overdeveloped plot structure. *Ironweed*, K.'s third novel in the series, departs substantially from his earlier fiction in its lyrical style, poetically charged with language that often approaches the surreal. Amidst the bleakness of vagrant existence the main characters seek the significance of their lives. The inner dialogue, supply crafted and imaginative, produces both heartfelt and satirical perceptions, and contributes to the novel's lyricism. Plot construction also shows an advance over K.'s previous novels. For example, the economical device of a returning ghost allows K. to eschew the rhetorical flourishes on the father-son theme evident in *Billy Phelan*. The characters of *Ironweed* speak a variety of rhetorical idioms and at times seem Joycean in their texture and social context.

K.'s interest in the formative years of American history produced *Quinn's Book* (1988), a wideranging novel centered on Daniel Quinn, a Civil War reporter whose curiosity leads him to describe the tumultuous social life of that era. Spanning the years 1849 to 1864, the plot has been criticized for lacking cohesiveness, much as *Legs* and *Billy Phelan* had been. However, its compelling scenes reflect many of the social and political tensions of the period, so that the episodic structure seems less chaotic. K.'s gift for presenting strong, colorful characters in fast-paced scenes is evident, even though his 19-c. dialogue often seems anachronistic.

K.'s gift for situating interesting historical characters has offered a deep appreciation of American popular culture. Part of his ability to create personable and forceful characters results from a journalist's ear for dialogue grounded in idioms evocative of the attitudes and experiences of certain American professions and historical periods. In one novel, *Ironweed*, the subjective dimensions of human life are given lyric stature even as its characters are framed within a realistic social milieu.

FURTHER WORKS: *O Albany!: An Urban Tapestry* (1983); *The Cotton Club* (1984, with Francis Ford Coppola); *Charlie Malarkey and the Belly Button Machine* (1986, with Brendan Christopher Kennedy); *Ironweed* (screenplay, 1987); *Very Old Bones* (1992); *Riding the Yellow Trolley Car* (1993); *The Flaming Corsage* (1996)

BIBLIOGRAPHY: Croyden, M., "The Sudden Fame of W. K.," *NYTMag* (26 Aug. 1984), 33ff.; Murtaugh, D. M., "Fathers and Their Sons," *Commonweal*, 116 (26 Aug. 1984): 32–35; Bonetti, K., "An Interview with W. K.," *Mississippi Review*, 8, 2 (1985): 71–86; Thompson, D., "The Man Has Legs: W. K. Interviewed," *Film Comment*, 21 (Mar.–Apr. 1985): 54–59; Whittaker, S., "The Lawyer As Narrator in W. K.'s *Legs*," *Legal Studies Forum*, 9, 2 (1985): 157–64; Black, D., "The Fusion of Past and Present in W. K.'s *Ironweed*," *Crit*, 27 (Spring 1986): 177–84; Clark, P. P., "Classical Myths in W. K.'s *Ironweed*," *Crit*, 27, 3 (Spring 1986): 167–76; Robertson, M., "The Reporter As Novelist: The Case of W. K.," *Columbia Journalism Review*, 24 (Jan.–Feb. 1986): 49–50; McCaffery, L., and Gregory, S., eds., *Alive and Writing; Interviews* *with American Authors of the 1980s* (1987): 157–74; Parini, J., "Man of Ironweed," *Horizon*, 30 (Dec. 1987): 35–36

—WILLIAM OVER

KENYAN LITERATURE

Kenya has produced written literature in five languages—English, Swahili, Kamba, Kikuyu, and Luo—but most Kenyan authors writing today express themselves in either English or Swahili.

In English

The earliest literary works in English were ethnographies and autobiographical narratives, the prototype being Jomo Kenyatta's (1893–1978) *Facing Mount Kenya* (1938), an anthropological account of traditional Kikuyu life and culture. Muga Gicaru (b. 1920) in *Land of Sunshine: Scenes of Life in Kenya before Mau Mau* (1958) and R. Mugo Gatheru (b. 1925) in *Child of Two Worlds* (1964) described growing up in a Kikuyu village during the interwar years, when educational opportunities were scarce and nationalistic feelings were beginning to spread throughout the country. The struggle for political independence, which precipitated a Kikuyu civil war in the 1950s known as Mau Mau, was recorded in autobiographical works by Josiah Kariuki (b. 1929), Karari Njama (b. 1926), and Waruhiu Itote (b. 1922). In all these life histories the experiences of the narrator were treated as if typical of the Kikuyu people as a whole; the individual was a representative of his community, his ethnic group, and, in a larger sense, his nation.

The emergence of James Ngugi, now known as NGUGI WA THIONG'O, as Kenya's first novelist may have been the consequence of the same ethnic autobiographical impulse, for he too was a Kikuyu writing about the impact of Western education and colonial political unrest on the lives of his people, ordinary rural citizens who had been deprived of their land by white settlers. In *The River Between* (1965) he tells of the rise of Kikuyu independent schools under the leadership of a "man of two worlds" who tries to unite his community through mass education. In *Weep Not, Child* (1964) he portrays a Kikuyu family split apart by the pressures of Mau Mau; the hero, a young boy, is nearly driven to suicide when he loses his opportunity for further education. In both works Ngugi stresses the importance of fusing old and new, traditional and Western, so that Africans could progress politically without losing their cultural identity.

Ngugi's later novels, *A Grain of Wheat* (1967) and *Petals of Blood* (1977), deal with postcolonial social problems in Kenya that have their roots in the past. Like Chinua ACHEBE of Nigeria, Ngugi attempts to understand present realities in his country by searching for their origins in earlier times. He has written fictional chronicles of his nation's history.

A number of Kenyan authors have followed in Ngugi's footsteps by writing nationalistic novels about Mau Mau and its aftermath. Of these, the most talented is Meja Mwangi (b. 1948), whose *Carcase for Hounds* (1974) and *Taste of Death* (1975) elevated the armed struggle to legendary status by focusing on the exploits of heroic freedom fighters. More recently Mwangi has turned his attention to urban problems in Nairobi, examining the human consequences of economic exploitation in the postcolonial era by detailing the lives of laborers, vagabonds, and slum dwellers, who face their daily battle for survival with ingenuity and resilient humor.

Mwangi's latest novels have less in common with Ngugi's sober historical reappraisals than they do with the humorous literature that emerged in Kenya in the 1970s. The book that started the trend toward lighter fiction was Charles Mangua's (b. 1939) *Son of Woman* (1971), a picaresque novel that pokes fun at every stratum of Kenyan society by viewing it from the gutter through the eyes of an opportunistic trickster. In *A Tail in the Mouth* (1972) Mangua went a step further in irreverence and satirized even the Mau Mau freedom fighters. Mangua's refreshingly flippant novels broke sales records in Kenya and encouraged the development of an indigenous popular literature.

The most successful popular writer to emerge in Kenya in recent years has been David Maillu (b. 1939), who built a publishing house, Comb Books, on earnings from his first "mini-novels," *Unfit for Human Consumption* (1973) and *Troubles* (1974), and his best-selling narrative poems, *My Dear Bottle* (1973) and *After 4:30* (1974). Although Maillu has been criticized for writing mildly pornographic works, he has maintained that he is a serious moralist who chooses to clothe his social messages in frank, sexually explicit humor. He has tended to concentrate on urban characters—civil servants, politicians, secretaries, prostitutes—who suffer misfortunes because they cannot purge themselves of bad habits and insatiable appetites. He is truly a writer for the masses.

Other writers of fiction worthy of mention are Grace OGOT, whose tales of traditional Luo life skillfully evoke the past; the half-brothers Leonard Kibera (b. 1942) and Samuel Kahiga (b. 1946), whose short stories and novelettes deal with psychological aspects of social change; and Mwangi Ruheni (b. 1934), who specializes in domestic comedies and crime fiction. Such writers have contributed thematic diversity to Kenyan fiction.

Kenya has not produced as many dramatists or poets as it has novelists, but the plays of Francis IMBUGA and the poetry of Jared Angira (b. 1947) have earned a measure of public recognition. Imbuga has explored poignant human dimensions of social and political turmoil in modern Africa, sometimes tracing the roots of a personal tragedy to profound changes in the cultural values of contemporary society. Angira has brooded on the predicament of modern man in the Third World; his verse has remained simple, direct yet quite resourceful in projecting sharp images in which the new generation of Africans can see themselves and their experience reflected.

In Swahili

Kenya is not as rich in Swahili-language literature as Tanzania (see TANZANIAN LITERATURE), but a significant number of plays, poems, and novelettes are available. The oldest and possibly most famous work is James Juma Mbotela's (dates n.a.) *Uhuru wa watumwa* (1934; *The Freeing of the Slaves in East Africa*, 1956), a narrative based on reminiscences about the slave trade. More recent examples include Ahmad Nassir bin Juma Bhali's (b. 1936) *Poems from Kenya: Gnomic Verses in Swahili* (1966), short enigmatic poems published in a bilingual edition, and J. N. Somba's (b. 1930) novel, *Kuishi kwingi ni kuona mengi* (1968; to live long is to see much), a story about the life of an average man in modern society. Kenyan publishers have also been active in bringing out

Swahili translations of literary works written by African authors in English.

In Kikuyu

Although the production of literature in other Kenyan languages has been negligible, a start has been made in Kikuyu with the publication of two new works by Ngugi wa Thiong'o: a play co-authored by Ngugi wa Mirii (b. 1951) about the exploitation of peasants and workers in independent Kenya, *Ngaahika ndeenda* (1980; I will marry when I want), the public performance of which in 1977 led to Ngugi wa Thiong'o's arrest and detention for nearly a year; and a protest novel about neocolonialism, *Caitaani mūtharaba-Inī* (1980; the Devil on the Cross), which was the first piece of full-length fiction to appear in Kikuyu. Because he now seeks to address himself primarily to a local audience, Ngugi has declared his intention to continue writing in his mother tongue rather than in English. If other writers follow suit, there may be a surge in the production of African-language literature in Kenya in the years to come.

BIBLIOGRAPHY: Liyong, T. lo, *The Last Word: Cultural Synthesism* 1969; Ngugi wa Thiong'o, *Homecoming: Essays on African and Caribbean Literature, Culture and Politics* (1972); p'Bitek, O., *Africa's Cultural Revolution* (1973); Gurr, A., and A. Calder, eds., *Writers in East Africa* (1974); Cook, D., ed., *In Black and White: Writings from East Africa with Broadcast Discussion and Commentary* (1976); Roscoe, A., *Uhuru's Fire: African Literature East to South* (1977); Wanjala, C., *The Season of Harvest: Some Notes on East African Literature* (1978); Wanjala, C., *For Home and Freedom* (1980); Lindfors, B., ed. *Mazungumzo: Interviews with East African Writers, Publishers, Editors and Scholars* (1980); Ngugi wa Thiong'o, *Writers in Politics* (1981)

—BERNTH LINDFORS

Kenyan Literature since 1980

Kenyan literature in English has its roots in autobiographical narratives that recount the personal and group histories of the authors. Although most African literature in European languages could also in some way lay claim to this putative genealogy, Kenya's experience as a settler colony perhaps gives the country its unique position in East Africa. Life in colonial Kenya was characterized by the expropriation of land by the settlers. The alienation of the land was later to enhance the proliferation of books panegyric of communal life and of its ties to the land. In those books, the struggle for the land and the Mau Mau movement occupy a special place.

With independence, however, came a host of new problems. The new state was unable to deliver on its promises. People were left to believe that political independence would be a panacea for all of their misery and deprivation. Without the promised solutions in sight, dashed hopes and unrealized dreams marked the Kenyan landscape. Themes dealing with this new reality are a major component of African postindependent literature. As the new realities took hold of an unsuspecting populace, some writers looked for a way out. Others found consolation in a nostalgic search for a golden past that perhaps never existed. The strength of

Kenyan literature of this time lies in its avoidance of romanticization of the past. NGUGI WA THIONG'O's *Petals of Blood* (1977), which sets the pace for the literature of this era, shows his understanding of the dynamics of postindependent Kenya, and reflects his basic understanding that a romanticization of the past does not only breed a prisoner to a remote past but also blurs one's vision of the present and future—that by ruminating on a wistful past one loses twice. Most other Kenyan writers have successfully managed to steer away from an undue fascination with the past and are now trying to come to grips with the socioeconomic problems of the here and now.

The reluctance to delve into the past in search of clues and answers for contemporary issues may reflect three things. First, it reveals the need for a new analysis of Kenyan society as old issues such as white versus black, familiarized by some of the early books, become obsolete. Secondly, a revival of such issues as the Mau Mau will ironically show how independent Kenya is not yet free; it is perhaps in this sense that writers are wary of stepping on the government's toes. Finally, the reluctance to deal with the past may emanate from practical considerations on the part of publishers as to what is popular with the reading public. As a result of these new realities, Kenyan literature of the past decade has turned inward and in the process has become more reflective of the country's ethnic diversity.

With the compartmentalization of Kenyan society, the individual as an embodiment of communal values, typical of the more immediate postindependent literature, gave way to a portrayal of a more pronounced individual character. David Maillu, by some accounts Kenya's most successful popular writer, typifies authors who create such a character. In *Ayah* (1986; housemaid) he deals with the fate of a housemaid who is both exploited by a mean wife and raped by an unscrupulous master. In *Untouchable* (1987) he depicts the contumacy of two lovers who are determined to have their way in an environment that is not yet ready for an interracial relationship.

Asenath Bole Odaga (dates n.a.), like her more famous compatriot Grace Ogot, deals with Luo social realities in her novels and in her studies on the oral literature. In *A Bridge of Time* (1987) the disintegration of the family is shown first through a devastating power struggle between a man, his son, and his brother, and later through a heinous love triangle between the son, his cousin, and the beauty of the village. In her latest novel, *Riana* (1991), the eponymous heroine's defiance of such social institutions as polygamy and levirate among her people attests to women coming of age in Luo land and, by extension, Kenya.

In an attempt to reverse the thematic trend in African literature in which most writers attempting to show the inequality between town and village all too often focus on the influx of people from rural to urban centers, Meja Mwangi, undeniably one of the most talented writers on the East African literary scene, adopts the countryside as the setting of his latest novel *Striving for the Wind* (1991). Rampant corruption, flagrant injustice, and squalid living conditions caused by class and gender difference are realistically depicted. Reminiscent of Maillu's *After 4:30* (1974) but without its alleged pornographic aspects, Mwangi's novel, as well as Odaga's *Riana*, emphasize the need for an urgent reappraisal of the lot of women in Kenyan society. This preoccupation with women's issues, as we shall see later on, is a tendency that Kenyan literature in English shares with that in Swahili.

H(enry) R. Ole Kulet (b. 1946) has left behind the themes of his first two books, *Is It Possible?* (1971) and *To Become a Man*

(1972). In both novels he had skillfully depicted the corrosive effects of colonial education and of culture shock on the Maasai. Kulet now champions the environmental cause, which has of late become an international concern since the African elephant is threatened with extinction. In *The Hunter* (1985) Kulet shows the intricacies and dangers involved in divulging the guarded secrets of the mafialike poaching business in Kenya. In *Daughter of Maa* (1987) he depicts how the arrival of a woman teacher at a village is viewed both with suspicion by the wives and with admiration by the husbands who surreptitiously covet her.

The keen observer of Kenyan literature cannot miss noticing the paucity of English drama and poetry writing. With the exception of Ngugi, Micere Mugo (b. 1942), Francis Imbuga, Jared Angira, and Jonathan Kariara (b. 1935), Kenya has not produced well-known dramatists and poets.

A discussion of Kenyan literature would be incomplete without a look at other languages, especially at the literature written in Swahili. Of the forty-six Kenyan languages, Swahili has certainly produced the most works. Writing in Swahili cuts across ethnic lines. In a marked difference with Kenyan literature in English, Swahili literature does abound with poetry and drama. Prose fiction, perhaps indicative of an overall tradition in Swahili literature, has lagged behind poetry and drama. Two recent novels in Swahili worthy of mention are Angaluki Muaka's (b. 1958) *Ushuhuda wa mwanachuo* (1986; testimony of a student), a story about the role of students in society, how they formulate and express the aspirations of the people, and how the university as an institution is a microcosm of Kenyan society; and Ari Katini Mwachofi's (dates n.a.) *Mama ee* (1987; O mother), which shows the valiant struggle of women against male chauvinism and the dominant culture that produces it.

Two plays that also espouse the cause of women are Chacha Nyaigoti Chacha's (b. 1952) *Mke mwenza* (1982; cowife), which raises social and emotional issues such as jealousy and infertility; and Alamin Mazrui's (b. 1948) *Kilio cha haki* (1981; a cry for justice) about the exploitation of workers and the rise of a woman leader who spearheads the struggle for their rights.

Ahmed Sheikh Nabhany (b. 1927), one of the leading contemporary Swahili poets, has two recent collections of poems: *Umbuji wa mnazi* (1985; compositions about the coconut) and *Umbuji wa Kiwandeyo* (1985; compositions about Lamu), which deals with various aspects of life, language, and culture. Alamin Mazrui has also a collection of poems, *Chembe cha moyo* (1988; arrow in my heart). These love and hate poems are heavily laden with symbolism.

Writing in Kikuyu vies for second place in Kenyan literature of indigenous languages. Ngugi's commitment to writing in his mother tongue no doubt enhances its development. His latest novel, *Matigari* (1987; *Matigari*, 1989), shows a close affinity with the Ng'ano (narrative) tradition of his Kikuyu culture. The eponymous hero is endowed with superhuman qualities that frustrate his opponent's endeavors to label him as one thing or another. The omnipresence of Matigari and his immunity to death are adeptly employed to reveal the vulnerability and frailty of those in power. The novel is also a pertinent reminder that the Mau Mau movement is far from being jettisoned from Kenyan history.

Other Kenyan languages, such as Dholou and Kamba, have also produced written literatures. It is hoped, however, that the drive for the production of indigenous literatures would not lead to further fragmentation of Kenyan society. Rather, the proliferation of written indigenous literatures will, one hopes, contribute to the forging of a new Kenyan national consciousness.

BIBLIOGRAPHY: Thiong'o, Ngugi wa, *Homecoming: Essays on African and Caribbean Literature, Culture and Politics* (1972); Baker, H. A., Jr., *The Journey Back* (1980); Killam, G. D., ed., *The Writing of East and Central Africa* (1984); Ngara, E., *Art and Ideology in the African Novel* (1985); Jeyifo, B., ed., *Wole Soyinka: Art, Dialogue and Outrage* (1988); Priebe, R. K., *Myth, Realism and the West African Writer* (1988); Wanjiku, M. K., and K. W. Muthi, *Gikuyu Oral Literature* (1988); Ngara, E., and A. Morrison, *Literature, Language and the Nation* (1989); Smith, A., *East African Writing in English* (1989); Harrow, K. W., ed., *Faces of Islam in African Literature* (1991)

—ALI JIMALE AHMED

KEROUAC, Jack

American novelist, essayist, short-story writer, and poet, b. 12 March 1922, Lowell, Mass.; d. 21 Oct. 1969; St. Petersburg, Fla.

Born Jean Louis Lebris de Kerouac, K. grew up in Pawtucketville, a French-Canadian community in Lowell, Massachusetts. A star athlete in high school, he attended Columbia University on a football scholarship. There his predilection for spontaneous, unconventional behavior began to emerge. After breaking his leg in a freshman football game, K. dropped out of Columbia to work at a series of odd jobs that included shipping out on a Merchant Marine vessel to Greenland. Back at Columbia the following fall, he abruptly quit the football team after the season's first game. K. then enlisted in the Navy, only to be discharged on psychiatric grounds after six months. In 1944 he met Allen GINSBERG and William BURROUGHS in New York City, and the alliances that resulted in the beat movement began to be formed.

K.'s first novel, *The Town and the City* (1950), is an autobiographical account of the decline of his own family. Despite its generally positive critical reception, K. judged the novel a failure because he felt he had not yet discovered his authentic voice. With the development of his theory of "spontaneous composition" in 1951, that voice emerged. K. attempted to abandon altogether conscious control of language so that the very "sound of the mind" could flow unfettered by traditional notions of craft. In marathon sessions that frequently lasted days, he attempted to write swiftly, "excitedly," in a semi-trance that resembled YEATS's later "automatic writing."

The result of K.'s new aesthetic was *On the Road* (1957). Because of its formal singularity, it was slow in finding a publisher. Finally, Malcolm COWLEY persuaded Viking Press to publish the novel, but only after Cowley himself heavily revised K.'s original manuscript. It was an overnight sensation, catapulting K. into sudden fame after years of obscurity; yet, ironically, it is largely not the novel K. wrote. Remaining is K.'s vigorous chronicling of his travels across America and Mexico with his fellow beats, particularly Neal Cassady (1926–1968), the prototype for Dean Moriarty in the novel. Remaining also is the celebration of alcohol, drugs, jazz, and unbridled sex that gained the work its early notoriety. But except for a certain looseness of structure, the novel as published is relatively conventional in form, its stylistic wildness subdued by the editors.

The Dharma Bums (1958), K.'s next published novel, contains an excellent portrait of the poet Gary Snyder (b. 1930), K.'s friend, on whom Jaffe Ryder, the novel's protagonist, is based, and is

Jack Kerouac

informed throughout by K.'s interest in Zen Buddhism. But perhaps because it was written at Viking's request for a sequel to *On the Road* it too lacks the stylistic spontaneity of K.'s more essential works, which are the twelve novels he wrote between 1951, when he developed his theory of spontaneous prose, and 1957, when *On the Road* at last appeared. Each of these novels is informed by K.'s new aesthetic; none was published until after the success of *On the Road*. Possibly the most important of these is the posthumously published *Visions of Cody* (1973), which grew out of the 1951 manuscript of *On the Road* and at one point even bore that title. The novel's shifting points of view, its occasional parody and imitation of other works of literature, and its digressive nature and rambling style lend it the improvisational quality of jazz and make it the most representative example of K.'s spontaneous writing. Other successful novels of this period include *Dr. Sax* (1959), an expressionistic meditation on death; *The Subterraneans* (1958), an autobiographical account of K.'s affair with a mulatto woman that was written in only three days; and *Maggie Cassidy* (1959), K.'s nostalgic evocation of the provincial roots from which he never fully escaped.

With the passing of the 1950s, K.'s significance came increasingly to be regarded as less literary than sociological. Alcoholic and largely forgotten, he died at the age of forty-seven, only a few months after Neal Cassady's nude corpse was discovered in Mexico. It now appears certain that his place in modern letters will be determined less by his role as a leader of the beat movement than by how the degree of success of his literary experiments is perceived.

FURTHER WORKS: *Mexico City Blues* (1959); *The Scripture of the Golden Eternity* (1960); *Tristessa* (1960); *Lonesome Traveler* (1960); *Book of Dreams* (1961); *Big Sur* (1962); *Visions of Gerard* (1963); *Desolation Angels* (1965); *Satori in Paris* (1966); *Vanity of Duluoz* (1968); *Scattered Poems* (1971); *Pic* (1971)

BIBLIOGRAPHY: Duffey, B., "The Three Worlds of J. K.," in Waldmeir, J. J., ed., *Recent American Fiction* (1963): 175–84; Webb, H. M., Jr., "The Singular Worlds of J. K.," in Moore, H. T., ed., *Contemporary American Novelists* (1964): 120–33; Charters, A., *K.* (1972); Dardess, G., "The Logic of Spontaneity: A Reconsideration of K.'s 'Spontaneous Prose Method,'" *Boundary 2*, 2 (1975): 719–43; Hipkiss, R. A., *J. K.: Prophet of a New Romanticism* (1976); Tytell, J., *Naked Angels: The Lives and Literature of the Beat Generation* (1976): 52–78: 140–211; Donaldson, S., ed. *"On the Road": Text and Criticism* (1979): 311–605

—CHARLES B. HARRIS

KESEY, Ken

American novelist, b. 17 Sept. 1935, La Junta, Col.

K. attended the University of Oregon and Stanford University. In 1966 he was found guilty of possession of marijuana, and in 1967 he spent five months in jail in California.

K. quickly became one of the most exciting American novelists of the 1960s, not only because of his writing but also because of his life style. Tom Wolfe's (b. 1931) *The Electric Kool-Aid Acid Test* (1968) chronicles the activities of K. and his followers, who live the counterculture life style. Roaming the country in their Day-Glo-painted bus and tripping on hallucinogenic drugs, the Merry Pranksters, the name K. gave to his communal group, seemed to many to be vigorously challenging American mores.

K.'s protagonists are good men. Harder than ever to find in the age of the antihero, K.'s good man proves to be as distressing to the society around him as have some good men in the past. The story of a K. novel becomes the story of one man's sensitizing those who know him to the point that they not only realize their own flaws but also simultaneously admire and hate the protagonist who has shown them the truth.

K.'s first novel, *One Flew over the Cuckoo's Nest* (1962), implicitly questions the ability of society to diagnose its own insanity. The setting is the ward of a mental hospital, a ward filled mainly with voluntarily admitted patients who in fact are reasonably normal but who do not feel themselves strong enough to make it in the world outside. The representative of social authority in this microcosm is the Big Nurse, Miss Ratched, a coldly efficient despot, whose goal is the coercion of the men under her domination into a condition of sterile, automated tidiness. To Chief Bromden, the hulking Columbia River Indian who acts as the tale's narrator, she is an agent of the "Combine." Chief Bromden's paranoid delusion has assumed the metaphor of an omnipotent, omniscient, force—the Combine—that manipulates him through the wiring system that he imagines is being systematically installed in each of the inmates.

Into this hospital comes Randal Patrick McMurphy, ex-marine, brawler, card shark, and odds-watching gambler. Having claimed insanity to escape from the rigors of a prison work farm, McMurphy at first views his stay in the hospital as merely a long poker game, just one more ploy in the life of a confirmed hedonist. In a modern fable that alternates between light comedy and BLACK HUMOR, McMurphy wins all his rounds with the Big Nurse but the last. She fashions an eventual triumph of sorts by getting the doctors to perform a lobotomy on McMurphy. Before then, however, he has pulled his fellow inmates, sometimes against their will, back to a condition of self-respect.

McMurphy is reincarnated in K.'s second novel, *Sometimes a Great Notion* (1964), in the person of Hank Stamper, raw and aggressive scion of an Oregon lumber empire. The struggle is again with a society unwilling to accommodate a strong individualist, but the issues are deepened and complicated by the fact that Hank's principal antagonist turns out to be his cerebral, introspective half-brother, Lee, and by K.'s development of Lee as an equally appealing character. K. manipulates the clash of fraternal egos to a powerful climax, before reconciling the brothers to a tragic understanding of their own vulnerability to an indifferent fate and to a group of townspeople who have been made intolerably uncomfortable by the sight of the Stampers' strength.

Lingering lovingly over the Oregon land and the people it nurtures and assaults, K. is occasionally guilty of marring *Sometimes a Great Notion* with stretches of prolixity. But such lapses are few, and the novel is remarkable for the skill with which K. manages the narrative.

Since 1964, K. has published very little. *Kesey's Garage Sale* (1973) is a collection of fugitive pieces by K. and by his friends. If, as he sometimes indicated, he has decided to move beyond the novel, it is a decision that his audience can only regret, for K.'s voice and themes have been a special kind of stimulus reminding his age of the evil as well as of the good, of which it is capable.

FURTHER WORKS: *Demon Box* (1986); *The Further Inquiry* (1990); *Sailor Song* (1992); *Last Go Round* (1994)

BIBLIOGRAPHY: Malin, I., "K. K.: *One Flew over the Cuckoo's Nest*," *Crit*, 5, 2 (1962): 81–84; Fiedler, L., *The Return of the Vanishing American* (1968): 177–87; Barsness, J. A., "K. K.: The Hero in Modern Dress," *BRMMLA*, 22, 1 (1969): 27–33; Olderman, R. M., *Beyond the Waste Land: A Study of the American Novel in the Nineteen-Sixties* (1972): 35–51; special K. issue *Lex et Scientia*, 13: 1–2 (1977); Pratt, J. C., ed., *"One Flew over the Cuckoo's Nest": Text and Criticism* (1977); Strelow, M., ed., *K.* (1977)

—CHARLES LARSON

KHÁI-HƯNG

(anagrammatized pseud. of [Trần] Khánh Giư) Vietnamese novelist, short-story writer, and dramatist, b. 1896, Hai-duong; d. 1947, Nam-dinh

K.-H. was the cofounder in 1933 of the "Self-Reliant" literary group and also one of its most prolific writers. Son of a provincial mandarin, he had a traditional education in Sino-Vietnamese letters followed by a French education, and chose first to be a teacher. Later the French authorities arrested him for his anticolonial politics and deported him to the highlands of northern Vietnam. Upon his release in 1943, he resumed his political activities, especially after the "August revolution" of 1945, but as a member of the Vietnamese Nationalist Party he was murdered by the communist Vietminh shortly after the French-Vietnamese hostilities broke out in December 1946. The exact date of K.-H.'s death is unknown.

His first three novels were idealistic, but later he dealt with local customs and mores, with emphasis on psychological characterizations. *Hồn bướ mơ tiên* (1933; butterfly soul dreaming of immortals) is about the pure love between Ngọc and a Buddhist novice, who actually is a disguised beautiful young woman. Lan, the latter, torn between love and religion, decides that she is more dedicated to her religious faith and plans to escape to the highlands and enter a remote temple. But the young man talks her out of it, swears that in his continuing friendship he would control his desire and that he would remain a bachelor and "only live in the dream world of idealistic platonic love." He further expresses his noble sentiment to Lan, "A family? I don't have a family any more: my extended family now is humankind, the universe, while my small family is our two souls hiding under the merciful shadow of Buddha." In *Nửa chừng xuân* (1934; unfinished spring), Mai, a pretty, intelligent, and noble girl in love with a mandarin's son, is determined to end the "illicit life" they have spent together. In the light of her sacrifice, Lộc, her husband, is just an ordinary young man, who has given a son to this young woman, but abandoned her after his manipulating mother made him suspect her of being unfaithful. When he argues that he is going to convert his love for his family into love for humanity and to devote his talent and energy to help society, the reader realizes that the author simply does not want a reunion to take place, so that their love could become idealized.

In his third novel, *Trống Mái* (1936; rooster and hen), K.-H. gave the idealization of his fiction a new twist, the praise of physical beauty: Hiền, a city girl, falls in love with a humble fisherman, or rather with his well-built physique. The author wants her to like Vọi the way an artist likes a beautiful statue, but critics have found this case of platonic love unrealistic. *Thử-tự* (1940: heir) belongs to a different category: It is a psychological novel, in which the author examines various corrupt practices in traditional Vietnamese society, particularly that of choosing at any price a descendant to be one's heir, reflecting the ancestral cult. In contrast, *Hạnh* (1940: Hanh) is a short novel with an educational focus since it features a shy and weak schoolteacher with an inferiority complex, afraid to face women in general. K.-H.'s short stories reveal him to be a keen, observant writer about the young Vietnamese generation of his time. His style went from floweriness to simplicity, and was definitely typical of the unfettered, flowing style, slightly influenced by French writings, that won K.-H.—and his associates—the admiration of readers, especially female readers. K.-H. showed that he perfectly understood Vietnamese women, their feelings, prejudices, and maneuvers.

FURTHER WORKS: *Gánh hàng hoa* (1934, with Nhất-Linh); *Đợi mưa gió* (1934, with Nhất-Linh); *Dọc đường gió bụi* (1936); *Anh phải sống* (1937, with Nhất-Linh); *Tục-luy* (1937); *Tiếng suối reo* (1937); *Gia-đình* (1938); *Thoát-ly* (1939); *Đợi-chờ* (1939); *Tiêu-sơn tráng-sĩ* (1940); *Đẹp* (1940); *Đời Mưlệch* (1941); *Nhưng ngày vui* (1941); *Đồng bênh* (1942); *Băn-khoăn* (1943)

BIBLIOGRAPHY: Durand, M. M. and Huân Nguyễn-Trần Huân, *An Introduction to Vietnamese Literature* (1985): 182–91 and passim; Bùi Xuân-Bào *Le roman vietnamien contemporain* (1972): 143–64 and passim; Huỳnh Sanh Thông, "Main Trends of Vietnamese

Literature between the Two World Wars," *The Vietnam Forum*, 3 (Winter-Spring 1984): 99–125

—DINH-HOA NGUYEN

al-KHĀL, Yūsuf

Lebanese poet and critic, b.1917, Tripoli; d.1987, Paris, France

Born in a Christian family from Tripoli, where he attended secondary school, K. graduated in 1944 from the American University of Beirut in philosophy and English, and went into teaching. He left Beirut in 1948 for the U.S., where he worked at the United Nations office first, then started an export business, while editing at the same time the Arabic paper *al-Hudā*. There he made the acquaintance of American poets like Archibald MACLEISH, Ezra POUND, and T. S. ELIOT. Back in Beirut in 1955, after a stay in Libya and Geneva, he advocated a new poetic mentality in addition to the new forms introduced by the young Iraqi poets Badr Shākir AL-SAYYĀB and Nāzik AL-MALĀIKA. It was this combination of a new mentality and the new form that marked the work of K. and his colleagues at the literary review *Shi'r* which from 1957 to 1964 was the most important forum for ideas on change and MODERNISM in Arabic literature.

However, the new review, founded in January 1957, did not fit in well with the spirit of *iltizām* or commitment that was propagated by the group of poets and writers at the other Beirutian review, *al-Ādāb*, started in 1953 by Suhayl Idrīs and still existing today. K. had to stop the experiment after a serious conflict with his most talented Syrian colleague, ADŪNĪS (pseud. of 'Alī Ahmad Sa'īd), and after persistent rumors from outside that the *Shi'r* group was infiltrated by Syrian nationalist elements. In 1967 K. started publishing the review again in a new form and with another editorial board, but it was no longer the avant-garde review it had been. K. also founded an art gallery, Gallery One, and a publishing house, Dār Majallat Shi'r, which published work of the main representatives of the New Poetry propagated by *Shi'r*. For a short time he edited also the literary revue *Adab* which existed from 1965 to 1966. In the 1970s K. devoted himself to a new translation of the Bible. During the Lebanese civil war he lived in Paris, where he died after having been decorated with the Lebanese Order of Merit. He expressed his bitterness about the Lebanese situation in *Rasā'il ilā Dūn Kīshūt* (1979; letters to Don Quixote).

As a poet, K. followed first Sa'īd 'AQL and his symbolist interpretation of reality in his first volumes, *Hurriyyah* (1945; liberty) and *Hīrūdiya* (1954; Herodias). Then he started to translate poetry of American poets, which he published together with Adūnīs in an anthology in 1958, notably Eliot's *The Waste Land* (1922). This reading fundamentally transformed his ideas about poetry. In 1958 he published in free verse *al-Bi'r almahjūrah* (the forsaken well), followed in 1960 by *Qasā'id fī l-arba'īn* (poems at the age of forty). In the first selection, dedicated to Pound, K. presents the poet as a new Christ in his struggle to revive Arabic poetry, whose task it is to redeem people from the past and to face the reality of the present. In its vision, life in the Arab world is marked by sterility, and the poet prays for another and better world in which people will find the well and drink from it. In the second selection of poems one notes a metaphysical dimension and a hopeful vision of the world, which will transcend suffering and death. By his reliance on fertility myths K. ranges himself in the group of so-called Tammuzists, which include also AL-SAYYĀB, Adūnīs, Jabrā Ibrāhīm JABRĀ, and Khalīl HĀWĪ. In later criticism K. advocated the use of the vernacular for serious literary purposes, but he never published poetry in dialect like, for example, Sa'īd 'Aql or Mīshāl Trād (b. 1913).

FURTHER WORKS: *Al a'māl al-shi'riyya al-kāmila* (1973); *Al-Wilāda al-thaniyya* (1981)

BIBLIOGRAPHY: Jargy, S., "Poètes arabes d'avantgarde," *Orient*, 18 (1961): 147–72; Badawi, M. M., *A Critical Introduction to Modern Arabic Poetry* (1975): 241–45; Moreh, S., *Modern Arabic Poetry 1800–1970* (1976): 278–88; Jayyusi, S. K., *Trends and Movements in Modern Arabic Poetry* (1977), Vol. 2: 569–73; Kheir Beik, K., *Le mouvement moderniste de la poésie arabe contemporaine* (1978), passim; Zeidan, J., "Myth and Symbol in the Poetry of Adūnīs and Y. al-K.", *JArabL*, 10 (1979): 70–94; Jayyusi, S. K., ed. *Modern Arabic Poetry: An Anthology* (1987): 295–99; Allen, R., ed. *Modern Arabic Literature* (1987): 180–83

—ED C. M. DE MOOR

KHAN, Ismith

Trinidadian novelist and short-story writer, b. 16 Mar. 1926, Port of Spain, Trinidad

Like Zampi, the introspective obeah man of *The Obeah Man* (1964), his second novel, K. is the product of a complex racial, economic, political, and social matrix. He is a Muslim of Pathan ancestry, but his sensibilities are strongly Trinidadian and West Indian, and his fiction is therefore West Indian in tone, characterization, and theme. K. attended Port of Spain's Queen's Royal College, alma mater of a number of distinguished Trinidadian writers, and later worked as a reporter for the *Trinidad Guardian*, as did novelist Sam SELVON and Nobel Prize-winning poet Derek WALCOTT. He studied sociology in the U.S., earning a B.A. degree and later an M.A. in creative writing from Johns Hopkins University. He has taught creative writing at Johns Hopkins and various institutions in southern California and Medgar Evers College.

K. seems to have been strongly influenced by Kale Khan, his anticolonialist grandfather, a ferocious Pathan who emigrated to Trinidad in the 19th c. and set up as a jeweler. Kale Khan's disaffected voice is prominent in K.'s first novel, *The Jumbie Bird* (1961), which depicts British colonialism as a moribund political and social system. The novel dramatizes the generational conflict between members of Kale Khan's family, the grandfather, who, like Johnny of Selvon's *An Island is a World* (1955), dreams of returning to India, and the son and grandson who must find a stable place in a pluralistic and amorphous society.

The Obeah Man explores the psychic scars of West Indian amorphousness and the cultural void created by a self-serving colonialism. The obeah man's metaphorical journey toward a self-affirming identity is an attempt to reconcile the duality of his human nature that is conveyed in the novel's antithesis between the isolated and pristine Blue Basin, where Zampi practices the chthonic art of obeah, and the hedonistic worlds of Trinidad's carnival and

rumshops. Zampi's quest for wholeness is closely linked with obeah which he regards as an authentic vocation demanding discipline and self-possession, the antithesis of darkness and witchcraft. Obeah, furthermore, is a synthesis of incongruities and conflicts, the lens through which he sees the emptiness of his former self-indulgent life that is embodied in the rumshops and their habitués, Massahood, the egotistical stickman, Hop-and-Drop, the amoral cripple, and the sensual Zolda, Zampi's discarded lover. The novel traces a symbolic journey from darkness to enlightenment, which culminates in Zampi's realization that he requires love, and not only the spiritual gratifications of obeah, for wholeness. Because Zampi's quest is ultimately concerned with existence and personal destiny, it transcends the boundaries of West Indianness and colonialism.

In *The Crucifixion* (1987) K. treats with compassion and sensitivity a well-known Trinidadian folk figure of the 1930s and 1940s: the self-ordained preacher who is both eccentric and charlatan. K.'s Manko resembles the fanatical Man-Man, the con artist/preacher of V. S. NAIPAUL's *Miguel Street* (1959), and Taffy, the religious crack-pot of Earl LOVELACE's *The Dragon Can't Dance* (1979). Naipaul's Man-Man has some of the characteristics of the picaresque rogue who is able to adjust and adapt his survival skills as circumstances require. K.'s Manko is more complex, and his adoption of a holy man's persona, which culminates in his symbolic crucifixion, is not so much a pose as a pathetic attempt at self-definition. Moreover, Manko and the impoverished yard dwellers with whom he lives are depicted, notwithstanding their warts, as desperate, victimized human beings.

K.'s work is notable for its accurate and engaging portrait of impoverished, discarded and dispossessed men and women, and his fiction also paints a compelling and vivid picture of the exhilarating world of Port of Spain's rumshops, a distinctive Trinidadian cultural phenomenon now in danger of extinction.

FURTHER WORKS: *A Day in the Country and Other Stories* (1990)

BIBLIOGRAPHY: Ramchand, K., "Obeah and the Supernatural in West Indian Literature," *Jamaica Journal*, 3 (1969): 52-54; Brown, L., "The Calypso Tradition in West Indian Literature," *MBL*, 2 (1971): 127-43; Davies, B., "The Personal Sense of a Society-Minority View: Aspects of the East Indian Novel in the West Indies," *SNNTS*, 4 (1972): 284-95; Lacovia, R., "I. K. and the Theory of Rasa," *BlackI*, 1 (1972): 23-27; Cobham, R., " *The Jumbie Bird* by I. K.: A New Assessment," *JCL*, 21 (1986): 240-49; Juneja, R., "Representing History in *The Jumbie Bird*," *WLWE*, 30 (1990): 17-28; Boxill, A., "I. K.," in Nelson, E., ed., *Writers of the Indian Diaspora* (1993): 153-58

—HAROLD BARRATT

KHANDEKAR, Vishnu Sakharam

Indian novelist, short-story writer, essayist, and critic (writing in Marathi), b. 11 Jan. 1898, Sangli; d. 2 Sept. 1976, Miraj

After finishing secondary school in Sangli, K. spent some time at college in Poona, but had to abandon his studies because of financial pressures. An idealistic commitment to uplifting the rural populace led him to become a school-teacher in the small coastal village of Shiroda in 1920. From 1938 until his death he lived in the upcountry town of Kolhapur, where for some time he wrote film scripts, but later devoted himself wholly to his literary writing, becoming one of the few Marathi writers to have lived by their pen.

The spirit of the idealistic teacher pervades K.'s vast output, which includes fifteen novels. His early novels, such as *Don dhruva* (1934; the two poles) and *Pandhare dhag* (1940; white clouds), recommend the Marxist path for the abolition of the "two poles" of poverty and wealth. K. was also attracted to the teachings of Gandhi but found his philosophy of nonviolent change, symbolized by the "white clouds" of Gandhian homespun clothes, inadequate for effecting a revolution. After 1942, disheartened to see Marxist as well as Gandhian ideals corrupted, K. did not write a novel for several years; he produced only three in the later period. In *Yayati* (1959; *Yayati*, 1978), he devotes himself to castigating the hedonistic materialism of modern times, seeing in Yayati, the mythic king who "borrowed" his son's youth to satisfy his own lust, the symbol of modern man.

While few Marathi writers have become as dear to middle-class readers as K., several critics have passed severe judgments on him. Written according to a thesis, his fiction generally lacks a dynamic, living quality. The thesis itself being a "teachable" simplification, the portrayal of life seldom achieves any depth or complexity. K.'s genuine feeling for the downtrodden does not result in a palpable depiction of their life, the author being circumscribed by his own middle-class background. His extremely ornate style, studded with epigrammatic sentences, similes, metaphors, and allegorical constructions, appears contrived. But with all his faults, K. remains a writer with an exemplary commitment to humanistic values.

FURTHER WORKS: *Rankache rajya* (1928); *Navamallika* (1929); *Dhundhurmas* (1929); *Hridayachi hak* (1930); *Kanchan-mrig* (1931); *Gadkari: Vyakti ani vangmaya* (1932); *Ulka* (1934); *Jivankala* (1934); *Dattak* (1934); *Vayulahari* (1936); *Vidyutprakash* (1937); *Davabindu* (1937); *Navachandrika* (1937); *Don mane* (1938); *Poojan* (1938); *Chandanyat* (1938); *Hirava chapha* (1939); *Rikama devhara* (1939); *Sukhacha shodh* (1939); *Pakalya* (1939); *Samadhivaril phule* (1939); *Hastacha paus* (1939); *Pahile prem* (1940); *Jalalela mohor* (1941); *Surya-kamale* (1941); *Kalika* (1941); *Avinash* (1941); *Krauncha-vadha* (1942); *Oonpaus* (1942; *Cultured moti* (1942); *Mandakini* (1942); *Gharatyabaher* (1944); *Nava pratakkal* (1944); *Pahilya-vahilya* (1944); *Pahili lat* (1944); *Phule ani dagad* (1944); *Stri ani purush* (1944); *Mrigajalatalya kalya* (1944); *Sayankal* (1944); *Surya-kamal* (1944); *Gokarnichi phule* (1944); *Jivanakala* (1944); *Vanabhojana* (1944); *Kalpalata* (1945); *Manjirya* (1945); *Marathicha natya-sansar* (1945); *Nave kiran* (1946); *Tisara prahar* (1946); *Goph ani gophan* (1946); *Phule ani kate* (1946); *Teen sammelane* (1947); *Sanjawat* (1948); *Soneri savalya* (1948); *Jhim-jhim* (1948); *V. M. Joshi: Vyakti ani vichar* (1948); *Ashru ani hasya* (1949); *Agarkar: Vyakti ani vichar* (1949); *Preeticha shodh* (1952); *Ashru* (1953); *Prasad* (1957); *Abhishek* (1958); *Manjhadhar* (1959); *Keshavasut: Kavya ani kala* (1959); *Murali* (1960); *Vanadevata* (1960); *Usshap* (1961); *Rimjhim* (1961); *Te divas, tee manase* (1961); *Rang ani gandh* (1961); *Resha ani rang* (1961); *Amritavel* (1967); *Dhagaädache chandane* (1972); *Dhwaj phadakat thevuya* (1975)

BIBLIOGRAPHY: Sardesai, G., "V. S. K.: A Social Humanist," *IndL*, 11 (1968): 92–97; Bhagwat, A. K., "V. S. K.," in Bhagwat, A. K.,

ed., *Maharashtra—A Profile: V. S. K. Felicitation Volume*, (1977): 1–18

—VILAS SARANG

KHANTY LITERATURE
See Finno-Ugric Literatures of the Soviet Union

al-KHARRĀT, Edwar

(also spelled Edward in English) Egyptian novelist, short-story writer, translator, and critic, b. 16 Mar. 1926, Alexandria

K. was born into a Coptic family and brought up and educated in Alexandria at Coptic and state schools. After his father's death in 1943, K. worked as a storeman for the British navy to help support his family while he completed his studies. He graduated in law from Alexandria University in 1946 and went to work as a clerk in the Egyptian National Bank. Active in a Trotskyist movement opposed to King Farouk and the British presence in Egypt, K. was arrested and held in concentration camps from 1948 to 1950. After his release he worked for an insurance company until 1955, when he resigned to finish writing his first collection of short stories. Subsequently he worked as press and public-relations officer for the Romanian embassy in Cairo and in 1959 joined the staff of the Afro-Asian Peoples' Solidarity Organization and the Afro-Asian Writers' Union, eventually becoming assistant secretary-general of both organizations. In 1983 he resigned to devote himself to writing.

The stories in K.'s first collection, *Hitān 'āliyah* (1959; high walls), like much of his later work, are poetically rooted in the daily life of Alexandria or the Egyptian countryside. However, their concern with isolation and guilt and the introspective, experimental nature of the writing were out of keeping with the prevailing tradition in Egyptian fiction, which was still outward-looking, positive, and inspired by national pride. During the 1960s, with the changing political and cultural climate, K.'s work began to receive more critical acclaim, and, as a critic and as a writer, he became an influential figure in the "new wave" of Egyptian writing, the so-called Sixties Generation. He was on the editorial board of the avant-garde periodical *Galīrī* 68, where many of the best short-story writers and critics published their work in the late 1960s.

K. is fluent in English and French and has translated works of fiction into Arabic, including those of American and African writers. He demonstrated his continuing concern with the state of new writing, the publishing industry, and related social issues in Egypt when he compiled *Mukhtārāt al-qissah al-qasīrah fī l-sab'īnīyāt* (1982; an anthology of the short story in the 1970s), which has an extensive critical introduction.

His second collection, *Sa'āt al-kibriyā'* (1972; hours of pride), which won the State Prize for the short story, anticipates the radical stylistic features that were to characterize K.'s work increasingly over the next two decades, with characters whose identities merge at some points, contradictory accounts of the same events, abrupt movements back and forth in time and space, and an iconoclastic use of Christian and Pharaonic allusions and symbols. Female characters are almost always at the center of the action, sometimes assuming superhuman proportions as saint-whore figures for the invariably male narrator, and arousing in him feelings of compassion, guilt, suspicion, ecstasy, and moral bewilderment.

K.'s first novel, *Rāma wa'l-tinnīn* (1979; Rama and the dragon), was a literary event in the Arab world, acknowledged by critics and other novelists as having effectively severed connections with the structure of the modern novel in Arabic established by Najīb MAHFŪZ. Each chapter is autonomous and yet related to the others. Legends from Eastern and Western traditions are used to illuminate and expand both each other and the new text, which is a blend of poetry, fiction, history, and philosophical debates on love, sex, and communication or its impossibility. Narrative traditions are ignored, questioned, or inverted, and the language is poetic and metaphorical throughout, but accessible, even demotic, in a way that much of experimental literary language is not.

From *Rāma wa'l-tinnīn* onwards, K.'s works are increasingly hard to classify in terms of genre. Although usually described as novels, they are more like interlocking stories with recurring autobiographical elements, such as the memories of wartime Alexandria in *Turābuhā za'farān* (1986; *City of Saffron*, 1989), which are worked and reworked in different combinations and contexts in a vivid portrayal of the alternating blissful security and bottomless terror of childhood experiences.

Sometimes the scenes and images are violently juxtaposed or change abruptly in ways that are not always successful, however much the essentially cerebral context of words and silent imaginative responses may be stretched and modified in experimental writing. In addition, the dreamlike or surreal episodes appear to have too tenuous a relationship with the perceived meanings of the text and the physical reality so carefully and often exquisitely constructed by K. But he sees the novel form as being open to almost unlimited adaptations and developments. Through it he returns again and again to such subjects as the ambiguities of moral responsibility and choice, the spiritual aspects of sexual passion and human suffering, and the relationship between love and knowledge, treating them in such a fashion that the meanings remain fluid and open to varying interpretations. The immediately accessible sense and imaginative power of his writing come from the masterly way he evokes the distinctive qualities of places, characters, and events through a wealth of description of textures, smells, tastes, and sounds.

FURTHER WORKS: *Ikhtināqāt al-'ishq wa-al-sabāh* (1983); *Mahattat al-sikka al-hadīd* (1985); *Al-za-man al-ākhar* (1985); *Adlā al-sahrā* (1987); *Yā banāt iskandariyyah* (1990); *Makhlūqāt al-ashwāq al-tā irah* (1990); *Amwāj al-layālī* (1991); *Hijarat Bubillu* (1992); *Yaqin al-'atash* (1996); *Al-Hassasiyya al-jadida* (1993); *Al-Kitaba 'abra al-naw'iyya* (1994)

BIBLIOGRAPHY: Cobham, C., "'An Open Wound' by K.," *JArabL*, 15 (1984): 121–34; Ayyād, S., and Witherspoon, N., "Elation and Solitude," *Reflections and Deflections* (1986): 255–58; Barbulesco, L., and Cardinal, P., "Portrait: Entretien et questionnaire," *L'Islam en question* (1986): 87–92; Fontaine, J., "Le nouveau roman égyptien (1975–1985)," *IBLA*, 158 (1986): 245–58; al-Shārūnī, Y., Hāfiz, S., and 'Atiyya, N., "K.," in Allen, R., ed. *Modern Arabic Literature* (1987): 183–87; Cardinal, P., "K., les clés d'Égypte," *Liberation*, 9 Mar. 1988, 38; K., , "The Mashriq," in Ostle, R. C., ed. *Modern Literature in the Near and Middle East 1850–1970* (1991): 180–92

—CATHERINE COBHAM

KHATIBI, Abdelkebir

Moroccan novelist and essayist (writing in French), b. 1938, El Jadida

After attending Koranic school and the École Franco-Musulmane, K. went at the age of twelve to boarding school in Marrakesh where he discovered French literature and culture, an experience which he has described in his autobiographical novel. *La mémoire tatouée* (1971; the tatooed memory). K. studied sociology at the Sorbonne (1958–1964). His 1965 doctorat de 3e Cycle entailed a thesis on *Le roman maghrébin* (1968; rev. ed., 1979; the Maghrebian novel). He directed the Institut de Sociologie in Rabat from 1966 until it was integrated into the university in 1970. He is currently a university research professor at the Institute of Scientific Research in Rabat. K.'s dual vision as writer and sociologist has played a significant role in defining his writing, which often links creative impulses and such social phenomena as the cinema, urban layout or planning, onomastics, art appreciation, tattoos, superstition, the acts of reading and writing, and psychoanalysis.

The publication of K.'s first and best-known work, *La mémoire tatouée*, signaled a new approach to writing in Morocco. The fragmented postmodern structure of the work, so different from the earlier well-wrought novels of writers like Driss CHRAIBI of Morocco, Mouloud FERAOUN, Mohammed DIB, and Mouloud MAMMERI of Algeria, and Albert MEMMI of Tunisia, reflects K.'s interest in modern linguistics and the critical theory of Roland BARTHES, Jacques DERRIDA, and others.

With the possible exception of *La mémoire tatouée* and *Un été à Stockholm* (1991; a summer in Stockholm), K.'s works defy easy classification by genre, and even those two works do not have the tight structural integrity we associate with the conventional novel. His works labeled "novels" often seem to be essays, and his essays include highly poetic, oneiric, or anecdotal passages, and in most of the works there is a sense of ritual and drama due to K.'s extensive use of dialogue—the "images" liminary to *La mémoire tatouée*—framing of characters in stagelike or still scenes: *Le livre du sang* (1979; the book of blood) and *Ombres japonaises* (1988; Japanese shadow play). Paradoxically, actual drama, *Le prophète voilé* (1979; the veiled prophet), and poetry, *Le lutteur de classe à la manière taoïste* (1976; the ranking Taostyle wrestler) and *Dédicace à l'année qui vient* (1986; a dedication for the coming year), are not K.'s strongest suits.

Both K.'s creative works and theoretical writings, which reinforce one another, have had considerable influence on Maghrebian writers of his generation. Tahar BEN JELLOUN'S first novel, *Harrouda* (1973; Harrouda), was inspired in part by *La mémoire tatouée*, and Nabile Fares (b. 1941) of Algeria and Abdelwahab Meddeb (b. 1946) of Tunisia may well have been encouraged in the pursuit of their own particular idioms as a result of K.'s success in exploiting code mixing and the use of "intersemiotics" in his works.

In such works as *La blessure du nom propre* (1974; the wound of the proper noun/name), *Amour bilingue* (1983; *Love in Two Languages*, 1990), and various essays on bilingualism and diglossia, especially *Maghreb pluriel* (1983; plural Maghreb), and the papers of a conference organized by K. and published under the title *Du bilinguisme* (1985; on bilingualism), K. has championed a constructive interpretation of interference in Maghrebian writing, in which the writer's mother tongue acts upon the acquired French in which he or she writes, providing a discourse based on "interior calligraphy" and resulting in an aesthetics of the "palimpsest" prominent, if not unique, in francophone and other bilingual literatures. It is when K. indulges in his passion for bilingualism and what he terms the "captation" of hidden psycholinguistic impulses—as in his reflections on parapraxis and word associations in *Amour bilingue* and *Par-dessus l'épaule* (1988; over one's shoulder)—or in the development of his narrative on a nonlinear basis—as in *Le livre du sang* and the passages reminiscent of vintage K. in the second half of *Un été à Stockholm*—that he is at his best. Even as K. brings into question the standard recipes that long governed literature, he loads language with a dynamics beyond entertainment and didacticism, giving it an importance akin to that generally accorded religion.

FURTHER WORKS: *Vomito blanco* (1974); *L'art calligraphique arabe* (1976, with Mohamed Sijelmassi); *De la mille et troisième nuit* (1980); *Le même livre* (1985, with Jacques Hassoun); *Figures de l'étranger dans la littérature française* (1987)

BIBLIOGRAPHY: Gontard, M., *Violence du texte* (1981): 80–114; Déjeux, J., *Dictionnaire des auteurs maghrébins de langue française* (1984): 242–43; Memmi, A., *Écrivains francophones du Maghreb* (1985): 194–99; Tenkoul, A., *Littérature Maghrébine d'écriture française* (1985): 131–44; Buci-Glucksmann, C., et al., *Imaginaires de l'autre: K. et la mémoire littéraire* (1987); special K. issue, *CelfanR*, 8: 1–2 (Nov. 1988–Feb. 1989); Sellin, E., "Obsession with the White Page, the Inability to Communicate, and Surface Aesthetics in the Development of Contemporary Maghrebian Fiction: The 'Mal de la page blanche' in K., Farès, and Meddeb," *IJMES*, 20, 2 (May 1988): 165–73

—ERIC SELLIN

KHLEBNIKOV, Velemir Vladimirovich

(pseud. of Viktor K.) Russian poet, dramatist, short-story writer, and essayist, b. 9 Nov. 1885, Tundutovo; d. 28 June 1922, Novgorod

K. was born in the Astrakhan district, the son of an ornithologist father and historian mother; his early associations with science were to have lasting effects on his work. K. studied mathematics and biology at Kazan University, and his first published work was a scientific article. In 1906, K. was imprisoned for one month for his involvement in student revolutionary activities. In 1909 he studied Sanskrit and Slavic historical philology at St. Petersburg University.

His literary associations began in 1908, when he became acquainted with Vyacheslav IVANOV and Mikhail KUZMIN, and soon became the center of a group that represented the beginnings of Russian FUTURISM.

K. spent much of his adult life a penniless wanderer, living for a time in various Russian and Ukrainian cities and obsessively computing mathematical formulas to derive the cyclical laws of history. In 1921 he traveled to Tehran with the Red Army as an adjutant to the general staff. His Persian experiences are recorded in the long poem "Truba Gul Mully" (written 1921, pub. 1928; Gul Mullah's pipe). He died after a month's illness aggravated by malnutrition.

K. is the modern Russian poet of the epic. Pagan Slavic mythology and the folk epic—as in "I i E" (1913; I and E), "Deti Vydry" (1913; the children of Vydra), and the play *Devy bog* (1912; a maiden's god)—and fantastic utopian dreams—as in the "super tale" *Ladomir* (1920; partial tr., *Goodworld*, 1976)—are the basis of much of his work. K.'s cosmogony is a unique poetic world whose meaning only gradually becomes clear to the reader after he learns K.'s system of myths and pagan view of the world. K.'s attraction to the epic was part of his preoccupation with the nature of time, and such long poems as "Gibel Atlantidy" (1912; the destruction of Atlantis), "Deti Vydry," and "Sinie okovy" (written 1922, pub. 1928; blue chains); the "super tale" *Zangezi* (1922; partial tr., *Zangezi*, 1976), a mixture of prose and poetry arranged in twenty sections called "planes"; and the play *Mirskontsa* (1913; *World from the End*, 1976) are all organized by his theory of historical repetition and are in part explained by it. By juxtaposing numbers connected with various historical events, K. tried to discern an underlying, rationally deducible periodicity. In this he shared a basic futurist-utopian vision of man freed by the discovery of the laws of existence to realize his creative potential.

At the heart of all K.'s poetry is his philosophy of language. Russian futurism was oriented toward the word in its material uniqueness—the physical aspect of the word on the page. Instrumentation—the manipulation of rhyme, alliteration, vowel harmonies—became a vehicle to transform meaning, to revitalize long-forgotten relationships among words themselves. On the one hand, associative freedom, even accident (for example, typographical errors) played an important role in the creative process in order to expose as arbitrary the encrustations of conventional meanings so that the real, "interior" meanings of words might be more perceptible. The result is the apparent disconnectedness, randomness of associations, and unmotivated semantic shifts that so often occur in K.'s writings. On the other hand, K. viewed his task to be a scientific distillation of language aimed at the determination of original meanings. "Nasha osnova" (1920; our base), K.'s most important theoretical essay, deals with neologisms formed by the manipulation of existing roots. Ultimately, *Zaum* ("transrational language") was an attempt to achieve a language of universal comprehensibility that would lead to world peace. His poem "Zaklyatie smekhom" (1910; "Incantation by Laughter," 1976) was based on the rich variety of Russian prefixes and suffixes used with the root word for laughter. *Zangezi* is a kind of poetic testament and compendium of *zaum* forms.

K.'s fiction is characterized by this same concentration on language and time. His most important prose piece, the autobiographical story "Ka" (1916; "Ka," 1976), contains violent, unmotivated shifts in time and the simultaneous interpenetration of historical periods.

K. would have liked to think of himself as the N. I. Lobachevsky (1792–1856)—a great mathematician—of the poetic word, suggesting new ways to view poetic time and space. He remains a difficult and eccentric master whose writing is fundamental to Russian modernism.

FURTHER WORKS: *Bitvy 1915–1917: Novoe uchenie o voyne* (1915); *Noch v okope* (1921); *Sobranie proizvedeny* (5 vols., 1928–1933); *Sobranie sochineny* (4 vols., 1968–1972). FURTHER WORKS IN ENGLISH: *Snake Train: Poetry and Prose* (1976)

BIBLIOGRAPHY: Markov, V., *The Longer Poems of K.* (1962); Markov, V., *Russian Futurism* (1968), passim; Baran, H., "K.'s Poem 'Bekh,'" *RusL*, No. 6 (1974): 5–19; special K. issue, *RusL*, 9, 1 (1981)

—GERALD PIROG

KHODASEVICH, Vladislav Felitsianovich

Russian poet and essayist, b. 16 May 1886, Moscow; d. 14 June 1939, Paris

K., one of the leading figures of Russian émigré literature in the 1920s and 1930s, was a descendant of the SYMBOLISTS who longed for a return to Pushkin. The last of six children of a Polish father and a Jewish mother—he had a lifelong fascination with Jewish culture—he described himself in his fanciful autobiographical sketch "Mladenchestvo" (1933, repub. 1965; infancy) as physically weak but mentally sharp. Brought up in the atmosphere of literary "Decadence," he was dissatisfied with what he felt was the 20th c.'s blindness to the great "classical" tradition of Russian harmony and versification. Never very political, he grew unhappy with the tendentiousness of the new Soviet age, and emigrated to western Europe in 1922, becoming ever more pessimistic in his life of poverty. His jaundiced outlook and miserable circumstances are poignantly described by his widow, Nina Berberova (b. 1900) in her chronicle of émigré literary life, *The Italics Are Mine* (1969). His death in 1939 marked the end of the European phase of Russian émigré culture in this century: World War II either killed or further scattered its representatives.

K. was not a prolific writer. His entire collected verse amounts to five small volumes of mostly short poems: *Molodost* (1908; youth); *Shchastlivy domik* (1914; the happy little house); *Putem zerna* (1920; the way of the grain); *Tyazhelaya lira* (1921; the heavy lyre); and *Evropeyskaya noch* (1927; European night). The last three constitute his mature verse, and were collected by K. himself in 1927 and republished with notes and additions by his widow in 1961. They show an unrelenting progression toward gloom and hopelessness, which the great critic D. S. Mirsky (1890–1939?) characterized as some of the most pessimistic verse in the history of Russian literature.

K.'s poetry is built on mystical solitude: the poet is always turning inward. Torn between his real physical needs and hatred of all the putrefaction he sees around him, K. seeks to deny his own physical self and to enter a completely solipsistic universe in which he exists alone with his verse, his soul, and his mental inventions. In his great "Ballada" (1921; ballad), as he sits in a chair rocking back and forth in meager surroundings in a St. Petersburg rooming house, he becomes Orpheus, transcending the real world to move into a world of pure creation, like Cincinnatus in *Invitation to a Beheading* by Vladimir NABOKOV, whose work K. was among the first to discover and champion.

K. emigrated first to Berlin (he was to spend the last fifteen years of his life in Paris), where with fellow émigrés Andrey Bely and Maxim Gorky he undertook the publication of a journal to appear simultaneously in Europe and the U.S.S.R. It failed, and K. felt increasingly isolated and hopeless. His verse assumed a cruel sharpness in its presentation of the ugly, prosaic, even gruesome detail. In "Pered zerkalom" (1924; before the mirror) the truth speaks to him and it speaks constant torment. The poet looks at himself and sees the deformity of pain. Indeed, deformity is everywhere, as he writes in "Dachnoe" (1923; suburbia). The world is full of grotesque shapes. Nothing makes sense anymore, and K. cannot bear what his poetic eye perceives.

So pervasive did this discordance become that K. literally silenced himself. After 1927, for all intents and purposes, he ceased writing poetry, devoting himself instead to the composition of several hundred critical essays of a general cultural and specifically literary nature, as a columnist for a Paris émigré daily, *Renaissance*. These essays sparkle with wit and intelligence and give a very sad picture of the émigré literary scene. Unlike his rival critics in emigration, Georgy Adamovich (1894–1972) and Marc Slonim (1894–1976), K. maintained that a Russian émigré literature was possible, but what it needed was a new method, a way not to follow the past or, as he put it, the same old tracks. Even here, however, K. was torn. Full of belief in this literary future, he was as full of doubt about its realization, for as he once put it, in the essay "Krovavaya pishcha" (1932; a food of blood), "to a very great degree, one can call the history of Russian literature the history of the destruction of Russian writers." So long as the emigration realized, as he wrote in "Podvig" (1932; the exploit), that "culture does not live either in refrigerators or in idle recollections . . . [and that it is preserved not by] those who think of the past, but by those who work for the present and future," it had hope.

Curiously, and without realizing the contradiction, K. placed this hope in a renewal of the past, a reconstruction of the Pushkin tradition. He wrote much about Pushkin, although he never produced a complete, full-length book on him. His love of Pushkinian metrics, moreover, was so overwhelming that he passed over too hurriedly much of the experimentation that was going on all around him. As a result, much of his imposing reasoning and classically honed verse was ignored by younger poets; he had but little influence, unlike his contemporary, Georgy Ivanov (1894–1958). But there is today a great renewed interest in his work, both in the West and the U.S.S.R., as Nadezhda Mandelshtam (1899–1980) has pointed out in her memoirs.

K. combines a symbolist mystical yearning for a kingdom of beauty that lies beyond the ugliness of the real with a classical sense of form derived from Pushkin. The tension produced by this unusual mixture makes of him an original, while his grotesque perception of the physical allies him to his Western contemporaries, who were portraying the very same decay that would culminate in World War II.

FURTHER WORKS: *Derzhavin* (1931); *O Pushkine* (1937); *Nekropol* (1939); *Literaturnye stati i vospominania* (1954)

BIBLIOGRAPHY: Nabokov, V., "On Hodasevich" (1939), *Strong Opinions* (1973): 223–27; Hughes, R., "K.: Irony and Dislocation: A Poet in Exile," *TriQ*, 28 (1973): 52–66; Smith, G. S., "Stanza Rhythm and Stress Load in the Iambic Tetrameter of V. F. K.," *SEEJ*, 24 (1980): 25–36; Bethea, D. M., *K.: His Life and Art* (1983)

—PHILIPPE RADLEY

KHOWAR LITERATURE
See Pakistani Literature

KIHLMAN, Christer Alfred

Finnish novelist (writing in Swedish), b. 14 June 1930, Helsinki

K.'s family background is important for an understanding of his work: His great-grandfather, Alfred Kihlman (1825–1914), was a provincial schoolmaster who, called to the Swedish Normal Lyceum, a new "model school" in Helsinki, carried on a distinguished pedagogical and political career while simultaneously becoming an industrialist; the "Kihlman Mansion," from the 1890s, still stands in the capital. His son Lorenzo (1861–1941) was a jurist remembered in particular for his opposition to Czarist rule; Lorenzo's sons were the critic and editor Erik (1895–1933) and the translator and novelist Bertel (1898–1977), who assumed the editorship of the important journal *Nya Argus* after Erik's death in a car accident. Thus Bertel's son, Christer, seemed destined for a life of literary activity and public responsibility. As an angry young man, revolting against his background (variously called "aristocratic" and "bourgeois" by him), he published the little magazine *Arena* together with Jörn DONNER, was a member of the circle around the poet Gunnar BJÖRLING, and brought out two verse books of his own. Employed as a reviewer by the Helsinki afternoon paper *Nya Pressen* and occasionally by Stockholm's *Dagens Nyheter*, he caught general Scandinavian attention with an article, "Svenskhetens slagskugga" (1959; "The Shadow Cast by Swedishness," 1986), on what he considered the privileged, artificial, and sterile life led by Finland's Swedish-speaking patricianate.

The attack was a forerunner of the novel *Se upp salige!* (1960; pay heed, o blest!), in which K. depicted the allegedly rotten establishment of a small town, Lexå, modeled on Porvoo (Swedish: Borgå), a place of historical and cultural importance, where the venerated national poet Johan Ludvig Runeberg (1804–1877) had dwelt. A well-meaning newspaper editor, the scion of an eminent family, undertakes numerous efforts, egged on by a leftist Finnish friend, to reveal the manifold hypocrisies of his milieu, but these projects all fall flat. Simultaneously, erotically fascinated by the friend's adolescent daughter, he neglects his son, who commits suicide. The book was received in some quarters as "the best Finland-Swedish novel in a very long time" (in it, K. had displayed his wonderfully pliant style to the full); but other voices called it a hateful and distorted parody on K.'s own cultural tradition.

Den blå modern (1962; *The Blue Mother*, 1990) is a kind of sequel; much of it likewise takes place in Lexå, and more is learned about the circumstances surrounding the death of the editor's son. Its main focus, though, is on two brothers and their male cousin, all members of the Lindermann family. One brother is an author and an alcoholic, sporadically unfaithful to his wife; the other is a homosexual whose fantasies of himself as commandant at Auschwitz represent the most shocking passages of the book. The depiction of the larger social and economic background is shadowy (in contrast to Donner's later portrayals of somewhat the same world in his novels); what matters to K. is the plumbing of tormented souls: The soft blue mother of the title may be a dream, for the brothers' actual mother has been selfish and uncaring,

partially responsible for their emotional deformations. Again, the novel caused a sensation; some critics found it turgid, in thrall to the torrents of words K. had found in William Faulkner and the Swedish novelist Lars AHLIN. The story was continued with *Madeleine* (1965; Madeleine); after the black comedy of *Se upp salige!* and the horrors of *Den blå modern*, the narrative, in diary form, has a curious idyllic tone—the marital storm eventually passes by.

Madeleine opens and closes on the day of John F. Kennedy's assassination, an event which—as K. asserted, not altogether logically—gave the final blow to his "belief and trust in a liberal bourgeois order of society." This claim was made in *Människan som skalv* (1971; the human being who trembled), a confession of K.'s alcoholism and his bisexuality, culminating in an encounter à trois between K.'s wife, a male friend, and himself. K. declared that, by his candor, he meant to contribute to a cleansing of a society defiled by capitalism. The book became a best-seller in Swedish and Finnish, a success that persuaded K. to go back on his pledge in 1966 to write no more novels since a Finland-Swedish author could not live by his pen alone. Subsequently, his production continued apace, divided between confessional and creative literature. Cultivating the former genre, he twice told about his involvements, during trips to South America, with male prostitutes: first in *Alla mina söner* (1980; *All My Sons*, 1984), where he likened himself to Saul and his ward (who had ambitions as a vocalist) to David, and again in *Livsdrömmen rena: Bok om maktlöshet* (1982; the pure dream of life: book about powerlessness), in which the author experiences the bliss of an automobile trip with a young companion through Uruguay, the living-out of a boyhood dream. *På drift i förlustens landskap* (1986; adrift in the landscape of loss) was much less ecstatic in tone, complaining bitterly about the infidelity of a neglected wife and about K.'s writer's block.

A decade before, K. had returned to the novel with *Dyre prins* (1975; *Sweet Prince*, 1983), about Donald Blaadh, a financial genius who comes out of nowhere after the Russo-Finnish War of 1941–1944, makes an opportunistic first marriage to a communist, and then weds a member of the wealthy Lindermann clan. The book has been called both a "Finland-Swedish *Buddenbrooks*" and a soap opera. Slowly, Donald realizes that he has neglected his children in pursuit of his career as an international financier—two of his six offspring commit suicide. (It was in search of more models for the Blaadh-Bladh family that K. first went to South America.) In *Gerdt Bladhs undergång* (1987; *The Death of Gerdt Bladh*, 1989) another branch of the clan has center stage. Recovered from his spiritual crisis, Donald lives in Spain with a new mistress, while his nephew Gerdt is the head of a great Helsinki department store. The old concerns of K. reappear (Gerdt has a weakness for young boys and is cuckolded by his wife); but the Finland-Swedish establishment, rapidly losing power in actual fact, is treated more gently than before, and an element of the supernatural has been added to K.'s complex intrigue. In Gerdt's youth, an admired older cousin committed suicide, and his energetic soul entered Gerdt's flabby body, transforming the boy into a "masculine" achiever, but leaving him, in fact, with two spirits, which cause "an ambivalence in his emotional life."

K.'s oeuvre offers serious problems of evaluation. The homosexual-bisexual thematology grows tedious, as do the ponderous essays, or editorials, that K. often allots to his characters or his narrative voice. Furthermore, in his constant earnestness, he can veer off into unintentional comedy. Yet, to balance these weaknesses, there are the incomparable grace and genuine evocative strength of K.'s prose, and his unfailing ability to recreate atmospheres and capture subtle emotional reactions. In much, he will remind an American reader of John CHEEVER, although he has never reached Cheever's mastery of narrative form.

FURTHER WORKS: *Rummen vid havet* (1951); *Munkmonolog* (1953); *Inblandningar utmaningar* (1969); *De nakna och de saliga* (1983, with Henrik Tikkanen)

BIBLIOGRAPHY: Schoolfield, G. C., "The Postwar Novel of Swedish Finland," *SS*, 34 (1962): 85–110; Svedberg, I., "Extending the Bounds of Reality: An Approach to the Work of C. K.," *BF*, 10 (1976): 7–10; Lillquist, H., "Die Bedingungen des Überlebens: Zum literarischen Werke C. Ks," *Jahrbuch für finnisch-deutsche Literaturbeziehungen*, 13 (1979): 80–89; Tate, J., "C. K.: Chronicles of Crisis," *BF*, 16 (1982): 141–43; Schoolfield, G. C., Afterword to *The Blue Mother* (1990): 281–308

—GEORGE C. SCHOOLFIELD

KIKUYU LITERATURE
See Kenyan Literature

KILLENS, John Oliver

American novelist, short-story writer, essayist, dramatist, and screenwriter, b. 14 Jan. 1916, Macon, Ga.; d. 27 Oct. 1987, Brooklyn, N.Y.

K., who attended a number of colleges and universities, served on the staff of the National Labor Relations Board from 1936 to 1942 and again in 1946. He served in the Pacific Amphibian Forces of the U.S. Army during World War II.

K.'s importance to African-American literature rests not only on his accomplishments as a writer, but also on his influence as a cofounder of the Harlem Writer's Guild—with Rosa Guy (b. 1922) and John H. Clarke (b. 1915)—as writer-in-residence at Fisk University, as professor of creative writing at the New School, as director of the Brooklyn Writers' Workshop, and, more generally, as a force in the Black Arts movement that emerged as an aesthetic extension of the Black Power movement in the 1960s and 1970s. K. was also active in the civil rights movement and was, by the late 1960s, identified with that movement's more militant wing, which had moved away from the commitment to nonviolence articulated by Martin Luther King, Jr.; this development in K.'s social and political attitudes is reflected in *Black Man's Burden*, a book of essays published in 1965.

K.'s early fiction is closely linked to the social, political, and artistic commitments suggested by these affiliations and activities. His themes in his first three novels include the struggle for black dignity in a racist society; the developing awareness of a black identity in individual characters; the gradual coming into being of a black communal consciousness; the translation of communal consciousness into political perception and action; and the troubled

search for the ground on which a healthy and vital relation of black and white might be based. It is a limitation of all three of these novels that they may in varying degrees be read as illustrations of these thematic concerns rather than as fully created examples of the novelist's art. The writing is frequently stiff, the dialogue explanatory or exclamatory, the situations dictated by the desire to make a point, the manner didactic, the tone painfully high-minded. Yet the three taken together represent a not ignoble attempt to move the African-American novel beyond the legacy of Richard WRIGHT and away from the influence of Ralph ELLISON, whose *Invisible Man* (1952) K. denounced as a "vicious distortion of Negro life." K. is not concerned, as Wright to a degree was, with victimhood and its causes. For K., literary realism is an instrument for social change through an affirmation of personal and communal awareness, commitment, and action. The emphasis on community, and on the black family as a source of strength, distances K. as well from the emphasis on the physical and spiritual solitude of the protagonist that is often a feature of the work of Wright and Ellison, and of K.'s younger contemporary James BALDWIN.

And Then We Heard the Thunder (1962) is K.'s most impressive novel in the mode of socially committed realism that characterizes his early work. Drawing on his own experience, during the war, K. attempts a "Big War" novel, of the sort of this time associated with writers like Norman MAILER and James JONES. But K.'s version is told from a black perspective, and K. examines unblinkingly the many ironies, comic and savage, involved in asking African-Americans to sacrifice themselves for a democracy whose benefits they are discouraged from claiming as their own. The novel reaches a powerful (and factually based) climax as a battle breaks out between black and white American troops in the streets of Bainbridge, Australia. K.'s development as an artist in the years since the publication of *Youngblood* (1954) is reflected in formal terms in his decision to end the novel as the battle is still in progress and as the fate of his protagonist is still in doubt; the openness of the ending is powerfully appropriate to the unfolding of the novel's themes. And if, as some critics observed, K.'s characters still have a tendency to become mouthpieces for attitudes and positions K. wants to affirm or expose, they transcend this function often enough to give this novel an occasional vitality beyond anything one finds elsewhere in K.'s earlier work. Finally, the novel is informed throughout by a comic sense, especially in the portrayal of character, that prevents the ruthless high-mindedness, to which the K. of this period is constantly tempted, from taking over.

K.'s third novel, *Sippi* (1967), does not sustain the level of accomplishment achieved in *And Then We Heard the Thunder* and suggests that K. had gone as far as he could with the sort of realism these works represent. His fourth novel, *The Cotillion; or, One Good Bull Is Half the Herd* (1971), turns away from the formal strategies and, to a lesser degree, from the thematic emphases of the earlier work. K. here takes a comic-satiric look at absurdities within the black community. His primary target is the sort of absurdity that arises when black people try to imitate the hollow frivolities (the cotillion, or formal display of debutantes) of a decadent white society. But he looks with an equally jaundiced eye on the fashions, fads, and role-playing that may substitute for an authentic racial consciousness. At the same time, K. celebrates all that is beautiful and life-giving in black culture and continues to explore the familiar themes of the growth and interaction of personal and racial awareness. The novel is written in what the narrator calls "Afro-Americanese." K.'s formal and stylistic experiments are not uniformly successful, but they do represent the author's willingness to try new ways and to explore new possibilities for African-American fiction.

The possibilities opened up in *The Cotillion* were, however, not to be developed by K. himself. The remaining novels published in his lifetime were intended for the "young adult" audience. A novel based on the life of Pushkin, the Russian poet who was of partly African ancestry, was published posthumously.

K. produced at least two novels that stand every chance of living on as significant works of African-American literature; they deserve to be read by audiences of varying racial and ethnic backgrounds, and in fact K. has been translated into more than a dozen languages. His effort to build on the legacy of Richard Wright, constitutes an honorable contribution to the development of an authentic African-American literature. And even K.'s hostility toward Ellison, though perhaps misguided in itself, may have served the useful function of suggesting to younger black writers and critics that they need not be intimidated by "official" accounts of the African-American literary tradition, especially insofar as those accounts are the handiwork of white academicians. His role in the encouragement of younger writers and his interaction with writers of his own generation must figure in any attempt to evaluate his importance to the literary culture of his time. His ultimate rank is yet to be determined, but we may confidently say this much: He was one of the liberators.

FURTHER WORKS: *Slaves* (1969); *Great Gittin' Up Morning: A Biography of Denmark Vesey* (1972); *A Man Ain't Nothin' But a Man: The Adventures of John Henry* (1975); *The Great Black Russian: A Novel on the Life and Times of Alexander Pushkin* (1988)

BIBLIOGRAPHY: Berry, A., "Crossroads, Georgia," *Masses and Mainstream*, Sept. 1954: 16–19; Ihde, H., "Black Writer's Burden: Remarks on J. O. K.," *ZAA*, 16 (1968): 117–37; Wiggins, W., "Black Folktales in the Novels of J. O. K.," *Black Scholar*, 3 (1971): 50–58; Wiggins, W., "Structure and Dynamics of Folklore: The Case of J. O. K.," *KFQ*, 17 (1972): 92–118; Klotman, P., "The White Bitch Archetype in Contemporary Black Fiction," *Bulletin of the Midwest MLA*, 6 (1973): 96–110; Gayle, A., Jr., *The Way of the New World: The Black Novel in America* (1975): 260–77; Bigsby, C. W. E., "Judgment Day Is Coming! The Apocalyptic Dream in Recent Afro-American Fiction," in Lee, A. R., ed., *Black Fiction: New Studies in the Afro-American Novel since 1945* (1980): 149–72; Gayle, A., Jr., Foreword to *Youngblood* (1982): 7–10; Watkins, M., Introduction to *And Then We Heard the Thunder* (1983): v–xvi; Bell, B. W., *The Afro-American Novel and Its Tradition* (1987): 245–53; Gayle, A., Jr., Foreword to *'Sippi* (1988): 5–10; Harris, N., *Connecting Times: The Sixties in Afro-American Fiction* (1988): 140–65

—W. P. KENNEY

KILPI, Eeva

Finnish novelist, short-story writer, and poet, b. 18 Feb. 1928, Hiitola

When K. was twelve years old, the family had to leave their Carelian hometown of Hiitola as a result of the Finnish Winter War

John Oliver Killens

in 1940. This experience, the topic of K.'s two long novels *Elämä edestakaisin* (1964; life back and forth) and *Elämän evakkona* (1983; refugees of life) as well as of her two memoir books, *Talvisodan aika* (1989; time of Winter War) and *Välirauha* (1990; provisionary peace), shaped K.'s outlook on life. As the theme of loss and pain or separation it structures much of K.'s production.

K.'s first collection of short stories, *Noidanlukko* (1959; noidanlukko), the name of a flower that never blooms, dealt with idyllic childhood experiences, which, however, were cut short by the war. In the autobiographical series of books, starting with *Talvisodan aika*, she returned to her childhood Carelia, but now in the documentary mode, focusing not only on the loss of the land itself but on what it meant for a girl to grow up in the midst of the family's many moves and the whole nation's attempts to come to terms with its new truncated existence. Ibsen's words "Kun det tapte evig eies" ("Only what is lost, is forever owned") describe admirably K.'s attitude to the lost province of Carelia. For K.'s and her parents' generation, Carelia functioned as the seat of authentic values; its shared loss gave the former Carelians a sense of togetherness, and the shared memories bestowed their lives with meaning. Realizing that with the demise of her fathers and mothers disappeared also the values of the era they represented, K. has felt compelled to record her own Carelian experiences based on diaries, old letters, and other documentary sources.

Women as creators and centers of creativity but also as the deprived ones, whose lives consist of a series of losses, are the protagonists of many of K.'s novels and short stories. The lost childhood experience of unity with one's environment can be recaptured through love and the sexual experience. But for a woman even love leads to losses, of lovers, of a husband, and, for the mother, of her sons. Finally, she has to face the increasing signs of physical deterioration, the augurs of old age and death. It is particularly this perspective of a middle-aged woman, rather scantily treated in literature, that gains prominence in K.'s works. More openly than perhaps any other Finnish woman writer of her generation K. has dealt with female sexuality. At times her attitude approaches the traditional male one where a one-night stand serves to validate the aging woman's self-worth and prowess. But more often, like in the erotic novel *Tamara* (1972; *Tamara*, 1978) and the fictional diary *Naisen Päiväkirja* (1978; a woman's diary), the sex act is the one experience that at least momentarily reestablishes a feeling of lost unity by erasing all alienating boundaries between male and female, body and soul, life and death. Identification with nature and its cycles of life and death, from trees to insects, offers a similar experience of almost pantheistic oneness with the universe. Stylistically K.'s detailed descriptions of nature are superb in their sensitivity and beauty.

While a male critic's retort that K.'s meticulous reporting of the female's bodily functions leaves readers cold greatly misjudged the sociological makeup of the readership, it did accurately reveal how K.'s works address women in particular. Both in her psychological analysis of the different phases in a woman's life and her openly confessional treatment of female sexuality, she has been the forerunner of the many women writers of the 1980s who have been both bolder and stylistically more experimental in their depictions of today's Finnish women. Also in her attunement and deference to nature K. anticipated the ecological consciousness of the 1990s. A good indication of the exceptionally warm reception K. has enjoyed among readers in Sweden are the numerous and almost instantaneous Swedish translations of her works.

FURTHER WORKS: *Kukkivan maan rannat* (1960); *Nainen kuvastimessa* (1962); *Uudet jumalat* (1965); *Lapikkaita* (1966); *Rakkauden ja kuoleman pöytä* (1967); *Kesä ja keski-ikäinen nainen* (1970); *Hyvän yön tarinoita* (1971); *Laulu rakkaudesta ja muita runoja* (1972); *Häätanhu* (1973); *Ihmisen ääni* (1976); *Terveisin* (1976); *Runoja 1972–1976* (1978); *Se mitä ei koskaan sanota* (1979); *Ennen kuolemaa* (1982); *Kuolema ja nuori rakastaja* (1986); *Animalia* (1987); *Kootut novellit* (1987)

BIBLIOGRAPHY: Deschner, M., "E. K.: Home and Solitude," *BF*, 3 (1984): 118–28

—VIRPI ZUCK

KILPI, Volter

Finnish novelist and essayist, b. 12 Dec. 1874, Kustavi; d. 13 June 1939, Turku

K.'s father was a merchant-ship captain based at Kustavi, on the coast north of Turku; he maintained his connection with the Kustavi district throughout his life. His family name was really Ericsson, but he and two brothers adopted the Finnish name he is known by. Following a university education, K. became a librarian

and was eventually appointed director of the Turku University Library. He began to lose his hearing at a rather early age and became progressively deafer throughout his life. He married the playwright Helga Vanhakartano in 1907.

K.'s first creative writings were neoromantic. *Bathseba* (1900; Bathsheba) is a sentimental poetic narrative in which a leading theme is the difficulty of human communication. His essays in *Ihmisestä ja elämästä* (1902; on man and life) voice the aestheticism common at the time and show the influence of Goethe, Schopenhauer, and Nietzsche. During the 1918 civil war and its aftermath, he published right-wing political pamphlets advocating a monarchy for Finland.

K. found his most original vein much later in the novel *Alastalon salissa* (1933; in the hall of Alastalo), the product of long labor. In it his aestheticism was left behind, although his preoccupation with the inner life only deepens. The prologue is a prolonged meditation on death inspired by the sight of an old churchyard and recalling a church service attended as a child. All the older people who were then present are now buried there. Memories of a wedding, of men, women, and girls, of an autumn Sunday morning press into the narrator's consciousness. This long, nostalgic book has been compared to the works of PROUST and JOYCE, and the rendering of the thought processes of the characters anticipates the "subconversations" of Nathalie SARRAUTE. Nevertheless, the characters and setting are entirely K.'s own. The time is around 1860. A group of merchant seamen and farmers come to Captain Mattsson's house to discuss a new shipbuilding venture. One of the men in attendance is Pukkila, his resentful rival. Another memorable character is Härkäniemi, a philosophical bachelor. Primarily through interior monologue the varied life of the community is unveiled. Much humor enlivens the novel, and a long sailor's yarn narrated by Härkäniemi lends variety.

K.'s book of short stories *Pitäjän pienempiä* (1934; humbler folk of the parish) parallels on a humbler level the depiction of the more prosperous class in *Alastalon salissa*. One especially effective story is "Merimiehenleski" (a seaman's widow), written in the form of a sequence of meditations of an old woman. She had lost her husband at sea many years before. There are no children to break the long silences left in her hut by his repeated departures and his final permanent absence. She is consoled by memories of her husband and by religious piety, but her prayers finally turn into imprecations against an unlistening God.

There is an autobiographical aspect to the novel *Kirkolle* (1937; on the way to church). A boat takes a large group of islanders to church. The gathering, the journey, and the arrival provide the action, but the main purpose of the book is the analysis of the churchgoers' feelings and the description of the midsummer Sunday setting. If the physical destination is a Christian church, the spiritual destination is agnostic in nature. Only the present existence is real, in all its paradoxical richness. The title of a book of meditations, *Suljetuilla porteilla* (1938; at closed gates), is perhaps unintentionally significant, for the author's difficult style has become almost hermetic. But an unfinished, posthumously published work shows a renewed clarity of expression: *Gulliverin matka Fantomimian mantereelle* (1944; Gulliver's journey to Fantomimia) is an interesting attempt to transport Gulliver into the modern world, where time-travel seems a familiar possibility.

K. is never likely to be popular. Even for Finnish readers, there is an obstacle in his handling of the language, his penchant for coinages and compounds of his own creation. Nonetheless, K. was a highly individual writer whose experiments in novelistic technique may justify comparison with the much better-known vanguard of the major currents of world literature.

FURTHER WORKS: *Parsifal* (1902); *Antinous* (1903); *Nykyaikaisista taidepyrinnöistä* (1905); *Kansallista itsetutkistelua* (1917); *Tulevaisuuden edessä* (1918)

BIBLIOGRAPHY: Ahokas, J., *A History of Finnish Literature* (1973): 209–17

—REINO VIRTANEN

KIMBUNDU LITERATURE

See Angolan Literature

KINCAID, Jamaica

Antiguan novelist and short-story writer, b. 25 May 1949, St. John's

Born Elaine Potter Richardson, K. grew up on the small island of Antigua. Her education on the island included attending government schools and an apprenticeship to a seamstress. Her father, a carpenter, was a native of Antigua and her mother, described by K. as a literate and cultured woman, was a native of Dominica. At the age of sixteen K. went to the U.S. to pursue her education. She worked as an au pair, a receptionist, and as a magazine writer for *Art Direction* while she attended classes. In 1973 she changed her name to Jamaica Kincaid. She submitted freelance articles to magazines and her name appeared in one of the "Talk of the Town" pieces in the *New Yorker*. She became a contributor to the *New Yorker*, and beginning in 1976, she became a staff writer for the magazine. K. received the Morton Dauwen Zabel Award for fiction in 1984, a Guggenheim Fellowship in 1989, and honorary degrees from Williams College and Long Island College in 1981. Her first volume of stories, *At the Bottom of the River*, appeared in 1983. After a visit to Antigua in 1985, an informal ban on her visiting island was affected. The ban on visiting was apparently lifted in 1992. In addition to *At the Bottom of the River*, K. has published four novels, *Annie John* (1985), *Lucy* (1990), *The Autobiography of My Mother* (1996), and *The Autobiography of My Brother* (1997); an extended essay entitled *A Small Place* (1988); and numerous stories and pieces for publication.

K.'s fiction is marked by two characteristic signatures: an almost palpable disdain of mother characters and language characterized by direct speech avoidance leading Merle HODGE to describe her works as "novels of introspection, only one central character is drawn in depth." K. stands apart from other Caribbean writers in these two features. Coupled with an assured though detached tone and remarkably vivid portraits of setting, K.'s canon is a study of post-colonial wrangling.

One can not read K.'s works without noting what H. Adlai Murdock termed "the protagonist's almost palpable hatred for her mother." *At the Bottom of the River*, *Annie John*, and *Lucy* might be viewed as a continuous novel during which the narrator outlines a series of conflicts between mother and daughter. On a literal level, the ongoing conflicts are informed by the question of how the protagonist will be in the world: a model Caribbean daughter or an individual who rejects the values of her mother (especially those imposed by colonialism). On a figurative level, the conflicts concern the Caribbean individual's struggle to overcome colonial influence, male privilege, and class privilege. It is not until the publication of *A Small Place* in which the mother is cast as opposition to the government, that the conflicts between the mother and daughter appear to be resolved. The resolution is a treatise on the dynamics of a small, formerly colonized, and presently exploited, as well as corrupt, island as they shape the character of its inhabitants.

In all of K.'s works the evocation of the mother is filtered through the body politics of a developing Caribbean daughter. The mother rarely speaks directly and when she does her words and actions are framed through the perception of the daughter. There is no compromise in the works, no attempts to explain or allow the mother to explain her actions or motivations. K. remains focused on the goal of expelling the values of the mothers that she associates as those of the oppressors. Margaret Homans uses the term "matrophobia'" to refer to the fear of becoming like one's mother and suggests that it is actually the mother's cultural powerlessness that the daughter is rejecting. The daughter then denies her love for and identification with the mother only insofar as the mother stands for a situation that the daughter wishes to rectify.

In *The Autobiography of My Mother* and *The Autobiography of My Brother* K. again translates the personal into narratives evocative of an entire society. *The Autobiography of My Mother* is the story of a motherless child who attempts to create herself in the absence of a maternal figure. *The Autobiography of my Brother* recounts the anguish of her brother Devon's life in Antigua before he died of AIDS in 1996 at the age of thirty-three. Here again the subject behind the subject is a mother figure who changes after the death of the brother.

K. is best known for her slim volumes of fiction, but in 1988 she published an astoundingly penetrating essay *A Small Place*. The piece was rejected by the new editorial board of the *New Yorker* as being too angry, and K. published it as a book. The essay addresses, among other things, the persona of the tourist, the persona of the native, island corruption, and the legacy of slavery in the Caribbean. K. Wrote it after a visit to her country and observed the situation with the eyes of an adult, some nineteen years after she had originally left the island-country. In this work the figurative meaning of the previous mother-daughter relationships are brought into greater focus. Here she makes the larger political connection between the Caribbean mother and the history of the island.

In addition to her understated prose style and her frank treatment of subject matter, K.'s works are important for its insistent focus on the individual's experience. Merle Hodge has distinguished her writing from that of writers who concern themselves with the collective experience of the Caribbean. Hodge believes that K.'s narratives expand into universal experience while approaching the mythological in its dimensions.

BIBLIOGRAPHY: Homans, M., *Women Writers and Poetic Identity* (1980); Dutton, W., "Merge and Separate: J. K.'s Fiction," *WLT*, 63 (Summer 1989): 406-10; Cudjoe, S. R., "J. K. and the Modernist Project: An Interview," *Caribbean Women Writers: Essays from the First International Conference* (1990): 215-31; Murdoch, H. A., "Severing the (M)other Connection: The Representation of

Cultural Identity in J. K.'s *Annie John*," *Callaloo*, 13 (Spring 1990): 325-40; Hodge, M., "Caribbean Writers and Caribbean Language: A Study of J. K.'s *Annie John*," in Newson, A. S., and L. Strong-Leek, eds., *Winds of Change: The Transforming Voices of Caribbean Women Writers and Scholars* (1998): 47-53

—ADELE S. NEWSON

KINGSTON, Maxine Hong

American autobiographer, novelist, journalist, and short-story writer, b. 27 Oct. 1940, Stockton, California

Maxine Ting Ting Hong was born in the U.S., the eldest child of Chinese immigrant parents. Her father arrived in the U.S. in 1924, her mother in 1939. Immersed from birth in Cantonese language and culture, K. began public school in America unable to speak English. However, by age nine she had become fluent enough in English to begin writing poetry. Having inherited her mother's gifts in the art of "talk-story" (storytelling), her writings eventually took the form of narrative. She married Earll Kingston in 1962.

K.'s *The Woman Warrior: Memoirs of a Girlhood Among Ghosts* is her first and most acclaimed work, winning a National Book Critics Circle Award for the best nonfiction book of 1976. *Woman Warrior* challenges categorization, for K. mixes her memories and life experiences with myth, creating in the process a text that is neither, and both, autobiography and novel. Through this extraordinary textual hybrid, K. explores her own identity, her relationship to her mother, and the traditional subject position of women in Chinese culture. Using a five-part structure, K. explores alternating visions of female subjectivity and the problems of self-representation, ultimately writing her self into and through the feminist, mythic image of a woman warrior. K.'s mother is the source of some of K.'s visions, offering her daughter both repressive cultural maxims and powerful and independent visions of womanhood. Thus, as K.'s mother performs it, female storytelling, and implicitly then female self-representation, is laced with cultural contradictions and ambiguities—a veritable minefield for K. as she seeks to author, indeed, to authorize, her self. K. manages to negotiate and neutralize that minefield in *Woman Warrior*, creating in the process a space for independent female self-authorship.

The book's first section, "No Name Woman," dissects and reconstitutes the forbidden story of K.'s paternal aunt, related to her as a "cautionary tale" by her mother. Against her mother's instructions, K. relates the brief story of No-Name aunt in the public forum of autobiography, breaking the culturally imposed, limiting silence her family had approved. K. searches for a new story for No-Name aunt, a narrative that will transform her mother's "cautionary tale" and give her aunt back both history and existence. K. experiments with several narratives, each successively more empowered, before finding one that suits her. Although she begins by imagining No-Name aunt as the passive, silenced victim of rape, K. ultimately settles on a story that presents her as a rebellious and desiring woman who ignored cultural prohibitions and sought out and claimed sexual pleasure. In a final spiteful act this No-Name aunt commits suicide by literally and figuratively polluting the family well with her illegitimate child. In the second section K. completes her appropriation of her mother's stories with the legend of Fa Mu

Lan, woman warrior. K.'s identification with Fa Mu Lan is implicit given the title of her autobiography; through the legend, K. portrays herself as arising, powerful, and battle-ready, out of a discourse-tradition handed down by her mother. In *Woman Warrior's* third section K. subsumes her mother's biography to her own autobiography. Her mother's story is not unlike Fa Mu Lan's narrative of female independence and power, yet it also resonates with the story of No Name Woman in its final capitulation to traditional images of a female subjectivity. Even as K. recounts her mother's independent life in China and draws her mother's character as warrior-like, she presents her readers with traditional Chinese misogyny in stories of bound feet, of girls sold into slavery, and of female infanticide. The dangers of the traditional cultural position of Chinese women is examined more fully in the fourth section, with the story of K.'s maternal aunt, Moon Orchid, whose husband abandons her for an English-speaking, Chinese-American wife. In the fifth section K. resolves her relationship with her mother when as equals they both relate the story of female authorial power embodied in the narrative of the Chinese poet Ts'ai Yen, her mother telling the beginning, K. the end.

K.'s second book, *China Men* (1980), won both a National Books Critics Circle Award and an American Book Award, and is considered by many critics to complete her autobiography. As *Woman Warrior* focused on K.'s relationship with her mother and her mother's history, so *China Men* focuses on K.'s relationship to her father and her father's history. In *China Men* K. again blurs the line between fact and fiction, combining historical fact, myth, and memory to write in epic form the history of a family of immigrant Chinese male sojourners.

In her first novel, *Tripmaster Monkey: His Fake Book* (1989), K. answers critics who have judged her work harshly, charging that she has played into prevailing American stereotypes that construe Asian Americans as effeminate, exotic, and passive. *Tripmaster Monkey* examines the significance of traditional Chinese texts to a contemporary, emergent Chinese-American literature, the legitimacy of claims that only certain specific texts can embody ethnic consciousness—the claim that some texts are "true" Chinese while others are "fake"—and exactly who can make such judgements. Set in San Francisco during the politically turbulent 1960s, the book's protagonist is a fifth-generation Chinese American hippie poet-playwright, aptly named by his father Wittman Ah Sing, after poet Walt Whitman. Wittman, who wants to be the "first bad-jazz China Man bluesman of America" exhibits both the fierce but narrowminded idealism and the unexamined sexism of K.'s most severe reviewers, yet K. does not appear to treat Wittman harshly. Instead, in *Tripmaster Monkey*, K. often finds common ground with her protagonist, allowing Wittman in a final, protracted rant, to voice her own exasperation with anti-American racism.

FURTHER WORKS: *Hawaii One Summer* (1987); *Through the Black Curtain* (1987)

BIBLIOGRAPHY: Smith, S., "M. H. K.'s 'Woman Warrior': Filiality and Woman's Autobiographical Storytelling," *A Poetics of Women's Autobiography: Marginality and Fictions of Self-Representation* (1987): 150-73; Leonard, J., "Of Thee Ah Sing" *The Nation*, 248 (1989): 768-72; Cheung, K., *Articulate Silences: Hisaye Yamamoto, M. H. K., Joy Kogawa* (1993); Pollack, H., ed., *Having Our Way: Women Rewriting Tradition in Twentieth-Century America* (1995); Smith, J., "Rethinking American Culture: M. H. K.'s

Cross-Cultural Tripmaster Monkey," *MLS*, 26, 4 (1996): 71-81; Chu, P., " *Tripmaster Monkey*, Frank Chin, and the Chinese Heroic Tradition," *ArQ*, 53, 3 (1997): 110-39

—MARSHA WATSON

KINNELL, Galway

American poet and translator, b. 1 Feb. 1927, Providence, R.I.

A Princeton graduate, K. has taught at many universities in the U.S. and abroad; he spent three years at the University of Hawaii, but then returned to the east coast. Clearly K. teachers more out of necessity than a fully developed sense of vocation; he seldom writes reviews or essays, although his novel *Black Light* (1966) is very powerful. For K., poetry is the first and last concern.

K.'s early poetry was filled with a miraculous sense of the commonplace. His long poem, "The Avenue Bearing the Initial of Christ into the New World," in *What a Kingdom It Was* (1960), celebrated the diversity of urban life, turning the welter of sensations into a Whitmanesque embrace of change and transformation. Allied in sensibility to the poetry of Robert BLY and James Wright (1927–1980), K. avoided irony in favor of an intensity created out of an imagery of incandescent attentiveness. Thematically his early poetry revolved around questions of suffering and death, using an essentially religious consciousness to question the human condition. Yet the religious fervor of the poetry never inhibited a full acceptance of the secular notions of pleasure and joy.

In *Body Rags* (1967) and *The Book of Nightmares* (1971) K. brought to fullest expression his sense of what he calls the "poetics of the physical world" by dealing with the courage, pain, and rage of "torn love." The main influences of this poetry, besides the obvious presence of Whitman, are the flower and animal poems of D. H. LAWRENCE and the natural-ecstatic sequences of Theodore ROETHKE. K.'s attention is often drawn to ways of registering both long-term and intense awareness of suffering and loss: the lines of the human face, the consuming power of fire, and the manifold forms of music and song, all appear often in his poems, and in many guises. His subjects can as readily be drawn from scenes of urban alienation as from the natural landscape of New England.

K. has also translated the poems of Villon—*The Poems of François Villon* (1965; rev. version, 1977)—and Yves BONNEFOY—*On the Motion and Immobility of Douve* (1968). These translations reflect the same qualities that animate his poems: states of extreme desire and moments of great subjective power are presented in a language dense with human urgency.

FURTHER WORKS: *First Poems, 1946–1954* (1954); *Flower Herding on Mount Monadnock* (1964); *The Avenue Bearing the Initial of Christ into the New World: Poems 1946–64* (1974); *Mortal Acts, Mortal Words* (1980); *Selected Poems* (1982); *The Past* (1985); *Imperfect Thirst* (1994)

BIBLIOGRAPHY: Howard, R., *Alone with America* (1969): 258–71; Davie, D., "Slogging for the Absolute," *Parnassus*, 3, 1 (1974): 9–22; McKenzie, J., "To the Roots: An Interview with K.," in Boyers, R., ed., *Contemporary Poetry in America* (1974): 240–55; Lieberman, L., *Unassigned Frequencies: American Poetry in*

Review (1977): 212–14; Molesworth, C., *The Fierce Embrace: A Study in Contemporary American Poetry* (1979): 98–111

—CHARLES MOLESWORTH

KINOSHITA Junji

Japanese dramatist, b. 2 Aug. 1914, Tokyo

Born in the Hongō district of Tokyo to a middle-class family, K. moved at the age of five with his family to ancestral holdings in the prefecture of Kumamoto on the island of Kyushu. There he was raised and educated at the Kumamoto Fifth High School in the prewar educational system. He returned to Tokyo in 1936 to enter the graduate school of Tokyo Imperial University, where he studied English literature and drama. He has lived in Tokyo since. K. is best known for his drama, but he has also published novels, criticism of drama and politics, and translations of Shakespeare, John Millington SYNGE, and other English-language dramatists.

K. is considered the foremost postwar dramatist of Shingeki or the "New Theater" tradition of modern realistic drama of Japan. Arising from productions of Shakespeare, Ibsen, and other European dramatists in translation in the first decade of the 20th c., the New Theater had become inextricably involved with leftist politics in the 1930s when K. first became active in it through the introduction of his mentors, the director Okakura Shirō and the actress Yamamoto Yasue. His first play, *Fūrō* (1939; wind and waves), recounted modern Kumamoto history in the epic style of the socialist dramatists of the 1930s, who, in turn, had learned their art from a variety of sources—Anton CHEKHOV, SOCIALIST REALISM, proletarian literature, and the old history plays of the Kabuki.

During World War II K. began experimenting with a new form of drama based on Japanese folktales. Soon after, he published *Yūzuru* (1949; *The Twilight Crane*, 1956), the most famous of these, which has become a standard play in the modern Japanese repertory. The genre, known by the neologism *minwageki* or "folktale drama" was considered by many to be the first indigenous form of modern drama and thus equivalent to other purely Japanese forms such as the Nō and Kabuki. Throughout the 1950s, K. continued to write folktale drama, which he produced in conjunction with *Budō no kai* or the Grapes Company, founded together with Okakura and Yamamoto. By the end of the decade, he had adapted the form for a variety of subjects, the most famous being *Onnyoro seisuiki* (1957; the rise and fall of Onnyoro), an ironic comedy, based on a play from the post-1949 Chinese revolutionary theater, recounting an instance of "self-criticism" by an "unself-conscious" peasant.

Even while he worked with folktales, K. continued to explore themes of modern Japanese history, especially the Pacific War and its effect on Japan, through plays in the realistic mode. Seen in the context of his entire work, these plays form the core of his career, with the folktale plays as his introduction to the art of writing for the theater. In 1960 the attempt by a broad coalition of political forces left of center to block passage of the Japan-U.S. Mutual Security Treaty in the Japanese Diet was frustrated. As one deeply involved in the movement, K. wrote a series of plays that helped provide a historical framework for the intellectual currents and social forces that had led to the 1960 defeat. These are best represented in the plays *Ottō to yobareru Nihonjin* (1962; a Japanese called Otto) and *Okinawa* (1963; Okinawa). K.'s work exploring the effects of the Pacific War on contemporary Japan culminated in *Kami to hito to no aida* (1970; *Between God and Man*, 1979), a two part play recreating in Part I the International Military Tribunal for the Far East (the Tokyo War Crimes Trials), and in Part II, the war crimes trial of a common soldier who manages to break out of the debilitating psychology of guilt that had marked virtually all of K.'s earlier heroes and, in his judgment, the Japanese people.

Since 1970 K. has produced only one more play, the epic *Shigosen no matsuri* (1978; requiem on the meridian), a choral rendition of a medieval Japanese military epic. Among its many other aspects, this last play highlights K.'s mastery of the various styles of classical and modern Japanese and his ability to feature language itself as a major element of interest throughout his drama. In the 1970s and 1980s, theater in Japan shifted focus from the text to production, and from the dramatist to the actor, as has been true in many contemporary theaters around the world. K.'s theater, the New Theater of Japan, had been created to feature the dramatist and the written word as the primary focus of theatrical activity, and it is possible that K. may be the last of the historian dramatists of modern Japan.

FURTHER WORKS: *Rajio dorama senshū* (1953); *Watashi no Shēkusupia* (1953); *Engeki no dentō to minwa* (1956); *Geijutsu to shakai e no me* (1956); *Nihon no minwa* (1960); *Minwagekishū* (3 vols., 1961); *K. sakuhinshū* (8 vols., 1962–1971); *Fuyu no jidai* (1964); *Nihon ga Nihon de aru tame ni wa* (1965); *Hanawaka/Yoki na jigoku yaburi* (1966); *Mugen kidō* (1966); *Yumemi kozō* (1966); *Dorama no sekai* (1967); *Shiroi yoru no utage* (1967); *Dorama to no taiwa* (1968); *Zuisō Shēkusupia* (1969); *K. hyōronshū* (12 vols., 1972); *Shēkusupia no sekai* (1973); *Bōkyaku ni tsuite* (1974); *Rekishi ni tsuite* (1976); *Unmei no kochiragawa* (1976); *Koten o yakusu* (1978); *Rakutenteki na Nihonjin* (1980); *Zuisōshū: Ryokaku* (1980); *Dorama ga naritatsu toki* (1981); *Gikyoku no Nihongo* (1982); *K. gikyokusen* (3 vols., 1982); *Giron shinokoshita koto* (1986); *K. shū* (16 vols., 1988). FURTHER WORKS IN ENGLISH: *To Be or Not To Be* (1972)

BIBLIOGRAPHY: Scott, A. C., *Twilight Crane, in Playbook, 5 Plays for a New Theater* (1956): 129–59; Mori, A., "Le dramaturge japonais K.," in Jacquot, J., ed., *Les théâtres d'Asie* (1961): 185–202; Gangloff, E. J., *Between God and Man: A Judgment on War Crimes* (1979)

—ERIC J. GANGLOFF

KINSELLA, Thomas

Irish poet, translator, and publisher, b. 4 May 1928, Dublin

One of the major poets working in the English language, K. was born in Dublin into a socialist family. After graduating from University College, Dublin, with a degree in public administration (1949), he became a civil servant and remained one for nearly twenty years, until his parallel career as a poet branched into the twin professions of American academic and Irish publisher. He is still, first and foremost, what he has been since the publication of his first major collection of poetry, *Another September* (1958), a modern Irish poet of the first rank.

Winner of the Guinness Poetry Prize (1958), *Another September* inaugurates what would become an archetypal career for a successful poet of the post-World War II generation. The volume brims with talent and influence, its prosodic expertise and lyrical precision of feeling and statement recalling W. H. AUDEN and William Butler YEATS in similar modes. The poise and pitch of rhyme remind the reader that K. is an Irish poet, familiar with the assonant architecture of Celtic bardic verse. The flint in the poems is the existential theme of ordeal as order, the images resolving in irony, as at the close of the collection's signature poem, "Baggot Street Deserta," where a cigarette flicked out a window rounds out a contemplation of the stars.

The collected *Poems* (1956) and *Moralities* (1960) exhibit the same virtues in service of the same themes. With *Downstream* (1962), K. moves on, gaining perspective with maturity. The struggle, often bitter, to create a self—and a poem—is reimagined as a quest, the poet in motion, reflecting on his passage, often through darkness, always bearing a burden of history. K. steps surely from poetic detachment to political engagement, Ireland's mythic and nationalist past providing a poetic heritage. The shallows of a river ford give rise to warrior, not Wordsworthian, associations in "A Country Walk," and the heroes of the 1916 Irish Uprising are remembered in a litany of names, as in Yeats, though in a typical early Kinsellan twist, the names are read from shop windows, reducing history and heroism to commodity.

In 1965 K., now a recognized poet and member of the Irish Academy of Letters, left the civil service to accept an invitation to be poet in residence at Southern Illinois University, a post that led to a professorship and began an academic career, primarily in America. *Wormwood* (1966), a short sequence of short poems full of nightmares, cold dawns, and bare, scarred trees, that traces and ultimately praises the existential ordeal of marriage, won the Dennis Devlin Memorial Award (1966). In *Nightwalker and Other Poems* (1968), K. is questing again, expanding his imagery into the gothic, extending his poetic form with fragments of liturgical and narrative forms, folktale, and allegory. The poems explore the psychological and political resonance of the theme of decay as devouring, but it is another theme, the dislocation of poetry and the inherent homelessness of poets, that sets K. wandering, through his heritage, invoking forebears from itinerant Irish bards of the 18th c. to Keats (1795–1821) to Yeats to Austin CLARKE, and through the two longer entries, "Phoenix Park" and "Nightwalker." Rhyme, a homing device, is abandoned, as K. gives up his poetry to the journey and rediscovers old ironies in fresh imagery, as when at the end of the title poem he stands in a desert of lunar dust and sees the earth, full, in the sky.

K. laments in *Nightwalker* the near destruction of the Irish language in the 18th c. and satirizes its institutionalization in the 20th. An Irish poet's heritage is bilingual, and most major Irish poets are translators, too. A Guggenheim fellowship in 1968 helped K. finish his prose and verse translation of the ancient epic cycle of heroic tales, *The Táin* (1969), source of the Cuchulain myth so important to Yeats and Ireland's literary revival. K.'s method is the reasonable reconstruction from various sources of the stories of warriors involved in the great cattle raid of Cooley, and the faithful translation of the language, even in attempting obscure prophetic verse. Over a decade later in *An Duanaire* (1981; the poem book), edited by Seán Ó Tuama, K. translated a selection of the extant works of latter-day cultural warriors, the dispossessed Irish poets of the 17th to 19th cs. Drawn by the drama of their struggle to retain possession of their language and bardic status, K. engages in his own struggle to suggest an untranslatable prosody (in both bardic syllabic verse and later accentual forms) while recreating the images and ideas, the politics and pathos of the originals. His resolute scholarship and dexterous poetic technique bridge the vernaculars of Irish verse and bring all-but-forgotten voices memorably to life.

His own poetry underwent a major development in the 1970s; he began publishing it himself. After relocating his American academic affiliation in 1971 to Temple University in Philadelphia, he established Peppercanister Press in Dublin in 1972. Since then, most of K.'s verse has first appeared as occasional poetry or works in progress in series of limited editions published by Peppercanister. His work has become at once more public and more private, responsive to events, sensitive to the graphic potential of the page and concrete presence of the poem, allusive to his personal life and previous work. The first of the Peppercanister poems was "Butcher's Dozen," a broadside criticizing the official report on the deaths of thirteen Civil Rights demonstrators in Derry on "Bloody Sunday"; the second was "A Selected Life," a short sequence occasioned by the death of K.'s friend, the composer and musical scholar Sean O'Riada.

Both these works were included in K.'s next collection, *Notes from the Land of the Dead and Other Poems* (1973). The poetic quest begun in *Downstream* continues here, turning inward, the poet adopting C. G. JUNG as a psychoanalytic guide/mentor. A dreaming consciousness and mythic resonance throw imagery into even stronger relief than in *Nightwalker* and put a metonymic stress on language. The rhythm of creation and destruction replaces rhyme, cracks syntax, and echoes across recurrent ellipses, ungrammatical enjambments and anomalies of typeface, illustration, and layout. This dynamic of a publisher's care and a poet's exploration characterizes all K.'s subsequent work: *Peppercanister Poems, 1972–1978* (1979), including poems in memory of O'Riada, John F. Kennedy on the tenth anniversary of his assassination, and the poet's father; and *Blood and Family* (1988), a refined volume of works within works, sequences taking geographical pattern ("Settings"), musical form ("Her Vertical Smile"), and fractured chronological order ("St. Catherine's Clock"), among other structures. Both volumes include self-reflexive commentary and notes, and the poems have begun to quote themselves.

K.'s progress as a modern poet, from prosody to experiment to self-reference, is typical, though his professional stature in its international acclaim is eminent. His participation, as an Irish poet, in the mythic and political history of his country is typical, though few, if any, contemporaries have made so important or impressive an impact. As an essayist—*Davis, Mangan, Ferguson? Tradition and the Irish Writer* (1970, with W. B. Yeats)—editor—*The New Oxford Book of Irish Verse* (1986)—translator, publisher, and teacher, he has practiced and studied poetry in all its aspects and made a significant contribution from every quarter, and that is unique. Judging by the poetry alone, however, K. is a major figure, regardless of label, among writers in English in the second half of the 20th c.

FURTHER WORKS: *The Starlit Eye* (1952); *Three Legendary Sonnets* (1952); *Per Imaginem* (1953); *Death of a Queen* (1956); *Poems and Translations* (1961); *Nightwalker* (1967); *Poems* (1968, with Anne Sexton and Douglas Livingstone); *Tear* (1969); *Finistère* (1972); *New Poems* (1973); *Vertical Man* (1973); *The Good Fight* (1973); *Selected Poems 1956–1968* (1973); *One* (1974); *A Technical Supplement* (1976); *Song of the Night and Other Poems* (1978);

The Messenger (1978); *One and Other Poems* (1979); *Poems 1956–1973* (1979); *Fifteen Dead* (1979); *Songs of the Psyche* (1985); *Out of Ireland* (1987); *St. Catherine's Clock* (1987)

BIBLIOGRAPHY: Rosenthal, M. L., *The New Poets: American and British Poetry since World War II* (1967): 283–97; Skelton, R., "The Poetry of T. K.," *Éire*, 2 (1967): 86–108; Bedient, C., *Eight Contemporary Poets* (1974): 119–38; Harmon, M., *The Poetry of T. K.: "With Darkness for a Nest"* (1974); Kersnowski, F. L., *The Outsiders: Poets of Contemporary Ireland* (1975): 73–84; Young, V., "Raptures of Distress," *Parnassus*, 3 (1975): 75–80; McGuiness, A. E., "'Bright Quincunx Newly Risen': T. K.'s Inward 'I,'" *Éire*, 4 (1980): 106–25; John, B., "Imaginative Bedrock: K.'s *One* and the *Lebor Gabála Erenn*," *Éire*, 1 (1985): 109–32; Johnston, D., *Irish Poetry after Joyce* (1985): 97–120; Garratt, R. F., *Modern Irish Poetry: Tradition and Continuity from Yeats to Heaney* (1986): 167–97; Skelton, R., *Celtic Contraries* (1990): 183–209

—DENNIS PAOLI

KIPLING, Rudyard

English short-story writer, novelist, and poet, b. 30 Dec. 1865, Bombay, India; d. 18 Jan. 1936, London

K. was born into a family of artists and politicians in British-ruled India. His childhood in India and his schooling in England,

Rudyard Kipling

when he was separated from his parents, provided much material for his early work, such as the story "Baa Baa Black Sheep" (1888). He worked as a journalist in India from 1882 to 1889 and at the same time began writing poetry and stories. He returned to England, then came to America (in 1892), where he lived for four years. Eventually, he settled permanently in Sussex, England. The death of his only son in World War I darkened his later life and work, as can be seen in books such as *The Irish Guards in the Great War* (1923), written as a memorial to his son.

K. is readily acknowledged as a good second-rank poet and versifier; in T. S. ELIOT's words, K. as a poet seems to be a "laureate without laurels." The poems in a very early work, *Departmental Ditties* (1886) show both K.'s romantic and his satirical tendencies. They are marked by acute observation, effective scenic presentation, and a sharp, racy style, which are in refreshing contrast to the then popular gushing style and Victorian verbosity. Wordplay and jollity are characteristic of K.'s early verse.

K.'s adoration of the British Empire produced some fine poems depicting the average British soldier's (Tommy's) life—his sense of community, his sufferings and joys. *Barrack-Room Ballads* (1892) contains some of the best known of these poems, including "Danny Deever," a deeply moving poem that became very popular among British servicemen. In these poems and other writings K. developed his idea—to him, a moral concept—of the "white man's burden," a mystique of the Empire, basing his ideas on what he called the "call to duty" and fulfillment of "the Law," which he believed British institutions embodied.

K. dealt with many other themes in his verse. "The Sons of Martha" (1907) expresses his faith in activism. In "The Gods of the Copy book Headings" (1919) he satirized man's slavishness to the gods of the marketplace. A notable late poem is "The Waster" (1930), about a man who "suffers unspeakable things, in body and soul and mind."

K.'s masterpiece, and his supreme achievement in fiction, is *Kim* (1901). It is so sprawling and discursive that at first the reader might overlook the continuity of its them. It portrays the young orphan Kim on the Grand Trunk Road, his association with Mahbub Ali, the man of many parts, and his deep attachment to the Tibetan lama, and traces the various stages of the boy's spiritual growth. *Kim* is episodic and kaleidoscopic; it encompasses the wonderful spectacle, the vision that reveals the mysteries of the Wheel of Life and of Buddhism. It is no conventional English novel, nor is it a modern psychological novel; it has a form of its own molded by its picaresque façade and its visionary and prophetic quality.

The novels *The Light That Failed* (1891) and *Captains Courageous* (1897) are also distinctive both in structure and meaning. *Captains Courageous* is the story of Harvey Cheyne, the spoiled child of an American millionaire, who falls into the sea, is rescued by the fisherman Manuel, and learns the art of roughing it. Cheyne's experience is part of America's great pioneering tradition. Transformed by the fishermen's rugged life, he develops a faith in activism and acquires moral values. *The Light That Failed* unfolds the complexities of the relationships between the painter Dick Heldar, two contrasting women, Maisie and Bessie, and Dick's friend Torpenhow. Dick's eyesight fails (hence the title), he bids goodbye to Bessie, goes to Port Said, and is killed by enemy fire. The novel presents the themes of love, war, and death in the context of Dick's personal predicament.

Realism, acute observation of men and landscapes, creation of atmosphere, exploration of myth, the animal world, fantasy, and

the abnormal and paranormal are the significant qualities of K. as a writer of short stories, a great many of which were written for children. The sweep of his imagination is very wide and covers many continents. Stories such as "The Phantom 'Rickshaw" (1888) vividly demonstrate how K. explores the supernatural world. "The Miracle of Puran Bhagat" in *The Second Jungle Book* (1895) is an extraordinary tale of the transformation of Sir Puran Dass into a saffron-robed Buddhist *sanyasi*, who has renounced worldly life. The theme of "The Bridge-Builders" (1898) is the bridge between the human and divine worlds—the characters Findlayson and Peroo both see the vision of Hindu gods in the Ganges—and the story sings the gospel of work.

During the last two decades of his life K. suffered from ill health and a steep decline in popularity. The later K. seems pessimistic and inclined to explore in greater depth the darker elements of human experience, as can be observed in such stories as "Mary Postgate" (1915), "The Gardener" (1926), and particularly "Dayspring Mishandled" (1928). These later tales, full of pathos and tragedy, and his later poems, too, reveal a sense of bitterness and a belief in the powerlessness of man in an uncertain world.

An artistic reporter for posterity of imperial England, an unusually skillful short-story writer, a novelist with an individualistic sense of the form of fiction, and a poet of haunting rhythms—K. achieved a reputation not equaled in his early years by any other Englishman except Thomas HARDY. His work also aroused controversies, and he became an object of severely adverse criticism. Nonetheless, he was the first Englishman to receive the Nobel Prize for literature (1907), at the age of forty-two. His popularity was phenomenal; so was the reaction against him in the 1940s. A K. revival is now under way, however, and the stage is set for a more balanced appraisal of his achievement.

FURTHER WORKS: *Schoolboy Lyrics* (1881); *The Phantom 'Rickshaw* (1888); *Plain Tales from the Hills* (1888); *Wee Willie Winkie* (1888); *Soldiers Three* (1888); *Life's Handicap* (1891); *The Naulahka* (1892, with Charles Wolcott Balestier); *Many Inventions* (1893); *The Jungle Book* (1894); *The Seven Seas* (1896); *Soldier Tales* (1896); *Recessional* (1897); *The Day's Work* (1898); *Ballad of East and West* (1899); *Stalky & Co.* (1899); *The White Man's Burden* (1899); *The K. Reader* (1900); *Just So Stories* (1902); *Traffics and Discoveries* (1904); *Puck of Pook's Hill* (1906); *Collected Verse* (1907); *Actions and Reactions* (1909); *Rewards and Fairies* (1910); *For All We Have and Are* (1914); *A Diversity of Creatures* (1917); *The Graves of the Fallen* (1919); *The Years Between* (1919); *Letters of Travel 1892–1913* (1920); *A Choice of the Songs from the Verse of R. K.* (1925); *Sea and Sussex* (1926); *Debits and Credits* (1926); *R. K.'s Verse 1885–1926* (1927); *The One-Volume K., Authorized* (1928); *A Book of Words: Selections from Speeches and Addresses Delivered between 1906 and 1927* (1928); *Limits and Renewals* (1932); *R. K.'s Verse 1885–1932* (1933); *All the Mowgli Stories* (1933); *Something of Myself* (1937); *Uncollected Prose I and II* (1938); *Complete Works* (35 vols., 1937–39); *R. K.'s Verse* (1940); *A Choice of K.'s Verse* (1941); *R. K. to Rider Haggard: The Record of a Friendship* (1965); *American Notes: R. K.'s West* (1981)

BIBLIOGRAPHY: Carrington, C., *R. K.: His Life and Work* (1955); Tompkins, J. M. S., *The Art of R. K.* (1959); Bodelsen, C. A., *Aspects of R. K.'s Art* (1964); Rutherford, A., ed., *K.'s Mind and Art* (1964); Connell, L., *K. in India* (1966); Dobrée, B., *R. K.: Realist and Fabulist* (1967); Rao, K. B., *R. K.'s India* (1967);

Shahane, V. A., *R. K.: Activist and Artist* (1973); Amis, K., *R. K. and His World* (1975); Wilson, A., *The Strange Ride of R. K.* (1977); Bloom, H., ed., *R. K.* (1987); Kemp, S., *K.'s Hidden Narratives* (1988)

—V. A. SHAHANE

KIPPHARDT, Heinar

German dramatist, b. 8 Mar. 1922, Heidersdorf; d. 18 Nov. 1982, Munich

K. qualified in medicine at Düsseldorf University and was dramatic adviser at the Deutsches Theater in East Berlin from 1951 to 1959. In 1959 he left East Germany for West Germany, because two of his more critical theater plays were censored. His primary concerns are with social injustice, mass hysteria, and individual accountability.

His early plays are satirical comedies that criticize the preoccupations and major social trends in both Germanies after the war: *Shakespeare dringend gesucht* (1954; desperately seeking Shakespeare) parodies the positivist portrayal of heroic socialist workers by East German writers in the 1950s; *Die Stühle des Herrn Szmil* (1958; the chairs of Mr. Szmil) criticizes profiteering and persistent capitalist and bourgeois practices under socialism, while lip service is being paid to socialist rhetoric; *Die Nacht, in der der Chef geschlachtet wurde* (1967; the night the boss was butchered) attacks the grotesque manifestations of materialism and egoism in West Germany during the "economic miracle" wonder years. The play *Der Hund des Generals* (1964; the general's dog) first appeared as a story and is a satire on war and Prussian discipline. K. is best known for two of his documentary plays, *In der Sache J. Robert Oppenheimer* (1964; in the matter of J. Robert Oppenheimer) and *Bruder Eichmann* (1983; brother Eichmann). The earlier play details the effects of McCarthyist hysteria in the U.S. in the trial against the inventor of the atom bomb who was accused of being a communist sympathizer and delaying the development of the hydrogen bomb, while the later play follows the Israeli trial of Adolf Eichmann, one of the most notorious Nazi officials. K.'s montage technique allows him to link an analysis of past injustices with their contemporary equivalents, for instance, anti-Semitism under the Nazis and xenophobia toward minorities, especially Turkish foreign workers, in present-day Germany. The play *Joel Brand: Die Geschichte eines Geschäfts* (1965; Joel Brand: the history of a deal) concerns the Nazi proposal to barter Hungarian Jews for trucks. The novel *März* (1976; März) is interested in schizophrenia and artistic creativity and indicts modern psychiatry's treatment of the poet Alexander März; it was made into a play in 1980. The poems *Angelsbrucker Notizen* (1977; notes from Angelsbruck) and the collection of diary entries *Traumprotokolle* (1981; dream notes) contain much autobiographical information about K.'s family, his own struggle with depression and feelings of inadequacy, and the Nazis' deportation of his father to Buchenwald. K. is one of the foremost leftist playwrights of the 1960s along with Peter WEISS, Hans Magnus ENZENSBERGER, and Rolf HOCHHUTH, who used documentary material in their art because they felt that people needed to be exposed to historicopolitical facts rather than fiction to be educated as citizens of a more democratic society. The 1960s in West Germany brought many Nazi warcrime trials, which resulted in a public reckoning with the Nazi

inheritance. K. is exemplary in linking his condemnation of Nazi practices with more recent processes of exclusion and repression in German society.

FURTHER WORKS: *Der Mann des Tages und andere Erzählungen* (1977); *Theaterstücke, Band 1 und 2* (1978)

BIBLIOGRAPHY: Kowal, M., "K. and the Documentary Theater," *American-German Review*, 5 (1966–1967): 20–30; Hilzinger, K. H., *Die Dramaturgie des dokumentarischen Theaters* (1976): 16–25, 70–76; Bartelheimer, L., and Nutz, M., *Materialien H. K. In der Sache Robert J. Oppenheimer* (1981); Carl, R. P., "Dokumentarisches Theater," in Durzak, M., ed., *Deutsche Gegenwartsliteratur* (1981): 99–127; Muschg, A., *Literatur als Therapie?* (1981); Naumann, U., ed., *H. K. Bruder Eichmann: Schauspiel und Materialien* (1983); Meyer, S., *Kunst als Widerstand* (1989)

—HELGA DRUXES

KIRK, Hans Rudolf

Danish novelist, b. 11 Jan. 1889, Hadsund; d. 16 June 1962, Copenhagen

Although K. grew up in a conservative middle-class milieu as the son of a doctor, he never lost sight of the fact that his family came from a long line of impoverished fisherfolk from western Jutland. He studied law at the University of Copenhagen, receiving a degree in 1922. Between 1923 and 1925 he held a position as a local government official. Thereafter he became a journalist and devoted himself entirely to writing. During the German occupation K. was interned in a concentration camp, from 1941 to 1943. After the war he became a major contributor to the communist newspaper *Land og folk*.

Since his early youth K. had been a convinced Marxist. In his writing he analyzes the relationship between the distribution of capital and people's outlook on life, illustrating how economic and social conditions determine the beliefs and habits of groups within society. His first and finest work, *Fiskerne* (1928; *The Fishermen*, 1951), is a novel that tells of the move by a whole community of fishermen from desperately poor homes on the west coast of Jutland to a fertile island. Belonging to a stern, pietistic movement within the Danish Lutheran church called "Indre Mission," whose religious fellowship gave the poor and oppressed the strength to face their harsh existence, the fishermen and their families form a sharp contrast to the well-to-do farmers of the island, whose faith is based on more traditional Christianity. The dramatic confrontation between the two groups and the gradual takeover of the entire parish by the newcomers is the theme of the book. Their radical and zealous religiosity is regarded by K. as a deflection of the energy that should have been used in the class struggle.

This view is further elaborated by K. in his next two novels, *Daglejerne* (1936; the laborers) and *De nye tider* (1939; new times), in which he sets out to expose the exploitation of the poor by those in power, and to show the development of a new, classless society by way of its liberation from religious and capitalist ties. With *Borgmesteren går af* (1941; the mayor resigns), a biting satire on government bureaucracy, K.'s writing changed character. The setting is no longer the old rural society, and the tendentiousness of his presentation becomes obvious. In *Slaven* (1948; the slave), a historical novel set in the 17th c., he formulates his ideas about the evils of capitalist society. The book describes the events on board a ship sailing from South America to Spain on which all social and economic classes are present. *Vredens søn* (1950; the son of wrath) presents Jesus as a purely historical figure. As a leader of the oppressed he could have liberated the Jewish people, in K.'s opinion, if he had embraced a social revolution rather than a religious one.

K. introduced the novel with a collective protagonist to Denmark and was also the first to signal the beginning of a new social and political awareness in the literature of the 1930s. His early novels, in particular *Fiskerne*, are distinguished by the author's intimate knowledge of the people about whom he writes and by the objectivity of his narration. In his later works, however, K.'s analysis of society became increasingly one-sided and dogmatic, and his characters turned into lifeless mouthpieces for his political ideas.

FURTHER WORKS: *Djævelens penge* (1952); *Klitgaard & sønner* (1952); *Skyggespil* (1953); *Borgerlige noveller* (1958); *Danmarksrejsen* (1966); *Breve fra Horserød* (1967)

BIBLIOGRAPHY: Mawby, J., *Writers and Politics in Modern Scandinavia* (1978): 14–21

—MARIANNE FORSSBLAD

KIRSCH, Sarah

(formerly Ingrid Bernstein) German poet and short-story writer, b. 16 Apr. 1935, Limlingerode

At an early age K. changed her given name to Sarah in protest against the persecution of the Jews during the years of the Third Reich. After completing her secondary education, she began an apprenticeship in forestry, then worked briefly in a sugar factory, before studying biology in Halle, where she received her degree in 1959. During her brief marriage to the author Rainer Kirsch (b. 1934), she became closely associated with members of the younger generation of East German writers, and from 1963 to 1965 she attended the Johannes R. Becher Literary Institute in Leipzig. Since then, she has devoted herself exclusively to her writing. In 1977 she moved to West Berlin, and since 1983 she has made her home in Schleswig-Holstein. She has received many awards for her poetry, including the Heinrich Heine Prize (1973), the Petrarch Prize (1976), the Austrian State Prize for Literature (1981), and the Friedrich Hölderlin Prize (1984).

K.'s poems focus on the fundamental elements of natural human experience, from personal encounters with the external world of lakes and forests, animals and birds, sun and moon, days and seasons, to intense inner confrontations with love, loneliness, uncertainty, and longing for self-realization and fulfillment. In language that is often reserved, even hesitant, sometimes terse and dissonant, she evokes images that are remarkable for their richness and depth, their fairy-tale quality, their successful communication of changes in mood and tone. Especially characteristic of her poetry are lines that draw the reader beneath the surface of apparently idyllic landscapes into undercurrents of disappointment, disillusionment, disenchantment, and despair. Even her love

songs discreetly juxtapose individual moments of happiness with sadness and pain. Tendencies in her best works are related to currents found in German romanticism and in the writings of the poet Johannes BOBROWSKI that focus on the increasing alienation of human beings from the natural world.

The poems of K.'s East German period, in *Gespräch mit dem Saurier* (1965; conversation with the saurian), coauthored with Rainer Kirsch, *Landaufenthalt* (1967; a stay in the country), *Zaubersprüche* (1973; magic spells), and *Rückenwind* (1976; tail wind), reflect her artistic progress from cautious and triflingly simple creations to more meaningful explorations of weighty problems. Even in her earliest writings, she occasionally succeeded in combining imagination, originality, and power of expression in the reproduction of subjective experience, but her lyrics took on the character of fresh, unique poetic utterance only as they became the product of increased reflection about more complex existential questions of personal identity and purpose.

Important tendencies of K.'s more mature verse include refinement of perception and awareness, heightened poetic sensitivity, broadening of theme and substance, integration of the private dimension into a deeper penetration of the general human condition, and greater density of imagery. In *La Pagerie* (1980; the pagery), a series of prose poems based upon her experiences in the Provence region of France, she demonstrated a special facility for combining delicate language with cynicism, while the creations of *Erdreich* (1982; earth realm), with their images of canyons, highways, and other landscapes encountered during a trip to the U.S., are critically ironic, almost apocalyptic interpretations of perceived threats to the contemporary world.

The tone of later collections suggests a return to an emphasis on private experience with nature and self. Some of K.'s best and most complex nature poems appear in *Katzenleben* (1984; *Catlives*, 1990), an almost idyllic documentation of her new life in rural Schleswig-Holstein. The intimacy of the poet's relationship to the surrounding world grows more intense in the prose poems of *Irrstern* (1987; wandering star), with their sometimes startling arrays of images, unusual observations, and predominantly elegiac mood. An inclination toward retreat into self becomes especially pronounced in the melancholy songs of resignation found in *Schneewärme* (1989; snow warmth).

More recently, in collections such as *Erlkönigs Tochter* (1992; Elf King's Daughter) and *Bodenlos* (1996; Bottomless), there has been an intensification of the tendency toward gloom and pessimism. Although many of the poems still contain powerful nature and landscape images, the dominant color is black, and the most characteristic themes are darkness, despair, loneliness, longing, cold, worry, and death.

Two of the most representative collections of K.'s prose writings are *Die ungeheuren berghohen Wellen auf See* (1973; the monstrous mountainhigh waves at sea) and *Allerlei-Rauh* (1988; pot-pourri-raw). The stories in the earlier book offer an unexpected mixture of satire and straight narration of factual substance. With their impact weakened by contrived endings in which characters always make the best of their situations, these pieces reflect external limiting factors that K. could not ignore and still be permitted to publish in East Germany. From that perspective, *Allerlei-Rauh*, with its elements of chronicle, fairy tale, legend, autobiography, and reflection about personal experience of nature and contemporary life in Schleswig-Holstein, documents K.'s progress toward richer, deeper literary expression and toward a prose that forms a definite complement to her poetry.

The two collections of diary-like prose texts, *Spreu* (1991; Chaff) and *Das simple Leben* (1994; The Simple Life), contain brief reflections and pointed impressions that give significant insight into the poet's life and creative approach. Their value lies more in what they reveal about K.'s thought processes and attitudes toward encounters with people and surroundings, than in their specific content.

The major strength of K.'s writing lies in her ability to relate deeply private concerns to the general human condition of her time, and to convey her feelings about those relationships in a manner that enables her readers to share in her experiences on an intimate level. That fact alone has made her one of the most important poets in contemporary Germany.

FURTHER WORKS: *Die betrunkene Sonne—Der Stärkste* (1963, with Rainer Kirsch); *Berlin-Sonnenseite* (1964, with Thomas Billhardt and Rainer Kirsch); *Gedichte* (1967); *Hansel und Gretel* (1972); *Die Pantherfrau* (1973; *The Panther Woman*, 1989); *Es war dieser merkwürdige Sommer* (1974); *Caroline im Wassertropfen* (1975, with Erdmut Oelschläger); *Zwischen Herbst und Winter* (1975, with Ingrid Schuppau); *Die betrunkene Sonne* (1975; *The Drunken Sun*, 1978); *Blitz aus heiterm Himmel* (1975); *Musik auf dem Wasser* (1977); *Wiepersdorf* (1977); *Sommergedichte* (1978); *Wintergedichte* (1978); *Katzenkopfpflaster* (1978); *Ein Sommerregen* (1978, with Kota Taniuchi); *Erklärung einiger Dinge* (1978, with Urs Widmer and Elke Erb); *Sieben Häute* (1979); *Drachensteigen* (1979); *Wind* (1979, with Kota Taniuchi); *Schatten* (1979, with Kota Taniuchi); *Hans mein Igel* (1980); *Papiersterne* (1981); *Landwege* (1985); *Hundert Gedichte* (1985); *Galoschen* (1987); *Lyrik* (1987, with A. R. Renck); *Luft und Wasser* (1988); *Die Flut* (1990); *Schwingrasen* (1991); *Ich Carusoe* (1995); *Nachtsommer* (1995); *Sechs Gedichte* (1995); *Luftspringerin* (1997). **FURTHER WORKS IN ENGLISH:** *Conjurations* (1985)

BIBLIOGRAPHY: Wittkowski, W., "S. K.: 'Der Milchmann Schäuffele,'" *GQ*, 54 (1981): 311–17; Figge, S. G., "'Der Wunsch nach Welt': The Travel Motif in the Poetry of S. K.," in Gerber, M., ed., *Studies in GDR Culture and Society* (1981), Vol. 1: 167–84; Armster, C., "'Merkwürdiges Beispiel weiblicher Entschlossenheit': A Woman's Story—by S. K.," in Gerber, M., ed., *Studies in GDR Culture and Society* (1982), Vol. 2: 243–50; Fehn, A., "Authorial Voice in S. K.'s *Die Pantherfrau*," in Woodmansee, M., and Lohnes, W. F. W., eds., *Erkennen und Deuten* (1983): 335–46; Post, L., "The Poetry of S. K.," *RaJAH*, (1986): 81–94; Melin, C., "Landscape As Writing and Revelation in S. K.'s 'Death Valley,'" *GR*, 4 (1987): 199–204; Mabee, B., *Die Poetik von S. K.* (1989); Wagener, H., *S. K.* (1989); Arnold, H. L., *S.K.* (1989); Cosentino, C., *Ein Spiegel mit mir darin* (1990); Heidenreich, W., *S. K.* (1995); Hopwood, M., and D. Basker, eds., *S. K.* (1997)

—LOWELL A. BANGERTER

KIŠ, Danilo

Serbian novelist, short-story writer, and essayist, b. 22 Feb. 1935, Subotica, Yugoslavia; d. 15 Oct. 1989, Paris, France

K. was one of the best-known of contemporary Serbian writers internationally. Born in Subotica of a Jewish father and a Montenegrin mother, he and his family were subjected to persecution by the Nazis during World War II, during which time most of his relatives perished, including his father. He studied literature at the University of Belgrade and later taught Serbo-Croatian for several years at French universities. He spent the last years of his life in Paris.

K. was most successful in novels, but he also wrote short stories and was a discerning essayist and a passionate polemicist. He belongs to a group of young Serbian writers who entered the literary scene in the mid-1960s and immediately asserted themselves as the new wave of Serbian letters. His first work, a short novel, *Mansarda* (1962; the attic), is typical of a beginner, yet it shows remarkable maturity in depicting the growing pains of young people searching for their identity amid the tragic combination of love and suicide. His next novel, *Psalam 44* (1962; psalm 44), employs a theme that would dominate K.'s writings for the rest of his career: the suffering of people, especially the Jews and other minorities, during war-time, most often during World War II. In this and other works, he does not dwell on suffering in itself but shows instead the degrading compromises the victims are forced to make, almost invariably leading to most tragic consequences. K. reaches the apex in this respect in his next two novels, *Bašta, pepeo* (1965; *Garden, Ashes*, 1975) and *Peščanik* (1972; *Hourglass*, 1990). In the first, he weaves a story of his childhood and his reminiscences of his remarkable father, who was, among other things, an eccentric, an incorrigible dreamer, a frustrated genius, a poet, a philosopher, a grotesque Don Quixote, and a drunkard who squandered his many gifts. The fact that his father ended tragically during the Nazi terror only enhanced the aura of pathos and unreality to the already unreal experiences of a growing boy. *Peščanik* continues to build a monument to the remarkable father, except that now the father is telling his own story in a dazzling variety of narrative devices.

From his personal vantage point, K. moves to a more general depiction of human's inhumanity to humans in his next novel, *Grobnica za Borisa Davidovića* (1976; *A Tomb for Boris Davidovich*, 1978). In seven seemingly unrelated stories K. follows the paths of several people, all of whom end up as victims of persecution. The victims are again mostly Jews, but this time they suffer not only at the hands of Nazis but also of the Soviet authorities asserting their party discipline. K.'s mixture of historical facts and fiction caused a furor in Yugoslav literary circles and led to accusations of plagiarism, which he was able to refute easily. With this work, K. cemented his reputation as a champion of human rights and a defender of basic human dignity against the forces of evil.

By choosing a significant subject matter and by employing a remarkable artistic prowess, K. built a reputation as one of the best among contemporary writers. He is especially adept at transcending regional boundaries and appealing to readers everywhere, as attested by numerous translations of his works into many languages.

FURTHER WORKS: *Noć i magla* (1968); *Papagaj* (1969); *Rani jadi* (1969); *Po-etika* (1972); *Po-etika, druga knjiga* (1974); *Drveni sanduk Tomasa Wulfa* (1974); *Čas anatomije* (1978); *Enciklopedija mrtvih* (1983; *The Encyclopedia of the Dead*, 1989)

BIBLIOGRAPHY: Vitanović, S., "Thematic Unity in D. K.'s Literary Works," *Relations*: 9–10 (1979): 66–69; Bynum, D. E., "Philosophical Fun and Merriment in the First Fiction of D. K.," *Serbian Studies*, 2, 4 (1984): 3–20; Czarny, N., "Imaginary—Real Lives: On D. K.," *CCur*, 3 (1984): 279–84; White, E., "D. K.: The Obligations of Form," *SWR*, 71, 3 (1986): 363–77; Gorjup, B., "D. K.: From 'Enchantment' to 'Documentation,'" *CSP*, 29, 4

(1987): 387–94; Shishkoff, S., "Košava in a Coffee pot; or, A Dissection of a Literary Cause Cèlébre," *CCur,* 6 (1987), 340–71; Oja, M. F., "Fictional History and Historical Fiction: Solzhenitsyn and K. as Exemplars," *History and Theory,* 27 (1988): 111–24; Matvejević, P., "D. K.: Encyclopedia of the Dead," *CCur,* 7 (1988): 337–49; Birnbaum, M. D., "The Fiction of D. K.," *CCur,* 8 (1989): 345–60

—VASA D. MIHAILOVICH

KISHIDA Kunio

Japanese dramatist and critic, b. 2 Nov. 1890, Tokyo; d. 5 March 1954, Tokyo

Born into a samurai family, K. went through military school and received a commission. He disappointed his father, a military officer, however, by resigning in order to take up the study of French literature at Tokyo University in 1916 instead of carrying on the family tradition. He left the university before graduation and went to France in 1920, determined to learn the craft of playwriting. In Paris he studied with the famous director Jacques Copeau at the Théâtre du Vieux Colombier.

K. returned to Japan in 1922 to try to create a truly modern Japanese drama based on the creation of poetic and psychologically accurate dialogue he found in the European works he discovered while living in Paris. K.'s efforts to replace a Japanese drama still heavily dependent on more traditional means of expression also led him into drama criticism, theater management, and stage direction, but all these activities shared the same purpose: to create a contemporary drama responsive to the psychological realities that he felt were crucial to portray if the Japanese theater were to become a viable form of modern literary expression.

K.'s early one-act plays are marked by a highly effective fusion of realistic dialogue and elegant fantasy. *Chiroru no aki* (1924; autumn in the Tyrol) places a Japanese protagonist in a European setting, in which he develops an affection for a European woman staying in the same small Austrian hotel. *Buranko* (1925; the swing) shows a young Tokyo couple coming to grips with the shifting roles of sense and sensibility in a marriage. The most successful of his early plays, *Kamifūsen* (1925; paper balloon), is a more lyrical examination of the same predicament.

By the late 1920s K.'s reputation had grown to the point that he was asked to write full-length plays for production in Tokyo, and much of his best work dates from this period. *Ochiba nikki* (1927; diary of fallen leaves) remains one of K.'s most poignant statements about the meaning of his French experience. The protagonist of the play is an elderly Japanese woman, of great wit and charm, whose son had married a French woman some years before; her granddaughter, Henriette, now stays with her. K.'s grasp of the nuances of the differences in cultures and his genuine ability to create effective stage personality makes the old lady, whose death scene concludes the play, one of his most moving creations. France figures again in *Ushiyama hoteru* (1929; Ushiyama Hotel), which chronicles in a sardonic, almost nihilistic fashion, the lives of a group of Japanese living in a dingy hotel in Vietnam, then a French colony.

After a long series of experiments, K. reached the final phase of his development in *Sawa shi no futari musume* (1935; Mr. Sawa's two daughters), which combines evocative dialogue with trenchant commentary on the social and psychological climate of the time. Like the characters in the earlier plays of K., those presented here are sophisticated and worldly (Mr. Sawa himself has lived in Europe), but their attempts at self-understanding are altogether Japanese.

By the beginning of World War II, K. had stopped writing, although he continued certain theatrical and cultural activities until 1944. After the end of the war he wrote a few short pieces but was hampered by ill health and heavy duties with the Bungakuza, an important acting troupe. He died while directing a play for the Bungakuza.

K.'s plays remain among the most respected modern classics of the Japanese stage and are still admired for their subtle dialogue, vivid atmosphere, and an emphasis on the centrality for the drama of individual psychology, a concept at variance with the Marxist dramaturgy popular in influential theater circles in Tokyo before the government suppression in the late 1930s. The Kishida Prize, the most important drama award in Japan, indicates the esteem in which K.'s work is still held. K.'s plays provide the best theatrical record of the Japanese in search of their own spiritual identity during the difficult decades between the two world wars.

FURTHER WORKS: *Furui omocha* (1924); *Hazakura* (1925); *Mura de ichi ban kuri no ki* (1926); *Mama sensei to sono otto* (1930); *Asamayama* (1931); *Shokugyō* (1935); *Saigetsu* (1935); *Fūzoku jihyō* (1936); *Zenshū* (10 vols., 1955)

BIBLIOGRAPHY: Japan UNESCO Commission, ed., *Theatre in Japan* (1963): 213–41; Ortolani, B., "Shingeki: The Maturing New Drama of Japan," in Roggendorf, J., ed., *Studies in Japanese Culture* (1963): 163–85; Rimer, J. T., *Toward a Modern Japanese Theatre: K. K.* (1974)

—J. THOMAS RIMER

KIZER, Carolyn

American poet, translator, and essayist, b. 10 Dec. 1925, Spokane, Washington

K. was born in Spokane, Washington, to exceptional parents. Her father was a lawyer who devoted time to liberal causes, and her mother, who earned a Ph.D. in biology from Stanford, was an activist, and, according to K., a very involved parent. Both encouraged their daughter's artistic propensities from an early age, and although appreciative, in her work K. deals with the difficulty of escaping this sometimes stifling atmosphere of expectation. K. studied at Sarah Lawrence College, Columbia University, and the University of Washington in Seattle, and also spent time in China where she developed her appreciation for Eastern poetic forms. Since completing her education, she actively crossed the boundaries between art and politics, working for the State Department in Pakistan, directing literary programs at the National Endowment for the Arts, and serving as poet-in-residence and lecturer at many universities, including the University of North Carolina, Columbia,

Washington University, Barnard, Princeton, Ohio University, Kinnaird College for Women, and the Iowa Writers Workshop.

K.'s early work was quite formal. Her first book, *The Ungrateful Garden* (1961), dealt mainly with the relationship between humans and nature. Beautiful natural images were often juxtaposed with horrific ones, challenging the tradition of the "nature poem." While it was acknowledged as the work of an important new poet, some critics complained of the poet's clear delight in verbal gymnastics, arguing that the content of the poems did not live up to their formal intricacy. The criticism was not repeated after her second collection, *Knock upon Silence* (1965), which was more relaxed than the first. The Eastern influence on K.'s style was more evident in this book, which was divided into four sections, including Chinese imitations and translations of Tu Fu, an eighth-century Chinese poet. In addition, *Knock upon Silence* included two long poems: "A Month in the Summer" and "Pro Femina." "A Month in the Summer" records the end of a love affair through journal entries and haiku poems. "Pro Femina," a satire about women in the style of Juvenal or Alexander Pope, has become one of K.'s best-known poems. In *Midnight Was My Cry: New and Selected Poems* (1971), K. included many poems from her first two volumes as well as new poems, admired for their maturity and affirmative tone. Unlike her earlier poems, they often dealt with social and political realities.

It would be thirteen years before the publication of K.'s next two books, *Yin: New Poems* and *Mermaids in the Basement*, both appearing in 1984. In these books the poet turns to personal concerns as well as explicitly addressing feminist issues. *Yin* includes an account of her father's final illness and an imagined diary by "Fanny," the wife of Robert Louis Stevenson. It was widely praised and won the Pulitzer Prize. K.'s next volume, *The Nearness of You* (1986), was dedicated to "the men I love," and provides a companion volume to the previous two collections, turning the poet's feminine perspective to contemplation of the roles and relationships of men. Like its companion volumes, it appeared more personal than the poet's early work, and less concerned with formal rigor.

K.'s 1987 collection of translations, *Carrying Over*, shows her range in its subtitle: *Poems from the Chinese, Urdu, Macedonian, Yiddish, and French African*. She has edited the works of neglected romantic poet John Clare, and a collection of poems by women, and published collections of essays as well. She also contributed to American poetry by founding *Poetry Northwest*, which she edited from 1959 until 1965. For these activities as well as for her highly praised poems, she has become one of America's foremost poetic voices.

FURTHER WORKS: *Proses: On Poems & Poets* (1993); *Harping On: Poems 1985-1995* (1996); *Picking and Choosing: Prose on Prose* (1996)

BIBLIOGRAPHY: Bangs, C.-J., "Women Poets and the 'Northwest School,'" *Women, Women Writers and the West* (1979): 71-82; Cheung, D., "C. K. and Her Chinese Imitations," in Tay, W., ed., *China and the West: Comparative Literature Studies* (1980): 77-84; Ingersoll, E., and S. Rubin, "'The Very Separateness of Things:' A Conversation with C. K.," *WR*, 11 (1986): 87-101; Rigsbee, D., ed., *An Answering Music: On the Poetry of C. K.* (1990); Bayes, R., "Franklin Street Days: C. K. in North Carolina, 1970-1974," *Pembroke*, 23 (1991): 130-36

—ANNE-LISE FRANÇOIS

KLEIN, A(braham) M(oses)

Canadian poet and novelist, b. 14 Feb. 1909, Montreal, Quebec; d. 20 Aug. 1972, Montreal, Quebec

After attending McGill University, K. studied law at the University of Montreal. After 1933 he practiced law in Montreal, was involved in Zionist organizations, and, from 1939 to 1955, edited the *Canadian Jewish Chronicle*. In the late 1940s he made many speeches for the Canadian Jewish Congress and, in 1949, ran unsuccessfully for parliament as the CCF (socialist) candidate. After two nervous breakdowns in the 1950s, K. became ever more reclusive, rarely seeing anyone outside his immediate family until his death.

K.'s first collection of poems, *Hath Not a Jew...* (1940), contained poems written in the late 1920s and early 1930s. These deal with the situation of the Jews throughout history and are written in a language that is deliberately archaic, in the manner of Edmund Spenser, Shakespeare, and Christopher Marlowe. Much of this hybrid verse is surprisingly fresh, colorful, and scintillating, especially in the poems for children, based on Jewish folklore and Hasidic tales from Poland, the land from which K.'s family had emigrated. There is almost no reference to Canada or identifiable mention of Montreal.

In the early 1930s, however, K. turned away from his exclusively Jewish concerns and wrote biting satires about the relations between urban rich and poor. These poems (in *Collected Poems*, 1974) were not included in the four collections published during his lifetime, but they foreshadowed his fusion of private vision and public observation in *The Rocking Chair* (1948). This collection, which explores the French-Canadian community and sensibility, is a landmark in the history of Canadian poetry.

Stylistically K. benefited from acquaintance with the work of Gerard Manley Hopkins (1844–1889), YEATS, AUDEN, and Dylan THOMAS, while remaining distinctively original (probably because of his mastery of a variety of languages). In a rich, sometimes even ornate language, he applies his very considerable insight into the nature of minority groups to the French-Canadians, Canadians in general, Canadian Indians, and even to the scattered Canadian poets. He expresses the collective Canadian consciousness, a tapestry of minority groups, each in its own cultural garrison (or ghetto) and surrounded by a vast and forbidding landscape. He also articulates the attempt of each cultural or regional community to achieve some harmony with the land and, perhaps through the land, with a larger order of things in the universe. "Portrait of the Poet as Landscape" is a key poem that has provided direction for later poets such as Irving LAYTON, Leonard COHEN, and Margaret ATWOOD.

K.'s novella, *The Second Scroll* (1951), is a Zionist version of the quest romance. Influenced by JOYCE, about whom he hoped to write a book, and perhaps by Dante, K. developed another version of the personal odyssey that holds spiritual significance for mankind at large. The messianic redemption in store for man appears to be foreshadowed in the reunion of the Jews with their Holy Land. The utopian Israel of this book may bear little resemblance to the reality of today, but the vision and some of the language, particularly in a brilliant recreation of Michelangelo's Sistine Chapel paintings as prophecy of Israel's tragedy and triumph, remain compelling and, by analogy, relevant to the Canadian attempt to achieve community.

There remains much unpublished work, including poems, a novel, and several versions of a folk play. K.'s was essentially a religious sensibility, and his great theme was the transcendence of evil through imaginative sympathy. While he was intensely concerned about the fate of Jewry, he was also able to interpret Canadians to themselves, and to affirm the value of cultural coexistence in the world at large.

FURTHER WORKS: *Poems* (1944); *The Hitleriad* (1944)

BIBLIOGRAPHY: Pacey, D., *Ten Canadian Poets* (1958): 254–92; Marshall, T., ed., *A. M. K.* (1970); Waddington, M., *A. M. K.* (1970); Rosenblatt, J., ed., special K. issue, *Jewish Dialog*, Passover, 1973; Fischer, G., *In Search of Jerusalem: Religion and Ethics in the Writings of A. M. K.* (1975); Mayne, S., ed., *The A. M. K. Symposium* (1975)

—TOM MARSHALL

KLÍMA, Ivan

Czechoslovak short-story writer, novelist, dramatist, and essayist (writing in Czech), b. 14 Sept. 1931, Prague

As a Jew, K. spent three years of his boyhood, during the German occupation, in the Terezín (Theresienstadt) concentration camp. Having completed his secondary education after the war, he went to study Czech and theory of literature at Charles University in Prague. From 1956 to 1963 he worked as an editor, first on a weekly magazine, later in a publishing house. In 1964 he joined the editorial staff of the Writers' Union journal *Literární noviny*. His controversial articles often brought him into conflict with the political authorities, and in 1967 he was expelled from the Communist Party. After the suppression of the Prague Spring reform movement, K.'s work was banned in Czechoslovakia, but continued to be published abroad in translation. In 1988 he became the first previously banned writer whose name was allowed to appear in print again, and the overthrow of the communist régime in the following year put an end to all restrictions.

K.'s first work of fiction was a collection of short stories, *Bezvadný den* (1960; a perfect day), in which he, like other young writers of the day, treated contemporary life with a frankness that would hardly have been tolerated a few years earlier. The wronged, abandoned, and betrayed characters in the short stories, victims of circumstances that were not supposed to exist in a socialist society, signaled K.'s concern with social ethics. In the novel *Hodina ticha* (1963; hour of silence), he tried to expose the damage inflicted in human terms on a farming community in eastern Slovakia by a callous collectivization drive. Although K. presented the excesses of Stalinism as a good idea badly executed, he was addressing a subject that was still regarded as risky and sensitive. Soon, however, writers like Ludvík VACULÍK and Milan KUNDERA were able to take an even more critical view of the recent past.

In the mid-1960s eastern European audiences and dramatists, such as Slawomir MROŻEK and Václav HAVEL, discovered that many aspects of everyday life under communism lent themselves to presentation on stage in terms of the THEATER OF THE ABSURD. When K. turned to drama, he, too, adopted some of its devices in *Zámek* (1964; the castle) and *Mistr* (1967; the master) and combined them with a Kafkaesque sense of a sealed world infested with

intangible evil. The influence of Franz KAFKA grew even more perceptible in a number of short stories and plays that were inspired by real-life experience. In *Cukrárna Myriam* (1968; Café Myriam), for instance, the poisoning of old people becomes an established and tolerated means of solving the housing shortage. A similarly haunting model situation, apparently abstracted from the 1950s show trials, was the basis of a meticulously constructed novella (originally a radio play), *Porota* (1969; "The Jury," in *A Ship Named Hope*, 1970).

During the 1970s and 1980s, when his work could only be published abroad, K.'s subjects became less sinister, although a young woman desensitized to the point of anomie appears again as the central character in *Milostné léto* (1979; rev. ed., 1985; *A Summer Affair*, 1987), the story of an older man's infatuation that inescapably leads to disaster. Some of the figures in *Má veselá jitra* (1979; *My Merry Mornings*, 1985) show similar signs of alienation, but there is also a touch of humor in the seven short stories that contemplate the ironies and peculiarities of life in a decaying socialist society. Another collection of short stories, *Moje první lásky* (1985; *My First Loves*, 1986), stands out as being least affected by the author's tendency to intellectualize in fiction social and ethical issues, a trait that is strongly detectable in *Soudce z milosti* (1986; *Judge on Trial*, 1991). The theme of conscience and moral fortitude in the face of pressure and persecution is combined in this novel, unusually for K., with that of religious faith.

A moral conflict of a private character is at the center of *Láska a smetí* (1988; *Love and Garbage*, 1990). A writer, who has taken on the job of a street sweeper, reminisces about his love affair with a life-hungry sculptress that he broke off, faced with deep feelings of guilt toward his wife and unable to continue living a lie. Although there is no hint of politics, the debris, both human and physical, that surrounds the narrator, seems to be symbolic of the disintegrating communist system. *Ostrov mrtvých králů* (1992; The Island of Dead Kings) is possibly the first Czech literary text, dealing with the fall of communism in Czechoslovakia. The hero of this novella is a Czech company director on holiday in Greece during the November 1989 Democratic Revolution. The dramatic events make the hero reassess his life. The volume also includes a number of earlier short stories by K., originally published in the 1960s. *Čekání na tmu, čekání na světlo* (1993; *Waiting for the Dark, Waiting for the Light*, 1994) is a novel of disillusionment, set in Czechoslovakia before, during, and after the 1989 Democratic Revolution. The work deals with ambiguities of reality and identity, pointing out that people are incapable of change, regardless of revolutions. The description of life in the final years of communism, especially the portrait of the communist president, includes some grotesque features. The novel is a story of Pavel, a middle-aged Czech TV cameraman who feels that if he lived in a free country, he would make an important film, an impassioned portrait of his times. But when freedom does come, Pavel dissipates his talents in small lucrative jobs, commercials, and pornographic movies. *Milostné rozhovory* (1995; Lover's Conversations) consists of dialogues and short stories mostly written in the 1990s, dealing with the theme of flawed love in a flawed world.

K. has been one of the most prolific and erudite Czech writers of the second half of the 20th c. With the exception of poetry, he has been active in all literary genres as well as in quality journalism. While aiming to provide an artistic comment on his times in carefully worked-out novels, plays, and short stories, he has not attempted entirely to hide their ideational framework. His authorial intentions have been allowed to show in places through the narrative conducted in a clear, unperturbed style, which reflected his preference for subtle sensitivity and refined reasoning. In this respect as well as in others, K.'s work paralleled trends manifest in contemporary Western fiction and in translation became an integral part of it.

FURTHER WORKS: *Mezi třemi hranicemi* (1960); *Karel Čapek* (1962); *Milenci na jednu noc* (1964); *Návštěva u nesmrtelné tetky* (1965); *Kokrhací hodiny* (1965); *Klára a dva páni* (1969; *Klara and Two Men*, 1983); *Ženich pro Marcelu* (1969); *Milenci na jeden den* (1969); *Pokoj pro dva* (1971); *Malomocní* (1972); *Ministr a anděl* (1990; *The President and the Angel*, 1979); *Franz a Felice* (1990; *Franz and Felice*, 1986); *Moje zlatá řemesla* (1990; *My Golden Trades*, 1992); *Markétin zvěřinec* (1990); *Už se blíží meče* (1990); *Hry* (1991). FURTHER WORKS IN ENGLISH: *The Games* (1985); *The Spirit of Prague* (1994)

BIBLIOGRAPHY: Mihailovich, V. D., et al., eds., *Modern Slavic Literatures* (1976), Vol. 2: 130–35; Goetz-Stankiewicz, M., *The Silenced Theatre* (1979): 117–45; Hájek, I., "Profile of I. K.," *IonC*, 12 (1983): 39–41; Goetz-Stankiewicz, M., "K. Under Kafka's Gaze—Kafka Under K.'s Pen," *CCur*, 5 (1986): 333–36; Roth, P., "A Conversation in Prague," *NYRB*, 12 Apr. 1990: 14–22

—IGOR HÁJEK

KLYUEV, Nikolay Alexeevich

Russian poet, b. 1887, Vytegra; d. Aug. 1937?, Siberia

Born to peasant parents, K. was steeped from childhood in northern Russian folk traditions. His family was associated with the illegal religious sectarians, God's People *(Khlysty)*, for whom K. was chosen to be a composer of ritual songs. It is likely that in 1906 or 1907 he went to Iran, India, and central Asia on secret sectarian business.

Although K. had no formal education, he was well-read in religious and mystical literature. K. began a correspondence with Alexandr BLOK in 1907 and participated in Vyacheslav IVANOV's "Tower", as this literary salon was called, in St. Petersburg. K. met Sergey YESENIN in 1915 and began a stormy literary and intimate relationship lasting until Yesenin's suicide, which inspired one of K.'s greatest poems, "Plach o Yesenine" (1927; "Lament for Esenin," 1977).

After 1924 K. wandered about Russia visiting monasteries and shrines. He was arrested in 1933 on charges of *"kulak* [well-to-do peasant] agitation" manifested by his dissemination of his powerful epic poem about village life under Soviet rule, "Pogorelshchina" (written 1926–28?, pub. 1954; "The Burned Ruins," 1977). Little is known about K.'s last years, after he was exiled to Siberia.

One of the first representatives of the so-called "peasant poets," K. wrote poetry characterized by vivid local color, an abundance of archaic and peasant language, daring and sometimes sexual imagery, and a deep understanding of Russian nature and art, especially icon painting and folk songs, as can be seen in works such as

Lesnye byli (1913; true forest stories), *Mirskie dumy* (1916; secular thoughts), and "Pesni zaonezhya" (1916; songs of the Onega region). K. successfully combined folk mannerisms with the sensibilities and poetic techniques of Russian SYMBOLISM. Much of his poetry—for example, *Bratskie pesni* (1912; brotherly songs)-is influenced by the ecstatic sectarian traditions. Deeply embedded in his work is an apocalyptic eschatology based on a mystic faith in the Russian peasantry and a profound opposition to the technical civilization of the West. The island of Kizhi in Lake Onega in his native region is connected in K.'s poetry with an ancient utopian peasant culture. His *Izbyanye pesni* (1920; songs of the peasant hut), however, written on the death of his mother, contains some of K.'s best and most accessible lyrics. They are written with a touching directness, unburdened by metaphysical and mystical import.

K.'s most accomplished works are his long poems: *Chetvyorty Rim* (1922; "The Fourth Rome," 1977), *Mat Subbota* (1922; "Mother Sabbath," 1977), "Zaozere" (1927; beyond the lake), "Plach o Yesenine," "Derevnya" (1927; the village), and "Pogorelschchina." They all express K.'s vision of a mysticism of Mother Earth and his grief over the destruction of what he believed to be the deepest wellsprings of the Russian spirit.

K. has been called by some one of the most decadent of the Russian symbolists "an Oscar Wilde or Paul Verlaine in bast shoes," and by others a truly national poet sprung from the soil of ancient Russia. In the former U.S.S.R. he is condemned as a *kulak* poet, although a small volume of his poetry has recently been published there. He is unquestionably a major figure in modern Russian poetry and awaits deep and comprehensive study.

FURTHER WORKS: *Sosen perezvon* (1912); *Lviny khleb* (1922); *Lenin* (1924); *Izba i pole* (1928); *Polnoe sobranie sochineny* (2 vols., 1954); *Sochinenia* (2 vols., 1969); *Stikhotvorenia i poemy* (1977). FURTHER WORKS IN ENGLISH: *Poems* (1977)

BIBLIOGRAPHY: Trostky, L., *Literature and Revolution* [first pub. 1923] (1971): 59–66; Zavalashin, V., *Early Soviet Writers* (1958): 91–100; Stammler, H., "N. K." (in German), in N. K., *Sochinenia* (1969), Vol. II: 7–50; McVay, G., "Yesenin's Posthumous Fame and the Fate of His Friends," *MLR*, 67 (1972): 595–97; McVay, G., *Esenin: A Life* (1976): 58–71, 169–71, 284–87; Ivask, G., "Russian Modernist Poets and the Mystic Sectarians," in Gibian, G., and Tjalsma, H. W., eds., *Russian Modernism* (1976): 85–106; Glad, J., Introduction to N. A. K., *Poems* (1977): ix–xx

—GERALD PIROG

KOBAYASHI Hideo

Japanese literary critic, b. 11 Apr. 1902, Tokyo; d. 1 Mar. 1983, Tokyo

K. is regarded as Japan's first modern literary and cultural critic, and by many its greatest and most influential. He was born in Tokyo at a time of that city's most rapid expansion, and lived there through the turbulence of both the 1923 earthquake and World War II. He studied French literature at the University of Tokyo, and already as a student began to translate and write essays on Charles

Baudelaire (1821–1867), Arthur Rimbaud (1854–1891), and André GIDE. He was also attracted to the critical writings of Montaigne and Paul VALÉRY. His own mature work is noted for its style, and read not just as commentary or criticism, but as literature.

K. wrote on a wide range of subjects, but always from a personal angle—that of an urban intellectual working to describe, but not define, the fast-changing contours of modern Japanese culture. His work in the late 1920s and the 1930s, most of it focused on contemporary Japanese, French, and Russian literature, seems most directly to address issues of Japan's complex, cross-cultural "modernity". His later work, addressed more to premodern or "classical" Japanese literature and aesthetics, can yet be seen as a continuing effort to record the culture of modern urban life, which by turns denies, invents, or takes refuge in the past.

The Japanese literary world that K. first entered was fraught with competing schools and ideologies: Marxism, aestheticism, populism. An early, prize-winning essay, "Samazamaru ishō" (1929; "Multiple Designs," 1995), marked the young critic as hostile to any and all ideological systems and fixed critical positions. He confronted, in particular, critics who lacked self-criticism, who presented their beliefs without irony or any skeptical distance. For K., the object of criticism did not exist in isolation from the values, tastes, and style of the critic. And in modern Japan, where under the impact of translated literatures and ideas these values and tastes were undergoing incessant change and transformation, K. could not help but be skeptical of the "stability" of any announced position. whether it be reactionary or avant-garde, cosmopolitan or nationalist.

Throughout the 1930s, even after the government moved to censor and ban radical, especially proletarian, writing, K. resisted the trend to define a "pure" Japanese culture, insulated and beyond any Western or outside influence. In "Kokyō ushinatta bungaku" (1933; "Literature of the Lost Home," 1995), he describes the culturally homeless situation of modern, urban Japanese, who respond as readily to the image of a Moroccan desert in a Western film, as they do to the city before their eyes. He observes, too, that Western culture is so much part of the education and cultural pursuits of modern Japanese that categorical distinctions between the "purely Japanese" and the foreign could no longer be made.

From this vantage, K. wrote about the tradition of novel writing in the West, and the modern phenomenon of the Japanese *shishōsetsu* or the "I-novel," as related but historically determined events, and with confidence that he could comprehend Rousseau or Gide as thoroughly as he could Tayama Katai (1871–1930) or SHIGA Naoya. Similarly, the great study *Dostoevsky no seikatsu* (1939; life of Dostoevsky) demonstrates K.'s capacity to read foreign culture as expressive of tensions deeply felt in modern Japanese life—in this case, how Dostoevsky's portraits of youth "possessed" by imported ideas rendered them as homeless in their own land as 20th-c. Japanese are in their own.

The coming of war and the intense government pressure on writers moved K. toward more reflective, meditative topics and themes. His wartime writing, some of it accommodationist in tone, was not the work of a propagandist but of a writer who had grown weary of his century. The essays collected in *Mujō to iu koto* (1946; on evanescence) mark K.'s "return" to the classics of medieval Japan. No doubt he was drawn to this period of warfare and cultural upheaval because of its resemblance to his own, and to its poets and tellers of tales because of a spirituality that allowed them to stand apart and observe the passing tragedy of worldly ambition.

Following the war, after the American occupation and the ensuing "economic miracle" had transformed a shattered country into a prosperous one, K. assumed a nearly legendary status for the integrity of his writing style and his iconoclastic, if by now highly refined and classical, tastes. His studies of Mozart, van Gogh, and the great 18th-c. scholar Motoori Norinaga (1730–1801) might be regarded together as the work of a mature critic, trying to provide perduring models of cultural conduct to a fashion-conscious youth culture of unstable and eclectic tastes.

Given the challenges to the political and cultural establishment that emerged in Japan in the 1960s, it is not surprising that K. would be denounced for his postwar conservatism. Still, it is a measure of K.'s real force and influence on Japanese letters in this century that both his admirers and his critics acknowledge the singularity of his style and his achievement. He remains the critical standard against which successive generations of Japanese critics have to measure themselves.

FURTHER WORKS: *Kobayashi Hideo Zenshū* (15 vols., 1979). FURTHER WORKS IN ENGLISH: *Literature of the Lost Home* (1995)

BIBLIOGRAPHY: Seidensticker, E., "K. H.," in Shively, D. H., ed., *Tradition and Modernization in Japanese Culture* (1971): 419–61; Keene, D., *Dawn to the West: Japanese Literature of the Modern Era* (1984): 582–610

—PAUL ANDERER

KOEPPEN, Wolfgang

West German novelist and essayist, b. 23 June 1906, Greifswald; d. 1996, Munich

The impoverished descendant of Pomeranian country squires, K. was raised as an only child by his mother. He studied philosophy, literature, and theater arts at the universities of Hamburg, Greifswald, Berlin, and Würzburg, worked as a seaman, actor, assistant theater director, and freelance journalist, and traveled widely in Germany, France, Italy, and the Netherlands. His eventual job as a journalist and critic for the *Börsen-Courier* in Berlin lasted only until Hitler's rise to power. Still, K. managed to publish his first novel, *Eine unglückliche Liebe* (1934; an unhappy love) in Germany, then spent considerable time in Holland while writing his next novel, *Die Mauer schwankt* (1934; the wall sways), which, in spite of its disguised criticism of the Nazi régime, was reissued in 1939 in Germany under the title *Die Pflicht* (duty). Generally, however, K. kept a low profile throughout the period of the Third Reich, trying to be neither used nor persecuted by the people in power. Since the end of World War II K. has lived predominantly in Munich as an independent writer, journalist, and critic and has traveled extensively throughout Europe, America, and the Soviet Union.

K.'s most important literary contribution has been a series of three novels that present a critical assessment of the psychological, social, and political situation in West Germany during the 1950s. In contrast to the two prewar novels, which concentrate on one person's alienation from his bourgeois environment, without much overt reference to current events, this postwar trilogy depicts revealing cross sections of West German society by following a diverse cast of characters for a day or two at quite clearly defined points in historical time and space.

In *Tauben im Gras* (1951; pigeons in the grass) it is obviously Munich in the spring of 1951, still under American military government but on the way toward physical recovery. The emotional recovery of the individuals from the shock and disruption of the war is less certain. A once hopeful writer is unable to produce, while his immature wife gradually pawns her crumbling inheritance. The collapse of the old order has left the people uprooted and confused but has also given them a chance for change and new beginnings, as in the case of a young war widow who has fallen in love with a black GI and dreams of life in a U.S. paradise. Whether such liberated attitudes will withstand the mounting pressures of the return of authoritarianism and of bigotry in Germany is left open to question.

Restoration of the old authoritarian law and order appears to be in full swing in *Das Treibhaus* (1953; *The Bonn Parliament*, 1953) as we follow Keetenheuve, a former emigrant and now member of the Bonn parliament, in his attempt to defeat proposals to reinstitute the German army and military conscription. His idealistic hopes for a liberal and truly democratic Germany have been eroded in this atmosphere of intrigue, opportunism, and pragmatic wheeling and dealing. He fails both socially and politically and ends in suicide.

Der Tod in Rom (1954; *Death in Rome*, 1961), the most pessimistic of the three novels, centers on the reemergence of Nazism in various forms. Judejahn, a former SS general and thus the embodiment of death and destruction, is in Rome to discuss his possible return to Germany with his former fellow Nazi, Pfaffrath, now a big-city mayor in West Germany. These and other figures in the novel typify certain tendencies in postwar Germany: opportunism, religious revival, hedonism, aesthetic nihilism, and, behind it all, the specter of a neo-Nazi movement.

K.'s style, in its rhetorical, learned, and provocative brilliance, is the dominant feature of his works. Huge cumulative sentences, long, evocative stream-of-consciousness passages overflowing with cleverly chosen details (including news headlines, slogans, and popular hit songs), and montages of quickly shifting scenes and moods create an overall poetic effect in a manner reminiscent of JOYCE, FAULKNER and DÖBLIN, with moments of lyrical beauty, biting satire, loneliness, and despair.

K.'s trilogy had a highly controversial reception. But public interest soon waned, and K. turned to writing sophisticated literary travelogues, such as *Nach Rußland und anderswohin: Empfindsame Reisen* (1958; to Russia and other places: sentimental journeys), which, being less provocative in tone and content, received widespread acclaim among critics and the general public and led to various literary awards, beginning with the Büchner Prize in 1962. More recently K. has moved toward a blend of the psychological novel and social criticism in his semifictional autobiography *Jugend* (1976; youth). There is a special youthfulness in K.'s relentless stylistic and topical nonconformism even as he reaches old age, and it may continue to irritate potential readers, but K.'s work clearly deserves more attention than it has received so far.

FURTHER WORKS: *Amerikafahrt* (1959); *New York* (1961); *Reisen nach Frankreich* (1961); *Romanisches Café: Erzählende Prosa* (1972)

BIBLIOGRAPHY: Bance, C. F., "*Der Tod in Rom* and *Die Rote*: Two Italian Episodes," *FMLS*, 3 (1967): 126–34; Demetz, P., "W. K.,"
Postwar German Literature (1972): 168–72; Erlach, D., *W. K. als zeitkritischer Erzähler* (1973); Craven, S., "W. K. and the Human Condition," *GL&L*, 29 (1976): 201–15; Greiner, U., ed., *Über W. K.* (1976)

—EBERHARD FREY

KOESTLER, Arthur

English novelist, essayist, and science writer, b. 5 Sept. 1905, Budapest, Hungary; d. 3 Mar. 1983, Munich

As a child, K. saw his family and native land disintegrate as a result of World War I. Much of his early manhood was spent in the Weimar Republic, and he watched his first career (as a journalist) and German society destroyed by the Third Reich. While wandering across Europe in the 1930s (with a brief sojourn in Palestine during the British Mandate), he experienced the famines and chaos of the Soviet Union, the Stalinist purges and double-think in the Communist Party (he joined in 1931 and resigned in 1938), the horror of the Spanish Civil War (during which he was captured by Franco's troops and sentenced to death), and the political corruption, paralysis, and fall of the French Third Republic. Escape to and settlement in Britain in 1940 marked his seventh country and sixth language since birth. He later became a British citizen, and except for travels to America and the Continent, he remained in that country. He was made a Commander of the Order of the British Empire in 1972 and a Companion of Literature in 1974.

K.'s early life explains the apocalyptic element in his work. In everything that he has written he has viewed the world and himself as moving toward destruction, only to be saved by rebirth in a new form. K. and his heroes tend to be embattled and persecuted: K. in prison in Spain in his memoir *Spanish Testament* (1937), rewritten as *Dialogue with Death* (1942); K. fleeing occupied France in his memoir *Scum of the Earth* (1941); Rubashov, the old Bolshevik, caught in Stalin's purges in the novel *Darkness at Noon* (1941); and even Spartacus, the slave leader, hunted by the Romans and attacked by his own followers in *The Gladiators* (1939). Of K.'s over thirty books, these remain his most vividly written.

At the beginning of his literary career, readers and critics hailed K.'s works because his apocalyptic mood confirmed and explained their sense of the times. In 1941 *Darkness at Noon* was welcomed as much for its apparent answer to "The Riddle of Moscow's Trials" (the title of the front-page *New York Times Book Review* piece) as for its psychological intensity. The novel is autobiographical in many ways, a testament to its author's Communist Party experiences and an announcement of his rebirth in a post-Communist phase. All of this lies beneath the political and intellectual drama of Rubashov's downfall and the decay of the Russian Revolution. The novel is considered one of the most powerful political fictions of the century.

When K. turned his talent full force to anti-Communism, many readers were willing to follow and others to join. In his book of essays *The Yogi and the Commissar* (1945), one of the first Cold War tracts, he articulated widely held fears about Stalinism and Communism. When, a few years later, hundreds of thousands of readers felt enlightened by his memoir of his Communist Party experiences in the collection of essays edited by Richard Crossman called *The God That Failed* (1949), and enthusiastic audiences greeted his speaking tours of Europe and America, he was at the height of his popularity.

K.'s next works, however, especially his two volumes of memoirs *Arrow in the Blue* (1951) and *The Invisible Writing* (1954), were less orthodox in their anti-Communism and more penetrating in their psychological analysis of the true-believer syndrome—they received a very mixed reception. K. was attacked by the same public who had earlier championed his works. There is an analogy between the public's response to K.'s writings on Communism and his version of his affair with Communism: in the beginning, the embrace was too passionate and when disillusion came, the split was rancorous.

Then, in the preface to his book of essays *Trail of the Dinosaur* (1955), K. declared his literary-political career over. He was finished with "these questions" and he wanted "a vocational change." Since that time, K.'s subjects have included science and mysticism, capital punishment (he opposes it), and extrasensory perception. He has baffled many of his former followers with his postpolitical writings. But the premises and themes of his recent work resemble those of his political writing. His central scientific theory—bisociation, that is, the collision of opposites, synthesis, and new form—is analogous to his political-literary structure of dialectic and apocalyptic transformation. He continues, at a distance and in muted tones, his autobiography: his topic may be science or mysticism, but his subject is his lifelong narrative of the self.

Throughout his long career, K.'s influence has been felt on many fronts. From 1937 to 1955, he was a committed writer, one of the main representatives of a whole generation of politically active European authors. Since 1956 he immersed himself mainly in questions of science and mysticism, and a large public, including many young persons, followed his explorations. K.'s work and his reputation as one of the most diverse and often protean writers of our century continues.

FURTHER WORKS: *Arrival and Departure* (1943); *Twilight Bar: An Escapade in Four Acts* (1945); *Thieves in the Night: Chronicle of an Experiment* (1946); *Promise and Fulfillment: Palestine, 1917–1949* (1949); *Insight and Outlook: An Inquiry into the Common Foundations of Science, Art, and Social Ethics* (1949); *The Age of Longing* (1951); *Reflections on Hanging* (1957); *The Sleepwalkers: A History of Man's Changing Vision of the Universe* (1959); *The Lotus and the Robot* (1961); *The Act of Creation* (1964); *The Ghost in the Machine* (1968); *Drinkers of Infinity: Essays, 1955–1967* (1969); *The Case of the Mid-Wife Toad* (1972); *The Roots of Coincidence* (1972); *The Call Girls* (1973); *The Heel of Achilles: Essays, 1968–1973* (1975); *The Thirteenth Tribe* (1976); *Janus: A Summing Up* (1978); *Bricks to Babel* (1981)

BIBLIOGRAPHY: Orwell, G., "A. K." *Dickens, Dali, and Others* (1946): 31–45; Pritchett, V. S., "K.: A Guilty Figure," *Harper's*, Jan. 1948: 84–92; Deutscher, I., "The Ex-Communist's Conscience," *Heretics and Renegades* (1957): 112–131; Aiken, H. D., "The Metaphysics of A. K.," *NYRB*, 17 Dec. 1964: 22–25; Calder, J., *Chronicles of Conscience: A Study of A. K. and George Orwell* (1968); Toulmin, S., "The Book of Arthur," *NYRB*, 11 Apr. 1968: 16–21; Harris, H., ed., *Astride the Two Cultures: A. K. at Seventy* (1975); Sperber, M., "Looking Back on K.'s Spanish War," *DR*, 57 (1977): 152–63; Sperber, M., ed., *A. K.: A Collection of Critical Essays* (1977); Hamilton, I. *K.* (1982)

—MURRAY A. SPERBER

KOLB, Annette

German novelist, and essayist, b. 2 Feb. 1870, Munich; d. 3 Dec. 1967, Munich

Reference works traditionally cite K.'s date of birth incorrectly as 1875, an error she encouraged by consciously misrepresenting her age. K.'s mother was a celebrated French pianist, her father a Bavarian landscape architect (rumored to have been an illegitimate son of the noble Wittelsbach family). Although raised in Bavaria, K. grew up bilingual (in German and French) and bicultural, and her mother's cosmopolitan salon encouraged her to pursue her political ideals as well as music and literature.

The Bavarian locale, an aristocratic milieu, music, and Franco-German politics and cultural relations are constant elements in her work. During World War I she won notoriety with her pacifist essays *Dreizehn Briefe einer Deutsch-Französin* (1916; thirteen letters of a Franco-German woman), condemning both French and German chauvinism. Denounced in both countries, she fled to Switzerland for safety, returning to Berlin and thence to Badenweiler near the Alsatian border only after the war. During this period she devoted herself to German-French rapprochement.

With *Das Beschwerdebuch* (1932; the register of grievances) she began to warn against totalitarianism, indeed to predict Hitler's ascent to power. In 1933, a persona non grata to the Nazi regime in Germany, K. emigrated, finally arriving in the U.S., where she spent four and a half difficult years. She had contact with the émigré circle around Thomas MANN, whose wife Katja had been her childhood friend. Mann incorporated K. into his novel *Doctor Faustus* (1947) as Jeanette Scheurl. K. eventually returned to Munich, still promulgating German-French understanding and championing both Adenauer and De Gaulle. In her later years, she won acclaim as a humanitarian and a grande dame of European letters.

K.'s three novels draw on her family back-ground for settings and incorporate her political ideals. The romantic tale *Das Exemplar* (1913; the paragon) is written in informal, flowing language that captures the melancholy tone of love and renunciation. There is a sociopolitical component in K.'s satirical portrayal of the English aristocracy; the most convincing element of the narrative is the psychological (although perhaps overly sentimentalized) portrait of the heroine Mariclée, whose lofty, romantic obsession for her "paragon" strengthens her when she renounces him to gain her own independence.

Daphne Herbst (1928; Daphne Herbst) depicts in a mature, disciplined style a young woman too delicate for the harshness of modern life. A gentle lament for Munich court society, the novel is nonetheless critical of the attitudes that hastened its demise. The death of Daphne, whose heightened emotions enervate and alienate her, symbolizes the decline of old values.

Overt autobiographical detail forms the backbone of K.'s last novel, *Die Schaukel* (1934; the swing). It is a mosaic of impressionistic flashbacks and foreshadowings that distance the reader from the narrative and underscore the insecurity of the stately serene Munich of K.'s youth. It is a nostalgic picture where "the swing stands still" in a time and place seemingly untouched by world events.

K.'s Franco-German allegiance and her political role as mediator of both cultures place her above convenient national categories. Her German revels in Gallic conceits, using foreign words, frequent rhetorical questions, and exclamation points for emphasis. Her diction, although sometimes archaic, is musical and elegant and a fitting medium for the values of tolerance, humanity, and grace—tempered with a dash of pessimism—with which she tried to inspire the 20th c.

FURTHER WORKS: *Kurze Aufsätze* (1899); *L'Âme aux deux Patries: Sieben Studien* (1906); *Wege und Umwege* (1914); *Die Last* (1918); *Zarastro: Westliche Tage* (1921); *Were Njedin: Erzählungen und Skizzen* (1924); *Spitzbögen* (1925); *Veder Napoli e partire* (1925); *Versuch über Briand* (1929); *Kleine Fanfare* (1930); *Festspieltage in Salzburg* (1937); *Mozart: Sein Leben* (1937); *Glückliche Reise* (1940); *Franz Schubert: Sein Leben* (1941); *König Ludwig II. von Bayern und Richard Wagner* (1947); *Blätter in den Wind* (1954); *Memento* (1960); *1907–1964: Zeitbilder* (1964)

BIBLIOGRAPHY: Rinser, L., *Der Schwerpunkt* (1960): 9–22; Soergel, A., and Hohoff, C., *Dichtung und Dichter der Zeit* (1961), Vol. I: 677–82; Rauenhorst, D., *A. K.: Ihr Leben und Werk* (1969); Lemp, R., *A. K.: Leben und Werk einer Europäerin* (1970); Benyoetz, E., *A. K. und Israel* (1970)

—THOMAS SVEND HANSEN

KOLMAR, Gertrud

(pseud. of Gertrud Chodziesner) German poet, b. 10 Dec. 1894, Berlin; d. 1943, Auschwitz, Poland

K.'s father was a well-to-do Jewish lawyer. The introverted child's home environment fostered in her love of nature, gardening, and the animal world. She was interested in history as well, particularly in the French Revolution (in 1933 she made Robespierre the subject of a scholarly essay and a poetic cycle). Fluent in French, English, and Russian, she became a translator and interpreter, working as a postal censor and with prisoners of war during World War I. Having experienced an unhappy love affair at that time, she never married. In the postwar period K. worked as a teacher and private tutor, specializing in the education of deafmute, sick, and otherwise handicapped children. After the death of her mother in 1930 the poet devoted herself to the care of her aged father; thus she chose not to emigrate after the Nazis' accession to power. The letters she wrote between 1938 and 1943 to her younger sister, who had escaped to Switzerland, were published posthumously and reflect the quiet, heroic courage, the dignity, and the resigned wisdom of a sensitive soul. Some of her poetry from those years is on Jewish themes. From 1941 on K. had to do forced labor in two Berlin factories. Her father was sent to Theresienstadt concentration camp in September 1942, and K. was deported in late February of the following year. The date and place of her death are uncertain, but she is presumed to have perished at Auschwitz.

K.'s first publication was *Gedichte* (poems), a book of forty poems issued in 1917, which caused no great stir. She did not publish again until 1930, when two of her poems appeared in the prestigious *Insel-Almanach*. The poet had no use for "modernity," kept aloof from the literary marketplace, and cultivated a low-pressure timelessness, creating quietly and self-effacingly in the manner of Emily Dickinson and developing a poetic idiom all her own, which combined visionary fervor with formal discipline. She excelled as a nature poet but also produced powerful, sensual, often lengthy poems on love, sexuality, motherhood, and children. Her explorations of female sexuality were quite novel and daring for someone of her generation and background. "Weibliches Bildnis" (partial trans., "Image of Woman," 1975), a cycle of seventy-five poems on which she worked for a decade, presents a typology of womanhood. That she favored the cyclical form is evidenced also by "kind" (child), "Tierträume" (partial trans., "Animal Dreams," 1975), "Das Wort der Stummen" (words of the silent), and *Die Frau und die Tiere* (1938; woman and animals; pub. under the name Chodziesner). Except for the last mentioned, these cycles were not published in her lifetime; they are included in *Das lyrische Werk* (1955; enl. ed., 1960; the poetic work).

The poetic sequence "Alte Stadtwappen" (old city coats of arms) came into being in 1927–28; eighteen of these fifty-three poems were issued in 1934 as *Preußische Wappen* (partial trans., "Prussian Coats of Arms," 1975). These poems are fanciful and symbolic depictions of the human situation generally, as well as poignant attempts to distill from various emblems the essence and the genius of the poet's now misguided land. The cycle "Bild der Rose" (partial trans., "Rose Sonnets," 1975) contains mostly sonnets, and in the late sequence "Welten" (1947; partial trans.,"Worlds," 1975), K. abandons her customary conservative form, strict meters, and regular rhyme schemes in favor of free-flowing unrhymed verse.

K.'s two plays were never published, but her works of fiction *Susanne* (Susanne) and *Eine Mutter* (a mother) did appear in 1959 and 1965 respectively. The latter, a short novel written in 1930–31, is a strange mixture of soap-opera melodrama, detective story, and symbolic fairy tale, presenting its Jewish protagonist as the archetypal woman.

FURTHER WORKS: *Tag-und Tierträume* (1963); *Das Bildnis Robespierres* (1965); *Die Kerze von Arras* (1968); *Briefe an die Schwester Hilde* (1970). FURTHER WORKS IN ENGLISH: *Dark Soliloquy: The Selected Poems of G. K.* (1975); *A Jewish Mother from Berlin and Susanna* (1997)

BIBLIOGRAPHY: Kayser, R., "Das lyrische Werk von G. K.," *GQ*, 33 (1960): 1–3; Picard, J., "G. K.: Reminiscences," *Jewish Frontier*, Mar. 1960: 12–17; Wallmann, J. P., "Deutsche Lyrik unter jüdischem Dreigestirn," *Merkur*, 20 (1966): 1119–94; Blumenthal, B. G., "G. K.: Love's Service to the Earth," *GQ*, 42 (1969): 485–88; Hamburger, M., "The Poetry of G. K.," *BUJ*, 24, 2 (1976): 65–67; Langer, L. L., "Survival through Art: The Career of G. K.," *Leo Baeck Institute Yearbook*, 23 (1978): 247–58; Langmann, E., "The Poetry of G. K.," *Seminar*, 2 (1978): 117-32; Eben, M. C., "G. K. An Appraisal," *German Life and Letters*, 37, 2 (1984): 197-210; Eichmann-Leutenegger, B., *G. K. Leben und Werk in Texten und Bildern* (1993); Woltman, J., *G. K. Leven und Werk* (1995); Frantz, B. C., *G. K.'s Prose* (1997)

—HARRY ZOHN

KOMI LITERATURE

See Finno-Ugric Literatures of the Soviet Union

KOMUNYAKAA, Yusef

American poet, b. 29 Apr. 1947, Bogalusa, Louisiana

Growing up in a small Southern town seventy miles north of New Orleans, where, as an African American, he was forbidden to use the library, K. developed early on a rich inner life that spoke of the promise of liberating imagination along with the painful reality of racial conflict. The son of a carpenter and the grandson of a stowaway from the West Indies who, according to family tradition, brought the K. name from West Africa, K. was drafted into the U.S. Army and sent to Vietnam where he served two tours of duty as a journalist for the military newspaper, *Southern Cross*. His job required him to be in battles, and he received a Bronze Star for bravery. Both his wartime and childhood experiences figure prominently in his poetry; K. writes with a compelling power, speaking in a variety of voices about racism, death, love, lust, and a poet's experience of the Vietnam War. In 1994 K. won the Pulitzer Prize for *Neon Vernacular* (1993). In the same year he was awarded the Kingsley Tufts Poetry Prize by the Claremont Graduate School, and the William Faulkner Prize by the University of Rennes. In 1991 he was presented with the *Kenyon Review* Award for excellence in poetry, and in 1990 he received the Thomas Forcade Award in literature and art dedicated to the reconciliation of Vietnam and America, given by the William Joiner Foundation. The *Village Voice* chose K.'s *Magic City* (1992) as one of the twenty-five best books published that year. In 1997 K. was awarded the Hanes Poetry Prize.

Called by another Pulitzer Prize-winner, Gwendolyn BROOKS, as "the best young black poet in America," K. has written ten books of poetry. Throughout his work K. crafts tightly constructed poems that convey (chiefly in the earlier poems) a sense of congestion, of secret lives, of heat, of madness. There are also the emotions of despair and anger engendered in a black man's perception of himself located in the deep South. In *Copacetic* (1984), blues and jazz rhythms help to tease out inferences and connections. K. speaks of the hidden motives in the heart as it runs to hide from the pain of exclusion, and of the effects of love and society failing in large and in small, personal ways. These poems carry with them strong poetic force, vitality in life and in jazz, and an ultimately optimistic stance in spite of the pain and contraction of daily living. In *I Apologize for the Eyes in My Head* (1986) K. speaks about racism and the transitory nature of life, employing violent and blood-soaked images, making reference to frustration, betrayal, and aching longing.

Another major theme in K.'s works concerns his experiences in Vietnam. His poetic reactions to the war are primarily found in *Dien Cai Dau* (1988). The claustrophobia of tunnels, the stolen jazz cadences of Hanoi Hannah, the tortured moral questions, and the troubling unethical acts in the war paint a landscape of nightmare and idealism blasted. The collection ends with what may be K.'s finest poem, "Facing It," a powerful elegy involving a visit to the Vietnam Veterans Memorial in Washington, D.C.

Magic City (1992) and *Neon Vernacular* speak of painful disruptions, racial injustices, and incoherence at the center of significant experiences, but also of gifts of self-insight and the possibility of joy. K. is able to distill experience into packed, concrete packages that end in uncertainty, with emotion and the heat of its turmoil staggering through a delicate and finely nuanced sensibility. *Thieves of Paradise* (1997) speaks about the joy and sorrow of memory, the power of sensation, and the responsibility of vision. His language is taut and sinewy, as he returns over and over again to a theme that runs through so much of his poetry: the sadness of failed ideals, the pain of moral failure, and the potential for transformation, often seemingly only inches beyond one's grasp. K. speaks of these issues at once learnedly, invoking classical allusions on occasion, while also invoking the voice of the street, often utilizing jazz and the blues as reference points for his allusions and in the rhythms of his lines. In "Anodyne," the final poem of the collection, K. speaks of all that haunts him, deeply through his bones. Yet the rhythm of music and the force of truth-telling gives him enough energy to outlast at least one hundred angels.

Although disdaining the label of jazz poet, K. quite self-consciously employs music in many of his poems as a structural device and as a method for discovery. He speaks of jazz as a method whereby one may approach the emotional mystery behind events and objects. Focusing on that emotional mystery is a major aspect of K.'s poetry, which necessitates indeterminacy. Yet K. strives after the hard and ugly truths as well, in a significant voice that is clear and distinctive, multilayered and psychologically complex. In being willing to confront large and difficult issues in American society like racism and the aftermath of the Vietnam War, not from any particular ideological stance but the perspective of a highly sensitive poetic soul, K., as he continues to write, is evolving into one of the most serious and significant poets this country has produced in recent years.

FURTHER WORKS: *Dedications and Other Darkhorses* (1977); *Lost in the Bonewheel Factory* (1979); *Toys in a Field* (1986); *February in Sydney* (1989); *The Jazz Poetry Anthology* (1991, with Sascha Feinstein); *The Second Set: The Jazz Poetry Anthology*, Vol. 2 (1996, with Sascha Feinstein)

BIBLIOGRAPHY: Kelley, R., "Jazz and Poetry: A Conversation," *GaR*, 46 (Winter 1992): 645-61; Aubert, A., "K.: The Unified Vision—Canonization and Humanity," *AAR*, 27 (Spring 1993): 119-23; Ringnalda, D., "Rejecting 'Sweet Geometry': K.'s Duende," *JAC*, 16 (Fall 1993): 21-28; Stein, K., "Vietnam and the 'Voice Within': Public and Private History in K.'s *Dien Cai Dau*," *MassR*, 36 (1995), 541-61; Conley, S., "About K.," *Ploughshares*, 23 (1997), 202-7

—BRIAN ADLER

KONRÁD, George (György)

Hungarian novelist and essayist, b. 2 Apr. 1933, Debrecen

K. is a writer whose works reveal a great deal about his life and career. Although he received a degree in literature at the University of Budapest, he worked for years as a social worker and then as a town planner at Budapest's Institute of Urban Planning. His first two novels, *A látogató* (1969; *The Case Worker*, 1974) and *A városalapító* (1977; *The City Builder*, 1977), were products of these professional activities. His celebrated essays on dissidence and censorship, notably "A függetlenség lassú munkája" (1977; "The Long Work of Liberty," 1978), "Az állami ember és a cenzúra" (1981; "Censorship and State-Owned Citizens," 1983), written in the 1970s and early 1980s, reflected his own situation at the time. His most recent fiction, *Kerti mulatság* (1989; *Feast in the Garden*, 1992), is directly autobiographical, chronicling his childhood in a prewar market town in eastern Hungary, his miraculous survival of the Nazi Holocaust, his youthful infatuation with socialism, as well as his years as a barely tolerated dissident intellectual.

A látogató, which secured K.'s place as a major contemporary novelist, is a sociologically precise and at the same time stunningly lyrical and provocatively nonpolitical examination of urban squalor and degradation. The city is Budapest, though it may well be any other metropolis. The case worker himself is a universal figure, a lonely, doubt-ridden man trying to comprehend the scope and texture of human misery. At once compassionate and detached, he listens to the horror stories of his clients and does what he can, which is not much. Still, he is no mere observer and recorder. His daily dealings with the dregs of society do not make him indifferent—they simply teach him the limits of his effectiveness and turn his anguish into quiet stoicism. What makes the novel an extraordinary achievement—what transforms the sociological content of the work into art—is K.'s success in revealing, with his physical descriptions even more effectively than with the actual case histories, the true state of his charges. Almost in the manner of the French *nouveau roman*, K. constructs a world of precisely observed objects, but his objects speak, and their tales of woe remain vivid.

A városalapító, K.'s second novel, is more abstract and elusive, outlining the political, social, and economic history of an unnamed Eastern European city, where rulers and ruling classes kept changing but where the intoxication with power remained constant. The central consciousness is that of a builder who sees everything from the vantage point of his profession. As a young city planner he had been "eager to sketch out the most daring visions of our collective history"; as a middle-aged, middle-echelon executive, however, he is content with his modest share of power and is glad that years of repression and regimentation have not dehumanized him completely.

In *A cinkos* (1978; *The Loser*, 1982) K. uses yet another approach. This novel fairly teems with narrative; scores upon scores of self-contained stories as well as realist mininovels crowd its pages. Yet, in its own way, *A cinkos* is also a piece of experimental fiction, an attempted synthesis of Eastern European history. Everything important that happened in Hungary in the last sixty-odd years is somehow worked into the novel. The hero—whom we see alternately as a pampered child, an underground communist, a prisoner, a cabinet minister, an academic, a mental patient—is a composite figure, and others in the novel likewise become characters in a grim political parable.

All of K.'s fictions—the traditional narratives as well as the allegories—are also reflective and meditative. This is especially true of his latest novel, *Kerti mulatság*, a many-faceted, self-consciously stylized and somewhat diffuse recreation of personal and family history. In his political essays and cultural-historical inquiries—*Antipolitika* (1983; *Antipolitics*, 1984) or *Az autonómia kísértése* (1980; the temptation of autonomy)—an always judicious and eloquent K. is able to make self-evident truths pressingly relevant. K. coauthored two studies with the noted sociologist Iván Szelényi (b. 1936): *Új lakótelepek szociológiai problémái* (1969; the sociological problems of new housing estates) and *Az értelmiség útja az osztályhatalomhoz* (1978; *The Intellectuals on the Road to Class Power*, 1979); and though his contributions to both were much more than stylistic, there are few examples of "hard" sociology or books of political philosophy that are as literate and readable as these two works.

In his novels K. delves into private misery and public oppression, and details these corruptions with the concern of a moralist. Not only does he demonstrate a somewhat old-fashioned belief in the moral value of literature, he places the highest premium on human freedom. His quest for individual freedom met with considerable opposition in his own country. While his works were acclaimed in the West—he received prestigious literary prizes in Austria, Switzerland, and Germany, and was elected president of PEN, the international writers organization—he was under a publication ban during most of the 1970s and early 1980s. His works began to appear in Hungary again only after the dramatic political changes of the late 1980s.

FURTHER WORKS: *Kitörés* (1975, with Péter Bacsó and Péter Zimre); *Európa köldökén* (1990); *Az újjászületés melankóliája* (1991); *Kő óra* (1994); *The Melancholy of Rebirth* (1995)

BIBLIOGRAPHY: Howe, I., on *The Case Worker, NYTBR*, 27 Jan. 1974: 1; Kauffmann, S., "G. K.," *Salmagundi*, 57 (1982): 87–91; Sanders, I., "Freedom's Captives: Notes on G. K.'s Novels," *WLT*, 57, 2 (Spring 1983): 210–14; Birnbaum, M. D., "The Tropics of Love and Loyalty in G. K.'s *The Loser*," *CCur*, 7 (1988): 271–94

—IVAN SANDERS

KONWICKI, Tadeusz

Polish novelist and film director, b. 22 June 1926, Nowa Wilejka

Born in Poland's northeastern region, K. spent World War II in that territory occupied first by the Soviets, then the Germans, and then by the Soviets again. In 1944 he joined the Polish underground Home Army and fought against the Soviet occupiers. In 1945 he moved to central Poland, entered the Jagiellonian University in Cracow, and soon emerged as a journalist and novelist whose fiction gained full recognition after 1956. In 1950 and 1954 he was awarded state prizes in literature; his movie *Ostatni dzień lata* (shown in the U.S. under the title *Last Day of Summer*) won the Grand Prize at the Venice Film Festival in 1960, and his novel *Nic albo nic* (1971; nothing or nothing) was selected in a readers' poll as the novel of the year.

K.'s early short stories in *Przy budowie* (1950; at the building site) and an unfinished novel, *Władza* (Vol. 1, 1954; power) followed the rigid dictates of SOCIALIST REALISM prevailing in Poland in the early 1950s. As soon as some artistic freedom was reestablished in 1956, K. published his semiautobiographical novel *Rojsty* (1956; marshes), which he had completed as early as 1948. The novel contained some of the central motifs that were expanded in his subsequent fiction and in the films he began to direct and produce in 1954: a guilt complex stemming from a killing, sexual frustrations, a fear of being persecuted by the authorities, and an all-embracing nostalgia for the lost land of his youth. These themes were given a coherent artistic form in the dreamlike plot of his novel *Sennik współczesny* (1963; *A Dreambook for Our Time*, 1969) and were further explored in other novels.

Another important theme in K.'s fiction is a highly critical attitude toward certain social problems in contemporary Poland, which is often juxtaposed with the previous ones. K. blends the present and the past into a nightmarish vision of life constantly threatened with destruction and death. When his criticism of political conditions in Poland became too vocal in 1976, the authorities banned reprints of all his already published work as well as publication of any works he might write in the future. K. responded with a novel, *Kompleks polski* (1977; *The Polish Complex*, 1981), published in a literary quarterly, *Zapis*, issued illegally, that is, without official censorship. Another major novel, *Mala apokalipsa* (1979; small apocalypse), was also published in *Zapis*. Together with a number of major Polish writers he has become a member of the literary opposition. K.'s films, released between 1956 and 1976, explored similar problems and themes.

K., an accomplished literary artist, has cast a sharp, critical, and often satirical eye on modern Poland. In his mature works he has become more and more preoccupied with philosophical and moral dilemmas beyond the borders of his own country and thus has become more universal.

FURTHER WORKS: *Powrót* (1954); *Z oblężonego miasta* (1956); *Dziura w niebie* (1959); *Ostatni dzień lata* (1966); *Wniebowstąpienie* (1967); *Zwierzoczłowiekoupiór* (1969; *Anthropos-Specter-Beast*, 1977); *Jak daleko stąd, jak blisko* (1972); *Kronika wypadków miłosnych* (1974); *Kalendarz i klepsydra* (1976)

BIBLIOGRAPHY: Miłosz, C., *The History of Polish Literature* (1969: 499–501; Krzyżanowski, J. R., "The Haunted World of T. K.," *BA*, 48 (1974): 485–90; Krzyzżanowski, J. R., "The Polish Complex," *PolR*, 25 (1980): 98–110

—JERZY R. KRZYŻANOWSKI

KOREAN LITERATURE

The appearance of the first truly modern literature in Korea was preceded by the transitional dominance of a "new literature" of enlightenment. The modern literary movement was launched by Ch'oe Nam-sŏn (1890–1957) and Yi Kwang-su (1892–?). The "new poetry" movement dates back to the publication of "Hae esŏ pada ege" (1908; "From the Sea to the Children," 1964), by Ch'oe Nam-sŏn in *Sonyŏn*, the first literary journal aimed at producing cultural reform by introducing Western civilization to the masses. Inspired by Byron's *Childe Harold's Pilgrimage*, Ch'oe celebrates, in clean masculine diction, the strength of the young people who will carry out the necessary social and literary revolution. However, neither Ch'oe nor his contemporaries succeeded in going beyond the bounds of traditional prosody, with its set alternation of four and three syllables, or in modernizing traditional forms of speech and allusion. In his stories, Yi Kwangsu adopted a prose style that approximated the everyday speech of the common people. Yet his stories, which dealt with the enlightened pioneers who championed Western science and civilization, still followed the conventional theme of the "reproval of vice and promotion of virtue."

In 1919, shortly before the unsuccessful movement for independence from Japan, translations from such Western poets as Paul Verlaine (1844–1896), Remy de Gourmont (1858–1915), and Fyodor SOLOGUB began to exert a powerful influence on Korean poetry. The indirection and suggestiveness of French SYMBOLISM were introduced by Kim Ŏk (1895–?), the principal translator. Against the didacticism of the age Kim set Mallarmé (1842–1898); against its rhetoric and sentimentality he set Verlaine, concluding in the process that free verse was the supreme creation of the symbolists. Kim's fascination with symbolism culminated, in March 1921, in the publication of *Onoe ŭi mudo* (dance of anguish), the first Korean collection of translations from Western poetry. Kim's translations from English, French, Esperanto, as well as from Japanese, were written in a melliflous, dreamy style. The exotic and melancholy beauty of autumn, as well as expressions of ennui and anguish, all appealed to poets who sought to express their frustration and despair at the collapse of the independence movement of 1919.

The movement for literary naturalism was launched in the 1920s by a group of young writers who rallied around a new definition of universal reality in hopes of rectifying defects of form and content in fiction. Yŏm Sang-sŏp (1897–1963), the first to introduce psychological analysis and scientific documentation into his stories, defined naturalism as an expression of awakened individuality. Naturalism's purpose, Yŏm asserted, was to expose the sordid aspects of reality, especially the sorrow and disillusionment occurring as authority figures are debased and one's idols are shattered. Many works of naturalist fiction were first-person narratives. A desire to portray reality led writers to touch upon certain problems, but only those encountered by the writers, members of the intelligentsia, who were offering themselves as the subjects of case studies. Most stories written in this vein dealt with the miseries of the urban poor, or with the characters' attempts to cope with socioeconomic pressures. The disharmony between the writer and his society often induced the writer to turn to nature; and the land and the simple folk furnished themes and motifs for some of the better Korean stories in the Zolaesque tradition, among them "Pul" (1925; "Fire," 1974) by Hyŏn Chin-gŏn (1900–1943) and "Kamja" (1925; "Potato," 1974) by Kim Tong-in (1900–1951). But the most persistent theme in these stories is the assault on orthodox moral codes.

Naturalism in Korea was never a unified literary movement. Naturalist writers were productive over a span of several decades and wrote works that diverged widely in their treatment of basic themes. "Nalgae" (1936; "Wings," 1974) by Yi Sang (1910–1937), which traces the ceaseless activity of the hero's mind, is a stream-of-consciousness story. Others wrote panoramic novels, case studies of emancipated women, or historical novels.

The 1920s produced several major poets. Han Yong-un (1879–1944), revolutionary, reformer, monk, poet, and prophet, published *Nim ŭi ch'immuk* (1926; the silence of love) comprising eighty-eight meditative poems. Han and succeeding poets of resistance against the Japanese were constantly aware of their country's plight. Han sought insights into the terrible fate he and his country faced, and he found Buddhist contemplative poetry the lyric genre most congenial to this pursuit. Kim So-wŏl (1902–1934), a nature and folk poet, used simplicity, directness, and terse phrasing to good effect, as in his "Ch'ohon" (1925; "Summons of the Soul," 1964), an impassioned plea to his love that she return to him. Many of his poems in *Chindallaekkot* (1925; *Azaleas*, 1980) were set to music.

The Manchurian incident of 1931 and the Japanese invasion of China in 1937 induced the military authorities to impose wartime restrictions. The grinding poverty of the lower classes at home and abroad, especially in the Korean settlements in southern Manchuria, was the chief concern of the writers of the "new tendency" movement, a movement in opposition to the romantic and decadent writers of the day, which later became proletarian in spirit. Writers of the class-conscious Korean Artist Proletariat Federation (KAPF), organized in 1925, asserted the importance of propaganda and regarded literature as a means to the political ends of socialism. The movement also attracted fellow travelers, who emerged from the shadows with the Russian slogan *V narod* ("To the people") on their lips.

Modern Korean literature attained its maturity in the 1930s through the efforts of a group of extraordinarily talented writers. They drew freely upon European examples to enrich their art. Translation of Western literature continued, and works by I. A. RICHARDS, T. S. ELIOT, and T. E. Hulme (1883–1917) were introduced. This artistic and critical activity was a protest against the reduction of literature to journalism by influential magazines of the day, and to its use as propaganda by leftist writers.

The first truly successful poet of modern Korea was Chŏng Chi-yong (b. 1903), a master of his medium and a continuing presence. A student of Blake and Whitman, Chŏng rendered details with IMAGISTIC precision. His first published collection of poems, *Chŏng Chi-yong sijip* (1935; the poems of Chŏng Chi-yong), was followed by *Paengnoktam* (1941; White Deer Lake), which marks the high point of his career. The collection symbolically represents the progress of the spirit to lucidity, the fusion of man and nature.

A poetry of resistance, voicing a sorrow for the ruined nation with defiance but without violence or hatred, is the legacy of Yi Yuksa (1904–1944) and Yun Tong-ju (1917–1945). In such poems as the posthumously published "Kwangya" (1946; "The Wide Plain," 1980) and "Ch'ŏngp'odo" (1939; "Deep-Purple Grapes," 1980) Yi Yuksa sang of his winter of discontent and trial, and of his hopes for Korea's future. The poetry of Yun Tong-ju, an unimpassioned witness to Korea's national humiliation, expresses sorrow in response to relentless tyranny.

Korean fiction of the 1930s took shape in the void created by the compulsory dissolution of KAPF in 1935. Barred from all involvement with social or political issues, writers became preoccupied with technical perfection and the pursuit of pure art. Some, such as Yi Hyo-sŏk (1907–1942), returned to nature and sex; others retreated to the labyrinth of primitive mysticism, superstition, and shamanism, for example Kim Tong-ni (b. 1913); still others sympathetically portrayed characters born out of their time, defeated and lonely. Narrative sophistication and subtlety were achieved through a denial of the writer's commitment to his art or to himself. A notable exception was Yŏm Sang-sŏp (1897–1963), who produced a document of the time in his novel *Samdae* (1932; three generations), a dialogue between liberalism and socialism and a study in the disintegration of traditional values and social classes.

The early 1940s brought disaster to all branches of Korean literature, as the Japanese suppressed all writings in Korean. The Sino-Japanese war extended into the Pacific in 1941. Censorship, which had begun with the Japanese annexation of Korea in 1910, was intensified. Korea was liberated on 14 August 1945, and the Republic of Korea (South Korea) was born on 15 August 1948. On the literary scene the controversy between left and right that had raged in the late 1920s and early 1930s was revived. There were frantic groupings and regroupings, and most of the hardcore leftist writers, such as Yi Ki-yŏng (b. 1896) and Han Sŏr-ya (b. 1900), had gone to North Korea by 1948.

Some poets who came of age in the 1940s also went north, while others gave up writing entirely. In general, though, the liberation of 1945 produced a flowering of poetry of all kinds. Some poets, like PAK Tu-Jin, Shin Tong-yŏp (1930–1969), and Hwang Tong-gyu (b. 1938), were determined to bear witness to the events of their age. Some, like Sŏ Chong-Ju, Pak Mogwŏl (1916–1978), and Shin Kyŏng-nim (b. 1936), sought to further assimilate traditional Korean values. Still others, like Kim Su-yŏng (1921–1968), Kim Ch'un-su (b. 1922), Hwang Tong-gyu, and Chŏng Hyŏnjong (b. 1939), have drawn variously on Western traditions to enrich their work. All have sought to voice their own authentic testimony regarding the moments of crisis their culture has known.

The single overwhelming reality in Korean fiction since the Korean War has been the division of the country. As a symbol not only of Korea's trials but of the division of mankind and his alienation from himself and his world, the thirty-eighth parallel torments the conscience of every protagonist in modern Korean fiction in search of his destiny. Among South Korean writers, Hwang Sun-wŏn (b. 1915) and O Yŏng-su (b. 1914) have attempted to capture the images of the people in lyrical prose. Sŏnu Hwi (b. 1922) shows historical consciousness in his works, while Chŏn Kwang-yong (b. 1919) depicts a hapless human type all too common during Korea's years of servitude. Son Ch'ang-sŏp (b. 1946) has delved relentlessly into the conscience of the lost generation of the Korean War, Kim Sŭng-ok (b. 1941) into the inaction, self-deception, and boredom of the alienated generation of the 1960s. Yi Pŏm-sŏn (b. 1920) has studied the defeat and disintegration of good people; Sŏ Chŏng-in (b. 1938), the frustration of the educated; Yi Hoch'ŏl (b. 1932), the ways in which modern society negates man's freedom and individuality. Noteworthy writers of the *roman-fleuve* include Hwang Sun-wŏn, An Su-gil (b. 1911), and Pak Kyŏng-ni (b. 1927), the mother-in-law of the poet Kim Chi-ha (b. 1941). Pak's multivolume *T'oji* (1969 ff.; land) has been acclaimed for its commanding style and narrative techniques. In general, these works explore complex contemporary realities and universal types of humanity.

The "new" drama movement, which began in 1908, saw the rise and fall of small theater groups, such as the T'owŏrhoe, organized in 1923 by a group of Korean students studying in Tokyo, and finally the Kŭk Yesul Yŏn'guhoe (Theatrical Arts Research Society), organized in 1931 (dissolved by the Japanese in 1938) by members of a Western literature research society. Through their experimental theater, the members of the society staged contemporary Western plays and encouraged the writing of original plays, such as Yu Ch'i-jin's (b. 1905) *T'omak* (1933; clay hut). The paucity of first-rate playwrights and actors, the dearth of plays that satisfy dramatic possibilities, and the general living standards of the audience have caused the relative inactivity in the field. Domestic plays and historical pieces continue to be written and staged, but the future of the dramatic arts in contemporary Korea is uncertain.

In the 20th c. a number of Koreans have written in Western languages or in Japanese. Li Mirok (1899–1950), who wrote in German, and Younghill Kang (1903–1972) and Richard E. Kim (b. 1932), writing in English, have produced autobiographical accounts of their formative years. *The Diving Gourd* (1962), a novel, and *Love in Winter* (1969), a collection of short stories, by Yong Ik Kim (b. 1920) combine traditional subjects and modern techniques in portrayals of the farmers and fisherfolk of the south. Among Korean writers born or residing in Japan, Yi Hoe-sŏng (b. 1935; known in Japan as Li Kaisei) is outstanding. His story "Kinuta o utsu onna" (1970; "A Woman Who Ironed Clothes," 1977), a kind of short *Bildungsroman*, won the coveted Akutagawa Prize in 1972.

Modern South Korean writers are constantly occupied with the complex realities of modern urban life, and with the lives and emotions of a people enduring continuous uncertainty and repression. That lively literary activity continues in such a setting attests to the resilience, strength, and tenacity of 20th-c Korean writers.

BIBLIOGRAPHY: Lee, P. H., *Korean Literature: Topics and Themes* (1965): 101–19; Lee, P. H., Introduction to *Flowers of Fire: Twentieth-Century Korean Stories* (1974): xiii–xxv; Pihl, M. R., "Engineers of the Human Soul: North Korean Literature Today," *Korean Studies*, 1 (1977): 63–110; Kim, C., "Images of Man in Postwar Korean Fiction," *Korean Studies*, 2 (1978): 1–27; Lee, P. H., Introduction to *The Silence of Love: Twentieth-Century Korean Poetry* (1980): xi–xix; Lee, P. H., "Literature and Folklore," in H. Kim, ed., *Studies on Korea: A Scholar's Guide* (1980): 165–75

—PETER H. LEE

KOSINSKI, Jerzy

American novelist, essayist, and critic, b. 14 June 1933, Łódź, Poland; d. 3 May 1991, New York, N.Y.

K., who was very reticent about his past, admitted he was a mute for a time during his childhood in war-torn Poland. He earned degrees in history and political science in Łódź and taught at the Polish Academy of Sciences in Warsaw from 1955 to 1957. Disillusioned by the collectivist communist state, K. created dossiers for people he invented in the communist bureaucracy, who then "recommended" his traveling to the U.S. After arriving in America in 1957 K. continued his graduate studies in history and political science. He was a professor of English at Wesleyan, Princeton, and Yale universities, and served as president of the American Center of PEN for many years, beginning in 1973.

The Painted Bird (1965), K.'s first novel, depicts a brutally violent peasant world of Eastern Europe during World War II and a lost boy's struggle for survival. The novel traces the boy's growing acceptance of violence and revenge as the only way to contend with his environment. But he does not stop at this point; instead he develops a spirit of retaliation against everyone he encounters. The surrealistic, gothic setting suggests a Bosch painting. K.'s descriptions of this world and the horrors of Nazism are presented in a powerful, stunning language.

K.'s work illuminates the quest for identity, which is constantly threatened by the encroachments of modern society. His fictional characters find themselves trapped in an external world that is beyond their comprehension and control. They struggle against the constant danger of dissolution for a glimpse of self-recognition. Such ideas place the works of K. in the direct line of those of KAFKA, BECKETT, and ROBBE-GRILLET.

Steps (1968) records, in a cinematic series of disjointed fragments, the sensitive protagonist's inability to come to grips with the world and society. The novel both suggests and denies the possibility of regaining individual selfhood in a world that accepts only collective forms of behavior. This collectivism, against which an individualistic ethic is struggling to reassert itself, provides the background of all of K.'s novels.

K.'s third novel, *Being There* (1971), is a spare allegory and comic story of a man of limited mind, named Chance, who is propelled into positions of great power by his accidental appearance on television. K. explores the pervasive power of television over the modern consciousness and its ability to manipulate our emotional responses. Television becomes the source of all Chance's values and actions, creating him in its own image.

In *The Devil Tree* (1973) K. continued his experiments with fragmented form. Events are presented starkly and simplistically like scenes in a documentary film, although a significantly revised and expanded version was published in 1981. In this novel K. uses a flat, contemporary language that reflects the despair of his wealthy and aimless protagonist. An exemplar of the rootlessness of modern man, the protagonist wanders from Bangkok to Africa, and slides unintentionally from sexual exploits to murder.

Cockpit (1975) is K.'s longest and structurally most complex novel and carries to the extreme the tradition of the picaresque fictional mode. Its protagonist, Tarden, is a former agent of a powerful security agency of the American government. Now a fugitive, Tarden has successfully erased his presence from the world of dossiers and transcripts, and projecting into alternative identities, he continues to move freely across the contemporary landscape, testing his independence from the world and attempting to control its effects. Celebrating the private self as an institution of the highest order, *Cockpit* is an inventive extension of the novel of incident, which became K.'s trademark.

Blind Date (1977) is the most obviously philosophical of K.'s novels. The main character, George Levanter, a businessman, lives by his wits. As a survivor of World War II and a defector from Eastern Europe, he gets involved in several violent and sexual adventures. K. discusses the ideas of Jacques Monod, the French biologist and philosopher who views life as a series of random chances, the blind dates of the title. Such a philosophic perspective, however, weakens the narrative strength of the novel.

In *Passion Play* (1979) K. harnesses his usual obsessions about the fragmentation of contemporary existence to the oldest recorded ballgame, polo, and produces a kind of toughened code of individual responsibility and control somewhat akin to HEMINGWAY's. Fabian, the champion polo player, leads an itinerant life of sport and sex but acknowledges a degree of self-discipline and celebration unusual in a K. hero. K.'s descriptions of polo matches and sexual encounters in the novel match his finest writing.

K. wrote two volumes of social psychology under the pen name Joseph Novak. *The Future Is Ours, Comrade* (1960) analyzes the individual and collective behavior of Soviet citizens in their daily interactions. In *No Third Path* (1961), in which the psychology of the Soviet citizen is examined, K. scrutinized wider questions about the makeup of *homo sovieticus*.

K.'s fiction depicts in precise and graphic prose the awful "thereness," the brute factuality of the modern world. The wasteland of *The Painted Bird* and *Steps* pictures this world as effectively in its time as ELIOT's *The Waste Land* communicated the spiritual milieu of the 1920s.

K.'s genius lies in his ability to recreate a sense of primitive and dark reality by means of violent and sexual images. The charge of self-indulgence is often mitigated by the taut, objective qualities of his prose. In his ability to reveal the springs of modern life, he was one of the most skillful novelists of our time.

FURTHER WORKS: *Notes of the Author* (1965); *The Art of the Self* (1968); *Pinball* (1982)

BIBLIOGRAPHY: Cahill, D., "J. K.: Retreat from Violence," *TCL*, 18 (1972): 121–32; Plimpton, G., and Landesman, R., Interview with K., *Paris Review*, No. 54 (1972): 183–207; Cahill, D. J., Interview with K., *NAR*, 258, 1 (1973): 56–66; Klinkowitz, J., Interview with K., *Fiction International*, No. 1 (1973): 31–48; Coale, S., "The Quest for the Elusive Self: The Fiction of J. K.," *Crit*, 14, 3 (1973): 25–37; Sanders, I., "The Gifts of Strangeness: Alienation and Creation in J. K.'s Fiction," *PolR*, 19: 3–4 (1974): 171–89; Coale, S., "The Cinematic Self of J. K.," *MFS*, 20 (1974): 359–70; Klinkowitz, J., "J. K.," *Literary Disruptions: The Making of a Post-Contemporary American Fiction* (1975): 82–101; Cunningham, L., "The Moral Universe of J. K.," *America*, 139 (1978): 327–29

—SAMUEL C. COALE

KOSSAK, Zofia

Polish novelist and short-story writer, b. 8 Aug. 1890, Kośmin; d. 9 April 1968, Górki Wielkie

K. studied art in Warsaw and Geneva, but she never pursued it professionally. Instead, in 1922, she began a literary career with a volume of World War I memoirs titled *Pożoga* (*The Blaze*, 1927). During World War II K. was active in the Polish Underground, and in 1943–44 she was a prisoner in Auschwitz. She left Poland after the war and resided in England until 1956. After a few months in France she returned to Poland at the beginning of 1957 and lived there until her death.

In 1928 K. was acclaimed as the "new SIENKIEWICZ". The work that caused such acclaim, *Złota wolność* (golden freedom), a historical novel about politics, patriotism, and religious conflict in 18th-c. Poland, was soon followed by three others: *Krzyżowcy* (1935; *Angels in the Dust*, 1947), *Król trędowaty* (1937; *The Leper King*, 1945), and *Bez oręża* (2 vols., 1937; *Blessed Are the Meek*, 1944; *The Meek Shall Inherit*, 1948). These were historical novels dealing with the Crusades. As early as the publication of these three books, critics cooled in their opinion of K.'s works, but the public received them enthusiastically. The numerous novels that followed all reflected K.'s preoccupation and fascination with religion and history. Her shorter works of narrower scope, such as *Beatum scelus* (1930; Latin: the blessed guilt), a tale of a miraculous painting of the Madonna, or *Szaleńcy boży* (1932; God's madmen), a colorful collection of the lives of the saints, also give evidence of her abiding interest in these two subjects.

While living in England, K. wrote her memoirs about Auschwitz, *Z otchłani: Wspomnienia z lagru* (1946; from the abyss: memoirs from the camp). This book, so different in subject and character from her other works, has a stark and piercing vividness. While her historical novels could be compared to panoramic oil paintings, full of color and large in scale, her memoirs from the camp resemble black and white, brutally direct sketches. Their narrative is halting, unlike the flowing narrative of her historical novels; and a great sense of pain and of probing into the limits of human endurance is evident.

During the final eleven years of K.'s life, after her return to Poland in 1957, she wrote a number of short stories for young people and still more historical novels, most notable of which is the three-volume novel *Dziedzictwo* (1961–67; heredity). As always, K.'s chief focus is religion and history.

The steady and consistent decline in critics' favorable response to K.'s novels and tales was caused by what they uniformly regarded as K.'s shallow knowledge of history and her limited familiarity with philosophy and theology. K.'s knowledge of Catholic doctrine was considered minimal and her treatment of history often more fantastic than factual. Nevertheless, no critic ever found her wanting in narrative talent or in vivid imagination. K. demonstrated considerable literary skills, and her knowledge and love of the visual arts is evident in all of her writings. The panoramic quality of her historical novels, the appeal of colors, the richness of detail, and the likability of her characters account for her considerable popularity among readers. The wealth of factual material assembled by K. in her historical novels and the faithful rendition of the language of a given historical period she described balance the shortcomings in K.'s interpretation of history and in her understanding of philosophy and theology. K. was neither a critic's nor a scholar's writer, but her works fared extremely well with her readers, and the passing of time does not diminish their popularity.

FURTHER WORKS: *Kłopoty Kacperka góreckiego skrzata* (1926; rev. version, 1946; *The Troubles of a Gnome*, 1928); *Wielcy i mali* (1927); *Legnickie pole* (1930; expanded 1946; final version 1962); *Nieznany kraj* (1932); *Trembowla* (1939); *Przymierze* (1946; *The Covenant*, 1951); *Puszkarz Orbano* (1947); *Gród nad jeziorem* (1947); *Suknia Dejaniry* (1948); *Z miłości* (1958); *Bursztyny* (1958); *Warna* (1958); *Pątniczym szlakiem* (1959); *Topsy i Lupus* (1959); *Troja północy* (1960)

BIBLIOGRAPHY: Kridl, M., *A Survey of Polish Literature and Culture* (1956), p. 499; Gillon, A., and Krzyżankowski, L., *Modern Polish Literature* (1964), p. 170

—MALGORZATA PRUSKA-CARROLL

KOSTENKO, Lina

Ukrainian poet, literary critic, and screenwriter, b. 19 Mar. 1930, Rzhyshchiv, Kiev region

Born into a family of teachers, K. completed her secondary education in Kiev and was admitted in 1952 to the prestigious Gorky Institute of Literature in Moscow, from which she graduated with distinction (1956). Attracted to literature very early in life, K. began to write poetry as a child and published her first poems at the age of fifteen in the Kiev-based literary journal *Dnipro*. Later she joined the journal's editorial board, holding a position until 1966, when she was dismissed for defending fellow writers persecuted by the Soviet régime. In the early 1960s she was also employed by the Dovzhenko Film Studios in Kiev as a scriptwriter. In 1958 K. became a member of the Union of Writers of Ukraine. Today, she is a leading Ukrainian poet whose works enjoy immense popularity, both in Ukraine and abroad.

K. belongs to the so-called *"shestydesyatnyky,"* the generation of Ukrainian poets who began to publish during the period of the first thaw in the 1960s. K.'s three collections of poetry, *Prominnya zemli* (1957; the rays of earth), *Vitryla* (1959; sails), and *Mandrivky sertsya* (1961; *Wanderings of the Heart*, 1990), established her reputation as the premier Ukrainian poet both in Ukraine and in the diaspora, and at the same time unleashed a flood of criticism from many influential Soviet critics. Already in 1958, K. was accused of "formalism," "linguistic trickery, and a pessimism unworthy of a Soviet poet," "mannerism," "modernism," "sickly sorrow and skepticism," and a number of other "sins." After these attacks, K. did not publish for three years. The appearance of her third collection muted the criticism; and her work received considerable praise from various critics including those who had attacked it previously. However, soon the critical mood changed once more. In a *Pravda* article published 14 April 1963, Andry Skaba (b. 1905) attacked the ideological content of the poetry produced by the generation of young Ukrainian poets, singling out K., Ivan Drach (b. 1936), and Mykola Vinhranovsky (b. 1936). The viciousness of these attacks silenced K. for the next ten years. But while she did not publish, she continued to write, and her previous work was widely reprinted, read, and discussed by the Ukrainian émigré community in the West.

K.'s poetry is characterized by a sense of authenticity of expression, an innovative powerful use of language, refreshingly striking, an at times almost exotic imagery coupled with traditional metaphors cast in classical verse, and an uncompromising, almost violent individualism. Recognizing no other law than her own poetic and philosophical convictions, she has been known to refuse even the slightest editorial changes, insisting on the inviolability of her poetic word. Thoroughly nonpolitical, highly lyrical, at times profoundly speculative, the thematic range of her poetry includes autobiography, Ukrainian history, and, more recently, life in medieval Europe. Her early love poetry, such as the poem "Bila symfoniya" (1962; "The White Symphony," 1969), in which unauthentic puppy love is contrasted with a more mature relationship, is a good example of her ability to judge human experience and to understand human nature. Her historical novel inverse, *Marusya Churay* (1979; Marusya Churay), a poetic biography of the legendary 17th-c. Ukrainian folksinger, was instrumental in reviving knowledge about Ukraine's distant past and its rich customs and traditions that had been all but forgotten in the age of SOCIALIST REALISM. In that sense, K.'s poetry has performed a most important function: that of keeping alive the spirit of Ukrainian national identity during the dark days of enforced Russification and Sovietization of the Ukrainian people. In 1987, as a result of the policies of *glasnost* and *perestroika,* K. was finally awarded the coveted Shevchenko Prize for this work. *Marusya Churay* and her dramatic poem *Snih u Florentsiyi* (1989; snow in Florence), a subtle analysis of the interaction between religion and art, are now being staged in various theaters in Ukraine and performed by amateur groups in Ukrainian communities living in the West.

K. has been the leading poetical voice of Ukrainian literature for more than three decades. While remaining firm and constant in her convictions, she has grown in wisdom and knowledge. The political changes in the late 1980s enabled her to travel in the West and to establish direct contact with Ukrainian émigré intellectuals and poets and with many Western writers, which will no doubt have an impact on her future writings. Her popularity has now reached new heights. The latest collection of her poetry, *Vybrane* (1989; selected works), published in an edition of 60,000 copies and containing many of her previously banned poems, was immediately sold out; she continues to enjoy esteem and popularity both in Ukraine and abroad. Despite her considerable success, K. maintains a strong sense of self-criticism: "Poetry and popularity—is an ever-present polarity," she notes, reminding her readers and herself of the poet's true calling—to be a *vox humana,* to speak the truth and to serve the muse and the people.

Free from any didactic or dogmatic overtones, blessed with revealing insight, informed by ethical and moral concerns, K.'s poetry assures its author a prominent place in the pantheon of Ukrainian poetry.

FURTHER WORKS: *Nad berehamy vichnoyi riky* (1977); *Nepovtornist* (1980); *Skifska baba* (1981); *Sad netanuchykh skulptur* (1987); *Buzynovy tsar* (1987); *Vybryne* (1989)

BIBLIOGRAPHY: Luckyj, G. S. N., Introduction to *Four Ukrainian Poets* (1969): i–iv; Marshal, H., "Soviet National Poets," *Bulletin of the Center for Soviet and East European Studies,* 12 (1973): 1–2; Ovcharenko, M. M., "The Poets of Spirit and Truth: L. K. and Vasyl Symonenko," *UkrR,* 20 (1973): 71–82; Mihailovich, V. D., et al., eds., *Modern Slavic Literatures* (1976), Vol. 2: 481–83; Naydan, M. M., "Floating Flowers: The Poetry of L. K.," *Ulbandus Review,* 1 (1977): 138–39; Naydan, M. M., Afterword to *Selected Works* (1990): 141–50

—LEONID RUDNYTZKY

KOSZTOLÁNYI, Dezső

Hungarian poet, novelist, short-story writer, essayist, critic, and translator, b. 29 March 1885, Szabadka (now Subotica, Yugoslavia); d. 3 Nov. 1936, Budapest

K. was born to educated middle-class parents; his father was the principal of a secondary school. He studied at the universities of Budapest and Vienna from 1903 to 1906. Having already published extensively, K. became a staff member of *Budapesti napló* in 1906 and a regular contributor to the literary journal *Nyugat* from its founding in 1908. A prolific writer, he supported himself entirely by his pen. In addition to numerous volumes of poetry and short stories, five novels, and nine short plays, he published some forty volumes of translations and enough essays and journalism to fill thirty volumes. In 1913 he married the actress and author Ilona Harmos, who later wrote his biography. In his later years he worked zealously in the cause of Hungarian linguistic purity. K. received many honors both at home and abroad; he was a Chevalier of the French Legion of Honor and the first president of the Hungarian PEN Club. After years of suffering, he died of throat cancer.

In his first volume of poems, *Négy fal között* (1907; between four walls), his chief themes emerged: childhood memories, love of family, awareness of the fleeting nature of things, death, and a tug-of-war between God and the "Nihil" (nothingness). There is also an interesting juxtaposition between the idyllic but melancholy spirit of the Hungarian countryside and the exciting intellectual ferment of the metropolis, Budapest.

If his first volume made his name known, the second made him famous. *A szegény kis gyermek panaszai* (1910; the complaints of the poor little child) combines novelty of subject matter with a virtuosity of poetic form. The poet of twenty-five looks back on himself as a child, speaks in the voice of that child, and in a series of poems of great insight and charm, recreates a whole submerged world. It remains his most universally loved volume. But if he never surpassed this collection, he nevertheless maintained a very high level throughout his career. *Öszi koncert; Kártya* (1911; fall concert; cards)—two books in one volume—contains his longest poem, celebrating his love for his wife. *Mágia* (1912; magic), *Lánc,*

lánc, eszterlánc... (1914; ring around the rosy), and *Mák* (1916; poppy) are full of magic and enchantment; they close his early period, which was noted for its strongly Parnassian, SYMBOLIST and impressionist elements.

In *Kenyér és bor* (1920; bread and wine) a change is evident. The difficulties of the war years, and the collapse and chaos that followed, caused K. to lose the bittersweet melancholy of the basically happy person he had been, and it was replaced by true despair. The title of his next volume expressed this shift best: *A bús férfi panaszai* (1924; the complaints of the sad man) is an eloquent statement of the human predicament. His next volume, *Meztelenül* (1928; naked), contained free verse poems. Although K. was as great a master of free verse as of rhyme and the traditional verse forms, this volume never achieved the acclaim or popularity it deserved.

In 1935, on the occasion of his fiftieth birthday, *Összegyűjtött költeményei* (collected poems) was published. This book contained a whole new volume of poetry, *Számadás* (the summing-up), which some critics consider his greatest poetic achievement. A posthumous volume, *Szeptemberi áhitat* (1939; September devotion), brought out his previously uncollected poems, including the last poem published (1935) in his lifetime, the beautiful title poem.

K., one of the two or three greatest Hungarian poets of his age, and one of the perhaps half a dozen greatest Hungarian poets of all time, was almost as important as a writer of fiction. In his early volumes of short stories he moved from realism in the manner of Maupassant to a sometimes fantastic romanticism and then back to realism. In 1921 he published a short novel, *A rossz orvos* (the bad doctor), an in-depth psychological study of the disintegration of a family. A divorced couple's only child dies because of the incompetence of a "society doctor." Although the mother remarries, the memory of the dead child links the parents by indestructible ties of mutual reproach.

K.'s first full-length novel was *A véres költő* (1922; later retitled *Nero, a véres költő; The Bloody Poet*, 1927), which examines the character of Nero from youthful promise to utter depravity. K. perceives Nero primarily as a dilettante poet who cannot accept the fact that he lacks the artistic genius he admires in others. The novel was enthusiastically read—in German translation—by Thomas MANN, and subsequent editions carried his Prefatory Letter.

A visit to his native Szabadka filled him with pity for his now destitute family and provided the inspiration for two compassionate novels, *Pacsirta* (1924; Lark) and *Aranysárkány* (1925; the golden kite). "Pacsirta" is the affectionate nickname of an ugly spinster pitied and doted upon by her parents. In no other work did K.'s deep Christian compassion emerge as movingly as in this family portrait. At the same time he gives a delightful picture of life in a small country town at the turn of the century. In *Aranysárkány* a golden kite flown by a group of schoolboys symbolizes a way of life that has forever vanished. But K.'s palette soon darkens: the hero, an upright teacher, is destroyed by forces he cannot control. K.'s last novel, *Édes Anna* (1926; *Wonder Maid*, 1947), the story of a "perfect servant" who murders her masters, is a fascinating sociological study in aberrant behavior.

He concluded his fiction writing career with two triumphant volumes of short fiction. *Esti Kornél* (1933; Kornél Esti) is sometimes called an episodic novel, but it is best considered a short-story cycle, told by or about a delightful ne'er-do-well, the author's naughty alter ego. K. immortalized this charming creature not only in *Esti Kornél* but also in a famous poem, "Esti Kornél éneke" (1935; "song of Kornél Esti") and in seventeen more short

stories in his next—and last—collection, the gigantic *Tengerszem* (1936; tarn). The majority of Hungarian critics considers *Tengerszem* K.'s crowning achievement in fiction.

As a translator, K. was best noted for his 1914 volume *Modern költők* (modern poets); with this he helped to create the taste with which he expected himself and his contemporaries to be judged. The posthumously published *Idegen költők* (1942; foreign poets) further consolidated his reputation as a supreme interpreter of lyric and narrative poetry of many lands and tongues. His translations of four of Shakespeare's plays have also been justly praised; they are faithful, brilliant, and eminently actable.

As a journalist and essayist, K. was known for his wit, originality, beautiful style, and breadth of interests, and he invented several new journalistic genres. Indeed, there are critics in present-day Hungary who maintain that K.'s true significance is just now emerging, and that it lies in his activities as an essayist.

FURTHER WORKS: *Boszorkányos esték* (1908); *Lótoszevők* (1910); *A vonat megáll* (1911); *Bolondok* (1911); *Beteg lelkek* (1912); *Mécs* (1913); *Öcsém* (1915); *Tinta* (1916); *Bűbájosok* (1916); *Káin* (1918); *Katona-arcok* (1918); *Páva* (1919); *Béla, a buta* (1920); *Tintaleves papirgaluskával* (1917); *Alakok* (1929); *Szent Imre himnuszok* (1930); *Zsivalygó természet* (1930); *Kínai és japán versek* (1931); *Bölcsőtől a koporsóig* (1934); *A bábjátékos* (1940); *Hátrahagyott művei* (11 vols., 1940–1948); *Novellái* (3 vols., 1943); *Írók, festők, tudósok* (2 vols., 1958); *Babits-Juhász-K. levelezése* (1950); *Összegyűjtött versei* (2 vols., 1962); *Elbeszélései* (1965); *Mostoha és egyéb kiadatlan művek* (1965); *Álom és ólom* (1969); *Füst* (1970); *Nyelv és lélek* (1971); *Hattyú* (1972); *Én, te, ő* (1973); *Sötét bújócska* (1974); *Ércnél maradóbb* (1975); *Patália* (1976); *Egy ég alatt* (1976); *Látjátok, feleim* (1977); *Színházi esték* (2 vols., 1978)

BIBLIOGRAPHY: Klaniczay, T., and et al., *History of Hungarian Literature* (1964): 212–14; Reményi, J., *Hungarian Writers and Literature* (1964): 252–65; Sőtér, I., "The Place of Hungarian Poetry in Europe," *NHQ*, 25 (1967): 34–43; Brunauer, D. H., and Brunauer, S., *D. K.* (1982)

—DALMA H. BRUNAUER

KÖTLUM, Jóhannes úr

See Jóhannes úr Kötlum

KOTSYUBYNSKY, Mykhaylo

Ukrainian novelist and short-story writer, b. 17 Sept. 1864, Vinnytsya; d. 25 Apr. 1913, Chernihiv

Son of a petty government official and his sickly wife, K. completed his secondary education at the Sharhorod Religious Boarding School in 1880 and continued his studies at the Kamyanets-Podilsky Theological Seminary, from which he was expelled for his political activities in 1882. Unable to pursue university studies and under constant police surveillance, K. became a self-taught scholar, passed his teacher's examination in 1891, and supported himself and his family, after his father lost his position and his mother went blind, by teaching and private tutoring. From 1892 to 1897, he worked for an agricultural commission engaged in grape-phylloxera control in Moldavia and in the Crimea, and in 1898 he moved to Chernihiv, where he became a government clerk. While fighting off poverty, K. was extremely active in Ukrainian cultural and political life and developed contacts with leading intellectuals, such as the writer Ivan FRANKO and the ethnographer and literary scholar Volodymyr Hnatyuk (1871–1926) in western Ukraine, at that time part of the Austro-Hungarian Empire.

An avid reader, K. was drawn to literature early in life. Influenced by Ukraine's national bard, Taras Schevchenko (1814–1861), as well as West European writers and thinkers, K. became Ukraine's leading prose writer of all time. His extensive travels to West European countries, including a sojourn (1909–1911) on the isle of Capri, are reflected in his works. K. gained considerable fame in his later years; many of his stories were translated into several European languages during his lifetime, and a three-volume Russian edition of his collected works was published in 1911–1914.

K.'s early stories, such as "Andry Soloveyko" (1884; "Andry Soloveyko"), "21 hrudnya, na Vvedeniye" (1885; "the 21st of December of the day of presentation"), "Na viru" (1891; a common-law marriage), are steeped in 19th-c. ethnographic realism and reflect the populist ideas prevalent at that time, but his later work is characterized by a sophisticated impressionistic style and subtle psychological probings into the human soul. Among his best are the short stories "Lyalechka" (1901; "the dolly"), an ironic account of an intellectual's assessment of his life, "Tsvit yabluni" (1902; "Apple Blossom," 1973), a story about a writer who plans to use artistic observations made of his dying daughter, and "Podarunok na imenyny" (1912; "The Birthday Present," 1973), a psychological study of a boy whose father takes him to a hanging for his birthday.

K.'s most famous works are the novella "Intermezzo" (1909; "intermezzo"), a stylistic masterpiece in which elements of REALISM and IMPRESSIONISM serve to heighten the psychological effect, and the pastoral novel *Tini zabutykh predkiv* (1911; *Shadows of Forgotten Ancestors*, 1981), which, set in the Carpathian mountains, presents a hauntingly beautiful slice of life of the Hutsul folk by exploring local legends and beliefs. This work, along with four other stories of K., was made into a successful film of the same title in 1967.

A consummate stylist, unsurpassed as a writer of Ukrainian prose, K. has become a classic writer of Ukrainian literature. His work is required reading in schools and the subject of countless scholarly investigations. In both Vinnytsya and Chernihiv, K. museums have been established to honor his memory and his lasting achievement.

FURTHER WORKS: *V putakh shaytana i inshi opovidannya* (1899); *Po-lyudskomu: opovidannya z bessarabskoho zhyttya* (1900); *Opovidannya* (1903); *Poyedynok i inshi opovidannya* (1903); *Debyut* (1911); *Lysty do Volodymyra Hnatyuka* (1914); *Tvory* (1924); *Tvory* (5 vols., 1925); *Vybrani tvory* (1927); *Tvory* (5 vols., 1930); *Vybrani tvory* (1934); *Vybrani tvory* (1936); *Vybrani opovidannya* (1937); *Vybrani tvory*, (4 vols., 1948); *Opovidannya. Novely. Povisti* (1953); *Povisti ta opovidannya* (1954); *Tvory* (3 vols., 1955); *Vybrani tvory* (1957); *Tvory* (6 vols., 1962); *Tvory* (7 vols., 1975). FURTHER WORKS IN ENGLISH: *Chrysalis and Other Stories* (1958); *Fata Morgana* (1976; rev. ed., 1980)

BIBLIOGRAPHY: Kalenichenko, N., Introduction to *The Birthday Present and Other Stories* (1973): 3–10; Mihailovich, V. D., et al., eds., *Modern Slavic Literatures* (1976), Vol. 2: 483–86; Kolesnyk, P., Introduction to *Fata Morgana and Other Stories* (1976): 5–10; Yaremenko, V., Introduction to *Fata Morgana and Other Stories* (1980): 5–11; Rubchak, B., "The Music of Satan and the Bedevilled World: An Essay on M. K.," in *Shadows of Forgotten Ancestors* (1981): 77–121; Nowosad, M. E., "Mysterious and Irrational Elements in the Works of M. K. and Theodor Storm," in Bristol, E., ed., *East European Literature: Selected Papers from the Second World Congress for Soviet and East European Studies* (1982): 43–56

—LEONID RUDNYTZKY

KOUROUMA, Ahmadou

Ivoirian novelist (writing in French), b. 1927, Boundiali, Côte d'Ivoire

K. was reared in Malinke land, on the border between Côte d'Ivoire and Guinea. In his twenties he sided with the independence movement: he was expelled from the Higher Technical School in Bamako for leading a student strike; when drafted by the French and ordered to help control nationalist demonstrations in Abidjan, he refused to do so and was consequently sent to Indochina. K.'s combat experience was limited; instead, he worked mostly as an interpreter in Saigon. In 1954 he left the army and went to France to study at the Institute for Actuaries in Lyon. He returned to Abidjan in 1961; but by 1963 was exiled for speaking out against governmental abuses and was never again allowed to practice his profession in Côte d'Ivoire. He worked successfully as an actuary in Algeria, Cameroon, and Togo. In 1992 he retired and returned to Côte d'Ivoire intending to devote himself full-time to writing.

He had first turned to writing to voice his disappointment with the arbitrariness, corruption, and nepotism of the Ivoirian government after independence. Completely unknown, he could not find a publisher for *Les soleils des indépendances* (1968; *The Suns of Independence*, 1980) and submitted his manuscript to a Canadian literary competition. He won and his novel was published by the University of Montreal Press. It attracted much attention and critical acclaim and was reissued in Paris in 1970.

This novel indicts both colonialism and the African bourgeoisie that rules after independence. Its hero is Fama, the last legitimate heir of the Dumbuya dynasty, who lost his chiefdom under the French and then was impoverished by independence, even though he had supported it. K's criticism of the régime is muted, however. Unfairly though he may have been treated, the illiterate Fama, unrealistically enamored of his aristocratic past, is not viable in the modern world.

Alongside Fama is his wife Salimata, a victim of both the present and the past. The couple has no children in accordance with traditional beliefs this is the worst possible tragedy. In despair, Salimata seeks help from both marabouts and fetishists, only to find that they injure and exploit her. Thus K., while exposing abuses under independence, also denounces traditional practices. K. presents Salimata as an important character at a time when most African novelists assigned women marginal roles. He is also ahead of his time when he questions the custom of excision and the automatic assumption that childlessness is the woman's fault.

K.'s style reflects the improvisational traits of oral literature. The omniscient narrator addresses both fictional characters and readers directly. With his use of pronouns: we, you, thou, he elicits response. With storytelling techniques such as rhetorical questions, repetition, autocorrection, exclamations, digressions, and songs he evokes oral presentation; an effect corroborated by redundance as several adjectives qualify a noun, three animals convey one image, multiple verbs describe one action.

The narrative is captivating, the characters are finely drawn, the milieu comes alive, but K's special contribution is the language in which he writes. As he has said, he writes in Malinke using French words. He discards the foreign connotations which make French unsuitable to express African reality. He peppers the text with Malinke words, with proverbs which reflect indigenous speech, with animal imagery. He distorts French syntax and structure, and invents words so as to adapt language to Fama's thought patterns.

In language, style, and content K's second novel, *Monnè, outrages et défis* (1990; *Monnew*, 1993), is consonant with *Les soleils des indépendances*. K. now paints Fama's beloved fabled past; he warns readers that they are entering a very different cultural world. Indeed French doesn't even have a word for "*monnè*" because the French have never experienced the outrage, defiance, and contempt that the Malinke have encountered since the 1850s.

The novel illuminates K's view of colonization and of African history. It is the story of Djigui Keita, king of Soba in northwest Côte d'Ivoire, surrounded by his griots, his court, and his people. The kingdom is not paradise, but it has remained stable for centuries and is comprehensible to all. Change occurs with the long foretold arrival of strangers who occupy the land. The previously powerful king, now confused and helpless, becomes merely an observer of the suffering of his people subjected to forced labor and taxes.

The vicissitudes of French history are reflected in Soba. Both world wars come and go; de Gaulle's followers are a little better than Petain's, but instability has set in for good and matters don't improve with independence. Djigui cannot understand the changes, let alone adapt to them, he is paralyzed by ineffective islamic and indigenous rituals and by a total inability to communicate with the intruders.

Linguistic differences cause a shift of power from governmental entities to the interpreter. It is he who speaks both languages and thereby controls events by mistranslating, admonishing or sweet-talking as he sees fit. Words are the very subject of the novel. Repeatedly K. illustrates the effects of the impossibility of translating words since underlying concepts differ. For instance, the Malinke have no word "civilization," and cannot fathom what the French mean when they claim that they have come to "civilize" them. The author's efforts to "Africanize" the French language are less daring and colorful in *Monnè*, but the consequences of linguistic barriers grow more dire because they directly affect an entire people, not just specific individuals.

The two novels, which represent the totality of K.'s writings to date, form a whole which depicts the author's view of his people's plight. As he did in *Les soleils des indépendances,* K. exposes in *Monnè* the consequences of forcible, incomprehensible change. The problems of cultural and linguistic incompatibility he describes are deeply rooted in Malinke land, but they are also universal, as current events prove daily. The poignancy and relevance of K's works are undeniable.

BIBLIOGRAPHY: Echenim, K., "La structure narrative de *Les soleils des indépendances*," *PA*, 107 (1978): 139-61; Koné, A.,"L'effet du réel dans les romans de K.," *EF*, 31, 1 (1995): 13-22; Joseph, G., "Free Indirect Discourse in *Les soleils des indépendances*," *AJS*, 6, 1 (1988-89): 69-84; Harrow, K., *Thresholds of Change in African Literature* (1994): 257-90; Midihouan, G. O., "A. K.; or, The Bitter Knowledge of Black Humiliation," *RAL*, 25, 3 (1994): 231-34; Poller, N., "An Authentic K.," *RAL*, 25, 3 (1994): 235-43; Gassama, M., *La langue d'A. K.; ou, le français sous le soleil d'Afrique* (1995)

—NATALIE SANDOMIRSKY

KRAMER, Theodor

Austrian poet, b. 1 Jan. 1897, Niederhollabrunn; d. 3 April 1958, Vienna

K., the son of a Jewish country doctor, was educated in Vienna. From October 1915 to the end of World War I he served in the army, and after being seriously wounded in Volhynia he was stationed in Italy as an officer. Following a brief period at the University of Vienna, K. worked in the book trade and contributed poetry to a number of periodicals and newspapers, winning various prizes. Illness forced him to become a freelance writer in 1931, and two years later he married the actress Inge Halberstam. In July 1939 K. emigrated to England, and from January 1943 on he was employed as a librarian at the County Technical College in Guildford (Surrey). His wife having left him and his mother having perished at Auschwitz, the poet became increasingly lonely and depressed. He was afflicted with a variety of ailments but continued to create prolifically. K. died six months after his return to Vienna.

K. wrote poetry exclusively. Playing, as he put it, the accordion rather than the harp and making music on an "organ of dust," this powerful social realist strove to be the voice of the underprivileged and inarticulate. His sociopsychologically observed typology of rural and urban outsiders and outcasts of society includes peasants and prostitutes, ditch diggers and drunkards, hired hands and hunchbacks. It was the poet's aim to give an unvarnished and unsentimental picture of their world and to express in his poetic "landscapes" and "cityscapes" even complex and abstruse situations, relationships, and feelings with directness and folk-song simplicity. His bittersweet poems are written in a variety of forms, including the cyclical, but most of them are short, have simple rhymes, and abound in colloquialisms. Despite the naturalistic bleakness and elegiac tone of these poems, K.'s great sensitivity and empathy make much of his poetry poignant and hauntingly beautiful. A childlike faith and tenderness often shine through the decay, the dissolution, and the despair.

K.'s first collection, *Die Gaunerzinke* (1929; the tramp's mark—the title refers to the marks made on certain houses by vagrants to serve as a guide for other tramps and thieves), was widely noticed and praised, but in exile the poet had to endure a decade of disappointment trying to find a publisher for what he regarded as his best and most mature work, the collection *Lob der Verzweiflung* (1972; in praise of despair). Since the early 1980s the T. K. Society of Vienna has attempted to focus attention on K. and other exiled writers by organizing symposia, lectures, and readings as well as publishing a journal and monographs.

FURTHER WORKS: *Kalendarium* (1930); *Wir lagen in Wolhynien im Morast* (1931); *Mit der Ziehharmonika* (1936); *Verbannt aus Österreich* (1943); *Die untere Schenke* (1946); *Wien 1938: Die grünen Kader* (1946); *Vom schwarzen Wein* (1956); *Einer bezeugt es...* (1960); *Gesammelte Gedichte* (3 vols., 1984–87); *Orgel aus Staub* (1983, 1991); *Der Braten resch, der Rotwein herb* (1988); *Lass still bein dir mich liegen* (1994); *Spätes Lied* (1996); *Unser Land* (1996). **FURTHER WORKS IN ENGLISH:** *Love in London* (1995)

BIBLIOGRAPHY: Zohn, H., "T. K., Neglected Austrian Poet," *GL&L*, 9, 2 (1956): 11–24; Schmied, W., "T. K.," *WZ*, 3, 1 (1957): 1–16; Chvojka, E., "T. K.," *Akzente*, 9 (1962): 143–57; Zohn, H., "T.K.'s letzte Jahre," *Wiener Juden in der deutschen Literatur* (1964): 73–82; Zohn, H., "Lob der Verzweiflung," *MAL*, 6 (1973): 211–16; Klinger, K., "Lebenslängliche Isolation: T. K.," in Spiel, H., ed., *Die zeitgenössische Literatur Österreichs* (1976): 352–57; Herz-Kestranek, M., *Oh, käm's auf mich nicht an!* (1987); Herz-Kestranek, M., *Über K. hinaus und zu ihm zurück* (1990); Strigl, D., "*Wo niemand zuhaus ist, dort bin ich zuhaus*," (1993); Chvojka, E., et al., "*Vielleicht hab ich es leicht, weil schwer, gehabt.*" *Eine Lebenschronik* (1997)

—HARRY ZOHN

KRASKO, Ivan

(pseud. of Ján Botto; other pseuds.: Janko Cigáň and Bohdan J. Potokinov) Czechoslovak poet (writing in Slovak), b. 12 July 1876, Lukovištia; d. 3 March 1958, Bratislava

After attending high school in Slovakia and Romania, K. studied engineering in Prague, worked in the chemical industry in Bohemia, and served as a soldier in Poland and Russia during World War I. Between 1918 and 1938 he was a civil servant and politician: he was a member of Parliament (1920–29) and a senator of the Agrarian Party (1929–39).

K. turned to literature during his university years and soon was hailed by leading poets and critics as an important new talent. He introduced MODERNISM and SYMBOLISM into Slovak poetry. He was a gifted representative of the tragic view of life, common in European poetry at the turn of the century. His poems show an affinity to those of Verlaine, Baudelaire, Rimbaud, and Mallarmé in their self-centered lyricism and despair. His rhythms, structure, and diction differed from the poetic style of the two leading Slovak poets, Hviezdoslav (pseud. of Pavol Országh, 1849–1921) and Svetozár Hurban Vajanský (1847–1916). Their traditional attitude toward national struggles and their introspective lyricism found some echo in K.'s poetry, but K.'s verse generally lacks the spark of hope and faith in his nation's future and resurrection that were present in the work of the older poets.

K.'s two slender collections of poems, *Noxet solitudo* (1909; Latin: night and solitude) and *Verše* (1912; poems), reflect his pessimism, the unfortunate situation of the Slovak people at the turn of the century, and the spiritual crisis of modern man. An example of his despairing mood is the poem "Jehovah" (1909; "Jehovah," 1924), in which K. curses his people and invokes Jehovah's vengeance on the Slovak nation for its idleness. Other poems in the 1909 volume reflect similar attitudes. K.'s feeling of belonging to his enslaved nation is expressed in "Otrok" ("The

Slave," 1924), in which he returns to his roots with a protest against enslavement and a dim hope that resurrection of his people is still possible. There is, however, none of the visionary quality of the previous generation of Slovak poets. K. rarely moves from a defeatist attitude to a call for action and struggle. His deep attachment to his homeland, from which he was separated in his youth, is also expressed in the poems "Otcova rol'a" ("father's field"), "Baníci" ("miners"), and "Vesper dominicae." K. writes in gentle terms of his return home, where his mother, in tears, remembers him while she is praying. Poems that express K.'s compassion for the sad fate of his nation and his protest against its enslavement are not, however, dominant in his poetry. Most characteristic of his work are personal lyrics, imbued with a tragic and pessimistic view of life, replete with dark metaphors, and only rarely turning from despair to a hope of overcoming destiny.

Although K. did not resume writing after World War I, his poetry strongly influenced the generation of Slovak poets between the wars. Moreover, many Slovak poets of today echo his introspective lyricism, his sympathy for humanity, and his concise clarity.

BIBLIOGRAPHY: Krčméry, Š., "A Survey of Modern Slovak Literature," *SEER*, 7 (1928–29): 160–70; Selver, P., "The Literature of the Slovaks," *Slavonic Review*, 12 (1934): 691–703; Mráz, A., *Die Literatur der Slowaken* (1943): 152; Noge, J., *An Outline of Slovakian Literature* (1968): 49–51; Richter, L., *Slowakische Literatur* (1979): 51–56

—JOSEPH M. KIRSCHBAUM

KRAUS, Karl

Austrian satirist, cultural critic, aphorist, and poet, b. 28 April 1874, Gitschin, Moravia, Austro-Hungarian Empire (now Jičín, Czechoslovakia); d. 12 June 1936, Vienna

When K. was three years old, his father, who was a wealthy manufacturer, moved with his family to Vienna. K.'s school and university years coincided with the heyday of the Viennese Burgtheater and the lively literary activity so characteristic of the Austro-Hungarian capital. From both K. received decisive impressions. Although he matriculated in the law school at the university, he attended only philosophical and literary lectures without ever working toward a degree. He resisted his strong inclinations toward the stage; his dramatic gifts, however, subsequently evolved into his uncommon accomplishments as a reader of his own works and those of others.

K.'s bent for polemics and satire is manifest in his early pamphlets, *Die demolierte Literatur* (1896; the demolished literature) and *Eine Krone für Zion* (1898; a crown for Zion). An event of decisive importance for his literary career was his founding of *Die Fackel* in 1899. The early contributors to this periodical included August STRINDBERG, Frank WEDEKIND, Georg TRAKL, Otto STOESSL, Detlev von Liliencron (1844–1909), Peter Altenberg (1859–1919), Richard Dehmel (1863–1920), Else Lasker-Schüler (1876–1945), and Berthold Viertel (1885–1953), but from 1911 to the time of K.'s death in 1936, *Die Fackel* was written exclusively by K. himself. It was, in a sense, a spiritual diary, but it was also a militantly ethical periodical that began before long to play a unique role in the world of German letters. As conceived by K., the concern of his fighting mission, although pursued in *Die Fackel* by purely literary means, was less with literary matters than with generally spiritual and ethical matters. His writing posed a constant challenge to the prevailing corruption of the spirit in all domains of public life—in politics, law and justice, literature, and art. K. came to be the accuser of everything that was rotten in the state of Austria. His most embittered hatred had its target in the press, which he attacked with a persistence that might suggest that he considered such activity the purpose of his life. Indeed, to unmask the press as the embodiment of intellectual prostitution, as the instrument par excellence of the trivialization and mechanization of life, as a menace to the already sorely imperiled state of peace, was to him a fate-imposed obligation.

That K. saw the press and the dangers of its enormous power as he did—the Vienna press of his age showed journalism in its ugliest form—followed inevitably from the ethical imperative that was the supreme law of his life and his every endeavor. Because he measured everything by absolute standards, condoning no compromise however trivial, he was bound to regard the journalist who works under the aegis of day-to-day contingencies rather than of ultimate principles as the embodiment of everything evil. The slightest deviation from absolute integrity signified to him man's dehumanization, which, undermining society, must finally lead to its general collapse.

K.'s polemical essays, in which he fought against the enslavement of man's natural drives by state and church, appeared in book form in the volumes *Sittlichkeit und Kriminalität* (1908; morality and criminality) and *Die chinesische Mauer* (1910; the great wall of China). Like all his writing, these essays were first published in *Die Fackel*.

K.'s conception of language was of central importance to him and is of similar importance in any evaluation of his work. The word and the thing, he held, were one. In language he saw the magic passkey to unlock all doors. Indeed, his feared and fearful attacks—the purpose of which was to unmask the hypocrisy and the corruption of his age by making them, through the instrumentality of his mordant wit, a laughingstock for his readers—used language as a means to destroy the adversary. Purity of language was to him the measure of the writer's integrity.

K. was thus not only the merciless and incorruptible critic of his age but also the teacher of a new and wakeful awareness of language. There are many whose ears he trained to discern the hollow ring of vacuous phrases, of puff and lie, of shamelessness and perfidy that assaulted them from the columns of the daily press, particularly in that time of war. And there are many whom he strengthened in the integrity of their conduct.

The drama *Die letzten Tage der Menschheit* (abridged tr., *The Last Days of Mankind*, 1974) was written during World War I, first appeared as a special issue of *Die Fackel*, and was published in book form in 1922. It bursts all conventional dimensions and was a climax in K.'s creative career. In K.'s words, "by earthly measurements" a performance would require some ten nights on the stage. It is actually intended to be read rather than performed; the imagination of the reader has to provide the stage. K. never doubted that Austria's declaration of war in 1914 marked the beginning of the end of that state. This satirical tragedy evolves through the prophetic power of its creator into an apocalyptic warning of an impending world-engulfing disaster. It represents a vast fresco of events at the front as well as behind the lines and back home. A

more powerful denunciation of war has never been written. The work has no single hero, although each scene, in this immense concert of scenes, has a hero of its own. There is no unity of time, place, or action, but the unity of the idea is for that very reason all the more compelling. On the basis of *Die letzten Tage der Menschheit*, professors at the Sorbonne in Paris repeatedly proposed K. for the Nobel Peace Prize.

K. was one of the very few who never succumbed even for a moment to the chauvinistic poison that filled the air in those years. The only writer of rank to stand firmly against the Austrians who were embracing the war en masse, he challenged with absolute courage the powers that be. In Berlin, where the tide of enthusiasm for war was running high, he read in public his sketch "Kant und ein Kantianer" (1917; "A Kantian and Kant," 1977), in which he contrasted the philosopher with Emperor Wilhelm II, who liked to fancy himself as fashioned in the mold of Kant and as one who embodied Kant's categorical imperative, but who was here referred to as a "second-class stage hero." The hope that the war would end in a German victory was to K. absolute treason, high treason against the spirit.

In his satirical sketches, epigrams, and dramas, K. waged a relentless war of cultural criticism against which the press, his favorite target, had no defense but that of trying to ignore the attacker. His other victims, hopelessly discredited and held up as laughingstocks, also preferred on the whole to limit themselves to reproaching him with the negative character of his criticism, which they claimed "could only destroy but not build up." To be sure, the great satirist must have a clear conception of absolute values. His endeavor to remove the worthless must be inspired by the desire to make room for the worthwhile; and a profound faith in positive values and affirmative truths is actually the basic prerequisite for his creativity.

K. was always ready to praise excellence where he saw it. He admired the great satirists of the past like Georg Christoph Lichtenberg (1742–1799) and Johann Nestroy (1801–1862) and contemporary writers as well: Strindberg, Wedekind, Altenberg, Trakl, Lasker-Schüler, and others. He revived interest in the great poets of the German baroque, and through his public readings of Shakespeare's plays he successfully opposed the trend of abandoning Shakespeare's works to the commercialized theater of the big city, with its optical illusions and sound effects. In his "Theater der Dichtung" ("literary theater"), what he called his public readings, standing alone at the lectern, he revealed the true power of the works of GOETHE, HAUPTMANN, and many other writers.

In matters of form K. was no innovator. He said of himself that he was one who continued in the tradition of Shakespeare (in the Schlegel-Tieck translation) and the "lambent flame of language" of the older Goethe, both of whom exerted the strongest influence on him. In matters of content, however, his work is far removed from the poetry of the neoclassicists and neoromanticists. It bears the imprint of his age, having its roots in the past and at the same time pointing the way to the future.

Many of K.'s poems are cerebral, their content frequently identical with his militant prose. Yet among his poems there are pieces of great lyrical power in which beauty of language and emotional content merge in perfect harmony. They are to be found in K.'s nine volumes of *Worte in Versen* (1916–30; words in verse). A collection of penetrating essays on questions of language, which K. was preparing for publication during the years 1933 and 1934, appeared only after his death under the title of *Die Sprache* (1937; language). The collected volumes *Sprüche und Widersprüche*

(1909; aphorisms and contradictions), *Pro domo et mundo* (1912; Latin: for home and world), and *Nachts* (1918; at night) prove K. to be one of the greatest masters of the aphorism.

K. died when Austria was facing the menace of Nazism at its western borders—this was two years before the forced Anschluss. The outbreak of barbarism in neighboring Germany may have precipitated his death. His last work, written during this time, was not published until 1952: through an analysis of language and speech, *Die dritte Walpurgisnacht* (the third Walpurgis Night) portrays the horror of the Hitler era—the dictatorship of the Führer and his literary henchmen. In this work K. provides a perceptive analysis of the diabolical nature of the Third Reich.

During his lifetime the impact of K.'s work was essentially restricted to Vienna. Since the end of World War II wider circles in the realm of German letters have begun to bear witness to his importance and have acknowledged his influence, although not as yet in full proportion to his extraordinary contribution to the artistic and intellectual life of his age. Although K.'s works condemned his time and although he foresaw prophetically the dangers inherent in modern civilization, leading to an ultimate apocalypse, his work in its totality is nevertheless a profession of faith in man and in the worth of life. He was deeply confident that his work would endure and that through it he would live on when he was gone. In this, too, he has proved to be prophetic.

FURTHER WORKS: *Heine und die Folgen* (1910); *Nestroy und die Nachwelt* (1912); *Weltgericht* (1919); *Ausgewählte Gedichte* (1920); *Literatur; oder, Man wird doch da sehn* (1921); *Untergang der Welt durch schwarze Magie* (1922); *Traumstück* (1923); *Wolkenkuckucksheim* (1923); *Traumtheater* (1924); *Epigramme* (1927); *Die Unüberwindlichen* (1928); *Literatur und Lüge* (1929); *Zeitstrophen* (1931); *Shakespeares Sonette* ([translations] 1933); *Shakespeares Dramen* ([translations] 2 vols., 1934–1935). FURTHER WORKS IN ENGLISH: *Poems* (1930); *In These Great Times* (1976); *Half Truths and One- and One-Half Truths: Selected Aphorisms* (1976); *No Compromise: Selected Writings* (1977)

BIBLIOGRAPHY: Liegler, L., *K. K. und sein Werk* (1920); Heller, E., *The Disinherited Mind* (1952; new ed., 1971): 235–56; Muschg, W., *Von Trakl zu Brecht* (1961): 174–97; Daviau, D., "The Heritage of K. K.," *BA*, 38 (1964): 248–56; Schick, P., *K. K. in Selbstzeugnissen und Bilddokumenten* (1965); Field, F., *The Last Days of Mankind: K. K. and His Vienna* (1967); Iggers, W. A., *K. K.: A Viennese Critic of the Twentieth Century* (1967); Weigel, H., *K. K.; oder, Die Macht der Ohnmacht* (1968); Zohn, H., *K. K.* (1971); Janik, A., and Toulmin, S., *Wittgenstein's Vienna* (1973): 67–91; Williams, C. E., *The Broken Eagle: The Politics of Austrian Literature from Empire to Anschluss* (1974): 187–235; Stern, J. P., "K. K. and the Idea of Literature," *Encounter*, Aug. 1975: 37–48; Grimstad, K., *Masks of the Prophet: The Theatrical World of K. K.* (1981)

—FREDERICK UNGAR

At the beginning of April 1899 the first issue of his [K.'s] *Fackel* appeared, and the most bitter and persistent attacks ever launched against the press dated from that time. The warning voice of conscience had awakened, and it spoke to a deluded time; that voice wanted to prove how deeply that time had sunk into bondage and how dangerous was the enemy, who was on the point of destroying an old culture. It was unavoidable that against the assault of such an enlightener the solid resistance of all those who considered the tendencies of the new epoch the expression of their own nature was marshaled. And nobody will find it surprising that the lowest, most underhanded and perfidious means ever used by a tyranny over the mind were brought into action against K. K., to force him into silence or at least to make the motives of his fight suspect. But for many . . . he was a spiritual liberator. One listened to these unaccustomed harangues, one felt joy at this young, self-intoxicating power; and not a few have to thank this daring fighter for the fact that they would remain true to themselves and were not pulled down into a God-estranged time.

Leopold Liegler, *K. K. und sein Werk* (1920), p. 51

K.'s work, as that of few other writers, stands totally devoted to one basic idea that language is of crucial importance to human existence. Every aspect of his endeavors, his public readings, his adaptations of Shakespeare and Offenbach, his poems, dramas, essays, and aphorisms serve the one purpose of revitalizing the word. This cannot be otherwise, for any contradictions or discrepancies in K.'s work (and life) would render him guilty of the same hypocrisy with which he charged his contemporaries. However, this cohesiveness demands that any judgment of K.'s writings involve them as a unit. If his central idea concerning language possesses continued validity, as the increasing attention today to the role of language would indicate, then so do all of his works which exemplify only this idea.

Despite the outward lack of success of his lifelong crusade on behalf of language, K.'s dedication to his principles continued with undiminished vigor to the end of his life. . . .

Donald Daviau, "The Heritage of K. K.," *BA*, 38 (1964), 255

Like Wittgenstein and Schoenberg, both of whom admired his work greatly, the satirist was obsessed with problems of language. To K. language is not merely the medium of thought: thought and language are related in a complex and semimystical dialectic which he, as a poet, was never concerned to analyse in any philosophical way. Thought, he asserts, does not possess an independent existence in this world, but through the prism of the material circumstances of life is dispersed and scattered among the elements of language. Or, to vary the metaphor, the world is sifted through the sieve of language. Above all, the function of words is not decorative: this is the burden of the satirist's attack on the Impressionists in Austria, an attack exemplified by K.'s description of Hofmannsthal in his attempt to revivify the baroque drama as "living among golden goblets in which there is no wine."

K. practised what he preached. With a style of extraordinary concentration, allusiveness and wit, with a moral fanaticism that bordered on the pathological, the satirist elevated language to apocalyptic significance and intensity. Since he was convinced that words are possessed of an innate magical potency by which they can revenge themselves on societies and individuals who pervert them or use them idly, K. would agonise for hours over the revision of his work and claimed in one of his epigrams that he worked longer on a single word than other men on a novel.

Frank Field, *The Last Days of Mankind: K. K. and His Vienna* (1967), pp. 12–13

K. K.'s satire is more deeply rooted in its own medium than the work of any other recent writer of German prose. "The German language," he said, "is the profoundest of all languages, but German speech is the shallowest." The genius of K. K. could not have arisen from the ground of another language; for the inspiration of his satirical work is the contrast between his faith in words and the speech of the faithless: and it is German that offers the biggest scope for this faith as well as its blasphemers.

His thinking was a voyage of exploration in a landscape of words. No other Western language allows adventures on such a scale, for every other language has been more thoroughly explored, surveyed and ordered. What in modern English may be a wrestle with words, is a vast conflagration in German, with victories more glorious and defeats more devastating; and what, in the workaday life of words, is a relaxed walk through an English park, is in German a venture into exposed territory. While the English writer or speaker, over long stretches of his verbal enterprise, is protected by the tact and wisdom of the linguistic convention itself, his German counterpart risks revealing himself as an idiot or a scoundrel through the ring and rhythm of his first sentence. Had Hitler's speeches been accessible to the West in their unspeakable original, we might have been spared a war. For this war was partly caused by Hitler's innocent translators, unavoidably missing in smooth and diplomatic French or English the resonance of the infernal sphere. Only German, in all its notorious long-windedness, offers such shortcuts to the termini of mankind. It was K. K. who knew them all.

Erich Heller, *The Disinherited Mind*, new 3rd ed. (1971), pp. 236–37

K. appeared to his contemporaries, by turns, as a prophetic thinker, a passionate Jewish prophet in the Old Testament sense, a pacifist in the spirit of Christianity, a well-intentioned educator, a benign sponsor of young or neglected poets, a social revolutionary, a conservative guardian of the German and Austrian tradition, an exalted model, a sadistic slanderer, and a cynical mocker of all values. To some he was a breathtaking incarnation of the absolute, an infallible oracle, a prophet desperately trying to show mankind the right way of pointing it back to the "origin" which, to him, was forever the goal; to others, he was an embittered, monomaniacal misanthrope, a man who directed his cannon fire at sparrows, an object of fear, vituperation, and blind hatred. This ambivalence is seen in K.'s relationship to some of his contemporaries, for in a number of instances apostles turned apostates, disciples became defectors, friends changed to foes, and those once championed were later chastised. Only relatively few disciples had the strength of character and the absolute integrity that K. demanded of them. More often than not, such falls from grace took place under unedifying circumstances and had both personal and literary repercussions, sometimes leading to acrimonious polemics and public pillorying.

Harry Zohn, *K. K.* (1971), pp. 88–89

K.'s response to the political developments of his time is more sustained, more perceptive, more urgent and more direct than that of any contemporary Austrian writer. He descends into the political arena in a way completely alien to his fellow writers. It is possible to quote many instances of K.'s contempt for and condemnation of "politics" as a degrading and immoral human activity, and he frequently takes pride in declaring his indifference to political issues. He warns that his concern lies with the form of his satirical statements rather than with their content. Charges of "aestheticism" were levelled against him during his lifetime. . . .

One way and another, K. dominates any study of the politics of Austrian literature during this period [1914–1938]. For all his involvement in the Viennese environment, there is something profoundly un-Viennese about his sheer intransigence and the absoluteness of his ethical and cultural values; he manifests none of that fickleness, inconsistency, arbitrariness, easy-going complaisance and mental slovenliness for which . . . he castigated his fellow citizens. . . .

C. E. Williams, *The Broken Eagle: The Politics of Austrian Literature from Empire to Anschluss* (1974), pp. 232, 235

Literature, K. believes, must take issue with the world of which it is a part. In the event, it is committed to being a critique of the press and all aspects of life that appear to be dominated and determined by the language of the press. Thus stylistic form—the linguistic intensity which derives from the verbal exploits and the self-conscious and language-conscious turns I have mentioned—spills over into content, the meta-language of quotation and critique is mode of writing and theme at once. Quotation is to K. what slices of social life were to the naturalists—what the interrelation of institution and individual was to the European realists—what nature was to the poetry of Weimar. Quotation is a major source of literary inspiration. Its function in K.'s work anticipated the "documentary theatre," but went far beyond its present-day users.

J. P. Stern, "K. K. and the Idea of Literature," *Encounter*, Aug. 1975, 42–43

KRĖVĖ, Vincas

(formerly Vincas Krėvė-Mickevičius) Lithuanian prose writer and dramatist, b. 19 Oct. 1882, Subartonys; d. 7 July 1954, Marple Township (near Philadelphia), Pa., U.S.A.

In his youth K. attended the theological seminary at Vilnius (1898–1900), then studied philology at the universities of Kiev and Lvov. After earning his doctorate at Lvov in 1908 he taught in Baku until 1920, and served there briefly (1919–20) as the Lithuanian consul to the then independent republic of Azerbaijan.

After his return to Lithuania in 1920 K. played a major role in political, cultural, and academic life. He was professor of Slavic literatures at the University of Lithuania (1922–43), dean of the Faculty of Humanities there (1925–37), the first president of the Lithuanian Academy of Arts and Sciences (1941), and editor of numerous literary journals and academic publications. In 1940, during the first weeks of the Soviet occupation, K. served as Foreign Minister and Acting Prime Minister of Lithuania. However, after having realized what the Soviet plans for the country were, he resigned from the two posts and, shortly before the second Soviet occupation of 1944, went into exile. After a sojourn in Austria, K. emigrated in 1947 to the U.S. to join the faculty of the University of Pennsylvania, where he taught Slavic and Lithuanian literatures until his retirement in 1953.

Essentially a late romanticist with touches of realism, K. first drew inspiration and material for his works from Lithuanian folklore and from the distant past of Lithuania. These sources found their best expression in *Dainavos šalies senu̧ žmoniu̧ padavimai* (1912; the old folktales of Dainava) and two plays, *Šarūnas* (1911; Šarūnas) and *Skirgaila* (1925; Skirgaila). In the folktale book he created, in a highly stylized rhythmic prose akin to folk literature, legends of ages long gone by, while in the two plays he revived, in a heroic style, both the legendary and historical past. For these dramas K. chose some of the most crucial and problematic periods of Lithuanian history and evolved his own interpretation of them. Moreover, these momentous periods of history are not introduced just for their own sake. They serve more as background and influencing factors on the leading characters, who are not helpless puppets controlled by the forces of history but conscious architects of the present and future. Men of flesh and blood, of manifold and complicated egos, with deep-rooted personal problems, the legendary prince Šarūnas and the historical Skirgaila are tragic figures struggling valiantly with their own times. While *Šarūnas* is a closet drama of epic design and proportions, *Skirgaila* is a tragedy of masterfully knit compact composition and Shakespearean overtones, a masterpiece of its genre.

K. also explored with a keen eye and deep psychological insight the rustic life of Lithuania as it existed at the turn of the century. To this category belong the collection of short stories *Šiaudinėj pastogėj* (2 vols., 1921–22; under the thatched roof); its sequel, *Raganius* (1939; the sorcerer); and the play *Žentas* (1921; the son-in-law), all more realistic than romantic in approach and treatment of the subject. *Šiaudinėj pastogėj* contains some of the best examples of the Lithuanian short story. Their characters, in contrast to the heroic figures of Šarūnas and Skirgaila, are simple country folk almost untouched by modern civilization and its inhibitions, although they have their own peculiar beliefs and philosophies.

A writer of diverse interests and wide erudition, K. was particularly well acquainted with Oriental thought and literature, as well as with the history of early Christianity. Two works were the creative outgrowth of these interests: the collection *Rytų pasakos* (1930; tales of the Orient), which introduced the Oriental style to Lithuanian literature, and a biblical epic in prose, *Dangaus ir žemės sūnūs* (2 vols., 1949, 1963; the sons of heaven and the earth). K. worked on this epic on and off throughout his entire literary life. In this work, employing a quasibiblical style, K. paints a wide and vivid panorama of the world of the Jews in the time of Christ and gives a rather unorthodox interpretation of the wellsprings of Christianity. Of particular interest is the tragedy of Herod, woven into the epic in the form of playlike dialogues. As conceived by K., Herod's tragedy lies primarily in the collision of the two widely different worlds—the Jewish and the Hellenistic—within himself and his milieu. This interpretation of Herod's doom adds a new dimension and contributes substantially to the treatment of the Herod theme in world literature.

One of the pathfinders of modern Lithuanian literature and its foremost representative, K. attained the stature of a classic in his own lifetime.

FURTHER WORKS: *Sutemose* (1921); *Likimo keliai* (2 vols., 1926, 1929); *Mindaugo mirtis* (1935); *Miglose* (1944); *Pagunda* (1950; *The Temptation*, 1965); *Raštai* (6 vols., 1956–1963); *Likimo žaismas* (1965). FURTHER WORKS IN ENGLISH: *The Herdsman and the Linden Tree* (1964)

BIBLIOGRAPHY: Senn, A., "On the Sources of a Lithuanian Tale ['Gilšė']," in Schirokauer, A. and Paulsen, W., *Corona* (1941): 8–22; Maciūnas, V., "V. K.'s Place in Lithuanian Literature," *Studi baltici*, 9 (1952): 11–23; Senn, A., "V. K.: Lithuania's Creator of Heroes," in *World Literatures* (1956): 170–84; Senn, A., "V. K. and Lithuanian Folklore," in Halle, M., et al., comps., *For Roman Jakobson* (1956): 444–48; Ostrauskas, K., "V. K.: A Lithuanian Classic," *BA*, 38 (1964): 265–67; special K. issue, *Lituanus*, 11, 3 (1965); Senn, A. E., "V. K.'s Journey to America," *JBalS*, 7 (1976): 255–63

—KOSTAS OSTRAUSKAS

KRISTENSEN, Tom

Danish poet, novelist, and critic, b. 4 Aug. 1893, London, England; d. 2 June 1974, Svendborg

K.'s father was a craftsman who hoped for success in America, but who never got any farther than London. In 1896 the family returned to Copenhagen, where life for some years proved to be financially quite insecure. The family moved from lodging to lodging (an experience reflected in the novel *En anden* (1923; another), and the young K. gained a detailed knowledge of the various neighborhoods of the fast-growing capital of Denmark. He entered the university and eventually received a degree in Danish, English, and German literature and languages, but instead of pursuing a teaching career, he began to test his talent as a poet and a critic.

K.'s debut was with the striking collection of poems *Fribytterdrømme* (1920; dreams of a freebooter), in which chaotic inner and outer worlds are charted with an exquisite sense of form and rhythm. These poems have been seen as a major contribution to Danish EXPRESSIONISM, but K.'s use of expressionistic techniques is actually quite moderate, and he records his obsession with colors and contours and his fascination with action and violence with a strict adherence to traditional meter. Some of these poems reveal an aesthetic intoxication with a many-splendored outer reality, be it the streets of Copenhagen, the grubby life in sleazy taverns, or the exotic settings of the Far East. Other poems show that K.'s ebullient enthusiasm for chaos and color exists together with a deep-seated anguish, an inner emptiness that cannot be filled by any philosophy, religion, or political conviction. Thus K.'s aestheticism borders on nihilism.

K.'s later collections of poetry, *Mirakler* (1922; miracles) and *Påfuglefjeren* (1922; the peacock feather), expressed the same duality; but gradually the intensity of the early poetry gave way to a more classical diction, as in *Den sidste lygte* (1954; the last streetlight). From the beginning to the end, these texts suggest, however, that it is only through the creative act that K. can find that moment of rest for which he yearns. These poignant, well-wrought poems, with their mixture of sensuousness, humor, and intellectualism, place K. as one of the best Danish poets of the 20th c.

K.'s first novel, *Livets arabesk* (1921; the arabesque of life), is one of the few expressionistic novels written in Denmark; it depicts an illusory revolution that, through the degeneration of the protagonist, shows how the hollow bourgeois tradition is crumbling. The revolution is, however, rendered from an aesthetic viewpoint rather than from a political one, and the text becomes at places a veritable orgy in the forms and colors of physical and psychic violence. Much more subdued is *En anden*, in which one of K.'s quite nihilistic characters subjects himself to a Freudian investigation of his childhood and later life in the Far East.

Hærværk (1930; *Havoc*, 1968) is a superior, intricately composed *roman à clef*, which brilliantly captures the mood of the newspaper rooms and bars of Copenhagen. Its protagonist is a gifted journalist who very determinedly ruins his marriage and career in an attempt to find meaning through debauchery. This haunting odyssey through low life does not, however, lead to self-destruction, and the protagonist emerges as a quite undaunted survivor. Perhaps the novel testifies to the strength of the nihilist.

After this tour de force K. mainly produced nonfiction: travel books; collections of an autobiographical nature, which recall, with a good portion of self-irony, the milieu of the young poet and his compatriots; and collections of his literary criticism written for the newspaper *Politiken*. In these articles K. shows himself once again to be a masterful stylist and also a keen and sympathetic observer of the literary scene. Among his major interests were American and English literature, and his writings on the so-called "lost generation" testify to a close identification with authors who, like himself, vainly sought a foothold in a world without redeeming values. As a critic he may remind his readers of Edmund WILSON, another searcher for ideological positions, for like Wilson, K.'s writings are eminently pedagogical: without ever becoming popular in a vulgar fashion, he writes with both an admirable clarity and an elegant turn of phrase that raise his journalism to the level of superior literary criticism.

FURTHER WORKS: *Bokserdrengen* (1925); *En kavaler i Spanien* (1926); *Verdslige sange* (1927); *Vindrosen* (1934); *Mod den yderste rand* (1936); *Digte i døgnet* (1940); *Mellem Scylla og Charybdis* (1943); *Hvad er Heta* (1946; rev. ed., 1959); *Mellem krigene* (1946); *En omvej til Andorra* (1947); *Rejse i Italien* (1951); *Til dags dato* (1953); *Det skabende øje* (1956); *Oplevelser med lyrik* (1957); *Den evige uro* (1958); *Mord i pantomimeteatret* (1962); *I min Tid* (1963); *Åbenhjertige fortielser* (1966); *Fra Holger Drachmann til Benny Andersen* (1967); *Hvad var mit ærinde* (1968); *Blandt københavnere* (1973); *Med disse øjne* (1973)

BIBLIOGRAPHY: Byram, M. A., "The Reality of T. K.'s *Hærværk*," *Scan*, 15 (1976): 29–37; Rossel, S., *A History of Danish Literature* (1992): 327-33

—NIELS INGWERSEN

KRISTEVA, Julia

French-Bulgarian literary theoretician and critic (writing in French), b. 24 June 1941, Sliven, Bulgaria

A literary critic, semiotician, psychoanalyst, and professor at the University of Paris VII, K. is one of the most important and

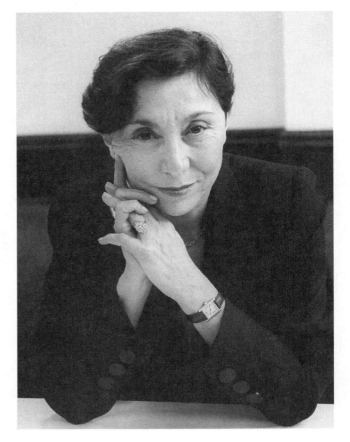

Julia Kristeva

original thinkers in France today. Educated in Bulgaria, K. emigrated to France in 1965. As a doctoral fellow at L'École Pratique des Hautes Études in Paris, she studied under Lucien Goldmann (1913–1970) and Roland BARTHES. Shortly after, she met Philippe SOLLERS, whom she married.

K. chose one of the most propitious moments to make her debut on the Parisian intellectual scene. The years 1965–1966 were marked by what can only be called an explosion of French intellectual thought. Undaunted by the impact of BARTHES, Michel FOUCAULT, Jacques LACAN, Émile Benveniste (1902–1976), and Louis Althusser (1918–1990), K. succeeded in conquering the Parisian intelligentsia with such publications as "Bakhtine, le mot, le dialogue et le roman" (1967; "Word, Dialogue, and Novel," 1980) and "Pour une sémiologie des paragrammes" (1967; for a semiology of paragrams).

In 1970 she published the doctoral dissertation she had written under Goldmann in 1966–1967, *Le texte du roman, Approche sémiologique d'une structure discursive transformationnelle* (the text of the novel, a semiological approach to a transformational discursive structure). This work analyzes the origins of the novel in the late Middle Ages from the perspective of Bakhtinian "postformalism," which K. was among the first to introduce in France. Her background in Russian formalism and training in linguistics made her invaluable to the *Tel Quel* team, whose editorial board she joined in 1970.

K. wrote an introduction to linguistics entitled *Le langage, cet inconnu* (1969; *Language: The Unknown*, 1989) under the name of Joyaux (the family name of Sollers). With *Séméiotiké, recherches pour une sémanalyse* (1969; semiotics, research for a sémanalysis) she firmly established her reputation in France and abroad. In this volume of essays she brings literary practice and psychoanalysis to bear on semiotic theory, and thereby formulates an original "textual semiotics" that makes subjectivity a fundamental concern of language.

La révolution du langage poétique, L'avantgarde à la fin du XIXe siècle. Lautréamont et Mallarmé (1974; *Revolution in Poetic Language*, 1984) is still considered her major theoretical work. The culmination of years of research, this state-doctoral thesis (*doctoral d'état*) draws on linguistics, philosophy, pschoanalysis, and avant-garde literature to elaborate a theoretical discourse centered on the question of subjectivity in language and history. K. demonstrates how the epistemological and sociopolitical transformations of the latter part of the 19th c. can be discerned in avant-garde "texts of rupture," where the subversion of language reciprocally implies the subversion of the writing subject, and both imply a critique of the existing sociopolitical order.

In the spring of 1974 K. traveled to China with other members of the *Tel Quel* team. Upon her return to Paris, she published *Des Chinoises* (1974; *About Chinese Women*, 1977), which is as much about K. and the West as it is about the evolution of Chinese women under Mao Tse-Tung. A highly subjective work, it allows us to understand the impact that the Chinese Cultural Revolution had on French intellectuals during the late 1960s and early 1970s. K.'s interest in non-Western cultures is also the basis for the collective work that she coedited in 1975, *La traversée des signes* (the traverse of signs).

Polylogue (polylogue), a collection of essays published in 1977, reflects K.'s growing interest in questions pertaining to the place of femininity and motherhood in Western thought and culture. *Folle vérité* (1979; mad truth) is a collective work resulting from a

seminar on psychotic discourse and truth directed by K. at a hospital in Paris. K.'s work as a practicing psychoanalyst has greatly influenced all her subsequent publications. In *Pouvoirs de l'horreur, essai sur l'abjection* (1980; *Powers of Horror: An Essay on Abjection*, 1982) K. scrutinizes both biblical writings and contemporary literary texts to reveal the abjection that underlies religious, moral, and political codes. *Histoires d'amour* (1983; *Tales of Love*, 1987) stems from K.'s experiences as a psychoanalyst and a mother. She examines the notion of love in relation to psychoanalysis, literature, religion, and philosophy. In analyzing discourses on love from the ancient Greeks to the moderns, K. traces the evolution of subjectivity in the West. K.'s work on the psychoanalytic dimensions of love in *Histoires d'amour* and *Au commencement était l'amour: Psychanalyse et foi* (1985; *In the Beginning Was Love: Psychoanalysis and Faith*, 1987) led to her study on loss, mourning, and absence in *Soleil noir: dépression et mélancholie* (1987; *Black Sun: Depression and Melancholia*, 1989). She examines the melancholic imaginary from both clinical and aesthetic perspectives.

In 1990 K. published *Les samouraïs* (*The Samurai*, 1992), a semiautobiographical novel on the passions underlying Parisian intellectual life in the 1960s and 1970s. *Etrangers à nous-mêmes* (1988; *Strangers to Ourselves*, 1991) and *Lettre ouverte à Harlem Désir* (1990; open letter to Harlem Désir) are works that reflect the political preoccupations of the 1980s and 1990s. Arguing that being a foreigner seems to have become the normal condition for the citizen at the end of the 20th c., K. turns to the question of exile, which has been one of her fundamental preoccupations as a foreigner living in France. She contends that we shall never be able to tolerate others so long as we have not yet come to terms with the otherness that lies within us.

K. has further examined the relationships between literature and psychoanalysis in such works as *Les nouvelles maladies de l'âme*, (1993; *New Maladies of the Soul*, 1995), *Sens et non-sens de la révolte* (1996; Meaning and Non-Meaning of Revolt), and *La révolte intime* (1997; Intimate Revolt). She has also brought new insights to Proust in *Le temps sensible: Proust et l'expérience littéraire* (1994; *Time and Sense: Proust and the Experience of Literature*, 1996).

As a psychoanalyst and writer, K. brings new insights to the study of Western thought and culture. Interdisciplinary in perspective, K.'s work provides an original response to the contemporary debate on the human subject and its relation to language, sexuality, and politics.

FURTHER WORKS: *Visions capitales* (1998); *Contre la dépression nationale* (1998); *Le féminin et le sacré* (1998, with Catherine Clément). FURTHER WORKS IN ENGLISH: *Desire in Language, A Semiotic Approach to Literature and Art* (1980); *The K. Reader* (1986)

BIBLIOGRAPHY: Lewis, P., "Revolutionary Semiotics," *Diacritics*, 4, 3 (1974): 28–32; Roudiez, L. S., Introduction to *Desire in Language* (1980): 1–20; Pajaczkowska, C., "Introduction to K.," *m/f*, 5–6 (1981): 149–57; Roudiez, L. S., Introduction to *Revolution in Poetic Language* (1984): 1–10; Barthes, R., "K.'s *Séméiotiké*," *The Rustle of Language* (1986): 168–71; Jardine, A., "Opaque Texts and Transparent Contexts: The Political Difference of J. K.," in Miller, N. K., ed., *The Poetics of Gender* (1986): 96–115; Moi, T., Introduction to *The K. Reader* (1986): 1–22; Lechte, J., *J. K.*

(1990); Fletcher, J., and Benjamin, A., eds., *Abjection, Melancholia, and Love: The Work of J. K.* (1990); Oliver, K., *Reading K.: Unraveling the Double-Bind* (1993); Volat-Shapiro, H., *J. K.” Œuvres et critique, 1966-1994* (1996); Smith, A., *J. K.: Readings of Exile and Estrangement* (1996); Reineke, M., *Sacrificed Lives: K. on Women and Violence* (1997); Smith, A.-M., *J. K.: Speaking the Unspeakable*

—DANIELLE MARX-SCOURAS

KRLEŽA, Miroslav

Yugoslav novelist, short-story writer, dramatist, poet, essayist, travel writer, and memoirist (writing in Croatian), b. 7 July 1893, Zagreb; d. 29 Dec. 1981, Zagreb

Upon finishing the lower grades of secondary school in Zagreb, K. was sent to a preparatory military school in Peczuj (1908) and later to the Military Academy in Budapest. His attempt to join the Serbian army as a volunteer in the Balkan Wars (1912) proved disastrous. Suspected by the Serbs of being an Austrian spy (Croatia was at the time part of the Austro-Hungarian Empire), K. was forced to return to Austria-Hungary, where he was treated as a deserter, thrown out of the academy, and in 1914 sent to the front as a common soldier.

After World War I K. returned to Zagreb, where he lived as a professional writer in open and extremely vocal opposition to the monarchist régime of Yugoslavia. During World War II he chose to live in seclusion and to remain silent, although he could not escape occasional harassment by the pro-Nazi Croatian government. K. greeted the postwar Communist régime with enthusiasm, immediately resuming his prominent role in Yugoslav political, cultural, and literary life, only this time on the side of the establishment. K. was vice-president of the Yugoslav Academy of Arts and Sciences from 1947 to 1957 and president of the Union of Yugoslav Writers from 1958 to 1961; since 1951 he served as director of the Yugoslav Lexicographic Institute in Zagreb and the editor-in-chief of the *Encyclopedia Yugoslavica*.

K.'s literary career, which spans a period of almost seventy years, began just before World War I with lyrical poetry and plays of EXPRESSIONIST orientation. During the war K. changed from an idealistic lyricist with a pagan enchantment with youth, life, and nature to an embittered and pessimistic individual whose poetry and prose—from 1914 to around 1922—reflected his strong antiwar feelings, particularly his profound disgust with senseless deaths of his countrymen sent to fight for the sake of a doomed empire that had oppressed them for centuries. In the early 1920s, deeply impressed by the outcome of the Soviet revolution and by its ideology, K. became an eloquent spokesman for revolution, and consequently became more and more concerned with the social ills plaguing Croatia and the rest of Europe after World War I.

In the late 1920s and early 1930s, K.'s literary activities reached their peak, and it was in that period that he produced most of his best works in poetry, fiction, and drama. After World War II K. stayed predominantly in the realm of prose and drama, although a fine group of philosophical poems, written mainly during the war, is found integrated in his memoirs and diaries.

K.'s most praised poetic work, *Balade Petrice Kerempuha* (1936; the ballads of Petritsa Kerempuh), is a collection of poems that represents the synthesis of K.'s entire poetic œuvre. Written in the Croatian *kajkavski* dialect, the "ballads" are, in K.'s own words, "a free variation on the old theme of *jacqueries* [peasants' revolts]." Through them, K. masterfully summarizes some thousand years of his unfortunate nation's history. At the same time, he expresses his impatience with his nation's lack of rebellious spirit and its slavish acceptance of the oppressive conditions of life imposed upon it by its various masters.

Another masterpiece, the Glembaj saga, is a complex work consisting of eleven prose fragments and three of K.'s most outstanding plays, *Gospoda Glembajevi* (1928; the patrician Glembajs), *U agoniji* (1928; revised second-act ending and a third act added 1959; in agony), and *Leda* (1930; Leda). The plays and six narratives were published together in *Glembajevi* (1932; the Glembajs), the remaining five narratives as part of *Novele* (1937; novellas). By focusing on individual members of the Glembaj family from various generations and on their ruthless climb to the top of the Austro-Hungarian socioeconomic elite, the short stories trace a century and a half of the family history filled with gruesome murders, greed, lust, alcoholism, and venereal diseases that eventually manifest themselves in madness, suicidal mania, and vices of all kinds. The short stories provide the necessary background for the morbid and grotesque drama of the last degenerate Glembaj offspring, a drama that coincides with the fall of Austria-Hungary and is portrayed in the three plays, which are set in Zagreb between 1913 and 1924.

Of K.'s four novels, his first, *Povratak Filipa Latinovicza* (1932; *The Return of Philip Latinovicz*, 1959), is the most popular and the most widely acclaimed. Its protagonist, Filip, is a typical K. hero, a deeply disturbed and disillusioned intellectual who cannot seem to find his place in life. In search of inner peace, Filip, a painter, returns home after twenty-three years of living abroad. He hopes that contact with his native soil will inspire him to create a painting of ultimate beauty and perfection and give his life a meaning and a direction it has never had. At home, Filip is haunted by traumatic childhood experiences and is unable to become reconciled with his mother, a former prostitute, whom he cannot forgive for her lack of love and affection. Ironically, he comforts himself with Bobočka, a newcomer in the town who has the same notorious reputation his mother once had. In Bobočka's circle Filip experiences a sort of a catharsis, as he realizes that his problems are not unique and that the world is full of unfortunate loners and drifters of his kind. The fact that Filip survives, while some other characters die a violent death, gives an optimistic touch to this otherwise gloomy novel in which, under heavy clouds, everything, including human beings, seems to rot in muddy soil drenched with human blood.

The satirical and allegorical novel *Banket u Blitvi* (3 vols., 1938, 1939, 1962; a banquet in Blitvia) treats the deplorable political situation in Europe in the interwar period through the conflict of the Blitvian (a play on words on *Litva*, Serbo-Croatian for Lithuania) dictator Barutanski (*barut* means "gunpowder") and an idealistic intellectual, Niels Nielsen, who believes that a man must fight for a better world even at the risk of his life. K. does not fail, however, to underline one of the classic Communist theses that individual efforts "in the struggle against crimes and lies end up as romantic adventures."

It has been pointed out many times that throughout his life K. stood in the forefront of the struggle against human stupidity, mediocrity, petit-bourgeois mentality, and backwardness in general. He has believed that the world we live in can and must be reformed until the new man emerges, free from all the prejudices and ready to live in harmony with himself and his fellow men. Like many outspoken men, K. has been a very controversial figure, especially in the interwar period, when he was attacked from many sides. Many may not like his baroque style or the dark colors of his moods; others may resent his arrogance and intellectual snobbery, or disagree with his political views, but few could deny that K. always stood firmly behind his ideas and defended them fiercely and fearlessly no matter how dangerous and how powerful were his opponents. Furthermore, it is hard not to admire K.'s enormous creative energy, reflected in over forty volumes of an extremely diversified œuvre and in his extensive participation in many aspects of his nation's cultural and political life. Today, K. is still the most impressive literary figure in Yugoslavia and a true giant of Croatian literature.

FURTHER WORKS: *Legenda* (1914); *Maskerata* (1914); *Zaratustra i mladić* (1914); *Podnevna simfonija* (1916); *Pan* (1917); *Tri simfonije* (1917); *Saloma* (1918 enl. with rev. end, 1963); *Hrvatska rapsodija* (1918; includes *Kraljevo* and *Cristoval Colon*); *Pjesme* (3 vols., 1918–1919); *Lirika* (1919); *Michelangelo Buonarroti* (1919); *Eppur si muove* (1919); *Tri kavalira gospodjice Melanije* (1920); *Hrvatska rapsodija* (1921; includes *Smrt Franje Kadavera* and *Veliki meštar sviju hulja*); *Magyar kiřalyi honvéd novela-Kraljevsko-ugarska domobranska novela* (1921); *Hrvatski bog Mars* (1922); *Galicija* (1922); *Adam i Eva* (1922); *Golgota* (1922); *Vučjak* (1923); *Vražji otok* (1923); *Novele* (1924); *Izlet u Rusiju* (1926); *Knjiga pjesama* (1931); *Moj obračun s njima* (1932); *Eseji* I (1932); *Sabrana djela* (9 vols., 1932–1934); *Hiljadu i jedna smrt* (1933); *Simfonije* (1933); *Legende* (1933); *U logoru* (1934; includes *Vučjak*); *Evropa danas* (1935); *Pjesme u tmini* (1937); *Deset krvavih godina* (1937); *Djela* (12 vols., 1937–1939); *Eppur si muove* (1938); *Knjiga proze* (1938); *Na rubu pameti* (1938; *On the Edge of Reason*, 1976); *Knjiga studija i putopisa* (1939); *Dijalektički antibarbarus* (1939); *Francisco José Goya y Lucientes* (1948); *Djetinjstvo u Agramu godine 1902–1903* (1952); *O Erazmu Rotterdamskom* (1953); *Kalendar jedne parlamentarne komedije* (1953); *Sabrana djela* (1953 ff.); *Davni dani* (1956); *Aretej* (1959); *Eseji* (6 vols., 1961–1967); *Poezija* (1967); *Izabrana dela* (1969 ff.); *99 varijacija* (1972); *Djetinjstvo i drugi spisi* (1972); *Put u raj* (1973); *M. K.: Jubilarno izdanje* (1973 ff.); *Pet stoljeća hrvatske književnosti*, Vols. 91–94 (1973); *Dnevnik* (5 vols., 1977). FURTHER WORKS IN ENGLISH: *The Cricket beneath the Waterfall, and Other Stories* (1972)

BIBLIOGRAPHY: Šinko, E., "M. K. and His Work: The Outline of a Study," *Yugoslavia*, 15 (1959): 59–64; Kadić, A., "M. K.," *BA*, 37 (1963): 396–400; Matković, M., "M. K.," *The Bridge*, No. 1 (1966): 15–23; Vaupotić, M., *Contemporary Croatian Literature* (1966): 34–35, 92–99, 158–61, 184–85; Kadić, A., "K.'s Tormented Visionaries," *SEER*, 45 (1967): 46–64; Pawel, E., "Three Generations," *PR*, 34 (1967): 606–13; Schneider, S., *Studien zur Romantechnik M. K.s* (1969); Suvin, D., "Voyage to the Stars and Pannonian Mire: M. K.'s Expressionist Vision and the Croatian Plebeian Consciousness in the Epoch of World War One," *Mosaic*, 6 (1973): 169–83; Ferguson, A., "A Critical Literary Approach to M. K.'s *The Return of Philip Latinovicz*," *JCS*, Nos. 14–15 (1973–74): 134–44; Eekman, T., *Thirty Years of Yugoslav Literature (1945-1975)* (1978)

—BILJANA ŠLJIVIĆ-ŠIMŠIĆ

KROETZ, Franz Xaver

German dramatist, b. 25 Feb. 1946, Munich

K. spent his childhood in Simbach on the Inn in Lower Bavaria and attended acting school in Munich. In 1972 K. joined the West German Communist Party, and his work took on an overtly political orientation.

K.'s plays deal primarily with the inarticulate working classes, and his dialogue is written in a terse, seemingly disconnected manner often in a Lower Bavarian dialect full of mundane aphorisms and clichés. The subject matter of his work usually includes shocking incidents of violence and overt sexual acts. These events, however, are couched in the same banal, heavy, unspectacular mood as his dialogue.

In his best known work, *Stallerhof* (1971; *Farmyard*, 1976), Sepp, a middle-aged hired hand, seduces Beppi, the farmer Staller's mentally retarded daughter. Staller apparently kills Sepp's dog and orders Sepp off the farm. Beppi is discovered to be pregnant. Staller's wife prepares to abort the child but relents, and at the end of the play the labor pains begin. Typically, the play is heavily punctuated with pauses and progresses by short stichomythic scenes, most set in different locales. The tone is fatalistic, and the characters do not achieve any perception; nor does the environment impinge upon them, as in strictly naturalistic plays.

After K. joined the Communist Party, his work moved from this rather abstract, universalized portrait of lower class life to an attempt to draw conclusions about it. His monodrama *Wunschkonzert* (1972; *Request Concert*, 1975) depicts the loneliness of a middle-aged woman who performs the meticulous ritual of an evening at home and then just as meticulously commits suicide. The solo character does not speak. The only sound is the radio airing a request concert. In his notes K. assigns the cause for the character's resignation and muteness to "exploitation and repression," which, if not self-directed, would have led to a "revolutionary situation."

K.'s work is strongly influenced by the *Volksstück* (literally, "folk play," but characterized by a lower-middle-class or proletarian milieu and the use of dialect) as exemplified in the plays of Ödön von HORVÁTH and Marieluise FLEISSER, and he is perhaps indebted directly to Georg Büchner's (1813–1837) *Woyzeck*.

Nevertheless K.'s contribution to drama and his style are distinctive. He eschews exposition, letting the event speak for itself without comment or sentiment. He sees the use of language in the theater as an artificial convention, asserting that "the most important action of my characters is their silence . . . Their problems lie so far back and are so advanced that they are no longer able to express them in words."

K. is part of a vanguard of new dramatists including the playwright-filmmaker Rainer Werner Fassbinder (b. 1946), who directed a film version of K.'s *Wildwechsel* (1973; wildgame path) for German television. Their intention is to move the German drama away from self-congratulatory bourgeois attitudes and its traditionally heavy reliance upon language and towards a sparer, more elemental concern with the deeper recesses of the human being as an inchoate social animal.

FURTHER WORKS: *Heimarbeit* (1971); *Hartnäckig* (1971); *Männersache* (1971; *Men's Business*, 1976); *Michi's Blut* (1971; *Michi's Blood*, 1976); *Geisterbahn* (1972); *Lieber Fritz* (1972); *Oberösterreich* (1972); *Dolomitenstadt Lienz* (1972); *Ein Mann, ein Wörterbuch* (1973; *A Man, A Dictionary*, 1976); *Maria Magdalena* (1973); *Agnes Bernauer* (1975); *Das Nest* (1976); *Mensch Meier* (1978); *Der Stramme Max* (1979); *Nicht Fisch nicht Fleisch* (1981)

BIBLIOGRAPHY: Gilman, R., Introduction to F. X. K., *Farmyard, and Four Plays* (1976): 7–23; Klaic, D., "The Theatre of F. X. K.," *Y/T*: 6, 1 (1974): 94–97

—PETER SANDER

KROLOW, Karl

German poet and essayist, b. 11 March 1915, Hanover

After studying Germanic and Romance philology, art history, and philosophy in Göttingen and Breslau (now Wrocław, Poland), K. began his literary career in Göttingen in 1942. He subsequently moved to Hanover, then in 1956 to Darmstadt. In 1966 he became vice-president of the German Academy for Language and Literature, of which he had been a member since 1954. Among the awards that K. has received for his writings are the Büchner Prize (1956), the Rainer Maria Rilke Poetry Prize (1977), the Hessian Culture Prize (1983), and the Bad Homburg Hölderlin Prize (1988).

Influenced in his early writing by Annette von Droste-Hülshoff (1797–1848), Oskar Loerke (1884–1938), and Wilhelm Lehmann (1882–1968), K. created nature and landscape poems that combine graphic precision with visual sensitivity, keen images and metaphors with simplicity and clarity of diction and expression. The poems of *Hochgelobtes, gutes Leben* (1943; highly lauded, good life) and *Gedichte* (1948; poems) feature a profusion of natural detail captured in simple, conventional forms. Four-line stanzas with traditional rhyme schemes abound. To the extent that man is visible in the poetry of the 1940s, he appears as a Robinson Crusoe-type, coping with the everyday problems of the postwar world. Political or social commentary is either absent or presented very indirectly through the isolated symbolic human figures.

During the early 1950s K. began to experiment with new techniques, forms, and themes. *Die Zeichen der Welt* (1952; the signs of the world) contains songlike long forms, hymns and odes that document K.'s movement from rhymed lyrics to unrhymed free rhythms. Unlike the earlier nature poems, the creations of this second period place heavy emphasis on the artificial components of human existence. Civilization, culture, and technology are the substance of poems dealing specifically with war, politics, literature, art, and music. In *Wind und Zeit* (1954; wind and time), K. employed short free-forms, abstractions, and the precise language and perceptual mode of mathematics to intensify his focus on the rigid artificiality of modern civilization.

The appearance of *Tage und Nächte* (1956; days and nights) marked the beginning of a third phase in K.'s poetic development. Under the influence of modern French and Spanish poetry, DADA-ISM, and especially the writings of Hans Arp (1887–1966), K. wrote surrealistic poems that incline toward the absurd. He began to view poetry as a grotesque play of words. As a result, in the collections of the late 1950s and the 1960s, the thematic emphasis on culture reached a peak and then receded. The poems of this period are noteworthy for their laconic, dry language and a tendency toward anecdotal narration.

Later poems, those contained, for example, in *Zeitvergehen* (1972; the passing of time) and *Der Einfachheit halber* (1977; for simplicity's sake), reflect a tempered synthesis of important aspects of earlier creative directions. They reveal a decline in the surrealistic element, coupled with a refinement of the mathematical precision of the early 1950s and a perfecting of the short, hasty, terse poetic miniature form that characterizes K.'s works of the late 1960s.

In the collections of his advanced years, such as *Schönen Dank und vorüber* (1984; thank you very much and it's finished), *Als es soweit war* (1988; when it got to that point), *Ich höre mich sagen* (1992; I hear myself say), and *Die zweite Zeit* (1995; the second time), K. focuses his lyrics very clearly on questions and feelings that arise from a sensitive consciousness of impending death. Vivid and sometimes harsh images of terminal illness, agony, mourning, and decay are mixed with more traditional winter motifs of cold and snow, but there are also powerful reflections upon past experience that project a deep longing for those things of life that can no longer be reclaimed.

Marked above all by an air of resignation and melancholy, K.'s lyric creations are eminently representative of the mainstream of postwar German poetry. As such, they are poems that are powerful for their innate humanity and their precise penetration of modern existence.

FURTHER WORKS: *Heimsuchung* (1948); *Auf Erden* (1949); *Von nahen und fernen Dingen* (1953); *Verzauberung* (1956); *Fremde Körper* (1959; *Foreign Bodies*, 1969); *Tessin* (1959); *Schatten eines Mannes* (1959); *Aspekte zeitgenössischer deutscher Lyrik* (1961); *Ausgewählte Gedichte* (1962); *Die Rolle des Autors im experimentalen Gedicht* (1962); *Unsichtbare Hände* (1962; *Invisible Hands*, 1969); *Schattengefecht* (1964); *Corrida de toros* (1964); *Reise durch die Nacht* (1964); *Gesammelte Gedichte* (1965); *Landschaften für mich* (1966); *Poetisches Tagebuch* (1966); *Das Problem des langen und kurzen Gedichts heute* (1966); *Unter uns Lesern* (1967); *Minuten Aufzeichnungen* (1968); *Alltägliche Gedichte* (1969); *Bürgerliche Gedichte* (1970); *Nichts weiter als Leben* (1970); *Deutschland deine Niedersachsen: ein Land, das es nicht gibt* (1972); *Zu des Rheins gestreckten Hügeln: Goethereise 1972* (1972); *Ein Gedicht entsteht* (1973); *Miteinander* (1974); *Gesammelte Gedichte* (1975); *Ein Lesebuch* (1975); *Bremen Color* (1976, with Jochen Mönch); *Das andere Leben* (1979); *Sterblich* (1980); *Gedichte* (1980); *Im Gehen* (1981); *Herbstsonett mit Hegel* (1981); *Zwischen Null und Unendlich* (1982); *Herodot; oder, Der Beginn von Geschichte* (1983); *Melanie—Geschicte eines Namens* (1983); *Fremde Körper* (1985); *Nacht-Leben; oder, Geschont Kindheit* (1985); *Unumwunden* (1985); *Gesammelte Gedichte* (4 vols., 1985–); *Die andere Seite der Welt* (1987); *In Kupfer gestochen* (1987); *Auf Erden* (1989); *Sätze in die Nacht* (1990, with Uta Franck); *Meine Gedichte* (1990); *Wenn die Schwermut Fortschritte macht* (1990); *Etwas brennt* (1994); *Gedichte, die von Liebe reden* (1997). FURTHER WORKS IN ENGLISH: *Leave Taking, and Other Poems* (1968); *Poems against Death* (1969); *Invisible Hands* (1969); *Foreign Bodies* (1969); *Bremen Color* (1976); *On Accountr of: Selected Poems* (1985); *What'll We Do with This Life: Selected Poems By K. K. 1950-1990* (1993)

BIBLIOGRAPHY: Domandi, A. K., ed., *A Library of Literary Criticism: Modern German Literature* (1972), Vol. II: 71–76; Fritz, W. H., ed., *Über K. K.* (1972); Rümmler, A., *Die Entwicklung der*

Metaphorik in der Lyrik K. K.s (1972); Paulus, R., *K. K. Bibliographie* (1972); Anderle, M., "Die Entwicklung der Lyrik K. K.s unter französischem und spanischem Einfluß," *Seminar*, 13 (1977): 172–88; Kolter, G., *Die Rezeption westdeutscher Nachkriegslyrik am Beispiel K. K.s* (1977); Paulus, R., *Der Lyriker K. K.* (1983); Arnold, H. L., ed., *K. K.* (1983); Hillebrand, B., *Vernunft ist etwas Sicheres* (1985); Profit, B. B., *Ein Portrait meines Selbst: K. K.'s Autobiographical Poems* (1991); Profit, V. B., *Menschlich* (1996)

—LOWELL A. BANGERTER

KRUCZKOWSKI, Leon

Polish novelist, dramatist, and journalist, b. 28 June 1900, Cracow, d. 1 Aug. 1962, Warsaw

K. grew up in modest surroundings, but his father, a bookbinder, managed to provide his seven children with education. K. finished a technical college in Cracow in 1918, and after two years of military service earned his living by teaching, while being actively engaged in cultural and educational socialist organizations. He began his writing career in 1918 with a volume of verse, but it was only after the success of his first novel, *Kordian i cham* (1932; Kordian and the boor) that he was able to dedicate himself fully to writing. As an officer in the Polish army, he was captured by the Germans during the 1939 campaign and spent the war in a prison camp, returning to Poland in 1945. Consistent and outspoken in his Marxist convictions as novelist before and as playwright after World War II, K. also remained a journalist throughout his career.

K. was an outstanding representative of the trend known as the "literature of the fact" in the 1920s in Russia; in Poland the phrase was the trademark of a group of progressive writers known as "The Suburbs," who believed in literature's duty to create "social documents." *Kordian i cham*, a historical novel, was meant as such a social documentation of the Polish insurrection of 1830–31. Moreover, it was based on an actual document, the diary of a village teacher, Deczyński, which K. fictionalized, changing certain facts to emphasize his thesis: that the nobility and the peasant masses fought for different concepts of a free Poland. This new approach to Poland's history, permeated with Marxist spirit, was K.'s answer to Stefan ŻEROMSKI'S famous historical novel *Popioły* (1904; *Ashes*, 1928), set in the time of the Napoleonic wars. It also refuted the heroic image of Kordian, the hero of the 1830 insurrection, as portrayed in Juliusz Słowacki's (1809–1849) play by that name (1834). K.'s Kordian, a young officer, is puny compared to the valiant "boor" Deczyński.

K.'s second novel, *Pawie pióra* (1935; peacock feathers), is also conceived in terms of the class struggle, this time between the village poor and the *kulaks* (wealthy farmers). Set on the eve of World War I, the novel portrays the awakening class consciousness of the Polish peasantry, presented as a collective hero. It echoes Stanisław WYSPIAŃSKI's *Wesele* (1901; the wedding) in its satire on the intelligentsia's fraternization with the village, and polemicizes against the program of the Peasant Party in interwar Poland.

K.'s third novel, *Sidła* (1937; the trap), is his least successful. It deals with the psychological effects of unemployment undermining the middle-class hero's self-respect and ruining his marriage,

and shows the emerging struggle between the revolutionary elements and the forces of Nazism in the Poland of the 1930s. Psychological analysis and creative imagination are not K.'s strong points, and these weaknesses could account for his preference for social and historical documents. His works also reflect a journalist's passion for participation in current events.

K. turned to the drama after 1945. His plays deal with philosophical and ethical problems, especially those created by the war and its aftermath. He believed that great theater, from its beginnings to today, has been, in his words, "a tribunal or a tribune," that is, a kind of court or a platform from which to express one's views. His own plays, particularly *Odwety* (1948; retributions) and *Niemcy* (1949; the Germans) are meant to be both. *Odwety*, which introduces the first Communist hero in Polish literature, portrays the moral tragedy of the postwar "lost generation"; *Niemcy* shows the impossibility of remaining neutral in a world of evil, the fallacy of an individual's claim to freedom from responsibility for the Nazi crimes. The characters, as is usual with K., are sharply divided into heroes and villains. *Śmierć gubernatora* (1961; death of the governor), whose plot is borrowed from a Russian short story by Leonid ANDREEV is less dependent than other of K.'s works on the dictates of SOCIALIST REALISM, of which K. was a convinced advocate and an acclaimed master. The message of this play is that power—any power—subjugating individual free will is evil; and this idea does not fit well in the Marxist conception of man and the world.

At the source of K.'s successful career—literary and, in the postwar period, political—lies his unswerving adherence to socialist beliefs as much as a humanitarian concern for suffering and social injustice.

FURTHER WORKS: *Bohater naszych czasów* (1935); *Przygoda z Vaterlandem* (1938); *Spotkania i konfrontacje* (1950); *Śród swoich i obcych* (1954); *Odwiedziny* (1955); *Pierwszy dzień wolności* (1960)

BIBLIOGRAPHY: Krzyżanowski, J., *A History of Polish Literature* (1978): 644–45; Miłosz, C., *The History of Polish Literature* (1969): 427–28, 512

—XENIA GASIOROWSKA

KRÚDY, Gyula

Hungarian novelist, b. 21 Oct. 1878, Nyíregyháza; d. 12 May, 1933, Budapest

K. was one of the great loners of modern Hungarian literature. An amazingly prolific writer who produced over sixty novels and three thousand short stories, he nevertheless remained an unaffiliated and curiously anachronistic figure all his life. He was married twice (his first wife, a writer, was seven years his senior; his second, twenty-one years his junior), but domestic life did not seem to suit his temperament. His bohemian habits also took their toll. His health rapidly declined in the 1920s, and he died in great poverty at the age of fifty-five.

K.'s early work reveals the influence of Kálmán Mikszáth's (1847–1910) anecdotal realism, as well as the social consciousness of the Russian realist masters; but he was among the first to abandon an essentially 19th-c. narrative mode, which was to dominate Hungarian fiction for many more years, in favor of a more diffuse, impressionistic, and lyrical prose style. K.'s family belonged to the provincial nobility, but by the turn of the century, this class was past its prime. Unlike Mikszáth, K. had no more stories to tell about it. Instead, he tried to hold on to a fast-vanishing, decadent world by fantasizing about the lives of its heroes. The accent in his fiction was no longer on the narrative but on mood, language, and a subjective authorial point of view.

As an adventurous, robust young writer, K. took turn-of-the-century Budapest by storm. He had the air and habits of an aristocrat and lived the life of a bohemian artist. His drinking, gambling, and womanizing became the stuff from which his fiction was made. K.'s treatment of high life and low life in the big city differed greatly, however, from that of other urban writers who dealt with this subject. He romanticized the present by inventing a kind of "instant" past. In his pages the Hungarian countryside became a quaintly seductive place; his Budapest was filled with inns, music halls, and brothels that really existed only in K.'s mind.

In his first literary success, *A vörös postakocsi* (1914; *The Crimson Coach*, 1967), which has remained his best loved and most frequently republished novel, K. presented the amorous adventures of Szindbád, who in different disguises appears in much of his fiction and who is the fictionalized and idealized alter ego of K. himself. Szindbád is a great seducer of woman, but he is also a chivalrous and gentle man, a rake with a heart, a somber hedonist.

There are autobiographical elements in almost all K.'s writings—the novel *N. N.* (1922; N.N.) is perhaps the most poignant evocation of his childhood—but autobiography becomes fable and legend as the author imaginatively recreates the past. Because his tone is always nostalgic and elegiac, the past thus evoked becomes dreamlike, other-worldly; and in novels such as *Asszonyságok díja* (1920; women's prize), *Hét bagoly* (1922; seven owls), and *Boldogult úrfikoromban* (1930; in my late lamented youth) it is invariably contrasted with a present that is harsh and prosaic. The inability to adjust to a changed world lends tragic dignity to many of K.'s characters. For example his best short story, "Utolsó szivar az Arabs szürkében" (1928; "The Last Cigar at the Grey Arab," 1966) is a masterful study of a melancholy aristocrat, about to fight a senseless duel with a young journalist.

As stylized and deliberately archaizing as his writings may appear, K. was a natural writer. In scores of novels he wrote about the same people and described similar settings; but the profusion of images and impressions enliven even his weaker writings—his many sketchy short stories or his stilted historical fiction. K.'s wistful, decadent sensibility and ironic sentimentality still evoke admiration; and his sophisticated mingling of reality and myth, past and present, lend an air of modernity to his fiction that few readers were aware of when the works first appeared.

FURTHER WORKS: *A podolini kísértet* (1906); *A bűvös erszény* (1908); *Szindbád ifjúsága* (1911); *Szindbád naplója* (1912); *Napraforgó* (1918); *Az útitárs* (1919); *Kleofásné kakasa* (1920); *Őszi versenyek* (1922); *Pesti nőrabló* (1922); *Jockey Club* (1925); *Valakit elvisz az ördög* (1928); *Az élet álom* (1931); *A tiszaeszlári Solymosi Eszter* (1931)

BIBLIOGRAPHY: Reményi, J., *Hungarian Writers and Literature* (1964): 229–38

—IVAN SANDERS

KRYNICKI, Ryszard

Polish poet, b. 28 June 1943, Sankt Valentin, Austria

K., one of the most significant figures of the New Wave in Polish poetry, began his literary career in the late 1960s under a banner of revolt against cultural and political uniformity. He graduated from Adam Mickiewicz University in Poznań (1967). During his student years, K., along with Stanislaw BARAŃCZAK, established the poetic group "Attempts." Both writers were considered the most outstanding representatives of the so-called "linguistic current" in poetry. They focused on a critique of the official language saturated with communist newspeak. By exposing this contaminated language they intended to reveal the captive conscience of the common individual under communism.

K.'s first volume of poetry, *Akt urodzenia* (1969; a birth certificate), was a promising representation of "linguistic poetics." Following the chief theoretician of the prewar Polish avant-garde, Tadeusz Peiper (1891–1969), in this volume K. adopted a style known as an "arrangement of blossoming." Each "blossoming poem" consisted of a whole set of ever more developed sentence structures reflecting the psychological process of cognition.

In the early 1970s, K., like Barańczak and Adam ZAGAJEWSKI, rejected the concept of the poet isolated from social realities and attempted to introduce political topics, such as the workers' bloody protests in December 1970, into his verses. His second volume, *Organizm zbiorowy* (1975; a collective organism), bears traces of such attempts. As a result of K.'s involvement in protests against restrictions of civil liberties, his name was put on the censor's Black List in December 1975. Consequently, his next volume, *Nasze życie rośnie* (1978; our life grows), could only be published in the West.

K.'s poetry of the mid-1970s is characterized by the intertwining of two different kinds of sensitivity: visionary and ethical. While reading these works, one is impressed by the quality of strangeness. The internal world of the poet is placed on the border between a waking and a dreamlike state. This visionary imagination is backed by a feeling of ethical chaos and by the image of reality in which intimate experiences can no longer be a protective shelter against the storm of history. Many of K.'s poems have drawn from the prophetic tradition through both the use of devices and the poet's ethical passion.

In the late 1970s, K.'s name frequently appeared in the uncensored quarterly *Zapis* among the names of its editors and contributors. After Wojciech Jaruzelski's declaration of martial law in December 1981, K. chose to remain in Poland. During the 1980s, he published several volumes of poetry in the underground: *Niewiele więcej* (1980; not much more), *Jeżeli w jakimś kraju* (1983; if in some country), and *Niewiele więcej i nowe wiersze* (1984; not much more and new poems). These independent publishing activities did not fail to have an impact on the formation of K.'s literary language. Freedom from censorship contributed to the literalness and simplicity of the poet's recent works.

Since his debut in 1969, K.'s poetics has come a long way. His early visionary works often assumed a verbose form, rich in both wordplay and paradox. All of those devices were gradually replaced by a means typical of poetic aphorisms and, when martial law had been imposed on Poland, by moral or even political slogans. Published under the changing political circumstances K.'s more recent collections of poetry, *Niepodlegli nicości* (1989; Independent of Nothingness) and *Magnetyczny punkt. Wybrane wiersze I przekłady* (1996; Magnetic Point: Selected Poems and Translations), contain some of his old and new works. The new poems included in these volumes represent an ecumenical position toward cognitive and ethical values, a position that no longer depends on any political encouragement or restrictions, but on the revelation of difficult, timeless truths.

K. has won several significant literary awards, among them the Kościelskis Prize (1973) and the Jurzykowski Prize (1989).

FURTHER WORKS IN ENGLISH: *Citizen R. K. Does Not Live* (1985)

BIBLIOGRAPHY: Barańczak, S., Foreword to *Citizen R. K. Does Not Live* (1985): 7–9; Witkowski, T., "R. K.: Between Metaphysics and Politics," *Studium Papers*, 14: 1–2 (1990), 70; Witkowski, T., "Between Poetry and Politics: Two Generations," *Periphery*, 2 (1996): 38-43; Witkoeski, T., "Politics for Art's Sake," *Periphery*, 3 (1997): 62-68

—TADEUSZ WITKOWSKI

KUKRIT Pramoj

Thai novelist, philosopher, historian, and journalist, b. 20 April 1911, Sing Buri; d. 9 Oct. 1995, Bangkok

K., the youngest son of Prince Khamop, received his early education in Thailand. At the age of fifteen he was sent to England to complete his secondary schooling; he then went to Oxford, from which he graduated in 1933. Returning to Thailand, he worked in the ministry of finance and later in banking; he also taught at two Thai universities. K. entered politics in 1946, serving as a cabinet minister for a time. His experiences as a politician, as well as his several months as a Buddhist monk, have colored his literary works. He was also active in Thai theater, acting and directing.

K. did not reach prominence as a literary figure until the early 1950s. His major works were written between 1950, when he left active politics, and 1973, when he returned to it (he was prime minister, 1975–76). In 1950 he founded the now greatly respected newspaper *Siam Rath*, in which all of his major works were to appear first. Because of this newspaper serialization, it is almost impossible to set exact dates to his works.

Sam kok chabab nai thun (c. 1949–51; three kingdoms: a capitalist's version) was K.'s first major novel. It retells the story of the Chinese classic of the 14th through 17th cs., *Three Kingdoms*, but from the point of view of the traditional villain, Tsao Tsao, rather than that of the hero, Liu Pei, to prove that the concept of heroism or villainy depends on the narrator's political point of view.

K.'s greatest novel, *Si phaendin* (1953; *Four Reigns*, 1981), tells the life story of a Thai upper-class woman, Poly, from 1892, when she goes to live in the Grand Palace as a servant of a royal princess at the age of ten, until her death in 1946 as a married woman outside the palace, with children and grandchildren. But the story of Ploy is a pretext for analyzing and commenting on the times and ever-shifting fashions. The book is, indeed, a detailed social record.

Another novel, *Phai daeng* (1953; *Red Bamboo*, 1961), tells of a Buddhist monk's conflicts with a local communist agitator in a fictitious town in central Thailand. *Huang maharnob* (early 1950s; the deep ocean) is K.'s most important nonfiction work. In it he shows the truth of Buddhist doctrine as proved by biology, and vice versa. The book has been criticized because K. assumes the truth of Buddhist teachings *a priori*. This is one of the strangest books of philosophy in Thai, and a puzzling work to many readers.

K.'s writings are always didactic, but his style is so fluent and humorous that he has an enormous readership in Thailand.

FURTHER WORKS: *Thok khmer* (early 1950s); *Lai chivit* (1950s); *Phuen non* (3 vols., 1950s–1960s); *Tsu hsi t'ai hao* (1950s); *Lok suan tua khong phom* (c. 1961–1962); *Yiu* (1968); *Khrong kraduk nai tu* (1971); *Tueng khong khon rak ma* (1978); *K. pho krua hua pa* (1979); *Tob panha hua jai* (1980)

BIBLIOGRAPHY: Wyatt, D. K., "K. P. and *Red Bamboo*," *Solidarity*, 5, 6 (1970): 68–73

—AYUMONGOL SONAKUL

KUKUČÍN, Martin

(pseud. of Matej Bencúr) Czechoslovak novelist and short-story writer (writing in Slovak), b. 17 May 1860, Jasenová; d. 21 May 1928, Zagreb, Yugoslavia

K. spent his early years in Slovakia, where he taught school briefly, and studied medicine in Prague. Because of his disappointment with social and political developments in Slovakia, he spent his adult life as an émigré, first in Dalmatia and later in Chile. He made two short visits to Slovakia, and died in self-imposed exile in Yugoslavia.

Early in his career K. enriched Slovak literature with a number of well-written short stories about the village people he knew from his youth. He describes their philosophy of life, their sorrows and joys, their humor and misery with perfection of detail and a deep knowledge of their psychology. His "village heroes" are portrayed with profound humanism and humor, even if their fates are tragic, and K.'s deeply ethical view of life transcends the descriptive realism of his characters. In his stories he reflected the moral and religious concepts of his people and their spiritual heritage. The gentry and the middle class in Slovakia had lost a sense of Slovak identity by the end of the 19th c., and K. portrayed the patient heroism of the village people as a means of arousing a sense of nationhood. An example of K.'s masterful narrative technique is his short story "Neprebudený" (1886; "unawakened," or "the village idiot"), in which the tragic end of a village idiot, who falls in love with the village belle, is presented by contrasting innocence and cruelty in the semifeudal world of a poor village.

While living in Dalmatia, K. produced his great novel *Dom v stráni* (2 vols., 1903–4; house on a hillside). With warm realism, K. depicts a conflict between two social classes—a landowning family and the patriarchal family of a simple farmer—against the background of the beautiful Dalmatian countryside. The great love of two young people, the children respectively of a proud peasant and of a no less proud landowner, fails to change the existing human relations and social order, which are stronger than human feelings. The structure, style, and psychological analysis of this novel make it one of the best examples of Slovak realism. It has been translated into several languages.

During his years in South America K. prepared material for a five-volume novel, *Mat' volá* (1926–27; motherland calls). This sad saga of Croatian immigrants in South America, with its central theme of the struggle for a livelihood and for human dignity, is different in style and structure from his previous works. K. evolved in this work from depicting the life of individuals or communities to the description of universal concepts of a new social order based on Christian principles.

K. also wrote historical novels and three plays. He was mainly attracted by the stormy events in Slovakia in the 19th c., and he portrayed the events and historical figures realistically. In several nonfiction books he described his travels and life in Chile, Argentina, France, and Yugoslavia.

In K.'s short stories, which influenced a number of writers, Slovak realism reached its purest literary form. K. is deservedly credited with helping to replace romanticism, which anachronistically prevailed in Slovak literature, with a moderate realism tempered by humanism, humor, and sympathy for simple people.

FURTHER WORKS: *Dedinský jarmok* (1883); *Obecné trampoty* (1884); *Z teplého hniezda* (1885); *Ryšavá jalovica* (1885); *Na obecnom salaši* (1887); *Zápisky zo smutného domu* (1888); *Na podkonickom bále* (1891); *Dies irae* (1892); *Ked' báčik z Chocholova umrie* (1894); *Vel'kou lyžicou* (1895); *Svadba* (1895); *Mladé letá* (1899); *Komasácia* (1899); *Bacuchovie dvor* (1923); *Obet'* (1924); *Lukáš Blahosej Krasoň* (1929); *Bohumil Valizlost' Zábor* (1930). FURTHER WORKS IN ENGLISH: *Seven Slovak Stories by M. K.* (1979)

BIBLIOGRAPHY: Krčméry, S., "A Survey of Modern Slovak Literature," *SEER*, 7 (1928–1929): 160–70; Selver, P., "The Literature of the Slovaks," *SlavonicR*, 12 (1934): 691–703; Mráz, A., *Die Literatur der Slowaken* (1943): 140–44; Potoček, C. J., *M. K.: A Link between Two Worlds* (1943); Noge, J., *An Outline of Slovakian Literature* (1968): 35–38; Rudinsky, N. L., "M. K., 1860–1923" and "Preliminary Notes on M. K.'s Criticism of Americanized Slovaks and His Opposition to the Slovak Gentry," *Slovak Studies*, 18 (1978): 7–64, 153–65

—JOSEPH M. KIRSCHBAUM

KUMIN, Maxine

American poet, essayist, novelist, short-story writer, and children's-book author, b. 6 June 1925, Philadelphia, Pa.

Although she has published essays and fiction, as well as a notable body of books for children, several in collaboration with fellow poet Anne SEXTON, K. is best known as a poet. Her work combines urban sophistication, an intellectual awareness of the universe, with deep knowledge of and feeling for both nature and rural life. Her biography reflects a similar duality: After living for many years in the Boston area, where she was a student at Radcliffe College (A.B., 1946; M.A., 1948) and then taught creative writing at institutions in the region, including Tufts and Brandeis universities, the University of Massachusetts, and Newton College, she moved to a farm in New Hampshire, where she gardens extensively and raises Arabian and quarter horses.

One of the words most commonly used in reviews and commentaries on K.'s work is "survival." She does write about personal and social grief, but the emphasis is on things that grow, continuity between generations, and other forces that insist on life—apprehended emotionally, though unsentimentally. The title of K.'s first

Maxine Kumin

published collection of poems, *Halfway* (1961), suggests the traditional midpoint in the biblically allotted human lifespan of threescore and ten, Dante's "middle of the journey." K. was at midlife, rhetorically, if not actuarially, but at the beginning of a poetic career that, over the next thirty years, was to witness the publication of eleven collections of her poems.

Halfway introduces themes that recur in K.'s work, particularly in *Up Country: Poems of New England* (1972), awarded the Pulitzer Prize for poetry in 1973, *Our Ground Time Here Will Be Brief* (1982), and *Nurture: Poems New and Selected* (1989). The particular survival of which she speaks in poems about fruits and vegetables, children, and animals is, throughout, what Sandra M. Gilbert (b. 1936) and Susan Gubar (b. 1944), writing in *The Norton Anthology of Literature by Women* (1985), call "a redemptive choice for sanity." K.'s close association with Anne Sexton and her references to her friend since the latter's suicide underscore the sense in which both physical and psychic survival represent conscious choices for her.

K.'s two collections of essays make a deliberate effort to connect the poet's experience of language with the lived experience of the natural world of New England. Thus, *To Make a Prairie* (1979) is subtitled "Essays on Poets, Poetry and Country Living," whereas the same relationship, at once metaphysical and metaphorical, is implied by the title of *In Deep: Country Essays* (1987). By contrast, K.'s fiction tends to concentrate on interpersonal relations; once more, a title, this time of a collection of short stories, *Why Can't We Live Together Like Civilized Human Beings?*

(1982), suggests both subject and tone. The children's books that K. has published, the earliest of them predating her first collection of poems, are fantasies or nature stories, all represented with a poet's ear and a poet's wit. Illustrated (by other hands), they both stress and stimulate the imagination.

FURTHER WORKS: *Sebastian and the Dragon* (1960); *Spring Things* (1961); *Summer Story* (1961); *Follow the Fall* (1961); *A Winter Friend* (1961); *Mittens in May* (1962); *No One Writes a Letter to the Snail* (1962); *Eggs of Things* (1963, with Anne Sexton); *Archibald the Traveling Poodle* (1963); *More Eggs of Things* (1964, with Anne Sexton); *Speedy Digs Downside Up* (1964); *The Beach Before Breakfast* (1964); *The Privilege* (1965); *Through Dooms of Love* (1965); *Paul Bunyan* (1966); *Faraway Farm* (1967); *Wonderful Babies of 1809 and Other Years* (1968); *The Passions of Uxport* (1968); *When Grandmother Was Young* (1969); *When Mother Was Young* (1970); *The Nightmare Factory* (1970); *The Abduction* (1971); *When Great-Grandmother Was Young* (1971); *Joey and the Birthday Present* (1971, with Anne Sexton); *Tilting the Barn Swallow* (1972); *The Designated Heir* (1974); *House, Bridge, Fountain, Gate* (1975); *The Wizard's Tears* (1975, with Anne Sexton); *What Color Is Caesar?* (1978); *The Retrieval System* (1978); *Closing the Ring* (1984); *The Microscope* (1984); *The Long Approach* (1985); *Looking for Luck* (1992); *Women, Animals and Vegetables: Essays and Stories* (1994); *Connecting the Dots* (1996)

BIBLIOGRAPHY: Green, C., *A Writer Is Essentially a Spy* (1972); Booth, P., "M. K.'s Survival," *APR*, 7, 6 (Nov.-Dec. 1978): 18–19; Estess, S. P., "Past Halfway: *The Retrieval System* by M. K.," *IowaR*, 10, 4 (Autumn 1979): 99–109; Hammond, K., "An Interview with M. K.," *WHR*, 33, 1 (Winter 1979): 2–15; Armitage, S., "An Interview with M. K.," *Paintbrush*: 7–8 (1980–81): 48–58; George, D. H., "K. on K. and Sexton: An Interview," *Poesis* 6, 2 (1985): 1–18; Harris, P., "Poetry Chronicle: Hunger, Hope, and Nurture: Poetry from Michael Ryan, the Chinese Democracy Movement, and M. K.," *VQR*: 67, 3 (1991): 455–77; Grosholz, E., *Telling the Barn Swallow: Poets on the Poetry of M. K.* (1997)

—LILLIAN S. ROBINSON

KUNANBAEV, Abai

Kazakh poet, b. 10 Aug., 1845, Chingis-Tau (now Karaul); d. 6 July, 1904, Chingis-Tau

K., who can easily be called the founder of modern Kazakh literature, was born into the family of a prominent feudal lord. He received a traditional education at a Kazakh *maktep* under Mullah Akhmet-Riza before he entered the Semipalatinsk school for a Russian education. The new school impacted K., influencing his world view, which thus far had been limited to the thoughts of Eastern authors like Abu al-Qasim Firdowsi (935-1020 or 26), Nizami Ganjavi (1141-1209), Muslih al-Din Sa'di (1213-1292), and Alisher Navo'i (1441-1501). Through the works of Ivan Andrevich Krilov (1769-1844), Alexandr Sergevich Pushkin (1799-1837), and Mikhail Urivich Lermontov (1814-1841), K. became familiar with methods and means that reshaped not only his own literary views but the views and the lifestyle of his whole tribe which was still nomadizing outside Semipalatinsk.

K. is one of the early promoters of the Russian language and culture among the Kazakhs. This is apparent from the themes of his poetry that deal with resistance against oppression and support of the weak, especially women. This to the point that Soviet commentators find in him the epitomé of progress in dismantling the Islamic *Shari'a* law among the Kazakhs. K.'s early poems are poignant examples of his stance against oppression and the tyranny of the *bais*, his own father included. Neither is his contribution to Kazakh poetry confined to the social themes he had developed. K. was also instrumental in introducing both the *musaddas* and the *musamman* meters as well as several thematic innovations into Kazakh verse. His treatment of the four seasons of the year, which includes "Bahor" (1890; Spring), "Zhoz" (1886; Summer), "Kuz" (1889; Fall), and "Qïsh" (1888; Winter), is one such innovation.

In addition, K.'s literary legacy includes a number of ballads with Eastern and Western themes. These fictional pieces include "Masqut" (1887; Mas'ud) and "Ezim Etsimesi" (A Word About Azim), exploring Eastern themes, while "Iskandir" (Alexander) examines the exploits of Alexander the Great. In this latter work K. compares Alexander's destructive measures with the constructive wisdom of Aristotle, Alexander's teacher.

Finally, being a musician, K. has adapted some of his own lyric poetry to music. In these pieces, he employs the Kazakh vernacular for the expression of the progressive aspects of the literatures of the East and the West.

K.'s life is the subject of two major works by the Kazakh author and academician Mukhtar Auezov (1897-1961). Entitled *Abai* (1942-47; *Abai*, 1992) and *Abai Zholï* (1952-56; The Path of Abai), these works examine the life of the poet as well as the history that shaped that life and the lives of his Kazakh contemporaries. The saga begins with K. as a boy returning to his *aul* from Semipalatinsk. There he observes the execution of a man and a woman who had been found guilty by the *Shari'a* law. He further discovers that his own father, Kunanbai, had been cunningly plotting the elimination of the innocents. Right there, K.'s path lies in front of him. Education of the Kazakhs in the Russian tradition by distancing them from the connivance of the likes of Kunanbai.

The task, however, was not easy. Neither was K.'s education sufficient to fathom the depth of the cultures involved. According to Auezov, K. joined forces with E. P. Mikhailov (dates n.a.), a political exile and a clever individual. Through Mikhailov, K. became aware of the unhappiness of the Russian masses and their struggle to free themselves from serfdom; a situation very similar to that of his own people trying to extricate themselves from the shackles of the *bais* and the *mullahs*.

The saga ends when K. masterfully foils all the intrigue that his enemies advance against him. Using his poetic and musical talents, he reaches the youths of the *auls* and communicates his message to them. With their help, he exposes the political machinations of the enemies of the people and opens the way for a smooth transition for the Kazakhs into a sedentary, law-abiding existence.

K. enriched the existing poetic forms by introducing new genres. The intellectual content of his poetry, some of which he himself put to music, endeared them to the Kazakh people while the humanist aspect served as a guide for the Kazakhs who, at the time, were on the verge of giving up their nomadic lifestyle for settlement in villages and towns.

FURTHER WORKS: *Qazaq akïnï Ibrahim Qünanbay üghlynïq, ölengy* (2 vols., 1909); *Shgharmaringïng byr todïq tolïq jïnagha*(1961)

BIBLIOGRAPHY: Akhmetov, Z., *Lermontov i Abai* (1954); Tazhibaev, T., *Filosofskie Psikholocheskie i Pedagogicheskie Vzglyadi Abaya Kunanbayeva* (1957); Karataev, M. S., *Rozhdennaia Oktiabrem* (1958); Auezov, M., *A. K.:Stat'i i issledovannia* (1967); Jünger, H., ed., *The Literatures of the Soviet Peoples: A Historical and Biographical Survey* (1970): 99; Auezov, M., *Put' Abaya* (2 vols., 1971); Diusenbaev, I. T., "A. K.," *Great Soviet Encyclopeia*, 3rd ed. (1973), Vol. 1: 2

—IRAJ BASHIRI

KUNDERA, Milan

Czechoslovak novelist, essayist, dramatist, and poet (writing in Czech and French) b. 1 April 1929, Brno

K. comes from a highly cultured middle class background. His father was a famous pianist and musicologist, an expert on the composer Leoš Janáček. As a result of the Nazi occupation, political consciousness came early for K. When he joined the Communist Party at the age of eighteen, he had no doubts about the course history had to take in order to fulfill the promise of the Liberation. This was in 1947, one year before the Communist seizure of power in Czechoslovakia. K.'s relationship with the Party, however, was to be problematic and unsteady; in 1950 he was dropped from membership, but was reinstated in 1956, after the "thaw," only to be dropped once more in 1970, as a result of his participation in the Prague Spring of 1968. Since 1969 his writings have not been allowed to be published in his homeland, and he has lived and published abroad since 1975, having received an extended travel visa from the Czechoslovak government. He has taught at the University of Rennes in France and now lives in Paris.

K.'s first publications, three books of verse, were in tune with the spirit of the times and won him the approbation of the official cultural establishment. The most publicized of his poetic cycles, *Poslední máj* (1955; the last May), celebrates the wartime martyrdom of the young Communist militant and writer Julius Fučík (1903–1943).

In the 1960s K. shifted to prose, having discovered the ambiguities of history and the uses of the language of irony. His three series of short stories under the title *Směšné lásky* (1963, 1965, 1968; *Laughable Loves*, 1974) established him as a modern master of the black comedy of the bedroom. In the setting of a people's democracy, the pursuit by K.'s Don Juan-like character of the "golden apple of eternal desire" can never break with the literary convention of farce. But his metaphysical anguish makes him a spiritual descendant of Mozart's Don Giovanni, although cloaked in darker meanings by overtones of Kierkegaard's interpretation of the Don Juan figure in his *Diary of a Seducer*.

Under the influence of the Kraus-Krejča actors' workshop, K. tried his hand at drama. His first play, *Majitelé klíčů* (1962; the owners of the keys), was an immediate if much debated success. The action, set in the period of the Nazi occupation, confronts the values of personal heroism in the name of a public cause with the attitudes of cowardly privatism, stemming from the necessary but questionable instinct for survival. During the ensuing controversy, K. protested in the essay "Slovo máautor" (1962; the word belongs to the author), published as an afterword to the play, that his heart was firmly on the side of heroism, but the implications of his play were considerably more ambivalent.

Milan Kundera

In his first novel, *Žert* (1967; *The Joke*, 1974), K.'s obsessive master theme of the ironic interplay between erotic and political potencies and their mutual interchangeability emerged. Since its plot describes the wrecking of the career of a young Czech Party intellectual during the Stalinist purges, the novel was immediately read as a manifestation of the new political thaw. K. was allowed to transform his novel into a script for a film, which he directed himself and which played successfully to international audiences.

In June 1967 K. delivered a major address at the Fourth Congress of Czechoslovak Writers. He reminded his colleagues of their extraordinary historical burden. Czech culture and even the Czech nation itself, he warned, existed not by the force of historical necessity but rather by the grace of its literature.

K.'s second novel was first published in France as *La vie est ailleurs* (1973; *Life Is Elsewhere*, 1974), where it was honored with the Médicis Prize for the best foreign novel. The original Czech text, under the title *Život je jinde*, even though completed in 1970, saw light only in 1979, when it was published by the émigré press run by Josef ŠKVORECKÝ. It is a chronicle of the early fame and premature demise of Jaromil, a Communist poet of distinctly bourgeois origins. In the career of this character K. examines the peculiar modern relation between poetry and revolutionary power. He diagnoses both forces as unclean, born of resentment and fear of impotence.

Valčík na rozloučenou (1979; *The Farewell Party*, 1976) has had a similar publishing history. This novel is another sexual comedy with a philosophical thrust. In a Bohemian spa that claims to cure infertility, men and women perform their mating dances with grim singlemindedness, as practiced gladiators of a society out of joint with nature and indifferent to history.

The novel *Kniha smíchu a zapomnění* was first published in France as *Le livre du rire et de l'oubli* (1979; *The Book of Laughter and Forgetting*, 1980). It is a polyphonic treatment of the theme of loss of memory and also seems to be an act of exorcism directed at the author's homeland, which he sees as petrified in a sleep resembling death. K. dubs Gustav Husák, the Czechoslovak president installed by the Russians, as the "president of forgetting."

K.'s significance as a writer cannot be divorced from the meaning of his people's recent historical experiences. His message of disillusionment falls on ready ears in the most sophisticated Western circles precisely because it is thoroughly existential, rather than ideological. It has to do with life's everyday texture and taste. The message is all the more effective because it comes from a true insider, a man whose social sensibility was bred in the international left's best hopes for humanity. For his countrymen, K.'s skepticism has the sting of a particularly Czech anxiety, a submerged deathwish, perhaps, in a culture perpetually in danger of being again overrun and delivered into oblivion.

The tragic days of August 1968 in Prague, when the Soviet tanks rolled in, figure in *Nesnesitelná lehkost bytí* (1985; *The Unbearable Lightness of Being*, 1984), encoded within the paradoxical treatment of the binary categories of light and heavy. Initially published in French translation as *L'Insoutenable légereté de l'être* (1984), this novel, which opens with a meditation on Nietzsche's myth of eternal recurrence, established K. as the postmodernist master of philosophical fiction.

Immortality (1991; *L'Immortalité*, 1990; *Nesmrtelnost*, 1993), Opus Seven of K.'s novelistic *oeuvre*, completes the great sequence of his Czech novels. A vast diachronic composition, it confronts Goethe's privileged moment at mid-point of the European Modern Era with the terminal decade of the 20c. In K.'s retrospective vision, our time assumes the redundant quality of an epilogue, with imagology supplanting ideology and all higher forms of culture bowing out.

Nesmrtelnost, appearing in Paris while communism was collapsing in Prague, is also poised on the cusp of K.'s personal history. It signals his transition from being a Czech writer in exile to his new, freely assumed identity as a European novelist writing in French.

Until then, K. had used French for essays, most notably those comprising the seven chapters of his seminal *L'art du roman* (1986; *The Art of the Novel*, 1988). Even earlier, he had translated the Czech text of a play completed in Prague in 1971, *Jacques it son maître, hommage à Denis Diderot en trois actes*, (1981). In 1993, a second book of essays in French (*Les testaments trahis*; *Testaments Betrayed*, 1995) continues K.'s meditation on the history of the European novel which he has called his only home.

La lenteur (1995; *Slowness*, 1996) the first of K.'s French novels is conceived as an hommage to the language and the spirit of Vivant Kenon's 18c. novella *Point de lendemain*. Formally inventive and rich in comic improvisation, the novel pits a large cast of contemporary, mostly grotesque characters against the dream of Denon's lovers.

In *L' Identité* (1997; *Identity*, 1998) the spatial and temporal scope narrows, as K. Takes a plunge into the inner world of an aging couple bound together by obsessional love. With sinister elegance, the stripped down linear narrative choreographs the theme of necessity as a descent into a nightmarish climax.

FURTHER WORKS: *Člověk zahrada širá* (1953); *Monology* (1957); *Umění románu: Cesta Vladislava Vančury za velkou epikou* (1960); *Sestřičko mych sestřiček* (1963); *Dvě uši dvě svatby* (1968); *Ptákovina* (1969)

BIBLIOGRAPHY: Roth, P., "Introducing M. K.," in M. K., *Laughable Loves* (1974): 1–16; Doležel, L., "A Scheme of Narrative Times" [on *The Joke*], in Matejka, L., and Titunik, I. R., eds., *Semiotics of Art: Prague School Contributions* (1976): 209–17; Harkins, W. E., Supplement to Novák, A., *Czech Literature* (1976): 349–55; Trensky, P. I., *Czech Drama since World War II* (1978): 73–84; Banerjee, M. N., on *Život je jinde* and *Le livre du rire et de l'oubli, WLT*, 54 (1980): 131–32; Updike, J., on *The Book of Laughter and Forgetting, NYTBR*, 30 Nov. 1980: 74–78; Adams, R. M., in *NYRB*, 5 Feb. 1981: 22–23; Jungmann, M., "K.'s Paradoxes," in Goetz-Stankiewicz, M., ed., *Good-bye, Samizdat* (1985); Banerjee, M. N., *Terminal Paradox: The Novels of M. K.* (1992); Longinovic, T. Z., *Borderline Culture* (1993); Misurella, F., *Understanding M. K.: Public Events, Private Affairs* (1993); O'Brien, J., *M. K. and Feminism* (1995); Chvatik, K., *Le monde romanesque de M. K.* (1995); Le Grand, E., *K. ou la mémoire du désir* (1996)

—MARIA NĚMCOVÁ BANERJEE

KUNERT, Günter

German poet, short-story writer, and novelist, b. 6 March 1929, Berlin

During his youth in Berlin, then the capital of Nazi Germany, K. experienced racial discrimination and other hardships because of his Jewish mother. After the war he briefly attended the Berlin Academy for Applied Arts before turning to writing. His first poems, published in the magazine *Ulenspiegel* in 1948, won him the praise and support of Johannes R. Becher (1891–1958), the EXPRESSIONIST poet who had become Minister of Culture in the newly founded German Democratic Republic. Initially promoted by the East Berlin cultural establishment, K. enjoyed considerable literary success, received various prizes, and was able to travel extensively in Europe and the U.S., even spending a semester (Fall 1972) as writer-in-residence at the University of Texas, Austin. Because of his stubbornly independent political attitudes, however, he gradually fell out of favor with the East German régime. In 1979 he was permitted to emigrate to West Germany.

K.'s early writings were much indebted to Bertolt BRECHT and the Americans Carl SANDBURG and Edgar Lee MASTERS; his later works show the increasing influence of Franz KAFKA. Quite unlike the lofty, rhetorical sentiments and extreme pathos of Becher, from the outset K.'s poetic stance has been cool and distanced, devoid of any shrill emotionality, and his diction is laconic, matter of fact, even colloquial. In his early poems, published in the volumes *Wegschilder und Mauerinschriften* (1950; road signs and wall inscriptions), *Unter diesem Himmel* (1955; under this sky), *Tagwerke* (1960; daily chores), and *Das Kreuzbrave Liederbuch* (1961; the well-behaved songbook)—selections from these volumes were later included in *Erinnerung an einen Planeten* (1963; memories of a planet)—he favored the traditional genres of song, ballad, and sonnet, but he also began to experiment with two newer forms, familiar from the poetry of Brecht: the dialectical minimal poem (a sparse poem of only five to ten lines characterized by extreme reduction of language and a dialectical logical structure) and the longer poem with epic qualities, employing a "gestic" style, fragmented sentences, and unrhymed verses with irregular rhythms. These two forms are dominant in his later poetry, collected in *Der ungebetene Gast* (1965; the uninvited guest), *Verkündigung des Wetters* (1966; weather announcement), *Warnung vor Spiegeln* (1970; beware of mirrors), *Unterwegs nach Utopia* (1977; on the way to utopia), *Verlangen nach Bomarzo: reisegedichte* (1978; longing for Bomarzo: travel poems), and *Abtötungsverfahren* (1980; procedures for mortification).

Although primarily known as a poet, K. has also written masterful, Kafkaesque short stories and miniature prose sketches reminiscent of Brecht's Keuner stories, published in the collections *Tagträume* (1964; daydreams), *Die Beerdigung findet in aller Stille statt* (1968; a private funeral will be held), and *Tagträume in Berlin und andernorts* (1972; daydreams in Berlin and elsewhere). His attempts at longer forms such as radio and television plays— for example, *Der Kaiser von Hondu* (1959; the emperor of Hondu) and *Ehrenhändel* (1972; affairs of honor)—and the novel *Im Namen der Hüte* (1967; in the name of hats) have been less successful. Recent experiments, however, with forms such as the short, Kafkaesque detective novel—*Gast aus England* (1973; guest from England)—and the satirical travel diary—*Der andere Planet: ansichten von Amerika* (1974; the other planet: views of America)—reveal promising new dimensions to his talents.

Because of his avowed desire to provoke his reader into self-awareness, K. has attempted to avoid any clearly defined ideological stance and has thus been able to appeal to audiences in both East and West. His major concerns—the conflict between individual self-realization and collective social goals, the threat of stagnation and persistent inhumanity undermining genuine efforts for positive social change, the dehumanizing effects of necessary technological advances—find poetic statement in moods ranging from unreserved confidence in the future, sardonic humor about human frailties, acerbic satire of present conditions, and dark despair about the ultimate futility of human endeavor. Recurrent themes and images—the pilot, for example, as a symbol for man's cosmic aspirations, as opposed to the buccaneer who perishes in his search for El Dorado—emerge in ever new variations to express a dialectical tension between the ideal and the real, between hope and disillusionment. Not surprisingly, in both his poetry and prose K. shows a marked preference for the parable, a form that can lend concrete expression to an abstract idea without becoming politically too explicit.

While K.'s early works proclaim an optimistic faith in social progress and collective human regeneration, his stance since the early 1960s has become increasingly skeptical, even bitter, often verging on profound melancholy. His struggle to achieve a balance between social preoccupations and the needs of the individual is in many respects paradigmatic for life in East Germany. It will therefore be interesting to see to what extent living in the West will affect his poetic production.

FURTHER WORKS: *Der ewige Detektiv* (1954); *Vom König Midas* (1958); *Die Weltreise im Zimmer* (1961); *Unschuld der Natur* (1966); *Kramen in Fächern* (1968); *Betonformen Ortsangaben* (1969); *Ortsangaben* (1971); *Notizen in Kreide* (1970); *Offener Ausgang* (1972); *Die geheime Bibliothek* (1973); *Im weiteren Fortgang* (1974); *Der Mittelpunkt der Erde* (1975); *Das kleine Aber* (1976); *Warum schreiben? Notizen zur Literatur* (1976);

Jeder Wunsch ein Treffer (1976); *Keine Affäre* (1976); *Ein anderer K.: Hörspiel* (1977; *A Different K.: A Radio Play*, 1977); *Camera obscura* (1978); *Unruhiger Schlaf* (1978); *Die Schreie der Fledermäuse: Geschichten, Gedichte, Aufsätze* (1979); *Ein englisches Tagebuch* (1980); *Ziellose Umtriebe: Nachrichten vom Reisen und vom Daheimsein* (1981)

BIBLIOGRAPHY: Demetz, P., *Postwar German Literature* (1970): 89–92; Flores, J., *Poetry in East Germany* (1971): 280–92; Hofacker, E. P., "G. K. and the East German Image of Man," *Monatshefte*, 66 (1974): 366–80; Hilton, I., "G. K.: The Way Ahead," *BA*, 50 (1976): 46–54; Kahn, L., "Orpheus in the East: G. K.'s Orpheus Cycle," *MLQ*, 38 (1977): 78–96; Jonsson, D., *Widersprüche— Hoffnungen: Literatur und Kulturpolitik: Die Prosa G. K.s* (1978); Krüger, M., ed., *K. lesen* (1979)

—HELENE SCHER

al-KŪNĪ, Ibrāhīm

(also spelled al-Kawnī or al-Koni), Libyan novelist and short-story writer, b. 1948, Libya

Born in the southern Libyan desert into a family of the Tuareg, the renowned traversers of the desert wastes of the Sahara, K. was educated in Libya and then worked as a journalist there before traveling to Moscow to study at the Gorky Institute. There he devoted himself to the study of literary traditions of the world, and, most notably, of Russia; his comments to colleagues make it abundantly clear that he feels a special affinity for the works and vision of Dostoevsky. During the 1980s K. lived in Poland, and more recently he has made Switzerland his place of residence.

While it would appear that K. has been writing since at least the 1970s, it was only in the 1980s and even more in the 1990s that he achieved a wide recognition for his contributions to the tradition of Arabic fiction. His output during this period has been prolific; K. is a writer with an absolute sense of literary purpose and a fresh vision through which to convey it. While dates of publication may not be an entirely accurate reflection of chronology, it appears that K. began his career with the short story genre, publishing a number of collections, from *Al-salāt khārij nitāq al-awqāt al-khamsah* (1974; Prayer Outside the Framework of the Normal Five Times) to *Al-qafas* (1990; The Cage) and *Dīwān al-nathr al-barrī* (1991; Collection of Prose from the Wild). Between 1989 and 1998 K. published a remarkable series of novels, some of them, such as *Al-khusūf* (1989; The Eclipse) and *Al-majūs* (2 vols., 1991, 1992; The Magi), in two or more volumes. These works have helped to establish K.'s reputation as a new and different voice in contemporary Arabic fiction. In 1970 he gave the clearest possible evidence of his extensive knowledge of the history and politics of the region that provides him with his fictional inspiration by publishing a historical study entitled *Thawrat al-sahrā al-kubrā* (Revolution of the Great Sahara).

The desert existence and the values and customs that it fosters are, of course, a deeply embedded part of the Arab sense of self-identity and heritage. Within the modern Arabic literary tradition the novel has tended to follow the example of its Western forebears by concentrating on the institution of the city and its variety of inhabitants. In the worlds created by novelists the desert has been an alien place, to be crossed—as illustrated in the work of Ghassān

KANAFĀNĪ—or polluted and destroyed—as illustrated in the work of 'Abd al-Raḥmān MUNĪF. It is in this regard that K. provides the Arabic novel with a new optic, as the desert—with all its pristine beauty and, when it so chooses, overwhelming savagery—becomes the venue for novels that recount the lives and loves of its peoples, past and present. Its denizens and the fascinating histories of its peoples and places are invoked to create a fabled world through which the reader of contemporary Arabic novels can contemplate the relationship of a complex and uncertain present, with most of its most powerful hegemonic forces situated outside the region, to a past in which values were placed into a very different set of balances. In shorter novels, such as *Al-tibr* (1990; Gold) and *Nazīf al-hajar* (1990; The Bleeding Rocks), we are introduced to the lives and travails of individual (mostly male) characters as they endeavor to adapt themselves to the foibles of other men and to the vicissitudes of desert existence. In *Al-tibr* the focus is the chain of events that surround a man's devotion to his prized camel and the troubles it caused him. In *Nazīf al-hajar* the main character, Asūf, serves as guardian to a remote and ancient shrine carved in the rocks of a deep desert ravine; in that environment he finds himself battling against the crazed instincts of a hunter who comes in quest of the fabled moufflon and seeks to destroy the delicate balance of the environment the animal symbolizes. In the longer works, such as *Al-majūs*, the fictional world expands to incorporate virtually the entire history of the southern desert region and the relationship between animalistic faiths of Africa and the Sūfī sects seeking to spread the word of Islam. Here the historical references range from the city of Timbuktu (in contemporary Mali) to the Nigerian city of Kano in the South, while in the realm of fantasy the novel includes references to the magical city of Wāw, itself the subject of a recent novel, *Wāw al-sughrā* (1997; Minor Wāw).

In all these works what strikes the reader initially is K.'s unique ability to create an atmosphere that is almost tactile and to develop a repertoire of unusual and picturesque imagery in order to describe the desert and its peoples, and in particular the disturbingly randomized and often cruel way in which it can inflict death on human and animals. Here indeed we find ourselves in a world almost completely unfamiliar to the novel and its readership. Yet, such is K.'s instinct for the potential of contemporary narrative and so broad is his erudition—the extent of his reading is evidenced by the wide variety of citations that characterize his chapter headings—that his rapidly growing list of fictional works manages to integrate the most ancient Arab venues and values into the realm of modern fiction. As such he takes his place as one of the most significant contemporary writers of fiction in the Arab world.

FURTHER WORKS: *Jur'ah min dam* (1983); *Shajarat al-rattām* (1986); *Al-bi'r* (1989); *Al-wāhah* (1989); *Akhbār al-Tūfān* (1989); *Nidā' al-waqwāq* (1989); *Watan al-ru'ā al-samāwiyyah* (1991); *Al-waqā'i' al-mafqūdah min sīrat al-majū s* (1992); *Kharīf al-darwīsh* (1994); *Al-fam* (1994); *Al-saharah* (2 vols., 1994, 1995); *Fitnat al-zu'ān* (1995); *Barr al-khayt'ūr* (1996); *'Ashb al-layl* (1997); *Al-dumyah* (1998)

BIBLIOGRAPHY: Allen, R., *The Arabic Novel* (1994): 244-58; Allen, R., *Tradition and Modernity in Arabic Literature* (1997): 151-59; Machut-Mendecka, E., "The Visionary Art of I. al-K.," *RAL*, 28 (Fall 1997): 141-49

—ROGER ALLEN

KUNIKIDA Doppo

(pseud. of Kunikida Tetsuo; known as Doppo) Japanese short-story writer, b. 15 July 1871, Chōshi; d. 23 June 1908, Chigasaki

K. grew up with a sense of pride in his samurai heritage mingled with an awareness that samurai ideals were ill-suited to the competitive modern age; due in part to his father's financial insecurity, he was unable to finish college, and he supported himself as a teacher and then as a war correspondent.

K. is remembered for his literary works (including some marginally successful experiments in modern verse), but in fact he spent the greater part of his brief professional life as a journalist, distinguishing himself initially with lively accounts of his shipboard experiences during the Sino-Japanese War of 1894–95. He met his first wife, a willful "modern" woman who shared his Christian faith, at a reception for newly returned war correspondents, and when she deserted him after six months of marriage, both his religious faith and the romanticized view of love he had absorbed from his reading in the English romantics were destroyed. Perhaps as a result of this early disillusionment, he became the first writer of his generation to break away from puerile sentimentalism.

From his earliest attempt at fiction, the prose-poem "Takibi" (1896; "The Bonfire," 1970), to his last important story, "Take no kido" (1908; "The Bamboo Gate," 1972), there is a remarkable consistency of theme and imagery in K.'s writing. Lonely wanderers or figures in the distance symbolize the endless stream of humanity drifting into and out of the world, but individually leaving no mark upon it. Early stories, such as "Gen oji" (1897; "Old Gen," 1955) and "Wasureenu hitobito" (1898; "Unforgettable People," 1972), and the lyrical essay "Musashino" (1898; "Musashino") express this theme in a voice close to song, while later stories, such as "Shōjikimono" (1903; "An Honest Man," 1972) and "Take no kido," attempt to invest the symbolic characters with individual personalities and place them in a dramatic context.

Turgenev's *Sportsman's Sketches* first provided K. with a Western model of poetic fiction, while the example of Maupassant brought to his later work a greater command of detached narration. In contrast to the so-called naturalists, with whom he is usually grouped, however, K. never relinquished the view of the moral nature of man he learned from his reading of Wordsworth. He was being praised as a pioneer naturalist near the end of his life (he died young of tuberculosis), but he firmly rejected the label.

As much as K. owed to his Western models, he left an entirely original and coherent body of works that draw from his own experience and imaginative power. Written in a period of Japanese literature that was primarily transitional and derivative, his stories not only served as models for such later masters as SHIGA Naoya and AKUTAGAWA Ryūnosuke but they continue to be read and enjoyed in their own right.

FURTHER WORKS: *Musashino* (1901); *D.-shū* (1905); *Unmei* (1906); *Tōsei* (1907); *Byōshōroku* (1908); *D.-shū dai-ni* (1908); *Azamukazaru no ki* (2 vols., 1908–1909); *Aitei tsūshin* (1908); *Nagisa* (1908); *K. D. zenshū* (10 vols., 1964–1967)

BIBLIOGRAPHY: McClellan, E., "The Impressionistic Technique in Some Modern Japanese Novelists," *ChiR*, 57 (1965): 48–60; Rubin, J., "Five Stories by K. D.," *MN*, 27 (1972): 273–341

—JAY RUBIN

KUNZE, Reiner

German poet and prose writer, b. 16 Aug. 1933, Oelsnitz

The son of a miner, K. studied philosophy and journalism in Leipzig from 1951 to 1955 and then became a teacher. He turned to professional writing soon after the East German government forced him to abandon his academic career in 1959. Although he repeatedly affirmed his support of the principles of Marxism, he continued to come under political attack because of his criticism of the policies of the régime. Most of his books were published in the West; only occasionally, during times of cultural thaw, did his works appear in the German Democratic Republic (GDR). After years of increasingly severe harassment he was forced to emigrate to West Germany in 1977. Among his literary awards is the prestigious Büchner Prize (1977).

K. established his reputation with the poetry collection *Sensible Wege* (1969; sensitive paths). These poems show an increased maturity and stylistic control, compared with his earlier works. Some are directly political or topical, and many contain indirect or veiled criticism of the repressive atmosphere in the GDR. Irony and understatement are typical characteristics. Communication is a favorite theme, both in its general human aspects and in contexts specifically applicable to the poet, who lived in virtual isolation in a small East German town. The poems of *Zimmerlautstärke* (1972; with volume turned down) are similar in style and theme. The irony is sharper, however, and references to politics—for example SOLZHENITSYN, the Russian invasion of Czechoslovakia— more pointed.

K.'s most successful work is *Die wunderbaren Jahre* (1976; *The Wonderful Years*, 1977), a collection of short prose sketches. Written in a laconic style reminiscent of the poetry, these texts paint a devastating picture of life in East Germany—of the Communist Party and its policies, of the difficulty of maintaining a sense of human dignity—as well as in post-1968 Czechoslovakia. On a deeper level, these specific issues reflect K.'s concern with the delicate balance between individual freedom and responsibility to others. K. directed a film version of this book, for which he also wrote the screenplay, published as *Der Film "Die wunderbaren Jahre"* (1979; the film *The Wonderful Years*).

Like many writers who were pressured into leaving the GDR in the late 1970s, K. remains dedicated to the principles of socialism, and he is less than happy in his role as a symbol of resistance to political oppression. His considerable literary talent should ensure his continued success, whatever the themes of his future works may be.

FURTHER WORKS: *Vögel über dem Tau* (1959); *Wesen und Bedeutung der Reportage* (1960); *Aber die Nachtigall jubelt* (1962); *Widmungen* (1963); *Poesiealbum 11* (1968); *Der Löwe Leopold* (1970); *Brief mit blauem Siegel* (1973); *Das Kätzchen* (1979); *Auf eigene Hoffnung* (1981). FURTHER WORKS IN ENGLISH: *With Volume Turned Down* (1973)

BIBLIOGRAPHY: Piontek, H., *Männer die Gedichte machen* (1970): 203–20; Wallmann, J., "Der Fall R. K.," *NDH*, No. 136 (1972): 93–115; Mytze, A., ed., *Über R. K.* (1976); Wallmann, J., ed., *R. K.: Materialien und Dokumente* (1977); Linn, M., "R. K.'s *Die Wunderbaren Jahre*," *DU*, 30, 6 (1978): 70–81

—JERRY GLENN

KUO Mo-jo

Chinese poet, dramatist, and essayist, b. 16 Nov. 1892, Tung-he, Ssu-ch'uan Province; d. 12 June 1978, Peking

K. was trained in medicine in Japan but never practiced. Instead, he became interested in literature and cofounded the Creation Society, which advocated the concept of "art for art's sake" during the height of the new literature movement in the early 1920s. Soon thereafter K. fled to Japan, where he stayed for ten years to escape the purge of Communists. When he returned to China in 1937, he became a prominent scholar of ancient Chinese social history and was a key figure in the national defense literature movement of the 1930s. After 1949 he was active in the upper echelons of the government of the People's Republic and became president of the Chinese Academy of Science.

K.'s prominence in literature came after the publication of *Nü-shen* (1921; partial tr., *Selected Poems from the Goddesses*, 1958), a poetry collection full of impulsive outbursts echoing the feelings of reform-minded intellectuals in search of a new China. The language was uninhibited, and K. was particularly criticized for his frequent use of foreign words. He continued with his poetry writing, collected in *Hsing k'ung* (1923; starry sky), *P'ing* (1927; vase), *Hui-fu* (1928; recovery), *Chan sheng chi* (1938; battle cries), and other volumes, but none received the same acclaim as *Nüshen*. Nevertheless, he remained consistent in his slogan-like outcries, especially on nationalism. After 1949 K. published more poems in collections such as *Hsin-hua chung* (1953; in praise of new China), *Ch'ang ch'un chi* (1959; forever spring), and *Tung feng chi* (1963; east wind). In most of these, K. glorified political causes. His poems of the 1970s were written in a more formal, classical style.

K.'s most celebrated dramatic work is *Ch'ü Yüan* (1942; *Ch'ü Yüan*, 1955). It is a creative reconstruction of the political defeat of China's first known poet-statesman, Ch'ü Yüan (c. 343–290 B.C.), whose loyalty led to his despair and self-destruction. K. utilized this historical play as propaganda for nationalism during the war with Japan. In *Ts'ai Wen-chi* (1956; Ts'ai Wen-chi), K. dramatized the return from the Huns to the Chinese kingdom of Ts'ai Yen (c. A.D. 162–239), a famous Han poetess. By using Ts'ai's return to vindicate the villainous image of statesman Ts'ao Ts'ao (A.D. 155–220), K. was in line with the current political issue of redefining Ts'ao's role in Chinese history.

K. also wrote a few essays of literary criticism and some short stories, none of which were outstanding. He often wrote stories with a very strong tendency toward autobiography, and he sometimes just retold historical anecdotes.

A prolific writer, K. was the only one to survive the numerous political purges against writers because his versatility and flexibility enabled him to adapt easily to every new political tide. K.'s early poetry shows a lack of discipline, and his later poems lost the impulsive energy that was his earlier trademark. His plays and later poetry reveal how he followed the Maoist doctrine that creative writing should support political and revolutionary activities.

FURTHER WORKS: *M. shih chi* (1935); *M. hsüan chi* (1936); *K. M. wen chi* (1949); *M. wen chi* (1957); *M. shih tz'u hsüan* (1977)

BIBLIOGRAPHY: Moy, C., "K. M. and the Creation Society," *Papers on China* (Harvard), 4 (1950): 131–59; Schultz, W., "K. M. and the Romantic Aesthetic: 1918–1925," *JOL* 6, 2 (1955): 49–81; Průšek, J., *Three Sketches of Chinese Literature* (1969): 99–140;

Gálik, M., "Studies in Modern Chinese Literary Criticism: IV: The Proletarian Criticism of K. M.," *AAS*, 6 (1970): 145–60; Roy, D. T., *K. M.: The Early Years* (1971); Lee, L. O., "K. M.," *The Romantic Generation of Modern Chinese Writers* (1973): 177–200

—MARLON K. HOM

KUPRIN, Alexandr Ivanovich

Russian short-story writer, novelist, and essayist, b. 8 Sept. 1870, Narovchat; d. 25 Aug. 1938, Leningrad

K.'s father, a minor official, died when Alexandr was only one year old. His mother had to work hard in order to survive, and K.'s childhood and youth were thorny. He graduated from a Moscow Cadet Corps School in 1887, finished officer school, and became a lieutenant in the army. In 1894 he left the military and became a "free man," but with no means of support. He then worked as a land surveyor, carpenter, tutor, actor, estate manager, and newspaper reporter. He traveled extensively in Russia, mixing thoroughly with the people and learning about all walks of life. He has often been called the "poet of life" and the *bytovik* (realist). In 1889 he published his first short story. Opposed to the 1917 Bolshevik revolution, he emigrated to France. But he returned in 1937 to the U.S.S.R., where he died a year later.

K.'s rich life experience is reflected in his stories, which have lively plots and little philosophy and didacticism, and which are realistic, with some romantic coloration. Fame throughout Russia came to K. with his *Poedinok* (1905; *The Duel*, 1916), published during the Russo-Japanese War. In this novel K. depicts officers negatively, seeing their life as senseless and brutal, and their conduct as unscrupulous. The hero, an idealistic lieutenant, loses his struggle against the traditional routine and dies in a duel. *Poedinok*, along with the shorter works "Shtabs-Kapitan Rybnikov" (1906; "Captain Rybnikov," 1916) and "Gambrinus" (1907; "Gambrinus," 1925), appealed to the radical and antimilitaristic intelligentsia; the social and political aspects of these works should not, however, obscure their aesthetic merit.

A sizable number of K.'s stories deal with love. An early novelette, *Olesya* (1898; *Olessia*, 1909), is a delightful tale about a girl living in the wilderness and her genuine love for a man who tries to escape from the conventions and hypocrisies of civilized society. This romantic episode develops against the background of a primeval forest. Realistic details are interwoven with witchcraft, and beautiful descriptions of nature are mingled with depictions of base human traits. *Sulamif* (1908; *Sulamith: A Prose Poem of Antiquity*, 1923), a stylized biblical narrative, and "Granatovy braslet" (1911; "The Bracelet of Garnets," 1917), sweet and melodramatic, are real hymns of boundless, passionate love, while the novel *Yama* (1912; *Yama: The Pit*, 1922) is a moralistic, somewhat sentimental story about the life of prostitutes, dedicated to "young people and mothers." K. emphasizes the evil of prostitution, but does not attempt to solve this age-old social problem.

The diversity of subjects in K.'s novels and stories can easily be traced through all of his writing. Among the best-known works are "Molokh" (1896; Moloch), a story about factory workers, their managers, and engineers; "Allez!" (1897; "Allez!," 1920) and "V tsirke" (1902; at the circus), dealing with circus life; "Kak ya byl

aktyorom" (1908; "How I Became an Actor," 1920); "Listrigony" (1908–11; "The Laestrygonians," 1917), a charming series of sketches about Balaklava Greek fishermen in the Crimea; and "Izumrud" (1907; "Emerald," 1920), about a race horse, a story reminiscent of Tolstoy's "Yardstick."

K.'s literary output in exile was insignificant. He published an autobiographical novel, *Yunkera* (1928–30; the cadets) and a novelette, *Zhaneta* (1934; Zhaneta). In *Yunkera* the older K. paints a sunny picture of the young Moscow cadets—a picture completely different from that given in *Poedinok*, while in *Zhaneta* K. shows the reader the hopeless existence of an aging Russian émigré professor—helpless, degraded, and crushed by the burden of life.

K. admired strong, healthy, enterprising, adventurous people. He loved children and animals; he felt deeply about nature. In some respects K.'s writing could be compared to that of Jack LONDON, KIPLING, and Bret Harte. In K.'s works one will find neither sophisticated psychological analysis of the protagonists, nor stylistic innovations, nor social "messages" à la GORKY. In K.'s stories, however, the reader always feels humaneness, compassion, sincerity, and truthfulness. His narration flows easily, his sentences are unconstrained, and his syntax lacks the pretentiousness so much in vogue with his contemporaries, the SYMBOLISTS. All these qualities have secured him a firm and respectable place in Russian literature.

FURTHER WORKS: *Izbrannoe* (1937); *Izbrannye sochinenia* (1947); *Sobranie sochineny v shesti tomakh* (1957–1958); *Sobranie sochineny v devyati tomakh* (1964). FURTHER WORKS IN ENGLISH: *A Slav Soul, and Other Stories* (1916); *The River of Life, and Other Stories* (1916); *The Bracelet of Garnets, and Other Stories* (1917); *Sasha, and Other Stories* (1920); *Gambrinus, and Other Stories* (1925); *The Garnet Bracelet, and Other Stories* (n.d., 195?)

BIBLIOGRAPHY: Phelps, W. L., "K.'s Picture of Garrison Life," *Essays on Russian Novelists* (1911): 278–84; Jackson, R. L., "A. I. K.'s 'River of Life,'" *Dostoevsky's Underground Man in Russian Literature* (1958): 108–12; Slonim, M., "A. I. K.," *From Chekhov to the Revolution* (1962): 173–77; Williams, G., "Romashov and Nazanskij; Enemies of the People," *CSP*, 9 (1967): 194–200; Luker, N. J. I., *A. K.* (1978)

—SERGE KRYZYTSKI

KURDISH LITERATURE

Kurdish literature in the 20th c. has been profoundly influenced by conditions over which Kurdish writers themselves have had little control. Lack of political unity and of national independence, together with social and economic underdevelopment, have impeded the growth of a modern literature. The partitioning of Kurdistan, as the area inhabited by the Kurds was commonly known, among Turkey, Syria, Iraq, and Iran after World War I frustrated attempts to create a single literary language, while literary manifestations of Kurdish national sentiment often brought severe repression. The condition of Kurdish letters has been most bleak in Turkey. In Iraq, however, the southern Kurdish dialect, Sorani, has been recognized as an official language. Newspapers and books have appeared in relative abundance, and a cohesive body of intellectuals has formed who have been the principal animators of modern Kurdish literature.

Kurdish literature is a young literature still in the process of formation. Its development has received little systematic attention, even from Kurdish intellectuals. The first anthology, a slender volume of poetry, was published only in 1938, and the two volumes of the first serious history of Kurdish literature, *Shi'r u edebiyatî kurdî* (Kurdish poetry and literature), by Refik Hilmi did not appear until 1941 and 1956 respectively. Western scholars have virtually ignored the subject.

Kurdish newspapers and journals have played an important role in literary development; they have served as gathering places for intellectuals and have offered an outlet for their work. The most important periodicals have been *Jin* (1920–63), *Gelawêj* (1939–49), and *Dengi gêtî taze* (1943–47), all Iraqi, which published classical and contemporary poetry and short fiction, and in which questions of modern language and literary development were debated.

In the first two decades of the century poetry was the preferred means of literary expression. Although classical meters and traditional subjects still predominated, innovation was apparent in the work of leading poets. Reza Talabani (1842–1910) was famous for his satirical, often obscene, verse. Because of his attachment to Sufism, his work abounds in religious subjects and adheres to classical norms, but in his later years he turned to contemporary social conditions for themes and to the vernacular for new forms of expression. Adab (1859–1916) was also a transitional figure. He sang of beauty, love, and the joy of life in traditional Eastern fashion, but in his *Divan* (1936; collection) many poems portray genuine human emotions in realistic surroundings.

Two main tendencies were apparent in poetry between the two world wars: civic verse, inspired by the struggles for political independence and cultural revival, and romanticism, which perpetuated the themes of the past. There was much innovation in form and content. Ahmad Muhtar (1897–1935) preserved the classical techniques, and his love poetry remained abstract and melancholy, but, increasingly, he focused his attention on the hard life of the common people and, implicitly, called for social reform. Other poets, such as Dildar Yunus (1918–1948), altered the centuries-old poetical canons. Alongside the *aruz* (the quantitative Arabic meter), a seven- and nine-syllable verse came into use. Rhyme became freer and the poems more conceptual, and the Kurdish vocabulary and syntax were strengthened at the expense of foreign models.

Prose writers, more rapidly than poets, embraced the new political and social themes and sought new techniques to express them. In the process the Kurdish short story was born. It was a distinctive literary form with little plot and character development but great emphasis on the author's message.

All the stages through which Kurdish literature passed in the first half of the 20th c. are reflected in the work of Tawfik Piramerd (1867–1950), perhaps the outstanding figure in modern Kurdish literature. He possessed a superb knowledge of Kurdish classical poetry, which he skillfully adapted to the new tendencies of the post-World War I era. He favored simple meters that resembled the rhythms of the Kurdish oral tradition, as in *Pend y pêshînan* (1936; proverbs), his own reworking of folk poetry in nearly 6500 *beyts* (couplets). Piramerd was also a master of the short story. He found inspiration in the Kurdish past, and his adaptation of the national legend, *Duwanze suwar y Meriwan* (1935; the twelve horsemen of Meriwan), has become a classic.

Since World War II patriotic and social themes have dominated both poetry and prose, with realism emerging as a distinct literary

current. The outstanding poet of the early postwar period was Abdulla Goran (1904–1962). His youthful poems were romantic songs of love and nature written in traditional *gazels* (short lyrical poems often of a mystical-religious content), *qasidas* (longer poems of a meditative or didactic character), and quatrains. Later he abandoned the *aruz* completely and used a variety of rhythms and rhymes in such works as *Behesht u yadgar* (1950; paradise and memories), in which affection for the homeland sets the tone. Goran also helped to create a new genre in Kurdish literature—the verse drama. His *Gul y xönawi* (1950; the bloody rose), which describes the plight of two lovers separated by social class, has enjoyed enormous popularity. The leading prose writer of the postwar period has been Shakir Fattah (b. 1910), many of whose short stories, such as *Shebengeberoj* (1947; sunflower), attacked the patriarchal and religious structure of Kurdish society.

Kurdish poetry and short fiction have achieved high artistic levels, but the novel and a modern theater have yet to make their appearance. Subjects for both abound and only await authors capable of transforming legend and new social situations into sustained works of art.

Kurdish literature in the Soviet Union stands apart from the main currents described. Only in the 1930s were the first genuine literary works produced, and since then Kurdish literature has reflected the general vicissitudes of Soviet literature. The outstanding writer is Arabe Shamo (Arab Shamilov, b. 1897), whose novels have described his own life and that of Kurdish refugees from Turkey.

Since the 1970s Kurdish writers in Turkish, Iraqi, and Iranian Kurdistan have been forced to pursue their creative vocation under the most difficult political and social conditions. Many have taken refuge in Western Europe, where, especially in France, Sweden, and Germany, important centers of Kurdish literary activity have emerged. In spite of adversity, Kurdish literature has displayed remarkable vitality. Poetry has maintained its primacy. Cigerxwin (1903–1984), the most famous dialect writer, published two volumes of poems, *Sefaq* (1982; The Dawn) and *Hevi* (1983; Hope), which were inspired by recent Kurdish history and display an admirable classical form and purity of language. Cuwamer, the greatest living Kurdish poet who carries on the tradition of Goran, is in *Helo* (1986; The Eagle) inspired by Kurdish history and the struggles of the *peshmerga* (Kurdish resistance fighters) and modernizes the *beyt*. With striking effect. S. Bekes experimented with the drama, a rare genre in Kurdish literature, in *Asik* (1978; The Gazelle), which he composed in free verse on themes drawn from contemporary problems of Kurdish society. Prose has been distinguished by collections of short stories, the notable *Pekenini geda* (1972; The Beggar's Smile) by Hesen Qizilci (1914–1985), a master of the genre, and by an occasional novel, especially *Heres* (1985; The Avalanche) by Muhammad Mukri, which, in recounting the struggles of a family to overcome political persecution and economic hardship, mirrors the destiny of the Kurds as a whole.

BIBLIOGRAPHY: Edmonds, C. J., "A Kurdish Newspaper: 'Rozh-i-Kurdistan,'" *Journal of the Central Asian Society*, 12 (1925): 83–90; Edmonds, C. J., "A Kurdish Lampoonist: Shaikh Riza Talabani," *Journal of the Royal Central Asian Society*, 22 (1935): 111–23; Bois, T., *Connaissance des Kurdes* (1965): 128–40; Hassanpour, A., *Nationalism and Language in Kurdistan, 1918–1985* (1992)

—KEITH HITCHINS

KUSHNER, Tony

American playwright and essayist, b. 16 July 1956, New York, New York

Born in New York City, K. is the son of two classical musicians. When he was a child, his family moved to a small town in Louisiana, but K. returned to New York to attend Columbia University. From an early age, he had sensed that he was gay; while in college he underwent therapy to be "cured." Instead, he learned to embrace his sexual identity, and soon became a vocal advocate for gay rights, joining ACT UP (AIDS Coalition to Unleash Power), a militant AIDS activist group formed in the 1980s.

In 1984 K. earned an M.F.A. in directing from New York University and began his writing career with a play for youth, *Yes, Yes, No, No* (perf. 1985, pub. 1987). In 1987 his first full-length adult play was performed, *A Bright Room Called Day* (1991). Tracing the story of a group of liberal friends in Weimar Germany whose community is threatened by Hitler's rise to power, the play includes commentary by a contemporary American woman who draws parallels between proto-Nazi Germany and Ronald Reagan's America. Many critics felt the parallel between Nazi Germany and contemporary America was strained and exaggerated.

But in 1991, K. secured his literary reputation with *Angels in America* (1992). Subtitled "A Gay Fantasia in National Themes," K.'s two-part epic was immediately acclaimed in the theater world. K.'s far-reaching style in the play, which lasts some seven hours, intertwines historical reference with personal narratives, philosophical ideas with popular culture references, and fantastic events with realistic stories. In this way the playwright hopes to weave the experience of being gay together with the historical and cultural question of what it means to be an American at the end of the 20th c. Like much 1980s activism, *Angels in America* takes up the contention that the personal is political.

Part 1, *Millennium Approaches*, follows the story of Prior, a young man struggling with AIDS who is visited by an angel proclaiming him a prophet. Prior's story is interwoven with others, including those of Joe, a closeted gay Mormon attorney, and Harper, his depressed wife, as well as Roy Cohn, the actual conservative attorney who lived a secret gay life. Part 2, *Perestroika*, is even more fantastic, with some scenes among the same characters, and others ranging from Russia to Heaven, where God appoints the now-dead Cohn his attorney, to defend himself against charges of having abandoned Heaven.

Rarely has a single play vaulted a playwright into the public eye as quickly as *Angels in America*. Many critics see it the defining play for an age of corporate mergers, global economies, renewed racial conflict, and AIDS. It is also, like K.'s other works, a very personal act of mourning.

K.'s next play, *Slavs! Thinking About the Longstanding Problems of Virtue and Happiness* (perf. 1994, pub. 1995), utilized much material edited from *Angels in America*, resulting in a play that seems more like outtakes than a complete picture in itself.

Since *Angels in America*, K. has moved into other forms of writing as well as directing. As in his plays, he considers pressing issues of public justice, seen in the light of historical and cultural contexts. While very focused on the politics of identity, K.'s works raise questions about the broadest political ideas: the meaning of citizenship, the nature of progress, and the definition of justice. He is also willing to question the authorship process itself: heavily influenced in his work by interaction with a close friend, Kimberly

Flynn, K. questioned the process by which plays are ascribed to single authors, pointing out ways in which all creative work is highly collaborative.

FURTHER WORKS: *Three Plays for Young Audiences* (1987); *The Illusion* (1991); *A Meditation from Angels in America* (1994); *Thinking About the Longstanding Problems of Virtue and Happiness* (1995); *T. K. in Conversation* (1997)

BIBLIOGRAPHY: Rogoff, G., "Angels in America, Devils in the Wings," *Theater*, 24, 2 (1993): 21-29; Savran, D., "T. K. Considers the Longstanding Problems of Virtue and Happiness," *AmerT*, 11, 8 (1994): 100-04; Kiefer, D., "Angels in America and the Failure of Revelation," *AD*, 4, 1 (1994): 21-38; McNulty, C., " *Angels in America*: T. K.'s Theses on the Philosophy of History," *MD*, 39, 1 (1996), 84-96; Geis, D., and S. Kruger, eds., *Approaching the Millennium: Essays on Angels in America* (1997)

—GINGER STRAND

KUWAITI LITERATURE

The development of Arabic literature in Kuwait was initiated by 'Abd al-Jalīl al-Tabātabā'ī (1776-1853), who guided emerging Kuwaiti authors to seek opportunities in the literary world. After al-Tabātabā'ī's death in 1853, his son Ahmad continued what his father had established until his death in 1878. Numerous Kuwaiti authors benefitted from al-Tabātabā'ī mentorships, most notably the late-19th-c. poet Khālid ibn 'Abd Allāh al-'Adsānī (1834-1898).

Al-'Adsānī was the *Imām* in the *Sūq's* mosque (the central market) and such a prestigious position was only obtainable by a few people in Kuwaiti society at that time. Despite being a cleric in the mosque, al-'Adsānī was a close friend of 'Abd Allāh al-Faraj (1836-1901), who was, in addition to being a distinguished poet, a well-known musician. Al-Faraj's songs and melodies spread throughout the Gulf states and still influence contemporary composers in the region. Al-Faraj's poetry and music enriched the literary movement of that era. However, poetry as an art form in al-Tabātabā'ī's period was a reflection of its political and historical context; at that time, most of the Arab states were under Ottoman colonial rule. Consequently, literature in Arabic remained passive, was copied, and lost much of its originality and identity.

In the 1860s, as a result of the previous period, young Kuwaiti men found themselves thirsty for knowledge that went beyond theological information or, geographically speaking, beyond Mecca and Medina. These young men found in Egypt a place that could capture their dreams and quench their thirst with the Nile of knowledge. The first generation of Kuwaitis who traveled seeking knowledge in the second half of the 19th c. planted the seeds for the period of enlightenment that was led by 'Abd al-'Azīz al-Rushayd (1883-1939). If al-Tabātabā'ī created literary form in Kuwait, it was al-Rushayd who carried it forward. In his time, al-Rushayd found educational conditions much improved. The first public school in Kuwait (al-Mubārikiyyah) was founded in 1911. Al-Rushayd taught at al-Mubārikiyyah for a period of time and then left for Ihsa, Mecca, and finally Medina, where he interacted with the intelligentsia of the time from throughout the Arab and Islamic world. While in Kuwait, 'Abd al-'Azīz al-Rushayd founded the journal *al-Kuwait*, which first appeared in February 1928. *Al-Kuwait* concentrated mainly on religious, ethical, and educational reformation, and rarely discussed political issues in his journal; however, the journal is noteworthy for introducing the short story as a genre into Kuwaiti literature. In addition to *al-Kuwait*, al-Rushayd also founded the literary journals *al-Kuwait wal Iraqi* and *al-Tawhid*.

Poetry

Kuwaiti poetry at the beginning of the 20th c. was a reflection of society and the country's political power structure at that time. It wasn't until Fahd al-'Askar (1913-1951) that poetry in Kuwait developed into an authentic art form. Al-'Askar gave Kuwaiti poetry a life and transformed it from a powerful tool for powerful people to an art in the hands of the common people. Influenced by the romantic school of Arabic literature, al-'Askar talked about societal problems and wrote his poems in the language of the people. Another important figure in Kuwaitian poetry is Ahmad al-'Udwānī (1923-1990). Khālid Sa'ūd al-Zayd describes al-'Udwānī as the most profound poet in Kuwait because of his understanding of both Arabic and Western literature. He was largely influenced by Sufism, the mystical school of Islam, which is manifested in his poems. Al-'Udwānī's style goes from the classical tradition to free verse; and sometimes he breaks the traditional rules of prosody, especially in his late work. His poems were collected recently in two volumes as *Ash'ār Ahmad al-'Udwānī* (1996; Poems of Ahmad al-'Udwānī).

Muhammad al-Fāyiz (1938-1991) is known for his first work, *Mudhakkirāt Bahhār* (1962; Memoirs of a Sailor), where the sailor is a metaphor for the Kuwait of the past, a past distinguished from the present by its caring, love, and togetherness. Al-Fāyiz published eleven works of poetry, the last in 1988 entitled *Tasqut Al-Harb* (Down with War), in which he condemns the civil war in Lebanon. In the same generation is Khālid Sa'ūd al-Zayd (b. 1937) who started what can be called "the Kuwaiti poem as story" in his first collection, *Salawāt fī Ma'bad Mahjūr* (1970; Prayers in an Abandoned Temple). He is well known for his Sufi poems, especially those about the Prophet Muhammad and al-Hallāj, a Sūfī martyr. Al-Zayd, who was a member of the resistance during the Iraqi invasion, wrote a long poem describing what he saw during the invasion, called *Al-khamīs al-Aswad* (1995; Black Thursday), in which he celebrates the Kuwaiti martyrs as well as the prisoners of war.

Su'ād āl-Sabāh (b. 1942), who started writing poetry as early as 1964, published nine poetry collections and other books related to her call for women's liberation from men's hegemony. In addition, al-Sabāh wrote *Barqiyyah 'ājilah ilā Watanī* (1992; An Urgent Telegram to My Country) and *Hal Tasmahūna lī an Uhibba Watanī* (1990; Would You Permit Me to Love My Country), in which she describes her resistance to the Iraqi invasion of Kuwait. As part of the same generation 'Abd Allāh al-'Utaybī (1942-1995) started his career as a poet as early as the 1960s; however, he only published his first *dīwān* in 1988 under the title *Mazār al-Hulm* (Shrine of the Dream). His poems focus on two main issues: women and domestic problems. Al-'Utaybī is famous among Kuwaitis for his poems that became operettas, performed especially on the national day, February 25. Al-'Utaybī's *Tā'ir al-Bushrā* (1993; The Bird of Good Augury), is an illustration of the Iraqi invasion and a song for his beloved country when the bird of good augury brought the news of Kuwait's liberation.

Khalīf al-Wuqayyān (b.1941) published his first poetry collection in 1974 under the title *al-Mubhirun ma'a al-Riyāh*, (Sailing with the Winds). His poems confront all forms of falseness in society. His final work, an anthology entitled *Dīwān Khalīfah al-Wuqayyān* (1995; Poems of Khalīfah al-Wuqayyān) brings together all his poems. Al-Wuqayyān also wrote about the Iraqi invasion of Kuwait, using children as a metaphor for life, as well as flowers and light as opposed to weapons of war. From the same generation is Ya'qūb al-Subay'ī (b. 1945), whose favorite topic is women, notably in *Idā'at al-Shayb al-Aswad* (1997; The Illuminations of the Black Gray Hair). Influenced by Khalil GIBRAN, Jannah al-Quraynī's (b. 1956) poems are distinguished by sadness.

Fiction

Kuwaiti short stories were born from the womb of the press. The literary journal *al-Kuwait* published the story "Munīrah" by Khālid al-Farag (1898-1954) in 1929, but the publication of short stories was suspended for eighteen years when *al-Kuwait* failed due to financial problems. The short story appeared again in *al-Bi'thah*, a journal founded by Kuwaiti students in Egypt. In 1947 *al-Bi'thah* published an issue devoted to the short story, which provided increased recognition for the genre. One of the stories published in the issue was 'Abd al-'Azīz Husayn's (1920-1996) "Dhi'b al-Sahrā" (The Desert Wolf), about an old Bedouin man who made a journey in the desert sixty years prior to the story being written. The story asserts that Kuwait was then at the beginning of modernity, when oil would start flowing. The author, while envisioning the future, warned from the quiet safety of the village of a transformation that was coming after the profusion of oil in Kuwait. The village would lose its virtues and become an empty desert.

The virtues that the peaceful village possessed disappeared with oil development in the area; and the economic changes that occurred dramatically showed what was hidden in society. A peaceful society was no longer the norm; the larger society was an empty cup; and the balance between authority and the people was disturbed. Fahd al-Duwayrī (b. 1924), who started writing in 1948, continued the tradition that started with 'Abd al-'Azīz Husayn. His first stories were collected in *Min al-Wāqi'* (From the Real World), in which al-Duwayrī employs techniques involving dialogue between the narrator and his/her audience. Issues about contemporary Kuwait were the main concerns in al-Duwayrī's stories. His last story, which he did not finish, was entitled "Rīh al-Shimāl" (The North Wind), and was published in the newspaper *Al-Watan* from February 18, 1992 to April 28, 1992. In 1984 Khālid Sa'ūd al-Zayd published a book about al-Duwayrī in which he collected the author's short stories.

On November 29, 1962, Sulaymān al-Shattī (b. 1943) published the first contribution to the Kuwaiti short story from his generation entitled *Al-Daffah* (The Helm), which would figuratively become the helm for his generation that guided the ship of stories. The conflict between members of society and governmental authority was illustrated in his first collection, *al-Sawt al khāfit* (1970; The Whispering Voice). Al-Shattī stressed the importance of democracy for the new society in Kuwait. "Al-Shay' al-Jadīd" (The New Thing) is one story in this collection; what he meant by the new thing was freedom, the freedom that parliament's members no longer represented at the heart of the nation, because they had lost their connection with the people. In his second collection, *Rijāl min al-Raff al-'Ālī* (Men from Upper Shelves), Sulaymān al-Shattī introduced characters that had the element of one man. 'Abd Allāh al-Dāyir is one of these characters who searched for a nation, an idea, that would solve the problems of his generation. The name al-Dāyir from its very connotation in Arabic refers to the idea of search, a search that continues to run in circles and still does not find the answer.

Ismā'īl Fahd ISMĀ'ĪL is another distinguished Kuwaiti short story writer and novelist. Indeed, he is more well known in other parts of the Arab world than in his native Kuwait. Perhaps the reason for such recognition outside Kuwait is due to the fact that Ismā'īl's early works rarely discussed issues related to Kuwait's society. Rather, Iraq and Egypt received the main focus of his writing. In addition, most of his works were published in Beirut, Lebanon, which made it difficult for readers in Kuwait to buy them. It was not until the Iraqi invasion of Kuwait that Ismā'īl wrote his most important work in terms of both size and quality, *Ahdathiyyāt Zaman al-'Uzlah* (1997; Events in the Time of Exile), published in seven volumes. Being a member of the resistance during the Iraqi invasion, Ismā'īl wrote of the life of the people that he knew: their struggles, fears, courage, love, and unity. Another important Kuwaiti short story writer is Sulaymān al-Khulayfī (b. 1946). The drastic social changes occurring in Kuwait after the profusion of oil influenced not only the topics that al-Khulayfī dealt with, but also the way he wrote his stories. His earlier works are *Hadamah* (1974; Destruction) and *al-Majmū'ah al-Thāniya* (1978; The Second Collection), which emphasizes two issues, sex and religious hypocrisy.

From the generation writing in the 1980s Muhammad al-'Ajmī (b. 1956) illustrates political and social concerns such as unemployment, especially among some Arab workers who find it difficult to find proper places to live and at the same time save money for their families. Another prominent Kuwaiti short story writer and novelist is Walīd al-Rujayb (b. 1954) whose main concern is writing about issues related to the working class. He is also well known for his novel *Badriyyah*, which he published in 1988, and a collection of short stories was published in 1994 entitled *al-Rīh Tahuzzuhā al-ashjār* (The Trees Are Shaken by the Wind). In this collection al-Rujayb describes the elite in society and how their consciousness reflects on societal issues.

The first short story written by Diyā' Hāshim al-Badr, a Kuwaiti woman, appeared in the journal *al-Bi'thah* in 1952. However, her contribution did not last but rather inspired many doubts by male writers who saw literary writing as a man's specialty. Such discouragement did not last forever. Many female writers contributed, in terms of both quantity and quality, a few years later. Their stories differed according to the topics they were discussing. Some emphasized the feminine world of the body and others conspired to break down the society's patriarchal hegemony. The work of Laylā al-'Uthmān (b. 1945) represents the woman's world of the past where patriarchalism prevailed. The past for al-'Uthmān is important in order to criticize the present consciousness. One character in her stories illustrates the group; such a person or group becomes her representation or an instance of her psychological surroundings. Women in al-'Uthmān's stories are the main characters and that men play minor roles. However, her representations of the female world can be taken beyond local boundaries to apply it to other Arab countries. Al-'Uthmān, in addition to short stories, wrote novels such as *al-Mar'ah wal-Qittah* (1985; The Woman and the Cat) and *Wasmiyyah Takhruju min al-Bahr* (1986; Wasmiyyah Comes from the Sea). The world of her novels is similar to that expressed in her short stories.

'Āliyah Shu'ayb (b. 1964) in her first short story collection published in 1989, *Imra'ah Tatazawwaj al-Bahr* (A Woman Who Married the Sea), illustrates the inner world of the woman through love and hate, present and future, and body and mind. This topic of the body is frequently raised in Shu'ayb's work, such as her second short story collection *Bilā Wajh* (1991; Without a Face). Shu'ayb's writing style is complex, making her reader think and go beyond accepted norms as if to say "This is how complex we women are." Among other distinguished female writers in Kuwait is Tayyibah al-Ibrāhīm. In addition to stories reflecting societal problems, she writes science fiction. Indeed, her novel *al-Insān al-muta'addid* (1980; The Multiple Human Being) explains cloning in a scientific way.

Drama

The establishment of drama in Kuwait started early compared to other Arab countries of the Gulf region; the first dramatic presentation was in 1922 on the al-Ahmadiyyah school stage. However, the real contribution to drama is credited to Hamad al-Rujayb (b. 1924), who was sent on a scholarship to Egypt, where he met his influential mentor Zakī Tulaymāt (d. 1982). Al-Rujayb published his first contributions to drama in the journal *al-Bi'thah*. He wrote *Man al-Jānī* (1947; Who Is the Criminal?), *Law Zād al-Saqqa* (1947; If the Carrier of Water Exceeds), and Kharūf Niyām Niyām (1949; Sleeping, Sleeping, Sheep). In addition, he cooperated with the distinguished poet Ahmad al-'Udwānī in creating the idea for the first drama written in poetic form, *Mahzalah fī mahzalah* (1948; Ridicule After Ridicule).

Though Kuwaiti drama began within the sphere of classical literary Arabic, it was Muhammad al-Nashmī (1927-1984) who took it to the level of colloquial Arabic. In 1943 Hamad al-Rujayb chose the actor and dramatist al-Nashmī to play a part in his drama. At the intermission the troupe performed a short work entitled *Umm 'Anbar* (The Mother of Anbar), and enjoyed a positive response from the audience for their performance, which was in vernacular instead of standard literary Arabic. The actors found that the dialect used was more appealing to the audience, and improved understanding and their interaction with them. In addition, the dialect freed the actors from the strictness that the written text imposed. Afterwards, al-Nashmi established a group of actors that performed using vernacular Arabic texts instead of classical ones.

In 1954 al-Nashmī founded Firqat al-Kashshāf al-Watanī (National Scout Theater), the first theater that brought together all Kuwaiti actors. Al-Nashmī wrote *Mudīr Fashil* (1955; The Unsuccessful Director), which was to be his first drama with this group. This play was highly successful with the audience. Indeed, occasionally, the audience asked specific actors to repeat specific scenes, and the actors did so in order to please their audience. After performing this drama, al-Nashmī and his group called themselves *al-Masrah al-Sha'bī* (The People's Theater).

In 1961 another theater was founded in Kuwait, *al-Masrah al-'Arabī* (The Arabian Theater), the result of Zakī Tulaymāt's intention to establish a theater focused on the written text, as opposed to al-Nashmī's theater. In 1962 *al-Masrah al-'Arabī* performed its first drama, *Saqr Quraysh* (Hawk of the Quraysh), by the distinguished Egyptian writer Mahmūd TAYMŪR. In the same year the theater introduced two other works by Tawfīq AL-HAKĪM. Zakī Tulaymāt encouraged his Kuwaiti students to write their own dramas. In 1963 Sa'd al-Faraj (b. 1941) wrote his first work for the group entitled *Istarthūnī wa-Anā Hayy* (They Inherited Me While I Was Still Alive).

By 1964 there were four theaters in Kuwait sponsored officially by the government: al-Masrah al-Sha'bī; al-Masrah al-'Arabī; Masrah al-Khalij al-'Arabī (The Arabian Gulf Theater); and al-Masrah al-Kuwaitī (The Kuwaiti Theater). These four theaters still exist, in addition to several private theaters. Among the four, Masrah al-Khalij al-'Arabī is the most distinguished, born as a result of the changes that occurred in Kuwaiti society after the oil profusion. Among the most important contemporary Kuwaiti dramatists was Saqr al-Rushūd (1940-1979), who was in addition a distinguished director. Al-Rushūd and 'Abd al-'Azīz al-Surayyi' (b. 1939) coauthored *1, 2, 3, 4 . . . boom* (1973), *Shayātīn laylat al-Jum'ah* (1973: The Friday Night Satans), and *Buhamdūn al-Mahattah* (1974; Buhamdun's Station). With al-Rushūd's death in 1979, Kuwait's drama gradually lost much of its seriousness and originality; at present, most of the work performed on Kuwaiti stages is geared toward profit rather than creativity. However, there remains a commitment on the part of young Kuwaiti dramatists to continue the tradition that began with Zāki Tulaymāt and Saqr al-Rushūd, most notably Fu'ād al-Shattī, who has established a major reputation in directing for the stage the work of the distinguished Syrian dramatist Sa'dallāh WANNŪS.

BIBLIOGRAPHY: Allen, R., *The Arabic Novel* (1982); Allen, R., ed., *Modern Arabic Literature* (1987); Badawi, M. M., ed., *Modern Arabic Literature* (1992); Jayyusi, S. K., ed., *The Literature of Modern Arabia: An Anthology* (1988)

—ALI A. AL-JAFAR

KUZMIN, Mikhail Alexeevich

Russian poet, novelist, dramatist, translator, and critic, b. 6 Oct. 1872, Yaroslavl; d. 1 March 1936, Leningrad

K.'s family was of the minor nobility. His interests in European culture, classical antiquity, and philosophy lasted throughout his life and influenced his art. K.'s life and work were characterized by a peasant/dandy dichotomy. At one time traveling with a group of Old Believers, at another owning 365 waistcoats, he exhibited a wide range of interests and knowledge. From 1891 to 1894 K. studied musical composition with Rimsky-Korsakov in the St. Petersburg Conservatory. After the revolution, while taking an active part in the development of cultural affairs for the Bolshevik government, he nevertheless came under increasing attack. After 1929 K. was no longer permitted to publish. He died on the eve of the Stalinist purges, in which he probably would have been included. His work is still not published in the Soviet Union.

K.'s writings are typified by a calm acceptance of life and an awareness of its perpetual change. His art is also strongly autobiographical; his first novel, *Krilya* (1906; *Wings*, 1972), caused a scandal because of its homosexual theme. Love, homosexual or heterosexual, is an important theme in much of K.'s work. Influenced by the philosophy of Plotinus, he saw love as the means through which man improves himself. Religion is also an important aspect of much of his work.

His first collection of poetry, *Seti* (1908; nets), evidences many characteristics of his early work, for example, clarity of form and use of prosaic detail, in striking contrast to the then current SYMBOLIST style. There is also an emphasis on the concrete over the abstract, and a celebration of the present. K.'s later verse differs in many respects from his early work. The poetry, while maintaining the earlier clear form, became increasingly elliptical and metaphorical. The sharp juxtaposition of images in the poems of the 1920s reflects his growing interest in German EXPRESSIONISM and the cinema of the period.

K.'s drama was also innovative. Breaking with Stanislavskian realism, he gave his early plays rococo settings. His later plays are more abstract than his earlier ones. His dramatic works revolve around love and personal relationships, including homosexual ones, a fact that caused some difficulties with the censors.

K. was a central figure in the literary and artistic world of his period. The time has come for a serious and objective appraisal of this multifaceted man about whom so little has been heard for the last fifty years.

FURTHER WORKS: *O Alexee, cheloveke Bozhem* (1907); *Priklyuchenia Eme-Lebyofa* (1907); *Tri pesy: Opasnaya predostorozhnost, Dva pastukakh, Vybor nevesty* (1907); *Komedia o Evdoky iz Gelopolia* (1907); *Alexandryskie pesni* (1908; *Alexandrine Songs*, 1980); *Komedia o Martiniane* (1908); *Nezhny Iosif* (1909); *Podvigi velikovo Alexandra* (1909); *O prekrasnoy yastnosti* (1910); *Puteshestvie sera Dzhona Firfaxa po Turtsy i drugim zamechatelnim stranam* (1910); *Gollandka Liza* (1911); *Osennie ozera* (1912); *Glinyanie golubki* (1914); *Plavayushchie puteshestvuyushchie* (1914); *Tikhy strazh* (1915); *Venetsianskie bezumtsy* (1915; "Venetian Madcaps," 1973); *Voennie rasskazy* (1915); *Chudeshnaya zhizn Iosifa Balzamo, grafa Kaliostro* (1916); *Vozhaty* (1918); *Dvum* (1918); *Zanaveshennye kartinki* (1920); *Ekho* (1921); *Nezdeshnie vechera* (1921); *Vtornik Meri* (1921); *Lesok* (1922); *Paraboly* (1923); *Uslovnosti* (1923); *Novy gul* (1924); *Sobranie stikhov* (3 vols., 1977); *Forel razbyvaet lyod* (1929); *The Trout Breaks the Ice*, (1980). FURTHER WORKS IN ENGLISH: *Wings: Poetry and Prose of M. K.* (1972); *Selected Prose and Poetry* (1980)

BIBLIOGRAPHY: Field, A., "M. K.: Notes on a Decadent's Prose," *RusR*, 22 (1963): 289–300; Green, M., "M. K. and the Theater," *RLT*, 7 (1973): 243–66; Malmstad, J. E., "The Mystery of Iniquity: M. K.'s Dark Streets Lead to Dark Thoughts," *SlavR*, 34 (1975): 44–64; Granoien, N., "*Wings* and the World of Art," *RLT*, 11 (1975): 393–405; Karlinsky, S., "Russia's Gay Literature and History: 11th–20th Centuries," *Gay Sunshine*, No. 29/30 (1976): 9–11; Malmstad, J. E., and Shmakov, G., "M. K.'s 'The Trout Breaks through the Ice,'" in Gibian, G., Tjalsma, H. W., eds., *Russian Modernism* (1976): 132–64; Malmstad, J. E., "M. K.: A Chronicle of His Life and Times," in M. K., *Sobranie stikhov* (1977), Vol. 3: 17–313

—JOHN R. RANCK

KYRGYZ LITERATURE

During the early Islamic period, the Turkic Kyrgyz were a major power along the Yenisei River, where they had developed a "runic" script and established an elaborate civilization. Their kingdom, however, was overthrown by the Uyghurs who, in turn, were swept into the Qipchak plains by the forces of Chingiz Khan in the 13th c. In subsequent centuries, tribes of the Kyrgyz moved south and established a unique mountain-dwelling pastoral exist-ence in the grasslands of the Tian Shan. Influenced by Muslim traders as well as by their neighbors, the Kyrgyz accepted Islam in the 18th c.

Between 1876 and 1916, when the Kyrgyz homeland was incorporated into the Russian Empire and when Muslim Central Asians rose against the dictatorial pressures of Russia, Russian peasants routinely displaced the Kyrgyz and confiscated their grazing lands. The revolt, however, was a precursor to the revolu-tion that established Soviet rule in Central Asia. Recognized as a people in 1924, the Kyrgyz were assigned republic status. During the Soviet period, too, especially after the demise of the Basmachi movement, the Kyrgyz suffered. Dominated ideologically by Com-munism, the Kyrgyz lost control over their land holdings and herds to the collectives; furthermore, most of their able intellectuals were purged by Stalin.

Today Kyrgyzstan's population is made up of Kyrgyzes, Rus-sians, Uzbeks, Ukrainians, and Germans with the highest birthrate occurring among the Kyrgyz. The republic has a democratic government with a growing market economy. Through privatization, the state-held enterprises have been divided among small concerns in the public sector. Agriculture, livestock raising, mining, and manufacturing have also been privatized. Kyrgyz intellectuals have advocated political, cultural, and economic reforms since the late 1960s.

One of the fallacies created by the Soviet system was the view that, before being forced to settle, the tribal peoples of Central Asia, the Kyrgyz included, did not have either a viable literature or an alphabet with which to write down their literatures. From this argument it also followed that neither the Arabic nor the Latin script that superseded it in the late 1920s were capable of providing the Central Asians with a vibrant literature. Only after the introduc-tion of Cyrillic in the 1940s and after an extensive involvement of the natives in Russian literature were the republics' modern litera-tures given the seal of Soviet approval. However, the rich literary heritage of the Kyrgyz underscores the absurdity of this claim.

Take, for instance *Manas*, a celebrated Kyrgyz epic among a long line of Central Asian epics. Over centuries *Manas*, a glorifica-tion of the exploits of the Kyrgyz hero of the same name, has served not only as a national icon and a symbol of Kyrgyz pride but also as a record of events preserving the history of the Kyrgyz as a people. The epic is estimated by some to contain almost a million *bayts*, describing the culture of the nomadic Kyrgyz, including the maintenance of traditional values, recognition of valor, defense of Islam, and promotion of individualism. A single performance of *Manas* may take up to six months. Unfortunately, only a portion of the epic entitled "The Memorial Feast for Kökötöy Khan" is available in English. Originally collected by the Kazakh Chokan Valikhanov (dates n.a.) in 1856, the episode, which is centered on the honor system, documents the ceremonies that mark the depar-ture of one leader and the installation of another.

Even though the Kyrgyz may not have had an alphabet of their own before 1924, they had a rich and vibrant tradition of oral transmission perpetuated by the *manaschis* and the *akins*, guardi-ans of the accuracy and authenticity of the deeds of their Kyrgyz ancestors. The *manaschi* recounted the exploits of the warrior class and the deeds of the religious elite while the *akin* informed about the lighter social, political, and educational aspects of the culture. Indeed, to a great extent, the foundation of present-day Kyrgyz literature is based on the recollections of the *manaschis* and the *akins*.

The earliest reference to the exploits of *Manas* appears in Saif al-Din Akhshikendi's *Majmu at-Tavarikh* (16th c.; A Compendi-um of Histories). Several episodes from the epic, especially *Ma-nas*'s marches against the enemies of the Kyrgyz, are documented. Today those episodes, and many more, are recited by the *manaschis* who might not be familiar with either Persian, the language in which Akhshikendi wrote, or the circumstances that brought the episodes to that author's attention. They tell the story because an audience requests it. This audience, the actual judge of the authen-ticity of the epic, especially of the details down to the ornaments of the hero's saddle, participates in the creation of the epic and suggests alterations and improvements based on experience.

The *manaschi*, a person of extremely rich spiritual inner world, has played a prominent role in the transmission of the vital values of the Kyrgyz across generations. He is not only fully familiar with the aspirations of the Kyrgyz as a people, but is equally informed about their legends, tales, and family histories. His persona, which carries an aura of mystery, has a magical attraction for the Kyrgyz.

Traditionally Singer, son of Yryman, is recognized as the first *manaschi* followed by Tolubay-Synchy and the 14th c. Togtogul (dates n.a.). The work of these early *manaschis*, in turn, was enhanced by the narrator Nauruz (dates n.a.). In the 19th c., Keldibek, son of Baryboz, Balyk and his son Naimanbai, Tynybek, and Choyuke (dates n.a.) continued the tradition. In more recent times, Sagynbai, son of Orozbek (1867-1930), Moldo Togolok (1860-1942), and Toktogol Satilganov (1864-1933) have enhanced the performance of the epic and promoted it among the Kyrgyz.

The Soviets also have a major share in the study of *Manas*. In fact, in this respect, they have played a dual role. On the one hand, they have tried to understand the elements that constitute the identity of *Manas* among the Kyrgyz, especially what makes the epic resilient as the mainstay of Kyrgyz nationalism; on the other hand, they have devised ways to suppress the epic, distancing the Kyrgyz from their main source of identity. As a result, between 1924 and 1953, especially in the 1940s, many studies and record-ings were made of the epic. Oddly enough, during the same period, the Kyrgyz themselves were prohibited from performing, singing, listening to, or otherwise engaging in *Manas*-related activities.

The Kyrgyz *akin* has a dual responsibility. He has to transmit the creations of *akins* and poets of the past with a great degree of accuracy and, when circumstances require, to spontaneously create poems of his own. To accomplish this task, he categorizes the songs into distinct genres. A song may be an *opmaida* (working song) or a *koshok* (lament). Some songs fall into the category of *term* (words of wisdom). He then puts these songs to music, which he sings as he plays on the *komuz*. Spontaneous creation, however, remains his most tasking requirement, for which he prepares by constantly working with the creations of the past masters, participating in poetry festivals and competitions, and by providing spontaneous verses fitting prevailing circumstances.

Moldo Togolok is perhaps the best example of *akins* who have made a successful transition to the so-called modern scene. His *Ösgörüsh* (1918; Revolution) and *Atkantan ve Süigenbai* (1923; Atkantan and Suigenbai) are examples of this smooth transition. Integrating his rich life experiences as a laborer, physician, and teacher with oral traditions and a socialist spirit, he rose against injustice in general and against the maltreatment of Kyrgyz women in particular. His fairy-tale allegory, "The Tale of the Birds," brilliantly depicts the interactions obtaining among the various Kyrgyz social strata.

Toktogol Satilganov, however, is the consummate Kyrgyz *akin*. One of the founders of modern Kyrgyz literature, he captivated his audiences with his lyrics which were centered on the themes of social justice and equality. In this endeavor, he was greatly helped by his musical talent. He sang his own lyrics as he played on the Kyrgyz's beloved *komuz*. *Alymakan* (n.d.; Alymakan), *Besh Kaman* (n.d.; The Five Boars), and *Kandai yal Tuudu Eken Lenindei Uuldu* (1919; What Wife Has Given Birth to a Son Like Lenin!) linked the traditional poetry of the people with the poetry of the Soviet period. His legacy was successfully continued by Kalyk Akiev (1883-1953), Usenbaev (1894-1963), and Osmonkul Bolebolaev (1888-1967).

The modern era of Kyrgyz literature coincides with the period of the Soviet administrative divisions of Central Asia and the establishment of unity among peoples who shared the same language and common ancestor. In this context, the first Kyrgyz newspaper, *Erkin-too*, the precursor of *Sovettik Kirgizstan*, is of great importance. A copy of the first issue of this newspaper, which carries the first printed work of a professional writer, Alai Tokombaev (b. 1904), is available at the National Kyrgyz Library. The piece entitled "Oktiabr'din Kelen Kezi" (When October Came) was published on November 7, 1924. *Erkin-too* was soon joined by the monthly Jangï *Madaniyat Jolunda* and the Komsomol organ *Leninchil Jash*. The editors of these newspapers, one of whom, Kasim Tinistanov (b. 1900?), disappeared in mid-1930s, played a major role in shaping national Kyrgyz literature. Soviet authorities were troubled most by Tinistanov's *Kasïm Ïrlarïngïng Jïynagï* (1925; Collection of Poems by Kasim), especially by the poet's overt praise for the Kyrgyz homeland and cultural heritage.

The first theater was established in 1926. Then, in 1927, the literary circle Kyzyl Uchkun, a publishing house, and the Writers Union came into existence. These developments encouraged young writers like Tokombaev and Mukai Elebaev (1905-1943) to integrate the efforts of Moldo Togolok and Toktogol Satilganov with the principles of socialist realism into a new and exciting series of works. Under their auspices, the art of the *manaschi* and the *akin*, too, gave way to the more precisely defined genres of music, poetry, drama, and fiction.

The 1920s saw the gradual development of Kyrgyz prose fiction led by Kasimali Bayalinov's (b. 1902) *Ajar* (1927; Ajar). Bayalinov deals with the theme of the plight of women in prerevolutionary society and the unsavory consequences of the 1916 Muslim uprising against Russian rule. Other works that deal with the theme of the position and role of women include Molodogazi Tokobaev's play *Kaygïlu Kakey* (1927; Ill-Fated Kakey), a May-December arranged marriage that ends in the girl's suicide, and Sidik Karashev's (dates n.a.) *Töraga Zeynep* (1929; Chairman Zeynap), account of the rise of an ordinary young woman to the head of the village soviet.

In the 1930s, recognized as the era of translations in Kyrgyz literature, the genre was greatly influenced, indeed directed, by the works of leading Russian authors like Maxim GORKY and Mikhail SHOLOKHOV. The influence of the former is easily traceable in Elebaev's *Uzak Jöl* (1936; The Long Road), while the latter influenced Tugelbai Sidikbekov's (b. 1912) *Keng Suu* (1937-38; Keng Suu). Sidikbekov wrote two novels, *Keng Suu* and *Temir* (1939-40; Temir), both of which deal with the approved themes of collectivization of land and the plight of women. The landmark contributions, however, were Joomart Bokobaev's (1910-1944) *Altïn Kïz* (1937; The Golden Girl) and Kasymaly Dzhantoshev's (b. 1904) *Kanybek* (1939-48; Kanibek)

The period also witnessed treatment of themes that were frowned upon, especially themes that bordered on national and religious sentiments. Naamatov's (dates n.a.) play entitled *Onaltïnjï Jïl* (1929; Year 16 [i.e., 1916]), staged in Frunze, was denounced as an example of nationalist falsification of history. Naamatov could well have followed the example of Joomart Turusbekov (1910-1943) whose musical play *Ajal Orduna* (1935; Instead of Death) on the same theme was applauded. Rather than presenting the conflict as an ethnic clash between the Muslims and the Russians, Turusbekov presents it as a local conflict among the social classes.

The 1940s were dominated by stories about the Patriotic War. The contributions of Alikul Osomonv (1915-1950), especially his *Jenishbek* (1946; Jenishbek), are examples of the literature of this time as is the novel by Tugelbai Sidikbekov (b. 1912) who, after many attempts at expressing himself in verse, had turned to writing novels. His *Bidin Samandïn Kishileri* (1946; People of Our Days) successfully describes a civil war that raged among the farmers within Kyrgyzstan during World War II.

Short-story writing, too, was picked up at this time, especially in the 1950s, and used as an effective medium of expression. Tokombaev's *Charlangan Churok* (1941; The Wounded Heart) is a telling example, as are his psychological studies of the Soviet farmers at the height of collectivization. His *Kuunum Sïrï* (1950; The Secret of the Melody), and *Os Kosum Menen* (1953; With My Own Eyes) further illustrate his understanding of the distinction between myth and reality in life.

The 1960s was a period of retrospection in Kyrgyz literature, especially that it followed the rehabilitation of *Manas* after the death of Stalin. With respect to a desire for democratic institutions, the Kyrgyz intellectuals were in the forefront of forces seeking drastic changes to the Soviets' dogmatic treatment of themes. Chingiz Aitmatov (b. 1928) was the most vocal member of this group that also included Sagindik Omurbaev (b. 1930), Shabdanday Abdiramonov (b. 1930), and Tolegen Kasimbekov (b. 1931). While Kasimbekov dwelled on the past and portrayed the atrocities of the Amirs and khans of the prerevolutionary Central Asia, Aitmatov examined the changes dictated by the Soviet system. More importantly, he clearly delineated the Kyrgyz nature of the means employed for downgrading not only Islam but the ethnic values of his people. In *Zhamila* (1958; *Jamila*, 1969), for instance, he employed the *akin* tradition to indicate the Soviets' subtle use of the Kyrgyz's own institutions to lure the youth away from their Islamic heritage and plant them in a supposedly superior socialist and communist cultural setting. Similarly, in *Gulsarat* (1966; *Farewell, Gul'sary*, 1969), he not only presents a realistic portrayal of the difficult circumstances created for the Kyrgyz by the kolkhoz and sovkhoz systems but, in contrast, illustrates the Kyrgyz values that had suffered in the process. Innocent Tanabai Bukasov's expulsion from the Party ends his life as we know it even though the Communist Party did not consider any of Bukasov's inherent values, his experience, devotion to work and truth, even his age, of any significance. Aitmatov's image of the mankurt appears not only in *Kïlïm Karïtar bir Kün* (1981; *The Day Lasts More Than a Hundred Years*, 1983), but in his other works as well, albeit symbolically. Indeed, Aitmatov's dexterity lies in symbolic presentation whereby he expresses his opinion and is praised for it. He has won both the Lenin Prize (1963) and the State Prize (1968) for literature.

Neither was fiction the only means of expression. Many poets appeared among whom the names of Sooronbai Jusuev (b. 1921), Jalil Sadikov (b. 1932), and Bayilda Sarnogoev (b. 1932) are worthy of note. Like Aitmatov who often tended to leave the ordinary and reach for higher values, Suyunbai Eraliev (b. 1921) abandoned the traditional meters and rhyme scheme for the blank verse. But his attempt at inaugurating a "new" phase for Kyrgyz poetry met with stiff resistance. His innovations in "Jüldüzlarga Sayakat" (1966; Journey to the Stars) received a most severe criticism.

The influence of Russian literature on the literatures of the republics is profound. Kyrgyzstan is not an exception. We can trace the early stages of this influence in Aitmatov's *Zhamila* and the *Ak Keme* (1970; *The White Ship*, n.d.). The more profound changes, however, came when Aitmatov, Kadyr Omurkulov (b. 1941), Cholpanbai Nusupov (b. 1957), and others began to write in Russian as well as in Kyrgyz. These writers have an almost native command of the Russian language and are profoundly affected by Russian literature and culture. Unlike their predecessor's, however, they are loyal to their ethnic Kyrgyz background and Islamic heritage. Islam, in fact, has become a recurring theme as much in the writings of young authors like Murad Aliev (dates n.a.) as well as in the reprints of the poetry of Ozibek Mambetiminov (dates n.a.), a Basmach rebel who was killed by the Red Army over seventy years ago.

Since the fall of the Soviet Union, the Kyrgyz writers' situation has changed. The government subsidies that allowed the publishers to concentrate on artistic values have been discontinued, the exclusive market where the Soviets sold their publications has evaporated, even people's attitude towards reading literature has changed. In addition, with censorship discontinued, the wellspring of exciting thematic conflicts, poetic and fictional, also dried up. This is not to mention shortage of paper, which has limited publication to governmentally sanctioned manuals and monographs. All this gloom, however, should not mean that exciting literature is not being produced. As the social and economic situation in present-day Kyrgyzstan improves, contemporary Kyrgyz literature will have increased accessibility to popular and critical reception.

BIBLIOGRAPHY: Kerimdzhanova, B., and Sh. Umetaliev, *Kirgizskaia sovetskaia literatura* (1955); Begaliev, S. O., *O Poetike eposa "Manas"* (1968); Samaganov, D., *Pisateli Sovetskogo Kirgizstana: Bibliograficheskii spravochnik* (1969); Bobulov, K., *Razvitie realizma v kirgizskoi proze* (1969); Sadykov, A., *Kyrgyz sovet adabiyatyndagy uluttuk zhana internatsionaldyk problema* (1969); Jünger, H. ed., *The Literatures of the Soviet Peoples: A Historical and Bibliographical Survey* (1970): 68-70; Kudurbaeva, R. Z., "[Kirghiz] Literature," *Great Soviet Encyclopeia*, 3rd ed. (1976): 500-2; Hatto, A. T., The Memorial Feast for *Kökötöy Khan: A Kirgiz Epic Poem* (1977); Hatto, A. T., ed., *Traditions of Heroic and Epic Poetry* (1980); Allworth, E. "The Changing Intellectual and Literary Community," "The Focus on Literature," and "The New Central Asians," in Allworth, E., ed., *Central Asia: 120 Years of Russian Rule* (1989): 349-97, 397-34, 527-73; Paksoy, H. B., *Alpamysh: Central Asian Identity Under Russian Rule* (1989); Rashid, A., *The Resurgence of Central Asia: Islam or Nationalism* (1994)

—IRAJ BASHIRI

DATE DUE
